# BRITISH UNION-CATALOGUE OF PERIODICALS

incorporating
World List of Scientific Periodicals

## *NEW PERIODICAL TITLES*

### 1969–1973

Edited for the British Library

by

Mrs J. Gascoigne, A.L.A.

**BUTTERWORTHS**

LONDON · BOSTON
Sydney · Wellington · Durban · Toronto

THE BUTTERWORTH GROUP

UNITED KINGDOM: Butterworth & Co (Publishers) Ltd
London: 88 Kingsway, WC2B 6AB

AUSTRALIA: Butterworths Pty Ltd
Sydney: 586 Pacific Highway, NSW 2067
Also at Melbourne, Brisbane, Adelaide and
Perth

SOUTH AFRICA: Butterworth & Co (South Africa) (Pty) Ltd
Durban: 152–154 Gale Street

NEW ZEALAND: Butterworths of New Zealand Ltd
Wellington: 26–28 Waring Taylor Street, 1

CANADA: Butterworth & Co (Canada) Ltd
Toronto: 2265 Midland Avenue,
Scarborough, Ontario M1P 4S1

USA: Butterworth (Publishers) Inc
Boston: 19 Cummings Park,
Woburn, Mass. 01801

DISTRIBUTORS FOR THE USA AND
CANADA
Archon Books, The Shoe String Press, Inc.
995 Sherman Avenue, Hamden, Connecticut
06514

First published 1976

ISBN 0 408 70796 8
ISSN 0007-1919

Typeset by Computaprint Ltd., London
Printed in Great Britain by Page Bros (Norwich) Ltd, Norwich.

# Introduction

## 1. ABOUT THE PUBLICATION

The *British Union-Catalogue of Periodicals* (*BUCOP*) appeared originally in four volumes from 1955–1958, with a Supplement published in 1962, bringing the coverage of serial publications in British libraries down to 1960. The *World List of Scientific Periodicals (WLSP)* appeared in its fourth edition in three volumes issued 1963–1965, covering scientific, technical and medical serials in British libraries for the period 1900–1960. The current computer-produced publication, which unites *BUCOP* and *WLSP* and carries the secondary title 'New Periodical Titles' began to appear in 1964. It is published in quarterly issues, which are cumulated annually into two volumes: one including all the titles appearing in the quarterlies, and the other (in effect continuing *WLSP*) including the scientific, technical and medical titles only.

This volume is a Cumulation of the Annual Volumes of *BUCOP* for 1969–1973, including revised information and holdings added since then.

## 2. SCOPE

2.1 The current publication (referred to below as *BUCOP*) is concerned with recording new periodical titles for the period in and after 1960. This embraces periodicals and serials which began publication for the first time, or which changed their titles, or which began a new series. Serials which ceased publication in this period are also noted. Where it has not proved possible to establish the commencing date of a particular new title of which we have been notified, the publication date may be taken as that of the earliest issue in our records.

2.2 *BUCOP* includes all periodicals and most categories of serial publications, with certain reservations, as described below:

2.2.1 *Reports.* Administrative reports are in general excluded, but research and development reports are included, as well as the annual reports of research organizations and learned societies.

2.2.2 *Monographic series.* Publishers' series, and un-numbered series are excluded, but monographic series issued by a learned body or research organization are included under the series title. Since libraries normally record their holdings of such material by specific, individual entries, it should be pointed out that these entries are likely to be partial, at best, as far as the recorded holdings are concerned.

2.2.3 *Limited interest.* Material of ephemeral, or of narrowly local or sectional interest, is normally excluded.

2.2.4 *Newspapers.* These are included, unless they fall into the 'limited interest' category.

2.2.5 *Editions.* Works issued in successive editions are not normally regarded as serials, except where the changes from issue to issue, as in the case of certain statistical publications, suggest that they qualify for entry here.

2.2.6 *Conference proceedings.* These are not regarded as serials, except where they form part of an editorially independent serial publication with an individual title; e.g. the 'Advances in . . .' type of title.

2.2.7 *Reprints.* These are not regarded as new publications.

## 3. TEXT

3.1 The main text of *BUCOP* comprises the following sections: New Periodical Titles (NPT), which gives main entries for each title, with publication details, and indication by symbols of libraries holding the title (but a title can be included where no U.K. holdings are known); Index of Sponsoring Bodies (ISB), listing the bodies responsible for the titles in NPT, with the titles issued by them; and in the cumulations only, an Index of Library Symbols (ILS) providing a key to the holding libraries indicated by symbols in NPT.

3.2 The NPT entry comprises the following elements, as required, in the order shown:
*Title* with title abbreviation.
*Sponsoring body* (or bodies); publisher.
*Imprint* (place of publication; numbers and dates of first and last issues).
*Remarks* (frequency of publication, previous and subsequent titles, etc).
*Holding libraries.*

3.3 The ISB section lists the sponsoring bodies, in the form in which they appear in the second element of the NPT entry, as headings, with the titles, in the form in which they appear in the first element of the NPT entry, below.

3.4 The ILS gives the name and address of the library concerned after the symbol by which it is indicated in NPT, together with information, where known, on the library's policy concerning loans and access and on its facilities for making photocopies/micro-films.
Details of the NPT entry, and of the ILS code for loans/access/photocopying/microfilming appear below.

## 4. TITLE

4.1 Serials are entered under their published titles. The 'corporate author' approach is never used: its place is supplied by the ISB which also shows 'distinctive' titles issued under the sponsorship of a body.

4.2 Separate entries are made in the case of a title change; but not in the case of a change in the name of the sponsoring body, except where the body name forms part of the title. However, a uniform title may be used in the case of a title change, if the circumstances appear to justify it; e.g. where the change is slight, not materially altering the position of the title in an alphabetical sequence, and where the numbering is continuous over the change. The use of a uniform title is indicated by a following asterisk; e.g.:

HISTORICAL STUDIES.* [originally HISTORICAL STUDIES, AUSTRALIA & NEW ZEALAND.]

4.3 A title which is inadequate without the name of the sponsoring body (which may appear in a separate position on the title-page) attached to it, is expanded according to the following pattern: Title word or phrase, Subordinate body (where required), Parent body; e.g.:

OCCASIONAL PUBLICATION, GRADUATE SCHOOL OF CONTEMPORARY EUROPEAN STUDIES, UNIVERSITY OF READING.

However, where the normal pattern for a concrete title in a particular language happens to take the opposite form (e.g. Hungarian, Japanese, Turkish, etc.), then that pattern is followed in expanding the title, thus:

(EOTVOS LORAND TUDOMANYEGYETEMI) KONYVTAR EVKONYVEI.

4.4 Where a serial has alternative titles in two or more languages, and these are also the languages of the text, preference is normally given to the English title where there is one. All the titles concerned are shown in the NPT entry thus:

INTERNATIONAL YEARBOOK OF CARTO-GRAPHY. = ANNUAIRE INTERNATIONALE DE CARTOGRAPHIE. = INTERNATIONALES JAHRBUCH FUR KARTOGRAPHIE.

References are made from the alternative titles. However, alternative titles are not shown, nor are references made, in the case of United Nations publications, and those of U.N. agencies.

4.5 Where a serial gives an alternative title in another language, but this is not one of the languages of the text, the vernacular form is preferred. The alternative title is shown in such cases as if it were a subtitle, but references are made as required.

4.6 A separate entry is made for each subdivision of a main title, and the secondary title is shown, where there is one, as follows:

JOURNAL OF POLYMER SCIENCE: PART A: GENERAL PAPERS.

4.7 A separate entry is made for each successive series of a main title, with the series indication attached to the main title in the same form as in 4.6. This indication may be reduced to NS (for 'new series',

'nuova seria', etc.), 2S for 'second series', etc. E.g.:

MEDICAL WORLD NEWSLETTER: NS.

4.8 A serial which is issued as part of a more general series is entered under the more specific title, if it is independently numbered, and is not lettered or numbered as part of the main title, with the series indicated in brackets after the title, thus:

FAR EASTERN AFFAIRS. (ST. ANTONY'S PAPERS.)

4.9 Additions to the title: official or authoritative serials whose contents pertain to a particular area, and this is not otherwise clear from the title, may have the name of that area added to the end and used as an additional filer word. The usual English form is normally used in such cases, e.g.:

BOLETIN ESTADISTICO (CHILE).

4.10 Omissions from the title: serial numbers and dates, together with the phrase containing them, are omitted from the title. Lengthy titles may be reduced to a significant phrase, if this is adequate for identification, and does not materially affect the placing of the title in an alphabetical sequence.

4.11 Absence of title: if a serial is issued without a title, but with the name of the sponsoring body, then the name of the body in brackets is used as the title, e.g.:

(LIST & INDEX SOCIETY).

4.12 If an alphabetical and/or numerical code is the only distinguishing feature of a serial (e.g. in the case of a research and development report series), the code is used as the title.

4.13 Subtitles are shown following the main title where the title consists of a single word, where the subtitle contains the name of the sponsoring body and might be assumed to be the main title, or where there is room to include it in the same line as the title. Otherwise, it is disregarded, or, if it contains useful information, it is given in the 'Remarks' section following S/T:.

4.14 References are made in cases where a published title deviates from the 'normal' pattern (cf. 4.3), e.g.:

JOURNAL, AMERICAN INSTITUTE OF AERO-NAUTICS & ASTRONAUTICS.
SEE: AIAA JOURNAL.

4.15 The following devices are used in the right hand margin opposite the last line of the title as required: XXX, to indicate a change of title (normally against the superseded title), or to show that the title has ceased publication; 000, to indicate a reference (primarily for the use of BUCOP editorial staff).

5. SPONSORING BODY

5.1 Sponsoring bodies are entered as the second element of the NPT entry and as headings in the ISB under the names by which they are normally identified in their publications, or, where this varies, under their official names. The native form is normally used; but an English form is preferred in the case of international organizations, or where English is an official language of the country concerned.

5.2 In the case of changes of name of a body, the form used in association with a particular title is used. Where there has been a change of name in association with a title which is itself unchanged, the latest form of name is normally preferred. A uniform name, with references, may be used if justified by circumstances. Such cases are indicated by an asterisk (cf. 4.2).

5.3 Additions to the name: an identifying characteristic which may be abbreviated, may be added if required to distinguish between bodies of the same name in different places, or where amplification appears desirable. A place-name (normally preference is given to a larger over a smaller unit) or the name of a superior body may be used; e.g.:

CORPUS CHRISTI COLLEGE (UNIV. OF CAMBRIDGE).
CORPUS CHRISTI COLLEGE (UNIV. OF OXFORD).

NATIONAL RESEARCH COUNCIL (CANADA).
NATIONAL RESEARCH COUNCIL (US).
MANCHESTER COLLEGE (OXFORD).

5.4 Omissions from the name: certain elements in a body's official name, of an 'honorific' nature, or which are often dispensed with when the name is shown in publications, may be omitted from the form used in *BUCOP*. Where such elements appear to have become an integral part of the name, and affect the placing of the name in an alphabetical list, they are retained, e.g.:

UNIVERSITA DI GENOVA. *Not* UNIVERSITA DEGLI STUDI DI GENOVA.

GOSUDARSTVENNAJA BIBLIOTEKA SSSR. *Not* GOSUDARSTVENNAJA ORDENA LENINA BIBLIOTEKA SSSR IMENI V.I. LENINA.

*But*

UNIWERSYTET IM. ADAMA MICKIEWICZA W POZNANIU.

5.5 Subordinate bodies are entered directly under their own names, if these are adequate for identification (with an added identifying characteristic if necessary) and unless the name itself implies subordination. *But* bodies subordinate to a commercial firm are always entered under the name of the parent body, whether their names are distinctive or not.

5.6 A subordinate body whose name does not (necessarily) imply subordination, but whose identification requires the addition of the name of the parent body is entered as an extension of the parent body's name the whole name then filing as a unit. But if such a name has been made distinctive by the inclusion of a place or personal name, it is entered directly under

that name; e.g.:

UNIVERSITY OF LONDON: INSTITUTE OF EDUCATION:
COURTAULD INSTITUTE OF ART.

But libraries with distinctive names are entered as an extension of the parent body's name, unless they are well known under their own names; e.g.:

UNIVERSITY OF LEEDS: BROTHERTON LIBRARY.

BODLEIAN LIBRARY.

5.7 A subordinate body whose name implies subordination is omitted from the name of the sponsoring body, and mentioned in the 'Remarks' section only; *except* where such a body is one of the departments, etc., of a government, or where it indicates a branch of the parent body located in another area. An example of the latter case:

ROYAL ASIATIC SOCIETY (HONG KONG BRANCH).

5.8 Where there is a hierarchy of subordinate bodies, and the specific sponsoring body cannot be entered directly under its own name (cf. 5.6), intermediary bodies between the parent body and the subordinate body concerned may be omitted from the entry.

5.9 In the case of 'jurisdictional' entries, the name of the jurisdiction, in its English form, is inserted before the body's actual name. This name is enclosed in brackets if it represents the name of a place. But if the official name of the body begins with the jurisdictional name in any form, it is entered directly under that name. Entries with an added jurisdictional name are filed as a unit. The title of an officer may be used instead of the name of his department if this appears to be the better known form. The name of a subordinate body may be given immediately after the jurisdictional name if the name is adequate for identification. Examples:

UNITED NATIONS: HIGH COMMISSIONER FOR REFUGEES.

(UNITED STATES) BUREAU OF MINES.
(UNITED STATES) DEPARTMENT OF STATE.
UNITED STATES INFORMATION SERVICE.

5.10 Bodies created and controlled by a government are entered directly under their names where they are of one of the types described in rule 78A of the *Anglo-American Cataloguing Rules; British Text* (London, The Library Association, 1967). However, contrary to rule 84 of that publication, *BUCOP* also enters armed forces directly under their names if these seem adequate for identification. An added identifier is normally used in these cases. E.g.:

AERONAUTICAL RESEARCH COUNCIL (GB).
NATIONAL AERONAUTICS & SPACE ADMINISTRATION (US).

ROYAL AIR FORCE (GB).
WARREN SPRING LABORATORY.

5.11 A body may be entered under an acronym or group of initials (regarded as a word), particularly if it is an international organization, if it is well known by those initials. E.g.:

GATT.
NATO.
UNESCO.

5.12 The name of a commercial publisher, or a university press, may appear in the entry enclosed in square brackets, in place of or together with the name of a sponsoring body.

5.13 If the vernacular form of the name of a body, or part of it, cannot be determined at the time of a title's inclusion, the name or part concerned is shown in round brackets.

5.14 The following devices are used in the right-hand margin opposite the last line of the body's name as required (cf. 4.15): XXX, to indicate a change in the body's name (normally against the superseded name); 000, to indicate a reference.

6. IMPRINT

The 'imprint' element of the NPT entry comprises:

6.1 Place of publication. Normally a specific city, or cities, or the name of a country in brackets if the place is variable, or cannot be determined. A serial published simultaneously in several places may be shown by one place only followed by &C.

6.2 The issue numbering and date of the first (and last) issue for that particular *title*. The numbers and dates are shown together for each issue concerned. Months are indicated according to the following abbreviated forms: JA, F, MR, AP, MY, JE, JL AG, S, OC, N, D. A day is shown with a month thus: 15/JL (to avoid confusion with issue numbers). A year of publication differing from the year pertaining to the contents of a work (normally affecting annuals) is shown in brackets after the date pertaining to the text. Volumes and issues are shown thus: 1(1). Some examples:

1(1), OC 1960–
[title in progress]
1(1), OC 1960– 3(4), JA 1964.//
[ceased publication]
1(1), OC 1960– 3(4), JA 1964.
[ceased publication, continued by another title]
1(1), OC 1960– 3(4) JA 1964 . . .
[ceased publication, continued by another title with continuous numbering]
3(5), F 1965–
[first issue of a new title continues numbering from a previous title]
1, 1959/60 (1962)–
[contents of first issue concern 1959/60, actual publication date 1962]

NO. 1, 1960– *or* [NO.]1, 1960–
[issues consecutively numbered without volume numbering]
1960 (1)–
[issues numbered from 1 each year, without volume numbering]

7. REMARKS

This section of the NPT includes the following information:

7.1 An indication of the frequency of publication, shown by a suitable abbreviation. Note the use of forms such as 2M, 2A for bi-monthly and biennial respectively, and 2/M, 2/A for semi-monthly and semi-annual, etc.

7.2 The language(s) of the text, if not indicated by the language of the title. These are shown by suitable abbreviations, e.g. ENGL., FR., GER., ITAL., JAP., RUSS. A form such as ENGL. = FR. shows that the same text is given in the languages named.

7.3 In the case of a title change, previous and subsequent titles, shown following the abbreviations PREV and SUBS. All the previous titles from the first issue of a particular sequence of numbering are shown where the numbering continues through several changes.

7.4 Other information of importance in relation to the title is given as required.

8. HOLDINGS

8.1 Holding libraries are represented by symbols, for which the key is given in the ILS. The symbol comprises two letters representing the place where the library is located, e.g. LO for London, and one letter indicating the type of library, as follows: N, National libraries, museums and art galleries, major government libraries; P, Public and county libraries; U, University libraries, including departmental and university college libraries; C, 'Collegiate' libraries, that is, educational institutions not of university status; S, special libraries in general, learned societies and professional associations; M, Medical libraries (including dentistry and veterinary science), and including university medical libraries; R, Research associations research stations, and the like, not covered by other categories; T, Trade and technological associations, major technical libraries; F, commercial firms, with their laboratories and research stations. The number in the library symbol distinguishes libraries of the same category in the same place.

8.2 Holding libraries in the NPT entry are shown in groups, as categorized by a, b and c below. A selection principle is exercised by the computer: if at least twelve libraries are represented in category a, categories b and c are not printed; if at least twelve libraries are represented in categories a and b together, category c is not printed.

(a) Libraries with complete runs from the first issue to the title shown to date. These are printed four to a line, the symbols alone being shown.

(b) Libraries with a continuous run from some issue after the first of that title. These are printed two to a line, with an open entry from the first issue held.

(c) Libraries with partial, or temporary holdings, with a specific indication of the holding. These are printed one to a line.

A library's holding may appear in both the b and c categories above if warranted. A single asterisk follows the symbol or precedes the holding to indicate issues missing in the run shown. A double asterisk follows the symbol to indicate that the title is held, but the precise holding is not known.

9. ARRANGEMENT OF ENTRIES

9.1 The order of filing of title (NPT) and sponsoring bodies (ISB) is alphabetical, word-by-word, with numerals preceding letters.

9.2 Articles are disregarded in the filing order throughout; unless they form an integral part of a place-name (cf. LOS ANGELES). They are not normally shown at the beginning of a title, unless it seems useful to indicate them; cf. AL-ANDALUS, filed as ANDALUS.

9.3 Prepositions and conjunctions are disregarded in the filing order, except where they begin a title.

9.4 Groups of initials are filed as if they were words whether they form a vocable or not.

9.5 Hyphenated words are filed as single words, unless each element also constitutes a word which can occur in isolation. Compound words which sometimes occur as separate words, or with a hyphen, or as single words, are normally filed as single words. Words with detached prefixes are filed as complete single words, E.g.:

| | | |
|---|---|---|
| INTER-AMERICAN | files as | INTERAMERICAN |
| FAR-EAST | files as | FAR EAST |
| YEAR BOOK | files as | YEARBOOK |
| YEAR-BOOK | files as | YEARBOOK |
| PAN AMERICAN | files as | PANAMERICAN |

9.6 Diacritical marks are omitted in *BUCOP*, and neither the spelling nor the filing is modified to indicate their presence.

OSTERREICHISCHE is shown and filed as OSTERREICHISCHE and not as OESTER-REICHISCHE

9.7 The filing is modified as appropriate to interfile cognate forms in the same or different languages; e.g. plurals are normally filed with and as the singular forms. Words like ARCHIV, ARCHIVE, ARCHIVES, ARCHIVIOS, etc., are interfiled., as are BOLETIM and BOLETIN, etc., JAPAN and JAPANESE are interfiled. Words with different, inflected endings are interfiled, e.g. DEUTSCHE, DEUTSCHER DEUTSCHES.

Normally this procedure affects words which differ only in their endings; in some cases, however, it is extended to words where the variation occurs near the beginning. E.g. AARBOK files with ARBOK; NIHON with NIPPON; SWENSKA with SVENSKA; etc.

10. TRANSLITERATION

Non-roman alphabets are transliterated, or other forms of script transcribed, according to systems generally established in the United Kingdom. However, the Hanyu Pinyin system is normally used in preference to the Wade-Giles for Chinese, especially for mainland China publications, which often carry a transcription in the Hanyu Pinyin form. The British Standard *BS 2979*: 1958 is used for Cyrillic according to the 'British' system, but with the modification that the letter y is used for the vowel sound shown in the standard as $\bar{y}$; otherwise, j is used in place of y, for instance in the forms ja, ju and (Ukranian) ji, and also for the short i.

11. ILS CODING

An indication is given in the ILS after the library's name and address of their policy concerning loans and access, and their facilities for making photocopies and microfilms, as follows:

L   The library lends most of its serials, either direct to other libraries, or through the British Library Lending Division.

*L   The library makes certain conditions concerning the loan of its serials, or will lend only some of its holdings.

XL   The library lends only to authorized users, or does not lend.

F   The library will lend its serials to libraries in foreign countries.

*F   The library will lend to foreign countries in special circumstances.

XF   The library will not lend its serials abroad.

A   The library permits access to callers in general.

*A   Access for reference is permitted to individuals suitably introduced.

XA   Access is restricted to authorized users of the library.

P   The library has photocopying facilities.

*P   The library has limited photocopying facilities.

XP   The library has no photocopying facilities.

M   The library has microfilming facilities.

*M   The library has limited microfilming facilities.

XM   The library has no microfilming facilities.

12. TITLE ABBREVIATIONS

12.1 The title abbreviations given in the NPT entry immediately after the full title (following the ++ sign) accord with the revised British Standard, *BS 4148*: 1969, and its associated *Word-Abbreviation List*. The revised British standard conforms in all particulars to the revised American standard in this field, *Z39.5*–1969.

12.2 The major differences from the previous standard, and from earlier British practice, are as follows:

(a) There is no distinction between word forms implied by the use of upper and lower case; in *BUCOP* the abbreviation like the rest of the main text, is in upper case throughout.

(b) Full stops are used after all abbreviations, even where the last letter of the original word is retained.

(c) The final element only of a compound word is abbreviated, unless hyphenation occurs; in such a case each element affected may be abbreviated.

12.3 Abbreviations have been assigned to titles in all subject fields, but not to all titles; in some cases it appears unsuitable to assign an abbreviated form but users of *BUCOP* are invited to query any such decision with the editor if they wish.

12.4 The added identifier required in some cases to distinguish or to clarify abbreviations, may be a place—and normally a larger unit, such as a country, is preferred over a city—or an abbreviation for the name of the sponsoring body. The body is always shown in an added identifier in an abbreviated form based on the full name where it appears in the title in the form of initials. In such a case it need not necessarily be regarded as part of the abbreviation, unless distinction is required. E.g.:

AIAA JOURNAL.
  + +AIAA J. (AM. INST. AERONAUT. & ASTRONAUT.)

12.5 Where it has been established, the Coden for a title appears after the abbreviation in square brackets. E.g.:

JOURNAL OF MACROMOLECULAR CHEMISTRY.
  ++ J. MACROMOL. CHEM. [JMCC-A]

12.6 The ampersand (&) is used for 'and' and its equivalent in all languages in the title abbreviation, but has no filing significance.

13    INTERNATIONAL STANDARD SERIAL NUMBERS.

The International Standard Serial Number relating to a title appears as the final element of the NPT entry for that title. E.g.:

PARNASSUS. POETRY IN REVIEW.
  NEW YORK 1, 1972–
  OX/U-I.

  ISSN 0048-3028

# New Periodical Titles

III PLANO DE FOMENTO: PROGRAMA DE EXECUCAO.
(PORTUGAL) PRESIDENCIA DO CONSELHO.
*LISBON 1968-*
A. III PLANO COVERS YEARS 1968-1973.
*LO/U-3.*

20TH CENTURY STUDIES.
*++20TH CENTURY STUD.*
UNIVERSITY OF KENT: FACULTY OF HUMANITIES.
*CANTERBURY 1, MR 1969-*
*CB/U-1. DB/U-1. ED/N-1. LO/U-2. LO/U-3.*
*ISSN 0041-4638*

365 DAYS OF THE YEAR. INDEPENDENT POETRY
REVIEW.
*WARNDON, WORCS. NO.1, 1969-*
*LO/U-2.*

2000.
*LONDON 1(1), JE 1971-*
M.
*ED/N-1. OX/U16.*

A' BHRATACH UR. NEW BANNER.
CELTIC LEAGUE IN GLASGOW.
*GLASGOW 1, 1971-*
*ED/N-1.*

AA NOTES.
ARCHITECTURAL ASSOCIATION.
*LONDON NO.1, N 1968-*
*ED/N-1. OX/U-1.*
*ISSN 0044-8648*

AAQ. ARCHITECTURAL ASSOCIATION QUARTERLY.
ARCHITECTURAL ASSOCIATION.
[PERGAMON PRESS]
*OXFORD &C 1, WINTER 1968/69-*
*ED/N-1. ED/U-1. OX/U-1. SH/U-1.*
*ISSN 0001-0189*

AARP. ART & ARCHAEOLOGY RESEARCH PAPERS.
*LONDON NO.1, JE 1972-*
*CA/U-1. ED/N-1. LO/N12. LO/U17.*

AARTHIK JAGAT. ECONOMIC JOURNAL OF THE ...
TRIBHUVAN UNIVERSITY ECONOMIC SOCIETY.
*TRIPURESWOR 1(1), 1965-*
*LO/U14.*

AAVSO JOURNAL.
*++AAVSO J.*
AMERICAN ASSOCIATION OF VARIABLE STAR OBSERVERS
*CAMBRIDGE, MASS. 1, SPRING 1972-*
*2/A.*

ABACO. ESTUDIOS SOBRE LITERATURA ESPANOLA.
[CASTALIA]
*MADRID 1, 1968-*
*DB/U-2. LO/U-2. LO/U11. LO/U17. SW/U-1.*
*HL/U-1. 1, 1969- 3, 1970.*
*MA/U-1. NO.1-2, 1969.*

ABBA SALAMA.
ASSOCIATION OF ETHIO-HELLENIC STUDIES.
*ADDIS ABABA 1, 1970-*
*OX/U-1.*
*LO/U14. 3, 1972-*

ABBIA. REVUE CULTURELLE CAMEROUNAISE.
*YAOUNDE NO.1, ?1963-*
ALSO S/T IN ENGL.: CAMEROON CULTURAL REVIEW.
*LO/U-2.*
*AD/U-1. 16, 1967-*
*ISSN 0001-3102*

ABC POL SCI. ADVANCE BIBLIOGRAPHY OF CONT-
ENTS: POLITICAL SCIENCE & GOVERNMENT.
AMERICAN BIBLIOGRAPHICAL CENTRE.
[ABC-CLIO INC.]
*SANTA BARBARA(CALIF.) 1(1), 1969-*
*AD/U-1. DB/U-2. EX/U-1. LO/N-1.*
*ISSN 0001-0456*

A.B.C. WORLD AIRWAYS & SHIPPING GUIDE.
[SKINNER]
*LONDON 1(1), 1969-*
*OX/U-1.*

ABHANDLUNGEN, ARBEITSGEMEINSCHAFT FUR TIER-
UND PFLANZENGEOGRAPHISCHE HEIMATFORSCHUNG IM
SAARLAND.
*++ABH. ARBEITSGEM. TIER- & PFLANZENGEOGR.*
*HEIMATFORSCH. SAARLAND.*
*SAARBRUCKEN 1, 1969-*
*LO/N-2.*

ABHANDLUNGEN ZUR KARST- UND HOHLENKUNDE:
REIHE A: SPELAOLOGIE.
*++ABH. KARST- & HOHLENKD., A.*
VERBAND DER DEUTSCHEN HOHLEN- UND KARSTFORSCHER
*MUNICH HEFT 1, 1966-*
*LO/N13.*
*ISSN 0567-4956*

ABHANDLUNGEN ZUR KARST- UND HOHLENKUNDE:
REIHE F: GESCHICHTE DER SPELAOLOGIE, BIO-
GRAPHIEN.
*++ABH. KARST- & HOHLENKD., F.*
VERBAND DER DEUTSCHEN HOHLEN- UND KARSTFORSCHER
*MUNICH HEFT 1, 1967-*
*LO/N13.*
*ISSN 0567-4972*

ABHANDLUNGEN, SAECHSISCHE AKADEMIE DER WISSEN-
SCHAFTEN (LEIPZIG): PHILOLOGISCHE-HISTORISCHE
KLASSE.                                              000
SEE: ONOMASTICA SLAVOGERMANICA.

ABHANDLUNGEN, ZENTRALES GEOLOGISCHES INSTITUT
(BERLIN).
*++ABH. ZENT. GEOL. INST. (BERL.).*
*BERLIN 1, 1966-*
*LO/N-2.*

ABORTION BIBLIOGRAPHY.
*++ABORT. BIBLIOGR.*
[WHITSTON PUBL. CO.]
*TROY, N.Y. 1, 1970(1972)-*
ANNU.
*LO/N13.*

ABOUT THIS ...
CHICHESTER POETS CO-OPERATIVE.
*CHICHESTER NO.1, 1968-*
S/T: AN OCCASIONAL PUBLICATION OF POETRY BY
MEMBERS OF THE ...
*LO/U-2.*

ABOUT WINE.
[VINTAGE PUBL.]
*LONDON NO.1, JA 1972-*
2W.
*ED/N-1.*

ABRIDGED INDEX MEDICUS.
NATIONAL LIBRARY OF MEDICINE (US).
*BETHESDA, MD. 1, JA 1970-*
M. PRECEDED BY A PILOT ISSUE DATED AG 1969.
SPONS. BODY ALSO: AMERICAN MEDICAL ASSOCIA-
TION. SUPERSEDES SAME TITLE ISSUED BY THE
ASSOCIATION FROM 1, 1968.
*AD/U-1. XS/R10.*
*ISSN 0001-3331*

ABSEES. SOVIET & EAST EUROPEAN ABSTRACTS
SERIES.                                              XXX
NATIONAL ASSOCIATION FOR SOVIET & EAST EUROPEAN
STUDIES.
*GLASGOW NO.1(27), JL 1970-*
Q. SPONS. BODY ALSO INSTITUTE OF SOVIET &
EAST EUROPEAN STUDIES, UNIVERSITY OF GLASGOW.
PREV: SOVIET STUDIES: INFORMATION SUPPLEMENT
FROM NO.1, 1964- 26, 1970.
*DB/U-2. DB/U-2. LD/U-1. LO/N-1. MA/P-1. OX/U-1.*
*RE/U-1. SH/U-1. SW/U-1. BH/P-1. LO/U-1. LO/U11.*
*NW/U-1.*
*CV/C-1. 2, 1971-*
*ISSN 0044-5622*

**ABSTRACTS FOR THE ADVANCEMENT OF INDUSTRIAL UTILIZATION OF CEREAL GRAINS.**          XXX
+ +ABSTR. ADV. IND. UTIL. CEREAL GRAINS.
WASHINGTON STATE UNIVERSITY: DIVISION OF INDUS-
TRIAL RESEARCH.
*PULLMAN, WASH. 8(43), 1969- 10(60), 1971.//*
PREV: ABSTRACTS FOR THE ADVANCEMENT OF INDUS-
TRIAL UTILIZATION OF WHEAT FROM 1(1), 1962-
7(42), 1969. DIVISION SUBORD. TO: COLLEGE OF
ENGINEERING.
*LO/N14.*
*ISSN 0001-3420*

**ABSTRACTS OF ALTERNATIVES TO LABORATORY ANIMALS.**          XXX
+ +ABSTR. ALTERNATIVES LAB. ANIM.
FUND FOR THE REPLACEMENT OF ANIMALS IN MEDICAL
EXPERIMENTS.
*LONDON 1(1-2), JE 1973 ...*
2A.
SUBS: ATLA ABSTRACTS.
*CA/U-1.   ED/N-1.   MA/U-1.   OX/U-8.*

**ABSTRACTS OF THE ANNUAL MEETING OF THE AMER-ICAN SOCIETY FOR MICROBIOLOGY.**          XXX
+ +ABSTR. ANNU. MEET. AM. SOC. MICROBIOL.
*WASHINGTON, D.C. 1972-*
PREV: BACTERIOLOGICAL PROCEEDINGS FROM 1950-
1971.
*LD/U-1.*

**ABSTRACTS IN ANTHROPOLOGY.**
+ +ABSTR. ANTHROPOL.
[GREENWOOD P.]
*WESTPORT, CONN. 1, F 1970-*
Q.
*BH/U-1.   BN/U-1.   CA/U-1.   CA/U-3.   LO/N-2.   LO/S10.
MA/U-1.
AD/U-1. 4, 1973-*
*ISSN 0001-3455*

**ABSTRACTS OF ARTICLES TO BE PUBLISHED IN THE PHYSICAL REVIEW.**          XXX
+ +ABSTR. ARTIC. PUBL. PHYS. REV.
AMERICAN PHYSICAL SOCIETY.
*FARMINGDALE, N.Y. 1961- 1969.*
SUPPL. TO PHYSICAL REVIEW LETTERS. SUBS:
PHYSICAL REVIEW ABSTRACTS.
*LO/N14.*

**ABSTRACTS, CEMENT RESEARCH INSTITUTE OF INDIA.**
SEE: CRI ABSTRACTS.

**ABSTRACTS ON CRIMINOLOGY & PENOLOGY.**          XXX
+ +ABSTR. CRIMINOL. & PENOL.
CRIMINOLOGICA FOUNDATION.
[KLUWER]
*DEVENTER 9, 1969-*
PREV: EXCERPTA CRIMINOLOGICA FROM 1, 1961-
8, 1968.
*BH/U-1.   CB/U-1.   GL/U-1.   LO/U-2.   LO/U-3.   NO/U-1.
OX/U17.   RE/U-1.   SO/U-1.
LO/U-4. 10, 1970-*
*ISSN 0001-3684*

**ABSTRACTS OF ENTOMOLOGY.**
+ +ABSTR. ENTOMOL.
*PHILADELPHIA 1, 1970-*
ISSUED BY BIOSCIENCES INFORMATION SERVICE OF
BIOLOGICAL ABSTRACTS.
*DB/U-2.   LO/N-2.   LO/N14.*
*ISSN 0001-3579*

**ABSTRACTS, HIGHWAY RESEARCH INFORMATION SERVICE (US).**          000
SEE: HRIS ABSTRACTS.

**ABSTRACTS OF HOSPITAL MANAGEMENT STUDIES.**
+ +ABSTR. HOSP. MANAGE. STUD.
UNIVERSITY OF MICHIGAN: COOPERATIVE INFORMATION
CENTRE FOR HOSPITAL STUDIES.
*ANN ARBOR 1, 1964-*
*RE/U-1.   XY/N-1.*
*ISSN 0001-3595*

**ABSTRACTS OF HUNGARIAN ECONOMIC LITERATURE.**
+ +ABSTR. HUNG. ECON. LIT.
VILAGGAZDASAGI TUDOMANYOS TANACS.
*BUDAPEST 1(1), 1971-*
2M.
*OX/U16.*
*ISSN 3344-5800*

**ABSTRACTS ON HYGIENE.**
+ +ABSTR. HYG.
*LONDON 43, 1968-*
PREV: BULLETIN OF HYGIENE., FROM 1, 1926.
*CR/M-1.   LO/M-1.   LO/U-1.   XS/T11.*
*ISSN 0001-3692*

**ABSTRACTS, INSTITUTE OF MARINE ENGINEERS: MARINE ENGINEERING/SHIPBUILDING.**
+ +ABSTR. INST. MAR. ENG., MAR. ENG./SHIPBUILD.
*LONDON 1(1), 1971-*
*OX/U-8.*
*GL/U-2. 3, 1973-*

**ABSTRACTS, INSTITUTE OF PETROLEUM.**          XXX
+ +ABSTR. INST. PETROL.
*LONDON MR 1969- 1972.*
TO END OF 1968 PART OF: JOURNAL OF THE INST.
OF PETROLEUM. SUBS: INTERNATIONAL PETROLEUM
ABSTRACTS.
*BR/U-3.   EX/U-1.   GL/U-1.   GL/U-2.   LO/N-7.   LO/N14.
MA/U-1.   RE/U-1.*
*ISSN 0020-305X*

**ABSTRACT, NATIONAL CITIZENS' ADVICE BUREAUX COUNCIL.**
+ +ABSTR. NAT. CITIZENS' ADVICE BUR. COUNC. (GB).
*LONDON NO.1, 1967-*
*OX/U-1.*

**ABSTRACTS ON POLICE SCIENCE.**
+ +ABSTR. POLICE SCI.
CRIMINOLOGICA FOUNDATION.
*LEIDEN 1, 1973-*
2M.
*HL/U-1.   LO/N14.   MA/U-1.   SH/U-1.   SO/U-1.*

**ABSTRACTS WITH PROGRAMS, GEOLOGICAL SOCIETY OF AMERICA.**          XXX
+ +ABSTR. PROGRAMS GEOL. SOC. AM.
*BOULDER 1, 1969-*
7/A. PREV: ABSTRACTS OF PAPERS SUBMITTED FOR
MEETINGS ... FROM 1961- 1968.
*AD/U-2.   LO/N-2.   SO/U-1.
OX/U-8. 3(1), 1971-          SH/U-1. F 1971-*

**ABSTRACTS OF PUBLISHED PAPERS, DIVISION OF APPLIED GEOMECHANICS, CSIRO (AUSTRALIA).**
+ +ABSTR. PUBL. PAP. DIV. APPL. GEOMECH. CSIRO
(AUST.).
*MELBOURNE NO.1, 1972-*
*LD/U-1.*

**ABSTRACTS & REVIEWS IN BEHAVIORAL BIOLOGY.**          XXX
+ +ABSTR. & REV. BEHAV. BIOL.
NATIONAL EDUCATIONAL CONSULTANTS (US).
*BALTIMORE, MD. 9, 1972-*
PREV: COMMUNICATIONS IN BEHAVIORAL BIOLOGY:
PART B: ABSTRACTS & INDEX FROM 1(1), 1968-
8(6), 1971.
*GL/U-1.   LO/N-2.   LO/N13.*

**ABSTRACTS OF ROMANIAN SCIENTIFIC & TECHNICAL LITERATURE.**          XXX
+ +ABSTR. ROM. SCI. & TECH. LIT.
INSTITUTUL CENTRAL DE DOCUMENTARE TEHNICA.
*BUCHAREST 7, 1971-*
PREV: ABSTRACTS OF RUMANIAN TECHNICAL LITERAT-
URE FROM 1, 1965- 6, 1970.
*LO/N14.*

**ABU TECHNICAL REVIEW.**
+ +ABU TECH. REV.
ASIAN BROADCASTING UNION.
*TOKYO NO.1, 1969-*
*LO/N-7.*   LO/N13.*

**ACADEMIC WRITER'S GUIDE TO PERIODICALS.**
+ +ACAD. WRIT. GUIDE PERIOD.
[KENT STATE UNIV. P.]
*KENT, OHIO 1, 1971-*
*OX/U-1.*

**ACADIENSIS. JOURNAL OF THE HISTORY OF THE ATLANTIC REGION.**
UNIVERSITY OF NEW BRUNSWICK: DEPARTMENT OF
HISTORY.
*FREDERICTON 1, 1971-*
2/A.
*LO/U-1.   OX/U-9.   OX/U-9.*
*ISSN 0044-5851*

ACCESS. KEY TO THE SOURCE LITERATURE OF THE
CHEMICAL SCIENCES.                                    xxx
AMERICAN CHEMICAL SOCIETY.
*EASTON, PA. 1969.*
PREV: THE SOCIETY'S LIST OF PERIODICALS ABSTR-
ACTED BY CHEMICAL ABSTRACTS. SUBS: CHEMICAL
ABSTRACTS SERVICE SOURCE INDEX.
*GL/U-1. LO/N14. XS/R10.*

ACCESSIBLE.
NATIONAL LIBRARY OF CANADA: RESEARCH & PLANNING
BRANCH.
*OTTAWA NO.1, [1972]-*
*ED/N-1.*
*OX/U-1. 1(4), 1973-*

ACCESSION BULLETIN, SOLID WASTE INFORMATION
RETRIEVAL SYSTEM.
*+ +ACCESS. BULL. SOLID WASTE INF. RETR. SYST.*
*ROCKVILLE, MD. 1, 1971-*
*LO/N13.*

ACCESSIONS LIST, AMERICAN LIBRARIES BOOK
PROCUREMENT CENTER: CEYLON.
*+ +ACCESS. LIST AM. LIBR. BOOK PROCURE. CENT.,*
*CEYLON.*
*NEW DELHI 1(1), MR 1967-*
*Q.*
*LO/N-3.*

ACCESSIONS LIST, AMERICAN LIBRARIES BOOK
PROCUREMENT CENTER: INDIA.
*+ +ACCESS. LIST AM. LIBR. BOOK PROCURE. CENT.,*
*INDIA.*
*NEW DELHI 1, JL 1962-*
*M.* HEAD OF TITLE: LIBRARY OF CONGRESS PUBLIC
LAW 480 PROJECT. CENTER SUBORD. TO LIBRARY
OF CONGRESS (US).
*LO/N-3.*

ACCESSIONS LIST, AMERICAN LIBRARIES BOOK
PROCUREMENT CENTER: INDONESIA.
*+ +ACCESS. LIST AM. LIBR. BOOK PROCURE. CENT.,*
*INDONESIA.*
*DJAKARTA 1, JL 1964-*
AT HEAD OF TITLE: THE LIBRARY OF CONGRESS
PUBLIC LAW 480 PROJECT. CENTER SUBORD. TO
LIBRARY OF CONGRESS (US).
*LO/N-3.*
*LO/N-2. 5(5/6), 1970-*

ACCESSIONS LIST, AMERICAN LIBRARIES BOOK
PROCUREMENT CENTER: ISRAEL.
*+ +ACCESS. LIST AM. LIBR. BOOK PROCURE. CENT.,*
*ISRAEL.*
*TEL-AVIV 1, AP 1964-*
AT HEAD OF TITLE: LIBRARY OF CONGRESS PUBLIC
LAW 480 PROJECT. CENTER SUBORD. TO LIBRARY
OF CONGRESS (US).
*LO/N-3.*

ACCESSIONS LIST, AMERICAN LIBRARIES BOOK
PROCUREMENT CENTER: MIDDLE EAST.
*+ +ACCESS. LIST AM. LIBR. BOOK PROCURE. CENT.,*
*MIDDLE EAST.*
*CAIRO 1, JA 1963-*
AT HEAD OF TITLE: LIBRARY OF CONGRESS PUBLIC
LAW 480 PROJECT. CENTER SUBORD. TO LIBRARY
OF CONGRESS (US).
*LO/N-3.*
*LO/N-2. 4, 1966-*

ACCESSIONS LIST, AMERICAN LIBRARIES BOOK
PROCUREMENT CENTER: NEPAL.
*+ +ACCESS. LIST AM. LIBR. BOOK PROCUR. CENT.,*
*NEPAL.*
*NEW DELHI 1(1), MR 1967-*
*3/A.*
*LO/N-3.*
*LO/N-2. 5, 1970-*

ACCIDENT ANALYSIS & PREVENTION.
*+ +ACCIDENT ANAL. & PREV.*
[PERGAMON]
*NEW YORK &C 1, 1969-*
*BH/P-1.    LD/U-1.    LO/N14.*
*NW/U-1. 2, 1970-*                    *SH/C-5. 2, 1970-*
*SH/U-1. JL 1971-*
*ISSN 0001-4575*

ACCOUNTANCY AGE.
*+ +ACCOUNT. AGE.*
[HAYMARKET PRESS.]
*LONDON 1(1), D 1969-*
*W.*
*ED/N-1    GL/U-3.    LO/U-1. *    OX/U-1.*
*MA/P-1. 1(2), 1969-*
*ISSN 0001-4672*

ACCOUNTANCY IRELAND.
*+ +ACCOUNT. IREL.*
INSTITUTE OF CHARTERED ACCOUNTANTS IN IRELAND.
*DUBLIN 1(1), JE 1969-*
*DB/U-2.*
*ISSN 0001-4699*

ACCOUNTANTS WEEK.                                    xxx
*+ +ACCOUNT. WEEK.*
[MORGAN-GRAMPIAN]
*LONDON NO.1, S 1970- 95, OC 1972.*
SUBS: ACCOUNTANTS WEEKLY.
*ED/N-1.    GL/U-2.    LO/U-1.    OX/U-1.*
*LO/N35. 2 YEARS ONLY.*

ACCOUNTANTS WEEKLY.                                    xxx
*+ +ACCOUNT. WKLY.*
[MORGAN-GRAMPIAN]
*LONDON 1(1), OC 1972-*
PREV: ACCOUNTANTS WEEK FROM NO.1, S 1970- 95,
OC 1972.
*LO/U-1.*
*SO/U-1. 1(2), 1972-*

ACCOUNTING AND BUSINESS RESEARCH.
*+ +ACCOUNT. & BUS. RES.*
INSTITUTE OF CHARTERED ACCOUNTANTS IN
ENGLAND & WALES.
*LONDON NO.1, 1970-*
*AD/U-1.    BH/U-3.    DB/U-2.    DN/U-1.    ED/N-1.    EX/U-1.*
*GL/U-1.    GL/U-3.    HL/U-1.    LO/N-7.    LO/U-3.    LO/U12.*
*MA/U-1.    NO/U-1.    NW/U-1.    OX/U-1.    OX/U-8.*
*OX/U16.    SH/C-5.    SH/U-1.    SO/U-1.    SW/U-1.*
*XS/R10.    XS/T-4.*
*ISSN 0001-4788*

ACCOUNTING & DATA PROCESSING ABSTRACTS.              xxx
*+ +ACC. & DATA PROCESS. ABSTR.*
INSTITUTE OF CHARTERED ACCOUNTANTS IN
ENGLAND & WALES.
*LONDON 1, 1970/71 (1970)-*
PREV: LIBRARIAN'S DIGEST OF ARTICLES, INSTIT-
UTE ... FROM JA 1954- 1969.
*CB/U-1.    ED/N-1.    GL/U-3.    LO/N14.    MA/U-1.    OX/U-1.*
*SH/U-1.    SO/U-1.    XS/R10.*
*NW/U-1. 1(5), 1971-*                    *SH/C-5. 1(12), 1971-*
*ISSN 0001-4796*

ACCOUNTING RESEARCH STUDY.
*+ +ACC. RES. STUD.*
AMERICAN INSTITUTE OF CERTIFIED PUBLIC ACCOUNT-
ANTS.
*NEW YORK NO.1, 1961-*
*GL/U-1.*

ACCOUNTS OF CHEMICAL RESEARCH.
*+ +ACC. CHEM. RES.*
AMERICAN CHEMICAL SOCIETY.
*WASHINGTON, DC 1(1), JA 1968-*
*M.*
*AD/U-1.    BH/U-1.    BH/U-3.    BL/U-1.    BN/U-2.    CB/U-1.*
*CR/U-1.    DB/U-1.    DB/U-2.    GL/U-2.    HL/U-1.    LO/N14.*
*LO/S-3.    LO/U-2.    LO/U-5.    LO/U11.    LO/U21.    MA/T-2.*
*OX/U-1.    OX/U-8.    RE/R-1.    RE/U-1.    SH/U-1.    SO/U-1.*
*XY/N-1.*
*ISSN 0001-4842*

ACE. ARTICLES IN CIVIL ENGINEERING.
UNIVERSITY OF BRADFORD LIBRARY.
*BRADFORD 1, 1969-*
*BH/P-1.    BL/U-1.    ED/U-1.    GL/U-2.    LO/N14.*
*LO/N-7. 1970-*
*GL/U-2. 1, 1969- 2(25), 1970.*
*SO/U-1. CURRENT YEAR ONLY.*

ACHIEVEMENTS IN TEACHING.
*+ +ACHIEV. TEACH.*
UNIVERSITY OF NEWCASTLE UPON TYNE:
INSTITUTE OF EDUCATION.
*NEWCASTLE UPON TYNE NO.1, 1967-*
*OX/U-1.*

ACQUA ED ARIA.
SOCIETA EDITRICE RIVISTE TECNICHE.
*MILANO 1(1), 1968-*
*LO/N14.*

ACQUA INDUSTRIALE.                                    xxx
SUBS (1970): INQUINAMENTO.

ACRIDA.
ASSOCIATION D'ACRIDOLOGIE.
*PARIS 1, 1972-*
FROM 1974 A SUPPLEMENT ENTITLED: ACRIDOLOGICAL
ABSTRACTS ALSO PUBL.
*CA/U-2.    LO/N-2.    LO/N13.    OX/U-8.*
*CA/U-1. 3, 1974-*
*ISSN 0300-4686*

**ACTA AGRARIA & SILVESTRIA: SERIA LESNA.**
++ACTA AGR. & SILVEST., SER. LES.
POLSKA AKADEMIA NAUK: KOMISJA NAUK ROLNICZNYCH
I LESNYCH.
KRAKOW 1, 1961-
SUMM. IN ENG. & RUSS.
DB/S-1.

**ACTA AGRARIA & SILVESTRIA: SERIA ROLNICZA.**
++ACTA AGR. & SILVEST., SER. ROLN. [ASRZ-A]
POLSKA AKADEMIA NAUK: KOMISJA NAUK ROLNICZNYCH
I LESNYCH.
KRAKOW 1, 1961-
SUMM. IN ENG. & RUSS.
DB/S-1.

**ACTA AMAZONICA.**
INSTITUTO NACIONAL DE PESQUISAS DA AMAZONIA
(BRAZIL).
MANAOS NO.1, AP 1971-
3/A. ENGL. OR PORT. SUMM. IN THE OTHER LANG.
LO/N-2.    OX/U-3.
ISSN 0044-5967

**ACTA ARCHAEOLOGICA LODZIENSIA.**                                    XXX
++ACTA ARCHAEOL. LODZ.
LODZKIE TOWARZYSTWO NAUKOWE.
LODZ NO.11(46), 1962-
PREV: ACTA ARCHAEOLOGICA UNIVERSITATIS LODZ-
IENSIS FROM 1, 1951- 10, 1961. NUMB. ALSO AS
PART OF MAIN SERIES: PRACE WYDZIALU 2: LODZKIE
TOWARZYSTWO NAUKOWE. NO.11 OF ABOVE = NO.46
OF PRACE. MONOGR.
BL/U-1.    CA/U-1.    LO/N-3.    OX/U-1.
ISSN 0065-0986

**ACTA ARCHAEOLOGICA UNIVERSITATIS LODZIENSIS.**     XXX
SUBS (1962): ACTA ARCHAEOLOGICA LODZIENSIA.

**ACTA BIOLOGIAE EXPERIMENTALIS.**                                    XXX
SUBS (1970):  ACTA NEUROBIOLOGIAE EXPERIMENT-
ALIS.

**ACTA BIOLOGICA JUGOSLAVICA: SERIJA D: EKOLO-
JIA.**
++ACTA BIOL. JUGOSLAV., D.
SAVEZ BIOLOSKIH DRUSTAVA JUGOSLAVIJE.
BELGRADE 1, 1966-
LO/N-2.
LO/N13. 4, 1969-

**ACTA BOTANICA ISLANDICA.  TIMARIT UM ISLENZKA
GRASAFRAEDI.**                                                        XXX
++ACTA BOT. ISL.
[BOKAUTGAFA MENNINGARSJODS]
REYKJAVIK 1, 1972-
PREV: FLORA. TIMARIT UM ISLENSKA GRASAFRAEDI
AKUREYRI FROM 1, 1963- 6, 1968.
LD/U-1.    LO/N-2.

**ACTA CARTOGRAPHICA.**
++ACTA CARTOGR.
AMSTERDAM  1, 1967-
LO/S13.    OX/U-1.
LV/U-1.  1, 1967- 2, 1968.

**ACTA CIENTIFICA, INSTITUTO DE INVESTIGACIONES
CIENTIFICAS Y TECNICAS DE LAS FUERZAS ARMADAS
(BUENOS AIRES).**
++ACTA CIENT. INST. INVEST. CIENT. & TEC.
FUERZAS ARMADAS (BUENOS AIRES).
BUENOS AIRES 1, 1967-
LO/N13.

**ACTA CRIMINOLOGICA. ETUDES SUR LA
CONDUITE ANTISOCIALE.**
++ACTA CRIMINOL.
UNIVERSITE DE MONTREAL: DEPARTEMENT DE
CRIMINOLOGIE.
MONTREAL 1, 1968-
A. ENGL. & FR.
OX/U15.

**ACTA CRYSTALLOGRAPHICA.**                                           XXX
++ACTA CRYSTALLOGR. [ACCR-A]
INTERNATIONAL UNION OF CRYSTALLOGRAPHY.
COPENHAGEN &C  1, 1948-23, 1967...
SUB: ISSUED WITH ABOVE TITLE IN SECTIONS:A & B
BN/U-2.

**ACTA CRYSTALLOGRAPHICA: SECTION A.**
++ACTA CRYSTALLOGR., A.
INTERNATIONAL UNION OF CRYSTALLOGRAPHY.
COPENHAGEN &C A24. 1968-
PREV: PART OF ACTA CRYSTALLOGRAPHICA.
BN/U-2.    RE/U-1.

**ACTA CRYSTALLOGRAPHICA: SECTION B.**
++ACTA CRYSTALLOGR., B.
INTERNATIONAL UNION OF CRYSTALLOGRAPHY.
COPENHAGEN &C  B24, 1968-
PREV. PART OF ACTA CRYSTALLOGRAPHICA.
BN/U-2.    RE/U-1.

**ACTA EMBRYOLOGIAE EXPERIMENTALIS.**                         XXX
++ACTA EMBRYOL. EXP.
ISTITUTO DI ZOOLOGIA (PALERMO).
PALERMO NO.1, 1969-
ENGL., FR., GER., OR ITAL.
PREV: ACTA EMBRYOLOGIAE ET MORPHOLOGIAE
EXPERIMENTALIS FROM 1, F 1957- 10, D 1968.
LO/N-2.
ISSN 0065-1184

**ACTA EMBRYOLOGIAE ET MORPHOLOGIAE
EXPERIMENTALIS.**                                                     XXX
SUBS (1969): ACTA EMBRYOLOGIAE EXPERIMENTALIS.

**ACTA ENTOMOLOGICA LITUANICA.**
++ACTA ENTOMOL. LITU.
[MINTIS]
VILNIUS  1, 1970-
LO/N13.

**ACTA ETHNOMUSICOLOGICA.**
++ACTA ETHNOMUSICOL.
[AKADEMISK FORLAG]
COPENHAGEN NO.1, 1969-
LO/N-1.

**ACTA FACULTATIS RERUM NATURALIUM UNIVERS-
ITATIS COMENIANAE: GENETICA.**
++ACTA FACUL. RERUM NAT. UNIV. COMENIANAE, GENET
[AFNG-A]
UNIVERZITA KOMENSKEHO (BRATISLAVA): PRIRODO-
VEDECKA FAKULTA.
BRATISLAVA  1, 1966-
CA/U-2.

**ACTA FACULTATIS RERUM NATURALIUM UNIVERSIT-
ATIS COMENIANAE: PHYSIOLOGIA PLANTARUM.**
++ACTA FACUL. RERUM NAT. UNIV. COMENIANAE,
PHYSIOL. PLANT.
UNIVERZITA KOMENSKEHO (BRATISLAVA): PRIRODO-
VEDECKA FAKULTA.
BRATISLAVA  NO.1, 1970-
CA/U-2.

**ACTA GENETICA ET STATISTICA MEDICA.**                       XXX
SUBS (1969): HUMAN HEREDITY.

**ACTA GEOBOTANICA BARCINONENSIA.**
++ACTA GEOBOT. BARCINON.
UNIVERSIDAD DE BARCELONA.
BARCELONA  1, 1964-
CA/U-1.

**ACTA GEODAETICA, GEOPHYSICA ET MONTANISTICA.**
++ACTA GEODAET. GEOPHYS. & MONTAN.
MAGYAR TUDOMANYOS AKADEMIA.
[AKADEMIAI KIADO]
BUDAPEST  1, 1966-
PAPERS IN ENGL., GER., FR., RUSS.  WITH SUMM.
LO/N-4.    LO/N13.    XS/N-1.
ISSN 0001-5679

**ACTA GEOLOGICA HISPANICA.**
++ACTA GEOL. HISPANICA.
INSTITUTO NACIONAL DE GEOLOGIA (SPAIN).
MADRID 1, 1966-
LO/N-2.
CA/U14. 8, 1973-

**ACTA GERMANICA.  ZUR SPRACHE UND DICHTUNG
DEUTSCHLANDS, OSTERREICHS UND DER SCHWEIZ.**
++ACTA GER.
SUDAFRIKANISCHEN GERMANISTENVERBANDES.
CAPE TOWN 1, 1966-
CB/U-1.    ED/N-1.    HL/U-1.    MA/U-1.

**ACTA HERPETOLOGICA JAPONICA.**                                  000
SEE (1964): HACHURUIGAKU ZASSHI.
AND (1967): HACHU RYOSEIRUIGAKU ZASSHI.

**ACTA HISTOCHEMICA ET CYTOCHEMICA.**
++ACTA HISTOCHEM. & CYTOCHEM. (JAP.)
(JAPAN SOCIETY OF HISTOCHEMISTRY & CYTO-
CHEMISTRY).
KYOTO  1, MR 1968-
S/T: OFFICIAL JOURNAL OF THE JAPAN SOCIETY ...
LO/U-2.    OX/U-8.
ISSN 0044-5991

**ACTA HISTORICA LITUANICA.**
++*ACTA HIST. LITUAN.*
LIETUVOS TSR MOKSLU AKADEMIJA ISTORIJOS.
*VILNIUS [VOL.]1, 1967-*
MONOGR. IN LITH. WITH RUSS. SUMM.
*LO/N-3.   OX/U-1.*

**ACTA INFORMATICA.**
++*ACTA INF.*
[SPRINGER]
*BERLIN &C.  1, 1971-*
Q. ENGL. & GER.
*GL/U-1.   GL/U-2.   LO/N14.   LO/U-2.   RE/U-1.   SH/U-1.*
*SW/U-1.   XS/R10.*
*CB/U-1.  4, 1974-*
*ISSN 0001-5903*

**ACTA INSTITUTI ROMANI FINLANDIAE.**
++*ACTA INST. ROM. FINL.*
INSTITUTUM ROMANUM FINLANDIAE.
*HELSINKI  1, 1963-*
MONOGR.  VOL.1 ISSUED IN 2 PARTS.  INST.
LOCATED IN ROME.
*LO/N-1.*
*MA/U-1.  1- 2(1-3).*

**ACTA JUGOSLAVIAE HISTORICA.**
++*ACTA JUGOSL. HIST.*
SAVEZ DRUSTAVA ISTORICARA JUGOSLAVIJE.
*BELGRADE  1, 1970-*
ENGL. OR FR.
*CA/U-1.   OX/U-1.*

**ACTA NEUROBIOLOGIAE EXPERIMENTALIS.**        XXX
++*ACTA NEUROBIOL. EXP.*
POLSKA AKADEMIA NAUK: INSTYTUT BIOLOGII
DOSWIADCZALNEJ IM. N. NENCKIEGO.
[POLSKIE WYDAWNICTWA NAUKOWE]
*WARSAW 30, 1970-*
PREV:  ACTA BIOLOGIAE EXPERIMENTALIS FROM 1,
1928- 29, 1969.
*DB/S-1.   GL/U-1.   LO/N14.*

**ACTA NEUROVEGETATIVA: SUPPLEMENTUM.**        XXX
SUBS (1969): JOURNAL OF NEURO-VISCERAL RELA-
TIONS: SUPPLEMENTUM.

**ACTA PARASITOLOGICA IUGOSLAVICA.**
++*ACTA PARASITOL. IUGOSL.*
DRUSTVO PARAZITOLOGA JUGOSLAVIJE.
*ZABREB  1, 1970-*
2/A.
*LO/N-2.   LO/N13.*

**ACTA PHYSICA POLONICA: SERIES A: GENERAL
PHYSICS, SOLID STATE PHYSICS, APPLIED PHYSICS.**
++*ACTA PHYS. POLON., A.*
POLSKA AKADEMIA NAUK: INSTYTUT FIZYKI.
*WARSAW A37(1), 1970-*
SPONS. BODY ALSO: POLSKIE TOWARZYSTWO FIZYCZNE
ISSUED AS SINGLE TITLE FROM 1, 1932- THEN
FROM 1970 CONTINUED IN TWO SERIES.  SER. A
CONTINUES NUMBERING OF ORIGINAL.
*ED/U-1.   GL/U-2.   LO/N-4.   LO/N14.   XS/R10.*

**ACTA PHYSICA POLONICA: B: ELEMENTARY PARTICLE
PHYSICS, NUCLEAR PHYSICS, THEORY OF RELAT-
IVITY, FIELD THEORY.**                          XXX
++*ACTA PHYS. POL., B.*
POLSKA AKADEMIA NAUK: INSTYTUT FIZYKI.
*WARSAW  B1, JA/MR 1970-*
SPONS. BODY ALSO POLSKIE TOWARZYSTWO FIZYCZNE.
FROM 1, 1932- ISSUED AS A SINGLE TITLE THEN
FROM 1970 CONTINUED IN TWO SERIES.
*CB/U-1.   GL/U-1.   GL/U-2.   LO/N-4.   LO/N14.   LO/U-2.*
*SH/U-1.*
*SF/U-1.  B5, 1974-*

**ACTA PHYTOTAXONOMICA BARCINONENSIA.**
++*ACTA PHYTOTAXON. BARCINON.*
UNIVERSIDAD DE BARCELONA.
*BARCELONA   1, 1968-*
ISSUED BY THE BODY'S FACULTAD DE CIENCIAS:
DEPARTAMENTO DE BOTANICA.
*CA/U-7.   LO/N-2.*

**ACTA RADIOBOTANIKA ET GENETIKA.**
++*ACTA RADIOBOT. & GENET.*
HOSHASEN IKUSHUJU.
*IBARAKI  1, AG 1967-*
*CA/U11.*

**ACTA REGIAE SOCIETATIS SCIENTIARUM ET LITTER-
ARUM GOTHOBURGENSIS: BOTANICA.**
++*ACTA R. SOC. SCI. & LITT. GOTHOBURG., BOT.*
GOTEBORGS KUNGLIGA VETENSKAPS- OCH VITTERHETS-
SAMHALLE.
*GOTEBORG  1, 1972-*
*CA/U-2.   DB/S-1.   LO/N-2.   LO/N13.*

**ACTA REGIAE SOCIETATIS SCIENTIARUM ET LITTER-
ARUM GOTHOBURGENSIS: GEOPHYSICA.**
++*ACTA REGIAE SOC. SCI. & LITT. GOTHOBURG.,*
*GEOPHYS.*
GOTEBORGS KUNGLIGA VETENSKAPS-OCH VITTERHETS-
SAMHALLE.
*GOTEBORG  1, 1968-*
*AD/U-1.   CA/U-2.   DB/S-1.   GL/U-1.   LO/N-2.   LO/N13.*
*OX/U-8.*

**ACTA REGIAE SOCIETATIS SCIENTIARUM ET LITTER-
ARUM GOTHOBURGENSIS: HUMANIORA.**
++*ACTA REGIAE SOC. SCI. & LITT. GOTHOBURG.,*
*HUMANIORA.*
GOTEBORGS KUNGLIGA VETENSKAPS-OCH VITTERHETS
SAMHALLE.
*GOTEBORG  NO.1, 1967-*
*CA/U-1.   LO/N-1.   LO/U-2.*

**ACTA RHEUMATOLOGICA SCANDINAVICA.**          XXX
SUBS (1972): SCANDINAVIAN JOURNAL OF
RHEUMATOLOGY.

**ACTA SCIENTIARUM LITTERARUMQUE, UNIVERSITAS
JAGELLONICA CRACOVIENSIS: SCHEDAE ...[VARIOUS
SERIES].**                                      000
SEE: ZESZYTY NAUKOWE UNIWERSYTETU JAGIELLON-
SKIEGO: PRACE ...[VARIOUS SERIES].

**ACTA SOCIETATIS LINGUISTICAE EUROPAEAE.**     000
SEE: FOLIA LINGUISTICA.

**ACTA SOCIOLOGICA, CENTRO DE ESTUDIOS DEL DES-
ARROLLO, UNIVERSIDAD NACIONAL AUTONOMA DE
MEXICO.  SERIE PROMOCION SOCIAL.**
++*ACTA SOCIOL. CENT. ESTUD. DESARROLLO UNIV.*
*NAC. AUTON. MEX., PROMOC. SOC.*
*MEXICO  1, 1969-*
*OX/U-1.*

**ACTA SOCIO-MEDICA SCANDINAVICA.**            XXX
++*ACTA SOCIO-MED. SCAND.*
NORDISK SOCIALMEDICINSK FOERENING.
*STOCKHOLM  1, 1969- 4, 1972.*
SUBS: SCANDINAVIAN JOURNAL OF SOCIAL MEDICINE.
3/A.  ENGL., FR. & GER.
*CO/U-1.*
*SH/U-1.  1971-*
*ISSN 0044-6041*

**ACTA SYMBOLICA.**
++*ACTA SYMB.*
UNIVERSITY OF AKRON: DEPARTMENT OF SPEECH
PATHOLOGY & AUDIOLOGY.
*AKRON, OHIO  1(1), 1970-*
2/A.  S/T: AN INTERDISCIPLINARY JOURNAL OF
THEORY & RESEARCH ON SYMBOLIC PROCESSES,
COMMUNICATION DISORDERS, & BEHAVIORAL SCIENCE.
*LO/N-1.  2(1), 1971-*

**ACTA UNIVERSITATIS BERGENSIS: SERIES MEDICA:
NS.**
++*ACTA UNIV. BERGENSIS, MED., NS.*
[NORWEGIAN UNIV. P.]
*BERGEN  NO.1, 1967-*
*AB/U-1.   NW/U-1.*

**ACTA UNIVERSITATIS CAROLINE: IURIDICA:
MONOGRAPHIA.**
++*ACTA UNIV. CAROL., IURIDICA, MONOGR.*
KARLOVA UNIVERSITA V PRAZE.
*PRAGUE  1, 1963-*
ENGL. & FR. SUMM. & SOME ARTICLES.
*CA/U-1.   LO/U-3.   OX/U-1.*

**ACTA UNIVERSITATIS CAROLINAE; PHILOLOGICA:
GERMANISTICA PRAGENSIA.**
++*ACTA UNIV. CAROL., PHILOL., GER. PRAG.*
KARLOVA UNIVERSITA V PRAZE.
*PRAGUE  [NO.]1, 1960-*
ALSO NUMBERED AS PART OF MAIN SERIES OF ACTA,
NO.1 = 3.  ISSUED BY THE FILOSOFICKA FAKULTA
(OF THE UNIV.)
*LO/N-3.  NO.1, 1960.*

**ACTA UNIVERSITATIS CAROLINAE; PHILOLOGICA; MONOGRAPHIA.**
+ +ACTA UNIV. CAROL., PHILOL., MONOGR.
KARLOVA UNIVERSITA V PRAZE.
 PRAGUE   NO.1, 1961-
 SUMM. IN VARIOUS LANGS.
 AD/U-1.    CA/U-1.    LO/N-1.
 LO/N-3. NOS. 10 & 12, 1966.
 LO/U15.  1969- 1971.
 SA/U-1.  1969- 1971.

**ACTA UNIVERSITATIS CAROLINAE:  PHILOSOPHICA ET HISTORICA:  MONOGRAPHIAE.**
+ +ACTA UNIV. CAROLINAE, PHIL. & HIST., MONOGR.
KARLOVA UNIVERSITA V PRAZE.
 PRAGUE  1, 1962-
 GER. & RUSS. SUMM.
 LO/U-3.

**ACTA UNIVERSITATIS PALACKIANAE OLOMUCENSIS: HISTORICA.**                                        XXX
+ +ACTA UNIV. PALACKI. OLOMUC., HIST.
PALACKEHO, UNIVERSITA: FILOSOFICKA FAKULTA.
 OLOMOUC  1, 1960-
 RUSS., GER. OR ENGL. SUMM.  ALSO CALLED:
 SBORNIK PRACI HISTORICKYCH.  PREV: HISTORIE,
 SBORNIK VYSOKA SKOLA PEDAGOGICKA V OLOMOUCI
 FROM 1, 1954- 6, 1959.
 BL/U-1.

**ACTA UNIVERSITATIS STOCKHOLMIENSIS: STOCKHOLM SLAVIC STUDIES.**                                   000
 SEE: STOCKHOLM SLAVIC STUDIES.

**ACTA UNIVERSITATIS STOCKHOLMIENSIS: STOCKHOLM STUDIES IN LINGUISTICS.**                           000
 SEE: STOCKHOLM STUDIES IN LINGUISTICS.

**ACTA UNIVERSITATIS STOCKHOLMIENSIS:  STOCKHOLM THEATRICAL HISTORY.**                              000
 SEE: STOCKHOLM STUDIES IN THEATRICAL HISTORY.

**ACTA UNIVERSITATIS WRATISLAVENSIS.**                                                             XXX
+ +ACTA UNIV. WRATISLAV.
UNIWERSYTET WROCLAWSKI.
 WROCLAW &C.  NO.1, JE 1962-
 PREV: ZESZYTY NAUKOWE UNIWERSYTETU WROCLAW-
 SKIEGO; SERIA A: NAUKI SPOLECZNE., (&) SERIA
 B: NAUKI PRZYRODNICZE.  INDIVIDUAL ISSUES ARE
 ALSO PARTS OF OTHER SERIES.
 LO/N13.    LO/U-1.    OX/U-1.

**ACTES DU PREMIER CONGRES INTERNATIONAL DES ETUDES BALKANIQUES ET SUD-EST EUROPEENNES.**
+ +ACTES PREMIER CONGR. INT. ETUD. BALKAN. & SUD-EST EUR.
ASSOCIATION INTERNATIONALE DES ETUDES BALKANIQ-
UES ET SUD-EST EUROPEENNES.
 SOFIA  1, 1967-
 OX/U-1.

**ACTINIDES REVIEWS.**                                                                             XXX
+ +ACTINIDES REV. [ACTN-A]
[ELSEVIER]
 AMSTERDAM  1, 1967- 1971.//
 LO/N14.

**ACTION.  AN ENGLISH-ARABIC NEWSPAPER.**
[ARABIC ENGLISH NEWSPAPER, INC.]
 NEW YORK  1, MY 1969-
 SO/U-1.

**ACTION WORLD.**
 LONDON  NO.1, [OC 1972]-
 ED/N-1.

**ACTIVATED CARBON ABSTRACTS.**                                                                    XXX
+ +ACT. CARBON ABSTR.
WITCO CHEMICAL CO.
[LITTLE INC.]
 [NEW YORK]  1, 1967- 4(1), 1970. //
 LO/N14.

**ACTIVITIES OF OECD.**
+ +ACT. OECD.
 PARIS  1970-
 REPORT BY THE SECRETARY GENERAL.
 LO/N-1.    OX/U17.    RE/U-1.
 LO/U12.  1972-

**ACTUALITES HEMATOLOGIQUES.**
+ +ACTUAL. HEMATOL.
 [MASSON]
 PARIS  1, 1967-
 LO/N13.    OX/U-8.

**ACTUALITES DE PHYSIOLOGIE PATHOLOGIQUE.**
+ +ACTUAL. PHYSIOL. PATHOL. (FR.).
[MASSON]
 PARIS  1, 1966-
 LO/N13.

**ACTUALITES DE PHYTOCHIMIE FONDAMENTALE.**
+ +ACTUAL. PHYTOCHIM. FONDAM.
[MASSON]
 PARIS  1, 1964-
 LO/N13.

**AD LIB.  SOUTHAMPTON UNIVERSITY LIBRARY INFORMATION BULLETIN.**
 SOUTHAMPTON  1(1), N 1969-
 SO/U-1.

**A.D.A.S.  QUARTERLY REVIEW.**                                                                    XXX
AGRICULTURAL DEVELOPMENT & ADVISORY SERVICE                                                        XXX
(GB).
 LONDON  NO.1, 1971-
 PREV: N.A.A.S. QUARTERLY REVIEW FROM NO.1,
 1948- 91, 1971.
 BH/P-1.    BH/U-1.    BN/U-2.    ED/N-1.    GL/U-1.    LO/N-6.
 LO/N14.    SO/U-1.
 ISSN 0027-5670

**ADMINISTRATION. QUARTERLY REVIEW OF THE INST-ITUTE OF ADMINISTRATION, UNIVERSITY OF IFE.**
 IBADAN  1, 1966-
 Q.
 OX/U-9.
 HL/U-1.  2, 1968-                    LO/N17.  3, 1968-
 LO/U-3.* 1(3), 1967-

**ADMINISTRATIVE SCIENCE REVIEW.**
+ +ADM. SCI. REV.
NATIONAL INSTITUTE OF PUBLIC ADMINISTRATION
(PAKISTAN).
 DACCA  1(1), MR 1967-
 Q.
 LO/U-8.  3(2), 1969-
 ISSN 0001-8406

**ADOLESCENCE.  AN INTERNATIONAL QUARTERLY ...**
[LIBRA PUBLISHERS]
 NEW YORK  1(1), SPRING 1966-
 MA/U-1.  3(9), 1968-                 OX/U-8.  1(5), 1967-
 ISSN 0001-8449

**ADPA.  AUTOMATIC DATA PROCESSING FOR ARCHIVAL MANAGEMENT.**
INTERNATIONAL COUNCIL ON ARCHIVES.
 OTTAWA  1(1), 1972-
 ENGL. & FR.
 ED/N-1.    LO/N12.    LO/U-1.    OX/U-1.
 LO/N-4.  1(1), 1972.

**ADVANCE.**
CHRISTIAN ENDEAVOUR UNION.
 WORCESTER  1, 1971-
 ED/N-1.    OX/U-1.

**ADVANCED STUDIES IN PURE MATHEMATICS.**
+ +ADV. STUD. PURE MATH.
 PARIS &C.  1, 1968-
 OX/U-8.

**ADVANCED TECHNOLOGY/LIBRARIES.**                                                                 XXX
+ +ADV. TECHNOL./LIBR.
(UNITED STATES) DEPARTMENT OF THE ARMY: OFFICE
OF THE CHIEF OF ENGINEERS.
 WHITE PLAINS, N.Y.  1, 1972-
 MON. PREV: MICROGRAPHICS FROM 1, 1970-
 5(10), 1972.
 GL/U-2.    LO/U-1.
 ISSN 0044-636X

**ADVANCEMENT OF SCIENCE.**                                                                        XXX
+ +ADV. SCI. [ADSC-A]
BRITISH ASSOCIATION FOR THE ADVANCEMENT OF
SCIENCE.
 LONDON  1, 1939- 27(134), 1971.//
 PREV: REPORT OF THE ANNUAL MEETING OF THE
 BRITISH ASSOCIATION FOR THE ADVANCEMENT OF
 SCIENCE FROM 1932- 1938.
 BR/U-1.    ED/N-1.    GL/U-1.    LC/U-1.    LO/N14.    LO/U-2.
 LO/U-3.
 ISSN 0001-866X

**ADVANCES IN ACTIVATION ANALYSIS.**
+ +ADV. ACTIV. ANAL.
[ACADEMIC P.]
 LONDON  1, 1969-
 AB/U-1.    ED/N-1.    GL/U-1.    LO/N-4.    LO/S-3.    LO/U12.
 XS/C-2.    XS/R10.

**ADVANCES IN AEROSOL PHYSICS.**
+ +ADV. AEROSOL PHYS.
[ISRAEL PROGRAM FOR SCIENTIFIC TRANSLATIONS]
*JERUSALEM; LONDON NO.1, 1969(1971)-*
ENGL. LANG. TRANSL. OF: FIZIKA AERODISPERSNYKH
SISTEM. DATING & NUMBERING OF ISSUES FOLLOW
ORIGINAL.
*LO/N14.*
*CA/U-1. NO.5, 1973-*          *SO/U-1. NO.5, 1973- ˙*

**ADVANCES IN ALICYCLIC CHEMISTRY: SUPPLEMENT.**
+ +ADV. ALICYCL. CHEM., SUPPL.
[ACADEMIC PRESS]
*NEW YORK &C [NO.]1, 1968-*
*BH/U-1.    LO/N14.    LO/U20.*

**ADVANCES IN ANIMAL PHYSIOLOGY & ANIMAL
NUTRITION.**                                                                    000
  SEE: FORTSCHRITTE IN DER TIERPHYSIOLOGIE UND
  TIERENAHRUNG.

**ADVANCES IN APPLIED MICROBIOLOGY: SUPPLEMENT.**
+ +ADV. APPL. MICROBIOL., SUPPL.
[ACADEMIC PRESS]
*NEW YORK &C [NO.]1, 1968-*
*LO/N-4.    LO/N14.    LV/U-1.*

**ADVANCES IN APPLIED PROBABILITY.**
+ +ADV. APPL. PROBAB.
APPLIED PROBABILITY TRUST.
*[SHEFFIELD] 1, 1969-*
*BR/U-3.    CB/U-1.    HL/U-1.    LO/N-4.    LO/N14.    LO/U-3.*
*LO/U12.    LO/U13.    OX/U16.    SH/U-1.    SW/U-1.*
*NW/U-1. 3, 1971-*
*ISSN 0001-8678*

**ADVANCES IN BIOCHEMICAL ENGINEERING.**
+ +ADV. BIOCHEM. ENG.
[SPRINGER]
*BERLIN 1, 1971-*
*ED/N-1.    HL/U-1.    LO/N-2.    LO/N14.    LO/U-2.*
*ISSN 0065-2210*

**ADVANCES IN BIOCHEMICAL PSYCHOPHARMACOLOGY.**
+ +ADV. BIOCHEM. PSYCHOPHARMACOL.
[RAVEN P.]
*NEW YORK 1, 1969-*
*GL/U-2.    HL/U-1.    LO/N13.    SO/U-1.    XS/C-2.*
*OX/U-8. 2, 1970-*
*ISSN 0065-2229*

**ADVANCES IN BIOMEDICAL ENGINEERING.**
+ +ADV. BIOMED. ENG.
[ACADEMIC P.]
*LONDON &C. 1, 1971-*
*GL/U-2.    LO/N14.    LO/U-2.    NW/U-1.    SF/U-1.    SW/U-1.*

**ADVANCES IN BIOMEDICAL ENGINEERING & MEDICAL
PHYSICS.**
+ +ADV. BIOMED. ENG. & MED. PHYS.
[INTERSCIENCE]
*LONDON &C 1, 1968-*
*GL/U-2.    LO/N14.    SO/U-1.*

**ADVANCES IN BIOPHYSICS.**
+ +ADV. BIOPHYS.
BIOPHYSICAL SOCIETY OF JAPAN.
[UNIV. OF TOKYO P.]
*TOKYO & C. 1, 1970-*
ANNU.
*BT/U-1.    CA/U-1.    GL/U-1.    LD/U-1.    LO/N-2.    LO/N-4.*
*LO/N13.    LO/U-2.    NW/U-1.    SH/U-1.*
*ISSN 0065-227X*

**ADVANCES IN CARBOHYDRATE CHEMISTRY & BIOCHEM-
ISTRY.˙**
+ +ADV. CARBOHYD. CHEM. & BIOCHEM.
[ACADEMIC P]
*NEW YORK &C. 1, 1945-*
TITLE EXPANDED FROM ADVANCES IN CARBOHYDRATE
CHEMISTRY WITH 24, 1969.
*HL/U-1.    LO/N14.*
*ISSN 0065-2318*

**ADVANCES IN CATALYSIS.**                                                   XXX
+ +ADV. CATAL.
[ACADEMIC P.]
*NEW YORK; LONDON 22, 1972-*
PREV: ADVANCES IN CATALYSIS & RELATED SUBJECTS
FROM 1, 1948- 21, 1970.
*LO/N14.*

**ADVANCES IN CATALYSIS & RELATED SUBJECTS.**              XXX
  SUBS (1972): ADVANCES IN CATALYSIS.

**ADVANCES IN CELL BIOLOGY.**
+ +ADV. CELL BIOL.
[NORTH-HOLLAND]
*AMSTERDAM 1, 1970-*
*BT/U-1.    CA/U-1.    CA/U-6.    LO/N-2.    LO/N13.    LO/U-2.*
*OX/U-1.    SH/C-5.    SH/U-1.    SO/U-1.    XS/C-2    XS/C-2.*
*ISSN 0065-2369*

**ADVANCES IN CELL & MOLECULAR BIOLOGY.**
+ +ADV. CELL & MOL. BIOL.
[ACADEMIC P.]
*NEW YORK & LONDON 1, 1971-*
*BL/U-1.    CA/U-1.    CA/U-2.    CA/U-6.    CA/U-7. ˙    DN/U-1.*
*ED/N-1.    GL/U-1.    LD/U-1.    LO/M11.    LO/N-2.    LO/N13.*
*NW/U-1.    SO/U-1.*
*ISSN 0065-2350*

**ADVANCES IN CHEMORECEPTION.**
+ +ADV. CHEMORECEPT.
[APPLETON-CENTURY-CROFTS]
*NEW YORK 1, 1970-*
*LO/N-2.    MA/U-1.*

**ADVANCES IN CONTACT LENSES.**                                           XXX
+ +ADV. CONTACT LENSES.
EXCERPTA MEDICA FOUNDATION.
*AMSTERDAM; NEW YORK 1, 1970- 2, 1971.//*
PUBL. FOR NATIONAL EYE RESEARCH FOUNDATION
(US).
*LO/N14.*
*BH/U-3. 2, 1971.*

**ADVANCES IN CORROSION SCIENCE & TECHNOLOGY.**
+ +ADV. CORROS. SCI. & TECHNOL.
[PLENUM P.]
*NEW YORK &C. 1, 1970-*
*LO/N-4.    LO/N14.    LO/T-3.    XS/T-7.*
*BL/U-1. 4, 1974-*
*ISSN 0065-2474*

**ADVANCES IN CYCLIC NUCLEOTIDE RESEARCH.**
+ +ADV. CYCLIC NUCLEOTIDE RES.
[RAVEN P.]
*NEW YORK 1, 1972-*
*CA/U-6.    GL/U-1.    LO/N13.    OX/U-8.*
*ISSN 0084-5930*

**ADVANCES IN CYTOPHARMACOLOGY.**
+ +ADV. CYTOPHARMACOL.
[NORTH-HOLLAND]
*AMSTERDAM 1, 1971-*
*LO/U-2.*
*ISSN 0084-5949*

**ADVANCES IN EDUCATIONAL PSYCHOLOGY.**
+ +ADV. EDUC. PSYCHOL.
[UNIVERSITY OF LONDON P.]
*LONDON 1, 1972-*
*GL/U-1.    SA/U-1.    SW/U-1.*
*ISSN 0306-3720*

**ADVANCES IN ENVIRONMENTAL SCIENCES & TECHNOLOGY.**
+ +ADV. ENVIRON. SCI. & TECHNOL.
[WILEY-INTERSCIENCE]
*NEW YORK 1, 1969-*
VOL.1 ENTITLED: ADVANCES IN ENVIRONMENTAL
SCIENCES.
*GL/U-1.    GL/U-2.    LD/U-1.    LO/N-2.    LO/N-4.    LO/N13.*
*LO/U-2.    MA/U-1.    NW/U-1.    SF/U-1.    XS/R10.*
*XW/T-1.*
*RE/U-1. 4, 1974-*
*ISSN 0065-2563*

**ADVANCES IN HIGH TEMPERATURE CHEMISTRY.**
+ +ADV. HIGH TEMP. CHEM.
[ACADEMIC PRESS]
*NEW YORK &C 1, 1967-*
*GL/U-2.    LD/U-1.    MA/U-1.    XS/C-2.*

**ADVANCES IN HUMAN GENETICS. (NEW YORK)**
+ +ADV. HUM. GENET. (N.Y.)
[PLENUM]
*NEW YORK 1, 1970-*
*BL/U-1.    GL/U-1.    LD/U-1.    LO/U-2.    NW/U-1.    SO/U-1.*
*XS/C-2.*

**ADVANCES IN HUMAN GENETICS. (STUTTGART).**                000
  SEE: FORTSCHRITTE DER ALLGEMEINEN UND KLINIS-
  CHEN HUMANGENETIK.

**ADVANCES IN INFORMATION SYSTEMS SCIENCE.**
+ +ADV. INF. SYST. SCI.
[PLENUM PRESS]
*NEW YORK 1, 1969-*
*CB/U-1.    LO/N14.    LO/U28.    NW/U-1.    SH/C-5.*
*SH/U-1.*
*DR/U-1. 1, 1969.*
*GL/U-1. 4, 1972.*

**ADVANCES IN LIBRARIANSHIP.**
++ADV. LIBR.
[ACADEMIC P.]
NEW YORK 1, 1970-
BH/U-1.    BT/U-1.    CV/C-1.    DB/U-2.    DB/U-2.    ED/N-1.
EX/U-1.    LD/U-1.    LN/U-2.    LO/N-2.    LO/N-3.    LO/N-4.
LO/N14.    LO/U-1.    LO/U-4.    LO/U20.    MA/U-1.    SH/U-1.
SO/U-1.    XS/C-2.

**ADVANCES IN MACROMOLECULAR CHEMISTRY.**
++ADV. MACROMOL. CHEM.
[ACADEMIC PRESS]
LONDON &C 1, 1968-
BH/U-1.    CA/U-1.    CB/U-1.    ED/N-1.    GL/U-1.    GL/U-2.
LO/N-4.    LO/N14.    LO/S-3.    LO/U22.    LV/P-1.    MA/U-1.
OX/U-8.
XS/C-2. 1, 1968.

**ADVANCES IN MENTAL SCIENCE.**
++ADV. MENT. SCI.
[UNIV. TEXAS P.]
AUSTIN, TEX. &C. 1, 1969-
LO/N-1.
ISSN 0572-3132

**ADVANCES IN METABOLIC DISORDERS: SUPPLEMENT.**
++ADV. METAB. DISORD., SUPPL.
[ACADEMIC P.]
NEW YORK 1, 1970-
LO/U20.

**ADVANCES IN MICROBIOLOGY OF THE SEA.**    XXX
++ADV. MICROBIOL. SEA.
LONDON 1, 1968.//
CR/U-1.    DB/U-2.    DN/U-1.    ED/N-1.    GL/U-1.    HL/U-1.
LO/C-4.    LO/N13.    LO/U-2.    LO/U-4.    MA/U-1.    MA/U-1.
SO/U-1.    SW/U-1.    XS/C-2.

**ADVANCES IN MICROCIRCULATION.**
++ADV. MICROCIRC.
[S. KARGER]
BASLE &C. 1, 1968-
NW/U-1.    OX/U-8.

**ADVANCES IN MICROWAVES: SUPPLEMENT.**
++ADV. MICROWAVES, SUPPL.
[ACADEMIC P.]
NEW YORK 1, 1970-
LO/N-4.    LO/N13.    LO/U20.

**ADVANCES IN MOLECULAR RELAXATION PROCESSES.**
++ADV. MOL. RELAX. PROCESSES.
[ELSEVIER]
AMSTERDAM 1(1), N 1967-
S/T: AN INTERNATIONAL JOURNAL.
GL/U-1.    LO/N14.    LO/U12.    XS/R10.
CB/U-1. 2, 1970-
ISSN 0001-8716

**ADVANCES IN MOLTEN SALT CHEMISTRY.**
++ADV. MOLTEN SALT CHEM.
[PLENUM P.]
NEW YORK; LONDON 1, 1971-
BH/U-3.    LO/N14.    LO/S-3.    OX/U-8.    SO/U-1.    SW/U-1.
XS/R10.
ISSN 0065-2954

**ADVANCES IN NEPHROLOGY FROM THE NECKER HOSPITAL.**
++ADV. NEPHROL. NECKER HOSP.
[YEAR BOOK MEDICAL PUBL.]
CHICAGO 1, 1971-
LO/N13.    OX/U-8.
ISSN 0084-5957

**ADVANCES IN NUCLEAR PHYSICS.**
++ADV. NUCL. PHYS.
[PLENUM PRESS]
NEW YORK &C 1, 1968-
BH/U-1.    LO/C-4.    LO/N14.    LO/U-2.    LO/U20.    SH/U-1.
SO/U-1.

**ADVANCES IN OBSTETRICS & GYNECOLOGY.**
++ADV. OBSTET. & GYNECOL.
[WILLIAMS & WILKINS]
BALTIMORE 1, 1967-
BL/U-1.    BN/U-2.    OX/U-8.

**ADVANCES IN PARTICLE PHYSICS.**    XXX
++ADV. PARTIC. PHYS.
[INTERSCIENCE]
NEW YORK &C. 1- 2, 1968.//
BH/U-1.    CB/U-1.    LD/U-1.    LO/C-4.    LO/N14.    LO/U-2.
LV/P-1.    LV/U-1.    MA/U-1.    SO/U-1.    XS/R10.

**ADVANCES IN PHARMACOLOGY & CHEMOTHERAPY.**    XXX
++ADV. PHARMACOL. & CHEMOTHER.
[ACADEMIC P.]
NEW YORK &C. 7, 1969-
INCORP: ADVANCES IN PHARMACOLOGY FROM 1, 1962
- 6, 1968, OF WHICH THE VOL. NUMBERING IS RE-
TAINED; & ADVANCES IN CHEMOTHERAPY FROM 1,
1964- 3, 1968.
GL/U-1.    HL/U-1.    LO/M-1.    LO/N14.    LO/U-2.    SO/U-1.
XS/C-2.

**ADVANCES IN PLASMA PHYSICS.**
++ADV. PLASMA PHYS.
NEW YORK &C 1, 1968-
BH/U-1.    ED/N-1.    GL/U-2.    LO/N-4.    LO/U22.    OX/U-8.
SO/U-1.
HL/U-1. 1, 1968- 5, 1974.

**ADVANCES IN PRIMATOLOGY.**
++ADV. PRIMATOL.
[APPLETON-CENTURY-CROFTS]
NEW YORK 1, 1970-
LO/N-2.    MA/U-1.    OX/U-8.
ISSN 0587-4416

**ADVANCES IN PROBABILITY & RELATED TOPICS.**
++ADV. PROBAB. & RELAT. TOP.
[DEKKER]
NEW YORK 1, 1971- [2, 1970]. //
VOL.2 PUB. 1970.
HL/U-1.    LO/N14.    LO/U28.    MA/U-1.    NW/U-1.
OX/U16.    XS/C-2.
ISSN 0065-3217

**ADVANCES IN PSYCHOBIOLOGY.**
++ADV. PSYCHOBIOL.
[WILEY-INTERSCIENCE]
NEW YORK &C. 1, 1972-
AD/U-1.    BL/U-1.    CA/U-1.    DB/U-2.    ED/N-1.    LO/N14.
RE/U-1.    SH/U-1.
ISSN 0065-3241

**ADVANCES IN PSYCHOLOGICAL ASSESSMENT.**
++ADV. PSYCHOL. ASSESS.
[SCIENCE & BEHAVIOR BOOKS INC.]
PALO ALTO 1, 1968-
LD/U-1.    LO/U-2.    SH/U-1.    SO/U-1.
OX/U-8. 1, 1970-
BT/U-1. 1, 1968.
ISSN 0065-325X

**ADVANCES IN QUANTUM ELECTRONICS.**
++ADV. QUANTUM ELECTRON.
[ACADEMIC P.]
LONDON &C. 1, 1970-
CB/U-1.    DN/U-1.    GL/U-1.    HL/U-1.    LD/U-1.    LO/N-4.
LO/N14.    SO/U-1.    XS/R10.    XS/R10.
ISSN 0065-3292

**ADVANCES IN RADIATION CHEMISTRY.**
++ADV. RADIAT. CHEM.
[WILEY-INTERSCIENCE]
NEW YORK &C. 1, 1969-
BH/U-1.    ED/N-1.    GL/U-1.    LD/U-1.    LO/N-4.    LO/N14.
LO/S-3.    LO/U12.    OX/U-1.    SF/U-1.    XS/C-2.

**ADVANCES IN RAMAN SPECTROSCOPY.**
++ADV. RAMAN SPECTROSC.
[HEYDEN]
LONDON 1, 1973-
CA/U-1.    LO/N14.    LO/U-2.

**ADVANCES IN STEROID BIOCHEMISTRY & PHARMACOLOGY.**
++ADV. STEROID BIOCHEM. & PHARMACOL.
[ACADEMIC P.]
LONDON 1, 1970-
BH/U-3.    ED/N-1.    GL/U-1.    LD/U-1.    LO/N13.    LO/S-3.
LO/U-2.    LO/U13.    LO/U28.    OX/U-8.    SH/U-1.    XS/C-2.
HL/U-1. 1 1970.
ISSN 0065-339X

**ADVANCES IN URETHANE SCIENCE & TECHNOLOGY.**
++ADV. URETHANE SCI. & TECHNOL.
[TECHNOMIC]
STAMFORD, CONN. 1, 1971-
LO/N14.
ISSN 0044-6378

**ADVANCES IN VETERINARY SCIENCE.**    XXX
SUBS (1969): ADVANCES IN VETERINARY SCIENCE &
COMPARATIVE MEDICINE.

**ADVANCES IN VETERINARY SCIENCE & COMPARATIVE MEDICINE.** XXX
+ +ADV. VET. SCI. & COMP. MED.
*NEW YORK 13, 1969-*
PREV: ADVANCES IN VETERINARY SCIENCE FROM 1, 1953- 12, 1968.
*BN/U-2.*
*ISSN 0065-3519*

**ADVERSE DRUG REACTION BULLETIN.**
+ +ADVERSE DRUG REACT. BULL.
ORGANISATION FOR POSTGRADUATE MEDICAL EDUCATION: NEWCASTLE REGION.
*NEWCASTLE UPON TYNE NO.1, N 1966-*
*BL/U-1.   CR/M-1.   LD/U-1.   NW/U-1.*
*AD/U-1. NO.26, 1971-   BH/U-3. NO.26, 1971-*
*ED/N-1. NO.28, 1971-   GL/U-1. NO.14, 1969-*
*LO/M-1. NO.14, 1969-   SO/U-1. NO.31, 1971-*
*ISSN 0044-6394*

**ADVERSE REACTIONS TITLES.**
+ +ADVERSE REACT. TITLES.
EXCERPTA MEDICA FOUNDATION.
*AMSTERDAM &C. 1, 1966-*
MON.
*OX/U-8. 5(1), 1970-*
*ISSN 0001-8848*

**ADVOCATE. JOURNAL OF THE LAW STUDENTS ...**
UNIVERSITY OF IFE: LAW STUDENTS SOCIETY.
*ILE-IFE 1, 1968-*
*BL/U-1.   OX/U15.*

**A.E.I. DISCUSSION PAPER.**
+ +A.E.I. DISCUSS. PAP.
UNIVERSITY OF OXFORD: INSTITUTE OF AGRICULTURAL ECONOMICS.
*OXFORD NO.1, 1971-*
*OX/U-1.*

**AEQUATIONES MATHEMATICAE.**
+ +AEQUAT. MATH.
UNIVERSITY OF WATERLOO (ONTARIO).
[BIRKHAUSER VERLAG]
*BASEL 1(1/2), 1968-*
PAPERS IN ENGL., FR., GER., ITAL., RUSS.
*BR/U-3.   LO/N-4.   LO/N14.   LO/U-2.   OX/U-8.   SO/U-1.*
*SW/U-1.*
*GL/U-1.*
*ISSN 0001-9054*

**AERONAUTICAL JOURNAL.** XXX
+ +AERONAUT. J. [AENJ-A]
ROYAL AERONAUTICAL SOCIETY.
*LONDON 72(685), JA 1968-*
PREV: JOURNAL, ROYAL ... FROM 27(145), 1923- 71, 1967.
*BH/P-1.   BL/U-1.   HL/U-1.   LO/U13.   RE/U-1.*
*ISSN 0001-9240*

**AEROPLANE MONTHLY.**
+ +AEROPL. MON.]
[IPC TRANSPORT P.]
*LONDON 1(1), MY 1973-*
*CA/U-1.   ED/N-1.   OX/U-1.*

**AEROSPACE.**
ROYAL AERONAUTICAL SOCIETY.
*LONDON S 1969-*
M.
*LO/U-1. AP 1970-*
*ISSN 0001-933X*

**AEROSPACE INTERNATIONAL.**
+ +AEROSP. INT.
AIR FORCE ASSOCIATION.
*WASHINGTON, DC 2(11), N 1966-*
PREV: AIR FORCE/SPACE DIGEST INTERNATIONAL., 1(1), 1965- 2(10), 1966.
*BR/U-3.*
*BL/U-1. 3,1967-*
*ISSN 0001-9372*

**AEROSPACE REVIEW.**
+ +AEROSP. REV.
[TREVOR-HOBBS LTD.]
*LONDON 1(1), N 1970-*
*ED/N-1.   LO/N14.   OX/U-1.*
*ISSN 0015-4865*

**AEROSPAZIO.** XXX
[EDITORIALE VELOCITA SRL]
*BOLOGNA 1, 1967- 5, 1971.*
*BOLOGNA 1, 1967-*
SUBS: AEROSPAZIO-EUROPA.
*LO/N14.*
*ISSN 0001-9437*

**AEROSPAZIO-EUROPA.** XXX
[BRETON SOL]
*MONZA 1, 1971-*
PREV: AEROSPAZIO FROM 1, 1967- 5, 1971.
*LO/N14.*

**AEROTECNICA.** XXX
SUBS (1971): PART OF AEROTECNICA - MISSILI E SPAZIO.

**AEROTECNICA - MISSILI E SPAZIO.** XXX
ASSOCIAZIONE ITALIANA DI AERONAUTICA E ASTRONAUTICA.
[TAMBURINI EDITORE]
*MILAN 50, 1971-*
INCORP: MISSILI E SPAZIO FROM 1, 1959- 11, 1969; & AEROTECNICA FROM 1, 1920/21- 49, 1969 OF WHICH VOLUME NUMBERING IS CONTINUED.
*LO/N14.*

**AEU REPORTS.**
+ +AEU REP. (AM. ETHICAL UNION).
AMERICAN ETHICAL UNION.
*NEW YORK 1(1), JL 1967-*
Q.
*OX/U-1.*
*ISSN 0001-1118*

**AFFARI ESTERI.** XXX
ASSOCIAZIONE ITALIANA PER GLI STUDI DI POLITICA ESTERA.
*ROME 1(1), JA 1969-*
Q. PREV: ESTERI FROM 1, JA 1950- 19(24), D 1968.
*OX/U-1.*
*ISSN 0001-964X*

**AFRICA. AN INTERNATIONAL BUSINESS, ECONOMIC & POLITICAL MONTHLY.**
[AFRICA JOURNAL LTD.]
*LONDON NO.1, MY 1971-*
*ED/N-1.   LO/S14.   LO/U-8.   LO/U14.   XY/N-1.*
*ISSN 0044-6475*

**AFRICAN ABSTRACTS.** XXX
INTERNATIONAL AFRICAN INSTITUTE.
*LONDON 1, JA 1950- 23, 1972.//*
Q. SPONS. BODIES ALSO: UNESCO; & THE FORD FOUNDATION.
*BH/P-1.   LO/U-1.   LO/U-3.*
*ISSN 0001-9895*

**AFRICAN ADMINISTRATIVE STUDIES.** 000
SEE: CAHIERS AFRICAINS D'ADMINISTRATION PUBLIQUE.

**AFRICAN ARTS. ARTS D'AFRIQUE.**
+ +AFR. ARTS.
UNIVERSITY OF CALIFORNIA (LOS ANGELES): AFRICAN STUDIES CENTER.
*LOS ANGELES 1(1), 1967-*
Q. ENGL. OR FR.
*OX/U-8.*
*ISSN 0001-9933*

**AFRICAN BUSINESS MONTHLY.**
+ +AFR. BUS. MON.
*ADDIS ABABA 1(1), JA 1967-*
*LO/N17.*

**AFRICA CONTEMPORARY RECORD.**
+ +AFR. CONTEMP. REC.
[AFRICA RESEARCH LTD.]
*LONDON 1968-69(1969)-*
S/T: ANNUAL SURVEY & DOCUMENTS.
*CV/C-1.   DB/U-2.   EX/U-1.   GL/U-1.   LO/N17.*
*LO/S26. *   LO/U-2.   LO/U-3.   LO/U12.   SH/U-1.*

**AFRICA ECONOMIC DIGEST.**
+ +AFR. ECON. DIG.
[AFRICA RESEARCH LTD.]
*EXETER 1(1), 1/JA 1965- 2(50), 23/D 1966.//*
VOL.1 COMPRISES NOS.1-51, VOL.2 NOS.1-50.
PREV: DIGEST OF ECONOMIC INTELLIGENCE FROM AFRICA.
*AD/U-1.   BH/U-1.   HL/U-1.   LO/P20.   LV/U-1.*
*MA/P-1. 2,1966.*

**AFRICAN ECONOMIC INDICATORS. = INDICATEURS ECONOMIQUES AFRICAINS.**
+ +AFR. ECON. INDIC.
UNITED NATIONS: ECONOMIC COMMISSION FOR AFRICA.
*ADDIS ABABA [1], 1968-*
*LO/U-3.*

**AFRICAN HISTORICAL STUDIES.**                                    XXX
++AFR. HIST. STUD.
BOSTON UNIVERSITY: AFRICAN STUDIES CENTER.
*BOSTON  1(1), 1968- 4(3), D 1971.*
SUBS: INTERNATIONAL JOURNAL OF AFRICAN HISTOR-
ICAL STUDIES.
*AD/U-1.     BL/U-1.     CB/U-1.     ED/U-1.     LO/N17.     LO/U-8.*
*ISSN 0001-9992*

**AFRICA INDEX. SELECTED ARTICLES ON SOCIO-
ECONOMIC DEVELOPMENT.**
++AFR. INDEX.
UNITED NATIONS: ECONOMIC COMMISSION FOR AFRICA.
*ADDIS ABABA  NO.1, AP 1971-*
Q.
*LO/U-8.     LO/S14.     OX/U24.*

**AFRICAN JOURNAL OF MEDICAL SCIENCES.**
++AFR. J. MED. SCI.
*OXFORD &C.  1(1), 1970-*
*ED/N-1.     LO/N13.     OX/U-1.*
*ISSN 0002-0028*

**AFRICAN JOURNAL OF PHARMACY & PHARMACEUTICAL
SCIENCES.**
++AFR. J. PHARM. & PHARM. SCI.
NIGERIAN PHARMACEUTICAL & MEDICAL COMPANY.
*APAPA  1(1), 1971-*
FROM 1(11), 1971 INCORPORATES WEST AFRICAN
PHARMACIST.
*BL/U-1.*
*ED/N-1.  2, D 1971-*                       *LO/N14.  1(2), 1971-*
*LO/R-6.  3, 1973-*
*ISSN 0044-6564*

**AFRICAN JOURNAL OF TROPICAL HYDROBIOLOGY &
FISHERIES.**
++AFR. J. TROP. HYDROBIOL. & FISH.
EAST AFRICAN FISHERIES RESEARCH ORGANIZATIONS.
*NAIROBI  1, 1971-*
ENGL. & FR.
*BN/U-2.     CA/U-1.     HL/U-1.     LO/N-2.     LO/R-5.     OX/U-1.*
*OX/U-8.*
*ISSN 0002-0036*

**AFRICAN LANGUAGE REVIEW.**                                        XXX
++AFR. LANG. REV.
FOURAH BAY COLLEGE: DEPARTMENT OF MODERN
EUROPEAN AFRICAN LANGUAGES.
*FOURAH BAY  6, 1967-*
PREV: SIERRA LEONE LANGUAGE REVIEW FROM NO.
1, 1962- 5, 1966. SPONS. BODY ALSO:
UNIVERSITY COLLEGE OF SIERRA LEONE.
*BH/U-1.*
*ISSN 0065-3977*

**AFRICAN LAW REPORTS: MALAWI SERIES.**
++AFR. LAW REP., MALAWI SER.
*DOBBS FERRY, N.Y.  1, 1968-*
*OX/U15.*
*BL/U-1  5, 1968/70(1971)-*
*ISSN 0568-1383*

**AFRICAN LAW STUDIES.**
++AFR. LAW STUD.
COLUMBIA UNIVERSITY: AFRICAN LAW CENTER.
*NEW YORK  NO.1, 1969-*
*LO/U14.     OX/U15.*
*ISSN 0002-0060*

**AFRICANA LIBRARY JOURNAL.**
++AFR. LIBR. J.
*NEW YORK  1, 1970-*
Q.
*AD/U-1.     BH/U-1.     CB/U-1.     ED/N-1.     LO/N-2.     LO/U-8.*
*LO/U14.     OX/U-9.     SH/U-1.*
*ISSN 0002-0303*

**AFRICAN LITERATURE TODAY.**
++AFR. LIT. TODAY.
*LONDON  NO.1, 1968-*
S/T: A JOURNAL OF EXPLANATORY CRITICISM.
*BH/U-1.     ED/N-1.     LO/S26.     OX/U-1.*
*CB/U-1.  CURRENT YEAR ONLY.*
*NW/U-1.  NO.1, 1968- NO.4, 1972.*

**AFRICANA MARBURGENSIA.**
++AFR. MARB.
MARBURGER UNIVERSITAT.
*MARBURG  1, 1968-*
S/T: UBER LAUFENDE UND ABGESCHLOSSENE ARBEITEN
AUS ALLEN WISSENSCHAFTSBEREICHEN AN DER
MARBURGER UNIVERSITAT.
*LO/N-1.*
*ISSN 0002-0311*

**AFRICAN PHILOSOPHICAL JOURNAL. CAHIERS PHIL-
OSOPHIQUES AFRICAINS.**
++AFR. PHILOS. J.
*LUBUMBASHI  1, 1972-*
*OX/U-1.*

**AFRICAN POPULATION NEWSLETTER.**
++AFR. POPULAT. NEWSL.
UNITED NATIONS: ECONOMIC COMMISSION FOR AFRICA.
*ADDIS ABABA  1(1), MY 1970-*
PROD. BY COMMISSION'S POPULATION PROGRAMME
CENTRE.
*LO/S14.     LO/U-8.*
*LO/N-1.  1(2), 1970-*                    *OX/U16.  1(2), 1970-*

**AFRICAN RED FAMILY.**
++AFR. RED FAM.
*LONDON  1(1), OC/D 1972-*
*CA/U-1.     LO/U-3.*

**AFRICAN RELIGIOUS RESEARCH.**
++AFR. RELIG. RES.
UNIVERSITY OF CALIFORNIA AT LOS ANGELES:
AFRICAN STUDIES CENTER.
*LOS ANGELES  1(1), AP 1971-*
S/T: A NEWSLETTER FOR THE HISTORICAL STUDY OF
AFRICAN RELIGIOUS SYSTEMS.
*LO/S10.*
*LO/U14.  1(2), 1971-*
*ISSN 0044-6602*

**AFRICANA RESEARCH BULLETIN.**
++AFR. RES. BULL.
*FREETOWN  1, 1970-*
INSTITUTE SUBORD. TO FOURAH BAY COLLEGE.
*AD/U-1.     LD/U-1.*
*LO/U-3.  2(1), 1971-*

**AFRICAN REVIEW.**
++AFR. REV.
UNIVERSITY COLLEGE, DAR-ES-SALAAM:
DEPARTMENT OF POLITICAL SCIENCE.
*DAR-ES-SALAAM  1(1), 1971-*
Q.
*AD/U-1.     EX/U-1.     LD/U-1.     LO/U-3.     LO/U-8.     LO/U14.*
*MA/U-1.     OX/U-9.     SH/U-1.     SO/U-1.     XY/N-1.*
*ISSN 0002-0117*

**AFRICAN SCHOLAR. JOURNAL OF RESEARCH &
ANALYSIS.**
++AFR. SCH.
AFRICAN ACADEMY OF POLITICAL & SOCIAL SCIENCES.
*WASHINGTON, D.C.  1(1), AG/N /968-*
*OX/U-9.*
*ISSN 0002-0141*

**AFRICAN SCIENTIST.**
++AFR. SCI.
[EAST AFRICAN PUBL. HO.]
*NAIROBI  1, 1969-*
*LO/N-2.*
*ISSN 0002-015X*

**AFRICAN SOCIAL RESEARCH DOCUMENTS.**
++AFR. SOC. RES. DOC.
RIJKSUNIVERSITEIT TE LEIDEN: AFRIKA-STUDIE-
CENTRUM.
*LEIDEN &C.  1, 1970-*
SPONS. BODY ALSO: AFRICAN STUDIES CENTRE,
UNIVERSITY OF CAMBRIDGE.
*LO/N-1.     OX/U-9.*

**AFRICA SOUTH OF THE SAHARA.**
++AFR. SOUTH SAHARA.
[EUROPA PUBL.]
*LONDON  [1], 1971-*
*BH/U-1.     EX/U-1.     GL/U-1.     LO/S14.     LO/U12.*
*NW/U-1.  CURRENT VOLUME.*

**AFRICA IN SOVIET STUDIES.**
++AFR. SOV. STUD.
*MOSCOW  [NO.1], 1969-*
*BH/U-1.     LO/U14.     OX/U-1.     OX/U-9.*

**AFRICAN STATESMAN.**
++AFR. STATESMAN.
COMMITTEE OF TEN.
*LAGOS  1(1), OC/D 1965-*
S/T: A QUARTERLY JOURNAL OF THE COMMITTEE ...
*LO/N17.*

**AFRICAN STUDIES BULLETIN.**                                        XXX
SUBS (1970): AFRICAN STUDIES REVIEW.

**AFRICAN STUDIES NEWSLETTER.***
+ +AFR. STUD. NEWSL.
AFRICAN STUDIES ASSOCIATION.
*LOS ANGELES 1(1), 1968-*
TITLE VARIES: 1(1) AS AFRICAN STUDIES ASSO-
CIATION NEWSLETTER.
*AD/U-1. BH/U-1.* LO/U-8. OX/U-9. 2(4), 1969-*
*SH/U-1. 1971-*
*ISSN 0002-0214*

**AFRICAN STUDIES REVIEW.**                                                    XXX
+ +AFR. STUD. REV.
AFRICAN STUDIES ASSOCIATION.
*EAST LANSING, MICH. 13, AP 1970-*
PREV: AFRICAN STUDIES BULLETIN FROM 1(1), AP
1958- 12, 1969.
*BH/U-1.   ED/N-1.   LO/U-3.   SH/U-1.*

**AFRICAN TARGET. = OBJECTIFS AFRICAINS.**
+ +AFR. TARGETS.
UNITED NATIONS: ECONOMIC COMMISSION FOR AFRICA.
*ADDIS ABABA [1], 1968-*
Q.
*LO/U-3.*
*LO/N-1. 4(1), 1970-        LO/U-8. 4(1), 1970-*
*ISSN 0002-0230*

**AFRIKANSKIJ SBORNIK.**
+ +AFR. SB.
AKADEMIJA NAUK SSSR: INSTITUT AFRIKI.
*MOSCOW VYP.1, 1963-*
*BH/U-1.   CC/U-1.   LO/U14.   OX/U-1.*
*BT/U-1. 2, 1964-            SW/U-1. 2, 1964-*

**AFRIQUE INDUSTRIE INFORMATIONS.**
+ +AFR. IND. INF.
*PARIS NO.1, 1970-*
*LO/U-14.*

**AFRISCOPE. AN INDIGENOUS MONTHLY ON AFRICA'S
SOCIAL & ECONOMIC DEVELOPMENT.**
[PAN AFRISCOPE PUBLS.]
*LAGOS 1(1), JE 1971-*
*LO/R-6. 1(2), 1971-         LO/U-8. 2(1), 1972-*
*OX/U-9. 1(2), 1971-*
*ISSN 0044-667X*

**AFRO-AMERICAN STUDIES.**
+ +AFRO-AM. STUD.
[GORDON & BREACH]
*LONDON 1(1), MY 1970-*
*AD/U-1.   ED/N-1.   OX/U-1.*
*ISSN 0002-0575*

**AFRO-ASIAN SOLIDARITY. JOURNAL OF ...**
AFRO-ASIAN PEOPLE'S SOLIDARITY MOVEMENT.
*LONDON 1(1), JA 1970-*
*LO/U-3.*

**AFRO-ASIAN WRITER.**
PERMANENT BUREAU OF AFRO-ASIAN WRITERS.
*CAIRO 1(1), 1966-*
*LO/U14.*

**AFTERIMAGE.**
[NARCIS PUBL. LTD.]
*LONDON NO.1, AP 1970-*
*ED/N-1.   EX/U-1.   OX/U-1.*

**AGARD EXTENDED SUMMARIES.**
+ +AGARD EXT. SUMM. (ADVIS. GROUP AEROSP. RES.
& DEV.)
ADVISORY GROUP FOR AEROSPACE RESEARCH &
DEVELOPMENT.
*NEUILLY-SUR-SEINE [NO.]1, JE 1968-*
*LO/N14.   LO/U-2.*

**AGE & AGEING.**
BRITISH GERIATRICS SOCIETY.
*LONDON 1, 1972-*
SPONS. BODY ALSO BRITISH SOCIETY FOR RESEARCH
ON AGEING.
*BL/U-1.   CA/U-1.   CO/U-1.   ED/N-1.   GL/U-1.   LO/N-1.*
*LO/N13.   LO/N31.   SO/U-1.*
*ISSN 0002-0729*

**AGE CONCERN TODAY.**                                                        XXX
AGE CONCERN.
*LONDON NO.1, SPRING 1972-*
Q. PREV: QUARTERLY BULLETIN, NATIONAL OLD
PEOPLE'S WELFARE COUNCIL FROM NO.1, MY 1948-
8, D 1971.
*BH/P-1.   CA/U-1.   CO/U-1.   ED/N-1.   LO/U-3.*

**AGENTS & ACTIONS.**
[BIRKHAUSER VERLAG]
*BASLE 1, 1969-*
*LO/N14.   LO/U-2.   OX/U-8.   SO/U-1.*

**AGENTZIA.**
[EDITIONS AGENTZIA]
*PARIS 1, 1968-*
*LO/U-2.***

**AGING & HUMAN DEVELOPMENT.**
+ +AGING & HUM. DEV.
[GREENWOOD PERIODICALS]
*WESTPORT, CONN. 1(1), F 1970-*
Q. S/T: AN INTERNATIONAL JOURNAL OF
PSYCHOSOCIAL GERONTOLOGY.
*LO/U-3.   SO/U-1.*
*ISSN 0002-0974*

**AGO. THE NEW ARCHAEOLOGICAL MAGAZINE.**
ARCHAEOLOGICAL CENTRE.
*BOURNEMOUTH NO.1, 1970-*
*CR/N-1.   LO/N-1.   LO/N-4.   OX/U-1.   SO/U-1.*
*ED/N-1. NO.5, 1970-*

**AGORA. A JOURNAL IN THE HUMANITIES & SOCIAL
SCIENCES.**
STATE UNIVERSITY OF NEW YORK COLLEGE AT POTSDAM
*NEW YORK 1, 1969-*
*CB/U-1. 1(2), 1970-*
*ISSN 0002-1016*

**AGRARTECHNIK.**                                                             XXX
[VERLAG TECHNIK]
*BERLIN 23, 1973-*
PREV: DEUTSCHE AGRARTECHNIK FROM 1, JA 1951-
22, 1972.
*LO/N14.*

**AGRICULTURAL ECONOMICS REPORT, DEPARTMENT OF
LAND ECONOMY, UNIVERSITY OF CAMBRIDGE.**
+ +AGRIC. ECON. REP. DEP. LAND ECON. UNIV. CAMB.
*CAMBRIDGE 65, 1969-*
PREV: REPORT, FARM ECONOMICS BRANCH, CAMBRIDGE
UNIVERSITY FROM 1, 1925-64, 1966.
*BN/U-2.*

**AGRICULTURAL EDUCATION & TRAINING.**
+ +AGRIC. EDUC. & TRAIN.
FOOD & AGRICULTURE ORGANIZATION OF THE U.N.
*ROME 1967-*
S/T: ANNUAL REVIEW OF SELECTED DEVELOPMENTS.
*LO/U-3.*
*OX/U-8. 1968-*

**AGRICULTURAL ENGINEER.**                                                    XXX
+ +AGRIC. ENG.
INSTITUTION OF AGRICULTURAL ENGINEERS.
*RICKMANSWORTH 27, 1972-*
PREV: JOURNAL & PROCEEDINGS, INSTITUTION ...
FROM 16, 1960- 26, 1971.
*ED/N-1.   LO/N14.*

**AGRICULTURAL ENTERPRISE STUDIES IN ENGLAND &
WALES: ECONOMIC REPORT.**
+ +AGRIC. ENTERP. STUD. ENGL. & WALES, ECON. REP.
(GREAT BRITAIN) MINISTRY OF AGRICULTURE,
FISHERIES & FOOD.
*EXETER NO.1, 1970-*
*LO/N-1.*

**AGRICULTURAL & GARDEN MACHINERY SERVICE.**
+ +AGRIC. & GARD. MACH. SERV.
BRITISH AGRICULTURAL & GARDEN MACHINERY
ASSOCIATION.
*RICKMANSWORTH 1, 1972-*
*LO/N-4.   LO/N-6.   LO/N14.   OX/U-8.*
*ED/N-1. 1(2), 1972-*

**AGRICULTURAL INSTITUTE REVIEW.**                                            XXX
SUBS (1969): A.I.C. REVIEW.

**AGRICULTURAL JOURNAL, DEPARTMENT OF AGRICUL-
URE (FIJI).**                                                                 XXX
SUBS (1970): FIJI AGRICULTURAL JOURNAL: NS.

**AGRICULTURAL SCIENCE, HONG KONG.**
+ +AGRIC. SCI. H.K.
(HONG KONG) DEPARTMENT OF AGRICULTURE &
FISHERIES.
*HONG KONG 1, 1968-*
*LO/N-2.*

**AGRICULTURAL SUPPLY INDUSTRY.**
+ +AGRIC. SUPPLY IND.
[MAGAZINES FOR INDUSTRY]
*LONDON 1(1), AP 1971-*
WKLY.
*OX/U24.*

**AGRICULTURAL WORKING PEOPLE OF KOREA.**
++AGR. WORK. PEOPLE KOREA.
UNION OF AGRICULTURAL WORKING PEOPLE OF KOREA.
PYONGYANG NO.1, 1968-
OX/U-1.

**AGROBOREALIS.**
ALASKA AGRICULTURAL EXPERIMENT STATION.
COLLEGE, ALASKA 1, AP 1969-
CA/U11.
ISSN 0002-1822

**AGROCIENCIA.**
MEXICO 1, 1966-
LO/N-2.

**AGROLOGIST.** XXX
AGRICULTURAL INSTITUTE OF CANADA.
OTTAWA 1, 1972-
PREV: A.I.C. REVIEW FROM 24(3), 1969- 26, 1971
LO/N14.
ISSN 0044-684X

**AGROMETEOROLOGICAL REPORT.**
++AGROMETEOROL. REP. (ZAMBIA).
(ZAMBIA) DEPARTMENT OF METEOROLOGY.
LUSAKA NO.1, 1970-
XS/N-1.

**AGRO-PECUARIA.**
LISBON 1, 1969-
S/T: REVISTA TECNICA DE INFORMACAO E DE
FOMENTO AGRICOLA E PECUARIO.
LO/N13.

**AGROTEHNICAR.**
['GOSPODARSKI LIST - AGROTEHNICAR']
ZAGREB 1, 1965-
LO/N13. 5, 1969-
ISSN 0002-1989

**AHIJUNA. HISTORIA Y LETRAS, POLITICA,
ECONOMIA.**
BUENOS AIRES 1(1), 1967-
LO/N-1.
ISSN 0002-2039

**AHSB (S) REPORT, UNITED KINGDOM ATOMIC
ENERGY AUTHORITY.** XXX
SUBS (1971): SRD REPORT, UNITED KINGDOM
ATOMIC ENERGY AUTHORITY.

**A.I.C. REVIEW.** XXX
++A.I.C. REV. (AGRIC. INST. CAN.).
AGRICULTURAL INSTITUTE OF CANADA.
OTTAWA 24(3), 1969- 26, 1971.
PREV: AGRICULTURAL INSTITUTE REVIEW FROM
1, 1945- 24(2), 1969. SUBS: AGROLOGIST.
CA/U11. LO/N14.
ISSN 0002-1504

**AICHE MONOGRAPH SERIES.** XXX
++AICHE MONOGR. SER.
AMERICAN INSTITUTE OF CHEMICAL ENGINEERS.
NEW YORK NO.7, 1972-
PREV: CHEMICAL ENGINEERING PROGRESS MONOGRAPH
SERIES FROM NO.1, 1951- NO.6, 1969. ISSUES
ALSO BEAR VOL. NUMBERING, VOL.68, ETC., OF
CHEMICAL ENGINEERING PROGRESS.
LO/N14.

**AICHI KOGYO DAIGAKU KENKYU HOKOKU. BULLETIN
OF AICHI INSTITUTE OF TECHNOLOGY.**
AICHI KOGYO DAIGAKU.
[NAGOYA] 1, 1965-
ENGL. SUMM.
LO/N14.

**AICHI-KEN NOGYO SOGO SHIKENJO KENKYU HOKOKU: D:
SANGYO. RESEARCH BULLETIN OF THE AICHI-KEN
AGRICULTURAL RESEARCH CENTER: SERIES D:
SERICULTURE.**
NAGAKUTE NO.1, 1970-
JAP. WITH ENGL. SUMM.
LO/N13.

**AIDC JOURNAL.**
++AIDC J. (AM. IND. DEVELOP. COUNC.).
AMERICAN INDUSTRIAL DEVELOPMENT COUNCIL.
BOSTON 1, JA 1966-
XY/N-1.**
ISSN 0001-155X

**AIDS TO READERS.**
NATIONAL REFERENCE LIBRARY OF SCIENCE & INVEN-
TION.
LONDON NO.1, 1968-
GL/U-1.

**AIDS TO RESEARCH IN EDUCATION.**
++AIDS RES. EDUC.
UNIVERSITY OF HULL: INSTITUTE OF EDUCATION.
HULL NO.1, 1970-
LO/N-1.

**AIIE TRANSACTIONS.**
++AIIE TRANS. (AM. INST. IND. ENG.)
AMERICAN INSTITUTE OF INDUSTRIAL ENGINEERS.
NEW YORK 1, 1969-
DB/U-2. GL/U-2. LO/N14.

**AIP INFORMATION PROGRAM NEWSLETTER.** XXX
SUBS (1970): AIP INFORMATION & PUBLICATION
NEWSLETTER.

**AIP INFORMATION & PUBLICATION NEWSLETTER.** XXX
++AIP INF. & PUBL. NEWSL. (AM. INST. PHYS.).
AMERICAN INSTITUTE OF PHYSICS.
NEW YORK 1(1), MR 1970-
PREV: AIP INFORMATION PROGRAM NEWSLETTER FROM
1, JE 1967.
RE/U-1. XS/R10. XS/R10.
ISSN 0001-1657

**AIR BRITAIN NEWS.**
[AIR BRITAIN HISTORIANS LTD.]
MAIDENHEAD 1(1), JA 1972-
ED/N-1. 2, 1973-

**AIR-CUSHION & HYDROFOIL SYSTEMS BIBLIOGRAPHY
SERVICE.**
++AIR-CUSHION & HYDROFOIL SYST. BIBLIOGR. SERV.
[ROBERT TRILLO LTD.]
SOUTHAMPTON, HANTS. NO.1, 1972-
ED/N-1. LO/N-4. LO/N14. OX/U-1.

**AIR ENTHUSIAST.**
[PILOT P. LTD.]
BROMLEY, KENT 1, 1971-
MON.
LO/N-4. LO/N14. LO/N35.
ISSN 0044-6963

**AIR FORCE SCIENTIFIC RESEARCH BIBLIOGRAPHY.**
++AIR FORCE SCI. RES. BIBLIOGR.
LIBRARY OF CONGRESS (US).
[USGPO]
WASHINGTON, DC 1, 1950/1956 (1961)-
COMP. BY THE SCIENCE & TECHNOLOGY DIVISION OF
THE LIBR. OF CONGR. SUPPORTED BY THE USAF
OFFICE (SUBORD. TO THE AIR FORCE OFFICE OF
SCIENTIFIC RESEARCH).
BN/U-2. LO/N14.

**AIR FORCE/SPACE DIGEST INTERNATIONAL.** XXX
++AIR FORCE/SPACE DIG. INT.
AIR FORCE ASSOCIATION.
WASH., DC 1(1), JA 1965- 2(10), OC 1966...
SUBS: AEROSPACE INTERNATIONAL.
BR/U-3. 2, 1966-

**AIR POLLUTION ABSTRACTS (RESEARCH TRIANGLE
PARK).** XXX
++AIR POLLUT. ABSTR. (RES. TRIANGLE PARK).
(UNITED STATES) AIR POLLUTION CONTROL OFFICE:
ENVIRONMENTAL PROTECTION AGENCY.
RESEARCH TRIANGLE PARK 2(2), 1971-
PREV: NAPCA ABSTRACTS BULLETIN FROM 1, 1970-
2(1), 1971.
LO/N14. XS/R10.
MA/U-1. 4(9), 1973- RE/U-1. 4, 1973-
ISSN 0027-5956

**AIR POLLUTION DIGEST.** 000
SEE: AIR QUALITY CONTROL DIGEST.

**AIR POLLUTION TRANSLATIONS.**
++AIR POLLUT. TRANSL.
NATIONAL AIR POLLUTION CONTROL ADMINISTRATION
(US).
ARLINGTON, VA. 1, 1969-
S/T: A BIBLIOGRAPHY WITH ABSTRACTS.
LO/N14.
BT/U-1. 1, 1969.

**AIR QUALITY CONTROL DIGEST. = AIR POLLUTION
DIGEST.** XXX
++AIR QUAL. CONTROL DIG.
DETROIT 1, 1969- 2(6), 1971 ...
SUBS: UDS AIR QUALITY CONTROL DIGEST.
LO/N14.
ISSN 0002-2527

**AIR TRANSPORTATION.** XXX
SUBS (1970): CARGO AIRLIFT.

AIR & TRAVEL TRAINING WORLD.                    XXX
+ + AIR & TRAVEL TRAIN. WORLD.
AIR TRANSPORT & TRAVEL INDUSTRY TRAINING BOARD.
 STAINES 1(1), F 1972-
6/A. PREV: NEWS, AIR TRANSPORT ... FROM 1(1),
1970- 2(9), 1971.
 ED/N-1.    LO/N-1.    OX/U-1.

AIRCRAFT ILLUSTRATED.
+ + AIRCR. ILLUS.
 LONDON 1, MR 1968-
 Q.
 LO/N14.    LO/P-7.
 ISSN 0002-2675

AIRCRAFT PROFILES.
+ + AIRCR. PROFILES.
[PROFILE PUBL.]
 LEATHERHEAD, SY. NO.1, 1965-
 ED/N-1.
 ISSN 0568-3793

AIRPORT FORUM.
[BAUVERLAG GMBH]
 WIESBADEN 1971-
 2M.
 LD/U-1.    LO/N14.
 ISSN 0002-2802

AIRPORTS INTERNATIONAL.
+ + AIRPORTS INT.
INTERNATIONAL CIVIL AIRPORT ASSOCIATION.
[WHS ADVERTISING, LTD.]
 LONDON NO.1, 1968-
 LO/N14.
 SO/U-1 NO.18, 1971-
 SW/U-1. NO.29, AG 1973-
 ISSN 0002-2853

AKADEMIKA. JERNAL ILMU KEMANUSIAAN DAN SAINS
KEMASYARAKATAN.
UNIVERSITI KEBANGSAAN MALAYSIA.
 KUALA LUMPUR NO.1, 1972-
 ENGL. S/T: JOURNAL OF HUMANITIES & SOCIAL
 SCIENCES.
 LO/U14.

ALA BULLETIN.                                   XXX
 SUBS (1970): AMERICAN LIBRARIES.

ALABAMA MARINE RESOURCES BULLETIN.*
+ + ALA. MAR. RESOUR. BULL.
ALABAMA MARINE RESOURCES LABORATORY.
 DAUPHIN ISLAND NO.1, 1963-
 TITLE VARIES. NO.1 AS MARINE RESOURCES
 BULLETIN. AS ABOVE FROM NO.2, 1969.
 LO/N13.

ALASKA.                                         XXX
[ALASKA NORTHWEST PUBL. CO.]
 EDMONDS, WASH. 35(10), 1969-
 PREV: ALASKA SPORTSMAN FROM 1(1), 1935-
 35(9), 1969.
 CA/U12.
 ISSN 0002-4562

ALASKA GEOGRAPHIC.
+ + ALASKA GEOGR.
ALASKA GEOGRAPHIC SOCIETY.
 ANCHORAGE 1(1), 1972-
 Q.
 LO/S13.

ALASKA'S HEALTH & WELFARE.*
(ALASKA) DEPARTMENT OF HEALTH & WELFARE.
 JUNEAU 1, 1943-
 TITLE EXPANDED FROM ALASKA'S HEALTH WITH
 18, F 1961.
 CA/U12.*
 ISSN 0002-4597

ALASKA INDUSTRY.
+ + ALASKA IND.
[ALASKA INDUSTRIAL PUBL. INC.]
 ANCHORAGE 1(1), 1969-
 M.
 CA/U12.*
 ISSN 0002-449X

ALASKA JOURNAL. HISTORY & ARTS OF THE NORTH.
+ + ALASKA J.
 JUNEAU, ALASKA 1(1), 1971-
 Q.
 CA/U12.
 ISSN 0002-4503

ALASKA SPORTSMAN.                               XXX
 SUBS (1969): ALASKA.

ALBATROSS.
[ALBATROSS P.]
 MADISON, WISC. NO.1, 1970-
 LO/U-2.

ALBERT DTZ. DRUCKMASCHINENTECHNISCHE ZEIT-
SCHRIFT.
ALBERT-FRANKENTHAL AG.
 FRANKENTHAL 1, 1971-
 LO/N14.

ALBERTA ANTHROPOLOGIST.                         XXX
 SUBS (1969): WESTERN CANADIAN JOURNAL OF
 ANTHROPOLOGY.

ALBION.
 LONDON NO.1, MY 1968-
 ED/N-1.    LO/U-2.

ALBION (MANCHESTER).
 MANCHESTER NO.1, 1972-
 ED/N-1.

ALBION (SEATTLE).
CONFERENCE ON BRITISH STUDIES: PACIFIC NORTH-
WEST SECTION.
[WASHINGTON STATE UNIV. P.]
 SEATTLE 1(1), 1969-
 LO/U-1.    OX/U-1.
 ED/N-1. 6, 1974-          NO/U-1. 3, 1971-
 ISSN 0587-2766

ALBISWERK-BERICHTE.                             XXX
 SUBS (1972): SIEMENS-ALBIS BERICHTE.

ALBRECHT-THAER-ARCHIV.                          XXX
 SUBS (1971): ARCHIV FUR BODENFRUCHTBARKEIT UND
 PFLANZENPRODUKTION.

A.L.C. POLICY PAPERS.
+ + A.L.C. POLICY PAP. (ASSOC. LIBERAL COUNC.).
ASSOCIATION OF LIBERAL COUNCILLORS.
 LONDON 1, [1969]-
 OX/U-1.

ALCHERINGA. ETHNOPOETICS.
 NEW YORK 1(1), 1970-
 2/A.
 OX/U-1.
 ISSN 0044-7218

ALCOHOLISM IN INDUSTRY.
+ + ALC. IND.
COUNSELLING & REHABILITATION EMPLOYEES
SERVICES.
 LONDON 1, SPRING 1968-
 ED/N-1.

ALDEBARAN REVIEW.
+ + ALDEBARAN REV.
 BERKELEY, CALIF 1, 1967-
 LO/U-2.**

ALEC REPORT.
+ + ALEC REP. (ASIAN LABOR EDUC. CENT.).
UNIVERSITY OF THE PHILIPPINES: ASIAN LABOR
EDUCATION CENTER.
 QUEZON CITY 1, 1969-
 HL/U-1.
 ISSN 0001-1762

ALGEBRA & LOGIC.
[CONSULTANTS BUREAU]
 NEW YORK &C. 7(1), JA/F 1968(1970)-
 ENGL. TRANSL. OF ALGEBRA I LOGIKA. VOL. NUMB-
 ERING FOLLOWS ORIG.
 LO/N14.    OX/U-8.
 ISSN 0002-5232

ALGEBRA I LOGIKA (ENGL. TRANSL.).              000
 SEE: ALGEBRA & LOGIC.

ALGEBRA UNIVERSALIS.
+ + ALGEBRA UNIVERS.
 WINNIPEG &C. 1/1, 1971-
 CA/U-2.    DB/S-1.    LO/N14.    OX/U-8.    SW/U-1.
 ISSN 0002-5240

ALGOLOGICAL STUDIES.
+ + ALGOL. STUD.
CESKOSLOVENSKA AKADEMIE VED: MIKROBIOLOGICKY
USTAV.
[SCHWEIZERBART'SCHE VERLAGSBUCHHANDLUNG]
 STUTTGART NO.1, 1970-
 PROD. BY ALGOLOGICAL LABORATORIES.
 GL/U-2.    LO/N-4.    OX/U-8.    SW/U-1.

**ALGORITMY I ALGORITMICHESKIE JAZYKI.**
+ +ALGORITMY & ALGORITM. JAZYKI.
AKADEMIJA NAUK SSSR: VYCHISLITEL'NYJ TSENTR.
*MOSCOW 1, 1967-*
*BH/U-1. LO/N13.*

**ALIPHATIC, ALICYCLIC, & SATURATED HETERO-**
**CYCLIC CHEMISTRY.** XXX
+ +ALIPHATIC, ALICYCLIC, & SATUR. HETEROCYCLIC
CHEM.
CHEMICAL SOCIETY.
*LONDON 1, 1970/71(1973) ...*
SUBS. PART OF: ALIPHATIC CHEMISTRY;
ALICYCLIC CHEMISTRY; & SATURATED
HETEROCYCLIC CHEMISTRY.
*GL/U-1. HL/U-1. LO/S-3. MA/U-1.*
*ISSN 0302-4164*

**ALJUMINIEVYE SPLAVY.**
[OBORONGIZ]
*MOSCOW 1, 1963-*
*LO/N13.* *

**ALKAHEST. AMERICAN COLLEGE POETRY.**
[WESLEYAN U.P.]
*MIDDLETOWN, CONN. NO.1, 1968-*
*LO/U-2. OX/U-1.*
*ISSN 0002-5488*

**ALKALOIDS. A REVIEW OF THE LITERATURE.**
CHEMICAL SOCIETY.
*LONDON 1, JA 1969/JE 1970(1971)-*
*BH/U-3. BL/U-1. ED/N-1. GL/U-2. LO/N14. LO/S-3.*
*LO/U-2. LO/U12.*
*ISSN 0305-9707*

**ALLAHABAD LAW REVIEW.**
ALLAHABAD LAW AGENCY.
*ALLAHABAD 1, 1969-*
*LO/U14.*

**ALLERGIE UND ASTHMA.** XXX
SUBS (1971): ALLERGIE UND IMMUNOLOGIE.

**ALLERGIE UND IMMUNOLOGIE.** XXX
+ +ALLERG. & IMMUNOL.
[JOHANN AMBROSIUS BARTH]
*LEIPZIG 17, 1971-*
PREV: ALLERGIE UND ASTHMA FROM 1, MY 1955- 16,
1970.
*LO/N13.*
*ISSN 0002-5755*

**ALLGEMEINE DEUTSCHE WEINFACHZEITUNG.** XXX
+ +ALLG. DTSCH. WEINFACHZTG.
[DIEMER UND MEINIGER]
*MAINZ 107, 1971- 110, 1974 ...*
PREV: DEUTSCHE WEIN-ZEITUNG FROM 91, 1955-
106, 1970. SUBS: WEINWIRTSCHAFT.
*LO/N14.*
*ISSN 0012-0960*

**ALLGEMEINE STATISTIK DES AUSLANDES; LANDER-**
**BERICHTE: PAKISTAN.**
+ +ALLG. STAT. AUSL., LANDESBER., PAK.
(GERMANY, WEST) STATISTISCHES BUNDESAMT.
*WIESBADEN 1966-*
*LO/U-3.*

**ALMANACCO BOMPIANI.** XXX
+ +ALM. BOMPIANI.
*MILAN 1971-*
PREV: ALMANACCO LETTERARIO BOMPIANI FROM
1938- 1970.
*GL/U-1.*

**ALMANACCO LETTERARIO BOMPIANI.** XXX
SUBS (1971): ALMANACCO BOMPIANI.

**ALPHA. REVISTA LITERARIA DE LOS AMIGOS DEL**
**ARTE.**
*BARRANCO, PERU 1(1), 1965-*
Q.
*LO/N-1.* *
*ISSN 0002-6379*

**ALTER ORIENT UND ALTES TESTAMENT. SONDERREIHE.**
[BUTZON & BERCHER]
*KEVELAER; NEUKIRCHEN-VLUYN 1, 1971-*
*GL/U-1. OX/U-1.*

**ALTERN UND ENTWICKLUNG.**
[SCHATTANER]
*STUTTGART 1, 1971-*
*LO/N13.*

**ALTERNATIVE.**
UNION MOVEMENT.
*LONDON NO.1, 1972-*
*ED/N-1.*

**ALTERNATIVE PRESS INDEX.**
CARLETON COLLEGE: RADICAL RESEARCH CENTER.
*NORTHFIELD, MINN. 1, 1969-*
Q.
*CA/U-1. 2(4), 1970-*
*ISSN 0002-662X*

**ALTO MEDIOEVO.**
CENTRO INTERNAZIONALE DELLE ARTI E DEL COSTUME.
*VENICE 1, 1967-*
*OX/U-1.*

**ALUMINIUM (DUSSELDORF). [ENGLISH TRANSLATION].**
[METAL INFORMATION SERVICES]
*STONEHOUSE, GLOS. 48(2), 1972-*
TRANSLATION OF THE TECHNICAL ARTICLES IN
ALUMINIUM (DUSSELDORF). DATING & NUMBERING
OF ISSUES FOLLOW ORIGINAL.
*LO/N14.*

**ALUMINIUM AGE.** 000
SEE: ARUMI EJI.

**AMA DRUG EVALUATIONS.** XXX
AMERICAN MEDICAL ASSOCIATION.
*CHICAGO 1, 1971-*
PREV: NEW DRUGS FROM 1965- 1967.
*GL/U-1. NW/U-1. SH/U-1.*
*LD/U-1. CURRENT COPY ONLY.*
*LO/U-1. [CURRENT COPY ONLY].*

**AMARU.**
UNIVERSIDAD NACIONAL DE INGENIERIA (PERU).
*LIMA NO.1, 1967-*
*CC/U-1. LO/U11.*
*ISSN 0002-6778*

**AMBIO. A JOURNAL OF THE HUMAN ENVIRONMENT,**
**RESEARCH & MANAGEMENT.**
KUNGLIGA SVENSKA VETENSKAPSAKADEMIEN.
[UNIVERSITETSFORLAGET]
*STOCKHOLM 1(1), F 1972-*
6/A.
*AD/U-1. BN/U-2. CA/U-1. LD/U-1. LO/N-2. LO/R-5.*
*MA/U-1. NO/U-1. OX/U-8. RE/U-1. XS/R10.*
*XS/U-1. 3, 1974-*
*ISSN 0044-7447*

**AMDEL BULLETIN.**
+ +AMDEL BULL. (AUST. MINER. DEV. LABS.)
AUSTRALIAN MINERAL DEVELOPMENT LABORATORIES.
*PARKSIDE, S.AUST. NO.1, 1966-*
*LO/N14.*

**AMERICA LATINA. REVISTA TEORICA-POLITICA.**
+ +AM. LAT. (URUG.).
*MONTEVIDEO NO.1, 1968-*
*CC/U-1. NO.1, 1968.*

**AMERICAN BIBLIOGRAPHY OF AGRICULTURAL ECON-**
**OMICS.**
+ +AM. BIBLIOGR. AGRIC. ECON.
AMERICAN AGRICULTURAL ECONOMICS ASSOCIATION.
*WASHINGTON, D.C. 1(1), 1971-*
6/A.
*BL/U-1. DB/U-2. OX/U24. RE/U-1. SH/U-1.*
*ISSN 0002-7669*

**AMERICAN BIRDS.** XXX
+ +AM. BIRDS.
NATIONAL AUDUBON SOCIETY.
*NEW YORK 25(1), F 1971-*
PREV: AUDUBON FIELD NOTES FROM 1, 1947- 24,
1970.
*LO/N-2.*
*ISSN 0004-7686*

**AMERICAN BULLETIN OF INTERNATIONAL LICENSING &**
**JOINT VENTURE OPPORTUNITIES.**
+ +AM. BULL. INT. LICENS. & JOINT VENTURE OPPORT-
UNITIES.
[INTERNATIONAL ADVANCEMENT, INC.]
*LOS ANGELES 1, 1971-*
*LO/N14.*

**AMERICAN CLASSICAL REVIEW.**
+ +AM. CLASS. REV.
CITY UNIVERSITY OF NEW YORK: QUEEN'S COLLEGE.
*FLUSHING, N.Y. 1(1), 1971-*
*EX/U-1. NO/U-1. OX/U-1.*
*ISSN 0044-7633*

**AMERICAN COSMETICS & PERFUMERY.**                    XXX
++AM. COSMET. & PERFUM.
[ALLURED PUBL. CORP.]
OAK PARK, ILL. 87, 1972 ...
PREV: AMERICAN PERFUMER & COSMETICS FROM
77(6), 1962- 86, 1971. SUBS: COSMETICS &
PERFUMERY.
LO/N14.    LO/S-3.

**AMERICAN DOCUMENTATION.**                            XXX
SUBS(1970): JOURNAL OF THE AMERICAN
SOCIETY FOR INFORMATION SCIENCE.

**AMERICAN EXILE IN BRITAIN.**
++AM. EXILE BR.
UNION OF AMERICAN EXILES IN BRITAIN.
LONDON   NO.1, 5/MR 1969-
M.
LO/U-3.

**AMERICAN FARMER.**                                   XXX
++AM. FARMER.
AMERICAN FARM BUREAU FEDERATION.
LAWRENCE, KANS. 47(2), 1972-
PREV: NATION'S AGRICULTURE FROM 11(4), 1935-
47(1), 1972.
LO/N13.

**AMERICAN FISH FARMER.**
++AM. FISH FARM.
LITTLE ROCK, ARKANSAS  1, D 1969-
M.
LO/R-5.  1970-                    LV/U-1.  1(3), 1970-
ISSN 0002-8479

**AMERICAN HORTICULTURAL MAGAZINE.**                   XXX
++AM. HORTIC. MAG.
AMERICAN HORTICULTURAL SOCIETY.
WASHINGTON, D.C. 39(1), JA 1960- 50, 1971 ...
PREV: NATIONAL HORTICULTURAL MAGAZINE FROM 1,
AG 1922- 38, D 1959. SUBS: AMERICAN HORTI-
CULTURALIST.
LO/N-2.
LO/N14. 41, 1962-
ISSN 0002-8800

**AMERICAN HORTICULTURALIST.**                         XXX
++AM. HORTIC.
AMERICAN HORTICULTURAL SOCIETY.
ALEXANDRIA, VA. 51, 1972-
PREV: AMERICAN HORTICULTURAL MAGAZINE FROM
39(1), JA 1960- 50, 1971.
LO/N-2.

**AMERICAN JOURNAL OF AGRICULTURAL ECONOMICS.**        XXX
++AM. J. AGRIC. ECON. [AJAE-B]
AMERICAN AGRICULTURAL ECONOMICS ASSOCIATION.
LEXINGTON 50(1), F 1968-
5/A. PREV: JOURNAL OF FARM ECONOMICS FROM 1,
1919- 49(5), 1967.
GL/U-2.    LO/N17.    LO/U-3.    OX/U16.    RE/U-1.    SO/U-1.
LO/N10. 53, 1971-
ISSN 0002-9092

**AMERICAN JOURNAL OF ART THERAPY.**                   XXX
++AM. J. ART THER.
WASHINGTON, D.C. 9(1), OC 1969-
PREV:  BULLETIN OF ART THERAPY FROM 1, 1961-
8, 1969.
GL/U-1. 9, 1969- 11, 1972.
ISSN 0007-4764

**AMERICAN JOURNAL OF JURISPRUDENCE.**                 XXX
++AM. J. JURISPRUDENCE.
UNIVERSITY OF NOTRE DAME: LAW SCHOOL.
NOTRE DAME, IND. 14, 1969-
PREV:  NATURAL LAW FORUM FROM 1, 1956- 13,
1968.
BL/U-1.    CV/C-1.    DN/U-1.

**AMERICAN JOURNAL OF PUBLIC HEALTH.**
++AM. J. PUBLIC HEALTH.
AMERICAN PUBLIC HEALTH ASSOCIATION.
NEW YORK 61, 1971-
PREV: AS PART OF AMERICAN JOURNAL OF PUBLIC
HEALTH & THE NATION'S HEALTH FROM 18, 1928.
NATION'S HEALTH CONTINUED AS SEPARATE TITLE.
LD/U-1.    LO/N13.

**AMERICAN LAW REPORTS: FEDERAL, CASES & ANNOTA-
TIONS.**
++AM. LAW REP., FED. CASES & ANNOT.
ROCHESTER, N.Y. &C. 1, 1969-
NO/U-1.    OX/U-1.    RE/U-1.    SO/U-1.

**AMERICAN LIBRARIES.  BULLETIN OF THE ...**           XXX
++AM. LIBR.
AMERICAN LIBRARY ASSOCIATION.
CHICAGO 1(1), JA 1970-
PREV:  ALA BULLETIN FROM 1, JA 1907- 63(11),
D 1969.
BH/U-1.    ED/N-1.    GL/U-2.    HL/U-1.
LO/N14.  LAST THREE YEARS.
ISSN 0002-9769

**AMERICAN LITERARY ANTHOLOGY.**
++AM. LIT. ANTHOL.
[FARRAR, STRAUS & GIROUX]
NEW YORK 1, 1968-
S/T: ANNUAL COLLECTION OF THE BEST FROM THE
LITERARY MAGAZINES.
LO/U-2.    OX/U-1.

**AMERICAN LITERARY REALISM, 1870-1910.**
++AM. LIT. REALISM 1870-1910.
UNIVERSITY OF TEXAS AT ARLINGTON:
DEPARTMENT OF ENGLISH.
ARLINGTON, TEX.  NO.1, 1967-
OX/U-1
ISSN 0002-9823

**AMERICAN MUSICAL DIGEST.**
++AM. MUSICAL DIG.
MUSIC CRITICS ASSOCIATION.
NEW YORK  1, OC 1969-
ED/N-1.
ISSN 0003-0120

**AMERICAN PAINT & WALLCOVERINGS DEALER.**             XXX
++AM. PAINT & WALLCOVER. DEALER.
[AMERICAN PAINT JOURNAL CO.]
ST. LOUIS, MO. 63(12), 1971-
PREV: AMERICAN PAINT & WALLPAPER DEALER FROM
46, D 1952- 63(11), 1971.
LO/N13.

**AMERICAN PAINT & WALLPAPER DEALER.**                 XXX
SUBS (1971): AMERICAN PAINT & WALLCOVERINGS
DEALER.

**AMERICAN PERFUMER.**                                 XXX
SUBS (1962): AMERICAN PERFUMER & COSMETICS.

**AMERICAN PERFUMER & COSMETICS.**                     XXX
++AM. PERFUM. & COSMET. [APRC-A]
[ALLURED PUBL. CORP.]
OAK PARK, ILL. 77(6), 1962-86, 1971 ...
PREV: AMERICAN PERFUMER FROM 75(7), JL 1960-
77(5), 1962. SUBS: AMERICAN COSMETICS &
PERFUMERY.
LO/N14.
ISSN 0003-0392

**AMERICAN PHILOSOPHICAL QUARTERLY; MONOGRAPH
SERIES.**
++AM. PHIL. Q., MONOGR. SER.
[BLACKWELL]
OXFORD  NO.1, 1968-
GL/U-1.    LO/U-1.    LO/U-3.    MA/U-1.

**AMERICAN POETRY REVIEW.**
++AM. POETRY REV.
PHILADELPHIA 1, 1972-
OX/U-1.
EX/U-1. 2(1), 1973-

**AMERICAN POLITICS QUARTERLY.**
++AM. POLIT. Q.
[SAGE PUBL.]
BEVERLY HILLS 1, JA 1973-
Q.
AD/U-1.    OX/U-9.    SH/U-1.    SW/U-1.
ISSN 0044-7803

**AMERICAN PROFESSIONAL PHARMACIST.**                  XXX
SUBS (1969): PHARMACY TIMES.

**AMERICAN STUDIES.  AN INTERDISCIPLINARY
JOURNAL.**                                             XXX
++AM. STUD. (LAWRENCE, KANS.).
MIDCONTINENT AMERICAN STUDIES ASSOCIATION.
LAWRENCE, KANS. 12, 1971-
SPONS. BODY ALSO UNIVERSITY OF KANSAS. PREV:
MIDCONTINENT AMERICAN STUDIES JOURNAL FROM 3,
1962- 11, 1970.
CB/U-1.    ED/N-1.    LD/U-1.    NO/U-1.    NW/U-1.    OX/U-1.
CA/U-1. 8, 1970-
ISSN 0026-3079

**AMERICAN STUDIES IN PAPYROLOGY.**
++AM. STUD. PAPYROL.
AMERICAN SOCIETY OF PAPYROLOGISTS.
*NEW HAVEN 1, 1966-*
BL/U-1.
*ISSN 0569-8642*

**AMERICAN STUDIES IN SCANDINAVIA.**
++AM. STUD. SCAND.
NORDISKA SALLSKAPET FOR AMERIKASTUDIER.
*UPPSALA NO.1, 1968-*
2/A. ISSUED UNDER THE BODY'S ENGL. FORM OF
NAME: NORDIC ASSOCIATION FOR AMERICAN STUDIES.
OX/U-1.

**AMERICAN SURVEYOR & PHOTOGRAMMETRIST.**          XXX
++AM. SURV. & PHOTOGRAMM.
[FARRAR PUBL. CO.]
*WASHINGTON, D.C. 3(11), N 1964- 9(4), 1970.//*
PREV: NATIONAL SURVEYOR FROM 1, MY 1962-
3(10), 1964.
LO/N13.
*ISSN 0003-1364*

**AMERICAN TRANSCENDENTAL QUARTERLY.**
++AM. TRANSCEND. Q.
EMERSON SOCIETY.
*HARTFORD, CONN. NO.1, 1969-*
ED. FOR THE EMERSON SOC. & FRIENDS ...
INDIV. ISSUES CAN APPEAR IN SEVERAL PARTS.
LO/N-1.   LO/N-3.
*ISSN 0003-1410*

**AMERICANA (1973).**
AMERICAN HERITAGE SOCIETY.
*NEW YORK 1, MR 1973-*
2M.
AD/U-1.   OX/U-9.

**AMERICA'S TEXTILES REPORTER/BULLETIN.**          XXX
++AM. TEXT. REP. BULL.
[CLARK PUBL. CO.]
*GREENVILLE, S.C. 97(9), 1971-*
M. PREV: TEXTILE BULLETIN FROM MR 1933-
97(8), 1971.
LO/N14. 97(12), 1971-

**AMGUEDDFA. BULLETIN OF THE NATIONAL MUSEUM
OF WALES.**
*CARDIFF [NO.]1, 1969-*
CA/U-1.   CR/N-1.   DB/U-2.   LO/N-2.   LO/U-2.   OX/U-2.
*ISSN 0003-1682*

**AMINO-ACID PEPTIDE & PROTEIN ABSTRACTS.**
++AMINO-ACID PEPT. & PROTEIN ABSTR.
[INFORMATION RETRIEVAL LTD.]
*LONDON 1(1), JA 1972-*
M.
CA/U-1.   GL/U-2.   LO/N14.   MA/U-1.   SH/U-1.
ED/N-1. 1(2), 1972-
*ISSN 0044-8125*

**AMINO-ACIDS, PEPTIDES & PROTEINS.**
++AMINO-ACIDS, PEPT. & PROTEINS.
CHEMICAL SOCIETY.
*LONDON 1, 1968 (1969)-*
A. S/T: A SPECIALIST PERIODICAL REPORT.
BH/U-1.   CB/U-1.   GL/U-2.   LO/C-4.   LO/N14.   LO/S-3.
LO/U12.   LO/U13.   LO/U20.   NW/U-1.   OX/U-8.
SH/U-1.   SO/U-1.
*ISSN 0044-8125*

**AMISTAD. WRITINGS ON BLACK HISTORY & CULTURE.**
[RANDOM HOUSE]
*NEW YORK 1, 1970-*
OX/U-1.
*ISSN 0003-1879*

**AMS NEWSLETTER.**
++AMS NEWSL. (AM. MUSICOL. SOC. INC.).
AMERICAN MUSICOLOGICAL SOCIETY, INC.
*DENTON, TEX. 1, 1971-*
ED/N-1.

**AMSTERDAMER BEITRAGE ZUR ALTEREN GERMANISTIK.**
++AMST. BEITR. ALTEREN GER.
[RODOPI NV]
*AMSTERDAM 1, 1972-*
ANNU. ENGL. & GER.
MA/U-1.   NO/U-1.   SH/U-1.

**ANAESTHESIA & ANALGESIA.**
++ANAESTH. & ANALG.
[MORGAN PUBL.]
*EWELL, SURREY 1(1), JA/F 1972-*
6/A.
ED/N-1.   LO/N14.   MA/U-1.   OX/U-8.

**ANAESTHESIA & INTENSIVE CARE.**
++ANAESTH. & INTENSIVE CARE.
AUSTRALIAN SOCIETY OF ANAESTHETISTS.
*POTTS POINT, N.S.W. 1, 1972-*
BL/U-1.

**ANAIS DA ESCOLA NACIONAL DE SAUDE PUBLICA E
DE MEDICINA TROPICAL.**                               XXX
++AN. ESC. NAC. SAUDE PUBLICA & MED. TROP.
*LISBON 1, 1967-*
PREV: ANAIS DO INSTITUTO DE MEDICINA TROPICAL
FROM 1, 1943.
GL/U-1.   LO/N-2.   LO/U-3.

**ANAIS DA FACULDADE DE FARMACIA E ODONTOLOGIA DA
UNIVERSIDADE DE SAO PAULO: FARMACIA.**                XXX
SUBS (1963) PART OF: REVISTA DA FACULDADE DE
ODONTOLOGIA DE SAO PAULO.

**ANAIS DA FACULDADE DE FARMACIA E ODONTOLOGIA DA
UNIVERSIDADE DE SAO PAULO: ODONTOLOGIA.**             XXX
SUBS (1963) PART OF: REVISTA DA FACULDADE DE
ODONTOLOGIA DE SAO PAOLO.

**ANAIS DE HISTORIA.**
++AN. HIST. (BR.).
(ASSIS, BRAZIL) FACULDADE DE FILOSOFIA,
CIENCIAS DE LETTRAS: DEPARTAMENTO DE HISTORIA.
*ASSIS, BRAZ. 1, 1968/69-*
CC/U-1.   LO/U19.

**ANAIS DO INSTITUTO DE MEDICINA TROPICAL.**          XXX
SUBS (1967): ANAIS DA ESCOLA NACIONAL DE
SAUDE PUBLICA E DE MEDICINA TROPICAL.

**ANALECTA.**
[ANALECTA INC.]
*DEMAREST, N.J. 1, 1967-*
Q.
OX/U-1.
*ISSN 0569-9770*

**ANALECTA ANSELMIANA. UNTERSUCHUNGEN UBER PERSON
UND WERK ANSELMS VON CANTERBURY.**
[MINERVA]
*FRANKFURT AM MAIN 1, 1969-*
GL/U-1.   LO/U17.   MA/U-1.

**ANALECTA HUSSERLIANA. YEARBOOK OF PHENOMENOL-
OGICAL RESEARCH.**
++AN. HUSSERLIANA.
[REIDEL; HUMANITIES P.]
*DORDRECHT; NEW YORK 1, 1971-*
ENGL. & GER.
BL/U-1.   DB/U-2.   DR/U-1.   GL/U-1.   LO/U-1.   OX/U-1.
SW/U-1.

**ANALECTA LINGUISTICA. INTERNATIONAL BULLETIN
OF LINGUISTICS.**
++ANALECTA LINGUIST.
[J. BENJAMINS N.V.]
*AMSTERDAM 1(1), 1971-*
DB/U-2.   EX/U-1.   OX/U-1.
*ISSN 0044-8176*

**ANALES DE LA ACADEMIA NACIONAL DE CIENCIAS
EXACTAS, FISICAS Y NATURALES (ARGENTINA).
SUPLEMENTO.**
++AN. ACAD. NAC. CIENC. EXACTAS FIS. NATUR.
(ARGENT.), SUPL.
*BUENOS AIRES NO.1, 1968-*
LO/N-4.

**ANALES CIENTIFICOS, UNIVERSIDAD NACIONAL DEL
CENTRO DEL PERU.**
++AN. CIENT. UNIV. NAC. CENT. PERU.
*HUANCAYO 1, 1972-*
OX/U-1.

**ANALES DE LA FACULTAD LATINOAMERICANA DE
CIENCIAS SOCIALES.**
++AN. FAC. LAT.AM. CIEN. SOC.
FACULTAD LATINOAMERICANA DE CIENCIAS SOCIALES.
*SANTIAGO DE CHILE 1(1), JA/D 1964.//*
LO/U-3.

**ANALI FILOLOSKOG FAKULTETA, BEOGRADSKI UNI-
VERZITET.**
++AN. FILOL. FAK. BEOGRAD. UNIV.
*BELGRADE KNJ.1, 1961 (1962)-*
ADDED TITLE IN FR.: ANNALES DE LA FACULTE DE
PHILOLOGIE, UNIVERSITE DE BELGRADE.
CA/U-1.   LO/N-3.   OX/U-1.

ANALELE, INSTITUTUL DE CERCETARI PENTRU
IMBUNATATIRI FUNCIARE SI PEDOLOGIE:
SERIA HIDROTECHNICA.
+ +AN. INST. CERCET. PENTRU IMBUNATATIRI
FUNCIARE & PEDOL., HIDROTECH.
BUCHAREST 1, 1968-
ENGL. SUMM.
LO/N13.

ANALELE, INSTITUTUL DE CERCETARI PENTRU
POMICULTURA PITESTI.
+ +AN. INST. CERCET. PENTRU POMICULT. PITESTI.
BUCHAREST 1, 1968-
ENGL. SUMM.
LO/N13.

ANALELE, INSTITUTUL DE CERCETARI PENTRU
VITICULTURA SI VINIFICATIE.
+ +AN. INST. CERCET. PENTRU VITICULT. &
VINIFICATE.
BUCHAREST 1, 1968-
ENGL. SUMM.
LO/N13.

ANALES, INSTITUTO DE ESTUDIOS MADRILENOS,
CONSEJO SUPERIOR DE INVESTIGACIONES
CIENTIFICAS (SPAIN).
+ +AN. INST. ESTUD. MADR. CONS. SUPER. INVEST.
CIENT. (SPAIN).
MADRID 1, 1966-
OX/U-1.    SH/U-1.

ANALES DEL INSTITUTO NACIONAL DE INVESTIGA-
CIONES BIOLOGICO-PESQUERAS.
+ +AN. INST. NAC. INVEST. BIOL.-PESQ. (MEX.)
INSTITUTO NACIONAL DE INVESTIGACIONES
BIOLOGICO-PESQUERAS (MEXICO).
MEXICO, DF 1, 1965-
LO/N-2.

ANALES, INSTITUTO DE LA PATAGONIA.
+ +AN. INST. PATAGONIA.
PUNTA ARENAS 1, 1970-
LO/N-2.

ANALES INTERNACIONALES DE CRIMINOLOGIA.    000
SEE: ANNALES INTERNATIONALES DE CRIMINOLOGIE.

ANALES DE LA SOCIEDAD MEXICANA DE HISTORIA
DE LA CIENCIA Y DE LA TECNOLOGIA.
+ +AN. SOC. MEX. HIST. CIENC. & TECNOL.
MEXICO, D.F. NO.1, 1969-
LO/M24.

ANALES DE SOCIOLOGIA.
+ +AN. SOCIOL. (SP.)
CENTRO DE ESTUDIOS ECONOMICOS Y SOCIALES
(BARCELONA).
BARCELONA 1(1), JE 1966-
ISSUED BY THE CENTRO'S DEPARTAMENTO DE
SOCIOLOGIA. CENTRO A SUBORD BODY 'DE LA
DELEGACION DEL CONSEJO SUPERIOR DE INVESTI-
GACIONES CIENTIFICAS.' 2/A.
LO/U-3.
ISSN 0003-2522

ANALES TOLEDANOS.
+ +AN. TOLEDANOS.
INSTITUTO PROVINCIAL DE INVESTIGACIONES Y EST-
UDIOS TOLEDANOS.
TOLEDO 1, 1967-
LO/N-1.    OX/U-1.

ANALES, UNIVERSIDAD DE LA PATAGONIA SAN JUAN
BOSCO.
+ +AN. UNIV. PATAGONIA SAN JUAN BOSCO.
COMODORO RIVADAVIA NO.1, 1964-
LO/N-2.

ANALELE UNIVERSITATII DIN TIMISOARA: SERIA
STIINTE FIZICE-CHIMICE.    XXX
+ +AN. UNIV. TIMISOARA, STIINTE FIZ.-CHIM.
TIMISOARA 7, 1969-
PREV: PART ANALELE UNIVERSITII DIN TIMISOARA:
SERIA STIINTE MATEMATICE-FIZICE FROM 1, 1963-
6, 1968.
GL/U-1.
CA/U-2. 8, 1970-

ANALELE UNIVERSITATII DIN TIMISOARA: SERIA
STIINTE MATEMATICE.    XXX
+ +AN. UNIV. TIMISOARA, STIINTE MAT.
TIMISOARA 7, 1969-
PREV: ANALELE UNIVERSITATII DIN
TIMISOARA: SERIA STIINTE MATEMATICE-FIZICE
FROM 1, 1963- 6, 1968.
GL/U-1.
CA/U-2. 7, 1969-

ANALUSIS.    XXX
SOCIETE DE PRODUCTIONS DOCUMENTAIRES.
RUEIL-MALMAISON 1, 1972-
MON. FR. PREV. PART OF: CHIMIE ANALYTIQUE
FROM 1, 1896- 54(3), 1972; & METHODS PHYSIQUE
D'ANALYSE FROM 1, 1965- 8(1), 1972.
LO/N14.    LO/S-3.
NW/U-1.    1(5), 1972-
XS/R10.    1(2), 1972- [5 YEARS ONLY].

ANALYTICAL LETTERS.
+ +ANAL. LETT.
[DEKKER]
NEW YORK 1, 1967-
BH/U-1.    LO/N14.    LO/S-3.    OX/U-8.
ISSN 0003-2719

ANALYTICAL PROFILES OF DRUG SUBSTANCES.
+ +ANAL. PROFILES DRUG SUBST.
ACADEMY OF PHARMACEUTICAL SCIENCES: PHARMACEUT-
ICAL ANALYSIS & CONTROL SECTION.
[ACADEMIC P.]
NEW YORK; LONDON 1, 1972-
LO/N14.

ANAN KOGYO KOTO SENMON GAKKO KENKYU KIYO.
RESEARCH REPORTS OF THE ANAN TECHNICAL
COLLEGE.
ANAN NO.1, 1965-
ENGL. SUMM.
LO/N14.

ANATOLICA. ANNUAIRE INTERNATIONAL POUR LES
CIVILISATIONS DE L'ASIE ANTERIEURE.
NEDERLANDS HISTORISCH-ARCHEOLOGISCH INSTITUUT
IN HET NABIJE OOSTEN.
LEYDEN NO.1, 1967-
BH/U-1.    GL/U-1.    LO/U17.    MA/U-1.    SH/U-1.

ANCIENT SOCIETY.
+ +ANCIENT SOC.
UNIVERSITE CATHOLIQUE DE LOUVAIN.
LOUVAIN 1, 1970-
ENGL. GER. FR. ITAL. DUTCH.
BL/U-1.    GL/U-1.    LO/U-1.    LO/U-2.    NO/U-1.    OX/U-1.
SH/U-1.
ISSN 0066-1619

ANDOVER DOCUMENTS.
+ +ANDOVER DOC.
ANDOVER LOCAL ARCHIVES COMMITTEE.
ANDOVER NO.1, 1968-
OX/U-1.

ANESTHESIA PROGRESS.
+ +ANESTH. PROG.
AMERICAN DENTAL SOCIETY OF ANESTHESIOLOGY.
WELLESLY, MASS. 13, 1966-
PREV: JOURNAL, AM. DENT. SOC. ANESTHESIOL.
FROM 5, 1958-12, 1965.
LO/M34.    XY/N-1.
ISSN 0003-3006

ANGEWANDTE METEOROLOGIE.    XXX
+ +ANGEW. METEOROL.
(GERMANY, EAST) METEOROLOGISCHER DIENST.
[AKADEMIE-VERLAG GMBH]
EAST BERLIN 1, JE 1951- 5(12), 1970.//
SUPPL. TO ZEITSCHRIFT FUR METEOROLOGIE.
LO/N14.    4(1), 1960-
ISSN 0570-0868

ANGLIA.
UNIVERSIDAD NACIONAL AUTONOMA DE MEXICO: CENTRO
DE ESTUDIOS ANGLOAMERICANOS.
MEXICO, D.F. 1, 1968-
OX/U-1.

ANGLICA WRATISLAVIENSIA.
+ +ANGLICA WRATISLAV.
UNIWERSYTET WROCLAWSKI.
WROCLAW 1, 1971-
MONOGR. ALSO NUMBERED AS: ACTA UNIVERSITATIS
WRATISLAVIENSIS. NO. 1 ABOVE = NO.146 OF THE
ACTA.
LO/N-3.

ANGLIJA, ZHURNAL O SEVODNJASHCHEJ ZHIZNI V
VELIKOBRITANII.
+ +ANGLIJA ZH. SEVODNJASHCHEJ ZHIZNI VELIKOBR.
(GREAT BRITAIN) CENTRAL OFFICE OF INFORMATION.
LONDON 1(1), 1962-
OX/U-1.

**ANGLO-AMERICAN CATALOGUING RULES AMENDMENT BULLETIN.**
++ANGLO-AM. CAT. RULES AMEND. BULL.
LIBRARY ASSOCIATION: CATALOGUING & INDEXING
GROUP.
LONDON NO.1, JA 1970-
CA/U-2.    CR/M-1.    LO/N17.    LO/U-2.    LO/U13.    RE/U-1.

**ANGLO-AMERICAN LAW REVIEW.**
++ANGLO-AM. LAW REV.
[JUSTICE OF THE PEACE]
CHICHESTER 1(1) JA/MR 1972-
Q.
BL/U-1.    CA/U-1.    CA/U13.    CR/U-1.    ED/N-1.    LO/U12.
LO/U28.    MA/U-1.    SH/U-1.    SO/U-1.
NO/U-1. 2, 1973-

**ANGLO-SAXON ENGLAND.**
++ANGLO-SAXON ENGL.
[CAMBRIDGE U.P.]
CAMBRIDGE 1, 1972-
BL/U-1.    BN/U-1.    CA/U-1.    GL/U-1.    LD/U-1.    LO/U-1.
NO/U-1.    OX/U-1.    SH/U-1.
HL/U-1. 1, 1972- 2, 1973.

**ANIMAL BEHAVIOUR MONOGRAPHS.**
++ANIM. BEHAV. MONOGR.
[BAILLIERE, TINDALL & CASSELL]
LONDON 1, 1968-
BH/U-1.    GL/U-1.    LD/U-1.    LO/N-2.    LO/N13.
ED/N-1. 4, 1971-                      MA/U-1. 3, 1970-
GL/U-1. 1, 1968- 3, 1970.
ISSN 0066-1856

**ANIMAL BLOOD GROUPS & BIOCHEMICAL GENETICS.**
++ANIM. BLOOD GROUPS & BIOCHEM. GENET.
EUROPEAN SOCIETY FOR ANIMAL BLOOD GROUP
RESEARCH.
[CENTRE FOR AGRICULTURAL PUBL. & DOCUMENTATION]
WAGENINGEN 1, 1970-
BL/U-1.    LO/N13.
SW/U-1.
ISSN 0003-3480

**ANIMAL LEARNING & BEHAVIOR.**                                              XXX
++ANIM. LEARN. & BEHAV.
PSYCHONOMIC SOCIETY.
AUSTIN, TEX. 1, 1973-
Q. PREV. PART OF: PSYCHONOMIC SCIENCE FROM
1, 1964- 29(6), JA 1973.
BN/U-1.    GL/U-1.    GL/U-2.    LD/U-1.    LO/U-4.    MA/U-1.
RE/U-1.    SH/U-1.    SO/U-1.
ISSN 0090-4996

**ANIMAL SCIENCE (SOFIA).**                                                   000
SEE: ZHIVOTNOVUDNI NAUKI.

**ANN ARBOR REVIEW.**
++ANN ARBOR REV.
ANN ARBOR, MICH. NO.1, 1967-
Q.
OX/U-1.
ISSN 0003-3731

**ANNALES: MUSEES, EDUCATION, ACTION CULTUR-ELLE.**
++ANN., MUS. EDUC. ACTION CULT.
INTERNATIONAL COUNCIL OF MUSEUMS.
LONDON NO.1, 1969-
LO/N-2.

**ANNALES DE L'ABEILLE.**                                                     XXX
SUBS (1970) PART OF: APIDOLOGIE.

**ANNALES D'ASTROPHYSIQUE.**                                                  XXX
SUBS: ASTRONOMY & ASTROPHYSICS.

**ANNALS OF CLINICAL BIOCHEMISTRY.**                                          XXX
++ANN. CLIN. BIOCHEM.
ASSOCIATION OF CLINICAL BIOCHEMISTS.
LONDON 6, 1969-
PREV: PROCEEDINGS, ASSOCIATION ... FROM 1,
1960- 6, 1968.
GL/U-1.    LO/N13.    NW/U-1.
ISSN 0004-5632

**ANNALS OF CLINICAL LABORATORY SCIENCE.**
++ANN. CLIN. LAB. SCI.
ASSOCIATION OF CLINICAL SCIENTISTS.
PHILADELPHIA 1(1), 1971-
OX/U-8.

**ANNALS OF CLINICAL RESEARCH.**                                             XXX
++ANN. CLIN. RES.
SUOMALAINEN LAAKARISEURA DUODECIM.
HELSINKI 1, 1969-
INCORP: ANNALES MEDICINAE INTERNAE FENNIAE
FROM 35, 1946- 57, 1968; & ANNALES PAEDIATRIAE
FENNIAE FROM 1, 1954/55- 14, 1968.
BL/U-1.
OX/U-8. 3(4), 1971-
ISSN 0003-4762

**ANNALS OF CLINICAL RESEARCH. SUPPLEMENT.**                                 XXX
++ANN. CLIN. RES., SUPPL.
SUOMALAINEN LAAKARISEURA DUODECIM.
HELSINKI 1, 1969-
PREV: ANNALES MEDICINAE INTERNAE FENNIAE.
SUPPLEMENTUM FROM 1(1), 1947.
BL/U-1.
OX/U-8. 3(4), 1971-
ISSN 0066-2291

**ANNALES, ECOLE DES SCIENCES, UNIVERSITE D'ABIDJAN.**
++ANN. EC. SCI. UNIV. ABIDJAN.
ABIDJAN 1, 1965-
LO/N-2.

**ANNALES OF ECONOMIC & SOCIAL MEASUREMENT.**
++ANN. ECON. & SOC. MEAS.
NATIONAL BUREAU OF ECONOMIC RESEARCH (US).
NEW YORK 1(1), JA 1972-
AD/U-1. 1, 1972- *    BL/U-1.    CA/U38.    GL/U-1.    LO/U-3.
OX/U-3.    OX/U-8.    OX/U16.    OX/U17.    SH/U-1.
SO/U-1.
EX/U-1. 2, 1973-                      HL/U-1. 2, 1973-
ISSN 0044-832X

**ANNALES D'EMBRYOLOGIE ET DE MORPHOGENESE.**
++ANN. EMBRYOL. & MORPHOGEN.
CENTRE NATIONAL DE LA RECHERCHE SCIENTIFIQUE.
PARIS 1, MR 1968-
Q.
LO/N-2.    LO/N13.    LO/U-2.
OX/U-8. 5, 1972-
ISSN 0003-4258

**ANNALES DE EPIPHYTIES.**                                                   XXX
SUBS (1969) PART OF: ANNALES DE PHYTOPATH-
OLOGIE; & ANNALES DE ZOOLOGIE - ECOLOGIE
ANIMALE.

**ANNALES D'ETUDES INTERNATIONALES. ANNALS OF INTERNATIONAL STUDIES.**
++ANN. ETUD. INT.
INSTITUT UNIVERSITAIRE DE HAUTES ETUDES INTER-
NATIONALES: ASSOCIATION DES ANCIENS.
GENEVA [NO.1], 1970-
AD/U-1.    LO/U-3.    OX/U-1.

**ANNALES, FACULTE DE DROIT ET DES SCIENCES ECONOMIQUES, UNIVERSITE DE CLERMONT-FERRAND.**
++ANN. FAC. DROIT & SCI. ECON. UNIV. CLERMONT-
FERRAND.
PARIS 1, 1964-
OX/U-1.

**ANNALES, FACULTE DES LETTRES ET SCIENCES HUMAINES, UNIVERSITE DE DAKAR.**
++ANN. FAC. LETT. & SCI. HUM. UNIV. DAKAR.
DAKAR NO.1, 1971-
OX/U-1.

**ANNALES DE LA FACULTE DES LETTRES ET SCIENCES HUMAINES, UNIVERSITE FEDERALE DU CAMEROUN.**
++ANN. FAC. LETT. & SCI. HUM. UNIV. FED.
CAMEROUN.
YAOUNDE 1(1), 1969-
LO/N-1.    LO/U14.

**ANNALES DE LA FACULTE DES LETTRES ET SCIENCES HUMAINES, UNIVERSITE DE NICE.**
++ANN. FAC. LETT. & SCI. HUM. UNIV. NICE.
[MONACO P.]
PARIS 1, 1967-
CA/U-1.

**ANNALES, FACULTE DE MEDECINE, UNIVERSITE D'ABIDJAN.**
++ANN. FAC. MED. UNIV. ABIDJAN.
ABIDJAN 1, 1965-
LO/N-2.

**ANNALES DE LA FACULTE DE PHILOLOGIE, UNI-VERSITE DE BELGRADE.**          000
SEE: ANALI FILOLOSKOG FAKULTETA, BEOGRADSKI
UNIVERZITET.

ANNALI DELLA FACOLTA DI SCIENZE AGRARIE DELLA
UNIVERSITA DEGLI STUDI DI TORINO.
++ANN. FAC. SCI. AGRAR. UNIV. STUDI TORINO.
TURIN 1, 1961/62(1962)-
BL/U-1.    LO/N-2.    LO/N13.    RE/U-1.

ANNALI DELLA FONDAZIONE LUIGI EINAUDI.
++ANN. FOND. LUIGI EINAUDI.
FONDAZIONE LUIGI EINAUDI.
TORINO  1, 1967-
ANNU.
LO/U-3.    OX/U-1.    RE/U-1.

ANNALES DE GENETIQUE ET DE SELECTION ANIMALE.
++ANN. GENET. & SEL. ANIM.
INSTITUT NATIONAL DE LA RECHERCHE AGRONOMIQUE
(FRANCE).
PARIS 1, 1969-
CA/U11.    LO/N13.
RE/U-1.  2, 1970-
ISSN 0003-4002

ANNALES D'HYDROBIOLOGIE.                              XXX
++ANN. HYDROBIOL.
INSTITUT NATIONAL DE LA RECHERCHE AGRONOM-
IQUE (FRANCE).
PARIS 1, 1970-
PREV: RECHERCHES D'HYDROBIOLOGIE CONTINENTALE
FROM NO.1, 1969.
DB/S-1.    LO/N-4.    LO/N13.    OX/U-8.
ISSN 0046-4937

ANNALES D'IMMUNOLOGIE.                                XXX
++ANN. IMMUNOL. (PARIS).
INSTITUT PASTEUR (PARIS).
PARIS 124C(1), 1973-
PREV. PART OF: ANNALES DE L'INSTITUT PASTEUR
FROM 1, 1887- 123, 1972.
GL/U-1.    GL/U-2.    LD/U-1.    LO/N-2.    LO/N-4.    LO/N13.
LO/N14.    LO/U-1.    NW/U-1.    RE/U-1.

ANNALS OF IMMUNOLOGY.                                 XXX
++ANN. IMMUNOL.(POZNAN).
POZNANSKIE TOWARZYSTWO PRZYJACIOL NAUK.
POZNAN 1, 1969-
PREV: BULLETIN DE LA SOCIETE DES AMIS DES
SCIENCES ET DES LETTRES DE POZNAN, SER.C -
MEDECINE FROM 1, 1949. BODY NAME IN FRENCH
SOCIETE DES AMIS ...
DB/S-1.    LO/N13.
ISSN 0044-8338

ANNALES, INSTITUT BELGE DU PETROLE.
++ANN. INST. BELG. PETROLE.
BRUSSELS 1, 1967-
FR. & FLEMISH.
LO/N14.
ISSN 0020-2185

ANNALES DE L'INSTITUT NATIONAL DE RECHERCHES
FORESTIERES DE TUNISIE.
++ANN. INST. NAT. RECH. FOR. TUNISIE.
ARIANA  1, 1968-
OX/U-3.

ANNALES, INSTITUT NATIONAL DE LA STATISTIQUE
ET DES ETUDES ECONOMIQUES (FRANCE).
++ANN. INST. NAT. STATIST. ETUD. ECON. (FR.).
PARIS NO.1, 1969-
LO/U-1.    LO/U-3.    OX/U-1.

ANNALES DE L'INSTITUT PASTEUR.                        XXX
SUBS (1973): PART OF: ANNALES D'IMMUNOLOGIE;
& ANNALES DE MICROBIOLOGIE.

ANNALES, INTERNATIONAL COUNCIL OF MUSEUMS.           000
SEE: ANNUAL, INTERNATIONAL COUNCIL OF MUSEUMS.

ANNALES INTERNATIONALES DE CRIMINOLOGIE.
INTERNATIONAL ANNALS OF CRIMINOLOGY. ANALES
INTERNACIONALES DE CRIMINOLOGIA.                      XXX
++ANN. INT. CRIMINOL.
SOCIETE INTERNATIONALE DE CRIMINOLOGIE.
PARIS 1962-
2/A. PREV: BULLETIN DE LA SOCIETE ...
ED/U-1.
LO/U-3.  7, 1968-
RE/U-1. CURRENT YEAR ONLY.
ISSN 0003-4452

ANNALS OF INTERNATIONAL STUDIES.                     000
SEE: ANNALES D'ETUDES INTERNATIONALES.

ANNALS OF THE IQSY.
INTERNATIONAL COUNCIL OF SCIENTIFIC UNIONS:
SPECIAL COMMITTEE FOR THE INTERNATIONAL YEARS
OF THE QUIET SUN.
[MASSACHUSETTS INSTITUTE OF TECHNOLOGY P.]
CAMBRIDGE, MASS. & C.  1, 1968-
CA/U12.    GL/U-1.

ANNALI, ISTITUTO ITALIANO PER GLI STUDI
STORICI.
++ANN. IST. ITAL. GLI STUD. STORICI.
ISTITUTO ITALIANO PER GLI STUDI STORICI.
NAPOLI 1, 1968-
CA/U-1.    OX/U-1.

ANNALI, ISTITUTO SPERIMENTALE AGRONOMICO.
++ANN. IST. SPER. AGRON.
BARI 1, 1970-
LO/N13.

ANNALI, ISTITUTO SPERIMENTALE PER L'ASSES-
TAMENTO FORESTALE E PER L'ALPICOLTURA.
++ANN. IST. SPER. ASSESTAMENTO FOR. ALPICOLT.
TRENTO 1, 1970-
LO/N13.

ANNALI DELL'ISTITUTO SPERIMENTALE PER LA
SELVICOLTURA.
++ANN. IST. SPER. SELVICOLT.
AREZZO 1, 1970-
LO/N13.    OX/U-3.

ANNALI, ISTITUTO SPERIMENTALE PER LA VALORIZ-
ZAZIONE TECNOLOGICA DEI PRODOTTI AGRICOLI.
++ANN. IST. SPER. VALORIZZAZIONE TECNOL. PROD.
AGRIC.
MILAN  1, 1970-
LO/N13.

ANNALI DELL' ISTITUTO SPERIMENTALE PER LA ZOO-
TECNIA (ROME).                                        XXX
++ANN. IST. SPER. ZOOTEC. (ROME).
ROME 1, 1968-
PREV: ANNALI DELL' ISTITUTO SPERIMENTALE
ZOOTECNICO DI ROMA FROM 1, 1933- 11, 1967.
CA/U11.

ANNALI DELL' ISTITUTO SPERIMENTALE ZOOTECNICO
DI ROMA.                                              XXX
SUBS (1968): ANNALI DELL' ISTITUTO SPERIMENT-
ALE PER LA ZOOTECNIA (ROME).

ANNALI DELL' ISTITUTO DI STUDI DANTESCHI.
++ANN. IST. STUDI DANTESCHI.
[VITA E PENSIERO]
MILAN 1, 1967-
CB/U-1.    SH/U-1.

ANNALES MALGACHES: MEDECINE.
++ANN. MALGACHES, MED.
UNIVERSITE DE MADAGASCAR.
TANANARIVE 1, 1963-
LO/N-2.

ANNALES MAROCAINES DE SOCIOLOGIE. = MOROCCAN
ANNALS OF SOCIOLOGY.
++ANN. MAROC. SOCIOL.
INSTITUT DE SOCIOLOGIE DE RABAT.
RABAT  1968-
A. ENGL., FR., ARAB.
LO/U-3.

ANNALS OF MATHEMATICAL LOGIC.
++ANN. MATH. LOGIC.
[NORTH-HOLLAND PUBL. CO.]
AMSTERDAM 1, 1970-
AD/U-1.    BR/U-3.    GL/U-1.    HL/U-1.    LD/U-1.    LO/N14.
LO/U-2.    LO/U-4.    MA/U-1.    OX/U-8.    SW/U-1.
BL/U-1.  5, 1972-              DN/U-1. 3(1), 1971-
ISSN 0003-4843

ANNALS OF MATHEMATICAL STATISTICS.                    XXX
SUBS (1973): PART OF ANNALS OF STATISTICS; &
ANNALS OF PROBABILITY.

ANNALES MEDICINAE INTERNAE FENNIAE.                   XXX
SUBS (1969): PART OF ANNALS OF CLINICAL
RESEARCH.

ANNALES MEDICINAE INTERNAE FENNIAE. SUPPLE-
MENTUM.
SUBS (1969): ANNALS OF CLINICAL RESEARCH.
SUPPLEMENT.

ANNALES DE MICROBIOLOGIE: A.                                    XXX
++ANN. MICROBIOL., A.
INSTITUT PASTEUR (PARIS).
 PARIS 124A(1), JA 1973-
 PREV. PART OF: ANNALES DE L'INSTITUT PASTEUR
 FROM 1, 1887- 123, 1972. SPONS. BODY ALSO:
 SOCIETE FRANCAISE DE MICROBIOLOGIE.
 BD/U-1.     BL/U-1.     GL/U-2.    LD/U-1.    LO/N-2.    LO/N-4.
 LO/N14.     NW/U-1.    RE/U-1.

ANNALES DE MICROBIOLOGIE: B.                                    XXX
++ANN. MICROBIOL., B.
INSTITUT PASTEUR (PARIS).
 PARIS 124B(1), JL 1973-
 PREV. PART OF: ANNALES DE L'INSTITUT PASTEUR
 FROM 1, 1887- 123, 1972. SPONS. BODY ALSO:
 SOCIETE FRANCAISE DE MICROBIOLOGIE.
 GL/U-2.     LO/N14.

ANNALES DES MUSEES.                                            000
 SEE: MUSEUMS ANNUAL.

ANNALS, OKLAHOMA ACADEMY OF SCIENCE.
++ANN. OKLA. ACAD. SCI.
 ARDMORE NO.1, 1970-
 LO/N-2.     LO/N-4.    LO/N13.    OX/U-1.

ANNALES PAEDIATRIAE FENNIAE.                                   XXX
 SUBS (1969): PART OF ANNALS OF CLINICAL RE-
 SEARCH.

ANNALS OF PHYSICAL MEDICINE.                                   XXX
 SUBS (1970): RHEUMATOLOGY & PHYSICAL MEDICINE.

ANNALES DE PHYSIQUE BIOLOGIQUE ET MEDICALE.
++ANN. PHYS. BIOL. & MED.
SOCIETE FRANCAISE DE PHYSIQUE BIOLOGIQUE ET
MEDICALE.
 [GAUTHIER-VILLARS]
 PARIS  1, 1967-
 ENGL. SUMM.
 LO/N14.
 ISSN 0029-0793

ANNALES DE PHYTOPATHOLOGIE.                                    XXX
++ANN. PHYTOPATHOL.
INSTITUT NATIONAL DE LA RECHERCHE AGRONOMIQUE
(FRANCE).
 PARIS 1(1), 1969-
 PREV. PART OF: ANNALES DES EPIPHYTIES
 FROM 1, 1950- 19, 1968.
 CA/U11.    LO/N-2.    LO/N14.    LO/R-2.    LO/R-6.    OX/U-8.
 XS/R-2.
 ISSN 0003-4177

ANNALS OF PROBABILITY.                                         XXX
++ANN. PROBAB.
INSTITUTE OF MATHEMATICAL STATISTICS.
 BALTIMORE 1, 1973-
 PREV. PART OF: ANNALS OF MATHEMATICAL STATIST-
 ICS FROM 1, 1930- 43, 1972.
 BR/U-1.    CA/U-2.    EX/U-1.    GL/U-2.    LD/U-1.    LO/N-4.
 LO/N13.    LO/R-5.    LO/U-3.    SF/U-1.    SH/U-1.    SO/U-1.

ANNALES DE RECHERCHES VETERINAIRES.
++ANN. RECH. VET.
INSTITUT NATIONAL DE LA RECHERCHE AGRONOM-
IQUE (FRANCE).
 PARIS  1, 1970-
 LO/M18.    LO/N13.
 ISSN 0003-4193

ANNALS OF REGIONAL SCIENCE.
++ANN. REG. SCI. (WASH.)
WESTERN REGIONAL SCIENCE ASSOCIATION.
 BELLINGHAM, WASH.   1(1), D 1967-
 ANNU. SPONS. BODY ALSO: WESTERN WASHINGTON
 STATE COLLEGE.
 AD/U-1.    CB/U-1.    GL/U-2.    LC/U-1.    LN/U-2.    LO/U-3.
 NO/U-1.

ANNALS, SOCIETE BELGE D'HISTOIRE DES HOPI-
TAUX.
++ANN. SOC. BELGE HIST. HOP.
 BRUSSELS 1, 1963-
 OX/U-8.

ANNALS, SOUTHEASTERN CONFERENCE ON LATIN AMER-
ICAN STUDIES.
++ANN. SOUTHEAST. CONF. LAT. AM. STUD.
 CARROLLTON, GA.   1(1), MR 1970-
 OX/U-1.

ANNALES, STATION BIOLOGIQUE (BESSE-EN-CHAN-
DESSE).
++ANN. STAT. BIOL. (BESSE-EN-CHANDESSE).
 BESSE-EN-CHANDESSE  NO.1, 1966-
 LO/N-2.

ANNALS OF STATISTICS.                                          XXX
++ANN. STAT.
INSTITUTE OF MATHEMATICAL STATISTICS.
 BALTIMORE 1, 1973-
 2M. PREV. PART OF ANNALS OF MATHEMATICAL
 STATISTICS FROM 1, 1930- 43, 1972.
 CA/U-2.    GL/U-1.    GL/U-2.    LD/U-1.    LO/N-4.    LO/R-5.
 LO/U-3.    OX/U16.    SF/U-1.    SH/U-1.

ANNALI DI STORIA ECONOMICA E SOCIALE, UNIVER-
SITA DEGLI STUDI DI NAPOLI.                                    XXX
++ANN. STOR. ECON. & SOC. UNIV. NAPOLI.
 NAPLES  1, 1960- 8, 1967.
 ANNU. SUBS: CAHIERS INTERNATIONAUX D'HISTOIRE
 ECONOMIQUE ET SOCIALE.
 LO/U-3.
 ISSN 0066-2283

ANNALS OF SYSTEMS RESEARCH.
++ANN. SYST. RES.
 [H.E. STENFERT KROESE]
 LEIDEN 1, 1971-
 LO/N13.

ANNALES DE L'UNIVERSITE D'ABIDJAN:
SERIE D: LETTRES ET SCIENCES HUMAINES.
 ABIDJAN 1, 1965-
 AD/U-1.    LO/S10.
 BH/U-1. 2, 1969-                       OX/U-1. 2, 1969-

ANNALES, UNIVERSITE D'ABIDJAN:  SERIE E:
ECOLOGIE.                                                      XXX
++ANN. UNIV. ABIDJAN, E.
 ABIDJAN 1, 1968- 3(1), 1970.//
 BH/U-1.    LO/N-2.    LO/R-6.
 ISSN 0587-4122

ANNALES DE L'UNIVERSITE D'ABIDJAN:
SERIE F: ETHNOSOCIOLOGIE.
++ANN. UNIV. ABIDJAN, F.
 ABIDJAN 1, 1969-
 BH/U-1.    LO/S10.    LO/U14.    OX/U-1.

ANNALES, UNIVERSITE D'ABIDJAN: SERIE G: GEOGR-
APHIE.
++ANN. UNIV. ABIDJAN, G.
 ABIDJAN 1, 1969- 2(2), 1970.//
 LO/N-2.    LO/R-6.    LO/S13.    LO/U14.    OX/U-1.

ANNALES DE L'UNIVERSITE D'ABIDJAN:
SERIE H: LINGUISTIQUE.
++ANN. UNIV. ABIDJAN, H.
 ABIDJAN 1, 1968-
 AD/U-1.    BH/U-1.    LO/S10.    OX/U-1.    SH/U-1.
 ISSN 0587-4130

ANNALES UNIVERSITATIS MARIAE CURIE-SKLODOWSKA:
SECTIO H: OECONOMIA.
++ANN. UNIV. MARIAE CURIE-SKLODOWSKA, H.
 LUBLIN 1, 1967-
 LO/U-3.
 OX/U16. 5, 1971-

ANNALES DE ZOOLOGIE - ECOLOGIE ANIMALE.                        XXX
++ANN. ZOOL., ECOL. ANIM.
INSTITUT NATIONAL DE LA RECHERCHE AGRONOMIQUE
(FRANCE).
 PARIS 1, 1969-
 PREV. PART OF: ANNALES DES EPIPHYTIES FROM
 1, 1950- 19, 1968.
 CA/U11.    LO/N-2.    LO/N14.    LO/R-6.    LO/S26.
 OX/U-1.    XS/R-2.
 ISSN 0003-4231

ANNEE POLITIQUE AU CONGO.
++ANNEE POLIT. CONGO.
CONGO (DEMOCRATIC REPUBLIC) OFFICE NATIONAL DE
LA RECHERCHE ET DU DEVELOPPEMENT.
 KINSHASA 1968-
 LO/U-3.
 LD/U-1. 1968.
 OX/U-9. 1968.

ANNOUNCED REPRINTS.
++ANNOUNCED REPR.
 [NCR MICROCARD EDITIONS]
 WASHINGTON D.C. 1(1), F 1969-
 EX/U-1.    LO/N-3.
 ISSN 0003-5106

ANNUAIRE DE DROIT AERIEN ET SPATIAL.                           000
 SEE: YEARBOOK OF AIR & SPACE LAW.

ANNUAIRE DE L'EGYPTOLOGIE.
++ANNU. EGYPTOL.
INSTITUT ORIENTALE FRANCAIS DU CAIRE.
 CAIRO 1, 1971-
 OX/U-1.

ANNUAIRE DE MUSEE DE TORUN.
SEE: ROCZNIK MUZEUM W TORUNIU.                    000

ANNUAIRE DE L'UNIVERSITE DE SOFIA: ETUDES DE LA
CHAIRE D'ECONOMIE POLITIQUE.                      000
SEE: GODISHNIK NA SOFIJSKIJA UNIVERSITET:
KATEDRA POLITICHESKA IKONOMIJA.

ANNUAL ABSTRACT OF GREATER LONDON STATISTICS.
+ +ANNU. ABSTR. GREATER LOND. STAT.
GREATER LONDON COUNCIL.
  LONDON 1, 1966-
SUB SERIES OF THE COUNCIL'S PUBLICATIONS.
  BT/U-1.    HL/U-1.    LO/U-3.    OX/U-1.    OX/U16.
  BH/U-1. 2, 1967-               LO/U-2. 2, 1969-
  LO/U11. 2, 1967-              LO/U12. 2, 1969-
  OX/U17. 2, 1967-              RE/U-1. 7, 1972-
  EX/U-1. 1, 1966- 3, 1968; 7, 1972-
  LO/U-4. 4, 1969.

ANNUAL BIBLIOGRAPHY OF SCOTTISH LITERATURE.
+ +ANNU. BIBLIOGR. SCOTT. LIT.
LIBRARY ASSOCIATION: UNIVERSITY, COLLEGE &
RESEARCH SECTION.
  ABERDEEN NO.1, 1969(1970)-
S/T: SUPPLEMENT TO BIBLIOTHECK. PRODUCED BY
SECTION'S SCOTTISH GROUP.
  DB/U-2.    ED/N-1.    GL/U-1.    GL/U-2.    NW/U-1.    OX/U-1.

ANNUAL BULLETIN OF GENERAL ENERGY STATISTICS
FOR EUROPE.
+ +ANNU. BULL. GEN. ENERGY STAT. EUR.
UNITED NATIONS: ECONOMIC COMMISSION FOR EUROPE.
  NEW YORK 1, 1968(1970)-
ENGL., FR. & RUSS.
  BH/U-1.    MA/P-1.    OX/U16.

ANNUAL, CHURCH SERVICE SOCIETY.                   XXX
SUBS (1971): LITURGICAL STUDIES.

ANNUAL CONSTRUCTOR.                               000
SEE: CONSTRUCTOR ANNUAL.

ANNUAL DIRECTORY OF BOOKSELLERS IN THE BRIT-
ISH ISLES SPECIALISING IN ANTIQUARIAN & OUT-
OF-PRINT BOOKS.
+ +ANNU. DIR. BOOKSELL. BR. ISLES SPEC. ANTIQ. &
O.P. BOOKS.
[CLIQUE LTD.]
  LONDON 1970-
  LO/U-3.    OX/U-1.
  BT/U-1. 1970.
  ISSN 0066-3913

ANNUAL, INTERNATIONAL COUNCIL OF MUSEUMS.        XXX
+ +ANNU. INT. COUNC. MUS.
  PARIS NO.1, 1969- NO.2, 1970 ...
SUBS: MUSEUMS' ANNUAL.
  LO/N-2.    LO/N-4.

ANNUAL JOURNAL, ROYAL NEW ZEALAND INSTITUTE
OF HORTICULTURE.                                 XXX
+ +ANNU. J. R. N.Z. INST. HORTIC.
  WELLINGTON, N.Z. NO.1, 1973-
PREV: JOURNAL OF THE ROYAL NEW ZEALAND INST-
ITUTE OF HORTICULTURE: NS FROM 1, 1968- 4,
1971.
  LO/N-2.

ANNUAL LECTURES, UNIVERSITY OF LAGOS.
+ +ANNU. LECT. UNIV. LAGOS.
  LAGOS NO.1, 1968-
MONOGR.
  HL/U-1.

ANNUAL PLAN (INDIA).
(INDIA) PLANNING COMMISSION.
  NEW DELHI 1966/67-
  LO/S14.
  LO/N10. CURRENT VOLUME.
  ISSN 0537-0299

ANNUAL PROGRESS IN CHILD PSYCHIATRY & CHILD
DEVELOPMENT.
+ +ANNU. PROG. CHILD PSYCHIATRY & CHILD DEV.
[BRUNNER/MAZEL; BUTTERWORTHS]
  NEW YORK; LONDON 1, 1968-
  DB/U-2.    LO/M33.    MA/U-1.    XY/N-1.
  CA/U-1. 4, 1971-             GL/U-2. 4, 1971-
  OX/U-8. 4, 1971-            SH/U-1. 4, 1971-
  ISSN 0066-4030

ANNUAL REPORT, AGRICULTURAL EXPERIMENT STAT-
IONS (GEORGIA).                                  XXX
SUBS (1970): BIENNIAL REPORT, AGRICULTURAL
EXPERIMENT STATIONS (GEORGIA).

ANNUAL REPORTS ON ANALYTICAL ATOMIC SPECTROS-
COPY.
+ +ANNU. REP. ANAL. AT. SPECROSC.
SOCIETY FOR ANALYTICAL CHEMISTRY.
  LONDON 1, 1971(1972)-
  LO/N14.    LO/S-3.    OX/U-8.    XS/R10.

ANNUAL REPORT, BRITISH IRON & STEEL RESEARCH
ASSOCIATION.                                     XXX
SUBS (1971): STEELRESEARCH.

ANNUAL REPORT, CANADIAN RADIO-TELEVISION COMM-
ISSION.
+ +ANNU. REP. CAN. RADIO-TELEV. COMM.
  OTTAWA 1, 1968/9.
  LO/U-3.
  ISSN 0068-9556

ANNUAL REPORT, CENTRE FOR ENVIRONMENTAL
STUDIES.
+ +ANNU. REP. CENT. ENVIRON. STUD.
  LONDON 1, 1967/68(1968)-
  BL/U-1.    BN/U-2.
  OX/U-1 5, 1972-

ANNUAL REPORT, CITY UNIVERSITY (LONDON).
+ +ANNU. REP. CITY UNIV. (LOND.).
  LONDON 1, 1966/67 (1967)-
ACTUAL TITLE: ANNUAL REPORT TO THE COURT.
  BH/U-1.

ANNUAL REPORT, DARESBURY NUCLEAR PHYSICS LAB-
ORATORY.                                         XXX
+ +ANNU. REP. DARESBURY NUCL. PHYS. LAB.
  DARESBURY, LANCS. 1968-
PREV: PROGRESS REPORT, DARESBURY ...: 4 GE V
ELECTRON SYNCHROTRON FROM 1, 1964- 6, 1967.
  BH/U-1.    LO/N-4.    LO/N14.
  OX/U-8. 1970(1971)-

ANNUAL REPORT, DECIMAL CURRENCY BOARD (GB).
+ +ANNU. REP. DECIMAL CURR. BOARD (GB).
  LONDON 1, 1967/68(1968)-
  GL/U-1.

ANNUAL REPORT, DITTON & COVENT GARDEN
LABORATORIES.                                    XXX
+ +ANNU. REP. DITTON & COVENT GARD. LABS.
  LONDON 1959/60- 1964/65.
PUBL. BY HMSO FOR AGRICULTURAL RESEARCH
COUNCIL. PREV REPORTS CONTAINED IN: FOOD
INVESTIGATION. SUBS (IN PART): ANNUAL
REPORT, DITTON LABORATORY.
  LO/N14.    OX/U-8.
  LO/U-2. 1963/4-                MA/P-1. 1962/3-

ANNUAL REPORT, DITTON LABORATORY.
+ +ANNU. REP. DITTON LAB.
  LONDON 1965/66 (1966)-
PUBL. BY HMSO FOR AGRICULTURAL RESEARCH
COUNCIL. PREV PART OF: ANNUAL REPORT,
DITTON & COVENT GARDEN LABORATORIES.
  BH/U-1.    LO/N14.    LO/U-2.    OX/U-8.
  BL/U-1. 1967/68(1968)-

ANNUAL REPORT, DIVISION OF COAL RESEARCH,
CSIRO (AUSTRALIA).                               XXX
+ +ANNU. REP. DIV. COAL RES. CSIRO (AUST.).
  CHATSWOOD, NSW 12TH, 1960- 18TH, 1965/66.
PREV: ANNUAL REPORT, COAL RESEARCH SECTION,
CSIRO (AUST.) SUBS: ANNUAL REPORT, DIVISION
OF MINERAL CHEMISTRY, CSIRO (AUST.)
  LO/N14.
  LO/U-2. 14, 1962-

ANNUAL REPORT, DIVISION OF MINERAL CHEMISTRY,
CSIRO (AUSTRALIA).                               XXX
+ +ANNU. REP. DIV. MIN. CHEM. CSIRO (AUST.).
  [SYDNEY] 1966/1967.
PREV: ANNUAL REPORT, DIVISION OF COAL
RESEARCH, CSIRO (AUSTRALIA). SUBS: MINERAL
CHEMISTRY RESEARCH REPORT, DIVISION OF MINERAL
CHEMISTRY, CSIRO (AUSTRALIA).
  LO/N14.    LO/U-5.

ANNUAL REPORT, DONCASTER & DISTRICT DEVELOP-
MENT COUNCIL.
+ +ANNU. REP. DONCASTER & DIST. DEVELOP. COUNC.
  DONCASTER 1, 1969-
FIRST ISSUE ALSO ENTITLED: INDUSTRY IS COMING.
  LD/U-1.    LO/U-3.

ANNUAL REPORT, HUMAN SCIENCES RESEARCH
COUNCIL (SOUTH AFRICA).
+ +ANNU. REP. HUM. SCI. RES. COUNC. (S. AFR.)
  PRETORIA 1ST, 1969/70 (1970)-
  BL/U-1.

**ANNUAL REPORT OF HYDROLOGICAL RESEARCH IN THE AREA OF LAKE BIWA.**
++*ANNU. REP. HYDROL. RES. AREA LAKE BIWA.*
KYOTO DAIGAKU: BOSAI KENKYUJO.
*KYOTO 1, 1967-*
BODY SUBORD. TO: DISASTER PREVENTION RESEARCH INSTITUTE.
*LO/N-4.    LO/N13.    XN/S-1.    XS/N-1.*

**ANNUAL REPORT, INSTITUTE FOR FERMENTATION (JAPAN).**                                                000
  SEE: HAKKO KENKYUJO NEMPO.

**ANNUAL REPORT, INSTITUTE OF JUDICIAL ADMINIS-TRATION, UNIVERSITY OF BIRMINGHAM.**
++*ANNU. REP. INST. JUDICIAL ADM. UNIV. BIRMING-HAM.*
*BIRMINGHAM NO.1, 1968/69(1969)-*
*BH/U-1.*
*LO/U12. 1969/70(1970).*

**ANNUAL REPORT OF THE LAW REFORM COMMISSION OF CANADA.**
++*ANNU. REP. LAW REFORM COMM. CAN.*
*OTTAWA 1ST, 1971/72-*
FR. TITLE: RAPPORT ANNUEL DE LA COMMISSION DE REFORME DU DROIT.
*LO/N-1.*

**ANNUAL REPORT, LONG ASHTON AGRICULTURAL & HORTICULTURAL STATION.**                                  XXX
  SUBS (1968): REPORT, LONG ASHTON RESEARCH STATION.

**ANNUAL REPORT, MARINE BIOCHEMISTRY UNIT, CSIRO (AUSTRALIA).**
++*ANNU. REP. MAR. BIOCHEM. UNIT CSIRO (AUST.).*
*SYDNEY 1971/72(1972)-*
*LO/N14.*

**ANNUAL REPORT, MEAT & LIVESTOCK COMMISSION.**
++*ANNU. REP. MEAT & LIVESTOCK COMM.*
*LONDON 1, 1968-*
*BL/U-1.    CA/U11.    OX/U-8.*

**ANNUAL REPORT, METRICATION BOARD (GREAT BRITAIN).**
++*ANNU. REP. METRIC. BOARD (GB).*
*LONDON 1ST, 1969-*
*BH/U-1.    LO/U-3.    OX/U-8.*

**ANNUAL REPORT OF THE NATIONAL INSTITUTE OF SCIENTIFIC INVESTIGATION (KOREA).**                       000
  SEE: KUNGNIP KWAHAK SUSA YONGUSO YONBO.

**ANNUAL REPORT OF THE NATIONAL VETERINARY ASSAY LABORATORY.**                                        000
  SEE: DOBUTSU IYAKUHIN KENSAJO NENPO.

**ANNUAL REPORT OF NATURAL SCIENCE & HOME ECONOMICS, KINJO GAKUIN COLLEGE.**                           000
  SEE: KINJO GAKUIN DAIGAKU RONSHU KASEIGAKU TOKUSHU.

**ANNUAL REPORT, NEW ZEALAND AGRICULTURAL ENGIN-EERING INSTITUTE.**
++*ANNU. REP. N.Z. AGRIC. ENG. INST.*
*CANTERBURY, N.Z. 1965/66(1966)-*
*LO/N14. 1969/71(1971)-*

**ANNUAL REPORT, NIGERIAN INSTITUTE FOR OIL PALM RESEARCH.**
++*ANNU. REP. NIGER. INST. OIL PALM RES.*
*BENIN CITY 1ST, 1964/65-*
INST. LOCATED 'NEAR BENIN CITY'. PREV: ANNUAL REPORT, WEST AFRICAN INSTITUTE FOR OIL PALM RESEARCH., TO 12TH, 1963/64.
*LO/N14.    LO/R-6.*

**ANNUAL REPORTS ON NMR SPECTROSCOPY.**                                                                XXX
++*ANNU. REP. NMR SPECTROSC.*
[ACADEMIC P.]
*LONDON 3, 1970-*
PREV: ANNUAL REVIEW ON NMR SPECTROSCOPY FROM 1, 1968- 2, 1969.
*GL/U-1.    HL/U-1.    LD/U-1.    LO/N14.    LO/U13.    XS/C-2.*
*XS/R10.*
*LO/U-2. 3, 1970-*
*ISSN 0066-4103*

**ANNUAL REPORT OF THE NOTO MARINE LABORATORY.**                                                       000
  SEE: NOTO RINKAI JIKKENJO NEMPO.

**ANNUAL REPORT, OAK RIDGE ASSOCIATED UNIVER-SITIES.**
++*ANNU. REP. OAK RIDGE ASSOC. UNIV.*
*OAK RIDGE, TENN. 1ST, 1965/66-*
PREV: A. REP., OAK RIDGE INSTITUTE OF NUCLEAR STUDIES. NAME OF BODY CHANGED 1/JA 1966 - 1ST REP. ABOVE ALSO KNOWN AS 20TH OF PREV. NAME/TITLE.
*LO/N14.*

**ANNUAL REPORTS IN ORGANIC SYNTHESIS.**
++*ANNU. REP. ORG. SYNTH.*
[ACADEMIC P.]
*NEW YORK &C. 1970(1971)-*
ABSTRACTS.
*GL/U-1.    LO/N14.    LO/S-3.*
*ISSN 0066-409X*

**ANNUAL REPORTS ON THE PROGRESS OF CHEMISTRY: SECTION A: GENERAL, PHYSICAL & INORGANIC CHEMISTRY.**   XXX
++*ANNU. REP. PROGR. CHEM., A.*
CHEMICAL SOCIETY.
*LONDON 64, 1968(1969)-*
PREV. AS SINGLE PUBL. WITH ABOVE MAIN TITLE FROM 1, 1904(1905). THEN FROM ABOVE NO. ISSUED IN SECTIONS A & B.
*LO/N14.*

**ANNUAL REPORTS ON THE PROGRESS OF CHEMISTRY: SECTION B: ORGANIC CHEMISTRY.**                         XXX
++*ANNU. REP. PROGR. CHEM., B.*
CHEMICAL SOCIETY.
*LONDON 64, 1968(1969)-*
SEE REMARKS FOR SECTION A.
*LO/N14.*

**ANNUAL REPORT ON RESEARCH, MOSS LANDING MARINE LABORATORIES.**
++*ANNU. REP. RES. MOSS LAND. MAR. LAB.*
*MOSS LANDING, CALIF. NO.1, 1970-*
*LO/N-2.    LO/N13.*

**ANNUAL REPORTS OF THE RESEARCH REACTOR INST-ITUTE, KYOTO UNIVERSITY.**
++*ANNU. REP. RES. REACT. INST. KYOTO UNIV.*
KYOTO DAIGAKU: GENSHIRO JIKKENJO.
*OSAKA 1, 1968-*
*CA/U-2. 2, 1969-*

**ANNUAL REPORT, SADO MARINE BIOLOGICAL STATION.**
  SEE: SADO RINKAI JIKENJO KENKYU NEMPO.

**ANNUAL REPORT, SHEEP DEVELOPMENT ASSOCIATION LTD.**
++*ANNU. REP. SHEEP DEVELOP. ASSOC. LTD.*
*WHEATLEY, OXF. 1, 1964-*
*CA/U11.*

**ANNUAL REPORT OF THE SHOWA PHARMACEUTICAL COLLEGE.**                                                 000
  SEE: SHOWA YAKKA DAIGAKU KIYO.

**ANNUAL REPORT, SUSSEX NATURALISTS' TRUST, LTD.**
++*ANNU. REP. SUSSEX NATUR. TRUST LTD.*
*BRIGHTON NO.1, 1961-*
*LO/N-2.***

**ANNUAL REPORT, TRENT RIVER AUTHORITY.**
++*ANNU. REP. TRENT RIVER AUTH.*
*NOTTINGHAM 1ST, 1966/67-*
PREV: ANNUAL REPORT, TRENT RIVER BOARD.
*BH/U-1.    LO/R-5.*

**ANNUAL REPORT, UNIVERSITY OF ASTON IN BIRMINGHAM.**
++*ANNU. REP. UNIV. ASTON BIRM.*
*BIRMINGHAM 1, 1966/67-*
*BL/U-1.    LO/N-1.*

**ANNUAL REPORT, WEST AFRICAN INSTITUTE FOR OIL PALM RESEARCH.**                                       XXX
  SUBS (1965): ANNUAL REPORT, NIGERIAN INSTI-TUTE FOR OIL PALM RESEARCH.

**ANNUAL REPORT, WEST COUNTRY TOURIST BOARD.**
++*ANNU. REP. WEST CTRY. TOURIST BOARD.*
*EXETER 1ST, 1972-*
*LO/N-1.*

**ANNUAL REPORT, WILDFOWL TRUST.**                                                                     XXX
  SUBS (1968): WILDFOWL.

ANNUAL REVIEW OF ANTHROPOLOGY.
++ANNU. REV. ANTHROPOL.
[ANNUAL REVIEWS INC.]
PALO ALTO, CALIF. 1, 1972-
BN/U-1.   DB/U-2.   HL/U-1.   LD/U-1.   LO/N-2.   LO/N13.
MA/U-1.
ISSN 0084-6570

ANNUAL REVIEW OF BIOPHYSICS & BIOENGINEERING.
++ANNU. REV. BIOPHYS. & BIOENG.
[ANNUAL REVIEWS INC.]
PALO ALTO, CALIF. 1, 1972-
BN/U-2.   CA/M-2.   DB/U-2.   EX/U-1.   LD/U-1.   LO/N-4.
LO/N14.   LO/U-2.   MA/U-1.
CA/U-2. 3, 1974-          SA/U-1. 3, 1974-
ISSN 0084-6589

ANNUAL REVIEW OF EARTH & PLANETARY SCIENCES.
++ANNU. REV. EARTH & PLANET. SCI.
[ANNUAL REVIEWS, INC.]
PALO ALTO, CALIF. 1, 1973-
LD/U-1.   LO/N-2.   OX/U-8.
CA/U-2. 2, 1974-
ISSN 0084-6597

ANNUAL REVIEW OF ECOLOGY & SYSTEMATICS.
++ANNU. REV. ECOL. & SYST.
[ANNUAL REVIEWS, INC.]
PALO ALTO, CALIF. 1, 1970-
AD/U-1.   AD/U-3.   BH/U-1.   BN/U-2.   CA/U-2.   CA/U11.
DB/U-1.   DB/U-2.   GL/U-1.   LC/U-1.   LD/U-1.   LO/N-2.
LO/N13.   LO/R-5.   LO/U11.   MA/U-1.   NW/U-1.
OX/U-8.   RE/U-1.   SF/U-1.   XY/N-1.
ISSN 0066-4162

ANNUAL REVIEW OF THE ECONOMIC COUNCIL OF
CANADA.
++ANNU. REV. ECON. COUNC. CAN.
OTTAWA 1, 1964(1965)-
LO/N10.
LO/U12. 5, 1968-          LV/U-1. 5, 1968-
SH/U-1. 5, 1968-

ANNUAL REVIEW OF FLUID MECHANICS.
++ANNU. REV. FLUID MECH.
[ANNUAL REVIEWS INC.]
PALO ALTO (CALIF.) 1, 1969-
BH/U-1.   BL/U-1.   EX/U-1.   LO/N-4.   LO/N14.   NW/U-1.
OX/U-8.   RE/U-1.   SF/U-1.   SH/U-3.
LD/U-1. 2, 1970-          LO/U12. 5, 1973-
SO/U-1. 2, 1970-
DR/U-1. 1, 1969.
LO/U13. 1, 1969- 2, 1970.
ISSN 0066-4189

ANNUAL REVIEWS OF INDUSTRIAL & ENGINEERING
CHEMISTRY.
++ANNU. REV. IND. & ENG. CHEM.
AMERICAN CHEMICAL SOCIETY.
WASHINGTON, D.C. 1970(1972)-
LO/N14.   LO/S-3.
SW/U-1. 1970.

ANNUAL REVIEW OF MATERIALS SCIENCE.
++ANNU. REV. MATER. SCI.
[ANNUAL REVIEWS INC.]
PALO ALTO, CALIF. 1, 1971-
DB/U-2.   LO/N-4.   LO/N14.   MA/U-1.   OX/U-8.
XS/R10.
LD/U-1. 2, 1972.
ISSN 0084-6600

ANNUAL REVIEW OF NMR SPECTROSCOPY.                    XXX
++ANNU. REV. NMR SPECTROSC.
[ACADEMIC PRESS]
NEW YORK &C 1, 1968- 2, 1969 ...
SUBS: ANNUAL REPORTS ON NMR SPECTROSCOPY.
BL/U-1.   CB/U-1.   CO/U-1.   CR/U-1.   DB/U-2.   GL/U-1.
HL/U-1.   LD/U-1.   LC/U-1.   LO/M22.   LO/N-4.   LO/N14.
LO/S-3.   LO/U-2.   LO/U-4.   LO/U12.   LO/U20.   OX/U-8.
XS/R10.
SW/U-1. 2, 1969.
ISSN 0066-4235

ANNUAL REVIEW OF PHOTOCHEMISTRY.                      000
SEE: ANNUAL SURVEY OF PHOTOCHEMISTRY.

ANNUAL REVIEW, REDESDALE EXPERIMENTAL
HUSBANDRY FARM.
++ANNU. REV. REDESDALE EXP. HUSB. FARM.
OTTERBURN NO.1, 1967/68 (1968)-
LO/N13.

ANNUAL REVIEW OF THE SCHIZOPHRENIC SYNDROME.        XXX
++ANNU. REV. SCHIZOPHRENIC SYNDROME.
[BRUNNER/MAZEL; BUTTERWORTHS]
NEW YORK; LONDON 2, 1972-
PREV: SCHIZOPHRENIC SYNDROME FROM 1, 1971.
GL/U-1.   LO/U-1.
SO/U-1. 1972.

ANNUAL REVIEW OF YASHIROGAKUIN UNIVERSITY.          000
SEE: YASHIRO GAKUIN DAIGAKU KIYO.

ANNUAL STATISTICAL BULLETIN, DEPARTMENT OF
STATISTICS (SWAZILAND).
++ANNU. STAT. BULL. DEP. STAT. (SWAZILAND).
MBABANE 1, 1966-
LO/N-1.

ANNUAL SUMMARY OF INFORMATION ON NATURAL
DISASTERS.
++ANNU. SUMM. INF. NATUR. DISASTERS.
UNESCO.
PARIS NO.1, 1966(1970)-
BH/U-1.   LO/N13.   LO/U-1.
ISSN 0066-4383

ANNUAL SURVEY OF AFRICAN LAW.
++ANNU. SURV. AFR. LAW.
[CASS]
LONDON 1, 1967(1970)-
BL/U-1.   CR/U-1.   EX/U-1.   MA/U-1.   OX/U-1.
ISSN 0066-4405

ANNUAL SURVEY OF ORGANOMETALLIC CHEMISTRY.
++ANNU. SURV. ORGANOMETAL. CHEM.
[ELSEVIER]
AMSTERDAM &C 1, 1964 (1965)- 3, 1966 (67)...
SUBS: ORGANOMETALLIC CHEMISTRY REVIEWS;
SECTION B: ANNUAL SURVEYS.
BH/U-1.   BL/U-1.   CO/U-1.   GL/U-2.   HL/U-1.   LB/U-1.
LD/U-1.   LO/N-4.   LO/N14.   LO/S-3.   LO/U-2.   LO/U13.
SO/U-1.   XS/C-2.
MA/U-1. 3,1966-          SH/U-1.

ANNUAL SURVEY OF PHOTOCHEMISTRY. SURVEY OF
1967- LITERATURE.
++ANNU. SURV. PHOTOCHEM.
[WILEY]
NEW YORK 1, 1969-
COVER TITLE: 1967- ANNUAL REVIEW OF PHOTOCHEM-
ISTRY.
AD/U-1.   GL/U-1.   HL/U-1.   LD/U-1.   LO/N14.   LO/S-3.
LO/U-2.   MA/U-1.   OX/U-8.
SO/U-1. 1, 1969.
XS/C-2. 1, 1969.
XS/R10. 1, 1969.
ISSN 0066-4421

ANNUARIO ASTRONOMICO, OSSERVATORIO ASTRON-
OMICO DI TRIESTE.                                   XXX
++ANNU. ASTRON. OSS. ASTRON. TRIESTE.
TRIESTE 1936(1937)- 1969(1970). //
LO/N13. 1959(1960)-

ANNUARIUM HISTORIAE CONCILIORUM.
++ANNU. HIST. CONCIL.
AMSTERDAM 1(1), 1969-
S/T: INTERNATIONALE ZEITSCHRIFT FUR KONZILIEN-
GESCHICHTSFORSCHUNG.
AD/U-1.   GL/U-1.   HL/U-1.   LO/N-1.   MA/S-1.   OX/U-1.
ISSN 0003-5157

ANNUARIUM HISTORIAE CONCILIORUM: SUPPLEMENTUM.
++ANNU. HIST. CONCIL., SUPPL.
AMSTERDAM 1, 1972-
GL/U-1.
LO/N-1. 1972.

ANTAEUS.
TANGIER &C. NO.1, 1970-
OX/U-1.
ISSN 0003-5319

ANTENNY. SBORNIK.
NAUCHNO-TEKHNICHESKOE OBSHCHESTVO RADIOTEKHNIKI
I ELEKTROSVJAZI: ANTENNAJA SEKTSIJA.
MOSCOW 1, 1966-
LO/N13.

ANTHOLOGIE AUTOMOBILE.
++ANTHOL. AUTOMOB.
[SOCIETE D'EDITIONS ET D'ETUDES TECHNIQUES]
PARIS NO.1, S/OC 1968-
2M.
LO/N-4. W NOS.2- 12;18.
ISSN 0587-3282

ANTHOS. POETRY, REVIEWS, STORIES, ARTICLES.
WHITEHALL MUSICAL & DRAMATIC SOCIETY.
 *DUBLIN NO.1, S 1972-*
 Q.
 *BL/U-1.     CA/U-1.     DB/U-2.     ED/N-1.     OX/U-1.*

ANTHROPOLOGICAL INDEX TO CURRENT PERIODICALS
IN THE LIBRARY OF THE ROYAL ANTHROPOLOGICAL
INSTITUTE.
 *+ +ANTHROPOL. INDEX CURR. PERIOD. LIBR. R.
 ANTHROPOL. INST.*
 ROYAL ANTHROPOLOGICAL INSTITUTE.
 *LONDON   6(1), JA/MR 1968-*
 PREV: INDEX TO CURRENT PERIODICALS RECEIVED
 IN THE LIBRARY OF THE ROYAL ANTHROPOLOGICAL
 INSTITUTE., FROM 1(1), JA/MR 1963.
 *BH/P-1.     DB/U-2.     ED/N-1.     GL/U-1.     HL/U-1.     LO/N-3.
 LO/U12.*
 *ISSN 0003-5467*

ANTHROPOLOGY OF THE NORTH.
 *+ +ANTHROPOL. NORTH. [ANNO-A]*
 [UNIV. OF TORONTO P.]
 *TORONTO   1, 1961-*
 S/T: TRANSLATIONS FROM RUSSIAN SOURCES.
 *OX/U-1.*
 *ISSN 0066-4715*

ANTIBIOTICA ET CHEMOTHERAPIA.                                              XXX
 SUBS (1971): ANTIBIOTICS & CHEMOTHERAPY.

ANTIBIOTICS & CHEMOTHERAPY (BASLE).                                        XXX
 *+ +ANTIBIOT. & CHEMOTHER.*
 [KARGER]
 *BASLE &C.   17, 1971-*
 PREV: ANTIBIOTICA ET CHEMOTHERAPIA FROM 1,
 1954- 16, 1970.
 *LO/N14.     LO/U-2.*
 *ISSN 0066-474X*

ANTICHITA VIVA.
 *FLORENCE   1, 1962-*
 *LO/U17.  8, 1969-                      OX/U-1.  8(1), 1969-*
 *ISSN 0003-5645*

ANTICHTHON. JOURNAL OF THE ...
 AUSTRALIAN SOCIETY FOR CLASSICAL STUDIES.
 *SYDNEY   1, 1967-*
 *BN/U-1.     CO/U-1.     DB/S-1.     EX/U-1.     LO/U-2.     MA/U-1.
 OX/U-1.     OX/U-2.     RE/U-1.     SH/U-1.*
 *BL/U-1.  3, 1969-                       BL/U-1.  3, 1969-
 GL/U-1.  5, 1971-                        NO/U-1.  3, 1969-
 NW/U-1.  4, 1970-*
 *ISSN 0066-4774*

ANTICIPATED CAPITAL EXPENDITURE OF THE PUBLIC
SECTOR.
 *+ +ANTICIP. CAPITAL EXPEND. PUBLIC SECTOR.*
 *PRETORIA   1968/1970, 1969-*
 IN AFRIKAANS & ENGL.
 *LO/U-3.*

ANTIGONISH REVIEW.
 *+ +ANTIGONISH REV.*
 ST. FRANCIS XAVIER UNIVERSITY: DEPARTMENT OF
 ENGLISH.
 *ANTIGONISH, NOVA SCOTIA   1(1), 1970-*
 *EX/U-1.     LO/N-1.     LO/U-2.*
 *ISSN 0003-5661*

ANTIKE WELT. ZEITSCHRIFT FUR ARCHAOLOGIE UND
URGESCHICHTE.
 [RAGGI]
 *ZURICH   1(1), 1970-*
 *OX/U-2.*
 *ISSN 0003-570X*

ANTIPODE. A RADICAL JOURNAL OF GEOGRAPHY.
 *WORCESTER, MASS.   1, AG 1969-*
 *LO/S13.     RE/U-1.*
 *MA/U-1.  6, 1974-                       SF/U-1.  5, 1973-
 SH/U-1.  6, 1974-*
 *ISSN 0066-4812*

ANTIQUAAR. TIJDSCHRIFT VAN DE NEDERLANDSCHE
VEREENIGING VAN ANTIQUAREN.
 *THE HAGUE   1(1), 1969- 4(6), 1973. //*
 ENGL. S/T: ANTIQUAREN. BULLETIN OF THE ANTIQ-
 UARIAN BOOKSELLERS' ASSOCIATION OF THE NETH-
 ERLANDS.
 *ED/N-1.     LO/N-1.*
 *ISSN 0003-5777*

ANTIQUAREN. BULLETIN OF THE ANTIQUARIAN BOOK-          000
SELLERS' ASSOCIATION OF THE NETHERLANDS.
 SEE: ANTIQUAAR. TIJDSCHRIFT VAN DE NEDER-
 LANDSCHE VEREENIGING VAN ANTIQUAREN.

ANTIQUITAS.
 UNIWERSYTET WROCLAWSKI.
 *WROCLAW   NO.1, AG 1963-*
 ALSO NUMBERED AS PART OF: ACTA UNIVERSITATIS
 WRATISLAVIENSIS., NO.1 ABOVE = NO.11 OF THE
 ACTA.
 *LO/N-3.*

ANTIQUITES AFRICAINES.
 *+ +ANTIQUITES AFR.*
 CENTRE NATIONAL DE LA RECHERCHE SCIENTIFIQUE.
 *PARIS   1, 1967-*
 *LO/U17.     LO/U17.     OX/U-1.     OX/U-2.
 GL/U-1.  1970-*
 *ISSN 0066-4871*

ANTS FOREFOOT.
 [COACH HOUSE P.]
 *TORONTO   NO.1, FALL 1967-*
 *EX/U-1.*
 *LO/U-2.  NO.2, 1968-*
 *ISSN 0003-6153*

ANUARIO DE BIBLIOTECOLOGIA Y ARCHIVOLOGIA:S2.          XXX
 *+ +ANU. BIBL. & ARCH., S2. (MEX.).*
 UNIVERSIDAD NACIONAL AUTONOMA DE MEXICO.
 *MEXICO, D.F.   1, 1969-*
 PREV: ANUARIO DE BIBLIOTECONOMIA Y ARCHIVON-
 OMIA FROM 1, 1961- 5, 1965.
 *OX/U-1.*

ANUARIO DE BIBLIOTECONOMIA Y ARCHIVONOMIA.             XXX
 *+ +ANU. BIBL. & ARCH. (MEX.).*
 UNIVERSIDAD NACIONAL AUTONOMA DE MEXICO:
 FACULTAD DE FILOSOFIA Y LETRAS.
 *MEXICO, D.F.   1, 1961- 5, 1965.*
 SUBS: ANUARIO DE BIBLIOTECOLOGIA Y ARCHIVOL-
 OGIA: 2S.
 *OX/U-1.*
 *ISSN 0570-4049*

ANUARIO FILOSOFICO.
 *+ +ANU. FILOS.*
 UNIVERSIDAD DE NAVARRA: SECCION DE FILOSOFIA.
 *PAMPLONA   1, 1968-*
 *OX/U-1.*
 *LO/U-2.  2, 1969-
 GL/U-1.  1, 1968- 2, 1969; 5, 1972.*
 *ISSN 0066-5215*

ANUARIO MARTIANO.
 *+ +ANU. MARTIANO.*
 CONSEJO NACIONAL DE CULTURA (CUBA): DEPARTA-
 MENTO COLECCION CUBANA.
 *HAVANA   NO.1, 1969-*
 *LO/U-1.     OX/U-1.*
 *ISSN 0066-524X*

ANUARIO DE SOCIOLOGIA DE LOS PUEBLOS IBERICOS.
 *+ +ANU. SOCIOL. PUEBLOS IBER.*
 ASOCIACION DE SOCIOLOGOS DE LENGUA ESPANOLA Y
 PORTUGUESA.
 *MADRID   1967-*
 A. SPONS. BODIES ALSO:  INSTITUTO DE ESTUDIOS
 SINDICALES, SOCIALES Y COOPERATIVOS; & INSTI-
 TUTO DE CULTURA HISPANICA.
 *LD/U-1.     LO/U-3.
 CB/U-1.  1967.
 NW/U-1.  1967.
 SO/U-1.  1, 1967- 2, 1968.*
 *ISSN 0066-5134*

ANVESAK.
 SARDAR PATEL INSTITUTE OF SOCIAL & ECONOMIC
 RESEARCH.
 *AHMEDABAD   1(1), JE 1971-*
 *OX/U16.*

ANZEIGER FUR SLAVISCHE PHILOLOGIE.
 *+ +ANZ. SLAV. PHILOL.*
 *WIESBADEN   1, 1966-*
 *SA/U-1.*

APCA ABSTRACTS.                                                           XXX
 SUBS (1971): NAPCA ABSTRACTS BULLETIN.

APE ENGINEERING.                                                          XXX
 *+ +APE ENG.*
 AMALGAMATED POWER ENGINEERING, LTD.
 *BEDFORD   NO.12, 1973-*
 PREV: APEX FROM NO.1, 1969- 11, 1972.
 *ED/N-1.     LO/N14.     LO/N35.*

**A.P.E.A. JOURNAL.**
AUSTRALIAN PETROLEUM EXPLORATION ASSOCIATION.
[TECHNICAL & INDUSTRIAL P.]
*SYDNEY  1, 1961-*
A.
*LO/N-2.\**
*LO/N-5.  13, 1973-          SH/U-1.  1969-*
*ISSN 0084-7534*

**APEX (BEDFORD).**                                          XXX
AMALGAMATED POWER ENGINEERING LTD.
*BEDFORD  NO.1, 1969- 11, 1972 ...*
SUBS: APE ENGINEERING.
*BL/U-1.     ED/N-1.     LO/N14.     OX/U-8.*
*ISSN 0570-4626*

**APEX (LONDON).**                                           XXX
CLERICAL & ADMINISTRATIVE WORKERS UNION.
*LONDON  13(7), 1973-*
PREV: CLERK:NS FROM 1, 1961- 13(6), 1973.
*NO/U-1.*
*HL/U-1.  13(7), 1973-*

**APHRA.**
*SPRINGTOWN, PA.  1, 1969-*
Q.
*LO/U-2.  1(2), 1969-*
*ISSN 0003-6447*

**APIDOLOGIE.**                                              XXX
INSTITUT NATIONAL DE LA RECHERCHE AGRONOM-
IQUE (FRANCE).
[DEUTSCHER IMKERBUND]
*BONN  1, 1970-*
INCORP: ANNALES DE L'ABEILLE FROM 1, JA/MR
1958- 11, 1968; & ZEITSCHRIFT FUR BIENENFOR-
SCHUNG FROM 1, JL 1950- 9, 1969. SPONS BODY
ALSO ARBEITSGEMEINSCHAFT DER INSTITUTE FUR
BIENENFORSCHUNG.
*LO/N-2.     LO/N14.*
*ISSN 0044-8435*

**APIS BULLETIN.**
QUEEN'S UNIVERSITY OF BELFAST: ARCHITECTURE &
PLANNING INFORMATION SERVICE.
*BELFAST  1(1), S 1971-*
*CA/U-1.     ED/N-1.     LO/N-1.     OX/U-1.*

**APLOMB ZERO.**
[SOUTH ST. PUBL.]
*SHERBORNE, DORSET.  NO.1, 1969-*
*LO/U-2.*
*ISSN 0003-651X*

**APOCALYPSE.  POEMS, SHORT STORIES, ESSAYS,
LINE DRAWINGS.**
*LIVERPOOL  NO.1, [AP 1968]-*
*ED/N-1.     LO/U-2.*
*ISSN 0570-4677*

**APPALACHIA.**
(UNITED STATES) APPALACHIAN REGIONAL COMMISSION
*WASHINGTON, D.C.  1, S 1967-*
*XY/N-1.*
*ISSN 0003-6595*

**APPLIANCE ENGINEER.**
*+ +APPLIANCE ENG.*
[DANA CHASE PUBL.]
*ELMHURST, ILL.  1, 1967-*
*LO/N14.\**
*ISSN 0003-6773*

**APPLICABLE ANALYSIS.**
*+ +APPL. ANAL.*
[GORDON & BREACH]
*NEW YORK &C.  1, 1971-*
*BR/U-1.     ED/N-1.     LO/N14.     SW/U-1.     XY/N-1.*
*GL/U-2.  3, 1973-                    RE/U-1.  3, 1973-*
*SH/U-1.  1972-*
*ISSN 0003-6811*

**APPLICAZIONI BIO-MEDICHE DEL CALCOLO ELET-
TRONICO.**
*+ +APPL. BIO-MED. CALCOLO ELETTRON.*
UNIVERSITA DI MILANO: CENTRO G. ZAMBON.
*MILAN  1, 1966-*
Q.
*CA/U-2.*

**APPLIED ACOUSTICS.**
*+ +APPL. ACOUST.*
*AMSTERDAM &C  1(1), 1968-*
*ED/N-1.     ED/N-1.     LO/N-4.     OX/U-8.     SO/U-1.*
*ISSN 0003-682X*

**APPLIED ECONOMICS.**
*+ +APPL. ECON. (GB).*
*OXFORD  1(1), JA 1969-*
Q.
*BH/U-1.     CB/U-1.     ED/N-1.     LD/U-1.     LO/U-3.     LO/U12.*
*MA/U-1.     OX/U16.     SH/U-1.     SO/U-1.*
*ISSN 0003-6846*

**APPLIED ENTOMOLOGY & ZOOLOGY.**
*+ +APPL. ENTOMOL. & ZOOL. (JAP.)*
NIPPON OYO-DOBUTSI-KONCHU GAKKAI.
*TOKYO  1, MR 1966-*
Q. BODY NAMED IN ENGL.: JAPANESE SOCIETY OF
APPLIED ENTOMOLOGY & ZOOLOGY.
*LO/N-2.     LO/N13.*
*ISSN 0003-6862*

**APPLIED ERGONOMICS.**
*+ +APPL. ERGON.*
*GUILDFORD  1, D 1969-*
S/T: THE JOURNAL ON THE TECHNOLOGY OF MAN'S
RELATIONS WITH MACHINES, ENVIRONMENT & WORK
SYSTEMS.
*BH/U-3     BT/C-1.     DB/U-2.     ED/N-1.     LO/N14.     LO/U-2.*
*OX/U-8.     SH/U-3.     SW/U-1.*
*LD/U-1.  1(2), 1970-                 SO/U-1.  3, 1972-*
*ISSN 0003-6870*

**APPLIED MATHEMATICAL SCIENCES.**
*+ +APPL. MATH. SCI.*
[SPRINGER]
*NEW YORK &C.  1, 1971-*
*LO/N14.*
*ISSN 0066-5452*

**APPLIED MINERALOGY.**
*+ +APPL. MINERAL.*
[SPRINGER]
*NEW YORK; VIENNA  1, 1971-*
*OX/U-8.*
*ISSN 0066-5487*

**APPLIED PHYSICS.**
*+ +APPL. PHYS.*
[SPRINGER]
*BERLIN &C.  1, 1973-*
*CA/U-2.     LO/N-4.     LO/N14.     SH/U-1.     SO/U-1.     XS/R10.*

**APPLIED PHYSICS & ENGINEERING.**
*+ +APPL. PHYS. & ENG.*
[SPRINGER]
*BERLIN &C.  1, 1967-*
*OX/U-8.*
*ISSN 0066-5509*

**APPLIED SOCIAL STUDIES.**                                  XXX
*+ +APPL. SOC. STUD.*
[PERGAMON PRESS]
*OXFORD &C  1, 1969- 3, 1971.//*
3/A. S/T: AN INTERNATIONAL JOURNAL OF SOCIAL
WORK EDUCATION, ADMINISTRATION & RESEARCH.
*BL/U-1.     BN/U-1.     CB/U-1.     ED/N-1.     LD/U-1.     LO/U-3.*
*LO/U-4.     LV/U-1.     SH/U-1.     SO/U-1.*
*SH/C-5.  3(3), 1971-*
*ISSN 0003-7001*

**APPLIED SOLID STATE SCIENCE.**
*+ +APPL. SOLID STATE SCI.*
[ACADEMIC P.]
*NEW YORK  1, 1969-*
S/T: ADVANCES IN MATERIALS & DEVICE RESEARCH.
*CB/U-1.     GL/U-1.     GL/U-2.     LO/C-4.     LO/N-4.     LO/N14.*
*LO/U-2.     LO/U11.     OX/U-8.     SF/U-1.     XS/R10.*

**APPLIED SPECTROSCOPY REVIEWS.**
*+ +APPL. SPECTROSC. REV.*
[DEKKER]
*BALTIMORE  1, 1967-*
2/A. PUBL. IN LONDON BY ARNOLD.
*BH/U-1.     BH/U-3.     BN/U-2.     CA/U-1.     LO/N-4.     LO/N14.*
*LO/U13.     LO/U21.     LO/U22.     MA/U-1.     OX/U-1.*
*SL/U-1.     XY/N-1.*
*LD/U-1.  1, 1968- 4, 1971.*
*ISSN 0570-4928*

**APPRAISAL.**
CHILDREN'S SCIENCE BOOK REVIEW COMMITTEE.
*CAMBRIDGE, MASS.  1, 1967/68-*
*DB/U-2.*
*ISSN 0003-7052*

**APPRECIATIONS IN HISTORY.**
*+ +APPRECIATIONS HIST.*
HISTORICAL ASSOCIATION.
*LONDON  NO.1, 1971-*
*LO/U-1.     MA/U-1.     NW/U-1.*

**APPRENTICE. OXFORD & CAMBRIDGE POETRY.**
UNIVERSITY OF CAMBRIDGE: MAGDALENE COLLEGE.
*CAMBRIDGE [NO.], 1 OC 1971-*
*ED/N-1.*

**APPROACHES TO SEMIOTICS.**
INTERNATIONAL ASSOCIATION FOR SEMIOTIC STUDIES.
*THE HAGUE &C. 1, 1969-*
SUPPL. TO SEMIOTICA.
*OX/U-1.*
*CA/U-1. 1972-*
*ISSN 0066-5576*

**AQUACULTURE.**
[ELSEVIER SCIENTIFIC PUBL. CO.]
*AMSTERDAM 1(1), MY 1972-*
*LO/N-2.    LO/R-6.    OX/U-8.*
*ISSN 0044-8486*

**AQUARIEN MAGAZIN.**
*STUTTGART JA 1967-*
S/T: NEUE MONATSHEFTE FUR AQUARIEN- UND
VIVARIENKUNDE. ADDED TITLE: AQUARIEN UND
TERRARIEN.
*LO/N-2. 1968(1)-*
*ISSN 0003-7257*

**AQUARIENFREUND.**
*WILHELMSHAVEN 1, 1972-*
*LO/N-2.*

**AQUARIUM DIGEST INTERNATIONAL.**
*++AQUARIUM DIG. INT.*
*MELLE, WEST GER.; HAYWARD, CALIF. 1, 1972-*
*LO/N-2.    LO/N13.*

**AQUATIC BIOLOGY ABSTRACTS.**                          XXX
*++AQUAT. BIOL. ABSTR.*
*LONDON    1(1), JA 1969- 3(6), 1971.*
SUBS. PART OF: AQUATIC SCIENCES & FISHERIES
ABSTRACTS.
*CA/U-1.    GL/U-1.    LO/N-2.    LO/U12.    LO/U13.    OX/U-1.*
*SO/U-1.*
*ED/N-1. 1(3),1969-    LO/N-6. 2, 1970-*
*LO/R-6. 3(1), 1971-    NW/U-1. 3, 1971-*
*ISSN 0003-7311*

**AQUATIC SCIENCES & FISHERIES ABSTRACTS.**           XXX
*++AQUAT. SCI. & FISH. ABSTR.*
[INFORMATION RETRIEVAL LTD.]
*LONDON    1(1),JL 1971-*
INCORP: AQUATIC BIOLOGY ABSTRACTS FROM 1(1),
JA 1969- 3(6), 1971; & CURRENT BIBLIOGRAPHY
FOR AQUATIC SCIENCES AND FISHERIES
FROM 2, 1959- 17, 1971.
*BN/U-2.    ED/N-1.    GL/U-1.    HL/U-1.    LO/N-2.    LO/N13.*
*LO/R-5.    LO/R-6.    LO/U12.    NW/U-1.    SO/U-1.*
*BL/U-1. 4, 1974-    CR/N-1. 3, 1973-*
*LO/U-4. 2, 1972-*
*0044-8516*

**AQUILA. CHESTNUT HILL STUDIES IN MODERN
LANGUAGES & LITERATURES.**
[NIJHOFF]
*THE HAGUE 1, 1968-*
*EX/U-1.    LO/N-1.    MA/U-1.    SH/U-1.    SW/U-1.*
*ISSN 0587-3428*

**ARAB HORSE NEWS.**
ARAB HORSE SOCIETY OF AUSTRALASIA.
*KELLYVILLE, N.S.W. 1, 1967-*
*LO/N13.*

**ARAB OIL & GAS. PETROLE ET LE GAZ ARABES.**
ARAB PETROLEUM RESEARCH CENTRE.
*BEIRUT 1(1), 1969-*
2/M. ENGL. & FR.
*LO/U14. 1971-*
*ISSN 0031-6369*

**ARANETA JOURNAL OF AGRICULTURE.**                    XXX
    **SUBS (1972): ARANETA RESEARCH JOURNAL.**

**ARANETA RESEARCH JOURNAL.**                          XXX
*++ARANETA RES. J.*
ARANETA INSTITUTE OF AGRICULTURE.
*MALABON, PHILIPP. 19(1), 1972-*
PREV: ARANETA JOURNAL OF AGRICULTURE FROM 1(1)
1953- 18(4), 1971.
*LO/R-6.*

**ARBEIDSMARKEDET. (NORWAY)**                          XXX
    **SUBS (1966): PLAN OG ARBEID.**

**ARBEITEN AUS DEM GEOLOGISCH-PALAONTOLOGISCHEN
INSTITUT, WESTFALISCHE WILHELMS-UNIVERSITAT.**
*++ARB. GEOL.-PALAONTOL. INST. WESTFAL. WILHELMS
UNIV.*
*MUNSTER 1, 1965-*
*LO/N-2.*

**ARBEITEN, INSTITUT FUR EISENBAHNWESEN, SPEZ-
IALBAHNEN UND VERKEHRSWIRTSCHAFT.**
*++ARB. INST. EISENBAHNWES. SPEZIALBAHNEN &
VERKEHRSWIRTSCH.*
*VIENNA 1, 1971-*
*LO/N13.*

**ARBEITSVORBEREITUNG.**
[VERLAG DIE ARBEITSVORBEREITUNG GMBH]
*VIERNHEIM    1963-*
*LO/N14.*
*ISSN 0003-780X*

**ARBORETUM & BOTANICAL GARDEN BULLETIN.**             XXX
*++ARBORETUM & BOT. GARD. BULL.*
AMERICAN ASSOCIATION OF BOTANICAL GARDENS
& ARBORETA.
*UNIVERSITY PARK, N.MEX. 1(1), JA 1967- 7(4),
            1973 ...*
SUBS: BULLETIN, AMERICAN ASSOCIATION OF
BOTANICAL GARDENS & ARBORETA.
*LO/N13. 1(4), 1967-*
*ISSN 0570-5975*

**ARC INDEX OF AGRICULTURAL & FOOD RESEARCH.**         XXX
*++ARC INDEX AGRIC. & FOOD RES.*
AGRICULTURAL RESEARCH COUNCIL.
*LONDON 6TH ED., 1971(1972)-*
PREV: INDEX OF AGRICULTURAL RESEARCH FROM
1951- 5TH ED., 1969.
*LO/N14.    LO/U12.*

**ARCHAEOLOGY ABROAD.**
*++ARCHAEOL. ABROAD.*
[ARCHAEOLOGY ABROAD SERVICE]
*LONDON NO.1, F 1972-*
Q.
*BL/U-1.    ED/N-1.    LO/U17.    OX/U-1.*
*CA/U-1. NO.2, 1972-*

**ARCHAIOLOGIKA ANALEKTA EX ATHENON. = ATHENS
ANNALS OF ARCHAEOLOGY.**                               XXX
*++ARCHAIOLOGIKA AN. ATHENON.*
(GREECE) GENERAL INSPECTORATE OF ANTIQUITIES
& RESTORATION.
[TAP]
*ATHENS 1, 1968-*
GREEK, ENGL., FR., OR ITAL. SUMM. IN GER.
*BL/U-1.    BN/U-1.    ED/U-1.    LO/U-4.    NW/U-1.    OX/U-2.*
*SH/U-1.*
*SO/U-1. 6, 1973-*
*ISSN 0004-6604*

**ARCHAEOLOGICUM BELGII SPECULUM.**
*++ARCHAEOL. BELG. SPECULUM.*
*BRUSSELS 1, 1968-*
*BL/U-1.    OX/U-2.*

**ARCHAEOLOGISCHES KORRESPONDENZBLATT.**
*++ARCHAOL. KORRESP.*
ROMISCH-GERMANISCHES ZENTRALMUSEUM.
*MAINZ AM RHEIN 1, 1971-*
*DB/S-1.    DB/U-2.    LO/U-2.    LO/U17.*
*MA/U-1. 3, 1973-*

**ARCHEOLOGIE MEDIEVALE.**
*++ARCHEOL. MEDIEV.*
CENTRE DE RECHERCHES ARCHEOLOGIQUES MEDIEVALES.
*CAEN 1, 1971-*
*BL/U-1.    LO/U17.    NO/U-1.*

**ARCHAEOLOGISCHE MITTEILUNGEN AUS IRAN: NEUE
FOLGE.**
*++ARCHAEOL. MITT. IRAN., NF.*
DEUTSCHES ARCHAOLOGISCHES INSTITUT: ABTEILUNG
TEHERAN.
*BERLIN 1, 1968-*
PREV. SERIES FROM 1, 1929- 9, 1938.
*OX/U-2.*
*NW/U-1. 2, 1969-*
*ISSN 0066-6033*

**ARCHAEOLOGICAL NEWSBULLETIN FOR NORTHUMBER-
LAND, CUMBERLAND & WESTMORLAND.**
*++ARCHEOL. NEWSBULL. NORTHUMBERL. CUMBERL. &
WESTMORL.*
UNIVERSITY OF NEWCASTLE UPON TYNE: DEPARTMENT
OF ADULT EDUCATION.
*NEWCASTLE UPON TYNE NO.1, JA 1968-*
*NW/U-1. (W.NO.9 & 10).*

ARCHEOLOGIA SLASKA.                                       XXX
  SUBS (1965): STUDIA ARCHEOLOGICZNE, UNIWERS-
YTET WROCLAWSKI.

ARCHAEOLOGICA SLOVACA - CATALOGI.
+ +ARCHAEOL. SLOVACA, CAT.
SLOVENSKA AKADEMIA VIED.
  BRATISLAVA 1, 1968-
  GL/U-1.   LO/U-2.

ARCHEOLOGISCHE STUDIEN, NEDERLANDS HISTORISCH
INSTITUUT TE ROME.
+ +ARCHEOL. STUD. NED. HIST. INST. ROME.
  THE HAGUE 1, 1965-
  OX/U-1.

ARCHEOLOGICKE STUDIJNI MATERIALY.
+ +ARCHEOL. STUD. MATER. (CZECH.).
CESKOSLOVENSKA AKADEMIE VED: ARCHEOLOGICKY
USTAV.
  PRAGUE 1, 1964-
  CA/U-1.   DB/S-1.

ARCHAOLOGISCHE VEROFFENTLICHUNGEN, ABTEILUNG
KAIRO, DEUTSCHES ARCHAOLOGISCHES INSTITUT.
+ +ARCHAOLOG. VEROFF. ABT. KAIRO DTSCH. ARCHAOL.
INST.
  BERLIN NO.1, 1970-
  CA/U-1.   LO/N-1.

ARCHAEOLOGIA VIVA.
+ +ARCHAEOL. VIVA.
[PUBL. D'ART ET D'ARCHEOLOGIE]
  PARIS 1, S/N 1968-
  Q. ENGLISH ED.
  LO/N15.   OX/U-2.   SH/U-1.
  ISSN 0003-8024

ARCHAOGRAPHIE.
[HESSLING]
  BERLIN 1, 1969-
  BL/U-1.   CA/U-3.   LO/N14.   OX/U-2.
  ISSN 0587-3460

ARCHEOCIVILISATION: NS.                                   XXX
ECOLE PRATIQUE DES HAUTES ETUDES (PARIS):
CENTRE D'ETUDES PRE-ET PROTOHISTORIQUES.
  PARIS 1, 1966-
  2/A. ENGL. & FR. PREV: ANTIQUITES NATIONALES
ET INTERNATIONALES FROM 1, MY 1960- 4, 1968.
  BL/U-1.   LO/S10.
  ISSN 0003-8156

ARCHITECT (1971).                                         XXX
[IPC BUILDING & CONTRACT JOURNALS]
  LONDON 1, F 1971-
  INCORP: ARCHITECT & BUILDING NEWS: NS FROM
1(1), S 1968- 7(8), JA 1971 & INDUSTRIALISED
BUILDING SYSTEMS & COMPONENTS FROM 1, 1963- 7,
1970.
  BH/P-1.   DB/U-2.   ED/N-1.   LO/N14.   LO/U-4.   RE/U-1.
  LO/U28. 2, 1972-
  ISSN 0003-8415

ARCHITECT & BUILDING NEWS: NS.                            XXX
+ +ARCHIT. & BUILD. NEWS., NS.
[BUILDING & CONTRACT JOURNALS LTD.]
  LONDON 1(1), S 1968- 7(8), JA 1971.
  SUBS. PART OF: ARCHITECT.
  AB/N-1.   BH/P-1.   CA/U-1.   LO/U-2.
  ISSN 0570-6416

ARCHITECTURA. JOURNAL OF THE HISTORY OF
ARCHITECTURE.
[DEUTSCHER KUNSTVERLAG]
  MUNICH 1, 1971-
  LO/N-1.   OX/U-1.
  ISSN 0044-863X

ARCHITECTURAL ASSOCIATION QUARTERLY.                      000
  SEE: AAQ.

ARCHITECTURE - BATIMENT - CONSTRUCTION.                   XXX
  SUBS (1969): ARCHITECTURE CONCEPT.

ARCHITECTURE CANADA.                                      XXX
+ +ARCHIT. CAN.
ROYAL ARCHITECTURAL INSTITUTE OF CANADA.
  TORONTO 43(7), JL 1966- 46(530), 1969...
  PREV: JOURNAL, ROYAL ARCHITECTURAL INSTITUTE
OF CANADA FROM 1, 1924- 43(6), 1966. SUBS:
ARCHITECTURE CANADA NEWSMAGAZINE.
  BL/U-1.
  ISSN 0003-8679

ARCHITECTURE CANADA NEWSMAGAZINE.                         XXX
+ +ARCHIT. CAN. NEWSMAG.
ROYAL ARCHITECTURAL INSTITUTE OF CANADA.
  TORONTO 47(531), 1970-
  PREV: ARCHITECTURE CANADA FROM 43(7), JL
1966- 46(530), 1969.
  LO/N13.

ARCHITECTURE CONCEPT.                                     XXX
+ +ARCH. CONC.
[EDITIONS SOUTHAM]
  MONTREAL 24(271), JA/F 1969-
  PREV: ARCHITECTURE - BATIMENT - CONSTRUCTION
FROM 1, 1946- 23(270), 1968.
  ISSN 0003-8687

ARCHITECTURAL HISTORY & THE FINE & APPLIED
ARTS.
+ +ARCHIT. HIST. & FINE & APPL. ARTS.
HISTORICAL MANUSCRIPTS COMMISSION.
  LONDON 1, 1969-
  S/T: SOURCES IN THE NATIONAL REGISTER OF
ARCHIVES.
  BL/U-1.

ARCHITECTURAL RESEARCH & TEACHING.                        XXX
+ +ARCHIT. RES. & TEACH.
  LONDON 1, MY 1970- 2(3), JE 1973 ...
  SUBS: JOURNAL OF ARCHITECTURAL RESEARCH.
  BL/U-1.   DB/U-2.   ED/N-1.   ED/U-1.   LO/U-2.   OX/U-1.
  SH/U-1.
  ISSN 0003-8601

ARCHITECTURE WEST MIDLANDS.
+ +ARCHIT. WEST MIDL.
ROYAL INSTITUTE OF BRITISH ARCHITECTS: WEST
MIDLANDS REGION.
  BIRMINGHAM NO.1, JL/AG 1970-
  ED/N-1.   LO/N-1.   OX/U-1.

ARCHITEKTURA A URBANIZMUS.
SLOVENSKA AKADEMIA VIED: USTAV STAVEBNICTVA A'
ARCHITEKTURY.
  BRATISLAVA 1(1), 1967-
  SPONS. BODY ALSO: CESKOSLOVENSKA AKADEMIE VED:
KABINET TEORIE ARCHITEKTURY A TVORBY ZIVOTNEHO
PROSTREDIA.
  OX/U-1.

ARCHIWUM AKUSTYKI.
+ +ARCH. AKUST.
POLSKA AKADEMIA NAUK: KOMITET AKUSTYKI.
  WARSAW; WROCLAW 1, D 1966-
  ENGL. & RUSS. SUMM. SPONS. BODY ALSO POLSKIE
TOWARZYSTWO AKUSTYCZNE.
  LO/N13.
  ISSN 0066-6823

ARCHIV FUR BODENFRUCHTBARKEIT UND PFLANZEN-
PRODUKTION.                                               XXX
+ +ARCH. BODENFRUCHTBARKEIT & PFLANZENPROD.
[AKADEMIE-VERLAG]
  BERLIN 15, 1971-
  PREV: ALBRECHT-THAER-ARCHIV FROM 1, 1956- 14,
1970. INCORP: ZEITSCHRIFT FUR LANDESKULTUR
FROM 1, 1960- 11, 1970.
  LO/N13.

ARCHIVES OF BRITISH HISTORY & CULTURE.
+ +ARCH. BR. HIST. & CULT.
CONFERENCE OF BRITISH STUDIES, WEST VIRGINIA
UNIVERSITY.
  MORGANTOWN, W.VA. 1/2, 1971-
  OX/U-1.

ARCHIVES FOR DERMATOLOGICAL RESEARCH.                     000
  SEE: ARCHIV FUR DERMATOLOGISCHE FORSCHUNG.

ARCHIV FUR DERMATOLOGISCHE FORSCHUNG. ARCHIVES
FOR DERMATOLOGICAL RESEARCH.                              XXX
+ +ARCH. DERMATOL. FORSCH.
[SPRINGER]
  BERLIN &C. 240, 1971-
  PREV: ARCHIV FUR KLINISCHE UND EXPERIMENTELLE
DERMATOLOGIE FROM 201, 1955- 239, 1970.
  LD/U-1.
  ISSN 0003-9187

ARCHIV DER ELEKTRISCHEN UBERTRAGUNG.                      XXX
  SUBS (1971): ARCHIV FUR ELEKTRONIK UND
UBERTRAGUNGSTECHNIK.

**ARCHIV FUR ELEKTRONIK UND UBERTRAGUNGSTECHNIK.**
++ARCH. ELEKTRON. & UBERTRAGUNGSTECH.
[HIRZEL]
 STUTTGART 25, 1971-
 PREV: ARCHIV DER ELEKTRISCHEN UBERTRAGUNG
 FROM 1, 1947- 24, 1970.
 LO/N14.
 ISSN 0001-1096

**ARCHIVES OF ENVIRONMENTAL CONTAMINATION &
TOXICOLOGY.**
++ARCH. ENVIRON. CONTAM. & TOXICOL.
[SPRINGER]
 NEW YORK &C. 1(1), 1973-
 Q.
 LO/N14.     OX/U-8.
 ISSN 0090-4341

**ARCHIV FUR EXPERIMENTELLE PATHOLOGIE UND
PHARMAKOLOGIE.**                                                     XXX
 SUBS (1966): ARCHIV FUR PHARMAKOLOGIE UND
 EXPERIMENTELLE PATHOLOGIE.

**ARCHIV FUR FORSTWESEN.**                                           XXX
++ARCH. FORSTWES. [AFOR-A]
DEUTSCHE AKADEMIE DER LANDWIRTSCHAFTSWISSEN-
SCHAFT ZU BERLIN.
 BERLIN 1, 1952- 20(2), 1971.//
 OX/U-3.
 DB/U-2. 15, 1966-              LO/N14. 4, 1955-
 ISSN 0570-6718

**ARCHIVES, FOUNDATION OF THANATOLOGY.**
++ARCH. FOUND. THANATOL.
 NEW YORK 1, AP 1969-
 LO/S18.

**ARCHIV FUR DIE GESAMTE PSYCHOLOGIE.**                              XXX
 SUBS (1970): ARCHIV FUR PSYCHOLOGIE.

**ARCHIVOS DE HISTORIA POTOSINA.**
++ARCH. HIST. POTOSINA.
ACADEMIA DE HISTORIA POTOSINA.
 SAN LUIS POTOSI 1(1), JL/S 1969-
 Q.
 LO/N-1. 1(2), 1969-          OX/U-1. 1(3), 1970-
 ISSN 0004-055X

**ARCHIV FUR KIRCHENGESCHICHTE VON BOHMEN-
MAHREN-SCHLESIEN.**
++ARCH. KIRCHENGESCH. BOHMEN-MAHREN-SCHLESIEN.
KOENIG-STEINER INSTITUT FUR KIRCHEN- UND
GEISTESGESCHICHTE DER SUDETENLAENDER.
 KONIGSTEIN 1, 1967-
 OX/U-1.
 ISSN 0570-6726

**ARCHIV FUR KLINISCHE UND EXPERIMENTELLE
DERMATOLOGIE.**                                                      XXX
 SUBS (1971): ARCHIV FUR DERMATOLOGISCHE
 FORSCHUNG.

**ARCHIV FUR KLINISCHE MEDIZIN.**                                    XXX
++ARCH. KLIN. MED. [AKME-A]
[SPRINGER]
 BERLIN &C. 212, 1966- 216, 1969.
 INCORP: DEUTSCHES ARCHIV FUR KLINISCHE MEDI-
 ZIN FROM 1, 1865- 211, 1965, OF WHICH VOL.
 NUMBERING IS RETAINED; & ZEITSCHRIFT FUR
 KLINISCHE MEDIZIN FROM 1, 1879- 158(7), 1965.
 SUBS: EUROPEAN JOURNAL OF CLINICAL INVESTIGAT-
 ION.
 LD/U-1.

**ARCHIVUM LINGUISTICUM: NS.**
++ARCH. LINGUIST., NS.
[SCHOLAR P.]
 MENSTON 1, 1970-
 PREV. SERIES FROM 1, 1949. S/T: A REVIEW OF
 COMPARATIVE PHILOLOGY & GENERAL LINGUISTICS.
 HL/U-1. LO/U-2.
 ISSN 0004-0703

**ARCHIVES OF MASS SPECTRAL DATA.**                                  XXX
++ARCH. MASS SPECTRAL DATA.
[INTERSCIENCE]
 NEW YORK 1(1), JA/MR 1970- 3, 1972. //
 Q.
 GL/U-1.     LO/N14.
 ISSN 0587-1735

**ARCHIV FUR METEOROLOGIE, GEOPHYSIK UND
BIOKLIMATOLOGIE; SUPPLEMENTUM.**
++ARCH. METEOROL. GEOPHYS. & BIOKLIMATOL.,
 SUPPL.
 VIENNA &C [NO.]1, 1966-
 ENGL., FR., GER.
 LO/N-4.

**ARCHIVES NEERLANDAISES DE ZOOLOGIE.**                              000
 SEE: NETHERLANDS JOURNAL OF ZOOLOGY.

**ARCHIVES OF PHARMACOLOGY.**                                        XXX
++ARCH. PHARMACOL.
[SPRINGER]
 BERLIN &C. 272, 1972-
 PREV: ARCHIV FUR PHARMAKOLOGIE UND EXPERIMENT-
 ELLE PATHOLOGIE FROM 254(1), 1966- 271, 1971.
 LD/U-1.     LO/U-1.*

**ARCHIV FUR PHARMAKOLOGIE UND EXPERIMENTELLE
PATHOLOGIE.**                                                        XXX
++ARCH. PHARMAKOL. EXP. PATHOL.
[SPRINGER]
 BERLIN &C. 254(1), 1966- 271, 1971...
 PREV: ARCHIV FUR EXPERIMENTELLE PATHOLOGIE UND
 PHARMAKOLOGIE FROM 1, 1873- 253, 1965.
 SUBS: ARCHIVES OF PHARMACOLOGY.
 LD/U-1.

**ARCHIV FUR PSYCHOLOGIE.**                                          XXX
++ARCH. PSYCHOL.
DEUTSCHE GESELLSCHAFT FUR PSYCHOLOGIE.
 LEIPZIG 122, 1970-
 PREV: ARCHIV FUR DIE GESAMTE PSYCHOLOGIE FROM
 113, 1961- 121, 1969.
 OX/U-1.
 ISSN 0066-6475

**ARCHIV FUR REFORMATIONSGESCHICHTE: BEIHEFT:
LITERATURBERICHT.**
VEREIN FUR REFORMATIONSGESCHICHTE.
 GUTERSLOH 1, 1972-
 SPONS. BODY ALSO: AMERICAN SOCIETY FOR REFORM-
 ATION RESEARCH.
 GL/U-1.

**ARCHIVIO DEL RICAMBIO.**                                           XXX
++ARCH. RICAMB.
 ROME &C. 24, 1960- [28, 1964].
 PREV: ARCHIVIO PER LO STUDIO DELLA FISIOPAT-
 OLOGIA E CLINICA DEL RICAMBIO FROM 1, 1933-
 23, 1959. SUBS: METABOLISMO.

**ARCHIVOS, SECCION DE ARCHIVOS Y MICROFILMES,
ACADEMIA COLOMBIANA DE HISTORIA.**
++ARCH. SECC. ARCH. MICROFILMES ACAD. COLOMBIANA
 HIST.
 BOGOTA 1(1), 1967-
 OX/U-1.

**ARCHIVES OF SEXUAL BEHAVIOUR.**
++ARCH. SEX. BEHAV.
[PLENUM PUBL. CORP.]
 NEW YORK 1(1), 1971-
 Q.
 OX/U-8.     XY/N-1.
 ISSN 0004-0002

**ARCHIVIO PER LO STUDIO DELLA FISIOPATOLOGIA E
CLINICA DEL RICAMBIO.**                                              XXX
 SUBS (1960): ARCHIVIO DEL RICAMBIO.

**ARCHIVES & THE USER.**
++ARCH & USER.
BRITISH RECORDS ASSOCIATION.
 LONDON NO.1, 1970-
 BH/U-1.     ED/N-1.     GL/U-1.
 ISSN 0066-653X

**ARCHIV FUR ZUCHTUNGSFORSCHUNG.**
++ARCH. ZUCHTUNGSFORSCH.
DEUTSCHE AKADEMIE DER LANDWIRTSCHAFTSWIS-
SENSCHAFTEN ZU BERLIN.
 BERLIN 1, 1971-
 Q.
 CA/U11.     LO/N14.     XS/R-2.

**ARCTIC & ALPINE RESEARCH.**
++ARCTIC ALPINE RES.
UNIVERSITY OF COLORADO: INSTITUTE OF ARCTIC &
ALPINE RESEARCH.
 BOULDER (COLO.) 1(1), W 1969-
 CA/U-2.     CA/U12.     LO/N-2.     LO/S13.     MA/U-1.
 NR/U-1.
 RE/U-1. 2, 1970-
 ISSN 0004-0851

**ARCTOS. ACTA PHILOLOGICA FENNICA. SUPPLEMEN-
TUM.**
KLASSILLUS-FILOLOGINEN YHDISTYS.
 HELSINKI 1, 1968-
 OX/U-1.

**AREA.**
INSTITUTE OF BRITISH GEOGRAPHERS.
*LONDON 1(1), 1969-*
*AD/U-1.     BH/U-1.     GL/U-1.     GL/U-2.     HL/U-1.     LO/N13.*
*LO/R-5.     LO/S13.     LO/U-1.     LO/U12.     SO/U-1.*
*SF/U-1. 3, 1971-             SW/U-1. 3, 1971-*
*ISSN 0004-0894*

**AREA DEVELOPMENT IN JAPAN.**
*+ + AREA DEV. JAP.*
JAPAN CENTER FOR AREA DEVELOPMENT RESEARCH.
*TOKYO 1, 1968-*
A.
*LO/U-3.*

**AREALY RASTENIJ FLORY SSSR.**
*+ + AREALY RAST. FLORY SSSR.*
LENINGRADSKIJ GOSUDARSTVENNYJ UNIVERSITET.
*LENINGRAD 1, 1969-*
*LO/N13.*

**ARELS JOURNAL.**
*+ + ARELS J.*
ASSOCIATION OF RECOGNISED ENGLISH LANGUAGE
SCHOOLS.
*LONDON 1(1), SUMMER 1972-*
*CA/U-1.     ED/N-1.*

**ARENA. AN INDEPENDENT STUDENT PUBLICATION.**
*COTTINGHAM, YORKS. NO.1, 1966-*
*HL/U-1.     LO/U-2.*

**AREPO.**
OXFORD UNIVERSITY CLASSICAL SOCIETY.
*OXFORD NO.1, 1968-*
*OX/U-1.     OX/U-2.*
*ISSN 0004-0967*

**ARETHUSA.**
STATE UNIVERSITY OF NEW YORK.
*BUFFALO, NY 1(1), FALL 1968-*
*2/A. ISSUED BY THE BODY'S DEP. OF CLASSICS.*
*CB/U-1.     EX/U-1.     HL/U-1.     LO/U-2.     MA/U-1.     OX/U-2.*
*SH/U-1.*
*NW/U-1.*
*ISSN 0004-0975*

**ARGAMON.**
ISRAEL MALACOLOGICAL SOCIETY.
*HAIFA 1, 1970-*
*LO/N-2.*

**ARGENTINA.**
(ARGENTINA) SECRETARIA DE DIFUSION Y TURISMO.
*BUENOS AIRES 1(1), 1969-*
*OX/U-1.*
*ISSN 0572-4015*

**ARHIV ZA RUDARSTVO I TEHNOLOGIJU.**                          XXX
*+ + ARH. RUD. & TEHNOL.*
SARAJEVSKI UNIVERZITET: INSTITUT ZA RUDARSKA
I HEMIJSKO-TEHNOLOSKA ISTRAZIVANJA.
*TUZLA 6(1), 1968-*
ENGL., FR. & GER. SUMM. PREV: ARHIV ZA TEHN-
OLOGIJU FROM 1, 1963- 5, 1967.
*LO/N13.*

**ARHIV ZA TEHNOLOGIJU. TECHNOLOGICA ACTA.**          XXX
*+ + ARH. TEHNOL.*
SARAJEVSKI UNIVERZITET: INSTITUT ZA RUDARSKA
I HEMIJSKO-TEHNOLOSKA ISTRAZIVANJA.
*TUZLA 1(1), 1963- 5, 1967...*
Q. ENGL., FR., GER. & RUSS. SUBS: ARHIV ZA
RUDARSTVO I TEHNOLOGIJU.
*LO/N13.*

**ARIEL. A REVIEW OF INTERNATIONAL ENGLISH
LITERATURE.**
UNIVERSITY OF CALGARY.
*CALGARY 1, 1970-*
*AD/U-1.     BH/P-1.     BL/U-1.     CB/U-1.     DB/U-2.     GL/U-1.*
*LD/U-1.     LO/U-1.     LO/U-2.     MA/U-1.**     NW/U-1.*
*OX/U-1.     SO/U-1.*
*EX/U-1. 3, 1972-*
*ISSN 0G04-1327*

**ARITHMOI. NEWSLETTER OF THE ...**
CENTER FOR COMPUTER ORIENTATED RESEARCH IN
BIBLICAL & RELATED ANCIENT LITERATURE.
*PELLA, IOWA 1, MR 1971-*
*NO/U-1.*

**ARIZONA FORESTRY NOTES.**
*+ + ARIZ. FOR. NOTES.*
NORTHERN ARIZONA UNIVERSITY; SCHOOL OF FORESTRY
*FLAGSTAFF NO.1, MY 1966-*
*OX/U-3.*

**ARIZONIANA.**                                                 XXX
ARIZONA PIONEERS' HISTORICAL SOCIETY.
*TUCSON, ARIZ. 1, 1960- 5, 1964 ...*
PREV: NEWSLETTER, ARIZONA PIONEERS' HISTORICAL
SOCIETY FROM OC 1955- OC 1959. SUBS: JOURNAL
OF ARIZONA HISTORY.

**ARK RIVER REVIEW.**
*+ + ARK RIVER REV.*
*WICHITA, KAN. 1(1), SPRING 1971-*
Q.
*LO/U-2.*

**ARKEOLOGISKE MEDDELELSER FRA HISTORISK MUSEUM,
UNIVERSITETET I BERGEN.**
*+ + ARKEOL. MEDD. HIST. MUS. UNIV. BERGEN.*
*BERGEN NO.1, 1971-*
*LO/U-2.*

**ARKHEOLOGICHESKIE OTKRYTIJA.**
*+ + ARKHEOL. OTKRYTIJA.*
AKADEMIJA NAUK SSSR: INSTITUT ARKHEOLOGII.
*MOSCOW 1, 1965(1966)-*
A.
*BH/U-1.     CA/U-1.     LO/N-3.     LO/U15.     OX/U-1.     XY/N-1.*

**ARKHEOLOGICHESKIE PAMJATNIKI MOLDAVII.**
*+ + ARKHEOL. PAMJATNIKI MOLD.*
AKADEMIJA NAUK MOLDAVSKOJ SSR: INSTITUT ISTORII
*KISHINEV 1, 1967-*
*OX/U-1.*

**ARKHEOLOGIJA I ETNOGRAFIJA BASHKIRII.**
*+ + ARKHEOL. & ETNOGR. BASHK.*
AKADEMIJA NAUK SSSR (BASHKIRSKIJ FILIAL):
INSTITUT ISTORII, JAZYKA I LITERATURY.
*UFA 1, 1962-*
*OX/U-1.*

**ARKHITEKTURA I STROITEL'STVO MOSKVY.**                       XXX
SUBS (1960): STROITEL'STVO I ARKHITEKTURA
MOSKVY.

**ARKIV FOR FYSIK.**                                            XXX
SUBS (1970): PHYSICA SCRIPTA.

**ARKIV FOR KEMI.**                                             XXX
SUBS (1971): CHEMICA SCRIPTA.

**ARKIV FOR ZOOLOGI.**                                          XXX
SUBS (1971): ZOOLOGICA SCRIPTA.

**ARKTICHESKAJA FLORA SSSR. FLORA ARCTICA URSS.**
*+ + ARKT. FLORA SSSR.*
AKADEMIJA NAUK SSSR: BOTANICHESKIJ INSTITUT.
*MOSCOW; LENINGRAD 1, 1960-*
*CA/U12.     OX/U-8.*

**ARLINGTON QUARTERLY.**
*+ + ARLINGTON Q.*
UNIVERSITY OF TEXAS AT ARLINGTON.
*ARLINGTON, TEX. 1(1), 1967-*
*OX/U-1.*
*LO/N-1. 1(2), 1968-*
*ISSN 0004-2137*

**ARLIS NEWSLETTER.**
*+ + ARLIS NEWSL.*
ART LIBRARIES SOCIETY.
*ST. ALBANS NO.1, 1969-*
*4/A.*
*GL/U-2.*
*SH/P-1. JE 1974-*
*ED/N-1. NO.10, F 1972-*
*LO/N12. NO.10, F 1972-*

**ARMADILLO PAPERS.**
*+ + ARMADILLO PAP.*
*AUSTIN, TEX. NO.1, N 1969-*
*GL/U-1.*

**ARMCHAIR NATURALIST.**
*+ + ARMCHAIR NAT.*
*POYNTON, CHESHIRE NO.1, 1973-*
*LO/N-2.*

**ARMIES & WEAPONS.**
[ALLAN]
*SHEPPERTON 1, N 1972-*
*6/A.*
*CA/U-1.     ED/N-1.*

**ARMOUR IN PROFILE.**
[PROFILE PUBLS. LTD.]
*LEATHERHEAD 1(1), 1968-*
*LO/N14.*

**ARMS CONTROL & DISARMAMENT (LONDON).** XXX
++ARMS CONTROL & DISARM. (LOND).
(GREAT BRITAIN) FOREIGN OFFICE.
  LONDON NO.1, AP 1967- 8, 1970 ...
  S/T: NOTES ON CURRENT DEVELOPMENTS. SUBS:
  ARMS LIMITATION & DISARMAMENT.
  ED/N-1. LO/N-1. LO/S14. OX/U-1. RE/U-1.

**ARMS CONTROL & DISARMAMENT (NEW YORK).** XXX
++ARMS CONTROL & DISARM. (NEW YORK).
HUDSON INSTITUTE.
[PERGAMON P.]
  NEW YORK &C. 1968-
  SUBS: ARMS CONTROL & NATIONAL SECURITY.
  GL/U-1. GL/U-3. HL/U-1. LO/S14. LO/U-3. SO/U-1.

**ARMS CONTROL & NATIONAL SECURITY.** XXX
++ARMS CONTROL & NATL. SECUR.
HUDSON INSTITUTE.
[PERGAMON P.]
  NEW YORK &C. 1, 1969-
  ANNU. PREV: ARMS CONTROL & DISARMAMENT.
  ED/N-1. HL/U-1. LO/N-1. LO/N17. · LO/S14. LO/U-3.
  OX/U-1.
  ISSN 0004-2447

**ARMS LIMITATION & DISARMAMENT.** XXX
++ARMS LIMITATION & DISARM.
(GREAT BRITAIN) FOREIGN OFFICE.
  LONDON NO.9, D 1970-
  S/T: NOTES ON CURRENT DEVELOPMENTS. PREV:
  ARMS CONTROL & DISARMAMENT (LONDON) FROM NO.1,
  AP 1967- 8, 1970.
  ED/N-1. LO/N-1. LO/S14. OX/U-1. RE/U-1.

**ARMY LOGISTICIAN.**
++ARMY LOGIST.
(UNITED STATES) ARMY: LOGISTICS MANAGEMENT
CENTRE.
  FORT LEE, VA. 1(1), S/OC 1969-
  LO/N-1.
  LO/N13. 1(2), 1969-
  ISSN 0004-2528

**AROMATIC & HETEROAROMATIC CHEMISTRY.**
++AROMAT. & HETEROAROMAT. CHEM.
CHEMICAL SOCIETY.
  LONDON 1, 1973-
  BH/U-3. CA/U-1. ED/N-1. LO/N14. LO/S-3. LO/U-2.
  LO/U12. MA/U-1. NW/U-1. RE/U-1. SF/U-1.
  ISSN 0305-9715

**ARQUIVOS, CENTRO CULTURAL PORTUGUES.**
++ARQ. CENT. CULT. PORT.
  PARIS 1, 1969-
  OX/U-1.
  SO/U-1. 7, 1973-

**ARQUIVOS DE CIENCIAS DO MAR.** XXX
++ARQ. CIENC. MAR. (BRAZ.).
UNIVERSIDADE FEDERAL DO CEARA: LABORATORIO DE
CIENCIAS DO MAR.
  FORTALEZA 9, 1969-
  PREV: ARQUIVOS, ESTACAO DE BIOLOGIA MARINHA,
  UNIVERSIDADE FEDERAL DO CEARA FROM 1, JE 1961-
  8(2), 1968.
  LO/N13.
  ISSN 0041-8854

**ARQUIVOS, ESTACAO DE BIOLOGIA MARINHA, UNI-
VERSIDADE FEDERAL DO CEARA.** XXX
  SUBS (1969): ARQUIVOS DE CIENCIAS DO MAR.

**ARQUIVOS DE HISTORIA DA CULTURA PORTUGUESA.**
++ARQ. HIST. CULT. PORT.
INSTITUTO DE ALTA CULTURA (PORTUGAL).
  LISBON 1, 1967-
  OX/U-1.
  ISSN 0587-3568

**ARRIVE. QUARTERLY JOURNAL OF THE ...** XXX
PEDESTRIANS' ASSOCIATION FOR ROAD SAFETY.
  LONDON NO.1, 1970-
  PREV: PEDESTRIAN FROM 1, 1951- 74, 1969.
  ED/N-1. LO/U-3. OX/U-1.
  ISSN 0031-3874

**ARS.**
SLOVENSKA AKADEMIA VIED: USTAV DEJIN UMENIA.
  BRATISLAVA 1(1), 1966-
  GER. OR SLOVAK WITH SUMM. IN OTHER LANGUAGE.
  OX/U-1.
  ISSN 0044-9008

**ARSENAL.**
  CHICAGO 1, 1970-
  LO/U-2. OX/U-1.

**ARSSKRIFT, SYDSVENSKA MEDICINHISTORISKA
SALLSKAPET.**
++ARSSKRIFT SYDSVEN. MEDICINHIST. SALLSKAPET.
  LUND 1964-
  LO/N-1. 1968-

**ART & ARCHAEOLOGY RESEARCH PAPERS (LONDON).** 000
  SEE: AARP. ART & ARCHAEOLOGY RESEARCH PAPERS.

**ART-LANGUAGE. JOURNAL OF CONCEPTUAL ART.**
[ART & LANGUAGE P.]
  COVENTRY 1(1), MY 1969-
  BT/C-1. ED/N-1. LO/N15. NO/U-1. OX/U-1.
  ISSN 0587-3584

**ART PSYCHOTHERAPY.**
++ART PSYCHOTHER.
[PERGAMON]
  NEW YORK; LONDON 1(1), AP 1973-
  Q. S/T: AN INTERNATIONAL JOURNAL.
  CA/U-1. ED/N-1.
  ISSN 0090-9092

**ARTE & POESIA.**
[DE LUCA]
  ROME 1, 1969-
  CB/U-1. MA/U-1.
  ISSN 0004-3419

**ARTI MUSICES.**
MUZICKA AKADEMIJA U ZAGREBU: MUZIKOLOSKI ZAVOD.
  ZAGREB 1, 1969-
  OX/U-1.
  CA/U-1. 3, 1972-
  LO/U-1. 1970 SPECIAL ISSUE; 2, 1971-
  ISSN 0587-5455

**ARTIFEX. JOURNAL OF THE CRAFTS.**
ART WORKERS' GUILD.
[ORIEL PRESS]
  NEWCASTLE UPON TYNE 1, 1968-
  LO/N14. OX/U-1.
  MA/U-1. 5, 1971-
  ISSN 0004-3699

**ARTIFICIAL INTELLIGENCE.**
++ARTIF. INTELL.
BRITISH COMPUTER SOCIETY.
[AMERICAN ELSEVIER PUBL. CO.]
  NEW YORK 1(1/2), 1970-
  Q. S/T: AN INTERNATIONAL JOURNAL.
  BH/U-3. HL/U-1. LD/U-1. LO/N14. LO/U12. LO/U18.
  MA/U-1. OX/U-8. SH/U-1. SW/U-1.
  GL/U-1. 1, 1970- 2, 1971.
  ISSN 0004-3702

**ARTIFICIAL KIDNEY BIBLIOGRAPHY.**
++ARTIF. KIDNEY BIBLIOGR.
  BETHESDA 1, 1967-
  LD/U-1. LO/M-1. LO/N13.
  ISSN 0004-3710

**ARTIKKELINDEKS FOR BYGG. SCANDINAVIAN BUILD-
ING ABSTRACTS.** XXX
STUDIESELSKAPET FOR NORSK INDUSTRI.
  OSLO 1, 1968- 4(2), 1971 ...
  DAN., NORW. & SWED. SUBS: NORDISKT ARTIKEL-
  INDEX FOR BYGG.
  LO/N14.
  ISSN 0004-377X

**ARTIKKEL INDEKS FOR SKIP.**
STUDIESELSKAPET FOR NORSK INDUSTRI.
  OSLO 1, 1968-
  LO/N14.

**ARTIKKEL-INDEKS, STUDIESELSKAPET FOR NORSK
INDUSTRI.** XXX
  SUBS (1970): POLYTEKNISK ARTIKKEL-INDEKS.

**ARTS D'AFRIQUE (LOS ANGELES).** 000
  SEE: AFRICAN ARTS.

**ARTS OF ASIA.**
[ARTS OF ASIA PUBL.]
  HONG KONG 1(1), JA/F 1971-
  LO/N15.
  ISSN 0004-4083

**ARTS BULLETIN. (1970).**
++ARTS BULL. (ARTS COUNC. G.B.).
ARTS COUNCIL OF GREAT BRITAIN.
  LONDON NO.1, 1970- 9, OC 1972. //
  ED/N-1. HL/U-1. MA/P-1. OX/U-1. RE/U-1.
  BH/P-1. 1, 1970- 5, 1971.

**ARTS DIARY.**
GREATER LONDON ARTS ASSOCIATION.
LONDON NO.1, 1967-
OX/U-1.

**ARTS IN IRELAND.**
+ +ARTS IREL.
DUBLIN 1, 1972-
DB/U-2.

**ARTS ET TRADITIONS POPULAIRES.**                      XXX
SUBS (1971): ETHNOLOGIE FRANCAISE: NS.

**ARUMI EJI. ALUMINIUM AGE.**
KEIKINZOKU ATSUEN KOGYOKAI.
TOKYO NO.1, 1964-
LO/N13.*

**ARUP JOURNAL.**                                       XXX
+ +ARUP J.
ARUP ASSOCIATES.
LONDON 1, 1966-
PREV: ARUP NEWSLETTER FROM 1, 1944- 38, 1965.
BL/U-1.

**ARUP NEWSLETTER.**                                    XXX
SUBS (1966): ARUP JOURNAL.

**ASAHIKAWA KOGYO KOTO SENMON GAKKO KENKYU
HOBUN. JOURNAL OF THE ASAHIKAWA TECHNICAL
COLLEGE.**
SAPPORO NO.1, 1964-
JAP. OR ENGL.
LO/N13.

**A.S.C. NEWSLETTER.**
MICHIGAN STATE UNIVERSITY: AFRICAN STUDIES
CENTER.
EAST LANSING NO.1, MY/JE 1970-
2M.
LO/U-8.

**ASCENT. A JOURNAL OF THE ARTS IN NEW ZEALAND.**
CHRISTCHURCH, NZ 1(1), N 1967-
ED/N-1.   LO/S26.
ISSN 0004-427X

**ASCW JOURNAL.**                                       XXX
SUBS (1968, PART OF): ASTMS JOURNAL.

**ASIA PACIFIC RECORD.**
+ +ASIA PAC. REC.
[ASIA PACIFIC P.]
SINGAPORE 1, AP 1970- 2(4), JY 1971. //
S/T: BASIC DOCUMENTS & VITAL SPEECHES.
LO/U-8.   LO/U14.
CB/U-1. 1(2), 1970-
LO/S14. 1(3), JE 1970-

**ASIA QUARTERLY. A JOURNAL FROM EUROPE.**              XXX
+ +ASIA Q.
UNIVERSITE LIBRE DE BRUXELLES: CENTRE D'ETUDE
DU SUD-EST ASIATIQUE ET DE L'EXTREME-ORIENT.
BRUSSELS 1971, NO.1-
PREV: REVUE DU SUD-EST ASIATIQUE ET DE
L'EXTREME-ORIENT FROM 1968- 1970.
HL/U-1.   LO/N-1.   LO/U-8.   OX/U-1.
ISSN 0035-2683

**ASIA RESEARCH BULLETIN.**
+ +ASIA RES. BULL.
[STRAITS TIMES P.]
SINGAPORE 1(1), JE 1971-
MON.
AD/U-1.   CA/U-1.   LO/U-8.
ISSN 0044-9172

**ASIAN ECONOMIES.**
+ +ASIAN ECON.
RESEARCH INSTITUTE OF ASIAN ECONOMICS.
SEOUL NO.1, JE 1972-
Q.
LO/U-3.

**ASIAN INDUSTRIAL DEVELOPMENT NEWS.**
+ +ASIAN IND. DEV. NEWS.
UNITED NATIONS: ECONOMIC COMMISSION FOR ASIA &
THE FAR EAST.
BANGKOK &C NO.2, 1967-
2/A. PREV, NO.1, 1965: INDUSTRIAL DEVELOPMENT
IN ASIA & THE FAR EAST.
BH/U-1.   ED/N-1.   LO/N17.   LO/S14.   LO/U-3.   MA/U-1.
OX/U16.   OX/U17.
ISSN 0004-4571

**ASIAN LAW SERIES, SCHOOL OF LAW, UNIVERSITY
OF WASHINGTON.**
+ +ASIAN LAW SER. SCH. LAW UNIV. WASH.
SEATTLE NO.1, 1969-
LO/N-1.   LO/N-3.

**ASIAN MASS COMMUNICATION BULLETIN.**
+ +ASIAN MASS COMMUN. BULL.
ASIAN MASS COMMUNICATION RESEARCH & INFORMAT-
ION CENTRE.
SINGAPORE 1(1), 1971-
LO/U14.

**ASIAN OUTLOOK.**                                      XXX
TAIPEI 1(1), AG 1965-
M. PREV: FREE CHINA & ASIA FROM JA 1956- AU
1965.
OX/U-1.
ISSN 0004-4628

**ASIAN POPULATION PROGRAMME NEWS.**
+ +ASIAN POPUL. PROGRAMME NEWS.
UNITED NATIONS: ECONOMIC COMMISSION FOR ASIA &
THE FAR EAST.
BANGKOK 1(1), SPRING 1971-
ENGL. SPONS. BY COMMISSION'S POPULATION
DIVISION.
LO/U-3.
LO/U14. 1(3), 1972-            OX/U16. 2(1), 1973-
ISSN 0084-6821

**ASIAN REVIEW. THE JOURNAL OF THE ...**
+ +ASIAN REV.
ROYAL SOCIETY FOR INDIA, PAKISTAN & CEYLON.
LONDON 1(1), N 1967- 2, JE 1969 ...
SUBS: SOUTH ASIAN REVIEW FROM 3(1), 1969.
LO/N17.*   LO/S14.   LO/U14.   RE/U-1.   SO/U-1.

**ASIAN STUDIES PROFESSIONAL REVIEW.**
+ +ASIAN STUD. PROF. REV.
ASSOCIATION FOR ASIAN STUDIES.
ANN ARBOR 1(1), 1971-
2/A.
LO/U-3.   LO/U-8.   LO/U14.   OX/U-1.   SH/U-1.
ISSN 0044-9245

**ASIAN TRADE UNIONIST.**
INTERNATIONAL CONFEDERATION OF FREE TRADE
UNIONS: ASIAN TRADE UNION COLLEGE.
NEW DELHI 1(1), S 1963- 6(4), D 1968.//
Q. SUPERSEDES AN EARLIER PUBL. OF THE SAME
TITLE, ISSUED 1(1), MR 1956- 3, MR 1958.
LO/U-3.
ISSN 0571-3153

**ASIE DU SUD-EST & MONDE INDONESIEN.**
+ +ASIE SUD-EST & MONDE INDONES.
ECOLE PRATIQUE DES HAUTES ETUDES (PARIS):
CENTRE DE DOCUMENTATION ET DE RECHERCHES.
PARIS 1, 1970-
LO/U14.

**ASLIB INFORMATION.**                                  XXX
+ +ASLIB INF.
LONDON 1, 1973-
MON. PREV: PART OF ASLIB PROCEEDINGS FROM
1957- 1972.
CA/U-1.   CA/U-2.   ED/N-1.   GL/U-2.   LO/N-2.   LO/N-6.
LO/R-6.   LO/U-3.   NO/U-1.   OX/U-1.   SO/U-1.   XS/R10.
ISSN 0305-0033

**ASLIB OCCASIONAL PUBLICATIONS.**
+ +ASLIB OCC. PUBL.
LONDON NO.1, 1968-
BN/U-2.   HL/U-1.   LO/N-4.   LO/U12.   OX/U-1.

**ASM NEWS.**
AMERICAN SOCIETY FOR METALS.
METALS PARK, OHIO 1(1), MR 1970-
LD/U-1.

**ASM NEWS QUARTERLY.**
+ +ASM NEWS Q. (AM. SOC. METALS).
AMERICAN SOCIETY FOR METALS.
METALS PARK, OHIO 1(1), FALL 1968-
XS/R10.

**ASM REVIEW OF METAL LITERATURE.**                     XXX
SUBS. (1968) PART OF: METALS ABSTRACTS; &
METALS ABSTRACTS INDEX.

**ASPECTS OF HOMOGENEOUS CATALYSIS.**
[MANFREDI]
MILAN 1, 1970-
S/T: A SERIES OF ADVANCES.
LD/U-1.   LO/S-3.   LO/U-1.

ASPERGILLUS NEWS LETTER.
+ +ASPERG. NEWS LETT.
UNIVERSITY OF SHEFFIELD.
SHEFFIELD 1, 1960-
ISSUED BY THE BODY'S DEP. OF GENETICS.
CA/U15.   LO/N13.

ASRCT NEWSLETTER.
+ +ASRCT NEWSL. (APPL. SCI. RES. CORP. THAIL.)
APPLIED SCIENTIFIC RESEARCH CORPORATION OF
THAILAND.
BANGKOK   NO.1, JL 1966-
2M. ENGL. & THAI.
LO/U13.
ISSN 0001-2629

ASSEMBLY & FASTENER ENGINEERING (LONDON).          XXX
+ +ASSEM. & FASTENER ENG. (LOND.). [AFAE-A]
[GRAMPIAN P.]
LONDON 7(8), AU 1969- 9(12), D 1971 ...
PREV: ASSEMBLY & FASTENER METHODS FROM 1,
1963- 7(7), JL 1969.  SUBS: SUB-ASSEMBLY-
COMPONENTS-FASTENING.
BH/P-1.   GL/U-2.   LO/N14.

ASSET.                                                            XXX
SUBS (1968, PART OF): ASTMS JOURNAL.

ASSIZE.  JOURNAL OF ...
QUEEN MARY COLLEGE LAW SOCIETY.
LONDON NO.1, MY 1967-
LO/U-2.

(ASSOCIATION FORET-CELLULOSE).
ASSOCIATION FORET-CELLULOSE.
PARIS 1, [1966]-
OX/U-3.

ASSURANCES ET TECHNIQUES DE L'EXPERTISE AUTO-
MOBILE.
+ +ASSUR. & TECH. EXPERTISE AUTO.
[EDITIONS TECHNIQUES POUR L'AUTOMOBILE ET
L'INDUSTRIE]
BOULOGNE-SUR-SEINE NO.1, 1966-
ISSUED AS SUPPL. TO:  REVUE TECHNIQUE AUTOMO-
BILE.
LO/N14.

ASTHETIK UND KOMMUNIKATION.
+ +ASTHET. & KOMMUN.
INSTITUT FUR EXPERIMENTELLE KUNST UND ASTHETIK.
FRANKFURT 1(1), D 1970-
S/T: BEITRAGE ZUR POLITISCHEN ERZIEHUNG.
LO/N-1.

ASTM STANDARDIZATION NEWS.                                       XXX
+ +ASTM STAND. NEWS.
AMERICAN SOCIETY FOR TESTING & MATERIALS.
PHILADELPHIA 1, 1973-
PREV: MATERIALS RESEARCH & STANDARDS FROM 1,
1961- 12, 1973.
BL/U-1.   BR/U-1.   GL/U-1.   LD/U-1.   LO/N-4.   LO/N14.
LO/N35.   OX/U-8.   SW/U-1.
LO/U-2. 1(7), 1973-

ASTMS JOURNAL.
+ +ASTMS J. (ASS. SCI. TECH. & MANAG. STAFFS).
ASSOCIATION OF SCIENTIFIC, TECHNICAL &
MANAGERIAL STAFFS.
LONDON [NO.]1, [MR] 1968-
2M (APPROX.) PREV: ASCW JOURNAL., (ASS. OF
SCIENTIFIC WORKERS)., (&) ASSET., (ASS. OF
SUPERVISORY STAFFS EXECUTIVES & TECHNICIANS).
ED/N-1.   HL/U-1.   LO/U-3.   OX/U-1.   OX/U17.
ISSN 0001-2653

ASTROLABIO.  PROBLEMI DELLA VITA ITALIANA.
ROME   1, MR 1963-
2/M.
GL/U-2. 6,1968-
ISSN 0004-6132

ASTRONOMICAL PAPERS TRANSLATED FROM THE
RUSSIAN.
+ +ASTRON. PAP. TRANSL. RUSS.
SMITHSONIAN INSTITUTION: ASTROPHYSICAL
OBSERVATORY.
CAMBRIDGE, MASS. NO.1, N 1962-
ALSO NUMBERED AS PART OF: TT REPORT SERIES.
TRANSL. OF PAPERS FROM VARIOUS SOURCES, INCL.
SOME PUBL. BY: AKADEMIJA NAUK SSSR: ASTRONO-
MICHESKIJ SOVET.  NOT PUBL. IN STRICT CHRONOL.
ORDER.
ED/R-3.*
CA/U-2. *7,1967-

ASTRONOMICHESKIJ VESTNIK.
+ +ASTRON. VESTN.
VSESOJUZNOE ASTRONOMO-GEODEZICHESKOE
OBSHCHESTVO.
MOSCOW 1(1), JA/MR 1967-
PREV: BJULLETEN' VSESOJUZNOGO ASTRONOMO-
GEODEZICHESKOGO OBSHCHESTVA.
ED/R-3.   LO/N13.
OX/U-1.  3(1), 1969-

ASTRONOMISCHER JAHRESBERICHT.                                    XXX
SUBS (1969): ASTRONOMY & ASTROPHYSICS
ABSTRACTS.

ASTRONOMISK TIDSSKRIFT.                                          XXX
+ +ASTRON. TIDSSKR.
ASTRONOMISK SELSKAB.
COPENHAGEN 1, 1968-
4A. SPONS. BODIES ALSO NORSK ASTRONOMISK
SELSKAB; & SVENSKA ASTRONOMISKA SAELLSKAPET.
PREV: NORSK ASTRONOMISK TIDSSKRIFT FROM N.S.
1, 1920- 1967.
LO/N13.
ISSN 0004-6345

ASTRONOMY & ASTROPHYSICS.                                        XXX
+ +ASTRON. & ASTROPHYS.
[SPRINGER VERLAG]
BERLIN &C. 1(1), 1969-
S/T: A EUROPEAN JOURNAL.  PREV: ANNALES
D'ASTROPHYSIQUE.
BH/U-1.   BL/U-1.   CR/U-1.   LO/U12.   LV/U-1.   MA/U-1.
NW/U-1.   OX/U-8.   SO/U-1.
ISSN 0004-6361

ASTRONOMY & ASTROPHYSICS. SUPPLEMENT SERIES.
+ +ASTRON. & ASTROPHYS., SUPPL. SER.
LEIDEN OBSERVATORY.
[SPRINGER VERLAG]
LEIDEN 1, 1970-
AD/U-1.   LO/N14.   LO/U12.   MA/U-1.   NW/U-1.
SO/U-1.
ISSN 0587-2065

ASTRONOMY & ASTROPHYSICS ABSTRACTS.                              XXX
+ +ASTRON. & ASTROPHYS. ABSTR.
ASTRONOMISCHES RECHEN-INSTITUT (HEIDELBERG).
[SPRINGER VERLAG]
BERLIN &C. 1, 1969-
2/A. PREV: ASTRONOMISCHER JAHRESBERICHT FROM
1, 1900- 68, 1968.
AD/U-1.   CA/U-2.   LD/U-1.   LO/N-4.   LO/N13.   LO/U-2.
LO/U12.   MA/U-1.   OX/U-8   SH/U-1.
ISSN 0067-0022

ASTRONOMY & SPACE.
+ +ASTRON. & SP.
[DAVID & CHARLES]
NEWTON ABBOT 1, 1971-
ED/N-1.   LO/N14.   XY/N-1.
ISSN 0044-9822

ASTROPHYSICAL ABSTRACTS.
+ +ASTROPHYS. ABSTR.
[GORDON & BREACH]
LONDON &C 1, 1969-
ED/N-1.   LO/N14.   OX/U-8.
ISSN 0587-5668

ASTURIENSIA MEDIEVALIA.
OVIEDO 1, 1972-
CA/U-1.   OX/U-1.

ASTURNATURA.
OVIEDO 1, 1973-
LO/N-2.

ASW NEWS.                                                        XXX
SUBS (1970): PART OF SOCIAL WORK TODAY.

ASYLUM.
BOOTLE, LANCS. [NO.]3, 1968-
PREV: MATRIX., 1-2, 1967.
LO/U-2.
ED/N-1. 4, 1968-
ISSN 0004-6426

ATALANTA NORVEGICA.*
+ +ATALANTA NORVEG.
NORSK LEPIDOPTERISK SELSKAP.
OSLO 1(1), AP 1967-
TITLE VARIES: ATALANTA FROM 1(1), 1967- 1(2),
1969.
LO/N-2.
LO/N14. 1(2), 1969-

**ATE.  JOURNAL OF THE ASSOCIATION OF TEACHERS OF ENGLISH.**
*DUBLIN  NO.1, 1970-*
*DB/U-2.*

**ATEISTICHESKIE CHTENIJA.**
*+ +ATEISTCHESK. CHTENIJA.*
[IZDATEL'STVO POLITICHESKOJ LITERATURY]
*MOSCOW  VYP.1, 1966-*
*BH/U-1.　　CC/U-1.　　GL/U-1.*
*ISSN 0571-7418*

**ATHANOR.**
[LEROY]
*NEW YORK  1(1), 1971-*
*Q.*
*LO/U-2.*
*ISSN 0044-9857*

**ATHENS ANNALS OF ARCHAEOLOGY.**　　　　000
SEE: ARCHAIOLOGIKA ANALEKTA EX ATHENON.

**ATHEROSCLEROSIS.**　　　　　　　　　　XXX
[ELSEVIER]
*AMSTERDAM  11, 1970-*
S/T: INTERNATIONAL JOURNAL FOR RESEARCH &
INVESTIGATION ON ATHEROSCLEROSIS & RELATED
DISEASES.  PREV: JOURNAL OF ATHEROSCLEROSIS
RESEARCH FROM 1, 1961- 10, 1969.
*CR/M-1.　　DB/U-2.　　LD/U-1.　　SO/U-1.*
*ISSN 0021-9150*

**ATLANTA NORVEGICA.**
*+ +ATLANTA NORV.*
NORWEGIAN LEPIDOPTEROLOGICAL SOCIETY.
*OSLO  1, 1967-*
*Q.  VARIOUS LANG.*
*CA/U-6.*

**ATLANTIC PAPERS.**
*+ +ATL. PAP.*
ATLANTIC INSTITUTE.
*BOULOGNE-SUR-SEINE  NO.1, 1969-*
*BH/U-1.　　BT/U-1.　　LO/N17.　　OX/U-1.*
*ISSN 0571-7795*

**ATLANTICA & ICELAND REVIEW.**　　　　XXX
*+ +ATL. & ICELAND REV.*
*REYKJAVIK  NO.1, 1968-*
PREV: ICELAND REVIEW FROM 1, AG/S 1963- 5,
1967.
*ED/N-1.*

**ATLANTICHESKIJ OKEAN.  RYBOPOISKOVYE ISSLE-
DOVANIJA.**
*+ +ATL. OKEAN.*
ATLANTICHESKIJ NAUCHNO-ISSLEDOVATEL'SKIJ
INSTITUT RYBNOGO KHOZJAJSTVA I OKEANOGRAFII.
*KALININGRAD  1, 1969-*
*LO/N13.*

**ATLANTIS.**
*DUBLIN  1, 1970-*
*BL/U-1.　　CB/U-1.　　CO/U-1.　　DB/U-2.　　ED/N-1.　　LO/N-1.*
*OX/U-1.*
*ISSN 0004-6884*

**ATLAS.  SUPPLEMENT TO THE ELSEVIER JOURNALS
IN THE GEOSCIENCES.**
*+ +[ATLS-A]*
[ELSEVIER]
*[AMSTERDAM]  1, 1965-*
*GL/U-1.  2, 1966-*
*LO/N13.  1, 1965; 2, 1966.*
*ISSN 0571-7914*

**A.T.M. BULLETIN.**　　　　　　　　　　XXX
*+ +A.T.M. BULL. (ASSOC. TEACH. MANAGE.).*
ASSOCIATION OF TEACHERS OF MANAGEMENT.
*BIRMINGHAM  [1], 1961- 9, 1969.*
SUBS: MANAGEMENT EDUCATION & DEVELOPMENT.
*CV/C-1.  1963-　　　　　GL/U-2.  4, 1964-*
*ISSN 0571-6659*

**A.T.M. OCCASIONAL PAPERS.**　　　　XXX
*OXFORD  NO.1, 1965- 6, 1969.*
SUBS: MANAGEMENT, EDUCATION & DEVELOPMENT.
*LO/N-1.　　OX/U-1.*
*ISSN 0066-9709*

**ATMOSPHERIC TURBIDITY DATA FOR THE WORLD.**
*+ +ATMOS. TURBIDITY DATA WORLD.*
(UNITED STATES) NATIONAL OCEANIC & ATMOSPHERIC
ADMINISTRATION: ENVIRONMENTAL DATA SERVICE.
*WASHINGTON  1, JL/D 1971-*
*XS/N-1.*

**ATOMES.**　　　　　　　　　　　　　　XXX
SUBS (1970): RECHERCHE.

**ATOMIC ABSORPTION & FLAME EMISSION SPECTRO-
SCOPY ABSTRACTS.**
*+ +AT. ABSORP. & FLAME EMISS. SPECTROSC. ABSTR.*
SCIENCE & TECHNOLOGY AGENCY.
*LONDON  1(1), JA/F 1969-*
*2M.*
*LO/N14.　　XS/R10.*
*CA/U-1.  3, 1972-　　　　　ED/N-1.  3, 1971-*
*LO/N-6.  2, 1970-　　　　　LO/U28.  4, 1972-*
*ISSN 0004-7074*

**ATOMIC DATA.**　　　　　　　　　　XXX
*+ +AT. DATA.*
[ACADEMIC P.]
*NEW YORK  1(1), S 1969- 5, 1973.*
SUBS. INCORP. IN: ATOMIC DATA & NUCLEAR DATA
TABLES.
*LO/N-4.　　LO/N14.　　LO/U-2.　　LO/U13.　　MA/U-1.*
*OX/U-8.　　XS/R10.*
*LO/U11.  3, 1971-*
*SH/U-1.  1, 1969/70.*
*ISSN 0004-7082*

**ATOMIC ENERGY CONFERENCES.**　　　XXX
SUBS (1969): MEETINGS ON ATOMIC ENERGY.

**ATOMINDEX.**　　　　　　　　　　　XXX
SUBS (1970): INIS ATOMINDEX.

**ATR.  AUSTRALIAN TELECOMMUNICATION RESEARCH.**
TELECOMMUNICATION SOCIETY OF AUSTRALIA.
*MELBOURNE  1, 1967-*
*LO/N14.*
*ISSN 0001-2777*

**ATTI, CENTRO STUDI E DOCUMENTAZIONE SULL'
ITALIA ROMANA.**
*+ +ATTI CENT. STUDI & DOC. ITAL. ROM.*
*MILAN  1, 1967/68(1969)-*
*BL/U-1.　　LO/N-1.　　OX/U-2.*
*BH/U-1.  1, 1967/68(1969).*

**ATTILA.**
*BRIGHTON  NO.1, MY 1971-*
*ED/N-1.  2, 1973-*

**AUARA.**
ANNAMALAI UNIVERSITY.
*ANNAMALAINAGAR  1, 1969-*
*A.*
*LO/N-2.*

**AUCKLAND UNIVERSITY LAW REVIEW.**
*+ +AUCKL. UNIV. LAW REV.*
UNIVERSITY OF AUCKLAND: LAW STUDENTS' SOCIETY.
*AUCKLAND  1, MY 1965-*
*OX/U15.  1967-*
*ISSN 0067-0510*

**AUDIENCE.**
[HILL PUBL. CO. INC.]
*BOSTON, MASS.  1, 1971-*
*6/A.*
*OX/U-1.  1(6), 1971-*
*ISSN 0004-749X*

**AUDIO (LONDON).**
[IPC MAGAZINES LTD.]
*LONDON  1972-*
*CA/U-1.　　LO/N14.*

**AUDIO AMATEUR.**
*+ +AUDIO AMAT.*
[DELL]
*SWATHMORE, PA.  1, 1970-*
*Q.*
*LO/N14.*
*ISSN 0004-7546*

**AUDIO ANNUAL.**　　　　　　　　　　XXX
*+ +AUDIO ANNU.*
[LINK HOUSE PUBL.]
*LONDON  1968- 1971.*
SUBS: HI-FI NEWS & RECORD REVIEW ANNUAL.
*LO/N14.*
*ISSN 0067-0545*

**AUDIO VISUAL.**                                               XXX
[CURRENT AFFAIRS LTD.]
*CROYDON 1(1), JA 1972-*
M. INCORP: FILM USER FROM 1, N 1946; &
INDUSTRIAL SCREEN FROM 1, MR/AP 1957.
*BL/U-1.    BN/U-1.    LN/U-2.    OX/U-1.    RE/U-1.    SO/U-1.*
*ED/N-1. NO.13, 1973.*
*LO/U-2. 3(27), MR 1974-*
*LO/U28. CURRENT YR. ONLY.*

**AUDIO-VISUAL MEDIA. MOYENS AUDIO-VISUELS.**     XXX
INTERNATIONAL COUNCIL FOR THE ADVANCEMENT OF
AUDIO-VISUAL MEDIA IN EDUCATION.
[PERGAMON]
*OXFORD 1(1), 1967- 4(4), 1970.*
Q. PREV: ICEF REVIEW. SUBS: EDUCATIONAL
MEDIA INTERNATIONAL.
*BL/U-1.    DB/U-2.    LO/N17.*
*NR/U-1. 2, 1968-*
*ISSN 0571-8716*

**AUDIOLOGY. JOURNAL OF AUDITORY COMMUNICATION**     XXX
[KARGER]
*BASLE &C. 10(1), 1971-*
PREV: INTERNATIONAL AUDIOLOGY FROM 1, 1962-
9, 1970.
*LO/N13.    SO/U-1.*
*ISSN 0020-6091*

**AUDUBON FIELD NOTES.**                               XXX
SUBS (1971): AMERICAN BIRDS.

**AUGUSTINIAN STUDIES.**
+ +*AUGUSTINIAN STUD.*
VILLANOVA UNIVERSITY: AUGUSTINIAN INSTITUTE.
*VILLANOVA, P.A. 1, 1970-*
A.
*OX/U-1.*

**AUSTRALASIAN ANNALS OF MEDICINE.**                   XXX
SUBS (1971): AUSTRALIAN & NEW ZEALAND JOURNAL
OF MEDICINE.

**AUSTRALIAN ACADEMIC & RESEARCH LIBRARIES.**
+ +*AUST. ACAD. & RES. LIBR.*
LIBRARY ASSOCIATION OF AUSTRALIA: UNIVERSITY
& COLLEGE LIBRARIES SECTION.
*BUNDOORA, VIC. 1(1), 1970-*
Q.
*BH/U-1.    SH/U-1.*
*ISSN 0004-8623*

**AUSTRALIAN BOOK AUCTION RECORDS.**
+ +*AUST. BOOK AUCTION REC.*
*SYDNEY 1, 1969/70(1971)-*
*OX/U-1.*

**AUSTRALIAN COMPUTER JOURNAL.**
+ +*AUST. COMPUT. J.*
AUSTRALIAN COMPUTER SOCIETY.
[AUSTRALIAN TRADE PUBL.]
*CHIPPENDALE , N.S.W. 1, 1967-*
2/A.
*CA/U-2.*    CA/U-2.**    LO/N14.    SW/U-1.*
*CB/U-1. 2(2), 1970-        LO/U28. 3, 1971-*
*SH/U-1. 1972-             SO/U-1. 2, 1970-*
*XS/R10. 2(1), 1970-        XY/N-1. MY 1969-*
*BR/F-1. 1(1), 1967.*
*ISSN 0004-8917*

**AUSTRALIAN CURRENT LAW REVIEW.**                     XXX
+ +*AUST. CURR. LAW REV.*
[BUTTERWORTHS]
*SYDNEY &C. 1(1), 1969-*
S/T: TOPICAL COMMENT ON THE LAW. PREV:
AUSTRALIAN LAWYER FROM 1, JA 1960- 7, 1967/68.
*OX/U15.*
*ISSN 0045-0413*

**AUSTRALIAN ECONOMIC HISTORY REVIEW.**                XXX
+ +*AUST. ECON. HIST. REV.*
UNIVERSITY OF SYDNEY: DEPARTMENT OF ECONOMICS.
[SYDNEY U.P.]
*SYDNEY 7(1), MR 1967-*
2/A. PREV: BUSINESS ARCHIVES & HISTORY FROM
2, 1962- 6, 1966.
*LO/U-8.    OX/U-9.*
*DB/S-1. 9, MR 1969-            SW/U-1. 12, 1972-*
*ISSN 0004-8992*

**AUSTRALIAN ECONOMIC NEWS DIGEST.**
+ +*AUST. ECON. NEWS DIG.*
AUSTRALIAN NEWS & INFORMATION BUREAU.
*LONDON 1(1), OC 1970-*
M.
*LO/S14.*

**AUSTRALIAN ECONOMIC REVIEW.**
+ +*AUST. ECON. REV.*
INSTITUTE OF APPLIED ECONOMIC RESEARCH (AUST-
RALIA).
*MELBOURNE 1(1), MR 1968-*
Q.
*LO/U-3.    LO/U-8.    OX/U-9*
*ISSN 0004-9018*

**AUSTRALIAN ENTOMOLOGICAL MAGAZINE.**
+ +*AUST. ENTOMOL. MAG.*
[AUSTRALIAN ENTOMOLOGICAL P.]
*GREENWICH, N.S.W. 1, JL 1972-*
Q.
*LO/N-2.    LO/N13.*

**AUSTRALIAN EXTERNAL TERRITORIES.**                   XXX
+ +*AUST. EXTERNAL TERR. [AEXT-A]*
(AUSTRALIA) DEPARTMENT OF EXTERNAL TERRITOR-
IES.                                                   XXX
*CANBERRA 8(3), JE 1968- 12(2), AP/JE 1972.//*
2M. PREV: AUSTRALIAN TERRITORIES FROM 1(1),
D 1960- 8(2), 1968.
*LO/U-3.    LO/U14.*
*ISSN 0004-9069*

**AUSTRALIAN FISHERIES.**                              XXX
+ +*AUST. FISH.*
(AUSTRALIA) DEPARTMENT OF PRIMARY INDUSTRY:
FISHERIES BRANCH.
*CANBERRA 28(1), JA 1969-*
PREV: AUSTRALIAN FISHERIES NEWSLETTER FROM
24(1), JA 1965- 27(12), D 1968.
*BN/U-2.    HL/U-1.*
*ISSN 0004-9115*

**AUSTRALIAN GEOMECHANICS JOURNAL.**
INSTITUTION OF ENGINEERS (AUSTRALIA).
*SYDNEY G1, 1971-*
SPONS. BODY ALSO AUSTRALASIAN INSTITUTE OF
MINING & METALLURGY.
*AD/U-2.    BL/U-1.    LO/N-4.    LO/N14.    NW/U-1.    SH/U-3.*
*SO/U-1.*

**AUSTRALIAN JOURNAL OF BIBLICAL ARCHAEOLOGY.**
UNIVERSITY OF SYDNEY.
*SYDNEY 1(1), 1968-*
SPONS. BODY ALSO: AUSTRALIAN SOCIETY FOR
BIBLICAL ARCHAEOLOGY.
*MA/S-1.    OX/U-1.    OX/U-2.    SH/U-1.*
*ISSN 0084-747X*

**AUSTRALIAN JOURNAL OF BOTANY: SUPPLEMENTARY
SERIES.**
+ +*AUST. J. BOT., SUPPL. SER.*
CSIRO (AUSTRALIA).
*MELBOURNE NO.1, 1971-*
*AD/U-3.    CA/U-2.    LO/N-2.    LO/N-4.    LO/N14.    LO/R-6.*

**AUSTRALIAN JOURNAL OF FORENSIC SCIENCES.**
+ +*AUST. J. FORENSIC SCI.*
AUSTRALIAN ACADEMY OF FORENSIC SCIENCES.
*SYDNEY 1, 1968-*
*LO/N13.*
*ISSN 0045-0618*

**AUSTRALIAN JOURNAL OF SCIENCE.**                     XXX
SUBS (1970): SEARCH.

**AUSTRALIAN JOURNAL OF ZOOLOGY: SUPPLEMENTARY
SERIES.**
+ +*AUST. J. ZOOL., SUPPL. SER.*
CSIRO (AUSTRALIA).
*MELBOURNE NO.1, 1971-*
*AD/U-3.    BL/U-1.    LD/U-1.    LO/N14.    LO/R-6.*

**AUSTRALIAN LAWYER.**                                 XXX
SUBS (1969): AUSTRALIAN CURRENT LAW REVIEW.

**AUSTRALIAN LEFT REVIEW.**
+ +*AUST. LEFT REV.*
*SYDNEY 1(1), JE/JL 1966-*
S/T: A MARXIST JOURNAL OF INFORMATION.
*LO/N-1.*
*OX/U-9. 1967-*
*ISSN 0004-9638*

**AUSTRALIAN MARINE SCIENCES NEWSLETTER.**
+ +*AUST. MAR. SCI. NEWSL.*
AUSTRALIAN MARINE SCIENCES ASSOCIATION.
*SYDNEY & C. NO.1, 1963-*
*LO/N-2.*
*ISSN 0587-5854*

AUSTRALIAN & NEW ZEALAND JOURNAL OF CRIMIN-
OLOGY.
+ +AUST. & N.Z. J. CRIMINOL.
AUSTRALIAN & NEW ZEALAND SOCIETY OF CRIMINOLOGY
MELBOURNE   1, 1968-
Q.
LO/U-3.    OX/U15.
ISSN 0004-8658

AUSTRALIAN & NEW ZEALAND JOURNAL OF MEDICINE.      XXX
+ +AUST. & N.Z. J. MED.
ROYAL AUSTRALASIAN COLLEGE OF PHYSICIANS.
SYDNEY 1, F 1971-
PREV: AUSTRALASIAN ANNALS OF MEDICINE FROM
1, 1952.
GL/U-1.    LO/M13.    LO/N31.    LO/U-1.    NW/U-1.
OX/U-8.
ISSN 0004-8291

AUSTRALIAN PARKS.
+ +AUST. PARKS.
AUSTRALIAN INSTITUTE OF PARKS & RECREATION.
MELBOURNE 1(1), AG 1964-
Q.
LO/N-2.  6(3), 1970-
ISSN 0004-9956

AUSTRALIAN PLANNING INSTITUTE JOURNAL.      XXX
SUBS (1970): ROYAL AUSTRALIAN PLANNING ...

AUSTRALIAN PLASTICS & RUBBER.      XXX
+ +AUST. PLAST. & RUBBER.
[BELL PUBL.]
SYDNEY 23(8), 1972-
PREV: PLASTICS IN AUSTRALIA FROM 12, 1961-
23(7), 1972.
LO/N13.
ISSN 0005-0016

AUSTRALIAN PSYCHOLOGIST.
+ +AUST. PSYCHOL.
BRISBANE   1, 1966-
XY/N-1.
ISSN 0005-0067

AUSTRALIAN TELECOMMUNICATION RESEARCH.      000
SEE: ATR.

AUSTRIAN HISTORICAL BIBLIOGRAPHY. = OSTERREICH-
ISCHE HISTORISCHE BIBLIOGRAPHIE.
+ +AUSTRIAN HIST. BIBLIOGR.
[CLIO P.]
SANTA BARBARA  [NO.1], 1965(1967)-
DB/U-1.    OX/U-1.
ISSN 0067-236X

AUTHENTIC REPORTS.
+ +AUTHENTIC REP.
WASSENAAR  1, 1969-
OX/U-1.

AUTO ZEITUNG.
+ +AUTO ZTG.
[HEINRICH BAUER FACHZEITSCHRIFTEN VERLAG]
COLOGNE NO.1, 1973-
LO/N14.

AUTOCAMPING.
LONDON  1(1), 1967-
OX/U-1.

AUTOMATIC CONTROL (1969- 1971).      XXX
[FARADAY P.]
NEW YORK  3, JA/F 1969(1970)- 5, 1971(1973).
ENGL. TRANSL. OF AVTOMATIKA I VYCHISLITEL'NAJA
TEKHNIKA.  DATING & NUMBERING OF ISSUES FOLLOW
ORIGINAL. SUBS: AUTOMATIC CONTROL & COMPUTER
SCIENCES FROM 6, 1972(1973).
LO/N14.
ISSN 0005-1047

AUTOMATIC CONTROL & COMPUTER SCIENCES.      XXX
+ +AUTOM. CONTROL & COMPUT. SCI.
[ALLERTON P]
NEW YORK  6, 1972(1973)-
ENGL. LANG. TRANSL. OF AVTOMATIKA I VYCHIS-
LITEL'NAJA TEKHNIKA.  DATING & NUMBERING OF
ISSUES FOLLOW ORIGINAL.  PREV: AUTOMATIC
CONTROL (1969- 1971) FROM 3, 1969(1970)- 5,
1971(1973).
LO/N14.

AUTOMATIC DOCUMENTATION & MATHEMATICAL
LINGUISTICS.
+ +AUTOM. DOC. & MATH. LING.
[FARADAY PRESS]
NEW YORK   1, 1967 (1968)-
Q.  A TRANSL. OF SELECTED MAJOR ARTICLES FROM:
NAUCHNO-TEKHNICHESKAJA INFORMATSIJA.  ISSUES
NUMBERED & DATED AS IN ORIG.
LO/N14.
ISSN 0005-1055

AUTOMATIC MONITORING & MEASURING.      XXX
+ +AUTOM. MONIT. & MEAS.
[CONSULTANTS BUREAU]
NEW YORK; LONDON  1970-
PREV: AUTOMETRY FROM 1966- 1969.
ENGL. TRANSL. OF AVTOMETRIYA.
LO/N-4.    LO/N14.
CA/U-1.  1971, 1973-
ED/N-1.  NO.5, OC/S 1971-
ISSN 0005-1292

AUTOMATION COUNCIL NEWS.
+ +AUTOM. COUN. NEWS.
UNITED KINGDOM AUTOMATION COUNCIL.
LONDON  NO.1, JA 1968-
LO/U12.
LO/N14.  CURRENT ISSUES ONLY.
ISSN 0005-1187

AUTOMATION PROJECT REPORT, LIBRARY,
UNIVERSITY OF SOUTHAMPTON.
+ +AUTOM. PROJ. REP. LIBR. UNIV. SOUTHAMPTON.
SOUTHAMPTON NO.1, 1970-
LO/N-1.

AUTOMATIQUE ET INFORMATIQUE INDUSTRIELLES.
+ +AUTOM. & INF. IND.
[SOCIETE DES EDITIONS RADIO]
PARIS NO.1, 1972-
LO/N14.

AUTOMATIZACIJA POSLOVANJA.
+ +AUTOM. POSLOVANJA. [APJA-B]
ZAVOD ZA EKONOMSKE EKSPERTIZE.
BELGRADE  1, 1963-
MON.  ENGL. CONT. LISTS.
LO/N13.
ISSN 0005-1268

AUTOMOBILE ABSTRACTS.      XXX
+ +AUTOMOB. ABSTR. [AUTA-B]
MOTOR INDUSTRY RESEARCH ASSOCIATION.
LINDLEY, NUNEATON  1968- 1971...
PREV: MIRA MONTHLY SUMMARY FROM AP- D 1967.
SUBS: MIRA ABSTRACTS.
BR/U-1.    GL/U-1.    LO/N14.
ISSN 0005-1357

AUTOMOBILE CONNOISSEUR.
+ +AUTO. CONNOISSEUR.
[SPEED & SPORTS PUBL. LTD.]
LONDON  NO.1, 1969-
ED/N-1.
ISSN 0045-1061

AUTOMOTIVE ENGINEERING.      XXX
+ +AUTOMOT. ENG.
SOCIETY OF AUTOMOTIVE ENGINEERS, INC.
NEW YORK  78(8), 1970-
PREV:  SAE JOURNAL FROM 22, 1928- 78(7), 1970.
GL/U-1.    LO/N14.

AUTOMOTIVE RESEARCH PUBLICATIONS.
+ +AUTOMOT. RES. PUBL.
MOTOR INDUSTRY RESEARCH ASSOCIATION.
LINDLEY, WARWICKS.  1970(1)-
Q.
LO/N14.  1972-                    OX/U-8.  1971-
SH/U-1.  1972-
GL/U-2.  [CURRENT 5 YEARS ONLY]

AUTOTRANSPORT.      XXX
[VOGT-SCHILD]
SOLOTHURN  1973-
PREV: SCHWEIZER AUTO-VERKEHR FROM 1, 1934- 34,
1972.
LO/N13.

AVANT GARDE.
[AVANT GARDE MEDIA, INC.]
NEW YORK  1, JA 1968-
2M.
LO/U-2.  NO.2, 5, 6, 1968- 1969.
ISSN 0005-1918

**AVIATION RESEARCH MONOGRAPHS.**
*+ +AVIAT. RES. MONOGR.*
UNIVERSITY OF ILLINOIS: AVIATION RESEARCH
LABORATORY.
*URBANA, ILL. 1, JL 1971-*
LABORATORY SUBORD. TO INSTITUTE OF AVIATION.
*LO/N14.*

**AVTOMATIKA. STROKOVNO GLASILO ZA AVTOMATI-
ZACIJO.**
POSLOVNO ZDRUZENJE AVTOMACIJA.
*LJUBLJANA 1(1), 1960-*
*LO/N-7. 2(3/4),1961-*

**AVTOMATIKA I IZCHISLITELNA TEKHNIKA.**
*+ +AVTOM. & IZCHISLITELNA TEKH.*
DURZHAVEN KOMITET ZA NAUKA I TEKHNICHESKI
PROGRES.
*SOFIA 1(1), 1967-*
2M. ENGL. SUMM.
*LO/N14.*
*LO/N13. 4, 1970-*                          *XS/T-4. 1970-*

**AVTOMATIKA I VYCHISLITEL'NAJA TEKHNIKA.**
*+ +AVTOM. VYCHISL. TEK.*
LATVIJAS PSR ZINATNU AKADEMIJA: INSTITUT ELEKT
RONIKI I VYCHISLITEL'NOJ TEKHNIKI.
*RIGA 8, 1965-*
PREV: TRUDY INSTITUTA ELETRONIKI I VYCHISLIT-
EL'NOJ TEKHNIKI FROM 1, 1961- 7, 1964.
*LO/N14. SW/U-1.*
*XS/T-4. 1970-*

**AVTOMATIKA I VYCHISLITEL'NAJA TEKHNIKA (ENGL.
TRANSL.).**                                                             **000**
  SEE: AUTOMATIC CONTROL (1969- 1971); &
  AUTOMATIC CONTROL & COMPUTER SCIENCES.

**AVTOMATIZATSIJA PROIZVODSTVENNYKH PROTSESSOV
V MASHINOSTROENII I PRIBOROSTROENII.**
*+ +AVTOM. PROIZ. PROTSESSOV MASHINOSTR. & PRIB-
OROSTR,*
L'VOVSKIJ POLITEKHNICHESKIJ INSTITUT.
*L'VOV VYP. 1, 1965-*
S/T: MEZHVEDOMSTVENNYJ RESPUBLIKANSKIJ
NAUCHNO-TEKHNICHESKIJ SBORNIK.
*BH/U-1.*

**AVTOMOBIL'NYJ TRANSPORT. MEZHVEDOMSTVENNYJ
RESPUBLIKANSKIJ NAUCHNO-TEKHNICHESKIJ SBORNIK.**
(UKRAINE) MINISTERSTVO VYSSHEGO I SREDNEGO
SPETSIAL'NOGO OBRAZOVANIJA.
*KIEV 1965-*
*BH/U-1. 1966-*                          *LO/N13. 1970-*

**AWARD JOURNAL. MAGAZINE OF THE DUKE OF
EDINBURGH'S AWARD.**
*LONDON NO.1, S 1970-*
3/A.
*OX/U-1.*

**AWARDS FOR COMMONWEALTH UNIVERSITY STAFF.**           **XXX**
*+ +AWARDS COMMONW. UNIV. STAFF.*
ASSOCIATION OF COMMONWEALTH UNIVERSITIES.
*LONDON 1972/74(1971)-*
2A. PREV: PART OF UNITED KINDOM POSTGRADUATE
AWARDS FROM 1949- 1969/71(1969).
*CA/U-2.*

**AWRE PAMPHLET.**
*+ +AWRE PAM. (AT. WEAP. RES. ESTAB.)*
ATOMIC WEAPONS RESEARCH ESTABLISHMENT.
*ALDERMASTON NO.1, 1967-*
*LO/N14.*

**AYACUCHO ARCHAEOLOGICAL-BOTANICAL PROJECT:
REPORTS.**
*+ +AYACUCHO ARCHAEOL.-BOT. PROJ., REP.*
ROBERT S. PEABODY FOUNDATION FOR ARCHAEOLOGY.
*ANDOVER, MASS. NO.1, 1969-*
*CA/U-1.*

**A.Y.R.S. AIRS.**                                                   **XXX**
AMATEUR YACHT RESEARCH SOCIETY.
[JOHN MORWOOD]
*HYTHE, KENT NO.1, D 1971-*
PREV: A.Y.R.S. PUBLICATION FROM NO.1, 1955-
NO.77, 1971.
*ED/N-1. LO/N14.*

**A.Y.R.S. PUBLICATION.**                                            **XXX**
  SUBS (1971): A.Y.R.S. AIRS.

**AZERBAJDZHANSKIJ ETNOGRAFICHESKIJ SBORNIK.**
*+ +AZERB. ETNOGR. SB.*
AKADEMIJA NAUK AZERBAJDZHANSKOJ SSR: INSTITUT
ISTORII.
*BAKU VYP.1, 1964-*
RUSS. & AZERB. S/T: ISSLEDOVANIJA I MATERIALY
*LO/U14.*
*BH/U-1. 2,1965.*

**AZIONE NONVIOLENTA.**
MOVIMENTO NONVIOLENTO PER LA PACE.
*PERUGIA 1(1), JA 1964-*
*XW/S-1.*

**BA SHIRU.**
UNIVERSITY OF WISCONSIN: DEPARTMENT OF AFRICAN
LANGUAGES & LITERATURE.
*MADISON, WIS. [NO.1], 1970-*
*LO/U14.*
*ISSN 0045-1282*

**BACH. QUARTERLY JOURNAL OF THE ...**
RIEMENSCHNEIDER BACH INSTITUTE.
*BEREA, OHIO 1, 1970-*
*ED/N-1. SH/U-1.*
*ISSN 0005-3600*

**BACIE NEWS.**                                                      **XXX**
BRITISH ASSOCIATION FOR COMMERCIAL & INDUSTRIAL
EDUCATION.
*LONDON 1, 1970- 4(6), 1973.*
PREV: BACIE MEMORANDA FROM 1960-1969. SUBS
PART OF: BACIE JOURNAL.
*ED/N-1. LO/N17. OX/U-1.*
*GL/U-2. 4, 1973-*
*ISSN 0005-2620*

**BACKGROUND BRIEFING.**
*+ +BACKGROUND BRIEF.*
(GREAT BRITAIN) DEPARTMENT OF EMPLOYMENT:
INFORMATION BRANCH.
*LONDON NO.1, AG 1970-*
NO.2 NOT PUBL.
*LO/N-1.*

**BACTERIOLOGICAL PROCEEDINGS.**                                     **XXX**
  SUBS (1972): ABSTRACTS OF THE ANNUAL MEET-
  ING OF THE AMERICAN SOCIETY FOR MICROBIOLOGY.

**BAIE NEWSLETTER.**
*+ +BAIE NEWSL.*
BRITISH ASSOCIATION OF INDUSTRIAL EDITORS.
*LONDON NO.1, 1972- 11, D 1972.//*
MON.
*ED/N-1. OX/U-1.*

**BAKER & BAKERY MANAGEMENT.**                                       **XXX**
*+ +BAKER & BAKERY MANAGE.*
[TRADE PUBL. LTD.]
*LONDON 1970(5)- 1971(3) ...*
PREV: BAKER FROM 1954- AP 1970.
SUBS: BAKERY MANAGEMENT.
*LO/R-6.*

**BAKERY MANAGEMENT.**                                               **XXX**
*+ +BAKERY MANAGE.*
[TRADE PUBL. LTD.]
*LONDON 1971(4)- N/D 1973. //*
PREV: BAKER & BAKERY MANAGEMENT FROM 1970
(5) -1971(3).
*LO/R-6.*
*ED/N-1. 1971(7)-*

**BALCANICA.**
SRPSKA AKADEMIJA NAUKA I UMETNOSTI: BALKAN-
OLOSKI INSTITUT.
*BELGRADE 1, 1970-*
ANNU. ENGL., FR., GER., OR RUSS. ADDED T.P.:
BALKANIKA.
*OX/U-1.*

**BALKANSKIJ ISTORICHESKIJ SBORNIK.**
*+ +BALKAN. ISTOR. SB.*
AKADEMIJA NAUK MOLDAVSKOJ SSR: INSTITUT ISTORII
*KISHINEV 1, 1968-*
A.
*CC/U-1. OX/U-1.*

**BANAA JOURNAL.**
*+ +BANAA J.*
BRITISH ANIMAL NURSING AUXILIARIES ASSOCIATION.
[NEWTON MANN]
*MATLOCK, DERBY. 1, 1973-*
*LO/N13.*

**BANGLADESH DOCUMENTS.**
++BANGLADESH DOC.
(BANGLADESH) MINISTRY OF FOREIGN AFFAIRS:
EXTERNAL PUBLICITY DIVISION.
DACCA 1(1), 1972-
LO/U14.

**BANGLADESH ECONOMIC REVIEW.**                    XXX
++BANGLADESH ECON. REV.
BANGLADESH INSTITUTE OF DEVELOPMENT ECONOMICS.
DACCA 1(1), JA 1973-
Q. PREV: PAKISTAN DEVELOPMENT REVIEW FROM
1(1), 1961- 11(1), MR 1971.
LO/N12.     LO/S14.     LO/U-8.     MA/U-1.     OX/U-1.
OX/U16.     RE/U-1.     SO/U-1.     SW/U-1.

**BANK OF CANADA REVIEW. = REVUE DE LA BANQUE
DU CANADA.**                                       XXX
++BANK CAN. REV.
OTTAWA  D 1971-
M. PREV: STATISTICAL SUMMARY, BANK ... FROM
1937- N 1971.
CA/U-1.     GL/U-1.     GL/U-1.     LO/U-3.
ISSN 0045-1460

**BANK OF ENGLAND STATISTICAL ABSTRACT.**
++BANK ENGL. STAT. ABSTR.
BANK OF ENGLAND.
LONDON NO.1, 1970(1971)-
ISSUED BY ECONOMIC INTELLIGENCE DEPARTMENT.
AD/U-1.     CB/U-1.     CR/U-1.     LD/U-1.     LO/N-1.
OX/U-1.     SO/U-1.

**BANK I KREDYT.**                                 XXX
PANSTWOWE WYDAWNICTWA EKONOMICZNE.
WARSAW 1(1), JA 1970-
M. PREV: WIADOMOSCI NARODOWEGO BANKU POLSK-
IEGO FROM 1(1), 1945- 25(12), 1969.
BH/U-1.     OX/U-1.

**BANK OFFICER.**                                  XXX
SUBS (1970): NUBE NEWS.

**BANQUE DES MOTS.**
CONSEIL INTERNATIONAL DE LA LANGUE FRANCAISE.
[PRESSES UNIVERSITAIRES DE FRANCE]
PARIS NO.1, 1971-
S/T: REVUE SEMESTRIELLE DE TERMINOLOGIE
FRANCAISE PUBLIEE PAR LE CONSEIL ...
CA/U-1.     LO/N-1.     LO/U-2.     MA/U-1.     SA/U-1.
EX/U-1. NO.5, 1973-

**BAR. ZEITSCHRIFT FUR ANGEWANDTE PNEUMATIK.**     XXX
[MARTONAIR DRUCKLUFTSTEUERUNGEN GMBH]
ALPEN 1971(2)-
PREV: ZEITSCHRIFT FUR ANGEWANDTE DRUCKLUFT-
TECHNIK FROM 1966- 1971(1).
LO/N14.

**BARGFRUEHLIG. MUSIKALISCH-VOLKSKUNDLICHE
ZEITSCHRIFT DER ...**
EIDGENOSSISCHEN JODLER-DIRIGENTEN-VEREINIGUNG.
KRIENS 1(1), [1970]-
LO/N-1.

**BASF DIGEST.**                                   XXX
++BASF DIG. (BAD. ANILIN- & SODA-FABR.)
BADISCHE ANILIN- UND SODA-FABRIK.
LUDWIGSHAFEN/RHEIN   1963- 1967 (1).
PARTIAL TRANSL. OF: BASF. (1951).  SUBS (AS A
COMPLETE TRANSL.): BASF REVIEW.
LO/U-2.

**BASF REVIEW.**
++BASF REV. (BAD. ANILIN- & SODA-FABR.)
BADISCHE ANILIN- UND SODA-FABRIK.
LUDWIGSHAFEN/RHEIN  17(3), 1967-
COMPLETE ENGL. TRANSL. OF: BASF. (1951).
NUMBERED AS ORIG.  PREV: BASF DIGEST., 1963-
1967 (1).
LO/U-2.
ISSN 0005-2655

**BASIC TEXTS, FOOD & AGRICULTURE ORGANIZATION
(UN).**
++BASIC TEXTS FAO (UN).
ROME 1, 1960-
ENGL., FR. & GER.
LO/U-2. 1966-

**BASIS. JAHRBUCH FUR DEUTSCHE GEGENWARTSLITER-
ATUR.**
[ATHENAEUM]
FRANKFURT/MAIN 1, 1970-
CA/U-1.     CB/U-1.     DB/U-2.     GL/U-1.     HL/U-1.     LD/U-1.
LO/N-1.     NW/U-1.     SH/U-1.     SW/U-1.
BL/U-1. 4, 1973-                     MA/U-1. 2, 1971-

**BATTELLE INFORMATION.**
++BATTELLE INF.
BATTELLE-INSTITUT; GEMEINNUTZIGE LABORATORIEN
FUR VERTRAGSFORSCHUNG.
FRANKFURT/MAIN  [NO.]1, [1968]-
LO/N-4.     LO/N14.     XS/R10.

**BATTELLE RESEARCH OUTLOOK.**                     XXX
++BATTELLE RES. OUTLOOK.
BATTELLE MEMORIAL INSTITUTE: COLUMBUS LABORAT-
ORIES.
COLUMBUS, OHIO  1, 1969- 4, 1972 ...
Q.  SUBS: RESEARCH OUTLOOK.
DB/U-2.     LO/N-4.     XS/R10.
ISSN 0522-4810

**BAUMASCHINEN DIENST.**                           XXX
++BAUMASCH. DIENST.
[WALTER SCHULTZ]
BAD WORISHOFEN  1, 1965- 3(5), 1967 ...
SUBS: BAUMASCHINENDIENST MIT BAUMASCHINEN-
MARKT.
LO/N14.

**BAUMASCHINENDIENST MIT BAUMASCHINENMARKT.**      XXX
[WALTER SCHULTZ]
BAD WORISHOFEN  3(6), 1967- 7, 1971 ...
PREV: BAUMASCHINEN DIENST FROM 1, 1965- 3(5),
1967.  SUBS: BD MIT BAUMASCHINENDIENST.
LO/N14.

**BAYN AL-NAHRAYN.  MESOPOTAMIA QUARTERLY.**
MOSUL UNIVERSITY.
MOSUL  1(1), 1973-
ARABIC.
LO/U14.

**BBC ENGINEERING.**                               XXX
++BBC ENG.
BRITISH BROADCASTING CORPORATION.
LONDON  NO.81, 1970-
PREV: BBC ENGINEERING DIVISION MONOGRAPH FROM
NO.1, 1955- 80, 1969.
BH/U-1.     DB/U-2.     ED/N-1.     LO/N-4.     LO/N14.     LO/U-2.
OX/U-8.
LD/U-1. NO.82, 1970-

**BBC ENGINEERING DIVISION MONOGRAPH.**            XXX
SUBS (1970): BBC ENGINEERING.

**B.B.G.O.A.**                                     XXX
SUBS (1971): GEOFISICA PANAMERICANA.

**BCE & PROCESS TECHNOLOGY.**                      XXX
++BCE & PROCESS TECHNOL.
[ENGINEERING CHEMICAL & MARINE P. LTD.]
LONDON  16(9), D 1971- 17(9), 1972 ...
PREV: BRITISH CHEMICAL ENGINEERING FROM 1(1),
MY 1956- 16(8), AG 1971. SUBS: PROCESS
TECHNOLOGY INTERNATIONAL.
BH/P-1.     ED/N-1.     LO/N14.

**BD MIT BAUMASCHINENDIENST.**                     XXX
[WALTER SCHULTZ]
BAD WORISHOFEN  8(1-10), 1972 ...
PREV: BAUMASCHINENDIENST MIT BAUMASCHINENMARKT
FROM 3(6), 1967- 7, 1971. SUBS: BD FUR
BAUSTOFFE UND BAUMASCHINEN.
LO/N14.

**BD FUR BAUSTOFFE UND BAUMASCHINEN.**             XXX
++BD BAUSTOFFE & BAUMASCH.
[WALTER SCHULTZ]
BAD WORISHOFEN  8(11), 1972-
PREV: BD MIT BAUMASCHINENDIENST FROM 8(1- 10),
1972.
LO/N14.

**BDA RESEARCH NOTES.**
++BDA RES. NOTES.
BRICK DEVELOPMENT ASSOCIATION.
LONDON  1, 1970-
BL/U-1.

**BDA TECHNICAL NOTE.**
++BDA TECH. NOTE (BRICK DEVELOP. ASS.).
BRICK DEVELOPMENT ASSOCIATION.
LONDON  1, 1970-
PREV:  CPTB TECHNICAL NOTE FROM 1, 1962- 2(7),
1969. ISSUED AS SUPPL. TO BRICK BULLETIN.
BL/U-1.     LO/N14.

**BEDRIJFSONTWIKKELING. EDITIE AKKERBOUW.**     XXX
(NETHERLANDS) MINISTERIE VAN LANDBOUW EN
VISSERIJ: DIRECTIE BEDRIJFSONTWIKKELING.
  *THE HAGUE 1, 1970- 2, 1971...*
  MON. PREV: LANDBOUWVOORLICHTING FROM 10, 1953-
  26, 1969. SUBS. PART OF: BEDRIJFSONTWIKKELING.
  *CA/U11.    LO/N14.*
  *ISSN 0023-7817*

**BEDRIJFSONTWIKKELING. EDITIE TUINBOUW.**     XXX
(NETHERLANDS) MINISTERIE VAN LANDBOUW EN
VISSERIJ: DIRECTIE BEDRIJFSONTWIKKELING.
  *THE HAGUE 1, 1970- 2, 1971...*
  MON. PREV: MEDEDELINGEN VAN DE DIRECTIE
  TUINBOUW FROM 1, 1937. SUBS. PART OF: BED-
  RIJFSONTWIKKELING.
  *CA/U11.    LO/N13.    XS/R-2.*
  *ISSN 0025-6854*

**BEDRIJFSONTWIKKELING. EDITIE VEEHOUDERIJ.**     XXX
(NETHERLANDS) MINISTERIE VAN LANDBOUW EN
VISSERIJ: DIRECTIE BEDRIJFSONTWIKKELING.
  *THE HAGUE 1, 1970- 2, 1971...*
  MON. PREV: VEETEELT- EN ZUIVEL BERICHTEN FROM
  1, 1958- 12, 1969. SUBS. PART OF: BEDRIJFS-
  ONTWIKKELING.
  *CA/U11.    LO/N13.*
  *ISSN 0042-3033*

**BEE.**     000
  SEE: BULLETIN OF ENVIRONMENTAL EDUCATION.

**BEHAVIOR GENETICS.**
  *+ +BEHAV. GENET.*
  [GREENWOOD PERIODICALS]
  *WESTPORT, CONN.  1, F 1970-*
  Q.
  *LO/N13.    MA/U-1.    SH/U-1.*
  *BL/U-1.  4, 1974-          OX/U-8.  2(1), 1972-*
  *ISSN 0001-8244*

**BEHAVIOR RESEARCH METHODS & INSTRUMENTATION.**
  *+ +BEHAV. RES. METH. & INSTRUM.*
  PSYCHONOMIC SOCIETY.
  [PSYCHONOMIC JOURNALS INC.]
  *MADISON, (WIS.)  1(1), 1968-*
  *BL/U-1.    BN/U-1.    OX/U-8.*
  *GL/U-2.  6, 1974-          MA/U-1.  2, 1970-*
  *SH/U-1.  1972-*
  *ISSN 0005-7878*

**BEHAVIOR THERAPY.**
  *+ +BEHAV. THER.*
  [ACADEMIC P.]
  *HANOVER, PA.  1, 1970-*
  *BN/U-1.    CB/U-1.    SH/U-1.*
  *ISSN 0005-7894*

**BEHAVIORAL BIOLOGY.**     XXX
  *+ +BEHAV. BIOL.*
  [ACADEMIC P.]
  *NEW YORK &C.  7(1), F 1972-*
  6/A.  PREV: COMMUNICATIONS IN BEHAVIORAL BIOL-
  OGY: PART A FROM 1(1), 1968- 6(5/6), 1971.
  *GL/U-1.  LO/N-2.  LO/N13.  MA/U-1.  OX/U-8.  SH/U-1.*
  *RE/U-1.  8, 1973-*

**BEHAVIOURAL BIOLOGY ABSTRACTS: SECTION A: ANIMAL
BEHAVIOUR.**     XXX
  *+ +BEHAV. BIOL. ABSTR., A.]*
  [INFORMATION RETRIEVAL LTD.]
  *LONDON  1(1), MY 1973- 1(4), N 1973 ...*
  SUBS: ANIMAL BEHAVIOUR ABSTRACTS.
  *ED/N-1.    EX/U-1.    GL/U-1.    HL/U-1.    LO/N-2.    LO/N-6.*
  *LO/N13.    LO/U-2.    SH/U-1.    SW/U-1.*

**BEHAVIORAL NEUROPSYCHIATRY.**     XXX
  *+ +BEHAV. NEUROPSYCHIATRY. [BENP-B]*
  INTERNATIONAL SOCIETY FOR EXISTENTIAL
  PSYCHIATRY.
  *NEW YORK  1(1), AP 1969-*
  M.  PREV: INTERNATIONAL JOURNAL OF NEUROPSY-
  CHIATRY FROM 1, JA/F 1965- 4(1), F 1968.
  INCLUDES A SEPARATELY PAGED SECTION PDM
  PHYSICIANS' DRUG MANUAL.
  *NW/U-1.  1(10), 1970-*
  *ISSN 0005-7932*

**BEHAVIORAL RESEARCH IN HIGHWAY SAFETY.**
  *+ +BEHAV. RES. HIGHW. SAF.*
  [BEHAVIORAL PUBL.]
  *NEW YORK  1, 1970-*
  *LO/N13.*
  *ISSN 0005-786X*

**BEHAVIOURAL SCIENCES & COMMUNITY DEVELOPMENT.**
  *+ +BEHAV. SCI. & COMMUNITY DEV.*
  NATIONAL INSTITUTE OF COMMUNITY DEVELOPMENT
  (INDIA).
  *HYDERABAD   1(1), 1967-*
  *LO/N17.*    SW/U-1.*
  *ISSN 0005-7843*

**BEHAVIORISM.  A FORUM FOR CRITICAL DISCUSSION.**
  UNIVERSITY OF NEVADA: DEPARTMENT OF PSYCHOLOGY.
  *RENO  1(1), FALL 1972-*
  2/A.
  *BN/U-1.    EX/U-1.*

**BEITRAGE ZUR ALGEBRA UND GEOMETRIE.**
  *+ +BEITR. ALGEBRA & GEOM.*
  [VEB DEUTSCHER VERLAG DER WISSENSCHAFTEN]
  *BERLIN  1, 1971-*
  *LO/N14.*

**BEITRAGE ZUR ANALYSIS.**
  *+ +BEITR. ANAL.*
  MARTIN-LUTHER-UNIVERSITAT HALLE-WITTENBERG.
  [VEB DEUTSCHER VERLAG DER WISSENSCHAFTEN]
  *BERLIN  1, 1971-*
  *LO/N14.*

**BEITRAGE ZUR AUSWARTIGEN UND INTERNATIONALEN
POLITIK.**
  *+ +BEITR. AUSWARTIGEN & INT. POLIT.*
  [WALTER DE GRUYTER & CO.]
  *BERLIN  1, 1966-*
  *LO/N-1.*
  *ISSN 0522-6287*

**BEITRAGE ZUR ELEKTRONENMIKROSKOPISCHEN DIREK-
TABBILDUNG VON OBERFLACHEN.**
  *+ +BEITR. ELEKTRONENMIKROSK. DIREKTABBILD. OBER-
  FLACHEN.*
  [REMY]
  *MUNSTER  1, 1968-*
  *CA/U-2.    LO/N14.*

**BEITRAGE ZUR GESCHICHTE DES JUNGDEUTSCHEN
ORDENS.**
  *+ +BEITR. GESCH. JUNGDTSCH. ORDENS.*
  [VERLAG WOLFGANG LOHMULLER]
  *MUNICH  1, 1970-*
  *LO/N-1.*

**BEITRAGE ZUR HISTORISCHEN SOZIALKUNDE.**
  *+ +BEITR. HIST. SOZIALKD.*
  ARBEITSGEMEINSCHAFT FUR HISTORISCHE SOZIAL-
  KUNDE.
  *VIENNA  1(1), 1971-*
  *LO/N-1.*
  *ISSN 0045-1681*

**BEITRAGE ZUR JAZZFORSCHUNG.  STUDIES IN JAZZ
RESEARCH.**
  *+ +BEITR. JAZZFORSCH.*
  HOCHSCHULE FUR MUSIK UND DARSTELLENDE KUNST IN
  GRAZ: INSTITUT FUR JAZZFORSCHUNG.
  *GRAZ  1, 1969-*
  SPONS. BODY ALSO INTERNATIONALEN GESELLSCHAFT
  FUR JAZZFORSCHUNG.
  *LO/N-1.    OX/U-1.*

**BEITRAGE ZUR KONFLIKTFORSCHUNG.**
  *+ +BEITR. KONFLIKTFORSCH.*
  [MARKUS-VERLAGSGESELLSCHAFT]
  *COLOGNE  1, 1971-*
  Q.
  *ED/N-1.    SH/U-1.    SO/U-1.*

**BEITRAGE ZUR LANDESPFLEGE.**     XXX
  SUBS (1969): LANDSCHAFT UND STADT.

**BEITRAGE ZUR NEOTROPISCHEN FAUNA.**     XXX
  SUBS (1971): STUDIES ON THE NEOTROPICAL FAUNA.

**BEITRAGE, OSTERREICHISCHE GESELLSCHAFT FUR
MUSIK.**
  *+ +BEITR. OSTERR. GES. MUSIK.*
  *KASSEL  1967-*
  ANNU.
  *LO/U-1.  1967- 1968/69.*

**BEITRAGE ZUR PATHOLOGIE.**     XXX
  *+ +BEITR. PATHOL.*
  [FISCHER]
  *STUTTGART  141, 1970-*
  PREV: BEITRAGE ZUR PATHOLOGISCHEN ANATOMIE
  UND ALLGEMEINEN PATHOLOGIE FROM 1, 1886-
  140, 1970.
  *GL/U-1.    LD/U-1.    LO/N13.*
  *ISSN 0005-8165*

BEITRAGE ZUR PATHOLOGISCHEN ANATOMIE UND ZUR
ALLGEMEINEN PATHOLOGIE.                                          xxx
  SUBS (1970): BEITRAGE ZUR PATHOLOGIE.

BEITRAGE ZUR POLITISCHEN BILDUNG.
++BEITR. POLIT. BILD.
[WERKBUND]
  WURZBURG NO.1, 1966-
MONOGR.
LO/N-1.

BEITRAGE ZUR RADIOASTRONOMIE.
++BEITR. RADIOASTRON.
[DUMMLER]
  BONN 1, 1968-
LO/N14.

BEITRAGE ZUR TECHNIKGESCHICHTE TIROLS.
++BEITR. TECHNIKGESCH. TIROLS.
OSTERREICHISCHER INGENIEUR- UND ARCHITEKTEN-
VEREIN: LANDESVEREIN TIROL.
  INNSBRUCK 1, 1969-
LO/N-4.
ISSN 0522-7143

BEITRAGE ZUR UR- UND FRUHGESCHICHTLICHEN ARCHAO-
LOGIE DES MITTELMEER-KULTURRAUMES.
++BEITR. UR- & FRUHGESCH. ARCHAOL. MITTELMEER-
  KULT.
[RUDOLF HABELT VERLAG]
  BONN 1, 1965-
CA/U-1.
ISSN 0067-5245

BELGIAN ENVIRONMENTAL RESEARCH INDEX.
++BELG. ENVIRON. RES. INDEX.
CENTRE NATIONAL DE DOCUMENTATION SCIENTIFIQUE
ET TECHNIQUE (BELGIUM).
  BRUSSELS 1/2, 1969/1970(1972)-
LO/N14.

BELGIAN PLASTICS.                                                xxx
++BELG. PLAST.
FEDERATION DES INDUSTRIES CHIMIQUES DE BELGIQUE
  BRUSSELS NO.1, 1969-
PREV: REVUE BELGE DES MATIERES PLASTIQUES
FROM NO.1, 1960.
LO/N13.
ISSN 0035-0842

BELGISCH TIJDSCHRIFT VOOR NIEUWSTE GESCHIEDENIS.
  SEE: REVUE BELGE D'HISTOIRE CONTEMPORAINE.

BELL JOURNAL OF ECONOMICS & MANAGEMENT
SCIENCE.
++BELL J. ECON. & MANAGE. SCI.
AMERICAN TELEPHONE & TELEGRAPH CO.
  NEW YORK 1, 1970-
2/A.
LO/U-3.    OX/U17.    SO/U-1.
BL/U-1. 2(2), 1971-             OX/U16. 4(1), 1973-
RE/U-1. 3, 1972-
ISSN 0005-8556

BENDIX TECHNICAL JOURNAL.
++BENDIX TECH. J.
BENDIX CORPORATION.
  DETROIT 1, SPRING 1968-
LO/N14.    LO/U-2.
ISSN 0005-8718

BENEFITS INTERNATIONAL.
++BENEFITS INT.
  LONDON 1, JL 1971-
ED/N-1.    OX/U-1.
ISSN 0045-172X

BENELUX-MERKENBLAD. RECUEIL DES MARQUES
BENELUX.
BENELUX-MERKENBUREAU.
  THE HAGUE 1, 1971-
DUTCH & FR.
LO/N14.

BENNINGTON REVIEW.                                               xxx
++BENNINGTON REV.
BENNINGTON COLLEGE.
  BENNINGTON, VT. 1, FALL 1966- 4(1), 1970.//
Q.
OX/U-1.
ISSN 0522-8999

BENZOLE BIBLIOGRAPHY.                                            xxx
++BENZOLE BIBLIOGR. [BZBI-A]
NATIONAL BENZOLE & ALLIED PRODUCTS ASSOCIATION.
  LONDON 1968-
PREV: REVIEW OF BENZOLE TECHNOLOGY FROM 1953-
1967.
BL/U-1.    LO/N14.

BERATENDE INGENIEURE.
++BERATENDE ING.
[HEYMANNS]
  COLOGNE 1971-
LO/N14.
ISSN 0005-8866

BERGBAU-REPORTER. = MINING REPORTER.
[VERLAG GLUCKAUF]
  ESSEN 1971-
LO/N14.

BERGBAUWISSENSCHAFTEN.                                           xxx
  SUBS (1971): BERGBAUWISSENSCHAFTEN UND
  VERFAHRENSTECHNIK IM BERGBAU UND HUTTENWESEN.

BERGBAUWISSENSCHAFTEN UND VERFAHRENSTECHNIK
IM BERGBAU UND HUTTENWESEN.                                      xxx
++BERGBAUWISS. VERFAHRENSTECH. BERGBAU &
  HUTTENWES.
[HERMANN HUBENER]
  GOSLAR 1, 1971-
PREV: BERGBAUWISSENSCHAFTEN FROM 1, 1954-17,
1970.
LO/N14.
ISSN 0005-8920

BERGFREIHEIT.                                                    xxx
  SUBS (1970): FUHRUNGSKRAFT.

BERICHT, DEUTSCHE FORSCHUNGSANSTALT FUR LUFT-
UND RAUMFAHRT.                                                   xxx
  SUBS (1964): FORSCHUNGSBERICHT, DEUTSCHE
  LUFT- UND RAUMFAHRT.

BERICHT, DEUTSCHE VERSUCHSANSTALT FUR LUFT-
UND RAUMFAHRT.                                                   xxx
  SUBS (1964): FORSCHUNGSBERICHT, DEUTSCHE
  LUFT- UND RAUMFAHRT.

BERICHT, FLUGWISSENSCHAFTLICHE FORSCHUNGSAN-
STALT.                                                           xxx
  SUBS (1964): FORSCHUNGSBERICHT, DEUTSCHE
  LUFT- UND RAUMFAHRT.

BERICHTE DER STUDIENGESELLSCHAFT ZUR FORDER-
UNG DER KERNENERGIEVERWERTUNG IN SCHIFFBAU
UND SCHIFFAHRT.
++BER. STUDIENGES. FORD. KERNENERGIEVERWERT.
  SCHIFFB. & SCHIFFAHRT.
STUDIENGESELLSCHAFT ZUR FORDERUNG DER KERN-
ENERGIEVERWERTUNG IN SCHIFFBAU UND SCHIFFAHRT.
[THIEMIG]
  MUNICH NO.1, 1965-
BODY LOCATED IN HAMBURG.
LO/N14.

BERICHTE, TECHNISCHE AKADEMIE (WUPPERTAL).
++BER. TECH. AKAD. (WUPPERTAL).
[VULKAN-VERLAG]
  ESSEN 1, 1969-
LO/N14.

BERITA KADJIAN SUMATERA. SUMATRA RESEARCH
BULLETIN.
UNIVERSITY OF HULL: SUMATRA RESEARCH COUNCIL.
  KINGSTON-UPON-HULL NO.1, 1971-
RESEARCH COUNCIL SUBORD. TO CENTRE FOR SOUTH
EAST ASIAN STUDIES.
ED/N-1.    LO/U-3.    LO/U14.    OX/U-1.

BERKSHIRE TRACTS.
++BERKS. TRACTS.
  UFFINGTON NO.1, 1968-
OX/U-1.

BESKONTAKTNYE ELEKTRICHESKIE MASHINY.
++BESKONTAKTN. ELEKTRI. MASH. [BEEM-B]
LATVIJAS PSR ZINATNU AKADEMIJA: ENERGETIKAS
INSTITUTAS.
  RIGA 1(12), 1962-
VOL.1- 3,(1962- 1963) PUBL. AS SUBSERIES TO:
TRUDY INSTITUTA ENERGETIKI AKADEMII NAUK
LATVIJSKOJ SSR VOLS. 12, 14, 16. EACH VOL. IS
DOUBLE NUMBERED.
LO/N14.

BETONSTEIN ZEITUNG.                                              xxx
  SUBS (1972): BETONWERK + FERTIGTEIL-TECHNIK.

**BETONWERK + FERTIGTEIL-TECHNIK.**                    XXX
*+ +BETONWERK + FERTIGTEIL-TECH.*
[BAUVERLAG GMBH]
  *WISEBADEN  38, 1972-*
  PREV: BETONSTEIN ZEITUNG FROM 1, 1935- 37,
  1971.
  *LO/N14.*

**BEYOND BAROQUE.  QUARTERLY ANTHOLOGY OF NASCENT
LITERARY TRENDS.**
[BEYOND BAROQUE ENTERPRISES]
  *VENICE, CALIF.  1(1), 1968-*
  *OX/U-1.*
  *ISSN 0006-0445*

**BIAS BULLETIN.**
*+ +BIAS BULL. (BRISTOL IND. ARCHAEOL. SOC.).*
BRISTOL INDUSTRIAL ARCHAEOLOGICAL SOCIETY.
  *BRISTOL  NO.1, 1967-*
  *BR/U-1.*

**BIAS JOURNAL.  JOURNAL OF THE BRISTOL INDUST-
RIAL ARCHAEOLOGICAL SOCIETY.**
*+ +BIAS J.*
  *BRISTOL  NO.1, 1968-*
  *BR/U-3.    LO/N-4.    LO/N14.*
  *CA/U-1.  6, 1973-*            *OX/U-1.*
  *ISSN 0306-1450*

**BIBLE.**
ST. PATRICK'S COLLEGE (MAYNOOTH).
  *MAYNOOTH, IRELAND  NO.1, SPRING 1967-*
  SUPPL. TO: FURROW.
  *ED/N-1.*
  *ISSN 0523-154X*

**BIBLICAL THEOLOGY BULLETIN.**
*+ +BIBLICAL THEOL. BULL.*
COLLEZIONE INTERNAZIONALE DEL GESU.
  *ROME  1(1), 1971-*
  *AD/U-1.    CA/U-1.    DB/U-2.    EX/U-1.    LD/U-1.    MA/U-1.*
  *OX/U-1.    SH/U-1.*
  *ISSN 0045-1843*

**BIBLIOGRAFIJA AFRIKI.**
*+ +BIBLIOGR. AFR.*
AKADEMIJA NAUK SSSR: INSTITUT AFRIKI.
  *MOSCOW  1, 1964-*
  S/T: DOREVOLJUTSIONNAJA I SOVETSKAJA LITERAT-
  URA NA RUSSKOM JAZYKE ORIGINAL'NAJA I
  PEREVODNAJA.
  *BT/U-1.    DR/U-1.    EX/U-1.    LO/U15.    OX/U-1.*

**BIBLIOGRAFIA ARGENTINA DE AGRONOMIA Y
VETERINARIA.**
*+ +BIBLIOGR. ARGENT. AGRON.& VET. [BAAV-A]*
UNIVERSIDAD NACIONAL DE BUENOS AIRES: FACULTAD
DE AGRONOMIA Y VETERINARIA.
  *BUENOS AIRES  1, 1967-*
  PRODUCED BY FACULTAD'S BIBLIOTECA CENTRAL.
  *LO/N-2.*
  *ISSN 0523-1647*

**BIBLIOGRAFIA ARGENTINA UNIVERSITARIA.**
*+ +BIBLIOGR. ARGENT. UNIV.*
UNIVERSIDAD NACIONAL DE LA PLATA: BIBLIOTECA.
  *LA PLATA  1, AG 1970-*
  *OX/U-1.*

**BIBLIOGRAFIA BRASILEIRA DE CIENCIAS AGRICOLAS.**
*+ +BIBLIOGR. BRAS. CIENC. AGRIC.*
INSTITUTO BRASILEIRO DE BIBLIOGRAFIA E
DOCUMENTACAO.
  *RIO DE JANEIRO  1, 1967/68(1969)-*
  *LO/N13.    OX/U-1.*
  *ISSN 0067-6594*

**BIBLIOGRAFIJA NA BULGARSKATA BIBLIOGRAFIJA,
KNIGOZNANIE I BIBLIOTECHNO DELO.**
*+ +BIBLIOGR. BULG. BIBLIOGR. KNIGOZN. & BIBL.*
*DELO.*
NARODNA BIBLIOTEKA 'KIRIL I METODY'.
  *SOFIA  1963(1965)-*
  ANNU.
  *OX/U-1.*

**BIBLIOGRAFIE EKONOMICKE LITERATURY: (KNIHY,
CLANKY, RECENZE).**                                  XXX
*+ +BIBLIOGR. EKON. LIT., KNIHY, CLANKY, RECENZE.*
STATNI KNIHOVNA CSSR.
  *PRAGUE  1(1), 1961- 3(12), 1963 ...*
  SUBS: NOVINKI LITERATURY, SPOLECENSKE VEDY:
  RADA 2: BIBLIOGRAFIE EKONOMICKE LITERATURY.
  *OX/U-1.  2, 1962-*
  *LO/N-3.  3(1-4, 6-12).*
  *ISSN 0006-1123*

**BIBLIOGRAFIA FILOSOFICA MEXICANA.**
UNIVERSIDAD NACIONAL AUTONOMA DE MEXICO:
INSTITUTO DE INVESTIGACIONES BIBLIOGRAFICAS.
  *MEXICO, D.F.  1(1), 1968 (1970)-*
  SPONS. BODY ALSO INSTITUTO DE INVESTIGACIONES
  FILOSOFICAS.
  *OX/U-1.*
  *ISSN 0572-6379*

**BIBLIOGRAFIA HISTORICA MEXICANA.**
COLEGIO DE MEXICO.
  *MEXICO  NO.1, 1967-*
  *LO/U-1.    LV/U-1.    SO/U-1.*
  *ISSN 0523-1795*

**BIBLIOGRAFIJA INOSTRANNOJ BIBLIOGRAFII PO
KHIMII.**
*+ +BIBLIOGR. INOSTR. BIBLIOGR. KHIM.*
AKADEMIJA NAUK SSSR: BIBLIOTEKA.
  *MOSCOW  1, 1966-*
  *OX/U-1.*

**BIBLIOGRAFIJA IZDANIJ AKADEMII NAUK LITOVSKOJ
SSR.**                                               000
  SEE: LIETUVOS TSR MOKSLU AKADEMIJOS LEIDI-
  NIU BIBLIOGRAFIJA.

**BIBLIOGRAFICKY KATALOG CSSR, CLANKY V SLOVEN-
SKYCH CASOPISOCH.**                                  XXX
  SUBS (1970): SLOVENSKA NARODNA BIBLIOGRAFIA:
  SERIA C: CLANKY.

**BIBLIOGRAFICKY KATALOG CSSR: SLOVENSKE KNIHY.**    XXX
  SUBS (1969): SLOVENSKA NARODNA BIBLIOGRAFIA:
  SERIA A: KNIHY.

**BIBLIOGRAFIA MEDICA DEL PROFESORADO DE LA
FACULTAD DE MEDICINA, UNIVERSIDAD CENTRAL DE
VENEZUELA.**
*+ +BIBLIOGR. MED. PROFESORADO FAC. MED. UNIV.*
*CENT. VENEZ.*
  *CARACAS  1, 1970-*
  ENGL. ABSTR.
  *LO/N13.*

**BIBLIOGRAFIA OFICIAL COLOMBIANA.**
*+ +BIBLIOGR. OFIC. COLOMB.*
ESCUELA INTERAMERICANA DE BIBLIOTECOLOGIA.
  *MEDELLIN  NO.1, 1964-*
  Q.
  *LO/U-3.    OX/U-1.*
  *ISSN 0067-6748*

**BIBLIOGRAFIA SLOVENSKYCH BIBLIOGRAFII.**
*+ +BIBLIOG. SLOV. BIBLIOGR. [BSVB-A]*
MATICA SLOVENSKA V MARTINE.
  *MARTIN  1961/1962(1965)-*
  *GL/U-1.    OX/U-1.*
  *ISSN 0523-1949*

**BIBLIOGRAFIA VENEZOLANA.**
*+ +BIBLIOGR. VENEZ.*
BIBLIOTECA NACIONAL: CENTRO BIBLIOGRAFICO
VENEZOLANO.
  *CARACAS  1(1), JA/MR 1970-*
  Q.
  *LO/U-1.*
  *ISSN 0006-1085*

**BIBLIOGRAFIA DE YACIMIENTOS PETROLIFEROS
FISCALES BOLIVIANOS.**
*+ +BIBLIOGR. YACIMIENTOS PETROL. FISCALES*
*BOLIVIAN.*
  *LA PAZ  1, 1961-*
  *LO/N13.*

**BIBLIOGRAPHIE AGRICOLE COURANTE ROUMAINE.**
*+ +BIBLIOGR. AGRIC. COURANTE ROUM.*
INSTITUTUL CENTRAL DE CERCETARI AGRICOLE.
  *BUCHAREST  1, 1967-*
  ISSUED BY THE BODY'S CENTRUL DE DOCUMENTARE
  AGRICOLA.  BODY NAMED IN FR.: INSTITUT CENTRAL
  DE RECHERCHES AGRICOLES.
  *CA/U11.    XS/U-1.*
  *BL/U-1.  2,1968-*
  *ISSN 0006-1301*

**BIBLIOGRAPHIES IN AGRICULTURAL HISTORY.**
*+ +BIBLIOGR. AGRIC. HIST.*
UNIVERSITY OF READING.
  *READING  NO.1, 1970-*
  MONOGR.
  *LO/N-1.*

**BIBLIOGRAPHIE DE L'ALGERIE.**
+ +BIBLIOGR. ALGERIE.
BIBLIOTHEQUE NATIONALE (ALGERIA).
ALGIERS 1(1), 1964-
OX/U-1.
ISSN 0523-2392

**BIBLIOGRAPHY ON THE APPLICATION OF COMPUTERS IN THE CONSTRUCTION INDUSTRY. SUPPLEMENT.**
+ +BIBLIOGR. APPL. COMPUT. CONSTR. IND., SUPPL.
(GREAT BRITAIN) MINISTRY OF PUBLIC BUILDING &
WORKS: COMMITTEE ON THE APPLICATION OF COMPUT-
ERS IN THE CONSTRUCTION INDUSTRY.
[H.M.S.O.]
LONDON 1ST, 1968-
LO/N14.

**BIBLIOGRAPHY OF ASIAN STUDIES.**                                              XXX
+ +BIBLIOGR. ASIAN STUD.
ASSOCIATION FOR ASIAN STUDIES.
CORAL GABLES, FLA. 1969-
PREV: PART OF JOURNAL OF ASIAN STUDIES.
CA/U-3.    LO/U-1.    LO/U-8.    NO/U-1.    OX/U-1.    RE/U-1.
CA/U-1. 1970-                    LO/U-3. 1970-

**BIBLIOGRAPHY TO THE AUGUSTAN POETRY.**
+ +BIBLIOGR. AUGUST. POETRY.
[VERLAG DR. H.A. GERSTENBERG]
HILDESHEIM NO.1, 1971-
CA/U-1.

**BIBLIOGRAPHIE, BANQUE CENTRALE DES ETATS DE L'AFRIQUE DE L'OUEST.**
+ +BIBLIOGR. BANQUE CENT. ETATS AFR. OUEST.
PARIS NO.1, 1968-
LV/U-1.

**BIBLIOGRAPHIES OF CHEMISTS.**
+ +BIBLIOGR. CHEM.
INTRA-SCIENCE RESEARCH FOUNDATION.
[GORDON & BREACH]
LONDON & CO. 1, 1971-
CA/U-1.    ED/N-1.    LO/N14.    XY/N-1.
ISSN 0045-1908

**BIBLIOGRAPHICAL CONTRIBUTIONS, UNIVERSITY OF KANSAS LIBRARIES.**
+ +BIBLIOGR. CONTRIB. UNIV. KANS. LIBR.
LAWRENCE (KANS.) 1, 1969-
DR/U-1.    GL/U-1.    LO/U-2.

**BIBLIOGRAPHIE DE LA COTE D'IVOIRE.**
+ +BIBLIOGR. COTE IVOIRE.
BIBLIOTHEQUE NATIONALE (IVORY COAST).
ABIDJAN 1969-
A.
LO/U-3.

**BIBLIOGRAPHY, DEPARTMENT OF THE INTERIOR (US).**
+ +BIBLIOGR. DEP. INTER. (US).
(UNITED STATES) DEPARTMENT OF THE INTERIOR.
WASHINGTON, D.C. NO.1, 1967-
LO/N-2.

**BIBLIOGRAPHIE D'ETUDES BALKANIQUES.**
+ +BIBLIOGR. ETUD. BALKAN.
BULGARSKA AKADEMIJA NA NAUKITE: (INSTITUT
D'ETUDES BALKANIQUES).
SOFIA 1966(1968)-
BODY NAME GIVEN WHOLLY IN FRENCH: ACADEMIE
BULGARE DES SCIENCES: INSTITUT D'ETUDES BALK-
ANIQUES.
LO/N-3.
ISSN 0523-2376

**BIBLIOGRAPHY OF FAMILY PLANNING & POPULATION.**
+ +BIBLIOGR. FAM. PLANN. & POPUL.
SIMON POPULATION TRUST.
CAMBRIDGE 1(1), JL 1972- 2(3), 1973.//
EXPERIMENTAL ISSUE DATED 0(0), S 1971.
BL/U-1.    CA/U-1.    DB/U-2.    ED/N-1.    GL/U-1.    LO/N13.
LO/U-3.

**BIBLIOGRAPHIES FRANCAISES DE SCIENCES SOCIALES.**                            XXX
+ +BIBLIOGR. FR. SCI. SOC.
FONDATION NATIONALE DES SCIENCES POLITIQUES
(FRANCE).
PARIS NO.1, 1960- 4, 1967.//
OX/U-1.
LO/N-1. NO.2, 1961-
ISSN 0523-2783

**BIBLIOGRAPHIE ZUR GESCHICHTE DES PIETISMUS.**
+ +BIBLIOGR. GESCH. PIETISMUS.
BERLIN 1, 1972-
CA/U-1.    OX/U-1.

**BIBLIOGRAPHY ON HIGH PRESSURE RESEARCH.***
+ +BIBLIOGR. HIGH PRESSURE RES.
HIGH PRESSURE DATA CENTER.
PROVO, UTAH 1, 1969-
TITLE REDUCED FROM BIBLIOGRAPHY ON HIGH PRES-
SURE RESEARCH IN CHEMISTRY & PHYSICS FROM
3(6), 1970.
LO/N-4.    LO/N14.
ISSN 0045-1932

**BIBLIOGRAPHY & INDEX OF GEOLOGY.***
+ +BIBLIOGR. & INDEX GEOL.
GEOLOGICAL SOCIETY OF AMERICA.
WASHINGTON, D.C. 1, 1933-
TITLE REDUCED FROM: BIBLIOGRAPHY & INDEX OF
GEOLOGY EXCLUSIVE OF NORTH AMERICA FROM 33,
1969.
BH/U-1.    BL/U-1.    BR/U-1.    GL/U-1.    HL/U-1.    LC/U-1.
LO/N-1.    LO/N-4.    LO/U-4.    LO/U-6.    LV/U-1.    MA/U-1.
LO/N13. 25, 1960-              SW/U-1. 2, 1935-
ISSN 0006-1522

**BIBLIOGRAPHY & INDEX OF MICROPALEONTOLOGY.**
+ +BIBLIOGR. & INDEX MICROPALEONTOL.
AMERICAN MUSEUM OF NATURAL HISTORY.
[MICROPALEONTOLOGY P.]
NEW YORK 1, 1972-
BH/U-3.    LO/N14.    MA/U-1.    OX/U-8.

**BIBLIOGRAPHIE DE LA LITTERATURE FRANCAISE DU MOYEN AGE A NOS JOURS.**          XXX
+ +BIBLIOGR. LITT. FR. MOYEN AGE NOS JOURS.
SOCIETE D'HISTOIRE LITTERAIRE DE LA FRANCE.
PARIS 1966(1967)-
PREV: BIBLIOGRAPHIE DE LA LITTERATURE FRANC-
AISE MODERNE (XVIE- XXE SIECLES) FROM 1962-
1965.
GL/U-1.    HL/U-1.    SO/U-1.
BL/U-1. 1972-
ISSN 0067-6942

**BIBLIOGRAPHY OF MARITIME & NAVAL HISTORY.**
+ +BIBLIOGR. MARIT. & NAV. HIST.
MARINE HISTORICAL ASSOCIATION.
MYSTIC, CONN. 1970(1971)-
AD/U-1.    LO/N-4.

**BIBLIOGRAPHIE MONDIALE DE DROIT SPATIAL ET MATIERES CONNEXES.**                000
SEE: WORLDWIDE BIBLIOGRAPHY OF SPACE LAW &
RELATED MATTERS.

**BIBLIOGRAPHIA MUSICOLOGICA.**
+ +BIBL. MUSICOLOGICA.
[JOACHIMSTHAL PUBL.]
UTRECHT 1, 1968 (1970)-
LO/N-1.    NW/U-1.    OX/U-1.
ISSN 0084-7844

**BIBLIOGRAPHY ON NEPAL.**
+ +BIBLIOGR. NEPAL.
(NEPAL) MINISTRY OF INFORMATION & BROADCASTING.
KATHMANDU NO.1, 1968-
PRODUCED BY MINISTRY'S DEPARTMENT OF INFORMAT-
ION.
LO/N-1.

**BIBLIOGRAPHIE OECUMENIQUE INTERNATIONALE.**                                    000
SEE: INTERNATIONALE OKUMENISCHE BIBLIOGRAPHIE

**BIBLIOGRAPHIE DU QUEBEC.**
+ +BIBLIOGR. QUEBEC.
BIBLIOTHEQUE NATIONALE (QUEBEC).
QUEBEC 1, 1969-
CB/U-1.    LO/N-1.    OX/U-9.
LO/U-8. 2, 1969-
ISSN 0006-1441

**BIBLIOGRAPHIE DER SCHWEIZERISCHEN AMTSDRUCK-SCHRIFTEN.**
+ +BIBLIOGR. SCHWEIZ. AMTSDRUCKSCHR.
SCHWEIZERISCHE LANDESBIBLIOTHEK.
BERN 1, 1968-
GER. & FR.
OX/U-1.

**BIBLIOGRAPHIE DES SCIENCES DE LA TERRE: CAHIER A: MINERALOGIE ET GEOCHIMIE.**    XXX
+ +BIBLIOGR. SCI. TERRE, A.
BUREAU DE RECHERCHES GEOLOGIQUES ET MINIERES
(FRANCE).
ORLEANS F 1968- 1971.
SUBS. PART OF: BULLETIN SIGNALETIQUE 220:
MINERALOGIE, GEOCHIMIE, GEOLOGIE
EXTRATERRESTRE. BIBLIOGRAPHIE DES SCIENCES
DE LA TERRE: CAHIER A.
LO/N14.
ISSN 0523-2538

D

BIBLIOGRAPHIE DES SCIENCES DE LA TERRE:
CAHIER B: GITOLOGIE ET ECONOMIE MINIERE.
+ +BIBLIOGR. SCI. TERRE, B.
BUREAU DE RECHERCHES GEOLOGIQUES ET MINIERES
(FRANCE).
  ORLEANS  F 1968- 1971.
  SUBS. PART OF: BULLETIN SIGNALETIQUE 221:
GITOLOGIE ECONOMIE MINIERE. BIBLIOGRAPHIE
DES SCIENCES DE LA TERRE: CAHIER B.
  LO/N14.
  ISSN 0523-2546

BIBLIOGRAPHIE DES SCIENCES DE LA TERRE:
CAHIER C: ROCHES CRISTALLINES.                                    XXX
+ +BIBLIOGR. SCI. TERRE, C.
BUREAU DE RECHERCHES GEOLOGIQUES ET MINIERES
(FRANCE).
  ORLEANS  F 1968- 1971.
  SUBS. PART OF: BULLETIN SIGNALETIQUE 222:
ROCHES CRISTALLINES. BIBLIOGRAPHIE DES
SCIENCES DE LA TERRE: CAHIER C.
  LO/N14.
  ISSN 0523-2554

BIBLIOGRAPHIE DES SCIENCES DE LA TERRE:
CAHIER D: ROCHES SEDIMENTAIRES.                                   XXX
+ +BIBLIOGR. SCI. TERRE, D.
BUREAU DE RECHERCHES GEOLOGIQUES ET MINIERES
(FRANCE).
  ORLEANS  F 1968- 1971.
  SUBS. PART OF: BULLETIN SIGNALETIQUE 223:
ROCHES SEDIMENTAIRES, GEOLOGIE MARINE.
BIBLIOGRAPHIE DES SCIENCES DE LA TERRE:
CAHIER D.
  LO/N14.
  ISSN 0523-2562

BIBLIOGRAPHIE DES SCIENCES DE LA TERRE: CAH-
IER E: STRATIGRAPHIE ET GEOLOGIE REGIONALE.                       XXX
+ +BIBLIOGR. SCI. TERRE., E.
BUREAU DE RECHERCHES GEOLOGIQUES ET MINIERES
(FRANCE).
  ORLEANS  1968- 1971.
  SUBS: BULLETIN SIGNALETIQUE 224:
STRATIGRAPHIE, GEOLOGIE REGIONALE, GEOLOGIE
GENERALE. BIBLIOGRAPHE DES SCIENCES DE LA
TERRE: CAHIER E.
  GL/U-1.    LO/N-2.
  SW/U-1.  1970(1)-
  ISSN 0523-2570

BIBLIOGRAPHIE DES SCIENCES DE LA TERRE:
CAHIER F: TECTONIQUE ET GEOPHYSIQUE.                              XXX
+ +BIBLIOGR. SCI. TERRE, F.
BUREAU DE RECHERCHES GEOLOGIQUES ET MINIERES
(FRANCE).
  ORLEANS  F 1968- 1971.
  SUBS. PART OF: BULLETIN SIGNALETIQUE 225:
TECTONIQUE. BIBLIOGRAPHIE DES SCIENCES DE LA
TERRE: CAHIER F.
  LO/N14.
  ISSN 0523-2589

BIBLIOGRAPHIE DES SCIENCES DE LA TERRE:
CAHIER G: HYDROGEOLOGIE ET GEOLOGIE DE
L'INGENIEUR.                                                      XXX
+ +BIBLIOGR. SCI. TERRE, G.
BUREAU DE RECHERCHES GEOLOGIQUES ET MINIERES
(FRANCE).
  ORLEANS  F 1968- 1971.
  SUBS. PART OF: BULLETIN SIGNALETIQUE 226:
HYDROLOGIE, GEOLOGIE DE L'INGENIEUR,
FORMATIONS SUPERFICIELLES. BIBLIOGRAPHIE
DES SCIENCES DE LA TERRE: CAHIER G.
  LO/N14.
  ISSN 0523-2597

BIBLIOGRAPHIE DES SCIENCES DE LA TERRE: CAH-
IER H: PALEONTOLOGIE.                                             XXX
+ +BIBLIOGR. SCI. TERRE, H.
BUREAU DE RECHERCHES GEOLOGIQUES & MINIERES
(FRANCE).
  ORLEANS  1968- 1971.
  SUBS. PART OF: BULLETIN SIGNALETIQUE 227:
PALEONTOLOGIE. BIBLIOGRAPHIE DES SCIENCES
DE LA TERRE: CAHIER H.
  GL/U-1.    LO/N-2.
  SW/U-1.  1970(1)-
  ISSN 0523-2600

BIBLIOGRAPHIC SERIES, AMERICAN INSTITUTE OF
ISLAMIC STUDIES.
+ +BIBLIOGR. SER. AM. INST. ISLAMIC STUD.
  DENVER  1969-
  CA/U-1.
  ISSN 0065-8847

BIBLIOGRAPHICAL SERIES, DEPARTMENT OF ENGLISH,
UNIVERSITY OF SOUTH CAROLINA.
+ +BIBLIOGR. SER. DEP. ENGL. UNIV. S. CAROLINA.
  COLUMBIA  1, 1966-
  MON.
  OX/U-1.
  ISSN 0584-3480

BIBLIOGRAPHIC SERIES, LIBRARY, UNIVERSITY OF
PITTSBURGH.                                                       000
  SEE: UNIVERSITY OF PITTSBURGH LIBRARIES BIB-
LIOGRAPHIC SERIES.

BIBLIOGRAPHICAL SERIES, LIBRARY, YALE UNIVER-
SITY.
+ +BIBLIOGR. SER. LIBR. YALE UNIV.
  NEW HAVEN, CONN.  1, 1970-
  OX/U-1.

BIBLIOGRAPHIE ZUR SYMBOLIK, IKONOGRAPHIE &
MYTHOLOGIE.
+ +BIBLIOGR. SYMB. IKONOGR. & MYTHOL.
  BADEN-BADEN  1, 1968-
  DB/U-2.    OX/U-1.      RE/U-1.
  ISSN 0067-706X

BIBLIOTECA DELL' 'ARCHIVIO VENETO'.
+ +BIBL. ARCH. VENETO.
DEPUTAZIONE DI STORIA PATRIA PER LE VENEZIE.
  VENICE  1, 1966-
  OX/U-1.

BIBLIOTECONOMIA E BIBLIOGRAFIA.  SAGGI E STUDI.
+ +BIBLIOTECON. & BIBLIOGR.
  [LEO S. OLSCHKI]
  FLORENCE  1, 1964-
  OX/U-1.
  ISSN 0067-7531

BIBIOTEKOZNAWSTWO.                                                XXX
  SUBS (1970): PART OF STUDIA O KSIAZCE.

BIENNIAL REPORT, AGRICULTURAL EXPERIMENT
STATIONS (GEORGIA).
+ +BIENN. REP. AGRIC. EXP. STN. (GA.).
  ATHENS, GA.  1968/70(1970)-
  PREV: ANNUAL REPORT, AGRICULTURAL EXPERIMENT
STATIONS (GEORGIA) FROM [1888]- 1967/68(1968).
ALSO ENTITLED: SERVING GEORGIA THROUGH RES-
EARCH.
  LO/N14.

BIENNIAL REVIEWS, NATIONAL INSTITUTE FOR
RESEARCH IN DAIRYING.
+ +BIENN. REV. NAT. INST. RES. DAIRY.
  READING  [1], 1970-
  BL/U-1.    CA/U-1.    CA/U12.    LD/U-1.    OX/U-8.    RE/U-1.
  ISSN 0085-3798

BIFLASH MESURES.
+ +BIFLASH MES.
ASSOCIATION DES OUVRIERS EN INSTRUMENTS DE
PRECISION.
  [DUMESNIL PUBLICITE INDUSTRIES]
  PARIS  1, [1969]-
  LO/N14.

BIG A.  ARCHITECTURAL STUDENT MAGAZINE,
QUEEN'S UNIVERSITY BELFAST.
  BELFAST  NO.1, MR 1972- 2, 1972.//
  ED/N-1.    OX/U-1.

BIG FARM MANAGEMENT.
+ +BIG FARM MANAGE.
  [NORTHWOOD PUBL.]
  LONDON  1, 1971-
  PREV: FARM & COUNTRY FROM 1(1), 1874- 225
(4199), D 1970.
  BN/U-2.    ED/N-1.    LD/U-1.    OX/U-8.    RE/U-1.
  NO/U-1.  3, 1973-
  ISSN 0014-7818

BIG VENUS.
  LONDON  [NO.1], 1969-
  LO/U-2.

BIJDRAGEN VOOR DE GESCHIEDENIS DER NEDERLANDEN.
  SUBS (1970) PART OF: BIJDRAGEN EN MEDEDELINGEN
BETREFFENDE DE GESCHIEDENIS DER NEDERLANDEN.

BIJDRAGEN EN MEDEDELINGEN BETREFFENDE DE GES-
GESCHIEDENIS DER NEDERLANDEN.                          XXX
+ +BIJD. MEDED. BETREFFENDE GESCHIEDENIS NED.
HAGUE 85, 1970-
INCORP: BIJDRAGEN VOOR DE GESCHIEDENIS DER
NEDERLANDEN PREV. FROM 1, 1946- 22, 1969; &
BIJDRAGEN EN MEDEDELINGEN VAN HET HISTORISCH
GENOOTSCHAP PREV. FROM 1, 1877- 84, 1969 OF
WHICH VOL. NO. IS CONTINUED.
LO/U19.

BIJDRAGEN EN MEDEDELINGEN VAN HET HISTORISCH
GENOOTSCHAP.                                            XXX
SUBS (1970) PART OF: BIJDRAGEN EN MEDEDELINGEN
BETREFFENDE DE GESCHIEDENIS DER NEDERLANDEN.

BILTEN PREVODA JUGOSLOVENSKIH AUTORA I JUGOS-
LAVIKE.
+ +BILT. PREVODA JUGOSL. AUTORA & JUGOSL.
NARODNA BIBLIOTEKA SR SRBIJE.
BELGRADE 1, 1970-
LO/N-3.    LO/U15.

B.I.M. NOTES FOR COLLECTIVE SUBSCRIBERS.              XXX
SUBS (1971): B.I.M. QUARTERLY REVIEW ...

B.I.M.  QUARTERLY REVIEW OF SERVICES FOR
COLLECTIVE SUBSCRIBERS.                                XXX
+ +B.I.M. Q. REV. SERV. COLLECT. SUBSCRIB.
BRITISH INSTITUTE OF MANAGEMENT.
LONDON 1(1), 1971-
PREV: B.I.M. NOTES FOR COLLECTIVE SUBSCRIBERS
FROM JL 1947- 11(5), OC 1970.
ED/N-1.    OX/U-1.    RE/U-1.    SH/C-5.

BIMESTRE.
FLORENCE 1, MR/AP 1969-
6/A.
DB/U-2.
ISSN 0006-2790

BIMONTHLY REVIEW OF SCIENTIFIC PUBLICATIONS.
+ +BIMON. REV. SCI. PUBL.
POLSKA AKADEMIA NAUK: OSRODEK ROZPOWSZECHNIANIA
WYDANNICTW NAUKOWYCH.
WARSAW 1(45), 1969-
PREV: QUARTERLY REVIEW... FROM 1962.
HL/U-1.    LD/U-1.    LO/N-3.    LO/N-4.    LO/U-2.    NO/U-1.
NW/U-1.

BIO-ACOUSTICS BULLETIN.
+ +BIO-ACOUST. BULL.
CORNELL UNIVERSITY: LABORATORY OF ORNITHOLOGY.
ITHACA, NY  1, 1961-
LO/N-2.
ISSN 0520-1578

BIOCHEMICAL EDUCATION.
+ +BIOCHEM. EDUC.
INTERNATIONAL UNION OF BIOCHEMISTRY.
LEEDS 1, 1972-
LD/U-1.    LO/S-3.    MA/U-1.

BIOCHEMICAL JOURNAL.                                   XXX
SUBS (1973) PUBLISHED IN SERIES [BIOCHEMICAL
JOURNAL: CELLULAR ASPECTS; & BIOCHEMICAL
JOURNAL: MOLECULAR ASPECTS]

BIOCHEMICAL JOURNAL: CELLULAR ASPECTS.                XXX
+ +BIOCHEM. J., CELL. ASPECTS.
BIOCHEMICAL SOCIETY.
LONDON  132, 1973-
PREV: PART OF MAIN TITLE FROM 1, 1906- 130,
1972. ISSUES HAVE EVEN VOLUME NUMBERS ONLY;
ODD NUMBERS ARE ALLOCATED TO BIOCHEMICAL
JOURNAL: MOLECULAR ASPECTS.
GL/U-1.    LO/M31.    LO/N14.

BIOCHEMICAL JOURNAL: MOLECULAR ASPECTS.               XXX
+ +BIOCHEM. J., MOL. ASPECTS.
BIOCHEMICAL SOCIETY.
LONDON  131, 1973-
SEE NOTES FOR BIOCHEMICAL JOURNAL: CELLULAR
ASPECTS.
GL/U-1.    LO/M31.    LO/N14.

BIOCHEMICAL SYSTEMATICS.                               XXX
+ +BIOCHEM. SYST.
[PERGAMON]
OXFORD &C. 1(1- 4), JA- D 1973...
SUBS: BIOCHEMICAL SYSTEMATICS & ECOLOGY.
AD/U-2.    BL/U-1.    CA/U-2.    ED/N-1.    GL/U-1.
GL/U-2.    LO/N-2.    LO/N13.    MA/U-1.    OX/U-3.    OX/U-8.
ISSN 0045-2025

BIOCHEMISTRY OF DISEASE.
+ +BIOCHEM. DIS.
[DEKKAR]
NEW YORK 1, 1971-
CA/U-1.

BIOCHIMIE.                                             XXX
SOCIETE DE CHIMIE BIOLOGIQUE.
[MASSON]
PARIS 53, 1971-
PREV: BULLETIN, SOCIETE ... FROM 1, 1914- 52,
1970.
LD/U-1.    LO/N14.    LO/S-3.    LO/U-1.    NW/U-1.

BIOFEEDBACK & SELF-CONTROL.
[ALDINE]
CHICAGO &C. 1970(1971)-
ANNU.
HL/U-1.    OX/U-8.    SA/U-1.    SW/U-1.

BIOGEOGRAFIA.
UNIVERSIDADE DE SAO PAULO: INSTITUTO DE
GEOGRAFIA.
SAO PAULO NO.1, 1969-
LO/N-2.

BIOGEOGRAPHICA (THE HAGUE).
THE HAGUE 1, 1972-
LO/N-2.    LO/R-5.    OX/U-8.

BIOINORGANIC CHEMISTRY.
+ +BIOINORG. CHEM.
[AMERICAN ELSEVIER]
NEW YORK 1, 1971-
CA/U-2.    LO/N14.
ISSN 0006-3061

BIOLOGIA GALLO-HELLENICA.
+ +BIOL. GALLO-HELLEN.
GROUPE FRANCO-HELLENIQUE DE RECHERCHES BIOL-
OGIQUE.
[TOULOUSE] 1, 1967-
LO/N-2.
CA/U-2. 2, 1969-

BIOLOGIA NEONATORUM.                                   XXX
SUBS (1970): BIOLOGY OF THE NEONATE.

BIOLOGIA PESQUERA.
+ +BIOL. PESQ.
UNIVERSIDAD DE CHILE: ESTACION DE BIOLOGIA
MARINA.
VALPARAISO NO.1, 1961-
PUBL. UNDER AUSPICES OF MINISTERIO DE AGRICUL-
TURA (CHILE): DEPARTAMENTO DE PESCA Y CAZA.
LO/N13.
ISSN 0523-6533

BIOLOGICAL & CHEMICAL FACTORS IN ANIMAL
NUTRITION.                                             000
SEE: BIOLOGIZACE A CHEMIZACE VYZIVY ZVIRAT.

BIOLOGICAL CONSERVATION.
+ +BIOL. CONSERV.
[ELSEVIER]
BARKING &C  1(1), OC 1968-
Q.
BH/U-1.    CR/U-1.    ED/N-1.    GL/U-1.    GL/U-2.    LD/U-1.
LO/N-2.    LO/N13.    LO/U-2.    LO/U12.    OX/U-3.    OX/U-8.
SH/U-1.    XS/U-1.
BH/U-3. 6, 1974-                      LO/U13. 3, 1970/71-
ISSN 0006-3207.

BIOLOGICAL JOURNAL.
+ +BIOL. J. (UNIV. W. INDIES).
UNIVERSITY OF THE WEST INDIES: NATURAL HISTORY
SOCIETY.
ST. AUGUSTINE 1(1), 1966-
LO/N-2.    LO/N13.

BIOLOGICAL JOURNAL OF THE LINNEAN SOCIETY
OF LONDON.
+ +BIOL. J. LINNEAN SOC. LOND.
LINNEAN SOCIETY OF LONDON.
LONDON  1, 1969-
PREV: PROCEEDINGS OF THE LINNEAN SOCIETY OF
LONDON 1, N 1838- 179(2), JE 1968.
BH/P-1.    BH/U-1.    ED/N-1.    LD/U-1.    LO/N-2.    LO/N-4.
LO/R-6.    LO/U-2.    RE/U-1.    SO/U-1.    SW/U-1.
LO/U12. 2(1), 1970-
ISSN 0024-4066

BIOLOGICAL MEMBRANE ABSTRACTS.
+ +BIOL. MEMBRANE ABSTR.
[INFORMATION RETRIEVAL LTD.]
LONDON 1(1), JA 1973-
CA/U-1.    ED/N-1.    GL/U-1.    LO/N13.    MA/U-1.
ISSN 0300-5763

**BIOLOGICAL NOTES, OHIO BIOLOGICAL SURVEY.**
+ +BIOL. NOTES OHIO BIOL. SURV.
COLUMBUS, OHIO NO.1, 1964-
LO/N-2. NO.2, 1964-

**BIOLOGICAL PSYCHIATRY.**                                                   XXX
+ +BIOL. PSYCHIAT.
SOCIETY OF BIOLOGICAL PSYCHIATRY.
NEW YORK 1(1), 1969-
PREV: TITLE VARIES AS PROCEEDINGS OF SCIENTIF-
IC SESSIONS, SOCIETY... FROM 1, 1958(THIS VOL.
ALSO CALLED BIOLOGICAL PSYCHIATRY). THEN PROC.
OF THE ANNUAL CONVENTION & SCIENCE PROGRAM,
SOCIETY... ALSO CALLED RECENT ADVANCES IN
BIOLOGICAL PSYCHIATRY. VOLS. BEAR DUAL NUM.
13 OF PROC.= 1 OF ADVANCES.
LO/U-2.    NW/U-1.
ISSN 0006-3223

**BIOLOGICAL PSYCHOLOGY.**
+ +BIOL. PSYCHOL.
[NORTH HOLLAND]
AMSTERDAM 1, 1973-
Q.
OX/U-8.    SH/U-1.
AD/U-7. 2, 1974-
HL/U-1. 1(1), 1973; 2, 1974-

**BIOLOGICHESKIE RESURSY VODOEMOV MOLDAVII.**
+ +BIOL. RESUR. VODOEMOV MOLD. [BRVM-A]
AKADEMIJA NAUK MOLDAVSKOJ SSR: INSTITUT
ZOOLOGII.
KISHINEV [1], 1962-
VOL.1 IS UNNUMBERED.
LO/N-2. 6, 1970-

**BIOLOGICHESKOE DEISTVIE RADIATSII.**
+ +BIOL. DEISTVIE RADIATSII. [BDRF-A]
L'VOVSKIJ GOSUDARSTVENNYJ UNIVERSITET: PROBLEM-
NAJA LABORATORIJA RADIOBIOLOGII.
L'VOV 1, 1962-
ENGL. CONT. LISTS.
LO/N13.

**BIOLOGIE ET GASTRO-ENTEROLOGIE.**
+ +BIOL. & GASTRO-ENTEROL.
SOCIETE NATIONALE FRANCAISE DE GASTROENTEROL-
OGIE.
[MASSON]
PARIS 1, 1968-
ENGL. SUMM. SUPPL. TO ARCHIVES FRANCAISES DES
MALADIES DE L'APPAREIL DIGESTIF.
SH/U-1.
OX/U-8. 1970-
ISSN 0006-3258

**BIOLOGIE IN UNSERER ZEIT.**
+ +BIOL. UNSERER ZEIT.
[VERLAG CHEMIE GMBH.]
WEINHEIM 1, 1971-
LO/N-2.
ISSN 0045-205X

**BIOLOGIST.**
INSTITUTE OF BIOLOGY.
LONDON 16, 1969-
PREV: JOURNAL, INSTITUTE OF BIOLOGY FROM
1, 1953- 15(4), N 1968.
ED/N-1.    LO/N13.
ISSN 0006-3347

**BIOLOGIZACE A CHEMIZACE VYZIVY ZVIRAT.**
+ +BIOL. & CHEM. VYZIVY ZVIRAT.
CESKOSLOVENSKA AKADEMIE VED.
PRAGUE 1, 1965-
ENGL. SUMM. & TITLE ALSO IN ENGL.: BIOLOGICAL
& CHEMICAL FACTORS IN ANIMAL NUTRITION. SPONS.
BODY ALSO SPOJENE PODNIKY PRO ZDRAVOTNICKOU
VYROBU.
CA/U11.
BN/U-2. 3, 1967-                    LO/N13. 7, 1971-

**BIOLOGY OF THE NEONATE. FOETAL & NEONATAL
RESEARCH.**                                                                  XXX
+ +BIOL. NEONATE.
[KARGER]
BASLE 15, 1970-
PREV: BIOLOGIA NEONATORUM FROM 1, 1959-
14, 1969.
BL/U-1.    LO/M-1.    LO/U-2.    RE/U-1.    SO/U-1.
ISSN 0006-3126

**BIOLOGY OF REPRODUCTION.**
+ +BIOL. REPROD.
SOCIETY FOR THE STUDY OF REPRODUCTION.
NEW YORK 1, AP 1969-
SUPPLEMENTS ISSUED WITH NO.1, JE 1969.
DN/U-1.    GL/U-1.    HL/U-1.    LO/M17.    LO/M26.
LO/N-2.    LO/N13.    LO/U-2.    NW/U-1.    RE/U-1.    XY/N-1.
OX/U-1. 1(3), 1969-              SH/U-1. 1971-
ISSN 0006-3363

**BIOLOGY OF REPRODUCTION: SUPPLEMENT.**
+ +BIOL. REPROD., SUPPL.
SOCIETY FOR THE STUDY OF REPRODUCTION.
[ACADEMIC P.]
NEW YORK &C. [NO.]1, 1969-
LO/N13.
ISSN 0006-3363

**BIOMATHEMATICS (1969).**
[DEKKER]
NEW YORK 1, 1969-
OX/U-8.

**BIOMATHEMATICS (1970).**
[SPRINGER]
BERLIN &C. 1, 1970-
OX/U-8.

**BIO-MEDICAL APPLICATIONS OF POLYMERS.**
+ +BIO-MED. APPL. POLYM.
RUBBER & PLASTICS RESEARCH ASSOCIATION OF
GREAT BRITAIN.
SHREWSBURY 1, 1972-
LO/N14.

**BIOMEDICINE.**                                                             XXX
[EDITIONS MEDICALES FLAMMARION]
PARIS 18, 1973-
PREV: REVUE EUROPEENE D'ETUDES CLINIQUES ET
BIOLOGIQUES FROM 15, 1970- 17, 1972.
BL/U-1.    GL/U-1.    LD/U-1.    LO/N13.

**BIOMEMBRANES.**
[PLENUM P.]
NEW YORK; LONDON 1, 1971-
ANNU.
GL/U-1.    LO/N13.    LO/U28.    OX/U-8.    XY/N-1.
HL/U-1. 1, 1971.
LD/U-1. 1, 1971.

**BIOMETEOROLOGY.**
INTERNATIONAL SOCIETY OF BIOMETEOROLOGY.
[PERGAMON]
OXFORD &C 1, 1960-
COMPRISES PROCEEDINGS OF THE ... INTERNATIO-
NAL BIOCLIMATOLOGICAL [LATER: BIOMETEOROLOGI-
CAL] CONGRESS., FROM 2ND, 1960. SOME ISSUED
AS SUPPL. TO: INTERNATIONAL JOURNAL OF BIO-
METEOROLOGY.
LO/N14.
LO/U-2. 3, 1967.
ISSN 0067-8902

**BIOMETRIE HUMAINE (BIOTYPOLOGIE).**                                         000
SEE: REVUE DE LA SOCIETE DE BIOMETRIE HUMAINE
(BIOTYPOLOGIE).

**BIOMINERALISATION. FORSCHUNGSBERICHTE.**
[SCHATTAUER]
STUTTGART &C. 1, 1970-
CA/U-1.    LO/N13.

**BIOORGANIC CHEMISTRY.**
+ +BIOORG. CHEM.
[ACADEMIC P.]
LONDON &C. 1, 1971-
AD/U-1.    GL/U-1.    GL/U-2.    LD/U-1.    LO/S-3.    LO/U-2.
LO/U12.    SH/U-1.    XY/N-1.
ISSN 0045-2068

**BIOPHON. BIO-ACOUSTICS BULLETIN.**
INTERNATIONAL BIO-ACOUSTICS COUNCIL.
AARHUS 1, 1971-
LO/N-2.

**BIOPHYSICS SERIES, UNIVERSITY OF CALIFORNIA.**
+ +BIOPHYS. SER. UNIV. CALIF.
BERKELEY, CALIF. 1, 1968-
MONOGR.
HL/U-1.
ISSN 0067-8929

**BIOS.**
UNIVERSITY COLLEGE, SWANSEA: BIOLOGICAL SOCIETY
SWANSEA 1, 1967-
LO/N-2.    SW/U-1.

BIOS. BRASSERIE, MALTERIE, BIOTECHNIQUE.                          XXX
*NANCY 1970-*
PREV: BRASSERIE FROM 1, AG 1946- 24(273), 1969
*LO/N13.*

BIOS. SEMINARIO DE ESTUDIOS BIOLOGICAS.                          XXX
ESCUELA NACIONAL DE CIENCIAS BIOLOGICAS
(MEXICO): SEMINARIO DE ESTUDIOS BIOLOGICAS.
*MEXICO, D.F. 1(1-3), 1968. //*
*LO/N-2.*

BIOSPHERE.  BULLETIN OF THE ...                                  XXX
*[BIOS-B]*
INTERNATIONAL BIOLOGICAL PROGRAMME.
*LONDON NO.1, JA 1967- 10, 1971.//*
ENGL. & FR.
*LD/U-1.*    *LO/N13.***
*ISSN 0523-6878*

BIOSYNTHESIS.  A SPECIALIST PERIODICAL REPORT.
CHEMICAL SOCIETY.
*LONDON 1, 1972.*
*AD/U-1.    BH/U-3.    CA/U-1.    ED/N-1.    GL/U-1.    GL/U-2.*
*LO/N14.    LO/S-3.    LO/U12.    MA/U-1.    SF/U-1.*
*HL/U-1. 1, 1972.*
*ISSN 0301-0708*

BIOTECHNOLOGY & BIOENGINEERING SYMPOSIUM.
*+ +BIOTECHNOL. & BIOENG. SYMP.*
*[INTERSCIENCE]*
*NEW YORK NO.1, 1969-*
SUPPL. TO BIOTECHNOLOGY & BIOENGINEERING.
*BN/U-2.    LO/U-2.*
*LO/N-4. NO.2, 1971-*
*ISSN 0572-6565*

BIOTROPICA.
ASSOCIATION FOR TROPICAL BIOLOGY.
*WASHINGTON, D.C. 1, 1969-*
PREV: BULLETIN, ASSOCIATION FOR TROPICAL
BIOLOGY FROM 1, 1962- 8, 1967.
*AD/U-1.    LO/N-2.    LO/N-4.    LO/N13.    XS/R-2.*
*ISSN 0006-3606*

BIOTYPOLOGIE.                                                    XXX
SUBS (1966): REVUE DE LA SOCIETE DE BIOMETRIE
HUMAINE (BIOTYPOLOGIE).

BIRD REPORT, FOREIGN SECTION, ORNITHOLOGICAL
SOCIETY OF TURKEY.
*+ +BIRD REP. FOREIGN SECT. ORNITHOL. SOC. TURK.*
*SANDY, BEDS. NO.1, 1969-*
*LO/N-2.*

BIRDS OF THE WORLD.                                              XXX
*[IPC MAGAZINES LTD.]*
*LONDON 1(1), JL 1969- 10(12), 1971.//*
*BH/P-1.    ED/N-1.*

BISCUIT & CRACKER BAKER.                                         XXX
SUBS (1968): SNACK FOOD.

BIT. NORDISK TIDSKRIFT FOR INFORMATIONS-
BEHANDLING.
LUNDS UNIVERSITET.
*[REGNECENTRALEN]*
*COPENHAGEN 7(2), 1967-*
COVER AS T.P. SUBTITLE SEPARATED FROM TITLE
IN PUBL. PREV FROM 1,1961 AS ABOVE SUBTITLE.
PUBL. FOR THE UNIV.'S DEP. OF NUMERICAL
ANALYSIS.
*AD/U-1.    BN/U-2.    CB/U-1.    LD/U-1.    SA/U-1.    SO/U-1.*
*SW/U-1.    XY/N-1.*
*HL/U-1. 1(2), 1961-            LO/U-5. 8,1968-*
*MA/U-1. 8,1968-*
*ISSN 0006-3835*

B.I.T.A. BULLETIN.
*+ +B.I.T.A. BULL. (BR. IND. TRUCK ASS.).*
BRITISH INDUSTRIAL TRUCK ASSOCIATION.
*LONDON NO.1, 1967-*
*ED/N-1.*

BIULETENIS, VILNIAUS ASTRONOMIJAS OBSERVATOR-
IJA.
*+ +BIUL. VILNIAUS ASTRON. OBS.*
*VILNIUS NR.1, 1960-*
RUSS. WITH ENGL. & LITH. SUMM.
*LO/N13.*

BIULETYN CHLODNICZY.                                             XXX
SUBS (1966): CHLODNICTWO.

BIULETYN GEOLOGICZNY.
*+ +BIUL. GEOL.*
UNIWERSYTET WARSZAWSKI: WYDZIAL GEOLOGII.
*WARSAW 1, 1961-*
ENGL. & RUSS. SUMM.
*BR/U-1.    DB/S-1.    LO/N-2.*
*LO/N13. 10, 1968-*

BIULETYN INFORMACYJNY BIBLIOTEKI NARODOWEJ.
*+ +BIUL. INF. BIBL. NARODOWEJ.*
BIBLIOTEKA NARODOWA.
*WARSAW NR.1, 1964-*
*ED/N-1. 4(29), 1966-*

BIULETYN KOLA LWOWIAN.
KOLO LWOWIAN.
*LONDON 1(1), 1961-*
*LO/N-3.*

BIULETYN, KOMITET PRZESTRZENNEGO ZAGOSPODAROW-
ANIA KRAJU POLSKIEJ AKADEMII NAUK.
*+ +BIUL. KOM. PRZESTRZENNEGO ZAGOSPOD. KRAJU POL.*
*AKAD. NAUK.*
*WARSAW 1, AP 1960-*
*BH/U-1.*
*LO/N13. 45, 1967-*

BIULETYNE TOWARZYSTWA POLSKO-UKRAINSKIEGO.
*+ +BIUL. TOW. POL.-UKR.*
TOWARZYSTWO POLSKO-UKRAINSKIE.
*LONDON 1, 1967-*
ENGL. SUMM.
*ED/N-1.    OX/U-1.*

BJULLETEN' VERKHOVNOGO SUDA RSFSR.
*+ +BJULL. VERKHOVNOGO SUDA RSFSR.*
(RUSSIA RSFSR) VERKHOVNYJ SUD.
*MOSCOW 1961(1)-*
M.
*CC/U-1. 1967-*                                 *OX/U-1. 1964-*
*GL/U-1. 1964(8)- [W. 1966(2)].*

BJULLETEN' VSESOJUZNOGO ASTRONOMO-GEODEZI-
CHESKOGO OBSHCHESTVA.                                            XXX
SUBS (1967): ASTRONOMICHESKIJ VESTNIK.

BLACK DWARF.
*LONDON 13(1), 1968-*
CONTINUES VOLUME NUMBERING OF A PERIODICAL OF
THE SAME TITLE WHICH CEASED IN 1824.
*LO/U-2.*
*BH/P-1. 13(1-37), 1968-1970.*
*ISSN 0006-4157*

BLACK LINES.
UNIVERSITY OF PITTSBURGH: BLACK STUDIES DEP-
ARTMENT.
*PITTSBURGH 1(1), 1970-*
*OX/U-1.*
*ISSN 0045-2203*

BLACK PUDDING: MAGAZINE FOR FREE EXPRESSION.
BLACK KNIGHT ANARCHIST GROUP.
*LONDON 1, 1969-*
M.
*LO/U-3.*

BLACK REVIEW.
*+ +BLACK REV.*
*[MORROW & CO.]*
*NEW YORK NO.1, 1971-*
*LO/U-2.*

BLACK SCHOLAR.  JOURNAL OF BLACK STUDIES &
RESEARCH.
*+ +BLACK SCH.*
BLACK WORLD FOUNDATION.
*SAN FRANCISCO 1(1), N 1969-*
10/A.
*LO/U14. 1(2), 1969-*
*ISSN 0006-4246*

BLACKCOUNTRYMAN.
*TIPTON, STAFFS. 1(1), 1968-*
*BH/U-1.    OX/U-1.*
*ISSN 0006-4335*

BLACKMORE STUDIES.
*+ +BLACKMORE STUD.*
BLACKMORE SOCIETY.
*LONDON NO. 1, 1969-*
*ED/N-1.    LO/N-1.    OX/U-1.*
*ISSN 0006-4343*

**BLAKE NEWSLETTER.**
+ +BLAKE NEWSL.
BERKELEY, CALIF. NO.1, JE 1967-
Q.
LV/U-1.    OX/U-1.
ED/N-1.  NO. 2, FALL 1970-
ISSN 0006-453X

**BLAKE STUDIES.**
+ +BLAKE STUD.
UNIVERSITY OF TULSA.
TULSA 1, 1968-
BH/P-1.    CA/U-1.    ED/N-1.    LA/U-1.    LO/P20.    LO/U-1.
LV/U-1.    OX/U-1.    SW/U-1.
AD/U-1.  6, 1973-
ISSN 0006-4548

**BLECH.**                                                                                              XXX
SUBS (1970): BLECH, ROHRE, PROFILE.

**BLECH, ROHRE, PROFILE.**                                                                              XXX
[PROST & MEINER-VERLAG]
COBURG 17, 1970-
PREV: BLECH FROM 1, 1954- 16, 1969.
LO/N14.
ISSN 0006-4688

**BLINDMAKER.**                                                                                         XXX
SUBS (1972): BLINDS & SHUTTERS.

**BLINDS & SHUTTERS.**                                                                                  XXX
BRITISH BLIND & SHUTTER ASSOCIATION.
LONDON NO.81, AP 1972-
Q.  PREV: BLINDMAKER FROM NO.1, 1952- NO.80,
JA 1972.
ED/N-1.    LO/N14.
ISSN 0305-733X

**BLL ANNOUNCEMENT BULLETIN. A GUIDE TO BRITISH**
**REPORTS, TRANSLATIONS & THESES.**                                                                     XXX
+ +BLL ANNOUNCE. BULL.
BRITISH LIBRARY: LENDING DIVISION.                                                                      XXX
BOSTON SPA, YORKS.  BAB 73-6, JE 1973-
PREV: NLL ANNOUNCEMENT BULLETIN FROM 1(1),
1971- NAB 73-5, 1973.
BL/U-1.    BR/U-1.    ED/N-1.    LD/U-1.    LO/N-2.    LO/N-4.
LO/N14.    LO/R-5.    LO/U-1.    MA/U-1.    SO/U-1.    XS/R10.
XY/N-1.
ISSN 0301-2085

**BLL REVIEW.**                                                                                         XXX
+ +BLL REV.
BRITISH LIBRARY: LENDING DIVISION.                                                                      XXX
BOSTON SPA, YORKS.  1(1), JL 1973-
PREV: NLL REVIEW FROM 1(1), JA 1971- 2(6), AP
1973.
BR/U-1.    ED/N-1.    HL/U-1.    LD/U-1.    LO/N-2.    LO/N12.
LO/N14.    LO/N35.    LO/R-5.    LO/U-3.    LO/U14.
MA/P-1.    MA/U-1.    NO/U-1.    OX/U-1.    OX/U16.
SO/U-1.    XS/N-1.    XS/R10.
ISSN 0305-6503

**BLOOD GROUP NEWS.**                                                                                   XXX
ASSOCIATION FOR MUTUAL INFORMATION.
COPENHAGEN 1, 1948- 19, 1971.//
BL/U-1.    LO/N13.**    XS/N-1.
ISSN 0006-498X

**BLOOMSBURY GEOGRAPHER.**
+ +BLOOMSBURY GEOGR.
UNIVERSITY COLLEGE LONDON: GEOGRAPHICAL
SOCIETY.
LONDON 1, 1968-
LO/U-1.    OX/U-1.
ISSN 0067-9232

**BLUEPRINT.**
ENGINEERING INDUSTRY TRAINING BOARD.
LONDON NO.1, 1970-
ED/N-1.    OX/U-1.

**BLYTHSWOOD TRACT SOCIETY MAGAZINE.**
+ +BLYTHSWOOD TRACT SOC. MAG.
GLASGOW NO.1, D 1967-
ED/N-1.

**BNF ABSTRACTS.**                                                                                      XXX
+ +BNF ABSTR. (BR. NON-FERROUS MET. RES. ASS.).
BRITISH NON-FERROUS METALS RESEARCH ASSOCIATION
LONDON NO.486, 1970-
PREV:  BULLETIN, BRITISH ... FROM NO.1, 1921-
485, 1969.
LO/N-7.    LO/N14.    LO/R-6.    XS/R10.
OX/U-8.  1968- 1971.
ISSN 0005-3244

**BNF NEWS SHEET.**
BRITISH NUCLEAR FORUM.
LONDON NO.1, JL 1970-
XS/R10.

**BOARD MANUFACTURE & PRACTICE.**                                                                       XXX
+ +BOARD MFR. & PRACT.
[PRESSMEDIA LTD.]
SEVENOAKS, KENT 13, 1970-
INCORP:  BOARD MANUFACTURE FROM 8(11), 1965-
12, 1969; & BOARD PRACTICE FROM 8(11), 1965-
9(1/2), 1966.
LO/N14.
ED/N-1.  15, 1972-
ISSN 0006-534X

**BOARD OF TRADE JOURNAL.**                                                                             XXX
SUBS (1970): TRADE & INDUSTRY.

**BOAT NEWS.**
[EAST MIDLAND ALLIED P.]
PETERBOROUGH NO.1, 7/MR 1973-
WKLY.
OX/U-1.

**BOGOSLOVSKIE TRUDY. SBORNIK.**
+ +BOGOSLOVSKIE TR.
MOSKOVSKAJA PATRIARKHIJA.
MOSCOW SB. 1, 1960-
GL/U-1. *
LO/N-3.  2, 1961-

**BOKREVY.**
LUND 1(1/2), 1970-
10/A.
LO/N-1.
BL/U-1.  6, 1975-

**BOLETIN, ACADEMIA PORTENA DEL LUNFARDO**
**(BUENOS AIRES).**
+ +BOL. ACAD. PORTENA LUNFARDO (BUENOS AIRES).
BUENOS AIRES 1(1), 1966-
SH/U-1.

**BOLETIN ADUANERO.**
+ +BOL. ADUANERO.
LA PAZ 1(1), MR 1967-
Q.
CC/U-1.  1(1), 1967.

**BOLETIN DE LA ASOCIACION ESPANOLA DE ORIENT-**
**ALISTAS.**
+ +BOL. ASOC. ESP. ORIENT.
MADRID 1, 1965-
LO/N-1.    OX/U-1.

**BOLETIN BIBLIOGRAFICO, ACADEMIA COLOMBIANA DE**
**CIENCIAS EXACTAS, FISICAS Y NATURALES.**
+ +BOL. BIBLIOGR. ACAD. COLOMBIANA CIENC. EXACTAS
FIS. & NATUR.
BOGOTA 1, 1968-
LO/N-2.    LO/S13.

**BOLETIN BIBLIOGRAFICO DE LA ESCUELA NACIONAL**
**DE CIENCIAS BIOLOGICAS (MEXICO).**
+ +BOL. BIBLIOGR. ESC. NAC. CIENC. BIOL. (MEX.).
MEXICO NO.1, 1965-
CA/U-2.    DB/S-1.    LO/N-2.

**BOLETIN DEL CENTRO DE COOPERACION CIENTIFICA**
**PARA AMERICA LATINA: NS.**                                                                            XXX
+ +BOL. CENT. COOP. CIENT. AM. LAT., NS.
MONTEVIDEO NO. 1-2, 1966 ...
SUBS: BOLETIN DEL CENTRO REGIONAL DE LA
UNESCO PARA EL FOMENTO DE LA CIENCIA EN
AMERICA LATINA.
LO/N-2.

**BOLETIN DEL CENTRO DE INVESTIGACIONES BIOLOG-**
**ICAS, UNIVERSIDAD DEL ZULIA.**
+ +BOL. CENT. INVEST. BIOL. UNIV. ZULIA.
MARACAIBO 1, 1967-
LO/N-2.

**BOLETIN DEL CENTRO REGIONAL DE LA UNESCO PARA**
**EL FOMENTO DE LA CIENCIA EN AMERICA LATINA.**                                                         XXX
+ +BOL. CENT. REG. UNESCO FOM. CIENC. AM. LAT.
MONTEVIDEO NO.3, 1967- 6, 1968.
PREV: BOLETIN DEL CENTRO DE COOPERACION CIENT-
IFICA PARA AMERICA LATINA: NS., FROM NO.1-
2, 1966. SUBS: BOLETIN, OFICINA DE CIENCIAS
DE LA UNESCO PARA AMERICA LATINA.
LO/N-2.

BOLETIM DE CIENCIAS DO MAR.                                  XXX
++BOL. CIENC. MAR. (BRAZ.).
UNIVERSIDADE FEDERAL DO CEARA: LABORATORIO DE
CIENCIAS DO MAR.
FORTALEZA NO.21, 1969-
PREV: BOLETIM, ESTACAO DE BIOLOGIA MARINHA,
UNIVERSIDADE FEDERAL DO CEARA FROM NO.1,
1961- 20, 1968.
LO/N13.

BOLETIN CIENTIFICO Y TECNICO, INSTITUTO NA-
CIONAL DE PESCA DEL ECUADOR.
++BOL. CIENT. TEC. INST. NAC. PESCA ECUADOR.
[BCTP-A]
GUAYAQUIL 1, 1964-
LO/N13.*

BOLETIM CLIMATOLOGICO (BRAZIL).
++BOL. CLIMATOL. (BRAZ.).
(BRAZIL) MINISTERIO DA AGRICULTURA: ESCRITORIO
DE METEOROLOGIA.
RIO DE JANEIRO 1(1), JA 1970-
XS/N-1.

BOLETIN CLIMATOLOGICO MENSUAL (COLOMBIA).
++BOL. CLIMATOL. MENS. (COLOMBIA).
(COLOMBIA) SERVICIO COLOMBIANO DE METEOROLOGIA
E HIDROLOGIA.
BOGOTA 1(001), JA 1970-
XS/N-1.

BOLETIN, DEPARTAMENTO DE BIOLOGIA, UNIVER-
SIDAD DEL VALLE.
++BOL. DEP. BIOL. UNIV. VALLE.
CALI 1, 1968-
LO/N-2.

BOLETIN DE DOCUMENTACION LATINOAMERICANA.
++BOL. DOC. LATINOAM.
INSTITUT FUR IBEROAMERIKÁ-KUNDE: DOKUMENTAT-
IONSDIENST LATEINAMERIKA.
HAMBURG 1, 1972-
DOKUMENTATIONSDIENST SUBORD. TO: DOKUMENTAT-
IONS-LEITSTELLE.
OX/U-1.

BOLETIM ESPECIAL, ASSOCIACAO BRASILEIRA DE
PESQUISAS SOBRE PLANTAS AROMATICAS E OLEOS
ESSENCIAIS.
++BOL. ESPEC. ASS. BRAS. PESQUI. PLANTAS
AROMAT. & OLEOS ESSENCIAIS.
SAO PAULO NO.1, D 1965-
LO/N-2.

BOLETIM, ESTACAO DE BIOLOGIA MARINHA, UNIVER-     XXX
SIDADE FEDERAL DO CEARA.
++BOL. ESTAC. BIOL. MAR. UNIV. FED. CEARA.
FORTALEZA NO.1, 1961- 20, 1968 ...
SUBS: BOLETIM DE CIENCIAS DO MAR.
LO/N13.

BOLETIN ESTADISTICO (CHILE).
++BOL. ESTAD. (CHILE).
SANTIAGO 1(1), S 1971-
OX/U-1. OX/U-3.

BOLETIN ESTADISTICO. (URUGUAY)
++BOL. ESTADIST. (URUGUAY)
BANCO CENTRAL DEL URUGUAY: DEPARTAMENTO DE
INVESTIGACIONES ECONOMICAS.
MONTEVIDEO 1, 1967-
OX/U-1.

BOLETIN DE ESTUDIOS HISTORICOS SOBRE SAN
SEBASTIAN.
++BOL. ESTUD. HIST. SAN SEBASTIAN.
REAL SOCIEDAD VASCONGADA DE LOS AMIGOS DEL
PAIS.
SAN SEBASTIAN 1, 1967-
ED/N-1. OX/U-1.

BOLETIN DE INFORMACION CIENTIFICA CUBANA.
++BOL. INF. CIENT. CUBANA.
ACADEMIA DE CIENCIAS DE CUBA: INSTITUTO DE
DOCUMENTACION E INFORMACION CIENTIFICA Y
TECNICA.
HAVANA 1, 1969-
LO/N-2.

BOLETIN DE INFORMACIONES SOCIO JURIDICAS
(COLOMBIA).
++BOL. INF. SOCIO JURIDICAS. (COLOMB.).
(COLOMBIA) MINISTERIO DE JUSTICIA.
BOGOTA 1(1), N 1970-
M.
LO/U-3.

BOLETIN INFORMATIVO DE LA BIBLIOTECA, SOCIE-
DAD VENEZOLANA DE ESPELEOLOGIA.
++BULL. INF. BIBL. SOC. VENEZ. ESPELEOL.
CARACAS NO.1, 1967-
LO/N-2.

BOLETIN INFORMATIVO HISPANOAMERICANO DE
HISTORIA DE LA MEDICINA.
++BOL. INF. HISPANOAM. HIST. MED.
CARACAS NO.1, 1964-
2/A.
LO/M24. NO.4, JA/JE 1966.
ISSN 0523-9168

BOLETIN INFORMATIVO, INSTITUTO VENEZOLANO DE
INVESTIGACIONES CIENTIFICAS.
SEE: I.V.I.C.

BOLETIN INFORMATIVO, SOCIEDAD MEXICANA DE
MICOLOGIA.
++BOL. INF. SOC. MEX. MICOL.
MEXICO CITY NO.1, 1968-
LO/N-2.

BOLETIN, INSTITUTO ANTARCTICO CHILENO.
++BOL. INST. ANTARCT. CHILENO.
SANTIAGO DE CHILE NO.1, MY 1965-
CA/U12.
LO/N-2. NO.3,1968-

BOLETIM, INSTITUTO DE BIOLOGIA MARINHA, UNI-
VERSIDADE FEDERAL DO RIO GRANDE DO NORTE.
++BOL. INST. BIOL. MAR. UNIV. FED. RIO GRANDE
NORTE.
NATAL, BRAZ. 1, 1964-
LO/N-2.

BOLETIM, INSTITUTO GEOCIENCIAS, UNIVERSIDADE
FEDERAL DO RIO DE JANEIRO: GEOLOGIA.
++BOL. INST. GEOCIENC. UNIV. FED. RIO DE
JANEIRO, GEOL.
RIO DE JANEIRO NO.1, 1967-
LO/N-2.

BOLETIN DEL INSTITUTO DE GEOGRAFIA, UNIVERS-
IDAD NACIONAL AUTONOMA DE MEXICO.
++BOL. INST. GEOGR. UNIV. NAC. AUTON. MEXICO.
MEXICO CITY 1, 1969-
LO/S13.

BOLETIM DO INSTITUTO DE INVESTIGACAO CIENTI-
FICA DE ANGOLA.
++BOL. INST. INVEST. CIENT. ANGOLA.
INSTITUTO DE INVESTIGACAO CIENTIFICA DE ANGOLA.
LUANDA 1, 1962-
LO/N-2.

BOLETIN DEL INSTITUTO DE INVESTIGACIONES
BIBLIOGRAFICAS (MEXICO).
++BOL. INST. INVEST. BIBLIOGR. (MEX.).
MEXICO, D.F. 1, 1969-
ED/N-1. LO/U-2. OX/U-1.

BOLETIM, INSTITUTO 'LUIS DE CAMOES.'
++BOL. INST. 'LUIS CAMOES.'
MACAO 1, 1965-
Q.
LO/N-1. 4(2/3), 1970-

BOLETIN, LABORATORIO DE PALEONTOLOGIA DE VER-
TEBRADOS, UNIVERSIDAD DE LA REPUBLICA (URUG.).
++BOL. LAB. PALEONTOL. VERTEBR. UNIV. REPUB.
(URUG.).
MONTEVIDEO 1, 1965-
LO/N-2.

BOLETIM MENSAL, DIRECCAO DOS SERVICOS DE            000
ECONOMIA E ESTATISTICA GERAL (MOZAMBIQUE).
SEE: BOLETIM MENSAL DE ESTATISTICA (MOZAMB.)

BOLETIM MENSAL DE ESTATISTICA (MOZAMBIQUE).**
++BOL. MENS. ESTAT. (MOZAMB.)
(MOZAMBIQUE) DIRECCAO PROVINCIAL DOS SERVICOS
DE ESTATISTICA GERAL.
LOURENCO MARQUES 1(1), 1960-
ISSUING BODY VARIES - ORIG.: DIRECCAO DOS SER-
VICOS DE ECONOMIA E ESTATISTICA GERAL. AS
ABOVE FROM ?1964. TITLE VARIES - ORIG.:
BOLETIM MENSAL.
LO/U14. 6(7),1965-

BOLETIN METEOROLOGICO MENSUAL (COLOMBIA).
++BOL. METEOROL. MENS. (COLOMBIA).
BOGOTA NO.1, S 1968-
XS/N-1.

**BOLETIN, MUSEO DE ARTES PLASTICAS (LA PLATA).**
+ +BOL. MUS. ARTES PLAST. (LA PLATA).
LA PLATA NO.1, AP 1965-
LO/N-1.

**BOLETIN, MUSEO DEL HOMBRE DOMINICANO.**
+ +BOL. MUS. HOMBRE DOMIN.
SANTO DOMINGO 1, 1972-
OX/U-1.

**BOLETIN, MUSEO DEL MAR (COLOMBIA).**
+ +BOL. MUS. MAR (COLOMBIA).
BOGOTA NO.1, 1970-
LO/N-2.

**BOLETIN, OFICINA DE CIENCIAS DE LA UNESCO
PARA AMERICA LATINA.**                                                            XXX
+ +BOL. OF. CIENC. UNESCO AM. LAT.
UNESCO: OFICINA DE CIENCIAS PARA AMERICA
LATINA.
MONTEVIDEO NO.1, 1970-
PREV: BOLETIN DEL CENTRO REGIONAL DE LA
UNESCO PARA EL FOMENTO DE LA CIENCIA EN
AMERICA LATINA FROM 3, 1967- 6, 1968.
LO/N-2.

**BOLETIN DE PREHISTORIA DE CHILE.**
+ +BOL. PREHIST. CHILE. [BPHC-A]
UNIVERSIDAD DE CHILE: DEPARTAMENTO DE HISTORIA.
SANTIAGO DE CHILE 1(1), 1968-
CC/U-1. 1(1), 1968.
ISSN 0523-9044

**BOLETIM DA SOCIEDADE BRASILEIRA DE MATEMATICA.**
+ +BOL. SOC. BRAS. MAT.
RIO DE JANEIRO 1(1), 1970-
2/A.
CA/U-2.

**BOLETIN DE LA SOCIEDAD DOMINICANA DE
GEOGRAFIA.**
+ +BOL. SOC. DOMIN. GEOGR.
SANTO DOMINGO 1(1), 1970-
LO/N-1.    OX/U-1.

**BOLETIN, SOCIEDAD ESPANOLA DE CERAMICA Y
VIDRIO.**                                                                          XXX
+ +BOL. SOC. ESP. CERAM. & VIDRIO.
MADRID 11, 1972-
PREV: BOLETIN, SOCIEDAD ESPANOLA DE CERAMICA
FROM 1, 1961- 10, 1971.
LO/N14.

**BOLETIN DE LA SOCIEDAD ZOOLOGICA DEL URUGUAY.**
+ +BOL. SOC. ZOOL. URUG.
MONTEVIDEO 1, 1971-
LO/N-2.

**BOLIVAR.**
SOCIEDAD BOLIVARIANA DE LIMA.
LIMA 1, 1968-
OX/U-1.

**BOLLETTINO, ASSOCIAZONE DEGLI AFRICANISTI
ITALIANI.**
+ +BOLL. ASS. AFR. ITAL.
COMO 1(1), 1968-
OX/U-9.

**BOLLETTINO DEL CENTRO CAMUNO DI STUDI PRE-
ISTORICI.**
+ +BOLL. CENT. CAMUNO STUDI PREISTOR.
BRESCIA 1, 1964/65-
ANNU. ITAL. & ENGL.
DB/S-1. 5, 1970.
SH/U-1. 1, 1964/65- 4, 1968; 1970-
SW/U-1. 8, 1972.

**BOLLETTINO ODONTO-IMPLANTOLOGICO.**
+ +BOLL. ODONTO-IMPLANTOL.
SOCIETE ODONTOLOGIQUE DES IMPLANTS-AIGUILLES.
PALERMO N.1, 1968-
LO/N14.

**BOLLETTINO DI STUDI LATINI. PERIODICO QUADRI-
MESTRALE D'INFORMAZIONE BIBLIOGRAFICA.**
+ +BOLL. STUDI LAT.
[LIBRARIA SCIENTIFICA EDITRICE]
NAPLES 1, 1971-
Q.
LO/N-1.    OX/U-1.
LO/U-4. 1, 1971- 3, 1973.
ISSN 0006-6583

**BOLLETTINO DELLA UNIONE MATEMATICA ITALIANA;
SERIE 4.**                                                                         XXX
+ +BOLL. U. MAT. ITAL., SER. 4.
UNIONE MATEMATICA ITALIANA.
BOLOGNA 1(1), 1968-
PREV SERIES OF ABOVE TITLE: (1) 1922-38;
(2) 1939-43; (3) 1, 1946- 22, 1967.
LO/N-4.    LO/U-2.

**BONGO-MAN: JOURNAL OF AFRICAN YOUTH.**
KINGSTON [NO.1], 1968-
LO/U-3.

**BONNER SCHRIFTEN ZUR POLITIK UND ZEITGESCHICHTE.**
+ +BONN. SCHR. POLIT. & ZEITGESCH.
[DROSTE VERLAG]
DUSSELDORF 1, 1970-
LO/N-1.
CA/U-1. [2] 1970-

**BOOK ADDICT.**
KINGSTON, SURREY NO.1, AP 1972-
MON.
CA/U-1.    ED/N-1.    OX/U-1.

**BOOK COLLECTING & LIBRARY MONTHLY.**
+ +BOOK COLLECT. & LIBR. MON.
LONDON NO.1, MY 1968-
ED/N-1.    LO/N-3.    LO/U-2.    OX/U-1.
MA/P-1. NO. 26, JE 1970-
ISSN 0006-7210

**BOOK OF INVASIONS.**
[TARA TELEPHONE PUBL.]
DUBLIN 1, 1969-
ISSUED AS SUPPLEMENTS TO CAPELLA.
BL/U-1.    LO/U-2.

**BOOKDEALER.**
[FUDGE]
LONDON NO.1, OC 1971-
S/T: THE TRADE WEEKLY FOR BOOKS WANTED & FOR
SALE.
ED/N-1.    OX/U-1.
CA/U-1. NO.6, 1971-

**BOOKLIST.**                                                                       XXX
AMERICAN LIBRARY ASSOCIATION.
CHICAGO 66(1), S 1969-
PREV: BOOKLIST & SUBSCRIPTION BOOKS BULLETIN
FROM 53, S 1956- 65, 1969.
DB/U-2.
ISSN 0006-7385

**BOOKLIST & SUBSCRIPTION BOOKS BULLETIN.**                                         XXX
SUBS (1969): BOOKLIST.

**BOOKS IN CANADA.**
+ +BOOKS CAN.
[CANADIAN REVIEW OF BOOKS LTD.]
TORONTO 1, JL 1971-
18/A.
ED/N-1.
ISSN 0045-2564

**BOR'BA S GAZOM I PYL'JU V UGOL'NYKH SHAKHTAKH.**
+ +BOR'BA GAZOM & PYL'JU UGOL'N. SHAKHTAKH.
GOSUDARSTVENNYJ MAKEEVSKIJ NAUCHNO-ISSLEDO-
VATEL'SKIJ INSTITUT.
MOSCOW; KIEV [1] 1964-
VOL.1 UNNUMBERED.
LO/N13. 5, 1969-

**BOR'BA S KORROZIEJ V KHIMICHESKOJ I NEFTEPERERA-
BATYVAJUSHCHEJ PROMYSHLENNOSTI.**
+ +BOR'BA KORROZ. KHIM. & NEFTEPERERAB. PROM-ST.
[BKKN-A]
[MASHINOSTROENIE]
MOSCOW 1, 1967-
LO/N13.

**BOREAL EXPRESS. JOURNAL D'HISTOIRE DU CANADA.**
TROIS RIVIERES, P.Q. 1, 1962-
LO/N-1.* 3, [1967]-
ISSN 0524-0867

**BOREAS. AN INTERNATIONAL JOURNAL OF QUATERNARY
GEOLOGY.**
[UNIVERSITETSFORLAGET]
OSLO 1, 1972-
AD/U-1.    BL/U-1.    LO/N-2.    LO/N13.    LO/U-1.    SH/U-1.

**BOTANICA RHEDONICA: SERIE A.**
+ +BOT. RHEDONICA, A. [BHRA-B]
UNIVERSITE DE RENNES: LABORATOIRE DE BOTANIQUE.
RENNES NO.1, 1966-
LABORATOIRE SUBORD. TO FACULTE DES SCIENCES.
LO/N-2.

**BOTANICA RHEDONICA: SERIE B.**
+ +BOT. RHEDONICA, B.
UNIVERSITE DE RENNES: LABORATOIRE DE BOTANIQUE.
RENNES NO.1, 1966-
LO/N-2.

**BOTANICAL JOURNAL OF THE LINNEAN SOCIETY.**
+ +BOT. J. LINN. SOC.
[ACADEMIC P.]
LONDON 62, 1969-
PREV: JOURNAL OF THE LINNEAN SOCIETY. BOTANY
FROM 1, 1855- 61, 1968 ...
BH/U-1.     BN/U-2.     DB/S-1.     ED/N-1.     GL/U-1.     LD/U-1.
MA/U-1.     RE/U-1.
ISSN 0024-4074

**BOTANICAL JOURNAL OF THE LINNEAN SOCIETY:**
**SUPPLEMENT.**
+ +BOT. J. LINNEAN SOC., SUPPL.
[ACADEMIC P.]
LONDON NO.1, 1970-
GL/U-1.

**BOTANIKOS KLAUSIMAI.**
+ +BOT. KLAUSIMAI.
LIETUVOS TSR MOKSLU AKADEMIJA: BOTANIKOS
INSTITUTAS.
VILNA 1, 1961-
LITH. & RUSS. TITLE VARIES: VOL.1(1961) PUBL.
AS: STRAINPSNIU RINKINYS.
LO/N-2.     LO/N13.

**BOTANIQUE.**
[G.B. PATTIL]
NAGPUR 1, 1970-
LO/N-2.

**BOTANY BULLETIN, DEPARTMENT OF FORESTS (PAPUA**
**& NEW GUINEA).**
+ +BOT. BULL. DEP. FOR. (PAPUA & NEW GUINEA).
(PAPUA & NEW GUINEA): DEPARTMENT OF FORESTS.
LAE, NEW GUINEA NO.1, 1969-
PROD. BY DEPARTMENT'S DIVISION OF BOTANY.
LO/N-2.

**BOTSWANA NOTES & RECORDS.**
+ +BOTSWANA NOTES & REC.
NATIONAL MUSEUM & ART GALLERY (BOTSWANA).
GABERONES 1, 1968-
LO/N-2.     LO/N13.     LO/N17.     LO/U14.     OX/U-9.
ISSN 0525-5090

**BOUNDARY-LAYER METEOROLOGY.**
+ +BOUNDARY-LAYER METEOROL.
[REIDEL]
DORDRECHT 1(1), MR 1970-
S/T: AN INTERNATIONAL JOURNAL OF PHYSICAL &
BIOLOGICAL PROCESSES IN THE ATMOSPHERIC BOUND-
ARY LAYER.
AD/U-3.     BH/U-1.     BR/U-3.     HL/U-1.     LO/N-2.     LO/N14.
LO/U12.     MA/U-1.     OX/U-8.     SH/U-1.     XS/N-1.     XS/T-4.
LN/U-2. 2, 1971-
ISSN 0006-8314

**BPMA NEWS.**
BRITISH PREMIUM MANUFACTURERS ASSOCIATION.
LONDON NO.1, AP 1972-
ED/N-1.

**BRADEA.**
HERBARIUM BRADEANUM (RIO DE JANEIRO).
RIO DE JANEIRO 1, 1969-
LO/N-2.

**BRADFORD SEVEN.**
UNIVERSITY OF BRADFORD.
BRADFORD 1(1), 1969-
OX/U-1.

**BRAIN, BEHAVIOR & EVOLUTION.**
+ +BRAIN, BEHAV. & EVOL.
[S. KARGER]
BASEL &C 1, 1968-
AD/U-1.     CR/U-1.     LO/M12.     LO/N-4.     LO/N13.
OX/U-8. 1(3), 1968-
ISSN 0006-8977

**BRAIN BIOCHEMISTRY MONTHLY.**
+ +BRAIN BIOCHEM. MON.
[LITERATURE SEARCHERS]
KETTERING, OHIO NO.1, 1966-
LO/N13.
ISSN 0524-1871

**BRASIL: SERIES ESTATISTICAS RETROSPECTIVAS.**
+ +BRAZ., SER. ESTATIST. RETROSP.
INSTITUTO BRASILEIRO DE ESTATISTICA.
RIO DE JANEIRO 1970-
A.
LO/U-3.

**BRASIL FLORESTAL.**
RIO DE JANEIRO 1, 1970-
OX/U-3.
ISSN 0045-270X

**BRASSERIE.**                                                        XXX
**SUBS (1970): BIOS.**

**BRECHE. ACTION SURREALISTE.**                                      XXX
[TERRAIN VAGUE]
PARIS 1, OC 1961- 8, 1965.//
CB/U-1.     LO/U-2.     SH/U-1.
ISSN 0524-4226

**BRECHT HEUTE. BRECHT TODAY.**
INTERNATIONAL BRECHT SOCIETY.
[ATHENAEUM]
FRANKFURT AM MAIN 1, 1971-
BT/U-1.     EX/U-1.     SO/U-1.     SW/U-1.

**BRECHT TIMES.**
[BRECHT TIMES P.]
WELWYN, HERTS. NO.1, 1973-
3/A. S/T: WORK OF SOCIALIST POETS.
ED/N-1.     OX/U-1.
CA/U-1. NO.2, 1973-

**BRECHT TODAY.**                                                    000
SEE: BRECHT HEUTE.

**BRECONSHIRE BIRDS.**
BRECKNOCK COUNTY NATURALISTS' TRUST.
MERTHYR TYDFIL NO.1, 1962-
LO/N-2.

**BRENNSTOFF-CHEMIE.**                                               XXX
**SUBS (1970): PART ERDOL UND KOHLE, ERDGAS,**
**PETROCHEMIE VEREINIGT MIT BRENNSTOFF-CHEMIE.**

**BRETBY BROADSHEET.**                                               XXX
NATIONAL COAL BOARD (GB): CENTRAL ENGINEERING
ESTABLISHMENT.
STANHOPE BRETBY, STAFFS. NO.1, 1961- 46, 1969
SUBS: MINING RESEARCH & DEVELOPMENT REVIEW.
LO/N14.

**BRETBY REPORT.**                                                   XXX
+ +BRETBY REP.
NATIONAL COAL BOARD (GB): CENTRAL ENGINEERING
ESTABLISHMENT.
STANHOPE BRETBY, STAFFS. 1961(1962)- 1968/69.
SUBS: MRDE REPORT.
LO/N14.

**BREWERS' JOURNAL (LONDON).**                                       XXX
**SUBS (1971): INTERNATIONAL BREWERS' JOURNAL.**

**BRI OCCASIONAL REPORT.**                                           XXX
+ +BRI OCC. REP. (BUILD. RES. INST., TOKYO)
[BRIR-A]
BUILDING RESEARCH INSTITUTE (TOKYO).
TOKYO NO.1, MR 1960- 28, 1967.
SUBS: BRI RESEARCH PAPER.
XS/N-1.
LO/N14. NO.7, 1962-

**BRIG. JOURNAL OF THE ...**
UNIVERSITY OF STIRLING.
STIRLING 1, OC 1969-
ED/N-1.

**BRITAIN & ISRAEL.**
+ +BR. & ISR.
LONDON NO.1, N 1970-
ED/N-1.     LO/S14.
LO/U-3. NO.2, 1971-
SO/U-1. [W. NO.3, 1971]

**BRITAIN & OVERSEAS.**
+ +BR. & OVERSEAS.
COMMONWEALTH INDUSTRIES ASSOCIATION LTD.
LONDON 1(1), JA/F 1971-
S/T: A DIGEST OF NEWS & VIEWS ON BRITAIN'S
ECONOMY & OUR ROLE IN OVERSEAS TRADE PAYMENTS.
ED/N-1.     LO/U-3.     OX/U-1.     OX/U16.
ISSN 0045-2866

**BRITANNIA.**
SOCIETY FOR THE PROMOTION OF ROMAN STUDIES.
*LONDON 1, 1970-*
*BH/U-1.    BL/U-1.    BN/U-1.    CA/U-1.    CO/U-1.    LO/S-7.*
*LO/U-2.    LO/U12.    LO/U13.    MA/P-1.    NO/U-1.*
*NW/U-1.    OX/U-1.    SH/U-1.    SW/U-1.*
*ISSN 0007-0203*

**BRITISH AMNESTY NEWS.**
*++BR. AMNESTY NEWS.*
AMNESTY INTERNATIONAL: BRITISH SECTION.
*LONDON NO.1, MY 1970-*
M.
*LO/U-3.*
*OX/U-1.  9, 1971-*
*CB/U-1.  NO.5, 1971; NO. 10, 1972-*

**BRITISH BUSINESSMAN'S LAW.**
*++BR. BUSINESSMAN'S LAW.*
*LONDON 1(1), MR 1973-*
8/A. S/T: A FOCUS ON COMMERCIAL LAW, TAX &
ACCOUNTING PROBLEMS OF THE BUSINESSMAN & COMP-
ANY DIRECTOR, INCLUDING TAX & ESTATE PLANNING.
*CA/U-1.    ED/N-1.    MA/P-1.    OX/U15.    SO/U-1.*

**BRITISH CLINICAL JOURNAL.**
*++BR. CLIN. J.*
[ORIGEN PUBL. CO.]
*LONDON 1, JE 1973-*
*CA/U-1.    ED/N-1.*
*OX/U-8.  1(2), 1973-*
*ISSN 0302-2919*

**BRITISH & COMMONWEALTH REVIEW.**                    XXX
**SUBS (1970): CLANSMAN.**

**BRITISH ECONOMY SURVEY.**
*++BR. ECON. SURV.*
ECONOMICS ASSOCIATION: LONDON BRANCH.
[OXFORD UNIV. P.]
*OXFORD 1(1), 1971-*
*CA/U-1.    ED/N-1.    LO/N-1.    LO/U-3.    NW/U-1.    OX/U-1.*
*OX/U16.    SH/U-1.*
*GL/U-2.  2(1), AUTUMN 1972-*

**BRITISH EUROPEAN.**                                 XXX
*++BR. EUR.*
EUROPEAN MOVEMENT.
*LONDON 1(1- 8), 1971. //*
*ED/N-1.    OX/U-1.*
*LO/U-3.  1(2), F/MR 1971-*

**BRITISH FARMER.**                                   XXX
**SUBS (1971): PART OF BRITISH FARMER & STOCK-
BREEDER; & N.F.U. INSIGHT.**

**BRITISH FARMER & STOCKBREEDER.**                    XXX
*++BR. FARM. & STOCKBREEDER.*
NATIONAL FARMERS' UNION.
*LONDON 1(1), MR 1971-*
INCORP: FARMER & STOCKBREEDER FROM 1, 1889-
85(4233), 1971; & BRITISH FARMER FROM NO.1,
JL 1948- 688, 1971.
*ED/N-1.    LO/N-6.    LO/N13.    LO/R-5.    MA/P-1.    OX/U-8.*
*RE/U-1.*
*LD/U-1.  1(2), 1971-*
*ISSN 0007-0688*

**BRITISH GEOLOGICAL LITERATURE: NS.**
*++BR. GEOL. LIT., NS.*
[CORIDON P.]
*BOURNE END, BUCKS. NO.1, 1972-*
PREV. SERIES FROM 1, 1964- 5, 1968.
*CA/U-1.    CA/U-2.    ED/N-1.    LO/U-1.    SH/U-1.*

**BRITISH INDUSTRY.**                                 XXX
*++BR. IND.*
FEDERATION OF BRITISH INDUSTRIES.
*LONDON NO.1, 8/JA 1965- NO.16, 4/AG 1967.*
PREV. PART OF: FBI REVIEW; BRITISH INDUSTRIES;
BEC BULLETIN; & BRITISH MANUFACTURER.
SUBS: BRITISH INDUSTRY WEEK.
*BH/U-1.    LO/N10.    LO/U-3.    OX/U-1.*
*MA/U-1.  1966.               OX/U17.  22, 1966-*
*ISSN 0524-6113*

**BRITISH INDUSTRY WEEK.**                            XXX
*++BR. IND. WEEK.*
CONFEDERATION OF BRITISH INDUSTRY.
*LONDON 1, 1967- 5(92), 1969 ...*
PREV: BRITISH INDUSTRY FROM NO. 1, 1965-
16, 1967. SUBS: INDUSTRY WEEK.
*RE/U-1.*
*ISSN 0524-6121*

**BRITISH ISLES TOMATO SURVEY.**
*++BR. ISLES TOMATO SURV.*
WYE COLLEGE: DEPARTMENT OF ECONOMICS.
*WYE NO.1, 1968-*
*LO/U-1.*

**BRITISH JOURNAL OF APPLIED PHYSICS.**               XXX
**SUBS (1968): JOURNAL OF PHYSICS D: APPLIED
PHYSICS.**

**BRITISH JOURNAL OF AUDIOLOGY.**                     XXX
ROYAL NATIONAL INSTITUTE FOR THE DEAF.
*LONDON 7, 1973-*
PREV: SOUND FROM 1, 1967- 6, 1972. SPONS.
BODY ALSO: BRITISH SOCIETY OF AUDIOLOGY.
*LO/N14.*

**BRITISH JOURNAL OF DERMATOLOGY: SUPPLEMENTS.**
*++BR. J. DERMATOL., SUPPL.*
[LEWIS]
*LONDON NO.1, 1969-*
*LO/M-1.*

**BRITISH JOURNAL OF EDUCATIONAL TECHNOLOGY.**        XXX
*++BR. J. EDUC. TECHNOL.*
*LONDON 2(1), JA 1971-*
PREV: JOURNAL OF EDUCATIONAL TECHNOLOGY FROM
1, 1970.
*AD/U-1.    BN/U-1.    DN/U-1.    ED/N-1.    EX/U-1.    HL/U-1.*
*HL/U-2.    LD/U-1.    LO/U13.    OX/U-1.*
*LO/U-1.  2(2), 1971-             SH/C-5.  2(2), 1971-*
*ISSN 0007-1013*

**BRITISH JOURNAL OF GUIDANCE & COUNSELLING.**
*++BR. J. GUID. & COUNS.*
CAREERS RESEARCH & ADVISORY CENTRE.
*CAMBRIDGE 1, 1973-*
*AD/U-1.    BH/U-3.    CA/U-1.    ED/N-1.    GL/U-1.    HL/U-1.*
*HL/U-2.    LD/U-1.    MA/U-1.    OX/U-1.    SW/U-1.*

**BRITISH JOURNAL OF HOSPITAL MEDICINE.**
*++BR. J. HOSP. MED.*
[HOSPITAL MEDICINE PUBLICATIONS LTD.]
*LONDON 1, 1968-*
PREV: HOSPITAL MEDICINE FROM 1, OC 1966.
*GL/U-1.    LO/M-1.    SO/U-1.    ZW/N-1.*
*NW/U-1.  4, 1970-              XS/R10.  3, 1970-*
*SH/C-5.  5(6), JE 1971-*
*ISSN 0007-1064*

**BRITISH JOURNAL OF MENTAL SUBNORMALITY.**           XXX
*++BR. J. MENT. SUBNORM.*
MIDLAND SOCIETY FOR THE STUDY OF MENTAL
SUBNORMALITY.
*BIRMINGHAM 17, 1971-*
PREV: JOURNAL OF MENTAL SUBNORMALITY FROM 6,
1960- 16, 1970.
*ED/N-1.    HL/U-1.    LO/U-1.    LV/U-2.*

**BRITISH JOURNAL OF MUSIC THERAPY.**
*++BR. J. MUSIC THER.*
BRITISH SOCIETY OF MUSIC THERAPY.
*LONDON 1(1), 1969-*
*ED/N-1.  1(2), 1970-             OX/U-8.  1(2), 1969-*

**BRITISH JOURNAL OF PHARMACOLOGY.***
*++BR. J. PHARMACOL.*
BRITISH PHARMACOLOGICAL SOCIETY.
[MACMILLAN]
*LONDON 1, 1946-*
TITLE REDUCED FROM BRITISH JOURNAL OF PHARMA-
COLOGY & CHEMOTHERAPY WITH 34(1), S 1968.
*LD/U-1.    LO/M-1.    LO/U-1.*
*ISSN 0007-1188*

**BRITISH JOURNAL OF POLITICAL SCIENCE.**
*++BR. J. POLIT. SCI.*
[CAMBRIDGE UNIV. P.]
*CAMBRIDGE 1(1), JA 1971-*
Q.
*AD/U-1.    BH/U-3.    BL/U-1.    BN/U-1.    CA/U-1.    CB/U-1.*
*DB/U-2.    ED/N-1.    EX/U-1.    GL/U-2.    HL/U-1.    LO/N-5.*
*LO/U-3.    LO/U-4.    MA/U-1.    NO/U-1.    NW/U-1.    OX/U-1.*
*SH/U-1.    SO/U-1.*
*LD/U-1.  2, 1972-             SH/C-5.  1(3), 1971-*
*ISSN 0007-1234*

**BRITISH JOURNAL OF PROJECTIVE PSYCHOLOGY &
PERSONALITY STUDY.**                                  XXX
*++BR. J. PROJ. PSYCHOL. & PERSONALITY STUD.*
BRITISH RORSCHACH FORUM.
*LONDON 14, JE 1969-*
2/A. PREV: RORSCHACH NEWSLETTER FROM
1952- 1968. SPONS. BODY ALSO: SOCIETY FOR
PROJECTIVE TECHNIQUES.
*GL/U-1.*

**BRITISH JOURNAL OF PSYCHIATRIC SOCIAL WORK.**                    XXX
ASSOCIATION OF PSYCHIATRIC SOCIAL WORKERS.
*LONDON 1, 1947- 10(4), 1970.*
SUBS: BRITISH JOURNAL OF SOCIAL WORK.
*HL/U-1.*

**BRITISH JOURNAL OF SOCIAL PSYCHIATRY.**
*++BR. J. SOC. PSYCHIAT.*
*LONDON 1(1), WINTER 1966(1967)-*
*Q.*
*BH/U-1.    ED/N-1.    LO/U-3.*
*ISSN 0007-1307*

**BRITISH JOURNAL OF SOCIAL WORK.**                                XXX
*++BR. J. SOC. WORK.*
BRITISH ASSOCIATION OF SOCIAL WORKERS.
*LONDON 1, 1971-*
INCORP: BRITISH JOURNAL OF PSYCHIATRIC SOCIAL
WORK FROM 1, 1947- 10, 1970; & SOCIAL WORK
(LONDON) FROM 1, 1939- 27, 1970.
*AD/U-1.    BH/U-1.    BL/U-1.    BN/U-1.    CB/U-1.    CV/C-1.*
*DB/U-2.    DN/U-1.    ED/N-1.    EX/U-1.    GL/U-1.    HL/U-1.*
*LD/U-1.    LO/N-1.    LO/U20.    MA/U-1.    NO/U-1.*
*NW/U-1.    SH/C-5.    SO/U-1.    SW/U-1.    XY/N-1.*
*ISSN 0045-3102*

**BRITISH JOURNAL OF SPORTS MEDICINE.**
*++BR. J. SPORTS MED.*
BRITISH ASSOCIATION OF SPORT & MEDICINE.
*LOUGHBOROUGH 4(1), D 1968-*
PREV: BULLETIN OF THE BRITISH ASSOCIATION OF
SPORT & MEDICINE FROM 1, [1964]- 3, 1968.
*ED/N-1.    OX/U-8.*
*BH/U-1.    5, 1970-*

**BRITISH MEAT.**
*++BR. MEAT.*
MEAT & LIVESTOCK COMMISSION (GB).
*LONDON NO.1, 1971-*
*AD/U-1.*
*LD/U-1.    NO.3, 1973-*

**BRITISH MEDICAL BOOKLIST.**                                     XXX
SUBS (1972): PART OF BRITISH MEDICINE.

**BRITISH MEDICAL INDEX.**                                        XXX
SUBS (1972): PART OF BRITISH MEDICINE.

**BRITISH MEDICINE.**                                             XXX
*++BR. MED.*
BRITISH COUNCIL.
*LONDON 1(1) JA 1972-*
M. INCORP: BRITISH MEDICAL BOOKLIST FROM 1,
1950- 21, 1971; & BRITISH MEDICAL INDEX FROM
NO.1, JL 1967- 27, D 1971.
*AD/U-1.    BH/P-1.    CA/U-1.    GL/U-1.    LO/M13.    LO/N13.*
*LO/U-1.    LO/U-2.    SH/U-1.*
*ED/N-1.    1(2), 1972-*
*GL/U-2.    5 YEARS ONLY.*
*LD/U-1.    2 YEARS ONLY.*

**BRITISH MENSA MAGAZINE.**
*++BR. MENSA MAG.*
BRITISH MENSA LTD.
*LONDON 1(1), JE 1972-*
*M.*
*ED/N-1.*

**BRITISH MUSEUM SOCIETY BULLETIN.**
*++BR. MUS. SOC. BULL.*
*LONDON NO.1, [1969]-*
*ED/N-1.    LO/N-2.    LO/U-1.    OX/U-1.*
*ISSN 0525-5260*

**BRITISH PATRIOT.**
*++BR. PATRIOT.*
BRITISH CAMPAIGN TO STOP IMMIGRATION.
*BRADFORD NO.1[AP 1973]-*
*LO/U-3.*

**BRITISH PHYCOLOGICAL BULLETIN.**                                XXX
SUBS: (1969) BRITISH PHYCOLOGICAL JOURNAL.

**BRITISH PHYCOLOGICAL JOURNAL.**
*++BR. PHYCOL. J.*
BRITISH PHYCOLOGICAL SOCIETY.
*PLYMOUTH 4(1), AP 1969-*
PREV: BRITISH PHYCOLOGICAL BULLETIN FROM
1(7), 1959.
*BN/U-2.    GL/U-1.    LD/U-1.    LO/N13.    LO/U13.*
*NW/U-1.    RE/U-1.*
*ISSN 0007-1617*

**BRITISH PLASTICS.**                                             XXX
SUBS (1972): EUROPLASTICS MONTHLY: BRITISH
PLASTICS EDITION.

**BRITISH POLYMER JOURNAL.**
*++BR. POLYM. J.*
SOCIETY OF CHEMICAL INDUSTRY.
*LONDON 1(1), JA 1969-*
*BH/P-1.    ED/N-1.    LO/N-3.    LO/N14.    LO/S-3.    LO/U12.*
*OX/U-8.*
*SH/U-3.    3, 1971-*
*ISSN 0007-1641*

**BRITISH STEEL.**
*++BR. STEEL.*
BRITISH STEEL CORPORATION.
*LONDON AP 1968-*
Q. PREV: STEEL REVIEW, (BRITISH IRON & STEEL
FEDERATION) FROM NO.1, 1956- 47, 1968.
*BH/U-1.    CB/U-1.    ED/N-1.    LO/U-3.*
*ISSN 0007-182X*

**BRITISH STUDIES MONITOR.**
*++BR. STUD. MONIT.*
BOWDOIN COLLEGE.
*BRUNSWICK, MAINE 1, 1970-*
*AD/U-1.    CB/U-1.    ED/N-1.    EX/U-1.    LD/U-1.    LO/N-1.*
*SW/U-1.*
*ISSN 0007-1846*

**BRITISH SURVEY.**                                               XXX
SUBS (1969): WORLD SURVEY.

**BRITISH TRADE JOURNAL & EXPORT WORLD.**                         XXX
SUBS (1970): INDUSTRIAL EXPORTS (GREAT BRI-
TAIN).

**BRITISH UNION CATALOGUE OF LATIN AMERICANA;**
**NEW LATIN AMERICAN TITLES.**
*++BR. U. CAT. LAT. AM., NEW LAT. AM. TITLES.*
UNIVERSITY OF LONDON; INSTITUTE OF LATIN
AMERICAN STUDIES.
*LONDON 1(1), OC 1968-*
M. EXCEPT AG/S.
*ED/N-1.    GL/U-1.    LO/U-3.    LO/U11.*

**BRITISH VEGETARIAN.**                                           XXX
SUBS (1971): VEGETARIAN: NS.

**BRITISH WATER SUPPLY.**
*++BR. WAT. SUPPLY.*
BRITISH WATERWORKS ASSOCIATION.
*LONDON NO.1, 1969-*
PREV: JOURNAL, BRITISH WATERWORKS ASSOCIATION.
*BH/P-1.    BL/U-1.    BN/U-1.    ED/N-1.    LO/N-2.    LO/N14.*
*SH/U-3.*
*ISSN 0007-1943*

**BRITISH WELDING JOURNAL.**                                      XXX
SUBS (1969): METAL CONSTRUCTION & BRITISH
WELDING JOURNAL.

**BRJUSOVSKIE CHTENIJA.**
EREVANSKIJ GOSUDARSTVENNYJ PEDAGOGICHESKIJ
INSTITUT.
*EREVAN 1962(1963)-*
*A.*
*CC/U-1.    NO/U-1.    SW/U-1.*
*LO/N-3.    1963(1964).*

**BROADCAST JOURNAL.**                                            XXX
*++BROADCAST J.*
SOCIETY OF BROADCAST ENGINEERS.
*LOS ANGELES 1, 1964- 8, 1971.//*
*2M.*
*LO/N14.    3(2), 1966-*
*ISSN 0007-2001*

**BROADHEAD CLASSICAL LECTURES.**
*++BROADHEAD CLASSICAL LECT.*
UNIVERSITY OF CANTERBURY (NZ).
*CHRISTCHURCH, N.Z. NO.1, 1969-*
*LO/N-1.    OX/U-1.*

**BROADSHEET, ECONOMIC & SOCIAL RESEARCH INSTI-**
**TUTE (DUBLIN).**                                                000
SEE: ESRI BROADSHEETS.

**BROMELIADS. JOURNAL OF THE...**
BRITISH BROMELIAD SOCIETY.
*BRISTOL 1(1), 1969-*
*LO/N-2.    LO/N13.*
*ED/N-1.    1(2), 1969-                    OX/U-8.    1(2), 1969-*
*ISSN 0084-8107*

**BROOKHAVEN NATIONAL LABORATORY LECTURES IN**
**SCIENCE.**                                                      000
SEE: VISTAS IN RESEARCH.

**BROOKINGS PAPERS ON ECONOMIC ACTIVITY.**
++BROOKINGS PAP. ECON. ACT.
BROOKINGS INSTITUTION.
 WASHINGTON, D.C. 1, 1970-
 LO/U-2.   LO/U-3.   LO/U12.   MA/U-1.   OX/U16.
 SO/U-1. 1971-
 EX/U-1. NO.1, 1974-
 SH/U-1. NO.10, 1973-
 ISSN 0007-2303

**BROWNING NEWSLETTER.**
 BAYLOR UNIVERSITY: ARMSTRONG BROWNING LIBRARY.
 WACO, TEX. NO.1, 1968- 9, 1972.
 SUBS: STUDIES IN BROWNING & HIS CIRCLE.
 LO/U-1.   OX/U-1.
 ISSN 0007-2532

**BRUNA ALPINA.**
 ASSOCIAZIONE NAZIONALE ALLEVATORI DELLA RAZZA
 BRUNA ALPINA (ITALY).
 MILAN 1, JA/F 1963-
 LO/N13. 1966(1)-
 ISSN 0524-7527

**BRUNEI MUSEUM JOURNAL.**
++BRUNEI MUS. J.
 BRUNEI 1, 1969-
 AD/U-3.   CA/U-3.   LO/N-2.   LO/U-8.   LO/U14.
 ISSN 0068-2918

**BSBI ABSTRACTS.  ABSTRACTS OF LITERATURE
RELATING TO THE VASCULAR PLANTS OF THE
BRITISH ISLES.**
 BOTANICAL SOCIETY OF THE BRITISH ISLES.
 LONDON PART 1, MY 1971-
 AD/U-1.   BL/U-1.   ED/N-1.   HL/U-1.   LD/U-1.   LN/U-2.
 LO/N-2.   LO/N-4.   LO/R-5.   LO/U12.   MA/U-1.   NW/U-1.
 SH/U-1.   SO/U-1.

**BSBI NEWS.**
 BOTANICAL SOCIETY OF THE BRITISH ISLES.
 LONDON 1, 1972-
 LO/N-2.   RE/U-1.
 SO/U-1. 2(1), 1973-

**BSSRS NEWSHEET.**
 BRITISH SOCIETY FOR SOCIAL RESPONSIBILITY IN
 SCIENCE.
 LONDON NO.1, AP 1969-
 ED/N-1.

**B.T.T.A. REVIEW.**
 BRITISH THORACIC & TUBERCULOSIS ASSOCIATION.
 EDINBURGH &C. 1(1), 1971-
 SUPPL. TO TUBERCLE.
 LO/U-1.   NW/U-1.   OX/U-8.

**BUCK'S SAFETY MANAGEMENT AID.**
++BUCK'S SAF. MANAGE. AID.
 [DATA RETRIEVAL LTD.]
 HASTINGS 1(1), JL/AG 1971-
 LO/N14.   XY/N-1.
 ED/N-1. 1(2), 1971-

**BUDUCNOST.  THE FUTURE.**
 SOCIJALDEMOKRATSKA ZAJEDNICA JUGOSLOVENA VAN
 OTADZBINE.
 LONDON; VIENNA 1(1), D 1966-
 ED/N-1.   LO/U-3.   OX/U-1.

**BUILD INTERNATIONAL.**
++BUILD INT.
 BUILD FOUNDATION.
 ROTTERDAM 1(1), S 1968-
 PREV: CIB BULLETIN FROM 1954- 1966. PUBL.
 BY THE FOUNDATION UNDER THE AUSPICES OF THE
 INTERNATIONAL COUNCIL FOR BUILDING RESEARCH
 STUDIES & DOCUMENTATION.
 GL/U-2.   LO/N14.   LO/U-2.   SH/U-1.
 ISSN 0525-0021

**BUILDER & DECORATOR.**
++BUILD. & DECOR.
 [STRODE PUBL. LTD.]
 LONDON 1(1), AG 1972-
 MON.
 ED/N-1. 1(2), 1972-
 LO/N14. CURRENT BOX ONLY.

**BUILDING CENTRE INTELLIGENCE REPORT.**
++BUILD. CENT. INTELL. REP.
 LONDON 1, 1969-
 OX/U-8.

**BUILDING CONSTRUCTION [ILLUSTRATED].**          XXX
 SUBS (1970): BUILDING DESIGN & CONSTRUCTION.

**BUILDING DESIGN & CONSTRUCTION.**          XXX
++BLDG. DES. & CONSTR.
 [CAHNERS]
 CHICAGO 11, 1970-
 PREV: BUILDING CONSTRUCTION [ILLUSTRATED] FROM
 S 1957.
 LO/N14.
 ISSN 0007-3407

**BUILDING FORUM.**
++BUILD. FORUM.
 [WEST PUBL. CORP.]
 SYDNEY 1, 1969-
 XS/R19.
 ISSN 0007-3466

**BUILDING MAINTENANCE.**
++BUILD. MAINT.
 LONDON 1(1), 1967-
 LO/N14.   OX/U-8.
 ED/N-1. 1(2), 1967-
 ISSN 0007-3482

**BUILDING MAINTENANCE & MODERNIZATION.**          XXX
 SUBS (1970): BUILDING OPERATING MANAGEMENT.

**BUILDING OPERATING MANAGEMENT.**          XXX
++BUILD. OP. MANAGE.
 [TRADE P. PUBL. CO.]
 MILWAUKEE 17, 1970-
 PREV: BUILDING MAINTENANCE & MODERNIZATION
 FROM 1, 1954 - 16, 1969.
 LO/N14.

**BUILDING RESEARCH CURRENT PAPERS; CONSTRUC-
TION SERIES.**
++BUILD. RES. CURR. PAP., CONSTR. SER.
 BUILDING RESEARCH STATION (GB).
 WATFORD 1, 1962-
 LO/N-4.
 BR/U-3. 2,1963-

**BUILDING RESEARCH CURRENT PAPERS; ENGINEERING
SERIES.**
++BUILD. RES. CURR. PAP., ENG. SER.
 BUILDING RESEARCH STATION (GB).
 WATFORD 1, 1963-
 BR/U-3.   LO/N-4.

**BUILDING RESEARCH & PRACTICE.**
++BUILD. RES. & PRACT.
 INTERNATIONAL COUNCIL FOR BUILDING RESEARCH
 STUDIES & DOCUMENTATION.
 LONDON 1, 1973-
 6/A.
 BL/U-1.   CA/U-1.   LO/R-6.   OX/U-8.   SH/U-1.

**BUILDING SERVICES ENGINEER.**          XXX
++BUILD. SERV. ENG.
 INSTITUTION OF HEATING & VENTILATING ENGINEERS.
 LONDON 39, N 1971-
 PREV: I.H.V.E. JOURNAL FROM 33, 1965- 39, 1971
 BH/P-1.   BL/U-1. *   BR/U-1.   ED/N-1.   LD/U-1.   LO/N14.
 NW/U-1.   XS/T-4.
 GL/U-1. 40, 1972-                    RE/U-1. 40, 1972-

**BUILDING TECHNOLOGY & COMMUNITY DEVELOPMENT.**
++BUILD. TECHNOL. & COMMUNITY DEV.
 VALTION TEKNILLINEN TUTKIMUSKESKUS.
 HELSINKI PUBLICATION 1, 1972-
 LO/N14. [W. PUBLICATION 2.]

**BUILDINGS FOR EDUCATION.**          XXX
++BUILD. EDUC.
 ASIAN REGIONAL INSTITUTE FOR SCHOOL BUILDING
 RESEARCH.
 COLOMBO 1(1), AP 1967- 2(4), D 1968.
 Q.  SUBS: NEWSLETTER ASIAN REGIONAL INSTITUTE
 FOR SCHOOL BUILDING RESEARCH.
 LO/N17.
 LD/U-2. 2(4), D 1968.
 ISSN 0572-7308

**BUILT ENVIRONMENT.**          XXX
++BUILT ENVIRON.
 [ARCHITECTURE & PLANNING PUBL.]
 LONDON 1(1), AP 1972-
 M. PREV: OAP JOURNAL FOR THE BUILT ENVIRON-
 MENT FROM 34, 1971- 35, 1972.
 BH/P-1.   DB/U-2.   ED/N-1.   GL/U-1.   LO/N14.   LO/R-5.
 LO/U-3.   OX/U-1.   RE/U-1.
 ISSN 0045-3463

BULGARIAN HORIZONS.
+ +BULG. HORIZ.
INFORMATION CENTRE OF LITERATURE, ART & SCIENCE
(SOFIA).
SOFIA 1, 1967-
S/T: QUARTERLY OF LITERATURE, ART & SCIENCE.
BL/U-1. 14, [1971}

BULGARSKA AKADEMIJA NA NAUKITE: INSTITUT ZA
BALKANISTIKA: SERIJA: IZVORI.
+ +BULG. AKAD. NAUK. INST. BALK., IZVORI.
SOFIA 1, 1966-
MONOGR.
LO/N-3.    OX/U-1.

BULGARSKI PLODOVE, ZELENCHUTSI I KONSERVI.
+ +BULG. PLODOVE ZELENCHUTSI & KONSERVI.
[BULGARPLOD]
SOFIA 1, 1966-
ENGL. CONT. LISTS.
LO/N13. 1971-

BULLETIN, AFRICAN STUDIES ASSOCIATION OF THE
WEST INDIES.
+ +BULL. AFR. STUD. ASSOC. WEST INDIES.
MONA, JAMAICA NO.1, 1967-
OX/U-9.

BULLETIN, AGRICULTURAL ADJUSTMENT UNIT, UNIV-
ERSITY OF NEWCASTLE UPON TYNE.
+ +BULL. AGR. ADJUST. UNIT UNIV. NEWCASTLE UPON
TYNE.
NEWCASTLE UPON TYNE NO.1, 1966/67 (1967)-
AGRICULTURAL ADJUSTMENT UNIT SUBORD. TO DEP-
ARTMENT OF AGRICULTURAL ECONOMICS.
AB/U-1.

BULLETIN OF THE AGRICULTURAL ENGINEERING
RESEARCH STATION.                                    000
SEE: NOGYO DOBOKU SHIKENJO HOKOKU.

BULLETIN OF AICHI INSTITUTE OF TECHNOLOGY.           000
SEE: AICHI KOGYO DAIGAKU KENKYU HOKOKU.

BULLETIN OF THE AKITA FRUIT-TREE EXPERIMENT
STATION.
+ +BULL. AKITA FRUIT-TREE EXP. STA.
AKITA 1, 1969-
XS/R-2.

BULLETIN OF THE ALLYN MUSEUM.
+ +BULL. ALLYN MUS.
SARASOTA, FLA. NO.1, N 1971-
LO/N-2.

BULLETIN OF THE AMERICAN ACADEMY OF BENARES.
+ +BULL. AM. ACAD. BENARES.
VARANASI 1, N 1967-
LO/U14.
ISSN 0569-2059

BULLETIN, AMERICAN ASTRONOMICAL SOCIETY.
+ +BULL. AM. ASTRON. SOC.
NEW YORK 1(1), 1969-
Q.
LO/N14.    LO/U-2.    SH/U-1.
ISSN 0002-7537

BULLETIN ANALYTIQUE, CENTRE D'ETUDES ET DE
RECHERCHES DE L'INDUSTRIE DES LIANTS HYDRAUL-
IQUES.                                               XXX
+ +BULL. ANAL. CENT. ETUD. RECH. IND. LIANTS
HYDRAUL.
PARIS 1969-
PREV: DOCUMENTATION BIBLIOGRAPHIQUE. BULLETIN
DE DOCUMENTATION, CENTRE ... FROM NO.1, 1949-
41, 1968.
LO/N14.

BULLETIN ANALYTIQUE DE LINGUISTIQUE FRANCAISE.
+ +BULL. ANAL. LINGUIST. FR.
CENTRE NATIONAL DE LA RECHERCHE SCIENTIFIQUE.
NANCY 1(1), 1969-
SPONS. BODY ALSO CENTRE DE RECHERCHE POUR
UN TRESOR DE LA LANGUE FRANCAISE.
DB/U-2.    LO/U-1.
EX/U-1. 1(4), 1969-              LD/U-1. 1(2), 1969-
SH/U-1. 1972-
ISSN 0007-408X

BULLETIN, APHID LABORATORY (SUWON).              •
+ +BULL. APHID LAB. (SUWON).
SUWON NO.1, 1969-
XS/R-2.

BULLETIN OF AQUATIC BIOLOGY.
+ +BULL. AQUATIC BIOL. [BAQB-A]
ZOOLOGICAL MUSEUM (AMSTERDAM): ICHTHYOLOGY
DEPARTMENT.
AMSTERDAM NO.1, 1957- 35, 1967.//
ENGL. & DUTCH.
LO/N14.
ISSN 0521-7229

BULLETIN, ARNOLD BAX SOCIETY.
+ +BULL. ARNOLD BAX SOC.
LONDON NO.1, F 1968-
CA/U-1.    ED/N-1.    LO/N-1.    OX/U-1.

BULLETIN OF THE ASIA INSTITUTE OF PAHLAVI
UNIVERSITY.
+ +BULL. ASIA INST. PAHLAVI UNIV.
SHIRAZ NO.1, 1969-
LO/U14.

BULLETIN, ASSOCIATION FOR COMMONWEALTH
LITERATURE & LANGUAGE STUDIES.
+ +BULL. ASS. COMMONW. LIT. & LANG. STUD.
LEEDS NO.3, MY 1967-
PUBL. FOR THE ASS. BY UNIV. OF LEEDS.
PREV: NEWS SHEET, ASSOCIATION ..., FROM [NO.
1], MY 1966- 2, 1966.
LO/S26.    LO/U-2.    LO/U-8.

BULLETIN, ASSOCIATION OF CONTEMPORARY
HISTORIANS.
+ +BULL. ASS. CONTEMP. HIST.
LONDON NO.1, JA 1969-
EX/U-1.    LO/U19.

BULLETIN, ASSOCIATION OF HISTORY TEACHERS IN
THE SOUTH WEST.
+ +BULL. ASS. HIST. TEACH. S.W.
BARNSTAPLE NO.1, F 1969-
CA/U-1.    EX/U-1.    LD/U-2.

BULLETIN, ASSOCIATION INTERNATIONALE D'ETUDES
DU SUD-EST EUROPEEN.
+ +BULL. ASS. INT. ETUD. SUD-EST EUR.
INTERNATIONAL ASSOCIATION OF SOUTH-EAST
EUROPEAN STUDIES.
BUCHAREST 1, 1963-
Q. IN FR., & BODY ON T.P. IN FR. FORM AS
INDICATED IN ABOVE TITLE.
LO/U15.
OX/U-1. 1- 3, 1965.
ISSN 0004-5551

BULLETIN, ASSOCIATION FOR LITERARY & LING-
UISTIC COMPUTING.
+ +BULL. ASSOC. LIT. & LINGUIST. COMPUT.
STOCKPORT, CHESHIRE 1(1), 1973-
3/A.
AD/U-1.    CA/U-1.    ED/N-1.    LD/U-1.    LO/U-2.    LO/U14.
OX/U-1.    SH/U-1.    SW/U-1.

BULLETIN OF THE ASSOCIATION OF MORAL WELFARE
WORKERS.                                             XXX
SUBS (1970): PART OF SOCIAL WORK TODAY.

BULLETIN OF ATMOSPHERIC ELECTRICITY.
+ +BULL. ATMOS. ELEC.
NATIONAL OBSERVATORY (GREECE): METEOROLOGICAL
INSTITUTE.
ATHENS 1, 1965-
XS/N-1.

BULLETIN OF THE AUSTRALIAN MATHEMATICAL SOC-
IETY.
+ +BULL. AUST. MATH. SOC.
[UNIV. OF QUEENSLAND P.]
ST. LUCIA, QUEENSL. 1, 1969-
AD/U-1.    LO/N-4.    LO/N13.    LO/U-2.    OX/U-8.    SW/U-1.
LO/U12. 8(1), 1973-              SH/U-1. 2(6), 1970-
ISSN 0004-9727

BULLETIN, AUSTRALIAN MINERAL DEVELOPMENT
LABORATORIES.                                        000
SEE: AMDEL BULLETIN.

BULLETIN, AUSTRALIAN & NEW ZEALAND ASSOCIA-
TION FOR MEDIEVAL & RENAISSANCE STUDIES.            XXX
+ +BULL. AUST. & N.Z. ASS. MEDIEV.
& RENAISS. STUD.
SYDNEY NO.1, 1968- 7, AU 1971.
SUBS: PARERGON.
LO/U19.    OX/U-1.

BULLETIN, AUSTRALIAN SOCIETY OF EXPLORATION
GEOPHYSICISTS.
+ +BULL. AUST. SOC. EXPLOR. GEOPHYS.
CROWS NEST, N.S.W. 1(1), S 1970-
Q.

BULLETIN, AUSTRALIAN SOCIETY FOR LIMNOLOGY.
+ +BULL. AUST. SOC. LIMNOL.
SYDNEY NO.1, OC 1969-
BN/U-2.   LO/N-2.
ISSN 0084-7607

BULLETIN, BALAI PENJELIDIKAN PERUSAHAAN
PERKEBUNAN GULA. BULLETIN, INDONESIAN SUGAR
EXPERIMENT STATION.
+ +BULL. BALAI PENJELIDIKAN PERUSAHAAN
PERKEBUNAN GULA.
PASURUAN NO.1, 1968-
LO/N13.

BULLETIN, BASILDON NATURAL HISTORY SOCIETY.
+ +BULL. BASILDON NAT. HIST. SOC.
BASILDON, ESSEX NO.1, 1968-
LO/N-2.

BULLETIN BELGE DE METROLOGIE.     XXX
SUBS (1971): BULLETIN DE METROLOGIE.

BULLETIN, B.I.A.S.     000
SEE: B.I.A.S. BULLETIN.

BULLETIN OF THE BIBLIOGRAPHICAL SOCIETY OF
AUSTRALIA & NEW ZEALAND.
+ +BULL. BIBLIOGR. SOC. AUST. & N.Z.
CLAYTON, VICTORIA NO.1, MR 1970-
CA/U-1.   NW/U-1.

BULLETIN DU BIBLIOPHILE.     XXX
+ +BULL. BIBLIOPHILE.
ASSOCIATION INTERNATIONALE DE BIBLIOPHILIE.
PARIS 1, 1969-
PREV: BIBLIOPHILIE FROM 1, 1965- 6, 1969.
EX/U-1.   LO/U-1.

BULLETIN BIOLOGIQUE (IVORY COAST).
+ +BULL. BIOL. (IVORY COAST).
ASSOCIATION SCIENTIFIQUE DE COTE D'IVOIRE.
ABIDJAN NO.1, 1967-
LO/N-2.

BULLETIN, BIRTH CONTROL CAMPAIGN.
LONDON NO.1, 1972-
Q.
ED/N-1.   LO/U-3.

BULLETIN, BRITISH ARACHNOLOGICAL SOCIETY.     XXX
+ +BULL. BR. ARACHNOL. SOC.
LOUGHBOROUGH 1, 1969-
PREV: BULLETIN, BRITISH SPIDER STUDY GROUP
FROM NO. 21, 1964- 40, 1968.
ED/N-1.   LO/N-2.   LO/N13.   MA/U-1.
ISSN 0524-4994

BULLETIN OF THE BRITISH ASSOCIATION FOR
AMERICAN STUDIES: NS.     XXX
+ +BULL. BR. ASS. AM. STUD., NS.
MANCHESTER NO.1, S 1960- 12/13, 1966.
PREV SERIES OF ABOVE TITLE, NO.1, 1956-
9, 1959. SUBS: JOURNAL OF AMERICAN STUDIES.
EX/U-1.   HL/U-1.   LO/N-1.   LO/U-2.   MA/U-1.
ISSN 0524-5001

BULLETIN, BRITISH ECOLOGICAL SOCIETY.
+ +BULL. BR. ECOL. SOC.
OXFORD &C. 1(1), JE 1970-
LO/N-2.   LO/R-5.   OX/U-3.

BULLETIN, BRITISH NON-FERROUS METALS RESEARCH
ASSOCIATION.     XXX
SUBS (1970): BNF ABSTRACTS.

BULLETIN, BRITISH PELARGONIUM & GERANIUM
SOCIETY.     XXX
+ +BULL. BR. PELARGONIUM & GERANIUM SOC.
LONDON 14(2), 1965- 16(1), 1967...
PREV: BULLETIN, GERANIUM SOCIETY FROM
[1], 1952- 13(1), 1964. SUBS: PELARGONIUM
NEWS.
LO/N13.

BULLETIN, BUREAU INTERNATIONAL DE L'EDITION
MECANIQUE.     XXX
SUBS (1968): BULLETIN, BUREAU INTERNATIONAL
DES SOCIETES GERANT LES DROITS D'ENREGISTRE-
MENT ET DE REPRODUCTION MECANIQUE.

BULLETIN, BUREAU INTERNATIONAL DES SOCIETES
GERANT LES DROITS D'ENREGISTREMENT ET DE REP-
RODUCTION MECANIQUE.     XXX
+ +BULL. BUR. INT. SOC. GERANT DROITS ENREGIST.
& REPROD. MEC.
PARIS NO.9, 1968-
PREV: BULLETIN, BUREAU INTERNATIONAL DE
L'EDITION MECANIQUE FROM NO.1, 1959- 8, 1962.
LO/N14.

BULLETIN DU BUREAU DE RECHERCHES GEOLOGIQUES
ET MINIERES: 2S: SECTION 2. GEOLOGIE
APPLIQUEE.     XXX
+ +BULL. BUR. RECH. GEOL. & MINIERES, 2S SECT. 2.
PARIS 1968(1)-
Q. PREV. PART OF ABOVE MAIN TITLE FROM
1961- 1967.
LO/N-4.
ISSN 0007-6090

BULLETIN, BUREAU DE RECHERCHES GEOLOGIQUES ET
MINIERES: 2S: SECTION 3: HYDROGEOLOGIE.
+ +BULL. BUR. RECH. GEOL. & MINIERES, 2S, SECT.3.
PARIS NO.1, 1968-
PREV: CHRONIQUE D'HYDROGEOLOGIE FROM NO.1,
MR 1963- 12, 1967.
LO/N-4.   LO/N13.

BULLETIN, BUREAU DE RECHERCHES GEOLOGIQUES ET
MINIERES: 2S: SECTION 4: GEOLOGIE ET
GENERALE.     XXX
+ +BULL. BUR. RECH. GEOL. & MINIERES (FR.), 2S,4.
PARIS 1968(1)-
Q. PREV. PART OF ABOVE MAIN TITLE
FROM 1961- 1967.
LO/N13.
ISSN 0007-6112

BULLETIN, BURNHAM ON CROUCH & DISTRICT LOCAL
HISTORY SOCIETY.
+ +BULL. BURNHAM CROUCH & DIST. LOCAL HIST. SOC.
BURNHAM NO.1, 1972-
ED/N-1.

BULLETIN, CANADIAN AMPHIBIAN & REPTILE CONS-
ERVATION SOCIETY.
+ +BULL. CAN. AMPHIBIAN & REPTILE CONSERV. SOC.
TORONTO 1, 1969-
LO/N-2.

BULLETIN, CANADIAN AMPHIBIAN & REPTILE CONS-
ERVATION SOCIETY: SUPPLEMENT.
+ +BULL. CAN. AMPHIBIAN & REPTILE CONSERV. SOC.,
SUPPL.
TORONTO NO.1, [1970]-
LO/N-2.

BULLETIN, CANADIAN BOTANICAL ASSOCIATION.
+ +BULL. CAN. BOT. ASSOC.
GUELPH, ONT. 1, JA 1968-
Q. ENGL. & FR.
LO/N-2. 4, 1971-
ISSN 0008-3046

BULLETIN, CENTRAL MARINE FISHERIES RESEARCH
INSTITUTE.
+ +BULL. CENT. MAR. FISH. RES. INST.
CENTRAL MARINE FISHERIES RESEARCH INSTITUTE
(INDIA).
MANDAPAM CAMP, INDIA NO.1, 1968-
BN/U-2.   LO/N-4.
ISSN 0577-084X

BULLETIN, CENTRE D'ETUDES ET DE DOCUMENTATION
EUROPEENNES (MONTREAL).
+ +BULL. CENT. ETUD. & DOC. EUR. (MONTREAL).
MONTREAL NO.1, 1968-
SH/U-1.

BULLETIN, CLEVELAND & TEESSIDE LOCAL HISTORY
SOCIETY.
+ +BULL. CLEVELAND & TEESSIDE LOCAL HIST. SOC.
MIDDLESBOROUGH NO.1, 1968-
OX/U-1.

BULLETIN, COMMISSION FOR THE GEOLOGICAL MAP
OF THE WORLD.
+ +BULL. COMM. GEOL. MAP WORLD.
PARIS NO.1, 1964-
ENGL. OR FR. NO.1 ALSO ENTITLED ANNUAL
REPORT, 1963.
LO/N-2. . LO/N13.

BULLETIN, COMMISSION GEOLOGIQUE DE FINLANDE.     XXX
SUBS (1971): BULLETIN, GEOLOGICAL SURVEY OF
FINLAND.

BULLETIN OF COMPUTER-AIDED ARCHITECTURAL
DESIGN.
+ +BULL. COMPUT.-AIDED ARCHIT. DES.
UNIVERSITY OF STRATHCLYDE: ARCHITECTURAL &
BUILDING AIDS COMPUTER UNIT.
*GLASGOW NO.1, 1969-*
*Q.*
*BL/U-1.    SH/U-1.*

BULLETIN OF CONCERNED ASIAN SCHOLARS.                              XXX
+ +BULL. CONCERNED ASIAN SCH.
COMMITTEE OF CONCERNED ASIAN SCHOLARS.
*CAMBRIDGE, MASS. 2(1), 1969-*
*Q.  PREV: CCAS NEWSLETTER FROM NO.1, 1968.*
*LO/U14.    MA/U-1.\**
*SH/U-1. 1971-*
*HL/U-1. 3(3- 4), 1971-*
*ISSN 0007-4810*

BULLETIN OF THE CONFERENCE OF SOCIALIST
ECONOMISTS.
+ +BULL. CONF. SOC. ECON.
*BRIGHTON 1(1), WINTER 1971-*
*BL/U-1.    CA/U-1.    LO/U-3.    LO/U12.    OX/U16.*

BULLETIN, CONNECTICUT HERPETOLOGICAL SOCIETY.
+ +BULL. CONN. HERPETOL. SOC.
*NEW LONDON 1, 1969-*
*LO/N-2.*

BULLETIN, CONSTRUCTION INDUSTRY RESEARCH &
INFORMATION ASSOCIATION.
   SEE: CIRIA BULLETIN.

BULLETIN, COUNCIL OF RESEARCH IN MUSIC EDUCA-
TION.
+ +BULL. COUNC. RES. MUSIC EDUC.
*URBANA, ILL. 1, 1963-*
*RE/U-2.*
*LO/U-1. NO.19, 1970-*
*LV/U-2. NO.19, 1970-*
*ISSN 0574-2722*

BULLETIN, CROYDON NATURAL HISTORY & SCIENT-
IFIC SOCIETY.
+ +BULL. CROYDON NAT. HIST. & SCI. SOC.
*CROYDON NO.1, 1967-*
*LO/U-1. W NOS.13- 16;18;20.*

BULLETIN OF CURRENT DOCUMENTATION.
+ +BULL. CURR. DOC.
ASSOCIATION OF COMMONWEALTH UNIVERSITIES.
*LONDON 1(1), JE 1971-*
*BL/U-1.    ED/N-1.    LO/N-1.    SH/U-1.*
*LO/U-2. 1(2), 1971-         LO/U28. 1, 1972-*
*MA/U-1. 1(2), 1971-         NO/U-1 1(2), D 1971-*
*OX/U16. 1(2), 1971-*

BULLETIN OF DAIDO TECHNICAL COLLEGE.                                000
   SEE: DAIDO KOGYO DAIGAKU KIYU.

BULLETIN OF THE DEPARTMENT OF GEOGRAPHY, UNI-
VERSITY OF TOKYO.
+ +BULL. DEP. GEOGR. UNIV. TOKYO.
TOKYO DAIGAKU: DEPARTMENT OF GEOGRAPHY.
*TOKYO 1, MR 1969-*
*LO/S13.    NO/U-1.*
*ISSN 0082-478X*

BULLETIN, DEPARTMENT OF MEDICINAL PLANTS,
MINISTRY OF FORESTS(NEPAL).
+ +BULL. DEP. MED. PLANTS MIN. FORESTS(NEPAL).
*NEPAL NO.1, 1967-*
*LO/N-2.*

BULLETIN, ECOLE NATIONALE SUPERIEURE D'AGRON-
OMIE ET DES INDUSTRIES ALIMENTAIRES (FRANCE).         XXX
+ +BULL. EC. NATL. SUPER. AGRON. & IND. ALIMENT.
*(FR.).*
*NANCY 14, 1972-*
PREV: BULLETIN, ECOLE NATIONALE SUPERIEURE
AGRONOMIQUE DE NANCY FROM 1, 1959- 13, 1971.
*LO/N14.*

BULLETIN, ECOLE NATIONALE SUPERIEURE AGRONOM-
IQUE DE NANCY.                                                     XXX
   SUBS (1972): BULLETIN, ECOLE NATIONALE
   SUPERIEURE D'AGRONOMIQUE ET DES INDUSTRIES
   ALIMENTAIRES (FRANCE).

BULLETIN, ECOLOGICAL RESEARCH COMMITTEE,
NATURAL SCIENCE RESEARCH COUNCIL (SWEDEN).
+ +BULL. ECOL. RES. COMM. NATL. SCI. RES. COUNC.
*(SWED.).*
(SWEDEN) STATENS NATURVETENSKAPLIGA FORSKNINGS-
RAD: ECOLOGICAL RESEARCH COMMITTEE.
*STOCKHOLM NO.1, 1968-*
ENGL. MONOGR. ISSUED UNDER THE COUNCIL'S
ENGLISH FORM OF NAME.
*LO/R-5. NO.6, 1971-*

BULLETIN OF ECONOMIC RESEARCH.                                     XXX
+ +BULL. ECON. RES.     .
UNIVERSITY OF YORK: DEPARTMENT OF ECONOMICS.
*HULL 23(1), MY 1971-*
*2/A.  PREV: YORKSHIRE BULLETIN OF ECONOMIC &*
SOCIAL RESEARCH FROM 1, 1948- 22, 1970.  ALSO
ISSUED JOINTLY BY DEPT. OF ECONOMICS OF UNIVS.
OF HULL, LEEDS, SHEFFIELD & BRADFORD.
*BH/P-1.    BN/U-1.    GL/U-1.    GL/U-1.    HL/U-1.    LO/U-1.*
*LO/U-3.    NO/U-1.    NW/U-1.*

BULLETIN, ECONOMICS DEPARTMENT, EDINBURGH &
EAST OF SCOTLAND COLLEGE OF AGRICULTURE.                           XXX
   SUBS (1970): REPORT, ECONOMICS DEPARTMENT,
   EAST OF SCOTLAND ...

BULLETIN OF EDUCATIONAL RESEARCH.
+ +BULL. EDUC. RES.
NEWCASTLE UPON TYNE POLYTECHNIC.
*NEWCASTLE UPON TYNE NO.1, 1971-*
*LD/U-1.    NW/U-1.*

BULLETIN, ELECTRICITY SUPPLY INDUSTRY TRAIN-
ING BOARD (G.B.).
+ +BULL. ELECTR. SUPPLY IND. TRAIN. BOARD (G.B.).
*LONDON NO.1, 1968-*
*LO/N-1.*

BULLETIN OF THE ENTOMOLOGICAL SOCIETY OF
CANADA.
+ +BULL. ENTOMOL. SOC. CAN.
*OTTAWA 1, 1969-*
*AD/U-1.    GL/U-1.*
*LO/R-5. 2(3), 1970-*
*MA/U-1. 1(2), 1969; 2, 1970; 3(2), 1971.*
*ISSN 0071-0741*

BULLETIN, ENTOMOLOGICAL SOCIETY OF NEW
ZEALAND.
+ +BULL. ENTOMOL. SOC. N.Z.
*NELSON NO.1, 1972-*
*LO/N-2.    LO/N13.*
*OX/U-8. NO.2, 1973-*

BULLETIN OF THE ENTOMOLOGICAL SOCIETY OF
NIGERIA.
+ +BULL. ENTOMOL. SOC. NIGER.
*IBADAN 1, 1967-*
*LO/N-2.*

BULLETIN OF ENVIRONMENTAL EDUCATION.
+ +BULL. ENVIRON. EDUC.
TOWN & COUNTRY PLANNING ASSOCIATION.
*LONDON NO.1, MY 1971-*
*M.*
*CA/U-1.    ED/N-1.    HL/U-1.    SH/U-1.*
*SW/U-1. NO.21, 1973-*
*ISSN 0045-1266*

BULLETIN DE L'ETUDE EN COMMUN DE LA MEDITERRA-
NEE.                                                               000
   SEE: NEWSLETTER OF THE COOPERATIVE INVESTI-
   GATION OF THE MEDITERRANEAN.

BULLETIN, EUGENICS SOCIETY.
+ +BULL. EUGEN. SOC.
*LONDON 1, 1969-*
*HL/U-1.    LO/N-1.    LO/S74.*

BULLETIN, EUROPEAN BANKS' INTERNATIONAL
COMPANY.                                                           000
   SEE: EBIC BULLETIN.

BULLETIN, FACULTY OF AGRICULTURE, UNIVERSITY
OF SHIMANE.
+ +BULL. FAC. AGR. UNIV. SHIMANE.
*MATSUE 1, 1967-*
*CA/U11.*

BULLETIN DE LA FACULTE D'AGRONOMIE, MINISTERE
DE L'EDUCATION NATIONALE (TUNISIA).                                XXX
+ +BULL. FAC. AGRON. MINIST. EDUC. NATL. (TUNIS.)
*TUNIS NO.22, 1969-*
PREV: BULLETIN DE L'ECOLE SUPERIEURE DE
TUNIS FROM NO.1, 1963- 21, 1968.
*XS/R-2.*

BULLETIN OF THE FACULTY OF ARTS, UNIVERSITY OF
BASRA.                                                                          000
   SEE: AL-MIRBAD.

BULLETIN OF THE FACULTY OF GENERAL EDUCATION,
UTSUNOMIYA UNIVERSITY: SECTION 2.                                               000
   SEE: UTSUNOMIYA DAIGAKU KYOYOBU KENKYU HOKOKU:
   DAI 2BU.

BULLETIN OF THE FACULTY OF SCIENCE, UNIVER-
SITY OF RIYAD.
   + +BULL. FAC. SCI. UNIV. RIYAD.
   RIYAD  1, 1969-
   A.
   CA/U-2.    LO/N-2.

BULLETIN, FAR SEAS' FISHERIES RESEARCH LABORA-
TORY.                                                                           000
   SEE:  ENYO SUISAN KENKYUJO KENKYU HOKOKU.

BULLETIN DE LA FEDERATION DES ENTREPRISES DE
BELGIQUE.                                                                       XXX
   + +BULL. FED. ENTREP. BELG.
   BRUSSELS  1/JA 1973-
   PREV: BULLETIN DE LA FEDERATION DES INDUSTRIES
   BELGES FROM 15/M, 1946- D 1972.
   LO/U-3.

BULLETIN DE LA FEDERATION DES INDUSTRIES
BELGES.                                                                         XXX
   SUBS (1973): BULLETIN DE LA FEDERATION DES
   ENTREPRISES DE BELGIQUE.

BULLETIN OF FISHERIES RESEARCH & DEVELOPMENT
AGENGY (KOREA).                                                                 000
   SEE: KUNGNIP SUSAN CHINHUNGWON YONGU POGO.

BULLETIN, GATESHEAD & DISTRICT LOCAL HISTORY
SOCIETY.
   + +BULL. GATESHEAD & DIST. LOCAL HIST. SOC.
   GATESHEAD  NO.1, 1969-
   LD/U-1.    OX/U-1.

BULLETIN, GEOGRAFISCH INSTITUUT, RIJKSUNIV-
ERSITEIT UTRECHT: SERIE II: SOCIALE GEOGRAFIE
ONTWIKKELINGSLANDEN.
   + +BULL. GEOGR. INST. RIJKSUNIV. UTRECHT, II.
   UTRECHT  NO.1, MR 1971-
   LO/S13.

BULLETIN, GEOGRAFISCH INSTITUUT, RIJKSUNIV-
ERSITEIT UTRECHT: SERIE III: HISTORISCHE
GEOGRAFIE.
   + +BULL. GEOGR. INST. RIJKSUNIV. UTRECHT, III.
   UTRECHT  NO.1, OC 1971-
   LO/S13.

BULLETIN, GEOLOGICAL, MINING & METALLURGICAL
SOCIETY OF LIBERIA.
   + +BULL. GEOL. MINING & MET. SOC. LIBERIA.
   MONROVIA  1, 1966-
   LO/N-2.

BULLETIN, GEOLOGICAL SOCIETY OF MALAYSIA.
   + +BULL. GEOL. SOC. MALAYS.
   KESATUAN KAJIBUMI MALAYSIA.
   KUALA LUMPUR  NO.1, 1968-
   CA/U14.    LO/N-2.

BULLETIN, GEOLOGICAL SOCIETY OF NORFOLK.                                        XXX
   + +BULL. GEOL. SOC. NORFOLK.
   NORWICH  NO.16, 1968-
   PREV: PARAMOUDRA CLUB BULLETIN FROM NO.1,
   1953- 15, 1967.
   LO/N-2.

BULLETIN, GEOLOGICAL SURVEY OF FINLAND.                                         XXX
   + +BULL. GEOL. SURV. FINL.
   OTANIEMI  NO..250, 1971-
   PREV: BULLETIN, COMMISSION GEOLOGIQUE DE
   FINLANDE FROM NO.1, 1895- 249, 1971.
   BR/U-1.    GL/U-1.    LO/N13.

BULLETIN, GEOLOGICAL SURVEY OF IRELAND.
   + +BULL. GEOL. SURV. IREL.
   DUBLIN  NO.1, N 1970-
   BH/U-1.    BR/U-3.    CO/U-1.    DB/S-1.    DB/U-2.    ED/N-1.
   LO/N-2.    LO/N-4.

BULLETIN, GEOLOGICAL SURVEY (LIBERIA).
   + +BULL. GEOL. SURV. (LIBERIA).
   MONROVIA  NO.1, 1967-
   LO/N-2.

BULLETIN, GERANIUM SOCIETY.                                                     XXX
   SUBS (1965): BULLETIN, BRITISH PELARGONIUM
   & GERANIUM SOCIETY.

BULLETIN, GLAMORGAN COUNTY NATURALISTS' TRUST.
   + +BULL. GLAMORGAN CTY. NAT. TRUST.
   [SWANSEA]  NO.1, 1962-
   LO/N-2.
   SW/U-1.  NO.10, 1971.

BULLETIN OF GRAIN TECHNOLOGY.
   + +BULL. GRAIN TECHNOL.  [BUGT-A]
   FOODGRAIN TECHNOLOGISTS' RESEARCH ASSOCIATION
   OF INDIA.
   HAPUR  1, 1963-
   Q.
   LO/N14.  3, 1965-
   ISSN 0007-4896

BULLETIN OF THE GROUP FOR THE STUDY OF IRISH
HISTORIC SETTLEMENT.
   + +BULL. GROUP STUD. IR. HIST. SETTLEMENT.
   BELFAST  NO.1, D 1970-
   BL/U-1.    ED/N-1.    LO/U-2.    OX/U-1.

BULLETIN, HIGH COMMISSIONER FOR REFUGEES,
UNITED NATIONS.                                                                 000
   SEE: HCR BULLETIN.

BULLETIN, HISTORICAL METALLURGY GROUP, IRON &
STEEL INSTITUTE.                                                                XXX
   + +BULL. HIST. METALL. GROUP. IRON & STEEL INST.
   LONDON  [1](1), 1963- 7, 1973...
   SUBS: HISTORICAL METALLURGY. VOL. NUMBERING
   COMMENCED WITH 1(9), 1967.
   CA/U-1.    NO/U-1.
   ED/N-1.  3, 1969-                              NW/U-1.  5, 1971-

BULLETIN, HISTORY OF EDUCATION SOCIETY.
   + +BULL. HIST. EDUC. SOC.
   [LEICESTER]  NO.1, 1968-
   ED/N-1.    MA/U-1.    OX/U-1.
   ISSN 0018-2699

BULLETIN OF HYGIENE.                                                            XXX
   SUBS (1968): ABSTRACTS ON HYGIENE.

BULLETIN, INDIAN GEOLOGISTS ASSOCIATION.
   + +BULL. INDIAN GEOL. ASS.
   CHANDIGARH  1, 1968-
   LO/N13.

BULLETIN OF THE INDIAN METEOROLOGICAL SOCIETY.
   SEE: VAYU MANDAL.

BULLETIN, INDIAN NATIONAL SCIENCE ACADEMY.                                      XXX
   + +BULL. INDIAN NATL. SCI. ACAD.
   NEW DELHI  NO.41, 1970-
   PREV: BULLETIN, NATIONAL INSTITUTE OF SCIENCES
   OF INDIA FROM NO.1, 1952- 40, 1969.
   LO/N14.

BULLETIN OF THE INDIAN SOCIETY FOR MALARIA &
OTHER COMMUNICABLE DISEASES.                                                    XXX
   + +BULL. INDIAN SOC. MALARIA & OTHER COMMUN. DIS.
   DELHI  1, MR/JE 1964-
   PREV:  BULLETIN OF THE NATIONAL SOCIETY OF
   INDIA FOR MALARIA & OTHER MOSQUITO-BORNE
   DISEASES FROM 1, JA 1953.
   LO/R-2.

BULLETIN, INDONESIAN SUGAR EXPERIMENT STATION                                   000
   SEE: BULLETIN, BALAI PENJELIDIKAN PERUSAHAAN
   PERKEBUNAN GULA.

BULLETIN, INDUSTRIAL ARCHAEOLOGY GROUP FOR
THE NORTH EAST.
   + +BULL. IND. ARCHAEOL. GROUP N. E.
   BARNARD CASTLE (DURHAM)  1, 1967-
   BN/U-1.    LO/N-4.

BULLETIN OF INDUSTRIAL ARTS INSTITUTE.                                          000
   SEE: SANGYO KOGEI SHIKENJO HOKOKU.

BULLETIN, INDUSTRIAL LAW SOCIETY.                                               XXX
   + +BULL. IND. LAW SOC.
   LONDON  NO.1, JA 1968- 12, 1972.
   SUBS: INDUSTRIAL LAW JOURNAL.
   HL/U-1.    LO/U-2.    OX/U15.
   ISSN 0579-4919

BULLETIN, INDUSTRIAL PRODUCTS RESEARCH INST-
ITUTE.                                                                          000
   SEE: SEIHIN KAGAKU KENKYUJO KENKYU HOKOKU.

BULLETIN D'INFORMATION, ASSOCIATION DES AMIS
D'ANDRE GIDE.
   + +BULL. INF. ASSOC. AMIS ANDRE GIDE.
   PARIS  NO.1, JL 1968-
   CB/U-1.  NO.6, 1970-                      EX/U-1.  NO.4, 1969-
   NW/U-1.  (W. NO.3-4,6)

BULLETIN D'INFORMATION ET DE COORDINATION,
ASSOCIATION INTERNATIONALE DES ETUDES
BYZANTINES.
+ +BULL. INF. & COORD. ASSOC. INT. ETUD.
BYZANTINES.
ATHENS; PARIS 1, 1964-
LO/U19.    OX/U-1.

BULLETIN D'INFORMATION, ECOLE DES SCIENCES DE
LA TERRE, UNIVERSITE DE GENEVE.
+ +BULL. INF. ECOLE SCI. TERRE UNIV. GENEVE.
GENEVA NO.1, 1969-
GL/U-1.    LO/N-2.

BULLETIN D'INFORMATION DE L'INSTITUT D'AMEN-
AGEMENT ET D'URBANISME DE LA REGION PARIS-
IENNE.
+ +BULL. INF. INST. AMENAGEMENT & URBANISME REG.
PARIS.
PARIS NO.1, S 1968-
Q.
CB/U-1.    LO/S13.

BULLETIN D'INFORMATION ET LIAISON.
+ +BULL. INF. LIAISON.
ASSOCIATION INTERNATIONALE D'ETUDE PATRISTIQUES
AMSTERDAM 1, 1968-
CA/U-1.    GL/U-1.    LO/U-1.    OX/U-1.
ISSN 0587-1999

BULLETIN, INSTITUTE OF CORNISH STUDIES.
+ +BULL. INST. CORN. STUD.
REDRUTH NO.1, JE 1972-
ED/N-1.    OX/U-1.

BULLETIN, INSTITUTE OF DEVELOPMENT STUDIES,
UNIVERSITY OF SUSSEX.
+ +BULL. INST. DEVELOP. STUD. UNIV. SUSSEX.
BRIGHTON 1(1), JE 1968-
3A.
LO/R-6.    LO/S74.    LO/U-8.
BT/U-1.  1(3), 1969-           GL/U-1.  2(3), 1970-
LD/U-1.  2(1), 1969-          LO/U-1.  2, 1969-
LO/U-3.  3, OC 1970-       LO/U14.  3, 1970-
OX/U24.  1(3), 1969-
ISSN 0572-5593

BULLETIN DE L'INSTITUT FRANCAIS D'ETUDES
ANDINES.
+ +BULL. INST. FR. ETUD. ANDINES.
LIMA 1, 1972-
LO/N-2.

BULLETIN, INSTITUT INTERNATIONAL D'ADMINIS-
TRATION PUBLIQUE.
+ +BULL. INST. INT. ADM. PUBLIQUE.
PARIS NO.1, 1967-
Q.
MA/U-1.
LO/N17. NO.8, 1968-
LD/U-1. NO.18, 1971-
ISSN 0020-2355

BULLETIN OF THE INSTITUTE OF JEWISH STUDIES.
+ +BULL. INST. JEW. STUD.
UNIVERSITY COLLEGE, LONDON: INSTITUTE OF JEWISH
STUDIES.
LONDON 1, 1973-
ED/N-1.    EX/U-1.    LO/U-1.    LO/U14.    MA/U-1.    OX/U-1.

BULLETIN, INSTITUTE OF MATHEMATICAL STATIST-
ICS.
+ +BULL. INST. MATH. STAT.
EAST LANSING, MICH 1(1), 1972-
AD/U-1.    EX/U-1.    LD/U-1.    LO/N-4.    LO/N13.    LO/U12.
RE/U-1.    SH/U-1.
MA/U-1.  1(2), 1972-

BULLETIN, INSTITUTE OF OCEANOGRAPHY & FISH-
ERIES (CAIRO).
+ +BULL. INST. OCEANOGR. & FISH (CAIRO).
CAIRO 1, 1970-
BN/U-2.    LO/N-2.

BULLETIN OF THE INSTITUTE OF PHYSICS (& THE
PHYSICAL SOCIETY).                                    XXX
SUBS (1968): PHYSICS BULLETIN.

BULLETIN DES INSTITUTS DE RECHERCHE DE L'
UNIVERSITE D'ABIDJAN.                                  XXX
+ +BULL. INST. RECH. UNIV. ABIDJAN.
ABIDJAN NO.2, 1968-
PREV: BULLETIN D'INFORMATION ET DE LIAISON
DES INSTITUTS D'ETHNO-SOCIOLOGIE ET DE GEOG-
RAPHIE TROPICALE, UNIVERSITE D'ABIDJAN FROM
NO.1, 1967.
BH/U-1.

BULLETIN OF THE INSTITUTE FOR RESEARCH IN
PRODUCTIVITY, WASEDA UNIVERSITY.                     000
SEE: WASEDA DAIGAKU SEISAN KENKYUJO KIYO.

BULLETIN, INSTITUTE OF TECHNICAL PUBLICITY &
PUBLICATIONS.                                         XXX
SUBS (1968): COMMUNICATOR OF TECHNICAL INF-
ORMATION.

BULLETIN, INSTITUTE FOR WORKERS' CONTROL.
+ +BULL. INST. WORK. CONTR.
NOTTINGHAM 1(1), 1968-
OX/U-1.

BULLETIN, INTERNATIONAL ASSOCIATION OF ENGIN-
EERING GEOLOGY.
+ +BULL. INT. ASS. ENG. GEOL.
PARIS NO.1, 1970-
SO/U-1.

BULLETIN, INTERNATIONAL ASSOCIATION OF LAW
LIBRARIES.
+ +BULL. INT. ASS. LAW LIBR.
THE HAGUE NO.1, S 1960- 30, 1972.
SUBS: INTERNATIONAL JOURNAL OF LAW LIBRARIES.
OX/U15.
LO/U-3. NO.16, MR 1966-
ISSN 0538-4524

BULLETIN OF THE INTERNATIONAL ASSOCIATION OF
SCIENTIFIC HYDROLOGY.                                 XXX
SUBS (1972): HYDROLOGICAL SCIENCES BULLETIN.

BULLETIN, INTERNATIONAL ASSOCIATION FOR SHELL
& SPATIAL STRUCTURES.
+ +BULL. INT. ASSOC. SHELL & SPAT. STRUCT.
MADRID NO.46, 1971-
PREV: BULLETIN, INTERNATIONAL ASSOCIATION FOR
SHELL STRUCTURES FROM NO.1, 1960- 45, 1971.
LO/N14.

BULLETIN, INTERNATIONAL BUREAU OF EDUCATION.        XXX
SUBS (1971): EDUCATIONAL DOCUMENTATION &
INFORMATION.

BULLETIN OF THE INTERNATIONAL COURT OF
JUSTICE.
+ +BULL. INT. COURT JUSTICE.
THE HAGUE  [NO.1], D 1969-
LO/S14.

BULLETIN, INTERNATIONAL FIELD YEAR FOR THE
GREAT LAKES.
INTERNATIONAL HYDROLOGICAL DECADE: UNITED
STATES NATIONAL COMMITTEE.
ROCKVILLE, MD. 1, 1972-
RESEARCH PROGRAM ORGANIZED BY THE UNITED
STATES & CANADIAN NATIONAL COMMITTEES FOR THE
INTERNATIONAL HYDROLOGICAL DECADE AT THE
CANADA CENTRE FOR INLAND WATERS & THE NATIONAL
OCEANIC & ATMOSPHERIC ADMINISTRATION.
BL/U-1.

BULLETIN, INTERNATIONAL INSTITUTE FOR LABOUR
STUDIES.
+ +BULL. INT. INST. LABOUR STUD.
GENEVA  1, OC 1966-
MON.
CC/U-1.    CV/U-1.    HL/U-1.    LO/N-1.    LO/N-3.    LO/S14.
LO/U-3. *    OX/U-1.    OX/U16.    RE/U-1.    XY/N-1.
ISSN 0435-2874

BULLETIN, INTERNATIONAL INSTITUTE OF
SEISMOLOGY & EARTHQUAKE ENGINEERING.
+ +BULL. INT. INST. SEISMOL. & EARTHQUAKE ENG.
TOKYO 1, 1964-
LO/N14.    XN/S-1.
ISSN 0074-655X

BULLETIN, INTERNATIONAL ORGANIZATION FOR
SEPTUAGINT & COGNATE STUDIES.
+ +BULL. INT. ORGAN. SEPTUAGINT & COGN. STUD.
PRINCETON, N.J. NO.1, 1968-
LO/U11.
BN/U-1. NO.6, FALL 1973-

BULLETIN, INTERNATIONAL PEAT SOCIETY.
+ +BULL. INT. PEAT SOC.
HELSINKI 1, 1970-
BL/U-1.    LO/N14.

BULLETIN, INTERNATIONAL RAILWAY CONGRESS
ASSOCIATION. ENGL. ED.                                XXX
SUBS (1970) PART OF: RAIL INTERNATIONAL.

BULLETIN OF THE INTERNATIONAL SOCIAL SECURITY
ASSOCIATION.                                                    XXX
++BULL. INT. SOC. SECUR. AS.
MONTREAL 1, 1948-19, 1966...
SUBS: INTERNATIONAL SOCIAL SECURITY REVIEW.
XY/N-1.**
BH/U-1. 12, 1959-            ED/U-1. 15, 1962-
LO/M10. 3, 1950-            MA/U-1. 8(7), 1955-
SW/U-1. 18, 1965-

BULLETIN, INTERNATIONAL SOCIETY OF ICHTHY-
OLOGY & HYDROBIOLOGY.
++BULL. INT. SOC. ICHTHYOL. & HYDROBIOL.
KANPUR NO.1, 1970-
LO/N-2.

BULLETIN, INTERNATIONAL UNION OF RAILWAYS.
ENGL. ED.                                                       XXX
SUBS (1970) PART OF: RAIL INTERNATIONAL.

BULLETIN, INTERNATIONAL WILDFOWL RESEARCH
BUREAU.                                                         XXX
++BULL. INT. WILDFOWL RES. BUR.
SLIMBRIDGE NO.27/28, JL/D 1969- 32, D 1971 ..
PREV: NEWSLETTER, INTERNATIONAL WILDFOWL
RESEARCH BUREAU FROM NO.1, 1955- 25/26, 1969.
SUBS: BULLETIN, INTERNATIONAL WATERFOWL
RESEARCH BUREAU.
LO/N-2.     LO/N13.     OX/U-8.

BULLETIN OF THE IRANIAN CULTURE FOUNDATION. =
NASHRIYAH-I BUNYAD-I FARHANG-I IRAN.
++BULL. IRAN. CULT. FOUND.
IRANIAN CULTURE FOUNDATION.
TEHERAN 1(1), 1969-
LO/U14.

BULLETIN, ISHIKAWA PREFECTURE COLLEGE OF
AGRICULTURE.                                                    000
SEE: ISHIKAWA-KEN NOGYO TANKI DAIGAKU KENKU
HOKOKU.

BULLETIN, ISRAEL EXPLORATION SOCIETY.                           XXX
SUBS (1968): QADMONIOT QUARTERLY FOR THE
ANTIQUITIES OF ERETZ-ISRAEL & BIBLICAL LANDS.

BULLETIN, I.T.D.G.                                              000
SEE: I.T.D.G. BULLETIN.

BULLETIN, JAPAN ENTOMOLOGICAL ACADEMY.
++BULL. JAP. ENTOMOL. ACAD.
NAGOYA 1, JA 1964-
LO/N-2.
ISSN 0448-8628

BULLETIN OF THE JAPAN SEA RESEARCH INSTITUTE.                   000
SEE: NIHON KAI-IKI KENKYUJO HOKOKU.

BULLETIN OF JSAE.
++BULL. JSAE. (JAP. SOC. AUTO. ENG.).
JIDOSHA GIJUTSUKAI.
TOKYO NO.1, 1969-
BODY NAME IN ENGL.: SOCIETY OF AUTOMOTIVE
ENGINEERS OF JAPAN.
LO/N-4.     LO/N14.     SO/U-1.

BULLETIN, KANAGAWA PREFECTURAL MUSEUM:
NATURAL SCIENCE.                                                000
SEE: KANAGAWA KENRITSU HAKUBUTSUKAN KENKYU
HOKOKU: SHIZEN KAGAKU.

BULLETIN OF KUSHIRO WOMEN'S JUNIOR COLLEGE.                     000
SEE: KUSHIRO JOSHI TANKI DAIGAKU KIYO.

BULLETIN OF THE KYOTO AGRICULTURAL EXPERIMENT
STATION.                                                        000
SEE: KYOTO FURITSU NOGYO SHIKENJO KENKYU
HOKOKU.

BULLETIN DE LIAISON, CENTRE D'ETUDES DES PROB-
LEMES DE LA MER.
++BULL. LIAISON CENT. ETUD. PROBL. MER.
RENNES 1, 1966-
NO/U-1.

BULLETIN DE LIAISON POUR LES ETUDES CHINOISES
EN EUROPE.
++BULL. LIAISON ETUD. CHIN. EUR.
ECOLE PRATIQUE DES HAUTES ETUDES (PARIS):
CENTRE DE DOCUMENTATION SUR L'EXTREME-ORIENT.
PARIS NO.1, 1968-
LO/N17.     LO/U14.     OX/U-1.
ISSN 0525-4361

BULLETIN, LIGUE DES BIBLIOTHEQUES EUROPEENNES
DE RECHERCHE.
++BULL. LIGUE BIBL. EUR. RECH.
LAUSANNE; BIRMINGHAM NO.1, 1972-
ENGL. & FR.
BN/U-1.     ED/N-1.     LD/U-1.     LO/N-1.     LO/N-4.     LO/U-1.
LO/U-3.     LO/U11.     NO/U-1.     NW/U-1.     OX/U-1.

BULLETIN OF THE LONDON MATHEMATICAL SOCIETY.
++BULL. LOND. MATH. SOC.
LONDON MATHEMATICAL SOCIETY.
LONDON 1(1), MR 1969-
FIRST ISSUE ACTUALLY NUMBERED: VOL.1, PART 1,
NO.1.
BH/U-1.     BL/U-1.     BR/U-3.     CB/U-1.     ED/N-1.     GL/U-1.
GL/U-2.     LO/N-1.     LO/N-4.     LO/N14.     LO/U-1.     LO/U-4.
LO/U11.     LO/U12.     LO/U13.     LV/U-1.     NW/U-1.
SH/U-1.     SO/U-1.     XS/R10.
ISSN 0024-6093

BULLETIN, LOS ANGELES COUNTY MUSEUM OF
NATURAL HISTORY: SCIENCE.
++BULL. LOS ANGELES COUNTY MUS. NAT. HIST. SCI.
LOS ANGELES NO.1, 1965-
LO/N13.
OX/U-8. NO.7, 1970-
ISSN 0076-0935

BULLETIN OF MARXIST STUDIES.                                    XXX
++BULL. MARXIST STUD.
RUGELEY, STAFFS. 1(1), 1968- 1(4), 1969 ...
Q. SUBS: MARXIST STUDIES.
ED/N-1. 1(4), 1969-            OX/U-1. 1(4), 1969-

BULLETIN, MARYLAND HERPETOLOGICAL SOCIETY.
++BULL. MD. HERPETOL. SOC.
[BALTIMORE] 1, 1965-
LO/N-2.
ISSN 0025-4231

BULLETIN OF MEDIEVAL CANON LAW: NS.
++BULL. MEDIEVAL CANON LAW, NS.
BERKELEY, CALIF. 1, 1971-
MA/U-1.

BULLETIN MENSUEL, ASSOCIATION BELGE DE MALAC-
OLOGIE, CONCHYLIOLOGIE ET PALEONTOLOGIE.
++BULL. MENS. ASS. BELGE MALACOL. CONCHYLIOL.
& PALEONTOL.
BRUSSELS NO.1, 1968-
LO/N-2.

BULLETIN, MENTAL HEALTH ASSOCIATION OF IRE-
LAND.
++BULL. MENT. HEALTH ASS. IR.
DUBLIN 1, 1969-
DB/U-2.

BULLETIN, METHODIST CHURCH MUSIC SOCIETY.
++BULL. METHODIST CHURCH MUSIC SOC.
AUDLEM, CHESHIRE 1(1), 1970-
M.
OX/U-1.

BULLETIN DE METROLOGIE.                                         XXX
++BULL. METROL.
(BELGIUM) SERVICE DE LA METROLOGIE.
BRUSSELS NO.370, 1971-
PREV: BULLETIN BELGE DE METROLOGIE FROM NO.
188, 1956- 369, 1971.
LO/N14.

BULLETIN, MICROBIOLOGY RESEARCH GROUP, SOUTH
AFRICAN COUNCIL FOR INDUSTRIAL RESEARCH.
++BULL. MICROBIOL. RES. GROUP S. AFR. COUNC.
SCI. & IND. RES.
PRETORIA 1, 1968-
LO/N-2.

BULLETIN, MINERALOGICAL SOCIETY OF GREAT
BRITAIN & IRELAND.                                              XXX
++BULL. MINERAL. SOC. G.B. & IR.
LONDON 1, F 1969-
PREV: NOTICES, MINERALOGICAL SOCIETY OF
GREAT BRITAIN & IRELAND FROM NO.1, 1877-
155, D 1968.
CA/U-1.     LO/N-4.     LV/U-1.     SH/U-1.
ED/N-1. NO.24, S 1974-

BULLETIN OF THE MORIOKA TOBACCO EXPERIMENT
STATION.
++BULL. MORIOKA TOB. EXP. STA.
JAPAN MONOPOLY CORPORATION: MORIOKA TOBACCO
EXPERIMENT STATION.
MORIOKA NO.1, 1964-
ENGL. ABSTR.
XN/S-1.

BULLETIN DU MUSEE NATIONAL DE VARSOVIE.                    000
  SEE: BULLETIN, MUZEUM NARODOWE W WARSZAWIE.

BULLETIN, MUZEUM NARODOWE W WARSZAWIE.
  + +BULL. MUZ. NAR. WARSZ.
  WARSAW  1(1/2), 1960-
  Q. VARIOUS LANGUAGES.
  ED/N-1.     OX/U-1.
  ISSN 0027-3791

BULLETIN OF THE NANSEI REGIONAL FISHERIES
RESEARCH LABORATORY.                                       000
  SEE: NANSEI KAIKU SUISAN KENKYUJO KENKYU
  HOKOKU.

BULLETIN OF THE NATIONAL ASSOCIATION OF
CLINICAL TUTORS.
  + +BULL. NATL. ASSOC. CLIN. TUT.
  [UPDATE PUBL. LTD.]
  LONDON  1(1), JA 1972-
  ED/N-1.

BULLETIN, NATIONAL AWAMI PARTY OF BANGLA DESH
(IN GREAT BRITAIN).
  + +BULL. NATL. AWAMI PARTY BANGLA DESH (GB).
  LONDON  NO.1, 1972-
  ED/N-1.     OX/U-1.

BULLETIN OF THE NATIONAL INSPECTION LABORATORY
FOR FEEDS & FERTILIZER (JAPAN).                            000
  SEE: TOKYO HISHIRYO KENSAJO SHIRYO KENKYU
  HOKOKU.

BULLETIN, NATIONAL INSTITUTE FOR HIGHER
EDUCATION (EIRE).
  + +BULL. NATL. INST. HIGHER EDUC. (EIRE).
  LIMERICK  1, 1972-
  DB/U-2.
  CA/U-1.  2, 1973-          ED/N-1.  2, 1973-

BULLETIN, NATIONAL INSTITUTE OF SCIENCES OF
INDIA.                                                     XXX
  SUBS (1970): BULLETIN, INDIAN NATIONAL SCI-
  ENCE ACADEMY.

BULLETIN OF THE NATIONAL MUSEUM OF WALES.                  000
  SEE: AMGUEDDFA.  BULLETIN OF THE NATIONAL
  MUSEUM OF WALES

BULLETIN, NATIONAL PORTS COUNCIL (GB).
  + +BULL. NATL. PORTS COUNC. (GB).
  LONDON  NO.1, 1972-
  LO/N-1.     LO/U-3.     SO/U-1.

BULLETIN, NATIONAL RESEARCH INSTITUTE FOR
POLLUTION & RESOURCES (JAPAN).                             000
  SEE: KOGAI SHIGEN KENKYUJO IHO.

BULLETIN OF THE NATIONAL SOCIETY OF INDIA FOR
MALARIA & OTHER MOSQUITO-BORNE DISEASES.                   XXX
  SUBS (1964): BULLETIN OF THE INDIAN SOCIETY
  FOR MALARIA & OTHER COMMUNICABLE DISEASES.

BULLETIN, NATURE CONSERVATION BRANCH (SOUTH
AFRICA).
  + +BULL. NAT. CONSERV. BRANCH (S. AFR.).
  PRETORIA  1, 1968-
  LO/N-2.

BULLETIN, NEW MILLS NATURAL HISTORY SOCIETY.
  + +BULL. NEW MILLS NAT. HIST. SOC.
  NEW MILLS  NO.1, 1971-
  LO/N-2.

BULLETIN, NEW YORK C.S. LEWIS SOCIETY.
  + +BULL. N.Y. C.S. LEWIS SOC.
  NEW YORK  NO.1, 1969-
  OX/U-1.

BULLETIN, NEW YORK STATE FLOWER GROWERS, INC.            XXX
  SUBS (1970): NYSFI BULLETIN.

BULLETIN OF THE NIIGATA UNIVERSITY FORESTS.               000
  SEE: NIIGATA DAIGAKU NOGAKUBU ENSHURIN
  HOKOKU.

BULLETIN, NORTH OF SCOTLAND COLLEGE OF AGRI-
CULTURE.
  + +BULL. N. SCOTL. COLL. AGR.
  ABERDEEN  NO.1, 1970-
  BL/U-1.     CA/U-1.     ED/N-1.

BULLETIN OF THE NORTHAMPTONSHIRE FEDERATION
OF ARCHAEOLOGICAL SOCIETIES.
  + +BULL. NORTHAMPS. FED. ARCHAEOL. SOC.
  LEICESTER  NO.1, D 1966-
  NO/U-1.  NO.2, 1967-          OX/U-2.  1967-

BULLETIN, NORTHAMPTONSHIRE NATURALISTS TRUST.
  + +BULL. NORTHAMPS. NATUR. TRUST.
  NORTHAMPTON  NO.1, OC 1967-
  BL/U-1.     ED/N-1.     LO/N13.     LO/R-5.     OX/U-8.

BULLETIN OF THE OCEAN RESEARCH INSTITUTE,
UNIVERSITY OF TOKYO.
  + +BULL. OCEAN RES. INST. UNIV. TOKYO.
  TOKYO DAIGAKU: OCEAN RESEARCH INSTITUTE.
  TOKYO  NO.1, 1967-
  ENGL.
  BN/U-1.     LO/N-2.     SO/U-1.     SW/U-1.
  ISSN 0564-6898

BULLETIN, OIL & NATURAL GAS COMMISSION(INDIA).
  + +BULL. OIL. & NATUR. GAS COMM. (INDIA).
  DEHRA DUN  1, 1964-
  LO/N-2.
  ISSN 0537-0094

BULLETIN, ONTARIO COLLEGE OF PHARMACY.                    XXX
  + +BULL. ONT. COLL. PHARM.  [BUON-A]
  TORONTO  1, 1952- 21(4), 1972.//
  XS/N-1.**
  LO/N14.  9, 1960-
  ISSN 0030-2856

BULLETIN, ORKNEY FIELD CLUB.
  + +BULL. ORKNEY FIELD CLUB.
  KIRKWALL  NO.1, 1968-
  LO/N-2.

BULLETIN ZUR OSTRECHTSFORSCHUNG IN DEN
LANDERN DES EUROPARATES.
  + +BULL. OSTRECHTSFORSCH. LANDERN EUR.
  DEUTSCHE GESELLSCHAFT FUR OSTEUROPAKUNDE.
  STUTTGART  1, JE 1968-
  2/A.
  LO/U-2.     OX/U15.

BULLETIN (OF THE) OTAGO MUSEUM.                            000
  SEE: OTAGO MUSEUM BULLETIN.

BULLETIN, OXFORDSHIRE BRANCH, COUNCIL FOR THE
PRESERVATION OF RURAL ENGLAND.
  + +BULL. OXF. BRA. COUNC. PRESERV. RUR. ENGL.
  OXFORD  1, 1966-
  OX/U-1.

BULLETIN OF THE PACIFIC ORCHID SOCIETY OF
HAWAII.                                                    XXX
  SUBS (1972): HAWAII ORCHID JOURNAL.

BULLETIN OF PEACE PROPOSALS.
  + +BULL. PEACE PROPOS.
  INTERNATIONAL PEACE RESEARCH INSTITUTE.
  OSLO  1(1), 1970-
  HL/U-1.     LO/N-1.     LO/N17.     LO/S74.     LO/U-2.     LO/U-3.
  OX/U-1.     SW/U-1.
  ISSN 0007-5035

BULLETIN PERIODIQUE, COMITE FRANCE-AMERIQUE
LATINE.
  + +BULL. PERIOD. COM. FR.-AM. LAT.
  PARIS  NO.1, 1971-
  OX/U-1.

BULLETIN, PSYCHONOMIC SOCIETY.                            XXX
  + +BULL. PSYCHONOMIC SOC.
  GOLETA, CALIF.  1, 1973-
  MON. PREV. PART OF: PSYCHONOMIC SCIENCE FROM
  1, 1964- 29(6), JA 1973.
  BN/U-1.     GL/U-1.     GL/U-2.     LD/U-1.     MA/U-1.     NW/U-1.
  SA/U-1.     SH/U-1.     SO/U-1.
  ISSN 0090-5054

BULLETIN OF RESEARCH INSTITUTE FOR POLYMERS &
TEXTILES (JAPAN).                                          000
  SEE: SENI KOBUNSHI ZAIRYO KENKYUJO KENKYU
  HOKOKU.

BULLETIN OF RESEARCH, OTANI COLLEGE OF TECHNOL-
OGY OF TOYAMA.                                             000
  SEE: TOYAMA KENRITSU OTANI GIJUTSU TANKI
  DAIGAKU KENKYU HOKOKU.

BULLETIN DE LA RILEM.                                      000
  SEE (PART OF): MATERIALS & STRUCTURES:
  TESTING & RESEARCH.

BULLETIN OF THE ROBERT OWEN BI-CENTENARY
ASSOCIATION.
  + +BULL. ROBERT OWEN BI-CENTEN. ASSOC.
  LONDON  NO.1, MY 1970-
  OX/U-1.

BULLETINS, ROYAL OBSERVATORY, GREENWICH:
SERIES D.                                                        XXX
  SUBS (1969) PART OF: GEOMAGNETIC BULLETINS.

BULLETIN, SADDLEWORTH HISTORICAL SOCIETY.
++BULL. SADDLEWORTH HIST. SOC.
  UPPERMILL 1(1), MR 1971-
  LO/N-1.
  MA/P-1.

BULLETIN OF THE SCHOOL OF EDUCATION, INDIANA
UNIVERSITY.                                                      XXX
  SUBS (1970): VIEWPOINTS.

BULLETIN, SCOTTISH BRANCH, GREAT BRITAIN -
U.S.S.R. ASSOCIATION.
++BULL. SCOTT. BR. G.B. - U.S.S.R. ASS.
  GREAT BRITAIN - U.S.S.R. ASSOCIATION: SCOTTISH
  BRANCH.
  EDINBURGH NO.1, OC 1968-
  ED/N-1.

BULLETIN OF THE SCOTTISH GEORGIAN SOCIETY.
++BULL. SCOTT. GEORGIAN SOC.
  EDINBURGH 1, 1972-
  AD/U-1.    CA/U-1.    ED/N-1.    LO/N-1.    MA/P-1.

BULLETIN OF THE SCOTTISH INSTITUTE OF MISS-
IONARY STUDIES.
++BULL. SCOTT. INST. MISSION. STUD.
  ABERDEEN 1, JE 1967-
  ED/N-1.    GL/U-1.    LO/U19.
  ISSN 0048-9778

BULLETIN OF THE SEIKEI UNIVERSITY.                              000
  SEE: SEIKEI DAIGAKU KENKYU HOKOKU.

BULLETIN SERVICE, NATIONAL INSTITUTE OF DRY-
CLEANING: FABRICS-FASHIONS.                                     XXX
  SUBS (1972): IFI BULLETIN SERVICE: FABRICS-
  FASHIONS BULLETIN.

BULLETIN SERVICE, NATIONAL INSTITUTE OF DRY-
CLEANING: PRACTICAL OPERATING TIPS.                             XXX
  SUBS (1972): IFI BULLETIN SERVICE: PRACT-
  ICAL OPERATING TIPS.

BULLETIN SERVICE, NATIONAL INSTITUTE OF DRY-
CLEANING: TECHNICAL.                                            XXX
  SUBS (1972): IFI BULLETIN SERVICE: TECH-
  NICAL BULLETIN.

BULLETIN OF THE SHIZUOKA PREFECTURE FORESTRY
EXPERIMENT STATION.                                             000
  SEE: SHIZUOKA-KEN RINGYO SHIKENJO KENKYU
  HOKOKU.

BULLETIN, SHROPSHIRE CONSERVATION TRUST.
++BULL. SHROPSHIRE CONSERV. TRUST.
  SHREWSBURY NO.1, 1963-
  LO/N-2.

BULLETIN FOR SOCIALIST SELF-MANAGEMENT.
++BULL. SOC. SELF-MANAGE.
  [BMS PUBL.]
  LONDON NO.1, S 1972-
  ED/N-1.

BULLETIN DE LA SOCIETE DES AMIS DES SCIENCES
ET DES LETTRES DE POZNAN, SER.C - MEDECINE.                     XXX
  SUBS (1969): ANNALS OF IMMUNOLOGY.

BULLETIN, SOCIETE DE CHIMIE BIOLOGIQUE.                         XXX
  SUBS (1971): BIOCHIMIE.

BULLETIN, SOCIETE D'ECOLOGIE (FRANCE).
++BULL. SOC. ECOL. (FR.).
  PARIS 1, 1969-
  LO/N-2.    LO/R-5.

BULLETIN, SOCIETE DES ETUDES RENANIENNES.
++BULL. SOC. ETUD. RENANIENNES.
  PARIS NO.1, 1970-
  LO/N-1.

BULLETIN, SOCIETE GEOGRAPHIQUE DE LIEGE.
++BULL. SOC. GEOGR. LIEGE.
  LIEGE NO.1, 1965-
  SO/U-1.
  ISSN 0583-8622

BULLETIN DE LA SOCIETE INTERNATIONALE DE
CRIMINOLOGIE.                                                   XXX
  SUBS (1962): ANNALES INTERNATIONALES DE
  CRIMINOLOGIE.

BULLETIN DE LA SOCIETE JULES VERNE: NS.
++BULL. SOC. JULES VERNE, NS.
  PARIS NO.1, JA 1967-
  PREV. SERIES FROM 1(1), N 1935- 3(13), D 1938.
  LO/N-1.
  CB/U-1. NO.9, 1969-

BULLETIN, SOCIETE LINNEENNE DE BORDEAUX.
++BULL. SOC. LINN. BORDEAUX.
  BORDEAUX 1, 1971-
  LO/N-2.

BULLETIN, SOCIETE DE PHARMACIE DE NANCY.                        XXX
  SUBS (1973): SCIENCES PHARMACEUTIQUES ET
  BIOLOGIQUES DE LORRAINE.

BULLETIN DE LA SOCIETE ROUMAINE DE LINGUIS-
TIQUE ROMANE.
++BULL. SOC. ROUM. LING. ROMANE.
  BUCHAREST 1, 1964-
  LO/U-2. 4, 1967.
  ISSN 0583-8800

BULLETIN, SOCIETY OF UNIVERSITY CARTOGRAPHERS.
++BULL. SOC. UNIV. CARTOGR.
  LIVERPOOL NO.1, D 1966-
  2/A.
  ED/N-1.
  SH/U-1. D 1970-
  ISSN 0036-1984

BULLETIN, SOIL SURVEY OF SCOTLAND.
++BULL. SOIL SURV. SCOTL.
  MACAULEY INSTITUTE FOR SOIL RESEARCH.
  ABERDEEN NO.1, 1969-
  DN/U-1.    GL/U-1.    GL/U-2.    LO/N13.    OX/U-8.

BULLETIN, SOUTH AFRICA WOOL TEXTILE RESEARCH              000
INSTITUTE.
  SEE: SAWTRI BULLETIN.

BULLETIN ON SOVIET & EAST EUROPEAN JEWISH
AFFAIRS.                                                         XXX
++BULL. SOV. & E. EUROP. JEW. AFF.
  INSTITUTE OF JEWISH AFFAIRS.
  LONDON NO.1, 1968- 6, D 1970.
  TITLE VARIES: NO.1-2 AS BULLETIN ON SOVIET
  JEWISH AFFAIRS. SUBS: SOVIET JEWISH AFFAIRS.
  LO/U-3.    SH/U-1.    SO/U-1.    SW/U-1.
  OX/U-1. 5, 1970-
  ISSN 0525-1559

BULLETIN DE STATISTIQUES DE SANTE ET DE
SECURITE SOCIALE.
++BULL. STAT. SANTE & SECUR. SOC.
  (FRANCE) MINISTERE DE LA SANTE PUBLIQUE ET DE
  SECURITE SOCIALE.
  PARIS NO.1, JA/F 1972-
  LO/N-1.

BULLETIN, SUGADAIRA BIOLOGICAL LABORATORY,
TOKYO UNIVERSITY OF EDUCATION.
++BULL. SUGADAIRA BIOL. LAB. TOKYO UNIV. EDUC.
  SUGADAIRA 1, 1967-
  ED/S-2.    LO/N-2.
  LO/U-2. NO.4, 1971-

BULLETIN TECHNIQUE, INSTITUT NATIONAL DES
INDUSTRIES EXTRACTIVES (BELGIUM): SECURITE ET
SALUBRITE.
++BULL. TECH. INST. NATL. IND. EXTR. (BELG.),
  SECUR. & SALUBRITE.
  LIEGE NO.1, 1970-
  DUTCH, ENGL., FR. & GER. SUMM.
  LO/N14.

BULLETIN, TEXAS ORNITHOLOGICAL SOCIETY.
++BULL. TEX. ORNITHOL. SOC.
  DALLAS 1, 1967-
  LO/N-2.    LO/N13.
  ISSN 0040-4543

BULLETIN OF THE TEXTILE RESEARCH INSTITUTE
(JAPAN).                                                         000
  SEE: SENI KOGYO SHIKENJO KENKYU HOKOKU.

BULLETIN TRIMESTRIEL D'INFORMATION, CENTRE
D'ETUDES ET DE DOCUMENTATION EUROPEENNES
(MONTREAL).
++BULL. TRIM. INF. CENT. ETUD. & DOC. EUR.
  (MONTREAL).
  MONTREAL 1, 1968-
  BH/U-1.

BULLETIN, UNIVERSITE D'ABIDJAN.
++BULL. UNIV. ABIDJAN.
  ABIDJAN 1, 1968-
  OX/U-1.

**BULLETIN OF THE UNIVERSITY OF LONDON.**                    XXX
++BULL. UNIV. LOND.
LONDON NO.1, OC 1971-
PREV: GAZETTE, UNIVERSITY ... FROM N 1901- JL
1971.
ED/N-1.    LO/M-3.    LO/U-1.    LO/U-3.    LO/U12.

**BULLETIN OF THE UTSUNOMIYA UNIVERSITY FORESTS**           000
SEE: UTSUNOMIYA DAIGAKU NOGAKUBU ENSHURIN
HOKOKU.

**BULLETIN, WELSH HYMN SOCIETY.**                           000
SEE: BWELTIN, CYMDEITHAS EMYNAU CYMRU.

**BULLETIN, WILDLIFE DISEASE ASSOCIATION.**                 XXX
++BULL. WILDL. DIS. ASS.
CHICAGO 1, 1965- 5, 1969 ...
PREV: NEWSLETTER, WILDLIFE ... FROM NO.1-39,
1964. SUBS: JOURNAL OF WILDLIFE DISEASES.
LO/N-2.
LO/N13. 1(2), 1965- 5, 1969.

**BUMP.**
UNIVERSITY OF EDINBURGH: STUDENT PUBLICATIONS
BOARD.
EDINBURGH NO.1, 1972-
ED/N-1.    OX/U-1.

**BURIED HISTORY. A QUARTERLY JOURNAL OF BIB-
LICAL ARCHAEOLOGY.**
++BURIED HIST.
AUSTRALIAN INSTITUTE OF ARCHAEOLOGY.
MELBOURNE NO.1, MR 1964-
CA/S-1.
ISSN 0007-6260

**BURISA NEWSLETTER.**
++BURISA NEWSL.
BRITISH URBAN & REGIONAL INFORMATION SYSTEMS
ASSOCIATION.
LIVERPOOL NO.1, OC 1972-
6/A.
CA/U-1.    ED/N-1.    LO/U-3.    OX/U-1.
GL/U-2. NO.2, 1972-          SH/U-1. NO.8, 1973-

**BURKE NEWSLETTER.**                                       XXX
SUBS (1967): STUDIES IN BURKE & HIS TIME.

**BURMESE ART NEWSLETTER.**
++BURMESE ART NEWSL.
DENISON UNIVERSITY: DEPARTMENT OF VISUAL ARTS.
GRANVILLE, OHIO NO.1, 1968-
LO/U14.

**BUSARA.**                                                 XXX
UNIVERSITY COLLEGE, NAIROBI: DEPARTMENT OF
ENGLISH.
[EAST AFRICAN PUBL. HO.]
NAIROBI 1(1), 1968-
PREV: NEXUS FROM 1, 1966- 2(4), 1968.
BT/U-1.    LO/U14.
CA/U-1. 3(4), 1971-
ISSN 0007-6376

**BUSINESS. THE MANAGEMENT JOURNAL.**                       XXX
SUBS (1967): BUSINESS MANAGEMENT (LONDON).

**BUSINESS EQUIPMENT GUIDE.**                               XXX
++BUS. EQUIP. GUIDE.
[BUSINESS BOOKS LTD.]
CROYDON NO.16, 1971-
PREV: BUSINESS EQUIPMENT BUYERS' GUIDE FROM
NO.1, 1962- 15, 1970.
ED/N-1.    HL/U-1.    SH/C-5.    XS/C-2.
ISSN 0007-6716

**BUSINESS MANAGEMENT (LONDON).**                           XXX
++BUS. MANAGE.
[BUSINESS PUBL. LTD.]
LONDON 97(3), MR 1967- 100(9), S 1970.
MON. PREV: BUSINESS. THE MANAGEMENT JOURNAL
FROM 53(3), 1928- 97(2), F 1967.
SUBS: INDUSTRIAL MANAGEMENT.
BH/P-1.    BH/U-1.    CB/U-1.    GL/U-2.    HL/U-1.    MA/U-4.
SH/C-5. 100, 1970-

**BUSINESS MONITOR; CIVIL AVIATION SERIES.**
++BUS. MONIT., CIVIL AVIAT. SER.
(GREAT BRITAIN) BOARD OF TRADE.
LONDON JA 1968-
COMPRISES VARIOUS SUBSERIES: CA 1, AIRPORT
ACTIVITY (Q); CA 2, AIR PASSENGERS (Q); CA 3,
AIR FREIGHT & MAIL (Q); CA 4, AIRLINES (M);
CA 5, AIRLINES (Q).
LO/N-3.    LO/U-3.
LO/N-1. CA8, 1972-
GL/U-1. CA1, 1969- CA8, 1972.

**BUSINESS SYSTEMS.***                                      
++BUS. SYST.
LONDON. 1965-
PREV– SCOPE BUSINESS SYSTEMS & EQUIPMENT.
ABSORBED: SCOPE. TITLE REDUCED FROM
BUSINESS SYSTEMS & EQUIPMENT FROM S 1970.
CA/U-1.    ED/N-1.    ED/N-1.    LO/M27.    LO/N-1.
LO/N14.*    OX/U-1.    XY/N-1.
DB/U-1. OC 1964- AP 1966.
MA/P-1. (THREE YEAR FILE)

**BWELTIN, CYMDEITHAS EMYNAU CYMRU.**
[LLANDYBIE] 1, 1968-
CR/N-1.

**BXL CROSSLINK.**
BAKELITE XYLONITE LTD.
LONDON 1(1), 1971-
OX/U-1.

**BYDGOSTIANA.**
BYDGOSKIE TOWARZYSTWO NAUKOWE.
BYDGOSZCZ NR.1, MY 1963-
OX/U-1.
ISSN 0525-3217

**BYGGET MED GOLVET I CENTRUM.**
[AB CASCO]
STOCKHOLM 1, 1967-
LO/N14.

**BYGGFORSK INFORMERER OM BYGGSKADER.**
++BYGGFORSK INF. BYGGSKADER.
NORGES BYGGFORSKNINGSINSTITUTT.
OSLO 1, 1971-
LO/N14.

**BYGGREFERAT.**                                            XXX
INSTITUTET FOR BYGGDOKUMENTATION.
STOCKHOLM 1, 1972-
PREV: NORDISKT ARTIKELINDEX FOR BYGG FROM
4(3-12), 1971.
LO/N14.

**BYRON JOURNAL.**
++BYRON J.
BYRON SOCIETY.
LONDON NO.1, 1973-
ED/N-1.    LO/U-1.    OX/U-1.    SA/U-1.

**BYZANTINA (THESSALONIKI).**
THESSALONIKI 1, 1969-
LO/U17.    OX/U-1.

**BYZANTINA NEERLANDICA: SERIES A.**
++BYZANTINA NEER., A.
[BRILL]
LEYDEN 1, 1969-
HL/U-1.
ISSN 0525-4507

**BYZANTINA VINDOBONENSIA.**
++BYZANT. VINDOBON.
UNIVERSITAT WIEN.
GRAZ &C BD.1, 1966-
'HRSG. VOM KUNSTHISTORISCHEN INSTITUT UND DEM
INSTITUT FUR BYZANTINISTIK DER UNIVERSITAT
WIEN'.
OX/U-1.
ISSN 0525-3292

**CABLE TELEVISION ENGINEERING.**                           XXX
++CABLE TELEV. ENG.
SOCIETY OF CABLE TELEVISION ENGINEERS.           XXX
[SOLIHULL] 10, JA 1973-
PREV: RELAY ENGINEER FROM 9(1), JA 1971-
9(4), JE 1972 ...
ED/N-1.    LO/N14.

**CACL.**                                                   XXX
ROYAL UNITED SERVICE INSTITUTION: LIBRARY.
LONDON 1, 1970- 2, 1971. //
S/T: A BI-MONTHLY INDEX TO SIGNIFICANT ART-
ICLES IN THE FIELDS OF MILITARY SCIENCE & IN-
TERNATIONAL AFFAIRS IN PERIODICALS HELD IN ...
SO/U-1.

**CACOPHONY.**
BROMSGROVE, WORCS. 1, JE 1967-
ED/N-1. 1967-                    LO/U-2. [2], 1967-
ISSN 0574-9921

**CACTUS.**
PARIS NO.1, 1946- 88, 1967.//
LO/N14. 80, 1964- 88, 1967.

**CADERNOS DE GEOCIENCIAS, INSTITUTO DE GEOCIEN-
CIAS, UNIVERSIDADE CATOLICA DE PERNAMBUCO.**
++CAD. GEOCIENC. INST. GEOCIENC. UNIV. CATOL.
PERNAMBUCO.
PERNAMBUCO 1, 1969-
LO/N-2.

**CAFD NEWSLETTER.**                                                                    XXX
++CAFD NEWSL.
COUNCIL FOR ACADEMIC FREEDOM & DEMOCRACY.
LONDON NO.1, JA 1971- 10, MY 1972. //
2M.
ED/N-1.     LO/U-3.

**CAFRAD NEWS.**
CENTRE AFRICAIN DE FORMATION ET DE RECHERCHES
ADMINISTRATIVES POUR LE DEVELOPPEMENT.
TANGIER NO.1, AU 1967-
LO/S14.

**CAGI TECHNICAL DIGEST.**
++CAGI TECH. DIG. (COMPRESSED AIR & GAS INST.).
COMPRESSED AIR & GAS INSTITUTE.
CLEVELAND OHIO 1, 1968-
LO/N14.

**CAHIERS AFRICAINS D'ADMINISTRATION PUBLIQUE.
AFRICAN ADMINISTRATIVE STUDIES.**
++CAH. AFR. ADM. PUBLIQUE.
CENTRE AFRICAIN DE FORMATION ET DE RECHERCHES
ADMINISTRATIVES POUR LE DEVELOPPEMENT.
TANGIER NO.1, MY 1967-
PRELIM. ISSUE DATED NO.0, N 1966.
AD/U-1.     GL/U-1.     LO/U-3.     LO/U-8.
ISSN 0007-9588

**CAHIERS D'AGRICULTURE PRATIQUE DES PAYS
CHAUDS.**
++CAH. AGR. PRAT. PAYS CHAUDS.
INSTITUT DE RECHERCHES AGRONOMIQUES TROPICALES
ET DES CULTURES VIVRIERES (PARIS).
PARIS 1965-
SUPPLEMENT A L'AGRONOMIE TROPICALE FROM
20, 1965.
BH/U-1.     CA/U11.
ISSN 0007-9677

**CAHIERS ALBERT CAMUS.**
++CAH. ALBERT CAMUS.
[NRF/GALLIMARD]
PARIS 1, 1971-
EX/U-1.     GL/U-1.     LO/U-2.     LO/U13.     MA/U-1.
LO/N-1. 1, 1971.

**CAHIERS DES AMERIQUES LATINES. SERIE ART &
LITTERATURE.**
++CAH. AM. LAT. SER. ART & LITT.
PARIS 1, 1967-
LO/U-1.     LV/U-1.
LD/U-1. NO.3, 1969-
ISSN 0068-5100

**CAHIERS DES AMERIQUES LATINES. SERIE SCIENCE
DE L'HOMME.**
++CAH. AM. LAT. SER. SCI. HOMME.
PARIS 1, JA/JE 1968-
2/A.
CA/U-1.     LO/U-1.     LO/U-3.     LV/U-1.     OX/U-1.
ISSN 0008-0020

**CAHIERS ANDRE GIDE.**
++CAH. ANDRE GIDE.
ASSOCIATION DES AMIS D'ANDRE GIDE.
[GALLIMARD]
PARIS NO.1, 1969.
BL/U-1.     EX/U-1.     GL/U-1.     LO/U-2.     SO/U-1.
MA/U-1. NO.1, 1969.
ISSN 0068-4937

**CAHIERS CANADIENS DE MUSIQUE.**                                                       000
SEE: CANADA MUSIC BOOK.

**CAHIERS DU CEDAF.**
++CAH. CEDAF.
CENTRE D'ETUDES ET DE DOCUMENTATION AFRICAINES.
BRUSSELS NO.1, 1971-
AD/U-1.     LO/U-3.     OX/U-9.

**CAHIERS CHARLES MAURRAS.**
++CAH. CHARLES MAURRAS.
PARIS 1[1], AP 1960-
Q.
OX/U-1.
ISSN 0575-0425

**CAHIERS CONGOLAIS RECHERCHE ET DU DEVELOPPE-
MENT.**                                                                                 XXX
++CAH. CONGOLAIS RECH. & DEVELOP.
CENTRE DE RECHERCHE ET D'INFORMATION SOCIO-
POLITIQUES (BELGIUM).
LEOPOLDVILLE & BRUSSELS 13(1), JA/MR 1970-
PREV: ETUDES CONGOLAISES FROM 1, MR 1961-
12, 1969.
LO/S14.

**CAHIERS DADA SURREALISME.**                                                           XXX
++CAH. DADA SURREALISME.
ASSOCIATION INTERNATIONALE POUR L'ETUDE DE DADA
ET DU SURREALISME.                                                                      XXX
[LETTRES MODERNES]
PARIS NO.1, 1966-
A. PREV: REVUE DE L'ASSOCIATION POUR L'ETUDE
DU MOUVEMENT DADA.
CB/U-1.     LC/U-1.     LO/U-2.
SW/U-1. NO.1, 1966- 2, 1968.

**CAHIERS ELISABETHAINS.**
++CAH. ELISABETHAINS.
MONTPELLIER 1, 1972-
AD/U-1.     OX/U-1.

**CAHIERS ERNEST-RENAN.**                                                               000
SEE: CAHIERS RENANIENS.

**CAHIERS DE FANJEAUX.**
++CAH. FANJEAUX.
[EDOUARD PRIVAT]
TOULOUSE 1, 1966-
OX/U-1.
ED/N-1. 2, 1967-
SO/U-1. NO.4, 1969; 7, 1972.
ISSN 0575-061X

**CAHIERS DU GROUPE FRANCAIS DE RHEOLOGIE.**
++CAH. GROUPE FR. RHEOL.
PARIS 1, S 1965-
RE/U-1.

**CAHIERS D'HISTOIRE DE BIOGRAPHIE ET DE
GENEALOGIE.**
++CAH. HIST. BIOGR. & GENEAL.
[VOSGES]
RUPT SUR MOSELLE 1, 1965-
OX/U-1.

**CAHIERS DE L'INSTITUT INTERNATIONAL D'ETUDES
SOCIALES.**
++CAH. INST. INT. ETUD. SOC.
PARIS 1, 1966-
BH/U-1.     LO/N-3.
ISSN 0537-8184

**CAHIERS INTERNATIONAUX D'HISTOIRE ECONOMIQUE
ET SOCIALE. QUADERNI INTERNAZIONALI DI
STORIA ECONOMICA E SOCIALE. INTERNATIONAL
JOURNAL OF ECONOMIC & SOCIAL HISTORY.**                                                 XXX
++CAH. INT. HIST. ECON. & SOC.
ISTITUTO ITALIANO PER LA STORIA DEI MOVIMENTI
SOCIALI E DELLE STRUTTURE SOCIALI.
GENEVA 1, 1972-
ANNU. PREV: ANNALI DI STORIA ECONOMICA E SOC-
IALE, UNIVERSITA DEGLI STUDI DI NAPOLI FROM 1,
1960- 8, 1967.
LO/N-1.     LO/U-3.     OX/U-1.

**CAHIERS JEAN COCTEAU.**
++CAH. JEAN COCTEAU.
SOCIETE DES AMIS DE JEAN COCTEAU.
[GALLIMARD]
PARIS 1, 1969-
BT/U-1.     EX/U-1.     GL/U-1.     LO/U-2.
LO/N-1. 2, 1971-                              NW/U-1. 2, 1971-
ISSN 0068-5178

**CAHIERS MARCEL PROUST: NS.**
++CAH. MARCEL PROUST, NS.
[NRF/GALLIMARD]
PARIS 1, 1970-
PREV. SER. FROM 1, 1927- 8, 1935.
BL/U-1.     GL/U-1.     LO/U13.

**CAHIERS DE MARIEMONT. BULLETIN DU ...**
++CAH. MARIEMONT.
MUSEE DE MARIEMONT.
MORLANWELZ, BELG. 1, 1970-
LO/N-1.     LO/N15.     OX/U-1.

**CAHIERS DE LA METEOROLOGIE (ALGERIA).**
++CAH. METEOROL. (ALGER.).
(ALGERIA) METEOROLOGIE NATIONALE.
ALGIERS NO.1, 1970-
XS/N-1.

CAHIERS ORSTOM: SERIE GEOLOGIE.
++CAH. ORSTOM, GEOL.
OFFICE DE LA RECHERCHE SCIENTIFIQUE ET
TECHNIQUE OUTRE-MER (FRANCE).
PARIS 1, 1969-
DB/S-1.   LO/N-2.   LO/N13.

CAHIERS ORSTOM: SERIE SCIENCES HUMAINES.
++CAH. ORSTOM, SCI. HUM.
OFFICE DE LA RECHERCHE SCIENTIFIQUE ET TECH-
NIQUE OUTRE-MER (FRANCE).
PARIS 1, 1963-
Q.
BH/U-1.   3, 1966-
ISSN 0008-0403

CAHIERS PHILOSOPHIQUES AFRICAINS.                   000
  SEE: AFRICAN PHILOSOPHICAL JOURNAL.

CAHIERS DES RELIGIONS AFRICAINES.
++CAH. RELIG. AFR.
UNIVERSITE LOVANIUM DE KINSHASA: CENTRE
D'ETUDES DES RELIGIONS AFRICAINES.
KINSHASA 1, JL 1967-
AD/U-1. 2, 1968-              BH/C-3. 2(2), 1968-
ISSN 0008-0047

CAHIERS RENANIENS.
++CAH. RENANIENS.
SOCIETE DES ETUDES RENANIENNES.
[EDITIONS A.-G. NIZET]
PARIS NO.1, 1971-
NO.1 ENTITLED CAHIERS ERNEST-RENAN.
LO/N-1.   MA/U-1.

CAHIERS DE TOPOLOGIE ET GEOMETRIE
DIFFERENTIELLE.
++CAH. TOPOL. & GEOM. DIFFER.
[DUNOD]
PARIS 1, 1971-
Q. FR. & ENGL.
SH/U-1.
ISSN 0008-0004

CAHIERS DE LA VIE QUOTIDIENNE.
++CAH. VIE QUOTID.
COMITE NATIONAL FRANCAIS DE LIAISON POUR LA
READAPTATION DES HANDICAPES.
PARIS NO.1, [1967]-
LO/N14.
ISSN 0590-7543

CAHIERS ZAIROIS D'ETUDES POLITIQUES ET
SOCIALES.
++CAH. ZAIROIS ETUD. POLIT. & SOC.
UNIVERSITE NATIONALE DU ZAIRE: FACULTE DES
SCIENCES SOCIALES, POLITIQUES ET ADMINISTRAT-
IVES.
LUBUMBASHI NO.1, 1973-
LO/U14.

CALCIFIED TISSUE ABSTRACTS.
++CALCIF. TISSUE ABSTR.
[INFORMATION RETRIEVAL LTD.]
LONDON 1, AP 1969-
M.
GL/U-1.   LO/N13.   LO/U-2.   OX/U-8.   SF/U-1.
ED/N-1. 1(9), 1969-
ISSN 0008-0586

CALCUTTA JOURNAL.
++CALCUTTA J.
PATENT OFFICE TECHNICAL SOCIETY (INDIA).
CALCUTTA 1, 1967-
LO/N14.

CALIFORNIA BIRDS.                                   XXX
++CALIF. BIRDS.
CALIFORNIA FIELD ORNITHOLOGISTS.
SAN DIEGO 1, JA 1970- 3, 1970...
Q. SUBS: WESTERN BIRDS.
LO/N-2.
ISSN 0045-3897

CALIFORNIA CITROGRAPH.                              XXX
  SUBS (1969): CITROGRAPH.

CALIFORNIA HORTICULTURAL JOURNAL.                   XXX
++CALIF. HORTICULT. J.
PACIFIC HORTICULTURAL CORPORATION.
SAN FRANCISCO 29, 1968-
PREV: JOURNAL, CALIFORNIA HORTICULTURAL
SOCIETY FROM 1, 1940- 28, 1967.
LO/N14.

CALIFORNIA STUDIES IN CLASSICAL ANTIQUITY.
++CALIF. STUD. CLASSICAL ANTIQ.
[UNIVERSITY OF CALIFORNIA P.]
BERKELEY &C. 1, 1968-
CA/U-1.   DB/S-1.   GL/U-1.   LD/U-1.   LO/U-2.   LO/U17.
MA/U-1.   NO/U-1.   OX/U-2.
AD/U-1. 2, 1969-              OX/U-1. 2, 1969-
ISSN 0068-5895

CALITATEA PRODUCTIEI SI METROLOGIE.
++CALITATEA PROD. METROL.
BUCHAREST 1, 1971-
LO/N13.

CALVIN THEOLOGICAL JOURNAL.
++CALVIN THEOL. J.
GRAND RAPIDS, MICH. 1, 1966-
DB/U-2.   LO/U-1.
ISSN 0008-1795

CAMAC BULLETIN.
++CAMAC BULL.
COMMISSION OF THE EUROPEAN COMMUNITIES.
BRUSSELS ISSUE NO.1, 1971-
PRODUCED BY THE ESONE COMMITTEE (FOR A EUROP-
EAN STANDARD OF NUCLEAR ELECTRONICS). CAMAC
IS THE COMMITTEE'S MODULAR UNIT SYSTEM OF
ELECTRONICS FOR DATA HANDLING.
LO/N14.

CAMBRIAN LAW REVIEW.
++CAMBRIAN LAW REV.
UNIVERSITY COLLEGE OF WALES: DEPARTMENT OF LAW.
ABERYSTWYTH 1, 1970-
BL/U-1.   CR/U-1.   ED/N-1.   HL/U-1.   OX/U-1.

CAMBRIDGE JOURNAL OF EDUCATION.
++CAMB. J. EDUC.
UNIVERSITY OF CAMBRIDGE: INSTITUTE OF EDUCATION
CAMBRIDGE 1, 1971-
CA/U-1.   ED/N-1.   HL/U-2.   LV/U-2.
LO/U28. 2, 1972-
ISSN 0305-764X

CAMELANG. BULLETIN DE LA ...
UNIVERSITE FEDERALE DU CAMEROUN: SECTION DE
LINGUISTIQUE APPLIQUEE.
YAOUNDE NO.1, 1969-
LO/U14.

CAMPANIA SACRA. STUDI E DOCUMENTI.
PONTIFICIA FACOLTA TEOLOGICA DELL' ITALIA
MERIDIONELLE (NAPLES): SEZIONE DI CAPODIMONTE.
NAPLES 1, 1970-
LO/U17.

CANADA MUSIC BOOK. CAHIERS CANADIENS DE
MUSIQUE.
++CAN. MUSIC BOOK.
CANADIAN MUSIC COUNCIL.
MONTREAL 1, SPRING/SUMMER 1970-
2/A.
OX/U-1.

CANADA PENSION PLAN. STATISTICAL BULLETIN.
++CAN. PENSION PLAN.
(CANADA) DEPARTMENT OF NATIONAL HEALTH & WELF-
ARE: OFFICE OF PLANNING & DEVELOPMENT.
OTTAWA 1(1), 1969-
LO/U-3.

CANADA TODAY.
++CAN. TODAY.
(CANADA) HIGH COMMISSION IN LONDON.
LONDON 1(1), MY/JE 1973-
6/A.
ED/N-1.   NO/U-1.

CANADIAN AFFAIRS.
++CAN. AFF.
TORONTO 1, D 1967-
MON.
OX/U-9. 4(1), 1970-
ISSN 0008-283X

CANADIAN AGRICULTURAL INSECT PEST REVIEW.          XXX
++CAN. AGRIC. INSECT PEST REV. [CAIP-A]
(CANADA) DEPARTMENT OF AGRICULTURE: RESEARCH
BRANCH.
OTTAWA 46, 1968-
PREV: CANADIAN INSECT PEST REVIEW FROM 1,
1923- 45, 1967. PRODUCED BY DEPARTMENT'S
SCIENTIFIC INFORMATION SECTION.
BN/U-2.

**CANADIAN AGRICULTURAL OUTLOOK.**
+ +CAN. AGR. OUTLOOK.
(CANADA) DEPARTMENT OF AGRICULTURE: ECONOMICS
BRANCH.
 OTTAWA 1971-
 A.
 LO/U-3.

**CANADIAN AGRICULTURAL SITUATION.**
+ +CAN. AGR. SITUATION.
(CANADA) DEPARTMENT OF AGRICULTURE: ECONOMICS
BRANCH.
 OTTAWA 1970-
 A.
 LO/U-3.

**CANADIAN ANTIQUES COLLECTOR.**                                    XXX
+ +CAN. ANTIQUES COLLECT.
 WILLOWDALE, ONT. 1(4), S 1966-
 M. S/T: A JOURNAL OF ANTIQUES & FINE ARTS.
 PREV: CANADIAN COLLECTOR FROM 1(1), AP 1966-
 1(3), 1966.
 ISSN 0045-4346

**CANADIAN ARCHIVIST.**
+ +CAN. ARCH.
 CANADIAN HISTORICAL ASSOCIATION.
 CALGARY 1(1), 1963-
 CA/U12.*   LO/U19.*
 ISSN 0576-4491

**CANADIAN AUDUBON.**                                               XXX
 SUBS (1972): NATURE CANADA.

**CANADIAN BAR JOURNAL.**                                           XXX
 SUBS: (1970): JOURNAL OF THE CANADIAN BAR
 ASSOCIATION.

**CANADIAN CARTOGRAPHER.**
+ +CAN. CARTOGR.
[UNIV. OF TORONTO PRESS]
 TORONTO 5(1), 1968-
 PREV: CARTOGRAPHER FROM 1, 1964.
 BH/U-1.   BN/U-1.   CA/U12.   ED/N-1.   ED/U-1.   GL/U-2.
 LO/S13.   OX/U-1.
 LO/N13. 5, 1968-
 EX/U-1. 10(1), JE 1973-
 ISSN 0008-3129

**CANADIAN CATTLEMEN.**                                             XXX
 SUBS (1969): CATTLEMEN, THE BEEF MAGAZINE.

**CANADIAN COLLECTOR.**                                             XXX
+ +CAN. COLLECT.
 WILLOWDALE, ONT. 1(1), 1966- 1(3), 1966 ...
 SUBS: CANADIAN ANTIQUES COLLECTOR.
 OX/U-1.

**CANADIAN CRIMINAL CASES: NS.**
+ +CAN. CRIM. CASES.
 TORONTO 1, 1969-
 BL/U-1.
 ISSN 0008-3348

**CANADIAN DATASYSTEMS.**
+ +CAN. DATASYST.
[MACLEAN-HUNTER, LTD.]
 TORONTO 1(1), N 1969-
 M.
 LO/N14. 2(2), 1970-
 ISSN 0008-3364

**CANADIAN FEED & GRAIN JOURNAL.**                                  XXX
+ +CAN. FEED & GRAIN J. [CFGJ-A]
[PUBLIC P.]
 WINNIPEG 20(1), JA 1964- 23(9), 1967 ...
 PREV: CANADIAN GRAIN JOURNAL FROM 5, MR 1950-
 19, 1963. SUBS: FARM SUPPLY STORE.
 LO/N13. 21(7), 1965-

**CANADIAN FISHERMAN.**                                             XXX
 SUBS (1969): SEA HARVEST & OCEAN SCIENCE.

**CANADIAN FISHERMAN & OCEAN SCIENCE.**                             XXX
+ +CAN. FISHERMAN & OCEAN SCI.
[R.J. COOKE LTD.; MUIR PUBL. CO.]
 QUEBEC &C D 1970-
 PREV: SEA HARVEST & OCEAN SCIENCE FROM JE/JL
 1969- JE/JL 1970.
 LO/N13.

**CANADIAN GRAIN JOURNAL.**                                         XXX
 SUBS (1964): CANADIAN FEED & GRAIN JOURNAL.

**CANADIAN HISTORICAL READINGS.**
+ +CAN. HIST. READ.
[UNIV. TORONTO P.]
 TORONTO NO.1, 1967-
 OX/U-9.

**CANADIAN INSECT PEST REVIEW.**                                    XXX
 SUBS (1968): CANADIAN AGRICULTURAL INSECT
 PEST REVIEW.

**CANADIAN JOURNAL OF AFRICAN STUDIES. = JOUR-
NAL CANADIEN DES ETUDES AFRICAINES.**
+ +CAN. J. AFR. STUD.
 COMMITTEE ON AFRICAN STUDIES IN CANADA.
 MONTREAL NO.1, MR 1967-
 2/A. PUBL. BY LOYOLA COLLEGE FOR THE
 COMMITTEE.
 OX/U-9.
 BL/U-1. 3, 1969-               LO/N17. 3(1), 1969-
 LO/R-6. 3(1), 1969-           LO/S10. 6, 1972-
 ISSN 0008-3968

**CANADIAN JOURNAL OF BEHAVIOURAL SCIENCE.
=REVUE DES SCIENCES DU COMPORTEMENT.**
+ +CAN. J. BEHAV. SCI.
 CANADIAN PSYCHOLOGICAL ASSOCIATION.
[UNIVERSITY OF TORONTO PRESS]
 TORONTO 1(1), 1969-
 CO/U-1.   OX/U-8.
 ISSN 0008-400X

**CANADIAN JOURNAL OF CRIMINOLOGY & CORRECTIONS**   XXX
+ +CAN. J. CRIMINOL. & CORRECT.
 CANADIAN WELFARE COUNCIL.
 OTTAWA 13(1), 1971-
 PREV: CANADIAN JOURNAL OF CORRECTIONS FROM
 1(1), 1958.
 OX/U15.

**CANADIAN JOURNAL OF ECONOMICS. SUPPLEMENT. =
REVUE CANADIENNE D'ECONOMIQUE. SUPPLEMENT.**
+ +CAN. J. ECON., SUPPL.
 CANADIAN ECONOMICS ASSOCIATION.
 TORONTO NO.1, F 1968-
 AB/U-1.
 ISSN 0576-5552

**CANADIAN JOURNAL OF FOREST RESEARCH.**
+ +CAN. J. FOR. RES.
 NATIONAL RESEARCH COUNCIL (CANADA).
 OTTAWA 1(1), MR 1971-
 Q.
 AD/U-1.   DB/U-2.   LO/R-5.   OX/U-3.
 LD/U-1. 3, 1973-
 ISSN 0045-5067

**CANADIAN JOURNAL OF PHARMACEUTICAL SCIENCES.**
+ +CAN. J. PHARM. SCI.
 CANADIAN PHARMACEUTICAL ASSOCIATION.
 OTTAWA 1, 1966-
 LO/N14.   LO/S-3.
 MA/U-1. 3, 1968-
 ISSN 0008-4190

**CANADIAN JOURNAL OF PHILOSOPHY.**
+ +CAN. J. PHILOS.
[CANADIAN ASSOCIATION FOR PUBLISHING IN
PHILOSOPHY]
 EDMONTON 1(1), S 1971-
 Q.
 BN/U-1.   CA/U-1.   EX/U-1.   GL/U-1.   LD/U-1.   LO/U-2.
 NO/U-1.   OX/U-1.   RE/U-1.   SW/U-1.
 MA/U-1. 1(3), 1972-
 ISSN 0045-5091

**CANADIAN JOURNAL OF RADIOGRAPHY, RADIOTHERAPY,
NUCLEOGRAPHY.**                                                     XXX
+ +CAN. J. RADIOGR. RADIOTHER. NUCLEOGR.
 CANADIAN SOCIETY OF RADIOLOGICAL TECHNICIANS.
 OTTAWA 1, 1970-
 PREV: FOCAL SPOT FROM 1, 1944- 27(128), MY
 1970.
 LO/N14.
 ISSN 0015-4938

**CANADIAN JOURNAL OF SPECTROSCOPY.**                               XXX
+ +CAN. J. SPECTROSC.
 CANADIAN ASSOCIATION FOR APPLIED SPECTROSCOPY.
 MONTREAL 17, 1972-
 PREV: CANADIAN SPECTROSCOPY FROM 9, OC 1963-
 16, 1971.
 LO/N13.
 ISSN 0045-5105

**CANADIAN JOURNAL OF THEOLOGY.**                                   XXX
 SUBS (1971): STUDIES IN RELIGION.

CANADIAN LEGAL STUDIES. = ETUDES JURIDIQUES
AU CANADA.
+ + CAN. LEGAL STUD.
ASSOCIATION OF CANADIAN LAW TEACHERS.
TORONTO NO.1, 1964-
OX/U15.
ISSN 0576-5625

CANADIAN LIBRARY JOURNAL.    XXX
+ + CAN. LIBR. J.
CANADIAN LIBRARY ASSOCIATION.
OTTAWA 27, 1970-
PREV: CANADIAN LIBRARY FROM 16(6), MY 1960-
26, 1969.
LO/N14.
ED/N-1. 28(5), S/OC 1971-
ISSN 0008-4352

CANADIAN MACHINERY & MANUFACTURING NEWS.    XXX
SUBS (1961): CANADIAN MACHINERY & METALWORKING

CANADIAN MACHINERY & METALWORKING.    XXX
+ + CAN MACH. METALWORK.
[MACLEAN-HUNTER]
TORONTO 72, 1961-
PREV: CANADIAN MACHINERY & MANUFACTURING
NEWS FROM 1, 1905- 71, 1960.
LO/N14.*
ISSN 0008-4379

CANADIAN MATHEMATICAL MONOGRAPHS.
+ + CAN. MATH. MONOGR.
CANADIAN MATHEMATICAL CONGRESS.
LONDON &C. NO.1, 1970-
OX/U-8.

CANADIAN METALS.    XXX
SUBS (1957): CANADIAN METALWORKING.

CANADIAN METALWORKING/MACHINE PRODUCTION.*
+ + CAN. METALWORK./MACH. PROD.
[MACLEAN; SOUTHAM BUSINESS PUBL.]
TORONTO; DON MILLS, ONT. 20(5), 1957- 31, N
1969.
PREV: CANADIAN METALS FROM 13, JA 1950- 20
(4), AP 1957. TITLE EXPANDED FROM CANADIAN
METALWORKING WITH 27(3), JA 1964. SUBS:
CANADIAN METALWORKING PRODUCTION.
LO/N14.
ISSN 0008-4447

CANADIAN METALWORKING PRODUCTION.    XXX
+ + CAN. METALWORK. PROD.
[SOUTHAM BUSINESS PUBL.]
DON MILLS, ONT. D 1969- F 1971.
PREV: CANADIAN METALWORKING/MACHINE PRODUC-
TION FROM 20(5), 1957- 31, N 1969. SUBS:
SOUTHAM'S METALWORKING.
LO/N14.

CANADIAN MILLING & FEED.    XXX
SUBS (1967): FEED & FARM SUPPLY DEALER.

CANADIAN NOTES & QUERIES.
+ + CAN. NOTES & QUERIES.
MONTREAL NO.1, JL 1968-
ED/N-1.

CANADIAN NURSERYMAN.
+ + CAN. NURSERYMAN.
ONTARIO NURSERY TRADES ASSOCIATION.
BURLINGTON, ONT. 1(1), 1964-
LO/N13. 4(9), 1967-
ISSN 0008-459X

CANADIAN REVIEW OF AMERICAN STUDIES.
+ + CAN. REV. AM. STUD.
CANADIAN ASSOCIATION OF AMERICAN STUDIES.
TORONTO 1, 1970-
2/A.
EX/U-1.    HL/U-1.    NO/U-1.
OX/U-1. 4(1), 1973-
ISSN 0007-7720

CANDELABRUM. A MAGAZINE OF POETRY.
LONDON 1(1), 1970-
LO/U-2.

CANDY & BAKED SNACK INDUSTRY.    000
SEE: CANDY & SNACK INDUSTRY.

CANDY INDUSTRY.    XXX
+ + CANDY IND.
[MAGAZINES FOR INDUSTRY]
NEW YORK 130(11), 1968- 135, 1970 ...
PREV: CANDY INDUSTRY & CONFECTIONERS' JOURNAL
FROM 107(3), 1956- 130(10), 1968. SUBS:
CANDY & SNACK INDUSTRY.
LO/N14.

CANDY INDUSTRY & CONFECTIONERS' JOURNAL.    XXX
SUBS (1968): CANDY INDUSTRY.

CANDY & SNACK INDUSTRY.*
+ + CANDY & SNACK IND.
[MAGAZINES FOR INDUSTRY]
NEW YORK 136(1), 1971-
PREV: CANDY INDUSTRY FROM 130(11), 1968- 135,
1970. TITLE VARIES 136(1-5) AS CANDY & BAKED
SNACK INDUSTRY.
LO/N14.

CANNING TRADE.    XXX
SUBS (1971): FOOD PRODUCTION MANAGEMENT.

CANTERBURY ENGINEERING JOURNAL.
+ + CANTERBURY ENG. J.
UNIVERSITY OF CANTERBURY: SCHOOL OF ENGINEERING
CHRISTCHURCH, N.Z. NO.1, JE 1970-
LD/U-1.    LO/U-2.    LO/U12.    LO/U12.

CAPELLA.
[TARA TELEPHONE PUBL.]
DUBLIN 1, 1969-
DB/U-2.    LO/U-2.
ISSN 0045-5660

CAPITAL ISSUES WITH ADJUSTED STOCK MARKET
PRICES FOR CAPITAL GAINS TAX PURPOSES.
+ + CAP. ISSUES ADJUST. STOCK MARK. PRICES
CAP. GAINS TAX PURP.
[EXTEL STATISTICAL SERVICES LTD.]
[LONDON] [1965/66]-
A., WITH Q. CUMULATIVE SUPPLS.
MA/P-1.    SH/U-1.

CAPITOL STUDIES.
+ + CAPITOL STUD.
UNITED STATES CAPITOL HISTORICAL SOCIETY.
WASHINGTON, D.C. 1, 1972-
AD/U-1.
ISSN 0045-5687

CARA. TRAVEL MAGAZINE OF ...
AER LINGUS: PUBLICITY DEPARTMENT.
DUBLIN 1, 1968-
Q.
DB/U-2.    ED/N-1.
ISSN 0008-6088

CARBENES.
[WILEY-INTERSCIENCE]
NEW YORK; LONDON 1, 1973-
LO/N14.

CARBOHYDRATE CHEMISTRY: A REVIEW OF THE
LITERATURE.
+ + CARBOHYD. CHEM. REV. LIT.
CHEMICAL SOCIETY.
LONDON 1, 1967(1968)-
BH/U-1.    ED/N-1.    GL/U-1.    LO/U-2.    LO/U12.    LO/U13.
MA/U-1.    NW/U-1.    RE/U-1.    SF/U-1.    SW/U-1.
CA/U-1. 1, 1967- 2, 1968.
ISSN 0576-7172

CARBOHYDRATE METABOLISM ABSTRACTS.    XXX
+ + CARBOHYD. METAB. ABSTR.
[INFORMATION RETRIEVAL LTD.]
LONDON 1(1- 12), JA- D 1973...
MON. SUBS: CARBOHYDRATE CHEMISTRY & METABOLISM
ABSTRACTS.
AD/U-2.    ED/N-1.    LO/N13.    OX/U-8.
CA/U-1. 1(3), 1973-
ISSN 0300-1407

CARDIOLOGY TODAY.
+ + CARDIOL. TODAY.
EXCERPTA MEDICA FOUNDATION.
MACCLESFIELD, CHES. 1(1), JA 1973-
S/T: CURRENT WORLD NEWS & VIEWS ON CARDIOLOGY.
CA/U-1.    ED/N-1.    OX/U-8.
BL/U-1. 1(4), 1973-

CARDIOVASCULAR CLINICS.
+ + CARDIOVASC. CLIN.
[F.A.DAVIS]
PHILADELPHIA 1, 1969-
DB/U-1.    LO/M17.    LO/U12.    RE/U-1.
ISSN 0069-0384

**CARE IN THE HOME.**
ROYAL SOCIETY FOR THE PREVENTION OF ACCIDENTS.
*LONDON 1(1), AP 1972-*
Q. INCORPS. HOME SAFETY JOURNAL.
*ED/N-1.*

**CAREER.**
[DOMINION P. LTD.]
*LONDON 1(1), N 1968-*
S/T: MAGAZINE FOR THE FINAL YEAR UNDERGRAD-
UATE.
*OX/U-1.*
*ED/N-1. 1(4), MR 1969-*
*ISSN 0590-8000*

**CARET. A POETRY MAGAZINE.**
*BELFAST NO.1, 1972-*
*ED/N-1.*

**CARGESE LECTURES IN PHYSICS.**
*+ +CARGESE LECT. PHYS. [CLEP-A]*
INSTITUT D'ETUDES SCIENTIFIQUES DE CARGESE.
[GORDON & BREACH]
*NEW YORK &C. 1, 1966(1967)-*
*LO/N14. LO/U-2.*
*OX/U-8. 3, 1969-*

**CARGO AIRLIFT.** XXX
[IMPORT PUBL.]
*NEW YORK 56(2), 1970-*
PREV: AIR TRANSPORTATION 1, 1942- 56(1), 1970
*LO/N13.*

**CARIBBEAN INSIDER.**
*+ +CARIBB. INSIDER.*
[ANTILLES PUBL. CO.]
*PORT OF SPAIN 1, 1972-*
S/T: REGIONAL NEWS-MAGAZINE FOR THE CARIBBEAN.
*LO/U-8. 1(3), 1972-*
*ISSN 0045-5814*

**CARIBBEAN REVIEW.**
*+ +CARIBB. REV.*
[CARIBBEAN REVIEW INC.]
*HATO REY, P.R. 1(1), 1969-*
Q.
*LO/U-8.*
*ISSN 0008-6525*

**CARLETON NEWSLETTER.**
*+ +CARLETON NEWSL.*
UNIVERSITY OF FLORIDA.
*GAINESVILLE, FLA. 1(1), JL 1970-*
*DB/U-2.*

**CARLOVIANA. NS. JOURNAL OF THE ...**
OLD CARLOW SOCIETY.
*CARLOW 1, 1968-*
*BL/U-1.*
*OX/U-1. 1(18), 1969-*

**CARN. A LINK BETWEEN THE CELTIC NATIONS.**
*DUBLIN 1, 1973-*
*CA/U-1. ED/N-1.*

**CARNIVORE GENETICS NEWSLETTER.**
*+ +CARNIVORE GENET. NEWSL.*
*SOUTHBOROUGH, MASS. NO.1, S 1966-*
2/A. ENGL., FR. OR GER. EDITED BY BIBLIO-
GRAPHY CENTRE, LONDON.
*CA/U11. CA/U15. LO/N-2.*
*LO/N13. NO.4, 1968-*
*ISSN 0008-6711*

**CARRIAGE JOURNAL.**
*+ +CARRIAGE J.*
CARRIAGE ASSOCIATION.
*SHEBOYGAN, WIS. 1(1), 1963-*
Q.
*LO/N-4.*
*ISSN 0008-6916*

**CARS IN PROFILE.**
[PROFILE PUBL.]
*WINDSOR, BERKS. NO.1, 1972-*
*LO/N-1.*

**CARTOGRAPHER.** XXX
ONTARIO INSTITUTE OF CHARTERED CARTOGRAPHERS.
*OTTAWA 1, 1964- 4, 1967...*
2/A. SUBS: CANADIAN CARTOGRAPHER.
*BH/U-1.*
*AD/U-1. 2,1965-          CA/U12. 2,1965-*
*HL/U-1. 2,1965-*

**CAS OCCASIONAL PAPER.** XXX
*+ +CAS OCCAS. PAP. [CASO-B]*
CENTRE FOR ADMINISTRATIVE STUDIES. XXX
*LONDON NO.1, 1967- 13, 1970 ...*
SUBS: OCCASIONAL PAPER, CIVIL SERVICE COLLEGE.
*LO/N14.*

**CAS REPORT.**
*+ +CAS REP.*
AMERICAN CHEMICAL SOCIETY: CHEMICAL ABSTRACTS
SERVICE.
*COLUMBUS, OHIO NO.1, OC 1972-*
*XS/R10.*
*LO/N14. CURRENT BOX ONLY.*

**CASE CONFERENCE.** XXX
SUBS (1970): PART OF SOCIAL WORK TODAY.

**CASE STUDIES IN AFRICAN DIPLOMACY.**
*+ +CASE STUD. AFR. DIPL.*
UNIVERSITY COLLEGE, DAR-ES-SALAAM: INSTITUTE
OF PUBLIC ADMINISTRATION.
*DAR ES SALAAM NO.1, 1969-*
*GL/U-1.*

**CASE STUDIES ON HOSPITAL MANAGEMENT LAW & PRAC-
TICE.**
*+ +CASE STUD. HOSP. MANAGE. LAW & PRACT.*
[WHITE'S PUBL.]
*BECKENHAM, KENT 1, 1969-*
*OX/U-8.*

**CASE STUDIES ON TECHNOLOGICAL DEVELOPMENT.**
*+ +CASE STUD. TECHNOL. DEV.*
UNESCO.
*PARIS NO.1, 1971-*
*LO/N13.*

**CASI TRANSACTIONS.**
*+ +CASI TRANS. (CAN. AERONAUT. & SPACE INST.)*
CANADIAN AERONAUTICS & SPACE INSTITUTE.
*OTTAWA 1, 1968-*
*BR/U-3. LO/N14.*
*ISSN 0007-7852*

**CASOPIS SLEZSKEHO MUSEA: SERIE C: DENDROLOGIE.**
*+ +CAS. SLEZSKEHO MUS., C.*
*OPAVA 1, 1962-*
PREV: DENDROLOGICKY SBORNIK FROM 1958- 1961.
*OX/U-3.*

**CASSETTES & CARTRIDGES.**
[GENERAL GRAMAPHONE PUBL. LTD.]
*LONDON NO.1, AP 1973-*
MON.
*CA/U-1. ED/N-1. OX/U-1.*
*CB/U-1. 1975-*
*LO/N14. CURRENT BOX ONLY.*

**CAST - FOR ECONOMIC PRODUCTION.**
*+ +CAST ECON. PROD.*
[IPC INDUSTRIAL P. LTD.]
*LONDON 1(1), SUMMER 1972-*
Q.
*ED/N-1.*

**CASTING ENGINEERING.**
*+ +CAST. ENG.*
[CONTINENTAL COMMUNICATIONS, INC.]
*FAIRFIELD, CONN. 1, 1969-*
*XY/N-1.*
*ISSN 0008-7513*

**CASTLE ST. CIRCULAR.**
*+ +CASTLE ST. CIRC.*
LIVERPOOL COUNCIL OF SOCIAL SERVICE.
*LIVERPOOL 1(1), 1966-*
*OX/U-1.*
*ISSN 0045-592X*

**CASTORO.**
[LA NUOVA ITALIA]
*FLORENCE NO.1, JA 1967-*
MON.
*DB/U-2.**
*ISSN 0008-753X*

**CATALYST (BUFFALO, N.Y.).**
STATE UNIVERSITY OF NEW YORK; SOCIOLOGY CLUB.
*BUFFALO, N.Y. NO.1, SUMMER 1965-*
2/A. CLUB LOCATED AT THE UNIV.'S NORTON
UNION.
*GL/U-2. 3, 1967-              MA/U-1. 3, 1967-*
*SH/U-1. 3, 1967-*
*ISSN 0411-2393*

CATALYST (LONDON).
ART INFORMATION REGISTRY.
*LONDON 1970/1(1970)-*
*LO/U-2.*

CATALYST. FOR THE SCOTTISH VIEWPOINT.
1320 CLUB.
*ST. ANDREWS D 1967-*
*Q.*
*ED/N-1. LO/U-3.*
*ISSN 0045-5962*

CATALYST FOR ENVIRONMENTAL QUALITY.    XXX
*+ +CATAL. ENVIRON. QUAL.*
*NEW YORK 1, 1970-*
*Q. PREV: CONSERVATION CATALYST.*
*LO/N13. LO/R-5.*
*ISSN 0008-7688*

CATAMARAN & TRIMARAN INTERNATIONAL.    XXX
*+ +CATAMARAN & TRIMARAN INT.*
*[PURNELL]*
*LONDON &C 1(1), SPRING 1964-*
*ORIG. PUBL. TRURO, THEN FALMOUTH. 'NEWS'*
*DELETED FROM TITLE FROM 4(6), 1967, & FROM*
*SAME ISSUE PUBL. IN LONDON.*
*ED/N-1. 3(10), 1966-*
*LO/N14. 3(10), 1966-*
*ISSN 0576-9167*

CATERING & HOTEL MANAGEMENT.
*+ +CATER. & HOTEL MANAGE.*
*[BLANDFORD PUBL. LTD.]*
*LONDON NO.42, 1970-*
*PREV: CATERING MANAGEMENT FROM NO.1, 1948.*
*ED/N-1. LO/N-7.*
*ISSN 0018-6104*

CATONSVILLE ROADRUNNER: REVOLUTIONARY CHRIST-
IAN MONTHLY.
*LONDON NO.1, 1969-*
*LO/U-3.*
*ED/N-1. NO.9, D 1969-*
*ISSN 0008-8536*

CATTLEMEN. THE BEEF MAGAZINE.    XXX
*[PUBLIC P.]*
*WINNIPEG 32(6), 1969-*
*PREV: CANADIAN CATTLEMEN FROM 1, JE 1938-*
*32(5), 1969.*
*LO/N13.*
*ISSN 0008-3143*

CAUCASIAN & NEAR EASTERN STUDIES.    000
*SEE: KAVKAZSKO-BLIZHNE-VOSTOCHNYJ SBORNIK.*

CAUSES OF DEATH (AUSTRALIA).
(AUSTRALIA) COMMONWEALTH BUREAU OF CENSUS &
STATISTICS.
*CANBERRA BULLETIN NO.1, 1963 [1964]-*
*TO 1962 PART OF THE BUREAU'S PUBL.: DEMO-*
*GRAPHY.*
*BH/U-1.*

CAVE. MAGAZINE OF THE ARTS.
*DUNEDIN, N.Z. NO.1, 1972-*
*LO/U-2. OX/U-1.*

CAVES.    000
*SEE: PESHCHERY.*

CBI EDUCATION & TRAINING BULLETIN.
*+ +CBI EDUC. & TRAIN. BULL.*
CONFEDERATION OF BRITISH INDUSTRY.
*LONDON [1(1)], S 1966-*
*Q. NUMBERING COMMENCES WITH 1(9), JA 1969.*
*OX/U17.*
*ED/N-1. 2(10), 1972-    XS/T-4. 2(9), 1972-*

CBI EUROPE BRIEF.
*+ +CBI EUR. BRIEF.*
CONFEDERATION OF BRITISH INDUSTRY.
*LONDON NO.1, JA 1971-*
*LO/N10.*
*ED/N-1. NO.15, S 1972-*
*OX/U-1. NO.15, S 1972-*

CBI INDUSTRIAL RELATIONS BULLETIN.    XXX
*+ +CBI IND. RELAT. BULL.*
CONFEDERATION OF BRITISH INDUSTRY.
*LONDON NO.1, JA 1970- NO.10, OC 1973.*
SUBS. PART OF: CBI MEMBERS BULLETIN.
*ED/N-1. LO/N10. MA/P-1.*

CBI INDUSTRIAL TRENDS SURVEY.    XXX
*+ +CBI IND. TRENDS SURV.*
CONFEDERATION OF BRITISH INDUSTRY.    XXX
*LONDON NO.41, JE 1971-*
PREV: INDUSTRIAL TRENDS SURVEY FROM NO.22,
1965- 40, 1971.
*MA/U-1. OX/U16. OX/U17. SO/U-1.*
*BH/U-3. NO.44, 1972-    CA/U-1. NO.47, 1973-*
*ED/N-1. NO.47, 1973-*

CBI INFORMATIONS.
*+ +CBI INF.*
COMPAGNIE DES CONSEILS EN BREVETS D'INVENTION.
*PARIS NO.1, 1972-*
*LO/N14.*

CBI OVERSEAS TRADE BULLETIN.
*+ +CBI OVERSEAS TRADE BULL.*
CONFEDERATION OF BRITISH INDUSTRY.
*LONDON NO.1, 1972-*
*ED/N-1. OX/U-1.*
*XS/T-4. NO.11, 1972-*

CBI REVIEW.
*+ +CBI REV.*
CONFEDERATION OF BRITISH INDUSTRY.
*LONDON NO.1, JE 1971-*
*CA/U-1. ED/N-1. EX/U-1. LO/N-1. LO/U-3. LO/U28.*
*OX/U-8. XS/R10.*

CBI SMALLER FIRMS BULLETIN.
*+ +CBI SMALLER FIRMS BULL.*
CONFEDERATION OF BRITISH INDUSTRY.
*LONDON NO.1, JL 1970-*
*Q.*
*OX/U17.*
*ED/N-1. NO.8, 1972-*

CCAS NEWSLETTER.    XXX
SUBS (1969): BULLETIN OF CONCERNED ASIAN
SCHOLARS.

CEAA NEWSLETTER.
*+ +CEAA NEWSL.*
MODERN LANGUAGE ASSOCIATION OF AMERICA: CENTER
FOR EDITIONS OF AMERICAN AUTHORS.
*NEW YORK NO.1, 1968-*
*OX/U-1.*
*ISSN 0544-6686*

CE-BNL BIB.
CENTRAL ELECTRICITY GENERATING BOARD: BERKELEY
NUCLEAR LABORATORIES.
*[BERKELEY, GLOS.] 1, 1969-*
*LO/N14.*

CEH DESIGN GUIDE.
*+ +CEH DES. GUIDE.*
CENTRE ON ENVIRONMENT FOR THE HANDICAPPED.
*LONDON 1, 1973-*
*OX/U-8.*

CELESTIAL MECHANICS.
*+ +CELESTIAL MECH.*
*[REIDEL PUBL. CO.]*
*DORDRECHT 1, 1969-*
*LO/N14. OX/U-1. SA/U-1.*
*ISSN 0008-8714*

CELIK. STEEL. STAL.
UDRUZENJE JUGOSLOVENSKIH ZELEZARA.
*BELGRADE 1(1), 1965-*
ENGL. & RUSS. SUMM. & CONT. LISTS.
*LO/N13. 5(20), 1969-*

CELL DIFFERENTIATION.
*+ +CELL. DIFFER.*
*[NORTH HOLLAND]*
*AMSTERDAM 1, 1972-*
*6/A.*
*AD/U-1. CA/U-2. CA/U15. LO/N13. LO/U28.*
*MA/U-1. OX/U-8. SH/U-1. SO/U-1. SW/U-1.*
*ISSN 0045-6039*

CELLOSCOPE.
BRITISH CELLOPHANE LTD.
*LONDON NO.1, 1966-*
*OX/U-1.*

CELLULAR IMMUNOLOGY.
*+ +CELL. IMMUNOL.*
*[ACADEMIC P.]*
*NEW YORK 1, MY 1970-*
*2M.*
*BL/U-1. GL/U-1. LD/U-1. LO/M12. LO/N13.*
*NW/U-1. SH/U-1. SO/U-1.*
*ISSN 0008-8749*

**CELULOZA - PAPIR - GRAFIKA.**
++*CELUL. - PAP. - GRAF.*
SAVEZ KEMICARA I TEHNOLOGA HRVATSKE.
*ZAGREB  1, MY 1961-*
Q. ENGL. & GER. SUMM. & CONTENTS LISTS.
*LO/N13.  4, 1964-*

**CEMENT & CONCRETE RESEARCH.**
++*CEM. & CONCR. RES.*
[PERGAMON P.]
*NEW YORK  1(1), JA 1971-*
ENGL., FR., GER. & RUSS. WITH SOME ABSTR. IN
OTHER LANG.
*AD/U-3.     ED/N-1.     LO/N14.     SH/C-5.     XS/R10.*
*GL/U-1.  4, 1974-                           GL/U-2.  2, 1972-*
*LD/U-1.  2, 1972-                           LO/U28.  2, 1972-*
*OX/U-8.  1(3), 1971-*
*ISSN 0008-8846*

**CEMENT & LIME MANUFACTURE.**                                          XXX
  **SUBS (1970): CEMENT TECHNOLOGY.**

**CEMENT TECHNOLOGY.**                                                  XXX
++*CEM. TECHNOL.*
CEMENT & CONCRETE ASSOCIATION.
*SLOUGH  1, 1970-*
PREV: CEMENT & LIME MANUFACTURE FROM 10, 1937-
42, 1969.
*ED/N-1.     GL/U-2.     LO/N14.     OX/U-8.     SH/C-5.*
*CO/U-1.  1(2), 1970-*
*EX/U-1.  2(1), JA F 1971-*
*ISSN 0008-8854*

**CENSORSHIP TODAY.**
*LOS ANGELES  1(1), 1968-*
*OX/U-1.*
*ISSN 0577-0025*

**CENSUS CENTENARY MONOGRAPH.**
++*CENSUS CENTEN. MONOGR. (INDIA).*
(INDIA) OFFICE OF THE REGISTRAR GENERAL.
*NEW DELHI  NO.1, 1972-*
*LO/N-1.*

**CENSUS DATA NEWS.**
(CANADA) STATISTICS CANADA: CENSUS DIVISION.                            XXX
*OTTAWA  1(1), 1971-*
*GL/U-1.     OX/U17.*

**CENSUS STUDIES.**
++*CENSUS STUD. (INDIA).  [CNSS-B]*
INSTITUTE OF ECONOMIC GROWTH (DELHI):
DEMOGRAPHIC RESEARCH CENTRE.
[ASIA PUBL. HOUSE]
*BOMBAY &C.  NO.1, [1969]-*
*LO/N-1.*
*ISSN 0070-3311*

**CENTRAL AFRICA RESEARCH BULLETIN.**
++*CENT. AFR. RES. BULL.*
CENTRAL AFRICA RESEARCH OFFICE.
*LONDON  1, F 1968-*
M.
*OX/U-9.*

**CENTRAL EUROPEAN HISTORY.**
++*CENT. EUR. HIST.*
EMORY UNIVERSITY.
*ATLANTA  1, MR 1968-*
*BT/U-1.     RE/U-1.     SH/U-1.     SW/U-1.     XY/N-1.***
*ISSN 0008-9389*

**CENTER DIARY.**                                                       XXX
++*CENT. DIARY.*
CENTER FOR THE STUDY OF DEMOCRATIC INSTITUTIONS
*SANTA BARBARA  NO.1, OC 1963 - 18, MY/JE 1967.*
SUBS: CENTER MAGAZINE.
*ISSN 0577-0165*

**CENTER DISCUSSION PAPERS, CENTER FOR LATIN
AMERICAN STUDIES, UNIVERSITY OF WISCONSIN
(MILWAUKEE).**
++*CENT. DISCUSS. PAP. CENT. LAT. AM. STUD. UNIV.
WIS. (MILW.).*
*MILWAUKEE  1, 1968-*
*OX/U-1.*

**CENTER MAGAZINE. A PUBLICATION OF THE ...**                           XXX
++*CENT. MAG.*
CENTER FOR THE STUDY OF DEMOCRATIC INSTITUTIONS
*SANTA BARBARA  1(1), OC/N 1967-*
PREV: CENTER DIARY FROM NO.1, 1963 - 18, 1967.
*LO/U-3.**
*ISSN 0008-9125*

**CENTRI MECCANOGRAFICI ED ELETTRONICI.**                               XXX
++*CENT. MECCANOGR. ELETTRON.*
ISTITUTO PER GLI STUDI ECONOMICI ED ORGANIZ-
ZATIVI: CENTRI MECCANOGRAFICI ED ELETTRONICI.
*MILAN  7, 1967- 11, 1971 ...*
PREV: BOLLETTINO D'INFORMAZIONE PER I CENTRI
MECCANOGRAFICI FROM 1, JA 1960- 6, 1966.
SUBS: MANAGEMENT E INFORMATICA.
*LO/N14.*

**CENTRE POINT.**
INNER LONDON TEACHERS' ASSOCIATION.
*LONDON  1(1), 1967-*
*OX/U-1.*

**CENTRE OF SOUTH ASIAN STUDIES NEWSLETTER.**
++*CENT. SOUTH ASIAN STUD. NEWSL.*
UNIVERSITY OF LONDON: CENTRE OF SOUTH ASIAN
STUDIES.
*LONDON  NO.1, OC 1969-*
CENTRE SUBORD. TO SCHOOL OF ORIENTAL &
AFRICAN STUDIES.
*LO/U14.*

**CERA BULLETIN.**                                                      XXX
++*CERA BULL. (CIVIL ENG. RES. ASS.)*
CIVIL ENGINEERING RESEARCH ASSOCIATION.
*LONDON  NO.1, MR 1964- 3, 1966...*
2/A. PREV: CERC BULLETIN. (CIVIL ENGINEERING
RESEARCH COUNCIL); NO.1, MR 1963. SUBS: CIRIA
BULLETIN.
*LO/N14.*
*BL/U-1.  NO.2, 1965-                      OX/U-8.  NO.3, 1966-*

**CERAMIC-METAL SYSTEMS BIBLIOGRAPHY &
ABSTRACTS.**                                                            XXX
++*CERAM.-MET. SYST. BIBLIOGR. & ABSTR.*
AMERICAN CERAMIC SOCIETY: CERAMIC-METAL SYSTEMS
DIVISION.
*COLUMBUS, OHIO  1970(1971)-*
PREV: CERAMIC-METAL SYSTEMS & ENAMEL BIBLIO-
GRAPHY & ABSTRACTS FROM 1960/1(1962)- 1969
(1970).
*LO/N14.*

**CERAMIC REVIEW. MAGAZINE OF THE CRAFTSMEN
POTTERS ASSOCIATION OF GREAT BRITAIN.**
++*CERAM. REV.*
CRAFTSMEN POTTERS ASSOCIATION OF GREAT
BRITAIN.
*LONDON  NO.1, F 1970-*
*ED/N-1.     LO/N-1.     LO/N14.     OX/U-1.*
*LC/C-1.  N/D 1971.*
*LD/U-1.  NO.13, 1971-*

**CERC BULLETIN.**                                                      XXX
++*CERC BULL.*
CIVIL ENGINEERING RESEARCH COUNCIL.
*LONDON  NO.1, MR 1963.*
SUBS: CERA BULLETIN. (CIVIL ENGINEERING
RESEARCH ASSOCIATION).
*LO/N14.*
*ISSN 0529-8474*

**CEREAL RUSTS BULLETIN.**
++*CEREAL RUSTS BULL.*
EUROPEAN & MEDITERRANEAN CEREAL RUSTS
FOUNDATION.
*WAGENINGEN  1, 1973-*
*AD/U-1.     BL/U-1.     LO/N-6.*
*XS/U-1.  2, 1974-*

**CERES. THE JOURNAL OF THE ...**                                       XXX
HOME-GROWN CEREALS AUTHORITY.
*LONDON  NO.1, JA 1968- NO.6, MY 1969.//*
Q. NOTE SAME TITLE ADOPTED SAME YEAR BY FAO.
*AB/U-2.     CA/U-1.     CA/U11.     ED/N-1.     LD/U-1.     OX/U-1.*
*XE/F-2.     XS/R-4.     XS/U-1.     ZS/U-1.*
*ISSN 0577-344X*

**CERTIFIED ACCOUNTANT.**                                               XXX
++*CERTIF. ACCOUNT.*
ASSOCIATION OF CERTIFIED & CORPORATE
ACCOUNTANTS.
*LONDON  64, 1972-*
PREV: CERTIFIED ACCOUNTANTS JOURNAL.
*ED/N-1.     GL/U-1.     LD/U-1.     LN/U-2.     LO/U-3.     LO/U28.*
*RE/U-1.     SA/U-1.*

**CERTIFIED ACCOUNTANTS JOURNAL.**                                      XXX
  **SUBS (1972): CERTIFIED ACCOUNTANT.**

**CESKOSLOVENSKA DEFEKTOLOGIA.**
++*CESK. DEFEKTOL.*
KARLOVA UNIVERSITA V PRAZE.
*PRAGUE  2, 1968-*
MONOGR.
*CA/U-1.     OX/U-1.*

**CESKOSLOVENSKA OCHRANA PRIRODY. NATURE CONS-
ERVATION IN CZECHOSLOVAKIA.**
*+ +CESK. OCHR. PRIR.*
SLOVENSKY USTAV PAMIATKOVEJ STAROSTLIVOSTI A
OCHRANY PRIRODY.
*BRATISLAVA 1, 1963-*
ENGL. GER. & RUSS. SUMM.
*LO/N-2.*

**CESKOSLOVENSKA VLASTIVEDA: DIL 1: GEOLOGIE,
FIZICKY ZEMEPIS.**
*+ +CESK. VLASTIVEDA, 1.*
CESKOSLOVENSKA SPOLECNOST PRO SIRENI POLITICK-
YCH A VEDECKYCH ZNALOSTI.
*PRAGUE 1, 1963-*
*LA/U-1.    OX/U-1.*

**CESKOSLOVENSKA VLASTIVEDA: DIL 2: DEJINY DO
R.1781.**
*+ +CESK. VLASTIVEDA, 2.*
CESKOSLOVENSKA SPOLECNOST PRO SIRENI POLITICK-
YCH A VEDECKYCH ZNALOSTI.
*PRAGUE 1, 1963-*
*LA/U-1.    OX/U-1.*

**CESKOSLOVENSKA VLASTIVEDA: DIL 3: LIDOVA
KULTURA.**
*+ +CESK. VLASTIVEDA, 3.*
CESKOSLOVENSKA SPOLECNOST PRO SIRENI POLITICK-
YCH A VEDECKYCH ZNALOSTI.
*PRAGUE 1, 1963-*
*LA/U-1.    OX/U-1.*

**CETOLOGY.**
[BIOLOGICAL SYSTEMS, INC.]
*ST. AUGUSTINE, FLA.   NO.1, MY 1971-*
*LO/N-2.*

**CEYLON COOPERATIVE REVIEW.**
*+ +CEYLON COOP. REV.*
COOPERATIVE FEDERATION OF CEYLON.
*COLOMBO   1(1), MR 1967-*
*Q.*
*LO/U-8.*

**CEYLON JOURNAL OF THE HUMANITIES.**                    XXX
*+ +CEYLON J. HUMANITIES.*
UNIVERSITY OF CEYLON.
*PERADENIYA   1(1), 1970-*
PREV. PART OF: UNIVERSITY OF CEYLON REVIEW
FROM 1, AP 1943- 25(1/2), AP/OC 1967.
*LO/N12.    LO/U-1.    LO/U14.    OX/U-1.*
*ISSN 0009-0840*

**CEYLON NEWS-LETTER.**                                  XXX
SUBS (1973): SRI LANKA NEWS-LETTER.

**CEYLON TODAY.**                                        XXX
SUBS (1972): SRI LANKA TODAY.

**CHAJ.  KULTURA I PROIZVODSTVO.**
GOSUDARSTVENNYJ KOMITET SOVETA MINISTROV GRUZ-
INSKOJ SSR PO KOORDINATSII NAUCHNO ISSLE-
DOVATEL'SKIKH RABOT: INSTITUT NAUCHNO-TEKHNICH-
ESKOJ INFORMATSII I PROPAGANDY.
*TIFLES   1, 1963-*
*LO/N13.   1(6), 1966-*

**CHANCELLOR COLLEGE FORUM.**
*+ +CHANCELLOR COLL. FORUM.*
UNIVERSITY OF MALAWI.
*LIMBE   1(1), 1969-*
*LO/U14.*

**CHANGES IN EMPLOYMENT STRUCTURE.**
*+ +CHANGES EMPLOYMENT STRUCT.*
OECD.
*PARIS   1, 1966-*
*GL/U-1.*

**CHANNEL.**
BRITISH HYDROMECHANICS RESEARCH ASSOCIATION.
*CRANFIELD   1, 1968-*
S/T: CIVIL HYDRAULICS & AERODYNAMICS: NOTES
& NEW ENGINEERING LITERATURE.
*BR/U-3.    LO/N-4.    LO/N14.    SF/U-1.    SH/U-3.    SW/U-1.*
*AD/U-1.  3, 1974-          ED/N-1.  1(8), 1968-*
*LO/U12.  2(1), 1969-       LV/U-1.  2, 1969-*
*XS/R10.  3(1), 1970-*
*ISSN 0009-1445*

**CHAPBOOK MISCELLANY.**
*+ +CHAPBOOK MISC.*
[SCHILLER LTD.]
*NEW YORK   1[1], 1970-*
*OX/U-1.*

**CHAPMAN.  POETRY MAGAZINE.**
*HAMILTON, LANARKSHIRE NO.1, S 1970-*
*ED/N-1.    OX/U-1.*
*AD/U-1.  2(2), 1972-*

**CHAPTER.**
WHITE PANTHER PARTY.
[INTERNATIONAL TIMES]
*LONDON   NO.1, 1972-*
*Q.*
*CA/U-1.   NO.2, [1973]-*
*ED/N-1.   NO.2, [1973]-*

**CHAUFFAGE AU MAZOUT.**                                 XXX
SUBS (1960): GAZ ET MAZOUT.

**CHELEN OPIT V SELSKOTO STOPANSTVO.**
*+ +CHELEN OPIT SELSKOTO STOP.*
BULGARSKA KOMUNISTICHESKA PARTIJA: OKRUZHEN
KOMITET.
*SOFIA   1, 1965-*
*OX/U-1.*

**CHELOVEK I OBSHCHESTVO.**
*+ +CHELOVEK & O-VO.*
LENINGRADSKIJ GOSUDARSTVENNYJ UNIVERSITET:
NAUCHNO-ISSLEDOVATEL'SKIJ INSTITUT KOMPLEKSNYKH
SOTSIAL'NYKH ISSLEDOVANIJ.
*LENINGRAD   1, 1966-*
*BH/U-1.    CC/U-1.    GL/U-1.    LO/U-2.    LO/U-3.*
*LO/U15. *   OX/U-1.*

**CHELTENHAM PAPERS.**
*+ +CHELTENHAM PAP.*
GLOUCESTERSHIRE COLLEGE OF ART.
*CHELTENHAM   NO.1, 1970-*
*LO/N-1.*

**CHELYS.**
VIOLA DA GAMBA SOCIETY.
*LONDON &C.   1, 1970-*
*OX/U-8.*

**CHEM 26.**                                             XXX
[HALE PUBL. CO.]
*STAMFORD, CONN.   6(7), 1970- 10(8), 1974 ...*
PREV: CHEMICALS 26 FROM 1(1), 1965- 6(6),
1970. SUBS: PAPER PROCESSING.
*LO/N14.*
*ISSN 0009-2762*

**CHEMBOOKS.  CHEMISTRY BOOKS, SERIES, PROCEED-
INGS, JOURNALS.**
[KARGER LIBRI]
*BASLE   1, MR/AP 1969-*
*BL/U-1.*

**CHEMICA SCRIPTA.**                                     XXX
*+ +CHEM. SCR.*
KUNGLIGA SVENSKA VETENSKAPS-AKADEMIEN.
*STOCKHOLM   1, 1971-*
PREV: ARKIV FOR KEMI FROM 1, S 1949- 32, 1969.
*CA/U-2.    DB/S-1.    GL/U-1.    LO/N-1.    LO/S-3.    LO/U11.*
*LO/U20.    MA/U-1.    NW/U-1.    SF/U-1.*
*ISSN 0004-2056*

**CHEMICAL ABSTRACTS SERVICE SOURCE INDEX.**            XXX
*+ +CHEM. ABSTR. SERV. SOURCE INDEX.*
AMERICAN CHEMICAL SOCIETY.
*COLUMBUS, OHIO   1970-*
PREV: ACCESS FROM 1969.
*LO/N14.    MA/U-1.*
*GL/U-2.  NO.4, 1970-*
*ISSN 0001-0634*

**CHEMICAL ABSTRACTS SERVICE SOURCE INDEX
QUARTERLY.**                                             XXX
*+ +CHEM. ABSTR. SERV. SOURCE INDEX Q.*
AMERICAN CHEMICAL SOCIETY.
*COLUMBUS, OHIO   1970(4)-*
PREV: ACCESS QUARTERLY. THE 4TH ISSUE OF EACH
YEAR IS CUMULATED FOR THE 12 MONTH PERIOD OC-S
*LO/N14.    LO/S-3.*
*LD/U-1.  1972(4)-*

**CHEMICAL AGE (LONDON).**                               XXX
SUBS (1972): CHEMICAL AGE INTERNATIONAL.

**CHEMICAL AGE INTERNATIONAL.**                          XXX
*+ +CHEM. AGE INT.*
[BENN BROS.]
*LONDON   105(2774), 1972- 108(2844/45), 1974...*
PREV: CHEMICAL AGE (LONDON) FROM 1(1), 1919-
105(2773), 1972. SUBS: CHEMICAL AGE (LONDON,
1974).
*ED/N-1.    LO/N13.    LO/N35.    XS/R10.*
*BL/U-1.  106(2790), 1973-*
*ISSN 0300-3248*

**CHEMICAL-BIOLOGICAL ACTIVITIES.**
++CHEM.-BIOL. ACT. [CBAC-A]
AMERICAN CHEMICAL SOCIETY.
EASTON, PA. 1, 1965-
PRELIMINARY ISSUE DATED S 1962.
SO/U-1. 1, 1965- 12, 1970.
ISSN 0009-238X

**CHEMICAL ECONOMY & ENGINEERING REVIEW.** XXX
++CHEM. ECON. & ENG. REV.
KAGAKU KEIZAI KENKYUJO.
TOKYO 1, 1969-
PREV: JAPAN CHEMICAL QUARTERLY FROM 1, 1965.
LO/N-7. LO/S-3.
ISSN 0009-2436

**CHEMICAL ENGINEERING COMMUNICATIONS.**
++CHEM. ENG. COMMUN.
[GORDON & BREACH]
NEW YORK; LONDON 1(1), JL 1973-
S/T: AN INTERNATIONAL JOURNAL OF CHEMICAL
ENGINEERING & APPLIED CHEMISTRY.
CA/U-1. ED/N-1. EX/U-1. GL/U-2. LO/S-3. LO/U-2.
OX/U-8. SF/U-1. SW/U-1.

**CHEMICAL ENGINEERING, JAPAN.** XXX
++CHEM. ENG., JAP.
KAGAKU KOGAKU KYOKAI.
TOKYO 1, AUTUMN 1963- 5, 1967.
ACTUAL TITLE CONTINUES: ... ABRIDGED EDITION
IN ENGLISH; I.E. OF: KAGAKU KOGAKU. NAME OF
BODY IN ENGL.: SOCIETY OF CHEMICAL ENGINEERS.
SUBS: JOURNAL OF CHEMICAL ENGINEERING OF
JAPAN. 1 ABOVE = 27 OF ORIG.
LO/N-4. LO/N14.
SW/U-1. 4, 1966-

**CHEMICAL ENGINEERING JOURNAL.**
++CHEM. ENG. J.
[ELSEVIER]
LONDON 1(1), JA 1970-
BH/U-1. BH/U-3. DB/U-1. LD/U-1. LO/N14. LO/R-6.
LO/S-3. SF/U-1. SH/U-3. SW/U-1. XS/R10.
ED/N-1. 1(4), OC 1970-
ISSN 0009-2487

**CHEMICAL ENGINEERING PROGRESS MONOGRAPH
SERIES.** XXX
SUBS (1972): AICHE MONOGRAPH SERIES.

**CHEMICAL INDUSTRY DEVELOPMENTS.** XXX
++CHEM. IND. DEV.
[COLOUR PUBLICATIONS PRIVATE, LTD.]
BOMBAY 6, 1972-
PREV: CHEMICAL PROCESSING & ENGINEERING FROM
1, 1967- 5, 1971.
LO/N14.

**CHEMICAL INSTRUMENTATION.**
++CHEM. INSTRUM.
[DEKKER]
NEW YORK 1, 1968-
LO/N14. LO/S-3.
ISSN 0009-2592

**CHEMICAL MARKETING REPORTER.** XXX
++CHEM. MARK. REP.
[SCHNELL PUBL. CO.]
NEW YORK 201, 1972-
PREV: OIL, PAINT & DRUG REPORTER FROM 1, 1871-
200, 1971.
LO/N13.

**CHEMICAL PHYSICS.**
++CHEM. PHYS.
[NORTH HOLLAND]
AMSTERDAM 1, JA/F 1973-
10/A.
BL/U-1. CA/U-2. LD/U-1. LD/U-1. LO/N-4. LO/N14.
LO/S-3. LO/U-2. LO/U-4. MA/U-1.
LO/U12. 3(1), 1974-

**CHEMICALS & PLASTICS INDUSTRIES REVIEW.**
++CHEM. & PLAST. IND. REV.
[GOWER ECONOMIC PUBL.]
EPPING, ESSEX 1972-
LO/N-1. OX/U-1. SW/U-1.

**CHEMICAL & PROCESS ENGINEERING.** XXX
SUBS (1972) PART OF: PROCESS ENGINEERING.

**CHEMICAL PROCESS REVIEW.**
++CHEM. PROC. REV.
NOYES DEVELOPMENT CORPORATION.
PARK RIDGE, NJ NO.1, JA 1967-
LO/N14.
ISSN 0069-3014

**CHEMICAL PROCESSING & ENGINEERING.** XXX
++CHEM. PROCESS. & ENG.
[COLOUR PUBLICATIONS PRIVATE, LTD.]
BOMBAY 1, 1967- 5, 1971 ...
SUBS: CHEMICAL INDUSTRY DEVELOPMENTS.
LO/N14. 3(2), 1969-

**CHEMICAL SOCIETY REVIEWS.** XXX
++CHEM. SOC. REV.
CHEMICAL SOCIETY.
LONDON 1, 1972-
INCORP: QUARTERLY REVIEWS OF THE CHEMICAL
SOCIETY FROM 1, 1947- 25, 1971; & RIC REVIEWS
FROM 1, 1968- 4, 1971.
AD/U-1. BH/U-3. ED/N-1. GL/U-1. LD/U-1. LO/N14.
LO/R-6. LO/S-3. LO/U-1. LO/U-2. LO/U-4. LO/U13.
NW/U-1. SH/U-1. SO/U-1. SW/U-1.
ISSN 0306-0012

**CHEMICAL TECHNOLOGY.** XXX
++CHEM. TECHNOL.
AMERICAN CHEMICAL SOCIETY.
WASHINGTON, D.C. JA 1971-
PREV: INDUSTRIAL & ENGINEERING CHEMISTRY FROM
15, 1923- 62(12), D 1970. MONTHLY ISSUES HAVE
COVER TITLE CHEMTECH.
AD/U-3. BH/P-1. LO/N-4. LO/N14. LO/S-3. LO/U20.
MA/P-1. SF/U-1. SO/U-1. XE/F-2.
OX/U-8. MR 1971-
GL/U-2. FIVE YEARS ONLY.
ISSN 0009-2703

**CHEMICAL THERMODYNAMICS.**
++CHEM. THERMODYN.
CHEMICAL SOCIETY.
LONDON 1, 1973-
CA/U-1. ED/N-1. HL/U-1. LO/N-2. LO/N14. LO/S-3.
LO/U-2. MA/P-1. MA/U-1. NW/U-1. RE/U-1.
ISSN 0305-9731

**CHEMICO-BIOLOGICAL INTERACTIONS.**
++CHEMICO-BIOL. INTERACTIONS.
[ELSEVIER PUBLISHING CO.]
AMSTERDAM 1, 1969-
S/T: INTERNATIONAL JOURNAL DEVOTED TO STUDIES
OF THE MECHANISMS BY WHICH EXOGENOUS CHEMICALS
PRODUCE CHANGES IN BIOLOGICAL SYSTEMS.
AD/U-1. BH/U-1. CA/U-2. DB/U-2. GL/U-2. LD/U-1.
LO/N-2. LO/N14. LO/S-3. LO/U12. LO/U20.
OX/U-8. SH/U-1.
BL/U-1. 6, 1973-
ISSN 0009-2797

**CHEMIE MIKROBIOLOGIE TECHNOLOGIE DER LEBENSMIT-
TEL. FOOD CHEMISTRY MICROBIOLOGY TECHNOLOGY.
CHIMIE MICROBIOLOGIE TECHNOLOGIE ALIMENTAIRE.**
++CHEM. MIKROBIOL. TECHNOL. LEBENSM.
[HANS CARL]
NUREMBERG 1, 1971-
BL/U-1. LO/N14.

**CHEMIEFASERN. ZEITSCHRIFT FUR MODERN TEXTIL-
VERARBEITUNG.** XXX
[CMFS-A]
[DEUTSCHER FACHVERLAG GMBH]
FRANKFURT AM MAIN 10(4), AP 1960- 22(1), 1972
PREV: REYON, ZELLWOLLE UND ANDERE CHEMIEFASERN
FROM 1952- 1960. SUBS: CHEMIEFASERN/TEXTIL-
INDUSTRIE.
LO/N14.

**CHEMIEFASERN/TEXTIL-INDUSTRIE.** XXX
[DEUTSCHER FACHVERLAG GMBH]
FRANKFURT AM MAIN 22(2), 1972-
PREV: CHEMIEFASERN FROM 10(4), AP 1960- 22(1),
1972. INCORP: TEXTIL-INDUSTRIE FROM 72, 1970-
74(1), 1972.
LO/N14.

**CHEMISTRY & BIOCHEMISTRY OF AMINO ACIDS,
PEPTIDES & PROTEINS.**
++CHEM. & BIOCHEM. AMINO ACIDS PEPTIDES &
PROTEINS.
[DEKKER]
NEW YORK 1, 1971-
GL/U-1. LO/N13. LO/S-3. LO/U-2. SF/U-1.

**CHEMISTRY & BIOLOGY.** 000
SEE: KAGAKU TO SEIBUTSU.

**CHEMISTRY & INDUSTRY.**
++CHEM. & IND.
SOCIETY OF CHEMICAL INDUSTRY.
LONDON NO.1, 1970-
ISSUES SUPPL. ENTITLED: CHEMISTRY & INDUSTRY
BULLETIN.
HL/U-1.
ISSN 0009-3068

**CHEMISTRY & INDUSTRY BULLETIN.**
+ +CHEM. & IND. BULL.
SOCIETY OF CHEMICAL INDUSTRY.
LONDON JA 1972-
SUPPL. TO CHEMISTRY & INDUSTRY.
CA/U-1.    XS/R10.

**CHEMISTRY LETTERS.**
+ +CHEM. LETT.
CHEMICAL SOCIETY OF JAPAN.
TOKYO NO.1, 1972-
JAP., ENGL., GER. OR FR.
LO/N14.    LO/S-3.
GL/U-1.  1973-                          LD/U-1.  1973-

**CHEMISTRY IN NEW ZEALAND.**                                    XXX
+ +CHEM. N.Z.
NEW ZEALAND INSTITUTE OF CHEMISTRY.
WELLINGTON, N.Z. 32, 1968-
PREV: JOURNAL OF THE NEW ZEALAND INSTITUTE OF
CHEMISTRY FROM 1, 1936- 31, 1967.
LO/N13.    LO/S-3.

**CHEMISTRY, OIL & GAS IN RUMANIA. NEWS & COM-
MENTARIES.**
+ +CHEM. OIL & GAS RUM.
CENTRUL DE DOCUMENTAIRE AL INDUSTREI PETROLVLUI
SI CHIMENIE.
BUCHAREST 1, 1965-
XY/N-1.**

**CHEMORECEPTION ABSTRACTS. CHEMICAL SENSE &
APPLIED TECHNIQUES.**
+ +CHEMORECEPT. ABSTR.
EUROPEAN CHEMORECEPTION RESEARCH ORGANIZATION.
[INFORMATION RETRIEVAL LTD.]
LONDON 1(1), JA 1973-
Q.
CA/U-1.    ED/N-1.    OX/U-8.

**CHEMOSPHERE. CHEMISTRY, PHYSICS & BIOLOGY AS
FOCUSED ON ENVIRONMENTAL PROBLEMS.**
[PERGAMON P.]
OXFORD 1(1), JA 1972-
6/A.
CA/U-1.    ED/N-1.    SH/U-1.    XS/R10.
ISSN 0045-6535

**CHEMSCAN: RADIATION & PHOTOCHEMISTRY.**                        XXX
+ +CHEMSCAN, RADIAT. & PHOTOCHEM.
CHEMICAL SOCIETY.
LONDON NO.20, 1969- 26, 1970.
SUBS: MACROPROFILE: RADIATION & PHOTOCHEMISTRY
CONTAINS SELECTED ENTRIES FROM, & FOLLOWS
NUMBERING OF CHEMICAL TITLES.
ED/N-1.    OX/U-1.    XS/R10.

**CHEMSCAN: STEROIDS.**                                          XXX
CHEMICAL SOCIETY.
LONDON NO.20, 1969- 26, 1970.
SUBS: MACROPROFILE: STEROIDS. CONTAINS
SELECTED ENTRIES FROM, & FOLLOWS NUMBERING OF
CHEMICAL TITLES.
ED/N-1.    OX/U-1.
CR/M-1.  1970-

**CHEMTECH.**                                                    000
SEE: CHEMICAL TECHNOLOGY.

**CHESHIRE HISTORY NEWSLETTER.**
+ +CHESHIRE HIST. NEWSL.
CHESHIRE COUNTY COUNCIL.
CHESTER NO.1, S 1971-
2/A.
ED/N-1.    LO/N-1.

**CHESIL. THE MAGAZINE OF CHESIL POETS.**
[WORD & ACTION]
WAREHAM, DORSET NO.1, F 1973-
CA/U-1.    ED/N-1.    LO/U-2.

**CHESS PLAYER. DER SCHACHSPIELER.**
NOTTINGHAM 1(1), 1971-
MON.
ED/N-1.
ISSN 0045-6594

**CHEST. JOURNAL OF CIRCULATION, RESPIRATION &
RELATED SYSTEMS.**                                              XXX
AMERICAN COLLEGE OF CHEST PHYSICIANS.
CHICAGO 57, 1970-
PREV: DISEASES OF THE CHEST FROM 1, 1935-
56, 1969.
CR/M-1.    NW/U-1.
ISSN 0012-3692

**CHEST & HEART. NEWS BULLETIN OF ...**
CHEST & HEART ASSOCIATION.
LONDON 1, JE 1969-
ED/N-1.    OX/U-8.

**CHI NEWS.**                                                    XXX
CHICAGO BRIDGE & IRON COMPANY.
OAK BROOK, ILL. 58(3), 1972-
PREV: WATER TOWER FROM 1, S 1914- 58(2), 1971.
LO/N14.

**CHIBA-KEN NOGYO SHIKENJO TOKUBETSU HOKOKU.
SPECIAL BULLETIN OF THE CHIBA-KEN AGRICULTUR-
AL EXPERIMENT STATION.**
CHIBA NO.1, 1961-
ENGL. SUMM.
LO/N13.

**CHIJIL KWANGSANG. GEOLOGY & ORE DEPOSIT.**
KUNGNIP CHIJIL CHOSASO.
SEOUL [NO.]1, 1966-
LO/N13.

**CHILDREN TODAY.**
+ +CHILD. TODAY.
(UNITED STATES) OFFICE OF CHILD DEVELOPMENT:
CHILDREN'S BUREAU.
WASHINGTON, D.C. 1, 1972-
DB/U-2.    LD/U-2.    LO/U28.

**CHILDREN'S BOOK REVIEW.**                                      XXX
+ +CHILD. BOOK REV.
[FIVE OWL P.]
BROXBOURNE, HERTS. 1(1), F 1971-
PREV: CHILDREN'S BOOK NEWS FROM 1, S/OC
1965- 5(6), D 1970.
BH/P-1.    DB/U-2.    ED/N-1.    GL/U-2.    HL/U-2.
ISSN 0009-1626

**CHILDREN'S LITERATURE IN EDUCATION.**
+ +CHILD. LIT. EDUC.
[WARD LOCK]
LONDON 1, MR 1970-
DB/U-2.    HL/U-2.    MA/U-1.    OX/U-1.
BL/U-1. 13, 1974-

**CHILDREN'S RIGHTS.**                                           XXX
[CHILDREN'S RIGHTS PUBL. LTD.]
NO.1, JA 1972 - 6, JL/AG 1972.
MON. SUBS: KIDS.
BH/U-1.    ED/N-1.    LO/U-3.

**CHIMICA (MILANO).***                                           XXX
SUBS (1969): NUOVA CHIMICA.

**CHIMIE ANALYTIQUE.**                                           XXX
SUBS (1972) PART OF: ANALUSIS.

**CHIMIE MICROBIOLOGIE TECHNOLOGIE ALIMENTAIRE.**                000
SEE: CHEMIE MIKROBIOLOGIE TECHNOLOGIE DER
LEBENSMITTEL.

**CHIMIKA CHRONIKA: NS.**
+ +CHIM. CHRON., NS.
GREEK CHEMISTS ASSOCIATION: SCIENTIFIC
COMMITTEE.
ATHENS 1, 1972-
PREVIOUS SERIES FROM 1955.
LD/U-1.

**CHINA MAINLAND REVIEW.**
+ +CHINA MAINL. REV.
UNIVERSITY OF HONG KONG: INSTITUTE OF MAINLAND
STUDIES.
HONG KONG 1(1), 1965-
LO/U-2.    LO/U-3.    OX/U-1.
ISSN 0577-8857

**CHINA NOW.**
SOCIETY FOR ANGLO-CHINESE UNDERSTANDING.
LONDON NO.1, MY 1970-
ED/N-1.    LO/U14.    OX/U-1.
ISSN 0045-6764

**CHINA'S MEDICINE.**                                            XXX
+ +CHINA. MED.
CHINESE MEDICAL ASSOCIATION.
PEKING 1966(1)-
PREV: CHINESE MEDICAL JOURNAL FROM 81, JA
1962- 85(9), 1966.
OX/U-8.
SO/U-1. 1966- 1968.
ISSN 0577-8921

**CHINESE ARTS.**                                                000
SEE: HSIN I-LIN.

**CHINESE ECONOMIC STUDIES.**
+ +CHIN. ECON. STUD.
[INTERNATIONAL ARTS & SCIENCES PRESS]
WHITE PLAINS, NY  1(1), FALL 1967-
S/T: A JOURNAL OF TRANSLATIONS.
LD/U-1.    LO/U-3.    OX/U16.
ISSN 0009-4552

**CHINESE EDUCATION.  A JOURNAL OF TRANSLATIONS.**
+ +CHIN. EDUC.
[INTERNATIONAL ARTS & SCIENCES P.]
WHITE PLAINS, N.Y.  1, 1968-
Q.
CA/U-1.    XY/N-1.
ISSN 0009-4560

**CHINESE LAW & GOVERNMENT.**
+ +CHIN. LAW & GOV.
[INTERNATIONAL ARTS & SCIENCES PRESS]
WHITE PLAINS, NY  1, 1968-
S/T: A JOURNAL OF TRANSLATIONS.
LD/U-1.    LO/U-3.
ISSN 0009-4609

**CHINESE SCHOLARS.**                                    000
SEE: CHUNG-KUO HSUEH-JEN.

**CHINESE SOCIOLOGY & ANTHROPOLOGY.**
+ +CHIN. SOCIOL. & ANTHROPOL.
[INTERNATIONAL ARTS & SCIENCES PRESS]
WHITE PLAINS, NY  1(1), FALL 1968-
S/T: A JOURNAL OF TRANSLATIONS.
CB/U-1.    LD/U-1.    LO/U-3.    LO/U14.    MA/U-1.    RE/U-1.
ISSN 0009-4625

**CHINESE STUDIES IN HISTORY.**                          XXX
+ +CHIN. STUD. HIST.
[INTERNATIONAL ARTS & SCIENCES P.]
NEW YORK  3(1), 1969-
PREV: PART CHINESE STUDIES IN HISTORY & PHIL-
OSOPHY FROM 1, 1967- 2, 1968 OF WHICH VOL.
NUMBERING IS CONTINUED.
SH/U-1.  1971-
LD/U-1.  3(1), 1969- 3(3), 1970.
ISSN 0009-4633

**CHINESE STUDIES IN HISTORY & PHILOSOPHY.**             XXX
+ +CHIN. STUD. HIST. & PHIL.
[INTERNATIONAL ARTS & SCIENCES P.]
NEW YORK  1(1), 1967- 2, 1968 ...
Q. SUBS. PART OF: CHINESE STUDIES IN HISTORY;
& CHINESE STUDIES IN PHILOSOPHY.
OX/U-1.

**CHINESE STUDIES IN PHILOSOPHY.**                       XXX
+ +CHIN. STUD. PHILOS.
[INTERNATIONAL ARTS & SCIENCES P.]
NEW YORK  1(1), 1969-
PREV: PART CHINESE STUDIES IN HISTORY & PHIL-
OSOPHY FROM 1, 1967- 2, 1968.
LD/U-1.    LO/U14.
ISSN 0023-8627

**CHIRIMO.  A THRICE YEARLY REVIEW OF RHODESIAN
& INTERNATIONAL POETRY.**
SALISBURY, RHOD.  NO.1, 1968-
LO/U14.    SO/U-1.
ISSN 0009-4684

**CHIRON. MITTEILUNGEN DER ...**
DEUTSCHES ARCHAOLOGISCHES INSTITUT: KOMMISSION
FUR ALTE GESCHICHTE UND EPIGRAPHIK. .
[BECK]
MUNICH  1, 1971-
CA/U-1.    GL/U-1.    LD/U-1.    LO/U17.    NO/U-1.    OX/U-2.
SH/U-1.    SW/U-1.
ISSN 0069-3715

**CHIRURGIA PLASTICA.**                                  XXX
+ +CHIR. PLAST.
[SPRINGER]
BERLIN  1, 1971-
PREV: CHIRURGIA PLASTICA ET RECONSTRUCTIVA
FROM 1, 1966 TO 8, 1970.
LO/N13.    OX/U-8.

**CHLODNICTWO.**                                         XXX
ZESPOL DO SPRAW CHLODNICTWA I NACZELNA ORGAN-
IZACJA TECHNICZNA.
WARSZAW  1(1), 1966-
M.  PREV: BIULETYN CHLODNICZY FROM 1(1), 1960-
5(32), 1965. ENGL., FR. & RUSS. SUMM. & CONT.
LISTS.
LO/N13.**

**CHONGORI CHAWON CHOSA POGO.  PROGRESS REPORT
OF THE SARDINES RESOURCES INVESTIGATIONS.**
KUNGNIP SUSAN CHINHUNGWON.
PUSAN  NO.1, 1965-
LO/N13.

**CHRISTIAN (LONDON).**
INSTITUTE OF CHRISTIAN STUDIES.
LONDON  1(1), 1973-
CA/U-1.    ED/N-1.    OX/U-1.

**CHRISTIAN ATTITUDES ON JEWS & JUDAISM.**
+ +CHRIST. ATTIT. JEWS & JUDAISM.
INSTITUTE OF JEWISH AFFAIRS.
LONDON  NO.1, JE 1968-
PUBL. BY THE INST. IN ASS. WITH THE WORLD
JEWISH CONGRESS. S/T: A PERIODICAL SURVEY.
ED/N-1.    LO/N-1.    SO/U-1.
ISSN 0009-5249

**CHRISTIAN BRETHREN RESEARCH FELLOWSHIP BROAD-
SHEET.**
+ +CHRIST. BRETHREN RES. FELLOWSHIP BROADSH.
PINNER, MIDDX.  NO.1, 1969-
ED/N-1.

**CHRISTIAN GUARDIAN WEEKLY.**
+ +CHRIST. GUARD. W.
LONDON  1, 1969-
ED/N-1.
ISSN 0578-0004

**CHRISTIAN HEALING.**
+ +CHRIST. HEAL.
CHURCHES' COUNCIL OF HEALING IN IRELAND.
DUBLIN; BELFAST  1, 1973-
DB/U-2.    ED/N-1.

**CHRISTMAS BROADSIDE.**
STATE UNIVERSITY OF NEW YORK: LOCKWOOD MEMORIAL
LIBRARY.
BUFFALO, N.Y.  NO.1, 1968-
LO/U-2.

**CHRISTUS REX.**                                        XXX
SUBS (1972): PART OF SOCIAL STUDIES.

**CHROMATOGRAPHIA.  AN INTERNATIONAL JOURNAL FOR
RAPID COMMUNICATION IN CHROMATOGRAPHY & RELATED
TECHNIQUES.**
[FRIEDRICH VIEWEG; PERGAMON]
BRUNSWICK, GER. & OXFORD  NO.1/2, 1968-
2M. ENGL., FR. & GER.
CA/U-1.    ED/N-1.    LO/N14.    LO/S31.    OX/U-8.
GL/U-2.  3/4, 1968-
ISSN 0009-5893

**CHROMOSOME ATLAS: FISH, AMPHIBIANS, REPTILES &
BIRDS.**
[SPRINGER]
BERLIN &C.  1, 1971-
A.
OX/U-8.

**CHRONICLE.**                                           XXX
ROTARY INTERNATIONAL OF GREAT BRITAIN &
IRELAND: DISTRICT 102.
FALKIRK  NO.1, S 1972-
PREV: MAGAZINE OF DISTRICT 102 ... FROM NO.1,
S 1951- NO.65, JL 1971.
ED/N-1.

**CHRONICLE, PORTLAND C.S. LEWIS SOCIETY.**
+ +CHRON. PORTLAND C.S. LEWIS SOC.
PORTLAND, OREG.  1, 1972-
OX/U-1.

**CHRONIQUE D'HYDROGEOLOGIE.**                           XXX
+ +CHRON. HYDROGEOL.
BUREAU DE RECHERCHES GEOLOGIQUES ET MINIERES.
PARIS  NO.1, MR 1963- 12, 1967.
SUBS: BULLETIN, BUREAU DE RECHERCHES GEOLO-
GIQUES ET MINIERES: 2S: SECTION 3: HYDRO-
GEOLOGIE.
LO/N13.

**CHRONIQUE DE L'IRSAC.  INFORMATIONS DE ...**           XXX
+ +CHRON. IRSAC. (INST. RECH. SCI. AFR. CENT.).
INSTITUT POUR LA RECHERCHE SCIENTIFIQUE EN
AFRIQUE CENTRALE (CONGO).
LWIRO-BUKAVU  1(1), AP 1966-
3/A.  PREV:  FOLIA SCIENTIFICA AFRICAE
CENTRALIS FROM 1, 1955- 6, 1960.
BL/U-1.    LO/N-2.    LO/N17.    LO/U14.

CHRONOLOGIE DES COMMUNAUTES EUROPEENNES.
+ +CHRONOL. COMMUNAUTES EUR.
UNIVERSITE LIBRE DE BRUXELLES: INSTITUT D'ETUDE
EUROPEENNES.
[PRESSES UNIVERSITAIRES DE BRUXELLES]
 BRUSSELS  NO.1, 1969-
 LO/N-1.
 ISSN 0069-3952

CHTO CHITAT'.                                          XXX
 SUBS (1961): V MIRE KNIG.

CHUNG-HUA MIN-KUO CH'I-K'AN LUN-WEN SO-YIN.
MONTHLY INDEX TO PERIODICALS PUBLISHED IN
TAIWAN.
 CHUNG-YANG T'U-SHU-KUAN (TAIWAN).
 TAIPEH  NO.1, 1970-
 LO/U14.

CHUNG-KUO HSUEH-JEN.  CHINESE SCHOLARS.
HSIN-YA YEN-CHIU-SO.
 HONG KONG  NO.1, 1970-
 LO/U14.

CHURCH GROWTH BULLETIN.
+ +CHURCH GROWTH BULL.
INSTITUTE OF CHURCH GROWTH.
 PASADENA  1(1), S 1964-
 2M.
 BH/C-3.  4(5), 1968-
 ISSN 0009-6385

CHURCH QUARTERLY.
+ +CHURCH Q.
SOCIETY FOR THE PROMOTION OF CHRISTIAN KNOW-
LEDGE.
[EPWORTH PRESS]
 LONDON  1(2), JL 1968- 4, JL 1971. //
 INCORP: CHURCH QUARTERLY REVIEW; & LONDON
 QUARTERLY & HOLBORN REVIEW.
 BH/P-1.  BN/U-1.  ED/N-1.  ED/P-1.  GL/U-1.  HL/U-1.
 LO/U-1.  LO/U11.  MA/U-1.*  NW/U-1.  OX/U-1.
 ISSN 0009-6547

CHURCH QUARTERLY REVIEW.                               XXX
 SUBS (1968) PART OF: CHURCH QUARTERLY.

CHURCH & STATE.
 DUBLIN  1, 1973-
 DB/U-2.

CHYMIA.                                                XXX
 SUBS (1969):  HISTORICAL STUDIES IN THE PHYS-
 ICAL SCIENCES.

CIB BULLETIN.                                          XXX
 SUBS (1968): BUILD INTERNATIONAL.

CIBA-BLATTER.                                          XXX
 SUBS (1971): CIBA-GEIGY ZEITSCHRIFT.

CIBA-GEIGY JOURNAL.                                    XXX
+ +CIBA-GEIGY J.
 BASLE  NO.1, 1971-
 PREV: CIBA JOURNAL FROM NO.1, 1957- 55, 1970.
 GL/U-1.  LO/N-4.  LO/N-4.  LO/N14.

CIBA-GEIGY REVIEW.                                     XXX
 BASLE  1971-
 Q. PREV: CIBA-REVIEW FROM [NO.]1, S 1937-
 141, 1970. ENGL. ED. OF CIBA-GEIGY RUNDSCHAU.
 AD/U-1.  BH/P-1.  CA/U-2.  CV/C-1.  LD/U-1.  LO/N-4.
 LO/N14.  SF/U-1.

CIBA-GEIGY RUNDSCHAU.                                  XXX
 BASLE  1971-
 PREV: CIBA-RUNDSCHAU FROM 1(1), 1936- 10(13),
 1970. ENGL. ED. ISSUED AS CIBA-GEIGY REVIEW.
 LO/N14.

CIBA-GEIGY TECHNICAL NOTES.                            XXX
+ +CIBA-GEIGY TECH. NOTES.
 DUXFORD, CAMBS.  1971-
 PREV: TECHNICAL NOTES, CIBA (A.R.L.), LTD.
 FROM [NO.], 187, 1958- 264, 1970.
 LO/N14.

CIBA-GEIGY ZEITSCHRIFT.                                XXX
+ +CIBA-GEIGY Z.
 BASLE  1, 1971-
 PREV: CIBA-BLATTER.
 LO/N14.

CIBA JOURNAL.                                          XXX
 SUBS (1971): CIBA-GEIGY JOURNAL.

CIBA-REVIEW.                                           XXX
 SUBS (1971): CIBA-GEIGY REVIEW.

CIBA-RUNDSCHAU.                                        XXX
 SUBS (1971): CIBA-GEIGY RUNDSCHAU.

CICINDELA.  A QUARTERLY JOURNAL DEVOTED TO
CICINDELIDAE.
 OSSEO, MINN.  1, 1969-
 LO/N-2.

CIENCIAS BIOLOGICAS.
+ +CIENC. BIOL.
UNIVERSIDADE DE LUANDA: FACULDADE DE CIENCIAS.
 LUANDA  1, 1970-
 LO/N-2.

CIENCIA SOCIAL.
+ +CIENC. SOC.
UNIVERSIDAD NACIONAL DEL CENTRO DEL PERU:
DEPARTAMENTO DE CIENCIAS SOCIALES.
 HUANCAYO  1(1), 1971-
 OX/U-1.

CII EUROLETTER.
+ +CII EUROLETT.
CONFEDERATION OF IRISH INDUSTRY.
 DUBLIN  1, 1973-
 DB/U-2.    OX/U-1.

CIIG BULLETIN.
CONSTRUCTION INDUSTRY INFORMATION GROUP.
 LONDON  1(1), 1970-
 OX/U-1.

CILT REPORTS & PAPERS.
+ +CILT REP. & PAP. (CENT. INF. LANG. TEACH.).
CENTRE FOR INFORMATION ON LANGUAGE TEACHING.
 LONDON  1, AP 1969-
 OX/U-1.

CINEASTE.
 NEW YORK  1(1), 1967-
 Q.
 OX/U-1.
 ISSN 0009-7004

CINEMA.
 CAMBRIDGE  NO.1, 1968-
 OX/U-1.
 HL/U-1.  NO.4, 1969-

CINEMA ITALIANS.
+ +CINEMA ITAL.
 ROME  1(1), 15/N 1967-
 S/T: PERIODICO DELL'ENTE AUTONOMO DI GESTIONE
 PER IL CINEMA.
 LO/N-1.

CINEMA X.
[ROSLAND PRODUCTIONS LTD.]
 LONDON  1(1), AG 1968-
 M.  S/T:  INTERNATIONAL GUIDE FOR ADULT
 AUDIENCES.
 OX/U-1.

CIPA JOURNAL.                                          XXX
+ +CIPA J.
CHARTERED INSTITUTE OF PATENT AGENTS.
 LONDON  1, 1971-
 PREV: TRANSACTIONS, CHARTERED ... FROM 10,
 1891- 88, 1969/70.
 BH/P-1.  ED/N-1.  LO/N14.

CIR STUDIES.                                           000
 SEE: STUDIES, COMMISSION ON INDUSTRIAL
 RELATIONS (GB).

CIRCE.  CAHIERS DU CENTRE ...
CENTRE DE RECHERCHE SUR L'IMAGINAIRE.
[LETTRES MODERNES]
 PARIS  NO.1, 1970-
 MONOGR.
 LO/N-1.
 ISSN 0069-4177

CIRCULAR, ENGINEERING EXPERIMENT STATION,
OREGON STATE COLLEGE.                                  XXX
 SUBS (1962): CIRCULAR, ENGINEERING EXPER-
 IMENT STATION, OREGON STATE UNIVERSITY.

CIRCULAR, ENGINEERING EXPERIMENT STATION,
OREGON STATE UNIVERSITY.                               XXX
+ +CIRC. ENG. EXP. STN. OREG. STATE UNIV.
 CORVALLIS  NO.28, 1962-
 PREV: CIRCULAR, ENGINEERING EXPERIMENT STATION
 OREGON STATE COLLEGE FROM NO.4, 1938-27, 1960.
 LO/N14.

F

**CIRIA.**                                                                            XXX
CONSTRUCTION INDUSTRY RESEARCH & INFORMATION
ASSOCIATION.
*LONDON 1969/70(1970)-*
PREV. CIRIA BULLETIN FROM NO.4, JL 1967- 6, JL
1969.
*LO/N14.*

**CIRIA BULLETIN.**                                                                   XXX
*+ +CIRIA BULL. (CONSTR. IND. RES. & INF. ASS.)*
CONSTRUCTION INDUSTRY RESEARCH & INFORMATION
ASSOCIATION.
*LONDON NO.4, JL 1967- 6, JL 1969.*
PREV: CERA BULLETIN, (CIVIL ENGINEERING
RESEARCH ASSOCIATION), FROM NO.1, MR 1964- 3,
JL 1966. SUBS: CIRIA.
*BL/U-1.    ED/N-1.    LO/N14.    OX/U-8.*
*ISSN 0069-9209*

**CIRIA REPORT.**                                                                     XXX
*+ +CIRIA REP.*
CONSTRUCTION INDUSTRY RESEARCH & INFORMATION
ASSOCIATION.
*LONDON NO.15, AP 1969-*
PREV: CIRIA RESEARCH REPORT FROM NO.10, S
1967- 14, JE 1968.
*BL/U-1.    LO/N14.    OX/U-8.    XS/R10.*

**CIRIA RESEARCH REPORT.**                                                            XXX
SUBS (1969): CIRIA REPORT.

**CISTERCIAN STUDIES.**
*+ +CISTERCIAN STUD.*
ABBAYE DE SCOURMONT.
*BEERNEM, BELG. 1(1), 1966-*
Q.
*OX/U-1.*
*ISSN 0578-3216*

**CITE NEWSLETTER.**
*+ +CITE NEWSL. (CENT. INF. TEACH. ENGL.)*
CENTRE FOR INFORMATION ON THE TEACHING OF
ENGLISH.
*EDINBURGH 1, 1968-*
*BH/U-1.    ED/N-1.*

**CITIZENS OF EUROPE.  NS.**
*+ +CITIZENS EUR. NS.*
EUROPEAN-ATLANTIC MOVEMENT.
*LONDON NO.1, N 1969-*
S/T: A BULLETIN OF CONTEMPORARY EUROPEAN
STUDIES FOR TEACHERS.
*ED/N-1.    LO/N-1.    OX/U-1.*

**CITROGRAPH.**
*LOS ANGELES 54(5), MR 1969-*
PREV: CALIFORNIA CITROGRAPH FROM 1, OC 1915-
54(4), F 1969.
*XS/R-2.*

**CITY.**
URBAN AMERICA.
*WASHINGTON, DC   1(1), AP 1967-*
2M.
*SH/U-1.  2(1),1968-*
*ISSN 0009-7675*

**CIVIC REVIEW.**
*+ +CIVIC REV.*
HULL CITY COUNCIL: DEVELOPMENT COMMITTEE.
*HULL NO.1, 1965-*
*HL/U-1.*

**CIVIL AIR TRANSPORT NEWS.**
*+ +CIVIL AIR TRANSP. NEWS.*
CIVIL AIR TRANSPORT INDUSTRY TRAINING BOARD.
*STAINES NO.1, 1968-*
*LO/N-1.    OX/U-1.*

**CIVIL ENGINEERING TECHNICIAN.  JOURNAL OF ...**
*+ +CIVIL ENG. TECH.*
SOCIETY OF CIVIL ENGINEERING TECHNICIANS.
*LONDON NO.1, N 1968-*
*ED/N-1.    LO/N14.    OX/U-8.*

**CIVIL SERVICE COLLEGE STUDIES.**
*+ +CIV. SERV. COLL. STUD.*
(GREAT BRITAIN) CIVIL SERVICE DEPARTMENT:
CIVIL SERVICE COLLEGE.
*LONDON 1, 1971-*
*GL/U-1.    LO/N-1.    OX/U-1.*

**CIVIL SERVICE MAGAZINE, UNITED REPUBLIC OF
TANZANIA.**
*+ +CIVIL SERV. MAG., U. REPUB. TANZANIA.*
(TANZANIA) MINISTRY OF INFORMATION & TOURISM.
*DAR-ES-SALAAM NO.1, MR 1965-*
2M.
*LO/U-8.*
*ISSN 0578-3844*

**CIVILTA MANTOVANA.**
*MANTUA 1, 1966-*
2M.
*LO/U17.*

**CLANSMAN.**                                                                         XXX
*LONDON NO.1, 1970-*
PREV: BRITISH & COMMONWEALTH REVIEW.
*ED/N-1.*
*ISSN 0007-0254*

**CLAPHAM OMNIBUS.  THE MAGAZINE OF LSE LAW
SOCIETY.**
LONDON SCHOOL OF ECONOMICS & POLITICAL SCIENCE:
LAW SOCIETY.
*LONDON NO.1, 1970-*
*LO/U-3.*

**CLARETIANUM.  COMMENTARIA THEOLOGICA.**
COLLEGIUM INTERNATIONALIS CLARETIANUM DE URBE.
*ROME 1, 1961-*
ANNU.  VARIOUS LANGS. VOL.1 ENTITLED:
THEOLOGICA.
*MA/S-1.*
*ISSN 0578-4182*

**CLAUDEL NEWSLETTER.**
*+ +CLAUDEL NEWSL.*
UNIVERSITY OF RHODE ISLAND: DEPARTMENT OF
LANGUAGES.
*KINGSTON, R.I. NO.1, AP 1968-*
*LO/N-1.    LO/U-1.*

**CLEAN AIR. JOURNAL OF THE ...**
NATIONAL SOCIETY FOR CLEAN AIR.
*BRIGHTON 1, 1971-*
INCORP: SMOKELESS AIR.
*BH/P-1.    CV/C-1.    ED/N-1.    LD/U-1.    LO/N14.    XS/N-1.*
*XS/T-4.*

**CLES POUR LES ARTS.**
ASSOCIATION POUR L'INFORMATION CULTURELLE
(BELGIUM).
*NAMUR NO.1, 1970-*
*OX/U-1.*
*ISSN 0045-7140*

**CLES POUR LA MUSIQUE.**
ASSOCIATION POUR L'INFORMATION MUSICALE
(BELGIUM).
*BRUSSELS NO.1, 1969-*
*OX/U-1.*

**CLES POUR LE SPECTACLE.**
ASSOCIATION POUR L'INFORMATION CULTURELLE
(BELGIUM).
*NAMUR NO.1, 1970-*
M.
*OX/U-1.*

**CLIMATE CONTROL.**
*+ +CLIM. CONTROL. [CLCO-A]*
ALL INDIA AIR CONDITIONING & REFRIGERATION
ASSOCIATION.
*NEW DELHI 1, 1968-*
2M.
*LO/N14.  5, 1972-*

**CLIMATE DATA PUBLICATION.**
*+ +CLIM. DATA PUBL.*
(ZAMBIA) DEPARTMENT OF METEOROLOGY.
*LUSAKA NO.1, 1967-*
*XS/N-1.*

**CLIMATIC RESEARCH UNIT MONTHLY BULLETIN.**                                          000
SEE: CRUMB. CLIMATIC RESEARCH UNIT MONTHLY
BULLETIN.

**CLIMATISATION, CHAUFFAGE ET PLOMBERIE.**
*+ +CLIM. CHAUFF. & PLOMB.*
[MACLEAN HUNTER]
*MONTREAL 1, 1962-*
M.
*LO/N14.  6, 1967-*
*ISSN 0578-5081*

**CLIMATOLOGICAL NOTE.**
+ +CLIMATOL. NOTE (EIRE).
(EIRE) METEOROLOGICAL SERVICE.
 DUBLIN NO.1, F 1972-
 DB/U-2.    LO/N-1.

**CLIMATOLOGICAL NOTES, DEPARTMENT OF GEOGRAPHY, HOSEI UNIVERSITY.**
+ +CLIMAT. NOTES DEP. GEOGR. HOSEI UNIV.
 TOKYO NO.1, 1969-
 XS/N-1.

**CLINICAL ALLERGY. JOURNAL OF THE BRITISH ALLERGY SOCIETY.**
+ +CLIN. ALLERGY.
 OXFORD 1, 1971-
 AD/U-1.    BL/U-1.    CA/M-1.    CA/U-1.    ED/N-1.    GL/U-1.
 LD/U-1.    LO/N13.    OX/U-1.    SO/U-1.    XY/N-1.
 LO/M11.  2, 1972-
 ISSN 0009-9090

**CLINICAL ENDOCRINOLOGY (1972).**
+ +CLIN. ENDOCRINOL. (1972)
[BLACKWELL]
 OXFORD &C.  1, 1972-
 AD/U-1.    BH/U-3.    BL/U-1.    CA/U-1.    ED/N-1.    GL/U-1.
 LD/U-1.    LO/M31.    LO/N13.    OX/U-8.
 LO/M11.  2, 1973-              SH/U-1.  2, 1973-
 ISSN 0300-0664

**CLINICAL GENETICS.**
+ +CLIN. GENET.
 COPENHAGEN  1(1), 1970-
 6A.
 AD/U-1.    BL/U-1.    DB/U-2.    GL/U-1.    LD/U-1.    LO/N14.
 NW/U-1.    OX/U-8.    SH/U-1.
 ISSN 0009-9103

**CLINICAL IMMUNOBIOLOGY & IMMUNOPATHOLOGY.**
+ +CLIN. IMMUNOBIOL. & IMMUNOPATHOL.
[ACADEMIC P.]
 NEW YORK  1, 1972-
 CA/U-1.    GL/U-1.    MA/U-1.

**CLINICAL SCIENCE.**                                               XXX
 SUBS (1973): CLINICAL SCIENCE & MOLECULAR
 MEDICINE.

**CLINICAL SCIENCE & MOLECULAR MEDICINE.**                          XXX
 MEDICAL RESEARCH SOCIETY.
[BLACKWELL SCI. PUBL.]
 LONDON 45, 1973-
 PREV: CLINICAL SCIENCE FROM 1, JL 1933- 44(6),
 1973. ADDIT. SPONS. BODY: BIOCHEMICAL SOCIETY
 GL/U-1.    LD/U-1.    LO/M31.    LO/N13.    SO/U-1.

**CLINICAL TOXICOLOGY.**
+ +CLIN. TOXICOL.
 AMERICAN ACADEMY OF CLINICAL TOXICOLOGY.
[DEKKER]
 NEW YORK  1, MR 1968-
 AD/U-1.    LO/N14.    RE/U-1.    XY/N-1.
 LO/M11.  3, 1970-              LO/M32.  2(1), 1969-
 ISSN 0009-9309

**CLINICS IN ENDOCRINOLOGY & METABOLISM.**
+ +CLIN. ENDOCRINOL. & METAB.
[SAUNDERS]
 LONDON  1(1), MR 1972-
 3/A.
 AD/U-1.    BL/U-1.    CA/U-1.    ED/N-1.    GL/U-1.    NW/U-1.
 SH/U-1.
 CA/M-7.  3, 1974-              LO/M11.  2, 1973-
 ISSN 0300-595X

**CLINICS IN GASTROENTEROLOGY.**
+ +CLIN. GASTROENTEROL.
[W.B. SAUNDERS CO.]
 LONDON; PHILADELPHIA  1, JA 1972-
 3/A.
 BL/U-1.    CA/U-1.    DB/U-2.    ED/N-1.    LD/U-1.    LO/N31.
 SO/U-1.
 ISSN 0300-5089

**CLINICS IN HAEMATOLOGY.**
+ +CLIN. HAEMATOL.
[SAUNDERS]
 LONDON  1(1), F 1972-
 3/A.
 CA/U-1.    DB/U-2.    ED/N-1.    LD/U-1.    SO/U-1.

**CLIP-KIT: STUDIES IN ENVIRONMENTAL DESIGN.**
+ +CLIP-KIT, STUD. ENVIRON. DES.
 LONDON  1, 1966-
 ED/N-1.
 ISSN 0009-9392

**CLOTHING RESEARCH JOURNAL.**                                      XXX
+ +CLOTH. RES. J.
 CLOTHING INSTITUTE.
 LONDON  1(1), JA 1973-
 3/A.  PREV: TECHNOLOGICAL REPORT, CLOTHING
 INSTITUTE.
 CA/U-1.    ED/N-1.    LO/N14.

**CLOUD MARAUDER.  A MAGAZINE OF POETRY.**
 OAKLAND, CALIF.  1(1), 1968-
 OX/U-1.
 ISSN 0009-9481

**COA REPORT AERO.**                                                XXX
+ +COA REP. AERO (COLL. AERONAUT.).                                 XXX
 COLLEGE OF AERONAUTICS (CRANFIELD).
 CRANFIELD  NO.163, 1963- 211, 1969.
 PREV:  REPORT, COLLEGE ... FROM 1, 1946- 162,
 1963.  SUBS:  CRANFIELD REPORT AERO.
 LO/N14.

**COA REPORT E & C.**
+ +COA REP. E & C. (COLL. AERONAUT.)
 COLLEGE OF AERONAUTICS (CRANFIELD).
 CRANFIELD  NO.1, JE 1964-
 LO/N-4.
 ISSN 0590-0522

**COA REPORT M & P.**
+ +COA REP. M & P. (COLL. AERONAUT.)
 COLLEGE OF AERONAUTICS (CRANFIELD).
 CRANFIELD  [NO.]1, MY 1964-
 LO/N-4.
 ISSN 0590-0530

**COA REPORT MAT.**
+ +COA REP. MAT. (COLL. AERONAUT.)
 COLLEGE OF AERONAUTICS (CRANFIELD).
 CRANFIELD  NO.1, MR 1966-
 LO/N-4.    LO/N14.
 ISSN 0590-0549

**COARSE GRAINS QUARTERLY.**                                        XXX
 SUBS (1970): COARSE GRAINS REVIEW.

**COARSE GRAINS REVIEW.**                                           XXX
+ +COARSE GRAINS REV.
 (CANADA) DOMINION BUREAU OF STATISTICS:
 AGRICULTURAL BRANCH.
 OTTAWA  30, 1970-
 PREV: COARSE GRAINS QUARTERLY FROM N 1941- 29,
 1970.
 LO/N13.

**COASTAL PRESERVATION & DEVELOPMENT: SPECIAL STUDY REPORTS.**
+ +COASTAL PRESERV. & DEV., SPEC. STUDY REP.
 COUNTRYSIDE COMMISSION (GB).
 LONDON  1, 1969-
 OX/U-1.

**COATING.**
[VIW VERLAG FUR INDUSTRIELLE WERBUNG]
 ZURICH  1, OC 1968-
 LO/N14.
 ISSN 0590-8450

**COBALT.**                                                         XXX
 SUBS (1973): COBALT & COBALT ABSTRACTS.

**COBALT & COBALT ABSTRACTS.**                                      XXX
+ +COBALT & COBALT ABSTR.
 CENTRE D'INFORMATION DU COBALT.
 BRUSSELS  1973-
 PREV: COBALT FROM NO.1, 1958- 57, 1972.
 BR/U-1.    LD/U-1.    LO/N35.

**COBI NEWSLETTER.**
+ +COBI NEWSL.
 INSTITUTE OF BIOLOGY: COMMITTEE ON BIOLOGICAL
 INFORMATION.
 LONDON  NO.1, 1973-
 LO/N-2.    LO/N-6.

**COCCIDIOLOGIST'S NEWSLETTER.**
+ +COCCIDOL. NEWSL.
 BELTSVILLE, MD.  1, 1973-
 LO/N-2.

**COCOMUNITY.**
 ASIAN COCONUT COMMUNITY.
 DJAKARTA  1(1), MY 1971-
 LO/R-6.

**CODATA BULLETIN.**
+ +CODATA BULL. (COMM. DATA SCI. & TECHNOL.).
COMMITTEE ON DATA FOR SCIENCE & TECHNOLOGY.
*FRANKFURT/MAIN NO.1, 1969-*
*LO/N-2.     LO/N14.*
*BH/U-1. NO.2, 1970-          SH/P-1. NO.3, 1971-*
*XS/N-1. NO.2, 1970-*

**CODATA NEWSLETTER.**
+ +CODATA NEWSL. (COMM. DATA SCI. & TECHNOL.).
COMMITTEE ON DATA FOR SCIENCE & TECHNOLOGY.
*FRANKFURT/MAIN 1, O 1968-*
*LO/U-2.     XS/R10.*
*BH/U-1. NO.2, 1969-          XS/N-1. NO.5, 1970-*
*ISSN 0007-8767*

**COGNITION. INTERNATIONAL JOURNAL OF COGNITIVE PSYCHOLOGY.**
[MOUTON]
*THE HAGUE 1, 1972-*
*Q. FR. SUMM.*
*CA/M-3.   CA/U-1.   DB/U-2.   LD/U-2.   LO/U-1.   LO/U-4*
*LV/U-2.   MA/U-1.   SH/U-1.   SO/U-1.   SW/U-1.*
*ISSN 0010-0277*

**COGNITIVE PSYCHOLOGY.**
+ +COGNITIVE PSYCHOL.
[ACADEMIC P.]
*NEW YORK 1, JA 1970-*
*Q.*
*BH/U-1.    BH/U-3.    BN/U-1.    DB/U-2.   HL/U-1.   LO/N-1.*
*LO/U-1.    LO/U-2.    LO/U-4.    MA/U-1.   OX/U-8.   RE/U-1.*
*DN/U-1. 2, 1971-                GL/U-2. 3, 1972-*
*SH/U-1. JA 1971-                SO/U-1. 6, 1974-*
*ISSN 0010-0285*

**COGNITIVE STUDIES.**
+ +COGNITIVE STUD.
[BRUNNER/MAZEL]
*NEW YORK 1, 1970-*
*ANNU.*
*AD/U-1.    BT/U-1.    NW/U-1.*
*ISSN 0069-4975*

**COIN INVESTOR.**
[MORLAND LEE]
*LONDON NO.1, JA 1969-*
*ED/N-1.*

**COINS.**                                                              XXX
[LINK HOUSE PUBL.]
*LONDON 7(1), JA 1970-*
M. PREV: COINS AND MEDALS FROM
1,1964- 6, 1969.
*CA/U-1.*
*ISSN 0010-048X*

**COINS, MEDALS & CURRENCY.**
[INDEPENDENT MAGAZINES, LTD.]
*LONDON 1(1), 1/MY 1967-*
S/T: INTERNATIONAL WEEKLY NEWSPAPER FOR
NUMISMATISTS.
*OX/U-2.*
*ED/N-1. 2(4), 1968-          OX/U-1. 2(4), 1968-*
*ISSN 0010-0498*

**COLLANA DI STUDI SULL'EUROPA ORIENTALE.**
+ +COLLANA STUDI EUR. ORIENT.
UNIVERSITA DEGLI STUDI DI PADOVA.
*PADUA 1, 1964-*
*CA/U-1. 2, 1964-*

**COLLECTED CONTRIBUTIONS, BEDFORD INSTITUTE.**
+ +COLLECT. CONTRIB. BEDFORD INST.
*DARTMOUTH, NOVA SCOTIA 1, 1968-*
*BN/U-2.    CA/U12.    LO/N-2.*

**COLLECTED PAPERS, CARWORTH EUROPE.**
+ +COLLECT. PAP. CARWORTH EUR.
*ALCONBURY, HUNTS. 1, 1967-*
VOL.1 = PROC. OF A SYMP. ON THE FUTURE OF THE
DEFINED LAB. ANIMAL; (CARWORTH EUROPE);
CAMBRIDGE, 1966.
*OX/U-8.*
*ED/N-1. 2, 1968-*
*ISSN 0576-842X*

**COLLECTED REPRINTS, DEPARTMENT OF OCEANOGR-APHY, UNIVERSITY OF CAPE TOWN.**
+ +COLLECT. REPR. DEP. OCEANOGR. UNIV. CAPE TOWN.
*RONDEBOSCH 1, 1962-*
*BN/U-2.*
*ISSN 0528-046X*

**COLLECTED REPRINTS, GREAT LAKES RESEARCH DIVISION, UNIVERSITY OF MICHIGAN.**
+ +COLLECT. REPR. GREAT LAKES RES. DIV. UNIV. MICH.
*ANN ARBOR 1, 1956-66(1967)-*
*BN/U-2.*

**COLLECTED REPRINTS, RESEARCH INSTITUTE OF NORTH PACIFIC FISHERIES, HOKKAIDO UNIVERSITY.**
+ +COLLECT. REPR. RES. INST. NORTH PAC. FISH. HOKKAIDO UNIV.
HOKKAIDO DAIGAKU: RESEARCH INSTITUTE OF
NORTH PACIFIC FISHERIES.
*HAKODATE 1, 1968-*
INST. SUBORD. TO: FACULTY OF FISHERIES.
*LO/N-2.*

**COLLECTED REPRINTS, UNIVERSITY OF TOKYO.**
+ +COLLECT. REPR. UNIV. TOKYO.
*TOKYO 1, 1969-*
*LO/N-2.*

**COLLECTION.**
*HOVE, SUSSEX NO.1, 1968-*
*CB/U-1.    ED/N-1.    LO/U-2.*

**COLLECTION L'EROTISME POPULAIRE.**
+ +COLLECT. EROTISME POP.
[G.-P. MAISONNEUVE & LAROSE]
*PARIS NO.1, 1970-*
ALSO ENTITLED : EROTISME POPULAIRE.
*LO/U-1.*

**COLLECTION DES PUBLICATIONS, FACULTE DES SCIENCES APPLIQUEES, UNIVERSITE DE LIEGE.**
+ +COLLECT. PUBL. FAC. SCI. APPL. UNIV. LIEGE.
*LIEGE NO.1, 1966-*
*BH/U-1.*
*ISSN 0075-9333*

**COLLEGE STUDENT SURVEY.**
+ +COLL. STUD. SURV.
*OSHKOSH, WIS. 1, 1967-*
*XY/N-1.*
*ISSN 0010-1184*

**COLLOID SCIENCE.**
+ +COLLOID SCI.
CHEMICAL SOCIETY.
*LONDON 1, 1970/71(1973)-*
*CA/U-1.    ED/N-1.    GL/U-2.   HL/U-1.   LO/S-3.   LO/U-2.*
*MA/U-1.    MA/U-1.    RE/U-1.   SH/U-1.   XS/R10.*
*ISSN 0305-9723*

**COLOMBIA TODAY.**
+ +COLOMB. TODAY.
COLOMBIA INFORMATION SERVICE.
*NEW YORK 1(1), N 1965-*
*SW/U-1.\**
*OX/U-1. 6(3), 1971-*
*ISSN 0010-1397*

**COLOMBO LAW REVIEW.**
+ +COLOMBO LAW REV.
UNIVERSITY OF COLOMBO: FACULTY OF LAW.
*COLOMBO 1, OC 1969-*
*ANNU.*
*BL/U-1.    OX/U15.*
*ISSN 0069-5939*

**COLOMBO PLAN NEWS LETTER.**
+ +COLOMBO PLAN NEWS LETT.
COLOMBO PLAN INFORMATION DEPARTMENT.
*COLOMBO 1(1), 1970-*
*LO/N10.    LO/U-3.    LO/U14.*
*HL/U-1. 2(1), 1971-\**
*ISSN 0010-1419*

**COLOQUOI LETRAS.**
+ +COLOQ. LET.
FUNDACAO CALOUSTE GULBENKIAN.
*LISBON NO.1, MR 1971-*
*Q.*
*ED/N-1.    LD/U-1.*

**COLOR.**
[PRINTMINT]
*BERKELEY, CALIF. [NO.], 1971-*
*LO/U-2.*

**COLORADO FARM & HOME RESEARCH.**                                    XXX
SUBS (1969): CSU RESEARCH.

COLUMBIA FORUM: NS.
*NEW YORK N.S. 1, 1971-*
PREV. SERIES FROM AUTUMN 1968. PREV: COLUMBIA
UNIVERSITY FORUM FROM 1, 1957- 11(2), SUMMER
1968.
*OX/U-1. 1971-*                                              XXX

COLUMBIA JOURNALISM REVIEW.
*++COLUMBIA JOURNALISM REV.*
COLUMBIA UNIVERSITY: GRADUATE SCHOOL OF
JOURNALISM.
*NEW YORK 1, 1962-*
Q. PILOT ISSUE DATED FALL 1961.
*OX/U-1. 10(1), 1971-*
*ISSN 0010-194X*

COLUMBIA STUDIES IN ECONOMICS.
*++COLUMBIA STUD. ECON.*
COLUMBIA UNIVERSTIY: SCHOOL OF INTERNATIONAL
AFFAIRS.
*NEW YORK 1, 1968-*
MONOGR.
*HL/U-1.\*\**
*ISSN 0069-6331*

COLUMBIA SURVEY OF HUMAN RIGHTS LAW.
*++COLUMBIA SURV. HUM. RIGHTS LAW.*
COLUMBIA UNIVERSITY: SCHOOL OF LAW.
*NEW YORK 1, 1967/1968- 3, 1971 ...*
SUBS : COLUMBIA HUMAN RIGHTS LAW REVIEW.
*OX/U15.*
*ISSN 0010-2008*                                             XXX

COLUMBIA UNIVERSITY FORUM.
SUBS (1968): COLUMBIA FORUM.                                 XXX

COLUMN. PYE UNICAM CHROMATOGRAPHY BULLETIN.
*CAMBRIDGE 1(1), 1965-*
S/T VARIES. 1(1) AS W.G. PYE JOURNAL OF GAS
CHROMATOGRAPHY; 1(2)- 2(3) AS W.G. PYE
CHROMATOGRAPHY BULLETIN.
*LO/N14.    XN/S-1.*
*CA/U-1. NO.13, 1971-*
*CA/U-2. NO.13, 1971-*
*ED/N-1. NO.13, 1971-*
*OX/U-8. NO.13, 1971-*
*ISSN 0010-2075*

COMBUSTION SCIENCE & TECHNOLOGY.
*++COMBUST. SCI. & TECHNOL.*
[GORDON & BREACH]
*NEW YORK &C 1, 1969-*
INCORP: PYRODYNAMICS.
*BH/U-1.    LO/N14.    NW/U-1.*
*LD/U-1. 1(3), 1969-              LO/U-2. 7, 1973-*
*ISSN 0010-2202*

COMENTARIOS BIBLIOGRAFICOS AMERICANOS.
*++COMENT. BIBLIOGR. AM.*
[PARINO]
*MONTEVIDEO 1968(1969)-*
A. VOL. FOR 1968 THEN 2M. FROM 1969.
*LO/N-1.*
*OX/U-1. 1969-*
*ISSN 0007-7917*

COMIC MEDIA.
*LONDON 1(1), 1972-*
6/A.
*ED/N-1. 2, 1973-*

COMMENTATIONES SCIENTIARUM SOCIALIUM.
*++COMMENTAT. SCI. SOC.*
SOCIETAS SCIENTIARUM FENNICA.
*HELSINKI 1, 1972-*
*BL/U-1.    DB/S-1.    GL/U-1.    LO/N-1.    OX/U-1.    SH/U-1.*

COMMENTS ON ASTROPHYSICS & SPACE PHYSICS.
*++COMMENTS ASTROPHYS. & SPACE PHYS.*
[GORDON & BREACH]
*NEW YORK &C 1, JA/F 1969-*
S/T: A JOURNAL OF CRITICAL DISCUSSION OF THE
CURRENT LITERATURE.
*BH/U-1.    CO/U-1.    LO/N14.    LO/U-2.*
*CB/U-1. 11, 1970-              OX/U-8. 1(2), 1969-*
*SO/U-1. 5, 1973-*
*ISSN 0010-2679*

COMMENTS ON ATOMIC & MOLECULAR PHYSICS.
*++COMMENTS AT. & MOL. PHYS.*
[GORDON & BREACH]
*NEW YORK &C. 1, 1969-*
S/T: A JOURNAL OF CRITICAL DISCUSSION OF THE
CURRENT LITERATURE.
*BH/U-1.    CO/U-1.    ED/N-1.    LO/N-4.    LO/N14.    XS/R10.*
*LO/U20. 3, 1971-*
*ISSN 0010-2687*

COMMENTS ON CONTEMPORARY PSYCHIATRY.
*++COMMENTS CONTEMP. PSYCHIATRY.*
[GORDON & BREACH]
*LONDON 1(1), JL/AU 1971-*
6/A.
*CA/U-1.    ED/N-1.    LO/N-1.    OX/U-8.*

COMMENTS ON EARTH SCIENCES: GEOPHYSICS.
*++COMMENTS EARTH SCI., GEOPHYS.*
[GORDON & BREACH]
*LONDON 1(1), JE/JL 1970-*
2/M. S/T: A JOURNAL OF CRITICAL DISCUSSION
OF THE CURRENT LITERATURE.
*LO/N14.    OX/U-8.*
*ED/N-1. 1(2), 1970-*
*ISSN 0010-2695*

COMMENTS ON PLASMA PHYSICS & CONTROLLED FUSION.
*++COMMENTS PLASMA PHYS. & CONTROLLED FUSION.*
[GORDON & BREACH]
*LONDON 1(1), JA/F 1972-*
6/A. S/T: A JOURNAL OF CRITICAL DISCUSSION OF
THE CURRENT LITERATURE.
*CA/U-1.    ED/N-1.*
*ISSN 0374-2806*

COMMERCE (NEPAL).
NEPAL ECONOMIC & COMMERCE RESEARCH CENTRE.
*KATHMANDU 1(1), S 1972-*
*LO/U-3.*

COMMERCE. JOURNAL OF THE ...
LONDON CHAMBER OF COMMERCE.
*LONDON. NO.1, JA 1962- 1364, 1970...*
M. CALLED (NS) OF PREV TITLE: CHAMBER OF
COMMERCE JOURNAL. SUBS: COMMERCE INTERNATIONAL
*ED/N-1.    MA/P-1.*
*XY/F-1. (1963)-*                                           XXX

COMMERCE INTERNATIONAL.
*++COMMER. INT.*
LONDON CHAMBER OF COMMERCE.
[INVESTMENT PUBL. COMMERCIAL LTD.]
*LONDON 101(1365), 1970-*
PREV: COMMERCE FROM 1, 1962.
*LO/N-7.    LO/N14.*
*ISSN 0010-2733*                                            XXX

COMMERCE TODAY.
*++COMMER. TODAY.*
(UNITED STATES) DEPARTMENT OF COMMERCE.
*WASHINGTON, D.C. 1(1), OC 1970-*
2M.
*CB/U-2.    GL/U-3.    LO/S14.    OX/U17.*
*LO/N-6. 1(18)-*
*ISSN 0020-6385*

COMMERCIAL FISHERIES REVIEW.
SUBS (1972): MARINE FISHERIES REVIEW.                       XXX

COMMERCIAL FISHING.
*++COMMERC. FISH.*
[COMMERCIAL FISHING ENTERPRISES LTD.]
*FLEETWOOD, LANCS. 1, 1970-*
*ED/N-1.    LO/N14.    OX/U-8.*

COMMERCIAL TRANSPORT.
*++COMMER. TRANSP.*
*RATHCOOLE, DUBLIN 1, 1972-*
*DB/U-2.*

COMMODITY RESEARCH REPORTS, BUREAU OF AGRI-
CULTURAL ECONOMICS (AUSTRALIA).
*++COMMOD. RES. REP. BUR. AGR. ECON. (AUST.).*
*CANBERRA NO.1, 1966-*
MONOGR.
*HL/U-1.\*\**

COMMON MARKET LEGISLATION DIGEST.
*++COMMON MARK. LEGIS. DIG.*
[NEWSLETTERS FOR BUSINESS]
*HARROW, MIDDX. 1(1), JA 1973-*
MON.
*OX/U15.*
*CA/U-1. NO.7, 1973-              ED/N-1. NO.7, 1973-*

COMMON MARKET NEWS LETTER.
[EURODATA PUBL. CO.]
*LONDON 1(1), N 1971-*
S/T: THE FORTNIGHTLY BUSINESS, INDUSTRIAL &
POLITICAL INFORMATION SERVICE ON THE EUROPEAN
COMMUNITY.
*LO/U-3.*
*ED/N-1. 1(3), 1971-              LO/N-6. 1(8), 1972-*

**COMMONWEALTH DIARY OF COMING EVENTS.**
++*COMMONW. DIARY COMING EVENTS.*
COMMONWEALTH SECRETARIAT.
*LONDON NO.1, JA 1972-*
*ED/N-1.    LO/N-1.*
*LO/S14.  AP 1972-*
*OX/U16.  [CURRENT ISSUES ONLY]*

**COMMONWEALTH OFFICE YEAR BOOK.**    XXX
++*COMMONW. OFF. YEAR BOOK.*    XXX
(GREAT BRITAIN) COMMONWEALTH OFFICE.
*LONDON  1967- 1968...*
PREV: COMMONWEALTH RELATIONS OFFICE YEAR BOOK
FROM 1966.  SUBS: YEAR BOOK OF THE COMMONW-
EALTH.
*BH/U-1.    BT/U-1.    GL/U-1.    LO/U-3.    RE/U-1.*

**COMMONWEALTH RECORD OF RECENT EVENTS.**
++*COMMONW. REC. RECENT EVENTS.*
COMMONWEALTH SECRETARIAT.
*LONDON  NO.1, F 1972-*
*Q.*
*ED/N-1.    LO/N-1.    LO/S14.    LO/U-8.*
*LO/U-3.  [CURRENT ISSUES ONLY]*

**COMMONWEALTH RELATIONS OFFICE LIST.**    XXX
SUBS (1966): COMMONWEALTH RELATIONS OFFICE
YEAR BOOK.

**COMMONWEALTH RELATIONS OFFICE YEAR BOOK.**    XXX
++*COMMONW. RELAT. OFF. YEARB.*
(GREAT BRITAIN) COMMONWEALTH RELATIONS OFFICE.
*LONDON  1966...*
PREV: COMMONWEALTH RELATIONS OFF. LIST FROM
1952.  SUBS: COMMONWEALTH OFFICE YEAR BOOK.
*BH/U-1.    SO/U-1.*

**COMMUNICATIONS.**
ECOLE PRATIQUE DES HAUTES ETUDES (PARIS):
CENTRE D'ETUDES DES COMMUNICATIONS DE MASSE.
*PARIS   NO.1, 1961-*
*MA/U-1.  7; 9,1961-*

**COMMUNICATIONS, AFRIKA-STUDIECENTRUM, RIJKS-**
**UNIVERSITEIT TE LEIDEN.**
++*COMMUN. AFR.-STUDIECENT. RIJKSUNIV. LEIDEN.*
[MOUTON]
*THE HAGUE  1, 1970-*
*CA/U-1.    LO/N-1.*

**COMMUNICATIONS IN BEHAVIORAL BIOLOGY: PART A.**    XXX
++*COMMUN. BEHAV. BIOL., A.*
[ACADEMIC PRESS]
*NEW YORK &C  1(1), 1968- 6(5/6), 1971 ...*
SUBS: BEHAVIORAL BIOLOGY.
*GL/U-1.    LO/N-2.    LO/N13.    MA/U-1.    OX/U-8.*

**COMMUNICATIONS IN BEHAVIORAL BIOLOGY: PART B:**
**ABSTRACTS & INDEX.**    XXX
++*COMMUN. BEHAV. BIOL., B.*
[ACADEMIC PRESS]
*NEW YORK &C  1(1), JA 1968- 8(6), 1971 ...*
SUBS: ABSTRACTS & REVIEWS IN BEHAVIORAL
BIOLOGY.
*BN/U-1.    GL/U-1.    LO/N13.    MA/U-1.    OX/U-8.    SH/U-1.*

**COMMUNICATIONS OF THE DEPARTMENT OF SILVI-**    000
**CULTURE, STATE AGRICULTURAL UNIVERSITY AT GHENT.**
SEE: SYLVA GANDAVENSIS.

**COMMUNICATIONS DESIGNER'S DIGEST.**    XXX
++*COMMUN. DES. DIG.*
DOUGLAS COMMUNICATIONS, INC.
*NEW YORK  1, 1967- N/D 1971.*
SUBS: COMMUNICATIONS EQUIPMENT AND SYSTEMS
DESIGN.
*LO/N14.*

**COMMUNICATIONS EQUIPMENT & SYSTEMS DESIGN.**    XXX
++*COMMUN. EQUIP. & SYST. DES.*
[COMMUNICATION TRENDS]
*PHILADELPHIA  1972-*
PREV: COMMUNICATIONS DESIGNER'S DIGEST FROM 1,
1967- N/D 1971.
*LO/N14.*

**COMMUNICATIONS IN SOIL SCIENCE & PLANT ANALYSIS.**
++*COMMUN. SOIL SCI. & PLANT ANAL.*
[DEKKER]
*NEW YORK  1(1), JA 1970-*
*2M.*
*BL/U-1.    HL/U-1.    LO/N13.    XS/R-2.*
*NW/U-1.  2, 1971-              OX/U-8.  1(2), 1970-*
*ISSN 0010-3624*

**COMMUNICATOR OF TECHNICAL INFORMATION. JOUR-**
**NAL OF THE ...**
++*COMMUN. TECH. INF.*
INSTITUTE OF TECHNICAL PUBLICITY & PUBLICATIONS
LTD.
*COVENTRY  NO.1, OC 1968-*
PREV: BULLETIN OF THE INSTITUTE ... FROM NO.
1, 1966.
*ED/N-1.    OX/U-8.*
*LO/N35.  NO.11, D 1971-*
*ISSN 0045-768X*

**COMMUNIQUES ON DEVELOPMENT ISSUES, OVERSEAS**
**DEVELOPMENT COUNCIL (US).**
++*COMMUNIQUES DEV. ISSUES OVERSEAS DEV. COUNC.*
*(US).*
*WASHINGTON, D.C.  NO.1, 1970-*
*OX/U16.*

**COMMUNIST COMMENT.**
IRISH COMMUNIST ORGANISATION.
*CORK  1, JL 1969-*
*HL/U-1.**    LO/U-3.*
*CA/U-1.  NO.48, 1972-*
*ED/N-1.  NO.48, 1972-*

**COMMUNIST VIEWPOINT.**
++*COMMUNIST VIEWP.*
COMMUNIST PARTY OF CANADA.
*TORONTO   1(1), MR/AP 1969-*
*2M.  S/T: THEORETICAL & POLITICAL JOURNAL OF*
THE ...
*LO/U-3.*
*ISSN 0010-3756*

**COMMUNITY (NEWCASTLE UNDER LYME).**
*NEWCASTLE UNDER LYME  NO.1, AUTUMN 1971-*
*3/A.*
*CA/U-1.    ED/N-1.*

**COMMUNITY.  QUARTERLY JOURNAL OF ...**    XXX
COMMUNITY RELATIONS COMMISSION.
*LONDON  1(1), JA 1970- 2(2), AP 1971.*
SUBS: NEW COMMUNITY.
*BH/P-1.    BH/U-1.    BL/U-1.    CB/U-1.    ED/N-1.    HL/U-1.*
*LO/N-1.    LO/N17.    LO/U-3.    OX/U-1.    SW/U-1.*
*OX/U17.  2, 1971-*

**COMMUNITY ACTION.**
*LONDON  [NO.1], F 1972-*
*2M.*
*LO/U-3.*
*ED/N-1.  NO.2, 1972-              LO/U-2.  NO.2, 1972-*
*SH/U-1.  NO.2, 1972-*

**COMMUNITY DEVELOPMENT DIGEST.**
++*COMMUNITY DEV. DIG.*
SEATO.
*BANGKOK  NO.1, JA/JE 1969-*
*2/A.*
*LO/N17.*

**COMMUNITY FORUM.**
NORTHERN IRELAND COMMUNITY RELATIONS COMMISSION
*BELFAST  1, 1971-*
*Q.*
*DB/U-2.    ED/N-1.    LD/U-1.    LO/N-1.    LO/U-3.*
*CO/U-1.  3(1) 1973-*

**COMMUNITY HEALTH.**
ROYAL INSTITUTE OF PUBLIC HEALTH & HYGIENE.
*BRISTOL  NO.1, 1969-*
*DN/U-1.    GL/U-1.    LO/U-1.    OX/U-8.    SO/U-1.*
*BL/U-1.  6, 1974-*
*ISSN 0010-3837*

**COMMUNITY MEDICINE.**    XXX
++*COMMUNITY MED.*
[MACMILLAN]
*LONDON  126, 1971- 129(19), 1973.*
PREV: MEDICAL OFFICER FROM 1, 1908- 125, 1971.
SUBS. INCORP. IN: HEALTH & SOCIAL SERVICE
JOURNAL.
*LD/U-1.    LO/N-6.    NW/U-1.    SO/U-1.*
*ED/N-1.  128(6), 1972-*

**COMPAIR JOURNAL.**
++*COMPAIR J.*
INTERNATIONAL COMPRESSED AIR CORPORATION, LTD.
*SLOUGH  1, 1971-*
*LO/N14.*

**COMPARATIVE & GENERAL PHARMACOLOGY.**
+ +COMP. & GEN. PHARMACOL.
[SCIENTECHNICA (PUBL.) LTD.]
*BRISTOL 1, MR 1970-*
*ED/N-1.   LO/N13.   LO/U-2.   NW/U-1.   OX/U-8.   SH/U-1.*
*SO/U-1.*
*CO/U-1.   2(5), MR 1971-*
*ISSN 0010-4035*

**COMPARATIVE GROUP STUDIES.**                                    XXX
+ +COMP. GROUP STUD.
[SAGE PUBL.]
*LONDON & BEVERLEY HILLS   1, 1970- 3, 1972 ...*
Q.  SUBS: SMALL GROUP BEHAVIOR.
*ISSN 0010-4108*

**COMPARATIVE & INTERNATIONAL LAW JOURNAL OF
SOUTHERN AFRICA.**
+ +COMP. & INT. LAW J. SOUTH. AFR.
*PRETORIA   1, 1968-*
*BL/U-1.   LO/U-3.   SH/U-1.*
*EX/U-1.   6(1), MR 1973-*
*ISSN 0010-4051*

**COMPARATIVE POLITICS.**
+ +COMP. POLIT.
CITY UNIVERSITY OF NEW YORK.
[UNIV. OF CHICAGO PRESS]
*CHICAGO   1(1), 1968-*
EDITED AT THE CITY UNIV. ...
*BH/U-1.   BL/U-1.*   CB/U-1.   GL/U-3.   LO/U-3.   LO/U-8.*
*LO/U14.   RE/U-1.   SH/U-1.   SW/U-1.*
*CV/C-1.   3, 1970-*
*ISSN 0010-4159*

**COMPASS.**
IRISH ASSOCIATION FOR CURRICULUM DEVELOPMENT.
*DUBLIN   1, 1972-*
*DB/U-2.*

**COMPENDIUM OF UNIVERSITY ENTRANCE REQUIRE-
MENTS FOR FIRST DEGREE COURSES IN THE UNITED
KINGDOM ...**
+ +COMPEND. UNIV. ENTR. REQUIR. FIRST DEGREE
COURSES UK.
COMMITTEE OF VICE-CHANCELLORS & PRINCIPALS
OF THE UNIVERSITIES OF THE UNITED KINGDOM.
[ASSOCIATION OF COMMONWEALTH UNIVERSITIES]
*LONDON   1963-*
ANNU. TITLE CONTINUES ... (EXCLUDING PART-
TIME & EXTERNAL DEGREE COURSES).
*LO/U28.   1968/69-*
*OX/U17.   1964; 1967/68-*
*ISSN 0571-625X*

**COMPOSANTS MECANIQUES ET ELECTRIQUES.**          XXX
+ +COMPOSANTS MEC. & ELECTR.   [CMEE-A]
[UNION FRANCAISE DE PUBLICATIONS TECHNIQUES]
*PARIS   NO.1, 1967- 40, 1972 ...*
SUBS: COMPOSANTS MECANIQUES ELECTRIQUES ET
ELECTRONIQUES.
*LO/N14.*

**COMPOSANTS MECANIQUES, ELECTRIQUES ET ELECTRON-
IQUES.**                                                          XXX
+ +COMPOSANTS MEC. ELECTR. & ELECTRON.
[UNION FRANCAISE DE PUBLICATIONS TECHNIQUES]
*PARIS   NO.41, 1973-*
PREV: COMPOSANTS MECANIQUES ET ELECTRIQUES
FROM NO.1, 1967- 40, 1972.
*LO/N14.*

**COMPOSITES. THE TECHNOLOGY OF COMPOSITE
MATERIALS.**
[ILIFFE]
*GUILDFORD   1(1), S 1969-*
*GL/U-2.   LO/N14.   MA/U-1.   OX/U-8.   XS/R10.*
*CA/U-1.   2, 1971-                     LD/U-1.   3(1), 1972-*
*LO/N-2.   3(1), 1972-                  SH/U-3.   3(1), 1972-*
*ISSN 0010-4361*

**COMPREHENSIVE CHEMICAL KINETICS.**
+ +COMPR. CHEM. KINET.
[ELSEVIER]
*AMSTERDAM &C.   1, 1969-*
*CO/U-1.   GL/U-1.*

**COMPTES RENDUS DE L'ACADEMIE DES SCIENCES
AGRICOLES EN BULGARIE.**                                          000
   SEE: DOKLADY AKADEMII SEL'SKO-KHOZJAJSTVENNYKH
   NAUK V BOLGARII.

**COMPUTER.**                                                     XXX
INSTITUTE OF ELECTRICAL & ELECTRONICS ENGIN-
EERS: COMPUTER SOCIETY.
*NORTHRIDGE, CALIF.   3(5), 1970-*
2M.  PREV: COMPUTER GROUP NEWS FROM 1(1), JL
1966- 3(4), 1970.
*BN/U-2.   CA/U-2.   HL/U-1.   LD/U-1.   LO/N13.   LO/N14.*
*NW/U-1.   RE/U-1.*
*EX/U-1.   4(1), 1971-              MA/U-1.   4, 1971-*
*SH/U-1.   7, 1974-*
*ISSN 0018-9162*

**COMPUTER AIDED DESIGN.**
+ +COMPUT. AIDED DES.
[HEYWOOD-TEMPLE IND. PUBLS. LTD.]
*LONDON   1(1), AUTUMN 1968-*
*CA/U-1.   CV/C-1.   ED/N-1.   EX/U-1.   LO/N-4.   LO/N14.*
*LO/U22.   OX/U-8.   SO/U-1.   SW/U-1.*
*ED/U-1.   2, 1969-                 GL/U-2.   4(3), 1972-*
*LD/U-1.   5, 1973-                 NW/U-1.   2(2), 1970-*
*XS/R10.   1(4), 1969-*
*ISSN 0010-4485*

**COMPUTER APPLICATIONS IN THE NATURAL & SOCIAL
SCIENCES.**
+ +COMPUT. APPL. NATUR. & SOC. SCI.
UNIVERSITY OF NOTTINGHAM.
*NOTTINGHAM   NO.1, 1969-*
*GL/U-1.   OX/U-8.   SH/U-1.*

**COMPUTER BULLETIN.**                                            XXX
+ +COMPUT. BULL.
BRITISH COMPUTER SOCIETY.
*LONDON   1, JE 1957- 16, 1972.*
*        S.2  NO.1, S 1974-*
*BH/P-1.   CA/U-1.*   HL/U-1.   LO/N14.   LO/R-5.*
*SW/U-1.*
*ED/N-1.   S.2. NO.1, 1974-*
*OX/U-8.   S.2. NO.1, 1974-*
*XS/R10.   S.2. NO.1, 1974-*
*ISSN 0010-4531*

**COMPUTER DIGEST (LONDON).**
+ +COMPUT. DIG. (LOND.).
[SPECIAL INTEREST PUBL.]
*LONDON   1(1), D 1972-*
WKLY.
*OX/U-8.*
*ISSN 0305-9405*

**COMPUTER EDUCATION.**
+ +COMPUT. EDUC.
COMPUTER EDUCATION GROUP.
*LONDON   1, 1969-*
SPONS. BODY ALSO: SCHOOLS COUNCIL (GB):
PROJECT TECHNOLOGY.
*ED/N-1.   LO/N-1.   I V/U-2.   MA/U-4.   OX/U-1.   XY/N-1.*
*HL/U-2.   11, JL 1972-*
*LO/C-8.   (ONE YEAR).*
*ISSN 0010-4590*

**COMPUTER EXECUTIVE. JOURNAL OF THE ...**        XXX
+ +COMPUT. EXECUTIVE.
VISIBLE RECORD (EDP) SOCIETY.
[MSOR LTD., PUBL. DIVISION]
*CROYDON, SURREY   NO.2, F/MR 1972-*
MON.  PREV: JOURNAL OF THE VISIBLE RECORD
(EDP) SOCIETY FROM NO.1, JA 1972.
*ED/N-1.*

**COMPUTER GRAPHICS & IMAGE PROCESSING.**
+ +COMPUT. GRAPHICS & IMAGE PROCESS.
[ACADEMIC P.]
*NEW YORK   1, 1972-*
Q.
*AD/U-1.   CA/U-2.   SH/U-1.*

**COMPUTER INFORMATION.**
+ +COMPUT. INF.
ASLIB: COMPUTER INFORMATION GROUP.
*LONDON   NO.1, AP 1972-*
*BL/U-1.   XS/T-4.*

**COMPUTER & INFORMATION SYSTEMS.**               XXX
+ +COMPUT. & INF. SYST.
[CAMBRIDGE SCIENTIFIC ABSTR. INC.]
*WASHINGTON, D.C.   6(1), 1969-*
PREV: INFORMATION PROCESSING JOURNAL FROM 1,
1962- 5, 1968.
*BH/U-1.   GL/U-2.   SO/U-1.*
*SH/C-5.   7(10), 1970-*
*ISSN 0010-4507*

**COMPUTER MANAGEMENT.** XXX
+ +COMPUT. MANAGE.
[SPECIAL INTEREST PUBL. LTD.]
 LONDON 5, 1970-
 PREV: MECHANISED ACCOUNTING & COMPUTER MANAGE-
 MENT FROM 1, 1966- 4(12), 1969.
 ED/N-1.    GL/U-3.    LO/N-7.    LO/N14.    MA/P-1.    OX/U-8.
 BH/U-3.  [CURRENT YEAR.]
 LO/U21.  [CURRENT YEAR.].
 ISSN 0010-4639

**COMPUTER METHODS IN APPLIED MECHANICS &
ENGINEERING.**
+ +COMPUT. METHODS APPL. MECH. & ENG.
[NORTH-HOLLAND PUBL. CO.]
 AMSTERDAM  1, 1972-
 LO/N14.    SW/U-1.
 ISSN 0045-7760

**COMPUTER PHYSICS COMMUNICATIONS.**
+ +COMPUT. PHYS. COMMUN.
[NORTH HOLLAND PUBL. CO.]
 AMSTERDAM  1, 1969-
 BL/U-1.    CA/U-2.    GL/U-1.    GL/U-2.    LO/N14.    LO/U-2.
 LO/U11.    LO/U13.    XS/R10.
 MA/U-1.  5, 1973-

**COMPUTER PROGRAM ABSTRACTS.**
+ +COMPUT. PROGR. ABSTR.
NATIONAL AERONAUTICS & SPACE ADMINISTRATION
(US).
 WASHINGTON, D.C.  1, 1967-
 LO/N14.
 XS/R10.  2(2), 15/JL 1970-
 ISSN 0045-785X

**COMPUTER PROGRAMS IN BIOMEDICINE.**
+ +COMPUT. PROGR. BIOMED.
[NORTH-HOLLAND PUBL. CO.]
 AMSTERDAM  1, 1970-
 BL/U-1.    LO/N13.    OX/U-8.    SH/U-1.
 ISSN 0010-468X

**COMPUTER PROGRAMS IN SCIENCE & TECHNOLOGY.**
+ +COMPUT. PROGRAMS SCI. & TECHNOL.
[SCIENCE ASSOCIATES/INTERNATIONAL]
 NEW YORK  1, JL 1971-
 Q.
 AD/U-1.    XS/T-4.    XY/N-1.
 LO/N14.  1, 1971- 73.
 ISSN 0045-7868

**COMPUTER YEARBOOK.** XXX
+ +COMPUT. YEARB.
[AMERICAN DATA PROCESSING]
 DETROIT  1972-
 PREV: COMPUTER YEARBOOK & DIRECTORY FROM 1,
 1966- 3, 1969.
 LO/N14.

**COMPUTERS IN BIOLOGY & MEDICINE.**
+ +COMPUT. BIOL. & MED.
[PERGAMON P.]
 NEW YORK &C.  1, 1970-
 LO/N-2.    LO/N14.    LO/R-5.    NW/U-1.    SH/U-1.
 LO/M12.  1(1), 1970.
 ISSN 0010-4825

**COMPUTERS IN CHEMICAL & BIOCHEMICAL RESEARCH.**
+ +COMPUT. CHEM. & BIOCHEM. RES.
[ACADEMIC P.]
 NEW YORK &C.  1, 1972-
 CA/U-1.    LO/N14.

**COMPUTERS IN THE ENVIRONMENTAL SCIENCES.** XXX
+ +COMPUT. ENVIRON. SCI.
UNIVERSITY OF EAST ANGLIA: SCHOOL OF ENVIRON-
MENTAL SCIENCES.
 NORWICH  1971- 1973.//
 PREV: COMPUTERS IN GEOGRAPHY FROM [1], 1970.
 CV/C-1.    LO/N-2.    LO/N14.    OX/U-1.    SH/U-1.    SO/U-1.
 XY/N-1.
 BL/U-1.  1974-
 ISSN 0300-0842

**COMPUTERS IN EUROPE.** XXX
+ +COMPUT. EUR.
[COMPUTER CONSULTANTS LTD.]
 LLANDUDNO  1971-
 PREV: EUROPEAN COMPUTER USERS HANDBOOK FROM
 1963- 1969/70.
 LO/N14.

**COMPUTERS & FLUIDS.  AN INTERNATIONAL JOURNAL.**
+ +COMPUT. & FLUIDS.
[PERGAMON P.]
 OXFORD; NEW YORK  1(1), 1973-
 CA/U-1.    CA/U-4.    ED/N-1.    GL/U-2.    LD/U-1.    MA/U-1.
 OX/U-8.    SF/U-1.    SH/U-3.    SW/U-1.    XS/N-1.
 ISSN 0045-7930

**COMPUTERS IN GEOGRAPHY.** XXX
+ +COMPUT. GEOGR.
UNIVERSITY OF EAST ANGLIA: SCHOOL OF ENVIRON-
MENTAL SCIENCES.
 NORWICH  [1], 1970.
 SUBS: COMPUTERS IN THE ENVIRONMENTAL SCIENCES.
 CV/C-1.    OX/U-1.    SH/U-1.

**COMPUTERS & STRUCTURES.**
+ +COMPUT. & STRUCT.
[PERGAMON P.]
 OXFORD  1(1/2), AG 1971-
 AD/U-1.    CA/U-1.    DB/U-2.    ED/N-1.    GL/U-2.    LO/N14.
 LO/N14.    NW/U-1.*    OX/U-8.    SH/U-3.    XS/R10.
 XY/N-1.
 LO/N35.  1(3), 1971-              SO/U-1.  2, 1972-
 ISSN 0045-7949

**COMPUTERS U.K.  AN ANNUAL SURVEY OF THE COM-
PUTER INDUSTRY IN GREAT BRITAIN.**
+ +COMPUT. U.K.
[DIGEST DATA BOOKS]
 CROYDON  1966-
 TITLE OF FIRST ISSUE: COMPUTERS. ANNUAL
 SURVEY.
 LO/N14.  1966-              XS/C-2.  1967-

**COMPUTING REPORT IN SCIENCE & ENGINEERING.**
+ +COMPUT. REP. SCI. & ENG.
IBM CORPORATION: DATA PROCESSING DIVISION.
 WHITE PLAINS, N.Y.  5(2), 1969-
 PREV:  COMPUTING REPORT FOR THE SCIENTIST &
 ENGINEER FROM 1(1), JA 1966- 5(1), 1969.
 LO/N14.
 ISSN 0010-4876

**COMPUTING SURVEYS.**
+ +COMPUT. SURV.
ASSOCIATION FOR COMPUTING MACHINERY.
 BALTIMORE, MD  1(1), MR 1969-
 BH/U-1.    BN/U-2.    CB/U-1.    GL/U-1.    LD/U-1.    LO/N14.
 LO/U11.    LO/U12.    OX/U-8.    RE/U-1.    SO/U-1.
 SW/U-1.    XS/R10.
 DR/U-1.  3, 1971-              LO/N-7.  3, 1971-
 LO/U-2.  2, 1970-
 ISSN 0010-4892

**COMSAT TECHNICAL REVIEW.**
+ +COMSAT TECH. REV.
COMMUNICATIONS SATELLITE CORPORATION.
 WASHINGTON, D.C.  1, 1971-
 2/A.  ENGL., FR. & SPAN. ABSTR.
 BL/U-1.    LO/N14.
 LO/N35.  2(1), 1972-

**COMUNICACIONES DEL MUSEO ARGENTINO DE CIEN-
CIAS NATURALES 'BERNARDINO RIVADAVIA' E INST-
ITUTO NACIONAL DE INVESTIGACION DE LAS CIEN-
CIAS NATURALES: ECOLOGIA.**
+ +COMUN. MUS. ARG. CIENC. NAT. & INST. NAC.
INVEST. CIENC. NAT., ECOL.
 BUENOS AIRES  1, 1968-
 BL/U-1.    LO/N-2.

**COMUNICACIONES DEL MUSEO ARGENTINO DE CIEN-
CIAS NATURALES 'BERNARDINO RIVADAVIA' E INST-
ITUTO NACIONAL DE INVESTIGACION DE LAS CIEN-
CIAS NATURALES: PALEONTOLOGIA.**
+ +COMUN. MUS. ARG. CIENC. NAT. & INST. NAC.
INVEST. CIENC. NAT., PALEONTOL.
 BUENOS AIRES  1, 1966-
 LO/N-2.    LO/N13.

**COMUNICACIONES DEL MUSEO ARGENTINO DE CIEN-
CIAS NATURALES 'BERNARDINO RIVADAVIA' E INST-
ITUTO NACIONAL DE INVESTIGACION DE LAS CIEN-
CIAS NATURALES: PARASITOLOGIA.**
+ +COMUN. MUS. ARG. CIENC. NAT. & INST. NAC.
INVEST. CIENC. NAT., PARASITOL.
 BUENOS AIRES  1, 1965-
 BL/U-1.

**COMUNICACIONES PALEONTOLOGICAS DEL MUSEO
DE HISTORIA NATURAL DE MONTEVIDEO.**
+ +COMUN. PALEONTOL. MUS. HIST. NAT.
MONTEVIDEO.
 MONTEVIDEO  1(1), 1970-
 CA/U-2.    LO/N-2.    LO/N13.

COMUNICADES, INSTITUTO DE ESTUDIOS SINDICALES,
SOCIALES Y COOPERATIVOS.
+ +COMUN. INST. ESTUD. SINDICALES SOC. & COOP.
  MADRID  1(1), 1966-
  NW/U-1.     OX/U-1.
  HL/U-1.  NO.10, 1969-

CONCERN.
  NATIONAL BUREAU FOR CO-OPERATION IN CHILD CARE.
  LONDON  NO.1, 1969-
  Q.
  LO/U-3.

CONCERNED THEATRE JAPAN.
  TOKYO  1(1), 1970-
  Q.  1(1) PRECEDED BY A SPECIAL INTRODUCTORY
  ISSUE DATED OC 1969.
  BH/P-1.     OX/U-1.
  ISSN 0010-518X

CONCERNING POETRY.
+ +CONCERN. POETRY.
  WESTERN WASHINGTON STATE COLLEGE: ENGLISH
  DEPARTMENT.
  WASHINGTON  1, 1968-
  OX/U-1.
  ISSN 0010-5201

CONCH.  A BIAFRAN JOURNAL OF LITERARY & CULTURAL
ANALYSIS.
  [ANOZIE]
  PARIS  1(1), 1969-
  LO/U14.

CONCHIGLIA. REVISTA MENSILE DELLA MERAVIGLIE
DEL MARE.
  ROME  1, 1969-
  LO/N-2.

CONCHIGLIE.
  [CGLI-A]
  UNIONE MALACOLOGICA ITALIANA.
  MILAN  1, 1965-
  LO/N-2.
  ISSN 0588-9758

CONCRETE BUILDING & CONCRETE PRODUCTS.            XXX
  SUBS (1970): PRECAST CONCRETE.

CONCRETE MATERIALS, TECHNOLOGY & CONSTRUCTION
ABSTRACTS.
+ +CONCR. MATER. TECHNOL. & CONSTR. ABSTR.
  CEMENT & CONCRETE ASSOCIATION.
  LONDON  M.1, 1968-
  PART REPLACEMENT OF THE FOLLOWING TITLES IN
  WHICH ABOVE ABSTR. PREV. APPEARED: FORMWORK
  ABSTR.; LIGHTWEIGHT AGGREGATE & LIGHTWEIGHT
  CONCR. ABSTR.; PRECAST CONCR. ABSTR.; & READY
  MIXED CONCR. ABSTR.
  GL/U-1.     LO/N14.     OX/U-8.

CONCRETE/BETON.
  CONCRETE SOCIETY OF SOUTHERN AFRICA.
  JOHANNESBURG NO.1, 1971-
  LO/N14.

CONCURRENCE.  A REVIEW FOR THE ENCOUNTER OF
COMMITMENTS.
  [HERDER]
  FREIBURG/BREISGAU  NO.1, SPRING 1969-
  ED/N-1.     MA/U-1.     SO/U-1.

CONDITIONAL REFLEX.
+ +COND. REFLEX.
  [LIPPINCOTT]
  PHILADELPHIA  1, JA/MR 1966-
  Q.  S/T: A PAVLOVIAN JOURNAL OF RESEARCH &
  THERAPY.
  EX/U-1.  3, 1968-                SH/U-1.  3, 1968-
  ISSN 0010-5392

CONFERENCES ET TRAVAUX, INSTITUT DE PHONET-
IQUE, UNIVERSITE LIBRE DE BRUXELLES.
+ +CONF. & TRAV. INST. PHONETIQUE UNIV. LIBRE
  BRUX.
  [PRESSES UNIVERSITAIRES DE BRUXELLES]
  BRUSSELS  1, 1970-
  MONOGR.
  LO/N-1.

CONFLICT STUDIES.
+ +CONFLICT STUD.
  CURRENT AFFAIRS RESEARCH SERVICES CENTRE.
  LONDON  1, D 1969-
  ED/N-1.     LO/N17.     LO/U14.     OX/U-1.
  MA/P-1.  NO.4, MY 1970-

CONFRONTATION.
  OHIO UNIVERSITY: BLACK STUDIES INSTITUTE.
  ATHENS, OHIO  1(1), 1970-
  OX/U-1.

CONFRUCTA.  INTERNATIONALE ZEITSCHRIFT FUR TECH-
NOLOGIE DER OBST- UND GEMUSE-VERARBEITUNG.        XXX
  [SIGURD HORN]
  FRANKFURT/MAIN  15, 1970-
  PREV:  FRUCHTSAFT-INDUSTRIE FROM 1, JA 1956-
  14, 1969.
  LO/N14.
  ISSN 0016-2213

CONNAISSANCE DES VOYAGES.
+ +CONN. VOYAGES.
  SOCIETE NOUVELLE D'EDITION GEOGRAPHIQUE ET
  TOURISTIQUE.
  PARIS  NO.1, 1970- 18, 1973.//
  Q.
  OX/U-1.
  ISSN 0010-6011

CONNECTICUT LAW REVIEW.
+ +CONN. LAW REV.
  UNIVERSITY OF CONNECTICUT: SCHOOL OF LAW.
  HARTFORD, CONN.  1(1), 1968-
  OX/U15.
  ISSN 0010-6151

CONNECTIVE TISSUE RESEARCH.
+ +CONNECT. TISSUE RES.
  [GORDON & BREACH]
  LONDON  1(1), 1972-
  CA/U-1.     DB/U-2.     GL/U-1.     LO/N13.     OX/U-8.
  ED/N-1.  1(2), 1972-

CONPARLIST.
  INSTITUTE OF CONSTITUTIONAL & PARLIAMENTARY
  STUDIES (INDIA).
  NEW DELHI  1(1), JA 1969-
  M.
  LO/N-1.
  LO/N12.  3(7), 1971-
  ISSN 0010-6313

CONRAD.  CONSTRUCTION RESEARCH & DEVELOPMENT
JOURNAL.
  (GREAT BRITAIN) MINISTRY OF PUBLIC BUILDING &
  WORKS.
  LONDON  1(1), AP 1969-
  Q.
  ED/N-1.     LO/N14.     LO/U-2.     OX/U-1.     XS/R10.
  MA/P-1.  2, 1970-            SF/U-1.  2, 1970-

CONRADIANA.
  UNIVERSITY OF MARYLAND.
  COLLEGE PARK, MD.  1, 1968-
  ISSUED BY THE BODY'S DEPARTMENT OF ENGLISH.
  OX/U-1.
  ISSN 0010-6356

CONSERVA.                                         XXX
  SUBS (1970): VOEDINGSMIDDELENTECHNOLOGIE.

CONSERVATION CATALYST.                            XXX
  SUBS (1970): CATALYST FOR ENVIRONMENTAL
  QUALITY.

CONSERVATION PROGRESS.
+ +CONSERV. PROGR.
  LONDON  NO.17, 1970-
  PREV: PROGRESS IN CREATING CONSERVATION AREAS
  FROM NO.1, 1968-
  XS/U-1.

CONSERVATION REVIEW.
+ +CONSERV. REV.
  SOCIETY FOR THE PROMOTION OF NATURE RESERVES.
  ALFORD, ABERDEEN  NO.1, 1970-
  ED/N-1.     LO/N-2.     LO/R-5.     LO/U-1.     OX/U-8.     SO/U-1.

CONSOLIDATED BUILDING REFERENCES TO ARTICLES
IN PERIODICALS.
  SUBS (1970) PART OF: CONSTRUCTION REFERENCES.

CONSTRUCTIEMATERIALEN.
  THE HAGUE  1, JA 1967- 3, 1969.
  M.  PREV IN PART: METALEN EN ANDERE CONSTRUC-
  TIE-MATERIALEN. SUBS. PART OF: CONSTRUCTEUR.
  LO/N14.
  ISSN 0589-4719

**CONSTRUCTION (LONDON).**
(GREAT BRITAIN) DEPARTMENT OF THE ENVIRONMENT.
*LONDON NO.1, MR 1972-*
Q.
*CA/U-1. DB/U-2. ED/N-1. LO/N14. SH/U-1. XS/R10.*
*BH/U-3. FIVE YEARS ONLY.*

**CONSTRUCTION & BUILDING MATERIALS REVIEW.**
*+ +CONSTR. & BUILD. MATER. REV.*
[GOWER ECONOMIC PUBL.]
*LONDON 1971-*
ANNU.
*ED/N-1. RE/U-1.*

**CONSTRUCTION MACHINERY & EQUIPMENT SALES.**
*+ +CONSTR. MACH. & EQUIP. SALES.*
(CANADA) DOMINION BUREAU OF STATISTICS.
*OTTAWA 1ST, 1967-*
*LO/U-3.*

**CONSTRUCTION PROGRESS.**
*+ +CONSTR. PROG.*
COSTAIN GROUP.
*LONDON NO.1, 1964-*
*LO/N14. OX/U-8.*

**CONSTRUCTION REFERENCES.** XXX
*+ +CONSTR. REF.*
(GREAT BRITAIN) DEPARTMENT OF THE ENVIRONMENT:
LIBRARY SERVICE. XXX
*LONDON NO.1, 1970-*
INCORP: CONSOLIDATED BUILDING REFERENCES TO
ARTICLES IN PERIODICALS FROM NO.5, 1949(1951)-
25, 1969; & CONSOLIDATED ACCESSIONS LIST,
LIBRARY, MINISTRY OF PUBLIC BUILDINGS & WORKS
(G.B.). FROM NO.35, 1963- 50, 1969.
*BH/U-1. GL/U-1. LD/U-1. LO/N14. OX/U-1. SF/U-1.*

**CONSTRUCTION RESEARCH & DEVELOPMENT JOURNAL.** 000
SEE: CONRAD.

**CONSTRUCTOR ANNUAL.**
*+ +CONSTR. ANNU.*
ASSOCIATED GENERAL CONTRACTORS OF AMERICA.
*WASHINGTON, D.C. 1, 1969-*
COVER TITLE: ANNUAL CONSTRUCTOR.
*LO/N13.*

**CONTACT (BROMLEY).** XXX
ELECTRICAL, ELECTRONIC & TELECOMMUNICATION
UNION.
*BROMLEY 1, 1969-*
PREV: ELECTRON.
*BH/U-1. ED/N-1. OX/U-1. OX/U17.*
*BH/P-1. 1(5), D 1969-*
*ISSN 0010-7255*

**CONTACT (DUBLIN).**
*DUBLIN NO.1, 1968-*
*OX/U-1.*

**CONTACT (LONDON).**
CENTRAL COUNCIL FOR THE DISABLED.
*LONDON NO.1, AP 1970-*
*ED/N-1. OX/U-8.*

**CONTACT. NEWSLETTER OF THE NATIONAL ASSOC-
IATION OF PRISON VISITORS.**
[AMBASSADOR PUBL. SERV.]
*LONDON NO.1, JA 1972-*
*ED/N-1. LO/U-3. OX/U15.*

**CONTACT LENS.**
[CNTL-B]
*HARROW, MIDDX. 1, 1966-*
Q.
*LO/N14.*
*ISSN 0010-7271*

**CONTACT LENS MEDICAL BULLETIN.**
*+ +CONTACT LENS MED. BULL.*
CONTACT LENS ASSOCIATION OF OPHTHALMOLOGISTS.
[KARGER]
*BASLE &C. 1, 1968-*
*LO/N14.\**
*ISSN 0010-728X*

**CONTACT POINT.**
BRITISH DENTAL ASSOCIATION: WESTERN COUNTIES
BRANCH.
*KINGSBRIDGE 1(1), 1970-*
*OX/U-8.*

**CONTACTBRIEF NEDERLANDSE LIBELLENONDERZOEKERS.**
*+ +CONTACTBRIEF NED. LIBELLENONDERZOEKERS.*
*UTRECHT NO.1, 1970-*
*LO/N-2.*

**CONTACTS.**
[SMOOTHIE PUBS.]
*BRIGHTON, SX. NO.1, SPRING 1972-*
*ED/N-1. LO/U-2.*

**CONTAINERISATION INTERNATIONAL. THE JOURNAL OF
INTERNATIONAL CONTAINERISATION & UNIT LOADING.**
*+ +CONTAINERISATION INT.*
[NATIONAL MAGAZINE CO.]
*LONDON 1, 1967-*
*ED/N-1. 3(6), 1969- OX/U-1. 1969-*
*LD/U-1. W.2(8), (11), 1968; 4(7), 1970.*
*LO/N14. CURRENT BOX ONLY.*
*LO/P-6. ONE YEAR.*
*ISSN 0010-7379*

**CONTAINERS ACTUALITES.**
*+ +CONTAINERS ACTUAL.*
*PARIS NO.1, 1969-*
*LO/N14.\**

**CONTAMINATION CONTROL INTERNATIONAL.**
*+ +CONTAM. CONTR. INT.*
[BLACKWENT]
*LOS ANGELES 1(1), MY 1968-*
*XS/R10.*

**CONTEMPORARY AFFAIRS: A QUARTERLY MAGAZINE.**
*+ +COMTEMP. AFF.*
(PAKISTAN) BUREAU OF NATIONAL RESEARCH & REFER-
ENCE.
*RAWALPINDI 1(1), 1969-*
*LO/U-3. LO/U14.*
*LO/N12. 1, SPRING 1969- 2(3), AUTUMN 1970.*
*LO/U-8. 1(3), 1969; 2(5), 1970-*
*ISSN 0010-745X*

**CONTEMPORARY POLAND.**
*+ +CONTEMP. POL.*
[POLSKA AGENCJA INTERPRESS]
*WARSAW 1(1), 1967-*
PUBLISHER NAMED AS POLISH AGENCY INTERPRESS.
*BH/U-1. SO/U-1.\**
*MA/U-1. 1(1-8), 1967.*
*ISSN 0010-7522*

**CONTEMPORARY SOCIOLOGY.**
*+ +CONTEMP. SOCIOL.*
AMERICAN SOCIOLOGICAL ASSOCIATION.
*ALBANY, N.Y. 1, JA 1972-*
2M. PREV: THE BOOK REVIEW SECTION OF THE
AMERICAN SOCIOLOGICAL REVIEW.
*CA/U-1. EX/U-1. OX/U-1. RE/U-1. SH/U-1.*
*GL/U-1. 1(4), 1972- LD/U-1. 2, 1973-*
*LO/U-3. 1(4), 1972-*

**CONTEMPORARY SWEDISH POETRY IN ENGLISH:
MANUSCRIPT SERIES.**
*+ +CONTEMP. SWED. POETRY ENGL., MANUSCR. SER.*
[ANGLO-AMERICAN CENTER]
*MULLSJO NO.1, 1971-*
*LO/N-1.*

**CONTEMPORARY TOPICS IN IMMUNOBIOLOGY.**
*+ +CONTEMP. TOP. IMMUNOBIOL.*
[PLENUM P.]
*NEW YORK; LONDON 1, 1972-*
*GL/U-1. OX/U-8.*

**CONTENTS OF CONTEMPORARY MATHEMATICAL
JOURNALS.**
*+ +CONTENTS CONTEMP. MATH. J.*
AMERICAN MATHEMATICAL SOCIETY.
*PROVIDENCE, RI. 1, 10/JA 1969- 6(26), 1974 ...*
2W. SUBS: CURRENT MATHEMATICAL PUBLICATIONS.
*BR/U-3. DB/U-2. ED/U-1. HL/U-1. LO/N14. LO/U-4.*
*SH/U-1.*
*CB/U-1. 1(3-4), 1969-*
*LN/U-2. 3(21), 1971-*
*XS/R10. 1(11), 30/MY 1969-*
*ISSN 0010-759X*

**CONTENTS OF CURRENT LEGAL PERIODICALS.**
*+ +CONTENTS CURR. LEG. PERIOD.*
[LAW PUBL. INC.]
*LOS ANGELES 1, 1972-*
MON.
*OX/U-1.*
*SH/U-1. 2, 1973-*

**CONTENTS OF RECENT ECONOMIC JOURNALS.**
+ +CONTENTS RECENT ECON. J.
(GREAT BRITAIN) DEPARTMENT OF TRADE & INDUSTRY.
 LONDON  8/JA 1971-
 ED/N-1.    LO/S14.    NO/U-1.    OX/U-1.    OX/U16.
 LO/U12.  26/MR 1971-          SH/C-5.  2/JL 1971-
 GL/U-2.  [CURRENT 3 YEARS].
 SO/U-1.  (CURRENT YEAR).
 SW/U-1.  (CURRENT 12 MONTHS).
 ISSN 0045-8368

**CONTEXT.**
HARVARD UNIVERSITY: LABORATORY FOR COMPUTER
GRAPHICS.
 CAMBRIDGE, MASS.  1, F 1968-
LABORATORY SUBORD. TO: GRADUATE SCHOOL OF
DESIGN.
 OX/U-1.

**CONTRACEPTION.**
[GERON-X INC.]
 LOS ALTOS, CALIF.  1, JA 1970-
 M.
 LO/S74.     SO/U-1.
 CA/M-7.  9, 1974-            CA/U-2.  7, 1973-
 MA/U-1.  1(6), 1970-
 ISSN 0010-7824

**CONTRACT CARPETING.**
+ +CONTRACT CARPET.
[A4 PUBL., LTD.]
 EDENBRIDGE, KENT  1970-
 ANNU.
 LO/N14.  CURRENT ISSUE.
 ISSN 0069-9578

**CONTRACTORS' PLANT REVIEW.**
+ +CONTRACT. PLANT REV.
[WHEATLAND JOURNALS LTD.]
 LONDON  1, 1962-
 M.  S/T: OFFICIAL JOURNAL OF THE CONTRACTORS'
MECHANICAL PLANT ENGINEERS.
 ED/N-1.  8(8), 1969-            LO/N14.  3, 1964-
 SH/C-5.  10, 1971-

**CONTREPOINT.**
 PARIS  NO.1, MY 1970-
 Q.
 LO/U-3.
 OX/U-1.  NO.2, 1970-
 ISSN 0010-7964

**CONTRIBUTIONS TO ASIAN STUDIES.**
+ +CONTRIB. ASIAN STUD.
CANADIAN ASSOCIATION FOR SOUTH ASIAN STUDIES.
 LEIDEN  1, JA 1971-
 A.
 LO/N-1.    LO/U-3.    LO/U14.    OX/U13.

**CONTRIBUTIONS FROM THE BOLUS HERBARIUM.**
+ +CONTRIB. BOLUS HERBARIUM.
UNIVERSITY OF CAPE TOWN: BOLUS HERBARIUM.
 CAPE TOWN NO.1, 1969-
 LO/N-2.

**CONTRIBUTIONS FROM BOYCE THOMPSON INSTITUTE
FOR PLANT RESEARCH.**                                          XXX
+ +CONTRIB. BOYCE THOMPSON INST. PLANT RES.
 NEW YORK  1, 1925- 24(14), 1971.//
 OX/U-3.*

**CONTRIBUTIONS FROM THE CUSHMAN FOUNDATION FOR
FORAMINIFERAL RESEARCH.**                                      XXX
 SUBS (1970): JOURNAL OF FORAMINIFERAL RES-
 EARCH.

**CONTRIBUTIONS, HAWAII INSTITUTE OF MARINE
BIOLOGY, UNIVERSITY OF HAWAII.***
+ +CONTRIB. HAWAII INST. MAR. BIOL. UNIV. HAWAII.
[KANEOHE]  1965 (1967)-
PREV: CONTRIBUTIONS OF THE HAWAII MARINE
LABORATORY, UNIVERSITY OF HAWAII FROM 1954-
1965.
 BN/U-2.

**CONTRIBUTIONS, HERBARIUM AUSTRALIENSE.**
+ +CONTRIB. HERB. AUST.
 MELBOURNE  NO.1, 1972-
 AD/U-1.    CA/U-2.

**CONTRIBUTIONS TO INDIAN SOCIOLOGY; (NS).**
+ +CONTR. INDIAN SOCIOL., N.S.
 BOMBAY &C  NO.1, 1967-
 PREV SERIES (PARIS), NO.1, 1957- 9, 1966.
 CA/U-3.    LO/U-3.    SW/U-1.

**CONTRIBUTIONS TO THE NATURAL NIDALITY OF
DISEASES.**                                                     000
 SEE: VOPROSY PRIRODNOJ OCHAGOVOSTI BOLEZNEJ.

**CONTRIBUTIONS, NATURE CONSERVANCY (US).**
+ +CONTRIB. NAT. CONSERV. (US).
 ARLINGTON, VA.  NO.1, 1970-
 LO/N-2.

**CONTRIBUTIONS OF THE OBSERVATORY, NEW
MEXICO STATE UNIVERSITY.**
+ +CONTRIB. OBS. N.M. STATE UNIV.
NEW MEXICO STATE UNIVERSITY; OBSERVATORY.
 LAS CRUCES, N.M.  1(1), MY 1967-
 ED/R-3.

**CONTRIBUTIONS AU RENOUVEAU DU FOLKLORE EN
WALLONIE.**
+ +CONTRIB. RENOUVEAU FOLKLORE WALLONIE.
COMMISSION ROYALE BELGE DE FOLKLORE.
 BRUSSELS  1, 1964-
 LO/N-1.

**CONTRIBUTIONS IN SCIENCE.**
+ +CONTRIB. SCI. (SANTA BARBARA, CALIF.).
MUSEUM OF NATURAL HISTORY (SANTA BARBARA,
CALIF.).
 SANTA BARBARA, CALIF.  NO.1, 1970- 3, 1971.//
 LO/N-2.    LO/N13.

**CONTRIBUCION TECNICA, CENTRO DE INVESTIGACION
DE BIOLOGIA MARINA.**
+ +CONTRIB. TEC. CENT. INVEST. BIOL. MAR. (ARG.)
 BUENOS AIRES  NO.1, 1965-
 LO/N-2.    LO/N13.

**CONTRIBUTIONS, VIRGIN ISLANDS ECOLOGICAL
RESEARCH STATION, CARIBBEAN RESEARCH
INSTITUTE.**
+ +CONTRIB. V.I. ECOL. RES. STAT. CARIBB. RES.
 INST.
 ST. THOMAS  NO.1, 1969-
 LO/N-2.

**CONTROL (LONDON).**                                          XXX
 SUBS (1969) PART OF: CONTROL & INSTRUMENTATION

**CONTROL & DYNAMIC SYSTEMS.  ADVANCES IN THEORY
& APPLICATIONS.**                                              XXX
+ +CONTROL & DYN. SYST.
[ACADEMIC P.]
 NEW YORK; LONDON  9, 1973-
PREV: ADVANCES IN CONTROL SYSTEMS FROM 1,
1964- 8, 1971.
 BR/U-1.    ED/N-1.    LD/U-1.    LO/N14.

**CONTROL & INSTRUMENTATION.**                                 XXX
+ +CONTROL & INSTRUM.
[MORGAN-GRAMPIAN]
 LONDON  1, JA 1969-
PREV. PART OF: CONTROL FROM 1(1), 1958- 3,
(129), 1969; & MEASUREMENT & INSTRUMENT REVIEW
FROM 15, 1968- 16, 1969. S/T: THE JOURNAL OF
AUTOMATION, CONTROL & INSTRUMENTATION
TECHNOLOGY.
 BH/U-1.    BN/U-2.    DB/U-2.    ED/N-1.    GL/U-1.    LO/N-4.
 LO/N14.    LO/U-2.    MA/U-1.    NW/U-1.    OX/U-8.    RE/U-1.
 SW/U-1.    XE/F-2.    XS/R10.
 LD/U-1.  1(3), 1969-
 ISSN 0010-8022

**CONWAY PAPERS.**
+ +CONWAY PAP.
SOUTH PLACE ETHICAL SOCIETY.
 LONDON  NO.1, 1971-
 LO/N-1.

**COOPERATION CANADA.**
+ +COOP. CAN.
CANADIAN INTERNATIONAL DEVELOPMENT AGENCY.
 OTTAWA  NO.1, MR/AP 1972-
 2M.  ENGL. & FR.
 LO/U-3.

**COPPER.**
INTERNATIONAL COPPER COUNCIL.
 GENEVA  NO.1, 1970-
 BH/U-1.    LO/U-2.
 ISSN 0010-857X

**COPPER INFORMATION: ARCHITECTURAL SERIES.**
+ +COPPER INF., ARCHIT.
SOUTH AFRICAN COPPER DEVELOPMENT ASSOCIATION.
 JOHANNESBURG  NO.1, 1970-
 LO/N14.

COPPER INFORMATION: ENGINEERING SERIES.
++COPPER INF., ENG.
SOUTH AFRICAN COPPER DEVELOPMENT ASSOCIATION.
JOHANNESBURG NO.1, 1970-
LO/N14.

COPPERBELT OF ZAMBIA MINING INDUSTRY YEAR
BOOK.                                                    XXX
++COPPERBELT ZAMBIA MIN. IND. YEAR BOOK.
COPPER INDUSTRY SERVICE BUREAU (ZAMBIA).
KITWE 1964(1965)- 1968(1969).
PREV: YEAR BOOK, NORTHERN RHODESIA CHAMBER OF
MINES FROM 1956(1957)- 1963(1964). SUBS:
MINING YEAR BOOK OF ZAMBIA.
BH/U-1.    GL/U-1.    NW/U-1.
NW/U-1. 1967-

COPPERFIELD.
MCMASTER UNIVERSITY: DEPARTMENT OF ENGLISH.
HAMILTON, ONT. 1, 1969-
OX/U-1. 1970-
ISSN 0069-9942

CORDON BLEU COOKERY COURSE.
CORDON BLEU COOKERY SCHOOL.
LONDON 1, COURSE 1, 1968-
OX/U-1.

CORN.                                                    XXX
SUBS (1970): CORN ANNUAL.

CORN ANNUAL.                                             XXX
++CORN ANNU.
CORN REFINERS ASSOCIATION.
WASHINGTON, D.C. 1970-
PREV: CORN FROM 1, 1945- 25(2), MR/AP 1969.
CA/U11.
LO/N13. CURRENT ISSUE ONLY.
ISSN 0069-9993

CORNELL INTERNATIONAL LAW JOURNAL.
++CORNELL INT. LAW J.
CORNELL SOCIETY OF INTERNATIONAL LAW.
ITHACA, N.Y. 1, 1968-
A. SOCIETY SUBORD. TO CORNELL UNIV. LAW
SCHOOL.
OX/UI5.
ISSN 0010-8812

CORNELL JOURNAL OF SOCIAL RELATIONS.
++CORNELL J. SOC. RELAT.
CORNELL UNIVERSITY: DEPARTMENT OF SOCIOLOGY.
ITHACA, N.Y. 1, 1966-
OX/U-1.    XY/N-1.
ISSN 0010-8820

CORNELL LIBRARY JOURNAL.
++CORNELL LIBR. J.
CORNELL UNIVERSITY.
ITHACA, N.Y. NO.1, WINTER 1966-
PUBL. BY THE LIBRARIES OF CORNELL UNIV.
BH/U-1.    DB/U-2.

CORNISH NATION.
++CORN. NAT.
CORNISH NATIONAL MOVEMENT.
REDRUTH 1(1), 1968-
2M.
ED/N-1.    LO/U-3.
OX/U-1. 1(5), 1969-
ISSN 0045-8570

CORNMARKET COMPUTER STAFF SURVEY.
++CORNMARK. COMPUT. STAFF SURV.
[CORNMARKET P.]
LONDON 1969-
A.
LO/U-3.

CORNMARKET SALARY SURVEY.
++CORNMARK. SALARY SURV.
[CORNMARKET P.]
LONDON JA 1965-
Q.
LO/U-3.*
OX/U-1. 1970-

CORRELATION.
ASTROLOGICAL ASSOCIATION.
BEACONSFIELD, BUCKS. 1, 1968-
SPONS. BODY ALSO INTERNATIONAL SOCIETY FOR
ASTROLOGICAL RESEARCH.
OX/U-1.

CORREIO DO LIVRO.
++CORR. LIVRO.
SAO PAULO 1, JE 1967-
OX/U-1.
ISSN 0010-907X

COSMATOM. A JOURNAL DEVOTED TO THE STUDY OF
FIVE-DIMENSIONAL SPACE-TIME-MASS.
[COSMATOM]
WORTHING, SX. 1(1), F 1973-
MON.
ED/N-1.    OX/U-8.

COSMETICS & PERFUMERY.                                   XXX
++COSMET. & PERFUM.
[ALLURED PUBL. CORP]
OAK PARK, ILL. 88, 1973-
PREV: AMERICAN COSMETICS & PERFUMERY FROM 87,
1972.
LD/U-1.    LO/N14.    LO/R-6.    LO/S-3.

COSMIC ELECTRODYNAMICS.                                  XXX
++COSMIC ELECTRODYN.
[REIDEL]
DORDRECHT 1, 1970- 3, 1973.
SUBS. INCORP. IN: ASTROPHYSICS AND SPACE
SCIENCE.
LD/U-1.    LO/N14.
ISSN 0010-9509

COSMOS.
[ARTS CENTRE]
MICKLEGATE, YORKS. NO.1, [1969]-
ED/N-1.    LO/U-2.    OX/U-1.

COSTERUS. ESSAYS IN ENGLISH & AMERICAN LANG-
UAGE & LITERATURE.
[EDITIONS RODOPI]
AMSTERDAM 1, 1972-
DB/U-2.    OX/U-1.

COSTO DE LA CONSTRUCCION (EN LA CAPITAL
FEDERAL).
++COSTO CONSTR. (CAPITAL FED.).
INSTITUTO NACIONAL DE ESTADISTICA Y CENSOS DE
REPUBLICA ARGENTINA.
BUENOS AIRES NO.1, 1969-
ED/N-1.    LO/U-2.    OX/U-1.

COSTUME.
COSTUME SOCIETY.
LONDON 1, 1968-
GL/U-1.
BH/P-1. 2, 1968-              OX/U-1. 1(2), 1968-

COTTON RESEARCH REPORTS.                                 XXX
++COTTON RES. REP.                                       XXX
COTTON RESEARCH CORPORATION.
LONDON 1970/71(1972)-
PREV: PROGRESS REPORTS FROM EXPERIMENT STAT-
IONS, COTTON RESEARCH CORPORATION FROM 1964/65
(1966)- 1969/70(1972). REPORTS FOR UGANDA,
1970/71 HAVE EARLIER TITLE.
LO/N-2.    LO/N14.

COUNCIL. NEWSLETTER OF THE ...
NATIONAL COUNCIL OF WOMEN OF GREAT BRITAIN.
LONDON 1, S 1972-
LO/U-3.
CA/U-1. 1(4), 1973-          ED/N-1. F 1974-

COUNCIL CLEANSING & CLEARWAYS.
++COUNC. CLEAN. & CLEARWAYS.
LONDON MY 1971-
LO/N14.    OX/U-8.

COUNTER MEASURES.
++COUNTER MEAS.
BEDFORD, MASS. NO.1, 1972-
OX/U-1.

COUNTERPOINTE. THE SCOTTISH BALLET MAGAZINE.
EDINBURGH NO.1, 1972-
CA/U-1.    ED/N-1.    OX/U-1.

COUNTRY. COUNTRY MUSIC MONTHLY.
[HANOVER BOOKS LTD.]
LONDON 1(1), MR 1972-
ED/N-1.

COUNTRY PROFILES.
++CTRY. PROFILES.
COLUMBIA UNIVERSITY: INTERNATIONAL INSTITUTE
FOR THE STUDY OF HUMAN REPRODUCTION.
NEW YORK NO.1, MY 1969-
LO/N17.    RE/U-1.    SO/U-1.

**COUPURE.**
[TERRAIN VAGUE]
*PARIS NO.1, 1969-*
*CB/U-1.*

**COURRIER DE LA NATURE.**
*+ +COURR. NATURE.*
SOCIETE NATIONALE DE PROTECTION DE LA NATURE ET
D'ACCLIMATATION (FRANCE).
*PARIS NO.1/2, 1967-*
*LO/N-2.*

**COURS ET DOCUMENTS DE BIOLOGIE.**
*+ +COURS & DOC. BIOL.*
[GORDON & BREACH SCIENCE PUBL.]
*PARIS 1, 1969-*
*CA/U-1. 2, 1971-*

**COURSE COMPARISON BULLETIN, CRAC.**                            000
   **SEE: CRAC, COURSE ...**

**COURSES FOR TEACHERS.**
[EYE PUBL.]
*LONDON 1(1), JA 1971-*
*CA/U-1. 3(2), 1973-*            *ED/N-1. 3, 1973-*
*OX/U-1. 3(1), 1973-*

**CRAB GRASS.**
*BELFAST 1, 1970-*
A PUBL. BY ARCHITECTURE STUDENTS AT QUEENS
UNIVERSITY, BELFAST.
*BL/U-1.*

**CRAC COURSE COMPARISON BULLETIN.**
*+ +CRAC COURSE COMP. BULL. (CAREERS RES. & ADVIS.*
*CENT.).*
CAREERS RESEARCH & ADVISORY CENTRE.
*CAMBRIDGE NO.1, 1966-*
*OX/U-1.*

**CRAFT TEACHER NEWS.**
*READING NO.1, 1971-*
*ED/N-1.*

**CRAFTWORK. SCOTLAND'S CRAFT MAGAZINE.**
SMALL INDUSTRIES COUNCIL FOR RURAL AREAS OF
SCOTLAND.
*EDINBURGH 1(1), SUMMER 1972-*
*CA/U-1. OX/U-1.*

**CRANBROOK MAGAZINE.**
*+ +CRANBROOK MAG.*
(CRANBROOK) PUBLIC AFFAIRS OFFICE.
*BLOOMFIELD HILLS, MICH. 1, 1969-*
*LO/N-2.*
*ISSN 0011-0795*

**CRANFIELD CTS REPORT.**
*+ +CRANFIELD CTS REP.*
CRANFIELD CENTRE FOR TRANSPORT STUDIES.
*CRANFIELD, BEDS. 1, 1972-*
*CA/U-1. GL/U-1. LO/N-4. LO/N14.*

**CRANFIELD REPORT AERO.**                                       XXX
*+ +CRANFIELD REP. AERO.*
CRANFIELD INSTITUTE OF TECHNOLOGY.                               XXX
*CRANFIELD, BEDS. NO.1, 1970-*
PREV: COA REPORT AERO FROM NO.163, 1963-
211, 1969.
*GL/U-1. LO/N14.*

**CRANFIELD REPORT A.S.A.E.**                                    XXX
*+ +CRANFIELD REP. A.S.A.E.*
CRANFIELD INSTITUTE OF TECHNOLOGY.
*CRANFIELD, BEDS. NO.1, 1970-*
PREV: ASAE REPORT FROM NO.1, 1966- 5, 1969.
*LO/N14.*

**CRANFIELD REPORT E & C.**                                      XXX
*+ +CRANFIELD REP. E & C.*
CRANFIELD INSTITUTE OF TECHNOLOGY.
*CRANFIELD, BEDS. NO.1, 1970-*
PREV: COA REPORT E & C FROM NO.1, 1964- 7,
1966.
*LO/N-4. LO/N14.*
*BR/U-3. 2, 1971-*

**CRANFIELD REPORT M & P.**                                      XXX
*+ +CRANFIELD REP. M & P.*
CRANFIELD INSTITUTE OF TECHNOLOGY.                               XXX
*CRANFIELD, BEDS. NO.1, F 1971-*
PREV: COA REPORT M & P FROM NO.1, 1964- 2,
1965.
*BR/U-3. GL/U-1. LO/N-4. LO/N14. NW/U-1. SO/U-1.*

**CRANFIELD REPORT MAT.**                                        XXX
*+ +CRANFIELD REP. MAT.*                                         XXX
CRANFIELD INSTITUTE OF TECHNOLOGY.
*CRANFIELD, BEDS. NO.1, 1970-*
PREV: COA REPORT MAT. FROM NO.1, 1966- 6,
1968.
*LO/N-4. LO/N14.*

**CRANFIELD REPORT SME.**
*+ +CRANFIELD REP. SME.*
CRANFIELD INSTITUTE OF TECHNOLOGY: SCHOOL OF
MECHANICAL ENGINEERING.
*CRANFIELD, BEDS. NO.1, 1972-*
*BL/U-1. BR/U-1. LO/N-4. LO/N14.*
*CA/U-1. NO.3, 1973-*

**CRANIA BOHEMICA. MATERIALY PREHISTORICKE A
HISTORICKE ANTROPOLOGIE.**
*+ +CRANIA BOHEM. [CBMP-B]*
CESKOSLOVENSKA AKADEMIE VED: ANTROPOLOGICKE
ODDELENI.
*PRAGUE 1, 1964-*
ANTROPOLOGICKE ODDELENI SUBORD. TO ARCHEOLOG-
ICKY USTAV.
*CA/U-1. OX/U-8.*
*ISSN 0590-0565*

**CRC CRITICAL REVIEWS IN ANALYTICAL CHEMISTRY.**
*+ +CRC CRIT. REV. ANAL. CHEM. (CHEM. RUBB. CO.).*
CHEMICAL RUBBER COMPANY (CLEVELAND).
*CLEVELAND 1, 1970-*
*LO/N14. LO/S-3. SH/U-1. XS/R10.*
*LO/U28. 2(2), 1971-*
*ISSN 0007-8980*

**CRC CRITICAL REVIEWS IN BIOCHEMISTRY.**
*+ +CRC CRIT. REV. BIOCHEM. (CHEM. RUBB. CO.).*
CHEMICAL RUBBER COMPANY (CLEVELAND).
*CLEVELAND 1, 1972-*
*GL/U-1. GL/U-2. HL/U-1. * LO/N14. LO/R-6. LO/S-3.*
*MA/U-1.*
*ISSN 0045-6411*

**CRC CRITICAL REVIEWS IN BIOENGINEERING.**
*+ +CRC CRIT. REV. BIOENG. (CHEM. RUBB. CO.).*
CHEMICAL RUBBER COMPANY (CLEVELAND).
*CLEVELAND 1, 1972-*
*GL/U-2.*
*ISSN 0045-642X*

**CRC CRITICAL REVIEWS IN CLINICAL LABORATORY
SCIENCES.**
*+ +CRC CRIT. REV. CLIN. LAB. SCI. (CHEM. RUBB.*
*CO.).*
CHEMICAL RUBBER COMPANY (CLEVELAND).
*CLEVELAND 1, 1970-*
*BL/U-1. LO/N14. NW/U-1. SH/U-1.*
*CA/M-7. 5, 1974-            OX/U-8. 2, 1971-*

**CRC CRITICAL REVIEWS IN CLINICAL RADIOLOGY &
NUCLEAR MEDICINE.**                                             XXX
*+ +CRC CRIT. REV. CLIN. RADIOL. & NUCL. MED.*
*(CHEM. RUBB. CO.).*
CHEMICAL RUBBER COMPANY (CLEVELAND).
*CLEVELAND, OHIO 4, 1973-*
PREV: CRC CRITICAL REVIEWS IN RADIOLOGICAL
SCIENCES FROM 1, 1970- 3, 1972.
*LO/N14. OX/U-8.*
*LD/U-1. 5, 1974-*

**CRC CRITICAL REVIEWS IN ENVIRONMENTAL CONTROL.**
*+ +CRC CRIT. REV. ENVIRON. CONTR. (CHEM. RUBB.*
*CO.).*
CHEMICAL RUBBER COMPANY (CLEVELAND).
*CLEVELAND 1, 1970-*
*BL/U-1. DB/U-2. LO/N-6. LO/N14. LO/U12. XS/R10.*
*LO/U28. 2, 1971-*
*ISSN 0007-8999*

**CRC CRITICAL REVIEWS IN FOOD TECHNOLOGY.**
*+ +CRC CRIT. REV. FOOD TECHNOL. (CHEM. RUBB. CO.)*
CHEMICAL RUBBER COMPANY (CLEVELAND).
*CLEVELAND 1, 1970-*
*DB/U-2. GL/U-2. LO/N-6. LO/N14. LO/R-6.*
*ISSN 0007-9006*

**CRC CRITICAL REVIEWS IN MACROMOLECULAR
SCIENCE.**                                                      XXX
*+ +CRC CRIT. REV. MACROMOL. SCI.(CHEM. RUBB. CO.)*
CHEMICAL RUBBER COMPANY (CLEVELAND).
*CLEVELAND 1(1- 4), 1972- 1973.*
SUBS. INCORP. IN: CRC CRITICAL REVIEWS IN
SOLID STATE SCIENCES.
*LO/N14.*
*LO/S-3. 1, 1972.*
*ISSN 0045-6438*

**CRC CRITICAL REVIEWS IN MICROBIOLOGY.**
*+ +CRC CRIT. REV. MICROBIOL. (CHEM. RUBB. CO.).*
CHEMICAL RUBBER COMPANY (CLEVELAND).
*CLEVELAND 1, 1971-*
*BN/U-2. CA/U-1. GL/U-1. GL/U-2. MA/U-1.*
*HL/U-1. 3, 1973-*
*ISSN 0045-6454*

**CRC CRITICAL REVIEWS IN RADIOLOGICAL SCIENCES.**
*+ +CRC CRIT. REV. RADIOL. SCI. (CHEM. RUBB. CO.).*
CHEMICAL RUBBER COMPANY (CLEVELAND).
*CLEVELAND 1, 1970- 3, 1972 ...*
SUBS: CRC CRITICAL REVIEWS IN CLINICAL
RADIOLOGY AND NUCLEAR MEDICINE.
*LO/N14.*
*ISSN 0007-9014*

**CRC CRITICAL REVIEWS IN SOLID STATE SCIENCES.**
*+ +CRC CRIT. REV. SOLID STATE SCI. (CHEM. RUBB.
CO.).*
CHEMICAL RUBBER COMPANY (CLEVELAND).
*CLEVELAND 1, 1970-*
FROM 1974 INCORPORATES: CRC CRITICAL REVIEWS
IN MACROMOLECULAR SCIENCE.
*AD/U-1. DN/U-1. LO/N14. SH/U-1. XS/R10.*
*CA/U-2. 4, 1973-*
*ISSN 0011-085X*

**CRC CRITICAL REVIEWS IN TOXICOLOGY.**
*+ +CRC CRIT. REV. TOXICOL. (CHEM. RUBB. CO.).*
CHEMICAL RUBBER COMPANY (CLEVELAND).
*CLEVELAND 1, 1971-*
*GL/U-2. LO/N14.*
*ISSN 0045-6446*

**C.R.C. NEWS.**                                                    XXX
COMMUNITY RELATIONS COMMISSION (GB).
*LONDON S 1969- OC 1971.//*
MON. PREV: COMMUNITY RELATIONS NEWS FROM
1, JE 1969- 2, JY/AG 1969.
*ED/N-1. LO/U-3.*
*LO/N-1. MY 1971-* *OX/U-1. JA 1970-*

**CRE YEARBOOK.**
*+ +CRE YEARB.*
STANDING CONFERENCE OF RECTORS & VICE-CHANCEL-
LORS OF THE EUROPEAN UNIVERSITIES.
*GENEVA 1972-*
S/T: YEARBOOK OF THE EUROPEAN UNIVERSITIES.
*LO/N-1. LO/U-1.*

**CREACION & CRITICA.**
*+ +CREACION & CRIT.*
[EDITORIAL JURIDICA]
*LIMA NO.1, JA 1971-*
*LO/N-1.*

**CREATION (PARIS).**
ASSOCIATION DE RECHERCHE SUR LA POESIE FRANC-
AISE MODERNE ET CONTEMPORAINE.
*PARIS 1, 1971-*
*EX/U-1.*

**CREATION. JOURNAL OF THE ...**
EVOLUTION PROTEST MOVEMENT.
*STOKE, HANTS. 1(1), OC 1971-*
*2/A.*
*ED/N-1.*

**CREATION & DETECTION OF THE EXCITED STATE.**
*+ +CREAT. & DETECT. EXCITED STATE.*
[DEKKER]
*NEW YORK 1, 1971-*
*OX/U-8.*

**CREATIVE PLASTICS.**
*+ +CREATIVE PLAST.*
DU PONT OF CANADA LTD.
*MONTREAL 1, 1963-*
PUBL. BY THE FIRM'S PLASTICS DEP.
*LO/N14. CURRENT ISSUES ONLY.*
*ISSN 0011-0906*

**CRI ABSTRACTS.**
*+ +CRI ABSTR. (CEM. RES. INST. INDIA).*
CEMENT RESEARCH INSTITUTE OF INDIA.
*DELHI 1, JA 1968-*
*Q.*
*LO/N-7. LO/N14.*

**CRIME & DETECTION.**                                              XXX
*+ +CRIME & DETECT.*
[TALLIS PRESS]
*OXFORD. NO.1, 1966- 4, 1967...*
Q. 1-4 ALSO CALLED VOL.1. SUBS: CRIMINOLO-
GIST.
*AD/U-1. BH/U-1.*
*ED/N-1. NO.3,1967-* *GL/U-2. NO.3,1967-*

**CRIMINAL LAW BULLETIN.**
*+ +CRIM. LAW BULL. [CRLB-A]*
STATE UNIVERSITY OF NEW YORK AT ALBANY.
*ALBANY, N.Y. &C. 1, F 1965-*
MON.
*OX/U15. 7(1), 1971-* *SH/U-1. 9, 1973-*
*ISSN 0011-1317*

**CRIMINALOGICA.**
AMERICAN SOCIETY OF CRIMINOLOGY.
*LOUISVILLE, KY. 1, MY 1963-*
*XY-N-1.* **

**CRIMINOLOGIST.**
[FORENSIC PUBL. CO.]
*LONDON NO.5, AG 1967-*
PREV: CRIME & DETECTION FROM NO.1, 1966-
4, 1967.
*BH/U-1. ED/N-1. GL/U-2. HL/U-1.*
*CO/U-1. NO.7, F 1968-*
*ISSN 0011-1376*

**CRITIC.**
[ARCHETYPE]
*LONDON 1[1], 1/MR 1968-*
*LV/P-1.*
*HL/U-1. 1(2),1968-*
*MA/P-1. 1(1-12), 1/MR- 17/MY 1968.*

**CRITICA.**
*MEXICO, DF 1, JA 1967-*
*LA/U-1.*
*ISSN 0011-1503*

**CRITICA SOCIOLOGICA.**
*+ +CRIT. SOCIOL.*
*ROME 1967(1)-*
*LO/U-3.*
*ISSN 0011-1546*

**CRITICAL IDIOM.**
*+ +CRIT. IDIOM.*
[METHUEN]
*LONDON 1, 1969-*
*GL/U-1.*

**CRITICAL REVIEWS IN ... (CHEMICAL RUBBER COM-**                   000
**PANY, CLEVELAND).**
SEE: CRC CRITICAL REVIEWS IN ...

**CRITICAL REVIEWS IN TRIBOLOGY.**
*+ +CRIT. REV. TRIBOL.*
[IPC SCIENCE & TECHNOLOGY P.]
*GUILDFORD 1, 1970(1972)-*
*CA/U-1. LD/U-1. SF/U-1. SH/U-1. SH/U-3. SO/U-1.*

**CRITIQUE. A NEW JOURNAL OF SOVIET STUDIES &**
**SOCIALIST THEORY.**
*GLASGOW 1(1), SPRING 1973-*
*2/A.*
*CA/U-1. ED/N-1. GL/U-1. LD/U-1. LO/U-3. OX/U-1.*
*SA/U-1. SH/U-1. SW/U-1.*

**CROATICA. PRINOSI PROUCAVANJU HRVATSKE**
**KNJIZEVNOSTI.**
INSTITUT ZA ZNANOST O KNJIZEVNOSTI: FILOZOFSKOG
FAKULTETA.
*ZAGREB 1, 1970-*
SPONS. BODY ALSO JUGOSLAVENSKA AKADEMIJA
ZNANOSTI I UMJETNOSTI: INSTITUT ZA KNJIZEVNOST
I TEATROLOGIJU.
*NO/U-1.*

**CROI. NEWSLETTER OF THE IRISH HEART**
**FOUNDATION.**
*DUBLIN [NO.1], 1968-*
*DB/U-2.*

**CRONACHE ERCOLANESI.**
*+ +CRON. ERCOLANESI.*
CENTRO INTERNAZIONALE PER LO STUDIO DEI PAPIRI
ERCOLANESI.
*NAPLES 1, 1971-*
*LD/U-1. MA/U-1. OX/U-1.*

**CRONICILE MEDIEVALE ALE ROMINIEI.**
*+ +CRON. MEDIEV. ROM.*
ACADEMIA REPUBLICII SOCIALISTE ROMANIA;
INSTITUTUL DE ISTORIE 'N. IORGA'.
*BUCHAREST 1, 1963-*
MONOGR., HARDBOUND.
*LO/N-3. 1, 4, 1963; 5, 1965; 6, 1967.*

CRONICILE MEDIEVALE ALE ROMINIEI, SUPLIMENT.
++CRON. MEDIEV. ROM., SUPL.
ACADEMIA REPUBLICII SOCIALISTE ROMANIA:
INSTITUTUL DE ISTORIE 'N. IORGA'.
*BUCHAREST 1, 1965-*
MONOGR., PAPERBOUND.
*LO/N-3. [NO.]1, 1965.*

CROSBY HISTORICAL PUBLICATIONS.
++CROSBY HIST. PUBL.
CROSBY PUBLIC LIBRARIES.
*CROSBY, LANCS. NO.1, 1972-*
*LO/N-1.*

CROSS TALK. MAGAZINE OF THE ...                    XXX
BRITISH RED CROSS SOCIETY.
*LONDON NO.1, JA 1972-*
MON. PREV: NEWS REVIEW, BRITISH RED CROSS
SOCIETY FROM 1957- D 1971.
*ED/N-1.   LO/N-1.*

CROSSCURRENTS. RECENT AUSTRALIAN POETRY.
*HEIDELBERG WEST, VICTORIA NO.1, 1968-*
*LO/U-2.*

CROSSWORD.
*OXFORD 1, 1969-*
*OX/U-1.*

CRREL IN ALASKA: ANNUAL REPORT.
(UNITED STATES) ARMY: COLD REGIONS RESEARCH &
ENGINEERING LABORATORY.
*HANOVER, N.H. (1970)1971-*
*CA/U12.   LO/N13.   XS/N-1.*

CRUMB. CLIMATIC RESEARCH UNIT MONTHLY
BULLETIN.
UNIVERSITY OF EAST ANGLIA: CLIMATIC RESEARCH
UNIT.
*NORWICH 1(1), JA 1972-*
*EX/U-1.   XS/N-1.*
*ISSN 0306-1388*

CRYOGENIC ENGINEERING NEWS.                        XXX
++CRYOG. ENG. NEWS.
[BUSINESS COMMUNICATIONS INC.]
*CLEVELAND 1, 1965- 4(5), 1969 ...*
MON. SUBS: CRYOGENICS & INDUSTRIAL GASES.
*SO/U-1. 3,1968-*

CRYOGENICS & INDUSTRIAL GASES.                     XXX
++CRYOG. & IND. GASES.
[BUSINESS COMMUNICATIONS INC.]
*CLEVELAND, OHIO 4(6), JE 1969-*
PREV: CRYOGENIC ENGINEERING NEWS FROM 1,
1965- 4(5), 1969.
*SO/U-1.*
*ISSN 0011-2283*

CRYSTAL LATTICE DEFECTS.
++CRYST. LATTICE DEFECTS.
[GORDON & BREACH]
*NEW YORK &C. 1, 1969-*
*BH/U-1.   LO/N14.   LO/U20.   OX/U-8.   XS/R10.*
*ISSN 0011-2305*

CRYSTAL STRUCTURE COMMUNICATIONS.
++CRYST. STRUCT. COMMUN.
UNIVERSITY OF PARMA: X-RAY CRYSTALLOGRAPHY
GROUP.
*PARMA 1, 1972-*
S/T: AN INTERNATIONAL QUARTERLY REPORT CONT-
AINING RESULTS OF CRYSTAL STRUCTURE ANALYSES.
*CA/U-1.   LD/U-1.   LO/N14.   LO/U28.   OX/U-8.   SH/U-1.*

CRYSTIC MONOGRAPH.
++CRYSTIC MONOGR.
SCOTT BADER & COMPANY: CRYSTIC RESEARCH CENTRE.
*WELLINGBOROUGH, NORTHANTS. NO.1, 1971-*
*CA/U-1.   LO/N14.*

CSS NEWSLETTER.                                    000
SEE: NEWSLETTER, CIVIL SERVICE SOCIETY.

CSTC REVUE.
++CSTC REV.
CENTRE SCIENTIFIQUE ET TECHNIQUE DE LA CONST-
RUCTION (BELGIUM).
*BRUSSELS 1, 1966-*
*BL/U-1.   LO/N13. [W. NO.4, 1966; NO.2, 1967].*

CSU RESEARCH.                                      XXX
++CSU RES.
AGRICULTURAL EXPERIMENT STATION, FORT COLLINS,
COLO.
*FORT COLLINS, COLO. 20(1), OC 1969-*
PREV: COLORADO FARM & HOME RESEARCH FROM
1950- 19(4), 1969.
*CA/U11.*

CTFA COSMETIC JOURNAL.                             XXX
++CTFA COSMET. J.
COSMETIC, TOILETRY & FRAGRANCE ASSOCIATION.
*WASHINGTON, D.C. 3, 1971-*
PREV: TGA COSMETIC JOURNAL FROM 1, 1969- 2,
1970.
*LO/N14.*

CUADERNOS DE ARAGON.
++CUAD. ARAGON.
CONSEJO SUPERIOR DE INVESTIGACIONES CIENTIFICAS
(SPAIN): INSTITUCION FERNANDO EL CATOLICO.
*ZARAGOZA 1, 1966-*
*OX/U-1. 2, 1967-*
*ISSN 0519-1626*

CUADERNOS DE ARTE Y LITERATURA.
++CUAD. ARTE & LIT.
UNIVERSIDAD DE GRANADA: FACULTAD DE LETRAS.
*GRANADA NO.1, 1967-*
*HL/U-1.*

CUADERNOS BIBLIOGRAFICOS.
++CUAD. BIBLIOGR. (SPAIN).
CONSEJO SUPERIOR DE INVESTIGACIONES CIENTIFICAS
(SPAIN).
*MADRID 1, 1961-*
*ED/N-1.*

CUADERNOS DE BOTANICA CANARIA.*
++CUAD. BOT. CANARIA.
MUSEO CANARIO.
*LAS PALMAS DE GRAN CANARIA 1, MY 1967-*
TITLE EXTENDED FROM: CUADERNOS DE BOTANICA
FROM 5, 1969.
*LO/N-2.*
*LO/N13. 5, 1969-*
*ISSN 0011-2372*

CUADERNOS DE ETNOLOGIA Y ETNOGRAFIA DE
NAVARRA.
++CUAD. ETNOL. & ETNOGR. NAVARRA.
INSTITUCION 'PRINCIPE DE VIANA'.
*PAMPLONA 1(1), JA/AP 1969-*
Q.
*LO/N-1.*

CUADERNOS DE FILOLOGIA CLASICA.
++CUAD. FILOL. CLASICA.
UNIVERSIDAD DE MADRID: FACULTAD DE FILOSOFIA Y
LETRAS.
*MADRID 1, 1971-*
*OX/U-1.*
*MA/U-1. 4, 1972-*

CUADERNOS GEOGRAFICOS DEL SUR (CHILE).
++CUAD. GEOGR. SUR (CHILE).
UNIVERSIDAD DE CONCEPCION (CHILE): INSTITUTO
CENTRAL DE GEOGRAFIA.
*CONCEPCION, CHILE 1, 1971-*
A.
*LO/S13.*

CUADERNOS DE MARCHA.
++CUAD. MARCHA.
[TALLERES GRAFICOS '33']
*MONTEVIDEO NO.1, MY 1967-*
MON.
*CC/U-1.*

CUADERNOS PREHISPANICOS.
++CUAD. PREHISP. (VALLADOLID).
UNIVERSIDAD DE VALLADOLID: SEMINARIO
AMERICANISTA.
*VALLADOLID 1(1), 1973-*
*OX/U-1.*

CUADERNOS DEL SUR. TEXTOS COMENTADOS.
++CUAD. SUR.
UNIVERSIDAD NACIONAL DEL SUR (ARGENTINA):
INSTITUTO DE HUMANIDADES.
*BAHIA BLANCA NO.1, 1965-*
MONOGR.
*LO/N-1.*

CUBA EN EL BALLET.
BALLET NACIONAL DE CUBA.
*HAVANA 1(1), 1970-*
*OX/U-1.*

**CUBAN STUDIES NEWSLETTER.**
+ +CUBAN STUD. NEWSL.
UNIVERSITY OF PITTSBURGH: CENTER FOR LATIN
AMERICAN STUDIES.
*PITTSBURGH 1(1), 1970-*
2A. CENTER SUBORD. TO UNIVERSITY CENTER FOR
INTERNATIONAL STUDIES.
*OX/U-1.*
*ISSN 0011-2631*

**CULTA BONONIA. REVISTA DI STUDI BOLOGNESI.**
*BOLOGNE 1, 1969-*
2/A.
*DB/U-2. LO/N-1. LO/U17.*
*HL/U-1. 3(2), 1971-*

**CULTURA.**
(BRAZIL) MINISTERIO DA EDUCACAO E CULTURA:
DIRECTORIA DE DOCUMENTACAO E DIVULGACAO.
*BRAZIL NO.1, JA/MR 1971-*
ENGL. & FR. SUMM.
*OX/U-1.*
*LO/U-1. 1(2), 1971-*

**CULTURAL HERMENEUTICS.**
+ +CULT. HERMENEUTICS.
[REIDEL]
*DORDRECHT 1(1), AP 1973-*
Q.
*DB/U-2. SW/U-1.*
*ISSN 0011-2860*

**CULTURE VIVANTE.**
+ +CULT. VIVANTE.
QUEBEC (PROVINCE) MINISTERE DES AFFAIRES CULT-
URELLES.
*QUEBEC 1, 1966-*
*BH/U-1.*

**CULTURES ET DEVELOPPEMENT. REVUE INTERNAT-
IONALE DES SCIENCES DU DEVELOPPEMENT.**
+ +CULT. & DEVELOP.
UNIVERSITE CATHOLIQUE DE LOUVAIN: INSTITUT
D'ETUDES DES PAYS EN DEVELOPPEMENT.
*LOUVAIN 1(1), 1968-*
*LO/U14. MA/U-1.*
*LO/N17. 1(2), 1968-*
*ISSN 0011-295X*

**CUMBERLAND RECORD SERIES.** XXX
SUBS (1968): PUBLICATIONS, RECORD OFFICE,
CUMBERLAND, WESTMORLAND & CARLISLE JOINT
ARCHIVES COMMITTEE.

**CUMBERLAND & WESTMORLAND INDUSTRIAL & COMMER-
CIAL REVIEW.**
+ +CUMBERLAND & WESTMORLAND IND. & COMMER. REV.
[W.PARR & CO.]
*WILMSLOW 1(1), AG 1969-*
*ED/N-1. OX/U-1.*

**CURRENT.**
[CURRENT INC.]
*NEW YORK 1, MY 1960-*
*XY/N-1.***

**CURRENT ABSTRACTS OF CHEMISTRY & INDEX CHEM-
ICUS.** XXX
+ +CURR. ABSTR. CHEM. & INDEX CHEM.
INSTITUTE FOR SCIENTIFIC INFORMATION.
*PHILADELPHIA 36(319), JA 1970-*
PREV: INDEX CHEMICUS FROM 1, 1960- 35, 1970.
*LO/N14. LO/S-3.*
*ISSN 0011-3158*

**CURRENT ABSTRACTS OF THE SOVIET PRESS.**
+ +CURR. ABSTR. SOV. P.
JOINT COMMITTEE ON SLAVIC STUDIES.
*NEW YORK 1(1), AP 1968-*
*OX/U-1.*
*ISSN 0011-3166*

**CURRENT ADVANCES IN PLANT SCIENCE.**
+ +CURR. ADV. PLANT SCI.
[SCIENCES, ENGINEERING, MEDICAL & BUSINESS DATA
LTD.]
*OXFORD 1(1), JL 1972-*
S/T: A MONTHLY SUBJECT CATEGORISED LISTING OF
TITLES IN PLANT SCIENCE COMPILED FROM CURRENT
LITERATURE.
*BL/U-1. BN/U-2. CA/U-7. ED/N-1. GL/U-1. LO/N13.*
*OX/U-8. SH/U-1.*
*LO/N-6. 1(3), 1972-*
*MA/U-1. 2, 1973-* *MA/U-1. 2, 1973-*

**CURRENT AFRICANIST RESEARCH. INTERNATIONAL
BULLETIN. = RECHERCHE AFRICANISTE EN COURS.
BULLETIN INTERNATIONALE.**
+ +CURR. AFR. RES.
INTERNATIONAL AFRICAN INSTITUTE: RESEARCH
INFORMATION LIAISON UNIT.
*LONDON NO.1, N 1971-*
ENGL.
*CA/U-1. LO/U-3. OX/U-1.*

**CURRENT BIBLIOGRAPHY FOR AQUATIC SCIENCES AND
FISHERIES.** XXX
SUBS (1971) PART OF: AQUATIC SCIENCES AND
FISHERIES ABSTRACTS.

**CURRENT BIBLIOGRAPHY, AUSTRALIAN INSTITUTE OF
ABORIGINAL STUDIES.** XXX
+ +CURR. BIBLIOGR. AUST. INST. ABORIG. STUD.
*CANBERRA NO.10, 1967-*
PREV: BIBLIOGRAPHY, AUSTRALIAN ... SERIES A
FROM NO.1, 1961/S 1962- 9, 1967.
*CA/U-3.*
*OX/U-8. 2(2), 1970-*

**CURRENT BIBLIOGRAPHY OF EPIDEMIOLOGY.**
+ +CURR. BIBLIOGR. EPIDEMIOL.
AMERICAN PUBLIC HEALTH ASSOCIATION.
*NEW YORK 1, 1969-*
*BL/U-1. SO/U-1.*
*ISSN 0011-3247*

**CURRENT CARIBBEAN BIBLIOGRAPHY.**
+ +CURR. CARIB. BIBLIOGR.
CARIBBEAN ECONOMIC DEVELOPMENT CORPORATION.
*HATO REY, P.R. JA 1969-*
CUMULATED A. BODY NAMED: CORPORACION DE
DESAROLLO ECONOMICO DEL CARIBE.
*LO/U-3.*

**CURRENT CONTENTS: AGRICULTURAL, FOOD & VETER-
INARY SCIENCES.**
+ +CURR. CONT., AGR. FOOD & VET. SCI.
INSTITUTE FOR SCIENTIFIC INFORMATION.
*PHILADELPHIA 1(1), 1970- 3, 1972 ...*
WKLY. SUBS: CURRENT CONTENTS: AGRICULTURE,
BIOLOGY & ENVIRONMENTAL SCIENCES.
*LO/N-6.*
*CO/U-1. 1(26), 1970- NW/U-1. 2, 1971-*
*CA/U-2. [CURRENT YEAR ONLY]*
*GL/U-1. [CURRENT YEAR ONLY]*
*LO/U28. [CURRENT YEAR ONLY]*
*ISSN 0011-3379*

**CURRENT CONTENTS: BEHAVIORAL, SOCIAL & MANAG-
EMENT SCIENCES.**
+ +CURR. CONTENTS, BEHAV. SOC. & MANAGE. SCI.
INSTITUTE FOR SCIENTIFIC INFORMATION.
*PHILADELPHIA 1, MR 1969-*
*GL/U-1.*
*CA/U-1. 4, 1972- CR/M-1. 1971-*
*SH/U-1. 1972-*
*OX/U17. 2(35), S 1970-*
*SH/C-5. 3(40), 1971-*

**CURRENT CONTENTS: CHEMICAL SCIENCES.** XXX
+ +CURR. CONT., CHEM. SCI. [CCCS-B]
INSTITUTE FOR SCIENTIFIC INFORMATION.
*PHILADELPHIA 1(1), F 1967- 4(52), D 1970.*
WKLY. SUBS: PART OF CURRENT CONTENTS: PHYS-
ICAL & CHEMICAL SCIENCES.
*CR/U-1.*
*SH/C-5. 4, 1970-*
*CA/U-2. 1 YEAR ONLY.*
*LO/N13. (CURRENT YEAR)*
*LO/U-2. 3 YEARS ONLY.*
*SH/U-1. 1970.*

**CURRENT CONTENTS: CLINICAL PRACTICE.**
+ +CURR. CONTENTS, CLIN. PRACT.
INSTITUTE FOR SCIENTIFIC INFORMATION.
*PHILADELPHIA 1, JA 1973-*
*AD/U-1.*
*BL/U-1. 2 YEARS.*
*GL/U-1. CURRENT YEAR.*

**CURRENT CONTENTS: EDUCATION.**
+ +CURR. CONT., EDUC.
INSTITUTE FOR SCIENTIFIC INFORMATION.
*PHILADELPHIA, PA. 1(1), JA 1969-*
W.
*BL/C-1. 1(48), 1969-*

**CURRENT CONTENTS: ENGINEERING & TECHNOLOGY.**
+ +CURR. CONT., ENG. & TECHNOL.
INSTITUTE FOR SCIENTIFIC INFORMATION.
PHILADELPHIA 1(1), JA 1970-
WKLY.
NW/U-1.
DR/U-1. 2, 1971-          MA/U-1. 2, 1971-
XS/R10. 1(26), 1970-
BH/U-3. ONE YEAR ONLY.
GL/U-2. TWO YEARS ONLY FROM 1970.
LO/N14. CURRENT YEAR ONLY.
ISSN 0011-3395

**CURRENT CONTENTS IN MANAGEMENT.**          XXX
+ +CURR. CONTENTS MANAGE.
MANCHESTER BUSINESS SCHOOL.
MANCHESTER NO.1, 1972- 29, 1974 ...
WKLY. SUBS: CONTENTS PAGES IN MANAGEMENT.
ED/N-1.    MA/U-1.
GL/U-2. NO.1, 1973-
CA/U-1. NO.1; 15, 1972-
XS/R10. NO.16, 1972-

**CURRENT CONTENTS: PHYSICAL & CHEMICAL
SCIENCES.**          XXX
+ +CURR. CONTENTS, PHYS. & CHEM. SCI.
INSTITUTE FOR SCIENTIFIC INFORMATION.
PHILADELPHIA 11(1), JA 1971-
INCORP: CURRENT CONTENTS: CHEMICAL SCIENCES
FROM 1(1), F 1967- 4(52), D 1970; & CURRENT
CONTENTS: PHYSICAL SCIENCES.
CA/U-2.**
GL/U-1. 2 YEARS.
LO/N14. CURRENT YEAR.
LO/U12. 2 YEARS.
LO/U28. CURR. YEAR.
NW/U-1. 12 MONTHS.
XS/R10. 3 MONTHS.
XS/T-4. 2 YEARS.

**CURRENT CONTENTS: PHYSICAL SCIENCES.**          XXX
**SUBS (1971): PART OF CURRENT CONTENTS:
PHYSICAL & CHEMICAL SCIENCES.**

**CURRENT INDEX TO CONFERENCE PAPERS IN CHEMISTRY.**
+ +CURR. INDEX CONF. PAP. CHEM.
[CCM INFORMATION CORP.]
NEW YORK 1, 1969- 1970 ...
PREPARED BY WORLD MEETINGS INFORMATION CENTER.
SUBS. PART OF: CURRENT INDEX TO CONFERENCE
PAPERS: SCIENCE & TECHNOLOGY.
LO/N14.    LO/S-3.    OX/U-8.

**CURRENT INDEX TO CONFERENCE PAPERS IN ENGIN-
EERING.**          XXX
+ +CURR. INDEX CONF. PAP. ENG.
[CCM INFORMATION CORP.]
NEW YORK 1, 1969- 1970 ...
SUBS. PART OF: CURRENT INDEX TO CONFERENCE
PAPERS: SCIENCE & TECHNOLOGY.
LO/N14.    OX/U-8.

**CURRENT INDEX TO CONFERENCE PAPERS: SCIENCE &
TECHNOLOGY.**          XXX
+ +CURR. INDEX CONF. PAP., SCI. & TECHNOL.
[CCM INFORMATION CORP.]
NEW YORK 2, 1971-
PREV. ISSUED IN THREE SERIES: CHEMISTRY,
ENGINEERING, & LIFE SCIENCES FROM 1, 1969- 70.
LO/N14.
GL/U-2. 2, 1971- 3(2), 1972.

**CURRENT INDEX TO JOURNALS IN EDUCATION.**
+ +CURR. INDEX J. EDUC.
CCM INFORMATION SCIENCES INC.
NEW YORK 1, 1969-
M.
DB/U-2.    SH/U-1.
AD/U-1. 6, 1974-
DN/U-1. 3(1), JA 1971-
ISSN 0011-3565

**CURRENT ISSUES IN COMMERCE & FINANCE.**
+ +CURR. ISSUES COMMER. & FINANC.
[QUEST RESEARCH PUBL.]
LONDON 1(1), MY 1973-
2W.
CA/U-1.    ED/N-1.    OX/U-1.

**CURRENT LEATHER LITERATURE.**
+ +CURR. LEATHER LIT.
CENTRAL LEATHER RESEARCH INSTITUTE (INDIA).
MADRAS 1, 1968-
LO/N14.

**CURRENT LITERATURE ON SCIENCE OF SCIENCE.**
+ +CURR. LIT. SCI. SCI.
COUNCIL OF SCIENTIFIC & INDUSTRIAL RESEARCH
(INDIA).
NEW DELHI 1, JA 1972-
DB/S-1.
XS/R10. 1(8), 1972-

**CURRENT LITERATURE ON VENEREAL DISEASE:
ABSTRACTS & BIBLIOGRAPHY.**          XXX
+ +CURR. LIT. VENER. DIS., ABSTR. & BIBLIOGR.
(UNITED STATES) PUBLIC HEALTH SERVICE: COM-
MUNICABLE DISEASE CENTER.
ATLANTA, GA. 1968(2)-
PREV: ABSTRACTS OF CURRENT LITERATURE ON
VENEREAL DISEASE FROM 1962(3)- 1968(1).
PRODUCED BY CENTER'S VENEREAL DISEASE BRANCH.
LD/U-1.
ISSN 0001-3544

**CURRENT MEDICAL RESEARCH & OPINION.**
+ +CURR. MED. RES. & OPIN.
LONDON 1, 1972-
BL/U-1.    CA/U-1.    CO/U-1.    ED/N-1.    GL/U-1.

**CURRENT PACKAGING ABSTRACTS.**          XXX
+ +CURR. PACKAG. ABSTR.
UNIVERSITY OF CALIFORNIA: PACKAGING LIBRARY.
DAVIS, CALIF. 5(2), 1973-
PREV: PACKAGING BULLETIN FROM 1, 1969- 5(1),
1973.
LO/N14.

**CURRENT PAPERS ON COMPUTERS & CONTROL.**          XXX
+ +CURR. PAP. COMPUT. & CONTROL.
INSTITUTION OF ELECTRICAL ENGINEERS.
LONDON NO.32, JA 1969-
PREV: CURRENT PAPERS ON CONTROL FROM
1, 1966- 31, 1968.
BR/U-3.    LO/U12.    RE/U-1.
EX/U-1. NO.56, JA 1971-
GL/U-1. RETAINED ONE YEAR.
LO/N-4. RETAINED TWO YEARS.
LO/N14. CURRENT ISSUES ONLY.
LO/U13. LAST TWO YEARS.
ISSN 0011-3794

**CURRENT PAPERS ON CONTROL.**          XXX
+ +CURR. PAP. CONTR.
INSTITUTION OF ELECTRICAL ENGINEERS.
LONDON. NO.1, JE 1966-31, 1968...
M.
SUBS: CURRENT PAPERS ON COMPUTERS & CONTROL.
BL/P-1.    DB/U-2.    ED/N-1.    LO/N-1.    XS/T-7.
BR/U-1. 26,1968-

**CURRENT PAPERS IN ELECTRICAL & ELECTRONICS
ENGINEERING.**
+ +CURR. PAP. ELEC. ELECTRON. ENG.
INSTITUTION OF ELECTRICAL ENGINEERS.
LONDON NO.54, JA 1969-
PREV: CURRENT PAPERS IN ELECTROTECHNOLOGY
FROM NO.30, JA 1967.
ED/N-1.    XS/R10.
BN/U-1. CURRENT YEAR ONLY.
GL/U-1. CURRENT YEAR ONLY.
LO/N14. CURRENT ISSUES ONLY.
LO/N35. NO.90, JA 1972-
LO/U13. CURRENT YEAR ONLY.
ISSN 0011-3778

**CURRENT POPULATION RESEARCH.**
+ +CURR. POPULAT. RES.
NATIONAL INSTITUTE OF CHILD HEALTH & HUMAN
DEVELOPMENT (US).
WASHINGTON, D.C. REPORT NO.1, 1966(1968)-
ISSUED BY INSTITUTE'S SCIENTIFIC INFORMATION
CENTERS BRANCH.
LO/N13.

**CURRENT RESEARCH IN FRENCH STUDIES AT UNIV-
ERSITIES & UNIVERSITY COLLEGES IN THE UNITED
KINGDOM.**          XXX
+ +CURR. RES. FR. STUD. UNIV. & UNIV. COLL. U.K.
ASSOCIATION OF UNIVERSITY PROFESSORS OF FRENCH.
LONDON 1969/70(1970)-
A. PREV: LIST OF CURRENT RESEARCH IN FRENCH
STUDIES FROM 1960/61- 1966/67.
BH/U-1.    BL/U-1.    CB/U-1.    GL/U-1.    LD/U-1.    LO/U-2.
LO/U11.    LO/U12.    OX/U-1.    SH/U-1.

**CURRENT RESEARCH NOTES IN QUANTITATIVE &
THEORETICAL GEOGRAPHY.**
+ +CURR. RES. NOTES QUANT. & THEOR. GEOGR.
UNIVERSITY OF HAWAII: SOCIAL SCIENCE RESEARCH
INSTITUTE.
HONOLULU NO.1, AG 1972-
LO/S13. NO.1, 1972.

**CURRENT TISSUE CULTURE LITERATURE.**     XXX
+ +CURR. TISSUE CULT. LIT. [CTCL-A]
TISSUE CULTURE ASSOCIATION.
[OCTOBER HOUSE, INC.]
NEW YORK 1, 1961- 5, 1965 ...
3/A. SUBS: INDEX OF TISSUE CULTURE.
GL/U-2. 5, 1965.*        LO/N14. 5, 1965.
LD/U-1 5(1- 3), 1965.

**CURRENT TITLES IN IMMUNOLOGY, TRANSPLANTATION &**
**ALLERGY.**
+ +CURR. TITLES IMMUNOL. TRANSPLANT. & ALLERGY.
[SCIENCES, ENGINEERING, MEDICAL & BUSINESS DATA
LTD.]
OXFORD 1(1), MY 1973-
2W.
AD/U-1.   CA/U-1.   LO/N13.
ED/N-1. 1(8), 1973-

**CURRENT TOPICS IN ANTHROPOLOGY.**
+ +CURR. TOP. ANTHROPOL.
[ADDISON-WESLEY PUBL. CO.]
READING, MASS 1, 1971-
CA/U-1.   CA/U-3.   OX/U-1.

**CURRENT TOPICS IN CELLULAR REGULATION.**
+ +CURR. TOP. CELL. REGUL.
[ACADEMIC P.]
NEW YORK &C. 1, 1969-
BH/U-1.   CA/U-1.   CV/U-1.   DN/U-1.   ED/N-1.   HL/U-1.
LO/N13.   LO/U-2.   LO/U20.   LO/U21.   MA/U-1.
NW/U-1.   OX/U-8.   RE/U-1.
SO/U-1. 1, 1969- 6, 1973.

**CURRENT TOPICS IN CLINICAL & COMMUNITY PSYCH-**
**OLOGY.**
+ +CURR. TOP. CLIN. & COMMUNITY PSYCHOL.
[ACADEMIC P.]
NEW YORK 1, 1969-
BH/U-1.   CV/C-1.   LO/U-1.
SH/U-1. 1970-

**CURRENT TOPICS IN COMPARATIVE PATHOBIOLOGY.**
+ +CURR. TOP. COMP. PATHOBIOL.
[ACADEMIC P.]
NEW YORK; LONDON 1, 1971-
CA/U-1.   ED/N-1.   LO/N-2.   LO/N13.   OX/U-8.

**CURRENT TOPICS IN EXPERIMENTAL ENDOCRINOLOGY.**
+ +CURR. TOP. EXP. ENDOCRINOL.
[ACADEMIC P.]
NEW YORK; LONDON 1, 1971-
CA/U-1.   GL/U-1.   LO/N13.

**CURRENT TOPICS IN MEMBRANES & TRANSPORT.**
+ +CURR. TOP. MEMBRANES & TRANSP.
[ACADEMIC P.]
NEW YORK, LONDON 1, 1970-
BH/U-3.   DN/U-1.   GL/U-1.   LD/U-1.   LO/N13.   SO/U-1.

**CURRENT TOPICS IN PATHOLOGY.**     XXX
+ +CURR. TOP. PATHOL.
[SPRINGER]
BERLIN &C. 51, 1970-
PREV: ERGEBNISSE DER ALLGEMEINEN PATHOLOGIE
UND PATHOLOGISCHEN ANATOMIE FROM 37, 1954-
50, 1968.
LO/N13.   NW/U-1.

**CURRENT TOPICS IN SURGICAL RESEARCH.**
+ +CURR. TOP. SURG. RES.
ASSOCIATION FOR ACADEMIC SURGERY.
NEW YORK &C. 1, 1969-
LO/N13.   OX/U-8.

**CURRENTS IN MODERN BIOLOGY BIOSYSTEMS.**     XXX
+ +CURR. MOD. BIOL. BIOSYST.
[NORTH-HOLLAND PUBL. CO.]
AMSTERDAM 5, 1972-
PREV: CURRENTS IN MODERN BIOLOGY FROM 1, 1967-
4, 1972.
RE/U-1.   SO/U-1.

**CYLCHGRAWN MEDDYGOL CYMRU.**     000
SEE: WELSH MEDICAL GAZETTE.

**CYPRUS BULLETIN.**
+ +CYPRUS BULL.
(CYPRUS) PUBLIC INFORMATION OFFICE.
NICOSIA 20/JA 1964-
ISSUED EVERY 2-3 DAYS.
LO/U-3.
LO/S26. ONE YEAR FILE.

**CYRENIANS NEWSLETTER.**
+ +CYRENIANS NEWSL.
CANTERBURY, KENT MY 1970-
OX/U-1.

**CYTOBIOLOGIE. ZEITSCHRIFT FUR EXPERIMENTELLE**
**ZELLFORSCHUNG.**
[WISSENSCHAFTLICHE VERLAGSGESELLSCHAFT]
STUTTGART 1, 1969-
AD/U-1.   LO/N-2.   LO/N13.   LO/U-2.   LO/U12.   OX/U-8.
SH/U-1.

**CYTOBIOS.**
[FACULTY PRESS]
CAMBRIDGE 1, 1969-
CA/U-1.   GL/U-1.   LO/U-2.   MA/U-1.   NW/U-1.   OX/U-8.
ISSN 0011-4529

**CYTOGENETICS & CELL GENETICS.**
+ +CYTOGENET. & CELL GENET.
[KARGER]
BASEL 12, 1973-
PREV: CYTOGENETICS FROM 1, 1962- 11, 1972.
GL/U-1.   LO/N-2.   LO/N13.

**CZ CHEMIE-TECHNIK.**
[HUTHIG]
HEIDELBERG 1, 1972-
LO/N14.   LO/S-3.

**CZECHOSLOVAK CHEMISTRY ABSTRACTS.**
+ +CZECH. CHEM. ABSTR.
SCIENCE & TECHNOLOGY AGENCY.
LONDON 1, 1967-
LO/N14.

**CZECHOSLOVAKIA INTERNATIONAL.**
+ +CZECH. INT.
INTERNATIONAL CONFEDERATION FOR DISARMAMENT &
PEACE.
LONDON 1(1), OC 1968-
XW/S-1.

**CZECHOSLOVAK SCIENCE & TECHNOLOGY DIGEST.**
+ +CZECH. SCI. & TECHNOL. DIG.
[SCIENTIFIC INFORMATION CONSULTANTS LTD.]
LONDON NO.1, 1970-
2M.
ED/N-1.   LO/N14.   OX/U-8.
ISSN 0045-947X

**CZECHOSLOVAK SCIENTIFIC & TECHNICAL**
**PERIODICALS CONTENTS.**
+ +CZECH. SCI. & TECH. PERIOD. CONTENTS.
(CZECHOSLOVAKIA) CENTRAL OFFICE OF SCIENTIFIC,
TECHNICAL & ECONOMIC INFORMATION.
PRAGUE 1, 1971-
CA/U-1.   LO/N-2.
CA/U-2. (ONE YEAR ONLY).
ISSN 0045-9488

**D E; DESIGN & ENVIRONMENT.**     000
SEE: DESIGN & ENVIRONMENT.

**DACHSHUND CLUB NEWSLETTER.**
+ +DACHSHUND CLUB NEWSL.
DACHSHUND CLUB.
MAIDENHEAD [NO.1], 1969-
OX/U-8. 1970-

**DAIDO KOGYO DAIGAKU KIYU. BULLETIN OF DAIDO**
**TECHNICAL COLLEGE.**
DAIDO KOGYO DAIGAKU.
NAGOYA NO.1, 1965-
LO/N13.

**DAIRY HERD MANAGEMENT.**
+ +DAIRY HERD MANAGE.
[MILLER PUBL. CO.]
MINNEAPOLIS 1, OC 1965-
2M.
LO/N14. 6, 1969-
ISSN 0011-5614

**DAIRY RESEARCH REVIEW SERIES.**
+ +DAIRY RES. REV. SER.
NATIONAL DAIRYING RESEARCH CENTRE (EIRE).
FERMOY, CO. CORK NO.1, 1965-
LO/N13.

**DAIRYING.**     XXX
ROYAL ASSOCIATION OF BRITISH DAIRY FARMERS.
LONDON 1970-
PREV: JOURNAL, ROYAL ASSOCIATION ... FROM 65,
1961- 73, 1969.
CA/U11.   ED/N-1.   LO/N-6.   LO/N14.
OX/U-8. JA 1971-

**DAIRYNEWS.**
IRISH CREAMERY MANAGERS' ASSOCIATION.
DUBLIN NO.1, JL 1972-
DB/U-2.

**DAMASCUS ECONOMIC LETTER.**
+ +DAMASCUS ECON. LETT.
DAMASCUS [NO.1], JL 1972-
MON. S/T: AN INDEPENDENT SURVEY COVERING POL-
ITICAL, ECONOMIC, LITERARY, SOCIAL & OTHER
ASPECTS OF DEVELOPMENT IN, & RELATING TO, THE
SYRIAN ARAB REPUBLIC.
LO/U-3.

**DAMASCUS ROAD.**
ALLENTOWN, PA. [NO.]1, [1961]-
LO/U-2.

**DAMILICA.**
MADRAS 1, 1970-
3/A. TAMIL OR ENGLISH. JOURNAL OF THE TAMIL
NADU STATE DEPARTMENT OF ARCHAEOLOGY.
LO/N12.     OX/U13.

**DANISH FOREIGN OFFICE JOURNAL.**                              XXX
   SUBS (1969): DANISH JOURNAL.

**DANISH JOURNAL.**                                            XXX
+ +DAN. J.
(DENMARK) UDENRIGSMINISTERIUM.
COPENHAGEN NO.65, 1969-
PREV: DANISH FOREIGN OFFICE JOURNAL FROM
NO.1, 1920- 64, 1968.
BH/U-1.     LO/U-1.     LO/U-3.     RE/U-1.
LD/U-1. NO.66, 1969-
ISSN 0011-6084

**DANSK LANDBRUG.**                                            XXX
   SUBS (1970): NYE DANSK LANDBRUG.

**DAPHNIS.  ZEITSCHRIFT FUR MITTLERE DEUTSCHE
LITERATUR.**
[DE GRUYTER]
BERLIN; NEW YORK 1, 1972-
AD/U-1.     CA/U-1.     ED/N-1.     LD/U-1.     MA/U-1.     SH/U-1.
SO/U-1.     SW/U-1.

**DARLITE. A MAGAZINE OF ORIGINAL WRITING ...**
UNIVERSITY COLLEGE, DAR-ES-SALAAM: DEPARTMENT
OF LITERATURE.
DAR-ES-SALAAM 1(1), 1966-
3/A.
LO/N17.

**DARPON.**
WOKING   [NO.1], MY 1968-
FOR BENGALI READERS IN ENGLAND.
ED/N-1.
ISSN 0011-6718

**DATA DYNAMICS.**                                             XXX
+ +DATA DYN.
[NORTH AMERICAN PUBL CO ]
PHILADELPHIA, PA. 13(7), 1971-
PREV: DATA PROCESSING MAGAZINE FROM 6(7),
1964- 13(6), 1971.
LO/N14.     LO/N35.

**DATA LINGUISTICA.**
+ +DATA LINGUIST.
STOCKHOLM NO.1, 1970-
CA/U-1.

**DATA MANAGEMENT. (CROYDON).**
+ +DATA MANAGE. (CROYDON).
[BUSINESS EQUIPMENT DIGEST LTD.]
CROYDON 1, 1969-
LO/N14.
ED/N-1. 1(2), 1969-               LO/N-7. 2(3), 1970-
OX/U-8. 1(2), 1969-
ISSN 0011-6831

**DATA MANAGEMENT. (PARK RIDGE).**                             XXX
+ +DATA MANAGE. (PARK RIDGE).
DATA PROCESSING MANAGEMENT ASSOCIATION.
PARK RIDGE, ILL. 8(4), 1970-
PREV:  JOURNAL OF DATA MANAGEMENT FROM 1(1),
1963- 8(3), 1970.
LO/N14.
LO/N-5. 8(9), S 1970-
ISSN 0022-0329

**DATA OF OCEANOGRAPHIC OBSERVATIONS & EXPLOR-
ATORY FISHINGS.**
+ +DATA OCEANOGR. OBS. & EXPLOR. FISH.
SHIMONOSEKI UNIVERSITY OF FISHERIES.
SHIMONOSEKI NO.1, 1965-
BN/U-2.

**DATA PROCESSING MONOGRAPH SERIES.**
+ +DATA PROC. MONOGR. SER.
AMERICAN DATA PROCESSING, INC.
DETROIT 1, 1967-
LO/N14.

**DATENVERARBEITUNG IN DER MEDIZIN. MITTEILUNGS-
BLATT DER INTERNATIONALEN GESELLSCHAFT FUR
PROSPEKTIVE MEDIZIN.**
+ +DATENVERARB. MED.
MUNICH 1/2, 1968-
GL/U-1.
ISSN 0418-422X

**DATR.  SUSSEX'S ONLY LITERARY MAGAZINE.**
[SMOOTHER PUBL.]
BRIGHTON NO.1, 1971-
ED/N-1.     OX/U-1.

**DAVIDSONIA.**
UNIVERSITY OF BRITISH COLUMBIA: BOTANICAL
GARDEN.
VANCOUVER 1, 1970-
Q.
LO/N-2.
ISSN 0045-9739

**DB.  SOUND ENGINEERING MAGAZINE.**
[SAGAMORE PUBL. CO.]
PLAINVIEW, N.Y. 1, N 1967-
M.
LO/N14.

**DDR VERKEHR.**
[VEB VERLAG FUR VERKEHRSWESEN]
BERLIN  1, 1968-
LO/N14.
ISSN 0011-4820

**DE.  IUS JOURNAL ON THE DEMOCRATIZATION &
REFORM OF EDUCATION.**
INTERNATIONAL UNION OF STUDENTS.
PRAGUE NO.1/2, 1971-
Q.
LO/U-3.
OX/U-1. 1973-

**DE ARTE.**
UNIVERSITY OF SOUTH AFRICA: DEPARTMENT OF
FINE ARTS.
PRETORIA NO.1, 1967-
LO/U-2.
ISSN 0004-3389

**DE LEONIST.**                                                XXX
DANIEL DE LEON LEAGUE.
NEW YORK  1969- S/OC 1970.
SUBS: SOCIALIST RECONSTRUCTION.
ED/N-1.     LO/U-3.

**DE PROPRIETIBUS: SERIES DIDACTICA.**
+ +DE PROPR., DIDACT.
THE HAGUE 1, 1972-
OX/U-1.

**DEAN BIBLIOGRAPHY OF FISHES.**
+ +DEAN BIBLIOGR. FISH.
AMERICAN MUSEUM OF NATURAL HISTORY.
NEW YORK  1, 1968(1971)-
LO/N-2.     SO/U-1.
ISSN 0070-3117

**DEBATE.  A DIGEST OF PARLIAMENTARY DEBATES &
QUESTIONS.**
[NEW EDUCATIONAL P.]
HAILSHAM, SUSSEX 1, N 1971-
ED/N-1.     MA/U-1.     NW/U-1.     OX/U-1.

**DECANTER.  AN INDEPENDENT MAGAZINE PRODUCED
BY STUDENTS OF THE UNIVERSITY OF EAST ANGLIA.**
NORWICH NO.1, JL 1965-
LO/U-2.

**DECIMAL CURRENCY BOARD NEWSLETTER.**
+ +DECIM. CURR. BOARD NEWSL.
DECIMAL CURRENCY BOARD (GB).
LONDON   NO.1, JL 1968-
LO/N-4.     LO/U-3.     XS/R10.
HL/U-2. 2,1968-
SO/U-1. CURRENT THREE YEARS.

**DECIMAL CURRENCY & METRICATION NEWS.**
+ +DECIM. CURR. & METRICATION NEWS.
[ROVIPRESS LTD]
LONDON  1, D 1968-
M.
ED/N-1.     GL/U-3.     OX/U-8.     XS/R10.
ISSN 0011-7293

**DECIMAL POINTS.**
+ +DECIM. POINTS.
BURROUGHS MACHINES LTD.
  LONDON NO.1, MY 1969-
  S/T: A MANAGEMENT GUIDE TO DECIMALISATION.
  GL/U-3.

**DECUSCOPE. NEWSLETTER FOR DIGITAL EQUIPMENT COMPUTER USERS SOCIETY.**
  MAYNARD, MASS. 1, 1962-
  LO/N14. 10, 1971-
  ISSN 0011-7447

**DEFAZET-AKTUELL. DEUTSCHE FARBEN-ZEITSCHRIFT.**
[WISSENSCHAFTLICHE VERLAGSGESELLSCHAFT.]
  STUTTGART 25(10), 1971-
  PREV: DEUTSCHE FARBEN-ZEITSCHRIFT FROM 5,
  1951- 25(9), 1971.
  LO/N14.

**DEFENCE.**
[WHITTON P.]
  LONDON 1(1), JL 1970-
  AD/U-1.    ED/N-1.

**DEJINY VED A TECHNIKY.**
+ +DEJINY VED A TECH.
CESKOSLOVENSKA SPOLECNOST PRO DEJINY VED A
TECHNIKY.
  PRAGUE 1, 1968-
  CA/U-1.    LO/N-4.

**DELIKT EN DELINKWENT.**                                    XXX
[BRILL]
  LEIDEN [1](1), N 1970-
  10/A. PREV: TIJDSCHRIFT VOOR STRAFRECHT FROM
  1, 1886- 79(4), 1970.
  LO/N-1.
  ISSN 0045-9879

**DELIRANTE. REVUE DE POESIE.**
  PARIS NO.1, JL/S 1967-
  Q.
  CB/U-1.
  LD/U-1. NO.1, 1967- 3, 1968.
  ISSN 0011-7889

**DEMOGRAFIA Y ECONOMIA.**
+ +DEMOGR. & ECON. (MEX.)
COLEGIO DE MEXICO.
  MEXICO, DF [1], 1967-
  3/A.
  GL/U-1.    LO/U-3.
  ISSN 0011-8257

**DEMOGRAPHIC STATISTICS (JAMAICA).**
+ +DEMOGR. STAT. (JAM.).
(JAMAICA) DEPARTMENT OF STATISTICS: DEMOGRAPHIC
& SOCIAL STATISTICS UNIT.
  KINGSTON, JAM. MR 1971-
  Q.
  LO/N-1.    LO/U-3.    LO/U-8.

**DEMONSTRATIO MATHEMATICA.**
+ +DEMONSTR. MATH.
POLITECHNIKA WARSZAWSKA: INSTYTUT MATEMATYKI.
  WARSAW 1, 1969-
  GL/U-1.

**DENDROFLORA.**
KONINKLIJKE VERENIGING VOOR BOSKOOPSE CULTUREN.
  BOSKOOP, NETH. NO.1, 1964-
  LO/N-2.

**DENDROLOGICKY SBORNIK.**                                   XXX
  SUBS (1962): CASOPIS SLEZSKEHO MUSEA: SERIE C.

**DENKI KENTEIJO GIHO. JEMIC TECHNICAL REPORT.**
NIHON DENKI KEIKI KENTEIJO.
  TOKYO 1, 1966-
  Q. JAP., ENGL. SUMM. 'JEMIC' (ENGL. NAME OF
  BODY) = JAPANESE ELECTRIC METERS INSPECTION
  CORPORATION.
  LO/N14.

**DENSHI TSUSHIN GAKKAI RONBUNSHI (ENGL. TRANSL.).**                                            000
  SEE: SYSTEMS, COMPUTERS, CONTROLS.

**DENSHI ZAIRYO. ELECTRONIC PARTS & MATERIALS.**
KOGYO CHOSAKAI K.K.
  TOKYO 1, 1962-
  M. JAP. ADDED ENGL. TITLE VARIES; 1-2 AS:
  ELECTRONIC MATERIALS & PARTS. AS ABOVE FROM
  VOL. 3.
  LO/N13.

**DENTAL NEWS.**                                             XXX
  SUBS: DENTAL PRACTICE.

**DENTAL PRACTICE.**                                         XXX
+ +DENT. PRACT.
[HAYMARKET P.]
  LONDON 1(1), S 1969-
  PREV: DENTAL NEWS FROM 1, 1964- 6(8), AG 1969
  OX/U-8.
  ISSN 0011-8710

**DENTAL PRACTITIONER & DENTAL RECORD.**                     XXX
  SUBS (1972): JOURNAL OF DENTISTRY.

**DENTAL UPDATE.**
[UPDATE PUBL. LTD.]
  LONDON 1, 1973-
  LD/U-1.    LO/M31.

**DENVER JOURNAL OF INTERNATIONAL LAW & POLICY.**
+ +DENVER J. INT. LAW & POLICY.
UNIVERSITY OF DENVER: COLLEGE OF LAW.
  DENVER 1(1), 1971-
  2/A.
  LO/S14.    OX/U-1.    OX/U15.

**DEPARTMENT OF EMPLOYMENT GAZETTE (GB).**                   XXX
+ +DEP. EMPLOY. GAZ. (GB).
(GREAT BRITAIN) DEPARTMENT OF EMPLOYMENT.
  LONDON 79(1), JA 1971-
  PREV: EMPLOYMENT & PRODUCTIVITY GAZETTE FROM
  76(6), JE 1968- 78, 1970.
  BH/P-1.    DN/U-1.    GL/U-3.    LD/U-1.    LO/N-7.    LO/U-2.
  NO/U-1.    NW/U-1.    XS/R10.

**DERECHO DE LA INTEGRACION.**
INSTITUTO PARA LA INTEGRACION DE AMERICA
LATINA.
  BUENOS AIRES NO.1, OC 1967-
  SPONS. BODY ALSO: INTER-AMERICAN
  DEVELOPMENT BANK
  LO/S14.    LO/U-3.

**DESALINATION ABSTRACTS.**
+ +DESAL. ABSTR.
CENTRE OF SCIENTIFIC & TECHNOLOGICAL INFORMA-
TION (ISRAEL).
  TEL AVIV 1, 1966(1968)-
  Q.
  LO/N14.
  GL/U-1. 6, 1971-
  XS/R10. 3(1), JA 1968-
  ISSN 0011-9172

**DESARROLLO ADMINISTRATIVO.**
+ +DESARRO. ADM.
UNIVERSIDAD CENTRAL DEL ECUADOR: INSTITUTO DE
ESTUDIOS ADMINISTRATIVOS.
  QUITO 1, 1969-
  LO/U-3.    OX/U-1.
  ISSN 0011-9202

**DESARROLLO RURAL EN LAS AMERICAS.**
+ +DESARRO. RURAL AM.
CENTRO INTERAMERICANO DE DESARROLLO RURAL Y
REFORMA AGRARIA (COLOMBIA).
  BOGOTA 1, 1969-
  BL/U-1.    OX/U-1.    OX/U24.
  ISSN 0046-0028

**DESCRIPTIONS OF PLANT VIRUSES.**
COMMONWEALTH MYCOLOGICAL INSTITUTE.
  LONDON 1, JE 1970-
  SPONS. BODY ALSO ASSOCIATION OF APPLIED
  BIOLOGISTS.
  BL/U-1.    LO/U13.    OX/U-3.

**DESIGN & ART DIRECTION ...**
+ +DES. & ART DIR.
DESIGNERS & ART DIRECTORS ASSOCIATION OF
LONDON.
[STUDIO VISTA]
  LONDON 1963-
  S/T: THE ANNUAL OF THE ... EXHIBITION OF THE
  ... ASSOCIATION ...  TITLE CONTINUES WITH
  LAST TWO DIGITS OF YEAR, E.G.: DESIGN & ART
  DIRECTION '66. (= FOURTH EXHIBITION).
  BT/C-1.**

**DESIGN EDUCATION.**
+ +DES. EDUC.
(HORNSEY) COLLEGE OF ART; ADVANCED STUDIES
GROUP.
  LONDON 1, 1966-
  OX/U-1.

**DESIGN ENGINEERING (LONDON).**                          XXX
+ +DES. ENG. (LOND.).
[MORGAN-GRAMPIAN]
LONDON 1973-
PREV: DESIGN ENGINEERING, MATERIALS & COMPON-
ENTS FROM S 1964- 1972.
LO/N14.
SF/U-1. S 1974-

**DESIGN & ENVIRONMENT.**
+ +DES. & ENVIRON.
[R.C. PUBL.]
NEW YORK 1, 1970-
Q. COVER TITLE: D E; DESIGN & ENVIRONMENT.
LO/U-2.    SH/U-1.
ISSN 0011-930X

**DESIGN RESEARCH REPORT.**
+ +DES. RES. REP.
UNIVERSITY OF MANCHESTER: INSTITUTE OF SCIENCE
& TECHNOLOGY.
MANCHESTER  NO.1, 1963/6 (1967)-
LO/U-2.

**DESIGN STUDY, GREATER LONDON COUNCIL.**
+ +DES. STUDY GREATER LOND. COUNC.
LONDON NO.1, 1969-
LO/N-1.

**DESIGNER BOOKBINDERS REVIEW.**
+ +DES. BOOKBINDERS REV.
LONDON 1, 1973-
CA/U-1.    ED/N-1.    OX/U-1.

**DESPATCH FROM IRELAND.**
+ +DESPATCH IREL.
STUDENT CHRISTIAN MOVEMENT.
BELFAST  NO.1, 11/OC 1971- 22/JE 1973. //
ED/N-1.
LO/U-3. [W.2(10)]

**DESTINY.**
[IPC MAGAZINES]
LONDON NO.1, OC 1972-
ED/N-1.

**DET. DIE EISENBAHNTECHNIK.**                            XXX
[VEB VERLAG TECHNIK]
BERLIN 21, 1973-
ENGL. SUMM.  PREV: DEUTSCHE EISENBAHNTECHNIK
FROM 2, 1954- 20, 1972.
LO/N14.

**DETALI MASHIN I POD'EMNO-TRANSPORTNYE MASHINY.**
+ +DETALI MASH. & POD'EMNO-TRANSP. MASH.
(UKRAINE) MINISTERSTVO VYSSHOJI I SREDN'OJI
SPETSIAL'NOJI OS'VITY.
KIEV SB.1, 1965-
LO/N13. 3, 1966-

**DETERGENTS & SPECIALTIES.**                             XXX
+ +DETERGENTS & SPEC.
[DORLAND PUBL. CO.]
DENVILLE, N.J. 6(1), JA 1969- 8(11), 1971...
PREV: DETERGENT AGE FROM 1, 1964- 5, 1968.
SUBS: HOUSEHOLD PERSONAL PRODUCTS INDUSTRY.
LO/N14.
ISSN 1100-958X

**DETRITUS.**
UNIVERSITY COLLEGE OF RHODESIA: MENNELL SOCIETY
SALISBURY 1, 1966-
LO/N-2.

**DEUTSCHE AGRARTECHNIK.**                                XXX
SUBS (1973): AGRARTECHNIK.

**DEUTSCHES ARCHIV FUR KLINISCHE MEDIZIN.**               XXX
SUBS (1966): PART OF ARCHIV FUR KLINISCHE
MEDIZIN.

**DEUTSCHE EISENBAHNTECHNIK.**                            XXX
SUBS (1973): DET.

**DEUTSCHE FARBEN-ZEITSCHRIFT.**                          XXX
SUBS (1971): DEFAZET-AKTUELL. DEUTSCHE
FARBEN-ZEITSCHRIFT.

**DEUTSCHE GESCHICHTE SEIT DEM ERSTEN WELTKRIEG.**
+ +DTSCH. GESCH. ERSTEN WELTKRIEG.
INSTITUT FUR ZEITGESCHICHTE (MUNICH).
[DEUTSCHE VERLAGS-ANSTALT]
STUTTGART [1971]-
LO/N-1.

**DEUTSCHE TEXTILTECHNIK.**                               XXX
SUBS (1973): TEXTILTECHNIK.

**DEUTSCHE WEIN-ZEITUNG.**                                XXX
SUBS (1971): ALLGEMEINE DEUTSCHE WEINFACH-
ZEITUNG.

**DEUTSCHE ZEITSCHRIFT FUR DIE GESAMTE GERICHT-
LICHE MEDIZIN.**                                          XXX
SUBS. (1970) PART OF: ZEITSCHRIFT FUR RECHTS-
MEDIZIN; & ZENTRALBLATT FUR DIE GESAMTE
RECHTSMEDIZIN UND IHRE GRENZGEBIETE.

**DEUTSCHLAND ARCHIV. ZEITSCHRIFT FUR FRAGEN
DER DDR UND DER DEUTSCHLANDPOLITIK.**
+ +DEUT. ARCH.
COLOGNE 1(1), AP 1968-
LO/U-3.
ISSN 0012-1428

**DEVELOPING COUNTRIES, PRODUCE & TRADE.**
+ +DEV. COUNTRIES, PROD. & TRADE.
COMMISSION OF THE EUROPEAN COMMUNITIES.
BRUSSELS 1, 1964-
GL/U-1. 2, 1966-
LO/R-6. 2/MR 1965- 6/JA 1967.

**DEVELOPMENT ADMINISTRATION.**
+ +DEVELOP. ADM.
INTERNATIONAL INSTITUTE OF ADMINISTRATIVE
SCIENCES.
BRUSSELS NO.1, MR 1966-
2/A. S/T: SUMMARIES OF SELECTED ARTICLES.
LO/N17.

**DEVELOPMENT & CHANGE.**
+ +DEVELOP. & CHANGE.
INSTITUTE OF SOCIAL STUDIES (HAGUE).
THE HAGUE 1, 1969-
BH/U-1.    CA/U-1.    DB/U-2.    HL/U-1.    LO/N17.    LO/S74.
LO/U-3.    OX/U16.
LO/U14. 2(1), 1970- [W.2(2)]
ISSN 0012-155X

**DEVELOPMENT DIALOGUE.**
+ +DEV. DIALOGUE.
DAG HAMMARSKJOLD FOUNDATION.
UPPSALA NO.1, 1972-
AD/U-1.    LO/U-8.    LO/U14.

**DEVELOPMENT DIGEST FOR YORKSHIRE & HUMBERSIDE.**
+ +DEVELOP. DIG. YORKS. & HUMBERSIDE.
DONCASTER & DISTRICT DEVELOPMENT COUNCIL.
DONCASTER [1], AG 1969-
HL/U-1.    LD/U-1.    SH/U-1.

**DEVELOPMENT FORUM.**
+ +DEV. FORUM.
UNITED NATIONS: CENTRE FOR ECONOMIC & SOCIAL
INFORMATION.
GENEVA 1(1), F 1973-
MON.
LO/R-5.    LO/R-6.    LO/S14.    LO/U-3.
CA/U-1. 1(2), 1973-                OX/U-1. 1(2), 1973-

**DEVELOPMENT, GROWTH & DIFFERENTIATION.**               XXX
+ +DEVELOP. GROWTH & DIFFERENT.
JAPANESE SOCIETY OF DEVELOPMENTAL BIOLOGISTS.
NAGOYA 11(1), JE 1969-
PREV: EMBRYOLOGIA FROM 1, 1950.
GL/U-1.    LO/U-2.
ISSN 0012-1592

**DEVELOPMENT & MATERIALS BULLETIN: 2S.**
+ +DEVELOP. & MATER. BULL., 2S.
GREATER LONDON COUNCIL.
LONDON NO.1, JA 1967-
BH/P-1.    LO/N14.    LO/U-2.    XS/R10.
ED/N-1. NO.5, 1967-

**DEVELOPMENT PAPERS, OVERSEAS DEVELOPMENT
COUNCIL (US).**
+ +DEV. PAP. OVERSEAS DEV. COUNC. (US).
WASHINGTON, D.C. NO.1, 1970-
OX/U16.

**DEVELOPMENT STUDIES, DEPARTMENT OF AGRICUL-
TURAL ECONOMICS, UNIVERSITY OF READING.**
+ +DEVELOP. STUD. DEP. AGR. ECON. UNIV. READING.
READING NO.1, S 1966-
LO/S13.

**DEVELOPMENTAL BIOLOGY: SUPPLEMENT.**
+ +DEVELOP. BIOL., SUPPL.
SOCIETY FOR DEVELOPMENTAL BIOLOGY.
NEW YORK &C. 1, 1967-
GL/U-1.

**DEVELOPMENTAL PSYCHOLOGY.**
+ +DEV. PSYCHOL.
AMERICAN PSYCHOLOGICAL ASSOCIATION.
*RICHMOND, VA. 1, 1969-*
*BL/U-1.    DB/U-2.    GL/U-2.    LO/U-1.    LO/U-2.    SH/U-1.*
*SO/U-1.*
*LO/N-1. 2, 1970-            OX/U-8. 4(1), 1971-*
*RE/U-1. 2, 1970-            SA/U-1. 2, 1970-*
*ISSN 0012-1649*

**DEVENIR HISTORICO.**
+ +DEVENIR HIST.
[EDICION MUNDO ACTUAL]
*BUENOS AIRES 1(1), JA/MR 1970-*
*OX/U-1.*
*ISSN 0012-1665*

**DEVON HISTORIAN.**
+ +DEVON HIST.
STANDING CONFERENCE FOR DEVON HISTORY.
*EXETER NO.1, 1970-*
*EX/U-1.    LO/N-1.    OX/U-1.*
*ISSN 0305-8549*

**DFVLR NACHRICHTEN.**
+ +DFVLR NACHR.
DEUTSCHE FORSCHUNGS- UND VERSUCHSANSTALT FUR
LUFT- UND RAUMFAHRT.
*PORZ-WAHN 1, 1969-*
*LO/N-4.    LO/N14.*
*ISSN 0011-4901*

**D.H. LAWRENCE REVIEW.**
+ +D.H. LAWRENCE REV.
[UNIVERSITY OF ARKANSAS]
*FAYETTEVILLE, ARK. 1, 1968-*
*CA/U-1.    LO/U-2.    NO/U-1.*    OX/U-1.
*HL/U-1. [W. 1(2), 1968].*
*ISSN 0011-4936*

**DHANA.**
MAKERERE UNIVERSITY.
[EAST AFRICAN LITERATURE BUREAU]
*NAIROBI 1(1), 1971-*
*2/A.*
*LO/U-2.    LO/U14.*

**DIAGRAMA. REVISTA DE CULTURA.**
*MIRAFLORES NO.1, S/OC [1971]-*
*LO/N-1.*

**DIALEKTOLOGICHESKIE MATERIALY PO GOVORAM
EVENKOV JAKUTSKOJ ASSR.**
+ +DIALEKTOL. MATER. GOVORAM EVENKOV JAKUTSKOJ
ASSR.
AKADEMIJA NAUK SSSR (SIBIRSKOE OTDELENIE):
JAKUTSKIJ FILIAL INSTITUTA JAZYKA, LITERATURY I
ISTORII.
*MOSCOW; LENINGRAD 1, 1962-*
*CA/U-1.    OX/U-1.*
*CC/U-1. 3, 1968.*

**DIALOGHI DI ARCHEOLOGIA.**
+ +DIALOGHI ARCHEOL.
*MILAN 1, 1966-*
*3/A.*
*OX/U-2.*

**DIALOGOS. REVISTA DEL DEPARTAMENTO DE FILOS-
OFIA, UNIVERSIDAD DE PUERTO RICO.**
UNIVERSITY OF PUERTO RICO: DEPARTMENT OF
PHILOSOPHY.
*[RIO PIEDRAS] 1(1), S 1964-*
*RE/U-1.*
*LO/U-1. 3(6), 1966; 4(7), 1967; 5(10), 1968-*

**DIALOGUE (CALCUTTA).**
[SATYABRATA PAL]
*CALCUTTA 1, [1968-]*
*LO/U-2.*

**DIALOGUE (CAPE TOWN).**
UNIVERSITY OF CAPE TOWN: STUDENTS REPRESENTA-
TIVE COUNCIL.
*CAPE TOWN 1(1), 1968-*
*LO/N-1.    LO/U28.    OX/U-1.*

**DIALOGUE (LONDON).**
SCHOOLS COUNCIL FOR THE CURRICULUM & EXAMIN-
ATIONS.
*LONDON NO.1, 1968-*
*OX/U-1.*
*ISSN 0420-0381*

**DIAMOND RESEARCH.**
+ +DIAMOND RES. [DIAR-B]
INDUSTRIAL DIAMOND INFORMATION BUREAU.
*LONDON [NO.1], 1964-*
SUPPL TO INDUSTRIAL DIAMOND REVIEW.
*LO/N-2.*
*LO/U-2. [NO.2] 1965-*
*ISSN 0070-4679*

**DIANA'S BIMONTHLY.**
+ +DIANA'S BIMON.
*PROVIDENCE, R.I. 1, 1972-*
*OX/U-1.*
*ISSN 0046-0222*

**DICKENS STUDIES.**                                    XXX
+ +DICKENS STUD.
EMERSON COLLEGE.
*BOSTON, MASS. 1, JA 1965- 5, MY 1969.*
SUBS: DICKENS STUDIES ANNUAL.
*AD/U-1.    LO/U-4.    NO/U-1.    SO/U-1.*
*ISSN 0419-1099*

**DICKENS STUDIES ANNUAL.**                             XXX
+ +DICKENS STUD. A.
[SOUTHERN ILLINOIS UNIV. P.]
*CARBONDALE, ILL. 1, 1970-*
PREV: DICKENS STUDIES FROM 1, JA 1965 -
5, MY 1969.
*CB/U-1.    LO/U-1.    NO/U-1.    NW/U-1.    OX/U-1.*

**DICKENS STUDIES NEWSLETTER.**
+ +DICKENS STUD. NEWSL.
*CARBONDALE, ILL. 1(1), MR 1970-*
*Q.*
*LO/N-1.    LO/N-3.*    LO/U-1.    OX/U-1.    SO/U-1.*
*ED/N-1. 2(3), S 1971-*
*LD/U-1. 1(2), S 1970-*
*ISSN 0012-2432*

**DICKSON MOUNDS MUSEUM ANTHROPOLOGICAL STUDIES.**
+ +DICKSON MOUNDS MUS. ANTHROPOL. STUD.
ILLINOIS STATE MUSEUM.
*SPRINGFIELD, ILL. NO.1, 1971-*
*LO/N-2.*

**DICTIONARY OF AFRICAN BIOGRAPHY.**
+ +DICTIONARY AFR. BIOGR.
[MELROSE P.]
*LONDON 1, 1970-*
*ANNU.*
*GL/U-1.    LO/U-3.*

**DIDASKALIA.**
*LISBON 1, 1971-*
*OX/U-1.*

**DIELECTRIC & RELATED MOLECULAR PROCESSES.**
+ +DIELECTR. & RELAT. MOL. PROCESSES.
CHEMICAL SOCIETY.
*LONDON 1, 1966/71(1972)-*
S/T: A REVIEW OF SELECTED DEVELOPMENTS.
*GL/U-2.    HL/U-1.    LO/N-4.    LO/N14.    LO/S-3.    LO/U-2.*
*NW/U-1.*
*ISSN 0305-974X*

**DIESEL & GAS TURBINE PROGRESS - WORLDWIDE
EDITION.**
+ +DIESEL & GAS TURBINE PROG. - WORLDWIDE ED.
DIESEL ENGINES INC.
*MILWAUKEE 1, 1969-*
*LO/N14.*
*ISSN 0012-2602*

**DIFFERENTIATION.**
[MACMILLAN JOURNALS LTD.]
*LONDON 1, 1973-*
*2M.*
*BL/U-1.    CA/U-1.    CA/U-2.    ED/N-1.    GL/U-1.    LO/M-3.*
*LO/M12.    LO/N-2.    MA/U-1.    OX/U-8.    SH/U-1.*
*ISSN 0301-4681*

**DIFFUSION MONOGRAPH SERIES.**
+ +DIFFUS. MONOGR. SER.
DIFFUSION INFORMATION CENTER.
*BAY VILLAGE, OHIO NO.1, 1972-*
ISSUED AS A SUPPL. TO: DIFFUSION DATA.
*BH/U-3.    GL/U-2.    LO/N14.    LO/N14.*

**DIGEST OF BUILDING LAND PRICES.**
+ +DIG. BUILD. LAND PRICES.
HOUSE-BUILDERS FEDERATION ADVISORY SERVICE.
[ESTATES GAZETTE]
*LONDON NO.1, JA 1973-*
*3/A.*
*CA/U-1.    ED/N-1.    SW/U-1.*

**DIGEST OF ECONOMIC INTELLIGENCE FROM AFRICA.**   XXX
++DIG. ECON. INTELL. AFR.
[AFRICA RESEARCH LTD]
  EXETER &C.  NO. 1, 1964- 35, 1964.
  AS (W) SUPPL TO– AFRICA RESEARCH BULLETINS.
  SUBS– AFRICA ECONOMIC DIGEST.
  BH/U-1.    ED/N-1.

**DIGEST OF HEALTH STATISTICS FOR ENGLAND &
WALES.**
++DIG. HEALTH STAT. ENGL. & WALES.
(GREAT BRITAIN) DEPARTMENT OF HEALTH & SOCIAL
SECURITY.
  LONDON [1], 1969-
  BH/U-1.    BL/U-1.    CR/M-1.    LO/U-3.    OX/U-8.    SO/U-1.

**DIGEST OF SCOTTISH STATISTICS.**   XXX
  SUBS (1971): PART OF SCOTTISH ABSTRACT OF
  STATISTICS; & SCOTTISH ECONOMIC BULLETIN.

**DIGESTION. INTERNATIONAL JOURNAL OF GASTROEN-
TEROLOGY.**
[S. KARGER]
  BASLE  1(1), 1968-
  PREV: GASTROENTEROLOGIA FROM 1, 1895.
  GL/U-1.
  DB/U-2.  5, 1972-            DN/U-1.  3, 1970-
  ISSN 0012-2823

**DIJALEKTIKA.  CASOPIS ZA OPSTE PROBLEME MATE-
MATICKIH. PRIRODNIH I TEHNICKIH NAUKA.**
  [DCOP-A]
BEOGRADSKI UNIVERZITET.
  BELGRADE 1(1), 1966-
  OX/U-1.
  ISSN 0419-1349

**DIMENSION. CONTEMPORARY GERMAN ARTS & LETTERS.**
UNIVERSITY OF TEXAS: DEPARTMENT OF GERMANIC
LANGUAGES.
  AUSTIN  1, 1968-
  LO/U-2.    OX/U-1.
  ED/N-1.  1(3), 1968-
  SW/U-1.  1(2), 1968; 2, 1969-
  ISSN 0012-2882

**DIMENSIONS ECONOMIQUES DE LA BOURGOGNE.**
++DIMENS. ECON. BOURGOGNE.
INSTITUT NATIONAL DE LA STATISTIQUE ET DES
ETUDES ECONOMIQUES (FRANCE): DIRECTION REGION-
ALE DE DIJON.
  DIJON [NO.1], JA 1972-
  S/T: REVUE MENSUELLE.
  LO/U-3.

**DINAMIKA I PROCHNOST' MASHIN.**
++DIN. & PROCHN. MASH.
KHAR'KOVSKIJ POLITEKHNICHESKIJ INSTITUT.
  KHAR'KOV 1, 1965-
  2A.  S/T: RESPUBLIKANSKIJ MEZHVEDOMSTVENNYJ
  NAUCHNO-TEKHNICHESKIJ SBORNIK.
  LO/N13.* 2, 1965-
  BH/U-1. 7, 1967- 9, 1968.
  ISSN 0419-1544

**DINERS CLUB MAGAZINE. (LONDON)**   XXX
  SUBS (1966): SIGNATURE.

**DINI NA MILA.  REVEALED RELIGION & TRADITIONAL
CUSTOM.**
  KAMPALA  1(1), 1965-
  ENGL.
  BH/C-3.
  LO/U14.  1(4), 1966-
  ISSN 0419-1609

**DINTERIA.  BEITRAGE ZUR FLORA VON SUDWEST-
AFRIKA.**
SOUTH WEST AFRICA SCIENTIFIC SOCIETY.
  WINDHOEK  NO.1, 1969-
  BODY NAME IN GERMAN: S.W.A. WISSENSCHAFTLICHE
  GESELLSCHAFT.
  LO/N-2.    LO/N13.
  ISSN 0012-3013

**DIRECT CURRENT.**   XXX
++DIRECT CURR.  [DICU-A]
[GARRAWAY]
  LONDON  1, 1952- 12(1), F 1967.
  S/T: INTERNATIONAL CONVERSION EQUIPMENT
  JOURNAL. SUBS: DIRECT CURRENT: NS.
  BR/U-1.    CA/U-1.    ED/N-1.    ED/U-3.    LO/F-1.    LO/N-1.
  LO/N-4.    LO/N14.    LO/U-2.    LO/U-6.    MA/U-3.    NO/U-1.
  OX/U-8.    XS/T-4.    XY/N-1.**
  BL/U-1. 6, 1961-                BN/U-2. 5(4), 1961-
  CV/C-1. 1961-                   DN/U-1. 1958-
  LC/U-1. 8, 1963-               LD/U-1. 1963-
  SW/U-1. 8, 1963-              XE/C-3. 1964-
  XS/R10. 4, 1959-             XW/C-4. 1963-
  CO/U-1. 5(4), MR 1961-

**DIRECT CURRENT: NS.**   XXX
++DIRECT CURR., NS.
[PERGAMON PRESS]
  OXFORD &C.  1(1), 1969- 1(4), 1970 ...
  PREV SERIES PUBL BY GARRAWAY LTD. LONDON,
  1, 1952- 12(1), F 1967.  SUBS: DIRECT CURRENT
  & POWER ELECTRONICS.
  ED/N-1.    GL/U-2.*    LO/N14.    LO/U12.    OX/U-8.
  SW/U-1.
  ISSN 0419-1811

**DIRECT ENERGY CONVERSION DIGEST.**   XXX
  SUBS (1966): ENERGY CONVERSION DIGEST.

**DIRECTORY OF COMMERCIAL MICROFILM SERVICES IN
THE UNITED KINGDOM.**
++DIR. COMMER. MICROFILM SERV. U.K.
NATIONAL REPROGRAPHIC CENTRE FOR DOCUMENTATION
(GB).
  HATFIELD  1ST, 1969-
  OX/U-1.

**DIRECTORY OF PUBLISHED PROCEEDINGS: SERIES SEMT.
SCIENCE/ENGINEERING/MEDICINE/TECHNOLOGY.**
++DIR. PUBL. PROC., SEMT. [DPPS-A]
[INTERDOK CORP.]
  WHITE PLAINS, N.Y.  1, S 1965-
  TITLE VARIES:  DIRECTORY OF PUBLISHED PROCEED-
  INGS FROM 1, 1965- 3(4), 1967.
  GL/U-1.
  ISSN 0012-3293

**DIS POLITIKA.  FOREIGN POLICY.**
++DIS POLIT.
  ANKARA  1, 1971-
  Q.  TURK. & ENGL.
  OX/U-1.

**DISCOURS SOCIAL.**
++DISCOURS SOC.
INSTITUT DE LITTERATURE ET DE TECHNIQUES ART-
ISTIQUES DE MASSE.
  BORDEAUX  1, 1970-
  OX/U-1.
  ISSN 0012-3595

**DISCOVERING ANTIQUES.**
++DISCOV. ANTIQUES.
[PURNELL]
  LONDON  NO.1, OC 1970-
  ED/N-1.    OX/U-1.
  BH/P-1.  OC 1970- AP 1972.
  ISSN 0012-3617

**DISCRETE MATHEMATICS.**
++DISCRETE MATH.
[NORTH-HOLLAND PUBL. CO.]
  AMSTERDAM  1, MY 1971-
  Q.
  AD/U-1.    CA/U-2.    GL/U-1.    LO/N-4.    LO/N14.    SH/U-1.
  SW/U-1.    XY/N-1.
  BL/U-1.  7, 1974-
  ISSN 0012-365X

**DISCUSSION PAPER, BRISTOL BRANCH, BRITISH
INSTITUTE OF MANAGEMENT.**
++DISCUSS. PAP. BRISTOL BRANCH BR. INST. MANAGE.
  BRISTOL  NO.1, 1972-
  LO/N-1.    OX/U-1.

**DISCUSSION PAPER, BRITISH ASSOCIATION OF SOC-
IAL WORKERS.**
++DISCUSS. PAP. BR. ASSOC. SOC. WORK.
  LONDON  NO.1, 1971-
  NW/U-1.    OX/U-1.

DISCUSSION PAPERS IN BUSINESS & ORGANISATION.
+ +DISCUSS. PAP. BUS. & ORG.
GRADUATE CENTRE FOR MANAGEMENT STUDIES (BIR-
MINGHAM).
BIRMINGHAM NO.1, 1966-
CENTRE SUBORD. TO UNIVERSITY OF BIRMINGHAM
(&) UNIVERSITY OF ASTON IN BIRMINGHAM.
BH/U-1.

DISCUSSION PAPERS, CENTRE FOR RUSSIAN & EAST
EUROPEAN STUDIES, UNIVERSITY OF BIRMINGHAM:
SERIES RC/A.
+ +DISCUSS. PAP. CENT. RUSS. & E. EUR. STUD.
UNIV. BIRMINGHAM, RC/A.
BIRMINGHAM NO.1, 1965-
BH/U-1.
SO/U-1. NO.8, 1966-*

DISCUSSION PAPERS, CENTRE FOR RUSSIAN & EAST
EUROPEAN STUDIES, UNIVERSITY OF BIRMINGHAM:
SERIES RC/B.
+ +DISCUSS. PAP. CENT. RUSS. & E. EUR. STUD.
UNIV. BIRMINGHAM, RC/B.
BIRMINGHAM NO.1, 1968-
BH/U-1.
SO/U-1. NO.1, 1968.

DISCUSSION PAPERS, CENTRE FOR RUSSIAN & EAST
EUROPEAN STUDIES, UNIVERSITY OF BIRMINGHAM:
SERIES RC/C: SOCIOLOGY & POLITICAL SCIENCE.
+ +DISCUSS. PAP. CENT. RUSS. & E. EUR. STUD.
UNIV. BIRMINGHAM, RC/C.
BIRMINGHAM NO.1, 1964-
BH/U-1.

DISCUSSION PAPERS, DEPARTMENT OF ECONOMICS,
UNIVERSITY OF ESSEX.
+ +DISCUSS. PAP. DEP. ECON. UNIV. ESSEX.
COLCHESTER NO.1, 1969-
SO/U-1.

DISCUSSION PAPERS, DEPARTMENT OF GEOGRAPHY,
RUTGERS UNIVERSITY.
+ +DISCUSS. PAP. DEP. GEOGR. RUTGERS UNIV.
NEW BRUNSWICK, N.J. 1, JA 1970-
LO/S13.

DISCUSSION PAPERS IN ECONOMICS, UNIVERSITY OF
KEELE.
+ +DISCUSS. PAP. ECON. UNIV. KEELE.
KEELE NO.1, 1973-
OX/U16.

DISCUSSION PAPERS IN ECONOMICS, UNIVERSITY
OF READING.
+ +DISCUSS. PAP. ECON. UNIV. READ.
READING NO.1, 1967-
ISSUED BY THE UNIV.'S DEP. OF ECONOMICS.
BH/U-1.

DISCUSSION PAPERS, FACULTY OF COMMERCE &
SOCIAL SCIENCE, UNIVERSITY OF BIRMINGHAM;
SERIES E: SOCIAL SCIENCE METHODOLOGY.
+ +DISCUSS. PAP. FAC. COMMER. & SOC. SCI. UNIV.
BIRM., SER. E.
UNIVERSITY OF BIRMINGHAM.
BIRMINGHAM NO.1, AP 1966-
BH/U-1.

DISCUSSION PAPER SERIES, DEPARTMENT OF GEOGR-
APHY, UNIVERSITY OF TORONTO.
+ +DISCUSS. PAP. SER. DEP. GEOGR. UNIV. TORONTO.
TORONTO NO.1, 1969-
LO/S13.

DISCUSSION PAPER SERIES, DEPARTMENT OF TOWN
PLANNING, UNIVERSITY COLLEGE LONDON.
+ +DISCUSS. PAP. SER. DEP. TOWN PLANN. UNIV.
COLL. LONDON.
LONDON 1, 1968-
LO/U-2.

DISCUSSION PAPER SERIES, INSTITUTE OF ECONO-
MIC RESEARCH, HARVARD UNIVERSITY.
+ +DISCUSS. PAP. SER. INST. ECON. RES. HARVARD
UNIV.
CAMBRIDGE, MASS. NO.1, 1967-
OX/U16.
SO/U-1. NO.25, 1968-*
ISSN 0441-635X

DISEASES OF THE CHEST.                                    XXX
SUBS (1970): CHEST.

DISPOSABLES INTERNATIONAL.                               XXX
+ +DISPOSABLES INT.
[STONHILL & GILLIS LTD.]
LONDON NO.3, 1970-
PREV: PAPER DISPOSABLES INTERNATIONAL FROM
NO.1, 1969- 2, 1970.
ED/N-1.     LO/R-6.
LO/N14. [CURRENT BOX]
ISSN 0046-0370

DISPOSABLES & NONWOVENS.
[TEXTILE BUSINESS P. LTD.]
LONDON 1, 1970-
ED/N-1.     LO/N14.     LO/R-6.     OX/U-1.
ISSN 0012-3811

DISSERTATION ABSTRACTS INTERNATIONAL: PART A:
THE HUMANITIES & SOCIAL SCIENCES.                        XXX
+ +DISS. ABSTR. INT., A.
[UNIVERSITY MICROFILMS]
ANN ARBOR 30(1), 1969-
PREV: DISSERTATION ABSTRACTS: A... FROM 27(1),
1966- 29, 1969.
GL/U-2.     HL/U-1.     LO/N-4.     LO/N14.
BH/P-1. 30(5), N 1969-
LO/U-3. 30(7), JA 1970-

DISSERTATION ABSTRACTS INTERNATIONAL: PART B:
THE SCIENCES & ENGINEERING.                              XXX
+ +DISS. ABSTR. INT., B.
[UNIVERSITY MICROFILMS]
ANN ARBOR 30(1), JL 1969-
PREV: DISSERTATION ABSTRACTS: B: ... FROM
27(1), JL 1966- 29(12), JE 1969.
HL/U-1.     LO/N-4.     XS/R10.
BH/P-1. 30(5), N 1969-

DISSERTATION SERIES, LATIN AMERICAN STUDIES
PROGRAM, CORNELL UNIVERSITY.
+ +DISS. SER. LAT. AM. STUD. PROGRAM CORNELL UNIV
ITHACA NO.1, 1967-
GL/U-1.

DISSERTATION SERIES, MODERN HUMANITIES
RESEARCH ASSOCIATION.
+ +DISS. SER. MOD. HUM. RES. ASSOC.
CAMBRIDGE 1, 1970-
LO/U-1.
LO/N-1. 1, 1970.

DISSERTATIONEN, TECHNISCHE HOCHSCHULE(VIENNA).
+ +DISS. TECH. HOCHSCH. (VIENNA).
VIENNA [NO.]1, 1968-
LO/N13.

DISSERTATIONEN, TIERARZTLICHE HOCHSCHULE
(VIENNA).
+ +DISS. TIERARZTL. HOCHSCH. (VIENNA).
VIENNA 1, 1970-
LO/N-2.

DISSERTATIONES UNIVERSITATIS VARSAVIENSIS.             000
SEE: ROZPRAWY UNIWERSYTETU WARSZAWSKIEGO.

DISTRICT BANK REVIEW.                                    XXX
SUBS (1968): PART OF QUARTERLY REVIEW, NAT-
IONAL WESTMINSTER BANK.

DISTRICT COUNCILS REVIEW.                                XXX
+ +DIST. COUNC. REV.
RURAL DISTRICT COUNCILS ASSOCIATION.
[MUNICIPAL PUBL. CO.]
LONDON 1, 1972-
PREV: RURAL DISTRICT REVIEW FROM 55, 1949- 77,
D 1971.
ED/N-1.     LO/U-3.     OX/U-1.     SO/U-1.
NO/U-1. 1975-

DIVISION OF SOILS TECHNICAL PAPER, CSIRO
(AUSTRALIA).                                             000
SEE: TECHNICAL PAPER, DIVISION OF SOILS,
CSIRO (AUSTRALIA).

DIW-BEITRAGE ZUR STRUKTURFORSCHUNG.
+ +DIW-BEITR. STRUKTURFORSCH. (DEUT. INST.
WIRTSCHAFTSFORSCH.).
DEUTSCHES INSTITUT FUR WIRTSCHAFTSFORSCHUNG.
BERLIN 1, 1967-
LO/U21.
ISSN 0522-9472

DIX-HUITIEME SIECLE.
SOCIETE FRANCAISE D'ETUDE DU XVIIIE SIECLE.
PARIS NO.1, 1969-
A.
CB/U-1.     DB/U-2.     EX/U-1.     GL/U-1.     LD/U-1.     LO/U13.
MA/U-1.     OX/U-1.     SH/U-1.     SO/U-1.
NO/U-1. 2, 1970-                    NW/U-1. 2, 1970-

**DKB ECONOMIC REPORT.**
+ +DKB ECON. REP.
DAIICHI KANGYO GINKO.
*TOKYO 1(1), OC/N 1971-*
MON. ISSUED UNDER THE BANK'S ENGL. FORM OF
NAME DAI-ICHI KANGYO BANK LTD.
*LO/U14. 2(6), 1972- [W.2(7)].*

**DMG BULLETIN.**
+ +DMG BULL.
DESIGN METHODS GROUP.
*BERKELEY, CALIF. 72-1, 1972-*
8/A.
*DB/U-2. SH/U-1.*

**DMG OCCASIONAL NEWSLETTER.**
+ +DMG OCCAS. NEWSL.
DESIGN METHODS GROUP.
*BERKELEY, CALIF. 1, 1972-*
*SH/U-1.*

**DMG OCCASIONAL PAPER.**
+ +DMG OCCAS. PAP.
DESIGN METHODS GROUP.
*BERKELEY, CALIF. NO.1, 1972-*
*DB/U-2.*

**DO TEMPO E DA HISTORIA.**
UNIVERSIDADE DE LISBOA: INSTITUTO DE ALTA
CULTURA.
*LISBON 1, 1965-*
*SO/U-1. 1, 1965- 5, 1972.*
*ISSN 0419-4896*

**DOBOKU GAKKAI ROMBUN HOKOKUSHU (ENGL. TRANSL)**          000
SEE: TRANSACTIONS OF THE JAPAN SOCIETY OF
CIVIL ENGINEERS.

**DOBUTSU IYAKUHIN KENSAJO NENPO. ANNUAL
REPORT OF THE NATIONAL VETERINARY ASSAY
LABORATORY.**
DOBUTSU IYAKUHIN KENSAJO.
*TOKYO NO.1, 1960-*
JAP., SOME ENGL. SUMM.
*LO/N13.*

**DOCTOR. NEWS, RESEARCH, FINANCE, ENTERTAIN-
MENTS, HOBBIES.**
*TWICKENHAM 1(1), JA 1971-*
2M.
*ED/N-1.*

**DOCUMENTA CHOPINIANA.**
+ +DOC. CHOPINIANA.
TOWARZYSTWO IM. FRYDERYKA CHOPINA.
*KRAKOW 1, 1970-*
*OX/U-1.*

**DOCUMENTATION: WEAR, FRICTION & LUBRICATION.**          000
SEE: DOKUMENTATION: VERSCHLEISS, REIBUNG UND
SCHMIERUNG.

**DOCUMENTATION BIBLIOGRAPHIQUE. BULLETIN DE
DOCUMENTATION, CENTRE D'ETUDES ET DE
RECHERCHES DE L'INDUSTRIE DES LIANTS HYDRAUL-
IQUES.**                                                   XXX
SUBS (1969): BULLETIN ANALYTIQUE, CENTRE ...

**DOCUMENTOS. REVISTA DE INFORMACION POLITICA.**
UNIVERSIDAD CENTRAL DE VENEZUELA: INSTITUTO DE
ESTUDIOS POLITICOS.
*CARACAS NO.1, JA/AP 1960-*
*OX/U-1.*
*ISSN 0012-4753*

**DOCUMENTOS DE POLEMICA.**
+ +DOC. POLEMICA.
*BUENOS AIRES 1, 1972-*
*OX/U-1.*

**DOCUMENTS D'HISTORIE MAGREBINE.**
+ +DOC. HIST. MAGREBINE.
*PARIS 1, 1972-*
*LO/N-1. OX/U-1.*

**DOCUMENTS SCIENTIFIQUES ET TECHNIQUES, CENTRE
TECHNIQUE DES INDUSTRIES AERAULIQUES ET
THERMIQUES.**
+ +DOC. SCI. & TECH. CENT. TECH. IND. AERAUL. &
THERM. (FR.).
*PARIS NO.1, 1964-*
*LO/N14.*

**DOG IN RESEARCH.**
+ +DOG RES.
[LITERATURE SEARCHERS]
*KETTERING, OHIO NO.1, 1966-*
*LO/N13.*
*ISSN 0419-5787*

**DOKLADY AKADEMII SEL'SKO-KHOZJAJSTVENNYKH
NAUK V BOLGARII.**
+ +DOKL. AKAD. S-KH. NAUK BOLG. [COAL-B]
*SOFIA 1(1), 1968-*
RUSS., ENGL., FR., & GER. TITLE ALSO IN FR.:
COMPTES RENDUS DE L'ACADEMIE DES SCIENCES
AGRICOLES EN BULGARIE.
*LO/N13. XS/R-2.*

**DOKLADY NA NAUCHNYKH KONFERENTSIJAKH, JARO-
SLAVSKIJ GOSUDARSTVENNYJ PEDAGOGICHESKIJ
INSTITUT.**
+ +DOKL. NAUCHN. KONF. JAROSLAV. GOS. PEDAGOG.
INST.
*JAROSLAVL' 1, 1962-*
*LO/N13.* *SA/U-1.*

**DOKLADY OTDELENIJ I KOMISSIJ GEOGRAFICHESKOGO
OBSHCHESTVA SSSR.**
+ +DOKL. OTD. & KOM. GEOGR. O-VA. SSSR.
*LENINGRAD VYP.1, 1967-*
*CC/U-1. OX/U-1.*
*BH/U-1. 1968- LO/N13. 1968-*
*LO/U15. 10, 1969.*

**DOKUMENTATION: VERSCHLEISS, REIBUNG UND
SCHMIERUNG. DOCUMENTATION: WEAR, FRICTION &
LUBRICATION.**
+ +DOK., VERSCHLEISS REIBUNG & SCHMIERUNG.
BUNDESANSTALT FUR MATERIALPRUEFUNG.
*BERLIN NO.1/4, 1967-*
*SW/U-1.*

**DOMBI. REVUE CONGOLAISE DES LETTRES ET DES
ARTS, CREATION ET CRITIQUE.**
*KINSHASA-KALINA 1(1), 1970-*
*LO/U14.*
*ISSN 0046-0532*

**DOMESTIC HEATING. THE JOURNAL OF THE ...**
+ +DOM. HEAT.
DOMESTIC HEATING SOCIETY.
*MELTON MOWBRAY &C 1, WINTER 1967/68-*
*ED/N-1. LO/N14.*
*ISSN 0012-5318*

**DOPOVIDI AKADEMIJI NAUK UKRAJINS'KOJI RSR:
SERIJA A: FIZYKO-TEKHNICHNI TA MATEMATYCHNI
NAUKY.**                                                   XXX
+ +DOPOV. AKAD. NAUK UKR. RSR, A.
*KIEV 1(29), JA 1967-*
PREV. AS PART OF ABOVE MAIN TITLE FROM 1939-
1966. THEN ISSUED IN SUBJECT SECTIONS WHICH
CONTINUE PREV. NUMBERING. VOL.1 OF ABOVE ALSO
CALLED VOL.2.
*LO/N-2. LO/N14. OX/U-8.*

**DOWN HERE. A MAGAZINE FROM THE EAST VILLAGE.**
*NEW YORK 1(1), 1966-*
Q.
*LO/U-2.*

**DRAMA IN EDUCATION. THE ANNUAL SURVEY.**
+ +DRAMA EDUC.
[PITMAN]
*LONDON 1, 1972-*
*GL/U-1. LD/U-1. OX/U-1. SW/U-1.*

**DRIFTSFORMER I LANDBRUKET.**
NORGES LANDBRUKSOKONOMISKE INSTITUTT.
*OSLO NO.1, 1970-*
*LO/N13.*

**DRIFTTEKNIK.**                                            XXX
SVENSKA DRIFTPERSONALFORBUNDET.
*JOHANNESHOV 14(2), 1973-*
PREV: SLAM.
*LO/N14.*

**DROITS DE L'HOMME. PARIS, 1968**                          000
SEE: HUMAN RIGHTS.

**DRUCKLUFT - PRAXIS.**
+ +DRUCKLUFT PRAX.
[KRAUSSKOPF-VERLAG FUR WIRTSCHAFT]
*MAINZ 1, 1969-*
*LO/N14.*
*ISSN 0012-6497*

**DRUGS.**
[KARGER]
BASLE &C. 1, 1971-
GL/U-1.   GL/U-2.   LO/N14.   LO/U-2.   SH/U-1.
LO/M11. 3, 1972-
ISSN 0012-6667

**DRUGS IN CURRENT USE & NEW DRUGS.***
+ +DRUGS CURR. USE & NEW DRUGS.
[SPRINGER]
NEW YORK 1969-
PREV: DRUGS IN CURRENT USE FROM 1955- 1968.
LO/N14.

**DRUG DEPENDENCE.**
+ +DRUG DEPEND. [DRDP-A]
NATIONAL CLEARINGHOUSE FOR MENTAL HEALTH
INFORMATION (US).
CHEVY CHASE, MD. NO.1, 1969-
PREP. JOINTLY WITH DIV. OF NARCOTIC ADDICT-
ION & DRUG ABUSE.
AD/U-1.   GL/U-1.       NW/U-1.       SO/U-1.
LD/U-1. NO.2, 1969-              OX/U-8. NO.3, 1970-
ISSN 0070-7368

**DRUG INTELLIGENCE (CINCINNATI).**                      XXX
+ +DRUG INTELL. (CINCI.).
CINCINNATI 1, JA 1967- 3(5), 1969 ...
SUBS: DRUG INTELLIGENCE & CLINICAL PHARMACY.
LO/N14.

**DRUG INTELLIGENCE & CLINICAL PHARMACY.**           XXX
+ +DRUG INTELL. & CLIN. PHARM.
[FRANCKE]
CINCINNATI 3(6), 1969-
PREV: DRUG INTELLIGENCE (CINCINNATI) FROM
1, JA 1967- 3(5), 1969.
LO/N14.
BH/U-3. 5, 1971-                GL/U-2. 5, N 1971-
ISSN 0012-6578

**DRUG LITERATURE INDEX.**
+ +DRUG LIT. INDEX.
EXCERPTA MEDICA FOUNDATION.
AMSTERDAM; LONDON 1, 1969 (1970)-
GL/U-2.   LO/N14.   OX/U-1.

**DRUG METABOLISM & DISPOSITION.**
+ +DRUG METAB. & DISPOSIT.
AMERICAN SOCIETY FOR PHARMACOLOGY & EXPERI-
MENTAL THERAPEUTICS.
[WILLIAMS & WILKINS]
BALTIMORE 1(1), 1973-
S/T: THE BIOLOGICAL FATE OF CHEMICALS.
CA/M-7.   MA/U-1.   OX/U-8.   SH/U-1.
ISSN 0090-9556

**DRUG METABOLISM REVIEWS.**
+ +DRUG METAB. REV.
[DEKKER]
NEW YORK 1, 1972-
2/A.
AD/U-1.   GL/U-1.   SO/U-1.
ISSN 0012-6594

**DRUGS & SOCIETY.**
+ +DRUGS & SOC.
INSTITUTE FOR THE STUDY OF DRUG DEPENDENCE.
LONDON 1(1), OC 1971- 3(3), D 1973. //
CA/U-1.   ED/N-1.   LO/U-3.   MA/P-1.   OX/U-8.
ISSN 0046-0761

**DRUID.**
DRUID ORDER.
LONDON NO.1, 1965-
ED/N-1. 2, 1966-
ISSN 0012-6705

**DRUNKEN BOAT.**
PISCATAWAY 1(1), 1969-
OX/U-1.

**DU PONT INNOVATION.**
DU PONT DE NEMOURS & CO.
WILMINGTON, DEL. 1, 1969-
LO/N14.
ISSN 0020-1626

**DUBLIN BIBLIOGRAPHICAL SERIES.**
+ +DUBLIN BIBLIOGR. SER.
[MUSEUM BOOKSHOP]
DUBLIN NO.1, 1966-
OX/U-1.
ISSN 0419-7917

**DUBLIN UNIVERSITY LAW REVIEW.**
+ +DUBLIN UNIV. LAW REV.
TRINITY COLLEGE (DUBLIN).
DUBLIN 1(1), [1968]-
2/A.
BL/U-1.   CO/U-1.   DB/U-2.   ED/N-1.   LO/U-3.   LV/U-1.
MA/U-1.   OX/U15.   SH/U-1.
ISSN 0012-6896

**DUQUESNE HISPANIC REVIEW.**
+ +DUQUESNE HISPANIC REV.
DUQUESNE UNIVERSITY: DEPARTMENT OF MODERN
LANGUAGES.
[DUQUESNE U.P.]
PITTSBURGH 1(1), 1962-
3/A.  SPAN.  S/T: REVISTA HISPANICA DE LA
UNIVERSIDAD DE DUQUESNE.
ED/N-1.
CR/U-1. 3, 1964-                    LO/U-2. 6(2), 1967-
MA/U-1. 10, 1971-
ISSN 0012-7191

**DURIUS.  BOLETIN CASTELLANO DE ESTUDIOS
CLASSICOS.**
VALLADOLID 1, 1973-
NO/U-1.

**DUTCH QUARTERLY REVIEW OF ANGLO-AMERICAN
LETTERS.**
+ +DUTCH Q. REV. ANGLO-AM. LETT.
ASSEN 1, 1971-
ED/N-1.
GL/U-1. 1972-                      LO/U-1. 2, 1972-
SA/U-1.
ISSN 0046-0842

**DYN. THE JOURNAL OF THE ...**
DURHAM UNIVERSITY ANTHROPOLOGICAL SOCIETY.
DURHAM 1, 1970-
CA/U-3.   ED/N-1.

**DYNAMIC MASS SPECTROMETRY.**
+ +DYN. MASS SPECTROM.
[HEYDEN]
LONDON 1, 1970-
CA/U-1.   CB/U-1.   ED/N-1.   LO/N-4.   LO/N14.   LO/S-3.

**DZIEJE POLSKIEJ GRANICY ZACHODNIEJ.**
+ +DZIEJE POL. GRANICY ZACHODNIEJ.
INSTYTUT ZACHODNI (POZNAN).
POZNAN 1, 1961-
MONOGR.
LO/N-3. 5(1970).

**EALING OCCASIONAL PAPERS IN THE HISTORY OF
LIBRARIES.**
+ +EALING OCCAS. PAP. HIST. LIBR.
EALING TECHNICAL COLLEGE: SCHOOL OF LIBRARIAN-
SHIP.
LONDON NO.1, 1972-
CA/U-1. .  LO/N-1.

**EARIC INFORMATION CIRCULAR.**
+ +EARIC INF. CIRC. (E. AFR. RES. INF. CENT.).
EAST AFRICAN RESEARCH INFORMATION CENTRE.
NAIROBI NO.1, 1968-
OX/U-9.

**EARLY CHILD DEVELOPMENT & CARE.**
[GORDON & BREACH]
LONDON 1(1), JL 1971-
CA/U-1.   ED/N-1.   LD/U-1.   OX/U-1.   SH/U-1.   SW/U-1.
MA/U-1. 1(2), 1972-
ISSN 0300-4430

**EARLY MUSIC.**
[OXFORD UNIV. P.]
LONDON 1, 1973-
Q.
BL/U-1.   CA/U-1.   HL/U-1.   LD/U-1.   LO/U-1.   MA/U-1.
NO/U-1.   SH/U-1.
ISSN 0306-1078

**EARTH & EXTRATERRESTRIAL SCIENCES.**
+ +EARTH & EXTRATERR. SCI.
[GORDON & BREACH]
NEW YORK &C. 1(1), 1969-
ED/N-1.   GL/U-1.   LC/U-1.   LO/N-4.   OX/U-1.   OX/U-8.
XY/N-1.
DB/U-1. 1(1), AG 1969- 1(5), JL 1970.

**EARTH SCIENCE BULLETIN.**
+ +EARTH SCI. BULL.
WYOMING GEOLOGICAL ASSOCIATION.
CASPER 1, MR 1968-
XY/N-1.**
LO/N-2. 1(2), 1968-
ISSN 0012-8236

**EARTH SCIENCES NEWSLETTER.**
+ +EARTH SCI. NEWSL.
NATIONAL ACADEMY OF SCIENCES (US): DIVISION OF
EARTH SCIENCES.
*WASHINGTON, D.C. NO.1, 1967-*
LO/N-2. NO.1, 1967- 4, 1968.
LO/N13. CURRENT YEAR ONLY.

**EARTH SCIENCES RESEARCH CATALOG.**
+ +EARTH SCI. RES. CAT.
AMERICAN ASSOCIATION OF PETROLEUM GEOLOGISTS.
*TULSA 1, 1970-*
OX/U-8.

**EARTH SCIENCE SERIES, IDAHO BUREAU OF MINES &
GEOLOGY.**
+ +EARTH SCI. SER. IDAHO BUR. MINES & GEOL.
*MOSCOW, IDAHO NO.1, 1967-*
LO/N-2.

**EARTHQUAKE ENGINEERING & STRUCTURAL DYNAMICS.**
+ +EARTHQUAKE ENG. & STRUCT. DYN.
INTERNATIONAL ASSOCIATION FOR EARTHQUAKE
ENGINEERING. ·
[WILEY]
*LONDON 1, 1972-*
CA/U-1. ED/N-1. LO/N14.

**EAST AFRICAN ECONOMIC REVIEW. N.S.**                        XXX
+ +EAST AFR. ECON. REV., NS.
ECONOMICS CLUB OF KENYA.
*NAIROBI 1, D 1964- 4(2), D 1968.*
PREV: SERIES 1, 1954- 11, 1964. SUBS:
EASTERN AFRICA ECONOMIC REVIEW.
HL/U-1. OX/U16.
BN/U-2. 3(1), 1967-

**EAST AFRICAN JOURNAL OF RURAL DEVELOPMENT.**
+ +EAST AFR. J. RURAL DEV.
EAST AFRICAN AGRICULTURAL ECONOMIC SOCIETY.
*KAMPALA, UGANDA 1(1), JA 1968-*
PUBL. JOINTLY BY THE SOC. & THE DEP. OF RURAL   ·
ECONOMY & EXTENSION, MAKARERE UNIV. COLL. 2/A
LO/N-1. LO/N17. LO/U-8. LV/U-1. MA/U-1. OX/U16.
XS/U-1.
ISSN 0012-8333

**EAST AFRICAN MANAGEMENT JOURNAL.**
+ +EAST AFR. MANAGE. J.
EAST AFRICAN MANAGEMENT FOUNDATION.
*NAIROBI 1(1), OC 1966-*
Q. S/T: THE JOURNAL OF THE ... FOUNDATION.
LO/U-3.
ISSN 0012-8341

**EAST AFRICAN REPORT ON TRADE & INDUSTRY.**
+ +EAST AFR. REP. TRADE & IND.
KENYA ASSOCIATION OF MANUFACTURERS.
[NEWS PUBL. LTD.]
*NAIROBI 1(1), JA 1970-*
MON. INCLUDES KENYA EXPORT NEWS
LO/U-8.

**EAST ASIAN OCCASIONAL PAPERS.**
+ +EAST ASIAN OCCAS. PAP.
UNIVERSITY OF HAWAII: ASIAN STUDIES PROGRAM.
*HONOLULU 1, 1969-*
SUBSERIES OF ASIAN STUDIES AT HAWAII.
LO/U14. SH/U-1.
ISSN 0070-8054

**EAST COAST YACHTSMAN.**
+ +EAST COAST YACHTSM.
*COLCHESTER 1, SPRING 1968-*
ED/N-1.

**EAST EUROPEAN METALS REVIEW.**
+ +EAST EUR. METALS REV.
METAL INFORMATION SERVICES.
*STONEHOUSE, GLOS. 1, 1969-*
LO/N14.

**EAST MIDLANDS BIBLIOGRAPHY.**                               XXX
+ +EAST MIDL. BIBLIOGR.
LIBRARY ASSOCIATION: EAST MIDLANDS BRANCH.
*DERBY 8(3), 1970-*
Q. PREV: NORTH MIDLAND BIBLIOGRAPHY FROM
1, 1963- 8(2), 1970.
BH/U-1. LO/N-3. LO/U-1. OX/U-1.
ISSN 0029-2885

**EAST RIDING ARCHAEOLOGIST.**
+ +EAST RID. ARCHAEOL.
EAST RIDING ARCHAEOLOGICAL SOCIETY.
*HULL 1, 1968-*
S/T: A JOURNAL OF THE ... SOCIETY.
CA/U-3. CR/N-1. LO/P-6. OX/U-1. SH/U-1.

**EAST YORKSHIRE FIELD STUDIES.**
HULL GEOLOGICAL SOCIETY.
*HULL [NO.]1, 1968-*
SPONS. BODIES ALSO: HULL SCIENTIFIC & FIELD
NATURALISTS' CLUB; & FIELD STUDIES ASSOCIATION
(HULL & E. YORKS.).
LO/N-2. LO/N13.

**EASTERN AFRICA ECONOMIC REVIEW.**
+ +EAST. AFR. ECON. REV.
[OXFORD UNIV. P.]
*NAIROBI 1, 1969-*
PREV: EAST AFRICAN ECONOMIC REVIEW FROM 1, JL
1954- N.S. 4(2), D 1968
BH/U-1. BN/U-2. CB/U-1. ED/U-1. GL/U-1. GL/U-2.
HL/U-1. LD/U-1. LO/N17. LO/R-6. LO/U14. MA/U-1.
OX/N-9. OX/U16. RE/U-1.
LO/N35. 4(1), 1972-
ISSN 0012-866X

**EASTERN AFRICA LAW REVIEW.**
+ +EAST. AFR. LAW REV.
UNIVERSITY COLLEGE, DAR-ES-SALAAM: FACULTY
OF LAW.
*DAR-ES-SALAAM 1(1), 1968-*
CR/U-1. OX/U15.
ISSN 0012-8678

**EASTERN EUROPE.**
+ +EAST. EUR.
LONDON CHAMBER OF COMMERCE & INDUSTRY, INC.
*LONDON 1(1), 1971-*
OX/U-1.

**EASTMAN ORGANIC CHEMICAL BULLETIN.**                        XXX
+ +EASTMAN ORG. CHEM. BULL.
EASTMAN KODAK.
*ROCHESTER, N.Y. 41, 1969-*
PREV: ORGANIC CHEMICAL BULLETIN FROM 20, 1948-
40, 1968.
LO/N14.
ISSN 0012-897X

**EASTWORD.**
EASTERN ARTS ASSOCIATION.
*CAMBRIDGE 1(1), AP 1972-*
M.
ED/N-1.

**EASY.**
[FLEETWAY PUBL.]
*LONDON 1(1), F 1968-*
S/T: HIS & HER DO-IT-YOURSELF WEEKLY.
OX/U-1. 1(3), 1968-

**EATON PAPER.**
+ +EATON PAP.
INSTITUTE OF ECONOMIC AFFAIRS (GB).
*LONDON [NO.]1, 1963-*
BT/U-1. MA/U-1.*

**EAU.**                                                       XXX
SUBS (1970): ·PART OF TECHNIQUES ET SCIENCES
MUNICIPALES - L'EAU.

**EBIC BULLETIN.**
+ +EBIC BULL. (EUR. BANKS' INT. CO.).
EUROPEAN BANKS' INTERNATIONAL COMPANY.
*BRUSSELS NO.1, 1970-*
LO/S14.

**ECMA STANDARDS.**
EUROPEAN COMPUTER MANUFACTURERS ASSOCIATION.
*GENEVA NO.1, 1965-*
BN/U-1.

**ECOLOGIA. RIVISTA DI STUDI E ANALISI SULL'
INQUINAMENTO, LA PIANIFICAZIONE E LA CONSERVAZ-
IONE AMBIENTALE.**
*MILAN 1, 1971-*
2M. ENGL. OR ITAL.
LO/N-2.*

**ECOLOGICAL NEWS.**                                          000
SEE: WIADOMOSCI EKOLOGICZNE.

**ECOLOGICAL STUDIES.**
+ +ECOL. STUD.
[SPRINGER]
*BERLIN &C. 1, 1970-*
GL/U-1. LO/N-2. OX/U-8.

**ECOLOGIST.**
[ECOSYSTEMS LTD.]
*LONDON 1(1), JL 1970-*
M. S/T: MAN & THE ENVIRONMENT, THE QUALITY
OF LIFE, POLLUTION, CONSERVATION.
*BL/U-1. DB/U-2. ED/P-1. EX/U-1. GL/U-2. LO/N-2.*
*LO/N13. LO/N17. LO/R-5. LO/U-1. LO/U-2. LO/U-3.*
*LO/U28. MA/P-1. SH/U-1.*
*BH/U-3. 2, 1972-          GL/U-1. 2(1), 1972-*
*SH/C-5. 1(7), 1971-       SO/U-1. 4, 1974-*
*XS/R10. 2(1), 1972-*
*LO/N35. 1(13), 1971-*
*XS/T-4. 2(1), JA 1972-*
*ISSN 0012-9631*

**ECOLOGY. TRANSLATION OF EKOLOGIJA.**                           XXX
[CONSULTANTS BUREAU]
*NEW YORK &C. [1], 1970.*
SUBS: SOVIET JOURNAL OF ECOLOGY.
*LO/N-2. LO/N13.*

**ECOLOGY OF FOOD & NUTRITION.**
++*ECOL. FOOD & NUTR.*
[GORDON & BREACH]
*NEW YORK &C. 1, 1971-*
S/T: AN INTERNATIONAL JOURNAL.
*BH/U-3. CA/U-1. ED/N-1. LD/U-1.*
*ISSN 0367-0244*

**ECOLOGY LAW QUARTERLY.**
++*ECOL. LAW Q.*
UNIVERSITY OF CALIFORNIA: SCHOOL OF LAW.
*BERKELEY 1, WINTER 1971-*
Q.
*CA/U13.*

**ECONOMIA Y DESARROLLO.**
++*ECON. & DESARROLLO (CUBA).*
UNIVERSIDAD DE LA HABANA: INSTITUTO DE ECONOMIA
*HAVANA NO.1, JA/MR 1970-*
Q. S/T: PUBLICACION TRIMESTRAL DEL ...
*LO/U-3. OX/U-1.*

**ECONOMIA PUBBLICA.**
++*ECON. PUBBLICA.*
[CIRIEC]
*MILAN 1(1), MY 1971-*
*CA/U-1. OX/U16.*

**ECONOMIC AGE.**
++*ECON. AGE.*
ECONOMIC RESEARCH COUNCIL (GB).
*LONDON 1(1), N/D 1968-*
2M.
*BH/U-1. BN/U-1. DB/U-2. GL/U-1. GL/U-2. LO/U-3.*
*MA/P-1. OX/U16.*

**ECONOMIC ANALYSIS & POLICY.**
++*ECON. ANAL. & POLICY.*
ECONOMIC SOCIETY OF AUSTRALIA & NEW ZEALAND:
QUEENSLAND BRANCH.
*ST. LUCIA 1(1), 1970-*
2/A.
*OX/U-1.*
*AD/U-1. 2, 1971-*

**ECONOMIC & COMMERCIAL NEWS (INDIA).**
++*ECON. & COMMER. NEWS (INDIA).*
(INDIA) MINISTRY OF FOREIGN TRADE.
*NEW DELHI 1(1), JE 1971-*
W.
*GL/U-1. LO/U-3.\**

**ECONOMIC DIGEST, ECONOMIC INFORMATION SERVICE,
MEAT & LIVESTOCK COMMISSION.**
++*ECON. DIG. ECON. INF. SERV. MEAT & LIVESTOCK
COMM.*
*BLETCHLEY 1, 1969-*
*OX/U21.*

**ECONOMIC & FINANCIAL REVIEW, CENTRAL BANK OF
KENYA.**
++*ECON. & FINAN. REV. CENT. BANK KENYA.*
*NAIROBI 1(1), 1968-*
*LD/U-1. LO/S14. LO/U-3. LO/U14. OX/U-9.*

**ECONOMIC & FINANCIAL REVIEW, RESERVE BANK OF
MALAWI.**
++*ECON. & FINAN. REV. RESERVE BANK MALAWI.*
*BLANTYRE 1(1), 1968-*
Q.
*LD/U-1. 1(2), 1968-          LO/U14. 1(3), 1969-*
*LO/U-8. 2(2), D 1969-*

**ECONOMIC GEOLOGY REPORT (JAMAICA).**
++*ECON. GEOL. REP. (JAMAICA).*
(JAMAICA) GEOLOGICAL SURVEY.
*KINGSTON NO.1, 1967-*
*LO/N-2.*

**ECONOMIC JOURNAL.**
++*ECON. J.*
GOVERNMENT COLLEGE (LAHORE): DEPARTMENT OF
ECONOMICS.
*LAHORE 1, 1968-*
2/A.
*OX/U13. 2, 1969-*
*LO/N12. 2(2); 4(2); 5, 1969-*
*ISSN 0424-2815*

**ECONOMIC JOURNAL OF THE ECONOMIC SOCIETY,
TRIBHUVAN UNIVERSITY.**                                          000
SEE: AARTHIK JAGAT.

**ECONOMIC & POLITICAL WEEKLY.**
++*ECON. & POLIT. WKLY. (INDIA).*
SAMEEKSHA TRUST.
*BOMBAY 1(1), 20/AG 1966-*
*LO/U-8.*
*ISSN 0012-9976*

**ECONOMIC PROGRESS REPORT. (GB).**
++*ECON. PROG. REP. (GB).*
(GREAT BRITAIN) TREASURY: INFORMATION DIVISION.
*LONDON 1, 1970-*
PREV: DEA PROGRESS REPORT FROM NO.1 1965-
56, 1969.
*BH/U-1. BL/U-1. GL/U-2. GL/U-3. HL/U-1. LD/U-1.*
*LO/N-3. LO/N-5. LO/N-7. LO/U-3. LO/U-3. OX/U-1.*
*OX/U16. RE/U-1. SO/U-1.*
*LO/N-4. NO.4, 1970-*
*CV/C-1. FIVE YEARS.*

**ECONOMIC REPORT, ECONOMICS DEPARTMENT,
EDINBURGH & EAST OF SCOTLAND COLLEGE OF
AGRICULTURE.**                                                   XXX
SUBS (1970): REPORT, ECONOMICS DEPARTMENT,
EAST OF SCOTLAND ...

**ECONOMIC REVIEW (DUBLIN).**
++*ECON. REV. (DUBLIN).*
CONFEDERATION OF IRISH INDUSTRY.
*DUBLIN JA 1971-*
Q.
*CA/U-1.*
*ED/N-1. OC 1971-*

**ECONOMIC SITUATION IN THE (EUROPEAN ECONOMIC)
COMMUNITY.**
++*ECON. SITUAT. (EUR. ECON.) COMMUNITY.*
EUROPEAN ECONOMIC COMMUNITY.
*BRUSSELS 1961-*
DUTCH, ENGL., FR., GER., ITAL. ISSUED BY THE
COMMUNITY'S COMMISSION.
*BH/U-1. 1962-          HL/U-1. 1974(1)-*
*LO/N-5, 1970(1)-      LO/P-6. 1962/1963-*
*SW/U-1. 1963-*
*ISSN 0013-0346*

**ECONOMIC & SOCIAL REVIEW.**
++*ECON. & SOC. REV.*
ECONOMIC & SOCIAL STUDIES.
*DUBLIN 1(1), OC 1969-*
Q.
*BL/U-1. CO/U-1. DB/S-1. DB/U-2. ED/N-1. LO/N-1.*
*LO/N17. LO/U-3. LO/U20. MA/U-1. NO/U-1.*
*SH/U-1. 5, 1973-*
*GL/U-2. 4(1), OC 1972-*
*ISSN 0012-9984*

**ECONOMIC STUDIES.**                                            XXX
++*ECON. STUD.*
[PERGAMON]
*OXFORD 4, 1969-*
Q. PREV: JOURNAL OF ECONOMIC STUDIES FROM
1, 1965- 3, 1968.
*ED/N-1. ED/U-2. HL/U-1. LD/U-1. LO/U-3. SO/U-1.*
*XS/U-1.*
*ISSN 0449-2420*

**ECONOMIC TRENDS.**
++*ECON. TRENDS.*
CONFEDERATION OF IRISH INDUSTRY.
*DUBLIN 1973-*
*CA/U-1. ED/N-1. OX/U-1.*

**ECONOMICA AFRICANA.**
++*ECON. AFR. [EAFC-A]*
UNIVERSITY OF MALAWI: CHANCELLOR COLLEGE
ECONOMICS SOCIETY.
*LIMBE 1(1), JL 1968-*
*LO/U-3.*

ECONOMIE DE L'ENERGIE.
+ +ECON. ENERG.
CENTRE NATIONAL DE LA RECHERCHE SCIENTIFIQUE
(FRANCE).
*PARIS 1971-*
MON. CONSISTS OF ABSTR.
XS/T-4.
LO/N14. 1972-
ISSN 0046-1202

ECONOMIE ET STATISTIQUE. REVUE MENSUELLE.
+ +ECON. STAT. (FR.).
INSTITUT NATIONAL DE LA STATISTIQUE ET DES
ETUDES ECONOMIQUES (FRANCE).
*PARIS 1, 1969-*
BH/U-1.    BT/U-1.    LO/U-1.    LO/U-3.    OX/U-1.    RE/U-1.

ECONOMY & SOCIETY.
+ +ECON. & SOC.
[ROUTLEDGE & KEGAN PAUL]
*LONDON 1(1), F 1972-*
Q.
CA/U-1.     ED/N-1.    EX/U-1.    GL/U-1.    GL/U-2.    LD/U-1.
LO/U-2.     LO/U-3.    LO/U-4.    MA/P-1.    MA/U-1.    NO/U-1.
OX/U16.     OX/U17.    SO/U-1.

ECY NEWSLETTER.                                              XXX
+ +ECY NEWSL.
EUROPEAN CONSERVATION YEAR SECRETARIAT.
*LONDON NO.1- 6, 1970.//*
MON.
LO/N-2.     LO/N-6.

EDDIES.
[UNDERCURRENTS]
*LONDON NO.1, OC 1972*
MON.
ED/N-1. NO.4, 1973-

EDGE. AN INDEPENDENT PERIODICAL.                             XXX
*EDMONTON, ALTA. NO.1, AUTUMN 1963- 9, 1969.//*
LO/U-2. 2,SPR 1964-

EDGE HILL FORUM ON TEACHER EDUCATION.
+ +EDGE HILL FORUM TEACH. EDUC.
EDGE HILL COLLEGE OF EDUCATION.
*ORMSKIRK, LANCS. NO.1, SUMMER 1972-*
ED/N-1.

EDINBURGH WEEKLY.
+ +EDINB. WKLY.
*EDINBURGH 1, 30/S 1966-*
ED/N-1.

EDINBURGH WORKING PAPERS IN LINGUISTICS.
+ +EDINB. WORK. PAP. LINGUIST.
*EDINBURGH 1, 1972-*
SH/U-1.

EDITERRA CIRCULAR LETTER.
+ +EDITERRA CIRC. LETT.
EUROPEAN ASSOCIATION OF EARTH SCIENCE EDITORS.
*UTRECHT M 1, 1969-*
LO/N-2.

EDN. ELECTRICAL DESIGN NEWS.                                 XXX
[ROGERS PUBL. CO.]
*DENVER, COLO. 7(5), 1962- 16(9), 1971 ...*
PREV: ELECTRICAL DESIGN NEWS FROM 1, MY 1956-
7(4), 1962. SUBS: EDN/EEE.
LO/N14.

EDN/EEE.                                                     XXX
[ROGERS PUBL. CO.]
*DENVER, COLO. 16(10), 1971-*
PREV: EDN. ELECTRICAL DESIGN NEWS FROM 7(5),
1962- 16(9), 1971.
LO/N14.

EDUCACAO (BRAZIL).
(BRAZIL) MINISTERIO DA EDUCACAO E CULTURA:
DIRETORIA DE DOCUMENTACAO E DIVULGACAO.
*BRASILIA 1, AP/JE 1971-*
Q. ENGL. & FR. SUMM.
OX/U-1.
LO/U-3. 1(2), 1971-
ISSN 0013-1024

EDUCATION 3 - 13.
[COLLINS]
*GLASGOW 1(1), AP 1973-*
CA/U-1.     ED/N-1.    HL/U-2.    LD/U-2.    SW/U-1.
ISSN 0300-4279

EDUCATION IN DEVELOPING COUNTRIES OF THE COM-
MONWEALTH. ABSTRACTS OF CURRENT RESEARCH.
+ +EDUC. DEV. COUNTRIES COMMONW.
COMMONWEALTH SECRETARIAT.
*LONDON 1969(1970)-*
ANNU.
LO/U-3.     LO/U14.

EDUCATION FOR DEVELOPMENT. JOURNAL OF ...
+ +EDUC. DEVELOP.
UNIVERSITY COLLEGE OF SOUTH WALES & MONMOUTH-
SHIRE: FACULTY OF EDUCATION.
*CARDIFF 1, 1970-*
ED/N-1.     HL/U-2.

EDUCATION IN EASTERN AFRICA.
+ +EDUC. EAST. AFR.
REGIONAL COUNCIL FOR EDUCATION (NAIROBI).
*NAIROBI 1(1), 1970-*
2/A.
LD/U-2.     LO/N-1.    OX/U-9.    XY/N-1.
HL/U-2. 2, 1971-
ISSN 0046-1423

EDUCATION ENVIRONMENT.
+ +EDUC. ENVIRON.
*DUBLIN 1(1), AP 1973-*
BL/U-1.     CO/U-1.    DB/U-1.
ED/N-1. 1(3), OC 1973-

EDUCATION FOR EUROPE.
+ +EDUC. EUR.
*GENEVA 1, 1972-*
OX/U-1.

EDUCATION FOR A MULTI-CULTURAL SOCIETY.
+ +EDUC. MULTI-CULT. SOC.
COMMUNITY RELATIONS COMMISSION (G.B.).
*[LONDON] NO.1, 1970-*
LO/N-1.

EDUCATION FOR PLANNING.
+ +EDUC. PLANN.
OXFORD POLYTECHNIC: DEPARTMENT OF TOWN PLANNING
*OXFORD 1(1), 1971-*
OX/U16. 1(2), 1971-

EDUCATION PLANNING PAPER.
+ +EDUC. PLANN. PAP.
(GREAT BRITAIN) DEPARTMENT OF EDUCATION &
SCIENCE.
*LONDON NO.1, 1970-*
LO/N-1.     OX/U-1.

EDUCATION & SOCIAL SCIENCE.
+ +EDUC. & SOC. SCI.
[PERGAMON]
*LONDON 1(1), 1969-*
Q.
DB/U-2.     ED/N-1.    HL/U-2.    LD/U-2.    LO/U-3.    MA/U-1.
OX/U-1.

EDUCATION TIMES.
+ +EDUC. TIMES.
[IRISH TIMES LTD.]
*DUBLIN 1, 1973-*
BL/U-1.     CA/U-1.

EDUCATION & TRAINING.                                        XXX
+ +EDUC. & TRAIN.
*LONDON 11(9), S 1969-*
PREV: TECHNICAL EDUCATION & INDUSTRIAL TRAIN-
ING* FROM 1, 1959- 11(8), 1969.
BH/P-1.     CV/C-1.    DB/U-2.    XS/R10.
LO/N-7. 12, 1970-              LO/U11. 12, 1970-
LO/U20. 12, 1970-
GL/U-2. THREE YEARS ONLY.
ISSN 0040-0912

EDUCATION & TRAINING OF THE MENTALLY
RETARDED.
+ +EDUC. & TRAIN. MENT. RETARD. [ETMR-B]
COUNCIL FOR EXCEPTIONAL CHILDREN: DIVISION OF
MENTAL RETARDATION.
*WASHINGTON, D.C. 1, 1966-*
LV/U-2.
ISSN 0013-1237

EDUCATION & URBAN SOCIETY.
+ +EDUC. & URBAN SOC.
[SAGE PUBL. INC.]
*BEVERLY HILLS 1(1), N 1968-*
Q. S/T: AN INDEPENDENT QUARTERLY WITH IMPLI-
CATIONS FOR PUBLIC POLICY.
LO/U-3.
ISSN 0013-1245

**EDUCATIONAL ADMINISTRATION BULLETIN.**
+ +EDUC. ADMIN. BULL.
BRITISH EDUCATIONAL ADMINISTRATION SOCIETY.
BRISTOL 1(1), SUMMER 1972-
HL/U-2.    LD/U-1.    MA/U-1.

**EDUCATIONAL BROADCASTING INTERNATIONAL.**    XXX
+ +EDUC. BROADCAST. INT.
CENTRE FOR EDUCATIONAL DEVELOPMENT OVERSEAS.
WREXHAM 5(1), MR 1971-
Q.  PREV: EDUCATIONAL TELEVISION INTERNATIONAL
FROM 1(1), MR 1967- 4, 1970.
ED/N-1.    LD/U-2.
HL/U-1. 7(3), 1974-              HL/U-2. 6, 1973-
MA/U-1. 6, 1973-
ISSN 0013-1970

**EDUCATIONAL DOCUMENTATION & INFORMATION.**    XXX
+ +EDUC. DOC. & INF.
INTERNATIONAL BUREAU OF EDUCATION.
GENEVA NO.178, 1971-
PREV: BULLETIN, INTERNATIONAL BUREAU OF
EDUCATION FROM NO.1, 1927- 177, 1970.
BH/P-1.    LD/U-1.    LN/U-2.    LO/U-1.*

**EDUCATIONAL EXCHANGE.**
+ +EDUC. EXCH.
CENTRAL BUREAU FOR EDUCATIONAL VISITS &
EXCHANGES.
LONDON NO.1, 1969-
3/A.
ED/N-1. NO.7, 1971-
ISSN 0046-1490

**EDUCATIONAL FLUID MECHANICS.**
+ +EDUC. FLUID MECH.
ARMFIELD HYDRAULIC ENGINEERING CO. LTD.
RINGWOOD, HANTS. NO.1, [1967]-
ISSUED BY THE FIRM'S TECHNICAL EDUCATIONAL
EQUIPMENT DIVISION.
BR/U-3.    LO/N14.

**EDUCATIONAL MEDIA INTERNATIONAL.**    XXX
+ +EDUC. MEDIA INT.
INTERNATIONAL COUNCIL FOR EDUCATIONAL MEDIA.
LONDON NO.1, MR 1971-
PREV: AUDIO-VISUAL MEDIA FROM 1(1), 1967-
4(4), 1970.
EX/U-1.    LD/U-2.    LO/U28.    OX/U-1.
ED/N-1. NO.2, 1971-              LO/N35. NO.2, 1972-
SH/U-1. NO.1, 1973-
ISSN 0004-7597

**EDUCATIONAL PHILOSOPHY & THEORY.**
+ +EDUC. PHIL. & THEOR.
UNIVERSITY OF NEW SOUTH WALES.
RANDWICK, N.S.W. 1, 1969-
BN/U-1.    CA/U-1.    LO/N-1.    OX/U-1.
ISSN 0013-1857

**EDUCATIONAL RESEARCH NEWS.**
+ +EDUC. RES. NEWS.
NATIONAL FOUNDATION FOR EDUCATIONAL RESEARCH
IN ENGLAND & WALES.
LONDON NO.1, S 1967-
ED/N-1.
CB/U-1. 2, 1968-

**EDUCATIONAL SERIES, GEOLOGICAL SURVEY (NORTH
DAKOTA).**
+ +EDUC. SER. GEOL. SURV. (N.D.).
GRAND FORKS, N.D. NO.1, [1972]-
LO/N-2.

**EDUCATIONAL SERIES, IOWA GEOLOGICAL SURVEY.**
+ +EDUC. SER. IOWA GEOL. SURV.
IOWA CITY 1, 1967-
ED/S-2.    GL/U-1.
ISSN 0578-6037

**EDUCATIONAL STUDIES IN MATHEMATICS.**
+ +EDUC. STUD. MATH.
[D REIDEL]
DORDRECHT 1, MY 1968-
Q. ENGL., FR.
DB/U-2.    GL/U-1.    HL/U-1.    LD/U-2.    LO/U-2.    LV/U-2.
OX/U-8.    SH/U-1.    SW/U-1.
ISSN 0013-1954

**EDUCATIONAL TELEVISION INTERNATIONAL.**    XXX
+ +EDUC. TELEV. INT.
CENTRE FOR EDUCATIONAL TELEVISION OVERSEAS.
[PERGAMON P.]
LONDON 1(1), MR 1967- 4, 1970...
Q.  PREV: CETO NEWS FROM NO.1, JL 1963- 13,
D 1966. SUBS: EDUCATIONAL BROADCASTING
INTERNATIONAL.
ED/N-1.    LD/U-2.    LO/N17.
GL/U-2. 2, 1968-

**EDV IN MEDIZIN UND BIOLOGIE.**
+ +EDV MED. & BIOL.
[FISCHER; ULMER]
STUTTGART 1970-
LO/N14.

**E.E.C. BEEF & VEAL CIRCULAR.**
UNIVERSITY OF EXETER: DEPARTMENT OF
AGRICULTURAL ECONOMICS.
EXETER NO.1, JA 1969-
M.
CA/U11.    MA/P-1.    OX/U24.*
ED/N-1. NO.3, MR 1969-

**EEF NEWS.**
ENGINEERING EMPLOYERS' FEDERATION.
LONDON 1, S 1969-
ED/N-1.    OX/U-1.    OX/U16.

**EEG-EMG.  ZEITSCHRIFT FUR ELEKTROENZEPHALO-
GRAPHIE, ELEKTROMYOGRAPHIE UND VERWANDTE
GEBIETE.**
[THIEME]
STUTTGART 1, 1970-
LO/N13.

**E.E.N.T. DIGEST.**    XXX
SUBS (1971): PART OF OPHTHALMOLOGY DIGEST; &
O.R.L. DIGEST.

**EESTI NSV TRUKITOODANGU STATISTIKA. STATIST-
IKA PECHATI ESTONSKOJ SSR.**
+ +EESTI NSV TRUKITOODANGU STAT.
(ESTONIAN SSR) RIIKLIK RAAMATUPALAT.
TALLINN 1961/1962(1963)-
ESTON. & RUSS.
BH/U-1.    CC/U-1.    OX/U-1.

**EFFEKTIVNOST' UDOBRENIJ V USLOVIJAKH MOLDAVII.**
+ +EFF. UDOBR. USLOVIJAKH MOLD.  [EUVM-A]
MOLDAVSKIJ NAUCHNO-ISSLEDOVATEL'SKIJ INSTITUT
POCHVOVEDENIJA I AGROKHIMII.
KISHINEV [1], 1961-
VOL.1 UNNUMBERED.
LO/N13. 5, 1970-
ISSN 0424-6551

**E.G.**
NORWICH SCHOOL OF ART: DEPARTMENT OF GRAPHIC
DESIGN.
NORWICH 1, 1968-
ED/N-1.

**EGLISE CANADIENNE. DOCUMENTS ET INFORMATIONS.**
+ +EGLISE CAN.
[EDITIONS FIDES]
MONTREAL 1(1), JA 1968-
MON.
LO/N-1.
ISSN 0013-2322

**EGLISE ET THEOLOGIE.**
+ +EGLISE & THEOL.
ST. PAUL UNIVERSITY: FACULTY OF THEOLOGY.
OTTAWA 1(1), 1970-
ENGL. OR FR.
LO/N-1.
ISSN 0013-2349

**EGYPTIAN JOURNAL OF GENETICS & CYTOLOGY.**
+ +EGYPT. J. GENET. & CYTOL.
EGYPTIAN SOCIETY OF GENETICS.
ALEXANDRIA 1, 1972-
2/A.
AD/U-1.    CA/U15.    LO/N-2.    LO/N13.    SW/U-1.
ISSN 0046-161X

**EGYPTOLOGY TITLES.**    XXX
+ +EGYPTOL. TITLES.
UNIVERSITY OF CAMBRIDGE: FACULTY OF ORIENTAL
STUDIES.
CAMBRIDGE NO.1, 1972-
SPONS. BODY ALSO BROOKLYN MUSEUM: WILBOUR
LIBRARY OF EGYPTOLOGY. TWO PRELIMINARY LISTS
ISSUED IN 1971. PREV: WILBOUR LIBRARY OF
EGYPTOLOGY ACQUISITIONS LIST.
CA/U-1.    ED/N-1.    LO/U-2.

**EIKON.**
[EIKON P.]
*PORTSMOUTH, N.H. 1(1), 1967-*
*LO/U-2.   OX/U-1.*

**EINSHTEINOVSKIJ SBORNIK.**
*+ +EINSHTEINOVSKIJ SB. [EINS-A]*
AKADEMIJA NAUK SSSR: EINSHTEINOVSKIJ KOMITET.
*MOSCOW 1966-*
ANNU.
*LO/N13.*
*ISSN 0424-7035*

**EKOLOGIA POLSKA: SERIA B.**                                     XXX
SUBS (1970): WIADOMOSCI EKOLOGICZNE.

**EKOLOGIJA.**
AKADEMIJA NAUK SSSR.
*SVERDLOVSK 1(1), 1970-*
2M.
*LO/N13.   OX/U-8.*
*LO/N-2. 3, 1971-*

**EKOLOGIJA (ENGL. TRANSL.).**                                    000
SEE: ECOLOGY. TRANSLATION OF EKOLOGIJA.

**EKONOMICHESKAJA NAUKA I KHOZJAJSTVENNAJA**
**PRAKTIKA.**
*+ +EKON. NAUK. & KHOZ. PRAKT.*
[EKONOMICHESKIJ EZHEGODNIK]
*MOSCOW 1965-*
A. TITLE VARIES: EKONOMICHESKIJ EZHEGODNIK:
EKONOMICHESKAJA NAUKA I KHOZJAJSTVENNAJA
PRAKTIKA.
*BH/U-1.   OX/U-1.   SW/U-1.*
*CC/U-1. 1966-*
*XW/C-3. 1965.*
*ISSN 0424-7310*

**EKONOMICHESKIJ EZHEGODNIK.**                                    000
SEE: EKONOMICHESKAJA NAUKA I KHOZJAJSTVENNAJA
PRAKTIKA.

**EKONOMIKA I KUL'TURA LITOVSKOJ SSR.**
*+ +EKON. & KUL'T. LITOV. SSR.*
(LITHUANIA) CENTRINE STATISTIKOS VALDYBA.
*VILNIUS 1963(1964)-*
ANNU. S/T: STATISTICHESKIJ EZHEGODNIK.
*BH/U-1.   CC/U-1.   GL/U-1.   LO/U-3.   LO/U15.   OX/U-1.*
*SW/U-1.*

**EKONOMIKA NEFTEDOBYVAJUSHCHEJ PROMYSHLENNOSTI.**
*+ +EKON. NEFTEDOBYVAJUSHCHEJ PROM-ST.*
VSESOJUZNYJ NAUCHNO-ISSLEDOVATEL'SKIJ INSTITUT
ORGANIZATSII, UPRAVLENIJA I EKONOMIKI NEFTE-
GAZOVOJ PROMYSHLENNOSTI.
*MOSCOW 1966-*
*LO/N13. 1967-*
*ISSN 0028-1158*

**EKONOMIKA I ORGANIZATSIJA SIL'S'KOHO HOSPOD-**
**ARSTVA.**
*+ +EKON. & ORG. SIL'S'KOHO HOSPOD.*
(UKRAINE) MINISTERSTVO SIL'S'KOHO HOSPODARSTVA.
*KIEV 1, 1964-*
S/T: RESPUBLIKANS'KYJ MIZHVIDOMCHYJ TEMA-
TYCHNYJ NAUKOVYJ ZBIRNYK.  VOLS. 10- 13 (1967)
PUBL. AS:  EKONOMIKA I ORGANIZATSIJA SEL'
SKOGO KHOZJAJSTVA.  RESPUBLIKANSKIJ MEZH-
VEDOMSTVENNYJ TEMATICHESKIJ NAUCHNYJ SBORNIK.
*BH/U-1. 11, 1967-          CC/U-1. 10, 1967-*
*ISSN 0424-7418*

**EKONOMIKO-MATEMATICHESKIE METODY.**
*+ +EKON.-MAT. METODY. [EMTM-B]*
AKADEMIJA NAUK SSSR: NAUCHNYJ SOVET PO PRIMEN-
ENIJU MATEMATICHESKIKH METODOV I VYCHISLITEL-
'NOJ TEKHNIKI V EKONOMICHESKIKH ISSLEDOVANIJAKH
I PLANIROVANII.
*MOSCOW 1, 1963-*
*LO/U-3.*
*ISSN 0424-7477*

**EKONOMIKO-MATEMATICHESKIE MODELI.**
*+ +EKON.-MAT. MODELI.*
AKADEMIJA NAUK SSSR: TSENTRAL'NYJ EKONOMIKO-
MATEMATICHESKIJ INSTITUT.
*MOSCOW 2, 1969-*
*BH/U-1.   CC/U-1.*
*ISSN 0531-7940*

**EKONOMSKA MISAO.**
*+ +EKON. MISAO.*
SAVEZ EKONOMISTA SR SRBIJE ZA PITANJA EKONOMSKE
TEORIJE I PRAKSE.
*BELGRADE 1(1), 1968-*
*OX/U-1. 3(1), 1970-*
*ISSN 0013-323X*

**EKRAN.**                                                        XXX
[IZDATEL'STVO ISKUSSTVO]
*MOSCOW 1964-*
A. PREV: EZHEGODNIK KINO FROM 1955- 1963.
*HL/U-1.*
*CC/U-1. 1970-*
*LO/U15. 1968- 1971.*
*ISSN 0424-7582*

**EKSPERIMENTAL'NAJA KHIRURGIJA I ANESTEZIOLOG-**
**IJA (ENGL. TRANSL.).**                                          000
SEE: EXPERIMENTAL SURGERY & ANESTHESIOLOGY.

**ELDO-ESRO SCIENTIFIC & TECHNICAL REVIEW.**                      XXX
EUROPEAN SPACE RESEARCH ORGANIZATION.
[GAUTHIER-VILLARS]
*PARIS 2, 1970-*
PREV: ELDO/ESRO TECHNICAL REVIEW FROM 1, 1969.
*LO/N14.*

**ELDO/ESRO TECHNICAL REVIEW. = REVUE TECHNIQUE**
**CECLES/CERS.**
*+ +ELDO/ESRO TECH. REV.*
EUROPEAN SPACE RESEARCH ORGANISATION.
[GAUTHIER-VILLARS]
*PARIS 1, 1969 ...*
SPONS. BODY ALSO: EUROPEAN SPACE RESEARCH
ORGANISATION. SUBS: ELDO/ESRO SCIENTIFIC &
TECHNICAL REVIEW.
*BL/U-1.   LD/U-1.   LO/N-5.*
*OX/U-8. 1(2), 1969-*
*ISSN 0013-4090*

**ELECTRA.**                                                      XXX
INTERNATIONAL CONFERENCE ON LARGE ELECTRONIC
SYSTEMS.
*PARIS NO.1, 1967-*
ENGL., FR. BODY NAMED IN FR.: CONFERENCE
INTERNATIONALE DES GRANDS RESEAUX ELECTRIQUES
A HAUTE TENSION. PREV SERIES UNDER ABOVE
TITLE: NO.1, 1931- 13, 1933; NO.1, 1946.
*LO/N14.*

**ELECTRIC COMFORT CONDITIONING JOURNAL.**                        XXX
*+ +ELEC. COMFORT COND. J.*
[ELECTRICAL INFORMATION PUBL.]
*MADISON, WIS. 16, 1970-*
PREV: ELECTRIC HEATING JOURNAL FROM 1, 1957.
*LO/N14.*

**ELECTRIC HEATING JOURNAL.**                                     XXX
SUBS (1970): ELECTRIC COMFORT CONDITIONING
JOURNAL.

**ELECTRICAL DESIGN NEWS.**                                       XXX
SUBS (1962): EDN. ELECTRICAL DESIGN NEWS.

**ELECTRICAL & ELECTRONICS MANUFACTURER.**                        XXX
*+ +ELECTR. & ELECTRON. MANUF. [EEMA-B]*
[TRADE NEWS LTD.]
*LONDON 10(1), MY 1966- 15(1), 1971 ...*
PREV: ELECTRICAL MANUFACTURER. SUBS:
ELECTRONICS MANUFACTURER.
*LO/N14.*

**ELECTRICAL & ELECTRONICS TECHNICIAN ENGINEER.**                 XXX
*+ +ELEC. & ELECTRON. TECH. ENG.*
INSTITUTION OF ELECTRICAL & ELECTRONICS TECH-
NICIAN ENGINEERS.
*LONDON 1, 1966- 7(3), 1972.*
2M. SUBS: ELECTROTECHNOLOGY (LONDON).
*BL/U-1. 3, 1968-          LO/N-7. 6(1), 1971-*
*LO/N14. 4(2), 1969-       OX/U-8. 5(1), 1970-*
*ISSN 0013-421X*

**ELECTRICAL MANUFACTURER.**                                      XXX
SUBS (1966): ELECTRICAL & ELECTRONICS
MANUFACTURER.

**ELECTRICAL WEST.**                                              XXX
*+ +ELECTR. WEST. [ELEW-A]*
[MILLER FREEMAN PUBL.]
*SAN FRANCISCO 1, 1887- 137(7), 1970.//*
*LO/N14. 131, 1964-*

**ELECTRICITE ELECTRONIQUE MODERNE: EDITION**
**ORANGE: MEDICAL.**
*+ +ELECTR. ELECTRON. MOD., ED. ORANGE, MED.*
*PARIS 1, 1971-*
*LO/N14.*

**ELECTRO OPTICS.**
*+ +ELECTRO OPT.*
[MILTON PUBL. CO.]
*LONDON 1, 1971-*
*BL/U-1.   ED/N-1.   LO/N-4.   LO/N14.   OX/U-8.*
*XS/R10. 2(7), 1972-*
*ISSN 0013-4589*

**ELECTROCHEMISTRY. A SPECIALIST PERIODICAL REPORT.**
CHEMICAL SOCIETY.
*LONDON 1, 1970-*
*LO/S-3.    LO/U-2.    LO/U13.    MA/U-1.    NW/U-1.    RE/U-1.*
*XS/R10.*
*ISSN 0305-9979*

**ELECTRODEPOSITION & SURFACE TREATMENT.**
++*ELECTRODEPOSIT. & SURF. TREAT.*
[ELSEVIER SEQUOIA]
*LAUSANNE 1, 1972-*
*LO/N14.    LO/N35.*

**ELECTRODIAGNOSTIC-THERAPIE. REVUE EUROPEENE D'ELECTROPHYSIOLOGIE APPLIQUEE.**
++*ELECTRODIAGN.-THER.*
*CHARLEROI 1, 1964-*
Q. RUNNING TITLE: REVUE ELECTRODIAGNOSTIC-
THERAPIE.
*LO/N13. 2, 1965-*
*ISSN 0424-8120*

**ELECTROMYOGRAPHY & CLINICAL NEUROPHYSIOLOGY.**    XXX
++*ELECTROMYOGR. & CLIN. NEUROPHYSIOL.*
UNIVERSITE CATHOLIQUE DE LOUVAIN: EMG
LABORATORY.
*LOUVAIN 12, 1972-*
PREV: ELECTROMYOGRAPHY FROM 1, 1961- 11, 1971.
*BL/U-1.*

**ELECTRON (MONTREAL).**
[TOMAR PUBL.]
*MONTREAL 1, 1964-*
MON.
*LO/N14. 5, 1968-*
*ISSN 0013-4759*

**ELECTRON. JOURNAL FOR ENGINEERS & MANAGERS IN ELECTRONICS.**
[IPC ELECTRICAL-ELECTRONIC P. LTD.]
*LONDON NO.1, AP 1972-*
2W.
*CA/U-1.    ED/N-1.    LO/N14.*

**ELECTRON SPIN RESONANCE.**
++*ELECTRON SPIN RESON.*
CHEMICAL SOCIETY.
*LONDON 1, 1973-*
*BH/U-3.    CA/U-1.    ED/N-1.    HL/U-1.    LO/N14.    LO/S-3.*
*LO/U-2.    LO/U12.    MA/U-1.    RE/U-1.*
*ISSN 0305-9758*

**ELECTRON TECHNOLOGY.**
++*ELECTRON TECHNOL.*
INSTYTUT TECHNOLOGII ELEKTRONOWEJ (WARSAW).
[POLISH SCIENTIFIC PUBL.]
*WARSAW 1, 1968-*
Q.
*LO/N-7.**    XY/N-1.*
*LO/N13. 2, 1969-*
*ISSN 0070-9816*

**ELECTRONIC CERAMICS.**    000
SEE: EREKUTORONIKU SERAMIKUSU.

**ELECTRONIC INSTRUMENT DIGEST.**
++*ELECTRON. INSTRUM. DIG.*
[KIVER PUBL.]
*CHICAGO 1, 1965- 7(7), 1971...*
SUBS: ELECTRONIC INSTRUMENTATION.
*LO/N14. 3, 1967-*
*ISSN 0013-4929*

**ELECTRONIC INSTRUMENTATION.**    XXX
++*ELECTRON. INSTRUM.*
[KIVER]
*CHICAGO 7(8), 1971- 8, 1972.//*
PREV: ELECTRONIC INSTRUMENT DIGEST FROM 1,
1965- 7(7), 1971.
*LO/N14.**

**ELECTRONIC MATERIALS & PARTS (TOKYO).**    000
SEE: DENSHI ZAIRYO.

**ELECTRONIC PARTS & MATERIALS (TOKYO).**    000
SEE: DENSHI ZAIRYO.

**ELECTRONIC PRODUCTS OF JAPAN.**
++*ELECTRON. PROD. JAP.*
[JAPAN OVERSEAS PUBL. INC.]
*TOKYO 1, 1967-*
*LO/N14.*

**ELECTRONIC STRUCTURE & MAGNETISM OF INORGANIC COMPOUNDS.**
++*ELECTRON. STRUCT. & MAGN. INORG. COMPD.*
CHEMICAL SOCIETY.
*LONDON 1, 1970-*
S/T: A REVIEW OF THE LITERATURE.
*BH/U-3.    BL/U-1.    ED/N-1.    GL/U-2.    LO/N-4.    LO/N14.*
*LO/S-3.    LO/U12.    MA/U-1.    NW/U-1.    SF/U-1.*
*RE/U-1.*
*ISSN 0305-9766*

**ELECTRONICS & COMMUNICATIONS ABSTRACTS JOURNAL.**    XXX
++*ELECTRON. & COMMUN. ABSTR. J.*
[CAMBRIDGE SCIENTIFIC ABSTRACTS, INC.]
*RIVERDALE, MD. 4(1), 1972-*
PREV: ELECTRONICS ABSTRACTS JOURNAL FROM 1,
1966- 3, 1972.
*BN/U-2.    LO/N14.    LO/N35.    XS/R10.*

**ELECTRONICS & INSTRUMENTATION.**    XXX
++*ELECTRON. & INSTRUM.*
[THOMSON PUBL. S.A.]
*JOHANNESBURG 1, 1970-*
INCORP: ELECTRONICS IN SOUTHERN AFRICA FROM
1, 1967- 3(4), 1970; & INSTRUMENTATION, ELEC-
TRONICS & NUCLEONICS FROM 1, ?1969- 2, 1970.
*LO/N14.*
*ISSN 0013-5186*

**ELECTRONICS MANUFACTURER. JOURNAL OF CIRCUIT PROCESS TECHNOLOGY.**    XXX
++*ELECTRON. MANUF.*
[TRADE NEWS LTD.]
*LONDON 15(2), 1971-*
PREV: ELECTRICAL & ELECTRONICS MANUFACTURER
FROM 10(1), MY 1966- 15(1), 1971.
*LO/N14.*

**ELECTRONICS MATERIALS REVIEW.**
++*ELECTRON. MATER. REV.*
NOYES DEVELOPMENT CORPORATION.
*PARKRIDGE, N.J. NO.1, 1969- 12, 1971. //*
*LO/N14.*

**ELECTRONICS POST.**    XXX
++*ELECTRON. POST. [ELPS-A]*
E.M.I. ELECTRONICS, LTD.
*HAYES, MIDDX. SPRING 1960- NO.23, SUMMER
1969.//*
*LO/N13.*

**ELECTRONICS IN SOUTHERN AFRICA.**    XXX
++*ELECTRON. SOUTH. AFR.*
SOUTH AFRICAN INSTITUTE OF ELECTRONIC & RADIO
ENGINEERS.
[THOMSON NEWSPAPERS SOUTH AFRICA (PTY) LTD.]
*CAPE TOWN 1, 1967- 3(4), 1970.*
SUBS. PART OF: ELECTRONICS & INSTRUMENTATION.
*LO/U14. 1(5), 1968-**

**ELECTRONICS TODAY INTERNATIONAL.**
++*ELECTRON. TODAY INT.*
[WHITEHALL P. LTD.]
*LONDON 1(1), AP 1972-*
MON.
*CA/U-1.    ED/N-1.    LO/N14.*

**ELECTRONICS WORLD.**    XXX
SUBS (1972): POPULAR ELECTRONICS INCLUDING
ELECTRONICS WORLD.

**ELECTRO-OPTICAL SYSTEMS DESIGN.**
++*ELECTRO-OPT. SYST. DES.*
[MILTON S. KIVER PUBL.]
*CHICAGO 1(1), JL/AG 1969-*
2M.
*LO/N14. 2, 1970-**

**ELECTROSTATICS ABSTRACTS.**
++*ELECTROSTAT. ABSTR.*
ELECTRICAL RESEARCH ASSOCIATION.
*LEATHERHEAD 1, 1971-*
*ED/N-1.    LO/N14.    OX/U-8.    XY/N-1.*
*ISSN 0046-1768*

**ELECTROTECHNOLOGY (LONDON).**    XXX
INSTITUTION OF ELECTRICAL & ELECTRONICS TECH-
NICIAN ENGINEERS.
*LONDON 1, 1973-*
PREV: ELECTRICAL & ELECTRONICS TECHNICIAN
ENGINEER FROM 1, 1966- 7(3), 1972.
*ED/N-1.    LO/N14.    LO/N35.*

**ELECTRO-TECHNOLOGY NEWSLETTER.**
+ +ELECTRO-TECHNOL. NEWSL.
  BEVERLY SHORES, IND.  85(5), 1970-
  PREV: ELECTRO-TECHNOLOGY FROM 66(4), 1960-
  85(4), 1970.
  LO/N14.*

**ELEGANCE SUISSE.**
  SCHWEIZERISCHE ZENTRALE FUR HANDELSFORDERUNG.
  LAUSANNE NR.1, 1968-
  ISSUED AS SUPPLEMENT TO:  TEXTILES SUISSES.
  LO/N13.
  ISSN 0013-5356

**ELEKTRO.  ELECKTOTEKNISK TIDSSKRIFT.**                       XXX
  [INGENIORFORLAGET]
  OSLO  83, 1970-
  PREV: ELEKTROTEKNISK TIDSSKRIFT FROM 1, 1888-
  82, 1969.
  LO/N14.
  ISSN 0013-550X

**ELEKTRO-STANDARD.**                                          XXX
  SUBS (1968): RATIO.

**ELEKTROENERGETIKA I AVTOMATIKA.**
+ +ELEKTROENERG. & AVTOM.
  AKADEMIJA NAUK MOLDAVSKOJ SSR: OTDEL
  ENERGETICHESKOJ KIBERNETIKI.
  KISHINEV  1, 1965-
  LO/N13.
  ISSN 0424-8534

**ELEKTROENERGIJA, MINISTERSTVO NA ELEKTRIFIKAT-**
**SIJATA (BULGARIA).**
  SUBS (1966): ENERGETIKA (SOFIA).

**ELEKTROFIZICHESKAJA APPARATURA.**
+ +ELEKTROFIZ. APPAR.
  NAUCHNO-ISSLEDOVATEL'SKIJ INSTITUT ELEKTROFIZI-
  CHESKOJ APPARATURY [IM. D.V. EFREMOVA].
  MOSCOW  1, 1963-
  XS/R10.
  LO/N13.  4, 1966-
  ISSN 0422-9398

**ELEKTROMASHINOSTROENIE I ELEKTROOBORUDOVANIE.**
+ +ELEKTROMASHINOST. & ELEKTROOBORUDOVANIE.
  ODESSKIJ POLITEKHNICHESKIJ INSTITUT.
  KHAR'KOV VYP. 1, 1965-
  S/T: RESPUBLIKANSKIJ, MEZHVUDOMSTVENNYJ,
  NAUCHNO-TEKHNICHESKIJ SBORNIK.
  LO/N13. VYP. 2, 1966-
  ISSN 0424-8589

**ELEKTRONIKA.**
  POLSKA AKADEMIA NAUK: KOMITET ELEKTRONIKI I
  TELEKOMUNIKACJI.                                             XXX
  WARSAW  11(1), 1970-
  PREV: PRZEGLAD ELEKTRONIKI FROM 1(1), 1960-
  10(12), 1969.
  LO/N14.   XS/R10.
  ISSN 0033-2089

**ELEKTRONIKER.**
  [AG AARGAUER TAGBLATT]
  AARAU  1, 1961-
  FROM 7(6), 1968- CONTAINS SUPPLEMENT:  ELEK-
  TRONIK INFORMATIONEN.
  LO/N14.
  ISSN 0531-9218

**ELEKTRONNYE I IONNYE PROTSESSY V TVERDYKH**
**TELAKH.**
+ +ELEKTRONNYE & IONNYE PROTSESSY TVERD. TELAKH.
  [EIPT-A]
  AKADEMIJA NAUK GRUZINSKOJ SSR: INSTITUT FIZIKI.
  TIFLIS  1, 1964-
  LO/N13.  1968-
  ISSN 0424-8694

**ELEMENTS.**
  DOW CHEMICAL EUROPE.
  ZURICH NO.1, 1969-
  ALSO FR., GER., ITAL. & DUTCH EDITIONS.
  BL/U-1.   OX/U-8.

**ELEMENTS, PRODUITS, SERVICES.**
+ +ELEM., PROD., SERV.(FR.).
  [EDITIONS LOGITEC]
  PARIS NO.1, 1969-
  LO/N14.
  ISSN 0013-6026

**ELIZABETH.**                                                 XXX
  [ELIZABETH P.]
  NEW ROCHELLE, N.Y.  1, MR 1961- 18, D 1971.//
  S/T: A MAGAZINE OF MODERN ELIZABETHAN & META-
  PHYSICAL POETRY.
  OX/U-1.
  ISSN 0013-6247

**ELM NEWSLETTER.**                                            XXX
+ +ELM NEWSL.
  FORESTRY COMMISSION (GB).
  LONDON  NO.1, JE 1972-
  S/T: A PERIODIC ROUNDUP ABOUT DUTCH ELM
  DISEASE.
  CA/U-1.   ED/N-1.   LO/N-1.   OX/U-3.

**ELTEKNIK.**                                                  XXX
  SUBS (1972): ELTEKNIK MED AKTUELL ELEKTRONIK.

**ELTEKNIK MED AKTUELL ELEKTRONIK.**                           XXX
+ +ELTEK. AKTUELL ELECTRON.
  SVENSKA ELEKTROINGENJORERS RIKSFORENING.
  STOCKHOLM 15(9), 1972-
  PREV: EKTEKNIK FROM 1, 1958- 15(7/8), 1972.
  LO/N14.

**EMAJL.  KERAMIKA-STAKLO.**
  UDRUZENJE EMAJLIRACA JUGOSLAVIJE.
  ZAGREB  1(1), 1965-
  GER. SUMM.
  LO/N13. 5(16), 1969-
  ISSN 0013-6506

**EMBASSY.  INTERNATIONAL MAGAZINE FOR THE**
**DIPLOMATIC WORLD.**
  [NOVEL PUBL. LTD.]
  LONDON  1(1), 1971-
  M.
  ED/N-1.
  ISSN 0046-1857

**EMBRYOLOGIA.**                                               XXX
  SUBS (1969): DEVELOPMENT, GROWTH & DIFFERENT-
  IATION.

**EMERSON SOCIETY QUARTERLY.**                                 XXX
  SUBS (1972): E.S.Q.

**ENCHORIA.  ZEITSCHRIFT FUR DEMOTISTIK UND**
**KOPTOLOGIE.**
  WIESBADEN  1, 1971-
  ANNU.
  CA/U-1.   LO/N-1.

**ENDOCRINOLOGIA EXPERIMENTALIS.**
+ +ENDOCRINOL. EXP.
  SLOVENSKA AKADEMIA VIED: ENDOCRINOLOGICKY
  USTAV.
  BRATISLAVA  1, 1964-
  VARIOUS LANGUAGES.
  XS/R12.
  OX/U-8. 5(3), 1971-
  ISSN 0013-7200

**ENDOCRINOLOGY INDEX.**
+ +ENDOCRINOL. INDEX.
  NATIONAL INSTITUTE OF ARTHRITIS & METABOLIC
  DISEASES (U.S.).
  WASHINGTON, D.C.  1, JA/F 1968-
  6/A. SPONS. BODY ALSO NATIONAL INSTITUTES OF
  HEALTH (U.S.), & (UNITED STATES) DEPARTMENT
  OF HEALTH, EDUCATION & WELFARE: PUBLIC HEALTH
  SERVICE.
  CR/M-1.   LO/N13.   LO/U-1.
  OX/U-8. 2, 1969-            SO/U-1. 2, 1969-
  ISSN 0013-7235

**ENDOSCOPY.**
  [THIEME]
  STUTTGART  1(1), AP 1969-
  ENGL. OR GER. WITH ENGL. SUMM.
  OX/U-8.
  ISSN 0013-726X

**ENERGETIKA (SOFIA).**                                        XXX
  (BULGARIA) MINISTERSTVO NA ENERGETIKATA I
  GORIVATA.
  SOFIA  17(1), 1966-
  GER. & RUSS. SUMM. & CONT. LISTS.  PREV:
  ELEKTROENERGIJA, MINISTERSTVO NA ELEKTRIFIK-
  ATSIJATA (BULGARIA) FROM 1(1), 1950- 16, 1965.
  LO/N13.
  ISSN 0424-9860

**ENERGETIKA I ELEKTRIFIKATSIJA.**                                          XXX
+ +*ENERG. & ELEKTRIF.*
NAUCHNO-TEKHNICHESKOE OBSHCHESTVO ENERGOPROMY-
SHLENNOSTI UKRAINSKOJ SSR: OBLSTNYE PRAVLENIJA.
*KIEV NO.1(25), 1966-*
S/T: NAUCHNOPROIZVODSTVENNYJ SBORNIK. PREV:
ENERGETIKA I ELEKTROTEKHNICHESKAJA PROMYSH-
LENNOST' FROM NO.1, 1960- 24, 1965.
*LO/N13.*
*ISSN 0424-9879*

**ENERGETIKA I ELEKTROTEKHNICHESKAJA PROMYSHLEN-
NOST'.**                                                                    XXX
+ +*ENERG. & ELEKTROTEK. PROM-ST.*
GOSUDARSTVENNYJ KOMITET SOVETA MINISTROV
UKRAINSKOJ SSR PO KOORDINATSII NAUCHNO-ISSLE-
DOVATEL'SKIKH RABOT: INSTITUT TEKHNICHESKOJ
INFORMATSII.
*KIEV NO.1, 1960- 24, 1965 ...*
S/T: NAUCHNO-TEKHNICHESKIJ SBORNIK. SUBS:
ENERGETIKA I ELEKTRIFIKATSIJA.
*ISSN 0423-1120*

**ENERGIE FLUIDE, HYDRAULIQUE, PNEUMATIQUE,
ASSERVISSEMENTS, LUBRIFICATION.**                                           XXX
+ +*ENERG. FLUIDE HYDRAUL. PNEUM. ASSERVISSEMENTS
LUBRIF.*
[UNION FRANCAISE DE PUBLICATIONS TECHNIQUES]
*PARIS 11(46), 1972-*
PREV: ENERGIE FLUIDE ET LUBRIFICATION + HYDR-
AULIQUE, PNEUMATIQUE ET ASSERVISSEMENTS FROM
NO.43, 1968- 10(45), 1971.
*LO/N14.*

**ENERGIE FLUIDE ET LUBRIFICATION.**                                        XXX
+ +*ENERG. FLUIDE & LUBRIF.*
SOCIETE DE PUBLICATIONS MECANIQUES.
*PARIS 1, 1962- 6(63), 1967.*
SUBS: ENERGIE FLUIDE ET LUBRIFICATION + HYDR-
AULIQUE, PNEUMATIQUE ET ASSERVISSEMENTS.
*LO/N14.*

**ENERGIE FLUIDE ET LUBRIFICATION + HYDRAULIQUE,
PNEUMATIQUE ET ASSERVISSEMENTS.**                                           XXX
+ +*ENERG. FLUIDE & LUBRIF. + HYDRAUL. PNEUM. &
ASSERVISSEMENTS.*
SYNDICAT DES CONSTRUCTEURS DE TRANSMISSIONS
HYDRAULIQUES ET PNEUMATIQUES.
[UNION FRANCAISE DE PUBLICATIONS TECHNIQUES]
*PARIS NO.43, 1968- 10(45), 1971 ...*
PREV: ENERGIE FLUIDE ET LUBRIFICATION FROM
1, 1962- 6(63), 1967; & HYDRAULIQUE, PNEUM-
ATIQUE & ASSERVISSEMENTS FROM NO.7, 1964- 42,
1967. SPONSORED BY ABOVE BODY FROM 1969.
SUBS: ENERGIE FLUIDE, HYDRAULIQUE, PNEUMATIQUE
ASSERVISSEMENTS, LUBRIFICATION.
*LO/N14.*
*ISSN 0013-7367*

**ENERGY & CHARACTER. THE JOURNAL OF BIOENERGETIC
RESEARCH.**
*ABBOTSBURY, DORSET 1(1), 1970-*
*OX/U-8.*
*ED/N-1. 2, 1971-*
*ISSN 0013-7472*

**ENERGY CONVERSION.**                                                      XXX
+ +*ENERGY CONVERS.*
[PERGAMON]
*OXFORD 8(1), AG 1968-*
PREV: ADVANCED ENERGY CONVERSION FROM 1, 1961-
7, 1968.
*GL/U-1.    LO/N14.    OX/U-8.*
*ISSN 0013-7480*

**ENERGY CONVERSION DIGEST.**                                               XXX
+ +*ENERGY CONVERS. DIG.*
[INDUSTRY REPORTS INC.]
*WASHINGTON, D.C. 5(10), N 1966-*
PREV: DIRECT ENERGY CONVERSION DIGEST FROM
1, F 1962- 5(9), 1966.
*XS/R10.*

**ENERGY DIGEST (LONDON).**                                                 XXX
+ +*ENERGY DIG. (LOND.).*
[TURRET P.]
*LONDON 1, 1972-*
PREV: JOURNAL OF FUEL & HEAT TECHNOLOGY FROM
14(7), 1966- 19(3), 1972.
*ED/N-1.    LD/U-1.    LO/N14.    OX/U-1.    SF/U-1.*

**ENERGY POLICY.**
[IPC SCIENCE & TECHNOLOGY P. LTD.]
*GUILDFORD 1, 1973-*
*Q.*
*BH/U-3.    CA/U-1.    ED/N-1.    EX/U-1.    GL/U-2.    HL/U-1.*
*LD/U-1.    LO/N14.    LO/U-2.    LO/U-3.    LO/U12.    MA/U-1.*
*SF/U-1.    SH/U-1.    SW/U-1.    XS/R10.*
*ISSN 0301-4215*

**ENERGY WORLD.**
INSTITUTE OF FUEL.
*LONDON NO.1, 1973-*
*BH/U-3.    CA/U-1.    ED/N-1.    EX/U-1.    GL/U-1.    GL/U-2.*
*LD/U-1.    LO/N14.    MA/U-1.    SF/U-1.    SH/P-1.    SH/U-3.*
*SO/U-1.    XS/R10.*

**ENGELHARDTIA.**
LONG ISLAND HERPETOLOGICAL SOCIETY.
*NEW YORK 1, 1968-*
*Q.*
*LO/N-2.*

**ENGINEERING & BOILERHOUSE REVIEW.**                                       XXX
SUBS (1969): PART OF WORKS ENGINEERING &
FACTORY SERVICES.

**ENGINEERING CYBERNETICS.**
+ +*ENG. CYBERN.*
[SCRIPTA TECHNICA INC.]
*WASHINGTON, D.C. 1, 1968-*
ENGL. TRANSL. OF TEKHNICHESKAYA KIBERNETIKA.
*LO/N-4.*
*ISSN 0013-788X*

**ENGINEERING EDUCATION.**                                                  XXX
+ +*ENG. EDUC.*
AMERICAN SOCIETY FOR ENGINEERING EDUCATION.
*WASHINGTON, D.C. 60, 1969/70(1969)-*
PREV: JOURNAL OF ENGINEERING EDUCATION FROM
NS. 15, 1924.
*BH/U-1.    LO/N13.    SF/U-1.*
*ISSN 0022-0809*

**ENGINEERING FRACTURE MECHANICS.**
+ +*ENG. FRACTURE MECH.*
[PERGAMON PRESS]
*OXFORD &C 1, JE 1968-*
*BR/U-3.    ED/N-1.    GL/U-1.    GL/U-2.    LO/N-4.    LO/N14.*
*MA/U-1.    OX/U-8.    SW/U-1.    XS/R10.*
*ISSN 0013-7944*

**ENGINEERING ISSUES.**                                                     XXX
+ +*ENG. ISSUES.*
AMERICAN SOCIETY OF CIVIL ENGINEERS.
*NEW YORK 97, OC 1971-*
PREV: JOURNAL OF PROFESSIONAL ACTIVITIES,
AMERICAN ... FROM 92(2), D 1966.
*GL/U-1.    SO/U-1.*

**ENGINEERING IN MEDICINE.**
+ +*ENG. MED.*
INSTITUTION OF MECHANICAL ENGINEERS: MEDICAL
ENGINEERING WORKING PARTY.
*LONDON 1(1), OC 1971-*
SPONS. BODY ALSO: COMMITTEE FOR RESEARCH INTO
APPARATUS FOR THE DISABLED, NATIONAL FUND FOR
RESEARCH INTO CRIPPLING DISEASES.
*BL/U-1.    GL/U-2.    LD/U-1.    LO/N14.    LO/U28.    SF/U-1.*
*SH/U-3.    SW/U-1.    XS/T-4.*
*ED/N-1. 1(2), 1972-          XS/R10. 1(2), 1972-*
*ISSN 0046-2039*

**ENGINEERING PRODUCTION.**                                                 XXX
+ +*ENG. PROD.*
[ENGINEERING, CHEMICAL & MARINE P. LTD.]
*LONDON 1(1), MR 1970-*
PREV: ENGINEERING NEWS FROM NO.1, 1961- NO.
441, 1970.
*BN/U-2.    ED/N-1.    LO/N-4.    LO/N14.    OX/U-8.    XS/R10.*
*ISSN 0013-8053*

**ENGLISH ELECTRIC JOURNAL.**                                               XXX
SUBS (1969): PART OF JOURNAL OF SCIENCE &
TECHNOLOGY (1969).

**ENGLISH FOR IMMIGRANTS.**                                                 XXX
+ +*ENGL. IMMIGR.*
ASSOCIATION OF TEACHERS OF ENGLISH TO PUPILS
FROM OVERSEAS.
[OXFORD UNIV. PRESS]
*OXFORD 1, SUMMER 1967- 4, 1971.*
ANNU. SUBS: MULTIRACIAL SCHOOL.
*ED/N-1. 2, 1968-*
*ISSN 0013-824X*

ENGLISH LITERARY RENAISSANCE.
+ +ENGL. LIT. RENAISSANCE.
UNIVERSITY OF MASSACHUSETTS: DEPARTMENT OF
ENGLISH.
*AMHERST, MASS. 1, 1971-*
Q.
*CB/U-1.    CV/U-1.    ED/N-1.    ED/N-1.    LO/U-1.    LV/U-1.
NO/U-1.    OX/U-1.    SO/U-1.    YK/U-1.*
*ISSN 0013-8312*

ENLIGHTENMENT ESSAYS.
*CHICAGO  1, 1970-*
S/T: DEVOTED TO STUDIES IN THE HISTORY,
LITERATURE, AND PHILOSOPHY OF THE AMERICAN,
BRITISH AND CONTINENTAL ENLIGHTENMENT.
*ED/N-1.*
*ISSN 0013-8479*

ENQUETES ET DOCUMENTS, CENTRE DE RECHERCHES
SUR L'HISTOIRE DE LA FRANCE ATLANTIQUE, UNIV-
ERSITE DE NANTES.
+ +ENQUETES & DOC. CENT. RECH. HIST. FR. ATL.
*UNIV. NANTES.
NANTES  1, 1971-*
*OX/U-1.*

ENQUIRY.  A QUARTERLY JOURNAL OF LITERATURE &
THE ARTS.
*HONG KONG  1(1), 1967-*
*LO/N-1.*

ENTENTE AFRICAINE.
+ +ENTENTE AFR.
[PRESSE AFRICAINE ASSOCIEE]
*PARIS  NO.1, JL 1969-*
Q.  ENGL.
*BH/U-1.*
*LO/U14.  NO.3, 1970-*
*ISSN 0013-8630*

ENTERPRISE.  THE INDECO JOURNAL.
INDECO LTD.
*LUSAKA  NO.1, 1969-*
*LO/N17.    LO/R-6.    LO/U-3.
LO/U14.  1970-*
*ISSN 0425-0974*

ENTOMOLOGEN.
*LUND  1, 1972-*
*LO/N-2.*

ENTOMOLOGICA SCANDINAVICA.
+ +ENTOMOL. SCAND.
SOCIETAS ENTOMOLOGICA SCANDINAVICA.
*COPENHAGEN  1, 1970-*
*LO/N-2.    LO/N13.*
*ISSN 0013-8711*

ENTOMOLOGY ABSTRACTS.
+ +ENTOMOL. ABSTR.
[INFORMATION RETRIEVAL LTD.]
*LONDON  1, 1969-*
*AD/U-1.    DN/U-1.    EX/U-1.    GL/U-1.    LO/N-2.    LO/N13.
OX/U-8.    SH/U-1.*
*BH/U-1.  2, 1970-*          *ED/N-1.  1(3), 1970-*
*MA/U-1.  2, 1970-*
*ISSN 0013-8924*

ENTOMOLOGY CIRCULAR, DIVISION OF PLANT IND-
USTRY, DEPARTMENT OF AGRICULTURE (FLORIDA).
+ +ENTOMOL. CIRC. DIV. PLANT IND. DEP. AGRIC.
(FLA.).
*GAINESVILLE  NO.1, 1962-*
*LO/N-2.*

ENVIRONMENT & BEHAVIOR.
+ +ENVIRON. & BEHAV. [EVBH-A]
[SAGE PUBL.]
*BEVERLY HILLS, CALIF.  1(1), JE 1969-*
Q.  NOT PUBL. S 1969- MR 1970.
*LO/U-1.    LO/U-3.    LO/U12.    SH/U-1.
GL/U-2.  3, 1971-          LD/U-1.  4, 1972-
LO/U-2.  2, 1970-          MA/U-1.  3, 1971-
NO/U-1.  6, 1974-          SH/C-5.  3, 1971-
BL/U-1.  [W.3, 1971]*
*ISSN 0013-9165*

ENVIRONMENT INDEX.
+ +ENVIRON. INDEX.
ENVIRONMENT INFORMATION CENTER.
*NEW YORK  1, 1971-*
ANNU.  S/T: GUIDE TO THE KEY ENVIRONMENTAL
LITERATURE OF THE YEAR.
*DB/U-2.*
*LO/N14.  2, 1972-          SH/U-1.  3, 1972-*

ENVIRONMENT & INDUSTRY.
+ +ENVIRON. & IND.
[CURRENT PUBL.]
*MAIDENHEAD, BERKS.  NO.1, F 1971-*
MON.
*LO/R-5.    XY/N-1.*
*LO/N14.  [CURRENT BOX ONLY]*

ENVIRONMENT INFORMATION ACCESS.                      XXX
+ +ENVIRON. INF. ACCESS.
ENVIRONMENT INFORMATION CENTER OF ECOLOGY FORUM
*NEW YORK  1, JA 1971- 3, 1973...*
2/W. SUBS: ENVIRONMENT ABSTRACT.
*LO/N13.*

ENVIRONMENT & PLANNING.
+ +ENVIRON. & PLANN.
[PION PUBL.]
*LONDON  1, 1969-*
S/T: INTERNATIONAL JOURNAL OF URBAN & REGIONAL
RESEARCH.
*BL/U-1.    CA/U-1.    ED/N-1.    HL/U-1.    LD/U-1.    LO/N-1.
LO/U-1.    LO/U-2.    LO/U-3.    MA/U-1.    OX/U-1.    RE/U-1.
SH/U-1.    SO/U-1.
GL/U-1.  3(1), 1971-          LO/U20.  2, 1970-
SH/C-5.  3, 1971-
BT/U-1.  1(1), 1969.*
*ISSN 0013-9173*

ENVIRONMENT REPORT.
+ +ENVIRON. REP.
[TRENDS PUBL. INC.]
*WASHINGTON, D.C.  1, MY 1970-*
2/M.
*LO/R-5.*
*ISSN 0013-9205*

ENVIRONMENT SCOTLAND. THE MAGAZINE OF THE ...
+ +ENVIRON. SCOTL.
SCOTTISH CIVIC TRUST.
*GLASGOW  1, 1969-*
*ED/N-1.    OX/U-1.*

ENVIRONMENT THIS MONTH.                              XXX
+ +ENVIRON. THIS MON.
[MTP ENVIRONMENT LTD.]
*LANCASTER  1(1- 2), 1972.*
MON. S/T: THE INTERNATIONAL JOURNAL OF ENVIRON
MENTAL SCIENCE. SUBS: ENVIRONMENT & CHANGE.
*CA/U-1.    ED/N-1.    HL/U-1.    LO/N-2.    LO/N14.    MA/U-1.
XS/R10.*

ENVIRONMENTAL BIOLOGY & MEDICINE.
+ +ENVIRON. BIOL. & MED.
[GORDON & BREACH]
*NEW YORK &C.  1, 1971-*
*ED/N-1.    LO/N-2.    LO/N13.    OX/U-8.    XY/N-1.*
*ISSN 0046-2233*

ENVIRONMENTAL BULLETIN.
+ +ENVIRON. BULL.
UNITED KINGDOM SCIENTIFIC MISSION (US).
*WASHINGTON, D.C.  NO.1, 1971-*
*LO/N-2.    LO/N-4.    LO/U28.    NW/U-1.
LO/R-5.  NO.5, 1971-
LD/U-1.  NO.3, S 1971-
LO/U-3.  [CURRENT ISSUES ONLY]
SO/U-1.  [CURRENT YEAR ONLY]*

ENVIRONMENTAL CONTROL MANAGEMENT.                    XXX
+ +ENVIRON. CONTROL MANAGE.
[A.M. BEST CO.]
*MORRISTOWN, N.J.  138(4), 1969- 139(2), 1970...*
PREV: SAFETY MAINTENANCE FROM 1, 1901. SUBS:
ENVIRONMENTAL CONTROL & SAFETY MANAGEMENT.
*LO/N14.*

ENVIRONMENTAL CONTROL AND SAFETY MANAGEMENT.         XXX
+ +ENVIRON. CONTR. SAF. MANAGE.
[A.M. BEST CO.]
*MORRISTOWN, N.J.  139(3), 1970-*
PREV: ENVIRONMENTAL CONTROL MANAGEMENT FROM
138(4), 1969- 139(2), 1970.
*LO/N14.*
*ISSN 0036-2514*

ENVIRONMENTAL EDUCATION.
+ +ENVIRON. EDUC.
DEMBAR EDUCATIONAL RESEARCH SERVICES.
*MADISON, WIS.  1, 1969-*
Q.
*LO/R-5.*
*CA/U-1.  1972-          HL/U-2.  1972/73-*
*ISSN 0013-9254*

**ENVIRONMENTAL ENTOMOLOGY.**
+ +ENVIRON. ENTOMOL.
ENTOMOLOGICAL SOCIETY OF AMERICA.
COLLEGE PARK, MA. 1, 1972-
LO/N-2.    LO/N13.    LO/R-5.    LO/R-6.
ISSN 0046-225X

**ENVIRONMENTAL FORUM ANTHOLOGY.**
+ +ENVIRON. FORUM ANTHOL.
[ENVIRONMENTAL FORUM]
LONDON NO.1, 1971-
S/T: POETRY, MUSIC, ARCHITECTURE, GRAPHICS.
LO/U-2.

**ENVIRONMENTAL GEOLOGY SERIES, DIVISION OF
GEOLOGY, STATE DEVELOPMENT BOARD (SOUTH
CAROLINA).**
+ +ENVIRON. GEOL. SER. DIV. GEOL. STATE DEV.
BOARD (S.C.)
COLUMBIA, S.C. 1, 1970-
LO/N-2.

**ENVIRONMENTAL GEOLOGY SERIES, DIVISION OF
GEOLOGY (TENNESSEE).**
+ +ENVIRON. GEOL. SER. DIV. GEOL. (TENN.).
NASHVILLE NO.1, 1972-
LO/N-2.

**ENVIRONMENTAL HEALTH (AMSTERDAM).**                    000
SEE: EXCERPTA MEDICA: SECTION 46: ENVIRON-
MENTAL HEALTH.

**ENVIRONMENTAL HEALTH (LONDON).**                    XXX
+ +ENVIRON. HEALTH. (LOND.).
ASSOCIATION OF PUBLIC HEALTH INSPECTORS.
LONDON 77, 1969-
PREV: PUBLIC HEALTH INSPECTOR FROM 73, OC
1964- 76, D 1968.
ED/N-1.    GL/U-1.    LD/U-1.    LO/N14.    RE/U-1.
ISSN 0013-9270

**ENVIRONMENTAL LETTERS.**
+ +ENVIRON. LETT.
[DEKKER]
NEW YORK 1(1), 1971-
DB/U-2.    LO/N14.    LO/R-5.    XY/N-1.
LD/U-1. 3, 1972-    XS/R10. 8(1), 1975-
ISSN 0013-9300

**ENVIRONMENTAL PHYSIOLOGY.**                    XXX
+ +ENVIRON. PHYSIOL.
[MUNKSGAARD]
COPENHAGEN 1, 1971...
Q. S/T: NUTRITION, POLLUTION, TOXICOLOGY.
SUBS : ENVIRONMENTAL PHYSIOLOGY AND
BIOCHEMISTRY.
AD/U-1.    BL/U-1.    CA/U-1.    GL/U-2.    LO/N13.    OX/U-8.
SO/U-1.

**ENVIRONMENTAL POLLUTION.**
+ +ENVIRON. POLLUT.
[ELSEVIER]
LONDON 1, 1970-
AD/U-1.    BL/U-1.    CR/N-1.    DB/U-2.    DN/U-1.    EX/U-1.
GL/U-2.    HL/U-1.    LO/N-2.    LO/N-5.    LO/N13.    LO/U-2.
LO/U12.    NW/U-1.    OX/U-8.    SH/U-1.    SW/U-1.
XS/R10.

**ENVIRONMENTAL POLLUTION MANAGEMENT.**
+ +ENVIRON. POLLUT. MANAGE.
[NATIONAL MAGAZINE CO. LTD.]
LONDON 1, OC 1971-
BH/U-3.**    ED/N-1.    GL/U-2.    SF/U-1.
XS/R10. 3(5), 1973-
NW/U-1. 1(3), D 1971; 2, 1972-

**ENVIRONMENTAL QUALITY.**
+ +ENVIRON. QUAL.
COUNCIL ON ENVIRONMENTAL QUALITY (US).
[ENVIRONMENTAL AWARENESS ASSOCIATES]
LOS ANGELES 1, 1970-
2M.
LD/U-1.    LO/R-5.
LO/N-2. 3, 1972-
ISSN 0013-9335

**ENVIRONMENTAL QUALITY & SAFETY.**
+ +ENVIRON. QUAL. & SAF.
STUTTGART &C. 1, 1972-
CA/U-1.    LO/N14.    OX/U-8.    RE/U-1.

**ENVIRONMENTAL SPACE SCIENCES.**
+ +ENVIRON. SPACE SCI.
[CONSULTANTS BUREAU]
NEW YORK 1(1), JA/F 1967(1968)-
TRANSL. OF KOSMICHESKAJA BIOLOGIJA I MEDITSINA
OX/U-8.    XY/N-1.
ISSN 0013-9378

**ENVIRONMENTAL TEST EQUIPMENT.**
+ +ENVIRON. TEST EQUIP.
SEVENOAKS, KENT NO.1, MY 1968-
2M.
ED/N-1.

**ENVOY. INTERNATIONAL MAGAZINE OF LEISURE.**
[GOURLAY PUBL. LTD.]
LONDON 1(1), MY 1967-
M.
OX/U-1. 1(9-12), 1968.
ISSN 0425-1407

**ENYO SUISAN KENKYUJO KENKYU HOKOKU. BULLETIN,
FAR SEAS' FISHERIES RESEARCH LABORATORY.**
ENYO SUISAN KENKYUJO.
SHIMIZU [NO.]1, 1969-
LO/N-2.    LO/N13.

**ENZYME.**                    XXX
[KARGER]
BASLE 12, 1971-
PREV: ENZYMOLOGIA BIOLOGICA ET CLINICA FROM 1,
1961- 11, 1970.
LO/N13.    LO/U-2.    NW/U-1.
ISSN 0013-9432

**ENZYMOLOGIA.**                    XXX
SUBS (1973): MOLECULAR & CELLULAR BIOCHEMISTRY

**EOLAS.**
(EIRE) GOVERNMENT INFORMATION BUREAU.
DUBLIN 1(1), AP 1972-
ENGL. OR IR.
DB/U-2.    LO/N-1.

**EOS. TRANSACTIONS, AMERICAN GEOPHYSICAL
UNION.**                    XXX
WASHINGTON, D.C. 50, 1969-
PREV: TRANSACTIONS, AMERICAN ... FROM 1, 1920-
49, 1968.
BH/P-1.    RE/U-1.

**EPETERIS.**
CYPRUS RESEARCH CENTRE.
NICOSIA 1, 1967/68-
LO/U-8.
ISSN 0071-0954

**EPHEMERE. REVUE TRIMESTRIELLE.**                    XXX
FONDATION MAEGHT.
PARIS NO.1, 1967- 19/20, 1973. //
BL/U-1.    LO/U13.
ISSN 0013-9483

**EPIDEMIOLOGIJA, MIKROBIOLOGIJA I INFEKTSIOZNI
BOLESTI.**
+ +EPIDEMIOL. MIKROBIOL. & INFEKTS. BOLESTI.
NAUCHNO DRUZHESTVO NA KHIGIENISTI, EPIDEMIOL-
OZI, MIKROBIOLOZI, INFEKTSIONISTI I ORGANIZ-
ATORI NA ZDRAVEOPAZVANETO.
SOFIA 1(1), 1964-
ENGL. SUMM.
LO/N13. 7(1), 1970-
ISSN 0425-1482

**EPIGRAPHISCHE STUDIEN.**
+ +EPIGRAPHISCHE STUD.
LANDSCHAFTVERBAND RHEINLAND.
[BOEHLAU-VERLAG]
COLOGNE 1, 1967-
SUBSERIES OF BONNER JAHRBUECHER. BEIHEFT.
AD/U-1.    HL/U-1.
BL/U-1. [W.5 & 6]
ISSN 0071-0989

**EPILEPSY ABSTRACTS.**
+ +EPILEPSY ABSTR. [EPIA-A]
EXCERPTA MEDICA FOUNDATION.
AMSTERDAM &C. 1, N 1967(1968)-
VOL.1- 3 PUBL. BY THE NATIONAL INSTITUTE OF
NEUROLOGICAL DISEASES & STROKE (US).
OX/U-8.
AD/U-1.                    BL/U-1. 5, 1972-
LD/U-1. 5, 1972-    NW/U-1. 4, 1971-
XN/S-1. 1(14), 1968-
ISSN 0013-9599

**EPIPHYTES.**
NATIONAL CACTUS & SUCCULENT SOCIETY (GB):
EPIPHYTIC PLANT STUDY GROUP.
BRISTOL 1(1), F 1968-
LO/N13.

EPISTEME. RIVISTA CRITICA DI STORIA DELLE
SCIENZE MEDICHE E BIOLOGICHE.
 MILAN   1(1), JA/AP 1967-
 Q. VARIOUS LANGS.
 LO/M24.   LO/N-4.
 ISSN 0013-9637

EPOCH. ENVIRONMENT - POLLUTION + CONSERVATION =
HEALTH.
 HOWEY FOUNDATION.
 CROYDON  1(1), AUTUMN 1972-
 CA/U-1.   ED/N-1.
 ISSN 0301-0643

EPWORTH WITNESS & JOURNAL OF THE ...
 + + EPWORTH WITNESS & J.
 LINCOLNSHIRE METHODIST HISTORY SOCIETY.
 EPWORTH  1, 1963-
 HL/U-1.*

EQUALITY.
 FRANKFURT/MAIN  1, MY 1965-
 Q.
 XW/S-1.
 LO/U-2  8, 1967; 11, 1968.

EQUINE VETERINARY JOURNAL.
 + + EQUINE VET. J.
 BRITISH EQUINE VETERINARY ASSOCIATION.
 LONDON   1(1), JL 1968-
 ED/N-1.   LO/M15.   LO/M18.   LO/N13.   OX/U-8.

EQUITY ANNUAL.
 + + EQUITY ANNU.
 IRISH ACTORS' EQUITY ASSOCIATION.
 DUBLIN  1(1), 1971/72-
 DB/U-2.

EQUIVALENCES. REVUE DE L'ECOLE SUPERIEURE DE
TRADUCTEURS ET D'INTERPRETES DE BRUXELLES.
 BRUSSELS  1(1), 1970-
 LO/N-1.

ERA JOURNAL. INNOVATION IN ELECTROTECHNOLOGY.       XXX
 + + ERA J. (ELEC. RES. ASS.)
 ELECTRICAL RESEARCH ASSOCIATION.
 LEATHERHEAD  1, 1969- 8, 1972. //
 BL/U-1.   BR/U-1.   ED/N-1.   LO/N14.   OX/U-8.   XS/R10.
 CV/C-1.   FIVE YEARS.
 ISSN 0012-7876

ERASMUS IN ENGLISH.
 [UNIV. TORONTO P.]
 TORONTO  1, 1970-
 BL/U-1.   DN/U-1.   ED/N-1.   HL/U-1.   OX/U-1.   SH/U-1.
 SO/U-1.

ERASMUS REVIEW.
 + + ERASMUS REV.
 [RUBIN PUBL.]
 BAYSIDE, NEW YORK  1, 1971-
 5/A.
 OX/U-1.
 ISSN 0046-2411

ERDOL UND KOHLE, ERDGAS, PETROCHEMIE VEREINIGT
MIT BRENNSTOFF-CHEMIE.*
 + + ERDOL & KOHLE ERDGAS PETROCHEM. VER. BRENNST.-
 CHEM.
 DEUTSCHE GESELLSCHAFT FUR MINERALOLWISSENSCH-
 AFT UND KOHLECHEMIE.
 [INDUSTRIEVERLAG VON HERNHAUSSEN]
 HAMBURG  1, 1948-
 AS ERDOL UND KOHLE FROM 1, 1948- 13(7), 1960;
 & ERDOL UND KOHLE, ERDGAS, PETROCHEMIE FROM
 13(8), 1960- 22, 1969. TITLE EXPANDED TO
 ABOVE FROM 23, 1970. INCORP: BRENNSTOFF-
 CHEMIE FROM 1970.
 LO/N14.
 NW/U-1.  23, 1970-

EREKUTORONIKU SERAMIKUSU. ELECTRONIC CERAMICS.
 [GAKKENSHA]
 TOKYO  1(1), 1970-
 LO/N14.

ERGEBNISSE DER ALLGEMEIN PATHOLOGIE UND PATHO-
LOGISCHEN ANATOMIE.                                 XXX
 SUBS (1970):  CURRENT TOPICS IN PATHOLOGY.

ERGEBNISSE DER ANGIOLOGIE.
 + + ERGEB. ANGIOL.
 [SCHATTAUER]
 STUTTGART &C.  1, 1969-
 LO/N13.

ERIN'S RAINBOW.
 [RAINBOW MAGAZINE]
 ARMAGH  1(1), 1972-
 ED/N-1.

EROTISME POPULAIRE.                                 000
 SEE: COLLECTION L'EROTISME POPULAIRE.

ERRATICA. A MAGAZINE OF LITERATURE.
 [ERRATICA P.]
 MILWAUKEE, WIS.  1, 1971-
 LO/U-2.
 ISSN 0046-2470

ERYTHROPOIETIN & ERYTHROPOIESIS MONTHLY.
 + + ERYTHROPOIETIN & ERYTHROPOIESIS M.
 [LITERATURE SEARCHERS]
 KETTERING, OHIO  NO.1, 1967-
 LO/N13.

ESAKIA. OCCASIONAL PAPERS OF THE HIKOSAN
BIOLOGICAL LABORATORY IN ENTOMOLOGY.
 KYUSHU DAIGAKU NOGAKUBU FUZOKU HIKOSAN SEIBUT-
 SUGAKU KENKYUSHO.
 HIKOSAN  NO.1, 1960-
 LO/N13.

ESCRITOS DEL VEDAT.
 INSTITUTO PONTIFICIO DE TEOLOGIA.
 TORRENTE  1, 1971-
 ANNU.
 MA/S-1.

L'ESPACE GEOGRAPHIQUE.
 + + ESPACE GEOGR.
 PARIS  1(1), JA/MR 1972-
 Q.
 HL/U-1.   LO/S13.   MA/U-1.
 ISSN 0046-2497

ESPACES ET SOCIETES.
 + + ESPACES & SOC.
 [EDITIONS ANTHROPOS]
 PARIS  NO.1, N 1970-
 S/T: REVUE CRITIQUE INTERNATIONALE DE L'AMEN-
 AGEMENT DE L'ARCHITECTURE ET DE L'URBANIZATION
 MA/U-1.
 ISSN 0014-0481

ESPANA, HOY. REVISTA DE ACTUALIDAD PERMANENTE.
 + + ESP. HOY.
 MADRID  NO.1, MR 1970-
 LO/U12.
 LD/U-1.  NO.9, 1971- [W. 12; 14; 16]

ESPELEOLOGIA.
 SOCIEDADE EXCURSIONISTA E ESPELEOLOGICA
 (BRAZIL).
 OURO PRETO, BRASIL  NO.1, 1969-
 LO/N-2.

E.S.Q.                                              XXX
 EMERSON SOCIETY.
 PULLMAN  18(67), 1972-
 PREV: EMERSON SOCIETY QUARTERLY FROM 1, 1955-
 65/66, 1971.
 OX/U-1.
 ISSN 0013-6670

ESRI BROADSHEETS.
 ECONOMIC & SOCIAL RESEARCH INSTITUTE (DUBLIN).
 DUBLIN  NO.1, OC 1969-
 DB/U-2.   OX/U16.
 MA/U-1.  NO.3, 1970-

ESSA.                                               XXX
 (UNITED STATES) ENVIRONMENTAL SCIENCE SERVICES
 ADMINISTRATION: OFFICE OF PUBLIC INFORMATION.
 ROCKVILLE, MD.  5(1- 3), 1970. //
 PREV: ESSA WORLD FROM 1(1), 1966- 4, 1969.
 LO/N13.

ESSA PROFESSIONAL PAPER.
 + + ESSA PROF. PAP. (ENVIRON. SCI. SERV. ADMIN.,
 US.).
 (UNITED STATES) ENVIRONMENTAL SCIENCE SERVICES
 ADMINISTRATION.
 ROCKVILLE, MD.  [NO.]1, 1967-
 LO/N13.   XS/N-1.*

ESSA WORLD.                                         XXX
 (UNITED STATES) ENVIRONMENTAL SCIENCE SERVICES
 ADMINISTRATION: OFFICE OF PUBLIC INFORMATION.
 ROCKVILLE, MD.  1(1), 1966- 4, 1969 ...
 SUBS: ESSA.
 LO/N13.  3(4), 1968-              XS/N-1.  1(4), 1966-
 ISSN 0012-8007

**ESSAYS IN CHEMISTRY.**
+ +ESSAYS CHEM.
[ACADEMIC P.]
LONDON &C.   1, 1970-
ED/N-1.     GL/U-1.     HL/U-1.     LO/N14.     LO/U-2.     LO/U13.
LO/U20.     SH/U-1.     SO/U-1.
CA/U-1.   1, 1970.
ISSN 0071-1373

**ESSAYS IN PHYSICS.**
+ +ESSAYS PHYS.
[ACADEMIC P.]
LONDON &C.   1, 1970-
BH/U-3.     ED/N-1.     GL/U-1.     LD/U-1.     LO/N-4.     LO/N14.
LO/U20.     MA/U-1.     SF/U-1.     XS/R10.
ISSN 0071-1438

**ESSAYS IN TOXICOLOGY.**
+ +ESSAYS TOXICOL.
[ACADEMIC P.]
NEW YORK &C.   1, 1969-
GL/U-1.     LD/U-1.     LO/N14.     LO/U20.     SO/U-1.
CA/U-1.

**ESSEX MAMMAL NEWS.**                                                      XXX
ESSEX MAMMAL GROUP.
WOODFORD GREEN   NO.1 1967- 14, 1972.//
LO/R-5.

**ESSRA MAGAZINE.**
+ +ESSRA MAG.
ECONOMIC & SOCIAL SCIENCE RESEARCH ASSOCIATION.
LONDON   1, SPRING 1971-
ED/N-1.     LO/U-3.

**ESTADISTICA CONTINUA: COMERCIO AGRARIO
EXTERIOR (PERU).**
+ +ESTAD. CONTIN., COMER. AGRAR. EXTER. (PERU).
(PERU) OFICINA DE ESTADISTICA.
LIMA   1(1), JA 1970-
OX/U16.

**ESTAMPAGE, FORGE ET BOULONNERIE.**                          XXX
SUBS (1969): PART OF FORMAGE ET TRAITEMENTS
DES METAUX.

**ESTATISTICAS INTERNAS.**
+ +ESTATIST. INT. (PORT.).
FUNDO DE DESENVOLVIMENTO DA MAO-DE-OBRA
(PORTUGAL).
LISBON   NO.1, 1968-
LO/U-3.

**ESTERI.**                                                                          XXX
SUBS (1969): AFFARI ESTERI.

**ESTETIKA.   CASOPIS PRO ESTETIKU A TEORII
UMENI.**
CESKOSLOVENSKA AKADEMIE VED: USTAV PRO CESKOU
LITERATURU.
PRAGUE   1(1), AP 1964-
Q.
CA/U-1.     OX/U-1.
ISSN 0014-1291

**ESTETIKA I ZHIZN'.**
AKADEMIJA NAUK SSSR: INSTITUT FILOSOFII.
MOSCOW   1, 1971-
BH/U-1.     GL/U-1.

**ESTRO.**
TUSCON, ARIZ.   1, 1965-
LO/U-2.

**ESTUARINE & COASTAL MARINE SCIENCE.**
+ +ESTUAR. & COAST. MAR. SCI.
ESTUARINE & BRACKISH WATER SCIENCES
ASSOCIATION.
LONDON   1, 1973-
CA/U-1.     CA/U-2.     ED/N-1.     EX/U-1.     GL/U-2.     LO/N-2.
LO/N13.     LO/R-5.     OX/U-8.     SH/U-1.
ISSN 0302-3524

**ESTUDIOS ANDINOS.**
+ +ESTUD. ANDINOS.
INSTITUTO BOLIVIANO DE ESTUDIO Y ACCION SOCIAL.
LA PAZ   1(1), 1970-
LO/U-3.     OX/U-1.
ISSN 0014-1429

**ESTUDIOS SOBRE LA ECONOMIA ARGENTINA.**
+ +ESTUD. ECON. ARGENT.
CONFEDERACION GENERAL ECONOMICA: INSTITUTO
DE INVESTIGACIONES ECONOMICAS Y FINANCIERAS.
BUENOS AIRES   1, MY 1968-
4/A.
LO/U-3.

**ESTUDIOS DE HISTORIA DE LAS INSTITUCIONES
POLITICAS Y SOCIALES.**
+ +ESTUD. HIST. INST. POLIT. & SOC. (CHILE).
UNIVERSIDAD CATOLICA DE CHILE: FACULTAD DE
CIENCIAS JURIDICAS, POLITICAS Y SOCIALES.
SANTIAGO DE CHILE   NO.1, 1966-
LO/U-1.     OX/U-1.
ISSN 0425-3558

**ESTUDIOS ORIENTALES.**
+ +ESTUD. ORIENT. (COL. MEX.)
COLEGIO DE MEXICO.
MEXICO, DF   1(1), JA 1966-
LO/U14.
ISSN 0014-1534

**ESTUDIOS ORTEGUIANOS.**
+ +ESTUD. ORTEGUIANOS.
[EDICIONES DE LA REVISTA DE OCCIDENTE]
MADRID   1, 1966-
AB/U-1.
ISSN 0425-3760

**ESTUDIOS SINDICALES Y COOPERATIVOS.**
+ +ESTUD. SINDICALES & COOP.
INSTITUTO DE ESTUDIOS SINDICALES, SOCIALES Y
COOPERATIVOS.
MADRID   1(1), 1967-
GL/U-1. 4(13), 1970-
NW/U-1. 5(17), 1971-
OX/U-1. 2(5/6), 1968-
SO/U-1. NOS. 5/6, 10/11, 13/14, JA/JE 1968-
AP/JE 1970.
ISSN 0014-1542

**ESTUDOS HISTORICOS.**
+ +ESTUD. HIST. (FAC. FIL. CIENC. & LETRAS
MARILIA).
FACULDADE DE FILOSOFIA, CIENCIAS E LETRAS DE
MARILIA (BRAZIL).
MARILIA, BRAZ.   NO.1, 1963-
FACULDADE AN AUTONOMOUS BODY.  ISSUED BY THE
DEPARTMENTO DE HISTORIA DA FACULDADE ...
LO/N-1.     LO/U11.     OX/U-1.
LO/U-1.   [W. NO.3, 1964; 4, 1965].

**ESTUDOS LEOPOLDENSES.**
+ +ESTUD. LEOPOLD.
FACULDADE DE FILOSOFIA, CIENCIAS E LETRAS DE
SAO LEOPOLDO (BRAZIL).
SAO LEOPOLDO, BRAZ.   NO.1, 1966-
PORT., ENGL.  FACULDADE AN AUTONOMOUS BODY.
LO/N-2.
ISSN 0014-1607

**ETHIOPIAN PUBLICATIONS.**
+ +ETHIOP. PUBL.
HAILE SELLASSIE I UNIVERSITY: INSTITUTE OF
ETHIOPIAN STUDIES.
ADDIS ABABA   1963/1964(JL 1965)-
ANNU. PUBL. JL OF EACH YEAR.  S/T: BOOKS, PAM-
PHLETS, ANNUALS & PERIODICAL ARTICLES PUB-
LISHED IN ...; FROM 2ND ISSUE, S/T CONTINUES
WITH RELEVANT YEARS, E.G. [2ND]: ... 1957
ETHIOPIAN & 1965 GREGORIAN CALENDAR.
LO/N-3.     SH/U-1.
LO/S10.   1965(66)-
BH/U-1.   1969.

**ETHNICA.   REVISTA DE ANTROPOLOGIA.**
CENTRO DE ETNOLOGIA PENINSULAR.
BARCELONA   1, JA/JE 1971-
2/A.
LO/S10.     OX/U-1.

**ETHNIES.**
[MOUTON]
THE HAGUE   1, 1971-
ANNU.
CA/U-1.     GL/U-1.

**ETHNOLOGIA SCANDINAVICA.**                                      XXX
+ +ETHNOL. SCAND.
KUNGLIGA GUSTAV ADOLFS AKADEMIEN.
STOCKHOLM   1, 1971-
ENGL. & GER.  PREV: FOLK-LIV FROM 1, 1937- 32,
1970.
AD/U-1.     BL/U-1.     LO/S10.     OX/U-1.     RE/U-1.
CO/U-1.   1972-                                   LD/U-1.   1972-

**ETHNOLOGIE FRANCAISE: NS.**                                    XXX
+ +ETHNOL. FR., NS.
SOCIETE D'ETHNOGRAPHIE FRANCAISE.
PARIS   1, 1971-
PREV: ARTS ET TRADITIONS POPULAIRES FROM 1,
JA/MR 1953- 18(4), 1970.
GL/U-1.     LO/N-1.  · LO/S10.     OX/U-1.     RE/U-1.
ISSN 0046-2616

ETHNOLOGISCHE ZEITSCHRIFT ZURICH.
+ +ETHNOL. Z. ZUR.
[LANG]
 BERN 1, 1970-
 2/A. S/T: EINE ZEITSCHRIFT DER SAMMLUNG FUR
 VOELKERKUNDE DER UNIVERSITAET ZURICH.
 DB/U-2.    LO/N-1.    LO/S10.    LO/S30.    OX/U-1.
 LO/U14.  1971-
 ISSN 0014-181X

ETHNOMEDIZIN.  ETHNOMEDICINE.
 ARBEITSGEMEINSCHAFT ETHNOMEDIZIN.
 [HELMUT BUSKE]
 HAMBURG  1(1), 1971-
 LO/S10.    OX/U-8.

ETIMOLOGIJA.
 AKADEMIJA NAUK SSSR: INSTITUT RUSSKOGO JAZYKA.
 MOSCOW  1963-
 ANNU. S/T: VARIES.
 ED/U-1.
 BH/U-1.  1966(1968)-          BL/U-1.  1964(1965)-
 CC/U-1.  1964(1965)-          NO/U-1.  1965(1967)-
 SA/U-1.  1964(1965)-
 ISSN 0425-4635

ETNOGRAFICHESKIJ SBORNIK (ULAN-UDE).
+ +ETNOGR. SB. (ULAN-UDE).
 AKADEMIJA NAUK SSSR (SIBIRSKOE OTDELENIE):
 BURJATSKIJ KOMPLEKSNYJ NAUCHNO-ISSLEDOVATEL'-
 SKIJ INSTITUT.
 ULAN-UDE  1, 1960-
 BH/U-1.    LO/U-3.    LO/U15.    OX/U-1.

ETUDES AFRICAINES.                                        XXX
+ +ETUD. AFR.
 CENTRE DE RECHERCHE ET D'INFORMATION SOCIO-
 POLITIQUES (BELGIUM).
 BRUSSELS  NO.1, 1969-
 PREV: COURRIER AFRICAIN FROM NO.1, 1960- 86/
 87, 1968.
 OX/U-9.

ETUDES BAUDELAIRIENNES.
+ +ETUD. BAUDELAIRIENNES.
 [A LA BACONNIERE]
 NEUCHATEL  1, 1969-
 AD/U-1.    GL/U-1.    MA/U-1.

ETUDES CINEMATOGRAPHIQUES.
+ +ETUD. CINEMATOGR.
 [M.J. MINARD-LETTRES MODERNES]
 PARIS  NO.1/2, 1960-
 3/A.
 OX/U-1.
 ISSN 0014-1992

ETUDE DES COLLECTIONS DU MUSEE.
+ +ETUDE COLLECT. MUS. (GUIMET).
 MUSEE GUIMET.
 [PRESSES UNIV. DE FRANCE]
 PARIS  1, 1971-
 LO/N-1.

ETUDES ET DOCUMENTS CONCERNANT LE SUD-EST
EUROPEEN.
+ +ETUD. & DOC. CONCERNANT SUD-EST EUR.
 INTERNATIONAL ASSOCIATION OF SOUTH-EAST
 EUROPEAN STUDIES.
 BUCHAREST  1, 1966-
 OX/U-1.  3, 1971-
 ISSN 0425-4988

ETUDES & DOCUMENTS, SOCIETE D'HISTOIRE ET D'
ART DU DIOCESE DE MEAUX.
+ +ETUD. & DOC. SOC. HIST. ART DIOCESE MEAUX.
 MEAUX  1, 1966-
 OX/U-1.

ETUDES FOREZIENNES.
+ +ETUD. FOREZIENNES.
 ST. ETIENNE  1, 1968-
 OX/U-1.
 ISSN 0071-206X

ETUDES FREUDIENNES.
+ +ETUD. FREUDIENNES.
 [EDITIONS DENCEL]
 PARIS  NO.1/2, N 1969-
 3/A.
 LO/N-1.
 ISSN 0014-2107

ETUDES GOBINIENNES.
+ +ETUD. GOBINIENNES.
 [KLINCKSIECK]
 PARIS  1966-
 A.
 CB/U-1.    SH/U-1.    SO/U-1.

ETUDES D'HISTOIRE AFRICAINE.
+ +ETUD. HIST. AFR. (KINSHASA).
 UNIVERSITE LOVANIUM DE KINSHASA.
 KINSHASA  1, 1970-
 AD/U-1.    CA/U-1.    LD/U-1.    LO/N-1.    LO/U-3.    LO/U14.
 OX/U-1.

ETUDES INTERNATIONALES.  REVUE TRIMESTRIELLE.
+ +ETUD. INT.
 CANADIAN INSTITUTE OF INTERNATIONAL AFFAIRS.
 [PRESSES DE L'UNIV. LAVAL]
 QUEBEC  1(1), 1970-
 LO/N-1.    LO/U-3.*
 ISSN 0014-2123

ETUDES IRLANDAISES.
+ +ETUD. IRL.
 UNIVERSITE DE LILLE: CENTRE D'ETUDES ET DE
 RECHERCHES IRLANDAISES.
 LILLE  1, N 1972-
 DB/S-1.

ETUDES JURIDIQUES AU CANADA.                             000
 SEE: CANADIAN LEGAL STUDIES.

ETUDES LITTERAIRES.
+ +ETUD. LITT. (UNIV. LAVAL).
 UNIVERSITE LAVAL.
 QUEBEC  1, AP 1968-
 3/A.
 BL/U-1.    DB/U-2.    EX/U-1.
 ISSN 0014-214X

ETUDES MALIENNES.
+ +ETUD. MALIENNES.
 INSTITUT DES SCIENCES HUMAINES DU MALI.
 BAMAKO, MALI  NO.1, [1969]-
 BH/U-1.    LO/N14.    LO/S10.

ETUDES PALMYRENIENNES.                                   000
 SEE: STUDIA PALMYRENSKIE.

ETUDES DE PHOTO-INTERPRETATION.
+ +ETUD. PHOTO-INTERPRET.
 INSTITUT GEOGRAPHIQUE NATIONAL (FRANCE).
 PARIS  NO.1, 1964-
 ENGL. SUMM.
 LO/N13.  NO.3, 1967-
 ISSN 0532-4637

ETUDES DE PHYSIOLOGIE ET DE PSYCHOLOGIE DE
TRAVAIL.
/  / ETUD. PHYSIOL. & PSYCHOL. TRAV.
 EUROPEAN COAL & STEEL COMMUNITY: HIGH AUTHORITY
 LUXEMBOURG  1, 1967-
 GL/U-1.  2, 1967-

ETUDES POLEMOLOGIQUES.                                   XXX
+ +ETUD. POLEMOL.
 INSTITUT FRANCAIS DE POLEMOLOGIE.
 PARIS  NO.1, JL 1971-
 PREV: GUERRES ET PAIX FROM 1, 1966- 4(6), 1970
 LO/N-1.
 OX/U-1.  2, 1971-
 ISSN 0046-2640

ETUDES PREHISTORIQUES (LYONS).
+ +ETUD. PREHIST. (LYONS).
 SOCIETE PREHISTORIQUE DE L'ARDECHE.
 LYONS  NO.1, MR 1971-
 DB/U-1.
 ISSN 0049-111X

ETUDES RIMBAUDIENNES.
+ +ETUD. RIMBAUDIENNES.
 [MINARD]
 PARIS  1, 1968(1969)-
 ANNU. SUBSERIES OF AVANT-SIECLE.
 LO/N-1.    LO/U-2.    SO/U-1.

ETUDES ROMANES DE L'UNIVERSITE D'ODENSE.
+ +ETUD. ROM. UNIV. ODENSE.
 ODENSE  1971-
 CA/U-1.    LO/N-1.

ETUDES TEILHARDIENNES.
+ +ETUD. TEILHARDIENNES.
 ASSOCIATION DES AMIS DE PIERRE TEILHARD DE
 CHARDIN: CENTRE BELGE D'ETUDE ET D'INFORM.
 BRUSSELS  1, 1968-
 LO/N-1.    OX/U-1.

**ETUDE DU TRAVAIL.**                                                                      XXX
SUBS (1973): PRODUCTION ET GESTION: ETUDE
DU TRAVAIL.

**ETYKA.**
POLSKA AKADEMIA NAUK: INSTYTUT FILOZOFII I
SOCJOLOGII.
*WARSAW NO 1, D 1966-*
ENGL. & FR. SUMM.
*OX/U-1.*
*BH/U-1. 5, 1969-*                      *LO/N-3. NO 2, 1967-*
*ISSN 0014-2263*

**ETZ-REPORT.**
[VDE VERLAG]
*BERLIN 1, 1970-*
*LO/N14.*

**EUGENICS QUARTERLY.**                                                              XXX
SUBS (1969): SOCIAL BIOLOGY.

**EUGENICS REVIEW.**                                                                      XXX
SUBS (1969): JOURNAL OF BIOSOCIAL SCIENCE.

**EURATOM. REVIEW OF THE EUROPEAN ATOMIC ENERGY
COMMUNITY.**                                                                                    XXX
EUROPEAN ATOMIC ENERGY COMMUNITY.
*LEYDEN 7(1), MR 1968- 7(4), D 1968...*
PREV: EURATOM BULLETIN FROM 1(1), 1962- 6(4),
D 1967. SUBS: EURO SPECTRA.
*BN/U-2.*

**EURATOM BULLETIN. Q.**                                                               XXX
*++EURATOM BULL.*
EUROPEAN ATOMIC ENERGY COMMUNITY.
*LEIDEN [1(1)], 1962- 6(4), 1967 ...*
SUBS: EURATOM.
*BN/U-2.     DB/U-2.     XS/R10.     XS/T-9.*
*BL/U-1. (1964)-*                    *LO/N-7. 1963-*
*ZS/T-1. (ONE YEAR FILE)*

**EURATOM INFORMATION.**                                                           XXX
*++EURATOM INF. [EUIN-A]*
EUROPEAN ATOMIC ENERGY COMMUNITY.
*DUSSELDORF. 1, 1963- 7, 1969...*
SUBS: EURO ABSTRACTS.
*LO/N-4.     LO/N-7.     LO/N-9.     XS/R10.     XS/T-3.     XS/T-9.*
*CA/U-2. 5,1967-*                    *ED/N-1. 3(10),1965-*
*MA/P-1. 2(5),1964-*
*ZS/T-1. (ONE YEAR FILE)*

**EURO ABSTRACTS.**
*++EURO ABSTR.*
COMMISSION OF THE EUROPEAN COMMUNITIES.
[HANDELSBLATT]
*DUSSELDORF &C. 8, 1970-*
ENGL., FR., GER., ITAL., & DUTCH. PREV: EUR-
ATOM INFORMATION FROM 1, 1963- 7, 1969.
*CA/U15.     DB/U-2.     ED/N-1.     LO/N-4.     LO/N14.*
*XS/R10.*
*ISSN 0014-2352*

**EURO SPECTRA. SCIENTIFIC & TECHNICAL REVIEW
OF THE EUROPEAN COMMUNITIES.**                                          XXX
EUROPEAN ATOMIC ENERGY COMMUNITY.
*LEIDEN 8(1), MR 1969-*
PREV: EURATOM FROM 7(1), 1968- 7(4), 1968.
*BH/U-1.     BL/U-1.     BN/U-2.     GL/U-1.     LO/N14.     XS/R10.*
*ISSN 0014-2360*

**EUROCLAY.**                                                                                        XXX
[LONDON & SHEFFIELD PUBL. CO.]
*LONDON NO.1, 1973-*
PREV: CLAYCRAFT & STRUCTURAL CERAMICS FROM
37(4), 1964- 46(6), 1973.
*ED/N-1.     LO/N14.*
*ISSN 0306-1841*

**EURO-FARM BUSINESS.**                                                             XXX
*++EURO-FARM BUS.*
[FARM BUSINESS LTD.]
*WARWICK 1(1), JA 1972-*
M. PREV: FARM BUSINESS FROM 1960- 1971.
*ED/N-1.     LO/N-6.*

**EUROFRUIT.**
[MARKET INTELLIGENCE LTD.]
*LONDON NO.1, F 1973-*
MON.
*CA/U-1.     ED/N-1.     LO/N-6.     LO/R-6.     OX/U-1.*

**EUROLAW COMMERCIAL INTELLIGENCE.**
*++EUROLAW COMMER. INTELL.*
*LONDON NO.1, N 1972-*
S/T: SURVEY OF EUROPEAN COMMERCIAL LAW DEVEL-
OPMENTS.
*BL/U-1.     ED/N-1.     EX/U-1.     SO/U-1.*
*LO/U-2. 1973-*
*ISSN 0305-9561*

**EUROMONEY. JOURNAL OF THE INTERNATIONAL MONEY
& BOND MARKETS.**
[EUROMONEY PUBL.]
*LONDON 1(1), 1969-*
M.
*OX/U-1.*
*BL/U-1. 1973-*                    *CA/U-1.* 1(2), 1969-*
*ED/N-1. 1(2), 1969-*            *OX/U16. 1(2), 1969-*
*OX/U17. 1(2), 1969-*
*ISSN 0014-2433*

**EUROMONITOR REVIEW.**
*++EUROMONIT. REV.*
*LONDON 1, AG 1968-*
S/T: QUARTERLY JOURNAL OF MARKET INTELLIGENCE
IN EUROPE.
*ED/N-1.     LO/P-6.*
*ISSN 0014-2441*

**EUROPA.**
*BRUSSELS 1(1), 1971-*
*OX/U-1.*

**EUROPAISCHE HOCHSCHULSCHRIFTEN: REIHE 17:
ERDWISSENSCHAFTEN.**
*++EUR. HOCHSCH., 17.*
[VERLAG HERBERT LANG]
*BONN 1, 1969-*
*LO/N-2.*
*ISSN 0531-8149*

**EUROPE DE DEMAIN.**
*++EUR. DEMAIN.*
[PRESSES UNIVERSITAIRES DE FRANCE]
*PARIS 1, 1964-*
*GL/U-1.*

**EUROPEAN CIVIL ENGINEERING.**
*++EUR. CIV. ENG.*
(CZECHOSLOVAKIA) MINISTERSTVO STAVEBNICTVI:
(RESEARCH INSTITUTE OF ENGINEERING,
BRATISLAVA).
*BRATISLAVA 1, 1970-*
*GL/U-1.*
*ISSN 0014-2883*

**EUROPEAN CIVIL ENGINEERING ABSTRACTS.**
*++EUR. CIVIL ENG. ABSTR.*
CONSTRUCTION INDUSTRY TRANSLATION & INFORMATION
SERVICES.
*DUBLIN 1, 1972- 2, 1973.*
SUBS. INCORP. IN: I.C.E. ABSTRACTS.
*BL/U-1.     LO/N14.*
*CA/U-1. 1(2), 1972-*                    *ED/N-1. 1(2), 1972-*
*ISSN 0046-273X*

**EUROPEAN COMMUNITY INFORMATION.**
*++EUR. COMMUNITY INF.*
[FT BUSINESS ENTERPRISES]
*LONDON NO.1, JA 1972-*
MON.
*CA/U-1.     ED/N-1.     LO/N-1.     OX/U-1.     OX/U17.*
*LO/N-6. NO.4, 1972-*              *MA/U-1. NO.3, 1972-*
*ISSN 0046-2748*

**EUROPEAN CONSERVATION YEAR NEWSLETTER.**                   000
SEE: ECY NEWSLETTER.

**EUROPEAN CURRICULUM STUDIES.**
*++EUR. CURRIC. STUD.*
COUNCIL FOR CULTURAL CO-OPERATION.
*STRASBOURG NO.1, 1968-*
*GL/U-1.*

**EUROPEAN DEMOGRAPHIC INFORMATION BULLETIN.**
*++EUR. DEMOGR. INF. BULL.*
EUROPEAN CENTRE FOR POPULATION STUDIES.
[NIJHOFF]
*THE HAGUE 1, 1970-*
Q.
*DB/U-2.     ED/N-1.     LO/N-1.     LO/S74.     OX/U-1.     OX/U17.*
*SH/U-1.     SO/U-1.*
*ISSN 0046-2756*

NPT/ 113

EURO                        EURO

**EUROPEAN ECONOMIC REVIEW.**
++EUR. ECON. REV.
EUROPEAN SCIENTIFIC ASSOCIATION OF APPLIED
ECONOMICS.
*WHITE PLAINS, N.Y. 1(1), 1969-*
Q.
BH/U-1. ED/U-1. EX/U-1. GL/U-1. HL/U-1. LO/N-7.
LO/N-7. LO/U-3. MA/U-1. NO/U-1. OX/U-1. OX/U16.
SH/U-1. SO/U-1.
*ISSN 0014-2921*

**EUROPEAN INTELLIGENCE.**       XXX
++EUR. INTELL.
*TUNBRIDGE WELLS NO.1, 1969-*
S/T: A WEEKLY REPORT ON THE ECONOMY OF THE
COMMON MARKET. PREV: OPERA MUNDI EUROPE FROM
1, 1959.
BH/U-1. ED/N-1. OX/U-1. RE/U-1.
*ISSN 0030-3593*

**EUROPEAN JOURNAL OF CLINICAL INVESTIGATION.** XXX
++EUR. J. CLIN. INVEST.
EUROPEAN SOCIETY FOR CLINICAL INVESTIGATION.
[SPRINGER]
*BERLIN &C. 1, 1970-*
PREV: ARCHIV FUR KLINISCHE MEDIZIN FROM
212, 1966- 216, 1969.
AD/U-1. CR/M-1. LD/U-1. LO/N13. NW/U-1.
OX/U-8.
BL/U-1. 4, 1974-
*ISSN 0014-2972*

**EUROPEAN JOURNAL OF FOREST PATHOLOGY.**
++EUR. J. FOREST PATHOL.
[P. PAREY]
*HAMBURG; BERLIN 1(1), S 1971-*
CA/U-7. LD/U-1. LO/N13. OX/U-3.

**EUROPEAN JOURNAL OF IMMUNOLOGY.**
++EUR. J. IMMUNOL.
*WEINHEIM 1, JA 1971-*
Q.
AD/U-1. BL/U-1. CA/M-1. GL/U-1. GL/U-2. LO/M12.
LO/N13. LO/U-2.
*ISSN 0014-2980*

**EUROPEAN JOURNAL OF MARKETING.**   XXX
++EUR. J. MARK.
[BUSINESS PUBL. LTD.]
*LONDON 5(2), 1971-*
Q. PREV: BRITISH JOURNAL OF MARKETING FROM
SPRING 1967- 5(1), 1971.
BT/U-1. CV/C-1. ED/N-1. LO/U28. MA/P-1.
RE/U-1. 6, 1972-

**EUROPEAN JOURNAL OF POLITICAL RESEARCH.**
++EUR. J. POLIT. RES.
EUROPEAN CONSORTIUM FOR POLITICAL RESEARCH.
*AMSTERDAM 1(1), AP 1973-*
Q.
BH/U-3. BL/U-3. EX/U-1. GL/U-1. GL/U-2. HL/U-1.
LO/U-3. OX/U-1. SH/U-1.
SF/U-1. 2(1), 1974-

**EUROPEAN JOURNAL OF SOCIAL PSYCHOLOGY.**
++EUR. J. SOC. PSYCHOL.
[MOUTON]
*THE HAGUE 1(1), 1971-*
Q.
AD/U-1. BH/U-3. DB/U-1. DN/U-1. GL/U-2. LO/N-1.
LO/U-3. LO/U-4. SH/U-1. SW/U-1.
*ISSN 0046-2772*

**EUROPEAN JOURNAL OF TOXICOLOGY.**   000
SEE: JOURNAL EUROPEEN DE TOXICOLOGIE.

**EUROPEAN LAW DIGEST.**
++EUR. LAW DIG.
[COMMON LAW REPORTS LTD.]
*LONDON 1, 1973-*
BL/U-1. CB/U-1. ED/N-1. GL/U-1. HL/U-1. LD/U-1.
LO/N14. LO/U-1. MA/P-1. MA/U-1. SH/U-1. SO/U-1.
*ISSN 0305-8476*

**EUROPEAN LAW NEWSLETTER.**
++EUR. LAW NEWSL.
[FINANCIAL TIMES LTD.]
*LONDON JL 1972-*
MON.
ED/N-1.
AD/U-1. 1973-
*ISSN 0300-2233*

**EUROPEAN MARKETING RESEARCH REVIEW.**
++EUR. MARKET. RES. REV.
EUROPEAN SOCIETY FOR OPINION SURVEYS &
MARKET RESEARCH.
*BRUSSELS 1, SUMMER 1966- 7, 1972.*
SUBS: EUROPEAN RESEARCH.
NO/U-1. XY/N-1.
*ISSN 0014-3014*

**EUROPEAN MARXIST REVIEW.**
++EUR. MARXIST REV.
FOURTH INTERNATIONAL: EUROPEAN BUREAU.
*LONDON 1, MY 1968-*
BUREAU PART OF THE INTERNATIONAL SECRETARIAT.
SPONS. BODY ALSO REVOLUTIONARY WORKERS PARTY.
ED/N-1. LO/U-3. OX/U-1.

**EUROPEAN MONOGRAPHS IN SOCIAL PSYCHOLOGY.**
++EUR. MONOGR. SOC. PSYCHOL.
*LONDON &C. 1, 1971-*
OX/U-1.

**EUROPEAN NEUROLOGY.**       XXX
++EUR. NEUROL.
[KARGER]
*BASLE &C 1, 1968-*
PREV: SECTION B OF PSYCHIATRIA ET NEUROLOGIA
FROM 133, JA/F 1957- 154, 1967.
LD/U-1. LV/U-1. OX/U-8.
*ISSN 0014-3022*

**EUROPEAN POLITICS. A COMPARATIVE GOVERNMENT
BIENNIAL.**
++EUR. POLIT.
[VAN NOSTRAND CO.]
*PRINCETON, N.J. 1, 1966-*
LO/U-3.
*ISSN 0531-4380*

**EUROPEAN POTATO JOURNAL.**    XXX
SUBS (1970): POTATO RESEARCH.

**EUROPEAN RUBBER JOURNAL.**    XXX
++EUR. RUBBER J.
[MACLAREN]
*LONDON 155(6), 1973-*
PREV: RUBBER JOURNAL FROM 146(3), 1964- 155
(5), 1973.
LO/N14. LO/R-6.
*ISSN 0305-2222*

**EUROPEAN STUDIES. TEACHERS' SERIES.**
++EUR. STUD., TEACH. SER.
UNIVERSITY OF SUSSEX: CENTRE FOR CONTEMPORARY
EUROPEAN STUDIES & EUROPEAN COMMUNITY INFORM-
ATION SERVICE.
*LONDON 1, 1968-*
BH/U-1. GL/U-1. LO/N-1. LO/U28. OX/U-1. XS/T-4.
LO/U-3. CURRENT ISSUES ONLY.

**EUROPEAN STUDIES REVIEW.**
++EUR. STUD. REV.
[MACMILLAN]
*LONDON 1(1), JA 1971-*
Q.
BN/U-1. HL/U-1. LD/U-1. LO/N-1. LO/S-7. LO/U-1.
LO/U-2. LO/U-3. LO/U-4. LO/U12. LO/U19. MA/U-1.
NO/U-1. NW/U-1. OX/U-1. SH/U-1. SW/U-1.
XY/N-1.
BL/U-1. 2, 1972-    EX/U-1. 2(1), 1972-
SO/U-1. 2, 1972-
*ISSN 0014-3111*

**EUROPEAN SURGICAL RESEARCH.**
++EUR. SURG. RES.
EUROPEAN SOCIETY FOR EXPERIMENTAL SURGERY.
*BASLE &C. 1(1), 1969-*
LV/U-1. OX/U-8.
*ISSN 0014-312X*

**EUROPEAN TRAINING.**
++EUR. TRAIN.
UNIVERSITY OF BRADFORD: MANAGEMENT CENTRE.
*BRADFORD 1(1), 1972-*
BH/U-3. BH/U-3. ED/N-1. LO/N35. OX/U-1. SF/U-1.
XS/R10.
*ISSN 0046-2810*

**EUROPEAN WHEAT ANEUPLOID CO-OPERATIVE NEWSL-
ETTER.**
++EUR. WHEAT ANEUPLOID CO-OP. NEWSL.
*CAMBRIDGE 1, 1967/8 [1969]-*
CA/U11.

EUROPHYSICS NEWS. BULLETIN OF THE...
+ +EUROPHYS. NEWS.
EUROPEAN PHYSICAL SOCIETY.
GENEVA NO.1, 1968-
BL/U-1.    ED/N-1.    LO/U-2.
GL/U-1.  2, 1969-
LD/U-1.  [W. NO.8, MR 1970].
LO/N14.  CURRENT BOX ONLY.
XS/R10.  CURRENT FIVE YEARS.

EUROPLASTICS MONTHLY: BRITISH PLASTICS EDIT-
ION.                                                    XXX
+ +EUROPLAST. MON., BR. PLAST. ED.
[IPC BUSINESS P.]
LONDON 45(4), 1972-
 PREV: BRITISH PLASTICS FROM 17, 1945- 45(3),
1972.
BH/P-1.    LD/U-1.    LO/N-4.    LO/N14.    LO/U28.    XS/R10.

EUROPROPERTY.
EUROPEAN PROPERTY OWNERS ASSOCIATION.
LONDON 1, 1968-
ED/N-1.

EUROTEST-SCHRIFTEN.
+ +EUROTEST-SCHR.
[ZEITSCHRIFTVERLAG OTTO BRAUN & CO.]
VIENNA 1, 1968-
LO/N-1.

EVANGELISCH-KATHOLISCHER KOMMENTAR ZUM NEUEN
TESTAMENT.
+ +EVANG.-KATHOL. KOMMENT. NEUEN TESTAMENT.
[NEUKIRCHENER VERLAG]
NEUKIRCHEN 1, 1969-
OX/U-1.

EVANGELISCHE KOMMENTARE.
+ +EVANG. KOMMENT.
[KREUZ-VERLAG]
STUTTGART 1(1), JA 1968-
OX/U-1.
CA/U-1. 3(11), 1970-
ISSN 0300-4236

EVENEMENTS DU MOIS EN TUNISIE.
CENTRE DE DOCUMENTATION NATIONALE (TUNIS).
TUNIS 1, 1967-
LO/U14.

EVERYDAY ELECTRONICS.
+ +EVERYDAY ELECTRON.
[IPC MAGAZINES]
LONDON 1(1), OC 1971-
ED/N-1.    OX/U-8.
LO/N14. [CURRENT BOX ONLY]

EX TERRA AURUM: SERIES A.
BUCHAREST 1, 1971-
OX/U-1.

EXCERPTA INDONESICA.
+ +EXCERPTA INDONES.
KONINKLIJK INSTITUUT VOOR TAAL-, LAND- EN
VOLKENKUNDE.
LEYDEN 1, 1970-
S/T: ABSTRACTS OF SELECTED PERIODICAL
ARTICLES ON INDONESIA. PRODUCED BY INSTITUTE'S
CENTRE FOR DOCUMENTATION ON MODERN INDONESIA.
HL/U-1.    LO/U14.    OX/U-1.
ISSN 0046-0885

EXCERPTA MEDICA, SECTION 28: UROLOGY
& NEPHROLOGY.                                          XXX
+ +EXCERPTA MED., 28.
EXCERPTA MEDICA FOUNDATION.
AMSTERDAM 1, 1967-
PREV: PART OF: EXCERPTA MEDICA: SECTION 9:
SURGERY. SERIES TITLE VARIES, 1, 1967- 2,
1968: UROLOGY.
LO/N13.    SH/U-1.
ISSN 0014-4320

EXCERPTA MEDICA: SECTION 34: PLASTIC SURGERY.
+ +EXCERPTA MED., 34.
EXCERPTA MEDICA FOUNDATION.
AMSTERDAM 1, 1970-
AD/U-1.    LD/U-1.    LO/N13.
ISSN 0014-438X

EXCERPTA MEDICA: SECTION 35: OCCUPATIONAL
HEALTH & INDUSTRIAL MEDICINE.
+ +EXCERPTA MED., 35.
EXCERPTA MEDICA FOUNDATION.
AMSTERDAM 1(1), JA 1971-
M.
AD/U-1.    DB/U-1.    LO/N13.    NW/U-1.    XS/R10.
XS/T-7.
BL/U-1. 1972-                           LD/U-1. 2, 1972-
SO/U-1. 2, 1972-
ISSN 0014-4398

EXCERPTA MEDICA: SECTION 36: HEALTH ECONOMICS.
+ +EXCERPTA MED., 36.
EXCERPTA MEDICA FOUNDATION.
AMSTERDAM 1, 1971- 2, 1972...
SUBS: EXCERPTA MEDICA: SECTION 36: HEALTH
ECONOMICS & HOSPITAL ADMINISTRATION.
AD/U-1.    LO/N13.    NW/U-1.
BL/U-1. 1972-                           LD/U-1. 2, 1972-
SO/U-1. 2, 1972-
ISSN 0014-4401

EXCERPTA MEDICA: SECTION 46: ENVIRONMENTAL
HEALTH.                                                XXX
+ +EXCERPTA MED., 46.
EXCERPTA MEDICA FOUNDATION.
AMSTERDAM 1, JA 1971- 2(2), F 1972 ...
MON. SUBS: EXCERPTA MEDICA: SECTION 46:
ENVIRONMENTAL HEALTH & POLLUTION CONTROL.
BH/U-3.    LO/R-5.    NW/U-1.
BL/U-1. 2, 1972-                        LD/U-1. 2, 1972-
ISSN 0046-2268

EXCERPTA MEDICA: SECTION 47: VIROLOGY.
+ +EXCERPTA MED., 47.
AMSTERDAM 1, 1971-
AD/U-3.    BL/U-1.    LO/N13.    NW/U-1.    SO/U-1.
ISSN 0031-6520

EXCERPTA MEDICA: SECTION 48: GASTROENTEROLOGY.
+ +EXCERPTA MED., 48.
AMSTERDAM 1, 1971-
AD/U-3.    LO/N13.    NW/U-1.
BL/U-1. 1972-                           LD/U-1. 2, 1972-
SO/U-1. 2, 1972-
ISSN 0031-3580

EXPATRIATE REVIEW.
+ +EXPATRIATE REV.
NEW YORK &C. NO.1, 1971-
LO/U-2.    OX/U-1.

EXPERIMENTAL SURGERY & ANESTHESIOLOGY.
+ +EXP. SURG. & ANESTHESIOL.
[CAMBRIDGE SCIENTIFIC ABSTRACTS, INC.]
RIVERDALE, MD. 1, 1971-
ENGL. TRANSL. OF: EKSPERIMENTAL'NAJA KHIRUR-
GIJA I ANESTEZIOLOGIJA FROM 16, 1971.
LO/N13.
ISSN 0046-2934

EXPERIMENTATION ANIMALE.
+ +EXP. ANIM.
[VIGOT FRERES]
PARIS 1, 1968-
LO/N13.
ISSN 0014-4916

EXPERIMENTELLE PATHOLOGIE.
+ +EXP. PATHOL.
[FISCHER]
VIENNA 1, 1967-
LO/U-2.
ISSN 0014-4908

EXPERIMENTS IN PHYSIOLOGY & BIOCHEMISTRY.
+ +EXP. PHYSIOL. & BIOCHEM.
[ACADEMIC PRESS]
NEW YORK &C 1, 1968-
GL/U-1.    LO/N13.    LO/U-2.    LV/P-1.

EXPORT ACTION. EXPORT NEWS FROM NEW ZEALAND.
[SHORTLAND PUBL. LTD.]
AUCKLAND 1(1), AG 1968-
ED/N-1.
LO/N-3. 1(2), N 1968.

EXPORT CLUB NEWS.
BRITISH NATIONAL EXPORT COUNCIL.
LONDON 1, F 1969-
OX/U-1.
ED/N-1. 2, 1969-

EXPORT DIRECTION.
+ +EXPORT DIR.
[SPECIAL INTEREST PUBL.]
LONDON 1, F 1970-
M. S/T: JOURNAL FOR EXPORT DECISION MAKERS.
ED/N-1. 2(3), AP 1971-
ISSN 0014-5130

EXPORT TIMES.
LONDON NO.1, S 1969-
ED/N-1.   GL/U-2.   OX/U-1.
ISSN 0046-2950

EXPRESSION (LIMBE).
UNIVERSITY OF MALAWI.
LIMBE NO.1, 1968-
LO/U14.

EXTENSION BULLETIN, NEW ZEALAND AGRICULTURAL
ENGINEERING INSTITUTE.
+ +EXT. BULL. N.Z. AGR. ENG. INST.
WELLINGTON, N.Z. 1, 1965-
CA/U11.

EXTERNAL AFFAIRS.                                    XXX
SUBS (1972): INTERNATIONAL PERSPECTIVES.

EXTRA.
TEGUCIGALPA 1, AG 1965-
MON.
OX/U-1.
ISSN 0531-6227

EZHEGODNIK GERMANSKOJ ISTORII.
+ +EZHEG. GER. ISTOR.
AKADEMIJA NAUK SSSR: KOMISSIJA ISTORIKOV SSSR &
GDR.
MOSCOW 1968(1969)-
KOMISSIJA SUBORD. TO: INSTITUT VSEOBSHCHEJ
ISTORII.  TITLE ALSO IN GER.: JAHRBUCH FUR
DEUTSCHE GESCHICHTE.
CA/U-1.   CC/U-1.
LO/U15.  1968/69; 1969/70.

EZHEGODNIK KINO.                                     XXX
SUBS (1964): EKRAN.

FACET.
GLASGOW SCHOOL OF ART.
GLASGOW NO.1, F 1968-
ED/N-1.

FACILITIES FOR ATMOSPHERIC RESEARCH.                 XXX
+ +FACIL. ATMOS. RES.
NATIONAL CENTER FOR ATMOSPHERIC RESEARCH (US).
BOULDER, COLO. NO.1, FALL 1966- 22, 1972.
SUBS: ATMOSPHERIC TECHNOLOGY.
LO/N13.   XS/N-1.
ISSN 0014-6420

FACTORY (LONDON).
[MORGAN-GRAMPIAN]
LONDON 1(1), S 1972-
S/T: THE JOURNAL OF WORKS MANAGEMENT.
CA/U-1.   ED/N-1.

FACTORY (NEW YORK).                                  XXX
SUBS (1968): MODERN MANUFACTURING.

FACTORY MUTUAL RECORD.                               XXX
SUBS (1971): RECORD, FACTORY MUTUAL ENGIN-
EERING CORPORATION.

FACTORY & PLANT.                                     XXX
SUBS (1969): INDUSTRIAL MANAGEMENT.

FACTS ABOUT THE PALESTINE PROBLEM.
+ +FACTS ABOUT PALEST. PROBL.
ARAB WOMEN'S INFORMATION COMMITTEE.
BEIRUT 1, 1968-
SO/U-1.

FACTSHEETS ON BRITAIN AND EUROPE.                    XXX
+ +FACTSHEETS BR. & EUR.
(GREAT BRITAIN) CENTRAL OFFICE OF INFORMATION.
LONDON NO.1- 12, 1971.//
GRATIS.
BH/P-1.   LO/N-1.   LO/U-3.

FACTUAL NEWS INFORMATION.
+ +FACTUAL NEWS INF.
INDEPENDENT WORLD WIDE RIGHT-WING NEWS & INFOR-
MATION SERVICE.
SLOUGH 1, S 1969-
ED/N-1.   OX/U-1.

FACULTY.THE UNIVERSITY WEEKLY.
[CITY MAGAZINES LTD.]
LONDON 1, OC 1970-
GL/U-2.   HL/U-1.   LO/M24.   LO/U13.   SF/U-1.   SH/C-1.

FACULTY PAPERS, SEOUL NATIONAL UNIVERSITY:
HUMANITIES & SOCIAL SCIENCES.
+ +FAC. PAP. SEOUL NATL. UNIV., HUM. & SOC. SCI.
SEOUL 1, 1971-
OX/U-1.

FAMILY CIRCLE.
+ +FAM. CIRCLE.
[STANDBROOK PUBL.]
LONDON 1(1), OC 1964-
INCORP: TRIO.
LO/N-1.

FAMILY IN HISTORICAL PERSPECTIVE.
+ +FAM. HIST. PERSPECT.
NEWBERRY LIBRARY.
CHICAGO NO.1, 1972-
OX/U-1.

FAMILY LAW.
+ +FAM. LAW.
[BUTTERWORTHS]
CHICHESTER 1(1), JA/F 1971-
2M.
BN/U-1.   DN/U-1.   ED/N-1.   EX/U-1.   HL/U-1.   LO/U-3.
LO/U12.   MA/U-1.   OX/U-1.   SH/U-1.   SO/U-1.
LO/U-2. 3, 1973-              NO/U-1. 3, 1973-
RE/U-1. 4, 1974-
ISSN 0014-7281

FAMILY LAW QUARTERLY.
+ +FAM. LAW Q.
AMERICAN BAR ASSOCIATION.
CHICAGO 1(1), 1967-
PUBL BY THE ASSOCIATION'S SECTION OF FAMILY
LAW.
LO/U-3.   OX/U15.
LO/U-2. 8, 1974-
ISSN 0014-729X

FAMILY PLANNING MISCELLANY.
+ +FAM. PLANN. MISC.
FAMILY PLANNING ASSOCIATION.
LONDON NO.1, JA 1967-
S/T: AN INFORMATION SHEET ISSUED BY THE ...
ASSOCIATION.
LO/U-3.
ED/N-1. 2,1967-

FAMILY PLANNING PERSPECTIVES.
+ +FAM. PLANN. PERSPECT.
PLANNED PARENTHOOD-WORLD POPULATION.
NEW YORK 1, 1969-
Q.
LO/S74.
ISSN 0014-7354

FANTASTIKA.
VSESOJUZNYJ LENINSKIJ KOMMUNISTICHESKIJ SOJUZ
MOLODEZHI: TSENTRAL'NYJ KOMITET.
MOSCOW 1962(1)-
BH/U-1.
CB/U-1. 1966-             HL/U-1. 1965-
LO/U12. 1966-            YK/U-1. 1968-
ISSN 0427-9832

FAO FISHERIES SYNOPSIS.
+ +FAO FISH. SYNOP.
FOOD & AGRICULTURE ORGANIZATION (UN).
ROME NO.1, 1965-
LO/N13.**
ISSN 0014-5602

FAR POINT.
[MANITOBA UNIV. P.]
WINNIPEG NO.1, 1968-
LO/U-2.   OX/U-1.
ISSN 0014-7621

FARADAY SPECIAL DISCUSSIONS OF THE CHEMICAL
SOCIETY.                                             XXX
+ +FARADAY SPEC. DISCUSS. CHEM. SOC.
CHEMICAL SOCIETY: FARADAY DIVISION.
LONDON NO.2, 1972(1973)-
PREV: SPECIAL DISCUSSIONS OF THE FARADAY
SOCIETY FROM NO.1, 1970(1971).
LO/N14.   LO/S-3.
GL/U-1. NO.53, 1972-

FARM BUILDING REPORT.                                    XXX
++FARM BUILD. REP.
SCOTTISH FARM BUILDINGS INVESTIGATION UNIT.
*ABERDEEN NO.1, 1966- 4, 1969.*
SUBS: FARM BUILDING RESEARCH & DEVELOPMENT
STUDIES.
*LO/N14.*

FARM BUILDING RESEARCH & DEVELOPMENT STUDIES.          XXX
++FARM BUILD. RES. & DEV. STUD.
SCOTTISH FARM BUILDINGS INVESTIGATION UNIT.
*ABERDEEN NO.1, 1971-*
PREV: FARM BUILDING REPORT FROM NO.1, 1966- 4,
1969.
*LO/N14.*

FARM ECONOMIST.                                          XXX
SUBS (1972): OXFORD AGRARIAN STUDIES.

FARM ENGINEERING INDUSTRY.
++FARM ENG. IND.
[FARM ENGINEERING INDUSTRY PUBL. LTD.]
*LONDON 1, 1969-*
*LO/N14.    OX/U-8.*
*ED/N-1.  1(3), 1969-*
*ISSN 0014-794X*

FARM & FOOD RESEARCH.                                    XXX
++FARM & FOOD RES.
FORAS TALUNTAIS.
*DUBLIN 1, 1970-*
PREV: FARM RESEARCH NEWS FROM 1, 1960- 10(6),
1969.
*BN/U-2.    CA/U-1.    DB/U-2.    ED/N-1.    LO/N13.    OX/U-8.*
*XS/R-2.*
*ISSN 0046-3302*

FARM MANAGEMENT REVIEW.                                  XXX
++FARM MANAGE. REV.
NORTH OF SCOTLAND COLLEGE OF AGRICULTURE:
AGRICULTURAL ECONOMICS DIVISION.
*ABERDEEN NO.1, OC 1972-*
PREV: FARM MANAGEMENT QUARTERLY FROM NO.1,
1964- NO.16, 1971.
*ED/N-1.    LD/U-1.    LO/N-6.    OX/U-3.    OX/U-8.*

FARM SUPPLY STORE.                                       XXX
[PUBLIC P.]
*WINNIPEG 23(10), 1967- 25, 1969.//*
PREV: CANADIAN FEED & GRAIN JOURNAL FROM
20(1), JA 1964- 23(9), 1967.
*LO/N13.*

FARMACEUT (NOVI SAD).
FARMACEUTSKO DRUSTVO VOJVODINE.
*NOVI SAD 1, 1966-*
*LO/N13.  5(4), 1970-*

FARMACEUTICKY OBZOR.                                     XXX
++FARM. OBZOR.
SLOVENSKY USTAV PRE DOSKOLOVANIE LEKAROV.
*BRATISLAVA 30(1), 1961-*
PREV: FARMACIA FROM 1(1), 1931- 29, 1960.
FROM VOL. 35 ENGL. SUMM. & CONT. LISTS.
*LO/N13.*    XY/N-1.*

FARMACIA.                                                XXX
SUBS(1961): FARMACEUTICKY OBZOR.

FARMER & STOCKBREEDER.                                   XXX
SUBS (1971): PART OF BRITISH FARMER & STOCK-
BREEDER.

FARMING BUSINESS.
++FARM. BUS.
AGRICULTURAL CENTRAL CO-OPERATIVE ASSOCIATION
LTD.
*LONDON 1(1), 1964-*
Q.
*ED/U-2.    LO/N-6.**    OX/U-1.    OX/U-3.*
*ED/N-1. MR 1971-            LO/N17. 2(3), 1965-*

FARMING PRACTICE.                                        XXX
++FARM. PRACT.
ROYAL AGRICULTURAL SOCIETY OF ENGLAND.
*LONDON 1(5), 1969-*
PREV: PRACTICE WITH SCIENCE FROM 1(1), 1967-
1(4), 1968.
*CA/U11.    LO/N13.*

FARNHAM PAPERS.
++FARNHAM PAP.
WORKERS' EDUCATIONAL ASSOCIATION: FARNHAM
BRANCH.
*FARNHAM 1, [1967]-*
*OX/U-1.*

FASCICULI HISTORICI.                                     XXX
++FASC. HIST.
UNIWERSYTET WARSZAWSKI: INSTYTUT HISTORYCZNY.
*WARSAW 1, 1968-*
ENGL. FR. & GER.  PREV: ZESZYTY HISTORYCZNE
FROM 1, 1960- 3, 1963.
*LO/S-9.    OX/U-1.*
*ISSN 0071-4038*

FASHION.                                                 XXX
[FLEETWAY PUBL.]
*LONDON 1968- 1969.*
MON. SUBS. PART OF: FLAIR WITH FASHION.
*OX/U-1.*

FATEH. INFORMATION OF THE ...
PALESTINE NATIONAL LIBERATION MOVEMENT.
*BEIRUT 1(1), OC 1969-*
W.
*LO/U-3.*
*ED/N-1. 2(8), 1970-*

FAULKNER CONCORDANCE NEWSLETTER.
++FAULKNER CONCORDANCE NEWSL.
*COLLEGE PARK, MO. NO.1, D 1972-*
*EX/U-1.    OX/U-1.*

FAUNA. THE ZOOLOGICAL MAGAZINE.
[FAUNA P.]
*RANCHO MIRAGE, CALIF. NO.1, JA/F 1971-*
*LO/N-2.    LO/N13.*
*ISSN 0046-337X*

FAUNA BULLETIN.
++FAUNA BULL.
(WESTERN AUSTRALIA) DEPARTMENT OF FISHERIES
& FAUNA.
*PERTH 1(1), 1967-*
*LO/N17.*

FAUNA CARIBAEA.
UNIVERSITY OF MIAMI: INSTITUTE OF MARINE
SCIENCE.
*CORAL GABLES NO.1, 1967-*
*OX/U-8.*
*ISSN 0430-1218*

FAUNA NA TRAKIJA.
BULGARSKA AKADEMIJA NA NAUKITE: ZOOLOGICHESKIJ
INSTITUT S MUZEJ.
*SOFIA 1, 1964-*
S/T: SBORNIK OT STATII.
*LO/N-2.    XY/N-1.*
*ISSN 0428-0644*

FAUNISTISCH-FLORISTISCHE NOTIZEN AUS DEM
SAARLAND.
++FAUN.-FLORIST. NOT. SAARLAND.
ARBEITSGEMEINSCHAFT FUR TIER- UND PFLANZENGEO-
GRAPHISCHE HEIMATFORSCHUNG IM SAARLAND.
*SAARBRUCKEN 1, 1968-*
*LO/N-2.*

FEATURES.
INTERNATIONAL CONFEDERATION OF FREE TRADE
UNIONS.
*BRUSSELS NO.1, 7/MR 1963-*
*OX/U17. *1963-1964.*

FEBS LETTERS.
++FEBS LETT.
FEDERATION OF EUROPEAN BIOCHEMICAL SOCIETIES.
*AMSTERDAM 1, 1968-*
*BH/U-1.    BL/U-1.    GL/U-1.    GL/U-2.    LO/U-4.    LO/U11.*
*LV/U-1.*
*CB/U-1. 6, 1970-*
*ISSN 0014-5793*

FEDERAL FISHERIES OCCASIONAL PAPER (NIGERIA).
++FED. FISH. OCC. PAP. (NIGERIA).
(NIGERIA) FEDERAL FISHERIES SERVICE.
*MAIDUGURI NO.1, 1961-*
PROD. BY THE SERVICE'S DEPT. OF FISHERIES
RESEARCH.
*OX/U-8. NO.11, 1968-*

FEDERATION NEWS.
++FED. NEWS.
WORLD STUDENT CHRISTIAN FEDERATION.
*GENEVA NO.1, 1968-*
*LO/U-3.*

FEDERATION RESEARCH PAPER.
++FED. RES. PAP.
ENGINEERING EMPLOYERS' FEDERATION.
*LONDON 1, 1968-*
*OX/U-8.*

FEED BAG.                                                                    XXX
  SUBS (1970): FEED INDUSTRY.

FEED & FARM SUPPLIES.                                                        XXX
  [TURRET P., LTD.]
  LONDON 67(6), JE 1970- 70(3), 1973.
  PREV: FERTILISER FEED & PESTICIDE JOURNAL
  FROM 66(1), JA 1969- 67(5), MY 1970. SUBS.
  PART OF: JOURNAL OF FLOUR & ANIMAL FEED
  MILLING.
  BN/U-2.    GL/U-1.

FEED & FARM SUPPLY DEALER.                                                   XXX
  [SAMFORD EVANS PUBL.]
  WINNIPEG 48(10), 1967-
  PREV: CANADIAN MILLING & FEED FROM 1, 1920-
  48(9), 1967.
  LO/N13.
  ISSN 0046-3604

FEED FORUM.                                                                  XXX
  BRITISH GLUES & CHEMICALS LTD: AGRICULTURAL
  DEPARTMENT.
  LONDON 1, 1966- 4(1), 1969.//
  LO/N13.
  ISSN 0430-280X

FEED INDUSTRY.                                                               XXX
  + +FEED IND.
  [COMMUNICATIONS MARKETING]
  EDINA, MINN. 46(4), 1970- 47, 1971 ...
  PREV: FEED BAG FROM 1, AG 1925- 46(3), 1969.
  SUBS: FEED INDUSTRY REVIEW.
  LO/N13.
  ISSN 0014-9535

FEED INDUSTRY REVIEW.                                                        XXX
  + +FEED IND. REV.
  [COMMUNICATIONS MARKETING]
  EDINA, MINN. 48, 1972-
  PREV: FEED INDUSTRY FROM 46(4), 1970- 47, 1971
  LO/N13.

FEEDBACK. THE GLASGOW JOURNAL OF PSYCHOLOGY.
  UNIVERSITY OF GLASGOW: DEPARTMENT OF PSYCHOLOGY
  [GLASGOW] 1, 1968-
  GL/U-1.    GL/U-2.
  ISSN 0014-9608

FEEDBACK. JOURNAL OF THE ...
  LOUGHBOROUGH UNIVERSITY OF TECHNOLOGY: SOCIAL
  SCIENCE SOCIETY.
  LOUGHBOROUGH 1(1), 1971-
  ED/N-1.    OX/U-1.

FEINISC.
  CUMANN NA GAEILGE (NEW YORK).
  NEW YORK 1, 1968-
  BL/U-1.    DB/U-2.    MA/U-1.

FEINWERKTECHNIK.                                                             XXX
  SUBS (1972): FEINWERKTECHNIK + MICRONIC.

FEINWERKTECHNIK + MICRONIC.                                                  XXX
  [HANSER]
  MUNICH 76, 1972-
  PREV: FEINWERKTECHNIK FROM 53, 1949- 75, 1971.
  LO/N14.

FELLOWSHIP OF RECONCILIATION QUARTERLY.                                     XXX
  + +FELLOWSHIP RECONCIL. Q.
  LONDON 1, 1967- 4, 1968...
  SUBS: RECONCILIATION QUARTERLY.
  ED/N-1.    OX/U-1.

FELSMECHANIK.                                                                000
  SEE: ROCK MECHANICS.

FERNSEH + FILMTECHNIKUM.                                                     XXX
  + +FERNSEH + FILMTECH.
  [VERLAG HORST AXTMANN GMBH]
  WIESBADEN 21(4), 1970-
  PREV: FILMTECHNIKUM FROM 1, 1950(?)- 21(3),
  1970.
  LO/N14.
  ISSN 0015-1424

FERNWARME INTERNATIONAL.
  + +FERNWARME INT.
  ARBEITSGEMEINSCHAFT FERNWARME.
  FRANKFURT AM MAIN 1, 1972-
  LO/N14.

FERROELECTRICS.
  NEW YORK 1(1), MR 1970-
  ED/N-1.    LO/N14.    LO/U12.    OX/U-8.    XS/R10.
  XS/T-4.
  BH/U-3.                          HL/U-1. 4(1), 1972-
  ISSN 0015-0193

FERTIGUNG.
  [VERLAG TECHNISCHE RUNDSCHAU]
  BERN 1, 1970-
  LO/N14.

FERTILIZER ABSTRACTS.
  + +FERT. ABSTR. [FERA-A]
  TENNESSEE VALLEY AUTHORITY.
  MUSCLE SHOALS, ALA. 1, JA 1968-
  VOLUME 1(1) PRECEDED BY AN ISSUE NUMBERED 0 OC
  1967.
  XE/F-2.
  ISSN 0015-0290

FERTILISER FEED & PESTICIDE JOURNAL.                                        XXX
  + +FERT. FEED & PESTIC. J.
  [TURRET P., LTD.]
  LONDON 66(1), JA 1969- 67(5), MY 1970 ...
  PREV: FERTILISER & FEEDING STUFFS JOURNAL
  FROM 41, 1954- 65, 1968. SUBS: FEED & FARM
  SUPPLIES.
  BN/U-2.    ED/N-1.    GL/U-1.    LO/N14.    RE/U-1.
  XS/R-2.  [W. 66(4); (5); (10)]

FERTILISER & FEEDING STUFFS JOURNAL.                                        XXX
  SUBS (1969): FERTILISER FEED & PESTICIDE
  JOURNAL.

FERTILIZER INTERNATIONAL.
  + +FERT. INT.
  BRITISH SULPHUR CORPORATION.
  LONDON NO.1, JL 1969-
  INCORP: WORLD OF N.P.K.S.
  ED/N-1.    OX/U-1.    XE/F-2.
  LO/N14. CURRENT BOX ONLY.
  ISSN 0015-0304

FERTILIZER PROGRESS.
  + +FERT. PROGR.
  FERTILIZER INSTITUTE.
  WASHINGTON, D.C. 1, 1970-
  2M.
  XE/F-2.
  ISSN 0002-1598

FESTIVUS.
  SAN DIEGO SHELL CLUB.
  SAN DIEGO [1, 1970]-
  LO/N-2.

FIAT JUSTITIA.
  MALAYSIAN & SINGAPORE LAW STUDENT'S SOCIETY.
  LONDON 1, 1966-
  BL/U-1.

FIBRE CHEMISTRY.
  + +FIBRE CHEM. [FICY-A]
  [CONSULTANTS BUREAU]
  LONDON; NEW YORK JA/F 1969-
  ENGL. TRANSL. OF: KHIMICHESKIE VOLOKNA. DATING
  & NUMBERING OF ISSUES FOLLOW ORIGINAL.
  CA/U-1.    ED/N-1.    LO/N14.
  ISSN 0015-0541

FIBRE E COLORI.                                                             XXX
  SUBS (1970): PART OF TEXTILIA.

FIBRE REVIEW.
  + +FIBRE REV.
  (AUSTRALIA) BUREAU OF AGRICULTURAL ECONOMICS.
  CANBERRA 1971-72(1972)-
  S/T: A REVIEW OF EVENTS & STATISTICS RELATING
  TO WOOL & COMPETING FIBRES.
  CA/U-1.    CA/U11.    LD/U-1.

FIBRE SCIENCE & TECHNOLOGY.
  + +FIBRE SCI. & TECHNOL.
  [ELSEVIER]
  AMSTERDAM &C 1(1), JL 1968-
  ED/N-1.    LO/N-4.    LO/N14.    OX/U-8.    SW/U-1.
  XS/R10.
  ISSN 0015-0568

FICTION.
  NEW YORK 1(1), 1972-
  OX/U-1.
  ISSN 0046-3736

**FID YEARBOOK.**
INTERNATIONAL FEDERATION FOR DOCUMENTATION.
*THE HAGUE 1969-*
*LO/U-3.*
*LO/N-2. 1970-*
*ISSN 0074-5839*

**FIELD. CONTEMPORARY POETRY & POETICS.**
OBERLIN COLLEGE.
*OBERLIN, OHIO NO.1, 1969-*
*LO/U-2.   OX/U-1.*
*ISSN 0015-0657*

**FIELDS & QUANTA.**
[GORDON & BREACH]
*NEW YORK; LONDON 1(1), OC 1970-*
Q. 1(2) DATED MR 1971.
*LO/N14.    OX/U-8.    XY/N-1.*
*ED/N-1. 1(2), 1971-*
*ISSN 0046-3744*

**FIELDWORKER.**
*LONDON 1, 1970-*
*LO/N-1.    LO/R-5.*

**FIJI AGRICULTURAL JOURNAL: NS.**
*++FIJI AGR. J., NS.*
(FIJI) DEPARTMENT OF AGRICULTURE.
*SUVA 32, 1970-*
2/A. PREV: AGRICULTURAL JOURNAL, DEPARTMENT
OF AGRICULTURE, FIJI FROM 1, 1928- 31, 1961.
*XS/R-2.*
*ISSN 0015-0886*

**FIJI TIMBERS & THEIR USES.**
(FIJI) DEPARTMENT OF FORESTRY.
*SUVA 1, 1966-*
*OX/U-3.*

**AL-FIKR AL-ISLAMI.**
*BEIRUT 1(1), 1969-*
M.
*LO/U14.*

**FILM USER.**                                                          XXX
SUBS (1972): PART OF AUDIO VISUAL.

**FILMS ILLUSTRATED.**
*++FILMS ILLUS.*
[INDEPENDENT MAGAZINES LTD.]
M.
*OX/U-1.*

**FILMTECHNIKUM.**                                                     XXX
SUBS (1970): FERNSEH + FILMTECHNIKUM.

**FILOLOSKI PREGLED. REVUE DE PHILOLOGIE.**
*BELGRADE 1963(1/2)-*
VARIOUS LANGUAGES.
*CA/U-1.    OX/U-1.*
*ISSN 0015-1807*

**FILOSOFSKIE NAUKI, URAL'SKIJ GOSUDARSTVENNYJ
UNIVERSITET [IM. A.M. GOR'KOGO].**
*++FIL. NAUK URAL. GOS. UNIV.*
*SVERDLOVSK 1, 1966-*
*BH/U-1.    YK/U-1.*

**FILOSOFSKIE VOPROSY MEDITSINY I BIOLOGII.**
*++FILOS. VOPR. MED. & BIOL.*
(UKRAINE) MINISTERSTVO ZDRAVOOKHRANENIJA USSR:
KIEVSKIJ MEDITSINSKI INSTITUT.
*KIEV [1], 1965-*
VOL.1 UNNUMBERED. S/T: RESPUBLIKANSKIJ MEZH-
VEDOMSTVENNYJ SBORNIK.
*BH/U-1.*
*ISSN 0430-4667*

**FINANCIAL TIMES EUROPEAN LAW NEWSLETTER.**              000
SEE: EUROPEAN LAW NEWSLETTER.

**FINANCIAL TIMES WORLD BUSINESS SERVICE.**
*++FINANC. TIMES WORLD BUS. SERV.*
[FINANCIAL TIMES LTD.]
*LONDON [NO.1], MR 1973-*
S/T: A WEEKLY DIGEST OF WORLD BUSINESS
INFORMATION.
*CA/U-1.    ED/N-1.    OX/U-1.*

**FINANCNE STUDIE. CASOPIS PRE OTAZKY FINANC-
NEJ TEORIE A HOSPODARSKEJ POLITIKY.**
*++FINANC. STUD.*
USTAV PRE VYSKUM FINANCII V BRATISLAVE.
*BRATISLAVA 1(1), 1968-*
Q. ENGL. & RUSS. SUMM.
*BH/U-1.    LO/U-3.*
*ISSN 0046-3906*

**FINANSOVA STATISTIKA, STATISTICHESKIJ SBORNIK.**
*++FINANSOVA STAT. STAT. SB.*
(BULGARIA) MINISTERSTVO SUVET: TSENTRALNO
STATISTICHESKO UPRAVLENIE.
*SOFIA 1968-*
*OX/U-1.*

**FINISHER NEWS.**
KODAK LTD.
*LONDON NO.1, OC 1969-*
*ED/N-1.*

**FINNISH PSYCHIATRY.**                                               000
SEE: PSYCHIATRICA FENNICA.

**FIRE JOURNAL.**                                                      XXX
*++FIRE J.  [FIJO-A]*
NATIONAL FIRE PROTECTION ASSOCIATION.
*BOSTON 59, 1965-*
PREV: QUARTERLY, NATIONAL ... FROM 1, JL
1907- 58, 1964.
*LO/N14.*
*ISSN 0015-2617*

**FIRE PREVENTION.**                                                   XXX
*++FIRE PREV.*
FIRE PROTECTION ASSOCIATION.
*LONDON NO.90, AP 1971-*
Q. PREV: F.P.A. JOURNAL FROM NO.1, AP 1948-
89, D 1970.
*BH/P-1.    ED/N-1.    LO/U-2.    RE/U-1.*

**FIRE PREVENTION SCIENCE & TECHNOLOGY.**
*++FIRE PREV. SCI. & TECHNOL.*
FIRE PROTECTION ASSOCIATION.
*LONDON NO.1, MR 1972-*
*XS/R10.*
*ISSN 0305-7844*

**FIRE SURVEYOR.**
*++FIRE SURV.*
INCORPORATED ASSOCIATION OF ARCHITECTS &
SURVEYORS.
*LONDON 1, 1972-*
S/T: JOURNAL OF THE FIRE SURVEYORS' SECTION OF
THE ASSOCIATION.
*LO/N14.    XS/R10.*
*CA/U-1. 1(2), 1972-              ED/N-1. 1(2), 1972-*

**FIRM & FORESTER.**
WORCESTERSHIRE & SHERWOOD FORESTERS REGIMENT.
*WORCESTER 1(1), 1970-*
*BH/P-1.    OX/U-1.*

**FISCHEREI-MAGAZIN.**
*++FISCH.-MAG.*
[A.GANTENBEIN]
*BIRSFELDEN 1, 1969-*
*LO/N13.*

**FISH DISTRIBUTION REPORT.**
*++FISH DISTRIB. REP.*
(UNITED STATES) BUREAU OF SPORT FISHERIES &
WILDLIFE.
*WASHINGTON, D.C. NO.1, 1967-*
*LO/N-2.*

**FISH FARMING INTERNATIONAL.**
*++FISH FARM. INT.*
[FISHING NEWS (BOOKS)]
*WEST BYFLEET, SURREY NO.1, 1973-*
*CA/U-1.    ED/N-1.    HL/U-1.    LO/N13.    LO/R-6.    OX/U-8.*

**FISH INDUSTRY REVIEW.**
*++FISH IND. REV.*
WHITE FISH AUTHORITY (GB).
*LONDON 1(1), 1971-*
Q.
*LO/N-6.    LO/N14.    OX/U16.*
*CA/U-1. 1(2), 1971-              ED/N-1. 1(2), 1971-*
*LO/R-6. 2(2), 1972-*

**FISH PHYSIOLOGY.**
*++FISH PHYSIOL.*
[ACADEMIC P.]
*NEW YORK &C. 1, 1969-*
*GL/U-1.*

**FISHERIES RESEARCH BULLETIN.**
*++FISH. RES. BULL. (N.Z.).*
(NEW ZEALAND) MARINE DEPARTMENT: FISHERIES
RESEARCH DIVISION.
*WELLINGTON, N.Z. NO.1, 1968-*
MONOGR. CALLED 'NEW SERIES' OF PREV: FISHERIES
BULLETIN; NO.1, 1927- 12, 1957.
*LO/N-2.    LO/N-6.    LV/U-1.    XY/N-1.*
*LO/S19. 1(1), 1968.*

FISHERIES RESEARCH BULLETIN (ZAMBIA).                    XXX
+ +FISH. RES. BULL. (ZAMBIA).
(ZAMBIA) DEPARTMENT OF WILDLIFE, FISHERIES &
NATIONAL PARKS: FISHERIES RESEARCH DIVISION.            XXX
CHILANGA  NO.1, 1962/63-
PREV: PART OF REPORT, JOINT FISHERIES RESEARCH
ORGANIZATION (NORTHERN RHODESIA & NYASALAND)
FROM NO.8, 1958- 11, 1961.

FISHERIES YEAR-BOOK & DIRECTORY.                         XXX
SUBS (1970):  FISHING INDUSTRY INDEX INTER-
NATIONAL.

FISHERY BULLETIN, FISH & WILDLIFE SERVICE
(US).                                                    XXX
SUBS(1971): FISHERY BULLETIN OF THE NATIONAL
OCEANIC & ATMOSPHERIC ADMINISTRATION (US).

FISHERY BULLETIN OF THE NATIONAL OCEANIC &
ATMOSPHERIC ADMINISTRATION (US).                         XXX
+ +FISH. BULL. NATL. OCEANIC & ATMOS. ADM. (US).
WASHINGTON, D.C. 68(2), 1971-
PREV: FISHERY BULLETIN, FISH & WILDLIFE SER-
VICE(US) FROM 50(35), 1941- 68(1), 1970.
LO/N-2.

FISHERY FACTS (US),
(UNITED STATES) DEPARTMENT OF COMMERCE.
SEATTLE  1, 1972-
SPONS. BODIES ALSO: NATIONAL OCEANIC & ATMOS-
PHERIC ADMINISTRATION; & THE NATIONAL MARINE
FISHERIES SERVICE.
BL/U-1.   LO/N-2.

FISHERY TECHNOLOGY.
+ +FISH. TECHNOL.
SOCIETY OF FISHERIES TECHNOLOGISTS (INDIA).
ERNAKULAM, COCHIN  1(1), 1964-
2/A.
LO/N13.  1(2), 1964-
ISSN 0015-3001

FISHING INDUSTRY INDEX INTERNATIONAL.                    XXX
+ +FISH. IND. INDEX INT.
[HAYMARKET P.]
LONDON  1970-
PREV: FISHERIES YEAR-BOOK & DIRECTORY FROM
1952.
LO/N14.

FISONS FERTILIZER & AGRICULTURAL NEWS.
+ +FISONS FERT. & AGRIC. NEWS.
FISONS LTD.
FELIXSTOWE  NO.1, 1968-
ABSTRACTED BY THE BODY'S TECHNICAL INFORMATION
DEPARTMENT.
LO/N14.

FITOPATALOGIA.
ASOCIACION LATINO-AMERICANA DE FITOPATALOGIA.
SANTIAGO  1, 1966-
LO/N-2.

FITZGERALD/HEMINGWAY ANNUAL.
+ +FITZGERALD/HEMINGWAY ANNU.
[MICROCARD EDITIONS]
WASHINGTON, D.C.  1969-
AD/U-1.   EX/U-1.   LO/N-1.   LO/U-1.   MA/U-1.   OX/U-1.
ISSN 0071-5654

FIZIKA AERODISPERSNYKH SISTEM (ENGL. TRANSL.)            000
SEE: ADVANCES IN AEROSOL PHYSICS.

FIZIKA I KHIMIJA OBRABOTKI MATERIALOV.
+ +FIZ. & KHIM. OBRAB. MATER.
AKADEMIJA NAUK SSSR: OTDELENIE FIZIKO-KHIMII I
TEKHNOLOGII NEORGANICHESKIKH MATERIALOV.
MOSCOW  1967(1)-
2M.
LO/N13.
XS/R10.  1968(1)-
ISSN 0015-3214

FIZIKA I TEKHNIKA POLUPROVODNIKOV.
+ +FIZ. TEK. POLUPROV.
AKADEMIJA NAUK SSSR.
MOSCOW &C  1(1), 1967-
CA/U-2.   LO/N14.
XS/T-4.  3(1), 1969-
ISSN 0015-3222

FIZIKO-MATEMATICHESKIE NAUKI V STRANAKH
VOSTOKA.                                                 XXX
+ +FIZ.-MAT. NAUKI STRANAKH VOSTOKA. [FMNV-A]
AKADEMIJA NAUK SSSR: INSTITUT ISTORII ESTESTVO-
ZNANIJA I TEKHNIKI.
MOSCOW  1(4), 1966-
PREV: IZ ISTORII NAUKI I TEKHNIKI V STRANAKH
VOSTOKA FROM 1, 1960- 3, 1963.
LO/N-4.   LO/U14.
ISSN 0430-6279

FIZIKO-TEKHNICHESKIE PROBLEMY RAZRABOTKI
POLEZNYKH ISKOPAEMYKH.
+ +FIZ.-TEKH. PROBL. RAZRAB. POLEZN. ISKOP.
[FTRI-A]
AKADEMIJA NAUK SSSR (SIBIRSKOE OTDELENIE).
NOVOSIBIRSK  1, 1965-
LO/N14.
ISSN 0015-3273

FIZIOLOGIJA I BIOKHIMIJA KUL'TURNYKH RASTENIJ
(ENGL. TRANSL.).                                         000
SEE: PHYSIOLOGY & BIOCHEMISTRY OF CULTIVATED
PLANTS.

FIZIOLOGIJA NA RASTENIJATA.
+ +FIZIOL. RAST.
AKADEMIJA NA SELSKOSTOPANSKITE NAUKI.
SOFIA  1, 1970-
ENGL. SUMM.  TITLE ALSO IN ENGL.: PLANT
PHYSIOLOGY.
LO/N13.

FIZIOLOGIJA VODOOBMENA I USTOJCHIVOSTI
RASTENIJ.
+ +FIZIOL. VODOOBMENA & USTOJCH. RAST. [FVUR-A]
KAZANSKIJ GOSUDARSTVENNYJ UNIVERSITET: BIOLOGI-
CHESKIJ NAUCHNO-ISSLEDOVATEL'SKIJ INSTITUT.
KAZAN'  1, 1968-
LO/N13.
ISSN 0430-6309

FLAME NOTES.
BECKMAN INSTRUMENTS INC.
FULLERTON, CALIF.  1, 1966-
LO/N14.
ISSN 0015-346X

FLAVOUR INDUSTRY.                                        XXX
+ +FLAVOUR IND.
[UNITED TRADE P.]
LONDON  1, 1970- 5, 1974 ...
PREV: PERFUMERY & ESSENTIAL OIL RECORD FROM
1, 1910- 60(11/12), N/D 1969. SUBS: INTER-
NATIONAL FLAVOURS AND FOOD ADDITIVES.
LO/N14.   LO/S-3.   LO/U28.   OX/U-1.
ISSN 0015-3532

FLINDERS JOURNAL OF HISTORY & POLITICS.
+ +FLINDERS J. HIST. & POLIT.
FLINDERS UNIVERSITY OF SOUTH AUSTRALIA: HISTORY
& POLITICS SOCIETY.
BEDFORD PARK, S. AUST.  1, JL 1969-
LO/U-3.   LO/U-8.

FLOORING (1966- 69).                                     XXX
[METCALFE PUBL. (LONDON)]
CAMBRIDGE  11, 1966- 14, 1969 ...
PREV: FLOORING & FINISHES NEWS FROM 8, 1963.
SUBS: FLOORING & CARPET SPECIFIER.
LO/N14.

FLOORING & CARPET SPECIFIER.                             XXX
+ +FLOOR. & CARPET SPECIFIER.
[METCALFE PUBL. (LONDON) LTD.]
CAMBRIDGE  15, 1970- 16(2/3), 1971 ...
PREV: FLOORING (1966-69) FROM 11, 1966 - 14,
1969. SUBS: FLOORING & FLOOR COVERINGS.
ED/N-1.   HL/U-1.   LO/N14.
ISSN 0015-377X

FLOORING & FINISHES NEWS.                                XXX
SUBS: FLOORING (1966- 69).

FLOORING & FLOORCOVERINGS.                               XXX
+ +FLOOR. & FLOORCOVER.
[METCALFE PUBL. (LONDON) LTD.]
LONDON  16(4), MY 1971-
PREV: FLOORING & CARPET SPECIFIER FROM 15,
1970- 16(2/3), 1971.
LO/N14.
ED/N-1.  16(5), MY 1971-

FLORA ARCTICA URSS.                                      000
SEE: ARKTICHESKAJA FLORA SSSR.

FLORIDA QUARTERLY.
+ +FLA. Q.
UNIVERSITY OF FLORIDA.
*GAINSVILLE, FLA. 1(1), 1967-*
3/A.
*LO/U-1.*
*ISSN 0015-4253*

FLORISTISCHE MITTEILUNGEN DES BOTANISCHEN
INSTITUTS UND DES BOTANISCHEN GARTENS DER
UNIVERSITAT ROSTOCK.
+ +FLORIST. MITT. BOT. INST. BOT. GARTENS UNIV.
ROSTOCK.
*ROSTOCK 1, 1965-*
*LO/N-2.*

FLOWER SCENE & THE LOVE GENERATION.
*NOTTINGHAM NO.1, OC [1967]-*
M.
*ED/N-1.*

FLOWERS FROM THE PRINTSHOP.
[EMBER PRESS]
*THAMES DITTON 1, 1966-*
*LO/U-2.*

FLUGSCHRIFT, KURATORIUM FUR TECHNIK UND                            XXX
BAUWESEN IN DER LANDWIRTSCHAFT.
+ +FLUGSCHR. KURATORIUM TECH. BAUW. LANDW.
[WOLFRATSHAUSEN BEI MUNCHEN]
*MUNICH 19, 1970-*
PREV: FLUGSCHRIFT, KURATORIUM FUR TECHNIK
IN DER LANDWIRTSCHAFT FROM NO.1, 1956-
18, 1968-
*LO/N14.*

FLUGSCHRIFT, KURATORIUM FUR TECHNIK IN DER                         XXX
LANDWIRTSCHAFT.
SUBS (1970): FLUGSCHRIFT, KURATORIUM FUR
TECHNIK UND BAUWESEN IN DER LANDWIRTSCHAFT.

FLUID DYNAMICS TRANSACTIONS.
+ +FLUID DYN. TRANS.
SYMPOSIUM ON FLUID DYNAMICS.
*NEW YORK 1, 1964-*
*BR/U-3.*

FLUID MECHANICS. SOVIET RESEARCH.
+ +FLUID MECH.
[SCRIPTA PUBL. CORP.]
*WASHINGTON, D.C. 1, JA/F 1972-*
CONSISTS OF TRANSLATIONS OF RUSSIAN PAPERS.
*GL/U-2. LO/N14. SH/U-1. SH/U-3.*

FLUID MECHANICS CURRENT INDEX.
+ +FLUID MECH. CURR. INDEX.
[FLUID MECHANICS]
*OAK RIDGE, TENN. 1, JA 1972-*
*LO/N14.*

FLUIDICS INTERNATIONAL.
+ +FLUIDICS INT.
[PRODUCT JOURNALS LTD.]
*WEST WICKHAM (KENT) 1, JL 1968-*
*BH/U-1. LO/N-4.*
*GL/U-1. 1969-*

FLUIDICS QUARTERLY.
+ +FLUIDICS Q.
FLUID AMPLIFIER ASSOCIATES.
*ANN ARBOR, MICH. 1, 1967-*
*EX/U-1. GL/U-1. LO/N14. NW/U-1.*
*ISSN 0015-4687*

FLUORESCENCE NEWS.
+ +FLUORESC. NEWS.
AMERICAN INSTRUMENT COMPANY: BIOCHEMICAL
INSTRUMENTATION DIVISION.
*SILVER SPRING, MD. 1(1), 1966-*
*LO/N14.*
*ISSN 0015-4709*

FLUORIDE.
*[FLUO-A]*
INTERNATIONAL SOCIETY FOR FLUORIDE RESEARCH.
*DETROIT 1, 1968-*
*LO/R-5.*
*OX/U-8. 4(4), 1971-*
*LD/U-1. 4(3), 1971- [W. 4(4): 5(1)].*
*ISSN 0015-4725*

FLUORINE CHEMISTRY REVIEWS.
+ +FLUORINE CHEM. REV.
[MARCEL DEKKER INC.]
*BALTIMORE 1, 1967-*
2/A.
*BH/U-1. GL/U-1. LO/N-4. NW/U-1. SW/U-1.*

FLUOROCARBON & RELATED CHEMISTRY.
+ +FLUOROCARBON & RELAT. CHEM.
CHEMICAL SOCIETY.
*LONDON 1, 1971-*
S/T: A REVIEW OF THE LITERATURE.
*ED/N-1. GL/U-1. GL/U-2. LO/N14. LO/S-3. LO/U-2.*
*LO/U-4. LO/U28. MA/U-1. NW/U-1. SF/U-1. SH/U-1.*
*XS/C-2.*
*ISSN 0301-8938*

FLYING SAUCER REVIEW CASE HISTORIES: SUPPLEMENT.
+ +FLY. SAUCER REV. CASE HIST., SUPPL.
[FLYING SAUCER SERVICE LTD.]
*LONDON NO.1, OC 1970-*
*OX/U-1.*

FMF REVIEW.                                                              XXX
FOOD MANUFACTURERS' FEDERATION.
*LONDON AP 1972- N/D 1974.*
PREV: FOOD WORLD FROM F 1966- MR 1972.
SUBS: WORLD FOOD REVIEW.
*ED/N-1. LO/N-6. LO/N14. LO/R-6.*
*ISSN 0305-7283*

FOCAL SPOT.                                                              XXX
SUBS (1970): CANADIAN JOURNAL OF RADIO-
GRAPHY, RADIOTHERAPY, NUCLEOGRAPHY.

FOCUS.
UNIVERSITY OF OXFORD: CATHOLIC CHAPLAINCY.
*OXFORD NO.1, 1969-*
*OX/U-1.*

FOCUS ON FILM.
[TANTIVY]
*LONDON NO.1, JA/F 1970-*
*BH/P-1. ED/N-1. EX/U-1. HL/U-1. OX/U-1.*
*ISSN 0015-5128*

FOCUS ON LOCAL GOVERNMENT.
+ +FOCUS LOCAL GOV.
CONSERVATIVE CENTRAL OFFICE.
*LONDON 1(1), 1972-*
*ED/N-1. LO/U-3.*

FOCUS ON PRAYER.                                                         XXX
INTERNATIONAL SOCIETY FOR THE EVANGELIZATION
OF THE JEWS.
*EASTBOURNE NO.1, 1971- 6, 1973.*
SUBS: PRAYER FOCUS.
*ED/N-1. OX/U-1.*

FOCUS ON ROBERT GRAVES.
*HEMPSTEAD, N.Y. NO.1, JA 1972-*
*OX/U-1.*

FOCUS ON SOCIAL WORK & SERVICE IN SCOTLAND.
+ +FOCUS SOC. WORK & SERV. SCOTL.
*EDINBURGH [NO.1], JA 1972-*
M.
*ED/N-1.*

FOGRA PRAXIS REPORT.
+ +FOGRA PRAX. REP.
DEUTSCHE GESELLSCHAFT FUR FORSCHUNG IM
GRAPHISCHEN GEWERBE.
*MUNICH 1, 1966-*
*LO/N14.*

FOLGER LIBRARY NEWSLETTER.
+ +FOLGER LIBR. NEWSL.
*WASHINGTON 1, 1969-*
*ED/N-1. MA/S-1.*
*OX/U-1. 1(2), 1969-              SO/U-1. JE 1970-*
*ISSN 0015-5438*

FOLIA FARMACEUTIKA.                                                     XXX
+ +FOLIA FARM.
ALGEMENE NEDERLANDSE PHARMACEUTISCHE STUDENTEN
VERENIGING.
*AMSTERDAM 61, 1973-*
PREV: FOLIA PHARMACEUTICA.
*LO/N14.*

FOLIA GEOGRAPHICA. SERIES GEOGRAPHICA-
OECONOMICA.
+ +FOLIA GEOGR., GEOGR.-OECON.
POLSKA AKADEMIA NAUK (ODDZIAL W KRAKOWIE),
KOMISJA NAUK GEOGRAFICZNYCH.
*KRAKOW 1, 1968 (1969)-*
ENGL. SUMM.
*LO/S13.*
*LD/U-1. [W. 3, 1970].*

**FOLIA GEOGRAPHICA. SERIES GEOGRAPHICA-PHYSICA.**
+ +FOLIA GEOGR., GEOGR.-PHYS.
POLSKA AKADEMIA NAUK (ODDZIAL W KRAKOWIE),
KOMISJA NAUK GEOGRAFICZNYCH.
*KRAKOW  1, 1967-*
ENGL. SUMM.
*LD/U-1.    LO/S13.*

**FOLIA HISTOCHEMICA ET CYTOCHEMICA.**
+ +FOLIA HISTOCHEM. & CYTOCHEM. [FHCY-A]
POLSKIE TOWARZYSTWO HISTOCHEMIKOW I CYTOCHEM-
IKOW.
*KRAKOW  1(1), 1963-*
ENGL. WITH RUSS. CONT. LISTS & SUMM.
*LO/N13.    OX/U-8.*
*ISSN 0015-5586*

**FOLIA HISTOCHEMICA ET CYTOCHEMICA: SUPPLEMENT.**
+ +FOLIA HISTOCHEM. & CYTOCHEM., SUPPL.
POLSKIE TOWARZYSTWO HISTOCHEMIKOW I CYTOCHEM-
IKOW.
*KRAKOW  NO.1, 1963-*
*OX/U-8.*

**FOLIA LINGUISTICA.  ACTA SOCIETATIS
LINGUISTICAE EUROPAEAE.**
+ +FOLIA LINGUIST. [FOLI-B]
EUROPEAN SOCIETY OF LINGUISTICS.
*THE HAGUE  1, 1967-*
*LO/U11.    RE/U-1.*
*ISSN 0430-862X*

**FOLIA MEDICA LODZIENSIA.**
+ +FOLIA MED. LODZ. [FOML-A]
LODZKIE TOWARZYSTWO NAUKOWE: WYDZIAT IV NAUK
LEKARSKICH.
*LODZ  1, 1966-*
*OX/U-8.*
*ISSN 0071-6731*

**FOLIA MENDELIANA.**
MORAVSKE MUZEUM V BRNE.
*BRNO  NO.1, 1966-*
ENGL. OR GER.
*LO/N-2.*
*LO/M24.  NO.4, 1969-*

**FOLIA OECONOMICA CRACOVIENSIA.**
+ +FOLIA OECON. CRACOV.
POLSKA AKADEMIA NAUK (ODDZIAL W KRAKOWIE):
KOMISJA NAUK EKONOMICZNYCH.
*CRACOW  1, 1960-*
ENGL. & RUSS. SUMM.
*OX/U-1.*
*ISSN 0071-674X*

**FOLIA PHARMACEUTICA.**                                                    XXX
SUBS (1973): FOLIA FARMACEUTIKA.

**FOLIA SCIENTIFICA AFRICAE CENTRALIS.**                          XXX
SUBS (1966): CHRONIQUES DE L'IRSAC.

**FOLK LITERATURE OF THE SEPHARDIC JEWS.**
+ +FOLK LIT. SEPHARDIC JEWS.
*BERKELEY, CALIF. &C.  1, 1971-*
*OX/U-1.*
*ISSN 0071-6758*

**FOLK-LIV.**                                                                           XXX
SUBS (1971): ETHNOLOGIA SCANDINAVICA.

**FOLKLORE RESEARCH CENTER STUDIES.**
+ +FOLKLORE RES. CENT. STUD.
HEBREW UNIVERSITY OF JERUSALEM: FOLKLORE RES-
EARCH CENTER.
*JERUSALEM  1, 1970-*
CENTER SUBORD. TO INSTITUTE OF JEWISH STUDIES.
*LO/S10.    OX/U-1.*

**FONTANE BLATTER.  (KREIS DER FREUNDE THEODOR
FONTANES).**
BRANDENBURGISCHEN LANDES- UND HOCHSHULBIBLIO-
THEK.
*POTSDAM, GER.  1(1), 1965-*
*OX/U-1.*
*ISSN 0015-6175*

**FONTI E RICERCHE DI STORIA ECCLESIASTICA
PADOVANA.**
+ +FONTI & RIC. STOR. ECCLESIASTICA PADOVANA.
ISTITUTO PER LA STORIA ECCLESIASTICA PADOVANA.
*PADUA  1, 1967-*
*OX/U-1.*
*ISSN 0532-0100*

**FOOD CHEMISTRY MICROBIOLOGY TECHNOLOGY.**       000
SEE: CHEMIE MIKROBIOLOGIE TECHNOLOGIE DER
LEBENSMITTEL.

**FOOD INDUSTRY STUDIES.**
+ +FOOD IND. STUD.
UNITED NATIONS: INDUSTRIAL DEVELOPMENT ORGAN-
ISATION.
*NEW YORK  NO.1, 1969-*
*LO/N13.*

**FOOD IRRADIATION INFORMATION.  INFORMATIONS
SUR L'IRRADIATION DES DENREES.**                                  XXX
+ +FOOD IRRADIAT. INF.
INTERNATIONAL PROJECT IN THE FIELD OF FOOD
IRRADIATION.
*KARLSRUHE  NO.1, 1972-*
PREV: FOOD IRRADIATION FROM 1, 1960- 11, 1971.
*DB/U-2.    LD/U-1.    LO/N-6.    LO/N14.    LO/R-6.    XS/R10.*

**FOOD PACKAGING DESIGN & TECHNOLOGY.**
+ +FOOD PACKAG. DES. & TECHNOL.
[FACTORY PUBLS. LTD.]
*LONDON    MY 1966-*
*ED/N-1.    LO/N14.    LV/P-1.*

**FOOD PROCESSING INDUSTRY.**
+ +FOOD PROCESS. IND.
[HARLEQUIN P.]
*LONDON  38(456), S 1969-*
PREV: FOOD PROCESSING & MARKETING FROM 33
(396), 1964.
*ED/N-1.    LV/P-1.*
*ISSN 0015-6531*

**FOOD PROCESSING REVIEW.**
+ +FOOD PROCESS. REV.
NOYES DEVELOPMENT CORPORATION.
*PARK RIDGE, NJ  NO.1, 1968-*
*LO/N14.*

**FOOD PRODUCTION MANAGEMENT.  CANNED, GLASSED &
FROZEN FOODS.**                                                                 XXX
+ +FOOD PROD. MANAGE.
[CANNING TRADE, INC.]
*BALTIMORE  94, 1971-*
PREV: CANNING TRADE FROM 14, MY 1912- 93, 1971
*LO/N13.*

**FOOD PROGRESS.**
+ +FOOD PROG.
INSTITUTE FOR INDUSTRIAL RESEARCH & STANDARDS
(EIRE).
*DUBLIN  NO.1, 1971-*
*DB/U-2.    LO/N13.*

**FOOD SCIENCE + TECHNOLOGY.**                                     000
SEE: LEBENSMITTEL-WISSENSCHAFT + TECHNOLOGIE.

**FOOD SCIENCE & TECHNOLOGY ABSTRACTS.**
+ +FOOD SCI. & TECHNOL. ABSTR.
INTERNATIONAL FOOD INFORMATION SERVICES.
[SHINFIELD]  1, 1969-
*GL/U-2.    LO/N14.    RE/U-1.*
*ISSN 0015-6574*

**FOOD WORLD.**                                                                    XXX
FOOD MANUFACTURERS' FEDERATION.
*LONDON  F 1966- MR 1972.*
PREV: FMF REVIEW FROM 1958- JA 1966.  SUBS:
FMF REVIEW.
*ED/N-1.*
*LO/N14.  1969-                          LO/R-6.  JA 1971-*
*ISSN 0015-668X*

**FOOTBALL LEAGUE REVIEW.**
+ +FOOTB. LEAG. REV.
FOOTBALL LEAGUE.
*LEICESTER  NO.1, AG 1966-*
*ED/N-1.*

**FOOTLIGHTS.**
EASTBOURNE THEATRE COMPANY.
*EASTBOURNE  NO.1, 1969-*
*LO/N-1.*

**FOOTWEAR DIGEST.**                                                         XXX
+ +FOOTWEAR DIG.
SHOE & ALLIED TRADES RESEARCH ASSOCIATION.
*KETTERING, NORTHANTS.  JA/F 1972-*
PREV: SHOEMAKING PROGRESS FROM 1, 1971.
*ED/N-1.    LO/N14.    OX/U-1.*

I

**FOR YOUR CURRENT INFORMATION: ECONOMICS.**    XXX
++FOR YOUR CURR. INF., ECON.
(GREAT BRITAIN) DEPARTMENT OF TRADE &
INDUSTRY.    XXX
  LONDON NO.1, S 1970- 9, D 1971.
  SUBS: FOR YOUR CURRENT INFORMATION: INDUSTRY &
  MANAGEMENT. PRODUCED BY DEPARTMENT'S INFOR-
  MATION SERVICES UNIT. NO.1 & 2, SPONS. BY
  MINISTRY OF TECHNOLOGY.
  LO/N-1.

**FOR YOUR CURRENT INFORMATION: INDUSTRY &
MANAGEMENT.**    XXX
++FOR YOUR CURR. INF., IND. & MANAGE.
(GREAT BRITAIN) DEPARTMENT OF TRADE &
INDUSTRY.    XXX
  LONDON NO.1- 6, JA/S 1972.//
  PREV: FOR YOUR CURRENT INFORMATION: ECONOMICS
  FROM NO.1, S 1970- 9, D 1971. PRODUCED BY
  DEPARTMENT'S INFORMATION SERVICES UNIT.
  LO/N-1.

**FORCES.**
HYDRO-QUEBEC.
  MONTREAL NO.1, WINTER 1967-
  3/A.
  BH/U-1.   BL/U-1. *
  ISSN 0015-6957

**FOREGROUND CHEMISTRY.**
++FOREGROUND CHEM.
[HEINEMAN EDUCATIONAL]
  LONDON NO.1, 1968-
  MONOGR.
  LO/U28.   OX/U-8.

**FOREIGN BULLETIN OF THE ITALIAN COMMUNIST**    XXX
**PARTY.**
++FOR. BULL. IT. COMMUNIST PARTY.
PARTITO COMUNISTA ITALIANO.
  ROME 1960- JA/AP 1970.
  SUBS: ITALIAN COMMUNISTS. PUBL. BY THE FOREIGN
  SECTION OF THE CENTRAL COMMITTEE OF C.P.I.
  LO/U-3.*
  ISSN 0479-6543

**FOREIGN COMPOUND METABOLISM IN MAMMALS.**
++FOREIGN COMPD. METAB. MAMMALS.
CHEMICAL SOCIETY.
  LONDON 1, 1970-
  S/T: A SPECIALIST PERIODICAL REPORT.
  BH/U-3.   BL/U-1.   GL/U-1.   GL/U-2.   LO/N14.   LO/S-3.
  LO/U12.   MA/U-1.   NW/U-1.   RE/U-1.
  ISSN 0300-3493

**FOREIGN LANGUAGE ANNALS.**
++FOREIGN LANG. ANN.
MODERN LANGUAGE ASSOCIATION OF AMERICA.
  NEW YORK 1, 1966-
  XY/N-1.
  ISSN 0015-718X

**FOREIGN POLICY.**    XXX
[NATIONAL AFFAIRS INC.]
  NEW YORK 1(1), 1970/71-
  Q. INCORP: INTERNATIONAL CONCILIATION FROM
  NO.7, 1972.
  LO/S14.   LO/U-3.   SO/U-1.
  AD/U-1. 10, 1973-      BL/U-1. 14, 1974-
  ISSN 0015-7228

**FOREIGN POLICY (ANKARA).**    000
SEE: DIS POLITIKA.

**FOREIGN TRADE REVIEW (INDIA).**
++FOREIGN TRADE REV. (INDIA).
INDIAN INSTITUTE OF FOREIGN TRADE.
  NEW DELHI 1(1), AP/JE 1966-
  Q.
  LO/N10.
  LO/R-6. 3(2), 1968-
  ISSN 0015-7325

**FOREIGN TRADE STATISTICAL DIGEST (SUDAN).**
++FOREIGN TRADE STAT. DIG.(SUDAN).
BANK OF SUDAN.
  KHARTOUM 1(1), 1969-
  Q.
  LO/U14.   OX/U-9.

**FORENSIC PHOTOGRAPHY.**
++FORENSIC PHOTOGR.
  BOGNOR REGIS 1(1), AG 1972-
  Q.
  CA/U-1.   ED/N-1.   LO/N14.

**FORENSIC SCIENCE.**    XXX
++FORENSIC SCI.
  LAUSANNE 1, 1972-
  PREV: JOURNAL OF FORENSIC MEDICINE FROM 1,
  1953- 18, 1971.
  BL/U-1.   DB/U-2.   NW/U-1.   OX/U15.
  GL/U-2. 1(2), JL 1972-

**FORESIGHT. U.F.O.'S, OCCULT, CONTROVERSY,
PSYCHIC RESEARCH.**
[FORESIGHT ORGANIZATION]
  BIRMINGHAM NO.1, AG 1970-
  CA/U-1. NO.16, F/MR 1973-
  ED/N-1. NO.16, F/MR 1973-

**FORESTS & FOREST PRODUCTS.**
++FORESTS & FOREST PROD. (AUST.)
(AUSTRALIA) COMMONWEALTH BUREAU OF CENSUS &
STATISTICS.
  CANBERRA NO.1, 1967/8 [1968]-
  A.
  LO/U-3.

**FOREST INDUSTRIES EQUIPMENT REVIEW.**
++FOREST IND. EQUIP. REV.
  AUCKLAND 1(1), N 1969-
  OX/U-3.

**FOREST RESEARCH SERIES, DEPARTMENT OF FOR-
ESTRY, CLEMSON UNIVERSITY.**
++FOR. RES. SER. DEP. FOR. CLEMSON UNIV.
  CLEMSON, S.C. 1, 1961-
  OX/U-3.

**FOREST TREE IMPROVEMENT.**
++FOR. TREE IMPROV.
[AKADEMISK FORLAG]
  COPENHAGEN NO.1, 1970-
  AD/U-1.   LO/N13.   OX/U-3.

**FORESTRY & HOME GROWN TIMBER.**
++FOR. & HOME GROWN TIMBER.
[BENN]
  LONDON 1(1), F 1972-
  Q.
  AD/U-1.   ED/N-1.   LO/R-5.   OX/U-3.

**FORMA.**
  OXFORD 1, 1971-
  BL/U-1.   CA/U-1.   ED/N-1.

**FORMA ET FUNCTIO.**
[PERGAMON; VIEWEG & SOHN]
  OXFORD; BRAUNSCHWEIG 1(1), 1969-
  S/T: AN INTERNATIONAL JOURNAL OF FUNCTIONAL
  BIOLOGY. ENGL., FR. & GER.
  LO/N-2.   LO/N13.   SF/U-1.
  ED/N-1. 1970-          MA/U-1. 2, 1970-
  OX/U-8. 2(1), 1970-
  ISSN 0015-7716

**FORMAGE DES MATERIAUX.**    XXX
++FORMAGE MATER.
  PARIS 1, AP/JE 1969- 4(15), 1972...
  Q. SUBS: METAUX DEFORMATION.
  LO/N14.
  ISSN 0015-7724

**FORMAGE ET TRAITEMENTS DES METAUX.**    XXX
++FORMAGE & TRAIT. METAUX.
[COMPAGNIE FRANCAISE D'EDITIONS]
  PARIS NO.1, JA/F 1969-
  M. PREV: ESTAMPAGE, FORGE & BOULONNERIE; &
  METAUX EN FEUILLES.
  LO/N14.
  ISSN 0015-7732

**FORMAT. COMPUTER LABORATORY NEWSLETTER.**
UNIVERSITY COLLEGE, DUBLIN: COMPUTER LABORATORY
  DUBLIN 1(1), JA 1970-
  DB/U-2.

**FORSCHUNGEN ZUR ANTIKEN SKLAVEREI.**
++FORSCH. ANTIKEN SKLAV.
AKADEMIE DER WISSENSCHAFTEN UND DER LITERATUR:
KOMMISSION FUR GESCHICHTE DES ALTERTUMS.
  WIESBADEN 1, 1967-
  OX/U-1.

FORSCHUNGSBERICHT, DEUTSCHE LUFT- UND RAUM-
FAHRT.                                                                    xxx
+ +FORSCHUNGSBER. DEUT. LUFT- & RAUMFAHRT.
MUNICH 64-01, S 1964-
INCORP: BERICHT, DEUTSCHE VERSUCHSANST. FUR
LUFT- UND RAUMFAHRT (DVL-BERICHT); BER., DEUT.
FORSCHUNGSANST. FUR LUFT- UND RAUMFAHRT (DFL-
BERICHT; BER., FLUGWISSENSCHAFTLICHE FORSCH-
UNGSANST. (FFM-BERICHT); & IN PART BER., DEUT.
FORSCHUNGSANST. FUR HUBSCHRAUBER UND VERTI-
KALFLUGTECH.; MITT., FORSCHUNGSINST. FUR
PHYSIK DER STRAHLANTRIEBE.
LO/N14.

FORSCHUNGSBERICHTE, OSTERREICHISCHES INSTITUT
FUR WIRTSCHAFTSFORSCHUNG.
+ +FORSCHUNGSBER. OSTERR. INST. WIRTSCHAFTS-
FORSCH.
VIENNA NO.1, 1972-
CA/U-1.

FORSKNING OCH FRAMSTEG.
+ +FORSK. FRAMSTEG.
SALLSKAPET FOR FORSKNINGSINFORMATION.
STOCKHOLM 1, 1969-
LO/N14.
ISSN 0015-7937

FORSKNINGSRAPPORT, NATURGEOGRAFISKA INSTITUT-
IONEN, STOCKHOLMS UNIVERSITET.
+ +FORSKNINGSRAPP. NATURGEOGR. INST. STOCKH.
UNIV.
STOCKHOLM 1, 1968-
CA/U12.

FORTNIGHT. AN INDEPENDENT REVIEW FOR NORTHERN
IRELAND.
BELFAST 1, 1970-
BL/U-1.    ED/N-1.
CO/U-1. NO.59, 1973-
ISSN 0046-4694

FORTSCHRITTE DER ALLGEMEINEN UND KLINISCHEN
HUMANGENETIK. ADVANCES IN HUMAN GENETICS.
+ +FORTSCHR. ALLG. & KLIN. HUMANGENET.
[THIEME]
STUTTGART 1, 1969-
LO/N13.    OX/U-8.

FORTSCHRITTE DER PFLANZENZUCHTUNG.
+ +FORTSCHR. PFLANZENZUCHT.
[PAUL PAREY]
BERLIN &C. 1, 1971-
SUPPL. TO ZEITSCHRIFT FUR PFLANZENZUCHTUNG.
CA/U-1.    GL/U-1.    LO/N13.

FORTSCHRITTE IN DER TIERPHYSIOLOGIE UND TIERE-
NAHRUNG. ADVANCES IN ANIMAL PHYSIOLOGY & ANIMAL
NUTRITION.
+ +FORTSCHR. TIERPHYSIOL. & TIERENAHR.
HAMBURG NO.1, 1972-
AD/U-1.    CA/U11.    GL/U-1.

FORTSCHRITTSBERICHTE UBER KOLLOIDE UND
POLYMERE.                                                                 xxx
+ +FORTSCHRITTSBER. KOLLOIDE & POLYM.
[STEINKOPF]
DARMSTADT 55, 1971-
PREV: KOLLOID-BEIHEFTE. SUPPLEMENTA ZUR
KOLLOID-ZEITSCHRIFT UND ZEITSCHRIFT FUR
POLYMERE.
LO/N14.    MA/U-1.    NW/U-1.
ISSN 0071-8017

FORUM. CASOPIS ODJELA ZA SUVREMENU KNJIZEV-
NOST JUGOSLAVENSKE AKADEMIJE ZNANOSTI I
UMJETNOSTI.
ZAGREB 1, JA 1962-
CA/U-1.
ISSN 0015-8445

FORUM. VYBER VEDECKYCH A TECHNICKYCH PRAC
ZVL.
ZAVODY NA VYROBU LOZISK.
POVAZSKA BYSTRICA 1, 1968-
ENGL. SUMM.
LO/N13. 2, 1969-                      LO/N14. 2, 1969-
LO/N-3. 4, 1970.

FORUM ITALICUM.
+ +FORUM ITAL.
STATE UNIVERSITY OF NEW YORK.
BUFFALO 1, 1967-
CB/U-1.*
AD/U-1. 5, 1971-                      CA/U-1. 7, 1973-
LD/U-1. 4, 1970-                      MA/U-1. 2, 1968-
ISSN 0014-5858

FOSSIL MAMMALS OF AFRICA.                                                 xxx
SUBS (1969): FOSSIL VERTEBRATES OF AFRICA.

FOSSIL VERTEBRATES OF AFRICA.
+ +FOSSIL VERTEBRATES AFR.
NEW YORK 1, 1969-
PREV: FOSSIL MAMMALS OF AFRICA FROM 1, 1951.
BL/U-1.    BN/U-2.    GL/U-1.    LO/N13.    LO/U12.

FOUNDATIONS OF LANGUAGE.
+ +FOUND. LANG.
[REIDEL]
DORDRECHT 1(1), 1965-
Q. S/T: INTERNATIONAL JOURNAL OF LANGUAGE &
PHILOSOPHY.
CR/U-1.    LO/N-3.
ISSN 0015-900X

FOUNDATIONS OF PHYSICS.
+ +FOUND. PHYS.
[PLENUM P.]
NEW YORK, LONDON 1(1), 1970-
Q.
LO/N-4.    LO/N14.    LO/U13.    RE/U-1.    SH/U-1.
OX/U-8. 1(2), 1970-                SO/U-1. 3, 1973-
ISSN 0015-9018

FOUR-IN-HAND LETTER QUARTERLY.
+ +FOUR-IN-HAND LETT. Q.
LONDON 1, 1969-
ED/N-1.    OX/U-1.

FOURPOSTER.                                                                xxx
HEAL ORGANISATION.
LONDON NO.20, OC 1962-
PREV: FOURPOSTER BROADSHEET FROM MR 1965- JL
1962.
LO/N-1.

FOURPOSTER BROADSHEET.                                                     xxx
SUBS (1962): FOURPOSTER.

FOWNES STREET JOURNAL.
+ +FOWNES ST. J.
WOMEN'S LIBERATION MOVEMENT.
DUBLIN 1, 1972-
DB/U-2.

F.P.A. CENTRE. NEWS ABOUT FIRE PREVENTION
INFORMATION & ACTIVITIES.                                                 xxx
FIRE PROTECTION ASSOCIATION.
LONDON MY 1969-
PREV: F.P.A. NEWS FROM MR 1967- N 1968.
ED/N-1. S 1969-                      LO/N-4. MR 1970-
LO/N13. CURRENT BOX.

F.P.A. JOURNAL.                                                            xxx
SUBS (1971): FIRE PREVENTION.

FPA NEWS.                                                                  xxx
FIRE PROTECTION ASSOCIATION.
LONDON MR 1967- N 1968 ...
S/T: A QUARTERLY REPORT OF WORK IN HAND.
SUBS: FPA CENTRE.
ED/N-1.    LO/N-4.

FRACTIONS. NEWS OF BIOCHEMICAL INSTRUMENTAT-
ION.
BECKMAN INSTRUMENTS, INC.: SPINCO DIVISION.
PALO ALTO, CALIF. NO.1, 1972-
LO/N14.

FRAGMENTA COLEOPTEROLOGICA.
+ +FRAGMENTA COLEOPTEROL.
KYOTO 1, 1961-
LO/N-2.

FRAGMENTA COLEOPTEROLOGICA JAPONICA.                                       000
SEE: KOCHUGAKU SHOSHI.

FRAGMENTA MINERALOGICA ET PALAEONTOLOGICA.
+ +FRAGM. MINERAL. & PALAEONTOL.
TERMESZETTUDOMANYI MUZEUM.
BUDAPEST 1, 1969-
LO/N-2.    LO/N13.

FRAMEWORKS JOURNAL.
+ +FRAMEWORKS J.
[FRAMEWORKS P.]
LONDON 1(1), JE 1972-
CA/U-1.    ED/N-1.    OX/U-1.

FREE CHINA & ASIA.                                                         xxx
SUBS (1965): ASIAN OUTLOOK.

**FREE PALESTINE.**
LONDON   1(1), JE 1968-
M.
LO/U-3.   LO/U14.
ED/N-1.   1(4),1968-

**FREEDOM. INTERNATIONAL EDITION.**
CHURCH OF SCIENTOLOGY.
EAST GRINSTEAD   NO.1, MY 1969-
OX/U-8.

**FREEDOM SCIENTOLOGY.**
++FREEDOM SCIENTOL.
CHURCH OF SCIENTOLOGY.
EAST GRINSTEAD   NO.1, AU 1968-
ED/N-1.   2, 1968-

**FREIGHT. JOURNAL OF THE ...**
FREIGHT TRANSPORT ASSOCIATION LTD.
CROYDON   1(1), 1969-
M.
OX/U-1.
ED/N-1.   1(3), 1969-
ISSN 0016-0849

**FREIGHT MANAGEMENT.**
++FREIGHT MANAGE.
[TEMPLE PRESS]
LONDON   (1), 1966-
S/T: PHYSICAL DISTRIBUTION ECONOMICS.
CA/U-1.   ED/N-1.   OX/U-1.   XY/N-1.
LO/N-7. N 1968-
LO/N14. [W. 3(3), 1969].
ISSN 0016-0873

**FREIGHT TRANSPORT EQUIPMENT.**
++FREIGHT TRANSP. EQUIP.
[MORGAN-GRAMPIAN]
LONDON   NO.1, N 1972-
CA/U-1.   ED/N-1.

**FREIGHT TRANSPORT SERVICES.**
++FREIGHT TRANSP. SERV.
[MORGAN-GRAMPIAN]
LONDON   NO.1, N 1972-
ED/N-1.

**FREIGHTWAY.**
NATIONAL FREIGHT FOUNDATION LTD.
LONDON   1, 1970-
OX/U-1.   SF/U-1.
ISSN 0300-4201

**FRENCH CANADIAN & ACADIAN GENEALOGICAL REVIEW.**
++FR. CAN. & ACADIAN GENEAL. REV.
CENTRE CANADIEN DES RECHERCHES GENEALOGIQUES.
QUEBEC   1(1), 1968-
Q.
OX/U-1.
ISSN 0016-1047

**FREQUENCY.**
BROOKLINE, MASS.   1, 1962- 6(11), 1968.
SUBS: FREQUENCY TECHNOLOGY.
LO/N-9.

**FREQUENCY TECHNOLOGY.**
++FREQ. TECHNOL.
[FREQUENCY INC.]
NORWOOD (MASS.)   6(12), D 1968-
PREV: FREQUENCY FROM 1, 1962- 6(11), 1968.
BN/U-2.   LO/N14.

**FRESHWATER BIOLOGY.**
++FRESHWATER BIOL.
[BLACKWELL]
OXFORD   1, 1971-
BH/U-3.   BN/U-2.   CR/N-1.   ED/N-1.   GL/U-1.   HL/U-1.
LO/N-2.   LO/N-6.   LO/N13.   LO/R-5.   LO/U-4.
BL/U-1. 4, 1974-            LO/U12. 4, 1974-
ISSN 0046-5070

**FRI NEWSLETTER.**
++FRI NEWSL. (FULMER RES. INST.)
FULMER RESEARCH INSTITUTE.
STOKE POGES   NO.1, AP 1968-
ED/N-1.

**FRIDERICIANA. ZEITSCHRIFT DER...**
UNIVERSITAT KARLSRUHE.
KARLSRUHE   1, 1967-
ED/S-2.

**FRINGE. OXFORD'S RADICAL MAGAZINE.**
OXFORD LIBERAL CLUB.
OXFORD   NO.1, 1966 - 2, 1967.//
LO/U-3.

**FRITZSCHE - D & O LIBRARY BULLETIN.**                         XXX
++FRITZSCHE - D & O LIBR. BULL.
FRITZSCHE DODGE & OLCOTT, INC.
NEW YORK   13(7), 1969-
FRITZSCHE LIBRARY BULLETIN FROM 1, N 1957-
13(6), 1969.
LO/N14.

**FRITZSCHE LIBRARY BULLETIN.**                                 XXX
SUBS (1969):  FRITZSCHE - D & O LIBRARY
BULLETIN.

**FRNM. BULLETIN OF THE FOUNDATION FOR RESEARCH
ON THE NATURE OF MAN.**                                         XXX
DURHAM, N.C.   NO.1, 1965- 14, 1969 ...
TITLE VARIES. NOS. 1- 4 ISSUED AS FRNM BULL-
ETIN.  SUBS: PARAPSYCHOLOGY BULLETIN.
GL/U-1.*

**FRONT PAGE.**
[SPOTLIGHT PUBL.]
LONDON   NO.1, MY 1972-
MON.
CA/U-1.   OX/U-1.
ED/N-1.   3, 1972-

**FRONT SHEET.**
NATIONAL ASSOCIATION FOR THE CARE & RESETTLE-
MENT OF OFFENDERS: SOUTH WALES & SEVERN VALLEY
REGION.
[CHELTENHAM] NO.1, N 1971- 11, D 1973.
ISSUED ON A RESTRICTED BASIS IN WEST COUNTRY.
SUBS: FRONTSHEET. NEWSPAPER FOR THOSE IN
PRISON.
LO/U-3.

**FRONTIERS. A MAGAZINE OF THE ARTS.**
CHRISTCHURCH, N.Z.   1(1), 1968-
LO/U-2.

**FRONTIERS OF HORMONE RESEARCH.**
++FRONT. HORM. RES.
BASEL &C.   1, 1972-
OX/U-8.

**FRONTIERS IN NEUROENDOCRINOLOGY.**
++FRONT. NEUROENDOCRINOL. [FNED-A]
[OXFORD UNIV. P.]
OXFORD &C.   1969-
LO/N-1.
ISSN 0532-7466

**FRUCHTSAFT-INDUSTRIE.**                                       XXX
SUBS (1970):  CONFRUCTA.

**FRUHE PLAKET IN EUROPE UND DER USA.**
++FRUHE PLAKET EUR. & USA.
BERLIN   1, 1973-
OX/U-1.   LO/U-3.

**FT ABSTRACTS IN SCIENCE & TECHNOLOGY.**
++FT ABSTR. SCI. & TECH.
[MICROINFO LTD.]
ALTON, HANTS.   1(1), JA 1972-
S/T: A MONTHLY REVIEW OF DEVELOPMENTS &
SIGNIFICANT EVENTS IN SCIENCE & TECHNOLOGY
REPORTED IN THE DAILY COLUMNS OF THE FINANCIAL
TIMES.
LO/N35.   MA/U-1.   XS/R10.   XS/T-4.
ED/N-1. 1(5), 1972-          SO/U-1. 2(5), 1973-
ISSN 0046-3000

**FTAT RECORD.**                                                XXX
++FTAT REC.
FURNITURE, TIMBER & ALLIED TRADES UNION.
LONDON   OC 1971-
MON. PREV: NUFTO RECORD FROM 5, 1906-
39, 1940; N.S., 1941- 1971.
LO/U-3.   OX/U-1.

**FUEL EFFICIENCY.**                                            XXX
SUBS (1966):  JOURNAL OF FUEL & HEAT TECHNOL.

**FUENTES.**
INSTITUTO NACIONAL DE INVESTIGACIONES Y
ARCHIVOS LITERARIOS (URUGUAY).
MONTEVIDEO   1(1), AG 1961-
CC/U-1.   1(1), 1961.
ISSN 0532-7849

**FUENTES CARTOGRAFICAS ESPANOLES.**
++FUENTES CARTOGR. ESP.
MADRID   1, 1972-
OX/U-1.

FUENTES HISTORICAS ARAGONESAS.
+ +FUENTES HIST. ARAGONESAS.
CONSEJO SUPERIOR DE INVESTIGACIONES CIENTIFICAS
(SPAIN): INSTITUCION FERNANDO EL CATOLICO.
 SARAGOSSA 1, 1962-
 OX/U-1.
 ISSN 0532-7873

FUHRUNGSKRAFT.                                                          XXX
[KARTENBERG]
 ESSEN 35(10), 1970-
 PREV: BERGFREIHEIT FROM 1, JA 1921- 35(9),
 1970.
 LO/N14.

FUJI SEITETSU GIHO.  TECHNICAL REPORT, FUJI
STEEL.                                                                 XXX
 [FSTG-A]
FUJI SEITETSU K.K.
 TOKYO 1(1), 1952- 18, 1969.//
 JAP. WITH ENGL. SUMM.  ENGL. TITLE VARIES.
 TECHNICAL REPORT, FUJI IRON & STEEL CO. FROM
 1, 1952- 12, 1963.  AS ABOVE FROM 13, 1964.
 LO/N14.  9(3), 1960- [W. 18(1)].
 ISSN 0429-8306

FUJIKURA TECHNICAL REVIEW.
+ +FUJIKURA TECH. REV.
FUJIKURA CABLE WORKS, LTD.
 TOKYO 1, 1969-
 LO/N14.

FUKAURA RINKAI JISSHUJO HOKOKU.  REPORT,
FUKAURA MARINE BIOLOGICAL LABORATORY.
 HIROSAKI UNIVERSITY: FACULTY OF SCIENCE.
 HIROSAKI NO.1, 1969-
 LO/N13.

FULDBLODSAVL.
FORENINGEN AF FULDBLODSOPDRAETTERE I DANMARK.
 COPENHAGEN 1, JA 1969-
 LO/N13.

FUNDAMENTA:  MONOGRAPHIEN ZUR URGESCHICHTE:
REIHE A.
+ +FUNDAM., MONOGR. URGESCH., A.
[BOEHLAU]
 COLOGNE 1, 1965-
 OX/U-1.
 ISSN 0532-8586

FUNKTSIONAL'NYJ ANALIZ I EGO PRILOZHENIJA.
+ +FUNKTS. ANAL. & EGO PRILOZH.
AKADEMIJA NAUK SSSR.
 MOSCOW 1(1), 1967-
 Q.
 LO/N13.   SH/U-1.
 ISSN 0016-285X

FUR TRADE JOURNAL.                                                     XXX
+ +FUR TRADE J.
[CLAY PUBL. CO.]
 BEWDLEY, ONT.  49(9), 1971-
 PREV: FUR TRADE JOURNAL OF CANADA FROM 1, S
 1923- 49(8), 1971.
 LO/N14.

FUR TRADE JOURNAL OF CANADA.                                           XXX
 SUBS (1971): FUR TRADE JOURNAL.

FURNISHING IRELAND.
+ +FURNISH. IREL.
BLACKROCK, CO. DUBLIN 1, 1972-
DB/U-2.

FURNITURE DESIGN.                                                      XXX
+ +FURNITURE DES.
[NTP BUSINESS J. LTD.]
 LONDON 1965- JA/F 1968.//
 2M.
 LO/N14.
 OX/U-1.  1967-

FURNITURE INDEX.
NORTH CAROLINA STATE UNIVERSITY AT RALEIGH:
SCHOOL OF ENGINEERING.
 RALEIGH, N.C.  1, 1970-
 PROD. BY SCHOOL'S INDUSTRIAL EXTENSION SERVICE
 LO/N14.
 ISSN 0046-5321

FUSE.
 SAN DIEGO, CALIF.  NO.[1], 1971-
 LO/U-2.
 ISSN 0046-5356

FUSILIER.
 ROYAL REGIMENT OF FUSILIERS.
 LONDON 1(1), 1968-
 ED/N-1.   OX/U-1.
 ISSN 0016-3147

FUTURE.                                                                000
 SEE: BUDUCNOST.

FUTURIST.  A NEWSLETTER FOR TOMORROW'S WORLD.
 WORLD FUTURE SOCIETY.
 WASHINGTON, D.C.  1(1), 1967-
 Q.
 LO/U-3.  2, 1968-                    SH/U-1.  AP 1968-
 XS/R10.  2(3), 1968-
 ISSN 0016-3317

F.W.P. JOURNAL.                                                        XXX
 SOUTH AFRICAN INSTITUTE FOR PRODUCTION
 ENGINEERING.
 JOHANNESBURG 12(6), 1972-
 PREV: FOUNDING, WELDING, PRODUCTION ENGINEER-
 ING JOURNAL & METAL INDUSTRY DIGEST FROM 1, AP
 1961- 12(5), 1972.
 LO/N14.

FYZIKALNY CASOPIS.                                                     XXX
+ +FYZ. CAS.
SLOVENSKA AKADEMIA VIED: FYZIKALNY USTAV.
 BRATISLAVA 17, 1967- 22, 1972 ...
 VARIOUS LANGUAGES. PREV. PART OF: MATEMATICKO-
 FYZIKALNY CASOPIS FROM 1, 1951- 16,
 1966. SUBS: ACTA PHYSICA SLOVACA.
 DB/S-1.   LD/U-1.   LO/N14.

GAELIC WEEKLY NEWS.
+ +GAELIC WKLY. NEWS.
 DUBLIN 1, AP 1968-
 ED/N-1.

GAME RESEARCH IN OHIO.
+ +GAME RES. OHIO.
(OHIO) DEPARTMENT OF NATURAL RESOURCES;
DIVISION OF WILDLIFE.
 COLUMBUS, OHIO  1, 1962-
 A.
 LO/R-5.

GAMES & PUZZLES.
[EDU - GAMES]
 LONDON NO.1, MY 1972-
 M.
 ED/N-1.

GAMING NEWSLETTER.                                                     XXX
+ +GAMING NEWSL.
NATIONAL GAMING COUNCIL (US).
 WASHINGTON, D.C.  1(1), MR/AP 1969- 1(4),
                        1969/70.//
 2M.
 SH/U-1.

GANNET.  NEWSLETTER OF THE GANNET CLUB OF THE
ROYAL ZOOLOGICAL SOCIETY OF SCOTLAND.
 EDINBURGH NO.1, JE 1972-
 ED/N-1.
 CA/U-1.  NO.2, 1973-

GARDAR.  ARSBOK FOR SAMFUNDET SVERIGE-ISLAND
I LUND-MALMO.
[GLEERUPS]
 LUND 1, 1970-
 CA/U-1.   LO/U-2.   NO/U-1.   OX/U-1.
 OX/U-1.  2, 1970-

GARDENERS CHRONICLE.*
+ +GARD. CHRON.
[HAYMARKET PUBL. GROUP]
 LONDON 155, 1964-166(14), 1969...
 TITLE VARIES. PREV: GARDENERS CHRONICLE & GAR-
 DENING ILLUSTRATED FROM 1, 1841.  AS ABOVE FROM
 155, 1964-164(26), 1968.  THEN GARDENERS CHRON.
 & NEW HORTICULTURIST FROM 165, 1969.  SUBS:
 GARDENERS CHRONICLE/HORTICULTURAL TRADE JOUR-
 NAL.
 BH/P-1.   ED/N-1.   LO/N-2.   LO/N14.

GARDENERS CHRONICLE/HORTICULTURAL TRADE JOURNAL.
+ +GARD. CHRON./HORT. TRADE J.
[HAYMARKET PUBL. GROUP]
 LONDON 166(15), 1969-
 PREV: GARDENERS CHRONICLE FROM 155, 1964-
 166(14), 1969.
 LO/N14.
 ISSN 0016-4682

**GARDENERS YEARBOOK.**
*+ +GARD. YEARB.*
[COLLINS]
*LONDON &C.  1968-*
*OX/U-8.*
*ISSN 0435-1215*

**GARP SPECIAL REPORT.**
WORLD METEOROLOGICAL ORGANIZATION.
*GENEVA  NO.1, 1970-*
SPONS. BODY ALSO:  INTERNATIONAL COUNCIL OF
SCIENTIFIC UNIONS.
*LO/N-4.*

**GAS & LIQUID CHROMATOGRAPHY ABSTRACTS.**                                        XXX
*+ +GAS & LIQ. CHROMATOGR. ABSTR.*
GAS CHROMATOGRAPHY DISCUSSION GROUP.
[APPLIED SCIENCE PUBL.]
*LONDON &C.  1970(1971)-*
PREV: GAS CHROMATOGRAPHY ABSTRACTS FROM 1958
(1960)- 1969(1970).
*XS/R10.*
*ISSN 0301-388X*

**GAS + SANITAIR MERCUUR.**
*AMSTERDAM  1(1), 1965-*
SUPPL. TO: ELECTRO RADIO MERCUUR.
*LO/N14.*
*ISSN 0016-4860*

**GASNYTT.**                                                                        XXX
SVENSKA GASFORENINGEN.
*STOCKHOLM  1970-*
PREV:  MANADSBLAD, SVENSKA GASFORENINGEN FROM
35(6), 1968- 36, 1969.
*LO/N14.*
*ISSN 0039-6834*

**GASTROENTEROLOGIA.**                                                              XXX
SUBS (1968): DIGESTION.

**GASTROENTEROLOGIA JAPONICA.**
*+ +GASTROENTEROL. JAP.*
JAPANESE SOCIETY OF GASTROENTEROLOGY.
*TOKYO  1, 1966-*
*OX/U-8. 5(2), 1970-*
*ISSN 0435-1339*

**G.A.T.F. BULLETIN.**                                                              000
SEE:  TECHNICAL SERVICE REPORT, GRAPHIC ARTS
TECHNICAL FOUNDATION, INC.

**GAZ ET MAZOUT.**                                                                  XXX
[CHAUD-FROID-PLOMBERIE]
*PARIS  5(17), 1960- 17(63), 1972 ...*
PREV: CHAUFFAGE AU MAZOUT FROM [1]1, S 1956-
5(16), 1960.  SUBS: GAZ - MAZOUT - ELECTRICITE
*LO/N14.*

**GAZ - MAZOUT - ELECTRICITE.**                                                     XXX
[EDITIONS PARISIENNES]
*PARIS  17(64), 1972-*
PREV: GAZ ET MAZOUT FROM 5(17), 1960- 17(63),
1972.
*LO/N14.*

**GAZETTE, INCORPORATED LAW SOCIETY OF IRELAND.**
*+ +GAZ. INC. LAW SOC. IREL.*
*DUBLIN  1, 1971-*
*DB/U-2.*

**GAZETTE, UNIVERSITY COLLEGE OF CAPE COAST.**
*+ +GAZ. UNIV. COLL. CAPE COAST.*
*CAPE COAST, GHANA  1(1), OC/D 1969-*
*LO/N17.*

**GAZETTE, UNIVERSITY OF LONDON.**                                                  XXX
SUBS (1971): BULLETIN ...

**GAZETTE, UNIVERSITY OF WARWICK.**
*+ +GAZ. UNIV. WARWICK.*
*COVENTRY  1, 1967-*
*LO/U-1.\**

**GAZETTE, VEGETARIAN SOCIETY OF THE UNITED
KINGDOM LTD.**
*ALTRINGHAM, CHES.  NO.1, 1970-*
*ED/N-1.    OX/U-8.*

**GAZOVAJA KHROMATOGRAFIJA.  SBORNIK STATEJ.**
*+ +GAZOV. KHROMATOGR.*
(RUSSIA USSR) MINISTERSTVO KHIMICHESKOJ PRO-
MYSHLENNOSTI: NAUCHNO-ISSLEDOVATEL'SKIJ INST-
ITUT TEKHNIKO-EKONOMICHESKIKH ISSEDOVANIJ.
*MOSCOW  1, 1964-*
*LO/N13.\*\**
*ISSN 0435-1541*

**GAZOVOE DELO.  NAUCHNO-TEKHNICHESKIJ SBORNIK.**                                    XXX
*+ +GAZOV. DELO.*
VSESOJUZNYJ NAUCHNO-ISSLEDOVATEL'SKIJ INSTITUT
ORGANIZATSII, UPRAVLENIJA I EKONOMIKI NEFTE-
GAZOVOJ PROMYSHLENNOSTI.
*MOSCOW  1, 1963-*
PREV: NOVOSTI NEFTIANOJ I GAZOVOJ TEKHNIKI:
SERIJA GAZOVOE DELO FROM 1952- 1962.
*LO/N13.  1970-*
*ISSN 0028-1166*

**G.E.C. - A.E.I. JOURNAL OF SCIENCE & TECH-
NOLOGY.**                                                                           XXX
*+ +G.E.C. - A.E.I. J. SCI. & TECHNOL.*
GENERAL ELECTRIC CO. LTD.
*LONDON  35(2),- 35(3), 1968 ...*
SUBS: PART OF JOURNAL OF SCIENCE & TECHNOLOGY
(1969).
*BH/P-1.    LO/N14.    MA/P-1.    RE/U-1.    XS/R10.*

**GELIOTEKHNIKA, AKADEMIJA NAUK UZBEKSKOJ SSR.**
*+ +GELIOTEKH. AKAD. NAUK UZB. SSR.*
*TASHKENT  1965-*
*CA/U11.*
*LO/N13.  1966-*

**GEMEENTEWERKEN.**                                                                  XXX
[SAMSON UITGEVERIJ]
*ALPHEN AAN DEN RIJN  1, 1972-*
PREV: TECHNISCH GEMEENTEBLAD FROM 1914- 57,
1971.
*LO/N13.*
*ISSN 0046-5577*

**GEMS.  THE BRITISH LAPIDARY MAGAZINE.**
*LONDON  [NO.] 1, 1969-*
*CR/N-1.    LO/N-2.*
*ED/P-1.  4, 1972-*
*ED/N-1.  3(3), MY/JE 1971-*
*ISSN 0016-6251*

**GENERAL RELATIVITY & GRAVITATION.**
*+ +GEN. RELATIV. & GRAVITAT.*
[PLENUM P.]
*LONDON  1(1), 1970-*
*CA/U-1.    ED/N-1.    GL/U-1.    NW/U-1.    OX/U-8.    XS/R10.*
*XY/N-1.*
*SO/U-1. 4, 1973-*
*MA/U-1. [W. 2(3), 1971].*
*ISSN 0001-7701*

**GENERAL REPORT ON THE ACTIVITIES OF THE
COMMUNITIES.**                                                                      XXX
*+ +GEN. REP. ACTIV. COMMUNITIES.*
COMMISSION OF THE EUROPEAN COMMUNITIES.
*BRUSSELS  1, 1967-*
TITLE IN FRENCH:  RAPPORT GENERAL SUR L'ACTI-
VITE DES COMMUNAUTES- INCORP: REPORTS OF THE
INDIVID. COMMUNITY COMMISSIONS PREV. ISSUED
SEPARATELY UNDER THE TITLE: GENERAL REPORT ...
COMMUNITY.  EUROPEAN COAL & STEEL COMMUNITY
FROM 1, 1952; EUROPEAN ECONOMIC COMMUNITY FROM
1, 1958; EUROPEAN ATOMIC ENERGY COMMUNITY FROM
1, 1958.
*BH/U-1.    LO/N10.    LO/P-6.    LO/S14.    OX/U16.*
*OX/U17.*

**GENERAL TECHNICAL REPORT, INTERMOUNTAIN
FOREST & RANGE EXPERIMENT STATION (US).**
*+ +GEN. TECH. REP. INTERMT. FOR. & RANGE EXP.
STN. (US).*
*OGDEN, UTAH  INT-1, 1972-*
STATION PART OF U.S. FOREST SERVICE.
*LO/N13.    OX/U-3.*

**GENERAL TECHNICAL REPORT, NORTHEASTERN FOREST
EXPERIMENT STATION (US).**
*+ +GEN. TECH. REP. NORTHEAST. FOR. EXP. STN.(US).*
*DARBY, PA.  NE-1, 1973-*
STATION PART OF U.S. FOREST SERVICE.
*LO/N14.    OX/U-3.*

**GENERAL TECHNICAL REPORT, PACIFIC NORTHWEST
FOREST & RANGE EXPERIMENT STATION (US).**
*+ +GEN. TECH. REP. PAC. NORTHWEST FOR. & RANGE
EXP. STAT. (US).*
*PORTLAND, OREG.  PNW-1, 1972-*
STATION PART OF U.S. FOREST SERVICE.
*OX/U-3.*

**GENERAL TECHNICAL REPORT, ROCKY MOUNTAIN
FOREST & RANGE EXPERIMENT STATION (US).**
*+ +GEN. TECH. REP. ROCKY MT. FOR. & RANGE EXP.
STN. (US).*
*FORT COLLINS, COLO.  RM1, 1972-*
STATION PART OF U.S. FOREST SERVICE.
*LO/N13.    OX/U-3.*

**GENERAL TOPOLOGY & ITS APPLICATIONS.**
*+ +GEN. TOPOL. & APPL.*
[NORTH HOLLAND PUBL. CO.]
*AMSTERDAM 1, AP 1971-*
*Q.*
*AD/U-1. BN/U-2. CA/U-2. EX/U-1. GL/U-1. HL/U-1.*
*LO/N-4. LO/N13. LO/N14. SH/U-1. SW/U-1.*
*XY/N-1.*
*BL/U-1. 3, 1973-*
*ISSN 0016-660X*

**GENESIS: GRASP.**
*NEW YORK 1(1), 1968-*
*Q.*
*LO/U-2.*

**GENETICS ABSTRACTS.**
*+ +GENET. ABSTR.*
[INFORMATION RETRIEVAL LTD.]
*LONDON 1(1), N 1968-*
*BH/U-1. BL/U-1. CA/U15. GL/U-1. LO/U12. OX/U-8.*
*ED/N-1. 1(4), 1969-*
*ISSN 0016-674X*

**GENETICS LECTURES, GENETICS INSTITUTE, OREGON STATE UNIVERSITY.**
*+ +GENET. LECT. GENET. INST. OREG. STATE UNIV.*
*CORVALLIS, OREG. 1, 1969-*
*LO/N-2. LO/N13.*

**GENETICS & PHYSIOLOGY NOTES.**
*+ +GENET. & PHYSIOL. NOTES.*
INSTITUTE OF PAPER CHEMISTRY.
*APPLETON, WIS. 1, 1967-*
*OX/U-3.*

**GENETICS & PLANT BREEDING.** 000
SEE: GENETIKA & SELEKTSIJA.

**GENETIKA & SELEKTSIJA. GENETICS & PLANT BREEDING.**
*+ +GENET. & SEL.*
AKADEMIJA NA SELSKOSTOPANSKITE NAUKI.
*SOFIA 1, 1968-*
*2M. ENGL. SUMM. & CONT. LISTS.*
*CA/U11. LO/N13.*
*ISSN 0016-6766*

**GENETIKA A SLECHTENI.**
*+ +GENET. SLECHTENI.*
(CZECHOSLOVAKIA) MINISTERSTVO ZEMEDELSTVI,
LESNIHO A VODNIHO HOSPODARSTVI: USTAV
VEDECKOTECHNICKYCH INFORMACI.
*PRAGUE 1(38), 1965-*
*ENGL. SUMM. & CONT. LISTS.*
*CA/U11. LO/N13.*
*ISSN 0036-5378*

**GENIE BIOLOGIQUE ET MEDICAL.**
[GEORGES THOMAS]
*NANCY 1, 1970-*
*LO/N13.*

**GENRE.**
UNIVERSITY OF ILLINOIS AT CHICAGO CIRCLE:
DEPARTMENT OF ENGLISH.
*CHICAGO 1(1), JA 1968-*
*LD/U-1. LO/N-1.*
*BT/C-1. 3(4), 1970- CA/U-1. 5(2), 1972-*
*OX/U-1. 1(4), 1968-*
*ISSN 0435-3110*

**GEO ABSTRACTS: A: LAND FORMS & THE QUATERNARY** XXX
*+ +GEO ABSTR., A.*
*NORWICH 1972-*
PREV: GEOGRAPHICAL ABSTRACTS: A FROM 1966-
1971. EDITED AT THE UNIV. OF EAST ANGLIA.
*BN/U-2. CA/U-2. GL/U-1. LN/U-2. LO/N-2. LO/N13.*
*LO/R-5. LO/U-1. LO/U28. RE/U-1. SA/U-1.*
*ISSN 0305-1897*

**GEO ABSTRACTS: B: BIOGEOGRAPHY & CLIMATOLOGY.** XXX
*+ +GEO ABSTR., B.*
*NORWICH 1972- 1973.*
PREV: GEOGRAPHICAL ABSTRACTS: B FROM 1966-
1971. EDITED AT THE UNIV. OF EAST ANGLIA.
SUBS. PART OF: GEO ABSTRACTS: B: CLIMATOLOGY
& HYDROLOGY; & ECOLOGICAL ABSTRACTS.
*ED/N-1. GL/U-1. LN/U-2. LO/N-2. LO/N13. LO/R-5.*
*LO/U-1. LO/U-3. LO/U12. LO/U28. RE/U-1. SA/U-1.*
*ISSN 0305-1900*

**GEO ABSTRACTS: C: ECONOMIC GEOGRAPHY.** XXX
*NORWICH 1972-*
PREV: GEOGRAPHICAL ABSTRACTS: C FROM 1966-
1971. EDITED AT THE UNIV. OF EAST ANGLIA.
*AD/U-1. CA/U-2. ED/N-1. GL/U-1. HL/U-1. LN/U-2.*
*LO/N13. LO/R-5. LO/U-1. LO/U-1. LO/U-3. LO/U28.*
*RE/U-1. SA/U-1.*
*ISSN 0305-1919*

**GEO ABSTRACTS: D: SOCIAL GEOGRAPHY & CARTOGRAPHY.** XXX
*+ +GEO ABSTR., D.*
*NORWICH 1972- 1973.*
PREV: GEOGRAPHICAL ABSTRACTS: D FROM 1966-
1971. EDITED AT THE UNIV. OF EAST ANGLIA.
SUBS: GEO ABSTRACTS: D: SOCIAL & HISTORICAL
GEOGRAPHY.
*ED/N-1. GL/U-1. LN/U-2. LO/N13. LO/R-5. LO/U-1.*
*LO/U-3. LO/U12. LO/U28. RE/U-1. SA/U-1.*
*ISSN 0305-1927*

**GEO ABSTRACTS: E: SEDIMENTOLOGY.**
*+ +GEO ABSTR., E.*
*NORWICH 1972-*
EDITED AT THE UNIVERSITY OF EAST ANGLIA.
*AD/U-1. BH/U-3. CA/U-1. CA/U-2. ED/N-1. GL/U-2.*
*LN/U-2. LO/N-2. LO/N-4. LO/N13. LO/R-5. LO/S13.*
*LO/U-1. LO/U28. SA/U-1. SF/U-1. SO/U-1.*
*ISSN 0305-1935*

**GEO ABSTRACTS: F: REGIONAL & COMMUNITY PLANNING.**
*+ +GEO ABSTR., F.*
*NORWICH 1972-*
EDITED AT UNIV. OF EAST ANGLIA.
*AD/U-1. ED/N-1. GL/U-2. LN/U-2. LO/N-4. LO/N13.*
*LO/R-5. LO/S13. LO/U-1. LO/U-3. LO/U28. MA/U-1.*
*SA/U-1. SF/U-1. SO/U-1.*
*ISSN 0305-1943*

**GEOBIOS.**
UNIVERSITE DE LYON: DEPARTEMENT DES SCIENCES DE
LA TERRE.
*LYONS NO.1, 1968-*
BODY PART OF FACULTE DES SCIENCES.
*LO/N-2. LO/U-2. SW/U-1.*
*MA/U-1. NO.2, 1969-*
*ISSN 0016-6995*

**GEOCHEMICAL JOURNAL.**
*+ +GEOCHEM. J. (JAP.)*
(GEOCHEMICAL SOCIETY OF JAPAN).
*NAGOYA 1, D 1966-*
*Q.*
*LO/N-2. OX/U-8.*
*ISSN 0016-7002*

**GEOCHIMICA ET COSMOCHIMICA ACTA: SUPPLEMENT.**
*+ +GEOCHIM. & COSMOCHIM. ACTA, SUPPL.*
[PERGAMON]
*NEW YORK; OXFORD 1, 1970-*
*LO/N-4.*

**GEOCOM BULLETIN.**
*+ +GEOCOM BULL.*
*CALGARY 1, 15/JA 1968-*
*LO/N-2. LO/N14.*
*LO/N-1. 2(1), JA 1969- MA/U-1. 3, 1970-*

**GEOFISICA E METEOROLOGIA.** XXX
SUBS (1972): RIVISTA ITALIANA DI GEOFISICA.

**GEOFISICA PANAMERICANA.** XXX
*+ +GEOFIS. PANAM.*
INSTITUTO PANAMERICANO DE GEOGRAFIA E HISTORIA:
COMISION DE GEOFISICA.
*LA PAZ, BOLIVIA 1, 1971-*
PREV: B.B.G.O.A. FROM 1, 1958- 4, 1968.
*LO/N14.*

**GEOFORUM. JOURNAL OF PHYSICAL, HUMAN & REGIONAL GEOSCIENCES.**
[PERGAMON]
*OXFORD NO.1, 1970-*
*BH/U-1. CA/U-5. DB/U-2. GL/U-1. GL/U-2. LO/N-7.*
*LO/N13. LO/R-5. LO/S13. LO/U12. NO/U-1.*
*CA/U-1. NO.9, 1972- MA/U-1. NO.2, 1970-*
*OX/U-1. NO.9, 1972- SH/C-5. NO.5, 1971-*
*SO/U-1. NO.4, 1970-*
*ISSN 0016-7185*

**GEOGRAFIJA I KHOZJAJSTVO MOLDAVII.**
*+ +GEOGR. & KHOZ. MOLD.*
AKADEMIJA NAUK MOLDAVSKOJ SSR: OTDEL GEOGRAFII.
*KISHINEV 2, 1969-*
VOL.1 PUBL. IN 1970.
*CC/U-1. LO/N-3. OX/U-1.*

**GEOGRAFISCH TIJDSCHRIFT: NS.**
+ +GEOGR. TIJDSCHR., NS.
KONINKLIJK NEDERLANDS AARDRIJKSKUNDIG
GENOOTSCHAP.
 AMSTERDAM 1, 1967-
 5/A. PREV. SERIES FROM 1, JA 1948.
 BH/U-1. LO/N13. LO/U-3.
 GL/U-2. 2, 1968-
 ISSN 0016-7215

**GEOGRAFSKI RAZGLEDI.**
+ +GEOGR. RAZGLEDI.
GEOGRAFSKO DRUSTVO NA SR MAKEDONIJA.
 SKOPJE 1, 1962-
 TITLE ALSO IN FRENCH: REVUE GEOGRAPHIQUE.
 OX/U-1.
 ISSN 0435-3722

**GEOGRAPHIC BULLETIN.**
+ +GEOGR. BULL.
(UNITED STATES) BUREAU OF INTELLIGENCE &
RESEARCH.
 WASHINGTON, D.C. 1, 1963-
 SO/U-1.

**GEOGRAPHIC PUBLICATIONS, DEPARTMENT OF GEOL-
OGY-GEOGRAPHY, UNIVERSITY OF MISSOURI.**
+ +GEOGR. PUBL. DEP. GEOL.-GEOGR. UNIV. MO.
 KANSAS CITY, MO. NO.1, 1972-
 MONOGR.
 LO/S13. NO.1, 1972.

**GEOGRAPHICAL ANALYSIS.**
+ +GEOGR. ANAL.
[OHIO STATE UNIV PRESS]
 COLUMBUS 1, JA 1969-
 S/T: AN INTERNATIONAL JOURNAL OF THEORET-
ICAL GEOGRAPHY.
 AD/U-1. BL/U-1. DB/U-2. EX/U-1. LD/U-1. LO/N-1.
 LO/S13. LO/U-1. LO/U-2. LO/U-3. LO/U11. NO/U-1.
 NW/U-1. OX/U-1. RE/U-1. SH/U-1.
 BH/U-1. 2, 1970-     SF/U-1. 3, 1971-
 SH/C-5. 3, 1971-     SO/U-1. 2, 1970-
 ISSN 0016-7363

**GEOGRAPHICAL EDUCATION. JOURNAL OF THE ...**
+ +GEOGR. EDUC.(AUST.).
AUSTRALIAN GEOGRAPHY TEACHERS' ASSOCIATION.
 WATTLE PARK, S. AUST. 1(1), JE 1969-
 LO/S13.

**GEOGRAPHICAL KNOWLEDGE.**
+ +GEOGR. KNOWL.
SOCIETY FOR GEOGRAPHICAL STUDIES.
 KANPUR 1(1), JA 1968-
 LO/S13.
 ISSN 0016-7401

**GEOGRAPHICAL PUBLICATIONS, DEPARTMENT OF
GEOGRAPHY, UNIVERSITY OF GUELPH.**
+ +GEOGR. PUBL. DEP. GEOGR. UNIV. GUELPH.
 DON MILLS, ONT. NO.1, 1971-
 LO/S13. NO.1, 1971.

**GEOKHIMICHESKIE ISSLEDOVANIJA.**
+ +GEOKHIM. ISSLED.
AKADEMIJA NAUK SSSR: INSTITUT MINERALOGII,
GEOKHIMII I KRISTALLOKHIMII REDKIKH ELEMENTOV.
 MOSCOW 1, 1970-
 LO/N13.

**GEOLOGIA APPLICATA E IDROGEOLOGIA.**
+ +GEOL. APPL. & IDROGEOL.
UNIVERSITA DI BARI; ISTITUTO DE GEOLOGIA
APPLICATA ALL'INGENERIA.
 BARI 1, 1966-
 LO/N-2. LO/N14.

**GEOLOGICA ET PALAEONTOLOGICA.**
+ +GEOL. & PALAEONTOL.
 MARBURG 1, 1967-
 BL/U-1. BR/U-3. GL/U-1. GL/U-1. LO/N-2. OX/U-8.

**GEOLOGICAL NEWSLETTER.**                                    XXX
+ +GEOL. NEWSL.
INTERNATIONAL UNION OF GEOLOGICAL SCIENCES.
 ANTWERP 1(1), AP 1967-
 PREV: CIRCULAR LETTER, INTERNATIONAL UNION...
 FROM NO.1, 1960- 18, F 1967.
 BH/U-1. CA/U14. LO/U-2. SH/U-1.
 DB/S-1. NO.4, 1969.     DB/U-2. 1969-
 DR/U-1. 1971-     GL/U-2. 1974-
 SW/U-1. 1969-
 ISSN 0047-1267

**GEOLOGICAL NEWSLETTER, UNIVERSITY OF LONDON.**
+ +GEOL. NEWSL. UNIV. LOND.
 LONDON NO.1, 1968-
 LO/N-2.

**GEOLOGICAL STUDIES.**
+ +GEOL. STUD.
(MYSORE) DEPARTMENT OF MINES & GEOLOGY.
 BANGALORE 1, 1967-
 LO/N-4.

**GEOLOGIE ALPINE.**                                          XXX
+ +GEOL. ALPINE.
UNIVERSITE DE GRENOBLE: LABORATOIRE DE GEOLOGIE
 GRENOBLE 42, 1966-
 PREV: TRAVAUX DU LABORATOIRE DE GEOLOGIE DE LA
 FACULTE DES SCIENCES DE GRENOBLE FROM 1, 1890-
 41, 1965.
 LO/N-2.
 LO/U-2. 44, 1968-

**GEOLOGIJA I GEOKHIMIJA GORJUCHIKH ISKOPAEMYKH.**
+ +GEOL. & GEOKHIM. GORJUCHIKH ISKOP. [GGGI-A]
AKADEMIJA NAUK UKRAJINS'KOJI RSR: INSTYTUT
HEOLOHIJI I HEOKHIMIJI HORJUCHYKH KOPALYN.
 KIEV 1, 1965-
 S/T: RESPUBLIKANSKIJ MEZHVEDOMSTVENNYJ SBORNIK
 VOL.5-8(1966) UNNUMBERED, HAVE DISTINCTIVE
 TITLES. TITLE ALSO IN UKR.: HEOLOHIJA I
 HEOKHIMIJA HORJUCHYKH KOPALYN.
 GL/U-1. LO/N13.
 ISSN 0435-4117

**GEOLOGIJA MESTOROZHDENIJ TVERDYKH POLEZNYKH
ISKOPAEMYKH.**
+ +GEOL. MESTOROZHD. TVERD. POLEZN. ISKOP.
VSESOJUZNYJ NAUCHNO-ISSLEDOVATEL'SKIJ INSTITUT
MINERAL'NOGO SYR'JA.
 MOSCOW 1, 1966-
 LO/N13. [W. VYP.2]
 ISSN 0435-415X

**GEOLOGIJAS INSTITUTAS DARBAI.**                             000
 SEE: TRUDY INSTITUTA GEOLOGII, GOSUDARSTVEN-
 NYJ GEOLOGICHESKIJ KOMITET SSSR.

**GEOLOGUES. REVUE TRIMESTRIELLE DE L'...**
UNION FRANCAISE DES GEOLOGUES.
 PARIS NO.1, JA/MR 1966-
 LO/N-2.
 ISSN 0016-7916

**GEOLOGY. JOURNAL OF THE ASSOCIATION OF ...**
ASSOCIATION OF TEACHERS OF GEOLOGY.
 [CHELTENHAM] 1, 1969-
 ED/N-1. LO/N-1. LO/N-2. OX/U-8.
 SH/U-1. 2, 1970-

**GEOLOGY & ORE DEPOSIT.**                                    000
 SEE: CHIJIL KWANGSANG.

**GEOLOGY & PALAEONTOLOGY OF SOUTHEAST ASIA.**
+ +GEOL. PALAEONTOL. SOUTHEAST. ASIA.
[UNIVERSITY OF TOKYO PRESS]
 TOKYO 1, 1964-
 LO/N13.

**GEOLOGY & SCENERY. GEOLOGICAL GUIDE BOOK.**
(ONTARIO) DEPARTMENT OF MINES.
 TORONTO NO.1, 1968-
 LO/N-2.

**GEOLOSKI GLASNIK - POSEBNA IZDANJA.**
+ +GEOL. GLAS. - POSEBNA IZD.
GEOLOSKI ZAVOD U SARAJEVU.
 SARAJEVO 1, 1963-
 ENGL., GER. OR FR. SUMM. & CONT. LISTS.
 SUPPL. TO: GEOLOSKI GLASNIK.
 BR/U-1. LO/N-2.
 LO/N13. 2, 1964-
 ISSN 0435-4257

**GEOMAGNETIC BULLETINS.**                                    XXX
+ +GEOMAGN. BULL.
INSTITUTE OF GEOLOGICAL SCIENCES (GB).
 HAILSHAM, SUSSEX NO.1, 1969-
 INCORP: OBSERVATORIES' YEAR BOOK FROM 1922-
 1967(1969); & BULLETINS, ROYAL OBSERVATORY,
 GREENWICH: SERIES D FROM NO.17, 1960- 153,
 1971.
 BH/U-1. LO/N-4. LO/N13. MA/P-1.

**GEOMAGNETIC SURVEY INFORMATION.**
+ +GEOMAG. SURV. INF.
UNITED STATES NAVAL OCEANOGRAPHIC OFFICE.
 WASHINGTON, D.C. NO.1, S 1963-
 CA/U12.

**GEOMAGNETIZM I AERONOMIJA.**
++GEOMAGN. & AERON.
AKADEMIJA NAUK SSSR.
 MOSCOW 1, 1961-
 ENGL. CONT. LISTS.
 LO/N13.
 ISSN 0016-7940

**GEOMEDICAL MONOGRAPH SERIES.**                    000
  SEE: MEDIZINISCHE LANDERKUNDE.

**GEOMETRIAE DEDICATA.**
++GEOM. DEDICATA.
[REIDEL]
 DORDRECHT 1, 1972-
 Q. ENGL. & GER.
 CA/U-2.   GL/U-1.   LO/N14.   OX/U-8.   SH/U-1.   SW/U-1.
 ISSN 0046-5755

**GEOMORFOLOGIA.**
UNIVERSIDADE DE SAO PAULO: INSTITUTO DE
GEOGRAFIA.
 SAO PAULO NO.1, 1966-
 LO/N-2.

**GEOMORFOLOGIJA.**
[GMFL-A]
AKADEMIJA NAUK SSSR.
 MOSCOW 1970(1)-
 ENGL. SUMM.
 LO/N13.   OX/U-8.
 LO/N-2.  1971-

**GEOMORFOLOGIJA (ENGL. TRANSL.).**                  000
  SEE: GEOMORPHOLOGY.

**GEOMORPHOLOGICAL REPORT, DEPARTMENT OF
GEOGRAPHY, UNIVERSITY OF NOTTINGHAM.**
++GEOMORPHOL. REP. DEP. GEOGR. UNIV. NOTTINGHAM.
 NOTTINGHAM NO.1, 1970-
 MONOGR.
 LO/N-1.   LO/N-2.   LO/U-2.

**GEOMORPHOLOGY.**
[CONSULTANTS BUREAU]
 NEW YORK &C. NO.1, 1970-
 ENGL. TRANSL. OF GEOMORFOLOGIJA. DATING &
 NUMBERING OF ISSUES FOLLOW ORIGINAL.
 LO/N13.   OX/U-8.

**GEOPHILE.**
CAMBRIDGESHIRE COLLEGE OF ARTS & TECHNOLOGY:
GEOGRAPHY DEPARTMENT.
 CAMBRIDGE 1, 1967/68-
 A.
 LO/S13.

**GEOPHYSICA GOTHOBURGENSIA.**
++GEOPHYS. GOTHOBURGENSIA.
GOTEBORGS UNIVERSITET.
 GOTEBORG 1, 1968-
 GL/U-1.   OX/U-8.

**GEOPHYSICAL FLUID DYNAMICS.**
++GEOPHYS. FLUID DYN.
[GORDON & BREACH]
 LONDON 1, AP 1970-
 S/T: A JOURNAL OF ATMOSPHERIC OCEANOGRAPHIC
 INTERACTION.
 BR/U-1.   ED/N-1.   EX/U-1.   LO/N-4.   LO/N13.   OX/U-8.
 GL/U-2. 2, 1971-            MA/U-1. 3, 1972-
 NW/U-1. 2, 1971-
 ISSN 0016-7991

**GEOPHYSICAL REPORTS, DEPARTMENT OF GEOLOGY,
UNIVERSITY OF READING.**
++GEOPHYS. REP. DEP. GEOL. UNIV. READING.
 READING 1, 1967-
 DB/S-1.

**GEOPHYSICAL SURVEYS.**
++GEOPHYS. SURV.
[D. REIDEL]
 DORDRECHT 1, 1972-
 S/T: INTERNATIONAL JOURNAL OF GEOPHYSICS.
 LO/N14.   SW/U-1.
 ISSN 0046-5763

**GEOPHYSIK UND GEOLOGIE. GEOPHYSIKALISCHE
VEROFFENTLICHUNGEN DER KARL-MARX-UNIVERSITAT,
LEIPZIG.**                                          xxx
++GEOPHYS. & GEOL.
[AKADEMIE-VERLAG]
 LEIPZIG & BERLIN 1, 1959- 15, 1970.
             N.S. 1, 1974-
 PREV. PART OF: VEROFFENTLICHUNGEN, GEOPHYSIK-
 ALISCHES INSTITUT, KARL-MARX-UNIVERSITAT,
 LEIPZIG: 2S: SPEZIALARBEITEN; & GEOPHYSIK UND
 GEOLOGIE. BEITRAGE ZUR SYNTHESE ZWEIER WISSEN-
 SCHAFTEN FROM 1, 1959- 15, 1970.
 CA/U-2. 1, 1974-
 LO/U-2. 1, 1959- 15, 1970.
 LV/U-1. 2, 1960- 15, 1970.
 OX/U-8. 1, 1959- 15, 1970.

**GEOPHYSIKALISCHE ABHANDLUNGEN.**
++GEOPHYS. ABH.
FREIE UNIVERSITAT: INSTITUT FUR METEOROLOGIE
UND GEOPHYSIK.
[REIMER]
 BERLIN 1, 1965-
 LO/N13.

**GEOSCIENCE DOCUMENTATION.**
++GEOSCI. DOC.
[GEO-SERVICES]
 LONDON &C. 1, JL 1969-
 S/T: GEO-SERVICES' BIMONTHLY JOURNAL FOR THE
 STUDY OF GEOSCIENCE LITERATURE.
 CA/U14.   ED/N-1.   GL/U-1.   LO/N-2.   LO/N13.   LO/S17.
 MA/U-1.   OX/U-1.   SH/U-1.   SH/U-3.
 ISSN 0016-8483

**GEOSCIENCE & MAN.**
++GEOSCI. & MAN.
LOUISIANA STATE UNIVERSITY: SCHOOL OF GEO-
SCIENCE.
 BATON ROUGE, LA. 1, 1970-
 LO/N-2.

**GEOSCIENCES BULLETIN: SERIES A.**
++GEOSCI. BULL., A.
RAND CORPORATION.
 SANTA MONICA 1(1), JA 1970- 3(12), D 1972. //
 SUBSER. OF THE CORPORATION'S RESEARCH
 MEMORANDUM.
 OX/U16. 1(6), 1970-
 ISSN 0534-0136

**GEOSCOPE.**
UNIVERSITY OF OTTAWA: GEOGRAPHERS' ASSOCIATION.
 OTTAWA NO.1, 1970-
 2/A. ENGL. OR FR.
 LO/S13.
 ISSN 0046-581X

**GEOTECHNICAL ABSTRACTS.**
++GEOTECH. ABSTR.
INTERNATIONAL SOCIETY FOR SOIL MECHANICS &
FOUNDATION ENGINEERING.
 ESSEN 1970-
 ENGL. ED. OF DOKUMENTATION BODENMECHANIK UND
 GRUNDBAU. PROD. FOR THE SOCIETY BY DEUTSCHE
 GESELLSCHAFT FUR ERD- UND GRUNDBAU.
 BH/U-3.   CV/C-1.   GL/U-2.   LO/N14.   LO/U11.
 BL/U-1. 1973-
 ISSN 0016-8491

**GEOTECHNICAL ENGINEERING.**                        xxx
++GEOTECH. ENG.
SOUTHEAST ASIAN SOCIETY OF SOIL ENGINEERING.
 BANGKOK 2, JE 1971-
 2/A. PREV: JOURNAL OF THE SOUTHEAST ASIAN
 SOCIETY OF SOIL ENGINEERING FROM 1, JE 1970.
 CA/U-4.
 ISSN 0046-5828

**GEOTECTONICS.**
AMERICAN GEOPHYSICAL UNION.
 WASHINGTON, D.C. 1967 (1)-
 2M. TRANSL. OF: GEOTEKTONIKA.
 SH/U-1.
 ISSN 0016-8521

**GEOTEKTONIKA.**
AKADEMIJA NAUK SSSR: GEOLOGICHESKIJ INSTITUT.
 MOSCOW 1965(1)-
 2M. ENGL. SUMM. & CONT. LISTS. TITLE ALSO IN
 ENGL.: GEOTECTONICS.
 LO/N-4. 1972-              LO/N13. 1966-
 OX/U-8. 1968-
 ISSN 0016-853X

**GEOTEKTONIKA; (ENGL. TRANSL.)**                   000
  SEE: GEOTECTONICS.

**GEOTHERMICS.**
INTERNATIONAL INSTITUTE FOR GEOTHERMAL RESEARCH
*PISA 1, 1972-*
*LO/N14.*
*CA/U-1. 3(2), 1974-*

**GEOTITLES WEEKLY.**
*+ +GEOTITLES WKLY.*
[GEOSERVICES PUBL.]
*LONDON &C. 1(1), 1969-*
*LO/N-2.*
*MA/U-1. 3, 1970-*
*CA/U14. 1(12), 1969-*
*ED/N-1. 3(25), 1970-*
*LO/N13. 3(25), 1970-*
*LO/S17. 3(25), 1970-*
*OX/U-8. 3(25), 1970-*
*ISSN 0016-8564*

**GERMAN-AMERICAN STUDIES.**
*+ +GER.-AM. STUD.*
SOCIETY FOR GERMAN-AMERICAN STUDIES.
*YOUNGSTOWN, OHIO 1(1), 1969-*
*LO/N-1.*
*ISSN 0046-5836*

**GERMAN MEDICAL MONTHLY.**　　　　　　XXX
SUBS (1971): GERMAN MEDICINE.

**GERMAN MEDICINE.**　　　　　　XXX
*+ +GER. MED.*
[THIEME]
*STUTTGART 1, 1971- 3, 1973.//*
PREV: GERMAN MEDICAL MONTHLY FROM 1, 1956- 15,
D 1970.
*DB/U-2. LO/N13. NW/U-1.*
*LD/U-1. 3, 1973-*
*ISSN 0046-5844*

**GERMAN STUDIES: SECTION 1: PHILOSOPHY & HISTORY.**
SEE: PHILOSOPHY & HISTORY.　　　000

**GERMAN STUDIES: SECTION 2: MODERN LAW & SOCIETY.**
SEE: MODERN LAW & SOCIETY.　　　000

**GERMAN STUDIES: SECTION 3. LITERATURE,
MUSIC, FINE ARTS.**　　　000
SEE: LITERATURE, MUSIC, FINE ARTS.

**GERMANISTICA PRAGENSIA.**　　　000
SEE: ACTA UNIVERSITATIS CAROLINAE; PHILO-
LOGICA: GERMANISTICA PRAGENSIA.

**GERMANISTIK.**
[THESEN VERLAG]
*FRANKFURT AM MAIN NO.1, 1970-*
A SERIES OF THESES.
*LO/N-1.*
*ISSN 0016-8912*

**GERMANISTISCHE ABHANDLUNGEN.**
*+ +GER. ABH.*
*STUTTGART 1, 1962-*
*CA/U-1.*
*LC/U-1. 4, 196 - 8, 1967.*
*LO/U-2. 1, 1962- 8, 1967.*

**GERONTOLOGY. OCCUPATIONAL & SOCIAL ASPECTS
OF HUMAN AGEING.**
*GUILDFORD 1(1), AP 1970. //*
*ED/N-1. HL/U-1. LO/N-1. LO/U-3. OX/U-1. XS/R10.*

**GESAMTVERZEICHNIS OSTERREICHISCHER
DISSERTATIONEN.**
*+ +GESAMTVERZ. OSTERR. DISS.*
NOTRING DER WISSENSCHAFTLICHEN VERBANDE
OSTERREICHS.
*VIENNA 1, 1966(1967)-*
*LO/U-1.*
*ISSN 0072-4165*

**GHANA. A CURRENT BIBLIOGRAPHY.**
RESEARCH LIBRARY ON AFRICAN AFFAIRS (ACCRA).
*ACCRA 1(1), S/OC 1967-*
2M.
*LO/N17. LO/U-8. OX/U-1.*

**GHANA JOURNAL OF AGRICULTURAL SCIENCES.**
*+ +GHANA J. AGR. SCI.*
GHANA ACADEMY OF SCIENCES: CROP RESEARCH
INSTITUTE.
*ACCRA 1, 1968-*
*LO/N-2. LO/N17. LO/U14.*

**GHANA JOURNAL OF SOCIOLOGY.**
*+ +GHANA J. SOCIOL.*
GHANA SOCIOLOGICAL ASSOCIATION.
*LEGON 1(1), 1965-*
*EX/U-1. 4(2), 1968-　　　　LO/U14. 3(2), 1967-*
*OX/U-9. 3(2), 1967-*
*ISSN 0435-9380*

**GHANA NATIONAL BIBLIOGRAPHY.**
*+ +GHANA NAT. BIBLIOGR.*
GHANA LIBRARY BOARD.
*ACCRA [NO.1], 1965(1968)-*
*BH/U-1. EX/U-1. MA/U-1.*

**GHANA SOCIAL SCIENCE JOURNAL.**
*+ +GHANA SOC. SCI. J.*
[GHANA PUBLISHING CORP.]
*[ACCRA] 1, 1971-*
*EX/U-1. LO/U-8.*
*ISSN 0046-5925*

**GIBBONS STAMP MONTHLY.**　　　　XXX
SUBS (1970): STAMP MONTHLY.

**GIDRAVLICHESKIE MASHINY.**
*+ +GIDRAVL. MASH.*
(UKRAINE) MINISTERSTVO VYSSHOJI I SEREDN'OJI
SPETSIAL'NOJI OS'VITY.
*KIEV 1, 1967-*
S/T: RESPUBLIKANSKIJ MEZHVEDOMSTVENNYJ
NAUCHNO-TEKHNICHESKIJ SBORNIK.
*LO/N13.*

**GIDRAVLIKA I GIDROTEKHNIKA.**
*+ +GIDRAVL. & GIDROTEKH. [GIGI-A]*
(UKRAINE) MINISTERSTVO VYSSHOJI I SREDN'OJI
SPETSIAL'NOJI OS'VITY.
*KIEV 1, 1965-*
S/T: MEZHVEDOMSTVENNYJ RESPUBLIKANSKIJ
NAUCHNO-TEKHNICHESKIJ SBORNIK.
*LO/N13. 3, 1966-*
*ISSN 0435-9666*

**GIDROBIOLOGICHESKIJ ZHURNAL.**
*+ +GIDROBIOL. ZH.*
AKADEMIJA NAUK UKRAJINS'KOJI RSR: (OTDELENIE
OBSHCHEJ BIOLOGII).
*KIEV 1, 1965-*
2M. ENGL. SUMM. & CONT. LISTS. TITLE ALSO IN
ENGL.: HYDROBIOLOGICAL JOURNAL.
*LO/N13.*
*LO/N-2. 3, 1967-*
*ISSN 0435-9682*

**GIDROBIOLOGICHESKIJ ZHURNAL (ENGL. TRANSL.).**　　000
SEE: HYDROBIOLOGICAL JOURNAL.

**GIESSENER BEITRAGE ZUR ENTWICKLUNGSFORSCHUNG;
REIHE 1: SYMPOSIEN.**
*+ +GIESSEN. BEITR. ENTWICKL.FORSCH., REIHE 1.*
JUSTUS LIEBIG-UNIVERSITAT IN GIESSEN; TROPEN
INSTITUT.
[GUSTAV FISCHER]
*STUTTGART BD.1, 1965-*
*LO/N13.*

**GIFU KOGYO KOTO SEMMON GAKKO KIYO. MEMOIR OF
GIFU TECHNICAL COLLEGE.**
GIFU KOGYO KOTO SEMMON GAKKO.
*GIFU NO.1, 1965-*
JAP. & ENGL.
*LO/N13. XN/S-1.*

**GIGIENA I SANITARIJA (ENGL. TRANSL.).**　　000
SEE: HYGIENE & SANITATION.

**GISPARK.**
GUYANA INSTITUTE FOR SOCIAL RESEARCH & ACTION.
*GEORGETOWN, GUYANA NO.1, JE 1973-*
*LO/U-8.*

**GISRA.**
GUYANA INSTITUTE FOR SOCIAL RESEARCH & ACTION.
*GEORGETOWN 1(1), 1970-*
*LO/U-8. OX/U-9.*

**GLASERS ANNALEN.**　　000
SEE: ZEITSCHRIFT FUR EISENBAHNWESEN UND
VERKEHRSTECHNIK.

**GLASGOW ARCHAEOLOGICAL JOURNAL.**
*+ +GLASGOW ARCHEOL. J.*
GLASGOW ARCHAEOLOGICAL SOCIETY.
*GLASGOW 1, 1969-*
PREV: TRANSACTIONS OF THE GLASGOW ARCHAEOL-
OGICAL SOCIETY FROM 1, 1857.
*BL/U-1. ED/N-1. GL/U-1. LO/N-1. OX/U-1. OX/U-2.*

GLASGOW DENTAL JOURNAL. JOURNAL OF THE ...
+ +GLASG. DENT. J.
UNIVERSITY OF GLASGOW: DENTAL HOSPITAL & SCHOOL
GLASGOW 1(1), 1969-
BL/U-1. GL/U-1. LD/U-1.
CA/U-1. 3, 1972- ED/N-1. 1(2), 1970-
ISSN 0046-600X

GLASGOW NEWS.
+ +GLASG. NEWS.
GLASGOW NO.1, 11/OC 1971-
ED/N-1. LO/U-3.

GLASNIK ARHIVA I DRUSTVA ARHIVISTA BOSNE I
HERCEGOVINE.
+ +GLAS. ARH. & DRUS. ARH. BOSNE & HERCEGOVINE.
DRZAVNI ARHIV NR BOSNE I HERCEGOVINE.
SARAJEVO 1(1), 1961-
OX/U-1.

GLASNIK MATEMATICKI, DRUSTVO MATEMATICARA I
FIZICARA SR HRVATSKE: SERIJA 3.                          XXX
+ +GLAS. MAT. DRUS. MAT. & FIZ. SR HRVAT., 3.
ZAGREB TOM 1(21), 1966-
ENGL., FR., GER. & RUSS. PREV: GLASNIK
MATEMATICKO-FIZICKI I ASTRONOMSKI: SERIJA 2
FROM 1, 1946- 20, 1965.
CA/U-2. DB/S-1. LD/U-1. LO/N-4. LO/N13.
ISSN 0017-095X

GLASNIK MATEMATICKO-FIZICKI I ASTRONOMSKI:
SERIJA 2.                                                XXX
SUBS (1966): GLASNIK MATEMATICKI, DRUSTVO
MATEMATICARA I FIZICARA SR HRVATSKE: SERIJA 3.

GLASNIK, PRIVREDNA KOMORA BOSNE I HERCEGOVINE.
+ +GLAS. PRIVREDNA KOMORA BOSNE & HERCEGOVINE.
SARAJEVO 1, 1963-
MON.
OX/U-1.
ISSN 0017-0968

GLASNIK UNIVERZITETA U NISU.
+ +GLAS. UNIV. NISU.
NIS 1(1), 1965-
OX/U-1.

GLENBOW. A NEWSLETTER OF THE GLENBOW-ALBERTA
INSTITUTE.
CALGARY 1(1), JA 1968-
LO/N-1.
ISSN 0017-1174

GLJATSIOLOGICHESKIE ISSLEDOVANIJA V KAZAKHST-
ANE.
+ +GLJATSIOL. ISSLED. KAZ.
AKADEMIJA NAUK KAZAKHSKOJ SSR: SEKTOR FIZICH-
ESKOJ GEOGRAFII.
ALMA-ATA VYP.1, [1961 ?]-
BH/U-1. 5, 1965- LO/N13. 7, 1968-

GLJATSIOLOGIJA ALTAJA.
+ +GLJATSIOL. ALTAJA.
TOMSK VYP.1, 1962-
CA/U12. LO/N13.

GLOUCESTERSHIRE HISTORICAL STUDIES.
+ +GLOUCS. HIST. STUD.
UNIVERSITY OF BRISTOL: DEPARTMENT OF EXTRA-
MURAL STUDIES.
BRISTOL 1, 1966/67-
ED/N-1.
LO/N-4. 2, 1968-
ISSN 0533-8697

GODISHNIK, OBSHCHESTVENA KULTURNO-PROSVETNA
ORGANIZATSIJA NA EVREITE V NARODNA REPUBLIKA
BULGARIJA.
+ +GOD. OBSHCHESTV. KULT.-PROSVETNA ORGAN.
EVREITE NARODNA REPUB. BULG.
SOFIA 1(1), 1966-
OX/U-1. 4(1), 1969-

GODISHNIK NA SOFIJSKIJA UNIVERSITET: KATEDRA
POLITICHESKA IKONOMIJA.
+ +GOD. SOFIJ. UNIV. KATEDRA POLIT. IKON.
SOFIA TOM 1, 1962-
FR., GER., OR RUSS. SUMM. TITLE ALSO IN
FRENCH: ANNUAIRE DE L'UNIVERSITE DE SOFIA:
ETUDES DE LA CHAIRE D'ECONOMIE POLITIQUE.
LO/N-3. TOM 2(1963). LO/U-3. TOM 5, 1966-

GOING METRIC.
METRICATION BOARD.(GB).
LONDON NO.1, JL 1971-
BH/U-1. CA/U-1. ED/N-1. LO/N-4. LO/N-6. LO/N-7.
LO/U-3. LO/U28. NW/U-1. OX/U16. SO/U-1.
XS/N-1. XS/R10. XS/T-4.
LO/N35. NO.3, 1972-

GOLD BULLETIN.
+ +GOLD BULL.
CHAMBER OF MINES OF SOUTH AFRICA: RESEARCH
ORGANISATION.
JOHANNESBURG NO.1, 1968-
GL/U-2. LO/N14. SO/U-1.*
ISSN 0017-1557

GOLDSMITH TODAY. BULLETIN OF THE ...
WORSHIPFUL COMPANY OF GOLDSMITHS.
LONDON NO.1, [1967]-
ED/N-1.

GONDWANA NEWSLETTER.
+ +GONDWANA NEWSL.
UNIVERSIDADE DO RIO GRANDE DO SUL: CENTRO DE
INVESTIGACAO DO GONDWANA.
PORTO ALEGRE NO.1, 1969-
LO/N-2.

GOOD ELF.
LONDON NO.1, 1970-
LO/U-2.

GOODWIN SERIES, SOUTH AFRICAN ARCHAEOLOGICAL
SOCIETY.
+ +GOODWIN SER. S. AFR. ARCHAEOL. SOC.
CLAREMONT 1, 1972-
CA/U-3. LO/N-2.

GORNAJA ELEKTROMEKHANIKA I AVTOMATIKA.
+ +GORNAJA ELEKTROMEKH. & AVTOM.
DNEPROPETROVSKIJ GORNYJ INSTITUT [IM. ARTEMA].
KHAR'KOV 1, 1965-
S/T: RESPUBLIKANSKIJ MEZHVEDOMSTVENNYJ NAUCHNO
TEKHNICHESKIJ SBORNIK.
LO/N14.

GORNOSLASKIE STUDIA SOCJOLOGICZNE, SLASKI
INSTYTUT NAUKOWY.
+ +GORNOSLASK. STUD. SOCJOLOGICZNE SLASK. INST.
NAUK.
KATOWICE 1, 1963-
BH/U-1. LO/U-3. OX/U-1.
ISSN 0072-5013

GORSKOSTOPANSKA NAUKA.
+ +GORSKOSTOP. NAUKA. [GONA-A]
AKADEMIJA NA SELSKOSTOPANSKITE NAUKI.
SOFIA 1, 1964-
OX/U-3.

GORTA NEWS.
FREEDOM FROM HUNGER COUNCIL OF IRELAND.
DUBLIN NO.1, 1970-
DB/U-2.

GOSPODARKA I ADMINISTRACJA TERENOWA.               XXX
+ +GOSPOD. & ADM. TERENOWA.
[ROBOTNICZA SPOLDZIELNIA WYDAWNICZA 'PRASA
KRAJOWA']
WARSAW 1(1), 1960- 13, 1972.
SUBS. PART OF: RADA NARODOWA, GOSPODARKA,
ADMINISTRACJA.
OX/U-1.
BH/U-1. 10(1), 1970-
ISSN 0434-2151

GOSPORT RECORDS.
+ +GOSPORT REC.
GOSPORT HISTORIC RECORDS & MUSEUM SOCIETY.
GOSPORT NO.1, MR 1971-
ED/N-1. LO/N-1. OX/U-1. SO/U-1.

GOTHIQUE.
GOTHIQUE FILM SOCIETY.
LONDON 1(1), JL 1965-
ED/N-1. 1968-
ISSN 0017-2472

GOTTINGER ARBEITEN ZUR GEOLOGIE UND PALAONTO-
LOGIE.
+ +GOTTINGER ARB. GEOL. & PALAONTOL.
GEOLOGISCH-PALAONTOLOGISCHES INSTITUT (GOTTIN-
GEN).
GOTTINGEN NO.1, 1969-
LO/U-2.

**GOVERNMENT & BUSINESS.**
++GOV. & BUS.
ECONOMISTS ADVISORY GROUP.
*LONDON [NO.1], MR. 1970-*
Q.
*GL/U-2. 1971- OX/U-1. JE/D 1971-*

**GOVERNMENT PENSION & SUPERANNUATION SCHEMES (AUSTRALIA).**
++GOV. PENSION & SUPERANNUATION SCHEMES (AUST.)
(AUSTRALIA) COMMONWEALTH BUREAU OF CENSUS &
STATISTICS.
*CANBERRA BULLETIN NO.1, 1963/64 (1966)-*
MIMEOGRAPHED.
*LO/S24.*

**GOVERNMENT REPORTS ANNOUNCEMENTS (US).** XXX
++GOV. REP. ANNOUNCE. (US).
NATIONAL TECHNICAL INFORMATION SERVICE (US).
*SPRINGFIELD, VA. 71(6), 1971-*
2/M. PREV: U.S. GOVERNMENT RESEARCH & DEVELOP-
MENT REPORTS FROM 40(1), 5/JA 1965- 71(5),
1971.
*LO/N-3. LO/N-4. NW/U-1.*

**GOVERNMENT REPORTS INDEX (US).** XXX
++GOV. REP. INDEX (US).
NATIONAL TECHNICAL INFORMATION SERVICE (US).
*SPRINGFIELD, VA. 71, 1971-*
ANNU. PREV: U.S. GOVERNMENT RESEARCH & DEVEL-
OPMENT REPORTS INDEX FROM 68(1), 1968- 71(5),
1971
*CA/U-2. LO/N-3. LO/N-4. XS/R10.*

**GOWER BIRDS.**
GOWER ORNITHOLOGICAL SOCIETY.
*SWANSEA 1, 1968-*
A.
*LO/R-5.*

**GRABUNGEN, OSTERREICHISCHES ARCHAOLOGISCHES INSTITUT.**
++GRAB. OST. ARCHAOL. INST.
*VIENNA 1965-*
ISSUED AS 'BEILAGE' TO: JAHRESHEFTE DES
OSTERREICHISCHEN ARCHAOLOGISCHEN INSTITUTES
IN WIEN (FROM 47, 1965). 'WIRD NUR MIT DEM
HAUPTBLATT ABGEGEBEN'.
*OX/U-2. 1966-*

**GRADINARSKA I LOZARSKA NAUKA.**
++GRADINAR. & LOZAR. NAUKA.
AKADEMIJA NA SELSKOSTOPANSKITE NAUKI.
*SOFIJA 1(1), 1964-*
ENGL., FR., GER. & RUSS. SUMM. PUBL. ORIG.
AS: IZVESTIJA NA AKADEMIJATA NA SELSKOSTOPAN-
SKITE NAUKIGRADINARSKA I LOZARSKA NAUKA.
*CA/U11. LO/N13. XS/R-2. XS/R-6.*
ISSN 0436-2624

**GRAFIK. ET TIDSSKRIFT OM GRAFIK OG GRAFIKERE.**
*VEMMELEV 1(1), [1970]-*
*LO/N-1.*

**GRANA. INTERNATIONAL JOURNAL OF PALYNOLOGY.** XXX
[ALMQVIST & WIKSELL]
*STOCKHOLM 10, 1970-*
PREV: GRANA PALYNOLOGICA: NS FROM 1, JL 1954-
9, 1969.
*LO/N13. SO/U-1.*
*BH/U-1. 11, 1970-*
ISSN 0017-3134

**GRANA PALYNOLOGICA: NS.** XXX
SUBS (1970): GRANA.

**GRANDE RONDE REVIEW.**
++GRANDE RONDE REV.
[GRANDE RONDE P.]
*LA GRANDE, OR. 1, 1964-*
*OX/U-1.*
ISSN 0017-3150

**GRANITE. A JOURNAL OF POETRY, FICTION, POETICS, & THOUGHT.**
[GRANITE PUBL.]
*HANOVER, N.H. NO.1, 1971-*
*OX/U-1.*
ISSN 0046-6298

**GRANMA WEEKLY REVIEW.**
++GRANMA W. REV.
COMMUNIST PARTY OF CUBA.
*HAVANA 1(1), 1966-*
*LO/U-3. OX/U-1.*
ISSN 0436-3132

**GRAPEVINE.**
UNIVERSITY OF READING: SIBLY HALL.
*READING 1, 1968-*
*RE/U-1.*

**GRAPEVINE. NEWSLETTER OF THE SCOTTISH CIVIC TRUST.**
*GLASGOW NO.1, MY 1972-*
6/A.
*ED/N-1.*
ISSN 0305-2192

**GRAPHIC TECHNOLOGY.** XXX
++GRAPHIC TECHNOL. [GRTC-A]
*LONDON. 1, MY/JE 1961-971, 1968...*
2M. INCORPS: PROCESS. SUBS: PRINTING TRADES
JOURNAL.
*BH/P-1. BL/P-1. GL/P-1. LO/F-9. LV/P-1. OX/U-1.*
*LO/N-7. 2,1961- 6,1962. 11- 14,1963.*
*LO/NU4. NO.1, 1961- 24, 1967. [W. 22, 1967].*

**GRASS.**
BRITISH ASSOCIATION OF GREEN CROP DRIERS.
*TUNBRIDGE WELLS 1, 1972-*
*AD/U-1. LO/R-6.*

**GRAZER FORSCHUNGEN ZUR WIRTSCHAFTS- UND SOZIALGESCHICHTE.**
++GRAZER FORSCH. WIRTSCH. & SOZIALGESCH.
UNIVERSITAT GRAZ: LEHRKANZEL FUR WIRTSCHAFTS-
UND SOZIALGESCHICHTE.
*GRAZ 1, 1971-*
*LO/N-1.*

**GREAT BEAR PAMPHLETS.**
[SOMETHING ELSE PRESS]
*NEW YORK NO.1, 1965-*
*LO/U-2.*

**GREAT LAKES ENTOMOLOGIST.** XXX
++GREAT LAKES ENTOMOL.
MICHIGAN ENTOMOLOGICAL SOCIETY.
*EAST LANSING, MICH. 5, 1972-*
PREV: MICHICAN ENTOMOLOGIST FROM 1(1), JL
1966- 4, 1971.
*LO/N-2. LO/N13.*

**GREATER LONDON ARTS.**
GREATER LONDON ARTS ASSOCIATION.
*LONDON 1(1), MR 1968-*
*ED/N-1. 1(3),1968-*

**GREBE. JOURNAL OF HERTFORDSHIRE & MIDDLESEX TRUST FOR NATURE CONSERVATION.**
*ST. ALBANS 1, 1970-*
*ED/N-1. LO/N-2. LO/N13. LO/R-5. OX/U-8.*

**GREEK OBSERVER.**
++GREEK OBS.
*LONDON NO.1, MR 1969-*
S/T: A MONTHLY MAGAZINE OF GREEK AFFAIRS.
*ED/N-1. LO/U-3. OX/U-1.*
ISSN 0017-3886

**GREEK REPORT.**
++GREEK REP.
*LONDON NO.1, F 1969-*
M. S/T: UNCENSORED INFORMATION & DOCUMENTS
ABOUT GREEK AFFAIRS.
*ED/N-1. LO/U-3. OX/U-1.*
ISSN 0017-3908

**GREENFIELD REVIEW.**
++GREENFIELD REV.
GREENFIELD CENTER.
*NEW YORK 1(1), 1970-*
*LO/U-2. OX/U-1.*
ISSN 0017-4041

**GREENSWARD. JOURNAL OF THE ...** XXX
SOUTH WEST & CENTRAL SCOTLAND GRASSLAND
SOCIETIES.
*AYR NO.4, 1964-*
PREV: JOURNAL, SOUTH WEST SCOTLAND GRASSLAND
SOCIETY FROM NO.1, 1962- 3, 1964.
*LO/N13.*
ISSN 0017-4092

**GREYHOUND MAGAZINE.**
++GREYHOUND MAG.
[GREYHOUND MAGAZINE CO. LTD.]
*LONDON 1(1), 1968-*
M.
*OX/U-1.*
*ED/N-1. 1(5), F 1969-*

GRIFFIN. THE JOURNAL OF THE GEOGRAPHY
DEPARTMENT OF THE NORTH-WESTERN POLYTECHNIC.          XXX
*LONDON 1, AP 1970- 2, 1971.*
SUBS: NORTH LONDON GEOGRAPHER.
*LO/N-1.   LO/S13.*

GRIFFON.
AMERICAN SCHOOL OF CLASSICAL STUDIES AT ATHENS:
GENNADIUS LIBRARY.
*ATHENS NO.1, AP 1965-*
*LO/N-1.   OX/U-1.*
*ISSN 0017-4246*

GRILLPARZER-FORUM FORCHTENSTEIN: VORTRAGE,
FORSCHUNGEN, BERICHTE.
GRILLPARZER-FORUM FORCHTENSTEIN.
*VIENNA &C   1965 (1966)-*
NAME OF BODY APPARENTLY INTENDED AS MAIN
TITLE.
*CB/U-1.   SO/U-1.*

GROPE.
*NEW YORK   1(1), JA 1964-*
*LO/U-2.*

GROUND ENGINEERING.
+ +GROUND ENG.
[ILIFFE]
*LONDON   1(1), JA 1968-*
*DB/U-2.   SO/U-1.*
*CA/U-1.  2, 1969-          ED/N-1.  2, 1969-*
*LO/N-4.  2(3), 1969-        LO/N14. 1(3), 1968-*
*LV/U-1.  2, 1969-           OX/U-8, 2(1), 1969-*
*ISSN 0017-4653*

GROUND WATER YEARBOOK.                                XXX
+ + GROUND WATER YEARB.
WATER RESOURCES BOARD (G.B.).
*LONDON   1964/66(1970)-*
PREV: SURFACE WATER YEARBOOK OF GREAT BRITAIN
FROM 1935/36(1938)- 1964/65(1968).
*BH/U-1.   EX/U-1.   LD/U-1.   LO/U-1.   OX/U-8.   SO/U-1.*
*SW/U-1.*

GROUP ANALYSIS.
+ +GROUP ANAL.
INSTITUTE OF GROUP ANALYSIS.
[PERGAMON]
*OXFORD &C   1(1), N 1967-*
3/A.  S/T: INTERNATIONAL PANEL & CORRESPOND-
ENCE.
*OX/U-8.*
*ED/N-1.  1(2),1968-*

GROWTH.                                               XXX
IRISH MANAGEMENT INSTITUTE: SMALL BUSINESS
DIVISION.
*DUBLIN   1, 1971- 72.//*
*BL/U-1.   DB/U-2.*
*ED/N-1.  1(2), 1971-*

GROWTH & CHANGE. JOURNAL OF REGIONAL DEVEL-
OPMENT.
UNIVERSITY OF KENTUCKY: COLLEGE OF BUSINESS &
ECONOMICS.
*LEXINGTON  1, JA 1970-*
Q.
*CB/U-1.   OX/U-1.*
*CA/U-1.  4(3), 1973-*
*ISSN 0017-4815*

GROWTH OF WORLD INDUSTRY.
+ +GROWTH WORLD IND.
UNITED NATIONS: DEPARTMENT OF ECONOMIC & SOCIAL
AFFAIRS: STATISTICAL OFFICE.
*NEW YORK  1, 1967-*
A.  IN ENG. & FR.
*LO/U-3.*

GRUNDFRAGEN DER LITERATURWISSENSCHAFT.
+ +GRUNDFRAGEN LITERATURWISS.
[BAYERISCHER SCHULBUCH VERLAG]
*MUNICH  NO.1, 1970-*
*LO/N-1.*

GRUZINSKIJ FOL'KLOR, MATERIALY I ISSLEDO-
VANIJA.
+ +GRUZ. FOL'KLOR MATER. & ISSLED.
AKADEMIJA NAUK GRUZINSKOJ SSR: INSTITUT ISTORII
GRUZINSKOJ LITERATURY.
*TIFLIS  1/2, 1964-*
GEORG. & RUSS.
*OX/U-1.*

GUA PAPERS OF GEOLOGY.
+ +GUA PAP. GEOL.
[STICHTING GUA]
*AMSTERDAM  SERIES 1. NO.1, 1972-*
*LO/N13.*

GUERILLA.
*TORONTO  NO.1, JE 1970-*
2W.
*LO/U-2. 2(19), 1971-*
*ISSN 0017-5099*

GUERRILLA. A MONTHLY NEWSPAPER OF CONTEMPORARY
KULTURE.
*DETROIT  1(1), JA 1967-*
*LO/U-2.  1(2),1967-*

GUIA LATINOAMERICANA DE DIARIOS, REVISTAS Y
MEDIOS DE DIFUSION.
+ +GUIA LAT. DIARIOS REV. MEDIOS DIFUS.
BOLSA DE PRENSA.
*BUENOS AIRES  1(1), 1967-*
*OX/U-1.*

GUIDANCE SCOTLAND.
+ +GUID. SCOTL.
CAREERS RESEARCH & ADVISORY CENTRE (SCOTLAND).
*GLASGOW [NO.1]. 1973-*
2/A.  S/T: A CRAC SCOTLAND MAGAZINE FOR
ADVISERS IN SCHOOLS, COLLEGES & UNIVERSITIES.
*CA/U-1.*
*OX/U-1.  NO.2, 1973-*

GUIDE TO EEC TECHNICAL DIRECTIVES.
+ +GUIDE EEC TECH. DIR.
INSTITUTE FOR INDUSTRIAL RESEARCH & STANDARDS
(EIRE).
PROD. BY THE INSTITUTE'S TECHNICAL INFORMATION
DIVISION.
*ED/N-1.*

GUIDE LEAFLET, SCIENCE MUSEUM, ST. PAUL
INSTITUTE.
+ +GUIDE LEAFL. SCI. MUS. ST. PAUL INST.
ST. PAUL INSTITUTE; SCIENCE MUSEUM.
*ST. PAUL, MINN.  NO.1, 1966-*
*LO/N-4.*

GUIDE TO REPRINTS.
[MICROCARD EDITIONS INC.]
*WASHINGTON, DC  1967-*
A.
*LO/N-3.   SH/U-1.*
*BH/U-1.  1969-          CV/C-1.  1970-*
*SO/U-1.  CURRENT YEAR ONLY.*

GULF BIRD-WATCHERS' NEWSLETTER.
*[BAHRAIN] 1, 1969-*
*LO/N-2.*

GUNMA SYMPOSIA ON ENDOCRINOLOGY.
+ +GUNMA SYMP. ENDOCRINOL.
GUNMA DAIGAKU NAIBUNDI KENYUSHO.
*GUNMA  1, 1964-*
A.
*XN/S-1.*
*CA/M-2.  [W. VOL.2]*

GUYANA JOURNAL.
+ +GUYANA J.
(GUYANA) MINISTRY OF EXTERNAL AFFAIRS.
*GEORGETOWN  1(1), AP 1968-*
*LO/N-1.   LO/U-3.   OX/U-9*
*LO/U-8.  1(2), 1968-*
*ISSN 0046-6654*

GUYNEWS.
(GUYANA) MINISTRY OF INFORMATION & CULTURE.
*GEORGETOWN  1, N 1971-*
M.
*ED/N-1.   LO/U-3.   LO/U-8.   OX/U-9.*
*ISSN 0046-6662*

GYNAECOLOGIA.                                         XXX
SUBS (1970): GYNECOLOGIC INVESTIGATION.

GYNECOLOGIC INVESTIGATION.                            XXX
+ +GYNECOL. INVEST.
[KARGER]
*BASLE 1(1), 1970-*
2M.  PREV: GYNAECOLOGIA FROM 121, 1946- 168,
1969.
*AB/U-3.   LO/N13.   OX/U-8.*
*ISSN 0017-5986*

**GYNECOLOGIC ONCOLOGY.**
+ +GYNECOL. ONCOL.
SOCIETY OF GYNECOLOGIC ONCOLOGY.
[ACADEMIC P.]
NEW YORK 1, N 1972-
Q.
LO/M-3.   LO/N13.   OX/U-8.
BL/U-1. 2, 1974-
ISSN 0090-8258

**HABIS.**
UNIVERSIDAD DE SEVILLA.
SEVILLE 1, 1970-
MA/U-1.   OX/U-1.

**HABITAT AUSTRALIA.**
+ +HABITAT AUST.
AUSTRALIAN CONSERVATION FOUNDATION.
CARLETON, VICTORIA NO.1, 1973-
S/T: AUSTRALIA'S NATIONAL CONSERVATION
MAGAZINE.
LO/N-2.   LO/R-5.

**HACETTEPE BULLETIN OF SOCIAL SCIENCES &
HUMANITIES.**
+ +HACETTEPE BULL. SOC. SCI. & HUM.
HACETTEPE UNIVERSITY.
ANKARA 1, JE 1969-
2/A.

**HACHINOHE KOGYO KOTO SENMON GAKKO KIYO.
RESEARCH REPORTS, HACHINOHE TECHNICAL COLLEGE.**
HACHINOHE NO.1, 1966-
JAP. OR ENGL.
LO/N14.

**HACHU RYOSEIRUIGAKU ZASSHI.  ACTA HERPETO-
LOGICA JAPONICA.**
NIHON HACHU RYOSEIRUI GAKKAI.
TOKYO 2(3), 1967-
JAP., ENGL. PREV: HACHURUIGAKU ZASSHI.
LO/N13.

**HACHURUIGAKU ZASSHI.  ACTA HERPETOLOGICA
JAPONICA.**                                          XXX
NIHON HACHURI GAKKAI.
TOKYO 1(1), 1964- 2(2), 1967...
JAP., ENGL.   SUBS: HACHU RYOSEIRUIGAKU ZASSHI
LO/13.

**HACIENDA PUBLICA ESPANOLA.**
+ +HACIENDA PUBLICA ESP.
INSTITUTO DE ESTUDIOS FISCALES.
MADRID NO.1, 1970-
2M.
LD/U-1. NO.19; 26.

**HADARAT AL-ISLAM.**
DAMASCUS 1(1), 1960-
MA/U-1. 2(6,7), 1961-

**HAEMOSTASIS.**
[KARGER]
BASLE &C. 1(1), 1972-
LO/N13.   OX/U-8.   SH/U-1.

**HAFNIA. COPENHAGEN PAPERS IN THE HISTORY OF
ART.**
KOBENHAVNS UNIVERSITET.
COPENHAGEN 1, 1970-
OX/U-2.

**HAKKO KENKYUJO NEMPO.  ANNUAL REPORT, INSTI-
TUTE FOR FERMENTATION (JAPAN).**
HAKKO KENKYUJO.
OSAKA NO.1, 1961/62(1963)-
LO/N13.

**HALIOTIS.**
SOCIETY FRANCAISE DE MALACOLOGIE.
PARIS 1, 1971-
2A.
LO/N-2.   LO/N13.

**HALLAMSHIRE & OSGOLDCROSS POETRY EXPRESS.**
[HEADLAND POETRY]
SHEFFIELD 1(1), 1972-
LO/U-2.

**HAM RADIO MAGAZINE.***
+ +HAM RADIO MAG.
COMMUNICATIONS TECHNOLOGY, INC.
GREENVILLE, N.H. 1(1), 1968-
M. TITLE VARIES:  HAM RADIO FROM 1(1), 1968-
2(1), 1968.
LO/N14.

**HAMBURGER MATHEMATISCHE EINZELSCHRIFTEN: NS.**
+ +HAMB. MATH. EINZELSCHR., NS.
UNIVERSITAT HAMBURG: MATHEMATISCHES SEMINAR.
[VANDENHOECK UND RUPRECHT]
GOTTINGEN 1(1), 1970-
PREV. SERIES FROM 1, 1923.
LO/N14.   OX/U-8.

**HAMBURGER PHILOLOGISCHE STUDIEN.**
+ +HAMB. PHILOL. STUD.
[HELMUT BUSKE]
HAMBURG 1, 1966-
CA/U-1. 1967-
ISSN 0072-9582

**HAMBURGER ROMANISTISCHE DISSERTATIONEN.**
+ +HAMB. ROM. DISS.
UNIVERSITAT HAMBURG: SEMINAR FUR ROMANISCHE
SPRACHEN UND KULTUR.
HAMBURG NO.1, 1966-
LO/N-1.
ISSN 0440-1727

**HAND. JOURNAL OF THE BRITISH SOCIETY FOR
SURGERY OF THE HAND.**
BRENTWOOD 1, 1969-
AD/U-1.   BL/U-1.   CA/U-1.   ED/N-1.   LD/U-1.   LO/N-1.
OX/U-8.   SH/U-1.
BN/U-2. 3(1), 1971-

**HANDBOOK, AUSTRALIAN ENTOMOLOGICAL SOCIETY.**
+ +HANDB. AUST. ENTOMOL. SOC.
BRISBANE NO.1, 1966-
LO/N-2.   LO/N13.

**HANDBOOK OF SENSORY PHYSIOLOGY.**
+ +HANDB. SENS. PHYSIOL.
[SPRINGER]
BERLIN 1, 1971-
GL/U-1.

**HANDLINGAR.**                                       000
(NORMALLY APPEARS IN TITLES AFTER NAME OF A
BODY).

**HANDLIST, COMMITTEE FOR THE STUDY OF ANGLO-
IRISH LANGUAGE & LITERATURE, ROYAL IRISH
ACADEMY.**
+ +HANDL. COMM. STUD. ANGLO-IR. LANG. & LIT. R.
IR. ACAD.
DUBLIN NO.1 JE 1969-
DB/U-1.   LO/N-1.

**HANNON.  REVUE LIBANAISE DE GEOGRAPHIE.**
UNIVERSITE LIBANAISE: DEPARTEMENT DE GEOGRAPHIE
BEIRUT 1, 1966-
LO/U14.

**HARLOW CONSUMER.**
+ +HARLOW CONSUM.
HARLOW CONSUMER GROUP.
HARLOW NO.1, OC 1963-
3/A.
LO/U-3.*

**HARRIER COMMUNIQUE.**
HAWKER SIDDELEY GROUP LTD.
KINGSTON-UPON-THAMES NO.1, 1970-
OX/U-1.
LO/N14. [CURRENT BOX]

**HARTFORD STUDIES IN LITERATURE.**
+ +HARTFORD STUD. LIT.
UNIVERSITY OF HARTFORD.
WEST HARTFORD, CONN. 1(1), 1969-
ED/N-1.   OX/U-1.
ISSN 0017-7989

**HART'S TONGUE.**
HAILEYBURY BIOLOGICAL SOCIETY.
HERTFORD [NO.1], 1970-
LO/N-2.

**HARVARD ENGLISH STUDIES.**
+ +HARV. ENGL. STUD.
[HARVARD UNIV. P.]
CAMBRIDGE, MASS. 1, 1970-
LO/N-3.   LO/U-1.

**HARVARD STUDIES IN EAST ASIAN LAW.**
+ +HARVARD STUD. E. ASIAN LAW.
HARVARD UNIVERSITY: LAW SCHOOL.
CAMBRIDGE, MASS. 1, 1967-
OX/U15.

**HAUSTECHNISCHER ANZEIGER.**
+ +HAUSTECH. ANZ.
[GIRARDET]
ESSEN 1, 1970-
LO/N14.
ISSN 0046-693X

**HAUTES ETUDES BETTERAVIERES ET AGRICOLES.**
+ +HAUTES ETUD. BETTERAVIERES & AGR.
PARIS 1, 1969-
LO/N13.

**HAUTS POLYMERES.**
+ +HAUTS POLYM.
SOCIETE D'EXPANSION TECHNIQUE ET ECONOMIQUE.
PARIS 1, 1968-
LO/N14.

**HAVE YOU READ THIS?**
SHIRLEY INSTITUTE.
MANCHESTER [NO.1], JA 1973-
MON. DIGEST PRODUCED FOR BUSINESS & TECHNICAL
MANAGEMENT OF CURRENT ENGLISH-LANGUAGE
ARTICLES ON TEXTILE TECHNOLOGY.
CA/U-1.    ED/N-1.    OX/U-1.
ISSN 0306-1639

**HAWAII ORCHID JOURNAL.**                          XXX
+ +HAWAII ORCHID J.
HONOLULU ORCHID SOCIETY.
HONOLULU 1, 1972-
PREV: BULLETIN OF THE PACIFIC ORCHID SOCIETY
OF HAWAII FROM 1, 1941- 29, 1971. SPONS. BODY
ALSO: PACIFIC ORCHID SOCIETY.
LO/N-2.    LO/N13.

**HAWAIIAN JOURNAL OF HISTORY.**
+ +HAWAII. J. HIST.
HAWAIIAN HISTORICAL SOCIETY.
HONOLULU 1, 1967-
LO/U19.

**HAWKER SIDDELEY TECHNICAL REVIEW.**
+ +HAWKER SIDDELEY TECH. REV.
LONDON 1, 1964-
BR/U-3.    MA/P-1. *    XN/S-1.
LO/P-7. 1(2), 1964-

**HAWKEYE HERITAGE.**
IOWA GENEALOGICAL SOCIETY.
DES MOINES 1, 1966-
Q.
ED/N-1. 5(1), 1970; 6(2), 1971-

**HAYDN-STUDIEN.**
+ +HAYDN-STUD.
JOSEPH HAYDN-INSTITUT (COLOGNE).
COLOGNE 1, JE 1965-
Q.
CA/U-1.    LP/U-1.
ISSN 0440-5323

**HCR BULLETIN.**
+ +HCR BULL. (UN HIGH COMM. REFUGEES).
UNITED NATIONS; HIGH COMMISSIONER FOR REFUGEES.
GENEVA NO.1, JA/MR 1968-
S/T: QUARTERLY RECORD OF ACTIVITIES.
ED/N-1.    LO/U-3.
ISSN 0017-615X

**HEADLAND. A QUARTERLY MAGAZINE.**
ACKWORTH, YORKS. 1, 1970-
LO/U-2.    OX/U-8.
ISSN 0017-8748

**HEADLINES. STORIES THAT MADE FRONT PAGE NEWS.**
[IPC MAGAZINES]
LONDON NO.1, S 1971-
M.
ED/N-1.    OX/U-1.

**HEALTH ASPECTS OF PESTICIDES: ABSTRACT
BULLETIN.**                                          XXX
+ +HEALTH ASPECTS PESTIC., ABSTR. BULL.
(UNITED STATES) DEPARTMENT OF HEALTH,
EDUCATION & WELFARE: PUBLIC HEALTH SERVICE.
WASHINGTON, D.C. 1(1), S 1968- 6(12), D 1973
SUBS: PESTICIDES ABSTRACTS.
LO/N13.
ISSN 0017-8918

**HEALTH PHYSICS RESEARCH ABSTRACTS.**
+ +HEALTH PHYS. RES. ABSTR.
INTERNATIONAL ATOMIC ENERGY AGENCY.
VIENNA 1, 1967-
AD/U-1.

**HEALTH & SAFETY AT WORK.**
(GREAT BRITAIN) DEPARTMENT OF EMPLOYMENT &
PRODUCTIVITY.
[H.M.S.O.]
LONDON NO.20, 1970-
SPONS. BODY ALSO CENTRAL OFFICE OF INFORMATION
PREV: SAFETY, HEALTH & WELFARE, NS FROM 1,
1958. SOME ISSUES ARE REVISED ED. OF EARLIER
SERIES.
LO/N14.

**HEALTH SERVICE HYGIENE.***                         XXX
+ +HEALTH SERV. HYG.
[NORTHWOOD PUBL. LTD.]
LONDON 1(1), 1969-
ISSUED AS SUPPL. TO: HOSPITAL EQUIPMENT &
SUPPLIES. TITLE REDUCED FROM HEALTH SERVICE
HYGIENE & EQUIPMENT WITH 2(2).
LO/N14.

**HEALTH SERVICES RESEARCH.**
+ +HEALTH SERV. RES.
HOSPITAL RESEARCH & EDUCATIONAL TRUST.
CHICAGO 1, 1966-
AD/U-1.    LO/N13.
ISSN 0017-9124

**HEALTH TODAY.**
[NEWMAN TURNER PUBL.]
WEYBRIDGE 1(1), 1971-
Q.
ED/N-1.    OX/U-8.
ISSN 0302-2412

**HEALTH TRENDS: A QUARTERLY REVIEW FOR THE
MEDICAL PROFESSION.**
(GREAT BRITAIN) DEPARTMENT OF HEALTH & SOCIAL
SECURITY.
[HMSO]
LONDON 1, 1969-
PREV: MONTHLY BULLETIN OF THE MINISTRY OF
HEALTH & THE PUBLIC HEALTH LABORATORY SERVICE
FROM 1, 1943.
LO/N-1.    SW/U-1.
BH/U-3. 2, 1970-                    CR/M-1. 2, 1970-
CO/U-1. 3(1), F 1971-
LO/U-1. [W. 1(2)- 1(4), 1969].
LO/U-3. 3(1), F 1971-
NO/U-1. 3(3), AG 1971-
ISSN 0017-9132

**HEART BULLETIN: NS (LONDON).**                     XXX
+ +HEART BULL., NS (LOND.).
BRITISH HEART FOUNDATION.
LONDON 1(1), 1973-
PREV. SERIES FROM NO.1, JL 1967- 20, D 1972.
INCORP: HEART FROM 1(1), JE 1963- D 1972.
ED/N-1.    OX/U-1.

**HEAT & FLUID FLOW.**
INSTITUTION OF MECHANICAL ENGINEERS: THERMO-
DYNAMICS & FLUID MECHANICS GROUP.
LONDON 1(1), AP 1971-
M.
AD/U-1.    BR/U-3.    DB/U-2.    GL/U-1.    GL/U-2.    LD/U-1.
LO/N14.    SH/C-5.    SH/U-3.    XS/R10.    XS/T-7.    XY/N-1.
LO/U28. 2, 1972-                    OX/U-8. 3(1), 1973-
ISSN 0046-7138

**HEAT TECHNOLOGY.**
+ +HEAT TECHNOL.
SELAS CORPORATION.
DRESHER, PA. 1, 1970-
LO/N14.
ISSN 0017-9337

**HEAT TRANSFER. JAPANESE RESEARCH.**
KAGAKU KOGAKU KYOKAI.
[SCRIPTA PUBL. CORP.]
WASHINGTON, D.C. 1, 1972-
SPONS. BODY ALSO: HEAT TRANSFER DIVISION OF
AMERICAN SOCIETY OF MECHANICAL ENGINEERS.
CA/U-4.    LO/N14.    SH/U-3.

**HEAT TRANSFER-SOVIET RESEARCH.**
+ +HEAT TRANSFER-SOV. RES.
AMERICAN SOCIETY OF MECHANICAL ENGINEERS.
NEW YORK 1, 1969-
RUSSIAN TRANSLATIONS.
AD/U-1.    GL/U-1.    LO/N14.    OX/U-8.    SH/U-3.    XS/R10.
GL/U-2. 3, 1971-

**HEATWAVE.**
LONDON NO.1, JL 1966-
ENGL. SUCCESSOR TO ANGLO-AMERICAN ED. (PUBL.
IN LONDON, NO.6, MY 1966) OF: REBEL WORKER.
LO/U-2.    LO/U-3.
ED/N-1. 2, 1966-

**HELLENIC REVIEW.**
++HELLEN. REV.
LONDON 1(1), JE - 1(5), OC 1968. //
M.
ED/N-1.    LO/U-3.    OX/U-1.
ISSN 0018-0041

**HELLENIC SHIPPING INTERNATIONAL.**
++HELLEN. SHIP. INT.
CATERHAM, SURREY NO.1, JA/F 1970-
ED/N-1.
OX/U-1. 2(1), 1970-
ISSN 0018-005X

**HELMINTHOLOGICAL ABSTRACTS: SERIES A: ANIMAL
& HUMAN HELMINTHOLOGY.**                                    XXX
++HELMINTHOL. ABSTR., A.
COMMONWEALTH AGRICULTURAL BUREAU.
FARNHAM ROYAL, BUCKS. 39, 1970-
FROM 1, 1932- 38, 1969 ISSUED AS SINGLE TITLE
THEN FROM ABOVE NO. CONTINUED IN TWO SERIES.
GL/U-2.    LO/U13.    RE/U-1.    SO/U-1.    SW/U-1.
LO/U28. 41, 1972-
ISSN 0300-8339

**HELMINTHOLOGICAL ABSTRACTS: SERIES B: PLANT
NEMATOLOGY.**                                               XXX
++HELMINTHOL. ABSTR., B.
COMMONWEALTH AGRICULTURAL BUREAU.
FARNHAM ROYAL, BUCKS. 39, 1970-
REMARKS AS FOR SERIES A.
GL/U-1.    GL/U-2.    LO/U13.    OX/U-3.    RE/U-1.    SO/U-1.
SW/U-1.    XS/R-2.
ISSN 0300-8320

**HELP.**
[COMMUNITY PUBLS. GROUP LTD.]
LONDON NO.1, MY 1968-
ED/N-1.
LO/P-7. SIX MONTH FILE.

**HELVETIA ARCHAEOLOGICA.**                                 XXX
++HELV. ARCHAEOL.
SCHWEIZERISCHE GESELLSCHAFT FUR UR- UND
FRUHGESCHICHTE.
BASLE 1, 1970-
PREV: UR-SCHWEIZ FROM 1, JL 1937- 33(4), 1969.
LD/U-1.    NW/U-1.    OX/U-2.    SO/U-1.
ISSN 0018-0173

**HELVETICA PHYSIOLOGICA ET PHARMACOLOGICA ACTA.**
++HELV. PHYSIOL. & PHARMACOL. ACTA.
SCHWEIZERISCHE VEREIN FUR PHYSIOLOGIE, PHYS-
IOLOGISCHE CHEMIE UND PHARMAKOLOGIE.
BASEL 1, 1943- 26, 1969.//
INCLUDES: VERHANDLUNGEN DES SCHWEIZERISCHEN
VEREINS ...; & COMPTES RENDUS DE LA SOCIETE
SUISSE DE PHYSIOLOGIE, CHIMIE PHYSIOLOGIQUE
ET PHARMACOLOGIE.
BL/U-1.    DB/U-2.    GL/U-1.    LO/M25.    LO/M32.    SH/U-1.
XY/N-1.**
LO/N13. 3, 1945-          LO/U-1. 8, 1950-
NO/U-1. 11, 1953-

**HELVETICA PHYSIOLOGICA ET PHARMACOLOGICA ACTA:
SUPPLEMENT.**                                               XXX
++HELV. PHYSIOL. & PHARMACOL. ACTA, SUPPL.
SCHWEIZERISCHE VEREIN FUR PHYSIOLOGIE, PHYSIOL-
OGISCHE CHEMIE UND PHARMAKOLOGIE.
BASLE 1, 1943- 18, 1967. //
BL/U-1.    LD/U-1.    LO/M25.    LO/U-2.    LO/U-6.    NW/U-1.
LO/M29. 11, 1953-          LO/N-4. 2, 1944-
LO/U-1. 6, 1950-

**HEMATOLOGIC REVIEWS.**
++HEMATOL. REV.
[ARNOLD]
LONDON 1, 1968-
ALSO PUBL. NEW YORK, DEKKER.
CA/U-1.    LO/N13.

**HEMICRANIA. JOURNAL OF THE MIGRAINE TRUST.**
LONDON 1, 1969-
DB/U-2.    ED/N-1.    LD/U-1.    LO/M-1.    LO/N13.    NW/U-1.
OX/U-8.    SH/U-1.
ISSN 0046-7235

**HEMIJSKA VLAKNA.**
++HEM. VLAKNA. [HEVL-A]
INDUSTRIJA VISKOZNIH PROIZVODA 'VISKOZA'.
NOVI SAD 1(1), 1961-
LO/N13. 9(3), 1969-

**HEOLOHIJA I HEOKHIMIJA HORJUCHYKH KOPALYN.**            000
SEE: GEOLOGIJA I GEOKHIMIJA GORJUCHIKH
ISKOPAEMYKH.

**HERALDIQUE ET GENEALOGIE. BULLETIN DES ...**
++HER. & GENEAL.
SOCIETES FRANCAISE DE GENEALOGIE, D'HERALDIQUE
ET DE SIGILLOGRAPHIE.
PARIS 1, JA/F 1969-
2M.
ED/N-1.

**HERE NOW.**
HEBBURN, CO. DURHAM 1(1), SPRING 1972-
S/T: SOUTH TYNESIDE ARTS QUARTERLY.
CA/U-1. 2, 1973-          ED/N-1. 2, 1973-
OX/U-1. 2(1), 1973-
ISSN 0046-7294

**HERPETOLOGICAL REVIEW.**                                 XXX
++HERPET. REV.
SOCIETY FOR THE STUDY OF AMPHIBIANS &
REPTILES.
CINCINNATI 1, 1967- 4, 1972.
SUBS: HISS NEWS-JOURNAL.
LO/N-2.
OX/U-8. NO.7, 1969-
ISSN 0018-084X

**HERPETON. JOURNAL OF THE ...**
SOUTHWESTERN HERPETOLOGISTS' SOCIETY.
PASADENA, CALIF 1, 1966-
LO/N-2.

**HERTFORDSHIRE ARCHAEOLOGY. TRANSACTIONS OF ...**
++HERTS. ARCHAEOL.
ST. ALBANS & HERTFORDSHIRE ARCHITECTURAL &
ARCHAEOLOGICAL SOCIETY.
ST. ALBANS 1, 1968-
SPONS. BODY ALSO EAST HERTFORDSHIRE ARCHAEO-
LOGICAL SOCIETY.
BL/U-1.    CA/U-3.    ED/N-1.    LO/N15.    LO/S-7.    LO/U-2.
LO/U19.    OX/U-1.    OX/U-2.    SH/U-1.
SO/U-1. 1, 1968- 2, 1970.

**HERTIS OCCASIONAL PAPER.**
++HERTIS OCC. PAP.
HATFIELD NO.1, 1967-
OX/U-1.

**HERZOGIA. ZEITSCHRIFT DER BRYOLOGISCH-LICHEN-
OLOGISCHEN ARBEITSGEMEINSCHAFT FUR MITTELEUROPA.**
[CRAMER]
LEHRE 1, 1968-
LO/N-2.    LO/N13.
ISSN 0018-0971

**HETEROFONIA. REVISTA MUSICAL.**
MEXICO, D.F. 1, 1968-
2M.
LO/U-1.
ISSN 0018-1137

**HIDROMETEOROLOGINIAI STRAIPSNIAI.**
++HIDROMETEOROL. STRAIPSNIAI.
LIETUVOS TSR GEOGRAFINE DRAUGIJA: HIDROMETEOR-
OLOGIJOS SKYRIUS.
VILNA 1, 1968-
LITH. & RUSS. RUSSIAN TITLE: STAT'I PO
GIDROMETEOROLOGII.
LO/N-4.

**HI-FI ANSWERS.**
[HAYMARKET PUBL.]
LONDON 1(1), OC 1972-
MON.
ED/N-1.

**HI-FI NEWS & RECORD REVIEW.**
++HI-FI NEWS & REC. REV.
[LINK HOUSE PUBL.]
CROYDON 16, 1971-
PREV: HI-FI NEWS FROM 1, 1956.
LO/N14.*
ISSN 0018-1226

**HI-FI NEWS & RECORD REVIEW ANNUAL.**                     XXX
++HI-FI NEWS & REC. REV. ANNU.
[LINK HOUSE PUBL.]
LONDON 1972-
PREV: AUDIO ANNUAL FROM 1961.
LO/N14.

**HI-FI FOR PLEASURE.**
LONDON 1(1), JA 1973-
MON.
CA/U-1.    OX/U-1.
ED/N-1. 1(5), 1973-
LO/N14. CURRENT BOX ONLY.

**HIGH ENERGY CHEMISTRY.**
+ +HIGH ENERGY CHEM.
[CONSULTANTS BUREAU]
*NEW YORK   1, JA/F 1967-*
TRANSL. OF: KHIMIJA VYSOKIKH ENERGIJ. (AKA-
DEMIJA NAUK SSSR).  NUMBERING & DATING AS IN
ORIG.
*LO/N14.      LO/S-3.      OX/U-8.*
*MA/U-1.  7, 1973-*
ISSN 0018-1439

**HIGH ROAD.**
BRITISH LEYLAND MOTOR CORPORATION LTD.
*COVENTRY  1, 1969-*
S/T: THE CAR MAGAZINE OF BRITISH LEYLAND ...
*ED/N-1.*

**HIGH SPEED RAIL RESEARCH REPORT.**
+ +HIGH SPEED RAIL RES. REP.
RAILROAD ENGINEERING INDEX INSTITUTE.
*WIJNANDSRADE, NETH.  1, 1972.*
*LO/N14.*

**HIGH TEMPERATURE BULLETIN.**                                    XXX
+ +HIGH TEMP. BULL.
UNIVERSITY OF LEEDS: INFORMATION CENTRE ON HIGH
TEMPERATURE PROCESSES.
*LEEDS  NO.21, 1971-*
PREV: HIGH TEMPERATURE INFORMATION BULLETIN
FROM NO.1, 1967- NO.20, 1971.  INFORMATION
CENTRE SUBORD. TO DEPARTMENT OF FUEL SCIENCE.
*LD/U-1.      LO/N14.      XS/R10.*
*SH/U-3.  NO.25, 1972-*

**HIGH TEMPERATURES, HIGH PRESSURES.**
+ +HIGH TEMP. HIGH PRESS.
[PION]
*LONDON  1(1), 1969-*
S/T: INTERNATIONAL JOURNAL OF RESEARCH.
ENGL. FR. OR GER. WITH ENGL. SUMMARIES.
*AD/U-3.      BL/U-1.      ED/N-1.      HL/U-1.      LD/U-1.      LO/N14.*
*MA/U-1.      OX/U-8.      SH/U-1.      XS/R10.*
*ISSN 0018-1544*

**HIGH TEMPERATURE INFORMATION BULLETIN.**            XXX
+ +HIGH TEMP. INF. BULL.
UNIVERSITY OF LEEDS.
*LEEDS  NO.1, 1967- 20, 1971 ...*
ISSUED BY THE UNIV.'S DEP. OF FUEL SCIENCE.
SUBS: HIGH TEMPERATURE BULLETIN.
*GL/U-2.      SO/U-1.      XN/S-1.*
*LV/U-1.  8, 1969-               XS/R10.  8, 1969-*

**HIGH TEMPERATURE SCIENCE.**
+ +HIGH TEMP. SCI.
[ACADEMIC PRESS]
*NEW YORK &C  1(1), MY 1969-*
*LO/N14.      MA/U-1.      OX/U-8.      SH/U-3.      XS/R10.*
*ISSN 0022-1538*

**HIGHER EDUCATION.**
+ +HIGHER EDUC.
[ELSEVIER]
*AMSTERDAM  1, 1972-*
Q.
*AD/U-1.      BH/U-1.      BL/U-1.      GL/U-2.      LO/U11.      MA/U-1.*
*SF/U-1.      SH/U-1.      SW/U-1.*
*LO/U-2.  3(1), 1974-*
*ISSN 0018-1560*

**HIGHER EDUCATION APPOINTMENTS.**
+ +HIGHER EDUC. APPOINTMENTS.
[FORTH PUBL. CO. LTD.; CORNMARKET P.]
*EDINBURGH  1970-*
W.
*BH/U-3.  6 MONTHS ONLY.*
*BL/U-1.  CURRENT YEAR ONLY.*
*ED/N-1.  1(10), 1970-*

**HIGHER EDUCATION BULLETIN: NS.**
+ +HIGHER EDUC. BULL., NS.
UNIVERSITY OF LANCASTER: DEPARTMENT OF EDUCAT-
IONAL RESEARCH.
*LANCASTER  1, 1972-*
*MA/U-1.*

**HIGHER EDUCATION JOURNAL.**                                 XXX
  SUBS (1970): SECONDARY EDUCATION.

**HIGHER EDUCATION MONOGRAPH SERIES.**
+ +HIGHER EDUC. MONOGR. SER.
NATIONAL FOUNDATION FOR EDUCATIONAL RESEARCH
IN ENGLAND & WALES.
*LONDON  NO.1, 1969-*
*GL/U-1.      LO/N-1.      OX/U-1.*

**HIGHER EDUCATION REVIEW.**
+ +HIGHER EDUC. REV.
[CORNMARKET PRESS]
*SOUTHAMPTON  NO.1, 1968-*
3/A.
*ED/N-1.      GL/U-2.      HL/U-2.      LO/U-1.      LO/U-3.      LO/U11.*
*LV/U-1.      MA/U-1.      NW/U-1.      SH/U-1.      SW/U-1.*
*ISSN 0018-1609*

**HIGHLAND HOTELKEEPER & TOURISTMAKER.**
+ +HIGHL. HOTELKEEPER & TOURISTMAKER.
*INVERNESS  NO.1, MY 1969-*
*ED/N-1.      OX/U-1.*
*ISSN 0018-1617*

**HIGHWAY ENGINEER.**                                              XXX
+ +HIGHW. ENG.
INSTITUTION OF HIGHWAY ENGINEERS.
[WHITEHALL P. LTD.]
*LONDON  20, 1973-*
PREV: JOURNAL OF THE INSTITUTION OF HIGHWAY
ENGINEERS FROM 1, 1948- 19, 1972.
*BH/P-1.      GL/U-1.      LD/U-1.      LO/N14.*
*ED/N-1.  20(2), F 1973-*

**HIGHWAY RESEARCH CIRCULAR.**
+ +HIGHW. RES. CIRC.
HIGHWAY RESEARCH BOARD (US).
*WASHINGTON, DC   1, MR 1965-*
*LV/U-1.*

**HIGHWAYS DESIGN & CONSTRUCTION.**                  XXX
+ +HIGHW. DES. & CONSTR.
[IPC BUILDING CONTRACT JOURNALS]
*LONDON  39(1741), S 1971- 41(1759), 1973 ...*
PREV: HIGHWAYS & TRAFFIC ENGINEERING FROM
37(1731), 1969- 39(1740), 1971.  SUBS: HIGH-
WAYS & ROAD CONSTRUCTION.
*ED/N-1.      LO/N14.      SH/U-3.*

**HIGHWAYS & PUBLIC WORKS.**                                  XXX
  SUBS (1969): HIGHWAYS & TRAFFIC ENGINEERING.

**HIGHWAYS & ROAD CONSTRUCTION.**                    XXX
+ +HIGHW. & ROAD CONSTR.
[IPC BUILDING & CONTRACT JOURNALS LTD.]
*LONDON  41(1760), AP 1973-*
PREV: HIGHWAYS DESIGN & CONSTRUCTION FROM
39(1741), 1971- 41(1759), 1973.  INCORP: ROADS
& ROAD CONSTRUCTION FROM 1, 1923- 50(600),
1972.
*DB/U-2.      ED/N-1.      LO/N14.*

**HIGHWAYS & TRAFFIC ENGINEERING.**                  XXX
+ +HIGHW. & TRAFFIC ENG.
[BUILDING CONTRACT JOURNALS]
*LONDON  37(1713), 1969- 39(1740), 1971 ...*
PREV: HIGHWAYS & PUBLIC WORKS.  SUBS: HIGHWAYS
DESIGN & CONSTRUCTION.
*LO/N14.*

**HIRAM POETRY REVIEW.**
+ +HIRAM POETRY REV.
HIRAM COLLEGE.
*HIRAM, OHIO   NO.1, FALL/WINTER 1966-*
ISSUED BY THE COLLEGE'S  ENGLISH DEP.
*LO/U-2.*
*ISSN 0018-2036*

**HISPANIA ANTIQUA.  REVISTA DE HISTORIA
ANTIQUA.**
+ +HISP. ANTIQ.
COLEGIO UNIVERSITARIO DE ALAVA.
*ALAVA  1, 1971-*
*BL/U-1.      LO/N-1.      MA/U-1.      OX/U-1.*

**HISS NEWS-JOURNAL.**                                             XXX
+ +HISS NEWS-J.
[HERPETOLOGICAL INFORMATION SEARCH SYSTEMS]
*NEW YORK  1(1), JA- 1(5), 1973. //*
2M.  PREV: HERPETOLOGICAL REVIEW FROM 1, 1967-
4, 1972.
*LO/N-2.      LO/N13.*

**HISS TITLES & REVIEWS.**                                        XXX
+ +HISS TITLES & REV.
[HERPETOLOGICAL INFORMATION SEARCH SYSTEMS]
*NEW YORK  1(1- 2), 1973.//*
*LO/N13.      OX/U-8.*

**HISTOCHEMICAL JOURNAL.**
+ +HISTOCHEM. J.
[CHAPMAN & HALL]
*LONDON  1(1), AG 1968-*
*BN/U-2.      CR/M-1.      DN/U-1.      ED/N-1.      GL/U-1.      LD/U-1.*
*LO/N-4.      LO/N13.      LO/U-2.      LV/U-1.      OX/U-8.      SH/U-1.*
*SO/U-1.*
*ISSN 0018-2214*

**HISTOIRE ET BIOLOGIE. CAHIERS DU CERCLE D'ETUDE HISTORIQUE DES SCIENCES DE LA VIE.**
*+ +HIST. & BIOL.(FR.)*
MUSEUM NATIONAL D'HISTOIRE NATURELLE (FRANCE): LABORATOIRE D'ETHNOBOTANIQUE.
*PARIS NO.1, 1968- 2, 1969 ...*
SUBS: HISTOIRE ET NATURE.
*LO/M24.    LO/N-2.    LO/N-4.    OX/U-8.*

**HISTOIRE DE LA PHILOSOPHIE.**
*+ +HIST. PHILOS.*
*PARIS 1, 1972-*
*LO/N-1.    OX/U-1.*

**HISTOIRE SOCIALE. = SOCIAL HISTORY.**
UNIVERSITY OF OTTAWA.
*OTTAWA NO.1, AP 1968-*
SPONS. BODY ALSO CARLETON UNIVERSITY.
*HL/U-1.    LO/N-1.    LO/U-3.    SH/U-1.*
*ISSN 0018-2257*

**HISTOIRE ET SOCIOLOGIE DE L'EGLISE.**
*+ +HIST. & SOCIOL. EGLISE.*
*PARIS 1, 1962-*
*OX/U-1.*

**HISTORIA ARCHAEOLOGICA (PULA).**
*+ +HIST. ARCHAEOL. (PULA).*
ARHEOLOSKI MUZEJ ISTRE.
*PULA 1, 1970-*
SERBO-CROAT.  ENGL. OR GER. SUMM.
*OX/U-2.*

**HISTORIA Y CULTURA.**
*+ +HIST. & CULT. (PERU).*
MUSEO NACIONAL DE HISTORIA (PERU).
*LIMA 1, 1965-*
*LO/U-1.    LV/U-1.    OX/U-1.*
*ISSN 0073-2486*

**HISTORIA HOSPITALIUM.  MITTEILUNGEN ...**
*+ +HIST. HOSP. (GER.)*
DEUTSCHE GESELLSCHAFT FUR KRANKENHAUSGESCHICHTE
*DUSSELDORF HEFT 1, MR 1966-*
S/T: MITT. DER DEUTSCHEN GESELLSCHAFT ...
*LO/M24.*

**HISTORIA I TEORIA LITERATURY: STUDIA: HISTORIA LITERATURY.**
*+ +HIST. & TEOR. LIT., STUD., HIST. LIT. (POL.)*
POLSKA AKADEMIA NAUK: INSTYTUT BADAN LITERAC-KICH.
*WARSAW [NO.]1, (JE 1961)-*
MONOGR.  NOT ISSUED IN STRICT CHRONOL. ORDER: 2, 1961; 1, 1963.

**HISTORIA I TEORIA LITERATURY: STUDIA: TEORIA LITERATURY.**
*+ +HIST. & TEOR. LIT., STUD., TEOR. LIT. (POL.)*
POLSKA AKADEMIA NAUK: INSTYTUT BADAN LITERAC-KICH.
*WARSAW [NO.]1, (MY 1961)-*
MONOGR.  NOT ISSUED IN STRICT CHRONOL. ORDER: 2, 1961; 1, 1962.
*ED/N-1. ***
*CA/U-1.  NO.5, 1966.*
*XY/N-1.  NO.9, 1963-*

**HISTORICA (RIO DE JANEIRO).**
*RIO DE JANEIRO 1, 1972-*
*OX/U-1.*

**HISTORICAL JOURNAL.**
*+ +HIST. J.*
UNIVERSITY OF NEWCASTLE (N.S.W.).
*NEWCASTLE, N.S.W.  1(1), JA 1968-*
*GL/U-1.    LO/U-8.    OX/U-1.*

**HISTORICAL METHODS NEWSLETTER.**
*+ +HIST. METHODS NEWSL.*
UNIVERSITY OF PITTSBURGH: DEPARTMENT OF HISTORY
*PITTSBURGH 1(1), D 1967-*
S/T: QUANTITATIVE ANALYSIS OF SOCIAL, ECONOMIC & POLITICAL DEVELOPMENT.
*CB/U-1.    OX/U-1.*
*CA/U-1.  3(3), 1970-*

**HISTORICAL & POLITICAL STUDIES.**
*+ +HIST. & POLIT. STUD.*
UNIVERSITY OF OTAGO: POLITICAL SCIENCE SOCIETY.
*DUNEDIN 1, 1969-*
*GL/U-1.    LD/U-1.    LO/U-3.*

**HISTORICAL STUDIES.*.**                                                          XXX
*+ +HIST. STUD. (UNIV. MELB.)*
UNIVERSITY OF MELBOURNE.
*MELBOURNE 1(1), AP 1940-*
ISSUED BY THE UNIV.'S DEPARTMENT OF HISTORY.
ISSUES NUMBERED CONTINUOUSLY WITH VOL. NOS.
TITLE REDUCED FROM: HISTORICAL STUDIES, AUS-TRALIA & NEW ZEALAND; FROM 13(49), OC 1967.
2/A.
*BH/P-1.    BH/U-1.    BR/U-1.    CA/U-1.    DR/U-1.    LO/N-1.*
*LO/U-1.    LO/U-8.*    LO/U11.*    LV/U-1.    OX/U-9.*
*AD/U-1.  4-                          BL/U-1.  10,1961-*
*ED/U-1.  3(11)-                      EX/U-1.  13(49),1967-*
*GL/U-1.  5(17)-                      GL/U-2.  13(50),1968-*
*LC/U-1.  6,1953-                     LD/U-1.  4(13),1949-*
*LO/N-3.  12(46),1966-                LO/S26.  10,1962-*
*LV/P-1.  8(30)-                      NO/U-1.  8(31),1958-*
*NW/U-1.  4(13)-*
*ISSN 0018-2559*

**HISTORICAL STUDIES IN THE PHYSICAL SCIENCES.**              XXX
*+ +HIST. STUD. PHYS. SCI.*
[UNIVERSITY OF PENNSYLVANIA P.]
*PHILADELPHIA 1, 1969-*
AT HEAD OF TITLE, V.1- EDGAR F. SMITH MEMORIAL COLLECTION, UNIV. OF PENNSYLVANIA.  PREV: CHYMIA FROM 1, 1948- 12, 1967.
*AD/U-1.    BH/U-1.    CB/U-1.    EX/U-1.    LD/U-1.    LO/M24.*
*LO/N-4.    LO/U-1.    LO/U-2.    LO/U11.    MA/U-1.    OX/U-8.*
*ISSN 0073-2672*

**HISTORICKA DEMOGRAFIE.**
*+ +HIST. DEMOGR.*
CESKOSLOVENSKA AKADEMIE VED: KOMISE PRO HISTORICKOU DEMOGRAFII.
*PRAGUE 1, 1967-*
FR. SUMM.  KOMISE ... SUBORD. TO: 'HISTORICKY USTAV' OF CSAV.
*OX/U-1.*

**HISTORICKO-STATISTICKE PRAMENE A MONOGRAFIE.**
*+ +HIST.-STAT. PRAMENE MONOGR.*
SLOVENSKA ARCHIVNA SPRAVA.
*BRATISLAVA 1, 1966-*
GER. & RUSS. SUMM.
*OX/U-1.*

**HISTORIE, SBORNIK VYSOKA SKOLA PEDAGOGICKA V OLOMOUCI.**                XXX
SUBS (1960): ACTA UNIVERSITATIS PALACKIANAE OLOMUCENSIS: HISTORICA.

**HISTORISCHE FORSCHUNGEN (BERLIN).**
*+ +HIST. FORSCH. (BERL.).*
[DUNCKER & HUMBLOT]
*BERLIN 1, 1968-*
MONOGR.
*LO/N-1.*

**HISTORY.  REVIEWS OF NEW BOOKS.**
*WASHINGTON, D.C.  1, OC 1972-*
10/A.
*OX/U-1.*

**HISTORY FROM THE ARCHIVES.**
*+ +HIST. ARCH.*
LINDSEY COUNTY COUNCIL.
*LINCOLN NO.1, 1968-*
*OX/U-1.*

**HISTORY OF ECONOMIC THOUGHT NEWSLETTER.**
*+ +HIST. ECON. THOUGHT NEWSL.*
UNIVERSITY OF NOTTINGHAM.
*NOTTINGHAM &C.  NO.1, N 1968-*
ORIG. PUB. BY UNIV. OF NOTTINGHAM. SUBS. PLACE AND PUBLISHER VARY.
*ED/N-1.    LO/U-3.    OX/U17.*
*ISSN 0440-9884*

**HISTORY OF EDUCATION.**
*+ +HIST. EDUC.*
HISTORY OF EDUCATION SOCIETY.
[DAVID & CHARLES]
*NEWTON ABBOT 1, 1972-*
*BL/U-1.    CA/U-1.    CB/U-1.    ED/N-1.    HL/U-1.    LO/U28.*
*LV/U-2.    MA/U-1.*

**HISTORY OF MEDICINE.**
*+ +HIST. MED.*
[SQUIBB]
*TWICKENHAM 1, 1968-*
*BL/U-1.    LD/U-1.    LO/M24.*
*AD/U-1.  2, 1970-*                        *CA/U-1.  1(2), 1969-*
*ISSN 0046-7618*

**HISTORY OF POLITICAL ECONOMY.**
++HIST. POL. ECON.
DURHAM (N.C.) 1(1), 1969-
2/A.
BH/U-1.    EX/U-1.    LD/U-1.    LO/N-1.    LO/U-3.    LO/U-3.
OX/U-1.    OX/U17.    SW/U-1.
GL/U-1. 4, 1972-                    MA/U-1. 4, 1972-
SF/U-1. 6, 1974-                    SH/U-1. 2, 1970-
ISSN 0018-2702

**HISTORY OF SCIENCE SERIES.**
++HIST. SCI. SER.
UNIVERSITY OF TEXAS: HUMAN RESEARCH CENTER.
AUSTIN &C. NO.1, 1969-
OX/U-8.

**HISTORY OF SOCIALISM YEARBOOK.**
++HIST. SOC. YRB.
USTAV DEJIN SOCIALISMU.
PRAGUE 1, 1968-
ENGL. FR. & GER. ARTIC.
LO/U-3.

**HISTORY STUDIES.**                                                    XXX
++HIST. STUD.
[PERGAMON PRESS]
OXFORD &C   1(1), MY 1968- 1(2), OC 1968.//
3/A.
LO/P-6.    LO/S-7.    LO/U-1.    MA/P-1.    SW/U-1.

**HISTORY TEACHERS' NEWSLETTER.**
++HIST. TEACH. NEWSL.
HISTORICAL ASSOCIATION.
LONDON NO.1, 1970-
ED/N-1.    OX/U-1.

**HISTORY TODAY.**
++HIST. TODAY.
[OLIVER & BOYD]
EDINBURGH &C 1, 1967-
S/T: SELECTIONS FROM HISTORY TODAY.
OX/U-1.
ISSN 0018-2753

**HISTORY TRAIL.**
LANCASTER CITY MUSEUM & ART GALLERY.
LANCASTER NO.1, 1971-
LO/N-4.    OX/U-1.

**HISTORY IN ZAMBIA.**
++HIST. ZAMBIA.
HISTORICAL ASSOCIATION OF ZAMBIA.
LUSAKA NO.1, JE 1970-
2/A.
LO/U-8. NO.2, 1971-

**HOCHFREQUENZTECHNIK UND ELEKTROAKUSTIK.**          XXX
SUBS (1971): PART OF ZEITSCHRIFT FUR ELEKT-
RISCHE INFORMATIONS- UND ENERGIETECHNIK.

**HOFMANNSTHAL-BLATTER.**
HOFMANNSTHAL GESELLSCHAFT.
FRANKFURT AM MAIN 1, 1968-
DB/U-2.    LO/N-1.

**HOFSTRA LAW REVIEW.**
++HOFSTRA LAW REV.
HOFSTRA UNIVERSITY: SCHOOL OF LAW.
HOFSTRA, N.Y. 1, 1973-
OX/U15.

**HOKKAIDO JOSHI TANKI DAIGAKU KENKYU KIYO.**
HOKKAIDO JOSHI TANKI DAIGAKU.
EBETSU 1, 1968-
LO/N13.

**HOKKAIDO KOGYO KAIHATSU SHIKENJO HOKOKU.**
**REPORTS OF THE GOVERNMENT INDUSTRIAL DEVELOP-
MENT LABORATORY.**
HOKKAIDO KOGYO KAIHATSU SHIKENJO.
SAPPORO NO.1, 1966-
ENGL. SUMM.
LO/N13.

**HOKURIKU NOGYO KENKYU SHIRYO.**
HOKURIKU NOGYO SHIKENJO.
NIIGATA NO.1, 1970-
LO/N13.

**HOLECTECHNIEK.**
SAMENWERKENDE ELECTROTECHNISCHE FABRIEKEN HOLEC
N.V.
HENGELO 1, 1971-
DUTCH & ENGL.
LO/N14.
ISSN 0018-3512

**HOLOGRAPHY INDEX.**
++HOLOGR. INDEX.
UNIVERSITY OF STRATHCLYDE: ANDERSONIAN LIBRARY.
GLASGOW 1, MY 1969-
ED/N-1.    GL/U-1.    LO/N14.    OX/U-1.
BH/U-3. [FIVE YEARS ONLY].

**HOLZ- UND KUNSTSTOFFVERARBEITUNG.**               XXX
++HOLZ & KUNSTSTOFFVERARB.
[DRW-VERLAGS]
STUTTGART 6, 1971-
PREV: MODERNE HOLZVERARBEITUNG FROM 1, JA
1966- 5, 1970.
LO/N14.

**HOME LIGHTING & ACCESSORIES.**                   XXX
++HOME LIGHT. & ACCESSORIES.
[ROSENTHAL & SMYTHE]
CLIFTON, N.J. F 1971-
PREV: LAMP JOURNAL FROM 24, 1941- 54(1), 1971.
LO/N13.

**HOME OFFICE RESEARCH STUDIES.**
++HOME OFF. RES. STUD.
(GREAT BRITAIN) HOME OFFICE.
LONDON 1, 1969-
OX/U-1.

**HONEST ULSTERMAN.**
BELFAST NO.1, MY 1968-
BL/C-1.    BL/U-1.    DB/U-2.    OX/U-1.
ED/N-1. NO.3, 1968-
ISSN 0018-4543

**HONEYWELL COMPUTER JOURNAL.**
++HONEYWELL COMPUT. J.
HONEYWELL INC.: ELECTRONIC DATA PROCESSING
DIVISION.
WELLESLEY HILLS (MASS.) 1(1), F 1967-
LO/N14.    LO/U-2.
LD/U-1. 5, 1971-
ISSN 0046-7847

**HONG KONG FISHERIES BULLETIN.**
++HONG KONG FISH. BULL.
(HONG KONG) DEPARTMENT OF AGRICULTURE &
FISHERIES: FISHERIES BRANCH.
HONG KONG NO.1, 1970-
LO/N-2.    LO/N13.    LO/R-6.

**HONG KONG LAW JOURNAL.**
++HONG KONG LAW J.
HONG KONG 1, JA 1971-
3/A.
LO/U-3.    LO/U14.

**HOPKINS RESEARCH BULLETIN.**
++HOPKINS RES. BULL.
HOPKINS SOCIETY.
LONDON NO.1, SPRING 1970-
CA/U-1. NO.3, 1972-                CA/U-1. NO.3, 1972-
ED/N-1. NO.3, 1972-                NO/U-1. NO.5, 1974-
ISSN 0085-1604

**HORIZON. LONDON SCIENTOLOGY MAGAZINE.**
HUBBARD SCIENTOLOGY ORGANIZATION.
LONDON ISSUE [NO.]1, AG [1967]-
M.
ED/N-1.

**HORMONE & METABOLIC RESEARCH.**
++HORMONE METAB. RES.
[THIEME]
STUTTGART 1, JA 1969-
AD/U-1.    BH/U-1.    LO/N13.    LO/U-2.    SO/U-1.
BL/U-1. 6, 1974-                   LD/U-1. 5, 1973-
OX/U-8. 1(3), 1969-               SH/U-1. JA 1970-
ISSN 0018-5043

**HORMONES.**
[KARGER]
BASLE &C. 1, 1970-
CR/M-1.    LO/N13.    OX/U-8.    SH/U-1.
BH/U-3. 2, 1971-
ISSN 0018-5051

**HORMONES & BEHAVIOR.**
++HORM. & BEHAV.
[ACADEMIC P.]
NEW YORK 1(1), AP 1969-
BH/U-3.    GL/U-1.    LO/N13.    LO/U-2.    MA/U-1.
NW/U-1.    OX/U-8.
ISSN 0018-506X

HORTICULTURAL PROGRESS REPORT, AGRICULTURAL
EXPERIMENTAL STATION, CALHOUN, LOUISIANA.
++HORTIC. PROG. REP. AGRIC. EXP. STN. CALHOUN LA
  CALHOUN, LA. NO.1, 1969-
  LO/N13.

HORTICULTURAL REVIEW.
++HORT. REV.
 COMMONWEALTH AGRICULTURAL BUREAU.
  FARNHAM ROYAL 1, 1969-
  BH/U-1.   CA/U11.   ED/N-1.   OX/U-1.

HOSHASEN IKUSHUJO TEKUNIKARU NYUSU. TECH-
NICAL NEWS, INSTITUTE OF RADIATION BREEDING
(JAPAN).
  [IBARAKI] NO.1, 1969-
  JAP. WITH ENGL. TRANSL.
  LO/N13.

HOSPITAL.                                                                    XXX
  SUBS (1972): HOSPITAL & HEALTH SERVICES REVIEW

HOSPITAL BUILDING & ENGINEERING.                                             XXX
++HOSP. BLDG. & ENG.
 [NORTHWOOD PUBL. LTD]
  LONDON  1(1), JA 1968- 5, 1972.
  SUBS: HOSPITAL DEVELOPMENT.
  LO/N14.
  OX/U-1.  2(1), 1969-
  ED/N-1.  2(5), S 1969-
  ISSN 0018-5582

HOSPITAL DEVELOPMENT.                                                        XXX
++HOSP. DEV.
 [NORTHWOOD PUBL.]
  LONDON  1, 1973-
  PREV: HOSPITAL BUILDING & ENGINEERING FROM 1,
  1968- 5, 1972.
  ED/N-1.   LO/N14.

HOSPITAL ENGINEER.                                                           XXX
  SUBS (1970): HOSPITAL ENGINEERING.

HOSPITAL ENGINEERING.                                                        XXX
++HOSP. ENG.
 INSTITUTE OF HOSPITAL ENGINEERING.
 [P. PEREGRINUS LTD.]
  STEVENAGE  24, 1970-
  PREV: HOSPITAL ENGINEER FROM 1, 1946- 23,
  1969.
  LO/N14.
  ISSN 0046-7960

HOSPITAL & HEALTH SERVICES PURCHASING.                                       XXX
++HOSP. & HEALTH SERV. PURCH.
 INSTITUTE OF HEALTH SERVICE ADMINISTRATORS.
  LONDON  1972-
  PREV: HOSPITAL PURCHASING FROM 1968(8)-
  1971. SUPPL. TO HOSPITAL & HEALTH SERVICES
  REVIEW.
  LO/N14.

HOSPITAL & HEALTH SERVICES REVIEW.                                           XXX
++HOSP. & HEALTH SERV. REV.
 INSTITUTE OF HEALTH SERVICE ADMINISTRATORS.
  LONDON  68, 1972-
  PREV: HOSPITAL FROM 1, 1887- 67, 1971.
  ED/N-1.   LO/N14.

HOSPITAL MEDICINE.                                                           XXX
++HOSP. MED.
  LONDON  1(1), OC 1966- 2(12), S 1968.
  M.  S/T: THE REVIEW JOURNAL FOR HOSPITAL
  MEDICAL STAFF. SUBS: BRITISH JOURNAL OF HOSP-
  ITAL MEDICINE.
  ED/N-1.   LO/M-3.   OX/U-8.
  GL/U-1.  2, 1967- [W. 2(2)]

HOSPITAL PURCHASING.                                                         XXX
++HOSP. PURCHAS.
 INSTITUTE OF HOSPITAL ADMINISTRATORS.
  LONDON  1968(8)- 1971.
  MON. PREV: HOSPITAL PURCHASING GUIDE FROM
  1967(1)- 1968(7). SUBS: HOSPITAL & HEALTH
  SERVICES PURCHASING. SUPPL. TO HOSPITAL.
  ED/N-1.   LO/N14.   OX/U-8.
  SW/U-1.  JA 1970-
  ISSN 0018-5825

HOSPITAL PURCHASING GUIDE.                                                   XXX
++HOSP. PURCHAS. GUIDE.
 INSTITUTE OF HOSPITAL ADMINISTRATORS.
  LONDON  1967(1)- 1968(7).
  SUBS: HOSPITAL PURCHASING.
  OX/U-8.
  LO/N14.  NO.2, 1967-

HOSPITAL TIMES.
++HOSP. TIMES.
 [HAYMARKET P.]
  LONDON  1(1), 1969-
  W.
  CR/M-1.  1(12), 1970-          OX/U-1.  1(15), 1970-*

HOTEL & RESTAURANT CATERING.
++HOTEL & RESTAURANT CATER.
 [PRACTICAL P.]
  LONDON  1(1), N 1969-
  ED/N-1.   LO/N-7.   OX/U-1.
  LO/N14.  CURRENT BOX ONLY.
  LO/N35.  2(11), S 1971-
  SH/C-1.  2(7), MY 1971-
  ISSN 0018-6090

HOUSEHOLD & PERSONAL PRODUCTS INDUSTRY.                                      XXX
++HOUSEHOLD & PERS. PROD. IND.
 [DORLAND PUBL. CORP.]
  DENVILLE, N.J.  8(12), 1971-
  PREV: DETERGENTS & SPECIALTIES FROM 6(1),
  1969- 8(11), 1971.
  LO/N14.

HOUSEWIVES' VOICE.
 IRISH HOUSEWIVES' ASSOCIATION.
  DUBLIN  1, 1972-
  DB/U-2.

HOUSING, BUILDING & PLANNING.                                               XXX
  SUBS (1968) PART OF: INTERNATIONAL SOCIAL
  DEVELOPMENT REVIEW.

HOUSING & CONSTRUCTION STATISTICS (G.B.).                                    XXX
++HOUS. & CONSTR. STAT. (GB).
 (GREAT BRITAIN) DEPARTMENT OF THE ENVIRONMENT.
  LONDON  1, 1972-
  PREV: HOUSING STATISTICS (GREAT BRITAIN) FROM
  NO.1, 1966- NO.24, 1972. SPONS. BODIES ALSO:
  SCOTTISH DEVELOPMENT DEPARTMENT; & WELSH
  OFFICE.
  CA/U-1.   GL/U-1.   LO/U-2.   NW/U-1.

HOUSING FACTS & FIGURES.
++HOUS. FACTS & FIGURES.
 GREATER LONDON COUNCIL: INTELLIGENCE UNIT.
  LONDON  NO.1, 1973-
  BL/U-1.   GL/U-1.   LO/U-3.

HOVER COVER.
 HOVERMAIL COLLECTORS' CLUB.
  WINCHESTER  NO.1, AG 1971-
  Q.
  ED/N-1.

HOW TO USE THE RECORD OFFICE (NORTHERN IRE-
LAND).
++HOW USE REC. OFF. (N. IR.).
  BELFAST  LEAFLET NO.1, 1969-
  LO/N-1.   OX/U-1.

HRIS ABSTRACTS.
++HRIS ABSTR. (HIGHW. RES. INF. SERV.)
 HIGHWAY RESEARCH INFORMATION SERVICE (US).
  WASHINGTON, DC  1, 1968-
  PRECEDED BY 'EXPERIMENTAL ISSUE', OC 1967.
  HRIS PART OF HIGHWAY RESEARCH BOARD (US).
  LO/N14.   LV/U-1.
  LD/U-1.  3 MR 1970-
  ISSN 0017-6222

HRONIKA MEDUNARODNIH DOGADAJA.
++HRONIKA MEDUNAR. DOGADAJA.
 INSTITUT ZA MEDUNARODNU POLITIKU I PRIVREDU.
  BELGRADE  [1], 1963-
  A.
  LO/U-3.   OX/U-1.

HSIN I-LIN. = CHINESE ARTS.
  TAIPEH  1(1), 1969-
  LO/U14.

HSIN-SHE HSUEH-PAO. JOURNAL OF THE ISLAND
SOCIETY (SINGAPORE).
  SINGAPORE  1, 1970-
  LO/U14.

HSMHA HEALTH REPORTS.                                                        XXX
++HSMHA HEALTH REP.
 (UNITED STATES) HEALTH SERVICE & MENTAL HEALTH
 ADMINISTRATION.
  WASHINGTON, D.C.  86, 1971- 87(2), 1972...
  MON. PREV: PUBLIC HEALTH REPORTS FROM
  1, 1878- 85, 1970. SUBS: HEALTH SERVICES
  REPORTS.
  CA/U-2.   ED/N-1.   LD/U-1.   LO/U-1.   NW/U-1.

HUA-KANG FO-HSUEH HSUEH-PAO. = HWAKANG BUDD-
HIST JOURNAL.
  *TAIPEH  1(1), 1968-*
  *LO/U14.*

HUD CHALLENGE.
(UNITED STATES) DEPARTMENT OF HOUSING & URBAN
DEVELOPMENT.
  *WASHINGTON, D.C.  1, 1969-*
  *BL/U-1.*
  *ISSN 0017-6303*

HUMAN BIOLOGY IN OCEANIA.
*+ +HUM. BIOL. OCEANIA.*
UNIVERSITY OF SYDNEY.
  *SYDNEY  1, F 1971-*
  *CA/U-3.    LO/S10.*
  *LO/N-2.  1, 1971- 2(2), 1973.*
  *ISSN 0046-8142*

HUMAN CONTEXT.
[NIJHOFF]
  *THE HAGUE  1(1), AG 1968-*
  ADDED TITLES IN VARIOUS LANGS.: LE DOMAINE
  HUMAIN; DER MENSCH UND SEINE WELT; HOMBRE Y
  SOCIEDAD; IL MONDO VISSUTO DELL'UOMO.
  *CB/U-1.    CO/U-1.    DB/U-2.    LO/U-1.    LO/U-2.    SH/U-1.*
  *ISSN 0018-7151*

HUMAN ECOLOGY.
*+ +HUM. ECOL.*
[PLENUM]
  *LONDON; NEW YORK  1, MR 1972-*
  *2/A.*
  *CA/U-3.    LO/N-2.    NO/U-1.    SH/U-1.*
  *AD/U-1.  2, 1974-*

HUMAN HEREDITY.
*+ +HUMAN HERED.*
[S. KARGER]
  *BASLE  19, 1969-*
  PREV: ACTA GENETICA ET STATISTICA MEDICA FROM
  1, 1948 - 18, 1968.
  *BN/U-1.    GL/U-1.    LO/N13.*
  *CA/U-3.  19, 1969-              LO/N-2.  22, 1972-*
  *LO/S10.  19, 1969-*
  *ISSN 0001-5652*

HUMAN PATHOLOGY. A CLINICOPATHOLOGIC QUARTERLY.
*+ +HUMAN PATHOL.*
[W.B. SAUNDERS]
  *LONDON  1, 1970-*
  *AD/U-1.    CR/M-1.    DN/U-1.    LO/M-3.    LO/M11.*
  *LO/N13.    NW/U-1.    SH/U-1.*
  *ISSN 0046-8177*

HUMAN RIGHTS. = DROITS DE L'HOMME.
  *PARIS  1, MR 1968-*
  ENGL., FR. WITH SUMM. IN ALTERNATIVE LANG.
  Q. S/T: JOURNAL OF INTERNATIONAL & COMPARA-
  TIVE LAW; (&) REVUE DE DROIT INTERNATIONAL ET
  COMPARE.
  *CB/U-1.    LO/U-3.    SH/U-1.    SO/U-1.*

HUMAN RIGHTS BULLETIN.
*+ +HUMAN RIGHTS BULL.*
UNITED NATIONS: DIVISION OF HUMAN RIGHTS.
  *NEW YORK  NO.1, JL 1969-*
  *LO/S14.*
  *ISSN 0046-8193*

HUMAN SETTLEMENTS.
*+ +HUM. SETTLEMENTS.*
UNITED NATIONS: CENTRE FOR HOUSING BUILDING &
PLANNING.
  *NEW YORK  1(1), JA 1971-*
  Q. CENTRE SUBORD. TO DEPARTMENT OF ECONOMIC &
  SOCIAL AFFAIRS.
  *ED/N-1.    LO/S14.    LO/U-3.    MA/P-1.    OX/U-1.    RE/U-1.*
  *ISSN 0046-8231*

HUMAN WORLD. A QUARTERLY REVIEW OF ENGLISH
LETTERS.
*+ +HUM. WORLD.*
  *SWANSEA  NO.1, 1970- 15/16, MY/AG 1974. //*
  *CA/U-1.    DB/U-2.    ED/N-1.    EX/U-1.    LD/U-1.    LO/N-1.*
  *LO/U-2.    LO/U11.    LO/U12.    NW/U-1.    OX/U16.*
  *SW/U-1.*
  *ISSN 0018-7313*

HUMANIST.                                                              XXX
  SUBS (1972): NEW HUMANIST.

HUMANIST NEWSLETTER.
*+ +HUM. NEWSL.*
BRITISH HUMANIST ASSOCIATION.
  *LONDON  1(1), AG 1972-*
  *ED/N-1.*

HUMANITAS. TYDSKRIF VIR NAVORSING IN DIE
GEESTESWETENSKAPPE.
SOUTH AFRICAN HUMAN SCIENCES RESEARCH COUNCIL.
  *PRETORIA  1, 1971-*
  2/A. AFRIKAANS OR ENGL. WITH SUMM. IN
  ALTERNATIVE LANG. ENGL. S/T: JOURNAL FOR
  RESEARCH IN THE HUMAN SCIENCES.
  *BL/U-1.    LO/U-3.    LO/U-8.*
  *ISSN 0046-8258*

HUMANITIES NEWSLETTER.
*+ +HUM. NEWSL.*
UNIVERSITY OF SHEFFIELD: INSTITUTE OF EDUCATION
  *SHEFFIELD  1, 1972-*
  *BH/U-1.    SH/U-1.*

HUNGARIAN MUSIC.                                                      000
  SEE: MAGYAR ZENE.

HUNTER NATURAL HISTORY.
*+ +HUNTER NAT. HIST.*
NEWCASTLE N.S.W. FLORA & FAUNA PROTECTION
SOCIETY.
  *NEWCASTLE, N.S.W.  1, 1969-*
  *OX/U-8.*
  *ISSN 0046-8312*

HWAKANG BUDDHIST JOURNAL.                                             000
  SEE: HUA-KANG FO-HSUEH HSUEH-PAO.

HYDE PARK SOCIALIST.
*+ +HYDE PARK SOC.*
  *LONDON  NO.1, AUTUMN 1968-*
  Q.
  *ED/N-1.  NO.9, 1970-              LO/U-3. NO.3, 1969-**
  *OX/U-1.  NO.11, 1971-            OX/U17. NO.11, 1971-*
  *ISSN 0018-8123*

HYDRAULIC & AIR ENGINEERING.
*+ +HYDRAUL. & AIR ENG.*
[APPLIED TECHNOLOGY PUBL.]
  *NEW MALDEN, SURREY  1, 1973-*
  *LO/N14.    LO/N35.*

HYDRAULIQUE, PNEUMATIQUE ET ASSERVISSEMENTS.            XXX
*+ +HYDRAUL. PNEUM. & ASSERVISSEMENTS.*
SYNDICAT DES CONSTRUCTEURS DE TRANSMISSIONS
HYDRAULIQUES ET PNEUMATIQUES.
[COMPAGNIE FRANCAISE D'EDITIONS]
  *PARIS  NO.7, 1964- 42, 1967.*
  PREV: REVUE DES TRANSMISSIONS HYDRAULIQUES ET
  PNEUMATIQUES ET DES ASSERVISSEMENTS FROM NO.1,
  1963- 6, 1963. SUBS (1968): ENERGIE FLUIDE
  ET LUBRIFICATION + HYDRAULIQUE, PNEUMATIQUE...
  *LO/N14.*

HYDRO DELFT.
WATERLOOPKUNDIG LABORATORIUM (DELFT).
  *DELFT  1, OC 1965-*
  Q.
  *BL/U-1.    LO/N14. [W. NO.5, 1966].*

HYDROBIOLOGICAL JOURNAL.
*+ +HYDROBIOL. J.*
AMERICAN FISHERIES SOCIETY.
[SCRIPTA TECHNICA]
  *WASHINGTON, D.C.  5, 1969(1970)-*
  2M. TRANSL. OF GIDROBIOLOGICHESKIJ ZHURNAL.
  *LO/N-2.    LO/N14.*
  *ISSN 0018-8166*

HYDROGEN SERIES.
*+ +HYDROGEN SER.*
  *NEW YORK  1, 1971-*
  *OX/U-8.*

HYDROGRAPHIC NEWSLETTER.
*+ +HYDROGR. NEWSL.*
NETHERLANDS HYDROGRAPHIC OFFICE.
  *THE HAGUE  1, 1963-*
  *LO/N-2.    LO/U-2.*

HYDROLOGIC REPORT (NEW MEXICO).
*+ +HYDROL. REP. (NEW MEX.).*
(NEW MEXICO) STATE BUREAU OF MINES & MINERAL
RESOURCES.
  *SOCORRO  1, 1971-*
  *LO/N-2.*

HYDROLOGICAL SCIENCES BULLETIN.                                       XXX
*+ +HYDROL. SCI. BULL.*
INTERNATIONAL ASSOCIATION OF HYDROLOGICAL
SCIENCES.
  *WALLINGFORD, BERKS  17, 1972-*
  PREV: BULLETIN OF THE INTERNATIONAL ASSOCIAT-
  ION OF SCIENTIFIC HYDROLOGY FROM NO.1, 1952-
  16, 1971.
  *ED/N-1.    LO/N13.  -  SH/U-1.*

NPT/ 142

**HYDROLOGICAL STATION LIST.**
+ +HYDROL. STA. LIST (S. AFR.)
(SOUTH AFRICA) DEPARTMENT OF INDUSTRIES.
 CAPE TOWN  NO.1, 1968-
 ISSUED BY THE BODY'S DIVISION OF SEA FISHERIES
 LO/N-2.

**HYDROSPACE. MARINE TECHNOLOGY & OCEANIC MAN-**
**AGEMENT.**                                                            XXX
 [SPEARHEAD PUBL. LTD.]
 BROMLEY, KENT 2(3), 1969- 5, 1972.
 PREV: HYDROSPACE. QUARTERLY REVIEW OF OCEAN
 MANAGEMENT FROM 1, 1967. SUBS: OFFSHORE
 SERVICES.
 LO/N14.
 LO/U-4. 3(2), 1970-              XS/T-4. 3(2), 1970-
 LO/U28. 5, 1972.
 ISSN 0018-8212

**HYGIENE AUF DEM LANDE.**
+ +HYG. LANDE.
 [VEB VERLAG VOLK UND GESUNDHEIT]
 BERLIN  HEFT 1, 1961-
 LO/N13.

**HYGIENE & SANITATION.**                                              XXX
(UNITED STATES) DEPARTMENT OF HEALTH, EDUCATION
& WELFARE: PUBLIC HEALTH SERVICE.
 [ISRAEL PROGRAM FOR SCIENTIFIC TRANSLATIONS]
 JERUSALEM  29, 1964(1965)- 36, 1971(1972).//
 ENGL. LANG. TRANSL. OF GIGIENA I SANITARIJA.
 NUMBERING & DATING OF ISSUES FOLLOW ORIGINAL.
 SPONS. BODY ALSO: NATIONAL SCIENCE FOUNDATION
 (US).
 ZW/M-1.*
 LO/N13. [W. 29(3, 5 & 12)]

**IAG JOURNAL.**                                                        XXX
+ +IAG J.
INTERNATIONAL FEDERATION FOR INFORMATION PRO-
CESSING: ADMINISTRATIVE DATA PROCESSING GROUP.
 AMSTERDAM 1, 1968- 4, 1971.
 SUBS: MANAGEMENT INFORMATICS. ALSO ENTITLED:
 IAG QUARTERLY, & IAG QUARTERLY JOURNAL.
 CB/U-1.   LO/N14.
 ISSN 0018-8387

**IATA NEWS REVIEW.**
+ +IATA NEWS REV. (INT. AIR TRANSP. ASS.)
INTERNATIONAL AIR TRANSPORT ASSOCIATION.
 MONTREAL  1(1), 1966-
 OX/U-1.
 LO/U-2. 4, 1969-

**IATUL NEWSLETTER.**                                                   XXX
+ +IATUL NEWSL. (INT. ASS. TECHNOL. UNIV. LIBR.)
INTERNATIONAL ASSOCIATION OF TECHNOLOGICAL
UNIVERSITY LIBRARIES.
 DELFT  NO.1, MR 1963- 11, D 1965.
 TITLE VARIES.  SUBS: IATUL PROCEEDINGS.
 SO/U-1. [W. NO.6, 1964].

**IATUL PROCEEDINGS.**
+ +IATUL PROC. (INT. ASS. TECHNOL. UNIV. LIBR.)
INTERNATIONAL ASSOCIATION OF TECHNOLOGICAL
UNIVERSITY LIBRARIES.
 DELFT  1, 1966-
 PREV: IATUL NEWSLETTER.
 LO/N14.   LO/U11.   SO/U-1.
 ISSN 0018-8476

**IBA TECHNICAL REVIEW.**
+ +IBA TECH. REV.
INDEPENDENT BROADCASTING AUTHORITY.
 LONDON  NO.1, 1972-
 CA/U-1.   ED/N-1.   GL/U-2.   LD/U-1.   RE/U-1.   SF/U-1.
 LO/N14. NO.3, 1973-

**IBAK.**                                                               000
 SEE: INTERNATIONALE BIBLIOGRAPHIE DER
 ANTIQUARIATS- AUKTIONS- UND KUNSTKATALOGE.

**IBERIAN STUDIES.**
+ +IBERIAN STUD.
IBERIAN SOCIAL STUDIES ASSOCIATION.
 KEELE, STAFFS 1, 1972.
 AD/U-1.   CA/U-1.   ED/N-1.   EX/U-1.   LD/U-1.   LO/U-3.
 MA/U-1.   RE/U-1.   SF/U-1.
 SH/U-1. 2, 1973-

**IBERO-AMERICANA. RESEARCH NEWS & PRINCIPAL**
**ACQUISITIONS OF DOCUMENTATION ON LATIN-**
**AMERICA IN DENMARK, FINLAND, NORWAY & SWEDEN.**
LATINAMERIKA-INSTITUTET I STOCKHOLM.
 STOCKHOLM 1, 1972-
 2/A. SWED., SPAN. OR ENGL.
 LO/N-1.   OX/U-1.   SW/U-1.
 ISSN 0046-8444

**IBERO-AMERICANA PRAGENSIA.**
+ +IBERO-AM. PRAGENSIA.
KARLOVA UNIVERSITA V PRAZE: CENTRO DE ESTUDIOS
IBERO-AMERICANOS.
 PRAGUE 1, 1967-
 ANNU.
 SO/U-1.
 SH/U-1. 1, 1967- 6, 1972.

**IBEROROMANIA. ZEITSCHRIFT FUR SPANISCHE, POR-**
**TUGIESISCHE, UND KATALANISCHE SPRACHE UND LITER-**
**ATUR.**
 MUNICH  1(1), F 1969-
 3A.
 ED/N-1.   EX/U-1.   LO/U-1.   NO/U-1.   SH/U-1.   SO/U-1.
 SW/U-1.

**IBP INTER-AMERICAN NEWS.**
INTERNATIONAL BIOLOGICAL PROGRAMME.
 WASHINGTON, D.C.  1, 1968-
 LO/N-2.

**ICA BULLETIN.**                                                       XXX
 SUBS (1968):  MAGAZINE OF THE INSTITUTE OF
 CONTEMPORARY ARTS.

**ICASALS NEWSLETTER.**
+ +ICASALS NEWSL. (INT. CENT. ARID & SEMI-ARID
 LAND STUD.)
INTERNATIONAL CENTER FOR ARID & SEMI-ARID
LAND STUDIES.
 LUBBOCK, TEX.  1, 1967-
 ISSUED FOR ICASALS BY THE DIVISION OF INFOR-
 MATION SERVICES OF TEXAS TECHNOLOGICAL COLLEGE
 LO/N13.
 ISSN 0018-8808

**ICH REVISTA.**
UNIVERSIDADE FEDERAL DO RIO GRANDE DO NORTE:
INSTITUTO DE CIENCIAS HUMANAS.
 NATAL, BRAZ.  1(1), 1971-
 OX/U-1.

**ICI L'EUROPE. BULLETIN D'INFORMATION DE LA**
**DIRECTION DES AFFAIRES JURIDIQUES.**
+ +ICI EUR.
COUNCIL OF EUROPE: DIRECTORATE OF INFORMATION.
 STRASBOURG  NO.1, 1969-
 AB/U-1.   NW/U-1.
 ISSN 0536-2636

**ICI GRASSLAND MANAGEMENT GUIDE.**
+ +ICI GRASSL. MANAGE. GUIDE.
IMPERIAL CHEMICAL INDUSTRIES: FARM ADVISORY
SERVICE.
 BIRMINGHAM &C. NO.1, 1969-
 LO/N-1.

**ICN CALLING. NEWSLETTER OF THE ...**
+ +ICN CALL. (INT. COUN. NURSES).
INTERNATIONAL COUNCIL OF NURSES.
 GENEVA  NO.1, JA 1968-
 LO/M27.

**ICONOGRAPHIE MUSICALE.**
+ +ICONOGR. MUSICALE.
 GENEVA  1, 1972-
 CA/U-1.   LO/N-1.   OX/U-1.

**ICSSR NEWSLETTER.**
+ +ICSSR NEWSL.
INDIAN COUNCIL OF SOCIAL SCIENCE RESEARCH.
 NEW DELHI  1(1), N 1969-
 Q.
 LO/U-8. 1(2), 1970-
 ISSN 0018-9049

**IDC PROGRESS REPORT.**
+ +IDC PROG. REP. (INT. DOC. CENT.)
INTERNATIONAL DOCUMENTATION CENTRE.
 TUMBA, SWEDEN  NO.1, N 1965-
 LD/U-1.

**IDEALISTIC STUDIES.**
+ +IDEALISTIC STUD.
 [NIJHOFF]
 THE HAGUE  1, JA 1971-
 3/A.
 AD/U-1.   BH/P-1.   LO/N-1.   LO/U-1.   LO/U-3.   OX/U-1.
 ISSN 0046-8541

**IDEAS.**
GOLDSMITHS' COLLEGE: CURRICULUM LABORATORY.
 LONDON  NO.1, F 1967-
 ED/N-1.   OX/U-1.   SW/U-1.
 ISSN 0305-7348

**IDEOLOGIE. QUADERNI DI STORIA CONTEMPORANEA.**
[LA NUOVA ITALIA]
*PADOVA &C. 1, 1967-*
*OX/U-1.*
*ISSN 0019-1477*

**IDESIA.**
UNIVERSIDAD DEL NORTE: DEPARTAMENTO DE AGRICUL-
TURA.
*ARICA, CHILE NO.1, 1970-*
*LO/N-2.*

**IDLER. AN ENTERTAINMENT.**
[EDITORIAL ASSOCIATES]
*WHEATLEY, OXF. 1(1), 1966-*
*BH/P-1.     ED/N-1.     LO/U-2.*

**IDRC REPORTS.**
*+ +IDRC REP.*
INTERNATIONAL DEVELOPMENT RESEARCH CENTRE.
*OTTAWA 1(1), MR 1972-*
ENGL. & FR.
*LO/R-6.*
*XS/R10. (3 YEARS ONLY).*

**IEE MEDICAL ELECTRONICS MONOGRAPHS.**
*+ +IEE MED. ELECTRON. MONOGR.*
INSTITUTION OF ELECTRICAL ENGINEERS.
[PEREGRINUS]
*LONDON [NO.]1, 1971-*
*LO/N-4.     LO/N14.*
*SO/U-1. NO.1, 1971- 12, 1974.*
*ISSN 0305-9596*

**IEEE TRANSACTIONS ON COMMUNICATIONS.**          XXX
*+ +IEEE TRANS. COMMUN.*
INSTITUTE OF ELECTRICAL & ELECTRONICS ENGINEERS
*NEW YORK 20, 1972-*
PREV: IEEE TRANSACTIONS ON COMMUNICATION
TECHNOLOGY FROM 12(3), 1964- 19, 1971.
*BR/U-1.     GL/U-1.     LD/U-1.     LO/N14.     LO/N35.*

**IEEE TRANSACTIONS ON INDUSTRY APPLICATIONS.**     XXX
*+ +IEEE TRANS. IND. APPL.*
INSTITUTE OF ELECTRICAL & ELECTRONICS ENGINEERS
*NEW YORK IA-8, 1972-*
PREV: IEEE TRANSACTIONS ON INDUSTRY &
GENERAL APPLICATIONS FROM IGA-1, 1965- 7, 1971
*BR/U-1.     GL/U-1.     LO/N14.     RE/U-1.*
*LO/U-2. IA-10, 1974-*

**IEEE TRANSACTIONS ON MAN-MACHINE SYSTEMS.**      XXX
*+ +IEEE TRANS. MAN-MACH. SYST.*
INSTITUTE OF ELECTRICAL & ELECTRONICS ENGINEERS
*NEW YORK 9, 1968- 11, 1970.*
PREV: IEEE TRANSACTIONS ON HUMAN FACTORS IN
ELECTRONICS FROM 4, 1963- 8, 1967. SUBS: IEEE
TRANSACTIONS ON SYSTEMS, MAN & CYBERNETICS.
*BH/U-1.     BL/U-1.     CV/C-1.     GL/U-1.     HL/U-1.     NW/U-1.*

**IEEE TRANSACTIONS ON MANUFACTURING TECHNOLOGY.**
*+ +IEEE TRANS. MANUF. TECHNOL.*
INSTITUTE OF ELECTRICAL & ELECTRONICS ENGINEERS
*NEW YORK MFT-1, JE 1972-*
*AD/U-1.     BH/U-3.     GL/U-1.     LD/U-1.     LO/N35.*
*NW/U-1.     RE/U-1.     SF/U-1.     SO/U-1.     XS/T-4.*
*ISSN 0046-838X*

**IEEE TRANSACTIONS ON PARTS, HYBRIDS &**
**PACKAGING.**          XXX
*+ +IEEE TRANS. PT. HYBRIDS & PACKAG.*
INSTITUTE OF ELECTRICAL & ELECTRONICS ENGINEERS
*NEW YORK PHP 7(2), JE 1971-*
PREV: IEEE TRANSACTIONS ON PARTS, MATERIALS &
PACKAGING FROM PMP 1, 1965- 7(1), 1971.
*AD/U-1.     GL/U-1.     LD/U-1.     LO/N14.     LO/U-2.     LO/U28.*
*XS/R10.     XS/T-4.*

**IEEE TRANSACTIONS ON PLASMA SCIENCE.**
*+ +IEEE TRANS. PLASMA SCI.*
INSTITUTE OF ELECTRICAL & ELECTRONICS ENG-
INEERS: NUCLEAR & PLASMA SCIENCES SOCIETY.
*NEW YORK PS-1, 1973-*
*CB/U-1.     GL/U-1.     GL/U-2.     LD/U-1.     LO/N-4.     LO/N14.*
*MA/U-1.     MA/U-1.     RE/U-1.     SF/U-1.     SH/U-3.     SO/U-1.*
*LO/U-2. PS-2, 1974-*

**IEEE TRANSACTIONS ON PROFESSIONAL COMMUNICAT-**
**ION.**          XXX
*+ +IEEE TRANS. PROF. COMMUN.*
*NEW YORK PC-15, 1972-*
PREV: IEEE TRANSACTIONS ON ENGINEERING WRITING
& SPEECH FROM EWS-6, 1963- EWS-14, 1971.
*GL/U-1.     LD/U-1.     LO/N14.*

**IEEE TRANSACTIONS ON SYSTEMS, MAN, & CYBERNET-**
**ICS.**          XXX
*+ +IEEE TRANS. SYST. MAN & CYBERN.*
INSTITUTE OF ELECTRICAL & ELECTRONICS ENGINEERS
*NEW YORK SMC-1, 1971-*
INCORP: IEEE TRANSACTIONS ON SYSTEMS SCIENCE
& CYBERNETICS FROM SSC-1, 1965- 6(4), 1970; &
IEEE TRANSACTIONS ON MAN-MACHINE SYSTEMS FROM
MMS-9, 1968- 11, 1970.
*AD/U-1.     AD/U-3.     CB/U-1.     CV/C-1.     DR/U-1.     GL/U-1.*
*GL/U-2.     HL/U-1.     LD/U-1.     LO/N-4.     LO/N14.     LO/U-2.*
*LO/U28.     MA/U-1.     NW/U-1.     RE/U-1.     SH/C-5.*
*ISSN 0018-9472*

**IEEE TRANSACTIONS ON VEHICULAR COMMUNI-**
**CATIONS.**          XXX
*+ +IEEE TRANS. VEHIC. COMMUN. [IEVC-A]*
INSTITUTE OF ELECTRICAL & ELECTRONICS ENGINEERS
*NEW YORK VC-12, 1963- 15, 1966...*
PREV: PGVC-[NO.]1,1952- 13,1959; VC-9,1960-
11,1962: IRE TRANS. ON VEHICULAR COMMUNICA-
TIONS.* ('IRE' ADDED TO ORIG. TITLE, 1954).
SUBS: IEEE TRANS. ON VEHICULAR TECHNOLOGY.
*CV/C-1.     ED/U-1.     GL/U-2.     LC/U-1.     LD/U-1.     LO/N-4.*
*LO/N-7.     LO/N-9.     LO/T-1.     LO/U-6.     OX/U-1.     XW/C-4.*
*BL/U-1. 15,1966-                    HL/U-1. %1966[-*
*XL/C-1. 15,1966-*

**IEEE TRANSACTIONS ON VEHICULAR TECHNOLOGY.**
*+ +IEEE TRANS. VEHIC. TECHNOL.*
INSTITUTE OF ELECTRICAL & ELECTRONICS ENGINEERS
*NEW YORK VT-16, 1967-*
(PREV) PGVC-[NO.]1,1952- 13,1959; VC-9,1960-
11,1962: IRE TRANS. ON VEHIC. COMMUNICATIONS.*
('IRE' ADDED TO ORIG. TITLE, 1954). THEN
VC-12,1963- 15,1966: IEEE TRANS. ON VEHIC.
COMMUNICATIONS. THEN AS ABOVE.
*HL/U-1.     LD/U-1.     LO/N14.     MA/U-1.*
*ISSN 0018-9545*

**IFCEP JOURNAL OF MODERN INDIA. THE INDUSTRY,**
**FINANCE, COMMERCE, EXPORT-PROMOTION EXPER-**
**IENCE OF INDIA.**
*+ +IFCEP J. MOD. INDIA.*
INDIAN INSTITUTE OF ASIAN STUDIES.
*BOMBAY 1(1), MR 1972-*
M.
*LO/U-3.*

**IFI BULLETIN SERVICE: FABRICS-FASHIONS**
**BULLETIN.**          XXX
*+ +IFI BULL. SERV., FABR.-FASHIONS BULL.*          XXX
INTERNATIONAL FABRICARE INSTITUTE.
*SILVER SPRING, MD. NO.FF-210, 1972-*
PREV: BULLETIN SERVICE, NATIONAL INSTITUTE OF
DRYCLEANING: FABRICS-FASHIONS FROM NO.FF-1,
1954- FF-209, 1972.
*LO/N14.*

**IFI BULLETIN SERVICE: PRACTICAL OPERATING**
**TIPS BULLETIN.**          XXX
*+ +IFI BULL. SERV., PRACT. OPER. TIPS BULL.*          XXX
INTERNATIONAL FABRICARE INSTITUTE.
*SILVER SPRING, MD. NO.P-110, 1972-*
PREV: BULLETIN SERVICE, NATIONAL INSTITUTE OF
DRYCLEANING: PRACTICAL OPERATING TIPS FROM
[NO]P-6, 1953- 109, 1972.
*LO/N14.*

**IFI BULLETIN SERVICE: TECHNICAL BULLETIN.**          XXX
*+ +IFI BULL. SERV., TECH. BULL.*          XXX
INTERNATIONAL FABRICARE INSTITUTE.
*SILVER SPRING, MD. NO.T-481, 1972-*
PREV: BULLETIN SERVICE, NATIONAL INSTITUTE OF
DRYCLEANING: TECHNICAL FROM NO.T-319, 1953-
T-480, 1972.
*LO/N14.*

**IHERINGIA: ANTROPOLOGIA.**
MUSEU RIO-GRANDENSE DE CIENCIAS NATURAIS.
*PORTO ALEGRE NO.1, 1969-*
*LO/N-2.*

**IHERINGIA: SERIE GEOLOGIA.**
MUSEU RIO-GRANDENSE DE CIENCIAS NATURAIS.
*PORTO ALEGRE NO.1, 1967-*
*LO/N-2.     LO/N13.*

**IHI ENGINEERING REVIEW.**
*+ +IHI ENG. REV.*
ISHIKAWAJIMA-HARIMA HEAVY INDUSTRIES COMPANY,
LTD.
*TOKYO 1(1), 1968-*
*LO/N14.*

IIC. INTERNATIONAL REVIEW OF INDUSTRIAL PROPERTY
AND COPYRIGHT LAW.                                            000
  SEE: INTERNATIONAL REVIEW OF INDUSTRIAL
  PROPERTY AND COPYRIGHT LAW.


IKENGA.  JOURNAL OF AFRICAN STUDIES.
  UNIVERSITY OF NIGERIA: INSTITUTE OF AFRICAN
  STUDIES.
    NIGERIA  1, 1972-
    2/A.
    AD/U-1.    LO/U-3.    LO/U-8.


IKONOMICHESKI ZHIVOT.
  + +IKON. ZHIVOT.
  BULGARSKA KOMUNISTICHESKA PARTIJA: TSENTRALEN
  KOMITET.
    SOFIA  1(1), 1966-
    OX/U-1.  4(2), 1970-


IKORAK.  BULLETIN OF THE INSTITUTE ...
  UNIVERSITY OF NIGERIA: INSTITUTE OF AFRICAN
  STUDIES.
    NSUKKA  1(1), JL 1971-
    LO/U-8.    LO/U14.
    ISSN 0046-8592


ILEA CONTACT.
  INNER LONDON EDUCATION AUTHORITY.
    LONDON  1(1), AP 1972-
    WKLY.
    CA/U-1.    ED/N-1.
    ISSN 0306-1981


ILLMANI.
    LA PAZ  1, 1972-
    OX/U-1.


ILLUMINATING ENGINEERING.                                     XXX
  SUBS (1971): PART OF JOURNAL, ILLUMINATING
  ENGINEERING SOCIETY (NEW YORK); & LD & A.
  LIGHTING DESIGN & APPLICATION.


ILLUMINATIONS.
    SAN FRANCISCO   1, SUMMER 1965-
    LO/U-2.


'ILMIYAH.
    BEIRUT  1, 1967-
    M. IN ARABIC.
    LO/U14.  1(2), 1967-


ILO PUBLICATIONS.
  + +ILO PUBL. (INT. LABOUR ORGAN.).
  INTERNATIONAL LABOUR ORGANISATION.
    GENEVA  1, 1969-
    LO/N10. 1(3), 1969-              OX/U-1.  1(3), 1969-


ILR RESEARCH.                                                 XXX
  SUBS (1969): ISSUES IN INDUSTRIAL SOCIETY.


IMAGE.
  SUNDERLAND FOLK CENTRE.
    SUNDERLAND  NO.1, 1968-
    ED/N-1.    OX/U-1.


IMAGE (1971).
  [BAROQUE P.]
    LONDON  NO.1, D 1971-
    ED/N-1. NO.7, 1972-


IMAGE DYNAMICS IN SCIENCE & MEDICINE.                         XXX
  + +IMAGE DYN. SCI. & MED.
  [N. AMERICAN PUBL. CO.]
    PHILADELPHIA  4, 1969-
    PREV:  VISUAL/SONIC MEDICINE FROM 2(4), 1967-
    3, 1968.
    LO/N14.


IMAGO (MONTREAL).
  [BOWERING]
    MONTREAL  [NO.]1, 1964-
    LO/N-1.  [NO.]10, [1969]-
    ISSN 0085-1744


IMF SURVEY.
  + +IMF SURV.
  INTERNATIONAL MONETARY FUND.
    WASHINGTON, D.C.  1(1), AG 1972-
    2W.
    CA/U38.    ED/N-1.    LO/R-6.    LO/U-3.    MA/P-1.    OX/U-1.
    OX/U16.    OX/U17.    RE/U-1.    SH/U-1.
    ISSN 0047-083X


IMMANUEL.
  ECUMENICAL THEOLOGICAL RESEARCH FRATERNITY IN
  ISRAEL.
    JERUSALEM  1972-
    S/T: A SEMI-ANNUAL BULLETIN OF RELIGIOUS
    THOUGHT & RESEARCH IN ISRAEL.
    CA/U-1.    NO/U-1.    SH/U-1.


IMMUNOLOGICAL COMMUNICATIONS.
  + +IMMUNOL. COMMUN.
  [DEKKER]
    NEW YORK  1, 1972-
    2M.
    LD/U-1.    OX/U-1.    SW/U-1.
    ISSN 0090-0877


IMPACT.
  [CHURCH IN WALES PUBL.]
    PENARTH  1, 1969-
    ED/N-1.


IMPACT. VALVE REPORT.                                         XXX
    ESTES PARK, COLO:  1973(3)-
    PREV: VALVE INFORMATION REPORT FROM 1962- F
    1973.
    LO/N14.


IMPERIAL TOBACCO GROUP REVIEW.
  + +IMP. TOB. GR. REV.
    LONDON  NO.1, 1969-
    OX/U-1.


IMPRINT.
    BRISTOL  NO.1, 1967-
    A POETRY MAGAZINE.
    ED/N-1.    LO/U-2.    OX/U-1.
    ISSN 0019-3038


IMPULSE (SOUTH AFRICA).
  UNIVERSITY OF CAPE TOWN: SCIENCE STUDENTS'
  COUNCIL.
    RONDEBOSCH  1, S 1970-
    LO/N14.


IMS NEWSLETTER.                                               XXX
  + +IMS NEWSL.
  UNESCO.
    PARIS  NO.1, F 1973-
    PREV: INTERNATIONAL MARINE SCIENCE FROM 1,
    1963- 7, 1970.
    LO/N-2.    RE/U-1.    XS/R10.


IMS REPORT.
  + +IMS REP.
  NATIONAL PHYSICAL LABORATORY (G.B.): DIVISION
  OF INORGANIC & METALLIC STRUCTURE.
    TEDDINGTON  NO.1, 1967-
    LO/N14.


IN BRIEF.  AN OCCASIONAL BULLETIN.
  COMMITTEE OF VICE-CHANCELLORS & PRINCIPALS OF
  THE UNIVERSITIES OF THE UNITED KINGDOM.
    LONDON  NO.1, 1969-
    ED/N-1.    HL/U-1.    SO/U-1.


IN THE SHADE.
    APPLETON, WIS.  1, 1968-
    OX/U-1.


IN TOUCH.
  NETHERLANDS CHAMBER OF COMMERCE IN THE UNITED
  KINGDOM.
    LONDON &C.  NO.1, OC 1970-
    ED/N-1.    OX/U-1.
    ISSN 0019-3283


IN VITRO.
  TISSUE CULTURE ASSOCIATION.
    BOSTON, MASS.  1, 1965-
    LO/M-3.    LO/M10.    LO/M17.    OX/U-1.    XY/N-1.


INCO REPORTER.
  + +INCO REP.
  INTERNATIONAL NICKEL LTD.
    LONDON  NO.1, MY 1972-
    ED/N-1.    OX/U-1.


INCOMES DATA.
  [INCOMES DATA SERVICES]
    LONDON   REPORT [NO.]1, 1966-
    2/M.
    DB/U-2. 16,1967-              GL/U-2. 20,1967-
    LO/U-3. 37,1968-             MA/U-1. 19,1967-
    SH/U-1. 15,1967-
    ISSN 0019-3461

INCOMES DATA STUDY.
[INCOMES DATA SERVICES LTD.]
*LONDON NO.1, JA 1971-*
*BH/U-3.    LO/U-3.*
*XS/R10. NO.26, 1972-*

INCREMENTAL MOTION CONTROL SYSTEMS & DEVICES
NEWSLETTER.
*+ +INCREMENT. MOTION CONTROL SYST. & DEVICES
NEWSL.*
UNIVERSITY OF ILLINOIS: DEPARTMENT OF ELECTR-
ICAL ENGINEERING.
*URBANA, ILL. 1, 1972-*
SPONS. BODY ALSO: WARNER ELECTRIC BRAKE &
CLUTCH CO.
*LO/N14.*

INDEKS BIOLOGI PERTANIAN INDONESIA.  INDONES-
IAN BIOLOGICAL & AGRICULTURAL INDEX.
LEMBAGA PERPUSTAKAAN BIOLOGI DAN PERTANIAN.
*BOGOR 1, JA/F 1969-*
*LO/N13.*
*ISSN 0019-3593*

INDENT.  JOURNAL OF INTERNATIONAL DENTISTRY.
COOPER LABORATORIES INTERNATIONAL, INC.
*BEDFORD HILLS, N.Y. 1, 1973-*
ENGL. ED.
*LD/U-1.    MA/U-1.*

INDEX.  QUADERNI CAMERTI DI STUDI ROMANISTICI.
[EDIZIONI SCIENTIFICHE ITALIANE]
*NAPLES 1, 1970-*
ENGL. S/T: INTERNATIONAL JOURNAL OF ROMAN LAW.
*AD/U-1.*

INDEX.  A RUNNING CHRONICLE OF CENSORSHIP &
THE SUPPRESSION OF FREE EXPRESSION AROUND THE
WORLD.
WRITERS & SCHOLARS INTERNATIONAL.
*LONDON 1(1), 1972-*
*CA/U-1.    ED/N-1.    LO/U-2.    LO/U-3.*

INDEX OF AGRICULTURAL RESEARCH.                        XXX
SUBS (1972): ARC INDEX OF AGRICULTURAL &
FOOD RESEARCH.

INDEX TO AIR POLLUTION RESEARCH.
*+ +INDEX AIR POLLUT. RES.*
PENNSYLVANIA STATE UNIVERSITY; CENTER FOR
AIR ENVIRONMENT STUDIES.
*UNIVERSITY PARK, PA.    1965-*
*LO/N14. 1966-*

INDEX OF ARTICLES ON JEWISH STUDIES.
*+ +INDEX ARTIC. JEW. STUD.*
HEBREW UNIVERSITY OF JERUSALEM.
[MAGNES P.]
*JERUSALEM NO.1, 1966(1969)-*
A.
*LO/N-3.*

INDEX AL ARTICOLELOR APARUTE IN CURSUL ANULUI
... IN REVISTELE MEDICALE PUBLICATE DE USSM.
*+ +INDEX ARTIC. APARUTE CURS. ANUL. ... REV.
MED. PUBL. USSM. (U. SOC. STIINTE MED.)*
UNIUNE SOCIETATILOR DE STIINTE MEDICALE.
*BUCHAREST    1964 (1965)-*
*OX/U-8.*

INDEX BIBLIOGRAPHIQUE DE CHIMIE ET METALLUR-
GIE DES MATERIAUX NUCLEAIRES.                          000
SUBS (1968) PART OF: INDEX DE LA LITTERA-
TURE NUCLEAIRE FRANCAISE.

INDEX CHEMICUS.                                        XXX
*+ +INDEX CHEM. [IDXC-A]*
INSTITUTE FOR SCIENTIFIC INFORMATION.
*PHILADELPHIA 1, JA 1960- 35(318), 1969...*
SUBS: CURRENT ABSTRACTS OF CHEMISTRY & INDEX
CHEMICUS.
*BL/U-1.    GL/U-2.*
*GL/U-1. 24, 1967-              SH/U-1. 12,1964-*
*SO/U-1. 16,1965-*

INDEX OF CONFERENCE PROCEEDINGS RECEIVED BY
THE BLL.                                               XXX
*+ +INDEX CONF. PROC. RECEIVED BLL.*               XXX
BRITISH LIBRARY: LENDING DIVISION.
*BOSTON SPA, YORKS. ICP NO.69, JE 1973-*
PREV: INDEX OF CONFERENCE PROCEEDINGS RECEIVED
BY THE NLL FROM NO.1, 1969- 68, 1973.
*BL/U-1.    ED/N-1.    HL/U-1.    LO/N-2.    LO/N-4.    LO/N14.*
*LO/R-5.    LO/R-6.    LO/U-1.    MA/U-1.    XS/R10.    XY/N-1.*
*RE/U-1. 1974-*
*BR/U-1. NO.76, 1974-*
*ISSN 0300-9971*

INDEX TO CURRENT MALAYSIAN, SINGAPORE & BRUN-
EI PERIODICALS.
*+ +INDEX CURR. MALAYSIAN SINGAPORE & BRUNEI
PERIOD.*
JOINT STANDING COMMITTEE ON LIBRARY COOPERATION
& BIBLIOGRAPHICAL SERVICES (MALAYA).
*KUALA LUMPUR &C. [1], 1967(1969)-*
*LO/N14.    LO/U14.*
*ISSN 0019-3984*

INDEX TO CURRENT PERIODICALS RECEIVED IN THE
LIBRARY OF THE ROYAL ANTHROPOLOGICAL
INSTITUTE.                                             XXX
*+ +INDEX CURR. PERIOD. RCD. LIBR. R. ANTHROPOL.
INST.*
ROYAL ANTHROPOLOGICAL INSTITUTE.
*LONDON    1(1), JA/MR 1963- 5(4), OC/D 1967...*
SUBS: ANTHROPOLOGICAL INDEX TO CURRENT PERI-
ODICALS IN THE LIBRARY OF THE ROYAL ANTHRO-
POLOGICAL INSTITUTE.
*BH/P-1.    BL/U-1.    ED/U-1.    GL/U-1.    HL/U-1.    LO/N-2.*
*LO/N12.**    LO/S10.    LO/U-1.    LO/U-2.    LO/U-3.*
*LO/U-4.    LO/U-5.    LO/U12.    NO/U-1.    OX/U-1.    OX/U-2.*
*SA/U-1.    SH/U-1.    XM/P-4.*

INDEX TO CURRENT URBAN DOCUMENTS.
*+ +INDEX CURR. URBAN DOC.*
[GREENWOOD P. INC.]
*WESTPORT, CONN. 1(1/2), JL/OC 1972-*
Q.
*ISSN 0046-8908*

INDEX TO DOUBLE TAXATION AGREEMENTS.
*+ +INDEX DOUBLE TAX. AGREEMENTS.*
[BUTTERWORTH]
*LONDON    NO.1, 1/MR 1968-*
BY RONALD DIBDEN.
*CB/U-1.    ED/N-1.*

INDEX INDIA.
UNIVERSITY OF RAJASTHAN: LIBRARY.
*JAIPUR 1, MR 1967-*
Q.
*LO/N-1.    LO/N17.    OX/U13.*
*ISSN 0019-3844*

INDEX TO INDIAN LEGAL PERIODICALS.
*+ +INDEX INDIAN LEGAL PERIOD.*
INDIAN LAW INSTITUTE.
*NEW DELHI    1, JA/JE 1963-*
2/A.
*BL/U-1.*
*ISSN 0019-4034*

INDEX OF INVESTIGATIVE DERMATOPATHOLOGY &
DERMATOLOGY.                                           XXX
*+ +INDEX INVEST. DERMATOPATHOL. & DERMATOL.*
UNIVERSITIES ASSOCIATED FOR RESEARCH & EDUCAT-
ION IN PATHOLOGY.
*BETHESDA, MD.    1(1), MR 1969- 2, 1970...*
MON. SUBS: INDEX OF DERMATOLOGY.
*OX/U-8. 1(5), 1969-*

INDEX DE LA LITTERATURE NUCLEAIRE FRANCAISE.
*+ +INDEX LITT. NUCL. FR.*
COMMISSARIAT A L'ENERGIE ATOMIQUE (FRANCE).
*GIF-SUR-YVETTE    1, 1968-*
ISSUED BY THE BODY'S SERVICE CENTRAL DE DOCU-
MENTATION.  PREV: INDEX BIBLIOGRAPHIQUE DE
CHIMIE ET METALLURGIE DES MATERIAUX NUCLEAIRES
(&) PHYSINDEX: (SERIE A-F).
*LO/N14.*
*ISSN 0019-3836*

INDEX OF MATHEMATICAL PAPERS.
*+ +INDEX MATH. PAP.*
AMERICAN MATHEMATICAL SOCIETY.
*PROVIDENCE, R.I.    1, 1970-*
*AD/U-1.    LO/N14.    SH/U-1.*
*CA/U-2. 1972-                        RE/U-1 3, 1972-*
*SO/U-1. 3, 1972-*
*ISSN 0019-3917*

INDEX TO OFFICE EQUIPMENT & SUPPLIES.
*+ +INDEX OFF. EQUIP. & SUPPLIES.*
*CROYDON    NO.1, 1967-*
*ED/N-1.    HL/U-1.*
*LO/N14.  CURRENT ISSUES ONLY.*
*ISSN 0019-4085*

INDEX RADIOHYGIENICUS.
*+ +INDEX RADIOHYG.*
USTAV HYGIENY PRACE A CHOROB Z POVOLANI.
*PRAGUE 1, AG 1965-*
*LO/N13.*
*ISSN 0019-395X*

**INDEX OF RHEUMATOLOGY.**
+ +INDEX RHEUMATOL. [INRH-A]
AMERICAN RHEUMATISM ASSOCIATION.
*NEW YORK   1, 1965-*
*LV/U-1.*
*ISSN 0019-3933*

**INDEX TO TECHNICAL PAPERS, RCA CORPORATION.**          XXX
+ +INDEX TECH. PAP. RCA CORP.
RADIO CORPORATION OF AMERICA.
*CAMDEN, N.J.  1969(1970)-*
PREV: RCA TECHNICAL PAPERS INDEX FROM 1,
1919/45(1945)- 1968(1969).
*LO/N14.*
*ISSN 0073-6015*

**INDEX OF TISSUE CULTURE.**          XXX
TISSUE CULTURE ASSOCIATION.
[OCTOBER HOUSE, INC.]
*NEW YORK  [6/9], 1966/69(1970)-*
PREV: CURRENT TISSUE CULTURE LITERATURE FROM
1, 1961- 5, 1965.  SPONS. BODY ALSO NATIONAL
LIBRARY OF MEDICINE (US).
*LD/U-1.    GL/U-2.    LO/N14.*

**INDIAN ADMINISTRATIVE & MANAGEMENT REVIEW.**
+ +INDIAN ADM. & MANAGE. REV.
[PADMA SETH]
*NEW DELHI   1(1), OC/D 1968-*
Q.  S/T: AN INTER-DISCIPLINARY QUARTERLY.
*LO/N17.    LO/U-3.*
*ISSN 0019-4298*

**INDIAN BOOKS.**
[MUKHERJI BOOK HOUSE]
*CALCUTTA  1, JA 1968-*
*LO/N14. 2, 1969-                    LO/S14. 4, 1971-*
*ISSN 0019-445X*

**INDIAN DEMOGRAPHIC BULLETIN.**          XXX
+ +INDIAN DEMOGR. BULL.
(INDIA) OFFICE OF THE REGISTRAR GENERAL.
*NEW DELHI   1(1), 1968-*
PREV: INDIAN POPULATION BULLETIN FROM 1, AP
1960- JA 1967.
*LO/U-3.*

**INDIAN GEOTECHNICAL JOURNAL.**          XXX
+ +INDIAN GEOTECH. J.
INDIAN GEOTECHNICAL SOCIETY.
*NEW DELHI  1, 1971-*
PREV: INDIAN NATIONAL SOCIETY OF SOIL MECHAN-
ICS & FOUNDATION ENGINEERING, JOURNAL.
*LO/N14.*
*ISSN 0046-8983*

**INDIAN HISTORIAN.**
+ +INDIAN HIST.
AMERICAN INDIAN HISTORICAL SOCIETY.
*SAN FRANCISCO  1(1), 1967-*
*MA/U-1.*
*ISSN 0019-4840*

**INDIAN JOURNAL OF AGRICULTURAL CHEMISTRY.**
+ +INDIAN J. AGRIC. CHEM.
INDIAN SOCIETY OF AGRICULTURAL CHEMISTS.
*ALLAHABAD  1, 1968-*
SPONS. BODY ALSO DEPARTMENT OF CHEMISTRY,
UNIVERSITY OF ALLAHABAD.
*LO/N14.*
*LO/S-3.  4, 1971-*

**INDIAN JOURNAL OF ANIMAL SCIENCES.**          XXX
+ +INDIAN J. ANIM. SCI.
INDIAN COUNCIL OF AGRICULTURAL RESEARCH.
*NEW DELHI  39, 1969-*
PREV:  INDIAN JOURNAL OF VETERINARY SCIENCE &
ANIMAL HUSBANDRY FROM 1, MR 1931- 38(4), 1968.
*LO/N13.*

**INDIAN JOURNAL OF BIOCHEMISTRY & BIOPHYSICS.**
+ +INDIAN J. BIOCHEM. & BIOPHYS.
COUNCIL OF SCIENTIFIC & INDUSTRIAL RESEARCH
(INDIA).
*NEW DELHI  8, 1970-*
PREV: INDIAN JOURNAL OF BIOCHEMISTRY FROM 1,
1964- 7, 1970.
*CA/U-2.    LO/M12.    LO/N13.    LO/S-3.    LO/U-2.*
*LV/U-1.  2, 1965-*

**INDIAN JOURNAL OF CHEMICAL EDUCATION.**
+ +INDIAN J. CHEM. EDUC.
NATIONAL COUNCIL OF SCIENCE EDUCATION (INDIA).
*NEW DELHI  1, 1970-*
3/A.
*LO/S-3.*

**INDIAN JOURNAL OF ENVIRONMENTAL HEALTH.**          XXX
+ +INDIAN J. ENVIRON. HEALTH.
CENTRAL PUBLIC HEALTH ENGINEERING RESEARCH
INSTITUTE (INDIA).
*NAGPUR  13(3), 1971-*
PREV: ENVIRONMENTAL HEALTH FROM 6, 1964- 13(2)
1971.
*LO/N14.*

**INDIAN JOURNAL OF EXPERIMENTAL PSYCHOLOGY.**
+ +INDIAN J. EXP. PSYCHOL. [IJEP-A]
MADRAS PSYCHOLOGY SOCIETY.
*MADRAS  1, JA 1967-*
2/A.  ENGL.
*SH/U-1.  7, 1973-*
*ISSN 0019-5197*

**INDIAN JOURNAL OF MARINE SCIENCES.**
+ +INDIAN J. MAR. SCI.
COUNCIL OF SCIENTIFIC & INDUSTRIAL RESEARCH
(INDIA).
*NEW DELHI  1(1), 1972-*
*LO/N-2.    LO/N13.    OX/U-8.*

**INDIAN JOURNAL OF NEMATOLOGY.**
+ +INDIAN J. NEMATOL.
*NEW DELHI  1, 1971-*
*LO/N-2.    LO/N13.*

**INDIAN JOURNAL OF NUTRITION & DIETETICS.**          XXX
+ +INDIAN J. NUTR. & DIET.
SRI AVINASHILINGHAM HOME COLLEGE.
*COIMBATORE  7, 1970-*
PREV:  JOURNAL OF NUTRITION & DIETETICS FROM
1, JA 1964- 6, 1969.
*CA/U-1.    LO/N13.    LO/R-6.*
*ISSN 0022-3174*

**INDIAN JOURNAL OF PURE & APPLIED MATHEMATICS.**
+ +INDIAN J. PURE & APPL. MATH.
NATIONAL INSTITUTE OF SCIENCES OF INDIA.
*NEW DELHI  1(1), JA 1970-*
Q.
*BR/U-1.    CA/U-1.    CA/U-2.    ED/S-2.    GL/U-1.    GL/U-2.*
*LD/U-1.    LO/N-4.    LO/N14.    LO/U-2.    OX/U-8.    SH/U-1.*
*MA/U-1.  1(2), 1970-*
*ISSN 0019-5588*

**INDIAN JOURNAL OF RADIO & SPACE PHYSICS.**
+ +INDIAN J. RADIO & SPACE PHYS.
COUNCIL OF SCIENTIFIC & INDUSTRIAL RESEARCH
(INDIA).
*NEW DELHI  1, 1972-*
SPONS. BODY ALSO: INDIAN NATIONAL SCIENCE
ACADEMY.
*LO/N14.*

**INDIAN JOURNAL OF REGIONAL SCIENCE.**
+ +INDIAN J. REG. SCI.
REGIONAL SCIENCE ASSOCIATION (INDIA).
*KHARAGPUR  1, 1968-*
PUBL. FOR ASSOC. BY INDIAN INSTITUTE OF TECH-
NOLOGY.
*CB/U-1.    LO/U-3.*
*ISSN 0046-9017*

**INDIAN JOURNAL OF SERICULTURE.**
+ +INDIAN J. SERICULT.
CENTRAL SILK BOARD (INDIA).
*BOMBAY  1, JL 1962-*
*LO/N13.*

**INDIAN JOURNAL OF VETERINARY SCIENCE & ANIMAL
HUSBANDRY.**          XXX
SUBS (1969):  INDIAN JOURNAL OF ANIMAL
SCIENCES.

**INDIAN LIBRARY SCIENCE ABSTRACTS.**
+ +INDIAN LIBR. SCI. ABSTR.
INDIAN ASSOCIATION OF SPECIAL LIBRARIES &
INFORMATION CENTRES.
*CALCUTTA  1(1), JA/MR 1967-*
Q.
*SH/U-1.  1(2), 1967-*
*ISSN 0019-5790*

**INDIAN NUMISMATIC CHRONICLE.**
+ +INDIAN NUMISMAT. CHRON.
BIHAR RESEARCH SOCIETY.
*PATNA  1, 1960-*
*OX/U13.*
*ISSN 0537-2348*

INDIAN POLITICAL SCIENCE REVIEW.
+ +INDIAN POLIT. SCI. REV.
UNIVERSITY OF DELHI: DEPARTMENT OF POLITICAL
SCIENCE.
DELHI 1, OC/MR 1966/67-
LO/U-3.*   OX/U13.
ISSN 0019-6126

INDIAN SILK.
CENTRAL SILK BOARD (INDIA).
BOMBAY  1(1), 1962-
M.
LO/N13. 4(10),1966-
ISSN 0019-6355

INDIAN WIRE INDUSTRY JOURNAL.                                    XXX
+ +INDIAN WIRE IND. J.
INDIAN WIRE ASSOCIATION.
BOMBAY  1, 1957- 12, 1969.//
M.
LO/N13. 3, 1960-
ISSN 0445-8222

INDIAN ZOOLOGIST.
+ +INDIAN ZOOL.
SOCIETY OF INDIAN ZOOLOGISTS.
DHARWAR 1, 1970-
LO/N-2.

INDIANA FOLKLORE.
+ +INDIANA FOLK.
HOOSIER FOLKLORE SOCIETY.
BLOOMINGTON, INDIANA 1, FALL 1968-
2/A.
LO/S30. 2, 1969-
ISSN 0019-6614

INDIANA UNIVERSITY MATHEMATICS JOURNAL.          XXX
+ +INDIANA UNIV. MATH. J.
BLOOMINGTON, INDIANA 20, 1970-
PREV: JOURNAL OF MATHEMATICS & MECHANICS FROM
6, 1957- 19, 1970.
HL/U-1.   LD/U-1.   LO/N14.   LO/U-2.   LO/U11.   NW/U-1.
SF/U-1.   SO/U-1.   XS/R10.
CB/U-1. 1974-
BN/U-2. 21(1), 1971-
LO/N-7. 20(11), 1971-
ISSN 0022-2518

INDICADORES ECONOMICO-SOCIAIS.                             XXX
+ +INDIC. ECON.-SOC. (PORT.).
INSTITUTO NACIONAL DE ESTATISTICA (PORTUGAL).
LISBON  ANO 1, JA 1973-
MON. PORT. & ENGL. ENGL. TITLE: SOCIAL-
ECONOMIC INDICATORS. PREV: INDICADORES ESTAT-
ISTICOS A CURTO PRAZO FROM ANO 1, F 1969- 1972
LO/N-1.   LO/U-3.   OX/U-1.
ED/N-1. 1(2), 1973-

INDICADORES ESTATISTICOS A CURTO PRAZO. =
SHORT TERM STATISTICAL INDICATORS.               XXX
+ +INDIC. ESTATIST. CURZO PRAZO.
INSTITUTO NACIONAL DE ESTATISTICA (PORTUGAL)
LISBON 1(1), F 1969- 1972.
M. SUBS: INDICADORES ECONOMICO-SOCIAIS.
ED/N-1.   LO/U-3.   OX/U16.

INDICATEURS ECONOMIQUES AFRICAINS.               000
SEE: AFRICAN ECONOMIC INDICATORS.

INDICE CULTURAL DE VENEZUELA.
+ +INDICE CULT. VENEZ.
(VENEZUELA) OFICINA CENTRAL DE INFORMACION.
CARACAS  NO.1, MR 1969-
M.
ED/N-1.
ISSN 0019-6991

INDO.  AFRICAN TRADE JOURNAL.
[AFRICA PUBL. (INDIA)]
NEW DELHI 1(1), JL 1965-
M.
LO/N17.

INDO-BRITISH REVIEW.
+ +INDO-BR. REV.
INDO-BRITISH HISTORICAL SOCIETY.
MADRAS  1, 1968-
OX/U13.
ISSN 0019-7211

INDONESIAN BIOLOGICAL & AGRICULTURAL INDEX.      000
SEE: INDEKS BIOLOGI PERTANIAN INDONESIA.

INDONESIAN NEWS.
+ +INDOS. NEWS.
(INDONESIA) EMBASSY (GB).
LONDON  1, 1970-
LO/U14.   OX/U-1.

INDUS.
[INDS-B]
WEST PAKISTAN WATER & POWER DEVELOPMENT
AUTHORITY.
LAHORE  1(1), F 1960-
OX/U16. 3(2), 1968-*
ISSN 0537-4715

INDUSTRIA.  JAPAN'S ECONOMY, INDUSTRY &
TECHNOLOGY.
DIAMOND LEAD CO.
TOKYO  1, OC 1971-
2M.
LO/U14.
SH/U-1. 2, 1972-

INDUSTRIAL ACCIDENT PREVENTION BULLETIN.         000
SEE: INDUSTRIAL SAFETY BULLETIN.

INDUSTRIAL AERODYNAMICS ABSTRACTS.
+ +IND. AERODYN. ABSTR.
BRITISH HYDROMECHANICS RESEARCH ASSOCIATION.
CRANFIELD  1(1), JA/F 1970-
S/T:  WORLD LITERATURE OF NON-AERONAUTICAL
AERODYNAMICS.
AD/U-1.   ED/N-1.   GL/U-2.   LO/N14.   LO/20.   OX/U-8.
SW/U-1.
BH/U-3. 2, 1971-              SO/U-1. 3, 1972-
ISSN 0019-7823

INDUSTRIAL & COMMERCIAL TRAINING.
+ +IND. & COMMER. TRAIN.
[JOHN WELLENS]
GUILSBOROUGH  1(1), N 1969-
AB/U-1.   ED/N-1.   LO/N-7.   LO/N17.   OX/U-1.   SF/U-1.
XS/R10.
GL/U-2. 4, 1972-              MA/P-1. 2, 1970-
ISSN 0019-7858

INDUSTRIAL COURT REPORTS.                                     XXX
+ +IND. COURT REP.
INCORPORATED COUNCIL OF LAW REPORTING FOR
ENGLAND & WALES.
LONDON  NO.1, 1972-
PREV: REPORTS OF RESTRICTIVE PRACTICES
CASES FROM 1, 1958- 1972.
CA/U-1.   CA/U13.   ED/N-1.   GL/U-1.   LO/U-1.   LO/U-3.
LO/U12.   LO/U12.   NW/U-1.

INDUSTRIAL DEVELOPMENT ABSTRACTS.
+ +IND. DEV. ABSTR.
UNITED NATIONS.
NEW YORK  1971(1/2)-
ABSTRACTS PUBL. OF THE UNITED NATIONS
INDUSTRIAL DEVELOPMENT ORGANIZATION.
LD/U-1.   LO/N10.   LO/N14.   LO/U-3.   NO/U-1.
OX/U16.   RE/U-1.

INDUSTRIAL DEVELOPMENT IN ASIA & THE FAR EAST.
+ +IND. DEV. ASIA & FAR E.
UNITED NATIONS: ECONOMIC COMMISSION FOR ASIA &
THE FAR EAST.
BANGKOK  NO.1, 1965...
SUBS: ASIAN INDUSTRIAL DEVELOPMENT NEWS.
ED/N-1.   HL/U-1.   LO/N17.   LO/S14.   LO/U-3.   MA/U-1.
OX/U16.   OX/U17.

INDUSTRIAL ENGINEERING.
+ +IND. ENG.
AMERICAN INSTITUTE OF INDUSTRIAL ENGINEERS.
NEW YORK  1, 1969-
PREV: JOURNAL OF INDUSTRIAL ENGINEERING FROM
1, JE 1949.
BH/U-1.   DB/U-2.   LO/N14.   SW/U-1.
BL/U-8. 5, 1973-            CV/C-1. 3, 1971-
ISSN 0019-8234

INDUSTRIAL ENGINEERING ABSTRACTS.
+ +IND. ENG. ABSTR.
BRITISH ALUMINIUM CO. LTD.
LONDON  NO.1, 1966-
LO/N14.

INDUSTRIAL & ENGINEERING CHEMISTRY.              XXX
SUBS (1971): CHEMICAL TECHNOLOGY.

INDUSTRIAL EXPORTS (GREAT BRITAIN).                XXX
+ +IND. EXPORTS (GB).
[BENN BROS.]
 LONDON  128, 1970-
 PREV:  BRITISH TRADE JOURNAL & EXPORT WORLD
 FROM 1929.
 ED/N-1.    LO/N-7.


INDUSTRIAL HERITAGE.
+ +IND. HERITAGE.
DURHAM UNIVERSITY GROUP FOR INDUSTRIAL ARCH-
AEOLOGY.
 DURHAM  NO.1, 1970-
 LO/N14.


INDUSTRIAL LAW JOURNAL.                            XXX
+ +IND. LAW J.
INDUSTRIAL LAW SOCIETY.
[SWEET & MAXWELL]
 LONDON  1(1), MR 1972-
 Q. PREV: BULLETIN, INDUSTRIAL LAW SOCIETY
 FROM NO.1, JA 1968- 12, 1972.
 AD/U-1.    CA/U-1.    CA/U13.    ED/N-1.    GL/U-1.    LO/U-3.
 LO/U11.    LO/U12.    MA/P-1.    ·MA/U-1.    SH/U-1.
 SO/U-1.
 EX/U-1.  2(1), 1973-
 ISSN 0305-9332


INDUSTRIAL MANAGEMENT (LONDON).                    XXX
+ +IND. MANAGE. (LONDON)
[BUSINESS PUBL. LTD.]
 LONDON  1(1), N 1970-
 MON. PREV: BUSINESS MANAGEMENT FROM 97(3), MR
 1967- 100(9), S 1970.
 BH/P-1.    DB/U-2.    LO/C31.    LO/N14.    MA/U-4.
 XS/R10.
 OX/U-1.  F 1971-                OX/U16.  1(8), 1971-
 SH/C-5.  1(6), 1971-
 ED/N-1.  1(2), F 1971-
 ISSN 0007-6929


INDUSTRIAL MANAGEMENT (SYDNEY).                    XXX
+ +IND. MANAGE. (SYDNEY).
[TAIT]
 SYDNEY  57(10), 1969-
 PREV: FACTORY & PLANT.
 LO/N14.


INDUSTRIAL MANAGEMENT REVIEW.                      XXX
 SUBS (1970): SLOAN MANAGEMENT REVIEW.


INDUSTRIAL MARKETING MANAGEMENT.
+ +IND. MARK. MANAGE.
EUROPEAN ASSOCIATION FOR INDUSTRIAL MARKETING
RESEARCH.
 AMSTERDAM  1(1), S 1971-
 MA/U-4.    XS/R10.    XY/N-1.
 ISSN 0019-8501


INDUSTRIAL MARKETING RESEARCH ABSTRACTS.
+ +IND. MARK. RES. ABSTR.
INDUSTRIAL MARKETING RESEARCH ASSOCIATION.
 LONDON  1(1), 1969-
 OX/U16.
 ED/N-1.  2, 1970-
 MA/U-4.  1, 1969- 2, 1970.
 ISSN 0019-0047


INDUSTRIAL MINERALS.
+ +IND. MINER.
[METAL BULLETIN LTD.]
 LONDON  NO.1, 1967-
 ED/N-1.    OX/U-8.
 MA/P-1.  NO.1, 1967- 15, 1968.
 ISSN 0019-8544


INDUSTRIAL OILS REVIEW.
+ +IND. OILS REV.
BURMAH-CASTROL INDUSTRIAL LTD.
 LONDON  NO.1, 1970-
 ED/N-1.    OX/U-1.


INDUSTRIAL PROCESS DESIGN FOR POLLUTION
CONTROL.                                           XXX
 + +IND. PROCESS DES. POLLUT. CONTROL.
 AMERICAN INSTITUTE OF CHEMICAL ENGINEERS.
 NEW YORK  4, 1972-
 PREV: INDUSTRIAL PROCESS DESIGN FOR WATER
 POLLUTION CONTROL FROM 1, 1967- 3, 1971.
 LO/N14.


INDUSTRIAL PROCESS DESIGN FOR WATER POLLUTION
CONTROL.*                                          XXX
 + +IND. PROCESS DES. WAT. POLLUT. CONTR.
 AMERICAN INSTITUTE OF CHEMICAL ENGINEERS.
 NEW YORK  1, 1967- 3, 1971...
 NO.1 PUBL. AS INDUSTRIAL PROCESS DESIGN FOR
 POLLUTION CONTROL. AS ABOVE FROM 2, 1970.
 SUBS: INDUSTRIAL PROCESS DESIGN FOR POLLUTION
 CONTROL.
 LO/N14.


INDUSTRIAL & PROCESS HEATING.                      XXX
+ +IND. & PROCESS HEAT. [IPRH-A]
[FACTORY PUBL. LTD.]
 LONDON  1, 1961- 9, 1969...
 SUBS: INDUSTRIAL PROCESS HEATING.
 LO/N14.  1967- 1969.


INDUSTRIAL PROCESS HEATING.                        XXX
+ +IND. PROCESS HEAT.
[FACTORY PUBL. LTD.]
 LONDON  10, 1970-
 PREV: INDUSTRIAL & PROCESS HEATING FROM 1,
 1961- 9, 1969.
 LO/N-7.    LO/N14.
 ISSN 0019-7947


INDUSTRIAL PROPERTY.  MONTHLY REVIEW OF THE
INTERNATIONAL ...
+ +IND. PROPERTY.
INTERNATIONAL BUREAU FOR THE PROTECTION OF
INDUSTRIAL PROPERTY.
 GENEVA  1962-
 LO/U-3.
 ISSN 0019-8625


INDUSTRIAL QUALITY CONTROL.                        XXX
 SUBS (1968): QUALITY PROGRESS.


INDUSTRIAL RELATIONS BULLETIN.
+ +IND. RELAT. BULL.
FABIAN SOCIETY: TRADE UNION & INDUSTRIAL
RELATIONS COMMITTEE.
 LONDON  NO.1, JL 1971- 3, 1972.//
 ED/N-1.    GL/U-2.    LO/U-3.    OX/U-1.    OX/U17.


INDUSTRIAL RELATIONS JOURNAL.
+ +IND. RELAT. J.
[BUSINESS PUBL. LTD.]
 LONDON  NO.1, 1970-
 Q.
 BH/P-1.    BH/U-3.    EX/U-1.    LA/U-1.    LO/N10.    LO/N17.
 LO/P-6.    MA/P-1.    MA/U-1.    MA/U-4.    OX/U-1.    XS/R10.
 XY/N-1.
 AD/U-1.  3, 1972-                BH/U-3.  1(3), 1970-
 CB/U-1.  2, 1971-                GL/U-1.  3(1), 1972-
 LO/U12.  2(2), 1971-            NW/U-1.  2, 1971-
 OX/U16.  2(1), 1971-            SO/U-1.  5, 1974-
 XS/T-4.  2(4), 1971-
 BN/U-1.  1(3), D 1970-
 ED/N-1.  1(2), S 1970-
 LO/U-3.  1(2), S 1970-[W. 2(2), 1971].
 ISSN 0019-8692


INDUSTRIAL RELATIONS LAW REPORTS.
+ +IND. RELAT. LAW REP.
[ECLIPSE PUBL.]
 LONDON  1(1), S 1972-
 MON.
 BH/U-3.    CA/U13.    ED/N-1.    GL/U-2.    LD/U-1.    LO/U-2.
 LO/U12.    MA/P-1.    OX/U15.    SH/U-1.    SO/U-1.
 EX/U-1.  2(1), JA 1973-


INDUSTRIAL RELATIONS REVIEW & REPORT.
+ +IND. RELAT. REV. & REP.
 LONDON  NO.1, F 1971-
 2M.
 LO/U-3.    LO/U12.
 BH/U-3.  23, 1972-              CB/U-1.  1974-
 MA/U-4.  NO.2, F 1971-
 SH/U-1.  NO.54, 1973-
 ISSN 0046-9246


INDUSTRIAL RESEARCH & DEVELOPMENT NEWS.            XXX
+ +IND. RES. & DEVELOP. NEWS.
UNITED NATIONS: INDUSTRIAL DEVELOPMENT ORGAN-
IZATION.
 NEW YORK  2, 1967-
 2/A.  PREV: INDUSTRIAL RESEARCH NEWS FROM
 1, 1966.
 LO/U-3.
 XS/T-4.  6(1), 1972-
 ISSN 0019-8730

**INDUSTRIAL RESEARCH NEWS.** XXX
+ +IND. RES. NEWS.
UNITED NATIONS: INDUSTRIAL DEVELOPMENT
ORGANIZATION.
*NEW YORK 1(1- 2), 1966...*
SUBS: INDUSTRIAL RESEARCH & DEVELOPMENT NEWS.
*LO/U-3.*

**INDUSTRIAL REVIEW.** XXX
+ +IND. REV.
GUYANA DEVELOPMENT CORPORATION.
*GEORGETOWN 3(1), JA/MR 1968-*
Q. PREV: QUARTERLY NEWS BULLETIN, GUYANA
INDUSTRIAL DEVELOPMENT CORPORATION FROM 1,
1966 - 2(4), 1967.
*LO/U-8.*

**INDUSTRIAL SAFETY BULLETIN.** XXX
+ +IND. SAF. BULL.
ROYAL SOCIETY FOR THE PREVENTION OF ACCIDENTS.
*LONDON 34(372), JA 1966- 34(383), 1966...*
PREV: INDUSTRIAL ACCIDENT PREVENTION BULLETIN
FROM 8(92), D 1940- 33(371), D 1965. SUBS:
PART OCCUPATIONAL SAFETY BULLETIN.
*LO/N14.*

**INDUSTRIAL & SCIENTIFIC COMMUNICATION.**
+ +IND. & SCI. COMMUN.
[PERGAMON]
*POTTERS BAR, HERTS. 1, 1970-*
*LO/N14.*

**INDUSTRIAL & SCIENTIFIC INSTRUMENTS.**
+ +IND. & SCI. INSTRUM.
[HANOVER PRESS LTD.]
*LONDON 1(1), 1969-*
S/T: POSTAL FACTFINDER SERVICE.
*LO/N-4.*

**INDUSTRIAL SCREEN.** XXX
SUBS (1972): PART OF AUDIO VISUAL.

**INDUSTRIAL TRENDS ENQUIRY.** XXX
SUBS (1965): INDUSTRIAL TRENDS SURVEY.

**INDUSTRIAL TRENDS SURVEY.** XXX
+ +IND. TRENDS SURV. XXX
CONFEDERATION OF BRITISH INDUSTRY.
*LONDON NO.22, 1965- 40, 1971 ...*
PREV: INDUSTRIAL TRENDS ENQUIRY FROM NO.1, F
1958- 21, N 1964. SUBS: CBI INDUSTRIAL TRENDS
SURVEY.
*OX/U17.*
*MA/U-1. NO.31, 1968- SO/U-1. NO.28, 1966-*

**INDUSTRIAL & WELFARE CATERING.** XXX
+ +IND. & WELFARE CATER.
[PRACTICAL P. LTD.]
*LONDON 1(1), 1969- 6(1/2), 1974.*
SUBS: STAFF AND WELFARE CATERING.
*ED/N-1. LO/N14. OX/U-1.*
*SH/C-5. 2(5/6), MR/AP 1971-*
*ISSN 0019-7693*

**INDUSTRIE LAITIERE SUISSE.** XXX
SUBS (1970): PRODUCTEUR DE LAIT.

**INDUSTRIE MINERALE: REVUE DE LA ...** XXX
+ +IND. MINER. (FR.).
SOCIETE DE L'INDUSTRIE MINERALE.
*SAINT-ETIENNE OC 1971-*
PREV: REVUE DE L'INDUSTRIE MINERALE FROM 1(1),
1921- 53(2), 1971.
*LD/U-1. LO/N14.*

**INDUSTRIE DES VOIES FERREES ET DES TRANSPORTS**
**AUTOMOBILES.** XXX
SUBS (1970): REVUE DES TRANSPORTS PUBLICS
URBAINS ET REGIONAUX.

**INDUSTRIEFEUERUNG.**
[VULKAN-VERLAG DR. W. CLASSEN]
*ESSEN 1, 1972-*
*LO/N14.*

**INDUSTRIES THERMIQUES (ET AERAULIQUES).** XXX
+ +IND. THERM. (& AERAULIQUES). [INTH-A]
SOCIETE DE DIFFUSION DES TECHNIQUES DU
BATIMENT ET DES TRAVAUX PUBLICS.
*PARIS. 1, 1955- 15, 1969.*
TITLE EXTENDED FROM 9, 1963. SUBS: PROMOCLIM,
INDUSTRIES THERMIQUES ET AERAULIQUES.
*LO/N-9. 9,1963- LV/U-1. 1964-*
*XS/T-2. 1961. 1962(1-7).*

**INDUSTRY WEEK. (CLEVELAND).** XXX
+ +IND. WEEK. (CLEVELAND).
[PENTON PUBL. CO.]
*CLEVELAND 166(1), JA 1970-*
PREV: STEEL FROM 87, 1930- 165, 1969.
*LO/N14.*
*ISSN 0039-0895*

**INDUSTRY WEEK. (LONDON).** XXX
+ +IND. WEEK. (LOND.).
CONFEDERATION OF BRITISH INDUSTRY.
*LONDON 5(93), 1969- 6(138), 1970.//*
PREV: BRITISH INDUSTRY WEEK FROM 1, 1967-
5(92), 1969.
*ED/N-1. GL/U-3. LO/N-7. LO/U-3. OX/U16. RE/U-1.*

**INFECTION.**
*MUNICH 1(1), 1973-*
*OX/U-8.*

**INFECTION & IMMUNITY.**
+ +INFEC. & IMMUNITY.
AMERICAN SOCIETY FOR MICROBIOLOGY.
*BETHESDA, MD. 1, JA 1970-*
M.
*DN/U-1. LD/U-1. LO/M12. LO/N13. LO/U-1. LO/U-2.*
*NW/U-1. OX/U-8. RE/U-1. SO/U-1.*
*BL/U-1. 5, 1972- CA/M-7. 9, 1974-*
*LO/M-3. 7, 1973- LO/M11. 3, 1971-*
*ISSN 0019-9567*

**INFEKTSIONNYE ZABOLEVANIJA KUL'TURNYKH**
**RASTENIJ MOLDAVII.**
+ +INFEKTS. ZABOL. KUL'T. RAST. MOLD. [IZKR-A]
AKADEMIJA NAUK MOLDAVSKOJ SSR: INSTITUT BIO-
KHIMII I FIZIOLOGII RASTENIJ.
*KISHINEV 1, 1962-*
*LO/N13. 2, 1963- 6, 1966.*
*ISSN 0446-1371*

**INFOR. CANADIAN JOURNAL OF OPERATIONAL**
**RESEARCH & INFORMATION PROCESSING.**
CANADIAN OPERATIONAL RESEARCH SOCIETY.
*OTTAWA 9, 1971-*
PREV: CORS JOURNAL FROM 1, D 1963- 8, 1970.
*BH/U-1. CR/U-1. HL/U-1. LO/N14.*
*BL/U-1. 12, 1974-*

**INFORMACJA BIEZACA.**
+ +INF. BIEZACA.
GLOWNA BIBLIOTEKA LEKARSKA.
*WARSAW 1(1), 1971-*
S/T: PRZEGLAD ZAWARTOSCI OBCOJEZYCZNYCH
CZASOPISM MEDYOZNYCH.
*LO/N-3.*

**INFORMATION.**
[TAYLOR & FRANCIS LTD.]
*LONDON NO.1, JA-JE 1969 (1970)-*
S/T: COMPRISING A COMPREHENSIVE LIST OF SCI-
ENTIFIC ARTICLES FROM INTERNATIONAL JOURNALS
PUBL. BY TAYLOR & FRANCIS.
*LD/U-1. LO/N-7. LO/N31. OX/U-1.*

**INFORMATION BROCHURE, IMPERIAL TOBACCO GROUP LTD**
+ +INF. BROCHURE IMP. TOB. GROUP LTD.
*NOTTINGHAM NO.1, 1969-*
*OX/U-1.*

**INFORMATION BULLETIN, BRITISH NUTRITION FOUN-**
**DATION LTD.**
+ +INF. BULL. BR. NUTR. FOUND. LTD.
*LONDON 1, 1968-*
*BH/U-1. BL/U-1. CA/U11. GL/U-2. OX/U-8. SO/U-1.*
*XS/U-1.*
*LO/N14. [CURRENT BOX ONLY].*

**INFORMATION BULLETIN, INTERNATIONAL SOLID**
**WASTES & PUBLIC CLEANSING ASSOCIATION.**
+ +INF. BULL. INT. SOLID WASTES & PUBLIC CLEAN.
ASS.
*ZURICH NO.1, 1969-*
*LO/N13.*

**INFORMATION BULLETIN, INTERNATIONAL UNION OF**
**PURE & APPLIED CHEMISTRY.** 000
SEE: INTERNATIONAL UNION OF PURE & APPLIED
CHEMISTRY ...

**INFORMATION BULLETIN ON ISOTOPIC GENERATORS.** XXX
+ +INF. BULL. ISOTOP. GENERATORS.
EUROPEAN NUCLEAR ENERGY AGENCY.
*PARIS NO.8, 1969-*
PREV: NEWSLETTER, ISOTOPIC GENERATOR INFORMA-
TION CENTRE FROM NO.1, 1966.
*LO/N14. XS/R10.*
*ISSN 0019-9982*

**INFORMATION BULLETIN, NONDESTRUCTIVE TESTING
CENTRE.**                                                    XXX
+ +INF. BULL. NONDESTRUCT. TEST. CENT. (GB).
HARWELL JE/JL 1967- 1969.
SUBS. PART OF: NON-DESTRUCTIVE TESTING.
LO/N14.

**INFORMATION CIRCULAR, GEOLOGICAL SURVEY OF
IRELAND.**
+ +INF. CIRC. GEOL. SURV. IRE.
(EIRE) GEOLOGICAL SURVEY.
DUBLIN 1, 1969-
BH/U-1.    DB/S-1.    GL/U-1.    LO/N-2.

**INFORMATION CIRCULAR, SOUTH PACIFIC
COMMISSION.**
+ +INF. CIRC. SOUTH PAC. COMM.
NOUMEA NO.1, S 1968-
OX/U-8. NO.5, 1969-
LO/U-3. NO.28, JA 1971-
ISSN 0081-282X

**INFORMATION, DEPARTMENT OF AUDIO VISUAL
COMMUNICATION, BRITISH MEDICAL ASSOCIATION.**
LONDON 1, 1969-
BL/U-1.
LO/U12. NO.3, JA 1970- [W. 4, 6, 7].

**INFORMATION DISPLAY. JOURNAL OF THE ...**             XXX
+ +INF. DISPLAY. [INFD-A]
SOCIETY FOR INFORMATION DISPLAY.
BEVERLY HILLS, CALIF. 1, S/OC 1964- 9, 1972 .
2M. SUBS: SID JOURNAL.
LO/N13. 2,1965-
ISSN 0020-0042

**INFORMATION FORESTRY.**
+ +INF. FOR.
VICTORIA, B.C. 1(1), MR 1972-
OX/U-3.

**INFORMATIONS, INTERNATIONAL ANTONIO VIVALDI
SOCIETY.**
+ +INF. INT. ANTONIO VIVALDI SOC.
COPENHAGEN NO.1, 1972-
ED/N-1.    LO/N-1.

**INFORMATIONS SUR L'IRRADIATION DES DENRÉES.**        XXX
SEE: FOOD IRRADIATION INFORMATION.

**INFORMATION ON LAND REFORM, LAND SETTLEMENT &
COOPERATIVES.**                                             XXX
+ +INF. LAND REFORM LAND SETTLE. & COOP.
FOOD & AGRICULTURAL ORGANIZATION (UN): AGRARIAN
RESEARCH & INTELLIGENCE SERVICE.
ROME [1964] (1)- 1967 (2).
SUBS: LAND REFORM, LAND SETTLEMENT & COOPER-
ATIVES. AGRARIAN RES. & INTELL. SERV. SUBORD.
TO RURAL INSTITUTIONS & SERVICES DIV.
LD/U-1.*    LO/U-3.    RE/U-1.
BN/U-2.    1965(2)-

**INFORMATION LETTER, STOCKHOLM CONFERENCE ON
VIETNAM.**
+ +INF. LETT. STOCKHOLM CONF. VIETNAM.
STOCKHOLM NO.1, MY 1968-
LO/U-3.

**INFORMATIONEN AUS ORTHODONTIE UND KIEFERORTHO-
PADIE.**
+ +INF. ORTHODONT. KIEFERORTHOP.
[ZAHNARZTLICH-MEDIZINISCHES SCHRIFTTUM]
MUNICH 1(1), MR 1969-
Q.
LO/N14.

**INFORMATION PAPER, CERAMICS GLASS & MINERAL
PRODUCTS INDUSTRY TRAINING BOARD.**
+ +INF. PAP. CERAM. GLASS & MINER. PROD. IND.
TRAIN. BOARD.
HARROW, MIDDX. NO.1, 1968-
LO/N-1.    OX/U-1.

**[INFORMATION PAPER] INTERGOVERNMENTAL OCEAN-
OGRAPHIC COMMISSION.**
PARIS &C. 1970-
PREV: INTERNATIONAL MARINE SCIENCE FROM 1,
1963- 7, 1970.
LO/N13.

**INFORMATION PROCESSING LETTERS.**
+ +INF. PROCESS. LETT.
[NORTH-HOLLAND PUBL. CO.]
AMSTERDAM 1, 1971-
LO/N-4.    LO/N14.    LO/U28.    OX/U-8.    RE/U-1.    SA/U-1.
SF/U-1.    SH/U-1.    SW/U-1.    XY/N-1.
LD/U-1. 2, 1973-
ISSN 0020-0190

**INFORMATION REVIEW (ROME).**                          000
SEE: RIVISTA DELL'INFORMAZIONE.

**INFORMATION SAMPLER DIGEST.**
+ +INF. SAMPL. DIG.
WAYNE STATE UNIVERSITY: SCIENTIFIC & TECHNICAL
INFORMATION CENTER.
DETROIT 1, 1969-
LO/N14.

**INFORMATION SCIENCE ABSTRACTS.**                      XXX
+ +INF. SCI. ABSTR.
AMERICAN CHEMICAL SOCIETY.
[DOCUMENTATION ABSTRACTS, INC.]
PHILADELPHIA, PA. 4(1), MR 1969-
2M. PREV: DOCUMENTATION ABSTRACTS FROM 1,
1966- 3, 1968. SPONS. BODIES ALSO AMERICAN
DOCUMENTATION INSTITUTE & SPECIAL LIBRARIES
ASSOCIATION.
BH/U-1.    DB/U-2.    GL/U-2.    LO/N-3.    LO/N14.    NO/U-1.
ISSN 0020-0239

**INFORMATION SCIENCES.**
+ +INF. SCI.
[AMERICAN ELSEVIER PUBL. CO.]
NEW YORK 1(1), 1968-
S/T: AN INTERNATIONAL JOURNAL.
LO/N-4.    LO/N14.    LO/U-6.    SH/U-1.
BL/U-1. 5, 1973-
ISSN 0020-0255

**INFORMATION-SHEET, CENTRE FOR SOUTH-EAST
ASIAN STUDIES, UNIVERSITY OF HULL.**
+ +INF.-SHEET CENT. SOUTH-EAST ASIAN STUD.
UNIV. HULL.
HULL NO.1, 1969-
HL/U-1.    LO/U-8.

**INFORMATION SHEET, LIBRARY, UNIVERSITY OF
SOUTHAMPTON.**
+ +INF. SHEET LIBR. UNIV. SOUTHAMPTON.
SOUTHAMPTON NO.1, D 1972-
SO/U-1.

**INFORMATION SYSTEMS INNOVATIONS.**
+ +INF. SYST. INNOVAT.
SMITHSONIAN INSTITUTION.
WASHINGTON, D.C. 1, 1969-
LO/N-2.

**INFORMATORE BOTANICO ITALIANO.**
+ +INF. BOT. ITAL.
SOCIETA BOTANICA ITALIANA.
FLORENCE 1, 1969-
LO/N-4.
ISSN 0020-0697

**INFORME ANUAL, CORPORACION VENEZOLANA DE
GUAYANA.**
+ +INFORME ANU. CORP. VENEZ. GUAYANA.
CARACAS 1, 1968-
A.
LO/U-3.

**INFOSYSTEMS.**                                          XXX
[HITCHCOCK PUBL. CO.]
WHEATON, ILL. 19(7), 1972-
PREV: BUSINESS AUTOMATION FROM 6, 1961-
19(6), 1972.
LO/N14.

**INGEGNERIA.**                                           XXX
[HOEPLI]
MILAN 1970-
PREV: RIVISTA DI INGEGNERIA FROM 1, JA 1951-
1969.
LO/N14.
ISSN 0035-6263

**INGEGNERIA ELETTRONICA.**                              XXX
+ +ING. ELETTRON.
[EDIZIONI I.E.N.S.]
MILAN 10, 1972-
PREV: INGEGNERIA ELETTRONICA E STRUMENTI FROM
8, 1970- 9, 1971.
LO/N14.

**INGEGNERIA ELETTRONICA NUCLEARE E STRUMENTI.**        XXX
SUBS (1970): INGEGNERIA ELETTRONICA E STRU-
MENTI.

INGEGNERIA ELETTRONICA E STRUMENTI.    XXX
+ +ING. ELETTRON. STRUM.
[EDIZIONI I.E.N.S.]
MILAN 8, 1970- 9, 1971 ...
PREV: INGEGNERIA ELETTRONICA NUCLEARE E STRU-
MENTI FROM 1, 1963- 7, 1969. SUBS: INGEGNERIA
ELETTRONICA.
LO/N14.

INGENIERIA FORESTAL (ARGENTINA).
UNIVERSIDAD NACIONAL DE LA PLATA: ESCUELA
SUPERIOR DE BOSQUE.
BUENOS AIRES  1(1), 1968- 1(3), 1969.//
ESCUELA SUBORD TO:  FACULTAD DE AGRONOMIA.
SPONS. BODY ALSO:  INSTITUTE DE ORDENACION DE
VERTIENTES A INGENIERIA FORESTAL.
OX/U-3.

IN'GU MUNJE NONJIP. JOURNAL OF POPULATION
STUDIES.
IN'GU MUNJE YON'GUSO.
SEOUL  NO.1, 1965-
LO/S74.

INIS ATOMINDEX.    XXX
INTERNATIONAL ATOMIC ENERGY AGENCY.
VIENNA  1, MY 1970-
PREV: ATOMINDEX FROM 1, OC 1959- 11(30), 15/MR
1970. ALSO ENTITLED INIS ATOMINDEKS.
DB/U-2.    LO/N14.
ISSN 0004-7139

INITIATION A LA LINGUISTIQUE: SERIES A: LECTURES
+ +INITIATION LINGUIST., A.
[KLINCKSIECK]
PARIS  1, 1970-
CA/U-1.
ISSN 0073-8018

INJURY.
BRISTOL  1(1), JL 1969-
S/T: BRITISH JOURNAL OF ACCIDENT SURGERY.
BN/U-2.    LO/M-1.    LO/N-1.    NW/U-1.    OX/U-8.
SO/U-1.  3, 1972.
ISSN 0020-1383

INKLINS.
ABERDEEN COLLEGE OF EDUCATION.
ABERDEEN  NO.1, 1968-
ED/N-1.
OX/U-1.  NO.3, 1970-

INLOGOV.
UNIVERSITY OF BIRMINGHAM: CLEARINGHOUSE FOR
LOCAL AUTHORITY SOCIAL SERVICES RESEARCH.
BIRMINGHAM  1, 1972-
CLEARINGHOUSE SUBORD. TO: INSTITUTE OF LOCAL
GOVERNMENT STUDIES.
OX/U-1.

INNOVATION IN EDUCATION.
+ +INNOVAT. EDUC.
OECD: CENTRE FOR EDUCATIONAL RESEARCH &
INNOVATION.
PARIS  NO.1, JE 1972-
DB/U-2.

INNSBRUCKER BEITRAGE ZUR SPRACHWISSENSCHAFT.
+ +INNSB. BEITR. SPRACHWISS.
INNSBRUCK  1, 1970-
OX/U-1.

INORGANIC CHEMISTRY OF THE TRANSITION ELEM-
ENTS.
+ +INORG. CHEM. TRANSIT. ELEM.
CHEMICAL SOCIETY.
LONDON  1, 1972-
LO/N14.    LO/S-3.    LO/U-2.    LO/U12.    MA/U-1.    SF/U-1.
SO/U-1.    XS/R10.
ISSN 0305-9774

INORGANIC MACROMOLECULES REVIEWS.
+ +INORG. MACROMOL. REV.
[ELSEVIER]
AMSTERDAM  1, 1970- 1(4), AP 1972.//
GL/U-1.    LO/N14.    LO/S-3.    MA/P-1.    OX/U-8.    XS/RIO.
ISSN 0020-1677

INORGANIC REACTION MECHANISMS.
+ +INORG. REACT. MECH.
CHEMICAL SOCIETY.
LONDON  1, JA 1969/AG 1970(1971)-
S/T: A REVIEW OF THE LITERATURE.
BH/U-3.    ED/N-1.    GL/U-1.    GL/U-2.    LO/N14.    LO/S-3.
LO/U12.
ISSN 0305-8255

IN-PLANT PRINTER.
LONDON  NO.1, MR 1969-
OX/U-1.

INQUINAMENTO.    XXX
[ETAS/KOMPASS]
MILAN  12, 1970-
PREV: ACQUA INDUSTRIALE FROM 1, 1959- 11,
1969.
LO/N13.
ISSN 0001-4982

INSCRIPTILE MEDIEVALE ALE ROMANIEI.
+ +INSCRIP. MEDIEV. ROM.
ACADEMIA REPUBLICII SOCIALISTE ROMANIA:
INSTITUTUL DE ISTORIE 'N ORGA'.
BUCHAREST  1, 1965.
LO/N-3.  1, 1965.

INSECT BIOCHEMISTRY.
+ +INSECT BIOCHEM.
BRISTOL  1, MR 1971-
Q.
LO/N-1.    LO/N-2.    SH/U-1.    XY/N-1.
ISSN 0020-1790

INSECT PEST BULLETIN.
+ +INSECT PEST BULL.
(NEW SOUTH WALES) DEPARTMENT OF AGRICULTURE:
ENTOMOLOGY BRANCH.
SYDNEY  NO.1, 1970-
LO/N13.

INSECT PEST SURVEY (TASMANIA).
+ +INSECT PEST SURV. (TASMAN.).
HOBART  NO.1, 1969-
LO/N-2.    LO/N13.

INSECT WORLD DIGEST.
+ +INSECT WORLD DIG.
[WORLD DIGESTS, INC.]
TALLAHASSEE  1, JA/F 1973-
2M.
LO/N-2.

INSECTA MATSUMURANA: SUPPLEMENT.
HOKKAIDO DAIGAKU NOGAKUBU KONCHUGAKU KYOSHITSU.
SAPPORO  NO.1, JL 1966-
LO/N-2.

INSECTS OF VIRGINIA.
+ +INSECTS VA.
VIRGINIA POLYTECHNIC INSTITUTE.
BLACKSBURG, VA.  NO.1, 1969-
LO/N-2.

INSIGHT.
CAPE COAST (GHANA)  1(1), MR 1966-
OX/U-9.

INSIGHT MAGAZINE.
+ +INSIGHT MAG.
BOURNEMOUTH  NO.1, 1967-
OX/U-1.

INSIGHT & OPINION.  QUARTERLY FOR CURRENT AFRI-
CAN THINKING.
+ +INSIGHT & OPIN.
[INSIGHT PUBL.]
ACCRA  1(1), 1966-
BH/U-1.  3(1), 1968-          ED/U-1.  4(1), 1969-
EX/U-1.  3(1), 1968-          LO/U-8.  5(1), 1970-
LD/U-1.  3(1), 1968.
ISSN 0020-1960

INSPEC MATTERS.
INSTITUTION OF ELECTRICAL ENGINEERS.
LONDON  NO.1, 1972-
LO/N35.    OX/U-8.
XS/R10.  NO.2, 1972-
ED/N-1.  NO.2, D 1972-

INSTANT RESEARCH ON PEACE & VIOLENCE.
+ +INSTANT RES. PEACE & VIOLENCE.
TAMPERE PEACE RESEARCH INSTITUTE.
TAMPERE  1, 1972-
Q.  RUSS. SUMM.
LO/U-3.
ISSN 0046-967X

INSTEAD.  A PAPER BY & FOR THE STAFF &
STUDENTS OF U.C.D.
UNIVERSITY COLLEGE, DUBLIN.
DUBLIN  1(1), 1/D 1971-
DB/U-2.

**INSTITUTIONEN FOR LANTBRUKETS BYGGNADSTEKNIK, HANDLINGAR.**    XXX
++*INST. LANTBRUKETS BYGGNADSTEK. HANDL.*
*LUND NO.112, 1969-*
PREV: STATENS LANDBRUKSBYGGNADSFORSOK (SWEDEN), HANDLINGAR.
*LO/N14.*

**INSTITUTO DE PESQUISAS E EXPERIMENTACAO AGROP-ECUARIAS DO NORTE (BRAZIL): SERIE CULTURAS DA AMAZONIA.**    XXX
*BELEM 1, 1970- 2, 1971.//*
*LO/N-2.*

**INSTITUTO DE PESQUISAS E EXPERIMENTACAO AGROP-ECUARIAS DO NORTE (BRAZIL): SERIE ESTUDOS SOBRE BUBALINOS.**    XXX
*BELEM 1, 1970- 2, 1971.//*
*LO/N-2.*    *LO/N13.*

**INSTITUTO DE PESQUISAS E EXPERIMENTACAO AGROP-ECUARIAS DO NORTE (BRAZIL): SERIE FITOTECNIA.**    XXX
*BELEM 1, 1970- 2, 1971.//*
*LO/N-2.*

**INSTITUTO DE PESQUISAS E EXPERIMENTACAO AGROP-ECUARIAS DO NORTE (BRAZIL): SERIE QUIMICA DE SOLOS.**    XXX
*BELEM 1, 1970.//*
*LO/N-2.*

**INSTITUTO DE PESQUISAS E EXPERIMENTACAO AGROP-ECUARIAS DO NORTE (BRAZIL): SERIE TECNOLOGIA.**    XXX
*BELEM 1, 1970.//*
*LO/N-2.*

**INSTRUCTIONAL SCIENCE.**
++*INSTR. SCI.*
[ELSEVIER]
*AMSTERDAM 1, 1972-*
Q.
*EX/U-1.*    *HL/U-2.*    *LO/U28.*    *MA/U-1.*    *SH/U-1.*    *SW/U-1.*
*ISSN 0020-4277*

**INSTRUMENT ABSTRACTS.**    XXX
SUBS(1968): SIRA ABSTRACTS & REVIEWS.

**INSTRUMENT CONSTRUCTION.**    XXX
SUBS (1967): SOVIET JOURNAL OF INSTRUMENT-ATION & CONTROL.

**INSTRUMENT MAINTENANCE MANAGEMENT.**
++*INSTRUM. MAINT. MANAGE.*
INSTRUMENT SOCIETY OF AMERICA.
*PITTSBURGH, PA. 1, 1966-*
COMPRISES PROC. OF THE NATIONAL ISA INSTRU-MENTATION MAINTENANCE SYMPOSIUM (ORG. BY THE INSTALLATION, OPERATION & MAINTENANCE DIV. OF ISA), FROM 1ST, 1966.
*LO/N14.*

**INSTRUMENT PRACTICE.**    XXX
SUBS (1972): PROCESS INSTRUMENTATION.

**INSTRUMENT TECHNOLOGY IN SOUTHERN AFRICA.**
++*INSTRUM. TECHNOL. S. AFR.*
INSTRUMENT & CONTROL SOCIETY OF SOUTHERN AFRICA
*JOHANNESBURG 1, 1964-*
PAPERS MAINLY IN ENGL.
*LO/N14. 1(2), 1964-***

**INSTRUMENTATION, ELECTRONICS & NUCLEONICS.**    XXX
SUBS (1970): PART OF ELECTRONICS & INSTRU-MENTATION.

**INSTRUMENTATION IN THE FOOD & BEVERAGE INDUSTRY.**
++*INSTRUM. FOOD & BEVERAGE IND.*
INSTRUMENT SOCIETY OF AMERICA.
*PITTSBURGH 1, 1972-*
CONSISTS OF THE PROCEEDINGS OF THE 1ST, 1972, INTERNATIONAL ISA FOOD INSTRUMENTATION DIVIS-ION SYMPOSIUM.
*LO/N14.*

**INSTRUMENTATION INTELLIGENCE.**    XXX
++*INSTRUM. INTELL.*
KODAK LTD.
*LONDON 1967- 1973.*
S/T: AN OCCASIONAL NEWSLETTER ISSUED FOR INSTRUMENTATION ENGINEERS BY KODAK LTD. SUBS: LIGHT READING.
*ED/N-1.*    *OX/U-8.*
*LO/N14. CURRENT YEAR ONLY.*

**INSTRUMENTATION TECHNOLOGY.**
++*INSTRUM. TECHNOL.*
INSTRUMENT SOCIETY OF AMERICA.
*PITTSBURGH, PA. 14, 1967-*
PREV: ISA JOURNAL FROM 1, 1954- 13, 1966.
*LO/N14.*
*BL/U-1. 14,1967-*
*ISSN 0020-4382*

**INSULA. BOLETIM DO ...**
UNIVERSIDADE FEDERAL DE SANTA CATARINA: CENTRO DE PESQUISAS E ESTUDOS BOTANICAS.
*FLORIANOPLIS, BRAZIL NO.1, 1969-*
*LO/N-2.*

**INSULATION/CIRCUITS.***    XXX
[LAKE PUBL. CO.]
*LIBERTYVILLE, ILL. 16(3), 1970-*
PUBL. AS INSULATION FROM 1, MY 1955- 16(2), 1970.
*LO/N14.*
*ISSN 0020-4544*

**INTEGRATED EDUCATION.**
++*INTEGR. EDUC.*
*CHICAGO 1, JA 1963-*
*MA/U-1. 6,1968-*
*ISSN 0020-4862*

**INTEGRATION. BEITRAGE ZUR EUROPAFORSCHUNG.**
COMMISSION OF THE EUROPEAN COMMUNITIES.
*BRUSSELS NO.1, 1969-*
Q.
*LO/S14. NO.1, 1969- NO.3/4, 1971.*

**INTELLIGENCE REPORT, BUILDING CENTRE TRUST.**
++*INTELL. REP. BUILD. CEN. TRUST.*
*[LONDON] 1, 1969-*
*LO/N14.*

**INTERAMERICANA REVIEW (PUERTO RICO).**    000
SEE: REVISTA INTERAMERICANA.

**INTERCHANGE. A JOURNAL OF EDUCATIONAL STUDIES.**
ONTARIO INSTITUTE FOR STUDIES IN EDUCATION.
*TORONTO 1(1), AP 1970-*
*BH/U-2.*    *DB/U-2.*    *HL/U-2.*    *LO/N-1.*    *SW/U-1.*
*ISSN 0020-5230*

**INTERCOM. THE JOURNAL OF THE ...**
(GREAT BRITAIN) HOME OFFICE: DIRECTORATE OF TELECOMMUNICATIONS.
[H.M.S.O.]
*LONDON NO.1, 1972-*
*CA/U-1.*    *ED/N-1.*    *LD/U-1.*    *LO/N-1.*    *OX/U-8.*
*GL/U-2. 10 YEARS ONLY.*

**INTERCULTURAL EDUCATION.**
++*INTERCULT. EDUC.*
*NEW YORK 1(1), D 1969-*
M. AN INFORMATION SERVICE OF EDUCATION & WORLD AFFAIRS.
*LO/U14.*
*ISSN 0020-532X*

**INTERFACE. JOURNAL OF NEW MUSIC RESEARCH.**
*AMSTERDAM 1(1), 1972-*
*LO/U-1.*    *OX/U-1.*

**INTERGYPS.**
GYPSUM PRODUCTS DEVELOPMENT ASSOCIATION.
*LONDON 1, 1971-*
*BL/U-1.*

**INTERLEX.**
*MONTREAL 1(1), 1971-*
*OX/U15.*

**INTERMET BULLETIN.**
UNIVERSITY OF UTAH: DEPARTMENT OF MINING, METALLURGICAL & FUEL ENGINEERING.
*SALT LAKE CITY 1, JL 1971-*
Q.
*SH/U-1.*
*LO/N14. 2, 1972-*

**INTERMOUNTAIN ECONOMIC REVIEW.**
++*INTERMT. ECON. REV.*
UNIVERSITY OF UTAH: DEPARTMENT OF ECONOMICS.
*SALT LAKE CITY MR 1970-*
2/A. PRELIMINARY ISSUE MR 1970.
*ISSN 0020-5664*

INTERNATIONAL.
INTERNATIONAL MARXIST GROUP.
*LONDON 1, JL 1970-*
*ED/N-1.   OX/U-1.   OX/U16.*
*ISSN 0020-5788*

INTERNATIONAL. A SURVEY OF BRITISH & WORLD
AFFAIRS.
*LONDON 1(1), MY 1968-*
Q. INCORP: WEEK.
*LO/U-3.*
*OX/U-1.  1(3), 1968-*
*ED/N-1.  1(4), AG 1968-*
*ISSN 0020-5788*

INTERNATIONAL AFFAIRS BULLETIN.
*+ +INT. AFF. BULL.*
COMMUNIST PARTY OF GREAT BRITAIN: INTERNATIONAL
DEPARTMENT.
*LONDON 1(1), 1966-*
2M.
*LO/U-3.*

INTERNATIONAL AFRICAN BIBLIOGRAPHY.                    XXX
*+ +INT. AFR. BIBLIOGR.*
INTERNATIONAL AFRICAN INSTITUTE.
*LONDON 1(1), JA 1971-*
Q. ENGL. & FR. PREV. PART OF: AFRICA.
*CA/U-1.   ED/N-1.   LD/U-1.   LO/N-1.   LO/N-2.   LO/S10.*
*LO/U-1.   LO/U-3.   LO/U-8.   NO/U-1.   OX/U-9   XY/N-1.*
*CB/U-1.  4, 1974-*
*ISSN 0020-5877*

INTERNATIONAL AIR-EQUIPMENT NEWS.
*+ +INT. AIR EQUIP. NEWS.*
[INFORMATION SERVICE PUBL.]
*LONDON 1, D 1967-*
2M.
*LO/P-7.  3, AP 1968.*
*ISSN 0538-4222*

INTERNATIONAL ANARCHISM.
*+ +INT. ANARCHISM.*
*LUND, E. YORKS. 1(1), MY 1969-*
M.
*ED/N-1.   OX/U-1.*

INTERNATIONAL ANNALS OF CRIMINOLOGY.                   000
SEE: ANNALES INTERNATIONALES DE CRIMINOLOGIE.

INTERNATIONAL ARCHIVES OF ETHNOGRAPHY.                 000
SEE: TROPICAL MAN.

INTERNATIONALES ASIEN FORUM.
*+ +INT. ASIEN FORUM.*
[WELTFORUM]
*MUNICH NO.1, 1970-*
*LO/U14.   OX/U-1.*
*ISSN 0020-9449*

INTERNATIONAL BAR JOURNAL.                             XXX
*+ +INT. BAR J.*
INTERNATIONAL BAR ASSOCIATION.
*LONDON &C. NO.1, JE 1970-*
PREV: INTERNATIONAL BAR NEWS FROM 1958.
*ED/N-1.  2, N 1970-           MA/U-1. AP 1971-*
*ISSN 0047-0589*

INTERNATIONAL BEHAVIOURAL SCIENTIST.
*+ +INT. BEHAV. SCI.*
DELTA TAU KAPPA.
*MEERUT 1(1), MR 1969-*
Q.
*LO/N-1.*
*ISSN 0020-613X*

INTERNATIONALE BIBLIOGRAPHIE DER ANTIQUARIATS-
AUKTIONS- UND KUNSTKATALOGE. (IBAK)
*+ +INT. BIBLIOGR. ANTIQ. AUKT. & KUNSTKAT.*
KARL MARX-UNIVERSITAT (LEIPZIG); BIBLIOTHEK.
*LEIPZIG [BD.1] 1960/61 (1965)-*
PUBL. BY 'UNIVERSITATSBIBLIOTHEK LEIPZIG'.
ALSO KNOWN AS 'IBAK'.
*BH/U-1.*

INTERNATIONAL BIBLIOGRAPHY, INFORMATION,
DOCUMENTATION.
*+ +INT. BIBLIOGR. INF. DOC.*
[BOWKER CO. & UNIPUB]
*NEW YORK 1, MR 1973-*
Q.
*AD/U-1.   ED/N-1.   GL/U-1.   GL/U-2.   HL/U-1.   LO/N14.*
*LO/U-1.   NO/U-1.   OX/U-1.   SW/U-1.*
*SH/P-1.  1974-*

INTERNATIONAL BREWERS' JOURNAL.                        XXX
*+ +INT. BREW. J.*
[W.REED]
*LONDON 104(1228), JA 1968- 106(1263), 1970.*
PREV: BREWERS' JOURNAL (LONDON) FROM 1, 1865.
SUBS: INTERNATIONAL BREWING & DISTILLING.
*LO/N14.*

INTERNATIONAL BREWING & DISTILLING.                    XXX
*+ +INT. BREW. & DISTILL.*
[W. REED]
*LONDON 1, 1971- 3, 1973 ...*
PREV: INTERNATIONAL BREWERS' JOURNAL.
SUBS: BREWING & DISTILLING INTERNATIONAL.
*ED/N-1.   LO/N14.   OX/U-1.*
*ISSN 0020-6210*

INTERNATIONAL BRIEFING.                                XXX
*+ +INT. BRIEF.*
LABOUR PARTY (GB).
*LONDON NO.1, 1970-*
PREV: OVERSEAS REVIEW FROM 1, 1946.
*CB/U-1.   OX/U17.   SW/U-1.*

INTERNATIONAL BULLETIN OF BACTERIOLOGICAL
NOMENCLATURE & TAXONOMY.
SUBS (1966): INTERNATIONAL JOURNAL OF SYSTEM-
ATIC BACTERIOLOGY.

INTERNATIONAL BUSINESSMEN'S WHO'S WHO.
*+ +INT. BUSINESSMEN'S WHO'S WHO.*
[BURKE'S PEERAGE LTD.]
*LONDON [NO.1], 1967-*
*LO/N17.   MA/U-1.   XS/C-2.*

INTERNATIONAL CANADA.
*+ +INT. CAN.*
CANADIAN INSTITUTE OF INTERNATIONAL AFFAIRS.
*TORONTO 1(1), MY 1970-*
*LO/S14.   OX/U-9.*
*ISSN 0027-0512*

INTERNATIONAL CATALOGUING. QUARTERLY
BULLETIN OF THE ...
*+ +INT. CAT.*
INTERNATIONAL FEDERATION OF LIBRARY ASSOCIAT-
IONS: COMMITTEE ON CATALOGUING.
*LONDON 1(1), JA/MR 1972-*
Q.
*CA/U-1.   ED/N-1.   LO/N-1.   LO/N35.   LO/U-2.   SH/U-1.*
*SO/U-1.*
*BL/U-1. 1973-*
*ISSN 0047-0635*

INTERNATIONAL CIVIL ENGINEERING MONTHLY.
*+ +INT. CIVIL ENG. M.*
[ISRAEL DISCOUNT BANK]
*TEL AVIV 1(1), JA 1969-*
*BR/U-3.   LO/N-4.   LO/N14.   LO/U12.*
*ISSN 0020-6377*

INTERNATIONAL CONCILIATION.                            XXX
SUBS (1972) INCORP. IN: FOREIGN POLICY.

INTERNATIONAL CURRENCY REVIEW.
*+ +INT. CURRENCY REV.*
*LONDON [NO.1], F 1969-*
2/M.
*BL/U-1.   CB/U-1.   EX/U-1.   LQ/U-3.*
*BN/U-1.  5, 1973-              MA/P-1.  N 1970- *
*SW/U-1.  1, 1969- 4, 1972.*
*ISSN 0020-6490*

INTERNATIONAL DIAMOND ANNUAL.                          XXX
*+ +INT. DIAMOND A.*
[DIAMOND ANNUAL (PTY) LTD.]
*JOHANNESBURG 1, 1971...*
SUBS: INTERNATIONAL DIAMONDS.
*LO/N14.*

INTERNATIONAL DIAMONDS.                                XXX
*+ +INT. DIAMONDS.*
[DIAMOND ANNUAL (PTY) LTD.]
*JOHANNESBURG NO.2, 1972-*
PREV: INTERNATIONAL DIAMOND ANNUAL FROM 1,
1971.
*LO/N14.*

INTERNATIONAL DOCUMENTS ON PALESTINE.
*+ +INT. DOC. PALEST.*
INSTITUTE FOR PALESTINE STUDIES.
*BEIRUT 1967(1970)-*
ANNU.
*MA/U-1.*

INTERNATIONAL ECUMENICAL BIBLIOGRAPHY.                 000
SEE: INTERNATIONALE OKUMENISCHE BIBLIOGRAPHIE

L

INTERNATIONAL EDUCATION YEAR 1970 BULLETIN.
++INT. EDUC. YEAR 1970 BULL.
UNESCO.
PARIS NO.1, JL/AG 1969-
M.
LO/N-3.

INTERNATIONAL FILM GUIDE.
++INT. FILM GUIDE.
[TANTIVY P.]
LONDON &C. 1964-
ANNU.
GL/U-1. 1972(1971)-          OX/U-1. 1967-
ISSN 0074-6053

INTERNATIONAL FREIGHTING WEEKLY.
++INT. FREIGHT. WKLY.
LONDON NO.1, 1970-
ED/N-1.
LO/N14. [CURRENT BOX ONLY].
ISSN 0032-5007

INTERNATIONAL HISTORICAL STATISTICS.                    000
SEE: STATISTIQUES INTERNATIONALES RETROSPEC-
TIVES.

INTERNATIONAL JOURNAL OF THE ADDICTIONS.
++INT. J. ADDICT.
INSTITUTE FOR THE STUDY OF DRUG ADDICTION.
NEW YORK 1, 1966-
LO/M17.   LO/M33.   XY/N-1.**
AD/U-1. 5, 1970-         CA/U37. 4, 1969-
LO/M27. 2(1), 1967-      LO/M32. 3, 1968-

INTERNATIONAL JOURNAL OF BIOCHEMISTRY.
++INT. J. BIOCHEM.
[SCIENTECHNICA]
BRISTOL 1, F 1970-
BH/U-1.   BL/U-1.   ED/N-1.   LO/N13.   LO/S-3.   LO/U-2.
SO/U-1.
ISSN 0020-711X

INTERNATIONAL JOURNAL OF BIO-MEDICAL COMPUTING.
++INT. J. BIO-MED. COMPUT.
[ELSEVIER]
AMSTERDAM 1, JA 1970-
Q.
AD/U-1.   CR/M-1.   DN/U-1.   ED/N-1.   GL/U-1.   LO/N13.
LO/U-2.   OX/U-8.   SH/U-1.   SO/U-1.
LO/U28. 2, 1971-
ISSN 0020-7101

INTERNATIONAL JOURNAL OF CHEMICAL KINETICS.
++INT. J. CHEM. KINET.
[INTERSCIENCE PUBL.]
EASTON (P.A.) 1, JA 1969-
AD/U-1.   BH/U-1.   CC/U-1.   HL/U-1.   LA/U-1.   LO/N14.
LO/S-3.   LO/U-2.   MA/U-4.   OX/U-8.   RE/U-1.   SF/U-1.
SH/U-1.   SW/U-1.
LD/U-1. 2, 1970-         LO/U12. 6(1), 1974-
XS/R10. 5(1), 1973-

INTERNATIONAL JOURNAL OF CHRONOBIOLOGY.
++INT. J. CHRONOBIOL.
[WILEY-INTERSCIENCE]
LONDON 1(1), 1973-
Q.
CA/U-1.   CA/U-2.   ED/N-1.   LO/N-2.   MA/U-1.   OX/U-8.
ISSN 0300-9998

INTERNATIONAL JOURNAL OF CIRCUIT THEORY &
APPLICATIONS.
++INT. J. CIRCUIT THEORY & APPL.
[WILEY]
LONDON 1(1), MR 1973-
BL/U-1.   CA/U-1.   ED/N-1.   GL/U-2.   HL/U-1.   LD/U-1.
LO/N14.   LO/N35.   OX/U-8.   RE/U-1.   SF/U-1.   SO/U-1.
SW/U-1.

INTERNATIONAL JOURNAL OF COMPUTER & INFORMATION
SCIENCES.
++INT. J. COMPUT. & INF. SCI.
[PLENUM]
NEW YORK; LONDON 1, 1972-
LO/N14.
CA/U-1. 3, 1974-         ED/N-1. 3, 1974-

INTERNATIONAL JOURNAL OF CRIMINOLOGY & PENOLOGY.
++INT. J. CRIMINOL. & PENOL.
[SEMINAR P.]
NEW YORK 1, 1973-
Q.
AD/U-1.   CA/U-1.   ED/N-1.   EX/U-1.   HL/U-1.   LO/U-3.
OX/U15.   SH/U-1.   SW/U-1.
ISSN 0306-3208

INTERNATIONAL JOURNAL OF DRAVIDIAN LINGUISTICS.
++INT. J. DRAVIDIAN LINGUIST.
UNIVERSITY OF KERALA: DEPARTMENT OF LINGUISTICS
TRIVANDRUM 1, 1972-
2/A.
LO/N12.   OX/U13.

INTERNATIONAL JOURNAL OF EARLY CHILDHOOD.
++INT. J. EARLY CHILDHOOD.
WORLD ORGANISATION FOR EARLY CHILDHOOD
EDUCATION.
OSLO 1, 1969-
DB/U-2.
CA/U-1. 4, 1972-         CO/U-1. 4, 1972-
ED/N-1. 4, 1972-         EX/U-1. 4, 1972-
SH/U-1. 4, 1972-
ISSN 0020-7187

INTERNATIONAL JOURNAL OF EARTHQUAKE ENGINEER-
ING & STRUCTURAL DYNAMICS.
++INT. J. EARTHQUAKE ENG. & STRUCT. DYN.
INTERNATIONAL ASSOCIATION FOR EARTHQUAKE
ENGINEERING.
[WILEY]
CHICHESTER 1(1), JL/S 1972-
Q.
BR/U-1.   SH/U-1.   SH/U-3.

INTERNATIONAL JOURNAL OF ECONOMIC & SOCIAL
HISTORY.                                               000
SEE: CAHIERS INTERNATIONAUX D'HISTOIRE ECON-
OMIQUE ET SOCIALE.

INTERNATIONAL JOURNAL OF ENVIRONMENTAL
ANALYTICAL CHEMISTRY.
++INT. J. ENVIRON. ANAL. CHEM.
[GORDON & BREACH]
LONDON 1, 1971-
LO/N14.   LO/U28.   SW/U-1.
ED/N-1. 1(3), 1972-

INTERNATIONAL JOURNAL OF ENVIRONMENTAL STUDIES.
++INT. J. ENVIRON. STUD.
[GORDON & BREACH]
LONDON 1(1), OC 1970-
LO/N-2.   LO/N13.   LO/R-5.   LO/U28.   OX/U-1.   XS/R10.
GL/U-2. 1971-              SH/C-5. 2, 1971-
ISSN 0020-7233

INTERNATIONAL JOURNAL OF EPIDEMIOLOGY.
++INT. J. EPIDEMIOL.
OXFORD 1, 1972-
AD/M-1.   BL/U-1.   CA/U-1.   ED/N-1.   LD/U-1.   OX/U-8.
SH/U-1.
ISSN 0300-5771

INTERNATIONAL JOURNAL OF FARM BUILDING RESEARCH.
++INT. J. FARM BUILD. RES.
[FARM JOURNALS LTD]
LONDON 1, JL 1966-
DB/U-2.   ED/N-1.   LO/N14.
ISSN 0020-7241

INTERNATIONAL JOURNAL OF FRACTURE.                     XXX
++INT. J. FRACT.
[NOORDHOFF]
LEIDEN 9, 1973-
PREV: INTERNATIONAL JOURNAL OF FRACTURE
MECHANICS FROM 1, 1965- 8, 1972.
BR/U-1.   GL/U-1.   LO/N14.   XS/R10.
AD/U-2. 10, 1974-

INTERNATIONAL JOURNAL OF GAME THEORY.
++INT. J. GAME THEORY.
INSTITUTE FOR ADVANCED STUDIES (VIENNA).
[PHYSICA-VERLAG]
VIENNA 1(1), 1971-
Q.
CA/U-1.   CA/U-2.   LO/N-4.   LO/N14.   NO/U-1.   OX/U-8.
SH/U-1.
ISSN 0020-7276

INTERNATIONAL JOURNAL OF HEALTH SERVICES.
++INT. J. HEALTH SERV.
[GREENWOOD PERS. INC.]
WESTPORT, CONN. 1, F 1971-
Q. S/T: PLANNING, ADMINISTRATION, EVALUATION.
AD/U-1.   SW/U-1.
ISSN 0020-7314

INTERNATIONAL JOURNAL OF INSECT MORPHOLOGY
& EMBRYOLOGY.
++INT. J. INSECT MORPHOL. & EMBRYOL.
[PERGAMON P.]
OXFORD &C. 1, 1971-
ED/N-1.   LO/N13.   MA/U-1.   OX/U-8.   SH/U-1.   XY/N-1.
ISSN 0020-7322

INTERNATIONAL JOURNAL OF LAW LIBRARIES.   XXX
++INT. J. LAW LIBR.
INTERNATIONAL ASSOCIATION OF LAW LIBRARIES.
 KARLSRUHE 1(1), 1973-
 3/A. PREV: BULLETIN, INTERNATIONAL ASSOCIATION
 OF LAW LIBRARIES FROM 1, 1960- 30, 1972.
 BL/U-1.   LO/U-3.   LO/U11.   LO/U14.   OX/U15.
 SH/U-1.
 SO/U-1.

INTERNATIONAL JOURNAL OF MAGNETISM.
++INT. J. MAGN.
[GORDON & BREACH]
 LONDON; NEW YORK 1, OC 1970-
 Q.
 CA/U-1.   ED/N-1.   LO/N14.   OX/U-8.   SF/U-1.   SH/U-1.
 SO/U-1.   XS/R10.
 MA/U-1. 3, 1972-
 ISSN 0020-7365

INTERNATIONAL JOURNAL OF MAN-MACHINE STUDIES.
++INT. J. MAN-MACH. STUD.
[ACADEMIC PRESS]
 LONDON 1, 1969-
 CB/U-1.   DB/U-2.   ED/N-1.   EX/U-1.   GL/U-1.   LD/U-1.
 LO/N-4.   LO/N14.   OX/U-8.   SW/U-1.
 BL/U-1. 6, 1974-   RE/U-1. 2, 1970-
 ISSN 0020-7573

INTERNATIONAL JOURNAL OF MASS SPECTROMETRY &
ION PHYSICS.
++INT. J. MASS SPECTROM. & ION PHYS.
[ELSEVIER]
 AMSTERDAM 1, 1968-
 BL/U-1. *   GL/U-1.   LO/N14.   LO/S-3.   LV/U-1.
 SH/U-1.   SO/U-1.
 ISSN 0020-7381

INTERNATIONAL JOURNAL OF MATHEMATICAL EDUCATION
IN SCIENCE & TECHNOLOGY.
++INT. J. MATH. EDUC. SCI. & TECHNOL.
[WILEY]
 CHICHESTER 1(1), JA/MR 1970-
 AD/U-1.   BH/U-3.   CB/U-1.   CV/U-1.   DB/U-2.   ED/N-1.
 HL/U-1.   LB/U-1.   LO/N-4.   LO/N14.   LO/U12.   LO/U13.
 LO/U21.   OX/U-1.   SH/C-5.   SH/U-1.   XY/N-1.
 ISSN 0020-739X

INTERNATIONAL JOURNAL OF MIDDLE EAST STUDIES.
++INT. J. MIDDLE EAST STUD.
[CAMBRIDGE UNIV. P.]
 LONDON 1, 1970-
 Q.
 DB/U-2.   ED/N-1.   EX/U-1.   LO/N-1.   LO/N17.   LO/S-7.
 LO/U-3.   LO/U14.   MA/U-1.   OX/U-1.
 ISSN 0020-7438

INTERNATIONAL JOURNAL OF NAUTICAL ARCHAEOLOGY
& UNDERWATER EXPLORATION.
++INT. J. NAUT. ARCHAEOL. & UNDERWATER EXPLOR.
COUNCIL FOR NAUTICAL ARCHAEOLOGY.
 LONDON 1, 1972-
 ANNU.
 BL/U-1.   CA/U-1.   CA/U-3.   CR/N-1.   ED/N-1.   SH/U-1.
 SH/P-1. 1974-
 ISSN 0305-7445

INTERNATIONAL JOURNAL OF NEURO-PHARMACOLOGY.   XXX
++INT. J. NEURO-PHARMACOL. [IJNE-A]
[PERGAMON PRESS]
 OXFORD &C 1, N 1962-8, 1969...
 Q. PRELIM ISSUE, NUMBERED 0(0). SUBS:
NEUROPHARMACOLOGY.
 AD/U-1.   CA/M-5.   GL/U-1.   LD/U-1.   LO/M25.   LO/U-2.
 OX/U-8.   SO/U-1.   XS/F16.
 ED/U-1. 6,1967-

INTERNATIONAL JOURNAL OF NEUROSCIENCE.
++INT. J. NEUROSCI.
[GORDON & BREACH]
 LONDON; NEW YORK 1(1), OC 1970-
 2M.
 AD/U-1.   LO/U-2.   OX/U-8.
 ED/N-1. 1(2), D 1970-
 ISSN 0020-7454

INTERNATIONAL JOURNAL OF NONDESTRUCTIVE TEST-
ING.
++INT. J. NONDESTRUCT. TEST.
[GORDON & BREACH]
 NEW YORK 1(1), JE 1969-
 ED/N-1.   LO/N-4.   LO/N14.   OX/U-8.   XS/R10.
 BL/U-1 2, 1970-
 ISSN 0020-7470

INTERNATIONAL JOURNAL OF NUCLEAR MEDICINE &
BIOLOGY.
++INT. J. NUCL. MED. & BIOL.
[PERGAMON]
 NEW YORK & OXFORD 1(1), JA 1973-
 MON.
 CA/M-7.   CA/U-1.   ED/N-1.   OX/U-8.   XS/R10.
 ISSN 0047-0740

INTERNATIONAL JOURNAL FOR NUMERICAL METHODS
IN ENGINEERING.
++INT. J. NUMER. METH. ENG.
[WILEY]
 CHICHESTER 1, 1969-
 BL/U-1.   BR/U-3.   CA/U-1.   DB/U-2.   GL/U-1.   GL/U-2.
 LO/N-4.   LO/N14.   LV/U-1.   OX/U-8.   RE/U-1.
 MA/U-1. 2, 1970-   NW/U-1. 2, 1970-
 ISSN 0029-5981

INTERNATIONAL JOURNAL OF OCEANOGRAPHY &
LIMNOLOGY.
++INT. J. OCEANOGR. & LIMNOL.
[OMNIPRESS]
 HADDONFIELD, NJ 1, JA 1967-
 Q.
 SO/U-1.
 LO/N-2. 1(1-4), 1967.

INTERNATIONAL JOURNAL OF OFFENDER THERAPY.   XXX
 SUBS (1972): INTERNATIONAL JOURNAL OF
 OFFENDER THERAPY & COMPARATIVE CRIMINOLOGY.

INTERNATIONAL JOURNAL OF OFFENDER THERAPY &
COMPARATIVE CRIMINOLOGY.   XXX
++INT. J. OFFENDER THER. & COMP. CRIMINOL.
ASSOCIATION FOR PSYCHIATRIC TREATMENT OF
OFFENDERS.
 LONDON 16, 1972-
 3/A. PREV: INTERNATIONAL JOURNAL OF OFFENDER
 THERAPY FROM 1, 1957- 15, 1971.
 ED/N-1.

INTERNATIONAL JOURNAL OF ORAL SURGERY.
++INT. J. ORAL SURG.
INTERNATIONAL ASSOCIATION OF ORAL SURGEONS.
[MUNKSGAARD]
 COPENHAGEN 1, 1972-
 2M.
 AD/U-1.   GL/U-1.   LD/U-1.   OX/U-8.   SH/U-1.
 CA/U-1. 3, 1974-

INTERNATIONAL JOURNAL OF PARASITOLOGY.
++INT. J. PARASITOL.
AUSTRALIAN SOCIETY FOR PARASITOLOGY.
[PERGAMON]
 OXFORD 1(1), MY 1971-
 Q.
 BL/U-1.   BN/U-2.   GL/U-1.   LO/M12.   LO/N-1.   LO/N-2.
 LO/N13.   LO/U28.   SH/U-1.   XY/N-1.
 HL/U-1. 4, 1974-
 BH/U-1. 1, 1971/72.
 NW/U-1. [W. 1(2-4), 1971]
 ISSN 0020-7519

INTERNATIONAL JOURNAL OF PEPTIDE & PROTEIN
RESEARCH.   XXX
++INT. J. PEPTIDE & PROTEIN RES.
[MUNKSGAARD]
 COPENHAGEN 4(2), 1972-
 PREV: INTERNATIONAL JOURNAL OF PROTEIN RE-
 SEARCH FROM 1(1), JA 1969- 4(1), 1972.
 GL/U-1.   LD/U-1.   LO/N-4.   LO/N11.   LO/N13.   LO/S-3.
 BL/U-1. 5, 1973-
 ISSN 0020-7551

INTERNATIONAL JOURNAL FOR THE PHILOSOPHY OF
RELIGION.
++INT. J. PHIL. RELIG.
[NIJHOFF]
 THE HAGUE 1(1), MR 1970-
 Q.
 BH/P-1.   DB/U-2.   DR/U-1.   EX/U-1.   HL/U-1.   LO/U-1.
 LO/U14.   OX/U-1.
 ISSN 0020-7047

INTERNATIONAL JOURNAL OF PHYSICAL DISTRIBUTION.
++INT. J. PHYS. DISTRIB.
[IPC TRANSPORT P.]
 LONDON 1, OC 1970-
 ENGL., GER. OR FR. SUMM.
 DB/U-2.   ED/N-1.   MA/P-1.   OX/U-1.
 BH/U-3. 3, 1972/73-   NO/U-1. 3, 1973-
 ISSN 0020-7527

INTERNATIONAL JOURNAL OF POLITICS.
++INT. J. POLIT.
[INTERNATIONAL ARTS & SCIENCES P.]
WHITE PLAINS, N.Y. 1(1), 1971-
Q. S/T: A JOURNAL OF TRANSLATIONS.
LO/U-3. OX/U-1. XY/N-1.
ISSN 0013-8783

INTERNATIONAL JOURNAL OF POLYMERIC MATERIALS.
++INT. J. POLYM. MAT.
[GORDON & BREACH]
NEW YORK 1(1), S 1971-
Q.
LO/N14. LO/N35. LO/U12. XY/N-1.
CA/U-1. 1972- ED/N-1. 1(2), 1972-
LD/U-1. 1(2), 1972-

INTERNATIONAL JOURNAL OF PRESSURE VESSELS &
PIPING.                                                          000
  SEE: PRESSURE VESSELS & PIPING.

INTERNATIONAL JOURNAL OF PROTEIN RESEARCH.        XXX
++INT. J. PROT. RES.
[MUNKSGAARD]
COPENHAGEN 1(1), JA 1969- 4(1), 1972 ...
SUBS: INTERNATIONAL JOURNAL OF PEPTIDE &
PROTEIN RESEARCH.
BH/U-1. CR/U-1. GL/U-1. GL/U-2. LO/N-4. LO/S-3.
LO/U-2. LO/U11. LV/U-1. NW/U-1. OX/U-8.
CB/U-1. 2, 1970-

INTERNATIONAL JOURNAL OF PSYCHOBIOLOGY.
++INT. J. PSYCHOBIOL.
[GREENWOOD]
WESTPORT, CONN. 1, JA 1970- 2, 1972.//
Q.
HL/U-1.** LO/N13. LO/U-1. SH/U-1.
ISSN 0020-7586

INTERNATIONAL JOURNAL FOR RADIATION PHYSICS
& CHEMISTRY.
++INT. J. RADIAT. PHYS. CHEM.
[PERGAMON PRESS]
OXFORD &C. 1(1), JA 1969-
ENGL., FR., GER., RUSS.
BH/U-1. DB/U-1. DB/U-2. LO/N14. LO/S-3. LO/U12.
OX/U-8. XS/R10.
ED/N-1. 1(2), 1969- LD/U-1. 5, 1973-
ISSN 0020-7055

INTERNATIONAL JOURNAL OF SOCIOLOGY.
++INT. J. SOCIOL.
[INTERNATIONAL ARTS & SCIENCES P.]
NEW YORK 1, 1971-
Q. S/T: A JOURNAL OF TRANSLATIONS.
GL/U-2. MA/U-1. OX/U-1. XY/N-1.
ISSN 0020-7659

INTERNATIONAL JOURNAL OF SOCIOLOGY OF THE FAMILY
++INT. J. SOCIOL. FAM.
[LUCKNOW PUBL. HOUSE]
MYSORE &C. 1(1), MR 1971-
2/A.
EX/U-1. MA/U-1.
ISSN 0020-7667

INTERNATIONAL JOURNAL OF SULFUR CHEMISTRY:
PART A: ORIGINAL EXPERIMENTAL & THEORETICAL
STUDIES.
++INT. J. SULFUR CHEM., A.
INTRA-SCIENCE RESEARCH FOUNDATION.
[GORDON & BREACH]
LONDON 1, 1971-
CA/U-1. ED/N-1. LO/N14. LO/S-3. LO/U28. SF/U-1.
HL/U-1. 2, 1971-
ISSN 0094-9337

INTERNATIONAL JOURNAL OF SULFUR CHEMISTRY:
PART B: QUARTERLY REPORTS ON SULFUR CHEMISTRY.
++INT. J. SULFUR CHEM., B.
INTRA-SCIENCE RESEARCH FOUNDATION.
SANTA MONICA 6, 1971-
PREV: QUARTERLY REPORTS ON SULFUR CHEMISTRY
FROM 1, MR 1966- 5, 1970.
CA/U-1. HL/U-1. LO/S-3. LO/U11.
ISSN 0094-9345

INTERNATIONAL JOURNAL OF SULFUR CHEMISTRY:
PART C: MECHANISMS OF REACTIONS OF SULFUR
COMPOUNDS.                                                      XXX
++INT. J. SULFUR CHEM., C.
INTRA-SCIENCE RESEARCH FOUNDATION.
[GORDON & BREACH]
SANTA MONICA 6, 1971-
PREV: MECHANISMS OF REACTIONS OF SULFUR COM-
POUNDS FROM 1, 1966- 5, 1970.
ED/N-1. LO/S-3. LO/U11. LO/U28. SF/U-1.
HL/U-1. 7, 1971-
ISSN 0094-9353

INTERNATIONAL JOURNAL OF SYSTEMATIC BACTERIO-
LOGY.
++INT. J. SYST. BACTERIOL.
INTERNATIONAL COMMITTEE ON BACTERIOLOGICAL
NOMENCLATURE; JUDICIAL COMMISSION.
[IOWA STATE UNIV. PRESS]
AMES, IOWA 16, 1966-
COMMITTEE SUBORD. TO: INTERNATIONAL ASSOCIA-
TION OF MICROBIOLOGICAL SOCIETIES. PREV:
INTERNATIONAL BULLETIN OF BACTERIOLOGICAL
NOMENCLATURE & TAXONOMY., FROM 1, 1951.
BL/U-1. GL/U-2. LO/N-2. LO/N13. SW/U-1. XS/T11.
ISSN 0020-7713

INTERNATIONAL JOURNAL OF SYSTEMS SCIENCE.
++INT. J. SYST. SCI.
LONDON 1, JL 1970-
DB/U-2. ED/N-1. GL/U-1. HL/U-1. LO/N-4. LO/N14.
MA/U-1. NW/U-1. OX/U-8. SF/U-1. SH/U-3.
CA/U-4. 5, 1974-
SO/U-1. 1, JL 1970- 2(3), N 1971.
ISSN 0020-7721

INTERNATIONAL JOURNAL OF THEORETICAL PHYSICS.
++INT. J. THEOR. PHYS.
[PLENUM PRESS]
LONDON &C 1(1), MY 1968-
BH/U-1. ED/N-1. LO/N14. LO/U-4. LO/U11. SO/U-1.
SW/U-1. XS/R10.
LD/U-1. 2(2), 1969-
MA/U-1. [W. 8(3)].
ISSN 0020-7748

INTERNATIONAL JOURNAL FOR VITAMIN & NUTRITION
RESEARCH.                                                       XXX
++INT. J. VITAM. & NUTR. RES.
[HANS HUBER]
BERN &C. 41, 1971-
PREV: INTERNATIONALE ZEITSCHRIFT FUR VITAMIN-
FORSCHUNG FROM 19, 1947- 40, 1970.
LO/N-4. LO/N13.

INTERNATIONALE KATHOLISCHE ZEITSCHRIFT.
++INT. KATHOL. Z.
FRANKFURT AM MAIN 1, JA/F 1972-
LO/N-1. OX/U-1.

INTERNATIONAL LABORATORY.
++INT. LAB.
[INTERNATIONAL SCIENTIFIC COMMUNICATIONS]
GREENS FARMS, CONN. 1971-
2M.
SH/U-1. *
LO/N14. S/OC 1974- LO/R-6. J/F 1973-
XS/R10. JA/F 1973-
ISSN 0010-2164

INTERNATIONAL LAWYER.
++INT. LAWYER.
AMERICAN BAR ASSOCIATION: SECTION OF INTERNAT-
IONAL & COMPARATIVE LAW.
CHICAGO 1(1), 1966-
OX/U15.
ISSN 0020-7810

INTERNATIONAL LIBRARY REVIEW.
++INT. LIBR. REV.
[ACADEMIC PRESS]
NEW YORK &C. 1, 1969-
BL/U-1. CR/U-1. GL/U-1. LO/N-1. LO/N-3. LO/N14.
LO/U-2. LO/U-3. LO/U14. MA/P-1. OX/U-1. SH/U-1.
ED/N-1. 2, 1970- NW/U-1. 2, 1970-
ISSN 0020-7837

INTERNATIONAL LOGIC REVIEW. RASSEGNA INTER-
NATIONALE DI LOGICA.
++INT. LOGIC REV.
BOLOGNA NO.1, MY 1970-
2/A.
LO/U-1.
SO/U-1. NO.1, 1970- 3, 1971; NO.5, 1972.
ISSN 0048-6779

INTERNATIONAL MEDICAL DIGEST.                                   XXX
  SUBS (1970): NOTES & TIPS.

**INTERNATIONAL MEDICAL TRIBUNE OF GREAT BRITAIN.**
+ +INT. MED. TRIB. G.B.
LONDON  1, 7/AP 1966-
W.
ED/N-1.
LO/M-3.  THREE MONTH FILE.
ISSN 0020-7942

**INTERNATIONAL METALLURGICAL REVIEWS.**                    XXX
INSTITUTE OF METALS.
LONDON  17, MR 1972-
PREV: METALLURGICAL REVIEWS, INCORP. IN METALS
& MATERIALS FROM 1967- 1971.
BR/U-3.   ED/N-1.   LO/N-4.   LO/N14.   MA/U-1.   NW/U-1.
XS/R10.

**INTERNATIONAL MICROFILM JOURNAL OF LEGAL
MEDICINE.**
+ +INT. MICROF. J. LEGAL MED.
NEW YORK  1, FALL 1965-
XY/N-1.

**INTERNATIONAL NEUROSCIENCES ABSTRACTS.**
+ +INT. NEUROSCI. ABSTR.
NORTH HOLLYWOOD, CALIF.  1, JA 1969-
LO/N13.   LO/U-2.
ISSN 0020-8078

**INTERNATIONAL NEWSLETTER ON PLANT PATHOLOGY.**
+ +INT. NEWSL. PLANT PATHOL.
INTERNATIONAL SOCIETY FOR PLANT PATHOLOGY.
WAGENINGEN  1, 1970-
2/A.
LO/N-6.   LO/U12.
LO/R-6.  2(2), 1972-

**INTERNATIONAL NEWSLETTER, SOCIETY FOR RE-
SEARCH INTO HIGHER EDUCATION.**
+ +INT. NEWSL. SOC. RES. HIGHER EDUC.
LONDON NO.1, 1972-
GL/U-2.

**INTERNATIONAL NUCLEAR INFORMATION SYSTEM REF-
ERENCE SERIES.**
+ +INT. NUCL. INF. SYST. REF. SER.
INTERNATIONAL ATOMIC ENERGY AGENCY.
VIENNA  IAEA-INIS-1, 1969-
LO/N-4.

**INTERNATIONALE OKUMENISCHE BIBLIOGRAPHIE. =
INTERNATIONAL ECUMENICAL BIBLIOGRAPHY = BIBLIO-
GRAPHIE OECUMENIQUE INTERNATIONALE.**
+ +INT. OKUMENISCHE BIBLIOGR.
[MATTHIAS-GRUENEWALD]
MAINZ &C.  1/2, 1962/63-
SA/U-1.
BL/U-1.  3/4, 1970-                    OX/U-1.  1967-

**INTERNATIONAL PAINTING & DECORATING JOURNAL.**      XXX
+ +INT. PAINT. & DECOR. J.
[SUTHERLAND PUBL. CO.]
SOUTHPORT  93(1104), 1973-
PREV: PAINTING & DECORATING JOURNAL FROM
89(1059), 1969- 92(1103), 1972.
LO/N14.

**INTERNATIONAL PERSPECTIVES.**                         XXX
+ +INT. PERSPECT.
(CANADA) DEPARTMENT OF EXTERNAL AFFAIRS.
OTTAWA  [NO.1], JA/F 1972-
PREV: EXTERNAL AFFAIRS 1, JA 1949- 23(12),
D 1971.
CA/U-1.   ED/N-1.   GL/U-1.   LO/U-1.   LO/U-3.   LO/U-8.

**INTERNATIONAL PETROLEUM ABSTRACTS.**                  XXX
+ +INT. PET. ABSTR.
INSTITUTE OF PETROLEUM.
[APPLIED SCIENCE PUBL.]
LONDON  1(1), MR 1973-
PREV: ABSTRACTS, INSTITUTE OF PETROLEUM FROM
MR 1969- 1972.
AD/U-2.   CA/U-1.   ED/N-1.   GL/U-1.   LO/N-4.   LO/N14.
MA/P-1.   MA/U-1.   OX/U-8.   RE/U-1.   SF/U-1.

**INTERNATIONAL PHARMACOPSYCHIATRY: TOPICAL
PROBLEMS.**
+ +INT. PHARMACOPSYCHIAT.
[KARGER]
BASLE  1, 1968-
LO/U-2.   SH/U-1.
ISSN 0020-8272

**INTERNATIONAL PROSPECT. JOURNAL OF WORLD SERVICE**
+ +INT. PROSPECT.
CANTERBURY  NO.1, OC/D 1969-
2M.
ED/N-1.   LO/N17.
ISSN 0020-8418

**INTERNATIONAL REVIEW OF THE AESTHETICS &
SOCIOLOGY OF MUSIC.**                                   XXX
+ +INT. REV. AESTHET. & SOCIOL. MUSIC.
ZAGREB MUSIC ACADEMY: INSTITUTE OF MUSICOLOGY.
ZAGREB  2(1), 1971-
PREV: INTERNATIONAL REVIEW OF MUSIC AESTHETICS
& SOCIOLOGY FROM 1, 1970.
ED/N-1.   LO/U-1.   LO/U13.
SH/U-1.  3, 1972-

**INTERNATIONAL REVIEW OF CYTOLOGY: SUPPLEMENT.**
+ +INT. REV. CYTOL., SUPPL.
[ACADEMIC P.]
NEW YORK; LONDON  [NO.]1, 1969-
CA/U-3.   GL/U-1.

**INTERNATIONAL REVIEW OF EAST-WEST TRADE.**
+ +INT. REV. E.-W. TRADE.
[SYMPOSIUM P.]
WHITE PLAINS, N.Y.  1(1), AP 1970-
LA/U-1.   OX/U16.
ISSN 0020-8558

**INTERNATIONAL REVIEW OF THE HISTORY OF
BANKING.**                                              000
SEE:  REVUE INTERNATIONALE D'HISTOIRE DE LA
BANQUE.

**INTERNATIONAL REVIEW OF INDUSTRIAL PROPERTY &
COPYRIGHT LAW.**                                        XXX
+ +INT. REV. IND. PROP. & COPYR. LAW.
MAX-PLANCK-INSTITUT FUR AUSLANDISCHES UND
INTERNATIONALES PATENT- URHEBER-UND
WETTBEWERBSRECHT.
[VERLAG CHEMIE]
WEINHEIM/BERGSTR.  1, 1970-
LO/N-5.   LO/N14.
LO/U-2.  5, 1974-                    SO/U-1.  5, 1974-
ISSN 0018-9855

**INTERNATIONAL REVIEW OF MUSIC AESTHETICS &
SOCIOLOGY.**
+ +INT. REV. MUSIC AESTHET. & SOCIOL.
ZAGREB MUSIC ACADEMY: INSTITUTE OF MUSICOLOGY.
ZAGREB  1, 1970-
2/A.
DB/U-2.   ED/N-1.   HL/U-1.   LO/U13.   NW/U-1.   OX/U-1.
ISSN 0047-1208

**INTERNATIONAL REVIEW OF SOCIOLOGY.**
+ +INT. REV. SOCIOL.
[LUCKNOW PUBL. HOUSE]
LUCKNOW  1(1), MR 1971-
EX/U-1.

**INTERNATIONAL ROPEWAY REVIEW.**                       XXX
SUBS (1972): LIFT.

**INTERNATIONAL SOCIAL DEVELOPMENT REVIEW.**
+ +INT. SOC. DEV. REV.
UNITED NATIONS: DEPARTMENT OF ECONOMIC &
SOCIAL AFFAIRS.
NEW YORK  NO.1, 1968-
SUPERSEDES THE DEP.'S: HOUSING, BUILDING &
PLANNING; POPULATION BULLETIN OF THE UNITED
NATIONS; INTERNATIONAL SOCIAL SERVICE REVIEW.
LO/N17.   LO/U-3.   LO/U-8.   MU/P-1.   OX/U16.
OX/U21.   RE/U-1.   LV/U-1.

**INTERNATIONAL SOCIAL SECURITY REVIEW.**
+ +INT. SOC. SECUR. REV.
INTERNATIONAL SOCIAL SECURITY ASSOCIATION.
GENEVA  YEAR 20, 1967-
PREV: BULLETIN OF THE INTERNATIONAL SOCIAL
SECURITY ASSOCIATION., YEAR 1, 1948- 19, 1966.
BH/U-1.   HL/U-1.   LO/U-3.
ISSN 0020-871X

**INTERNATIONAL SOCIAL SERVICE REVIEW.**               XXX
SUBS (1968) PART OF: INTERNATIONAL SOCIAL
DEVELOPMENT REVIEW.

**INTERNATIONAL STATISTICAL REVIEW.  REVUE INT-
ERNATIONALE DE STATISTIQUE.**                           XXX
+ +INT. STAT. REV.
INTERNATIONAL STATISTICAL INSTITUTE.
LONDON  40, 1972-
PREV: REVIEW OF THE INTERNATIONAL STATISTICAL
INSTITUTE FROM 1, JA 1933- 39, 1971, OF WHICH
NUMBERING IS CONTINUED.
LD/U-1.   LO/N-1.   LO/N10.   RE/U-1.

**INTERNATIONAL STUDIES.**
+ +INT. STUD.
KOREAN INSTITUTE OF INTERNATIONAL STUDIES.
SEOUL  1(1), 1970-
Q.
LO/S14.

**INTERNATIONAL STUDIES IN ECONOMICS: MONOGRAPH.**
++INT. STUD. ECON., MONOGR.
IOWA STATE UNIVERSITY OF SCIENCE & TECHNOLOGY:
DEPARTMENT OF ECONOMICS & SOCIOLOGY.
  AMES  NO.1, 1966-
  OX/U-1.
  ISSN 0539-0478

**INTERNATIONAL STUDIES IN EDUCATION: MONOGRAPH.**
++INT. STUD. EDUC., MONOGR.
IOWA STATE UNIVERSITY OF SCIENCE & TECHNOLOGY.
  AMES  NO.1, 1969-
  OX/U-1.

**INTERNATIONAL STUDIES IN INDUSTRIAL DEMOCRACY.**
++INT. STUD. IND. DEMOCR.
INSTITUTE FOR WORKERS' CONTROL.
  NOTTINGHAM  NO.1 [1971]-
  LQ/N-1.

**INTERNATIONAL STUDIES OF MANAGEMENT &
ORGANIZATION.**
++INT. STUD. MANAGE. & ORGAN.
[INTERNATIONAL ARTS & SCIENCES P.]
  NEW YORK  1(1), 1971-
  Q.  S/T:  A JOURNAL OF TRANSLATIONS.
  LO/U-3.
  SH/U-1.  3, 1973-
  SW/U-1.  1, 1971- 3, 1974.
  ISSN 0020-8825

**INTERNATIONAL STUDIES IN SOCIOLOGY & SOCIAL
ANTHROPOLOGY.**
++INT. STUD. SOCIOL. & SOC. ANTHROPOL.
[BRILL]
  LEIDEN  1, 1963-
  CA/U-1.    LC/U-1.
  ISSN 0074-8684

**INTERNATIONAL SURGERY.**                    XXX
++INT. SURG. [INTS-A]
INTERNATIONAL COLLEGE OF SURGEONS.
  CHICAGO  45, 1966-
  PREV:  JOURNAL, COLLEGE ... FROM 1(3), JA
  1939- 44, 1965.
  LO/M-1.
  ISSN 0020-8868

**INTERNATIONAL SURGICAL DIGEST.**            XXX
  SUBS (1970): NOTES & TIPS.

**INTERNATIONAL TEXTILE MACHINERY.**
++INT. TEXT. MACH.
SKINNER & CO.
  MANCHESTER  S 1967-
  LO/N14.

**INTERNATIONAL TOURISM QUARTERLY.**
++INT. TOURISM Q.
ECONOMIST INTELLIGENCE UNIT.
  LONDON  NO.1, 1971-
  ED/N-1.    GL/U-2.    LO/N-1.    LO/U-3.    OX/U-1.    SH/C-5.

**INTERNATIONAL TRADE FORUM; SUPPLEMENT.**
++INT. TRADE FORUM, SUPPL.
GATT INTERNATIONAL TRADE CENTRE.
  GENEVA  1, AG 1965-
  LV/U-1.

**INTERNATIONAL UNION OF PURE & APPLIED CHEM-
ISTRY INFORMATION BULLETIN.**
++INT. U. PURE & APPL. CHEM. INF. BULL.
  OXFORD  NO.1, D 1969-
  ED/N-1.    XS/R10.
  LO/N-6.  1971-                    LO/U-1.  NO.42, 1972-

**INTERNATIONAL UROLOGY & NEPHROLOGY.**
++INT. UROL. & NEPHROL.
[AKADEMIAI KIADO]
  BUDAPEST  1, 1969-
  VOL.1 CALLED UROLOGY & NEPHROLOGY.  AN
  INTERNATIONAL QUARTERLY.
  NW/U-1.    OX/U-8.
  ISSN 0042-1162

**INTERNATIONAL YEAR FOR HUMAN RIGHTS NEWS-
LETTER.**
++INT. YEAR HUM. RIGHTS NEWSL.
UNITED NATIONS: OFFICE OF PUBLIC INFORMATION.
  NEW YORK  NO.1, JL 1967-
  ED/N-1.    MA/P-1.

**INTERNATIONAL YEARBOOK FOR CHILD PSYCHIATRY &
ALLIED DISCIPLINES.**
++INT. YEARB. CHILD PSYCHIATR. & ALLIED DISCIP.
[WILEY INTERSCIENCE]
  NEW YORK &C.  1, 1970-
  OX/U-1.
  LO/N-1.  1, 1970.

**INTERNATIONALE ZEITSCHRIFT FUR VITAMIN-
FORSCHUNG.**                                  XXX
  SUBS (1971): INTERNATIONAL JOURNAL FOR VITAMIN
  & NUTRITION RESEARCH.

**INTERNATIONALIST.**                         XXX
THIRD WORLD FIRST EDUCATIONAL TRUST.
[ADAMSON COMMUNICATIONS LTD.]
  EWELME, OXON.  NO.1, 1970- 7, N 1972.
  3/A. SUBS: NEW INTERNATIONALIST.
  ED/N-1.    LO/U-3.    LO/U14.    OX/U-1.

**INTERPERSONAL DEVELOPMENT.**
++INTERPERS. DEV.
[KARGER]
  BASLE &C.  1(1), 1970-
  Q.
  OX/U-8.
  ISSN 0047-1283

**INTERPLAY. THE MAGAZINE OF EUROPEAN/AMERICAN
AFFAIRS.**
[WELKIN CORP.]
  NEW YORK  1(1), JE/JL 1967-
  EX/U-1.    LO/N17.

**INTERPRETATION.  A JOURNAL OF POLITICAL PHIL-
OSOPHY.**
[NIJHOFF]
  THE HAGUE  1, 1970-
  EDITED AT QUEEN'S COLLEGE OF THE CITY UNIVER-
  SITY OF NEW YORK.
  DB/U-2.    ED/N-1.    HL/U-1.    LO/N-1.    LO/U-3.    MA/U-1.
  SO/U-1.    SW/U-1.
  CB/U-1.  1971-
  ISSN 0020-9635

**INTERVIROLOGY.**
INTERNATIONAL ASSOCIATION OF MICROBIOLOGICAL
SOCIETIES: VIROLOGY SECTION.
  BASLE &C.  1(1), 1973-
  BL/U-1.    LO/N13.    OX/U-8.

**INTO THE WEST COUNTRY.**
++INTO WEST CTRY.
WEST COUNTRY TOURIST BOARD.
  EXETER  NO.1, JE 1972-
  S/T: NEWS FROM THE WEST COUNTRY TOURIST BOARD.
  LO/N-1.

**INTRAMURAL LAW JOURNAL.**                   XXX
++INTRAMURAL LAW J.
QUEEN'S UNIVERSITY (KINGSTON, ONT.): FACULTY OF
LAW.
  KINGSTON, ONT.  1(1), 1968- 1(2), 1969 ...
  SUBS: QUEEN'S INTRAMURAL LAW JOURNAL.
  OX/U15.

**INTRA-SCIENCE CHEMISTRY REPORTS.**
++INTRA-SCI. CHEM. REP.
INTRA-SCIENCE RESEARCH FOUNDATION.
  SANTA MONICA, CALIF.  1(1), 1967-
  LO/N14.*    LO/S-3.    LO/U11.
  ISSN 0020-9848

**INTRODUCTIONS A LA BIOLOGIE AFRICAINE.**
++INTROD. BIOL. AFR.
UNIVERSITE D'ABIDJAN.
  ABIDJAN  1, 1968-
  LO/N-2.

**INTRODUCTIONS TO GERMAN LITERATURE.**
++INTROD. GER. LIT.
[CRESSET PRESS]
  LONDON  1, 1968-
  GL/U-1.

**INTRODUKTSIJA I AKKLIMATIZATSIJA RASTENIJ.**
++INTROD. & AKKLIM. RAST.
AKADEMIJA NAUK UZBEKSKOJ SSR: BOTANICZESKIJ
SAD.
  TASHKENT  1, 1962-
  LO/N13.  4, 1966-
  ISSN 0535-4978

**INVENTARIA ARCHAEOLOGICA.**
++INVENTARIA ARCHAEOL.
ACADEMIA REPUBLICII SOCIALISTE ROMANIA: INSTIT-
UTUL DE ARCHEOLOGIE.
BUCHAREST NO.1, 1966-
DB/S-1.
ISSN 0539-2306

**INVENTORY OF COLLECTIONS, ILLINOIS STATE
MUSEUM.**
++INVENTORY COLLECT. ILL. STATE MUS.
SPRINGFIELD, ILL. NO.1, 1969-
LO/N-2.

**INVENTORY SERIES, NATIONAL ARCHIVES (US).**
++INVENT. SER. NATL. ARCH. (US).
WASHINGTON, D.C. NO.1, 1970-
LO/U19.

**INVESTIGACION Y PROGRESO AGRICOLA.**
++INVEST. PROG. AGR. (CHILE).
INSTITUTO DE INVESTIGACIONES AGROPECUARIAS
(CHILE).
SANTIAGO DE CHILE 1, 1967-
LO/N13.

**INVESTIGACIONES AGROPECUARIAS DEL PERU.**
++INVEST. AGROPECU. PERU.
(PERU) DIRECCION GENERAL DE INVESTIGACIONES
AGROPECUARIAS.
LIMA 1, 1970-
LO/N13.

**INVESTIGACIONES MARINAS (CHILE).**
++INVEST. MAR.(CHILE).
UNIVERSIDAD CATOLICA DE VALPARAISO: DIVISION
DE INVESTIGACIONES DEL MAR.
VALPARAISO 1, 1970-
LO/N13.
ISSN 0020-997X

**INVESTIGATIONS SUPPORTED BY THE HUMAN
SCIENCES COMMITTEE.** XXX
SUBS (1967): RESEARCH SUPPORTED BY THE SSRC.

**INVESTMENT PROMOTION NEWSLETTER.**
++INVESTMENT PROMOT. NEWSL.
UNITED NATIONS: ECONOMIC COMMISSION FOR AFRICA.
ADDIS ABABA 1(1), JE 1973-
LO/S14.

**INVESTMENT SPECIAL.**
++INVEST. SPEC.
[ECOUTEL RESEARCH]
LONDON 1(1), 1967-
OX/U-1.

**INZHENERNAJA GEODEZIJA.**
++INZH. GEOD.
KYJIVS'KYJ INZHENERNO-BUDIVEL'NYJ INSTYTUT.
KIEV 1, 1965-
LO/N13. 3, 1966-
ISSN 0578-5898

**INZHENERNYJ ZHURNAL: MEKHANIKA TVERDOGO TELA.** XXX
++INZH. ZH., MEK. TVERD. TELA.
AKADEMIJA NAUK SSSR: INSTITUT MEKHANIKI.
MOSCOW 1, JA/F 1966- 1968.
PREV: INZHENERNYJ ZHURNAL FROM 1961- 1965.
SUBS: IZVESTIJA AKADEMII NAUK SSSR: MEKHANIKA
TVERDOGO TELA.
LO/N13.

**INZYNIERIA CHEMICZNA.** XXX
++INZ. CHEM.
POLSKA AKADEMIA NAUK: KOMITET HYDRO-TERMODYN-
AMIKI MASZYN I INZYNIERII CHEMICZNEJ.
WROCLAW 1, 1971-
ENGL. & RUSS. SUMM. PREV: CHEMIA STOSOWANA:
SERIA B FROM 1964- 1970.
LO/N14. LO/S-3. LO/S14.

**ION EXCHANGE & MEMBRANES.**
++ION EXCH. & MEMBR.
[GORDON & BREACH]
NEW YORK; LONDON &C. 1, 1972-
S/T: SCIENCE & TECHNOLOGY OF DYNAMIC
MACROMOLECULES.
ED/N-1. GL/U-1. LO/N14. XS/R10.
CA/U-1. 1(2), 1972-

**ION EXCHANGE & SOLVENT EXTRACTION.** XXX
++ION EXCH. & SOLVENT EXTR.
[DEKKER]
NEW YORK 3, 1973-
INCORP: SOLVENT EXTRACTION REVIEWS FROM 1(1-2)
1971; & ION EXCHANGE FROM 1, 1966- 2, 1969.
EX/U-1. GL/U-1. LO/N14. LO/S-3. LO/U-2.
OX/U-8. 1(2), 1972-

**IOWA REVIEW.**
++IOWA REV.
UNIVERSITY OF IOWA: SCHOOL OF LETTERS & THE
GRADUATE COLLEGE.
IOWA CITY 1(1), 1970-
Q.
LO/U-2. OX/U-1.
LO/N-1. 1(2), 1970-
ISSN 0021-065X

**IOWA STATE ENGINEERING RESEARCH.**
++IOWA STATE ENG. RES.
IOWA STATE UNIVERSITY OF SCIENCE & TECHNOLOGY:
ENGINEERING RESEARCH INSTITUTE.
AMES, IOWA 1, 1966-
LO/N14.

**IOWA STATE JOURNAL OF RESEARCH.** XXX
++IOWA STATE J. RES.
IOWA STATE UNIVERSITY: GRADUATE COLLEGE.
AMES, IOWA 47, 1972-
PREV: IOWA STATE JOURNAL OF SCIENCE FROM
34(1), AG 1959- 46, 1972.
LO/N-2. LO/N14.

**IOWA STATE JOURNAL OF SCIENCE.** XXX
SUBS (1972): IOWA STATE JOURNAL OF RESEARCH.

**IPW BERICHTE.**
++IPW BER.
INSTITUT FUR INTERNATIONALE POLITIK UND
WIRTSCHAFT.
BERLIN 1(1), AP 1972-
MON.
LO/S14. LO/U-3.
ISSN 0046-970X

**IR & T JOURNAL.** XXX
++IR & T J.
INTERNATIONAL RESEARCH & TECHNOLOGY CORP-
ORATION.
WASHINGTON, D.C. 1(1), S 1967- 6, JE 1968.
MON. SUBS: IR & T NUCLEAR JOURNAL.
ISSN 0538-947X

**IR & T NUCLEAR JOURNAL.** XXX
++IR & T NUCL. J.
INTERNATIONAL RESEARCH & TECHNOLOGY CORPORATION
WASHINGTON, D.C. 1, 1969-
MON. PREV: IR & T JOURNAL FROM 1(1), 1967-
6, JE 1968.
XS/R10.
ISSN 0579-5575

**IRANDOC SCIENCE & SOCIAL SCIENCE ABSTRACT
BULLETIN.**
++IRANDOC SCI. & SOC. SCI. ABSTR. BULL.
TEHRAN 1(1), 1970-
CENTRE SUBORD. TO: INSTITUTE FOR RESEARCH &
PLANNING IN SCIENCE & EDUCATION.
LO/N-4.

**IRANIAN JOURNAL OF PLANT PATHOLOGY.**
++IRAN. J. PLANT PATHOL.
PLANT PESTS & DISEASES RESEARCH INSTITUTE
(IRAN).
TEHRAN 1, 1964-
Q. FARSI WITH ENGL. SUMM.
LO/N-2. 4, 1967-
ISSN 0006-2774

**IRANIAN STUDIES.**
++IRAN. STUD.
SOCIETY FOR IRANIAN CULTURE & SOCIAL STUDIES.
NEW HAVEN, CONN. 1, 1967-
LO/U14.
ISSN 0021-0862

**IRAQI JOURNAL OF AGRICULTURAL SCIENCE.**
++IRAQI J. AGR. SCI.
UNIVERSITY OF BAGHDAD: COLLEGE OF AGRICULTURE.
ABU-GHRAIB 1, 1966-
ENGL. WITH ARABIC SUMM.
LO/N13.
LO/R-6. 2(1), 1967-

**IRELAND EAST TOURISM NEWS.**
+ +IREL. EAST TOURISM NEWS.
 DUN LAOGHAIRE, CO. DUBLIN  NO.1, [1969]-
 DB/U-2.

**IRISH ANCESTOR.**
+ +IR. ANCESTOR.
 DUBLIN  1(1), 1969-
 BL/U-1.  CO/U-1.  DB/S-1.  DB/U-2.  ED/N-1.  MA/S-1.
 ISSN 0047-1437

**IRISH ARCHIVES BULLETIN.**
+ +IR. ARCH. BULL.
 IRISH SOCIETY FOR ARCHIVES.
 DUBLIN  1(1), MY 1971-
 BL/U-1.  CO/U-1.  DB/S-1.  DB/U-2.  ED/N-1.  LD/U-1.
 LO/N-1.  LO/U-1.  OX/U-1.

**IRISH BACON NEWS.**
+ +IR. BACON NEWS.
 IRISH PIGS & BACON COMMISSION.
 DUBLIN  1, 1966/67-
 DB/U-2.
 ISSN 0047-1445

**IRISH BAKERY WORLD.**
+ +IR. BAKERY WORLD.
 [JEMMA PUBL. LTD.]
 BLACKROCK, CO. DUBLIN  1(1), AG/S 1971-
 2M.
 DB/U-2.  1(2), 1971-

**IRISH BOOKLORE.**
+ +IR. BOOKLORE.
 BELFAST  1, 1971-
 2/A.
 DB/U-2.  LO/N-1.  LO/U-3.  OX/U-1.
 ED/N-1.  1(2), 1971-  LD/U-1.  2, 1972-
 MA/U-1.  2, 1972-
 ISSN 0044-8346

**IRISH CATERING REVIEW.**
+ +IR. CATER. REV.
 DUBLIN  NO.1, MR 1969-
 DB/U-2.
 ISSN 0021-1095

**IRISH CLOTHING INDUSTRY.**
+ +IR. CLOTH. IND.
 FEDERATION OF IRISH INDUSTRIES: CLOTHING SECTOR
 DUBLIN  1, 1970-
 DB/U-2.

**IRISH COMMUNIST.**
+ +IR. COMMUNIST.
 IRISH COMMUNIST ORGANISATION.
 LONDON  NO.1, D 1965-
 MON.
 LO/U-3.
 CA/U-1.  NO.73; 77, 1972-
 ED/N-1.  NO.73, 1972-

**IRISH CO-OPERATIVE REVIEW.**
+ +IR. CO-OP. REV.
 IRISH AGRICULTURAL ORGANISATION SOCIETY LTD.
 DUBLIN  1, JA 1968-
 S/T: OFFICIAL JOURNAL OF THE IRISH AGRICUL-
 TURAL CO-OPERATIVE MOVEMENT.
 DB/S-1.  DB/U-2.

**IRISH DECIMAL MONTHLY. = MIOSACHAN DEACHUIL.**
+ +IR. DECIMAL MON.
 IRISH DECIMAL CURRENCY BOARD.
 DUBLIN  NO.1, MY 1969-
 DB/U-2.
 LO/U-3.  NO.1, MY 1969- 17, OC 1970. [W. 12]

**IRISH FARMING NEWS.**
+ +IR. FARM. NEWS.
 IRISH FARMING NEWS COOPERATIVE SOCIETY LTD.
 LIMERICK & DUBLIN  1, 1967-
 DB/U-2.
 ISSN 0021-1176

**IRISH HOSPITAL. OFFICIAL JOURNAL OF THE ...**
+ +IR. HOSP.
 INSTITUTE OF HOSPITAL ADMINISTRATORS (EIRE).
 DUBLIN  1, 1962-
 CO/U-1.

**IRISH HOUSEHOLDER & GARDENER.**
+ +IR. HOUSEHOLDER & GARD.
 [CREATION HOUSE]
 DUBLIN  1(1), AG 1972-
 MON.
 DB/U-2.  OX/U-1.

**IRISH JOURNAL OF PSYCHOLOGY.**
+ +IR. J. PSYCHOL.
 PSYCHOLOGICAL SOCIETY OF IRELAND.
 DUN LAOIRE  1, 1971-
 3/A.
 BL/U-1.  BL/U-2.  DB/S-1.  DB/U-2.  LN/U-2.  LO/N-1.
 SH/U-1.
 CA/U-1.  1(3), 1972-  ED/N-1.  1(3), 1972-
 OX/U-1.  1(3), 1972-

**IRISH JURIST: NS.**
+ +IR. JURIST, NS.
 UNIVERSITY COLLEGE, DUBLIN.
 DUBLIN  1(1), 1966-
 PREVIOUS SERIES FROM 1, AP 1935.
 CR/U-1.  DB/S-1.  HL/U-1.  MA/U-1.  SH/U-1.  SW/U-1.
 CA/U-1.  6, 1971-
 ISSN 0021-1273

**IRISH LIVESTOCK & MEAT IN THE COMMON MARKET.**
+ +IR. LIVEST. & MEAT COMMON MARK.
 IRISH LIVESTOCK & MEAT BOARD.
 DUBLIN  1, 1972-
 BL/U-1.

**IRISH MEDICAL LABORATORY TECHNOLOGIST.**
+ +IR. MED. LAB. TECHNOL.
 MEDICAL LABORATORY TECHNOLOGISTS' ASSOCIATION.
 DUBLIN  1, 1968-
 DB/U-2.

**IRISH PACKAGING & PRINTING.**
+ +IR. PACKAG. & PRINT.
 IRISH PACKAGING INSTITUTE.
 DUBLIN  1(1), 1970-
 DB/U-2.

**IRISH PHOTO NEWS & MOVIE MAKER.**
+ +IR. PHOTO NEWS & MOVIE MAK.
 DUBLIN  1, 1970-
 DB/U-2.

**IRISH SPELEOLOGY. JOURNAL OF THE ...**                    XXX
+ +IR. SPELEOL.
 IRISH SPELEOLOGICAL ASSOCIATION.
 DUBLIN  NO.3, 1969-
 PREV: JOURNAL OF THE SPELEOLOGICAL SOCIETY OF
 IRELAND FROM NO.1, 1969.
 DB/S-1.

**IRISH UNIVERSITY REVIEW.**                                XXX
+ +IR. UNIV. REV.
 SHANNON  1(1), 1970-
 PREV: UNIVERSITY REVIEW (DUBLIN) FROM 1,1954-
 5, 1968.
 AD/U-1.  DB/U-2.  OX/U-1.
 DB/S-1.  1, 1970.
 ISSN 0021-1427

**IRISH VEGETARIAN STUDIES.**
+ +IR. VEG. STUD.
 FORAS TALUNTAIS.
 DUBLIN  NO.1, 1967-
 OX/U-8.

**IRON ORE & ALLOYING METALS.**
+ +IRON ORE & ALLOY. METALS.
 COMMONWEALTH SECRETARIAT.
 LONDON  1(1), MY 1969-
 Q.
 BH/U-1.  ED/N-1.  MA/P-1.  OX/U-8.  XS/R10.

**IRON & STEEL (LONDON).**                                  XXX
 SUBS (1973): IRON & STEEL INTERNATIONAL.

**IRON & STEEL INTERNATIONAL.**                             XXX
+ +IRON & STEEL INT.
 [IPC SCIENCE & TECHNOLOGY P.]
 GUILDFORD  46(3), 1973-
 PREV: IRON & STEEL (LONDON) FROM 12(6), 1939-
 46(2), 1973.
 ED/N-1.  LO/N-4.  LO/N14.
 XS/T-4.  47(1), F 1974-

**IRONBRIDGE QUARTERLY.**
+ +IRONBRIDGE Q.
 IRONBRIDGE GORGE MUSEUM TRUST LIMITED.
 IRONBRIDGE (SHROPSHIRE)  1(1), 1971-
 ED/N-1.  LO/N-4.

**IRONWOOD.**
 [IRONWOOD P.]
 TUCSON, ARIZ.  NO.1, 1972-
 2/A.
 OX/U-1.
 ISSN 0047-150X

**IRREGULAR SERIALS & ANNUALS.**
+ +IRREGULAR SER. & ANNU.
[RR BOWKER CO.]
NEW YORK &C 1967-
S/T: AN INTERNATIONAL DIRECTORY.
LO/N-3.     LO/N14.
BT/U-1. 1967.

**IRRIGATION ENGINEERING & MAINTENANCE.** XXX
**SUBS (1967): WORLD IRRIGATION.**

**IRRIGATION FARMER.** XXX
+ +IRRIG. FARMER.
[IRRIGATION PUBL. ASSOCIATES]
HAWTHORN, VICTORIA 5, 1969- 8, 1973.
PREV: WATER IN AUSTRALIA FROM 1, 1965- 4, 1969
SUBS: IRRIGATION FARMER DIGEST.
LO/N14. [W. 7(8), 1972]
ISSN 0043-1214

**IRRIGATION JOURNAL.** XXX
+ +IRRIG. J.
[WATER WELL JOURNAL PUBL. CO.]
COLUMBUS, OHIO 1(1- 3), JA/F- MY/JE 1971;
    21(4), JL/AG 1971-
PREV: WORLD IRRIGATION FROM 17(6), OC/D 1967-
20, 1970, FROM WHICH NUMBERING IS CONT. WITH
ISSUE FOR JL/AG 1971.
LO/N14. CURRENT BOX.

**ISA INSTRUMENTATION INDEX.**
+ +ISA INSTRUM. INDEX. (INSTRUM. SOC. AM.)
INSTRUMENT SOCIETY OF AMERICA
PITTSBURGH, PA. ISSUE 1, 1967-
INDEXES ISA PUBLS. ISSUES CUMULATE A.
LO/N-4.     LO/N14.

**ISA JOURNAL.** XXX
**SUBS (1967): INSTRUMENTATION TECHNOLOGY.**

**ISAA. SOUTH AFRICAN ARCHITECTURAL RECORD.** XXX
INSTITUTE OF SOUTH AFRICAN ARCHITECTS.
JOHANNESBURG 48, 1963- 53, 1968 ...
PREV: SOUTH AFRICAN ARCHITECTURAL RECORD FROM
9, 1924- 47, 1962. SUBS: PLAN (JOHANNESBURG)
LO/N13.

**ISHIKAWA-KEN NOGYO TANKI DAIGAKU KENKYU
HOKOKU. BULLETIN, ISHIKAWA PREFECTURE COLLEGE
OF AGRICULTURE.**
ISHIKAWA-KEN NOGYO TANKI DAIGAKU.
ISHIKAWA NO.1, 1972-
LO/N13.

**ISHIKAWA-KEN NOGYO TANKI DAIGAKU TOKUBETSU
KENKYU HOKOKU. SPECIAL BULLETIN OF THE AGRI-
CULTURAL COLLEGE OF ISHIKAWA PREFECTURE.**
ISHIKAWA-KEN NOGYO TANKI DAIGAKU.
NONOICHI 1, 1971-
LO/N13.

**ISKUSSTVO KNIGI.**
['ISKUSSTVO']
MOSCOW 1, 1960-
ANNU.
LO/U15.     OX/U-1.
NR/U-1. 6, 1970-
ISSN 0578-8013

**ISLAM & THE MODERN AGE.**
+ +ISLAM & MOD. AGE.
ISLAM & THE MODERN AGE SOCIETY.
NEW DELHI 1, MY 1970-
Q.
BH/C-3.
ISSN 0021-1826

**ISLANDS. A NEW ZEALAND QUARTERLY OF ARTS &
LETTERS.**
CHRISTCHURCH, N.Z. 1, 1972-
AD/U-1.     ED/N-1.     LD/U-1.     OX/U-1.
CA/U-1. 3, 1974-          SH/U-1. 1974-

**ISLENZKAR LANDBUNADAR RANNSOKNIR. = JOURNAL
OF AGRICULTURAL RESEARCH IN ICELAND.**
+ +ISL. LANDBUNADAR RANNSOKNIR.
REYKJAVIK 1, 1969-
CA/U11.     DB/S-1.

**ISMEC BULLETIN. INFORMATION SERVICE IN MECH-
ANICAL ENGINEERING.**
INSTITUTION OF MECHANICAL ENGINEERS.
LONDON 1(1), JL 1973-
2M. SPONS. BODY ALSO: INSTITUTION OF ELECT-
RICAL ENGINEERS.
BH/U-3.     ED/N-1.     GL/U-2.     LD/U-1.     LO/N14.     LO/N35.
MA/U-1.     OX/U-8.     SO/U-1.

**ISO INFORMATION.**
+ +ISO INF. (INT. SOC. ORGANBUILDERS).
INTERNATIONAL SOCIETY OF ORGANBUILDERS.
LAUFFEN/NECKAR NO.1, 1969-
ENGL., FR.
LO/N14.

**ISOTOPE.**
(SOUTH AFRICA) ATOMIC ENERGY BOARD.
PRETORIA 1, 1969-
AFRIKAANS & ENGL.
LO/N14.
ISSN 0021-1893

**ISOTOPE IN INDUSTRIE UND LANDWIRTSCHAFT.**
+ +ISOTOPE IND. & LANDW.
OSTERREICHISCHE STUDIENGESELLSCHAFT FUR
ATOMENERGIE.
VIENNA & C. 1964(1)- 1971(2/3). //
LO/N14. 1967(2/3)-

**ISOTOPE & RADIATION RESEARCH.**
+ +ISOT. & RADIAT. RES.
MIDDLE EAST REGIONAL RADIOSCOPE CENTRE FOR
THE ARAB COUNTRIES.
CAIRO 1, 1968-
LO/N13.
ISSN 0021-1907

**ISOTOPENPRAXIS.**
+ +[IPRX-A]
[AKADEMIE-VERLAG]
BERLIN 1, OC 1965-
ISSUED AS 'BEILAGE ZUR KERNENERGIE'. SUMM. IN
ENGL. & RUSS.
LO/N14.
ISSN 0021-1915

**ISRAEL BOOK WORLD.**
+ +ISR. BOOK WORLD.
TEL AVIV NO.1, AU 1970-
SO/U-1.
ISSN 0021-1974

**ISRAEL JOURNAL OF ENTOMOLOGY.**
+ +ISR. J. ENTOMOL.
ISRAEL SOCIETY OF ENTOMOLOGY.
REHOVOT 1, 1966-
A.
LO/N-2.

**ISRAEL MUSEUM NEWS.**
+ +ISR. MUS. NEWS.
ISRAEL MUSEUM.
JERUSALEM 1, S 1965-
OX/U-2.
ISSN 0021-227X

**ISRAEL ORIENTAL STUDIES.**
+ +ISR. ORIENT. STUD.
TEL AVIV UNIVERSITY.
TEL AVIV 1, 1971-
BL/U-1.     CA/U-1.     MA/U-1.     OX/U-1.

**ISRAEL & PALESTINE.**
+ +ISR. & PALEST.
PARIS NO.1, JE 1971-
M. ENGL. & FR.
LO/N-1.     SO/U-1.

**ISRAEL QUARTERLY OF ECONOMICS.**
+ +ISR. Q. ECON.
[ACADEMIC P.]
JERUSALEM 1(1), 1971/72-
Q.
LO/U-3.     OX/U16.
CA/U-1. 1(4), 1972-

**ISRAEL STUDIES IN CRIMINOLOGY.**
+ +ISR. STUD. CRIMINOL.
TEL-AVIV UNIVERSITY: INSTITUTE OF CRIMINOLOGY &
CRIMINAL LAW.
[GOMEH PUBL. HOUSE]
TEL-AVIV 1, 1970-
INSTITUTE SUBORD. TO FACULTY OF LAW.
LO/N-1.     OX/U-1.     OX/U15.
ISSN 0075-1391

**ISRAEL YEARBOOK ON HUMAN RIGHTS.**
+ +ISR. YEARB. HUM. RIGHTS.
TEL-AVIV UNIVERSITY: FACULTY OF LAW.
TEL-AVIV 1, 1971-
LO/U14.     OX/U15.

**ISSLEDOVANIJA DAL'NEVOSTOCHNYKH MOREJ SSSR.** XXX
**SUBS (1962): ISSLEDOVANIJA FAUNY MOREJ.**

**ISSLEDOVANIJA FAUNY MOREJ.**                                                          XXX
++ISSLED. FAUNY MOREJ.
AKADEMIJA NAUK SSSR: ZOOLOGICHESKIJ INSTITUT.
 MOSCOW &C  1(9), 1962...
 PREV: ISSLEDOVANIJA DAL'NEVOSTOCHNYKH MOREJ
 SSSR. CONT. NUMBERING IN PARENTHESIS.
 CA/U12.      XY/N-1.

**ISSLEDOVANIJA PO GENETIKE.**
++ISSLED. GENET.
LENINGRADSKIJ GOSUDARSTVENNYJ UNIVERSITET.
 LENINGRAD  1, 1961-
 LO/N13.
 ISSN 0578-9508

**ISSLEDOVANIJA PO INTEGRO-DIFFERENTSIAL'NYM
URAVNENIJAM V KIRGIZII.**
++ISSLED. INTERGRO-DIFFER. URAVN. KIRG.
AKADEMIJA NAUK KIRGIZSKOJ SSR: INSTITUT FIZIKI,
MATEMATIKI I MEKHANIKI.
 FRUNZE  1, 1961-
 LO/N13.  6, 1969-
 ISSN 0578-9516

**ISSLEDOVANIJA PO OBSHCHEJ ALGEBRE.**
++ISSLED. OBSHCH. ALGEBRE.
KISHINEVSKIJ UNIVERSITET: KAFEDRA ALGEBRY I
GEOMETRII.
 KISHINEV  1, 1968-
 CA/U-2.    LO/N13.

**ISSLEDOVANIE PLAZMENNYKH SGUSTKOV.**
++ISSLED. PLAZMENNYKH SGUSTKOV.
AKADEMIJA NAUK UKRAJINS'KOJI RSR: FIZYKO-
TEKHNICHNYJ INSTYTUT.
 KIEV  [1], 1965-
 S/T: FIZIKA PLAZMY I PROBLEMY UPRAVLJAEMOGO
 TERMOJADERNOGO SINTEZA.
 LO/N13.
 BH/U-1.  4(1969) ONLY.

**ISSLEDOVANIJA PO STROITEL'STVU.**                                                    000
 SEE: UURIMUSI EHITUSE ALALT.

**ISSLEDOVANIJA PO TEORII CHISEL.**
++ISSLED. TEOR. CHISEL.  [ISTC-A]
SARATOVSKIJ GOSUDARSTVENNYJ UNIVERSITET.
 SARATOV  1, 1966-
 LO/N13.*
 ISSN 0578-9567

**ISSLEDOVANIJA PO UPRUGOSTI I PLASTICHNOSTI.**
++ISSLED. UPRUGOSTI & PLAST.
LENINGRADSKIJ GOSUDARSTVENNYJ UNIVERSITET:
MATEMATIKO-MAKHANICHESKIJ FAKUL'TET.
 LENINGRAD  SB.1, 1961-
 LO/N13.  SB.3, 1964-
 BH/U-1.  SB.4 ONLY.

**ISSUE. A QUARTERLY JOURNAL OF OPINION.**
AFRICAN STUDIES ASSOCIATION.
 WALTHAM, MASS  1, 1971-
 OX/U-1.
 LO/U-8.  2(1), 1972-           SH/U-1.  3, 1973-
 ISSN 0047-1607

**ISSUES IN CRIMINOLOGY.**
++ISSUES CRIMINOL.
UNIVERSITY OF CALIFORNIA: SCHOOL OF CRIMINO-
LOGY.
 BERKELEY  1(1), 1965-
 CA/U16.
 CB/U-1.  5, 1970-            SH/U-1.  7, 1972-
 ISSN 0021-2385

**ISSUES IN INDUSTRIAL SOCIETY.**                                                       XXX
++ISSUES IND. SOC.
NEW YORK STATE SCHOOL OF INDUSTRIAL & LABOR
RELATIONS.
 ITHACA, N.Y.  1, 1969-
 PREV: ILR RESEARCH FROM 1(1), 1954- 13(2),
 1967.  SCHOOL PART OF CORNELL UNIVERSITY.
 LO/U-3.    OX/U17.

**ISTITUTO DI PETROGRAFIA QUADERNI.**                                                   000
 SEE: QUADERNI, ...

**ISTORIJA I METODOLOGIJA ESTESTVENNYKH NAUK.**
++ISTOR. & METOD. ESTESTV. NAUK.
MOSKOVSKIJ GOSUDARSTVENNYJ UNIVERSITET:
SEKTSIJA ISTORII ESTESTVOZNANIJA.
 MOSCOW  VYP.1, 1960-
 SEKTSIJA ... SUBORD. TO:  UCHENYJ SOVET PO
 ESTESTVENNYM NAUKAM.
 OX/U-8.
 CC/U-1.  1968-                LO/N-4. VYP.2, 1963-
 LO/U15.  9, 1970.
 ISSN 0579-0204

**ISTORIJA RABOCHEGO KLASSA LENINGRADA. SBORNIK
STATEJ.**
++ISTOR. RAB. KL. LENINGR.
LENINGRADSKIJ GOSUDARSTVENNYJ UNIVERSITET.
 LENINGRAD  1, 1962-
 OX/U-1.
 ISSN 0579-0220

**ISVR TECHNICAL REPORT.**
++ISVR TECH. REP. (UNIV. SOUTHAMP., INST. SOUND
 & VIBR. RES.)
UNIVERSITY OF SOUTHAMPTON: INSTITUTE OF SOUND &
VIBRATION RESEARCH.
 SOUTHAMPTON  [NO.]1, 1967-
 LO/N14.

**ITA FOUNDATION PUBLICATION.**
++ITA FOUND. PUBL. (INITIAL TEACH. ALPHABET).
 LONDON  NO.1, 1967-
 OX/U-1.

**ITALIAN AFFAIRS.**                                                                   XXX
 SUBS (1964): ITALY; DOCUMENTS & NOTES.

**ITALIAN COMMUNISTS.**                                                                XXX
++ITAL. COMMUNISTS.
PARTITO COMUNISTA ITALIANO.
 ROME  1, 1972-
 2M. PREV: FOREIGN BULLETIN OF THE ITALIAN
 COMMUNIST PARTY FROM 1960- JA/AP 1970.
 PUBL. BY THE FOREIGN SECTION
 OF THE CENTRAL COMMITTEE OF C.P.I.
 LO/U-3.    OX/U-1.
 GL/U-1.  1972(2/3)-

**ITALIANISTICA.  REVISTA DI LETTERATURA ITALIANA.**
[MARZORATI]
 MILAN  1(1), 1972-
 CA/U-1.    DB/U-2.    ED/N-1.    LO/N-1.    LO/U-2.    LO/U-4.
 MA/U-1.

**ITALY; DOCUMENTS & NOTES.**
(ITALY) CONSIGLIO DEI MINISTRI.
 ROME  13, 1964-
 BODY GIVEN IN ENGL. AS: PRESIDENCY OF THE
 COUNCIL OF MINISTERS. (INFORMATION SERVICE,
 I.E. SERVIZIO DELLE INFORMAZIONE).  ALSO
 NUMBERED AS FROM NEW SERIES NO.1.  PREV:
 ITALIAN AFFAIRS. DOCUMENTS & NOTES., FROM
 1, 1952.
 BH/U-1.    LO/P20.    MA/U-1.
 ISSN 0021-3063

**ITC JOURNAL.**                                                                       XXX
INTERNATIONAL INSTITUTE FOR AERIAL SURVEY &
EARTH SCIENCES.                                                                        XXX
 ENSCHEDE  1973-
 INCORP: THE INSTITUTE'S PUBLICATIONS: SERIES A
 FROM NO.39, 1967- 53, 1972; & SERIES B FROM
 NO.40, 1966- 67, 1972.
 LO/N14.    SH/U-1.    SW/U-1.

**I.T.D.G. BULLETIN.**
++I.T.D.G. BULL. (INTERMED. TECHNOL. DEV. GROUP
 LTD.).
INTERMEDIATE TECHNOLOGY DEVELOPMENT GROUP LTD.
 LONDON  NO.1, 1966-
 OX/U-1.

**ITF DOCUMENTATION.**
++ITF DOC. (INT. TRANSP. WORKERS' FED.).
INTERNATIONAL TRANSPORT WORKERS FEDERATION.
 LONDON  NO.1, AP 1967-
 ED/N-1.

**ITOGI NAUKI: GEOGRAFIJA SSSR.**
++ITOGI NAUKI, GEOGR. SSSR.
AKADEMIJA NAUK SSSR: INSTITUT NAUCHNOJ INFOR-
MATSII.
 MOSCOW  VYP.1, 1965-
 BH/U-1.    CC/U-1.    SW/U-1.
 GL/U-1.  7, 1969.
 LO/U15.  6, 1968- 8, 1970.
 ISSN 0579-1529

**ITOGI NAUKI: MATEMATICHESKIJ ANALIZ.**
++ITOGI NAUKI, MAT. ANAL.
AKADEMIJA NAUK SSSR: INSTITUT NAUCHNOJ
INFORMATSII.
 MOSCOW  1, 1962(1964)-
 BH/U-1.  1967-                CA/U-1.  1963-
 LA/U-1.  1967-
 ISSN 0579-160X

ITOGI NAUKI: ORGANIZATSIJA UPRAVLENIJA.
++ITOGI NAUKI, ORGAN. UPR.
AKADEMIJA NAUK SSSR.
 MOSCOW 1, 1971-
 SPONS. BODY ALSO: VSESOJUZNYJ INSTITUT
 NAUCHNOJ I TEKHNICHESKOJ INFORMATSII.
 BH/U-1.

ITOGI NAUKI: SERIJA MATEMATIKA: (ENGL.
TRANSL.)                                             000
 SEE: PROGRESS IN MATHEMATICS.

ITOGI NAUKI: ZOOLOGIJA.
++ITOGI NAUKI, ZOOL. [IZOO-A]
AKADEMIJA NAUK SSSR: INSTITUT NAUCHNOJ
INFORMATSII.
 MOSCOW 1963-
 LO/N-2. 1964-               XS/R14. 1966-
 ISSN 0579-1839

ITOGI NAUKI I TEKHNIKI: METALLOVEDENIE I TER-
MICHESKAJA OBRABOTKA.
++ITOGI NAUKI & TEKH, METALLOVED. & TERM. OBRAB.
AKADEMIJA NAUK SSSR: VSESOJUZNYJ INSTITUT
NAUCHNOJ I TEKHNICHESKOJ INFORMATSII.
 MOSCOW 1965-
 BH/U-1. 1966(1967)-

ITOGI NAUKI I TEKHNIKI: METALLURGIJA.
++ITOGI NAUKI & TEKH., METALL.
AKADEMIJA NAUK SSSR: VSESOJUZNYJ INSTITUT
NAUCHNOJ I TEKHNICHESKOJ INFORMATSII.
 MOSCOW 1962-
 BH/U-1. 1966(1967)-
 ISSN 0579-1979

ITOGI NAUKI I TEKHNIKI - SERIJA: PROMYSHLENNYJ
TRANSPORT.
++ITOGI NAUKI & TEKH., PROM. TRANSP.
AKADEMIJA NAUK SSSR: INSTITUT NAUCHNOJ
INFORMATSII.
 MOSCOW 1964/1965 (1966)-
 BH/U-1.

ITV EDUCATION NEWS.
++ITV EDUC. NEWS.
INDEPENDENT TELEVISION AUTHORITY.
 LONDON NO.1, JE 1970-
 ED/N-1.

I.V.I.C. BOLETIN INFORMATIVO, INSTITUTO
VENEZOLANO DE INVESTIGACIONES CIENTIFICAS.
 CARACAS 1(1), D 1965-
 LO/N13. 1(2), 1966-

I.W.G.I.A. DOCUMENTS.
INTERNATIONAL WORK GROUP FOR INDIGENOUS AFFAIRS
 COPENHAGEN 1, 1971-
 CA/U-3.   OX/U-1.

IZ ISTORII BIOLOGICHESKIKH NAUK. MEMORABILIA
HISTORIAE NATURALIS.                                 XXX
++IZ ISTOR. BIOL. NAUK.
AKADEMIJA NAUK SSSR: INSTITUT ISTORII ESTESTVO-
ZNANIJA I TEKHNIKI (LENINGRADSKOE OTDELENIE).
 MOSCOW 1, 1966-
 PREV: PART OF 'TRUDY INSTITUTA ISTORII ESTEST-
 VOZNANIJA I TEKHNIKI AN SSSR FROM 1954- 1965.
 LO/N-2.   OX/U-8.   XY/N-1.

IZ ISTORII KUL'TURNOGO STROITEL'STVA V TAD-
ZHIKISTANE.
++IZ ISTOR. KUL'T. STROIT. TADZH.
 DUSHANBE VYP. 1, 1968-
 GL/U-1.   LO/N-3.

IZOTOPY V SSSR.
++IZOT. SSSR.
GOSUDARSTVENNYJ KOMITET PO ISPOL'ZOVANIJU
ATOMNOJ ENERGII SSSR.
 MOSCOW 1, 1965-
 SPONS. BODY ALSO: VSESOJUZNOE OB'EDINENIE
 IZOTOP.
 XS/R10.

IZVESTIJA AKADEMII NAUK ARMJANSKOJ SSR:
OBSHCHESTVENNYE NAUKI.                               XXX
 SUBS (1966): VESTNIK OBSHCHESTVENNYKH NAUK,
 AKADEMIJA NAUK ARMJANSKOJ SSR.

IZVESTIJA AKADEMII NAUK AZERBAJDZHANSKOJ SSR:
SERIJA NAUK O ZEMLE.
++IZV. AKAD. NAUK AZERB. SSR, NAUK ZEMLE.
 BAKU 1966(1)-
 LO/N13. 1966(4)-         LO/U-2. 1967(3)-

IZVESTIJA AKADEMII NAUK KAZAKHSKOJ SSR:
SERIJA BIOLOGICHESKIKH NAUK.                         XXX
++IZV. AKAD. NAUK KAZ. SSR, BIOL. NAUK.
 ALMA-ATA 1, 1963-
 PREV: IZVESTIJA AKADEMII NAUK KAZAKHSKOJ SSR:
 SERIJA BOTANIKI I POCHVOVEDENIJA FROM 1958-
 1962.
 LO/N-2.   LO/N13.

IZVESTIJA AKADEMII NAUK KAZAKHSKOJ SSR:
SERIJA BOTANIKI I POCHVOVEDENIJA.                    XXX
 SUBS (1963): IZVESTIJA AKADEMII NAUK
 KAZAKHSKOJ SSR: SERIJA BIOLOGICHESKIKH
 NAUK.

IZVESTIJA AKADEMII NAUK LATVIJSKOJ SSR: SERIJA
KHIMICHESKAJA.                                       000
 SEE: LATVIJAS PSR ZINATNU AKADEMIJAS VESTIS:
 KIMIJAS SERIJA.

IZVESTIJA AKADEMII NAUK MOLDAVSKOJ SSR:
SERIJA BIOLOGICHESKOKH I KHIMICHESKIKH NAUK.         XXX
++IZV. AKAD. NAUK MOLD. SSR, BIOL. & KHIM. NAUK.
 [IMBK-B]
 KISHINEV 1968(1)-
 PREV: AS PART OF ABOVE MAIN TITLE FROM 1961-
 1967, THEN IN 3 SERIES.
 LO/N13.
 LO/N-2. 1969(3)-

IZVESTIJA AKADEMII NAUK MOLDAVSKOJ SSR:
SERIJA FIZIKO-TEKHNICHESKIKH I MATEMATICHES-
KIKH NAUK.                                           XXX
++IZV. AKAD. NAUK MOLD. SSR, FIZ.-TEKH. & MAT.
 NAUK. [IZFM-B]
 KISHINEV 1968(1)-
 PREV: AS PART OF ABOVE MAIN TITLE FROM 1961-
 1967, THEN IN 3 SERIES.
 LO/N-2.   LO/N13.

IZVESTIJA AKADEMII NAUK MOLDAVSKOJ SSR:
SERIJA OBSHCHESTVENNYKH NAUK.                        XXX
++IZV. AKAD. NAUK MOLD. SSR, OBSHCHESTV. NAUK.
 [IZMO-B]
 KISHINEV 1968(1)-
 PREV: AS PART OF ABOVE MAIN TITLE FROM 1961-
 1967, THEN ISSUED IN 3 SERIES.
 CC/U-1.   LO/N-3.

IZVESTIJA AKADEMII NAUK SSSR: MEKHANIKA TVER-
DOGO TELA.                                           XXX
++IZV. AKAD. NAUK SSSR, MEKH. TVERD. TELA.
 MOSCOW 1969-
 PREV: INZHENERNYJ ZHURNAL: MEKHANIKA TVERDOGO
 TELA FROM 1966- 1968.
 LO/N-4.   LO/N-7.   LO/N14.

IZVESTIJA AKADEMII NAUK SSSR: SERIJA EKONOM-
ICHESKAJA.
++IZV. AKAD. NAUK SSSR, EKON.
 MOSCOW 1, 1970-
 CC/U-1.   OX/U-1.

IZVESTIJA AKADEMII NAUK SSSR: SERIJA MATEMATI-
CHESKAJA. (ENGL. TRANSL.)                            000
 SEE: MATHEMATICS OF THE USSR - IZVESTIJA.

IZVESTIJA AKADEMII NAUK TADZHIKSKOJ SSR: OTD-
ELENIE FIZIKO-MATEMATICHESKIKH I GEOLOGO-KHIM-
ICHESKIKH NAUK.                                      XXX
++IZV. AKAD. NAUK TADZH. SSR, OTD. FIZ.-MAT. &
 GEOL.-KHIM. NAUK.
 DUSHANBE 24, 1967-
 PREV: IZVESTIJA AKADEMII ...: OTDELENIE FIZ-
 IKOTEKHNICHESKIKH I KHIMICHESKIKH NAUK FROM
 1(14), 1964- 23, 1967.
 LO/N13.

IZVESTIJA AKADEMII NAUK TADZHIKSKOJ SSR: OTD-
ELENIE FIZIKO-TEKHNICHESKIKH I KHIMICHESKIKH
NAUK.                                                XXX
++IZV. AKAD. NAUK TADZH. SSR, OTD. FIZ.-TEKH. &
 KHIM. NAUK. [ITFK-A]
 DUSHANBE 1(14), 1964- 23, 1967-
 PREV: IZVESTIJA AKADEMII ...: OTDELENIE GEOL-
 OGO-KHIMICHESKIKH I TEKHNICHESKIKH NAUK FROM
 1, 1959- 13, 1964. SUBS: IZVESTIJA AKADEMII..
 OTDELENIE FIZIKO-MATEMATICHESKIKH I GEOLOGO-
 KHIMICHESKIKH NAUK.
 LO/N13. 19, 1966- 23, 1967.

IZVESTIJA AKADEMII NAUK TADZHIKSKOJ SSR:
OTDELENIE GEOLOGO-KHIMICHESKIKH I TEKHN-
ICHESKIKH NAUK.                                      XXX
 SUBS (1964): IZVESTIJA AKADEMII ...: OTDEL-
 ENIE FIZIKO-TEKHNICHESKIKH I KHIMICHESKIKH
 NAUK.

IZVESTIJA AKADEMII NAUK TURKMENSKOJ SSR:
SERIJA BIOLOGICHESKIKH NAUK.                                    XXX
+ +IZV. AKAD. NAUK TURKM. SSR, BIOL. NAUK.
ASHKHABAD 1960(1)-
PREV: PART OF IZVESTIJA AKADEMII NAUK TURKMEN-
SKOJ SSR FROM 1952- 1959.
LO/N13. 1960-
LO/N-3. 1961- 1963. 1966(1-2).

IZVESTIJA AKADEMII NAUK TURKMENSKOJ SSR:
SERIJA FIZIKO-TEKHNICHESKIKH, KHIMICHESKIKH
I GEOLOGICHESKIKH NAUK.                                         XXX
+ +IZV. AKAD. NAUK TURKM. SSR, FIZ.-TEKH. KHIM.
& GEOL. NAUK.
ASHKHABAD 1960(1)-
PREV: PART OF IZVESTIJA AKADEMII NAUK TURKMEN-
SKOJ SSR FROM 1952- 1959.
LO/N13. 1960-
LO/N-3. 1961- 1963.
SH/U-1. 1960(6). 1963(1)-

IZVESTIJA AKADEMII NAUK TURKMENSKOJ SSR:
SERIJA OBSHCHESTVENNYKH NAUK.                                   XXX
+ +IZV. AKAD. NAUK TURKM. SSR, OBSHCHEST. NAUK.
ASHKHABAD 1960(1)-
PREV: IZVESTIJA AKADEMII NAUK TURKMENSKOJ
SSR FROM 1952- 1959.
LO/N13. 1960-
LO/N-3. 1960-                    LO/U14. 1970-
SW/U-1. 1970-
GL/U-1. [W. 1962- 65]

IZVESTIJA NA GEOLOGICHESKIJA INSTITUT, BUL-
GARSKA AKADEMIJA NA NAUKITE: SERIJA GEOTEK-
TONIKA, STRATIGRAFIJA I LITOLOGIJA.                             XXX
+ +IZV. GEOL. INST. BULG. AKAD. NAUK., GEOTEKTON-
IKA STRATIGR. & LITOL.
SOFIA KN. 16, 1967-
PREV: IZVESTIJA NA GEOLOGICHESKIJA INSTITUT,
BULGARSKA AKADEMIJA NA NAUKITE FROM 1, 1951-
15, 1966. THEN ISSUED IN SUBJECT SECTIONS
WHICH CONTINUE PREV. NUMBERING.
LO/N-2.    LO/N14.    LO/U-2.

IZVESTIJA NA GEOLOGICHESKIJA INSTITUT, BUL-
GARSKA AKADEMIJA NA NAUKITE: SERIJA INZHEN-
ERNA GEOLOGIJA I KHIDROGEOLOGIJA.                               XXX
+ +IZV. GEOL. INST. BULG. AKAD. NAUK., INZH.
GEOL. & KHIDROGEOL.
SOFIA KN. 16, 1967-
PREV: IZVESTIJA NA GEOLOGICHESKIJA INSTITUT,
BULGARSKA AKADEMIJA NA NAUKITE FROM 1, 1951-
15, 1966. THEN ISSUED IN SUBJECT SECTIONS
WHICH CONTINUE PREV. NUMBERING.
LO/N-2.    LO/N14.    LO/U-2.

IZVESTIJA NA GEOLOGICHESKIJA INSTITUT, BUL-
GARSKA AKADEMIJA NA NAUKITE: SERIJA PALEON-
TOLOGIJA.                                                       XXX
+ +IZV. GEOL. INST. BULG. AKAD. NAUK., PALEONTOL.
SOFIA KN. 16, 1967-
PREV: IZVESTIJA NA GEOLOGICHESKIJA INSTITUT,
BULGARSKA AKADEMIJA NA NAUKITE FROM 1, 1951-
15, 1966. THEN ISSUED IN SUBJECT SECTIONS
WHICH CONTINUE PREV. NUMBERING.
LO/N-2.    LO/N14.    LO/U-2.

IZVESTIJA NA OTDELENIETO ZA KHIMICHESKI
NAUKI, BULGARSKA AKADEMIJA NA NAUKITE.                          XXX
+ +IZV. OTD. KHIM. NAUK. BULG. AKAD. NAUK.
SOFIA 1, 1968-
BULG., ENGL., FR., GER. OR RUSS.  PREV: IZ-
VESTIJA NA INSTITUTA PO FIZIKOKHIMIJA, BUL-
GARSKA AKADEMIJA NA NAUKITE FROM 1, 1960- 6,
1967; & IZVESTIJA NA INSTITUTA PO ORGANICHNA
KHIMIJA, BULGARSKA AKADEMIJA NA NAUKITE FROM
1, 1964- 3, 1967.
BH/U-1.    DB/S-1.    LO/N14.

IZVESTIJA SIBIRSKOGO OTDELENIJA AKADEMII
NAUK SSSR; SERIJA BIOLOGO-MEDITSINSKIKH NAUK.
+ +IZV. SIB. OTD. AKAD. NAUK SSSR, BIOL. MED.
NAUK. [IZSB-A]
AKADEMIJA NAUK SSSR (SIBIRSKOE OTDELENIE).
NOVOSIBIRSK 1963 (1)-
ALSO NUMBERED AS PART OF GEN. SERIES (ABOVE
MAIN TITLE), ALSO FROM NO.1 EACH YEAR.
BH/U-1.    LO/N14.    OX/U-8.
LO/N-3. 1965 (1).

IZVESTIJA SIBIRSKOGO OTDELENIJA AKADEMII
NAUK SSSR; SERIJA KHIMICHESKIKH NAUK.
+ +IZV. SIB. OTD. AKAD. NAUK SSSR, KHIM. NAUK.
AKADEMIJA NAUK SSSR (SIBIRSKOE OTDELENIE).
NOVOSIBIRSK 1963 (1)-
ALSO NUMBERED AS PART OF GEN. SERIES (ABOVE
MAIN TITLE), WHICH IS NUMBERED FROM 1 EACH YR.
BH/U-1.    LO/N14.
XS/R10. 1968(1)-
LO/N-3. 1965 (1).

IZVESTIJA, SIBIRSKOGO OTDELENIJA, AKADEMII NAUK
SSSR: SERIJA KHIMICHESKIKH NAUK (ENGL.
TRANSL.).                                                       000
SEE: SIBERIAN CHEMISTRY JOURNAL.

IZVESTIJA SIBIRSKOGO OTDELENIJA AKADEMII
NAUK SSSR; SERIJA OBSHCHESTVENNYKH NAUK.
+ +IZV. SIB. OTD. AKAD. NAUK SSSR, OBSHCHEST.
NAUK.
AKADEMIJA NAUK SSSR (SIBIRSKOE OTDELENIE).
NOVOSIBIRSK 1963 (1)-
ALSO NUMBERED AS PART OF GEN. SERIES (ABOVE
MAIN TITLE), WHICH NUMBERS FROM 1 EACH YEAR.
BH/U-1.    LO/N14.    OX/U-1.
CC/U-1. 1964(1)-              GL/U-1. 1964-
LO/U-3. JA 1972-              SW/U-1. 1966(1)-

IZVESTIJA SIBIRSKOGO OTDELENIJA AKADEMII
NAUK SSSR; SERIJA TEKHNICHESKIKH NAUK.
+ +IZV. SIB. OTD. AKAD. NAUK SSSR, TEKH. NAUK.
AKADEMIJA NAUK SSSR (SIBIRSKOE OTDELENIE).
NOVOSIBIRSK 1963 (1)-
ALSO NUMBERED AS PART OF GEN. SERIES (ABOVE
MAIN TITLE), WHICH NUMBERS FROM 1 EACH YEAR.
BH/U-1.    LO/N14.
CA/U-2. 1965(1)-              XS/R10. 1968(3)-

IZVESTIJA NA TSENTRALNIJA NAUCHNOIZSLEDOVATELSKI
VETERINAREN INSTITUT PO VIRUSOLOGIJA.                           000
SEE: IZVESTIJA NA VETERINARNIJA INSTITUT PO
VIRUSOLOGIJA.

IZVESTIJA UZBEKISTANSKOGO FILIALA GEOGRAFICH-
ESKOGO OBSHCHESTVA SSSR.                                        XXX
SUBS (1963): IZVESTIJA UZBEKISTANSKOGO GEOG-
RAFICHESKOGO OBSHCHESTVA.

IZVESTIJA UZBEKISTANSKOGO GEOGRAFICHESKOGO
OBSHCHESTVA.                                                    XXX
+ +IZV. UZB. GEOGR. O-VA.
TASHKENT 7, 1963-
PREV: IZVESTIJA UZBEKISTANSKOGO FILIALA GEOG-
RAFICHESKOGO OBSHCHESTVA SSSR: FROM 1, 1955-
6, 1962.
LO/N-3. TOM 10(1967).

IZVESTIJA NA VETERINARNIJA INSTITUT PO VIRUS-
OLOGIJA.
+ +IZV. VET. INST. VIRUSOL.
AKADEMIJA NA SELSKOSTOPANSKITE NAUKI: VETERIN-
AREN INSTITUT PO VIRUSOLOGIJA.
SOFIA 1, 1962-
ENGL. SUMM. VOL.1 PUBL. AS: IZVESTIJA NA
TSENTRALNIJA NAUCHNOIZSLEDOVATELSKI VETERIN-
AREN INSTITUT PO VIRUSOLOGIJA.
LO/N13.

IZVESTIJA NA VETERINARNOKHIGIENNIJA INSTITUT
ZA ZHIVOTINSKI PRODUKTI.
+ +IZV. VETERINARNOKHIG. INST. ZHIVOTIN. PROD.
AKADEMIJA NA SELSKOSTOPANSKITE NAUKI: VETERIN-
ARNOKHIGIENEN INSTITUT ZA ZHIVOTINSKI PRODUKTI.
SOFIA 1, 1961-
GER. & RUSS. SUMM.  INSTITUT SUBORD. TO:
OTDELENIE ZA ZHIVOTNOVUDSTVO I VETERINARNI
MEDITSINA. BODY NAME VARIES: TSENTRALEN
NAUCHNO-IZSLEDOVATELSKI VETERINAROKHIGIENICH-
ESKI INSTITUT ZA ZHIVOTINSKI PRODUKTO FROM 1-2
LO/N13. 3, 1963.

IZVOARE ORIENTALE PRIVIND ISTORIA ROMANIEI.
+ +IZVO. ORIENT. PRIV. ISTOR. ROM.
ACADEMIA REPUBLICII SOCIALISTE ROMANIA.
BUCHAREST 1, 1966-
ISSUED BY THE ACADEMY'S 'INSTITUTUL DE
ISTORIE 'N. IORGA' SI INSTITUTUL DE STUDII
SUD-EST EUROPENE'.
LO/N-3. 1, 1966.

JACK LONDON NEWSLETTER.
+ +JACK LONDON NEWSL.
CARBONDALE, ILL. 1(1), JL/D 1967-
2/A.
OX/U-1.
ISSN 0021-3837

JACOB BURCHKHARDT STUDIEN.
+ +JACOB BURCHKHARDT STUD.
ASSEN 1, 1970-
OX/U-1.

JADAVPUR JOURNAL OF COMPARATIVE LITERATURE.
+ +JADAVPUR J. COMP. LIT.
UNIVERSITY OF CALCUTTA: DEPARTMENT OF COMPARA-
TIVE LITERATURE.
CALCUTTA 1, 1961-
LO/U14. 3, 1963-
DB/U-1. 6, 1966- 8, 1968.

JADD-O-JEHAD.
COMMITTEE OF WEST PAKISTANIS IN SOLIDARITY WITH
BENGAL & KASHMIR.
LONDON 1(1), 1971-
ED/N-1. 1(2), 1971-

JADERNAJA GEOFIZIKA.
+ +JAD. GEOFIZ.
GOSUDARSTVENNOE NAUCHNO-TEKHNICHESKOE IZDATEL'-
STVO NEFTJANOJ I GORNO-TOPLIVNOJ PROMYSHLEN-
NOSTI.
MOSCOW 1961-
LO/N13. 1961; 1963.

JADERNYJ MAGNITNYJ REZONANS.
+ +JAD. MAGN. REZONANS.
LENINGRADSKIJ GOSUDARSTVENNYJ UNIVERSITET.
LENINGRAD 1, 1965-
LO/N13.

JAHRBUCH FUR GEOLOGIE.
+ +JAHRB. GEOL.
ZENTRALES GEOLOGISCHES INSTITUT.
[AKADEMIE VERLAG]
BERLIN 1, 1965(1967)-
ENGL. & RUSS. SUMM. & CONTENTS LISTS.
LO/N-2.    LO/N13.

JAHRBUCH DES INSTITUTS FUR DEUTSCHE GESCH-
ICHTE.
+ +JAHRB. INST. DTSCH. GESCH.
TEL-AVIV UNIVERSITY: INSTITUTE FOR GERMAN
HISTORY.
TEL-AVIV 1, 1972-
LO/N-1.    LO/U-2.    OX/U-1.

JAHRBUCH FUR INTERNATIONALE GERMANISTIK.
+ +JAHRB. INT. GER.
[GEHLEN]
BAD HOMBURG 1, 1969-
BN/U-1.    CB/U-1.    EX/U-1.    LO/U-1.    LO/U-2.    LO/U-4.
LO/U13.    SH/U-1.    SW/U-1.

JAHRBUCH DER KARL-MAY-GESELLSCHAFT.
+ +JAHRB. KARL-MAY-GES.
[HANSA-VERLAG]
HAMBURG 1970-
LO/N-1.

JAHRBUCH DES KUNSTHISTORISCHEN INSTITUTES
DER UNIVERSITAT GRAZ.
+ +JAHRB. KUNSTHIST. INST. UNIV. GRAZ.
UNIVERSITAT GRAZ; KUNSTHISTORISCHES INSTITUT.
GRAZ 1, 1965-
OX/U-2.

JAHRBUCH DER OSTERREICHISCHEN BYZANTINISCHEN
GESELLSCHAFT.                                              XXX
SUBS (1969): JAHRBUCH DER OSTERREICHISCHEN
BYZANTINISTIK.

JAHRBUCH DER OSTERREICHISCHEN BYZANTINISTIK.    XXX
+ +JAHRB. OSTERR. BYZANTINISTIK.
[H. BOEHLAU VERLAG]
VIENNA 18, 1969-
PREV: JAHRBUCH DER OSTERREICHISCHEN BYZANTIN-
ISCHEN GESELLSCHAFT FROM 1, 1951- 17, 1968.
CA/U-1.    OX/U-1.
ISSN 0075-2355

JAHRBUCH DER WIRTSCHAFT OSTEUROPAS. YEARBOOK
OF EAST-EUROPEAN ECONOMICS.
+ +JAHRB. WIRT. OSTEUR.
OSTEUROPA-INSTITUT (MUNICH).
MUNICH &C. 1, 1970-
BH/U-1.    CA/U-1.    GL/U-1.    OX/U-1.    SH/U-1.
ISSN 0449-5225

JAHRESBERICHT, KESTNER MUSEUM.
+ +JAHRESBER. KESTNER MUS.
HANOVER 1, 1964/65(1965)-
OX/U-2.

JAHRESHEFTE DES OSTERREICHISCHEN ARCHAOLOGISCHEN
INSTITUTES IN WIEN; BEILAGE: GRABUNGEN.
SEE: GRABUNGEN, OSTERREICHISCHES ARCHAOLOG-
ISCHES INSTITUT.

JAMAICA ARCHITECT. A REVIEW OF ARCHITECTURE
IN THE TROPICS.
+ +JAM. ARCHIT.
JAMAICAN SOCIETY OF ARCHITECTS.
KINGSTON 1(1), F 1967-
Q.
LO/N17.

JAMAICA TODAY.
JAMAICA INFORMATION SERVICE.
KINGSTON 1(1), JA 1969-
LO/N17.

JAMAICAN ACCESSIONS.                                      XXX
+ +JAMAICAN ACCESS.
INSTITUTE OF JAMAICA: WEST INDIA REFERENCE
LIBRARY.
KINGSTON 1964 (1965)- 1967 (1968)...
SUBS (1968): JAMAICAN NATIONAL BIBLIOGRAPHY.
LO/N14.    SO/U-1.

JAMAICAN NATIONAL BIBLIOGRAPHY.                          XXX
+ +JAMAICAN NAT. BIBLIOGR.
INSTITUTE OF JAMAICA: WEST INDIA REFERENCE
LIBRARY.
KINGSTON 1968 (1969)-
PREV: JAMAICAN ACCESSIONS FROM 1964- 1967.
GL/U-1.    HL/U-1.    LO/N-3.    LO/N14.    LO/N14.    OX/U-1.
OX/U-9.

JANUA LINGUARUM: SERIES CRITICA.
[MOUTON & CO.]
THE HAGUE &C. 1, 1972-
CA/U-1.    OX/U-1.
ISSN 0075-3092

JAPAN AGRICULTURAL RESEARCH QUARTERLY.             000
SEE: JARQ.

JAPAN CHEMICAL QUARTERLY.                                XXX
+ +JAP. CHEM. Q. [JCHQ-A]
KAGAKU KEIZAI KENKYUJO.
TOKYO  1, JL 1965- 5(4), OC 1969.
BODY NAMED IN PUBL.: CHEMICAL ECONOMY RESEARCH
INSTITUTE.  SUBS: CHEMICAL ECONOMY & ENGINEER-
ING REVIEW.
LO/S-3.  2,1966-

JAPANESE ECONOMIC STUDIES.  A JOURNAL OF
TRANSLATIONS.
+ +JAP. ECON. STUD.
[INTERNATIONAL ARTS & SCIENCES P.]
WHITE PLAINS, N.Y.  1(1), 1972-
Q.
CA/U-1.    LO/U-3.
SH/U-1.  1(3), 1973-
ISSN 0021-4841

JAPANESE JOURNAL OF CLINICAL ELECTRON
MICROSCOPY.
+ +JAP. J. CLIN. ELECTRON MICROSC.
CLINICAL ELECTRON MICROSCOPY SOCIETY OF JAPAN.
TOKYO 1(1), 1969-
Q. ENGL. & JAP.  ENGL. SUMM.
GL/U-1.
ISSN 0021-4981

JAPANESE JOURNAL OF CLINICAL ONCOLOGY.
+ +JAP. J. CLIN. ONCOL.
TOKYO 1(1), 1971-
TOKYO 1(1), 1971-
LO/N13.    OX/U-8.

JAPANESE JOURNAL OF EXPERIMENTAL MECHANICS.    000
SEE: ORYOKU TO HIZUMI.

JAPANESE JOURNAL OF SURGERY.
+ +JAP. J. SURG.
JAPAN SURGICAL SOCIETY.
TOKYO 1(1), MR 1971-
Q. ENGL., FR. & GER.
SH/U-1.
OX/U-8. 1(2), 1971-
ISSN 0047-1909

JAPANESE NUCLEAR MEDICINE.
+ +JAP. NUCL. MED.
JAPAN RADIOISOTOPE ASSOCIATION.
TOKYO 1, 1961-
XN/S-1.**

JAPAN PESTICIDE INFORMATION.
+ +JAP. PESTIC. INF.
 TOKYO 1, 1969-
 CA/U11.   LO/N-2.   LO/N13.   LO/R-6.

JAPANISCHE STUDIEN ZUR DEUTSCHEN SPRACHE UND
LITERATUR = ETUDES JAPONAISES EN LANGUE ET
LITTERATURE ALLEMANDES = JAPANESE STUDIES IN
GERMAN LANGUAGE & LITERATURE.
+ +JAP. STUD. DTSCH. SPRACHE & LIT.
 [H. LANG]
 BERN & FRANKFURT AM MAIN NO.1, 1971-
 LO/N-1.
 ISSN 0021-4841

JARE SCIENTIFIC REPORTS; SPECIAL ISSUE.
+ +JARE SCI. REP., SPEC. ISSUE. (JAP. ANTARCT.
 RES. EXPED.)
 JAPANESE ANTARCTIC RESEARCH EXPEDITION.
 TOKYO  NO.1, F 1967-
 PUBL. FOR JARE BY  NATIONAL SCIENCE MUSEUM
 (JAPAN); DEP. OF POLAR RESEARCH.
 DB/S-1.   LO/N-4.

JARQ. JAPAN AGRICULTURAL RESEARCH QUARTERLY.
 NORIN-SHO NORIN SUISAN GIJUTSU KAIGI.
 TOKYO  1(1), 1960-
 XN/S-1.
 LO/N17.  1(4), 1967-
 ISSN 0021-3551

JASIS.                                                  000
 SEE: JOURNAL OF THE AMERICAN SOCIETY FOR
 INFORMATION SCIENCE.

JAZZ RESEARCH.                                          000
 SEE: JAZZFORSCHUNG.

JAZZFORSCHUNG.  JAZZ RESEARCH.
 HOCHSCHULE FUER MUSIK UND DARSTELLENDE KUNST:
 INSTITUT FUER JAZZ FORSCHUNG.
 [VERLAG UNIVERSAL EDITION]
 GRAZ  1, 1969-
 A.
 LO/N-1.   OX/U-1.

JEMIC TECHNICAL REPORT.                                 000
 SEE: DENKI KENTEIJO GIHO.

JERUSALEM STUDIES IN GEOGRAPHY.
+ +JERUSALEM STUD. GEOGR.
 HEBREW UNIVERSITY OF JERUSALEM: DEPARTMENT OF
 GEOGRAPHY.
 JERUSALEM  NO.1, 1970-
 AD/U-1.   LO/S13.   SH/U-1.

JEWEL OF AFRICA.  A LITERARY & CULTURAL
MAGAZINE FROM ZAMBIA.
+ +JEWEL AFR.
 MPHALA CREATIVE SOCIETY.
 LUSAKA  1(1), 1967?-
 LO/U14.  2(1), 1969-
 ISSN 0021-6259

JEWISH SOCIAL WORK FORUM.
+ +JEW. SOC. WORK FORUM.
 WURZWEILER SCHOOL OF SOCIAL WORK.
 NEW YORK  1(1), 1964-
 2/A.  PRODUCED BY SCHOOL'S ALUMNI ASSOCIATION.
 CB/U-1.*
 ISSN 0021-6712

JEWISH VEGETARIAN.
+ +JEW. VEG.
 JEWISH VEGETARIAN & NATURAL HEALTH SOCIETY.
 LONDON   NO.1, S 1966-
 ED/N-1.
 ISSN 0021-681X

JOB SAFETY & HEALTH.                                    XXX
+ +JOB SAF. & HEALTH.
 (UNITED STATES) OCCUPATIONAL SAFETY & HEALTH
 ADMINISTRATION.
 WASHINGTON, D.C.  1, 1972-
 PREV: SAFETY STANDARDS FROM 1, AG 1951- 21,
 1972.
 LO/N14.

JOLA TECHNICAL COMMUNICATIONS.
+ +JOLA TECH. COMMUN.
 AMERICAN LIBRARY ASSOCIATION: INFORMATION
 SCIENCE & AUTOMATION DIVISION.
 CHICAGO  1(1), OC 1969-
 ISSUED AS A NEWS SUPPL. TO JOURNAL OF LIBRARY
 AUTOMATION.
 BH/U-1.   BL/U-1.   LO/N-3.   LO/N-7.   LO/U-2.   XS/R10.
 ISSN 0021-3748

JOURNAL OF ABSTRACTS, BRITISH SHIP RESEARCH
ASSOCIATION.                                            XXX
+ +J. ABSTR. BR. SHIP RES. ASS.
 LONDON 23, 1968-
 PREV:  JOURNAL, BRITISH SHIP RES. ASS.* FROM
 1, AP 1946- 22, 1967.
 LO/N14.

JOURNAL OF ADHESION.
+ +J. ADHES.
 PROGRAM DESIGN, INC.
 [TECHNOMIC PUBL. CO.]
 STAMFORD, CONN.  1, 1969-
 LO/N14.   XS/R10.
 CA/U-1.  4(4), AG 1972-
 ED/N-1.  4(4), AG 1972-
 ISSN 0021-8464

JOURNAL OF AEROSOL SCIENCE.
+ +J. AEROSOL SCI.
 [PERGAMON]
 OXFORD &C.  1, 1970-
 ED/N-1.   EX/U-1.   LO/U-1.   LO/N14.   LO/U-2.   MA/U-1.
 NW/U-1.   OX/U-8.
 SO/U-1.  2, 1971-
 ISSN 0021-8502

JOURNAL OF AESTHETIC EDUCATION.
+ +J. AESTHET. EDUC.
 (ILLINOIS) SUPERINTENDENT OF PUBLIC
 INSTRUCTION.
 SPRINGFIELD, ILL.  [1], SPRING 1966-
 ISSUED AS A COOPERATIVE VENTURE OF THE OFFICE
 OF THE SUPERINTENDENT ... & THE UNIVERSITY
 OF ILLINOIS
 CB/U-1.  2,1968-
 ISSN 0021-8510

JOURNAL OF AFRICAN & ASIAN STUDIES.
+ +J. AFR. & ASIAN STUD.
 ASSOCIATION FOR THE STUDY OF AFRICAN & ASIAN
 AFFAIRS.
 DELHI  1(1), 1967-

DEVELOPMENT.
+ +J. AGRIC. ECON. & DEV.
 FARM ECONOMICS ASSOCIATION OF THE PHILIPPINES.
 LAGUNA  1(1), JA 1971-
 2/A.
 LO/U-3.   OX/U24.

JOURNAL OF AGRICULTURAL LABOUR SCIENCE.
+ +J. AGRIC. LABOUR SCI.
 BRITISH SOCIETY FOR AGRICULTURAL LABOUR SCIENCE
 READING  1(1), 1972-
 2/A.
 BL/U-1.   LO/N-6.   OX/U-3.   RE/U-1.

JOURNAL OF AGRICULTURAL RESEARCH.              XXX
+ +J. AGRIC. RES.
 (PUNJAB, PAKISTAN) DEPARTMENT OF AGRICULTURE.
 LAHORE  8(3), S 1970-
 PREV: WEST PAKISTAN JOURNAL OF AGRICULTURAL
 RESEARCH FROM 1, 1962- 8(2), 1970.
 LO/R-6.

JOURNAL OF AGRICULTURAL RESEARCH IN ICELAND.       000
 SEE:  ISLENZKAR LANDBUNADAR RANNSOKNIR.

JOURNAL OF ALLERGY.                                    XXX
 SUBS (1971): JOURNAL OF ALLERGY & CLINICAL
 IMMUNOLOGY.

JOURNAL OF ALLERGY & CLINICAL IMMUNOLOGY.          XXX
+ +J. ALLERGY & CLIN. IMMUNOL.
 AMERICAN ACADEMY OF ALLERGY.
 ST. LOUIS  48(1), 1971-
 PREV: JOURNAL OF ALLERGY FROM 1, N 1929-47(6),
 1971.  INCORP: ALLERGY ABSTRACTS.
 GL/U-1.   LO/N-1.

JOURNAL, AMERICAN ASSOCIATION OF VARIABLE STAR
OBSERVERS.                                             000
 SEE: AAVSO JOURNAL.

JOURNAL, AMERICAN DENTAL SOCIETY OF ANESTHES-      XXX
IOLOGY.
 SUBS (1966): ANESTHESIA PROGRESS.

JOURNAL OF THE AMERICAN FORENSIC ASSOCIATION.
+ +J. AM. FORENS. ASS.
 AMERICAN FORENSIC ASSOCIATION.
 COLUMBIA, MO.   1(1), JA 1964-
 GL/U-2.  4(1),1967-
 ISSN 0002-8533

**JOURNAL, AMERICAN SOCIETY FOR HORTICULTURAL SCIENCE.**
+ +J. AM. SOC. HORT. SCI.
GENEVA (N.Y.) 94(1), 1969-
PREV: PROCEEDINGS, AMERICAN SOCIETY FOR
HORTICULTURAL SCIENCE FROM 1, 1903-93, 1968.
BN/U-2.   GL/U-1.   LO/N14.   XS/R-2.
ISSN 0003-1062

**JOURNAL OF THE AMERICAN SOCIETY FOR INFORMA-TION SCIENCE.**            XXX
+ +J. AM. SOC. INF. SCI.
WASHINGTON, D.C. 21(1), JA/F 1970-
2M.   PREV: AMERICAN DOCUMENTATION FROM 1,
1950- 20, 1969.  ALSO KNOWN AS JASIS.
BH/U-1.   BL/U-1.   LO/N-4.   LO/U-3.   NW/U-1.   RE/U-1.
ED/N-1.  22, 1971-
ISSN 0002-8231

**JOURNAL OF ANCIENT INDIAN HISTORY.**
+ +J. ANCIENT INDIAN HIST.
UNIVERSITY OF CALCUTTA: DEPARTMENT OF ANCIENT
INDIAN HISTORY & CULTURE.
CALCUTTA 1, 1968-
LO/U14.   OX/U13.

**JOURNAL OF THE ANCIENT NEAR EASTERN SOCIETY OF COLUMBIA UNIVERSITY.**
+ +J. ANC. NEAR EAST. SOC. COLUMBIA UNIV.
NEW YORK 1(1), 1968-
LO/U14. 1(2), 1969-            MA/U-1. 4(2), 1972-
OX/U-2.  1969-

**JOURNAL OF THE ANTHROPOLOGICAL SOCIETY OF OXFORD.**
+ +J. ANTHROPOL. SOC. OXFORD.
OXFORD UNIVERSITY ANTHROPOLOGICAL SOCIETY.
OXFORD 1, 1970-
CA/U-3.   CB/U-1.   ED/N-1.   LO/S10.   LO/U-2.   LO/U14.
OX/U-1.
ISSN 0044-8370

**JOURNAL OF APPLIED BEHAVIOR ANALYSIS.**
+ +J. APPL. BEHAV. ANAL.
SOCIETY FOR THE EXPERIMENTAL ANALYSIS OF
BEHAVIOR.
ANN ARBOR 1(1), SPRING 1968-
BN/U-1.   EX/U-1.   LD/U-1.   MA/U-1.   OX/U-8.
SO/U-1.  7, 1974-
ISSN 0021-8855

**JOURNAL OF APPLIED CHEMISTRY & BIOTECHNOLOGY.**   XXX
+ +J. APPL. CHEM. & BIOTECHNOL.
SOCIETY OF CHEMICAL INDUSTRY.
LONDON 21, 1971-
ISSUED WITH ABSTRACTS.  TITLE EXPANDED FROM
JOURNAL OF APPLIED CHEMISTRY WITH ABOVE NO.
BH/P-1.   GL/U-1.   LD/U-1.   LO/N-7.   LO/N14.   LO/U-1.

**JOURNAL OF APPLIED EDUCATIONAL STUDIES.**
+ +J. APPL. EDUC. STUD.
OXFORD UNIVERSITY ADVANCED STUDIES IN EDUCATION
SOCIETY.
OXFORD 1, 1972-
CA/U-1.   ED/N-1.   LD/U-1.   OX/U-1.
HL/U-2.  3, 1974-
ISSN 0301-7079

**JOURNAL OF APPLIED ELECTROCHEMISTRY.**
+ +J. APPL. ELECTROCHEM.
[CHAPMAN & HALL]
LONDON 1, 1971-
AD/U-1.   BH/U-3.   EX/U-1.   LO/N-4.   LO/N14.   LO/S-3.
OX/U-8.   SH/C-5.
LD/U-1. 2, 1972-            SO/U-1. 4, 1974-

**JOURNAL OF APPLIED SOCIAL PSYCHOLOGY.**
+ +J. APPL. SOC. PSYCHOL.
[SCRIPTA PUBL. CORP.]
WASHINGTON, D.C. 1(1), JA/MR 1971-
Q.
AD/U-1.   BN/U-1.   DB/U-2.   EX/U-1.   LO/U-1.   LO/U-3.
LO/U28.   SH/U-1.   XY/N-1.
ISSN 0021-9029

**JOURNAL OF APPROXIMATION THEORY.**
+ +J. APPROX. THEORY.
NEW YORK 1, 1968-
Q.
AD/U-1.   CA/U-2.   HL/U-1.   LO/N14.   LO/U-2.   SH/U-1.
SW/U-1.   XS/R10.
CB/U-1. 2, 1969-            GL/U-1. 5, 1972-
MA/U-1. 5, 1972-
ISSN 0021-9045

**JOURNAL OF ARABIC LITERATURE.**
+ +J. ARABIC LIT.
[BRILL]
LEIDEN 1, 1970-
ANNU.
AD/U-1.   DB/U-2.   LO/N-1.   MA/U-1.   OX/U-1.

**JOURNAL OF ARIZONA HISTORY.**            XXX
+ +J. ARIZ. HIST.
ARIZONA PIONEERS' HISTORICAL SOCIETY.
TUCSON, ARIZ. 6(1), SPRING 1965-
PREV: ARIZONIANA FROM 1, 1960- 5, 1964.
LO/U-1.  13, 1972-

**JOURNAL OF THE ASAHIKAWA TECHNICAL COLLEGE.**   000
SEE: ASAHIKAWA KOGYO KOTO SEMMON GAKKO
KENKYU HOBUN.

**JOURNAL OF ASIAN HISTORY.**
+ +J. ASIAN HIST.
[OTTO HARRASSOWITZ]
WIESBADEN 1, 1967-
2/A.  TEXT IN ENGL., FR., GER. OR RUSS.
LO/N-1.   SH/U-1.
ISSN 0021-910X

**JOURNAL OF THE ASIATIC SOCIETY.**
+ +J. ASIAT. SOC. [JOAS-A]
ASIATIC SOCIETY (CALCUTTA).
CALCUTTA 1(1), 1959(1961)-
CALLED SERIES 4.  PREV (SERIES 3): JOURNAL
OF THE ROYAL ASIATIC SOCIETY OF BENGAL; [TWO
PARTS]: SCIENCE (&) LETTERS., 1,1935- 24,1958.
LO/N-1.   LO/N-4.

**JOURNAL OF THE ASSOCIATION FOR THE ADVANCE-MENT OF AGRICULTURAL SCIENCES IN AFRICA.**
+ +J. ASSOC. ADV. AGRIC. SCI. AFR.
ADDIS ABABA 1(1), AG 1971-
LO/R-6.   OX/U-3.

**JOURNAL OF THE ASSOCIATION OF LAW TEACHERS.**
+ +J. ASSOC. LAW TEACH.
ASSOCIATION OF LAW TEACHERS.
[SWEET & MAXWELL]
LONDON 1, 1967- 4, 1970 ...
SUBS: LAW TEACHER.
CB/U-1.   ED/N-1.   LO/U12.   LV/U-1.   SH/U-1.
LO/U11.  3, 1969-
SH/C-5.  4, 1970-
SO/U-1.  1, 1967; 3, 1969.
ISSN 0044-9628

**JOURNAL OF ATHEROSCLEROSIS RESEARCH.**   XXX
+ +J. ATHEROSCLER. RES. [JASR-A]
[ELSEVIER]
AMSTERDAM. 1, JA/F 1961- 10, 1969...
2M.  SUBS: ATHEROSCLEROSIS.
AD/U-1.   BH/U-1.   DB/U-2.   ED/U-1.   GL/M-1.   LD/U-1.
LO/M-2.   LO/M17.   LO/M32.   NW/U-1.   OX/U-8.
LO/M11.  1964-            LV/U-1.  1963-
SH/U-1.  6,1966-

**JOURNAL, AUSTRALIAN ENTOMOLOGICAL SOCIETY.**   XXX
+ +J. AUST. ENTOMOL. SOC.
BRISBANE 6, JE 1967-
PREV:  JOURNAL, ENTOMOLOGICAL SOCIETY OF
QUEENSLAND FROM 1, 1962- 5, 1966.
LO/N13.
MA/U-1.  1968-
ISSN 0004-9050

**JOURNAL OF AUTISM & CHILDHOOD SCHIZOPHRENIA.**
+ +J. AUTISM & CHILD. SCHIZOPHR.
[SCRIPTA PUBL. CORP.]
WASHINGTON, D.C. 1, JA/MR 1971-
Q.
BN/U-1.   DB/U-2.   LO/U-4.   MA/U-1.   OX/U-8.   XY/N-1.
ISSN 0021-9185

**JOURNAL OF AUTOMOTIVE ENGINEERING.**
+ +J. AUTOMOT. ENG.
INSTITUTION OF MECHANICAL ENGINEERS: AUTOMOBILE
DIVISION.
LONDON 1, MR 1970-
AD/U-2.   BL/U-1.   GL/U-2.   LO/N14.   SH/U-3.   SO/U-1.
XS/R10.
BH/P-1. 2, JA 1971-            ED/N-1. 2, 1971-
LO/U20. 2, 1971-
MA/P-1. 1(2), AP 1970-
ISSN 0047-2247

**JOURNAL OF THE BALINT SOCIETY.**
+ +J. BALINT SOC.
LONDON 1(1), JE 1971-
AD/U-1.   ED/N-1.

JOURNAL OF BEHAVIOR THERAPY & EXPERIMENTAL
PSYCHIATRY.
++J. BEHAV. THER. & EXP. PSYCHIAT.
BEHAVIOR THERAPY SOCIETY.
[PERGAMON P.]
 NEW YORK &C. 1(1), MR 1970-
 Q.
 CR/U-1.   ED/N-1.   LO/U-2.   OX/U-8.   SH/U-1.
 HL/U-1 ·1(3), 1970-                LO/M11. 2, 1971-
 ISSN 0005-7916

JOURNAL OF BIOENERGETICS.
++J. BIOENERG.
[PLENUM P.]
 LONDON &C. 1(1), JA 1970-
 2M.
 CA/U-1.   ED/N-1.   HL/U-1.   LO/N13.   LO/U-2.   LO/U11.
 NW/U-1.   OX/U-8.   SH/U-1.
 GL/U-1. 3, 1972-

JOURNAL OF BIOLOGICAL STANDARDIZATION.
++J. BIOL. STAND.
 LONDON 1, 1973-
 CA/U-1.   ED/N-1.   LO/N-2.   OX/U-8.
 ISSN 0092-1157

JOURNAL OF BIOMECHANICS.
++J. BIOMECH.
[PERGAMON]
 OXFORD &C 1, 1968-
 ED/N-1.   LO/N-4.   LO/N14.   LO/U12.   OX/U-8.
 ISSN 0021-9290

JOURNAL OF BIOMEDICAL MATERIALS RESEARCH.
++J. BIOMED. MATER. RES.
[INTERSCIENCE]
 NEW YORK &C   1, MR 1967-
 Q.
 GL/U-2.   LO/N14.
 ISSN 0021-9304

JOURNAL OF BIOMEDICAL SYSTEMS.
++J. BIOMED. SYST.
[TECHNICAL ECONOMICS, INC.]
 BERKELEY, CALIF. 1, 1970-
 LO/N13.   OX/U-8.
 ISSN 0021-9312

JOURNAL OF BIOSOCIAL SCIENCE.
++J. BIOSOC. SCI.
 OXFORD   1(1), JA 1969-
 Q. PREV: EUGENICS REVIEW FROM 1, 1909-60, 1968.
 AD/U-1.   BH/U-1.   BH/U-3.   CA/U-3.   CA/U11.   CB/U-1.
 CR/M-1.   DB/U-2.   ED/U-1.   LD/U-1.   LO/S10.   LO/U-2.
 LO/U-3.   LO/U-4.   RE/U-1.   SH/U-1.   SO/U-1.   SW/U-1.
 ISSN 0021-9320

JOURNAL, BIRLA INSTITUTE OF TECHNOLOGY &
SCIENCE.
++J. BIRLA INST. TECHNOL. & SCI.
 PILANI 1, 1967-
 LO/N14.

JOURNAL OF BLACK POETRY.
++J. BLACK POETRY.
 SAN FRANCISCO 1, 1966-
 Q.
 LO/U-2. 1(15), 1971-              OX/U-1. 1(11), 1969-
 ISSN 0021-9339

JOURNAL OF BLACK STUDIES.
++J. BLACK STUD.
[SAGE PUBL.]
 BEVERLY HILLS 1(1), S 1970-
 Q.
 CA/U-1.   OX/U-1.   SH/U-1.
 AD/U-1. 2, 1971/72-
 ISSN 0021-9347

JOURNAL, BRISTOL INDUSTRIAL ARCHAEOLOGICAL
SOCIETY.                                              000
 SEE: BIAS JOURNAL.

JOURNAL, BRITISH DAIRY FARMERS' ASSOCIATION.         XXX
 SUBS (1961): JOURNAL, ROYAL ASSOCIATION OF
 BRITISH DAIRY FARMERS.

JOURNAL OF THE BRITISH ENDODONTIC SOCIETY.
++J. BR. ENDODONT. SOC.
 BRITISH ENDODONTIC SOCIETY.
 LONDON   1(1), SPRING 1967-
 Q.
 SH/U-1.
 ED/N-1. 1(2), 1967-              LO/N14. 2, 1968-
 OX/U-8.
 ISSN 0007-0653

JOURNAL OF THE BRITISH INTERPLANETARY SOCIETY.
++J. BR. INTERPLANET. SOC. [JBIS-A]
 BRITISH INTERPLANETARY SOCIETY.
 LONDON  1, 1934- 20, 1965...
       21, 1968-
 RESUMED PUBL. AS INDEP. JOURNAL.  FROM 1966-67
 PART OF THE SOCIETY'S: SPACEFLIGHT.
 ED/N-1.    MA/U-1.    LO/U-1.
 GL/U-1. 17,1959-               LO/N-7. 6,1947-
 LO/P-7. *6,1947-               LO/U-6. 12,1953-
 SH/U-1. 19,1964-               SH/U-3. 12,1953-
 SW/U-1. 12,1953-               XE/C-3. (1957)-
 XS/N-2. (1950)-                XW/C-4. (1959)-
 XW/P-5. 19,1963-              YK/U-1. 19,1963-

JOURNAL, BRITISH SHIP RESEARCH ASSOCIATION.*        XXX
 SUBS (1968): JOURNAL OF ABSTRACTS, BRITISH
 SHIP RESEARCH ASSOCIATION

JOURNAL, BRITISH SOCIETY FOR PHENOMENOLOGY.
++J. BR. SOC. PHENOMENOL.
 MANCHESTER 1(1), 1970-
 BN/U-1.    CB/U-1.    DB/U-2.    ED/N-1.    EX/U-1.   GL/U-1.
 HL/U-1.    LD/U-1.    LO/U-1.    LO/U-2.    MA/U-1.   NO/U-1.
 OX/U-1.    RE/U-1.    SH/U-1.
 AD/U-1.
 ISSN 0007-1773

JOURNAL, BRITISH WATERWORKS ASSOCIATION.            XXX
 SUBS (1969): BRITISH WATER SUPPLY.

JOURNAL OF BRYOLOGY.                                 XXX
++J. BRYOL.
 BRITISH BRYOLOGICAL SOCIETY.
 LONDON 7, 1972-
 PREV: TRANSACTIONS, BRITISH BRYOLOGICAL SOC-
 IETY FROM 1, 1946- 6(2), 1971.
 ED/N-1.    GL/U-1.    LO/R-5.    LO/U13.    MA/U-1.    NW/U-1.
 RE/U-1.

JOURNAL OF BUSINESS FINANCE.                         XXX
++J. BUS. FINAN.
[BUSINESS PUBL. LTD.]
 LONDON 1, 1969- 5(2), 1973.
 SUBS: JOURNAL OF GENERAL MANAGEMENT.
 CB/U-1.    ED/N-1.    EX/U-1.    LO/U-3. 2(1), 1970-    NO/U-1.
 OX/U-1.    RE/U-1.    SW/U-1.
 BH/U-3.  4, 1972-              BN/U-1. 2(2), 1970-
 GL/U-1. 1(2), 1969-           LO/U-3. 2(1), 1970-
 NW/U-1. 1(2), 1969-           OX/U16. 2(1), 1970-
 SF/U-1.  3, 1971-             SH/C-5. 2, 1970-
 XS/T-4. 3(4), 1971-
 ISSN 0021-9452

JOURNAL OF BUSINESS POLICY.                          XXX
++J. BUS. POLICY.
[BUSINESS PUBL.]
 LONDON 1(1), 1970- 3(1), 1973.
 Q. SUBS. INCORP. IN: JOURNAL OF GENERAL
 MANAGEMENT.
 CB/U-1.    LO/N-5.    OX/U-1.    OX/U17.    RE/U-1.    SH/U-1.
 SW/U-1.
 XS/R10. 3(3), 1973-
 ISSN 0021-9479

JOURNAL OF BUSINESS & SOCIAL STUDIES.
++J. BUS. & SOC. STUD. (UNIV. LAGOS).
 UNIVERSITY OF LAGOS.
 LAGOS   1(1), S 1968-
 S/T: PUBLICATION OF THE SCHOOLS OF ADMINI-
 STRATION & SOCIAL STUDIES, UNIV. OF LAGOS.
 ED/U-1.    LO/U-3.
 ISSN 0021-9428

JOURNAL, BUTLER SOCIETY.
++J. BUTLER SOC.
 KILKENNY 1, 1968-
 BL/U-1.    DB/S-1.    DB/U-2.    ED/N-1.    OX/U-1.

JOURNAL OF BYELORUSSIAN STUDIES.
++J. BYELORUSS. STUD.
 ANGLO-BYELORUSSIAN SOCIETY.
 LONDON 1, 1965-
 BH/U-1.    CA/U-1.    DB/U-2.    RE/U-1.
 ED/N-1(2), 1966-              LD/U-1.
 MA/S-1. 3, 1967-

JOURNAL, CALIFORNIA HORTICULTURAL SOCIETY.          XXX
 SUBS (1968): CALIFORNIA HORTICULTURAL JOURNAL.

JOURNAL OF THE CAMBORNE-REDRUTH NATURAL
HISTORY SOCIETY.
++J. CAMBORNE-REDRUTH NAT. HIST. SOC.
 CAMBORNE, CORNWALL 1(1), 1969-
 ED/N-1.
 LO/R-5. 2(1), 1969-              OX/U-8. 2(1), 1969-

**JOURNAL OF CAMEROON AFFAIRS.**
+ +J. CAMEROON AFF.
CAMEROON STUDENTS ASSOCIATION OF ARTS &
SCIENCES.
 HUNTINGDON, PA.  1, JA/F 1972-
 AD/U-1.    LO/U14.

**JOURNAL OF THE CANADIAN BAR ASSOCIATION.**          XXX
+ +J. CAN. BAR ASS.
 OTTAWA  1, 1970-
 PREV:  CANADIAN BAR JOURNAL FROM 1, 1958- 12,
 1969.
 LO/U-2.

**JOURNAL OF CANADIAN FICTION.**
+ +J. CAN. FICTION.
 [BELLROCK P.]
 FREDERICTON  1, 1972-
 Q.
 LD/U-1.    OX/U-1.
 ISSN 0047-2255

**JOURNAL, CANADIAN INSTITUTE OF FOOD SCIENCE &**
**TECHNOLOGY.**                                        XXX
+ +J. CAN. INST. FOOD SCI. & TECHNOL.
 OTTAWA  5, 1972-
 PREV: JOURNAL, CANADIAN INSTITUTE OF FOOD
 TECHNOLOGY FROM 1, 1968- 4, 1971.
 LO/N14.

**JOURNAL, CANADIAN INSTITUTE OF FOOD**
**TECHNOLOGY.**                                        XXX
+ +J. CAN. INST. FOOD TECHNOL.
 OTTAWA  1, JA 1968- 4, 1971 ...
 SUBS: JOURNAL, CANADIAN INSTITUTE OF FOOD
 SCIENCE & TECHNOLOGY.
 LO/N14.
 ISSN 0008-3860

**JOURNAL, CANADIAN SOCIETY OF EXPLORATION GEO-**
**PHYSICISTS.**
+ +J. CAN. SOC. EXPLOR. GEOPHYS.
 CALGARY  1, 1965-
 LO/N14.
 ISSN 0008-5022

**JOURNAL, CANADIAN SOCIETY OF FORENSIC SCIENCE.**
+ +J. CAN. SOC. FORENSIC SCI.
 OTTAWA  1, MR 1968-
 LO/N13.  1(3), 1968-
 ISSN 0008-5030

**JOURNAL, CANTERBURY BOTANICAL SOCIETY.**
+ +J. CANTERBURY BOT. SOC.
 CHRISTCHURCH, N.Z.  NO.1, 1968-
 LO/N-2.

**JOURNAL, CAREERS RESEARCH & ADVISORY CENTRE.**
+ +J. CAREERS RES. & ADVIS. CENT.
 CAMBRIDGE  1, 1964-
 BH/P-1.    BH/U-1.    CA/U-1.    DB/U-1.    LA/U-1.    OX/U-1.
 XY/N-1.**

**JOURNAL OF CARIBBEAN HISTORY.**                      XXX
+ +J. CARIBB. HIST.
 UNIVERSITY OF THE WEST INDIES: DEPARTMENT OF
 HISTORY.
 BARBADOS  1, N 1970- 5, N 1972.//
 BH/P-1.    ED/N-1.    LO/U-8.    LO/U19.    MA/U-1.    NO/U-1.
 OX/U-9.
 ISSN 0047-2263

**JOURNAL OF THE CATCH SOCIETY OF AMERICA.**
+ +J. CATCH SOC. AM.
 FREDONIA, NEW YORK  1(1), 1969-
 LO/N-1.

**JOURNAL OF CERAMIC HISTORY.**
+ +J. CERAM. HIST.
 STAFFORD  NO.1, 1968-
 ED/N-1.    LO/N-1.    OX/U-1.

**JOURNAL OF CEYLON LAW.**
+ +J. CEYLON LAW.
 INCORPORATED COUNCIL OF LEGAL EDUCATION
 (CEYLON).
 COLOMBO  1(1), JE 1970-
 OX/U15.

**JOURNAL, CHARTERED INSTITUTE OF TRANSPORT.**        XXX
+ +J. CHART. INST. TRANSP.
 LONDON  34(4), 1971-
 PREV: JOURNAL, INSTITUTE OF TRANSPORT FROM 1,
 1920- 34(3), 1971.
 BH/P-1.    ED/N-1.    GL/U-1.    LO/N14.    LO/U-1.    NO/U-1.
 RE/U-1.

**JOURNAL OF CHEMICAL ENGINEERING OF JAPAN.**
+ +J. CHEM. ENG. JAP.
 KAGAKU KOGAKU KYOKAI.
 TOKYO  1(1), F 1968-
 BODY IN ENGL.: SOCIETY OF CHEMICAL ENGINEERS.
 PREV: CHEMICAL ENGINEERING, JAPAN.  BOTH PREV
 & ABOVE ARE ENGL. EDS. OF THE BODY'S: KAGAKU
 KOGAKU.
 EX/U-1.    GL/U-2.    LO/N14.    LO/S-3.    LO/U-2.    NW/U-1.
 OX/U-8.  3(1), 1970.        XS/R10.  2(1), 1969-
 ISSN 0021-9592

**JOURNAL OF THE CHEMICAL SOCIETY: CHEMICAL**
**COMMUNICATIONS.**                                    XXX
+ +J. CHEM. SOC., CHEM. COMMUN.
 LONDON  1972(1)-
 2/M. PREV: CHEMICAL COMMUNICATIONS FROM
 1965(1)- 1971(24).
 BH/P-1.    CA/U-2.    LN/U-2.    LO/N14.    LO/U11.    MA/U-1.
 ISSN 0022-4936

**JOURNAL OF THE CHEMICAL SOCIETY: DALTON TRANS-**
**ACTIONS: INORGANIC CHEMISTRY.**
+ +J. CHEM. SOC., DALTON TRANS.
 LONDON  1972-
 PREV: PART OF JOURNAL, CHEMICAL SOCIETY: A
 FROM 1966- 1971.
 CA/U-2.    ED/N-1.    GL/U-1.    HL/U-1.    LN/U-2.    LO/N-4.
 LO/N14.    LO/U13.    MA/U-1.    RE/U-1.    SO/U-1.
 XS/R10.
 LO/R-6.  1, 1972- 23, 1973.
 ISSN 0300-9246

**JOURNAL OF THE CHEMICAL SOCIETY: FARADAY**
**TRANSACTIONS 1: [PHYSICAL CHEMISTRY].**              XXX
+ +J. CHEM. SOC., FARADAY TRANS. 1.
 LONDON  68(589), 1972-
 PREV. PART OF: TRANSACTIONS, FARADAY SOCIETY
 FROM 1, 1905- 67(588), 1971; & JOURNAL, CHEM-
 ICAL SOCIETY: A FROM 1966- 1971.  ISSUES BEAR
 ODD NUMBERS ONLY, EVEN NUMBERS ADDED TO ...
 FARADAY TRANSACTIONS 2...
 BH/U-1.    CA/U-2.    ED/N-1.    GL/U-1.    HL/U-1.    LN/U-2.
 LO/N14.    LO/N35.    MA/U-1.    RE/U-1.    SO/U-1.
 XS/R10.
 ISSN 0300-9599

**JOURNAL OF THE CHEMICAL SOCIETY: FARADAY**
**TRANSACTIONS 2: [CHEMICAL PHYSICS].**                XXX
+ +J. CHEM. SOC., FARADAY TRANS. 2.
 LONDON  68(590), 1972-
 PREV. PART OF: TRANSACTIONS, FARADAY SOCIETY
 FROM 1, 1905- 67(588) 1971; &: JOURNAL CHEM-
 ICAL SOCIETY: A FROM 1966- 1971. ISSUES BEAR
 EVEN NUMBERS ONLY, ODD NUMBERS ADDED TO ...
 FARADAY TRANSACTIONS 1 ...
 CA/U-2.    ED/N-1.    GL/U-1.    HL/U-1.    LN/U-2.    LO/N14.
 LO/N35.    MA/U-1.    SO/U-1.    XS/R10.
 ISSN 0300-9238

**JOURNAL OF THE CHEMICAL SOCIETY: PERKIN TRANS-**
**ACTIONS 1: ORGANIC & BIO-ORGANIC CHEMISTRY.**
+ +J. CHEM. SOC., PERKIN TRANS. 1.
 LONDON  1972-
 PREV: JOURNAL, CHEMICAL SOCIETY: C FROM 1966-
 1971.
 CA/U-2.    ED/N-1.    GL/U-2.    HL/U-1.    LN/U-2.    LO/N-4.
 LO/N14.    LO/U28.    MA/U-1.    RE/U-1.    SO/U-1.
 ISSN 0300-922X

**JOURNAL OF THE CHEMICAL SOCIETY: PERKIN TRANS-**
**ACTIONS 2: PHYSICAL ORGANIC CHEMISTRY.**
+ +J. CHEM. SOC., PERKIN TRANS. 2.
 LONDON  1972-
 PREV: JOURNAL, CHEMICAL SOCIETY: B FROM 1966-
 1971.
 CA/U-2.    ED/N-1.    GL/U-2.    LN/U-2.    LO/N-4.    LO/N14.
 MA/U-1.    RE/U-1.    SO/U-1.    XS/R10.
 ISSN 0300-9580

**JOURNAL OF CHEMICAL THERMODYNAMICS.**
+ +J. CHEM. THERMODYN.
 [ACADEMIC PRESS]
 LONDON &C  1(1), 1969-
 CA/U-1.    DB/U-2.    ED/N-1.    GL/U-2.    LO/N-4.    LO/N14.
 LO/S-3.    MA/U-1.    OX/U-8.    SH/U-1.    XS/R10.
 BL/U-1.  5, 1973-        CB/U-1.  2, 1970-
 ISSN 0021-9614

**JOURNAL OF CHROMATOGRAPHIC SCIENCE.**
+ +J. CHROMATOGR. SCI.
 EVANSTON (ILL.)  7(1), 1969-
 PREV: JOURNAL OF GAS CHROMATOGRAPHY FROM
 1, 1963.
 BH/U-1.    HL/U-1.    LO/N-4.    LO/N14.    LO/S-3.    NW/U-1.
 SO/U-1.    XS/R10.    ZW/N-1.
 ISSN 0021-9665

M

JOURNAL OF CLINICAL PHARMACOLOGY & THE JOURNAL OF NEW DRUGS.          XXX
++J. CLIN. PHARMACOL. & J. NEW DRUGS.
[HALL ASSOCIATES]
NEW YORK  7, 1967- 10, 1970 ...
2M.  PREV: JOURNAL OF NEW DRUGS FROM 1, JA/F
1961- 6, N/D 1966.  SUBS: JOURNAL OF CLINICAL
PHARMACOLOGY & NEW DRUGS.
OX/U-8. 10(1), 1970-

JOURNAL OF COATED FIBROUS MATERIALS.          XXX
++J. COATED FIBROUS MATER.
[TECHNOMIC PUBL. CO.]
WESTPORT, CONN.  1, 1971- 2, 1973...
SUBS: JOURNAL OF COATED FABRICS.
LO/N14.    OX/U-8.
ISSN 0047-2298

JOURNAL OF COLLEGE SCIENCE TEACHING.
++J. COLL. SCI. TEACH.
NATIONAL SCIENCE TEACHERS ASSOCIATION (US).
WASHINGTON, D.C.  1(1), OC 1971-
Q.
LN/U-2.  1(2), 1971-
ISSN 0047-231X

JOURNAL OF COLOR & APPEARANCE.
++J. COLOR & APPEARANCE.
[GORDON & BREACH]
NEW YORK  1, 1971-
LO/N14.    MA/U-1.
CA/U-1.  1(6), 1972-          ED/N-1.  1(6), 1972-
GL/U-2.  2, 1973-              OX/U-8.  1(6), 1972-

JOURNAL OF COMBINATORIAL THEORY: SERIES A.          XXX
++J. COMB. THEORY, A.
[ACADEMIC P.]
NEW YORK; LONDON  10, 1971-
AS PART OF ABOVE MAIN TITLE FROM 1, 1966-
9, 1970. THEN WITH ABOVE NO. CONTINUED IN
TWO SERIES.
BR/U-1.    CB/U-1.    EX/U-1.    GL/U-1.    GL/U-2.    LO/U11.
RE/U-1.

JOURNAL OF COMBINATORIAL THEORY: SERIES B.          XXX
++J. COMB. THEORY, B.
[ACADEMIC P.]
NEW YORK; LONDON  10, 1971-
SEE REMARKS FOR SERIES A.
BR/U-1.    EX/U-1.    GL/U-1.    GL/U-2.    LO/U11.    RE/U-1.

JOURNAL OF COMMUNICABLE DISEASES.
++J. COMMUN. DIS. (INDIA).
INDIAN SOCIETY FOR MALARIA & OTHER COMMUNICABLE
DISEASES.
DELHI  1, 1969-
LO/N-2.
ISSN 0019-5138

JOURNAL OF COMMUNICATION DISORDERS.
++J. COMMUN. DISORD.
[NORTH-HOLLAND PUBL. CO.]
AMSTERDAM  1, MY 1967-
LO/N13.
ISSN 0021-9924

JOURNAL OF COMPARATIVE ADMINISTRATION.
++J. COMP. ADM.
[SAGE PUBLICATIONS]
BEVERLY HILLS  1(1), MY 1969- 5, 1974 ...
SUBS: ADMINISTRATION AND SOCIETY.
EX/U-1.    GL/U-1.    HL/U-1.    LO/U-3.    LO/U-8.
ISSN 0021-9932

JOURNAL OF COMPARATIVE FAMILY STUDIES.
++J. COMP. FAM. STUD.
UNIVERSITY OF CALGARY: DEPARTMENT OF SOCIOLOGY
& ANTHROPOLOGY.
CALGARY  1(1), 1970-
2/A.
CA/U-3.    LO/N-1.    LO/U-3.    OX/U-1.
ISSN 0047-2323

JOURNAL OF COMPARATIVE PATHOLOGY.*          XXX
++J. COMP. PATHOL. [JCVP-A]
[LIVERPOOL UNIV. P.]
LIVERPOOL  75, 1965-
Q.  PREV: JOURNAL OF COMPARATIVE PATHOLOGY &
THERAPEUTICS FROM 1, 1888- 74, 1964.
LO/M-1.    SH/U-1.
ISSN 0021-9975

JOURNAL OF COMPARATIVE PHYSIOLOGY.          XXX
++J. COMP. PHYSIOL.
[SPRINGER]
BERLIN & C.  77(1), 1972- 92(4), 1974 ...
PREV: ZEITSCHRIFT FUR VERGLEICHENDE PHYSIOL-
OGIE FROM 21, 1935- 76, 1972. SUBS. PART OF:
JOURNAL OF COMPARATIVE PHYSIOLOGY: A: SENSORY,
NEURAL AND BEHAVIOURAL PHYSIOLOGY; & JOURNAL
OF COMPARATIVE PHYSIOLOGY: B: METABOLIC &
TRANSPORT FUNCTIONS.
GL/U-1.    LO/N-4.    LO/N13.    LO/U28.    OX/U-8.

JOURNAL OF CONSTITUTIONAL & PARLIAMENTARY
STUDIES (INDIA).
++J. CONST. & PARLIAMENT. STUD. (INDIA).
INSTITUTE OF CONSTITUTIONAL & PARLIAMENTARY
STUDIES (INDIA).
NEW DELHI  1(1), JA/MR 1967-
Q.
LO/N-1.    LO/U-8.    LO/U14.    OX/U13.
ISSN 0022-0043

JOURNAL OF CONSULTING & CLINICAL PSYCHOLOGY.*          XXX
++J. CONSULT. & CLIN. PSYCHOL.
AMERICAN PSYCHOLOGICAL ASSOCIATION.
LANCASTER, PA.  32, 1968-
PREV: JOURNAL OF CONSULTING PSYCHOLOGY.,
FROM 1, 1937.
LO/U-2.    SO/U-1.
ISSN 0022-006X

JOURNAL OF CONTEMPORARY ASIA.
++J. CONTEMP. ASIA.
LONDON  1(1), 1970-
CB/U-1.    HL/U-1.    LO/U-3.    LO/U14.    OX/U-1.    SH/U-1.
ISSN 0047-2336

JOURNAL OF COOPERATIVE EDUCATION.
++J. COOP. EDUC.
COOPERATIVE EDUCATION ASSOCIATION.
PHILADELPHIA  1, 1964-
SF/U-1.  9, 1973-
ISSN 0022-0132

JOURNAL OF COORDINATION CHEMISTRY.
++J. COORD. CHEM.
[GORDON & BREACH]
LONDON  1(1), AG 1971-
BH/U-3.    LO/N14.    LO/S-3.    LO/U11.
ED/N-1.  1(2), 1971-          GL/U-1.  3, 1973-
XY/N-1.  1, 1971.

JOURNAL OF CRIMINAL JUSTICE.
++J. CRIM. JUSTICE.
[PERGAMON]
NEW YORK; OXFORD  1, 1973-
CA/U-1.    ED/N-1.    HL/U-1.    OX/U-1.    SH/U-1.
ISSN 0047-2352

JOURNAL OF CROATIAN STUDIES.
++J. CROAT. STUD.
CROATION ACADEMY OF AMERICA.
NEW YORK  1, 1960-
MA/U-1.

JOURNAL OF CROSS CULTURAL PSYCHOLOGY.
++J. CROSS CULT. PSYCHOL.
WESTERN WASHINGTON STATE COLLEGE: CENTER FOR
CROSS CULTURAL RESEARCH.
BELLINGHAM, WASH.  1, 1970-
AB/U-1.    DB/U-1.    DB/U-2.    GL/U-2.    HL/U-1.
LO/U20.  2, 1971-
ISSN 0022-0221

JOURNAL OF CRYSTAL & MOLECULAR STRUCTURE.
++J. CRYST. & MOL. STRUCT.
[PLENUM PUBL. CO.]
LONDON &C.  1(1/2), JA 1971-
CA/U-1.    ED/N-1.    GL/U-1.    LO/N14.    OX/U-8.    XS/R10.
BL/U-1.  4, 1974-

JOURNAL OF CURRENT LASER ABSTRACTS.
++J. CURR. LASER ABSTR.
INSTITUTE FOR LASER DOCUMENTATION (VANCOUVER).
VANCOUVER, BC  4, 1967-
PREV: LASER/MASER INTERNATIONAL; FROM 1,1964.
BL/U-1.    LO/N14.
ISSN 0022-0264

JOURNAL OF CURRICULUM STUDIES.
++J. CURRIC. STUD.
GLASGOW  1(1), N 1968-
2/A.
BL/U-1.    DB/U-2.    ED/N-1.    EX/U-1.    GL/U-1.    HL/U-2.
LO/U11.    MA/U-1.    OX/U-1.    SH/U-1.    SW/U-1.
GL/U-2.  5(1), MY 1973-
ISSN 0022-0272

**JOURNAL OF CYBERNETICS.**
+ +J. CYBERN.
[SCRIPTA PUBL. CO.]
WASHINGTON, D.C. 1, 1971-
CB/U-1.   LO/N-4.   LO/N14.   LO/U28.
CO/U-1. 2(1), 1972-
XY/N-1. 1(1), 1971.
ISSN 0022-0280

**JOURNAL OF DENTISTRY.**                                    XXX
+ +J. DENT.
[J. WRIGHT]
BRISTOL 1(1), OC 1972-
PREV: DENTAL PRACTITIONER & DENTAL RECORD FROM
1, 1950- 22, 1971/72.
DB/U-2.   ED/N-1.   GL/U-1.   LD/U-1.   OX/U-8.   SH/U-1.
ISSN 0300-5712

**JOURNAL OF DEVELOPMENT PLANNING.**
+ +J. DEVELOP. PLANN.
UNITED NATIONS: DEPARTMENT OF ECONOMIC & SOCIAL
AFFAIRS.
NEW YORK NO.1, 1969-
BH/U-1.   CB/U-1.   ED/N-1.   LO/U-3.   LO/U14.   MA/P-1.
MA/U-1.   OX/U16.   OX/U17.
LO/U-8. NO.2, 1970-

**JOURNAL OF DIFFERENTIAL GEOMETRY.**
+ +J. DIFFERENT. GEOMETRY.
LEHIGH UNIVERSITY (PA).
PROVIDENCE (R.I.) 1, 1967-
AD/U-1.   HL/U-1.   LO/N14.   LO/U-2.   LO/U11.   MA/U-1.
OX/U-8.   SH/U-1.   SO/U-1.   SW/U-1.
GL/U-1. 1968-           LD/U-1. 4(4), 1970-
ISSN 0022-040X

**JOURNAL OF EARTH SCIENCES.**                              XXX
+ +J. EARTH SCI.
LEEDS GEOLOGICAL ASSOCIATION.
LEEDS 8(1), 1970-
PREV: TRANSACTIONS, LEEDS GEOLOGICAL ASSOCIAT-
ION FROM 1, 1883- 7, 1955/67(1968).
ED/N-1.   HL/U-1.   LD/U-1.   LO/N-4.   LO/N13.   LO/R-5.
LO/U12.   NW/U-1.   RE/U-1.   SO/U-1.

**JOURNAL OF EAST AFRICAN STUDIES.**
+ +J. EAST AFR. STUD.
WILMINGTON COLLEGE.
WILMINGTON, OHIO 1(1), 1971-
LO/U-8. 2(1), 1973-

**JOURNAL OF EASTERN AFRICAN RESEARCH &
DEVELOPMENT.**
+ +J. EAST. AFR. RES. & DEV.
EAST AFRICAN LITERATURE BUREAU.
NAIROBI 1(1), 1971-
2/A. ENGL. & SWAHILLI.
NO/U-1. 4, 1974-           OX/U-9. 1(2), 1971-

**JOURNAL OF ECONOMETRICS.**
+ +J. ECONOMETRICS.
[NORTH-HOLLAND]
AMSTERDAM 1(1), MR 1973-
Q.
AD/U-1.   DB/U-2.   EX/U-1.   LO/U-3.   LO/U12.   MA/U-1.
OX/U-1.   OX/U16.   OX/U17.   SH/U-1.   SO/U-1.
BH/U-3. 2, 1974-

**JOURNAL OF ECONOMIC ABSTRACTS.**                          XXX
+ +J. ECON. ABSTR. [JLEA-A]
AMERICAN ECONOMIC ASSOCIATION.
CAMBRIDGE, MASS. 1, JA 1963-6, 1968.
SUBS: JOURNAL OF ECONOMIC LITERATURE.
BH/U-1.   BL/U-1.   ED/U-1.   GL/C-1.   GL/P-1.   HL/U-1.
LA/U-1.   LC/U-1.   LD/P-1.   LO/U-2.   LO/U-3.   LV/P-1.
NO/P-1.   NO/U-1.   OX/U11.   SA/U-1.   SH/U-1.   SO/U-1.
SW/U-1.
LO/C-8. 1, AP 1963-       LO/U-1. 4,1966-

**JOURNAL OF ECONOMIC EDUCATION.**
+ +J. ECON. EDUC.
JOINT COUNCIL ON ECONOMIC EDUCATION.
NEW YORK 1, 1969-
2/A.
BH/U-2.   MA/U-1.
XY/N-1. 1971-
ISSN 0022-0485

**JOURNAL OF ECONOMIC ISSUES.**
+ +J. ECON. ISSUES.
ASSOCIATION FOR EVOLUTIONARY ECONOMICS.
AUSTIN, TEX. 1(1/2), JE 1967-
Q. SPONS. BODY ALSO: UNIVERSITY OF TEXAS.
CB/U-1.   LO/N-7.   LO/U-3.
NO/U-1. 3, 1969-
ISSN 0021-3624

**JOURNAL OF ECONOMIC LITERATURE.**                         XXX
+ +J. ECON. LIT.
AMERICAN ECONOMIC ASSOCIATION.
EVANSTON (ILL.) 7, 1969-
PREV: JOURNAL OF ECONOMIC ABSTRACTS FROM 1,
1963- 6, 1968.
BL/U-1.   CB/U-1.   CO/U-1.   GL/U-1.   LO/U-1.   LO/U-3.
NO/U-1.   OX/U17.   RE/U-1.
CA/U-1. 8, 1970-
LO/N17. 8(1), MR 1970-
LO/R-6. 8(1), MR 1970-
OX/U24. 9(1), MR 1971-
ISSN 0022-0515

**JOURNAL OF ECONOMIC THEORY.**
+ +J. ECON. THEORY.
LONDON 1(1), JE 1969-
Q.
AD/U-1.   GL/U-1.   LO/N10.   LO/U-2.   LO/U-3.   LO/U12.
OX/U17.   SH/U-1.   SO/U-1.
CA/U-1. 3, 1971-         CB/U-1. 2, 1970-
MA/U-1. 3, 1971-         OX/U16. 2(1), 1970-
ISSN 0022-0531

**JOURNAL OF EDUCATION FOR INDUSTRY & COMMERCE.**
+ +J. EDUC. IND. & COMMER.
(GREAT BRITAIN) DEPARTMENT OF EDUCATION &
SCIENCE.
LONDON NO.1, AP 1966-
Q.
MA/P-1. NO.1, AP 1966- 4, JA 1967. (W. NO.3,
OC 1966)

**JOURNAL OF EDUCATION FOR SOCIAL WORK.**
+ +J. EDUC. SOC. WORK.
COUNCIL ON SOCIAL WORK EDUCATION.
NEW YORK 1, 1965-
AD/U-1. 3, 1967-          LV/U-1. 2(5), 1966-
NO/U-1. 5, 1969-         XY/N-1. 5(1), 1969-
ISSN 0022-0612

**JOURNAL OF EDUCATIONAL ADMINISTRATION &
HISTORY.**
+ +J. EDUC. ADMIN. & HIST.
UNIVERSITY OF LEEDS.
LEEDS 1(1), D 1968-
2/A.
AD/U-1.   BN/U-1.   CB/U-1.   DB/U-2.   ED/N-1.   EX/U-1.
GL/U-2.   HL/U-2.   LO/P-6.   LO/U-1.   MA/U-1.   SH/U-1.
SW/U-1.
CO/U-1. 2(2), JE 1970-
ISSN 0022-0620

**JOURNAL OF EDUCATIONAL TECHNOLOGY.**
+ +J. EDUC. TECHNOL.
NATIONAL COUNCIL FOR EDUCATIONAL TECHNOLOGY(GB)
[COUNCILS & EDUCATION P.]
LONDON 1(1), 1970- 1(3), D 1970 ...
SUBS: BRITISH JOURNAL OF EDUCATIONAL
TECHNOLOGY.
AD/U-1.   BN/U-1.   DN/U-1.   ED/N-1.   HL/U-1.   HL/U-2.
LD/U-1.   LO/N-1.   LOS/74.   LO/U11.   OX/U-1.
ISSN 0022-0698

**JOURNAL OF ELASTICITY.**
+ +J. ELASTICITY.
[WOLTERS-NOORDHOFF]
GRONINGEN 1(1), 1971-
AD/U-1.   BR/U-1.   GL/U-1.   LD/U-1.   LO/N14.   LO/U28.
SH/U-1.   SH/U-3.
GL/U-2. 3(1), 1973-      MA/U-1. 4, 1974-
SO/U-1. 4, 1974-

**JOURNAL OF ELASTOPLASTICS.**
+ +J. ELASTOPLAST.
[TECHNOMIC PUBL. CO.]
STAMFORD, CONN. 1, 1969- 5, 1973 ...
SUBS: JOURNAL OF ELASTOMERS AND PLASTICS.
LO/N14.   OX/U-8.
ISSN 0022-071X

**JOURNAL OF ELECTROCARDIOLOGY.**
+ +J. ELECTROCARDIOL.
RESEARCH IN ELECTROCARDIOLOGY INC.
KETTERING, OHIO 1(1), 1968-
Q.
LO/N13.   OX/U-8.
ISSN 0022-0736

**JOURNAL OF ELECTRON SPECTROSCOPY & RELATED
PHENOMENA.**
+ +J. ELECTRON SPECTROSCOP. & RELAT. PHENOM.
[ELSEVIER]
AMSTERDAM 1, 1972-
BL/U-1.   CA/U-2.   GL/U-2.   LO/N14.   LO/S-3.   LO/U12.
MA/U-1.   OX/U-3.   XS/R10.   XS/R10.

JOURNAL OF ELECTRONIC MATERIALS.
++J. ELECTRON. MATER.
AMERICAN INSTITUTE OF MINING, METALLURGICAL &
PETROLEUM ENGINEERS: METALLURGICAL SOCIETY.
NEW YORK [1], 1973-
Q.
LO/N14.
CA/U-2. 2, 1973-

JOURNAL OF ENGINEERING EDUCATION.    XXX
SUBS (1969): ENGINEERING EDUCATION.

JOURNAL, ENGLISH PLACE NAME SOCIETY.
++J. ENGL. PLACE NAME SOC.
LONDON 1, 1968/69 (1969)-
BH/U-1.    BL/U-1.    ED/N-1.    GL/U-1.    LD/U-1.    LO/N-3.
LO/U-1.    LO/U-4.    LO/U12.    LO/U13.    MA/S-1.
NO/U-1.    NW/U-1.    OX/U-1.    RE/U-1.    SO/U-1.
SW/U-1.

JOURNAL OF ENTOMOLOGY: SERIES A: GENERAL ENT-
OMOLOGY.    XXX
++J. ENTOMOL., A.
ROYAL ENTOMOLOGICAL SOCIETY OF LONDON.
LONDON 46, 1971-
PREV: PROCEEDINGS, ROYAL ... SERIES A: GENERAL
ENTOMOLOGY FROM 11, 1936- 45, 1970.
BH/P-1.    ED/N-1.    GL/U-1.    HL/U-1.    LD/U-1.    LO/N-4.
LO/N14.    NW/U-1.    SO/U-1.
ISSN 0047-2409

JOURNAL OF ENTOMOLOGY: SERIES B: TAXONOMY.    XXX
++J. ENTOMOL., B.
ROYAL ENTOMOLOGICAL SOCIETY OF LONDON.
LONDON 40, 1971-
PREV: PROCEEDINGS, ROYAL ... SERIES B:
TAXONOMY FROM 5, 1936- 39, 1970.
BH/P-1.    GL/U-1.    HL/U-1.    LD/U-1.    LO/N-4.    LO/R-5.
NW/U-1.    SO/U-1.
ISSN 0047-2417

JOURNAL OF ENVIRONMENTAL MANAGEMENT.
++J. ENVIRON. MANAGE.
[ACADEMIC P.]
LONDON &C. 1, 1973-
AD/U-3.    BL/U-1.    CA/U-1.    ED/N-1.    EX/U-1.    GL/U-2.
HL/U-1.    LO/N14.    LO/R-5.    MA/U-1.    OX/U-1.    OX/U-3.
SH/U-1.
LO/U-4. 3, 1975-
ISSN 0301-4797

JOURNAL OF ENVIRONMENTAL PLANNING & POLLUTION
CONTROL.
++J. ENVIRON. PLANN. & POLLUT. CONTROL.
[MERCURY HOUSE BUSINESS PUBL. LTD.]
LONDON 1(1), 1972-
Q.
BH/U-3.    LO/N13.    LO/R-5.    LO/U-4.    OX/U-1.    XS/R10.
CA/U-1. 1(2), 1972/73-
ED/N-1. 1(2), 1972/73-

JOURNAL OF ENVIRONMENTAL QUALITY.
++J. ENVIRON. QUAL.
AMERICAN SOCIETY OF AGRONOMY.
MADISON, WIS. 1, 1972-
Q.
AD/U-3.    CA/U-1.    LO/N-6.    LO/N13.    OX/U-8.    RE/U-1.
BL/U-1. 4, 1975-
ISSN 0047-2425

JOURNAL OF ENVIRONMENTAL SYSTEMS.
++J. ENVIRON. SYST.
[BAYWOOD PUBL. CO.]
FARMINGDALE, N.Y. 1(1), MR 1971-
Q.
XY/N-1.
ISSN 0047-2433

JOURNAL OF EUROPEAN ECONOMIC HISTORY.
++J. EUR. ECON. HIST.
BANCO DI ROMA.
ROME 1(1), 1972-
3/A.
CA/U-1.    EX/U-1.    LO/N-1.    LO/N-3.    MA/U-1.    SH/U-1.
SW/U-1.
AD/U-1. 2, 1973-                OX/U-1. 2(1), 1973-

JOURNAL OF EUROPEAN STUDIES.
++J. EUR. STUD.
[SEMINAR P.]
LONDON 1(1), MR 1971-
Q.
AD/U-1.    DB/U-2.    ED/N-1.    LO/N-1.    MA/U-1.    RE/U-1.
ISSN 0047-2441

JOURNAL EUROPEEN DE TOXICOLOGIE. EUROPEAN
JOURNAL OF TOXICOLOGY.
++J. EUR. TOXICOL.
[EDITIONS DIMEO]
ARCUEIL 1, 1968-
LO/N13.
ISSN 0021-8219

JOURNAL OF EVOLUTIONARY BIOCHEMISTRY & PHYSIOL-
OGY.
++J. EVOL. BIOCHEM. & PHYSIOL.
[CONSULTANTS BUREAU]
NEW YORK &C. 5(1), 1969-
2M. TRANSL. OF: ZHURNAL EVOLYUTSIONNOJ
BIOKHIMII I FIZIOLOGII.
LO/N-2.    LO/N13.    LO/U-2.    OX/U-8.
ISSN 0022-0930

JOURNAL OF EXPERIMENTAL SOCIAL PSYCHOLOGY;
SUPPLEMENT.
++J. EXP. SOC. PSYCHOL., SUPPL.
[ACADEMIC PRESS]
NEW YORK 1, 1966-
AD/U-1.
CA/U-1. 10, 1974-

JOURNAL OF FARM ECONOMICS.    XXX
SUBS (1968): AMERICAN JOURNAL OF
AGRICULTURAL ECONOMICS.

JOURNAL OF FIRE & FLAMMABILITY.
++J. FIRE & FLAMMABILITY.
[TECHNOMIC PUBL. CO.]
STAMFORD, CONN. 1, 1970-
LO/N14.
ISSN 0022-1104

JOURNAL OF FISH BIOLOGY.
++J. FISH BIOL.
FISHERIES SOCIETY OF THE BRITISH ISLES.
LONDON 1(1), JA 1969-
BH/U-3.    BL/U-1.    CO/U-1.    DB/U-2.    ED/N-1.    EX/U-1.
LO/N-2.    LO/N12.    LO/R-5.    LO/R-6.    LO/U-2.    LO/U12.
LV/U-1.    OX/U-8.    SH/U-1.
LO/U13. 2, 1970-                  NW/U-1. 3, 1971-
RE/U-1. 2, 1970-
ISSN 0022-1112

JOURNAL OF FLOUR & ANIMAL FEED MILLING.    XXX
++J. FLOUR & ANIM. FEED MILL.
[TURRET P.]
LONDON 155(4), AP 1973-
PREV: MILLING FROM 1, 1891- 155(3), 1973.
INCORP. FEED & FARM SUPPLIES FROM 67(6), 1970-
70(3), 1973.
BL/U-1.    ED/N-1.    GL/U-1.    LD/U-1.    LO/N-6.    LO/R-6.
ISSN 0305-716X

JOURNAL OF FLUORINE CHEMISTRY.
++J. FLUORINE CHEM.
[ELSEVIER SEQUOIA S.A.]
LAUSANNE 1, 1971/72-
LO/N14.    LO/S-3.    LO/U-4.    NW/U-1.    OX/U-8.    SF/U-1.
ISSN 0022-1139

JOURNAL OF THE FOLKLORE INSTITUTE, INDIANA
UNIVERSITY.    XXX
++J. FOLKLORE INST. INDIANA UNIV.
[MOUTON]
THE HAGUE & BLOOMINGTON 1, 1964-
PREV: MIDWEST FOLKLORE FROM 1, 1951- 13, 1963.
CR/U-1.    SH/U-1.
BL/U-1. 6, 1969- [W. 7,8]

JOURNAL OF FORAMINIFERAL RESEARCH.    XXX
++J. FORAMINER. RES.
CUSHMAN FOUNDATION FOR FORAMINIFERAL RESEARCH.
WASHINGTON, D.C. 1, 1971-
PREV: CONTRIBUTIONS FROM THE CUSHMAN ... FROM
1, 1950- 21, 1970.
DB/S-1.    HL/U-1.    LO/N-2.    LO/N14.    OX/U-8.    SO/U-1.

JOURNAL OF FORENSIC MEDICINE.    XXX
SUBS (1972): FORENSIC SCIENCE.

JOURNAL OF THE FORESTRY COMMISSION (GB).    XXX
++J. FOR. COMM. (GB).
LONDON NO.1, 1922- 36, 1969. //
OX/U-3.
LO/N13. NO.2, 1923-            XS/R-2. NO.32, 1963-*

JOURNAL OF FUEL & HEAT TECHNOLOGY.
+ +J. FUEL & HEAT TECHNOL.
[ARROW PRESS]
  LONDON  14(7), 1966- 19(3), 1972.
  (PREV) 1, 1952- 2, 1954: FUEL ECONOMIST. THEN
  3, 1954- 14(6), 1966: FUEL EFFICIENCY.  THEN
  AS ABOVE. SUBS: ENERGY DIGEST (LONDON).
  ED/N-1.     LO/N14.
  XS/T11.  TWO YEAR FILE.
  ISSN 0022-121X

JOURNAL OF GENERAL EDUCATION DEPARTMENT, NIIGATA
UNIVERSITY.                                                        000
  SEE:  NIIGATA DAIGAKU KYOYOBU KENKYU KIYO.

JOURNAL FOR GENERAL PHILOSOPHY OF SCIENCE.         000
  SEE: ZEITSCHRIFT FUR ALLGEMEINE WISSENSCHAFTS-
  THEORIE.

JOURNAL OF GEOCHEMICAL EXPLORATION.
+ +J. GEOCHEM. EXPLOR.
  ASSOCIATION OF EXPLORATION GEOCHEMISTS.
  [ELSEVIER]
  AMSTERDAM  1, 1972-
  BR/U-1.     LO/N-4.        LO/N14.
  GL/U-2.  3, 1974-                        RE/U-1.  4, 1975-

JOURNAL OF THE GEOGRAPHICAL ASSOCIATION OF
TANZANIA.
+ +J. GEOGR. ASS. TANZANIA.
  DAR ES SALAAM  NO.1, D 1967-
  LO/S13.
  ISSN 0016-738X

JOURNAL, GEOLOGICAL SOCIETY OF IRAQ.
+ +J. GEOL. SOC. IRAQ.
  BAGDAD  1, 1968-
  LO/N-2.

JOURNAL, GEOLOGICAL SOCIETY OF LONDON.       XXX
+ +J. GEOL. SOC. LOND.
  LONDON  127, 1971-
  PREV: QUARTERLY JOURNAL ... FROM 1, 1845-
  126, 1970.
  BH/P-1.    DN/U-1.    GL/U-1.    HL/U-1.    LD/U-1.    LO/N14.
  LO/R-5.    LO/U-1.    LO/U-2.    NW/U-1.    SO/U-1.
  ISSN 0016-7649

JOURNAL, GEOLOGICAL SOCIETY OF THE PHILIP-
PINES.                                                              XXX
+ +J. GEOL. SOC. PHILIPP.
  MANILA  23(2), 1969-
  PREV: PHILIPPINE GEOLOGIST FROM 1, D 1946-
  23(1), 1969.
  LO/N13.

JOURNAL OF GEOMETRY.
+ +J. GEOM.
  [BIRKHAUSER]
  BASLE  1, 1971-
  CA/U-1.    CA/U-2.    LO/N13.    SH/U-1.
  GL/U-1.  4, 1974-
  ISSN 0047-2468

JOURNAL, GEORGIA ENTOMOLOGICAL SOCIETY.
+ +J. GEORGIA ENTOMOL. SOC.
  ATHENS, GA.  1, 1966-
  LO/N-2.
  ISSN 0016-8238

JOURNAL OF THE GUILD OF AIR PILOTS & AIR
NAVIGATORS.
+ +J. GUILD AIR PILOTS & AIR NAVIG.
  LONDON  1(1), 1972-
  ED/N-1.    OX/U-1.

JOURNAL OF THE HAMPSHIRE & ISLE OF WIGHT
NATURALISTS' TRUST LTD.
+ +J. HANTS. & ISLE WIGHT NATUR. TRUST LTD.
  PORTSMOUTH  1, MR 1967-
  SO/U-1.

JOURNAL OF HEALTH & SOCIAL BEHAVIOUR.         XXX
+ +J. HEALTH & SOC. BEHAV.
  AMERICAN SOCIOLOGICAL ASSOCIATION.
  NEW YORK  8, 1967-
  PREV: JOURNAL OF HEALTH & HUMAN BEHAVIOUR FROM
  1, 1960- 7, 1966.
  NW/U-1.  11, 1970-                  SW/U-1.  9, 1968-
  ISSN 0022-1465

JOURNAL, HERPETOLOGICAL ASSOCIATION OF AFRICA.
+ +J. HERPETOL. ASSOC. AFR.
  [UMTALI]  NO.1, 1965-
  LO/N-2.

JOURNAL OF HERPETOLOGY.                             XXX
+ +J. HERPETOL.
  SOCIETY FOR THE STUDY OF AMPHIBIANS & REPTILES.
  CINCINNATI, OHIO  1, MR 1968-
  PREV:  JOURNAL, OHIO HERPETOLOGICAL SOCIETY
  FROM 2(2), 1959- 5(4), D 1966.
  LO/N-2.     LO/N13.
  OX/U-8.  3, 1969-
  ISSN 0022-1511

JOURNAL, HILLINGDON NATURAL HISTORY SOCIETY.
+ +J. HILLINGDON NAT. HIST. SOC.
  WEST DRAYTON, MIDDX.  NO.1, 1970(1971)-
  LO/N-2.

JOURNAL OF HISTORICAL STUDIES.                    XXX
+ +J. HIST. STUD.
  PRINCETON, N.J.  1, AUTUMN 1967- 2(4),
                   WINTER 1969/1970. //
  Q.
  LO/S-7.    LO/U-1.    NO/U-1.    OX/U-1.    XY/N-1.

JOURNAL FOR THE HISTORY OF ASTRONOMY.
+ +J. HIST. ASTRON.
  LONDON  1(1), 1970-
  2A.
  AB/U-1.    CB/U-1.    ED/N-1.    ED/U-1.    GL/U-1.    LO/N-4.
  LO/U-1.    LO/U-2.    LO/U-4.    LO/U11.    NW/U-1.    SH/U-1.
  SO/U-1.
  RE/U-1.  6, 1975-
  EX/U-1.  2(1), F 1971-
  ISSN 0021-8286

JOURNAL OF THE HISTORY OF BIOLOGY.
+ +J. HIST. BIOL.
  [BELLKNAP PRESS]
  CAMBRIDGE, MASS.  1(1), 1968-
  DB/U-2.    ED/U-1.    LO/M24.    LO/N-4.    LO/U-2.
  ISSN 0022-5010

JOURNAL OF HISTORY & POLITICAL SCIENCE.
+ +J. HIST. & POLIT. SCI.
  GOVERNMENT COLLEGE (LAHORE): DEPARTMENT OF
  HISTORY.
  LAHORE  1, 1971/72-
  SPONS. BODY ALSO COLLEGE'S DEPARTMENT OF POL-
  ITICAL SCIENCE.
  LO/N12.    LO/U-8.

JOURNAL, HONG KONG BRANCH, ROYAL ASIATIC SOC-
IETY OF GREAT BRITAIN & IRELAND.
+ +J. HONG KONG BR. R. ASIAT. SOC. G.B. & IR.
  HONG KONG  1, 1960/61(1961)-
  OX/U-1.
  CB/U-1.  2, 1962-                    LO/S10.  2, 1962-

JOURNAL OF HUMAN EVOLUTION.
+ +J. HUM. EVOL.
  [ACADEMIC P.]
  LONDON  1(1), JA 1972-
  CA/U-1.    CA/U-3.    ED/N-1.    LO/N-2.    LO/S10.    OX/U-8.
  SH/U-1.
  ISSN 0047-2484

JOURNAL OF THE HYDROGRAPHIC SOCIETY.         XXX
+ +J. HYDROGR. SOC.
  LONDON  1(1), OC 1972 ...
  SUBS: HYDROGRAPHIC JOURNAL.
  CA/U-1.    ED/N-1.    LO/S13.

JOURNAL OF HYDRONAUTICS.
+ +J. HYDRONAUT.
  AMERICAN INSTITUTE OF AERONAUTICS & ASTRO-
  NAUTICS.
  EASTON, PA.  1, JL 1967-
  Q.
  BL/U-1.    LO/N14.    SO/U-1.
  LO/N-4.  4(1), 1970-                LV/U-1.  2(3), 1968-
  ISSN 0022-1716

JOURNAL, ILLUMINATING ENGINEERING SOCIETY
(NEW YORK).                                                     XXX
+ +J. ILLUM. ENG. SOC. (N.Y.).
  NEW YORK  1, 1971-
  Q.  PREV: PART OF ILLUMINATING ENGINEERING
  FROM 34(6), JE 1940- 66(5), 1971.
  LO/N-4.    LO/N14.    MA/U-1.    SF/U-1.    SH/U-1.

JOURNAL OF IMMUNOLOGICAL METHODS.
+ +J. IMMUNOL. METHODS.
  [NORTH-HOLLAND]
  AMSTERDAM  1, 1971-
  Q.
  AD/U-1.    BL/U-1.    CA/M-1.    GL/U-1.    LD/U-1.    LO/M12.
  LO/N13.    OX/U-8.    RE/U-1.    SF/U-1.    SH/U-1.    SO/U-1.
  XY/N-1.
  ISSN 0022-1759

JOURNAL OF IMPERIAL & COMMONWEALTH HISTORY.
+ +J. IMP. & COMMONW. HIST.
[CASS]
LONDON  1(1), OC 1972-
Q.
CA/U-1.    ED/N-1.    EX/U-1.    LD/U-1.    LO/U-3.    LO/U-8.
LO/U13.    MA/U-1.    OX/U-9.    SH/U-1.    SO/U-1.

JOURNAL OF THE INDIAN ACADEMY OF WOOD SCIENCE.
+ +J. INDIAN ACAD. WOOD SCI.
BANGALORE  1(1), JA/JE 1970-
LO/R-6.    OX/U-3.

JOURNAL OF INDIAN PHILOSOPHY.
+ +J. INDIAN PHILOS.
[REIDEL]
DORDRECHT  1(1), OC 1970-
A.
LO/U14.    SW/U-1.
MA/U-1.  2, 1972-
ISSN 0022-1791

JOURNAL OF INDO-EUROPEAN STUDIES.
+ +J. INDO-EUR. STUD.
HATTIESBURG, MISS.  1, 1973-
LO/S10.    LO/U-1.    LO/U12.    LO/U14.    OX/U-1.    RE/U-1.
SH/U-1.
ISSN 0092-2323

JOURNAL, INDUSTRIAL ARCHAEOLOGY SOCIETY,
PORTSMOUTH COLLEGE OF TECHNOLOGY.
+ +J. IND. ARCHAEOL. SOC. PORTSMOUTH COLL.
TECHNOL.
PORTSMOUTH  1, 1968-
LO/N-4.

JOURNAL OF INDUSTRIAL ENGINEERING.          XXX
SUBS (1969): INDUSTRIAL ENGINEERING.

JOURNAL OF INDUSTRIAL PSYCHOLOGY. Q.          XXX
+ +J. IND. PSYCHOL.
MONTPELIER, VT.  1, MR 1963- 6, 1968.//
XY/N-1.

JOURNAL, INSTITUTE OF BIOLOGY.          XXX
SUBS (1969): BIOLOGIST.

JOURNAL OF THE INSTITUTION OF COMPUTER
SCIENCES.
+ +J. INST. COMPUT. SCI.
LONDON  1(1), JA 1970-
BN/U-2.    SW/U-1.
CA/U-1.  3, 1972-          ED/N-1.  3, 1972-

JOURNAL, INSTITUTE OF ECONOMIC RESEARCH,
KARNATAK UNIVERSITY.
+ +J. INST. ECON. RES. KARNATAK UNIV.
DHARWAR  1, 1966-
2/A.
LO/U-3.

JOURNAL, INSTITUTION OF GENERAL TECHNICIAN
ENGINEERS.          XXX
+ +J. INST. GEN. TECH. ENG.
LONDON  82, 1971-
PREV: JOURNAL & RECORD OF TRANSACTIONS,
JUNIOR INSTITUTION OF ENGINEERS FROM 16,
1905, - 81, 1970.
BH/P-1.    LO/N13.    NW/U-1.

JOURNAL OF THE INSTITUTION OF HIGHWAY
ENGINEERS.          XXX
SUBS (1973): HIGHWAY ENGINEER.

JOURNAL, INSTITUTE OF LANDSCAPE ARCHITECTS.          XXX
SUBS (1971): LANDSCAPE DESIGN.

JOURNAL, INSTITUTION OF LOCOMOTIVE ENGINEERS.          XXX
SUBS (1970): RAILWAY DIVISION JOURNAL,
INSTITUTION OF MECHANICAL ENGINEERS.

JOURNAL, INSTITUTE OF MATERIALS HANDLING.          XXX
SUBS (1968): MATERIALS HANDLING AND
MANAGEMENT.

JOURNAL OF THE INSTITUTE OF NAVIGATION.          XXX
SUBS (1972): JOURNAL OF NAVIGATION.

JOURNAL, INSTITUTION OF NUCLEAR ENGINEERS.          XXX
+ +J. INST. NUCL. ENG.
LONDON  12, 1971-
PREV: NUCLEAR ENERGY FROM 12(119), AP 1958-
[NS]11, 1970.
ED/N-1.    LO/N14.    NW/U-1.    XS/R10.

JOURNAL, INSTITUTION OF PUBLIC HEALTH
ENGINEERS.          XXX
SUBS (1973): PUBLIC HEALTH ENGINEER.

JOURNAL, INSTITUTION OF THE RUBBER INDUSTRY.          XXX
+ +J. INST. RUBBER IND.
LONDON  1(1), 1967- 9(1), 1975 ...
PREV. PART OF: THE INSTITUTION'S TRANSACTIONS
FROM 1(1), 1925- 42(6), 1966; & ITS PROCEED-
INGS FROM 1, 1954- 13, 1966. SUBS: RUBBER
INDUSTRY.
LO/N14.
ISSN 0538-012X

JOURNAL, INSTITUTE OF TRANSPORT.          XXX
SUBS (1971): JOURNAL, CHARTERED INSTITUTE OF
TRANSPORT.

JOURNAL OF INTER-AMERICAN STUDIES & WORLD
AFFAIRS.*
+ +J. INTER-AM. STUD. & WORLD AFF.
UNIVERSITY OF MIAMI: CENTER FOR ADVANCED INTER-
NATIONAL STUDIES.
CORAL GABLES, FLA.  12(1), JA 1970-
TITLE EXPANDED FROM JOURNAL OF INTER-AMERICAN
STUDIES WITH 12(1), JA 1970.
AB/U-1.    CC/U-1.*    HL/U-1.**    LO/S14.    LO/S27.**
LO/U-2.**    LO/U-3.
ED/U-1.  5, 1963-          LC/U-1.  5, 1963-
MA/U-1.  4, 1962-

JOURNAL OF INTERDISCIPLINARY CYCLE RESEARCH.
+ +J. INTERDISCIP. CYCLE RES.
[SWETS EN ZEITLINGER]
AMSTERDAM  1, 1970-
ED/U-1.    HL/U-1.    LO/N13.    LO/U-2.    OX/U-8.    SO/U-1.
BH/U-3.  3, 1972-
ISSN 0022-1945

JOURNAL OF INTERDISCIPLINARY HISTORY.
+ +J. INTERDISCIPLINARY HIST.
MASSACHUSETTS INSTITUTE OF TECHNOLOGY: SCHOOL
OF HUMANITIES & SOCIAL SCIENCES.
CAMBRIDGE, MASS.  1(1), 1970-
Q.
AD/U-1.    DB/U-2.    LO/N-1.    LO/U-3.    LO/U19.    LO/U28.
MA/P-1.    NO/U-1.    OX/U17.    SW/U-1.
BL/U-1.  3, 1972-          EX/U-1.  4(1), 1973-
GL/U-2.  5(1), 1974-
ISSN 0022-1953

JOURNAL, INTERNATIONAL ASSOCIATION FOR MATHE-
MATICAL GEOLOGY.
+ +J. INT. ASS. MATH. GEOL.
[PLENUM P.]
NEW YORK  1, 1969-
GL/U-2.    LO/N-2.    LO/N-4.    LO/N14.    OX/U-1.
HL/U-1.  2, 1970-          RE/U-1.  7, 1975-

JOURNAL OF INTERNATIONAL BUSINESS STUDIES.
+ +J. INT. BUS. STUD.
ASSOCIATION FOR EDUCATION IN INTERNATIONAL
BUSINESS.
ATLANTA  1, SPRING 1970-
2/A.  SPONS. BODY ALSO: SCHOOL OF BUSINESS
ADMINISTRATION, GEORGIA STATE UNIVERSITY.
RE/U-1.
BH/U-3.  4, 1973-
ISSN 0047-2506

JOURNAL, INTERNATIONAL COLLEGE OF SURGEONS.          XXX
SUBS (1966): INTERNATIONAL SURGERY.

JOURNAL, INTERNATIONAL COMMISSION OF JURISTS.          XXX
SUBS. (1969) PART OF: REVIEW, INTERNATIONAL
COMMISSION OF JURISTS.

JOURNAL OF INTERNATIONAL ECONOMICS.
+ +J. INT. ECON.
[NORTH-HOLLAND PUBL. CO.]
AMSTERDAM  1(1), F 1971-
Q.
AD/U-1.    CA/U-1.    CB/U-1.    CO/U-1.    EX/U-1.    GL/U-1.
HL/U-1.    LO/N-1.    LO/N-7.    LO/U-3.    LO/U20.    MA/U-1.
NW/U-1.    OX/U-1.    OX/U15.    OX/U17.    SH/U-1.
SW/U-1.
GL/U-2.  3, 1973-
XY/N-1.  1(1), 1971-
ISSN 0022-1996

JOURNAL INTERNATIONAL DE L'ENFANCE PRE-SCOL-
AIRE.          000
SEE: INTERNATIONAL JOURNAL OF EARLY CHILDHOOD.

JOURNAL OF INTERNATIONAL LAW & ECONOMICS.                    XXX
+ +J. INT. LAW & ECON.
GEORGE WASHINGTON UNIVERSITY: NATIONAL LAW
CENTER.
 WASHINGTON, D.C. 5(2), JA 1971-
 PREV: JOURNAL OF LAW & ECONOMIC DEVELOPMENT
 FROM 2(2), 1967- 5(1), 1970.
 LO/U24.    OX/U15.
 ISSN 0022-2003

JOURNAL OF INTERNATIONAL MEDICAL RESEARCH.
+ +J. INT. MED. RES.
[CAMBRIDGE MEDICAL PUBL.]
 NORTHAMPTON 1, 1972-
 AD/U-1.    BL/U-1.    CA/U-1.    ED/N-1.    LO/M31.
 ISSN 0300-0605

JOURNAL OF THE INTERNATIONAL PHONETIC ASSOC-
IATION.
+ +J. INT. PHONETIC ASSOC.
 LONDON 1(1), JE 1971-
 2/A. PREV: MAITRE PHONETIQUE FROM 1, 1886-
 85, 1970.
 BH/P-1.    BN/U-1.    GL/U-1.    LD/U-1.    LO/N-1.    LO/U-2.
 LO/U14.    NO/U-1.    NW/U-1.    SH/U-1.    SO/U-1.
 ED/N-1. 2, 1972-

JOURNAL OF INTERNATIONAL RESEARCH COMMUNICAT-
IONS: MEDICAL SCIENCE.
+ +J. INT. RES. COMMUN., MED. SCI.
[MTP INTERNATIONAL RESEARCH COMMUNICATIONS LTD]
 LANCASTER 1(1), MR 1973-
 MON.
 AD/U-1.    MA/U-1.    OX/U-8.    SO/U-1.
 ISSN 0030-5569

JOURNAL OF THE IRI.                                          000
 SEE: JOURNAL, INSTITUTION OF THE RUBBER
 INDUSTRY.

JOURNAL, IRISH BAPTIST HISTORICAL SOCIETY.
+ +J. IR. BAPTIST HIST. SOC.
 BELFAST 1, 1969-
 BL/U-1.    ED/N-1.    LO/N-1.    OX/U-1.

JOURNAL OF THE IRISH COLLEGES OF PHYSICIANS &
SURGEONS.                                                    XXX
+ +J. IR. COLL. PHYSICIANS & SURG.
 DUBLIN 1, 1971-
 PREV: JOURNAL OF THE ROYAL COLLEGE OF SURGEONS
 IN IRELAND FROM 1, 1964- 6(4), 1971.
 ED/N-1.    LO/M13.    LO/N-1.    NW/U-1.

JOURNAL OF IRISH PHILATELY.
+ +J. IR. PHILATELY.
EIRE PHILATELIC ASSOCIATION.
 DUBLIN 1, 1972-
 SPONS. BODY ALSO IRISH PHILATELIC CIRCLE.
 DB/U-2.

JOURNAL OF THE ISLAND SOCIETY (SINGAPORE).                   000
 SEE: HSIN-SHE HSUEH-PAO.

JOURNAL, JAPAN HYDRAULICS & PNEUMATICS
SOCIETY.                                                     000
 SEE: YUATSU TO KUKIATSU.

JOURNAL OF THE JAPANESE SOCIETY OF PEDIATRIC
SURGEONS.                                                    000
 SEE: NIHON SHONI GEKKA GAKKAI ZASSHI.

JOURNAL, JAPAN STATISTICAL SOCIETY.                          000
 SEE: NIHON TOKEI GAKKAI.

JOURNAL, KERRY ARCHAEOLOGICAL & HISTORICAL
SOCIETY.
+ +J. KERRY ARCHAEOL. & HIST. SOC.
 TRALEE 1, 1968-
 BL/U-1.    CO/U-1.    DB/S-1.    DB/U-2.    OX/U-1.
 OX/U-2. [W.VOL.2.]

JOURNAL OF THE KOREAN SOCIETY OF PROFESSIONAL
ENGINEERS.                                                   000
 SEE: KISULSA.

JOURNAL, KUWAIT MEDICAL ASSOCIATION.
+ +J. KUWAIT MED. ASS.
 KUWAIT 1, 1967-
 Q.
 AD/U-1.
 ISSN 0023-5776

JOURNAL, LANCASHIRE & CHESHIRE BRANCH, WESLEY
HISTORICAL SOCIETY.
+ +J. LANCS. & CHESHIRE BRA. WESLEY HIST. SOC.
 MANCHESTER 1, 1965-
 MA/S-1.

JOURNAL OF THE LANGUAGE ASSOCIATION OF EAST-
ERN AFRICA.
+ +J. LANG. ASSOC. EAST. AFR.
[EAST AFRICAN PUBL. HOUSE]
 NAIROBI 1(1), 1970-
 LO/N-1.    LO/U14.    MA/U-1.
 ISSN 0023-8325

JOURNAL OF LATIN AMERICAN STUDIES.
+ +J. LAT. AM. STUD.
[CAMBRIDGE UNIV PRESS]
 LONDON 1(1), MY 1969-
 CC/U-1.    DB/U-2.    ED/N-1.    ED/U-1.    EX/U-1.    LO/N-1.
 LO/N17.    LO/S-7.    LO/U-1.    LO/U-2.    LO/U-3.    LO/U13.
 NW/U-1.    OX/U-1.    RE/U-1.    SH/U-1.
 LO/U20. 3, 1971-                      MA/U-1. 3, 1971-
 ISSN 0022-216X

JOURNAL OF LAW & ECONOMIC DEVELOPMENT.                       XXX
+ +J. LAW & ECON. DEV. [JLED-A]
GEORGE WASHINGTON UNIVERSITY: INTERNATIONAL
LAW SOCIETY.
 WASHINGTON, D.C. 2(2), 1967- 5(1), 1970 ...
 PREV: STUDIES IN LAW & ECONOMIC DEVELOPMENT
 FROM 1(1), AP 1966- 2(1), MY 1967. SUBS:
 JOURNAL OF INTERNATIONAL LAW & ECONOMICS.
 LO/U24.
 ISSN 0022-2003

JOURNAL OF LEGAL MEDICINE.                                   000
 SEE: ZEITSCHRIFT FUR RECHTSMEDIZIN.

JOURNAL OF LEGAL STUDIES.
+ +J. LEG. STUD.
UNIVERSITY OF CHICAGO: LAW SCHOOL.
 CHICAGO 1, JA 1972-
 2/A.
 BL/U-1.    CA/U13.    CB/U-1.    CR/U-1.    LO/U12.
 OX/U15.    SH/U-1.
 ISSN 0047-2530

JOURNAL OF LEISURE RESEARCH.
+ +J. LEISURE RES.
NATIONAL RECREATION & PARK ASSOCIATION (US).
 WASHINGTON, D.C. 1, 1969-
 Q.
 AD/U-1.    HL/U-1.    LO/N-1.    LO/R-5.    LO/U-2.    RE/U-1.
 XS/U-1.
 BH/U-1. 3, 1971-           LD/U-1. 2, 1970-
 MA/U-1. 2, 1970-          SH/C-5. 3, 1971-
 SH/U-1. 1970-
 LO/U-3. [W. 1(3), 1969]
 ISSN 0022-2216

JOURNAL OF LIBRARIANSHIP.
+ +J. LIBR. (GB).
LIBRARY ASSOCIATION.
 LONDON 1(1), JA 1969-
 Q.
 AD/U-1.    BN/U-1.    CB/U-1.    DB/U-2.    ED/N-1.    ED/P-1.
 ED/U-1.    EX/U-1.    GL/U-2.    LO/M24.    LO/N-2.    LO/N-3.
 LO/N-4.    LO/N14.    LO/P-6.    LO/S-7.    LO/U-3.    LO/U12.
 LO/U13.    LV/U-1.    MA/U-1.    RE/U-1.    XS/R10.
 ISSN 0022-2232

JOURNAL OF THE LINNEAN SOCIETY. BOTANY.                      XXX
 SUBS (1969): BOTANICAL JOURNAL OF THE LINN-
 EAN SOCIETY.

JOURNAL OF THE LINNEAN SOCIETY. ZOOLOGY.                     XXX
 SUBS (1969): ZOOLOGICAL JOURNAL OF THE LINN-
 EAN SOCIETY.

JOURNAL OF LITERARY SEMANTICS.
+ +J. LIT. SEMANTICS.
 THE HAGUE 1, 1972-
 CA/U-1.    DB/U-2.    LO/U13.    NO/U-1.    SA/U-1.

JOURNAL, LONDON MATHEMATICAL SOCIETY: 2S.
+ +J. LOND. MATH. SOC., 2S.
[HODGSON]
 LONDON 1, 1969-
 LO/U11.
 ISSN 0024-6107

JOURNAL, LOUISIANA SOCIETY FOR HORTICULTURAL
RESEARCH.                                                    XXX
+ +J. LA. SOC. HORT. RES.
 LAFAYETTE 11, 1970-
 PREV: LSHR NEWS LETTER FROM 8(3), 1967- 10,
 1969.
 LO/N13.

**JOURNAL OF LOW TEMPERATURE PHYSICS.**
+ +*J. LOW TEMP. PHYS.*
[PLENUM P.]
*NEW YORK  1(1), F 1969-*
BH/U-1.    CA/U-1.    CA/U-2.    CB/U-1.    HL/U-1.    LO/N-4.
LO/U-1.    LO/U12.    SF/U-1.**    XS/R10.
AD/U-3.  1973-                LO/N-7.  2, 1970-
LO/N14.  1(3), 1969-         NW/U-1.  2, 1970-
OX/U-8.  1(4), 1969-
ISSN 0022-2291

**JOURNAL OF LUBRICATION TECHNOLOGY. (TRANS-ACTIONS OF THE ASME: SERIES F).**
+ +*J. LUBRIC. TECHNOL.*
AMERICAN SOCIETY OF MECHANICAL ENGINEERS.
*NEW YORK  89F, 1967-*
Q.  PUBL. A. AS: TRANS. ASME: SER. F.  NUMBER-
ING AS FROM 1, 1880 OF: TRANSACTIONS OF THE
AM. SOC. MECH. ENG.  PREV PART OF: J. OF
BASIC ENGINEERING. (TRANS. OF THE ASME: SER.
D.)
LO/N14.    SO/U-1.    XS/R10.    XS/T-7.
ISSN 0022-2305

**JOURNAL OF LUMINESCENCE.**
+ +*J. LUMIN.*
[NORTH-HOLLAND]
*AMSTERDAM  1, 1970-*
HL/U-1.    LO/N-4.    LO/N14.    LO/S-3.    OX/U-8.    XS/R10.
BL/U-1.  6, 1973-
ISSN 0022-2313

**JOURNAL OF MACROMOLECULAR SCIENCE: PART C: REV-IEWS IN MACROMOLECULAR CHEMISTRY.**                    XXX
+ +*J. MACROMOL. SCI., C.*
[DEKKER]
*NEW YORK  C 1, 1967-*
PREV: REVIEWS IN MACROMOLECULAR CHEMISTRY FROM
1, 1966.
BH/U-1.    LO/N14.    RE/U-1.
LO/U12.  C5(1), 1970-        OX/U-8.  C4(1), 1970-
SH/C-5.  C5, 1970/71-
ISSN 0022-2356

**JOURNAL OF MACROMOLECULAR SCIENCE: PART D: REV-IEWS IN POLYMER TECHNOLOGY.**                         XXX
+ +*J. MACROMOL. SCI., D.*
[DEKKER]
*NEW YORK  D1, 1971...*
2/A. SUBS: POLYMER- PLASTICS TECHNOLOGY
& ENGINEERING
LO/N-4.    LO/N14.    OX/U-8.
ISSN 0022-2321

**JOURNAL OF MAGNETIC RESONANCE.**
+ +*J. MAGN. RESON.*
[ACADEMIC PRESS]
*NEW YORK &C  1(1), JA 1969-*
AD/U-1.    HL/U-1.    LO/N-4.    LO/N14.    LO/S-3.    LO/U12.
MA/U-1.    NW/U-1.    OX/U-8.    SH/U-1.    SO/U-1.
XS/R10.
LD/U-1.  4, 1971-
BN/U-2.  4(1), F 1971-
ISSN 0022-2364

**JOURNAL, MARINE TECHNOLOGY SOCIETY.**
+ +*J. MAR. TECHNOL. SOC.*
*WASHINGTON, D.C.  3(1), JA 1969-*
PREV: JOURNAL OF OCEAN TECHNOLOGY FROM 1, JE
1966.
BN/U-2.

**JOURNAL OF MARITIME LAW & COMMERCE.**
+ +*J. MAR. LAW & COMMER.*
*SILVER SPRING, MD.  1(1), OC 1969-*
LO/U-3.    OX/U-1.
LO/U-2.  6, 1974-
SO/U-1.  1, 1969- [W. VOL.4]
ISSN 0022-2410

**JOURNAL POUR LES MATERIAUX D'ENREGISTREMENT DES SIGNAUX.**                                            000
   SEE: JOURNAL FUR SIGNALAUFZEICHUNGSMATERIALIEN

**JOURNAL OF MATHEMATICAL & PHYSICAL SCIENCES.**
+ +*J. MATH. PHYS. SCI.*
INDIAN INSTITUTE OF TECHNOLOGY.
*MADRAS  NO.1, JE 1967-*
LO/N14.    LO/U-2.
ISSN 0047-2557

**JOURNAL OF MATHEMATICAL SOCIOLOGY.**
+ +*J. MATH. SOCIOL.*
[GORDON & BREACH]
*LONDON; NEW YORK  1(1), JA 1971-*
2/A.
AD/U-1.    ED/N-1.    LO/N-1.    LO/U-3.    OX/U-1.    OX/U17.
SO/U-1.  3, 1973-
ISSN 0022-250X

**JOURNAL OF MATHEMATICS & MECHANICS.**                 XXX
   SUBS (1970): INDIANA UNIVERSITY MATHEMAT-ICS JOURNAL.

**JOURNAL OF MATHEMATICS & PHYSICS.**                   XXX
   SUBS: (1969): STUDIES IN APPLIED MATHEMATICS.

**JOURNAL OF MAXILLOFACIAL SURGERY.**
EUROPEAN ASSOCIATION FOR MAXILLOFACIAL SURGERY.
[G.THIEME]
*STUTTGART  1, 1973-*
LD/U-1.    MA/U-1.
SH/U-1.  1(3), S 1973-

**JOURNAL OF MECHANOCHEMISTRY & CELL MOTILITY.**
+ +*J. MECHANOCHEM. & CELL MOTILITY.*
[GORDON & BREACH]
*NEW YORK &C.  1, 1971-*
HL/U-1.    LO/N14.
CA/U-1.  1(3), 1972-        CA/U-2.  2, 1973-
ED/N-1.  1(3), 1972-        OX/U-8.  1(3), 1972-

**JOURNAL DE MEDECINE DE MONTPELLIER.**                 XXX
+ +*J. MED. MONTPELLIER.*
UNIVERSITE DE MONTPELLIER: FACULTE DE MEDECINE.
*MONTPELLIER  1, JA 1966-*
PREV: MONTPELLIER MEDICAL FROM 1, 1858.
BH/U-1.
ISSN 0021-7891

**JOURNAL OF MEDICAL LABORATORY TECHNOLOGY.**          XXX
   SUBS (1971): MEDICAL LABORATORY TECHNOLOGY.

**JOURNAL OF MEDICAL MICROBIOLOGY.**
+ +*J. MED. MICROBIOL.*
PATHOLOGICAL SOCIETY OF GREAT BRITAIN &
IRELAND.
[LIVINGSTONE]
*EDINBURGH  1(1), AG 1968-*
S/T: AN OFFICIAL JOURNAL OF THE ... SOCIETY ..
GL/U-2.    LD/U-1.    LO/M-1.    LO/M18.    LO/N13.    LO/U-1.
LO/U-2.    OX/U-8.    RE/U-1.    SH/U-1.    SO/U-1.
CR/M-1.  1970-
ISSN 0022-2615

**JOURNAL OF MEDICAL PRIMATOLOGY.**
+ +*J. MED. PRIMATOL.*
*BASLE &C.  1(1), 1972-*
LO/N13.    OX/U-8.
CA/U-1.  1(3), 1972-
ISSN 0047-2565

**JOURNAL OF MEDICINE, EXPERIMENTAL & CLINICAL.**      XXX
+ +*J. MED. EXP. & CLIN.*
[KARGER]
*BASEL &C.  1, 1970-*
PREV: MEDICINA EXPERIMENTALIS FROM 18, 1968-
19, 1969.
GL/U-1.    LO/N13.    LO/U-2.

**JOURNAL OF MEDIEVAL & RENAISSANCE STUDIES.**
+ +*J. MEDIEVAL & RENAISS. STUD.*
[DUKE UNIV. P.]
*DURHAM, N.C.  1, 1971-*
AD/U-1.    DB/U-2.    ED/N-1.    EX/U-1.    LO/M24.    LO/N-1.
LO/U-1.    LO/U17.    NO/U-1.    OX/U-1.
ISSN 0047-2573

**JOURNAL OF MEMBRANE BIOLOGY.**
+ +*J. MEMBRANE BIOL.*
[SPRINGER]
*NEW YORK  1, 1969-*
S/T: AN INTERNATIONAL JOURNAL FOR STUDIES ON
THE STRUCTURE, FUNCTION & THE GENESIS OF
BIOMEMBRANES.
CB/U-1.    DB/U-2.    DN/U-1.    LD/U-1.    LO/U-2.    NW/U-1.
OX/U-8.    SH/U-1.    SO/U-1.
BH/U-3.  2, 1970-            LO/U20.  4, 1971-
ISSN 0022-2631

JOURNAL OF MICROBIOLOGY OF THE UNITED ARAB
REPUBLIC. MAGALLAT AL-MIKROBIYOLOCIYA LI-AL-
GUMHURIYYAT AL-'ARABIYYAT AL-MUTTAHIDAH.
+ +J. MICROBIOL. U.A.R. [JMBU-A]
NATIONAL INFORMATION & DOCUMENTATION CENTRE
(U.A.R).
CAIRO 1(1), 1966- 4, 1969(1970) ...
EDITED BY THE SOCIETY OF APPLIED MICROBIOLOGY.
SUBS: UNITED ARAB REPUBLIC JOURNAL OF
MICROBIOLOGY FROM 5, 1970.
BN/U-2.    DB/S-1.    LD/U-1.    LO/N-2.    LO/N13.
ISSN 0022-2704

JOURNAL OF MICROGRAPHICS.                           XXX
+ +J. MICROGR.
NATIONAL MICROFILM ASSOCIATION (U.S.).
ANNAPOLIS, MD. 3, 1969-
PREV: NMA JOURNAL FROM 1, 1967 - 2, 1969.
LO/N-4.    LO/N-7.    LO/N14.
ISSN 0022-2712

JOURNAL OF MICROSCOPY.
+ +J. MICROSC.
ROYAL MICROSCOPICAL SOCIETY.
OXFORD &C 89(1), 1969-
PREV: JOURNAL, ROYAL MICROSCOPICAL SOCIETY
FROM 1, 1878-3, 1880; THEN AS SERIES 2, 1(1),
1881- 88(4), 1968.
AD/U-1.    BH/U-1.    BN/U-2.    ED/N-1.    GL/U-1    LO/N14.
NW/U-1.    XS/R10.
ISSN 0022-2720

JOURNAL, MINING AND GEOLOGICAL SOCIETY,
UNIVERSITY OF NEW SOUTH WALES.
+ +J. MIN. & GEOL. SOC. UNIV. NSW.
SYDNEY 1, 1963-
LO/N-2. 4, 1966-

JOURNAL OF MINING & GEOLOGY.                        XXX
+ +J. MIN. & GEOL.
NIGERIAN MINING, GEOLOGICAL & METALLURGICAL
SOCIETY.
IBADAN 3, 1968-
PREV: JOURNAL, NIGERIAN ... FROM 1(1), D
1963- 2, 1967.
LO/N13.
ISSN 0022-2763

JOURNAL OF MODERN LITERATURE.
+ +J. MOD. LIT.
TEMPLE UNIVERSITY.
PHILADELPHIA 1, 1970-
ED/N-1.    GL/U-2.    HL/U-1.    LO/N-1.    LO/U-2.    OX/U-1.
ISSN 0022-281X

JOURNAL OF MOLECULAR & CELLULAR CARDIOLOGY.
+ +J. MOL. & CELL. CARDIOL.
[ACADEMIC P.]
LONDON &C. 1, 1970-
BL/U-1.    CR/M-1.    LO/N13.    SH/U-1.
GL/U-2. 4, 1972-
ISSN 0022-2828

JOURNAL OF MOLECULAR EVOLUTION.
+ +J. MOL. EVOL.
[SPRINGER]
BERLIN &C. 1, 1971-
Q.
AD/U-1.    CA/U-1.    GL/U-1.    LO/M12.    LO/N13.
MA/U-1.    OX/U-8.    XY/N-1.
LD/U-1. 2, 1972-
ISSN 0022-2844

JOURNAL OF MONEY, CREDIT & BANKING.
+ +J. MONEY CREDIT & BANK.
COLUMBUS (OHIO), 1, 1969-
LO/U-3.    MA/U-1.    OX/U17.    RE/U-1.    SW/U-1.
XY/N-1.
GL/U-2. 4, 1972-                       NO/U-1. 4, 1972-
DR/U-1. 1(2), 1969- [W. 2(1)]
EX/U-1. 3(1), F 1971-
SO/U-1. 1(2), MY 1969-
ISSN 0022-2879

JOURNAL OF MORAL EDUCATION.
+ +J. MORAL EDUC.
[PEMBERTON]
LONDON 1(1), OC 1971-
3/A.
BN/U-1.    CA/U-1.    ED/N-1.    HL/U-2.    LD/U-1.    LN/U-2.
MA/U-1.    SH/U-1.    SW/U-1.
EX/U-1. 3(1), 1973-
ISSN 0305-7240

JOURNAL OF THE MOSCOW PATRIARCHATE.
+ +J. MOSC. PATRIARCHATE.
MOSCOW NO.1, N 1972-
MON. ENGL. LANG. ED. OF ZHURNAL MOSKOVSKOI
PATRIARKHII.
BH/P-1.    OX/U-1.

JOURNAL OF MOTOR BEHAVIOR.
+ +J. MOTOR BEHAV.
[JOURNAL PUBL. AFFILIATES]
COLLEGE PARK, M.D. 1, MR 1969-
LD/U-1.    LO/N13.    LO/U-2.    OX/U-8.    SH/U-1.
SO/U-1. 5, 1973-
ISSN 0022-2895

JOURNAL OF THE MOUNT SINAI HOSPITAL.               XXX
SUBS (1970): MOUNT SINAI JOURNAL OF
MEDICINE.

JOURNAL OF MULTIVARIATE ANALYSIS.
+ +J. MULTIVARIATE ANAL.
[ACADEMIC P.]
NEW YORK; LONDON 1, 1971-
Q. ENGL., FR. & GER.
CA/U-2.    EX/U-1.    LO/N14.    LO/R-5.    LO/U28.
OX/U16.    SH/U-1.    SO/U-1.
XY/N-1. 1(1), 1971.
ISSN 0047-259X

JOURNAL OF NANYANG UNIVERSITY.
+ +J. NANYANG UNIV.
SINGAPORE 1, 1967-
CHIN. & ENGL.
LO/N-2.    OX/U-1.
CB/U-1. 2, 1968-              LO/N17. 2, 1968-

JOURNAL OF NARRATIVE TECHNIQUE.
+ +J. NARRATIVE TECH.
EASTERN MICHIGAN UNIVERSITY: DEPARTMENT OF
ENGLISH.
YPSILANTI, MICH. 1, 1971-
3/A.
GL/U-2.    LO/U-1.
ISSN 0022-2925

JOURNAL, NATIONAL AGRICULTURAL SOCIETY OF
CEYLON.
+ +J. NATL. AGRIC. SOC. CEYLON.
PERADENIYA 1, 1964-
CA/U11. 4, 1967-              LO/R-6. 3, 1966-

JOURNAL, NATIONAL ASSOCIATION OF CYCLE TRADERS.
SEE: N.A. JOURNAL.

JOURNAL OF NATIONAL ECONOMICS: SUPPLEMENT.        000
SEE: ZEITSCHRIFT FUR NATIONALOKONOMIE:
SUPPLEMENTUM.

JOURNAL OF THE NATIONAL FEDERATION OF CLAIM-
ANTS UNIONS.
+ +J. NAT. FED. CLAIMANTS UNIONS.
BIRMINGHAM [NO.]1, AG 1970-
BH/P-1.    LO/U-3.    OX/U-1.    OX/U17.

JOURNAL, NATIONAL MICROFILM ASSOCIATION.         000
SEE: NMA JOURNAL.

JOURNAL, NATIONAL UNION OF SHEET METAL WORK-
ERS, COPPERSMITHS, HEATING & DOMESTIC ENGIN-
EERS: N.S.
+ +J. NAT. UNION SHEET METAL WORK. COPPERSMITHS
HEAT. & DOM. ENG., N.S.
LONDON NO.1, F 1970-
ED/N-1.    OX/U-8.

JOURNAL OF NAVIGATION.                             XXX
+ +J. NAVIG.
INSTITUTE OF NAVIGATION.
LONDON 25(1), JA 1972-
PREV: JOURNAL OF THE INSTITUTE OF NAVIGATION
FROM 1, 1948- 24(4), OC 1971.
BH/P-1.    ED/N-1.    GL/U-1.    LO/N-4.    LO/N14.    NW/U-1.

JOURNAL OF NEMATOLOGY.
+ +J. NEMATOL.
SOCIETY OF NEMATOLOGISTS.
RIVERSIDE, CALIF. 1, 1969-
CA/U-1.    LO/N13.    NW/U-1.
ISSN 0022-300X

JOURNAL OF NEUROBIOLOGY.
+ +J. NEUROBIOL.
[WILEY-INTERSCIENCE]
NEW YORK 1, 1969-
S/T: AN INTERNATIONAL JOURNAL.
AD/U-1.    LO/N13.    LO/U-2.
ISSN 0022-3034

JOURNAL OF NEUROCYTOLOGY.
+ +J. NEUROCYTOL.
[CHAPMAN & HALL]
LONDON 1(1), JL 1972-
BL/U-1.    ED/N-1.    GL/U-1.    LO/N-2.    LO/U-2.

JOURNAL OF NEURO-VISCERAL RELATIONS: SUPPLEMEN-
TUM.                                                          XXX
+ +J. NEURO-VISCERAL RELAT., SUPPL.
[SPRINGER]
VIENNA &C. [NO.]9, 1969-
PREV: ACTA NEUROVEGETATIVA: SUPPLEMENTUM
FROM 1, 1952.
LO/N13.

JOURNAL OF THE NEW AFRICAN LITERATURE.
+ +J. NEW AFR. LIT.
HOOVER INSTITUTION ON WAR, REVOLUTION &
PEACE.
STANFORD, CALIF.  NO.1, SPRING 1966-
S/T: A BIANNUAL INTERNATIONAL PUBLICATION.
INSTITUTION LOCATED AT STANFORD UNIVERSITY.
LO/U14.

JOURNAL OF THE NEW ZEALAND INSTITUTE OF
CHEMISTRY.                                                   XXX
SUBS (1968): CHEMISTRY IN NEW ZEALAND.

JOURNAL OF THE NIGERIAN MINING, GEOLOGICAL &
METALLURGICAL SOCIETY.                                       XXX
+ +J. NIGER. MIN. GEOL. & MET. SOC.
IBADAN  1(1), D 1963- 2, 1967.
1(1) CALLED 'SPECIAL INAUGURAL ISSUE'. SUBS:
JOURNAL OF MINING AND GEOLOGY.
LO/N-2.

JOURNAL OF NON-CRYSTALLINE SOLIDS.
+ +J. NON-CRYST. SOLIDS.
[NORTH-HOLLAND PUBL. CO.]
AMSTERDAM  1, 1968-
AD/U-1.    BH/U-1.    LO/N14.    OX/U-8.    SH/U-1.    XS/T-4.
SH/U-3.  12, M 1973-
DN/U-1.  5(1), S 1970-
ISSN 0022-3093

JOURNAL OF NONMETALS.
+ +J. NONMET.
[GORDON & BREACH]
LONDON  1(1), D 1972-
CA/U-1.    ED/N-1.    LO/N14.    LO/N35.    LO/S-3.    MA/U-1.
SO/U-1.    XS/R10.

JOURNAL, NORTHAMPTON MUSEUM & ART GALLERY.
+ +J. NORTHANTS. MUS. & ART GALLERY.
NORTHAMPTON  1, 1967-
OX/U-2.
OX/U-1.  5, 1969-

JOURNAL OF THE NORTHEASTERN POLITICAL SCIENCE
ASSOCIATIONS.                                                000
SEE: POLITY. THE JOURNAL OF ...

JOURNAL OF NORTHWEST SEMITIC LANGUAGES.
+ +J. NORTHWEST SEMITIC LANG.
[BRILL]
LEIDEN  1, 1971-
BL/U-1.    EX/U-1.    LO/U-1.    LO/U14.    MA/U-1.    OX/U-1.
SH/U-1.

JOURNAL OF NUMBER THEORY.
+ +J. NUMBER THEORY.
[ACADEMIC PRESS]
NEW YORK &C  1, JA 1969-
BR/U-3.    LO/N14.    LO/U-2.    OX/U-8.    SH/U-1.    SO/U-1.
SW/U-1.
ISSN 0022-314X

JOURNAL OF NUTRITION EDUCATION.
+ +J. NUTR. EDUC. [JNUE-B]
SOCIETY FOR NUTRITION EDUCATION.
BERKELEY, CALIF  1, 1969-
Q.
LO/N-6.  2(3), 1971-                   SO/U-1.  1(3), 1970-
ISSN 0022-3182

JOURNAL, OCEANOLOGICAL SOCIETY OF KOREA.
+ +J. OCEANOL. SOC. KOREA.
SEOUL  1, 1966-
LO/N-2.

JOURNAL, OHIO HERPETOLOGICAL SOCIETY.                        XXX
SUBS (1968): JOURNAL OF HERPETOLOGY.

JOURNAL OF THE OLD ATHLONE SOCIETY.
+ +J. OLD ATHLONE SOC.
ATHLONE  1, 1969-
BL/U-1.    CO/U-1.    DB/S-1.    DB/U-2.    ED/N-1.    LO/N-1.

JOURNAL OF THE OLD WEXFORD SOCIETY.
+ +J. OLD WEXFORD SOC.
WEXFORD  1, 1968-
CA/U-1.    DB/S-1.    ED/N-1.    OX/U-1.
BL/U-1.  2, 1969-

JOURNAL OF OPTICS.
+ +J. OPT.
OPTICAL SOCIETY OF INDIA.
CALCUTTA  1, 1972-
Q.
CA/U-2.

JOURNAL OF ORAL PATHOLOGY.
+ +J. ORAL PATHOL.
[MUNKESGAARD]
COPENHAGEN  1(1), 1972-
6/A.
GL/U-1.    LD/U-1.    SH/U-1.    SO/U-1.

JOURNAL OF PALESTINE STUDIES.
+ +J. PALEST. STUD.
INSTITUTE FOR PALESTINE STUDIES.
BEIRUT  1(1), 1971-
S/T: A QUARTERLY ON PALESTINE AFFAIRS & THE
ARAB-ISRAELI CONFLICT.  SPONS. BODY ALSO:
KUWAIT UNIVERSITY.
CA/U-1.    LO/U-3.    LO/U14.    SH/U-1.    SO/U-1.
MA/U-1.  1(2), 1972-
ISSN 0047-2654

JOURNAL, PAPUA & NEW GUINEA SOCIETY.
+ +J. PAPUA & NEW GUINEA SOC.
PORT MORESBY  1(1), 1967-
LO/U-8.
ISSN 0031-1499

JOURNAL OF PATHOLOGY.*
+ +J. PATHOL.
PATHOLOGICAL SOCIETY OF GREAT BRITAIN & IRELAND
EDINBURGH  97(1), JA 1969-
PREV: JOURNAL OF PATHOLOGY & BACTERIOLOGY
FROM 45(2), 1937- 96(2), 1968.
BN/U-2.    LD/U-1.    LO/M-1.    LO/U-1.    LO/U-2.    OX/U-8.
RE/U-1.    ZW/M-1.
ISSN 0022-3417

JOURNAL OF PERIODONTOLOGY.                                   XXX
SUBS (1969): JOURNAL OF PERIODONTOLOGY -
PERIODONTICS.

JOURNAL OF PERIODONTOLOGY - PERIODONTICS.                    XXX
+ +J. PERIOD. - PERIOD.
AMERICAN ACADEMY OF PERIODONTOLOGY.
CHICAGO  40, 1969-
INCORP: JOURNAL OF PERIODONTOLOGY FROM 1,
1930- 39, 1968, OF WHICH VOL. NUMBERING IS RE-
TAINED; & PERIODONTICS FROM 1, 1963- 6, 1968.
LD/U-1.

JOURNAL OF PERSONALITY ASSESSMENT.                           XXX
+ +J. PERS. ASSESS.
SOCIETY FOR PERSONALITY ASSESSMENT.
BURBANK, CALIF.  35, 1971-
PREV: JOURNAL OF PROJECTIVE TECHNIQUES &
PERSONALITY ASSESSMENT FROM 27(2), JE 1963-
34, 1970.
DR/U-1.    GL/U-1.    LD/U-1.    LO/N13.    LO/U-1.    MA/U-1.
NW/U-1.
ISSN 0022-3891

JOURNAL DE PHARMACOLOGIE.
+ +J. PHARMACOL. (FR.).
ASSOCIATION DES PHARMACOLOGISTES.
[MASSON]
PARIS  1, JA 1970-
GL/U-1.    LO/N14.    LO/U-2.    OX/U-8.
ISSN 0021-793X

JOURNAL OF PHENOMENOLOGICAL PSYCHOLOGY.
+ +J. PHENOMENOL. PSYCHOL.
[DUQUESNE UNIV. P.]
PITTSBURGH  1, 1970-
2A.
AD/U-1.
ISSN 0047-2662

JOURNAL OF PHILIPPINE LIBRARIANSHIP.
+ +J. PHILIPPINE LIBR.
UNIVERSITY OF THE PHILIPPINES: INSTITUTE OF
LIBRARY SCIENCE.
QUEZON CITY  1, 1968-
BL/U-1.    OX/U-1.
ISSN 0022-359X

**JOURNAL OF PHILOSOPHICAL LOGIC.**
+ +J. PHILOS. LOGIC.
[REIDEL]
  DORDRECHT 1, 1972-
  BL/U-1.    BN/U-1.    CA/U-1.    CB/U-1.    LO/U-1.    LO/U-2.
  LO/U-4.    MA/U-1.    OX/U-1.    SW/U-1.
  ISSN 0022-3611

**JOURNAL OF PHONETICS.**
+ +J. PHONET.
[SEMINAR P.]
  LONDON; NEW YORK 1, 1973-
  AD/U-1.    BN/U-1.    CA/U-1.    ED/N-1.    LD/U-1.    LO/U14.
  NO/U-1.
  SH/U-1.  2, 1974-
  ISSN 0095-4470

**JOURNAL OF PHOTOCHEMISTRY.**
+ +J. PHOTOCHEM.
[ELSEVIER SEQUOIA]
  LAUSANNE 1, 1972-
  LD/U-1.    LO/N14.    SO/S-3.    LO/U-2.    MA/U-1.    XS/R10.
  SF/U-1.  2, 1973/74-
  ISSN 0047-2670

**JOURNAL OF PHYSICAL & CHEMICAL REFERENCE DATA.**
  NATIONAL BUREAU OF STANDARDS (US).
  WASHINGTON, D.C. 1, 1972-
  SPONS. BODIES ALSO: AMERICAN INSTITUTE OF
  PHYSICS; & AMERICAN CHEMICAL SOCIETY.
  AD/U-1.    BH/U-3.    CA/U-2.    LO/N14.    LO/U12.
  MA/U-1.    OX/U-8.    XS/R10.
  RE/U-1.  3, 1974-
  ISSN 0047-2689

**JOURNAL OF PHYSICAL OCEANOGRAPHY.**
+ +J. PHYS. OCEANOGR.
  AMERICAN METEOROLOGICAL SOCIETY.
  LANCASTER, PA.  1(1), 1971-
  LO/N-4.    LO/N14.    SH/U-1.    XS/N-1.
  SO/U-1.  2, 1972-              XS/R10.  2, 1972-
  XY/N-1.  1(1), 1971.
  ISSN 0022-3670

**JOURNAL OF PHYSICS; A: GENERAL. PROCEEDINGS**
**OF THE PHYSICAL SOCIETY.**                              XXX
+ +J. PHYS., A.
  INSTITUTE OF PHYSICS & THE PHYSICAL SOCIETY.
  LONDON 1, 1968- 5, 1972 ...
  CALLED 'SERIES 2' OF PREV: PROCEEDINGS OF THE
  PHYSICAL SOCIETY OF LONDON TO 92, 1967,
  OF WHICH ABOVE IS A PART CONTINUATION.
  SUBS: JOURNAL OF PHYSICS: A: MATHEMATICAL,
  NUCLEAR & GENERAL.
  BN/U-2.    CB/U-1.    GL/U-2.    HL/U-1.    LO/F-1.    LO/N14.
  LO/U-2.    LO/U13.    MA/P-1.    MA/U-1.    SO/U-1.    XS/N-1.
  ISSN 0022-3689

**JOURNAL OF PHYSICS; B: ATOMIC & MOLECULAR**
**PHYSICS. PROCEEDINGS OF THE PHYSICAL SOCIETY.**
+ +J. PHYS., B. (GB)
  INSTITUTE OF PHYSICS & THE PHYSICAL SOCIETY.
  LONDON 1, 1968-
  CALLED 'SERIES 2' OF PREV: PROCEEDINGS OF THE
  PHYSICAL SOCIETY OF LONDON TO 92, 1967,
  OF WHICH ABOVE IS A PART CONTINUATION.
  BN/U-2.    CB/U-1.    ED/N-1.    GL/U-2.    HL/U-1.    LO/F-1.
  LO/U-2.    LO/N14.    LO/U13.    MA/P-1.    SO/U-1.
  ISSN 0022-3700

**JOURNAL OF PHYSICS: C: SOLID STATE PHYSICS.**
**PROCEEDINGS OF THE PHYSICAL SOCIETY.**                  XXX
+ +J. PHYS., C.
  INSTITUTE OF PHYSICS & THE PHYSICAL SOCIETY.
  LONDON 1, 1968-
  CALLED 'SERIES 2' OF PREV: PROCEEDINGS OF THE
  PHYSICAL SOCIETY OF LONDON TO 92, 1967,
  OF WHICH ABOVE IS A PART CONTINUATION.
  ISSUES SUPPL. METAL PHYSICS (LONDON).
  BN/U-2.    CB/U-1.    ED/N-1.    GL/U-2.    HL/U-1.    LO/F-1.
  LO/N14.    LO/U-1.    LO/U-2.    LO/U13.    MA/P-1.
  MA/U-1.    SO/U-1.    XS/N-1.
  ISSN 0022-3719

**JOURNAL OF PHYSICS D: APPLIED PHYSICS.**               XXX
+ +J. PHYS., D.
  INSTITUTE OF PHYSICS & THE PHYSICAL SOCIETY.
  LONDON 1, 1968-
  PREV: BRITISH JOURNAL OF APPLIED PHYSICS FROM
  1, 1950- 18, 1967. SERIES TITLE FROM 1, 1968-
  2, 1969: BRITISH JOURNAL OF APPLIED PHYSICS.
  AS ABOVE FROM 3(1), JA 1970.
  BH/U-1.    BN/U-1.    BN/U-2.    GL/U-2.    HL/U-1.    LO/F-1.
  LO/U13.
  BH/P-1.  3(1), 1970-        CB/U-1.  3(1), 1970-
  ED/N-1.  3(1), 1970-        LO/N-5.  3(1), 1970-
  LO/N14.  2, 1969-           XS/R10.  3(1), 1970-
  ISSN 0022-3727

**JOURNAL OF PHYSICS E: SCIENTIFIC INSTRUMENTS.**        XXX
+ +J. PHYS. E.
  INSTITUTE OF PHYSICS & THE PHYSICAL SOCIETY.
  LONDON 1, 1968-
  PREV: JOURNAL OF SCIENTIFIC INSTRUMENTS FROM
  1, 1923- 44, 1967. SERIES TITLE FROM 1,
  1968- 2, 1969: JOURNAL OF SCIENTIFIC INSTRU-
  MENTS. AS ABOVE FROM 3(1), JA.1970.
  BH/U-1.    BN/U-1.    BR/U-3.    GL/U-2.    HL/U-1.    LO/F-1.
  LO/N14.    LO/S-3.    LO/U11.    LO/U13.
  BH/P-1.  3, 1970-           BH/U-1.
  CB/U-1.  3, 1970-           ED/N-1.  3, 1970-
  LO/N-5.  3, 1970-           RE/U-1.  3, 1970-
  XS/R10.  3, 1970-
  ISSN 0022-3735

**JOURNAL OF PHYSICS: F: METAL PHYSICS.**               XXX
+ +J. PHYS., F.
  INSTITUTE OF PHYSICS & THE PHYSICAL SOCIETY.
[PHYSICS TRUST PUBL.]
  LONDON 1(1), JA 1971-
  PREV: METAL PHYSICS (LONDON) FROM NO.1-3, 1970
  AD/U-1.    CB/U-1.    CO/U-1.    DB/U-2.    GL/U-1.    GL/U-2.
  HL/U-1.    LD/U-1.    LO/U-1.    LO/U-2.    LO/U11.    RE/U-1.
  SF/U-1.    SH/C-5.    SH/U-1.    SO/U-1.    XS/R10.
  LO/N-4.  4, 1974-
  ISSN 0305-4608

**JOURNALS OF PIERRE MENARD.**
+ +J. PIERRE MENARD.
  OXFORD NO.1, JA 1969-
  ED/N-1.    LO/U-2.    OX/U-1.

**JOURNAL OF POLITICAL & MILITARY SOCIOLOGY.**
+ +J. POLIT. & MIL. SOCIOL.
  NORTHERN ILLINOIS UNIVERSITY: DEPARTMENT OF
  SOCIOLOGY.
  DEKALB 1, 1973-
  BH/U-3.    CA/U-1.    LO/U14.
  ISSN 0047-2697

**JOURNAL OF POPULAR CULTURE.**
+ +J. POP. CULT.
  MODERN LANGUAGE ASSOCIATION OF AMERICA.
  OHIO 1(1), 1967-
  EX/U-1.    OX/U-1.
  LO/N-1.  3(1), 1969-           LO/U-2.  3(2), 1969-
  CB/U-1. [W. 1(1-3), 1967.]
  ISSN 0022-3840

**JOURNAL OF POPULATION STUDIES.**            OOO
**SEE: IN'GU MUNJE NONJIP.**

**JOURNAL, PRESBYTERIAN HISTORICAL SOCIETY OF**
**ENGLAND.**                                              XXX
  SUBS(1973): JOURNAL, UNITED REFORMED CHURCH
  HISTORY SOCIETY.

**JOURNAL & PROCEEDINGS, INSTITUTION OF AGRI-**
**CULTURAL ENGINEERS.**                                   XXX
+ +J. & PROC. INST. AGRIC. ENG.
  LONDON 16, 1960- 26, 1971...
  PREV: JOURNAL AND PROCEEDINGS, INSTITUTION OF
  BRITISH AGRICULTURAL ENGINEERS FROM 14, 1958-
  15, 1959. SUBS: AGRICULTURAL ENGINEER.
  LO/N14.

**JOURNAL & PROCEEDINGS, INSTITUTION OF BRITISH**
**AGRICULTURAL ENGINEERS.**                               XXX
  SUBS (1960): JOURNAL & PROCEEDINGS, INSTIT-
  UTION OF AGRICULTURAL ENGINEERS.

**JOURNAL & PROCEEDINGS, INSTITUTE OF ROAD TRANS-**
**PORT ENGINEERS.**                                       XXX
  SUBS (1970): TRANSPORT ENGINEER.

**JOURNAL OF PROFESSIONAL ACTIVITIES.**                  XXX
  SUBS (1972): ENGINEERING ISSUES.

**JOURNAL OF PSYCHEDELIC DRUGS.**
+ +J. PSYCHEDELIC DRUGS.
  HAIGHT-ASHBURY MEDICAL CLINIC.
  SAN FRANCISCO 1(1), 1967-
  SPONS. BODY ALSO UNIVERSITY OF CALIFORNIA:
  MEDICAL CENTER PSYCHOPHARMACOLOGY STUDY GROUP.
  LO/N-1.  1(2), 1967/68-
  ISSN 0022-393X

**JOURNAL OF PSYCHOLINGUISTIC RESEARCH.**
+ +J. PSYCHOLINGUIST. RES.
[PLENUM P.]
  NEW YORK 1(1), 1971-
  Q.
  LO/N-1.    LO/U-1.    OX/U-1.    SH/U-1.    SO/U-1.    XY/N-1.
  ISSN 0090-6905

JOURNAL OF PUBLIC ECONOMICS.
*++J. PUBLIC ECON.*
[NORTH-HOLLAND PUBL. CO.]
*AMSTERDAM  1(1), AP 1972-*
*Q.*
*AD/U-1.    BN/U-1.    EX/U-1.    LO/U-3.    LO/U12.    NO/U-1.*
*OX/U17.    SH/U-1.    SO/U-1.*
*ISSN 0047-2727*

JOURNAL OF PURCHASING.
*++J. PURCHAS.*
NATIONAL ASSOCIATION OF PURCHASING AGENTS.
*NEW YORK   1, MY 1965-*
*XY/N-1.*
*ISSN 0022-4030*

JOURNAL OF PURE & APPLIED ALGEBRA.
*++J. PURE & APPL. ALGEBRA.*
[NORTH-HOLLAND PUBL. CO.]
*AMSTERDAM  1, JA 1971-*
*Q.*
*AD/U-1.    CA/U-2.    LO/N14.    LO/U-4.    LO/U12.*
*NW/U-1.    SH/U-1.    SW/U-1.    XY/N-1.*
*BH/U-3.  4, 1974-*
*MA/U-1.  3, 1973-*          *GL/U-1.  4, 1974-*
*ISSN 0022-4049*

JOURNAL OF QUALITY TECHNOLOGY.
*++J. QUAL. TECHNOL.*
AMERICAN SOCIETY FOR QUALITY CONTROL.
*MILWAUKEE  1, 1969-*
PREV PART OF: INDUSTRIAL QUALITY CONTROL FROM
1, JL 1944.
*BH/U-1.    LO/N-4.    LO/N14.    SH/U-1.    SW/U-1.*
*CB/U-1.  2(2), 1970-*
*ISSN 0022-4065*

JOURNAL OF RADIOANALYTICAL CHEMISTRY.
*++J. RADIOANAL. CHEM.*
[ELSEVIER / AKADEMIAI KIADO]
*AMSTERDAM / BUDAPEST  1, 1968-*
*LO/N14.    LO/S-3.*
*ISSN 0022-4081*

JOURNAL, RAILWAY DIVISION, INSTITUTION OF
MECHANICAL ENGINEERS.                                    000
  SEE:  RAILWAY DIVISION JOURNAL ...

JOURNAL OF RAMAN SPECTROSCOPY.
*++J. RAMAN SPECTROSC.*
[REIDEL]
*DORDRECHT  1(1), AP 1973-*
*6/A.  S/T: AN INTERNATIONAL JOURNAL FOR ORIG-*
INAL WORK IN ALL ASPECTS OF RAMAN SPECTROSCOPY
INCLUDING HIGHER ORDER PROCESSES, & ALSO
BRILLOUIN- & RAYLEIGH SCATTERING.
*BL/U-1.    GL/U-1.    LO/N14.    LO/S-3.    LO/U-2.    OX/U-8.*
*XS/R10.*

JOURNAL & RECORD OF TRANSACTIONS, JUNIOR
INSTITUTION OF ENGINEERS.                                XXX
  SUBS (1971): JOURNAL, INSTITUTION OF
  GENERAL TECHNICIAN ENGINEERS.

JOURNAL OF RECREATIONAL MATHEMATICS.
*++J. RECREAT. MATH.*
[GREENWOOD]
*WESTPORT, CONN.  1(1), 1968-*
*LO/U14.    XS/R10.*
*LO/U11.  4, 1971-*
*ISSN 0022-412X*

JOURNAL OF REFRIGERATION.                                XXX
*++J. REFRIG.  [JREF-A]*
[FOXLOW PUBL.]
*LONDON  1, 1957- 12, 1969.//*
FROM 8, 1965 CONTAINS MONTHLY ISSUES OF PROCE-
EDINGS, INSTITUTE OF REFRIGERATION. CONTAINS
SUPPL. REFRIGERATION TECHNICIAN FROM 8(5)-
8(11), 1965.
*LO/N14.*
*ISSN 0022-4138*

JOURNAL, REGIONAL ENGLISH LANGUAGE CENTRE
(SINGAPORE).
  SEE: R.E.L.C. JOURNAL.

JOURNAL, REGISTERED PLUMBERS ASSOCIATION.               XXX
  SUBS (1970): PLUMBING.

JOURNAL OF RELIGION IN AFRICA. RELIGION EN
AFRIQUE.
*++J. RELIG. AFR.*
[BRILL]
*LEYDEN  1, 1967-*
*BH/C-3.    BH/U-1.       GL/U-1.    LO/U11.*
*BL/U-1.  3, 1970-*          *LD/U-1.  4, 1971-*
*ISSN 0022-4200*

JOURNAL OF RELIGION IN AFRICA: SUPPLEMENTS.            000
  SEE: STUDIES ON RELIGION IN AFRICA.

JOURNAL OF REMOTE SENSING.
*++J. REMOTE SENS.*
INTERNATIONAL REMOTE SENSING INSTITUTE.
*SACRAMENTO, CALIF.  1, 1970-*
*LO/N14.*
*LO/U-2.  2, 1971-*
*ISSN 0047-2743*

JOURNAL OF REPRINTS FOR ANTITRUST LAW & ECON-
OMICS.
*++J. REPR. ANTITRUST LAW & ECON.*
[FEDERAL LEGAL PUBL. INC.]
*NEW YORK  1, 1969-*
*Q.  S/T: SELECTED REPRINTS IN THE FIELD OF*
INDUSTRIAL ORGANISATION & ANTITRUST LAW.
*EX/U-1.    LO/U-2.    LO/U-3.*
*ISSN 0022-4243*

JOURNAL OF REPRODUCTION & FERTILITY: SUPPLE-
MENT.
*++J. REPROD. & FERT., SUPPL.*
SOCIETY FOR THE STUDY OF FERTILITY.
[BLACKWELL]
*OXFORD &C.  NO.1, 1966-*
*CR/U-1.  NO.2, 1967-*          *LO/N13.  NO.2, 1967-*
*LO/U-1.  NO.13, 1971-*

JOURNAL OF RESEARCH & DEVELOPMENT IN EDUCAT-
ION.
*++J. RES. & DEVELOP. EDUC.*
UNIVERSITY OF GEORGIA: COLLEGE OF EDUCATION.
*ATHENS, GA.  1(1), 1967-*
*DB/U-2.    SO/U-1.*
*ISSN 0022-426X*

JOURNAL OF RESEARCH, HARYANA AGRICULTURAL
UNIVERSITY.
*++J. RES. HARYANA AGRIC. UNIV.*
*HARYANA, INDIA  1, 1971-*
*BL/U-1.*

JOURNAL OF THE RESEARCH SOCIETY OF PAKISTAN.
*++J. RES. SOC. PAK.*
*LAHORE  1, JL 1964-*
URDU WITH ENGL. SUMM.
*OX/U13.*

JOURNAL OF RESEARCH OF THE UNITED STATES
GEOLOGICAL SURVEY.
*++J. RES. U.S. GEOL. SURV.*
(UNITED STATES) DEPARTMENT OF THE INTERIOR:
GEOLOGICAL SURVEY.
*WASHINGTON, D.C.  1, 1973-*
*2M.*
*BL/U-1.    CA/U-2.    CA/U14.    LD/U-1.    LO/N-2.    LO/N13.*
*LO/U-1.    MA/U-1.    RE/U-1.    SA/U-1.    SW/U-1.*

JOURNAL OF RESEARCH, UNIVERSITY OF THE PAN-
JAB: HUMANITIES.
*++J. RES. UNIV. PANJAB, HUM.*
*LAHORE   1, JA 1966-*
*BL/U-1.*

JOURNAL, ROYAL AERONAUTICAL SOCIETY.                    XXX
  SUBS (1968): AERONAUTICAL JOURNAL.

JOURNAL, ROYAL ARCHITECTURAL INSTITUTE OF
CANADA.                                                  XXX
  SUBS (1966):  ARCHITECTURE CANADA.

JOURNAL OF THE ROYAL ASIATIC SOCIETY OF
BENGAL.                                                  XXX
  SUBS (1961): JOURNAL OF THE ASIATIC SOCIETY.

JOURNAL, ROYAL ASSOCIATION OF BRITISH DAIRY
FARMERS.                                                 XXX
*++J. R. ASS. BR. DAIRY FARMERS.*
*LONDON  65, 1961- 73, 1969.*
PREV:  JOURNAL, BRITISH DAIRY FARMERS' ASSO-
CIATION FROM 1, 1877- 64, 1960. SUBS:  DAIRY-
ING.
*CA/U11.    LO/N-6.    LO/N14.*

JOURNAL OF THE ROYAL MICROSCOPICAL SOCIETY.            XXX
  SUBS: (1969) JOURNAL OF MICROSCOPY.

JOURNAL, ROYAL NEW ZEALAND INSTITUTE OF
HORTICULTURE: NS.                                        XXX
*++J. R. N.Z. INST. HORT., NS.*
*WELLINGTON  1, 1968- 4, 1971.*
PREV. SERIES FROM 1, 1929. SUBS: ANNUAL
JOURNAL, ROYAL NEW ZEALAND INSTITUTE OF
HORTICULTURE.
*LO/N-2.    LO/N13.*
*ISSN 0557-6601*

JOURNAL OF THE ROYAL SOCIETY OF NEW ZEALAND.          XXX
+ +J. R. SOC. N.Z.
 WELLINGTON 1, 1971-
 PREV: TRANSACTIONS ... ISSUED IN THREE SERIES:
 BIOLOGICAL SCIENCES; EARTH SCIENCES; & GENERAL
 CA/U-2.   DB/S-1.   GL/U-1.   HL/U-1.   LD/U-1.   LO/N-2.
 LO/N-4.   LO/N14.   NW/U-1.

JOURNAL, ROYAL TOWN PLANNING INSTITUTE.          XXX
+ +J. R. TOWN PLANN. INST.
 LONDON 57(6), 1971-
 PREV: JOURNAL, TOWN PLANNING INSTITUTE FROM
 10, 1924- 57(5), 1971.
 BH/P-1.   CV/C-1.   ED/N-1.   GL/U-1.   LO/R-5.   LO/U28.
 NO/U-1.   NW/U-1.
 ISSN 0048-8739

JOURNAL, ROYAL UNITED SERVICE INSTITUTION.          XXX
 SUBS(1971): JOURNAL, ROYAL UNITED SERVICE
 INSTITUTE FOR DEFENCE STUDIES.

JOURNAL, ROYAL UNITED SERVICE INSTITUTE FOR
DEFENCE STUDIES.          XXX
+ +J. R. UNITED SERV. INST. DEF. STUD.
 LONDON 116(662- 664), 1971...
 Q. PREV: JOURNAL, ROYAL UNITED SERVICE INST-
 ITUTION FROM 1, 1857- 116(661), 1971.
 SUBS: RUSI.
 ED/N-1.   LO/S14.   LO/U-1.

JOURNAL OF SAITAMA UNIVERSITY ...          000
 SEE: SAITAMA DAIGAKU KIYO ...

JOURNAL OF SCIENCE & TECHNOLOGY (1969).          XXX
+ +J. SCI. & TECHNOL. (1969).          XXX
 GENERAL ELECTRIC & ENGLISH ELECTRIC CO.
 LONDON 36(1), 1969- 39(1), 1972 ...
 INCORP: GEC-AEI JOURNAL OF SCIENCE & TECHNOL-
 OGY FROM 35(2-3), 1968; & ENGLISH ELECTRIC
 JOURNAL 1, 1920- 23(6), 1968. SUBS: GEC
 JOURNAL OF SCIENCE AND TECHNOLOGY (1972).
 BH/P-1.   ED/N-1.   GL/U-1.   LO/N14.   LO/U-2.   MA/P-1.
 XS/R10.
 BR/U-3. 37, 1970-
 ISSN 0022-4421

JOURNAL OF SCIENTIFIC INSTRUMENTS.          XXX
 SUBS (1968): JOURNAL OF PHYSICS E: JOURNAL OF
 SCIENTIFIC INSTRUMENTS.

JOURNAL, SCIENTIFIC RESEARCH COUNCIL(JAMAICA).
+ +J. SCI. RES. COUNC. (JAMAICA).
 KINGSTON, JAMAICA 1, 1970-
 BL/U-1.   LO/N13.   SH/U-1.
 ISSN 0036-8822

JOURNAL OF THE SCOTTISH ASSOCIATION OF
GEOGRAPHY TEACHERS.
+ +J. SCOTT. ASSOC. GEOGR. TEACH.
 GLASGOW NO.1, OC 1971-
 OX/U-1.
 ED/N-1. NO.2, 1973-
 LO/S13. NO.1, 1971.

JOURNAL OF THE SCOTTISH LABOUR HISTORY
SOCIETY.
+ +J. SCOTT. LAB. HIST. SOC.
 [GLASGOW] NO.1, MY 1969-
 AD/U-1.   ED/N-1.   ED/P-1.   GL/U-2.   LO/U-3.   OX/U-1.
 OX/U17.

JOURNAL, SEMPERVIVUM SOCIETY.
+ +J. SEMPERVIVUM SOC.
 BISHOPS STORTFORD 1, 1970-
 LO/N-2.

JOURNAL OF SEX RESEARCH.
+ +J. SEX RES.
 SOCIETY FOR THE SCIENTIFIC STUDY OF SEX.
 NEW YORK 1(1), MR 1965-
 3/A.
 XY/N-1.
 CB/U-1. 1973-                    LO/N-1. 6(1), 1970-
 LO/S74. 6, 1970-                 LO/U-1. 1971-
 ISSN 0022-4499

JOURNAL OF SIGNAL RECORDING MATERIALS.          000
 SEE: JOURNAL FUR SIGNALAUFZEICHUNGSMATERIALIEN

JOURNAL FUR SIGNALAUFZEICHUNGSMATERIALIEN.
+ +J. SIGNALAUFZEICHNUNGSMATER.
 CHEMISCHE GESELLSCHAFT IN DER DDR.
 [AKADEMIE VERLAG]
 BERLIN 1, 1973-
 ALSO ENTITLED ZHURNAL MATERIALY REGISTRATSII
 INFORMATSII; JOURNAL OF SIGNAL RECORDING
 MATERIALS; & JOURNAL POUR LES MATERIAUX
 D'ENREGISTREMENT DES SIGNAUX.
 LO/N14.

JOURNAL, SINGAPORE NATIONAL ACADEMY OF
SCIENCE.
+ +J. SINGAPORE NATL. ACAD. SCI.
 SINGAPORE 1, 1969-
 LO/N-2. 2, 1970-

JOURNAL OF SOCIAL HISTORY.
+ +J. SOC. HIST.
 UNIVERSITY OF CALIFORNIA.
 BERKELEY 1, 1967-
 DB/U-2.   NO/U-1.
 BH/U-3. 7, 1973-              ED/N-1. 1(2), 1967-
 LO/U-2. 3, 1969-             LO/U20. 4, 1971-
 LO/U-3. [W. 1(2), 1967.]
 ISSN 0022-4529

JOURNAL OF SOCIAL POLICY.
+ +J. SOC. POLICY.
 SOCIAL ADMINISTRATION ASSOCIATION.
 [CAMBRIDGE U.P.]
 LONDON 1, 1972-
 AD/U-1.   BL/U-1.   BN/U-1.   ED/N-1.   GL/U-1.   LD/U-1.
 LN/U-2.   LO/S-7.   LO/U-2.   LO/U-3.   LO/U-3.   LO/U-4.
 LO/U12.   LO/U28.   MA/U-1.   NO/U-1.   OX/U17.
 SH/U-1.
 ISSN 0047-2794

JOURNAL OF SOCIAL SCIENCE.
+ +J. SOC. SCI.
 UNIVERSITY OF MALAWI.
 LIMBE 1, 1972-
 AD/U-1.   LO/U-3.   LO/U14.

JOURNAL, SOCIETY OF ENVIRONMENTAL ENGINEERS.          XXX
+ +J. SOC. ENVIRON. ENG.
 LONDON NO.52, 1972-
 PREV: ENVIRONMENTAL ENGINEERING FROM NO.15,
 1965- NO.51, 1971.
 LO/N14.   LO/U-2.
 CA/U-4. 1973-

JOURNAL OF THE SOCIETY OF LEATHER TECHNOLOG-
ISTS & CHEMISTS.          XXX
+ +J. SOC. LEATHER TECHNOL. & CHEM.
 REDBOURNE, HERTS. 57, 1973-
 PREV: JOURNAL OF THE SOCIETY OF LEATHER
 TRADES' CHEMISTS FROM 32, 1948- 56, 1972.
 ED/N-1.   LD/U-1.   LO/N14.   LO/R-6.   LO/S-3.

JOURNAL OF THE SOCIETY OF LEATHER TRADES'
CHEMISTS.          XXX
 SUBS (1973): JOURNAL OF THE SOCIETY OF
 LEATHER TECHNOLOGISTS & CHEMISTS.

JOURNAL OF THE SOIL ASSOCIATION.          XXX
+ +J. SOIL ASSOC.
 HAUGHLEY, SUFFOLK 15(2), AP 1968- 17(2), 1972
 PREV: MOTHER EARTH FROM 1, 1946- 15(1), 1968.
 SUBS: PART OF SOIL ASSOCIATION.
 ED/N-1.   GL/U-1.   LO/N14.   XS/U-1.

JOURNAL OF SOLID STATE CHEMISTRY.
+ +J. SOLID STATE CHEM.
 [ACADEMIC P.]
 NEW YORK 1(1), JE 1969-
 AD/U-3.   BH/U-1.   LO/N14.   LO/S-3.   MA/U-1.
 NW/U-1.   XS/R10.
 LD/U-1. 2, 1970-              OX/U-8. 2(1), 1970-
 SH/U-1. 1972-

JOURNAL OF SOLUTION CHEMISTRY.
+ +J. SOLUTION CHEM.
 [PLENUM P.]
 NEW YORK 1, 1972-
 LO/N14.   LO/S-3.   NW/U-1.   OX/U-8.   RE/U-1.
 ED/N-1. 3, 1974-

JOURNAL, SOUTHEAST ASIAN SOCIETY OF SOIL
ENGINEERING.          XXX
+ +J. SOUTHEAST ASIAN SOC. SOIL ENG.
 BANGKOK 1(1- 2), JE/D 1970...
 SUBS: GEOTECHNICAL ENGINEERING.
 SH/U-3.

**JOURNAL OF SOUTHEAST ASIAN STUDIES.**
++J. SOUTHEAST ASIAN STUD.
UNIVERSITY OF SINGAPORE: DEPARTMENT OF HISTORY.
[MCGRAW HILL]
  SINGAPORE 1(1), 1970-
  2/A. PREV: JOURNAL OF SOUTHEAST ASIAN
  HISTORY FROM 1, 1960.
  CB/U-1.    ED/N-1.    LO/N17.    LO/U-1.    LO/U-3.    LO/U-8.
  LO/U14.    OX/U-9.
  ISSN 0022-4634

**JOURNAL OF SPECIALIST MEDICINE.**
++J. SPEC. MED.
[N.C. MAGAZINES LTD.]
  LONDON 1(1), 1970-
  BN/U-2.    CR/M-1.    ED/N-1.    OX/U-8.
  LD/U-1. CURRENT YEAR.

**JOURNAL OF THE SPELEOLOGICAL SOCIETY OF IRE-**          XXX
**LAND.**
++J. SPELEOL. SOC. IREL.
  DUBLIN NO.1 - 2, 1969...
  SUBS: IRISH SPELEOLOGY.
  DB/U-2.

**JOURNAL OF THE STAFFORDSHIRE INDUSTRIAL**
**ARCHAEOLOGY SOCIETY.**
  STAFFORD NO.1, 1970-
  SPONS. BODY ALSO NORTH STAFFORDSHIRE
  POLYTECHNIC.
  LO/N-4.

**JOURNAL OF STATISTICAL COMPUTATION & SIMULATION.**
++J. STAT. COMPUT. & SIMULAT.
[GORDON & BREACH]
  NEW YORK; LONDON 1(1), JA 1972-
  CB/U-1.    ED/N-1.    LO/N14.    SH/U-1.
  CA/U-1. 2, 1973-                   OX/U-8. 2, 1973-

**JOURNAL OF STATISTICAL PHYSICS.**
++J. STAT. PHYS.
[PLENUM P.]
  NEW YORK &C 1, 1969-
  LO/N14.    LO/U-2.    LO/U-4.    OX/U-8.    SW/U-1.
  SO/U-1. 7, 1973-
  ISSN 0022-4715

**JOURNAL OF STEROID BIOCHEMISTRY.**
++J. STEROID BIOCHEM.
[PERGAMON]
  OXFORD 1(1), N 1969-
  Q.
  DN/U-1.    ED/N-1.    GL/U-1.    LO/N13.    LO/S-3.    LO/U-1.
  NW/U-1.    OX/U-8.    SH/U-1.
  ISSN 0022-4731

**JOURNAL OF STRUCTURAL LEARNING.**
++J. STRUCT. LEARN.
INTERNATIONAL STUDY GROUP FOR MATHEMATICS
LEARNING.
[GORDON & BREACH]
  NEW YORK 1, JA 1968-
  EX/U-1.
  HL/U-2. 1969-                    LN/U-2. 3, 1971-
  LO/U20. 3, 1971-
  ED/N-1. 2(2), 1970-
  ISSN 0022-4774

**JOURNAL OF STRUCTURAL MECHANICS.**
++J. STRUCT. MECH.
[DEKKER]
  NEW YORK 1, 1972-
  Q.
  BL/U-1.    CA/U-4.    GL/U-1.    GL/U-2.    LO/N14.    MA/U-1.
  SH/U-3. 2, 1973-

**JOURNAL FOR THE STUDY OF JUDAISM IN THE PERSIAN,**
**HELLENISTIC & ROMAN PERIOD.**
++J. STUD. JUDAISM PERSIAN HELL. & ROM. PERIOD.
[BRILL]
  LEIDEN 1, 1970-
  BN/U-1.    DB/U-2.    EX/U-1.    LO/U-2.    LO/U11.    MA/U-1.
  OX/U-1.    SH/U-1.
  ISSN 0047-2212

**JOURNAL OF SUBMICROSCOPIC CYTOLOGY.**
++J. SUBMICROSC. CYTOL.
UNIVERSITA DI BOLOGNA: CENTRO DI MICROSCOPIA
ELETTRONICA.
  BOLOGNA 1, 1969-
  CA/U-1.    LO/N-2.    LO/N13.
  ISSN 0022-4782

**JOURNAL, SULPHUR INSTITUTE.**
++J. SULPHUR INST.
  WASHINGTON, D.C. 1, 1965-
  LO/N14.
  ISSN 0039-4904

**JOURNAL OF SUPRAMOLECULAR STRUCTURE.**
++J. SUPRAMOL. STRUCT.
  NEW YORK 1, 1972-
  AD/U-1.    CA/U-2.    GL/U-1.    LO/M12.    LO/N13.
  LO/N14.    MA/U-1.    SH/U-1.
  HL/U-1. 1(1), 1972; 2, 1974-
  ISSN 0091-7419

**JOURNAL OF SURGICAL ONCOLOGY.**
++J. SURG. ONCOL.
[PLENUM PUBL. CORP.]
  NEW YORK 1(1), 1969-
  Q.
  LO/M-3.    LO/N13.    OX/U-8.
  ISSN 0022-4790

**JOURNAL OF SYSTEMS ENGINEERING.**
++J. SYST. ENG.
UNIVERSITY OF LANCASTER: DEPARTMENT OF SYSTEMS
ENGINEERING.
  LANCASTER 1(1), 1969-
  2/A.
  AD/U-1.    BH/U-1.    CB/U-1.    ED/N-1.    EX/U-1.    GL/R-1.
  LA/U-1.    LD/U-1.    LO/N-6.    LO/N-7.    LO/N14.    LO/U-2.
  OX/U-1.    SW/U-1.    XS/R10.
  ISSN 0022-4820

**JOURNAL OF TAMIL STUDIES.**
++J. TAMIL STUD.
INTERNATIONAL ASSOCIATION OF TAMIL RESEARCH.
  MADRAS 1(1), 1969-
  LO/U14.    OX/U13.

**JOURNAL OF TESTING & EVALUATION.**
++J. TEST. & EVAL.
AMERICAN SOCIETY FOR TESTING & MATERIALS.
  PHILADELPHIA 1, 1973-
  PREV: JOURNAL OF MATERIALS FROM 1, 1966- 7,
  1972.
  BL/U-1.    LD/U-1.    LO/N-4.    LO/N14.    LO/S-3.    XS/R10.

**JOURNAL OF TEXTURE STUDIES.**
++J. TEXTURE STUD.
[REIDEL PUBLISHING CO.]
  DORDRECHT 1(1), N 1969-
  Q. S/T: AN INTERNATIONAL JOURNAL OF RHEOLOGY,
  PSYCHORHEOLOGY, PHYSICAL & SENSORY TESTING OF
  FOODS & PHARMACEUTICALS.
  LD/U-1.    OX/U-8.
  BL/U-1. 6, 1975-                    RE/U-1. 5, 1974-
  LO/R-6. 3(1), MR 1972-
  ISSN 0022-4901

**JOURNAL FOR THE THEORY OF SOCIAL BEHAVIOUR.**
++J. THEORY SOC. BEHAV.
[BLACKWELL]
  OXFORD 1, AP 1971-
  2/A.
  AD/U-1.    CA/U-1.    ED/N-1.    LD/U-1.    LO/N-1.    LO/U-2.
  LO/U-4.    MA/U-1.    NO/U-1.    OX/U-1.    OX/U17.
  SH/U-1.
  SO/U-1. 4, 1974-
  ISSN 0021-8308

**JOURNAL OF THERMAL ANALYSIS.**
++J. THERM. ANAL.
[HEYDEN]
  LONDON &C 1, 1969-
  ENGL., FR., GER.
  BL/U-1.    GL/U-1.    LO/N14.    LO/S-3.
  ED/N-1. 2(3), 1970-                SF/U-1. 2, 1970-
  ISSN 0022-5215

**JOURNAL, TOWN PLANNING INSTITUTE.**                     XXX
  SUBS (1971): JOURNAL, ROYAL ...

**JOURNAL OF TROPICAL PEDIATRICS & ENVIRONMENTAL**
**CHILD HEALTH.**                                          XXX
++J. TROP. PEDIATR. & ENVIRON. CHILD HEALTH.
[AMBERLEY HOUSE]
  LONDON 17, MR 1971-
  Q. PREV: JOURNAL OF TROPICAL PEDIATRICS FROM
  1, JE 1955- 16, 1970.
  ED/N-1.
  ISSN 0300-9920

**JOURNAL OF TYPOGRAPHIC RESEARCH.**                      XXX
++J. TYPOGR. RES.
[CASE WESTERN RESERVE UNIV. PRESS]
  CLEVELAND, OHIO 1(1), JA 1967-4, 1970 ...
  Q. SUBS: VISIBLE LANGUAGE.
  ED/N-1.    LO/N14.
  LO/U-2. 2, 1968-

JOURNAL, UNITED REFORMED CHURCH HISTORY
SOCIETY.                                                    XXX
+ +J. UNITED REFORMED CHURCH HIST. SOC.
  LONDON 1(1), 1973-
  PREV. PART OF: TRANSACTIONS, CONGREGATIONAL
  HISTORICAL SOCIETY FROM 1, 1901- 20, 1972; &
  JOURNAL, PRESBYTERIAN HISTORICAL SOCIETY OF
  ENGLAND FROM 1, 1914- 14, 1972.
  AD/U-1.    ED/N-1.    HL/U-1.    LO/U-1.    MA/P-1.    MA/S-1.
  OX/U-1.    SH/U-1.

JOURNAL OF THE UNIVERSITY COLLEGE, DURBAN.
+ +J. UNIV. COLL. DURBAN.
  DURBAN 1(1), 1965-
  LO/U14.

JOURNAL OF URBAN ANALYSIS.
+ +J. URBAN ANAL.
  [GORDON & BREACH]
  LONDON 1, 1972-
  ED/N-1.    NO/U-1.    OX/U-1.    SH/U-1.
  ISSN 0091-1909

JOURNAL OF THE VARENDRA RESEARCH MUSEUM.
+ +J. VARENDRA RES. MUS.
  RAJSHAHI 1(1), 1972-
  CA/U-1.    OX/U13.

JOURNAL OF THE VETERINARY CONTROL & RESEARCH
INSTITUTE PENDIK.                                          000
  SEE: PENDIK VETERINER KONTROL VE ARASTIRMA
  ENSTITUSU DERGI.

JOURNAL OF THE VISIBLE RECORD (EDP) SOCIETY.               XXX
+ +J. VISIBLE REC. (EDP) SOC.
  LONDON NO.1, JA 1972 ...
  MON. SUBS: COMPUTER EXECUTIVE. JOURNAL OF
  THE VISIBLE RECORD (EDP) SOCIETY.
  CA/U-1.    ED/N-1.

JOURNAL OF VOCATIONAL BEHAVIOR.
+ +J. VOCAT. BEHAV.
  [ACADEMIC P.]
  NEW YORK &C. 1(1), JA 1971-
  BH/U-3.    OX/U-8.    SH/U-1.
  HL/U-1. 1(2), 1971; 4, 1974-
  ISSN 0001-8791

JOURNAL OF THE WATFORD & DISTRICT INDUSTRIAL
HISTORY SOCIETY.
+ +J. WATFORD & DIST. IND. HIST. SOC.
  HEMEL HEMPSTEAD, HERTS. NO.1, 1971-
  LO/N-4.
  ED/N-1. NO.2, 1972-

JOURNAL OF WEST MIDLANDS REGIONAL STUDIES.                 XXX
+ +J. WEST MIDL. REG. STUD.
  WOLVERHAMPTON COLLEGE OF TECHNOLOGY.
  WOLVERHAMPTON 1, D 1967- 2, 1968...
  SUBS: WEST MIDLANDS STUDIES.
  BH/P-1.    BH/U-1.    SO/U-1.

JOURNAL OF WILDLIFE DISEASES.                              XXX
+ +J. WILD. DIS.
  WILDLIFE DISEASE ASSOCIATION.
  AMES, IOWA 6, 1970-
  PREV: BULLETIN, WILDLIFE DISEASE ASSOCIATION
  FROM 1, 1965.
  LO/N-2.    LO/N13.
  ISSN 0583-8800

JOURNAL, WOLVERTON & DISTRICT ARCHAEOLOGICAL
SOCIETY.                                                   XXX
+ +J. WOLVERTON & DIST. ARCHAEOL. SOC.
  [WOLVERTON] NO.1, 1968- 2, 1969.
  PREV: NEWS LETTER, WOLVERTON & DISTRICT
  ARCHAEOLOGICAL SOCIETY. SUBS: WOLVERTON HISTO-
  RICAL JOURNAL.
  BH/U-1.    LV/U-1.

JOURNAL, YALOVA HORTICULTURAL RESEARCH &
TRAINING CENTER.                                           000
  SEE: YALOVA BAHCE KULTURLERI ARASTIRMA VE
  EGITIM MERKEZI DERGI.

JPL QUARTERLY TECHNICAL REVIEW.
+ +JPL Q. TECH. REV.
  CALIFORNIA INSTITUTE OF TECHNOLOGY: JET
  PROPULSION LABORATORY.
  PASADENA 1, AP 1971-
  CV/C-1.

JUGOSLAVISCHE ERFINDER-ZEITSCHRIFT.                        000
  SEE: JUGOSLOVENSKO PRONALAZASTVO.

JUGOSLOVENSKI ISTORIJSKI CASOPIS.
+ +JUGOSL. ISTOR. CAS.
  SAVEZ ISTORIJSKIH DRUSTAVA JUGOSLAVIJE.
  BELGRADE 1, 1962-
  CA/U-1.    OX/U-1.
  NO/U-1. 1970-
  ISSN 0449-3931

JUGOSLOVENSKO PRONALAZASTVO.
+ +JUGOSL. PRONALAZASTVO. [JUPR-A]
  UDRUZENJE JUGOSLOVENSKIH PRONALAZACA.
  BELGRADE 1, JA 1960-
  MON.
  LO/N14.**
  0448-0341

JUGOSLOVENSKO VINOGRADARSTVO I VINARSTVO.
+ +JUGOSL. VINOGRAD. & VINAR. [JVIV-A]
  INSTITUT ZA SPOLJNU TRGOVINU.
  BELGRADE 1, 1967-
  MON.
  LO/N13. [W. 1(7) & (8)]
  ISSN 0022-6130

JUGOSLOVENSKO VOCARSTVO.
+ +JUGOSL. VOCARSTVO.
  JUGOSLOVENSKO NAUCHNO VOCARSKO DRUSTVO.
  CACAK 1(1), 1967-
  ENGL., FR., OR GER. SUMM. & CONT. LISTS.
  LO/N13.
  ISSN 0022-6092

JUNIOR PHILIPPINE SCIENTIST.
+ +JUNIOR PHILIPPINE SCI.
  UNIVERSITY OF SAN CARLOS (PHILIPPINES).
  CEBU CITY [NO.]1, 1964-
  LO/N-2.

JURIMETRICS JOURNAL.                                       XXX
+ +JURIMETRICS J. [JURJ-A]
  AMERICAN BAR ASSOCIATION: SPECIAL COMMITTEE ON
  ELECTRONIC DATA RETRIEVAL.
  CHICAGO S 1966-
  Q. PREV: MULL. MODERN USES OF LOGIC IN LAW
  FROM S 1959- JE 1966.
  LO/U-3.    NO/U-1.
  CR/U-1. 12, 1971-
  ISSN 0022-6793

JUSTICE.
  INTERNATIONAL COMMISSION OF JURISTS: AUSTRALIAN
  SECTION.
  SYDNEY NO.1, 1968-
  OX/U15.

JUSTICE OF THE PEACE.                                      XXX
  [JUSTICE OF THE PEACE LTD.]
  CHICHESTER; LONDON 135(47), N 1971-
  W. PREV: PART OF JUSTICE OF THE PEACE & LOCAL
  GOVERNMENT REVIEW FROM 1, 1837- 135(46), 1971.
  LO/U12.    SO/U-1.

JUSTICE OF THE PEACE & LOCAL GOVERNMENT
REVIEW.                                                    XXX
  SUBS (1971): PART OF JUSTICE OF THE PEACE; &
  LOCAL GOVERNMENT REVIEW.

JUTE CHRONICLE.
+ +JUTE CHRON.
  INDIAN JUTE MILLS ASSOCIATION.
  CALCUTTA 1(1), 1966-
  2M.
  LO/N14.*
  ISSN 0022-7110

JYDSK LANDBRUG.                                            XXX
  SUBS (1970): NYE DANSK LANDBRUG.

JYVASKYLA STUDIES IN THE ARTS.
+ +JYVASKYLA STUD. ARTS.
  JYVASKYLAN YLIOPISTO.
  JYVASKYLA NO.1, 1967-
  FINN.
  LO/N-3.    NW/U-1.    OX/U-1.
  ISSN 0075-4633

K SOBYTIJAM V CHEKHOSLOVAKII: FAKTY, DOKUM-
ENTY, SVIDETEL'STVA PRESSY I OCHEVIDTSEV.
+ +K SOBYTIJAM CHEKH., FAKTY DOK. SVIDETEL'STVA
  PRESSY & OCHEVIDTSEV.
  [PRESS-GRUPPA SOVETSKIKH ZHURNALISTOV]
  MOSCOW 1, 1968-
  ALSO PUBL. IN ENGL.: ON EVENTS IN CZECHOSLOV-
  AKIA.
  CA/U-1.    CC/U-1.    GL/U-1.    HL/U-1.    OX/U-1.

KAGAKU KOGAKU: (ENGL. ED.)　　　　000
　SEE (1963): CHEMICAL ENGINEERING, JAPAN.
　　(1968): JOURNAL OF CHEMICAL ENGINEERING
　　OF JAPAN.

KAGAKU TO SEIBUTSU.　CHEMISTRY & BIOLOGY.
　NIHON NOGEI KAGAKKAI.
　TOKYO 1(1), 1962-
　LO/N13.
　ISSN 0453-073X

KAGOSHIMA DAIGAKU KOGAKUBU KENKYU HOKOKU.
RESEARCH REPORTS, FACULTY OF ENGINEERING,
KAGOSHIMA UNIVERSITY.
　FUKUOKA NO.1, 1961-
　ENGL. SUMM.
　LO/N13.
　ISSN 0451-212X

KAGOSHIMA KOGYO KOTO SENMON GAKKO KENKYU
HOKOKU.　RESEARCH REPORT OF KAGOSHIMA TECH-
NICAL COLLEGE.
　KAGOSHIMA 1, 1965-
　SOME ENGL. SUMM.
　LO/N13.

KAIYO KAGAKU.　MARINE SCIENCES.
　KAIYO SHUPPAN K.K.
　TOKYO 1, 1969-
　ENGL. SUMM.
　LO/N13.

KAJIAN EKONOMI MALAYSIA.　MALAYSIAN ECONOMIC
STUDIES.
　PERSATUAN EKONOMI MALAYSIA.
　KUALA LUMPUR 1, 1964-
　HL/U-1.　LO/U14.
　ISSN 0022-782X

KALEIDOSCOPE.
　CHICAGO 1(1), 1968-
　LO/U-2.

KALENDAR' KHOZJAJSTVENNIKA.
　[IZDATEL'STVO 'EKONOMIKA'].
　MOSCOW 1965-
　A.
　BH/U-1.
　CC/U-1. 1969(1968)-
　ISSN 0453-1205

KALMIA.
　PHILADELPHIA 1, MR 1969-
　LO/N-2.
　ISSN 0453-1388

KANAGAWA KENRITSU HAKUBUTSUKAN KENKYU HOKOKU:
SHIZEN KAGAKU.
　YOKOHAMA 1, 1968-
　LO/N-2.
　ISSN 0453-1906

KANO STUDIES.
　+ +KANO STUD.
　ABDULLAH BAYERO COLLEGE (KANO).
　KANO, NIGERIA 1, 1965-
　CA/U-1.　LO/U14.　OX/U-1.

KANSAS KIN.
　+ +KANS. KIN.
　RILEY COUNTY (KANSAS) GENEALOGICAL SOCIETY.
　MANHATTAN, KANS. 1, 1963-
　ED/N-1. 4(4), 1966-
　ISSN 0451-4084

KARACHI LAW JOURNAL.
　+ +KARACHI LAW J.
　SIND MUSLIM LAW COLLEGE (KARACHI).
　KARACHI 1, 1964-
　OX/U15.
　ISSN 0075-5095

KARTOFEL', OVOSHCHYE I BAKHCHEVYE KULTURY.　　000
　SEE: KARTOPLJA, OVOCHEVI TA BASHTANNI KUL'TURY

KARTOPLJA, OVOCHEVI TA BASHTANNI KUL'TURY.
　+ +KARTOPLJA OVOCHEVI BASHTANNI KULT. [KOBK-B]
　UKRAJINS'KYJ NAUCHNO-DOSLIDNYJ INSTYTUT
　OVOCHIVNYTSTVA I KARTOPLI.
　KIEV 1, 1964-
　RUSS. SUMM. & TITLE: KARTOFEL', OVOSHCHYE I
　BAKHCHEVYE KUL'TURY.
　LO/N13. 4, 1968-

KASETSART JOURNAL.　　　　XXX
　+ +KASETSART J.
　KASETSART UNIVERSITY (BANGKOK).
　BANGKOK 1, 1961- 6(2), 1966.//
　ENGL. SUMM.
　CA/M-3.**
　LO/N-2. 4, 1964-　　　LO/R-6. 7(1), 1973-
　ISSN 0075-5192

KATALIZ I KATALIZATORY.
　+ +KATALIZ & KATAL.
　AKADEMIJA NAUK UKRAJINS'KOJI RSR.
　KIEV [1], 1965-
　S/T: RESPUBLIKANSKIJ MEZHVEDOMSTENNYJ SBORNIK.
　LO/N13. 2, 1966-
　ISSN 0453-3585

KATALOG MIKROFILMOW ARCHIWALNYCH.
　+ +KAT. MIKROFILMOW ARCH.
　NACZELNA DYREKCJA ARCHIWOW PANSTWOWYCH:
　ARCHIWUM DOKUMENTACJI MECHANICZNEJ.
　WARSAW 1, 1961-
　OX/U-1.
　ISSN 0451-503X

KAVKAZSKIJ ETNOGRAFICHESKIJ SBORNIK.
　+ +KAZ. ETNOGR. SB.
　AKADEMIJA NAUK GRUZINSKOJ SSR: INSTITUT ISTORI.
　TBILISI 1, 1964-
　GEORG. & RUSS.
　LO/S10.　OX/U-1.

KAVKAZSKO-BLIZHNE-VOSTOCHNYJ SBORNIK.
　+ +KAVK.-BLIZHNE-VOST. SB.
　AKADEMIJA NAUK GRUZINSKOJ SSR: INSTITUT ISTORII
　TIFLIS 1, 1960-
　GEORG. & RUSS. WITH ENGL. SUMM.　TITLE ALSO IN
　ENGL.: CAUCASIAN & NEAR EASTERN STUDIES.
　TITLE VARIES: VOL.1 PUBL. AS: VOSTOCHNYJ
　SBORNIK.　ENGL. TITLE: ORIENTAL STUDIES.
　LO/U14.　OX/U-1.
　ISSN 0451-5633

KAWASAKI SEITETSU GIHO.　KAWASAKI STEEL TECH-
NICAL REPORT.
　KAWASAKI SEITETSU K.K.
　TOKYO 1(1), 1969-
　ENGL. SUMM.
　LO/N13.　XN/S-1.

KAWASAKI STEEL TECHNICAL REPORT.　　　000
　SEE: KAWASAKI SEITETSU GIHO.

KEEPSAKE POEM.
　[KEEPSAKE P.]
　RICHMOND, SURREY NO.1, 1972-
　LO/N-1.

KEIO ENGINEERING REPORTS.　　　XXX
　+ +KEIO ENG. REP.
　KEIO GIJUKU DAIGAKU FUJIHARA KINEN KOGAKUBU.
　TOKYO 24, 1971-
　PREV: KEIO GIJUKU DAIGAKU FUJIHARA KINEN
　KOGAKUBU KENYU HOKOKU FROM 1, 1948- 23, 1970.
　LO/N13.

KEIO GIJUKU DAIGAKU FUJIHARA KINEN KOGAKUBU
KENYU HOKOKU.　　　　XXX
　SUBS (1971): KEIO ENGINEERING REPORTS.

KELVIN HUGHES REVIEW.*　　　XXX
　+ +KELVIN HUGHES REV.
　KELVIN HUGHES DIVISION OF SMITHS INDUSTRIES,
　LTD.
　LONDON NO.1, 1952-
　NO.1-30 PUBL. AS KELVIN HUGHES MARINE REVIEW.
　AS ABOVE FROM NO.31, 1966.
　LO/N14. NO.11, 1955-

KEMIA UJABB EREDMENYEI.
　[AKADEMIAI KIADO]
　BUDAPEST 1, 1970-
　LO/N13.

KEMIO INTERNACIA.
　+ +KEMIO INT.
　URUGVAJA ESPERANTO-SOCIETO.
　MONTEVIDEO 1, MY 1965-
　PUBL. ON BEHALF OF: UNIVERSALA ESPERANTO
　ASOCIO; (& FROM 2, 1966) INTERNACIA SCIENCA
　ASOCIO ESPERANTISTA.
　LO/N13.
　ISSN 0022-9857

KENCHIKU KEMPO.
　TOHOKU KOGYO DAIGAKU.
　SENDAI NO.1, 1968-
　LO/N13.

KENT TECHNICAL REVIEW.
++KENT TECH. REV.
[GEORGE KENT, LTD]
 LUTON, BEDS. NO.1, 1970-
 BL/U-1.   LO/N14.

KENTUCKY ANCESTORS.
++KY. ANCESTORS.
KENTUCKY HISTORICAL SOCIETY.
 FRANKFORT, KY. 1(1), JL 1965-
 Q.
 LO/U-1.
 ISSN 0023-0103

KENYA EXPORT NEWS.                                     000
 SEE: EAST AFRICAN REPORT ON TRADE & INDUSTRY.

KENYA HIGH COURT DIGEST.
++KENYA HIGH COURT DIG.
UNIVERSITY OF NAIROBI: FACULTY OF LAW.
[KENYA HIGH COURT DIGEST]
 NAIROBI 1, MY 1971-
 BL/U-1.

KENYA JOURNAL OF ADULT EDUCATION.
++KENYA J. ADULT EDUC.
(KENYA) BOARD OF ADULT EDUCATION.
 NAIROBI D 1971-
 3/A.
 ED/N-1.   LO/U-3.   OX/U-9.
 CA/U-1. 3, 1974-            LO/N-1. 2(1), 1973-
 ISSN 0047-3340

KENYON REVIEW.                                         XXX
++KENYON REV.
KENYON COLLEGE.
 GAMBIER, OHIO [1], 1939- 32(1), 1970.//
 DB/U-2.   HL/U-1.   LD/U-1.   MA/U-1.   SO/U-1.   YK/U-1.

KETSKIJ SBORNIK. STUDIA KETICA.
++KETSKIJ SB.
MOSKOVSKIJ GOSUDARSTVENNYJ UNIVERSITET:
INSTITUT VOSTOCHNYJH JAZYKOV.
 MOSCOW 1, 1968-
 ADD. TITLE PAGE: STUDIA KETICA.
 CC/U-1.   OX/U-1.
 CA/U12. 2, 1969-            LO/N-3. 2, 1969-

KETT.
UNIVERSITY OF EAST ANGLIA.
 NORWICH 1(1), OC 1971-
 6/A.
 ED/N-1.

KEY FRAME.
FAIR ORGAN PRESERVATION SOCIETY.
 MANCHESTER NO.1, D 1964-
 ED/N-1. 1970-

KEY TO TURKISH SCIENCE: AGRICULTURE.
++KEY TURK. SCI., AGRIC.
[TURDOK]
 ANKARA 1(1), MY 1968-
 BL/U-1.   CA/U11.   LO/N14.   OX/U24.
 ISSN 0023-0871.

KEY TO TURKISH SCIENCE: APPLIED ECONOMICS.
++KEY TURK. SCI., APPL. ECON.
[TURDOK]
 ANKARA 1(1), AP 1969-
 BL/U-1.   LO/U-3.   OX/U24.
 ISSN 0023-088X

KEY TO TURKISH SCIENCE: BIOLOGICAL SCIENCES.
++KEY TURK. SCI., BIOL. SCI.
[TURDOK]
 ANKARA 1, 1969-
 LO/N14.
 ISSN 0023-0898

KEY TO TURKISH SCIENCE: CHEMISTRY.
++KEY TURK. SCI., CHEM.
[TURDOK]
 ANKARA 1, 1967-
 BL/U-1.   LO/N14.
 ISSN 0023-0901

KEY TO TURKISH SCIENCE: CIVIL ENGINEERING.
++KEY TURK. SCI., CIVIL ENG.
[TURDOK]
 ANKARA 1, 1971-
 LO/N14.

KEY TO TURKISH SCIENCE: EARTH SCIENCES.               XXX
++KEY TURK. SCI., EARTH SCI.
[TURDOK]
 ANKARA 3, 1971-
 PREV: KEY TO TURKISH SCIENCE: GEOLOGY FROM 1,
 1969- 2, 1970.
 LO/N14.

KEY TO TURKISH SCIENCE: ELECTRICAL & ELECTRONICS
ABSTRACTS.
++KEY TURK. SCI., ELEC. & ELECTRON. ABSTR.
[TURDOK]
 ANKARA 1, 1969-
 BL/U-1.   LO/N14.

KEY TO TURKISH SCIENCE: ENGINEERING.
++KEY TURK. SCI., ENG.
[TURDOK]
 ANKARA 1, 1967-
 BL/U-1.   LO/N14.
 ISSN 0023-091X

KEY TO TURKISH SCIENCE: GEOLOGY.                      XXX
++KEY TURK. SCI., GEOL.
[TURDOK]
 ANKARA 1, 1969- 2, 1970...
 SUBS: KEY TO TURKISH SCIENCE: EARTH SCIENCES
 BL/U-1.   LO/N-2.   LO/N14.
 ISSN 0023-0928

KEY TO TURKISH SCIENCE: MATHEMATICS & PHYSICAL
SCIENCES.*
++KEY TURK. SCI., MATH. & PHYS. SCI.
[TURDOK]
 ANKARA 1, 1969-
 1, 1969 SERIES TITLE AS PHYSICAL SCIENCES.
 BL/U-1.   LO/N14.

KEY TO TURKISH SCIENCE: MEDICINE.
++KEY TURK. SCI., MED.
[TURDOK]
 ANKARA 1, 1971-
 LO/N14.

KEY TO TURKISH SCIENCE: VETERINARY & ANIMAL
SCIENCES.
++KEY TURK. SCI., VET. & ANIM. SCI. [KTVA-A]
[TURDOK]
 ANKARA 1, 1967-
 BL/U-1.   LO/N14.
 LO/N-2 6, 1972-
 ISSN 0023-0944

KHARCHOVA PROMYSLOVIST'.
++KHARCHOVA PROMYSL.
DERZHAVNYJ KOMITET PO KOORDYNATSIJI NAUKOVO-
DOSLIDNYKH ROBIT URSR: INSTYTUT TEKHNICHNOJI
INFORMATSIJI.
 KIEV 1(1), 1960-
 Q. S/T: INFORMATSIJNYJ NAUKOVO-TEKHNICHNYJ
 ZBIRNYK. SPONS. BODY ALSO: UKRAJINS'KE
 NAUKOVO-TEKHNICHNE TOVARYSTVO KHARCHOVOJI
 PROMYSLOVOSTI.
 LO/N13. 7(25), 1966-
 ISSN 0453-7971

KHIMICHESKAJA PROMYSHLENNOST (ENGL. TRANSL.).        000
 SEE: SOVIET CHEMICAL INDUSTRY.

KHIMICHESKAJA TEKHNOLOGIJA.
++KHIM. TEKHNOL.
DNIPROPETROVS'KYJ KHIMIKO-TEKHNOLOHICHNYJ
INSTYTUT.
 KHAR'KOV VYP.1, 1965-
 LO/N13.
 ISSN 0453-8196

KHIMICHESKIE REAKTIVY I PREPARATY.                   000
 SEE: METODY POLUCHENIJA KHIMICHESKIKH REAKTI-
 VOV I PREPARATOV.

KHIMICHESKIE VOLOKNA (ENGLISH TRANSLATION).          000
 SEE: FIBRE CHEMISTRY.

KHIMIJA GETEROTSIKLICHESKIKH SOEDINENIJ.
++KHIM. GETEROTSIKL. SOEDIN.
LATVIJAS PSR ZINATNU AKADEMIJA.
 RIGA 1965(1)-
 ENGL. CONT. LISTS. TRANSL. PUBL. AS CHEMISTRY
 OF HETEROCYCLIC COMPOUNDS (BUCOP 1960-68).
 CA/U-2.   LO/S-3.
 LO/N13. 1966-
 ISSN 0453-8234

KHIMIJA GETEROTSIKLICHESKIKH SOEDINENIJ: SBORNIK.
++KHIM. GETEROTSIKL. SOEDIN., SB.
LATVIJAS PSR ZINATNU AKADEMIJA.
RIGA NO.1, 1967-
SUPPL. TO: KHIMIJA GETEROTSIKLICHESKIKH
SOEDINENIJ.
CA/U-2.   LO/N13.   LO/S-3.
ISSN 0454-8825

KHIMIJA PRIRODNYKH SOEDINENIJ.
++KHIM. PRIR. SOEDIN.
AKADEMIJA NAUK UZBEKSKOJ SSR.
TASHKENT 1, 1964-
TOM 1, 1964 PUBL. AS: NAUCHNYE TRUDY, TASHKEN-
TSKIJ GOSUDARSTVENNYJ UNIVERSITET [IM. V.I.
LENINA]: NOVAJA SERIJA, VYP. 263, KN. 13.
CA/U-2. 1965-              LO/N13. 1965-
LO/S-3. 1965-
ISSN 0023-1150

KHIMIJA V SEL'SKOM KHOZJAJSTVE.
(RUSSIA USSR) MINISTERSTVO KHIMICHESKOJ
PROMYSHLENNOSTI.
MOSCOW 1, N 1963-
M. S/T: NAUCHNO-TEKHNICHESKIJ ZHURNAL.
LO/N13. 4, 1966-
ISSN 0023-1185

KHIMIJA I TEKHNOLOGIJA GORJUCHIKH SLANTSEV I
PRODUKTOV IKH PERERABOTKI.                         XXX
++KHIM. & TEKHNOL. GORJUCH. SLANTS. & PROD.
PERERAB.
EESTI NSV POLEVKIVI UURIMISE INSTITUUT.
LENINGRAD 8, 1960- 13, 1964.
PREV: PART OF TRUDY VSESOJUZNOGO NAUCHNO-
ISSLEDOVATEL'SKOGO INSTITUTA PO PERERABOTKE
SLANTSEV 'VNIIPS' FROM 1, 1948- 7, 1959. SUBS:
DOBYCHA I PERERABOTKA GORJUCHIKH SLANTSEV.
LO/N13.

KHIMIJA I TEKHNOLOGIJA TOPLIVA I PRODUKTOV
EGO PERERABOTKI.                                   XXX
++KHIM. & TEKHNOL. TOPL. & PROD. PERERAB.
VSESOJUZNYJ NAUCHNO-ISSLEDOVATEL'SKIJ INSTITUT
PERERABOTKI I ISPOL'ZOVANIJA TOPLIVA.
LENINGRAD 8, 1960-
PREV: PART OF TRUDY VSESOJUZNOGO NAUCHNO-
ISSLEDOVATEL'SKOGO INSTITUTA PO PERERABOTKE
SLANTSEV 'VNIIPS' FROM 1, 1948- 7, 1959.
LO/N13.

KHIMIJA VYSOKIKH ENERGIJ.
++KHIM. VYS. ENERG.
AKADEMIJA NAUK SSSR.
MOSCOW 1(1), 1967-
CONTENTS LIST IN ENGL.
CA/U-2.   LO/N13.   LO/S-3.
ISSN 0023-1193

KHIMIKO-FARMATSEVTICHESKIJ ZHURNAL.
++KHIM.-FARM. ZH.
(RUSSIA USSR) MINISTERSTVO MEDITSINSKOJ PROMY-
SHLENNOSTI USSR.
MOSCOW 1(1), 1967-
ENGL. CONT. LISTS. BODY ORIG. AS: MINISTER-
STVO ZDRAVOKHRANENIJA SSSR. ENGL. TRANSLATION
PUBL. AS RUSSIAN CHEMICO-PHARMACEUTICAL
JOURNAL.
LO/N13.
ISSN 0023-1134

KHOLODIL'NAJA TEKHNIKA I TEKHNOLOGIJA.
++KHOLOD. TEKH. & TEKHNOL.
(UKRAINE) MINISTERSTVO VYSSHEGO I SREDNEGO
SPETSIAL'NOGO OBRAZOVANIJA.
KIEV 1, 1965-
S/T: RESPUBLIKANSKIJ MEZHVEDOMSTVENNYJ
NAUCHNO-TEKHNICHESKIJ SBORNIK.
BH/U-1.
LO/N13. 3, 1966-
ISSN 0453-8307

KHUDOZHESTVENNAJA LITERATURA, LITERATUROVED-
ENIE, ISKUSSTVO.                                   XXX
++KHUDOZHESTVENNAJA LIT. LIT. ISKUSSTVO.
GOSUDARSTVENNAJA BIBLIOTEKA SSSR IM. V.I.
LENINA.
MOSCOW JA/MR, 1963(1964)- 1966(1968) ...
A. S/T: REKOMENDATEL'NYJ UKAZETEL' LITERA-
TURY. ORIG. AS: REKOMENDATEL'NYJ UKAZATEL'
NOVINOK. PREV: NOVINKI KHUDOZHESTVENNOJ
LITERATURY FROM 1956- 1962. SUBS: LITERATURA
I ISKUSSTVO, GOSUDARSTVENNAJA BIBLIOTEKA SSSR.
BH/U-1.   CC/U-1.   LA/U-1.
HL/U-1. 1965(1966)-            SW/U-1. 1966-
LO/N-3. 1966(1968).
ISSN 0453-8366

KIARIO.
UNIVERSIDAD DE SAN MARCOS: CENTRO DE INVESTIG-
ACIONES DE SELVA.
LIMA NO.1, S 1969-
OX/U-1.
ISSN 0455-0412

KIBERNETIKA I DIAGNOSTIKA.
++KIBERN. & DIAGN. [KIBD-A]
RIGAS POLITEHNISKAIS INSTITUTS.
RIGA 1, 1966-
BH/U-1. 3, 1969-              CC/U-1. 2, 1968-
LO/N13. 2, 1968-
ISSN 0453-8404

KIBERNETIKA, OTDELENIE MATEMATIKI, MEKHANIKI
I KIBERNETIKI UKRAINSKOJ AKADEMII NAUK SSR.
++KIBERN. OTD. MAT. MEKH. & KIBERN. UKR. AKAD.
NAUK SSR.
AKADEMIJA NAUK UKRAJINS'KOJI RSR: OTDELENIE
MATEMATIKI, MEKHANIKI I KIBERNETIKI.
KIEV 1965(1)-
ENGL. CONT. LISTS.
CA/U-2.   LO/N13.

KIBERNETIKA I VYCHISLITEL'NAJA TEKHNIKA(KIEV)
++KIBERN. & VYCHISL. TEKH. (KIEV).
AKADEMIJA NAUK UKRAJINS'KOJI RSR: (INSTITUT
KIBERNETIKY).
KIEV 1, 1969-
S/T: RESPUBLIKANSKIJ MEZHVEDOMSTVENNYJ
SBORNIK.
BH/U-1.   LO/N13.

KIDNEY.
NATIONAL KIDNEY FOUNDATION (US).
MIAMI 1, 1967-
2M.
OX/U-8. 4(2), 1971-
ISSN 0023-1304

KIDNEY INTERNATIONAL.
++KIDNEY INT.
[SPRINGER]
NEW YORK &C. 1, 1972-
MON.
CA/M-2.   LO/M11.   LO/N13.   SH/U-1.   SO/U-1.
ISSN 0085-2538

KIDS.                                              XXX
[CHILDREN'S RIGHTS PUBL. LTD.]
LONDON NO.7, S 1972-
PREV: CHILDREN'S RIGHTS FROM NO.1, JA 1972-
NO.6, JL/AG 1972.
ED/N-1.

KIELER NOTIZEN ZUR PFLANZENKUNDE SCHLESWIG-
HOLSTEINS.
++KIEL. NOT. PFLANZENKUNDE SCHLESWIG-HOLSTEINS.
ARBEITSGEMEINSCHAFT FUR FLORISTIK IN SCHLESWIG-
HOLSTEIN UND HAMBURG.
KIEL 1, 1969-
LO/N-2.

KIMIA.
MALAYSIAN INSTITUTE OF CHEMISTRY.
PETALING JAYA, SELANGOR NO.1, 1970-
LO/N14.

KINEMA.
[TARASQUE P.]
NOTTINGHAM NO.1, JE 1968-
ED/N-1.   OX/U-1.

KINGSTON GEOGRAPHER. JOURNAL OF ...
++KINGSTON GEOGR.
GEOGRAPHICAL ASSOCIATION: KINGSTON BRANCH.
KINGSTON-UPON-THAMES 1(1), OC 1968-
LO/S13.

KINGSTON GEOLOGICAL REVIEW.
++KINGSTON GEOL. REV.
KINGSTON COLLEGE OF TECHNOLOGY: GEOLOGY CLUB.
KINGSTON-UPON-THAMES 1, 1968-
LO/N-2.

KINGSTON LAW REVIEW.
++KINGSTON LAW REV.
KINGSTON LAW REVIEW ASSOCIATION.
KINGSTON-UPON-THAMES 1, 1968-
BL/U-1.
CR/U-1. 2(2), 1970-          ED/N-1. 3, 1971/72-
ISSN 0453-8854

KINJO GAKUIN DAIGAKU RONSHU KASEIGAKU
TOKUSHU. ANNUAL REPORT OF NATURAL SCIENCE &
HOME ECONOMICS, KINJO GAKUIN COLLEGE.
*AICHI, JAP. NO.1, 1962-*
A. JAP. & ENGL.
*XN/S-1.*

KINOKALENDAR'.
[ISKUSSTVO]
*MOSCOW 1967-*
*LD/U-1.*
*ISSN 0453-8919*

KIRTLANDIA.
CLEVELAND MUSEUM OF NATURAL HISTORY.
*CLEVELAND, OHIO NO.1, D 1967-*
*LO/N-2.*
*NW/U-11. NO.5, 1969-*
*ISSN 0075-6245*

KIST. MAGAZINE OF THE...
NATURAL HISTORY & ANTIQUARIAN SOCIETY OF MID
ARGYLL.
*CRINAN NO.1, 1971-*
*CA/U-1. ED/N-1. LO/N-2.*

KISULSA. JOURNAL OF THE KOREAN SOCIETY OF
PROFESSIONAL ENGINEERS.
HANGUK KISULSAHOE.
*SEOUL 1, 1968-*
*LO/N13.*

KIVUNG. JOURNAL OF THE ...
UNIVERSITY OF PAPUA & NEW GUINEA: LINGUISTIC
SOCIETY.
*BOROKO 1(1), AP 1968-*
*LO/U-2.*
*ISSN 0023-1959*

KLEIO.
UNIVERSITY OF SOUTH AFRICA: DEPARTMENT OF
HISTORY.
*PRETORIA 1(1), 1969-*
AFRIKAANS & ENGL.
*MA/S-1. OX/U-9.*
*ISSN 0023-2084*

KLERONOMIA.
PATRIARCHAL INSTITUTE FOR PATRISTIC STUDIES
(THESSALONIKI).
*THESSALONIKI 1, 1969-*
*LO/U11.*

KLIMATOLOGISKE MEDDELELSER.
*+ + KLIMATOL. MEDD.*
DANSK METEOROLOGISK INSTITUT.
*CHARLOTTENLUND NO.1, 1971-*
*LO/N13.*

KNOWE. THE MONTHLY SUPPLEMENT TO AKROS.
[AKROS PUBL.]
*PENWORTHAM 1(1- 3), 1971.//*
*ED/N-1. LO/U-2. OX/U-1.*

KOBE MUNICIPAL HOSPITAL BULLETIN.                    000
SEE: KOBE-SHIRITSU BYOIN KIYO.

KOBE-SHIRITSU BYOIN KIYO. = KOBE MUNICIPAL
HOSPITAL BULLETIN.
KOBE-SHI EISEI-KYOKU.
*KOBE-SHI 1, 1961-*
*XN/S-1.*

KOBUNSHI KAGAKU: ENGLISH EDITION.
[RALPH MCELROY CO.]
*AUSTIN, TEX. 1, 1972-*
TRANSL. OF THE JAPANESE EDITION FROM 29(321),
1972.
*LO/N14.*

KOCHUGAKU SHOSHI. FRAGMENTA COLEOPTEROLOGICA
JAPONICA.
*TOKYO NO.1, 1964-*
*LO/N13.*

KOELTECHNIEK (LEIDEN &C.).                           XXX
SUBS (1970): KOELTECHNIEK - KLIMAATREGELING.

KOELTECHNIEK - KLIMAATREGELING.                      XXX
*+ + KOELTECH. - KLIMAATREGELING.*
NEDERLANDSE VERENIGING VOOR KOELTECHNIEK.
[VERENIGDE PERIODIEKE PERS]
*THE HAGUE 63(7), 1970-*
PREV: KOELTECHNIEK (LEIDEN &C.) FROM 51,
1958- 63(6), 1970.
*LO/N14.*

KOGAI (HAKUA SHOBO). POLLUTION CONTROL.
KOGYO GIJUTSUIN SHIGEN GIJUTSU SHIKENJO SANGYO
KOGAI BOSHI GIJUTSU-BU UKIMA BUNSHITSU.
*TOKYO 1, 1966-*
ENGL. SUMM.
*LO/N13.*

KOGAI KANKEI KENKYU SEIKA SHOROKU.
NORIN-SHO NORIN SUISAN GIJUTSU KAIGI.
*TOKYO NO.1, 1969-*
*LO/N13.*

KOGAI SHIGEN KENKYUJO HOKOKU.
*KAWAGUCHI 1, 1970-*
*LO/N13.*

KOGAI SHIGEN KENKYUJO IHO. BULLETIN, NATION-
AL RESEARCH INSTITUTE FOR POLLUTION & RESOUR-
CES (JAPAN).
*KAWAGUCHI 1, 1971-*
*LO/N13.*

KOGEI KENKYU.                                        XXX
SUBS (1965): SANGYO KOGEI SHIKENJO HOKOKU.

KOKAI JITSUYO SHINAN KOHO.
(JAPAN) PATENT OFFICE.
*TOKYO [NO.] 1, [1971]-*
TITLE IN ENGLISH: OPEN UTILITY MODEL
APPLICATION GAZETTE.
*LO/N14.*

KOKURITSU BOSAI KAGAKU GIJUTSU SENTA KENKYU
HOKOKU. REPORT OF THE NATIONAL RESEARCH
CENTER FOR DISASTER PREVENTION.
KOKURITSU BOSAI KAGAKU GIJUTSU SENTA.
*TOKYO NO.1, 1968-*
ENGL. SUMM.
*LO/N13.*

KOKURITSU SHINJU KENKYUJO SHIRYO. MATERIAL,
NATIONAL PEARL RESEARCH LABORATORY (JAPAN).
*KASHIKOJIMA NO.1, 1970-*
*LO/N13.*

KOKUSHIKAN DAIGAKU KOGAKUBU KIYO.
TRANSACTIONS, DEPARTMENT OF ENGINEERING,
KOKUSHIKAN UNIVERSITY.
*TOKYO NO.1, 1968-*
*LO/N13.*

KOLLOID-BEIHEFTE. SUPPLEMENTA ZUR KOLLOID-
ZEITSCHRIFT UND ZEITSCHRIFT FUR POLYMERE.      XXX
SUBS (1971): FORTSCHRITTSBERICHTE UBER
KOLLOIDE UND POLYMERE.

KOLO. CASOPIS ZA KNJIZEVNOST, UMJETNOST I
KULTURU: NS.
MATICA HRVATSKA.
*ZAGREB 1, 1963-*
PREV. SERIES FROM 1842- 1963.
*LO/N-3. 1963(3).*
*ISSN 0454-2371*

KOMMUNAL'NOE KHOZJAJSTVO.                            000
SEE: NAUKA I TEKHNIKA V GORODSKOM KHOZJAJSTVE

KOMMUNIST UZBEKISTANA.
*+ + KOMMUNIST UZB.*
KOMMUNISTICHESKAJA PARTIJA UZBEKISTANA.
*TASHKENT 1, JL 1960-*
FIRST ISSUE ALSO CALLED VOL. 32(7) AS CONT. OF
PARALLEL PUBLICATION IN UZBEK PUBLISHED SINCE
1925.
*CC/U-1. 1963-          OX/U-1. 1970-*

KOMMUNIST VOORUZHENNYKH SIL.                         XXX
GLAVNOE POLITICHESKOE UPRAVLENIE SOVETSKOJ
ARMII I VOENNO-MORSKOGO FLOTA.
*MOSCOW 1, OC 1960-*
S/T: VOENNO-POLITICHESKIJ ZHURNAL GLAVNOGO
POLITICHESKOGO UPRAVLENIJA SOVETSKOJ ARMII I
VOENNO-MORSKOGO FLOTA. INCORP: PROPAGANDIST I
AGITATOR FROM 1941- S 1960; & PARTIJNO-POLITI-
CHESKAJA RABOTA V SOVETSKOJ ARMII I VOENNO-
MORSKOM FLOTE FROM 1957- S 1960.
*CC/U-1. 1964-          OX/U-1. 1965-*
*SH/U-1. 1970-*
*ISSN 0454-2657*

KOMPLEKSNYE ISSLEDOVANIJA PRIRODY OKEANA.
*+ + KOMPLEKSN. ISSLED. PRIR. OKEANA.*
MOSKOVSKIJ GOSUDARSTVENNYJ UNIVERSITET.
*MOSCOW 1, 1970-*
*LO/N13.*

**KOMPLEKSNYE ISSLEDOVANIJA VODOKHRANILISHCH.**
*+ +KOMPLEKSN. ISSLED. VODOKHRAN.*
MOSKOVSKIJ GOSUDARSTVENNYJ UNIVERSITET: KAFEDRA
GIDROLOGII.
*MOSCOW 1, 1971-*
KAFEDRA GIDROLOGII SUBORD. TO: GEOGRAFICHESKIJ
FAKUL'TET.
*LO/N13.*

**KONCHU TO SHIZEN.  NATURE & INSECTS.**
NYU SAIENSU-SHA.
*TOKYO 1, 1966-*
MON.  JAP. OR ENGL.
*LO/N-2.*
*ISSN 0023-3218*

**KONSTITUTSIJA I SVOJSTVA MINERALOV.**
*+ +KONST. & SVOJSTVA MINER. [KSMU-A]*
AKADEMIJA NAUK UKRAJINS'KOJI RSR: INSTYTUT
HEOLOHICHNYKH NAUK.
*KIEV 1, 1966-*
S/T: RESPUBLIKANSKIJ MEZHVEDOMSTVENNYJ SBORNIK
SERIJA 'KHIMICHESKIJ SOSTAV I SVOJSTVA MINERA-
LOV'.  SPONS. BODY ALSO VSESOJUZNOE MINERAL-
OGICHESKOE OBSHCHESTVO: (UKRAINSKOE OTDELENIE)
*LO/N13.    LO/556.    XY/N-1.*
*ISSN 0454-3343*

**KONSTRUIROVANIE KRUPNYKH MASHIN.**                           XXX
*+ +KONSTR. KRUPNYKH MASH.*
NAUCHNO-ISSLEDOVATEL'SKIJ INSTITUT TJAZHELOGO
MASHINOSTROENIJA.
*MOSCOW 1, 1962- 2, 1963 ...*
S/T: SBORNIK STATEJ.  SUBS: PROIZVODSTVO
KRUPNYKH MASHIN.

**KONSTRUIROVANIE KRUPNYKH MASHIN: SBORNIK
STATEJ.**                                                     XXX
SUBS (1964): PROIZVODSTVO KRUPNYKH MASHIN.

**KOOLEWONG.  PROCEEDINGS OF THE ROYAL ZOOLOG-
ICAL SOCIETY OF NEW SOUTH WALES.**                            XXX
*MOSMAN, N.S.W.  1(1), MR 1972-*
Q.  PREV: PROCEEDINGS OF THE ROYAL ZOOLOGICAL
SOCIETY OF NEW SOUTH WALES FROM 1935/36- 1969/
70(1971).
*CA/U-2.    LO/N-2.    LO/N13.*

**KOREAN MEDICAL ABSTRACTS.**
*+ +KOREAN MED. ABSTR.*
*SEOUL 1, 1971-*
*LO/N13.*

**KOREAN NATURE.**
*+ +KOREAN NAT.*
KOREAN ASSOCIATION FOR THE PROTECTION OF NATURE
*PYONGYANG NO.1, 1965-*
Q.
*LO/N-2.*
*ED/N-1.  NO.24, 1972-*
*ISSN 0023-4036*

**KOREA OBSERVER.**
*+ +KOREA OBS.*
ACADEMY OF KOREAN STUDIES.
*SEOUL 1(1), OC 1968-*
Q.
*LO/U-3.    OX/U-1.*
*ISSN 0023-3919*

**KOREAN SCIENTIFIC ABSTRACTS.**
*+ +KOREAN SCI. ABSTR.*
KOREA SCIENTIFIC & TECHNOLOGICAL
INFORMATION CENTER.
*[SEOUL] 1, 1969-*
*LO/N14.*
*ISSN 0023-4052*

**KORROSION OCH METALLSKYDD.**
*+ +KORROS. METALLSKYDD.*
KUNGLIGA TEKNISKA HOGSKOLAN: INSTITUTIONEN
FOR TEKNISK ELEKTROKEMI OCH KORROSIONSLARA.
*STOCKHOLM 1, 1968-*
*LO/N14.*

**KORTTERMYN EKONOMIESE AANWYSERS (S. AFR.)**          000
SEE: SHORT TERM ECONOMIC INDICATORS (S. AFR.)

**KOSMICHESKAJA BIOLOGIJA I MEDITSINA.**               XXX
*+ +KOSM. BIOL. & MED.*
(RUSSIA USSR) MINISTERSTVO ZDRAVOOKHRANENIJA.
*MOSCOW 1, 1967- 7, 1973...*
ENGL. SUMM. & CONT. LISTS. SUBS: KOSMICHESKAJA
BIOLOGIJA & AVIAKOSMICHESKAJA MEDITSINA.
*LO/N13. 2, 1968-              OX/U-8. 3, 1969-*

**KOSMICHESKAJA BIOLOGIJA I MEDITSINA (ENGL.
TRANSL.).**                                                   000
SEE:  ENVIRONMENTAL SPACE SCIENCES.

**KOZHI, OBUVKI.**                                            XXX
*[KOZO-A]*
DURZHAVNA STROITELNA ORGANIZATSIJA: KOMITET PO
LEKATA PROMISHLENOST.                                         XXX
*SOFIA 4, 1963-*
ENGL. CONT. LISTS.  PREV: KOZHI, OBUVKI,
KAUCHUK, PLASTMASI FROM 1, 1960- 3, 1962.
*LO/N13.*

**KOZHI, OBUVKI, KAUCHUK, PLASTMASI.**                        XXX
*+ +KOZHI OBUVKI KAUCH. PLAST.  [KOKP-A]*
KOMITET PO LEKATA I KHRANITELNATA PROMISH-
LENOST.                                                       XXX
*SOFIA 1, 1960- 3, 1962 ...*
ENGL. CONT. LISTS.  SUBS: KOZHI, OBUVKI.
*LO/N13.*

**KRAGLIEVIANA.**
ASOCIACION KRAGLIEVIANA DEL URUGUAY.
*MONTEVIDEO 1, 1965-*
*LO/N-2.*

**KRAKOWSKIE STUDIA PRAWNICZE.**
*+ +KRAKOW. STUD. PRAWNICZE.*
POLSKA AKADEMIA NAUK (ODDZIAL W KRAKOWIE):
KOMISJA NAUK PRAWNYCH.
*BRESLAU &C.  1(1/2), 1968-*
ENGL., FR. OR GER. SUMM.
*OX/U-1.*
*ISSN 0023-4478*

**KRATKIE SOOBSHCHENIJA O DOKLADAKH I POLEVYKH
ISSLEDOVANIJAKH INSTITUTA ARKHEOLOGII.***                     XXX
*+ +KRATK. SOOBSHCH. DOKL. POLEVYKH ISSLED. INST.
ARKHEOL.*
AKADEMIJA NAUK SSSR: INSTITUT ARKHEOLOGII.
*MOSCOW 80, 1960-*
PREV: KRATKIE SOOBSHCHENIJA O DOKLADAKH I
POLEVYKH ISSLEDOVANIJAKH INSTITUTA MATERIAL-
'NOJ KUL'TURY FROM 1, 1939.
*BH/U-1.**    CC/U-1.    XY/N-1.*
*LO/N-3.  81, 1960-*

**KREDIT UND KAPITAL.**
*[DUNCKER & HUMBLOT]*
*BERLIN  HEFT 1, 1968-*
Q.
*LO/U-3.*
*ISSN 0023-4591*

**KRISHNAMURTI FOUNDATION BULLETIN.**
*+ +KRISHNAMURTI FOUND. BULL.*
*LONDON  NO.1, 1968-*
*ED/N-1.    OX/U-1.*
*ISSN 0047-3693*

**KRITIKA PHYLLA.**
*+ +KRIT. PHYLLA.*
*ATHENS  1, JA 1971-*
2M.
*CA/U-1.*

**KRITIKON LITTERARUM.**
*+ +KRIT. LITT.*
*FRANKFURT AM MAIN  1, 1972-*
*DB/U-2.    NO/U-1.    SH/U-1.*

**KRUGOZOR.**
GOSUDARSTVENNYJ KOMITET SOVETA MINISTROV SSSR
PO RADIOVESHCHANIJU I TELEVIDENIJU.
*MOSCOW AP, 1964-*
M.  S/T: EZHEMESJACHNYJ ZVUKOVOJ ZHURNAL.
INCLUDES GRAMOPHONE RECORDS.
*ED/N-1.  1968-                        SA/U-1.  1967-*

**KTBL-BAUSCHRIFTEN.**
KURATORIUM FUR TECHNIK UND BAUWESEN IN DER
LANDWIRTSCHAFT.
*FRANKFURT AM MAIN  1, 1969-*
*LO/N13.    LO/N14.*

**KULLABERGS NATUR.**
*+ +KULLABERGS NAT.*
*LUND 1, 1960-*
*LO/N-2.*
*ISSN 0452-7887*

KULTIVARIA LIMBII.
++KULTIV. LIMBII.
AKADEMIJA NAUK MOLDAVSKOJ SSR; INSTITUT
JAZYKA I LITERATURY.
 KISHINEV 1, 1961-
 MOLD.
 CC/U-1. 5, 1966-
 LO/N-3. 2, 1962.

KULTURA. TYGODNIK SPOLECZNO-KULTURALNY.          XXX
 WARSAW 1(1), JE 1963-
 W. PREV: PART OF NOWA KULTURA FROM 1(1),
 1950- 14(689), 1963; & PRZEGLAD KULTURALNY
 FROM 1(1), 1952- 12(561), 1963.
 GL/U-1.     LO/N-3.*     LO/S-9.
 ISSN 0454-5877

KULTURBRIEF.
 BONN 1(1), S 1971-
 ENGL.
 LO/N-1.     OX/U-1.

KULTURGEOGRAFISKE SKRIFTER, KULTURGEOGRAFISK
INSTITUT, AARHUS UNIVERSITET. = PUBLICATIONS OF
THE INSTITUTE OF ECONOMIC & APPLIED GEOGRAPHY,
UNIVERSITY OF AARHUS.
 ++KULTURGEOGR. SKR. KULTURGEOGR. INST. AARHUS
 UNIV.
 AARHUS 1, 1967-
 MONOGR. DAN., ENGL.
 LO/S13.

KULTURNI TVORBA.                                 XXX
 VYBOR SOCIALISTICKE KULTURY.
 PRAGUE 1, JA 1963- 6, AG 1968.
 S/T: TYDENIK PRO POLITIKU A KULTURU. PREV:
 KULTURA FROM 1(1), 1957- 6(52), 1962. SUBS:
 POLITIKA.
 LA/U-1.*
 MA/U-1. 1, 1963- 3, 1966.*
 ISSN 0454-5966

KUMQUAT.
 [KUMQUAT P.]
 MONTCLAIR, N.J. 1, 1967-
 OX/U-1.
 ISSN 0454-6253

KUNAN/HICHA/AHORA.
 INSTITUTO DE LENGUAS ABORIGINES.
 LIMA 1(1), MY 1962-
 LO/N-1. (ISOLATED ISSUES ONLY).
 ISSN 0454-630X

KUNG. THE MAGAZINE OF THE LONDON SCHOOL OF
ECONOMICS ANTHROPOLOGY SOCIETY.
 LONDON SCHOOL OF ECONOMICS & POLITICAL SCIENCE
 ANTHROPOLOGY SOCIETY.
 LONDON 1, 1966-
 LO/U-3. 1971/2-                    LO/U14. 1971/2-
 LO/S10. 1, 1966- 5, 1972.

KUNGNIP KWAHAK SUSA YONGUSO YONBO. ANNUAL
REPORT OF THE NATIONAL INSTITUTE OF SCIEN-
TIFIC INVESTIGATION.
 SEOUL [NO.]1, 1962-
 KOREAN OR ENGL.
 LO/N13.

KUNGNIP SUSAN CHINHUNGWON SAOP POGO. REPORT OF
THE RESULTS OF EXPLORATORY FISHING IN EAST SEA
OF KOREA.
 PUSAN [NO.]1, 1968-
 LO/N13.

KUNGNIP SUSAN CHINHUNGWON YONGU POGO. BULLE-
TIN OF FISHERIES RESEARCH & DEVELOPMENT
AGENCY (KOREA).
 KUNGNIP SUSAN CHINHUNGWON.
 PUSAN 1, 1967-
 ENGL. SUMM.
 LO/N13.

KUNSTJAHRBUCH.
 [FACKELTRAGER-VERLAG SCHMIDT-KUSTER]
 HANNOVER NO.1, 1970-
 LO/N-1.

KUNST-SPIEGEL. MITTEILUNGSBLATT DER LIGA GEGEN
ENTARTETE KUNST.
 VIENNA NO.1, S 1971-
 LO/N-1.

KURBISKERN. LITERATUR UND KRITIK.
 [DAMNITZ VERLAG]
 MUNICH 1, 1965-
 Q.
 LO/U-2.

KURDICA.
 COMMITTEE FOR THE ADVANCEMENT OF KURDISTAN (GB)
 LONDON NO.1, JL 1968-
 ED/N-1.     LO/U14.     OX/U-1.

KURZMITTEILUNGEN, DEUTSCHE DENDROLOGISCHE
GESELLSCHAFT.
 ++KURZMITT. DTSCH. DENDROL. GES.
 DARMSTADT 1, 1968-
 LO/N-2.

KUSHIRO JOSHI TANKI DAIGAKU KIYO. BULLETIN
OF KUSHIRO WOMEN'S JUNIOR COLLEGE.
 HOKKAIDO NO.1, 1965-
 A.
 XN/S-1.

KUZNECHNO-SHTAMPOVOCHNOE PROIZVODSTVO: (GER.
TRANSL.)                                          000
 SEE: UMFORMTECHNIK. [ARTICLES]

KVANTOVAJA ELEKTRONIKA (MOSCOW).                  000
 SEE: SOVIET JOURNAL OF QUANTUM ELECTRONICS.

KYANON KENKYU HOKOKU. RESEARCH REPORT OF
CANON CAMERA CO., INC.
 KYANON KAMERA K.K.
 TOKYO NO.1, 1962-
 ENGL. SUMM.
 LO/N13.

KYBERNETES. AN INTERNATIONAL JOURNAL OF
CYBERNETICS & GENERAL SYSTEMS.
 [GORDON & BREACH]
 LONDON 1(1), 1972-
 BH/U-1.   CA/U-1.   CB/U-1.   ED/N-1.   LO/N14.   LO/U28.
 SH/U-1.
 HL/U-1. 3, 1974-

KYOTO FURITSU NOGYO SHIKENJO KENKYU HOKOKU.
BULLETIN OF THE KYOTO AGRICULTURAL EXPERIMENT
STATION.
 KYOTO FURITSU NOGYO SHIKENJO.
 KYOTO NO.1, 1966-
 ENGL. SUMM.
 LO/N13.

KYOTO UNIVERSITY AFRICAN STUDIES.
 ++KYOTO UNIV. AFR. STUD.
 KYOTO DAIGAKU: COMMITTEE OF THE AFRICA PRIMAT-
 OLOGICAL EXPEDITION.
 KYOTO 1, 1966-
 LO/N-2.     LO/S10.     OX/U-9.

KYUSHU DAIGAKU RIGAKUBU SHIMABARA KAZAN ONSEN
KENKYUSHO KENKYU HOKOKU.
 FUKUOKA-SHI 1, 1965-
 XN/S-1.

KYUSHU KOGYO GIJUTSU SHIKENJO HOKOKU. REPORTS
OF THE GOVERNMENT INDUSTRIAL RESEARCH INSTI-
TUTE, KYUSHU.
 TOSU NO.1, 1969-
 ENGL. SUMM.
 LO/N13.

L & M NEWS.                                       XXX
 SUBS (1970): LINOTYPE NEWS.

LA TROBE LIBRARY JOURNAL.
 ++LA TROBE LIB. J.
 MELBOURNE 1(1), 1968-
 LO/N-2.     OX/U-1.     OX/U-9.
 ISSN 0041-3151

LAB. LABORATORY EQUIPMENT MAGAZINE.              XXX
 [MILTON PUBL. CO. LTD.]
 LONDON 1(1), S/OC 1971- 3(15), MY/JE 1973.
 MON. PREV: LABORATORY ELECTRONIC EQUIPMENT
 FROM 1(1), 1966- 6 (34), JL/AG 1971. SUBS:
 LABORATORY WEEKLY.
 ED/N-1.     LO/N14.**     LO/U-8.

LABORATORY ELECTRONIC EQUIPMENT.
 ++LAB. ELECTRON. EQUIP.
 [MILTON PUBL. CO.]
 LONDON 1(1), 1966-
 FROM 1968 ISSUES SUPPL.: LASER REVIEW.
 LO/N14.
 ED/N-1. 3(5), 1968-

**LABORATORY MEDICINE.**
+ +LAB. MED.
[LIPPINCOTT]
*PHILADELPHIA 1, JA 1970-*
PREV. SERIES AS LABORATORY MEDICINE. THE
BULLETIN OF PATHOLOGY FROM 10(9- 12), 1969.
INCORP. TECHNICAL BULLETIN, REGISTRY OF
MEDICAL TECHNOLOGISTS, AMERICAN SOCIETY OF
CLINICAL PATHOLOGISTS FROM 26, 1956- 39(12),
D 1969.
*XY/N-1.*
*DN/U-1. 2(1), 1971-*
*ISSN 0007-5027*

**LABORATORY PRIMATE NEWSLETTER.**
+ +LAB. PRIMATE NEWSL.
BROWN UNIVERSITY: PSYCHOLOGY DEPARTMENT.
*PROVIDENCE, R.I. 1, JA 1962-*
2M.
*ED/U-1.*
*ISSN 0023-6861*

**LABORATORY TECHNICAL REPORT, DIVISION OF
MECHANICAL ENGINEERING, NATIONAL RESEARCH
COUNCIL (CANADA).**
+ +LAB. TECH. REP. DIV. MECH. ENG. NATL. RES.
COUNC. (CAN.).
*OTTAWA LTR-CS-1, 1969-*
PROD. BY DIV'S. CONTROL SYSTEMS LABORATORY.
*LO/N14.*

**LABORATORY TECHNICAL REPORT, NATIONAL AERO-
NAUTICAL ESTABLISHMENT (CANADA).**
+ +LAB. TECH. REP. NATL. AERONAUT. ESTABL. (CAN.)
[LRAE-A]
NATIONAL RESEARCH COUNCIL (CANADA): NATIONAL
AERONAUTICAL ESTABLISHMENT.
*OTTAWA LTR-HA-1, 1970-*
*LO/N14. UNRESTRICTED ISSUES ONLY.*

**LABORATORY TECHNIQUES IN BIOCHEMISTRY & MOL-
ECULAR BIOLOGY.**
+ +LAB. TECH. BIOCHEM. & MOL. BIOL.
[NORTH-HOLLAND PUBL. CO.]
*AMSTERDAM &C. 1, 1969-*
*LO/N-4. LO/N13 LO/U-2. OX/U-8.*

**LABOUR CHALLENGE.**
NORTHERN IRELAND LABOUR PARTY.
*BELFAST 1, S 1970-*
*ED/N-1. OX/U-1.*

**LABOUR & INDUSTRIAL RELATIONS RESEARCH IN
CANADA. = RECHERCHE SUR LE TRAVAIL ET LES
RELATIONS INDUSTRIELLES AU CANADA.**
+ +LABOUR & IND. RELAT. RES. CAN.
(CANADA) DEPARTMENT OF LABOUR.
*OTTAWA 1968-*
A. ENGL. & FR.
*LO/U-3.*

**LABOUR NEWS (US).**                                                   XXX
(UNITED STATES) INFORMATION SERVICE (GB).
*LONDON JL/AG 1968- MY/JE 1972.//*
2M. COVER TITLE: LABOUR NEWS FROM THE UNITED
STATES.
*BH/P-1. OX/U-9.*

**LABOUR RESEARCH BULLETIN (BRITISH COLUMBIA).**
+ +LABOUR RES. BULL. (B.C.).
(BRITISH COLUMBIA) DEPARTMENT OF LABOUR:
RESEARCH BRANCH.
*VICTORIA, B.C. 1, 1973-*
MON.
*LO/U-3.*

**LACE CURTAIN. A MAGAZINE OF POETRY & CRITICISM.**
[ NEW WRITERS P.]
*DUBLIN 1, [1969]-*
*BL/U-1. DB/U-2. LO/U-1. LO/U-2.*

**LAG BULLETIN.**                                                        000
SEE: LEGAL ACTION GROUP BULLETIN.

**LAGASCALIA.**
*SEVILLA 1, 1971-*
*LO/N-2. LO/N13.*

**LAGOS NOTES & RECORDS.**
+ +LAGOS NOTES & REC.
UNIVERSITY OF LAGOS.
*LAGOS 1(1), JE 1967-*
2/A. S/T: UNIVERSITY OF LAGOS BULLETIN OF
AFRICAN STUDIES.
*LO/U-8. LO/U14.*
*LD/U-1. 1(1), JE 1967; 2(1), JE 1968.*

**LAITIERS DE HAUTS FOURNEAUX.**                                         XXX
+ +LAIT. HAUTS FOURNEAUX.
ASSOCIATION TECHNIQUE POUR LE DEVELOPPEMENT DES
LAITIERS DE HAUTS FOURNEAUX.
*PARIS 24(25), 1971-*
PREV: LAITIERS ET TARMACADAM.
*LO/N14.*

**LAITIERS ET TARMACADAM.**                                             XXX
SUBS (1971): LAITIERS DE HAUTS FOURNEAUX.

**LAKEHEAD UNIVERSITY REVIEW.**
+ +LAKEHEAD UNIV. REV.
*PORT ARTHUR, ONT. 1(1), 1968-*
2/A.
*OX/U-9.*
*ISSN 0023-7337*

**LAKOKRASOCHNYE MATERIALY I IKH PRIMENENIE.**
+ +LAKOKRAS. MATER. & IKH PRIMEN.
(RUSSIA USSR) MINISTERSTVO KHIMICHESKOJ PROM-
YSHLENNOSTI.
*MOSCOW 1, 1960-*
BODY ORIG. AS: GOSUDARSTVENNYJ KOMITET PO
KHIMII.
*LO/N13. 1961-*

**LAMP JOURNAL.**                                                       XXX
SUBS (1971): HOME LIGHTING & ACCESSORIES.

**LANCASHIRE LAD.**
+ +LANCS. LAD.
QUEEN'S LANCASHIRE REGIMENT.
*PRESTON 1(1), 1970-*
*OX/U-1.*

**LAND- UND MILCHWIRTSCHAFT.**                                          XXX
+ +LAND- & MILCHWIRT.
*BERNE 57(20), 1968-*
PREV: SCHWEIZERISCHES ZENTRALBLATT DER MILCH-
PRODUZENTEN FROM 1, 1912- 57(19), 1968.
*LO/N13.*

**LAND REFORM, LAND SETTLEMENT & COOPERATIVES.**
+ +LAND REFORM LAND SETTLE. & COOP.
FOOD & AGRICULTURAL ORGANIZATION (UN): RURAL
INSTITUTIONS DIVISION.
*ROME NO.1, 1969-*
PREV: INFORMATION ON LAND REFORM, LAND
SETTLEMENT & COOPERATIVIES FROM [1, 1964.]
*BN/U-2. LD/U-1. LO/N17. LO/U-2. SW/U-1.***

**LAND RESOURCES BIBLIOGRAPHY.**
+ +LAND RESOUR. BIBLIOGR.
(GREAT BRITAIN) FOREIGN & COMMONWEALTH OFFICE:
OVERSEAS DEVELOPMENT ADMINISTRATION.
*SURBITON NO.1, 1971-*
MONOGR. PROD. BY THE LAND RESOURCES DIVISION.
*GL/U-1. LO/N-1. LO/N-4. OX/U-3. CA/U-1. CA/U11.*

**LAND RESOURCE STUDY.**
+ +LAND RESOUR. STUD.
(GREAT BRITAIN) MINISTRY OF OVERSEAS DEVELOP-
MENT: LAND RESOURCES DIVISION.
*TOLWORTH 1, 1966-*
DIVISION SUBORD. TO MINISTRY DIRECTORATE OF
OVERSEAS SURVEYS.
*BN/U-2. CA/U11. GL/U-1.*

**LAND USE & BUILT FORM STUDIES REPORTS.**
+ +LAND USE & BUILT FORM STUD. REP.
UNIVERSITY OF CAMBRIDGE: CENTRE FOR LAND USE &
BUILT FORM STUDIES.
*CAMBRIDGE NO.1, 1968-*
CENTRE SUBORD. TO: SCHOOL OF ARCHITECTURE.
*MA/U-1. SH/U-1.*

**LAND & WATER LAW REVIEW.**
+ +LAND & WATER LAW REV.
UNIVERSITY OF WYOMING; COLLEGE OF LAW.
*LARAMIE 1, 1966-*
*BL/U-1.*
*ISSN 0023-7612*

**LANDBOUWVOORLICHTING.**                                               XXX
SUBS (1970): BEDRIJFSONTWIKKELING. EDITIE
AKKERBOUW.

**LANDSCAPE DESIGN.**                                                   XXX
+ +LANDSCAPE DES.
INSTITUTE OF LANDSCAPE ARCHITECTS.
*LONDON NO.93, 1971-*
PREV: JOURNAL, INSTITUTE OF LANDSCAPE
ARCHITECTS FROM NO.9, AP 1946- 92, 1970.
*BH/P-1. LO/R-5.*
*GL/U-2. NO. 106, 1974-*
*ISSN 0020-2908*

**LANDSCAPE RESEARCH NEWS.**
++*LANDSCAPE RES. NEWS.*
LANDSCAPE RESEARCH GROUP.
*LONDON 1(1), AG 1968-*
*ED/N-1.     LO/R-5.**     OX/U-1.*

**LANDSCHAFT UND STADT.**
[ULMER]
*STUTTGART 1, 1969-*
PREV: BEITRAGE ZUR LANDESPFLEGE FROM 1, 1963.
*LO/U-2.*
*ISSN 0023-8058*

**LANDSCHAFTSARCHITEKTUR.**                                    XXX
[VEB DEUTSCHER LANDWIRTSCHAFTSVERLAG]
*BERLIN 1, 1972-*
PREV: DEUTSCHE GARTENARCHITEKTUR FROM 1, 1960-
12, 1971.
*LO/N13.*

**LANGUAGE & AUTOMATION.**
++*LANG. & AUTOM.*
CENTER FOR APPLIED LINGUISTICS.
*WASHINGTON, D.C. NO.1, 1970-*
*Q.*
*OX/U-1.*
*ISSN 0023-8287*

**LANGUAGE SCIENCES.**
++*LANG. SCI.*
INDIANA UNIVERSITY: RESEARCH CENTER FOR THE
LANGUAGE SCIENCES.
*BLOOMINGTON, INDIANA NO.1, MY 1968-*
*CB/U-1.     NW/U-1.*
*LO/U14. NO.6, 8- 13, 1969- 1970.*
*ISSN 0023-8341*

**LANGUAGE IN SOCIETY.**
++*LANG. SOC.*
[CAMBRIDGE UNIV. P.]
*LONDON 1, AP 1972-*
*2/A.*
*BL/U-1.     CB/U-1.     ED/N-1.     GL/U-2.     LD/U-1.     LO/U-3.*
*MA/U-1.     NO/U-1.     OX/U-1.*
*EX/U-1. 2(1), 1973-          HL/U-1. 1(2), 1972-*
*ISSN 0047-4045*

**LANGUE FRANCAISE.**
++*LANG. FR.*
[LIBRAIRIE LAROUSSE]
*PARIS 1, F 1969-*
*Q.*
*CO/U-1.     DB/U-2.     HL/U-1.     LD/U-1.     LO/U-2.     LO/U12.*
*LO/U13.     SH/U-1.*
*RE/U-1. NO.9, 1971-*
*EX/U-1. NO.5, F 1970-*
*LO/U-4. NO.4, D 1969-*
*MA/U-1. NO.5, F 1970-*
*SO/U-1. NO.21, F 1974-*
*ISSN 0023-8368*

**LASER.**
[AARGAUER TAGBLATT AG]
*AARAU 1, AG 1969-*
*Q.*
*LO/N14.*
*LO/U13.  2, 1970-*

**LASER APPLICATIONS.**
[ACADEMIC P.]
*NEW YORK; LONDON 1, 1971-*
*GL/U-1.     LD/U-1.     LO/N14.     LO/U-8.     SO/U-1.*

**LASER APPLICATIONS IN MEDICINE & BIOLOGY.**
++*LASER APPL. MED. & BIOL.*
[PLENUM P.]
*NEW YORK &C. 1, 1971-*
*LO/N13.*

**LASER INTERACTION & RELATED PLASMA PHENOMENA.**
++*LASER INTERACT. & RELAT. PLASMA PHENOM.*
[PLENUM P]
*NEW YORK; LONDON [1], 1971-*
NUMBERING STARTS WITH VOL.2.
*LO/N14.*

**LASER/MASER INTERNATIONAL.**                                XXX
++*LASER/MASER INT.*
[PACIFIC IMPEX CO]
*VANCOUVER, BC 1, AP 1964-3, 1966...*
SUBS (1967): JOURNAL OF CURRENT LASER ABSTR.
*BL/U-1. 3,1966.*

**LASER-RAMAN SPECTROSCOPY ABSTRACTS.**
++*LASER-RAMAN SPECTROSC. ABSTR.*
[SCIENCE & TECHNOLOGY AGENCY]
*LONDON 1(1), JA/MR 1972-*
*Q.*
*CA/U-1.     ED/N-1.     OX/U-8.*
*ISSN 0047-410X*

**LATEST INFORMATION ON NATIONAL ACCOUNTS OF
LESS DEVELOPED COUNTRIES.**
++*LATEST INF. NAT. ACC. LESS DEVELOP. COUNT.*
OECD: DEVELOPMENT CENTRE.
*PARIS 1, JA 1969-*
IN ENGL. & FR.
*GL/U-1.     LD/U-1.*     *OX/U16.*

**LATIN AMERICAN JOURNAL OF CHEMICAL ENGINEERING
& APPLIED CHEMISTRY.**                                        000
   SEE: REVISTA LATINOAMERICANA DE INGENIERIA
   QUIMICA Y QUIMICA APLICADA.

**LATIN AMERICAN MONOGRAPHS (AUSTIN, TEX.).**
++*LAT. AM. MONOGR. (AUSTIN, TEX.)*
UNIVERSITY OF TEXAS: INSTITUTE OF LATIN
AMERICAN STUDIES.
*AUSTIN, TEX. &C. NO.1, 1964-*
*LO/U-1.**
*LO/N-3. (W. NO.2,3,5,8,10 & 11).*
*ISSN 0075-8086*

**LATIN AMERICA REVIEW OF BOOKS.**
++*LAT. AM. REV. BOOKS.*
[LATIN AMERICAN NEWSLETTERS LTD.]
*LONDON NO.1, SPRING 1973-*
*AD/U-1.     BL/U-1.     CA/U-1.     ED/N-1.     GL/U-1.     HL/U-1.*
*LD/U-1.     LO/U-1.     MA/U-1.     OX/U-1.     OX/U16.     SA/U-1.*
*SF/U-1.     SH/U-1.*

**LATIN AMERICAN STUDIES IN THE UNIVERSITIES
OF THE UNITED KINGDOM.**
++*LAT. AM. STUD. UNIV. U.K.*
UNIVERSITY OF LONDON: INSTITUTE OF LATIN
AMERICAN STUDIES.
*LONDON NO.1, 1966/67-*
*A.*
*CB/U-1. 2,1967/8-                    LO/U-3. 2,1967/8-*

**LATIN AMERICAN THEATRE REVIEW.**
++*LAT. AM. THEATRE REV.*
UNIVERSITY OF KANSAS: CENTRE OF LATIN AMERICAN
STUDIES.
*LAWRENCE, KANS. 1, 1967-*
S/T: A JOURNAL DEVOTED TO THE THEATRE & DRAMA
OF SPANISH & PORTUGUESE AMERICA. ISSUES ALSO
PUBLISHED AS NUMBERS WITHIN THE CENTRE'S OCC-
ASIONAL PUBLICATIONS.
*ED/N-1.     LO/U-1.     LO/U11.     LV/U-1.     OX/U19.*
*ISSN 0023-8813*

**LATIN AMERICAN URBAN RESEARCH.**
++*LAT. AM. URBAN RES.*
UNIVERSITY OF FLORIDA: CENTER FOR LATIN
AMERICAN STUDIES.
[SAGE PUBL.]
*BEVERLY HILLS, CALIF. 1, 1970-*
*AD/U-1.     EX/U-1.     GL/U-1.     LO/U-1.*
*ISSN 0075-8167*

**LATINO AMERICA. ANUARIO ESTUDIOS LATINOAMER-
ICANOS.**
++*LAT. AM. (MEX.).*
UNIVERSIDAD NACIONAL AUTONOMA DE MEXICO: CENTRO
DE ESTUDIOS LATINOAMERICANOS.
*MEXICO, D.F. 1, 1968-*
*CC/U-1.     LV/U-1.     OX/U-1.     OX/U18.*
*BH/U-1. 2, 1969.*
*LO/U-1. 1, 1968- 4, 1971.*
*ISSN 0460-1955*

**LATINSKAJA AMERIKA.**
++*LATINSKAJA AM.*
AKADEMIJA NAUK SSSR: INSTITUT LATINSKOJ
AMERIKI.
*MOSCOW 1, 1969-*
*GL/U-1.     OX/U-1.*
*ISSN 0460-1483*

**LATVIJAS PSR ZINATNU AKADEMIJAS VESTIS:
KIMIJAS SERIJA. = IZVESTIJA AKADEMII NAUK
LATVIJSKOJ SSR: SERIJA KHIMICHESKAJA.**
++*LATV. PSR ZINAT. AKAD. VESTIS, KIM. [LZAK-A]*
LATVIJAS PSR ZINATNU AKADEMIJA.
*RIGA 1969(1)-*
2M. LATV. & RUSS.
*LO/S-3.*

**LATVIJSKIJ MATEMATICHESKIJ EZHEGODNIK.**
*+ +LATV. MAT. EZHEG.*
LATVIJAS PSR ZINATNU AKADEMIJA.
*RIGA 1, 1965-*
A. ENGL. SUMM. SPONS. BODY ALSO LATVIJAS
UNIVERSITATE.
*GL/U-1.*
*LO/N13. 2, 1966-*
*ISSN 0458-8223*

**LAURELS.**
EAST MIDLAND ART ASSOCIATION.
*NOTTINGHAM 1, 1972-*
*CA/U-1. ED/N-1. LO/N-1. NO/U-1.*

**LAW BOOKS PUBLISHED.**
*+ +LAW BOOKS PUBL.*
[GLANVILLE]
*DOBBS FERRY, N.Y. 1, 1969-*
*Q. CUMULATES ANNUALLY. INTERIM SUPPLEMENT TO
LAW BOOKS IN PRINT.*
*BL/U-1. GL/U-2. LO/U-2. NO/U-1.*
*ISSN 0023-9240*

**LAW & COMPUTER TECHNOLOGY.**
*+ +LAW & COMPUT. TECHNOL.*
WORLD PEACE THROUGH LAW CENTER: SECTION ON LAW
& COMPUTER TECHNOLOGY.
*WASHINGTON, D.C. 1, 1968-*
*M.*
*DN/U-1.*
*OX/U15. 1(1-11), 1968.*
*ISSN 0023-9178*

**LAW GUARDIAN.**
*LONDON NO.1, F 1965-*
*M.*
*LO/U-2.*
*ISSN 0023-9259*

**LAW LIBRARIAN. BULLETIN OF THE ...**
*+ +LAW LIBR.*
BRITISH & IRISH ASSOCIATION OF LAW LIBRARIANS.
*LONDON 1(1), AP 1970-*
*BH/P-1. CA/U-1. DB/U-2. DN/U-1. ED/N-1. EX/U-1.*
*GL/U-2. HL/U-1. LO/N-1. LO/U-2. LO/U-3. LO/U11.*
*LO/U12. LO/U14. LO/U28. MA/U-1. NO/U-1.*
*NW/U-1. OX/U15. RE/U-1. SH/U-1. SO/U-1.*
*ISSN 0023-9275*

**LAW & POLICY IN INTERNATIONAL BUSINESS.**
*+ +LAW & POLICY INT. BUS.*
GEORGETOWN UNIVERSITY: LAW CENTRE.
*WASHINGTON, D.C. 1, 1969-*
*2/A.*
*OX/U15.*
*ISSN 0023-9208*

**LAW & THE SOCIAL ORDER.**                                    XXX
*+ +LAW & SOC. ORDER.*
ARIZONA STATE UNIVERSITY: COLLEGE OF LAW.
*TEMPE, ARIZ. 1, 1969- 5(4), 1973.*
*Q. S/T: ARIZONA STATE LAW JOURNAL. SUBS:
ARIZONA STATE LAW JOURNAL.*
*OX/U15.*
*ISSN 0023-9224*

**LAW & SOCIETY NEWSLETTER.**
*+ +LAW & SOC. NEWSL.*
INSTITUTE OF CONSTITUTIONAL & PARLIAMENTARY
STUDIES (INDIA): CENTRE FOR THE STUDY OF LAW &
SOCIETY.
*NEW DELHI 1(1), JA/MR 1971-*
*LO/N-1.*
*ISSN 0047-4169*

**LAW & SOCIETY REVIEW.**                                      XXX
*+ +LAW & SOC. REV.*
LAW & SOCIETY ASSOCIATION.
[SAGE PUBL. INC.]
*BEVERLY HILLS, CALIF. 1, N 1966-*
*GL/U-2. LO/N-1. LO/U28. MA/U-1.*
*AD/U-1. 5, 1970-               CA/U-1. 6, 1971-*
*CB/U-1. 8, 1973-               CR/U-1. 6, 1971-*
*LO/U-3. 5(1), 1970-*
*BL/U-1. 1(2), 1967- [W. 2(1)]*
*ISSN 0023-9216*

**LAWASIA.**
LAW ASSOCIATION FOR ASIA & THE WESTERN PACIFIC.
*SYDNEY 1(1), 1969-*
*LO/U14. OX/U15.*
*ISSN 0047-4207*

**LAWYER (LAGOS). JOURNAL OF THE ...**
UNIVERSITY OF LAGOS LAW SOCIETY.
*LAGOS 1(1), 1966-*
                                    *LO/N-1. 3(1), D 1968-*
*ISSN 0023-9437*

**LD & A. LIGHTING DESIGN & APPLICATION.**                    XXX
ILLUMINATING ENGINEERING SOCIETY.
*NEW YORK 1(1), 1971-*
PREV: PART OF ILLUMINATING ENGINEERING FROM
34(6), JE 1940- 66(5), 1971.
*LO/N-4. LO/N14. LO/N35. LO/U-2.*

**LEAD RESEARCH DIGEST.**                                      XXX
*+ +LEAD RES. DIG.*
INTERNATIONAL LEAD ZINC RESEARCH ORGANIZATION,
INC.
*NEW YORK NO.28, 1971-*
PREV: PART OF THE ORGANIZATION'S RESEARCH
DIGEST: PART 4: LEAD METALLURGY; & RESEARCH
DIGEST: PART 5: LEAD CHEMISTRY.
*LO/N14.*

**LEAFLET, NORTH OF SCOTLAND COLLEGE OF AGRI-
CULTURE. NS.**
*+ +LEAFL. N. SCOTL. COLL. AGR., NS.*
*ABERDEEN NO.1, 1969-*
*ED/N-1.*

**LEANDRA. REVISTA DE INFORMACAO CIENTIFICA.**
UNIVERSIDADE FEDERAL DE RIO DE JANEIRO:
DEPARTAMENTO DE BOTANICA.
*RIO DE JANEIRO 1, 1971-*
DEPARTAMENTO DE BOTANICA SUBORD. TO: INSTITUTO
DE BIOLOGIA.
*LO/N-2. LO/N13.*
*OX/U-8. 2(2), 1972-*

**LEARNING & MOTIVATION.**
*+ +LEARN. & MOTIV.*
[ACADEMIC P.]
*NEW YORK 1, 1970-*
*AD/U-1. BN/U-1. HL/U-1. LD/U-1. LO/N13.*
*ISSN 0023-9690*

**LEB NEWS.**
LONDON ELECTRICITY BOARD.
*LONDON NO.1, AG 1971-*
*LO/N-1.*

**LEBENSMITTEL-WISSENSCHAFT + TECHNOLOGIE. = FOOD
SCIENCE + TECHNOLOGY. = SCIENCE + TECHNOLOGIE
ALIMENTAIRE.**
*+ +LEBENSM.-WISS. + TECHNOL.*
[FORSTER VERLAG]
*ZURICH 1, 1968-*
GER. ENGL. OR FR. WITH SUMM. IN EACH LANG.
*BH/U-1. LO/N14.*
*LD/U-1. 6, 1973-*
*ISSN 0023-6438*

**LECTURE NOTE SERIES, LONDON MATHEMATICAL
SOCIETY.**
*+ +LECT. NOTE SER. LOND. MATH. SOC.*
*LONDON NO.1, 1971-*
*LO/N-4.*

**LECTURE NOTES IN ECONOMICS & MATHEMATICAL
SYSTEMS.**                                                     XXX
*+ +LECT. NOTES ECON. & MATH. SYST.*
[SPRINGER]
*BERLIN &C. NO.60, 1971-*
PREV: LECTURE NOTES IN OPERATIONS RESEARCH &
MATHEMATICAL SYSTEMS FROM NO.16, 1969-
59, 1971.
*LO/N13.*

**LECTURE NOTES IN OPERATIONS RESEARCH & MATHEMA-
TICAL ECONOMICS.**                                             XXX
*+ +LECT. NOTES OP. RES. & MATH. ECON.*
[SPRINGER]
*BERLIN &C. NO.1, 1967- 15, 1969...*
SUBS: LECTURE NOTES IN OPERATIONS RESEARCH &
MATHEMATICAL SYSTEMS.
*LO/N13. OX/U-8.*
*ISSN 0458-9343*

**LECTURE NOTES IN OPERATIONS RESEARCH & MATHE-
MATICAL SYSTEMS.**                                             XXX
*+ +LECT. NOTES OPER. RES. & MATH. SYST.*
[SPRINGER]
*BERLIN &C. NO.16, 1969- 59, 1971...*
PREV: LECTURE NOTES IN OPERATIONS RESEARCH &
MATHEMATICAL ECONOMICS FROM NO.1, 1967- 15,
1969. SUBS: LECTURE NOTES IN ECONOMICS &
MATHEMATICAL SYSTEMS.
*LO/N13. OX/U-8.*

**LECTURE NOTES IN PHYSICS.**
+ +*LECT. NOTES PHYS.*
[SPRINGER]
*BERLIN &C. [NO.]1, 1969-*
*LO/N14.     LO/U-2.     NW/U-1.*

**LECTURE SERIES, NIGERIAN INSTITUTE OF INTER-NATIONAL AFFAIRS.**
+ +*LECT. SER. NIGER. INST. INT. AFF.*
*LAGOS  NO.1, 1969-*
*OX/U-9.*
*ISSN 0078-0731*

**LECTURES IN MATHEMATICS, DEPARTMENT OF MATH-EMATICS, KYOTO UNIVERSITY.**
+ +*LECT. MATH. DEP. MATH. KYOTO UNIV.*
KYOTO DAIGAKU: DEPARTMENT OF MATHEMATICS.
*TOKYO  1, 1968-*
*OX/U-8.*

**LECTURES ON MATHEMATICS IN THE LIFE SCIENCES.**
+ +*LECT. MATH. LIFE SCI.*
AMERICAN MATHEMATICAL SOCIETY.
*PROVIDENCE, R.I. [NO.1] 1968-*
*LO/N-2.*

**LECTURES, ROYAL INSTITUTE OF PHILOSOPHY.**
+ +*LECT. R. INST. PHIL.*
[MACMILLAN]
*LONDON &C.  1, 1966/67 (1968)-*
*AD/U-1.     GL/U-1.     LO/U-2.     LO/U-3.     LO/U11.*
*HL/U-1.  1, 1966/67.*

**LEEDS STUDIES IN BIBLIOGRAPHY & TEXTUAL CRIT-ICISM: OCCASIONAL PAPER.**
+ +*LEEDS STUD. BIBLIOGR. & TEXTUAL CRITIC., OCC. PAP.*
*LEEDS  NO.1, 1969-*
*GL/U-1.     LO/N-1.     OX/U-1.*

**LEEDS STUDIES IN ENGLISH.  NS.**                    XXX
+ +*LEEDS STUD. ENGL., NS.*
UNIVERSITY OF LEEDS: SCHOOL OF ENGLISH.
*LEEDS  1, 1967-*
PREV. SERIES AS LEEDS STUDIES IN ENGLISH &
KINDRED LANGUAGES FROM 1, 1932- 8, 1952.
*BH/U-1.     DB/U-2.     ED/N-1.     HL/U-1.     LD/U-1.     LO/N-1.*
*LO/U-2.     SH/U-1.     SW/U-1.*
*LO/U13.  4, 1970-*

**LEFT.  JOURNAL OF THE ...**
LABOUR PARTY YOUNG SOCIALISTS (GB).
*LONDON  NO.1, OC 1968-*
*MON.*
*LO/U-3.*
*HL/U-1.  2, 1970-*
*ISSN 0024-0303*

**LEGAL ACTION GROUP BULLETIN.**
+ +*LEG. ACTION GROUP BULL.*
[LEGAL ACTION GROUP INFORMATION SERVICE]
*LONDON  NO.1, JA 1972-*
*CA/U-1.     LO/U-2.*     OX/U15.*
*BL/U-1.  1974-                          ED/N-1.  F 1972-*
*GL/U-2.  NO.5, 1972-                 LO/U12.  F 1972-*

**LEGIBILITY RESEARCH ABSTRACTS.**
+ +*LEGIBILITY RES. ABSTR.*
[LUND HUMPHRIES]
*LONDON  1970(1971)-*
*DB/U-2.     LO/N14.     RE/U-1.*

**LEGKAJA PROMYSHLENNOST'.  MEZHVEDOMSTVENNYJ RESPUBLIKANSKIJ NAUCHNO-TEKHNICHESKIJ SBORNIK.**
+ +*LEGK. PROM-ST. [LPRO-A]*
(UKRAINE) MINISTERSTVO VYSSHEGO I SREDNEGO
SPETSIAL'NOGO OBRAZOVANIJA.
*KIEV  1, 1965-*
*BH/U-1.*
*CC/U-1.  1966-                      LO/N13.  2, 1966-*
*ISSN 0458-970X*

**LEGON OBSERVER.  ORGAN OF THE ...**
+ +*LEGON OBS.*
LEGON COMMITTEE ON NATIONAL RECONSTRUCTION.
*LEGON  1(1), JL 1966-*
*LO/U-8.     LO/U14.     MA/U-1.**
*EX/U-1.  2(21), 1967-*
*LO/S26.  TWO YEAR FILE.*
*ISSN 0024-0540*

**LEICESTERSHIRE HISTORIAN.**
+ +*LEICS. HIST.*
LEICESTERSHIRE LOCAL HISTORY COUNCIL.
*LEICESTER  1(1), 1967-*
*OX/U-1.*
*NO/U-1.  1(6), 1970-*
*ED/N-1.  2(2), 1971/72-*
*LO/U-1.  [W. 1(2), 1968]*
*ISSN 0024-0664*

**LEISURE PAINTER.**
[REEVES & SONS LTD.]
*ENFIELD, MIDDX.  SPRING 1967-*
*ED/N-1.     XL/P-8.*
*ISSN 0024-0710*

**LEMBAGA PUSAT PERPUSTAKAAN BIOLOGI DAN PER-TANIAN SERI BIBLIOGRAFI.**
+ +*LEMBAGA PUSAT PERPUSTAKAAN BIOL. PERTANIAN SER. BIBLIOGR.*
*BOGOR  NO.1, 1967-*
*LO/N13.*

**LEMMING.**
SAN DIEGO COUNCIL FOR POETRY.
*SAN DIEGO, CALIF.  NO.1, 1971-*
*LO/U-2.*
*ISSN 0047-4398*

**LENAU-FORUM.**
INTERNATIONALE LENAU-GESELLSCHAFT.
*VIENNA  1, 1969-*
*DB/U-2.     LO/N-1.*
*ISSN 0024-0788*

**LENS.**
PHOTOGRAPHIC SOCIETY OF IRELAND.
*DUBLIN  [NO.1]  OC 1968-*
*DB/U-2.*

**LEPROSY MISSION IN ACTION.**
+ +*LEPR. MISSION ACTION.*
LEPROSY MISSION.
*LONDON  NO.1, 1970-*
*ED/N-1.     OX/U-8.*

**LERNA.**
AMERICAN SCHOOL OF CLASSICAL STUDIES AT ATHENS.
*PRINCETON, N.J.  1, 1969-*
*OX/U-1.*

**LESKOVACKI ZBORNIK.**
+ +*LESKOVACKI ZB.*
NARODNI MUZEJ.
*LESKOVAC  1, 1961-*
*OX/U-1.*

**LESOVEDENIE.**
AKADEMIJA NAUK SSSR.
*MOSCOW  1, 1967-*
ENGL. SUMM. & CONT. LISTS.
*LO/N13.     OX/U-3.*

**LESSING YEARBOOK.**
AMERICAN LESSING SOCIETY.
[HUEBER]
*MUNICH  1, 1969-*
ENGL. OR GER.
*LO/U17.     NO/U-1.     SA/U-1.     SH/U-1.     SW/U-1.*
*LD/U-1.  4, 1972.*
*ISSN 0075-8833*

**LETRAS DE DEUSTO.**
UNIVERSIDAD DE DEUSTO: FACULTAD DE FILOSOFIA
Y LETRAS.
*BILBOA  1(1), 1971-*
*ED/N-1.     LO/N-1.     OX/U-1.*

**LETTERE AL NUOVO CIMENTO.  RIVISTA INTERNAZ-IONALE DELLA...**
+ +*LETT. NUOVO CIM.*
SOCIETA ITALIANA DI FISICA.
[EDITRICE COMPOSITORI]
*BOLOGNA  1, 1969-*
PREV AS PART OF NUOVO CIMENTO.
*BH/U-1.     BH/U-3.     BL/U-1.     CB/U-1.**     DB/U-2.     LC/U-1.*
*LO/U-2.     LO/U-4.     LO/U12.     RE/U-1.     SH/U-1.     SO/U-1.*
*EX/U-1.  3(1), 1970-*
*ISSN 0024-1318*

**LETTERS IN APPLIED & ENGINEERING SCIENCES.**
+ +*LETT. APPL. & ENG. SCI.*
[PERGAMON]
*NEW YORK; LONDON  1, 1973-*
*CA/U-1.     ED/N-1.     LO/N14.     OX/U-8.*
*ISSN 0090-6913*

**LEVANT. JOURNAL OF THE...**
BRITISH SCHOOL OF ARCHAEOLOGY IN JERUSALEM.
*LONDON 1, 1969-*
*BH/U-1.     BL/U-1.     CA/U-3.     ED/N-1.     EX/U-1.     GL/U-1.*
*LO/N-1.     MA/U-1.     OX/U-1.     OX/U-2.     SH/U-1.*
*LD/U-1.  4, 1972-*

**LIBER BULLETIN.**                                                    000
SEE: BULLETIN, LIGUE DES BIBLIOTHEQUES EUROPE-
ENNES DE RECHERCHE.

**LIBERATED GUARDIAN.**                                                XXX
*NEW YORK  1, AP 1970- 3(8), F 1973.*
MON. SUBS: NEW YORK CITY STAR. S/T: A NATIONAL
LIBERATED PUBLICATION.
*LO/U-2.  2(5), 1971-          LO/U-3.  2(8), 1972-*
*ISSN 0024-1865*

**LIBERIAN ECONOMIC & MANAGEMENT REVIEW.**
*+ +LIBERIAN ECON. & MANAGE. REV.*
*MONROVIA  1, 1972-*
*OX/U-9.*

**LIBERIAN STUDIES JOURNAL.**
*+ +LIBERIAN STUD. J.*
DEPAUW UNIVERSITY: AFRICAN STUDIES CENTRE.
*GREENCASTLE, INDIANA  1, OC 1968-*
*2/A.*
*LO/N-1.     LO/U-1.     LO/U14.*
*ISSN 0024-1989*

**LIBERTARIAN STRUGGLE.**
ORGANISATION OF REVOLUTIONARY ANARCHISTS.
*LEEDS  1(1), F 1973-*
MON.
*LO/U-3.*

**LIBERTY.**                                                           XXX
YORKSHIRE ANARCHIST FEDERATION.
*SELBY, YORKS.  1(1) JA 1969- 1(3), MR 1969.//*
*LO/U-3.*

**LIBRARIAN'S DIGEST OF ARTICLES, INSTITUTE OF**
**CHARTERED ACCOUNTANTS IN ENGLAND & WALES.**       XXX
SUBS (1970): ACCOUNTING & DATA PROCESSING
ABSTRACTS.

**LIBRARIANS FOR SOCIAL CHANGE.**
*+ +LIBR. SOC. CHANGE.*
*BRIGHTON  NO.1, 1972-*
*Q.*
*ED/N-1.     LO/U-2.     LO/U-3.*
*ISSN 0305-165X*

**LIBRARIES INFORMATION BULLETIN, UNIVERSITY OF**
**CAMBRIDGE.**
*+ +LIBR. INF. BULL. UNIV. CAMB.*
UNIVERSITY OF CAMBRIDGE.
*CAMBRIDGE  NO.1, MR 1972-*
*ED/N-1.     LO/N-2.     OX/U-1.*

**LIBRARY ACTION.**
*+ +LIBR. ACTION.*
LIBRARY ACTION GROUP.
*LEEDS  NO.1, F 1971-*
*Q.*
*ED/N-1.     LD/U-1.*
*ISSN 0047-4525*

**LIBRARY ASSOCIATION RESEARCH PUBLICATIONS.**
*+ +LIBR. ASSOC. RES. PUBL.*
*LONDON  NO.1, 1969-*
*GL/U-1.     OX/U-1.*
*ISSN 0460-2137*

**LIBRARY BULLETIN, DEPARTMENT OF THE ENVIRON-**
**MENT (GB).**
*+ +LIBR. BULL. DEP. ENVIRON (GB).*
(GREAT BRITAIN) DEPARTMENT OF THE ENVIRONMENT.
*LONDON  NO.1, JA 1972-*
*DB/U-2.     MA/P-1.*

**LIBRARY BULLETIN, ECONOMICS LIBRARY, CENTRAL**
**BUREAU OF STATISTICS (GHANA).**
*+ +LIBR. BULL. ECON. LIBR. CENT. BUR. STATIST.*
*(GHANA).*
*ACCRA  1(1), 1970-*
*OX/U-9.*

**LIBRARY BULLETIN, INSTITUTE OF SOUTHEAST**
**ASIAN STUDIES (SINGAPORE).**
*+ +LIBR. BULL. INST. SOUTHEAST ASIAN STUD.*
*(SINGAPORE).*
*SINGAPORE  NO.1, 1971-*
*LO/N12.*
*ISSN 0073-9723*

**LIBRARY-COLLEGE JOURNAL.**
*+ +LIBR.-COLL. J.*
LIBRARY-COLLEGE ASSOCIATIONS, INC.
*NEW YORK  1, 1968-*
*GL/U-2.     LV/U-1.*
*ISSN 0024-225X*

**LIBRARY & INFORMATION SCIENCE ABSTRACTS.**        XXX
LIBRARY ASSOCIATION.
*LONDON  1, 1969-*
SPONS. BODY ALSO ASLIB.  PREV: LIBRARY SCIENCE
ABSTRACTS FROM 1, 1950.
*BH/P-1.     BH/U-1.     BN/U-1.     CB/U-1.     ED/N-1.     GL/U-1.*
*GL/U-2.     HL/U-1.     HL/U-1.     LO/N-4.     LO/N14.     LO/N17.*
*LO/P-6.     LO/U-2.     LO/U-3.     LO/U11.     LO/U12.     LV/P-1.*
*LV/U-1.     NR/P-1.     OX/U-1.     RE/U-1.     SH/U-1.     SW/U-1.*
*XS/R10.*
*ISSN 0024-2179*

**LIBRARY JOURNAL BOOK REVIEW.**
*+ +LIBR. J. BOOK REV.*
[BOWKER]
*NEW YORK &C.  1967(1968)-*
*A.*
*LO/N-3.  1969-*
*ISSN 0075-9082*

**LIBRARY JOURNAL/SCHOOL LIBRARY JOURNAL:**
**PREVIEWS.**
*+ +LIBR. J./SCH. LIBR. J., PREVIEWS.*
*NEW YORK  1(1), 1972-*
*LD/U-1.     LO/N-4.     OX/U-1.*
*NW/U-1.  1(5), 1973-          SF/U-1.  1(7), 1973-*
*ISSN 0000-0051*

**LIBRARY PROGRESS.**
*+ +LIBR. PROG.*
*TILBURG  1968-*
*A.*
*OX/U-1.  1970-*
*ISSN 0024-2497*

**LIBRARY PUBLICATIONS, BIRKBECK COLLEGE,**
**UNIVERSITY OF LONDON.**
*+ +LIBR. PUBL. BIRKBECK COLL. UNIV. LOND.*
*LONDON  [NO.1] 1970-*
NUMBERS 1 & 2 DO NOT BEAR THE SERIES TITLE &
NUMERATION.
*LO/N-1.*

**LIBRARY RESEARCH NEWS.**
*+ +LIBR. RES. NEWS.*
MCMASTER UNIVERSITY: MILLS MEMORIAL LIBRARY.
*HAMILTON, ONT.  1(1), 1968/69[1968]-*
*BL/U-1.     LD/U-1.     OX/U-1.     SO/U-1.*

**LIBRARY SCIENCE ABSTRACTS.**                                         XXX
SUBS (1969): LIBRARY & INFORMATION SCIENCE
ABSTRACTS.

**LIBRARY WORLD.**                                                     XXX
SUBS (1971): NEW LIBRARY WORLD.

**LIBRE.  REVISTA CRITICA TRIMESTRAL DEL MUNDO DE**
**HABLA ESPANOLA.**                                                    XXX
[EDITIONS LIBRES]
*PARIS  NO.1, S/N 1971-4, 1972. //*
*ED/N-1.     OX/U-1.*
*ISSN 0047-455X*

**LIBRO ABIERTO.**
*MEXICO, D.F.  1(1), 1971-*
*LO/U-1.     OX/U-1.*

**LIBROS.**
[GALERNA]
*BUENOS AIRES  NO.1, 1969-*
*M.*
*LO/U-1.     OX/U-1.*
*LO/N-1.  1(4), 1969-*
*ISSN 0024-2756*

**LIBYAN JOURNAL OF SCIENCE.**
*+ +LIBYAN J. SCI.*
UNIVERSITY OF LIBYA: FACULTY OF SCIENCE.
*TRIPOLI  1, 1971-*
*LO/N-2.     LO/N14.*

**LIETUVOS TSR AUKSTUJU MOKYKLU MOKSLO DARBAI:**
**BIOLOGIJA.**
*+ +LIET. TSR AUKST. MOKYKLU MOKSLO DARB., BIOL.*
*VILNIUS  1, 1961-*
TITLE ALSO IN RUSSIAN: NAUCHNYE TRUDY VYSSHIKH
UCHEBNYKH ZAVEDENIJ LITOVSKOJ SSR: BIOLOGIJA.
*LO/N13.  10, 1970-          OX/U-8.  2, 1962-*
*ISSN 0459-3383*

LIETUVOS TSR AUKSTUJU MOKYKLU MOKSLO DARBAI:
EKONOMIKA. = UCHENYE ZAPISKI VYSSHIKH UCHEB-
NYKH ZAVEDENIJ LITOVSKOJ SSR: EKONOMIKA.                    XXX
++LIET. TSR AUKST. MOKYK. MOKS. DARB., EKON.
LIETUVOS TSR AUKSTESNIS MOKYKLA.
 VILNIUS   2, 1962-
 PREV: VILNIAUS VALSTYBINIS /V. KAPSUKO VARDO/
 UNIVERSITETAS, MOKSLO DARBAI; EKONOMIKA. =
 UCHENYE ZAPISKI, VIL'NJUSSKIJ GOS. UNIVERSITET
 /IM. V. KAPSUKASA/; EKONOMIKA.
 LO/N-3.    OX/U-1.

LIETUVOS TSR AUKSTUJU MOKYKLU MOKSLO DARBAI:
ELEKTROTECHNIKA IR AUTOMATIKA = NAUCHNYE
TRUDY VYSSHIKH UCHEBNYKH ZAVEDENIJ LITOVSKOJ
SSR: ELEKTROTEKHNIKA I AVTOMATIKA.                          XXX
++LIET. TSR AUKST. MOKYKLU MOKSLO DARB. : ELEK-
 TROTECH. & AUTOM.
LIETUVOS TSR AUKSTESNIS MOKYKLA.
 VILNIUS  TOM 1, 1966-
 LITHUANIAN & RUSS.  PREV: PART OF LIETUVOS TSR
 AUKSTUJU MOKYKLU MOKSLO DARBAI: ELEKTROTECH-
 NIKA IR MECHANIKA.
 LO/N13.  5, 1969-
 ISSN 0459-3413

LIETUVOS TSR AUKSTUJU MOKYKLU MOKSLO DARBAI:
ELEKTROTECHNIKA IR MECHANIKA = NAUCHNYE TRUDY
VYSSHIKH UCHEBNYKH ZAVEDENIJ LITOVSKOJ SSR:
ELEKTROTEKHNIKA I MEKHANIKA.                                XXX
++LIET. TSR AUKST. MOKYKLU MOKSLO DARB., ELEK-
 TROTECH. & MECH. [LDEM-A]
LIETUVOS TSR AUKSTESNIS MOKYKLA.
 VILNIUS  1, 1962- 4, 1965.
 SUBS: WITH ABOVE MAIN TITLE ISSUED IN TWO SER-
 IES; ELEKTROTEKHNIKA IR AUTOMATIKA; & MECHAN-
 IKA.
 ISSN 0459-3421

LIETUVOS TSR AUKSTUJU MOKYKLU MOKSLO DARBAI:
FILOSOFIJA. = UCHENYE ZAPISKI VYSSHIKH UCHEB-
NYKH ZAVEDENIJ LITOVSKOJ SSR.
++LIET. TSR AUKST. MOKYK. MOKS. DARB., FILOS.
LIETUVOS TSR AUKSTESNIS MOKYKLA.
 VILNIUS   2(1), 1962-
 OX/U-1.
 LO/N-3.  2(2),1962-

LIETUVOS TSR AUKSTUJU MOKYKLU MOKSLO DARBAI:
GEOGRAFIJA IR GEOLOGIJA. = NAUCHNYE TRUDY
VYSSHIKH UCHEBNYKH ZAVEDENIJ LITOVSKOJ SSR:
GEOGRAFIJA I GEOLOGIJA.
++LIET. TSR AUKST. MOKSLO DARB.: GEOGR.
 & GEOL. [LAMG-A]
LIETUVOS TSR AUKSTESNIS MOKYKLA.
 VILNIUS  1, 1962-
 LO/N13.
 OX/U-1.  3, 1964-
 ISSN 0459-3448

LIETUVOS TSR AUKSTUJU MOKYKLU MOKSLO DARBAI:
ISTORIJA. = NAUCHNYE TRUDY VYSSHIKH UCHEBNYKH
ZAVEDENIJ LITOVSKOJ SSR: ISTORIJA.
++LIET. TSR AUKST. MOKYK. MOKS. DARB., ISTOR.
LIETUVOS TSR AUKSTESNIS MOKYKLA.
 VILNIUS  3, 1962-
 PREV: VILNIAUS VALSTYBINIS /V. KAPSUKO VARDO/
 UNIVERSITETAS, MOKSLO DARBAI. = UCHENYE
 ZAPISKI, VIL'NJUSSKIJ GOS. UNIV. /IM. V. KAP-
 SUKASA/: ISTORIJA.
 LO/N-3.

LIETUVOS TSR AUKSTUJU MOKYKLU MOKSLO DARBAI:
KALBOTYRA. = UCHENYE ZAPISKI VYSSHIKH UCHEB-
NYKH ZAVEDENIJ LITOVSKOJ SSR: JAZYKOZNANIE.     XXX
++LIET. TSR AUKST. MOKYK. MOKS. DARB., KALBOT.
LIETUVOS TSR AUKSTESNIS MOKYKLA.
 VILNIUS  3, 1961-
 PREV: VILNIAUS VALSTYBINIS /V. KAPSUKO VARDO/
 UNIVERSITETAS, MOKSLO DARBAI; KALBOTYRA. =
 UCHENYE ZAPISKI, VIL'NJUSSKIJ GOS. UNIV. /IM.
 V. KAPSUKASA/; JAZYKOZNANIE.
 LO/N-3.

LIETUVOS TSR AUKSTUJU MOKYKLU MOKSLO DARBAI:
LITERATURA. = NAUCHNYE TRUDY VYSSHIKH UCHEB-
NYKH ZAVEDENIJ LITOVSKOJ SSR: LITERATURA.       XXX
++LIET. TSR AUKST. MOKYK. MOKS. DARB., LIT.
LIETUVOS TSR AUKSTESNIS MOKYKLA.
 VILNIUS  3, 1962-
 PREV: VILNIAUS VALSTYBINIS /V. KAPSUKO VARDO/
 UNIVERSITETAS, MOKSLO DARBAI; LITERATURA. =
 UCHENYE ZAPISKI, VIL'NJUSSKIJ GOS. UNIV. /IM.
 V. KAPSUKASA/; LITERATURA.
 LO/N-3.

LIETUVOS TSR AUKSTUJU MOKYKLU MOKSLO DARBAI:
MECHANIKA. = NAUCHNYE TRUDY VYSSHIKH UCHEB-
NYKH ZAVEDENIJ LITOVSKOJ SSR: MEKHANIKA.         XXX
++LIET. TSR AUKST. MOKYKLU MOKSLO DARB., MECH.
 [LAMD-A]
 VILNIUS  1962(1). TOM 1, 1966-
 SINGLE ISSUE PUBL. IN 1962. IN 1963 MERGED
 INTO: LIETUVOS TSR AUKSTUJU MOKYKLU MOKSLO
 DARBAI: ELETROTECHNIKA IR MECHANIKA.  IN 1966
 RESUMED INDEPENDENT PUBLICATION COMMENCING
 WITH VOL. 1.
 ISSN 0457-8279

LIETUVOS TSR AUKSTUJU MOKYKLU MOKSLO DARBAI:
MECHANINE TECHNOLOGIJA.= NAUCHNYE TRUDY
VYSSHIKH UCHEBNYKH ZAVEDENIJ LITOVSKOJ SSR:
MEKHANICHESKAJA TEKHNOLOGIJA.
++LIET. TSR. AUKST. MODYKLU MOKSLO DARB., MECH.
 TECHNOL. [LAMT-B]
 VILNIUS  1, 1968-
 LITH. & RUSS.
 LO/N13.   OX/U-8.

LIETUVOS TSR AUKSTUJU MOKYKLU MOKSLO DARBAI:
MENOTYRA. = UCHENYE ZAPISKI VYSSHIKH UCHEBNYKH
ZAVEDENIJ LITOVSKOJ SSR: ISKUSSTVOVEDENIE.
++LIET. TSR AUKST. MOKYK. MOKS. DARB., MENOTYRA.
 VILNIUS  1, 1967-
 LO/N-3.

LIETUVOS TSR AUKSTUJU MOKYKLU MOKSLO DARBAI:
STATYBA IR ARCHITEKTURA.
++LIET. TSR AUKST. MOKYKLU MOKSLO DARB., STATYBA
 ARCHIT.
 VILNIUS  1, 1962-
 TITLE ALSO IN RUSSIAN: NAUCHNYE TRUDY VYSSHIKH
 UCHEBNYKH ZAVEDENIJ LITOVSKOJ SSR: STROITEL'-
 STVO I ARKHITEKTURA.
 OX/U-1.
 LO/N13.  4(2), 1965-
 ISSN 0457-8287

LIETUVOS TSR MOKSLU AKADEMIJOS /IR JOS/ DAR-
BUOTOJU KNYGU IR STRAIPSNIU BIBLIOGRAFIJA.       XXX
 SUBS (1965): LIETUVOS TSR MOKSLU AKADEMIJOS
 LEIDINIU BIBLIOGRAFIJA.

LIETUVOS TSR MOKSLU AKADEMIJOS LEIDINIU
BIBLIOGRAFIJA. = BIBLIOGRAFIJA IZDANIJ
AKADEMII NAUK LITOVSKOJ SSR.
++LIET. TSR MOKS. AKAD. LEID. BIBLIOGR.
LIETUVOS TSR MOKSLU AKADEMIJA; CENTRINE
BIBLIOTEKA.
 VILNIUS   1963 (1965)-
 PREV: LIETUVOS TSR MOKSLU AKADEMIJOS /IR JOS/
 DARBUOTOJU KNYGU IR STRAIPSNIU BIBLIOGRAFIJA.
 'IR JOS' DROPPED FROM PREV TITLE FROM 1959(61)
 CC/U-1.   LO/N-3.   LO/N-4.   LO/N14.   OX/U-1.

LIFE & WORSHIP.  QUARTERLY OF ...               XXX
++LIFE & WORSH.
SOCIETY OF ST. GREGORY.
 LONDON 39, 1970-
 PREV:  LITURGY FROM 13, 1944.
 ED/N-1.

LIFT. ELEVATOR LIFT & ROPEWAY ENGINEERING.      XXX
AERIAL ROPEWAY ENGINEERS SOCIETY.
 WESTERHAM, KENT 14, 1972-
 PREV: INTERNATIONAL ROPEWAY REVIEW FROM 1,
 1959- 13, 1971.  SPONS. BODY ALSO ORGANIZZAZ-
 IONE INTERNAZIONALE TRANSPORTI A FUNE.
 ED/N-1.   LO/N14.

LIGHT CRAFT, SMALL BOAT.                         000
 SUBS (1969): PART OF SMALL BOAT.

LIGHT ENGINEERING.                               XXX
++LIGHT ENG.
[FACTORY PUBL. LTD.]
 LONDON  JA- JY 1971.
 PREV:  LIGHT PRODUCTION ENGINEERING FROM JA
 1963- 1970. SUBS. PART OF: OEM DESIGN.
 LO/N14.   OX/U-8.
 ISSN 0024-337X

LIGHTING EQUIPMENT NEWS.
++LIGHT. EQUIP. NEWS.
[EQUIPMENT NEWS LTD.]
 LONDON  1, 1967-
 M.
 BL/U-1.   LO/N14.
 ISSN 0024-3418

**LIGHTING JOURNAL.**
+ +LIGHT. J.
BRITISH LIGHTING INDUSTRIES, LTD.
LONDON NO.1, 1968-
LO/N14.
ED/N-1. NO.6, 1971-

**LIGHTING RESEARCH & TECHNOLOGY.**　　　　XXX
+ +LIGHT. RES. & TECHNOL.
ILLUMINATING ENGINEERING SOCIETY.
LONDON 1(1), 1969-
PREV: TRANSACTIONS OF THE ILLUMINATING ENG-
INEERING SOCIETY FROM 1, 1936- 33(4), 1968.
ED/N-1. LO/N-4. LO/N14. LO/U-6. LV/U-1. SH/U-1.
ISSN 0024-3426

**LILLABULERO.**
CHAPEL HILL, N.C. 1(1), 1967-
OX/U-1.
ISSN 0024-3485

**LIMES U JUGOSLAVIJI.**
+ +LIMES JUGOSL.
ARHEOLOSKO DRUSTVO JUGOSLAVIJE.
BELGRADE 1, 1961-
OX/U-2.
ISSN 0459-4363

**LIMNOLOGICAL DATA REPORT: LAKE EYRIE.**
+ +LIMNOL. DATA REP., LAKE EYRIE.
CANADIAN OCEANOGRAPHIC DATA CENTRE.
OTTAWA NO.1, 1970-
LO/N13.

**LIMNOLOGICAL DATA REPORT: LAKE HURON, LAKE
SUPERIOR.**
+ +LIMNOL. DATA REP., LAKE HURON LAKE SUPER.
CANADIAN OCEANOGRAPHIC DATA CENTRE.
OTTAWA NO.1, 1970-
LO/N13.

**LINEAR & MULTILINEAR ALGEBRA.**
[GORDON & BREACH]
NEW YORK 1, 1973-
Q.
CA/U-1. ED/N-1. OX/U-8. SH/U-1. SW/U-1.

**LINGUISTIC INQUIRY.**
+ +LINGUIST. INQ.
[M.I.T. PRESS]
CAMBRIDGE, MASS. 1, JA 1970-
Q.
BH/U-1. BN/U-1. ED/U-1. LD/U-1. LO/N-1. LO/U-1.
LO/U-3. LO/U-4. NO/U-1. OX/U-1.
HL/U-1. 1(4), 1970- SH/U-1. 1972-
ISSN 0024-3892

**LINGUISTICS IN DOCUMENTATION: CURRENT AB-
STRACTS.**
+ +LINGUIST. DOC., CURR. ABSTR.
WASHINGTON, D.C. NO.1, 1970-
DB/U-2.

**LINGUISTIK UND DIDAKTIK.**
MUNICH NO.1, 1970-
LO/N-1.
ISSN 0047-472X

**LINGUISTIQUE FINNO-OUGRIENNE SOVIETIQUE.**　　000
SEE: SOVETSKOE FINNO-UGROVEDENIE.

**LINGUISTISCHE BERICHTE.**
+ +LINGUIST. BER.
[VIEWEG]
BRAUNSCHWEIG NO.1, 1969-
2M.
CB/U-1. DB/U-2. LO/U-1. SH/U-1.
LO/N-1. NO.3, 1969- NW/U-1. NO.5, 1970-
CA/U-1. NO.23, 1973-
NO/U-1. NO.11, 1971-
ISSN 0024-3930

**LINK (GUILDFORD).**
GUILDFORD INSTITUTE OF FURTHER EDUCATION.
GUILDFORD 1, 1968-
ED/N-1. OX/U-1.

**LINK (LONDON, 1971).**
NATIONAL CHRISTIAN EDUCATION COUNCIL.
LONDON NO.1, 1971-
OX/U-1.
ED/N-1. NO.6, 1972-

**LINOTYPE NEWS.**　　　　XXX
LINOTYPE & MACHINERY LTD.
ALTRINCHAM 1970(2)-
PREV: L & M NEWS FROM 1, 1927- 1970(1).
ED/N-1. LO/N14.

**LIPPISCHE STUDIEN.**
+ +LIPPISCHE STUD.
DETMOLD 1, 1972-
OX/U-1.

**LIPUNAN.**
UNIVERSITY OF THE PHILIPPINES; INSTITUTE OF
ASIAN STUDIES.
QUEZON CITY 1(1), 1965-
LO/U14.

**LIQUID SCINTILLATION COUNTING.**
+ +LIQ. SCINTILL. COUNT.
[HEYDEN]
LONDON &C. 1, 1971-
CONSISTS OF PROCEEDINGS OF 1970 INTERNATIONAL
SYMPOSIUM ON LIQUID SCINTILLATION COUNTING.
LO/N14.
ISSN 0302-3354

**LIST OF ARTICLES INDEXED, LIBRARY, INTER-
NATIONAL UNION FOR CHILD WELFARE.**
+ +LIST ARTIC. INDEXED LIBR. INT. UNION CHILD
WELFARE.
GENEVA NO.1, F/OC 1968-
ED/N-1. LO/U-3.

**LIST OF BOOKS RECEIVED FROM THE USSR (&
TRANSLATED BOOKS).**　　　　XXX
+ +LIST BOOKS RECEIV. USSR (& TRANSL. BOOKS).
NATIONAL LENDING LIBRARY FOR SCIENCE &
TECHNOLOGY.
LONDON. 1, OC 1957- 35, JL 1961...
BOSTON SPA. NO.36, 1961-196, 1974. //
1-35 ISSUED BY– GREAT BRITAIN, DEPT OF SCIEN-
TIFIC & INDUSTRIAL RESEARCH, LENDING LIBRARY
UNIT. TITLE EXPANDED FROM 36.
DB/U-2.** LO/U-5.* NO/U-1.
GL/U-1. 77,1965- XS/R10. (1962)-
YK/U-1. 83,1965-

**LIST OF FOREIGN ACCESSIONS, NATIONAL LIBRARY
OF SCOTLAND.**
+ +LIST FOREIGN ACCESS. NAT. LIBR. SCOTL.
EDINBURGH 1, D 1969-
ED/N-1. LD/U-1. OX/U-1.

**LIST OF OVERSEA STANDARDS.**　　　　XXX
+ +LIST OVERSEA STAND.
BRITISH STANDARDS INSTITUTION.
LONDON AP 1969- F 1974
PREV: OVERSEA & COMMONWEALTH STANDARDS FROM
1956- MR 1969. SUBS: WORLDWIDE LIST OF
PUBLISHED STANDARDS.
GL/U-1. LO/N14.

**LIST OF PUBLICATIONS DEPOSITED IN THE LIBRARY
OF THE NATIONAL ARCHIVES (RHODESIA).**　　　XXX
SUBS (1968): RHODESIA NATIONAL BIBLIOGR.

**LIST OF PUBLICATIONS & PATENTS WITH ABSTRACTS,
WESTERN MARKETING & NUTRITION RESEARCH DIVIS-
ION, DEPARTMENT OF AGRICULTURE (US).**　　　XXX
+ +LIST PUBL. & PAT. ABSTR. WEST. MARK. & NUTR.
RES. DIV. DEP. AGRIC. (US).
BERKELEY, CALIF. NO.31, JL/D 1970-
PREV: LIST OF PUBLICATIONS & PATENTS WITH
ABSTRACTS, WESTERN UTILIZATION RESEARCH &
DEVELOPMENT DIVISION, DEPARTMENT OF AGRICULT-
URE (US) FROM NO.3, JL/D 1956- NO.30, JA/JE
1970.
LO/N14.

**LIST OF PUBLICATIONS & PATENTS WITH ABSTRACTS,
WESTERN UTILIZATION RESEARCH & DEVELOPMENT
DIVISION, DEPARTMENT OF AGRICULTURE (US).**　　XXX
SUBS (1970): LIST OF PUBLICATIONS & PATENTS
WITH ABSTRACTS, WESTERN MARKETING & NUTRIT-
ION RESEARCH DIVISION, DEPARTMENT OF AGRI-
CULTURE (US).

**LIST OF PUBLICATIONS & PATENTS, SOUTHERN UTIL-
IZATION RESEARCH & DEVELOPMENT DIVISION, DEP-
ARTMENT OF AGRICULTURE (US).**　　　　XXX
SUBS (1971): PUBLICATIONS & PATENTS WITH
ABSTRACTS, SOUTHERN MARKETING & NUTRITION
RESEARCH DIVISION, DEPARTMENT ...

**LIST OF SCIENTIFIC REPORTS RELATING TO
THAILAND.**
+ +LIST SCI. REP. RELAT. THAILAND.
NATIONAL RESEARCH COUNCIL OF THAILAND.
BANGKOK NO.1, OC 1964-
LO/N-2.

**LISTY, SVAZ CESKOSLOVENSKYCH SPISOVATELU.**   XXX
*PRAGUE 1(1), 1968- 2(19), 1969.//*
W. PREV: LITERARNI LISTY FROM 1968(1-25).
*BH/U-1.   LA/U-1.*

**LITERARNI LISTY.**   XXX
*+ +LIT. LISTY.*
SVAZ CESKOSLOVENSKYCH SPISOVATELU.
*PRAGUE 1968(1 - 25).*
W. PREV: LITERARNI NOVINY FROM 1(1), 1952-
16(52), 1967. SUBS: LISTY, SVAZ CESKOSLOVEN-
SKYCH SPISOVATELU.
*BH/U-1.   LA/U-1.*

**LITERARNI NOVINY.**   XXX
SUBS (1968): LITERARNI LISTY.

**LITERARY MONOGRAPHS.**
*+ +LIT. MONOGR.*
UNIVERSITY OF WISCONSIN: DEPARTMENT OF ENGLISH.
*MADISON 1, 1967-*
*BH/U-1.*
*ISSN 0075-9902*

**LITERATUR UND GESCHICHTE.**
*+ +LIT. & GESCH.*
[LOTHAR STIEHM VERLAG]
*HEIDELBERG 1, 1970-*
*CA/U-1.   LO/U13.*

**LITERATUR IN DER GESELLSCHAFT.**
*+ +LIT. GES.*
[BERTELSMANN UNIVERSITATSVERLAG]
*DUSSELDORF 1, 1971-*
*CA/U-1.   LO/N-1.*

**LITERATUR UND REFLEXION.**
*+ +LIT. & REFLEXION.*
[VERLAG GEHLEN]
*BAD HOMBURG 1, 1970-*
*CA/U-1.*

**LITERATUR UND WIRKLICHKEIT.**
*+ +LIT. & WIRKLICHKEIT.*
[BOUVIER]
*BONN 1, 1967-*
*GL/U-1.*

**LITERATUR IN WISSENSCHAFT UND UNTERRICHT.**
*+ +LIT. WISS. & UNTERR.*
UNIVERSITAT KIEL: ENGLISCHES SEMINAR.
*KIEL 1, 1968-*
Q.
*OX/U-1.*
*ISSN 0024-4643*

**LITERATURA I ISKUSSTVO, GOSUDARSTVENNAJA
BIBLIOTEKA SSSR IM. V.I. LENINA.**   XXX
*+ +LIT. & ISKUSSTVO GOS. BIBL. SSSR IM. V.I.
LENINA.*
*MOSCOW 1967(1968)-*
S/T: REKOMENDATEL'NYJ UKAZATEL' LITERATURY.
PREV: KHUDOZHESTVENNAJA LITERATURA, LITERA-
TUROVEDENIE, ISKUSSTVO FROM 1963(1964)- 1966
(1968).
*BH/U-1.   CC/U-1.   LD/U-1.*

**LITERATURA I SOVREMENNOST'.**
*+ +LIT. & SOVREM.*
[GOSUDARSTVENNOE IZDATEL'STVO KHUDOZHESTVENNOJ
LITERATURY]
*MOSCOW [1], 1959/1960(1960)-*
A. S/T: STAT'I O LITERATURE.
*BH/U-1.   CC/U-1.   DR/U-1.   ED/U-1.   GL/U-1.   NO/U-1.*
*BT/U-1. 4, 1963-   LA/U-1. 8, 1968-*
*LV/U-1. 7, (1967)-   MA/U-1. 9, 1969-*
*NR/U-1. 6, 1965-*
*LO/U15. 3, 1962- 10, 1970.*
*ISSN 0459-5378*

**LITERATURA O STRANAKH AZII I AFRIKI.**
*+ +LIT. STRANAKH AZII & AFR.*
AKADEMIJA NAUK SSSR: INSTITUT NARODOV AZII.
*MOSCOW 1961-*
ANNU.
*CC/U-1.   DR/U-1.   LO/U14.   OX/U-1.*
*LO/U15. 1961- 1963.*

**LITERATURE & IDEOLOGY.**
*+ +LIT. & IDEOL.*
NECESSITY FOR CHANGE INSTITUTE OF IDEOLOGICAL
STUDIES.
*MONTREAL; DUBLIN NO.1, 1969-*
*OX/U-1.*
*LO/N-1. NO.3, 1969-*
*ISSN 0024-4740*

**LITERATURE & IDEOLOGY MONOGRAPH.**
*+ +LIT. & IDEOL. MONOGR.*
NECESSITY FOR CHANGE INSTITUTE OF IDEOLOGICAL
STUDIES.
[PROGRESSIVE BOOKS & PERIODICALS]
*MONTREAL; DUBLIN NO.1, 1969-*
*LO/N-1.   OX/U-1.*

**LITERATURE, MUSIC, FINE ARTS.**
*+ +LIT. MUSIC FINE ARTS.*
*TUBINGEN 1(1), 1968-*
2/A. ENGL. & GER. S/T: A REVIEW OF GERMAN-
LANGUAGE RESEARCH CONTRIBUTIONS ON LITERATURE,
MUSIC & FINE ARTS. PUBL. AS GERMAN STUDIES:
SECTION III.
*LO/S29.   MA/P-1.   SH/U-1.*
*LO/U-1. 5, 1972-*
*ISSN 0024-4775*

**LITERATURNYE VZAIMOSVJAZI. SBORNIK.**
*+ +LIT. VZAIMOSVJAZI.*
AKADEMIJA NAUK GRUZINSKOJ SSR: INSTITUT ISTORII
GRUZINSKOJ LITERATURY.
*TIFLIS 1, 1965-*
*OX/U-1.*

**LITHOLOGY & MINERAL RESOURCES.**
*+ +LITHOL. & MINER. RESOUR.*
[CONSULTANTS BUREAU]
*NEW YORK NO.1, 1966(1967)-*
2M. TRANSL. OF LITOLOGIJA I POLEZNYE ISKO-
PAEMYE. NUMBERING & DATING AS IN ORIG.
*LO/N14.*
*ISSN 0024-4902*

**LITOLOGIJA I POLEZNYE ISKOPAEMYE (ENGL.
TRANSL.).**   000
SEE: LITHOLOGY & MINERAL RESOURCES.

**LITORAL. REVISTA DE LA POESIA Y EL PENSAMIENTO.**
*TORREMOLINOS NO.1, MY 1968-*
MON.
*LO/N-1.*
*LO/U-2. NO.13/14, 1970-*

**LITTACK. A CRITICAL SURVEY.**
[EMBER P.]
*ESHER, SURREY 1(1), 1972-*
*CA/U-1.   ED/N-1.   LO/U-2.*
*SH/U-1. 1973-*

**LITTERARIA. TEORIA LITERATURY, METODOLOGIA,
KULTURA, HUMANISTYKA.**
WROCLAWSKIE TOWARZYSTWO NAUKOWE.
*WROCLAW 1, 1969-*
NUMBERED ALSO AS PART OF PRACE WROCLAWSKIEGO
TOWARZYSTWA NAUKOWEGO, SER. A. NO. 1 OF ABOVE
= NO. 134 OF PRACE ...
*LO/N-3.*

**LITTERATURE.**
UNIVERSITE DE PARIS: DEPARTEMENT DE LITTERATURE
FRANCAISE.
*PARIS NO.1, F 1971-*
Q.
*CB/U-1.   EX/U-1.   MA/U-1.   OX/U19.   SH/U-1.*
*ISSN 0047-4800*

**LITTLE SQUARE REVIEW.**
*+ +LITTLE SQUARE REV.*
*SANTA BARBARA, CALIF. NO.1, 1966-*
Q.
*LO/U-2.*
*ISSN 0024-5070*

**LITTLE WORD MACHINE.**
*+ +LITTLE WORD MACH.*
*SHIPLEY, YORKS. NO.1, 1972-*
*CA/U-1.   ED/N-1.   OX/U-1.*

**LITTLEMORE JOURNAL.**
*+ +LITTLEMORE J.*
*LITTLEMORE NO.1, 1968-*
*OX/U-1.*

**LITURGICAL STUDIES.**   XXX
*+ +LITURGICAL STUD.*
CHURCH SERVICE SOCIETY.
*EDINBURGH 1(1), MY 1971-*
PREV: ANNUAL, CHURCH SERVICE SOCIETY FROM 1,
1928- 40, 1970.
*AD/U-1.   ED/N-1.   GL/U-1.   OX/U-1.   SA/U-1.*

**LITURGY.**   XXX
SUBS (1970): LIFE & WORSHIP.

**LITURGY BULLETIN.**
++*LITURGY BULL.*
DIOCESE OF SOUTHWARK COMMISSION FOR THE LIT-
URGY: SUB-COMMITTEE FOR THE PROMOTION OF THE
LITURGY.
*LONDON NO.1, OC 1971-*
*ED/N-1. NO.4, 1972-*

**LITVA SEGODNJA.**
LITOVSKOE OBSHCHESTVO DRUZHBY I KUL'TURNYKH
SVIAZEJ S ZARUBEZHNYMI STRANAMI.
*VILNIUS 1, 1966-*
*CC/U-1. 5, 1971-*
*ISSN 0459-6005*

**LIVERPOOL.**
LIVERPOOL PUBLIC RELATIONS OFFICE.
*LIVERPOOL NO.1, JA 1966-*
S/T: AN INTERNATIONAL MAGAZINE ABOUT LIVER-
POOL, ITS INDUSTRY, ITS PEOPLE.
*MA/P-1.**

**LIVESTOCK FARMING.**                                    XXX
++*LIVESTOCK FARM.*
[ALAN EXLEY LTD.]
*BATTLE, SUSSEX 7(1), 1970-*
PREV: BEEF & SHEEP FARMING FROM 1, MR 1964-
6, 1969.
*CA/U11. ED/N-1. LO/N-6.*
*ISSN 0005-7746*

**LIVING JUDAISM. JOURNAL OF THE ...**                   XXX
REFORM SYNAGOGUES OF GREAT BRITAIN.
*LONDON 1, 1966-*
Q. PREV: SYNAGOGUE REVIEW FROM 10, 1935-
40, 1965-66.
*SO/U-1.*
*ISSN 0024-5267*

**LIVRE ANNUEL INTERNATIONAL DE PSYCHIATRIE
INFANTILE ET DES PROFESSIONS ASSOCIEES.**
++*LIVRE ANNU. INT. PSYCHIATR. INFANT. & PROF.
ASSOC.*
INTERNATIONAL ASSOCIATION FOR CHILD PSYCHIATRY
& ALLIED PROFESSIONS.
*PARIS 1, 1970-*
*LO/N-1.*

**LIVROS NOVOS.**
*SAO PAULO 1, 1972-*
*ED/N-1.*
*LO/U-2. 2, 1973-*

**LLAFUR. THE JOURNAL OF THE ...**
SOCIETY FOR THE STUDY OF WELSH LABOUR HISTORY.
*SWANSEA 1, 1972-*
*BL/U-1. LO/U-1. OX/U17. SH/U-1. SW/U-1.*
*ISSN 0306-0837*

**LLOYD'S LAW REPORTS.**
++*LLOYD'S LAW REP.*
CORPORATION OF LLOYD'S.
*LONDON 1(1), 1969-*
*DN/U-1. HL/U-1. LO/U11. SO/U-1. XS/C-2. XS/R10.*
*ISSN 0024-5488*

**LLYFRGELL.**
COLLEGE OF LIBRARIANSHIP, WALES.
*ABERYSTWYTH 1, 1972-*
*2/A.*
*ED/N-1.*

**LOCAL COUNCIL DIGEST.**
++*LOCAL COUNC. DIG.*
[POLITICO-STATS LTD.]
*BEXLEY HEATH 1, 17/JE 1967-*
*2/M.*
*BH/U-1. HL/U-1. LO/P-6. MA/P-1.*

**LOCAL GOVERNMENT REVIEW.**                              XXX
++*LOCAL GOV. REV.*
[JUSTICE OF THE PEACE LTD.]
*CHICHESTER; LONDON 136(1), N 1971-*
W. PREV: PART OF JUSTICE OF THE PEACE & LOCAL
GOVERNMENT REVIEW FROM 1, 1837- 135(46), 1971.
*ED/N-1. HL/U-1. LD/U-1. LO/U-3. LO/U12. LO/U28.*
*MA/P-1.* NO/U-1. NW/U-1.* SO/U-1.*

**LOCAL GOVERNMENT STUDIES.**
++*LOCAL GOV. STUD.*
UNIVERSITY OF BIRMINGHAM: INSTITUTE OF LOCAL
GOVERNMENT STUDIES.
*LONDON NO.1, OC 1971-*
*2/A.*
*EX/U-1. GL/U-1. LO/U-3. LO/U28. NO/U-1. NW/U-1.*
*SF/U-1. SH/U-1. SO/U-1.*
*ED/N-1. NO.2, 1972-*
*ISSN 0300-3930*

**LOCAL HISTORY PUBLICATION, DONCASTER ARTS &
MUSEUM SOCIETY.**
++*LOCAL HIST. PUBL. DONCASTER ARTS & MUS. SOC.*
*DONCASTER NO.1, 1972-*
*OX/U-1.*

**LOCAL POPULATION STUDIES. MAGAZINE & NEWS-
LETTER.**
UNIVERSITY OF NOTTINGHAM: DEPARTMENT OF ADULT
EDUCATION.
*NOTTINGHAM 1, 1968-*
SPONS. BODY ALSO CAMBRIDGE GROUP FOR THE
HISTORY OF POPULATION AND SOCIAL STRUCTURE.
*BN/U-1. ED/N-1. GL/U-2. HL/U-1. LO/P-6. LO/U-1.*
*LO/U-3. MA/U-1. NO/U-1.*
*AD/U-1. 2, 1969-*
*BH/U-3. NO.11, 1973-*
*ISSN 0460-2269*

**LOCKE NEWSLETTER.**
++*LOCKE NEWSL.*
*YORK 1, 1970-*
*BL/U-1. CB/U-1. ED/N-1. GL/U-1. LD/U-1. LO/U-1.*
*LV/U-1. NO/U-1. OX/U-1. SA/U-1. SO/U-1.*
*HL/U-1. NO.1, 1970-2, 1971.*

**LOCO PROFILE.**
[PROFILE PUBL.]
*WINDSOR, BERKS. NO.1, [1970]-*
*LO/N-1. LO/N-4. OX/U-1.*

**LOG BOOK.**
SHIP STAMP SOCIETY.
*TIMPERLEY 1(1), JE 1971-*
*ED/N-1. OX/U-1.*

**LOGGING RESEARCH REPORTS.**                             XXX
++*LOGG. RES. REP.*
PULP & PAPER RESEARCH INSTITUTE OF CANADA.
*POINTE CLAIRE, P.Q. LRR/45, 1971-*
PREV: WOODLANDS REPORTS FROM WR/30, 1970- 44,
1972.
*LO/N14.*

**LOGIKA, UNIWERSYTET WROCLAWSKI.**
++*LOGIKA UNIW. WROCL.*
*WROCLAW 1, 1969-*
NUMBERED ALSO AS PART OF PRACE FILOZOFICZNE,
UNIWERSYTET WROCLAWSKI, AND ACTA UNIVERSITATIS
WRATISLAVISENSIS. NO. 1 OF ABOVE = NO. 5 OF
'PRACE ...' & NO. 101 OF 'ACTA ...'.
*LO/N-3.*

**LONDON ARCHAEOLOGIST.**
++*LOND. ARCHAEOL.*
*WEST WICKHAM, KENT 1(1), D 1968-*
Q. SPONS. BY LEADING ARCHAEOLOGICAL SOCIETIES
IN & AROUND LONDON.
*ED/N-1. LO/N-1. LO/P-6. LO/U12. OX/U-2.*
*SH/U-1. 1969-*
*LO/N-4. 1(11), 1971-*
*ISSN 0024-5984*

**LONDON BULLETIN.**                                      XXX
++*LOND. BULL.*
BERTRAND RUSSELL PEACE FOUNDATION.
*LONDON NO.1, AG 1967-13, N/D 1969.*
M. SUBS: PART OF SPOKESMAN.
*LO/U-3.*

**LONDON EDUCATIONAL REVIEW.**
++*LOND. EDUC. REV.*
UNIVERSITY OF LONDON: INSTITUTE OF EDUCATION.
*LONDON 1(1), 1972-*
*3/A.* SAMPLE ISSUED IN 1971.
*ED/N-1. EX/U-1. HL/U-2. LO/U-1. LO/U11. LO/U26.*
*MA/U-1. SW/U-1.*
*ISSN 0300-385X*

**LONDON PRINTER.**
++*LOND. PRINT.*
LONDON MASTER PRINTERS ASSOCIATION.
*LONDON 1, 1966-*
Q.
*ED/N-1.*

**LONDON QUARTERLY & HOLBORN REVIEW.**                    XXX
SUBS (1968) PART OF: CHURCH QUARTERLY.

**LONDON RECUSANT.**
*ENFIELD, MIDDX. 1(1), JA 1971-*
*3/A.* S/T: A JOURNAL IN WHICH STUDIES WILL BE
PUBLISHED COVERING THE CATHOLIC HISTORY OF
LONDON.
*ED/N-1. LO/N-1.*

LONDON REVIEW OF PUBLIC ADMINISTRATION.
++LOND. REV. PUBLIC ADM.
ROYAL INSTITUTE OF PUBLIC ADMINISTRATION:
LONDON REGIONAL GROUP.
 HODDESDON, HERTS. NO.1, MR 1972-
 2/A.
 LO/U-1.      LO/U-3.

LONDONER. JOURNAL OF THE GEOGRAPHY SECTION,
CITY OF LONDON POLYTECHNIC.
 LONDON 1, JE 1972-
 LO/S13. 1, JE 1972.

LONG DISTANCE FOOTPATH GUIDE.
 COUNTRYSIDE COMMISSION (GB).
 LONDON NO.1, 1969-
 GL/U-1.      OX/U-1.

LONG RANGE PLANNING. JOURNAL OF THE ...
++LONG RANGE PLANN.
SOCIETY FOR LONG RANGE PLANNING.
[PERGAMON]
 OXFORD 1(1), S 1968-
 DN/U-1.   ED/N-1.   MA/P-1.   OX/U-1.   SH/U-1.   XS/R10.
 CV/C-1. 3, 1971-          DB/U-2. 1(3), 1969-
 GL/U-1. 2(3), 1970-       MA/U-1. 2(2), 1969-
 NO/U-1. 1(3), 1969-
 ISSN 0024-6301

LOOK 'N COOK.
[THORPE & PARTNERS (SALES) LTD.]
 LONDON 1(1), [1969]-
 ED/N-1.      OX/U-1.
 ISSN 0024-6395

LOOK AT FINLAND.
++LOOK FINL.
(FINLAND) ULKOASAINMINISTERIO.
 HELSINKI NO.1, 1967-
 Q. BODIES NAMED IN ENGL.: MINISTRY FOR
 FOREIGN AFFAIRS [ITS PRESS BUREAU] & FINNISH
 TRAVEL ASSOCIATION.
 LO/S14.
 OX/U-1. 1974(2)-

LORE & LANGUAGE.
++LORE & LANG.
SHEFFIELD SURVEY OF LANGUAGE & FOLKLORE.
 SHEFFIELD NO.1, JL 1969-
 ED/N-1.   LO/N-1.   OX/U-1.

LORENTZIA.
 UNIVERSIDAD NACIONAL DE CORDOBA: FACULTAD DE
 CIENCIAS EXACTAS, FISICAS Y NATURALES.
 CORDOBA, ARGENT. NO.1, 1970-
 PRODUCED BY FACULTAD'S MUSEO BOTANICO.
 LO/N-2.

LOTUS.
[JONATHAN HEMLEY]
 ATHENS, OHIO NO.1, 1968-
 LO/U-2.
 ISSN 0459-8261

LOUGHBOROUGH OCCASIONAL PAPERS IN SOCIAL
STUDIES.
++LOUGHBOROUGH OCCAS. PAP. SOC. STUD.
LOUGHBOROUGH COLLEGE OF FURTHER EDUCATION.
 LOUGHBOROUGH NO.1, [1969]-
 OX/U-1.

LOUVAIN STUDIES.
++LOUVAIN STUD.
 AMERICAN COLLEGE (LOUVAIN).
 LOUVAIN 1, 1966-
 BL/U-1.
 ISSN 0024-6964

LOW COST AUTOMATION REVIEW.
++LOW COST AUTOM. REV.
LOW COST AUTOMATION CENTRE.
 BELFAST NO.1, 1969-
 BL/U-1.   ED/N-1.   LO/N14.
 ISSN 0024-7049

LOYALIST LINKS.
LEAGUE OF ANGLICAN LOYALISTS.
 LONDON NO.1, 1971-
 ED/N-1. NO. 10, 1971-
 OX/U-1. NO.10, 1971-

LSHR NEWS LETTER.                                    XXX
++LSHR NEWS LETT. (LOUISIANA SOC. HORT. RES.).
 LAFAYETTE 8(3), 1967- 10, 1969 ...
 PREV: MONTHLY NEWS LETTER ... FROM 1, 1960-
 8(2), 1967. SUBS: JOURNAL, LOUISIANA ...
 LO/N13.

LTP PUBLICATIONS.
++LTP PUBL.
AMERICAN LIBRARY ASSOCIATION: LIBRARY TECHNO-
LOGY PROGRAM.
 CHICAGO NO.1, 1961-
 GL/U-1.

LUCRARI STIINTIFICE ALE INSTITUTUL DE CERCET-
ARI SI PROIECTARI PENTRU PASTRAREA SI VALOR-
IFICAREA LEGUMELOR SI FRUCTELOR.
++LUCR. STIINT. INST. CERCET. & PROIECT. PENTRU
 PASTRAREA & VALORIFICAREA LEGUMELOR & FRUCTEL.
 BUCHAREST 1, 1970-
 CA/U11.   XS/R-2.

LUCRARILE STIINTIFICE, INSTITUTUL DE CERCET-
ARI PENTRU NUTRITIE ANIMALA.
++LUCR. STIINT. INST. CERCET. NUTR. ANIM.
 BUCHAREST 1, 1972-
 BL/U-1.

LUDD'S MILL.
 HUDDERSFIELD NO.1, [1971]-
 ED/N-1.   LO/U-2.   LO/U-3.   OX/U-1.
 CA/U-1. NO.3, 1971-
 ISSN 0047-5157

LUDOVICO MAZIMILIANEA.
 BERLIN 1, 1971-
 CA/U-1.   OX/U-1.

LUG.
 DUBLIN NO.1, SPRING 1972-
 CO/U-1.   DB/U-2.   LO/N-1.

LUNA MONTHLY.
++LUNA MON.
[LUNA PUBL.]
 ORADELL, N.J. 1, 1969-
 OX/U-1.
 ISSN 0024-7375

LYDGATE NEWSLETTER.
++LYDGATE NEWSL.
 NEW YORK 1, 1972-
 OX/U-1.

LYING IN. THE JOURNAL OF REPRODUCTIVE MEDI-
CINE.                                                XXX
 CHICAGO LYING IN HOSPITAL.
 CHICAGO 1, JA/F 1968- 1(6), 1968 ...
 2M. SUBS: JOURNAL OF REPRODUCTIVE MEDICINE.
 XY/N-1.**

LYMPHOLOGY.
 INTERNATIONAL SOCIETY OF LYMPHOLOGY.
[GEORGE THIEME VERLAG]
 STUTTGART 1, MR 1968-
 LO/U-2.
 ISSN 0024-7766

LYNX-DRUCK.
[HARTMUT LUDKE VERLAG]
 HAMBURG NO.1, 1970-
 MONOGR.
 LO/N-1.

LYRIC. INTERNATIONAL POETRY QUARTERLY.
 LEEDS NO.1, MR 1968-
 ED/N-1.

M. A QUARTERLY REVIEW OF THE ...
 MONTREAL MUSEUM OF FINE ARTS.
 MONTREAL NO.1, JE 1969-
 ENGL. & FR.
 CR/N-1.   OX/U-2.
 ISSN 0027-0725

MABON.
 NORTH WALES ASSOCIATION FOR THE ARTS.
 BANGOR 1, 1969-
 2/A. ALSO A WELSH EDITION.
 BL/U-1.   ED/N-1.   LO/U-2.   LV/P-1.   MA/U-1.   SW/U-1.
 ISSN 0024-886X

MABU.
 LIMA NO.1, N 1971-
 LO/N-1.

MAC. POETRY MAGAZINE.
 MAYBOLE, AYRSHIRE NO.1, 1970-
 LO/U-2.

MACANA.
 UNIVERSIDAD DEL VALLE: DEPARTAMENTO DE
 BIBLIOTECAS.
 CALI, COLOMB. 1, OC 1971-
 OX/U-1.

**MACANA: SUPLEMENTO.**
 *CALI, COLOMB. 1, 1971-*
 *OX/U-1.*

**MCCUTCHEON'S PATENT REVIEW ON SOAPS, DETER-
GENTS & EMULSIFIERS.**
 *+ +MCCUTCHEON'S PAT. REV. SOAPS, DETERG. & EMULS.*
 [JOHN W. MCCUTCHEON INC.]
 *MORRISTOWN, NJ  1, 1966-*
 *LO/N14.*

**MACEDONIAN REVIEW.**
 *+ +MACEDONIAN REV.*
 *SKOPJE 1(1), 1971-*
 *CA/U-1.    OX/U-1.*

**MACHINE.  BOLLETINO DELL' ...**
 ISTITUTO ITALIANO PER LA STORIA DELLA TECNICA.
 *FLORENCE 1(1), D 1967-*
 *LO/N-4.*

**MACHINE AGE.**                                                                                    XXX
 *+ +MACH. AGE.*
 [ROWSE MUIR INTERNATIONAL LTD.]
 *LONDON  1(1), 1960- 3(29), 1962 ...*
 M.  SUBS:  MODERN INDUSTRY & MACHINE AGE.
 *LO/N14.*

**MACHINE DESIGN & CONTROL.**                                                            XXX
 *+ +MACH. DES. & CONTROL.*
 [DESIGN ENGINEERING PUBL.]
 *LONDON  6, MY 1968- 9, 1971.*
 PREV:  MACHINE DESIGN ENGINEERING FROM 1, F
 1963- 6(4), 1968. SUBS. PART OF: OEM DESIGN.
 *LO/N14.*

**MACHINE SHOP (SYDNEY).**                                                                XXX
 *+ +MACH. SHOP (SYDNEY).*
 [TECHNICAL & INDUSTRIAL P.]
 *SYDNEY 19(9), 1968-*
 PREV: MACHINE SHOP & METAL MANUFACTURE FROM
 17(6), 1966- 19(8), 1968.
 *LO/N13.*

**MACHINE SHOP & METAL MANUFACTURE.**                                    XXX
 *+ +MACH. SHOP & MET. MANUF.*
 [TECHNICAL & INDUSTRIAL P.]
 *SYDNEY 17(6), 1966- 19(8), 1968...*
 SUBS: MACHINE SHOP.
 *LO/N13.*

**MACHINE SHOP & METALWORKING.**                                              XXX
 SUBS (1966): MACHINE SHOP & METAL MANUFACTURE.

**MACROMOLECULES.**
 AMERICAN CHEMICAL SOCIETY.
 *WASHINGTON, D.C.  1, 1968-*
 *BH/U-1.    LO/N-4.    LO/N14.    LO/S-3.*
 *AD/U-1.  2, 1969-*
 *ISSN 0024-9297*

**MACROPROFILE: RADIATION & PHOTOCHEMISTRY.**              XXX
 UNITED KINGDOM CHEMICAL INFORMATION SERVICE.
 *NOTTINGHAM 1971-*
 PREV: CHEMSCAN: RADIATION & PHOTOCHEMISTRY
 FROM NO.20, 1969- 26, 1970.  CONTAINS SELECTED
 ENTRIES FROM CHEMICAL TITLES.
 *CR/M-1.    ED/N-1.    OX/U-1.    XS/R10.*
 *LO/N14. [CURRENT BOX ONLY]*

**MACROPROFILE: STEROIDS.**                                                           XXX
 UNITED KINGDOM CHEMICAL INFORMATION SERVICE.
 PREV: CHEMSCAN: STEROIDS FROM NO.20, 1969- 26,
 1970.  CONTAINS SELECTED ENTRIES FROM CHEMICAL
 TITLES.
 *CR/M-1.    ED/N-1.    LO/N14.    OX/U-1.*

**MADOQUA. JOURNAL OF NATURE CONSERVATION RES-
EARCH, SOUTH WEST AFRICA.**
 (SOUTH AFRICA) ADMINISTRATION OF SOUTH WEST
 AFRICA: NATURE CONSERVATION & TOURISM BRANCH.
 *WINDHOEK  1, 1969-*
 *LO/N-2.*
 *OX/U-8.  NO.2, 1970-*

**MAGALLAT AL-MIKROBIYOLOCIYA LI-AL-GUMHURIYYAT
AL-'ARABIYYAT AL-MUTTAHIDAH.**                                            000
 SEE: JOURNAL OF MICROBIOLOGY OF THE UNITED
 ARAB REPUBLIC.

**MAGAZIN ISTORIC.**
 *+ +MAG. ISTOR.*
 SOCIETATEA DE STIINTE ISTORICE SI FILOLOGICE
 DIN REPUBLICA SOCIALISTA ROMANIA.
 *BUCHAREST  1, AP 1967-*
 MON.
 *OX/U-1.*
 *ISSN 0541-881X*

**MAGAZINE OF DISTRICT 102, ROTARY INTERNATIONAL
OF GREAT BRITAIN & IRELAND.**                                            XXX
 SUBS (1972): CHRONICLE.

**MAGAZINE OF THE INSTITUTE OF CONTEMPORARY
ARTS.**                                                                                       XXX
 *+ +MAG. INST. CONTEMP. ARTS.*
 *LONDON NO.1, 1968-*
 PREV:  ICA BULLETIN.
 *CB/U-1.*
 *ED/N-1.  NO.1- 8, 1968.*

**MAGAZINE, SHETLAND PONY STUD-BOOK SOCIETY.**
 *+ +MAG. SHETLAND PONY STUD-BOOK SOC.*
 *STOWMARKET, SUFF.  1, 1968-.*
 *LO/N13.*

**MAGENIA FROG MAGAZINE.**
 *+ +MAGENIA FROG MAG.*
 *VANCOUVER NO.1, 1970-*
 *LO/U-2.    OX/U-1.*

**MAGNETIC RESONANCE REVIEW.**
 *+ +MAGN. RESONANCE REV.*
 [GORDON & BREACH]
 *LONDON 1(1), 1972-*
 S/T: QUARTERLY LITERATURE REVIEW JOURNAL.
 *ED/N-1.    LO/N14.*
 *CA/U-1.  1(4), 1972-*

**MAGNETOHYDRODYNAMICS & PLASMAS JOURNAL.**              XXX
 *+ +MAGNETOHYDRODYN. & PLASMAS J.*
 [CAMBRIDGE SCIENTIFIC ABSTR., INC.]
 *RIVERDALE, MD.  1(1), 1972...*
 SUBS. PART OF: SCIENCE RESEARCH ABSTRACTS:
 PART A: SUPERCONDUCTIVITY, MAGNETO-HYDRO-
 DYNAMICS & PLASMAS, THEORETICAL PHYSICS.
 *LO/N14.*

**MAGNITNAJA GIDRODINAMIKA.**
 *+ +MAGN. GIDRODIN.*
 LATVIJAS PSR ZINATNU AKADEMIJA.
 *RIGA  1965(1)-*
 Q.  RUSS. TEXT.  ENGL. SUMM. & CONT. LISTS.
 BODY NAME IN RUSS: AKADEMIJA NAUK LATVIJSKOJ
 SSR.
 *LO/N-4.    LO/N13.*
 *ISSN 0025-0015*

**MAGYAR ZENE.  HUNGARIAN MUSIC.**
 [KULTURA]
 *BUDAPEST  1, 1960-*
 2M.
 *OX/U-1.  7, 1966-*
 *ISSN 0025-0384*

**MAGYARORSZAG REGESZETI TOPOGRAFIAJA.**
 MAGYAR TUDOMANYOS AKADEMIA: REGESZET KUTATO
 INTEZET.
 *BUDAPEST  1, 1966-*
 *BL/U-1.*
 *ISSN 0076-2504*

**MAHASAGAR.**
 NATIONAL INSTITUTE OF OCEANOGRAPHY (INDIA).
 *NEW DELHI  1, MR/JE 1968-*
 4/A.
 *LO/N-2.*

**MAINE FARM RESEARCH.**                                                             XXX
 SUBS (1968):  RESEARCH IN THE LIFE SCIENCES.

**MAINLINE.  A MAGAZINE OF POETRY.**
 *WINDSOR, ONT.  NO.1, 1968-*
 3/A.
 *LO/N-1.*
 *LO/U-2.  NO.6, 1970-*
 *ISSN 0025-0821*

**MAINTENANCE.**
 [ILIFFE]
 *LONDON 5(7), 1967-*
 PREV: PRACTICAL MAINTENANCE & CLEANING FROM
 1, 1963.
 *ED/N-1.    LO/N14.*
 *ISSN 0025-0872*

**MAITRE PHONETIQUE.**                                                                 XXX
 SUBS (1971): JOURNAL OF THE INTERNATIONAL
 PHONETIC ASSOCIATION.

**MAITREYA.**
 [SHAMBALA PUBL.]
 *BERKELEY, CALIF  1, 1970-*
 *OX/U-1.  2, 1971-*
 *ISSN 0025-1011*

MAIZURU KOGYO KOTO SENMON GAKKO KIYO.
*MAIZURU-SHI 1, 1966-*
ENGL. ABSTR. SOME ARTIC. IN ENGL.
*XN/S-1.*

MAJI MAJI RESEARCH PAPERS.
*++MAJI MAJI RES. PAP.*
[EAST AFRICAN PUBL. HOUSE]
*NAIROBI NO.1, 1969-*
*LO/N-1. OX/U-9.*

MAJORITY RULE.
*++MAJOR. RULE.*
MOVEMENT FOR DEMOCRACY IN RHODESIA.
*LONDON NO.1, S 1968. //*
*LO/U-3. LO/U14.*

MAKERERE HISTORY PAPERS.
*++MAKERERE HIST. PAP.*
[LONGMANS OF UGANDA LTD.]
*KAMPALA NO.1, 1968-*
*BT/U-1. OX/U-9.*
*ISSN 0076-2903*

MALACOLOGICAL REVIEW.
*++MALACOL. REV.*
*WHITMORE LAKE, MICH. 1, 1968-*
ANNU.
*LO/N-2. LO/N13. OX/U-8. SH/U-1.*
*CA/U-1. 7, 1974- MA/U-1. 4, 1971-*

MALAYSIAN AGRICULTURAL RESEARCH.
*++MALAYS. AGRIC. RES.*
UNIVERSITY OF MALAYSIA: FACULTY OF AGRICULTURE.
*KUALA LUMPUR 1(1), JE 1972-*
*AD/U-1. LD/U-1. LO/R-6.*

MALAYSIAN DIGEST.                                          XXX
*++MALAYSIAN DIG.*
(MALAYSIA) FEDERAL DEPARTMENT OF INFORMATION.
*KUALA LUMPUR 1, 1969-*
PREV. PART OF: MALAYSIAN PRESS DIGEST FROM
1(1), 1968- 2(6), JE 1969; & WARTA MALAYSIA.
*CB/U-1. HL/U-1. OX/U-9.*
*ISSN 0047-5629*

MALAYSIAN ECONOMIC STUDIES.                              000
SEE: KAJIAN EKONOMI MALAYSIA.

MALAYSIAN MANAGEMENT REVIEW. JOURNAL OF THE...
*++MALAYS. MANAGE. REV.*
MALAYSIAN INSTITUTE OF MANAGEMENT.
*KUALA LUMPUR 1, JL 1966-*
*2/A.*
*HL/U-1. LO/U14.*
*ISSN 0025-1348*

MALAYSIAN PINEAPPLE.
*++MALAYS. PINEAPPLE.*
PINEAPPLE RESEARCH STATION (PEKAN NERIAS).
*PEKAN NERIAS, JOHORE 1, 1971-*
*LO/N13. LO/R-6.*

MALAYSIAN PRESS DIGEST.                                  XXX
*++MALAYS. PRESS DIG.*
(MALAYSIA) FEDERAL DEPARTMENT OF INFORMATION.
*KUALA LUMPUR 1(1), 1968- 2(6), JE 1969.*
SUBS. PART OF: MALAYSIAN DIGEST.
*CB/U-1. 1(7), 1968- ED/N-1. 1(9), 1968-*
*LO/S26. ONE YEAR FILE.*

MALLORN.
TOLKIEN SOCIETY.
*LONDON [NO.]1, N 1970-*
*CA/U-1. NO.6, 1972- ED/N-1. NO.6, 1972-*

MALOPOLSKIE STUDIA HISTORYCZNE.                          XXX
SUBS (1967): STUDIA HISTORYCZNE, KOMISJA NAUK
HISTORYCZNYCH, (ODDZIAL W KRAKOWIE) POLSKA
AKADEMIA NAUK.

MAMMAL REVIEW.
*++MAMMAL REV.*
MAMMAL SOCIETY OF THE BRITISH ISLES.
*LONDON 1, 1970-*
*CA/U11. LO/N-2. SH/U-1.*
*ED/N-1. 2, 1972-*

MAMMALIAN SPECIES.
*++MAMM. SPECIES.*
AMERICAN SOCIETY OF MAMMALOGISTS.
*STILLWATER, OKLA. NO.1, 1969-*
*LO/N-2. LO/N13. OX/U-1.*

MAN & HIS ENVIRONMENT.
*++MAN & HIS ENVIRON.*
[PERGAMON]
*OXFORD &C. 1, 1970.//*
*LO/N-2. LO/N14.*

MAN IN NEW GUINEA.
UNIVERSITY OF PAPUA & NEW GUINEA: DEPARTMENT
OF ANTHROPOLOGY & SOCIOLOGY.
*BOROKO 1(1), OC 1968-*
*LO/N-1. LO/U-8.*
*ISSN 0025-1577*

M.A.N. RESEARCH, ENGINEERING, MANUFACTURING.
MASCHINENFABRIK AUGSBURG-NURNBERG, A.G.
*AUGSBURG [NO.1], 1970-*
NUMBERING COMMENCES WITH NO.2.
*LO/N-4. LO/N14.*

MAN IN SOUTHEAST ASIA.
UNIVERSITY OF QUEENSLAND.
*BRISBANE NO.1, 1968-*
PROD. BY UNIV. DEPTS. OF ANTHROPOLOGY &
SOCIOLOGY; & GEOGRAPHY.
*HL/U-1.*

MANADSBLAD, SVENSKA GASFORENINGEN.*
*++MANADSBL. SVEN. GASFORENINGEN.*
*STOCKHOLM 35(6), 1968- 36, 1969.*
PREV: MANADSBLAD, SVENSKA GASVERKSFORENINGEN.
SUBS: GASNYTT.
*LO/N14.*

MANAGEMENT IN ACTION.                                    XXX
*++MANAGE. ACTION.*
ORGANISATION & METHODS SOCIETY.
[DISTINCTIVE PUBL. LTD.]
*CROYDON 1(1), OC 1969-*
PREV: OFFICE METHODS & MACHINES FROM 11(130),
1964- 16(189), 1969. INCORP: JOURNAL OF THE
ORGANISATION & METHODS SOCIETY.
*BL/U-1. DB/U-2. ED/N-1. GL/U-3. HL/U-1. LO/N-7.*
*LO/N14. NW/U-1. OX/U-1. XS/R10.*
*ISSN 0030-0217*

MANAGEMENT & DESIGN NOTES.
*++MANAGE. & DES. NOTES.*
COUNTRYSIDE COMMISSION (GB).
*LONDON NO.1, [1972]-*
*LO/N-1. NW/U-1.*

MANAGEMENT EDUCATION AND DEVELOPMENT.                    XXX
*++MANAGE. EDUC. & DEV.*
ASSOCIATION OF TEACHERS OF MANAGEMENT.
*LONDON 1, 1970-*
PREV: A.T.M. OCCASIONAL PAPERS FROM
1, 1965; & A.T.M. BULLETIN FROM 1961-9, 1969.
*BH/U-1. GL/U-2. MA/P-1.*
*CA/U-1. 3, 1972- ED/N-1. 3, 1972-*
*ISSN 0047-5688*

MANAGEMENT E INFORMATICA.                                XXX
*++MANAGE. & INF.*
[ANGELI]
*MILAN 12, 1970-*
PREV: CENTRI MECCANOGRAFICI ED ELETTRONICI
FROM 7, 1967- 11, 1971.
*LO/N14.*

MANAGEMENT JAPAN. IMAJ REVIEW.                           XXX
*++MANAGE. JAP.*
INTERNATIONAL MANAGEMENT ASSOCIATION OF JAPAN.
*TOKYO 1(1), MY 1967-*
Q. PREV: QUARTERLY REVIEW OF MANAGEMENT
FROM JA/MR 1964.
*DB/U-2.*
*ISSN 0025-1828*

MANAGEMENT MONOGRAPHS.
*++MANAGE. MONOGR.*
[IRISH UNIVERSITY P.]
*SHANNON NO.1, [1969]-*
*LO/N-1.*

MANAGEMENT BY OBJECTIVES.
*++MANAGE. OBJECTIVES.*
[CLASSIFIED MEDIA LTD.]
*LONDON 1(1), JL 1971-*
*ED/N-1. LO/N-6. LO/N35. OX/U-1. XS/R10.*
*ISSN 0047-5661*

MANAGEMENT OF PERSONNEL QUARTERLY.
*++MANAGE. PERSONNEL Q.*
UNIVERSITY OF MICHIGAN: BUREAU OF INDUSTRIAL
RELATIONS.
*ANN ARBOR, MICH. 1, 1961-*
*LV/U-1.*
*ISSN 0025-1852*

**MANAGEMENT IN PRINTING.**
+ +MANAGE. PRINT.
INSTITUTE OF MANAGEMENT IN PRINTING LTD.
 *LONDON 1(1), JL 1971-*
 6/A.
 CA/U-1.     ED/N-1.

**MANAGEMENT REPORTS OF THE INDUSTRIAL OPERA-
TIONS UNIT, MINISTRY OF TECHNOLOGY (G.B.).**
+ +MANAGE. REP. IND. OP. UNIT MIN. TECHNOL.
 (G.B.).
 *LONDON NO.1, 1967-*
 ED/S-1.

**MANAGEMENT SERVICES (N.H.S.).**
(GREAT BRITAIN) DEPARTMENT OF HEALTH & SOCIAL
SECURITY.
 *LONDON NO.1, 1970-*
 MONOGR.
 GL/U-1.     LO/N-1.     OX/U-8.

**MANAGEMENT SERVICES IN GOVERNMENT.**                          XXX
+ +MANAGE. SERV. GOV.
(GREAT BRITAIN) CIVIL SERVICE DEPARTMENT.                       XXX
 *LONDON 28, 1973-*
 PREV: O & M BULLETIN FROM 1, 1945- 27, 1972.
 DB/U-2.     ED/N-1.     LO/N-4     LO/N-6.     LO/N14.     LO/N35.
 LO/R-5.     OX/U16.     XS/R10.

**MANAGEMENT SKILLS.**
+ +MANAGE. SKILLS.
[NICHOLAS PAUL]
 *LONDON NO.1, 1970-*
 ED/N-1.     XS/R10.

**MANCUNIAN INDIAN.**
INDIAN ASSOCIATION OF MANCHESTER.
 *MANCHESTER 1(1), MR 1971-*
 M.
 ED/N-1.     LD/U-1.     LO/U 3.     OX/U-1.

**MANIFEST. A NEWSLETTER FOR THE ASSOCIATES OF
THE JAMES FORD BELL LIBRARY.**
UNIVERSITY OF MINNESOTA: LIBRARY.
 *MINNEAPOLIS F 1965-*
 3/A.
 LO/U-1. F 1968-
 ISSN 0542-5174

**MANIFOLD.**
UNIVERSITY OF WARWICK: MATHEMATICS INSTITUTE.
 *COVENTRY NO.1, SUMMER 1968-*
 ED/N-1.     LO/U-2.
 OX/U16. NO.4, SUMMER 1969- [W. NO.7.]

**MANITOBA ENTOMOLOGIST.**
+ +MANITOBA ENTOMOL.
ENTOMOLOGICAL SOCIETY OF MANITOBA.
 *WINNIPEG 1, 1967-*
 CA/U12.     LO/N-2.     LO/N13.

**MANNINAGH. A REVIEW OF MANX CULTURE.**
 *DOUGLAS, ISLE OF MAN NO.1, MY 1972-*
 DB/U-2.     ED/N-1.

**MANPOWER.**
(UNITED STATES) DEPARTMENT OF LABOR MANPOWER
ADMINISTRATION.
 *WASHINGTON, D.C. 1(1), JA 1969-*
 DB/U-2. 4(7), 1972-          OX/U-9. 1(2), 1969-
 ISSN 0025-2395

**MANPOWER PAPERS.**
+ +MANPOWER PAP.
(GREAT BRITAIN) DEPARTMENT OF EMPLOYMENT &
PRODUCTIVITY.
[H.M.S.O.]
 *LONDON NO.1, 1968-*
 EX/U-1.     GL/U-1.     OX/U-1.

**MANPOWER & UNEMPLOYMENT RESEARCH IN AFRICA. A
NEWSLETTER.**
+ +MANPOWER & UNEMPLOY. RES. AFR.
MCGILL UNIVERSITY: CENTRE FOR DEVELOPING-AREA
STUDIES.
 *MONTREAL 1(1), AP 1968-*
 LO/U-3.     LO/U-8.     OX/U-9.     OX/U17.
 LO/U14. 4(1), 1971-
 LO/N17. 2(1), AP 1969-
 ISSN 0025-2417

**MANTRA. MYSTICAL MAGAZINE.**
 *LONDON NO.1, S 1971-*
 Q.
 ED/N-1.     OX/U-1.

**MANUFACTURING ENGINEERING & MANAGEMENT.**          XXX
+ +MFG. ENG. & MANAGE.
SOCIETY OF MANUFACTURING ENGINEERS.
 *MILWAUKEE, WIS. 64, 1970-*
 PREV: TOOL & MANUFACTURING ENGINEER FROM 1,
 MY 1932- 63(6), 1969.
 CV/C-1.     LV/P-1.     LO/N14.     SF/U-1.
 ISSN 0040-9219

**MANUFACTURING MANAGEMENT.**                               XXX
+ +MANUF. MANAGE.
[MACLEAN-HUNTER LTD.]
 *LONDON NO.1, JA 1971- MR 1974.//*
 MON.
 ED/N-1.
 GL/U-2. 1973(1).
 LO/S-1. 1972- 73.

**MANUFACTURING OPTICIAN / INTERNATIONAL.**                 XXX
+ +MANUF. OPT. / INT. [MAOP-A]
[HATTON PRESS]
 *LONDON 1(1), OC 1947- 18, 1966...*
 *19, JL 1966-*
 TITLE EXTENDED BY ADDING 'INTERNATIONAL' FROM
 VOL.19, ALSO CALLED NEW SERIES.
 ED/N-1. 18(16), 1966-          LO/N14. 1(4), 1948-

**MANUSCRIPTA MATHEMATICA.**
+ +MANUSCRIPTA MATH.
[SPRINGER]
 *BERLIN 1(1), F 1969-*
 MAINLY IN GERMAN.
 BH/U-1.     BN/U-2.     DN/U-1.     ED/U-1.     GL/U-1.     LO/N14.
 SH/U-1.     SW/U-1.
 NW/U-1. 6, 1972-
 ISSN 0025-2611

**MANUTENTION, STOCKAGE.**                                  XXX
SUBS (1972): PART OF MTD. MANUTENTION/TRANS-
PORT/DISTRIBUTION.

**MANX LIFE.**
 *DOUGLAS, ISLE OF MAN 1, 1971-*
 ED/N-1.

**MAR Y PESCA.**
INSTITUTO NACIONAL DE LA PESCA (CUBA).
 *HAVANA NO.1, OC 1965-*
 M. S/T: LA REVISTA DEL HOMBRE DE MAR.
 LO/N13.
 ISSN 0025-2735

**MARC DOCUMENTATION SERVICE.**                             000
SEE: PUBLICATIONS, BNB MARC DOCUMENTATION
SERVICE.

**MARCH OF JAPAN'S ECONOMY.**
+ +MARCH JAP. ECON.
[ASAHI EVENING NEWS CO. LTD.]
 *TOKYO 1(1), 1967-*
 S/T: INDUSTRIAL COOPERATION FOR OVERSEAS
 DEVELOPMENT.
 LO/N17.
 ISSN 0542-660X

**MARCHE IVOIRIEN.**                                        XXX
CENTRE D'INFORMATION ET DE DOCUMENTATION
IVOIRIEN.
 *PARIS NO.1, JA 1967- 14, MR 1968.*
 MON. SUBS. INCORP. IN: REALITES IVOIRIENNES.
 LO/N17.
 LO/U14. NO.1, 1967- 14, 1968.
 ISSN 0542-6642

**MARGA.**
 *COLOMBO 1, 1971-*
 Q.
 ISSN 0047-5912

**MARGIN: QUARTERLY JOURNAL OF THE NATIONAL
COUNCIL OF APPLIED ECONOMIC RESEARCH.**
 *NEW DELHI 1(1), OC 1968-*
 LO/U-3.
 ISSN 0025-2921

**MARGINS. A REVIEW OF LITTLE MAGAZINES & SMALL
PRESS BOOKS.**
[MONDAY MORNING P.; HARPOON P.]
 *MILWAUKEE NO.1, 1972-*
 LO/U-2.     OX/U-1.

**MARINE BEHAVIOUR & PHYSIOLOGY.**
+ +MAR. BEHAV. & PHYSIOL.
[GORDON & BREACH]
 *LONDON 1(1), AP 1972-*
 BN/U-2.     CA/U-1.     ED/N-1.     LO/N13.     LO/U-2.     SW/U-1.
 RE/U-1. 2, 1973-

MARINE CHEMISTRY.
+ +MAR. CHEM.
[ELSEVIER]
AMSTERDAM 1, 1972-
LO/N-2.   LO/N14.   OX/U-8.   SO/U-1.   SW/U-1.

MARINE ENGINEER & NAVAL ARCHITECT.                    XXX
SUBS (1972): PART OF SHIPBUILDING & MARINE
ENGINEERING INTERNATIONAL.

MARINE ENGINEERS JOURNAL.                             XXX
+ +MAR. ENG. J.
INSTITUTE OF MARINE ENGINEERS.
LONDON N 1967- D 1970.
SUBS: MARINE ENGINEERS REVIEW.
XY/N-1.

MARINE ENGINEERS REVIEW.                              XXX
+ +MAR. ENG. REV.
INSTITUTE OF MARINE ENGINEERS.
[MARINE MEDIA MANAGEMENT]
LONDON JA 1971-
PREV: MARINE ENGINEERS JOURNAL FROM N 1967- D
1970.
GL/U-2.   LO/N14.   LO/U-1.   LO/U12.   OX/U-8.   SO/U-1.
LD/U-1.   JA 1972-
BR/U-1.   1, 1971- 4, 1974.
ISSN 0047-5955

MARINE FISHERIES REVIEW.                              XXX
+ +MAR. FISH. REV.
(UNITED STATES) NATIONAL MARINE FISHERIES
SERVICE.
WASHINGTON, D.C. 34(7/8), 1972-
PREV: COMMERCIAL FISHERIES REVIEW FROM 1, JA
1939- 34(5/6), 1972.
LO/N-6.   LO/N14.

MARINE GEOPHYSICAL RESEARCHES.
+ +MAR. GEOPHYS. RES.
[REIDEL PUBL. CO.]
DORDRECHT 1(1), AG 1970-
Q.   ENGL. OR FR. S/T: AN INTERNATIONAL JOURNAL
FOR THE STUDY OF THE EARTH BENEATH THE SEA.
AD/U-1.   BH/U-1.   BR/U-3.   GL/U-1.   LO/N-2.   LO/N14.
OX/U-8.   SW/U-1.
ISSN 0025-3235

MARINE INVERTEBRATES OF SCANDINAVIA.
+ +MAR. INVERTEBR. SCAND.
NORGES ALMENVITENSKAPELIGE FORSKNINGSRAAD.
OSLO NO.1, 1966-
LO/N-2.

MARINE POLLUTION BULLETIN. NS.
+ +MAR. POLLUT. BULL., NS.
[MACMILLAN (JOURNALS) LTD.]
LONDON 1(1), JA 1970-
PREV. SERIES 1968- 1969 PUBL. BY DEPT. OF
ZOOLOGY, UNIV. OF NEWCASTLE.
DN/U-1.   HL/U-1.   LO/N-2.   LO/N-4.   LO/N-7.   LO/N14.
MA/U-1.   NW/U-1.   OX/U-8.   SH/U-1.   SO/U-1.
AD/U-3.   4, 1973-              GL/U-1.   1(2), 1970-
LO/N-6.   1(2), 1970-          LO/U-4.   3, 1972-
LO/U20.   2, 1971-             XS/R10.   1(3), 1970-
EX/U-1.   2(1), JA 1971-
ISSN 0025-326X

MARINE RESOURCES BULLETIN.                            000
SEE:  ALABAMA MARINE RESOURCES BULLETIN.

MARINE SCIENCE CONTENTS TABLES.                       XXX
+ +MAR. SCI. CONT. TABL.
FOOD & AGRICULTURAL ORGANISATION (UN).
ROME 2(8), 1967-
M.  PREV:  CURRENT CONTENTS IN MARINE SCIENCES
FROM 1(1), MY 1966- 2(7), JL 1967.  ISSUED BY
THE FAO'S FISHERY RESOURCES & EXPLOITATION
DIVISION: BIOLOGICAL DATA SECTION.
GL/U-2.   LO/N-2.   LO/N13.   XS/R10.
CA/U-2.   5(7), 1970-
ISSN 0025-3308

MARINE SCIENCE PAPERS.                                XXX
+ +MAR. SCI. PAP.
(CANADA) DEPARTMENT OF THE ENVIRONMENT: MARINE
SCIENCES BRANCH.
OTTAWA NO.2, 1971-
PREV: PAPERS, MARINE SCIENCES BRANCH, DEPART-
MENT OF ENERGY, MINES & RESOURCES (CANADA)
FROM NO.1, 1971.
LO/N-2.
GL/U-1.   3, 1971-

MARINE SCIENCES.                                      000
SEE:  KAIYO KAGAKU.

MARINE TECHNOLOGY (DUSSELDORF).                       000
SEE: MEERESTECHNIK.

MARITIME HISTORY.
+ +MARIT. HIST.
[DAVID & CHARLES]
NEWTON ABBOT, DEVON 1(1), AP 1971-
AD/U-1.   ED/N-1.   EX/U-1.   LD/U-1.   LO/N-1.   LO/N-4.
LO/U-2.   LO/U19.   OX/U-1.   OX/U17.   SO/U-1.
XY/N-1.

MARITIME MONOGRAPHS & REPORTS.
+ +MARIT. MONOGR. & REP.
NATIONAL MARITIME MUSEUM (G.B.).
LONDON NO.1, 1970-
LO/N-1.

MARITIME STUDIES & MANAGEMENT.
+ +MARIT. STUD. & MANAGE.
[SCIENTECHNICA]
BRISTOL 1(1), JL 1973-
Q.
AD/U-1.   CA/U-1.   ED/N-1.   LO/N-1.   OX/U-1.   SO/U-1.
ISSN 0306-1957

MARKET RESEARCH IN BENELUX.
+ +MARK. RES. BENELUX.
[ERC MARKET RESEARCH PUBL. LTD.]
LONDON 1(1), 1971-
ED/N-1.
ISSN 0047-598X

MARKET RESEARCH IN GERMANY.
+ +MARK. RES. GER.
[ERC MARKET RESEARCH PUBL. LTD.]
LONDON 1(1), JA 1971-
ED/N-1.
ISSN 0047-5998

MARKET RESEARCH IN ITALY.
+ +MARK. RES. ITALY.
[ERC MARKET RESEARCH PUBL. LTD.]
LONDON 1(1), JA 1971-
ED/N-1.
ISSN 0047-6005

MARKETING REPORT, DEPARTMENT OF AGRICULTURAL
ECONOMICS, UNIVERSITY OF LEEDS.
+ +MARKET. REP. DEP. AGR. ECON. UNIV. LEEDS.
LEEDS 1, 1968-
CA/U11.

MARKETING WORLD. OFFICIAL JOURNAL OF THE ...
+ +MARKET. WORLD.
MARKETING SOCIETY.
OXFORD 1(1),JL 1969- 1(5), 1970. //
DB/U-2.   ED/N-1.   GL/U-2.   GL/U-3.   OX/U-1.
ISSN 0025-3812

MARSHALL MCLUHAN DEW-LINE NEWSLETTER.
+ +MARSHALL MCLUHAN DEW-LINE NEWSL.
[FIRST RUN LTD]
LONDON 1(1), MY 1969-
M.
ED/N-1.   OX/U-1.   SO/U-1.

MARXISMUS DIGEST.
+ +MARXISMUS DIG.
INSTITUT FUR MARXISTISCHE STUDIEN UND FORSCH-
UNGEN (FRANKFURT/MAIN).
FRANKFURT/MAIN 1, 1970-
S/T: THEORETISCHE BEITRAGE AUS MARXISTISCHEN
UND ANTIIMPERIALISTISCHEN ZEITSCHRIFTEN.
DB/U-2.   LO/U-3.
OX/U-1.   4, 1971-

MARXIST STUDIES NEWSLETTER.
+ +MARXIST STUD. NEWSL.
[B.M.S. PUBL.]
LONDON NO.1, AP 1970-
ED/N-1.   OX/U-1.

MARXISTISK KRITIK.
COPENHAGEN 1(1), 1968-
LO/N-1.
ISSN 0542-7819

MASHINOSTROENIE.                                      XXX
(BULGARIA) MINISTERSTVO NA TEZHKATA PROMISH-
LENOST.
SOFIA 1(9), 1960-
ENGL., GER. & RUSS. SUMM. & CONT. LISTS.
BODY VARIES.  PREV: TEZHKA PROMISHLENOST FROM
1, 1952- 8, 1959.
LO/N13.
BH/U-1.   1964-
ISSN 0025-455X

**MASHINOSTROENIE. INFORMATSIONNYJ NAUCHNO-TEKHN-ICHESKIJ SBORNIK.**　　　　xxx
DERZHAVNYJ KOMITET PO KOORDYNATSIJI NAUKOVO-
DOSLIDNYKH ROBIT: INSTYTUT TEKHNICHNOJI
INFORMATSIJI.
　KIEV 1, JA/F 1962- 1965...
　SUBS: TEKHNOLOGIJA I ORGANIZATSIJA PROIZVOD-
STVA.
　LO/N13.

**MASOWE BADANIA STATYSTYCZNE.**　　　　xxx
＋＋MASOWE BADANIA STAT.
(POLAND) GLOWNY URZAD STATYSTYCZNY.
　WARSAW NO.38, 1968-
　PREV: PART OF STATYSTYKA POLSKI: SPISY LUDNO-
SCI FROM NR. 1, 1967- 19, 1968; & STATYSTYKA
POLSKI: SPISY MIESZKAN I BUDYNKOW FROM NR. 1,
1967- 18, 1968. CONT. THE COMBINED NUMBERS OF
BOTH SERIES.
　BH/U-1.　LO/U-3.

**MASQUE.**
　LEICESTER 1(1), [1969]-
　NOTE IN 1(1), PROD. BY SIXTH-FORMERS OF LEIC-
ESTER CITY GRAMMAR SCHOOLS.
　LO/U-2.

**MASS SPECTROMETRY.**
＋＋MASS SPECTROM.
CHEMICAL SOCIETY.
　LONDON 1, 1971-
　S/T: A SPECIALIST PERIODICAL REPORT.
　BH/U-3.　GL/U-2.　LO/N14.　LO/S-3.　LO/U-2.　LO/U12.
　LO/U13.　NW/U-1.　SO/U-1.
　ISSN 0305-9987

**MASS WORKING PAPERS.**
BIRMINGHAM LIBRARIES CO-OPERATIVE MECHANISATION
PROJECT.
　BIRMINGHAM NO.1, 1970-
　SPONS. BODY ALSO LOUGHBOROUGH UNIVERSITY OF
TECHNOLOGY LIBRARY.
　LO/N14.

**MASSACHUSETTS STUDIES IN ENGLISH.**
＋＋MASS. STUD. ENGL.
UNIVERSITY OF MASSACHUSETTS: GRADUATE ENGLISH
PROGRAM.
　AMHERST, MASS. 1(1), SPRING 1967-
　LO/N-1.
　LO/U-1. 2(2), 1969-
　ISSN 0047-6161

**MASTER BUILDER (1971).**　　　　xxx
＋＋MASTER BUILD.
FEDERATION OF MASTER BUILDERS.
　LONDON 16, 1971-
　PREV: MASTER BUILDERS' JOURNAL FROM 1, 1955-
15, 1970.
　BL/U-1.　ED/N-1.
　LO/N13. 17, 1972-

**MASTER BUILDERS' JOURNAL.**　　　　xxx
　SUBS (1971): MASTER BUILDER (1971).

**MASTERA POETICHESKOGO PEREVODA.**
　MOSCOW VYP.1, 1963-
　BH/U-1.　CC/U-1.

**MASTERSTVO OCHERKISTA.**
KAZANSKIJ GOSUDARSTVENNYJ UNIVERSITET.
　KAZAN 1, 1970-
　GL/U-1.　MA/U-1.　NO/U-1.

**MATEKON.**　　　　xxx
[INTERNATIONAL ARTS & SCIENCES P.]
　WHITE PLAINS, N.Y. 6, 1970-
　PREV: MATHEMATICAL STUDIES IN ECONOMICS &
STATISTICS IN THE U.S.S.R. & EASTERN EUROPE
FROM 1, 1964- 5, 1970.
　HL/U-1.　LO/N13.　OX/U-1.　RE/U-1.
　SW/U-1. 6, 1970- 10(2), 1974.
　ISSN 0025-1127

**MATEMATECESKII SBORNIK: NS (ENGL. TRANSL.).**
　SEE: MATHEMATICS OF THE U.S.S.R. - SBORNIK.

**MATEMATICHESKIE ISSLEDOVANIJA.**
＋＋MAT. ISSLED. (AKAD. NAUK MOLD. SSR).
AKADEMIJA NAUK MOLDAVSKOJ SSR: INSTITUT
MATEMATIKI.
　KISHINEV 1(1), 1966-
　ISSUED BY 'INSTITUT MATEMATIKI S VYCHIS-
LITEL'NYM TSENTROM AN MSSR'.
　CA/U-2.　DB/S-1.
　GL/U-1. 1(1), 1966- 2(2), 1967.

**MATEMATICHESKIE METODY V EKONOMIKE.**
＋＋MAT. METOD. EKON.
LATVIJAS PSR ZINATNU AKADEMIJA: INSTITUT
EKONOMIKI.
　RIGA VYP.1, 1967-
　LO/U-3.　OX/U-1.
　LO/N-3. 4, 1969-

**MATEMATICHESKIE ZAMETKI.**
＋＋MAT. ZAMETKI.
AKADEMIJA NAUK SSSR: OTDELENIE MATEMATIKI.
　MOSCOW 1(1), 1967-
　M.
　CA/U-2.　LO/N14.　SH/U-1.
　LO/U-4. 1(5), 1967-　　　　OX/U-8. 1968-
　SW/U-1. 1(2), 1967-
　LO/U12. 11(1), 1972-

**MATEMATICHESKIE ZAMETKI (ENGL. TRANSL.).**　　　　000
　SEE: MATHEMATICAL NOTES.

**MATEMATICKO-FYZIKALNY CASOPIS.**　　　　xxx
　SUBS (1967) IN TWO SECTIONS: FYZIKALNY CASOPIS
　& MATEMATICKY CASOPIS.

**MATEMATICKY CASOPIS.**　　　　xxx
＋＋MAT. CAS.
SLOVENSKA AKADEMIA VIED.
　BRATISLAVA 17, 1967-
　VARIOUS LANGUAGES. PREV. PART OF MATEMATICKO-
FYZIKALNY CASOPIS FROM 1, 1951- 16, 1966...
　DB/S-1.　LD/U-1.　LO/N14.
　ISSN 0025-5173

**MATERIAL, NATIONAL PEARL RESEARCH LABORATORY
(JAPAN).**　　　　000
　SEE: KOKURITSU SHINJU KENKYUJO SHIRYO.

**MATERIAL UND ORGANISMEN. MATERIALS & ORGANISMS.
MATERIAUX ET ORGANISMES.**
＋＋MATER. & ORG.
[DUNCKER & HUMBLOT]
　BERLIN 1, 1965-
　ENGL. & GER. WITH ENGL., FR., GER. & SPAN.
SUMM.
　LO/N-2.　LO/N14.
　OX/U-8. 3(3), 1968-
　ISSN 0025-5270

**MATERIAL'NAJA KUL'TURA TADZHIKISTANA.**
＋＋MATER. KUL'T. TADZH.
AKADEMIJA NAUK TADZHIKSKOJ SSR: INSTITUT
ISTORII.
　DUSHANBE VYP.1, 1968-
　CA/U-1.　LO/N-3.　LO/S10.　LO/U14.　OX/U-1.

**MATERIAL'NAJA KUL'TURA USTRUSHANY.**
＋＋MATER. KUL'T. USTRUSHANY.
AKADEMIJA NAUK TADZHIKSKOJ SSR: INSTITUT
ISTORII.
　DUSHANBE VYP.1, 1966-
　MONOGR.
　LO/N-3.

**MATERIAL'NO-TEKHNICHESKOE SNABZHENIE.**
＋＋MATER.-TEKH. SNABZH.
GOSUDARSTVENNYJ KOMITET SOVETA MINISTROV SSSR
PO MATERIAL'NO-TEKHNICHESKOMU SNABZHENIJU.
　MOSCOW 1(1), 1966-
　M.
　BH/U-1.　LO/N14.

**MATERIALS APPLICATION NEWS FOR DESIGN & MANU-
FACTURING.**
＋＋MATER. APPL. NEWS DES. MANUF.
AMERICAN SOCIETY FOR METALS.
　MOUNT MORRIS, ILL. 1(1), JA/F 1967-
　XS/R10. 1(3), MY/JE 1967-

**MATERIALS ENGINEERING.**
＋＋MATER. ENG.
[REINHOLD]
　NEW YORK 65(4), AP 1967-
　PREV: METALS & ALLOYS FROM 1(1), 1929- 22(3),
1945; THEN MATERIALS AND METHODS FROM 22(4),
1946- 45, 1957; THEN MATERIALS IN DESIGN
ENGINEERING FROM 46(1), 1957- 65(3), 1967.
　LO/N14.　XS/R10.
　ISSN 0025-5319

MATERIALS HANDLING & MANAGEMENT.
INSTITUTE OF MATERIALS HANDLING.
[TEMPRINT P.]
 LONDON JA 1968-
 SPONS. BODY ALSO: ASSOCIATION OF STORES &
 MATERIALS CONTROLLERS. PREV: JOURNAL, INSTI-
 TUTE OF MATERIALS HANDLING FROM 1(1), MY 1958-
 7(4), OC 1967.
 LO/N14.    OX/U-1.

MATERIALS INFORMATION JAPAN.
+ +MATER. INF. JAP.
JRDI LABORATORY.
 TOKYO 1, F 1969-
 M. PRELIM. ISSUE NUMBERED 1, 1968.
 LO/N14.

MATERIALS & PROCESS TECHNOLOGY.                              000
 SEE: SAMPE JOURNAL.

MATERIALS PROTECTION & PERFORMANCE.*                         XXX
+ +MATER. PROT. & PERFORM.
NATIONAL ASSOCIATION OF CORROSION ENGINEERS.
 HOUSTON, TEX.  1, JA 1962-
 TITLE EXPANDED FROM MATERIALS PROTECTION WITH
 9(7), 1970.
 BH/P-1.    BH/U-1.    CV/F-1.    GL/U-1.    LO/F-1.    LO/F-9.
 LO/N-4.    LO/N-7.    LO/N14.    LO/S-3.    LO/T-1.    SH/U-3.
 SW/U-1.    XE/F-4.    XS/R10.    XY/N-1.    ZS/F-1.    ZS/T-1.
 CV/C-1.  2,1963-                  GL/U-2.
 LC/U-1.  2,1963-

MATERIALS & STRUCTURES: TESTING & RESEARCH. =
MATERIAUX ET CONSTRUCTIONS: ESSAIS ET RE-
CHERCHES.
+ +MATER. & STRUCT., TEST. & RES.
INTERNATIONAL ASSOCIATION OF TESTING &
RESEARCH LABORATORIES FOR MATERIALS &
STRUCTURES.
 PARIS  1(1), 1968-
 ENGL. & FR.  BODY IN FR: REUNION INTERNATIO-
 NALE DES LABORATOIRES D'ESSAIS ET DE RE-
 CHERCHES SUR LES MATERIAUX ET LES CONSTRUC-
 TIONS (RILEM).  ENGL. NAME ORIG: INTERNATIO-
 NAL UNION OF TESTING ...  CONTAINS AS SUPPL:
 RILEM BULLETIN. = BULLETIN DE LA RILEM.
 GL/U-2.    LO/N-4.    LO/N14.    MA/U-1.
 ISSN 0025-5432

MATERIALY DO DZIEJOW KOSCIOLA W POLSCE.                      000
 SEE:  MATERIALY ZRODLOWE DO DZIEJOW KOSCIOLA
 W POLSCE.

MATERIALY K FAUNE GRUZII.
+ +MATER. FAUNE GRUZ.  [MAFG-B]
AKADEMIJA NAUK GRUZINSKOJ SSR: INSTITUT
ZOOLOGII.
 TIFLIS  1, 1966-
 LO/N-2.
 ISSN 0543-0534

MATERIALY GLIATSIOLOGICHESKIKH ISSLEDOVANIJ.
[VARIOUS SUBSERIES].
 AKADEMIJA NAUK SSSR: INSTITUT GEOGRAFII.
 MOSCOW 1960-
 CA/U12.    XY/N-1.

MATERIALY PO GEOLOGII TJAN'-SHANJA.
+ +MATER. GEOL. TJAN'-SHANJA.
AKADEMIJA NAUK KIRGIZSKOJ SSR: INSTITUT
GEOLOGII.
 FRUNZE  VYP.1, 1961-
 LO/N13.
 LO/N-2.  4, 1964-

MATERIALY STAROZYTNE.                                        XXX
 SUBS (1971): PART OF MATERIALY STAROZYTNE I
 WCZESNOSREDNIOWIECZNE.

MATERIALY STAROZYTNE I WCZESNOSREDNIOWIECZNE.                XXX
+ +MATER. STAROZYTNE & WCZESNOSREDNICWIECZNE.
PANSTWOWE MUZEUM ARCHEOLOGICZNE.
 WROCLAW &C.  1, 1971-
 INCORP: MATERIALY STAROZYTNE FROM 1, 1956- 11,
 1968; & MATERIALY WCZESNOSREDNIOWIECZNE FROM
 1, 1949- 6, 1969.
 DB/S-1.    LO/U17.    SH/U-1.

MATERIALY I STUDIA DO HISTORII PRASY I
CZASOPISMIENNICTWA POLSKIEGO.
+ +MATER. & STUD. HIST. PRASY & CZAS. POL.
POLSKA AKADEMIA NAUK: PRACOWNIA HISTORII
CZASOPISMIENNICTWA POLSKIEGO XIX I XX WIEKU.
 WARSAW  ZESZYT 2, N 1965-
 MONOGR. ZESZYT 1 PUBL. MR 1966.
 LO/N-3*.    LO/U-3.    OX/U-1.

MATERIALY I STUDIA, KATEDRA HISTORII POW-
SZECHNEJ I STOSUNKOW MIEDZYNARODOWYCH, WYZSZA
SZKOLA NAUK SPOLECZNYCH.
+ +MATER. STUD. KATEDRA HIST. POWSZECHNEJ STOSUN-
 KOW MIEDZYNAR. WYZSZ. SZK. NAUK SPOLECZ.
 WARSAW  TOM 1, D 1960-
 ENGL. & RUSS. SUMM.
 LO/U-3.

MATERIALY I STUDIA, MIEDZYUCZELNIANY ZAKLAD
PODSTAWOWYCH PROBLEMOW ARCHITEKTURY, URBANIS-
TYKI I BUDOWNICTWA, MINISTERSTWO SZKOLNICTWA
WYZSZEGO:  SERIA 1: ZAGADNIENIA LUDNOSCIOWE.
 (POLAND) MINISTERSTWO SZKOLNICTWA WYZSZEGO:
 MIEDZYUCZELNIANY ZAKLAD PODSTAWOWYCH PROBLEMOW
 ARCHITEKTURY, URBANISTYKI I BUDOWNICTWA.
 WARSAW  ZESZYT 1, 1965-
 LO/U-3.

MATERIALY I STUDIA, MIEDZYUCZELNIANY ZAKLAD
PODSTAWOWYCH PROBLEMOW ARCHITEKTURY, URBANIS-
TYKI I BUDOWNICTWA, MINISTERSTWO SZKONICTWA
WYZSZEGO:  SERIA 4: ZAGADNIENIA SPOLECZNO-
GOSPODARCZE W KSZALTOWANIU PRZESTRZENNYM.
 WARSAW  ZESZYT 1, N 1963-
 MONOGR. SER.
 LO/N-3.    LO/U-3.

MATERIALY I STUDIA, MIEDZYUCZELNIANY ZAKLAD
PODSTAWOWYCH PROBLEMOW ARCHITEKTURY, URBANIS-
TYKI I BUDOWNICTWA, MINISTERSTWO SZKOLNICTWA
WYZSZEGO: SERIA 6: ZAGADNIENIA TEORII
ARCHITEKTURY.
 (POLAND) MINISTERSTWO SZKOLNICTWA WYZSZEGO:
 MIEDZYUCZELNIANY ZAKLAD PODSTAWOWYCH PROBLEMOW
 ARCHITEKTURY, URBANISTYKI I BUDOWNICTWA.
 WARSAW  ZESZYT 1, 1964-
 MONOGR. ZESZYT 1 PUBL. AS:  MATERIALY I
 STUDIA ...:  SERIA TEORII ARCHITEKTURY.
 LO/N-3.

MATERIALY I STUDIA Z NAJNOWSZEJ HISTORII
POLSKI.
+ +MATER. & STUD. NAJNOWSZEJ HIST. POL.
WYZSZA SZKOLA NAUK SPOLECZNYCH PRZY KC PZPR:
KATEDRA HISTORII POLSKI.
 WARSAW  1, 1963-
 BH/U-1.    CA/U-1.    OX/U-1.

MATERIALY WCZESNOSREDNIOWIECZNE.                             XXX
 SUBS (1971): PART OF MATERIALY STAROZYTNE I
 WCZESNOSREDNIOWIECZNE.

MATERIALY ZRODLOWE DO DZIEJOW KOSCIOLA W
POLSCE.
+ +MATER. ZRODLOWE DZIEJOW KOSCIOLA POL.
TOWARZYSTWO NAUKOWE KATOLICKIEGO UNIWERSYTETU
LUBELSKIEGO: INSTYTUT GEOGRAFII HISTORYCZNEJ
KOSCIOLA W POLSCE.
 LUBLIN  TOM 1, 1965-
 MONOGR.  TITLE ON COVER:  MATERIALY DO DZIEJOW
 KOSCIOLA W POLSCE.
 CA/U-1.    LO/N-3.
 ISSN 0076-5244

MATERIAUX ET CONSTRUCTIONS: ESSAIS ET RE-
CHERCHES.                                                    000
 SEE: MATERIALS & STRUCTURES: TESTING &
 RESEARCH.

MATERIAUX ET TECHNIQUES.                                     XXX
+ +MATER. & TECH. (FR.).
[DUNOD]
 PARIS  58, 1970-
 PREV: PRATIQUE DES INDUSTRIES MECANIQUES FROM
 6(8), 1923- 57, 1969.
 LO/N14.
 ISSN 0032-6895

MATERIELS NOUVEAUX ET TECHNIQUES MONDIALES.                  XXX
+ +MATER. NOUV. & TECH. MOND.
 PARIS  NO.189, 1971-
 PREV: REVUE FRANCAISE DES TECHNIQUES
 MONDIALES FROM NO.150, 1967- 188, 1970.
 LO/N13.

MATERNAL & CHILD CARE.
+ +MATERN. & CHILD CARE.
[BOUVERIE PUBL. CO. LTD.]
 LONDON  1, MY 1965-
 M.
 LO/M10.    LO/S18.    XY/N-1.
 CA/U-1.  3(21), 1967-           OX/U-1.  3, 1967-
 ISSN 0025-5475

**MATHEMATICA BALKANICA.**
+ +MATH. BALK.
UNION BALKANIQUE DES MATHEMATICIENS.
*BELGRADE 1, 1971-*
*CA/U-2.    DB/S-1.    GL/U-1.    LO/N-4.    LO/N-4.    LO/N14.*
*LO/U-2.*

**MATHEMATICAL ALGORITHMS.**
+ +MATH. ALGOR.
[MIT PRESS]
*CAMBRIDGE, MASS.  1(1), JA 1966-*
Q.  1(1) CALLED 'PRELIMINARY ISSUE'.
*LO/N14.*
ISSN 0025-5548

**MATHEMATICAL BIOSCIENCES: SUPPLEMENT.**
+ +MATH. BIOSCI., SUPPL.
¡AMERICAN ELSEVIER]
*NEW YORK NO.1, 1969-*
*GL/U-1.    LO/N14.*

**MATHEMATICAL CHRONICLE.**
+ +MATH. CHRON.
UNIVERSITY OF AUCKLAND: DEPARTMENT OF MATHEM-
ATICS.
*AUCKLAND  1(1), N 1969-*
*LO/N13.    OX/U-1.    OX/U-8.    SW/U-1.    SW/U-1.*
*XY/N-1.*
ISSN 0581-1155

**MATHEMATICAL NOTES.**
+ +MATH. NOTES.
[CONSULTANTS BUREAU]
*NEW YORK 1(1/2), 1967(1968)-*
M.  TRANSL. OF MATEMATICHESKIE ZAMETKI.
*CR/U-1.    OX/U-8.    RE/U-1.*
ISSN 0001-4346

**MATHEMATICAL PROGRAMMING.**
+ +MATH. PROGRAM.
[NORTH HOLLAND]
*AMSTERDAM  1(1), OC 1971-*
2M.
*DN/U-1.    GL/U-2.    LD/U-1.    LO/N14.    LO/U-3.    LO/U28.*
*OX/U-8.    SH/U-1.    XS/R10.*
*BL/U-1. 6, 1974-              MA/U-1. 2, 1972-*
ISSN 0025-5610

**MATHEMATICAL SPECTRUM.**
+ +MATH. SPECTRUM.
[OXFORD UNIV. PRESS]
*LONDON  1(1), 1968-*
2/A.
*BL/U-1.    BN/U-2.    LO/N-5.    LO/N14.    MA/U-1.    SW/U-1.*
*XS/R10.*
*BR/U-1. 4, 1971/1972-*
*SH/U-3. 3, 1970/1971-*

**MATHEMATICS REPORT, DEPARTMENT OF MATHEMATICS,
WESTERN MICHIGAN UNIVERSITY.**
+ +MATH. REP. DEP. MATH. WEST. MICH. UNIV.
*KALAMAZOO NO.1, 1968-*
*LO/N14.\**

**MATHEMATICS IN SCHOOL.**
+ +MATH. SCH.
MATHEMATICAL ASSOCIATION.
*LONDON  1, N 1971-*
*BN/U-1.    CA/U-1.    ED/N-1.*

**MATHEMATICS OF THE USSR - IZVESTIJA.**
+ +MATH. USSR. - IZV.
AMERICAN MATHEMATICAL SOCIETY.
*PROVIDENCE, R.I.  1(1), JA/F 1967-*
TRANSL. OF IZVESTIJA AKADEMII NAUK SSSR:
SERIJA MATEMATICHESKAJA FROM 31(1).
*LO/N-4.    LO/N14.    LO/U11.    NW/U-1.    OX/U-8.*
*AD/U-1. 3, 1969-*
ISSN 0025-5726

**MATHEMATICS OF THE USSR - SBORNIK.**
+ +MATH. USSR - SB. [MUSI-A]
AMERICAN MATHEMATICAL SOCIETY.
*PROVIDENCE, R.I.  1(1), 1967(1968)-*
ENGL. TRANSL. OF MATEMATECESKII SBORNIK: NS.
*HL/U-1.    LO/N-4.    LO/U11.    NW/U-1.*
ISSN 0025-5734

**MATHEMATIK UND WIRTSCHAFT.**
+ +MATH. & WIRT.
[VERLAG DIE WIRTSCHAFT]
*BERLIN 1, 1963-*
ANNU.
*LO/U-3. 3, 1966-*
ISSN 0543-1034

**MATHEMATISCHE OPERATIONSFORSCHUNG UND STATISTIK.**
+ +MATH. OPER. & STAT.
[AKADEMIE-VERLAG]
*BERLIN  1, 1970-*
*LO/N14.*
ISSN 0047-6277

**MATRIX.**                                                    XXX
*BOOTLE, LANCS. [NO.]1, 1967- 2, 1967 ...*
SUBS: ASYLUM.
*LO/U-2.*

**MATRUSRI.**
*BAPATLA  1(1), 1966-*
M.
*LO/N-1. 4(2), 1969-*

**MATSUE KOGYO KOTO SENMON GAKKO KENKYU KIYO.
RESEARCH REPORTS OF MATSUE TECHNICAL COLLEGE.**
MATSUE KOGYO KOTO SENMON GAKKO.
*MATSUE NO.1, 1966-*
JAP. OR ENGL.
*LO/N13.*

**MATSUSHITA DENKO GIHO.  MATSUSHITA ELECTRIC
WORKS TECHNICAL REPORT.**
*OSAKA NO.1, 1970-*
ENGL. SUMM.
*LO/N13.*

**MATSUSHITA ELECTRIC WORKS TECHNICAL REPORT.**        000
SEE:  MATSUSHITA DENKO GIHO.

**MATTHEWS WRIGHTSON REVIEW.**
MATTHEWS WRIGHTSON GROUP OF COMPANIES.
*LONDON NO.1, 1969-*
*LO/N14.*

**MAWAQIF; LI'L HURRIYAH WA'L IBDA' WA'L
TAGHIR.**
*BEIRUT 1(1), 1968-*
M.
*LO/U14.*

**MAWAZO.**
MAKERERE UNIVERSITY COLLEGE: FACULTIES OF ARTS
& SOCIAL SCIENCES.
*KAMPALA  1(1), JE 1967-*
*BH/U-1.    BL/U-1.    LO/N17.    LO/S26.    LO/U-8.    MA/U-1.*
*RE/U-1.*
*CB/U-1. 2, 1969-*
*LO/U-1. 1(1), JE 1967- [W. 1(4).]*
ISSN 0047-6293

**MAYNE STREET.**
[MAYNE STREET POETS]
*STOKE-ON-TRENT 1, MY 1969-*
*ED/N-1.    OX/U-1.*

**MAZUNGUMZO.  STUDENT JOURNAL OF AFRICAN
STUDIES.**
MICHIGAN STATE UNIVERSITY: AFRICAN STUDIES
CENTER.
*EAST LANSING  1, FALL 1970-*
*LD/U-1.*
ISSN 0047-6307

**MBA.  MASTERS IN BUSINESS ADMINISTRATION.**
[MBA ENTERP. INC.]
*CAMBRIDGE, MASS.  1, 1966-*
M.  S/T: THE MAGAZINE OF MANAGEMENT EDUCATION
FOR THE MASTERS IN BUSINESS ADMINISTRATION.
*MA/U-4. MR 1969-*
ISSN 0024-7952

**MCZ NEWSLETTER.**
+ +MCZ NEWSL.
HARVARD UNIVERSITY: MUSEUM OF COMPARATIVE
ZOOLOGY.
*CAMBRIDGE, MASS.  1, 1971-*
*LO/N-2.    LO/N13.*

**MEASUREMENT & INSTRUMENT REVIEW.**                    XXX
SUBS (1969) PART OF: CONTROL & INSTRUMENTATION

**MEASURING TOOLS.**                                    XXX
+ +MEAS. TOOLS.
[INDUSTRIAL REVIEWS LTD.]
*WINCHESTER NO.1, MY 1968- 13, MY/JE 1969.*
SUBS. PART OF: PRECISION TOOLS. S/T: METROLOGY
APPLIED TO MANUFACTURING.
*ED/N-1.    LO/N14.    OX/U-8.*

**MEAT (DULUTH, MINN.).**                               XXX
SUBS (1970): MEAT MANAGEMENT.

**MEAT MANAGEMENT.** XXX
++MEAT MANAGE.
[HARBRACE PUBL.]
DULUTH, MINN. 36(5), 1970- 37(5), 1971.//
PREV: MEAT (DULUTH, MINN.) FROM
1, 1934- 36(4), 1970.
LO/N13.

**MEAT SCIENCE REVIEW.**
++MEAT SCI. REV.
AMERICAN MEAT INSTITUTE FOUNDATION.
CHICAGO 1, 1967-
XY/N-1.**

**MEAT TRADER.**
NATIONAL FEDERATION OF MEAT TRADERS'
ASSOCIATIONS (GB).
WATFORD NO.1, 1966-
M.
OX/U-1.

**MEAT & WOOL.** XXX
[HEREFORD PRINT. CO.]
WELLINGTON, N.Z. 1, 1892- 197(2), 1970.//
LO/N13. 163, 1962-

**MECANIQUE - MATERIAUX ELECTRICITE.** XXX
++MEC. - MATER. ELECTR. (FR.).
[EDITIONS SCIENCE ET INDUSTRIE]
PARIS 53(233), 1970-
PREV: MECANIQUE - ELECTRICITE FROM 44(130),
1960.
LO/N14.
ISSN 0025-6439

**MECANIQUE DES ROCHES.** 000
SEE: ROCK MECHANICS.

**MECHANICAL ENGINEERING NEWS.**
++MECH. ENG. NEWS.
INSTITUTION OF MECHANICAL ENGINEERS.
LONDON NO.1, 1973-
BL/U-1. CA/U-1. ED/N-1. OX/U-8. SO/U-1. SW/U-1.
LO/N14. [CURRENT YEAR ONLY]

**MECHANICAL ENGINEERING SCIENCE.** XXX
++MECH. ENG. SCI. (GB).
INSTITUTION OF MECHANICAL ENGINEERS.
LONDON MONOGRAPH NO.1, 1965- NO.6, 1967. //
ED/N-1. GL/U-1. LO/N-4. LO/N14. LO/U-6. SO/U-1.

**MECHANISED ACCOUNTING & COMPUTER MANAGEMENT.** XXX
++MECH. ACC. & COMPUT. MANAGE.
[SPECIAL INTEREST PUBL. LTD.]
LONDON 1, 1966- 4, 1969...
SUBS: COMPUTER MANAGEMENT.
ED/N-1. 1(2), 1966- GL/U-3. 2(2), 1967-
LO/N14. 2, 1966-

**MECHANISM & MACHINE THEORY.** XXX
++MECH. & MACH. THEORY.
[PERGAMON]
OXFORD &C. 7, 1972-
PREV: JOURNAL OF MECHANISMS FROM 1, 1966- 6,
1971.
ED/N-1. LO/N14.
GL/U-2. 9, 1974- NW/U-1. 7, 1972-

**MECHANISMS OF AGEING & DEVELOPMENT.**
++MECH. AGE & DEV.
[ELSEVIER SEQUOIA]
LAUSANNE 1(1), 1972-
2/M.
AD/U-1. CA/U-2. LD/U-1. LO/U-2. MA/U-1. OX/U-8.
SH/U-1.
ISSN 0047-6374

**MECHANISMS OF MOLECULAR MIGRATIONS.**
++MECH. MOL. MIGRAT.
[INTERSCIENCE PUBL.]
NEW YORK 1, 1968-
LO/S-3. XS/C-2.

**MECHANISMS OF REACTIONS OF SULFUR COMPOUNDS.**
++MECH. REACT. SULFUR COMPOUNDS.
INTRA-SCIENCE RESEARCH FOUNDATION.
SANTA MONICA, CALIF. 1, 1966 (1967)- 5, 1970.
SUBS: INTERNATIONAL JOURNAL OF SULFUR CHEMI-
STRY: PART C: MECHANISMS OF REACTIONS OF
SULFUR COMPOUNDS.
LO/N14. LO/S-3.

**MECMAN TECHNIQUES.**
++MECMAN TECH.
MECMAN LTD.
READING NO.1, 1967-
LO/R-6.

**MEDDELANDEN, HISTORISKA INSTITUTIONEN, GOTEB-
ORGS UNIVERSITET.**
++MEDD. HIST. INST. GOTEBORGS UNIV.
GOTEBORGS NO.1, 1969-
BL/U-1. LO/U-2. OX/U-1.
LO/N-1. NO.5, 1972-

**MEDEDELINGEN VAN DE DIRECTIE TUINBOUW.** XXX
SUBS (1970): BEDRIJFSONTWIKKELING. EDITIE
TUINBOUW.

**MEDEDELINGEN VAN DE HYDROBIOLOGISCHE
VERENIGING.** XXX
++MEDED. HYDROBIOL. VER.
AMSTERDAM 1, 1967- 6, 1972.
SUBS: HYDROBIOLOGICAL BULLETIN.
LO/N-2.

**MEDEDELINGEN, WERKGROEP VOOR TERTIAIRE EN
KWARTAIRE GEOLOGIE.**
++MEDED. WERKGROEP TERTIAIRE & KWARTAIRE GEOL.
ROTTERDAM 1, 1964-
LO/N-2.

**MEDIEVAL INDIA.** XXX
ALIGARH MUSLIM UNIVERSITY: DEPARTMENT OF
HISTORY.
[ASIA PUBL. HOUSE]
LONDON 1, 1969-
S/T: A MISCELLANY. PREV: MEDIEVAL INDIA
QUARTERLY FROM 1, JL 1950.
LO/N-1. OX/U-1.
ISSN 0076-6119

**MEDIEVAL INDIA QUARTERLY.** XXX
SUBS (1969): MEDIEVAL INDIA.

**MEDIEVAL IRISH HISTORY SERIES.**
++MEDIEVAL IR. HIST. SER.
DUBLIN HISTORICAL ASSOCIATION.
DUNDALK 1, 1964-
GL/U-1.
ISSN 0543-324X

**MEDIAEVAL MANUSCRIPTS FROM THE LOW COUNTRIES IN
FACSIMILE.**
++MEDIAEVAL MANUSCR. LOW CTRIES. FACSIMILE.
[ROSENKILDE & BAGGER]
COPENHAGEN 1, 1971-
OX/U-1.

**MEDIAEVAL SCANDINAVIA.**
++MEDIAEV. SCAND.
[ODENSE UNIV. P.]
ODENSE 1, 1968-
S/T: A JOURNAL DEVOTED TO THE STUDY OF
MEDIAEVAL CIVILIZATION IN SCANDANAVIA AND
ICELAND.
DB/S-1. DB/U-2. ED/N-1. EX/U-1. HL/U-1. LO/N-1.
LO/U-4. LO/U12. LO/U13. OX/U-1. SO/U-1.
SW/U-1.

**MEDIEVALIA ET HUMANISTA: NS.**
CASE WESTERN RESERVE UNIVERSITY.
CLEVELAND NO.1, 1970-
PREV. SER. FROM 1, 1943- 17, 1966. S/T:
STUDIES IN MEDIEVAL & RENAISSANCE CULTURE.
EX/U-1. LO/U19.

**MEDICAL BEHAVIORAL SCIENCE.**
++MED. BEHAV. SCI.
WAKE FOREST UNIVERSITY: OVERSEAS RESEARCH
CENTER.
WINSTON-SALEM, N.C. NO.1, 1971-
S/T: JOURNAL OF CROSS-CULTURAL RESEARCH.
LO/N13.

**MEDICAL EQUIPMENT.**
++MED. EQUIP.
[MILTON PUBL. CO. LTD.]
LONDON 1, 1969-
LO/N14.
ISSN 0025-7249

**MEDICAL JOURNAL OF ZAMBIA.**
++MED. J. ZAMBIA.
[ASSOCIATED REVIEWS LTD.]
NDOLA 1, 1967-
Q. FROM 1969- 2M.
ED/U-1.
ISSN 0047-651X

**MEDICAL LABORATORY TECHNOLOGY.**   XXX
*++MED. LAB. TECHNOL.*
INSTITUTE OF MEDICAL LABORATORY TECHNOLOGY.
[ACADEMIC P.]
*LONDON 28(1), 1971-*
PREV: JOURNAL OF MEDICAL LABORATORY TECHNOLOGY
FROM 9, 1951- 27, 1970.
*ED/N-1.    GL/U-1.    RE/U-1.*
*SO/U-1.  29(3), 1972-*
*ISSN 0022-2607*

**MEDICAL MICROBIOLOGY & IMMUNOLOGY.**   XXX
*++MED. MICROBIOL. & IMMUNOL.*
[SPRINGER]
*BERLIN 157, 1971-*
PREV: ZEITSCHRIFT FUR MEDIZINISCHE MIKROBIOL-
OGIE UND IMMUNOLOGIE FROM 152, 1966- 156, 1971
*LD/U-1.    LO/N13.    SO/U-1.*

**MEDICAL MONOGRAPHS.**
*++MED. MONOGR.*
RADIOCHEMICAL CENTRE (AMERSHAM).
*AMERSHAM   NO.1, 1967-*
CENTRE PART OF UKAEA.
*LO/N-4.   LO/N14.*

**MEDICAL NEWS.**   XXX
*++MED. NEWS.*
[MEDICAL NEWS LTD.]
*LONDON  NO.1, OC 1962-NO.369, OC 1969.//*
SUBS: MEDICAL NEWS-TRIBUNE.
*BN/U-2.  NO.62, 1963-*

**MEDICAL NEWS-TRIBUNE.**
*++MED. NEWS-TRIB.*
[MEDICAL NEWS LTD.]
*LONDON  1(1), N 1969-*
PREV: MEDICAL NEWS FROM 1, OC 1962- 369, 1969.
*BN/U-2.    LO/N-7.    LO/U-2.*
*ISSN 0047-6544*

**MEDICAL OFFICER.**   XXX
  SUBS (1971): COMMUNITY MEDICINE.

**MEDICAL PROGRESS THROUGH TECHNOLOGY.**
*++MED. PROG. TECHNOL.*
[SPRINGER]
*BERLIN &C.  1, 1972-*
*LO/N13.*
*ISSN 0047-6552*

**MEDICAL TEACHER.**
*++MED. TEACH.*
[UPDATE PUBL.]
*LONDON  1, 1972-*
*BL/U-1.    GL/U-1.    LO/N31.    MA/U-1.    SO/U-1.*
*CA/U-11.  2(9), 1973-       ED/N-1.  2(9), 1973-*
*LD/U-1. [CURRENT YEAR ONLY]*
*OX/U-1.  2(9- 12), 1973.*

**MEDICAL TECHNICIAN.**
*++MED. TECH.*
[MORGAN PUBL.]
*EWELL, SURREY  1(1), JA 1971-*
*ED/N-1.    OX/U-1.*
*ISSN 0300-3868*

**MEDICINA EXPERIMENTALIS. INTERNATIONAL JOUR-
NAL OF EXPERIMENTAL MEDICINE.**   XXX
*++MED. EXP.*
[KARGER]
*BASLE  18, 1968- 19, 1969.*
PREV: AS ABOVE FROM 1, 1959- 11, 1964; THEN
PART MEDICINA ET PHARMACOLOGIA EXPERIMENTALIS
FROM 12(1), JA 1965- 17, 1967. SUBS: JOURNAL
OF MEDICINE.
*GL/U-1.    LO/N13.*

**MEDICINE TODAY & TOMORROW.**   XXX
  SUBS (1967): SOCIALISM & HEALTH.

**MEDITERRANEA. REVUE DES PROBLEMES AGRONO-
MIQUES MEDITERRANEENS.**
CENTRE INTERNATIONAL DE HAUTES ETUDES AGRONO-
MIQUES MEDITERRANEENNES.
*PARIS  [NO.]1, D 1963/JA 1964-*
Q. 'SOUS L'EGIDE DU CONSEIL DE L'EUROPE ET
DE L'O.C.D.E.'
*LO/U-3.*

**MEDITERRANEAN REVIEW (LONDON).**
*++MEDITERR. REV. (LOND.).*
*LONDON  1(1), 1969-*
S/T: A MAGAZINE OF ART, CULTURE, TRADE &
TRAVEL - FOR THE SECOND AGE OF THE RENAIS-
SANCE.
*LO/N-1.*
*ED/N-1.  2(2), 1970-        OX/U-1.  2(2), 1970-*

**MEDITERRANEAN REVIEW (NEW YORK).**
*++MEDITERR. REV. (N.Y.).*
DOWLING COLLEGE.
*NEW YORK  1, 1970-*
ENGL., FR., PORT., OR SPAN.
*OX/U-1.*
*ISSN 0025-8288*

**MEDIZINISCHE LANDERKUNDE. GEOMEDICAL MONO-
GRAPH SERIES.**
*++MED. LANDERKD. [MLGM-B]*
HEIDELBERGER AKADEMIE DER WISSENSCHAFTEN:
MATHEMATISCH-NATURWISSENSCHAFTLICHE KLASSE.
[SPRINGER]
*BERLIN &C.  1, 1967-*
ENGL. & GER.
*CA/U-2.    LO/N13.*
*ISSN 0076-6151*

**MEERESTECHNIK. MARINE TECHNOLOGY (DUSSELDORF).**
VEREIN DEUTSCHER INGENIEURE.
*DUSSELDORF  1, 1970-*
GER. & ENGL.
*LO/N14.    LO/U-4.    XS/R10.*
*GL/U-2.  2, 1971-*
*ISSN 0025-8644*

**MEETINGS ON ATOMIC ENERGY.**   XXX
*++MEET. AT. ENERGY.*
INTERNATIONAL ATOMIC ENERGY AGENCY.
*VIENNA  1(1), JA 1969-*
S/T: A QUARTERLY WORLD-WIDE LIST OF CONFEREN-
CES, EXHIBITIONS AND TRAINING COURSES IN ATOM-
IC ENERGY, TOGETHER WITH A SELECTIVE LIST OF
MEETINGS ON SPACE SCIENCE.  PREV: ATOMIC
ENERGY CONFERENCES.
*ED/N-1.    GL/U-2.    LO/N14.    XS/C-2.    XS/R10.*
*LO/N-4.  2(1), 1970-*
*ISSN 0047-6641*

**MEIJI DAIGAKU KAGAKU GIJUTSU KENKYUJO KIYO.
MEMOIRS OF THE INSTITUTE OF SCIENCES & TECH-
NOLOGY, MEIJI UNIVERSITY.**
*TOKYO  1, 1962-*
*LO/N13.\**
*XN/S-1.  7, 1968-*

**MEKHANIKA MASHIN.**   XXX
*++MEKH. MASH.*
AKADEMIJA NAUK SSSR: OTDELENIE MEKHANIKI I
PROTSESSOV UPRAVLENIJA.
*MOSCOW  VYP.1/2, 1966-*
PREV: TEORIJA MASHIN I MEKHANIZMOV FROM 1962-
1965. SPONS. BODY ALSO: GOSUDARSTVENNYJ
NAUCHNO-ISSLEDOVATEL'SKIJ INSTITUT MASHINO-
VEDENIJA.
*BH/U-1.    LO/N14.*
*ISSN 0543-4114*

**MEKHANIKA POLIMEROV.**
*++MEKH. POLIM. [MKPL-A]*
LATVIJAS PSR ZINATNU AKADEMIJA.
*RIGA  1, 1965-*
2M.  ENGL. SUMM.
*CA/U-2.    LO/S-3.*
*LO/N14.  5, 1969-                OX/U-1.  1967(2)-*

**MELANDERIA.**
WASHINGTON STATE ENTOMOLOGICAL SOCIETY.
*PULLMAN, WASH.  1, 1969-*
*CA/U11.    DB/S-1.    LO/N-2.    LO/N13.*
*ISSN 0076-6224*

**MELANESIAN LAW JOURNAL.**
*++MELANESIAN LAW J.*
UNIVERSITY OF PAPUA & NEW GUINEA: LAW FACULTY.
[LAW BOOK CO. LTD.]
*SYDNEY  1(1), 1970-*
A.
*OX/U15.*

**MELANGES D'ARCHEOLOGIE ET D'HISTOIRE.**   XXX
  SUBS (1971): PART OF MELANGES DE L'ECOLE
  FRANCAISE DE ROME: MOYEN AGE - TEMPS
  MODERNES; & MELANGES ... ROME: ANTIQUITE.

**MELANGES DE L'ECOLE FRANCAISE DE ROME:
ANTIQUITE.**   XXX
*++MELANGES EC. FR. ROME, ANTIQ.*
*ROME  83, 1971-*
PREV: PART OF MELANGES D'ARCHEOLOGIE ET D'
HISTOIRE FROM 1, 1881- 82, 1970.
*GL/U-1.*

**MELANGES DE L'ECOLE FRANCAISE DE ROME: MOYEN
AGE - TEMPS MODERNES.**                                          XXX
+ +MELANGES EC. FR. ROME, MOYEN AGE TEMPS MOD.
 ROME 83, 1971-
 PREV: PART OF MELANGES D'ARCHEOLOGIE ET
 D'HISTOIRE FROM 1, 1881- 82, 1970.
 GL/U-1.

**MELBOURNE SLAVONIC STUDIES.**
+ +MELBOURNE SLAV. STUD.
UNIVERSITY OF MELBOURNE: DEPARTMENT OF RUSSIAN
LANGUAGE & LITERATURE.
 MELBOURNE 1, 1967-
 CA/U-1.    NR/U-1.
 SH/U-1.   1968-

**MELIORATSIJA I VODNOE KHOZJAJSTVO.**                           XXX
+ +MELIOR. & VODN. KHOZ.
(UKRAINE) MINISTERSTVO MELIORATSII I VODNOGO
KHOZJAJSTVA.
 KIEV TOM 6, 1967-
 S/T: RESPUBLIKANSKIJ MEZHVEDOMSTVENNYJ
 NAUCHNO-TEKHNICHESKIJ SBORNIK. PREV: VODNOE
 KHOZJAJSTVO FROM 1, 1965- 5, 1966.
 LO/N13.
 BH/U-1. 7, 1968-

**MELTO. RECHERCHES ORIENTALES.**                                XXX
UNIVERSITE SAINT-ESPRIT.
 KASLIK 1(1), 1965- 5(2), 1969.
 SUBS. PART OF: PAROLE DE L'ORIENT.
 LO/U14.   MA/U-1.*

**MEMBRANES.**
[DEKKER]
 NEW YORK 1, 1972-
 LO/N14.
 ISSN 0076-6356

**MEMOIRES, BIOLOGICAL SOCIETY OF NEVADA.**
+ +MEM. BIOL. SOC. NEV.
 VERDI, NEV. 1, 1962-
 LO/N-2.

**MEMOIRS , DEPARTMENT OF AGRICULTURAL SCIENCE
& APPLIED BIOLOGY, UNIVERSITY OF CAMBRIDGE.**                    XXX
+ +MEM. DEP. AGRIC. SCI. & APPL. BIOL. UNIV.
 CAMB.
 CAMBRIDGE NO.42, 1970 ...
 PREV: MEMOIRS, SCHOOL OF AGRICULTURE, UNI-
 VERSITY OF CAMBRIDGE FROM NO.1, 1929- 41, 1969
 SUBS: MEMOIRS, DEPARTMENT OF APPLIED BIOLOGY,
 UNIVERSITY OF CAMBRIDGE.
 LO/N13.

**MEMOIRS, DEPARTMENT OF APPLIED BIOLOGY, UNIV-
ERSITY OF CAMBRIDGE.**                                          XXX
+ +MEM. DEP. APPL. BIOL. UNIV. CAMB.
 CAMBRIDGE NO.43, 1971-
 PREV: MEMOIRS, DEPARTMENT OF AGRICULTURAL SCI-
 ENCE & APPLIED BIOLOGY, UNIVERSITY OF CAMB-
 RIDGE FROM NO.42, 1970.
 LO/N14.

**MEMOIRS, ENTOMOLOGICAL SOCIETY OF QUEBEC.**
+ +MEM. ENTOMOL. SOC. QUE.
 QUEBEC NO.1, F 1968-
 ED/U-2.

**MEMOIRS, GEOLOGICAL SURVEY OF WYOMING.**
+ +MEM. GEOL. SURV. WYO.
 LARAMIE 1, 1968-
 GL/U-1.   LO/N-2.

**MEMOIR OF GIFU TECHNICAL COLLEGE.**                            000
 SEE:  GIFU KOGYO KOTO SEMMON GAKKO KIYO.

**MEMOIRES DE L'INSTITUT D'ETHNOLOGIE,
UNIVERSITE DE PARIS.**
+ +MEM. INST. ETHNOL. UNIV. PARIS.
 PARIS 1, 1969-
 CA/U-3.   LO/N-3.

**MEMOIRES, INSTITUT DE PREHISTOIRE, UNIVERSITE
DE BORDEAUX.**
+ +MEM. INST. PREHIST. UNIV. BORDEAUX.
 BORDEAUX NO.1, 1961-
 SUBSERIES OF ITS PUBLICATIONS.
 LO/N-2.

**MEMOIRS OF THE INSTITUTE OF SCIENCES & TECHNOL-
OGY, MEIJI UNIVERSITY.**                                        000
 SEE: MEIJI DAIGAKU KAGAKU GIJUTSU KENKYUJO
 KIYO.

**MEMOIRS OF THE KYUSHU INSTITUTE OF TECHNOLOGY:
ENGINEERING.**
+ +MEM. KYUSHU INST. TECHNOL., ENG.
KYUSHU KOGYO DAIGAKU.
 KYUSHU NO.1, 1971-
 LO/N14.

**MEMOIRS, MIYAKONOJO TECHNICAL COLLEGE.**                       000
 SEE: MIYAKONOJO KOGYO KOTO SENMON GAKKO
 KENKYU.

**MEMOIRS, MUSEUM OF ANTHROPOLOGY, UNIVERSITY
OF MICHIGAN.**
+ +MEM. MUS. ANTHROPOL. UNIV. MICHIGAN.
 ANN ARBOR 1, 1969-
 AD/U-1.   BH/U-1.    CA/U-3.   GL/U-1.   LO/N-1.   LO/N-2.
 LO/N-4.   MA/U-1.   OX/U-1.

**MEMOIRS OF THE NATIONAL SCIENCE MUSEUM TOKYO.**
+ +MEM. NAT. SCI. MUS. TOKYO.
 TOKYO 1, 1968-
 JAP. & ENGL. ARTIC. ENGL. ABSTR.
 LO/N-2.   XN/S-1.

**MEMOIRS, NORTHERN CAVERN & MINE RESEARCH
SOCIETY.**                                                      XXX
+ +MEM. NORTH. CAVERN & MINE RES. SOC.
 SKIPTON 1(1), 1964-
 PREV: TRANSACTIONS, NORTHERN CAVERN ... FROM
 1(1), 1960/61- 1(2), 1962/63.
 LO/N-2.

**MEMOIR, PALEONTOLOGICAL SOCIETY.**
+ +MEM. PALEONTOL. SOC.
 TULSA [NO.]1, 1968-
 ISSUED AS SUPPL. TO:  JOURNAL OF PALEONTOLOGY.
 BL/U-1.   LO/N13.
 ISSN 0078-8597

**MEMOIRES ET RECUEILS DE DOCUMENTS, CENTRE
INTERUNIVERSITAIRE D'ETUDE DE L'HISTOIRE DE
LA TAPISSERIE FLAMANDE.**
+ +MEM. & RECL. DOC. CENT. INTERUNIV. ETUD. HIST.
 TAPISSERIE FLAMANDE.
 GHENT 1, 1969-
 OX/U-1.

**MEMOIRS, SCHOOL OF AGRICULTURE, UNIVERSITY OF
CAMBRIDGE.**                                                    XXX
 SUBS (1970):  MEMOIRS, DEPARTMENT OF
 AGRICULTURAL SCIENCE & APPLIED BIOLOGY,
 UNIVERSITY OF CAMBRIDGE.

**MEMOIRS, SENDAI SHIRAYURI JUNIOR COLLEGE.**                    000
 SEE: SENDAI SHIRAYURI TANKI DAIGAKU KIYO.

**MEMORABILIA HISTORIAE NATURALIS.**                             000
 SEE: IZ ISTORII BIOLOGICHESKIKH NAUK.

**MEMORIA ANTIQUITATIS.**
+ +MEM. ANTIQ.
MUZEUL ARHEOLOGIC (PIATRA NIAMT).
 PIATRA NIAMT 1, 1969-
 CA/U-1.   DB/S-1.

**MEMORIE GEOPALAEONTOLOGICHE DELL'UNIVERSITA
DI FERRARA.**
+ +MEM. GEOPALAEONTOL. UNIV. FERRARA.
 FERRARA 1(1), 1964-
 LO/N-2.

**MEMORIE DELLA SOCIETA DEI NATURALISTI IN
NAPOLI.**
+ +MEM. SOC. NAT. NAPOLI.
 NAPLES 1, 1970-
 LO/N-2.

**MEMORY & COGNITION.**                                          XXX
+ +MEM. & COGNITION.
PSYCHONOMIC SOCIETY.
 AUSTIN, TEX. 1, 1973-
 MON. PREV. PART OF: PSYCHONOMIC SCIENCE FROM
 1, 1964- 29(6), JA 1973.
 AD/U-1.    BL/U-1.    BN/U-1.   GL/U-1.   GL/U-2.   LD/U-1.
 LO/U-4.    MA/U-1.   RE/U-1.   SA/U-1.   SH/U-1.   SO/U-1.
 ISSN 0090-502X

**MENDEL NEWSLETTER.**
+ +MENDEL NEWSL.
AMERICAN PHILOSOPHICAL SOCIETY.
 PHILADELPHIA NO.1, 1968-
 S/T: ARCHIVAL RESOURCES FOR THE HISTORY OF
 GENETICS & ALLIED SCIENCES.
 LO/M24.   LO/N-2.
 ISSN 0025-9241

**MENDELEEV CHEMISTRY JOURNAL.**
++*MENDELEEV CHEM. J.*
[FARADAY PRESS]
*NEW YORK 11, 1966(1968)-*
TRANSL. OF: ZHURNAL VSESOJUZNOGO KHIMICHES-
KOGO OBSHCHESTVA IMENI D.I. MENDELEEVA.
ISSUES NUMBERED & DATED AS ORIG.
*LO/N14.    LO/S-3.*
*ISSN 0025-925X*

**MENDELSSOHN STUDIEN.**
++*MENDELSSOHN STUD.*
MENDELSSOHN-GESELLSCHAFT.
[DUNCKER & HUMBLOT]
*BERLIN 1, 1972.*
ENGL. OR GER.
*CA/U-1.    LO/N-1.    LO/U-1.    OX/U-1.*

**MENSARIO, ARQUIVO NACIONAL (BRAZIL).**
++*MENS. ARQ. NAC. (BRAZ.).*
*RIO DE JANEIRO 1(1), 1970-*
*OX/U-1.*

**MENTAL HEALTH.**                                      XXX
SUBS (1971): MIND & MENTAL HEALTH MAGAZINE.

**MENTAL HEALTH DIGEST.**
++*MENT. HEALTH DIG.*
NATIONAL CLEARINGHOUSE FOR MENTAL HEALTH
INFORMATION (US).
*MARYLAND NO.1, 1967-*
SPONS. BODY ALSO NATIONAL INSTITUTE OF MENTAL
HEALTH (US).
*LO/N-3. 4, 1968-*
*ISSN 0025-9659*

**MENTAL RETARDATION (NEW YORK).**                      XXX
++*MENT. RETARD. (N.Y.).*
[GRUNE & STRATTON]
*NEW YORK &C. 1, 1969- 4, 1972.*
A. SUBS: MENTAL RETARDATION & DEVELOPMENT
DISABILITIES.
*OX/U-8.*
*ISSN 0076-647X*

**MENTAL RETARDATION ABSTRACTS.**
++*MENT. RETARD. ABSTR.*
NATIONAL CLEARINGHOUSE FOR MENTAL HEALTH
INFORMATION (US).
*BETHESDA, MD. 1(1), JA/MR 1964-*
*DB/U-2.    XY/N-1.***
*GL/U-2. 3(4), 1966-        LO/M-7. 2, 1965-*
*LO/M27. 2, 1965           OX/U-1. 4, 1967-*
*SH/U-1. 3(4), 1966-*
*ISSN 0025-9691*

**MENTAL WELFARE.**                                     XXX
SUBS (1970): PART OF SOCIAL WORK TODAY.

**MERCURY. THE JOURNAL OF THE ...**
ASTRONOMICAL SOCIETY OF THE PACIFIC.
*SAN FRANCISCO 1(1), 1972-*
*CA/U-2.    LO/N-4.    MA/U-1.*
*BL/U-1. 4, 1975-*
*ISSN 0047-6773*

**MEROVA TECHNIKA.**
++*MEROVA TECH. [MVTE-A]*
(CZECHOSLOVAKIA) URAD PRO NORMALIZACI A MERENI.
*PRAGUE 1, 1962-*
FR. & RUSS. SUMM.
*LO/N13. 9, 1970-*
*ISSN 0026-0142*

**MESOPOTAMIA. JOURNAL OF AGRICULTURE &
FORESTRY RESEARCH.**
UNIVERSITY OF BAGHDAD: COLLEGE OF AGRICULTURE.
*MOSUL 1(1), JE 1966- 2, 1967 ...*
SUBS. MESOPOTAMIA AGRICULTURE.
*BL/U-1.    LO/N-2.    OX/U-3.*

**MESOPOTAMIA QUARTERLY.**                              000
SEE: BAYN AL-NAHRAYN.

**MESSAGE D'EXTREME-ORIENT.**
*BRUSSELS NO.1, 1971-*
*LO/U14.*

**MESTER.**
UNIVERSITY OF CALIFORNIA (LOS ANGELES):
DEPARTMENT OF SPANISH & PORTUGUESE.
*LOS ANGELES 1(1), AP 1970-*
SPAN. OR PORT.
*LO/N-1.*
*ISSN 0026-0436*

**METABOLISMO.**
SOCIETA ITALIANA PER LO STUDIO DEL METABOLISMO
NORMALE E PATOLOGICO.
[CEPI]
*ROME 1, 1965-*
2M. ENGL. SUMM. PREV: ARCHIVIO PER LO
STUDIO DELLA FISIOPATOLOGIA E CLINICA DEL
RICAMBIO FROM 1, 1933- 23, 1959; THEN
ARCHIVIO DEL RICAMBIO FROM 24, 1960.
*LO/N13.*
*ISSN 0026-0509*

**METAL BULLETIN MONTHLY.**
++*METAL BULL. MON.*
[METAL BULLETIN LTD.]
*LONDON NO.1, JA 1971-*
S/T: THE WORLD OF STEEL & METALS.
*BH/P-1.    ED/N-1.    LO/N10.    LO/N13.    MA/P-1.    OX/U-1.*

**METAL CONSTRUCTION & BRITISH WELDING JOURNAL.**
++*METAL CONSTR. & BR. WELD. J.*
WELDING INSTITUTE.
*LONDON 1, 1969-*
PREV: BRITISH WELDING JOURNAL FROM 1, 1954- 15
1968.
*BH/U-1.    BN/U-1.    ED/N-1.    LO/F-1.    LO/N-4.    LO/N14.*
*LV/U-1.    MA/U-1.    SO/U-1.    XS/R10.    XS/T-4.*
*LD/U-1. 4(5), 1972-*
*ISSN 0020-0541*

**METAL FORMING.**                                      XXX
++*MET. FORM.*
[FUEL & METALLURGICAL JOURNALS LTD.]
*LONDON 33, N 1966- 38(7), 1971...*
PREV: METAL TREATMENT FROM 1, 1935- 33, OC
1966. SUBS (1971) PART OF: METALLURGIA &
METAL FORMING.
*LO/N14.*
*ISSN 0026-0622*

**METAL JOINING DIGEST.**                               XXX
++*METAL JOIN. DIG.*
WAYNE STATE UNIVERSITY: CENTER FOR APPLICATION
OF SCIENCE & TECHNOLOGY.
*DETROIT 1, 1967- 6(4), 1972 ...*
SUBS: UDS METAL JOINING DIGEST.
*LO/N14.*
*ISSN 0026-0630*

**METAL PHYSICS (LONDON).**                             XXX
++*METAL PHYS. (LOND.).*
.INSTITUTE OF PHYSICS & THE PHYSICAL SOCIETY.
*LONDON NO.1- 3, 1970.*
ISSUED AS SUPPL. TO JOURNAL OF PHYSICS: C:
SOLID STATE PHYSICS. SUBS: JOURNAL OF PHYSICS:
F: METAL PHYSICS.
*LD/U-1.    LO/N14.    NW/U-1.*

**METAL TREATMENT.**                                    XXX
SUBS (1966): METAL FORMING.

**METALLOGRAPHY. AN INTERNATIONAL JOURNAL.**
INTERNATIONAL METALLOGRAPHIC SOCIETY.
[ELSEVIER]
*NEW YORK 1(1), S 1968-*
*LO/N14.    SH/U-3.    XS/R10.*
*ISSN 0026-0800*

**METALLOVEDENIE I TERMICHESKAJA OBRABOTKA.**           XXX
++*METALLOVED. & TERM. OBRAB.*
NAUCHNO-TEKHNICHESKOE OBSHCHESTVO MASHINO-
STROITEL'NOJ PROMYSHLENNOSTI: SEKTSIJA METAL-
LOVEDENIJA I TERMICHESKOJ OBRABOTKI.
*MOSCOW 3, 1964-*
PREV: TRUDY SEKTSII METALLOVEDENIJA I TERMICH-
ESKOJ OBRABOTKI, NAUCHNO-TEKHNICHESKOE OBSH-
CHESTVO MASHINOSTROITEL'NOJ PROMYSHLENNOSTI
FROM 1, 1958- 2, 1960.
*LO/N13. 4, 1966-*

**METALLURGIA (MANCHESTER).**                           XXX
SUBS (1971) PART OF: METALLURGIA & METAL
FORMING.

**METALLURGIA & METAL FORMING.**                        XXX
++*METALL. & MET. FORM.*
[FUEL & METALLURGICAL JOURNALS LTD.]
*LONDON 38(8), 1971-*
INCORP: METALLURGIA (MANCHESTER) FROM NO.1,
1929- 501, 1971; & METAL FORMING FROM 33,
1966- 38(7), 1971.
*BH/P-1.    BH/U-1.    BR/U-1.    CV/C-1.    GL/U-1.    LO/N14.*
*LO/N35.    MA/U-1.    NW/U-1.    XS/R10.*

**METALLURGICAL ABSTRACTS.**                            XXX
SUBS. (1968) PART OF: METALS ABSTRACTS; &
METALS ABSTRACTS INDEX.

**METALLURGICAL REPORTS, CENTRE DE RECHERCHES
METALLURGIQUES (BELGIUM).**                                    XXX
*+ +METALL. REP. CENT. RECH. METALL. (BELG.).*
*BRUSSELS NO.1, 1966-*
PREV: [PUBLICATION] CENTRE NATIONAL ... BODY
AS CENTRE NATIONAL DE RECHERCHES METALLURGI-
QUES FROM 1, 1966- 25, 1970.
*LO/N14.*

**METALLURGICAL TRANSACTIONS.**                                XXX
*+ +MET. TRANS.*
AMERICAN SOCIETY FOR METALS.
*NEW YORK 1(1), JA 1970-*
SPONS. BODY ALSO AMERICAN INST. MINING, MET-
ALLURGICAL & PETROL. ENG. INCORP: TRANSACT-
IONS, METALLURGICAL SOCIETY OF AIME FROM 211,
1957- 245(12), 1969; & TRANSACTIONS QUARTERLY,
AMERICAN SOC. FOR METALS FROM 54(1), MR 1961-
62(4), D 1969.
*BH/P-1.    BH/U-3.    BL/U-1.    DB/U-2.    DN/U-1.    GL/U-1.*
*GL/U-2.    LD/U-1.    LO/N-4.    LO/N-5.    LO/N14.    LO/U12.*
*MA/U-1.    NW/U-1.    OX/U-8.    SW/U-1.    XS/R10.*
*ISSN 0026-086X*

**METALLURGICHESKAJA I GORNORUDNAJA PROMYSHLEN-
NOST'.**
*+ +METALLURG. & GORNORUDN. PROM-ST.*
(UKRAINE) MINISTERSTVO CHERNOJ METALLURGII
USSR.
*KIEV 1(1), 1960-*
2M. S/T: NAUCHNO-TEKHNICHESKIJ SBORNIK.
BODY ORIG. AS: GOSUDARSTVENNYJ KOMITET PO
KOORDINATSII NAUCHNO-ISSLEDOVATEL'SKIKH RABOT
USSR: INSTITUT TEKHNICHESKOJ INFORMATSII.
*LO/N13. 6(31), 1965-*

**METALS.**
[HEYWOOD-TEMPLE INDUSTRIAL PUBL.]
*LONDON 1, 1966- 2(20), 1968. //*
PREV: LIGHT METALS & METAL INDUSTRY FROM
27(317), 1964.
*LO/N14.    LO/R-6.*
*BH/P-1. [W. NO.17, 20.]*

**METALS ABSTRACTS.**                                          XXX
*+ +METALS ABSTR.*
AMERICAN SOCIETY FOR METALS.
*METALS PARK, OHIO &C. 1, 1968-*
INCORP. IN PART: METALLURGICAL ABSTRACTS; &
ASM REVIEW OF METAL LITERATURE FROM 1, 1944-
24(12), 1967. SPONS. BODY ALSO INSTITUTE OF
METALS.
*BL/U-1.    BN/U-1.    DB/U-1.    LO/N-4.    LO/N14.    LO/U-2.*
*MA/P-1.    MA/U-1.    XW/C-4.*
*ISSN 0026-0924*

**METALS ABSTRACTS INDEX.**                                    XXX
*+ +METALS ABSTR. INDEX.*
AMERICAN SOCIETY FOR METALS.
*METALS PARK, OHIO &C. 1, 1968-*
INCORP. IN PART: METALLURGICAL ABSTRACTS; &
ASM REVIEW OF METAL LITERATURE FROM 1, 1944-
24(12), 1967. SPONS. BODY ALSO INSTITUTE OF
METALS.
*BL/U-1.    DB/U-2.    LO/N-4.    LO/N-7. **    XW/C-4.*
*BH/P-1. 3, 1970-*
*ISSN 0026-0932*

**METALS AUSTRALIA.**
*+ +MET. AUST.*
AUSTRALIAN INSTITUTE OF METALS.
*SYDNEY 1, 1968/69-*
*LO/N14.**
*ISSN 0047-6897*

**METAPHILOSOPHY.**
[BLACKWELL]
*OXFORD 1(1), JA 1970-*
*ED/N-1.    GL/U-1.    LO/N-1.    LO/U-1.    LO/U-3.    LO/U-4.*
*OX/U-1.    SH/U-1.*
*NO/U-1. 5, 1974-*
*ISSN 0026-1068*

**METAUX DEFORMATION.**                                        XXX
*+ +MET. DEFORM.*
[PYC-EDITION]
*PARIS NO.16, 1973-*
PREV: FORMAGE DES MATERIAUX FROM 1(1), 1969-
4(15), 1972. ALSO ENTITLED TRAVAIL DES METAUX
PAR DEFORMATION.
*LO/N14.*

**METAUX EN FEUILLES.**                                        XXX
SUBS (1969): PART OF FORMAGE ET TRAITEMENTS
DES METAUX.

**'METEOR' FORSCHUNGSERGEBNISSE; REIHE A:
ALLGEMEINES PHYSIK UND CHEMIE DES MEERES.**
*+ +'METEOR' FORSCHUNGSERGEB., A.*
DEUTSCHE FORSCHUNGSGEMEINSCHAFT.
[BORNTRAEGER]
*BERLIN NO.1, 1966-*
*LO/N13.    LO/U-2.*

**'METEOR' FORSCHUNGSERGEBNISSE; REIHE B:
METEOROLOGIE UND AERONOMIE.**
*+ +'METEOR' FORSCHUNGSERGEB., B.*
DEUTSCHE FORSCHUNGSGEMEINSCHAFT.
[BORNTRAEGER]
*BERLIN NO.1, 1967-*
*LO/N13.    LO/U-2.*

**'METEOR' FORSCHUNGSERGEBNISSE: REIHE C: GEOL-
OGIE UND GEOPHYSIK.**
*+ +'METEOR' FORSCHUNGSERGEB., C.*
DEUTSCHE FORSCHUNGSGEMEINSCHAFT.
[BORNTRAEGER]
*BERLIN NO.1, 1968-*
*CA/U14.    LO/N13.    SW/U-1.*

**'METEOR' FORSCHUNGSERGEBNISSE: REIHE D:
BIOLOGIE.**
*+ +'METEOR' FORSCHUNGSERGEB., D.*
DEUTSCHE FORSCHUNGSGEMEINSCHAFT.
[BORNTRAEGER]
*BERLIN NO.1, 1967-*
*LO/N13.*

**METEOR NEWS.**
ASTRO-GATOR ASTRONOMY CLUB.
*JACKSONVILLE, FLA. NO.1, 1970-*
*LO/N13.*

**METEORNOE RASPROSTRANENIE RADIOVOLN.**
*+ +METEORNOE RASPROSTR. RADIOVOLN.*
KAZANSKIJ GOSUDARSTVENNYJ UNIVERSITET.
*KAZAN' 1, 1963-*
*LO/N13.*

**METEOROLOGIJA, KLIMATOLOGIJA I GIDROLOGIJA.**
ODESSKIJ GIDROMETEOROLOGICHESKIJ INSTITUT.
*KIEV VYP.1, 1965-*
S/T: MEZHVEDOMSTVENNYJ NAUCHNYJ SBORNIK.
ENGL., FR. OR GER. SUMM.
*BH/U-1. VYP.2, 1966-          LO/N13. VYP.3, 1968-*

**METEOROLOGY & HYDROLOGY (RUMANIA).**
*+ +METEOROL. & HYDROL. (RUM.).*
INSTITUTUL DE METEOROLOGIE SI HIDROLOGIE.
*BUCHAREST NO.1, 1971-*
*XS/N-1.*

**METHOD. JOURNAL OF THE PROFESSIONAL & EXECUTIVE**
[CRAFTSMAN PUBL.]
*LONDON 1, 1970-*
*ED/N-1.    LO/N14.    OX/U-1.*
*LO/N35. 2(2), 1972-*

**METHODS & ACHIEVEMENTS IN EXPERIMENTAL
PATHOLOGY.**
*+ +METH. & ACHIEVE. EXP. PATHOL.*
[S. KARGER (&C)]
*BASEL &C 1, 1966-*
*LO/N13.*

**METHODS IN FREE-RADICAL CHEMISTRY.**
*+ +METH. FREE-RADICAL CHEM.*
[MARCEL DEKKER]
*NEW YORK 1, 1969-*
*LO/N14.    LO/S-3.    LO/U-2.*

**METHODS IN IMMUNOLOGY & IMMUNOCHEMISTRY.**
*+ +METHODS IMMUNOL. & IMMUNOCHEM. [MIIM-B]*
[ACADEMIC P.]
*NEW YORK 1, 1967-*
*LO/M31.*
*ISSN 0076-6917*

**METHODS IN MICROBIOLOGY.**
*+ +METH. MICROBIOL.*
[ACADEMIC P.]
*LONDON 1, 1969-*
*GL/U-1.    HL/U-1.    LO/U20.    LV/P-1.*
*AD/U-1. 2, 1970.*

**METHODS IN MOLECULAR BIOLOGY.**
*+ +METHODS MOL. BIOL.*
[DEKKER]
*NEW YORK 1, 1971-*
*GL/U-1.    OX/U-8.*

**METHODS OF NEUROCHEMISTRY.**
+ +METH. NEUROCHEM.
[DEKKER]
NEW YORK 1, 1971-
LO/N13.   LO/U-2.   OX/U-8.

**METHODS IN PHARMACOLOGY.**
+ +METHODS PHARMACOL.
[MEREDITH CORP.]
NEW YORK 1, 1971-
LO/N13.   OX/U-8.
ISSN 0091-3030

**METHODS PHYSIQUE D'ANALYSE.**                     XXX
**SUBS(1972) PART OF: ANALUSIS.**

**METHODS IN PSYCHOBIOLOGY.**
+ +METHODS PSYCHOBIOL.
[ACADEMIC P.]
LONDON 1, 1971-
ANNU.
CA/U-1.   DB/U-2.   SH/U-1.   SO/U-1.

**METHODS IN SUBNUCLEAR PHYSICS.**
+ +METH. SUBNUCL. PHYS.
[GORDON & BREACH]
NEW YORK & C. 1, 1968-
CONSISTS OF THE PROC. OF THE INTERNATIONAL
SCHOOL OF ELEMENTARY PARTICLE PHYSICS,
HERCEG-NOVI, YUGOSLAVIA.
LO/N14.

**METODIK REKOMMENDATION, STATENS LANTBRUKSKEM-
ISKA LABORATORIUM (SWEDEN).**
+ +METOD. REKOM. STATENS LANTBRUKSKEM. LAB.
(SWED.).
UPPSALA [NR.]1, 1970-
LO/N14.

**METODY POLUCHENIJA KHIMICHESKIKH REAKTIVOV I
PREPARATOV.**
+ +METODY POLUCH. KHIM. REAKT. & PREP.
VSESOJUZNYJ NAUCHNO-ISSLEDOVATEL'SKIJ INSTITUT
KHIMICHESKIKH REAKTIVOV I OSOBO CHISTYKH KHIM-
ICHESKIKH VESHCHESTV.
MOSCOW VYP.1, 1960-
VYP.1 PUBL. AS: KHIMICHESKIE REAKTIVY I PREP-
ARATY.
LO/N13. VYP.8, 1964-

**METODY I PRAKTIKA OPREDELENIJA EKONOMICHESKOJ
EFFEKTIVNOSTI KAPITAL'NYKH VLOZHENIJ I
NOVOJ TEKHNIKI.**
+ +METODY & PRAKT. OPRED. EKON. EFF. KAPITAL'NYKH
VLOZHENIJ & NOVOJ TEKH.
AKADEMIJA NAUK SSSR: INSTITUT EKONOMIKI.
MOSCOW VYP.1, 1961-
S/T: SBORNIK NAUCHNOJ INFORMATSII. INSTITUT
SUBORD. TO: NAUCHNYJ SOVET PO PROBLEME
EKONOMICHESKOJ EFFEKTIVNOSTI KAPITAL'NYKH
VLOZHENIJ I NOVOJ TEKHNIKI.
BH/U-1.   CC/U-1.

**METODY VYCHISLENIJ.**
LENINGRADSKIJ GOSUDARSTVENNYJ UNIVERSITET:
KAFEDRA VYCHISLITEL'NOJ MATEMATIKI I VYCHISLI-
TEL'NYJ TSENTR LGU.
LENINGRAD 1, 1963-
LO/N13. 2, 1963-
BH/U-1. 5, 1968.

**METRICATION BULLETIN.**
+ +METRIC. BULL.
CONFEDERATION OF IRISH INDUSTRY.
DUBLIN 1, 1970-
DB/U-2.

**METRICATION IN THE CONSTRUCTION INDUSTRY.**
+ +METRIC. CONSTR. IND.
(GREAT BRITAIN) MINISTRY OF PUBLIC BUILDING &
WORKS.
LONDON &C. NO.1, 1970-
OX/U-8.

**METROLOGY & INSPECTION.**
+ +METROL & INSP.
[ENGINEERING, CHEMICAL & MARINE P. LTD.]
LONDON 1, 1969-
PUBL. FOR MACHINE SHOP & ENGINEERING MANUFACT-
URE.
ED/N-1.   LO/N14.
LO/N-4. 1(2), 1969-              LO/N-7. 3(4), 1971-
XS/R10. 1(3), 1969-
ISSN 0026-1408

**METRON. SIRA MEASUREMENT & CONTROL ABSTRACTS
& REVIEWS.**                                       XXX
BRITISH SCIENTIFIC INSTRUMENT RESEARCH
ASSOCIATION.
[PERGAMON]
OXFORD 1, JA 1969-
MON. PREV: SIRA ABSTRACTS & REVIEWS FROM 23,
1968.
BH/P-1.   BR/U-3.   CB/U-1.   ED/N-1.   LO/N-4.   LO/N14.
LO/U-2.   SH/U-3.   XS/R10.
MA/U-1. 2, 1970-              SO/U-1. 3, JA 1971-
XS/T-4. [CURRENT TWO YEARS]
ISSN 0026-1416

**METROPOLE.  LES CAHIERS D'URBANISME.**
MONTREAL NO.1, 1963-
FR. & ENGL.
LO/N-1.* NO.3, 1965-
ISSN 0026-1440

**METROPOLITAN MUSEUM JOURNAL.**
+ +METROP. MUS. J.
METROPOLITAN MUSEUM OF ART (NEW YORK).
NEW YORK 1, 1968-
DB/U-2.   LO/U-1.   LO/U17.   MA/U-1.   OX/U-1.

**METU.  STUDIES IN DEVELOPMENT.**
ANKARA 1, 1970(1971)-
BH/U-1.

**MEZHDUNARODNOE RABOCHEE DVIZHENIE.**
+ +MEZHDUNAR. RAB. DVIZHENIE.
AKADEMIJA NAUK SSSR: INSTITUT MEZHDUNARODNOGO
RABOCHEGO DVIZHENIJA.
MOSCOW 1970(1971)-
A.
BH/U-1.   LO/U-3.

**MEZHDUNARODNYJ EZHEGODNIK - POLITIKA I EKON-
OMIKA.**                                           XXX
+ +MEZHD. EZHEG. - POLIT. EKON.
AKADEMIJA NAUK SSSR: INSTITUT MIROVOJ EKONOMIKI
I MEZHDUNARODNYKH OTNOSHENIJ.
MOSCOW 1961-
A. PREV: MEZHDUNARODNYJ POLITIKO-EKONOMU-
CHESKIJ EZHEGODNIK FROM 1958- 1960.
CC/U-1.   LO/N-3.   NO/U-1.   SW/U-1.

**MEZHDUNARODNYJ POLITIKO-EKONOMICHESKIJ EZHE-
GODNIK.**                                          XXX
SUBS (1961):  MEZHDUNARODNYJ EZHEGODNIK -
POLITIKA I EKONOMIKA.

**MGA BULLETIN.**                                   XXX
SUBS (1973): MUSHROOM JOURNAL.

**MGG.**                                            000
SEE: MOLECULAR & GENERAL GENETICS.

**MICHIGAN ACADEMICIAN.**                           XXX
+ +MICH. ACAD.
MICHIGAN ACADEMY OF SCIENCE, ARTS & LETTERS.
ANN ARBOR 1, 1969-
Q. PREV: PAPERS ... FROM 1, 1921- 53, 1967.
BH/U-1.   GL/U-1.   LD/U-1.   LO/N-2.   LO/N-4.   LO/N13.
OX/U-1. 2(1), 1969-
ISSN 0026-2005

**MICHIGAN CONSERVATION.**                          XXX
SUBS (1969):  MICHIGAN NATURAL RESOURCES.

**MICHIGAN NATURAL RESOURCES.**                     XXX
+ +MICH. NATUR. RESOUR.
(MICHIGAN) DEPARTMENT OF NATURAL RESOURCES.
LANSING. MICH. 38, 1969-
PREV: MICHIGAN CONSERVATION FROM 1, OC 1931-
37(2), 1968.
LO/N13.
ISSN 0026-2358

**MICHIGAN SCIENCE IN ACTION.**
+ +MICH. SCI. ACTION.
MICHIGAN STATE UNIVERSITY: AGRICULTURAL
EXPERIMENT STATION.
EAST LANSING, MICH. [NO.]1, 1967-
LO/N-2.
LO/N14. [CURRENT BOX]

**MICROBIOLOGIA.**
SOCIETATEA DE STIINTE BIOLOGICE DIN REPUBLICA
SOCIALISTA ROMANIA: SECTIA DE MICROBIOLOGIE.
BUCHAREST 1, 1970-
CA/U11.   LO/N-4.   LO/N13.   OX/U-8.

**MICROBIOLOGY ABSTRACTS: SECTION C: ALGOLOGY, MYCOLOGY & PROTOZOOLOGY.**
++MICROBIOL. ABSTR., C.
[INFORMATION RETRIEVAL LTD.]
LONDON 1(1), JA 1972-
MON.
AD/U-2.    BH/U-3.    DB/U-2.    ED/N-1.    GL/U-1.    LO/N-2.
LO/N14.    SF/U-1.    XY/N-1.

**MICROBIOS.**
[FACULTY P.]
CAMBRIDGE 1, 1969-
CA/U-1.    GL/U-1.    GL/U-2.    LO/N-2.    LO/N13.    LO/U-2.
LO/U-4.    MA/U-1.    OX/U-8.
SH/U-1. 1, 1969- 1974.*
ISSN 0026-2633

**MICROFORM REVIEW.**
++MICROFORM REV.
WESTON, CONN. 1(1), JA 1972-
ED/N-1.    LO/N35.    OX/U-1.
ISSN 0002-6530

**MICROGRAPHICS. NEWS & VIEWS.**                          XXX
[MYERS]
PALOS VERDES PENINS., LOS ANG. 1(1), 1970-
                                    5, 1972.
2W. SUBS: ADVANCED TECHNOLOGY/LIBRARIES.
PRELIM. ISSUE JE 1970.
LO/U-1. [W.3(8), 1971]

**MICROINFO. MICROGRAPHICS NEWS BULLETIN.**
MICROINFO LTD.
ALTON, HANTS. 1, 1970-
LO/N-7.    LO/N14.    OX/U-1.
ISSN 0047-7192

**MICRON.**
[STRUCTURAL PUBL. LTD.]
WATFORD 1, 1969-
Q.
BH/U-1.    CA/U-2.    GL/U-1.    LO/N-2.    LO/N14.    MA/U-1.
XS/R10.
GL/U-2. 3, 1971-             LO/U-2. 2, 1970-
ED/N-1. 1(4), MR 1970-
ISSN 0047-7206

**MICRO-NEWS BULLETIN.**
++MICRO-NEWS BULL.
NATIONAL MICROFILM ASSOCIATION (US).
ANNAPOLIS, MD. [NO.1], 1967/68(1967)-
BL/U-1.    LO/N-4.    OX/U-1.
ISSN 0026-2544

**MICROSCOPICA ACTA.**                          XXX
++MICROSC. ACTA.
[S. HIRZEL]
STUTTGART 71, 1971-
Q. ENGL., FR. & GER. SUMM. PREV: ZEITSCHRIFT
FUR WISSENSCHAFTLICHE MIKROSKOPIE UND FUR MIK-
ROSKOPISCHE TECHNIK FROM 1, 1884- 70, 1970.
CA/U-2.    LO/N-4.    LO/N14.
ISSN 0044-376X

**MICROSTRUCTURES.**
INTERNATIONAL METALLOGRAPHIC SOCIETY.
LOS ANGELES 1(1), 1970-
2M.
LO/N14.    OX/U-8.
ISSN 0026-2846

**MICROVASCULAR RESEARCH.**
++MICROVASC. RES.
[ACADEMIC P.]
NEW YORK &C. 1(1), JE 1968-
AT HEAD OF TITLE: 1968- MVR.
CA/U-1.    GL/U-1.    LO/N13.    LO/U-2.    NW/U-1.    SO/U-1.
BL/U-1. 2, 1970-             OX/U-8. 2(1), 1970-
ISSN 0026-2862

**MIDDLE EAST INTERNATIONAL.**
++MIDDLE EAST INT.
[MORRIS PUBL.]
LONDON NO.1, AP 1971-
MON.
ED/N-1.    LO/N-1.
SH/U-1. JL 1971-
AD/U-1. NO.10, 1972-
ISSN 0047-7249

**MIDLAND HISTORY.**                          XXX
UNIVERSITY OF BIRMINGHAM.
[PHILLIMORE]
BIRMINGHAM 1, 1971-
PREV: UNIVERSITY OF BIRMINGHAM HISTORICAL
JOURNAL FROM 1, 1947/48- 12(2), 1970.
AD/U-1.    BH/U-1.    BL/U-1.    BN/U-1.    CA/U-1.    DB/S-1.
ED/N-1.    EX/U-1.    GL/U-2.    LO/N-3.    LO/S-7.    LO/U-1.
LO/U-2.    LO/U-3.    LO/U19.    NO/U-1.    NW/U-1.    SH/U-1.
SO/U-1.
ISSN 0047-729X

**MIDWEST FOLKLORE.**                          XXX
SUBS (1964): JOURNAL OF THE FOLKLORE
INSTITUTE, INDIANA UNIVERSITY.

**MIDWIFE & HEALTH VISITOR.**
[RECORDER P. LTD.]
LONDON 1, 1965-
MON.
LO/M-1.
LO/S74. 4, 1968-
ISSN 0020-3516

**MIE DAIGAKU NOGAKUBU ENSHURIN SHIRYO.
RESEARCH DATA, MIE UNIVERSITY FORESTS.**
TSU NO.1, 1968-
LO/N13.    XN/S-1.

**MIKOLOGIJA I FITOPATOLOGIJA.**
++MIKOL. & FITOPAT.
AKADEMIJA NAUK SSSR.
LENINGRAD 1(1), 1967-
2M. TITLE & CONT. LISTS ALSO IN ENGL.:
MYCOLOGY & PHYTOPATHOLOGY.
LO/N13.    LO/R-3.
XS/R-2. 1(1), 1967; 3, 1969-
ISSN 0026-3648

**MIKROELEMENTY V SEL'SKOM KHOZJAJSTVE I MEDIT-
SINE.**
++MIKROELEM. SEL'SK. KHOZ. & MED.
AKADEMIJA NAUK UKRAJINS'KOJI RSR: INSTYTUT
FIZIOLOHIJI ROSLYN.
KIEV 1, 1966-
XY/N-1.
LO/N13. 3, 1967-

**MIKROELEMENTY V SIBIRI.**
++MIKROELEM. SIB.
BURJATSKIJ KOMPLEKSNYJ NAUCHNO-ISSLEDOVAT-
EL'SKIJ INSTITUT: KOMISSIJA PO IZUCHENIJU MIK-
ROELEMENTOV.
ULAN-UDE TOM 1, 1962-
S/T: INFORMATSIONNYJ BJULLETEN'. VOL. 1 PUBL.
AS: MIKROELEMENTY V VOSTOCHNOJ SIBIRI I NA
DAL'NEM VOSTOKE.
XY/N-1.
LO/N13. 3, 1964-

**MIKROELEMENTY V VOSTOCHNOJ SIBIRI I NA DAL'NEM
VOSTOKE.**                          000
SEE: MIKROELEMENTY V SIBIRI.

**MIKROFAUNA DES MEERESBODENS.**
AKADEMIE DER WISSENSCHAFTEN UND DER LITERATUR:
MATHEMATISCH-NATURWISSENSCHAFTLICHE KLASSE.
MAINZ 1, 1970-
DB/S-1.    LO/N-2.    LO/N13.    LO/U-2. 1971(7)-

**MILITARGESCHICHTE.**                          XXX
DEUTSCHES INSTITUT FUR MILITARGESCHICHTE.   XXX
BERLIN 11, JA 1972-
2M. PREV: ZEITSCHRIFT FUR MILITARGESCHICHTE
FROM 1, 1962- 10, 1971.
OX/U-1.

**MILITARHISTORISCHE SCHRIFTENREIHE.**
++MILITARHIST. SCHRIFTENR.
HEERESGESCHICHTLICHEN MUSEUM (VIENNA).
VIENNA 1, 1964-
OX/U-1.
ISSN 0544-0781

**MILITARY MODELLING.**
++MIL. MODELL.
[MODEL & ALLIED PUBL.]
LONDON 1(1), JA 1971-
MON.
ED/N-1.    LO/N14.
ISSN 0026-4083

**MILITARY VEHICLE DATA.**
++MIL. VEH. DATA.
[BELLONA PUBL.]
BRACKNELL, BERKS. NO.1, [1970]-
LO/N-1.

**MILLENNIUM. A JOURNAL OF INTERNATIONAL STUDIES.**
LONDON SCHOOL OF ECONOMICS & POLITICAL SCIENCE.
[MILLENIUM PUBL. GROUP]
*LONDON [1], 1971-*
*LO/U-3.   LO/U-8.   SW/U-1.*
*ED/N-1. 2(3), 1973/74-          EX/U-1. 1(2), 1971-*
*LO/U-1. 1(2), 1971-             LO/U14. 1(2), 1971-*
*OX/U-1. 1(2), 1971-             SH/U-1. 2, 1972-*
*ISSN 0305-8298*

**MILLING.**                                                                          XXX
**SUBS (1973): JOURNAL OF FLOUR & ANIMAL FEED MILLING.**

**MILLNOTES.**
*READING NO.1, OC 1970-*
3/A. S/T: RESULTS OF RESEARCH & FIELDWORK ON
MILLS.
*ED/N-1.   LO/N-4.   OX/U-8.*

**MILTON NEWSLETTER.**                                                                XXX
*++MILTON NEWSL.*
OHIO UNIVERSITY: DEPARTMENT OF ENGLISH.
*ATHENS, OHIO 1, 1967- 3, 1969 ...*
SUBS: MILTON QUARTERLY.
*AD/U-1.   DB/U-2.   LO/N-3.   LO/U-1.*

**MILTON QUARTERLY.**                                                                 XXX
*++MILTON Q.*
OHIO UNIVERSITY: DEPARTMENT OF ENGLISH.
*ATHENS, OHIO 4, 1970-*
PREV: MILTON NEWSLETTER FROM 1, 1967- 3, 1969.
*LO/N-3.   LO/U-1.   OX/U-1.*
*ISSN 0026-4326*

**MILTON STUDIES.**
*++MILTON STUD.*
[PITTSBURGH UNIVERSITY PRESS]
*PITTSBURGH 1, 1969-*
*AD/U-1.   CB/U-1.   ED/N-1.   ED/U-1.   EX/U-1.   LO/U-2.*
*NW/U-1.   RE/U-1.*
*NO/U-1. 2, 1970-                SH/U-1. 4, 1972-*

**MIMEOGRAPHED PUBLICATION, COMMONWEALTH BUREAU**
**OF PASTURES & FIELDCROPS.**                                                         XXX
**SUBS (1968)  REVIEW SERIES, ...**

**MIND & MENTAL HEALTH MAGAZINE.**                                                    XXX
*++MIND & MENT. HEALTH MAG.*
NATIONAL ASSOCIATION OF MENTAL HEALTH (GB).
*LONDON AUTUMN 1971- WINTER 1972.//*
Q. PREV: MENTAL HEALTH FROM 1, JA 1940-
SUMMER 1971.
*BL/P-1.   BN/U-1.   ED/N-1.   LN/U-2.   SO/U-1.*

**MINDECO MINING YEAR BOOK.**                                                         XXX
*++MINDECO MIN. YEAR BOOK.*
COPPER INDUSTRY SERVICE BUREAU (ZAMBIA).
*KITWE 1970(1971)-*
PREV: MINING YEAR BOOK OF ZAMBIA FROM 1969.
*LD/U-1.*

**MINE & QUARRY.**                                                                    XXX
MINERALS ENGINEERING SOCIETY.
[ASHIRE PUBL. LTD.]
*LONDON 1, 1972-*
PREV: MINING & MINERALS ENGINEERING FROM 1,
1964- 8(3), 1972.
*ED/N-1.   LD/U-1.   LO/N-4.   LO/N14.   LV/P-1.   OX/U-8.*
*SH/U-1.   SH/U-3.*

**MINERAL CHEMISTRY RESEARCH REPORT, DIVISION**
**OF MINERAL CHEMISTRY, CSIRO (AUSTRALIA).**                                          XXX
*++MINER. CHEM. RES. REP. DIV. MINER. CHEM. CSIRO*
*(AUST.).*
*MELBOURNE; SYDNEY 1967/68(1968)-*
PREV: ANNUAL REPORT, DIVISION OF MINERAL
CHEMISTRY ... FROM 1966/67.
*GL/U-1.   LD/U-1.   OX/U-8.*

**MINERAL DIGEST.**
*++MINER. DIG.*
[MINERAL DIGEST, LTD.]
*NEW YORK 1, [1971]-*
*LO/N-2.*

**MINERAL EXPLORATION (AUSTRALIA).**
*++MINER. EXPLOR. (AUST.).*
(AUSTRALIA) COMMONWEALTH BUREAU OF CENSUS &
STATISTICS.
*CANBERRA NO.1, 1965(1967)-*
*BH/U-1.*

**MINERAL RESOURCES REPORT (NEW MEXICO).**
*++MINER. RESOUR. REP. (NEW MEX.).*
(NEW MEXICO) STATE BUREAU OF MINES & MINERAL
RESOURCES.
*SOCORRO 1, 1969-*
SPONS. BODY ALSO: NEW MEXICO INSTITUTE OF
MINING & TECHNOLOGY.
*LO/N-2.*

**MINERALOGICAL RECORD.**
*++MINERAL. REC.*
[MINERALOGICAL RECORD, INC.]
*BOWIE, MD. 1, 1970-*
*LO/N-2.   LO/N13.*
*ISSN 0026-4628*

**MINERALOGY & MATERIALS NEWS BULLETIN FOR**
**QUANTITATIVE MICROSCOPIC METHODS.**
*++MINERAL. & MATER. NEWS BULL. QUANT. MICROSC.*
*METHODS.*
MINERALOGICAL SOCIETY: APPLIED MINERALOGY GROUP
[POLYHEDRON PRINTERS]
*CAMBRIDGE 1970-*
Q.
*BL/U-1.   ED/N-1.   OX/U-8.   SH/U-1.*
*LD/U-1. [W. 1971(4)]*

**MINERALS QUARTERLY.**
*++MINER. Q.*
COMMONWEALTH SECRETARIAT.
*LONDON 1(1), AP 1969-*
*ED/N-1.   LO/U-3.   MA/P-1.   OX/U-8.*

**MINERALS, ROCKS & INORGANIC MATERIALS.**
*++MINER. ROCKS & INORG. MATER.*
[SPRINGER]
*BERLIN; NEW YORK 1, 1968-*
S/T: MONOGRAPH SERIES OF THEORETICAL & EXP-
ERIMENTAL STUDIES.
*OX/U-8.*
*ISSN 0076-8944*

**MINERALS SCIENCE & ENGINEERING.**
*++MINER. SCI. & ENG.*
NATIONAL INSTITUTE FOR METALLURGY (S. AFRICA).
*COTTESLOE, S. AFR. 1, 1969-*
*BR/U-3.   ED/S-2.   LD/U-1.        LO/N-2.      LO/N14.*
*DB/U-2. 4, 1972-                   GL/U-2. 3, 1971-*
*SW/U-1. 2, 1970                    XS/R10. 1(2), 1969-*
*HL/U-1. 4(2), 1972- [W. 4(3).]*
*LO/U-2. 3, 1971- [W. 3(3).]*
*ISSN 0026-4660*

**MINERVA IDROCLIMATOLOGICA.**
*++MINERVA IDROCLIMATOL.*
*TURIN 1, 1961-*
*LO/N13.*
*ISSN 0026-4792*

**MINIATURE AUTO.**                                                                   XXX
[KNIGHTSBRIDGE PUBLICATIONS (1962) LTD.]
*LONDON 1, 1965-*
PREV: MINIATURE AUTOWORLD FROM 1, JA 1965.
SUBS: PART OF MODEL CARS.
*LO/P-7.*
*ED/N-1. 2(5), 1966-*

**MINIATURE WARFARE.**
*LONDON 1(1), F 1968-*
MON. S/T: THE MAGAZINE FOR THE WARGAME ENTHUSI
AST.
*ED/N-1.*
*ISSN 0026-5136*

**MINING ELECTRICAL & MECHANICAL ENGINEER.**                                          XXX
**SUBS (1969): MINING TECHNOLOGY.**

**MINING REPORTER.**                                                                  000
SEE: BERGBAU-REPORTER.

**MINING RESEARCH & DEVELOPMENT REVIEW.**                                             XXX
*++MIN. RES. & DEV. REV.*
NATIONAL COAL BOARD (GB): MINING RESEARCH &
DEVELOPMENT ESTABLISHMENT.
*STANHOPE BRETBY, STAFFS. NO.1, 1970-*
PREV: BRETBY BROADSHEET FROM NO.1, 1961- 46,
1969.
*LO/N14.*

**MINING TECHNOLOGY.**                                                                XXX
*++MIN. TECHNOL.*
ASSOCIATION OF MINING ELECTRICAL & MECHANICAL
ENGINEERS.
*LONDON 51(583), 1969-*
PREV: MINING ELECTRICAL & MECHANICAL ENGINEER
FROM 1, 1920.
*BH/U-1.   GL/U-2.   LD/U-1.   LO/N14.*
*ISSN 0026-5276*

**MINING YEAR BOOK OF ZAMBIA.**                                            XXX
COPPER INDUSTRY SERVICE BUREAU (ZAMBIA).
*KITWE 1969(1970).*
PREV: COPPERBELT OF ZAMBIA MINING INDUSTRY
YEAR BOOK FROM 1964(1965)- 1968(1969).   SUBS:
MINDECO MINING YEAR BOOK.
*BH/U-1.     GL/U-1.     OX/U-9.*

**MINISTRY STUDIES.**
*+ +MIN. STUD.*
MINISTRY STUDIES BOARD (US).
*WASHINGTON, D.C. 1(1), MY 1967-*
Q.
*OX/U-1.*

**MINNESOTA SYMPOSIA ON CHILD PSYCHOLOGY.**
*+ +MINN. SYMP. CHILD PSYCHOL.*
UNIVERSITY OF MINNESOTA: INSTITUTE OF CHILD
DEVELOPMENT.
*MINNEAPOLIS 1, 1966-*
*GL/U-1. 1967-              OX/U-8. 1967-*
*ISSN 0076-9266*

**MINTEL. MARKET INTELLIGENCE.**
[OMIS LTD.]
*CROYDON NO.1, AP 1972-*
*ED/N-1.*

**MIOSACHAN DEACHUIL.**                                                    000
SEE: IRISH DECIMAL MONTHLY.

**MIRA ABSTRACTS.**                                                        XXX
*+ +MIRA ABSTR.*
MOTOR INDUSTRY RESEARCH ASSOCIATION.
*LINDLEY, NUNEATON 1972-*
PREV: AUTOMOBILE ABSTRACTS FROM 1968- 1971.
*ED/N-1.     GL/U-1.     LO/N14.     LO/N35.*

**MIRA MONTHLY SUMMARY.**                                                  XXX
*+ +MIRA MON. SUMM.*
MOTOR INDUSTRY RESEARCH ASSOCIATION.
*LINDLEY, NUNEATON AP- D 1967 ...*
PREV: MONTHLY SUMMARY OF AUTOMOBILE ENGINEER-
ING LITERATURE FROM 1955- MR 1967. SUBS:
AUTOMOBILE ABSTRACTS.
*GL/U-1.     LO/N14.*

**AL-MIRBAD. BULLETIN OF THE ...**
UNIVERSITY OF BASRA: FACULTY OF ARTS.
*BASRA NO.1, 1968-*
*LO/U14.*

**MISCELANEA, COMISION DE INVESTIGACION CIENT-
IFICA DE LA PROVINCIA DE BUENOS AIRES.**
*+ +MISC. COM. INVEST. CIENT. PROV. BUENOS AIRES.*
COMISION DE INVESTIGACION CIENTIFICA (BUENOS
AIRES, PROVINCIA).
*LA PLATA NO.1, 1969-*
*LO/N-2.*

**MISCELLANEA, ZAKLAD ANTROPOLOGII POLSKIEJ
AKADEMII NAUK.**
*+ +MISC. ZAKL. ANTROPOL. POL. AKAD. NAUK.*
POLSKA AKADEMIA NAUK: ZAKLAD ANTROPOLOGII.
*WROCLAW 1, 1960-*
ENGL. SUMM. NUMBERED ALSO AS PART OF MAIN
SERIES: MATERIALY I PRACE ANTROPOLOGICZNE.
NO.1 OF ABOVE = NO.15 OF MATERIALY...
*LO/N-2.     LO/N-3.*

**MISCELLANEOUS PAPER, FOREST RESEARCH INSTIT-
UTE (MALAYSIA).**
*+ +MISC. PAP. FOREST RES. INST. (MALAYSIA).*
(MALAYSIA) FOREST DEPARTMENT: FOREST RESEARCH
INSTITUTE.
*KUALA LUMPUR 1, 1972-*
*OX/U-3.*

**MISCELLANEOUS PAPERS IN THE NATURAL SCIENCES.**
*+ +MISC. PAP. NATUR. SCI.*
AMERICAN UNIVERSITY OF BEIRUT.
*BEIRUT NO.1, 1963-*
*LO/N-2.*

**MISCELLANEOUS PUBLICATION, AUSTRALIAN ENTOMOL-
OGICAL SOCIETY.**
*+ +MISC. PUB. AUST. ENTOMOL. SOC.*
*BRISBANE NO.1, 1968-*
*LO/N-2.*

**MISCELLANEOUS REPORTS, RESEARCH INSTITUTE FOR
NATURAL RESOURCES (TOKYO).**                                               000
SEE: SHIGEN KAGAKU KENKYUSHO IHO.

**MISSILI E SPAZIO.**                                                      XXX
SUBS (1971): PART OF AEROTECNICA - MISSILI E
SPAZIO.

**MISSISSIPPI VALLEY JOURNAL OF BUSINESS &
ECONOMICS.**
*+ +MISS. VAL. J. BUS. & ECON.*
LOUISIANA STATE UNIVERSITY: COLLEGE OF BUSINESS
ADMINISTRATION.
*NEW ORLEANS 1(1), 1965-*
3/A. PROD. BY COLLEGE'S DIV. OF BUSINESS &
ECONOMIC RESEARCH.
*CA/U-1.*
*LO/N10. 6(1), 1970-*
*ISSN 0026-6418*

**MITTEILUNGEN, DEUTSCHE GESELLSCHAFT FUR DIE
GESAMTE HYGIENE, GESELLSCHAFT FUR GESUNDHEITS-
SCHUTZ: SEKTION FUR GESCHICHTE DER MEDIZIN.**
*+ +MITT. DEUT. GES. GESAMTE HYG. GES. GESUNDHEIT-
SSCHUTZ, GESCH. MED.*
*BERLIN NO.1, 1967-*
*LO/M24.*

**MITTEILUNGEN, DEUTSCHE MALAKOZOOLOGISCHEN
GESELLSCHAFT.**
*+ +MITT. DEUT. MALAKOZOOL. GES.*
*FRANKFURT/MAIN 1, JL 1962-*
*LO/N-2.*

**MITTEILUNGEN, ENTOMOLOGISCHERVEREIN (STUTT-
GART).**
*+ +MITT. ENTOMOLOGISCHERVER. (STUTTGART).*
*STUTTGART 1, 1966-*
*LO/N13.*

**MITTEILUNGEN AUS DEM GEOLOGISCHES INSTITUT
DER TECHNISCHE HOCHSCHULE (HANNOVER).**                                    XXX
*+ +MITT. GEOL. INST. TECH. HOCHSCH. (HANNOVER).*
*HANNOVER 1, 1963- 7, 1968 ...*
SUBS: MITTEILUNGEN AUS DEM GEOLOGISCHES INST-
ITUT DER TECHNISCHEN UNIVERSITAT HANNOVER.
*LO/N-2.*
*LO/N13. W 3, 1965; 4, 1966.*

**MITTEILUNGEN AUS DEM GEOLOGISCHEN INSTITUT
DER TECHNISCHE UNIVERSITAT HANNOVER.**                                     XXX
*+ +MITT. GEOL. INST. TECH. UNIV. HANNOVER.*
*HANNOVER 8, 1968-*
PREV: MITTEILUNGEN AUS DEM GEOLOGISCHEN INST-
ITUT DER TECHNISCHE HOCHSCHULE (HANNOVER) FROM
1, 1963- 7, 1968.
*LO/N-2.*

**MITTEILUNG, INSTITUT FUR BAU VON LANDVERK-
EHRSWEGEN.**                                                               XXX
*+ +MITT. INST. BAU LANDVERKEHRSWEGEN.*
*MUNICH 14, 1970-*
PREV: MITTEILUNGEN, INSTITUT FUR EISENBAHNBAU
UND STRASSENBAU.
*LO/N14.*

**MITTEILUNGEN, INSTITUT FUR EISENBAHNBAU UND
STRASSENBAU.**                                                             XXX
SUBS (1970): MITTEILUNGEN, INSTITUT FUR BAU
VON LANDVERKEHRSWEGEN.

**MITTEILUNGEN, INSTITUT FUR HYDRAULIK UND GEW-
ASSERKUNDE, TECHNISCHE HOCHSCHULE MUNCHEN.**
*+ +MITT. INST. HYDRAUL. & GEWASSERK. TECH.
HOCHSCH. MUNCH.*
*MUNICH 1, 1968-*
*BL/U-1.*

**MITTEILUNGEN DES INSTITUTS FUR MEERESKUNDE,
UNIVERSITAT HAMBURG.**
*+ +MITT. INST. MEERESK. UNIV. HAMBURG.*
UNIVERSITAT HAMBURG: INSTITUT FUR MEERESKUNDE.
*HAMBURG 1, 1962-*
*XS/R11.*
*XS/N-1. 10, 1968-*

**MITTEILUNGEN, INSTITUT FUR TECHNOLOGIE DER
GESUNDHEITSBAUTEN.**
*+ +MITT. INST. TECHNOL. GESUNDHEITSBAUTEN.*
*BERLIN 1, 1965-*
*LO/N14.*

**MITTEILUNGEN, SOCIETAS URALO-ALTAICA.**
*+ +MITT. SOC. URALO-ALTAICA.*
*HAMBURG 1, 1968-*
*OX/U-1.*

**MITTEILUNGEN UBER TEXTILINDUSTRIE.**                                     XXX
SUBS (1971): MITTEX.

**MITTEILUNGEN, ZENTRALINSTITUT FUR SCHWEISS-
TECHNIK DER DEUTSCHEN DEMOKRATISCHEN
REPUBLIK.**
*++MITT. ZENTRALINST. SCHWEISSTECH. DTSCH.
DEMOKR. REPUB.
HALLE 1971-
LO/N14.*

**MITTEX.**                                                                                           XXX
VEREIN EHEMALIGER TEXTILFACHSCHULER ZURICH.
*ZURICH 78(3), 1971-*
PREV: MITTEILUNGEN UBER TEXTILINDUSTRIE
FROM 1, 1894- 78(2), 1971. SPONS. BODY ALSO:
ANGEHORIGER DER TEXTILINDUSTRIE.
*LO/N14.*

**MIYAKONOJO KOGYO KOTO SENMON GAKKO KENKYU. =
MEMOIRS OF MIYAKONOJO TECHNICAL COLLEGE.**
*MIYAKONOJO-SHI 1, 1966-*
ENGL. ABSTR.
*XN/S-1.*

**MIZHSLOV'JANS'KY FOL'KLORYSTYCHNY VZAEMYNY.**        XXX
SUBS (1965): SLOV'JANS'KE LITERATUROZNAVSTVO
I FOL'KLORYSTYKA.

**MIZHSLOV'JANS'KY LITERATURNY VZAEMYNY.**                XXX
SUBS (1965): SLOV'JANS'KE LITERATUROZNAVSTVO
I FOL'KLORYSTYKA.

**MLA ABSTRACTS OF ARTICLES IN SCHOLARLY
JOURNALS.**
*++MLA ABSTR. ARTIC. SCH. J.*
MODERN LANGUAGE ASSOCIATION OF AMERICA.
*NEW YORK 1, 1970-*
ANNU. COVER TITLE: MLA ABSTRACTS.
*CA/U-1.    DB/U-2.    ED/N-1.    EX/U-1.    RE/U-1.*

**MLA INDEX SERIES.**
*++MLA INDEX SER.*
MUSIC LIBRARY ASSOCIATION.
*NEW YORK &C. NO.1, 1964-*
*OX/U-1.
ISSN 0077-2445*

**MODE. THE FIRST MIDLANDS FASHION MEDIA.**
[ASSOCIATED PUBL. LTD.]
*STOURBRIDGE 1(1), 1972-*
Q.
*OX/U-1.*

**MODEL CARS.**
ELECTRIC CAR RACING ASSOCIATION.
[MODEL & ALLIED PUBLICATIONS LTD]
*HEMEL HEMSTEAD 1, 1964-*
FROM OC 1968 INCORPORATES MINIATURE AUTO.
*ED/N-1 5(11), 1968-          LO/P-7 5(10), 1968-
LO/N14 CURRENT YEAR ONLY.*

**MODEL RAILWAY NEWS.**                                                           XXX
SUBS (1971): MODEL RAILWAYS.

**MODEL RAILWAYS.**                                                                       XXX
*++MODEL RAILW.*
[MODEL & ALLIED PUBL.]
*HEMEL HEMPSTEAD 1, 1971-*
PREV: MODEL RAILWAY NEWS FROM 1, 1925-
47(560), 1971.
*ED/N-1.    LO/N-4.    LO/N-4.    LO/N14.    OX/U-1.
ISSN 0026-7368*

**MODEL REVIEW.**
*++MODEL REV.*
[RADIO CONTROL PUBL. CO.]
*HAMPTON HILL (MIDDX.) 1, 1969-*
*LO/N14.*

**MODERN AUSTRIAN LITERATURE.**                                      XXX
*++MOD. AUSTRIAN LIT.*
INTERNATIONAL ARTHUR SCHNITZLER RESEARCH
ASSOCIATION.
*NEW YORK 1, 1968-*
PREV: JOURNAL, INTERNATIONAL ARTHUR SCHNITZLER
RESEARCH ASSOCIATION FROM 1, 1962- 6, 1967.
*LO/U-1.*    LO/U10.
ISSN 0026-7503*

**MODERN CEYLON STUDIES.**                                                  XXX
*++MOD. CEYLON STUD.*
UNIVERSITY OF CEYLON.
*PERADENIYA 1(1), JA 1970-*
2/A. PREV. PART OF: UNIVERSITY OF CEYLON
REVIEW FROM 1, AP 1943- 25(1/2), AP/OC 1967.
S/T: A JOURNAL OF THE SOCIAL SCIENCES.
*AD/U-1.    LO/N12.    LO/N-1.    LO/U-3.    LO/U-8.    LO/U14.
ISSN 0026-7570*

**MODERN CHINA STUDIES. INTERNATIONAL BULLETIN.**
*++MOD. CHINA STUD.*
[RESEARCH PUBL.]
*LONDON NO.1, AG 1970-*
2/A.
*ED/N-1.    GL/U-1.    LD/U-1.    LO/S14.    LO/U14.    MA/U-1.
OX/U-1.
ISSN 0305-7429*

**MODERN GEOLOGY.**
*++MOD. GEOL.*
[GORDON & BREACH]
*NEW YORK &C. 1, N 1969-*
*ED/N-1.    HL/U-1.    LO/N14.    OX/U-8.
ISSN 0026-7775*

**MODERN GERIATRICS.**
*++MOD. GERIATR.*
[BARKER]
*LONDON 1(1), OC 1970-*
S/T: DEVOTED TO THE DISEASES OF MIDDLE AGE
& BEYOND.
*LD/U-1.    LO/M31.    LO/N-1.    OX/U-8.
SO/U-1. 4, 1974-
ISSN 0026-7783*

**MODERNE HEIZGERATE.**                                                         XXX
*++MOD. HEIZGERATE.*
[WARMETECHNISCHE RUNDSCHAU]
*STUTTGART 1, 1960- 2, 1961.//
LO/N14.*

**MODERNE HOLZVERARBEITUNG.**                                      XXX
*++MOD. HOLZVERARB.*
[DRW-VERLAGS]
*STUTTGART 1, JA 1966- 5, 1970...*
SUBS: HOLZ- UND KUNSTSTOFFVERARBEITUNG.
*LO/N14. 3, 1968-*

**MODERN INTERNATIONAL DRAMA.**
*++MOD. INT. DRAMA.*
PENNSYLVANIA STATE UNIVERSITY.
*UNIVERSITY PARK 1(1), S 1967-*
2/A. S/T: THE MAGAZINE OF CONTEMPORARY
INTERNATIONAL DRAMA IN TRANSLATION.
*LO/N-1.
ISSN 0026-7856*

**MODERNE JORDFLYTNING.**
*++MOD. JORDFLYTNING.*
[TEKNISK FORLAG A/S]
*COPENHAGEN 1(1), 1969-*
*LO/N14.
ISSN 0026-8623*

**MODERN LANGUAGES IN SCOTLAND.**
*++MOD. LANG. SCOTL.*
SCOTTISH CENTRE FOR MODERN LANGUAGES.
*ABERDEEN NO.1, 1973-*
S/T: JOURNAL OF THE SCOTTISH CENTRAL COMMITTEE
FOR MODERN LANGUAGES.
*AD/U-1.    CA/U-1.    ED/N-1.    LD/U-1.    OX/U-1.    SW/U-1.*

**MODERN LAW & SOCIETY.**
*++MOD. LAW & SOC.*
*TUBINGEN 1, 1968-*
2/A. S/T: A REVIEW OF GERMAN LANGUAGE RESEARCH
CONTRIBUTIONS ON LAW, POLITICAL SCIENCE,
SOCIOLOGY. ISSUED AS GERMAN STUDIES:
SECTION 2.
*LO/S29.    MA/P-1.
SH/U-1. 6, 1973-
CO/U-1. 4(1), 1971.
ISSN 0026-7953*

**MODERN MANAGEMENT & ADMINISTRATION IN GENERAL
PRACTICE.**
*++MOD. MANAGE. & ADM. GEN. PRACT.*
BUREAU OF MEDICAL PRACTITIONER AFFAIRS.
*LONDON 1, 1970-*
*BL/U-1.    LD/U-1.*

**MODERN MANUFACTURING.**                                              XXX
*++MOD. MFR.*
[MCGRAW-HILL]
*NEW YORK 126(6), 1968; 1(2), JL 1968-*
PREV: FACTORY FROM 117, 1959- 126(5), 1968.
*BH/P-1.    LO/N14.    MA/P-1.
ISSN 0026-802X*

**MODERN NUTRITION.**                                              XXX
+ +MOD. NUTR.
AMERICAN ACADEMY OF NUTRITION.
*LOS ANGELES 5, JA 1952- 21, 1968.//*
PREV: MONTHLY NEWSLETTER JOURNAL, AMERICAN
ACADEMY OF APPLIED NUTRITION FROM 1, 1948- 4,
1951.
*XY/N-1.\*\**
*LO/N13. 17, 1964-*

**MODERN OCCASIONS. A QUARTERLY OF LITERATURE
& IDEAS OF CULTURE & POLITICS.**
+ +MOD. OCCAS.
*CAMBRIDGE, MASS. 1(1), 1970-*
*OX/U-1.    SH/U-1.*
*CA/U-1. 1971-          NO/U-1. 1972-*
*ISSN 0026-8186*

**MODERN PLASTICS.**                                              XXX
SUBS (1971): MODERN PLASTICS INTERNATIONAL.

**MODERN PLASTICS INTERNATIONAL.**                                XXX
+ +MOD. PLAST. INT.
[MCGRAW-HILL]
*LAUSANNE 1(1), JA 1971-*
PREV: MODERN PLASTICS FROM 1, 1925- 47, 1970.
*BH/P-1.    LO/N-6.    LO/N14.    OX/U-8.    XS/R10.    XS/T-4.*
*MA/U-1. 1(3), 1971-*
*XS/R10. (5 YEARS).*
*ISSN 0026-8283*

**MODERNE PROBLEME DER PHARMACOPSYCHIATRIE.**                      000
SEE: MODERN PROBLEMS OF PHARMACOPSYCHIATRY.

**MODERN PROBLEMS OF PHARMACOPSYCHIATRY. = MODERNE
PROBLEME DER PHARMACOPSYCHIATRIE. = PROBLEMES
ACTUELS DE PHARMACOPSYCHIATRIE.**
+ +MOD. PROBL. PHARMACOPSYCHIAT.
[KARGER]
*BASLE 1, 1968-*
*LO/M17. 3, 1969-*

**MODERN SCOTTISH POETS.**
+ +MOD. SCOTT. POETS.
[JOHN HUMPRIES, CAITHNESS BOOKS]
*THURSO 1, 1968-*
*GL/U-1.    LO/U-2.*

**MODERN TRENDS IN BIOMECHANICS.**
+ +MOD. TRENDS BIOMECH.
[BUTTERWORTHS]
*LONDON 1, 1970-*
*CA/U-1.    GL/U-1.    LO/U-2.    LO/U20.    NW/U-1.*
*ISSN 0581-0302*

**MODERN TRENDS IN CARDIAC SURGERY.**
+ +MOD. TRENDS CARD. SURG.
[BUTTERWORTHS]
*LONDON [1], 1960-*
*GL/U-1.    NW/U-1.*
*ISSN 0544-6783*

**MODERN TRENDS IN DRUG DEPENDENCE & ALCOHOLISM.**
+ +MOD. TRENDS DRUG DEPEND. & ALCOHOL.
[BUTTERWORTHS]
*LONDON 1, 1970-*
*LO/U-2.    NW/U-1.*

**MODERN TRENDS IN HUMAN GENETICS.**
+ +MOD. TRENDS HUMAN GENET.
[BUTTERWORTHS]
*LONDON 1, 1970-*
*AD/U-1.    AD/U-3.    GL/U-1.    LO/N13.    LO/U-2.    NW/U-1.*

**MODERN TRENDS IN MENTAL HEALTH AND SUBNORMAL-
ITY.**
+ +MOD. TRENDS MENT. HEALTH & SUBNORMAL.
[BUTTERWORTHS]
*LONDON 1, 1968-*
*BN/U-1.    GL/U-1.*

**MODERN TRENDS IN PHYSIOLOGY.**
+ +MOD. TRENDS PHYSIOL.
[BUTTERWORTHS]
*LONDON 1, 1972-*
*CA/U-1.    GL/L'-1.    LO/U-2.    NW/U-1.*

**MODERN TRENDS IN RADIOTHERAPY.**
+ +MOD. TRENDS RADIOTHER.
[BUTTERWCRTHS]
*LONDON 1, 1967-*
*GL/U-1.    LO/N14.    NW/U-1.*

**MODERN TRENDS IN RHEUMATOLOGY.**
+ +MOD. TRENDS RHEUMATOL.
[BUTTERWORTH]
*LONDON 1, 1966-*
*GL/U-1.    LO/N13.    NW/U-1.*

**MODERN TRENDS IN SURGERY.**
+ +MOD. TRENDS SURG.
[BUTTERWORTH]
*LONDON 1, 1962-*
*BL/P-1.*

**MODERN TRENDS IN TOXICOLOGY.**
+ +MOD. TRENDS TOXICOL.
[BUTTERWORTHS]
*LONDON 1, 1968-*
*GL/U-1.    LO/N13.    OX/U-8.*

**MODERN TRENDS IN VASCULAR SURGERY.**
+ +MOD. TRENDS VASC. SURG.
[BUTTERWORTHS; APPLETON-CENTURY CROFTS]
*LONDON; NEW YORK 1, 1970-*
*GL/U-1.*

**MODERNE WELT.**                                                 XXX
+ +MOD. WELT.
ARBEITSKREIS FUR OST-WEST-FRAGEN.
*COLOGNE 1(1), JE 1959- 11(4), 1970.//*
S/T: ZEITSCHRIFT FUR VERGLEICHENDE GEISTES-
GESCHICHTLICHE UND SOZIALWISSENSCHAFTLICHE
FORSCHUNG.
*LO/N-3.    LO/U-3.*
*LO/S29. 8, 1967-*
*ISSN 0026-8674*

**MODERN WORLD.**
+ +MOD. WORLD.
STUDY GROUP ON EAST-WEST QUESTIONS (WOHRENDAMM)
[ECON VERLAG]
*DUSSELDORF 1965/66 (1967)-*
S/T: ANNUAL REVIEW OF INTERNATIONAL RELATIONS
& POLITICAL SCIENCE.
*LO/U10.    MA/U-1.*

**MODULAR QUARTERLY.**                                            XXX
+ +MODULAR Q. [MODQ-A]
MODULAR SOCIETY.
*LONDON 1955- 1970//*
PREV: TRANSACTIONS OF THE MODULAR SOCIETY FROM
1953- 1955. COMPRISES THE TRANSACTIONS OF THE
SOCIETY, NO.19-71; & OF THE INTERNATIONAL
MODULAR GROUP, NO.1-39. TRANSACTIONS CONT. IN
OAP JOURNAL FOR THE BUILT ENVIRONMENT.
*LO/N14. 1957-*
*ISSN 0544-7232*

**MOLECULAR BIOLOGY, BIOCHEMISTRY & BIOPHYSICS.
MOLEKULARBIOLOGIE, BIOCHEMIE UND BIOPHYSIK.**
+ +MOL. BIOL. BIOCHEM. & BIOPHYS.
[SPRINGER]
*BERLIN NO.1, 1967-*
*LO/U-2.*
*ISSN 0077-0221*

**MOLECULAR BIOLOGY REPORTS.**
+ +MOL. BIOL. REP.
[REIDEL]
*DORDRECHT 1(1), JE 1973-*
S/T: AN INTERNATIONAL JOURNAL FOR RAPID COM-
MUNICATIONS IN MOLECULAR BIOLOGY.
*CA/U-2.    LO/N14.    OX/U-8.    SH/U-1.*

**MOLECULAR & CELLULAR BIOCHEMISTRY.**                            XXX
+ +MOL. & CELL. BIOCHEM.
[W. JUNK]
*THE HAGUE 1, 1973-*
PREV: ENZYMOLOGIA FROM 1, 1936- 46, 1972.
*BL/U-1.    CR/U-1.    DB/U-2.    GL/U-1.    LD/U-1.    LO/N-4.*
*LO/N14.    LO/S-3.    LO/U-1.    MA/U-1.    OX/U-8.    RE/U-1.*
*SH/U-1.    SO/U-1.*
*ISSN 0300-8177*

**MOLECULAR CRYSTALS.**                                           XXX
+ +MOL. CRYST.
[GORDON & BREACH]
*LONDON &C 1, JA 1966- 5(3), F 1969 ...*
SUBS: MOLECULAR CRYSTALS & LIQUID CRYSTALS.
*BH/U-1.    BN/U-2.    ED/N-1.    GL/U-2.    LO/N-4.    LO/S-3.*
*LO/U-2.    LO/U11.*
*HL/U-1. 1, 1966; 3, 1968-*

**MOLECULAR CRYSTALS & LIQUID CRYSTALS.**                         XXX
+ +MOL. CRYST. LIQUID CRYST.
[GORDON & BREACH]
*LONDON 5(4), 1969-*
PREV: MOLECULAR CRYSTALS FROM 1(1), 1966-
5(3), F 1969.
*GL/U-2.    LO/N14.*
*ISSN 0026-8941*

**MOLECULAR EVOLUTION.**
++MOL. EVOL.
[NORTH-HOLLAND PUBL. CO.]
AMSTERDAM; NEW YORK 1, 1971-
CA/U-1.

**MOLECULAR & GENERAL GENETICS.**                    XXX
++MOLEC. & GEN. GENET.
[SPRINGER]
BERLIN &C 99(1), 1967-
PREV: ZEITSCHRIFT FUR VERERBUNGSLEHRE FROM
89(5), 1958- 98, 1966.
BH/U-1.    CA/U15.    LD/U-1.    LO/U-2.    MA/U-1.
ISSN 0026-8925

**MOLECULAR PHOTOCHEMISTRY.**
++MOL. PHOTOCHEM.
[DEKKER]
NEW YORK 1, JA 1969-
BH/U-1.    CA/U-2.    DN/U-1.    LO/S-3.    MA/U-1.    OX/U-1.
OX/U-8.    RE/U-1.    SF/U-1.
BH/U-3.    2, 1970-
GL/U-1.    2, 1970- 3, 1972.
ISSN 0026-8968

**MOLECULAR SPECTROSCOPY.**
++MOL. SPECTROSC.
CHEMICAL SOCIETY.
LONDON 1, 1971(1973)-
S/T: A REVIEW OF THE RECENT LITERATURE.
BL/U-1.    CA/U-1.    CB/U-1.    ED/N-1.    GL/U-1.    GL/U-2.
HL/U-1.    LO/N14.    LO/S-3.    LO/U-2.    LO/U12.    MA/U-1.
RE/U-1.    SO/U-1.
ISSN 0305-9782

**MOLECULAR STRUCTURES & DIMENSIONS.**
INTERNATIONAL UNION OF CRYSTALLOGRAPHY.
UTRECHT 1, 1970-
A.  SPONS. BODY ALSO CRYSTALLOGRAPHIC DATA
CENTRE (CAMBRIDGE).
BH/U-1.    CA/U-1.    LO/U11.    LO/N14.    SH/U-1.

**MOLEKULARBIOLOGIE, BIOCHEMIE UND BIOPHYSIK.**       000
SEE: MOLECULAR BIOLOGY, BIOCHEMISTRY & BIO-
PHYSICS.

**MOLLUSCAN DIGEST.**
++MOLLUSCAN DIG.
[PISMO BEACH, CALIF.] 1, 1971-
LO/N-2.

**MONARCHIST BOOK REVIEW.**
++MONARCHIST BOOK REV.
MONARCHIST PRESS ASSOCIATION.
LONDON 1968/69-
ANNU.  S/T: AN ANNOTATED LIST OF NEW & RE-
PRINTED BOOKS DEALING WITH VARIOUS ASPECTS OF
MONARCHY PUBLISHED IN GREAT BRITAIN.
LO/U-3.
ISSN 0077-0280

**MONATSBERICHTE, DEUTSCHE AKADEMIE DER WISSEN-**
**SCHAFTEN ZU BERLIN.**                              XXX
++MONATSBER. DTSCH. AKAD. WISS. BERL. [MDAW-A]
BERLIN 1, 1959- 13, 1971.//
LO/N-2.    LO/N-4.    LO/N14.
ISSN 0011-9814

**MONDA LINGVO-PROBLEMO.**
++MONDA LINGVO-PROBL.
CENTRO DE ESPLORO KAJ DOKUMENTADO PRI LA MONDA
LINGVO-PROBLEMO.
THE HAGUE 1, JA 1969-
S/T: SOCIA LINGVISTIKA, POLITIKA, JURA, PSIK-
OLOGIA, EKONOMIKA.  ARTICLES IN VARIOUS LANG.
WITH SUMM. IN ESPERANTO.
BD/U-1.    LO/U-2.    LO/U-3.    OX/U-1.
ISSN 0026-9344

**MONDE MODERNE.**
++MONDE MOD.
SOCIETE NOUVELLE D'EDITION ET DE DIFFUSION.
PARIS 1, 1972-
Q.
OX/U-1.

**MONDES EN DEVELOPPEMENT.**
++MONDES DEV.
[EDITIONS TECHNIQUES ET ECONOMIQUES]
PARIS NO.1, 1973-
LO/U14.    OX/U16.

**MONEY MANAGEMENT & UNITHOLDER.**                   XXX
++MONEY MANAGE. & UNITHOLDER.
FUNDEX LTD.
LONDON OC 1970-
M.  PREV: UNITHOLDER FROM 1, F 1963- S 1970.
BN/U-1.    MA/U-1.
ISSN 0028-6052

**MONEYSAVERS.**
MONEYSAVERS ASSOCIATION.
LONDON 1, D 1972-
ED/N-1.

**MONGOLIA SOCIETY BULLETIN.**                       XXX
++MONGOLIA SOC. BULL.
BLOOMINGTON, IND. 4(1), 1965-
2/A.  PREV: MONGOLIA SOCIETY NEWSLETTER FROM
1, 1962- 3, 1964.
LD/U-1.  4(1), 1965- 5(2), 1966.
ISSN 0026-9654

**MONGOLIA SOCIETY NEWSLETTER.**                     XXX
++MONGOLIA SOC. NEWSL.
NEW YORK &C. 1, 1962- 3, 1964 ...
2/A.  SUBS: MONGOLIA SOCIETY BULLETIN.
LD/U-1.  2(1), 1963.  3(2), 1964.

**MONMOUTHSHIRE WILDLIFE REPORT.**
++MONMOUTHSHIRE WILDL. REP.
MONMOUTHSHIRE NATURALISTS TRUST, LTD.
[NEWPORT] NO.1, 1964-
LO/N-2.

**MONOGRAM.  BRIGHTON FILM REVIEW.**
LONDON NO.1, AP 1971-
ED/N-1.

**MONOGRAPH, AUSTRALIAN ACADEMY OF THE**
**HUMANITIES.**
++MONOGR. AUST. ACAD. HUM.
[SYDNEY UNIV. P.]
SYDNEY NO.1, 1970-
LO/N-1.    OX/U-1.

**MONOGRAPH, BUREAU OF BUSINESS & ECONOMIC**
**RESEARCH, UNIVERSITY OF IDAHO.**
++MONOGR. BUR. BUS. & ECON. RES. UNIV. IDAHO.
MOSCOW, IDAHO NO.1, 1963-
BUREAU SUBORD. TO COLLEGE OF BUSINESS
ADMINISTRATION.
LO/N-1.

**MONOGRAPHS, CATHOLIC RECORD SOCIETY.**
++MONOGR. CATH. REC. SOC.
LONDON 1, 1966/67 (1968)-
LO/U-1.    SH/U-1.

**MONOGRAPHIE, CENTRE D'ETUDES ET DE RECHERCHES**
**DE L'INDUSTRIE DU BETON MANUFACTURE.**
++MONOGR. CENT. ETUD. & RECH. IND. BETON MFR.
EPERNON NO.1, 1970-
LO/N14.

**MONOGRAFIAS CIENTIFICAS 'AUGUSTO PI SUNER.'**
++MONOGR. CIENT. AUGUSTO PI SUNER.
INSTITUTO PEDAGOGICO NACIONAL (VENEZUELA).
CARACAS NO.1, 1970-
LO/N-2.

**MONOGRAFIAS, DEPARTMENT OF SCIENTIFIC AFFAIRS,**
**PAN-AMERICAN UNION.**                              000
SEE:  SERIE DE [VARIOUS SUBJECTS], DEPARTMENT
OF SCIENTIFIC AFFAIRS ...

**MONOGRAPHS ON DRUGS.**
++MONOGR. DRUGS.
[KARGER]
BASEL &C. 1, 1972-
DB/U-2.

**MONOGRAPHIES D'HISTOIRE SUISSE.**
SEE: MONOGRAPHIEN ZUR SCHWEIZER GESCHICHTE.

**MONOGRAPHS, INDIANA ACADEMY OF SCIENCE.**
++MONOGR. INDIANA ACAD. SCI.
INDIANAPOLIS NO.1, 1969-
DB/S-1.    ED/S-2.    LO/N-2.

**MONOGRAFIAS, INSTITUTO DE CIENCIAS DO HOMEM,**
**UNIVERSIDADE FEDERAL DE PERNAMBUCO.**
++MONOGR. INST. CIENC. HOMEM UNIV. FED.
PERNAMBUCO.
RECIFE 1, 1966-
ISSUED BY THE INST. DIVISAO DE HISTORIA.
OX/U-1.

MONOGRAPHIES, INSTITUT D'HISTOIRE A BEOGRAD SERIE 1: LES PAYS YOUGOSLAVES AU XX SIECLE. 000
SEE: POSEBNA IZDANJA, ISTORIJSKI INSTITUT, SRPSKA AKADEMIJA NAUKA I UMETNOSTI, SERIJA 1: JUGOSLOVENSKE ZEMIJE U XX VEKU.

MONOGRAPH, INSTITUTE OF WORK STUDY PRACTITIONERS.
++MONOGR. INST. WORK STUD. PRACT.
ENFIELD NO.1, 1967-
OX/U-1.

MONOGRAFIA, LABORATORIO DEL TRANSPORTE Y MECANICA DEL SUELO (MADRID).
++MONOGR. LAB. TRANSP. MEC. SUELO (MADR.).
MADRID 1, 1966-
LO/N14.

MONOGRAPHS ON THE LIFE OF THOMAS HARDY. XXX
++MONOGR. LIFE THOMAS HARDY.
BEAMINSTER, DORSET NO.1, 1962- 22, 1965 ...
SUBS: MONOGRAPHS ON THE LIFE, TIMES & WORKS OF THOMAS HARDY.
LO/U-1.

MONOGRAPHS ON THE LIFE, TIMES & WORKS OF THOMAS HARDY. XXX
++MONOGR. LIFE TIMES & WORKS THOMAS HARDY.
BEAMINSTER, DORSET NO.23, 1966- 72, 1971.
PREV: MONOGRAPHS ON THE LIFE OF THOMAS HARDY FROM NO.1, 1962- 22, 1965. SUBS: THOMAS HARDY YEAR BOOK.
LO/U-1.
ISSN 0544-8514

MONOGRAPHS ON MEDITERRANEAN ANTIQUITY.
++MONOGR. MEDITERR. ANTIQ.
NEW YORK UNIVERSITY: DEPARTMENT OF CLASSICS.
[BRILL]
LEIDEN 1967-
CA/U-1.

MONOGRAPH, NORFOLK REED GROWERS ASSOCIATION.
++MONOGR. NORFOLK REED GROW. ASSOC.
NORWICH NO.1, 1969-
OX/U-8.

MONOGRAPHS IN PAEDIATRICS.
++MONOGR. PAEDIATR.
[KARGER]
BASLE &C. 1, 1971-
OX/U-8.

MONOGRAPHS ON PLASTICS.
++MONOGR. PLAST.
NEW YORK 1, 1972-
OX/U-8.

MONOGRAPHS, RESEARCH DIVISION, VIRGINIA POLYTECHNIC INSTUTUTE.
++MONOGR. RES. DIV. VA. POLYTECH. INST.
BLACKSBURG, VA. 1, 1969-
LO/N-2.

MONOGRAPHIEN ZUR SCHWEIZER GESCHICHTE. = MONOGRAPHIES D'HISTOIRE SUISSE.
++MONOGR. SCHWEIZ. GESCH.
ALLGEMEINE GESCHICHTFORSCHENDE GESELLSCHAFT DER SCHWEIZ.
[FRANCKE]
BERN 1, 1968-
LO/N-1.

MONOGRAPH OF THE SCIENCE MUSEUM OF MINNESOTA.
++MONOGR. SCI. MUS. MINN.
SAINT PAUL INSTITUTE: SCIENCE MUSEUM.
ST. PAUL, MINN. 1, 1972-
LO/N-2.

MONOGRAPH SERIES, ASSOCIATION OF PUBLIC HEALTH INSPECTORS.
++MONOGR. SER. ASSOC. PUBLIC HEALTH INSP.
LONDON [1], 1972-
BL/U-1.

MONOGRAPH SERIES, CENTRE FOR LATIN AMERICAN STUDIES, UNIVERSITY OF LIVERPOOL.
++MONOGR. SER. CENT. LAT. AM. STUD. UNIV. LIVERP
LIVERPOOL NO.1, 1970-
LO/N-1.  LO/U-1.

MONOGRAPH SERIES, DEPARTMENT OF ENGLISH, UNIVERSITY OF TULSA.
++MONOGR. SER. DEP. ENGL. UNIV. TULSA.
TULSA NO.1, 1966-
LO/N-1.  LO/N-3.  OX/U-1.

MONOGRAPH SERIES, DEPARTMENT OF GEOGRAPHY, JAMES COOK UNIVERSITY OF NORTH QUEENSLAND.
++MONOGR. SER. DEP. GEOGR. JAMES COOK UNIV. NORTH QUEENSL.
TOWNSVILLE NO.1, 1970-
LO/N-2.  LO/S13.

MONOGRAPH SERIES, DIVISION OF MARINE FISHERIES, DEPARTMENT OF NATURAL RESOURCES (MASSACHUSETTS).
++MONOGR. SER. DIV. MAR. FISH. DEP. NATUR. RESOUR. (MASS.).
BOSTON NO.1, 1965-
LO/N14.
LO/N-2.  NO.2, 1966-

MONOGRAPH SERIES, INSTITUTE OF HUMAN BIOLOGY (PAPUA-NEW GUINEA).
++MONOGR. SER. INST. HUM. BIOL. (PAPUA-NEW GUINEA).
MADANG NO.1, 1970-
LO/N13.

MONOGRAPH SERIES, KOREA BRANCH, ROYAL ASIATIC SOCIETY OF GREAT BRITAIN & IRELAND.
++MONOGR. SER. KOREA BRANCH R. ASIAT. SOC. G.B. & IREL.
SEOUL NO.1, 1967-
LO/N-1.

MONOGRAPH SERIES, OVERSEAS DEVELOPMENT COUNCIL (US).
++MONOGR. SER. OVERSEAS DEV. COUNC. (US).
WASHINGTON, D.C. NO.1, 1970-
OX/U16.

MONOGRAPH SERIES, SOUTH PACIFIC REGIONAL COLLEGE OF TROPICAL AGRICULTURE.
++MONOGR. SER. SOUTH PAC. REG. COLL. TROP. AGRIC.
ALAFUA 1, 1970-
CA/U11.

MONOGRAPH, SIAM SOCIETY.
++MONOGR. SIAM SOC.
BANGKOK NO.1, 1962-
HL/U-1.**
LO/N-2.  NO.3, 1966.

MONOGRAFIE SLASKIE OSSOLINEUM.
++MONOGR. SLASK. OSSOLINEUM.
ZAKLAD NARODOWY IM. OSSOLINSKICH WE WROCLAWIU.
WROCLAW 1, 1960-
MONOGR.
BH/U-1.  LO/U-3.  OX/U-1.

MONOGRAPHIEN UND TEXTE ZUR NIETZSCHE-FORSCHUNG.
++MONOGR. & TEXTE NIETZSCHE-FORSCH.
BERLIN 1, 1972-
OX/U-1.

MONOGRAPHS IN VIROLOGY.
++MONOGR. VIROL.
[KARGER]
BASEL 1, 1968-
GL/U-1.

MONOTYPE BULLETIN. XXX
++MONOTYPE BULL.
MONOTYPE CORP. LTD.
LONDON NO.74, 1968- 88, 1973.
PREV: MONOTYPE TECHNICAL BULLETIN FROM NO.1, 1943- 73, 1967. SUBS. PART OF: MONOTYPE PICTORIAL.
ED/N-1.
LO/N14.  NO.74, 1968- 88, 1973.

MONOTYPE TECHNICAL BULLETIN. XXX
SUBS (1968): MONOTYPE BULLETIN.

MONTHLY BIBLIOGRAPHY OF MEDICAL REVIEWS.
++M. BIBLIOGR. MED. REV.
NATIONAL LIBRARY OF MEDICINE (US).
BETHESDA, MD. 1(1), JA 1968-
OX/U-8.  1(5), 1968-
ISSN 0027-0202

MONTHLY BULLETIN, CLIMATIC RESEARCH UNIT. 000
SEE: CRUMB. CLIMATIC RESEARCH UNIT MONTHLY BULLETIN.

MONTHLY BULLETIN OF THE MINISTRY OF HEALTH & THE PUBLIC HEALTH LABORATORY SERVICE. XXX
SUBS: (1969) HEALTH TRENDS.

MONTHLY ECONOMIC BULLETIN, GHANA COMMERCIAL
BANK.
++MON. ECON. BULL. GHANA COMMER. BANK.
ACCRA [1, 1971]-
ISSUED BY THE BANK'S ECONOMIC INTELLIGENCE
DEPARTMENT.
LO/U-8. 3(11), 1973-

MONTHLY INDEX TO PERIODICALS PUBLISHED IN
TAIWAN.                                                    000
SEE: CHUNG-HUA MIN-KUO CH'I-K'AN LUN-WEN SO-
YIN.

MONTHLY NEWSLETTER JOURNAL, AMERICAN ACADEMY
OF APPLIED NUTRITION.                                      XXX
SUBS (1952): MODERN NUTRITION.

MONTHLY NEWS LETTER, LOUISIANA SOCIETY FOR
HORTICULTURAL RESEARCH.                                    XXX
++M. NEWS LETT. LA. SOC. HORT. RES.
LAFAYETTE 1, 1960- 8(2), 1967 ...
SUBS: LSHR NEWS LETTER.
LO/N13. 3, 1962-

MONTHLY REVIEW, INSTITUTE OF TRADING STAND-
ARDS ADMINISTRATION.                                       XXX
++MON. REV. INST. TRAD. STAND. ADM.
SLOUGH, BUCKS 80(8), AG 1972-
PREV: MONTHLY REVIEW, INSTITUTE OF WEIGHTS &
MEASURES ADMINISTRATION FROM 1, 1893- 80(7),
1972.
ED/N-1.

MONTHLY REVIEW, INSTITUTE OF WEIGHTS & MEAS-
URES ADMINISTRATION.                                       XXX
SUBS (1972): MONTHLY REVIEW, INSTITUTE OF
TRADING STANDARDS ADMINISTRATION.

MONTHLY SELECTION OF RECENT PUBLICATIONS
(BOOKS, THESES ETC.) IN THE FIELDS OF SPORT,
PHYSICAL EDUCATION & RECREATION.
++MON. SEL. RECENT PUBL. (BOOKS THESES ETC.)
FIELDS SPORT PHYS. EDUC. & RECREAT.
QUEEN'S UNIVERSITY OF BELFAST: PHYSICAL EDUCAT-
ION CENTRE.
BELFAST NO.1, JA 1972-
SPONS. BODY ALSO: UNITED KINGDOM NATIONAL
DOCUMENTATION CENTRE FOR SPORT, PHYSICAL
EDUCATION & RECREATION.
BL/U-1.      OX/U-1.
ED/N-1. 2, 1972-                    HL/U-2. 3, 1973-
SH/P-1. 1974- [ONE YEAR FILED]

MONTHLY STATISTICAL BULLETIN OF BANGLADESH.
++MON. STAT. BULL. BANGLADESH.
(BANGLADESH) BUREAU OF STATISTICS.
DACCA 1(1), 1972-
LO/U14.

MONTHLY SUMMARY OF AUTOMOBILE ENGINEERING
LITERATURE.                                                XXX
SUBS (1967): MIRA MONTHLY SUMMARY.

MONTICOLA.
ARBEITSGEMEINSCHAFT FUR ALPENORNITHOLOGIE.
INNSBRUCK 1(1), 1966-
LO/N13.

MONTPELLIER MEDICAL.                                       XXX
SUBS (1966): JOURNAL DE MEDECINE DE MONT-
PELLIER.

MONUMENTUM.
CONSEIL INTERNATIONAL DES MONUMENTS ET DES
SITES.
LOUVAIN 1, 1967-
2/A. FR. WITH ENGL. SUMM.
RE/U-1. 1, 1967- 2, 1968.
ISSN 0027-0776

MOODIES AUSTRALIAN REVIEW.
++MOODIES AUST. REV.
[MOODIES SERVICES LTD.]
LONDON NO.1, OC 1970-
M.
ED/N-1.

MOODIES JAPANESE REVIEW.
++MOODIES JAP. REV.
[MOODIES SERVICES LTD.]
LONDON 1, 1973-
CA/U-1.      ED/N-1.      OX/U-1.

MOON. AN INTERNATIONAL JOURNAL OF LUNAR
STUDIES.
[REIDEL PUBL. CO.]
DORDRECHT 1(1), N 1969-
Q.
AD/U-1.      LO/N-4.      LO/U-2.      OX/U-8.      SH/U-1.
LO/U12. 3(1), 1971-
LO/N-2. 1, 1969- 11, 1974.
ISSN 0027-0903

MORAL EDUCATION.
++MORAL EDUC.
[PERGAMON]
OXFORD 1(1), 1969-
3/A.
CA/U-1.      HL/U-2.      LO/N-6.      LO/U11.      MA/U-1.      OX/U-1.
ED/N-1. 1(3), D 1969-
ISSN 0027-0997

MOROCCAN ANNALS OF SOCIOLOGY.                              000
SEE: ANNALES MAROCAINES DE SOCIOLOGIE.

MOSAIC. A JOURNAL FOR THE COMPARATIVE STUDY
OF LITERATURE & IDEAS.
[UNIVERSITY OF MANITOBA P.]
WINNIPEG 1(1), OC 1967-
BL/U-1.      ED/N-1.      OX/U-1.      SW/U-1.
CB/U-1. 2, 1968-                          DB/U-2. 5(4), 1972-
DN/U-1. 4(1), 1970-
BH/U-1. 1, 1967- 3, 1968.
HL/U-1. 1(3); 2(2), 1968-
ISSN 0027-1276

MOSAIC. QUARTERLY JOURNAL OF ...
NATIONAL SCIENCE FOUNDATION (US).
WASHINGTON, D.C. 1, 1970-
LO/N14.
ISSN 0027-1284

MOSCOW NEWSLETTER.
++MOSC. NEWSL.
(GREAT BRITAIN) DEPARTMENT OF TRADE & INDUSTRY.
LONDON NO.1, 1972-
LO/N35.      NW/U-1.      OX/U-8.      SH/U-1.
LO/U-3. [CURRENT ISSUES ONLY]

MOSCOW UNIVERSITY MATHEMATICS BULLETIN.
++MOSC. UNIV. MATH. BULL.
[FARADAY P.]
NEW YORK 24, 1969(1971)-
TRANSL. OF SECTION MATEMATIKA OF VESTNIK
MOSKOVSKOGO UNIVERSITETA: SERIJA 1:
MATEMATIKA, MEKHANIKA.
LO/N14.      LO/N14.
ISSN 0027-1322

MOSELLA.
CENTRE D'ETUDES GEOGRAPHIQUES (METZ).
METZ 1(1), 1971-
SPONS. BODY ALSO DEPARTMENT DE GEOGRAPHIE DE
LA FACULTE DES LETTRES DE METZ.
EX/U-1.      OX/U-1.
ISSN 0047-8164

MOSQUITO SYSTEMATICS.                                      XXX
++MOSQ. SYST.
RALEIGH, N.C. 4, 1972-
PREV: MOSQUITO SYSTEMATICS NEWSLETTER FROM 1,
1969- 3, 1971.
LO/N-2.

MOSQUITO SYSTEMATICS NEWSLETTER.                           XXX
++MOSQUITO SYST. NEWSL.
RALEIGH, N.C. NO.1, 1969- 3, 1971.
SUBS: MOSQUITO SYSTEMATICS.
LO/N-2.

MOTHER. A JOURNAL OF NEW LITERATURE.
NEW YORK NO.1, AP 1964-
AFTER NO.8, MY 1967 (ACCORDING TO NST) 'LATER
PARTS WILL NOT BE PRINTED BUT WILL BE ISSUED
AS LONG-PLAYING RECORDS.'
LO/U-2. 6, 1965-                          LO/U11. 7, 1966-

MOTHER EARTH.                                              XXX
SUBS (1968): JOURNAL OF THE SOIL ASSOCIATION.

MOTOR RACING THE INTERNATIONAL WAY.
++MOT. RAC. INT. WAY.
[BARNES]
LONDON &C. 1(1), 1970-
OX/U-1.

MOTUS. PERIODICAL OF THE ARTS.
UNIVERSITY COLLEGE, CORK: ARTS SOCIETY.
CORK 1, 1968-
BL/U-1.      LO/U-2.

**MOUNT SINAI JOURNAL OF MEDICINE.**          XXX
*+ +MOUNT SINAI J. MED.*
MOUNT SINAI HOSPITAL (NEW YORK).
*BALTIMORE 37, 1970-*
PREV: JOURNAL OF THE MOUNT SINAI HOSPITAL FROM
1, MY/JE 1934.
*LD/U-1.     LO/M-1.*

**MOUNT WILHELM STUDIES.**                     000
SEE: MT. WILHELM STUDIES.

**MOUNTAIN HOLIDAYS.**
*+ +MT. HOLIDAYS.*
MOUNTAINEERING ASSOCIATION.
*LONDON [1], JA 1967-*
*OX/U-1.*

**MOVE.**
*PRESTON   NO.1, D 1964-*
Q.
*ED/N-1.  6, 1966-                 LO/U-2.  5, 1966-*

**MOVEMENT.**
*LONDON  NO.1, JA 1973-*
MON.
*ED/N-1.    LO/U-3.    OX/U-1.*

**MOVEMENT. A SCOUT & GUIDE JOURNAL.**
[INDEPENDENT SCOUT & GUIDE PUBL.]
*SWINDON  1, 1969-*
*BH/U-1.    ED/N-1.*

**MOVOZNAVSTVO.  NAUKOVO TEORETYCHNYJ ZHURNAL.**
AKADEMIJA NAUK UKRAJINS'KOJI RSR: VIDDIL
LITERATURY, MOVY I MYSTETSVOZNAVSTVA.
*KIEV 1(1), 1967-*
2M.
*LO/N-3.  5(1), 1971-*

**MOYENS AUDIO-VISUELS.**                       000
SEE:  AUDIO-VISUAL MEDIA.

**MOZAIKA: RUSSIAN-ENGLISH.**
*WARSAW  NO.1, 1964-*
*LO/N-3.*
*GL/U-1. 1965-              HL/U-1. 1967-*

**MPA REVIEW.**
*+ +MPA REV.*
METROPOLITAN PENSIONS ASSOCIATION.
*LONDON  NO.1, 1968-*
*ED/N-1.*

**MRDE REPORT.**                                XXX
NATIONAL COAL BOARD (GB): MINING RESEARCH &
DEVELOPMENT ESTABLISHMENT.
*STANHOPE BRETBY, STAFFS.  1969/70-*
PREV: BRETBY REPORT FROM 1961- 1968/69.
*LO/N14.*

**MT. WILHELM STUDIES.**
*+ +MT. WILHELM STUD.*
AUSTRALIAN NATIONAL UNIVERSITY: DEPARTMENT OF
BIOGEOGRAPHY & GEOMORPHOLOGY.
*CANBERRA  1, 1969-*
*LO/N-2.*

**MTD.  MANUTENTION/TRANSPORT/DISTRIBUTION.**   XXX
[COMPAGNIE FRANCAISE D'EDITIONS]
*PARIS  NO.1, 1972-*
INCORP. MANUTENTION, STOCKAGE.
*LO/N14.*

**MTP INTERNATIONAL REVIEW OF SCIENCE: INORGANIC
CHEMISTRY.**
*+ +MTP INT. REV. SCI., INORG. CHEM.*
[BUTTERWORTHS; UNIVERSITY PARK P.]
*LONDON; BALTIMORE, MD.  SERIES 1, 1972-*
*ED/N-1.    GL/U-1.    LO/N14.    LO/S-3.*

**MTP INTERNATIONAL REVIEW OF SCIENCE: ORGANIC
CHEMISTRY.**
*+ +MTP INT. REV. SCI., ORG. CHEM.*
[BUTTERWORTHS; UNIVERSITY PARK P.]
*LONDON; BALTIMORE, MD.  SERIES 1, 1973-*
*BH/U-3.    ED/N-1.    GL/U-1.    LO/N14.*

**MTP INTERNATIONAL REVIEW OF SCIENCE: PHYSICAL
CHEMISTRY.**
*+ +MTP INT. REV. SCI., PHYS. CHEM.*
[BUTTERWORTHS; UNIV. PARK P]
*LONDON; BALTIMORE, MD.  SERIES 1, 1972-*
*ED/N-1.    GL/U-1.    LO/N14.    LO/S-3.*
*ED/U-1. 10, 1972.*
*ISSN 0076-177X*

**MULL.  MODERN USES OF LOGIC IN LAW.**         XXX
SUBS (1966): JURIMETRICS JOURNAL.

**MULL UND ABFALL.**
[E. SCHMIDT]
*BERLIN &C.  1, 1969-*
*LO/N14.*

**MULL - ABFALL - ABWASSER.**
[SCHWEIGER]
*DUREN  NO.1, 1966-*
*LO/N14.*

**MULTIHULL INTERNATIONAL.**
*+ +MULTIHULL INT.*
[MARINE MAGAZINES LTD.]
*FALMOUTH  NO.1, 1968-*
*ED/N-1.    LO/N14.*
*ISSN 0027-3155*

**MULTINATIONAL BUSINESS.**
*+ +MULTINATL. BUS.*
ECONOMIST INTELLIGENCE UNIT.
*LONDON  NO.1, N 1971-*
S/T: A QUARTERLY REVIEW OF NEWS & ANALYSIS.
*ED/N-1.    GL/U-2.    HL/U-2.    LO/U-3.    OX/U-1.*
*ISSN 0300-3922*

**MULTIRACIAL SCHOOL.  JOURNAL OF THE ...**     XXX
*+ +MULTIRACIAL SCH.*
ASSOCIATIONS FOR THE EDUCATION OF PUPILS FROM
OVERSEAS.
*OXFORD  1, 1971-*
PREV: ENGLISH FOR IMMIGRANTS FROM 1, 1967-
4, 1971.
*BL/U-1.    ED/N-1.    HL/U-2.    LD/U-2.    OX/U-1.*

**MULTIVARIATE BEHAVIORAL RESEARCH.**
*+ +MULTIVARIATE BEHAV. RES.*
SOCIETY OF MULTIVARIATE EXPERIMENTAL PSYCHOLOGY
*FORT WORTH  1, 1966-*
*GL/U-1.    GL/U-2.*
*ISSN 0027-3171*

**MUNCHENER ARCHAOLOGISCHE STUDIEN.**
*+ +MUNCH. ARCHAOL. STUD.*
[W. FINK]
*MUNICH  1, 1970-*
*CA/U-1.*

**MUNDUS ARTIUM.  A JOURNAL OF INTERNATIONAL
LITERATURE & THE ARTS.**
OHIO UNIVERSITY.
*ATHENS, OHIO  1, WINTER 1967-*
ISSUED BY THE UNIV.'S  DEP. OF ENGLISH.
3/A.
*LO/U-2.    NO/U-1.*
*ISSN 0027-3406*

**MUNICIPAL ENGINEERING.**                      XXX
*+ +MUNIC. ENG.*
[MUNICIPAL ENGINEERING PUBL. LTD.]
*LONDON  146(27), 1969-*
PREV:  MUNICIPAL ENGINEERING, CLEANSING &
PUBLIC HEALTH FROM 1, 1874- 146(26), 1969.
*LO/N14.*
*ISSN 0027-3457*

**MUNICIPAL ENGINEERING, CLEANSING & PUBLIC
HEALTH.**                                       XXX
SUBS (1969):  MUNICIPAL ENGINEERING.

**MUNRO EAGLE.**
CLAN MUNRO ASSOCIATION: AMERICAN BRANCH.
*DANSVILLE, N.Y.  NO.1, 1969-*
A.
*LO/N-1.*

**MUSCLE BIOLOGY.**
*+ +MUSCLE BIOL.*
INSTITUTE FOR MUSCLE BIOLOGY.
[DEKKER]
*NEW YORK  1, 1972-*
S/T: A SERIES OF ADVANCES.
*CA/U-1.    GL/U-1.    LO/N13.    SO/U-1.*

**MUSE.**
BIRMINGHAM POETRY CENTRE.
*BIRMINGHAM  NO.1, 1971-*
*ED/N-1.    LO/U-2.*

**MUSEUMS ANNUAL.**                             XXX
*+ +MUS. ANNU.*
INTERNATIONAL COUNCIL OF MUSEUMS.
*PARIS  NO.3, 1971-*
PREV: ANNUAL, INTERNATIONAL COUNCIL OF MUSEUMS
FROM NO.1, 1969- NO.2, 1970.
*LO/N-2.    LO/N-4.*

MUSEUM & ARCHIVES NOTES, PROVINCIAL MUSEUM &
ARCHIVES OF ALBERTA.
+ +MUS. & ARCH. NOTES PROV. MUS. & ARCH. ALBERTA.
EDMONTON NO.1, 1970-
LO/N-2.

MUSEUMS ASSOCIATION INFORMATION SHEET.
+ +MUS. ASSOC. INF. SHEET.
LONDON [NO.1], 1969-
ED/N-1.    LO/N-1.    LO/N-2.    OX/U-1.

MUSEUM BOOKLET, CAMBRIDGE & COUNTY FOLK
MUSEUM.
+ +MUS. BOOKLET CAMB. & CTY. FOLK MUS.
CAMBRIDGE NO.1, AG 1971-
LO/N-1.

MUSEUM CONTRIBUTIONS.
+ +MUS. CONTRIB.
UNIVERSITY OF MISSOURI.
COLUMBIA, MO. NO.1, [1970]-
LO/N-2.

MUSEUM NEWS.
+ +MUS. NEWS.
MUSEUMS ACTION MOVEMENT.
LONDON NO.1, 1972-
2/A.
CA/U-1.    ED/N-1.    OX/U-1.

MUSEUM STUDIES.
+ +MUS. STUD. (ART INST. CHICAGO).
CHICAGO 1, 1966-
ANNU.
LO/U17.    OX/U-2.
AD/U-1. 6, 1971-

MUSEUMSTEKNISKE STUDIER. STUDIES IN MUSEUM
TECHNOLOGY.
+ +MUSEUMSTEKNISKE STUD.
DANMARKS NATIONALMUSEET.
COPENHAGEN NO.1, 1970-
LO/N-1.

MUSHROOM.
HORNCHURCH 1, [1969-]
LO/U-2.

MUSHROOM JOURNAL.                                    XXX
+ +MUSHROOM J.
MUSHROOM GROWERS' ASSOCIATION.
LONDON NO.1, 1973-
PREV: MGA BULLETIN FROM NO.1, 1945- 276, 1972.
LO/N14.    OX/U-8.

MUSIC CATALOGING BULLETIN.
+ +MUSIC CAT. BULL.
MUSIC LIBRARY ASSOCIATION.
ANN ARBOR 1, JA 1970-
LO/U-2.
ISSN 0027-4283

MUSIC & COMMUNICATION.
+ +MUSIC & COMMUN.
INTERNATIONAL MUSIC COUNCIL.
FLORENCE 1, 1970-
OX/U-1.

MUSIC FORUM.
[COLUMBIA UNIV. P.]
NEW YORK &C 1, 1967-
GL/U-1.    LO/U-1.    LO/U11.    MA/U-1.    NO/U-1.

MUSIC INDEXES & BIBLIOGRAPHIES.
+ +MUSIC INDEXES & BIBLIOGR.
[J. BOONIN]
HACKENSACK, N.J. 1, 1970-
OX/U-1.

MUSIC NOW.
INTERNATIONAL SOCIETY FOR CONTEMPORARY MUSIC.
SYDNEY 1(1), 1969-
LO/N-1.    OX/U-1.

MUSIC SCENE.
[IPC MAGAZINES]
LONDON NO.1, N 1972-
ED/N-1.

MUSIKBIBLIOGRAPHISCHER DIENST.
+ +MUSIKBIBLIOGR. DIENST.
DEUTSCHER BUCHEREIVERBAND: ARBEITSSTELLE
FUR DAS BUCHEREIWESEN.
BERLIN 1, 1969/70-
2M.
LO/N-1.

MUSIQUE EN JEU.
PARIS 1, 1970-
OX/U-1.
MA/P-1. NO.9, 1972-

MUSK-OX.
UNIVERSITY OF SASKATCHEWAN: MUSK-OX CIRCLE.
SASKATOON NO.1, 1967-
LO/N-2.

MUSLIM HERALD.
LONDON 1(1), JA 1961-
S/T: A MONTHLY MAGAZINE DEVOTED TO THE CAUSE
OF ISLAM.
LO/N-1.
OX/U-1. 10(3), 1970-
BT/U-1. 8, 1968.

MUST.
EDINBURGH UNIVERSITY DRAMATIC SOCIETY.
EDINBURGH 1967-
ED/N-1.    LO/U-2.

MUZYKA I SOVREMENNOST'. SBORNIK STATEJ.
+ +MUZYKA & SOVREM.
MOSCOW 1962(1)-
OX/U-1. 1965(3)-

MYCOLOGY & PHYTOPATHOLOGY.                           000
SEE: MIKOLOGIJA I FITOPATOLOGIJA.

MYOTIS. MITTEILUNGSBLATT FUER FLEDERMAUS.
[MYMF-A]
ZOOLOGISCHES FORSCHUNGSINSTITUT.
BONN [NO.]1, 1963-
LO/N-2.

MYSORE JOURNAL OF AGRICULTURAL SCIENCES.
+ +MYSORE J. AGR. SCI.
UNIVERSITY OF AGRICULTURAL SCIENCES (BANGALORE)
BANGALORE 1, 1967-
LO/N-2.
LO/N13. 3(2), 1969-             LO/R-6. 4(1), 1970-
ISSN 0047-8539

NA ANTENIE.
RADIO WOLNA EUROPA: ROZGLOSNIA POLSKA.
LONDON 1, 1963-
FROM 1, 1963- 6, 1968 PUBL. AS SUPPLEMENT TO
'WIADOMOSCI' (LONDON).
LO/S-9.
LO/N-3. 7, 1969-             OX/U-1. 7, 1969-

N.A. JOURNAL.
+ +N.A. J. (NAT. ASS. CYCLE TRAD.).
NATIONAL ASSOCIATION OF CYCLE TRADERS.
LONDON 1, 1969-
OX/U-1.    LO/N14.

NAA RESEARCH STUDIES IN MANAGEMENT REPORTING.
+ +NAA RES. STUD. MANAGE. REP. [NRSM-A]
NATIONAL ASSOCIATION OF ACCOUNTANTS (US).
NEW YORK NO.1, 1968-
NW/U-1.

N.A.A.S. QUARTERLY REVIEW.                           XXX
SUBS (1971): A.D.A.S. QUARTERLY REVIEW.

NACHRICHTEN DER AKADEMIE DER WISSENSCHAFTEN
IN GOTTINGEN: PHILOLOGISCHE-HISTORISCHE
KLASSE.
+ +NACHR. AKAD. WISS. GOTTINGEN, PHILOL.-HIST.
KL.
[VANDENHOECK & RUPRECHT]
GOTTINGEN NO.1, 1970-
MONOGR.
LO/N-1.
BL/U-1. 1973-

NAGASAKI DAIGAKU KOGAKUBU KENKYU HOKOKU.
REPORTS, FACULTY OF ENGINEERING, NAGASAKI
UNIVERSITY.
NAGASAKI NO.1, 1971-
JAP. WITH ENGL. SUMM.
LO/N14.

NAIROBI HISTORICAL STUDIES.
+ +NAIROBI HIST. STUD.
UNIVERSITY COLLEGE, NAIROBI: DEPARTMENT OF
HISTORY.
[EAST AFRICAN PUBL. HOUSE]
NAIROBI 1, 1969-
OX/U-9.

NAMIBIA NEWS.
SOUTH WEST AFRICAN PEOPLES ORGANISATION IN
BRITAIN.
*LONDON 1(1), F 1968-*
2M.
*LO/U-8.*
*LO/U-3. 6, 1973-*

NANKAI-KU SUISAN KENKYUJO HOKOKU RINJIGO.
OCCASIONAL REPORT OF THE NANKAI REGIONAL FISH-
ERIES RESEARCH LABORATORY.
*KOCHI NO.1, 1962-*
*LO/N-2. LO/N13.*

NANSEI KAIKU SUISAN KENKYUJO KENKYU HOKOKU.
BULLETIN OF THE NANSEI REGIONAL FISHERIES
RESEARCH LABORATORY.
*HIROSHIMA NO.1, 1969-*
ENGL. SUMM.
*LO/N13.*
*LO/N-2. NO.2, 1969-*

NANSEI KAIKU SUISAN KENKYUJO NENJI HOKOKU.
*HIROSHIMA NO.1, 1968-*
*LO/N13.*

NANTA MATHEMATICA.
+ +NANTA MATH. [NAMA-B]
NANYANG UNIVERSITY: DEPARTMENT OF MATHEMATICS.
*SINGAPORE 1, 1966/67-*
ENGL. & CHIN.
*SH/U-1. SW/U-1.*

NANTIS NEWS.
NOTTINGHAM & NOTTINGHAMSHIRE TECHNICAL INFOR-
MATION SERVICE (NANTIS).
*NOTTINGHAM NO.1, JA 1971-*
MON.
*ED/N-1. OX/U-8.*
*ISSN 0027-593X*

NANYANG QUARTERLY.                                    XXX
+ +NANYANG Q.
SOUTH SEAS SOCIETY.
*SINGAPORE 1, MR 1971- 3, 1973...*
SUBS: REVIEW OF SOUTHEAST ASIAN STUDIES.
*OX/U-1.*

NAPCA ABSTRACTS BULLETIN.                             XXX
+ +NAPCA ABSTR. BULL.
(UNITED STATES) NATIONAL AIR POLLUTION CONTROL
ADMINISTRATION.
*RALEIGH, N.C. 1, 1970- 2(1), 1971...*
PREV: APCA ABSTRACTS FROM 1, 1955- 15(9), 1970
SUBS: AIR POLLUTION ABSTRACTS (RESEARCH
TRIANGLE PARK). ISSUED BY ADMINISTRATION'S
OFFICE OF TECHNICAL INFORMATION & PUBLICATIONS
*LO/N14. NW/U-1.*
*XS/N-1.\*\**

N.A.S. REPORT.
NATIONAL ASSOCIATION OF SCHOOLMASTERS (GB).
*HEMEL HEMPSTEAD NO.1, 1971-*
*ED/N-1. OX/U-1.*

NASHRIYAH-I BUNYAD-I FARHANG-I IRAN.                 000
SEE: BULLETIN OF THE IRANIAN CULTURE FOUNDAT-
ION.

NASSAU REVIEW.
+ +NASSAU REV.
NASSAU COMMUNITY COLLEGE.
*GARDEN CITY, N.Y. 1, 1964-*
*OX/U-1.*

NASTAVA ISTORIJE.
+ +NASTAVA ISTOR.
SAVEZ DRUSTAVA HISTORICARA JUGOSLAVIJE
(ZAGREB).
*ZAGREB 1, 1967-*
Q. TITLE ALSO IN CROATIAN: NASTAVA POVIJESTI;
MACEDONIAN: NASTAVA PO ISTORIJA; & SLOVENIAN:
POUK ZGODOVINE.
*OX/U-1.*

NASTAVA POVIJESTI.                                    000
SEE: NASTAVA ISTORIJE.

NATALIA.
NATAL SOCIETY.
*PIETERMARITZBURG 1, 1971-*
*OX/U-9.*
*ISSN 0085-3674*

NATHANIEL HAWTHORNE JOURNAL.
[NCR MICROCARD EDITIONS]
*WASHINGTON, D.C. 1970-*
ANNU.
*CA/U-1. OX/U-1.*
*HL/U-1. 1971-*

NATIONAL BIBLIOGRAPHY OF BOTSWANA.
+ +NATL. BIBLIOGR. BOTSWANA.
(BOTSWANA) NATIONAL LIBRARY SERVICE.
*GABERONES 1(1), 1969-*
*LO/N17. LO/U-1. LO/U-8. OX/U-9.*
*ED/N-1. 4, 1972- LO/U-3. 1(2), 1969-*
*XY/N-1. 1(2), 1969-*
*ISSN 0027-8777*

NATIONAL BUREAU REPORT.
+ +NATL. BUR. REP.
NATIONAL BUREAU OF ECONOMIC RESEARCH (US).
*NEW YORK NO.1, JA 1968-*
ALSO ISSUES SUPPLEMENTS.
*OX/U16.*
*CB/U-1. 3, 1968- OX/U17. 2, 1968-*
*SO/U-1. CURRENT YEAR ONLY.*

NATIONAL ELECTRONICS REVIEW (GB).                     XXX
+ +NATL. ELECTRON. REV. (GB).
NATIONAL ELECTRONICS COUNCIL (GB).
*LONDON 7(1), 1971-*
PREV: NEC REVIEW FROM 3(2), 1967- 6, 1970.
*ED/N-1. LO/N-7. LO/N14. SH/C-5.*
*SH/P-1. 1974-*

NATIONAL HORTICULTURAL MAGAZINE.                      XXX
SUBS (1960): AMERICAN HORTICULTURAL MAGAZINE.

NATIONAL LIBRARY NEWS. = NOUVELLES DE LA BIB-
LIOTHEQUE NATIONALE.
+ +NATL. LIBR. NEWS. (CAN.).
NATIONAL LIBRARY OF CANADA.
*OTTAWA 1, JA/MR 1969-*
ENGL. & FR.
*ED/N-1.*
*CA/U-1. 6, 1974-*
*ISSN 0027-9633*

NATIONAL LIBRARY OCCASIONAL PUBLICATION
(NIGERIA).
+ +NATL. LIBR. OCCAS. PUBL. (NIGER.).
NATIONAL LIBRARY OF NIGERIA.
*LAGOS NO.1, 1968-*
MONOGR.
*LO/N-1.*

NATIONAL MICRO-NEWS.                                  XXX
SUBS. (1967): NMA JOURNAL.

NATIONAL PALACE MUSEUM QUARTERLY.
+ +NATL. PALACE MUS. Q.
TAIPEI NATIONAL PALACE MUSEUM.
*TAIPEI 1(1), 1966-*
*OX/U-1.*

NATIONAL PROVINCIAL BANK REVIEW.                      XXX
SUBS (1968): PART OF QUARTERLY REVIEW,
NATIONAL WESTMINSTER BANK.

NATIONAL SWEDISH BUILDING RESEARCH SUMMARIES.         000
SEE: RAPPORT, STATENS INSTITUT FOR BYGGNADS-
FORSKNING: ENGLISH SUMMARIES.

NATIONAL WESTMINSTER. STAFF MAGAZINE OF...
+ +NATL. WESTMINSTER.
NATIONAL WESTMINSTER BANK GROUP.
*LONDON 1, AP 1969-*
*ED/N-1.*

NATIONALIST.
[MWANANCHI PUBL. CO.]
*DAR-ES-SALAAM NO.1, 1/AP 1964-*
*BT/U-1. MA/U-1.*

NATION'S AGRICULTURE.                                 XXX
SUBS (1972): AMERICAN FARMER.

NATION'S HEALTH.                                      XXX
AMERICAN PUBLIC HEALTH ASSOCIATION.
*NEW YORK MR 1971-*
PREV: PART AMERICAN JOURNAL OF PUBLIC HEALTH
PREV: PART AMERICAN JOURNAL OF PUBLIC HEALTH
& THE NATION'S HEALTH FROM 18, 1928- 60, 1970.
*LO/N13.*
*ISSN 0028-0496*

**NATIONSWERDUNG OSTERREICHS. SCHRIFTENREIHE DES OSTERREICHISCHEN NATIONALINSTITUTS.**
+ +NATIONSWERDUNG OSTERR.
[VERLAG KURT WEDL]
  VIENNA &C. 1, 1971-
  LO/N-1.

**NATO LATEST.**
NORTH ATLANTIC TREATY ORGANIZATION: INFORMATION
SERVICE.
  BRUSSELS 1, JE 1968-
  LO/S14.

**NATO LETTER.**                                                        XXX
  SUBS (1971): NATO REVIEW.

**NATO REVIEW.**                                                        XXX
+ +NATO REV.
  BRUSSELS 19(5/6), MY-JE 1971-
  PREV: NATO LETTER FROM [1], S 1953- 19(3/4),
  1971. PRODUCED BY THE ORGANIZATION'S INFOR-
  MATION SERVICE.
  AD/U-1.    BH/U-1.    ED/N-1.    LD/U-1.    LO/U-1.
  LO/U-3. [CURRENT ISSUES ONLY]

**NATURA BRESCIANA.**
+ +NAT. BRESCIA.
  MUSEO CIVICO DI STORIA NATURALE.
  BRESCIA NO.1, 1965-
  LO/N13.

**NATURAL GAS, L.N.G. & L.P.G.**                                        XXX
+ +NAT. GAS L.N.G. & L.P.G.
[SCIENTIFIC SURVEYS, LTD.]
  LONDON 2, 1969-
  PREV: NATURAL GAS & L.P.G. FROM 1, 1967- 68.
  LO/N14.

**NATURAL HISTORY DIVISION INFORMATION, PROVINCIAL MUSEUM & ARCHIVES OF ALBERTA.**
+ +NAT. HIST. DIV. INF. PROV. MUS. & ARCH.
ALBERTA.
  EDMONTON NO.1, 1971-
  LO/N-2.

**NATURAL LAW FORUM.**                                                  XXX
  SUBS (1969): AMERICAN JOURNAL OF
JURISPRUDENCE.

**NATURAL RESOURCES FORUM.**
+ +NAT. RESOUR. FORUM.
UNITED NATIONS: DEPARTMENT OF ECONOMIC & SOCIAL
AFFAIRS.
  NEW YORK 1, 1971-
  BH/U-1.    DN/U-1.    ED/N-1.    LO/N-2.    LO/N13.    MA/P-1.

**NATURAL RESOURCES LAWYER.**
+ +NAT. RESOUR. LAWYER.
AMERICAN BAR ASSOCIATION: SECTION OF NATURAL
RESOURCES LAW.
  CHICAGO 1(1), 1968-
  Q.
  OX/U15. 1(4), 1968-
  ISSN 0028-0747

**NATURALEZA.**
COMISION CIENTIFICA DE PROTECCION DE LA
NATURALEZA (SPAIN).
  MADRID NO.1, 1969-
  LO/N-2.

**NATURALEZA ECUATORIANA.**
+ +NAT. ECUATOR.
UNIVERSIDAD DE GUAYAQUIL: ESCUELA DE CIENCIAS
NATURALES.
  GUAYAQUIL 1, 1966-
  LO/N-2.

**NATURE: NEW BIOLOGY.**                                                XXX
[MACMILLAN]
  LONDON 229, 1971- 246, 1973.
  CONTAINS INFORMATION PREV. PUBL. IN NATURE.
  FROM VOL. 247(5435), JA 1974 CONTINUED AS PART
  OF NATURE.
  BH/P-1.    BH/U-3.    GL/U-1.    HL/U-1.    LO/N-4.    LO/N-6.
  LO/N14.    LO/U-1.    LO/U13.    OX/U-8.    SF/U-1.    SO/U-1.
  XS/R10.
  SH/C-5. 232(27), 7/JE 1971-
  ISSN 0369-4887

**NATURE: PHYSICAL SCIENCE.**                                           XXX
[MACMILLAN]
  LONDON 229, 1971- 246, 1973.
  SEE NOTE FOR NATURE: NEW BIOLOGY.
  BH/P-1.    BH/U-3.    CV/C-1.    GL/U-1.    HL/U-1.    LO/N-4.
  LO/N-6.    LO/N14.    LO/S-3.    LO/U-1.    LO/U13.    LO/U20.
  OX/U-8.    SF/U-1.    SH/U-3.    SO/U-1.    XS/R10.
  ISSN 0300-8746

**NATURE, AGRICULTURE, ENVIRONMENT.**
+ +NAT. AGRIC. ENVIRON.
ASSOCIATION VAROISE POUR LA SAUVEGARDE DE
L'AGRICULTURE, DE LA NATURE ET DE L'ENVIRONE-
MENT.
  TOULON NO.1, 1971-
  LO/N13.

**NATURE CANADA.**                                                      XXX
+ +NAT. CAN.
CANADIAN AUDUBON SOCIETY.
  OTTAWA 1, 1972-
  PREV: CANADIAN AUDUBON FROM 20, 1958- 33, 1971
  LO/N-2.    LO/R-5.

**NATURE CONSERVATION IN CZECHOSLOVAKIA.**                              000
  SEE: CESKOSLOVENSKA OCHRANA PRIRODY.

**NATURE & INSECTS.**                                                   000
  SEE: KONCHU TO SHIZEN.

**NATURE IN LANCASHIRE. JOURNAL OF THE ...**
+ +NAT. LANCS.
LANCASHIRE NATURALISTS' TRUST.
  BIRKENHEAD 1, 1970-
  SUPPL. ISSUED UNDER TITLE: NEWSLETTERS ...
  ED/N-1.    LO/N-2.    LO/N13.

**NATURKUNDLICHE JAHRESBERICHTE, MUSEUM HEINEANUM.**
+ +NATURKD. JAHRESBER. MUS. HEINEANUM.
  HALBERSTADT [NO.]1, 1966-
  LO/N13.

**NATUUR- EN STEDESCHOON.**
+ +NAT. & STEDESCHOON.
KONINKLIJKE VERENIGING VOOR NATUUR- EN STEDES-
CHOON.
  ANTWERP NO. 1, 1970-
  LO/N-2.

**NATUUREBEHOUD.**
VERENIGING TOT BEHOUD VAN NATUURMONUMENTEN IN
NEDERLAND.
  AMSTERDAM NO.1, 1970-
  LO/N-2.

**NAUCHNO-TEKHNICHESKAJA INFORMATSIJA, VSESO-JUZNYJ INSTITUT NAUCHNOJ I TEKHNICHESKOJ INFORMATSII.**
+ +NAUCHNO-TEKH. INF. VSES. INST. NAUCHNOJ &
TEKH. INF.
  MOSCOW 1963- 1966.
  SUBS: FROM 1967 ISSUED IN TWO SERIES: SERIJA
  1: ORGANIZATSIJA I METODIKA ORGANIZATSIONNOJ
  RABOTY. SERIJA 2: INFORMATSIONNYE PROTSESSY I
  SISTEMY.
  CC/U-1.    LO/N14.    SH/U-1.

**NAUCHNO-TEKHNICHESKAJA INFORMATSIJA, VSESO-JUZNYJ INSTITUT NAUCHNOJ I TEKHNICHESKOJ INFORMATSII: SERIJA 1: ORGANIZATSIJA I METOD-IKA INFORMATSIONNOJ RABOTY.**
+ +NAUCHNO-TEKH. INF. VSES. INST. NAUCHNOJ &
TEKH. INF., 1.
  MOSCOW 1967-
  PREV: AS PART OF ABOVE MAIN TITLE FROM 1963-
  1966. THEN WITH ABOVE NO. ISSUED IN TWO
  SERIES.
  BH/U-1.    LO/N14.    SH/U-1.

**NAUCHNO-TEKHNICHESKAJA INFORMATSIJA, VSESO-JUZNYJ INSTITUT NAUCHNOJ I TEKHNICHESKOJ INFORMATSII: SERIJA 2: INFORMATSIONNYE PROT-SESSY I SISTEMY.**
+ +NAUCHNO-TEKH. INF. VSES. INST. NAUCHNOJ &
TEKH. INF., 2.
  MOSCOW 1967-
  SEE REMARKS FOR SERIES 1.
  BH/U-1.    LO/N14.    SH/U-1.

**NAUCHNO-TEKHNICHESKAJA INFORMATSIJA; (ENGL. TRANSL., SELECTED ARTICLES).**                                  000
  SEE: AUTOMATIC DOCUMENTATION & MATHEMATICAL
LINGUISTICS.

**NAUCHNOE UPRAVLENIE OBSHCHESTVOM.**
+ +NAUCHN. UPR. O-VOM.
AKADEMIJA OBSHCHESTVENNYKH NAUK PRI TSK KPSS:
KAFEDRA NAUCHNOGO KOMMUNIZMA.
  MOSCOW 1, 1967-
  BH/U-1.    CC/U-1.

NAUCHNYE INFORMATSII ASTRONOMICHESKOGO SOVETA
AKADEMII NAUK SSSR.
++NAUCHN. INF. ASTRON. SOV. AKAD. NAUK SSSR.
[NIAS-B]
MOSCOW 1, 1965-
ENGL. SUMM.
ED/R-3. ED/S-2.
LO/N13. 5, 1967-

NAUCHNYE IZVESTIJA, KAZAKHSKIJ GOSUDARSTVENNYJ
MEDITSINSKIJ INSTITUT.                                          XXX
SUBS (1962): TRUDY, GOSUDARSTVENNYJ ...

NAUCHNYE SOOBSHCHENIJA, ARMJANSKIJ NAUCHNO-
ISSLEDOVATEL'SKIJ INSTITUT STROITEL'NYKH
MATERIALOV I SOORUZHENIJ.
++NAUCHN. SOOBSHCH. ARM. NAUCHNO-ISSLED. INST.
STROIT. MATER. & SOORUZH. [NSSS-A]
EREVAN 1, 1962-
ARM. & RUSS.
LO/N13. 4, 1964-

NAUCHNYE TRUDY, INSTITUT CHERNOJ METALLURGII.          XXX
++NAUCHN. TR. INST. CHERN. METALL. [NTIC-A]
GOSUDARSTVENNYJ KOMITET PO CHERNOJ I TSVETNOJ
METALLURGII PRI GOSPLANE SSSR: INSTITUT CHERNOJ
METALLURGII.
MOSCOW 21, 1965-
PREV: TRUDY DNEPROPETROVSKOGO INSTITUTA
CHERNOJ METALLURGII FROM 19, 1965- 20, 1965.
LO/N13. LO/S56.

NAUCHNYE TRUDY, KAZAKHSKIJ POLITEKHNICHESKIJ
INSTITUT.                                                       000
SEE: TRUDY, KAZAKHSKIJ ...

NAUCHNYE TRUDY, KHAR'KOVSKIJ ZOOVETERINARNYJ
INSTITUT.                                                       XXX
++NAUCHN. TR. KHARK. ZOOVET. INST. [NKZI-A]
KHARKOV 1(25), 1963-
PREV: SBORNIK TRUDOV, KHARKOVSKIJ ZOOTEKHNI-
CHESKIJ INSTITUT FROM 1, 1935- 1962. CONT.
NUMB. IN PARENTHESES.
LO/N13.

NAUCHNYE TRUDY, KRASNODARSKIJ NAUCHNO-
ISSLEDOVATEL'SKIJ INSTITUT SEL'SKOGO
KHOZJAJSTVA.                                                    000
SEE: TRUDY ...

NAUCHNYE TRUDY, NOVOSIBIRSKIJ GOSUDARSTVENNYJ
UNIVERSITET: FILOSOFSKAJA SERIJA.
++NAUCHNY. TR. NOVOSIB. GOS. UNIV., FIL.
NOVOSIBIRSK 1, 1965-
OX/U-1.

NAUCHNYE TRUDY, NOVOSIBIRSKIJ GOSUDARSTVENNYJ
UNIVERSITET: ISTORICHESKAJA SERIJA.
++NAUCH. TR. NOVOSIB. GOS. UNIV., ISTOR.
NOVOSIBIRSK VYP.1, 1967-
CA/U-1. GL/U-1. OX/U-1. SW/U-1.

NAUCHNYE TRUDY, NOVOSIBIRSKIJ GOSUDARSTVENNYJ
UNIVERSITET: SERIJA EKONOMICHESKAJA.
++NAUCHN. TR. NOVOSIB. GOS. UNIV., EKON.
NOVOSIBIRSK VYP. 1, 1964-
BH/U-1. OX/U-1.

NAUCHNYE TRUDY, PERMSKIJ NAUCHNO-ISSLEDO-
VATEL'SKIJ UGOL'NYJ INSTITUT.
++NAUCHN. TR. PERMSK. NAUCHNO-ISSLED. UGOL'N.
INST. [NTPU-A]
PERM' 1, 1960-
VOL.1 PUBL. AS: SBORNIK MATERIALOV, PERMSKIJ
NAUCHNO-ISSLEDOVATEL'SKIJ UGOL'NYJ INSTITUT.
LO/N13.

NAUCHNYE TRUDY, TSENTRAL'NYJ NAUCHNO-
ISSLEDOVATEL'SKIJ EKONOMICHESKIJ INSTITUT.
++NAUCHN. TR. TSENTR. NAUCHN-ISSLED. EKON. INST.
MOSCOW 1, 1969-
BH/U-1. CC/U-1. GL/U-1. LO/U-3.

NAUCHNYE TRUDY VYSSHIKH UCHEBNYKH ZAVEDENIJ
LITOVSKOJ SSR: BIOLOGIJA.                                       000
SEE: LIETUVOS TSR AUKSTUJU MOKYKLU MOKSLO
DARBAI: BIOLOGIJA.

NAUCHNYE TRUDY VYSSHIKH UCHEBNYKH ZAVEDENIJ
LITOVSKOJ SSR: ELEKTROTEKHNIKA I AVTOMATIKA.                    000
SEE: LIETUVOS TSR AUKSTUJU MOKYKLU MOKSLO DAR-
BAI: ELEKTROTECHNIKA IR AUTOMATIKA.

NAUCHNYE TRUDY VYSSHIKH UCHEBNYKH ZAVEDENIJ
LITOVSKOJ SSR: ELEKTROTEKHNIKA I MEKHANIKA.                     000
SEE: LIETUVOS TSR AUKSTUJU MOKYKLU MOKSLO DAR-
BAI: ELEKTROTECHNIKA IR MECHANIKA.

NAUCHNYE TRUDY VYSSHIKH UCHEBNYKH ZAVEDENIJ
LITOVSKOJ SSR: GEOGRAFIJA I GEOLOGIJA.                          000
SEE: LIETUVOS TSR AUKSTUJU MOKYKLU MOKSLO DAR-
BAI: GEOGRAFIJA IR GEOLOGIJA.

NAUCHNYE TRUDY VYSSHIKH UCHEBNYKH ZAVEDENIJ
LITOVSKOJ SSR: MEKHANICHESKAJA TEKHNOLOGIJA.                    000
SEE: LIETUVOS TSR AUKSTUJU MOKYKLU MOKSLO
DARBAI: MECHANINE TECHNOLOGIJA.

NAUCHNYE TRUDY VYSSHIKH UCHEBNYKH ZAVEDENIJ
LITOVSKOJ SSR: MEKHANIKA.                                       000
SEE: LIETUVOS TSR AUKSTUJU MOKYKLU MOKSLO
DARBAI: MECHANIKA.

NAUCHNYE TRUDY VYSSHIKH UCHEBNYKH ZAVEDENIJ
LITOVSKOJ SSR: STROITEL'STVO I ARKHITEKTURA.                    000
SEE: LIETUVOS TSR AUKSTUJU MOKYKLU MOKSLO
DARBAI: STATYBA IR ARCHITEKTURA.

NAUKA I CHELOVECHESTVO.
AKADEMIJA NAUK SSSR.
MOSCOW 1, 1962-
A. S/T: MEZHDUNARODNYJ EZHEGODNIK.
LO/N-3. LO/U-1. XY/N-1.
BD/U-1. 1965- CC/U-1. 2, 1963-
BH/U-1. 1964-
SW/U-1. 1965-

NAUKA I TEKHNIKA V GORODSKOM KHOZJAJSTVE.
++NAUK. & TEKH. GOR. KHOZ.
NAUCHNO-ISSLEDOVATEL'SKIJ I KONSTRUKTORSKO-
TEKHNOLOGICHESKIJ INSTITUT GORODSKOGO
KHOZJAJSTVA.
KIEV VYP.1, 1964-
TITLE VARIES. VOL. 1 & 2 (1964) AS KOMMUNAL'
NOE KHOZJAJSTVO.
CC/U-1. 10, 1968- LO/N13. VYP.5, 1966-
SW/U-1. 5, 1966-

NAUKI POLITYCZNE.
++NAUKI POLIT.
UNIWERSYTET WROCLAWSKI: INSTYTUT NAUK POLIT-
YCZNYCH.
WROCLAW 1, 1972-
ALSO NUMBERED AS: ACTA UNIVERSITATIS WRAT-
ISLAVIENSIS. NO.1 ABOVE = NO.153 OF THE ACTA.
LO/N-3.

NAUKOVI PRATSI Z ISTORII KPRS.
++NAUK. PR. ISTOR. KPRS.
KYJIVS'KYJ DERZHAVNYJ UNIVERSYTET.
KIEV 1, 1965-
UKR. S/T: MIZHVIDOMCHYJ NAUKOVYJ ZBIRNYK.
SW/U-1.
CC/U-1. 14, 1967-

NAUTAKARJA.
SUOMEN KOTIELAINJALOSTUSYHDISTYS.
HELSINKI 1971-
LO/N13.

NAUTOLOGIA.
[NTLG-A]
POLSKIE TOWARZYSTWO NAUTOLOGICZNE.
SZCZECIN &C. 1, 1966-
Q.
OX/U-1.
ISSN 0548-0523

NAVAL ARCHITECT.                                                XXX
++NAVAL ARCHIT.
ROYAL INSTITUTION OF NAVAL ARCHITECTS.
LONDON AP 1971-
PREV: TRANSACTIONS, ROYAL ... FROM 102, 1960-
113(1), 1971.
ED/N-1. GL/U-2. LO/N14. NW/U-1. SO/U-1.
BL/U-1. 1975- GL/U-1. 1974-
SO/U-1. 1971- 1972.
ISSN 0306-0209

NB: EDITION EUROPA.
INTERNATIONAL BOOK INFORMATION SERVICE.
NEW YORK 1(1), JA 1966-
ADDED TITLES IN ENGL. (NEW SCIENTIFIC BOOKS),
FR. (NOUVEAUX LIVRES SCIENTIFIQUES) & ITAL.
(NUOVI LIBRI SCIENTIFICI) & GER. (NEUE WISSEN-
SCHAFTLICHE BUCHER). ALSO IN AM. ED. (IN ENGL.
ONLY).
LO/N13. 1(5), 1966-

**NDT INFO. THE INFORMATION BULLETIN OF THE ...**
NONDESTRUCTIVE TESTING CENTRE (HARWELL).
[ILIFFE SCI. & TECHNOL. PUBLS.]
*GUILDFORD   1, MR 1968-*
PREV: INFORMATION BULLETIN, NONDESTRUCTIVE
TESTING CENTRE.
*ED/N-1.      LO/N14.      XS/R10.*
*SO/U-1.   CURRENT YEAR ONLY.*

**NEC REVIEW.**
*+ +NEC REV. (NAT. ELECTRON. COUN., G.B.)*
NATIONAL ELECTRONICS COUNCIL (GB).
*LONDON   3(2), OC 1967- 6, 1970.*
Q. PREV: NERC REVIEW FROM 1(1), JA 1965.
SUBS: NATIONAL ELECTRONICS REVIEW.
*BH/U-1.      ED/N-1.      LO/N14.*

**NEDELJA.**
*MOSCOW   1(1), 1960-*
SUPPLEMENT TO IZVESTIJA.
*SO/U-1.   8(14), 1967-*
*ISSN 0548-1007*

**NEDERLANDS GEODETISCH TIJDSCHRIFT.**                    XXX
*+ +NED. GEOD. TIJDSCHR.*
NEDERLANDSE VERENIGING VOOR GEODESIE.
*DELFT   1, 1970-*
PREV: TIJDSCHRIFT VOOR KADASTER EN LANDMEET-
KUNDE  FROM 1, 1885- 86, 1970.
*LO/N13.*
*ISSN 0040-7526*

**NEDERLANDSE PLUIMVEEHOUDERIJ.**                         XXX
SUBS (1972): PLUIMVEEHOUDERIJ.

**NEFTEGAZOVAJA GEOLOGIJA I GEOFIZIKA.**                  XXX
*+ +NEFTEGAZOV. GEOL. & GEOFIZ. [NGGS-A]*
VSESOJUZNYJ NAUCHNO-ISSLEDOVATEL'SKIJ INSTITUT
ORGANIZATSII, UPRAVLENIJA I EKONOMIKI NEFTE-
GAZOVOJ PROMYSHLENNOSTI.
*MOSCOW   1, 1963-*
MON.  PREV: NOVOSTI NEFTIIANOJ I GAZOVOJ
TEKHNIKI: GEOLOGIJA FROM 1946- 1962.
*LO/N13.   1970-*

**NEMATOLOGY CIRCULAR, DIVISION OF PLANT IND-
USTRY, DEPARTMENT OF AGRICULTURE (FLORIDA).**
*+ +NEMATOL. CIRC. DIV. PLANT IND. DEP. AGRIC.*
*(FLA.).*
(FLORIDA) DEPARTMENT OF AGRICULTURE: DIVISION
OF PLANT INDUSTRY.
*GAINESVILLE, FLA.   NO.1, 1962-*
*LO/N-2.*

**NEMOURIA.**
DELAWARE MUSEUM OF NATURAL HISTORY.
*GREENVILLE, DEL.   NO.1, 1970-*
*LO/N-2.*

**NEODIDAGMATA.**
UNIWERSYTET IM. ADAMA MICKIEWICZA W POZNANIU:
MIEDZYWYDZIALOWY ZAKLAD NOWYCH TECHNIK NAUCZAN-
IA.
*POZNAN   ZESZYT 1, 1970-*
FR. & RUSS. SUMM.
*LO/N-3.*

**NEO-HELLENIKA. ANNUAL PUBLICATION OF THE ...**
CENTER FOR NEO-HELLENIC STUDIES (AUSTIN).
*AMSTERDAM   1, 1970-*
*DB/U-2.      EX/U-1.      OX/U-1.*
*ISSN 0077-6521*

**NEPTUNE'S KINGDOM. POETRY BROADSHEET.**
*KILKEE, CO. CLARE   NO.1, 1972-*
*ED/N-1.      OX/U-1.*

**NERC NEWS JOURNAL.**
NATURAL ENVIRONMENT RESEARCH COUNCIL (GB).
*LONDON   NO.1, 1970-*
Q.
*CA/U12.      ED/N-1.      HL/U-1.      LD/U-1.      LO/N-2.      LO/N-4.*
*LO/N-6.      XS/N-1.*
*BH/U-1.   NO.2, 1971-                   GL/U-1.   NO.2, 1971-*
*LO/U12.   NO.2, 1971-*
*BH/U-3.   1971- [3 YEARS ONLY]*

**NERC REVIEW.**                                          XXX
*+ +NERC REV. (NAT. ELECTRON. RES. COUN., G.B.)*
NATIONAL ELECTRONICS RESEARCH COUNCIL (GB).
*LONDON   1, JA 1965- 3(1), 1967...*
S/T: QUARTERLY REVIEW OF PROGRESS IN ELECTRO-
NICS RESEARCH. SUBS: NEC REVIEW. (NAT. ELEC-
TRONICS COUNCIL).
*XS/R10.      BH/C-1.      BH/U-1.      BL/U-1.      CV/U-1.      GL/U-2.*
*LO/N-4.      LO/N-7.      LO/N14.      LO/U-2.      LV/P-1.      SH/U-1.*

**NEREM TECHNICAL APPLICATIONS PAPERS.**
*+ +NEREM TECH. APPL. PAP.*
INSTITUTE OF ELECTRICAL & ELECTRONICS ENGINEERS
*BOSTON, MASS.   1, 1970(1971)-*
PAPERS PRESENTED AT THE NORTHEAST ELECTRONICS
RESEARCH & ENGINEERING MEETING OF THE
INSTITUTE.
*LO/N14.*

**NETHERLANDS JOURNAL OF VETERINARY SCIENCE.**
*+ +NETH. J. VET. SCI.*
ROYAL NETHERLANDS VETERINARY ASSOCIATION.
*UTRECHT   1(1), AP 1968-*
2/A.
*LO/M15.      LO/M18.      LV/U-1.*
*ISSN 0047-9365*

**NETHERLANDS JOURNAL OF ZOOLOGY= ARCHIVES
NEERLANDAISES DE ZOOLOGIE.**
*+ +NETH. J. ZOOL.*
HOLLAND SOCIETY OF SCIENCES.
*LEYDEN   18(1), MY 1968-*
PREV: ALTERNATIVE TITLE AS MAIN TITLE FROM
1, 1934-17, 1967.  JOURNAL FORMS SERIES IV B
OF THE ARCHIVES NEERLANDAISES DES SCIENCES
EXACTES ET NATURELLES, PUBL. BY NETHERLANDS
ZOOLOGICAL SOCIETY.
*BL/U-1.      BN/U-2.      LD/U-1.      LO/N13.*
*ISSN 0028-2960*

**NETHERLANDS NITROGEN TECHNICAL BULLETIN.**            000
SEE: NN.

**NETHERLANDS YEARBOOK OF INTERNATIONAL LAW.**
*+ +NETH. YEARB. INT. LAW.*
INTER-UNIVERSITY INSTITUTE FOR INTERNATIONAL
LAW.
*LEIDEN   1, 1970-*
*BL/U-1.      LO/U-3.      MA/U-1.      NO/U-1.      OX/U15.*

**NETHERMERE NEWS.**
D.H. LAWRENCE ASSOCIATION.
*NOTTINGHAM   1, JA 1973-*
*NO/U-1.*

**NETSU KANRI.**                                          XXX
SUBS (1971): NETSU KANRI TO KOGAI.

**NETSU KANRI TO KOGAI.**                                 XXX
CHUO NETSU KANRI KYOGIKAI.
*TOKYO   23(10), 1971-*
PREV: NETSU KANRI FROM 1, 1949- 23(9), 1971.
*LO/N13.*

**NETWORKS. AN INTERNATIONAL JOURNAL.**
[INTERSCIENCE]
*NEW YORK   1, 1971-*
Q.
*AD/U-1.      LO/N14.      LO/U28.      OX/U-8.      SO/U-1.*
*BL/U-1.   5, 1975-                   SW/U-1.   3, 1973-*
*ISSN 0028-3045*

**NEUE HEFTE FUR PHILOSOPHIE.**
*+ +NEUE HEFTE PHILOS.*
[VANDENHOECK & RUPRECHT]
*GOTTINGEN   1, 1971-*
*OX/U-1.*

**NEUE WISSENSCHAFTLICHE BUCHER. (1966)**               000
SEE: NB: EDITION EUROPA.

**NEUE ZEITSCHRIFT FUR SYSTEMATISCHE THEOLOGIE
UND RELIGIONSPHILOSOPHIE.**                               XXX
*+ +NEUE Z. SYST. THEOL. & RELIGIONSPHILOS.*
[GRUYTER & CO.]
*BERLIN   5, 1963-*
PREV: NEUE ZEITSCHRIFT FUR SYSTEMATISCHE
THEOLOGIE FROM 1, 1959- 4, 1962.
*LO/U-1.*
*ISSN 0028-3517*

**NEUROBIOLOGY.**
[MUNKSGAARD]
*COPENHAGEN   1, 1971-*
*CA/U-2.      LO/N13.*

**NEUROPAEDIATRIE. JOURNAL OF PEDIATRIC NEURO-
BIOLOGY, NEUROLOGY & NEUROSURGERY.**
[HIPPOKRATES-VERLAG]
*STUTTGART   1, JL 1969-*
ENGL. OR GER.  SUMM. IN ENGL. & GER.,
FR. OR SPAN.
*AD/U-1.*
*MA/U-1.   4, 1973-*
*ISSN 0028-3797*

**NEUROPHARMACOLOGY.**  XXX
[PERGAMON]
*OXFORD  9, 1970-*
PREV: INTERNATIONAL JOURNAL OF NEUROPHARMACOL-
OGY FROM 1, 1962- 8, 1969.
*BL/U-1.   ED/N-1.   ED/U-1.   GL/U-1.   LO/U-2.   NW/U-1.*
*ISSN 0028-3908*

**NEURORADIOLOGY.**
[SPRINGER]
*BERLIN &C.  1(1), 1970-*
*Q.*
*AD/U-1.   OX/U-8.*
*ISSN 0028-3940*

**NEUROSCIENCE & BEHAVIORAL PHYSIOLOGY.**  XXX
*+ +NEUROSCI. & BEHAV. PHYSIOL.*
[SCRIPTA PUBL. CORP.]
*WASHINGTON, D.C. 5(1), JA/MR 1972-*
PREV: NEUROSCIENCE TRANSLATIONS FROM NO.1,
1967/68- NO.16, 1970/71.
*LO/N13.   SO/U-1.*

**NEUROSCIENCES RESEARCH.**
*+ +NEUROSCI. RES.*
[ACADEMIC P.]
*NEW YORK &C  1, 1968-*
*GL/U-1.   LO/U20.   NW/U-1.*
*SH/U-1.  1971-*

**NEUROSURGICAL BIBLIO-INDEX.**
*+ +NEUROSURG. BIBLIO-INDEX.*
AMERICAN ASSOCIATION OF NEUROLOGICAL SURGEONS.
*[CHICAGO]  NO.1, 1969-*
*Q.* DERIVED FROM THE INDEX MEDICUS, PUBL. BY
NATIONAL LIBRARY OF MEDICINE (US). ISSUED
AS SUPPL. TO JOURNAL OF NEUROSURGERY.
*LD/U-1.   NW/U-1.*

**NEUTRON ACTIVATION ANALYSIS ABSTRACTS.**
*+ +NEUTRON ACT. ANAL. ABSTR.*
[SCIENCE & TECHNOLOGY AGENCY]
*LONDON  1(1), JL/S 1971-*
*CA/U-1.   ED/N-1.   OX/U-8.   XS/R10.*
*ISSN 0047-9446*

**NEW ACADEMIC.**
*+ +NEW ACAD.*
[MACMILLAN (JOURNALS) LTD.]
*LONDON; WASHINGTON, D.C.  NO.1, MY 1971-*
*40/A.*
*OX/U-1.*

**NEW AMERICAN REVIEW.**  XXX
*+ +NEW AM. REV.*
[NEW AMERICAN LIBRARY INC.]
*NEW YORK  NO.1, 1967- 15, 1972.*
*3/A.* SUBS: AMERICAN REVIEW.
*OX/U-1.*
*ED/N-1.  NO.12, 1971-*
*ISSN 0028-4211*

**NEW ATLANTIS.**
*PADUA  NO.1, 1969-*
*2/A.  S/T:* AN INTERNATIONAL JOURNAL OF URBAN
& REGIONAL STUDIES.
*GL/U-1.   LO/U-3.   NW/U-1.   SH/U-1.*
*ISSN 0028-4246*

**NEW BANNER.**  000
  SEE: A' BHRATACH UR.

**NEW BELIZE.**
(BRITISH HONDURAS) GOVERNMENT INFORMATION
SERVICE.
*BELMOPEN  1(1), MR 1971-*
*Q.*
*LO/U-8.*

**NEW CANADA.**
*+ +NEW CAN.*
CANADIAN LIBERATION MOVEMENT.
*TORONTO  1(1), F 1970-*
*M.*
*LO/U-8.  2(5), 1971-*
*ISSN 0028-4386*

**NEW CHEMICAL PRODUCTS QUARTERLY.**
*+ +NEW CHEM. PROD. Q.*
NOYES DEVELOPMENT CORPORATION.
*PARK RIDGE, NJ  1, OC/D 1968-*
*LO/N14.*

**NEW CIVIL ENGINEER.**
*+ +NEW CIVIL ENG.*
INSTITUTION OF CIVIL ENGINEERS.
*LONDON  NO.1, MY 1972-*
*BH/U-3.   BL/U-1.   CA/U-1.   GL/U-2.   LO/N-4.*
*DB/U-2.  JL 1972-*                        *ED/N-1.  NO.3, 1972-*
*LO/U-2. [ONE YEAR ONLY]*
*MA/U-1.  NO.95, 1974-*
*SF/U-1.  NO. 141, 1/MY 1975-*
*SO/U-1.  NO.14, 1972-*
*XS/R10.  NO.22, 1973-*

**NEW COMMONWEALTH.**  XXX
  **SUBS (1966): NEW COMMONWEALTH, TRADE &
  COMMERCE.**

**NEW COMMONWEALTH, TRADE & COMMERCE.**  XXX
*+ +NEW COMMONW. TRADE & COMMER.*
*LONDON  44(12), 1966- 49(9), 1970 ...*
PREV: NEW COMMONWEALTH FROM 21, OC 1950- 44
(11), 1966.  SUBS: NEW COMMONWEALTH & WORLD
DEVELOPMENT.
*HL/U-1.   LO/U-3.*

**NEW COMMONWEALTH & WORLD DEVELOPMENT.**  XXX
*+ +NEW COMMONW. & WORLD DEV.*
*LONDON  49(10/11), 1970- NO.10/11/12, 1972.*
PREV: NEW COMMONWEALTH, TRADE & COMMERCE FROM
44(12), 1966- 49(9), 1970.  SUBS: INCORP. IN
WORLD DEVELOPMENT.
*HL/U-1.   LO/U-3.   NW/U-1.*

**NEW COMMUNITY.**  XXX
COMMUNITY RELATIONS COMMISSION (GB).
*LONDON  1(1), OC 1971-*
*Q.* PREV: COMMUNITY FROM 1, JA 1970- 2(2),
AP 1971.
*AD/U-1.   ED/N-1.   EX/U-1.   LO/U-4.   MA/P-1.   NO/U-1.*
*SH/U-1.*
*GL/U-2.  2(1), 1972/73-*
*HL/U-1.  1, 1971- 2, 1973.*
*ISSN 0047-9586*

**NEW DATA.  CAREERS, PRODUCTS, NEWS.**
[JUNIPER J. LTD.]
*LONDON  1(1), S 1969-*
*BL/U-1.*
*ED/N-1.  2(12), 10/MR 1970-*

**NEW DEMOCRAT.**
*+ +NEW DEMOCR.*
NEW DEMOCRATIC PARTY OF ONTARIO.
*TORONTO  1, S 1961-*
*LO/N-1.  7(1), 1967-*            *LO/U-8.  1973-*
*ISSN 0028-4564*

**NEW DIFFUSIONIST.  A STUDY OF INTER-RELATION-
SHIPS IN CULTURAL ANTHROPOLOGY.**
*+ +NEW DIFFUS.*
*HATFIELD, HERTS.  NO.1, OC 1970-*
*Q.*
*CA/U-3.   ED/N-1.   OX/U-1.*
*ISSN 0047-9608*

**NEW DIRECTIONS IN PSYCHOLOGY.**
*+ +NEW DIR. PSYCHOL.*
[HOLT, RINEHART & WINSTON]
*NEW YORK  [NO.]1, 1962-*
*LO/U-3.  3, [1967].*
*LO/U20.  3, [1967].*
*MA/P-1.  2, 1966.*

**NEW DIVINITY.**
*DUBLIN  1, 1970-*
*DB/U-2.   OX/U-1.*

**NEW DOCTOR.**
[PROFESSIONAL RESEARCH PUBLS.]
*BASINGSTOKE  1, JL/AG 1967-*
*ED/N-1.*

**NEW DRUGS.**  XXX
AMERICAN MEDICAL ASSOCIATION.
*CHICAGO  1965- 1967.*
PREV: NEW & NON OFFICAL DRUGS FROM 1958- 1964.
SUBS: AMA DRUG EVALUATIONS.
*AD/U-1.   LO/N10.*
*BN/U-1.  1967-*
*ISSN 0545-0985*

**NEW EDINBURGH REVIEW.**
*+ +NEW EDINBURGH REV.*
UNIVERSITY OF EDINBURGH: STUDENT PUBLICATIONS
BOARD.
*EDINBURGH  NO.1, 1969-*
*OX/U-1.*
*ISSN 0028-4645*

**NEW EDUCATION & PROGRAMMED LEARNING NEWS.***
+ +NEW EDUC. & PROGRAM. LEARN. NEWS.
LONDON 1, N 1964- 4(12), 1968.
ISSUED AS NEW EDUCATION FROM 1(1), 1964- 4(3),
1968. THEN TITLE EXPANDED AS ABOVE. SUBS:
PART OF NEW UNIVERSITY & NEW EDUCATION WITH
PROGRAMMED LEARNING NEWS.*
BH/P-1.   BH/U-1.   BL/U-1.   BN/U-1.   BR/U-3.   DB/U-2.
ED/N-1.   GL/U-2.   HL/U-1.   HL/U-2.   LO/U11.   MA/P-1.
OX/U-1.   SH/U-1.   SW/U-1.   YK/U-1.
LO/S26.  3 YEAR FILE.

**NEW ELECTRONICS.**
LONDON  1(1), 3/S 1968-
LO/F-1.   LO/N14.
ISSN 0047-9624

**NEW ENGLAND BUSINESS REVIEW.**                         XXX
SUBS (1969):  NEW ENGLAND ECONOMIC REVIEW.

**NEW ENGLAND ECONOMIC REVIEW.**                        XXX
+ +N. ENGL. ECON. REV.
FEDERAL RESERVE BANK OF BOSTON.
BOSTON  1969-
PREV:  NEW ENGLAND BUSINESS REVIEW FROM MR
1956- D 1968.
BH/U-1.
ISSN 0028-4726

**NEW ENGLAND LAW REVIEW.**                           . XXX
+ +NEW ENGL. LAW REV.
NEW ENGLAND SCHOOL OF LAW.                              XXX
BOSTON  4(2), 1969-
PREV: PORTIA LAW JOURNAL FROM 1, 1965- 4(1),
1968.
BL/U-1.  7, 1971-

**NEW ENGLAND MARINE RESOURCES INFORMATION.**
+ +NEW ENGL. MAR. RESOUR. INF.
NEW ENGLAND MARINE RESOURCES INFORMATION
PROGRAM.
NARRAGANSETT, R.I.  1, 1969-
LO/N-2.
ISSN 0047-9659

**NEW ENGLAND PAPERS ON EDUCATION.**
+ +NEW ENGL. PAP. EDUC.
UNIVERSITY OF NEW ENGLAND: DEPARTMENT OF EDUC-
ATION.
ARMIDALE, N.S.W.  NO.1, 1966-
OX/U-1.

**NEW GEOGRAPHY.**
+ +NEW GEOGR.
[ABELARD-SCHUMAN]
LONDON & C.  1966/67(1967)-
2A.
DB/U-2.

**NEW GERMAN STUDIES.**
+ +NEW GER. STUD.
UNIVERSITY OF HULL: DEPARTMENT OF GERMAN.
HULL  1, 1973-
3/A.
AD/U-1.   BL/U-1.   ED/N-1.   MA/U-1.   OX/U-1.   SH/U-1.
SO/U-1.   SW/U-1.
LO/U-4.  3, 1975-

**NEW GUINEA & AUSTRALIA, THE PACIFIC & SOUTH-
EAST ASIA.**
+ +NEW GUINEA & AUST. PAC. & SOUTH-EAST ASIA.
COUNCIL ON NEW GUINEA AFFAIRS.
SYDNEY  1(1), MR/AP 1965-
Q.
LO/N17.
LO/S26.  1(3), 1965-
ISSN 0028-5145

**NEW GUINEA PERIODICAL INDEX. GUIDE TO CURRENT
PERIODICAL LITERATURE ABOUT THE NEW GUINEA
ISLANDS.**
+ +NEW GUINEA PERIOD. INDEX.
UNIVERSITY OF PAPUA & NEW GUINEA: LIBRARY.
BOROKO  1(1), 1968-
Q.
LO/U-8.   LO/U-14.
ISSN 0028-5161

**NEW HEADLAND.**
[W. OXLEY]
EPPING  NO.1/2, AG 1972-
ED/N-1.

**NEW HUMANIST.**                                        XXX
+ +NEW HUM.
[RATIONALIST PRESS ASSOCIATION LTD.]
LONDON  88(1), MY 1972-
MON. PREV: HUMANIST FROM 1, 1885- 87(4), 1972.
BH/P-1.   ED/N-1.   LO/U-1.   LO/U28.
ISSN 0306-512X

**NEW INTERNATIONALIST.**                                XXX
+ +NEW INT.
WALLINGFORD, BERKS.  MR 1973-
MON. PREV: INTERNATIONALIST FROM NO.1, 1970-
7, N 1972.
AD/U-1.   LO/R-6.   MA/P-1.
LO/S14.  AP 1973-              SW/U-1.  AP 1973-
ISSN 0305-9529

**NEW LATIN AMERICAN TITLES.**
+ +NEW LAT. AM. TITLES.
UNIVERSITY OF LONDON: INSTITUTE OF LATIN AMER-
ICAN STUDIES.
LONDON  1(1), OC 1968-
S/T: BRITISH UNION CATALOGUE OF LATIN
AMERICANA.
GL/U-2.   LO/U23.   XS/U-1.*
EX/U-1.  5(1), 1972-        NW/U-1.  3, 1970-

**NEW LIBRARY WORLD.**                                   XXX
+ +NEW LIBR. WORLD.
[BINGLEY (JOURNALS) LTD.]
LONDON  73(853), JL 1971-
PREV: LIBRARY WORLD FROM 1, JL 1898- 72(852),
1971.
LD/U-1.   LO/N-3.   LO/N14.   NW/U-1.   SH/U-3.

**NEW LITERARY HISTORY.**
+ +NEW LIT. HIST.
UNIVERSITY OF VIRGINIA.
CHARLOTTESVILLE  1(1), OC 1969-
S/T: A JOURNAL OF THEORY AND INTERPRETATION.
CB/U-1.   DB/U-2.   DN/U-1.   HL/U-1.   LO/U-1.   LO/U-2.
LO/U17.   OX/U-1.
MA/U-1.  2, 1970-          SH/U-1.  1971-
ISSN 0028-6087

**NEW MALAYAN YOUTH.**
+ +NEW MALAY. YOUTH.
LONDON  1(1), 1972-
MON.  JOURNAL OF MALAYAN & SINGAPOREAN STUDENT
MOVEMENT.
LO/U-3.*

**NEW MEASURE.**                                         XXX
+ +NEW MEAS.
OXFORD.  1, 1965- 10, 1969.//
(A QUARTERLY MAGAZINE OF POETRY).
ED/N-1.   LO/U-1.   MA/P-1.

**NEW MIDDLE EAST.**
[NEW MIDDLE EAST PUBL. CO.]
LONDON  NO.1, OC 1968-
S/T:  INTERNATIONAL INDEPENDENT MONTHLY.
LO/N17.   LO/U-3.   LO/U14.   MA/U-1.   OX/U-1.
SO/U-1.
SH/U-1.  JA 1971-
ISSN 0028-6346

**NEW NIPPON ELECTRIC TECHNICAL REVIEW.**                000
SEE: SHIN NIHON DENKI GIHO.

**NEW & NON OFFICAL DRUGS.**                             XXX
SUBS (1965): NEW DRUGS.

**NEW NORTH.**
ABERDEEN UNIVERSITY LITERARY SOCIETY.
ABERDEEN   NO.1, MY 1967-
ED/N-1.   LO/U-2.

**NEW ORLEANS REVIEW.**
+ +NEW ORLEANS REV.
NEW ORLEANS CONSORTIUM.
NEW ORLEANS  1(1), 1968-
Q. S/T: A JOURNAL OF LITERATURE & CULTURE.
LO/U-2.   OX/U-1.
ISSN 0028-6400

**NEW POETRY (LONDON).**
[CATHAY BOOKS]
LONDON  NO.1/2, 1971-
ED/N-1.

**NEW PRIORITIES. A MAGAZINE FOR ACTIVISTS.**
[GORDON & BREACH]
NEW YORK; LONDON  1(1), 1971-
Q.
CA/U-1.   ED/N-1.   OX/U-9.

**NEW PRODUCTS: MEDICAL, SURGICAL.**
+ +NEW PROD., MED. SURG.
[STUART PHILLIPS PUBL.]
SUTTON, SURREY 1, 1969-
LO/N14.
ISSN 0047-9845

**NEW RENAISSANCE.**
ARLINGTON, MASS. 1, FALL 1968-
OX/U-1.
ISSN 0028-6575

**NEW SCIENTIFIC BOOKS.** (1966)                    000
SEE: NB: EDITION EUROPA.

**NEW SCIENTIST & SCIENCE JOURNAL.**               XXX
+ +NEW SCI. & SCI. J.
[IPC MAGAZINES]
LONDON 49(735), 1971-
INCORP: SCIENCE JOURNAL FROM ABOVE NO.
GL/U-1.   LO/N14.

**NEW SCOTLAND.**
+ +NEW SCOTL.
[NEW SCOTLAND PUBL.]
ELDERSLIE NO.1, JL 1968-
M.  S/T: A REVIEW OF POLITICAL & CURRENT
AFFAIRS IN SCOTLAND.
ED/N-1.  NO.2, 1968-          LO/U-3.  NO.5, 1968-
OX/U-1.  NO.2, 1968-

**NEW SLAVIC PUBLICATIONS.**
+ +NEW SLAVIC PUBL.
ASSOCIATION OF RESEARCH LIBRARIES: SLAVIC
BIBLIOGRAPHIC & DOCUMENTATION CENTER.
WASHINGTON, D.C. 1(1), MY 1970-
M.
LO/N-3.  1(2), 1970-          OX/U-1.  2(3), 1970-
ISSN 0028-6710

**NEW SOCIOLOGY.**
+ +NEW SOCIOL.
KINGSTON POLYTECHNIC: SCHOOL OF SOCIOLOGY.
KINGSTON UPON THAMES 1(1), 1971-
GL/U-1.   LD/U-1.   LO/U-3.

**NEW STATEMENTS.**
CANADIAN UNIVERSITY SERVICE.
OTTAWA 1(1), 1971- 2(2), 1974.//
OX/U-1.   OX/U16.

**NEW TECHNIQUES IN ASTRONOMY.**
+ +NEW TECH. ASTRON.
[GORDON & BREACH]
NEW YORK &C. [1], 1971-
ENGL. TRANSL., WITH ADDITIONAL MATERIAL, OF
NOVAJA TEKHNIKA V ASTRONOMIJ 1, 1963.
LO/N14.

**NEW TOWNS BULLETIN.**
+ +NEW TOWNS BULL.
NEW TOWNS ASSOCIATION.
LONDON [NO.1] AP 1972-
MON.
CA/U-1.

**NEW TRENDS IN BIOLOGY TEACHING.**
+ +NEW TRENDS BIOL. TEACH.
UNESCO.
PARIS 1, 1966 (1967)-
BL/U-1.   GL/U-1.

**NEW TRENDS IN CHEMISTRY TEACHING.**
+ +NEW TRENDS CHEM. TEACH.
UNESCO.
PARIS 1, 1964/1965 (1967)-
BL/U-1.   GL/U-1.   SW/U-1.

**NEW TRENDS IN CZECHOSLOVAK ECONOMICS.**
+ +NEW TRENDS CZECH. ECON.
PRAGUE NO.1, 1969-
LO/U-3.

**NEW TRENDS IN PHYSICS TEACHING.**
+ +NEW TRENDS PHYS. TEACH.
UNESCO.
PARIS 1, 1965/1966 (1968)-
GL/U-1.

**NEW UNIVERSITY & NEW EDUCATION WITH PROGRAMMED
LEARNING NEWS.***
+ +NEW UNIV. & NEW EDUC. PROGRAM. LEARN. NEWS.
[NEW UNIV. JOURNALS LTD.]
LONDON 1(1), N 1967-
M.  ISSUED AS NEW EDUCATION FROM 1(1), 1967-
2, 1968, THEN INCORP:  NEW EDUCATION & PRO-
GRAMMED LEARNING NEWS FROM 3, 1969.
BH/U-1.   EX/U-1.   GL/U-2.   GL/U-3.   HL/U-1.   LO/N17.
LO/U11.   OX/U-1.   SH/U-1.
BN/U-1.  3, 1969-             ED/N-1.  3, 1969-
HL/U-2.  3, 1969-            SW/U-1.  3, 1969-

**NEW YEATS PAPERS.**
+ +NEW YEATS PAP.
[DOLMEN P.]
DUBLIN NO.1, 1971-
GL/U-1.   LO/N-1.

**NEW YORK QUARTERLY.**
NEW YORK QUARTERLY POETRY REVIEW FOUNDATION,
INC.
NEW YORK NO.1, 1970-
LO/N-1.   OX/U-1.

**NEW YORK UNIVERSITY JOURNAL OF INTERNATIONAL
LAW & POLITICS.**
+ +N.Y. UNIV. J. INT. LAW & POLIT.
NEW YORK UNIVERSITY: INTERNATIONAL LAW SOCIETY.
NEW YORK 1(1), AP 1968-
OX/U15.   SH/U-1.
ISSN 0028-7873

**NEW YORK UNIVERSITY STUDIES IN COMPARATIVE
LITERATURE.**
+ +N.Y. UNIV. STUD. COMP. LIT.
[NEW YORK UNIVERSITY P.; UNIVERSITY OF LONDON
P.]
NEW YORK; LONDON 1, 1968-
LO/N-1.   LO/N-3.
ISSN 0077-9504

**NEW ZEALAND ABERDEEN ANGUS REVIEW.**             XXX
+ +N.Z. ABERDEEN ANGUS REV.
[MEAT & WOOL]
WELLINGTON, N.Z.  1, 1967- 3, 1969 ...
SUBS: NEW ZEALAND ANGUS REVIEW.
LO/N13.

**NEW ZEALAND ANGUS REVIEW.**
+ +N.Z. ANGUS REV.
[MEAT & WOOL]
WELLINGTON, N.Z.  4, 1970-
PREV: NEW ZEALAND ABERDEEN ANGUS REVIEW FROM
1, 1967- 3, 1969.
LO/N13.

**NEW ZEALAND JOURNAL OF FORESTRY SCIENCE.**
+ +N.Z. J. FOR. SCI.
FOREST RESEARCH INSTITUTE (NEW ZEALAND).
ROTORUA 1, 1971-
AD/U-1.   BN/U-2.   LO/N-2.   LO/N14.   LO/R-5.   OX/U-3.
ISSN 0048-0134

**NEW ZEALAND JOURNAL OF GEOGRAPHY.**             XXX
+ +N.Z. J. GEOGR.
NEW ZEALAND GEOGRAPHICAL SOCIETY.
CHRISTCHURCH NO.47, 1969-
PREV:  RECORD OF PROCEEDINGS OF THE SOCIETY &
ITS BRANCHES FROM NO.1, JA/MY 1946- 46, D
1968.
BH/U-1.   CB/U-1.   HL/U-1.   LO/S13.   LO/U-2.   RE/U-1.
SO/U-1.  NO.48, MY 1970-
ISSN 0028-8292

**NEW ZEALAND JOURNAL OF HEALTH, PHYSICAL EDU-
CATION & RECREATION.**
+ +N.Z. J. HEALTH PHYS. EDUC. & RECREAT.
NEW ZEALAND ASSOCIATION OF HEALTH, PHYSICAL
EDUCATION & RECREATION.
DUNEDIN NO.1, JL 1967-
LD/U-1.
ISSN 0028-8314

**NEW ZEALAND JOURNAL OF HISTORY.**
+ +N.Z. J. HIST.
UNIVERSITY OF AUCKLAND.
AUCKLAND 1(1), AP 1967-
2/A. ISSUED BY THE UNIV.'S HISTORY DEPARTMENT.
AD/U-1.   EX/U-1.   LO/N17.   LO/S-7.   LO/U-8.
GL/U-2.  2, 1968-
ISSN 0028-8322

NEWCASTLE HISTORY MONOGRAPHS.
+ +NEWCASTLE HIST. MONOGR.
NEWCASTLE, N.S.W., PUBLIC LIBRARY.
NEWCASTLE, N.S.W. NO.1, 1966-
  LO/N-1.
  ISSN 0078-0243

NEWCASTLE PAPERS IN ARCHITECTURE & BUILDING
SCIENCE.
+ +NEWCASTLE PAP. ARCHIT. & BUILD. SCI.
UNIVERSITY OF NEWCASTLE UPON TYNE: SCHOOL OF
ARCHITECTURE.
NEWCASTLE UPON TYNE NO.1, 1970-
ED/N-1.    LO/N14.    OX/U-1.

NEWS, AIR TRANSPORT & TRAVEL INDUSTRY TRAIN-
ING BOARD.                                              XXX
+ +NEWS AIR TRANSP. & TRAVEL IND. TRAIN. BOARD.
STAINES  1(1), 1970- 2(9), D 1971.
SUBS: AIR TRANSPORT TRAINING WORLD.
OX/U-1.

NEWS, BOTANICAL SOCIETY OF THE BRITISH ISLES.    000
SEE: B.S.B.I. NEWS.

NEWS OF THE BRITISH ASSOCIATION OF INDUSTRIAL
EDITORS.
+ +NEWS BR. ASSOC. IND. ED.
LONDON NO.1, JA 1973-
MON.
ED/N-1.

NEWS BULLETIN, CHESHIRE CONSERVATION TRUST.
+ +NEWS BULL. CHESHIRE CONSERV. TRUST.
[MOBBERLEY] NO.1, 1967-
LO/R-5.

NEWS BULLETIN, INTERNATIONAL INSTITUTE FOR
THE UNIFICATION OF PRIVATE LAW.
+ +NEWS BULL. INT. INST. UNIFICAT. PRIV. LAW.
ROME  1, AP 1969-
Q.
OX/U15.

NEWS BULLETIN, NORTHERN IRELAND BRANCH,
SCHOOL LIBRARY ASSOCIATION.
+ +NEWS BULL. NORTH. IREL. BRANCH SCHOOL LIBR.
ASSOC.
BELFAST  1, 1969-
BL/U-1.

NEWS, ENGINEERING EMPLOYERS' FEDERATION.        000
SEE: EEF NEWS.

NEWS, GEOLOGICAL SURVEY OF INDIA.
+ +NEWS GEOL. SURV. INDIA.
CALCUTTA  1, 1970-
LO/N-2.    SH/U-1.

NEWS, MOSS LANDING MARINE LABORATORIES.
+ +NEWS MOSS LAND. MAR. LAB.
MOSS LANDING, CALIF.  1, 1972-
LO/N-2.

NEWS, NATIONAL UNION OF TEACHERS.               000
SEE: N.U.T. NEWS.

NEWS [OF THE] PUBLIC HEALTH ENGINEERING DE-       000
PARTMENT, UNIV. OF NEW SOUTH WALES.
SEE: PH NEWS.

NEWS RELEASES, UNITED STATES ATOMIC ENERGY
COMMISSION.
+ +NEWS RELEASES U.S. AT. ENERGY COMM.
WASHINGTON, D.C.  1(1), JL 1970-
LO/S14.    XS/R10.

NEWS REVIEW, INTERNATIONAL AIR TRANSPORT ASS.    000
SEE: IATA NEWS REVIEW.

NEWS ON RUSSIAN MEDICINE & BIOCHEMISTRY.
+ +NEWS RUSS. MED. & BIOCHEM.
[HEYDEN]
  LONDON    JA 1968-
  ED/N-1.    LO/N14.    OX/U-8.

NEWS SHEET, ASSOCIATION FOR COMMONWEALTH
LITERATURE & LANGUAGE STUDIES.                  XXX
+ +NEWS SHEET ASS. COMMONW. LIT. & LANG. STUD.
LEEDS   [NO.1], MY 1966-2.//
PUBL. FOR THE ASS. BY UNIV. OF LEEDS.
SUBS: BULLETIN, ASSOCIATION ..., FROM NO.3,
MY 1967.
LO/U-2.

NEWS SHEET, NORGREN FLUIDICS.
+ +NEWS SHEET NORGREN FLUID.
SHIPSTON-ON-STOUR  NO.1, [1970]-
LO/N14.

NEWS, SOCIETY OF DYERS & COLOURISTS.             000
SEE: SDC NEWS.

NEWS, TUFTED CARPET MANUFACTURE'S ASSOCIATION    000
SEE: T.C.M.A. NEWS.

NEWSBRIEF RHODESIA '73.
+ +NEWSBRIEF RHOD. '73.
AFRICAN BUREAU FOR THE 1973 JUSTICE FOR
RHODESIA CAMPAIGN.
  LONDON  1(1), F 1973-
MON.
LO/U-3.    OX/U-1.
ED/N-1.  1(5), 1973-

NEWSLETTER, AFRICAN STUDIES ASSOCIATION.         000
SEE:  AFRICAN STUDIES NEWSLETTER.

NEWSLETTER, AFRICAN STUDIES CENTER, MICHIGAN
STATE UNIVERSITY.                               000
SEE: A.S.C. NEWSLETTER.

NEWSLETTER, AHMADI NATURAL HISTORY & FIELD
STUDIES GROUP.
+ +NEWSL. AHMADI NAT. HIST. & FIELD STUD. GROUP.
AHMADI, KUWAIT  NO.1, 1970-
LO/N-2.

NEWSLETTER, AMERICAN DIALECT SOCIETY.
+ +NEWSL. AM. DIALECT SOC.
WASHINGTON, D.C.  1(1), 1969-
BL/U-1.    MA/S-1.    OX/U-1.    SH/U-1.
ISSN 0002-8193

NEWSLETTER, AMERICAN MUSICOLOGICAL SOCIETY, INC.
SEE: AMS NEWSLETTER.

NEWSLETTER, AMERICAN SCHOOLS OF ORIENTAL RE-
SEARCH.
+ +NEWSL. AM. SCH. ORIENT. RES.
CAMBRIDGE, MASS.  1, 1969-
LO/S10.

NEWSLETTER, APPLIED SCIENTIFIC RESEARCH
CORPORATION OF THAILAND.                        000
SEE: ASRCT NEWSLETTER.

NEWSLETTER, ARCTIC INSTITUTE OF NORTH AMERICA.
+ +NEWSL. ARCTIC INST. NORTH AM.
MONTREAL  1968(1)- 1972(4).
PREV: ARCTIC NEWSLETTER. SUBS: INFORMATION
NORTH FROM SPRING 1973.
LD/U-1.    LO/N13.
LO/N-2.  1970(5)-              SO/U-1.  1972(1)-
ISSN 0066-6963

NEWSLETTER, ARIZONA PIONEERS' HISTORICAL
SOCIETY.                                        XXX
SUBS (1960): ARIZONIANA.

NEWSLETTER OF THE ASSOCIATION FOR AFRICAN
MICROPALEONTOLOGY & BIOSTRATIGRAPHY.
+ +NEWSL. ASSOC. AFR. MICROPALEONTOL. &
BIOSTRATIGR.
CAIRO  NO.1, 1968-
LO/N-2.

NEWSLETTER, ASSOCIATION OF BRITISH LIBRARY
SCHOOLS.
+ +NEWSL. ASSOC. BR. LIBR. SCH.
MANCHESTER  NO.1, 1967-
DB/U-2.

NEWSLETTER, ASSOCIATION OF MINNESOTA
ENTOMOLOGISTS.
+ +NEWSL. ASSOC. MINN. ENTOMOL.
ST. PAUL  1, 1966-
LO/N-2.

NEWSLETTER, BERMUDA BIOLOGICAL STATION FOR
RESEARCH.
+ +NEWSL. BERMUDA BIOL. STN. RES.
ST. GEORGE'S WEST  1, 1971-
LO/N-2.

NEWSLETTER, BIBLIOGRAPHICAL SOCIETY OF CANADA.
SUBS.(1962): PAPERS, BIBLIOGRAPHICAL SOCIETY
OF CANADA.

NEWSLETTER, BIOLOGICAL GROUP, ASLIB.
+ +NEWSL. BIOL. GROUP ASLIB.
LONDON  NO.1, 1970-
LO/N-2.    LO/N-4.

NEWSLETTER, BRITISH ARACHNOLOGICAL SOCIETY.
++NEWSL. BR. ARACHNOL. SOC.
LOUGHBOROUGH NO.1, 1971-
LO/N-2.    LO/R-5.

NEWSLETTER, BRITISH ESPERANTO ASSOCIATION.
++NEWSL. BR. ESPERANTO ASSOC.
LONDON 1(1), JA 1973-
MON.
ED/N-1.    OX/U-1.

NEWSLETTER, BRITISH PHYCOLOGICAL SOCIETY.
++NEWSL. BR. PHYCOL. SOC.
[LONDON] NO.1, 1971-
LO/N-2.

NEWSLETTER, BRITISH SOCIETY FOR EIGHTEENTH-
CENTURY STUDIES.
++NEWSL. BR. SOC. EIGHTEENTH-CENTURY STUD.
LONDON NO.1, MY 1972-
ED/N-1.    OX/U-1.    SH/U-1.

NEWSLETTER, BRITISH UNIVERSITIES FILM COUNCIL.
++NEWSL. BR. UNIV. FILM COUNC.
LONDON [NO.]1, 1967-
NOS. 1 & 2 UNNUMBERED.
LO/U-1.    LO/U-2.    LO/U11.    LO/U13.
BL/U-1. NO.4, 1968-        LO/S10. NO.9, 1970-
LV/U-1. NO.5, 1968-
CA/U-1. NO.21, 1974-
ED/N-1. NO.21, F 1974-
LO/U12. NO.8, N 1969-

NEWSLETTER, BRUNEL INDUSTRIAL LIAISON BUREAU.
++NEWSL. BRUNEL IND. LIAISON BUR.
BRUNEL UNIVERSITY: BRUNEL INDUSTRIAL LIAISON
BUREAU.
UXBRIDGE NO.1, N 1972-
ED/N-1.    OX/U-1.

NEWSLETTER, BUSINESS ARCHIVES COUNCIL OF
SCOTLAND.
++NEWSL. BUS. ARCH. COUNC. SCOTL.
GLASGOW NO.1, OC 1966-
ED/N-1.    GL/U-2.    HL/U-1.    LO/U-2.    LO/U-3.    MA/U-1.
GL/U-1. NO.3, 1968-        NO/U-1. NO.3, 1968-

NEWSLETTER, CENTER FOR CHINESE RESEARCH MATER-
IALS, ASSOCIATION OF RESEARCH LIBRARIES.
++NEWSL. CENT. CHIN. RES. MATER. ASSOC. RES.
LIBR.
WASHINGTON, D.C. NO.1, 1968-
OX/U-1.

NEWSLETTER, CENTER FOR EDITIONS OF AMERICAN
AUTHORS.                                              000
  SEE: CEAA NEWSLETTER.

NEWSLETTER, CENTRE FOR INFORMATION ON THE
TEACHING OF ENGLISH.                                 000
  SEE: CITE NEWSLETTER.

NEWSLETTER, CENTRE OF SOUTH ASIAN STUDIES.          000
  SEE: CENTRE OF ...

NEWSLETTER, CENTER FOR URBAN STUDIES, UNIVER-
SITY OF CHICAGO.
++NEWSL. CENT. URBAN STUD. UNIV. CHICAGO.
CHICAGO 1, 1968-
BL/U-1.

NEWSLETTER, CIVIL SERVICE SOCIETY.
++NEWSL. CIV. SERV. SOC.
DUBLIN NO.1, MR 1971-
NO.1 ISSUED AS CSS NEWSLETTER.
DB/U-2.

NEWSLETTER, COCKBURN ASSOCIATION.
++NEWSL. COCKBURN ASSOC.
EDINBURGH NO.1, 1972-
ED/N-1.    LO/U-3.    OX/U-1.

NEWSLETTER ON COMPARATIVE STUDIES OF             XXX
COMMUNISM.
++NEWSL. COMP. STUD. COMMUNISM.
AMERICAN COUNCIL OF LEARNED SOCIETIES DEVOTED
TO HUMANISTIC STUDIES: PLANNING GROUP ON
COMPARATIVE COMMUNIST STUDIES.
BUFFALO, N.Y. 1(1), F 1968- 6(4), 1973.//
LO/U-3.
LO/N-1. 2(2), 1969-
ISSN 0028-9469

NEWSLETTER FOR COMPUTER ARCHAEOLOGISTS.          XXX
++NEWSL. COMPUT. ARCHAEOL. [NCOA-A]
ARIZONA STATE UNIVERSITY: DEPARTMENT OF
ANTHROPOLOGY.
TEMPE, ARIZ. 1, JL 1965- JE 1966 ...
SUBS: NEWSLETTER OF COMPUTER ARCHAEOLOGY.
LO/S10.
LO/N-2. 1(2), 1965-

NEWSLETTER OF COMPUTER ARCHAEOLOGY.              XXX
++NEWSL. COMPUT. ARCHAEOL. [NCOA-B]
ARIZONA STATE UNIVERSITY: DEPARTMENT OF
ANTHROPOLOGY.
TEMPE, ARIZ. 2, JL 1966-
PREV: NEWSLETTER FOR COMPUTER ARCHAEOLOGISTS
FROM 1, JL 1965- JE 1966.
LO/N-2.    LO/S10.
SH/U-1. 2(3), 1967-              SO/U-1. 8(2), 1972-
ISSN 0028-9450

NEWSLETTER OF THE COOPERATIVE INVESTIGATION
OF THE MEDITERRANEAN. BULLETIN DE L'ĘTUDE EN
COMMUN DE LA MEDITERRANEE.
++NEWSL. COOP. INVEST. MEDITER.
MONACO NO.1, 1970-
LO/N-4.    LO/N14.

NEWSLETTER, COUNCIL FOR ACADEMIC FREEDOM &
DEMOCRACY.                                           000
  SEE: CAFD NEWSLETTER.

NEWSLETTER, DANISH-SCOTTISH SOCIETY.
++NEWSL. DAN.-SCOTT. SOC.
EDINBURGH NO.1, JL 1973-
ED/N-1.

NEWSLETTER, DECIMAL CURRENCY BOARD.                  000
  SEE: DECIMAL CURRENCY BOARD NEWSLETTER.

NEWSLETTER, DIVISION OF MECHANICAL ENGINEER-
ING, NATIONAL RESEARCH COUNCIL (CANADA):
COMPUTERS.
++NEWSL. DIV. MECH. ENG. NATL. RES. COUNC.
(CAN.), COMPUT.
OTTAWA 1, 1971-
LO/N14.

NEWSLETTER, DIVISION OF MECHANICAL ENGINEER-
ING, NATIONAL RESEARCH COUNCIL (CANADA):
ENGINEERING & BIOLOGICAL CONTROL SYSTEMS.
++NEWSL. DIV. MECH. ENG. NATL. RES. COUNC.
(CAN.), ENG. & BIOL. CONTROL SYST.
OTTAWA 1, 1971-
LO/N14.

NEWSLETTER, DIVISION OF MECHANICAL ENGINEER-
ING, NATIONAL RESEARCH COUNCIL (CANADA):
GENERAL.
++NEWSL. DIV. MECH. ENG. NATL. RES. COUNC.
(CAN.), GEN.
OTTAWA 1, 1973-
LO/N14.

NEWSLETTER, DIVISION OF MECHANICAL ENGINEER-
ING, NATIONAL RESEARCH COUNCIL (CANADA):
MANUFACTURING DEVELOPMENTS.
++NEWSL. DIV. MECH. ENG. NATL. RES. COUNC.
(CAN.), MANUF. DEV.
OTTAWA 1, 1969-
LO/N14.

NEWSLETTER, DIVISION OF MECHANICAL ENGINEER-
ING, NATIONAL RESEARCH COUNCIL (CANADA):
MEDICAL INSTRUMENTATION.
++NEWSL. DIV. MECH. ENG. NATL. RES. COUNC.
(CAN.), MED. INSTRUM.
OTTAWA 1, 1970-
LO/N14.

NEWSLETTER, DIVISION OF MECHANICAL ENGINEER-
ING, NATIONAL RESEARCH COUNCIL (CANADA):
STANDARDS & STANDARDIZATION IN THE ENGINEERING
INDUSTRIES.
++NEWSL. DIV. MECH. ENG. NATL. RES. COUNC.
(CAN.), STAND. & STAND. ENG. IND.
OTTAWA 1, 1972-
LO/N14.

NEWSLETTER, DIVISION OF MECHANICAL ENGINEER-
ING, NATIONAL RESEARCH COUNCIL (CANADA):
TRANSPORTATION.
++NEWSL. DIV. MECH. ENG. NATL. RES. COUNC.
(CAN.), TRANSP.
OTTAWA 1, 1969-
LO/N14.

NEWSLETTER, ECONOMIC DEVELOPMENT COMMITTEE
FOR FOOD MANUFACTURING.
++NEWSL. ECON. DEVELOP. COMM. FOOD MFG. (GB).
NATIONAL ECONOMIC DEVELOPMENT OFFICE (GB).
LONDON NO.1 1969-
LO/U-3.

NEWSLETTER, ECONOMIC DEVELOPMENT COMMITTEE
FOR MOTOR MANUFACTURING INDUSTRY.
++NEWSL. ECON. DEVELOP. COMM. MOT. MFR. IND.
NATIONAL ECONOMIC DEVELOPMENT OFFICE (GB).
LONDON [NO.1], JA 1969-
BH/U-1.

NEWSLETTER, EIGHTEENTH-CENTURY SHORT-TITLE
CATALOGUE COMMITTEE.
++NEWSL. EIGHTEENTH-CENTURY SHORT-TITLE CAT.
COMM.
IOWA CITY NO.1, 1970-
OX/U-1.

NEWS LETTER, ENVIRONMENTAL MUTAGEN SOCIETY.          XXX
++NEWS LETT. ENVIRON. MUTAGEN SOC.
OAK RIDGE, TENN. NO.1, 1969- 6, OC 1972.
SUBS: INCORP. IN: MUTATION RESEARCH, AS THE
SECTION ON ENVIRONMENTAL MUTAGENESIS
& RELATED SUBJECTS.
LO/N13.
ISSN 0013-9319

NEWSLETTER, FOLGER LIBRARY.                          000
SEE: FOLGER LIBRARY NEWSLETTER.

NEWSLETTER, FOLKESTONE NATURAL HISTORY
SOCIETY.
++NEWSL. FOLKESTONE NATUR. HIST. SOC.
FOLKESTONE NO.1, [1970]-
LO/N-2.

NEWSLETTER, FULMER RESEARCH INSTITUTE.              000
SEE: FRI NEWSLETTER.

NEWSLETTER, GENERAL STUDIES ASSOCIATION.
++NEWSL. GEN. STUD. ASSOC.
SEVENOAKS, KENT NO.1, JA 1972-
Q.
ED/N-1. NO.2, 1972-

NEWSLETTER, HAMPSHIRE FIELD CLUB &
ARCHAEOLOGICAL SOCIETY.                             XXX
++NEWSL. HANTS. FIELD CLUB & ARCHAEOL. SOC.
SOUTHAMPTON 1(1), 1965- 1(3), 1966 ...
SUBS: HAMPSHIRE ARCHAEOLOGY & LOCAL HISTORY
NEWSLETTER.
LO/N13.

NEWSLETTER, HEALTH EDUCATION COUNCIL (GB).
++NEWSL. HEALTH EDUC. COUNC. (GB).
WEMBLEY NO.1, 1973-
CA/U-1.    ED/N-1.    LO/N-1.    OX/U-8.

NEWSLETTER, HEREFORDSHIRE & RADNORSHIRE
NATURE TRUST, LTD.
++NEWSL. HEREFORD. & RADNOR. NAT. TRUST, LTD.
[HEREFORD] NO.1, 1963-
LO/N-2.

NEWSLETTER, HERPETOLOGICAL ASSOCIATION OF
RHODESIA.
++NEWSL. HERPETOL. ASSOC. RHOD.
UMTALI NO.1, 1963-
LO/N-2.

NEWSLETTER, INDUSTRIAL ARCHAEOLOGY SECTION,
DERBYSHIRE ARCHAEOLOGICAL & NATURAL HISTORY
SOCIETY.
++NEWSL. IND. ARCHAEOL. SECT. DERBY. ARCHAEOL. &
NAT. HIST. SOC.
DERBY NO.1, 1969-
LO/N-4.

NEWSLETTER, INSTITUTE OF DEVELOPMENT STUDIES,        XXX
UNIVERSITY OF SUSSEX.
++NEWSL. INST. DEVELOP. STUD. UNIV. SUSSEX.
BRIGHTON 1, JA 1968- 4, JA 1969.
SUBS: INCL. IN BULLETIN, INSTITUTE...
OX/U21.
OX/U-1. NO.2, 1968-
SO/U-1. [CURRENT YEAR ONLY]

NEWS LETTER, INSTITUTE OF JOURNALISTS.
++NEWS LETT. INST. JOURNALISTS.
LONDON NO.1, 1964-
ED/N-1.    OX/U-1.
BH/P-1. 7(6), 1970-

NEWSLETTER, INSTITUTE OF POLAR STUDIES, OHIO
STATE UNIVERSITY.
++NEWSL. INST. POLAR STUD. OHIO STATE UNIV.
COLUMBUS NO.1, 1969-
2A.
CA/U12.

NEWSLETTER, INSTITUTE OF SOUTHEAST ASIAN
STUDIES (SINGAPORE).
++NEWSL. INST. SE. ASIAN STUD. (SINGAPORE).
SINGAPORE NO.1, 1969-
HL/U-1.

NEWSLETTER, INTERNATIONAL ALBAN BERG SOCIETY.
++NEWSL. INT. ALBAN BERG SOC.
NEW YORK NO.1, 1968-
MA/U-1.

NEWSLETTER, INTERNATIONAL ASSOCIATION FOR THE
STUDY OF ANGLO-IRISH LITERATURE.
++NEWSL. INT. ASSOC. STUD. ANGLO-IR. LIT.
DUBLIN NO.1, 1971-
DB/S-1.    DB/U-2.

NEWSLETTER, INTERNATIONAL ASSOCIATION OF
TECHNOLOGICAL UNIVERSITY LIBRARIES.                 000
SEE: IATUL NEWSLETTER.

NEWSLETTER, INTERNATIONAL CENTER FOR ARID &
SEMI-ARID LAND STUDIES.                             000
SEE: ICASALS NEWSLETTER.

NEWSLETTER, INTERNATIONAL COUNCIL ON ARCHIVES.
++NEWSL. INT. COUNC. ARCH.
MADRID NO. 1, 1969.//
LO/U-1.    LO/U-8.

NEWSLETTER, INTERNATIONAL CROCODILIAN SOCIETY.
++NEWSL. INT. CROCODILIAN SOC.
SILVER SPRINGS, FLA. NO.1, 1969-
LO/N-2.

NEWSLETTER, INTERNATIONAL SOCIETY OF CHEMOTH-
ERAPY.
++NEWSL. INT. SOC. CHEMOTHER.
[MUNICH] NO.1, F 1969-
OX/U-8.

NEWSLETTER, INTERNATIONAL WILDFOWL RESEARCH
BUREAU.                                             XXX
SUBS (1970): BULLETIN, INTERNATIONAL WILD-
FOWL RESEARCH BUREAU.

NEWSLETTER, INTERNATIONAL YEAR FOR HUMAN
RIGHTS.                                             000
SEE: INTERNATIONAL YEAR FOR HUMAN RIGHTS
NEWSLETTER.

NEWSLETTER, IRISH WILDBIRD CONSERVANCY.             XXX
++NEWSL. IR. WILDBIRD CONSERV.
DUBLIN [NO.1], AP 1969- 19, 1974.
SUBS: I.W.C. NEWS.
DB/S-1.*    DB/U-2.
LO/N13. [CURRENT BOX ONLY]

NEWSLETTER, JAMAICAN GEOGRAPHICAL SOCIETY.
++NEWSL. JAMAICAN GEOGR. SOC.
KINGSTON NO.1, MY 1967-
LO/U-8.

NEWSLETTER, JAPAN LIBRARY GROUP.
++NEWSL. JAP. LIBR. GROUP.
SHEFFIELD NO.1, 1969-
OX/U-1.

NEWSLETTER, KESATUAN KAJIBUMI MALAYSIA.
++NEWSL. KESATUAN KAJIBUMI MALAYS.
KUALA LUMPUR NO.1, JL 1966-
LO/N-2.

NEWSLETTERS, LANCASHIRE NATURALISTS' TRUST.        000
SEE: NATURE IN LANCASHIRE.

NEWSLETTER, LATIN AMERICAN STUDIES ASSOCIA-
TION.
++NEWSL. LAT. AM. STUD. ASS.
WASHINGTON, D.C. 1(1), 1969-
OX/U-1.
ISSN 0023-8805

NEWSLETTER ON LIBRARY RESEARCH.
++NEWSL. LIBR. RES.
UNIVERSITY OF ILLINOIS: GRADUATE SCHOOL OF
LIBRARY SCIENCE.
URBANA NO.1, S 1972-
Q.
ED/N-1.    OX/U-1.

NEWSLETTER, LITERARY & LINGUISTIC GROUP,
UNIVERSITY OF MANCHESTER REGIONAL COMPUTER
CENTRE.                                                                 XXX
++NEWSL. LIT. & LINGUIST. GROUP, UNIV. MANCH.
 REG. COMPUT. CENT.
 MANCHESTER 1, 1971- 6, 1972.//
 CA/U-1.   HL/U-1.   MA/U-1.   SH/U-1.

NEWSLETTER, MAINE HISTORICAL SOCIETY.
++NEWSL. MAINE HIST. SOC.
 PORTLAND, MAINE 1, JE 1961-
 OX/U-9. 9(2), 1969-
 ISSN 0464-5820

NEWSLETTER, MENTAL HEALTH ASSOCIATION OF
IRELAND.
++NEWSL. MENT. HEALTH ASSOC. IREL.
 DUBLIN 1(1), 1973-
 DB/U-2.   ED/N-1.   OX/U-8.

NEWSLETTER, MISSOURI LIBRARY ASSOCIATION.
++NEWSL. MO. LIBR. ASS.
 COLUMBIA 1(1, F 1970-
 2M.
 OX/U-1.   1(2), 1970-
 ISSN 0024-8223

NEWSLETTER, MOSS LANDING LABORATORIES.
++NEWSL. MOSS LAND. LAB.
 MOSS LANDING (CALIF.) 1(1), 1968-
 LO/N-2.   1(1), 1968- 1(2), 1969.

NEWSLETTER, MUSIC LIBRARY ASSOCIATION.
++NEWSL. MUSIC LIBR. ASS.
 NEW YORK NO.1, F 1969-
 DB/U-2.

NEWSLETTER, NATIONAL CENTRAL LIBRARY (TAIPEI).
++NEWSL. NAT. CENT. LIBR. (TAIPEI).
 TAIPEI 1(1), 1969-
 OX/U-1.

NEWSLETTER OF THE NATIONAL GARDENS GUILD.
++NEWSL. NAT. GARD. GUILD.
 STANFORD-LE-HOPE NO.1, OC/D 1968-
 ED/N-1.   OX/U-8.

NEWSLETTER, NATIONAL UNION OF SOUTH AFRICAN
STUDENTS.
++NEWSL. NAT. UNION S. AFR. STUD.
 CAPE TOWN NO.1, 1970-
 OX/U-9.

NEWSLETTER, NEUTRON DATA COMPILATION CENTRE.
++NEWSL. NEUTRON DATA COMPIL. CENT.
 SACLAY CCDN - NW1, 1966-
 LO/N14.

NEWSLETTER, NORTHUMBERLAND LOCAL HISTORY
SOCIETY.
++NEWSL. NORTHUMBERL. LOCAL HIST. SOC.
 NEWCASTLE UPON TYNE NO.1, 1967-
 BN/U-1.

NEWSLETTER, NUCLEAR PHYSICS BOARD, SCIENCE
RESEARCH COUNCIL(GB).
++NEWSL. NUCL. PHYS. BOARD. SCI. RES. COUNC.(GB)
 LONDON NO.1, 1969-
 XS/R10.

NEWSLETTER, PEACE & CONFLICT RESEARCH
PROGRAMME.
++NEWSL. PEACE & CONFLICT RES. PROGRAMME.
 LANCASTER 1(1), MR 1971-
 LO/N-1.   OX/U-1.

NEWSLETTER, PERIVALE BIRD SANCTUARY.
++NEWSL. PERIVALE BIRD SANCTUARY.
 EALING 1, 1970-
 LO/N-2.

NEWSLETTER, PETER WARLOCK SOCIETY.                                      000
 SEE: PETER WARLOCK SOCIETY NEWSLETTER.

NEWSLETTER, PRINTING & PUBLISHING INDUSTRY
TRAINING BOARD.
++NEWSL. PRINT. & PUBL. IND. TRAIN. BOARD.
 LONDON NO.1, JA 1969-
 LO/N-1.

NEWSLETTER, QUEKETT MICROSCOPICAL CLUB.
++NEWSL. QUEKETT MICROSC. CLUB.
 LONDON NO.1, MR 1972-
 2/A.
 ED/N-1.

NEWSLETTER, ROYAL AUSTRALASIAN ORNITHOLOGISTS'
UNION.
++NEWSL. R. AUSTRALAS. ORNITHOL. UNION.
 MELBOURNE NO.1, 1969-
 LO/N-2.

NEWSLETTER, SCANDINAVIAN INSTITUTE OF ASIAN
STUDIES.
++NEWSL. SCAND. INST. ASIAN STUD.
 COPENHAGEN NO.1, S 1968-
 LO/U-8.
 LO/N-1.   NO.3, JA 1970-

NEWSLETTER, SCIENCE OF SCIENCE FOUNDATION.                              000
 SEE: SSF NEWSLETTER.

NEWSLETTER, SCOTTISH SOCIETY OF THE HISTORY
OF MEDICINE.
++NEWSL. SCOTT. SOC. HIST. MED.
 EDINBURGH NO.1, AP 1972-
 ED/N-1.
 LO/N-4.   NO.2, 1973-

NEWSLETTER OF THE SCOTTISH SOCIETY FOR
INDUSTRIAL ARCHAEOLOGY.
++NEWSL. SCOTT. SOC. IND. ARCHAEOL.
 GLASGOW NO.1, 1969-
 ED/N-1.   LO/N-4.
 OX/U-1.   NO.3(1), 1971-

NEWSLETTER, SCOTTISH WILDLIFE TRUST.
++NEWSL. SCOTT. WILDL. TRUST.
 EDINBURGH NO.1, 1965-
 LO/N-2.
 OX/U-8.   NO.18, 1971-

NEWSLETTER, SELBORNE SOCIETY.                                           XXX
++NEWSL. SELBORNE SOC.
 LONDON NO.1, 1970- 6, MY 1972...
 SUBS: PERIVALE NEWSLETTER.
 LO/N-2.
 LO/R-5.   NO.5, 1971-

NEWSLETTER, SLAVIC BIBLIOGRAPHIC & DOCUMENTAT-
ION CENTER, ASSOCIATION OF RESEARCH LIBRARIES.
++NEWSL. SLAVIC BIBLIOGR. & DOC. CENT. ASSOC.
 RES. LIBR.
 WASHINGTON, D.C. NO.1, JA 1970- 6, 1972. //
 BL/U-1. NO.3, 1971-           OX/U-1. NO.2, 1970-

NEWSLETTER, SOCIALIST LABOUR LEAGUE.                                    XXX
 SUBS (1969): WORKERS' PRESS.

NEWSLETTER, SOCIETY OF DESIGNER-CRAFTSMEN.
++NEWSL. SOC. DES.-CRAFTSMEN.
 LONDON NO.1, 1968-
 OX/U-1.

NEWSLETTER, SOCIETY FOR ETHNOMUSICOLOGY.                                000
 SEE: SEM NEWSLETTER.

NEWSLETTER, SOCIETY FOR PSYCHICAL RESEARCH.                             000
 SEE: S.P.R. NEWSLETTER.

NEWS LETTER, SOMERSET TRUST FOR NATURE
CONSERVATION.
++NEWS LETT. SOMERSET TRUST NAT. CONSERV.
 TAUNTON NO.1, 1964-
 LO/N-2.

NEWSLETTER, SOUTH AFRICAN INSTITUTE OF INTER-
NATIONAL AFFAIRS.
++NEWSL. S. AFR. INST. INT. AFF.
 JOHANNESBURG NO.1, F 1969-
 Q.
 LO/S14.*

NEWSLETTER, SOUTH-EAST ASIA LIBRARY GROUP.
++NEWSL. SOUTH-EAST ASIA LIBR. GROUP.
 HULL NO.1, JL 1968-
 HL/U-2.   LO/N12.   LO/U-8.

NEWSLETTER, SOUTHEAST ASIAN RESEARCH MATER-
IALS GROUP.
++NEWSL. SOUTHEAST ASIAN RES. MATER. GROUP.
 CANBERRA NO.1, JA 1972-
 LO/U-8.   OX/U-1.

NEWSLETTER, STANDING CONSULTATIVE COUNCIL ON
YOUTH & COMMUNITY SERVICE.
++NEWSL. STAND. CONSULT. COUNC. YOUTH & COM-
 MUNITY SERV.
 EDINBURGH 1, 1972-
 CA/U-1.   OX/U-1.

**NEWSLETTERS ON STRATIGRAPHY.**
++NEWSL. STRATIGR.
[BRILL]
LEIDEN 1, 1970-
GL/U-1.    HL/U-1.    LO/N-2.    LO/N13.    OX/U-8.    SH/U-3.

**NEWSLETTER, SUSSEX ARCHAEOLOGICAL SOCIETY.**          000
SEE: SUSSEX ...

**NEWSLETTER, TEXAS HERPETOLOGICAL SOCIETY.**
++NEWSL. TEX. HERPETOL. SOC.
SAN ANGELO, TEX. NO.1, 1972-
LO/N-2.

**NEWSLETTER OF TREE IMPROVEMENT & INTRODUCTION.**
++NEWSL. TREE IMPROV. & INTROD.
FOREST RESEARCH INSTITUTE (AUSTRALIA).
CANBERRA 1(1), AP 1968-
OX/U-3.

**NEWSLETTER, UNITED NATIONS INDUSTRIAL DEVELOP-
MENT ORGANIZATION.**                                      000
SEE: UNIDO NEWSLETTER.

**NEWSLETTER, UNIVERSITY ASSOCIATION FOR CONT-
EMPORARY EUROPEAN STUDIES.**
++NEWSL. UNIV. ASS. CONTEMP. EUR. STUD.
[LONDON] [NO.1], 1968-
ISSUES NO. 0 & 1 ARE REGARDED AS NO. 1 & 2.
OX/U17. MY 1969-

**NEWSLETTER, WARWICKSHIRE LOCAL HISTORY
SOCIETY.**
++NEWSL. WARKS. LOCAL HIST. SOC.
WARWICK 1, JL 1965-
BH/P-1.

**NEWSLETTER, WILDLIFE DISEASE ASSOCIATION.**          XXX
SUBS: BULLETIN, WILDLIFE ...

**NEWSLETTER, THE WORLD UNION OF JEWISH STUDIES.**
++NEWSL. WORLD UNION JEW. STUD.
JERUSALEM NO.1, 1970-
SO/U-1.

**NEXT WAVE POETS.**
[NEXT WAVE PUBL.]
LONDON NO.1, 1969-
LO/N-1.

**NEXUS.**                                                XXX
SUBS (1968): BUSARA.

**N.F.U. INSIGHT.**                                       XXX
NATIONAL FARMERS' UNION.
LONDON NO.1, AP 1971-
PREV: PART OF BRITISH FARMER FROM NO.1, JL
1948- 688, JA 1971.
ED/N-1.    MA/P-1.    OX/U-8.
LD/U-1. NO.37, 1972-

**NGS NEWS.**
NEW GLASGOW SOCIETY.
GLASGOW 1, 1968-
GL/U-1.

**NIAE NEWSLETTER.**
NATIONAL INSTITUTE OF AGRICULTURAL
ENGINEERING (GB).
SILSOE, BEDS. NO.1, 1970-
LO/N14.    OX/U-8.    XS/F-4.
LO/R-6. 3, 1971-

**NICO. REVUE PERIODIQUE DE CENTRE BELGE DE
PEDAGOGIE DE LA MATHEMATIQUE.**
BRUSSELS NO.1, N 1968-
DB/U-2.

**NIETZSCHE STUDIEN. INTERNATIONALES JAHRBUCH
FUR DIE NIETZSCHE-FORSCHUNG.**
++NIETZSCHE STUD.
BERLIN 1, 1972-
BT/U-1.    CA/U-1.    DB/U-2.    GL/U-2.    MA/U-1.    OX/U-1.

**NIEUWE UITGAVEN IN NEDERLAND.**                        XXX
++NIEUWE UITG. NED.
THE HAGUE 1, 1937- 27(12), JA 1966.//
M. NUMBERING OMITTED FOR A TIME FROM 2(10),
1938.
LC/U-1.**    LO/N-1.
BH/U-1. 16-              BL/U-1. 24,1962-
GL/U-1. *14(11)-        HL/U-1. 21,1959-
LA/U-1. 26,1964-        LO/N-3. 22,1960-
LO/N14. *2,1938-        LO/S22. 13-
LO/U-2. (1947)-         LO/U11. 22,1960-

**NIGERIA. BULLETIN ON FOREIGN AFFAIRS.**
NIGERIAN INSTITUTE OF INTERNATIONAL AFFAIRS.
LAGOS 1(1), JL 1971-
Q.
LO/U-8.

**NIGERIAN ENGINEER.**
++NIGER. ENG.
NIGERIAN SOCIETY OF ENGINEERS.
[LAGOS] 1, 1962-
LO/N13.

**NIGERIAN ENTOMOLOGISTS' MAGAZINE.**
++NIGER. ENTOMOL. MAG.
ENTOMOLOGICAL SOCIETY OF NIGERIA.
IBADAN 1(1), AG 1966-
LO/N-2.    LO/N13.

**NIGERIAN JOURNAL OF CONTEMPORARY LAW.**
++NIGER. J. CONTEMP. LAW.
NIGERIAN SOCIETY OF CONTEMPORARY LAW.
LAGOS 1(1), 1970-
BL/U-1.    LO/U14.
ISSN 0048-0401

**NIGERIAN JOURNAL OF FORESTRY.**
++NIGER. J. FOR.
FORESTRY ASSOCIATION OF NIGERIA.
IBADAN 1(1), JA 1971-
2/A.
AD/U-1.    LO/R-6.    OX/U-3.

**NIGERIAN JOURNAL OF ISLAM.**
++NIGER. J. ISLAM.
CONFERENCE OF MUSLIM LECTURERS & SENIOR STAFF
OF ALL NIGERIAN UNIVERSITIES.
ILE-IFE 1(1), 1970-
2/A.
AD/U-1.    BH/C-3.
ISSN 0029-0106

**NIGERIAN JOURNAL OF PUBLIC AFFAIRS.**
++NIGER. J. PUBLIC AFF.
AHMADU BELLO UNIVERSITY: INSTITUTE OF ADMIN-
ISTRATION.
ZARIA 1(1), OC 1970-
LO/U-8.
OX/U-9. 2(1), 1971-

**NIGERIAN MEDICAL JOURNAL.**
++NIGER. MED. J.
NIGERIAN MEDICAL ASSOCIATION.
LAGOS 1, 1971-
BL/U-1.

**NIHON KAI-IKI KENKYUJO HOKOKU. BULLETIN OF
THE JAPAN SEA RESEARCH INSTITUTE.**
NIHON KAI-IKI KENKYUJO.
KANAZAWA NO.1, 1969-
ENGL. SUMM.
LO/N13.

**NIHON KOGYO DAIGAKU KENKYU HOKOKU. REPORT
OF RESEARCHES, NIPPON INSTITUTE OF TECHNOLOGY.**
NIHON KOGYO DAIGAKU.
TOKYO 1, 1971-
LO/N13.

**NIHON SHONI GEKKA GAKKAI ZASSHI. JOURNAL OF
THE JAPANESE SOCIETY OF PEDIATRIC SURGEONS.**
NIHON SHONI GEKKA GAKKAI.
TOKYO 1(1), 1965-
WITH VOL.4(1) ENGLISH TITLE CHANGED FROM
JOURNAL, JAPANESE SOCIETY OF PEDIATRIC
SURGERY.
XS/N-1.

**NIHON TOKEI GAKKAI.**
NIHON TOKEI GAKKAISHI.
TOKYO 1, 1970-
ENGL. TITLE = JOURNAL, JAPAN STATISTICAL
SOCIETY.
LO/N13.

**NIHON YUNIBAKKU SOGO KENKYUJO, K.K. SOKEN
KIYO.**
TOKYO 1, 1971-
ALSO ENTITLED: REPORTS OF RESEARCH ACTIVITIES
ON COMPUTER SCIENCES & TECHNOLOGY.
LO/N14.

**NIIGATA DAIGAKU KYOYOBU KENKYU KIYO. JOURNAL
OF GENERAL EDUCATION DEPARTMENT, NIIGATA UNI-
VERSITY.**
NIIGATA NO.1, 1968-
LO/N13.

**NIIGATA DAIGAKU NOGAKUBU ENSHURIN HOKOKU.**
**BULLETIN OF THE NIIGATA UNIVERSITY FORESTS.**
NIIGATA DAIGAKU NOGAKUBU FUZOKU ENSHURIN.
*NIIGATA 1, 1962-*
BODY NAME MEANS 'NIIGATA UNIV. FAC. OF AGRI-
CULTURE (ATTACHED) FORESTS.'
*OX/U-3.*

**NINETEENTH CENTURY THEATRE RESEARCH.**
++*NINETEENTH CENTURY THEATRE RES.*
*EDMONTON, ALBERTA 1, 1973-*
2/A.
*LO/U-4.     SH/U-1.     SW/U-1.*

**NIPPON STEEL TECHNICAL REPORT OVERSEAS.**
++*NIPPON STEEL TECH. REP. OVERSEAS.*
SHIN NIHON SEITETSU K.K.
*TOKYO NO.1, 1972-*
CONTAINS TRANSL. OR ABRIDGMENTS OF ARTICLES IN
SEITETSU KENKYU FROM NO.272, 1972-.
*LO/N14.*

**NKANGA EDITIONS.**
++*NKANGA ED.*
*KAMPALA NO.1, 1968-*
*OX/U-9.*

**NLL ANNOUNCEMENT BULLETIN.**                                          XXX
++*NLL ANNOUNCE. BULL. (NAT. LEND. LIBR.)*
NATIONAL LENDING LIBRARY FOR SCIENCE & TECH-
NOLOGY.                                                                 XXX
*BOSTON SPA, YORKS. 1(1), 1971- 2(12), 1972.*
*NAB 73-1, JA 1973- NAB 73-5, MY 1973 ...*
MON. PREV: BRITISH RESEARCH & DEVELOPMENT
REPORTS FROM NO.1, JA 1966- 5(12), D 1970.
SUBS: BLL ANNOUNCEMENT BULLETIN.
*BH/U-1.     BN/U-2.     CB/U-1.     DB/U-2.     GL/U-1.     LD/U-1.*
*LO/N-3.     LO/N-4.     LO/N-7.     LO/N14.     LO/R-5.     LO/U-2.*
*LO/U12.     NO/U-1.     NW/U-1.     OX/U-1.     RE/U-1.     SA/U-1.*
*SW/U-1.     XS/N-1.*

**NLL REVIEW.**                                                         XXX
++*NLL REV.*
NATIONAL LENDING LIBRARY FOR SCIENCE &
TECHNOLOGY.
*LONDON 1, JA 1971- 2(6), AP 1973.*
PREV. PART OF: NLL TRANSLATIONS BULLETIN FROM
3, 1961- 12, 1970. SUBS: BLL REVIEW.
*BH/U-1.     BN/U-2.     BR/U-3.     DB/U-2.     ED/N-1.     GL/U-1.*
*LD/U-1.     LN/U-2.     LO/N-1.     LO/N-3.     LO/N-4.     LO/N14.*
*LO/U-1.     LO/U-2.     LO/U12.     LO/U14.     NO/U-1.     OX/U-1.*
*SF/U-1.     SH/U-1.     SO/U-1.     SW/U-1.     XS/N-1.     XS/R10.*
*ISSN 0027-6790*

**NMA JOURNAL.**                                                        XXX
++*NMA J. (NAT. MICROF. ASS.)*
NATIONAL MICROFILM ASSOCIATION (US).
*ANNAPOLIS, MD. 1(1), 1967- 2(4), 1969...*
Q. SUBS: JOURNAL OF MICROGRAPHICS. PREV:
NATIONAL MICRO-NEWS FROM NO.1, D 1953- 88,
JE 1967.
*BL/U-1.     LO/N-4.     LO/N14.     LO/U-2.     NW/U-1.     OX/U-1.*
*LO/N-1. 1(3), 1968-*

**NMR. BASIC PRINCIPLES & PROGRESS.**
[SPRINGER]
*BERLIN 1, 1969-*
*CA/U-1.     LO/N14.*

**NN. NETHERLANDS NITROGEN TECHNICAL BULLETIN.**
NETHERLANDS NITROGEN FERTILIZER INDUSTRY
AGRICULTURAL BUREAU.
*THE HAGUE NO.1, S 1966-*
*XE/F-2.*

**NOAA.**
NATIONAL OCEANIC & ATMOSPHERIC ADMINISTRATION
(US).
*ROCKVILLE, MD. 1(1), JA 1971-*
Q.
*XS/N-1.*
*ISSN 0014-0821*

**NOGYO DOBOKU SHIKENJO GIHO; C: ZOKO. TECH-
NICAL REPORT OF THE AGRICULTURAL ENGINEERING
RESEARCH STATION; C: CONSTRUCTION ENGINEERING.**
NORIN-SHO NOGYO DOBOKU SHIKENJO.
*HIRATSUKA NO.1, 1966-*
*LO/N13.*

**NOGYO DOBOKU SHIKENJO HOKOKU.**
NORIN-SHO NOGYO DOBOKU SHIKENJO.
*KANAGAWA 1, 1963-*
ENGL. ABSTRACTS.
*XN/S-1.*

**NOISE CONTROL & VIBRATION REDUCTION.**
++*NOISE CONTROL & VIB. REDUCT.*
[TRADE & TECHNICAL P.]
*LONDON 1, N 1970-*
*ED/N-1.     LD/U-1.     LO/N14.     OX/U-8.*

**NOISE & VIBRATION BULLETIN.**
++*NOISE & VIB. BULL.*
[MULTI-SCIENCE PUBL. CO. LTD.]
*LONDON 1, JA 1970-*
*OX/U-8.     SH/U-1.*
*ISSN 0029-0947*

**NON-IONIZING RADIATION.**
++*NON-IONIZ. RADIAT.*
[ILIFFE]
*GUILDFORD 1(1), JE 1969-*
*LO/N14.     OX/U-8.     XS/R10.*

**NOORDHOLLANDS GLORIE.**                                               XXX
++*NOORDHOLL. GLORIE.*
PROVINCIALE BOND VAN RUNDVEEFOKVERENIGINGEN IN
NOORDHOLLAND.
*ALKMAAR 1972-*
PREV: GLORY OF NOORDHOLLAND FROM 1964- 1971.
*LO/N13.*

**NORDEUROPA. JAHRBUCH FUR NORDISCHE STUDIEN.**
ERNST-MORITZ-ARNDT UNIVERSITAT GREIFSWALD.
*GREIFSWALD 1, 1966-*
ADDED S/T: WISSENSCHAFTLICHE ZEITSCHRIFT DER
ERNST-MORITZ-ARNDT ...
*DB/S-1.*

**NORDEUROPAEISK MEJERI-TIDSSKRIFT.**                                   XXX
++*NORDEUR. MEJERI-TIDSSKR.*
*COPENHAGEN 38, 1972-*
PREV: NORDISK MEJERI-TIDSSKRIFT FROM 1, 1935-
37, 1971.
*LO/N13.*

**NORDIC HYDROLOGY.**
++*NORD. HYDROL.*
[MUNKSGAARD]
*COPENHAGEN 1(1), 1970-*
Q.
*BH/U-1.     BH/U-3.     CA/U-2.     GL/U-2.     HL/U-1.     LO/N-2.*
*LO/N-4.     LO/N14.     OX/U-8.     XE/F-2.     XS/N-1.*
*ISSN 0029-1277*

**NORDISK ASTRONOMISK TIDSSKRIFT.**                                     XXX
SUBS (1968): ASTRONOMISK TIDSSKRIFT.

**NORDISK MEJERI-TIDSSKRIFT.**                                          XXX
SUBS (1972): NORDEUROPAEISK MEJERI-TIDSSKRIFT.

**NORDISKT ARTIKELINDEX FOR BYGG.**                                     XXX
++*NORD. ARTIKELINDEX BYGG.*
STUDIESELKAPET FOR NORSK INDUSTRI.
*OSLO 4(3-12), 1971.*
PREV: ARTIKKELINDEKS FOR BYGG FROM 1, 1968-
4(2), 1971. SUBS: BYGGREFERAT.
*LO/N14.*

**NORFOLK ARCHITECTS ASSOCIATION BROADSHEET.**
++*NORFOLK ARCHIT. ASSOC. BROADSHEET.*
*LYNG NO.1, 1971-*
*ED/N-1.*

**NORMALE UND PATHOLOGISCHE ANATOMIE.**                                 XXX
++*NORM. & PATHOL. ANAT.*
[THIEME]
*STUTTGART 21, 1970-*
PREV: ZWANGLOSE ABHANDLUNGEN AUS DEM GEBIET
DER NORMALEN UND PATHOLOGISCHEN ANATOMIE FROM
1, 1957- 20, 1969.
*LO/N13.*

**NORSK HVALFANGST-TIDENDE. = NORWEGIAN
WHALING GAZETTE.**                                                      XXX
++*NORSK HVALFANGST-TID. [NOHT-A]*
INTERNATIONAL ASSOCIATION OF WHALING COMPANIES.
*SANDEFJORD 1(1), 1912- 57(6), 1968.//*
NORWEG., ENGL. WLSP/4 HOLDINGS INCLUDED
BELOW.
*LO/N-1.*     *XY/N-1.***
*CA/U12. (1923)-*                      *LO/N-6. (1942)-*
*LO/N13. 53,1964-*                     *XS/R11. *(1927)-*

**NORTH EAST NEWS.**
NORTH EAST DEVELOPMENT COUNCIL.
*NEWCASTLE/TYNE NO.1, SUMMER 1963-*
S/T: A QUARTERLY REPORT ON DEVELOPMENT IN
NORTH EAST ENGLAND.
*HL/U-1.*
*ED/N-1. 8, 1966-*

**NORTH INDIA CHURCHMAN. OFFICIAL MAGAZINE OF THE CHURCH OF NORTH INDIA.**   XXX
*DELHI 1(1), F 1971-*
PREV: UNITED CHURCH REVIEW: NS FROM 1, D 1929-
41(10), 1970.
*BH/C-3.*

**NORTH MAGAZINE. A MONTHLY MAGAZINE FOR DURHAM, NORTHUMBERLAND & NORTH YORKSHIRE.**
*++NORTH MAG.*
*YORK 1(1), JL 1971-*
*ED/N-1.    OX/U-1.*

**NORTH SEA YACHTSMAN.**   000
**SUBS (1969): PART OF SMALL BOAT.**

**NORTH WALES FARMER.**
NATIONAL FARMERS' UNION.
*WREXHAM NO.1, 1970-*
S/T: OFFICIAL JOURNAL OF THE DENBIGHSHIRE,
FLINTSHIRE & MONTGOMERYSHIRE BRANCHES OF THE
NATIONAL ...
*OX/U-8.*

**NORTH WEST INDUSTRIAL REVIEW.**
*++NORTH WEST IND. REV.*
[W.PARR]
*WILMSLOW, CHESHIRE 1, JL 1969-*
*ED/N-1.    LV/P-1.    OX/U-1.*
*LO/U-1. 6, 1974-*

**NORTHCOTT MAGAZINE.**
*++NORTHCOTT MAG.*
[TOYNE]
*NEWTON ABBOT, DEVON. 1(1), AP 1969-*
*EX/U-1.    OX/U-1.*

**NORTHEAST ASIA JOURNAL OF THEOLOGY.**
*++NORTHEAST ASIA J. THEOL.*
*TOKYO 1, MR 1968-*
2/A.
*BH/C-3.*

**NORTHERN COUNTIES MAGAZINE.**
*++NORTH. COUNTIES MAG.*
[JOHN G. ECCLES]
*INVERNESS 1, JA 1969-*
*ED/N-1.    ED/P-1.    OX/U-1.*

**NORTHERN ENGINEER.**
*++NORTH. ENG.*
UNIVERSITY OF ALASKA: INSTITUTE OF ARCTIC EN-
VIRONMENTAL ENGINEERING.
*COLLEGE, ALASKA 1(1), 1968-*
Q.
*CA/U12.*
*ISSN 0029-3083*

**NORTHERN INDUSTRY. MANAGEMENT JOURNAL FOR THE NORTHERN REGION.**
*++NORTH. IND.*
[PAULL & GOODE PUBL. LTD.]
*SUNDERLAND 1(1), S 1970-*
*OX/U-1.*
*ED/N-1. 1(11), 1971-*
*ISSN 0048-0762*

**NORTHERN IRELAND LOCAL HISTORY.**
*++NORTH. IREL. LOCAL HIST.*
*BELFAST 1(1), N 1969-*
*BL/C-1.    DB/U-2.    OX/U-1.*
*BL/U-1.    1970-*

**NORTHERN OFFSHORE.**
*++NORTH. OFFSHORE.*
[SELVIGS FORLAG]
*OSLO 1, 1972-*
ENGL. S/T: THE NORWEGIAN JOURNAL OF OIL &
GAS.
*LO/N14.*

**NORTHERN SCOTLAND.**
*++NORTH. SCOTL.*
UNIVERSITY OF ABERDEEN: CENTRE FOR SCOTTISH
STUDIES.
*ABERDEEN 1(1), D 1972-*
ANNU. S/T: A HISTORICAL JOURNAL.
*AD/U-1.    BL/U-1.    CA/U-1.    DB/U-2.    EX/U-1.    GL/U-1.*
*LD/U-1.    LO/U-2.    OX/U-1.    SA/U-1.    SH/U-1.*

**NORTHWEST GEOLOGY.**
*++NORTHWEST GEOL.*
UNIVERSITY OF MONTANA.
*MISSOULA 1, 1972-*
*LO/N13.*

**NORWEB NEWS.**
NORTH WESTERN ELECTRICITY BOARD.
*MANCHESTER NO.1, MR 1971-*
S/T: STAFF NEWSPAPER OF THE NORTH WESTERN
ELECTRICITY BOARD.
*LO/N-1.*

**NORWEGIAN ARCHAEOLOGICAL REVIEW.**
*++NORW. ARCHAEOL. REV.*
*OSLO 1, 1968-*
*BL/U-1.    CA/U-3.    CR/N-1.    DB/U-2.    ED/N-1.    LO/U-2.*
*OX/U-1.    SH/U-1.*
*ISSN 0029-3652*

**NORWEGIAN JOURNAL OF BOTANY.**   XXX
*++NORW. J. BOT.*
[UNIVERSITETSFORLAGET]
*OSLO 18, 1971-*
PREV: NYTT MAGASIN FOR BOTANIKK FROM
1, 1952- 17, 1970.
*DB/S-1.    LO/N-4.    LO/N13.    NW/U-1.    OX/U-8.*

**NORWEGIAN JOURNAL OF ZOOLOGY.**   XXX
*++NORW. J. ZOOL.*
[UNIVERSITETSFORLAGET]
*OSLO 19, 1971-*
PREV: NYTT MAGASIN FOR ZOOLOGI FROM 1, 1953-
18, 1970.
*BN/U-2.    CA/U12.    DB/S-1.    LO/N-4.    LO/N13.*
*NW/U-1.    OX/U-8.*
*ISSN 0029-6864*

**NOTEBOOKS OF PIERRE MENARD.**
*++NOTEB. PIERRE MENARD.*
[PETER HOY]
*OXFORD NO.1, S 1969-*
M.
*ED/N-1.    OX/U-1.*

**NOTES ET DOCUMENTS VOLTAIQUES.**
*++NOTES & DOC. VOLTAIQUES.*
CENTRE VOLTAIQUE DE LA RECHERCHE SCIENTIFIQUE.
*OUAGADOUGOU, UPPER VOLTA 1, OC/D 1967-*
Q.
*LO/U14.*
*CA/U-1. 1(4), 1968-             ED/U-1. 2, 1968-*

**NOTE D'INFORMATION, BANQUE DE FRANCE.**
*++NOTE INF. BANQUE FR.*
*PARIS NO.1, OC 1971-*
*OX/U16.*

**NOTES & NEWS, NATIONAL YOUTH TEMPERANCE COUNCIL.**   XXX
**SUBS (1967): TREND.**

**NOTE TECHNIQUE, INSTITUT BELGE DE LA SOUDURE.**
*++NOTE TECH. INST. BELGE SOUDURE.*
*BRUSSELS NO.1, 1968-*
*LO/N14.*

**NOTES & TIPS.**   XXX
[HARPER & ROW]
*HAGERSTOWN, MD. 1, JL 1970-*
PREV PART: INTERNATIONAL MEDICAL DIGEST FROM
1, MR 1920- 86(6), JE 1970; INTERNATIONAL
SURGICAL DIGEST FROM 1, 1926- 79(6), 1970.
*AD/U-1.*
*SO/U-1. 1(7), 1971-*
*ISSN 0020-7934*

**NOTICES, MINERALOGICAL SOCIETY OF GREAT BRITAIN & IRELAND.**
**SUBS (1969): BULLETIN, MINERALOGICAL SOCIETY OF GREAT BRITAIN & IRELAND.**

**NOTI-CIAT.**
CENTRO INTERNACIONAL DE AGRICULTURE TROPICAL.
*CALI, COLOMBIA 1, 1971-*
*LO/R-6.*

**NOTICIERO TUBEROSAS.**
*++NOT. TUBEROSAS.*
SOCIEDAD LATINOAMERICANA DE TUBEROSAS.
*MARACAY, VENEZ. 1, MR 1971-*
*LO/R-6.*

**NOTIZIARIO DI GEOGRAFIA ECONOMICA, ISTITUTO DI GEOGRAFIA ECONOMICA, UNIVERSITA DI ROMA.**
*++NOTIZ. GEOGR. ECON. IST. GEOGR. ECON. UNIV. ROMA.*
*ROME 1(1/2), JA-JE 1970-*
*LO/S13.*

NOTO RINKAI JIKKENJO NEMPO. ANNUAL REPORT OF
THE NOTO MARINE LABORATORY.
 *OGI 1, 1961-*
 *JAP. OR ENGL.*
 *LO/N13.*

NOTTINGHAM LINGUISTIC CIRCULAR.
 *++NOTT. LINGUIST. CIRC.*
 NOTTINGHAM LINGUISTIC CIRCLE.
 *NOTTINGHAM 1, 1971-*
 *2/A.*
 *SH/U-1.*

NOUVEAUX LIVRES SCIENTIFIQUES. (1966)                    000
 SEE: NB: EDITION EUROPA.

NOUVELLES DE LA BIBLIOTHEQUE NATIONALE (CANADA).
 SEE: NATIONAL LIBRARY NEWS.

NOUVELLE CHINE.
 *++NOUV. CHINE.*
 *PARIS NO.1, MR 1971-*
 *LO/U14.*
 *ISSN 0048-0959*

NOUVELLES DE LA FAUNE.                                   000
 SEE: WILDLIFE NEWS.

NOUVELLE OPTIQUE.
 *++NOUV. OPT.*
 *MONTREAL 1, 1971-*
 *OX/U-1.*

NOUVELLE PRESSE MEDICALE.                                XXX
 *++NOUV. PRESSE MED.*
 [MASSON]
 *PARIS NO.1, 1972-*
 PREV: PRESSE MEDICALE FROM 1, 1893- 79, 1971.
 *LD/U-1.     OX/U-8.*

NOUVELLE REVUE DES DEUX MONDES.                          XXX
 *++NOUV. REV. DEUX MONDES.*
 *PARIS NO.1, 1972-*
 PREV: LA REVUE. LITTERATURE, HISTOIRE, ARTS
 & SCIENCES DES DEUX MONDES FROM JA 1948- 1971.
 *BH/P-1.     GL/U-1.*

NOUVELLE REVUE D'OPTIQUE.                                XXX
 *++NOUV. REV. OPT.*
 [MASSON]
 *PARIS 4, 1973-*
 PREV: NOUVELLE REVUE D'OPTIQUE APPLIQUEE FROM
 1, 1970- 3, 1972. GER. & ENGL. SUMM.
 *LO/N14.*

NOUVELLE REVUE D'OPTIQUE APPLIQUEE.                      XXX
 *++NOUV. REVUE OPT. APPL.*
 [MASSON & CIE]
 *PARIS 1(1), JA/F 1970- 3, 1972...*
 2M. ENGL. & GER. ABSTR. SUBS: NOUVELLE
 REVUE D'OPTIQUE.
 *LO/N-4.     LO/N14.     LO/U13.     NW/U-1.     OX/U-8.*
 *SH/U-1.*
 *ISSN 0029-4780*

NOVA BROADCAST SERIES.
 *++NOVA BROAD. SER.*
 [NOVA BROADCAST P.]
 *SAN FRANCISCO 1, 1968-*
 *OX/U-1.*

NOVAJA TEKHNIKA V ASTRONOMIJ (ENGL. TRANSL.).           000
 SEE: NEW TECHNIQUES IN ASTRONOMY.

NOVINKI KHUDOZHESTVENNOJ LITERATURY.                     XXX
 SUBS (1963): KHUDOZHESTVENNAJA LITERATURA,
 LITERATUROVEDENIE, ISKUSSTVO.

NOVINKY LITERATURY, PRIRODNI VEDY: RADA
CHEMICKA.
 *++NOVINKY LIT. PRIR. VEDY, CHEM. [NLPC-A]*
 STATNI KNIHOVNA CSSR.
 *PRAGUE 1, 1964-*
 *LO/N-3.** 

NOVINKY LITERATURY, PRIRODNI VEDY: RADA
GEOLOGICKO-GEOGRAFICKA.
 *++NOVINKY LIT. PRIR. VEDY, GEOL.-GEOGR.*
 STATNI KNIHOVNA CSSR.
 *PRAGUE 1, 1964-*
 *LO/N-3.** 

NOVINKY LITERATURY, SPOLECENSKE VEDY: RADA 2:
BIBLIOGRAFIE EKONOMICKE LITERATURY.                      XXX
 *++NOVINKY LIT. SPOLECENSKE VEDY, 2.*
 STATNI KNIHOVNA CSSR.
 *PRAGUE 4(1), 1964-*
 PREV: BIBLIOGRAFIE EKONOMICKE LITERATURY:
 (KNIHY, CLANKY, RECENZE) FROM 1(1), 1961-
 3(12), 1963.
 *LO/N-3. 4(1-3, 5-11).*

NOVITATES SYSTEMATICAE PLANTARUM NON VASCULAR-
IUM.                                                     000
 SEE: NOVOSTI SISTEMATIKI NIZSHIKH RASTENIJ.

NOVITATES SYSTEMATICAE PLANTARUM VASCULARUM.             000
 SEE: NOVOSTI SISTEMATIKI VYSSHIKH RASTENIJ.

NOVOE V SEL'SKOKHOZJAJSTVENNOJ NAUKE I PRAK-
TIKE.
 *++NOV. S-KH. NAUK & PRAKT.*
 TSENTRAL'NAJA NAUCHNAJA SEL'SKOHOZJAJSTVENNAJA
 BIBLIOTEKA.
 *MOSCOW 1961-*
 S/T: ANNOTIROVANNYJ UKAZATEL LITERATURY
 ZA ...
 *XY/N-1.*
 *BH/U-1. 1966-          CC/U-1. 1965-*

NOVOE I ZABYTOE.
 *++NOV. & ZABYTOE.*
 GOSUDARSTVENNYJ LITERATURNYJ MUZEJ.
 *MOSCOW 1, 1966-*
 *GL/U-1.     SW/U-1.*

NOVOSTI NEFTIANOJ I GAZOVOJ TEKHNIKI:
GEOLOGIJA.                                               XXX
 SUBS (1963): NEFTEGAZOVAJA GEOLOGIJA I
 GEOFIZIKA.

NOVOSTI NEFTIANOJ I GAZOVOJ TEKHNIKI: SERIJA
GAZOVOE DELO.                                            XXX
 SUBS (1963): GAZOVOE DELO.

NOVOSTI SISTEMATIKI NIZSHIKH RASTENIJ. NOVI-
TATES SYSTEMATICAE PLANTARUM NON VASCULARIUM.
 *++NOV. SIST. NIZSHIKH RAST.*
 AKADEMIJA NAUK SSSR: BOTANICHESKIJ INSTITUT.
 *MOSCOW; LENINGRAD 1964-*
 A. CONTENTS LISTS ALSO IN LATIN.
 *CA/U-2.     LO/N-1.     LO/N13.     XN/R-1.     XY/N-1.*

NOVOSTI SISTEMATIKI VYSSHIKH RASTENIJ. NOVI-
TATES SYSTEMATICAE PLANTARUM VASCULARIUM.
 *++NOV. SIST. VYSSH. RAST.*
 AKADEMIJA NAUK SSSR: BOTANICHESKIJ INSTITUT.
 *MOSCOW 1964-*
 A. CONTENT LISTS ALSO IN LATIN.
 *CA/U-2.     LO/N-2.     LO/N13.     LV/U-1.     XN/R-1.     XY/N-1.*
 *BD/U-1. 3, 1966- 4, 1967.*

NOVYE ISSLEDOVANIJA V PEDAGOGICHESKIKH
NAUKAKH.
 *++NOV. ISSLED. PEDAGOG. NAUKAKH.*
 AKADEMIJA PEDAGOGICHESKIKH NAUK RSFSR.
 *MOSCOW TOM 1, 1963-*
 CONT. LISTS IN ENGL. VOLS 1-3 ISSUED AS VOLS
 129, 133, 138 OF: IZVESTIJA AKADEMII PEDA-
 GOGICHESKIKH NAUK RSFSR.
 *BH/U-1.     CC/U-1.     HL/U-1.*
 *XY/N-1. 4, 1965-*

NOWA KULTURA.                                            XXX
 SUBS (1963): PART OF KULTURA.

NRC RESEARCH NEWS.                                       XXX
 SUBS (1969): SCIENCE DIMENSION.

NRCD BULLETIN.                                           XXX
 *++NRCD BULL. (NAT. REPROGR. CENT. DOC.)*
 NATIONAL REPROGRAPHIC CENTRE FOR DOCUMENTATION.
 *HATFIELD 1, 1967- 6, 1972/1973 ...*
 CENTRE LOCATED AT HATFIELD COLLEGE OF TECH-
 NOLOGY. 'D' IN TITLE ACTUALLY PRINTED WITH
 LOWER CASE LETTER. SUBS: REPROGRAPHICS
 QUARTERLY FROM 7, 1974.
 *BH/P-1.     BL/U-1.     GL/U-1.     GL/U-2.*
 *BH/U-1. 2, 1969-          ED/N-1. 1(4), 1968-*
 *LO/N-2. 2, 1969-          LO/N-4. 3(1), 1969-*

NSF FACTBOOK.
 NATIONAL SCIENCE FOUNDATION (US).
 [ACADEMIC MEDIA INC.]
 *ORANGE, N.J. 1971-*
 *LO/N14.*

**NU SCIENCE.**
++NU SCI.
UNIVERSITY OF NATAL: SCIENCE STUDENT'S COUNCIL.
*PIETERMARITZBURG 1, 1968-*
*LD/U-1.* *   LO/N-2.*

**NUBE NEWS. THE BANK OFFICER: JOURNAL OF ...**
NATIONAL UNION OF BANK EMPLOYEES.
*TWICKENHAM, MIDDX. NO.1, JA 1970-*
M. PREV: BANK OFFICER FROM 1, AG 1919- 1969.
*LO/U-3.     OX/U17.*
*ED/N-1. NO.33, S 1972-*

**NUCLEAR APPLICATIONS & TECHNOLOGY.***
++NUCL. APPL. & TECHNOL.
AMERICAN NUCLEAR SOCIETY.
*HINSDALE, ILL. 1, F 1965- 9, 1970...*
(APPLICATIONS OF THE NUCLEAR SCIENCES, NUCLEAR
ENGINEERING & RELATED ARTS). TITLE EXPANDED
FROM NUCLEAR APPLICATIONS WITH 7, 1969. SUBS:
NUCLEAR TECHNOLOGY.
*LO/N-4.     LO/N14.     OX/U-8.*
*XS/R10. 7(1), 1969-*
*ISSN 0550-3043*

**NUCLEAR DATA TABLES.**                                          XXX
++NUCL. DATA TABLES.
[ACADEMIC P.]
*NEW YORK &C. 9(4/5), 1971- 11, 1973...*
PREV: NUCLEAR DATA - SECTION A FROM 1(1),
1965- 8(3), 1971. SUBS: ATOMIC DATA & NUCLEAR
DATA TABLES.
*CA/U-2.     LO/N14.     OX/U-8.*

**NUCLEAR ENERGY.**                                              XXX
SUBS (1971): JOURNAL, INSTITUTION OF
NUCLEAR ENGINEERS.

**NUCLEAR ENGINEERING INTERNATIONAL.**                           XXX
++NUCL. ENG. INT.
[HEYWOOD-TEMPLE IND. PUBLS. (&C)]
*LONDON 1(1), AP 1956-*
ORIG. TITLE TO 13(149), 1968: NUCLEAR ENGIN-
EERING. AS ABOVE FROM 13(150), N 1968.
INCORP. NUCLEAR POWER AFTER AP. 1963.
*BH/U-1.     BN/U-2.     BR/U-3.     CA/U-4.     ED/P-1.*     GL/U-1.*
*LO/N-7.     LO/N14.     LO/U12.     LO/U20.     MA/F-1.*
*NO/U-1.     NW/U-1.     SH/U-3.     SW/U-1.     XE/F-3.***
*XS/N-2.     XS/R10.     XS/T-2.*     XW/C-3.     ZS/T-1.*
*BL/U-1. 5, 1960-              LO/P-6. 1957-*
*XE/C-3. 1960-                XW/P-5. 8, 1963-*
*XS/T-4. 1(1)- 5(50), JL 1960.*
*ISSN 0029-5507*

**NUCLEAR MAGNETIC RESONANCE.**
++NUCL. MAGN. RESONANCE.
CHEMICAL SOCIETY.
*LONDON 1, 1972-*
*ED/N-1.     LO/N14.     LO/S-3.     LO/U12.     MA/U-1.     SF/U-1.*
*XS/R10.*
*RE/U-1. 2, 1971/72-*

**NUCLEAR MAGNETIC RESONANCE SPECTROMETRY
ABSTRACTS.**
++NUCL. MAGN. RESONANCE SPECTROM. ABSTR.
[SCIENCE & TECHNOLOGY AGENCY]
*LONDON 1(1), JA/F 1971-*
6/A.
*CA/U-1.     ED/N-1.     OX/U-8.*
*LO/U28. 2, 1972-*

**NUCLEAR & PARTICLE PHYSICS ANNUAL.**                           XXX
++NUCL. & PARTIC. PHYS. ANNU.
[GORDON & BREACH]
*NEW YORK & C. 1, 1967(1969). //*
*LO/N-4.     LO/N14.*
*ISSN 0550-3035*

**NUCLEAR SCIENCE ABSTRACTS OF CZECHOSLOVAKIA.**
++NUCL. SCI. ABSTR. CZECH.
CZECHOSLOVAK ATOMIC ENERGY COMMISION.
*ZBRASLAV NAD VLTAVOU 1, 1969-*
PRODUCED BY COMMISSION'S CENTRE FOR SCIENTIFIC
& TECHNICAL INFORMATION.
*LO/N-4.     LO/N14.*

**NUCLEAR SCIENCE INFORMATION OF JAPAN.**                        XXX
++NUCL. SCI. INF. JAP.
KAGAKU GIJUTSUCHO GENSHIRYOKUKYOKU.
*TOKAI-MURA 1(1), MY 1970-*
2M. PREV: NUCLEAR SCIENCE ABSTRACTS OF JAPAN
FROM 1, MR 1961.
*XS/R10.*
*ISSN 0029-5620*

**NUCLEAR STANDARDS NEWS.**
++NUCL. STAND. NEWS.
AMERICAN NUCLEAR SOCIETY.
*HINSDALE, ILL. JL 1970-*
M.
*ISSN 0029-3055*

**NUCLEAR TECHNOLOGY.**                                          XXX
++NUCL. TECHNOL.
AMERICAN NUCLEAR SOCIETY.
*HINSDALE, ILL. 10, 1971-*
PREV: NUCLEAR APPLICATIONS & TECHNOLOGY FROM
1, F 1965- 9, 1970.
*LO/N14.     XS/R10.*
*ISSN 0029-5450*

**NUCLEIC ACIDS (1971).**                                        XXX
[LITERATURE SEARCHERS]
*GRESHAM, OREG. 3, 1971-*
PREV: NUCLEIC ACIDS MONTHLY FROM NO.1, OC
1965- 35, 1971.
*LO/N13.*

**NUCLEIC ACIDS ABSTRACTS.**
++NUCLEIC ACIDS ABSTR.
[INFORMATION RETRIEVAL LTD.]
*LONDON 1(1), JA 1971-*
*DB/U-2.     ED/N-1.     GL/U-2.     LO/M-3.     LO/N14.     SH/U-1.*
*GL/U-1. 4, 1974-*
*ISSN 0048-1041*

**NUCLEIC ACIDS MONTHLY.**                                       XXX
++NUCLEIC ACIDS MON. [NCAM-A]
[LITERATURE SEARCHERS]
*KETTERING, OHIO NO.1, OC 1965- 35, 1971.*
SUBS: NUCLEIC ACIDS (1971).
*LO/N13. NO.2, 1965-*

**NUCLEONICS.**                                                  XXX
++[NUCL-A]
[MCGRAW-HILL PUBL. CO.]
*NEW YORK 1(1), S 1947- 25(5), JE 1967.//*
M.
*BH/U-1.     GL/U-1.     LC/U-1.     LO/M12.*     LO/M19.*
*LO/N-7.     LO/N14.     LO/U-2.     XS/R10.     XW/C-4.**
*BL/U-1. 18,1960-              CA/U-4. 14,1956-*
*HL/U-1. 14,1956-             LA/U-1. 22(4),1964-*
*LO/C18. 21(3),1963-          LO/M-1. *12,1953-*
*XS/N-2. (1948)-*
*LO/M-2. 1,1947- 16,1958.*
*LO/U-4. 15,1957- 20,1962.*
*YK/U-1. 14,1956- 18,1960.*

**NUESTRA HISTORIA.**
++NUESTRA HIST.
CENTRO DE ESTUDIOS DE HISTORIA ARGENTINA.
*BUENOS AIRES 1(1), 1968-*
*OX/U-1.*
*ISSN 0029-571X*

**NUESTRA TIERRA.**
*MONTEVIDEO NO.1, 1969-*
NO.1 PRECEDED BY AN ISSUE CALLED NUMBER 0.
*LO/N-1.*

**NUEVA NARRATIVA HISPANOAMERICANA.**
++NUEVA NARRATIVA HISPANOAM.
ADELPHI UNIVERSITY: LATIN AMERICAN STUDIES
PROGRAM.
*GARDEN CITY, N.Y. 1, JA 1971-*
2/A.
*LO/U11.     MA/U-1.*
*ISSN 0048-1084*

**NUEVA SOCIEDAD. REVISTA DE PROBLEMAS SOCIALES,
POLITICOS, ECONOMICOS Y CULTURALES.**
++NUEVA SOC. (COSTA RICA).
*SAN JOSE, COSTA RICA 1, JL/AG 1972-*
2M.
*LO/U-3.*

**NUEVOS MERCADOS (BOGOTA).**
++NUEVOS MERC.
CENTRO INTERAMERICANO DE PROMOCION DE
EXPORTACIONES.
*BOGOTA NO.1, 1970-*
*OX/U-1.*

**NUFTO RECORD.**                                                XXX
SUBS (1971): FTAT RECORD.

**NUMAZU KOGYO KOTO SENMON GAKKO KENKYU HOKOKU.
RESEARCH REPORTS OF NUMAZU TECHNICAL COLLEGE.**
NUMAZU KOGYO KOTO SENMON GAKKO.
*NUMAZU NO.1, 1964-*
JAP. & ENGL.
*LO/N13.*

NUMISMATIC LITERATURE SUPPLEMENTS.
++NUMISMAT. LIT. SUPPL.
AMERICAN NUMISMATIC SOCIETY.
 NEW YORK 1, 1967-
 AD/U-1.

NUOVA CHIMICA.                                                           XXX
++NUOVA CHIM.
[NUOVA EDITORIALE CULTURALE CHIMICA]
 MILAN 45, 1969-
 PREV: CHIMICA FROM 1, 1924- 38, 1962.
 LO/N14.

NUOVA RIVISTA MUSICALE ITALIANA.                                        XXX
++NUOVA RIV. MUSIC. ITAL.
[RAI]
 TURIN 1, MY/JE 1967-
 2M. PREV: RIVISTA MUSICALE ITALIANA FROM 1,
 1894- 57(2), AP/JE 1955.
 ED/N-1.
 NO/U-1. 4, 1970-                    SH/U-1. 6, 1972-
 SO/U-1. 3, 1969-
 ISSN 0029-6228

NUOVI LIBRI SCIENTIFICI. (1966)                                         000
 SEE: NB: EDITION EUROPA.

NUOVI STUDI POLITICI.
++NOUVI STUDI POLIT.
[BULZONI]
 ROME 1, JA/F 1971-
 2M.
 OX/U-1.

NUOVO CIMENTO. SUPPLEMENTO.                                             XXX
 SUBS. (1969): RIVISTA DEL NUOVO CIMENTO.

NURNBERGER WERKSTUCKE ZUR STADT- UND LANDES-
GESCHICHTE NURNBERG.
++NURNB. WERKSTUCKE STADT & LANDESGESCH. NURNB.
STADT-ARCHIV NURNBERG.
 NUREMBERG 1, 1970-
 OX/U-1.

NURSING BIBLIOGRAPHY.
++NURS. BIBLIOGR.
ROYAL COLLEGE OF NURSING.
 LONDON NO.1, JA 1972-
 S/T: A MONTHLY LIST OF CURRENT PUBLICATIONS ON
 NURSING & ALLIED SUBJECTS.
 CA/U-1.      DB/U-2.      ED/N-1.      MA/P-1.      SO/U-1.

N.U.T. NEWS.
NATIONAL UNION OF TEACHERS.
 LONDON 1, MR 1969-
 ED/N-1.      OX/U-1.

NUTRITION & FOOD SCIENCE.                                               XXX
++NUTR. & FOOD SCI.
[FORBES PUBL.]
 LONDON NO.22, 1971-
 PREV: REVIEW OF NUTRITION & FOOD SCIENCE
 FROM NO.1, OC 1965- 21, 1970.
 ED/N-1.      LD/U-1.      LO/N14.      OX/U-1.      RE/U-1.
 ISSN 0034-6659

NUTRITION REPORTS INTERNATIONAL.
++NUTR. REP. INT.
[GERON-X INC.]
 LOS ALTOS, CALIF. 1, 1970-
 LO/N13.      SO/U-1.
 SF/U-1. 3, 1971-
 ISSN 0029-6635

NUYTSIA.
WESTERN AUSTRALIAN HERBARIUM.
[PERTH] 1, 1970-
 CA/U-7.      LO/N-2.      LO/N13.

NYANSKAFFET UDENLANDSK LITTERATUR.
++NYANSKAFFET UDENLANDSK LITT.
ODENSE UNIVERSITETSBIBLIOTEK.
 ODENSE 1(1), 1970-
 LO/N-1.

NYE DANSK LANDBRUG.                                                     XXX
++NYE DAN. LANDBRUG.
SAMVIRKENDE DANSKE LANDBOFORENINGER.
 COPENHAGEN 1, 1970-
 INCORP: DANSK LANDBRUG FROM 56, 1937- 88(12),
 1969; & JYDSK LANDBRUG.
 LO/N13.
 ISSN 0011-6351

NYQ.                                                                    000
 SEE: NEW YORK QUARTERLY.

NYSFI BULLETIN.                                                         XXX
NEW YORK STATE FLOWER INDUSTRIES, INC.               XXX
 PRATTSBURG, N.Y. NO.1, 1970-
 PREV: BULLETIN, NEW YORK STATE FLOWER GROWERS,
 INC. FROM NO.1, AG 1945- NO.295, 1970.
 LO/N13.

NYTT MAGASIN FOR BOTANIKK.                                             XXX
 SUBS (1971): NORWEGIAN JOURNAL OF BOTANY.

NYTT MAGASIN FOR ZOOLOGI.                                              XXX
 SUBS (1971): NORWEGIAN JOURNAL OF ZOOLOGY.

NZOI RECORDS.
++NZOI REC.
NEW ZEALAND OCEANOGRAPHIC INSTITUTE.
 WELLINGTON, N.Z. 1, 1972-
 LO/N-2.

O & M BULLETIN.                                                        XXX
 SUBS (1973): MANAGEMENT SERVICES IN
 GOVERNMENT.

OAP JOURNAL FOR THE BUILT ENVIRONMENT.                                 XXX
++OAP J. BUILT. ENVIRON.
[ARCHITECTURE & PLANNING PUBL.]
 LONDON 34, 1971- 35, 1972.
 CONT. OF, & ALSO ENTITLED OFFICIAL ARCHITECT-
 URE & PLANNING FROM 1, 1937- 33, 1970. INCORP:
 TRANSACTIONS OF THE MODULAR SOCIETY & OF THE
 INTERNATIONAL MODULAR GROUP, WHICH WERE PREV.
 PUBL. AS PART OF MODULAR QUARTERLY FROM 1955-
 1970.  SUBS: BUILT ENVIRONMENT.
 GL/U-1.      LO/N14.      LO/R-5.

OBJECTIFS AFRICAINS.                                                    000
 SEE: AFRICAN TARGETS.

OBJECTIVE: JUSTICE.
UNITED NATIONS: OFFICE OF PUBLIC INFORMATION.
 NEW YORK 1, 1969-
 S/T: A PERIODICAL REVIEW OF UNITED NATIONS
 ACTIVITY AGAINST APARTHEID, RACIAL DISCRIMINA-
 TION & COLONIALISM.
 AD/U-1.      ED/N-1.      MA/P-1.
 LO/U-3. 2, 1970-
 ISSN 0029-7593

OBLIQUES. LITTERATURE, THEATRE.
LES PILLES, FR. 1, 1972-
 Q.
 CA/U-1.      DB/U-2.      LO/N-1.

OBRABOTKA METALLOV DAVLENIEM V MASHINOST-
ROENII.
++OBRAB. MET. DAVLENIEM MASHINOST.
KHAR'KOVSKIJ GOSUDARSTVENNYJ UNIVERSITET.
 KHAR'KOV 1, 1967-
 S/T: RESPUBLIKANSKIJ MEZHVEDOMSTVENNYJ
 NAUCHNO-TEKHNICHESKIJ SBORNIK.
 BH/U-1. 4, 1969-              LO/N13. 4, 1969-

OBRADORS. QUASERNS D'INVENTARI DE LA
CREACION LITERARIA OCCITANA.
UNIVERSITE DE MONTPELLIER: FACULTAT DE LAS
LETRAS E SCIENCIAS HUMAINES.
 MONTPELLIER 1, JA 1969-
 PROD. BY CENTRE D'ESTUDIS OCCITANS.
 LO/N-1.

OBSERVATORIES' YEAR BOOK.                                              XXX
 SUBS. (1969): PART OF GEOMAGNETIC BULLETINS.

OBSHCHESTVENNOE PITANIE. MEZHVEDOMSTVENNYJ
RESPUBLIKANSKIJ NAUCHNO-TEKNICHESKIJ SBORNIK.
(UKRAINE) MINISTERSTVO TORGOVLI UKRAINSKOJ SSR.
 KIEV 1965-
 BH/U-1. 1966-                 CC/U-1. 1966-

OBZOR. A BULGARIAN REVIEW OF LITERATURE &
THE ARTS.
 SOFIA NO.1, WINTER 1967-
 DB/U-2.
 ED/N-1. NO.4, 1968-
 ISSN 0029-7852

OCCASIONAL PAPERS, AFRICAN STUDIES CENTRE
(CAMBRIDGE).
++OCCAS. PAP. AFR. STUD. CENT. (CAMB.).
 CAMBRIDGE NO.1, 1968-
 CA/U11.

OCCASIONAL PAPERS, ANTHROPOLOGY MUSEUM OF THE
UNIVERSITY OF QUEENSLAND.
++OCCAS. PAP. ANTHROPOL. MUS. UNIV. QUEENSL.
 ST. LUCIA 1, 1973-
 CA/U-3.

OCCASIONAL PAPERS, ASIAN INSTITUTE FOR ECONO-
MIC DEVELOPMENT & PLANNING, UNITED NATIONS.
++OCCAS. PAP. ASIAN INST. ECON. DEVELOP. &
PLANN. U.N.
BANGKOK 1(1), MY 1969-
LO/U-3.

OCCASIONAL PAPERS IN ASIAN & PACIFIC STUDIES.
++OCCAS. PAP. ASIAN & PAC. STUD.
LIBRARIES BOARD OF SOUTH AUSTRALIA.
ADELAIDE NO.1, 1967-
OX/U-1.

OCCASIONAL PAPERS, ASSOCIATION FOR SCOTTISH
LITERARY STUDIES.
++OCCAS. PAP. ASSOC. SCOTT. LIT. STUD.
ABERDEEN NO.1, S 1972-
CA/U-1. ED/N-1. GL/U-2. SO/U-1.

OCCASIONAL PAPERS, BANK OF SIERRA LEONE.
++OCCAS. PAP. BANK SIERRA LEONE.
FREETOWN 1, 1972-
CA/U-1. OX/U-9.

OCCASIONAL PAPERS, BRANCH & MOBILE LIBRARIES
GROUP, LIBRARY ASSOCIATION.
++OCCAS. PAP. BRANCH & MOBILE LIBR. GROUP
LIBR. ASSOC.
LONDON NO.1, 1969-
LO/N-1. OX/U-1.

OCCASIONAL PAPERS, BRITISH BUREAU OF TELEVIS-
ION ADVERTISING.
++OCCAS. PAP. BR. BUR. TELEV. ADVER.
LONDON 1, 1969-
OX/U-1.

OCCASIONAL PAPERS, BRITISH GEOMORPHOLOGICAL
RESEARCH GROUP.                                    XXX
++OCCAS. PAP. BR. GEOMORPHOL. RES. GROUP.
LONDON &C. NO.1, 1964- 6, 1968.//
LO/U-1. 1, 1964; 4, 1966- 6, 1968.

OCCASIONAL PAPERS, BRITISH INSTITUTE OF MAN-
AGEMENT: NS.
++OCCAS. PAP. BR. INST. MANAGE., NS.
LONDON NO.1, 1968-
PREVIOUS SERIES FROM NO.1, 1949.
OX/U-1.

OCCASIONAL PAPERS, CENTENNIAL MUSEUM
(VANCOUVER).
++OCCAS. PAP. CENTENNIAL MUS. (VANCOUVER).
VANCOUVER NO.1, 1969-
LO/N-2.

OCCASIONAL PAPERS, CENTRE OF ORIENTAL STUDIES,
AUSTRALIAN NATIONAL UNIVERSITY.
++OCCAS. PAP. CENT. ORIENT. STUD. AUST. NAT.
UNIV.
CANBERRA NO.1, 1963-
OX/U-1.

OCCASIONAL PAPERS, CHARTERED INSURANCE INSTI-
TUTE.
++OCCAS. PAP. CHART. INSUR. INST.
LONDON 1, 1966-
OX/U-1.

OCCASIONAL PAPER, CIVIL SERVICE COLLEGE.        XXX
++OCCAS. PAP. CIVIL SERV. COLL.
LONDON NO.14, 1970-
PREV: CAS OCCASIONAL PAPER FROM NO.1, 1967-
13, 1970. NO.14- 15 ALSO BEAR PREV. TITLE.
LO/N14.
GL/U-1. NO.16, 1971-

OCCASIONAL PAPERS, DEPARTMENT OF ENGLISH
LOCAL HISTORY, UNIVERSITY OF LEICESTER: 2S.
++OCCAS. PAP. DEP. ENGL. LOCAL HIST. UNIV.
LEIC., 2S.
LEICESTER NO.1, 1969-
PREV. SERIES FROM NO.1, 1952.
GL/U-1. MA/U-1.

OCCASIONAL PAPERS, DEPARTMENT OF GEOGRAPHY &
GEOLOGY, INDIANA STATE UNIVERSITY.              000
SEE: PROFESSIONAL PAPERS, DEPARTMENT OF
GEOGRAPHY & GEOLOGY, INDIANA STATE UNIVERSITY.

OCCASIONAL PAPERS, DEPARTMENT OF GEOGRAPHY,
UNIVERSITY COLLEGE, LONDON.
++OCCAS. PAP. DEP. GEOGR. UNIV. COLL. LOND.
LONDON NO.1, JL 1969-
LO/S13. LO/U-2.
CA/U-1. NO.15, 1973-

OCCASIONAL PAPERS, DEPARTMENT OF GEOGRAPHY,
UNIVERSITY OF NEBRASKA.
++OCCAS. PAP. DEP. GEOGR. UNIV. NEBR.
LINCOLN, NEBR. 1, 1971-
LO/S13.

OCCASIONAL PAPERS, DEPARTMENT OF GEOGRAPHY,
UNIVERSITY OF OTTAWA.
++OCCAS. PAP. DEP. GEOGR. UNIV. OTTAWA.
OTTAWA 1, 1971-
LO/S13.

OCCASIONAL PAPER, DEPARTMENT OF ICHTHYOLOGY,
RHODES UNIVERSITY.
++OCCAS. PAP. DEP. ICHTHYOL. RHODES UNIV.
GRAHAMSTOWN, S.AFR. NO.1, 1964-
LO/N13.

OCCASIONAL PAPER, DEPARTMENT OF SOCIOLOGY,
UNIVERSITY OF STRATHCLYDE.
++OCCAS. PAP. DEP. SOCIOL. UNIV. STRATHCLYDE.
GLASGOW NO.1, 1968-
GL/U-2.

OCCASIONAL PAPERS IN ECONOMIC & SOCIAL HIST-
ORY, UNIVERSITY OF HULL.
++OCCAS. PAP. ECON. & SOC. HIST. UNIV. HULL.
HULL NO.1, 1969-
MONOGR.
HL/U-1. OX/U-1.

OCCASIONAL PAPER, ENGINEERING INDUSTRY TRAIN-
ING BOARD (GB).
++OCCAS. PAP. ENG. IND. TRAIN. BOARD (GB).
LONDON NO.1, AP 1972-
LO/N-1.

OCCASIONAL PAPERS IN ESTATE MANAGEMENT.        XXX
++OCCAS. PAP. ESTATE MANAGE.
COLLEGE OF ESTATE MANAGEMENT.
LONDON NO.1- 3, 1966.//
LO/U-1.
ISSN 0078-3048

OCCASIONAL PAPERS, FISHERIES DEPARTMENT,
MINISTRY OF ANIMAL INDUSTRY, GAME & FISHERIES
(UGANDA).
++OCCAS. PAP. FISH. DEP. MINIST. ANIM. IND.
GAME & FISH. (UGANDA).
ENTEBBE NO.1, 1967-
LO/N13.

OCCASIONAL PAPERS, F.L. ALLAN MEMORIAL TRUST.
++OCCAS. PAP. F.L. ALLAN MEM. TRUST.
LONDON NO.1, 1967-
OX/U-1.

OCCASIONAL PAPERS IN GEOGRAPHY, DEPARTMENT OF
OF GEOLOGY & GEOGRAPHY, UNIVERSITY OF THE
WEST INDIES.
++OCCAS. PAP. GEOGR. DEP. GEOL. & GEOGR. UNIV.
WEST INDIES.
MONA, WEST INDIES NO.1, 1966-
OX/U-9.

OCCASIONAL PAPERS, GEOLOGICAL SURVEY OF FIJI.
++OCCAS. PAP. GEOL. SURV. FIJI.
SUVA NO.1, [1967]-
LO/N17.

OCCASIONAL PAPERS IN GERMAN STUDIES, UNIV-
ERSITY OF WARWICK.
++OCCAS. PAP. GER. STUD. UNIV. WARWICK.
COVENTRY NO.1, [1972]-
CA/U-1.

OCCASIONAL PAPERS IN GERONTOLOGY.
++OCCAS. PAP. GERONTOL.
ANN ARBOR, MICH. NO.1, 1968-
OX/U-8.

OCCASIONAL PAPERS, HORACE BARKS REFERENCE
LIBRARY & INFORMATION SERVICE.
++OCCAS. PAP. HORACE BARKS REF. LIBR. & INF.
SERV.
STOKE-ON-TRENT NO.1, 1969-
LO/N-1.

OCCASIONAL PAPER, ILKESTON & DISTRICT LOCAL
HISTORY SOCIETY.
++OCCAS. PAP. ILKESTON & DIST. LOCAL HIST. SOC.
ILKESTON NO.1, 1969-
OX/U-1.

OCCASIONAL PAPERS, INSTITUTE OF LATIN-
GLASGOW NO.1, 1971-
BT/U-1.    CA/U-5.    GL/U-1.    GL/U-2.    LO/N-1.    LO/U-2.
NO/U-1.    OX/U16.    SF/U-1.

OCCASIONAL PAPERS, INSTITUTE OF LOCAL GOVERN-
MENT STUDIES, UNIVERSITY OF BIRMINGHAM,
SERIES A.
++OCCAS. PAP. INST. LOCAL GOV. STUD. UNIV.
BIRMINGHAM, A.
BIRMINGHAM NO.1, 1969-
BH/U-1.    OX/U-1.

OCCASIONAL PAPERS, INSTITUTE OF SOCIAL,
ECONOMIC & GOVERNMENT RESEARCH, UNIVERSITY OF
ALASKA.
++OCCAS. PAP. INST. SOC. ECON. & GOV. RES.
UNIV. ALASKA.
FAIRBANKS NO.1, 1970-
CA/U12.

OCCASIONAL PAPER, IRISH COUNCIL OF THE EUROP-
EAN MOVEMENT.
++OCCAS. PAP. IR. COUNC. EUR. MOVEMENT.
DUBLIN NO.1, 1971-
DB/U-2.

OCCASIONAL PAPERS, KENYA INSTITUTE OF ADMIN-
ISTRATION.
++OCCAS. PAP. KENYA INST. ADM.
LOWER KABETE NO.1, 1968-
MA/U-1.    OX/U-9.

OCCASIONAL PAPERS IN LIBRARIANSHIP, LIBRARIES
BOARD OF SOUTH AUSTRALIA.
++OCCAS. PAP. LIBR. LIBR. BOARD SOUTH AUST.
(SOUTH AUSTRALIA) LIBRARIES BOARD.
ADELAIDE NO.1, 1965-
BL/U-1.    OX/U-1.

OCCASIONAL PAPER, LIBRARY, EDINBURGH COLLEGE
OF COMMERCE.
++OCCAS. PAP. LIBR. EDINB. COLL. COMMER.
EDINBURGH 1, 1969-
OX/U-1.

OCCASIONAL PAPERS, LIBRARY, KENT STATE UNIV-
ERSITY.
++OCCAS. PAP. LIBR. KENT STATE UNIV.
KENT, OHIO NO.1, 1968-
OX/U-1.

OCCASIONAL PAPERS, MAKERERE INSTITUTE OF
SOCIAL RESEARCH.
++OCCAS. PAP. MAKERERE INST. SOC. RES.
KAMPALA NO.1, 1967-
OX/U-9. NO.4, 1968-
ISSN 0076-2954

OCCASIONAL PAPERS, MILWAUKEE PUBLIC MUSEUM:
NATURAL HISTORY.
++OCCAS. PAP. MILWAUKEE PUBLIC MUS., NAT. HIST.
MILWAUKEE NO.1, 1968-
LO/N-2.

OCCASIONAL PAPERS, MUSEUM OF NATURAL HISTORY,
UNIVERSITY OF KANSAS.                                          xxx
++OCCAS. PAP. MUS. NAT. HIST. UNIV. KANS.
LAWRENCE, KANS. NO.1, AP 1971-
PREV: PUBLICATIONS, MUSEUM OF NATURAL HISTORY,
UNIVERSITY OF KANSAS FROM 1, 1946- 20, 1971.
AD/U-3.    CA/U-2.    DB/S-1.    LD/U-1.    LO/N13.    NW/U-1.
OX/U-8.    SH/U-1.

OCCASIONAL PAPERS, MUSEUM, TEXAS TECH
UNIVERSITY.
++OCCAS. PAP. MUS. TEX. TECH UNIV.
LUBBOCK NO.1, 1972-
LO/N-2.

OCCASIONAL PAPER, NATIONAL COUNCIL FOR
EDUCATIONAL TECHNOLOGY (GB).
++OCCAS. PAP. NATL. COUNC. EDUC. TECHNOL.(GB).
LONDON NO.1, 1969-
OX/U-1.

OCCASIONAL PAPER, NATIONAL PRICE'S COMMISSION,
DEPARTMENT OF INDUSTRY & COMMERCE (EIRE).
++OCCAS. PAP. NATL. PRICE'S COMM. DEP. IND. &
COMMER. (EIRE).
DUBLIN NO.1, 1972-
DB/U-2.    LO/N-1.

OCCASIONAL PAPERS, NATIONAL REPROGRAPHIC
CENTRE FOR DOCUMENTATION (GB).
++OCCAS. PAP. NATL. REPROGR. CENT. DOC.
HATFIELD NO.1, 1972-
CA/U-1.    SO/U-1.

OCCASIONAL PAPERS, NUMISMATIC SOCIETY OF
IRELAND.
++OCCAS. PAP. NUMIS. SOC. IREL.
BELFAST NO.1, 1965-
DB/S-1.
LO/N-1. NO.5, 1969-

OCCASIONAL PAPERS IN OLD COLONY STUDIES.
++OCCAS. PAP. OLD COLONY STUD.
[PLIMOUTH PLANTATION INC.]
PLYMOUTH, MASS. NO.1, 1969-
OX/U-9.
ISSN 0473-7482

OCCASIONAL PAPERS FROM THE OSAKA MUSEUM OF
NATURAL HISTORY.                                              000
SEE: SHIZENSHI KENKYU.

OCCASIONAL PAPER, OVERSEAS DEVELOPMENT
COUNCIL (US).
++OCCAS. PAP. OVERSEAS DEV. COUNC. (US).
WASHINGTON, D.C. NO.1, 1971-
OX/U16.

OCCASIONAL PAPER, PENAL RESEARCH INSTITUTE,
UNIVERSITY OF OXFORD.
++OCCAS. PAP. PENAL RES. INST. UNIV. OXF.
OXFORD NO.1, 1970-
LO/N-1.    OX/U15.

OCCASIONAL PAPERS, SAFFRON WALDEN HISTORICAL
& ARCHAEOLOGICAL SOCIETY.
++OCCAS. PAP. SAFFRON WALDEN HIST. & ARCHAEOL.
SOC.
SAFFRON WALDEN NO.1, 1967-
OX/U-1.

OCCASIONAL PAPERS, SALK INSTITUTE FOR
BIOLOGICAL STUDIES.
++OCCAS. PAP. SALK INST. BIOL. STUD.
SAN DIEGO NO.1, 1969-
LO/U-1.    OX/U-8.

OCCASIONAL PAPER SERIES, CENTRE FOR DEVELOP-
ING AREA STUDIES, MCGILL UNIVERSITY.
++OCCAS. PAP. SER. CENT. DEV.-AREA STUD. MCGILL
UNIV.
MONTREAL NO.1, 1968-
OX/U-9.

OCCASIONAL PAPERS IN SOCIAL RESEARCH.
++OCCAS. PAP. SOC. RES.
UNIVERSITY OF NOTTINGHAM: DEPARTMENT OF ADULT
EDUCATION.
NOTTINGHAM NO.1, 1968-
OX/U-1.
LO/N-1. NO.1, 1968.

OCCASIONAL PAPERS, SURVEY RESEARCH CENTRE,
UNIVERSITY OF STRATHCLYDE.
++OCCAS. PAP. SURV. RES. CENT. UNIV.
STRATHCLYDE.
GLASGOW 1, 1969-
CB/U-1.    GL/U-2.    MA/U-1.

OCCASIONAL PAPER, SUSSEX ARCHAEOLOGICAL
SOCIETY.
++OCCAS. PAP. SUSSEX ARCHAEOL. SOC.
[PHILLIMORE]
CHICHESTER 1, 1970-
BH/U-1.    BL/U-1.    LO/N-3.    LO/U-1.    LO/U-2.    OX/U-1.

OCCASIONAL PAPER, SUSSEX DIVISION,
ASSOCIATION OF ASSISTANT LIBRARIANS.
++OCCAS. PAP. SUSSEX DIV. ASSOC. ASSIST. LIBR.
LONDON NO.1, 1969-
LO/N-1.

OCCASIONAL PAPERS, TROPICAL SCIENCE CENTER
(COSTA RICA).
++OCCAS. PAP. TROP. SCI. CENT. (COSTA RICA).
SAN JOSE, COSTA RICA NO.1, [1963]-
LO/N-2.

OCCASIONAL PAPERS, UNIVERSITY OF LANCASTER
LIBRARY.                                                      000
SEE: UNIVERSITY OF LANCASTER LIBRARY ...

OCCASIONAL PAPERS OF THE WESTERN FOUNDATION
OF VERTEBRATE ZOOLOGY.
++OCCAS. PAP. WEST. FOUND. VERTEBR. ZOOL.
LOS ANGELES NO.1, 1968-
LO/U-2.

**OCCASIONAL PAPER, YOUTH SERVICE INFORMATION CENTRE, NATIONAL COMMERCIAL TEMPERANCE YOUTH LEAGUE.**
*++OCCAS. PAP. YOUTH SERV. INF. CENT. NATL.*
*COMMER. TEMPERANCE YOUTH LEAGUE.*
*LEICESTER [NO.]1, 1971-*
*LO/N-1.*

**OCCASIONAL PUBLICATION OF THE AFRICAN & AFRO-AMERICAN RESEARCH INSTITUTE, UNIVERSITY OF TEXAS.**
*++OCCAS. PUBL. AFR. & AFRO-AM. RES. INST. UNIV.*
*TEX.*
*AUSTIN, TEX. NO.1, 1970-*
*MONOGR.*
*CA/U-1.    LO/N-1.    OX/U-1.*
*DB/U-2. NO.4, 1972-*

**OCCASIONAL PUBLICATIONS, ASLIB.**    000
  SEE: ASLIB, OCCASIONAL ...

**OCCASIONAL PUBLICATION, BELFAST NATURALISTS' FIELD CLUB.**
*++OCCAS. PUBL. BELFAST NAT. FIELD CLUB.*
*BELFAST NO.1, 1968-*
*OX/U-8.*

**OCCASIONAL PUBLICATIONS, DORE VILLAGE SOCIETY.**
*++OCCAS. PUBL. DORE VILLAGE SOC.*
*DORE, DERBY. NO.1, 1969-*
*OX/U-1.*

**OCCASIONAL PUBLICATION, INSTITUTE OF MARINE SCIENCE, UNIVERSITY OF ALASKA.**
*++OCCAS. PUBL. INST. MAR. SCI. UNIV. ALASKA.*
*COLLEGE NO.1, 1970-*
*LO/N-2.    OX/U-8.*

**OCCASIONAL PUBLICATIONS, LIBRARY, UNIVERSITY OF WARWICK.**
*++OCCAS. PUBL. LIBR. UNIV. WARWICK.*
*COVENTRY NO.1, 1971-*
*LO/N-1.*

**OCCASIONAL PUBLICATIONS, LONDON RECORD SOCIETY.**
*++OCCAS. PUBL. LOND. REC. SOC.*
*LONDON NO.1, 1970-*
*BH/U-1.    LO/U-1.    OX/U-1.*

**OCCASIONAL PUBLICATIONS, NORTHERN CAVERN & MINE RESEARCH SOCIETY.**    XXX
*++OCCAS. PUBL. NORTH. CAVERN & MINE RES. SOC.*
*SKIPTON NO.5, 1972-*
PREV: INDIVIDUAL SURVEY SERIES, NORTHERN
CAVERN & MINE RESEARCH SOCIETY FROM NO.1,
1966- NO.4, 1970.
*LO/N-2.*

**OCCASIONAL PUBLICATIONS, URBAN STUDY GROUP, INSTITUTE OF BRITISH GEOGRAPHERS.**
*++OCCAS. PUBL. URBAN STUDY GROUP INST. BR.*
*GEOGR.*
*LONDON NO.1, 1972-*
*LO/S13.*

**OCCASIONAL PUBLICATION, WESSEX CAVE CLUB: SERIES 1.**
*++OCCAS. PUBL. WESSEX CAVE CLUB, 1.*
*PANGBOURNE NO.1, 1969-*
*LO/N13.*

**OCCASIONAL REPORT OF THE NANKAI REGIONAL FISHERIES RESEARCH LABORATORY.**    000
  SEE: NANKAI-KU SUISAN KENKYUJO HOKOKU RINJIGO.

**OCCASIONAL RESEARCH PAPERS, INSTITUTE OF EDUCATION, UNIVERSITY OF CAMBRIDGE.**
*++OCCAS. RES. PAP. INST. EDUC. UNIV. CAMB.*
*CAMBRIDGE NO.1, 1968-*
*OX/U-1.*

**OCCASIONAL WINDHOVER.**
*++OCCAS. WINDHOVER.*
ROEHAMPTON NEW ARTS CIRCLE.
*ROEHAMPTON [1], 1969-*
*LO/U-2.*

**OCCUPATIONAL HEALTH & INDUSTRIAL MEDICINE.**    000
  SEE: EXCERPTA MEDICA: SECTION 35.

**OCCUPATIONAL SAFETY BULLETIN.**    XXX
*++OCCUP. SAF. BULL.*
ROYAL SOCIETY FOR THE PREVENTION OF ACCIDENTS.
*LONDON 35(384), 1967- 39(433), 1971.*
INCORP: INDUSTRIAL SAFETY BULLETIN FROM 1,
1933- 34(383), 1966; & COMMERCE SAFETY BULLET-
IN FROM 1(1), JE 1965- 2(12), D 1966. SUBS:
OCCUPATIONAL SAFETY & HEALTH: SUPPLEMENT.
*ED/N-1.    LO/N14.    LO/S24.    XS/R10.*
*SW/U-1. 37. AG 1969-*

**OCCUPATIONAL SAFETY & HEALTH.**    XXX
*++OCCUP. SAF. & HEALTH.*
ROYAL SOCIETY FOR THE PREVENTION OF ACCIDENTS.
*LONDON 1, 1971-*
PREV: BRITISH JOURNAL OF OCCUPATIONAL SAFETY
FROM 7(79), 1967- 8(94), 1970.
*BH/P-1.    ED/N-1.    LO/N14.    MA/P-1.    OX/U-1.    XS/R10.*
*ISSN 0007-1153*

**OCCUPATIONAL SAFETY & HEALTH: SUPPLEMENT.**    XXX
*++OCCUP. SAF. & HEALTH, SUPPL.*
ROYAL SOCIETY FOR THE PREVENTION OF ACCIDENTS.
*LONDON 1, 1971-*
PREV. OCCUPATIONAL SAFETY BULLETIN FROM 35
(384), 1967- 39(433), 1971.
*ED/N-1.    LO/N14.*

**OCEAN ENGINEERING.**
*++OCEAN ENG.*
[PERGAMON]
*OXFORD & NEW YORK 1, 1968-*
*ED/N-1.    GL/U-2.    LO/N14.    OX/U-8.    SO/U-1.*
*ISSN 0029-8018*

**OCEAN INDUSTRY.**
*++OCEAN IND.*
[GULF PUBL. CO.]
*HOUSTON, TEX.  1(1), 1966-*
*LO/N14. 5, 1970-            XS/R10. 3(2), 1968-*
*BN/U-2. 2(1), 1967-*
*GL/U-2. 9(4), AP 1974-*
*ISSN 0029-8026*

**OCEAN MANAGEMENT.**
*++OCEAN MANAGE.*
*AMSTERDAM 1, 1973-*
*Q.*
*CA/U13.    GL/U-2.    LO/N-2.    LO/S14.    LO/U-3.    OX/U-8.*
*SW/U-1.*

**OCEANIC ABSTRACTS (1972).**    XXX
*++OCEANIC ABSTR. (1972).*
[POLLUTION ABSTRACTS]
*LA JOLLA, CALIF. 1972-*
INCORP: OCEANIC CITATION JOURNAL FROM 5(6),
1968- 8, 1971; & OCEANIC INDEX FROM 3, 1966-
8, 1971.
*LO/N13.*

**OCEANIC CITATION JOURNAL.**    XXX
*++OCEANIC CITAT. J.*
OCEANIC RESEARCH INSTITUTE (US).
*LA JOLLA, CALIF. 5(6), 1968- 8, 1971.*
PREV: OCEANIC INDEX - CITATION JOURNAL FROM
5(1-5), 1968. SUBS. PART OF: OCEANIC
ABSTRACTS (1972).
*LO/N13.    SW/U-1.*
*CA/U-2. 7, 1970-            XS/R10. 6, 1969-*

**OCEANIC COORDINATE INDEX.**    XXX
*++OCEANIC COORD. INDEX.*
MISSION BAY RESEARCH FOUNDATION OF SAN DIEGO.
*LA JOLLA, CALIF. 1, 1964- 2, 1965 ...*
SUBS: OCEANIC INDEX.
*LO/N13.*

**OCEANIC INDEX.**    XXX
OCEANIC RESEARCH INSTITUTE (US).
*LA JOLLA, CALIF. 3, 1966- 8, 1971.*
PREV: OCEANIC COORDINATE INDEX FROM 1, 1964-
2, 1965. SUBS. PART OF: OCEANIC ABSTRACTS
(1972). IN 1968 THE CITATION SECTION WAS
SUPERSEDED BY: OCEANIC INDEX - CITATION JOUR-
NAL.
*BN/U-2.    LO/N13.    SW/U-1.*
*LO/U-6. 5, 1968-*
*ISSN 0029-8093*

**OCEANIC INDEX - CITATION JOURNAL.**    XXX
*++OCEANIC INDEX - CITAT. J.*
OCEANIC RESEARCH INSTITUTE (US).
*LA JOLLA, CALIF. 5(1-5), 1968 ...*
PREV: THE CITATION SECTION OF OCEANIC INDEX.
SUBS: OCEANIC CITATION JOURNAL.
*LO/NJ3.*

**OCEANIC INSTRUMENTATION REPORTER.**
+ +OCEANIC INSTRUM. REP.
OCEAN ENGINEERING INFORMATION SERVICE.
*LA JOLLA, CALIF. 1, 1968-*
LO/N14. [CURRENT BOX ONLY]
ISSN 0029-8107

**OCEANOGRAPHIC DATA LISTS & INVENTORIES.**
+ +OCEANOGR. DATA LISTS & INVENT.
[A.F. HOST]
*COPENHAGEN NO.1, 1971-*
LO/N13.

**OCEANOLOGY (WASHINGTON, D.C.).**                    XXX
[ONLG-A]
AMERICAN GEOPHYSICAL UNION.
[SCRIPTA TECHNICA, INC.]
*WASHINGTON, D.C. 5, 1965(1966)-*
ENGL. LANG. TRANSL. OF OKEANOLOGIJA. DATING &
NUMBERING OF ISSUES FOLLOW ORIGINAL. PREV:
SOVIET OCEANOGRAPHY FROM 1961(1963)- 1964
(1966).
LO/N14.     SO/U-1.
EX/U-1. 6(1), 1966-

**OCEANOLOGY. THE WEEKLY OF OCEAN TECHNOLOGY.**
[OCWT-A]
[ZIFF-DAVIS PUBL. CO.]
*WASHINGTON, D.C. 1(1), 1966-*
LO/N17. 8(20), 1970-
ISSN 0029-8158

**OCEANOLOGY INTERNATIONAL.**                         XXX
+ +OCEAN. INT. [OCAN-B]
[INDUSTRIAL RESEARCH PUBL. CO.]
*BEVERLY SHORES, INDIANA 1(2), 1966- 6(11),*
*1971.*
PREV: OCEANOLOGY (NEW YORK) FROM 1(1), 1966.
SUBS. INCORP. IN: UNDERSEA TECHNOLOGY.
LO/N14. 3(5), 1968-          XS/R10. 5(1), 1970-
ISSN 0029-8166

**OCEANS.**
[TRIDENT PUBL.]
*SAN DIEGO 1, JA 1968(1969)-*
XS/R11.*
ISSN 0029-8174

**OCEANS INFORMATION.**
+ +OCEANS INF.
ASSOCIATION SCIENTIFIQUE ET TECHNIQUE POUR
L'EXPLOITATION DES OCEANS.
*PARIS NO.1, OC 1969-*
XS/R10.

**OCHERKI PO ARKHEOLOGII BELORUSSII.**
+ +OCHERKI ARKHEOL. BELORUSS.
AKADEMIJA NAUK BELORUSSKOJ SSR: (INSTYTUT
HISTORYI).
*MINSK 1, 1970-*
BH/U-1.

**OCHERKI PO ISTORII AZERBAJDZHANSKOJ FILOSOFII.**
+ +OCHERKI. ISTOR. AZERB. FILOS.
AKADEMIJA NAUK AZERBAJDZHANSKOJ SSR: SEKTOR
FILOSOFII.
*BAKU 1, 1966-*
OX/U-1.

**OCHERKI PO ISTORII LENINGRADSKOGO UNIVERSITETA.**
+ +OCHERKI ISTOR. LENINGR. UNIV.
LENINGRADSKIJ GOSUDARSTVENNYJ UNIVERSITET.
*LENINGRAD 1, 1962-*
OX/U-1.

**OCHERKI PO ISTORII RUSSKOGO JAZYKA I
LITERATURY XVIII VEKA (LOMONOVSKIE CHTENIJA).**
+ +OCHERKI ISTOR. RUSS. JAZYKA LIT. XVIII VEKA
LOMONOVSKIE CHTENIJA.
KAZANSKIJ GOSUDARSTVENNYJ UNIVERSITET.
*KAZAN VYP. 1, 1967-*
LO/N-3.

**OCHERKI PO SOVREMENNOJ SOVETSKOJ I
ZARUBEZHNOJ EKONOMIKE.**
+ +OCHERKI SOVREM. SOV. & ZARUBEZHNOJ EKON.
NAUCHNO-ISSLEDOVATEL'SKIJ EKONOMICHESKIJ
INSTITUT.
*MOSCOW 1, 1960-*
LO/U-3.   OX/U-1.

**OCTOBRE. = OKTOBER. = OTTOBRE.**
CENTRE LENINE (LAUSANNE).
*LAUSANNE 1(1), 25/MY 1964-*
FR., GER., ITAL. S/T IN FR. (PERIODIQUE DU
CENTRE LENINE, ORGANISATION DES MARXISTES-
LENINISTES DE SUISSE); GER. (ZEITSCHRIFT DES
LENINZENTRUMS, ...) & ITAL. (PERIODICO DEL
CENTRO LENIN, ...).
LO/U-3.
ISSN 0029-828X

**ODDA-TALA.**
*SAN FRANCISCO NO.1, 1968-*
OX/U-1.
ISSN 0029-8352

**O'DELL MEMORIAL MONOGRAPHS.**
+ +O'DELL MEM. MONOGR.
UNIVERSITY OF ABERDEEN: DEPARTMENT OF GEOGRAPHY
*ABERDEEN 1, 1968-*
BL/U-1.    BN/U-2.

**ODENSE UNIVERSITY CLASSICAL STUDIES.**
+ +ODENSE UNIV. CLASS. STUD.
ODENSE UNIVERSITET.
*ODENSE 1, 1971-*
LO/N-1.

**ODENSE UNIVERSITY STUDIES IN ENGLISH.**
+ +ODENSE UNIV. STUD. ENGL.
ODENSE UNIVERSITET.
*ODENSE [1] 1969-*
CA/U-1.   LO/N-1.
ISSN 0078-3293

**ODENSE UNIVERSITY STUDIES IN LINGUISTICS.**
+ +ODENSE UNIV. STUD. LINGUIST.
ODENSE UNIVERSITET.
*ODENSE 1, 1968-*
LO/N-1.

**ODENSE UNIVERSITY STUDIES IN LITERATURE.**
+ +ODENSE UNIV. STUD. LIT.
ODENSE UNIVERSITET.
*ODENSE 1, 1969-*
ENGL. SUMM.
CA/U-1.
ISSN 0078-3323

**ODENSE UNIVERSITY STUDIES IN PHILOSOPHY.**
+ +ODENSE UNIV. STUD. PHILOS.
ODENSE UNIVERSITET.
*ODENSE 1972-*
LO/N-1.

**ODIN RAZ V ZHIZNI.**
[AGENSTVO PECHATI NOVOSTI].
*MOSCOW 1964-*
A.
BH/U-1.    SW/U-1.

**ODONATOLOGICA.**
SOCIETAS INTERNATIONALIS ODONATOLOGICA.
*UTRECHT 1, 1972-*
LO/N-2.
SF/U-1. 3(1), 1974-

**ODONTOLOGISK TIDSKRIFT.**                           XXX
SUBS (1970): SCANDINAVIAN JOURNAL OF DENTAL
RESEARCH.

**ODRA, MIESIECZNIK SPOLECZNO-KULTURALNY.**
+ +ODRA MIES. SPOL.-KULT.
WROCLAWSKIE WYDAWNICTWO PRASOWE RSW 'PRASA'.
*WROCLAW 1(1), 1961-*
M. SUPERSEDES AN EARLIER PUBL. WITH THE
SAME TITLE.
LO/N-3. 3(10), 1963.

**ODYSSEUS. MAGAZINE OF THE ARTS.**
[TROUBADOR P.]
*PORTLAND, OREG. 1, 1971-*
OX/U-1.

**OECD FINANCIAL STATISTICS.**
+ +OECD FINANC. STAT.
*PARIS 1, 1970-*
2/A.
BH/U-1.   ED/N-1.   GL/U-1.   LO/N-3.   NO/U-1.   OX/U16.
RE/U-1.   SW/U-1.
ISSN 0048-2188

**OECD POPULATION ABSTRACTS.**
+ +OECD POPUL. ABSTR.
*PARIS NO.1, D 1970-*
PROD. BY THE POPULATION UNIT.
LO/S14.   LO/U-3.   OX/U24.
CA/U-1. NO.11, 1973

**OECOLOGIA.**
[SPRINGER VERLAG]
*BERLIN &C. 1, AP 1968-*
*AD/U-1.    CA/U-6.    GL/U-1.    LO/N-4.    LO/N13.    LO/R-5.*
*LO/S19.    LO/U-2.    LO/U-6.    NO/U-1.    OX/U-1.    OX/U-8.*
*XN/R-1.    XY/N-1.*
*BL/U-1.  12, 1973-*
*ISSN 0029-8549*

**OECOLOGIA PLANTARUM.**
*++OECOL. PLANT.*
[GAUTHIER-VILLARS]
*PARIS 1(1), 1966-*
*BN/U-2.    CA/U-7.    DN/U-1.    LO/U-2.*
*SH/U-1.  2, 1968-*
*ISSN 0029-8557*

**OEM DESIGN.**                                                    XXX
*++OEM DES.*
[MERCURY HOUSE BUSINESS PUBL.]
*LONDON 1, 1971-*
INCORP: PRODUCT DESIGN ENGINEERING; MACHINE
DESIGN & CONTROL; LIGHT ENGINEERING; &
PLASTICS IN ENGINEERING.
*ED/N-1.    LO/N14.    LO/N35.    OX/U-8.    SF/U-1.*
*SW/U-1.    XS/T-4.*
*HL/U-1.  3(1), 1974-*
*ISSN 0306-0381*

**OF SEA & SHORE.**
*PORT GAMBLE, WASH. 1, 1970-*
*LO/N-2.    LO/N13.*
*ISSN 0030-0055*

**OFFICIAL ARCHITECTURE & PLANNING.**                             XXX
SUBS (1971): OAP JOURNAL FOR THE BUILT
ENVIRONMENT.

**OFFSET PRINTING.**                                              XXX
*++OFFSET PRINT.*
[MACLEAN-HUNTER]
*LONDON NO.36, 1972-*
PREV: SMALL OFFSET PRINTING FROM NO.1, 1969-
35, 1971.
*ED/N-1.    LO/N14.    RE/U-1.*

**OFFSHORE SERVICES.**                                            XXX
*++OFFSHORE SERV.*
[SPEARHEAD PUBL.]
*KINGSTON-UPON-THAMES 1972-*
PREV: HYDROSPACE FROM 1, 1967- 5, 1972.
*ED/N-1.    LO/N14.    OX/U-8.    XS/R10.*

**OFFSHORE TECHNOLOGY.**
*++OFFSHORE TECHNOL.*
SCIENTIFIC SURVEYS (OFFSHORE) LTD.
*LONDON 1(1), MY 1969-*
*ED/N-1.    LO/N14.    OX/U-8.    XS/R10.*
*ISSN 0030-0616*

**OHIO OPPORTUNITY IN ACTION.**
(OHIO) OFFICE OF OPPORTUNITY.
*COLUMBUS, OHIO 1, 1965-*
M.
*CB/U-1.**

**OHMU: OCCASIONAL PAPERS OF THE ZOOLOGICAL
LABORATORY, KYUSHU IMPERIAL UNIVERSITY.**
*FUKUOKA 1, 1968-*
LAB. SUBORD. TO: FACULTY OF AGRICULTURE.
*LO/N-2.*

**OIDEAS.**
(EIRE) DEPARTMENT OF EDUCATION.
*DUBLIN [NO.]1, 1968-*
*BL/U-1.    DB/U-2.    ED/N-1.    LO/N-1.*

**OIL, PAINT & DRUG REPORTER.**                                   XXX
SUBS (1972): CHEMICAL MARKETING REPORTER.

**OKEANOLOGIJA (ENGL. TRANSL.).**                                 000
SEE: OCEANOLOGY (WASHINGTON, D.C.).

**OKHRANA PRIRODY NA DAL'NEM VOSTOKE.**
*++OKHR. PRIR. DAL'NEM VOSTOKE. [OPDV-A]*
AKADEMIJA NAUK SSSR (SIBIRSKOE OTDELENIE):
KOMISSIJA PO OKHRANE PRIRODY.
*VLADIVOSTOK 1, 1963-*
KOMISSIJA ... SUBORD. TO: DAL'NEVOSTOCHNYJ
FILIAL.
*LO/N-3.    OX/U-1.*

**OKHRANA PRIRODY MOLDAVII.**
*++OKHR. PRIR. MOLD.*
AKADEMIJA NAUK MOLDAVSKOJ SSR: KOMISSIJA PO
OKHRANE PRIRODY.
*KISHINEV 1, 1960-*
*LO/N-2.*
*LO/N13.  3, 1965-*

**OKHRANA PRIRODY NA URALE.**
*++OKHR. PRIR. URALE.*
AKADEMIJA NAUK SSSR (URAL'SKIJ FILIAL): KOMIS-
SIJA PO OKHRANE PRIRODY.
*SVERDLOVSK VYP.1, 1960-*
VYP.2 PUBL. IN PERM.
*LO/N13.    XY/N-1.*
*BH/U-1.  5 (1966).*

**OKTOBER.  LAUSANNE, 1964**                                      000
SEE: OCTOBRE (LAUSANNE).

**OLD ENGLISH NEWSLETTER.**
*++OLD ENGL. NEWSL.*
MODERN LANGUAGE ASSOCIATION OF AMERICA: OLD
ENGLISH GROUP.
*COLUMBUS, OHIO 1, AP 1967-*
PUBL. FOR MLAA BY CENTER FOR MEDIAEVAL &
RENAISSANCE STUDIES, OHIO STATE UNIVERSITY.
*CA/U-1.    EX/U-1.    LD/U-1.    LO/U-1.    MA/U-1.*
*ISSN 0030-1973*

**OLD MOTOR NEWS.**
*++OLD MOT. NEWS.*
OLD MOTOR CLUB.
*LONDON NO.1, MY 1971-*
*ED/N-1.    LO/N-4.    OX/U-1.*

**OLD TIME MUSIC.**
[OLD TIME MUSIC]
*LONDON NO.1, SUMMER 1971-*
Q.
*ED/N-1.*
*ISSN 0048-1653*

**OLE.**
SUBS (1967): OPEN SKULL.

**OMEGA.  THE INTERNATIONAL JOURNAL OF MANAGEMENT
SCIENCE.**
[PERGAMON P.]
*OXFORD 1(1), F 1973-*
2M.
*BH/U-3.    BL/U-1.    CA/U-4.    ED/N-1.    EX/U-1.    GL/U-1.*
*GL/U-2.    NO/U-1.    SH/U-1.    SW/U-1.  2, 1974-*
*CA/U-1.  1(2), 1973-              OX/U-1.  1(2), 1973-*
*XS/R10.  1(3), 1973-*
*ISSN 0305-0483*

**ON EVENTS IN CZECHOSLOVAKIA.**                                  000
SEE: K SOBYTIJAM V CHEKHOSLOVAKII: FAKTY,
DOKUMENTY, SVIDETEL'STVA PRESSY I OCHEVIDTSEV.

**ON THE MOVE.**
BIBLE CHURCHMEN'S MISSIONARY SOCIETY.
*LONDON NO.1, 1972-*
2/A.
*ED/N-1.  NO.2, 1972-*

**ON VIEW.  A GUIDE TO MUSEUM & GALLERY
ACQUISITIONS IN BRITAIN.**
[PLAISTOW PUBLS.]
*LONDON [1] 1966/67-*
*ED/N-1.*
*BL/U-1.  3, 1968/69-              LO/N-4.  3, 1968/69-*

**ONKOLOGIJA.**
NAUCHNO DRUZHESTVO NA ONKOLOZITE.
*SOFIA 1(1), 1964-*
ENGL. SUMM.
*LO/M-3.  2, 1965-              LO/N13.  7, 1970-*

**ONOMASTICA SLAVOGERMANICA.**
*++ONOMASTICA SLAVOGER.*
UNIWERSYTET WROCLAWSKI.
*WROCLAW; LEIPZIG 1, 1965-*
PUBL. ALTERNATELY IN WROCLAW & LEIPZIG.
VOL.1(1965) PUBL. AS: ABHANDLUNGEN, SAECHSIS-
CHE AKADEMIE DER WISSENSCHAFTEN (LEIPZIG):
PHILILOGISCHE-HISTORISCHE KLASSE.
*LO/N-3.  4 (1968).*

**ONTARIO EDUCATION/1966.**
*++ONT. EDUC./1966.*
(ONTARIO) DEPARTMENT OF EDUCATION.
*TORONTO 1(1), 1966-*
*XN/S-1.*

**ONTARIO FISH & WILDLIFE REVIEW.**
*+ +ONT. FISH. & WILDL. REV.*
(ONTARIO) DEPARTMENT OF LANDS & FORESTS.
*TORONTO    1(1), SUMMER 1961-*
Q.
*LO/N13.  2, 1963-*
*ISSN 0030-2929*

**ONTOGENEZ.**
AKADEMIJA NAUK SSSR.
*MOSCOW  1(1), 1970-*
2M.  ENGL. SUMM.
*CA/U-2.    LO/N13.    OX/U-8.*

**OPEN PLACES.**
*NEW YORK  NO.1, N 1966-*
*OX/U-1.*

**OPEN SKULL.**
*SAN FRANCISCO    1, JE 1967-*
PREV: OLEI
*LO/U-2.*

**OPEN UTILITY MODEL APPLICATION GAZETTE**
**(JAPAN).**                                                        000
    SEE: KOKAI JITSUYO SHINAN KOHO.

**OPERA MUNDI EUROPE.**                                   XXX
    SUBS (1969): EUROPEAN INTELLIGENCE.

**OPHTHALMIC RESEARCH.**
*+ +OPHTHALMIC RES.*
[KARGER]
*BASLE  1, 1970-*
*LO/N13.    OX/U-8.*
*ISSN 0030-3747*

**OPHTHALMIC SURGERY.**
*+ +OPHTHALMIC SURG.*
[SLACK INC.]
*PITMAN, N.J.  1, 1970-*
*LO/N14.*
*SO/U-1.  4, 1973-*
*ISSN 0022-023X*

**OPHTHALMOLOGY DIGEST.**                               XXX
*+ +OPHTHALMOL. DIG.*
[E.E.N.T. DIGEST]
*NORTHFIELD, ILL.  33(4), 1971-*
PREV: PART OF E.E.N.T. DIGEST FROM 21(6),
1959- 33(3), 1971.
*LO/N14.*
*ISSN 0048-1955*

**OPISTHOBRANCH NEWSLETTER.**
*+ +OPISTHOBRANCH NEWSL.*
*PISMO BEACH, CALIF.  1, 1969-*
*LO/N-2.*

**OPTICA APPLICATA.**
*+ +OPT. APPL.*
BRESLAU POLITECHNIKA.
*WROCLAW  1, 1971-*
*SW/U-1.*

**OPTICAL ENGINEERING.**                                   XXX
*+ +OPT. ENG.*
SOCIETY OF PHOTO-OPTICAL INSTRUMENTATION ENGIN-
EERS.
*REDONDO BEACH, CALIF.  11, 1972-*
PREV: SPIE JOURNAL FROM 1, OC/N 1962- 10, 1971
*LO/N14.*
*CA/U-2.  13, 1974-*
*ISSN 0036-1860*

**OPTICAL NEWS.**
*+ +OPT. NEWS.*
[HAYMARKET PRESS]
*LONDON   1(1), JA 1968-*
S/T: THE MONTHLY NEWSPAPER FOR THE OPHTHALMIC
OPTICIAN, THE DISPENSING OPTICIAN & THE
OPTICAL INDUSTRY.
*ED/N-1.    LO/N14.*

**OPTICAL WORLD.  OPTISCHE WELT.  L'OPTIQUE DANS**
**LE MONDE.**
*+ +OPT. WORLD.*
[OPTICAL WORLD LTD.]
*LONDON  1, 1972-*
ENGL. WITH FR. & GER. SUMM., & NEWS IN THE
THREE LANGUAGES.
*CA/U-1.    ED/N-1.    LO/N14.*

**OPTICS COMMUNICATIONS.**
*+ +OPT. COMMUN.*
[NORTH HOLLAND PUBL. HO.]
*AMSTERDAM  1, AP 1969-*
*CB/U-1.    LO/U-2.    SO/U-1.*
*BH/U-3. 13, 1975-              SH/U-3. 10, 1974-*
*ISSN 0030-4018*

**OPTICS & LASER TECHNOLOGY.**                      XXX
*+ +OPT. & LASER TECHNOL.*
[ILIFFE]
*GUILDFORD  2(3), 1970-*
PREV: OPTICS TECHNOLOGY FROM 1, 1968- 2, 1970.
*AD/U-1.    BH/U-1.    ED/N-1.    HL/U-1.    LO/N-7.    LO/N14.*
*LO/U-2.    XS/R10.*
*BL/U-1. 6, 1974-              SH/U-3. 4, F 1972*
*SO/U-1. 4, 1972-*
*EX/U-1. 3(2), MY 1971-*
*ISSN 0030-3992*

**OPTICS & SPECTROSCOPY: SUPPLEMENT.**
*+ +OPT. & SPECTROSC., SUPPL.*
OPTICAL SOCIETY OF AMERICA.
*WASHINGTON, DC [NO.]1, 1966-*
*AD/U-1.    LO/U20.*

**OPTICS TECHNOLOGY.**                        .           XXX
*+ +OPT. TECHNOL.*
[ILIFFE]
*GUILDFORD  1, N 1968- 2(2), 1970 ...*
SUBS: OPTICS & LASER TECHNOLOGY.
*AB/U-1.    BH/U-1.    ED/N-1.    HL/U-1.    LO/N14.    XS/R10.*

**OPTIKA I SPEKTROSKOPIJA: SBORNIK STATEJ.**
*+ +OPT. & SPEKTROSK., SB. STATEJ. [OPSP-A]*
AKADEMIJA NAUK SSSR.
*MOSCOW  TOM 1, 1963-*
ISSUED BY THE AKAD.'S  OTDELENIE FIZIKO-
MATEMATICHESKIKH NAUK.  AKAD. ALSO ISSUES:
OPTIKA I SPEKTROSKOPIJA., AS A 2M PUBL.,
SINCE 1956.
*LO/N14.    OX/U-8.    XY/N-1.*

**OPTIKO-MEKHANICHEKAIA PROMYSHLENNOST'; (ENGL.**
**TRANSL.)**
    SEE: SOVIET JOURNAL OF OPTICAL TECHNOLOGY.

**OPTIMAL'NOE PLANIROVANIE.**                      XXX
*+ +OPTIM. PLANIROVANIE.*
AKADEMIJA NAUK SSSR(SIBIRSKOE OTDELENIE):
INSTITUT MATEMATIKI.
*NOVOSIBIRSK  VYP.1, 1964- 17, 1970.*
SUBS: OPTIMIZATSIJA (NOVOSIBIRSK).
*GL/U-1.    LO/N13.*
*BH/U-1. 7, 1967-              CC/U-1. 14, 1969-*

**OPTIMUM.  A FORUM FOR MANAGEMENT.**
(CANADA) DEPARTMENT OF SUPPLY & SERVICES:
BUREAU OF MANAGEMENT CONSULTING.
*OTTAWA  1(1), 1970-*
Q.  ENGL. OR FR. WITH SUMM. IN ALTERNATIVE
LANG.
*LO/U-3.*
*LO/N35.  3, 1972-*
*ISSN 0475-1906*

**OPTIQUE DANS LE MONDE.**                        000
    SEE: OPTICAL WORLD.

**OPTISCHE WELT.**                                      000
    SEE: OPTICAL WORLD.

**OPTO-ELECTRONICS.**                                  XXX
[CHAPMAN & HALL]
*LONDON  1(1), F 1969- 6, 1974 ...*
SUBS: OPTICAL AND QUANTUM ELECTRONICS FROM
7, 1975.
*AD/U-3.    BH/U-1.    CA/U-2.    CB/U-1.    EX/U-1.    GL/U-1.*
*LO/N-4.    LO/N14.    LO/U-2.    LO/U11.    RE/U-1.    SW/U-1.*
*XS/R10.*
*ED/N-1. 2, 1970-              OX/U-8. 2, 1970-*
*SO/U-1. 3, F 1971-*
*BD/U-1. 1(4), 1969; 5(6), 1973.*
*ISSN 0030-4077*

**OPUSCULA SPARSA.**
UNIVERSIDAD DE BARCELONA: FACULTAD DE CIENCIAS.
*BARCELONA  NO.1, 1970-*
PROD. BY DEPARTMENTO DE BOTANICO OF THE
FACULTAD.
*LO/N-2.*

**ORAL HISTORY.**
*+ +ORAL HIST.*
ESSEX UNIVERSITY: DEPARTMENT OF SOCIOLOGY.
*LONDON  1(1), [1971]-*
*ED/N-1.    EX/U-1.    GL/U-1.    MA/P-1.*

**ORAL SCIENCES REVIEWS.**
+ +ORAL SCI. REV.
[MUNKSGAARD]
COPENHAGEN 1, 1972-
GL/U-1.    LD/U-1.    LO/N13.    MA/U-1.    SH/U-1.

**ORBIS MUSICAE.**
TEL-AVIV UNIVERSITY: DEPARTMENT OF MUSICOLOGY.
TEL-AVIV 1(1), AG 1971-
ED/N-1.    OX/U-1.

**ORBIT.**
ONTARIO INSTITUTE FOR STUDIES IN EDUCATION.
TORONTO 1, F 1970-
S/A.  TWO PRELIMINARY ISSUES IN OC & D 1969.
LD/U-1.
ISSN 0030-4433

**ORCHADIAN.**
AUSTRALASIAN NATIVE ORCHID SOCIETY.
SYDNEY 1, 1968-
LO/N-2.

**OREBROPROJEKTTE.**
[UTBILDNINGSFORLAGET]
STOCKHOLM NO.1, 1971-
MONOGR.
LO/N-1.

**ORGAN YEARBOOK.**
+ +ORGAN YEARB.
AMSTERDAM 1, 1970-
S/T: A JOURNAL FOR THE PLAYERS & HISTORIANS OF
KEYBOARD INSTRUMENTS.
DR/U-1.    MA/P-1.    NO/U-1.    SH/U-1.
LO/U-1. 2, 1971-

**ORGANIC CHEMICAL BULLETIN.**                                          XXX
SUBS (1969): EASTMAN ORGANIC CHEMICAL
BULLETIN.

**ORGANIC COMPOUNDS OF SULPHUR, SELENIUM &
TELLURIUM.**
+ +ORG. COMPOUNDS SULPHUR SELENIUM & TELLURIUM.
CHEMICAL SOCIETY.
LONDON 1, 1970-
A SPECIALIST PERIODICAL REPORT.
GL/U-1.    LO/S-3.    LO/U12.    MA/U-1.    NW/U-1.    SF/U-1.
RE/U-1. 2, 1970-
ISSN 0305-9812

**ORGANIC MAGNETIC RESONANCE.**
+ +ORG. MAGN. RESONANCE.
[HEYDEN & SON]
LONDON 1(1), F 1969-
CA/U-1.    CB/U-1.    ED/U-1.    GL/U-1.    LD/U-1.    LO/N14.
LO/S-3.    LO/U11.    SH/U-1.    XS/R10.
BL/U-1. 5, 1973-      LO/R-6. 6, 1974-
ISSN 0030-4921

**ORGANIC MAGNETIC RESONANCE: SPECTRAL SUPPLEM-
ENT.**
+ +ORG. MAGN. RESONANCE, SPECTRAL SUPPL.
[HEYDEN & SON]
LONDON 1, 1969-
LD/U-1.    LO/N14.    LO/S-3.

**ORGANIC METAL COATING REVIEW.**
+ +ORG. METAL COAT. REV.
EUROPEAN COIL COATING ASSOCIATION.
BRUSSELS [NO.1], 1969-
ENGL., FR. & GER.
LO/N14.

**ORGANIC PHOTOCHEMICAL SYNTHESES.**
+ +ORG. PHOTOCHEM. SYNTH.
[WILEY-INTERSCIENCE]
NEW YORK &C. 1, 1971-
LO/N14.

**ORGANIC PREPARATIONS & PROCEDURES.**                                  XXX
+ +ORG. PREP. & PROCED.
[MARCEL DEKKER]
NEW YORK 1(1), 1969- 2(4), N 1970 ...
S/T: AN INTERNATIONAL JOURNAL FOR RAPID
COMMUNICATION. SUBS: ORGANIC PREPARATIONS AND
PROCEDURES INTERNATIONAL.
LD/U-1.    LO/S-3.    OX/U-8.    SF/U-1.

**ORGANIC PREPARATIONS AND PROCEDURES
INTERNATIONAL.**                                                        XXX
+ +ORG. PREP. & PROCED. INT.
[MARCEL DEKKER]
NEW YORK 3(1), F 1971-
S/T: THE NEW JOURNAL FOR ORGANIC SYNTHESIS.
PREV. ORGANIC PREPARATIONS AND PROCEDURES
FROM 1(1), 1969- 2(4), N 1970 ...
DN/U-1.    LO/S-3.    SH/U-1.
ISSN 0030-4948

**ORGANIC REACTIVITY.**                                                 000
SEE: REAKTSIONNAJA SPOSOBNOST' ORGANICHESKIKH
SOEDINENIJ.

**ORGANIZATSIJA I PLANIROVANIE OTRASLEJ NAROD-
NOGO KHOZJAJSTVA.**
+ +ORGAN. & PLANIROVANIE OTRASLEJ NAR. KHOZ.
(UKRAINE) GOSPLAN: NAUCHNO-ISSLEDOVATEL'SKIJ
EKONOMICHESKIJ INSTITUT.
KIEV 1, 1965-
S/T: MEZHVEDOMSYVENNYJ NAUCHNYJ SBORNIK.
OX/U-1.
BH/U-1. 1967-                       CC/U-1. 1967-
GL/U-1. 3, 1965-

**ORGANOMETALLIC CHEMISTRY.**
+ +ORGANOMET. CHEM.
CHEMICAL SOCIETY.
LONDON 1, 1972-
BL/U-1.    CA/U-1.    ED/N-1.    GL/U-2.    HL/U-1.    LO/N14.
LO/S-3.    LO/U-2.    LO/U12.    MA/U-1.    SF/U-1.    SO/U-1.
ISSN 0301-0074

**ORGANOMETALLIC CHEMISTRY REVIEWS.**                                   XXX
+ +ORGANOMET. CHEM. REV.
AMSTERDAM 1(1), JA 1966- 2, 1967...
SUBS: ORGANOMETALLIC CHEMISTRY REVIEWS;
SECTION A: SUBJECT REVIEWS.
LO/N-4.    LO/N14.    LO/S-3.    LO/U-2.    LO/U12.    LO/U13.
MA/U-1.    SH/U-1.    SO/U-1.

**ORGANOMETALLIC CHEMISTRY REVIEWS; SECTION A:
SUBJECT REVIEWS.**                                                      XXX
+ +ORGANOMET. CHEM. REV., A.
[ELSEVIER]
AMSTERDAM 3(1), F 1968- 8(2), AG 1972.
PREV: ORGANOMETALLIC CHEMISTRY REVIEWS FROM
1, 1966- 2, 1967. SUBS. INCORP. IN: JOURNAL OF
ORGANOMETALLIC CHEMISTRY FROM 34, 1972.
BH/U-1.    LO/U-2.
CO/U-1. 4, 1969-
ISSN 0030-5111

**ORGANOMETALLIC CHEMISTRY REVIEWS; SECTION B:
ANNUAL SURVEYS.**                                                       XXX
+ +ORGANOMET. CHEM. REV., B.
[ELSEVIER]
AMSTERDAM 4, JE 1968- 8(2), AG 1972.
PREV: ANNUAL SURVEY OF ORGANOMETALLIC CHEMI-
STRY FROM 1, 1964 (1965)- 3, 1966 (1967).
SUBS. INCORP. IN: JOURNAL OF ORGANOMETALLIC
CHEMISTRY FROM 34, 1972.
BH/U-1.    LO/N14.    LO/U-2.    LO/U12.
ISSN 0030-512X

**ORGANOMETALLIC REACTIONS.**
+ +ORGANOMET. REACT.
[WILEY-INTERSCIENCE]
NEW YORK &C. 1, 1970-
ANNU.
ED/N-1.    GL/U-1.    LD/U-1.    LO/N14.    LO/S-3.    LO/U-2.
OX/U-8.    SH/U-1.    SO/U-1.

**ORGANOMETALLICS IN CHEMICAL SYNTHESIS.**
+ +ORGANOMET. CHEM. SYN.
LAUSANNE 1, 1970-
GL/U-1.    LO/S-3.    LO/U11.    OX/U-8.
ISSN 0030-5146

**ORGANOPHOSPHORUS CHEMISTRY.**
+ +ORGANOPHOSPHORUS CHEM.
CHEMICAL SOCIETY.
LONDON 1, 1970-
S/T: A SPECIALIST PERIODICAL REPORT.
BH/U-1.    BH/U-3.    GL/U-1.    GL/U-2.    LO/N14.    LO/S-3.
LO/U12.    LO/U13.    MA/U-1.    NW/U-1.    SF/U-1.
SH/U-1.
AD/U-1. 2, 1971-

**ORIEL.**
PLAID CYMRU.
CAERDYDD NO.1, AUTUMN 1968-
Q.  WELSH & ENGL.
SW/U-1. NO.2, 1968.

ORIENT.
SOCIETY FOR NEAR EASTERN STUDIES IN JAPAN.
*TOKYO 1, 1960-*
VARIOUS LANGS.
*OX/U-1.*
*LO/U-1. 2, 1962-*

ORIENT-PRESS. BOLLETTINO BIBLIOGRAFICO DI STUDI
ORIENTALISTICI.
[ORIENT-PRESS]
*ROME 1(1), JA/F 1970-*
2M.
*LO/U14.*

ORIENT SYRIEN.                                                       XXX
SUBS (1970): PART PAROLE DE L'ORIENT.

ORIENTACE. LITERATURA UMENI, KRITIKA.
[CESKOSLOVENSKY SPISOVATEL].
*PRAGUE 1(1), 1966-*
2M.
*LA/U-1.*

ORIENTAL INSECTS.
*+ +ORIENT. INSECTS.*
ASSOCIATION FOR THE STUDY OF ORIENTAL INSECTS.
*DELHI 1, 1968-*
*LO/N-2. LO/N13. .*
*ISSN 0030-5316*

ORIENTALIA LOVANIENSIA PERIODICA.
*+ +ORIENT. LOVANIENSIA PERIOD.*
INSTITUUT VOOR ORIENTALISTIEK (LOUVAIN).
*LOUVAIN 1, 1970-*
*LO/N-1. LO/U14. LO/U17. MA/S-1. MA/U-1.*
*OX/U-1. OX/U-2.*

ORIGINAL EQUIPMENT MANUFACTURE DESIGN.
*+ +ORIG. EQUIP. MANUF. DES.*
[MERCURY HOUSE BUSINESS PUBL.]
*LONDON 1, OC 1971-*
*SH/C-5.*

ORIGINI. PREISTORIA E PROTOSTORIA DELLE
CIVILTA ANTICHE.
UNIVERSITA DI ROMA: MUSEO DELLE ORIGINI.
*ROME 1, 1967-*
MUSEO SUBORD. TO: ISTITUTO DI PALETNOLOGIA.
*CA/U-3. DB/S-1. LO/S10. OX/U-2.*
*ISSN 0474-6805*

ORITA. IBADAN JOURNAL OF RELIGIOUS STUDIES.
UNIVERSITY OF IBADAN: DEPARTMENT OF RELIGIOUS
STUDIES.
*IBADAN 1(1), JE 1967-*
2/A.
*BH/C-3. OX/U-1.*
*ISSN 0030-5596*

O.R.L. DIGEST.                                                       XXX
*+ +O.R.L. DIG.*
[E.E.N.T. DIGEST]
*NORTHFIELD, ILL. 33(4), 1971-*
PREV: PART OF E.E.N.T. DIGEST FROM 21(6),
1959- 33(3), 1971.
*LO/N13.*
*ISSN 0048-1254*

ORNIS SCANDINAVICA.
*+ +ORNIS SCAND.*
SCANDINAVIAN ORNITHOLOGISTS' UNION.
*OSLO 1, 1970-*
*CA/U12. LO/N-2.*
*BL/U-1. 4, 1973-*
*ISSN 0030-5693*

ORTHODONTIST.                                                       XXX
BRITISH ASSOCIATION OF ORTHODONTISTS.
[HENRY EVAN &C.]
*LONDON 1, 1969- 4, 1972.*
SUBS. PART OF: BRITISH JOURNAL OF ORTHODONTICS
*ED/N-1. GL/U-1. LO/N14.*
*LD/U-1. 3, 1971-*
*ISSN 0048-2250*

ORTHOPEDIC CLINICS OF NORTH AMERICA.
*+ +ORTHOP. CLIN. NORTH AM.*
*PHILADELPHIA &C. 1, 1970-*
*DB/U-2. NW/U-1.*
*CA/U-1. 5, 1974-*
*ISSN 0030-5898*

ORTHOPAEDIC MEDICINE, SURGERY.
*+ +ORTHOP. MED. SURG.*
[STUART PHILLIPS PUBL.]
*LONDON 1, 1970-*
Q.
*ED/N-1. OX/U-8.*
*ISSN 0030-5855*

ORTHOPAEDICS: OXFORD.
NUFFIELD ORTHOPAEDIC CENTRE: DEPARTMENT OF
ORTHOPAEDIC SURGERY.
*OXFORD 1(1), AP 1968-*
2A.
*ISSN 0030-5863*

ORYOKU TO HIZUMI. JAPANESE JOURNAL OF EXPER-
IMENTAL MECHANICS.
[CHUO KAGAKUSHA]
*TOKYO 1, 1971-*
*LO/N13.*

OSLER LIBRARY NEWSLETTER.
*+ +OSLER LIBR. NEWSL.*
MCGILL UNIVERSITY: LIBRARY.
*MONTREAL NO.1, 1969-*
*LD/U-1. LO/M24. OX/U-1.*

OSTERREICHISCHE CHEMISCHPUTZER-, WASCHER- UND
FARBER-ZEITSCHRIFT.                                                 XXX
*+ +OSTER. CHEMISCHPUTZER- WASCHER- & FARBER-Z.*
[INDUSTRIE UND FACHVERLAG]
*VIENNA 22, 1970-*
PREV: OSTERREICHISCHE FARBER-, WASCHER UND
CHEMISCHPUTZER-ZEITSCHRIFT.
*LO/N14.*
*ISSN 0029-9367*

OSTERREICHISCHE FARBER-, WASCHER- UND CHEMISCH-
PUTZER-ZEITSCHRIFT.                                                 XXX
SUBS (1970): OSTERREICHISCHE CHEMISCHPUTZER-,
WASCHER- UND FARBER-ZEITSCHRIFT.

OSTERREICHISCHE FOTO-ZEITUNG.                                       XXX
*+ +OSTERR. FOTO-ZTG.*
[ABZ-DRUCK- UND VERLAGSANSTALT HAMANN & SINEK]
*VIENNA 25(2), 1973-*
PREV: OSTERREICHISCHE PHOTO-ZEITUNG FROM
[1957]- 25(1), 1973.
*LO/N14.*

OSTERREICHISCHE HISTORISCHE BIBLIOGRAPHIE.                          000
SEE: AUSTRIAN HISTORICAL BIBLIOGRAPHY.

OSTERREICHISCHES JAHRBUCH FUR SOZIOLOGIE.
*+ +OSTERR. JAHRB. SOZIOL.*
OSTERREICHISCHE GESELLSCHAFT FUR SOZIOLOGIE.
[SPRINGER-VERLAG]
*VIENNA & NEW YORK NO.1, [1970]-*
*LO/N-1.*

OSTERREICHISCHE PHOTO-ZEITUNG.                                      XXX
SUBS (1973): OSTERREICHISCHE FOTO-ZEITUNG.

OSTERREICHISCHE ZEITSCHRIFT FUR POLITIKWISS-
ENSCHAFT.
*+ +OSTERR. Z. POLITIKWISS.*
OSTERREICHISCHE GESELLSCHAFT FUR POLITIKWISSEN-
SCHAFT.
*VIENNA 1972-*
Q.
*LO/U-3. OX/U-1.*
*GL/U-2. 2, 1973-*

O-T IRELAND.
ASSOCIATION OF OCCUPATIONAL THERAPISTS OF
IRELAND.
*DUBLIN 1, 1973-*
*DB/U-2.*

OT/ITS RESEARCH REPORT.                                             XXX
*+ +OT/ITS RES. REP.*
INSTITUTE FOR TELECOMMUNICATION SCIENCES.
*BOULDER, COLO. 1, 1970- 12, 1971 ...*
SUBS: TELECOMMUNICATIONS RESEARCH &
ENGINEERING REPORT.
*LO/N14.*

OTAGO LAW REVIEW.
*+ +OTAGO LAW REV.*
UNIVERSITY OF OTAGO: LAW STUDENTS ASSOCIATION.
*DUNEDIN, N.Z. 1(1), 1965-*
*OX/U15.*
*BL/U-1. 2, 1969-*

**OTAGO MUSEUM BULLETIN.**
+ +OTAGO MUS. BULL.
OTAGO MUSEUM.
 DUNEDIN, N.Z.  NO.1, 1967-
 LO/N-2.

**OTAZKY MEZINARODNI POLITIKY.**
+ +OTAZKY MEZINAROD. POLIT.
KOMUNISTICKA STRANA CESKOSLOVENSKA.
 PRAGUE  1, 1961-
 'VYDALO ODDELENI PROPOAGANDY A AGITACE UV
 (USTREDNI VYBOR) KSC.'
 LO/N-3.  1-2, 1961.

**OTAZKY MEZINARODNICH VZTAHU.**
+ +OTAZKY MEZINAROD. VZTAHU.
USTAV PRO MEZINARODNI POLITIKU A EKONOMII.
 PRAGUE  1, 1961-
 LO/N-3.*

**OTBOR I PEREDACHA INFORMATSII.**
+ +OTBOR & PEREDACHA INF. [OTPI-A]
AKADEMIJA NAUK UKRAJINS'KOJI RSR: FIZYKO-
MEKHANICHNYJ INSTYTUT.
 KIEV VYP.[1], 1965-
 VOL. NUMBERING STARTED WITH NO.15, 1968.
 BH/U-1.  15, 1968-  LO/N13.

**OTHER BOOKS.  ACCESS TO SMALL PRESS FOR
LIBRARIES.**
 BERKELEY, CALIF.  1, 1972-
 LO/U-2.

**OTTAWA LAW REVIEW.**
+ +OTTAWA LAW REV.
UNIVERSITY OF OTTAWA.
 OTTAWA  1, 1966-
 2/A.  ISSUED BY THE BODY'S  FACULTY OF LAW,
 COMMON LAW SECTION.
 BL/U-1.   LO/N-1.
 LO/U24.  1, 1966- 2(1), 1967.
 ISSN 0048-2331

**OTTAWA NEWSLETTER.**
+ +OTTAWA NEWSL.
(GREAT BRITAIN) DEPARTMENT OF EDUCATION &
SCIENCE: INTERNATIONAL SCIENTIFIC RELATIONS
DIVISION.
 LONDON  1, 1968-
 LO/N14.   XN/S-1.
 LO/U-3. [CURRENT ISSUES ONLY]
 OX/U16.  NO.10, MR 1972-

**OTTOBRE.  LAUSANNE, 1964**                                  000
  SEE: OCTOBRE.

**OUTCAST.**                                                 XXX
 [AMERICAN POET P.]
 SANTA FE NO.1, 1966- 15, 1969.//
 OX/U-1.  NO.4; 8, 1967-
 ISSN 0474-912X

**OUTCROP.  MAGAZINE OF THE ...**
UNIVERSITY OF GLASGOW: GEOLOGICAL SOCIETY.
 GLASGOW  1(1), 1967-
 GL/U-1.

**OUTDOORS.**
PHYSICAL EDUCATION ASSOCIATION OF GREAT
BRITAIN & NORTHERN IRELAND.
 LONDON  1, 1969-
 LV/U-2.
 SW/U-1.  3, 1972-

**OVERFLOW.  LITERATURE & ART.**
 [OVERFLOW PUBL.]
 ANN ARBOR  1, 1967-
 OX/U-1.
 ISSN 0030-7408

**OVERSEA & COMMONWEALTH STANDARDS.**             XXX
  SUBS (1969): LIST OF OVERSEA STANDARDS.

**OVERSEAS DEVELOPMENT.**
+ +OVERSEAS DEV.
(GREAT BRITAIN) MINISTRY OF OVERSEAS DEVELOP-
MENT.
 [HMSO]
 LONDON  NO.1, N 1966-
 LO/U-3.   LO/U-8.
 ISSN 0030-7440

**OVERSEAS REVIEW.**                                         XXX
  SUBS (1970):  INTERNATIONAL BRIEFING.

**OXFORD AGRARIAN STUDIES.**                                 XXX
+ +OXF. AGRAR. STUD.
UNIVERSITY OF OXFORD: INSTITUTE OF AGRICULTURAL
ECONOMICS.
 OXFORD  1, 1972-
 PREV: FARM ECONOMIST FROM 1, 1928- 12(4), 1971
 BH/U-1.   DB/U-2.    ED/N-1.    GL/U-1.    LO/N-6.    LO/U-3.
 LO/U12.    OX/U-3.    SH/U-1.

**OXFORD INSTRUMENTS NEWSLETTER.**
+ +OXF. INSTRUM. NEWSL.
[OXFORD INSTRUMENTS]
 OXFORD  NO.1, 1971-
 ED/N-1.   OX/U-8.
 LO/N14.  CURRENT BOX ONLY.

**OXFORD WORKING PAPERS IN PLANNING & RESEARCH.**
+ +OXF. WORK. PAP. PLANN. & RES.
OXFORD POLYTECHNIC: DEPARTMENT OF TOWN PLANNING
 OXFORD  NO.1, 1970-
 OX/U16.
 BL/U-1.  3, 1970-

**OXIDATION OF METALS.**
+ +OXIDAT. METALS.
[PLENUM PUBL. CORP.]
 NEW YORK  1, 1969-
 CA/U-2.   LO/N14.    OX/U-1.    XS/R10.    XY/N-1.
 GL/U-1.  1970-                       MA/U-1.  4(2), 1972-
 NW/U-1.  3, 1971-
 ISSN 0030-770X

**OYAMA KOGYO KOTO SENMON GAKKO KENKYU KIYO.
RESEARCH REPORTS, OYAMA TECHNICAL COLLEGE.**
OYAMA KOGYO KOTO SENMON GAKKO.
 OYAMA  NO.1, 1969-
 LO/N13.

**OZILA.  FORUM LITTERAIRE CAMEROUNAIS.**
 YAOUNDE  NO.1, F 1970
 FR. OR ENGL.
 LO/N-1.

**PACIFIC BIRD OBSERVER.**
+ +PAC. BIRD OBSERV.
SMITHSONIAN INSTITUTION.
 WASHINGTON, DC  NO.1, 1965-
 S/T: NEWSLETTER OF THE PACIFIC OCEAN BIOLO-
 GICAL SURVEY PROGRAM OF THE SMITHSONIAN
 INSTITUTION.  ISSUED BY THE INSTN.'S  DIVISION
 OF BIRDS.
 LO/N-2.    LO/N13.*

**PACIFIC COMMUNITY.  AN ASIAN QUARTERLY REVIEW.**
+ +PAC. COMMUNITY.
PACIFIC NEWS COMMONWEALTH.
 TOKYO  1(1), OC 1969- NO.9, WINTER 1971. //
 LO/N17.   LO/U-3.    NO/U-1.    OX/U-1.    SH/U-1.
 LO/S14.  NO.4, AUTUMN 1969-
 ISSN 0030-8633

**PACIFIC GEOLOGY.**
+ +PAC. GEOL. [PCEO-B]
[TSUKIJI SHOKAN]
 TOKYO  [NO.]1, 1968-
 A.
 LO/N-2.    LO/N13.    OX/U-8.
 SO/U-1.  2, 1970- 3, 1971.

**PACIFIC ISLANDS STUDIES & NOTES.**
+ +PAC. ISL. STUD. & NOTES.
[KRAUSS]
 HONOLULU  NO.1, 1971-
 ED/U-1.    GL/U-1.    LO/N-2.    LO/U-1.

**PACIFIC PERSPECTIVE.**
+ +PAC. PERSPECT.
SOUTH PACIFIC SOCIAL SCIENCES ASSOCIATION.
 SUVA  1(1), 1972-
 2/A.
 LO/U-8.    LO/U14.

**PACIFIC SEARCH.  JOURNAL OF NATURAL SCIENCE IN
THE PACIFIC NORTHWEST.**
+ +PAC. SEARCH. [PSJN-A]
[PACIFIC SEARCH INC.]
 SEATTLE  1, OC 1966-
 M.
 LO/N-2.
 ISSN 0030-8897

**PACIFIC VIEWPOINT MONOGRAPH.**
+ +PAC. VIEWPOINT MONOGR.
VICTORIA UNIVERSITY OF WELLINGTON.
 WELLINGTON, NZ  1, 1967-
 ISSUED BY THE BODY'S  DEP. OF GEOGRAPHY.
 SH/U-1.

PACKAGING BULLETIN.                                    XXX
+ +PACKAG. BULL.
UNIVERSITY OF CALIFORNIA: PACKAGING LIBRARY.
 DAVIS, CALIF  1, 1969- 5(1), 1973 ...
 SUBS: CURRENT PACKAGING ABSTRACTS.
 LO/N14.

PACKAGING JOURNAL. (RES. ASS. PAP. & BOARD,
PRINT. & PACKAG. IND.) (1968)                          000
 SEE: PIRA PACKAGING JOURNAL.

PACKAGING & PRINTING PROGRESS.
+ +PACKAG. & PRINT. PROG.
 INSTITUTE FOR INDUSTRIAL RESEARCH & STANDARDS
 (EIRE).
 DUBLIN  1, 1973-
 DB/U-2.     LO/N14.
 CA/U-1.  1(3), 1973-              ED/N-1.  1(3), 1973-
 OX/U-1.  2(1), 1973-

PACKUNG UND TRANSPORT IM CHEMIEBETRIEB.                XXX
+ +PACKUNG & TRANSP. CHEMIEBTR. [PTCB-A]
 [HANDELSBLATT GMBH]
 DUSSELDORF  1968(1)- 1971(11) ...
 SUBS: PACKUNG UND TRANSPORT IN DER CHEMISCHEN
 INDUSTRIE.
 LO/N14.
 ISSN 0030-9184

PACKUNG UND TRANSPORT IN DER CHEMISCHEN
INDUSTRIE.                                             XXX
+ +PACKUNG & TRANSP. CHEM. IND.
 [HANDELSBLATT GMBH]
 DUSSELDORF  1971(12)-
 PREV: PACKUNG UND TRANSPORT IM CHEMIEBETRIEB
 FROM 1968(1)- 1971(11).
 LO/N14.

PAEDIATRICIAN.
 INTERNATIONAL COLLEGE OF PEDIATRICS.
 [KARGER]
 BASLE &C.  1(1), 1972/73-
 2M.
 AD/M-1.    LO/N-1.    OX/U-8.

PAG BULLETIN.
+ +PAG BULL.
 UNITED NATIONS: PROTEIN ADVISORY GROUP.
 NEW YORK  NO.1, OC 1967-
 SPONS. BY FAO/WHO/UNICEF PROTEIN ADVISORY
 GROUP.
 CA/U-1.**     OX/U-8.
 CA/U11.  1(8), 1969-           DB/U-2.  3, 1973-
 LD/U-1.  3, 1973-              LO/N-6.  NO.9, 1970-
 ED/N-1.  NO.11, 1971-
 LO/N-3.  NO.11, 1971-*

PAGE.
 COMPUTER ARTS SOCIETY.
 BRACKNELL, BERKS.  1, 1969-
 OX/U-1.
 ISSN 0030-9362

PAGES. INTERNATIONAL MAGAZINE OF THE ARTS.
 [HRS GRAPHICS]
 LONDON  NO.1, 1970-
 LO/N15.    LO/U-2.
 ED/N-1.  3, 1972-
 ISSN 0030-9389

PAIDEUMA.
 NATIONAL POETRY FOUNDATION (US).
 ORONO, MAINE  1, 1972-
 S/T: A JOURNAL DEVOTED TO EZRA POUND SCHOLAR-
 SHIP.
 CA/U-1.    ED/N-1.    OX/U-1.

PAINT, OIL & COLOUR JOURNAL.                           XXX
 SUBS (1971): POLYMERS, PAINT & COLOUR JOURNAL.

PAINT TECHNOLOGY.                                      XXX
 SUBS (1972): PIGMENT & RESIN TECHNOLOGY.

PAINTING & DECORATING.                                 XXX
 SUBS (1969): PAINTING & DECORATING JOURNAL.

PAINTING & DECORATING JOURNAL.                         XXX
+ +PAINT. & DECOR. J.
 [SUTHERLAND PUBL. CO.]
 SOUTHPORT  89(1059), 1969- 92(1103), 1972 ...
 PREV: PAINTING & DECORATING FROM 74(885),
 1954- 89(1058), 1969.  SUBS: INTERNATIONAL
 PAINTING & DECORATING JOURNAL.
 LO/N14.

PAIR.
 [C. DAVIES]
 LLANDYBIE  1, 1972-
 ED/N-1.

PAKISTAN BULLETIN.                                     XXX
+ +PAK. BULL.
 (PAKISTAN) HIGH COMMISSION, LONDON.
 LONDON  25, 1973-
 PREV: PAKISTAN NEWS FROM 1, 1947- 24, 1972.
 ED/N-1.    LD/U-1.

PAKISTAN ECONOMIC SURVEY.
+ +PAK. ECON. SURV.
 (PAKISTAN) OFFICE OF THE ECONOMIC ADVISER.
 ISLAMABAD &C.  1961/62-
 LO/N-1.  1968/69-              NO/U-1.  1971/72-
 SO/U-1.  1964/65-
 ISSN 0078-8082

PAKISTAN FORUM.
+ +PAK. FORUM.
 [MONTREAL]  1(1), OC/N 1970-
 S/T: AN INDEPENDENT MAGAZINE OF PAKISTANIS IN
 U.S.A. & CANADA.
 LO/N-1.

PAKISTAN JOURNAL OF BIOCHEMISTRY.
+ +PAK. J. BIOCHEM.
 PAKISTAN SOCIETY OF BIOCHEMISTS.
 LAHORE  1, 1968-
 LO/U-2.

PAKISTAN JOURNAL OF FAMILY PLANNING.
+ +PAK. J. FAM. PLANN.
 NATIONAL RESEARCH INSTITUTE OF FAMILY PLANNING
 (PAKISTAN).
 KARACHI  1, JL 1967-
 LO/S74.

PAKISTAN JOURNAL OF ZOOLOGY.
+ +PAK. J. ZOOL.
 ZOOLOGICAL SOCIETY OF PAKISTAN.
 JAMSHORO  1, 1969-
 LO/N-2.    OX/U-8.
 ISSN 0030-9362

PAKISTAN LIBRARY BULLETIN. QUARTERLY JOURNAL
OF THE ...
+ +PAK. LIBR. BULL.
 (PAKISTAN) LIBRARY PROMOTION BUREAU.
 [UNIV. OF KARACHI]
 KARACHI  1(1), S 1968-
 LO/U14.    OX/U13.
 ISSN 0030-9966

PAKISTAN MEDICAL REVIEW.
+ +PAK. MED. REV.
 KARACHI  1, AP 1966-
 LO/M32.**
 ISSN 0031-0018

PAKISTAN NEWS.                                         XXX
 SUBS (1973): PAKISTAN BULLETIN.

PALAEOECOLOGY OF AFRICA, & OF THE SURROUNDING
ISLANDS & ANTARCTICA.
+ +PALAEOECOL. AFR. & SURROUND. ISLES. & ANTARCT.
 [A.A. BALKEMA]
 CAPE TOWN  1, 1950/63 (1966)-
 LO/N-2.    LO/N13.

PALAEONTOLOGY & STRATIGRAPHY OF THE BALTIC &
THE BYELORUSSIA.                                       000
 SEE: PALEONTOLOGIJA I STRATIGRAFIJA PRIBALTIKI
 I BELORUSSII.

PALAEOVERTEBRATA.
 LABORATOIRE DE PALEONTOLOGIE (MONTPELLIER).
 MONTPELLIER  1, JE 1967-
 Q.
 LO/N-2.
 ISSN 0031-0247

PALEONTOLOGIA.
 UNIVERSIDADE DO RECIFE: INSTITUTO DE GEOLOGIA.
 RECIFE  NO.1, 1962-
 LO/N-2.

**PALEONTOLOGICAL JOURNAL.**
*+ +PALEONTOL. J. [PJOU-A]*
AMERICAN GEOLOGICAL INSTITUTE.
*WASHINGTON, D.C. 1967-*
Q. ENGL. LANG. TRANSL. OF PALEONTOLOGICHES-
KIJ ZHURNAL. NUMBERING & DATING OF ISSUES
FOLLOW ORIGINAL. PRIOR TO NO.1, 1967, SELECT-
ED PAPERS ONLY OF PALEONTOLOGICHESKIJ ZHURNAL
WERE PUBL. IN INTERNATIONAL GEOLOGY REVIEW.
*BR/U-1.    LO/N13.*
*BL/U-1.  6, 1972-*                    *EX/U-1.  8, 1974-*

**PALEONTOLOGICHESKIJ ZHURNAL (ENGL. TRANSL.).**          000
**SEE: PALEONTOLOGICAL JOURNAL.**

**PALEONTOLOGIJA, GEOLOGIJA I POLEZNYE ISKOP-**
**AEMYE MOLDAVII.**
*+ +PALEONTOL. GEOL. & POLEZN. ISKOP. MOLD.*
*[PSPB-B]*
AKADEMIJA NAUK MOLDAVSKOJ SSR: INSTITUT
GEOLOGII I POLEZNYKH ISKOPAEMYKH.
*KISHINEV  1, 1967-*
*LO/N-2.*
*LO/N13.  4, 1968-*

**PALEONTOLOGIJA I STRATIGRAFIJA BSSR (MINSK).**          XXX
**SUBS (1966): PALEONTOLOGIJA I STRATIGRAFIJA**
**PRIBALTIKI I BELORUSSII.**

**PALEONTOLOGIJA I STRATIGRAFIJA PRIBALTIKI I**
**BELORUSSII.  PALAEONTOLOGY & STRATIGRAPHY OF**
**THE BALTIC & THE BYELORUSSIA.**                         XXX
*+ +PALEONTOL. & STRATIFR. PRIBALT. & BELORUSS.*
AKADEMIJA NAUK BELORUSSKOJ SSR: INSTITUT
GEOLOGICHESKIKH NAUK (MINSK).
*VILNIUS  1(6), 1966-*
ENGL. SUMM. & T/P. PREV: PALEONTOLOGIJA I
STRATIGRAFIJA BSSR. (MINSK) FROM 1955- 1966.
CONT. PREV. NUMBERING IN PARENTHESES. SPONS.
BODIES ALSO GEOLOGIJOS INSTITUTAS (VILNIUS): &
GEOLOGIJAS INSTITUTS (RIGA).
*LO/N-2.    LO/N13.*

**PALMS.**
PALM SOCIETY.
*MELBOURNE, FLA.  1, 1969-*
*LO/N-2.    XS/R-2.*

**PAMATNIKY NASI MINULOSTI.**
CESKOSLOVENSKA AKADEMIE VED: ARCHEOLOGICKY
USTAV.
*PRAGUE  1, 1964-*
MONOGR.
*CA/U-1.    OX/U-1.*

**PAMETNITSI NA STARATA BULGARSKA PISMENOST.**
BULGARSKA AKADEMIJA NA NAUKITE: INSTITUT ZA
LITERATURA.
*SOFIA  1, 1963-*
*OX/U-1.*

**PAMIR. LITERATURNO-KHUDOZHESTVENNYJ I OBSH-**
**CHESTVENNO-POLITICHESKIJ ZHURNAL.**
SOJUZ PISATELEJ TADZHIKISTANA.
*DUSHANBE  1, 1968-*
2M.
*LO/N-3.  1970(1)-*

**PAMJATNIKI LITERATURY NARODOV VOSTOKA: PEREV-**
**ODY.**                                                  XXX
*+ +PAMJATNIKI LIT. NAR. VOSTOKA, PEREVODY.*
AKADEMIJA NAUK SSSR: INSTITUT NARODOV AZII.
*MOSCOW  1960- 1964.*
SUBS: PAMJATNIKI PIS'MENNOSTI VOSTOKA. VOL.
1(1961), VOL.2(1960), VOL.3(1960) IS ALSO
VOL.31 OF 'BIBLIOTHECA BUDDICA'. 2 PARTS IN
VOL.4(1962-63), CALLED PARTS 3-4 (PARTS 1-2
NEVER PUBLISHED).
*LO/N-3.  VOL.4.*

**PAMJATNIKI PIS'MENNOSTI VOSTOKA.**                      XXX
AKADEMIJA NAUK SSSR: INSTITUT NARODOV AZII.
*MOSCOW  1, 1965-*
MONOGR. PREV: PAMJATNIKI LITERATURY NARODOV
VOSTOKA: PEREVODY FROM 1960- 1964.
*CA/U-1.    CC/U-1.    OX/U-1.*
*LO/N-3.  3,1967.*

**PAMJATNIKI TURKMENISTANA.**
*+ +PAMJAT. TURKMEN.*
TURKMENSKOE RESPUBLIKANSKOE DOBROVOL'NOE OB-
SHCHESTVO OKHRANY PAMJATNIKOV ISTORII I
KUL'TURY.
*ASHKHABAD   1, 1966-*
ENGL. SUMM.
*DB/S-1.    OX/U-1.    XY/N-1.*

**PAN-AFRICAN JOURNAL.**
*+ +PAN-AFR. J.*
PAN-AFRICAN INSTITUTE.
*NEW YORK  1(1), 1968-*
Q.
*LO/U-8.  1(2-3),1968-*                    *OX/U-9  2(1), 1969-*

**PAN-AFRICANIST.**
NORTHWESTERN UNIVERSITY: PROGRAM OF AFRICAN
STUDIES.
*EVANSTON  1, MR 1971-*
*AD/U-1.    LO/U14.*
*OX/U-9.  3, 1971-*

**PAN AMERICAN REVIEW.**
*+ +PAN AM. REV.*
[FUNCH P.]
*EDINBURGH, TEX.  1(1), 1970-*
2A.
*OX/U-1.*
*ISSN 0031-059X*

**PANDEX CURRENT INDEX TO SCIENTIFIC & TECH-**
**NICAL LITERATURE.**
*+ +PANDEX CURR. INDEX SCI. TECH. LIT.*
CCM INFORMATION SCIENCES INC.
*NEW YORK  1(1), JA 1969-*
2W.
*OX/U-8.*
*ISSN 0031-0700*

**PANJAB UNIVERSITY JOURNAL OF MATHEMATICS.**
*+ +PANJAB UNIV. J. MATH.*
UNIVERSITY OF THE PANJAB: DEPARTMENT OF MATH-
EMATICS.
*LAHORE  1, 1967-*
VOL.1- 2 ALSO NUMBERED NO.1- 2.
*LO/N14.*

**PAPER, ARCHAEOLOGICAL SURVEY OF CANADA, NAT-**
**IONAL MUSEUM OF MAN (CANADA): MERCURY SERIES.**
*+ +PAP. ARCHAEOL. SURV. CAN. NATL. MUS. MAN*
*(CAN.), MERCURY SER.*
*OTTAWA  1, 1972-*
*BL/U-1.    DB/S-1.*
*SO/U-1.  NO.1- 2, JL 1972.*

**PAPER, ARCHITECTURAL ASSOCIATION.**
*+ +PAP. ARCHIT. ASSOC.*
*LONDON  NO.1, 1965-*
*LO/N14.\*\**

**PAPERS, BIBLIOGRAPHICAL SOCIETY OF CANADA.**            XXX
*+ +PAP. BIBLIOGR. SOC. CAN.*
*TORONTO  1, 1962-*
PREV: NEWSLETTER, BIBLIOGRAPHICAL SOCIETY OF
CANADA FROM N.S.1, 1955- 5, JE 1962.
*ED/N-1.*
*ISSN 0067-6896*

**PAPER & BOARD ABSTRACTS. (RES. ASS. PAP. &**
**BOARD, PRINT. & PACKAG. IND.)**                          000
**SEE: PIRA PAPER & BOARD ABSTRACTS.**

**PAPER & BOARD JOURNAL. (RES. ASS. PAP. &**
**BOARD, PRINT. & PACKAG. IND.)**                          000
**SEE: PIRA PAPER & BOARD JOURNAL.**

**PAPERS, BOROUGH OF TWICKENHAM LOCAL HISTORY**
**SOCIETY.**
*+ +PAP. BOROUGH TWICKENHAM LOCAL HIST. SOC.*
*TWICKENHAM  1, 1964-*
*LO/P-6.*

**PAPERS, CANADIAN CENTRE FOR FOLK CULTURE**
**STUDIES, NATIONAL MUSEUM OF MAN (CANADA):**
**MERCURY SERIES.**
*+ +PAP. CAN. CENT. FOLK CULT. STUD. NATL. MUS.*
*MAN (CAN.), MERCURY SER.*
*OTTAWA  NO.1, JL 1972-*
*CA/U-1.    DB/S-1.    SO/U-1.*

**PAPERS, DEPARTMENT OF GEOGRAPHY, UNIVERSITY**
**OF QUEENSLAND.**                                        XXX
*+ +PAP. DEP. GEOGR. UNIV. QUEENSL.*
*BRISBANE  1(1), 1960- 1(2), 1961.//*
*LO/U-1.*

**PAPER DISPOSABLES INTERNATIONAL.**                      XXX
*+ +PAP. DISPOSABLES INT.*
*LONDON  NO.1, 1969- 2, 1970 ...*
SUBS: DISPOSABLES INTERNATIONAL.
*ED/N-1.*
*LO/N14.  CURRENT BOX ONLY.*

**PAPERS IN EDUCATION.**
++PAP. EDUC.
ANSTEY COLLEGE OF PHYSICAL EDUCATION.
SUTTON COLDFIELD NO.1, 1969-
BH/U-1.

**PAPERS, ETHNOLOGY DIVISION, NATIONAL MUSEUM OF MAN (CANADA): MERCURY SERIES.**
++PAP. ETHNOL. DIV. NATL. MUS. MAN (CAN.), MERCURY SER.
OTTAWA 1, 1972-
BL/U-1.  CA/U-1.  CA/U-2.  DB/S-1.

**PAPERS ON FAR EASTERN HISTORY.**
++PAP. FAR EAST. HIST.
AUSTRALIAN NATIONAL UNIVERSITY: DEPARTMENT OF FAR EASTERN HISTORY.
CANBERRA 1, 1970-
BL/U-1.  LD/U-1.  OX/U-1.
SH/U-1. 5, 1972-

**PAPERS IN GEOGRAPHY, DEPARTMENT OF GEOGRAPHY, PENNSYLVANIA STATE UNIVERSITY.**
++PAP. GEOGR. DEP. GEOGR. PA. STA. UNIV.
UNIVERSITY PARK, PA. NO.1, JE 1969-
MONOGR.
LO/S13.
MA/U-1. NO.3, 1969-

**PAPERS, HISTORICAL ASSOCIATION OF TANZANIA.**
++PAP. HIST. ASS. TANZANIA.
DAR ES SALAAM NO.1, 1966-
OX/U-9.

**PAPERS, HISTORY DIVISION, NATIONAL MUSEUM OF MAN (CANADA): MERCURY SERIES.**
++PAP. HIST. DIV. NATL. MUS. MAN (CAN.), MERCURY SER.
OTTAWA 1, 1972-
BL/U-1.  DB/S-1.  LO/N-1.
SO/U-1. NO.1, 1972.

**PAPERS OF THE INSTITUTE OF JEWISH STUDIES LONDON.**
++PAP. INST. JEWISH STUD. LOND.
INSTITUTE OF JEWISH STUDIES (LONDON).
[MAGNES PRESS]
JERUSALEM 1, 1964-
LO/U-2.  LO/U14.  MA/U-1.

**PAPER, INSTITUTE OF PSYCHOLOGY (DUBLIN).**
++PAP. INST. PSYCHOL. (DUBLIN).
DUBLIN NO.1, MR 1971-
DB/U-2.  LO/N-1.

**PAPERS ON LANGUAGE & LITERATURE.**
++PAP. LANG. & LIT.
SOUTHERN ILLINOIS UNIVERSITY.
EDWARDSVILLE, ILL. 1, 1965-
Q. S/T: JOURNAL FOR SCHOLARS & CRITICS OF LANGUAGE & LITERATURE.
AD/U-1. 3(4), 1967-          BL/U-1. 6, 1970-
MA/U-1. 8, 1972-
ISSN 0031-1294

**PAPERS IN LINGUISTICS.**
++PAP. LINGUIST.
FLORIDA STATE UNIVERSITY: DEPARTMENT OF ENGLISH
TALLAHASSEE 1, JL 1969-
BN/U-1.  HL/U-1.
YK/U-1. 2, 1970-
ISSN 0555-9073

**PAPERS IN LINGUISTICS: MONOGRAPH SERIES.**
++PAP. LINGUIST., MONOGR. SER.
[LINGUISTIC RESEARCH, INC.]
CHAMPAIGN, ILL. [NO.]1, 1970-
BN/U-1.
LO/U-1. 3, 1972-          SH/U-1. 6, 1973-

**PAPERS, MARINE SCIENCES BRANCH, DEPARTMENT OF ENERGY, MINES & RESOURCES (CANADA).**          XXX
++PAP. MAR. SCI. BRA. DEP. ENERGY MINES & RESOUR. (CAN.).
OTTAWA [NO.]1, 1970 ...
SUBS: MARINE SCIENCE PAPERS, MARINE SCIENCES BRANCH, DEPT. OF THE ENVIRONMENT (CANADA).
LO/N-2.  LO/N14.  OX/U-8.

**PAPERS OF THE MICHIGAN ACADEMY OF SCIENCE, ARTS & LETTERS.**          XXX
SUBS (1969): MICHIGAN ACADEMICIAN.

**PAPERS ON MIGRATION & MOBILITY IN NORTHERN ENGLAND.**
++PAP. MIGR. & MOBILITY NORTH. ENGL.
UNIVERSITY OF NEWCASTLE UPON TYNE: DEPARTMENT OF GEOGRAPHY.
NEWCASTLE UPON TYNE NO.1, 1965-
MONOGR. NOS. 1-2 ENTITLED PAPERS ... IN NORTH EAST ENGLAND.
BH/U-1.*  HL/U-1.
DB/U-2. NO.4, 1967-

**PAPERS FOR STUDENTS, CONCHOLOGICAL SOCIETY OF GREAT BRITAIN & IRELAND.**
++PAP. STUD. CONCHOL. SOC. G.B. & IREL.
MANCHESTER NO.1, 1965-
LO/N-2.  LO/N13.

**PAPER TRAINING NEWS.**
++PAP. TRAIN. NEWS.
PAPER & PAPER PRODUCTS INDUSTRY TRAINING BOARD.
POTTERS BAR NO.1, SUMMER 1969-
ED/N-1.  LO/N-1.

**PAPER, WALTON & WEYBRIDGE HISTORICAL SOCIETY.**
++PAP. WALTON & WEYBRIDGE HIST. SOC.
WEYBRIDGE NO.1, 1966-
OX/U-1.

**PARAGUAY TODAY.**
++PARAG. TODAY.
[DIPLOMATIST PUBL. LTD.]
LONDON NO.1, [1965]-
Q.
OX/U-1.
ISSN 0031-1693

**PARAMOUDRA CLUB BULLETIN.**          XXX
SUBS (1968): BULLETIN, GEOLOGICAL SOCIETY OF NORFOLK.

**PARAPSYCHOLOGY BULLETIN.**          XXX
++PARAPSYCHOL. BULL.
FOUNDATION FOR RESEARCH ON THE NATURE OF MAN.
DURHAM, N.C. NO.15, 1970-
PREV: FRNM FROM NO.1, 1965- 14, 1969.
GL/U-1.  LO/U-1.
ISSN 0031-1790

**PARAZITOLOGICHESKIJ SBORNIK.**
++PARAZITOL. SB. (AKAD. NAUK GRUZ. SSR).
[PSAN-A]
AKADEMIJA NAUK GRUZINSKOJ SSR: INSTITUT ZOO-LOGII.
TBILISI [NO.]1, 1966-
IN GEORG. & RUSS.
LO/N-2.

**PARAZITOLOGIJA.**
AKADEMIJA NAUK SSSR.
LENINGRAD TOM 1, 1967-
2M.
LO/M-3.  LO/N-2.  LO/N13.  LO/R-2.

**PARAZITY ZHIVOTNYKH I RASTENIJ.**
++PARAZITY ZHIVOTN. & RAST.
AKADEMIJA NAUK MOLDAVSKOJ SSR: INSTITUT ZOOLOGII.
KISHINEV VYP.1, 1965-
LO/N-2. [W. 2, 3]  LO/N13.

**PARENT EDUCATOR.**          XXX
++PARENT EDUC.
BRITISH PARENT EDUCATION INFORMATION CIRCLE.
HALIFAX NO.13, MR 1973-
PREV: QUARTERLY JOURNAL OF THE BRITISH PARENT EDUCATION INFORMATION CIRCLE FROM NO.1, MR 1970- NO.12, D 1972.
LD/U-1.

**PARENTS REVIEW.**          XXX
SUBS (1966): PNEU.

**PARERGA.**
UNIVERSITY OF WASHINGTON: FAR EASTERN & RUSSIAN INSTITUTE.
SEATTLE NO.1, 1968-
LO/U14.

**PARERGON. BULLETIN OF THE AUSTRALIAN & NEW ZEALAND ASSOCIATION FOR MEDIEVAL & RENAIS-SANCE STUDIES.**          XXX
[CANBERRA] NO.1, D 1971-
PREV: BULLETIN, AUSTRALIAN ... FROM NO.1, 1968- 7, AG 1971.
LO/U19.  OX/U-1.
CA/U-1. NO.5, 1973-

**PARIS MAGAZINE.**
++PARIS MAG.
 PARIS   NO.1, OC 1967-
 Q.
 LO/U-2.

**PARK.**
 [FERRY PRESS]
 LONDON  NO.1, 1968-
 PREV. WIVENHOE PARK REVIEW FROM NO.1,
 WINTER 1965- 2, 1967. PREV. TITLE AND NUMBE-
 RING (FROM NO.3) ALSO SHOWN ON ABOVE.
 LO/U-2.
 OX/U-1.  NO.4/5, 1969-
 ISSN 0031-210X

**PARK ADMINISTRATION, HORTICULTURE & RECREAT-**          XXX
**ION.**
 SUBS (1969): PARKS & RECREATION.

**PARKINSON'S DISEASE & RELATED DISORDERS,**
**CITATIONS FROM THE LITERATURE.**
++PARKINSON'S DIS. & RELAT. DISORD., CITAT. LIT.
 NATIONAL INSTITUTE OF NEUROLOGICAL DISEASES &
 STROKE (US).
 BETHESDA, MD.  1(1), 1970-
 M.  SUPERSEDES IN PART A BIWEEKLY PUBLN. WITH
 THE SAME TITLE.  PUBL. BY THE PARKINSON
 INFORMATION CENTER FROM NO.1, 1963/64- NO.6,
 1970.
 BL/U-1.   OX/U-8.

**PARKS & RECREATION. OFFICIAL JOURNAL OF ...**
++PARKS & RECREAT.
 INSTITUTE OF PARKS & RECREATION ADMINISTRATION.
 LONDON  34(8), AG 1969-
 PREV: PARK ADMINISTRATION, HORTICULTURE &
 RECREATION FROM 1, 1936.
 LO/N13.   RE/U-1.   XS/R-2.
 ED/N-1.  37, 1972-            GL/U-2.  39, 1974-
 ISSN 0031-2223

**PARLIAMENT & SOCIAL WORK.**
++PARLIAMENT & SOC. WORK.
 BRITISH ASSOCIATION OF SOCIAL WORKERS.
 LONDON  1(1), 1970-
 WKLY. DURING PARLIAMENTARY SESSIONS.
 SW/U-1.
 ED/N-1.  2(7), 1971-          LO/U-3.* 1(4), 1970-
 NW/U-1.  1(16),1971-
 LO/U28.  CURRENT YEAR ONLY.
 NO/U-1.  1970- 1971.

**PARNASSUS.  POETRY IN REVIEW.**
 NEW YORK  1, 1972-
 LO/U-2.   OX/U-1.
 ISSN 0048-3028

**PARODONTOLOGIE & ACADEMY REVIEW.**
++PARODONTOL. & ACAD. REV.
 CALIFORNIA ACADEMY OF PERIODONTOLOGY.
 [ARPA INTERNATIONALE]
 ZURICH  1, MR 1967-
 Q.  PREV: PARODONTOLOGIE FROM 1, 1947- 20,
 1966; & ACADEMY REVIEW (CALIF.) FROM 1, 1953-
 14(2), 1966.
 LO/N13.

**PAROLE E METODI.**
 ISTITUTO DELL'ATLANTE LINGUISTICO ITALIANO.
 TURIN  [NO.]1, 1971-
 S/T: BOLLETTINO DELL'ATLANTE LINGUISTICO
 ITALIANO.
 MA/U-1.

**PAROLE DE L'ORIENT.**                                        XXX
 UNIVERSITE SAINT-ESPRIT.
 KASLIK  1, 1970-
 INCORP: MELTO FROM 1(1), 1965- 5(2), 1969; &
 ORIENT SYRIEN FROM 1, 1956- 12, 1967.
 LD/U-1.   LO/U14.   MA/U-1.
 OX/U-1.  2(1), 1971-

**PARTICLE ACCELERATORS.**
++PARTICLE ACCEL.
 [GORDON & BREACH]
 NEW YORK  1(1), MR 1970-
 ED/N-1.   LO/N-4.   LO/N14.   XS/R10.
 ISSN 0031-2460

**PARTICLE ANALYST.**
++PARTIC. ANAL.
 [ANN ARBOR SCIENCE PUBLISHERS INC.]
 ANN ARBOR  1, 5/JA 1968-
 2/M.
 LO/N14.

**PARTICLE SIZE ANALYSIS BIBLIOGRAPHY.**
++PART. SIZE ANAL. BIBLIOGR.
 POWDER ADVISORY CENTRE.
 NEWCASTLE-UPON-TYNE  NO.1, 1968/70 (1970)-
 LO/N-4.   LO/N14.

**PARTICLE TECHNOLOGY RESEARCH REVIEW.**
++PART. TECHNOL. RES. REV.
 POWDER ADVISORY CENTRE.
 LONDON  1, 1973-
 LO/N14.

**PARTICLES & NUCLEI.**                                         XXX
++PART. & NUCL.
 F.U. RESEARCH INSTITUTE INC.
 ATHENS, OHIO  1(1), OC 1970- 2, 1971 ...
 SUBS: SOVIET JOURNAL OF PARTICLES & NUCLEI.
 LO/N14.   LO/U12.
 ISSN 0031-2479

**PARTICULATE MATTER.**
++PARTICUL. MATTER.
 POWDER ADVISORY CENTRE.
 NEWCASTLE UPON TYNE  1, 1970-
 ED/N-1.   LO/N14.   OX/U-8.   XS/R10.
 ISSN 0031-2487

**PARTIJNO-POLITICHESKAJA RABOTA V SOVETSKOJ ARMII**
**I VOENNO-MORSKOM FLOTE.**                                     XXX
 SUBS (1960): PART KOMMUNIST VOORUZHENNYKH SIL.

**PASC JOURNAL.**                                               XXX
++PASC J.
 PAKISTAN ADMINISTRATIVE STAFF COLLEGE.
 LAHORE  1(1), 1963- 2, 1964 ...
 SUBS: QUARTERLY, PAKISTAN ...
 LO/N17.
 DB/U-2.  6, 1973-

**PATENT ABSTRACTS, RES. ASS. PAP. & BOARD, PRINT.**
**& PACKAG. IND.   (1969)**                                     000
 SEE: PIRA PATENT ABSTRACTS.

**PATENT LAW REVIEW.**
++PAT. LAW REV.
 [SAGE HILL PUBL.]
 ALBANY, N.Y.  1, 1969-
 MA/U-1.
 CA/U-1.  1973-

**PATENT LICENSING GAZETTE.**                                   XXX
++PAT. LICENS. GAZ.
 TECHNI RESEARCH ASSOCIATES.
 WILLOW GROVE, PA.  1, 1968- 7, 1974 ...
 SUBS: WORLD TECHNOLOGY.
 LO/N14.
 ISSN 0031-2878

**PATENT REVIEW ON SOAPS, DETERGENTS & EMUL-**
**SIFIERS (+) MCCUTCHEON'S ...**

**PATHOBIOLOGY ANNUAL.**
++PATHOBIOL. ANNU.
 [APPLETON-CENTURY-CROFTS]
 NEW YORK; LONDON  1, 1971-
 OX/U-8.

**PATHOLOGIE BIOLOGIE.**                                        XXX
++PATHOL. BIOL.
 [LA SEMAINE DES HOPITAUX]
 PARIS  17, 1969-
 PREV: PATHOLOGIE ET BIOLOGIE FROM 1, 1953- 16,
 1968.
 LD/U-1.
 ISSN 0031-3009

**PATHOLOGY.  JOURNAL OF THE ...**
 COLLEGE OF PATHOLOGISTS OF AUSTRALIA.
 [SYDNEY U.P.]
 SYDNEY  1, 1969-
 AD/U-1.   LO/M30.   LO/M32.   LO/N13.   NW/U-1.
 OX/U-8.   XY/N-1.
 ISSN 0031-3025

**PATHOLOGY CIRCULAR, DIVISION OF PLANT IND-**
**USTRY, DEPARTMENT OF AGRICULTURE (FLORIDA).**
++PATHOL. CIRC. DIV. PLANT IND. DEP. AGRIC.
 (FLA.).
 GAINESVILLE  NO.1, 1962-
 LO/N-2.

PATTERN RECOGNITION.  JOURNAL OF THE ...
+ +PATTERN RECOG.
PATTERN RECOGNITION SOCIETY.
[PERGAMON]
OXFORD &C   1, JL 1968-
ED/N-1.    GL/U-2.    LO/N14.
BH/U-1.  2, 1970-
ISSN 0031-3203

PAUSE.
MONMOUTH  1, 1969-
LO/U-2.

PCB.  PLASTICS PACKAGING PAPER CONVERTERS
BULLETIN.
[DELLFIELD PUBLS. LTD.]
LONDON   1, 1968-
VOL.1 PRECEDED BY 'INTRODUCTORY ISSUE'.
ED/N-1.    LO/N14.

PD NEWS.
POWELL DUFFRYN LTD.
LONDON  NO.1, 1967-
OX/U-1.

PEACE RESEARCH.
+ +PEACE RES.
CANADIAN PEACE RESEARCH INSTITUTE.
OAKVILLE, ONT.  1(1), N 1969-
S/T: A MONTHLY JOURNAL OF ORIGINAL RESEARCH
ON THE PROBLEM OF WAR.
BL/U-1.    LO/N-1.
ISSN 0008-4697

PEACE RESEARCH MONOGRAPHS.
+ +PEACE RES. MONOGR.
INTERNATIONAL PEACE RESEARCH INSTITUTE.
OSLO  NO.1, 1967-
LO/N-1.
ISSN 0553-4275

PEACE RESEARCH REVIEWS.
+ +PEACE RES. REV.
CANADIAN PEACE RESEARCH INSTITUTE.
CLARKSON, ONTARIO  1(1), F 1967-
LO/U-3.

PEDESTRIAN.                                                    XXX
SUBS (1970):  ARRIVE.

PEDIATRIC RADIOLOGY.
+ +PEDIATR. RADIOL.
[SPRINGER]
BERLIN &C.  1, 1973-
Q.
AD/U-1.    BL/U-1.    SH/U-1.

PEGASUS.
UNIVERSITY OF EXETER: DEPARTMENT OF CLASSICS.
EXETER [NO.1], 1964-
OX/U-1.    OX/U-2.*

PELARGONIUM NEWS.                                              XXX
BRITISH PELARGONIUM & GERANIUM SOCIETY.
BECKENHAM, KENT  16(2), 1967-
PREV: BULLETIN, BRITISH PELARGONIUM AND
GERANIUM SOCIETY FROM 14(2), 1965 - 16(1),
1967.
LO/N13.

PELICAN.
UNIVERSITY OF OXFORD: CORPUS CHRISTI COLLEGE.
OXFORD  1(1), 1969-
INCORP: PELICAN RECORD.
LO/N-1.    OX/U-1.

PELICAN RECORD.                                               XXX
SUBS (1969):  PART OF PELICAN.

PENDIK VETERINER KONTROL VE ARASTIRMA ENSTI-
TUSU DERGI.
+ +PENDIK VET. KONTR. ARASTIRMA ENST. DERG.
ISTANBUL  1, 1967-
LO/N13.

PENNINE POETS - POETRY SHEET.
[HALIFAX?]  NO.1, [1967]-
LO/U-2.

PENSAMIENTO CRITICO.
+ +PENSAMIENTO CRIT.
CENTRO DE ESTUDIOS LATINOAMERICANO (HAVANA).
HAVANA  NO.1, F 1967-
MON.
OX/U-1.  NO.5, 1967-
LO/U-3.  NO.6, 1967- [W. NO.15 & 16].
LV/U-1.  NO.7 & 9, 1967-
ISSN 0553-6146

PENSAMIENTO POLITICO.
+ +PENSAMIENTO POLIT.
MEXICO, D.F.  1(1), 1969-
OX/U-1.
ISSN 0031-4757

PENSIERO E LINGUAGGIO IN OPERAZIONI.  THOUGHT
& LANGUAGE IN OPERATIONS.
+ +PENSIERO & LINGUAGGIO OP.
UNIVERSITA DI MILANO: CENTRO DI CIBERNETICA E
DI ATTIVITA LINGUISTICHE.
MILAN  1, 1970-
Q.
LO/N-1.    LO/U-3.

PENSIERO POLITICO.
+ +PENSIERO POLIT.
FLORENCE   1, 1968-
3/A.  S/T: RIVISTA DI STORIA DELLE IDEE
POLITICHE E SOCIALI.
LO/U-3.    OX/U-1.
ISSN 0031-4846

PENTACOL. CHEMICAL JOURNAL OF THE UNIVERSITY
OF WALES.                                                     XXX
ABERYSTWYTH  9, 1970-
PREV: TETRACOL FROM 1, 1962- 8, 1969.
LO/N14.

PEQUENO UNIVERSO.
UNIVERSIDAD AUTONOMA DE SANTO DOMINGO: FACULTAD
DE HUMANIDADES.
SANTO DOMINGO  1, 1971-
OX/U-1.

PERCEPTION.
[PION LTD.]
LONDON  1, 1972-
Q.
AD/U-1.    BN/U-1.    CA/M-3.    CA/U-1.    ED/N-1.    GL/U-1.
LD/U-1.    LO/U-4.    SH/U-1.
ISSN 0301-0066

PERFORMANCE DATA FOR NEW PASSENGER CARS &
MOTORCYCLES.
+ +PERFORM. DATA NEW PASSENG. CARS & MOTORCYCLES.
NATIONAL HIGHWAY SAFETY BUREAU (US).
WASHINGTON, D.C.  1, JA 1970-
LO/N14.

PERFORMING ARTS IN CANADA.
+ +PERFORM. ARTS CAN.
[CANADIAN STAGE & ARTS PUBL.]
TORONTO  1961-
IRREG. VOL. NUMBERING.
ED/N-1.  8, 1971-
ISSN 0031-5230

PERFUMERY & ESSENTIAL OIL RECORD.                             XXX
SUBS (1970):  FLAVOUR INDUSTRY.

PERGAMON BOOK NEWS.
[PERGAMON PRESS]
OXFORD   1, AUTUMN/WINTER 1967-
ED/N-1.    OX/U-1.

PERIODICA MATHEMATICA HUNGARICA.
+ +PERIOD. MATH. HUNG.
JANOS BOLYAI MATHEMATICAL SOCIETY.
[AKADEMIAI KIADO]
BUDAPEST  1(1), 1971-
Q.  ENGL., GER. & FR.
CA/U-2.    LO/N13.    LO/U13.    OX/U-8.    SH/U-1.
SW/U-1.    XY/N-1.
GL/U-2.  2, 1972-
ISSN 0031-5303

PERIODICAL LITERATURE SURVEY IN THE FIELDS OF
GEOGRAPHY, GEOMORPHOLOGY & GEOLOGY: INTERIM
REPORT.
+ +PER. LIT. SURV. FIELDS GEOGR. GEOMORPHOL. &
GEOL., INTERIM REP.
UNIVERSITY OF EAST ANGLIA.
NORWICH [NO.]1, 1968-
GL/U-1.

PERIODICAL NEWS FROM THE NATIONAL REFERENCE
LIBRARY OF SCIENCE & INVENTION.                               XXX
+ +PERIOD. NEWS NAT. REF. LIBR. SCI. & INVENT.
LONDON  1970(1)- 1973(6) ...
SUBS: PERIODICALS NEWS FROM THE SCIENCE
REFERENCE LIBRARY.
CV/C-1.    ED/N-1.    GL/U-1.    LO/U13.*    NW/U-1.
SH/P-1.    SH/U-1.    XS/R-2.
LO/U-1. [CURRENT YEAR ONLY]
SO/U-1. [CURRENT YEAR ONLY]

**PERIODICALS NEWS FROM THE SCIENCE REFERENCE
LIBRARY.**                                                                         XXX
*+ +PERIOD. NEWS SCI. REF. LIB.*
*LONDON   1973(7)-*
SCIENCE REFERENCE LIBRARY SUBORD. TO
REFERENCE DIVISION, BRITISH LIBRARY. PREV.
PERIODICAL NEWS FROM THE NATIONAL REFERENCE
LIBRARY OF SCIENCE & INVENTION FROM 1970(1)-
1973(6).
*SH/P-1.*
*OX/U-8.   1973(8)-*

**PERIPATOI.  PHILOLOGISCH-HISTORISCHE STUDIEN ZUM
ARISTOTELISMUS.**
[WALTER DE GRUYTER & CO.]
*BERLIN   1, 1971-*
*LO/N-1.*

**PERISCOPIO.**
[EDITORIAL PRIMERA PLANA]
*BUENOS AIRES   1, S 1969-*
*CC/U-1.*
*ISSN 0555-9693*

**PERIVALE NEWSLETTER.**                                                            XXX
*+ +PERIVALE NEWSL.*
SELBORNE SOCIETY.
*LONDON   NO.7, N 1972-*
PREV: NEWSLETTER, SELBORNE SOCIETY FROM NO.1,
1970- 6, MY 1972.
*LO/R-5.*

**PERKIN-ELMER NMR QUARTERLY.**
*+ +PERKIN-ELMER NMR Q.*
*BEACONSFIELD, BUCKS.   NO.1, 1971-*
*CA/U-1.     ED/N-1.     LO/N14.*

**PERPUSTAKAAN.**                                                                   XXX
LIBRARY ASSOCIATION OF MALAYSIA.
*SINGAPORE   1(1), OC 1966-*
2/A.  PREV: PERPUSTAKAAN MALAYSIA. SPONS. BODY
ALSO LIBRARY ASSOCIATION OF SINGAPORE.
*HL/U-1.     LO/N17.*
*GL/U-2.  2, 1967-*
*ISSN 0031-5559*

**PERPUSTAKAAN MALAYSIA.**                                                          XXX
*+ +PERPUSTAKAAN MALAYS.*
LIBRARY ASSOCIATION OF MALAYSIA.
*SINGAPORE   1, 1965-1966.*
NATIVE NAME OF BODY: PERSATUAN PERPUSTAKAAN
MALAYSIA. PREV. MALAYAN LIBRARY JOURNAL; &
SINGAPORE LIBRARY JOURNAL. SUBS: PERPUSTAKAAN.
*ED/N-1.     LO/U-2.*
*HL/U-1.1,1965.*

**PERSONALITY. AN INTERNATIONAL JOURNAL.**
SOCIETY FOR PERSONALITY RESEARCH.
[PLENUM P.]
*NEW YORK   1(1), 1970-*
Q.
*LO/U-1.*
*SH/C-5.  1(2), 1970-*
*SH/U-1.  1, 1970- 2, 1971.*
*ISSN 0031-563X*

**PERSONNEL ADMINISTRATION.**                                                       XXX
**SUBS (1972): PERSONNEL ADMINISTRATION &
PUBLIC PERSONNEL REVIEW.**

**PERSONNEL ADMINISTRATION & PUBLIC PERSONNEL
REVIEW.**                                                                           XXX
*+ +PERS. ADM. & PUBLIC PERS. REV.*
INTERNATIONAL PERSONNEL MANAGEMENT ASSOCIAT-
ION.                                                                                XXX
*CHICAGO   1(1), JL/AG 1972-*
6/A.  INCORP: PERSONNEL ADMINISTRATION FROM 1,
S 1938- 35(3), JE 1972; & PUBLIC PERSONNEL
REVIEW FROM 1, AP 1940- 33(2), AP 1972.
*LO/U-3.*

**PERSONNEL MANAGEMENT (1969).**                                                    XXX
*+ +PERS. MANAGE. (1969).*
INSTITUTE OF PERSONNEL MANAGEMENT.
[BUSINESS PUBLS.]
*LONDON   1(1), MY 1969-*
PREV: PART OF: PERSONNEL. JOURNAL OF THE
INST. ... FROM 1(1), D 1967-2(4), AP 1969; &
PERSONNEL & TRAINING MANAGEMENT FROM 1967-
1969. ALSO ENTITLED PERSONNEL MANAGEMENT FROM
1952- 49(381), 1967.
*DB/U-2.     ED/N-1.     GL/U-2.    LO/N-2.    LO/N17.    LO/U-3.*
*LO/U20.     OX/U-1.     XS/R10.*
*ISSN 0031-5761*

**PERSONNEL REVIEW.**
*+ +PERS. REV.*
INSTITUTE OF PERSONNEL MANAGEMENT.
[GOWER P.]
*LONDON   1(1), 1971-*
*CA/U-1.     CR/U-1.     ED/N-1.     MA/P-1.     OX/U-1.     OX/U16.*
*XS/R10.*
*LO/N35.  1(2), 1972-*          *LO/U-3.  4, 1975-*
*ISSN 0048-3486*

**PERSONNEL & TRAINING MANAGEMENT.**                                                XXX
**SUBS (1969) PART OF: PERSONNEL MANAGEMENT.**

**PERSPECTIVA SOCIAL.**
*+ +PERSPECT. SOC.*
INSTITUTO CATOLICO DE ESTUDIOS SOCIALES DE
BARCELONA.
*BARCELONA   1, 1973-*
*LO/N-1.     OX/U-1.*

**PERSPECTIVE.**
*KARACHI   1, JL 1967-*
M.
*ED/N-1.     LO/U14.     OX/U13.*

**PERSPECTIVE (N.Z.).**
NEW ZEALAND GEOGRAPHICAL SOCIETY.
*CHRISTCHURCH   NO.1, 1965-*
Q.
*LO/U-8.  NO.2, 1965-*
*ISSN 0553-738X*

**PERSPECTIVE.  QUARTERLY REVIEW OF PROGRESS IN
PHOTOGRAPHY, CINEMATOGRAPHY, SOUND & IMAGE
RECORDING.**                                                                        XXX
*[PERS-A]*
[FOCAL P]
*LONDON   1, 1959- 8, 1966.//*
PREV: PROGRESS IN PHOTOGRAPHY FROM 1940/50
(1951)- 1955/58(1958).
*BH/P-1.     ED/N-1.     LO/N14.*
*ISSN 0553-7363*

**PERSPECTIVES.**
WORLD COUNCIL OF PEACE.
*VIENNA   NO.1, JA 1967-*
MON.
*LO/U-3.*
*ISSN 0553-7533*

**PERSPECTIVES IN GEOGRAPHY.**
*+ +PERSPECT. GEOGR.*
NORTHERN ILLINOIS UNIVERSITY: EARTH SCIENCE
DEPARTMENT.
*DEKALB   1, 1971-*
ANNU.  MONOGR.
*LO/U-2.*

**PERSPECTIVES ON HUMAN EVOLUTION.**
*+ +PERSPECT. HUM. EVOL.*
SOCIETY FOR THE STUDY OF HUMAN EVOLUTION.
*NEW YORK   1, 1968-*
*CA/U-3.     LO/N-2.     LO/N13.*

**PERSPECTIVES NIGERIENNES.**
*+ +PERSPECT. NIGER.*
CENTRE D'INFORMATION DU NIGER.
[EURAFOR PRESS]
*PARIS   NO.1, OC 1966-*
M.
*LO/N17.*
*ISSN 0031-6008*

**PERSPECTIVES IN OPTHALMOLOGY.**
*+ +PERSPECT. OPTHALMOL.*
EXCERPTA MEDICA FOUNDATION.
*AMSTERDAM   1, 1968-*
BASED ON THE 1967- POSTGRADUATE COURSES HELD
UNDER THE AUSPICES OF THE NETHERLANDS
OPTHALMOLOGICAL SOCIETY.
*LO/N13.*

**PESHCHERY.**                                                                      XXX
*[PESY-A]*
GEOGRAFICHESKOE OBSHCHESTVO SSSR (PERMSKIJ
OTDEL).
*PERM'   1(2), 1961-*
TITLE ALSO IN ENGL.: CAVES.  PREV: SPELEOL-
OGICHESKIJ BJULLETIN'. ONLY I ISSUE PUBL.
1947 OF WHICH NUMB. IS CONTINUED.  SPONS. BODY
ALSO: PERMSKIJ GOSUDARSTVENNYJ UNIVERSITET:
INSTITUT KARSTOVEDENIJA I SPELEOLOGII.
*LO/N13.  3(4), 1963-*
*LO/N-3.  5(6), 1965.*

PESQUISA AGROPECUARIA BRASILEIRA.                    XXX
+ +PESQUI. AGROPECU. BRAS. [PEAB-B]
(BRAZIL) DEPARTAMENTO DE PESQUISAS E EXPER-
IMENTACAO AGROPECUARIAS.
RIO DE JANEIRO  1, 1966- 2, 1967...
SUBS. PART OF: PESQUISA AGROPECUARIA BRAS-
ILEIRA: SERIE AGRONOMIA; & PESQUISA AGRO-
PECUARIA BRASILEIRA: SERIE VETERINARIA; &
PESQUISA AGROPECUARIA BRASILEIRA: SERIE
ZOOTECNICA.
CA/U11.    LO/N-2.
ISSN 0079-1121

PESQUISA AGROPECUARIA BRASILEIRA: SERIE
AGRONOMIA.                                           XXX
+ +PESQUI. AGROPECU. BRAS., AGRON.
(BRAZIL) MINISTERIO DA AGRICULTURA: ESCRITORIO
DE PESQUISAS E EXPERIMENTACAO.
RIO DE JANEIRO  3, 1968-
PREV. PART OF: PESQUISA AGROPECUARIA BRAS-
ILEIRA FROM 1, 1966- 2, 1967.
CA/U11.    LO/N-2.

PESQUISA AGROPECUARIA BRASILEIRA: SERIE
VETERINARIA.                                         XXX
+ +PESQUI. AGROPECU. BRAS., VET.
(BRAZIL) MINISTERIO DA AGRICULTURA: ESCRITORIO
DE PESQUISAS E EXPERIMENTACAO.
RIO DE JANEIRO  3, 1968-
PREV. PART OF: PESQUISA AGROPECUARIA BRAS-
ILEIRA FROM 1, 1966- 2, 1967.
CA/U11.    LO/N-2.

PESQUISAS, INSTITUTO DE GEOCIENCIAS, UNIV-
ERSIDADE FEDERAL DO RIO GRANDE DO SUL.
+ +PESQUI. INST. GEOCIENC. UNIV. FED. RIO GRANDE
   SUL.
PORTO ALEGRE  1, 1972-
LO/N-4.

PESTICIDE BIOCHEMISTRY & PHYSIOLOGY.
+ +PESTIC. BIOCHEM. & PHYSIOL.
LONDON  1, 1971-
BL/U-1.    LO/N-6.    LO/R-5.    SO/U-1.    XY/N-1.
RE/U-1.  3, 1973-
LO/U-2.  1, 1971.
ISSN 0048-3575

PESTICIDE SCIENCE.
+ +PESTIC. SCI.
SOCIETY OF CHEMICAL INDUSTRY.
LONDON  1(1), JA/F 1970-
AD/U-1.    BL/U-1.    CA/U11.    ED/N-1.    HL/U-1.    LO/N-1.
LO/N-2.    LO/N14.    LO/R-6.    LO/S-3.    LO/S26.    NW/U-1.
OX/U-8.    RE/U-1.    SO/U-1.    XS/R-2.    XS/U-1.
GL/U-1.  2(1), 1971-
ISSN 0031-613X

PESTICIDES.
[COLOUR PUBL. PVT., LTD.]
BOMBAY  1, S 1967-
LO/R-6.
LO/N14.  4, 1970-
ISSN 0031-6148

PETAHIM.  BI-MONTHLY JOURNAL OF JEWISH THOUGHT.
JERUSALEM  1, N 1967-
HEB. WITH ENGL. SUMM.
SO/U-1.  1, 1967- 7, 1974.*

PETER WARLOCK SOCIETY NEWSLETTER.
+ +PETER WARLOCK SOC. NEWSL.
PETER WARLOCK SOCIETY.
LONDON  1, 1966-
ED/N-1.

PETROLE ET LE GAZ ARABES.                            000
SEE: ARAB OIL & GAS.

PETROLEO INTERAMERICANO.                             XXX
SUBS (1971): PETROLEO Y PETROQUIMICA
INTERNACIONAL.

PETROLEO Y PETROQUIMICA INTERNACIONAL.               XXX
+ +PET. & PETROQUIM. INT.
[PETROLEUM PUBL. CO.]
TULSA, OKLA.  29(11), 1971-
PREV: PETROLEO INTERAMERICANO FROM 1, 1943-
29(10), 1971.
LO/N14.

PETROLEUM GEOLOGY OF TAIWAN.
+ +PETROL. GEOL. TAIWAN.
CHINESE PETROLEUM CORPORATION: TAIWAN PETROLEUM
EXPLORATION OFFICE.
MIAOLI  1, 1962-
LO/N-2.

PETROLEUM & PETROCHEMICAL INTERNATIONAL.             XXX
+ +PET. & PETROCHEM. INT.
[PETROLEUM PUBL. CO.]
LONDON  11(11), 1971-
PREV: OIL & GAS INTERNATIONAL FROM 1, 1960-
11(10), 1971.
LO/N14.
AD/U-1.  12, 1972-

PETROLEUM REVIEW.                                    XXX
+ +PET. REV. [PTRV-A]
INSTITUTE OF PETROLEUM.
LONDON  22(259), 1968-
PREV: REVIEW, INSTITUTE ... FROM 1, 1947-
21(258), 1967.
LO/N14.
ISSN 0020-3076

PETROS.
UNIVERSITY OF NATAL: STUDENTS GEOLOGICAL
SOCIETY.
DURBAN  1, 1969-
LO/N-2.

PFA TECHNICAL BULLETIN.
+ +PFA TECH. BULL.
CENTRAL ELECTRICITY GENERATING BOARD.
LONDON  NO.1, 1965-
LO/N14.

PFM PAPER.
RICKMANSWORTH  [NO.]1, 1970-
OX/U-1.

P.G. NEWSLETTER.
+ +P.G. NEWSL.
UNIVERSITY OF LEEDS: POST GRADUATE STUDENTS'
REPRESENTATIVE COUNCIL.
LEEDS  NO.1, S 1968-
LD/U-1.

PH NEWS.
UNIVERSITY OF NEW SOUTH WALES.
SYDNEY   1, 1967-
ISSUED BY THE BODY'S PUBLIC HEALTH ENGINEERING
DEPARTMENT.
LO/N14.

PHANEROGAMARUM MONOGRAPHIAE.
+ +PHANEROGAMARUM MONOGR.
[CRAMER VERLAG]
LEHRE, WEST GER.  1, 1969-
LO/N-2.    OX/U-8.

PHARMACEUTICAL HISTORIAN.  NEWSLETTER OF ...
+ +PHARM. HIST.
BRITISH SOCIETY FOR THE HISTORY OF PHARMACY.
LONDON  1(1), OC 1967-
ED/N-1.    LO/M24.    LO/N-4.    OX/U-8.

PHARMACOLOGIA CLINICA.
+ +PHARMACOL. CLIN.
[SPRINGER]
BERLIN  1, 1968-
HL/U-1.
LO/M11.  1970-

PHARMACOLOGICAL RESEARCH COMMUNICATIONS.
+ +PHARMACOL. RES. COMMUN.
[ACADEMIC PRESS]
LONDON  1, MR 1969-
PUBL. FOR THE ITALIAN PHARMACOLOGICAL SOCIETY.
ED/N-1.    GL/U-2.    LO/N14.    LO/U-2.
ISSN 0031-6989

PHARMACOLOGY.  INTERNATIONAL JOURNAL OF EX-
PERIMENTAL & CLINICAL PHARMACOLOGY.
[S. KARGER]
BASEL &C  1, 1968-
PREV PART OF: MEDICINA ET PHARMACOLOGIA
EXPERIMENTALIS.
AD/U-1.    LO/N13.    LO/U-2.    OX/U-8.
ISSN 0031-7012

PHARMACOLOGY FOR PHYSICIANS.                         XXX
+ +PHARMACOL. PHYSICIANS. [PCPH-B]
AMERICAN SOCIETY FOR PHARMACOLOGY &
EXPERIMENTAL THERAPEUTICS.
PHILADELPHIA  1(1), JA 1967- 3, 1969 ...
SUBS: RATIONAL DRUG THERAPY.
NW/U-1.  1(11), 1967-

**PHARMACOLOGY & THERAPEUTICS IN DENTISTRY.**
++PHARMACOL. & THER. DENT.
[HEALTH SCIENCE PUBL. CO.]
  NEW YORK 1, 1970-
  PREV: JOURNAL OF ORAL THERAPEUTICS &
  PHARMACOLOGY FROM 1, 1964- 4(6), 1968.
  LD/U-1.    LO/N13.
  ISSN 0001-4389

**PHARMACY TIMES.**                                         XXX
++PHARM. TIMES.
  PORT WASHINGTON, N.Y.  35(9), S 1969-
  PREV: AMERICAN PROFESSIONAL PHARMACIST FROM
  1, 1935 - 35(8), 1969.
  LO/N13.
  ISSN 0003-0627

**PHARMAZEUTISCHE ZENTRALHALLE.**                           XXX
++PHARM. ZENTRALH.
[STEINKOPFF]
  BERLIN  107, 1968- 108, 1969 ...
  PREV: PHARMAZEUTISCHE ZENTRALHALLE FUR
  DEUTSCHLAND FROM 1, 1859- 106, 1967. SUBS:
  ZENTRALBLATT FUR PHARMAZIE, PHARMAKOTHERAPIE
  UND LABORATORIUMSDIAGNOSTIK.
  LO/N14.

**PHASE.**
  EXETER  1, [1966]-
  POETRY MAGAZINE.
  ED/N-1.    LO/U-2.

**PHILIPPIA.**
  NATURKUNDEMUSEUM IM OTTONEUM ZU KASSEL.
  KASSEL 1, 1970-
  LO/N-2.

**PHILIPPINE ENTOMOLOGISTS.**
++PHILIPP. ENTOMOL.
  PHILIPPINE ASSOCIATION OF ENTOMOLOGISTS.
  COLLEGE, LAGUNA  1, 1968-
  LO/N-2.    LO/R-2.
  ISSN 0048-3753

**PHILIPPINE FORESTS.**
++PHILIPP. FOR.
  MANILA  1(1), JE/AG 1967-
  OX/U-3.

**PHILIPPINE GEOLOGIST.**                                   XXX
  SUBS (1969): JOURNAL, GEOLOGICAL SOCIETY OF
  THE PHILIPPINES.

**PHILIPPINE JOURNAL OF GEODESY & PHOTOGRAM-
METRY.**
++PHILIPP. J. GEOD. & PHOTOGRAMM.
  UNIVERSITY OF THE PHILIPPINES: TRAINING CENTER
  FOR APPLIED GEODESY & PHOTOGRAMMETRY.
  QUEZON CITY  1, 1966-
  CENTER PART OF THE UNIV.'S COLLEGE OF ENGIN-
  EERING.
  LO/N13.

**PHILIPPINE PROGRESS.**
++PHILIPP. PROGR.
  DEVELOPMENT BANK OF THE PHILIPPINES.
  MAKATI 1(1), S 1967-
  S/T: BUSINESS & ECONOMIC INFORMATION.
  LO/U-3. 4, 1970-              OX/U16. 1(12), 1968-
  ISSN 0031-7764

**PHILIPPINE REVIEW OF BUSINESS & ECONOMICS.**
++PHILIPP. REV. BUS. & ECON.
  UNIVERSITY OF THE PHILIPPINES: COLLEGE OF
  BUSINESS ADMINISTRATION.
  QUEZON CITY  1, F 1964-
  OX/U16.
  ISSN 0031-7780

**PHILIPPINES NUCLEAR JOURNAL.**
++PHILIPP. NUCL. J.
  PHILIPPINE ATOMIC ENERGY COMMISSION.
  MANILA  1, 1966-
  LO/N14.

**PHILLIPS COMMON MARKET NEWSLETTER.**
++PHILLIPS COMMON MARK. NEWSL.
[NEWSLETTERS FOR BUSINESS]
  HARROW, MIDDX.  NO.1, D 1972-
  ED/N-1.  1973-

**PHILLIPS PAY & PRICES NEWSLETTER.**
++PHILLIPS PAY & PRICES NEWSL.
[NEWSLETTERS FOR BUSINESS]
  HARROW, MIDDX.  NO.1, MR 1973-
  2W.
  ED/N-1.    OX/U-1.

**PHILOSOPHIA.  PHILOSOPHICAL QUARTERLY OF ISRAEL.**
[ISRAEL UNIVERSITIES P.]
  JERUSALEM 1, 1971-
  BL/U-1.    CA/U-1.    EX/U-1.    LO/U-1.    LO/U-2.    LO/U-4.
  NO/U-1.    OX/U-1.    SW/U-1.
  LD/U-1.  2, 1972-
  ISSN 0048-3893

**PHILOSOPHIA MATHEMATICA.**
++PHILOS. MATH.  [PHMA-B]
  ASSOCIATION FOR PHILOSOPHY OF MATHEMATICS.
  DEKALB, ILL.  1, JE 1964-
  OX/U-8.
  ISSN 0031-8019

**PHILOSOPHISCHE PERSPEKTIVEN.**
++PHILOS. PERSPEKT.
[KLOSTER-MANN]
  FRANKFURT AM MAIN 1, 1969-
  ANNU.
  CA/U-1.    OX/U-1.
  ISSN 0556-4980

**PHILOSOPHY & HISTORY.**
++PHILOS. & HIST.
  INSTITUTE FOR SCIENTIFIC COOPERATION
  (TUBINGEN).
  TUBINGEN 1, 1968-
  2/A. S/T: A REVIEW OF GERMAN LANGUAGE RESEARCH
  CONTRIBUTIONS ON PHILOSOPHY, HISTORY &
  CULTURAL DEVELOPMENTS. ISSUED AS GERMAN
  STUDIES: SECTION 1.
  LO/S29.    MA/P-1.
  CO/U-1. 4(1), 1971-              GL/U-1. 5, 1972-
  ISSN 0016-884X

**PHILOSOPHY & PUBLIC AFFAIRS.**
++PHILOS. & PUBLIC AFF.
[PRINCETON UNIV. P.]
  PRINCETON 1(1), 1971-
  Q.
  AD/U-1.    CA/U-1.    CA/U12.    EX/U-1.    GL/U-1.    HL/U-1.
  LD/U-1.    LO/U-2.    LO/U-3.    LO/U-4.    NO/U-1.    OX/U17.
  RE/U-1.    SO/U-1.    SW/U-1.
  CB/U-1. 3, 1973-                 MA/U-1. 3, 1973-
  BL/U-1.  [W. 1(1), 1(3)]
  ISSN 0048-3915

**PHILOSOPHY & RHETORIC.**
++PHILOS. & RHETORIC.
[PENNSYLVANIA STATE UNIV. P.]
  UNIVERSITY PARK, PA.  1, JA 1968-
  Q.
  BH/U-1. 2, 1969-                 GL/U-1. 3, 1970-
  LO/U-3. 2, 1969-                 OX/U-1. 2(1), 1969-
  ISSN 0031-8213

**PHILOSOPHY OF THE SOCIAL SCIENCES.**
++PHILOS. SOC. SCI.
  YORK UNIVERSITY, TORONTO.
[ABERDEEN UNIV. P.]
  TORONTO 1(1), 1971-
  Q.
  CA/U-1.    ED/N-1.    EX/U-1.    GL/U-1.    HL/U-1.    LO/N-1.
  LO/U-3.    MA/U-1.    NO/U-1.    RE/U-1. 2, 1972-    SH/U-1.
  XY/N-1.
  ED/U-1. 3(2/3), 1973.
  ISSN 0048-3931

**PHOENIX.  POETRY & PROSE MAGAZINE FROM THE ...**
  UNIVERSITY OF GLASGOW: DEPARTMENT OF ENGLISH
  LITERATURE.
  GLASGOW 1, N 1972-
  CA/U-1.    ED/N-1.    OX/U-1.

**PHONOGRAPHIC BULLETIN.**
++PHONOGR. BULL.
  INTERNATIONAL ASSOCIATION OF SOUND ARCHIVES.
  UTRECHT NO.1, 1971-
  ED/N-1.

**PHOSPHORUS & THE HEAVIER GROUP VA ELEMENTS.**
++PHOSPHORUS & HEAVIER GROUP VA ELEM.
[GORDON & BREACH]
  LONDON &C.  1, 1971-
  CA/U-1.    ED/N-1.    LO/N14.    LO/S-3.    LO/U11.    OX/U-8.

**PHOTO TECHNIQUE.**
++PHOTO TECH.
[FRASER PEARCE LTD.].
  CAMBRIDGE 1(1), N 1972-
  MON.
  CA/U-1.    LO/N14.
  ED/N-1. 1(5), 1973-

**PHOTOCHEMISTRY. A REVIEW OF THE LITERATURE.**
CHEMICAL SOCIETY.
*LONDON 1, JL 1968/JE 1969 (1970)-*
A SPECIALIST PERIODICAL REPORT.
*BH/U-1.    BH/U-3.    CB/U-1.    GL/U-1.    GL/U-2.    LO/N-4.*
*LO/N14.    LO/S-3.    LO/U-2.    LO/U12.    LO/U20.*
*MA/U-1.    RE/U-1.    SF/U-1.    SH/U-1.    SO/U-1.    XS/R10.*
*AD/U-1. 2, 1971-*

**PHOTOGRAMMETRIC JOURNAL OF FINLAND.**
*+ +PHOTOGRAMM. J. FINL.*
FINNISH SOCIETY OF PHOTOGRAMMETRY.
*OTANIEMI 1, 1967-*
ENGL. & GER. SPONS. BODY ALSO: TECHNICAL UNI-
VERSITY OF HELSINKI: INST. OF PHOTOGRAMMETRY.
*BL/U-1. 2, 1968-                LO/N13. 2, 1968-*

**PHOTOGRAPHIC TECHNOLOGY USSR.**
*+ +PHOTOGR. TECHNOL. USSR.*
[FOREIGN RESOURCES ASSOCIATES]
*FORT COLLINS, COLO. 1, 1973-*
ENGL. LANG. TRANSL. OF TECHNICAL ARTICLES
FROM ZHURNAL NAUCHNOJ I PRIKLADNOJ FOTOGRAFII
I KINEMATOGRAFII. TRANSL. BEGINS WITH TOM.
18, 1973.
*LO/N14.*

**PHOTOGRAPHY INDEX FOR AMATEURS.**
*+ +PHOTOGR. INDEX AMAT.*
HERTFORDSHIRE COUNTY LIBRARIES.
*STEVENAGE NO.1, AP/JE 1968-*
*ED/N-1.    ED/P-1.    OX/U-1.*

**PHOTOPHYSIOLOGY. CURRENT TOPICS.**
*[PHCT-B]*
[ACADEMIC P.]
*NEW YORK 1, 1964-*
*CA/U-1.    CA/U-7.    OX/U-8.*

**PHYSICA SCRIPTA.**                                                    XXX
*+ +PHYS. SCR.*
KUNGLIGA SVENSKA VETENSKAPSAKADEMIEN.
[ALMQUIST & WIKSELL]
*STOCKHOLM 1(1), 1970-*
MON. MAINLY IN ENGL. PREV: ARKIV FOR FYSIK
FROM 1, 1949- 40, 1970.
*BH/U-1.    CA/U-2.    CB/U-1.    DB/S-1.    DB/U-2.    GL/U-1.*
*GL/U-2.    LO/N-4.    LO/N14.    LO/S-3.    OX/U-8.    RE/U-1.*
*SO/U-1.    XS/R10.*
*LO/U-4. 5, 1972-                LO/U12. 9, 1974-*
*ISSN 0031-8949*

**PHYSICA STATUS SOLIDI: A: APPLIED RESEARCH.**
*+ +PHYS. STATUS SOLIDI, A.*
[AKADEMIE-VERLAG GMBH; ACADEMIC P.]
*BERLIN &C. 1, JA 1970-*
MON.
*AD/U-1.    GL/U-2.    HL/U-1.    LO/N14.    LO/U12.*
*NW/U-1.    XS/R10.*
*ISSN 0031-8965*

**PHYSICA STATUS SOLIDI: B: BASIC RESEARCH.**            XXX
*+ +PHYS. STATUS SOLIDI, B.*
[AKADEMIE-VERLAG; ACADEMIC P.]
*BERLIN &C. 43, 1971-*
PREV. AS ABOVE MAIN TITLE FROM 1, 1961- 42,
1970.
*HL/U-1.    LD/U-1.    LO/N14.    XS/T-4.*

**PHYSICAL & MATHEMATICAL SCIENCES RESEARCH**
**PAPERS.**                                                            000
**SEE: PHYSICAL SCIENCES RESEARCH PAPERS.**

**PHYSICAL METHODS IN MACROMOLECULAR CHEMISTRY.**
*+ +PHYS. METHODS MACROMOL. CHEM.*
[DEKKER]
*NEW YORK 1, 1969-*
*AD/U-1.    LO/N-4.    LO/S-3.*

**PHYSICAL REVIEW ABSTRACTS.**                              XXX
*+ +PHYS. REV. ABSTR.*
AMERICAN PHYSICAL SOCIETY.
*FARMINGDALE, N.Y. 1, JA 1970-*
PREV: ABSTRACTS OF ARTICLES TO BE PUBLISHED IN
THE PHYSICAL REVIEW FROM 1961- 1969.
*CO/U-1.    RE/U-1.    SO/U-1.*
*ISSN 0048-4024*

**PHYSICAL SCIENCES RESEARCH PAPERS.**
*+ +PHYS. SCI. RES. PAP.*
(UNITED STATES) AIR FORCE: CAMBRIDGE RESEARCH
LABORATORIES.                                                          XXX
*HANSCOM FIELD, MASS. NO.1, 1964-*
SOME ISSUES ENTITLED PHYSICAL & MATHEMATICAL
SCIENCES RESEARCH PAPERS.
*LO/N14. (UNRESTRICTED ISSUES ONLY).*

**PHYSICO-CHEMICAL MEASUREMENT UNIT BULLETIN.**
*+ +PHYSICO-CHEM. MEAS. UNIT. BULL.*
ATOMIC ENERGY RESEARCH ESTABLISHMENT.
*HARWELL NO.1, 1969-*
*XS/R10.*

**PHYSICS BULLETIN.**                                          XXX
*+ +PHYS. BULL.*
INSTITUTE OF PHYSICS & THE PHYSICAL SOCIETY.
*LONDON 19, 1968-*
PREV: BULLETIN OF THE INSTITUTE OF PHYSICS
(& THE PHYSICAL SOCIETY)., 1, 1950- 18, 1967.
PREV TITLE EXTENDED (WITH CHANGE IN NAME OF
BODY BY AMALGAMATION) FROM 12, 1960.
*ED/N-1.    LO/N13.    LO/U-2.*

**PHYSICS & CHEMISTRY IN SPACE.**
*+ +PHYS. & CHEM. SPACE.*
[SPRINGER]
*BERLIN &C. 1, 1970-*
*OX/U-8.*

**PHYSICS REPORTS. A REVIEW SECTION OF PHYSICS**
**LETTERS (SECTION C).**
*+ +PHYS. REP.*
[NORTH-HOLLAND]
*AMSTERDAM 1C(1), 1971-*
*BH/U-1.    BN/U-2.    CA/U-1.    DB/U-2.    EX/U-1.    GL/U-1.*
*GL/U-2.    LO/N-4.    LO/N14.    LO/U-1.    LO/U-2.    LO/U13.*
*MA/U-1.    SF/U-1.    SO/U-1.    XS/R10.*
*RE/U-1. 1(2), 1971-*

**PHYSICS OF SINTERING.**                                      XXX
*+ +PHYS. SINTER.*
BORIS KIDRIC INSTITUTE OF NUCLEAR SCIENCES.
*BELGRADE 1(1), JL 1969- 5, 1973...*
3A. S/T: JOURNAL OF THE INTERNATIONAL TEAM
FOR THE STUDY OF SINTERING. SUBS: SCIENCE OF
SINTERING.
*LD/U-1.    LO/N14.*
*LO/U21. 2(1), 1970-              XS/R10. 2(1), 1970-*
*CA/U-2. 1(1), 1969- 2(1), 1970.*
*ISSN 0031-9198*

**PHYSICS IN TECHNOLOGY.**                                    XXX
*+ +PHYS. TECHNOL.*
INSTITUTE OF PHYSICS & THE PHYSICAL SOCIETY.
*LONDON 4, 1973-*
PREV: REVIEW OF PHYSICS IN TECHNOLOGY FROM 1,
1970- 3, 1972.
*AD/U-3.    CO/U-1.    DB/U-2.    LO/N-4.    LO/N14.    SO/U-1.*
*XS/R10.*

**PHYSIKALISCHEN GRUNDLAGEN DER MEDIZIN: AB-**
**HANDLUNGEN AUS DER BIOPHYSIK.**
*+ +PHYS. GRUNDL. MED., ABH. BIOPHYS.*
[GEORG THIEME]
*LEIPZIG HEFT 1, 1960-*
*LO/N13.*

**PHYSIKALISCHE VERHANDLUNGEN.**
*+ +PHYS. VERH.*
*KARLSRUHE &C. 1, 1950- 19, 1968.//*
ISSUED AS SUPPLEMENT TO PHYSIKALISCHE BLATTER.
*LO/N14.*

**PHYSIOLOGICAL CHEMISTRY & PHYSICS.**
*+ +PHYSIOL. CHEM. & PHYS.*
[PACIFIC PUBL. CO.]
*PORTLAND, OREG. 1(1), JA/F 1969-*
*OX/U-1.    OX/U-8.*
*ISSN 0031-9325*

**PHYSIOLOGICAL PLANT PATHOLOGY.**
*+ +PHYSIOL. PLANT PATHOL.*
*LONDON 1(1), 1971-*
Q.
*AD/U-1.    AD/U-3.    BH/U-1.    BL/U-1.    BN/U-2.    CA/U-7.*
*ED/N-1.    EX/U-1.    GL/U-1.    LO/N-6.    LO/N13.    LO/R-6.*
*LO/U12.    MA/U-1.    OX/U-3.    OX/U-3.    SH/U-1.*
*SO/U-1.    XS/R-2.*
*ISSN 0048-4059*

**PHYSIOLOGICAL PSYCHOLOGY.**                                 XXX
*+ +PHYSIOL. PSYCHOL.*
PSYCHONOMIC SOCIETY.
*AUSTIN, TEX. 1(1), MR 1973-*
Q. PREV. PART OF: PSYCHONOMIC SCIENCE FROM
1, 1964- 29(6), JA 1973.
*AD/U-1.    BN/U-1.    GL/U-1.    GL/U-2.    LO/N13.    LO/U-4.*
*RE/U-1.    SH/U-1.    SO/U-1.    SW/U-1.*
*ISSN 0090-5046*

**PHYSIOLOGY & BIOCHEMISTRY OF CULTIVATED**
**PLANTS.**                                                        XXX
+ +PHYSIOL. & BIOCHEM. CULT. PLANTS.
[CONSULTANTS BUREAU]
  NEW YORK; LONDON 1, 1970- 2, 1971.//
  2M. ENGL. TRANSL. OF FIZIOLOGIJA I BIOKHIMIJA
  KUL'TURNYKH RASTENIJ. DATING & NUMBERING OF
  ISSUES FOLLOWS ORIGINAL.
  LO/N13.

**PHYTOPHYLACTICA.**
(SOUTH AFRICA) DEPARTMENT OF AGRICULTURE.
  PRETORIA 1, 1969-
  LO/N-2.

**PICTORIAL SCIENCE.**
+ +PICTORIAL SCI.
[EVANS BROS.]
  LONDON 1, 1968-
  ED/N-1.      HL/U-2.

**PIG INTERNATIONAL.**
+ +PIG INT.
[WATT PUBL. CO.]
  THE HAGUE &C. 1(1), 1971-
  Q.
  LO/N-6. 2(2), 1972-
  ISSN 0031-9767

**PIGMENT & RESIN TECHNOLOGY.**                                    XXX
+ +PIGM. & RESIN TECHNOL.
[SAWELL PUBL.]
  LONDON 1(1), JA 1972-
  PREV: PAINT TECHNOLOGY FROM 1(1), 1936-
  35(12), D 1971.
  BH/P-1.    ED/N-1.    LO/N14.    LO/N35.    LO/S-3.

**PIPING WORLD.**
[IAN CARMICHAEL ASSOCIATES]
  GLASGOW 1(1), 5/JL 1969-
  DEALS WITH BAGPIPING.
  LO/N-3. 1(1).

**PIRA NEWS.**
RESEARCH ASSOCIATION FOR THE PAPER & BOARD,
PRINTING & PACKAGING INDUSTRIES.
  LEATHERHEAD NO.1, 1968-
  ED/N-1.

**PIRA PACKAGING JOURNAL.**
+ +PIRA PACKAG. J.
RESEARCH ASSOCIATION FOR THE PAPER & BOARD,
PRINTING & PACKAGING INDUSTRIES.
  LEATHERHEAD 1, AUTUMN 1968-
  S/T: A TECHNICAL JOURNAL FOR PACKAGING &
  RELATED INDUSTRIES.
  ED/N-1.

**PIRA PAPER & BOARD ABSTRACTS.**
+ +PIRA PAP. & BOARD ABSTR.
RESEARCH ASSOCIATION FOR THE PAPER & BOARD,
PRINTING & PACKAGING INDUSTRIES.
  KENLEY 1, 1968-
  ED/N-1.

**PIRA PAPER & BOARD JOURNAL.**
+ +PIRA PAP. & BOARD J.
RESEARCH ASSOCIATION FOR THE PAPER & BOARD,
PRINTING & PACKAGING INDUSTRIES.
  LEATHERHEAD 1, SUMMER 1968-
  ED/N-1.

**PIRA PATENT ABSTRACTS.**
+ +PIRA PAT. ABSTR.
RESEARCH ASSOCIATION FOR THE PAPER & BOARD,
PRINTING & PACKAGING INDUSTRIES.
  LEATHERHEAD 1, 1969-
  PREP. BY THE BODY'S INFORMATION SECTION FROM
  COPIES OF ORIG. BR. PATENTS.
  LO/N14.

**PIRA PRINTING JOURNAL.**
+ +PIRA PRINT. J.
RESEARCH ASSOCIATION FOR THE PAPER & BOARD,
PRINTING & PACKAGING INDUSTRIES.
  LEATHERHEAD 1, 1968-
  S/T: A TECHNICAL JOURNAL FOR PRINTING &
  RELATED INDUSTRIES.
  ED/N-1.

**PISATEL' I ZHIZN'.**
SOJUZ PISATELEJ SSSR: LITERATURNYJ INSTITUT.
  MOSCOW 1961(1)-
  S/T: SBORNIK ISTORIKO-LITERATURNYKH, TEORETI-
  CHESKIKH I KRITICHESKIKH STATEJ.
  CC/U-1.
  BH/U-1. 1963-                         ED/U-1. 1963-

**PITTIERIA.**
UNIVERSIDAD DE LOS ANDES.
  MERIDA, VENEZ. NO.1, F 1967-
  LO/N-2.

**P.L.A. MONTHLY.**                                                XXX
  SUBS (1970): PORT OF LONDON.

**PLAN (JOHANNESBURG).**
INSTITUTE OF SOUTH AFRICAN ARCHITECTS.
  JOHANNESBURG 54(1), 1969-
  PREV: ISAA FROM 48, 1963- 53, 1968.
  LO/N13. 54(2), 1969-

**PLAN. MAGAZINE OF THE CONSTRUCTION INDUSTRY.**
[POMEROY P.]
  DUBLIN NO.1, OC 1969-
  BL/U-1.    DB/U-2.
  LO/N14. (CURRENT BOX)

**PLAN OG ARBEID. TIDSSKRIFT FOR DISTRIKTS-**
**UTBYGGING, REGIONPLANLEGGING OG SYSSELSETTING.**
(NORWAY) ARBEIDSDIREKTORATET.
  OSLO 1966(1)-
  6/A. PREV: ARBEIDSMARKEDET.
  LO/U13.
  SF/U-1. 1974(1),
  ISSN 0032-0609

**PLANET.**
[GWASG GOMER]
  LLANDYSUL NO.1, 1970-
  2M. ENGL. & WELSH.
  MA/U-1.
  MA/P-1. NO.14, OC/N 1972-

**PLANETARIUM.**
ARMAGH PLANETARIUM.
  ARMAGH 1, 1967-
  BL/U-1.

**PLANNING & COMPENSATION REPORTS.**                               XXX
  SUBS (1968): PROPERTY & COMPENSATION REP.

**PLANNING IN DURHAM.**
+ +PLANN. DURHAM.
DURHAM COUNTY COUNCIL: PLANNING COMMITTEE.
  DURHAM [NO.1], 1970-
  A.
  LO/U-3.

**PLANNING FAMILIAL.**
+ +PLANN. FAMILIAL.
FEDERATION NATIONAL DU MOVEMENT FRANCAIS POUR
LE PLANNING FAMILIAL.
  PARIS 1, MR 1964-
  M.
  LO/S74.

**PLANNING FOR FIRE SAFETY IN BUILDINGS SERIES.**
+ +PLANN. FIRE SAF. BUILD. SER.
FIRE PROTECTION ASSOCIATION.
  LONDON [NO.]1, 1965-
  LO/N-4.

**PLANNING RESEARCH STUDIES, BUILDING RESEARCH**
**GROUP, KWAME NKRUMAH UNIVERSITY OF SCIENCE &**
**TECHNOLOGY.**
+ +PLANN. RES. STUD. BUILD. RES. GROUP KWAME
NKRUMAH UNIV. SCI. & TECHNOL. [PRSS-B]
  KWAME NO.1, 1963-
  MONOGR.
  LO/N-1.

**PLANNING UNIT REPORT, BRITISH MEDICAL**
**ASSOCIATION.**
+ +PLANN. UNIT REP. BR. MED. ASSOC.
  LONDON NO.1, 1967-
  GL/U-1.    LO/N-1.

**PLANOWANIE GOSPODARKI NARODOWEJ W POLSCE**
**LUDOWEJ. MATERIALY DO BIBLIOGRAFII.**
+ +PLANOWANIE GOSPOD. NARODOWEJ POL. LUDOWEJ.
SZKOLA GLOWNA PLANOWANIA I STATYSTYKI.
  WARSAW 1, 1960-
  LO/U-3.    OX/U-1.

**PLANT FOODS FOR HUMAN NUTRITION.**
+ +PLANT FOODS HUM. NUTR.
[PERGAMON PRESS]
  OXFORD &C 1(1), MY 1968- 2, (3/4), MR 1972.
  Q. SUBS. PART OF: QUALITAS PLANTARUM - PLANT
  FOODS FOR HUMAN NUTRITION FROM 23(1/3), 21/S
  1973.
  BL/U-1.    CO/U-1.    ED/N-1.    GL/U-2.    LO/N14.    OX/U-8.
  SH/U-1.
  BH/U-1. 2, 1972-

PLANT PHYSIOLOGY.                                          000
  SEE: FIZIOLOGIJA NA RASTENIJATA.

PLANT SCIENCE LETTERS.
  ++PLANT SCI. LETT.
  [ELSEVIER]
  AMSTERDAM 1, 1973-
  S/T: AN INTERNATIONAL JOURNAL OF EXPERIMENTAL
  PLANT BIOLOGY.
  AD/U-3.    BL/U-1.   CA/U-7.   GL/U-1.   LO/N-2.   LO/N13.
  LO/U-2.    MA/U-1.   RE/U-1.   SH/U-1.   SW/U-1.
  LD/U-1. 2, 1974-              LO/R-6. 2(1), 1974-

PLANT SCIENCES - ENTOMOLOGY.
  ++PLANT SCI., ENTOMOL.
  NEW YORK (STATE) AGRICULTURAL EXPERIMENT
  STATION.
  GENEVA, N.Y. NO.1, 1972-
  FORMS PART OF NEW YORK'S FOOD & LIFE SCIENCES
  BULLETIN.
  LO/N13.

PLANTES MEDICINALES & PHYTOTHERAPIE.
  ++PLANT. MED. & PHYTOTHER.
  CENTRE D'ETUDE DES PLANTES MEDICINALES: FACULTE
  MIXTE DE MEDICINE ET DE PHARMACIE.
  ANGERS 1, 1967-
  LO/N-2.    XY/N-1.
  ISSN 0032-0994

PLASTER JACKET.
  FLORIDA STATE MUSEUM.
  GAINSVILLE NO.1, 1966-
  SPONS. BODY PART OF UNIVERSITY OF FLORIDA.
  LO/N-2.

PLASTICONSTRUCTION.
  [CARL HANSER]
  MUNICH 1, 1971-
  ENGL., FR. SUMM. & CONTENTS LISTS. CONTAINS
  SUPPL: BAUEN MIT KUNSTSTOFFEN.
  LO/N14.
  ISSN 0032-1117

PLASTICS IN ENGINEERING.
  ++PLAST. ENG.
  [FACTORY PUBLS. LTD.]
  LONDON JE 1968- 1971.
  SUBS. PART OF: OEM DESIGN.
  ED/N-1.    LO/N14.
  ISSN 0032-1192

PLASTICS PACKAGING PAPER CONVERTERS BULLETIN.
  SEE: PCB.

PLASTICS - RUBBERS - TEXTILES.
  ++PLAST. - RUBB. - TEXT.
  [RUBBER & TECHNICAL P.]
  LONDON 1, 1970-
  LO/N14.    MA/P-1.    XS/R10.
  ED/N-1. 1(3), 1970-          LO/U20. 2, 1971-
  ISSN 0035-9459

PLASTICS SOUTHERN AFRICA.
  ++PLAST. SOUTH. AFR.
  [GEORGE WARMAN & CO.]
  CAPE TOWN 1, 1971-
  LO/N14.

PLAY.
  INTER-ACTION TRUST.
  LONDON 1(1), 1969-
  OX/U-1.

PLESSE-ARCHIV.
  [E. GOLTZE KG.]
  GOTTINGEN 1, 1966-
  LO/N-2.

PLI KNOW HOW.                                              XXX
  [INDUSTRIAL OPPORTUNITIES LTD.]
  HAVANT, HANTS. NO.106, 1973-
  PREV: PRODUCT LICENSING INDEX FROM NO.15,
  1965- 105, 1973.
  LO/N14.    LO/N35.

PLUIMVEEHOUDERIJ.                                          XXX
  NEDERLANDSE ORGANISATIE VAN PLUIMVEEHOUDERS.
  [C. MISSET]
  DOETINCHEM 1, 1971-
  PREV: NEDERLANDSE PLUIMVEEHOUDERIJ FROM 1, JA
  1967- 4, 1970.
  LO/N13.

PLUMBING.                                                  XXX
  INSTITUTE OF PLUMBING.
  HORNCHURCH, ESSEX 1(1), 1970-
  Q. PREV: JOURNAL, REGISTERED PLUMBERS ASSOC-
  IATION.
  ED/N-1. 1(5), 1971-              OX/U-8. 1(5), 1971-
  LO/N14. [CURRENT BOX ONLY]

PLUMBING & HEATING JOURNAL.                                XXX
  ++PLUMB. & HEAT. J.
  [PLUMBING TRADE JOURNAL CO. LTD.]
  SOUTHPORT 49(4), S 1969-
  PREV: PLUMBING TRADE JOURNAL & HEATING REVIEW
  FROM 42(8), JA 1963- 49(3), AG 1969.
  ED/N-1.    XS/R10.
  ISSN 0032-1699

PLUMBING TRADE JOURNAL & HEATING REVIEW.*                  XXX
  ++PLUMB. TRADE J. & HEAT. REV.
  [PLUMBING TRADE JOURNAL CO. LTD.]
  SOUTHPORT 42(8), JA 1963- 49(3), AU 1969 ...
  M. PREV: PLUMBING TRADE JOURNAL FROM 1, 1921
  - 42(7), 1962. THEN TITLE EXPANDED AS ABOVE.
  LO/N-1.    LO/N-4.    MA/P-1.

PLURAL SOCIETIES.
  ++PLURAL SOC.
  FOUNDATION FOR THE STUDY OF PLURAL SOCIETIES.
  THE HAGUE 1(1), 1970-
  S/T: QUARTERLY JOURNAL.
  LO/U14.    OX/U-9.
  ISSN 0048-4482

PLUTONIUM - DOKUMENTATION.
  ++PLUTONIUM - DOK.
  GESELLSCHAFT FUR KERNFORSCHUNG.
  KARLSRUHE 1(1), JA 1967-
  XS/R10.
  ISSN 0032-1729

PLYWOOD WORLD.                                             XXX
  COUNCIL OF FOREST INDUSTRIES OF BRITISH
  COLUMBIA.
  VANCOUVER 1, 1961- 11, 1970.
  SUBS: WOOD WORLD.
  LO/N14. 7(3), 1967-

P/M PARTS ENGINEERING.
  ++P/M PARTS ENG.
  POWDER METALLURGY PARTS MANUFACTURERS ASSOCI-
  ATION.
  NEW YORK 1, 1966-
  PREV: POWDER METALLURGY QUARTERLY.
  LO/N14.

PNEU. JOURNAL OF THE ...
  PARENTS NATIONAL EDUCATIONAL UNION.
  LONDON 1, 1966-
  PREV: PARENTS REVIEW.
  ED/N-1.

P-NODAL SOLUTIONS FOR EARTHQUAKES.
  ++P-NODAL SOLUT. EARTHQUAKES.
  INTERNATIONAL SEISMOLOGICAL CENTRE.
  EDINBURGH 1, 1964 (1968)-
  ED/N-1.    LO/N13.

POCHVOZNANIE I AGROKHIMIJA. SOIL SCIENCE &
AGROCHEMISTRY.
  ++POCHVOZN. & AGROKHIM. [PVAG-A]
  AKADEMIJA NA SELSKOSTOPANSKITE NAUKI.
  SOFIA 1, 1966-
  ENGL. SUMM. & CONT. LISTS.
  LO/N13.    XS/R-2.

PODIUM.
  [G. GRASIL]
  BAD VOSLAU NO.1, AP 1971-
  Q.
  LO/N-1.

PODVIG. ALMANAKH.
  MOSCOW 1, 1968-
  CC/U-1.    SF/U-1.

POE NEWSLETTER. STUDIES ON EDGAR ALLAN POE.               XXX
  ++POE NEWSL.
  PULLMAN, WASH. 1, 1968- 3(2), 1970 ...
  SUBS: POE STUDIES.
  CA/U-1.    ED/N-1.    EX/U-1.
  ISSN 0032-1877

POE STUDIES.                                                                          XXX
+ +POE STUD.
WASHINGTON STATE UNIVERSITY: DEPARTMENT OF
ENGLISH.
*PULLMAN 4(1), JE 1971-*
PREV: POE NEWSLETTER FROM 1, 1968- 3(2), 1970.
*ED/N-1.    LO/U-1.*

POESIA & FICCAO.
SOCIEDADE DE LINGUA PORTUGUESA.
*LISBON 1, 1972-*
*MA/U-1.*

POESIE. ZEITSCHRIFT FUR LITERATUR.
*BASEL 1, 1972-*
*LO/N-1.*

POESIE PRESENTE. CAHIERS TRIMESTRIELS DE
POESIE.
[ROUGERIE]
*LIMOGES NO.1, MY 1971-*
*LO/N-1.*

POESIE UND WISSENSCHAFT.
+ +POESIE & WISS.
[STIEHM VERLAG]
*HEIDELBERG 1, 1967-*
*GL/U-1.*

POET (LONDON).
[DEREK MAGGS]
*LONDON 1, AUTUMN 1972-*
*Q.*
*ED/N-1.*

POETICS. INTERNATIONAL REVIEW FOR THE THEORY OF
LITERATURE.
[MOUTON]
*THE HAGUE NO.1, 1971-*
*DB/U-2.    ED/N-1.    HL/U-1.    LO/N-1.    LO/U-1.    LO/U-4.*
*MA/U-1.*
*OX/U-1. 1973-*
*LO/U14. NO.7, 1973.*
*ISSN 0048-4571*

POETIQUE. REVUE DE THEORIE ET D'ANALYSE
LITTERAIRES.
[SEUIL]
*[PARIS] NO.1, 1970-*
*AD/U-1.    ED/N-1.    GL/U-1.    HL/U-1.    LD/U-1.    LO/U-1.*
*LO/U-2.    MA/U-1.    RE/U-1.*
*BN/U-1. NO.9, 1972-*
*NO/U-1. NO.14, 1973; 21, 1975-*
*ISSN 0032-2024*

POETRY ...
HAVERING POETRY GROUP.
*UPMINSTER 2, 1966-*
ACTUAL TITLE CONTAINS NUMBER; E.G.: POETRY
ONE; POETRY TWO; &C.
*LO/U-2.*

POETRY: INTRODUCTION.
+ +POETRY, INTROD.
[FABER]
*LONDON 1, 1969-*
*LO/U-2.*

POETRY OF THE CIRCLE IN THE SQUARE.
BRISTOL ARTS CENTRE: POETRY CIRCLE.
*BRISTOL 1, [1966]-*
*LO/U-2.*

POETRY FORUM.
*FARNBOROUGH NO.1, [1970]-*
*Q.*
*ED/N-1.    OX/U-1.*

POETRY MAGAZINE.
+ +POETRY MAG.
POETRY SOCIETY OF AUSTRALIA.
*SYDNEY NO.1, 1964-*
*LO/U-2.*

POETRY NEW ZEALAND.
+ +POETRY N.Z.
[PEGASUS P.]
*CHRISTCHURCH, N.Z. 1, 1971-*
*LO/U-2.*

POETRY REVIEW.
+ +POETRY REV.
UNIVERSITY OF TAMPA.
*TAMPA, FLA. NO.1, 1964-*
*LO/U-1. NO.10,1967-*

POETRY ST. IVES.
*ST. IVES 1, 1965-*
*LO/U-2.*

POETRY SINGAPORE.
UNIVERSITY OF SINGAPORE.
*SINGAPORE NO.1, 1968-*
ISSUED BY THE BODY'S DEP. OF ENGLISH.
*LO/U-2.*
*ISSN 0032-2164*

POETRY WORKSHOP.
WOLVERHAMPTON COLLEGE OF ART.
*WOLVERHAMPTON 1(1), 1967-*
*LO/U-2.*

POETSDOOS.
*ST. ALBANS NO.1, 1966-*
*LO/U-2.*

POEZIJA.
SOCJETA TAL-POEZIJA.
*SAN GWANN, MALTA NO.1, 1971-*
*LO/U-2.    OX/U-1.*

POEZIJA. AL'MANAKH.
[MOLODAIA GVARDIIA]
*MOSCOW VYP. 1, 1968-*
*BH/U-1.    CC/U-1.    GL/U-1.    LO/U15.    MA/U-1.    NO/U-1.*
*NR/U-1.*
*LD/U-1. 5, 1971-*
*ISSN 0056-0519*

POGAMOGGAN.
[OMPHALOS PRESS]
*NEW YORK NO.1, 1964.//*
*LO/U-2.*

POINT.
*BILLESDON 1, AUTUMN 1967-*
THEOLOGICAL & SOCIOLOGICAL ARTICLES.
*ED/N-1.*

POINT (PARIS).
*PARIS NO.1, S 1972-*
*WKLY.*
*LO/U-3.*
*ED/N-1. NO.128, 1975-*

POINT TO POINT COMMUNICATION.                                   XXX
+ +POINT POINT COMMUN.
MARCONI'S WIRELESS TELEGRAPH COMPANY.
*CHELMSFORD, ESSEX 14(1), JA 1970- 18, 1974.*
PREV: POINT TO POINT TELECOMMUNICATION FROM
1, 1956- 13, 1969. SUBS: COMMUNICATION &
BROADCASTING.
*ED/N-1.    LO/N-4.    LO/N-7.*
*ISSN 0032-2334*

POINT TO POINT TELECOMMUNICATION.                              XXX
SUBS (1970): POINT TO POINT COMMUNICATION.

POINT THREE.
TOC H.
*LONDON JA 1968-*
M. PREV: TOC H JOURNAL.
*ED/N-1.*
*ISSN 0032-2326*

POINTE. MAGAZINE OF BALLET IN SCOTLAND.
*KIRKNEWTON 1, 1972-*
*ED/N-1.*

POKROKY VO VINOHRADNICKOM A VINARSKOM VYSKUME.
+ +POKROKY VINOHRAD. & VINARSK. VYSK. [PVVV-A]
VYSKUMNY USTAV PRE VINOHRADNICTVO A VINARSTVO.
*BRATISLAVA 1960-*
GER. & RUSS. SUMM.
*XS/R-2. 1963.*

POLAR NEWS.
(JAPAN POLAR RESEARCH ASSOCIATION).
*TOKYO 1(1), D 1965-*
*CA/U12.    LO/N-2.*
*ISSN 0023-6004*

POLEMICA. REFLEXIONES SOBRE TEMES SOCIALES
DE MEXICO.
PARTIDO REVOLUCIONARIO INSTITUCIONAL: COMITE
EJECUTIVO NACIONAL.
*MEXICO, D.F. 1, MR/AP 1969-*
*OX/U-1.*

POLICE. THE MONTHLY JOURNAL OF THE ...
POLICE FEDERATION.
*LONDON 1, 1968-*
*ED/N-1.    OX/U15.*
*ISSN 0032-2555*

**POLICY PAPERS, ASSOCIATION OF LIBERAL COUNCILLORS.**
SEE: A.L.C. POLICY PAPERS.

**POLICY & POLITICS.**
++POLICY & POLIT.
LONDON 1(1), S 1972-
Q. S/T: STUDIES OF LOCAL GOVERNMENT & ITS SERVICES.
AD/U-1. BL/U-1. CA/U-1. ED/N-1. ED/U-1. EX/U-1.
GL/U-1. GL/U-2. LD/U-1. LO/U-2. LO/U-3. LO/U-4.
NO/U-1. NW/U-1. SH/U-1.
SF/U-1. 2, 1973-
BN/U-1. 2, 1973/74-

**POLICY SCIENCES.**
++POLICY SCI.
[AMERICAN ELSEVIER]
NEW YORK 1, 1970-
CA/U-1. GL/U-2. LO/U-3. SH/U-1. SW/U-1.
ISSN 0032-2687

**POLIMEROS.**
(BRAZIL) MINISTERIO DA INDUSTRIA E DO COMERCIO.
RIO DE JANEIRO 1, 1971-
SPONS. BODY ALSO SUPERINTENDENCIA DA BORRACHA.
LO/N14.

**POLIMERY V MASHINOSTROENII. SBORNIK TRUDOV.**
++POLIM. MASHINOSTR.
LUGANSKIJ MASHINOSTROITEL'NYJ INSTITUT.
L'VOV 4, 1964-
NO DATA AVAILABLE REGARDING VOLS.1- 3.
LO/N13.

**POLISH CARTOGRAPHICAL REVIEW.**                                    000
SEE: POLSKI PRZEGLAD KARTOGRAFICZNY.

**POLISH PSYCHOLOGICAL BULLETIN.**
++POL. PSYCHOL. BULL.
POLSKIE TOWARZYSTWO PSYCHOLOGICZNE.
WARSAW 1(1), 1970-
LD/U-1. SH/U-1.

**POLISH ROUND TABLE. YEARBOOK.**
++POL. ROUND TABLE.
POLSKIE TOWARZYSTWO NAUK POLITYCZNYCH.
WARSAW 1, 1967-
BODY NAMED IN PUBL.: POLISH ASSOCIATION OF POLITICAL SCIENCES.
LO/U-3. OX/U-1.

**POLISH YEARBOOK OF INTERNATIONAL LAW.**
++POL. YEARB. INT. LAW.
POLSKI INSTYTUT SPRAW MIEDZYNARODOWYCH.
WROCLAW &C 1, 1966/67(1968)-
LO/S14. LO/U-3.
CA/U-1. 2, 1968-1969(1971)-

**POLITECNICA. REVISTA DE INFORMACION TECNICO-CIENTIFICA.**
ESCUELA POLITECNICA NACIONAL (ECUADOR).
QUITO 1(1), 1967-
LO/N13. 1(2), 1968-

**POLITEIA.**
UNIVERSIDAD CENTRAL DE VENEZUELA: INSTITUTO DE ESTUDIOS POLITICOS.
CARACAS 1, 1972-
ANNU.
OX/U-1.

**POLITICA DEL DIRITTO.**
++POLIT. DIRITTO.
[SOCIETA EDITRICE IL MULINO]
BOLOGNA [1], 1970-
2/M.
OX/U15.
ISSN 0032-3063

**POLITICAL COMPANION.**
++POLIT. COMPANION.
GLASGOW [NO.1], OC/D 1969-
Q.
BH/P-1. BH/U-1. CB/U-1. ED/N-1. GL/U-1. LO/U-3.
EX/U-1. NO 6, JA/MR 1971-
HL/U-1. NO.3, AP/JE 1970-
NO/U-1. NO.6, JA/MR 1971-
SO/U-1. NO.3, AP/JE 1970-
ISSN 0032-3152

**POLITICAL & ECONOMIC REVIEW.**
++POLIT. & ECON. REV.
INDIAN NATIONAL CONGRESS.
NEW DELHI 1, MR 1970-
W.
OX/U13.

**POLITICAL SCIENCE ANNUAL.**
++POLIT. SCI. ANNU.
[BOBBS-MERRILL CO. LTD.]
INDIANAPOLIS &C. 1, 1966-
OX/U-1.
GL/U-2. 2, 1969-                      MA/U-1. 2, 1970-
ISSN 0079-3043

**POLITICAL SCIENCE REVIEW.**
++POLIT. SCI. REV.
UNIVERSITY OF RAJASTHAN: DEPARTMENT OF POLITICAL SCIENCE.
JAIPUR 1, F 1962-
LO/U-8. 6(3-4), 1967. 7(1-2), 1968.

**POLITICAL SCIENTIST.**
++POLIT. SCI.
RANCHI UNIVERSITY: DEPARTMENT OF POLITICAL SCIENCE.
RANCHI 1(1), JL/D 1964-
2/A.
LO/U14.
ISSN 0032-3209

**POLITICAL THEORY.**
++POLIT. THEORY.
[SAGE PUBL.]
BEVERLY HILLS; LONDON 1(1), F 1973-
Q.
BL/U-1. CA/U-1. DB/U-2. EX/U-1. GL/U-1. HL/U-1.
LD/U-1. LO/U-3. LO/U12. MA/U-1. OX/U-1. RE/U-1.
SH/U-1. SO/U-1. SW/U-1.
ISSN 0090-5917

**POLITICAL YEAR.**
++POLIT. YEAR.
[PITMAN]
LONDON 1970- 1971.//
ANNU.
OX/U-1.
SH/U-1. 1971-

**POLITICKA MISAO.**
++POLIT. MISAO.
SVEUCILISTE U ZAGREBU.
ZAGREB 1965 (1)-
Q. ISSUED BY THE BODY'S FAKULTET POLITICKIH NAUKA. ENGL. & RUSS. SUMM.
LO/U-3.
OX/U-1. 6(1), 1969-
ISSN 0032-3241

**POLITICS & MONEY.**
++POLIT. & MONEY.
[P. & M. PUBL. CO.]
LONDON 1(1), JA 1970-
S/T: A MONTHLY ANALYSIS OF CURRENT TRENDS.
ED/N-1. OX/U-1.
ISSN 0032-3284

**POLITICS & SOCIETY.**
++POLIT. & SOC.
[GERON X INC.]
LOS ALTOS, CALIF. 1(1), N 1970-
Q.
DB/U-2. GL/U-2. OX/U-1. OX/U17.
MA/U-1. 2(2), 1972-                  NO/U-1. 2, 1971-
ISSN 0032-3292

**POLITIKA. TYDENIK.**                                                XXX
VYBOR SOCIALISTICKE KULTURY.
PRAGUE 1(1), 1968- 2(5), 1969.//
PREV: KULTURNI TVORBA FROM 1, JA 1963- 6, AG 1968.
BH/U-1.* LA/U-1.*

**POLITIKS.**
MERSEYSIDE POLITICS ASSOCIATION.
LIVERPOOL 1, S 1970-
3/A.
ED/N-1. D 1970-

**POLITIQUE ETRANGERE DE LA FRANCE: TEXTES ET DOCUMENTS.**
++POLIT. ETRANG. FR., TEXTES & DOC.
[DOCUMENTATION FRANCAISE]
PARIS 1966 (1967)-
LO/U-3. LO/U19.

**POLITIQUE INTERIEURE DE LA FRANCE.**
++POLIT. INTERIEURE FR.
(FRANCE) SECRETARIAT D'ETAT AUPRES DU PREMIER MINISTRE CHARGE DE L'INFORMATION.
PARIS 1(1), 1969-
Q.
LO/U-3.

POLITY. THE JOURNAL OF THE NORTHEASTERN
SCIENCE ASSOCIATIONS.
[UNIV. OF MASSACHUSETTS PRESS]
AMHERST, MASS. 1(1), FALL 1968-
CB/U-1.*    GL/U-2.    OX/U-1.    SW/U-1.
ISSN 0032-3497

POLJOPRIVREDNA TEHNIKA.
+ +POLJOPR. TEH. (YUG.)
INSTITUT ZA MEHANIZACIJU POLJOPRIVREDE.
BELGRADE   1, 1963-
SUMM. IN ENGL.
XS/R-6.
LO/N13.   3, 1965- [W. 4(5).]

POLLUTION.
[MICROINFO LTD.]
ALTON, HANTS.   1, 1971-
S/T: ENVIRONMENTAL NEWS BULLETIN.
ED/N-1.    LO/R-5.
LD/U-1.   2, 1972-         LO/U20.   2, 1972-
XS/R10.   4(1), JA 1974-
ISSN 0048-4784

POLLUTION ABSTRACTS.
+ +POLLUT. ABSTR.
LA JOLLA, CALIF.   1(1), MY 1970-
2M.
LO/N-2.    LO/N14.    LO/R-5.    LO/U12.    LO/U28.    SO/U-1.
XS/R10.
LD/U-1.   3, 1972-          OX/U-8.   2(1), 1971-
ISSN 0032-3624

POLLUTION CONTROL (LONDON).
+ +POLLUT. CONTROL (LOND.).
[FACTORY PUBL. LTD.]
LONDON   [NO.1], MR 1971-
Q.
ED/N-1.    LO/N14.    OX/U-8.    XS/R10.

POLLUTION CONTROL (TOKYO).                    000
SEE: KOGAI (HAKUA SHOBO).

POLLUTION CONTROL REVIEW.
+ +POLLUT. CONTROL REV.
[NOYES DATA CORP.]
PARK RIDGE, N.J.   NO.1, 1971-
LO/N14.

POLLUTION ENGINEERING.
+ +POLLUT. ENG.
[RICE-THOMPSON]
GREENWICH, CONN.   1, 1969-
LO/N14.
XS/R10.   6(9), 1974-
ISSN 0032-3640

POLLUTION MONITOR.
+ +POLLUT. MONIT.
[WEALDEN P. LTD.]
TONBRIDGE   NO.1, JE/JL 1971-
2M.
ED/N-1.    LD/U-1.    LO/N-6.    LO/N14.    LO/U28.    OX/U-8.
XE/F-2.    XS/R10.

POLLUTION TECHNOLOGY INTERNATIONAL.           XXX
+ +POLLUT. TECHNOL. INT.
[RHODES (PROMOTIONS)]
MANCHESTER   6, 1972-
PREV: WASTE DISPOSAL FROM 1, 1967- 5, 1971.
LO/N14.

POL'SKIJ KARTOGRAFICHESKIJ OBZOR.            000
SEE: POLSKI PRZEGLAD KARTOGRAFICZNY.

POLSKA LUDOWA. MATERIALY I STUDIA.           XXX
+ +POL. LUDOWA.
POLSKA AKADEMIA NAUK: INSTYTUT HISTORII.
WARSAW   1, S 1962- 7, 1968.
SUBS: DZIEJE NAJNOWSZE.
BH/U-1.    CA/U-1.    OX/U-1.

POLSKI PRZEGLAD KARTOGRAFICZNY.
+ +POL. PRZEGLAD KARTOGR.
POLSKIE TOWARZYSTWO GEOGRAFICZNE.
WARSAW   1, 1969-
Q.  ENGL. & RUSS. SUMM.  TITLE ALSO IN ENGL.:
POLISH CARTOGRAPHICAL REVIEW; & RUSS.:
POL'SKIJ KARTOGRAFICHESKIJ OBZOR.
LO/N13.    LO/S13.

POLUPROVODNIKOVAJA TEKHNIKA I MIKROELEKTRONIKA.
+ +POLUPROVODN. TEK. & MIKROELEKTRON. [PTMU-A]
AKADEMIJA NAUK UKRAJINS'KOJI RSR.
KIEV   1, 1966-
SO/U-1.
LO/N13.   2, 1967-

POLYMER JOURNAL (TOKYO).
+ +POLYM. J. (TOKYO).
SOCIETY OF POLYMER SCIENCE (JAPAN).
TOKYO   1, 1970-
LO/N14.    MA/U-1.
BL/U-1.   4, 1973-              LD/U-1.   2, 1971-
ISSN 0032-3896

POLYMER NEWS.
+ +POLYM. NEWS.
[GORDON & BREACH]
NEW YORK & C.   1, 1970-
ED/N-1.    LO/N14.
ISSN 0032-3918

POLYMER-PLASTICS TECHNOLOGY & ENGINEERING.    XXX
+ +POLYM.-PLAST. TECHNOL. & ENG.
[DEKKER]
NEW YORK   2(1), 1973-
PREV: JOURNAL OF MACROMOLECULAR SCIENCE: PART
D: REVIEWS IN POLYMER TECHNOLOGY FROM
D1(1), 1971.
LO/N-4.    LO/N14.

POLYMER SCIENCE & TECHNOLOGY:  GUIDES TO THE   XXX
JOURNAL & REPORT LITERATURE.
+ +POLYM. SCI. & TECHNOL., GUIDES J. & REP. LIT.
AMERICAN CHEMICAL SOCIETY.
WASHINGTON, D.C.   1, 1966- 9, 1971.
PUBL. BY SOCIETY'S CHEMICAL ABSTRACTS SERVICE.
AFTER 9, 1971 PUBLISHED IN COMPUTER-READABLE
FORM ONLY.
LO/N14.   2, 1967-

POLYMER SCIENCE & TECHNOLOGY:  GUIDES TO
PATENT LITERATURE.
+ +POLYM. SCI. & TECHNOL., GUIDES PAT. LIT.
AMERICAN CHEMICAL SOCIETY.
WASHINGTON, D.C.   1, 1966- 9, 1971.
PUBL. BY SOCIETY'S CHEMICAL ABSTRACTS SERVICE.
AFTER 9, 1971 PUBLISHED IN COMPUTER-READABLE
FORM ONLY.
LO/N14.   2, 1967-

POLYMERS, PAINT & COLOUR JOURNAL.             XXX
+ +POLYM. PAINT & COLOUR J.
[FUEL & METALLURGICAL JOURNALS]
LONDON   160(3801), 1971-
PREV: PAINT, OIL & COLOUR JOURNAL FROM 117
(2673), 1950- 160(3800), 1971.
ED/N-1.    LO/N14.    LO/N35.

POLYTEKNISK ARTIKKEL-INDEKS.                  XXX
+ +POLYTEK. ARTIKKEL-INDEKS.
STUDIESELSKAPET FOR NORSK INDUSTRI.
OSLO   21, 1970-
PREV: ARTIKKEL-INDEKS, STUDIESELSKAPET ...
FROM 1, 1949- 20, 1969.
LO/N13.

PONTO.  REVISTA DE POEMAS DE PROCESO.
ST. TEREZA, GUANABARA   1, [?1968]-
EACH ISSUE A FOLDER WITH LOOSE-LEAF CONTENTS.
LO/U-2.

POPULAR ARTS REVIEW.
+ +POP. ARTS REV.
GLASGOW   1(1), 1972-
CA/U-1.    ED/N-1.    OX/U-1.

POPULAR ELECTRONICS INCLUDING ELECTRONICS
WORLD.                                        XXX
+ +POP. ELECTRON. INCL. ELECTRON. WORLD.
[ZIFF-DAVIS PUBL. CO.]
NEW YORK   1, 1972- 4, 1973...
PREV: ELECTRONICS WORLD FROM 61(5), 1959- 86,
1971. SUBS: POPULAR ELECTRONICS.
LO/N14.

POPULAR HI-FI (1971).
+ +POP. HI-FI (1971).
[HAYMARKET PUBL.]
LONDON   1(1), MR 1971-
MON.
LO/N14.   1(11), 1971-
ED/N-1.   1(3), 1971-

POPULATION BULLETIN OF THE UNITED NATIONS.    XXX
SUBS (1968) PART OF: INTERNATIONAL SOCIAL
DEVELOPMENT REVIEW.

**POPULATION NEWSLETTER.**
*+ +POPUL. NEWSL.*
UNITED NATIONS: DEPARTMENT OF ECONOMIC &
SOCIAL AFFAIRS.
*NEW YORK   NO.1, AP 1968-*
Q.  ISSUED BY THE DEP.'S POPULATION DIVISION.
*ED/N-1.    LO/S14.    LO/U-3.*
*MA/P-1.  NO.2, 1968-*
*ISSN 0048-4849*

**POPULIER.**
NATIONALE POPULIEREN COMMISSIE (NETH.)
*WAGENINGEN   1(1), MY 1964-*
*OX/U-3.*

**PORFEYDD.**
*ABERTAWE   CYF 1, 1969-*
*CR/U-1.    SW/U-1.*
*ISSN 0048-4857*

**PORIO SEIWAKUCHIN KENKYU HOKOKU.**
JAKUDOKU SEI-PORIO-UIRUSU-WAKUCHIN KENKYU
KYOGIKAI.
*[TOKYO?]   [NO.1], 1962-*
*LO/N13.*

**POROMERICS PROGRESS.**                         XXX
*+ +POROMERICS PROG.*
SHOE & ALLIED TRADES RESEARCH ASSOCIATION.
*KETTERING, NORTHANTS.  1(1), F 1969- 3(2),*
*1971 ...*
SUBS: SHOE MATERIALS PROGRESS.
*OX/U-1.*
*ED/N-1.  3(1), 1971-          LO/N14.  2(6), 1970-*

**POROSHKOVAJA METALLURGIJA.**
*+ +POROSHK. METALL.*
AKADEMIJA NAUK UKRAJINS'KOJI RSR: INSTYTUT
METALLOKERAMIKY I SPETSIAL'NYKH SPLAVIV.
*KIEV  1, 1961-*
ENGL. SUMM.
*LO/N13.    XY/N-1.*

**PORT OF LONDON.**                              XXX
*+ +PORT LOND.*
PORT OF LONDON AUTHORITY.
*LONDON  45(537), 1970-*
PREV: P.L.A. MONTHLY FROM 1(1), 1925- 45(536),
1970.
*BH/P-1.    LO/N-4.    LO/N14.    LO/U-1.    LO/U-2.*
*SO/U-1.  48(566), 1973-*
*ISSN 0030-8064*

**PORTFOLIO.**
EAST LONDON ARTS MAGAZINE SOCIETY.
*LONDON  NO.1, 1970-*
*OX/U-1.*

**PORTIA LAW JOURNAL.**                          XXX
SUBS (1969): NEW ENGLAND LAW REVIEW.

**PORTSMOUTH PAPERS.**
*+ +PORTSMOUTH PAP.*
PORTSMOUTH CITY COUNCIL.
*PORTSMOUTH  NO.1, 1967-*
*LO/U-1.*

**PORTUGAL ECONOMIC INFORMATION.**
*+ +PORT. ECON. INF.*
PORTUGUESE NATIONAL TRADE OFFICE (LONDON).
*LONDON  NO.1, 1970- 6, 1971. //*
*LO/U-3.    OX/U-1.*

**PORTUGUES NA INGLATERRA.**
*+ +PORT. INGLATERRA.*
*LONDON  NO.1, N 1972-*
*LO/N-1.*

**POSEBNA IZDANJA, GEOLOSKI ZAVOD, SKOPJE.**
*+ +POSEBNA IZD. GEOL. ZAVOD, SKOPJE.*
*SKOPJE  1, 1965-*
ENGL. SUMM.
*DB/S-1.    ED/S-2.    LO/N13.*

**POSEBNA IZDANJA, INSTITUT ZA TEORIJU KNJIZEV-
NOSTI I UMETNOSTI.**
*+ +POSEBNA IZD. INST. TEOR. KNJIZEVNOSTI & UMET.*
*BELGRADE  1, 1962-*
MONOGR.
*NO/U-1.*

**POSEBNA IZDANJA, ISTORIJSKI INSTITUT, SRPSKA
ACADEMIJA NAUKA I UMETNOSTI, SERIJA 1:
JUGOSLOVENSKE ZEMIJE U XX VEKU. = MONOGRAPHIES,
INSTITUT D'HISTOIREA BEOGRAD - SERIE 1: LES
PAYS YOUGOSLAVES AU XX SIECLE.**
*+ +POSEBNA IZD. ISTOR. INST. SRP. ACAD. NAUKA*
*UMET., 1.*
*BELGRADE  1, 1962-*
ON SOME ISSUES BODY APPEARS AS: ISTORIJSKI
INSTITUT U BEOGRADA. SUMM. & T.P. ALSO IN FR.
*OX/U-1.*
*LO/N-3.  2, 1962-*

**POSEBNA IZDANJA, MATEMATICKI INSTITUT U
BEOGRADU.**
*+ +POSEBNA IZD. MAT. INST. BEOGR.*
*BELGRADE  1, 1963-*
SERBOCROAT OR FR.
*GL/U-1.    LO/N-4.    LO/U-2.*

**POSEBNA IZDANJA, ORIJENTALNI INSTITUT U
SARAJEVU.**
*+ +POSEB. IZD. ORIJENT. INST. SARAJEVU.*
*SARAJEVO  1, 1960-*
MONOGR.
*LO/N-3.  6,1968.*

**POSEBNO IZDANJE, PRIRODONAUCEN MUZEJ.**
*+ +POSEBNO IZD. PRIR. MUZ.*
*SKOPJE  1, 1964-*
TEXT IN GER. MACEDONIAN SUMM.
*DB/S-1.*

**POSTAL HISTORY INTERNATIONAL.**
*+ +POSTAL HIST. INT.*
[PROUD-BAILEY CO. LTD.]
*BRIGHTON  1(1), JA 1972-*
M.
*ED/N-1.*

**POSTEPY MIKROBIOLOGII.**
*+ +POSTEPY MIKROBIOL.*
POLSKA AKADEMIA NAUK: KOMITET MIKROBIOLOGI-
CZNY.
*WARSZAW  1(1), S 1962-*
TEXT PARTLY IN ENGL.  ENGL. CONT. LISTS.
*LO/N13.*

**POSTYLLA BOHEMICA.**
*+ +POSTYLLA BOHEM.*
*BREMEN  1, 1972-*
*OX/U-1.*

**POTATO QUARTERLY.**
*+ +POTATO Q.*
POTATO MARKETING BOARD.
*LONDON  NO.1, F 1972-*
*CA/U-1.    CA/U11.    ED/N-1.    LO/N-1.*
*BL/U-1.  4, 1972-*

**POTATO RESEARCH.**                             XXX
*+ +POTATO RES.*
EUROPEAN ASSOCIATION FOR POTATO RESEARCH.
*WAGENINGEN  13(1), MR 1970-*
PREV: EUROPEAN POTATO JOURNAL FROM 1, MR
1958- 12(4), D 1969.
*CA/U11.    LO/N-6.    LO/N14.*
*ISSN 0014-3065*

**POTTERY GAZETTE & GLASS TRADE REVIEW.**        XXX
SUBS (1970): TABLEWARE INTERNATIONAL +
POTTERY GAZETTE.

**POUK ZGODOVINE.**                              000
SEE: NASTAVA ISTORIJE.

**POULTRY MEAT: BROILER & TURKEY EDITION.**
*+ +POULT. MEAT., BROILER & TURK. ED.*
[WATT PUBL. CO.]
*MT. MORRIS, ILL.  1, 1964-*
PREV: POULTRY PROCESSING & MARKETING.
*LO/N13.*

**POULTRY PROCESSING & MARKETING.**             XXX
SUBS (1964): POULTRY MEAT: BROILER & TURKEY
EDITION.

**POULTRY TESTING.**
*+ +POULT. TEST.*
[NATIONAL POULTRY TESTS LTD.]
*GODALMING, SY.  1, 1971-*
M.
*LO/N-6.*

POUR L'ECOLE DU PEUPLE. CAHIERS ETUDIANTS EURO-
PEENS.
*ROME 1, [1970]-*
ENGL., FR., GER., OR ITAL. SUMM. IN OTHER
THREE LANG.
*LO/U-3.*

POVERTY. JOURNAL OF THE ...
CHILD POVERTY ACTION GROUP.
*LONDON NO.1, WINTER 1966-*
S/T VARIES. ORIG: QUARTERLY NEWSLETTER OF ...
*ED/N-1.      HL/U-1.      LO/U-3.      XL/P-8.*
*CB/U-1. NO.5, 1967-              MA/U-1. NO.4, 1967-*
*SH/C-5. NO.5, 1967-              SO/U-1. NO.5, 1967-*
*SW/U-1. NO.5, 1967-*
*AD/U-1. NO.5, 1967- [W. NO.8]*
*GL/U-2. NO.29, 1974-*
*ISSN 0032-5856*

POWDER METALLURGY INTERNATIONAL.
*+ +POWDER METALL. INT.*
[SCHMID]
*FREIBURG 1(1), S 1969-*
*LO/N14.      XS/R10.*
*LO/N35. 3, 1971-*
*ISSN 0048-5012*

POWDER METALLURGY QUARTERLY.                              XXX
SUBS (1966): P/M PARTS ENGINEERING.

POWDER METALLURGY SCIENCE & TECHNOLOGY.
*+ +POWDER METALL. SCI. & TECHNOL.*
FRANKLIN INSTITUTE RESEARCH LABORATORIES.
*PHILADELPHIA 1, 1968-*
*LO/N14.*
*ISSN 0048-5020*

POWER DRIVES.
[TRADE & TECHNICAL P.]
*MORDEN, SURREY 32(372), 1971-*
VOL. NUMBERING CONTINUES THAT OF POWER
TRANSMISSION (LONDON).
*LO/N14.*

POWER TRANSMISSION (LONDON).                              XXX
*+ +POWER TRANSM. (LOND.).*
[TRADE & TECHNICAL P.]
*LONDON 1(1), 1932- 31(371), 1962.//*
SUBS: INCORP. IN INTERNATIONAL POWER EQUIPMENT
NEWS. FROM 1971 VOL. NUMBERING RESUMED BY:
POWER DRIVES.
*LO/N14.*

POWER & WORKS ENGINEERING.                                XXX
SUBS (1967): WORKS ENGINEERING & FACTORY
SERVICES.

POWERBOAT & WATERSPORT.                                   XXX
[LERNHURST PUBL.]
*LONDON 2(2), 1969-*
PREV: WATERSPORT & POWERBOAT FROM [1], 1968-
2(1), 1969.
*LO/N14.*
*OX/U-1. 2(8), 1970-*

POZYVNYE ISTORII. UCHENYE ZAPISKI PO ISTORII
VLKSM.
*+ +POSYVNYE ISTOR.*
VSESOJUZNYJ LENINSKIJ KOMMUNISTICHESKIJ SOJUZ
MOLODEZHI: TSENTRAL'NYJ KOMITET.
*MOSCOW 1, 1969-*
*BH/U-1.      LO/U-3.*

PRACE BIALOSTOCKIEGO TOWARZYSTWA NAUKOWEGO.
*+ +PR. BIALOSTOCKIEGO TOW. NAUK.*
*BIALYSTOK 1, 1963-*
*LO/U-3.      OX/U-1.*
*LO/N-3. VOL.5 (1965).*

PRACE Z DEJIN UNIVERSITY KARLOVY.
*+ +PR. DEJIN UNIV. KARLOVY.*
KARLOVA UNIVERSITA V PRAZE.
*PRAGUE 1, 1966-*
*LA/U-1.      OX/U-1.*

PRACE GEOLOGICZNO-MINERALOGICZNE, UNIWERSYTET
WROCLAWSKI.
*+ +PR. GEOL.-MINER. UNIW. WROCLAW.*
*WROCLAW NO.1, 1969-*
ALSO NUMBERED AS: ACTA UNIVERSITATIS WRATI-
SLAVIENSIS; NO.1 ABOVE = NO.85 OF THE ACTA.
ENGL. & RUSS. SUMM.
*LO/N-3.*

PRACE INSTYTUTU AUTOMATYKI POLSKIEJ AKADEMII
NAUK.
*+ +PR. INST. AUTOM. POL. AKAD. NAUK.*
*WARSAW VYP.1, 1963-*
ENGL. SUMM.
*LO/N13. 82, 1969-*

PRACE INSTYTUTU GOSPODARKI WODNEJ. PROCEED-
INGS OF WATER ECONOMICS RESEARCH INSTITUTE.
TRUDY INSTITUTA VODNOGO KHOZJAJSTVA.
*+ +PR. INST. GOSPOD. WODNEJ.*
*WARSAW 1(1), JA 1961-*
POL. ENGL. & RUSS. ENGL. SUMM. & CONT. LISTS.
*LO/N13. 5(3), 1969-              NW/U-1. 4(3), 1967-*

PRACE INSTYTUTU MASZYN MATEMATYCZNYCH, POLSKA
AKADEMIA NAUK: SERIA A.
*+ +PR. INST. MASZ. MAT. POL. AKAD. NAUK, A.*
*WARSAW 1, 1962-*

PRACE INSTYTUTU MASZYN MATEMATYCZNYCH, POLSKA
AKADEMIA NAUK: SERIA B.
*+ +PR. INST. MASZ. MAT. POL. AKAD. NAUK, B.*
*WARSAW 1, 1963-*
ENGL. SUMM.
*LO/N13.*

PRACE KOMISJI ARCHEOLOGICZNEJ, ODDZIAL W
KRAKOWIE, POLSKA AKADEMIA NAUK.
*+ +PR. KOM. ARCHEOL. ODDZ. KRAKOW. POL. AKAD.*
*NAUK.*
*WROCLAW &C NO.1, 1960-*
*DB/S-1.      LO/U-2.      OX/U-1.*
*LO/N-3. NO.5, 1964.*

PRACE KOMISJI AUTOMATYKI, WYDZIAL NAUK TECH-
NICZNYCH, POZNANSKIE TOWARZYSTWO PRZYJACIOL
NAUK.
*+ +PR. KOM. AUTOM. WYDZ. NAUK TECH. POZNAN. TOW.*
*PRZYJACIOL NAUK.*
POZNANSKIE TOWARZYSTWO PRZYJACIOL NAUK: KOMISJA
AUTOMATYKI.
*POZNAN 1(1), OC 1969-*
ENGL. SUMM. KOMISJA AUTOMATYKI SUBORD. TO:
WYDZIAL NAUK TECHNICZNYCH OF POZNANSKIE ...
*DB/S-1.*

PRACE KOMISJA BUDOWNICTWA I ARCHITEKTURY,
POZNANSKIE TOWARZYSTWO PRZYJACIOL NAUK.
*+ +PR. KOM. BUDOWNICTWA & ARCHIT. POZNAN. TOW.*
*PRZJACIOL NAUK.*
*POZNAN 1(1), OC 1961-*
KOMISJA IS PART OF TOWARZYSTWO'S WYDZIAL NAUK
TECHNICZNYCH.
*DB/S-1.*

PRACE KOMISJI BUDOWY MASZYN I ELEKTROTECHNIKI,
POZNANSKIE TOWARZYSTWO PRZYJACIOL NAUK.
*+ +PR. KOM. BUDOWY MASZ. ELECTROTECH. POZNAN.*
*TOW. PRZYJ. NAUK.*
*POZNAN 1(1), F 1961-*
KOMISJA IS PART OF TOWARZYSTWO'S WYDZIAL NAUK
TECHNICZNYCH.
*DB/S-1.*
*LO/N13. 1, 1961- 2, 1963. [W. 2(1)]*

PRACE KOMISJI BUDOWY MASZYN, WYDZIAL NAUK
TECHNICZNYCH, POZNANSKIE TOWARZYSTWO PRZYJACIOL
NAUK.
*+ +PR. KOM. BUDOWY MASZ. WYDZ. NAUK TECH. POZNAN.*
*TOW. PRZYJACIOL NAUK.*
POZNANSKIE TOWARZYSTWO PRZYJACIOL NAUK: KOMISJA
BUDOWY MASZYN.
*POZNAN 1(1), 1969-*
ENGL. SUMM. KOMISJA ... SUBORD. TO: WYDZIAL
NAUK TECHNICZNYCH OF: POZNANSKIE TOW. PRZYJ.
NAUK.
*DB/S-1.*

PRACE KOMISJI CERAMICZNEJ, ODDZIAL W KRAKOWIE,
POLSKA AKADEMIA NAUK: CERAMIKA.                           XXX
*+ +PR. KOM. CERAM. ODDZ. KRAKOW. POL. AKAD. NAUK,*
*CERAM.*
*CRACOW 11, JL 1969-*
ENGL. & RUSS. SUMM. PREV: PRACE KOMISJI
NAUK TECHNICZNYCH, ODDZIAL W KRAKOWIE, POLSKA
AKADEMIA NAUK: CERAMIKA FROM 1, 1964- 10,
1968.
*DB/S-1.      LO/N13.      XM/T-1.*

PRACE KOMISJI ETNOGRAFICZNEJ, WYZIAL HISTORII
I NAUK SPOLECZNYCH, POZNANSKIE TOWARZYSTWO
PRZYJACIOL NAUK.
*+ +PR. KOM. ETHNOGR. WYZIAL HIST. NAUK SPOLECZ.*
*POZNAN. TOW. PRZYJ. NAUK.*
*POZNAN 1(1), 1968-*
ENGL. SUMM.
*BH/U-1.      DB/S-1.      ED/U-1.      OX/U-1.*

PRACE KOMISJI FILOLOGII KLASYCZNEJ, ODDZIAL W
KRAKOWIE, POLSKA AKADEMIA NAUK.
++PR. KOM. FIL. KLASYCZNEJ ODDZIAL KRAKOWIE
POL. AKAD. NAUK.
WROCLAW NR.2, D 1960-
MONOGR.
DB/S-1.    OX/U-1.

PRACE KOMISJI GORNICZO-GEODEZYJNEJ, ODDZIAL W          XXX
KRAKOWIE, POLSKA AKADEMIA NAUK: GEODEZJA.
++PR. KOM. GORN.-GEOD. ODDZ. KRAKOW. POL. AKAD.
NAUK, GEOD.
CRACOW 4, 1969-
MONOGR. ENGL. & RUSS. SUMM. PREV: PRACE
KOMISJI NAUK TECHNICZNYCH, ODDZIAL W KRAKOWIE,
POLSKA AKADEMIA NAUK: GEODEZJA FROM 1, 1964-
3, 1967.
DB/S-1.
LO/N13.  NO.7, 1969-

PRACE KOMISJI GORNICZO-GEODEZYJNEJ, ODDZIAL        XXX
W KRAKOWIE, POLSKA AKADEMIA NAUK: GORNICTWO.
++PR. KOM. GORN.-GEOD. ODDZ. KRAKOW. POL. AKAD.
NAUK, GORN.
CRACOW 7, JE 1969-
MONOGR. ENGL. & RUSS. SUMM. PREV: PRACE
KOMISJI NAUK TECHNICZNYCH, ODDZIAL W KRAKOWIE,
POLSKA AKADEMIA NAUK: GORNICTWO FROM 1, JL
1965- 6, 1968.
DB/S-1.

PRACE KOMISJI HISTORYCZNOLITERACKIEJ, ODDZIAL
W KRAKOWIE, POLSKA AKADEMIA NAUK.
++PR. KOM. HIST.LIT. ODDZ. KRAKOW. POL. AKAD.
NAUK.
WROCLAW &C NO.1, 1961-
MONOGR. FR. & RUSS. SUMM.
CA/U-1.    DB/S-1.    SW/U-1.
LO/N-3.  NO.12, 1964.

PRACE KOMISJI JEZYKOZNAWSTWA, ODDZIAL W
KRAKOWIE, POLSKA AKADEMIA NAUK.
++PR. KOM. JEZYKOZN. ODDZ. KRAKOW. POL. AKAD.
NAUK.
CRACOW NO.1, 1964-
CA/U-1.
ED/U-1.  NO.3, 1964.

PRACE KOMISJI JEZYKOZNAWCZEJ, POZNANSKIE
TOWARZYSTWO PRZYJACIOL NAUK.
++PR. KOM. JEZYKOZNAW. POZNAN. TOW. PRZYJAC.
NAUK.
POZNAN  1(1), N 1962-
MONOGR. KOMISJA PART OF THE TOWARZYSTWO'S
WYDZIAL FILOLOGICZNO-FILOZOFICZNY.
DB/S-1.

PRACE KOMISJI METALURGICZNO-ODLEWNICZEJ,
ODDZIAL W KRAKOWIE, POLSKA AKADEMIA NAUK:
METALURGIA.                                            XXX
++PR. KOM. MET.-ODLEW. ODDZ. KRAKOW. POL. AKAD.
NAUK, MET.
CRACOW 9, JL 1969-
MONOGR. ENGL. & RUSS. SUMM. PREV: PRACE
KOMISJI NAUK TECHNICZNYCH, ODDZIAL W KRAKOWIE,
POLSKA AKADEMIA NAUK: METALURGIA FROM 1, 1965-
8, 1968.
DB/S-1.
LO/N13.  NO.9, 1969-

PRACE KOMISJI NAUK EKONOMICZNYCH, ODDZIAL W
KRAKOWIE, POLSKA AKADEMIA NAUK.
++PR. KOM. NAUK EKON. ODDZ. KRAKOW. POLSKA AKAD.
NAUK.
CRACOW &C. NR.1, 1960-
BH/U-1.    LO/U-3.

PRACE KOMISJI NAUK EKONOMICZNYCH, WYDZIAL
HISTORII I NAUK SPOLECZNYCH, POZNANSKIE
TOWARZYSTWO PRZYJACIOL NAUK.
++PR. KOM. NAUK. EKON. WYDZ. HIST. NAUK SPOL.
POZNAN. TOW. PRZYJ. NAUK.
POZNAN 1(1), OC 1968-
MONOGR. ENGL. SUMM.
BH/U-1.    DB/S-1.    OX/U-1.

PRACE LABORATORIA RYBARSTVA, SLOVENSKA AKA-
DEMIA VIED.
++PR. LAB. RYBARST. SLOV. AKAD. VIED.
BRATISLAVA  ZV.1, 1962-
LO/N-2.    XN/R-1.

PRACE, MAZOWIECKI OSRODEK BADAN NAUKOWYCH.
++PR. MAZOWIECKI OSRODEK BADAN NAUK.
WROCLAW 1, 1967-
BH/U-1.    LO/U-3.    OX/U-1.

PRACE MONOGRAFICZNE, KOMISJA FILOLOGII
KLASYCZNEJ, ODDZIAL W KRAKOWIE, POLSKA
AKADEMIA NAUK.
++PR. MONOGR. KOMISJA FIL. KLASYCZNEJ ODDZIAL
KRAKOWIE POL. AKAD. NAUK.
WROCLAW 1, AP 1960-
DB/S-1.

PRACE OSRODKA METODYCZNEGO UNIWERSYTECKICH
STUDIOW DLA PRACUJACYCH, UNIWERSYTET IM.
ADAMA MICKIEWICZA W POZNANIU.
++PR. OSRODKA METOD. UNIW. STUD. PRACUJACYCH
UNIW. IM. ADAMA MICKIEWICZA POZNAN.
POZNAN NR. 1, 1967-
MONOGR.
LO/N-3. 12, 1970-

PRACE PSYCHOLOGICZNE, UNIWERSYTET WROCLAWSKI.
++PR. PSYCHOL. UNIW. WROCLAW.
WROCLAW 1, 1972-
ALSO NUMBERED AS: ACTA UNIVERSITATIS WRATI-
SLAVIENSIS. NO.1 ABOVE = NO.148 OF THE ACTA.
LO/N-3.

PRACE I STUDIA INSTYTUTU GEOGRAFICZNEGO UNIW-
ERSYTETU WARSZAWSKIEGO.
++PR. & STUD. INST. GEOGR. UNIW. WARSZAWSKIEGO.
UNIWERSYTET WARSZAWSKI: KATEDRA KLIMATOLOGII.
WARSAW 1, 1964-
ENGL. SUMM.  KATEDRA SUBORD. TO: INSTYTUT
GEOGRAFICZNY.
LO/N13.

PRACE VYZKUMNEHO USTAVU RYBARSKEHO VE VODNAN-
ECH.
++PR. VYZK. UST. RYBARSKEHO VOD.
CESKOSLOVENSKA AKADEMIE ZEMEDELSKYCH VED,
VYZKUMNY USTAV RYBARSKY VE VODNANECH.
VODNANY 1, 1962-
ENGL., FR. & RUSS. SUMM.
LO/N13.

PRACE WYDZIALU V: NAUK TECHNICZNYCH, LODZKIE
TOWARZYSTWO NAUKOWE.
++PR. WYDZ. V, NAUK TECH. LODZ. TOW. NAUK.
LODZ 1, MR 1963-
DB/S-1.    GL/U-1.

PRACE WYDZIALU BIOLOGII I NAUKI O ZIEMI,
UNIWERSYTET IM. ADAMA MICKIEWICZA W POZNANIU,
SERIA BIOLOGIA.
++PR. WYDZ. BIOL. NAUK. ZIEMI UNIW. IM. ADAMA
MICKIEWICZA POZNANIU, BIOL.
POZNAN 1, 1961-
BL/U-1.    DB/S-1.

PRACE WYDZIALU BIOLOGII I NAUK O ZIEMI,
UNIWERSYTET IM. ADAMA MICKIEWICZA W POZNANIU:
SERIA GEOGRAFIA.
++PR. WYDZ. BIOL. & NAUK ZIEMI UNIW. IM. ADAMA
MICKIEWICZA POZNANIU, GEOGR.
POZNAN 1, 1962-
MONOGR.
LO/S13.    OX/U-1.

PRACE WYDZIALU BIOLOGII I NAUKI O ZIEMI,
UNIWERSYTET IM. ADAMA MICKIEWICZA W POZNANIU,
SERIA GEOLOGIA.
++PR. WYDZ. BIOL. NAUKI ZIEMI UNIW. IM. ADAMA
MICKIEWICZA POZNANIU, GEOL.
POZNAN 1, F 1961-
MONOGR.
DB/S-1.    OX/U-8.

PRACE WYDZIALU FILOLOGICZNEGO, UNIWERSYTET
IM. ADAMA MICKIEWICZA W POZNANIU: SERIA
FILOLOGIA UGROFINSKA.
++PR. WYDZ. FILOL. UNIW. IM. ADAMA MICKIEWICZA
POZNAN., FIL. UGROFINSKA.
POZNAN NR. 1, 1969-
MONOGR. VARIOUS LANG.
GL/U-1.    LO/N-3.    OX/U-1.

PRACE WYDZIALU HUMANISTYCZNEGO, LUBELSKIE TOW-
ARZYSTWO NAUKOWE - MONOGRAFIE.
++PR. WYDZ. HUM. LUBELSKIE TOW. NAUK., MONOGR.
WROCLAW TOM 1, 1967-
CA/U-1.

PRACE WYDIALU NAUK HUMANISTYCZNYCH, BYDGOS-
KIE TOWARZYSTWO NAUKOWE - SERIA B.
++PR. WYDZ. NAUK HUM. BYDGOSKIE TOW. NAUK., B.
BYDGOSZCZ 1, JE 1965-
MONOGR.
CA/U-1.

**PRACTICA FARMACEUTICA.**
(RUMANIA) DIRECTIA GENERALA FARMACEUTICA.
(RUMANIA) MINISTERUL SANATATII.
[EDITURA MEDICALA]
*BUCHAREST  1, 1968-*
*LO/N13.*

**PRACTICAL AVIATION.**
+ +*PRACT. AVIAT.*
[PRACTAVIA LTD.]
*BOOKER, BUCKS.  NO.1, OC 1971-*
Q.
*ED/N-1.     OX/U-1.*

**PRACTICAL BOATING.**
+ +*PRACT. BOAT.*
*LONDON   1, 1967-*
S/T: POWER & SAIL.
*ED/N-1.*

**PRACTICAL CAMPER.**
+ +*PRACT. CAMPER.*
*LONDON  1, F 1967-*
*ED/N-1.*
*ISSN 0032-6356*

**PRACTICAL MAINTENANCE & CLEANING.**                                XXX
+ +*PRACT. MAINT. & CLEAN.*
[ILIFFE]
*LONDON   1(1), 1963- 5(6), 1967...*
SUBS: MAINTENANCE.
*ED/N-1.     LO/N-4.     OX/U-1.*
*LO/N-7. 3, 1965-                       LO/N14.  1(3), 1963-*
*LO/P20. (ONE YEAR FILE)*
*NO/P-1. (ONE YEAR FILE)*

**PRACTICAL TELEVISION & TELEVISION TIMES.***
+ +*PRACT. TELEV. & TELEV. TIMES.*
[NEWNES]
*LONDON  1(1), 1950- 20(240), 1965.*
TITLE VARIES: PUBL. AS PRACTICAL TELEVISION
FROM 1(1)- 1(4), 1950;  15(175), 1965- 20
(240), 1970.  PREV: SUPPL. TO PRACTICAL
WIRELESS.  SUBS: TELEVISION (LONDON).
*ED/P-1.*     LO/N14.**

**PRACTICE WITH SCIENCE.**
+ +*PRACT. SCI. (R. AGRIC. SOC.)*
ROYAL AGRICULTURAL SOCIETY OF ENGLAND.
*LONDON   1, 1967-*
S/T: NAC & RASE REVIEW.  PREV: RASE REVIEW.
*LD/U-1.*

**PRACTICE OF SURGERY.  CURRENT REVIEW.**
+ +*PRACT. SURG.*
[C.V. MOSBY CO.]
*ST. LOUIS, MO.  1, 1972-*
*CA/U-1.*

**PRAKSA.  CASOPIS ZA DRUSTVENA PITANJA.**
[NOVINSKO IZDAVACKO PREDUZECE 'POBJEDA']
*TITOGRAD  1(1), 1964-*
*OX/U-1.*
*LO/N13.  5, 1970-*

**PRAKTISCHE WINKE FUR DIE BLECHVERARBEITUNG
UND OBERFLACHENBEHANDLUNG.**
+ +*PRAKT. WINKE BLECHVERARB. & OBERFLACHENBEHANDL*
DEUTSCHE FORSCHUNGSGESELLSCHAFT FUR BLECHVER-
ARBEITUNG UND OBERFLACHENBEHANDLUNG.
*DUSSELDORF  1, 1970-*
*LO/N14.*

**PRATIQUE DES INDUSTRIES MECANIQUES.**                              XXX
SUBS (1970): MATERIAUX ET TECHNIQUES.

**PRAXIS.  FILIZOFSKI CASOPIS.**
HRVATSKO FILOZOFSKO DRUSTVO.
*ZAGREB  1, 1964-*
*OX/U-1.*

**PRAYER FOCUS.**                                                    XXX
INTERNATIONAL SOCIETY FOR THE EVANGELIZATION
OF THE JEWS.
*EASTBOURNE  NO.1, 1973-*
PREV: FOCUS ON PRAYER FROM NO.1, 1971- 6, 1973
*ED/N-1.*

**PRAZSKY SBORNIK HISTORICKY.**                                      XXX
+ +*PRAZSKY SB. HIST.*
PRAZSKA INFORMACNI SLUZBA.
*PRAGUE  1964-*
PREV: PRAZSKY SBORNIK VLASTIVEDNY FROM 1962-
1963.
*CA/U-1.     LA/U-1.     OX/U-1.*

**PRAZSKY SBORNIK VLASTIVEDNY.**                                     XXX
+ +*PRAZSKY SB. VLASTIV.*
PRAZSKA INFORMACNI SLUZBA.
*PRAGUE  1962- 1963.*
SUBS: PRAZSKY SBORNIK HISTORICKY.
*CA/U-1.     OX/U-1.*

**PRECAST CONCRETE.**                                                XXX
+ +*PRECAST CONCR.*
CEMENT & CONCRETE ASSOCIATION.
*LONDON  1, 1970-*
PREV: CONCRETE BUILDING & CONCRETE PRODUCTS
FROM 15, 1940- 44, 1969.
*DB/U-2.     LD/U-1.     LO/N14.     MA/U-1.     OX/U-1.*
*ED/N-1.  2(2), 1971-                      EX/U-1.  2, 1971-*
*SF/U-1.  2, 1971-*
*ISSN 0010-5325*

**PRECIGAZ.**
[L'AIR LIQUIDE]
*[PARIS?]  NO.1, [1966?]-*
*LO/N14.*

**PRECISION TOOLS.**                                                 XXX
+ +*PRECIS. TOOLS. [PRET-B]*
[PENTICE P. LTD.]
*WINCHESTER  NO.1- 3, 1969; APR 1972-*
INCORP: CUTTING TOOLS FROM NO.1, 1967- NO.31,
1969; & MEASURING TOOLS FROM NO.1, MY 1968-
NO.13, MY/JE 1969.
*BH/P-1.     ED/N-1.     LO/N14.     OX/U-8.*
*GL/U-2.  1972-                       XS/R10.  NO.2, 1969-*
*ISSN 0556-3011*

**PREMIERE.**
[TONIC PUBL. LTD.]
*LONDON  NO.1, JL 1969-*
*ED/N-1.*
*OX/U-1.  1970-*

**PREPARATION & PROPERTIES OF SOLID STATE
MATERIALS.**
+ +*PREP. & PROP. SOLID STATE MATER.*
[DEKKER]
*NEW YORK  1, 1971-*
*BH/U-3.     LD/U-1.     LO/N14.*

**PREPARATIVE BIOCHEMISTRY.**
+ +*PREP. BIOCHEM.*
[DEKKER]
*NEW YORK  1, JA 1971-*
Q.
*BN/U-2.     LO/S-3.     SH/U-1.*
*LO/N14.  2, 1972-                    XS/R10.  3(1), 1973-*
*ISSN 0032-7484*

**PRESENCE.  A MAGAZINE OF THE REVOLUTION.**
*BUFFALO, NY  NO.1, 1967-*
*LO/U-2.*

**PRESENCE FRANCOPHONE.  REVUE SEMESTRIELLE DU
CELEF.**
UNIVERSITE DE SHERBROOKE: CENTRE D'ETUDE DES
LITTERATURES D'EXPRESSION FRANCAISE.
*SHERBROOKE  NO.1, 1970-*
*LO/N-1.*
*ISSN 0048-5195*

**PRESENCE DU GROUPE CDF.**
CHARBONNAGES DE FRANCE.
[ETIENNE MORIN]
*NEUILLY-SUR-SEINE   1(1), 1966-*
IN ACTUAL TITLE 'D' IN 'CDF' IN LOWER CASE.
*LO/N14.*

**PRESENCIA.  TRIBUNA LIBERTARIA.**
*PARIS   N/D 1965-*
2M.
*LO/U-3.*
*LO/U-3.  1, 1965- 8, 1967.*

**PRESS RELEASES, INFORMATION DEPARTMENT, LEAG-
UE OF ARAB STATES.**
+ +*PRESS RELEASES INF. DEP. LEAGUE ARAB STATES.*
[CAIRO]  1, JA 1969-
*LO/U-3.*

**PRESSE MEDICALE.**                                                 XXX
SUBS (1972): NOUVELLE PRESSE MEDICALE.

**PRESS-UPS.  A MAGAZINE OF INFORMATION.**
*EDINBURGH  1, N/D 1970-*
*ED/N-1.     LO/U-2.*

PRESSURE VESSELS & PIPING.
[ADVANCED SCIENCE PUBL.]
 LONDON 1, 1973-
 S/T: AN INTERNATIONAL JOURNAL. COVER TITLE:
 INTERNATIONAL JOURNAL OF PRESSURE VESSELS &
 PIPING.
 BL/U-1.    ED/N-1.    GL/U-2.    LO/N14.    OX/U-8.    SH/U-3.
 XS/R10.
 CA/U-1.    1(2), 1973-

PRESUPUESTO (SPAIN).
 (SPAIN) MINISTERIO DE HACIENDA.
 [MADRID] [1], 1966-
 2A.  EACH ISSUE COVERS CURRENT & SUCCEEDING
 YEARS. PREV: PRESUPUESTOS GENERALES DES ESTADO
 (SPAIN).
 LO/U-3.

PRESUPUESTOS GENERALES DES ESTADO (SPAIN).          000
 SUBS (1966): PRESUPUESTO (SPAIN).

PRETORIA THEOLOGICAL STUDIES.
 ++PRETORIA THEOL. STUD.
 [BRILL]
 LEIDEN 1, 1971-
 OX/U-1.
 LO/N-1.    1, 1971.

PREUVES. LES IDEES QUI CHANGENT LE MONDE.
 SOCIETE D'ETUDES ET DE PUBLICATIONS ECONOMIQUES
 PARIS 1, 1970-
 Q.  SPONS. BODY ALSO ASSOCIATION INTERNATION-
 ALE POUR LA LIBERTE DE LA CULTURE.
 LO/N17.
 ISSN 0032-7980

PREVENT. THE JOURNAL FOR ALL WHO WOULD PREVENT
DISEASE.
 LONDON 1(1), D/JA 1972/73-
 6/A.
 BL/U-1.    CA/U-1.    CO/U-1.    DB/U-2.    ED/N-1.

PREVENTIVE MEDICINE.
 ++PREV. MED.
 AMERICAN HEALTH FOUNDATION.
 [ACADEMIC P.]
 NEW YORK 1, MR 1972-
 Q.

PREVIEW OF FORTHCOMING BOOKS.
 SOUTH CROYDON NO.1, 1968-
 SUPPL. TO: PUBLISHER.
 ED/N-1.
 OX/U-1. NO.1, 1968- 11, 1970.

PRIBOROSTROENIE.          XXX
 SUBS (1967): PRIBORY I SISTEMY UPRAVLENIJA.

PRIBOROSTROENIE, MEZHVEDOMSTVENNYJ RESPUBLIK-
AN SKIJ NAUCHNO-TEKHNNICHESKIJ SBORNIK.
 ++PRIBOROSTR. MEZHVEDOM. RESPUB. NAUCH.-TEKH. SB
 (RUSSIA USSR) MINISTERSTVO VYSSHEGO I SREDNEGO
 SPETSIAL'NOGO OBRAZOVANIJA USSR.
 KIEV 1, 1965-
 BH/U-1.

PRIBORY I METODY ANALIZA IZLUCHENIJ.          XXX
 SUBS (1962): VOPROSY DOZIMETRII I ZASHCHITY
 OT IZLUCHENIJ.

PRIBORY I SISTEMY AVTOMATIKI.
 ++PRIB. & SIST. AVTOM.
 KHAR'KOVSKIJ INSTITUT GORNOGO MASHINOSTRO-
 ENIJA, AVTOMATIKI I VYCHISLITEL'NOJ TEKHNIKI.
 KHAR'KOV 1, 1965-
 S/T: RESPUBLIKANSKIJ MEZHVEDOMSTVENNYJ
 NAUCHNO-TEKHNICHESKIJ SBORNIK. TITLE VARIES:
 VOL.1: PRIBORY I USTROISTVA SREDSTV AVTOMATIKI
 I TELEMEKHANIKI.
 BH/U-1.    9, 1969    LO/N13.    2, 1966-

PRIBORY I SISTEMY UPRAVLENIJA.
 ++PRIB. & SIST. UPR.
 (RUSSIA USSR) MINISTERSTVO PRIBOROSTROENIJA,
 SREDSTV AVTOMATIZATSII I SISTEM UPRAVLENIJA ...
 MOSCOW 1967 (1)-
 PREV: PRIBOROSTROENIE., TO 1966 (12).  NAME
 OF MIN. CONTINUES: ... I TSENTRAL'NOGO PRAV-
 LENIJA NAUCHNO-TEKHNICHESKOGO OBSHCHESTVA
 PRIBOROSTROITEL'NOJ PROMYSHLENNOSTI.
 BH/U-1.    LO/N14.

PRIBORY I SISTEMY UPRAVLENIJA; (ENGL. TRANSL.)
 SEE: SOVIET JOURNAL OF INSTRUMENTATION &
 CONTROL.

PRIBORY I USTROISTVA SREDSTV AVTOMATIKI I          000
TELEMEKHANIKI.
 SEE: PRIBORY I SISTEMY AVTOMATIKI.

PRIEM I OBRABOTKA INFORMATSII V STRUKTURNO-
SLOZHNYKH INFORMATSIONNYKH SISTEMAKH.
 ++PRIEM & OBRAB. INF. STRUKT. INF. SIST.
 KAZANSKIJ GOSUDARSTVENNYJ UNIVERSITET.
 KAZAN' 1, 1969-
 BH/U-1.    LO/N13.

PRIKLADNAJA GEOMETRIJA I INZHENERNAJA GRAFIKA.
 ++PRIKL. GEOM. & INZH. GRAFIKA. [PGIG-B]
 KIEVSKIJ INZHENERNO-STROITEL'NYJ INSTITUT.
 KIEV 1, 1956-
 S/T: MEZHVEDOMSTVENNYJ RESPUBLIKANSKIJ
 NAUCHNYJ SBORNIK.
 XY/N-1.
 LO/N13.    4, 1966-

PRIKLADNAJA MATEMATIKA I PROGRAMMIROVANIE.
 ++PRIKL. MAT. & PROGRAM.
 AKADEMIJA NAUK MOLDAVSKOJ SSR: INSTITUT MATEM-
 ATIKI S VYCHISLITEL'NYM TSENTROM.
 KISHINEV 1, 1969-
 LO/N13.

PRIKLADNAJA MEKHANIKA (ENGL. TRANSL.).          000
 SEE: SOVIET APPLIED MECHANICS.

PRILOZI ZA ISTORIJU SOCIJALIZMA.
 ++PRILOZI ISTOR. SOCIJALIZMA.
 INSTITUT ZA IZUCAVANJE RADNICKOG POKRETA.
 BELGRADE 1, 1964-
 TITLE ALSO IN ENGL., FR., GER. & RUSS. ENGL.
 OR RUSS. SUMM.
 OX/U-1.

PRIMARY MATHEMATICS.          XXX
 ++PRIMARY MATH. [PMTH-A]
 [PERGAMON]
 OXFORD 6, 1968-
 PREV: TEACHING ARITHMETIC FROM 1, 1963- 5,
 1967.
 BL/C-2.    LD/U-2.    LV/U-2.
 CO/U-1.    7, 1969-
 ISSN 0032-8294

PRIMATE BEHAVIOR. DEVELOPMENTS IN FIELD &
LABORATORY RESEARCH.
 ++PRIMATE BEHAV.
 [ACADEMIC P.]
 LONDON &C. 1, 1970-
 CA/U-3.    CA/U-6.    GL/U-1.    MA/U-1.

PRIMENENIE MATEMATIKI V EKONOMIKE.
 ++PRIMEN. MAT. EKON.
 LENINGRADSKIJ GOSUDARSTVENNYJ UNIVERSITET.
 LENINGRAD VYP.1, 1963-
 ISSUED BY THE BODY'S KAFEDRA I LABORATORIJA
 EKONOMIKO-MATEMATICHESKIKH METODOV.
 BH/U-1.    GL/U-1.    OX/U-1.
 CC/U-1.    2, 1964-
 LO/U-3.    1, 1963- 4, 1967.

PRIMITIVE ART SERIES.
 ++PRIMITIVE ART SER.
 MILWAUKEE PUBLIC MUSEUM.
 MILWAUKEE NO.1, 1961-
 LO/N-2.

PRINT OUT.
 [CREED & CO. LTD.]
 BRIGHTON NO.1, 1966-
 LO/N14.

PRINT OUT. THE NEWSLETTER OF THE ...
 ASSOCIATION OF SCIENTIFIC, TECHNICAL &
 MANAGERIAL STAFFS.
 LONDON [NO.1], OC/N 1971-
 Q.
 LO/U-3.

PRINT ROOM.          XXX
 [NORTHWOOD PUBLS. LTD.]
 LONDON 1, 1969- 3(30), 1971.
 SUBS. INCORP. IN: PRINTING EQUIPMENT & MATE-
 RIALS.
 LO/N14.
 OX/U-1.    1(2), 1969-
 ISSN 0032-8561

PRINTING ART.
 ++PRINT. ART.
 [STELLAR P.]
 HATFIELD, HERTS. 1, SPRING 1973-
 Q.
 DB/U-2.    MA/U-1.

PRINTING INDUSTRY.
++PRINT. IND.
[PRINTING INDUSTRY MAGAZINE LTD.]
 LONDON NO.1, S 1970-
S/T: THE PRINTER'S GUIDE TO PAPER PRICES,
EQUIPMENT & NEW PRODUCTS.
 ED/N-1.    LO/N14.    OX/U-1.
 ISSN 0019-3224

PRINTING JOURNAL, RES. ASS. PAP. & BOARD,
PRINT. & PACKAG. IND.  (1968)                        000
 SEE: PIRA PRINTING JOURNAL.

PRINTING MANAGEMENT.                                 XXX
++PRINT. MANAGE.
[PENTON PUBL. CO.]
 CLEVELAND, OHIO 100(12), 1970-
 PREV:  PRINTING PRODUCTION FROM 88(9), 1958-
 100(11), 1970.
 LO/N13.
 ISSN 0032-8650

PRINTING PRODUCTION.                                 XXX
 SUBS (1970):  PRINTING MANAGEMENT.

PRINTING TECHNOLOGY.                                 XXX
 SUBS (1973): PROFESSIONAL PRINTER.

PRINTING TRADES JOURNAL.
++PRINT. TRADES J.
[BENN]
 LONDON 972, 1968...
 PREV: GRAPHIC TECHNOLOGY FROM  1, MY/JE 1961.
 CA/U-1.    LO/N14.

PRIORITY NEWS.
ADVISORY CENTRE FOR EDUCATION FOR PRIORITY.
 CAMBRIDGE NO.1, 1972-
 LV/U-2.

PRIRODNAJA OBSTANOVKA I FAUNY PROSHLOGO.
++PRIR. OBSTANOVKA FAUNY PROSHLOGO.
AKADAMIJA NAUK UKRAJINS'KOJI RSR: INSTYTUT
ZOOLOHIJI.
 KIEV VYP.  1, 1963-
 LO/N-2.
 LO/N13.  3, 1967-

PRISPEVKY K DEJINAM KSC.                             XXX
 SUBS (1968): REVUE DEJIN SOCIALISMU.

PRIVATE LIBRARY: QUARTERLY JOURNAL OF THE
PRIVATE LIBRARIES ASSOCIATION. 2S.
++PRIV. LIBR. 2S.
 LONDON 2ND SERIES  1, 1968-
 1ST SERIES FROM  1(7), 1958- 8(4), 1967.
 LD/U-1.    LO/U-2.
 ISSN 0032-8893

PRIVATE PRINTER & PRIVATE PRESS.
++PRIV. PRINTER & PRIV. PRESS.
 OXFORD NO.1, F 1968-
 OX/U-1.

PROBABILISTIC METHODS IN APPLIED MATHEMATICS.
++PROBABIL. METH. APPL. MATH.
[ACADEMIC P.]
 NEW YORK  1, 1968-
 GL/U-1.

PROBLEMOS. FILOSOFIJOS, SOCIOLOGIJOS, LOGIKO-
OS, ESTETIKOS, ETIKOS IR ATEIZMO MOKSLINIS
LEIDINYS.
(LITHUANIA) LIETUVOS TSR AUKSTOJO IR SPECIAL-
IOJO VIDURINIO MOKSLO MINISTERIJA.
 VILNIUS  1, 1968-
 2/A.  ENGL. & RUSS. SUMM.
 LO/N-3.

PROBLEMES ACTUELS DE PHARMACOPSYCHIATRIE.           000
 SEE:  MODERN PROBLEMS OF PHARMACOPSYCHIATRY.

PROBLEMES ACTUELS RELATIFS A LA NUTRITION ET A
LA DIETETIQUE.
++PROBL. ACTUELS RELATIFS NUTR. DIET.
[MASSON]
 PARIS  1, 1964-
 LO/N13.

PROBLEMAS DEL DESARROLLO.  REVISTA LATINOAMER-
ICANA DE ECONOMIA.
++PROBL. DESARROLLO.
 UNIVERSIDAD NACIONAL AUTONOMA DE MEXICO:
INSTITUTO DE INVESTIGACIONES ECONOMICAS.
 MEXICO 1(1), OC/D 1969-
 Q.
 LO/U-3.

PROBLEMS OF DESERT DEVELOPMENT.                      000
 SEE: PROBLEMY OSVOENIJA PUSTYN'.

PROBLEMS OF ONTOGENESIS.                             000
 SEE: ZAGADNIENIA ONTOGENEZY.

PROBLEMY ANALITICHESKOJ KHIMII.
++PROBL. ANAL. KHIM.
 AKADEMIJA NAUK SSSR: INSTITUT GEOKHIMII I
ANALITICHESKOJ KHIMII.
 MOSCOW 1, 1970-
 LO/N13.

PROBLEMY ENDOKRINOLOGII.                             XXX
++PROBL. ENDOKRINOL. [PROE-A]
(RUSSIA USSR) MINISTERSTVO ZDRAVOOKHRANENIJA.
 MOSCOW 13(1), 1967-
 ENGL. SUMM. & CONT. LISTS.  PREV: PROBLEMY
 ENDOKRINOLOGII I GORMONOTERAPII FROM 1(1),
 1955- 12(6), 1966.  SPONS. BODY ALSO: VSESO-
 JUZNOE NAUCHNOE OBSHCHESTVO ENDOKRINOLOGOV.
 LO/N13.  14, 1968-

PROBLEMY ENDOKRINOLOGII I GORMONOTERAPII.           XXX
 SUBS (1967): PROBLEMY ENDOKRINOLOGII.

PROBLEMY GEOGRAFII MOLDAVII.
++PROBL. GEOGR. MOLD.
 AKADEMIJA NAUK MOLDAVSKOJ SSR: OTDEL GEOGRAFII.
 KISHINEV  1, 1966-
 SPONS. BODY ALSO: GEOGRAFICHESKOE OBSHCHESTVO
 MOLDAVII.
 OX/U-1.
 LO/U15.  5, 1970- 6, 1971.

PROBLEMY GEOLOGII MINERAL'NYKH MESTOROZHDENIJ,
PETROLOGII I MINERALOGII.
++PROBL. GEOL. MINER. MESTOROZHD. PETROL. &
MINERAL. [PCMM-A]
 AKADEMIJA NAUK SSSR: INSTITUT GEOLOGII RUDNYKH
MESTOROZHDENIJ, PETROGRAFII, MINERALOGII I
GEOKHIMII.
 MOSCOW 1, 1969-
 LO/N13.    XY/N-1.

PROBLEMI NA IZKUSTVOTO.
++PROBL. IZKUSTVOTO.
 BULGARSKA AKADEMIJA NA NAUKITE: INSTITUT ZA
IZKUSTVOZNANIE.
 SOFIA 1(1), 1968-
 Q.  S/T: TRIMESECHNO SPISANIE ZA ESTETIKA,
 TEORIJA, ISTORIJA I KRITIKA NA IZKUSTVOTO.
 ENGL., FR., GER. & RUSS. SUMM.
 LO/N-1.    LO/N-3.    LO/N15.    OX/U-1.    OX/U-2.
 ISSN 0032-9371

PROBLEMY KOSMICHESKOJ BIOLOGII.
++PROBL. KOSM. BIOL.
 AKADEMIJA NAUK SSSR: OTDELENIE BIOLOGICHESKIKH
NAUK.
 MOSCOW 1, 1962-
 ENGL. SUMM.
 LO/N13.    XY/N-1.

PROBLEMY KOSMICHESKOJ FIZIKI.
++PROBL. KOSM. FIZ.
 KYJIVS'KYJ DERZHAVNYJ UNIVERSYTET.
 KIEV 1, 1966-
 ENGL. SUMM.  S/T: MEZHVEDOMSTVENNYJ NAUCHNYJ
 SBORNIK.
 LO/U13.

PROBLEMY NAUCHNOGO KOMMUNIZMA.
++PROBL. NAUCH. KOMMUNIZMA.
 AKADEMIJA OBSHCHESTVENNYKH NAUK PRI TSK KPSS:
NAUCHNOGO KOMMUNIZMA.
 MOSCOW VYP. 1, 1966-
 BH/U-1.    CC/U-1.

PROBLEMY OBSHCHEJ ENERGETIKI I EDINOJ ENERG-
ETICHESKOJ SISTEMY.
++PROBL. OBSHCH. ENERG. & EDINOJ ENERG. SIST.
[POES-B]
 KAZAKHSKIJ NAUCHNO-ISSLEDOVATEL'SKIJ INSTITUT
 ALMA-ATA 1, 1965-
 BH/U-1.
 LO/N13. 2, 1966-

PROBLEMY OSVOENIJA PUSTYN'.
++PROBL. OSVOENIJA PUSTYN'.
 AKADEMIJA NAUK TURKMENSKOJ SSR: NAUCHNYJ SOVET
PO PROBLEME PUSTYN'.
 ASHKHABAD 1, 1967-
 ENGL. SUMM. & CONT. LISTS.  TITLE ALSO IN
 ENGL.: PROBLEMS OF DESERT DEVELOPMENT.
 OX/U-1.
 LO/N13.  1969-

PROBLEMY POLONII ZAGRANICZNEJ.
++PROBL. POL. ZAGRANICZ.
POLSKA AKADEMIA NAUK: KOMISJA POLONII ZAGRANI-
CZNEJ.
*WARSAW   TOM 1, 1960-*
ANNU. KOMISJA SUBORD TO THE AKADEMIA'S
KOMITET BADAN NAD KULTURA WSPOLCZESNA.
*LO/U-3.*

PROBLEMY PROCHNOSTI.
++PROBL. PROCHN.
AKADEMIJA NAUK UKRAJINS'KOJI RSR: INSTITUT
PROBLEM PROCHNOSTI.
*KIEV  1, 1969-*
S/T: EZHEMESJACHNYJ NAUCHNO-TEKHNICHESKIJ
ZHURNAL.  ENGL. TRANSL. PUBL. AS STRENGTH OF
MATERIALS.
*LO/N14.  2, 1970-*

PROBLEMY PROCHNOSTI (ENGL. TRANSL.).                      000
SEE: STRENGTH OF MATERIALS.

PROBLEMY PSIKHOLOGII SPORTA.
++PROBL. PSIKHOL. SPORTA.
INSTITUTY FIZICHESKOJ KUL'TURY.
*MOSCOW  1, 1960-*
S/T: SBORNIK RABOT INSTITUTOV FIZICHESKOJ
KUL'TURY.
*BH/U-1.  5, 1967-*

PROBLEMY RAZVITIJA EKONOMIKI DAGESTANA.
++PROBL. RAZVIT. EKON. DAGESTANA.
AKADEMIJA NAUK SSSR: (DAGESTANSKIJ FILIAL)
OTDEL EKONOMIKI.
*MAKHACHKALA 1964-*
VOL.1 UNNUMBERED, VOL.2, DATED 1964.
*CC/U-1.  GL/U-1.  LO/N-3.*

PROBLEMY REGIONAL'NOGO ZIMOVEDENIJA.
++PROBL. REG. ZIMOVEDENIJA.
AKADEMIJA NAUK SSSR.
*CHITA  1, 1966-*
SPONS. BODY ALSO: GEOGRAFICHESKOE OBSHCHESTVO
SSSR: ZABAJKAL'SKIJ OTDEL.
*CA/U12.  LO/N13.*

PROBLEMY SOVREMENNOJ EKONOMIKI KAZAKHSTANA.
++PROBL. SOVREM. EKON. KAZAKH.
AKADEMIJA NAUK KAZAKHSKOJ SSR: INSTITUT
EKONOMIKI.
*ALMA-ATA  VYP.1, 1965-*
S/T: SBORNIK STATEJ.
*LO/U-3.  SW/U-1.*
*BH/U-1.  2, 1966-*                *CC/U-1.  2, 1966-*

PROBLEMI SPOLJNE TRGOVINE I KONJUNKTURE.
++PROBL. SPOLJNE TRGOV. & KONJUNKT.
INSTITUT ZA SPOLJNU TRGOVINU.
*BELGRADE   1(1), 1962-*
*GL/U-1.  6, 1967-*

PROBLEMY TEPLOENERGETIKI I PRIKLADNOJ TEPLOF-
IZIKI.
++PROBL. TEPLOENERG. & PRIKL. TEPLOFIZ.
KAZAKHSKIJ NAUCHNO-ISSLEDOVATEL'SKIJ INSTITUT
ENERGETIKI.
*ALMA-ATA  VYP.1, 1964-*
*XY/N-1.*
*LO/N13.  5, 1969-*

PROCEDURES ALGOL EN ANALYSE NUMERIQUE.
++PROCED. ALGOL ANAL. NUMER.
CENTRE NATIONAL DE LA RECHERCHE SCIENTIFIQUE
(FRANCE).
*PARIS  [1], 1967-*
*LO/N14.*

PROCEEDINGS, AGRICULTURAL ECONOMICS SOCIETY
OF IRELAND.
++PROC. AGRIC. ECON. SOC. IREL.
*DUBLIN  1(1), 1969-*
*DB/U-2.*

PROCEEDINGS OF THE AMERICAN SOCIETY FOR EIGHT-
EENTH-CENTURY STUDIES.                                    000
SEE: STUDIES IN EIGHTEENTH CENTURY CULTURE.

PROCEEDINGS, AMERICAN SOCIETY FOR HORTICULT-
URAL SCIENCE.                                             XXX
SUBS: (1969) JOURNAL, AMERICAN SOCIETY FOR
HORTICULTURAL SCIENCE.

PROCEEDINGS OF THE ANNUAL CONVENTION &
SCIENCE PROGRAM, SOCIETY OF BIOLOGICAL
PSYCHIATRY.                                               XXX
SUBS(1969): BIOLOGICAL PSYCHIATRY.

PROCEEDINGS, ASSOCIATION OF AMERICAN GEOG-
RAPHERS.
++PROC. ASSOC. AM. GEOGR.
*LAWRENCE, KANSAS  1, 1969-*
*AD/U-1.    BH/U-1.    HL/U-1.    SA/U-1.    SH/U-1.*

PROCEEDINGS OF THE ASSOCIATION OF VETERINARY
ANAESTHETISTS.
++PROC. ASSOC. VET. ANAESTH.
*NESTON, CHESHIRE  NO.1, 1970-*
*CA/U-1.    ED/N-1.    GL/U-1.    OX/U-8.*

PROCEEDINGS, AUSTRALIAN ACADEMY OF THE
HUMANITIES.                                               XXX
++PROC. AUST. ACAD. HUM.
*SYDNEY  1, 1970-*
PREV: REPORT, AUSTRALIAN HUMANITIES RESEARCH
COUNCIL FROM 1956/57.
*OX/U-1.*

PROCEEDINGS, AUSTRALIAN ASSOCIATION OF NEURO-
LOGISTS.
++PROC. AUST. ASSOC. NEUROL.
*MELBOURNE  1, MY 1963-*
*LO/M32.*   XY/N-1.*

PROCEEDINGS OF THE AUSTRALIAN BIOCHEMICAL
SOCIETY.
++PROC. AUST. BIOCHEM. SOC.
*CARLTON, VICTORIA  1968-*
*LO/M12.    LO/N14.    LO/S-3.    LO/U-2.*

PROCEEDINGS, AUSTRALIAN PHYSIOLOGICAL SOCIETY.
++PROC. AUST. PHYSIOL. SOC.
*CANBERRA  F 1963-*
*LO/U-2.*

PROCEEDINGS OF THE COLORADO MUSEUM OF NATURAL
HISTORY.                                                  XXX
SUBS (1955): PROCEEDINGS OF THE DENVER
MUSEUM OF NATURAL HISTORY.

PROCEEDINGS, DENVER MUSEUM OF NATURAL HISTORY             XXX
++PROC. DENVER MUS. NAT. HIST.
*DENVER  NO.1, 1955- NO.12, 1966.//*
PREV: PROCEEDINGS OF THE COLORADO MUSEUM OF
NATURAL HISTORY FROM 1915- 1948.
*LO/N-2.*

PROCEEDINGS OF THE ECOLOGICAL SOCIETY OF
AUSTRALIA.
++PROC. ECOL. SOC. AUST.
*CANBERRA   1, 1966-*
*BN/U-2.    LO/N-2.    LO/U-2.*
*LO/U11.  4, 1969-*

PROCEEDINGS, GEOSCIENCE INFORMATION SOCIETY.
++PROC. GEOSCI. INF. SOC. (US).
*WASHINGTON, D.C.  1, 1969-*
*LO/N-2.    LO/N14.*

PROCEEDINGS, GRASSLAND SOCIETY OF SOUTHERN
AFRICA.
++PROC. GRASSL. SOC. SOUTH. AFR.
*PIETERMARITZBURG  1, 1966-*
*LO/N-2.*

PROCEEDINGS, INDIAN DIVISION, BRITISH INSTIT-
UTION OF RADIO ENGINEERS.                                 XXX
++PROC. INDIAN DIV. BR. INST. RADIO ENG.
*BANGALORE  1, 1963-*
SUBS: PROCEEDINGS, INDIAN DIVISION, INSTITUT-
ION OF ELECTRONIC & RADIO ENGINEERS.
*LO/N14.*

PROCEEDINGS, INDIAN DIVISION, INSTITUTION OF
ELECTRONIC & RADIO ENGINEERS.                             XXX
++PROC. INDIAN DIV. INST. ELECTRON. & RADIO ENG.
*BANGALORE  2, 1964-*
PREV: PROCEEDINGS, INDIAN DIVISION, BRITISH
INSTITUTION OF RADIO ENGINEERS FROM 1, 1963.
*LO/N14.*

PROCEEDINGS, INDIAN NATIONAL SCIENCE ACADEMY:
PART A: PHYSICAL SCIENCES.                                XXX
++PROC. INDIAN NAT. SCI. ACAD., A.
*NEW DELHI  36, 1970-*
PREV:  PROCEEDINGS, NATIONAL INSTITUTE OF
SCIENCES OF INDIA, A FROM 21, 1955- 35, 1969.
*LD/U-1.    LO/N14.*

PROCEEDINGS, INDIAN NATIONAL SCIENCE ACADEMY:
PART B: BIOLOGICAL SCIENCES.                              XXX
++PROC. INDIAN NAT. SCI. ACAD., B.
*NEW DELHI  36, 1970-*
PREV: PROCEEDINGS, NATIONAL INSTITUTE OF
SCIENCES OF INDIA: B: FROM 21, 1955- 35, 1969.
*DB/S-1.    NW/U-1.*

PROCEEDINGS, INSTITUTION OF CIVIL ENGINEERS:
PT 1, DESIGN & CONSTRUCTION.                          XXX
+ +PROC. INST. CIVIL ENG., 1.
  LONDON 52, 1972-
  PREV: PART OF MAIN TITLE FROM 1, 1952- 51,
  1972. PT 1 HAS EVEN VOLUME NUMBERS ONLY, ODD
  NUMBERS BEING ALLOTTED TO PT 2.
  LO/N14.

PROCEEDINGS, INSTITUTION OF CIVIL ENGINEERS:
PT 2: RESEARCH & THEORY.                              XXX
+ +PROC. INST. CIVIL ENG., 2.
  LONDON 53, 1972-
  SEE NOTES FOR PT 1.
  LO/N14.

PROCEEDINGS, INSTITUTION OF THE RUBBER
INDUSTRY.                                             XXX
  SUBS (1967) PART OF: JOURNAL, INSTITUTION
  OF THE RUBBER INDUSTRY.

PROCEEDINGS, INTERNATIONAL ASSOCIATION OF
TECHNOLOGICAL UNIVERSITY LIBRARIES.                   .000
  SEE: IATUL PROCEEDINGS.

PROCEEDINGS OF THE LINNEAN SOCIETY OF LONDON.         XXX
  SUBS (1969): BIOLOGICAL JOURNAL OF THE ...

PROCEEDINGS, MATHEMATICAL & PHYSICAL SOCIETY
OF A.R.E.                                             XXX
+ +PROC. MATH. & PHYS. SOC. A.R.E.
  CAIRO NO.33, 1969-
  PREV: PROCEEDINGS, MATHEMATICAL & PHYSICAL
  SOCIETY OF U.A.R. FROM 23, 1960- NO.32, 1968.
  LO/N14.

PROCEEDINGS OF THE MEETINGS, FEDERATION OF
EUROPEAN BIOCHEMICAL SOCIETIES.
+ +PROC. MEET. FED. EUR. BIOCHEM. SOCS.
  LONDON 1, 1964-
  BH/U-1.

PROCEEDINGS, NATIONAL INSTITUTE OF SCIENCES
OF INDIA: PART A: PHYSICAL SCIENCES.                  XXX
  SUBS (1970): PROCEEDINGS, INDIAN NATIONAL
  SCIENCE ACADEMY: PART A: PHYSICAL SCIENCES.

PROCEEDINGS, NATIONAL INSTITUTE OF SCIENCES
OF INDIA: PART B: BIOLOGICAL SCIENCES.                XXX
  SUBS (1970): PROCEEDINGS, INDIAN NATIONAL
  SCIENCE ACADEMY: PART B: BIOLOGICAL
  SCIENCES.

PROCEEDINGS, PEORIA ACADEMY OF SCIENCE.
+ +PROC. PEORIA ACAD. SCI.
  PEORIA, ILL. 1, 1968-
  LO/N-2.

PROCEEDINGS, ROYAL ENTOMOLOGICAL SOCIETY OF
LONDON: SERIES A: GENERAL ENTOMOLOGY.                 XXX
  SUBS (1971): JOURNAL OF ENTOMOLOGY: SERIES
  A: GENERAL ENTOMOLOGY.

PROCEEDINGS, ROYAL ENTOMOLOGICAL SOCIETY OF
LONDON: SERIES B: TAXONOMY.                           XXX
  SUBS (1971): JOURNAL OF ENTOMOLOGY: SERIES
  B: TAXONOMY.

PROCEEDINGS OF THE ROYAL ZOOLOGICAL SOCIETY
OF NEW SOUTH WALES.                                   XXX
  SUBS (1972): KOOLEWONG.

PROCEEDINGS, SCIENTIFIC COMMITTEE ON OCEANIC
RESEARCH.
+ +PROC. SCI. COMM. OCEAN. RES.
  LA JOLLA, CALIF. 1, 1965-
  CA/U12.

PROCEEDINGS OF THE SCIENTIFIC SECTION, TOILET
GOODS ASSOCIATION, INC.                               XXX
  SUBS (1969): TGA COSMETIC JOURNAL.

PROCEEDINGS OF SCIENTIFIC SESSIONS, SOCIETY
OF BIOLOGICAL PSYCHIATRY.                             XXX
  SUBS(1969): BIOLOGICAL PSYCHIATRY.

PROCEEDINGS OF THE SCOTTISH TARTANS SOCIETY.
+ +PROC. SCOTT. TARTANS SOC.
  SCOTTISH TARTANS SOCIETY.
  STIRLING 1967-
  ED/N-1. JE 1967-

PROCEEDINGS, SECTION OF SCIENCES, ISRAEL
ACADEMY OF SCIENCES & HUMANITIES.
+ +PROC. SECT. SCI. ISRAEL ACAD. SCI. & HUM.
  JERUSALEM NO.1, 1966-
  LO/N-2.

PROCEEDINGS, SOCIETY OF RELAY ENGINEERS.             XXX
  SUBS (1971): RELAY ENGINEER.

PROCEEDINGS OF THE SOCIETY FOR VETERINARY
ETHOLOGY.
+ +PROC. SOC. VET. ETHOL.
  SOCIETY FOR VETERINARY ETHOLOGY.
  LONDON 1, 1966-
  LO/M18.   LO/N-1.   OX/U-8.

PROCEEDINGS OF THE STEKLOV INSTITUTE OF MATH-
EMATICS.
+ +PROC. STEKLOV INST. MATH.
  AMERICAN MATHEMATICAL SOCIETY.
  PROVIDENCE, R.I. NO.64, 1965(1966)-
  ENGL. TRANSL. OF TRUDY MATEMATICHESKOGO
  INSTITUTA IMENI V.A. STEKLOVA.
  HL/U-1.**   LO/N-4.   LO/U-2.   XY/N-1.

PROCEEDINGS OF SYMPOSIA IN APPLIED MATHEMAT-
ICS OF THE AMERICAN MATHEMATICAL SOCIETY.            XXX
  SUBS (1969): SIAM-AMS PROCEEDINGS.

PROCEEDINGS & TRANSACTIONS OF THE BRITISH
ENTOMOLOGICAL & NATURAL HISTORY SOCIETY.             XXX
+ +PROC. & TRANS. BR. ENTOMOL. & NATUR. HIST.
  SOC.
  LONDON 1, OC 1968-
  PREV: PROC. & TRANS. OF THE SOUTH LONDON ENTO-
  MOLOGICAL & NATURAL HISTORY SOCIETY.
  DB/S-1.   ED/N-1.   LD/U-1.   LO/N-2.   LO/N13.

PROCEEDINGS & TRANSACTIONS OF THE SOUTH LON-
DON ENTOMOLOGICAL & NATURAL HISTORY SOCIETY.         XXX
  SUBS (1968): PROC. & TRANS. OF THE BRITISH
  ENTOMOLOGICAL & NATURAL HISTORY SOCIETY.

PROCEEDINGS OF WATER ECONOMICS RESEARCH INST-
ITUTE.                                                000
  SEE: PRACE INSTYTUTU GOSPODARKI WODNEJ.

PROCES. SOCIAAL CULTUREEL TIJDSCHRIFT.
  [UITGEVERIJ H. NELISSEN]
  BILTHOVEN, NETH. 1(1), JA 1969-
  M.
  LO/N-1.
  ISSN 0032-9584

PROCESS ENGINEERING.                                  XXX
+ +PROCESS ENG.
  [MORGAN-GRAMPIAN]
  LONDON AG 1972-
  INCORP: CHEMICAL & PROCESS ENGINEERING FROM
  33(4), 1952- 53(7), 1972; & PROCESS ENGINEER-
  ING PLANT & CONTROL FROM OC 1965- 1972.
  BH/P-1.   LO/N14.   LO/S-3.   MA/P-1.   MA/U-1.   SF/U-1.
  XS/R10.

PROCESS INSTRUMENTATION.                              XXX
+ +PROCESS INSTRUM.
  [UNITED TRADE P.]
  LONDON 1(1), AP 1972-
  PREV: INSTRUMENT PRACTICE FROM 1, 1946- 26(3),
  1972.
  BR/U-1.   ED/N-1.
  NW/U-1. 1(3), 1972-          SO/U-1. 1(4), 1972-
  SW/U-1. 1(3), 1972-          XS/R10. 1(5), 1972-

PROCESS TECHNOLOGY INTERNATIONAL.                     XXX
+ +PROCESS TECHNOL. INT.
  [IPC INDUSTRIAL P.]
  LONDON 17(10), 1972- 18(11), 1973.
  PREV: BRITISH CHEMICAL ENGINEERING & PROCESS
  TECHNOLOGY FROM 16(9), D 1971- 17(9), 1972.
  SUBS. PART OF: CHEMICAL PROCESSING, WHICH FROM
  1974 BECAME: PROCESSING. THE PLANT, EQUIPMENT
  & SYSTEMS JOURNAL FOR THE PROCESSING
  INDUSTRIES.
  BH/U-1.   ED/N-1.   LD/U-1.   LO/N14.   LO/R-6.   LO/S-3.
  XS/R10.

PRODUCTEUR DE LAIT.                                   XXX
+ +PROD. LAIT.
  UNION CENTRALE DES PRODUCTEURS SUISSES DE LAIT.
  BERNE 55(1), 1970-
  PREV: INDUSTRIE LAITIERE SUISSE.
  ISSN 0019-9125

PRODUCTION ET GESTION : L'ETUDE DU TRAVAIL.          XXX
+ +PROD. & GEST., ETUD. TRAV.
  BUREAU DES TEMPS ELEMENTAIRES.
  PARIS NO.250, 1973-
  PREV: ETUDE DU TRAVAIL FROM NO.1, 1948- 249,
  1973.
  LO/N14.

**PRODUCTION MACHINERY & EQUIPMENT.**
++PROD. MACH. & EQUIP.
[FIVE WINDSORS PUBL. CO.]
OAKVILLE, ONT.  1, 1971-
LO/U14.

**PRODUCTION TECHNOLOGY. ABSTRACTS AND REPORTS**   xxx
**FROM EASTERN EUROPE.**
++PROD. TECHNOL.
MACHINE TOOL INDUSTRY RESEARCH ASSOCIATION.
MACCLESFIELD  NO.26, 1969-
PREV: RUSSIAN MACHINE TOOLS FROM
NO.1, 1963- 25, 1968.
BH/U-1.    BL/U-1.    LO/N14.    LO/U20.
ISSN 0032-9886

**PROFESSIONAL ADMINISTRATION.**   xxx
++PROF. ADM.
CHARTERED INSTITUTE OF SECRETARIES & ADMINIST-
RATORS.
LONDON  1(1), AP 1971-
M.  PREV: CHARTERED SECRETARY FROM 1, JA
1961- 11(3), 1971.
ED/N-1.    GL/U-1.    GL/U-3.    LO/N-7.    LO/U-1.    OX/U-1.
SH/C-5.    SO/U-1.

**PROFESSIONAL PAPERS, DEPARTMENT OF GEOGRAPHY**   xxx
**& GEOLOGY, INDIANA STATE UNIVERSITY.**
++PROF. PAP. DEP. GEOGR. & GEOL. INDIANA STATE
UNIV.
TERRE HAUTE  NO.2, 1971-
NO.1, 1968 PUBL. AS OCCASIONAL PAPERS ...
LO/S13.

**PROFESSIONAL PAPERS SERIES, MARINE LABORATORY,**   xxx
**STATE BOARD OF CONSERVATION (FLORIDA).**
SUBS (1969):  PROFESSIONAL PAPERS SERIES,
MARINE RESEARCH LABORATORY, DEPARTMENT OF
NATURAL RESOURCES (FLORIDA).

**PROFESSIONAL PAPERS SERIES, MARINE RESEARCH**
**LABORATORY, DEPARTMENT OF NATURAL RESOURCES**
**(FLORIDA).**   xxx
++PROF. PAP. SER. MAR. RES. LAB. DEP. NATUR.
RESOUR. (FLA.).
ST. PETERSBURG, FLA.  NO.10, 1969-
PREV: PROFESSIONAL PAPERS SERIES, MARINE
LABORATORY, STATE BOARD OF CONSERVATION
(FLORIDA) FROM NO.1, 1960- 9, 1967.
LO/N13.

**PROFESSIONAL PRINTER.**   xxx
++PROF. PRINTER.
INSTITUTE OF PRINTING.   xxx
LONDON  17, 1973-
PREV: PRINTING TECHNOLOGY FROM 1, 1957- 16,
1972.
LO/N14.

**PROFILE.**
LABOUR YOUTH OF TASMANIA.
LAUNCESTON  1(1), OC 1971-
LO/U-8.

**PROGRAM REVIEW, FOREST MANAGEMENT INSTITUTE**
**(CANADA).**   xxx
++PROGRAM REV. FOR. MANAGE. INST. (CAN.).
OTTAWA  1967/69(1969)-
PREV: PROGRAM REVIEW, FOREST MANAGEMENT RES-
EARCH & SERVICES INSTITUTE (CANADA) FROM 1965/
66(1967).
LO/N14.
ISSN 0071-7495

**PROGRAM REVIEW, FOREST MANAGEMENT RESEARCH &**
**SERVICES INSTITUTE (CANADA).**   xxx
++PROGRAM REV. FOR. MANAGE. RES. & SERV. INST.
(CAN.).
OTTAWA  1965/66(1967).
SUBS: PROGRAM REVIEW, FOREST MANAGEMENT INST-
ITUTE (CANADA).  COVERS PERIOD 1/AP 1965- 31/
MR 1967.
LO/N14.

**PROGRAMMED INSTRUCTION IN INDUSTRY.**
++PROGR. INSTR. IND.
OXFORD  1, 1967-
ED/N-1.    OX/U-1.**

**PROGRAMMED LEARNING BULLETIN.**
++PROGR. LEARN. BULL.
MORAY HOUSE COLLEGE OF EDUCATION.
EDINBURGH  NO.1, 1970-
ED/N-1.    LO/N35.    SH/U-1.

**PROGRAMMED LEARNING NEWS.**
++PROGR. LEARN. NEWS.
ASSOCIATION FOR PROGRAMMED LEARNING.
LONDON  1, F 1967-
2M.
BH/U-1.    ED/N-1.

**PROGRAMMES IN PRINT.**   xxx
SUBS (1969): PART YEARBOOK OF EDUCATIONAL &
INSTRUCTIONAL TECHNOLOGY.

**PROGRAMMIROVANNOE OBUCHENIE.  MEZHVEDOMSTVEN-**
**NYJ NAUCHNYJ SBORNIK.**
++PROGRAM. OBUCHENIE.
KYJIVS'KYJ DERZHAVNYJ UNIVERSYTET.
KIEV  1, 1967-
BH/U-1.    CC/U-1.
ISSN 0555-3725

**PROGRESELE STIINTEI.**
++PROG. STIIN.
ACADEMIA REPUBLICII SOCIALISTE ROMANIA:
CENTRUL DE DOCUMENTARE STIINTIFICA.
BUCHAREST  1(1), 1965-
SUMM. IN ENGL., FR., GER., RUSS.
OX/U-8.
LO/N13  2, 1966-
ISSN 0033-0477

**PROGRESS IN AEROSPACE STUDIES.**   xxx
++PROG. AEROSP. STUD.
[PERGAMON]
OXFORD &C.  11, 1970-
PREV:  PROGRESS IN AERONAUTICAL SCIENCES FROM
1, 1961- 10, 1970.
LO/N14.

**PROGRESS AGAINST CANCER.**
++PROG. AGAINST CANCER.
NATIONAL ADVISORY CANCER COUNCIL (US).
WASHINGTON, D.C.  1966-
SPONS. BODY ALSO: NATIONAL CANCER INSTITUTE
(US).
LO/N13.

**PROGRESS IN ANALYTICAL CHEMISTRY.**
++PROG. ANAL. CHEM.
[PLENUM P.]
NEW YORK  1, 1968-
GL/U-1.    LO/N-4.    LO/S-3.
BT/U-1.  1, 1968.

**PROGRESS IN BIOORGANIC CHEMISTRY.**
++PROG. BIOORG. CHEM.
[WILEY-INTERSCIENCE]
NEW YORK  1, 1971-
CA/U-1.    CA/U-2.    ED/N-1.    LD/U-1.    LO/N14.    LO/S-3.
SF/U-1.    SO/U-1.

**PROGRESS IN CHEMICAL TOXICOLOGY.**
++PROG. CHEM. TOXICOL. [PCTX-A]
[ACADEMIC P.]
NEW YORK &C.  1, 1963-
LO/M-1.    LO/S-3.

**PROGRESS IN CLINICAL IMMUNOLOGY.**
++PROG. CLIN. IMMUNOL.
[GRUNE & STRATTON]
NEW YORK  1, 1972-
BL/U-1.    CA/U-1.    GL/U-1.

**PROGRESS [IN] CLINICAL PATHOLOGY.**
++PROG. CLIN. PATHOL.
[GRUNE & STRATTON]
NEW YORK   1, 1966-
NW/U-1.    SH/C-5.
CA/U-1.  4, 1972-                    ED/N-1.  4, 1972-

**PROGRESS IN CONSTRUCTION SCIENCE & TECHNOLOGY.**
++PROG. CONSTR. SCI. & TECHNOL.
[MEDICAL & TECHNICAL PUBL. CO.]
AYLESBURY, BUCKS.  [1], 1971-
CA/U-1.    LO/N14.    OX/U-8.

**PROGRESS IN CREATING CONSERVATION AREAS.**   xxx
++PROG. CREAT. CONSERV. AREAS.
LONDON  NO.1, JA 1968- 16, D 1969 ...
SUBS: CONSERVATION PROGRESS.
ED/N-1.

**PROGRESS IN DISTRIBUTION BULLETIN.**
++PROG. DISTRIB. BULL. (IR.)
IRISH NATIONAL PRODUCTIVITY COMMITTEE.
DUBLIN  NO.1, [1965]-
DB/U-2.    ED/N-1.

PROGRESS IN ELECTROCHEMISTRY OF ORGANIC
COMPOUNDS.
++PROG. ELECTROCHEM. ORG. COMP.
[PLENUM P.]
LONDON; NEW YORK 1, 1969(1971)-
ENGL. TRANSL. OF PROGRESS ELEKTROKHIMII ORGAN-
ICHESKIKH SOEDINENIJI.
BH/U-1. LO/N14. LO/S-3. SF/U-1.

PROGRESS ELEKTROKHIMII ORGANICHESKIKH
SOEDINENIJ (ENGL. TRANSL.).
SEE: PROGRESS IN ELECTROCHEMISTRY OF ORGANIC
COMPOUNDS.

PROGRESS IN EQUINE PRACTICE.
++PROG. EQUINE PRACT.
[AMERICAN VETERINARY PUBL.]
SANTA BARBARA, CALIF. &C [1], 1966-
ISSUED AS PART OF THE PUBLISHERS': MODERN
VETERINARY REFERENCE SERIES. CONSISTS OF
ABSTRACTS.
LO/N13.

PROGRESS IN FELINE PRACTICE (INCLUDING
CAGED BIRDS & EXOTIC ANIMALS).
++PROG. FELINE PRACT.
[AMERICAN VETERINARY PUBL.]
SANTA BARBARA, CALIF. [1], 1966-
ISSUED AS PART OF THE PUBLISHERS': MODERN
VETERINARY REFERENCE SERIES. CONSISTS OF
ABSTRACTS.
LO/N13.

PROGRESS IN GASTROENTEROLOGY.
++PROG. GASTROENTEROL.
[GRUNE & STRATTON]
NEW YORK &C 1, 1968-
BN/U-1. DB/U-2.

PROGRESS IN GEOGRAPHY: INTERNATIONAL REVIEWS
OF CURRENT RESEARCH.
++PROG. GEOG.
[EDWARD ARNOLD]
LONDON 1, 1969-
ANNU.
BH/U-1. ED/U-1. EX/U-1. GL/U-1. LD/U-1. LO/N-2.
LO/U-3. LO/U-4. LO/U11. LO/U12. NW/U-1. RE/U-1.
SO/U-1.
MA/U-1. 1, 1969.

PROGRESS IN HEAT & MASS TRANSFER.
++PROGR. HEAT & MASS TRANSFER.
[PERGAMON]
OXFORD 1, 1969-
BH/U-1. BR/U-1. GL/U-2. LB/U-1. LD/U-1. LO/N-4.
LO/U20. MA/U-1. OX/U-8. XS/R10.
HL/U-1. 1, 1969- 7, 1973.

PROGRESS IN HIGH TEMPERATURE PHYSICS &
CHEMISTRY.
++PROG. HIGH TEMP. PHYS. & CHEM.
[PERGAMON]
OXFORD &C 1, 1967-
LD/U-1. LO/N14. LV/P-1. XS/R10.

PROGRESS IN HISTOCHEMISTRY & CYTOCHEMISTRY.
++PROG. HISTOCHEM. & CYTOCHEM.
[FISCHER]
STUTTGART &C. 1, 1970-
LO/N13. OX/U-8.

PROGRESS IN LEARNING DISABILITIES.
++PROG. LEARN. DISABILITIES.
[GRUNE & STRATTON]
NEW YORK 1, 1968-
LO/U20.

PROGRESS IN LIBRARY SCIENCE.
++PROG. LIBR. SCI.
LONDON 1965- 1967. //
AD/U-1. BH/U-1. BL/P-1. CR/U-1. DB/U-2. LO/N-9.
LO/U-1. LO/U-2. LO/U13. MA/P-1. MA/U-1. SH/U-1.
SO/U-1. SW/U-1.
GL/U-1. 1966-

PROGRESS IN MATHEMATICS.
++PROG. MATH.
[PLENUM PRESS]
NEW YORK 1, 1968-
TRANSL. FROM: ITOGI NAUKI: SERIJA MATEMATIKA.
(FROM 1966).
AD/U-1. BN/U-2. CB/U-1. LO/N14.

PROGRESS IN MOLECULAR & SUBCELLULAR BIOLOGY.
[SPRINGER]
BERLIN &C. 1, 1969-
AD/U-2. BL/U-1. CA/U-1. GL/U-1. HL/U-1. LD/U-1.
LO/N-2. LO/N13. LO/U-2. LO/U-4. LO/U12. MA/U-1.
NW/U-1. SO/U-1. SW/U-1.
AD/U-1. 1, 1969.

PROGRESS IN NEUROBIOLOGY.
++PROG. NEUROBIOL.
[PERGAMON]
OXFORD 1, 1973-
CA/M-2. HL/U-1. LO/U-2. MA/U-1.
CA/U-1. 1(3), 1973- ED/N-1. 1(3), 1973-

PROGRESS IN NEUROLOGICAL SURGERY.
++PROG. NEUROL. SURG.
[KARGER]
BASLE 1, 1966-
GL/U-1.

PROGRESS IN NEUROPATHOLOGY.
++PROG. NEUROPATHOL.
[HEINEMANN MEDICAL BOOKS]
LONDON 1, 1971-
LO/N13.

PROGRESS NOTES, CANADIAN WILDLIFE SERVICE.
++PROG. NOTES CAN. WILDL. SERV.
OTTAWA NO.1, F 1967-
CA/U12. LO/N-2. LO/R-5.

PROGRESS IN ORGANIC COATINGS.
++PROG. ORG. COAT.
[ELSEVIER]
LAUSANNE 1, 1972-
GL/U-2. LO/N14. OX/U-8.
ISSN 0033-0655

PROGRESS IN PHOTOGRAPHY.                                          XXX
SUBS (1959): PERSPECTIVE. QUARTERLY REVIEW...

PROGRESS IN PHYSICAL THERAPY.
++PROG. PHYS. THER.
[ROYAL VANGORCUM LTD.]
AMSTERDAM 1(1), 1970-
CR/M-1. OX/U-8.
ISSN 0048-5519

PROGRESS IN PHYSIOLOGICAL SCIENCES.
++PROG. PHYSIOL. SCI.
[CONSULTANTS BUREAU]
NEW YORK; LONDON 1, 1970-
ENGL. TRANSL. OF USPEKHI FIZIOLOGICHESKIKH
NAUK. DATING & NUMBERING OF ISSUES FOLLOW
ORIGINAL.
LO/N13. LO/U-2.

PROGRESS IN PHYTOCHEMISTRY.
++PROG. PHYTOCHEM.
[INTERSCIENCE]
LONDON &C 1, 1968-
BH/U-1. BN/U-2. CR/U-1. DR/U-2. HL/U-1. LD/U-1.
LO/N14. LO/S-3. LO/U-2. LO/U-4. LO/U12. LV/U-1.
MA/U-1. SO/U-1. SW/U-1.
AD/U-1. 2, 1970-

PROGRESS IN PLANNING.
++PROGR. PLANN.
[PERGAMON]
OXFORD 1, 1973-
AD/U-1. CA/U-1. ED/N-1. LO/U-3. OX/U16. SO/U-1.

PROGRESS IN POLYMER SCIENCE, JAPAN.
++PROG. POLYM. SCI. JAP.
[KODANSHA LTD./ HALSTED PRESS]
TOKYO; NEW YORK 1, 1971-
CA/U-1. LO/N14.

PROGRESS IN QUANTUM ELECTRONICS.
++PROG. QUANTUM ELECTRON.
[PERGAMON]
OXFORD 1(1), 1969-
AD/U-1. BH/U-3.** LO/N-4. LO/N14. XS/R10.
ED/N-1. 1(4), 1971- LD/U-1. 1(4), 1971-

PROGRESS REPORT, COMMONWEALTH FOUNDATION.
++PROG. REP. COMMONW. FOUND.
LONDON 1ST, 1967-
OX/U-9.

**PROGRESS REPORT, DARESBURY NUCLEAR PHYSICS
LABORATORY: 4 GE V ELECTRON SYNCHROTRON.**                    XXX
*+ +PROG. REP. DARESBURY NUCL. PHYS. LAB., 4 GE V
ELECTRON SYNCHROTON.
DARESBURY, LANCS. 1, 1964- 6, 1967.
SUBS: ANNUAL REPORT, DARESBURY ...
LO/N14.
BH/U-1. 1965-*

**PROGRESS REPORTS FROM EXPERIMENT STATIONS,
COTTON RESEARCH CORPORATION.**                               XXX
*+ +PROG. REP. EXP. STN. COTTON RES. CORP.
LONDON 1964/65(1966)- 1969/70(1972).
PREV: PROGRESS REPORTS FROM EXPERIMENT STAT-
IONS, EMPIRE COTTON GROWING CORPORATION FROM
1933/34(1935)- 1964/65(1966). SUBS: COTTON
RESEARCH REPORTS.
CA/U15. LO/N14.*

**PROGRESS REPORTS FROM EXPERIMENT STATIONS,
EMPIRE COTTON GROWING CORPORATION.**                         XXX
  **SUBS (1966): PROGRESS REPORTS FROM EXPER-
  IMENT STATIONS, COTTON RESEARCH CORPORATION.**

**PROGRESS REPORT, INTERNATIONAL DOCUMENTA-
TION CENTRE.**                                               000
  **SEE: IDC PROGRESS REPORT.**

**PROGRESS REPORT, ROYAL INSTITUTION OF GREAT
BRITAIN.**
*+ +PROG. REP. R. INST. G.B.
LONDON [NO.1], 1969-
OX/U-8.*

**PROGRESS REPORT OF THE SARDINES RESOURCES
INVESTIGATIONS (SOUTH KOREA).**                              000
  **SEE: CHONGORI CHAWON CHOSA POGO.**

**PROGRESS IN RESPIRATION RESEARCH.**                        XXX
*+ +PROG. RESP. RES.
[BASLER DRUCK- UND VERLAGSANSTALT]
BASLE 3, 1969-
PREV: PROGRESS IN RESEARCH IN EMPHYSEMA &
CHRONIC BRONCHITIS FROM 1, 1963.
LO/N13.    NW/U-1.    OX/U-1.
SO/U-1. 3, 1969- 6, 1971.*

**PROGRESS IN SEPARATION & PURIFICATION.**
*+ +PROG. SEP. & PURIF.
[INTERSCIENCE]
LONDON &C 1, 1968-
BH/U-1.    GL/U-1.    LO/N14.    LO/S-3.    LO/U-2.    XW/C-4.
LD/U-1. 3, 1970-*

**PROGRESS IN SURFACE & MEMBRANE SCIENCE.**                  XXX
*+ +PROG. SURF. & MEMBRANE SCI.
[ACADEMIC P.]
NEW YORK; LONDON 4, 1971-
PREV: RECENT PROGRESS IN SURFACE SCIENCE FROM
1, 1964- 3, 1970.
ED/N-1.    GL/U-1.    LD/U-1.    LO/N14.    MA/P-1.    MA/U-1.
OX/U-8.    XS/R10.
SO/U-1. 8, 1974-*

**PROGRESS IN SURFACE SCIENCE.**
*+ +PROG. SURF. SCI.
[PERGAMON]
OXFORD 1, 1971-
ED/N-1.    GL/U-1.    LO/N14.    LO/S-3.    OX/U-8.
XS/R10.*
SO/U-1. 1, 1971- 4, 1972.*

**PROGRESS IN SWINE PRACTICE.**
*+ +PROG. SWINE PRACT.
[AMERICAN VETERINARY PUBL.]
SANTA BARBARA, CALIF. &C [1], 1966-
PART OF PUBLISHERS': MODERN VETERINARY REFER-
ENCE SERIES. CONSISTS OF ABSTRACTS.
LO/N13.*

**PROGRESS IN THIN-LAYER CHROMATOGRAPHY & RELATED
METHODS.**
*+ +PROG. THIN-LAYER CHROMATOGR. & RELATED METH.
[ANN ARBOR-HUMPHREY SCIENCE PUBL.]
ANN ARBOR &C. 1, 1970-
LD/U-1.    LO/S-3.    LO/U20.    OX/U-8.
ISSN 0079-6867*

**PROGRESS IN TOTAL SYNTHESIS.**
*+ +PROG. TOTAL SYNTH.
[APPLETON-CENTURY-CROFTS]
NEW YORK 1, 1971-
ANNU.
SF/U-1.*

**PROGRESS IN VACUUM MICROBALANCE TECHNIQUES.**              XXX
*+ +PROG. VAC. MICROBALANCE TECH.
[HEYDEN]
LONDON &C. 1, 1972-
PREV: VACUUM MICROBALANCE TECHNIQUES FROM 1,
1961- 8, 1969(1971).
CA/U-1.    LO/N14.*

**PROGRESS IN WATER TECHNOLOGY.**
*+ +PROG. WATER TECHNOL.*
INTERNATIONAL ASSOCIATION ON WATER POLLUTION
RESEARCH.
*[PERGAMON]
NEW YORK; OXFORD 1, 1972-
LO/N14.
CA/U-1. 2, 1973-*

**PROGRESSIVNAJA TEKHNOLOGIJA MASHINOSTROENIJA.**
BELORUSSKIJ POLITEKHNICHESKIJ INSTITUT.
*MINSK 1, 1970-*
SPONS. BODY ALSO: (BELORUSSIA) MINISTERSTVO
VYSSHEGO I SREDNEGO SPETSIAL'NOGO OBRAZOVANIJA
*BH/U-1.    LO/N13.*

**PROHEMIO. RIVISTA DE LINGUISTICA Y CRITICA
LITERARIA.**
CONSEJO SUPERIOR DE INVESTIGACIONES CIENTIFICAS
(SPAIN).
*BARCELONA &C. 1(1), AP 1970-*
SPONS. BODY ALSO UNIVERSITA DI PISA: ISTITUTO
DI LETTERATURA SPAGNOLA E ISPANO-AMERICANO.
*LO/N-1.
NO/U-1. 2(2), 1971-*

**PROIZVODSTVO I ISSLEDOVANIE STALEJ I SPLAVOV.**
*+ +PROIZVOD. & ISSLED. STALEJ & SPLAVOV.*
(RUSSIA USSR) MINISTERSTVO CHERNOJ METALLURGII.
*MOSCOW 1, 1968-*
SPONS. BODY ALSO: UKRAINSKIJ NAUCHNO-ISSLE-
DOVATEL'SKIJ INSTITUT SPETSIAL'NYKH STALEJ,
SPLAVOV I FERROSPLAVOV.
*LO/N13.*

**PROIZVODSTVO KRUPNYKH MASHIN.**
*+ +PROIZVOD. KRUPNYKH MASH. [PKMT-A]*
URAL'SKIJ MASHINOSTROITEL'NYJ ZAVOD: NAUCHNO-
ISSLEDOVATEL'SKIJ INSTITUT TJAZHELOGO MASHINO-
STROENIJA.
*MOSCOW 3, 1964-*
S/T: SBORNIK STATEJ. PREV: KONSTRUIROVANIE
KRUPNYKH MASHIN: SBORNIK STATEJ. FROM 1, 1962-
2, 1963.
*BH/U-1. 4, 1964-                    LO/N13. 5, 1964-*

**PROLOGUE.**
NATIONAL ARCHIVES (US).
*WASHINGTON, D.C. 1(1), 1967(1969)-*
S/T: THE JOURNAL OF THE NATIONAL ARCHIVES.
*AD/U-1.    BL/U-1.    HL/U-1. *    LO/N-1.    LO/U19.
OX/U-1.
ED/N-1. 2, 1970-*
ISSN 0033-1031

**PROMETEJ. ISTORIKO-BIOGRAFICHESKIJ AL'MANAKH
SERII 'ZHIZN' ZAMECHATEL'NYKH LUDEJ'.**
*MOSCOW TOM 1, 1966-
BH/U-1.    CA/U-1.    CC/U-1.    ED/N-1.    GL/U-1.    MA/U-1.
NO/U-1.    OX/U-1.*

**PROMOCLIM. INDUSTRIES THERMIQUES ET
AERAULIQUES.**
SOCIETE D'ETUDE ET DE DIFFUSION DES INDUSTRIES
THERMIQUES.
*PARIS 1, JA 1970-*
PREV: INDUSTRIES THERMIQUES ET AERAULIQUES
FROM 1, 1955- 15(699), 1969.
*LO/N14.    XS/T10.
MA/U-1. 2, 1971-*
ISSN 0019-9397

**PROOF. THE YEARBOOK OF AMERICAN BIBLIOGRAPHICAL
& TEXTUAL STUDIES.**
*[UNIV. SOUTH CAROLINA P.]
COLUMBIA, S.C. 1, 1971-
CA/U-1.    DB/U-2.    NO/U-1.    NW/U-1.    OX/U-1.
SW/U-1.*

**PROP.**
PRESERVATION OF THE RIGHTS OF PRISONERS.
*HULL NO.1, 1972-
ED/N-1.*

**PROPAGANDIST I AGITATOR.**                                 XXX
  **SUBS (1960): PART KOMMUNIST VOORUZHENNYKH SIL.**

**PROPERTY & COMPENSATION REPORTS.**
+ +PROP. & COMPENS. REP.
LONDON  19, 1968-
PREV: PLANNING & COMPENSATION REPORTS FROM
1, 1949/51.
BL/U-1.    ED/N-1.    LV/U-1.    NO/U-1.    SO/U-1.
ISSN 0033-1295

**PROPERTY & INVESTMENT REVIEW.**
+ +PROP. & INVESTMENT REV.
[NEWMAN BOOKS]
LONDON  S 1970-
MON.
ED/N-1.  JE 1972-

**PROPERTY IRELAND.**
+ +PROP. IREL.
OUGHTERARD, CO. GALWAY  1, 1970-
DB/U-2.

**PROPERTY JOURNAL: NS.**
+ +PROP. J., NS.
NATIONAL ASSOCIATION OF PROPERTY OWNERS.
LONDON  1, 1970-
MON. PREV: REAL ESTATE JOURNAL, NS FROM 1, JE
1950.
LO/U-3.
ISSN 0033-1309

**PROSE.**
[PROSE PUBL. INC.]
NEW YORK  NO.1, 1970-
2/A.
ED/N-1.    LO/N-1.    LO/U-2.    OX/U-1.
ISSN 0033-1457

**PROSPECCION SIGLO XXI - VENEZUELA ANO 2000.**
UNIVERSIDAD CATOLICA ANDRES BELLO: CENTRO DE
ESTUDIOS DEL FUTURO DE VENEZUELA.
CARACAS  NO.1, 1969-
LO/U-3.

**PROSPECT.**
PRINTING & PUBLISHING INDUSTRY TRAINING BOARD.
LONDON  NO.1, AP 1971-
BH/U-1.    LO/N-1.

**PROSPECTS IN EDUCATION.**                                          XXX
+ +PROSPECTS EDUC.
UNESCO.
PARIS  NO.1- 2, 1969.
      1(1), 1970- 1(4), 1970 ...
SUSPENDED 1971. SUBS: PROSPECTS. QUARTERLY
REVIEW OF EDUCATION.
DB/U-2.    LO/N-3.    LO/N-9.    LO/N17.    LO/S74.    LV/U-2.
BH/U-1.  1, 1970-                    OX/U-1.  1, 1970-
MA/P-1.  NO.1- 2, 1969.
ISSN 0033-1538

**PROSPECTUS: A JOURNAL OF LAW REFORM.**                             XXX
UNIVERSITY OF MICHIGAN: LAW SCHOOL.
ANN ARBOR, MICH.  1(1), AP 1968- 3, 1970 ...
2/A. SUBS: JOURNAL OF LAW REFORM FROM 4(1),
1970.
OX/U-1.

**PROSTAGLANDINS.**
[GERON-X INC.]
LOS ALTOS, CALIF.  1(1), JA 1972-
MON. ENG. ABSTR.
AD/U-2.    CA/U-2.    GL/U-1.    LO/N13.    LO/S74.    LO/U-2.
LO/N31.  2, 1972-

**PROTECTION OF NATURE.**                                            000
SEE: VARSTVO NARAVE.

**PROTECTIVE COATINGS ON METALS.**
+ +PROT. COAT. METALS.
[CONSULTANTS BUREAU]
NEW YORK  1, 1967 (1969)-
TRANS. OF ZASHCHITNYE POKRYTIYA NA METALLAKH.
DATING & NUMBERING OF ISSUES FOLLOW ORIGINAL.
LO/N14.

**PROTEIN SYNTHESIS. A SERIES OF ADVANCES.**
+ +PROTEIN SYNTH.
[DEKKER]
NEW YORK  1, 1971-
CA/U-1.    LD/U-1.    LO/S-3.

**PROVA RADICALE. TRIMESTRALE POLITICO.**
ROME  1, 1971-
Q.
LO/U-3.

**PRUDENTIA.**
UNIVERSITY OF AUCKLAND.
AUCKLAND  1, 1970-
S/T: A JOURNAL DEVOTED TO THE INTELLECTUAL
HISTORY OF THE HELLENISTIC & ROMAN PERIODS.
CA/S-1.
GL/U-1.  5, 1973-

**PRZEGLAD KULTURALNY.**                                             XXX
SUBS (1963): PART OF KULTURA.

**PRZEGLAD PENITENCJARNY.**
(POLAND) MINISTERSTWO SPRAWIEDLIWOSCI: OSRODEK
BADAN PRZESTEPCZOSCI.
WARSAW  1(1), 1963-
FR. & RUSS. SUMM.
CA/U-1.

**PRZEGLAD PRAWA I ADMINISTRACJI.**
+ +PRZEGL. PRAWA & ADM.
UNIWERSYTET WROCLAWSKI.
WROCLAW  1, 1972-
ALSO NUMBERED AS: ACTA UNIVERSITATIS WRATI-
SLAVIENSIS. NO.1 ABOVE = NO.144 OF THE ACTA.
LO/N-3.

**PRZESZLOSC DEMOGRAFICZNA POLSKI. MATERIALY I
STUDIA.**
+ +PRZESZLOSC DEMOGR. POL.
POLSKA AKADEMIA NAUK: SEKCJA DEMOGRAFII
HISTORYCZNEJ.
WARSAW  [1], S 1967-
SEKCJA DEMOGRAFII HISTORYCZNEJ SUBORD. TO
KOMITET NAUK DEMOGRAFICZNYCH.
BH/U-1.    LO/N-3.

**PS. NEWSLETTER OF THE ...**
AMERICAN POLITICAL SCIENCE ASSOCIATION.
WASHINGTON, D.C.  1, 1968-
BH/U-1.    CB/U-1.    GL/U-2.
EX/U-1.  4, 1971-

**PSICON. MAGAZINE OF THE ...**
PSYCHIC YOUTH GROUP.
LONDON  1, S/OC 1968-
ED/N-1.    OX/U-1.

**PSIKHOLOGIJA I TEKHNIKA.**
+ +PSIKHOL. & TEKH.
AKADEMIJA PEDAGOGICHESKIKH NAUK RSFSR.
MOSCOW  VYP.1, 1965-
BH/U-1.

**PSIONIC MEDICINE.**
+ +PSIONIC MED.
PSIONIC MEDICAL SOCIETY.
HINDHEAD, SURREY  1(1), 1969-
ED/N-1.    OX/U-8.
ISSN 0033-2585

**PSYCHIATRICA FENNICA. FINNISH PSYCHIATRY.
SUOMALAISTA PSYKIATRICAA.**
+ +PSYCHIATR. FENN.
HELSINGIN YLIOPISTOLLISEN KESKUSSAIRAALAN
PSYKIATRIAN KLINIKAN VUOSIKIRJA.
HELSINKI  1970-
ANNU.
LD/U-1.
BL/U-1.  1971-

**PSYCHIATRY & ART.**
+ +PSYCHIATR. & ART.
AMERICAN SOCIETY OF PSYCHOPATHOLOGY OF
EXPRESSION.
[KARGER]
BASLE  1, 1968-
GL/U-1.

**PSYCHIATRY & NEUROLOGY.**
+ +PSYCHIATR. & NEUROL.
[MORGAN PUBL.]
EWELL, SURREY  1, 1970-
LO/N-1.

**PSYCHIATRY & SOCIAL SCIENCE REVIEW.**
+ +PSYCHIATR. & SOC. SCI. REV.
[PSYCHIATRY & SOCIAL SCIENCE BOOK CENTER]
NEW YORK  1, 1967-
LO/S18.  3(6, 8), 1969-
ISSN 0033-2763

**PSYCHOLOGICAL MEDICINE.**
+ +PSYCHOL. MED.
BRITISH MEDICAL ASSOCIATION.
 LONDON 1(1), N 1970-
 AD/U-1.    BL/U-1.    CR/M-1.    DN/U-1.    EX/U-1.    LO/M11.
 LO/U-2.    OX/U-1.    SH/U-1.
 NW/U-1. 1971-
 ISSN 0033-2917

**PSYCHOLOGICAL MONOGRAPHS ON COGNITIVE PROCESSES.**
+ +PSYCHOL. MONOGR. COGNITIVE PROCESSES.
[HUTCHINSON EDUCATIONAL LTD.]
 LONDON 1, 1965-
 AD/U-1.
 ISSN 0079-7367

**PSYCHOLOGICAL STUDIES: MINOR SERIES.**
+ +PSYCHOL. STUD., MINOR SER.
[MOUTON & CO.]
 THE HAGUE 1, 1967-
 OX/U-1.

**PSYCHOLOGIE. SCHWEIZERISCHE ZEITSCHRIFT FUR PSYCHOLOGIE UND IHRE ANWENDUNGEN.**     XXX
 BERN 26(3), 1967-
 PREV: AS SUBTITLE SCHWEIZERISCHE ZEITSCHRIFT
 ... FROM 1, 1942- 26(2), 1967.
 LO/N13.

**PSYCHOLOGIE V EKONOMICKE PRAXI. PSYCHOLOGY IN ECONOMICS.**
+ +PSYCHOL. EKON. PRAXI.
KARLOVA UNIVERSITA V PRAZE.
 PRAGUE 1/2, 1966-
 S/T: CASOPIS PRO POMOC HOSPODARSKE PRAXI.
 ENGL. SUMM.
 LO/N13.

**PSYCHOLOGY IN ECONOMICS.**     000
 SEE: PSYCHOLOGIE V EKONOMICKE PRAXI.

**PSYCHOLOGY OF LEARNING & MOTIVATION.**
+ +PSYCHOL. LEARN. & MOTIV.
[ACADEMIC PRESS]
 NEW YORK &C 1, 1967-
 ANNU. S/T: ADVANCES IN RESEARCH & THEORY.
 BH/U-1.    BN/U-1.    GL/U-1.    LO/U-1.    LO/U-2.    LO/U-3.
 RE/U-1.

**PSYCHOLOGY OF MUSIC.**
+ +PSYCHOL. MUSIC.
SOCIETY FOR RESEARCH IN PSYCHOLOGY OF MUSIC &
MUSIC EDUCATION.
 LONDON 1, 1973-
 HL/U-2.    LD/U-2.    MA/U-1.    SH/U-1.

**PSYCHOLOGY TODAY.**
+ +PSYCHOL. TODAY.
[CRM INC.]
 DEL MAR, CALIF. 1, MY 1967-
 LV/U-1.    SH/U-1. 1972-
 AD/U-1. 1(5), 1967-           ED/N-1.**
 LO/S24. 1970-
 BH/U-3. N, 1970- [5 YEARS ONLY]
 EX/U-1. 4(1), JE 1970-
 GL/U-2. 1, 1967- 3, 1970.
 ISSN 0033-3107

**PSYCHOTHEQUE.**
[EDITIONS UNIVERSITAIRES]
 PARIS NO.1, 1969-
 MONOGR.
 LO/N-1.
 ISSN 0079-7448

**PUBBLICAZIONE, ISTITUTO DI ELETTRONICA E RADIO-CONTROLLI, UNIVERSITA DI PISA.**
+ +PUBBL. IST. ELETTRON. & RADIO-CONTROLL. UNIV. PISA.
 PISA NO.1, 1970-
 ISTITUTO SUBORD. TO FACOLTA DI INGEGNERIA.
 LO/N14.

**PUBBLICAZIONI DELL'ISTITUTO DI LINGUA E LETT-ERATURA ITALIANA, UNIVERSITA DI GENOVA.**
+ +PUBBL. IST. LINGUA & LETT. ITAL. UNIV. GENOVA.
 GENOA NO.1, 1971-
 ISTITUTO SUBORD. TO FACOLTA DI MAGISTERO.
 LO/N-1.

**PUBBLICAZIONI DELL' ISTITUTO SPERIMENTALE PER LA FRUTTICOLTURA.**
+ +PUBBL. IST. SPER. FRUTTICOLT.
 ROME 1, 1968-
 XS/R-2.

**PUBBLICAZIONI, ISTITUTO DI ZOOLOGIA, UNI-VERSITA DI SIENA.**
+ +PUBBL. IST. ZOOL. UNIV. SIENA.
UNIVERSITA DI SIENA: ISTITUTO DI ZOOLOGIA.
 SIENA 1, 1966-
 LO/N-2.

**PUBLIC AFFAIRS BULLETIN, PUBLIC AFFAIRS RES-EARCH BUREAU, SOUTHERN ILLINOIS UNIVERSITY.**
+ +PUBLIC AFF. BULL. PUBLIC AFF. RES. BUR. SOUTH. ILL. UNIV.
 CARBONDALE, ILL. 1(1), 1968-
 OX/U-9.

**PUBLIC AFFAIRS INFORMATION SERVICE: FOREIGN LANGUAGE INDEX.**
+ +PUBLIC AFF. INF. SERV., FOREIGN LANG. INDEX.
[PUBLIC AFFAIRS INFORMATION SERVICE, INC.]
 NEW YORK 1, 1968/1971-
 Q. JA 1970 CONSTITUTES A TRIAL ISSUE.
 GL/U-2.    LO/U-3.    SO/U-1.
 ISSN 0048-5810

**PUBLIC AUTHORITY FINANCE BULLETIN.**
+ +PUBLIC AUTH. FINANC. BULL.
(AUSTRALIA) COMMONWEALTH BUREAU OF CENSUS & STATISTICS.
 CANBERRA NO.1, 1969/70(1972)-
 LD/U-1.    LO/N-1.

**PUBLIC CHOICE.**     XXX
THOMAS JEFFERSON CENTER FOR POLITICAL ECONOMY.
[UNIV. OF VIRGINIA P.]
 CHARLOTTESVILLE, VA. 4, 1968-
 PREV: PAPERS ON NON-MARKET DECISION MAKING
 FROM 1, 1966- 3, 1967. CENTER PART OF UNIV-
 ERSITY OF VIRGINIA.
 EX/U-1.    GL/U-1.    LO/U-3.    MA/U-1.
 SF/U-1. 14, 1973-

**PUBLIC ENTERPRISE.**
+ +PUBLIC ENTERP.
PUBLIC ENTERPRISE GROUP.
 LONDON NO.1, 1971-
 ED/N-1.    GL/U-2.    NO/U-1.    OX/U-1.    OX/U16.
 OX/U17.

**PUBLIC FINANCE QUARTERLY.**
+ +PUBLIC FINANC. Q.
 BEVERLEY HILLS 1, 1973-
 Q.
 AD/U-1.    GL/U-1.    LO/U-3.    SW/U-1.
 BH/U-3. 2, 1974-              LO/U12. 2(1), 1974-
 SF/U-1. 3, 1975-
 ISSN 0048-5853

**PUBLIC HEALTH ENGINEER.**     XXX
+ +PUBLIC HEALTH ENG.     XXX
INSTITUTION OF PUBLIC HEALTH ENGINEERS.
[MUNICIPAL PUBL. CO.]
 LONDON 1, 1973-
 PREV: JOURNAL, INSTITUTION OF PUBLIC HEALTH
 ENGINEERS FROM 54, 1955- 71, 1972.
 BR/U-1.    GL/U-1.    LO/N-4.    LO/N14.    OX/U-8.    SH/U-3.

**PUBLIC HEALTH INSPECTOR.**     XXX
+ +PUBLIC HEALTH INSP.
ASSOCIATION OF PUBLIC HEALTH INSPECTORS.
 LONDON. 73, OC 1964- 76, D 1968...
 CONTAINS AS SUPPL: PUBLIC HEALTH INSPECTOR
 TRADE NEWS & BUYERS GUIDE. PREV: SANITARIAN
 FROM 1, 1932. SUBS: ENVIRONMENTAL HEALTH.
 ED/N-1.    LO/N14.

**PUBLIC HEALTH REPORTS.**     XXX
 SUBS (1971): HSMHA HEALTH REPORTS.

**PUBLIC OPINION.**
+ +PUBLIC OPIN.
THEMIS SOCIETY.
 HARROGATE NO.1, JL 1970-
 ED/N-1.    OX/U-1.

**PUBLIC PERSONNEL REVIEW.**     XXX
 SUBS (1972): PERSONNEL ADMINISTRATION &
 PUBLIC PERSONNEL REVIEW.

**PUBLIC SCHOOL LEAVER.**
+ +PUBLIC SCH. LEAVER.
 LONDON 1(1), 1969-
 ED/N-1.    OX/U-1.

**PUBLICATION, AMERICAN SOCIETY FOR OCEANO-GRAPHY.**
+ +PUBL. AM. SOC. OCEANOGR.
 HOUSTON NO.1, [1966?]-
 LO/N13. 1968-

**PUBLICATIONS IN ARCHAEOLOGY, NATIONAL MUSEUM OF MAN (CANADA).**
*++PUBL. ARCHAEOL. NATL. MUS. MAN (CAN.).*
*OTTAWA NO.1, 1970-*
*BL/U-1.    CR/N-1.    DB/S-1.    LO/N-2.*

**PUBLICATIONS OF THE ASTROPHYSICS BRANCH, NATIONAL RESEARCH COUNCIL (CANADA).**
*++PUBL. ASTROPHYS. BRANCH NATL. RES. COUNC. (CAN.).*
*OTTAWA   PAB1(1), 1971-*
BRANCH SUBORD. TO RADIO & ELECTRICAL ENGINEER-
ING DIVISION.
*LO/N-4.*

**PUBLICATIONS IN AUTOMATIC COMPUTATION, UNIVER- SITY OF CALIFORNIA.**
**SEE: UNIVERSITY OF CALIFORNIA ...**

000

**PUBLICACOES AVULSAS, INSTITUTO ANCHIETANO DE PESQUISAS UNIVERSIDADE DO VALE DO RIO DOS SINOS.**
*++PUBL. AVULSAS INST. ANCHIETANO PESQUI.*
*UNIV. VALE RIO SINOS.*
*SAO LEOPOLDO  1, 1970-*
*CA/U-3.*

**PUBLICATIONS IN BIOLOGICAL OCEANOGRAPHY, NAT- IONAL MUSEUM OF NATURAL SCIENCES (CANADA).**
*++PUBL. BIOL. OCEANOGR. NAT. MUS. NATUR. SCI. (CAN.).*
*OTTAWA  NO.1 1970-*
*CR/N-1.    DB/S-1.    ED/S-2.    LO/N-2.    LO/N13.    NW/U-1.*

**PUBLICATIONS, BIOLOGICAL RESEARCH CENTRE (BAGHDAD).**
*++PUBL. BIOL. RES. CENT. (BAGHDAD).*
*BAGHDAD  NO.1, 1967-*
*LO/N-2.*

**PUBLICATIONS, BNB MARC DOCUMENTATION SERVICE.**
*++PUBL. BNB MARC DOC. SERV.*
BRITISH NATIONAL BIBLIOGRAPHY.
*LONDON  1, 1968-*
*BH/U-1.    EX/U-1.    GL/U-1.    LO/N-2.*

**PUBLICATIONS IN BOTANY, NATIONAL MUSEUM OF NATURAL SCIENCES (CANADA).**
*++PUBL. BOT. NAT. MUS. NATUR. SCI. (CAN.).*
*OTTAWA  NO.1 1969-*
*BL/U-1.    CR/N-1.    ED/S-2.    LO/N-2.    LO/N13.    NW/U-1.*

**PUBLICATION, BUREAU FOR ECONOMIC POLICY & ANALYSIS (SOUTH AFRICA).**
*++PUBL. BUR. ECON. POLICY & ANAL. (S. AFR.).*
*PRETORIA NO.1, 1968-*
MONOGR.
*LO/N-1.*

**PUBLICATIONS, CAIRO UNIVERSITY HERBARIUM.**
*++PUBL. CAIRO UNIV. HERB.*
*CAIRO  NO.1, 1968-*
*LO/N-2.*

**PUBLICACIONES, CATEDRA DE PALEONTOLOGIA, UNIVERSIDAD DE BARCELONA.**
*++PUBL. CATEDRA PALEONTOL. UNIV. BARCELONA.*
*BARCELONA  NO.1, 1964-*
*LO/N-2.*

**PUBLICATION OF THE CENTRE OF ADVANCED STUDY IN GEOLOGY, PUNJAB UNIVERSITY.**
*++PUBL. CENT. ADV. STUDY GEOL. PUNJAB UNIV.*
*CHANDIGARH  NO.1, 1966-*
*LO/N-2.    SH/U-1.*

**PUBLICATIONS, CENTRE D'HISTOIRE RURALE DE L'UNIVERSITE CATHOLIQUE DE LOUVAIN.**
*++PUBL. CENT. HIST. RUR. UNIV. CATH. LOUVAIN.*
UNIVERSITE CATHOLIQUE DE LOUVAIN: CENTRE
D'HISTOIRE RURALE.
*LOUVAIN  NO.1, 1963-*
*LO/U19.\**

**PUBLICATIONS, CENTRE FOR MIDDLE EASTERN & ISLAMIC STUDIES, UNIVERSITY OF DURHAM.**
*++PUBL. CENT. MIDDLE EAST. & ISLAMIC STUD. UNIV. DURHAM.*
*DURHAM  NO.1, 1969-*
*BH/U-1.    LO/N-1.*

**PUBLICACIONES, CENTRO PIRENAICO DE BIOLOGIA EXPERIMENTAL.**
*++PUBL. CENT. PIRENAICO BIOL. EXP.*
*BARCELONA  1, 1964-*
*LO/N13.*
*LO/N-2. 1968-*

**PUBLICATIONS DU CENTRE DE RECHERCHE BRETONNE ET CELTIQUE DE LA FACULTE DES LETTRES ET SCIENCES HUMAINES DE BREST.**
*++PUBL. CENT. RECH. BRETONNE & CELTIQUE FAC. LETT. & SCI. HUM. BREST.*
*RENNES  1, 1970-*
MONOGR.
*LO/N-1.*

**PUBLICATIONS DU CENTRE DE RECHERCHES SAHA- RIENNES: SERIE GEOLOGIE.**
*++PUBL. CENT. RECH. SAHAR., SER. GEOL.*
CENTRE DE RECHERCHES SAHARIENNES.
*PARIS  NO.1, 1961- 2, 1962...*
PUBL. FOR THE CENTRE BY CNRS.  SUBS: PUBL. DU
CENTRE DE RECHERCHES SUR LES ZONES ARIDES:
SERIE GEOLOGIE.
*CA/U14.    LO/N-2.*

XXX

**PUBLICATIONS DU CENTRE DE RECHERCHES SUR LES ZONES ARIDES: SERIE GEOLOGIE.**
*++PUBL. CENT. RECH. ZONES ARIDES, SER. GEOL.*
CENTRE DE RECHERCHES SUR LES ZONES ARIDES.
*PARIS  NO.3, 1964-*
PUBL. FOR THE CENTRE BY CNRS.
*CA/U14.    LO/N-2.*

**PUBLICATIONS DU C.E.S.C.M.**
*++PUBL. C.E.S.C.M.*
UNIVERSITE DE POITIERS: CENTRE D'ETUDES
SUPERIEURES DE CIVILISATION MEDIEVALE.
*POITIERS  NO.1, 1960-*
*LO/N-1.*

**PUBLICACIONES, COMISION INTERNACIONAL PERMAN- ENTE DE FOLKLORE.**
*++PUBL. COM. INT. PERM. FOLKLORE.*
*BUENOS AIRES  1, 1962-*
*OX/U-1.*

**PUBLICACION, COMISION DE INVESTIGACION CIEN- TIFICA (BUENOS AIRES, PROVINCIA).**
*++PUBL. COM. INVEST. CIEN. (B.AIRES, PROV.)*
*BUENOS AIRES  NO.1, 1960-*
*LO/N-2.*

**PUBLICATION, COMMISSION ON COLLEGE GEOGRAPHY, ASSOCIATION OF AMERICAN GEOGRAPHERS.**
*++PUBL. COMM. COLL. GEOGR. ASSOC. AM. GEOGR.*
*WASHINGTON, D.C.  1, 1965-*
*LO/N-4.\*\**

**PUBLICATIONS OF THE CONTRACT RESEARCH UNIT, NEW ZEALAND INSTITUTE OF ECONOMIC RESEARCH.**
*++PUBL. CONTRACT RES. UNIT N.Z. INST. ECON. RES.*
*WELLINGTON  NO.1, 1968-*
*OX/U-9.*

**PUBLICATIONS, DEPARTMENT OF GEOLOGY, UNIV- ERSITY COLLEGE OF WALES.**
*++PUBL. DEP. GEOL. UNIV. COLL. WALES.*
*ABERYSTWYTH  NO.1, 1972-*
*CA/U-1.    LO/N-2.    LO/N13.*

**PUBLICACIONES, DEPARTAMENTO DE INGLES, UNIV- ERSIDAD DE VALLADOLID.**
*++PUBL. DEP. INGLES UNIV. VALLADOLID.*
*VALLADOLID  1, 1971-*
*OX/U-1.*

**PUBLICATIONS IN ETHNOLOGY, NATIONAL MUSEUM OF MAN (CANADA).**
*++PUBL. ETHNOL. NATL. MUS. MAN (CAN.).*
*OTTAWA  NO.1, 1970-*
*BL/U-1.    CA/U-2.    CR/N-1.    DB/S-1.    LO/N-2.    SO/U-1.*

**PUBLICATIONS IN FOLK CULTURE, NATIONAL MUSEUM OF MAN (CANADA).**
*++PUBL. FOLK CULT. NATL. MUS. MAN (CAN.).*
*OTTAWA  1, 1971-*
*BL/U-1.    CA/U-1.    CA/U-2.    DB/S-1.*

**PUBLICATIONS IN GEOGRAPHY, DEPARTMENT OF GEOGRAPHY, STATE UNIVERSITY OF NEW YORK.**
*++PUBL. GEOGR. DEP. GEOGR. STATE UNIV. N.Y.*
STATE UNIVERSITY OF NEW YORK: DEPARTMENT OF
GEOGRAPHY.
*ONEONTA, N.Y.  1, 1970-*
*LO/S13.*

**PUBLICATIONS IN GEOGRAPHY, DEPARTMENT OF GEOGRAPHY, UNIVERSITY OF NEWCASTLE (N.S.W.)**
*++PUBL. GEOGR. DEP. GEOGR. UNIV. NEWCASTLE (N.S.W.).*
*NEWCASTLE, N.S.W.  1, 1971-*
MONOGR.
*LO/S13.*

PUBLICACIONES GEOLOGICAS DEL ICAITI.
++PUBL. GEOL. ICAITI. (INST. CENTROAM. INVEST.
& TECNOL. IND.)
INSTITUTO CENTROAMERICANO DE INVESTIGACION Y
TECNOLOGIA INDUSTRIAL.
GUATEMALA, CA   NO.1, 1966-
LO/N-2.

PUBLICATION, HAMPSHIRE ARCHIVISTS' GROUP.
++PUBL. HANTS. ARCH. GROUP.
PORTSMOUTH  NO.1, 1970-
AD/U-1.    OX/U-1.

PUBLICATIONS IN HISTORY, NATIONAL MUSEUM OF
MAN (CANADA).
++PUBL. HIST. NATL. MUS. MAN (CAN).
OTTAWA  1, 1970-
BL/U-1.    DB/S-1.

PUBLICATIONS, INDIAN BRANCH, ANTHROPOS
INSTITUTE.
++PUBL. INDIAN BRANCH ANTHROPOS INST.
[ASIA PUBL. HOUSE]
LONDON  NO.1, [1966]-
MONOGR.
LO/N-1.

PUBLICATIONS DE L'INSTITUT D'ASTRONOMIE ET
GEOPHYSIQUE GEORGES LEMAITRE, UNIVERSITE
CATHOLIQUE DE LOUVAIN.
++PUBL. INST. ASTRON. & GEOPHYS. GEORGES
LEMAITRE UNIV. CATHOL. LOUV.
LOUVAIN  1, 1966/67-
ED/N-1.    ED/U-1.

PUBLICATIONS OF THE INSTITUTE OF ECONOMIC &
APPLIED GEOGRAPHY, UNIVERSITY OF AARHUS.          000
SEE: KULTURGEOGRAFISKE SKRIFTER, KULTUR-
GEOGRAFISK INSTITUT, AARHUS UNIVERSITET.

PUBLICACIONES DEL INSTITUTO DE GEOGRAFIA,
UNIVERSIDAD DE VALENCIA.
++PUBL. INST. GEOGR. UNIV. VALENCIA.
VALENCIA  1, 1966-
MONOGR.
LO/S13.

PUBLICATION, INTERNATIONAL CENTER FOR ARID &
SEMI-ARID LAND STUDIES.
++PUBL. INT. CENT. ARID & SEMI-ARID LAND STUD.
LUBBOCK, TEX.  NO.1, 1967-
LO/N13.

PUBLICATIONS, INTERNATIONAL INSTITUTE FOR
AERIAL SURVEY & EARTH SCIENCES: SERIES A:        XXX
[PHOTOGRAMMETRY].
++PUBL. INT. INST. AERIAL SURV. & EARTH SCI., A.
DELFT  NO.39, 1967- 53, 1972.
PREV: PUBLICATIONS, INTERNATIONAL TRAINING
CENTRE FOR AERIAL SURVEY: SERIES A FROM NO.1,
1960- 38, 1966.  SUBS: PART OF ITC JOURNAL.
LO/N14.
ISSN 0074-6371

PUBLICATIONS, INTERNATIONAL INSTITUTE FOR
AERIAL SURVEY & EARTH SCIENCES: SERIES B:        XXX
[PHOTO-INTERPRETATION].
++PUBL. INT. INST. AERIAL SURV. & EARTH SCI., B.
DELFT  NO.40, 1966- 67, 1972.
PREV: PUBLICATIONS, INTERNATIONAL TRAINING
CENTRE FOR AERIAL SURVEY: SERIES B FROM NO.1,
1960- 39, 1966.  SUBS: PART OF ITC JOURNAL.
LO/N14.
ISSN 0074-638X

PUBLICATION, IRON & STEEL INSTITUTE.             XXX
++PUBL. IRON & STEEL INST.
LONDON  NO.97, 1966-
PREV: [SPECIAL REPORT], IRON & STEEL INSTITUTE
FROM [NO.1], 1931- 96, 1966.
LO/N14.

[PUBLICATIONS] ISTITUTO DI FILOLOGIA ROMANZA,
UNIVERSITA DEGLI STUDI DI TORINO.
TURIN  NO.1, 1971-
MONOGR. ISTITUTO SUBORD. TO FACOLTA DI LETTERE
E FILOSOFIA.
LO/N-1.

PUBLICACIONES, LATINAMERIKA-INSTITUTET I
STOCKHOLM: SERIES A: MONOGRAFIAS.
++PUBL. LATINAM.-INST. STOCKH., A.
STOCKHOLM  NO.1, 1970-
LO/N-1.

PUBLICACIONES, LATINAMERIKA-INSTITUTET I
STOCKHOLM: SERIES B: INFORMES.
++PUBL. LATINAM.-INST. STOCKH., B.
STOCKHOLM  NO.1, 1970-
LO/N-1.

PUBLICACIONES, LATINAMERIKA-INSTITUTET I
STOCKHOLM: SERIES C: ARS REDOGORELSAR.
++PUBL. LATINAM.-INST. STOCKH., C.
STOCKHOLM  NO.1, 1970-
LO/N-1.

PUBLICATIONS, LIBRARY, UNIVERSITY OF READING.    XXX
SEE: READING UNIVERSITY LIBRARY PUBLICATIONS.

PUBLICATIONS IN LINGUISTICS, UNIVERSITY OF
ICELAND.
++PUBL. LINGUIST. UNIV. ICELAND.
HASKOLI ISLANDS.
[SNAEBJORN JONSSON CO.]
REYKJAVIK  1, 1972-
CA/U-1.    LO/U-2.

PUBLICATIONS, LONDON RECORD SOCIETY.
++PUBL. LOND. REC. SOC.
LONDON  1, 1965-
BH/U-1.    HL/U-1.    LV/U-1.    SO/U-1.
AB/U-1.  1, 1965; 2, 1966.

PUBLICATIONS, LUDLOW MUSEUM.
++PUBL. LUDLOW MUS.
LUDLOW  NO.1, 1968-
LO/N-2.

PUBLICATIONS, MODERN HUMANITIES RESEARCH
ASSOCIATION.
++PUBL. MOD. HUMANIT. RES. ASSOC.
CAMBRIDGE  1, 1969-
GL/U-1.    LO/N-1.    LO/U-1.    NW/U-1.

PUBLICATIONS MULTIGRAPHIEES, SOCIETE D'ARCH-
EOLOGIE ET D'HISTOIRE DE LA MANCHE.
++PUBL. MULTIGR. SOC. ARCHEOL. HIST. MANCHE.
SAINT-LO  1, 1966-
OX/U-1.

PUBLICATIONS IN MUSEOLOGY.
++PUBL. MUSEOL.
MILWAUKEE PUBLIC MUSEUM.
MILWAUKEE, WIS.  NO.1, 1960-
LO/N-2.

PUBLICATIONS, MUSEUM OF NATURAL HISTORY, UNIV-   XXX
ERSITY OF KANSAS.
SUBS (1971): OCCASIONAL PAPERS ...

PUBLICATIONS, NATURAL ENVIRONMENT RESEARCH
COUNCIL (GB): SERIES B.
++PUBL. NAT. ENVIRON. RES. COUNC. (GB), B.
LONDON  NO.1, 1971-
GL/U-1.    LO/N-2.    LO/N-4.    LO/N14.
LO/U28.  3, 1972-

PUBLICATIONS, NATURAL ENVIRONMENT RESEARCH
COUNCIL (GB): SERIES C.
++PUBL. NAT. ENVIRON. RES. COUNC. (GB), C.
LONDON  NO.1, 1970-
LO/N-2.    LO/N13.
GL/U-1.  4, 1971-

PUBLICATIONS, NATURAL ENVIRONMENT RESEARCH
COUNCIL (GB):  SERIES D.
++PUBL. NAT. ENVIRON. RES. COUNC. (GB), D.
LONDON  NO.1, 1970-
LO/N-2.    LO/N13.

PUBLICATIONS, NEW MEXICO ORNITHOLOGICAL
SOCIETY.
++PUBL. N.M. ORNITHOL. SOC.
CEDAR CREST, N.M.  NO.1, 1963-
LO/N-1.

PUBLICACIONES DEL OBSERVATORIO ASTRONOMICO
NACIONAL (COLOMBIA).
++PUBL. OBS. ASTRON. NAC. (COLOMBIA).
BOGOTA  NO.1, 1967-
ED/R-3.

PUBLICATIONS OF THE OWENS VALLEY RADIO
OBSERVATORY.
++PUBL. OWENS VALLEY RADIO OBS.
PASADENA, CALIF.  1(1), 1967-
OBS. SUBORD. TO: CALIFORNIA INSTITUTE OF
TECHNOLOGY.
ED/R-3.

PUBLICATION, OXFORD CITY & COUNTY MUSEUM.
+ +PUBL. OXF. CITY & CTY. MUS.
OXFORD NO.1, 1968-
MONOGR.
LO/N-1.

PUBLICATIONS IN PALAEONTOLOGY, NATIONAL MUS-
EUM OF NATURAL SCIENCES (CANADA).
+ +PUBL. PALAEONTOL. NAT. MUS. NATUR. SCI. (CAN.)
OTTAWA NO.1, 1970-
CA/U-2.    ED/S-2.    LO/N-2.    LO/N13.    NW/U-1.
CR/N-1. NO.3, 1970-

PUBLICATIONS & PATENTS WITH ABSTRACTS, SOUTH-
ERN MARKETING & NUTRITION RESEARCH DIVISION,
DEPARTMENT OF AGRICULTURE (US).
+ +PUBL. & PAT. ABSTR. SOUTH. MARK. & NUTR. RES.
DIV. DEP. AGRIC. (US).
NEW ORLEANS JL/D 1970[1971]-
PREV: LIST OF PUBLICATIONS & PATENTS, SOUTH-
ERN UTILIZATION RESEARCH & DEVELOPMENT DIVIS-
ION, DEPARTMENT ... FROM JL/D 1956 (1957)-
JA/JE 1970.
LO/N14.

PUBLICATIONS, PENNSYLVANIA-YALE EXPEDITION TO
EGYPT.
+ +PUBL. PA.-YALE EXPED. EGYPT.
NEW HAVEN &C. NO.1, 1963-
OX/U-1.

PUBLICATIONS, PROVINCIAL MUSEUM & ARCHIVES OF
ALBERTA.
+ +PUBL. PROV. MUS. & ARCH. ALBERTA.
EDMONTON NO.1, 1969-
LO/N-2.

PUBLICATIONS, RACHELWOOD WILDLIFE RESEARCH
PRESERVE.
+ +PUBL. RACHELWOOD WILDL. RES. PRESERV.
NEW FLORENCE, PA. NO.1, 1971-
LO/N-2.

PUBLICATIONS, RADCLIFFE LOCAL HISTORY SOCIETY.
+ +PUBL. RADCLIFFE LOCAL HIST. SOC.
RADCLIFFE, LANCS. [NO.]1, 1969-
MONOGR.
LO/N-1.

PUBLICATIONS, RECORD OFFICE, CUMBERLAND, WEST-
MORLAND & CARLISLE JOINT ARCHIVES COMMITTEE.
+ +PUBL. REC. OFF. CUMBERLAND WESTMORLAND &
CARLISLE JOINT ARCH. COMM.
CARLISLE 1, 1968-
PREV: CUMBERLAND RECORD SERIES FROM 1, 1953-
2, 1962.
LO/N15.    LO/U-1.

PUBLICATIONS, RENAISSANCE ENGLISH TEXT
SOCIETY.
+ +PUBL. RENAISSANCE ENGL. TEXT SOC.
CHICAGO 1, 1965-
LO/U-1.

[PUBLICATIONS] SCOTTISH RECORD SOCIETY. N.S.
EDINBURGH 1, 1969-
ED/P-1.    GL/U-1.    LO/N-1.    NO/U-1.
ED/U-1. 3, 1972-

PUBLICACAO, SOCIEDADE BRASILEIRA DE GEOLOGIA.
+ +PUBL. SOC. BRAS. GEOL.
RIO DE JANEIRO NO.1, 1966-
LO/N-2.

PUBLICATIONS, SOCIETY OF ANTIQUARIES OF
NEWCASTLE-UPON-TYNE: RECORD SERIES.
+ +PUBL. SOC. ANTIQ. NEWC.-TYNE, REC. SER.
NEWCASTLE-UPON-TYNE NO.1, 1968-
LO/U-1.    MA/U-1.

PUBLICATIONS, UNIVERSITY OF CALIFORNIA: NEAR          000
EASTERN STUDIES.
SEE: UNIVERSITY OF CALIFORNIA PUBLICATIONS ...

PUBLICATIONS, UNIVERSITE LIBANAISE: SECTION
DES SCIENCES CHIMIQUES.
+ +PUBL. UNIV. LIBANAISE, SCI. CHIM.
BEIRUT 1, 1964-
LO/N-2.

PUBLICATIONS, UTAH GEOLOGICAL ASSOCIATION.
+ +PUBL. UTAH GEOL. ASSOC.
SALT LAKE CITY [NO.]1, 1972-
LO/N-2.

PUBLICATIONS, WAIKATO BRANCH, NEW ZEALAND
GEOGRAPHICAL SOCIETY.
+ +PUBL. WAIKATO BRANCH N.Z. GEOGR. SOC.
HAMILTON, N.Z. 1, 1970-
MONOGR.
LO/S13.

PUBLICATION, WATER RESOURCES BOARD (GB).
+ +PUBL. WATER RESOUR. BOARD (GB).
LONDON [NO.1], 1966-
TITLE & NUMBERING START WITH NO.2.
LO/N14.

PUBLICATION, WATER RESOURCES RESEARCH CENTER,
UNIVERSITY OF ARKANSAS.
+ +PUBL. WATER RESOUR. RES. CENT. UNIV. ARKANSAS.
FAYETTEVILLE NO.1, 1967-
LO/N13.

[PUBLICATIONS] WILTSHIRE RECORD SOCIETY.          000
SEE: WILTSHIRE RECORD ...

PUBLICATIONS IN ZOOLOGY, NATIONAL MUSEUM OF
NATURAL SCIENCES (CANADA).
+ +PUBL. ZOOL. NATL. MUS. NAT. SCI. (CAN.).
OTTAWA 1, 1969-
BL/U-1.    CR/N-1.    ED/S-2.    LO/N-2.    LO/N13.    LO/U11.

PUBLIKASJONER, BOLIGINSTITUTTET FOR OSLO.
+ +PUBL. BOLIGINST. OSLO.
[OSLO] NO.1, [1970]-
MONOGR.
LO/N-1.

PUBLIKATIE, NEDERLANDS AKOESTISCH GENOOTSCHAP.
+ +PUBL. NED. AKOESTISCH GENOOT.
DELFT NO.1, 1962-
LO/N14.*

PUBLIKATSII OTDELENIJA STRUKTURNOJ I PRI-
KLADNOJ LINGVISTIKI, MOSKOVSKIJ GOS. UNIV.
+ +PUBL. OTD. STRUKT. & PRIKL. LING. MOSK. GOS.
UNIV.
MOSKOVSKIJ GOSUDARSTVENNYJ UNIVERSITET.
MOSCOW VYP.1, 1965-
MONOGR.
ED/U-1.
BH/U-1. 2, 1968.

PUBLISHER: PREVIEW OF FORTHCOMING BOOKS.     000
SEE: PREVIEW OF FORTHCOMING BOOKS.

PUBLISHERS' WORLD. A YEARBOOK FOR PUBLISHERS,
BOOKSELLERS, LIBRARIANS.                          XXX
+ +PUBL. WORLD.
[BOWKER & CO.]
NEW YORK 1, 1965- 5, 1970. //
XS/C-2.
LO/U-3. [NO.3], 1967-

PUMPS & OTHER FLUIDS MACHINERY ABSTRACTS.
+ +PUMPS & OTHER FLUIDS MACH. ABSTR.
BRITISH HYDROMECHANICS RESEARCH ASSOCIATION.
CRANFIELD 1, 1971-
ED/N-1.    GL/U-2.    LO/N14.    OX/U-8.    XY/N-1.
LO/U28. 2, 1972-                      SH/U-3. 4, 1974-
SO/U-1. 3, 1973-
ISSN 0302-2870

PUNJAB PAST AND PRESENT.
PUNJABI UNIVERSITY.
PATIALA 1, 1967-
OX/U13.

PUZZLER.
[SEYMOUR P.]
LONDON NO.1, N 1972-
MON.
ED/N-1.    OX/U-1.

PW QUARTERLY.
PRICE WATERHOUSE & CO.
[LONDON] 1, 1968-
S/T: A PUBLICATION OF ...
CB/U-1.

PYRENAE. CRONICA ARQUEOLOGICA.
UNIVERSIDAD DE BARCELONA: INSTITUTO DE
ARQUEOLOGIA Y PREHISTORIA.
BARCELONA 1, 1965-
CA/U-3.    LO/N-1.
CA/U-1. 7, 1971-
LO/U-1. 1, 1965- 3, 1967.

**PYRODYNAMICS.**                                                                XXX
[GORDON & BREACH SCI PUBLRS]
*NEW YORK. 1, JA/F 1964-6, 1969.///*
INCORP. INTO COMBUSTION SCIENCE & TECHNOLOGY.
*LO/N-4.    LO/N-9.    XY/N-1.*
*ED/N-1. 2,1965-*

**QADMONIOT QUARTERLY FOR THE ANTIQUITIES OF
ERETZ-ISRAEL & BIBLICAL LANDS.**
*+ +QADMONIOT Q. ANTIQ. ERETZ-ISRAEL & BIBLICAL
LANDS.*
ISRAEL EXPLORATION SOCIETY.
*JERUSALEM 1, 1968-*
HEBREW TEXT.  PREV: BULLETIN, ISRAEL EXPLOR-
ATION SOCIETY FROM 1, 1933.
*CA/U-1.    GL/U-1.    LO/U14.    LO/U17.*
*ISSN 0033-4839*

**QUADERNI AGRONOMIA, ISTITUTO DE AGRONOMIA
GENERALE E COLTIVAZIONI ERBACEE, UNIVERSITA
DI PALERMO.**
*+ +QUAD. AGRON. IST. AGRON. GEN. & COLTIV.
ERBACEE UNIV. PALERMO.*
*PALERMO 1, 1965-*
*XS/R-4.    XY/N-1.*

**QUADERNI INTERNAZIONALI DI STORIA ECONOMICA E
SOCIALE.**                                                                        000
SEE: CAHIERS INTERNATIONAUX D'HISTOIRE ECON-
OMIQUE ET SOCIALE.

**QUADERNI, ISTITUTO DI PETROGRAFIA, UNIVERSITA
DI ROMA.**
*+ +QUAD. IST. PETROGR. UNIV. ROMA.*
*ROME NO.1, 1968-*
*LO/N13.*

**QUADERNI, ISTITUTO ROMANO PER LA STORIA
D'ITALIA DAL FASCISMO ALLA RESISTENZA.**
*+ +QUAD. IST. ROM. STOR. ITAL. FASCISMO RESIST.*
*ROME 1, 1969-*
*OX/U-1.*

**QUADERNI, ISTITUTO STORICO DELLA RESISTENZA
IN TOSCANA.**
*+ +QUAD. IST. STOR. RESIST. TOSCANA.*
*FLORENCE 1, 1972-*
*OX/U-1.*

**QUADERNI, ISTITUTO DI TOPOGRAFIA ANTICA, UNIV-
ERSITA DI ROMA.**
*+ +QUAD. IST. TOPOGR. ANTICA UNIV. ROMA.*
*ROME 1, 1964-*
*ED/N-1. 5, 1968-*

**QUADERNI LIVORNESI.  RIVISTA QUADRIMESTRALE.**
*+ +QUAD. LIVORNESI.*
*LIVORNO NO.1, JA/AP 1972-.*
*LO/N-1.*

**QUADERNI DEL MUSEO PITRE.**
*+ +QUAD. MUS. PITRE.*
*PALERMO NO.1, 1969-*
MONOGR.
*LO/N-1.*

**QUADERNI DI POESIA.**
*+ +QUAD. POESIA.*
[REBELLATO]
*PADUA NO.1, 1971-*
*LO/N-1.*

**QUADERNI DI RELAZIONI INTERNAZIONALI.**
*+ +QUAD. RELAZ. INT.*
ISTITUTO PER GLI STUDI DI POLITICA INTERNAZ-
IONALI.
*MILAN NO.1, F 1972-*
SUPPL. TO RELAZIONI INTERNAZIONALI.
*LO/U-3.*

**QUADERNI DI SPERIMENTAZIONE.**
*+ +QUAD. SPER.*
ISTITUTO SPERIMENTALE PER LE COLTURE FORAGGERE.
*LODI NO.1, 1970-*
*LO/N13.*

**QUADERNI PER LA STORIA DELL'UNIVERSITA DI
PADOVA.**
*+ +QUAD. STOR. UNIV. PADOVA.*
UNIVERSITA DEGLI STUDI DI PADOVA: ISTITUTO
PER LA STORIA.
[ED. ANTENORE]
*PADUA 1, 1968-*
*HL/U-1.*

**QUADERNI STORICI.**
*+ +QUAD. STORICI.*
ISTITUTO DI STORIA E SOCIOLOGIA.
*ANCONA 1, 1966-*
3/A.
*SH/U-1. 1971-*
*DB/U-2. 8(22), 1973-*
*LO/N-1. NO.16, 1971-*

**QUADERNO, CENTRO DI STUDI E DI RICERCHE
ECONOMICO-SOCIALI DELLA TOSCANA.**
*+ +QUAD. CENT. STUD. RIC. ECON.-SOC. TOSCANA.*
*FLORENCE 1, 1968-*
*OX/U-1.*

**QUADERNO, ISTITUTO DI FISICA TECNICA,
UNIVERSITA DEGLI STUDI DI PADOVA.**
*+ +QUAD. IST. FIS. TEC. UNIV. STUDI PADOVA.*
*PADUA NO.1, 1966-*
ISTITUTO SUBORD. TO FACOLTA DI INGEGNERIA.
SPONS. BODY ALSO LABORATORIO PER LA TECNICA
DEL FREDDO, CONSIGLIO NAZIONALE DELLE RICERCHE
*LO/U13.*

**QUADERNO, MUSEI CIVICI DI STORIA ED ARTE
(TRIESTE).**
*+ +QUAD. MUS. CIV. STOR. & ARTE (TRIESTE).*
*TRIESTE NO.1, 1968-*
MONOGR.
*LO/N-1.*

**QUAERENDO.**
[THEATRUM ORBIS TERRARUM LTD.]
*AMSTERDAM 1, 1971-*
*AD/U-1.    ED/N-1.    LO/N-1.    LO/U-2.    MA/S-1.    OX/U-1.*
*RE/U-1.*
*ISSN 0014-9527*

**QUALITY MATTERS.  BULLETIN OF THE MEMBERS OF
THE ...**
*+ +QUAL. MATTERS.*
NATIONAL COUNCIL FOR QUALITY & RELIABILITY (GB)
*LONDON NO.1, JE 1972-*
*ED/N-1.*

**QUALITY PROGRESS.**
*+ +QUAL. PROG.*
AMERICAN SOCIETY FOR QUALITY CONTROL.
*MILWAUKEE, WIS. 1, 1968-*
PREV: INDUSTRIAL QUALITY CONTROL.
*BH/U-1.    DB/U-2.*
*ISSN 0033-524X*

**QUALITY TECHNOLOGY.**
*+ +QUAL. TECHNOL.*
ATOMIC ENERGY RESEARCH ESTABLISHMENT.
*HARWELL 1973-*
YEARBOOK OF THE NONDESTRUCTIVE TESTING CENTRE,
HARWELL.
*LO/N14.*

**QUARTERLY BULLETIN, BANK OF UGANDA.**
*+ +Q. BULL. BANK UGANDA.*
*KAMPALA 1(1), 1968-*
*LD/U-1.    LO/U14.*

**QUARTERLY BULLETIN OF THE BRITISH PARENT EDUC-
ATION INFORMATION CIRCLE.**                              XXX
*+ +Q. BULL. BR. PARENT EDUC. INF. CIRCLE.*
*HALIFAX NO.1, MR 1970-NO.12, 1972 ...*
SUBS: PARENT EDUCATOR.
*LD/U-1.*

**QUARTERLY BULLETIN, NATIONAL OLD PEOPLE'S
WELFARE COUNCIL.**                                             XXX
SUBS (1973): AGE CONCERN TODAY.

**QUARTERLY BULLETIN OF STATISTICS FOR ASIA &
THE FAR EAST.**                                                    XXX
*+ +Q. BULL. STAT. ASIA & FAR EAST.*
UNITED NATIONS: ECONOMIC COMMISSION FOR ASIA &
THE FAR EAST.
*BANGKOK 1(1), S 1971- 3(3), S 1973 ...*
MATERIAL PREV. PUBL. AS THE ASIAN ECONOMIC
STATISTICS SECTION IN ECONOMIC BULLETIN FOR
ASIA & THE FAR EAST. SUBS: QUARTERLY BULLETIN
OF STATISTICS FOR ASIA & THE PACIFIC.
*CA/U-1.    ED/N-1.    LO/S14.    LO/U-3.    SH/P-1.*

---

**QUARTERLY DENTAL REVIEW.**
*++Q. DENT. REV.*
[COMPANY PUBL. LTD.]
*LONDON 1, 1967-*
S/T: ABSTRACTS FROM CURRENT LITERATURE FOR THE
DENTAL PRACTITIONER.
*LD/U-1. LO/M31.*
*CA/U-1. 8, 1974-*                    *ED/N-1. 7(4), 1973-*
*GL/U-1. 4(4), 1970-*
*ISSN 0033-5479*

**QUARTERLY DIGEST OF STATISTICS (MALAWI).***        XXX
*++Q. DIG. STAT. (MALAWI).*
(MALAWI) MINISTRY OF FINANCE.
*ZOMBA AP 1964-*
PREV. PART OF: MONTHLY DIGEST OF STATISTICS
(RHODESIA & NYASALAND: FEDERATION). FOR 1964
ISSUES, JURISDICTION KNOWN AS: NYASALAND.
*HL/U-1.     LO/U-3.*
*LO/N17. AP 1965-*                    *LO/S26. AP 1965-*

**QUARTERLY ECONOMIC BULLETIN, BANK NEGARA
MALAYSIA.**
*++Q. ECON. BULL. BANK NEGARA MALAYSIA.*
*KUALA LUMPUR 1, 1968-*
*HL/U-1.     LO/U-3.*

**QUARTERLY ECONOMIC BULLETIN, NEPAL RASTRA
BANK.**
*++Q. ECON. BULL. NEPAL RASTRA BANK.*
*KATHMANDU NO.1, OC 1966-*
*LO/U-3.*

**QUARTERLY ECONOMIC REVIEW: THE ARABIAN
PENINSULA & JORDAN.**                                XXX
*++Q. ECON. REV., ARABIAN PENINSULA & JORDAN.*
ECONOMIST INTELLIGENCE UNIT.
*LONDON 1968(1)- 1970(4).*
SUBS: PART OF QUARTERLY ... SAUDI ARABIA,
JORDAN.
*LO/U-3.     OX/U-1.*

**QUARTERLY ECONOMIC REVIEW: CONTINENTAL
SOUTH EAST ASIA.**                                   XXX
SUBS. (1971) PART OF: QUARTERLY ECONOMIC
REVIEW: INDOCHINA: SOUTH VIETNAM, NORTH
VIETNAM, CAMBODIA, LAOS; & QUARTERLY
ECONOMIC REVIEW: THAILAND, BURMA.

**QUARTERLY ECONOMIC REVIEW: CZECHOSLOVAKIA,
HUNGARY.**                                           XXX
*++Q. ECON. REV., CZECH. HUNG.*
ECONOMIST INTELLIGENCE UNIT.
*LONDON JA 1971(1)-*
PREV: PART OF QUARTERLY ... EASTERN EUROPE,
NORTH; & EASTERN EUROPE, SOUTH FROM 1956(1)-
1970(4).
*LO/U-3.     OX/U-1.*
*SW/U-1. 1971- 1973.*

**QUARTERLY ECONOMIC REVIEW: EASTERN EUROPE,
NORTH.**
SUBS (1971): PART OF QUARTERLY ... POLAND,
EAST GERMANY; & ... CZECHOSLOVAKIA, HUNGARY.

**QUARTERLY ECONOMIC REVIEW: EASTERN EUROPE,
SOUTH.**                                             XXX
SUBS (1971): PART OF QUARTERLY ... RUMANIA,
BULGARIA, ALBANIA; & ... CZECHOSLOVAKIA,
HUNGARY.

**QUARTERLY ECONOMIC REVIEW: INDOCHINA: SOUTH
VIETNAM, NORTH VIETNAM, CAMBODIA, LAOS.**
*++Q. ECON. REV., INDOCHINA, SOUTH VIETNAM
NORTH VIETNAM CAMBODIA LAOS.*
ECONOMIST INTELLIGENCE UNIT.
*LONDON 1971(1)-*
PREV. PART OF: QUARTERLY ECONOMIC REVIEW:
CONTINENTAL SOUTH EAST ASIA FROM 1953(1)-
1970(4).
*HL/U-1.     LO/U-3.     OX/U-1.*

**QUARTERLY ECONOMIC REVIEW: MOROCCO.**              XXX
*++Q. ECON. REV., MOROCCO*
ECONOMIST INTELLIGENCE UNIT.
*LONDON F 1971(1)-*
PREV: PART OF QUARTERLY ... ALGERIA, MOROCCO
FROM AP 1960(1)- 1970(4).
*LO/U-3.     OX/U-1.*
*ISSN 0306-4840*

**QUARTERLY ECONOMIC REVIEW: OIL IN THE FAR
EAST & AUSTRALASIA.**
*++Q. ECON. REV., OIL FAR EAST & AUSTRALAS.*
ECONOMIST INTELLIGENCE UNIT.
*LONDON MR 1971(1)-*
*LO/U-3.     OX/U-1.*

**QUARTERLY ECONOMIC REVIEW: OIL IN LATIN
AMERICA & THE CARIBBEAN.**
*++Q. ECON. REV., OIL LAT. AM. & CARIBB.*
ECONOMIST INTELLIGENCE UNIT.
*LONDON JA 1971(1)-*
*LO/U-3.     OX/U-1.*
*ISSN 0306-4808*

**QUARTERLY ECONOMIC REVIEW: OIL IN THE MIDDLE
EAST.**                                              XXX
*++Q. ECON. REV., OIL MIDDLE EAST.*
ECONOMIST INTELLIGENCE UNIT.
*LONDON 1971(1)-*
PREV: QUARTERLY ... MIDDLE EAST OIL FROM
1968(1)- 1970(4).
*OX/U-1.*

**QUARTERLY ECONOMIC REVIEW: POLAND, EAST
GERMANY.**                                           XXX
*++Q. ECON. REV., POL. EAST GER.*
ECONOMIST INTELLIGENCE UNIT.
*LONDON JA 1971(1)-*
PREV: PART OF QUARTERLY ... EASTERN EUROPE,
NORTH FROM 1956(1)- 1970(4).
*LO/U-3.     OX/U-1.*
*SW/U-1. 1971- 1973.*
*ISSN 0306-4751*

**QUARTERLY ECONOMIC REVIEW: RUMANIA, BULGARIA,
ALBANIA.**                                           XXX
*++Q. ECON. REV., RUM. BULG. ALBANIA.*
ECONOMIST INTELLIGENCE UNIT.
*LONDON JA 1971(1)-*
PREV: PART OF QUARTERLY ... EASTERN EUROPE,
SOUTH FROM 1956(1)- 1970(4).
*LO/U-3.     OX/U-1.*
*SW/U-1. 1971- 1973.*

**QUARTERLY ECONOMIC REVIEW: SAUDI ARABIA,
ARABIA, JORDAN.**                                    XXX
*++Q. ECON. REV., SAUDI ARABIA JORDAN.*
ECONOMIST INTELLIGENCE UNIT.
*LONDON F 1971(1)-*
PREV: PART OF QUARTERLY ... ARABIAN PENINSULA
& JORDAN FROM 1968(1)- 1970(4).
*LO/U-3.     OX/U-1.*
*ISSN 0306-2694*

**QUARTERLY ECONOMIC REVIEW: THAILAND, BURMA.**      XXX
*++Q. ECON. REV., THAILAND BURMA.*
ECONOMIST INTELLIGENCE UNIT.
*LONDON 1971(1)-*
PREV. PART OF: QUARTERLY ECONOMIC REVIEW:
CONTINENTAL SOUTH EAST ASIA FROM 1953(1)-
1970(4).
*HL/U-1.     LO/U-3.**     OX/U-1.*

**QUARTERLY GEOLOGICAL NOTES (AUSTRALIA).**
*++Q. GEOL. NOTES (AUST.).*
*ADELAIDE NO.1, JA 1962-*
*LO/N-2.*

**QUARTERLY, ILLINOIS STATE GENEALOGICAL
SOCIETY.**
*++Q. ILL. STATE GENEAL. SOC.*
*SPRINGFIELD, ILL. 1, SPRING 1969-*
*ED/N-1. 1(3), 1969-**

**QUARTERLY JOURNAL, GEOLOGICAL SOCIETY OF
LONDON.**                                            XXX
SUBS (1971): JOURNAL ...

**QUARTERLY JOURNAL, INTERNATIONAL FEDERATION       000
FOR INFORMATION PROCESSING.**
SEE: IAG QUARTERLY JOURNAL.

**QUARTERLY JOURNAL OF MANAGEMENT DEVELOPMENT.**
*++Q. J. MANAGE. DEV.*
UNIVERSITY OF ALLAHABAD: MOTILAL NEHRU INSTIT-
UTE OF RESEARCH & BUSINESS ADMINISTRATION.
*ALLAHABAD 1(1), S 1970-*
*DB/U-2.*
*ISSN 0048-6183*

**QUARTERLY JOURNAL, MARA INSTITUTE OF TECHNOL-
OGY.**
*++Q. J. MARA INST. TECHNOL.*
*PETALING JAYA, MALAYSIA 1, 1969-*
*HL/U-1.*

**QUARTERLY JOURNAL, NATIONAL CENTRE FOR THE
PERFORMING ARTS (INDIA).**
*++Q. J. NATL. CENT. PERFORM. ARTS (INDIA).*
*BOMBAY 1, 1972-*
*ED/N-1.     LO/N12.*

QUARTERLY JOURNAL, PARSON WOODFORDE SOCIETY.
++Q. J. PARSON WOODFORDE SOC.
WINTERBOURNE STICKLAND 1(1), 1968-
OX/U-1.

QUARTERLY LITERATURE REPORTS: CLINICAL
BIOCHEMISTRY.
++Q. LIT. REP., CLIN. BIOCHEM.
[KOGAN PAGE]
LONDON [1], OC/D 1968 (1969)-
VOL. NUMBER. COMMENCES WITH VOL 1, NO. 2.
LO/M31.    LO/N14.
ISSN 0009-9139

QUARTERLY LITERATURE REPORTS: POLYMERS.
++Q. LIT. REP., POLYM.
[KOGAN PAGE]
LONDON 1, 1968 (1969)-
VOL. NUMBER. COMMENCES WITH 1(2), 1968.
LO/N14.    LO/S-3.    OX/U-8.
BL/U-8. 5, 1973-
ISSN 0032-3977

QUARTERLY LITERATURE REPORTS: SURFACE ACTIVITY.
++Q. LIT. REP., SURF. ACTIV.
[KOGAN PAGE]
LONDON 1, 1968 (1969)-
VOL. NUMBER. COMMENCES WITH 1(2), 1968.
LO/N14.    LO/S-3.    OX/U-8.
BL/U-1. 5, 1972-              GL/U-2. 5, 1972-
ISSN 0033-5681

QUARTERLY METEOROLOGICAL MAGAZINE (NIGERIA).
++Q. METEOROL. MAG. (NIGER.).
(NIGERIA) METEOROLOGICAL SERVICE.
LAGOS 1(1), 1971-
XS/N-1.

QUARTERLY, NATIONAL FIRE PROTECTION ASSOCIA-
TION.                                                           XXX
SUBS (1965): FIRE JOURNAL.

QUARTERLY NEWS BULLETIN, GUYANA INDUSTRIAL          XXX
DEVELOPMENT CORPORATION.
++Q. NEWS BULL. GUYANA IND. DEVELOP. CORP.
GEORGETOWN 1(1), JA/MR 1966 - 2(4), OC/D
1967...
SUBS: INDUSTRIAL REVIEW.
LO/U-8.

QUARTERLY NEWSLETTER, ASIAN DEVELOPMENT BANK.
++Q. NEWSL. ASIAN DEV. BANK.
MAKATI, PHILIPPINES NO.1, JA 1969-
HL/U-1.    LO/S14.

QUARTERLY NEWSLETTER OF THE BRITISH INSTITUTE
OF INTERNATIONAL & COMPARATIVE LAW.
++Q. NEWSL. BR. INST. INT. & COMP. LAW.
LONDON NO.1, F 1973-
CA/U-1.    DB/U-2.    ED/N-1.    LO/U12.    OX/U15.

QUARTERLY NEWSLETTER, FARNHAM MUSEUM SOCIETY.
++Q. NEWSL. FARNHAM MUS. SOC.
FARNHAM 1(1), 1965-
OX/U-1.
SO/U-1. 1(2), 1966-

QUARTERLY, ORANGE COUNTY CALIFORNIA GENEAL-
OGICAL SOCIETY.
++Q. ORANGE CTY. CALIF. GENEAL. SOC.
ORANGE, CALIF. 1, 1964-
ED/N-1. 3, 1966-
ISSN 0030-4263

QUARTERLY, PAKISTAN ADMINISTRATIVE STAFF
COLLEGE.                                                       XXX
++Q. PAK. ADM. STAFF COLL.
LAHORE 3, 1965-
PREV: PASC JOURNAL FROM 1(1), 1963- 2, 1964.
LO/N17.

QUARTERLY PROGRESS REPORT, CRYOGENIC DATA
CENTER.
++Q. PROG. REP. CRYOG. DATA CENT.
BOULDER, COLO. 1, 1965-
LO/N14.

QUARTERLY REPORTS, ELECTRONICS INSTRUMENTAT-
ION CENTRE, UNIVERSITY OF SOUTHAMPTON.
++Q. REP. ELECTRON. INSTRUM. CENT. UNIV.
SOUTHAMPTON.
SOUTHAMPTON NO.1, 1972-
CENTRE IS PART OF THE DEPARTMENT OF ELECTRON-
ICS.
SO/U-1.

QUARTERLY REVIEW, CENTRAL BANK OF MALTA.
++Q. REV. CENT. BANK MALTA.
VALETTA 1, S 1968-
LO/N-1.

QUARTERLY REVIEWS OF THE CHEMICAL SOCIETY.       XXX
SUBS (1972): PART OF CHEMICAL SOCIETY REVIEWS.

QUARTERLY REVIEW OF HISTORICAL STUDIES.
++Q. REV. HIST. STUD. (INDIA).
INSTITUTE OF HISTORICAL STUDIES (CALCUTTA).
CALCUTTA 1, AP/JE 1961-
LO/U14.    OX/U-1.
BT/U-1. 4, 1964/5-
ISSN 0033-5800

QUARTERLY REVIEW OF MANAGEMENT.                  XXX
SUBS (1967): MANAGEMENT JAPAN.

QUARTERLY REVIEW, NATIONAL WESTMINSTER BANK.
++Q. REV. NAT. WESTMINSTER BANK.
LONDON N 1968-
INCORP: NATIONAL PROVINCIAL BANK REVIEW;
WESTMINSTER BANK REVIEW; DISTRICT BANK REVIEW.
BH/U-1.    BN/U-1.    CB/U-1.    ED/N-1.    GL/U-1.    GL/U-3.
LO/P-6.    LO/U-2.    LO/U-3.    LV/U-1.    OX/U17.

QUARTERLY STATISTICAL BULLETIN OF LIBERIA.
++Q. STAT. BULL. LIBERIA.
(LIBERIA) DEPARTMENT OF PLANNING & ECONOMIC
AFFAIRS.
MONROVIA NO.1, 1969-
LD/U-1.

QUARTERLY STATISTICAL REVIEW, BANK OF ZAMBIA.
++Q. STAT. REV. BANK ZAMBIA.
LUSAKA 1(1), MR 1971-
Q.
LD/U-1.    LO/U-8.    OX/U-9.

QUARTO.
BRADFORD WRITER'S CIRCLE.
BRADFORD [NO.1, 1972]-
ED/N-1.

QUATERNARY RESEARCH. AN INTERDISCIPLINARY
JOURNAL.
++QUATERNARY RES.
[ACADEMIC P.]
NEW YORK 1, 1970-
Q. TEXT MAINLY IN ENGL. OCCAS. IN FR., GER.,
OR RUSS.
AD/U-1.    CA/U-1.    GL/U-1.    HL/U-1.    LD/U-1.    LO/N-2.
LON/13.    LO/U-1.    LO/U-4.    OX/U-9.    SH/U-1.    SO/U-1.

QUE FAIRE. CAHIERS DU CENTRE D'ETUDES ET
D'INITIATIVE REVOLUTIONNAIRE.
PARIS NO.1, F 1970-
LO/U-3.

QUEBEC NOUVEAU.
++QUE. NOUV.
MOUVEMENT NATIONAL DES QUEBECOIS.
QUEBEC 1(1), N 1972-
LO/U-8.

QUEEN'S INTRAMURAL LAW JOURNAL.                  XXX
++QUEEN'S INTRAMURAL LAW J.
QUEEN'S UNIVERSITY (KINGSTON, ONT.): FACULTY OF
LAW.
KINGSTON, ONT. 1(3), 1969- 1(4), 1970.
PREV: INTRAMURAL LAW JOURNAL FROM 1(1), 1968-
1(2), 1969.   SUBS: QUEENS LAW JOURNAL.
OX/U15.

QUEEN'S LAW JOURNAL.                             XXX
++QUEEN'S LAW J.
QUEEN'S UNIVERSITY (KINGSTON, ONT.): FACULTY OF
LAW.
KINGSTON, ONT. 1, 1971-
PREV: QUEEN'S INTRAMURAL LAW JOURNAL FROM
1(3), 1969- 1(4), 1970.
OX/U15.

QUEEN'S PAPERS IN PURE & APPLIED MATHEMATICS.
++QUEEN'S PAP. PURE & APPL. MATH.
QUEEN'S UNIVERSITY (KINGSTON, ONT.).
KINGSTON, ONT. NO.1, 1966-
GL/U-1.    OX/U-8.

QUELLEN UND STUDIEN ZUR GESCHICHTE DER
PHILOSOPHIE.                                     XXX
++QUELLEN & STUD. GESCH. PHILOS.
[WALTER DE GRUYTER & CO.]
BERLIN 1, 1960- 14, 1971.
SUBS: QUELLEN UND STUDIEN ZUR PHILOSOPHIE.
CA/U-1.    GL/U-1.    LO/N-1.    OX/U-1.
ISSN 0481-3618

T

**QUELLEN UND STUDIEN ZUR MUSIKGESCHICHTE SCHLESWIG-HOLSTEINS.**
+ +QUELLEN & STUD. MUSIKGESCH. SCHLESWIG-
HOLSTEINS.
[KARL WACHHOLTZ VERLAG]
NEUMUNSTER 1, 1971-
LO/N-1.    OX/U-1.

**QUELLEN UND STUDIEN ZUR PHILOSOPHIE.**                                     XXX
+ +QUELLEN & STUD. PHILOS.
[WALTER DE GRUYTER & CO.]
BERLIN 1, 1971-
ANNU. PREV: QUELLEN UND STUDIEN ZUR GES-
CHICHTE DER PHILOSOPHIE FROM 1, 1960- 14, 1971
GL/U-1.    LO/N-1.

**QUEST. HOUSE JOURNAL OF THE SCIENCE RESEARCH COUNCIL.**
LONDON 1(1), JA/MR 1968-
XS/R10.

**QUEST. MAGAZINE FOR THE PRACTISING OCCULTIST & MAGICIAN.**
LONDON NO.1, MR 1970-
ED/N-1.    OX/U-1.

**QUESTIONI DI ARCHIVISTICA E SCIENZE AUSILIARE DELLA STORIA.**
+ +QUEST. ARCH. & SCI. AUSILIARE STOR.
BOLOGNA 1, 1972-
OX/U-1.

**QUINTESSENCE INTERNATIONAL. JOURNAL OF PRAC-**                            XXX
**TICAL DENTISTRY.**
+ +QUINTESSENCE INT.
[HAASE]
BERLIN 1, OC 1969-
MON. FROM 3(9), 1972 INCORP: DENTAL DIGEST.
ED/U-1.    LD/U-1.    LO/M31.
MA/U-1. 2(10), 1971-
ISSN 0033-6572

**QUIXOTE.**
UNIVERSITY OF WISCONSIN: DEPARTMENT OF COMPARA-
TIVE LITERATURE.
[QUIXOTE P.]
MADISON, WIS. 1(1), 1965-
LO/U-2.
ISSN 0033-6629

**QUOI DE NEUF.**
FEDERATION FRANCAISE DE SPELEOLOGIE.
PARIS NO.1, 1970-
LO/N-2.
ISSN 0033-6645

**R & D. RESEARCH & DEVELOPMENT FOR INDUSTRY.**                             XXX
[HEYWOOD (NAT. TRADE PRESS)]
LONDON NO.1, S 1961- 41, 1965.//
MON.
AD/U-1.    BH/U-1.    BR/F-1.    BR/P-1.    BR/U-3.    ED/N-1.
LO/C14.    LO/F-9.    LO/M-2.    LO/M12.    LO/M29.
LO/N-7.    LO/N-8.    LO/N14.    LO/R-4.    LO/R-5.    LO/T-1.
LO/U13.    MA/C-1.    NO/U-1.    OX/U-8.    RE/F-1.    SH/U-3.
XE/F-2.    XE/F-4.    XS/C-3.    XS/F12.    XS/R-4.    XS/R10.
XS/T-2.    XS/T-4.    XS/T-9.    XW/C-4.    ZS/T-1.    ZW/F-1.

**R. & D. MANAGEMENT.**
+ +R. & D. MANAGE.
[BLACKWELL]
OXFORD 1, OC 1970-
3/A.
CR/U-1.    ED/N-1.    HL/U-1.    LO/N14.    LO/R-5.    MA/U-1.
OX/U-1.    OX/U16.    OX/U17.    XS/T-4.
GL/U-2. 4, 1973-
ISSN 0033-6807

**R & D PROJECTS IN DOCUMENTATION & LIBRARIAN-**
**SHIP.**
+ +R & D PROJ. DOC. & LIBR.
INTERNATIONAL FEDERATION FOR DOCUMENTATION.
THE HAGUE NO.1, 1971-
MON.
LO/N14.    OX/U-1.

**RABOTA KONSTRUKTSII ZHILYKH ZDANII IZ KRUP-**
**NORAZMERNYKH ELEMENTOV.**
+ +RAB. KONSTR. ZHILYKH ZDANII KRUPNORAZMERNYKH
ELEM.
TSENTRAL'NYJ NAUCHNO-ISSLEDOVATEL'SKIJ I PRO-
EKTNYJ INSTITUT TORGOVOGO I EKSPERIMENTAL'NOGO
PROEKTIROVANIJA ZHILISHCHA.
MOSCOW 2, 1965-
NO DATA AVAILABLE REGARDING VOL.1.
LO/N13.

**RACE RELATIONS.**
+ +RACE RELAT.
RACE RELATIONS BOARD (GB).
LONDON NO.1, 1967-
NS. NO.1, 1973-
LO/U-3.    OX/U-1.
CR/U-1. NO.8, 1970-
LO/U-4. N.S. NO.1, 1973-
ISSN 0033-7293

**RACE RELATIONS ABSTRACTS.**
+ +RACE RELAT. ABSTR.
INSTITUTE OF RACE RELATIONS.
LONDON 1(1), 1968- 2(2), 1970.
N.S. NO.1, 1973-
CB/U-1.    ED/N-1.    HL/U-1.    LO/N-1.    LO/U-1.    LO/U-3.
NO/U-1.    OX/U-1.    OX/U17.
AD/U-1. 1974-
ISSN 0033-7307

**RACE RELATIONS BULLETIN.**
+ +RACE RELAT. BULL.
INSTITUTE OF RACE RELATIONS.
LONDON NO.1, MY 1969- 38, D 1972 ...
PUBL. BY THE RUNNYMEDE TRUST IN COLLAB. WITH
THE INST. OF RACE RELATIONS. SUBS: RUNNYMEDE
TRUST BULLETIN.
AD/U-1.    ED/N-1.    LO/N17.    LO/U-1.    LO/U-3.    LV/U-1.
OX/U17.    RE/U-1.
CB/U-1. NO.10, 1970-
ISSN 0033-7323

**RACE RELATIONS BULLETIN: INDUSTRIAL SUPPLE-**                             XXX
**MENT.**
+ +RACE RELAT. BULL., IND. SUPPL.
INSTITUTE OF RACE RELATIONS.
LONDON NO.1, JE 1970- NO.28, D 1972 ...
MON. SPONS. BODY ALSO: RUNNYMEDE TRUST. SUBS:
RUNNYMEDE TRUST: INDUSTRIAL SUPPLEMENT.
OX/U-1.    OX/U17.
LD/U-1. NO.5, 1970-*

**RACE TODAY.**
INSTITUTE OF RACE RELATIONS.
[RESEARCH PUBL. SERVICES LTD.]
LONDON 1(1), MY 1969-
MON. PREV: INSTITUTE OF RACE RELATIONS NEWS
LETTER FROM AP/1960.
CB/U-1.    ED/N-1.    LD/U-2.    LO/N17.    LO/U-1.    LO/U-3.
MA/P-1.    OX/U-1.    OX/U17.    RE/U-1.
BL/U-1. 3, 1971-
SW/U-1. 3(10), OC 1971-
ISSN 0033-7358

**RACKHAM LITERARY STUDIES.**
+ +RACKHAM LIT. STUD.
UNIVERSITY OF MICHIGAN.
ANN ARBOR 1971-
OX/U-1.

**RADIATION DATA & REPORTS.**                                               XXX
+ +RADIAT. DATA & REP.
(UNITED STATES): ENVIRONMENTAL PROTECTION
AGENCY: OFFICE OF RADIATION PROGRAMS.
WASHINGTON, D.C. 13, 1972-
PREV: RADIOLOGICAL HEALTH DATA & REPORTS FROM
7, 1966- 12, 1971.
LO/N-6.    LO/N13.

**RADIATION EFFECTS.**
+ +RADIAT. EFFECTS.
[GORDON & BREACH]
NEW YORK 1(1), JA 1969-
CA/U-1.    ED/N-1.    LO/N14.    OX/U-8.    XS/R10.
ISSN 0033-7579

**RADIATION RESEARCH REVIEWS.**
+ +RADIAT. RES. REV.
[ELSEVIER]
AMSTERDAM 1, 1968- 5(3/4), 1974 .//
Q.
DB/U-2.    LD/U-1.    LO/N14.    LO/U11.    OX/U-8.    SH/U-1.
GL/U-1. 3, 1971-
XS/R10. 2(1), AG 1969-
ISSN 0033-7595

**RADIATSIONNAJA TEKHNIKA.**
+ +RADIATS. TEKH.
VSESOJUZNYJ NAUCHNO-ISSLEDOVATEL'SKIJ INSTITUT
RADIATSIONNOJ TEKHNIKI.
MOSCOW 1, 1967-
S/T: TRUDY VSESOJUZNOGO NAUCHNO-ISSLEDOVATEL'-
SKOGO INSTITUTA RADIATSIONNOJ TEKHNIKI.
XS/R10.
LO/N13. 2, 1968-

**RADICAL. A JOURNAL OF RADICAL THOUGHT & EXP-RESSION.**
UNIVERSITY OF CAPE TOWN: RADICAL STUDENT'S
SOCIETY.
*RONDEBOSCH NO.1, 1966-*
*LO/U14.*
*LD/U-U. 1970-              LO/U-2. 1968-*
*ISSN 0033-7609*

**RADICAL PHILOSOPHY.**
*++RADICAL PHILOS.*
RADICAL PHILOSOPHY GROUP.
*CANTERBURY NO.1, JA 1972-*
*3/A.*
*BL/U-1. BN/U-1. CA/U-1. ED/N-1. LO/U-2. LO/U-3.*
*MA/U-1.*
*EX/U-1. NO.2, 1972- [W. NO.4, 7]*
*ISSN 0300-2111*

**RADICAL SOFTWARE.**
[GORDON & BREACH]
*NEW YORK; LONDON 1(1), S 1970.*
*        2, OC 1972-*
*9/A.*
*CA/U-1.*
*ED/N-1. 2, 1972-           OX/U-1. 2, 1972-*

**RADIO CONSTRUCTOR.**                                    XXX
SUBS (1972): RADIO & ELECTRONICS CONSTRUCTOR.

**RADIO & ELECTRONICS CONSTRUCTOR.**                     XXX
*++RADIO & ELECTRON. CONSTR.*
[DATA PUBL.]
*LONDON 26, 1972-*
PREV: RADIO CONSTRUCTOR FROM 1, 1947- 25, 1972
*ED/N-1. LO/N14.*

**RADIO, ELEKTRONIK SCHAU.**                             XXX
*++RADIO ELEKTRON. SCHAU.*
[TECHNISCHER VERLAG ERB]
*VIENNA 47, 1971-*
PREV: RADIOSCHAU FROM 1, 1951- 20, 1970.
*LO/N14.*

**RADIO SKY.**
SOCIETY FOR AMATEUR RADIO ASTRONOMERS.
*[MANCHESTER] 1, 1966-*
*ED/N-1.*   *LO/N13.*

**RADIOCHEMICAL & RADIOANALYTICAL LETTERS.**
*++RADIOCHEM. & RADIOANAL. LETT.*
[ELSEVIER SEQUOIA; AKADEMIAI KIADO]
*LAUSANNE; BUDAPEST 1, 1969-*
*LO/N14. LO/S-3. XS/R10. BH/U-1.*
*OX/U-8. 1(3), 1969-*

**RADIOCHEMISTRY. (LONDON).**
CHEMICAL SOCIETY.
*LONDON 1, 1969/1971(1972)-*
A SPECIALIST PERIODICAL REPORT.
*ED/N-1. GL/U-1. HL/U-1. LO/N14. LO/S-3. LO/U12.*
*MA/U-1. NW/U-1.*
*ISSN 0301-0716*

**RADIOLOGICAL HEALTH DATA & REPORTS.**                  XXX
*++RADIOL. HEALTH DATA & REP.*
(UNITED STATES) PUBLIC HEALTH SERVICE.
*WASHINGTON, D.C. 7, 1966- 12, 1971 ...*
PREV: RADIOLOGICAL HEALTH DATA FROM 1, 1960-
6, 1965. SUBS: RADIATION DATA & REPORTS.
*XY/N-1.*
*ISSN 0033-8400*

**RADIOLOGICAL PROTECTION BULLETIN.**
*++RADIOL. PROT. BULL.*
NATIONAL RADIOLOGICAL PROTECTION BOARD (GB).
*HARWELL NO.1, 1972-*
*Q.*
*CA/U-1. ED/N-1. LO/N-6. LO/N14.*

**RADIOSCHAU.**                                          XXX
SUBS (1971): RADIO, ELEKTRONIK SCHAU.

**RAEC GAZETTE.**
*++RAEC GAZ.*
ROYAL ARMY EDUCATIONAL CORPS.
*ELTHAM 1(1), 1967-*
*CA/U-1. ED/N-1. OX/U-1.*
*ISSN 0033-670X*

**RAIL ENGINEERING INTERNATIONAL.**
*++RAIL ENG. INT.*
[SHAW PUBL. CO.]
*LONDON 1, 1971-*
*ED/N-1. LO/N-4. LO/N14.*
*ISSN 0048-6612*

**RAIL INTERNATIONAL. MONTHLY REVIEW.**                  XXX
*++RAIL INT.*
INTERNATIONAL RAILWAY CONGRESS ASSOCIATION.
*BRUSSELS 1(1), 1970-*
PREV PART OF: BULLETIN, INTERNATIONAL
RAILWAY CONGRESS ASSOCIATION. ENGL. ED.
FROM 1, 1896- 46, 1969; CYBERNETICS &
ELECTRONICS ON THE RAILWAYS FROM 1, 1964-
1969; & BULLETIN, INTERNATIONAL UNION OF
RAILWAYS. ENGL. ED. FROM 23, 1952- 40, 1969.
SPONS. BODY ALSO: INTERNATIONAL UNION OF
RAILWAYS.
*ED/N-1. LO/N-1. LO/N-4. OX/U17. SW/U-1.*
*LO/N14. 1(2), 1971-*
*ISSN 0020-8442*

**RAILWAY DIVISION JOURNAL, INSTITUTION OF
MECHANICAL ENGINEERS.**                                  XXX
*++RAILW. DIV. J. INST. MECH. ENG.*
*LONDON 1(1), 1970- 2, 1971.*
PREV: JOURNAL, INSTITUTION OF LOCOMOTIVE
ENGINEERS FROM 1, 1911- 59(328), 1969.
SUBS: REJ. THE RAILWAY ENGINEERING JOURNAL.
*BR/-3. ED/N-1. GL/U-2. LD/U-1. LO/N-4. LO/N14.*
*SW/U-1.*

**RAILWAY SIGNALING & COMMUNICATIONS.**                  XXX
SUBS (1970): RAILWAY SYSTEM CONTROLS.

**RAILWAY SYSTEM CONTROLS.**                             XXX
*++RY. SYST. CONTR.*
[SIMMONS-BOARDMAN]
*CHICAGO 1, 1970-*
PREV: RAILWAY SIGNALING & COMMUNICATIONS
FROM 42, 1949- 63(3), 1970.
*LO/N14.*
*ISSN 0033-7102*

**RAION E FIBRE NUOVE.**                                 XXX
SUBS (1970): PART OF TEXTILIA.

**RAJSHAHI UNIVERSITY STUDIES.**
*++RAJSHAHI UNIV. STUD.*
*RAJSHAHI 1, F 1961-*
*LO/N12.*
*LO/U14. 3, JA 1970-*
*ISSN 0483-9218*

**RAM. A COLLECTION OF VERSE.**
UNIVERSITY COLLEGE OF NORTH WALES.
*BANGOR NO.1, 1972-*
*Q.*
*ED/N-1.*

**RAMAN NEWSLETTER.**
*++RAMAN NEWSL.*
*WASHINGTON (D.C.) NO.1, 1968-*
*XS/R10.*

**RAMUS. CRITICAL STUDIES IN GREEK & ROMAN
LITERATURE.**
[AUREAL PUBL.]
*BERWICK, VICTORIA 1, 1972-*
PUBL. FOR MONASH UNIVERSITY, DEPARTMENT OF
CLASSICAL STUDIES.
*HL/U-1. LD/U-1. LO/U-2. MA/U-1. OX/U-1.*
*SO/U-1. 2, 1973-*

**RANGIERTECHNIK.**                                      XXX
SUBS (1972): RANGIERTECHNIK UND GLEISANSCH-LUSSTECHNIK.

**RANGIERTECHNIK UND GLEISANSCHLUSSTECHNIK.**            XXX
*++RANGIERTECH. & GLEISANSCHLUSSTECH.*
[HESTRA-VERLAG]
*DARMSTADT 1972-*
PREV: RANGIERTECHNIK FROM 18, 1958- 31, 1971.
*LO/N14.*

**RANK & FILE.**
*LONDON NO.1, MR/AP 1969-*
PRODUCED BY LEFT-WING TEACHERS WITHIN THE
NATIONAL UNION OF TEACHERS.
*LO/U-3.*
*ED/N-1. NO.18, 1972-*

**RAPPORT D'ACTIVITE, CENTRE NATIONAL D'ETUDES
SPATIALES.**
*++RAPP. ACTIV. CENT. NAT. ETUD. SPATIALES (FR.)*
*PARIS MR/S, 1962-*
*LO/N14. 1965/66-*
*ISSN 0069-2034*

RAPPORT D'ACTIVITE DE LA STATION ZOOLOGIQUE
DE NAPLES.
+ +RAPP. ACTIV. STA. ZOOL. NAPLES.
STAZIONE ZOOLOGICA DI NAPOLI.
NAPLES    1962/4-
LO/N-2.    LO/U-2.    SO/U-1.

RAPPORT, AFDELINGEN FOR BAERENDE KONSTRUKT-          XXX
IONER, DANMARKS TEKNISKE HOJSKOLE.
+ +RAPP. AFD. BAERENDE KONSTR. DAN. TEKH. HOJSK.
COPENHAGEN NO.11, 1970-
DAN. & ENGL. PREV: RAPPORT, LABORATORIET FOR
BYGNINGSTEKNIK, DANMARKS ... FROM NO.1, 1967-
10, 1969.
LO/N14.

RAPPORT, DANMARKS GEOLOGISKE UNDERSOGELSE.
+ +RAPP. DAN. GEOL. UNDERS.
DANMARKS GEOLOGISKE UNDERSOGELSE.
[REITZEL'S FORLAG]
COPENHAGEN NO.1, 1968-
SUMM. IN ENGL.
BH/U-1.    LO/N-2.    LO/N13.

RAPPORT, GENEESKUNDIGE RAAD, KONINKLIJKE
NEDERLANDSE AKADEMIE VAN WETENSCHAPPEN.
+ +RAPP. GENEESK. RAAD KON. NED. AKAD. WET.
THE HAGUE  NO.1, 1965-
LO/N13.

RAPPORT GENERAL SUR L'ACTIVITE DES COMMUNAUTES.
SEE: GENERAL REPORT ON THE ACTIVITIES OF THE
COMMUNITIES.

RAPPORT, INSTITUTT FOR FORBRENNINGSMOTORER,
NORGES TEKNISKE HOGSKOLE.
+ +RAPP. INST. FORBRENNINGSMOTORER NORG. TEK.
HOGSK.
TRONDEIM  NR. IF/R.1, 1967-
LO/N14.

RAPPORT, LABORATORIET FOR BYGNINGSTEKNIK,
DANMARKS TEKNISKE HOJSKOLE.
+ +RAPP. LAB. BYGNINGSTEK. DAN. TEK. HOJSK.
COPENHAGEN NO.1, 1967- 10, 1969.
IN ENGL. & DAN. SUBS: RAPPORT, AFDELINGEN FOR
BAERENDE KONSTRUKTIONER, DANMARKS TEKNISKE
HOJSKOLE.
LO/N14.

RAPPORT, NATUREGEOGRAFISKA INSTITUTIONEN, UNIV-
ERSITET I UPPSALA.
+ +RAPP. NATURGEOGR. INST. UNIV. UPPSALA.
UPPSALA  1, 1969-
MONOGR.
CA/U-1.    LO/S13.

RAPPORT, STATENS INSTITUT FOR BYGGNADSFORSK-
NING: ENGLISH SUMMARIES.
+ +RAPP. STATENS INST. BYGGNADSFORSK. ENGL. SUMM.
STOCKHOLM  1, 1969-
9/A. ALSO ENTITLED: NATIONAL SWEDISH BUILDING
RESEARCH SUMMARIES.
LO/N-4.
LO/N14.  1971*-
ISSN 0586-1764

RAPRA IN BRIEF.
RUBBER & PLASTICS RESEARCH ASSOCIATION OF
GREAT BRITAIN.
SHAWBURY, SALOP. NO.1, 1973-
S/T: A MONTHLY REVIEW OF CURRENT ACTIVITIES OF
THE ASSOCIATION.
ED/N-1.    OX/U-1.
XS/R10.   THREE YEARS.

RAPRA LITERATURE BULLETIN.
+ +RAPRA LIT. BULL. (RUBB. & PLAST. RES. ASS.)
RUBBER & PLASTICS RESEARCH ASSOCIATION OF
GREAT BRITAIN.
SHAWBURY, SALOP  ABSTRACT 1, 21/AP 1967-
XS/R10.  CURRENT YEAR ONLY.

RAPRA MEMBERS JOURNAL.
RUBBER & PLASTICS RESEARCH ASSOCIATION OF
GREAT BRITAIN.
SHAWBURY, SALOP  1(1), JA 1973-
OX/U-1.  1, 1973- 2(6), 1974.
XS/R10.  3 YEARS ONLY.

RARE EARTH BULLETIN.
+ +RARE EARTH BULL.
[MULTI-SCIENCE PUBL. CO.]
LONDON  1, 1973-
CONSISTS OF ABSTRACTS.
ED/N-1.    LO/N14.    OX/U-8.

RARE-EARTH INFORMATION CENTER NEWS.
+ +RARE-EARTH INF. CENT. NEWS (IOWA STATE UNIV.)
IOWA STATE UNIVERSITY: RARE-EARTH INFORMATION
CENTER.
AMES, IOWA  1(1), 1/MR 1966-
Q.  CENTER ATTACHED TO AMES LABORATORY (OF
THE UNIVERSITY).
SH/U-1.

RASE REVIEW.                                                           XXX
SUBS: PRACTICE WITH SCIENCE.

RASEN, TURF, GAZON.
[HORTUS]
BONN &C.  1, 1970-
S/T: INTERNATIONALE ZEITSCHRIFT FUR FORSCHUNG
UND PRAXIS.
LO/N13.

RASPRAVE I GRADA ZA POVIJEST NAUKA.
+ +RASPR. & GRADA POVIJEST NAUKA.
JUGOSLAVENSKA AKADEMIJA ZNANOSTI I UMJETNOSTI:
INSTITUT ZA POVIJEST PRIRODNIH, MATEMATICKIH I
MEDICINSKIH NAUKA.
ZAGREB  1, 1963-
LO/M24.    LO/N-4.    OX/U-8.

RASSEGNA INTERNATIONALE DI LOGICA.                                     000
SEE: INTERNATIONAL LOGIC REVIEW.

RASTER.  DRIEMAANDELIJKS TIJDSCHRIFT VOOR
LITTERATUUR.
[UITGEVERIJ VAN DITMAR]
AMSTERDAM  NO.1, AP 1967-
LO/N-1.
ISSN 0033-9938

RASTITEL'NYE RESURSY, AKADEMIJA NAUK SSSR.
+ +RAST. RESUR. AKAD. NAUK SSSR.
MOSCOW &C.  1(1), 1965-
CONTENTS LIST IN ENGL.
LO/N-2.
LO/N13.  2(3), 1966-              XS/R-2.   1970-

RASY I NARODY.  SOVREMENNYE, ETNICHESKIE I
RASOVYE PROBLEMY.
AKADEMIJA NAUK SSSR: INSTITUT ETNOGRAFII.
MOSCOW  1, 1971-
A.
CC/U-1.    LO/U-3.

RATIO.  ZEITSCHRIFT FUR RATIONALISIERUNG MIT
ELEKTROSTANDARD.
INSTITUT FUR RATIONALISIERUNG UND ORGANISATION
DER ELEKTROINDUSTRIE.
DRESDEN  [BD.]1, 1968-
M.  PREV: ELEKTRO-STANDARD.
LO/N13.

RATIONAL DRUG THERAPY.                                                 XXX
+ +RATION. DRUG THER.
AMERICAN SOCIETY FOR PHARMACOLOGY &
EXPERIMENTAL THERAPEUTICS.
PHILADELPHIA  4, 1970-
PREV: PHARMACOLOGY FOR PHYSICIANS FROM 1(1),
JA 1967- 3, 1969.
NW/U-1.
BL/U-1. 5, 1971-              LO/N11. 5, 1971-
ISSN 0031-7020

RATOON.
[J.R. RAMSAMMY]
QUEENSTOWN, GUYANA  NO.1, JA 1971-
LO/U-8.

RAVEN BANNER.  A FORUM FOR THE DISCUSSION &
PROPAGATION OF ODINIST PRINCIPLES.
ODINIST COMMITTEE.
LONDON  NO.1, 1973-
ED/N-1.    OX/U-1.

RAYMONDIANA.
UNIVERSIDAD NACIONAL MAYOR DE SAN MARCOS:
INSTITUTO DE BOTANICA.
LIMA  1, 1968-
LO/N-2.

RAZNOCHINNO-DEMOKRATICHESKOE DVIZHENIE V
POVOLZH'E I NA URALE.
+ +RAZNOCHINNO DEMOKR. DVIZHENIE POVOLZH'E URALE.
KAZANSKIJ GOSUDARSTVENNYJ UNIVERSITET.
KAZAN'  1, 1964-
MONOGR.
BH/U-1.    LO/N-3.

RAZON Y FABULA.
UNIVERSIDAD DE LOS ANDES.
*BOGOTA NO.1, MY 1967-*
6/A.
*LO/U-1.* LV/U-1. OX/U-1.*
*ED/N-1. NO.2, JL/AG 1967-*
*SH/U-1. JA/F 1971-*

REACTOR & FUEL-PROCESSING TECHNOLOGY.      XXX
SUBS (1970): REACTOR TECHNOLOGY.

REACTOR TECHNOLOGY. QUARTERLY TECHNICAL      XXX
PROGRESS REVIEW.
*+ +REACTOR TECHNOL.*
UNITED STATES ATOMIC ENERGY COMMISSION: DIVI-
SION OF TECHNICAL INFORMATION.
*WASHINGTON, D.C. 13(1), 1969/70-*
PREV: REACTOR & FUEL-PROCESSING TECHNOLOGY
FROM 10(3), 1967- 12(4), 1969.
*LO/N-4.*
*ISSN 0034-0332*

READING. A JOURNAL FOR THE STUDY & IMPROVE-
MENT OF READING & RELATED SKILLS.
UNITED KINGDOM READING ASSOCIATION.
*STOCKPORT, CHES. 1(2), MR 1967-*
3/A.
*BL/C-1.*
*GL/U-2. 5, 1971-*
*ISSN 0034-0472*

READING AREA NEWS.
SCHOOLS COUNCIL (GB): SIXTH FORM MATHS PROJECT.
*READING NO.1, 1971-*
*ED/N-1.*

READING GEOGRAPHER.
*+ +READING GEOGR.*
UNIVERSITY OF READING: DEPARTMENT OF GEOGRAPHY.
*READING 1, 1970-*
*BL/U-1. HL/U-1. RE/U-1.*
*LO/U-1. 2, 1971-*

READING UNIVERSITY LIBRARY PUBLICATIONS.
*+ +READING UNIV. LIBR. PUBL.*
*READING NO.1, 1969-*
*LO/N-1.*

READINGS IN POLITICAL ECONOMY.
*+ +READ. POLIT. ECON.*
INSTITUTE OF ECONOMIC AFFAIRS.
*[LONDON] NO.1, 1967-*
*DB/U-2. HL/U-1.*

REAKTSIONNAJA SPOSOBNOST' ORGANICHESKIKH
SOEDINENIJ.
*+ +REAKTS. SPOSOBNOST ORG. SOEDIN. [RSOT-A]*
TARTUSKIJ GOSUDARSTVENNYJ UNIVERSITET.
*TARTU 1(1), MY 1964-*
ENGL. SUMM. & TITLE: ORGANIC REACTIVITY.
*CA/U-2. GL/U-1. HL/U-1. LO/U-2.*
*LO/S-3. 6, 1969- OX/U-8. 6, 1969-*
*SF/U-1. 11, 1974-*

REALITES IVOIRIENNES.
CENTRE D'INFORMATION ET DE DOCUMENTATION
IVOIRIEN.
*PARIS NO.1, N 1965- 84, 1969.//*
WKLY. INCORP: MARCHE IVOIRIEN FROM 1968.
*LO/N17.*
*ISSN 0486-1078*

REALITY. A JOURNAL OF LIBERAL OPINION.      XXX
*PIETERMARITZBURG 1(1), JA/MR 1969-*
2M. PREV: TRANSKEI LIBERAL NEWS FROM 1, JA
1964.
*LO/U-3. OX/U16.*
*LO/U14. 1(4), 1970-*
*LO/U-8. 5(6), JA 1974-*
*ISSN 0034-0979*

REALTY REVIEW.
*+ +REALTY REV.*
SAN JOSE STATE COLLEGE: SCHOOL OF BUSINESS.
*SAN JOSE, CALIF. 1, 1964-*
*SH/C-5. MR 1971-*
*ISSN 0034-1061*

RECALL. REVIEW OF EDUCATIONAL CYBERNETICS &
APPLIED LINGUISTICS.
[LONGMAC LTD.]
*CAMBRIDGE &C. 1, 1969-*
3A.
*ED/N-1. OX/U-1. SH/U-1.*
*ISSN 0034-1150*

RECENT ADVANCES IN BIOLOGICAL PSYCHIATRY.      XXX
SUBS(1969): BIOLOGICAL PSYCHIATRY.

RECENT ADVANCES IN PHYTOCHEMISTRY.
*+ +RECENT ADV. PHYTOCHEM.*
PHYTOCHEMICAL SOCIETY OF NORTH AMERICA.
*NEW YORK &C 1, 1968-*
*BH/U-1. GL/U-1. LO/N-2. LO/N13. LO/U12. RE/U-1.*

RECENT DEVELOPMENT OF NEUROBIOLOGY IN HUNGARY.
*+ +RECENT DEV. NEUROBIOL. HUNG.*
[AKADEMIAI KIADO]
*BUDAPEST 1, 1967-*
*LO/N13.*

RECENT LITERATURE OF MAMMALOGY.
*+ +RECENT LIT. MAMMOL.*
AMERICAN SOCIETY OF MAMMALOGISTS.
*STILLWATER, OKLA. [NO.1], 1970-*
ISSUED AS SUPPL. TO: JOURNAL OF MAMMALOGY.
*LO/N13.*

RECENT POLAR LITERATURE.      XXX
*+ +RECENT POLAR LIT.*
SCOTT POLAR RESEARCH INSTITUTE.
*CAMBRIDGE NO.1, 1973-*
PREV. PART OF: POLAR RECORD FROM 1931- 1972.
*BL/U-1. CA/U-1. CA/U-2. CA/U12. LD/U-1. LO/N-2.*
*OX/U-1. OX/U10. SW/U-1. XS/N-1.*

RECENT RESULTS IN CANCER RESEARCH.
*+ +REC. RESULT. CANCER RES.*
[SPRINGER]
*BERLIN 1, 1966-*
*BN/U-1.*

RECENT SOCIOLOGY.
*+ +RECENT SOCIOL.*
[MACMILLAN CO.]
*LONDON &C. NO.1, 1969-*
ANNU.
*LO/N-1. LO/U-3. OX/U-1. OX/U17.*
*HL/U-1. 1, 1969- 2, 1970; 5, 1973.*
*ISSN 0080-0023*

RECERQUES.
*BARCELONA 1, 1970-*
*OX/U-1.*

RECHERCHE.      XXX
[SOCIETE D'EDITIONS SCIENTIFIQUES]
*PARIS 1, MY 1970-*
INDIVIDUAL ISSUES NUMBERED INDEPENDENTLY OF
VOL. NUMBERING. PREV: ATOMES FROM 1, 1946.
INCORP: NUCLEUS FROM JA 1971.
*BN/U-2. DB/S-1. LO/N14. LO/U20.*
*MA/U-1. 1(3), 1970-*
*LD/U-1. NO.1, MY; 4, S; 6, N 1970-*
*LO/U-2. 5(42), 1974-*
*XS/R10. 4(32), MR 1973-*
*ISSN 0029-5671*

RECHERCHE AFRICANISTE EN COURS. BULLETIN
INTERNATIONALE.      000
SEE: CURRENT AFRICANIST RESEARCH.

RECHERCHES AMERINDIENNES AU QUEBEC. BULLETIN
D'INFORMATION.
*+ +RECH. AMERINDIENNES QUE.*
SOCIETE DES RECHERCHES AMERINDIENNES AU QUEBEC.
*MONTREAL 1(1), JA 1971-*
*LO/S10.*
*LO/N-1. 2(1), 1972-*

RECHERCHES D'ECONOMIE ET DE SOCIOLOGIE
RURALES.
*+ +RECH. ECON. SOCIOL. RUR.*
INSTITUT NATIONAL DE LA RECHERCHE AGRONOMIQUE
(FRANCE): DEPARTEMENT D'ECONOMIE ET DE SOCIOL-
OGIE RURALES.
*PARIS NO.1, 1967-*
*LO/N13.*

RECHERCHE, ENSEIGNEMENT, DOCUMENTATION AFRIC-
ANISTES FRANCOPHONES.
*+ +RECH. ENSEIG. DOC. AFR. FRANCOPHONES.*
[CARDAN]
*PARIS 1(1), 1969-*
S/T: BULLETIN D'INFORMATION ET DE LIAISON.
*AD/U-1. BH/U-1. LO/U-8.*
*OX/U-1. 1(2), 1969-*

RECHERCHES GERMANIQUES.
*+ +RECH. GER.*
UNIVERSITE DE STRASBOURG.
*STRASBOURG 1, 1971-*
ANNU.
*BL/U-1. HL/U-1. LO/N-1. LO/U13. MA/S-1. MA/U-1.*
*NO/U-1. SH/U-1. SW/U-1.*

RECHERCHES D'HYDROBIOLOGIE CONTINENTALE.
++RECH. HYDROBIOL. CONTINENTALE.
INSTITUT NATIONAL DE LA RECHERCHE AGRONOMIQUE
(FRANCE).
PARIS NO.1, 1969.
SUBS: ANNALES D'HYDROBIOLOGIE.
DB/S-1.   LO/N-2.   LO/N-4.   LO/N13.   OX/U-8.

RECHERCHES SOCIOLOGIQUES.
++RECH. SOCIOL.
BRUSSELS NO.1, JE 1970-
OX/U-1.

RECHERCHE SUR LE TRAVAIL ET LES RELATIONS
INDUSTRIELLES AU CANADA.                               000
SEE: LABOUR & INDUSTRIAL RELATIONS RESEARCH
IN CANADA.

RECHTSTHEORIE.
[DUNCKER & HUMBLOT]
BERLIN 1(1), 1970-
OX/U15.
ISSN 0034-1398

RECLAIM. CONSERVATION BULLETIN.
CONFEDERATION OF IRISH INDUSTRY.
DUBLIN NO.1, MY 1971-
DB/U-2.

RECOIL.
UNIVERSITY COLLEGE, CORK: ENGINEERING SOCIETY.
CORK NO.1, 1972-
DB/U-2.   ED/N-1.

RECONCILIATION QUARTERLY.                              XXX
++RECONCIL. Q.
FELLOWSHIP OF RECONCILIATION.
LONDON 5, 1969-
PREV: FELLOWSHIP OF RECONCILIATION QUARTERLY
FROM 1, 1967.
OX/U-1.
ISSN 0034-1479

RECONSTRUCTION.
LAWRENCE (KANS.) 1(1), 1969-
LO/U-2.

RECORD BUYER.
[WORLD DISTRIBUTORS]
MANCHESTER NO.1, F 1969-
ED/N-1.   OX/U-1.

RECORD, FACTORY MUTUAL ENGINEERING CORPORAT-
ION.                                                  XXX
++REC. FACT. MUTUAL ENG. CORP.
BOSTON, MASS. 48, 1971-
PREV: FACTORY MUTUAL RECORD FROM 1, JE 1924-
47, 1970.
LO/N14.

RECORD OF PROCEEDINGS OF THE NEW ZEALAND GEO-
GRAPHICAL SOCIETY.                                    XXX
SUBS (1969): NEW ZEALAND JOURNAL OF
GEOGRAPHY.

RECORDS OF THE AUSTRALIAN ACADEMY OF SCIENCE.
++REC. AUST. ACAD. SCI.
CANBERRA 1(1), D 1966-
BL/U-1.   CA/U-2.   DB/U-2.   LO/M24.   LO/N-2.

RECORDS OF THE GEOLOGICAL SURVEY OF MALAWI.           XXX
++REC. GEOL. SURV. MALAWI.
ZOMBA 3, 1961-
PREV: RECORDS OF THE GEOLOGICAL SURVEY OF
NYASALAND FROM 1, 1959- 2, 1960.
BR/U-3.   LO/N-2.
GL/U-1. 3, 1961- 7, 1967.

RECORDS OF THE GEOLOGICAL SURVEY OF
NYASALAND.                                            XXX
SUBS (1961): RECORDS OF THE GEOLOGICAL
SURVEY OF MALAWI.

RECORDS, PUBLIC MUSEUM & ART GALLERY OF PAPUA
& NEW GUINEA.
++REC. PUBLIC MUS. & ART GALLERY PAPUA & NEW
GUINEA.
PORT MORESBY 1, 1970-
LO/N-2.

RECORDS, ZOOLOGICAL SURVEY OF PAKISTAN.
++REC. ZOOL. SURV. PAKISTAN.
ZOOLOGICAL SURVEY OF PAKISTAN.
KARACHI 1, 1969-
LO/N-2.

RECUEIL DES LOIS ET REGLEMENTS LIBANAIS ET DE
JURISPRUDENCE.
++RECL. LOIS & REGLEMENTS LIBAN. & JURISPRUD.
BEIRUT NO.1, 1970-
LO/U14.

RECUEIL DES MARQUES BENELUX.                          000
SEE: BENELUX-MERKENBLAD.

RECUEIL DE TRAVAUX, BUREAU INTERNATIONAL DES
POIDS ET MESURES.
++RECL. TRAV. BUR. INT. POIDS & MES.
SEVRES 1, 1966/67-
A.
LO/N13.

RECUEIL DE TRAVAUX, SECTION OCEANOGRAPHIE,
CENTRE DE NOUMEA, OFFICE DE LA RECHERCHE
SCIENTIFIQUE ET TECHNIQUE OUTRE-MER.
++RECL. TRAV. SECT. OCEANOGR. CENT. NOUMEA,
OFF. RECH. SCI. TECH. OUTRE-MER.
PARIS 1, 1969-
LO/N-2.

RECUEIL DES TRAVAUX DE LA SOCIETE PREHISTOR-
IQUE TCHECOSLOVAQUE.                                  000
SEE: SBORNIK CESKOSLOVENSKE SPOLECNOSTI
ARCHEOLOGICKE.

RED RAG. A MAGAZINE OF WOMEN'S LIBERATION.
LONDON NO.1, [1972]-
PRODUCED BY A MARXIST COLLECTIVE IN THE
WOMEN'S LIBERATION MOVEMENT.
LO/U-3.
CA/U-1. NO.3, 1973-          ED/N-1. NO.3, 1973-

RED VANGUARD. JOURNAL OF THE THEORY &
PRACTICE OF MARXISM-LENINISM.
MARXIST-LENINIST ORGANIZATION OF BRITAIN.
LONDON NO.1, 1970-
Q.
ED/N-1.   OX/U-1.
HL/U-1. NO.2, 1972-
ISSN 0011-1856

REFERATIVNYJ SBORNIK: ORGANIZATSIJA
UPRAVLENIJA PROMYSHLENNOST'JU.
++REF. SB., ORG. UPR. PROM-ST.
AKADEMIJA NAUK SSSR: VSESOJUZNYJ INSTITUT
NAUCHNOJ I TEKHNICHESKOJ INFORMATSII.
MOSCOW 1, 1967-
LO/N-3.*

REFERENCE LISTS, LIBRARY, UNITED NATIONS.
++REF. LISTS LIBR. U.N.
GENEVA NO.1, 1970-
ENGL., FR. & RUSS.
LO/N-1.

REFERENCE SERVICES REVIEW.
++REF. SERV. REV.
[PIERIAN P.]
ANN ARBOR, MICH. 1, 1973-
5/A.  PRELIM. ISSUE DATED N/D 1972.
CA/U-1.   DB/U-2.   ED/N-1.   GL/U-2.   OX/U-1.

REFORM.
UNITED REFORMED CHURCH.
LONDON [NO.1], N 1972-
MON.
CA/U-1.   ED/N-1.

REFRIGERATION & AIR CONDITIONING.                     XXX
++REFRIG. & AIR COND.
[REFRIGERATION P.]
LONDON 73(862), 1970-
PREV: MODERN REFRIGERATION & AIR CONDITIONING
FROM 67(798), 1964- 73(861), 1970.
LO/N-6.   LO/N-7.
ISSN 0026-8364

REGELUNGSTECHNIK.                                     XXX
SUBS (1970):  REGELUNGSTECHNIK UND PROZESS -
DATENVERARBEITUNG.

REGELUNGSTECHNIK UND PROZESS- DATENVERARBEITUNG.
++REGELUNGSTECH. & PROZESS- DATENVERARB.
MUNICH 18, 1970-
PREV: REGELUNGSTECHNIK FROM 1, 1953- 17(12).
1969.
LO/N-7.   LO/N14.
ISSN 0034-3226

**REGENSBURGER BEITRAGE ZUR MUSIKALISCHEN VOLKS-
UND VOLKERKUNDE.**
+ +REGENSB. BEITR. MUSIKALISCHEN VOLKS- &
VOLKERKD.
*REGENSBURG 1, 1969-*
OX/U-1.

**REGIONAL CONFERENCE SERIES IN MATHEMATICS.**
+ +REG. CONF. SER. MATH.
AMERICAN MATHEMATICAL SOCIETY.
*PROVIDENCE, R.I. NO.1, 1970-*
LO/N-4.    LO/N14.

**REGIONAL PAPERS, NATIONAL INSTITUTE OF ECON-
OMIC & SOCIAL RESEARCH (G.B.).**
+ +REG. PAP. NATL. INST. ECON. & SOC. RES. (G.B.)
*LONDON [NO.]1, 1970-*
LO/N-1.    OX/U-1.

**REGIONAL REVIEW QUARTERLY.**
+ +REG. REV. Q.
NATIONAL SERVICE TO REGIONAL COUNCILS (US).
*WASHINGTON, D.C. 1(1), S/OC 1968-*
LO/U-3.    OX/U-9.
ISSN 0034-3382

**REGIONAL & URBAN ECONOMICS. OPERATIONAL
METHODS.**
+ +REG. & URBAN ECON.
[NORTH-HOLLAND PUBL. CO.]
*AMSTERDAM 1(1), MY 1971-*
Q.
AD/U-1.    CB/U-1.    LD/U-1.    LN/U-2.    LO/N-7.    LO/U-3.
OX/U17.    RE/U-1.    SO/U-1.    XY/N-1.
BL/U-1. 4, 1974-
ISSN 0034-3331

**REGISTERED ARCHITECT. JOURNAL OF THE ...**
+ +REGIST. ARCHIT.
INSTITUTE OF REGISTERED ARCHITECTS.
*LONDON*
ED/N-1. JE 1965-

**REINIGER + WASCHER.**                                                   XXX
[NEUER MERKUR GMBH]
*MUNICH 23(4), 1970-*
PREV: WASCHER + REINIGER.
LO/N14.
ISSN 0034-3625

**REINSURANCE. THE MONTHLY INTERNATIONAL REIN-
SURANCE MAGAZINE.**
[BUCKLEY P.]
*LONDON 1, 1969-*
CA/U-1.
ISSN 0048-7171

**REJ. THE RAILWAY ENGINEERING JOURNAL.**          XXX
INSTITUTION OF MECHANICAL ENGINEERS.
*LONDON 1(1), JA 1972-*
6/A. PREV: RAILWAY DIVISION JOURNAL, INSTITU-
TION OF MECHANICAL ENGINEERS FROM 1(1), 1970-
2, 1971.
ED/N-1.    LO/N-4.    LO/N14.    OX/U-8.

**RELATORIOS E COMUNICACOES, INSTITUTO DE
INVESTIGACAO CIENTIFICA DE ANGOLA.**
+ +RELAT. & COMMUN. INST. INVEST. CIENT. ANGOLA.
*LUANDA 1, 1962-*
LO/N-2.

**RELAY ENGINEER.**                                                        XXX
+ +RELAY ENG.
SOCIETY OF RELAY ENGINEERS.
*SOLIHULL 9(1), JA 1971- 9(4), JL 1972 ...*
PREV: PROCEEDINGS, SOCIETY... FROM 1, 1946-
8(3), 1970. SUBS: CABLE TELEVISION ENGINEERING
LO/N14.    OX/U-8.
ISSN 0048-718X

**R.E.L.C. JOURNAL.**
REGIONAL ENGLISH LANGUAGE CENTRE (SINGAPORE).
*SINGAPORE 1, 1970-*
HL/U-2.
BN/U-1. 3, 1972-
ISSN 0033-6882

**RELEASE. THE MAGAZINE OF ...**
JORDANHILL COLLEGE OF EDUCATION.
*GLASGOW*
ED/N-1. F 1967-

**RELIGION. A JOURNAL OF RELIGION & RELIGIONS.**
[ORIEL P.]
*NEWCASTLE UPON TYNE 1(1), 1971-*
2/A.
AD/U-1.    BN/U-1.    CB/U-1.    DN/U-1.    ED/N-1.    GL/U-1.
GL/U-2.    HL/U-1.    LD/U-1.    LO/N-1.    LO/U-3.    MA/U-1.
NO/U-1.    SH/U-1.    SW/U-1.
ISSN 0048-721X

**RELIGION EN AFRIQUE.**                                                   000
SEE: JOURNAL OF RELIGION IN AFRICA.

**RELIGION IN COMMUNIST LANDS.**
+ +RELIG. COMMUNIST LANDS.
CENTRE FOR THE STUDY OF RELIGION & COMMUNISM.
*CHISLEHURST, KENT 1(1), JA/F 1973-*
6/A.
AD/U-1.    CA/U-1.    ED/N-1.    LO/S14.    LO/U-3.    OX/U-1.
EX/U-1. 1(6), N/D 1973-

**RELIGIOUS SITUATION.**
+ +RELIG. SITUATION.
[BEACON P.]
*BOSTON, MASS. 1968-*
A.
LO/U-3.

**RELIGIOUS STUDIES MONOGRAPHS.**
+ +RELIG. STUD. MONOGR.
SILLIMAN UNIVERSITY.
*DUMAGUETE CITY, PHILIPP. NO.1, 1968-*
HL/U-1.**

**REMOTE SENSING OF ENVIROMENT: AN INTER-
DISCIPLINARY JOURNAL.**
+ +REMOTE SENS. ENVIRON.
[AMERICAN ELSEVIER PUBL. CO.]
*NEW YORK 1(1), MR 1969-*
AD/U-3.    BH/U-3.    BN/U-2.    EX/U-1.    HL/U-1.    LD/U-1.
LO/N14.    LO/U-3.    LO/U-4.    MA/U-1.    OX/U-3.
NO/U-1. 2, OC 1971-        RE/U-1. 3, 1974-
ISSN 0034-4257

**RENAISSANCE. A BI-MONTHLY MAGAZINE OF THE ARTS.**
[OPEN CITY]
*[LOS ANGELES] NO.1, MY/JE [1968]-*
LO/U-2.

**RENAISSANCE NEWS.**                                                      XXX
SUBS (1967): RENAISSANCE QUARTERLY.

**RENAISSANCE QUARTERLY.**
+ +RENAISS. Q.
RENAISSANCE SOCIETY OF AMERICA.
*NEW YORK 20(1), 1967-*
PREV: RENAISSANCE NEWS FROM 1, 1948.
AD/U-1.    BH/P-1.    BH/U-1.    CR/U-1.    EX/U-1.    HL/U-1.
LD/U-1.    LO/N-3.    LO/U-1.    SO/U-1.
ED/N-1. 20, 1967-
ISSN 0034-4338

**RENAISSANCE & REFORMATION.**
+ +RENAISSANCE & REFORMAT.
UNIVERSITY OF TORONTO RENAISSANCE & REFORMATION
COLLOQUIUM.
*TORONTO 1, 1964-*
3/A. ENGL. & FR. SPONS. BODY ALSO CENTRE FOR
RENAISSANCE & REFORMATION STUDIES, VICTORIA
UNIVERSITY.
LD/U-1. 8, 1971-

**RENDICONTI DELL'ISTITUTO DI MATEMATICA
DELL'UNIVERSITA DI TRIESTE.**
+ +REND. IST. MAT. UNIV. TRIESTE.
*TRIESTE 1, 1969-*
GL/U-1.    LO/N14.    LO/U-2.

**RENDICONTI, SOCIETA ITALIANA DI MINERALOGIA
E PETROLOGIA.**                                                           XXX
+ +REND. SOC. ITAL. MINERAL. & PETROL.
*MILAN 24, 1968-*
ITAL., FR. & SPAN. WITH ENGL. SUMM. PREV:
RENDICONTI, SOCIETA MINERALOGICA ITALIANA FROM
1, 1941- 23, 1967.
LO/N14.

**RENDICONTI, SOCIETA MINERALOGICA ITALIANA.**           XXX
SUBS (1968): RENDICONTI, SOCIETA ITALIANA DI
MINERALOGIA E PETROLOGIA.

**RENNER RESEARCH REPORTS.**
+ +RENNER RES. REP.
TEXAS RESEARCH FOUNDATION: HOBLITZELLE
AGRICULTURAL LABORATORY.
*RENNER, TEX. 1, 1968- 1(11), AP 1972. //*
CA/U11.    LO/N-2.
LO/N13. 1(4), 1969-

RENTGENOGRAFIJA MINERAL'NOGO SYR'JA.
VSESOJUZNYJ NAUCHNO-ISSLEDOVATEL'SKIJ INSTITUT
MINERAL'NOGO SYR'JA (VIMS).
 *MOSCOW 1, 1962-*
 SPONS. BODY ALSO KOMISSIJA PO RENTGENOGRAFII
 MINERAL'NOGO SYR'JA, AKADEMIJA NAUK SSSR.
 *LO/N13.*

REPERTOIRE ANALYTIQUE DE LITTERATURE
FRANCAISE.
 *++REPERT. ANAL. LIT. FR.*
 UNIVERSITE DE BORDEAUX: SECTION DE LA LANGUE ET
 LITTERATURE FRANCAISE.
 *SAINT-MEDARD-EN-JALLES 1, 1970-*
 SECTION SUBORD. TO : FACULTE DES LETTRES ET
 SCIENCES HUMAINES.
 *EX/U-1.     GL/U-1.     HL/U-1.*

REPERTORIO DAS PUBLICACOES PERIODICAS
PORTUGUESAS.
 *++REPERT. PUBL. PERIOD. PORT.*
 BIBLIOTECA NACIONAL (PORTUGAL).
 *LISBON 1961(1964)-*
 *LV/U-1.     OX/U-1.*

REPORT, AUSTRALIAN HUMANITIES RESEARCH
COUNCIL.                                                                 XXX
 SUBS (1970): PROCEEDINGS, AUSTRALIAN ACAD-
 EMY OF THE HUMANITIES.

REPORTS, AYACUCHO ARCHAEOLOGICAL-BOTANICAL
PROJECT.                                                                 000
 SEE: AYACUCHO ...

REPORT, BUXTON FIELD CLUB.
 *++REP. BUXTON FIELD CLUB.*
 *BUXTON 1ST, 1969/71(1971)-*
 *LO/N-2.     LO/N13.*

REPORT, CALIFORNIA INSTITUTE OF INTERNATIONAL
STUDIES.                                                                 XXX
 *++REP. CALIF. INST. INT. STUD.*
 *STANFORD, CALIF.  1(1), 1970- 2, 1972 ...*
 SUBS: WORLD AFFAIRS REPORT FROM 3, 1973.
 *OX/U-1.*

REPORT, CENTRAL COUNCIL FOR AGRICULTURAL &
HORTICULTURAL CO-OPERATION.
 *++REP. CENT. COUNC. AGRIC. & HORTIC. CO-OP.*
 *LONDON 1ST, 1967/68(1968)-*
 *A.*
 *CA/U11.     OX/U24.*

REPORT, CIVIL SERVICE DEPARTMENT (GB).
 *++REP. CIVIL SERV. DEP. (GB).*
 (GREAT BRITAIN) CIVIL SERVICE DEPARTMENT.
 *LONDON 1, 1970-*
 *BH/U-1.     BL/U-1.     GL/U-1.     LO/N-2.     OX/U-1.*

REPORT, COLLEGE OF AERONAUTICS (CRANFIELD).             XXX
 SUBS (1963): COA REPORT AERO.

REPORT, COMPUTER CENTRE, TOKYO UNIVERSITY.
 *++REP. COMPUT. CENT. TOKYO UNIV.*
 TOKYO DAIGAKU: OGATA KEISANKEI SENTA.
 *TOKYO 1(1), 1968-*
 *LO/N14.     OX/U-8.     SW/U-1.     XN/S-1.*

REPORT, CONSTRUCTION INDUSTRY RESEARCH
INFORMATION ASSOCIATION.                                       000
 SEE: CIRIA REPORT.

REPORT, COUNTRYSIDE COMMISSION FOR SCOTLAND.
 *++REP. COUNTRYSIDE COMM. SCOTL.*
 COUNTRYSIDE COMMISSION FOR SCOTLAND.
 *PERTH 1, 1969-*
 *BL/U-1.     GL/U-1.     LO/N-1.     LO/N-2.     OX/U-1.*

REPORT, DEPARTMENT OF AGRICULTURAL MARKETING,
UNIVERSITY OF NEWCASTLE UPON TYNE.
 *++REP. DEP. AGR. MARK. UNIV. NEWCASTLE TYNE.*
 *NEWCASTLE UPON TYNE NO.1, AP 1965-*
 *BN/U-1.     BN/U-2.*

REPORT, DEPARTMENT OF APPLIED AGRICULTURAL
ECONOMICS, UNIVERSITY COLLEGE, DUBLIN.
 *++REP. DEP. APPL. AGR. ECON. UNIV. COLL. DUBLIN.*
 *DUBLIN 1, 1970-*
 *BL/U-1.     LO/N-1.*

REPORT, DEPARTMENT OF ATMOSPHERIC SCIENCE,
COLORADO STATE UNIVERSITY.
 *++REP. DEP. ATMOS. SCI. COLO. STATE UNIV.*
 *FORT COLLINS, COLO.  NO.1, 1968-*
 *XS/N-1.*

REPORT, DEPARTMENT OF ELECTRICAL ENGINEERING,
WEST HAM COLLEGE OF TECHNOLOGY.
 *++REP. DEP. ELEC. W. HAM COLL. TECHNOL.*
 *LONDON 1, 1967-*
 *DB/U-1.     OX/U-8.*

REPORT, DORMAN MUSEUM & MUNICIPAL ART GALLERY.
 *++REP. DORMAN MUS. & MUNIC. ART GALLERY.*
 *MIDDLESBROUGH 1, AP 1966-*
 *LO/N-2.*

REPORT, ECONOMICS DEPARTMENT, EAST OF
SCOTLAND COLLEGE OF AGRICULTURE.                           XXX
 *++REP. ECON. DEP. EAST SCOTL. COLL. AGRIC.*
 *EDINBURGH NO.96, 1970-*
 INCORP: BULLETIN, ECONOMICS DEPARTMENT,
 EDINBURGH & EAST OF SCOTLAND ... FROM 1946-
 1969; & ECONOMIC REPORT, ECONOMICS DEPARTMENT,
 EDINBURGH & EAST ... FROM NO.1, 1949- 95,
 1968, OF WHICH VOL. NUMBERING IS CONTINUED.
 *CA/U11.*

REPORTS, FACULTY OF ENGINEERING, NAGASAKI
UNIVERSITY.                                                               000
 SEE: NAGASAKI DAIGAKU KOGAKUBU KENKYU HOKOKU.

REPORTS OF THE FACULTY OF SCIENCE, KAGOSHIMA
UNIVERSITY.
 *++REP. FAC. SCI. KAGOSHIMA UNIV.*
 *KAGOSHIMA NO.1, 1968-*
 *LO/N-4.*

REPORTS OF FAMILY LAW.
 *++REP. FAM. LAW.*
 (CANADA) COURTS.
 *TORONTO 1, 1971-*
 *ANNU.*
 *SO/U-1.*

REPORT, FARM ECONOMICS BRANCH, CAMBRIDGE
UNIVERSITY.                                                              XXX
 SUBS: (1969) AGRICULTURAL ECONOMICS REPORT,
 DEPARTMENT OF LAND ECONOMY, UNIVERSITY OF
 CAMBRIDGE.

REPORTS ON THE FAUNA & FLORA OF WISCONSIN.
 *++REP. FAUNA & FLORA WIS.*
 WISCONSIN STATE UNIVERSITY: MUSEUM OF NATURAL
 HISTORY.
 *STEVENS POINT 1, 1969-*
 *LO/N-2.*

REPORT, FUKAURA MARINE BIOLOGICAL LABORATORY.       000
 SEE: FUKAURA RINKAI JISSHUJO HOKOKU.

REPORT, GEOLOGICAL SURVEY OF WESTERN AUSTRAL-
IA.
 *++REP. GEOL. SURV. W. AUST.*
 (WESTERN AUSTRALIA) GEOLOGICAL SURVEY.
 *[PERTH] 1, 1969-*
 *ED/S-2.     GL/U-1.     LO/N-2.*
 *ISSN 0085-8145*

REPORTS OF THE GOVERNMENT INDUSTRIAL DEVELOPMENT
LABORATORY.                                                             000
 SEE: HOKKAIDO KOGYO KAIHATSU SHIKENJO HOKOKU.

REPORTS OF THE GOVERNMENT INDUSTRIAL RESEARCH
INSTITUTE, KYUSHU.                                                     000
 SEE: KYUSHU KOGYO GIJUTSU SHIKENJO HOKOKU.

REPORT, GROUP FOR EUROPEAN SUPERCONDUCTING
SYNCHROTRON STUDIES.
 *++REP. GROUP EUR. SUPERCOND. SYNCHROTRON STUD.*
 *DIDCOT, BERKS.  GESSS-1, 1972-*
 *LO/N14.*

REPORTS, HAMILTON NATURAL HISTORY SOCIETY.
 *++REP. HAMILTON NATUR. HIST. SOC.*
 *HAMILTON, LANARK.  1, 1969-*
 *BL/U-1.     GL/U-1.     LO/N13.     OX/U-8.*

REPORTS ON HEALTH & SOCIAL SUBJECTS (GB).               XXX
 *++REP. HEALTH & SOC. SUBJ. (GB).*
 (GREAT BRITAIN) DEPARTMENT OF HEALTH & SOCIAL
 SECURITY.                                                                  XXX
 *LONDON NO.1, 1972-*
 PREV: REPORTS ON PUBLIC HEALTH & MEDICAL
 SUBJECTS (GB) FROM NO.1, 1920- 128, 1972.
 *GL/U-1.     LO/M27.     LO/N14.     NW/U-1.*

REPORT, HIGHLANDS & ISLANDS DEVELOPMENT BOARD.
 *++REP. HIGHL. & ISL. DEV. BOARD.*
 *INVERNESS 1ST 1/N, 1965- 31/D, 1966(1967)-*
 *LD/U-1.     LO/U-3.*
 *LO/U12. (W. 2ND. & 3RD.).*

REPORTS OF THE INSTITUTE FOR MEDICAL & DENTAL
ENGINEERING, TOKYO MEDICAL & DENTAL UNIVERSITY.
SEE: TOKYO IKA SHIKA DAIGAKU IYO KIZAI KEN-
KYUJO HOKOKU.

REPORT OF INVESTIGATIONS, DIVISION OF MINERAL
RESOURCES, DEPARTMENT OF CONSERVATION & ECON-
MIC DEVELOPMENT (VIRGINIA).
+ +REP. INVEST. DIV. MINER. RESOUR. DEP. CONSERV.
& ECON. DEV. (VA.).
CHARLOTTESVILLE [NO.]1, 1960-
LO/N14.

REPORT OF INVESTIGATIONS, GOVERNMENT CHEMICAL
LABORATORIES, WESTERN AUSTRALIA.
+ +REP. INVEST. GOV. CHEM. LAB. WEST. AUST.
(WESTERN AUSTRALIA) GOVERNMENT CHEMICAL LABOR-
ATORIES.
PERTH 1, 1968-
LO/N14.

REPORT, IRISH SOCIETY FOR THE PROTECTION OF
BIRDS.                                                    XXX
SUBS (1968): REPORT, IRISH WILDBIRD
CONSERVANCY.

REPORT, IRISH WILDBIRD CONSERVANCY.
DUBLIN [NO.1], 1968-
PREV: REPORT, IRISH SOCIETY FOR THE PROTECTION
OF BIRDS.
DB/U-2.    LO/N13.    LO/R-5.
LO/N-2.  1969-

REPORT, JOINT FISHERIES RESEARCH ORGANIZATION
(NORTHERN RHODESIA & NYASALAND).                          XXX
SUBS (1962): FISHERIES RESEARCH BULLETIN
(ZAMBIA).

REPORTS, LAND USE & BUILT FORM STUDIES.                  000
SEE: LAND USE ...

REPORT, LONG ASHTON RESEARCH STATION.
+ +REP. LONG ASHTON RES. STA.
BRISTOL 1968(1969)-
PREV: ANNUAL REPORT, LONG ASHTON AGRICULTURAL
& HORTICULTURAL STATION FROM 1913. STATION
SUBORD. TO UNIV. OF BRISTOL: DEPT. OF AGRI-
CULTURE & HORTICULTURE. ON T.P. UNDER BODY
NAME: NATIONAL FRUIT & CIDER CENTRE.
LO/N14.

REPORT OF MARINE GEOLOGY & GEOPHYSICS (KOREA,
SOUTH).
+ +REP. MAR. GEOL. & GEOPHYS. (KOREA, SOUTH).
(KOREA, SOUTH) GEOLOGICAL SURVEY.
SEOUL 1, 1970-
LO/N-2.

REPORTS ON MARINE SCIENCE AFFAIRS.
+ +REP. MAR. SCI. AFF.
WORLD METEOROLOGICAL ORGANIZATION.
GENEVA NO.1, 1970-
LO/N13.    XS/N-1.

REPORTS ON MATHEMATICAL PHYSICS.
+ +REP. MATH. PHYS.
[NORTH-HOLLAND PUBL. CO.; POLISH SCIENTIFIC
PUBL.]
AMSTERDAM; WARSAW 1, 1970-
CA/U-2.    CB/U-1.    LO/N14.    SA/U-1.
OX/U-8.  4(1), 1973-
ISSN 0034-4877

REPORT, MAURICE FALK INSTITUTE FOR ECONOMIC
RESEARCH IN ISRAEL.
+ +REP. MAURICE FALK INST. ECON. RES. ISR.
JERUSALEM [1], 1964/1966(1967)-
LO/S14.

REPORT, MODERN LANGUAGE ASSOCIATION OF AMERICA
CONFERENCE.                                               000
SEE: SHAKESPEAREAN RESEARCH & OPPORTUNITIES.

REPORT, NATIONAL BUREAU OF ECONOMIC RESEARCH.            000
SEE: NATIONAL BUREAU REPORT.

REPORT OF THE NATIONAL RESEARCH CENTER FOR
DISASTER PREVENTION (JAPAN).                              000
SEE: KOKURITSU BOSAI KAGAKU GIJUTSU SENTA
KENKYU HOKOKU.

REPORT, NORTH OF SCOTLAND COLLEGE OF AGRIC-
ULTURE.
+ +REP. N. SCOTL. COLL. AGR.
ABERDEEN [1], 1969-
OX/U-8.

[REPORT] OFFICE OF RADIATION PROGRAMS, ENVIR-
ONMENTAL PROTECTION AGENCY (US).
WASHINGTON, D.C. EPA/ORP 73-1, 1973-
LO/N14.

REPORTS ON ORGANISATION, BRITISH STEEL CORP-
ORATION.
+ +REP. ORG. BR. STEEL CORP.
[H.M.S.O.]
LONDON 1, AG 1967-
OX/U16.

REPORT ON OVERSEAS TRADE (GB).                           XXX
+ +REP. OVERSEAS TRADE (GB).
(GREAT BRITAIN) DEPARTMENT OF TRADE & INDUSTRY.
LONDON 1(1), F 1950- 22(2), F 1971. //
M.
LO/S14.

REPORTS ON POPULATION / FAMILY PLANNING.
POPULATION COUNCIL.
NEW YORK NO.1, 1969-
SPONS. BODY ALSO INTERNATIONAL INSTITUTE FOR
THE STUDY OF HUMAN REPRODUCTION.
LO/M17.    LO/M27.    RE/U-1.
BL/U-1.  1970-                      GL/U-1. NO.7, 1971-
OX/U16.  NO.12, 1972-

REPORTS ON PUBLIC HEALTH & MEDICAL SUBJECTS.             XXX
SUBS (1972): REPORTS ON HEALTH & SOCIAL
SUBJECTS.

REPORT, RANGELANDS RESEARCH UNIT, CSIRO
(AUSTRALIA).                                              XXX
+ +REP. RANGELANDS RES. UNIT, CSIRO (AUST.).
CANBERRA 1968/69(1970)-
PREV: ANNUAL REPORT, DIVISION OF LAND RESEARCH
& REGIONAL SURVEY, CSIRO (AUSTRALIA) FROM
1960/61(1961)- 1967/68(1969).
LO/N14.

REPORTS ON RESEARCH ACTIVITIES ON COMPUTER
SCIENCES & TECHNOLOGY.                                    000
SEE: NIHON YUNIBAKKU SOGO KENKYUJO, K.K. SOKEN
KIYO.

REPORTS OF THE RESEARCH INSTITUTE FOR
STRENGTH & FRACTURE OF MATERIALS, TOHOKU
UNIVERSITY.
+ +REP. RES. INST. STRENGTH & FRACT. MATER.,
TOHOKU UNIV.
TOHOKU DAIGAKU: RESEARCH INSTITUTE FOR
STRENGTH & FRACTURE OF MATERIALS.
SENDAI 1(1), 1965-
2/A.
CA/U-2.    GL/U-2.    LO/N-4.    SO/U-1.    SW/U-1.
BH/U-3.  5, 1969/70-

REPORT [OF] RESEARCH PROJECTS & POSTGRADUATE
STUDENTSHIP STUDIES SPONSORED BY THE POTATO            000
MARKETING BOARD.
SEE: RESEARCH PROJECTS ...

REPORTS ON RESEARCH IN SOUTHEAST ASIA: SOCIAL
SCIENCE SERIES.
+ +REP. RES. SOUTHEAST ASIA, SOC. SCI. SER.
KYOTO DAIGAKU TONAN AJIA KENKYU SENTA.
KYOTO S-1, 1967-
LO/N-1.

REPORT OF RESEARCHES, NIPPON INSTITUTE OF
TECHNOLOGY.                                               000
SEE: NIHON KOGYO DAIGAKU KENKYU HOKOKU.

REPORTS OF RESTRICTIVE PRACTICES CASES.                  XXX
SUBS: (1972): INDUSTRIAL COURT REPORTS.

REPORT OF THE RESULTS OF EXPLORATORY FISHING IN
EAST SEA OF KOREA.                                        000
SEE: KUNGNIP SUSAN CHINHUNGWON SAOP POGO.

REPORT, SCOTTISH TOURIST BOARD.
+ +REP. SCOTT. TOURIST BOARD.
EDINBURGH 1, 1969/70-
GL/U-1.

REPORT SERIES, LEICESTERSHIRE COUNTY LIBRARY.
+ +REP. SER. LEICS. COUNTY LIBR.
LEICESTER 1, 1969-
OX/U-1.

REPORT SERIES, SCHOOL OF ARCHITECTURE, NOVA
SCOTIA TECHNICAL COLLEGE.
+ +REP. SER. SCH. ARCHIT. NOVA SCOTIA TECH. COLL.
HALIFAX, NOVA SCOTIA 1, 1970-
BL/U-1.

REPORT OF SHIP RESEARCH INSTITUTE.                                    000
  SEE: SEMPAKU GIJUTSU KENKYUJO HOKOKU.

REPORT, STAMFORD SURVEY GROUP.
  ++REP. STAMFORD SURV. GROUP.
  NOTTINGHAM 1, 1970-
  OX/U-1.

REPORT, SUTTON BRIDGE EXPERIMENTAL STATION.
  ++REP. SUTTON BRIDGE EXP. STN.
  LONDON NO.1, 1967-
  BL/U-1.    LO/N13.
  BH/U-1.  NO.6, 1971-

REPORT, TOKYO METROPOLITAN INDUSTRIAL TECHNIC
INSTITUTE.                                                            000
  SEE: TOKYO TORITSU KOGYO GIJUTSU SENTA KENKYU
  HOKOKU.

REPORT OF UNIVERSITY MICROFILMS ACTIVITY.                            000
  SEE: RUMA.

[REPORT] WICKEN FEN GROUP.
  WICKEN FEN GROUP.
  [CAMBRIDGE] 1, 1969-
  LO/N13.

REPORT, WILDLIFE ECOLOGY UNIT, DEPARTMENT OF
AGRICULTURE, STOCK & FISHERIES (PAPUA & NEW
GUINEA).
  ++REP. WILDL. ECOL. UNIT DEP. AGR. STOCK FISH.
  (PAPUA & NEW GUINEA).
  PORT MORESBY 1968-1969(1969)-
  LO/N-2.

REPORTS ON WMO/IHD PROJECTS.
  WORLD METEOROLOGICAL ORGANIZATION.
  GENEVA NO.1, 1967-
  SPONS. BODY ALSO: INTERNATIONAL HYDROLOGICAL
  DECADE.
  LO/N13.    XS/N-1.

REPORTER.
  SVAZ CESKOSLOVENSKYCH NOVINARU.
  PRAGUE 1, 1966-
  BH/U-1.  4, 1969-*              LA/U-1.  3, 1968-*

REPRINT NEWS.                                                        XXX
  ++REPR. NEWS.
  [MICRO METHODS]
  EAST ARDSLEY NO.6, 1968- NO.10, 1971/72.//
  PREV: MICRONEWS FROM NO.1, 1960- NO.5, 1965.
  ED/N-1.    LO/U-1.

REPRINT REVIEW.
  ++REPRINT REV.
  [GARRATT FREEMAN ASSOCIATES]
  LONDON 1(1), N 1969-
  S/T: A SPECIALIST GUIDE FOR LIBRARIANS,
  PUBLISHERS AND BOOKSELLERS.
  OX/U-1.
  ED/N-1.  2, OC 1970-

REPRODUCTION METHODS.                                               XXX
  ++REPROD. METH.
  [GELLERT PUBL. CORP.]
  NEW YORK 9(9), 1969-
  PREV: RM. REPRODUCTION METHODS FOR BUSINESS
  & INDUSTRY FROM 1, MR/AP 1961- 9(8), 1969.
  LO/N14.
  ISSN 0033-6998

RES FACTA.
  [POLSKIE WYDAWNICTO MUZYCZNE]
  CRACOW 1, 1967-
  OX/U-1.

RESEARCH (LONDON).                                                  XXX
  [ASHBOURNE PUBL.]
  LONDON 1(1), MR 1968-
  M. PREV: RESEARCH TECHNIQUES & INSTRUMENTA-
  TION FROM 1, 1965.
  BL/U-1.    LO/N-4.    OX/U-8.    XS/R10.

RESEARCH ACTIVITIES OF THE ENGINEERING RES-
EARCH INSTITUTE, KYOTO UNIVERSITY.                                  XXX
  ++RES. ACTIV. ENG. RES. INST. KYOTO UNIV.
  KYOTO DAIGAKU: KOGAGU KENKYUJO.
  KYOTO NO.1, 1968- 4, 1970 ...
  SUBS: RESEARCH ACTIVITIES, INSTITUTE OF ATOMIC
  ENERGY, KYOTO UNIVERSITY.
  BH/U-1.    LO/N-4.    LO/N14.    XS/N-1.

RESEARCH ACTIVITIES, INSTITUTE OF ATOMIC
ENERGY, KYOTO UNIVERSITY.                                           XXX
  ++RES. ACT. INST. ATOMIC ENERGY KYOTO UNIV.
  KYOTO DAIGAKU: INSTITUTE OF ATOMIC ENERGY.        XXX
  KYOTO NO.5, 1971-
  PREV: RESEARCH ACTIVITIES, ENGINEERING RES-
  EARCH INSTITUTE, KYOTO UNIVERSITY FROM NO.1,
  1968- NO.4, 1971.
  LO/N14.

RESEARCH IN AFRICAN LITERATURES.
  ++RES. AFR. LIT.
  UNIVERSITY OF TEXAS: AFRICAN & AFRO-AMERICAN
  RESEARCH INSTITUTE.
  AUSTIN, TEX. 1, 1970-
  CB/U-1.    LD/U-1.    LO/N-1.    OX/U-1.    SW/U-1.
  DB/U-2.  1(2), 1970-
  ISSN 0034-5210

RESEARCH BIBLIOGRAPHY SERIES, ECONOMIC RES-
EARCH CENTRE, UNIVERSITY OF SINGAPORE.
  ++RES. BIBLIOGR. SER. ECON. RES. CENT. UNIV.
  SINGAPORE.
  SINGAPORE NO.1, 1967-
  OX/U-1.

RESEARCH BULLETIN OF THE AICHI-KEN AGRICULTURAL
RESEARCH CENTER: SERIES D: SERICULTURE.                             000
  SEE: AICHI-KEN NOGYO SOGO SHIKENJO KENKYU
  HOKOKU: D: SANGYO.

RESEARCH BULLETIN, BUNDA COLLEGE OF AGRICULT-
URE.
  ++RES. BULL. BUNDA COLL. AGRIC.
  L'LONGWE, MALAWI 1, S 1970-
  LO/R-6.

RESEARCH BULLETIN, CORBY HISTORICAL SOCIETY.
  ++RES. BULL. CORBY HIST. SOC.
  CORBY 1, 1968-
  OX/U-1.

RESEARCH BULLETIN, DEPARTMENT OF AGRICULTURE,
STOCK & FISHERIES (PAPUA & NEW GUINEA): CROP
PRODUCTION SERIES.
  ++RES. BULL. DEP. AGR. STOCK & FISH. (PAPUA &
  NEW GUINEA), CROP PROD. SER.
  PORT MORESBY NO.1, 1969-
  LO/N13.

RESEARCH BULLETIN, FACULTY OF AGRICULTURE,
UNIVERSITY OF IFE.
  ++RES. BULL. FAC. AGR. UNIV. IFE.
  ILE-IFE 1, 1968-
  CA/U11.

RESEARCH BULLETIN, HIROSHIMA INSTITUTE OF
TECHNOLOGY.
  ++RES. BULL. HIROSHIMA INST. TECHNOL.
  HIROSHIMA 1, 1966-
  JAP. OR ENGL.
  LO/N-2.    LO/N14.
  DB/S-1.  5, N 1970-

RESEARCH BULLETIN, INSTITUTE OF FOREST PROD-
UCTS, UNIVERSITY OF WASHINGTON.
  ++RES. BULL. INST. FOR. PROD. UNIV. WASH.
  SEATTLE, WASH. 1, 1965-
  INSTITUTE SUBORD. TO: COLLEGE OF FORESTRY.
  OX/U-3.

RESEARCH BULLETIN, INSTITUTE FOR THE STUDY OF
WORSHIP & RELIGIOUS ARCHITECTURE, UNIVERSITY
OF BIRMINGHAM.
  ++RES. BULL. INST. STUD. WORSHIP & RELIG.
  ARCHIT. UNIV. BIRMINGHAM.
  BIRMINGHAM [NO.1], 1966-
  BH/U-1.
  CA/U-1.  1969-

RESEARCH BULLETIN, MEGURO PARASITOLOGICAL
MUSEUM.
  ++RES. BULL. MEGURO PARASITOL. MUS.
  MEGURO KISEICHUKAN.
  TOKYO NO.1, 1967-
  LO/N-2.

RESEARCH BULLETIN, SCHOOL OF ENVIRONMENTAL
STUDIES, UNIVERSITY COLLEGE, LONDON.
  ++RES. BULL. SCH. ENVIRON. STUD. UNIV. COLL.
  LOND.
  LONDON NO.1, MY 1971-
  CA/U-1.    ED/N-1.    LO/N-1.    OX/U-1.

**RESEACH BULLETIN, WEST PAKISTAN UNIVERSITY OF ENGINEERING & TECHNOLOGY.**
+ +RES. BULL. WEST PAKISTAN UNIV. ENG. & TECHNOL.
 LAHORE  1, JE 1969-
 LD/U-1.

**RESEARCH & CLINICAL STUDIES IN HEADACHE. AN INTERNATIONAL REVIEW.**
+ +RES. & CLIN. STUD. HEADACHE.
[KARGER]
 BASLE  1, 1967-
 GL/U-1.    LD/U-1.    OX/U-1.    XY/N-1.

**RESEARCH COMMUNICATION IN CHEMICAL PATHOLOGY & PHARMACOLOGY.**
+ +RES. COMMUN. CHEM. PATHOL. & PHARMACOL.
[PJD PUBL. LTD.]
 NEW YORK  1(1), JA 1970-
 2M.
 GL/U-1.    OX/U-8.
 CA/U-2.  5, 1973-
 ISSN 0034-5164

**RESEARCH DATA, MIE UNIVERSITY FORESTS.**                              000
 SEE: MIE DAIGAKU NOGAKUBU ENSHURIN SHIRYO.

**RESEARCH DEVELOPMENT BULLETIN, WHITE FISH AUTHORITY.**
+ +RES. DEVELOP. BULL. WHITE FISH AUTH.
 LONDON  NO.1, AP 1964-
 XS/R10.

**RESEARCH DIGEST, INTERNATIONAL LEAD ZINC RE-**                        XXX
**SEARCH ORGANIZATION: PART 4: LEAD METALLURGY.**
 SUBS (1971): PART OF LEAD RESEARCH DIGEST.

**RESEARCH DIGEST, INTERNATIONAL LEAD ZINC RE-**                        XXX
**SEARCH ORGANIZATION: PART 5: LEAD CHEMISTRY.**
 SUBS (1971): PART OF LEAD RESEARCH DIGEST.

**RESEARCH IN EDUCATION (EDINBURGH).**
+ +RES. EDUC. (EDINB.).
 SCOTTISH COUNCIL FOR RESEARCH IN EDUCATION.
 EDINBURGH  1, 1968-
 CA/U-1.    CB/U-1.    OX/U-1.

**RESEARCH IN EDUCATION (MANCHESTER).**
+ +RES. EDUC. (MANCH.).
[MANCHESTER UNIV. PRESS]
 MANCHESTER  1, MY 1969-
 AB/U-1.    BL/U-1.    ED/N-1.    EX/U-1.    GL/U-2.    LO/N-1.
 LO/N17.    LO/U-2.    LO/U11.    LO/U28.    MA/P-1.
 MA/S-1.    OX/U-1.    OX/U17.    SH/U-1.    SW/U-1.
 ISSN 0034-5237

**RESEARCH IN EDUCATION (WASHINGTON, D.C.).**
+ +RES. EDUC. (WASHINGTON, D.C.).
 (UNITED STATES) EDUCATIONAL RESEARCH INFORMA-
 TION CENTER.
 WASHINGTON, D.C.  1, N 1966-
 LA/U-1.
 DB/U-2.  2(8), 1967-          GL/U-2.  6, 1971-
 LD/U-1.  6(3), 1971-         LO/U21.  2, 1967-
 SH/U-1.  1971-
 GL/U-1.  6(10), 1971-
 LB/U-1.  3(12), 1968-
 ISSN 0034-5229

**RESEARCH IN IMMUNOCHEMISTRY & IMMUNOBIOLOGY.**
+ +RES. IMMUNOCHEM. & IMMUNOBIOL.
[UNIVERSITY PARK P.]
 BALTIMORE, MD.  1, 1972-
 LO/N13.
 CA/U-1.  3, 1973-
 ISSN 0080-164X

**RESEARCH JOURNAL, MAHATMA PHULE AGRICULTURAL UNIVERSITY.**
+ +RES. J. MAHATMA PHULE AGRIC. UNIV.
 POONA, INDIA  1, 1970-
 LO/N13.

**RESEARCH IN THE LIFE SCIENCES.**                                      XXX
+ +RES. LIFE SCI.
 AGRICULTURAL EXPERIMENT STATION, ORONO, MAINE.
 ORONO  15(4), 1968-
 PREV: MAINE FARM RESEARCH FROM 1, AP 1953-
 15(3), 1967.
 CA/U11.

**RESEARCH MEMORANDA, CENTRE FOR URBAN & REGIONAL STUDIES, UNIVERSITY OF BIRMINGHAM.**
+ +RES. MEMO. CENT. URBAN & REG. STUD. UNIV.
 BIRMINGHAM.
 BIRMINGHAM  NO.1, 1967-
 BH/U-1.

**RESEARCH METHODS IN NEUROCHEMISTRY.**
+ +RES. METHODS NEUROCHEM.
[PLENUM P.]
 NEW YORK &C.  1, 1972-
 GL/U-1.    LO/N13.

**RESEARCH NOTES, DEPARTMENT OF LINGUISTICS & NIGERIAN LANGUAGES, UNIVERSITY OF IBADAN.**
+ +RES. NOTES DEP. LINGUIST. & NIGERIAN LANG.
 UNIV. IBADAN.
 IBADAN  1(1), 1967-
 LO/U14.

**RESEARCH NOTES, DIVISION FOREST RESEARCH, MINISTRY OF NATURAL RESOURCES & TOURISM.**
+ +RES. NOTES DIV. FOR. RES. MIN. NATUR. RESOUR.
 & TOURISM (ZAMBIA).
 KITWE  1, 1968-
 LO/N-2.

**RESEARCH NOTES, FORD FORESTRY CENTER, MICHI-GAN TECHNOLOGICAL UNIVERSITY.**
+ +RES. NOTES FORD FOR. CENT. MICH. TECHNOL UNIV.
 L'ANSE, MICH.  NO.1, 1966-
 LO/N14.

**RESEARCH NOTE, PRESTRESSED CONCRETE DEVELOP-MENT GROUP.**
+ +RES. NOTE PRESTRESS. CONCR. DEVELOP. GROUP.
 LONDON  PCR 1, 1965-
 LO/N14.

**RESEARCH NOTES, RESEARCH INSTITUTE FOR SOCIAL DEVELOPMENT (UNITED NATIONS).**
+ +RES. NOTES RES. INST. SOC. DEVELOP. (U.N.).
 GENEVA  NO.1, JE 1968-
 S/T:  A REVIEW OF RECENT & CURRENT STUDIES
 CONDUCTED AT THE INSTITUTE.
 LO/N17.    OX/U16.    OX/U17.
 LO/S14.  NO.3, D 1970-

**RESEARCH PAMPHLETS, FACULTY OF AGRICULTURE, UNIVERSITY OF ALEPPO.**
+ +RES. PAM. FAC. AGRIC. UNIV. ALEPPO.
 ALEPPO  NO.1, 1971-
 LO/N-2.

**RESEARCH PAPER, INSTITUTE OF ADVANCED ARCHIT-ECTURAL STUDIES, UNIVERSITY OF YORK.**
+ +RES. PAP. INST. ADV. ARCHIT. STUD. UNIV. YORK.
 YORK  NO.1, 1971-
 LO/N-1.

**RESEARCH PAPER, NORTHERN FOREST EXPERIMENT STATION (US).**                                                    XXX
+ +RES. PAP. NORTH. FOR. EXP. STAT. (US).
 JUNEAU, ALASKA  NOR-1, 1964- 3, 1967. //
 OX/U-3.

**RESEARCH PAPERS, SCHOOL OF GEOGRAPHY, UNIVER-SITY OF OXFORD.**
+ +RES. PAP. SCH. GEOGR. UNIV. OXF.
 OXFORD  NO.1, MY 1972-
 MONOGR.
 DB/U-2.    LO/S13.

**RESEARCH PAPER SERIES, INSTITUTE OF AGRICULT-URAL HISTORY, UNIVERSITY OF READING.**
+ +RES. PAP. SER. INST. AGRIC. HIST. UNIV.
 READING.
 READING  NO.1, 1970-
 MONOGR.
 LO/N-1.

**RESEARCH PAPERS, VALE OF EVESHAM HISTORICAL SOCIETY.**
+ +RES. PAP. VALE EVESHAM HIST. SOC.
 EVESHAM  1, 1967-
 DB/U-2.

**RESEARCH POLICY.**
+ +RES. POLICY.
[NORTH-HOLLAND]
 AMSTERDAM  1(1), N 1971-
 LO/N-6.    LO/N13.    LO/R-5.    MA/U-1.    OX/U-8.    SH/U-3.
 XS/R10.
 ISSN 0048-7333

**RESEARCH PROJECTS & POSTGRADUATE STUDENTSHIP STUDIES SPONSORED BY THE POTATO MARKETING BOARD: REPORT.**
+ +RES. PROJ. & POSTGRAD. STUD. STUD. SPONS.
 POTATO MARKET. BOARD, REP.
 LONDON  NO.1, 1967-
 LO/N13.
 GL/U-1.  NO.3 1972-

RESEARCH IN PROSTAGLANDINS.
++RES. PROSTAGLANDINS.
WORCESTER FOUNDATION FOR EXPERIMENTAL BIOLOGY.
SHREWSBURY, MASS. 1, JE 1971-
BL/U-1. DB/U-2. LD/U-1.* LO/M31. LO/N13.
CO/U-1. 2(1), 1972-
ISSN 0048-7309

RESEARCH PUBLICATIONS, DEPARTMENT OF GEOG-
RAPHY, UNIVERSITY OF TORONTO.
++RES. PUBL. DEP. GEOGR. UNIV. TORONTO.
TORONTO 1, 1968-
SH/U-1.

RESEARCH PUBLICATION, KANSAS AGRICULTURAL EXP-
ERIMENT STATION.                                     XXX
++RES. PUBL. KANS. AGRIC. EXP. STN.
MANHATTAN, KANS. NO.162, 1970-
PREV: TECHNICAL BULLETIN, KANSAS ... FROM NO.
1, 1916- 161, 1969.
LO/N13.

RESEARCH PUBLICATIONS, LIBRARY ASSOCIATION.      000
SEE: LIBRARY ASSOCIATION ...

RESEARCH PUBLICATION, NEW ZEALAND AGRICUL-
TURAL ENGINEERING INSTITUTE.
++RES. PUBL. N.Z. AGR. ENG. INST.
WELLINGTON, N.Z. 1, 1967-
CA/U11.

RESEARCH REPORT, AGRICULTURAL EXPERIMENT STA-
TION, BLACKSBURG, VIRGINIA.                          XXX
SUBS (1967): RESEARCH REPORT, RESEARCH
DIVISION, VIRGINIA POLYTECHNIC INSTITUTE.

RESEARCH REPORTS OF THE ANAN TECHNICAL COLLEGE
SEE: ANAN KOGYO KOTO SENMON GAKKO KENKYU KIYO.

RESEARCH REPORT OF CANON CAMERA CO., INC.        000
SEE: KYANON KENKYU HOKOKU.

RESEARCH REPORTS, DEPARTMENT OF ANTHROPOLOGY,
UNIVERSITY OF MASSACHUSETTS.
++RES. REP. DEP. ANTHROPOL. UNIV. MASS.
AMHERST NO.1, F 1968-
OX/U-1.

RESEARCH REPORT, DEPARTMENT OF APPLIED
GEOLOGY, UNIVERSITY OF STRATHCLYDE.
++RES. REP. DEP. APPL. GEOL. UNIV. STRATHCLYDE.
GLASGOW NO.1, 1970-
LO/N-2. LO/N13. OX/U-8.

RESEARCH REPORTS, FACULTY OF ENGINEERING,
KAGOSHIMA UNIVERSITY.                                000
SEE: KAGOSHIMA DAIGAKU KOGAKUBU KENKYU
HOKOKU.

RESEARCH REPORTS, FISH COMMISSION (OREGON).
++RES. REP. FISH COMM. (OREG.).
PORTLAND 1, 1969-
PREV: COMMISSION'S CONTRIBUTION & RESEARCH
BRIEFS.
LO/N-2. LO/N13.

RESEARCH REPORTS, HACHINOHE TECHNICAL COLLEGE    000
SEE: HACHINOHE KOGYO KOTO SEMMON GAKKO KIYO.

RESEARCH REPORT OF KAGOSHIMA TECHNICAL
COLLEGE.                                             000
SEE: KAGOSHIMA KOGYO KOTO SEMMON GAKKO
KENKYU HOKOKU.

RESEARCH REPORT, KANAGAWA PREFECTURAL MUSEUM:
NATURAL HISTORY.
++RES. REP. KANAGAWA PREFECT. MUS., NATUR. HIST.
KANAGWA KENRITSU HAKUBUTSUKAN.
YOKOHAMA NO.1, 1970-
LO/N-2.

RESEARCH REPORTS OF THE MAIZURU TECHNICAL
COLLEGE.                                             000
SEE: MAIZURU KOGYO KOTO SENMON GAKKO KIYO.

RESEARCH REPORTS OF MATSUE TECHNICAL COLLEGE.
SEE: MATSUE KOGYO KOTO SEMMON GAKKO KENKYU
KIYO.

RESEARCH REPORTS, OYAMA TECHNICAL COLLEGE.       000
SEE: OYAMA KOGYO KOTO SEMMON GAKKO KENKYU KIYO

RESEARCH REPORT, RESEARCH DIVISION, VIRGINIA
POLYTECHNIC INSTITUTE.                               XXX
++RES. REP. RES. DIV. VA. POLYTECH. INST.
BLACKSBURG, VA. NO.116, 1967-
PREV: RESEARCH REPORT, AGRICULTURAL EXPERIMENT
STATION, BLACKSBURG, VA. FROM NO.1, MR 1956-
115, 1966.
LO/N13.

RESEARCH REPORT, TAIWAN SUGAR EXPERIMENT STA-
TION.
++RES. REP. TAIWAN SUGAR EXP. STAT.
TAIWAN 1, 1968-
CA/U11.

RESEARCH REPORT, TAY ESTUARY RESEARCH CENTRE,
UNIVERSITY OF DUNDEE.
++RES. REP. TAY ESTUARY RES. CENT. UNIV. DUNDEE.
NEWPORT-ON-TAY NO.1, 1971-
CA/U-1. LO/N13.

RESEARCH REPORTS OF TSUYAMA TECHNICAL COLLEGE    000
SEE: TSUYAMA KOGYO KOTO SENMON GAKKO KIYO.

RESEARCH REPORT, WOLLONGONG UNIVERSITY
COLLEGE.
++RES. REP. WOLLONGONG UNIV. COLL.
WOLLONGONG UNIVERSITY COLLEGE.
WOLLONGONG, N.S.W. NO.1, 1967-
COLLEGE PART OF UNIVERSITY OF NEW SOUTH WALES.
BN/U-2. GL/U-1.
NW/U-1. NO.2, 1966/67-

RESEARCH IN REPRODUCTION.
++RES. REPROD.
INTERNATIONAL PLANNED PARENTHOOD FEDERATION.
LONDON 1, 1969-
CA/U-1. ED/N-1. LO/N13. OX/U-8. RE/U-1. SH/U-1.
BL/U-1. 4(4), 1972-
CR/M-1. (THREE YEARS ONLY)
LD/U-1. [ONE YEAR ONLY]

RESEARCH RESULTS DIGEST, NATIONAL COOPERATIVE
HIGHWAY RESEARCH PROGRAM (U.S).
++RES. RESULT. DIG. NAT. COOP. HIGHW. RES.
PROGR. (U.S.).
WASHINGTON, D.C. NO.1, 1968-
LV/U-1.
GL/U-1. NO.35, F 1972-

RESEARCH REVIEW, COMMONWEALTH BUREAU OF
HORTICULTURE & PLANTATION CROPS.
++RES. REV. COMMONW. BUR. HORT. & PLANT. CROPS.
FARNHAM ROYAL, BUCKS. NO.1, 1966-
BH/U-1. LO/N14.

RESEARCH REVIEW, INSTITUTE OF AFRICAN STUDIES,
UNIVERSITY OF GHANA.
++RES. REV. INST. AFR. STUD. UNIV. GHANA.
ACCRA 1(1), 1965-
OX/U-9.

RESEARCH SERIES, MUSEUM OF SYSTEMATIC BIOLOGY,
UNIVERSITY OF CALIFORNIA.
++RES. SER. MUS. SYST. BIOL. UNIV. CALIF.
IRVINE, CALIF. NO.1, 1968-
DB/S-1. LO/N-2.

RESEARCH IN SPECIAL EDUCATION. ABSTRACTS &
INFORMATION.
++RES. SPEC. EDUC.
ASSOCIATION FOR SPECIAL EDUCATION: RESEARCH
COMMITTEE.
WALLASEY, CHES. NO.1, JL 1967-
AD/U-1. BL/C-1. CA/U-1. ED/N-1. LO/N-1. LO/U-9.

RESEARCH ON STEROIDS.
++RES. STEROIDS.
INTERNATIONAL STUDY GROUP FOR STEROID HORMONES.
ROME 1, 1964-
GL/U-1.

RESEARCH STUDIES IN MANAGEMENT REPORTING.        000
SEE: NAA RESEARCH STUDIES IN MANAGEMENT
REPORTING.

RESEARCH STUDIES, ROYAL COMMISSION ON LOCAL
GOVERNMENT IN SCOTLAND.
++RES. STUD. R. COMM. LOCAL GOV. SCOTL.
EDINBURGH 1, 1969-
OX/U-1.

RESEARCH STUDIES, UNIVERSITY OF UDAIPUR.
++RES. STUD. UNIV. UDAIPUR.
UDAIPUR 1, 1963-
LO/N-2.

**RESEARCH SUPPORTED BY THE SSRC.**
+ +RES. SUPPORT. SSRC. (SOC. SCI. RES. COUN.)
SOCIAL SCIENCE RESEARCH COUNCIL (GB).
*LONDON 1967-*
A. PREV: INVESTIGATIONS SUPPORTED BY THE
HUMAN SCIENCES COMMITTEE.
HL/U-1.     LO/N14.     MA/U-4.     OX/U17.     SO/U-1.
ED/U-1. CURRENT ISSUE ONLY.
LO/U-3. LAST THREE ISSUES ONLY.

**RESEARCH IN THE TEACHING OF ENGLISH.**
+ +RES. TEACH. ENGL.
NATIONAL COUNCIL OF TEACHERS OF ENGLISH (US).
*CHAMPAIGN, ILL. 1, 1967-*
LO/U-9.
NW/U-2. 3, 1969-
ISSN 0034-527X

**RESEARCHER.**
UNIVERSITY OF THE EASTERN PHILIPPINES: RESEARCH
CENTRE.
*CATARMAN, SAMAR 1, 1965-*
S/T: TECHNICAL JOURNAL OF THE UNIVERSITY OF
THE EASTERN PHILIPPINES.
LO/N13.
ISSN 0048-7341

**RESHENIE ZADACH STROITEL'NOJ FIZIKI NA
TSIFROVYKH I ANALOGOVYKH MASHINAKH.**
+ +RESHENIE ZADACH STROIT. FIZ. TSIFROVYKH &
ANALOGOVYKH MASH.
NAUCHNO-ISSLEDOVATEL'SKIJ INSTITUT STROITEL'NOJ
FIZIKI: OTDEL INFORMATSIONNO-IZDATEL'SKOJ I
PATENTNO-LITSENZIONNOJ RABOTY.
*MOSCOW 1, 1968-*
LO/N13.

**RESOURCE PAPER, COMMISSION ON COLLEGE GEOG-
RAPHY, ASSOCIATION OF AMERICAN GEOGRAPHERS.**
+ +RESOUR. PAP. COMM. COLL. GEOGR. ASSOC. AM.
GEOGR.
*WASHINGTON, D.C. NO.1, 1968-*
DB/U-2.     LO/U-2.
ISSN 0066-9369

**RESOURCE PAPER, POLICY RESEARCH & CO-ORDINAT-
ION BRANCH, DEPARTMENT OF ENERGY, MINES &**
+ +RESOUR. PAP. POLICY RES. & CO-ORD. BRANCH DEP.
ENERGY MINES & RESOUR. (CAN.).
*OTTAWA NO.1, 1971-*
LO/N13.

**RESOURCES IN EDUCATION.**
+ +RESOUR. EDUC.
[EDUCATIONAL RESOURCES LTD.]
*LONDON 1, OC 1971-*
M.
CA/U-1.     LN/U-2.     OX/U-1.     SW/U-1.

**RESTAURATOR: INTERNATIONAL JOURNAL FOR THE
PRESERVATION OF LIBRARY & ARCHIVAL MATERIAL.**
[RESTAURATOR PRESS]
*COPENHAGEN 1, 1969-*
BH/U-1.     BN/U-1.     DB/U-2.     ED/N-1.     GL/U-1.     LO/N-1.
LO/N-4.     LO/N12.     LO/N14.     LO/P-6.     LO/U-1.     LO/U-2.
LV/U-1.     MA/S-1.     NW/U-1.
ISSN 0034-5806

**RESTAURATOR: SUPPLEMENT.**
[RESTAURATOR P.]
*COPENHAGEN NO.1, 1969-*
LO/N-4.

**RESULTS & PROBLEMS IN CELL DIFFERENTIATION.**
+ +RESULT. & PROBL. CELL DIFFERENT.
[SPRINGER]
*BERLIN 1, 1968-*
S/T: A SERIES OF TOPICAL VOLUMES IN DEVELOP-
MENTAL BIOLOGY.
GL/U-1.     LO/N13.

**RESURGENCE.**
*LONDON NO.1, MY/JE 1966-*
ED/N-1.     LO/U-3.     OX/U17.

**RESUSCITATION.**
[MIDDLESEX PUBL. CO. LTD.]
*LONDON 1(1), MR 1972-*
Q.
CA/U-1.     ED/N-1.     OX/U-8.

**RETIREMENT CHOICE.**
+ +RETIRE. CHOICE.
PRE-RETIREMENT ASSOCIATION.
*LONDON 1(1), OC 1972-*
MON.
SH/U-1.
CA/U-1. 1(4), 1973-          ED/N-1. 1(4), 1973-

**REVELATION.**
REVELATIONIST SOCIETY FOR PSYCHICAL & SPIRITUAL
STUDIES.
*ST. ANNES, LANCS. 1(1), JL 1972-*
Q.
ED/N-1.     OX/U-1.

**REVIEW. YUGOSLAV MONTHLY MAGAZINE.**          000
SEE: REVIJA. JUGOSLOVENSKI ILUSTROVANI
CASOPIS.

**REVIEWS IN AMERICAN HISTORY.**
+ +REV. AM. HIST.
*WESTPORT, CONN. 1, 1973-*
S/T: A QUARTERLY JOURNAL OF CRITICISM.
AD/U-1.     BL/U-1.     DB/U-2.     ED/N-1.     GL/U-1.     HL/U-1.
MA/U-1.     SA/U-1.
ISSN 0048-7511

**REVIEWS IN ANALYTICAL CHEMISTRY.**
+ +REV. ANAL. CHEM.
[FREUND PUBL. HOUSE]
*TEL-AVIV 1(1), 1971-*
Q.
LO/N14.     LO/S-3.     XY/N-1.
ISSN 0048-752X

**REVIEW OF APPLIED MYCOLOGY.**          XXX

**REVIEW OF BENZOLE TECHNOLOGY.**          XXX
SUBS (1968): BENZOLE BIBLIOGRAPHY.

**REVIEW OF CERAMIC TECHNOLOGY.**
+ +REV. CERAM. TECHNOL.
METALS & CERAMICS INFORMATION CENTER (U.S.).
*COLUMBUS, OHIO NO.1, JA 1972-*
LO/N14. NO.11, 1972-

**REVIEWS ON COATINGS & CORROSION.**
+ +REV. COAT & CORROS.
[FREUND]
*TEL-AVIV 1, 1972-*
LO/N14.

**REVIEWS ON ENVIRONMENTAL HEALTH.**
+ +REV. ENVIRON. HEALTH.
[FREUND]
*TEL-AVIV 1, 1972-*
DB/U-2.     LO/N14.
ISSN 0048-7554

**REVIEWS OF GEOPHYSICS & SPACE PHYSICS.***
+ +REV. GEOPHYS. & SPACE PHYS.
AMERICAN GEOPHYSICAL UNION.
*RICHMOND, VA. 1, F 1963-*
Q. TITLE EXTENDED FROM: REVIEWS OF GEOPHYS-
ICS FROM 8, 1970.
BH/U-1.     BL/U-1.     CA/U-2.     ED/R-3.     HL/U-1.     LD/U-1.
LO/N-4.     LO/N14.     LO/U-2.     SA/U-1.     SH/U-1.     SO/U-1.
XS/N-1.
DB/U-2. 2, 1964-               LO/N-7. 2, 1964-
MA/U-1. 4, 1966-               SW/U-1. 4, 1966-

**REVIEW OF GHANA LAW.**
+ +REV. GHANA LAW.
GENERAL LEGAL COUNCIL (GHANA).
*ACCRA 1(1), 1969-*
OX/15.
ISSN 0034-6578

**REVIEWS ON HIGH TEMPERATURE MATERIALS.**
+ +REV. HIGH TEMP. MATER.
[FREUND PUBL. HOUSE]
*TEL-AVIV 1(1), AG 1971-*
Q.
LO/N14.     XS/R10.     XY/N-1.

**REVIEW OF INCOME & WEALTH.**
+ +REV. INCOME & WEALTH.
INTERNATIONAL ASSOCIATION FOR RESEARCH IN
INCOME & WEALTH.
*NEW HAVEN, CONN. NO.1, 1969-*
GL/U-2.
ISSN 0034-6586

**REVIEW OF INDONESIAN & MALAYAN AFFAIRS.**
+ +REV. INDONES. & MALAY. AFF.
UNIVERSITY OF SYDNEY: DEPARTMENT OF INDONESIAN
& MALAYAN STUDIES.
*SYDNEY 1(1), MR 1967-*
Q. VOL.4(3-4), JE-D 1970 NOT PUBLISHED.
LO/U-3. 3, 1969-
LO/N12. 1(2), 1967- 4, 1971.

**REVIEW OF INDUSTRIAL RELATIONS RESEARCH.**
*+ +REV. IND. RELAT. RES.*
INDUSTRIAL RELATIONS RESEARCH ASSOCIATION.
*MADISON, WIS. 1, 1970-*
ANNU.
*GL/U-1.   LO/U-3.   OX/U17.*

**REVIEW, INSTITUTE OF HUMAN SCIENCES, BOSTON COLLEGE.**   XXX
**SUBS (1969): URBAN & SOCIAL CHANGE REVIEW.**

**REVIEW, INSTITUTE OF PETROLEUM.**   XXX
**SUBS (1968): PETROLEUM REVIEW.**

**REVIEW, INTERNATIONAL COMMISSION OF JURISTS.**
*+ +REV. INT. COMM. JURISTS.*
*GENEVA 1, MR 1969-*
IRREG. PREV. PART OF: BULLETIN, INTERNATIONAL
COMMISSION OF JURISTS FROM 1, 1954; & JOURNAL,
INTERNATIONAL COMMISSION OF JURISTS FROM 1,
1957- 9(2), 1968.
*BL/U-1.   CB/U-1.   LO/U-2.   LO/U14.   LV/U-1.   RE/U-1.*
*LO/U12. 2, 1969-*
*LO/U11. NO.1, 1969- 6, 1971.*

**REVIEW, INTERNATIONAL ORGANIZATION FOR ANCIENT LANGUAGES ANALYSIS BY COMPUTER.**
*+ +REV. INT. ORG. ANCIENT LANG. ANAL. COMPUT.*
*LIEGE NO.1, 1966-*
Q. ENGL. FR. & ITAL. WITH FR. SUMM. FR. TITLE:
REVUE, ORGANISATION INTERNATIONALE POUR
L'ETUDE DES LANGUES ANCIENNES PAR ORDINATEUR.
*CA/U-1.   DB/U-2.   HL/U-1.   MA/U-1.\**
*SA/U-1. 1973-*
*ISSN 0030-4972*

**REVIEW OF THE INTERNATIONAL STATISTICAL INSTITUTE.**   XXX
**SUBS (1972): INTERNATIONAL STATISTICAL REVIEW.**

**REVIEW OF METALS TECHNOLOGY.**
*+ +REV. MET. TECHNOL.*
METALS & CERAMICS INFORMATION CENTER (U.S.).
*COLUMBUS, OHIO JA 1972-*
*LO/N14. 1973-*

**REVIEW, NATIONAL ELECTRONICS COUNCIL (GB).**   000
**SEE: NEC REVIEW.**

**REVIEW OF NATIONAL LITERATURES.**
*+ +REV. NATL. LIT.*
ST. JOHN'S UNIVERSITY.
*JAMAICA, N.Y. 1, 1970-*
2/A.
*CB/U-1.   DB/U-2.   ED/N-1.   OX/U-1.*
*ISSN 0034-6640*

**REVIEW OF PARLIAMENT & PARLIAMENTARY DIGEST.**   XXX
*+ +REV. PARLIAMENT & PARLIAMENTARY DIG.*
[PARLIAMENTARY DIGEST LTD.]
*LONDON NO.1, 20/OC 1972- 13, F 1974.*
   *NO.1, MR 1974- 17, 2/AG 1974 ...*
WKLY. SUBS: REVIEW OF PARLIAMENT & POLITICAL
CHRONICLE.
*ED/N-1.   EX/U-1.   OX/U-1.   SO/U-1.*

**REVIEW OF PHYSICS IN TECHNOLOGY.**   XXX
*+ +REV. PHYS. TECHNOL.*
*LONDON 1, 1970- 3, 1972 ...*
SUBS: PHYSICS IN TECHNOLOGY.
*BH/U-3.   ED/N-1.   GL/U-2.   HL/U-1.   LO/N-4.   LO/N14.*
*SH/U-3.*
*SF/U-1. 2, 1971-*
*SH/C-5. 3, 1972.*
*ISSN 0034-6683*

**REVIEW OF PLANT PATHOLOGY.**   XXX
*+ +REV. PLANT PATHOL.*
COMMONWEALTH MYCOLOGICAL INSTITUTE.
*FARNHAM ROYAL, BUCKS. 49, 1970-*
PREV: REVIEW OF APPLIED MYCOLOGY FROM 1, 1922-
48, 1969.
*BH/U-1.   CA/U11.   ED/N-1.   GL/U-2.   HL/U-1.   LO/N-4.*
*LO/N14.   LO/N17.   LO/U-1.   LO/U-2.   LO/U11.*
*MA/U-1.   NW/U-1.   OX/U-3.   RE/U-1.   SO/U-1.   XS/R-2.*
*ISSN 0034-6438*

**REVIEW OF PLANT PROTECTION RESEARCH.**
*+ +REV. PLANT PROT. RES.*
NIPPON OYO-DOBUTSI-KONCHU GAKKAI.
*TOKYO 1, 1968-*
*LO/N-2.   NW/U-1.*

**REVIEWS IN POLYMER TECHNOLOGY.**
*+ +REV. POLYM. TECHNOL.*
[DEKKER]
*NEW YORK 1, 1972-*
*LO/U12.*

**REVIEWS ON REACTIVE SPECIES IN CHEMICAL REACTIONS.**
*+ +REV. REACT. SPECIES CHEM. REACT.*
[FREUND PUBL. HOUSE]
*TEL-AVIV 1, 1973-*
*LO/N14.*

**REVIEW OF REGIONAL STUDIES.**
*+ +REV. REG. STUD.*
SOUTHWESTERN REGIONAL SCIENCE ASSOCIATION.
*BLACKSBURG, VA. 1, 1970-*
Q. SPONS. BODIES ALSO COLLEGE OF BUSINESS,
VIRGINIA POLYTECHNIC INSTITUTE; & STATE
UNIVERSITY OF VIRGINIA.
*NO/U-1. 4, 1974-*                   *SH/U-1.*
*ISSN 0048-749X*

**REVIEW SERIES, COMMONWEALTH BUREAU OF PAST-URES & FIELD CROPS.**
*+ +REV. SER. COMMONW. BUR. PASTURES & FIELDCROPS.*
*FARNHAM ROYAL., BUCKS. NO. 1, 1968-*
PREV: MIMEOGRAPHED PUBLICATION, COMMONWEALTH
BUREAU OF PASTURES & FIELDCROPS FROM 1, 1961.
*BN/U-2.   CA/U11.   LO/N-1.   LO/N14.   OX/U-8.*

**REVIEWS ON SILICON, GERMANIUM, TIN & LEAD COMPOUNDS.**
*+ +REV. SILICON GERMANIUM TIN & LEAD COMPD.*
[FREUND]
*TEL-AVIV 1, 1972-*
*LO/N14.*
*ISSN 0048-7570*

**REVIEW OF SUBAQUATIC PHYSIOLOGY & HYPERBARIC MEDICINE.**   000
**SEE: REVUE DE PHYSIOLOGIE SUBAQUATIQUE ET MEDECINE HYPERBARE.**

**REVIEW, WARREN SPRING LABORATORY.**   XXX
*+ +REV. WARREN SPRING LAB.*
[HMSO]
*LONDON 1969/70(1971)-*
PREV: REPORT, WARREN ... FROM 1958- 1968(1969)
*LO/N-2.   LO/N14.   LO/R-5.   NW/U-1.*

**REVIJA. JUGOSLOVENSKI ILUSTROVANI CASOPIS.**
[NOVINSKO IZDAVACKO PREDUZECE 'BORBA'].
*BELGRADE 1, 1965-*
MON. PUBL. ALSO IN ENGL., FR., GER., RUSS., &
SPAN. ENGL. TITLE: REVIEW. YUGOSLAV MONTHLY
MAGAZINE.
*LO/N-1.   SW/U-1.*
*ISSN 0486-6231*

**REVISTA DE LA ACADEMIA NACIONAL DE CIENCIAS ECONOMICAS (PERU).**
*+ +REV. ACAD. NAC. CIENC. ECON. (PERU).*
*LIMA 1(1), 1971-*
*LO/N-1.   OX/U16.*

**REVISTA DE ADMINISTRACION PUBLICA (ARGENTINA).**
*+ +REV. ADM. PUBLICA (ARGENT.).*
INSTITUTO SUPERIOR DE ADMINISTRACION PUBLICA
(ARGENTINA).
*BUENOS AIRES 1(1), AP/JE 1961-*
*OX/U-1.*

**REVISTA DE AGRICULTURA (CUBA).**
*+ +REV. AGRIC. (CUBA). [RAGU-A]*
ACADEMIA DE CIENCIAS DE CUBA: INSTITUTO DE
AGRONOMIA.
*HAVANA 1, 1967-*
*LO/N13.*
*ISSN 0034-7671*

**REVISTA, ASOCIACION DE MEDICOS VETERINARIOS DEL PERU.**
*+ +REV. ASOC. MED. VET. PERU.*
*LIMA NO.1, 1961/62(1961)-*
*LO/N13.*

**REVISTA, BIBLIOTECA NACIONAL (URUGUAY).**
*+ +REV. BIBL. NAC. (URUG.).*
*MONTEVIDEO 1(1), 1966-*
*OX/U-1.*
*ED/N-1. NO.2, 1969-*

**REVISTA BRASILEIRA DE FISICA.**
*+ +REV. BRAS. FIS.*
SOCIEDADE BRASILEIRA DE FISICA.
*SAO PAULO 1, 1971-*
*3/A.*
*CA/U-1.    CA/U-2.    LO/N14.    LO/N-1.*

**REVISTA BRASILEIRA DE GEOCIENCIAS.**
*+ +REV. BRAS. GEOCIENC.*
SOCIEDADE BRASILEIRA DE FISICA.
*SAO PAULO 1, 1971-*
*LO/N-2.*

**REVISTA BRASILEIRA DE PESQUISAS MEDICAS E
BIOLOGICAS.**
*+ +REV. BRAS. PESQUI. MED. & BIOL.*
*SAO PAULO 1, JA/F 1968-*
ENGL. & PORT.
*LO/N-2.*
*ISSN 0034-7310*

**REVISTA BRASILEIRA DE TECNOLOGIA.**
*+ +REV. BRAS. TECNOL.*
CONSELHO NACIONAL DE PESQUISAS (BRAZIL).
[E. BLUCHER]
*SAO PAULO 1(1), 1970-*
Q. ENGL. OR PORT. WITH SUMM. IN OTHER LANG.
*LO/N14. 1(2), 1970-*
*ISSN 0048-7643*

**REVISTA DEL CENTRO DE ESTUDIOS EDUCATIVOS
(MEXICO).**
*+ +REV. CENT. ESTUD. EDUC. (MEX.).*
*MEXICO, D.F. 1(1), 1971-*
*LO/N-1.*

**REVISTA DE CIENCIAS AGRONOMICAS: SERIE A.**          XXX
*+ +REV. CIENC. AGRON., A.*
UNIVERSIDADE DE LOURENCO MARQUES: INSTITUTO
SUPERIOR DE AGRONOMIA.
*LOURENCO MARQUES 1, 1968-*
SUPERSEDES IN PART REVISTA DOS ESTUDOS GERAIS
UNIVERSITARIOS DE MOCAMBIQUE: SERIE 2:
CIENCIAS BIOLOGICAS E AGRONOMICAS FROM 1,
1964- 4, 1967.
*CA/U11.*

**REVISTA DE CIENCIAS BIOLOGICAS: SERIE A.**          XXX
*+ +REV. CIENC. BIOL., A.*
UNIVERSIDADE DE LOURENCO MARQUES.
*LOURENCO MARQUES 1, 1968-*
PREV. PART OF: REVISTA DOS ESTUDOS GERAIS
UNIVERSITARIOS DE MOCAMBIQUE: SERIE 2: CIEN-
CIAS BIOLOGICAS E AGRONOMICAS FROM 1, 1964- 4,
1967.
*DB/S-1.    LO/N-2.*
*RE/U-1. 2, 1969-*

**REVISTA DE CIENCIAS BIOLOGICAS: SERIE B.**
*+ +REV. CIENC. BIOL., B.*
UNIVERSIDADE DE LOURENCO MARQUES.
*LOURENCO MARQUES 1, 1970-*
PREV. PART OF: REVISTA DOS ESTUDOS GERAIS
UNIVERSITARIOS DE MOCAMBIQUE: SERIE 2: CIEN-
CIAS BIOLOGICAS E AGRONOMICAS FROM 1, 1964- 4,
1967.
*DB/S-1.    LO/N-2.    LO/N13.    RE/U-1.*

**REVISTA DE CIENCIAS ECONOMICAS Y SOCIALES.**
*+ +REV. CIENC. ECON. & SOC.*
*SANTO DOMINGO 1, 1972-*
*OX/U-1.*

**REVISTA DE CIENCIAS GEOLOGICAS: SERIE A.**          XXX
*+ +REV. CIENC. GEOL., A.*
UNIVERSIDADE DE LOURENCO MARQUES.
*LOURENCO MARQUES 1, 1968-*
PREV. PART OF: REVISTA DOS ESTUDOS GERAIS
UNIVERSITARIOS DE MOCAMBIQUE: SERIE 6:
CIENCIAS GEOLOGICAS FROM 2, 1965- 4, 1967.
*GL/U-1.*

**REVISTA DE CIENCIAS GEOLOGICAS: SERIE B.**          XXX
*+ +REV. CIENC. GEOL., B.*
UNIVERSIDADE DE LOURENCO MARQUES.
*LOURENCO MARQUES 1, 1968-*
PREV. PART OF: REVISTA DOS ESTUDOS GERAIS
UNIVERSITARIOS DE MOCAMBIQUE: SERIE 6:
CIENCIAS GEOLOGICAS FROM 2, 1965- 4, 1967.
*LO/N-2.*

**REVISTA DE CIENCIAS MATEMATICAS: SERIE B.**          XXX
*+ +REV. CIENC. MAT., B.*
UNIVERSIDADE DE LOURENCO MARQUES.
*LOURENCO MARQUES 1, 1970-*
PREV. PART OF: REVISTA DOS ESTUDOS GERAIS
UNIVERSITARIOS DE MOCAMBIQUE: SERIE 1:
CIENCIAS MATEMATICAS, FISICAS E QUIMICAS
FROM 1, 1964- 1967.
*LO/N13.*

**REVISTA DE CIENCIAS MEDICAS. SERIE A.**          XXX
*+ +REV. CIENC. MED., A.*
UNIVERSIDADE DE LOURENCO MARQUES: FACULDADE
DE MEDICINA.
*LOURENCO MARQUES 1, 1968-*
PREV. PART OF: REVISTA DOS ESTUDOS GERAIS
UNIVERSITARIOS DE MOCAMBIQUE: SERIE 3: MEDICAS
FROM 1, 1964- 4, 1967.
*GL/U-1. 1969-*

**REVISTA DE CIENCIA POLITICA.**
*+ +REV. CIENC. POL. (BRAZ.).*
INSTITUTO DE DIREITO PUBLICO E CIENCIA POLITICA
(BRAZIL).
*RIO DE JANEIRO 1(1), MR 1967-*
Q.
*LO/U-3. 5(1), 1971-*
*ISSN 0034-8023*

**REVISTA DE CIENCIAS VETERINARIAS: SERIE A.**          XXX
*+ +REV. CIENC. VET., A.*
UNIVERSIDADE DE LOURENCO MARQUES.
*LOURENCO MARQUES 1, 1968-*
PREV. PART OF: REVISTA DOS ESTUDOS GERAIS
UNIVERSITARIOS DE MOCAMBIQUE: SERIE 4:
CIENCIAS VETERINARIAS FROM 1, 1964- 3, 1966.
*LO/N-2.    LO/N13.*

**REVISTA DE CIENCIAS VETERINARIAS: SERIE B.**          XXX
*+ +REV. CIENC. VET., B.*
UNIVERSIDADE DE LOURENCO MARQUES.
*LOURENCO MARQUES 1, 1968-*
PREV. PART OF: REVISTA DOS ESTUDOS GERAIS
UNIVERSITARIOS DE MOCAMBIQUE: SERIE 4:
CIENCIAS VETERINARIAS FROM 1, 1964- 3, 1966.
*LO/N-2.    LO/N13.*

**REVISTA COLOMBIANA DE CIENCIA POLITICA.**
*+ +REV. COLOMB. CIENC. POLIT.*
*BOGOTA 1, 1971-*
*OX/U-1.*

**REVISTA COLOMBIANA DE FOLCLOR: SUPLEMENTO.**
*+ +REV. COLOMB. FOLCLOR, SUPL.*
INSTITUTO COLOMBIANO DE FOLCLOR.
*BOGOTA 1, 1970-*
*OX/U-1.*

**REVISTA CUBANA.**
*+ +REV. CUBANA.*
PATROCINADA POR CUBANOS EN EL DESTIERRO.
*NEW YORK 1(1), JA/JE 1968-*
*CA/U-1.    LO/N-1.*
*OX/U-1. 1(2), 1968-*

**REVISTA CUBANA DE CIENCIA AGRICOLA.**          XXX
*+ +REV. CUBANA CIENC. AGR.*
INSTITUTO DE CIENCIA ANIMAL (CUBA).
*HAVANA 1, N 1967- 6, 1972 ...*
ENGL. ED. SUBS: CUBAN JOURNAL OF AGRICULTURAL
SCIENCE.
*BL/U-1.    CA/U11.*
*ED/N-1. 2(3), 1968-                    LO/N13. 2, 1968-*
*XS/U-1. 2, 1968-*
*ISSN 0034-7485*

**REVISTA CUBANA DE CIENCIAS VETERINARIAS.**
*+ +REV. CUBANA CIENC. VET.*
CONSEJO CIENTIFICO VETERINARIO (CUBA).
*HAVANA 1, JA/JE 1970-*
ENGL. SUMM.
*LO/N-2.*
*ISSN 0048-7678*

**REVISTA DOMINICANA DE ARQUEOLOGIA Y ANTRO-
POLOGIA.**
*+ +REV. DOMIN. ARQUEOL. & ANTROPOL.*
UNIVERSISAD AUTONOMA DE SANTO DOMINGO: FACULTAD
DE HUMANIDADES.
*SANTO DOMINGO 1(1), 1971-*
*OX/U-1.*

REVISTA, ESCOLA DE COMUNICACOES CULTURAIS,
UNIVERSIDADE DE SAO PAULO.
*+ +REV. ESC. COMUN. CULT. UNIV. SAO PAULO.*
*SAO PAULO 1(1), 1968-*
COVER TITLE DATED 1, 1967.
*OX/U-1.*
*LO/U11.*

REVISTA ESPANOLA DE LINGUISTICA.
*+ +REV. ESP. LINGUIST.*
SOCIEDAD ESPANOLA DE LINGUISTICA.
*MADRID 1, 1971-*
2/A.
*CA/U-1.    MA/U-1.    OX/U-1.    SH/U-1.*
*NO/U-1. 2, 1972-*

REVISTA ESPANOLA DE MICROPALEONTOLOGIA.
*+ +REV. ESP. MICROPALEONTOL.*
CENTRO DE INVESTIGACION JUAN GAVALA.
*MADRID 1, 1969-*
*CA/U14.    HL/U-1.    LO/N-2.    LO/U-2.    OX/U-8.*

REVISTA ESPANOLA DE LA OPINION PUBLICA.
*+ +REV. ESP. OPIN. PUBLICA.*
INSTITUTO DE LA OPINION PUBLICA (SPAIN).
*MADRID 1, MY/AG 1965-*
Q. PRECEDED BY AN EXPERIMENTAL ISSUE CALLED
NO.0, AP 1965.
*LO/U-3.*
*BD/U-1. NO.27, 1972; NO.31- 33, 1973.*
*GL/U-1. NO.3, 1966- 21/22, 1970.** 
*ISSN 0034-9429*

REVISTA DOS ESTUDOS GERAIS UNIVERSITARIOS DE
MOCAMBIQUE: SERIE 1: CIENCIAS MATEMATICAS,
FISICAS E QUIMICAS.                                               XXX
*+ +REV. ESTUD. GER. UNIV. MOCAMBIQUE, 1.*
*LOURENCO MARQUES 1, 1964- 1967.*
SUBS. PART OF: REVISTA DE CIENCIAS MATEMAT-
ICAS: SERIE A & SERIE B; & REVISTA DE FISICA,
QUIMICA E ENGENHARIA: SERIE A & SERIE B.
*DB/S-1.    LO/U11.*
*LO/N13. 1, 1964.*

REVISTA DOS ESTUDOS GERAIS UNIVERSITARIOS DE
MOCAMBIQUE: SERIE 3: CIENCIAS MEDICAS.                            XXX
SUBS (1968) PART OF: REVISTA DE CIENCIAS
MEDICAS: SERIE A & SERIE B.

REVISTA DOS ESTUDOS GERAIS UNIVERSITARIOS DE
MOCAMBIQUE: SERIE 6: CIENCIAS GEOLOGICAS.                         XXX
SUBS (1968) PART OF: REVISTA DE CIENCIAS
GEOLOGICAS: SERIE A & SERIE B.

REVISTA DA FACULDADE DE ODONTOLOGIA DA
UNIVERSIDADE DE SAO PAULO.                                        XXX
*+ +REV. FAC. ODONTOL. UNIV. SAO PAULO. [ROUS-A]*
*SAO PAULO 1, 1963-*
2/A. PREV. PART OF: ANAIS DA FACULDADE DE
FARMACIA & ODONTOLOGIA DA UNIVERSIDADE DE SAO
PAULO: ODONTOLOGIA FROM 18, 1961- 19(2), JE/D
1962; & ANAIS DA FACULDADE DE FARMACIA E ODON-
TOLOGIA DA UNIVERSIDADE DE SAO PAULO: FARMACIA
FROM 18, 1961- 19(1), JA/JE 1962.
*LO/N13.*
*LO/M34. 4, 1966-*
*ISSN 0581-6866*

REVISTA DE FISICA, QUIMICA E ENGENHARIA:
SERIE A.                                                          XXX
*+ +REV. FIS. QUIM. & ENG., A.*
UNIVERSIDADE DE LOURENCO MARQUES.
*LOURENCO MARQUES 1 1969-*
ENGL. OR PORT. PREV. PART OF: REVISTA DOS
ESTUDOS GERAIS UNIVERSITARIOS DE MOCAMBIQUE:
SERIE 1: CIENCIAS MATEMATICAS, FISICAS E
QUIMICAS FROM 1, 1964- 1967.
*LO/N13.*

REVISTA FORESTAL DEL PERU.
*+ +REV. FOR. PERU.*
UNIVERSIDAD AGRARIA, LIMA: INSTITUTO DE INVES-
TIGACIONES FORESTALES.
*LIMA 1, 1967-*
*LO/N-2.    OX/U-3.*

REVISTA GEOGRAFICA DE VALPARAISO.
*+ +REV. GEOGR. VALPARAISO.*
UNIVERSIDAD CATOLICA DE VALPARAISO: DEPARTA-
MENTO DE GEOGRAFIA.
*VALPARAISO 1, 1967-*
*BH/U-1.*
*ISSN 0034-9577*

REVISTA DE HISTORIA ENTRERRIANA.
*+ +REV. HIST. ENTRERRIANA.*
ASOCIACION ENTRERRIANA GENERAL URQUIZA.
*BUENOS AIRES 1, 1966-*
*OX/U-1.*

REVISTA DEL INSTITUTO COLOMBIANO AGROPECUARIO.
*+ +REV. INST. COLOMB. AGROPECUAR.*
*BOGOTA 1(1), D 1966-*
2/A.
*XS/R-2.*

REVISTA DO INSTITUTO DE ESTUDOS BRASILEIROS,
UNIVERSIDADE DE SAO PAULO.
*+ +REV. INST. ESTUD. BRAS. UNIV. SAO PAULO.*
*SAO PAULO NO.1, 1966-*
*CC/U-1.    ED/U-1.*
*LO/U-1. NO.2, 1967-** 

REVISTA DE LA INTEGRACION.
*+ +REV. INTEGRACION.*
INSTITUTO PARA LA INTEGRACION DE AMERICA
LATINA.
*BUENOS AIRES NO.1, N 1967-*
*LO/U-3. NO.2, 1968-*
*OX/U18. NO.9- 14.*
*ISSN 0034-8422*

REVISTA INTERAMERICANA. INTERAMERICANA
REVIEW.
*+ +REV. INTERAM. (PUERTO RICO).*
INTERAMERICAN UNIVERSITY OF PUERTO RICO.
*SAN GERMAN, P.R. 1, SPRING 1971-*
Q. COVERTITLE: REVISTA INTERAMERICANA REVIEW.
*OX/U-1.*

REVISTA, JUNTA DE ESTUDIOS HISTORICOS DE
BAHIA BLANCA.
*+ +REV. JUNTA ESTUD. HIST. BAHIA BLANCA.*
*BAHIA BLANCA 1, D 1967-*
Q.
*OX/U-1.*

REVISTA LATINOAMERICANA DE CIENCIA POLITICA.
*+ +REV. LATINOAM. CIENC. POLIT.*
ESCUELA LATINOAMERICANA DE CIENCIA POLITICA Y
*SANTIAGO DE CHILE 1(1), AP 1970-*
3/A.
*LO/U-3.*
*GL/U-1. 1(1), 1970.*

REVISTA LATINOAMERICANA DE ESTUDIOS URBANO
REGIONALES.
UNIVERSIDAD CATOLICA DE CHILE: CENTRO INTERDIS-
CIPLINARIO DE DESARROLLO URBANO Y REGIONAL.
*SANTIAGO DE CHILE 1(1), OC 1970-*
3/A. SPONS. BODY ALSO: CONSEJO LATINOAMERICANO
DE CIENCIAS SOCIALES.
*LO/U-3.*
*ISSN 0048-7821*

REVISTA LATINOAMERICANA DE INGENIERIA QUIMICA
Y QUIMICA APLICADA = LATIN AMERICAN JOURNAL
OF CHEMICAL ENGINEERING & APPLIED CHEMISTRY.
*+ +REV. LATINOAM. ING. QUIM. & QUIM. APL.*
SOCIEDAD ARGENTINA DE INVESTIGADORES EN CIENCIA
DE LA INGENIERIA QUIMICA Y QUIMICA APLICADA.
*LA PLATA 1, 1971-*
*GL/U-1.    LD/U-1.    LO/N14.*

REVISTA DE LETRAS (BRAZIL).
*+ +REV. LET. (BRAZ.).*
FACULDADE DE FILOSOFIA, CIENCIAS E LETRAS
(ASSIS, BRAZIL).
*ASSIS, BRAZ. 1, 1960-*
*MA/U-1. 13, 1970/71-*
*ISSN 0080-2352*

REVISTA DE MEDICINA VETERINARIA (SAO PAULO).
*+ +REV. MED. VET. (SAO PAULO).*
SOCIEDADE PAULISTA DE MEDICINA VETERINARIA E
DOS MEDICOS VETERINARIOS BRASILEIROS.
*SAO PAULO 1, JL 1965-*
*LO/N13.*

REVISTA DE METEOROLOGIA MARITIMA (SPAIN).
*+ +REV. METEOROL. MARIT. (SPAIN).*
(SPAIN) SERVICIO METEOROLOGICO NACIONAL:
SECCION MARITIMA.
*MADRID NO.1, S 1970-*
*XS/N-1.*

REVISTA DE MICROBIOLOGIA.
+ +REV. MICROBIOL.
SOCIEDADE BRASILEIRA DE MICROBIOLOGIA.
  SAO PAULO  1, 1970-
  PORT. OR ENGL.
  LO/N13.
  ISSN 0001-3714

REVISTA, MUSEO ARGENTINO DE CIENCIAS NATUR-
ALES 'BERNARDINO RIVADAVIA' E INSTITUTO
NACIONAL DE INVESTIGACION DE LAS CIENCIAS
NATURALES:  ECOLOGIA.
+ +REV. MUS. ARGENT. CIENC. NATUR. & INST. NAC.
  INVEST. CIENC. NAT., ECOL.
  BUENOS AIRES  1, 1963-
  BL/U-1.

REVISTA, MUSEO ARGENTINO DE CIENCIAS NATUR-
ALES 'BERNARDINO RIVADAVIA' E INSTITUTO
NACIONAL DE INVESTIGACION DE LAS CIENCIAS
NATURALES:  ENTOMOLOGIA.
+ +REV. MUS. ARGENT. CIENC. NATUR. & INST. NAC.
  INVEST. CIENC. NAT., ENTOMOL.
  BUENOS AIRES  1, 1964-
  LO/N13.

REVISTA, MUSEO ARGENTINO DE CIENCIAS NATUR-
ALES 'BERNARDINO RIVADAVIA' E INSTITUTO
NACIONAL DE INVESTIGACION DE LAS CIENCIAS
NATURALES:  PARASITOLOGIA.
+ +REV. MUS. ARGENT. CIENC. NATUR. & INST. NAC.
  INVEST. CIENC. NAT., PARASITOL.
  BUENOS AIRES  1, 1968-
  DB/S-1.    LO/N13.

REVISTA NACIONAL DE CULTURA (BOLIVIA).
+ +REV. NAC. CULT. (BOLIVIA).
(BOLIVIA) MINISTERIO DE EDUCACION.
  LA PAZ  1(1), 1970-
  OX/U-1.

REVISTA PARAGUAYA DE SOCIOLOGIA.
+ +REV. PARAG. SOCIOL.
CENTRO PARAGUAYO DE ESTUDIOS SOCIOLOGICOS.
  ASUNCION  1(1), S/D 1964-
  LO/N-1.  1(2), 1965-          OX/U-1.  1(2), 1965-
  LO/U-3.  5(13), 1968-
  ISSN 0035-0354

REVISTA DE PLANEACION Y DESARROLLO.
+ +REV. PLANEACION DESARRO.
(COLOMBIA) DEPARTMENTO NACIONAL DE PLANEACION.
  BOGOTA  1, 1969-
  Q.  IN ENGL. & SPAN.
  LO/U-3.
  ISSN 0034-8686

REVISTA DE SAUDE PUBLICA (BRAZIL).
+ +REV. SAUDE PUBLICA (BRAZIL).
UNIVERSIDADE DE SAO PAULO: FACULDADE DE SAUDE
PUBLICA.
  SAO PAULO  NO.1, 1970-
  LO/N-2.
  ISSN 0034-8910

REVISTA SOCIALISTA.
+ +REV. SOC. (ARG.).
  BUENOS AIRES  1, JL/S 1971-
  OX/U-1.

REVISTA DE SOLDADURA.
+ +REV. SOLDADURA.
CENTRO NACIONAL DE INVESTIGACIONES METALURGICAS
(SPAIN).
  MADRID  1, 1971-
  LO/N14.
  ISSN 0048-7759

REVISTA THEOBROMA.
+ +REV. THEOBROMA.
CENTRO DE PESQUISAS DO CACAU.
  ITABUNA, BRAZ.  1(1), JA/MR 1971-
  LO/R-6.

REVISTA DA UNIVERSIDADE FEDERAL DO PARA.
+ +REV. UNIV. FED. PARA.
  BELEM, BRAZ.  SER.1.  1(1), 1971-
  LO/N-1.

REVISTA URUGUAYA DE CIENCIAS SOCIALES.
+ +REV. URUG. CIENC. SOC.
  MONTEVIDEO  1(1), AP/JE 1972-
  3/A.
  LO/N-1.    LO/U-3.

REVOLJUTSIONNOE DVIZHENIE V SIBIRI I NA
DAL'NEM VOSTOKE.
+ +REVOLJUTSIONNOE DVIZHENIE SIB. & DAL'NEM
  VOSTOKE.
TOMSKIJ GOSUDARSTVENNYJ UNIVERSITET.
  TOMSK  1, 1960-
  CA/U-1.    GL/U-1.    LO/U-3.    SW/U-1.
  ISSN 0484-8306

REVOLJUTSIONNO-ISTORICHESKIJ KALENDAR'-
SPRAVOCHNIK.
+ +REVOLJUTSIONNO-ISTOR. KAL.-SPRAV.
  MOSCOW  1964(1963)-
  A.
  BH/U-1.
  ISSN 0556-7076

REVUE. LITTERATURE, HISTOIRE, ARTS & SCIENCES
DES DEUX MONDES.                                        XXX
  SUBS (1972): NOUVELLE REVUE DES DEUX MONDES.

REVUE D'ACOUSTIQUE.
+ +REV. ACOUST.
GROUPEMENT DES ACOUSTICIENS DE LANGUE FRANCAISE
[INFORMATION PROPAGANDE FRANCAISES]
  PARIS  1(1), 1968-
  LO/N14.

REVUE AFRICAINE DE MANAGEMENT.
+ +REV. AFR. MANAGE.
INSTITUT SUPERIEUR DE GESTION DES ENTERPRISES
(TUNIS).
  TUNIS  1(1), 1971-
  LO/U14.

REVUE D'ALLEMAGNE.
+ +REV. ALLEMAGNE.
SOCIETE D'ETUDES ALLEMANDES.
  STRASBOURG  1(1), JA/MR 1969-
  LO/N-1.    OX/U-1.
  ISSN 0035-0974

REVUE ARCHEOLOGIQUE DE NARBONNAISE.
+ +REV. ARCHEOL. NARBONNAISE.
[EDITIONS E. DE BOCCARD]
  PARIS  1, 1968-
  A.
  CA/U-1.    NW/U-1.    OX/U-2.    SH/U-1.

REVUE DES ARCHEOLOGUES ET HISTORIENS D'ART DE
LOUVAIN.
+ +REV. ARCHEOL. & HIST. ART LOUVAIN.
UNIVERSITE CATHOLIQUE DE LOUVAIN: INSTITUT
SUPERIEUR D'ARCHEOLOGIE ET D'HISTOIRE DE L'ART.
  LOUVAIN  NO.1, 1968-
  A.  S/T: PUBLICATION DES ANCIENS ET DES
  ETUDIANTS DE L'INSTITUT ...
  DB/U-2.    MA/U-1.    OX/U-2.

REVUE DE L'ART.
+ +REV. ART.
COMITE FRANCAISE D'HISTOIRE DE L'ART.
  PARIS  1, 1968-
  Q.
  LO/U17.    NO/U-1.    OX/U-2.
  ISSN 0035-1326

REVUE DE L'ASSOCIATION POUR L'ETUDE DU
MOUVEMENT DADA.                                         XXX
+ +REV. ASSOC. ETUDE MOUVEMENT DADA.
  PARIS  NO.1, OC 1965.
  SUBS: CAHIERS DADA SURREALISME.
  CB/U-1.    LO/U-2.

REVUE DE L'ASSOCIATION FRANCAISE POUR
L'AVANCEMENT DES SCIENCES.
+ +REV. ASS. FR. AVAN. SCI.
  PARIS  1(1), 1969-
  LO/N-4.

REVUE BELGE D'HISTOIRE CONTEMPORAINE. BELGISCH
TIJDSCHRIFT VOOR NIEUWSTE GESCHIEDENIS.
+ +REV. BELG. HIST. CONTEMP.
  GHENT  1(1), 1969-
  LO/U-1.    OX/U-1.
  ISSN 0035-0869

REVUE CANADIENNE D'ECONOMIQUE. SUPPLEMENT.      000
  SEE: CANADIAN JOURNAL OF ECONOMICS. SUPPLE-
  MENT.

REVUE CANADIENNE DES SCIENCES DU COMPORTEMENT.
  SEE: CANADIAN JOURNAL OF BEHAVIOURAL SCIENCE.

REVUE, CENTRE SCIENTIFIQUE ET TECHNIQUE DE LA
CONSTRUCTION.                                           000
  SEE: CSTC REVUE.

REVUE DU CETHEDEC.
+ +REV. CETHEDEC.
CENTRE D'ETUDES THEORIQUES DE LA DETECTION ET
DES COMMUNICATIONS.
*PARIS [1], 1964-*
CONTAINS SUPPL. REVUE DU CETHEDEC. CAHIER.
*LO/N14.*

REVUE DU COMPORTEMENT ANIMAL.
+ +REV. COMPORTEMENT ANIM.
[CREPIN-LEBLOND]
*PARIS ?1, 1967-*
*LO/N-2. 4, 1970-*          *OX/U-8. 2(1), 1968-*
*SO/U-1. 4, 1970-*

REVUE DE CYTOLOGIE CLINIQUE.
+ +REV. CYTOL. CLIN.
[EDITIONS VARIA]
*PARIS 1, 1968-*
*LO/N13.*

REVUE DEJIN SOCIALISMU. PRISPEVKY K DEJINAM
KSC.                                                          XXX
+ +REV. DEJIN SOC.
USTAV DEJIN SOCIALISMU.
*PRAGUE 8, 1968-*
RUSS. & GER. CONT. LISTS. PREV: PRISPEVKY K
DEJINAM KSC FROM 1, 1957- 7, 1967.
*CA/U-1.*
*LA/U-1. 9, 1969-*
*ISSN 0556-7599*

REVUE DE DROIT SOCIAL. TIJDSCHRIFT VOOR SOCIAL
RECHT.
+ +REV. DROIT SOC.
[LARCIER]
*BRUSSELS NO.1, 1971-*
FR. & DUTCH.
*GL/U-1.*
*ISSN 0035-1113*

REVUE ECONOMIQUE, BANQUE NATIONALE DE PARIS.
+ +REV. ECON. BANQUE NAT. PARIS.
*PARIS NO.1, 1967-*
*LV/P-1.*

REVUE ECONOMIQUE DE MADAGASCAR.
+ +REV. ECON. MADAGASCAR.
UNIVERSITE DE MADAGASCAR.
*TANANARIVE NO.1, 1966-*
*LO/U-3.    OX/U-9.*
*ISSN 0080-2581*

REVUE ELECTRODIAGNOSTIC-THERAPIE.                             000
SEE: ELECTRODIAGNOSTIC-THERAPIE.

REVUE D'ELECTROENCEPHALOGRAPHIE ET DE NEURO-
PHYSIOLOGIE CLINIQUE.
+ +REV. ELECTROENCEPHALOGR. & NEUROPHYSIOL. CLIN.
[MASSON & CIE]
*PARIS 1(1), 1971-*
Q.
*LO/N13.    XY/N-1.*

REVUE D'EPIDEMIOLOGIE, MEDECINE SOCIALE ET
SANTE PUBLIQUE.                                               XXX
+ +REV. EPIDEMIOL. MED. SOC. & SANTE PUBLIQUE.
[MASSON]
*PARIS 19, 1971-*
PREV: REVUE D'HYGIENE ET DE MEDECINE
SOCIALE FROM 1, 1953- 18, 1970.
*LO/N13.*

REVUE DE L'EST. ECONOMIE ET TECHNIQUES DE
PLANIFICATION, DROIT ET SCIENCES SOCIALES.
+ +REV. EST.
CENTRE NATIONALE DE LA RECHERCHE SCIENTIFIQUE
(FRANCE).
*PARIS 1(1), JL 1970-*
*DB/U-2.    LO/U-3.    MA/U-1.*
*OX/U-1. 1(2), 1970-*
*ISSN 0035-1415*

REVUE EUROPEENNE D'ETUDES CLINIQUES ET BIOLOG-
IQUES.                                                        XXX
+ +REV. EUR. ETUD. CLIN. & BIOL.
[EDITIONS MEDICALES FLAMMARION]
*PARIS 15, 1970- 17, 1972 ...*
PREV: REVUE FRANCAISE D'ETUDES CLINIQUES ET
BIOLOGIQUES FROM 1, 1956- 14, 1969. SUBS:
BIOMEDICINE.
*BL/U-1.    LD/U-1.    NW/U-1.*
*ISSN 0035-3019*

REVUE FRANCAISE D'ETUDES CLINIQUES ET BIOLOG-
IQUES.                                                        XXX
SUBS (1970): REVUE EUROPEENNE D'ETUDES ...

REVUE FRANCAISE D'ETUDES POLITIQUES AFRICAINES.
+ +REV. FR. ETUD. POLIT. AFR.
SOCIETE AFRICAINE D'EDITION.
*DAKAR 25, 1968...*
PREV: LE MOIS EN AFRIQUE: REVUE FRANCAISE
D'ETUDES POLITIQUES AFRICAINES FROM 1, JA 1966
*MA/U-1.*

REVUE FRANCAISE DE PEDAGOGIE.
+ +REV. FR. PEDAGOG.
INSTITUT PEDAGOGIQUE NATIONAL (FRANCE).
*PARIS NO.1, OC/D 1967-*
*DB/U-2.    LV/U-2.*

REVUE FRANCAISE DE RADIODIFFUSION ET DE TELE-
VISION.                                                       XXX
+ +REV. FR. RADIODIFFUS. & TELEV.
INFORMATION PROPAGANDE FRANCAISES.
[E. BOURNAZEL]
*PARIS 1(1), 1967- 4(13), 1970 ...*
SUBS: REVUE TECHNIQUE DE RADIODIFFUSION ET
DE TELEVISION. PUBLISHED IN COOPERATION WITH
THE OFFICE DE RADIODIFFUSION TELEVISION
FRANCAISE. ENGL. SUMMARIES.
*LO/N14.*

REVUE FRANCAISE DES TECHNIQUES MONDIALES.        XXX
+ +REV. FR. TECH. MOND.
*PARIS NO.150, 1967- 188, 1970...*
PREV: TECHNIQUES MONDIALES FROM NO.1, 1950-
149, 1966. SUBS: MATERIELS NOUVEAUX ET
TECHNIQUES MONDIALES.
*LO/N13.*

REVUE D'HISTOIRE ET DE CIVILISATION DU
MAGHREB.
+ +REV. HIST. & CIVILIS. MAGHREB.
UNIVERSITE D'ALGER: FACULTE DES LETTRES ET
SCIENCES HUMAINES.
*ALGIERS NO.1, 1966-*
2/A.
*OX/U-1.*

REVUE D'HISTOIRE DES MINES ET DE LA METALL-
URGIE. REVUE SEMESTRIELLE...                                  XXX
+ +REV. HIST. MINES & METALL.
CENTRE DE RECHERCHES DE L'HISTOIRE DE LA SID-
ERURGIE(GENEVA).
[DROZ]
*GENEVA 1(1), 1969- 4, 1972. //*
PREV: REVUE D'HISTOIRE DE LA SIDERURGIE FROM
1, 1960.
*LO/N-1.    LO/N-4.    LO/U-1.    LO/U-2.    LO/U-3.*
*EX/U-1. 2(1), 1970-*

REVUE D'HISTOIRE DES TEXTES.                                  XXX
+ +REV. HIST. TEXTES.
CENTRE NATIONAL DE LA RECHERCHE SCIENTIFIQUE
(FRANCE): INSTITUT DE RECHERCHE ET D'HISTOIRE
DES TEXTES.
*PARIS 1, 1971-*
PREV: BULLETIN D'INFORMATION, INSTITUT DE
RECHERCHE ET D'HISTOIRE DES TEXTES FROM NO,1,
1952- 15, 1969.
*AD/U-1.    BL/U-1.    DB/U-2.    GL/U-1.    LD/U-1.    LO/N-1.*
*LO/U-1.    MA/U-1.    NO/U-1.    NW/U-1.    SH/U-1.*

REVUE D'HYGIENE ET DE MEDECINE SOCIALE.                       XXX
SUBS (1971): REVUE D'EPIDEMIOLOGIE, MEDECINE
SOCIALE ET SANTE PUBLIQUE.

REVUE D'IMMUNOLOGIE.*
+ +REV. IMMUNOL.
[MASSON ET CIE]
*PARIS 1, 1935-*
TITLE VARIES. AS ABOVE FROM 1, 1935- 9,
1945; & FROM 34, 1970. EXPANDED TO REVUE
D'IMMUNOLOGIE ET DE THERAPIE ANTIMICROBIENNE
FROM 10, 1946- 33, 1969.
*ED/U-1.    LO/M12.    LO/M17.    LO/N13.    OX/U-8.*
*LO/M10. 9, 1945;              LO/M32. 11, 1947-*
*LO/N-4. 12, 1948-*

REVUE DE L'INDUSTRIE MINERALE.                                XXX
SUBS (1971): INDUSTRIE MINERALE.

REVUE DE L'INSTITUT PASTEUR DE LYON.
+ +REV. INST. PASTEUR LYON.
INSTITUT PASTEUR DE LYON.
*LYON 1, 1967-*
'PUBLIEE PAR LA DIRECTION ET LE PERSONNEL
SCIENTIFIQUE DE L'INSTITUT ...'
*LD/U-1.    LO/N14.*
*ISSN 0020-2487*

REVUE INTERNATIONALE D'HISTOIRE DE LA BANQUE.
= RIVISTA INTERNAZIONALE DI STORIA DELLA
BANCA. = INTERNATIONAL REVIEW OF THE HISTORY
OF BANKING.
++REV. INT. HIST. BANQUE.
INSTITUT INTERNATIONAL D'HISTOIRE DE LA BANQUE.
  GENEVA  1, 1968-
  ANNU. ENGL., FR., GER., ITAL. OR SPAN.
  LO/U-3.     MA/U-1.     OX/U-1.
  ISSN 0030-4972

REVUE INTERNATIONALE DE STATISTIQUE.                    000
  SEE: INTERNATIONAL STATISTICAL REVIEW.

REVUE LIBANAISE DES SCIENCES POLITIQUES.
++REV. LIBAN. SCI. POLIT.
ASSOCIATION LIBANAISE DES SCIENCES POLITIQUES.
  BEIRUT  NO.1, JA/JE 1970-
  LO/N-1.
  ISSN 0557-9414

REVUE DE MEDECINE DE TOULOUSE.
++REV. MED. TOULOUSE. [RMDT-A]
UNIVERSITE DE TOULOUSE: FACULTE MIXTE DE
MEDECINE ET DE PHARMACIE.
  TOULOUSE  1, JA 1965-
  M. S/T: ENSEIGNEMENT, DOCUMENTS, INFORMA-
  TIONS. ISSUED IN COOP. WITH VARIOUS SCI. SOC.
  LO/M-1.

REVUE DE L'OCCIDENT MUSULMAN ET DE LA
MEDITERRANEE.
++REV. OCCIDENT MUSULMAN MEDITER.
ASSOCIATION POUR L'ETUDE DES SCIENCES HUMAINES
EN AFRIQUE DU NORD.
  AIX-EN-PROVINCE NO.1, 1966-
  2A.
  LO/U-3.
  LO/N-1.  NO.9, 1971-
  MA/U-1.  NO.11, 1972-
  ISSN 0035-1474

REVUE, ORGANISATION INTERNATIONALE POUR L'ETUDE
DES LANGUES ANCIENNES PAR ORDINATEUR.                    000
  SEE: REVIEW, INTERNATIONAL ORGANIZATION FOR
  ANCIENT LANGUAGES ANALYSIS BY COMPUTER.

REVUE DE PEDIATRIE.
++REV. PEDIAT.
  PARIS  1, 1965-
  Q. FR. & ENGL. SUMM.
  LO/M-1.*
  DB/U-2. 1(2), 1965-          LD/U-1. 1(2), 1965-*
  ISSN 0035-1644

REVUE DE PHYSIOLOGIE SUBAQUATIQUE ET MEDECINE
HYPERBARE. = REVIEW OF SUBAQUATIC PHYSIOLOGY &
HYPERBARIC MEDICINE.
++REV. PHYSIOL. SUBAQUAT. MED. HYPERBARE.
SOCIETE INTERNATIONALE D'EDITION MEDICALE.
  PARIS  1(1), MR/MY 1968-
  LO/N-4.

REVUE ROUMAINE D'EMBRYOLOGIE ET DE CYTOLOGIE:
SERIE DE CYTOLOGIE.
++REV. ROUM. EMBRYOL. CYTOL., CYTOL. [RECC-A]
ACADEMIA REPUBLICII POPULARE ROMINE.
  BUCHAREST  1, 1964-
  LO/N13.
  ISSN 0035-4007

REVUE ROUMAINE D'EMBRYOLOGIE ET DE CYTOLOGIE:
SERIE D'EMBRYOLOGIE.
++REV. ROUM. EMBRYOL. CYTOL., EMBRYOL. [RECY-A]
ACADEMIA REPUBLICII POPULARE ROMINE.
  BUCHAREST  1(1), 1964-
  ENGL., FR., GER.
  OX/U-1.
  LO/N13. 1(2), 1964-

REVUE ROUMAINE D'ETUDES INTERNATIONALES.
++REV. ROUM. ETUD. INT.
ASSOCIATION DE DROIT INTERNATIONAL ET DE RELAT-
IONS INTERNATIONALES DE LA REPUBLIQUE SOCIAL-
ISTE DE ROUMANIE.
  BUCHAREST  NO.1/2, 1967-
  OX/U-1.
  LO/S14. NO.3/4, 1968-
  ISSN 0048-8178

REVUE ROUMAINE DE VIROLOGIE.                             XXX
++REV. ROUM. VIROL.
[EDITIONS DE L'ACADEMIE]
  BUCHAREST  9, 1972-
  PREV: REVUE ROUMAINE D'INFRAMICROBIOLOGIE FROM
  1, 1964- 8, 1971.
  LO/N14.
  BL/U-1. 9, 1972-          DB/S-1. 9, 1972-

REVUE DU SECOND OEUVRE.
[EDITIONS PARISIENNES]
  PARIS  1(1), 1961-
  LO/N14.

REVUE SENEGALAISE DE DROIT.
++REV. SENEGAL. DROIT.
ASSOCIATION SENEGALAISE D'ETUDES ET DE
RECHERCHES JURIDIQUES.
  DAKAR  1, AG 1967-
  2/A.
  OX/U15.
  ISSN 0035-4112

REVUE DE LA SOCIETE DE BIOMETRIE HUMAINE            XXX
(BIOTYPOLOGIE).
++REV. SOC. BIOM. HUM. (BIOTYPOL.).
  PARIS  1(1/2), MY/JE 1966-
  PREV: BIOTYPOLOGIE FROM 1, 1932- 26(4), D
  1965. RUNNING TITLE: BIOMETRIE HUMAINE
  (BIOTYPOLOGIE).
  BH/U-1.     LO/N13.     OX/U-8.

REVUE SUISSE D'AGRICULTURE.
++REV. SUISSE AGR.
UNION DES SYNDICATS AGRICOLES ROMANDS.
  LAUSANNE  1, 1969-
  CA/U11.     LO/N13.     LO/R-6.*

REVUE SUISSE DE VITICULTURE ET ABORICULTURE.
++REV. SUISSE VITICULT. & ABORICULT.
  LAUSANNE  1, 1969-
  CA/U11.     LO/N13.     XS/R-2.
  ISSN 0035-4171

REVUE TECHNIQUE CECLES/CERS.                            000
  SEE: ELDO/ESRO TECHNICAL REVIEW.

REVUE TECHNIQUE, COMPAGNIE FRANCAISE THOMSON
  HOUSTON- HOTCHISS BRANDT.
  SUBS. (1969) PART OF: REVUE TECHNIQUE,
  THOMSON-CSF.

REVUE TECHNIQUE DE RADIODIFFUSION ET DE TELE-
VISION.                                                 XXX
++REV. TECH. RADIODIFFUS. & TELEV.
INFORMATION PROPAGANDE FRANCAISES.
[E. BOURNAZEL]
  PARIS  4(14), 1970- 8(35), 1974 ...
  PREV: REVUE FRANCAISE DE RADIODIFFUSION ET
  DE TELEVISION FROM 1(1), 1967- 4(13), 1970.
  SUBS: RADIODIFFUSION-TELEVISION.
  LO/N14.

REVUE TECHNIQUE, THOMSON-CSF.                           XXX
++REV. TECH. THOMSON-CSF.
[MASSON]
  PARIS  1, 1969-
  ENGL. & GER. SUMM. INCORP: ANNALES DE RADIO-
  ELECTRICITE FROM 1, JL 1945- 23(94), 1968;
  & REVUE TECHNIQUE, COMPAGNIE FRANCAISE THOMSON
  HOUSTON- HOTCHKISS BRANDT FROM NO.43, 1966-
  45, 1968.
  LC/U-1.     LO/N-4.     LO/N14.     SO/U-1.     SW/U-1.

REVUE THEOLOGIQUE DE LOUVAIN.
++REV. THEOL. LOUV.
UNIVERSITE CATHOLIQUE DE LOUVAIN: FACULTE DE
THEOLOGIE.
  LOUVAIN  1, 1970-
  DR/U-1.     LO/N-1.

REVUE DES TRANSMISSIONS HYDRAULIQUES ET PNEU-
MATIQUES ET DES ASSERVISSEMENTS.                        XXX
  SUBS (1964): HYDRAULIQUE, PNEUMATIQUE ET
  ASSERVISSEMENTS.

REVUE DES TRANSPORTS PUBLICS URBAINS ET REG-
IONAUX.                                                 XXX
++REV. TRANSP. PUBLICS URBAINS & REG.
UNION DES TRANSPORTS PUBLICS URBAINS ET REG-
IONAUX.                                                 XXX
  PARIS  59(661), 1970-
  PREV: INDUSTRIE DES VOIES FERREES ET DES
  TRANSPORTS AUTOMOBILES FROM 19, 1925- 58,1969.
  LO/N14.

REVUE TRIMESTRIELLE D'IMPLANTOLOGIE.
VIERTELJAHRIGE REVUE UBER IMPLANTOLOGIE.
++REV. TRIMEST. IMPLANTOL.
GROUPE D'ETUDE SUISSE POUR LES IMPLANTS.
  LAUSANNE  NO.1, OC 1967-
  FR., ENGL., GER. & SPAN.
  LO/N13.

REVUE, UNIVERSITE DE BUJUMBURA.   XXX
+ +REV. UNIV. BUJUMBURA.
BUJUMBURA, BURUNDI 1, 1967- 2, 1968.//
Q.
LO/N-2.

REVUE YOUGOSLAVE D'INVENTIONS.   000
SEE: JUGOSLOVENSKO PRONALAZASTVO.

REVUE DE ZOOLOGIE AGRICOLE ET APPLIQUE.   XXX
SUBS (1969): REVUE DE ZOOLOGIE AGRICOLE ET DE
PATHOLOGIE VEGETALE.

REVUE DE ZOOLOGIE AGRICOLE ET DE PATHOLOGIE
VEGETALE.
+ +REV. ZOOL. AGR. PATHOL. VEG.
SOCIETE D'ETUDE ET DE VULGARISATION DE LA
ZOOLOGIE AGRICOLE.
BORDEAUX 68, 1969-
PREV: REVUE DE ZOOLOGIE AGRICOLE ET APPLIQUEE
FROM 1, 1902.
LO/N14.
ISSN 0035-1806

REYON, ZELLWOLLE UND ANDERE CHEMIEFASERN.   XXX
SUBS (1960): CHEMIEFASERN.

RHEUMATOLOGY & PHYSICAL MEDICINE.   XXX
+ +RHEUMATOL. & PHYS. MED.
BRITISH ASSOCIATION OF PHYSICAL MEDICINE.
[BAILLIERE]
LONDON 10(7), AG 1970- 11(8), 1972...
PREV: ABSTRACTS OF PHYSICAL MEDICINE FROM 1,
JA 1952- 10(6), 1970. SUBS: RHEUMATOLOGY
& REHABILITATION.
ED/N-1.   LD/U-1.   NW/U-1.
ISSN 0003-4908

RHEUMATOLOGY & PHYSICAL MEDICINE: SUPPLEMENTS.
+ +RHEUMATOL. & PHYS. MED., SUPPL.
[BAILLIERE]
LONDON 1970-
NW/U-1.
ISSN 0003-4908

RHEUMATOLOGY & REHABILITATION.   XXX
+ +RHEUMATOL. & REHABIL.
BRITISH ASSOCIATION FOR RHEUMATOLOGY &
REHABILITATION.
[BAILLIERE]
LONDON 12, 1973-
PREV: RHEUMATOLOGY & PHYSICAL MEDICINE FROM
10(7), 1970- 11(8), 1972.
ED/N-1.   LD/U-1.
CA/M-7.   13, 1974-

RHIZOCRINUS.  OCCASIONAL PAPERS [OF THE] ...
UNIVERSITET I OSLO: ZOOLOGISK MUSEUM.
OSLO 1, 1969-
BL/U-1.   CR/N-1.   LO/N-2.

RHODE ISLAND AGRICULTURE.   XXX
SUBS (1970): RHODE ISLAND RESOURCES.

RHODE ISLAND RESOURCES.   XXX
+ +R.I. RESOUR.
AGRICULTURAL EXPERIMENT STATION, KINGSTON, R.I.
KINGSTON, R.I. 16(1), 1970-
SPONS. BODY ALSO: AGRICULTURAL EXTENSION
SERVICE, UNIVERSITY OF RHODE ISLAND.  PREV:
RHODE ISLAND AGRICULTURE FROM 1, 1954- 15(4),
1969.
CA/U12.   LO/N-6.
ISSN 0035-4635

RHODESIA NATIONAL BIBLIOGRAPHY.
+ +RHOD. NAT. BIBLIOGR.
NATIONAL ARCHIVES OF RHODESIA.
SALISBURY, RHOD.  1967 (1968)-
PREV: LIST OF PUBLICATIONS DEPOSITED IN THE
LIBRARY OF THE NATIONAL ARCHIVES.
LO/N-3.   LO/U19.

RHODESIA SCIENCE NEWS.
+ +RHOD. SCI. NEWS.
ASSOCIATION OF SCIENTIFIC SOCIETIES IN
RHODESIA.
SALISBURY, RHOD. 1, 1967-
LO/N-2.
LO/N13. [CURRENT BOX ONLY]
ISSN 0035-4732

RHODESIAN COMMENTARY.
+ +RHOD. COMMENT.
(RHODESIA) MINISTRY OF INFORMATION, IMMI-
GRATION & TOURISM.
SALISBURY, RHOD.  1(1), 21/JA 1966-
LO/U-3.   LO/U14.
LO/S14.  1(33), 1967-
ISSN 0035-4759

RHODESIAN HISTORY.
+ +RHOD. HIST.
CENTRAL AFRICA HISTORICAL ASSOCIATION.
SALISBURY 1, 1970-
AD/U-1.   BL/U-1.   CA/U-1.   LO/U-3.   LO/U-8.   OX/U-1.

RHODESIAN LIBRARIAN.
+ +RHOD. LIBR.
RHODESIA LIBRARY ASSOCIATION.
SALISBURY, RHOD.  1(1), 1969-
LD/U-1.   LO/N17.   LO/U-8.
OX/U-9.  1(2), 1969-
ISSN 0035-4848

RHODESIAN OUTLOOK.
+ +RHOD. OUTLOOK.
[MAXEY & CHRISTIE]
CHEAM NO.1, AP 1969.
ED/N-1.   LO/N17.   LO/U-3.

RHODESIAN REVIEW.
+ +RHOD. REV.
SOUTHERN AFRICA RESEARCH OFFICE.
LONDON 1(1), N 1971-
MON.
LO/U-3.

RHODODENDRON.
AUSTRALIAN RHODODENDRON SOCIETY.
OLINDA, VICTORIA 1, 1962-
LO/N-2.

RICERCHE DI AUTOMATICA.
+ +RIC. AUTOM.
ASSOCIAZIONE NAZIONALE ITALIANA PER
L'AUTOMAZIONE.
MILAN 1, S 1970-
3/A. ENGL. FROM 4, 1973 ISSUED BY THE NATIONAL
RESEARCH COUNCIL OF ITALY, AUTOMATIC CONTROL
AND SYSTEMS GROUP.
LO/N14.
BL/U-1.  3, 1972-
ISSN 0048-8291

RICERCHE DI BIOLOGIA DELLA SELVAGGINA.   XXX
+ +RIC. BIOL. SELVAGGINA.
UNIVERSITA DI BOLOGNA: LABORATORIO DI ZOOLOGIA
APPLICATA ALLA CACCIA.
BOLOGNA NO.51, 1971-
PREV: RICERCHE DI ZOOLOGIA APPLICATA ALLA
CACCIA FROM NO.1, 1930- NO.50, 1971.
LO/N-2.   LO/N-4.

RICERCHE DI ZOOLOGIA APPLICATA ALLA CACCIA.   XXX
SUBS (1971): RICERCHE DI BIOLOGIA DELLA
SELVAGGINA.

RIDING THE INTERNATIONAL WAY.
+ +RID. INT. WAY.
[KAYE & WARD]
LONDON NO.1, 1969-
LO/N-1.   OX/U-1.

RIDINGS BOOKLETS.
+ +RIDINGS BOOKL.
[RIDINGS PUBL. CO.]
DRIFFIELD(YORKS.) [NO.1], 1966-
LO/U-2.

RIFORMA UNIVERSITARIA.
+ +RIFORMA UNIV.
ROME 1, 1971-
OX/U-1.

RILEM BULLETIN. = BULLETIN DE LA RILEM.   000
SEE (PART OF): MATERIALS & STRUCTURES:
TESTING & RESEARCH.

**RILM ABSTRACTS OF MUSIC LITERATURE.**
++*RILM ABSTR. MUSIC LIT.*
INTERNATIONAL REPERTORY OF MUSIC LITERATURE.
*FLUSHING, NY   1(1), JA/AP 1967-*
Q.  'RILM' = FR. NAME OF BODY: REPERTOIRE
INTERNATIONAL DE LA LITTERATURE MUSICALE.
PUBL. BY  INTERNATIONAL RILM CENTER.  SPON-
SORED BY: INTERNATIONAL MUSICOLOGICAL SOCIETY;
INTERNATIONAL ASSOCIATION OF MUSIC LIBRARIES;
AMERICAN COUNCIL OF LEARNED SOCIETIES.
*BN/U-1.     ED/N-1.     LO/U-1.     LO/U-2.     MA/P-1.     MA/U-1.*
*NO/U-1.     SH/U-1.     SO/U-1.*
*ISSN 0033-6955*

**RINGKASAN PUBLIKASI DAN LAPORAN PENELITIAN**
**PERTANIAN.**
PANITIA KOORDINASI PENELITIAN PERTANIAN.
*BOGOR  1, 1971-*
*LO/N13.*

**RIVESTIMENTI.**
*VARESE  1, 1972-*
*LO/N14.*

**RIVISTA DI AGRONOMIA.**
++*RIV. AGRON.*
SOCIETA ITALIANA DI AGRONOMIA.
[EDAGRI COLE]
*BOLOGNA  NO.1, 1967-*
ENGL. SUMMARIES.
*LO/N14.*
*CA/U11.  5(2), 1971-*
*ISSN 0035-6034*

**RIVISTA DI DIRITTO INTERNAZIONALE PRIVATO E**
**PROCESSUALE.**
++*RIV. DIRITTO INT. PRIV. PROCESSUALE.*
[CASA EDITRICE DOTT. ANTONIO MILANI]
*PADUA  1, JA/MR 1965-*
*OX/U15.*
*ISSN 0035-6174*

**RIVISTA DELL'INFORMAZIONE.  INFORMATION**
**REVIEW.**
++*RIV. INF.*
ISTITUTO NAZIONALE DELL'INFORMAZIONE.
*ROME  1, 1970-*
*LO/N35.  2, 1971-*              *SH/U-1.  3, 1972-*

**RIVISTA DE INGEGNERIA.**
  SUBS (1970): INGEGNERIA.

**RIVISTA DI INGEGNERIA AGRARIA.**
++*RIV. ING. AGRAR.*
ASSOCIAZONE ITALIANA DI GENIO RURALE.
[EDAGRICOLE]
*BOLOGNA  1, 1970-*
SPONS. BODY ALSO: UTENTI MOTORI AGRICOLI.
[MORGEL-LIANA]
*BRESCIA  1(1), MR 1968-*
Q.
*LO/N-1.*
*ISSN 0035-6719*

**RIVISTA INTERNAZIONALE DI PSICOLOGIA E IPNOSI.**
++*RIV. INT. PSICOL. & IPNOSI.*
ISTITUTO DI INDAGINI PSICOLOGICHE.
*MILAN  13, 1972-*
PREV: RIVISTA DI PSICOLOGIA DELLA SCRITTURA
FROM 1, 1955- 12, 1971.
*LO/N13.*
*ISSN 0035-6743*

**RIVISTA INTERNAZIONALE DI STORIA DELLA BANCA.**
  SEE: REVUE INTERNATIONALE D'HISTOIRE DE LA
  BANQUE.

**RIVISTA ITALIANA DI GEOFISICA.**                           XXX
++*RIV. ITAL. GEOFIS.*
SOCIETA ITALIANA DI GEOFISICA E METEOROLQGIA.
*GENOA  21, 1972-*
PREV: GEOFISICA E METEOROLOGIA FROM 1, JA/F
1953- 20, 1971.
*LO/N13.*

**RIVISTA ITALIANA DI GEOTECNICA.**
++*RIV. ITAL. GEOTEC.*
ASSOCIAZIONE GEOTECNICA ITALIANA.
[EDIZIONI SCIENTIFICHE ITALIANE]
*NAPLES  1, 1967-*
SOME ENGL. SUMM.
*LO/N14.*

**RIVISTA ITALIANA DI PISCICOLTURA E ITTIOPATO-**
**LOGIA.**
++*RIV. ITAL. PISCICOLT. & ITTIOPATOL.*
ASSOCIAZIONE PISCICOLTORI ITALIANI.
*PADOVA  1, 1966-*
*LO/N13.\**

**RIVISTA ITALIANA DI SCIENZA POLITICA.**
[SOCIETA EDITRICE DI MULINO]
*BOLOGNA  1, 1971-*
*GL/U-2.     OX/U-1.*
*MA/U-1.  2, 1972-*
*ISSN 0048-8402*

**RIVISTA DI MEDICINA LEGALE E LEGISLAZIONE**
**SANITARIA.**                                                XXX
++*RIV. MED. LEG. & LEGISLAZIONE SANIT.*
*PAVIA  1, JA/F 1959- 5, 1963.//*
ENGL., FR., ITAL. & GER. SUMM.
*LO/N13.  2, 1960-*

**RIVISTA DEL NUOVO CIMENTO.**
++*RIV. NUOVO CIM.*
SOCIETA ITALIANA DI FISICA.
[EDITRICE COMPOSITORI]
*BOLOGNA  1(1), JA/MR 1969-*
ENGL. OR ITAL.  PREV: NUOVO CIMENTO. SUPPLE-
MENTO FROM 1, 1963- 6, 1968.
*BH/U-1.     BN/U-2.     CB/U-1.     CO/U-1.     ED/U-1.     GL/U-1.*
*LD/U-1.     LO/N14.     LO/U-1.     NW/U-1.     SH/U-1.     SO/U-1.*
*SW/U-1.     XS/R10.*
*ISSN 0035-5917*

**RIVISTA DI PSICOLOGIA DELLA SCRITTURA.**          XXX
  SUBS (1972): RIVISTA INTERNAZIONALE DI PSIC-
  OLOGIA E IPNOSI.

**RIVISTA DI SOCIOLOGIA.**
++*RIV. SOCIOLOG.*
LIBERA UNIVERSITA INTERNAZIONALE DEGLI STUDI
SOCIALI PRO DEO: ISTITUTO DI SOCIOLOGIA.
*ROME  1(1), 1963-*
*3/A.*
*LO/U-3.*
*ISSN 0035-6530*

**RIVISTA STORICA DELL'ANTICHITA.**
++*RIV. STOR. ANTICHITA.*
[PATRON]
*BOLOGNA  1, 1971-*
*2/A.*
*BL/U-1.     MA/U-1.*
*OX/U-1.  1972-*

**RIVISTA TESSILE - TEXTILIA.**                           XXX
  SUBS (1970): TEXTILIA.

**ROAD INTERNATIONAL.**                                   XXX
++*ROAD INT.  [ROIN-A]*
INTERNATIONAL ROAD FEDERATION.
*GENEVA  NO.1, N 1950- 81, 1971.//*
*LO/N13.     LO/U-3.*
*ISSN 0035-7219*
BRITISH TAR INDUSTRY ASSOCIATION.
*LONDON  1, 1947-*
*LO/N14.*
*LD/U-1.  23, 1969-*

**ROAD TRAFFIC REPORTS.**
++*ROAD TRAFFIC REP.*
[MASON]
*HAVANT, HANTS. JA 1970-*
*CA/U13.     ED/N-1.     EX/U-1.     LO/N-1.     NO/U-1.     SH/U-1.*
*SO/U-1.*

**ROADS & ROAD CONSTRUCTION.**                           XXX
  SUBS (1973): INCORP. IN HIGHWAYS & ROAD
  CONSTRUCTION.

**ROCENKA STATNI KNIHOVNY CSSR V PRAZE.**
++*ROC. STATNI KNIH. CSSR PRAZE.*
STATNI KNIHOVNA CSSR PRAZE.
*PRAGUE  1962/1963(1964)-*
ENGL., GER., RUSS. SUMM.
*LO/N-3.*

ROCK MECHANICS. = FELSMECHANIK. = MECANIQUE
DES ROCHES.
+ +ROCK MECH.
INTERNATIONAL SOCIETY OF ROCK MECHANICS.
VIENNA 1(1), 1969-
PREV. FELSMECHANIK UND INGENIEURGEOLOGIE. =
ROCKMECHANICS AND ENGINEERING GEOLOGY FROM 1,
1963.
BH/U-1.    BL/U-1.    DR/U-1.    GL/U-2.    LO/N-4.    LO/N14.
LO/U-2.    LO/U11.    NW/U-1.    OX/U-8.    SH/U-3.
SO/U-1.
AD/U-2. 6, 1974-                    EX/U-1. 4, 1972-
SH/C-5. 3, 1971-
ISSN 0035-7448

ROCK MECHANICS: SUPPLEMENTUM.                              XXX
+ +ROCK MECH., SUPPL.
INTERNATIONAL SOCIETY OF ROCK MECHANICS.
[SPRINGER]
VIENNA & NEW YORK [NO.1], 1970-
PREV: ROCK MECHANICS & ENGINEERING GEOLOGY:
SUPPLEMENTUM FROM 1, 1964- 5, 1969.
LO/N14.

ROCK MECHANICS ABSTRACTS.
+ +ROCK MECH. ABSTR.
AMERICAN INSTITUTE OF MINING, METALLURGICAL
& PETROLEUM ENGINEERS.
NEW YORK 1, 1970-
COMPILED BY ROCK MECHANICS INFORMATION SERVICE
IMPERIAL COLLEGE OF SCIENCE & TECHNOLOGY.
GL/U-2.    LO/N14.
ISSN 0035-7456

ROCK MECHANICS & ENGINEERING GEOLOGY: SUPPL-
EMENTUM.                                                   XXX
+ +ROCK MECH. & ENG. GEOL., SUPPL.
INTERNATIONAL SOCIETY OF ROCK MECHANICS.
VIENNA [NO.] 1, 1964- 5, 1969.
SUBS: ROCK MECHANICS: SUPPLEMENTUM.
LO/N14.

ROCKY MOUNTAIN JOURNAL OF MATHEMATICS.
+ +ROCKY MT. J. MATH.
ROCKY MOUNTAIN MATHEMATICS CONSORTIUM.
MISSOULA, MONT. 1, 1971-
AD/U-1.    CA/U-2.    DB/U-2.    LO/N14.    OX/U-8.    RE/U-1.
SH/U-1.    SW/U-1.
BL/U-1. 3, 1973-                    GL/U-1. 4, 1974-
ISSN 0035-7596

ROCZNIK BIBLIOTEKI NARODOWEJ.
+ +ROCZ. BIBL. NAR.
BIBLIOTEKA NARODOWA.
WARSAW 1, MR 1965-
ANNU. ENGL. SUMM.
LO/S-9.    OX/U-1.

ROCZNIK DOCHODU NARODOWEGO.
+ +ROCZ. DOCHODU NARODOWEGO.
(POLAND) GLOWNY URZAD STATYSTYCZNY.
WARSAW 1960/1965(1966)-
ISSUED AS PART OF SERIES: ROCZNIKI BRANZOWE.
LO/N10.    LO/U-3.
BH/U-1. (1969)-

ROCZNIK KOMISJI HISTORYCZNOLITERACKIEJ, ODD-
ZIAL W KRAKOWIE, POLSKA AKADEMIA NAUK.
+ +ROCZ. KOM. HISTORYCZNOLIT. ODDZ. KRAKOW. POL.
AKAD. NAUK.
POLSKA AKADEMIA NAUK (ODDZIAL W KRAKOWIE):
KOMISJA HISTORYCZNOLITERACKA.
WROCLAW [NO.]1, OC 1963-
DB/S-1.

ROCZNIK KOMISJI NAUK PEDAGOGICZNYCH, POLSKA
AKADEMIA NAUK.
+ +ROC. KOM. NAUK PEDAGOG. POL. AKAD. NAUK.
WROCLAW 1, D 1961-
A.
BH/U-1. 9, 1969-

ROCZNIK KULTURALNY KUJAW I POMORZA.
+ +ROC. KULT. KUJAW & POMORZA.
KUJAWSKO-POMORSKIE TOWARZYSTWO KULTURALNE.
BYDGOSZCZ 1, 1963/1964(1965)-
A.
OX/U-1.

ROCZNIK MAZOWIECKI.
+ +ROCZ. MAZOWIECKI.
(POLAND) WOJEWODZKA RADA NARODOWA.
WARSAW 1, 1967-
ANNU.
OX/U-1.
BH/U-1. 3, 1970-

ROCZNIK MUZEUM W TORUNIU.
+ +ROC. MUZ. TORUNIU.
TORUN 1(1), 1962-
A. ADDED TITLE PAGE IN FR.: ANNUAIRE DE MUSEE
DE TORUN.
OX/U-1.

ROCZNIK NADNOTECKI.
+ +ROC. NADNOTECK.
POZNAN 1, 1966-
A.
OX/U-1.

ROCZNIK PILSKI.
+ +ROC. PILSK.
POLSKIE TOWARZYSTWO HISTORYCZNE: KOLO W PILE.
POZNAN 1, 1960-
A.
OX/U-1.

ROCZNIK STATYSTYCZNY GOSPODARKI MIESZKANIOWEJ
I KOMUNALNEJ.
+ +ROCZ. STAT. GOSPOD. MIESZKANIOWEJ & KOMUNALNEJ
(POLAND) GLOWNY URZAD STATYSTYCZNY POLSKIEJ
RZECZYPOSPOLITEJ LUDOWEJ.
WARSAW 1965(1967)-
LO/U-3.

ROCZNIK STATYSTYKI HANDLU ZAGRANICZNEGO.
+ +ROCZ. STAT. HANDLU ZAGRANICZNEGO.
(POLAND) GLOWNY URZAD STATYSTYCZNY POLSKIEJ
RZECZYPOSPOLITEJ LUDOWEJ.
WARSAW 1, 1965(1966)-
BH/U-1.    LO/U-3.

ROCZNIK STATYSTYKI HANDLU ZAGRANICZNEGO:
SERIA ROCZNIKI BRANZOWE.
+ +ROCZ. STAT. HANDLU ZAGRANICZNEGO, ROCZ.
BRANZOWE.
(POLAND) GLOWNY URAZAD STATYSTYCZNY POLSKIEJ
RZECZYPOSPOLITEJ LUDOWEJ.
WARSAW 1, 1965(1966)-
BH/U-1.    CC/U-1.    LO/U-3.

ROCZNIK STATYSTYCZNY INWESTYCJI I SRODKOW
TRWALYCH.
+ +ROCZ. STAT. INWESTYCJI & SRODKOW TRWALYCH.
(POLAND) GLOWNY URZAD STATYSTYCZNY.
WARSAW 1, 1946/1966(1968)-
NUMB. ALSO AS PART OF ROCZNIKI BRANZOWE.
(NO.1 OF ABOVE = NO. 11).
BH/U-1.    LO/N10.

ROCZNIK STATYSTYCZNY SZKOLNICTWA.                          XXX
+ +ROCZ. STAT. SZK. [RSSZ-A]
(POLAND) GLOWNY URZAD STATYSTYCZNY.
WARSAW 1, 1944/45- 1966/67(1967).//
NUMB. ALSO AS PART OF ROCZNIKI BRANZOWE.
(NO.1 OF ABOVE = NO.7).
BH/U-1.

ROCZNIK TORUNSKI.
+ +ROC. TORUNSKI.
TOWARZYSTWO MILOSNIKOW TORUNIA.
TORUN 1, 1966-
A.
OX/U-1.

ROCZNIK ZIEM ZACHODNICH I POLNOCNYCH.
TOWARZYSTWO ROZWOJU ZIEM ZACHODNICH.
WARSAW 1, 1960-
A.
OX/U-1.

RODOPSKI SBORNIK.
+ +RODOPSKI SB.
BULGARSKA AKADEMIJA NA NAUKITE: PROBLEMNA
KOMISIJA ZA IZUCHAVANE MINALOTO, BITA I KULT-
URATA NA NASELENIETO V RODOPITE.
SOFIA 1, 1965-
FR. & RUSS. SUMM.
OX/U-2.

ROLLARIENSIA. JAARBOEK VAN ...
GESCHIED- EN OUDHEIDKUNDIG GENOOTSCHAP VAN
ROESELARE EN OMMELAND.
ROESELARE 1, 1969-
LO/N-1.

ROLLS-ROYCE JOURNAL.
+ +ROLLS-ROYCE J.
ROLLS-ROYCE LTD.
DERBY [NO.]1, [1968]-
BH/U-1.    BR/U-3.    ED/N-1.    LO/N-4.    LO/N14.    OX/U-8.

**ROLLS-ROYCE OWNER.**
[OWNER PUBL.]
*ST. LEONARDS-ON-SEA, SX. 1(1), AG 1963- 1(8),
           AG 1964. //*
*LO/P-7.*
*ISSN 0035-7952*

**ROMANIA LITERARA.**
*+ +ROM. LIT.*
UNIUNEA SCRIITORILOR DIN REPUBLICA SOCIALISA
ROMANIA.
*BUCHAREST 1(1), OC 1968-*
WKLY.
*BL/U-1. 36, 1973-                    MA/U-1. 5(1), 1972-*

**ROMANISCHE ENTYMOLOGIEN.**
*+ +ROM. ENTYMOL.*
*HEIDELBERG NO.1, WINTER 1968-*
*LO/U-3.*

**ROMANO DROM. THE PAPER OF THE...**
*+ +ROM. DROM.*
NATIONAL GYPSY COUNCIL.
*LONDON 1, JE 1969-*
*ED/N-1.    LO/U-3.*

**ROMANTISME.**
SOCIETE DES ETUDES ROMANTIQUES.
[FLAMMARION]
*PARIS 1, 1971-*
S/T: REVUE DE LA SOCIETE DES ETUDES
ROMANTIQUES.
*AD/U-1.    BN/U-1.    CA/U-1.    DB/U-2.    EX/U-1.    GL/U-1.*
*OX/U-1.*
*NO/U-1. 7, 1974-*
*ISSN 0048-8593*

**ROMASHKA.**
VSESOJUZNYJ LENINSKIJ KOMMUNISTICHESKIJ SOJUZ
MOLODEZHI.
*MOSCOW NO.1, 1967-*
*BH/U-1.    CC/U-1.*

**RORSCHACH NEWSLETTER.**                              XXX
  SUBS (1969): BRITISH JOURNAL OF PROJECTIVE
  PSYCHOLOGY & PERSONALITY STUDY.

**ROSCOE REVIEW.**
*+ +ROSCOE REV.*
UNIVERSITY OF MANCHESTER: DEPARTMENT OF EXTRA-
MURAL STUDIES.
*MANCHESTER [NO.1], 1968-*
*DB/U-2.*

**ROSE BULLETIN.**
*+ +ROSE BULL.*
ROYAL NATIONAL ROSE SOCIETY.
*LONDON 1, 1970-*
*LO/N-2.    RE/U-1.*
*ED/N-1. OC 1971-*

**ROST I USTOJCHIVOST' RASTENIJ: SERIJA:
FIZIOLOGIJA RASTENIJ.**
*+ +ROST & USTOICH. RAST., FIZIOL. RAST.*
AKADEMIJA NAUK UKRAJINS'KOJI RSR: INSTYTUT
FIZIOLOHIJI ROSLYN.
*KIEV 1, 1965-*
*LO/N13.*

**ROSTRUM. THEATRE & MUSIC QUARTERLY.**
[ROSTRUM PUBL.]
*CAMBRIDGE NO.1, 1971-*
*ED/N-1.    OX/U-1.*

**ROTUNDA. THE BULLETIN OF THE ...**
ROYAL ONTARIO MUSEUM.
*TORONTO 1(1), 1968-*
*GL/U-1.    LO/N-2.    LO/N-4.*
*ISSN 0035-8495*

**ROUND-UP OF ECONOMIC STATISTICS.**
*+ +ROUND-UP ECON. STAT. (AUST.).*
(AUSTRALIA) DEPARTMENT OF THE TREASURY.
*CANBERRA NO.1, F 1973-*
MON.
*LO/U-3.*

**ROUND-UP NEWSLETTER.**
*+ +ROUND-UP NEWSL.*
UNIVERSITY OF THE WEST INDIES: INSTITUTE OF
EDUCATION.
*KINGSTON &C. NO.1, 1968-*
*OX/U-9.*

**ROYAL AUSTRALIAN PLANNING INSTITUTE JOURNAL.**       XXX
*+ +R. AUST. PLANN. INST. J.*
*MELBOURNE 8(3), 1970-*
PREV: AUSTRALIAN PLANNING INSTITUTE JOURNAL
FROM 1, D 1958- 8(2), 1970.
*CV/C-1.*
*ISSN 0004-9999*

**ROYAL GREEN JACKETS CHRONICLE.**
*+ +R. GREEN JACKETS CHRON.*
*WINCHESTER 1, 1966-*
*OX/U-1.*

**ROYAL STUART PAPERS.**
*+ +R. STUART PAP.*
ROYAL STUART SOCIETY.
*REDBRIDGE, SURREY NO.1, [1972]-*
MONOGR.
*LO/N-1.*
*CA/U-1. NO.3, 1973-*

**ROZPRAWY UNIWERSYTETU WARSZAWSKIEGO. DISSER-
TATIONES UNIVERSITATIS VARSAVIENSIS.**
*+ +ROZPR. UNIW. WARSZ.*
*WARSAW 1, 1962-*
MONOGR.
*BH/U-1.    OX/U-1.*

**ROZPRAWY WYDZIALU 3: NAUK MATEMATYCZNYCH I
PRZYRODNICZYCH, GDANSKIE TOWARZYSTWO NAUKOWE.**
*+ +ROZPR. WYDZ. 3., NAUK MAT. & PRZYR. GDANSK.
TOW. NAUKE.*
*GDANSK 1, 1964-*
ENGL. & RUSS. SUMM.
*CA/U-1.    LO/N14.*

**ROZPRAWY, WYZSZA SZKOLA ROLNICZA W SZCZECINIE.XX**
*+ +ROZP. WYZSZA SZK. ROLN. SZCZECINIE.*
*SZCZECIN NO.1, 1966- 31, 1972.*
MONOGR. SUBS: ROZPRAWY, AKADEMIA ROLNICZA W
SZCZECINIE.
*LO/N-3.*

**RUFF CUT. FANZINE OF POETRY & PROSE.**
[FLANGEBUCKET P.]
*ISLEWORTH, MIDDX. NO.1, 1968-*
*ED/N-1.*

**RUMA. REPORT OF UNIVERSITY MICROFILMS ACTIVITY.**
[UNIVERSITY MICROFILMS LTD.]
*HIGH WYCOMBE, BUCKS. 1(1), 1970-*
*ED/N-1.    OX/U-1.*

**RUMANIAN STUDIES.**
*+ +RUM. STUD.*
*LONDON 1, 1970-*
S/T: AN INTERNATIONAL ANNUAL OF THE HUMANI-
TIES & SOCIAL SCIENCES.
*ED/N-1.    LO/U-3.    OX/U-1.*
*SO/U-1. 1, 1970- 2, 1973.*

**RUNNING MAN. A NEW LIBERTARIAN MAGAZINE.**
[RUNNING MAN PUBL.]
*LONDON 1(1), MY/JE 1968- 1(3/5), S/OC 1968.//*
*ED/N-1.    OX/U-1.*

**RUNNYMEDE TRUST: EUROPEAN SUPPLEMENT.**
*+ +RUNNYMEDE TRUST, EUR. SUPPL.*
*LONDON NO.1, JA 1973-*
MON.
*ED/N-1.    LD/U-1.    OX/U-1.*

**RUNNYMEDE TRUST: INDUSTRIAL SUPPLEMENT.**          XXX
*+ +RUNNYMEDE TRUST, IND. SUPPL.*
*LONDON NO.29, JA 1973-*
PREV: RACE RELATIONS BULLETIN: INDUSTRIAL
SUPPLEMENT FROM NO.1, JE 1970- NO.28, D 1972.
*ED/N-1.    LD/U-1.    OX/U-1.*

**RUNNYMEDE TRUST BULLETIN. A MONTHLY SUMMARY
OF RACE RELATIONS INFORMATION.**                     XXX
*+ +RUNNYMEDE TRUST BULL.*
*LONDON NO.39, JA 1973-*
PREV: RACE RELATIONS BULLETIN FROM NO.1, MY
1969- NO.38, D 1972.
*ED/N-1.    HL/U-1.    LD/U-1.    NO/U-1.*

**RURAL AFRICANA. RESEARCH NOTES ON LOCAL
POLITICS & POLITICAL ANTHROPOLOGY.**
*+ +RUR. AFR.*
MICHIGAN STATE UNIVERSITY: AFRICAN STUDIES
CENTER.
*EAST LANSING, MICH. 1, MR 1967-*
CENTER SUBORD. TO: POLITICAL SCIENCE DEPART-
MENT.
*LO/U-8.*
*OX/U24. NO.2, JE 1967-\**

**RURAL DISTRICT REVIEW.**                                                          XXX
  SUBS (1972): DISTRICT COUNCILS REVIEW.

**RURAL MEDICINE.**
  + +RUR. MED.
  [RURAL ENVIRONMENT PUBL.]
  *LONDON 1, 1969- 3, 1972. //*
  S/T: A QUARTERLY JOURNAL ABOUT ENVIRONMENTAL
  HEALTH & GENERAL PRACTICE IN THE COUNTRYSIDE.
  *LD/U-1.*
  *CA/U-1. 3(3), 1972-*
  *ED/N-1. 3, 1972.*

**RURAL STUDIES: YORKSHIRE EAST RIDING.**
  + +RURAL STUD., YORKS. E. RIDING.
  EAST RIDING ASSOCIATION FOR RURAL STUDIES.
  *[HULL] 1, 1967-*
  A.
  *HL/U-2.*

**RUSI. JOURNAL OF THE ROYAL UNITED SERVICES
INSTITUTE FOR DEFENCE STUDIES.**                          XXX
  *LONDON 117, 1972-*
  PREV: JOURNAL, ROYAL UNITED SERVICES INSTITUTE
  FOR DEFENCE STUDIES FROM 116(662)- 116(664),
  1971.
  *BH/P-1.    LO/U-1.*

**RUSKIN NEWSLETTER.**
  + +RUSKIN NEWSL.
  RUSKIN ASSOCIATION.
  *BEMBRIDGE 1, AUTUMN 1969-*
  2/A.
  *LO/N-1.    MA/S-1.*

**RUSSELL. THE JOURNAL OF THE...**
  BERTRAND RUSSELL ARCHIVES.
  [MACMASTER UNIV. LIB. P.]
  *HAMILTON, ONT. 1971-*
  *LO/U-1.    LO/U-3.    SH/U-1.    SW/U-1.*
  *ISSN 0036-0163*

**RUSSIAN LITERATURE.**
  + +RUSS. LIT.
  [MOUTON]
  *THE HAGUE 1971-*
  *BN/U-1.    CA/U-1.    GL/U-1.    LO/N-1.    RE/U-1.    SH/U-1.*

**RUSSIAN LITERATURE TRIQUARTERLY.**
  + +RUSS. LIT. TRIQ.
  *ANN ARBOR, MICH. 1, 1971-*
  *BN/U-1.    DB/U-2.    ED/N-1.    GL/U-1.    MA/U-1.    NO/U-1.*
  *RE/U-1.    SH/U-1.    SW/U-1.*
  *BL/U-1. 4, 1972-                SO/U-1. 7, 1973-*
  *ISSN 0048-881X*

**RUSSIAN ULTRASONICS.**
  + +RUSS. ULTRASON.
  [MULTI-SCIENCE PUBL. CO.]
  *BRENTWOOD, ESSEX 1, 1971-*
  TRANSLATIONS OF RUSSIAN PAPERS.
  *ED/N-1.    LO/N14.    LO/N35.*
  *ED/N-1. 1(2), 1971-                OX/U-8. 1(2), 1971-*
  *XY/N-1. 1(2), 1971-*
  *ISSN 0048-8828*

**RUSSKAJA RECH'.**
  AKADEMIJA NAUK SSSR: INSTITUT RUSSKOGO JAZYKA.
  *MOSCOW NO.1, 1967-*
  2M. S/T: NAUCHNO-POPULJARNYJ ZHURNAL.
  *RE/U-1.*
  *CC/U-1. 1969-*                SA/U-1. 2, 1968-*
  *SW/U-1. 3, 1967-*
  *ISSN 0036-0368*

**RUSSKIJ JAZYK ZA RUBEZHOM.**
  + +RUSS. JAZYK RUBEZHOM.
  MOSKOVSKIJ UNIVERSITET: NAUCHNO-METODICHESKIJ
  TSENTR RUSSKOGO JAZYKA.
  *MOSCOW 1, 1967-*
  WITH RECORDS.
  *BH/U-1.    CC/U-1.    ED/U-1.    HL/U-1.    NO/U-1.    RE/U-1.*
  *SH/U-1.*
  *SW/U-1. 1, 1968-*

**RUSSKIJ JAZYK I SOVETSKOE OBSHCHESTVO.**
  + +RUSS. JAZYK & SOV. O-VO.
  AKADEMIJA NAUK SSSR: INSTITUT RUSSKOGO JAZYKA.
  *MOSCOW [1], 1968-*
  *CC/U-1.    GL/U-1.*

**RUTGERS JOURNAL OF COMPUTERS & THE LAW.**
  + +RUTGERS J. COMPUT. & LAW.
  RUTGERS UNIVERSITY: SCHOOL OF LAW.
  *NEWARK, N.J. 1, 1970-*
  *BL/U-1. 3, 1973-                SH/U-1. 3, 1974-*
  *ISSN 0048-8844*

**RYA MAGAZINE.**
  + +RYA MAG. (R. YACHT. ASS.).
  ROYAL YACHTING ASSOCIATION.
  *LONDON NO.1, 1968-*
  *ED/N-1.    OX/U-1.*

**RYBNOE KHOZJAJSTVO. RESPUBLIKANSKIJ MEZHVE-
DOMSTVENNYJ TEMATICHESKIJ NAUCHNYJ SBORNIK.**
  UKRAINSKIJ NAUCHNO-ISSLEDOVATEL'SKIJ INSTITUT
  RYBNOGO KHOZJAJSTVA.
  *KIEV 1, 1965-*
  *LO/N13.*

**S NARODOM - ZA NAROD.**
  SOJUZ BOR'BY ZA OSVOBOZHDENIE NARODOV ROSSII.
  *MUNICH 1, MR 1962-*
  *LO/N-3.*

**SABRAO NEWSLETTER.**
  + +SABRAO NEWSL.
  *MISIMI 1, 1969-*
  *CA/U11.*

**SAD TRAFFIC.**
  *BARNSLEY 1(1), 1969-*
  *LO/U-2.*

**SADLER'S WELLS MAGAZINE.**
  + +SADLER'S WELLS MAG.
  SADLER'S WELLS OPERA.
  *LONDON 1, D 1965-*
  *ED/N-1.*

**SADO RINKAI JIKENJO KENKYU NEMPO.
ANNUAL REPORT, SADO MARINE BIOLOGICAL STATION.**
  *NIIGATA NO.1, 1971-*
  *CA/U-2.    LO/N13.    XN/S-1.*

**SADOI SHARK.**
  UNION OF WRITERS OF TAJIKISTAN.
  *DUSHANBE NO.1, 1966-*
  S/T: A LITERARY & SOCIO-POLITICAL JOURNAL.
  *LO/U14.*

**SAE JOURNAL.**                                                      XXX
  SUBS (1970): AUTOMOTIVE ENGINEERING.

**SAFETY, HEALTH & WELFARE. NS.**                         XXX
  SUBS (1970): HEALTH & SAFETY AT WORK.

**SAFETY MAINTENANCE.**                                      XXX
  SUBS (1969): ENVIRONMENTAL CONTROL MANAGEMENT.

**SAFETY STANDARDS.**                                         XXX
  SUBS (1972): JOB SAFETY & HEALTH.

**SAGE PROFESSIONAL PAPERS IN COMPARATIVE POLITICS**
  + +SAGE PROF. PAP. COMP. POLIT.
  [SAGE PUBL. INC.]
  *BEVERLY HILLS 1, 1970-*
  *OX/U-1.    OX/U17.*
  *CA/U-1. 3, 1972-                RE/U-1. 4, 1973-*
  *ISSN 0080-5343*

**SAGE RESEARCH PROGRESS SERIES ON WAR, REVOLUTION
& PEACEKEEPING.**
  + +SAGE RES. PROG. SER. WAR REVOLUTION &
  PEACEKEEP.
  [SAGE PUBL. INC.]
  *BEVERLY HILLS 1, 1971-*
  *GL/U-1.*
  *ISSN 0080-536X*

**SAGE URBAN STUDIES ABSTRACTS.**
  + +SAGE URBAN STUD. ABSTR.
  [SAGE PUBL.]
  *BEVERLY HILLS; LONDON 1(1), F 1973-*
  Q.
  *BL/U-1.    DB/U-2.    GL/U-2.    MA/U-1.    NO/U-1.    SH/U-1.*
  *ISSN 0090-5747*

**SAGITTARIUS. BEITRAGE ZUR ERFORSCHUNG UND
PRAXIS ALTER UND NEUER KIRCHENMUSIK.**
  INTERNATIONAL HEINRICH SCHUTZ-GESELLSCHAFT.
  [BAERENREITER]
  *KASSEL &C. 1, 1966-*
  *OX/U-1.*
  *ISSN 0080-5408*

**ST. ANDREWS REVIEW.**
  + +ST. ANDREWS REV.
  ST. ANDREWS PRESBYTERIAN COLLEGE (LAURINBURG,
  N.C.).
  *LAURINBURG, N.C. 1(1), 1970-*
  S/T: A TWICE-YEARLY MAGAZINE OF THE ARTS &
  HUMANITIES.
  *LO/U-2.    OX/U-1.*
  *ISSN 0036-2751*

**SAINT LOUIS QUARTERLY.** XXX
+ +*ST. LOUIS Q.*
SAINT LOUIS COLLEGE.
*BAGUIO CITY, PHILIPP. 1(1), MR 1963- 7(1),*
*1969.//*
S/T: AN INTERDISCIPLINARY JOURNAL IN THE
SCIENCES AND THE HUMANITIES.
*LO/N-3.*
*LD/U-1. 5(3- 4), 1967.*
*LO/U14. 7(1), 1969.*

**SAINT LOUIS UNIVERSITY RESEARCH JOURNAL.**
+ +*ST. LOUIS UNIV. RES. J.*
SAINT LOUIS UNIVERSITY (PHILIPPINES): GRADUATE
SCHOOL OF ARTS & SCIENCES.
*BAGUIO CITY 1, 1970-*
S/T: AN INTERDISCIPLINARY JOURNAL IN THE
SCIENCES & THE HUMANITIES.
*LO/U14.*
*ISSN 0036-3014*

**ST. LUKE'S HOSPITAL GAZETTE.**
+ +*ST. LUKE'S HOSP. GAZ.*
[ROYAL UNIVERSITY MEDICAL SCHOOL]
*VALLETTA, MALTA 1, JE 1966-*
*GL/U-1. LO/M-1.*
*ISSN 0036-3081*

**SAITAMA DAIGAKU KIYO; SHIZEN KAGAKU HEN. =**
**JOURNAL OF SAITAMA UNIVERSITY; NATURAL**
**SCIENCE.**
SAITAMA DAIGAKU; KYOYOBU.
*URAWA, JAP. NO.1, 1965-*
IN JAP. BODY ALSO CALLED IN ENGL.: SAITAMA
UNIVERSITY; COLLEGE OF LIBERAL ARTS.
*LO/N-2. LO/N13.*

**SAIVA SIDDHANTA MAHASAMAJAM.**
*MADRAS 1(1), 1966-*
*OX/U13.*

**SALES ENGINEER.** XXX
+ +*SALES ENG.*
INSTITUTION OF SALES ENGINEERS.
*LEAMINGTON, WARWICK. 1, 1967- 3(1), 1971.*
SUBS: SELLING ENGINEERING.
*CA/U-1. 2(2), 1969- ED/N-1. 2, 1969-*
*OX/U-1. 2(2), 1969-*
*ISSN 0048-9042*

**SALG NEWSLETTER.**
+ +*SALG NEWSL.*
SOUTH ASIA LIBRARY GROUP.
*LONDON NO.1, 1973-*
2/A.
*LO/N12. LO/U-1. LO/U-8. LO/U14.*

**SALMON NET. MAGAZINE OF THE ...**
SALMON NET FISHING ASSOCIATION OF SCOTLAND.
*[ABERDEEN] 1, 1965-*
*AD/U-1.*

**SAMADHI. CAHIERS D'ETUDES BOUDDHIQUES.**
INSTITUT BELGE DES HAUTES ETUDES BOUDDHIQUES:
CENTRE D'ETUDES BOUDDHIQUES ANANDA.
*BRUSSELS 1, 1967-*
Q.
*LO/N12.*
*CA/U-1. 7, 1973- LO/U14. 5(1), 1971-*
*ISSN 0036-3685*

**SAMFERDSEL, TRANSPORTEKONOMISK INSTITUTT,**
**NORGES TEKNISK-NATURVITENSKAPELIGE FORSK-**
**NINGSRAD.**
+ +*SAMFERDSEL TRANSP. INST. NORG. TEK.-NATURVIT-*
*ENSK. FORSK.*
*OSLO NR.1, 1968-*
*OX/U-1.*

**SAMMLUNG MUSIKWISSENSCHAFTLICHER ABHANDLUNGEN.**
+ +*SAMML.-MUSIKWISS. ABH.*
[LIBRAIRIE VALENTIN KOERNER]
*BADEN-BADEN 1, 1971-*
*LO/N-1.*

**SAMOLETOSTROENIE I TEKHNIKA VOZDUSHNOGO FLOTA.**
+ +*SAMOLETOSTR. & TEKH. VOZDUSHN. FLOTA. [STVO-B]*
KHAR'KOVSKIJ AVIATSIONNYJ INSTITUT.
*KHAR'KOV 1, 1965-*
S/T: RESPUBLIKANSKIJ MEZHVEDOMSTVENNYJ
NAUCHNO-TEKHNICHESKIJ SBORNIK.
*LO/N13. 2, 1965-**

**SAMPE JOURNAL.** XXX
+ +*SAMPE J.*
SOCIETY FOR THE ADVANCEMENT OF MATERIAL &
PROCESS ENGINEERING.
*LOS ANGELES 1, ?1965-*
ISSUE 7(6), 1972 ENTITLED: MATERIALS &
PROCESS TECHNOLOGY. SPONS. BODY: SOCIETY OF
AEROSPACE MATERIAL & PROCESS ENGINEERS
FROM 1, 1965- 8(5), 1972. FROM 8(6), 1973
SPONS. BODY AS ABOVE.
*LO/N14. 5, 1969-*
*ISSN 0036-0813*

**SAMPE QUARTERLY.**
+ +*SAMPE Q.*
SOCIETY FOR THE ADVANCEMENT OF MATERIAL &
PROCESS ENGINEERING.
*AZUSA, CALIF. 1(1), 1969(1970)-*
SPONS. BODY: SOCIETY OF AEROSPACE MATERIAL
& PROCESS ENGINEERS FROM 1(1), 1969(1970)-
4(1), 1972. FROM 4(2), 1973 SPONS.
BODY AS ABOVE.
*LO/N14. XS/R10.*
*ISSN 0036-0821*

**SAMPHIRE.**
*IPSWICH, SUFFOLK NO.1, 1968-*
*LO/U-1. LO/U-3.*
*ISSN 0036-388X*

**SAN CARLOS PUBLICATIONS: SERIES B: NATURAL**
**SCIENCES.**
+ +*SAN CARLOS PUBL., B. [SCBN-A]*
UNIVERSITY OF SAN CARLOS (PHILIPPINES).
*CEBU NO.1, 1964-*
*LO/N-2.*

**SAN FRANCISCO EARTHQUAKE.**
*SAN FRANCISCO 1(1), 1967-*
Q.
*OX/U-1.*
*LO/U-2. 1(2), 1968-*
*ISSN 0036-4126*

**SANGYO KOGEI SHIKENJO HOKOKU. BULLETIN OF**
**INDUSTRIAL ARTS INSTITUTE.** XXX
SANGYO KOGEI SHIKENJO. XXX
*TOKYO NO.42, 1965- 58, 1969 ...*
PREV: KOGEI KENKYU FROM NO.1, 1941- 41, 1963.

**SANTA FE LITERARIA.**
+ +*ST. FE LIT.*
*SANTA FE, ARGENT. 1(1), 1970-*
S/T: PANORAMA BIBLIOGRAFICO MENSUAL.
*LO/N-1.*
*ISSN 0036-4533*

**SANTIAGO. REVISTA DE LA UNIVERSIDAD DE**
**ORIENTE.**
*SANTIAGO DE CUBA 1(1), 1970-*
*LO/N-1.*
*ISSN 0048-9115*

**SAPPORO BULLETIN.**
+ +*SAPPORO BULL.*
HOKKAIDO DAIGAKU: BOTANIC GARDEN.
*SAPPORO NO.1, 1963-*
*LO/N-2. XN/S-1.*

**SARTONIA.**
RIJKSUNIVERSITEIT TE GENT: MUSEUM VOOR DE
GESCHIEDENIS VAN DE WETENSCHAPPEN.
*GHENT NO.1, 1966-*
*LO/M24.*

**SARTRYCK OCH PRELIMINARA RAPPORTER.**
+ +*SARTRYCK PRELIM. RAPP.*
INGENIORSVETENSKAPSAKADEMIEN: PALKOMMISSIONEN.
*STOCKHOLM 1, 1966-*
2&3, 1966 BEAR COMMISSION'S EARLIER NAME
PALKOMMITTEN.
*LO/N14.*

**SATIRE NEWSLETTER.**
+ +*SATIRE NEWSL.*
NEW YORK STATE COLLEGE.
*ONEONTA 1, 1963-*
*BT/U-1. CV/U-1. LO/U-1. OX/U-1.*
*CC/U-1. 5, 1967-*
*ISSN 0036-4967*

**SATIS. SCIENCE & TECHNOLOGY INFORMATION**
**SOURCES FOR TEACHERS.**
SCHOOLS COUNCIL (GB).
*LOUGHBOROUGH, LEICS. 1, 1969-*
*ED/N-1. LO/U11. LO/U12. OX/U-1.*
*SW/U-1. 3, 1971-*

SATURDAY REVIEW (SAN FRANCISCO).                                 XXX
  SUBS (1973): SATURDAY REVIEW OF THE ...
  (ARTS; EDUCATION; SCIENCES; & SOCIETY.

SATURDAY REVIEW OF THE ARTS.                                     XXX
  + + SATURDAY REV. ARTS.
  SAN FRANCISCO 1(1- 4), 1973.
  PREV: PART OF SATURDAY REVIEW (SAN FRANCISCO)
  FROM 1, AG 1924- 55(52), D 1972. SUBS. PART
  OF: SATURDAY REVIEW/WORLD.
  GL/U-1.     LO/U-1.      MA/P-1.**
  HL/U-1.  1(3- 4), 1973.

SATURDAY REVIEW OF EDUCATION.                                    XXX
  + + SATURDAY REV. EDUC.
  SAN FRANCISCO 1(1- 4), 1973.
  PREV: PART OF SATURDAY REVIEW (SAN FRANCISCO)
  FROM 1, AG 1924- 55(52), D 1972. SUBS. PART
  OF: SATURDAY REVIEW/WORLD.
  GL/U-1.     LO/U-1.      MA/P-1.**
  HL/U-1.  1(3- 4), 1973.
  OX/U-1.  1(4), 1973.

SATURDAY REVIEW OF THE SCIENCES.                                 XXX
  + + SATURDAY REV. SCI.
  SAN FRANCISCO 1(1- 4), 1973.
  PREV: PART OF SATURDAY REVIEW (SAN FRANCISCO)
  FROM 1, AG 1924- 55(52), D 1972. SUBS. PART
  OF: SATURDAY REVIEW/WORLD.
  GL/U-1.     LO/U-1.      MA/P-1.**
  HL/U-1.  1(3- 4), 1973.
  OX/U-1.  1(3- 4), 1973.

SATURDAY REVIEW OF THE SOCIETY.                                  XXX
  + + SATURDAY REV. SOC.
  SAN FRANCISCO 1(1- 4), 1973.
  PREV: PART OF SATURDAY REVIEW (SAN FRANCISCO)
  FROM 1, AG 1924- 55(52), D 1972. SUBS. PART
  OF: SATURDAY REVIEW/WORLD.
  GL/U-1.     LO/U-1.      MA/P-1.**
  OX/U-1.  1(4), 1973.

SAVACOU.  A JOURNAL OF THE ...
  CARIBBEAN ARTISTS MOVEMENT.
  KINGSTON, JAMAICA NO.1, JE 1970-
  Q.
  OX/U-9
  LO/U-8.  NO.2, 1970-
  LO/U-2.  NO.7- 8, 1973.
  ISSN 0036-5068

SAVANNA.
  AHMADU BELLO UNIVERSITY.
  ZARIA, NIGERIA  1(1), JE 1972-
  2/A. S/T: A JOURNAL OF THE ENVIRONMENTAL AND
  SOCIAL SCIENCES.
  AD/U-1.     BL/U-1.     LO/N-1.     LO/N13.     LO/S13.     LO/U-3.
  NO/U-1.     OX/U-9.     SH/U-1.     SW/U-1.

SAWTRI BULLETIN.
  + + SAWTRI BULL. (S. AFR. WOOL TEXT. RES. INST.).
  SOUTH AFRICA WOOL TEXTILE RESEARCH INSTITUTE.
  PORT ELIZABETH  1, 1967-
  LO/N14.

SBIRKA PRAMENU A PRIRUCEK K DEJINAM UNIVER-
SITY KARLOVY.
  + + SB. PRAMENU & PRIRUCEK DEJINAM UNIV. KARLOVY.
  KARLOVA UNIVERSITA V PRAZE.
  PRAGUE  1, 1961-
  CA/U-1.     LA/U-1.     OX/U-1.

SBORNIK, ARCHEOLOGICKY USTAV (POBOCKA V BRNE)
CESKOSLOVENSKA AKADEMIE VED.
  + + SB. ARCHEOL. USTAV (POBOCKA V BRNE) CESK.
  AKAD. VED.
  BRNO  1, 1960-
  OX/U-1.  2, 1963-                     OX/U-2.  2, 1963-

SBORNIK CESKOSLAVENSKE SPOLECNOSTI ARCHEOLOG-
ICKE. = RECUEIL DES TRAVAUX DE LA SOCIETE
PREHISTORIQUE TCHECOSLOVAQUE.
  + + SB. CESK. SPOL. ARCHAEOL.
  CESKOSLOVENSKA SPOLECNOST ARCHEOLOGICKA.
  BRNO  1, 1961-
  GER. SUMM.
  LO/S10.     OX/U-2.
  LO/N-3.

SBORNIK DOKLADOV I SOOBSHCHENIJ LINGVISTICH-
ESKOGO OBSHCHESTVA.
  + + SB. DOKL. & SOOBSHCH. LINGVISTICHESK. O-VA.
  GOSUDARSTVENNYJ PEDAGOGICHESKIJ INSTITUT:
  LINGVISTICHESKOE OBSHCHESTVO.
  KALININ  1, 1969-
  ENGL. CONT. LISTS & INTRODUCTION.
  CC/U-1.

SBORNIK FILOZOFICKEJ FAKULTY UNIVERZITY KOM-
ENSKEHO: GRAECOLATINA ET ORIENTALIA.
  + + SB. FILOZ. FAK. UNIV. KOMENSKEHO, GRAECOLAT. &
  ORIENT.
  BRATISLAVA  1, 1969-
  FR., GER., ENGL. OR LAT.
  LO/U14.     OX/U-1.
  CA/U-1.  1971-

SBORNIK FILOZOFICKEJ FAKULTY UNIVERZITY
KOMENSKEHO: MARXIZMUS-LENINIZMUS.
  + + SB. FIL. FAK. UNIV. KOMENSK., MARXIZM.-LENIN-
  IZM.
  BRATISLAVA  [NO.]1, 1962-
  ANNU. SUMM. IN GER. & RUSS.  ALSO NUMBERED AS
  PART OF GEN. SER. OF ABOVE MAIN TITLE, FROM
  ROC. 13.
  LO/U-3.     OX/U-1.

SBORNIK FILOZOFICKEJ FAKULTY UNIVERZITY
KOMENSKEHO: MUSAICA.
  + + SB. FIL. FAK. UNIV. KOMENSK., MUSAICA.
  BRATISLAVA  [NO.]1, 1961-
  A.  SUMM. IN ENGL., FR. & GER.  ALSO NUMBERED
  AS PART OF GEN. SER. OF ABOVE MAIN TITLE,
  FROM ROC. 12.  ON T.P. AS  ROC. 12(1).
  LO/N-3.
  SW/U-1.

SBORNIK FILOZOFICKEJ FAKULTY UNIVERZITY
KOMENSKEHO: OECONOMICA. (ORIG: POLITICKA
EKONOMIA).
  + + SB. FIL. FAK. UNIV. KOMENSK., OECON.
  BRATISLAVA  [NO.]1, 1963-
  A.  SUMM. IN GER. & RUSS.  SERIES TITLE VARIES
  FIRST ISSUE: ... POLITICKA EKONOMIA.  ALSO
  NUMBERED AS PART OF GEN. SER. OF ABOVE MAIN
  TITLE, FROM ROC. 14.
  LO/U-3.
  ED/N-1.  6, 1968-
  LO/N-3.  1- 2, 1964.

SBORNIK FILOZOFICKEJ FAKULTY UNIVERZITY
KOMENSKEHO: PHILOSOPHICA.
  + + SB. FIL. FAK. UNIV. KOMENSK., PHIL.
  BRATISLAVA  [NO.1], 1960-
  A.  SUMM. IN FR., GER., RUSS.  NUMBERED AS
  PART OF GEN. SER. OF ABOVE MAIN TITLE FROM
  ROC. 10.  ISSUES OF SUBSERIES NUMBERED FROM 3.
  OX/U-1.
  XY/N-1.  ROC 8/9, 1967/68(1969)-

SBORNIK FILOZOFICKEJ FAKULTY UNIVERZITY
KOMENSKEHO: PSYCHOLOGICA.
  + + SB. FIL. FAK. UNIV. KOMENSK., PSYCHOL.
  BRATISLAVA  [NO.]1, 1961-
  A.  SUMM. IN ENGL., FR., GER., RUSS.  ALSO
  NUMBERED AS PART OF GEN. SER. OF ABOVE MAIN
  TITLE, FROM ROC. 12.
  LD/U-1.     LO/N-3.

SBORNIK MATERIALOV, PERMSKIJ NAUCHNO-ISSLEDO-
VATEL'SKIJ UGOL'NYJ INSTITUT.                                    000
  SEE: NAUCHNE TRUDY ...

SBORNIK, MOSKOVSKIJ ... INSTITUT STALI I
SPLAVOV.*
  + + SB. MOSK. INST. STALI SPLAVOV. [SMSS-A]
  MOSCOW  1, 1932-
  MONOGR.  TITLE EXPANDED FROM SBORNIK, MOSKOV-
  SKIJ ... INSTITUT STALI WITH 40, 1962.
  BH/U-1.  40, 1962-                LO/N13.  23, 1946-*

SBORNIK NAUCHNO-ISSLEDOVATEL'SKIKH RABOT PO
LESNOMU KHOZJAJSTVU.                                             XXX
  + + SB. NAUCHNO-ISSLED. RAB. LESN. KHOZ. [SKLK-A]
  LENINGRADSKIJ NAUCHNO-ISSLEDOVATEL'SKIJ
  MOSCOW; LENINGRAD  6, 1959-
  ENGL SUMM.  PREV: SBORNIK RABOT PO LESNOMU
  KHOZJAJSTVU FROM 2, 1958- 5, 1962.
  LO/N13.

SBORNIK NAUCHNYKH RABOT, KIEVSKIJ TORGOVO-
EKONOMICHESKIJ INSTITUT.
  + + SB. NAUCHN. RAB. KIEV. TORG.-EKON. INST.
  KIEV  1, 1968-
  GL/U-1.

SBORNIK NAUCHNYKH RABOT, KURGANSKAJA OBLAST-
NAJA GOSUDARSTVENNAJA SEL'SKOKHOZJAJSTVENNAJA
OPYTNAJA STANTSIJA.
  + + SB. NAUCHN. RAB. KURGAN. OBL. GOS. S-KH. OPYTN
  STN.
  CHELJABINSK  1, 1966-
  LO/N13.

SBORNIK NAUCHNYKH TRUDOV, KAZAKHSKIJ GORNO-
METALLURGICHESKIJ INSTITUT.                                         XXX
  SUBS (1960): TRUDY, KAZAKHSKIJ POLITEKHNICH-
  ESKIJ INSTITUT.

SBORNIK NAUCHNYKH TRUDOV, KAZAKHSKIJ POLITEKH-
NICHESKIJ INSTITUT.                                                 000
  SEE: TRUDY, KAZAKHSKIJ POLITEKHNICHESKIJ
  INSTITUT.

SBORNIK PEDAGOGICKE FAKULTY UNIVERSITY
KARLOVY - HISTORIE.
+ +SB. PEDAGOG. FAK. UNIV. KARLOVY, HIST.
  PRAGUE  1, 1966-
  GER. SUMM.
  LO/N-3.

SBORNIK PRAC CHEMICKEJ FAKULTY SVST.
+ +SB. PR. CHEM. FAK. SVST.
  SLOVENSKA VYSOKA SKOLA TECHNICKA: CHEMICKA
  FAKULTA.
  BRATISLAVA  1, 1961-
  GER. & RUSS. SUMM.
  LO/S-3.

SBORNIK PRACI FILOSOFICKE FAKULTY BRNENSKE
UNIVERSITY: RADA HUDEBNEVEDNA H.
+ +SB. PR. FIL. FAK. BRN. UNIV., RADA HUDEBN. H.
  UNIVERSITA J.E. PURKYNE V BRNE.
  BRNO   CAST (H)1, 1966-
  VARIOUS LANGS.  SERIES BEGINS WITH ROC. 15 OF
  THE SBORNIK.
  LO/N-3.  2, 1967.

SBORNIK PRACI HISTORICKYCH.                                         000
  SEE: ACTA UNIVERSITATIS PALACKIANAE OLOMUC-
  ENSIS: HISTORICA.

SBORNIK PRACI, VYZKUMNY USTAV ZELEZORUDNYCH
DOLU A HRUDKOVEN N.P. EJPOVICE.
  HRUDKOVEN N.P. EJPOVICE.
  MNISEK  1, 1960-
  ENGL., GER. & RUSS. SUMM.

SBORNIK RABOT ASPIRANTOV, VORONEZHSKIJ GOSUD-
ARSTVENNYJ UNIVERSITET.
+ +SB. RAB. ASPIR. VORONEZH. GOS. UNIV.
  VORONEZH  1(1), 1965-
  GL/U-1.  3(1), 1967-

SBORNIK RABOT PO LESNOMU KHOZJAJSTVU.                               XXX
  SUBS (1963): SBORNIK NAUCHNO-ISSLEDOVATEL'-
  SKIKH RABOT PO LESNOMU KHOZJAJSTVU.

SBORNIK RABOT MOSKOVSKOJ GIDROMETEOROLOGI-
CHESKOJ OBSERVATORII.
+ +SB. RAB. MOSK. GIDROMETEOROL. OBS.
  MOSKOVSKAJA GIDROMETEOROLOGICHESKAJA OBSERV-
  ATORIJA.
  MOSCOW  1, 1960-
  SPONS. BODY ALSO: GLAVNOE UPRAVLENIE GIDRO-
  METEOROLOGICHESKOJ SLUZHBY PRI SOVETE
  MINISTROV SSSR.
  LO/N13.  3, 1968-
  BH/U-1.  3, 1968.

SBORNIK TRUDOV, DONETSKIJ NAUCHNO-ISSLEDO-
VATEL'SKIJ INSTITUT CHERNOJ METALLURGII.
+ +SB. TR. DONETSK. NAUCHNO-ISSLED. INST. CHERN.
  METALL.
  MOSCOW  2, 1965-
  NO DATA AVAILABLE REGARDING VOL.1.  TITLE
  VARIES: VOL2 'TRUDY'.
  LO/N13.

SBORNIK TRUDOV, KHAR'KOVSKIJ ZOOTEKHNICHESKIJ
INSTITUT.                                                          XXX
  SUBS (1963): NAUCHNYE TRUDY, KHAR'KOVSKIJ
  ZOOVETERINARNYJ INSTITUT.

SBORNIK UVTI: SOCIOLOGIE A HISTORIE
ZEMEDELSTVI.
+ +SB. UVTI, SOCIOL. & HIST. ZEMED.
  (CZECHOSLOVAKIA) MINISTERSTVO ZEMEDELSTVI,
  LESNIHO A VODNIHO HOSPODARSTVI: USTAV VEDECKO-
  TECHNICKYCH INFORMACI.
  PRAGUE  1(38), JL 1965-
  ENGL. SUMM. NUMBERED ALSO AS PART OF MAIN SER.
  LO/N-3.

SBORNIK VYSOKE SKOLY CHEMICKO-TECHNOLOGICKE
V PRAZE: POTRAVINARSKA TECHNOLOGIE.                                XXX
  SUBS (1966): SBORNIK VYSOKE SKOLY CHEMICKO-
  TECHNOLOGICKE V PRAZE: POTRAVINY.

SBORNIK VYSOKE SKOLY CHEMICKO-TECHNOLOGICKE
V PRAZE: POTRAVINY.                                                XXX
+ +SB. VYS. SK. CHEM.-TECHNOL. PRAZE, POTRAVINY.
  PRAGUE  9, 1966-
  PREV: SBORNIK VYSOKE SKOLY CHEMICKO-
  TECHNOLOGICKE V PRAZE: POTRAVINARSKA
  TECHNOLOGIE FROM 1, 1957- 8, 1964.
  LO/N13.   XM/R-1.   XS/F10.   XS/R-2.

SBORNIK VYSOKEJ SKOLY EKONOMICKEJ.
+ +SB. VYS. SK. EKON.
  BRATISLAVA  1, 1960-
  ENGL., GER. & RUSS. SUMM.
  BH/U-1.   LO/N-3.

SBORNIK VYSOKE SKOLY ZEMEDELSKE V BRNE: RADA
D: SPISY FAKULTY PROVOZNE EKONOMICKE.                              XXX
+ +SB. VYS. SK. ZEMED. BRNE, D.
  BRUENN  NO.1, 1965-
  ENGL. FR. GER. & RUSS. SUMM.  PART CONT. OF:
  SBORNIK BYSOKE SKOLY ZEMEDELSKE V BRNE: RADA
  A: SPISY FAKULTY AGRONOMICKE A FAKULTY
  PROVOZNE EKONOMICKE FROM 1953.
  LO/N13.

SCALE MODELS.
[MODEL & ALLIED PUBL. LTD.]
  HEMEL HEMPSTEAD, HERTS.  1(1), 1969-
  M.
  ED/N-1.   LO/N14.   OX/U-1.
  ISSN 0036-5432

SCAN.  SPECTROPHOTOMETRY, CHROMATOGRAPHY,
ANALYTICAL NEWS.                                                   XXX
  PYE UNICAM LTD.
  CAMBRIDGE  1973-
  3/A.  INCORP: COLUMN FROM 1(1), 1965- NO.15,
  1972; & SPECTROVISION FROM NO.1, 1956- NO.28,
  1972.
  CA/U-2.   ED/N-1.   LO/N14.   OX/U-8.

SCANDINAVIAN BUILDING ABSTRACTS.                                   000
  SEE: ARTIKKELINDEKS FOR BYGG.

SCANDINAVIAN FOREST ECONOMICS.
+ +SCAND. FOR. ECON.
  HELSINKI  1, 1973-
  OX/U-3.

SCANDINAVIAN JOURNAL OF DENTAL RESEARCH.                           XXX
+ +SCAND. J. DENT. RES.
  NORDISKA ODONTOLOGISKA FORENINGEN.
  [MUNKSGAARD]
  COPENHAGEN  78, 1970-
  PREV: ODONTOLOGISK TIDSKRIFT FROM 1, 1893-
  77, 1969.
  LD/U-1.
  ISSN 0029-845X

SCANDINAVIAN JOURNAL OF IMMUNOLOGY.
+ +SCAND. J. IMMUNOL.
  [UNIVERSITETSFORLAGET]
  OSLO  1, 1972-
  Q.
  AD/U-1.   CA/M-1.   LO/M12.   OX/U-8.

SCANDINAVIAN JOURNAL OF INFECTIOUS DISEASES.
+ +SCAND. J. INFEC. DIS.
  [ALMQVIST & WIKSELL]
  STOCKHOLM  1, 1969-
  GL/U-1.   LO/U-1.   NW/U-1.
  CA/M-7.  6, 1974-
  ISSN 0036-5548

SCANDINAVIAN JOURNAL OF INFECTIOUS DISEASES:
SUPPLEMENTUM.
+ +SCAND. J. INFEC. DIS., SUPPL.
  [ALMQVIST & WIKSELL]
  STOCKHOLM  1, 1970-
  BL/U-1.   LO/U-1.

SCANDINAVIAN JOURNAL OF METALLURGY.
+ +SCAND. J. METALL.
  [JERNKONTORET]
  STOCKHOLM  1, 1972-
  CONTINUES MATERIAL IN ENGLISH PREVIOUSLY PUBL.
  IN JERNKONTORETS ANNALER FROM 1, 1817.
  GL/U-2.   LD/U-1.   LO/N14.   LO/U28.   SH/U-3.
  XS/R10.

SCANDINAVIAN JOURNAL OF REHABILITATION MEDICINE.
+ +SCAND. J. REHABIL. MED.
  GOTHENBURG  1, 1969-
  LO/N13.   NW/U-1.
  ISSN 0036-5505

**SCANDINAVIAN JOURNAL OF RHEUMATOLOGY.**  XXX
++*SCAND. J. RHEUMATOL.*
SCANDINAVIAN SOCIETY OF RHEUMATOLOGISTS.
*STOCKHOLM 1(1), 1972-*
ENGL. PREV: ACTA RHEUMATOLOGICA SCANDINAVICA
FROM 1, 1955- 17(4), 1971.
*BL/U-1.*

**SCANDINAVIAN JOURNAL OF SOCIAL MEDICINE.**  XXX
++*SCAND. J. SOC. MED.*
NORDISK SOCIALMEDICINSK FOERENING.
[ALMQVIST & WIKSELL]
*STOCKHOLM 1, 1973-*
3/A. PREV: ACTA SOCIO-MEDICA SCANDINAVICA
FROM 1, 1969- 4, 1972.
*MA/U-1.    SH/U-1.*

**SCANDINAVIAN JOURNAL OF THORACIC & CARDIOVASCU-
LAR SURGERY: SUPPLEMENT.**
++*SCAND. J. THORAC. & CARDIOVASC. SURG., SUPPL.*
[ALMQVIST & WIKSELL]
*STOCKHOLM [NO.]1, 1969-*
*BL/U-1.*

**SCANDINAVIAN PUBLIC LIBRARY QUARTERLY.**
++*SCAND. PUBLIC LIBR. Q.*
*VALBY, DEN.  1, 1968-*
PUBL. BY SCANDINAVIAN STATE DIRECTORS OF
PUBLIC LIBRARIES. ENGL.
*DB/U-2.    ED/N-1.    ED/P-1.    GL/U-2.    LO/U-2.    LV/P-1.*
*OX/U-1.*
*ISSN 0036-5602*

**SCANDINAVIAN SHIP ABSTRACT JOURNAL.**
++*SCAND. SHIP ABSTR. J.*
NORWEGIAN CENTRE FOR INFORMATICS.
*OSLO  1, 1973-*
*LO/N14.*

**SCHACHSPEILER.**  000
SEE: CHESS PLAYER.

**SCHEDAE PHILOSOPHICAE.**  000
SEE: ZESZYTY NAUKOWE UNIWERSYTETU JAGIELLON-
SKIEGO: PRACE FILOZOFICZNE.

**SCHEIDEWEGE.  VIERTELJAHRESSCHRIFT FUR
SKEPTISCHES DENKEN.**
[KLOSTERMANN]
*FRANKFURT AM MAIN 1(1), 1971-*
*LO/N-1.    OX/U-1.*
*ISSN 0048-9336*

**SCHISM.  A JOURNAL OF DIVERGENT AMERICAN
OPINIONS.**
[SCHISM PUBL. CO.]
*MT. VERNON, OHIO 1(1), 1969-*
Q.
*OX/U-9.*
*ISSN 0036-6110*

**SCHIZOPHRENIA.**
AMERICAN SCHIZOPHRENIA FOUNDATION.
*MINNEAPOLIS 1(1), 1969-*
*OX/U-8.*
*ISSN 0036-6129*

**SCHIZOPHRENIC SYNDROME.**  XXX
[BRUNNER/MAZEL]
*NEW YORK &C. 1[1], 1971.*
SUBS: ANNUAL REVIEW OF THE SCHIZOPHRENIC
SYNDROME.
*GL/U-1.    LO/U-1.    OX/U-8.*

**SCHOLARLY PUBLISHING.**
[UNIVERSITY OF TORONTO P.]
*TORONTO 1, OC 1969-*
Q.
*CA/U-1.    CR/N-1.    LO/N15.    MA/U-1.    OX/U-1.*
*ED/N-1.  2, OC 1970-*
*LO/N-1.  1(4), JL 1970-*
*ISSN 0036-634X*

**SCHOOL LEAVER.**
++*SCH. LEAVER.*
[DOMINION P. LTD.]
*ED/N-1.    OX/U-1.*

**SCHOOL LIBRARIES.**  XXX
SUBS (1972): SCHOOL MEDIA QUARTERLY.

**SCHOOL MEDIA QUARTERLY.**  XXX
++*SCH. MEDIA Q.*
AMERICAN ASSOCIATION OF SCHOOL LIBRARIANS.
*FULTON, MO.  1, FALL 1972-*
PREV: SCHOOL LIBRARIES FROM 1, 1951- 21,
SUMMER 1972.
*DB/U-2.*

**SCHRIFTEN ZUR JUDENTUMSKUNDE.**
++*SCHR. JUDENTUMSKDE.*
SCHWEIZER EVANGELISCHEN JUDENMISSION.
[THEOLOGISCHER VERLAG]
*ZURICH 1, 1971-*
*CA/U-1.    LO/N-1.*

**SCHRIFTEN, OSTERREICHISCHE KULTURINSTITUT
(CAIRO).**
++*SCHR. OSTERR. KULTURINST. (CAIRO).*
*CAIRO 1, 1969-*
+*OXSOHR. VERFASSUNGSGESCH.*
[DUNCKER & HUMBLOT]
*BERLIN 1, 1961-*
*LO/N-1.*

**SCHRIFTEN, ZENTRALINSTITUT FUR WIRTSCHAFTS-
WISSENSCHAFTEN, DEUTSCHE AKADEMIE DER WISSEN-
SCHAFTEN ZU BERLIN.**
++*SCHR. ZENTRALINST. WIRTSCHAFTSWISS. DTSCH.
AKAD. WISS. BERL.*
*BERLIN 1, 1972-*
*OX/U-1.*

**SCHRIFTENREIHE DES FIRMENARCHIVS, BADISCHE
ANILIN-UND SODA-FABRIK.**
++*SCHRIFTENR. FIRMENARCH. BADISCHE ANILIN-
SODA-FABR.*
*LUDWIGSHAFEN AM RHEIN 1, 1968-*
*LO/N14.*

**SCHRIFTENREIHE, INTERNATIONALER STIFTUNG
MOZARTEUM.**
++*SCHRIFTENR. INT. STIFT. MOZARTEUM.*
*SALZBURG 1, 1966-*
*OX/U-1.*

**SCHRIFTENREIHE, LUDWIG-BULTZMANN INSTITUT FUR
GESCHICHTE DER ARBEITERBEWEGUNG.**
++*SCHRIFTENR. LUDWIG-BULTZMANN INST. GESCH.
ARBEITERBEWEGUNG.*
*VIENNA 1, 1972-*
*LO/N-1.    OX/U-1.*

**SCHRIFTENREIHE, NIEDERSACHSISCHE LANDESZENT-
RALE FUR POLITISCHE BILDUNG: BEITRAGE ZUR
POLITISCHEN BILDUNG AN VOLKSSCHULEN.**
++*SCHRIFTENR. NIEDERSACHS. LANDESZENT. POLIT.
BILD., BEITR. POLIT. BILD. VOLKSSCHUL.*
*HANNOVER 1, 1971-*
*OX/U-1.*

**SCHRIFTENREIHE SCHWEISSEN UND SCHNEIDEN.**
++*SCHRIFTENR. SCHWEISSEN & SCHNEIDEN.*
[DEUTSCHER VERLAG FUR SCHWEISSTECHNIK]
*DUSSELDORF 1, 1970-*
*LO/N14.*

**SCHRIFTENREIHE DER SCHWEIZERISCHEN GESELL-
SCHAFT FUR KOORDINATION UND FORDERUNG DER
BAUFORSCHUNG.**
++*SCHRIFTENR. SCHWEIZ. GES. KOORD. & FORD.
BAUFORSCH.*
SCHWEIZERISCHE GESELLSCHAFT FUR KOORDINATION
UND FORDERUNG DER BAUFORSCHUNG.
*ZURICH 1, 1965-*
MONOGR.
*LO/N14.*

**SCHRIFTENREIHE TECHNOLOGIEN.**
++*SCHRIFTENR. TECHNOL.*
(GERMANY, WEST) BUNDESMINSTER FUR BILDUNG UND
WISSENSCHAFT.
*BONN [NR]1, 1970-*
*LO/N13.*

**SCHRIFTENREIHE FUR VEGETATIONSKUNDE.**
++*SCHRIFTENR. VEG.*
BUNDESANSTALT FUR VEGETATIONSKUNDE, NATURSCHUTZ
& LANDSCHAFTSPFLEGE.
*BAD GODESBERG NO.1, 1966-*
*LO/N13.    LO/R-5.*

**SCHRIFTENREIHE DER WALCKER-STIFTUNG FUR ORGEL-
WISSENSCHAFTLICHE FORSCHUNG.**
++*SCHRIFTENR. WALCKER-STIFT. ORGELWISS. FORSCH.*
[MUSIKWISSENSCHAFTLICHE VERLAGS-GESELLSCHAFT]
*STUTTGART 1, 1970-*
MONOGR.
*LO/N-1.*

**SCHWEIZER AUTO-VERKEHR.**  XXX
SUBS (1973): AUTOTRANSPORT.

**SCHWEIZERISCHE ZEITSCHRIFT FUR PSYCHOLOGIE UND
IHRE ANWENDUNGEN.**  XXX
SUBS (1967): PSYCHOLOGIE.

SCHWEIZERISCHES ZENTRALBLATT DER MILCHPRODUZEN-
TEN.    XXX
  SUBS (1968):  LAND-UND MILCHWIRTSCHAFT.

SCIATH.  JOURNAL OF THE ...
  NATIONAL INDUSTRIAL SAFETY ORGANISATION (EIRE).
  *DUBLIN NO.1, MY 1968-*
  *DB/U-2.*

SCIENCE ABSTRACTS.    XXX
  *+ +SCI. ABSTR.*
  ESSO PETROLEUM CO. LTD.
  *LONDON NO.1, 1967...*
  SUBS: SCIENCE TEACHERS ABSTRACTS.
  *BN/U-1.    LO/U11.*

SCIENCE IN ACTION.
  *LONDON  1, 19/S 1968-*
  *2W.*
  *ED/N-1.*

SCIENCE & ARCHAEOLOGY.
  *+ +SCI. & ARCHAEOL.*
  [GEORGE STREET P.]
  *STAFFORD NO.1, 1970-*
  *ED/N-1.    LO/N-1.    LO/N-4.    LO/N14.    NO/U-1.    OX/U-2.*

SCIENCE BULLETIN.  LONDON, 1969    000
  SEE: SCIENCE POLICY & ORGANISATION BULLETIN.

SCIENCE DIMENSION.
  *+ +SCI. DIMENS.*
  NATIONAL RESEARCH COUNCIL (CANADA).
  *OTTAWA  1(1), AP 1969-*
  6/A.  ENGL. = FR.  BODY ALSO NAMED IN FR.:
  CONSEIL NATIONAL DE RECHERCHES DU CANADA.
  PREV: NRC RESEARCH NEWS.
  *LD/U-1.    LO/N-2.    XS/R10.*
  *LO/N-3.  1(1) ONLY.*
  *ISSN 0036-830X*

SCIENCE FICTION SPECIAL.
  *+ +SCI. FICTION SPEC.*
  [SIDGWICK & JACKSON]
  *LONDON NO.1, 1970-*
  *LO/N-1.*

SCIENCE-FICTION STUDIES.
  *+ +SCI.-FICTION STUD.*
  *TERRE HAUTE, INDIANA  1, 1973-*
  *Q.*
  *CA/U-1.    OX/U-1.    SH/U-1.*

SCIENCE FORUM.  A CANADIAN JOURNAL OF SCIENCE
& TECHNOLOGY.
  *+ +SCI. FORUM (CAN.)*
  *TORONTO  1, F 1968-*
  2M.  ENGL., FR.
  *ED/U-1.    LO/N14.*
  *ISSN 0036-8393*

SCIENCE & GOVERNMENT REPORT.
  *+ +SCI. & GOV. REP.*
  *WASHINGTON, D.C. NO.1, F 1971-*
  *2/M.*
  *MA/U-1.*
  *ISSN 0048-9581*

SCIENCE IN ICELAND. = SCIENTIA ISLANDICA.
  *+ +SCI. ICELAND.*
  VISINDAFELAG ISLENDINGA.
  *REYKJAVIK  1, 1968-*
  *LO/N-2.    LO/N-4.    LO/N13.*

SCIENCE & INDUSTRY.
  *+ +SCI. & IND. (PAKISTAN).*
  PAKISTAN COUNCIL OF SCIENTIFIC & INDUSTRIAL
  RESEARCH.
  *KARACHI  1(1), JA 1963- 9(3/4), 1972. //*
  *Q.*
  *LO/N-3.\**
  *LO/N-2.  5(3), 1967-*
  *LO/R-6.  5(3), 1967; 6(1/2), 1968-*

SCIENCE, MEDICINE & MAN.    XXX
  *+ +SCI. MED. & MAN.*
  [PERGAMON]
  *OXFORD  1(1), AP 1973- 1(4), D 1974 ...*
  MON. SUBS: ETHICS IN SCIENCE & MEDICINE.
  *CA/U-1.    ED/N-1.*
  *ISSN 0300-9955*

SCIENCE NOTES.
  (NEW JERSEY) STATE MUSEUM.
  *TRENTON, N.J. NO.1, 1971-*
  *LO/N-2.*

SCIENCE POLICY.
  *+ +SCI. POL.*
  SCIENCE POLICY FOUNDATION.
  *LONDON 1, 1972-*
  PREV: SCIENCE POLICY NEWS FROM 1(1), 1969- 3,
  1971.
  *DB/U-1.    ED/N-1.    LO/N-4.    LO/N13.    LO/N35.    LO/R-5.*
  *MA/U-1.    XS/R10.*
  *ISSN 0048-9700*

SCIENCE POLICY INFORMATION.    XXX
  *+ +SCI. POLICY INF.*
  OECD.
  *PARIS NO.1, JA 1967- 5, N 1968.*
  SUBS. PART OF: SCIENCE POLICY NEWS.
  *ED/N-1.    LO/U-3.    XS/R10.*

SCIENCE POLICY NEWS.    XXX
  SCIENCE OF SCIENCE FOUNDATION LTD.
  *LONDON 1(1), 1969- 3(3), 1971.*
  S/T:  A BIMONTHLY BULLETIN PUBLISHED BY THE
  SSF IN COLLABORATION WITH OECD. INCORP:  SSF
  NEWSLETTER; & SCIENCE POLICY INFORMATION.
  SUBS: SCIENCE POLICY.
  *ED/N-1.    LO/N-4.    LO/N17.    LO/R-5.    LO/U-3.    OX/U-8.*
  *XS/R10.*
  *GL/U-2.  KEPT FOR TWO YEARS ONLY.*

SCIENCE POLICY NEWS SUPPLEMENT:  LIST OF
CURRENT NATIONAL PUBLICATIONS.
  *+ +SCI. POLICY NEWS, SUPPL.*
  SCIENCE OF SCIENCE FOUNDATION LTD.
  *LONDON NO.1, 1969-*
  *LO/N-4.*

SCIENCE POLICY & ORGANISATION BULLETIN.    XXX
  *+ +SCI. POLICY & ORG. BULL.*
  (GREAT BRITAIN) DEPARTMENT OF EDUCATION &
  SCIENCE.
  *LONDON NO.1, F 1969- 4 1970.*
  TITLE SHOWN ON T.P. EQUIVALENT (MASTHEAD) WITH
  'SCIENCE' & 'BULLETIN' IN LARGE TYPE, WITH
  'POLICY AND ORGANISATION' IN SMALL TYPE
  BETWEEN THEM.
  *BL/U-1.    CB/U-1.    ED/N-1.    GL/U-2.    LO/N-1.    LO/N-2.*
  *LO/N-3.    LO/N-4.    LV/U-1.    OX/U-1.    SH/U-1.    XS/R10.*
  *LO/U-2.  CURRENT THREE YEARS.*

SCIENCE POLICY STUDIES.
  *+ +SCI. POLICY STUD.*
  (GREAT BRITAIN) DEPARTMENT OF EDUCATION &
  SCIENCE.
  *LONDON 1, 1967-*
  *GL/U-1.    LO/N-4.    LO/U-1.*

SCIENCE REPORTS, DEPARTMENT OF GEOGRAPHY &
METEOROLOGY, NATIONAL TAIWAN UNIVERSITY.
  *+ +SCI. REP. DEP. GEOGR. & METEOROL. NAT. TAIWAN
  UNIV.*
  *TAIPEI NO.1, AG 1962-*
  *LO/S13.*

SCIENCE REPORTS OF THE SHIMABARA INSTITUTE OF
VOLCANOLOGY & BALNEOLOGY, KYUSHU UNIVERSITY.    000
  SEE: KYUSHU DAIGAKU RIGAKUBU SHIMABARA KAZAN
  ONSEN KENKYUSHO KENKYU HOKOKU.

SCIENCE REPORTS OF THE TOKYO WOMEN'S CHRIST-
IAN COLLEGE.
  *+ +SCI. REP. TOKYO WOMEN'S CHRIST. COLL.*
  *TOKYO NO.1, 1967-*
  *XN/S-1.*

SCIENCE RESEARCH ABSTRACTS: PART A: SUPERCOND-
UCTIVITY, MAGNETOHYDRODYNAMICS & PLASMAS,
THEORETICAL PHYSICS.    XXX
  *+ +SCI. RES. ABSTR., A.*
  [CAMBRIDGE SCIENTIFIC ABSTRACTS]
  *RIVERDALE, MD.  1(2), 1972-*
  INCORP: MAGNETOHYDRODYNAMICS & PLASMAS JOURNAL
  FROM 1(1), 1972; & THEORETICAL PHYSICS JOURNAL
  FROM 1(1), 1972.
  *LO/N14.*

SCIENCE STUDIES.    XXX
  *+ +SCI. STUD.*
  [MACMILLAN JOURNALS LTD.]
  *BASINGSTOKE  1(1), JA 1971- 4, 1974...*
  S/T: RESEARCH IN THE SOCIAL & HISTORICAL
  DIMENSIONS OF SCIENCE & TECHNOLOGY. SUBS:
  SOCIAL STUDIES OF SCIENCE.
  *AD/U-1.    BH/U-3.    ED/N-1.    LD/U-1.    LO/N-1.    LO/N-7.*
  *LO/N13.    LO/U-1.    MA/U-1.    NO/U-1.    SH/C-5.*
  *XS/R10.*
  *DB/U-2.  3, 1973-              HL/U-1.  2, 1972-*
  *ISSN 0036-8539*

**SCIENCE TEACHERS ABSTRACTS.**
++SCI. TEACH. ABSTR.
ESSO PETROLEUM CO. LTD.
LONDON NO.2, 1967-
PREV: SCIENCE ABSTRACTS; FROM NO.1, 1967.
HL/U-2.    LO/U11.

**SCIENCE TEACHING EQUIPMENT.**
++SCI. TEACH. EQUIP.
[MILTON PUBL. CO.]
LONDON 1(1), 1968-
SUPPL. TO: EDUCATIONAL ELECTRONIC EQUIPMENT.
ED/N-1.    LO/N-4.    LO/N14.
ISSN 0036-8571

**SCIENCE + TECHNOLOGIE ALIMENTAIRE.**          000
SEE: LEBENSMITTEL-WISSENSCHAFT + TECHNOLOGIE.

**SCIENCE & TECHNOLOGY NEWSLETTER.**
++SCI. & TECHNOL. NEWSL.
SHELL PETROLEUM CO.
LONDON 1, 1965-
XN/S-1.
LO/N14. [CURRENT BOX ONLY]

**SCIENCE OF THE TOTAL ENVIRONMENT.**
++SCI. TOTAL ENVIRON.
[ELSEVIER]
AMSTERDAM 1(1), MY 1972-
Q. ENGL., FR. OR GER.
LO/N14.    OX/U-8.    XS/R10.
LO/R-6. 2(1), 1973-
ISSN 0048-9697

**SCIENCES PHARMACEUTIQUES ET BIOLOGIQUES DE
LORRAINE.**                                    XXX
++SCI. PHARM. & BIOL. LORRAINE.
SOCIETE DE PHARMACIE DE NANCY.
NANCY 1, 1973-
PREV: BULLETIN, SOCIETE DE PHARMACIE DE NANCY
FROM NO.1, MR 1949- 95, 1972.
LO/N13.

**SCIENCES SOCIALES AU CANADA.**                000
SEE: SOCIAL SCIENCES IN CANADA.

**SCIENTIA HORTICULTURAE.**
++SCI. HORTIC. (NETH.).
INTERNATIONAL SOCIETY FOR HORTICULTURAL SCIENCE
[ELSEVIER SCIENTIFIC PUBL. CO.]
AMSTERDAM 1(1), JA 1973-
GL/U-2.    LO/N-6.    LO/N13.    LO/R-6.    MA/U-1.

**SCIENTIA ISLANDICA.**                         000
SEE: SCIENCE IN ICELAND.

**SCIENTIFIC ERA.  MONTHLY DIGEST OF SCIENCE &
TECHNOLOGY.**
++SCI. ERA.
STAMFORD, LINCS. 1(1), AP 1972-
ED/N-1.    OX/U-8.

**SCIENTIFIC INFORMATION NOTES.**
++SCI. INF. NOTES.
SCIENCE ASSOCIATES/INTERNATIONAL.
NEW YORK 1(1/2), JA-F/MR-AP 1969-
PREV: AS ABOVE FROM 1, 1959- 10, 1968 ISSUED
BY NATIONAL SCIENCE FOUNDATION. SUBS:
INFORMATION: NEWS, SOURCES, PROFILES.
DB/U-2.    GL/U-2.    LO/N-2.    OX/U-8.    SO/U-1.    XS/R10.
LO/N14. [CURRENT BOX ONLY]
SW/U-1. 1, 1969.

**SCIENTIFIC NOTE, EUROPEAN SPACE RESEARCH ORG-
ANIZATION.**
++SCI. NOTE EUR. SPACE RES. ORG.
PARIS SN1, 1967-
NOT ISSUED IN NUMERICAL ORDER.
SO/U-1.
LO/N14. SN-12, 1967-

**SCIENTIFIC PUBLICATIONS, INTERNATIONAL AGENCY
FOR RESEARCH ON CANCER.**
++SCI. PUBL. INT. AGENCY RES. CANCER.
LYON NO.1, 1971-
LO/N13.

**SCIENTIFIC REPORT, ASSOCIATION OF CLINICAL
BIOCHEMISTS.**
++SCI. REP. ASS. CLIN. BIOCHEM.
LIVERPOOL NO.1, 1965-
LO/N14.

**SCIENTIFIC RESEARCHES, EAST REGIONAL LABORA-
TORIES, PAKISTAN COUNCIL OF SCIENTIFIC &
INDUSTRIAL RESEARCH.**                         XXX
++SCI. RES. E. REG. LABS. PAKISTAN COUN. SCI. &
IND. RES.
PAKISTAN COUNCIL OF SCIENTIFIC & INDUSTRIAL
RESEARCH: EAST REGIONAL LABORATORIES.
DACCA 1, JA 1964- 7(1), 1970.
Q. SUBS: SCIENTIFIC RESEARCHES B.C.S.I.R.
LABORATORIES, DACCA.
LO/N14.

**SCIENTIFIC RESULTS, ICEFIELD RANGES
RESEARCH PROJECT.**
++SCI. RESULTS ICEFIELD RANGES RES. PROJ.
NEW YORK 1, 1969-
LO/N-2.

**SCIENTOLOGY.**
EAST GRINSTEAD 1, 1968-
S/T: THE FIELD STAFF MEMBER MAGAZINE.
ED/N-1.

**SCIENZE SOCIALI.**
++SCI. SOC. (ITALY).
COMITATO PER LE SCIENZE POLITICHE E SOCIALI.
[SOCIETA EDITRICE IL MULINO]
BOLOGNA 1, AP 1971-
RE/U-1.

**SCI/TECH QUARTERLY INDEX.**
++SCI/TECH Q. INDEX.
[CCM INFORMATION CORP.]
NEW YORK 1(1), 1970-
S/T: GUIDE & INDEX TO SCIENTIFIC & TECHNICAL
DOCUMENTS TRANSLATED & PUBLISHED BY THE U.S.
JOINT PUBLICATIONS RESEARCH SERVICE.
LO/N14.    OX/U-8.

**SCOLIES.  CAHIERS DE RECHERCHES DE ...**
ECOLE NORMALE SUPERIEURE.
[PRESSES UNIV. DE FRANCE]
PARIS 1, 1971-
LO/U17.    OX/U-1.

**SCOOTERING & LIGHTWEIGHTS.**
++SCOOTER. & LIGHTWEIGHTS.
[R. MILWARD & SONS LTD]
NOTTINGHAM 1, JA 1968-
M.
LO/P-7.

**SCOPE.**
BRITISH MEDICAL STUDENTS' ASSOCIATION.
LONDON 1(1), 1969-
OX/U-1.
ED/N-1. 1(3), 1970-
CR/M-1. [TWO YEARS ONLY]
ISSN 0036-8989

**SCOPUS REVIEW.**
++SCOPUS REV.
HEBREW UNIVERSITY OF JERUSALEM.
JERUSALEM 1, 1969-
LO/U14.    SO/U-1.

**SCOTIA.**
LYTH 1, 1970-
OX/U-1.

**SCOTIA REVIEW.**
++SCOTIA REV.
[DAVID MORRISON]
WICK NO.1, AG 1972-
AD/U-1.    ED/N-1.

**SCOTNEWS. NEWSLETTER OF THE ...**
WORLD FEDERATION OF SCOTTISH SOCIETIES &
INDIVIDUALS.
EDINBURGH 1, AP 1969-
ED/N-1.    OX/U-1.

**SCOTTISH ABSTRACT OF STATISTICS.**           XXX
++SCOTT. ABSTR. STAT.
(GREAT BRITAIN) SCOTTISH OFFICE.
EDINBURGH NO.1, 1971-
PREV: PART OF DIGEST OF SCOTTISH STATISTICS
FROM NO.1, AP 1953- 37, AP 1971.
CR/U-1.    GL/U-1.    LO/U-3.    LO/U12.    MA/U-1.    OX/U-1.
OX/U16.    OX/U24.
SF/U-1. NO.2, 1972-

**SCOTTISH ARCHAEOLOGICAL FORUM.**
++SCOTT. ARCHAEOL. FORUM.
EDINBURGH 1969-
AD/U-1.    CA/U-3.    DB/S-1.    DB/U-2.    ED/N-1.    GL/U-1.
NW/U-1.    OX/U-1.

**SCOTTISH ECONOMIC BULLETIN.**                     XXX
+ +SCOTT. ECON. BULL.
(GREAT BRITAIN) SCOTTISH OFFICE.
EDINBURGH NO.1, 1971-
PREV: PART OF DIGEST OF SCOTTISH STATISTICS
FROM NO.1, AP 1953- 37, AP 1971.
AD/U-1.   BH/U-1.   GL/U-1.   LO/N-1.   LO/U-3.   LO/U12.
NW/U-1.   OX/U16.   OX/U24.

**SCOTTISH ECONOMIC REVIEW.**
+ +SCOTT. ECON. REV.
SCOTTISH COUNCIL (DEVELOPMENT & INDUSTRY).
EDINBURGH 1(1), JE 1969-
AD/U-1.   ED/N-1.   ED/N-1.   GL/U-2.   GL/U-3.   OX/U-1.
SO/U-1.

**SCOTTISH GARDENER.**
+ +SCOTT. GARD.
GLASGOW NO.1, F 1973-
ED/N-1.   GL/U-2.

**SCOTTISH LABOUR HISTORY SOCIETY JOURNAL.**        000
SEE: JOURNAL OF THE SCOTTISH LABOUR HISTORY
SOCIETY.

**SCOTTISH LIBRARY STUDIES.**
+ +SCOTT. LIBR. STUD.
SCOTTISH LIBRARY ASSOCIATION.
GLASGOW NO.1, 1971-
LO/N-1.

**SCOTTISH LITERARY NEWS.  NEWSLETTER OF THE ...**
+ +SCOTT. LIT. NEWS.
ASSOCIATION FOR SCOTTISH LITERARY STUDIES.
ABERDEEN 1, OC 1970-
AD/U-1.   ED/N-1.   GL/U-2.
GL/U-1. 1(2) 1971-              SH/U-1. AG, 1971-
SO/U-1. 2, 1971-
EX/U-1. 1(3/4), 1971-
ISSN 0048-9794

**SCOTTISH MARXIST.**
+ +SCOTT. MARXIST.
COMMUNIST PARTY OF GREAT BRITAIN: SCOTTISH
COMMITTEE.
GLASGOW NO.1, JE 1972-
ED/N-1.
HL/U-1. 2, 1972-               LO/U-3. 2, 1972-

**SCOTTISH THEATRE.**
+ +SCOTT. THEATRE.
INVERKEITHING 1, MR 1969-
S/T: SCOTLAND'S MONTHLY MAGAZINE OF THE STAGE.
ED/N-1.   GL/U-1.   GL/U-2.

**SCOTTISH VANGUARD.  JOURNAL OF THE ...**
WORKERS' PARTY OF SCOTLAND (MARXIST-LENINIST).
GLASGOW 1(1), 1967-
ED/N-1.   LO/U-3.   OX/U17.

**SCRAP & WASTE, RECLAMATION & DISPOSAL.**
+ +SCRAP & WASTE RECLAM. & DISPOSAL.
[FUEL & METALLURGICAL JOURNALS]
LONDON 1(1), S 1970-
LO/N14.   OX/U-1.   XS/R10.
ISSN 0048-9824

**SCREEN.  JOURNAL OF THE...**                      XXX
SOCIETY FOR EDUCATION IN FILM & TELEVISION.
LONDON 10, 1969-
PREV FROM 1, 1959: SCREEN EDUCATION.
ED/N-1.   EX/U-1.   LD/U-2.

**SCREEN EDUCATION.**                               XXX
SUBS (1969): SCREEN.  JOURNAL OF THE...

**SCRIBE.  JOURNAL OF THE DESCENDANTS OF BABY-**
**LONIAN JEWRY.**
COMMITTEE FOR DESCENDANTS OF BABYLONIAN JEWRY.
LONDON 1(1), S/OC 1971-
6/A.
SO/U-1.
ED/N-1. 2(7), 1972-
LO/U-2. 1(2,6); 2(8- 12)

**SCRIBLERIAN: A NEWSLETTER DEVOTED TO POPE,**
**SWIFT & THEIR CIRCLE.**
TEMPLE UNIVERSITY: DEPARTMENT OF ENGLISH.
PHILADELPHIA (P.A.) 1(1), 1968-
2/A.
BL/U-1.   DB/U-2.   ED/N-1.   GL/U-1.   LO/N-1.   LO/U-1.
MA/S-1.   NO/U-1.   OX/U-1.   SO/U-1.   SW/U-1.
AD/U-1. 1(2), 1969-           HL/U-1. 2, 1969-
LO/U13. 4, 1971/72-          MA/U-1. 5(2), 1973-
LO/N-3. 1(2), 1969.
ISSN 0036-9640

**SCRINIUM FRIBURGENSE.**
+ +SCRINIUM FRIB.
UNIVERSITE DE FRIBOURG: MEDIAEVISTISCHES
INSTITUT.
FREIBURG, SWITZ. NO.1, 1971-
LO/N-1.

**SCRIPT.**
DUBLIN 1, 1970-
DB/U-2.

**SCRIPT.  MAGAZINE ON ALTERNATIVE RADIO.**
LONDON REGION FREE RADIO CAMPAIGN.
LONDON NO.1, 1972-
6/A.
ED/N-1. NO.3, 1972-          OX/U-1. NO.3, 1972-

**SCRIPTA GEOBOTANICA.**
+ +SCR. GEOBOT.
GOTTINGEN 1, 1970-
LO/N-2.

**SCRIPTA GEOLOGICA.**
+ +SCR. GEOL.
RIJKSMUSEUM VAN GEOLOGIE EN MINERALOGIE.
LEIDEN [NO.]1, 1971-
ENGL; OCCASIONALLY FR., GER. OR SPAN.
LO/N-2.   LO/N13.   SO/U-1.

**SCRIPTA INSTITUTI DONNERIANI ABOENSIS.**
/ / SCR. INST. DONNER. ABO.
DONNER INSTITUTE FOR RESEARCH IN RELIGIOUS &
CULTURAL HISTORY (ABO AKADEMI).
STOCKHOLM 1, 1967-
ENGL., GER.  BODY LOCATED IN FINLAND (ABO).
DB/S-1.   ED/S-2.

**SCRIPTA JAPONICA III.**                           000
SEE: SYSTEMS, COMPUTERS, CONTROLS.

**SCRIPTA MERCATURAE.**
+ +SCR. MERCAT. (GER.)
MUNICH NO.1, 1967-
EX/U-1.   LO/N-1.   SH/U-1.
ISSN 0036-973X

**SCRIPTA THEOLOGICA.**
+ +SCR. THEOL. (SP.)
UNIVERSIDAD DE NAVARRA.
PAMPLONA 1(1), 1969-
MA/S-1.
ISSN 0036-9764

**SCRIPTS.  A MONTHLY OF PLAYS & THEATER PIECES.**
NEW YORK SHAKESPEARE FESTIVAL PUBLIC THEATER.
NEW YORK 1, N 1971-
OX/U-1.
ISSN 0006-5307

**SCRIPTURE BULLETIN.**
+ +SCRIPTURE BULL.
CATHOLIC BIBLICAL ASSOCIATION.
STRAWBERRY HILL, MIDDX. 1(1), 1969-
OX/U-1.
ED/N-1. 1(3), 1969-
ISSN 0036-9780

**SCRIPTURE IN CHURCH.**
[DOMINICAN PUBL.]
DUBLIN 1, 1971-
Q.
DB/U-2.

**SCSST NEWS.**
STANDING CONFERENCE ON SCHOOLS' SCIENCE &
TECHNOLOGY.
LONDON NO.1, F 1972-
ED/N-1.

**SCULPTURE INTERNATIONAL.**                        XXX
+ +SCULP. INT. (GB).
[STUDIO INTERNATIONAL]
NORTHAMPTON 1(1), 1966- 3(1), 1969.//
ENGL., SUMMARIES IN FR., SPAN., RUSS.
BH/P-1.   LV/P-1.   OX/U-1.

**SDC NEWS.**
SOCIETY OF DYERS & COLOURISTS.
BRADFORD 1, 1969-
ED/N-1.
LO/N14.  CURRENT BOX ONLY.

**SEA ANGLER (1972).**
[A.E. MORGAN PUBL.]
EWELL, SURREY NO.1, MR 1972-
M.
ED/N-1.

SEA HARVEST & OCEAN SCIENCE.                          XXX
+ +SEA HARVEST & OCEAN SCI.
[NATIONAL BUSINESS PUBL.]
GARDENVALE, QUE. JE/JL 1969- JE/JL 1970.
MON. PREV: CANADIAN FISHERMAN FROM 1, 1914-
56(4), AP 1969. SUBS: CANADIAN FISHERMAN &
OCEAN SCIENCE.
LO/N13.

SEA LETTER.
+ +SEA LETT.
SAN FRANCISCO MARITIME MUSEUM.
SAN FRANCISCO 1(1), 1960-
LO/N-4.
ISSN 0037-0010

SEARCH.                                              XXX
AUSTRALIAN & NEW ZEALAND ASSOCIATION FOR THE
ADVANCEMENT OF SCIENCE.
SYDNEY 1, 1970-
PREV: AUSTRALIAN JOURNAL OF SCIENCE FROM 1,
1938- 32, 1970.
CA/U-2.    DB/U-1.    ED/S-2.    LD/U-1.    LO/N-2.    LO/N-4.
LO/N14.    LO/U-2.    NW/U-1.    OX/U-8.    XS/R10.
ISSN 0004-9549

SEARCHER.
SOUTHERN CALIFORNIA GENEALOGICAL SOCIETY.
LONG BEACH, CALIF. 1, 1964-
MON.
ED/N-1. 7, 1970-
ISSN 0037-0401

SEAWEED RESEARCH & UTILISATION.
+ +SEAWEED RES. & UTIL.
MADURAI 1, 1971-
LO/N-2.

SECONDARY EDUCATION.                                 XXX
+ +SECOND. EDUC.
NATIONAL UNION OF TEACHERS.
LONDON 1(1), 1970-
PREV: HIGHER EDUCATION JOURNAL FROM 1, 1936-
17, 1970.
BH/U-1.    BN/U-1.    CR/M-1.    DB/U-2.    HL/U-2.    LV/U-1.
OX/U-1.    SW/U-1.
ISSN 0018-1595

SECURITIES LAW REVIEW.
+ +SECUR. LAW REV.
[SAGE HILL PUBL.]
ALBANY, N.Y. 1, 1969-
A.
HL/U-1.    MA/U-1.

SECURITY SURVEYOR. JOURNAL OF THE ...
+ +SECUR. SURV.
ASSOCIATION OF BURGLARY INSURANCE SURVEYORS.
LONDON 1(1), MY 1970-
LO/N-1.
ISSN 0306-6118

SEED.
UNITED NATIONS STUDENTS ASSOCIATION: EDINBURGH
BRANCH.
EDINBURGH NO.1, F 1972-
ED/N-1.
CA/U-1. 2, 1972-

SEED. JOURNAL OF ORGANIC LIVING.
LONDON 1(1), AP 1972-
ED/N-1. 2, 1972-

SEEK TRUTH TO SERVE THE PEOPLE.
PROGRESSIVE INTELLECTUALS' STUDY GROUP.
LONDON 1(1), N 1971-
2M.
LO/U-3.

SEIHIN KAGAKU KENKYUJO KENKYU HOKOKU. BULL-
ETIN, INDUSTRIAL PRODUCTS RESEARCH INSTITUTE.   XXX
SEIHIN KAGAKU KENKYUJO.                          XXX
TOKYO NO.59, 1969.
PREV: SANGYO KOGEI SHIKENJO HOKOKU FROM NO.
42, 1965- 58, 1969.
LO/N13.

SEIKAKEN NYUSU.
SEIHIN KAGAKU KENKYUJO.
TOKYO 1, 1969-
LO/N13.

SEIKEI DAIGAKU KENKYU HOKOKU. BULLETIN OF
THE SEIKEI UNIVERSITY.
SEIKEI DAIGAKU.
TOKYO 1(1), 1961-
XS/N-1.

SEISMOLOGICAL BULLETIN, INSTITUTE OF GEOLOG-
ICAL SCIENCES (GB).
+ +SEISMOL. BULL. INST. GEOL. SCI. (GB).
[H.M.S.O.]
LONDON NO.1, 1972-
GL/U-1.    GL/U-2.    LO/N-4.    LO/N14.    MA/U-1.    OX/U-8.

SEIZURE MAGAZINE.
+ +SEIZURE MAG.
EUGENE, OREG. 1, MR/AG 1972-
2/A.
OX/U-1.

SELECTED ANNUAL REVIEWS OF THE ANALYTICAL
SCIENCES.
+ +SEL. ANNU. REV. ANAL. SCI.
SOCIETY FOR ANALYTICAL CHEMISTRY.
LONDON 1, 1971-
CA/U-1.    LO/N14.    LO/S-3.    OX/U-8.    XS/R10.    XY/N-1.
ISSN 0300-9963

SELECTED LECTURES OF THE ROYAL SOCIETY.
+ +SEL. LECT. R. SOC.
ROYAL SOCIETY.
LONDON 1, 1967-
REPRINTED FROM: PROCEEDINGS OF THE ROYAL
SOCIETY.
BH/U-1.    HL/U-1.

SELECTED REFERENCES ON ENVIRONMENTAL QUALITY
AS IT RELATES TO HEALTH.
+ +SEL. REF. ENVIRON. QUAL. RELAT. HEALTH.
NATIONAL LIBRARY OF MEDICINE (US).
BETHESDA, MD. 1, JA 1971-
MON.
LO/N13.    LO/U-1.
ISSN 0049-0105

SELECTED WATER RESOURCES ABSTRACTS.
+ +SELEC. WATER RESOUR. ABSTR.
CLEARINGHOUSE FOR FEDERAL SCIENTIFIC & TECH-
NICAL INFORMATION (U.S.).
WASHINGTON, D.C. 1, 1968-
DB/U-2.
LO/N14. 2, 1969-                    LO/R-5. 2, 1969-
NW/U-1. 5, 1972-
ISSN 0037-136X

SELECTION DE SOMMAIRES DE LA PRESSE SCIENTIF-
IQUE ET TECHNIQUE DE LANGUE FRANCAISE.
+ +SEL. SOMM. P. SCI. & TECH. LANG. FR.
CENTRE DE DOCUMENTATION DE L'ARMEMENT.
PARIS NO.1, 1971-
LO/N13.

SELECTIONS FROM HISTORY TODAY.                       000
SEE: HISTORY TODAY.

SELECTIVE ORGANIC TRANSFORMATIONS.
+ +SEL. ORG. TRANSFORM.
[WILEY-INTERSCIENCE]
NEW YORK 1, 1970-
BL/U-1.    LO/S-3.    SH/U-1.
LD/U-1. 1, 1970.
ISSN 0080-8660

SELF-SERVICE. = LIBRE-SERVICE. = SELBST-
BEDIENUNG.
+ +SELF-SERV.
INTERNATIONAL SELF-SERVICE ORGANISATION.
COLOGNE 1961-
LO/N10. 1964-

SEL'SKAJA NOV'.
(RUSSIA USSR) MINISTERSTVO SEL'SKOGO
KHOZJAJSTVA.
MOSCOW 1966(1)-
M.
BH/U-1.    OX/U-1.
CC/U-1. 1968(1)-

SEL'SKOE KHOZJAJSTVO ROSSII.                         XXX
+ +SEL'SK. KHOZ. ROSS. [SKHR-A]
(RUSSIA RSFSR) MINISTERSTVO SEL'SKOGO
KHOZJAJSTVA.
MOSCOW 1966(1)-
PREV: KOLKHOZNO-SOVKHOZNOE PROIZVODSTVO RSFSR
FROM 1963(1)- 1965(8).
BH/U-1.    LO/N13.    OX/U-1.

SEL'SKOE KHOZJAJSTVO SEVERO-ZAPADNOJ ZONY.          XXX
SUBS (1963): SEL'SKOKHOZJAJSTVENNOE PROIZVOD-
STVO NECHERNOZEMNOJ ZONY.

**SEL'SKOHOZJAJSTVENNAJA BIOLOGIJA.**
++S-KH. BIOL. [SSBL-A]
VSESOJUZNAJA AKADEMIJA SEL'SKOHOZJAJSTVENNYKH
NAUK [IM. V.I. LENINA].
*MOSCOW 1, 1966-*
2M. ENGL. CONT. LISTS & SUMM.
CA/M-5.    CC/U-1.    LO/N13.    XS/R-2.

**SEL'SKOHOZJAJSTVENNOE PROIZVODSTVO NECHERNO-**                    XXX
**ZEMNOJ ZONY.**
++S-KH. PROIZVOD. NECHERNOZEMN. ZONY. [SPNZ-A]
(RUSSIA RSFSR) MINISTERSTVO SEL'SKOGO KHOZJAJ-
STVA.
*MOSCOW 1(1), JA 1963- 5(12), 1967.*
PREV: SEL'SKOE KHOZJAJSTVO SEVERO-ZAPADNOJ
ZONY FROM 1, JA 1958- 1962. SUBS: ZEMLJA
RODNAJA.
LO/N13.

**SEL'SKOHOZJAJSTVENNOE PROIZVODSTVO POVOL-**                      XXX
**ZH'JA.**
++S-KH. PROIZVOD. POVOLZH. [SPPO-A]
(RUSSIA RSFSR) MINISTERSTVO SEL'SKOGO KHOZJAJ-
STVA.
*SARATOV 1, JA 1963- 1967.*
M. SUBS: STEPNYE PROSTORY.
LO/N13.

**SEM NEWSLETTER.**
++SEM NEWSL. (SOC. ETHNOMUSICOL.)
SOCIETY FOR ETHNOMUSICOLOGY.
*MILWAUKEE 1, 1967-*
ED/N-1.    LO/S10.
ISSN 0036-1291

**SEMIGROUP FORUM.**
[SPRINGER-VERLAG NEW YORK INC.]
*NEW YORK 1, 1970-*
A.
BL/U-1.    BN/U-2    CA/U-2.    DN/U-1.    LO/N-4.    LO/N14.
OX/U-8.    SW/U-1.

**SEMINAIRE DE MATHEMATIQUES SUPERIEURES.**
++SEMIN. MATH. SUP.
UNIVERSITE DE MONTREAL: DEPARTEMENT DE MATHEM-
ATIQUES.
*MONTREAL 1, 1962-*
OX/U-8. 1965-

**SEMINARS IN DRUG TREATMENT.**
++SEMIN. DRUG TREAT.
[STRATTON]
*NEW YORK 1(1), JE 1971-*
Q.
XY/N-1.

**SEMINARS IN MATHEMATICS.**
++SEMIN. MATH. [SEMT-B]
[CONSULTANTS BUREAU]
*NEW YORK 1, 1966(1968)-*
ENGL. TRANSL. OF ZAPISKI NAUCHNYKH SEMINAROV.
OX/U-8.

**SEMINARS IN NUCLEAR MEDICINE.**
++SEMIN. NUCL. MED.
[STRATTON, INC.]
*NEW YORK 1(1), JA 1971-*
Q.
AD/U-1.    LO/M-3.    LO/N13.    OX/U-8.

**SEMIOTICA.**
ASSOCIATION INTERNATIONALE DE SEMIOTIQUE.
*THE HAGUE 1, 1969-*
Q.
BH/U-1.    HL/U-1.    LO/U-1.    LO/U-2.    LO/U-14.    MA/U-1.
NO/U-1.    OX/U-1.    SH/U-1.
ED/N-1. 10, 1974-                           LD/U-1. 5, 1972-
ISSN 0037-1998

**SEMITICS.**
UNIVERSITY OF SOUTH AFRICA.
*PRETORIA 1, 1970-*
BL/U-1.    CA/S-1.    DB/U-2.    LO/U11.    OX/U-1.    SH/U-1.
HL/U-1. 1, 1970- 2, 1972.

**SEMPAKU GIJUTSU KENKYUJO HOKOKU. REPORT OF**
**SHIP RESEARCH INSTITUTE.**
*TOKYO 1, 1964-*
ENGL. SUMM.
LO/N13.

**SENDAI SHIRAYURI TANKI DAIGAKU KIYO.**
**MEMOIRS, SENDAI SHIRAYURI JUNIOR COLLEGE.**
*IZUMI NO.1, 1970-*
LO/N13.    XN/S-1.

**SENECA REVIEW.**
++SENECA REV.
HOBART & WILLIAM SMITH COLLEGES: STUDENT
ASSOCIATIONS.
*GENEVA, N.Y. 1(1), 1970-*
LO/U-1.    LO/U-2.
ISSN 0037-2145

**SENI KOBUNSHI ZAIRYO KENKYUJO KENKYU HOKOKU.**
**BULLETIN OF RESEARCH INSTITUTE FOR POLYMERS**
**&TEXTILES (JAPAN).**                                              XXX
*YOKOHAMA NO.88, 1969-*
ENGL. SUMM. PREV: SENI KOGYO SHIKENJO
KENKYU HOKOKU FROM NO.1, 1920- 87, 1969.
LO/N14.

**SENI KOGYO SHIKENJO KENKYU HOKOKU. BULLETIN**
**OF THE TEXTILE RESEARCH INSTITUTE (JAPAN).**                      XXX
SUBS (1969): SENI KOBUNSHI ZAIRYO KENKYUJO
KENKYU HOKOKU.

**SENJER JAHRBUCH. BEITRAGE ZUR GEOGRAPHIE,**                       000
**ETHNOLOGIE, OKONOMIK, GESCHICHTE UND KULTUR.**
SEE: SENJSKI ZBORNIK. PRILOZI ZA GEOGRAFIJU,
ETNOLOGIJU, EKONOMIKU, POVIJEST I KULTURU.

**SENJSKI ZBORNIK. PRILOZI ZA GEOGRAFIJU,**
**ETNOLOGIJU, EKONOMIKU, POVIJEST I KULTURU.**
++SENJSKI ZB.
GRADSKI MUZEJ U SENJU: SENJSKO MUZEJSKO
DRUSTVO.
*SENJ 1, 1965-*
GER. TITLE: SENJER JAHRBUCH. BEITRAGE ZUR
GEOGRAPHIE, ETHNOLOGIE, OKONOMIK, GESCHICHTE
UND KULTUR.
OX/U-1.

**SEPARATION & PURIFICATION METHODS.**
++SEP. & PURIF. METHODS.
[DEKKER]
*NEW YORK 1, 1972-*
SUPPL. TO SEPARATION SCIENCE.
AD/U-1.    LO/N-4.    LO/N14.    LO/S-3.    OX/U-1.    SF/U-1.
SW/U-1. 1, 1973.

**SERAPIS.**
UNIVERSITY OF CHICAGO.
*CHICAGO 1, JE 1969-*
ANNU. S/T: STUDENT FORUM ON THE ANCIENT
WORLD.
CA/U-1.
ISSN 0586-7924

**SEREDNI VIKI NA UKRAJINI.**
++SEREDNI VIKI UKR.
AKADEMIJA NAUK UKRAJINS'KOJI RSR: INSTYTUT
ARKHEOLOHIJI.
*KIEV 1, 1971-*
CA/U-1.

**SERHB MAGAZINE.**
++SERHB MAG.
SOUTH EASTERN REGIONAL HOSPITAL BOARD
(SCOTLAND).
*EDINBURGH 1, 1968-*
ED/N-1.

**SERIA PRAC Z ZAKRESU DZIEJOW UNIWERSYTETU**
**POZNANSKIEGO.**
++SER. PR. ZAKR. DZIEJOW UNIW. POZNAN.
UNIWERSYTET IM. ADAMA MICKIEWICZA W POZNANIU.
*POZNAN NO.1, 1961-*
MONOGR.
LO/N-3.

**SERIA ZRODEL, WYDZIAL I: NAUK SPOLECZNYCH I**
**HUMANISTYCZNYCH, GDANSKIE TOWARZYSTWO NAUKOWE.**
++SER. ZROD. WYDZ. I, GDANSK. TOW. NAUK.
*GDANSK NO.1, 1960-*
MONOGR. FROM 1963 ALSO NUMBERED AS PART OF
(NEW) GEN. SERIES: STUDIA I MATERIALY DO
DZIEJOW GDANSKA.
LO/N-3. NO.6, 1964.

**SERIE ANTROPOLOGICA, DEPARTMENTO DE ANTROPO-**
**LOGIA, ACADEMIA DE CIENCIAS DE CUBA.**
++SER. ANTROPOL. DEP. ANTROPOL. ACAD. CIENC.
CUBA.
*HAVANA NO.1, 1968-*
OX/U-1.

**SERIE ARCHIVO NACIONAL, ACADEMIA DE CIENCIAS**
**DE CUBA.**
++SER. ARCH. NAC. ACAD. CIENC. CUBA.
*HAVANA 1, 1969-*
OX/U-1.

SERIE DE BIOLOGIA, DEPARTMENT OF SCIENTIFIC
AFFAIRS, PAN-AMERICAN UNION.
+ +SER. BIOL. DEP. SCI. AFF. PAN-AM. UNION.
WASHINGTON, D.C. NO.1, 1965-
MONOGR.
OX/U-8. 1966-

SERIE CIENTIFICA, INSTITUTO ANTARCTICO
CHILENO.
+ +SER. CIENT. INST. ANTARCT. CHILENO.
SANTIAGO 1, 1970-
LO/N-2.

SERIE CIENTIFICA, INSTITUTO DE INVESTIGACAO
AGRONOMICA DE ANGOLA: SELECTED SERIES.
+ +SER. CIENT. INST. INVEST. AGRON. ANGOLA, SEL.
SER.
NOVA LISBOA, ANGOLA 1, 1968-
OX/U-3.

SERIE DE CULTURAS MESOAMERICANAS.
+ +SER. CULT. MESOAM.
TUTO DE INVESTIGACIONES HISTORICAS.
OX/U-1.

SERIE DE FISICA, DEPARTMENT OF SCIENTIFIC
AFFAIRS, PAN-AMERICAN UNION.
+ +SER. FIS. DEP. SCI. AFF. PAN-AM. UNION.
WASHINGTON, D.C. NO.1, 1965-
MONOGR.
OX/U-8. 1968-

SERIE DE INVESTIGACION, INSTITUTO FORESTAL DE
CHILE.
+ +SER. INVEST. INST. FOR. CHILE.
SANTIAGO DE CHILE NO.1, 1970-
OX/U-3.

SERIE DE MATEMATICA, DEPARTMENT OF SCIENTIFIC
AFFAIRS, PAN-AMERICAN UNION.
+ +SER. MAT. DEP. SCI. AFF. PAN-AM. UNION.
WASHINGTON, D.C. NO.1, 1963-
MONOGR.
OX/U-8. 1968-

SERIE METEOROLOGICA, INSTITUTO DE
METEOROLOGIA, ACADEMIA DE CIENCIAS DE CUBA.
+ +SER. METEOROL. INST. METEOROL. ACAD. CIENC.
CUBA.
HAVANA 1, 1968-
BL/U-1.

SERIE OCEANOLOGICA, INSTITUTO DE OCEANOLOGIA,
ACADEMIA DE CIENCIAS DE CUBA.
+ +SER. OCEANOL. INST. OCEANOL. ACAD. CIENC.CUBA.
HAVANA 1, 1968-
LO/N-2.

SERIE DE QUIMICA, DEPARTMENT OF SCIENTIFIC
AFFAIRS, PAN-AMERICAN UNION.
+ +SER. QUIM. DEP. SCI. AFF. PAN-AM. UNION.
WASHINGTON, D.C. NO.1, 1965-
MONOGR.
OX/U-8. 1968-

SERIES HAEMOTOLOGICA.
+ +SER. HAEMATOL.
[MUNKSGAARD]
COPENHAGEN NO.1-11, 1965.
N.S. 1, 1968-
CR/M-1. GL/U-1. LD/U-1. LD/U-1. LO/N13.

SERIES ON ROCK & SOIL MECHANICS.
+ +SER. ROCK & SOIL MECH.
[TRANS TECH PUBL.]
CLEVELAND, OHIO 1, JA 1971-
BL/U-1.

SERMONS FOR TODAY.
[EPWORTH P.]
LONDON NO.1, 1968-
MONOGR.
OX/U-1.

SERVICE.
WOLVERHAMPTON CONSUMER GROUP.
WOLVERHAMPTON NO.1, 1968-
OX/U-1. OX/U-1.

SERVICE. NEWSLETTER OF THE ...
HOTEL & CATERING INDUSTRY TRAINING BOARD (GB).
LONDON NO.1, N 1967-
ED/N-1. LO/N-1.
LO/U-3. [CURRENT ISSUES ONLY]

SERVICE POINT.
LIBRARY ASSOCIATION: BRANCH & MOBILE LIBRARIES
GROUP.
BIRKENHEAD NO.1, S 1972-
CA/U-1. ED/N-1.
GL/U-2. NO.2, 1973-

SERVING GEORGIA THROUGH RESEARCH.                     000
SEE: BIENNIAL REPORT, AGRICULTURAL EXPERIMENT
STATIONS (GEORGIA).

SERVO-MECHANISMS.                                     XXX
(GREAT BRITAIN) MINISTRY OF AVIATION.
LONDON 1, JA 1965- 4(12), D 1968.//
S/T: BULLETIN OF AUTOMATIC & MANUAL CONTROL
ABSTRACTS. PREV: BIBLIOGRAPHY ON SERVOMECH-
ANISMS FROM 1961- 1964.
BH/P-1. BH/U-1. BL/U-1. BR/U-3. DB/U-2. ED/N-1.
LO/N-4. LO/N-7. LO/N14. LO/U11. LO/U12.
SH/U-3.

SESAME. THE NEWSPAPER OF THE OPEN UNIVERSITY.
BLETCHLEY, BUCKS. 1(1), MY 1972-
9/A.
ED/N-1. LD/U-1. LO/U-1.
BH/U-3. ONE YEAR ONLY.

SESHETA. POETRY MAGAZINE.
[SESHETA P.]
SUTTON NO.1, 1971-
3/A.
ED/N-1.

SESSUOLOGIA.
CENTRO ITALIANO DI SESSUOLOGIA.
[MINERVA MEDICA]
TORINO 1, 1960-
SUMM. IN ENGL.
LO/N13.
ISSN 0037-2838

SETTLEMENT NEWS.
IRISH COUNCIL FOR ITINERANT SETTLEMENT.
DUBLIN NO.1, MY/JE 1970-
DB/U-2.

SEVENTIES.                                            XXX
[SEVENTIES P.]
MADISON, MINN. NO.1, SPRING 1972-
PREV: SIXTIES FROM NO.4, 1960- NO.10, 1968.
LO/U-1.
ISSN 0037-5969

SEVERN & WYE REVIEW.
+ +SEVERN & WYE REV.
CHEPSTOW SOCIETY.
[PHILLIMORE]
CHICHESTER 1(1), 1970-
Q.
ED/N-1. LO/N-3. OX/U-1. SW/U-1.
ISSN 0049-0296

SEVERO-ZAPAD EVROPEJSKOJ CHASTI SSSR.
+ +SEV.-ZAPAD EVR. CHASTI SSSR. [SZEC-A]
LENINGRADSKIJ GOSUDARSTVENNYJ UNIVERSITET.
LENINGRAD [1], 1963-
BH/U-1. CC/U-1. LO/U-3.
GL/U-1. 4, 1965-                      LO/N13. 4, 1965-

SFINX.
UNIVERSITY OF OXFORD SPECULATIVE FICTION GROUP.
OXFORD NO.1, 1969-
OX/U-1.

SHAKESPEARE STUDIES: MONOGRAPH SERIES.
+ +SHAKESPEARE STUD., MONOGR. SER.
VANDERBILT UNIVERSITY: CENTER FOR SHAKESPEARE
STUDIES.
[WM. C. BROWN]
DUBUQUE, IOWA 1, 1969-
AD/U-1. BH/U-1. DB/U-2. LO/U-1. NW/U-1. OX/U-1.

SHAKESPEAREAN RESEARCH & OPPORTUNITIES.
+ +SHAKESPEAREAN RES. & OPPORTUNITIES.
MODERN LANGUAGE ASSOCIATION OF AMERICA.
NEW YORK &C. NO.1, 1965-
S/T: REPORT OF THE MODERN LANGUAGE ASSOCIATION
OF AMERICA CONFERENCE. TITLE VARIES. AS SHAKE-
SPEAREAN RESEARCH OPPORTUNITIES FROM NO.1,
1965- 3, 1967. AS ABOVE FROM NO.4, 1968/69.
NW/U-1.
BL/U-1. 2, 1966-                ED/N-1. 2, 1966-
GL/U-1. 2, 1966-               LO/U13. 3, 1967-
NO/U-1. 2, 1966-               SO/U-1. 3, 1967-
HL/U-1. 3, 1967- 5/6, 1970/71.
SH/U-1. 5/6, 1970/71-
ISSN 0080-9144

SHAMBHALA. OCCASIONAL PAPERS OF THE INSTIT-
UTE OF TIBETAN STUDIES.
*TRING, HERTS. NO.1, JA 1971-*
*OX/U-1.*

SHANTIH. NEW INTERNATIONAL WRITINGS.
*NEW YORK 1, 1971-*
*Q.*
*OX/U-1. 1(2), 1971.*
*ISSN 0037-329X*

SHEFFIELD PHILATELIST. N.S.
SHEFFIELD PHILATELIC SOCIETY.
*SHEFFIELD NO.1, 1969-*
*OX/U-1.*

SHIGEN KAGAKU KENKYUSHO IHO. MISCELLANEOUS
REPORTS, RESEARCH INSTITUTE FOR NATURAL
RESOURCES.
*TOKYO NO.1, 1943- 75, 1971. //*
*LO/N-2. NO.13, 1949-*

SHIKOKU NOGYO NO SHIN GIJUTSU.
SHIKOKU NOGYO SHIKENJO.
*KOGAWA 1, 1964-*
*LO/N13.\**

SHIN NIHON DENKI GIHO. NEW NIPPON ELECTRIC
TECHNICAL REVIEW.
SHIN NIHON DENKI K.K.
*OTSU 1, 1966-*
*ENGL. SUMM.*
*LO/N14.*

SHIPBUILDING INTERNATIONAL.                           XXX
*++SHIPBUILD. INT.*
*[WHITEHALL P. LTD.]*
*LONDON 7(7), 1964- 15(2), 1972.*
PREV: SHIPBUILDING EQUIPMENT FROM 1, 1958-
7(6), 1964. SUBS: PART OF SHIPBUILDING &
MARINE ENGINEERING INTERNATIONAL.
*LO/N14.*

SHIPBUILDING & MARINE ENGINEERING INTERNAT-
IONAL.                                                 XXX
*++SHIPBUILD. & MAR. ENG. INT.*
*[WHITEHALL P. LTD.]*
*LONDON 95(1156), JL 1972*
INCORP: MARINE ENGINEER & NAVAL ARCHITECT FROM
1, 1879- 95, 1972; & SHIPBUILDING INTERNAT-
IONAL FROM 7(7), 1964- 15(2), 1972.
*ED/N-1. GL/U-1. LO/N14.*
*NW/U-1. 95(1156- 1161), JL-D 1972.*

SHIPBUILDING & TRANSPORT REVIEW INTERNATIONAL.
*++SHIPBUILD. & TRANSP. REV. INT.*
*[SIJTHOFF PERS & ECONOMISCH DAGBLAD/HTC]*
*ROTTERDAM NO.1, 1972-*
*LO/N14.*

SHIPPING & SHIPBUILDING NEWS.
*++SHIPP. & SHIPBUILD. NEWS.*
*[ENGINEERING CHEMICAL & MARINE P.]*
*LONDON 1(1), 1971-*
*W.*
*OX/U-1.*
*LO/N-4. 1(7), 1971-          LO/N35. 2(1), 1972-*
*ISSN 0049-0377*

SHIRLEY LINK.                                          XXX
SHIRLEY INSTITUTE.
*MANCHESTER 1965- 1971.*
SUBS: TEXTILES (MANCHESTER).
*LO/N14. 1969-*
*ED/N-1. WINTER 1968/69-*
*LO/R-6. WINTER 1969/70-*
*OX/U-1. WINTER 1968/69-*
*ISSN 0037-3974*

SHIROARI.
TERMITE CONTROL ASSOCIATION OF JAPAN.
*TOKYO NO.1, 1962-*
*LO/N-2.*

SHIZENSHI KENKYU.
OSAKA SHIRITSU SHIZEN KAGAKU HAKUBUTSUKAN.
*OSAKA 1, 1968-*
*LO/N-2. LO/N13.*

SHIZUOKA-KEN RINGYO SHIKENJO KENKYU HOKOKU.
BULLETIN OF THE SHIZUOKA PREFECTURE FORESTRY
EXPERIMENT STATION.
SHIZUOKA-KEN RINGYO SHIKENJO.
*HAMAKITA NO.1, 1969-*
*LO/N13.*

SHOCK & VIBRATION DIGEST.
*++SHOCK & VIB. DIG. [SHVD-A]*
SHOCK & VIBRATION INFORMATION CENTER (US).
*WASHINGTON, D.C. 1, 1969-*
*MON.*
*LO/N14. SW/U-1.*
*XW/T-1. 5(1), 1973-*

SHOE MATERIALS PROGRESS.                               XXX
*++SHOE MATER. PROG.*
SHOE & ALLIED TRADES RESEARCH ASSOCIATION.
*KETTERING, NORTHANTS. 3(3), 1971-*
PREV: POROMERICS PROGRESS FROM 1(1), F 1969-
3(2), 1971.
*ED/N-1. LO/N14.*

SHOEMAKING PROGRESS.
*++SHOEMAK. PROG.*
SHOE & ALLIED TRADES RESEARCH ASSOCIATION.
*KETTERING, NORTHANTS. 1, 1971.*
SUBS: FOOTWEAR DIGEST.
*ED/N-1. LO/N14. OX/U-1.*

SHORT TERM ECONOMIC INDICATORS (SOUTH AFRICA).
= KORTTERMYN EKONOMIESE AANWYSERS.
*++SHORT TERM ECON. INDIC. (S. AFR.)*
(SOUTH AFRICA) BUREAU OF STATISTICS.
*PRETORIA JL 1967-*
*M. ENGL. = AFRIKAANS.*
*LO/U-3.*

SHORT TERM STATISTICAL INDICATORS.          OOO
SEE: INDICADORES ESTATISTICOS A CURTO PRAZO

SHOWA YAKKA DAIGAKU KIYO. ANNUAL REPORT OF
THE SHOWA PHARMACEUTICAL COLLEGE.
*TOKYO NO.1, 1963-*
*JAP. OR ENGL.*
*LO/N13.*

SHOYU TO GIJUTSU. SHOYU & TECHNICS.               XXX
NIHON SHOYU GIJUTSUKAI.
*TOKYO NO.1, 1952- 678, 1971.//*
*LO/N13. 562, 1968-*

SHOYU & TECHNICS.                                     000
SEE: SHOYU TO GIJUTSU.

SIAM JOURNAL ON COMPUTING.
*++SIAM J. COMPUT.*
SOCIETY FOR INDUSTRIAL & APPLIED MATHEMATICS.
*PHILADELPHIA 1, MR 1972-*
*Q.*
*DB/U-2. LO/N-4. LO/N14. SH/U-1.*

SIAM JOURNAL ON MATHEMATICAL ANALYSIS.
*++SIAM J. MATH. ANAL.*
SOCIETY FOR INDUSTRIAL & APPLIED MATHEMATICS.
*PHILADELPHIA 1(1), F 1970-*
*BH/U-3. DN/U-1. ED/U-1. LO/N14. OX/U-8. SH/U-1.*
*XS/R10. XS/T-4.*
*ISSN 0036-1410*

SIAM-AMS PROCEEDINGS.                                 XXX
*++SIAM-AMS PROC.*
AMERICAN MATHEMATICAL SOCIETY.
*PROVIDENCE, R.I. 1, 1969-*
PREV: PROCEEDINGS OF SYMPOSIA IN APPLIED
MATHEMATICS OF THE AMERICAN MATHEMATICAL
SOCIETY FROM 1, 1947 (1949).
*BH/U-1. BR/U-1. GL/U-1. LO/N-4. LO/N-4. LO/N13.*
*LO/U-2. NW/U-1. OX/U-8. RE/U-1.*
*BR/U-3. 2, 1970-*

SIBERIAN CHEMISTRY JOURNAL.                           XXX
*++SIB. CHEM. J. [SICJ-A]*
*[CONSULTANTS BUREAU]*
*NEW YORK 1967(1968)- 1970(1971).//*
ENGL. TRANSL. OF IZVESTIJA, SIBIRSKOGO OTDEL-
ENIJA, AKADEMII NAUK SSSR: SERIJA KHIMICHESK-
IKH NAUK. DATING & NUMBERING FOLLOW ORIGINAL.
*LO/N13.*
*ISSN 0583-1768*

SIBIR' I DAL'NYJ VOSTOK V PERIOD VOSSTANOV-
LENIJA NARODNOGO KHOZJAJSTVA.
*++SIB. & DAL'NYJ VOSTOK PERIOD VOSSTANOV. NAR.
KHOZ.*
(RUSSIA RSFSR) MINISTERSTVO VYSSHEGO I SREDNEGO
SPETSIAL'NOGO OBRAZOVANIJA.
*TOMSK 1, 1963-*
*OX/U-1.*
*LO/U-3. 4, 1965-*

**SICHERHEIT AM ARBEITSPLATZ.**                              XXX
LEDERINDUSTRIE-BERUFS-GENOSSENSCHAFT.
*MAINZ 1971-*
PREV: TECHNISCHER BERICHT, LEDERINDUSTRIE-
BERUFSGENOSSENSCHAFT FROM 1950-1969(1970).
*LO/N14.*

**SIECLE A MAINS.**
[CLAUDE ROYET-JOURNOUD]
*LONDON NO.1, S 1963-*
2- 3/A. NO.1, PUBL. IN ANTIBES.
*LO/N-1.*
*ISSN 0037-4628*

**SIEMENS DATA REPORT.**
*+ +SIEMENS DATA REP.*
SIEMENS UND HALSKE AG.
*MUNICH 1, 1966-*
*LO/N14.*
*ISSN 0037-4652*

**SIEMENS FORSCHUNGS- UND ENTWICKLUNGSBERICHTE.**
*+ +SIEMENS FORSCH.- & ENTWICKLUNGSBER.*
SIEMENS A.G.
[SPRINGER]
*BERLIN &C. 1(1), 1971-*
ENGL. & GER. SUMM. ALSO ENTITLED: SIEMENS
RESEARCH & DEVELOPMENT REPORTS.
*GL/U-1.    LO/N14.    LO/U12.    NW/U-1.    OX/U-8.*
*RE/U-1.    SF/U-1.*
*SA/U-1. 3, 1974-*
*HL/U-1. 1(1,4); 2, 1971-*

**SIEMENS RESEARCH & DEVELOPMENT REPORTS.**        000
SEE: SIEMENS FORSCHUNGS- UND ENTWICKLUNGS-
BERICHTE.

**SIEMENS-ALBIS BERICHTE.**                                  XXX
*+ +SIEMENS-ALBIS BER.*
SIEMENS-ALBIS, A.G.                                          XXX
*ZURICH 24, 1972-*
PREV: ALBISWERK-BERICHTE FROM 1, 1949- 23,
1971.
*LO/N14.*

**SIERRA LEONE CHAMBER OF COMMERCE JOURNAL.**
*+ +SIERRA LEONE CHAMB. COMMER. J.*
SIERRA LEONE CHAMBER OF COMMERCE.
*FREETOWN 1(1), 1965-*
*LO/N17.*
*EX/U-1. 1(4), 1968-*

**SIERRA LEONE LAW REPORTS.**
*+ +SIERRA LEONE LAW REP.*
(SIERRA LEONE) SUPREME COURT.
[SWEET & MAXWELL]
*LONDON 1, 1960/61 (1966)-*
A.
*OX/U15.*

**SIGNAL. APPROACHES TO CHILDREN'S BOOKS.**
[THIMBLE P.]
*STROUD, GLOS. NO.1, JA 1970-*
3/A.
*CB/U-2.    ED/N-1.    LO/N-1.    OX/U-1.*
*BL/U-1. NO.13, 1974-*
*ISSN 0037-4954*

**SIGNATURE.**
DINERS CLUB OF GREAT BRITAIN.
*LONDON 1(1), N 1966-*
6/A. PREV: DINERS CLUB MAGAZINE.
*ED/N-1.*

**SIGNO.**
BIBLIOTECA NACIONAL (SALVADOR).
*SAN SALVADOR 1, 1971-*
Q.
*OX/U-1.*

**SIGNUM NEWSLETTER.**
*+ +SIGNUM NEWSL.*
ASSOCIATION FOR COMPUTING MACHINERY: SPECIAL
INTEREST COMMITTEE ON NUMERICAL MATHEMATICS.
*NEW YORK 1, 1966-*
*AD/U-1. 9, 1974-*                *BN/U-2. 1(2), 1966-*

**SILLAGES.**
UNIVERSITE DE POITIERS: DEPARTEMENT D'ETUDES
PORTUGAISES ET BRESILIENNES.
*POITIERS 1, 1972-*
FR. & PORT.
*LD/U-1.    SH/U-1.*

**SILVER BULLETIN.**
*+ +SILVER BULL.*
[MORLANDS LEE LTD.]
*LONDON NO.1, AP 1969-*
S/T: THE MARKET IN OLD SILVER EXPLAINED BY
THE EXPERTS OF ART & ANTIQUES WEEKLY.
*CA/U-1.*
*ED/N-1. NO.2, 1969-*
*ISSN 0586-609X*

**SIMON STAR. NEWSLETTER OF THE SIMON
COMMUNITY.**                                                 XXX
*LONDON [1](1), 1964- 3(12), AP 1969.*
*N.S. NO.1, MR 1970-*
SUPERSEDED BY SOCIAL ACTION FROM MY 1969- F
1970.
*LO/U-3. **
*ED/N-1. N.S. NO.13, 1971-*

**SIMULATION COUNCILS PROCEEDINGS SERIES.**
*+ +SIMULAT. COUNC. PROC. SER.*
SIMULATION COUNCILS, INC.
*LA JOLLA, CALIF. 1, 1971-*
*LO/N14.*

**SIMULATION & GAMES.**
*+ +SIMULAT. & GAMES.*
*BEVERLY HILLS, CALIF. 1, 1970-*
Q. S/T: AN INTERNATIONAL JOURNAL OF THEORY,
DESIGN & RESEARCH.
*LO/U-3.    SH/U-1.*
*GL/U-2. 5, 1974-*
*ISSN 0037-5500*

**SIMULATION/ GAMING/ NEWS.**
*+ +SIMULAT. GAMING NEWS.*
STANFORD UNIVERSITY.
*STANFORD, CALIF. 1, F 1972-*
5/A.
*SH/U-1.*

**SIMULATION IN THE SERVICE OF SOCIETY.**
*+ +SIMULAT. SERV. SOC.*
*LA JOLLA, CALIF. 1, JA 1971-*
M.
*SH/U-1.*

**SIN NOMBRE. REVISTA TRIMESTRAL LITERARIA.**
[EDITORIAL SIN NOMBRE]
*SAN JUAN, P.R. 1, JE/S 1970-*
SUBTITLE VARIES.
*MA/U-1. 3, 1972-*                *NO/U-1. 4(2), 1973-*
*ISSN 0037-5527*

**SIND UNIVERSITY RESEARCH JOURNAL.**
*+ +SIND UNIV. RES. J.*
*HYDERABAD 1, 1965-*
*LO/N-2.*

**SINE. BULLETIN OF THE ...**
SCOTLAND-CHINA ASSOCIATION.
*EDINBURGH 1, 1972-*
*ED/N-1.*
*CA/U-1. 1(2), 1972-*

**SINGAPORE BOOK WORLD.**
NATIONAL BOOK DEVELOPMENT COUNCIL OF SINGAPORE.
*SINGAPORE 1, 1970-*
*HL/U-1.    LO/U-8.    LO/U14.    OX/U-1.*

**SINGAPORE PUBLIC HEALTH BULLETIN.**
(SINGAPORE) MINISTRY OF HEALTH: PUBLIC HEALTH
DIVISION.
*SINGAPORE NO.1, 1967-*
*LO/N13.*

**SINGAPORE STATISTICAL BULLETIN.**
*+ +SINGAPORE STAT. BULL.*
(SINGAPORE) NATIONAL STATISTICAL COMMISSION.
*SINGAPORE 1(1), JE 1972-*
*HL/U-1.    LO/N-1.    LO/U-3.*

**SINTESI GRAFICA DELLA VITA ECONOMICA
ITALIANA.**
*+ +SINT. GRAFICA VITA ECON. ITAL.*
ISTITUTO CENTRALE DI STATISTICA.
*ROME 1(1), 1967-*
*LO/N-1.*

**SINTESE POLITICA, ECONOMICA, SOCIAL.**             XXX
*+ +SINT. POLIT. ECON. SOC.*
PONTIFICIA UNIVERSIDADE CATOLICA DO RIO DE
JANIERO: INSTITUTO DE ESTUDOS POLITICOS E
SOCIAIS.
*RIO DE JANEIRO 1, JA/MR 1959- 39, JL/D 1968//*
*CC/U-1. 1(2), 1959-*                *LO/U-3. 5, 1960-*
*OX/U-1. 25, 1965-*
*ISSN 0037-5772*

**SIOCHAIN.**
GARDA SIOCHANA PENSIONERS ASSOCIATION.
*DUBLIN 1, 1972-*
*DB/U-2.*

**SIPAPU.**
*DAVIS, CALIF. 1(1), 1970-*
S/T: A NEWSLETTER FOR LIBRARIANS, SCHOLARS,
EDITORS & OTHERS CONCERNED WITH ETHNIC
STUDIES, THE COUNTER-CULTURE & THE UNDER-
GROUND PRESS.
*LO/U-2.*
ISSN 0037-5837

**SIPRI YEARBOOK OF WORLD ARMAMENTS & DISARM-
AMENTS.**
*+ +SIPRI YRB. WORLD ARMAM. & DISARM.*
STOCKHOLM INTERNATIONAL PEACE RESEARCH INST-
ITUTE.
*STOCKHOLM 1, 1968/69 (1969)-*
*LD/U-1.    LO/U-3.    OX/U-1.*
*SH/U-1. 4, 1973-*
*SW/U-1. 2, 1969/70.*

**SIRA ABSTRACTS & REVIEWS.**                    XXX
*+ +SIRA ABSTR. & REV.*
BRITISH SCIENTIFIC INSTRUMENT RESEARCH
ASSOCIATION.
[TAYLOR & FRANCIS]
*LONDON 23(1- 12), JA- D 1968.*
MON. PREV: INSTRUMENT ABSTRACTS FROM 14(5),
1959- 22, 1967. SUBS: METRON. SIRA MEASUREMENT
& CONTROL ABSTRACTS.
*BH/P-1.    ED/N-1.    HL/U-1.    LO/N14.*

**SIRIUS.**
SOCIETY FOR INVESTIGATION & RESEARCH INTO
UNIDENTIFIED FLYING OBJECT SIGHTINGS.
*LONDON 1, 1971-*
*ED/N-1.*

**SIS RYMD-INFORMATION.**
*+ +SIS RYMD-INF.*
SVENSKA INTERPLANETARISKA SALLSKAPET.
*STOCKHOLM 1, 1965-*
*LO/N14.*

**SISTEMA. REVISTA DE CIENCIAS SOCIALES.**
*MADRID 1, JA 1973-*
Q.
*OX/U-1.*

**SISTEMNYE ISSLEDOVANIJA.**
*+ +SIST. ISSLED.*
AKADEMIJA NAUK SSSR: INSTITUT ISTORII ESTEST-
VOZNANIJA I TEKHNIKI.
*MOSCOW 1, 1969-*
A. TITLE ALSO IN ENGL.: SYSTEMS RESEARCH.
*BH/U-1.    CC/U-1.    LO/N13.*

**SITUATION DE L'AGRICULTURE BELGE AU COURS DE
L'ANNEE.**
*+ +SITUAT. AGR. BELGE COURS ANN.*
INSTITUT ECONOMIQUE AGRICOLE (BELGIUM).
*BRUSSELS 1, 1961-*
*LO/U-3.*

**SIXTEENTH CENTURY ESSAYS & STUDIES.**          XXX
*+ +SIXTEENTH CENTURY ESSAYS & STUD.*
FOUNDATION FOR REFORMATION RESEARCH.
*ST. LOUIS, MO. 1, 1970- 2, 1971 ...*
ANNU. SUBS: SIXTEENTH CENTURY JOURNAL.
*MA/S-1.*

**SIXTEENTH CENTURY JOURNAL.**                   XXX
*+ +SIXTEENTH CENTURY J.*
FOUNDATION FOR REFORMATION RESEARCH.
*ST. LOUIS, MO. 3, 1972-*
2/A. PREV: SIXTEENTH CENTURY ESSAYS & STUDIES
FROM 1, 1970- 2, 1971.
*MA/S-1.*
*DB/U-2. 4, 1973-              LO/U-2. 5(1), 1974-*
ISSN 0080-987X

**SKANDINAVISTIK. ZEITSCHRIFT FUR SPRACHE, LIT-
ERATUR UND KULTUR DER NORDISCHEN LANDER.**
*GLUCKSTADT 1, 1971-*
*ED/N-1.    LD/U-1.    LO/N-1.    LO/U-2.*

**SKINNER'S COTTON & MAN-MADE FIBRES DIRECTORY
OF THE WORLD.**
*+ +SKINNER'S COTT. MAN-MADE FIBRES DIR. WORLD.*
[SKINNER & CO.]
*MANCHESTER 1964-*
ENGL., FR., GER., ITAL., SPAN., PORT.
*LO/N-14. 1967-*

**SKORSTENSFEJARMASTAREN.**
SVERIGES SKORSTENSFEJAREMASTARES RIKSFORBUND.
*STOCKHOLM 1, 1965-*
*LO/N14.*

**SKRIFTER, ISOTOPTEKNISKA LABORATORIET.**
*+ +SKR. ISOTOPTEK. LAB.*
*STOCKHOLM [NR.]1, 1960-*
*LO/N14.\**

**SKRIFTER FRA NORSK STADNAMNARKIV.**
*+ +SKR. NOR. STADNAMNARK.*
[UNIVERSITETSFORLAGET]
*OSLO 1, 1960-*
ENGL. SUMM.
*CA/U-1. 2, 1961-*

**SKRIFTER UTGIVNA AV LATINAMERIKA-INSTITUTET I
STOCKHOLM: SERIES C.**
*+ +SKR. LATINAM.-INST. STOCKH., C.*
*STOCKHOLM NO.1, 1970-*
MONOGR.
*LO/N-1.*

**SKRIFTSERIE, NORDISK INSTITUT FOR FOLKEDIGTN-
ING.**
*+ +SKRIFTSER. NORD. INST. FOLKEDIGTNING.*
*COPENHAGEN 1, 1962-*
*ED/N-1. 3, 1964-*
*LO/U-2. 3, 1964.*

**SLAM.**                                        XXX
SUBS (1973): DRIFTTEKNIK.

**SLAVICA WRATISLAVIENSIA. (ACTA UNIVERSITATIS
WRATISLAVIENSIS).**
*+ +SLAV. WRATISLAV.*
UNIWERSYTET WROCLAWSKI.
*WROCLAW NO.1, 1969-*
ALSO NUMBERED AS PART OF MAIN SERIES: ACTA
UNIVERSITATIS WRATISLAVIENSIS. NO.1 OF ABOVE
= NO. 106 OF ACTA. POL. & RUSS.
*LO/N-3.*

**SLOAN MANAGEMENT REVIEW.**                     XXX
*+ +SLOAN MANAGE. REV.*
ALFRED P. SLOAN SCHOOL OF MANAGEMENT.
*CAMBRIDGE, MASS. 12(1), 1970-*
PREV: INDUSTRIAL MANAGEMENT REVIEW FROM 1,
1959- 11(3), 1970.
*HL/U-1.    LO/N-7.*
*SH/U-1. 13, 1971-*
ISSN 0019-848X

**SLOUGH CONSUMER.**
*+ +SLOUGH CONSUM.*
SLOUGH CONSUMER GROUP.
*SLOUGH NO.1, 1968-*
*OX/U-1.*

**SLOVENSKA NARODNA BIBLIOGRAFIA: SERIA A:
KNIHY.**                                         XXX
*+ +SLOV. NAR. BIBLIOGR., A.*
MATICA SLOVENSKA V MARTINE.
*TURCIANSKY SV. MARTIN 20(13), 1969-*
PREV: BIBLIOGRAFICKY KATALOG CSSR: SLOVENSKE
KNIHY FROM 1(1), 1950- 20(12), 1969.
*GL/U-1.    LA/U-1.    LO/N-3.    OX/U-1.*

**SLOVENSKA NARODNA BIBLIOGRAFIA: SERIA C:
CLANKY.**                                        XXX
*+ +SLOV. NAR. BIBLIOGR., C.*
MATICA SLOVENSKA V MARTINE.
*MARTIN 16(1), JA 1970-*
M. PREV: BIBLIOGRAFICKY KATALOG CSSR, CLANKY
V SLOVENSKYCH CASOPISOCH FROM 1(1), 1955-
15(14), 1969.
*LA/U-1.    LO/N-3.    OX/U-1.*

**SLOV'JANS'KE LITERATUROZNAVSTVO I FOL'KLORYS-
TYKA.**
AKADEMIJA NAUK UKRAJINS'KOJI RSR.
*KIEV VYP.1, 1965-*
S/T: RESPUBLIKANS'KYJ MIZHVIDOMCHYJ ZBIRNYK.
PREV: MIZHSLOV'JANS'KY LITERATURNY FROM 1,
1958- 3, ?1964. & MIZHSOLV'JANS'KY FOL'KLORY-
STYCHNY VZAEMYNY FROM 1958- ?1964.
*LO/N-3.*
*BH/U-1. 5, 1970-*

**SLPMB RECORD. A NEWSLETTER FROM THE SIERRA
LEONE PRODUCE MARKETING BOARD.**
*FREETOWN 1, JE 1966-*
*LO/U-8.*

**SLR CAMERA.**
[HAYMARKET PRESS]
*LONDON 1(1), 1967.*
*LO/N14.*
*ED/N-1. 1(2), JL 1967.*
*SH/P-1. [FIVE YEARS]*
*ISSN 0036-1631*

**SMALL ANIMAL CLINICIAN.**
*++SMALL ANIM. CLIN.*
AMERICAN ANIMAL HOSPITAL ASSOCIATION.
*KANSAS CITY, MO. 2, JA 1961- 3, 1963.*
M. SUBS: PART OF VETERINARY MEDICINE/SMALL
ANIMAL CLINICIAN.
*LO/M18.*

**SMALL ARMS PROFILE.**
[PROFILE PUBL. LTD.]
*WINDSOR 1, AG 1971-*
M.
*ED/N-1.    LO/N14.*

**SMALL BOAT.**
[CARAVAN PUBL.]
*CROYDON 1(1), AP 1969-*
INCORP: LIGHT CRAFT, SMALL BOAT & NORTH SEA
YACHTSMAN.
*ED/N-1.    OX/U-1.*
*LO/N14. [CURRENT BOX ONLY]*
*ISSN 0037-718X*

**SMALL BUSINESS.**
*++SMALL BUS.*
AMERICAN INSTITUTE OF PLANNERS.
*WASHINGTON, D.C. NO.1, 1967-*
S/T: AN AMERICAN INSTITUTE OF PLANNERS
BACKGROUND PAPER.
*LO/U-2.*

**SMALL GROUP BEHAVIOR.**                                    XXX
*++SMALL GROUP BEHAV.*
[SAGE PUBL.]
*LONDON; BEVERLY HILLS 4(1), 1973-*
PREV: COMPARATIVE GROUP STUDIES FROM 1, 1970-
3, 1972.
*DB/U-2.    SH/U-1.*
*NO/U-1.  5, 1974-              SW/U-1.  4, 1973-*
*BD/U-1.  4(1- 4), 1973.*
*ISSN 0090-5526*

**SMALL OFFSET PRINTING.**                                  XXX
*++SMALL OFFSET PRINT.*
[MACLEAN-HUNTER LTD.]
*LONDON NO.1, 1969- 35, 1971 ...*
SUBS: OFFSET PRINTING.
*ED/N-1.    OX/U-1.*
*LO/N14. [W. NO.2;5 & 8, 1969]*
*ISSN 0037-7201*

**SMALL PRESS REVIEW.**
*++SMALL PRESS REV.*
*EL CERRITO, CALIF.  1(1), SPRING 1967-*
PUBL. IN CONJUNC. WITH: DIRECTORY OF LITTLE
MAGAZINES.
*HL/U-1.    LO/U-1.    LO/U-2.*
*ISSN 0037-7228*

**SMITHSONIAN.**
[SMITHSONIAN ASSOCIATES]
*WASHINGTON, D.C. 1(1), AP 1970-*
MON.
*LO/N-2.*
*LO/U-1. 1(8), 1970-*
*ISSN 0037-7333*

**SMITHSONIAN CONTRIBUTIONS TO BOTANY.**
*++SMITHSON. CONTRIB. BOT.*
SMITHSONIAN INSTITUTION.
*WASHINGTON 1, 1969-*
*BL/U-1.    DB/S-1.    ED/S-2.    LO/N-2.    LO/N-4.    LO/N13.*
*NW/U-1.    OX/U-8.*

**SMITHSONIAN CONTRIBUTIONS TO THE EARTH
SCIENCES.**
*++SMITHSON. CONTRIB. EARTH SCI.*
SMITHSONIAN INSTITUTION.
*WASHINGTON, D.C. NO.1, 1969-*
*BH/P-1.    BH/U-1.    BH/U-3.    BL/U-1.    GL/U-1.    LO/N-2.*
*LO/N-4.    LO/N14.    LO/U12.*    MA/U-1.    NW/U-1.*
*OX/U-8.    SH/U-1.***
*CA/U14. NO.2, 1970-              SO/U-1. NO.2, 1970-*

**SMITHSONIAN CONTRIBUTIONS TO PALEOBIOLOGY.**
*++SMITHSON. CONTRIB. PALEOBIOL.*
SMITHSONIAN INSTITUTION.
*WASHINGTON NO.1, 1969-*
*BH/P-1.    BH/U-1.    BH/U-3.    BL/U-1.    BN/U-2.    DB/S-1.*
*LO/N-2.    LO/N-4.    LO/N13.    LO/U-2.    NW/U-1.    OX/U-8.*
*CA/U14. NO.3, 1971-              LO/U-1. NO.3, 1971-*
*SO/U-1. NO.3, 1971-*

**SMITHSONIAN CONTRIBUTIONS TO ZOOLOGY.**
*++SMITHSON. CONTRIB. ZOOL.*
SMITHSONIAN INSTITUTION.
*WASHINGTON, D.C. 1, 1969-*
*BH/P-1.    BH/U-1.    BL/U-1.    BN/U-2.    DB/S-1.    ED/U-1.*
*GL/U-1.    LO/N-2.    LO/N-4.    LO/U-2.    LO/U12.***
*MA/U-1.**    NW/U-1.    OX/U-8.*

**SMM TECHNICAL PAPER.**
*++SMM TECH. PAP.*
[STONE MANGANESE MARINE LTD.]
*LONDON 1, 1964-*
*LO/N14.*

**SMOKELESS AIR.**                                          XXX
SUBS (1971): PART CLEAN AIR.

**SMRE TECHNICAL PAPER.**
*++SMRE TECH. PAP.*
SAFETY IN MINES RESEARCH ESTABLISHMENT.
*SHEFFIELD P1, 1973-*
*CA/U-1.    LO/N14.*

**SNACK FOOD.**                                             XXX
[AMERICAN TRADE PUBL. CO.]
*NEW YORK 57, 1968-*
PREV: BISCUIT & CRACKER BAKER FROM 39, 1950-
56, 1967.
*LO/N14.*
*ISSN 0037-7406*

**SNIC BULLETIN.**
*++SNIC BULL.*
SINGAPORE NATIONAL INSTITUTE OF CHEMISTRY.
*SINGAPORE 1, 1972-*
*LO/N14.*

**SOAG THEORY & PRACTICE.**
*++SOAG THEORY & PRACT.*
SOAG MACHINE TOOLS LTD.
*LONDON 1, 1961-*
*LO/N14.*    XN/S-1.*

**SOAP & CHEMICAL SPECIALTIES.**                            XXX
SUBS (1971): SOAP, COSMETICS, CHEMICAL
SPECIALITIES.

**SOAP, COSMETICS, CHEMICAL SPECIALTIES.**                  XXX
*++SOAP COSMET. CHEM. SPEC.*
·CHEMICAL SPECIALTIES MANUFACTURERS ASSOCIATION.
[MAC NAIR-DORLAND CO.]
*NEW YORK 47(7), 1971-*
PREV: SOAP & CHEMICAL SPECIALITIES FROM 30(5),
1954- 47(6), 1971.
*LO/N14.*
*LO/S-3. 49, 1973-*

**SOBRE LOS DERIVADOS DE LA CANA DE AZUCAR.**
*++SOBR. DERIV. CANA AZUCAR.*
INSTITUTO CUBANO DE INVESTIGACIONES DE LOS
DERIVADOS DE LA CANA DE AZUCAR.
*HAVANA 1, 1967-*
*LO/N14.*

**SOCIAL ACTION.**
*++SOC. ACTION.*
SIMON COMMUNITY TRUST RESEARCH.
*ST. LEONARDS-ON-SEA NO.1, MY 1969-*
SUPERSEDED SIMON STAR FROM MY 1969- F 1970.
*ED/N-1.    LO/U-3.    OX/U-1.*
*CV/C-1. ONE YEAR.*

**SOCIAL AUDIT.**
*++SOC. AUDIT.*
[SOCIAL AUDIT LTD.]
*LONDON 1(1), 1973-*
Q.
*BH/U-1.    CA/U-1.    CB/U-1.    ED/N-1.    GL/U-2.    HL/U-1.*
*LO/N-1.    LO/U-3.    LO/U12.    NW/U-1.    OX/U-1.*
*OX/U16.    OX/U17.    SH/U-1.*
*MA/U-1. 1(4), 1974-*

**SOCIAL BIOLOGY.**                                               XXX
++SOC. BIOL.
AMERICAN EUGENICS SOCIETY.
[UNIV. CHICAGO P.]
 CHICAGO 16(1), MR 1969-
 PREV: EUGENICS QUARTERLY FROM 1, 1954-15,1968.
 BH/U-1.    CA/U-1.    CA/U-3.    LD/U-1.
 ISSN 0037-766X

**SOCIAL CHANGE.**
++SOC. CHANGE.
[GORDON & BREACH]
 NEW YORK 1, 1973-
 AD/U-1.    CA/U-1.    ED/N-1.    OX/U-1.

**SOCIAL DEVELOPMENT NEWSLETTER.**
++SOC. DEV. NEWSL.
UNITED NATIONS: DEPARTMENT OF ECONOMIC & SOCIAL
AFFAIRS.
 NEW YORK NO.1, MY 1971-
 Q.
 LO/S14.    OX/U-3.    SW/U-1.

**SOCIAL-ECONOMIC INDICATORS (PORTUGAL).**                        000
  SEE: INDICADORES ECONOMICO-SOCIAIS.

**SOCIAL, ECONOMIC & POLITICAL STUDIES OF THE
MIDDLE EAST.**
++SOC. ECON. POLIT. STUD. MIDDLE EAST.
 LEIDEN 1, 1971-
 CA/U-1.

**SOCIAL HISTORY.**                        000
  SEE: HISTOIRE SOCIALE.

**SOCIAL INDICATORS FOR FIJI.**
++SOC. INDIC. FIJI.
(FIJI) BUREAU OF STATISTICS.
 SUVA NO.1, N 1972-
 ANNU.
 LO/U-3.

**SOCIAL POLICY.**
++SOC. POLICY.
[INTERNATIONAL ARTS & SCIENCES P.]
 WHITE PLAINS, N.Y. MY/JL 1970-
 AD/U-1.    CR/U-1.    HL/U-1.    LO/U-3.    LO/U-4.
 MA/U-1. 3(4/5), 1972-
 ISSN 0037-7783

**SOCIAL PRAXIS. INTERNATIONAL & INTERDISCIPLIN-
ARY QUARTERLY OF SOCIAL SCIENCES.**
++SOC. PRAX.
 THE HAGUE 1, 1973-
 FR. SUMM.
 HL/U-1.    LO/U-3.

**SOCIAL SCIENCE BULLETIN (KENYA).**
++SOC. SCI. BULL. (KENYA).
UNIVERSITY COLLEGE, NAIROBI: INSTITUTE FOR
DEVELOPMENT STUDIES.
 NAIROBI NO.1, 1965-
 Q.
 LO/N17.

**SOCIAL SCIENCE RESEARCH.**
++SOC. SCI. RES.
[SEMINAR P.]
 NEW YORK; & LONDON 1(1), AP 1972-
 S/T: A QUARTERLY JOURNAL OF SOCIAL SCIENCE
 METHODOLOGY & QUANTITATIVE RESEARCH.
 AD/U-1.    BD/U-1.    BL/U-1.    CA/U-1.    GL/U-1.    LO/U-3.
 MA/U-1.    OX/U17.    SH/U-3.    SO/U-1.
 LO/U-4. 3, 1974-
 ISSN 0049-089X

**SOCIAL SCIENCES IN CANADA. SCIENCES SOCIALES
AU CANADA.**
++SOC. SCI. CAN.
SOCIAL SCIENCE RESEARCH COUNCIL OF CANADA.
 OTTAWA 1(1), JA 1971-
 BH/P-1.    LO/N-1.    LO/U-3.    LO/U-8.    OX/U16.    OX/U17.
 BH/U-3. FIVE YEARS ONLY.
 ISSN 0049-092X

**SOCIAL SCIENTIST.**
++SOC. SCI.
INDIAN SCHOOL OF SOCIAL SCIENCES.
 NEW DELHI 1(1), AG 1972-
 MON.
 LD/U-1.    LO/U-3.

**SOCIAL SECURITY QUARTERLY.**
++SOC. SECUR. Q. (AUST.).
(AUSTRALIA) DEPARTMENT OF SOCIAL SECURITY.
 CANBERRA WINTER 1973-
 LO/U-3.

**SOCIAL STUDIES. IRISH JOURNAL OF SOCIOLOGY.**                   XXX
++SOC. STUD.
CHRISTUS REX SOCIETY.
 MAYNOOTH, CO. KILDARE 1(1), JA 1972-
 2M. INCORP. CHRISTUS REX. PRELIM. NO. 0(0)
 ISSUED IN 1971.
 AD/U-1.    DB/U-1.    ED/N-1.    LO/U-3.    OX/U-1.

**SOCIAL THEORY & PRACTICE.**
++SOC. THEORY & PRACT.
FLORIDA STATE UNIVERSITY: CENTRE FOR SOCIAL
PHILOSOPHY.
 TALLAHASSEE, FLA. 1, 1970-
 Q. CENTRE SUBORD. TO: DEPARTMENT OF PHILOS-
 OPHY.
 CA/U-1.    DB/U-2.    LO/U-1.    SW/U-1.
 GL/U-1. 3, 1974-
 ISSN 0037-802X

**SOCIAL TRENDS.**
(GREAT BRITAIN) CENTRAL STATISTICAL OFFICE.
 LONDON [NO.1], 1970-
 ANNU.
 CA/U-1.    CA/U-5.    CB/U-1.    DB/U-2.    LO/N-7.    LO/R-5.
 LO/U-3.    LO/U11.    LO/U12.    OX/U-1.    OX/U17.
 RE/U-1.    SF/U-1.    SW/U-1.    XS/R10.

**SOCIAL WORK (LONDON).**                                         XXX
  SUBS (1971): PART BRITISH JOURNAL OF SOCIAL
  WORK.

**SOCIAL WORK TODAY. JOURNAL OF THE ...**
++SOC. WORK TODAY.
BRITISH ASSOCIATION OF SOCIAL WORKERS.
 LONDON 1(1), AP 1970-
 INCORP: CASE CONFERENCE FROM 1, 1954- 16,
 1970; MEDICAL SOCIAL WORK FROM 18, 1965- 22,
 1969; MENTAL WELFARE; BULLETIN OF THE ASSOCIA-
 TION OF MORAL WELFARE WORKERS; & ASW NEWS.
 AD/U-1.    BH/U-1.    BN/U-1.    CB/U-1.    CV/C-1.    DB/U-1.
 DB/U-2.    ED/N-1.    ED/U-1.    EX/U-1.    GL/U-2.    LO/N-1.
 LO/U-1.    LO/U-3.    LO/U-4.    LO/U12.    MA/P-1.    NO/U-1.
 SO/U-1.
 MA/U-1. 1(5), 1970-          SH/P-1. 1975-
 ISSN 0037-8070

**SOCIALISM & HEALTH.**                                           XXX
++SOC. & HEALTH. [SOHE-A]
SOCIALIST MEDICAL ASSOCIATION.
 LONDON 1, JA/F 1967-
 PREV: MEDICINE TODAY & TOMORROW FROM [1], OC
 1937- 18, N/D 1966.
 LO/U-3.
 BH/P-1. 4(4), 1970-          SO/U-1. 6(4), 1972-
 SW/U-1. 2(2), 1968-          SW/U-1. 2(2), 1968-

**SOCIALIST AFFAIRS.**                                            XXX
++SOC. AFF.
 LONDON 21(1), JA 1971-
 M. PREV: SOCIALIST INTERNATIONAL INFORMATION
 FROM 1(27/28), JL 1951- 20, 1970.
 LO/S14.    OX/U-1.
 OX/U17. 2, 1952- 9, 1959.
 ISSN 0049-0946

**SOCIALIST INTERNATIONAL INFORMATION.**                          XXX
  SUBS (1971): SOCIALIST AFFAIRS.

**SOCIALIST REVOLUTION.**                                         XXX
++SOC. REVOLUTION.
[AGENDA PUBL. CO.]
 SAN FRANCISCO NO.1, JA/F 1970-
 PREV: STUDIES ON THE LEFT FROM 1, 1959- 7(2),
 MR/AP 1967.
 LO/N-1.    OX/U-1.
 BL/U-1. 1970-[W. NO.1].
 ISSN 0037-8240

**SOCIALIST VOICE.**
 LONDON 1(1), 1969-
 S/T: INTERNATIONAL SOCIALIST FORUM.
 ED/N-1.    OX/U-1.    OX/U17.
 ISSN 0037-8267

**SOCIALIST WOMAN.**
++SOC. WOMAN.
SOCIALIST WOMAN GROUPS.
 LONDON [NO.] 1, MR/AP 1971-
 2M.
 ED/N-1.    LO/U-3.

**SOCIALISTICKE ZEMEDELSTVI, CASOPIS PRO
VYROBNI ZEMEDELSKE SPRAVY A ORGANIZATORY
VYROBY.**
++SOC. ZEMED. CAS. PRO VYROBNI ZEMED. SPRAVY
ORGAN. VYROBY.
(CZECHOSLOVAKIA) MINISTERSTVO ZEMEDELSTVI,
LESNIHO A VODNIHO HOSPODARSTVI.
PRAGUE 1, AP 1964-
LO/N-3.*

**SOCIEDAD Y POLITICA.**
++SOC. & POLIT. (PERU).
LIMA 1(1), JE 1972-
Q.
CC/U-1.    LO/U-3.

**SOCIETAS. A REVIEW OF SOCIAL HISTORY.**
CONFERENCE GROUP FOR SOCIAL & ADMINISTRATIVE
HISTORY.
APPLETON, WIS. 1(1), 1971-
Q.
BH/P-1.    HL/U-1.    LO/N-1.    LO/U-3.
CV/U-1. 4, 1974-                DB/U-2. 4, 1974-
SH/U-1. 2, 1972-
ISSN 0037-8879

**SOCIETY.**                                                                                             XXX
RUTGERS UNIVERSITY.
NEW BRUNSWICK, N.J. 9(4), F 1972-
MON. PREV: TRANS-ACTION FROM 1, 1963- 9(3),
1972.
LO/U-1.    NO/U-1.
SH/U-1. 10, 1972-

**SOCIETY & LEISURE.**
++SOC. & LEISURE.
EUROPEAN CENTRE FOR LEISURE & EDUCATION.
PRAGUE NO.1, 1969-
ED/N-1.    OX/U-1.
SF/U-1. 5, 1973-
ISSN 0037-9670

**SOCIOLOGICAL ANALYSIS.**                                                                               XXX
++SOCIOL. ANAL.
UNIVERSITY OF SHEFFIELD: DEPARTMENT OF SOCIO-
LOGICAL STUDIES.
SHEFFIELD 1(1), OC 1970- 3, JE 1973 ...
3/A. SUBS: SOCIOLOGICAL ANALYSIS & THEORY.
ED/N-1.    LO/U-3.    OX/U-1.    RE/U-1.    SH/U-1.    SW/U-1.
ISSN 0049-1233

**SOCIOLOGICAL JOURNAL.**
++SOCIOL. J.
MAKERERE UNIVERSITY: SOCIOLOGICAL SOCIETY.
KAMPALA 1(1), OC 1970-
LO/U-8.

**SOCIOLOGICAL METHODOLOGY.**
++SOCIOL. METHODOL.
AMERICAN SOCIOLOGICAL ASSOCIATION.
[JOSSEY-BASS]
SAN FRANCISCO 1, 1969-
BL/U-1.    CA/U-1.    LO/N-1.    LO/U20.    OX/U17.
RE/U-1. 1972-                SF/U-1. 1972-
ISSN 0081-1750

**SOCIOLOGICAL METHODS & RESEARCH.**
++SOCIOL. METHODS & RES.
[SAGE PUBLS.]
BEVERLY HILLS, CALIF. 1, 1972/73-
AD/U-1.    EX/U-1.    LD/U-1.    LO/U-4.    MA/U-1.    NO/U-1.
OX/U17.    SH/U-1.    SO/U-1.
CA/U-1. 1(2), 1972-
ISSN 0049-1241

**SOCIOLOGICAL STUDIES.**
++SOCIOL. STUD.
[CAMBRIDGE UNIV. P.]
CAMBRIDGE 1, 1968-
MONOGR.
EX/U-1.    GL/U-1.    LV/U-1.    MA/U-1.    OX/U-1.    OX/U17.

**SOCIOLOGICAL THEORIES IN PROGRESS.**
++SOCIOL. THEOR. PROG.
[HOUGHTON MIFFLIN]
BOSTON, MASS. 1, 1966-
AD/U-1.    GL/U-1.    OX/U17.

**SOCIOLOGICAL YEARBOOK OF RELIGION IN BRITAIN.**
++SOCIOL. YEARB. RELIG. BR.
[SCM PRESS]
LONDON [1968]-
GL/U-1.    LD/U-1.    LO/U-3.    OX/U-1.

**SOCIOLOGIE ET SOCIETES.**
++SOCIOL. & SOC.
[LES PRESSES DE L'UNIVERSITE DE MONTREAL]
MONTREAL 1(1), MY 1969-
LO/N-1.    MA/U-1.
CB/U-1. 6, 1974-
ISSN 0038-030X

**SOCIOLOGIJA SELA.**
++SOCIOL. SELA.
AGRARNI INSTITUT.
ZAGREB 1, JL/S 1963-
Q. ENGL., & RUSS. SUMM.
BD/U-1.    OX/U-1.
ISSN 0038-0326

**SOFTWARE AGE.**                                                                                        XXX
[PRESS-TECH INC.]
EVANSTON, ILL. 1, S 1967- 5(2), 1971. //
2M.
XS/R10.
LO/N14. 1, 1967- 4(6), 1970.
ISSN 0038-061X

**SOFTWARE MONTHLY.**
++SOFTWARE MON.
[A.P. PUBL. LTD.]
LONDON 1(1), JE 1970-
S/T: A NEWSLETTER FROM SOFTWARE WORLD.
ED/N-1. 1(3), 1970-

**SOFTWARE PRACTICE AND EXPERIENCE.**
++SOFTWARE PRACT. & EXPER.
[WILEY-INTERSCIENCE]
LONDON 1(1), 1971-
Q.
CA/U-1.    CB/U-1.    ED/N-1.    GL/U-1.    GL/U-2.    LO/N14.
RE/U-1.    SH/U-1.    SO/U-1.
SH/C-5. 1(2), 1971-
ISSN 0038-0644

**SOFTWARE WORLD.**
[AP PUBL. LTD.]
LONDON 1(1), 1969-
LO/N14.    OX/U-8.    XS/R10.
ISSN 0038-0652

**SOIL ASSOCIATION.**                                                                                    XXX
++SOIL ASSOC.
STOWMARKET, SUFFOLK 1(1), AP 1973-
INCORP: JOURNAL OF THE SOIL ASSOCIATION FROM
15(2), AP 1968- 17(2), 1972; & SPAN. SOIL
ASSOCIATION NEWS FROM NO.1, 1967- 66, 1973.
ED/N-1.    GL/U-1.    LO/N-6.    LO/N14.    LO/R-5.    OX/U-8.

**SOIL BIOLOGY & BIOCHEMISTRY.**
++SOIL BIOL. & BIOCHEM.
[PERGAMON PRESS]
OXFORD &C. 1(1), AP 1969-
BL/U-1.    CA/U11.    ED/N-1.    HL/U-1.    LD/U-1.    LO/N-2.
LO/N13.    LO/R-5.    OX/U-3.    OX/U-8.    RE/U-1.    XS/R-2.
LO/U11. 3, 1971-                NW/U-1. 2, 1970-
ISSN 0038-0717

**SOIL BULLETIN (DUBLIN).**
++SOIL BULL. (DUBLIN).
DUBLIN 1, 1970-
BL/U-1.    DB/U-2.

**SOIL SCIENCE & AGROCHEMISTRY.**                                                                        000
SEE: POCHVOZNANIE I AGROKHIMIJA.

**SOIL & WATER.**
(NEW ZEALAND) SOIL CONSERVATION & RIVERS
CONTROL COUNCIL.
WELLINGTON 1, 1964-
CA/U11.    LO/N-6.    XS/R-4.
XY/N-1.
ISSN 0038-0695

**SOLAR ENERGY.**                                                                                        000
SEE: TAIYO ENERUGI.

**SOLID-LIQUID FLOW ABSTRACTS.**
++SOLID-LIQUID FLOW ABSTR.
[GORDON & BREACH]
LONDON &C. 1, 1968-
LO/N14.
GL/U-2. 5, 1974-
ISSN 0038-1063

**SOLID STATE SURFACE SCIENCE.**
++SOLID STATE SURF. SCI. [SSSS-B]
[DEKKER]
NEW YORK 1, 1969-
LO/N14.    LO/S-3.
ISSN 0081-1971

**SOLIDARITY (MELBOURNE).**
*MELBOURNE NO.1, 1970-*
*LO/U-2.*

**SOLO.**
*DUBLIN 1, 1972/73-*
*DB/U-2.*

**SOLON. A RIGHT WING JOURNAL: PHILOSOPHY - POL-
ITICS - MORALS.**                                          XXX
*SUNNINGDALE (BERKS.) 1(1), OC 1969- 1(4),*
*        OC 1970. //*
*3A.*
*ED/N-1.     LO/U-3.     MA/P-1.     OX/U-1.     OX/U17.*
*ISSN 0038-1187*

**SOLUTIONS. ELECTROPHORESIS, MEMBRANE FILTR-
ATION, ETC.**                                              XXX
*[HAWKSLEY & SONS, LTD.]*
*LANCING, SX. 1, MR 1969- 2(6), 1971. //*
*CA/U-2.     ED/N-1.     LO/N14.     OX/U-8.*

**SOLVENT EXTRACTION REVIEWS.**                            XXX
*++SOLVENT EXTR. REV.*
*[DEKKER]*
*NEW YORK 1(1- 2), 1971.*
*2/A. SUBS: ION EXCHANGE & SOLVENT EXTRACTION.*
*LO/N14.     LO/S-3.     OX/U-8.*
*XS/R10. 1, 1971.*
*ISSN 0038-125X*

**SOMENI.**
*TANZANIA LIBRARY ASSOCIATION.*
*DAR ES SALAAM NO.1, JL 1968-*
*Q.*
*LO/N17.*
*ISSN 0038-1292*

**SOMETHING ABOUT THE AUTHOR.**
*[GALE RESEARCH]*
*DETROIT 1, 1971-*
*S/T: FACTS & PICTURES ABOUT CONTEMPORARY*
*AUTHORS & ILLUSTRATORS OF BOOKS FOR YOUNG*
*PEOPLE.*
*DB/U-2.*

**SOMETHING ELSE NEWSLETTER.**
*++SOMETHING ELSE NEWSL.*
*[SOMETHING ELSE P.]*
*NEW YORK 1(1), 1966-*
*LO/U-2.*
*OX/U-1. 1(9), 1968-*
*ISSN 0038-1349*

**SONAR BANGLIA.**                                         XXX
*CANBERRA COMMITTEE FOR SUPPORT OF BANGLADESH.*
*CANBERRA NO.1, N 1971- 7, F 1972.//*
*LO/U-8.*

**SOOBSHCHENIJA PRIBALTIJSKOJ KOMISSII PO
IZUCHENIJU MIGRATSII PTITS.**
*++SOOBSHCH. PRIBALT. KOM. IZUCH. MIGRATSII PTITS*
*[SPIE-A]*
*PRIBALTIJSKAJA KOMISSIJA PO IZUCHENIJU*
*MIGRATSII PTITS.*
*TARTU NO.1, 1961-*
*ENGL. SUMM. & CONT. LISTS.*
*LO/N-2.*
*LO/N13. NO.2, 1963-*

**SOOBSHCHENIJA SHEMAKHINSKOJ ASTROFIZICHESKOJ
OBSERVATORII.**                                           XXX
*++SOOBSHCH. SHEMAKH. ASTROFIZ. OBS.*
*AKADEMIJA NAUK AZERBAJDZHANSKOJ SSR: SHEMAKH-*
*INSKAJA ASTROFIZICHESKAJA OBSERVATORIJA.*
*BAKU 1, 1965-*
*PREV: TRUDY SHEMAKHINSKOJ ASTROFIZICHESKOJ*
*OBSERVATORII AKADEMII NAUK AZERBAJDZHANSKOJ*
*SSR FROM 1, 1959- 3, 1964.*
*ED/R-3.     LO/N13.*

**SOOBSHCHENIJA PO VYCHISLITEL'NOJ TEKHNIKE.**
*++SOOBSHCH. VYCHISL. TEKH.*
*AKADEMIJA NAUK SSSR: VYCHISLITEL'NYJ TSENTR.*
*MOSCOW 1, 1962-*
*LO/N13.*
*BH/U-1. 5, 1968-*

**SOTSIALISTICHESKIJ REALIZM I PROBLEMY
ESTETIKI.**
*++SOTS. REALIZM & PROBL. ESTETIKI.*
*AKADEMIJA NAUK SSSR: INSTITUT FILOSOFII.*
*MOSCOW 1, 1967-*
*A.*
*LO/N-3. 2, 1970-*          *NO/U-1. 2, 1970-*
*CA/U-1. 1, 1967.*

**SOTSIALISTICHESKOE I KOMMUNISTICHESKOE STROIT-
EL'STVO V SIBIRI.**
*++SOTS. & KOMMUNIST. STROIT. SIB.*
*(RUSSIA, RSFSR) MINISTERSTVO VYSSHEGO I SRED-*
*NEGO SPETSIAL'NOGO OBRAZOVANIJA.*
*TOMSK VYP.1, 1962-*
*S/T: MEZHVUZOVSKIJ SBORNIK STATEJ.*
*GL/U-1.     LO/N-3.     LO/U-3.*
*BH/U-3. 1, 1962-*
*CC/U-1. 4, 1966- 5, 1967.*

**SOTSIOLOGICHESKIE ISSLEDOVANIJA.**
*++SOTSIOL. ISSLED.*
*URAL'SKIJ GOSUDARSTVENNYJ UNIVERSITET.*
*SVERDLOVSK 1, 1966-*
*CC/U-1.     GL/U-1.*

**SOUND. A QUARTERLY JOURNAL DEVOTED TO THE
STUDY OF AUDIOLOGY.**
*ROYAL NATIONAL INSTITUTE FOR THE DEAF.*
*LONDON 1(1), F 1967- 6, 1972 ...*
*SUBS: BRITISH JOURNAL OF AUDIOLOGY.*
*ED/N-1.     LO/N14.     MA/U-1.*

**SOUND & PICTURE TAPE RECORDING MAGAZINE.**               XXX
*++SOUND & PICT. TAPE RECORD. MAG.*
*[ANGLIA ECHO NEWSPAPERS]*
*LONDON 15(4), 1971-*
*PREV: TAPE RECORDING MAGAZINE FROM 6(1),*
*1962- 15(3), 1971.*
*LO/N13.*

**SOUND VERDICT.**
*LONDON BOROUGH OF CAMDEN: LIBRARIES & ARTS*
*DEPARTMENT.*
*LONDON NO.1, 1968(1969)-*
*LO/N14.     MA/P-1.     OX/U-1.*

**SOUNDINGS.**
*UNIVERSITY OF CALIFORNIA LIBRARY.*
*SANTA BARBARA 1(1), 1969-*
*2/A.*
*MA/S-1.     OX/U-1.*
*ISSN 0038-1853*

**SOUNDINGS. A MUSIC JOURNAL.**
*UNIVERSITY COLLEGE OF SOUTH WALES & MONMOUTH-*
*SHIRE.*
*CARDIFF NO.1, 1970-*
*AD/U-1.     BN/U-1.     DB/U-2.     ED/N-1.     EX/U-1.     LO/U13.*
*OX/U-1.*

**SOURCES & METHODS.**
*OECD.*
*PARIS NO.1, N 1967-*
*LO/S14.     MA/U-1.     OX/U17.*

**SOURCES & STUDIES FOR THE HISTORY OF THE
JESUITS.**
*++SOURCES & STUD. HIST. JESUITS.*
*INSTITUTUM HISTORICUM SOCIETATIS IESU.*
*ROME &C. 1, 1967-*
*LO/N-1.     OX/U-1.*

**SOUTH AFRICAN ARCHITECTURAL RECORD.**                    XXX
**SUBS (1963): ISAA.**

**SOUTH AFRICAN INDUSTRY & TRADE.**                        XXX
*++SOUTH AFR. IND. & TRADE. [SAIT-A]*
*[SOUTH AFRICAN PUBL. (PTY) LTD.]*
*CAPE TOWN 35(3), JL 1939- 66, 1970.//*
*PREV: INDUSTRY & TRADE FROM 35(1- 2), MY- JE*
*1939.*
*LO/N13. 56, 1960-*

**SOUTH AFRICA INTERNATIONAL.**
*++SOUTH AFR. INT.*
*SOUTH AFRICA FOUNDATION.*
*LONDON 1, 1970-*
*MON.*
*ED/N-1.     LO/U14.     RE/U-1.*
*AD/U-1. 3(3), 1973-*          *NO/U-1. 4, 1973-*
*ISSN 0015-5055*

**SOUTH AFRICAN JOURNAL OF AFRICAN AFFAIRS.**
*++SOUTH AFR. J. AFR. AFF.*
*AFRICA INSTITUTE OF SOUTH AFRICA.*
*PRETORIA 1, 1971-*
*ANNU.*
*LO/S14.*
*ED/N-1. 3(1), 1973-*

**SOUTH AFRICAN JOURNAL OF ANTARCTIC RESEARCH.**
++SOUTH AFR. J. ANTARCT. RES.
SOUTH AFRICAN COUNCIL FOR SCIENTIFIC & INDUST-
RIAL RESEARCH.
  PRETORIA 1971-
  CA/U12.    LO/S13.
  ISSN 0081-2455

**SOUTH AFRICAN JOURNAL OF DAIRY TECHNOLOGY.**
++SOUTH AFR. J. DAIRY TECHNOL.
SOUTH AFRICAN SOCIETY OF DAIRY TECHNOLOGY.
  PRETORIA 1, 1969-
  LO/N14.

**SOUTH AFRICAN STATISTICAL JOURNAL. = SUID-
AFRIKAANSE STATISTIESE TYDSKRIF.**
++SOUTH AFR. STATIST. J.
SOUTH AFRICAN STATISTICAL ASSOCIATION.
  CAPETOWN 1, 1967-
  BL/U-1.    LO/N-1.    LO/N14.    LO/U-3.
  EX/U-1. 8(1), 1974-
  ISSN 0038-271X

**SOUTH ASIA. JOURNAL OF SOUTH ASIAN STUDIES.**
[UNIV. WESTERN AUSTRALIA P.]
  NEDLANDS, W. AUST.  1, AG 1971-
  ANNU.
  AD/U-1.    LO/U-8.    LO/U14.    OX/U13.    SW/U-1.
  OX/U10.  1972-

**SOUTH ASIAN STUDIES.**
++SOUTH ASIAN STUD.
UNIVERSITY OF RAJASTHAN: SOUTH ASIA STUDIES
CENTRE.
  JAIPUR 1, 1965-
  2/A.  CENTRE SUBORD. TO: DEPARTMENT OF POLIT-
  ICAL SCIENCE.
  LO/N12.*
  LO/S14. 3(2), JL 1968- 7(2), JL 1972.
  ISSN 0038-285X

**SOUTH AUSTRALIAN YEAR BOOK.**
++SOUTH AUST. YEAR BOOK.
(AUSTRALIA) COMMONWEALTH BUREAU OF CENSUS &
STATISTICS: SOUTH AUSTRALIA OFFICE.
  ADELAIDE NO.1, 1966-
  LV/U-1.
  SW/U-1. 5, 1970-

**SOUTHEAST ASIA. AN INTERNATIONAL QUARTERLY.**
SOUTHERN ILLINOIS UNIVERSITY: CENTER FOR
VIETNAMESE STUDIES.
  CARBONDALE 1(1), 1971-
  HL/U-1.    OX/U-1.
  ISSN 0049-1551

**SOUTHEAST ASIA MICROFILMS NEWSLETTER.**
++SOUTHEAST ASIA MICROFILMS NEWSL.
SARBICA-CONSAL REGIONAL MICROFILM CLEARING
HOUSE.
  SINGAPORE NO.1, D 1972-
  2/A.  PUBL. BY THE INSTITUTE OF SOUTHEAST
  ASIAN STUDIES (SINGAPORE).
  LO/N12.    LO/N14.    LO/U-8.    LO/U14.

**SOUTHEAST ASIAN ARCHIVES. JOURNAL OF THE ...**
++SOUTHEAST ASIAN ARCH.
INTERNATIONAL COUNCIL ON ARCHIVES: SOUTHEAST
ASIAN REGIONAL BRANCH.
  KUALA LUMPUR 1, 1969-
  LO/U-8.    LO/U14.    OX/U-1.

**SOUTH EAST ASIAN JOURNAL OF SOCIOLOGY.**                      XXX
++SOUTH EAST ASIAN J. SOCIOL.
UNIVERSITY OF SINGAPORE: SOCIOLOGY SOCIETY.
  SINGAPORE 1(1), MY 1968- 4, 1971.
  SUBS. PART OF: SOUTH EAST ASIAN JOURNAL OF
  SOCIAL SCIENCE.
  LO/U-3.

**SOUTHEAST ASIAN JOURNAL OF TROPICAL MEDICINE
AND PUBLIC HEALTH.**
++SOUTHEAST ASIAN J. TROP. MED. & PUBLIC HEALTH.
SOUTHEAST ASIAN MINISTERS OF EDUCATION COUNCIL.
  BANGKOK 1, 1970-
  LO/N-2.
  SH/U-1. 1971-
  ISSN 0038-3619

**SOUTH HAMPSHIRE GEOGRAPHER.**
++SOUTH HANTS. GEOGR.
PORTSMOUTH COLLEGE OF TECHNOLOGY: GEOGRAPHICAL
SOCIETY.
  PORTSMOUTH NO.1, 1968-
  LO/N-1.    LO/S13.    OX/U-1.

**SOUTHAM'S METALWORKING.**                                    XXX
[SOUTHAM BUSINESS PUBL.]
  DON MILLS, ONT. 34(9), 1971-
  PREV: CANADIAN METALWORKING PRODUCTION FROM
  D 1969- F 1971.
  LO/N14.

**SOUTHERN CALIFORNIA LIT SCENE.**
++SOUTH. CALIF. LIT SCENE.
  LONG BEACH, CALIF. 1(1), 1970-
  M.  S/T: AN ADVENTURE IN PERSONAL JOURNALISM,
  A REGIONAL LITERARY MAGAZINE.
  LO/U-2.

**SOUTHERN HUMANITIES REVIEW.**
++SOUTH. HUM. REV.
AUBURN UNIVERSITY.
  AUBURN, ALA.  1, SPRING 1967-
  Q.
  HL/U-1.
  LO/U-1. 2(2); 7, 1973-
  ISSN 0038-4186

**SOUTHERN LITERARY JOURNAL.**
++SOUTH. LIT. J.
UNIVERSITY OF NORTH CAROLINA: DEPARTMENT OF
ENGLISH.
  CHAPEL HILL, N.C. 1(1), 1968-
  OX/U-1.
  MA/U-1. 4(2), 1972-
  ISSN 0038-4291

**SOVETSKAJA PECHAT'.**                                        XXX
**SUBS (1967): ZHURNALIST.**

**SOVETSKAJA TJURKOLOGIJA.**
++SOV. TJURKOLOGIJA.
AKADEMIJA NAUK AZERBAJDZHANSKOJ SSR.
  BAKU NO.1, 1970-
  2M. S/T: NAUCHNO-TEORETICHESKIJ ZHURNAL.
  SPONS. BODY ALSO AKADEMIJA NAUK SSSR.
  LO/N-3.    OX/U-1.
  LO/U14. NO.2, 1970-

**SOVETSKIE ARKHIVY.**                                         XXX
++SOV. ARKH. [SOAR-B]
(RUSSIA USSR) SOVET MINISTROV: GLAVNOE
ARKHIVNOE UPRAVLENIE.
  MOSCOW NO.1, 1966-
  PREV: VOPROSY ARKHIVOVEDENIJA FROM 1, 1956-
  10, 1965.
  BH/U-1.    CC/U-1.    LD/U-1.    OX/U-1.    SW/U-1.
  MA/U-1. 1967-

**SOVETSKOE FINNO-UGROVEDENIE.**
++SOV. FINNO-UGROVED.
EESTI NSV TEADUSTE AKADEEMIA.
  TALLIN 1, 1965-
  TITLE ALSO IN ENGL.: SOVIET FENNO-UGRIC
  STUDIES.  FR.: LA LINGUISTIQUE FINNO-OUGRIENNE
  SOVIETIQUE.  GER.: SOWJETISCHE FINNISCH-
  UGRISCHE SPRACHWISSENSCHAFT.  SOME ARTICLES IN
  ENGL., FR., OR GER. WITH SUMM. IN THE OTHER
  LANGUAGES.
  OX/U-1.
  LO/N-3. 4(2), 1968.
  ISSN 0038-5182

**SOVIET ANALYST.**
++SOV. ANAL.
  LONDON 1(1), MR 1972-
  S/T: A FORTNIGHTLY NEWSLETTER.
  DB/U-2.    ED/N-1.    LO/U-3.    MA/U-1.    OX/U-1.
  ISSN 0049-1713

**SOVIET APPLIED MECHANICS.**
++SOV. APPL. MECH.
[FARADAY P.]
  NEW YORK 2(1), 1966(1968)-
  M. TRANSL. OF PRIKLADNAJA MEKHANIKA.
  OX/U-8.    XY/N-1.
  ISSN 0038-5298

**SOVIET CHEMICAL INDUSTRY.**
++SOV. CHEM. IND.
[MCELROY SCIENTIFIC TRANSLATIONS]
  AUSTIN, TEX. 7, 1969-
  M. ENGL. TRANSL. OF KHIMICHESKAJA PROMYSHLEN-
  NOST.
  BH/U-3.    LO/N14.    LO/S-3.
  ISSN 0038-5344

**SOVIET CYBERNETICS REVIEW.**
++SOV. CYBERN. REV.
RAND CORPORATION.
  SANTA MONICA, CALIF. 1, 1971-
  LO/N14.    LO/U-3.    OX/U16.
  ISSN 0038-5352

SOVIET & EASTERN EUROPEAN FOREIGN TRADE.    XXX
+ +SOV. & EAST. EUR. FOREIGN TRADE
[INTERNATIONAL ARTS & SCIENCES P.]
 WHITE PLAINS, N.Y. 3(1), JA/F 1967-
 PREV: AMERICAN REVIEW OF SOVIET & EASTERN
EUROPEAN FOREIGN TRADE FROM 1, JA/F 1965- 2,
1966.
LO/U-3.   OX/U-1.   XY/N-1.
ISSN 0038-5263

SOVIET FENNO-UGRIC STUDIES.    000
 SEE: SOVETSKOE FINNO-UGROVEDENIE.

SOVIET JEWISH AFFAIRS.    XXX
+ +SOV. JEW. AFF.
INSTITUTE OF JEWISH AFFAIRS.
 LONDON NO.1, JE 1971-
2/A. PREV: BULLETIN ON SOVIET & EAST
EUROPEAN JEWISH AFFAIRS FROM NO.1, 1969- 6, D
1970.
ED/N-1.   GL/U-1.   LD/U-1.   LO/U-3.   LO/U14.   SH/U-1.
SO/U-1.
 ISSN 0038-545X

SOVIET JOURNAL OF ECOLOGY.    XXX
+ +SOV. J. ECOL.
[CONSULTANTS BUREAU]
 NEW YORK; LONDON 2, 1972-
EKOLOGIJA.
LO/N13.   LO/R-5.

SOVIET JOURNAL OF INSTRUMENTATION & CONTROL.    
+ +SOV. J. INSTRUM. CONTR.
[SCRIPTA TECHNICA LTD.]
 LONDON NO.1, JA 1967-
PREV: INSTRUMENT CONSTRUCTION; FROM NO.1,
1959. TRANSLATION OF PRIBORY I SISTEMY
UPRAVLENIJA.
BH/P-1.   ED/N-1.   LO/N-4.   LO/N14.   OX/U-8.   XS/R10.
ISSN 0038-5476

SOVIET JOURNAL OF OPTICAL TECHNOLOGY.    
+ +SOV. J. OPT. TECHNOL.
OPTICAL SOCIETY OF AMERICA.
 LANCASTER (P.A.) 34, JA/F 1967-
TRANSL. OF OPTIKO-MEKHANICHEKAIA PROMYSHLENN-
OST' PUBL. FOR THE SOC. BY THE AMERICAN
INSTITUTE OF PHYSICS.
CA/U-1.   LO/N-4.   LO/U21.   OX/U-1.   XY/N-1.**
LO/N-7.   35, 1968-
ISSN 0038-5514

SOVIET JOURNAL OF QUANTUM ELECTRONICS.    
+ +SOV. J. QUANTUM ELECTRON.
AMERICAN INSTITUTE OF PHYSICS.
 NEW YORK 1, 1971-
ENGL. TRANSL. OF KVANTOVAJA ELEKTRONIKA
(MOSCOW).
BL/U-1.   LO/N14.   OX/U-8.
MA/U-1.   2, 1972-
ISSN 0049-1748

SOVIET LASER RESEARCH: SPECIAL REPORTS.    
+ +SOV. LASER RES., SPEC. REP.
[SCIENTIFIC INFORMATION CONSULTANTS LTD.]
 LONDON 1, 1973-
COLLECTION OF TRANSLATED ARTICLES.
LO/N14.

SOVIET NEUROLOGY & PSYCHIATRY.    XXX
+ +SOV. NEUROL. & PSYCHIATR.
[INTERNATIONAL ARTS & SCIENCES PRESS]
 NEW YORK 1, 1968-
4/A. PREV: PART OF SOVIET PSYCHOLOGY &
PSYCHIATRY FROM 1, 1962.
LO/U-2.   OX/U-8.
ISSN 0038-559X

SOVIET PSYCHOLOGY.    XXX
+ +SOV. PSYCHOL.
[INTERNATIONAL ARTS & SCI. P.]
 WHITE PLAINS, N.Y. 5, F 1966-
SELECTED TRANSLATIONS FROM ORIGINAL SOVIET
SOURCES. PREV. PART OF: SOVIET PSYCHOLOGY &
PSYCHIATRY FROM 1, 1962- 4(3/4), 1966.
BN/U-2.   LO/N13.   MA/U-1.   SO/U-1.
ISSN 0038-5751

SOVIET PSYCHOLOGY & PSYCHIATRY.    XXX
+ +SOV. PSYCHOL. & PSYCHIATR.
[INTERNATIONAL ARTS & SCIENCES PRESS]
 NEW YORK. 1, 1962- 4(3/4), 1969 ...
Q. SELECTED ARTICLES IN ENGL. TRANSL.
SUBS. PART OF: SOVIET PSYCHOLOGY; & SOVIET
NEUROLOGY & PSYCHIATRY.
LC/U-1.   LO/N13.   LO/N14.   LO/U-1.   OX/U-1.
XY/N-1.**
 AB/U-1. 5, 1966-     AD/U-1. 5, 1966-
 EX/U-1. 4, 1965-     SO/U-1. 3, 1964-
 ISSN 0038-5476

SOVIET SCIENCE REVIEW.    XXX
+ +SOV. SCI. REV.
[ILIFFE]
 LONDON 1, JL 1970- 3, 1972. //
 DB/U-2.   EX/U-1.   LO/N-1.   LO/N-2.   LO/N-4.   LO/N-7.
 LO/N14.   OX/U-8.   XS/R10.
 ISSN 0038-5816

SOWJETISCHE FINNISCH-UGRISCHE SPRACHWISSEN-
SCHAFT.    000
 SEE: SOVETSKOE FINNO-UGROVEDENIE.

SOZIALORDNUNG DER GEGENWART.    XXX
+ +SOZIALORDNUNG GGW.
[E. SCHMIDT VERLAG]
 BERLIN 8, 1968-
PREV: SOZIALVERSICHERUNG DER GEGENWART FROM
1/2, 1961/62- 7, 1967. S/T: JAHRBUCH UND
NACHSCHLAGEWERK FUR WISSENSCHAFT UND PRAXIS
DER GESAMTEN SOZIALVERSICHERUNG, SOZIALGER-
ICHTSBARKEIT, BUNDESARBEITSVERWALTUNG, VER-
SORGUNG, SOZIALHILFE.
OX/U-1.

SOZIALVERSICHERUNG DER GEGENWART.    XXX
+ +SOZIALVERSICHER. GGW.
[E. SCHMIDT VERLAG]
 BERLIN 1/2, 1961/62- 7, 1967 ...
ANNU. SUBS: SOZIALORDNUNG DER GEGENWART.
+OXSOZIALWISS. JAHRB. POLIT.
[G. OLZOG]
 MUNICH &C. 1, 1969-
 LO/N-1.   OX/U-1.   OX/U17.
 ISSN 0587-0755

SPAIN TODAY (MADRID).
SPANISH INFORMATION SERVICE.
 MADRID NO.1, MR 1970-
PREV: THE WEEK IN SPAIN. ISSUED ALSO
IN SPAN., FR., GER. & ARABIC EDITIONS.
ED/N-1. *   OX/U-1.   LO/S14. *
 ISSN 0038-643X

SPAN. SOIL ASSOCIATION NEWS.    XXX
SOIL ASSOCIATION.
 STOWMARKET NO.1, 1967- 66, 1973.
SUBS. PART OF: SOIL ASSOCIATION.
BL/U-1.   BN/U-2.   LO/N-6.
ED/N-1. 2, 1967-

SPARROW.
 LOS ANGELES 1, 1972-
LO/U-2.   OX/U-1.

SPEAK.
PATAPHYSICAL SOCIETY.
 OXFORD 1, 1966-
LO/U-2.

SPEAK OUT.
NATIONAL COUNCIL FOR CIVIL LIBERTIES.
 LONDON NO.1, 1968-
LO/U-3.
OX/U17. NO.3 1972-

SPEAKERS' NOTES.
NORTH ATLANTIC TREATY ORGANIZATION: INFORMATION
SERVICE.
 BRUSSELS NO.SN/1, F 1968-
LO/S14.

SPECIAL BULLETIN OF THE AGRICULTURAL COLLEGE
OF ISHIKAWA PREFECTURE.    000
 SEE: ISHIKAWA-KEN NOGYO TANKI DAIGAKU
 TOKUBETSU KENKYU HOKOKU.

SPECIAL BULLETIN OF THE CHIBA-KEN AGRICULTURAL
EXPERIMENT STATION.    000
 SEE: CHIBA-KEN NOGYO SHIKENJO TOKUBETSU
 HOKOKU.

SPECIAL DISCUSSIONS OF THE FARADAY SOCIETY.                     XXX
++SPEC. DISCUSS. FARADAY SOC.
[ACADEMIC P.]
 LONDON &C.  NO.1, 1970(1971)...
 SUBS: FARADAY SPECIAL DISCUSSIONS OF THE
 CHEMICAL SOCIETY.
 BH/U-3.    LO/N14.    LO/S-3.

SPECIAL PAPERS, GEOLOGICAL SURVEY OF IRELAND.
++SPEC. PAP. GEOL. SURV. IREL.
(EIRE) GEOLOGICAL SURVEY.
 DUBLIN  NO.1, 1971-
 BR/U-1.    DB/U-2.    LO/N-2.
 ISSN 0085-1019

SPECIAL PUBLICATIONS, AMERICAN SOCIETY OF
MAMMALOGISTS.
++SPEC. PUBL. AM. SOC. MAMMAL.
 STILLWATER, OKLA.  NO.1, 1967-
 LO/N-2.    OX/U-8.

SPECIAL PUBLICATION, AUSTRALIAN CONSERVATION
FOUNDATION.
++SPEC. PUBL. AUST. CONSERV. FOUND.
 CANBERRA  1, 1968-
 LO/N-2.    LO/R-5.

SPECIAL PUBLICATIONS, BERMUDA BIOLOGICAL STA-
TION FOR RESEARCH.
++SPEC. PUBL. BERMUDA BIOL. STA. RES.
 ST. GEORGE'S WEST  NO.1, 1969-
 LO/N-2.

SPECIAL PUBLICATIONS, BRIGHAM YOUNG UNIVER-
SITY GEOLOGY STUDIES.
++SPEC. PUBL. BRIGHAM YOUNG UNIV. GEOL STUD.
 PROVO  NO.1, 1969-
 BH/U-1.

SPECIAL PUBLICATIONS, CENTRALINSTITUT FOR
NORDISK ASIEN-FORSKNING.
++SPEC. PUBL. CENTRALINST. NORD. ASIEN-FORSK.
 COPENHAGEN  1, 1969-
 OX/U-1.

SPECIAL PUBLICATION, COLORADO GEOLOGICAL
SURVEY.
++SPEC. PUBL. COLO. GEOL. SURV.
 DENVER  NO.1, 1969-
 LO/N-2.

SPECIAL PUBLICATION, DEPARTMENT OF GEOLOGY,
UNIVERSITY OF LEICESTER.
++SPEC. PUBL. DEP. GEOL. UNIV. LEIC.
 LEICESTER  NO.1, 1969-
 OX/U-8.

SPECIAL PUBLICATION, DEPARTMENT OF ICHTHYO-
LOGY, RHODES UNIVERSITY.
++SPEC. PUBL. DEP. ICHTHYOL. RHODES UNIV.
 GRAHAMSTOWN, S.AFR.  NO.1, AG 1967-
 LO/N-2.    LO/N13.

SPECIAL PUBLICATION, GEOLOGICAL SOCIETY OF
AUSTRALIA.
++SPEC. PUBL. GEOL. SOC. AUST.
 SYDNEY  NO.1, 1968-
 LO/N-2.    LO/N-4.    LO/N14.

SPECIAL PUBLICATIONS, GEOLOGICAL SOCIETY OF
SOUTH AFRICA.
++SPEC. PUBL. GEOL. SOC. SOUTH AFR.
 JOHANNESBURG  NO.1, 1970-
 LO/N-2.    OX/U-8.

SPECIAL PUBLICATIONS, GEOLOGICAL SURVEY
(GEORGIA).
++SPEC. PUBL. GEOL. SURV. (GA).
 ATLANTA  NO.1, AP 1963-
 LO/N-2.

SPECIAL PUBLICATION, GEOLOGICAL SURVEY OF
IRAN.
++SPEC. PUBL. GEOL. SURV. IRAN.
 TEHRAN  NO.1, 1964-
 LO/N-2.

SPECIAL PUBLICATIONS, INSTITUTE OF BRITISH
GEOGRAPHERS.
++SPEC. PUBL. INST. BR. GEOGR.
 LONDON  1, 1968-
 BH/U-1.    LO/N-1.    LO/R-5.    LO/S13.    LO/U-1.    NW/U-1.
 OX/U-1.

SPECIAL PUBLICATIONS, MANITOBA MUSEUM OF MAN
& NATURE.
++SPEC. PUBL. MANIT. MUS. MAN & NAT.
 WINNIPEG  NO.1, 1970-
 LO/N-2.

SPECIAL PUBLICATIONS, MUSEUM, TEXAS TECH
UNIVERSITY.
++SPEC. PUBL. MUS. TEX. TECH UNIV.
 LUBBOCK  NO.1, 1972-
 LO/N-2.

SPECIAL PUBLICATION, POWER ENGINEERING SOC-
IETY, INSTITUTE OF ELECTRICAL & ELECTRONICS
ENGINEERS.
++SPEC. PUBL. POWER ENG. SOC. INST. ELECTR. &
 ELECTRON. ENG. INC.
 NEW YORK  NO.1, 1970-
 CONFERENCE REPORTS.
 LO/N14.

SPECIAL PUBLICATIONS, SCANDINAVIAN INSTITUTE
++SPEC. PUBL. SCAND. INST. ASIAN STUD.
 COPENHAGEN  NO.1, 1969-
 LO/N-1.

SPECIAL PUBLICATIONS FROM THE SETO MARINE
BIOLOGICAL LABORATORY: SERIES 2.
++SPEC. PUBL. SETO MAR. BIOL. LAB., SER. 2.
 SETO RINKAI JIKKENJO (KYOTO DAIGAKU).
 SHIRAHAMA  NO.1, 1964-
 ORIG. SERIES FROM NO.1, 1959.
 LO/N13.

SPECIAL PUBLICATIONS, SOCIETY OF
NEMATOLOGISTS.
++SPEC. PUBL. SOC. NEMATOL.
 SOCIETY OF NEMATOLOGISTS.
 BELTSVILLE, MD.  NO.1, 1971-
 SUPPL. TO JOURNAL OF NEMATOLOGY.
 NW/U-1.

SPECIAL PUBLICATION, TUSSOCK GRASSLANDS &
MOUNTAIN LANDS INSTITUTE.
++SPEC. PUBL. TUSSOCK GRASSL. & MT. LANDS INST.
 CHRISTCHURCH, NZ  NO.1, 1962-
 INST. AT (BUT NOT CONSTITUENT PART OF):
 LINCOLN COLLEGE.
 LO/N13.*

SPECIAL PUBLICATIONS, UNITED STATES NATIONAL
SECTION, PAN AMERICAN INSTITUTE OF GEOGRAPHY
& HISTORY.                                                     XXX
++SPEC. PUBL. US NATL. SECT. PANAM. INST. GEOGR.
 & HIST.
 RIO DE JANEIRO  NO.1, S 1970- 6, JL 1971.//
 OX/U-1.

SPECIAL REPORT, AGRICULTURAL EXPERIMENT STAT-
ION, NEW YORK (STATE).
++SPEC. REP. AGRIC. EXP. STAT. N.Y. (STATE).
 GENEVA, N.Y.  NO.1, 1970-
 LO/N13.

SPECIAL REPORT, AQUATIC RESEARCH INSTITUTE.
++SPEC. REP. AQUAT. RES. INST.
 STOCKTON, CALIF.  NO.1, MY 1963-
 PLACE NAME ACTUALLY: PORT OF STOCKTON.
 LO/N-2.

SPECIAL REPORT, GEOLOGICAL SOCIETY OF LONDON.
++SPEC. REP. GEOL. SOC. LOND.
 LONDON  NO.1, 1971-
 LO/N-2.    LO/N13.    LO/U-1.

SPECIAL REPORT, HIGHLANDS & ISLANDS DEVELOP-
MENT BOARD.
++SPEC. REP. HIGHL. & ISL. DEVELOP. BOARD.
 INVERNESS  NO.1, 1969-
 OX/U-1.

SPECIAL REPORT, INTERNATIONAL CENTER FOR
ARID & SEMI-ARID LAND STUDIES.
++SPEC. REP. INT. CENT. ARID & SEMI-ARID LAND
 STUD.
 LUBBOCK, TEX.  NO.1, 1967-
 LO/N13.

[SPECIAL REPORT], IRON & STEEL INSTITUTE.                       XXX
 SUBS (1966): PUBLICATION, IRON & STEEL INST-
 ITUTE.

SPECIAL REPORT, NATIONAL INSPECTION LABORATORY
FOR FEEDS & FERTILIZER.                                         000
 SEE: TOKYO HISHIRYO KENSAJO TOKUBETSU HOKOKU.

SPECIAL SCIENTIFIC REPORT, MARINE LABORATORY,
STATE BOARD OF CONSERVATION (FLORIDA).                    XXX
SUBS (1969): SPECIAL SCIENTIFIC REPORT,
MARINE RESEARCH LABORATORY, DEPARTMENT OF
NATURAL RESOURCES (FLORIDA).

SPECIAL SCIENTIFIC REPORT, MARINE RESEARCH
LABORATORY, DEPARTMENT OF NATURAL RESOURCES
(FLORIDA).                                               XXX
++SPEC. SCI. REP. MAR. RES. LAB. DEP. NATUR.
RESOUR. (FLA.).
ST. PETERSBURG, FLA. NO.23, 1969-
PREV: SPECIAL SCIENTIFIC REPORT, MARINE
LABORATORY, STATE BOARD OF CONSERVATION
(FLORIDA) FROM NO.1, 1959- 22, 1969.
LO/N13.

SPECIAL SERIES IN ETHNOMUSICOLOGY.
++SPEC. SER. ETHNOMUSICOL.
SOCIETY FOR ETHNOMUSICOLOGY.
[WESLEYAN UNIVERSITY P.]
MIDDLETOWN, CONN. NO.1, 1966-
MONOGR.
LO/N-1.

SPECIAL SERIES, LIST & INDEX SOCIETY.
++SPEC. SER. LIST. & INDEX SOC.
LONDON 1, 1968-
BH/U-1.    CB/U-1.    GL/U-1.    LO/N-1.    LO/U11.

SPECIAL STEELS REVIEW.                                    XXX
++SPEC. STEEL REV.
BRITISH STEEL CORPORATION.
SHEFFIELD NO.1, 1969- 3, 1971 ...
PUBL. JOINTLY BY THE ALLOY & STAINLESS STEEL,
& SPECIAL STEEL PRODUCTS DIVISIONS OF THE
CORPORATION'S MIDLAND GROUP. PREV: ESC REVIEW
FROM 1, 1965. SUBS: SPECIAL STEELS TECHNICAL
REVIEW.
BL/U-1.    LO/N-7.    LO/N14.    OX/U-8.    XS/R10.

SPECIAL SURVEY, SOIL SURVEY OF GREAT BRITAIN.
++SPEC. SURV. SOIL SURV. G.B.
SOIL SURVEY OF GREAT BRITAIN (ENGLAND & WALES).
HARPENDEN 1, 1969-
OX/U-1.    CA/U11.

SPECIAL SYMPOSIA, AMERICAN SOCIETY OF LIMNOL-
OGY & OCEANOGRAPHY.
++SPEC. SYMP. AM. SOC. LIMNOL. & OCEANOGR.
LAWRENCE, KAN. 1, 1972-
OX/U-8.

SPECIALISED BIBLIOGRAPHY, CENTRE FOR
INFORMATION ON LANGUAGE TEACHING.
++SPEC. BIBLIOGR. CENT. INF. LANG. TEACH.
LO/N-1.

SPECIALITIES.                                             XXX
[ASHBOURNE PUBLS]
LONDON 1, S 1964- 4(12), D 1968.//
M.
OX/U-1.*
ED/N-1. 1(12),1965-                  LO/N14.  2,1966-

SPECTRA-PHYSICS LASER TECHNICAL BULLETIN.
++SPECTRA-PHYS. LASER TECH. BULL. [SPLT-A]
MOUNTAIN VIEW, CALIF. NO.1, 1965-
LO/N14.

SPECTROSCOPIC PROPERTIES OF INORGANIC &
ORGANOMETALLIC COMPOUNDS.
++SPECTROSC. PROP. INORG. & ORGANOMET. COMPD.
CHEMICAL SOCIETY.
LONDON 1, 1968-
BH/U-1.    GL/U-1.    GL/U-2.    LO/S-3.    LO/U-12.    NW/U-1.
OX/U-3.    XS/R10.

SPECTROSCOPY LETTERS.
++SPECTROSC. LETT.
[DEKKER]
NEW YORK 1(1), JA 1968-
S/T: AN INTERNATIONAL JOURNAL FOR RAPID
COMMUNICATION.
LO/N14.    OX/U-8.    XS/R10.
DB/U-2. 7, 1974-
ISSN 0038-7010

SPECTROVISION.                                            XXX
SUBS (1973): PART OF SCAN. SPECTROPHOTOMETRY,
CHROMATOGRAPHY, ANALYTICAL NEWS.

SPECULUM JURIS.
UNIVERSITY OF FORT HARE (S.AFR.)
FORT HARE 1965-
S/T: ANNUAL JOURNAL OF THE FACULTY OF LAW &
THE JURIDICAL SOCIETY OF THE UNIV. COLL. OF
FORT HARE.
BL/U-1.

SPEKTRUM.
DEUTSCHE AKADEMIE DER WISSENSCHAFTEN ZU BERLIN.
BERLIN 1(1), MY 1970-
M.
CA/U-2.
LO/U-1. 1, 1970- 3, 1972. [W.3(8- 11)]
ISSN 0049-1861

SPELEOLOGICHESKIJ BJULLETEN'.                             XXX
SUBS (1961): PESHCHERY.

SPENSER NEWSLETTER.
++SPENSER NEWSL.
UNIVERSITY OF WESTERN ONTARIO: DEPARTMENT OF
ENGLISH.
LONDON, ONT. 1, 1970-
3/A.
AD/U-1.    CB/U-1.    HL/U-1.    LO/U-1.
LO/N-1. 2(1), 1971-

SPERO.
FLINT, MICH. 1, 1965-
OX/U-1.
ISSN 0038-7363

SPERRY ENGINEERING REVIEW.                                XXX

SPERRY RAND ENGINEERING REVIEW.                           XXX
++SPERRY RAND ENG. REV. [SRER-A]                          XXX
SPERRY RAND CORPORATION.
GREAT NECK, N.Y. 20(3), 1968- 24, 1971.
PREV: SPERRY ENGINEERING REVIEW FROM 1, 1947-
20(2), 1967. SUBS: SPERRY TECHNOLOGY. VOL.
23(4), 1970 NOT PUBLISHED.
LO/N14.
ISSN 0038-7371

SPERRY TECHNOLOGY.                                        XXX
++SPERRY TECHNOL.
SPERRY RAND CORPORATION.
NEW YORK 1, 1972-
PREV: SPERRY RAND ENGINEERING REVIEW FROM
20(3), 1968- 24(1971).
LO/N14.    LO/N35.

SPINNER, WEBER, TEXTILVEREDLUNG.                          XXX
SUBS (1971): TEXTILBETRIEB.

SPODE HOUSE REVIEW.
++SPODE HOUSE REV.
HAWKESYARD PRIORY.
RUGELY, STAFFS. 1, D 1964-
LO/N-1.

SPOKEN ENGLISH.
++SPOKEN ENGL.
ENGLISH SPEAKING BOARD.
OXFORD 1(1), 1968-
3/A.
OX/U-1.    SH/U-1.
ISSN 0038-722X

SPOKESMAN.
BERTRAND RUSSELL PEACE FOUNDATION.
NOTTINGHAM [NO.1], MR 1970-
INCORP: LONDON BULLETIN FROM NO.14, 1970.
ED/N-1.    LO/N-1.    LO/U-3.    NO/U-1.    OX/U-1.    OX/U17.
ISSN 0024-5992

SPORTS DEVELOPMENT BULLETIN.
++SPORTS DEV. BULL.
CENTRAL COUNCIL FOR PHYSICAL RECREATION.
LONDON NO.1, OC 1967-
Q. PUBL. AS A SUPPL. TO: SPORT & RECREATION.
ED/N-1.    LO/U-3.

SPORTS INFORMATION MONTHLY BULLETIN.
++SPORTS INF. MON. BULL.
QUEEN'S UNIVERSITY OF BELFAST: PHYSICAL EDUCAT-
ION CENTRE.
BELFAST NO.1, JA 1972-
SPONS. BODY ALSO UNITED KINGDOM NATIONAL DOC-
UMENTATION CENTRE FOR SPORT, PHYSICAL EDUCAT-
ION & RECREATION.
BL/U-1.    OX/U-1.
ED/N-1. NO.2, 1972-                  HL/U-2. 3, 1973-

**S.P.R. NEWSLETTER.**
+ +S.P.R. NEWSL. (SOC. PSYCHICAL RES.)
SOCIETY FOR PSYCHICAL RESEARCH.
*LONDON 1, JE 1969-*
*ED/N-1.*

**SPRACHE DER GEGENWART.**
+ +SPRACHE GGW.
INSTITUT FUR DEUTSCHE SPRACHE.
*DUSSELDORF 1, 1967-*
*DB/U-1.    DR/U-1.*

**SPRACHKUNST. BEITRAGE SUR LITERATUR-
WISSENSCHAFT.**
[HERMANN BOEHLAUS]
*VIENNA 1(1/2), 1970-*
*Q.*
*GL/U-1.    LO/U11.*
*LO/U-2. 5(1), 1974-*           *SH/U-1. 5, 1974-*
*ISSN 0038-8483*

**SPRAVNI PRAVO.**
(CZECHOSLOVAKIA) MINISTERSTVO VNITRA.
*PRAGUE 1(1), 1968-*
SPRAVY A SPRAVNIHO PRAVA.
*LA/U-1.*

**SPRAVOCHNIK PROPAGANDISTA-MEZHDUNARODNIKA.**
+ +SPRAV. PROPAG.-MEZHDUNAR.
IZDATEL'STVO POLITICHESKOJ LITERATURY.
*MOSCOW [1], 1966-*
*A.*
*BH/U-1.    CC/U-1.    SA/U-1.*
*LO/N-3. 1967.*

**SPRAWY MIESZKANIOWE.**
INSTYTUT GOSPODARKI MIESZKANIOWEJ: KOMITET
BUDOWNICTWA, URBANISTYKI I ARCHITEKTURY.
*WARSAW 1, 1963-*
*Q. ENGL., FR. & RUSS. SUMM. & CONT. LISTS.*
*BH/U-1. 7, 1969-*               *BL/U-1. 7, 1969-*

**SPRINGHEAD JOURNAL.**
+ +SPRINGHEAD J.
GRAVESEND HISTORICAL SOCIETY: SPRINGHEAD
EXCAVATION COMMITTEE.
*GRAVESEND NO.1, 1968-*
*CB/U-1.*

**SQUASH PLAYER.**
[A.C.M. WEBB (PUBL.) LTD.]
*LONDON 1, OC 1971-*
*MON.*
*ED/N-1.*

**SRD REPORT, UNITED KINGDOM ATOMIC ENERGY
AUTHORITY.**                                                    XXX
+ +SRD REP. UK AT. ENERGY AUTH.
UNITED KINGDOM ATOMIC ENERGY AUTHORITY: SAFETY
& RELIABILITY DIRECTORATE.
*RISLEY (LANCS.) SRD R1, 1971-*
PREV: AHSB (S) REPORT, UNITED KINGDOM ATOMIC
ENERGY AUTHORITY.
*LO/N14.*

**SRI LANKA NEWS-LETTER.**                                      XXX
+ +SRI LANKA NEWSL.
(SRI LANKA) HIGH COMMISSION (LONDON).                           XXX
*LONDON NO.1, 1973-*
PREV: CEYLON NEWS-LETTER.
*LO/N12.    LO/S14.*

**SRI LANKA TODAY.**                                            XXX
(SRI LANKA) GOVERNMENT INFORMATION DEPART-
MENT.                                                           XXX
*COLOMBO 21(5/6), MY/JE 1972-*
PREV: CEYLON TODAY FROM 1, S 1952- 21(3/4),
1972.
*LD/U-1.    LD/U-1.    LO/S14.    XY/N-1.*

**SSEB NEWS.**
SOUTH OF SCOTLAND ELECTRICITY BOARD.
*GLASGOW NO.1, 1971-*
*LO/N-1.*

**SSF NEWSLETTER.**                                             XXX
+ +SSF NEWSL. (SCI. SCI. FOUND.)
SCIENCE OF SCIENCE FOUNDATION.
*LONDON 1(1), F 1966- 4(3), 1969.*
2M. SUBS: PART OF SCIENCE POLICY NEWS.
*LO/N-4. 2(3), 1967-*               *LO/N-4. 2(3), 1967-*
*LO/R-5. 3, 1967-*
*GL/U-2. TWO YEAR FILE.*

**SSHA JOURNAL.**
+ +SSHA J. (SCOTT. SPEC. HOUS. ASSOC.).
SCOTTISH SPECIAL HOUSING ASSOCIATION.
*EDINBURGH NO.1, MY 1970-*
*ED/N-1.*

**STADCHLO. NEWSLETTER OF THE ...**
IRISH PUBLISHERS' ASSOCIATION.
*DUBLIN 1, 1970-*
*BL/U-1.*

**STAFF RESEARCH STUDIES, BANK OF CANADA.**
+ +STAFF RES. STUD. BANK CAN.
*OTTAWA NO.1, 1969-*
*BH/U-1.    LD/U-1.*
*OX/U16. NO.3; 6; & 8, 1969-*

**STAFF STUDIES, CENTRAL BANK OF CEYLON.**
+ +STAFF STUD. CENT. BANK CEYLON.
*COLOMBO 1, 1971-*
*CA/U-1.    OX/U-9.    OX/U-9.*

**STAL (BELGRADE).**                                            000
SEE: CELIK.

**STAL IN ENGLISH.**                                            XXX
SUBS (1971): STEEL IN THE USSR.

**STAMP MONTHLY.**                                              XXX
+ +STAMP M.
[STANLEY GIBBONS]
*LONDON 1, JE 1970-*
PREV: GIBBONS STAMP MONTHLY FROM 1, 1927.
*BH/P-1.    ED/N-1.*
*0016-9676*

**STAMP OUT.**
EALING TECHNICAL COLLEGE: SCHOOL OF LIBRARIAN-
SHIP.
*EALING 1, D 1971-*
*ED/N-1.*

**STANKI I INSTRUMENT: (GER. TRANSL.)**                         000
SEE: UMFORMTECHNIK. [ARTICLES]

**STANKI I REZHUSHCHIE INSTRUMENTY.**
+ +STANKI & REZHUSHCHIE INSTRUM.
KHAR'KOVSKIJ POLITEKHNICHESKIJ INSTITUT.
*KHAR'KOV 1, 1966-*
S/T: RESPUBLIKANSKIJ MEZHVEDOMSTVENNYJ
NAUCHNO-TEKHNICHESKIJ SBORNIK.
*BH/U-1.    LO/N13.*

**STANZA. A MAGAZINE OF CONTEMPORARY POETRY &
CRITICISM.**
NORTHERN POETRY WORKSHOP.
*MANCHESTER NO.1, MY 1968-*
*ED/N-1.    LO/U-2.*

**STARDOCK.**
[GOTHIQUE PUBL.]
*LONDON NO.1, 1968-*
*ED/N-1.    OX/U-1.*

**STATEMENT, COUNCIL FOR NATIONAL ACADEMIC
AWARDS.**
+ +STAT. COUNC. NAT. ACAD. AWARDS.
*LONDON NO.1, 1964-*
*LV/U-2. NO.3, 1965.*
*SO/U-1. NO.2, 1965.*
*XS/C-2. NO.1, 1964.*

**STATENS LANDBRUKSBYGGNADSFORSOK (SWEDEN),
HANDLINGAR.**                                                   XXX
SUBS (1969): INSTITUTIONEN FOR LANTBRUKETS
BYGGNADSTEKNIK, HANDLINGAR.

**STAT'I PO GIDROMETEOROLOGII (VILNA).**                        000
SEE: HIDROMETEOROLOGINIAI STRAIPSNIAI.

**STATISTICAL BULLETIN FOR AFRICA.**
+ +STAT. BULL. AFR.
UNITED NATIONS: ECONOMIC COMMISSION FOR AFRICA.
*ADDIS ABABA NO.1, N 1965-*
*LD/U-1.*

**STATISTICAL MECHANICS.**
+ +STAT. MECH.
CHEMICAL SOCIETY.
*LONDON 1, 1973-*
*BH/U-3.    CB/U-1.    ED/N-1.    HL/U-1.    LO/N14.    LO/S-3.*
*LO/U-2.    MA/U-1.    RE/U-1.    SF/U-1.*
*GL/U-2. 1(1- 3), 1973.*
*ISSN 0305-9960*

**STATISTICAL NOTES ON TIN.**
+ +STAT. NOTES TIN.
INTERNATIONAL TIN COUNCIL.
LONDON 1(1), 1971-
Q.
LO/U-3.

**STATISTICAL OBSERVER.**
+ +STATIST. OBS. (CAN.).
(CANADA) DOMINION BUREAU OF STATISTICS:
INFORMATION DIVISION.
OTTAWA 1, 1968-
LO/U-3.

**STATISTICAL SUMMARY, BANK OF CANADA.**          XXX
  **SUBS (1971): BANK OF CANADA REVIEW.**

**STATISTICAL SUPPLEMENT TO SULPHUR, NITROGEN &**
**PHOSPHORUS & POTASSIUM.**
+ +STATIST. SUPPL. SULPHUR NITROGEN & PHOSPHORUS
& POTASSIUM.
BRITISH SULPHUR CORPORATION.
LONDON NO.1, 1970-
2/A.
OX/U-1.

**STATISTICS OF EDUCATION (GB): SPECIAL SERIES.**
+ +STATIST. EDUC. (GB), SPEC. SER.
(GREAT BRITAIN) DEPARTMENT OF EDUCATION &
SCIENCE.
LONDON NO.1, PT.1, 1968-
OX/U-1.

**STATISTICS OF SCIENCE & TECHNOLOGY.**          XXX
+ +STAT. SCI. & TECHNOL. [SSCT-B]
(GREAT BRITAIN) DEPARTMENT OF EDUCATION &
SCIENCE.
LONDON 1967- 1970. //
A. SPONS. BODY ALSO DEPARTMENT OF TRADE &
INDUSTRY.
BH/U-1.    EX/U-1.    GL/U-1.    MA/P-1.    SO/U-1.
LO/P-6. 1968-                    SH/U-1. 1968-
LO/U-2. 1967 & 1970.

**STATISTIKA & ELEKTRONNO-VYCHISLITEL'NAJA**
**TEKHNIKA V EKONOMIKE. SBORNIK STATEJ.**
+ +STAT. & ELEKTRON.-VYCHISL. TEKH. EKON.
[SETE-B]
NAUCHNO-ISSLEDOVATEL'SKIJ INSTITUT PO PROEKTIR-
OVANIJU VYCHISLITEL'NYKH TSENTROV I SISTEM
EKONOMICHESKOJ INFORMATSII.
MOSCOW 1, 1966-
BH/U-1.    CC/U-1.    OX/U-1.
LO/U-3. 2, 1968-

**STATISTIKA PECHATI ESTONSKOJ SSR.**          000
  **SEE: EESTI NSV TRUKITOODANGU STATISTIKA.**

**STATISTIQUES AGRICOLES (BELGIUM).**
+ +STAT. AGR. (BELG.).
INSTITUT NATIONAL DE STATISTIQUE (BELGIUM).
BRUSSELS NO.1, JA 1969-
M.
LO/U-3.

**STATISTIQUES DEMOGRAPHIQUES (BELGIUM).**
+ +STAT. DEMOGR. (BELG.).
INSTITUT NATIONAL DE STATISTIQUE (BELGIUM).
BRUSSELS NO.1, 1969-
LO/U-3.

**STATISTIQUES FINANCIERES, INSTITUT NATIONAL**
**DE STATISTIQUE (BELGIUM).**
+ +STAT. FINANC. INST. NATL. STAT. (BELG.).
BRUSSELS NO.1, 1972-
LO/N-1.

**STATISTIQUES INTERNATIONALES RETROSPECTIVES =**
**INTERNATIONAL HISTORICAL STATISTICS.**
+ +STAT. INT. RETROSP.
INSTITUT DE SOCIOLOGIE SOLVAY: CENTRE D'ECON-
OMIE POLITIQUE.
BRUSSELS 1, 1968-
LO/N-1.

**STATISTISCHE BEIHEFTE ZU DEN MONATSBERICHTEN**
**DER DEUTSCHEN BUNDESBANK. REIHE I: BANKENSTAT-**
**ISTIK NACH BANKENGRUPPEN.**
+ +STATIST. BEIH. MONATSBER. DEUT. BUNDESBANK, I.
FRANKFURT AM MAIN 1, S 1969-
RE/U-1.

**STATISTISCHE STUDIEN UND ERHEBUNGEN.**
+ +STAT. STUD. & ERHEB.
COMMISSION OF THE EUROPEAN COMMUNITIES.
[BRUSSELS] NO.1, 1968-
2M.
BH/U-1.    MA/P-1.

**STATYSTYKA POLSKI: SERIA L.**
+ +STAT. POL., L.
(POLAND) GLOWNY URZAD STATYSTYCZNY POLSKIEJ
RZECZYPOSPOLITEJ LUDOWEJ.
WARSAW 1, 1964-
BH/U-1.    LO/N-3.    LO/N10.

**STATYSTYKA POLSKI: SERIA M.**
+ +STAT. POL., M.
(POLAND) GLOWNY URZAD STATYSTYCZNY POLSKIEJ
RZECZYPOSPOLITEJ LUDOWEJ.
WARSAW 1, 1965-
BH/U-1.    LO/N-3.    LO/N10.

**STATYSTYKA POLSKI: SERIA R.**
+ +STAT. POL., R.
(POLAND) GLOWNY URZAD STATYSTYCZNY POLSKIEJ
RZECZYPOSPOLITEJ LUDOWEJ.
WARSAW 1/2, N 1963-
BH/U-1.

**STATYSTYKA POLSKI: SPISY LUDNOSCI.**          XXX
+ +STAT. POL., SPISY LUDNOSCI.
(POLAND) GLOWNY URZAD STATYSTYCZNY.
WARSAW 1, N 1967- 19, 1968.
SUBS: PART OF MASOWE BADANIA STATYSTYCZNE.
BH/U-1.    LO/U-3.

**STATYSTYKA POLSKI: SPISY MIESZKAN I BUDYNKOW.**   XXX
+ +STAT. POL., SPISY MIESZKAN & BUDYNKOW.
(POLAND) GLOWNY URZAD STATYSTYCZNY.
WARSAW NR.1, D 1967- 18, 1968.
SUBS: PART OF MASOWE BADANIA STATYSTYCZNE.
BH/U-1.    LO/U-3.

**STC NEWS BULLETIN.**          000
  **SEE: STC QUARTERLY REVIEW.**

**STC QUARTERLY REVIEW.**          XXX
+ +STC Q. REV. (STAND. TELEPH. & CABLES, LTD.).
STANDARD TELEPHONES & CABLES, LTD.
LONDON 14(2), 1968- 16, 1970...
PREV: STC NEWS BULLETIN FROM 1, 1954-
14(1), 1967. SUBS: STC REVIEW.
LO/N14.

**STC REVIEW.**          XXX
+ +STC REV. (STAND. TELEPH. & CABLES, LTD.).
STANDARD TELEPHONES & CABLES, LTD.
LONDON 17, 1971-
PREV: STC QUARTERLY REVIEW FROM 14(2),
1968- 16, 1970.
ED/N-1.    LO/N14.

**STEAM ALIVE? SERIES ON RAILWAY PRESERVATION.**
[ALLEN]
SHEPPERTON NO.1, [1969]-
ED/N-1.

**STEAM MAN.**
[STEAM MAN PUBL.]
LONDON NO.1, 1971-
Q. THE MAGAZINE DEVOTED TO ALL FORMS OF STEAM
ENGINE.
CR/N-1.    ED/N-1.    LO/N14.

**STEEL.**          XXX
  **SUBS (1970): INDUSTRY WEEK. (CLEVELAND).**

**STEEL (BELGRADE).**          000
  **SEE: CELIK.**

**STEEL & METALS INTERNATIONAL.**          XXX
+ +STEEL & METALS INT.
[INTERTECH P.]
LONDON 7, 1970-
PREV: STEEL INTERNATIONAL FROM 1(1), JE 1966-
6(33), 1970.
ED/N-1.    LO/N14.
ISSN 0039-0933

**STEEL METRICATION BULLETIN.**
+ +STEEL METRICAT. BULL.
BRITISH STEEL CORPORATION.
LONDON NO.1, JA 1971-
LO/N-1.

**STEEL RESEARCH.**          000
  **SEE: STEELRESEARCH.**

**STEEL REVIEW.**          XXX
  **SUBS (1968): BRITISH STEEL.**

**STEEL TIMES ANNUAL REVIEW OF THE STEEL INDUSTRY.**
+ +STEEL TIMES ANNU. REV. STEEL IND.
[FUEL & METALLURGICAL JOURNALS LTD.]
LONDON [1], OC 1969-
XS/R10.

**STEEL IN THE USSR.**                                                    XXX
IRON & STEEL INSTITUTE.
*LONDON 1, 1971-*
PREV. STAL IN ENGLISH FROM JA 1959- D 1970.
S/T: A SELECTION OF TRANSLATED MATERIAL FROM
STAL & IZVESTIJA VYSSHIKH UCHEBNYKH ZAVEDENII
CHERNAYA METALLURGIJA.
*BH/P-1.     BH/U-3.     ED/N-1.     GL/U-2.     LD/U-1.     LO/N14.*
*MA/U-1.     SH/C-5.*
*ISSN 0038-9218*

**STEELRESEARCH.**                                                        XXX
BRITISH STEEL CORPORATION.
*LONDON 1971-*
PREV: ANNUAL REPORT, BRITISH IRON & STEEL
RESEARCH ASSOCIATION FROM 1944(1945)- 1969
(1970).
*LO/N14.     RE/U-1.     XS/R10.*

**STEENSTRUPIA.**
KOBENHAVNS UNIVERSITET: ZOOLOGISKE MUSEUM.
*COPENHAGEN 1, 1970-*
*CA/U-2.     GL/U-1.     LO/N-2.     LO/N13.*

**STEINMETZ + BILDHAUER.**                                                XXX
[CALLWEY]
*MUNICH 1971-*
PREV: STEINMETZ UND STEINBILDHAUER FROM
1, 1884- 86, 1970.
*LO/N13.*

**STEINMETZ UND STEINBILDHAUER.**                                         XXX
**SUBS (1971): STEINMETZ + BILDHAUER.**

**STEPNYE PROSTORY.**
(RUSSIA RSFSR) MINISTERSTVO SEL'SKOGO KHOZJAJ-
STVA.
*SARATOV 1968(1)-*
PREV: SEL'SKOKHOZJAJSTVENNOE PROIZVODSTVO
POVOLZH'JA FROM 1, 1963- 1967.
*LO/N13.*

**STERBEECKIA.**
ANTWERPSE MYCOLOGISCHE KRING.
*ANTWERP 1(1), OC 1961-*
*LO/N-2.*

**STEREO HEADPHONES: AN OCCASIONAL MAGAZINE OF
THE NEW POETRIES.**
*KERSEY (SUFF.) 1(1), 1969-*
*ED/N-1.     LO/U-2.     OX/U-1.*
*ISSN 0039-1212*

**STEROIDOLOGIA.**                                                        XXX
[KARGER]
*BASLE &C. 1, 1970- 2, 1971...*
PREV: EUROPEAN JOURNAL OF STEROIDS FROM 1,
1966- 2, 1967. SUBS: STEROIDS & LIPIDS
RESEARCH.
*LO/N14.     LO/S-3.     OX/U-8.*
*CA/U-1. 2, 1971-*
*ISSN 0049-2221*

**STEROIDS & LIPIDS RESEARCH.**                                           XXX
*++STEROIDS & LIPIDS RES.*
[KARGER]
*BASLE &C. 3, 1972-*
PREV: STEROIDOLOGIA FROM 1, 1970- 2, 1971.
*LO/N14.     LO/S-3.*

**STIRPES.**
TEXAS STATE GENEALOGICAL SOCIETY.
*FORT WORTH 1, 1961-*
Q.
*ED/N-1.**
*ISSN 0039-1522*

**STOCHASTIC PROCESSES & THEIR APPLICATIONS.**
*++STOCHASTIC PROCESS. & APPL.*
[NORTH-HOLLAND]
*AMSTERDAM 1, 1973-*
Q.
*CA/U-1.     HL/U-1.     LO/N13.     MA/U-1.     OX/U-8.     SH/U-1.*
*SW/U-1.*
*EX/U-1. 2(1), 1974-*

**STOCHASTICS.**
[GORDON & BREACH]
*NEW YORK &C. 1, 1973-*
*CA/U-1.     ED/N-1.     LO/N14.     OX/U-8.     SH/U-1.*
*ISSN 0090-9491*

**STOCKHOLM PAPERS.**
*++STOCKH. PAP.*
STOCKHOLM INTERNATIONAL PEACE RESEARCH
INSTITUTE.
[ALMQVIST & WIKSELL]
*STOCKHOLM NO.1, 1969-*
MONOGR.
*LO/N-1.*

**STOCKHOLM SLAVIC STUDIES.**
*++STOCKH. SLAVIC STUD.*
[ALMQVIST & WIKSELL]
*STOCKHOLM NO.1, 1967-*
SECTION OF ACTA UNIVERSITATIS STOCKHOLMIENSIS.
*LO/N-1.*

**STOCKHOLM STUDIES IN LINGUISTICS.**
*++STOCKHOLM STUD. LINGUIST.*
STOCKHOLMS UNIVERSITET.
*STOCKHOLM NO.1, 1971-*
SECTION OF: ACTA UNIVERSITATIS STOCKHOLM-
IENSIS.
*DB/S-1.     LO/U-1.*

**STOCKHOLM STUDIES IN POLITICS.**
*++STOCKH. STUD. POLIT.*
STOCKHOLMS UNIVERSITET: STATSVETENSKAPLIGA
INSTITUTIONEN.
*STOCKHOLM 1, 1971-*
*LO/N-1.*
*ISSN 0085-6762*

**STOCKHOLM STUDIES IN THEATRICAL HISTORY.**
*++STOCKHOLM STUD. THEATRICAL HIST.*
STOCKHOLMS UNIVERSITET.
*STOCKHOLM NO.1, 1967-*
SECTION OF: ACTA UNIVERSITATIS STOCKHOLMIEN-
SIS.
*LO/U-1.*

**STOM. RIVISTA DI STOMATOLOGIA INFANTILE.**
[GIULIO EINAUDI EDITORE]
*TURIN 1, 1968-*
*LO/N13.*

**STORIA DELL' ARTE.**
*FLORENCE 1/2, 1969-*
*LO/U17.*
*CA/U-1. 5, 1970-*

**STORIA CONTEMPORANEA.**
*++STOR. CONTEMP.*
[SOCIETA EDITRICE IL MULINO]
*BOLOGNA 1(1), MR 1970-*
Q. ENGL. & RUSS. SUMM.
*OX/U-1. 1(2), 1970-*
*ISSN 0039-1875*

**STP NOTES.**
INTER-UNION COMMISSION ON SOLAR TERRESTRIAL
PHYSICS (ICSU).
*WASHINGTON, D.C. NO.1, AP 1968-*
*XS/N-1.*

**STRAIPSNIU RINKINYS.**                                                  000
**SEE: BOTANIKOS KLAUSIMAI.**

**STRATEGIC SURVEY.**
*++STRAT. SURV.*
INSTITUTE FOR STRATEGIC STUDIES (LONDON).
*LONDON 1966-*
A.
*LO/U-3.*

**STRATHSPEY EXPRESS.**                                                   XXX
STRATHSPEY RAILWAY ASSOCIATION.
*SAUCHIE NO.3, N 1972-*
PREV: STRATHSPEY RAILWAY NEWSLETTER FROM NO.1,
AP 1972- 2, AG 1972.
*ED/N-1.*

**STRATHSPEY RAILWAY NEWSLETTER.**                                        XXX
*++STRATHSPEY RAILW. NEWSL.*
*SAUCHIE NO.1, AP 1972- 2, AG 1972 ...*
SUBS: STRATHSPEY EXPRESS.
*ED/N-1.*

**STREET RESEARCH.**
*++STREET RES.*
*MANCHESTER BULLETIN NO.1, [AP 1972]-*
*ED/N-1.*

STRENGTH OF MATERIALS.
+ +STRENGTH MATER.
[CONSULTANTS BUREAU]
*NEW YORK &C.  NO.1, 1969(1970)-*
M.  TRANSL. OF PROBLEMY PROCHNOSTI.
*LO/N14.    OX/U-8.*
*XS/R10.  4(1), 1972-*
*ISSN 0039-2316*

STRESS.  AN INFORMATION BULLETIN ON LIBRARIES
& LOCAL GOVERNMENT REORGANISATION IN
YORKSHIRE.
LIBRARY ASSOCIATION: YORKSHIRE BRANCH.
*LEEDS NO.1, S 1972-*
*ED/N-1.   OX/U-1.*

STRIKER.
[CITY MAGAZINES LTD.]
*LONDON  NO.1, JA 1970-*
*OX/U-1.*

STRIP MILL PRODUCTS REVIEW.
+ +STRIP MILL PROD REV.
BRITISH STEEL CORPORATION: STRIP MILLS DIVISION
*LONDON  1, 1970-*
*ED/N-1.   LO/N-1.    LO/N14.*

STROITEL'STVO I ARKHITEKTURA (KIEV).
+ +STROIT. & ARKHIT. (KIEV).
ZONAL'NYJ NAUCHNO-ISSLEDOVATEL'SKIJ I
PROEKTNYJ INSTITUT TIPOVOGO I EKSPERIMENT-
AL'NOGO PROEKTIROVANIJA ZHILYKH OBSHCHEST-
VENNYKH ZDANIJ GORODA KIEVA.
*KIEV 1, 1964-*
S/T: MEZHVEDOMSTVENNYJ RESPUBLIKANSKIJ
NAUCHNYJ SBORNIK.
*BH/U-1.  6, 1968-                    LO/N13.  4, 1966-*
*XY/N-1.  2, 1965-*

STROITEL'STVO I ARKHITEKTURA MOSKVY.                    XXX
+ +STROIT. & ARKHIT. MOSK.
MOSKOVSKIJ GORODSKOJ SOVET DEPUTATOV TRUDJASH-
CHIKHSJA.
*MOSCOW  1960(1)-*
M.  PREV: ARKHITEKTURA I STROITEL'STVO MOSKVY
FROM 1952- 1959.
*LO/N13.***
*CC/U-1.***
*ISSN 0039-2421*

STROITEL'STVO I ARKHITEKTURA UZBEKISTANA.*
+ +STROIT. & ARKHIT. UZB. [SAUZ-A]
(UZBEKISTAN) MINISTERSTVO STROITEL'STVA I
GOSSTROJA.
*TASHKENT  1, 1960-*
PUBLICATION SUSPENDED DURING 1964 & TEMPOR-
ARILY SUBSTITUTED BY STROITEL'STVO I
ARKHITEKTURA SREDNEJ AZII.
*LO/N13.*
*LO/N-3  8(3), 1967.*

STRUCTURA.  SCHRIFTENREIHE ZUR LINGUISTIK.
[W. FINK VERLAG]
*MUNICH  1, 1970-*
*CA/U-1.*

STRUCTURE (DUBLIN).
*DUBLIN  1(1), 1972-*
Q.
*BL/U-1.   CA/U-1.   DB/U-2.   ED/N-1.   OX/U-1.*

STRUKTURA I ROL' VODY V ZHIVOM ORGANIZME.
+ +STRUKT. & ROL' VODY ZHIV. ORG.
*LENINGRAD  SB.1, 1966-*
*XY/N-1.*

STUDENT.
[CONNAUGHT PUBL.]
*LONDON  1, JA 1968-*
*ED/N-1.  1(2), 1968-*

STUDENT LIFE.
*LONDON   1(1), N 1967-*
4/A.
*ED/N-1.*

STUDENTS PROJECTS, COLLEGE OF LIBRARIANSHIP,
UNIVERSITY COLLEGE, ABERYSTWYTH.
+ +STUD. PROJ. COLL. LIBR. UNIV. COLL.
ABERYSTWYTH.
*ABERYSTWYTH  NO.1, 1970-*
*LO/N-1.*

STUDIES IN ADULT EDUCATION.
+ +STUD. ADULT EDUC.
[DAVID & CHARLES]
*NEWTON ABBOT  1(1), AP 1969-*
*ED/N-1.    HL/U-2.    LB/U-1.    LO/U-3.    OX/U-1.    SO/U-1.*
*GL/U-2.  6, 1974-*
*ISSN 0039-3525*

STUDIES IN AFRICAN ECONOMICS.
+ +STUD. AFR. ECON.
[OXFORD UNIV. PRESS]
*LONDON  1, 1967-*
*ED/N-1.    OX/U-9.*

STUDIA AMSTELODAMENSIA AD EPIGRAPHICUM, IUS
ANTIQUUM ET PAPYROLOGICAM PERTINENTIA.
+ +STUD. AMSTELODAMENSIA EPIGR. ANTIQ. & PAPYRO-
LOGICAM PERTINENTIA.
*AMSTERDAM  1, 1972-*
*CA/U-1.    OX/U-1.*

STUDIA ANGLICA POSNANIENSIA.
+ +STUD. ANGLICA POSNAN.
UNIWERSYTET IM ADAMA MICKIEWICZA W POZNANIU.
*POZNAN  1, 1968-*
S/T: AN INTERNATIONAL REVIEW OF ENGLISH
STUDIES.
*CB/U-1.    DB/U-1.    OX/U-1.*

STUDIEN ZUR ANTIKEN PHILOSOPHIE.
+ +STUD. ANITKEN PHILOS.
*AMSTERDAM  1, 1971-*
*OX/U-1.*

STUDIES IN APPLIED MATHEMATICS.                    XXX
+ +STUD. APPL. MATH.
MASSACHUSETTS INSTITUTE OF TECHNOLOGY: APPLIED
MATHEMATICS GROUP.
*CAMBRIDGE, MASS.  48(1), MR 1969-*
PREV: JOURNAL OF MATHEMATICS & PHYSICS FROM
1, 1921-47(4), 1968.
*BN/U-2.    GL/U-1.    NW/U-1.*
*XS/N-1.  2, 1971-*
*ISSN 0022-2526*

STUDIA ARCHEOLOGICZNE, UNIWERSYTET WROCLAWSKI    XXX
+ +STUD. ARCHEOL. UNIW. WROCLAW.
*WROCLAW  1, JE 1965-*
PREV: ARCHEOLOGIA SLASKA FROM 1, 1957- 1965.
ISSUES NUMBERED ALSO AS PART OF THE MAIN
SERIES: ACTA UNIVERSITATIS WRATISLAVIENSIS.
*DR/U-1.    LO/N-3.    OX/U-1.*

STUDIES IN ARCHITECTURAL HISTORY.
+ +STUD. ARCHIT. HIST.
UNIVERSITY OF VICTORIA: MALTWOOD MUSEUM.
*VICTORIA (B.C.)  1, 1968-*
*OX/U-1.*

STUDIA BIBLICA ET THEOLOGICA.
+ +STUD. BIBLICA & THEOL.
FULLER THEOLOGICAL SEMINARY.
*PASADENA, CALIF.  1, MR 1971-*
ANNU.
*CA/S-1.*

STUDIES IN BLACK LITERATURE.
+ +STUD. BLACK LIT.
MARY WASHINGTON COLLEGE: DEPARTMENT OF ENGLISH.
*FREDERICKSBURG, VA.  1(1), 1970-*
3/A.
*LD/U-1.  1(2), 1970-*
*ISSN 0039-3576*

STUDIES IN BURKE & HIS TIME.                    XXX
+ +STUD. BURKE & HIS TIME.
ALFRED UNIVERSITY.
*ALFRED, N.Y.  9(1), 1967-*
PREV: BURKE NEWSLETTER FROM NO.1, 1959- 29,
1967.
*OX/U-1.*
*ISSN 0039-3584*

STUDII SE CERCETARI DE INFRAMICROBIOLOGIE.      XXX
SUBS (1972): STUDII SI CERCETARI DE VIRUSOL-
OGIE.

STUDII SI CERCETARI DE MECANICA AGRICOLA.
+ +STUD. CERCET. MEC. AGRIC.
CONSILIUL SUPERIOR AL AGRICULTURII (RUMANIA).
*BUCAREST  1, 1967-*
*LO/N13.*

**STUDII SI CERCETARI DE VIRUSOLOGIE.**     **XXX**
++*STUD. CERCET. VIRUSOL.*
[EDITURA ACADEMIEI REPUBLICII SOCIALISTE
ROMANIA]
*BUCHAREST 23, 1972-*
PREV: STUDII SI CERCETARI DE INFRAMICROBIOL-
OGIE FROM 2, 1950- 22, 1971.
*LO/N13.*

**STUDIE, CESKOSLOVENSKA AKADEMIE VED.**
++*STUD. CESK. AKAD. VED.*
*PRAGUE 1, 1968-*
MONOGR.
*OX/U-1.*

**STUDIES, COMMISSION ON INDUSTRIAL RELATIONS
(GB).**
++*STUD. COMM. IND. RELAT. (GB).*
*LONDON 1, 1972-*
*CA/U-1.*

**STUDIES IN COMPARATIVE COMMUNISM.**
++*STUD. COMP. COMMUNISM.*
UNIVERSITY OF SOUTHERN CALIFORNIA: SCHOOL OF
POLITICS & INTERNATIONAL RELATIONS.
*LOS ANGELES 1, JL/OC 1968-*
ISSUED BY THE SCHOOL'S RESEARCH INSTITUTE.
*BH/U-1.*    *BL/U-1.*    *CB/U-1.*    *SW/U-1.*
*LO/N17. 2, 1969-*
*ISSN 0039-3592*

**STUDIES IN COMPARATIVE LITERATURE.**
++*STUD. COMP. LIT.*
UNIVERSITY OF SOUTHERN CALIFORNIA.
*LOS ANGELES [NO.]1, 1968-*
*MA/U-1.*

**STUDIES IN COMPARATIVE LITERATURE, NEW YORK
UNIVERSITY.**     **000**
SEE: NEW YORK UNIVERSITY STUDIES IN
COMPARATIVE LITERATURE.

**STUDIES IN COMPARATIVE RELIGION.**
++*STUD. COMP. RELIG.*
[TOMORROW PUBL. LTD.]
*BEDFONT 1(1), 1967-*
Q.
*OX/U-1.*
*SH/U-1. JL/OC 1968-*

**STUDIES IN CONTEMPORARY EUROPEAN ISSUES.**
++*STUD. CONTEMP. EUR. ISSUES.*
COLLEGE OF EUROPE.
*BRUGES [NO.]1, 1968-*
*LO/N-3.*

**STUDIA COPERNICANA.**
++*STUD. COPERNICANA.*
POLSKA AKADEMIA NAUK: ZAKLAD HISTORII NAUKI I
TECHNIKI.
*WROCLAW 1, JE 1970-*
MONOGR. VARIOUS LANGUAGES.
*CC/U-1.*    *LO/N-4.*

**STUDIA AD CORPUS HELLENISTICUM NOVI TESTAMENTI.**
++*STUD. CORPUS HELL. NOVI TESTAMENTI.*
[BRILL]
*LEIDEN 1, 1970-*
*CA/U-1.*

**STUDIA DEMOGRAFICZNE.**
++*STUD. DEMOGR.*
POLSKA AKADEMIA NAUK: KOMITET NAUK DEMOGRAFIC-
ZNYCH.
*WARSAW 1, 1963-*
Q. ENGL. & RUSS. SUMM.
*LO/N-3.*    *LO/U-3.*    *OX/U-1.*
*BH/U-3. 15, 1968-*
*ISSN 0039-3134*

**STUDIEN ZUR DEUTSCHEN LITERATUR.**
++*STUD. DEUT. LIT.*
[MAX NIEMEYER VERLAG]
*TUBINGEN 1, 1966-*
MONOGR.
*LO/U-2.*

**STUDIA Z DZIEJOW OSADNICTWA.**
++*STUD. DZIEJOW OSADNICTWA.*
POLSKA AKADEMIA NAUK: INSTYTUT HISTORII KULTURY
MATERIALNEJ.
*WARSAW; WROCLAW 1, 1963-*
FR. SUMM. MONOGR. SUBSER. OF: STUDIA I
MATERIALY Z HISTORII KULTURY MATERIALNEJ.
*OX/U-1.*

**STUDIA Z DZIEJOW POLSKI W OKRESIE OSWIECENIA.**     **XXX**
SUBS (1960): STUDIA I MATERIALY Z DZIEJOW
POLSKI W OKRESIE OSWIECENIA.

**STUDIA Z DZIEJOW RZEMIOSLA I PRZEMYSLU.**
++*STUD. DZIEJOW RZEMIOSLA & PRZEM.*
POLSKA AKADEMIA NAUK: INSTYTUT HISTORII KULTURY
MATERIALNEJ.
*WROCLAW 1, 1961-*
FR. SUMM. MONOGR. SUBSER. OF STUDIA I
MATERIALY Z HISTORII KULTURY MATERIALNEJ.
*OX/U-1.*

**STUDIA Z DZIEJOW ZSRR I EUROPY SRODKOWEJ.**
++*STUD. DZIEJOW ZSRR & EUR. SRODKOWEJ.*
POLSKA AKADEMIA NAUK: ZAKLAD HISTORII ZSRR I
EUROPY SRODKOWEJ.
*WROCLAW 1, 1965-*
ENGL. & RUSS. SUMM. ZAKLAD HISTORII ZSRR
SUBORD. TO: INSTYTUT HISTORII OF POLSKA
AKADEMIA NAUK.
*BH/U-1.*    *CA/U-1.*

**STUDIES IN EDUCATION (EXETER).**
++*STUD. EDUC. (EXETER).*
UNIVERSITY OF EXETER: ST. LUKE'S COLLEGE OF
EDUCATION.
*EXETER NO.1, 1970-*
*ED/N-1.*

**STUDIES IN EDUCATION (FERNHEAD, LANCS.).**
++*STUD. EDUC. (FERNHEAD, LANCS.).*
PADGATE COLLEGE OF EDUCATION.
*FERNHEAD, LANCS. NO.1, MY 1966-*
*DB/U-2.*    *ED/N-1.*

**STUDIES IN EIGHTEENTH CENTURY CULTURE.**
++*STUD. EIGHTEENTH CENTURY CULT.*
[CASE WESTERN RESERVE UNIV. P.]
*CLEVELAND &C. 1, 1971-*
VOL.1- ISSUED AS IST 1970- PROCEEDINGS OF THE
AMERICAN SOCIETY FOR EIGHTEENTH-CENTURY
STUDIES.
*CA/U-1.*    *MA/U-1.*    *OX/U-1.*

**STUDIEN ZUR ENGLISCHEN LITERATUR.**
++*STUD. ENGL. LIT.*
*BONN 1, 1969-*
*CA/U-1.*    *LO/U-1.*    *OX/U-1.*

**STUDIES IN ENGLISH, DEPARTMENT OF ENGLISH,
UNIVERSITY OF MISSISSIPPI.**
++*STUD. ENGL. DEP. ENGL. UNIV. MISS.*
*LAFAYETTE 1, 1960-*
*LO/U-1.*
*OX/U-1. 2, 1961-*

**STUDIES IN ENGLISH, UNIVERSITY OF CAPE TOWN.**
++*STUD. ENGL. UNIV. CAPE TOWN.*
*CAPE TOWN 1, F 1970-*
*BL/U-1.*    *ED/N-1.*    *ED/U-1.*    *GL/U-1.*    *HL/U-1.*    *OX/U-1.*

**STUDIES IN ENVIRONMENT THERAPY.**
++*STUD. ENVIRON. THER.*
PLANNED ENVIRONMENT THERAPY TRUST.
*WORTH, SX. 1, 1968-*
*OX/U-8.*

**STUDIA ESTETYCZNE.**
++*STUD. ESTETYCZNE.*
POLSKA AKADEMIA NAUK: INSTYTUT FILOZOFII I
SOCJOLOGII.
*WARSAW 1, 1964-*
ENGL., & RUSS. SUMM.
*OX/U-1.*

**STUDIES IN EXPORT PROMOTION.**
PAN-AMERICAN UNION.
*WASHINGTON, D.C. 1, 1966-*
SOME ISS. IN SPAN.
*OX/U-1.*

**STUDIES IN FAMILY PLANNING.**
++*STUD. FAM. PLANN.*
POPULATION COUNCIL.
*NEW YORK 1, JL 1963-*
*CA/U-1.*    *LO/M10.*    *LO/M17.*    *LO/U-3.*    *RE/U-1.*
*BT/U-1. 23, 1967-*
*ISSN 0039-3665*

**STUDIES IN GENERAL & COMPARATIVE LITERATURE.**
++*STUD. GEN. & COMP. LIT.*
[MOUTON]
*THE HAGUE 1, 1965-*
*LO/U-2.*

**STUDIA GEOLOGICA.**
++*STUD. GEOL.*
UNIVERSIDAD DE SALAMANCA.
*SALAMANCA 1, 1971-*
*LO/N-2.*

**STUDI GEOLOGICI CAMERTI.**
++*STUDI GEOL. CAMERTI.*
*CAMERINO 1, 1971-*
*LO/N-2.*

**STUDI GERMANICI. NS.**
++*STUD. GER. N.S. (ITAL.).*
ISTITUTO ITALIANO DI STUDI GERMANICI.
*ROME 1, 1963-*
PREV. SER. ISSUED 1935.
*LO/N-1.*
*MA/U-1. 4, 1966-*
*ISSN 0039-2952*

**STUDIEN ZUR GESCHICHTE DER OSTERREICHISCH-UNGARISCHEN MONARCHIE.**
++*STUD. GESCH. OSTERR.-UNG. MONARCHIE.*
OSTERREICHISCHE AKADEMIE DER WISSENSCHAFTEN.
*GRAZ &C 1, 1963-*
ISSUED BY THE AKADEMIE'S KOMMISSION FUR DIE
GESCHICHTE DER OSTERREICHISCH-UNGARISCHEN
MONARCHIE.
*OX/U-1.*

**STUDI DI GRAMMATICA ITALIANA.**
++*STUDI GRAMMATICA ITAL.*
ACCADEMIA DELLA CRUSCA.
*FLORENCE 1, 1972-*
*DB/U-1.     RE/U-1.*
*MA/U-1. 2, 1972-*

**STUDIA HELLENSKIE.**
++*STUD. HELLEN.*
KATOLICKI UNIWERSYTET LUBELSKI: TOWARZYSTWO
NAUKOWE.
*LUBLIN Z.1, 1967-*
MONOGR. FR. SUMM. NUMBERED ALSO AS PART OF
MAIN SERIES: ROZPRAWY WYDZIALU HISTORYCZNO-
FILOLOGICZNEGO, TOWARZYSTWO NAUKOWE KATOLIC-
KIEGO UNIWERSYTETU LUBELSKIEGO. NO.1 OF ABOVE
= NO.32 OF ROZPRAWY...
*LO/N-3.*

**STUDIES IN THE HISTORY OF CHRISTIAN THOUGHT.**
++*STUD. HIST. CHRIST. THOUGHT.*
[E.J. BRILL]
*LEIDEN 1, 1966-*
*GL/U-1.     OX/U-1.*
*HL/U-1. 4, 1968.*

**STUDIES IN HISTORY & PHILOSOPHY OF SCIENCE.**
++*STUD. HIST. & PHIL. SCI.*
*LONDON 1, 1970-*
Q.
*AD/U-1.     BN/U-1.     CB/U-1.     DN/U-1.     ED/N-1.     ED/U-1.*
*EX/U-1.     GL/U-1.     LO/M24.     LO/N-2.     LO/N-4.     LO/U-1.*
*LO/U-2.     LO/U-3.     MA/U-1.     NW/U-1.     OX/U-8.     RE/U-1.*
*SO/U-1.     SW/U-1.*
*DB/U-2. 1973                     NO/U-1. 1(4), 1971-*
*ISSN 0039-3681*

**STUDIA HISTORYCZNE, KOMISJA NAUK HISTORY-**
**CZNYCH, (ODDZIAL W KRAKOWIE) POLSKA AKADEMIA**
**NAUK.**                                                                 XXX
++*STUD. HIST. KOM. NAUK HIST. (ODDZ. KRAKOW.)*
*POLSKA AKAD. NAUK.*
*CRACOW 10(1/2), 1967-*
Q. CONTENTS LIST IN ENGL. & RUSS. PREV:
MALOPOLSKIE STUDIA HISTORYCZNE FROM 1(1),1958.
*LO/N-3.*

**STUDIA HISTORYCZNE, TOWARZYSTWO NAUKOWE KATOL-**
**ICKIEGO UNIWERSYTETU LUBELSKIEGO.**
++*STUD. HIST. TOW. NAUK. KATOL. UNIW. LUBEL.*
KATOLICKI UNIWERSYTET LUBELSKI: TOWARZYSTWO
NAUKOWE.
*LUBLIN 1, 1968-*
FR. OR GER. SUMM. NUMBERED ALSO AS PART OF
MAIN SERIES: ROZPRAWY WYDZIALU HISTORYCZNO-
FILOLOGICZNEGO, TOWARZYSTWO NAUKOWE KATOLICK-
IEGO UNIWERSYTETU LUBELSKIEGO. NO.1 OF ABOVE
= NO. 34 OF ROZPRAWY...
*LO/N-3.*

**STUDIES IN THE HUMANITIES.**
++*STUD. HUM.*
CORNELL UNIVERSITY: SOCIETY FOR THE HUMANITIES.
*ITHACA, N.Y. 1, 1967-*
*OX/U-1.*
*ISSN 0585-7279*

**STUDI ILLUSTRATIVI DELLA CARTA GEOLOGICA**
**D'ITALIA: FORMAZIONI GEOLOGICHE.**
++*STUDI ILLUS. CARTA GEOL. ITAL., FORM. GEOL.*
SERVIZIO GEOLOGICO D'ITALIA.
*ROME 1, 1968-*
*LO/N-4.*
*ISSN 0579-4153*

**STUDIES IN INTERNATIONAL AFFAIRS.**
++*STUD. INT. AFF.*
WASHINGTON CENTER OF FOREIGN POLICY RESEARCH.
[JOHNS HOPKINS P.]
*BALTIMORE, MD. 1, 1967-*
*HL/U-1.*

**STUDIES IN INTERNATIONAL SECURITY.**
++*STUD. INT. SECUR.*
INSTITUTE FOR STRATEGIC STUDIES (LONDON).
[WEIDENFELD & NICOLSON]
*LONDON 1, 1960-*
MONOGR.
*HL/U-1.***

**STUDI INTERNAZIONALI DI FILOSOFIA.**
++*STUDI INT. FILOS.*
*TURIN 1, 1969-*
A. REPLACES THE FASCICOLO INTERNAZIONALE.
ISSUED ANNUALLY WITH FILOSOFIA FROM 10, 1959-
19, 1968.
*BH/U-1.     GL/U-1.     HL/U-1.     OX/U-1.*
*LO/N-3. 3, 1971-*
*ISSN 0039-2979*

**STUDIES IN IOWA HISTORY.**
++*STUD. IOWA HIST.*
IOWA STATE HISTORICAL SOCIETY.
*IOWA CITY 1(1), 1969-*
*OX/U-9.*
*ISSN 0039-3703*

**STUDI ITALIANI DI LINGUISTICA TEORICA ED**
**APPLICATA.**
++*STUDI ITAL. LINGUIST. TEOR. & APPL.*
UNIVERSITA DI BOLOGNA: CENTRO INTERFACOLTA DI
LINGUISTICA TEORICA ED APPLICATA.
*BOLOGNA 1, 1972-*
*LO/N-1.     RE/U-1.     SH/U-1.*

**STUDIES IN JAZZ RESEARCH.**                                               000
SEE: BEITRAGE ZUR JAZZFORSCHUNG.

**STUDIA KETICA.**                                                          000
SEE: KETSKIJ SBORNIK.

**STUDIA KOMITETU PRZESTRZENNEGO ZAGOSPODARO-**
**WANIA KRAJU POLSKIEJ AKADEMII NAUK.**
++*STUD. KOM. PRZESTRZENNEGO ZAGOSPOD. KRAJU POL.*
*AKAD. NAUK.*
*WARSAW 1, 1961-*
MONOGR.
*BH/U-1.     HL/U-1.     LO/U-3.*

**STUDIA O KSIAZCE.**                                                       XXX
++*STUD. KSIAZCE.*
OGOLNOPOLSKI ORGAN SZKOL WYZSZYCH.
*WROCLAW &C. 1, 1970-*
INCORP: BIBLIOTEKOZNAWSTWO FROM 1, 1955- 6,
1970; ZESZYTY NAUKOWE UNIWERSYTETU IM. ADAMA
MICKIEWICZA: BIBLIOTEKA FROM 1, 1960- 9, 1970;
& ZESZYTY NAUKOWE UNIWERSYTETU MIKOLAJA
KOPERNIKA: NAUKI HUMANISTYCZNO-SPOLECZNE:
NAUKA O KSIAZCE FROM 1, 1962- 5, 1968.
*GL/U-1.     OX/U-1.*

**STUDIES IN LAW & ECONOMIC DEVELOPMENT.**                                  XXX
++*STUD. LAW & ECON. DEV.*
GEORGE WASHINGTON UNIVERSITY: INTERNATIONAL
LAW SOCIETY.
*WASHINGTON, D.C. 1(1), AP 1966- 2(1), MY*
*1967 ...*
SUBS: JOURNAL OF LAW & ECONOMIC DEVELOPMENT.
*LO/U24.*

**STUDIES IN LAW & ECONOMICS.**                                             000
SEE: STUDIA PRAWNO-EKONOMICZNE, LODSKIE TOWAR-
ZYSTWO NAUKOWE.

**STUDIES ON THE LEFT.**                                                    XXX
SUBS (1970): SOCIALIST REVOLUTION.

**STUDIA LEIBNITIANA. VIERTELJAHRSCHRIFT FUR**
**PHILOSOPHIE UND GESCHICHTE DER WISSENSCHAFTEN.**
++*STUD. LEIBNITIANA.*
GOTTFRIED-WILHELM-LEIBNIZ GESELLSCHAFT E.V.
*WIESBADEN 1(1), 1969-*
*LO/N-4.     LO/U17.     OX/U-1.*
*0039-3185*

**STUDIA LINGUISTICA GERMANICA.**
+ +STUD. LINGUIST. GER.
[DE GRUYTER]
  BERLIN  1, 1968-
  GL/U-1.

**STUDIES IN THE LITERARY IMAGINATION.**
+ +STUD. LIT. IMAGIN.
GEORGIA STATE COLLEGE: DEPARTMENT OF ENGLISH.
  ATLANTA  1, AP 1968-
  CA/U-1.    LO/N-1.    OX/U-1.
  RE/U-1.  4, 1971-
  ISSN 0039-3819

**STUDIA LITTERARIA.**
+ +STUD. LITT. (HUNG.)
KOSSUTH LAJOS TUDOMANYEGYETEM: MAGYAR
IRODALOMTORTENETI INTEZET.
[TAUKONYVKIADO]
  BUDAPEST  TOMUS 1, 1963-
  S/T: COMMUNICATIONES INSTITUTI HISTORIAE
  LITTERARUM HUNGARICUM IN UNIVERSITATE SCIEN-
  TIARUM DEBRECENIENSI DE LUDOVICO KOSSUTH
  NOMINATA.  A DEBRECENI KOSSUTH LAJOS TUDO-
  MANYEGYETEM MAGYAR IRODALOMTORTENETI INTEZETE-
  NEK KOZLEMENYEI.
  LO/N-3.  1, 1963.

**STUDIA I MATERIALY Z DZIEJOW POLSKI W OKRESIE
OSWIECENIA.**                                                          XXX
+ +STUD. & MATER. DZIEJOW POL. OKRESIE OSWIECENIA
POLSKA AKADEMIA NAUK: INSTYTUT HISTORII.
  WARSAW  3, 1960- 6, 1966.
  MONOGR.  PREV: STUDIA Z DZIEJOW POLSKI W
  OKRESIE OSWIECENIA FROM 1, 1957- 2, 1959.
  SUBS: STUDIA Z OKRESU OSWIECENIA.
  LO/N-3.    OX/U-1.

**STUDIES IN MEDIEVAL & REFORMATION THOUGHT.**
+ +STUD. MEDIEVAL & REFORMATION THOUGHT.
[E.J. BRILL]
  LEIDEN  1, 1966-
  GL/U-1.    OX/U-1.

**STUDI MEMORIE E DOCUMENTI, BIBLIOTECA DEL
MOVIMENTO OPERAIO ITALIANO.**
+ +STUDI MEM. & DOC. BIBL. MOV. OPERAIO ITAL.
  ROME  1, 1971-
  OX/U-1.

**STUDI MERIDIONALI.**
+ +STUDI MERID.
[CASA EDITRICE STUDI MERIDIONALI]
  ROME  1, OC/D 1968-
  Q.
  LO/U17.

**STUDIES IN MONETARY ECONOMICS.**
+ +STUD. MONETARY ECON.
MINNEAPOLIS FEDERAL RESERVE BANK.
  MINNEAPOLIS  NO.1, MR 1972-
  LO/U12.    OX/U16.

**STUDI MUSICALI.**
ACCADEMIA NAZIONALE DI SANTA CECILIA.
  ROME  1, 1972-
  2/A.
  CA/U-1.    LO/U-1.

**STUDIES IN NATURAL SCIENCES.**
+ +STUD. NAT. SCI.
EASTERN NEW MEXICO UNIVERSITY.
  PORTALES  1, 1971-
  LO/N-2.

**STUDIES OVER NEDERLAND IN OORLOGSTIJD.**
+ +STUD. NED. OORLOGSTIJD.
  THE HAGUE  1, 1972-
  OX/U-1.

**STUDIA NEERLANDICA.  DRIEMAANDELIJKS TIJDSCHRIFT
VOOR NEERLANDISTIEK.**
+ +STUD. NEERL.
[ATHENAEUM-POLAK & VAN GENNEP]
  AMSTERDAM  NO.1, 1970-
  Q.
  LO/N-1.

**STUDIES ON THE NEOTROPICAL FAUNA.**                                 XXX
+ +STUD. NEOTROP. FAUNA.
[SWETS & ZEITLINGER]
  AMSTERDAM  7, 1972-
  PREV: BEITRAGE ZUR NEOTROPISCHEN FAUNA FROM 1,
  1956- 6, 1971.
  LO/N-2.    LO/N13.
  OX/U-8.  6(1), 1969-

**STUDIES IN NIGERIAN LANGUAGES.**
+ +STUD. NIGER. LANG.
  ZARIA  1, 1971-
  LO/U14.    OX/U-1.

**STUDIES IN NONVIOLENCE.**
+ +STUD. NONVIOLENCE.
PEACE PLEDGE UNION: YOUTH ASSOCIATION.
  LONDON  1(1), JE 1969-
+XVBTSUD. NOVEL.
NORTH TEXAS STATE UNIVERSITY.
  DENTON, TEX.  1(1), 1969-
  Q.
  DB/U-2.    ED/N-1.    LO/N-1.    LO/U-1.    OX/U-1.
  NO/U-1.  3(3), 1971-            NW/U-1.  3(3), 1971-
  ISSN 0039-3827

**STUDIES IN OFFICIAL STATISTICS (GREAT BRIT-
AIN): RESEARCH SERIES.**
+ +STUD. OFF. STATIST. (G.B.), RES. SER.
(GREAT BRITAIN) CENTRAL STATISTICAL OFFICE.
[H.M.S.O.]
  LONDON  NO.1, 1968-
  GL/U-1.    LO/U-1.

**STUDIA Z OKRESU OSWIECENIA.**
+ +STUD. OKRESU OSWIECENIA.
POLSKA AKADEMIA NAUK; INSTYTUT BADAN LITERAC-
KICH.
  WROCLAW &C  TOM 1, AG 1964-
  MONOGR.
  CA/U-1.    LO/N-3.    NO/U-1.    OX/U-1.

**STUDIES IN OPTIMIZATION.**
+ +STUD. OPTIM.
SOCIETY FOR INDUSTRIAL & APPLIED MATHEMATICS.
  PHILADELPHIA  1, 1970-
  OX/U-8.

**STUDIA ORAWSKIE.**
+ +STUD. ORAWSKIE.
UNIWERSYTET JAGIELLONSKI.
  KRAKOW  NR.1, 1964-
  MONOGR.  NUMBERED ALSO AS PART OF THE MAIN
  SERIES: ZESZYTY NAUKOWE UNIWERSYTETU JAGIELL-
  ONSKIEGO, & SUBSERIES TO 'ZESZYTY ...': PRACE
  JEZYKOZNAWCZE. ADD. TITLE PAGE IN LATIN:
  STUDIA ORAVIENSIA.
  ED/U-1.    LO/N-3.

**STUDIEN ZUR OSTASIATISCHEN SCHRIFTKUNST.**
+ +STUD. OSTASIATISCHEN SCHRIFTKUNST.
[F. STEINER VERLAG]
  WIESBADEN  1, 1970-
  OX/U-1.

**STUDIA PALMYRENSKIE. = ETUDES PALMYRENIENNES.**
+ +STUD. PALMYRENSKIE.
UNIWERSYTET WARSZAWSKI: KATEDRA ARCHEOLOGII
SRODZIEMNOMORSKIEJ.
  WARSAW  [Z.] 1, 1966-
  KATEDRA SUBORD. TO WYDZIAL HISTORYCZNY, UNIW.
  WARSZAWSKI. TEXT PARTLY IN FR.
  CA/U-3.    OX/U-1.

**STUDI PARLAMENTARI E DI POLITICA COSTITU-
ZIONALE.**
+ +STUDI PARL. & POLIT. COST.
  ROME  1(1), 1968-
  Q.
  LO/U-3.

**STUDIA PHILONICA.**
+ +STUD. PHILONICA.
[PHILO INSTITUTE, INC.]
  CHICAGO  1, 1972-
  ANNU.
  LO/U17.    OX/U-1.

**STUDIEN ZUR PHILOSOPHIE UND LITERATUR DES
NEUNZEHNTEN JAHRHUNDERTS.**
+ +STUD. PHIL. & LIT. NEUNZEHN. JAHRH.
FRITZ-THYSSEN-STIFTUNG.
  FRANKFURT/MAIN  1, 1968-
  BODY LOCATED IN COLOGNE.
  LO/N-1.

**STUDI PIEMONTESI.**
+ +STUDI PIEMONT.
CENTRO STUDI PIEMONTESI.
  TURIN  1, MR 1972-
  2/A.  ENGL. SUMM.
  OX/U-1.

**STUDIA PRAWNO-EKONOMICZNE, LODSKIE TOWARZYSTWO NAUKOWE. STUDIES IN LAW & ECONOMICS.**
++STUD. PRAWNO-EKON. LODZK. TOW. NAUK.
LODZ 1, 1968-
ENGL. SUMM.
DB/S-1.     LO/N-3.     OX/U-1.

**STUDIES IN PRE-COLUMBIAN ART & ARCHAEOLOGY.**
++STUD. PRE-COLUMB. ART & ARCHAEOL.
DUMBARTON OAKS TRUSTEES.
HARVARD UNIVERSITY.
WASHINGTON, DC  NO.1, 1966-
PUBL. FOR HARVARD UNIV. 'A NEW SERIES ...
CONCERNED CHIEFLY WITH OBJECTS IN THE ROBERT
WOODS BLISS COLLECTION.'
CA/U-3.

**STUDIES IN PREHISTORIC ANTHROPOLOGY.**
++STUD. PREHIST. ANTHROPOL.
UNIVERSITY OF OTAGO: ANTHROPOLOGY DEPARTMENT.
DUNEDIN  1, 1969-
LO/N-1.

**STUDI E PROBLEMI DI CRITICA TESTUALE.**
++STUDI & PROBL. CRIT. TESTUALE.
BOLOGNA 1, OC 1970-
BH/U-1.     NO/U-1.     SW/U-1.
DB/U-2.  8, 1974-

**STUDIEN UND QUELLEN ZUR GESCHICHTE REGENSBURGS.**
++STUD. & QUELLEN GESCH. REGENSB.
[MITTELBAYERISCHE DRUCKEREI- UND VERLAGS-
GESELLSCHAFT]
REGENSBURG 1, 1970-
OX/U-1.

**STUDIES IN REGIONAL ECONOMIC INTEGRATION.**
++STUD. REG. ECON. INTEGRATION.
UNIVERSITY OF THE WEST INDIES: INSTITUTE OF
SOCIAL & ECONOMIC RESEARCH.
KINGSTON, JAM. 1, 1967-
MONOGR.
LO/N-3.     OX/U16.

**STUDIES IN REGIONAL SCIENCE.**
++STUD. REG. SCI.
LONDON [1], 1969-
BL/U-1.

**STUDIES IN RELIGION. SCIENCES RELIGIEUSES.**                    XXX
++STUD. RELIG.
CORPORATION FOR THE PUBLICATION OF ACADEMIC
STUDIES IN RELIGION IN CANADA.
[UNIV. OF TORONTO P.]
TORONTO 1, 1971-
PREV: CANADIAN JOURNAL OF THEOLOGY FROM 1, AP
1955- 16, 1970.
NW/U-1.     OX/U-1.
ISSN 0008-4298

**STUDIES ON RELIGION IN AFRICA.**
++STUD. RELIG. AFR.
[BRILL]
LEIDEN 1, 1970-
SUPPL. TO JOURNAL OF RELIGION IN AFRICA.
BH/U-1.

**STUDI E RICERCHE DI LETTERATURA INGLESE E AMERICANA.**
++STUDI & RIC. LETT. INGLESE & AM.
UNIVERSITA COMMERCIALE LUIGI BOCCONI: FACOLTA
DI LINGUE E LETTERATURE STRANIERE.
MILAN 1, 1967-
ANNU.
OX/U-1.

**STUDI RISORGIMENTALI.**
++STUDI RISORG.
ISTITUTO PER LA STORIA DEL RISORGIMENTO
ITALIANO (COMITATO DI CATANIA).
CATANIA  1, 1965-
OX/U-1.

**STUDIE O RUKOPISECH.**
++STUD. RUKOPISECH.
CESKOSLOVENSKA AKADEMIE VED: KOMISE PRO SOUPIS
RUKOPISU.
PRAGUE 1962-
OX/U-1.
LO/U-1. 1964-

**STUDIA SAMARITANA.**
++STUD. SAMARITANA.
[WALTER DE GRUYTER & CO.]
BERLIN 1, 1969-
MONOGR.
LO/N-1.

**STUDIES ON SELECTED DEVELOPMENT PROBLEMS IN VARIOUS COUNTRIES IN THE MIDDLE EAST.**
++STUD. SELEC. DEVELOP. PROBL. VARIOUS COUNT.
MIDDLE EAST.
UNITED NATIONS: ECONOMIC & SOCIAL OFFICE IN
BEIRUT.
NEW YORK 1, 1967-
A.
LO/U-2.     LO/U-3.

**STUDIES IN SEMITIC LANGUAGES & LINGUISTICS.**
++STUD. SEMITIC LANG. & LINGUIST.
[BRILL]
LEYDEN 1, 1967-
OX/U-1.

**STUDIES IN SOCIOLOGY.**
++STUD. SOCIOL.
[ALLEN & UNWIN]
LONDON 1, 1967-
MONOGR.
HL/U-1.**

**STUDIA SOCJOLOGICZNE.**
++STUD. SOCJOLOGICZNE.
POLSKA AKADEMIA NAUK: INSTYTUT FILOZOFII I
SOCJOLOGII.
WARSAW &C.  1(1), 1961-
Q.
LO/S-9.  1961-*
BH/U-1." 1964-                        LO/U-3.  1963-
OX/U-1.  1968-
ISSN 0039-3371

**STUDIES IN SPANISH LITERATURE.**
++STUD. SPAN. LIT.
[MOUTON]
THE HAGUE 1, 1971-
CA/U-1.

**STUDIES IN TECHNOLOGICAL MANPOWER.**
++STUD. TECHNOL. MANPOWER.
(GREAT BRITAIN) MINISTRY OF TECHNOLOGY.
LONDON  NO.1, 1970-
OX/U-1.

**STUDII TEHNICE SI ECONOMICE, INSTITUTUL GEO-LOGIC: SERIA A: PROSPECTIUNI SI EXPLORARI GEOLOGICE.**
++STUD. TEH. & ECON. INST. GEOL. (ROM.), SER. A.
BUCHAREST
NOTE THAT SAME TITLE (IN SER. A, B & C) PUBL.
BY SAME BODY PREVIOUSLY (SEE BUCOP/4V). AT
HEAD OF TITLE OF ABOVE (SUPERIOR BODY): COMI-
TETUL GEOLOGIC DE CERCETARI SI EXPLORARE A
BOGATILOR SOLULUI SI SUBSOLULUI.
BR/U-1. NO.8 1970-             LO/N-2. NO.7, 1967-

**STUDII TEHNICE SI ECONOMICE, INSTITUTUL GEO-LOGIC: SERIA B: CHIMIE.**
++STUD. TEH. & ECON. INST. GEOL. (ROM.), SER. B.
BUCHAREST
REMARKS AS FOR SER. A.
LO/N-2. NO.45, 1970-

**STUDII TEHNICE SI ECONOMICE, INSTITUTUL GEO-LOGIC: SERIA C: PEDOLOGIA.**
++STUD. TEH. & ECON. INST. GEOL. (ROM.), SER. C.
BUCHAREST
REMARKS AS FOR SER. A.
LO/N-2. NO.16 1970-

**STUDII TEHNICE SI ECONOMICE, INSTITUTUL GEO-LOGIC: SERIA D: PROSPECTIUNI GEOFIZICE.**
++STUD. TEH. & ECON. INST. GEOL. (ROM.), SER. D.
BUCHAREST
REMARKS AS FOR SER. A.
BR/U-1. NO.7, 1970-            LO/N-2. NO.7, 1970-
LO/N-2. NO.5,1966-

**STUDII TEHNICE SI ECONOMICE, INSTITUTUL GEO-LOGIC: SERIA F: GEOLOGIE TEHNICA.**
++STUD. TEH. & ECON. INST. GEOL. (ROM.), SER. F.
BUCHAREST
REMARKS AS FOR SER. A.
LO/N-2.
BR/U-1. NO.8, 1970-

**STUDII TEHNICE SI ECONOMICE, INSTITUTUL GEO-LOGIC: SERIA H: GEOLOGIE.**
++STUD. TEH. & ECON. INST. GEOL. (ROM.), SER. H.
BUCHAREST
REMARKS AS FOR SER. A.
LO/N-2. NO.3, 1967-            LO/U-2. NO.2,1965-

**STUDII TEHNICE SI ECONOMICE, INSTITITUL GEO-
LOGIC: SERIA I: MINERALOGIE-PETROGRAFIE.**
++*STUD. TEH. & ECON. INST. GEOL. (ROM.), SER. I.*
*BUCHAREST NO.1, 1965*
REMARKS AS FOR SER. A.
*LO/N-2.   NO.3, 1967-*

**STUDII TEHNICE SI ECONOMICE, INSTITUTUL GEO-
LOGIC: SERIA J: STRATIGRAFIE.**
++*STUD. TEH. & ECON. INST. GEOL. (ROM.), SER. J.*
*BUCHAREST NO.1, 1966-*
REMARKS AS FOR SER. A.
*LO/N-2.   LO/U-2.*

**STUDI E TESTI, ACCADEMIA LUCCHESE DI SCIENZE,
LETTERE E ARTI.**
++*STUDI & TESTI ACCAD. LUCCHESE, SCI. LETT. &
ARTI.*
*LUCCA 1, 1969-*
MONOGR.
*LO/N-1.*

**STUDIA THEODISCA.**
++*STUD. THEODISCA.*
*ASSEN NO.1, 1962-*
*CA/U-1.  2, 1962-*
*ISSN 0081-6957*

**STUDIES IN THE 20TH CENTURY.**
++*STUD. 20TH CENTURY.*
RUSSELL SAGE COLLEGE.
*NEW YORK NO.1, 1968-*
*2/A.*
*OX/U-1.*
*ISSN 0039-3835*

**STUDIES IN VERMONT GEOLOGY.**
++*STUD. IN VERMONT GEOL.*
(VERMONT) DEPARTMENT OF WATER RESOURCES.
*MONTPELIER NO.1, 1970-*
*LO/N-2.   LO/N13.*

**STUDIA IN VETERIS TESTAMENTI PSEUDEPIGRAPHA.**
++*STUD. VETERIS TESTAMENTI PSEUDEPIGR.*
[BRILL]
*LEYDEN 1, 1970-*
*CA/U-1.*

**STUDIA WARSZAWSKIE.**
++*STUD. WARSZ.*
POLSKA AKADEMIA NAUK: INSTYTUT HISTORII.
*WARSAW 1, JL 1968-*
MONOGR.
*BH/U-1.   CA/U-1.   LO/U15.*
*ISSN 0081-7023*

**STUDIA NAD ZAGADNIENIAMI GOSPODARCZYMI I
SPOLECZNYMI ZIEM ZACHODNICH.**
++*STUD. ZAGADNIENIAMI GOSPOD. & SPOLECZNYMI ZIEM
ZACHODNICH.*
INSTYTUT ZACHODNI.
*POZNAN 1, JE 1960-*
*BH/U-1.   ED/N-1.   LO/N-3.   LO/U-3.*

**STUDIO SOUND.**                                                    XXX
[LINK HOUSE PUBL.]
*CROYDON 13(4), 1971- 15(4), 1973 ...*
PREV: STUDIO SOUND & TAPE RECORDER FROM 12(2),
1970- 13(3), 1971.  SUBS: STUDIO SOUND &
BROADCAST ENGINEERING.
*LO/N14.*

**STUDIO SOUND & BROADCAST ENGINEERING.**            XXX
++*STUDIO SOUND & BROADCAST ENG.*
[LINK HOUSE PUBL.]
*CROYDON 15(5), 1973-*
PREV: STUDIO SOUND FROM 13(4), 1971- 15(4),
1973.
*LO/N14.*

**STUDIO SOUND & TAPE RECORDER.**                          XXX
++*STUDIO SOUND & TAPE REC.*
[LINK HOUSE PUBL. LTD.]
*CROYDON 12(2), 1970- 13(3), 1971 ...*
PREV:  TAPE RECORDER FROM 1, 1959- 12(1),
1970. SUBS: STUDIO SOUND.
*LO/N14.*

**STUDY PAPER, SCOTTISH ASSOCIATION FOR PUBLIC
TRANSPORT.**
++*STUDY PAP. SCOTT. ASSOC. PUBLIC TRANSP.*
*GLASGOW 1, 1972-*
*OX/U-1.*

**STUDY, SOCIAL SCIENCE RESEARCH UNIT, DEPART-
MENT OF HEALTH & SOCIAL SECURITY.**
++*STUDY SOC. SCI. RES. UNIT DEP. HEALTH & SOC.
SECUR. (GB).*
(GREAT BRITAIN) DEPARTMENT OF HEALTH & SOCIAL
SECURITY: SOCIAL SCIENCE RESEARCH UNIT.
[HMSO]
*LONDON NO.1, 1969-*
*GL/U-1.   LO/N-1.*

**STUTTGARTER BIBLISCHE MONOGRAPHIEN.**               XXX
++*STUTTG. BIBLISCHE MONOGR.*
[VERLAG KATHOLISCHES BIBELWERK]
*STUTTGART NO.1, 1967- 12, 1971.//*
NO.8 NOT PUBLISHED.
*OX/U-1.*

**STYLE.**
UNIVERSITY OF ARKANSAS.
*FAYETTEVILLE, ARK.  1, 1967-*
*BH/U-1.   HL/U-1.   LO/U-2.*
*ISSN 0039-4238*

**SUB-AQUA MAGAZINE.**
++*SUB-AQUA MAG.*
[PRENBOURNE PUBL. LTD.]
*▪EDHILL, SY.  JL/AG 1970-*
*6A.*
*ED/N-1.   LO/N14.*

**SUB-ASSEMBLY - COMPONENTS - FASTENING.**           XXX
++*SUB-ASSEM. -COMPON. -FASTENING.*
[MORGAN-GRAMPIAN]
*LONDON 10(1), JA 1972-*
PREV: ASSEMBLY & FASTENER ENGINEERING (LONDON)
FROM 7(8), AG 1969- 9, 1971.
*BH/P-1.   ED/N-1.   GL/U-2.   LO/N14.   LO/N35.*

**SUB-CELLULAR BIOCHEMISTRY.**
++*SUB-CELL. BIOCHEM.*
[PLENUM P.]
*LONDON &C.  1(1), S 1971-*
Q.
*CA/U-1.   ED/N-1.   EX/U-1.   GL/U-1.   LO/N-1.   LO/S-3.*
*MA/U-1.   OX/U-8.   XY/N-1.*
*HL/U-1.  1(3); 2, 1972-*
*ISSN 0306-0225*

**SUCHASNA UKRAINA.**                                            XXX
SUBS (1961): PART SUCHASNIST'.

**SUCHASNIST'.**
UKRAINS'KE TOVARYSTVO ZAKORDONNYKH STUDII.
*MUNICH 1, JA 1961-*
M.  ON COVER: SUCASNIST'.  INCORP: SUCHASNA
UKRAINA FROM 1, 1951- 10, 1960 &: UKRAINS'KA
LITERATURNA GAZETA FROM 1, 1955- 6, 1960.
*LO/U15.*

**SUCTION.**
*IOWA CITY NO.1, 1969-*
*OX/U-1.*

**SUDAN AGRICULTURAL JOURNAL.**
++*SUDAN AGRIC. J.*
SUDAN AGRICULTURAL SOCIETY.
*KHARTUM 1, 1965-*
*LO/N13.*

**SUDAN LAW REPORTS: CIVIL CASES.**
++*SUDAN LAW REP., CIVIL CASES.*
UNIVERSITY OF KHARTOUM: FACULTY OF LAW.
[OCEANA PUBL.]
*NEW YORK 1, 1969-*
*LO/U14.*

**SUDENE. BOLETIM DE RECURSOS NATURAIS.**
(BRAZIL) SUPERINTENDENCIA DO DESENVOLVIMENTO
DO NORDESTE.
*RECIFE 1, 1963-*
*LO/N-2.*

**SUDOSTROENIE I MORSKIE SOORUZHENIJA.**
++*SUDOSTR. & MORSK. SOORUZH. [SUMS-B]*
KHAR'KOVSKIJ GOSUDARSTVENNYJ UNIVERSITET.
*KHAR'KOV 1, 1965-*
S/T: RESPUBLIKANSKIJ MEZHVEDOMSTVENNYJ
NAUCHNO-TEKHNICHESKIJ SBORNIK.
*LO/N13. [W. VYP. 1, 3 & 6].*

SUECANA EXTRANEA: BOCKER OM SVERIGE & OCH
SVENSK SKONLITTERATUR PA FRAMMANDE SPRAK.
+ +SUEC. EXTRANEA, BOCKER SEVRIGE & SVEN.
 SKONLITT. FRANMMANDE SPRAK.
 KUNGLIGA BIBLIOTEKET (STOCKHOLM).
 STOCKHOLM 1963/1966(1968)-
 S/T:ALSO IN ENGL. BOOKS ON SWEDEN & SWEDISH
 LITERATURE IN FOREIGN LANGUAGES.
 GL/U-1.   LO/S14.   OX/U-1.   SO/U-1.
 BH/P-1.   1971(1) -

SUFFOLK LOCAL HISTORY NEWSLETTER.
+ +SUFFOLK LOCAL HIST. NEWSL.
 SUFFOLK RURAL COMMUNITY COUNCIL: SUFFOLK LOCAL
 HISTORY COUNCIL.
 IPSWICH NO.1, 1969-
 MA/S-1.   OX/U-1.

SUGAR TECHNOLOGY REVIEWS.
+ +SUGAR TECHNOL. REV.
 [ELSEVIER]
 AMSTERDAM 1, 1969-
 LO/N14.   SH/C-5.

SUID-AFRIKAANSE STATISTIESE TYDSKRIF.     OOO
 SEE: SOUTH AFRICAN STATISTICAL JOURNAL.

SUMAC.
 [SUMAC P.]
 FREMONT (MICH.) 1, 1969-
 LO/U-2.   1(2), 1969-
 ISSN 0039-4939

SUMITOMO KINZOKU.                          XXX
 SUBS (1969):SUMITOMO SEARCH.

SUMITOMO SEARCH.
 SUMITOMO METAL INDUSTRIES, LTD.
 OSAKA 1, 1969-
 PREV: SUMITOMO KINZOKU FROM 1, 1949.
 LO/N14.

SUNBIRD.
 QUEENSLAND ORNITHOLOGICAL SOCIETY.
 BRISBANE 1, 1970-
 LO/N-2.
 ISSN 0049-2493

SUNBURST.
 LONDON WRITERS & ARTISTS GROUP.
 LONDON 1(1), JL 1970-
 ED/N-1.

SUNG STUDIES NEWSLETTER.
+ +SUNG STUD. NEWSL.
 PRINCETON UNIVERSITY: DEPARTMENT OF EAST ASIAN
 STUDIES.
 PRINCETON NO.1, 1970-
 SEE:PSYCHIATRICA FENNICA.

SUPER MARKETING. FOR THE GROCERY BUYER.
 [IPC CONSUMER INDUSTRIES P. LTD.]
 LONDON NO.1, F 1972-
 W.
 ED/N-1.   OX/U-1.

SURFACE COATINGS DIGEST.                   XXX
+ +SURF. COAT. DIG.
 DETROIT 1, 1968- 4(1), 1972 ...
 SUBS: UDS SURFACE COATINGS DIGEST.
 LO/N14.

SURFACE & COLLOID SCIENCE.
+ +SURF. & COLLOID SCI.
 [WILEY-INTERSCIENCE]
 NEW YORK 1, 1969-
 CA/U-2.   ED/N-1.   LO/S-3.   LO/U20.

SURFACE & DEFECT PROPERTIES OF SOLIDS.
+ +SURF. & DEFECT PROP. SOLIDS.
 CHEMICAL SOCIETY.
 LONDON 1, 1972-
 CA/U-1.   ED/N-1.   GL/U-1.   LO/N14.   LO/S-3.   MA/U-1.
 XS/R10.
 RE/U-1.   2, 1972-
 ISSN 0305-3873

SURFACE WATER YEAR-BOOK OF GREAT BRITAIN.  XXX
 SUBS (1970): GROUND WATER YEARBOOK.

SURFACE WAVE ABSTRACTS.
+ +SURF. WAVE ABSTR.
 [MULTI-SCIENCE PUBL. CO.]
 BRENTWOOD, ESSEX 1, 1971-
 LO/N14.   LO/U12.   OX/U-8.
 ED/N-1.   1(3), 1971-           XY/N-1.   1(2), 1971-
 ISSN 0049-2639

SURGERY ANNUAL.
+ +SURG. ANNU.
 [BUTTERWORTHS]
 LONDON &C. 1, 1969-
 AD/U-1.   GL/U-1.   LD/U-1.   OX/U-8.
 LO/N-1.   2, 1970-

SURGICAL NEUROLOGY.
+ +SURG. NEUROL.
 [PAUL C. BUCY & ASSOC.)
 TRYON, N.C. 1(1), JA 1973-
 2M.
 OX/U-8.

SURVEYS OF AFRICAN ECONOMIES.
+ +SURV. AFR. ECON.
 INTERNATIONAL MONETARY FUND.
 WASHINGTON, D.C. 1, 1968-
 LO/U-2.   MA/U-1.   OX/U17.

SURVEY OF CURRENT AFFAIRS.                 XXX
+ +SURV. CURR. AFF.
 (GREAT BRITAIN) CENTRAL OFFICE OF INFORMATION.
 LONDON 1(1), JA 1971-
 MON. PREV: SURVEY OF BRITISH & COMMONWEALTH
 AFFAIRS FROM 1(1), JA 1967- 4 (26), 1970.
 BH/P-7.   BH/U-1.   ED/N-1.   GL/U-1.   LD/U-1.   LO/N-1.
 LO/N-7.   LO/S14.   LO/U-8.   MA/P-1.   NO/U-1.   NW/U-1.
 OX/U-1.   SO/U-1.
 LO/N35.   2(1), 1972-
 ISSN 0039-6214

SURVEY OF THE GERMAN PRESS.
+ +SURV. GER. PRESS.
 INSTITUTE OF JEWISH AFFAIRS.
 LONDON NO.1, 1966-
 LO/N-1.

SUSSEX AFRAS JOURNAL.
+ +SUSSEX AFRAS J.
 UNIVERSITY OF SUSSEX.
 FALMER, BRIGHTON NO.1, 1972-
 LO/U14.

SUSSEX ARCHAEOLOGICAL SOCIETY NEWSLETTER.
+ +SUSSEX ARCHAEOL. SOC. NEWSL.
 LEWES NO.1, S 1970-
 BL/U-1.   LO/N-1.   LO/N-3.   OX/U-1.
 LO/N15. NO.2, 1971-

SUSSEX INDUSTRIAL HISTORY.
+ +SUSSEX IND. HIST.
 SUSSEX INDUSTRIAL ARCHAEOLOGY STUDY GROUP.
 CHICHESTER NO.1, 1970/71-
 2/A.
 ED/N-1.   LO/N-4.   LO/U-3.
 SH/U-1.   1972-

SUVREMENI EKONOMSKI PROBLEMI.
+ +SUVREM. EKON. PROBL.
 JUGOSLAVENSKA AKADEMIJA ZNANOSTI I UMJETNOSTI.
 ZAGREB 1, 1962-
 GL/U-1.   OX/U-1.

SVENSK HAMNTIDNING.
+ +SVEN. HAMNTIDN.
 SVENSK HAMNFORBUNDET.
 STOCKHOLM 1, 1969-
 LO/N14.

SVENSK TIDSKRIFTSFORTECKNING.
+ +SVEN. TIDSKR.
 TIDNINGSAKTIEBOLAGET SVENSK BOKHANDEL.
 STOCKHOLM 1967/68(1968)-
 GL/U-1.   1970/71-
 LO/N-3.   1967/68.

SVODNYJ UKAZATEL' BIBLIOGRAFICHESKIKH SPISKOV
I KARTOTEK, SOSTAVLENNYKH BIBLIOTEKAMI SOVETS-
KOGO SOJUZA : OBSHCHESTVENNYE NAUKI, KHUDOZ-
HESTVENNAJA LITERATURA, ISKUSSTVO.
 GOSUDARSTVENNAJA BIBLIOTEKA SSSR IM. V.I.
 LENINA.
 MOSCOW 1, 1960(1961)-
 A.
 BH/U-1.   CA/U-1.   CC/U-1. 1962(1963)-
 OX/U-1.   1961(1962)-

SVODNYJ UKAZATEL' BIBLIOGRAFICHESKIKH SPISKOV
I KARTOTEK, SOSTAVLENNYKH BIBLIOTEKAMI SOVETS-
KOGO SOJUZA : SEL'SKOE KHOZJAJSTVO.
 VSESOJUZNAJA AKADEMIJA SEL'SKOKHOZJAJSTVENNYKH
 NAUK [IM. V.I. LENINA].
 MOSCOW 1960(1961)-
 A. SPONS. BODY ALSO: TSENTRAL'NAJA NAUCHNAJA
 SEL'SKOKHOZJAJSTVENNAJA BIBLIOTEKA.
 CC/U-1. 1965(1966)-
 BH/U-1. 1966(1967)-           XY/N-1. 1965(1966)-

**SWEDISH JOURNAL OF AGRICULTURAL RESEARCH.**                    XXX
++SWED. J. AGRIC. RES.
LANTBRUKSHOGSKOLAN (SWEDEN).
*STOCKHOLM 1, 1971-*
PREV: LANTBRUKSHOGSKOLANS ANNALER FROM 1,
1933- 36, 1970.
*BN/U-2.    LO/N13.    LO/R-6.    LO/U-1.    NW/U-1.    OX/U-8.
XS/R-2.
ISSN 0049-2701*

**SWEDISH STUDIES IN INTERNATIONAL RELATIONS.**
++SWED. STUD. INT. RELAT.
UTRIKESPOLITISKA INSTITUTET.
[LAROMEDELSFORLAGEN]
*STOCKHOLM NO.1, 1971-
LO/N-1.
BL/U-1. 3, 1971.*

**SWEET & MAXWELL'S STUDENTS' LAW REPORTER.**
++SWEET & MAXWELL'S STUD. LAW REP.
[SWEET & MAXWELL]
*LONDON 1(1), 1970-
3/A.
CR/U-1.    ED/N-1.    NO/U-1.    OX/U15.*

**SWIATOWID. TYCODNIK ILUSTROWANY, MAGAZYN
TURYSTYCZNY.**
*WARSAW 1(1), AP 1961-
W.
LO/N-3.* *

**SYCAMORE BROADSHEET.**
[SYCAMORE P.]
*OXFORD NO.1, 1968-
LO/N-1.*

**SYESIS.**
BRITISH COLUMBIA PROVINCIAL MUSEUM.
*VICTORIA (B.C.) 1, 1968-
LO/N-2.    LO/N13.    LO/S10.*

**SYLLOGEUS.**
NATIONAL MUSEUM OF NATURAL SCIENCES (CANADA).
*OTTAWA NO.1, 1972-
CA/U-1.    CA/U-2.    DB/S-1.    LO/N-2.    SO/U-1.*

**SYLVA GANDAVENSIS. MEDEDELINGEN VAN DE AFDEL-
ING VOOR BOSBOUW, RIJKSFACULTEIT LANDBOUWWET-
ENSCHAPPEN TE GENT.**
*GHENT NO.1, 1967-
BN/U-2.    OX/U-3.*

**SYMBIOSES.**
SOCIETE DE BIOLOGIE HUMAINE ET ANIMALE DU
CENTRE.
*OLIVET 1, 1970-
LO/N-2.    LO/N13.*

**SYMPLEGADES.**
[ORIEL P.]
*NEWCASTLE UPON TYNE NO.1, 1969-*
S/T: A SERIES OF PAPERS ON COMPUTERS, LIBRAR-
IES & INFORMATION PROCESSING. MONOGR.
*LO/N-3.    LO/U-1.*

**SYMPOSIA OF THE FARADAY SOCIETY.**
++SYMP. FARADAY SOC.
FARADAY SOCIETY.
*LONDON NO.1, 1967-
BH/U-1.    BN/U-2.    CB/U-1.    ED/S-2.    GL/U-2.    LO/M-3.
LO/S-3.    LO/U-2.    LO/U-5.    MA/U-1.    RE/U-1.    SH/U-1.
SO/U-1.*

**SYNAGOGUE REVIEW.**                                            XXX
SUBS (1966): LIVING JUDAISM.

**SYNOPSES OF THE BRITISH FAUNA: NS.**
++SYNOP. BR. FAUNA, NS.
LINNEAN SOCIETY OF LONDON.
*LONDON NO.1, 1970-*
PREV. SERIES FROM 1, 1944.
*LO/N-2.*

**SYNTEZA.**
CESKOSLOVENSKY VYSKUMNY USTAV PRACE.
*BRATISLAVA 1, JE 1968-*
S/T: CASOPIS PRE TEORIU A METODY VIED A PRACI.
*LO/U-3.
LO/N13. 4, 1971-*

**SYNTHESIS. ARCHITECTURAL RESEARCH REVIEW.**
OXFORD POLYTECHNIC: DEPARTMENT OF ARCHITECTURE.
*OXFORD 1, 1973-
BL/U-1.*

**SYNTHESIS. INTERNATIONAL JOURNAL OF METHODS IN
SYNTHETIC ORGANIC CHEMISTRY.**
[THIEME]
*STUTTGART &C. 1969(1)-
M.
DB/U-2.    ED/U-1.    GL/U-1.    HL/U-1.    LO/N-4.    LO/N14.
LO/S-3.    LO/U-2.    LO/U11.    OX/U-8.    SH/U-1.    SW/U-1.
DN/U-1.    1970-                   LD/U-1. 1972(1)-
LO/R-6.    1975(1)-                LO/U12. 1974(1)-
MA/U-1.    1970(1)-
ISSN 0039-7881*

**SYNTHESIS. MAGAZINE FOR INVENTORS.**
[SYNTHESIS, INC.]
*MANHATTAN BEACH, CALIF. NO.1, 1971-
LO/N14.*

**SYNTHESIS OF HIGHWAY PRACTICE.**
++SYNTH. HIGHW. PRACT.
NATIONAL COOPERATIVE HIGHWAY RESEARCH PROGRAM
(U.S.).
*WASHINGTON, D.C. [NO.]1, 1969-
SO/U-1.
GL/U-1. [NO.]9, 1972-*

**SYNTHESIS IN INORGANIC & METAL-ORGANIC
CHEMISTRY.**                                                     XXX
++SYNTH. INORG. & MET.-ORG. CHEM.
[DEKKER]
*NEW YORK 1, JA 1971- 3, 1973...*
Q. SUBS: SYNTHESIS AND REACTIVITY IN
INORGANIC & METAL-ORGANIC CHEMISTRY.
*GL/U-1.    LO/N14.    LO/S-3.    LO/U11.    SH/U-1.
ISSN 0039-789X*

**SYNTHESIS MICROBIOLOGICA.**
++SYN. MICROBIOL.
UNIVERSITA DI PARMA: ISTITUTO DI MICROBIOLOGIA
*PARMA 1(1), 1964-*
S/T: RASSEGNA BIBLIOGRAFICA BIMESTRALE; (&)
MICROBIOLOGICAL CURRENT LITERATURE. SUPPL.
TO: IGIENE MODERNA.
*LD/U-1.
CA/U15.  4, 1968-                   LO/N13.  1(5),  1965-
MA/U-1.  4, 1968-
ISSN 0039-7903*

**SYNTHETIC COMMUNICATIONS.**
++SYNTH. COMMUN.
[DEKKER]
*NEW YORK 1(1), 1971-
DB/U-1.    LO/N14.    LO/S-3.    OX/U-1.    OX/U-8.    SF/U-1.
XY/N-1.
LO/U-2.  3, 1973-                   LO/U28.  2, 1972-
MA/U-1.  2, 1972-
ISSN 0039-7911*

**SYNTHETIC PROCEDURES IN NUCLEIC ACID CHEM-
ISTRY.**
++SYN. PROC. NUCL. ACID CHEM.
*NEW YORK 1, 1968-
LO/S-3.*

**SYSTEM OF NATIONAL ACCOUNTS: FINANCIAL
ACCOUNTS.**
++SYST. NAT. ACC., FINAN. ACC.
(CANADA) DOMINION BUREAU OF STATISTICS.
*OTTAWA 1, 1968-
4/A.
LO/U-3.*

**SYSTEMS, COMPUTERS, CONTROLS. SCRIPTA
JAPONICA III.**
++SYST. COMPUT. & CONTROLS.
[SCRIPTA PUBL. CORP.]
*WASHINGTON, D.C. 1, 1970(1971)-*
TRANSLATION OF SOME ARTICLES FROM DENSHI
TSUSHIN GAKKAI RONBUNSHI, SERIES A, B, & C; &
OTHER PRIMARY JAPANESE PERIODICALS.
*LO/N-4.    LO/N14.    SO/U-1.*

**SYSTEMS RESEARCH.**                                            000
SEE: SISTEMNYE ISSLEDOVANIJA.

**SZLAKAMI NAUKI.**
LODZKIE TOWARZYSTWO NAUKOWE.
*LODZ 1, 1961-*
ENGL. SUMM.
*DB/S-1.    NO/U-1.
ISSN 0082-1314*

**SZOCIOLOGIA.**
MAGYAR TUDOMANYOS AKADEMIA SZOCIOLOGIAI
BIZOTTSAGANAK FOLYOIRATA.
*BUDAPEST 1972-
CA/U-1.    OX/U-1.*

**TAAMULI. A POLITICAL SCIENCE FORUM.**
UNIVERSITY COLLEGE, DAR ES SALAAM: DEPARTMENT
OF POLITICAL SCIENCE.
*DAR ES SALAAM 1, JL 1970-*
*2/A.*
*MA/U-1. 1971-*
*ISSN 0049-2817*

**TABLEWARE INTERNATIONAL.** XXX
*++TABLEWARE INT.*
[TRADE PUBL.]
*LONDON 1(7), 1971-*
PREV: TABLEWARE INTERNATIONAL + POTTERY
GAZETTE FROM 1(1- 6), 1970- 1971. ISSUES
SUPPLEMENT: TABLEWARE REFERENCE BOOK.
*LO/N14.*

**TABLEWARE INTERNATIONAL + POTTERY GAZETTE.** XXX
*++TABLEWARE INT. + POTTERY GAZ.*
[TRADE PUBL.]
*LONDON 1, 1970- 1(6), 1971...*
PREV: POTTERY GAZETTE & GLASS TRADE REVIEW
FROM 44(500), 1919- 95(118), 1970.
SUBS: TABLEWARE INTERNATIONAL.
*LO/N14.*

**TABULATA.**
SANTA BARBARA MALACOLOGICAL SOCIETY.
*SANTA BARBARA 1, 1967-*
*LO/N-2. LO/N13.*

**TAGUS.**
*OXFORD 1(1), 1970-*
*ED/N-1. LO/U-2.*
*ISSN 0039-8950*

**TAIYO ENERUGI. SOLAR ENERGY.** XXX
NIHON TAIYO ENERUGI RIYO KYOKAI.
*TOKYO 1, 1962- 3, 1966. //*
ENGL. SUMM.
*LO/N13.*

**TALANTA. PROCEEDINGS OF THE ...**
DUTCH ARCHAEOLOGICAL & HISTORICAL SOCIETY.
[WOLTERS-NOORDHOFF]
*GRONINGEN 1, 1969-*
*BL/U-1. OX/U-2.*

**TALOUSTIETEELLISEN SEURAN VUOSIKIRJA.**
YEARBOOK OF THE FINNISH SOCIETY FOR ECONOMIC
RESEARCH.
*HELSINKI 1963(1964)-*
*LO/N-1.*

**TAMKANG REVIEW.**
*++TAMKANG REV.*
TAMKANG COLLEGE OF ARTS & SCIENCES: WESTERN
LITERATURE RESEARCH INSTITUTE.
*TAIPEH 1(1), 1970-*
S/T: A JOURNAL DEVOTED TO COMPARATIVE STUDIES
BETWEEN CHINESE & FOREIGN LITERATURES.
*LO/U14.*
*ISSN 0049-2949*

**TANSY.**
*LAWRENCE, KANS. 1, 1970-*
*OX/U-1.*

**TANY MALAGASY.** 000
SEE: TERRE MALGACHE.

**TANZANIA ZAMANI.**
UNIVERSITY COLLEGE, DAR-ES-SALAAM.
*DAR-ES-SALAAM NO.1, JL 1967-*
S/T: A BULLETIN OF RESEARCH ON PRE COLÔNIAL
HISTORY.
*LD/U-1. OX/U-9.*
*ISSN 0039-9507*

**TAPE RECORDER.** XXX
SUBS (1970): STUDIO SOUND & TAPE RECORDER.

**TARGET. JOURNAL OF THE RANK & FILE BUSMEN.**
*LONDON 1(1), JL 1967-*
M. 'TO CARRY FORWARD THE TRADITIONS &
PRINCIPLES OF PLATFORM.'
*ED/N-1. OX/U17.*

**TARGET. THE TUBEMAN'S NEWSLETTER.**
*LONDON 1(1- 2), 1970.//*
*2M.*
*ED/N-1. LO/U-3.*

**TARTU RIIKLIK ULIKOOL, ILMUNUD TOODE BIBLIO-
GRAAFIA.**
TARTU RIIKLIK ULIKOOL: RAAMATUKOGU.
*TARTU 1960-*
A.
*GL/U-1. OX/U-1.*

**TASMANIAN UNIVERSITY LAW REVIEW.** XXX
SUBS (1964): UNIVERSITY OF TASMANIA LAW
REVIEW.

**TASMANIAN YEAR BOOK.**
*++TASMAN. YEAR BOOK.*
(AUSTRALIA) COMMONWEALTH BUREAU OF CENSUS &
STATISTICS: TASMANIAN OFFICE.
*HOBART NO.1, 1967-*
*LO/U-2. LO/U-3. MA/P-1.*
*LO/N17. 3, 1969-*

**TAT. SARVODAYA COMMUNITIES NEWSLETTER.**
TATHATA CENTRE.
*NEWENT, GLOS. NO.1, AG 1966-*
*XW/S-1.*

**TAWOW. CANADIAN INDIAN CULTURAL MAGAZINE.**
(CANADA) DEPARTMENT OF INDIAN AFFAIRS &
NORTHERN DEVELOPMENT.
*OTTAWA 1(1), 1970-*
Q.
*OX/U-9.*
*ISSN 0039-9930*

**TAYMAG. NEWSLETTER OF THE CITY OF DUNDEE
MUSEUMS & ART GALLERIES DEPARTMENT.**
DUNDEE MUSEUMS & ART GALLERIES DEPARTMENT.
*DUNDEE NO.1, S/OC 1968-*
*ED/N-1. ED/P-1.*
*OX/U-1. NO.3, 1969-*

**T.C.M.A. NEWS.**
TUFTED CARPET MANUFACTURER'S ASSOCIATION.
*MANCHESTER 1(1), 1966-*
*OX/U-1.*

**TEA IN EAST AFRICA.** XXX
*++TEA EAST AFR.*
KENYA TEA BOARD.
*NAIROBI 12(4), 1972- 13(3), 1972.*
*N.S. NO.1, 1973-*
PREV: TEA FROM 1, 1960- 12(3), 1971. SPONS.
BODIES ALSO: UGANDA TEA BOARD & TANZANIA TEA
AUTHORITY.
*LO/N14. LO/R-6.*

**TEACH-IN. THE JOURNAL FOR JUNIOR HOSPITAL
DOCTORS & SENIOR MEDICAL STUDENTS.** XXX
[UPDATE PUBL. LTD.]
*LONDON 1, 1972- 3(9), S 1974.*
SUBS: HOSPITAL UPDATE.
*BL/U-1. GL/U-1. MA/U-1. SO/U-1.*
*AD/M-1. 2, 1973- CA/U-1. 2(9), 1973-*
*LD/U-1. (ONE YEAR ONLY)*

**TEACHER. CURRENT IDEAS FOR UGANDA PRIMARY &
SECONDARY SCHOOLS.**
NATIONAL INSTITUTE OF EDUCATION (UGANDA).
*KAMPALA NO.1, 1970-*
*LD/U-1.*

**TEACHING EXCEPTIONAL CHILDREN.**
*++TEACH. EXCEPT. CHILD.*
COUNCIL FOR EXCEPTIONAL CHILDREN.
*WASHINGTON, D.C. 1, N 1968-*
Q.
*XY/N-1.*
*ISSN 0040-0599*

**TEACHING GEOGRAPHY.**
*++TEACH. GEOGR.*
GEOGRAPHICAL ASSOCIATION.
*SHEFFIELD NO.1, 1967-*
*LO/S13. OX/U-1.*

**TEACHING HISTORY.**
*++TEACH. HIST.*
HISTORICAL ASSOCIATION.
*LONDON 1(1), MY 1969-*
*DB/U-2. ED/N-1. LO/U11. OX/U-1. SH/U-1.*

**TEACHING POLITICS. JOURNAL OF THE POLITICS
ASSOCIATION.**
*++TEACH. POLIT.*
*LONDON 1, MY 1972-*
*CA/U-1. ED/N-1. HL/U-2. SW/U-1.*

TEATHBHA.  JOURNAL OF THE LONGFORD HISTORICAL
SOCIETY.
  LONGFORD 1, 1969-
  BL/U-1.     DB/S-1.     DB/U-2.     ED/N-1.     OX/U-1.

TECHNICAL BULLETIN, BRITISH GEOMORPHOLOGICAL
RESEARCH GROUP.
  ++TECH. BULL. BR. GEOMORPHOL. RES. GROUP.
  LONDON NO.1, 1968-
  AD/U-1.     DB/U-2.     LO/S13.     LO/U-2.     OX/U-8.

TECHNICAL BULLETIN, COMMITTEE FOR CO-ORDINA-
TION OF JOINT PROSPECTING FOR MINERAL RESOUR-
CES IN ASIAN OFFSHORE AREAS (UN).
  ++TECH. BULL. COMM. CO-ORD. JOINT PROSPECT.
  MINER. RESOUR. ASIAN OFFSHORE AREAS (UN).
  [BANGKOK] 1, 1968-
  COMM. SUBORD. TO:  ECONOMIC COMMISSION FOR
  ASIA & THE FAR EAST.
  LO/N-2.     OX/U-8.

TECHNICAL BULLETIN, DEPARTMENT OF AGRICULTURE,
WESTERN AUSTRALIA.
  ++TECH. BULL. DEP. AGR. WEST. AUST.
  PERTH NO.1, 1969-
  LO/N13.

TECHNICAL BULLETIN, KANSAS AGRICULTURAL
EXPERIMENT STATION.                                                XXX
  SUBS (1970): RESEARCH PUBLICATION, KANSAS ...

TECHNICAL BULLETIN, LAFAYETTE NATURAL HISTORY
MUSEUM.
  ++TECH. BULL. LAFAYETTE NAT. HIST. MUS.
  LAFAYETTE, LA. 1, 1969-
  LO/N-2.

TECHNICAL BULLETIN, LAND RESOURCES DIVISION,
MINISTRY OF OVERSEAS DEVELOPMENT (GB).
  ++TECH. BULL. LAND RESOUR. DIV. MIN. OVERSEAS
  DEVELOP. (GB).
  TOLWORTH NO.1, 1967-
  DIVISION SUBORD. TO MINISTRY'S DIRECTORATE OF
  OVERSEAS SURVEYS.
  BN/U-2.     CA/U11.     OX/U-8.

TECHNICAL BULLETIN, MINISTRY OF AGRICULTURE
(U.A.R.).
  ++TECH. BULL. MIN. AGR. (U.A.R.).
  CAIRO 1, 1967-
  CA/U11.

TECHNICAL BULLETIN, NATIONAL COUNCIL OF THE
PAPER INDUSTRY FOR AIR & STREAM IMPROVEMENT
(US).                                                              XXX
  ++TECH. BULL. NATL. COUNC. PAP. IND. AIR &
  STREAM IMPROV. (US).
  NEW YORK NO.213, 1968-
  PREV: TECHNICAL BULLETIN, NATIONAL COUNCIL FOR
  STREAM IMPROVEMENT OF THE PULP, PAPER & PAPER-
  BOARD INDUSTRIES (US) FROM NO.1, 1945- 212,
  1967.
  LO/N14.

TECHNICAL BULLETIN, NATIONAL COUNCIL FOR
STREAM IMPROVEMENT OF THE PULP, PAPER & PAPER-
BOARD INDUSTRIES (US).                                             XXX
  SUBS (1968): TECHNICAL BULLETIN, NATIONAL
  COUNCIL OF THE PAPER INDUSTRY FOR AIR &
  STREAM IMPROVEMENT (US).

TECHNICAL BULLETIN, REGISTRY OF MEDICAL
TECHNOLOGISTS, AMERICAN SOCIETY OF CLINICAL
PATHOLOGISTS.                                                      XXX
  SUBS. (1970) PART OF: LABORATORY MEDICINE.

TECHNICAL BULLETIN, ROYAL BOTANICAL GARDENS
(HAMILTON, ONT.).
  ++TECH. BULL. R. BOT. GARD. (HAMILTON, ONT.).
  HAMILTON, ONT. NO.1, 1963-
  LO/N-2.

TECHNICAL COMMUNICATION, COMMONWEALTH BUREAU
OF ANIMAL HEALTH.
  ++TECH. COMMUN. COMMONW. BUR. ANIM. HEALTH.
  FARNHAM ROYAL 1, 1969-
  CA/U11.     LO/N14.

TECHNICAL COMMUNICATIONS, COMMONWEALTH INST-
ITUTE OF BIOLOGICAL CONTROL.
  ++TECH. COMMUN. COMMONW. INST. BIOL. CONTROL.
  FARNHAM ROYAL NO.1, 1960-
  MA/U-1.

TECHNICAL DEPARTMENT BULLETIN, ASSOCIATED
OCTEL COMPANY.
  ++TECH. DEP. BULL. ASSOC. OCTEL CO.
  LONDON 1, 1970-
  LO/N14.

TECHNICAL DIGEST, COMPRESSED AIR & GAS INSTI-
TUTE.                                                              000
  SEE: CAGI TECHNICAL DIGEST.

[TECHNICAL DISCLOSURE], WELDING INSTITUTE.
  ABINGTON, CAMBS. [NO.1, 1970]-
  LO/N14.

TECHNICAL EVALUATION REPORTS, NATIONAL
REPROGRAPHIC CENTRE FOR DOCUMENTATION.
  ++TECH. EVAL. REP. NATL. REPROGR. CENT. DOC.
  HATFIELD NO.1, JE 1967-
  CENTRE LOCATED AT HATFIELD POLYTECHNIC.
  BL/U-1.     OX/U-1.

TECHNICAL INFORMATION SHEET, MASTIC ASPHALT
COUNCIL & EMPLOYERS' FEDERATION.
  ++TECH. INF. SH. MASTIC ASPHALT COUNC. & EMPLOY.
  FED.
  LONDON 1, 1969-
  LO/N14.

TECHNICAL JAPAN.
  ++TECH. JAP.
  [TOKYO NEWS SERVICE LTD.]
  TOKYO 1, 1968-
  LO/N14.

TECHNICAL MEMORANDUM, DIVISION OF WILD LIFE
RESEARCH, CSIRO (AUSTRALIA).
  ++TECH. MEMO. DIV. WILD LIFE RES. CSIRO.(AUST.).
  MELBOURNE NO.1, 1969-
  LO/N-2.

TECHNICAL MONOGRAPH, AGROCHEMICALS DIVISION,
CIBA.
  ++TECH. MONOGR. AGROCHEM. DIV. CIBA.
  BASLE 1, 1969-
  CA/U11.

TECHNICAL MONOGRAPH, SOIL SURVEY OF GREAT
BRITAIN.
  ++TECH. MONOGR. SOIL SURV. G.B.
  SOIL SURVEY OF GREAT BRITAIN (ENGLAND & WALES).
  HARPENDEN 1, 1969-
  CA/U11.     DN/U-1.     GL/U-1.     LO/N13.

TECHNICAL NEWS, INSTITUTE OF RADIATION BREEDING.
  SEE: HOSHASEN IKUSHUJO TEKUNIKARU NYUSU.

TECHNICAL NOTES, ASIAN REGIONAL INSTITUTE
FOR SCHOOL BUILDING RESEARCH.
  ++TECH. NOTES. ASIAN REG. INST. SCH. BUILD. RES.
  COLOMBO 1, 1970-
  BL/U-1.

TECHNICAL NOTES, CIBA (A.R.L.), LTD.                               XXX
  SUBS (1971): CIBA-GEIGY ...

TECHNICAL NOTE, CONSTRUCTION INDUSTRY RES-
EARCH & INFORMATION ASSOCIATION.
  ++TECH. NOTE CONSTR. IND. RES. & INF. ASSOC.
  LONDON NO.1, 1968-
  LO/N14. (NON-CONFIDENTIAL ISSUES ONLY).

TECHNICAL NOTE, COPPER DEVELOPMENT ASSOCIAT-
ION.
  ++TECH. NOTE COPPER DEV. ASSOC.
  LONDON TN 1, 1970-
  LO/N14.

TECHNICAL NOTES, DEPARTMENT OF INDIAN AFFAIRS
& NORTHERN DEVELOPMENT (CANADA).
  ++TECH. NOTES DEP. INDIAN AFF. & N. DEVELOP.
  (CAN.).
  OTTAWA 1, 1968-
  PROD. BY DEPT'S. NORTHERN SCIENCE RESEARCH
  GROUP.
  CA/U12.

TECHNICAL NOTE, FOREST PRODUCTS RESEARCH LAB-
ORATORY (GB).                                                      XXX
  ++TECH. NOTE FOR. PROD. RES. LAB. (GB).
  AYLESBURY NO.1, 1966- 53, 1971...
  SUBS: TECHNICAL NOTE, PRINCES RISBOROUGH
  LABORATORY, BUILDING RESEARCH ESTABLISHMENT
  (GB).
  BL/U-1.     LO/N14.

TECHNICAL NOTE, INTERDEPARTMENTAL SUB-COMM-
ITTEE FOR COMPONENT CO-ORDINATION, MINISTRY
OF PUBLIC BUILDING & WORKS (GB).
++TECH. NOTE INTER-DEP. SUB-COMM. COMPONENT
CO-ORD. MINIST. PUBLIC BUILD. & WORKS (GB).
LONDON NO.1, 1970-
COMMITTEE SUBORD. TO DIRECTORATE OF RESEARCH
& INFORMATION.
OX/U-8.

TECHNICAL NOTE, PRINCES RISBOROUGH LABORATORY,          XXX
BUILDING RESEARCH ESTABLISHMENT (GB).
++TECH. NOTE PRINCES RISBOROUGH LAB. BUILD. RES.
ESTABL. (GB).
PRINCES RISBOROUGH NO.54, 1972-
PREV: TECHNICAL NOTE, FOREST PRODUCTS RESEARCH
LABORATORY (GB) FROM NO.1, 1966- NO.53, 1971.
LO/N14.

TECHNICAL PAPERS, AGRICULTURAL ADJUSTMENT
UNIT, UNIVERSITY OF NEWCASTLE UPON TYNE.
++TECH. PAP. AGR. ADJUST. UNIT UNIV. NEWCASTLE
UPON TYNE.
NEWCASTLE UPON TYNE 1, 1968-
MONOGR. UNIT SUBORD. TO: DEPARTMENT OF
AGRICULTURAL ECONOMICS.
BL/U-1.    NW/U-1.

TECHNICAL PAPERS, ARCTIC INSTITUTE OF NORTH            XXX
AMERICA.
++TECH. PAP. ARCT. INST. NORTH AM.
MONTREAL NO.1, 1956- 23, 1969. //
LO/N-2.
OX/U-8. NO.5, 1960-

TECHNICAL PAPER, AUSTRALIAN WATER RESOURCES
COUNCIL.
++TECH. PAP. AUST. WATER RESOUR. COUNC.
CANBERRA NO.1, 1971-
LO/N13.    SO/U-1.

TECHNICAL PAPER, COMMISSION ON COLLEGE GEOGR-
APHY, ASSOCIATION OF AMERICAN GEOGRAPHERS.
++TECH. PAP. COMM. COLL. GEOGR. ASSOC. AM.
GEOGR.
WASHINGTON, D.C. NO.1, 1968-
DB/U-2.
ISSN 0066-9377

TECHNICAL PAPER, DEPARTMENT OF FORESTRY,
CLEMSON UNIVERSITY.
++TECH. PAP. DEP. FOR. CLEMSON UNIV.
CLEMSON, S.C. 1, 1973-
OX/U-3.

TECHNICAL PAPERS, DEVELOPMENT CENTRE, OECD.
++TECH. PAP. DEVELOP. CENT. OECD.
PARIS [NO.1], 1970-
LO/N13.

TECHNICAL PAPER, DIVISION OF APPLIED CHEM-
ISTRY, CSIRO (AUSTRALIA).
++TECH. PAP. DIV. APPL. CHEM. CSIRO (AUST.).
MELBOURNE NO.1, 1971- 4/5, 1974.
SUBS. PART OF: TECHNICAL PAPER, DIVISION OF
APPLIED ORGANIC CHEMISTRY, CSIRO (AUSTRALIA).
LO/N14.    MA/U-1.

TECHNICAL PAPER, DIVISION OF APPLIED MINERAL-
OGY, CSIRO (AUSTRALIA).
++TECH. PAP. DIV. APPL. MINERAL. CSIRO (AUST.).
MELBOURNE NO.1, 1971-
MA/U-1.

TECHNICAL PAPER, DIVISION OF FOOD PRESERVAT-          XXX
ION, CSIRO (AUSTRALIA).
SUBS (1972): TECHNICAL PAPER, DIVISION OF
FOOD RESEARCH ...

TECHNICAL PAPER, DIVISION OF FOOD RESEARCH,          XXX
CSIRO (AUSTRALIA).
++TECH. PAP. DIV. FOOD RES. CSIRO (AUST.).
MELBOURNE NO.36, 1972-
PREV: TECHNICAL PAPER, DIVISION OF FOOD
PRESERVATION ... FROM NO.1, 1956- 35, 1970.
LO/N14.

TECHNICAL PAPER, DIVISION OF HORTICULTURAL
RESEARCH, CSIRO (AUSTRALIA).
++TECH. PAP. DIV. HORTIC. RES. CSIRO.(AUST.).
MELBOURNE NO.1, 1970-
MA/U-1.    OX/U-8.

TECHNICAL PAPER, DIVISION OF SOILS, CSIRO
(AUSTRALIA).
++TECH. PAP. DIV. SOILS CSIRO (AUST.).
MELBOURNE NO.1, 1971-
AD/U-1.    BH/U-1.    BL/U-1.    BN/U-2.    GL/U-1.    LO/N13.
MA/U-1.

TECHNICAL PAPERS IN HYDROLOGY.
++TECH. PAP. HYDROL.
UNESCO.
PARIS NO.1, 1970-
NOS.3 & 4 PUBL. IN 1969.
LO/N13.    OX/U-8.
LO/U-1.    1970-
ISSN 0082-2310

TECHNICAL PROGRESS REPORT, BUREAU OF MINES
(UNITED STATES).
++TECH. PROG. REP. BUR. MINES (U.S.).
PITTSBURGH [NO.]1, 1968-
LO/N14.    1, 1968-*

TECHNICAL PUBLICATION, PRICE'S (BROMBOROUGH),
LTD.                                                   XXX
SUBS: TECHNICAL PUBLICATION, PRICE'S
CHEMICALS LTD.

TECHNICAL PUBLICATION, PRICE'S CHEMICALS, LTD.
++TECH. PUBL. PRICE'S CHEM. LTD.
BEBINGTON, CHES. NO.101, 1972-
PREV: TECHNICAL PUBLICATION, PRICE'S (BROM-
BOROUGH), LTD. FROM NO.1, 1958- 16, 1968.
ED/N-1.    LO/N14.

TECHNICAL REPORT, AGRICULTURAL DEVELOPMENT &
ADVISORY SERVICE (GB).                                 XXX
++TECH. REP. AGRIC. DEV. & ADVIS. SERV. (GB).
LONDON NO.27, 1971-
PREV: TECHNICAL REPORT, AGRICULTURAL LAND
SERVICE (GB) FROM NO.1, 1957- 26, 1970.
LO/N15.

TECHNICAL REPORT OF THE AGRICULTURAL ENGINEERING
RESEARCH STATION; C: CONSTRUCTION ENGINEERING.00
SEE: NOGYO DOBOKU SHIKENJO GIHO; C: ZOKO.

TECHNICAL REPORT, AGRICULTURAL LAND SERVICE
(GB).                                                  XXX
SUBS (1971): TECHNICAL REPORT, AGRICULTURAL
DEVELOPMENT & ADVISORY SERVICE (GB).

TECHNICAL REPORT, BOTSWANA CO-OPERATIVE DEVEL-
OPMENT CENTRE.
++TECH. REP. BOTSWANA COOP. DEV. CENT.
INTERNATIONAL LABOUR ORGANIZATION: BOTSWANA
CO-OPERATIVE DEVELOPMENT CENTRE.
GENEVA NO.1, 1971-
LO/N-1.

TECHNICAL REPORT, DEPARTMENT OF FISHERIES
(WASHINGTON, STATE).
++TECH. REP. DEP. FISH. (WASH. STATE).
OLYMPIA, WASH. NO.1, 1970-
LO/N13.

TECHNICAL REPORT, DIVISION OF APPLIED GEOMECH-
ANICS, CSIRO (AUSTRALIA).                              XXX
++TECH. REP. DIV. APPL. GEOMECH. CSIRO (AUST.).
MELBOURNE NO.12, 1970-
PREV: TECHNICAL REPORT, DIVISION OF SOIL
MECHANICS ... FROM NO.1, 1963- 11, 1969.
LO/N13.

TECHNICAL REPORT, DIVISION OF SOIL MECHANICS,
CSIRO (AUSTRALIA).                                     XXX
++TECH. REP. DIV. SOIL MECH. CSIRO (AUST.).
MELBOURNE NO.1, 1963- 11, 1969 ...
SUBS: TECHNICAL REPORT, DIVISION OF APPLIED
GEOMECHANICS ...
LO/N13.**
OX/U-8. NO.8, 1968-

TECHNICAL REPORTS, ENGINEERING RESEARCH INST-
ITUTE, KYOTO UNIVERSITY.                               XXX
SUBS (1971): TECHNICAL REPORTS, INSTITUTE
OF ATOMIC ENERGY, KYOTO UNIVERSITY.

TECHNICAL REPORT, FARM POWER & MACHINERY LAB-
ORATORY, KYOTO DAIGAKU.
++TECH. REP. FARM POWER & MACH. LAB. KYOTO
DAIGAKU.
KYOTO NO.1, 1972-
LO/N13.

TECHNICAL REPORT, FUJI STEEL.                          000
SEE: FUJI SEITETSU GIHO.

TECHNICAL REPORTS, GRASSLAND HUSBANDRY DIVIS-
ION, NORTH OF SCOTLAND COLLEGE OF AGRICULTURE.
++TECH. REP. GRASSL. HUSB. DIV. NORTH SCOTL.
COLL. AGRIC.
ABERDEEN NO.1, 1972-
AD/U-1.

TECHNICAL REPORTS, INSTITUTE OF ATOMIC ENERGY,
KYOTO UNIVERSITY.                                    XXX
++TECH. REP. INST. ATOMIC ENERGY KYOTO UNIV.
KYOTO DAIGAKU: INSTITUTE OF ATOMIC ENERGY.           XXX
KYOTO NO.153, 1971-
PREV: TECHNICAL REPORTS, ENGINEERING RESEARCH
INSTITUTE, KYOTO UNIVERSITY FROM 1(1), 1951-
NO.152, 1971.
GL/U-1.    LD/U-1.    LO/N14.    XS/R10.

TECHNICAL REPORT, INSTITUTE OF SOUND &
VIBRATION, UNIVERSITY OF SOUTHAMPTON.                000
SEE: ISVR TECHNICAL REPORT.

TECHNICAL REPORT, INTERNATIONAL PACIFIC HALI-
BUT COMMISSION.
++TECH. REP. INT. PAC. HALIBUT COMM.
SEATTLE NO.1, 1969-
LO/N-2.    LO/N13.
ISSN 0579-3920

TECHNICAL REPORT, JAPANESE ELECTRIC METERS
INSPECTION CORPORATION.                              000
SEE: DENKI KENTEIJO GIHO.  JEMIC TECHNICAL
REPORT.

TECHNICAL REPORTS, MARINE SCIENCES RESEARCH
LABORATORY, MEMORIAL UNIVERSITY OF NEWFOUND-
LAND.
++TECH. REP. MAR. SCI. RES. LAB. MEM. UNIV.
NEWFOUNDL.
ST. JOHN'S NO.1, 1969-
LO/N-2.

TECHNICAL REPORT, MATSUSHITA ELECTRIC WORKS.        000
SEE:  MATSUSHITA DENKO GIHO.

TECHNICAL REPORTS, MUSEUM OF ANTHROPOLOGY,
UNIVERSITY OF MICHIGAN.
++TECH. REP. MUS. ANTHROPOL. UNIV. MICH.
ANN ARBOR 1, 1971-
BL/U-1.    CA/U-3.    GL/U-1.    LO/N-2.    LO/N-4.

TECHNICAL REPORT, NEUTRON BEAM RESEARCH
COMMITTEE, SCIENCE RESEARCH COUNCIL (GB).
++TECH. REP. NEUTRON BEAM RES. COMM. SCI. RES.
COUNC. (GB).
LONDON NO.1, 1970-
LO/N14.

TECHNICAL REPORT, PLASTICS PIPE INSTITUTE.
++TECH. REP. PLAST. PIPE INST.
NEW YORK PPI-TR/I, 1968-
LO/N14.

TECHNICAL REPORT SERIES, COMPUTING LABORATORY,
UNIVERSITY OF NEWCASTLE UPON TYNE.
++TECH. REP. SER. COMPUT. LAB. UNIV. NEWCASTLE
UPON TYNE.
NEWCASTLE UPON TYNE NO.1, 1969-
LO/N14. NO.2 1969-
LO/N-4.  [W. NO.4]

TECHNICAL REPORT, TANZANIA NATIONAL INDUST-
RIAL TRAINING PROGRAMME.
++TECH. REP. TANZANIA NATL. IND. TRAIN.
PROGRAMME.
INTERNATIONAL LABOUR ORGANIZATION: TANZANIA
NATIONAL INDUSTRIAL TRAINING PROGRAMME.
GENEVA NO.1, 1971-
LO/N-1.

TECHNICAL REPORT, UNIVERSITY COMPUTING CENTER,
UNIVERSITY OF TENNESSEE.
++TECH. REP. UNIV. COMPUT. CENT. UNIV. TENN.
KNOXVILLE NO.1, 1965-
SOME REPORTS ISSUED IN COOPERATION WITH DEPT.
OF AGRONOMY, TENNESSEE AGRICULTURAL EXPERIMENT
STATION.
LO/N14.*

TECHNICAL & RESEARCH REPORTS, APPLIED
PSYCHOLOGY ADVISORY SERVICE.
++TECH. & RES. REP. APPL. PSYCHOL. ADVIS.
SERV.
BELFAST 1, 1969-
BL/U-1.

TECHNICAL REVIEW, ASIAN BROADCASTING UNION.        000
SEE:  ABU TECHNICAL REVIEW.

TECHNICAL REVIEW, BRITISH QUARRYING & SLAG
FEDERATION.
++TECH. REV. BR. QUARR. & SLAG FED.
LONDON 1, 1970-
BR/U-1.    LO/N14.
ED/N-1. 3, 1972-

TECHNICAL REVIEW, CAVE DIVING GROUP.
++TECH. REV. CAVE DIV. GROUP.
BRISTOL NO.1, 1966-
LO/N13.

TECHNICAL REVIEW, MITSUBISHI JUKOGYO K.K.
++TECH. REV. MITSUBISHI JUKOGYO K.K.
TOKYO 1, 1964-
LO/N13.

TECHNICAL & SCIENTIFIC BOOKS IN PRINT.
++TECH. & SCI. BOOKS PRINT.
[WHITAKER]
LONDON 1969/1970-
S/T: A REFERENCE CATALOGUE. PREV: TECHNICAL
BOOKS IN PRINT FROM 1966-68.
BN/U-2.

TECHNICAL SERIES, SOCIETY FOR APPLIED BACTER-
IOLOGY.
++TECH. SER. SOC. APPL. BACTERIOL.
LONDON &C. NO.1, 1966-
OX/U-8.

TECHNICAL SERVICE REPORT, GRAPHIC ARTS TECH-
NICAL FOUNDATION, INC.
++TECH. SERV. REP. GRAPHIC ARTS TECH. FOUND. INC
PITTSBURGH 1, 1967-
ALSO ENTITLED: G.A.T.F. BULLETIN.
LO/N14.

TECHNICON QUARTERLY.
++TECHNICON Q.
TECHNICON INSTRUMENTS CORPORATION.
NEW YORK 1, 1968-
LO/N14.

TECHNIKGESCHICHTE IN EINZELDARSTELLUNGEN.
++TECHNIKGESCH. EINZELDARSTELL.
VEREIN DEUTSCHER INGENIEURE.
DUSSELDORF NO.1, 1967-
LO/N-4.

TECHNIQUES OF BIOCHEMICAL & BIOPHYSICAL
MORPHOLOGY.
++TECH. BIOCHEM. & BIOPHYS. MORPHOL.
[WILEY-INTERSCIENCE]
NEW YORK 1, 1972-
CA/U-1.    GL/U-1.    MA/U-1.
ISSN 0082-2523

TECHNIQUES ELECTRONIQUES ET AUDIOVISUELLES.        XXX
++TECH. ELECTRON. & AUDIOV.
[SOCIETE DES EDITIONS RADIO]
PARIS NO.1, 1970- 12, 1971...
SUBS. PART OF: T.E.S.T. TECHNIQUES ELECTRON-
IQUES, SON, TELEVISION. NO.13 NOT PUBLISHED.
LO/N14.
ISSN 0033-7811

TECHNIQUES & METHODS OF ORGANIC & ORGANOMETAL-
LIC CHEMISTRY.
++TECH. & METHODS ORG. & ORGANOMET. CHEM.
[DEKKER]
NEW YORK 1, 1969-
LO/S-3.

TECHNIQUES & METHODS OF POLYMER EVALUATION.
++TECH. & METH. POLYM. EVAL.
[MARCEL DEKKER]
NEW YORK 1, 1966-
ED/N-1.    GL/U-1.    XY/N-1.
ISSN 0082-2434

TECHNIQUES MONDIALES.                               XXX
SUBS (1967): REVUE FRANCAISE DES TECHNIQUES
MONDIALES.

TECHNIQUES PHILIPS.                                 XXX
++TECH. PHILIPS. [TQPH-A]
COMPAGNIE FRANCAISE PHILIPS.
PARIS NO.1, JA/F 1968- 1971.//
2M. CONSISTS MAINLY OF PAPERS TRANSLATED FROM
PHILIPS TECHNICAL REVIEW.
LO/N13.

**TECHNIQUES ET SCIENCES MUNICIPALES - L'EAU.**                    XXX
++*TECH. SCI. MUNIC. EAU.*
ASSOCIATION GENERALE DES HYGIENISTES ET TECH-
NICIENS MUNICIPAUX.
*PARIS 65, 1970-*
PREV: TECHNIQUES ET SCIENCES MUNICIPALES
FROM 54, 1959- 64, 1969. THEN INCORP: EAU.
*LO/N14.*

**TECHNISCHER BERICHT, LEDERINDUSTRIE-BERUFS-
GENOSSENSCHAFT.**                                                  XXX
SUBS (1971): SICHERHEIT AM ARBEITSPLATZ.

**TECHNISCHE BERICHTE, NACHRICHTENTECHNISCHE
WERKE, A.G.**
++*TECH. BER. NACHRICHTENTECH. WERKE A.G.*
*VIENNA 1, 1970-*
*LO/N14.*

**TECHNISCH GEMEENTEBLAD.**                                        XXX
SUBS (1972): GEMEENTEWERKEN.

**TECHNOCRAT.**
FUJI MARKETING RESEARCH CO., LTD.
*TOKYO 1, 1968-*
*LO/N14.*
*ISSN 0040-1609*

**TECHNOLOGICA ACTA.**                                             XXX
SEE: ARHIV ZA TEHNOLOGIJU.

**TECHNOLOGICAL FORECASTING & SOCIAL CHANGE.***
++*TECHNOL. FORECAST. & SOC. CHANGE.*
[AMERICAN ELSEVIER]
*NEW YORK 1, JE 1969-*
TITLE EXPANDED FROM TECHNOLOGICAL FORECASTING
WITH 2, 1970.
*LO/N14.      XS/R10.*
*BH/U-3.  3, 1971/72-           GL/U-2.  5(1), 1973-*
*LO/N35.  3(1), 1971-          SW/U-1.  3, 1971-*
*ISSN 0040-1625*

**TECHNOLOGICAL REPORT, CLOTHING INSTITUTE.**                      XXX
SUBS (1973): CLOTHING RESEARCH JOURNAL.

**TECHNOLOGY IN AGRICULTURE.**                                     XXX
++*TECHNOL. AGR.*
INSTITUTE OF CORN & AGRICULTURAL MERCHANTS.
*LONDON   1(1), JL 1968- 2(6), N 1969.//*
*ED/N-1.      OX/U-8.*
*XS/U-1.  S 1968-*

**TECHNOLOGY & THE ENVIRONMENT.**
++*TECHNOL. & ENVIRON.*
(GREAT BRITAIN) DEPARTMENT OF TRADE & INDUSTRY.
*LONDON  [NO.1], N 1971-*
S/T: REPORTS FROM SCIENTIFIC COUNSELLORS.
PRODUCED BY DEPARTMENT'S OVERSEAS TECHNICAL
INFORMATION UNIT.
*LO/N-1.      LO/N-6.      LO/N14.      LO/N35.      LO/U-3.      LO/U28.*
*OX/U16.      SO/U-1.      XS/R10.      XS/T-4.*
*CA/U-1.  NO.4, 1972-           ED/N-1.  NO.4, 1972-*
*OX/U-1.  NO.6, 1973-*

**TECHNOLOGY IRELAND.**
++*TECHNOL. IRELAND.*
INSTITUTE FOR INDUSTRIAL RESEARCH & STANDARDS
(EIRE).
*DUBLIN  1, 1969-*
*BL/U-1.      CO/U-1.      DB/U-1.      ED/N-1.      LO/N14.      OX/U-8.*
*ISSN 0040-1676*

**TECNOLOGIA ALIMENTARIA.**
++*TECNOL. ALIMENT. (BRAZ.).*
*BUENOS AIRES   1(1), 1966-*
*LO/N14.*
*ISSN 0040-1943*

**TECNOLOGIE MECCANICHE.**
++*TECNOL. MECC.*
[STAMMER S.A.S.]
*MILAN  1, 1970-*
*LO/N14.*

**TEHNIKA HRONIKA.  MENIAIA EKDOSIS TON TEHNIKON
ERIMETETERION TES ELLADOS.**
++*TEH. HRONIKA.*
TEHNIKON ERIMETETERION TES ELLADOS.
*ATHENS  1, 1970-*
ENGL., FR. OR GER. SUMM.
*BL/U-1.*

**TEHNOLOGIJA MESA.**
++*TEHNOL. MESA. [TEME-A]*
JUGOSLOVENSKI INSTITUT ZA TEHNOLOGIJU MESA.
*BELGRADE  1, AG 1960-*
ENGL., FR., & GER. SUMM.
*LO/N13.  7, 1966-*

**TEILHARD STUDY LIBRARY.**
++*TEILHARD STUDY LIBR.*
PIERRE TEILHARD DE CHARDIN ASSOCIATION OF
GREAT BRITAIN & IRELAND.
[GARNSTONE P.]
*LONDON  1, 1967-*
*OX/U-1.*

**TEIRESIAS.  A REVIEW & CONTINUING BIBLIOGRAPHY
OF BOIOTIAN STUDIES.**
*MONTREAL  1, JE 1971-*
*CA/U-1.*

**TEKHNICHESKAYA KIBERNETIKA. (ENGL. TRANSL.)**                    000
SEE: ENGINEERING CYBERNETICS.

**TEKHNICHESKIE IZMERENIJA V MASHINOSTROENII.**
++*TEKH. IZMER. MASHINOSTR. [TAVM-A]*
NAUCHNO-ISSLEDOVATEL'SKIJ INSTITUT METROLOGII
VYSSHIKH UCHEBNYKH ZAVEDENIJ.
*MOSCOW  1, 1967-*
*BH/U-1.      LO/N13.*

**TEKHNOLOGIJA I AVTOMATIZATSIJA MASHINOSTROEN-
IJA.**
++*TEKHNOL. & AVTOM. MASHINOSTR. [TAVM-A]*
(UKRAINE) MINISTERSTVO VYSSHOJI I SEREDN'OJI
SPETSIAL'NOJI OS'VITY.
*KIEV  1, 1966-*
S/T: MEZHVEDOMSTVENNYJ RESPUBLIKANSKIJ
NAUCHNO-TEKHNICHESKIJ SBORNIK.  TITLE VARIES:
VOL.1 PUBL. AS: TEKHNOLOGIJA MASHINOSTROENIJA.
*BH/U-1.  2, 1967-                     LO/N13.  2, 1967-*

**TEKHNOLOGIJA ELEKTROMASHINOSTROENIJA.**
++*TEKHNOL. ELEKTROMASHINOSTR. [TEMS-A]*
[IZDATEL'STVO 'ENERGIJA']
*MOSCOW; LENINGRAD  1, 1965-*
*BH/U-1.*
*LO/N13.  4, 1967-*

**TEKHNOLOGIJA MASHINOSTROENIJA.**                                 000
SEE: TEKHNOLOGIJA I AVTOMATIZATSIJA MASHINO-
STROENIJA.

**TEKHNOLOGIJA I ORGANIZATSIJA PROIZVODSTVA.**                     XXX
++*TEKHNOL. & ORGAN. PROIZVOD.*
UKRAINSKIJ NAUCHNO-ISSLEDOVATEL'SKIJ INSTITUT
NAUCHNO-TEKHNICHESKOJ INFORMATSII I TEKHNIKO-
EKONOMICHESKIKH ISSLEDOVANIJ.
*KIEV  1966-*
2M.  PREV: MASHINOSTROENIE (KIEV) FROM 1960-
1965.
*LO/N13.*

**TEKNIKA.  PHILIPS TIDNING FOR ELEKTRONIK.**
SVENSKA AB PHILIPS.
*STOCKHOLM  1970-*
*LO/N14.*

**TEKNISK TIDSSKRIFT FOR TEXTIC- OG
BEKLAEDNINGSINDUSTRI.**                                            XXX
++*TEK. TIDSSKR. TEXTIC- OG BEKLAEDNINGSIND.*
[TEKNISK - FORLAG]
*COPENHAGEN  29(4), 1971-*
PREV: TIDSSKRIFT FOR TEXTILTEKNIK FROM
1, 1943- 29(3), 1971.
*LO/N13.*
*ISSN 0040-2621*

**TELECOMMUNICATIONS.**
[HORIZON HOUSE]
*DEDHAM, MASS.  1, JE 1967-*
M.
*LO/N14.*

**TELECOMMUNICATIONS RESEARCH & ENGINEERING
REPORT.**                                                          XXX
++*TELECOMMUN. RES. & ENG. REP.*
INSTITUTE FOR TELECOMMUNICATION SCIENCES.
*BOULDER, COLO.  13, 1971-*
PREV: OT/ITS RESEARCH REPORT FROM 1, 1970- 12,
1971.
*LO/N14.*

**TELEMETRY JOURNAL.**
++*TELEM. J. [TEJO-B]*
INTERNATIONAL FOUNDATION FOR TELEMETERING.
[VALUE ENGINEERING PUBL.]
*LOS ANGELES  1(1), AP/MY 1966-*
2M.
*LO/N14.  1(2), 1966-*            *XS/T-7.  6(1), 1970-*
*ISSN 0040-2621*

TELEVISION (LONDON).                                        XXX
[IPC MAGAZINES LTD.]
LONDON 21(241), 1970-
PREV: PRACTICAL TELEVISION FROM 15(175),
1965- 20(240), 1970.
LO/N14.
ISSN 0032-647X

TELEVISION (PARIS).                                         XXX
SUBS (1970): TELEVISION ET TECHNIQUES TELE-
VISUELLES.

TELEVISION QUARTERLY.
+ +TELEV. Q. [TVQU-A]
NATIONAL ACADEMY OF TELEVISION ARTS & SCIENCES
(US).
NEW YORK 1, F 1962-
EX/U-1.
HL/U-1. 8(1), 1969-

TELEVISION ET TECHNIQUES TELEVISUELLES.                     XXX
+ +TELEV. & TECH. TELEVISUELLES.
SOCIETE DES EDITIONS RADIO.
PARIS NO.205, 1970- 219, 1971.
PREV: TELEVISION (PARIS) FROM NO.1, 1939-
204, 1970. SUBS. PART OF: T.E.S.T. TECHNIQUES
ELECTRONIQUES, SON, TELEVISION.
LO/N14.

TELOS.
STATE UNIVERSITY OF NEW YORK: GRADUATE PHILO-
SOPHY ASSOCIATION.
BUFFALO, N.Y. 1(1), 1968-
CB/U-1.      OX/U-1.

TENDANCES DE LA CONJONCTURE.
+ +TENDANCES CONJONCT.
INSTITUT NATIONAL DE LA STATISTIQUE ET DES
ETUDES ECONOMIQUES (FRANCE).
PARIS NO.1, 1969-
BH/U-1.     OX/U-1.
BD/U-1. NO.2, 1974-

TENNESSEE POETRY JOURNAL.
+ +TENN. POETRY J.
MARTIN, TENN. 1(1), 1967-
3A.
OX/U-1.

TENNIS TALK.
NATIONAL ASSOCIATION OF YOUTH CLUBS.
LONDON NO.1, 1969-
ED/N-1.     OX/U-1.

TENNIS WORLD.
[TENNIS WORLD LTD.]
HINCKLEY, LEICS. 1, AP 1969-
ED/N-1.     OX/U-1.
ISSN 0040-3474

TEORETICHESKAJA ELEKTROTEKHNIKA, L'VOVSKIJ
GOSUDARSTVENNYJ UNIVERSITET.
+ +TEORETICHES. ELEKTROTEK. L'VOV. GOS. UNIV.
[TELT-A]
L'VOV 1, 1966-
ENGL. SUMM.
LO/N13.
CA/U-2. 3, 1967-

TEORETICHESKAJA I MATEMATICHESKAJA FIZIKA.
+ +TEOR. & MAT. FIZ. [TMFZ-A]
AKADEMIJA NAUK SSSR.
MOSCOW 1(1), 1969-
OX/U-8.
LO/N14. 2, 1970-

TEORETICHESKAJA I MATEMATICHESKAJA FIZIKA
(ENGL. TRANSL.).                                            000
SEE: THEORETICAL & MATHEMATICAL PHYSICS.

TEORETICHESKIE OSNOVY KHIMICHESKOJ TEKHNOLO-
GII.
+ +TEOR. OSN. KHIM. TEKNOL.
AKADEMIJA NAUK SSSR.
MOSCOW 1(1), 1967-
2M.
LO/S-3.     XS/R10.
ISSN 0040-3571

TEORIJA IN PRAKSA. REVIJA ZA DRUZBENA
VPRASANJA.
+ +TEOR. PRAKSA.
VISOKA SKOLA ZA POLITICNE VEDE.
LJUBLJANA 1, 1964-
OX/U-1. 7(1), 1970-
ISSN 0040-3598

TEORIJA I PRAKTIKA STOMATOLOGII.                            XXX
+ +TEOR. & PRAKT. STOMATOL.
MOSKOVSKIJ MEDITSINSKIJ STOMATOLOGICHESKIJ
INSTITUT.
MOSCOW 4, 1960-
PREV: TRUDY MOSKOVSKOGO MEDITSINSKOGO STOMAT-
OLOGICHESKOGO INSTITUTA FROM 1, 1958- 3, 1959.
LO/N13.

TEORIJA I RASCHET IMPUL'SNYKH I USILITEL'NYKH
SKHEM NA POLUPROVODNIKOVYKH PRIBORAKH.
+ +TEOR. & RASCHET IMPUL'SNYKH & USILITEL'NYKH
SKHEM POLUPROVODN. PRIB.
MOSKOVSKIJ INZHENERNO-FIZICHESKIJ INSTITUT.
MOSCOW 1, 1969-
LO/N13.

TERATOLOGY. JOURNAL OF ABNORMAL DEVELOPMENT.
TERATOLOGY SOCIETY.
PHILADELPHIA 1, F 1968-
SPONS. BODY ALSO: WISTAR INSTITUTE OF
ANATOMY & BIOLOGY.
BL/U-1.    DB/U-2.    LO/M17.    LO/U-2.    LV/U-1.    XY/N-1.
ISSN 0040-3709

TERATOLOGY LOOKOUT.
EUROPEAN TERATOLOGY SOCIETY.
STOCKHOLM 1, JA 1970-
SPONS. BODY ALSO: BIOMEDICAL DOCUMENTATION
CENTER.
LD/U-1.    LO/U-2.

TERPENOIDS & STEROIDS.
CHEMICAL SOCIETY.
LONDON 1, S 1969/AG 1970(1971)-
S/T: A REVIEW OF THE LITERATURE.
BH/U-3.    BL/U-1.    ED/N-1.    GL/U-2.    LO/N14.    LO/S-3.
LO/U12.    SO/U-1.
ISSN 0300-5992

TERRA AUSTRALIS.
+ +TERRA AUST.
AUSTRALIAN NATIONAL UNIVERSITY: RESEARCH SCHOOL
OF PACIFIC STUDIES.
CANBERRA 1, 1971-
ISSUED BY SCHOOL'S DEPT. OF PREHISTORY.
CA/U-1.    CA/U-3.    LO/N-2.

TERRAE INCOGNITAE. THE ANNALS OF THE ...
SOCIETY FOR THE HISTORY OF DISCOVERIES.
AMSTERDAM 1, 1969-
BL/U-1.    GL/U-1.    LO/N-2.    LO/S13.    LO/U-1.    LO/U17.
OX/U-1.
ED/N-1. 2, 1970-                       SF/U-1. 4, 1974-
ISSN 0082-2884

TERRE MALGACHE. TANY MALAGASY.
ECOLE NATIONALE SUPERIEURE AGRONOMIQUE
(MADAGASCAR).
TANANARIVE NO.1, 1967-
2/A.
LO/N-2.    OX/U24.
ISSN 0563-1637

TERTIARY TIMES.
TERTIARY RESEARCH GROUP.
BROMLEY, KENT 1, 1970-
ED/N-1.    LO/N-2.    LO/N13.    LO/U-2.    OX/U-8.

TESOL QUARTERLY. TEACHERS OF ENGLISH & SPEA-
KERS OF OTHER LANGUAGES.
+ +TESOL Q.
GEORGETOWN UNIVERSITY: INSTITUTE OF LANGUAGES &
LINGUISTICS.
WASHINGTON, D.C. 1, MR 1967-
BN/U-1.
MA/U-1. 6, 1972-
ISSN 0039-8322

T.E.S.T. TECHNIQUES ELECTRONIQUES, SON,
TELEVISION.                                                 XXX
[SOCIETE DES EDITIONS RADIO]
PARIS NO.14, 1972-
INCORP: TECHNIQUES ELECTRONIQUES ET AUDIO-
VISUELLES FROM NO.1, 1970- NO.12, 1971, OF
WHICH VOL. NUMBERING IS CONTINUED; & TELEVIS-
ION ET TECHNIQUES TELEVISUELLES FROM NO.205,
1970- NO.219, 1971.
LO/N14.

TEST- OCH MATERIALUTGAVOR, SLAVISKA
INSTITUTET, LUNDS UNIVERSITET.
+ +TEXT- OCH MATERIALUTGAVOR SLAVISKA INST. LUNDS
UNIV.
LUND NO.1, 1961-
LO/N-1.

TETHYS.
STATION MARINE D'ENDOUME.
 MARSEILLE 1(1), 1969-
 BN/U-2.    LO/N-2.    LO/N-4.
 ISSN 0040-4012

TETRADI PEREVODCHIKA: UCHENYE ZAPISKI.
MOSKOVSKIJ GOSUDARSTVENNYJ PEDAGOGICHESKIJ
INSTITUT INOSTRANNYKH JAZYKOV.
 MOSCOW 1, 1963-
 ED/U-1.    LO/N10.
 BH/U-1.  7, 1970-              CC/U-1.  4, 1967-
 GL/U-1.  4, 1967-             MA/U-1.  5, 1968-
 OX/U-1.  2, 1964-

TEXACO QUARTERLY.
+ +TEXACO Q.
TEXACO LTD.
 LONDON   1(1), OC 1968-

TEXAS ARCHITECTURAL SURVEY.
+ +TEX. ARCHIT. SURV.
AMON CARTER MUSEUM OF WESTERN ART.
 AUSTIN &C.  NO.1, 1966-
 SPONS. BODY ALSO: UNIVERSITY OF TEXAS: SCHOOL
 OF ARCHITECTURE.
 OX/U-1.

TEXTILBETRIEB.                                          XXX
[VOGEL]
 WURZBURG 89(10), 1971-
 PREV: SPINNER, WEBER, TEXTILVEREDLUNG FROM
 79(10), 1961- 89(9), 1971.
 LO/N14.

TEXTILE BULLETIN.                                       XXX
 SUBS (1971): AMERICA'S TEXTILES REPORTER/
 BULLETIN.

TEXTILE CHEMIST & COLORIST.
+ +TEXT. CHEM. & COLOR.
AMERICAN ASSOCIATION OF TEXTILE CHEMISTS &
COLORISTS.
 RESEARCH TRIANGLE PARK, N.C.  1, 1969-
 2W.
 GL/U-2.    LO/N14.
 ISSN 0040-490X

TEXTILE HISTORY.
+ +TEXT. HIST.
[DAVID & CHARLES]
 NEWTON ABBOT 1, D 1968-
 CB/U-1.    EX/U-1.    GL/U-2.    LO/N-1.    LO/N-4.    LO/U-2.
 LO/N-3.    MA/U-1.    SW/U-1.
 NW/U-1.  1970-

TEXTILE PROCESSING REVIEW.
+ +TEXT. PROCESS. REV.
[NOYES DEVELOPMENT CORP.]
 PARK RIDGE (N.J.) 1, 1969-
 LO/N14.

TEXTILE PROGRESS.
+ +TEXT. PROG.
TEXTILE INSTITUTE.
 MANCHESTER 1, 1969-
 BH/U-1.    ED/N-1.    GL/U-3.    LO/N-4.    LO/N14.    MA/P-1.
 OX/U-1.  2(2), 1970-
 ISSN 0040-5167

TEXTILES (MANCHESTER).                                  XXX
 SHIRLEY INSTITUTE.
 MANCHESTER 1, 1972-
 PREV: SHIRLEY LINK FROM 1965- 1971.
 ED/N-1.    LO/N14.    XS/R10.

TEXTILIA.                                               XXX
[PAN]
 MILAN 46(7), 1970-
 PREV: RIVISTA TESSILE - TEXTILIA FROM 36,
 1960- 46(6), 1970. INCORP; FIBRE E COLORI +
 RAION E FIBRE NUOVE.
 LO/N14.
 ISSN 0033-9067

TEXTIL-INDUSTRIE.                                       XXX
[LAPP]
 MONCHENGLADBACH 72, 1970- 74(1), 1972.
 PREV: ZEITSCHRIFT FUR DIE GESAMTE TEXTIL-
 INDUSTRIE FROM 1, 1897- 71, 1969. SUBS. INCORP
 IN: CHEMIEFASERN/TEXTILINDUSTRIE.
 LO/N14.

TEXTIL-PRAXIS.                                          XXX
 SUBS (1971): TEXTIL-PRAXIS INTERNATIONAL.

TEXTIL-PRAXIS: INTERNATIONAL EDITION.                   XXX
[KONRADIN-VERLAG R. KOHLHAMMER]
 STUTTGART NO.1, MR 1961- 1970.
 SUBS: INCORP. IN TEXTIL-PRAXIS INTERNATIONAL.
 LO/N14.

TEXTIL-PRAXIS INTERNATONAL.                             XXX
+ +TEXT.-PRAX. INT.
[KONRADIN-VERLAG R. KOHLHAMMER]
 STUTTGART 26, 1971-
 PREV: TEXTIL-PRAXIS FROM 1, AG 1946- 25, 1970.
 INCORP. TEXTIL-PRAXIS: INTERNATIONAL EDITION.
 LO/N14.
 ISSN 0040-4853

TEXTILTECHNIK.                                          XXX
KAMMER DER TECHNIK (LEIPZIG).
[VEB FACHBUCHVERLAG]
 LEIPZIG 23, 1973-
 PREV: DEUTSCHE TEXTILTECHNIK FROM 7, 1957-
 22, 1972.
 LO/N14.

TEXTURE.
[GORDON & BREACH]
 NEW YORK &C.  1, 1972-
 CA/U-1.    ED/N-1.    LO/N14.    OX/U-8.

TEZHKA PROMISHLENOST.                                   XXX
 SUBS (1960):  MASHINOSTROENIE.

TGA COSMETIC JOURNAL.                                   XXX
+ +TGA COSMET. J. (TOILET GOODS ASS.)
TOILET GOODS ASSOCIATION.
 WASHINGTON, D.C.  1, 1969- 2, 1970 ...
 PREV: PROCEEDINGS OF THE SCIENTIFIC SECTION,
 TOILET GOODS ASSOCIATION, INC. FROM 1, JA 1944
 SUBS: CTFA COSMETIC JOURNAL.
 LO/N14.

THAI NEWS.
(THAILAND) EMBASSY (GB).
 LONDON NO.1, 1970-
 LO/U14.

THEATRE DOCUMENTATION.                                  XXX
+ +THEATRE DOC.
THEATRE LIBRARY ASSOCIATION.
 NEW YORK 1, 1968- 4(1), 1972.
 2/A. SUBS: PERFORMING ARTS RESOURCES.
 GL/U-1.    LO/N-1.    LO/U-1.    LO/U13.    NW/U-1.    OX/U-1.
 NO/U-1.  2(1), 1969-
 ISSN 0040-5485

THEATRE QUARTERLY.
+ +THEATRE Q.
[METHUEN, EYRE & SPOTTISWOODE]
 LONDON 1(1), JA/MR 1971-
 BH/P-1.    BN/U-1.    CB/U-1.    CO/U-1.    DB/U-2.    ED/N-1.
 EX/U-1.    LD/U-1.    LO/U-1.    LO/U13.    NO/U-1.    NW/U-1.
 SH/U-1.    SW/U-1.
 LO/U28. 2, 1972-
 ISSN 0049-3600

THEATRE QUEBEC.
+ +THEATRE QUE.
CENTRE D'ESSAI DES AUTEURS DRAMATIQUES DE
MONTREAL.
 MONTREAL 1(1), [1969]-
 4/A.
 LO/N-1.

THEMES IN EDUCATION.
+ +THEMES EDUC.
UNIVERSITY OF EXETER: INSTITUTE OF EDUCATION.
 EXETER NO.1, 1967-

THEN.
[THEN LTD.]
 LONDON [NO.1] MY 1972-
 6/A.
 CA/U-1.

THEOKRATIA.
INSTITUTUM JUDAICUM DELITZSCHIANUM.
[BRILL]
 LONDON 1, 1967/69(1970)-
 AD/U-1.    DB/U-2.    LO/N-1.    OX/U-1.

THEOLOGICA (ROME).                                      000
 SEE: CLARETIANUM.

**THEOLOGICAL & RELIGIOUS INDEX.**
++THEOL. & RELIG. INDEX.
[THEOLOGICAL ABSTRACTING & BIBLIOGRAPHICAL
SERVICES]
*HARROGATE, YORKS. 1(1), 1971-*
Q.
*CA/U-1.    ED/N-1.    EX/U-1.    LD/U-1.    XY/N-1.*
*LO/U-1. [W. 1(1), 1971]*

**THEOLOGISCHE INTERVIEW.**
[PATMOS]
*DUSSELDORF NO.1, [1969]-*
MONOGR.
*LO/N-1.*

**THEORETICAL & MATHEMATICAL PHYSICS.**
++THEOR. & MATH. PHYS.
[CONSULTANTS BUREAU]
*NEW YORK 1(1), OC 1969-*
M. ENGL. TRANSL. OF TEORETICHESKAJA I MATEM-
ATICHESKAJA FIZIKA.
*LO/N14.    XS/R10.*
*OX/U-8. 2(1), 1970-*
*ISSN 0040-5779*

**THEORETICAL PHYSICS JOURNAL.**                    XXX
++THEOR. PHYS. J.
[CAMBRIDGE SCIENTIFIC ABSTRACTS]
*RIVERDALE, MD. 1, 1972...*
ALSO ENTITLED: THEORETICAL PHYSICS ABSTRACTS
JOURNAL. SUBS: SCIENCE RESEARCH ABSTRACTS:
PART A: SUPERCONDUCTIVITY, MAGNETO-
HYDRODYNAMICS & PLASMAS, THEORETICAL
PHYSICS.
*LO/N14.*
*ISSN 0049-3678*

**THEORETICAL POPULATION BIOLOGY.**
++THEOR. POPULAT. BIOL.
[ACADEMIC P.]
*NEW YORK &C. 1, 1970-*
*LD/U-1.    LO/N-2.    LO/N14.    LO/R-5.    LO/U-2.    MA/U-1.*
*OX/U-8.    RE/U-1.    SO/U-1.*
*GL/U-2. 1974-                LO/U13. 3, 1972-*
*SH/U-1. 1972-*
*ISSN 0040-5809*

**THEORETICAL PRACTICE.**                            XXX
++THEOR. PRACT.
*LONDON NO.1, JA 1971- 7 JA 1973.//*
5/A.
*CB/U-1.    ED/N-1.    LO/U-3.    MA/U-1.    OX/U-1.*

**THEORY & DECISION.**
++THEORY & DECIS.
[REIDEL]
*DORDRECHT 1(1), OC 1970-*
S/T: AN INTERNATIONAL JOURNAL FOR PHILOSOPHY
& METHODOLOGY OF THE SOCIAL SCIENCES.
*AD/U-1.    CA/U-1.    HL/U-1.    LO/U-3.    LO/U20.    OX/U16.*
*OX/U17.    SW/U-1.*
*ISSN 0040-5833*

**THEORY & EXPERIMENT IN EXOBIOLOGY.**
++THEORY & EXP. EXOBIOL.
[WOLTERS-NOORDHOFF]
*GRONINGEN 1, 1971-*
*LO/N13.*

**THERMAL ANALYSIS ABSTRACTS.**
++THERM. ANAL. ABSTR.
INTERNATIONAL CONFEDERATION FOR THERMAL
ANALYSIS.
[HEYDEN]
*LONDON &C. 1, 1972-*
*LO/N14.    LO/U28.*
*CA/U-1. 1(4), 1972-            ED/N-1. 1(4), 1972-*
*OX/U-8. 1(4), 1972-*

**THERMOCHIMICA ACTA.**
++THERMOCHIM. ACTA.
*AMSTERDAM 1, 1970-*
*AD/U-1.    CA/U-2.    DB/U-2.    GL/U-1.    LO/N-4.    LO/S-3.*
*LO/U12.    LO/U12.    OX/U-1.    SH/C-5.*
*BD/U-1. 5(2), 1972-        BL/U-1. 5, 1972-*
*LD/U-1. 2(2), 1971-*
*SF/U-1. 11(3), 1975-*
*ISSN 0040-6031.*

**THESAURUS MUSICUS.**
++THESAUR. MUSIC.
[ZENEMUKIADO VALLALAT]
*BUDAPEST 1, 1962-*
ENGL., GER., HUNG.
*OX/U-1.*

**THESPIS.**
INTERNATIONAL THEATRE INSTITUTE: GREEK CENTER.
*ATHENS 1, MY 1964-*
*BN/U-1. 1, 1964- 3, 1966.*

**THETA - PI.**                                      XXX
[BRILL]
*LEIDEN 1, 1972- 3, 1974. //*
S/T: A JOURNAL FOR GREEK & EARLY CHRISTIAN
PHILOSOPHY...
*CA/U-1.    OX/U-1.*

**THIN FILMS.**                                      XXX
[GORDON & BREACH SCIENCE PUBLISHERS]
*NEW YORK &C   1(1), JA 1968- 2(2), AG 1972.*
SUBS. INCORP. IN: ELECTROCOMPONENT SCIENCE &
TECHNOLOGY.
*ED/N-1.    LO/N14.    XS/R10.*

**THIN-LAYER CHROMATOGRAPHY ABSTRACTS.**
++THIN-LAYER CHROMATOGR. ABSTR.
[SCIENCE & TECHNOLOGY AGENCY]
*LONDON 1(1), JA/F 1971-*
6/A.
*CA/U-1.    ED/N-1.*

**THIRD WORLD. SOCIALISM & DEVELOPMENT.**            XXX
FABIAN SOCIETY.
*LONDON 1(1), S 1972-*
MON. PREV: VENTURE FROM 1, 1949- 24, 1972.
*CA/U-1.    ED/N-1.    LO/N-6.    LO/S14.    LO/U-3.    MA/U-1.*
*NW/U-1.    OX/U-9    SH/U-1.    SO/U-1.*

**THIRD WORLD REPORTS.**
++THIRD WORLD REP.
*LONDON 1(1), MR 1970-*
S/T: A MONTHLY NEWS SERVICE ON THE LIBERATION
MOVEMENTS.
*LO/U-3. 4(1), 1973-*
*ISSN 0049-3740*

**THIS ENGLAND.**
*GRIMSBY 1(1), MR 1968-*
Q.
*ED/N-1.    OX/U-1.*
*ISSN 0040-6171*

**THIS IS MALAWI.**
(MALAWI) DEPARTMENT OF INFORMATION.
*BLANTYRE 1, JA 1965-*
*CA/U-1. 2, 1966-                LO/U14. 1971-*
*ISSN 0563-4784*

**THOMAS HARDY YEAR BOOK.**                          XXX
[TOUCAN P.]
*ST. PETER PORT, GUERNSEY NO.1, 1970-*
PREV: MONOGRAPHS ON THE LIFE, TIMES & WORKS OF
THOMAS HARDY FROM NO.23, 1966- 72, 1971.
*GL/U-2.    HL/U-1.    LO/U-1.    OX/U-1.    SH/U-1.*
*ISSN 0082-416X*

**THORNFIELD JOURNAL.**
++THORNFIELD J.
UNIVERSITY COLLEGE, DUBLIN: PSYCHOLOGICAL
SOCIETY.
*DUBLIN 1, 1967-*
*DB/U-2.*
*CA/U-1. 5, 1972-                ED/N-1. 5, 1972-*

**THORNFIELD SERIES.**
UNIVERSITY COLLEGE, DUBLIN: DEPARTMENT OF
PSYCHOLOGY.
*DUBLIN NO.1, 1971-*
*DB/U-2.*

**THOUGHT & LANGUAGE IN OPERATIONS.**                000
SEE: PENSIERO E LINGUAGGIO IN OPERAZIONI.

**THROB. A MAGAZINE OF DECEPTIVE POETRY.**
[HORSEHEAD NEBULA P.]
*MANHATTAN BEACH, CALIF. NO.1, 1971-*
*LO/U-2.*

**THROMBOSIS RESEARCH.**
++THROMB. RES.
[PERGAMON P.]
*NEW YORK 1, F 1972-*
6/A.
*DB/U-2.    ED/N-1.    LO/N13.    OX/U-8.*
*BL/U-1. 4, 1974-*
*ISSN 0049-3848*

THUNDER. QUARTERLY THEORETICAL & DISCUSSION
JOURNAL OF THE PEOPLE'S PROGRESSIVE PARTY.
*GEORGETOWN, BRITISH GUIANA  1(1), JL/S 1969-*
Q. PREV PUBL. WITH SUBTITLE: ORGAN OF THE
PEOPLE'S PROGRESSIVE PARTY FROM 1, 1950.
PUBL. SUSPENDED JL- D 1970.
*LO/U-3.*
*ISSN 0040-6635*

TIDSSKRIFT FOR TEXTILTEKNIK.                           XXX
SUBS (1971): TEKNISK TIDSSKRIFT FOR TEXTIC-
OG BEKLAEDNINGSINDUSTRI.

TIDSSKRIFT FOR VOKSENOPPLAERING.
*++TIDSSKR. VOKSENOPPLAERING.*
[FOLKEUNIVERSITETET]
*OSLO  NO.1, 1966-*
*LO/N-1.*
*ISSN 0040-7216*

TIJDSCHRIFT VOOR KADASTER EN LANDMEETKUNDE.           XXX
SUBS(1970): NEDERLANDS GEODETISCH TIJDSCHRIFT.

TIJDSCHRIFT VOOR SOCIAL RECHT.                        000
SEE: REVUE DE DROIT SOCIAL.

TIJDSCHRIFT VOOR STRAFRECHT.                          XXX
SUBS (1970): DELIKT EN DELINKWENT.

TIMBERLAB NEWS: NEWSLETTER OF THE...
FOREST PRODUCTS RESEARCH LABORATORY.
[HMSO]
*LONDON  NO.1, MY 1969-*
SUPPL. TO TIMBER TRADES JOURNAL.
*ED/N-1.     LD/U-1.     OX/U-1.     SH/U-1.*
*LO/N14. [CURRENT BOX ONLY]*

TIME SALE. FOR THE COMPUTER INDUSTRY.
[MEDIA PROMOTION LTD.]
*LONDON  NO.1, 1972-*
*ED/N-1.     OX/U-1.*
*LO/N14. CURRENT BOX ONLY.*

TIMES HIGHER EDUCATION SUPPLEMENT.
*++TIMES HIGHER EDUC. SUPPL.*
[TIMES PUBL. CO. LTD.]
*LONDON  NO.1, 15 OC 1971-*
W.
*BH/U-1.     CA/U-1.     CA/U13.    DN/U-1.   ED/N-1.   EX/U-1.*
*GL/U-1.     HL/U-1.     HL/U-2.    LO/U-1.   LO/U-3.   LO/U-4.*
*LO/U12.     LV/U-2.     NO/U-1.    NW/U-1.   SF/U-1.   SO/U-1.*
*BH/U-3. (FIVE YEARS).*
*LO/N35. 2 YEARS ONLY.*
*OX/U16. (ONE YEAR).*
*XS/T-4. (3 MONTHS).*
*ISSN 0049-3929*

TINTENFISCH.  JAHRBUCH FUR LITERATUR.
[VERLAG KLAUS WAGENBACH]
*BERLIN  [NO.]1, 1968-*
SUBSERIES OF: QUARTHEFTE.
*CB/U-1.     LO/U-2.*

TIRE SCIENCE & TECHNOLOGY.
*++TIRE SCI. & TECHNOL.*
AMERICAN SOCIETY FOR TESTING & MATERIALS.
*PHILADELPHIA  1, 1973-*
*LO/N14.*
*ISSN 0090-8657*

TISSUE ANTIGENS.
*COPENHAGEN  1(1), 1971-*
S/T: HISTOCOMPATIBILITY & IMMUNOGENETICS.
*AD/U-1.     CA/M-1.     LO/M-3.     OX/U-8.*
*ISSN 0001-2815*

TISSUE & CELL.
[OLIVER & BOYD]
*EDINBURGH  1(1), 1969-*
*BN/U-2.     ED/N-1.     GL/U-1.    LD/U-1.   LO/N-2.   LO/U-2.*
*LV/U-1.     MA/U-1.     OX/U-8.    SH/U-1.   SW/U-1.*
*ISSN 0040-8160*

TISSUE CULTURE ABSTRACTS, BIBLIOGRAPHY &
METHODS.
*++TISSUE CULT. ABSTR. BIBLIOGR. & METHODS.*
BIO-CULT LABORATORIES LTD.
*PAISLEY  1(1), AG 1971-*
1(1) ENTITLED: TISSUE CULTURE ABSTRACTS &
METHODS.
*XS/R10.*

T.-I.-T. JOURNAL OF LIFE SCIENCES.
TOWER INTERNATIONAL TECHNOMEDICAL INSTITUTE.
*PHILADELPHIA  1, MR 1971-*
Q.
*CA/U-2.     OX/U-8.*
*ISSN 0039-8160*

TLUSZCZE I SRODKI PIORACE.                            XXX
SUBS:  TLUSZCZE, SRODKI PIORACE, KOSMETYKI.

TLUSZCZE, SRODKI PIORACE, KOSMETYKI.                  XXX
INSTYTUT CHEMII OGOLNEJ.
*WARSAW  10(1), 1966-*
2M. SPONS. BODY ALSO: ZJEDNOCZENIE PRZEMYSLU
CHEMII GOSPODARCZEJ.  PREV: TLUSZCZE I SRODKI
PIORACE FROM 1(1), 1957- 9(6), 1965.
*XY/N-1.  1967-*

TOC H JOURNAL.                                        XXX
SUBS (1968): POINT THREE.

TOCHER. TALES, MUSIC, SONG.
UNIVERSITY OF EDINBURGH: SCHOOL OF SCOTTISH
STUDIES.
*EDINBURGH  1, 1971-*
Q.
*DB/U-2.     ED/N-1.     GL/U-1.    LO/S10.   MA/P-1.   SH/U-1.*
*ISSN 0049-397X*

TODAY (1970).
SCRIPTURE UNION.
*LONDON  NO.1, 1970-*
*ED/N-1.     OX/U-1.*

TODAY (1971).
ROYAL SOCIETY FOR THE PREVENTION OF CRUELTY TO
ANIMALS.
*LONDON  NO.1, 1971-*
Q.
*ED/N-1.*

TOKSIKOLOGIA NOVYKH PROMYSHLENNYKH KHIMICH-
ESKIKH VESHCHESTV.
*++TOKSIKOL. NOVYKH PROM. KHIM. VESHCHESTV.*
[TPKV-A]
AKADEMIJA MEDITSINSKIKH NAUK SSSR.
*MOSCOW  1, 1961-*
ENGL. SUMM.
*LO/N13. 2, 1961-*

TOKYO HISHIRYO KENSAJO SHIRYO KENKYU HOKOKU.
BULLETIN OF NATIONAL INSPECTION LABORATORY
FOR FEEDS & FERTILIZER.
*TOKYO  NO.1, 1966-*
ENGL. SUMM.
*LO/N13.*

TOKYO HISHIRYO KENSAJO TOKUBETSU HOKOKU.
SPECIAL REPORT, NATIONAL INSPECTION LABORAT-
ORY FOR FEEDS & FERTILIZER.
*TOKYO  NO.1, 1969-*
ENGL. TITLE FROM NO.2.
*LO/N13.*

TOKYO IKA SHIKA DAIGAKU IYO KIZAI KENKYUJO
HOKOKU.  REPORTS OF THE INSTITUTE FOR MEDICAL
& DENTAL ENGINEERING, TOKYO MEDICAL & DENTAL
UNIVERSITY.
*TOKYO  1, 1967-*
ENGL. SUMM.
*LO/N13.*

TOKYO TORITSU KOGYO GIJUTSU SENTA KENKYU
HOKOKU.  REPORT, TOKYO METROPOLITAN INDUST-
RIAL TECHNIC INSTITUTE.                               XXX
*TOKYO  NO.1, 1971-*
PREV: TOKYO TORITSU KOGYO SHOREIKAN HOKOKU
FROM NO.1, 1952- 21, 1970.
*LO/N14.*

TOKYO TORITSU KOGYO SHOREIKAN HOKOKU.                 XXX
SUBS (1971): TOKYO TORITSU KOGYO GIJUTSU
SENTA KENKYU HOKOKU.

TOO MUCH.
UNIVERSITY COLLEGE HOSPITAL MEDICAL SCHOOL.
*LONDON  NO.1, N 1971-*
S/T: THE NEWSPAPER FROM THE MEDICAL SCHOOL,
UNIVERSITY COLLEGE HOSPITAL.
*ED/N-1.     LO/U-1.     OX/U-1.*

TOOL & MANUFACTURING ENGINEER.                        XXX
SUBS (1970): MANUFACTURING ENGINEERING &
MANAGEMENT.

TOOLS & TILLAGE.
[GAD]
*COPENHAGEN  1, 1968-*
S/T: A JOURNAL ON THE HISTORY OF THE IMPLE-
MENTS OF CULTIVATION & OTHER AGRICULTURAL
PROCESSES.
*AD/U-1.     BL/U-1.     CA/U-3.    EX/U-1.   LO/U-2.   NO/U-1.*

**TOPICAL TALKS.**
++TOP. TALKS.
SOUTH AFRICAN INSTITUTE OF RACE RELATIONS.
JOHANNESBURG NO.1, 1967-
OX/U-9.

**TOPICS IN CARBOCYCLIC CHEMISTRY.**                    XXX
++TOP. CARBOCYCLIC CHEM.
[LOGOS P.]
LONDON 1, 1969. //
BH/U-1.   GL/U-1.   HL/U-1.   LD/U-1.   LO/N-4.   LO/N14.
LO/S-3.   LO/U20.   MAU-1.   SF/U-1.   SO/U-1.

**TOPICS IN INORGANIC & GENERAL CHEMISTRY.**
++TOP. INORG. & GEN. CHEM.
[ELSEVIER]
AMSTERDAM &C. 1, 1964-
MONOGR.
GL/U-1.
ISSN 0082-495X

**TOPICS IN LIPID CHEMISTRY.**
++TOP. LIPID CHEM.
[LOGOS P.]
LONDON 1, 1970-
BH/U-3.   HL/U-1.   LO/N14.   LO/S-3.   XS/C-2.
LD/U-1. 1, 1970.

**TOPICS IN MEDICINAL CHEMISTRY.**
++TOP. MED. CHEM.
[INTERSCIENCE]
NEW YORK &C  1, 1967-
LO/N13.   SO/U-1.

**TOPICS IN OCEAN ENGINEERING.**
++TOP. OCEAN ENG.
[GULF PUBL.]
HOUSTON, TEXAS 1, 1969-
LO/N14.

**TOPICS IN PHARMACEUTICAL SCIENCES.**
++TOP. PHARM. SCI.
[INTERSCIENCE]
NEW YORK &C  1, 1968-
LD/U-1.   LO/N14.

**TOPIQUE. REVUE FREUDIENNE.**
[PRESSES UNIVERSITAIRES DE FRANCE]
PARIS 1, OC 1969-
OX/U-8.
ISSN 0040-9375

**TORNEDALICA.**
LULEA, SWED. NO.1, 1962-
LO/N-1. NO.2, 1963-

**TORONTO MEDIEVAL BIBLIOGRAPHIES.**
++TORONTO MEDIEVAL BIBLIOGR.
UNIVERSITY OF TORONTO: CENTRE FOR MEDIEVAL
STUDIES.
LO/N-1.

**TORQUE. FOR THE CULTURED DESPISERS & ADVO-
CATES OF TECHNOLOGY.**
UNIVERSITY COLLEGE, LONDON: FACULTY OF ENGIN-
EERING.
LONDON 1, 1969-
ED/N-1.   LO/U-2.

**TOTUS HOMO. REVISTA SCIENTIFICA
INTERDISCIPLINARE.**
ISTITUTO DI PSICO-SINTESI SCIENTIFICA.
MILAN NO.1, 1969-
3/A. ENGL., FR. OR ITAL.
LO/N-1.
DB/U-2. 4, 1972-

**TOVAROVEDENIE. MEZHVEDOMSTVENNYJ RESPUBLIK-
ANSKIJ NAUCHNO-TEKHNICHESKIJ SBORNIK.**
KIEV 1, 1965-
CC/U-1.

**TOWARDS ONE NIGERIA.**
(NIGERIA) FEDERAL MINISTRY OF INFORMATION.
LAGOS NO.1, 1967-
OX/U-9.

**TOWN PLANNING REPORTS.**
++TOWN PLANN. REP.
UNIVERSITY OF CANTERBURY: DEPARTMENT OF
PSYCHOLOGY & SOCIOLOGY.
CHRISTCHURCH, N.Z. NO.1, 1969-
HL/U-1.

**TOXIC SUBSTANCES. ANNUAL LIST.**
++TOXIC SUBST.
NATIONAL INSTITUTE FOR OCCUPATIONAL SAFETY &
HEALTH (US).
ROCKVILLE, MD. 1, 1971-
LO/N14.

**TOXICITY BIBLIOGRAPHY.**
++TOXIC. BIBLIOGR.
NATIONAL LIBRARY OF MEDICINE (U.S.).
BETHESEDA 1, 1968-
S/T: A BIBLIOGRAPHY COVERING REPORTS ON TOX-
ICITY STUDIES, ADVERSE DRUG REACTIONS, &
POISONING IN MAN & ANIMALS.
DB/U-2.   LD/U-1.*   LO/M-3.   LO/N14.
NW/U-1. 4, 1971-
ISSN 0041-0071

**TOXICOLOGICAL & ENVIRONMENTAL CHEMISTRY REVIEW.**
++TOXICOL. & ENVIRON. CHEM. REV.
[GORDON & BREACH]
NEW YORK &C. 1, 1972-
CA/U-1.   LO/N14.   LO/S-3.   OX/U-8.
ED/N-1. 1(3), 1973-

**TOXICOLOGY.**
[ELSEVIER]
AMSTERDAM 1, 1973-
Q.
DB/U-2.   LO/M11.   LO/N-2.   LO/R-6.   OX/U-8.

**TOXICOLOGY & APPLIED PHARMACOLOGY: SUPPLEMENT.**
++TOXICOL. & APPL. PHARMACOL., SUPPL.
[ACADEMIC P.]
NEW YORK &C. 1, 1962-
ED/N-1. 3, 1969-

**TOYAMA KENRITSU OTANI GIJUTSU TANKI DAIGAKU
KENKYU HOKOKU. BULLETIN OF RESEARCH, OTANI
COLLEGE OF TECHNOLOGY OF TOYAMA.**                    XXX
TOYAMA KENRITSU OTANI GIJUTSU TANKI DAIGAKU.
TOYAMA 1, 1967- 5, 1972 ...
SUBS: TOYAMA KENRITSU GIJUTSU TANKI DAIGAKU
KENKUYU HOKUKU.
LO/N13.

**TRABAJOS DEL DEPARTAMENTO DE BOTANICA Y FIS-
IOLOGIA VEGETAL, UNIVERSIDAD DE MADRID.**
++TRAB. DEP. BOT. FISIOL. VEG. UNIV. MADR.
MADRID NO.1, 1968-
LO/N-2.

**TRABALHOS, INSTITUTO DE INVESTIGACAO CIENTIF-
ICA DE MOCAMBIQUE.**
++TRAB. INST. INVEST. CIENT. MOCAMBIQUE.
LOURENCO MARQUES NO.1, 1961-
LO/N-2.

**TRACKS.**
UNIVERSITY OF WARWICK.
COVENTRY NO.1, 1967-
3/A.
LO/U-2.

**TRACT.**
[GRYPHON P.] .
LLANON, CARDIGAN. NO.1, 1972-
Q.
BN/U-1.
ED/N-1. NO.6, 1973-

**TRADE & INDUSTRY.**                    XXX
++TRADE & IND.
(GREAT BRITAIN) DEPARTMENT OF TRADE & INDUSTRY.
LONDON 1, 1970-
PREV: BOARD OF TRADE JOURNAL FROM 1, JL 1886-
199(3839), OC 1970.
GL/U-1.   HL/U-1.   LO/U-1.   LO/U-2.   LO/U-3.   LO/U20.
OX/U-1.   OX/U16.   RE/U-1.   SH/U-1.   SO/U-1.
ISSN 0006-5325

**TRAFODION, CYMDEITHAS EMYNWYR CYMRU.**
LLANDYBIE 1, 1969-
CR/N-1.

**TRAINING IN BUSINESS & INDUSTRY.**
++TRAIN. BUS. & IND.
[GELLART-WOLFMAN PUBL. CORP.]
NEW YORK 1, 1964-
XY/N-1.
ISSN 0041-0896

**TRAINING FOR INDUSTRY SERIES.**
++TRAIN. IND. SER.
UNITED NATIONS: INDUSTRIAL DEVELOPMENT
ORGANISATION.
NEW YORK 1, 1969-
GL/U-1.

TRAINING SYSTEMS IN INDUSTRY.
++TRAIN. SYST. IND.
[PERGAMON]
OXFORD 1(1), 1969-
ED/N-1.

TRAMS.                                                                      XXX
[TRAM-B]
TRAMWAY MUSEUM SOCIETY.
SHEFFIELD NO.1, AP 1961- NO.32, AP 1969.//
Q.
BH/P-1.

TRAMWAY TOPICS.
++TRAMW. TOP.
TRAMWAY MUSEUM SOCIETY.
HYDE, CHES. NO.1, SPRING 1968-
Q.
ED/N-1.
OX/U-1. NO.2, 1968-
MA/P-1. NO.1- 2, 1968.

TRANSACTIONS, AMERICAN GEOPHYSICAL UNION.            XXX
SUBS (1960): EOS.

TRANSACTIONS OF THE AMERICAN SOCIETY OF
MECHANICAL ENGINEERS: SERIES ...                     000
SEE (FOR REFS.): TRANSACTIONS OF THE ASME: ...

TRANSACTIONS, AMERICAN SOCIETY FOR METALS.           XXX
SUBS (1961): TRANSACTIONS QUARTERLY ...

TRANSACTIONS OF THE ASME: SERIES F.                  XXX
SEE: JOURNAL OF LUBRICATION TECHNOLOGY.

TRANSACTIONS, BIOCHEMICAL SOCIETY.
++TRANS. BIOCHEM. SOC.
LONDON 1(1), JA 1973-
CA/U-1.    CA/U-7.   EX/U-1.   GL/U-1.   GL/U-2.   LD/U-1.
LO/M-3.    LO/N-4.   LO/R-6.   LO/S-3.   MA/U-1.   SH/U-1.
SO/U-1.

TRANSACTIONS, BRITISH BRYOLOGICAL SOCIETY.           XXX
SUBS (1972): JOURNAL OF BRYOLOGY.

TRANSACTIONS, BRITISH CERAMIC SOCIETY.               XXX
SUBS (1971): PART OF TRANSACTIONS & JOURNAL,
BRITISH CERAMIC SOCIETY.

TRANSACTIONS, BRITISH SOCIETY FOR THE HISTORY
OF PHARMACY.
++TRANS. BR. SOC. HIST. PHARM.
LONDON 1, 1970-
AD/U-1.    BH/U-3.   ED/N-1.   LO/M24.   LO/N-1.   LO/N-4.
LO/U11.    OX/U-8.

TRANSACTIONS, CANADIAN AERONAUTICS & SPACE
INSTITUTE.                                           000
SEE: CASI TRANSACTIONS.

TRANSACTIONS, CHARTERED INSTITUTE OF PATENT
AGENTS.                                              XXX
SUBS (1971): CIPA JOURNAL.

TRANSACTIONS, CHIGWELL LOCAL HISTORY SOCIETY.
++TRANS. CHIGWELL LOCAL HIST. SOC.
LOUGHTON, ESSEX NO.1, 1970-
ED/N-1.

TRANSACTIONS, CONGREGATIONAL HISTORICAL
SOCIETY.                                             XXX
SUBS(1973): JOURNAL, UNITED REFORMED CHURCH
HISTORY SOCIETY.

TRANSACTIONS, DEPARTMENT OF ENGINEERING,
KOKUSHIKAN UNIVERSITY.                               000
SEE: KOKUSHIKAN DAIGAKU KOGAKUBU KIYO.

TRANSACTIONS, FARADAY SOCIETY.                       XXX
SUBS(1972): PART OF JOURNAL, CHEMICAL SOC-
IETY: FARADAY TRANSACTIONS 1; & ... 2.

TRANSACTIONS OF THE GLASGOW ARCHAEOLOGICAL           XXX
SOCIETY.
SUBS (1969): GLASGOW ARCHAEOLOGICAL JOURNAL.

TRANSACTIONS, INSTITUTION OF NAVAL ARCHITECTS        XXX
SUBS (1960): TRANSACTIONS, ROYAL ...

TRANSACTIONS, INSTITUTION OF THE RUBBER
INDUSTRY.                                            XXX
SUBS (1967) PART OF: JOURNAL, INSTITUTION
OF THE RUBBER INDUSTRY.

TRANSACTIONS, INTERNATIONAL MODULAR GROUP.           XXX
SUBS (1971): PART OF OAP JOURNAL FOR THE
BUILT ENVIRONMENT.

TRANSACTIONS OF THE JAPAN SOCIETY OF CIVIL
ENGINEERS.
++TRANS. JAP. SOC. CIVIL ENG. [DGRO-A]
DOBOKU GAKKAI.
TOKYO 1, 1969-
TRANSL. IN FULL OR AS ABSTR. OF: DOBOKU GAKKAI
ROMBUN HOKOKUSHU.
LO/N14.
CA/U-4. 3, 1972-                    GL/U-1. 4, 1973-

TRANSACTIONS & JOURNAL, BRITISH CERAMIC
SOCIETY.                                             XXX
++TRANS. & J. BR. CERAM. SOC.
STOKE-ON-TRENT 70, 1971-
INCORP: JOURNAL ... FROM 1, OC 1963- 7, 1970;
& TRANSACTIONS ... FROM 37, 1938- 69, 1969/70
THE NUMBERING OF WHICH IS CONTINUED.
BH/P-1.    ED/N-1.   LD/U-1.   LO/N13.   LO/N14.   LO/S-3.

TRANSACTIONS, LEEDS GEOLOGICAL ASSOCIATION.          XXX
SUBS (1970): JOURNAL OF EARTH SCIENCES.

TRANSACTIONS, MODULAR SOCIETY.                       XXX
SUBS (1971): PART OF OAP JOURNAL FOR THE
BUILT ENVIRONMENT.

TRANSACTIONS OF THE NEBRASKA ACADEMY OF
SCIENCES.
++TRANS. NEBR. ACAD. SCI.
LINCOLN, NEBR. 1, 1972-
ANNU.
AD/U-1.    CA/U-2.   LO/N14.
ISSN 0077-6351

TRANSACTIONS, PAPUA & NEW GUINEA SCIENTIFIC
SOCIETY.
++TRANS. PAPUA & NEW GUINEA SCI. SOC.
PORT MORESBY 1, 1960-
LO/N-2. 1, 1960- 10, 1969.
ISSN 0085-4700

TRANSACTIONS QUARTERLY, AMERICAN SOCIETY FOR
METALS.                                              XXX
++TRANS. Q. AM. SOC. METALS. [ASMQ-A]
NEW YORK 54(1), MR 1961- 62(4), D 1969.//
PREV: TRANSACTIONS, AMERICAN SOCIETY ... FROM
15, 1934- 53, 1960.
LO/N-7.
CV/C-1. 56, 1963-                   LO/U-2. 59, 1966-

TRANSACTIONS, ROYAL INSTITUTION OF NAVAL
ARCHITECTS.                                          XXX
++TRANS. R. INST. NAVAL ARCHIT.
LONDON 102, 1960- 113(1), 1971.
PREV: TRANSACTIONS, INSTITUTION OF NAVAL
ARCHITECTS FROM 1, 1860- 101, 1959. SUBS:
NAVAL ARCHITECT.
LO/N14.

TRANSACTIONS, ROYAL SOCIETY OF NEW ZEALAND:
BIOLOGICAL SCIENCES.                                 XXX
++TRANS. R. SOC. N.Z., BIOL. SCI.
WELLINGTON 11, 1968- 12, 1970.
INCORP: TRANSACTIONS ... BOTANY FROM 1, 1961-
3(17), 1968; & TRANSACTIONS ... ZOOLOGY FROM
1, 1961- 10(26), 1968. SUBS. PART OF:
JOURNAL OF THE ROYAL SOCIETY OF NEW ZEALAND.
GL/U-1.    GL/U-1.   LO/N14.   NW/U-1.

TRANSACTIONS, ROYAL SOCIETY OF NEW ZEALAND:
EARTH SCIENCES.                                      XXX
++TRANS. R. SOC. N.Z., EARTH SCI.
WELLINGTON 7, 1969- 8, 1970.
PREV: TRANSACTIONS, ROYAL SOCIETY OF NEW ZEA-
LAND: GEOLOGY FROM 1, 1961 - 6, 1969. SUBS.
PART OF: JOURNAL OF THE ROYAL SOCIETY OF
NEW ZEALAND
GL/U-2.    LD/U-1.   LO/N14.   MA/U-1.

TRANSACTIONS OF THE ROYAL SOCIETY OF NEW
ZEALAND: GEOLOGY.                                    XXX
++TRANS. R. SOC. N.Z., GEOL. [TRZG-A]
WELLINGTON, NZ. 1, 22/S 1961- 6, 1969...
TO 88, 1961 THE TRANS. APPEARED AS A SINGLE
PUBL. THEN DIVIDED INTO FOUR SECTIONS. SUBS:
TRANS. ROYAL SOCIETY OF NEW ZEALAND: EARTH
SCIENCES.
ED/U-1.    GL/U-1.   HL/U-1.   LO/N-4.   LO/U-2.   LV/U-1.
GL/U-2. 2, 1963/65-*

TRANSACTIONS, SOCIETY FOR ADVANCEMENT OF
ELECTROCHEMICAL SCIENCE & TECHNOLOGY (INDIA).
++TRANS. SOC. ADV. ELECTROCHEM. SCI. & TECHNOL.
(INDIA).
CECRINAGAR 1, JA 1966-
Q.
LO/N14.

TRANSACTIONS, TEESSIDE INDUSTRIAL ARCHAEOLOGY
GROUP.
++TRANS. TEESSIDE IND. ARCHAEOL. GROUP.
MIDDLESBROUGH 1, 1968-
BN/U-1.    LO/N-4.

TRANSACTIONS, WELSH HYMNMASTERS' SOCIETY.                    000
SEE: TRAFODION, CYMDEITHAS EMYNWYR CYMRU.

TRANSAFRICAN JOURNAL OF HISTORY.
++TRANSAFR. J. HIST.
[EAST AFRICAN PUBL. HOUSE]
NAIROBI &CO.  1(1), JA 1971-
PUBLISHED FOR THE DEPARTMENTS OF HISTORY OF
MAKERERE UNIVERSITY, UNIVERSITY OF NAIROBI,
UNIVERSITY OF DAR ES SALAAM, UNIVERSITY OF
ZAMBIA & UNIVERSITY OF MALAWI.
LO/U-3.    LO/U-8.    OX/U-9.
CA/U-1. 3, 1973-
ISSN 0041-106X

TRANSKEI LIBERAL NEWS.                                       XXX
SUBS (1969): REALITY.

TRANSLATION NEWS.
++TRANSL. NEWS.
EUROPEAN TRANSLATIONS CENTRE.
DELFT NO.1, 1971-
DB/U-1.    HL/U-1.**    LO/N-2.    SF/U-1.
ISSN 0046-2837

TRANSLATIONS REGISTER-INDEX.
++TRANS. REGIST.-INDEX.
SPECIAL LIBRARIES ASSOCIATION.
CHICAGO 1, 1967-
COMPILED BY THE ASSOCIATION'S TRANSLATIONS
CENTER.
DB/U-2.    LO/N14.    SO/U-1.
EX/U-1. 2(1), 1968-          GL/U-2. 4, 1970-
MA/P-1. 4, 1970-
ISSN 0041-1256

TRANSLOG.  JOURNAL OF MILITARY TRANSPORTA-
TION MANAGEMENT.                                             XXX
(UNITED STATES) MILITARY TRAFFIC MANAGEMENT &
TERMINAL SERVICE.
WASHINGTON, D.C. 1, F 1970-
M. PREV: TRANSPORTATION PROCEEDINGS FROM
1(1), F 1967- 3(12), JA 1970.
LO/N13.
ISSN 0041-1639

TRANSPLANTATION PROCEEDINGS.
++TRANSPLANT. PROC.
[HENRY M. STRATTON INC.]
NEW YORK 1, MR 1969-
LO/M-3.    OX/U-1.    OX/U-8.    SH/U-1.
NW/U-1. 2, 1970-
ISSN 0041-1345

TRANSPLANTATION REVIEWS.
++TRANSPLANT. REV.
[MUNKSGAARD]
COPENHAGEN 1, JE 1969-
BL/U-1.    DB/U-2.    GL/U-1.    LO/N13.    NW/U-1.    OX/U-8.
SH/U-1. 5, 1970.

TRANSPORT BOOKMAN.
++TRANSP. BOOKMAN.
LONDON NO.1, 1970-
ED/N-1.    LO/N-4.    OX/U-1.

TRANSPORT ENGINEER.                                          XXX
++TRANSP. ENG.
INSTITUTE OF ROAD TRANSPORT ENGINEERS.
LONDON 1970-
PREV: JOURNAL & PROCEEDINGS, INSTITUTE ...
FROM 1, 1947- 23(2), 1969.
ED/N-1.    LO/N-7.    LO/N14.
ISSN 0020-3122

TRANSPORT & MATERIALS HANDLING.
++TRANSP. & MATER. HANDL.
DUBLIN 1, 1972-
DB/U-2.    ED/N-1.    OX/U-1.

TRANSPORT RESEARCH BULLETIN.
++TRANSP. RES. BULL.
CHARTERED INSTITUTE OF TRANSPORT.
LONDON NO.1, 1971-
SUPPL. TO THE INSTITUTE'S JOURNAL.
LO/N14.

TRANSPORT TEKNIK.
++TRANSP. TEKH.
[AGRO TEKNISKA FORLAGET]
STOCKHOLM 1, 1969-
LO/N14.
ISSN 0041-154X

TRANSPORT THEORY & STATISTICAL PHYSICS.
++TRANSP. THEORY & STAT. PHYS.
[DEKKER]
NEW YORK 1, JA 1971-
Q.
AD/U-1.    GL/U-2.    LO/N14.    LO/U12.    SF/U-1.    XY/N-1.
SO/U-1. 3, 1973-
ISSN 0041-1450

TRANSPORT TRAINING. NEWSPAPER OF THE ...
++TRANSP. TRAIN.
ROAD TRANSPORT INDUSTRY BOARD.
LONDON 1, JL 1968-
ED/N-1.    OX/U-1.
LO/U-3. [CURRENT ISSUES ONLY]

TRANSPORTATION.
[ELSEVIER]
AMSTERDAM 1, MY 1972-
GL/U-1.    GL/U-2.    LO/N-1.    LO/N14.    SH/U-1.    SH/U-3.
ISSN 0049-4488

TRANSPORTATION BULLETIN.
++TRANSP. BULL.
UNITED KINGDOM SCIENTIFIC MISSION (US).
WASHINGTON, DC  NO.1, S 1966-
HL/U-1.    LO/N14.

TRANSPORTATION NOISE BULLETIN.
++TRANSP. NOISE BULL.
HIGHWAY RESEARCH BOARD (US).
WASHINGTON, D.C. 1, OC 1971-
LD/U-1.    SO/U-1.
LO/N14. 1(2), 1972-

TRANSPORTATION PLANNING & TECHNOLOGY.
++TRANSP. PLANN. & TECHNOL.
[GORDON & BREACH]
NEW YORK; LONDON 1, 1972-
CA/U-1.    ED/N-1.    GL/U-1.    LD/U-1.    LO/N14.    OX/U-1.
SH/U-3.

TRANSPORTATION PROCEEDINGS.                                  XXX
++TRANSP. PROC.
(UNITED STATES) MILITARY TRAFFIC MANAGEMENT &
TERMINAL SERVICE.
WASHINGTON, D.C. 1(1), F 1967- 3(12), JA 1970.
M. SUBS: TRANSLOG.
LO/N13.*

TRAVAIL DES METAUX PAR DEFORMATION.                         000
SEE: METAUX DEFORMATION.

TRAVAIL THEATRAL.
++TRAV. THEATRAL.
LAUSANNE NO.1, 1970-
CA/U-1.    GL/U-1.
DB/U-2. NO.10, 1973-
ISSN 0049-4534

TRAVAUX DE BIOLOGIE.
++TRAV. BIOL. (CAN.)
MONTREAL NO.1, 1966-
LO/N-2.

TRAVAUX DE DOCTORAT EN THEOLOGIE ET EN DROIT
CANONIQUE.
++TRAV. DOCT. THEOL. & DROIT CANON.
LOUVAIN 1, 1969-
OX/U-1.

TRAVAUX, FACULTE DES SCIENCES, UNIVERSITE DE
RENNES: SERIE OCEANOGRAPHIE BIOLOGIQUE.
++TRAV. FAC. SCI. UNIV. RENNES, OCEANOGR. BIOL.
RENNES 1, 1968-
LO/N-2.

TRAVAUX DES JEUNES SCIENTIFIQUES.
++TRAV. JEUNES SCI.
ASSOCIATION DES JEUNES SCIENTIFIQUES.
MONTREAL 1, 1964-
LO/N-2.

TRAVAUX ET JOURS.  REVUE TRIMESTRIELLE.
++TRAV. & JOURS.
UNIVERSITE ST. JOSEPH (BEIRUT).
BEIRUT NO.1, 1961-
LO/U14.
ISSN 0041-1930

TRAVAUX DU LABORATOIRE DE GEOLOGIE DE LA FAC-
ULTE DES SCIENCES DE GRENOBLE                                    XXX
 SUBS (1966): GEOLOGIE ALPINE.

TRAVAUX ET RECHERCHES DE SCIENCE POLITIQUE.
 ++TRAV. & RECH. SCI. POLIT.
 FONDATION NATIONALE DES SCIENCES POLITIQUES
 (FRANCE).
  PARIS 1, 1969-
  LO/N-1.    OX/U-1.
  ISSN 0041-2678

TRAVAUX, SECTION DE PHILOLOGIE ET HISTOIRE
ORIENTALE, UNIVERSITE CATHOLIQUE DE LOUVAIN.
 ++TRAV. SECT. PHILOL. & HIST. ORIENT. UNIV.
 CATHOL. LOUV.
  LOUVAIN 1, 1972-
  SECTION SUBORD. TO: FACULTE DE PHILOSOPHIE ET
  LETTRES.
  OX/U-1.

TRAVELLING.
 BRITISH RAILWAYS BOARD.
  LONDON  JA 1972-
  LO/N-1.    OX/U-1.

TREE TALKS.
 CENTRAL NEW YORK GENEALOGICAL SOCIETY.
  NEW YORK  1, MR 1961-
  ED/N-1.  3, 1963-
  ISSN 0041-2201

TREND.
 NATIONAL YOUTH TEMPERANCE COUNCIL.
  LONDON  NO.1, SUMMER 1967-
  Q. PREV: NOTES & NEWS, NATIONAL YOUTH TEMPER-
  ANCE COUNCIL.
  ED/N-1.

TRENDS & TOPICS.
 ASSOCIATION OF ARTS CENTRES IN SCOTLAND.
  EDINBURGH  NO.1, OC 1971-
  ED/N-1.    OX/U-1.

TRESORS INCONNUS DU MUSEE DE MARIEMONT.
 ++TRESORS INCONNUS MUS. MARIEMONT.
  MARIEMONT, BELG.  NO.1, 1966-
  LO/N-1.  NO.6, 1972-

TRIBOLOGY.
 [ILIFFE]
  GUILDFORD  1(1), JA 1968-
  Q.
  OX/U-8.
  LO/N-7.  3(3), 1970-            SH/C-5.  3(3), 1970-

TRIBOLOGY, LUBRICATION, FRICTION & WEAR.
 ++TRIBOL. LUBRIC. FRICT. & WEAR.
  GUILDFORD  1(1), 1968-
  LO/N-4.
  MA/P-1.  2, 1969-               RE/U-1.  2, 1969-
  ISSN 0041-2678

TRIBOLOGY NEWS.
 ++TRIBOL. NEWS.
 INSTITUTION OF MECHANICAL ENGINEERS.
  LONDON   ISSUE [NO.]1, N 1966-
  XS/R10.

TRIBOS. TRIBOLOGY ABSTRACTS.
 BRITISH HYDROMECHANICS RESEARCH ASSOCIATION.
  CRANFIELD  1(1/2), JA/F 1968-
  M., AFTER FIRST ISSUE. S/T. VARIES.
  BN/U-1.    GL/U-2.    LO/N14.    OX/U-8.    SW/U-1.
  XS/R10.
  ED/N-1.  1(5),1968-            LO/N-4.  2(1), 1969-

TRIO.                                                            XXX
 SUBS (1964): PART OF FAMILY CIRCLE.

TRI-QUARTERLY: SUPPLEMENT.
 NORTHWESTERN UNIVERSITY.
  EVANSTON, ILL.  NO.1, 1967-
  OX/U-1.

TROLL.  A MAGAZINE OF ARTICLES, REVIEWS,
ILLUSTRATIONS, POEMS, STORIES & LETTERS.
  [LONDON]  1, SUMMER 1965-
  OX/U-1.

TROPICAL AGRICULTURE RESEARCH SERIES (JAPAN).
 ++TROP. AGR. RES. SER. (JAP.).
 NORIN-SHO NORIN SUISAN GIJUTSU KAIGI.
  TOKYO  NO.1, 1967-
  LO/N13.

TROPICAL ANIMAL HEALTH & PRODUCTION.
 ++TROP. ANIM. HEALTH & PROD.
 UNIVERSITY OF EDINBURGH: CENTRE FOR TROPICAL
 VETERINARY MEDICINE.
 [E & S LIVINGSTONE LTD.]
  EDINBURGH &C  1(1), AU 1969-
  ED/N-1.    LO/M18.    LO/N13.    LO/N17.    OX/U-8.
  XS/U-1.
  GL/U-2.  2, 1970-
  ISSN 0049-4747

TROPICAL DOCTOR.
 ++TROP. DOC.
 ROYAL SOCIETY OF MEDICINE.
  LONDON  1(1), 1971-
  S/T: JOURNAL OF MODERN MEDICAL PRACTICE.
  CO/U-1.    ED/N-1.    LO/N-1.    OX/U-8.    XY/N-1.
  BL/U-1.  3, 1973-
  ISSN 0049-4755

TROPICAL GRASSLANDS.
 ++TROP. GRASSL.
 TROPICAL GRASSLAND SOCIETY OF AUSTRALIA.
  BRISBANE  1(1), MY 1967-
  BN/U-2.    LO/R-6.    XS/R-4.
  LO/N13.  2, 1968-
  ISSN 0049-4763

TROPICAL MAN.                                                    XXX
 ++TROP. MAN.
 KONINKLIJKE INSTITUUT VOOR DE TROPEN:
 (ANTHROPOLOGY DEPARTMENT).
 [BRILL]
  LEYDEN  1, 1968-
  PREV: INTERNATIONAL ARCHIVES OF ETHNOGRAPHY
  FROM 1, 1888.
  GL/U-1.    LON-17.    OX/U-8.

TROPICAL PEST BULLETIN.
 ++TROP. PEST BULL.
 CENTRE FOR OVERSEAS PEST RESEARCH.
  LONDON  1, 1972-
  CA/U11.    LO/N-2.    LO/S13.    LO/U-4.    OX/U-8.

TROPICAL STORAGE ABSTRACTS.
 ++TROP. STORAGE ABSTR.
 TROPICAL STORED PRODUCTS CENTRE.
  SLOUGH, BUCKS.  1, 1973-
  CA/U-1.    LO/N-6.    LO/N14.    LO/R-6.

TRUDOVE PO BULGARSKA DIALEKTOLOGIJA.
 ++TR. BULG. DIALEKTOL.
 BULGARSKA AKADEMIJA NA NAUKITE: INSTITUT ZA
 BULGARSKI EZIK.
  SOFIA  1, 1965-
  MONOGR.
  CA/U-1.    ED/N-1.

TRUDOVI NA KATEDRATA ZA ISTORIJA NA KNIZEV-
NOSTITE NA NARODITE NA FNR JUGOSLAVIJA.
 ++TR. KATEDRATA ISTOR. KNIZEVNOSTITE NAR. FNR
 JUGOSLAV.
 UNIVERZITET SKOPJE: KATEDRA ZA ISTORIJA NA
 KNIZEVNOSTITE NA NARODITE FNRJ.
  SKOPJE  GOD 1, 1960-
  6M.  KATEDRA ZA ISTORIJA ... SUBORD. TO: FILO-
  ZOFSKI FAKULTET OF THE UNIVERSITY.
  LO/N-3.

TRUDOVE VURKHU GEOLOGIJATA NA BULGARIJA:
SERIJA INZHENERNA GEOLOGIJA I KHIDROGEOLOGIJA.
 ++TR. VURKHU GEOL. BULG., INZH. GEOL. &
  KHIDROGEOL. [TVBK-A]
 BULGARSKA AKADEMIJA NA NAUKITE: GEOLOGICHESKI
 INSTITUT.
  SOFIA  1, 1962-
  ENGL., FR., GER. OR RUSS. SUMM.
  LO/N13.
  GL/U-1.  5, 1966-

TRUDY ALMA-ATINSKOGO GOSUDARSTVENNOGO NAUCHNO-
ISSLEDOVATEL'SKOGO INSTITUTA STROITEL'NYKH
MATERIALOV.                                                      XXX
 ++TR. ALMA-AT. GOS. NAUCHNO-ISSLED. INST. STROIT
  MATER. [TASM-B]
  ALMA-ATA  5(7), 1963-
  PREV: TRUDY KAZAKHSKOGO FILIALA AKADEMII
  STROITEL'STVA I ARKHITEKTURY SSSR FROM 1(3),
  1959- 4(6), 1962.
  LO/N13.  7(9), 1966-

**TRUDY ARKTICHESKOGO I ANTARKTICHESKOGO NAUCHNO-ISSLEDOVATEL'SKOGO INSTITUTA ...**     XXX
++TR. ARKT. & ANTARKT. NAUCH.-ISSLED. INST. [TAAI-A]
ARKTICHESKIJ I ANTARKTICHESKIJ NAUCHNO-ISSLEDOVATEL'SKIJ INSTITUT (LENINGRAD).
*LENINGRAD   TOM 218, (1960)-*
FULL TITLE CONTINUES: ... GLAVNOGO UPRAVLENIJA SEVERNOGO MOSKOGO PUTI MINISTERSTVA MORSKOGO FLOTA SSSR. NOT PUBL. IN STRICT CHRONOL. ORDER: 221, 1958; 219, 1957 &C. PREV: TRUDY ARKTICHESKOGO NAUCHNO-ISSLEDOVATEL'SKOGO INSTITUTA.
*BH/U-1.   CA/U12.*
*LO/N-2. 259,1964-            LON/13. 1961-*

**TRUDY, ARMJANSKAJA PROTIVOCHUMNAJA STANTSIJA.**
++TR. ARM. PROTIVOCHUMNAJA STN.
*EREVAN 1, 1960-*
*LO/N-2. 2, 1963-            LO/N13. 2, 1963-*

**TRUDY AZERBAJDZHANSKOGO NAUCHNO-ISSLEDOVATEL'-SKOGO INSTITUTA MEKHANIZATSII I ELEKTRIFIK-ATSII SEL'SKOGO KHOZJAJSTVA.**
++TR. AZERB. NAUCHNO-ISSLED. INST. MEKH. & ELEKTRIF. SEL'SK. KHOZ.
AZERBAJDZHANSKIJ NAUCHNO-ISSLEDOVATEL'SKIJ INSTITUT MEKHANIZATSII I ELEKTRIFIKATSII SEL'SKOGO KHOZJAJSTVA.
*KIROVABAD 1, 1961-*
*LO/N13.*

**TRUDY BURJATSKOGO INSTITUTA OBSHCHESTVENNYKH NAUK.**
++TR. BURJAT. INST. OBSHCHESTV. NAUK.
AKADEMIJA NAUK SSSR (SIBIRSKOE OTDELENIE): BURJATSKIJ INSTITUT OBSHCHESTVENNYKH NAUK.
*ULAN-UDE 3, 1967-*
MONOGR. BURJATSKIJ INSTITUT ... SUBORD. TO BURJATSKIJ FILIAL.
*LO/U14.*
*CC/U-1. 5, 1968-            GL/U-1. 3, 1967-*
*OX/U-1. 4, 1967-*

**TRUDY DAL'NEVOSTOCHNOGO TEKHNICHESKOGO INST-ITUTA RYBNOJ PROMYSHLENNOSTI I KHOZJAJSTVA.**
++TR. DAL'NEVOST. TEKH. INST. RYBN. PROM-ST. & KHOZ. [TDRP-A]
*VLADIVOSTOK 1, 1960-*
IRR. VOL. 2 PUBL. IN 1958.
*LO/N13. 3(1963) & 5(1967).*

**TRUDY DNEPROPETROVSKOGO INSTITUTA CHERNOJ METALLURGII.**     XXX
++TR. DNEPROPETR. INST. CHERN. METALL. [TDIC-A]
*KIEV 19, 1965- 20, 1965.*
PREV: TRUDY INSTITUTA CHERNOJ METALLURGII AKADEMII NAUK UKRAINSKOJ SSR FROM 1, 1947-18, 1962. SUBS: NAUCHNYE TRUDY, INSTITUT CHERNOJ METALLURGII GOSUDARSTVENNOGO KOMITETA PO CHERNOJI TSVETNOJ METALLURGII PRI GOSPLANE SSSR.
*LO/N13.   LO/S56.*

**TRUDY EL'BRUSSKOJ VYSOKOGORNOJ KOMPLEKSNOJ EKSPEDITSII.**     XXX
SUBS (1966): TRUDY, VYSOKOGORNYJ GEOFIZICH-ESKIJ INSTITUT (NAL'CHIK).

**TRUDY GEOLOGICHESKOGO INSTITUTA AKADEMII NAUK GRUZINSKOJ SSR: NOVAJA SERIJA.**
++TR. GEOL. INST. AKAD. NAUK. GRUZ. SSR, NS.
*TIFLIS 1, 1965-*
*LO/N13.   LO/N14.*

**TRUDY GIDROMETEOROLOGICHESKOGO NAUCHNO-ISSLE-DOVATEL'SKOGO TSENTRA SSSR.**
GLAVNOE UPRAVLENIE GIDROMETEOROLOGICHESKOJ SLUZHBY PRI SOVETE MINISTROV SSSR: GIDROMETEOR-OLOGICHESKIJ NAUCHNO-ISSLEDOVATEL'SKIJ TSENTR SSSR.
*MOSCOW 1, 1967-*
*BH/U-1.   LO/N13.*

**TRUDY, GOSUDARSTVENNYJ INSTITUT PO PROEKTIROVAN-IJU MORSKIKH PORTOV I SUDOREMONTNYKH PREDPRI-JATII.**     XXX
SUBS (1962): TRUDY, GOSUDARSTVENNYJ PROEKTNO-KONSTRUKTORSKIJ I NAUCHNO-ISSLEDOVATEL'SKIJ INSTITUT MORSKOGO TRANSPORTA.

**TRUDY, GOSUDARSTVENNYJ MEDITSINSKIJ INSTITUT.**     XXX
++TR. GOS. MED. INST.
*ALMA-ATA 20, 1962-*
PREV: NAUCHNYE IZVESTIJA, KAZAKHSKIJ GOSUD-ARSTVENNYJ MEDITSINSKIJ INSTITUT FROM 1, 1935-19, 1962.
*LO/N13. 22, 1965-*

**TRUDY, GOSUDARSTVENNYJ PROEKTNO-KONSTRUKTOR-SKIJ I NAUCHNO-ISSLEDOVATEL'SKIJ INSTITUT MORSKOGO TRANSPORTA.**     XXX
++TR. GOS. PROEKTNO-KONSTR. & NAUCHNO-ISSLED. INST. MORSK. TRANSP. [TGPN-A]
*MOSCOW 1(7), 1962-*
PREV: TRUDY, GOSUDARSTVENNYJ INSTITUT PO PRO-EKTIROVANIJU MORSKIKH PORTOV I SUDOREMONTNYKH PREDPRIJATII FROM 1, 1956- 6, 1959. CONT. NUMB. IN PARENTHESES.
*BH/U-1.   CC/U-1.*

**TRUDY, GOSUDARSTVENNYJ VSESOJUZNYJ INSTITUT PO PROEKTIROVANIJU I NAUCHNO-ISSLEDOVATEL'-SKIM RABOTAM 'JUZHGIPROTSEMENT'.**
++TR. GOS. VSES. INST. PROEKT. & NAUCHNO-ISSLED. RAB. JUZHGIPROTSEMENT.
*KIEV 1, 1960-*
*SW/U-1.*

**TRUDY GOSUDARSTVENNYKH ZAPOVEDNIKOV ESTONSKOJ SSR.**
++TR. GOS. ZAPOVEDNIKOV EST. SSR.
(ESTONIA) METSAMAJANDUSE JA LOODUSKAITSE MINISTEERIUM.
*TALLIN 1, 1968-*
RUSS. WITH ENGL. SUMM. BODY IN RUSS.: MINIST-ERSTVO LESNOGO KHOZJAJSTVA I OKHRANY PRIRODY ESTONSKOJ SSR.
*LO/N13.*

**TRUDY, GRUZINSKIJ NAUCHNO-ISSLEDOVATEL'SKIJ INSTITUT PISHCHEVOJ PROMYSHLENNOSTI.**
++TR. GRUZ. NAUCHNO-ISSLED. INST. PISHCH. PROM-ST. [TGNP-B]
*MOSCOW 1, 1965-*
RUSS. & GEORG.
*LO/N13.*

**TRUDY INSTITUTA CHERNOJ METALLURGII AKADEMII NAUK UKRAINSKOJ SSR.**     XXX
SUBS (1965): TRUDY DNEPROPETROVSKOGO INSTIT-UTA CHERNOJ METALLURGII.

**TRUDY INSTITUTA EKONOMIKI AKADEMII NAUK LATVIJSKOJ SSR.**
++TR. INST. EKON. AKAD. NAUK LATV. SSR.
*RIGA 1, 1961-*
RUSS.
*GL/U-1.   LO/U-3.   NR/U-1.   SW/U-1.*

**TRUDY, INSTITUT ELEKTRONIKI, AVTOMATIKI I TELEMEKHANIKI AKADEMII NAUK GRUZINSKOJ SSR.**
++TR. INST. ELEKTRON. AVTOM. & TELEMEKH. AKAD. NAUK GRUZ. SSR.
*TIFLIS 1, 1960-*
GEORG. & RUSS.
*BH/U-1.   LO/N13.*

**TRUDY INSTITUTA GEOLOGII I GEOFIZIKI, AKADEM-IJA NAUK SSSR (SIBIRSKOE OTDELENIE).**
++TR. INST. GEOL. & GEOFIZ. AKAD. NAUK SSSR (SIB. OTD.).
*NOVOSIBIRSK 1, 1960-*
*BH/U-1.   HL/U-1.   LO/N13.   OX/U-8.*

**TRUDY INSTITUTA GEOLOGII, GOSUDARSTVENNYJ GEOLOGICHESKIJ KOMITET SSSR.**
++TR. INST. GEOL. GOS. GEOL. KOM. SSSR.
*VILNA 1, 1965-*
LITH. SUMM. & TITLE: GEOLOGIJAS INSTITUTAS DARBAI.
*LO/N-2.   LO/N-4.*

**TRUDY INSTITUTA GEOLOGII KOMI FILIALA AKAD-EMII NAUK SSSR.**
++TR. INST. GEOL. KOMI FIL. AKAD. NAUK SSSR. [TGGS-A]
*SYKTYVKAR 1, 1960-*
IRR.
*CA/U12.   LO/N13.*

**TRUDY, INSTITUT GEOLOGII I RAZRABOTKI GORJU-CHIKH ISKOPAEMYKH AKADEMII NAUK SSSR.**
++TR. INST. GEOL. & RAZRAB. GORJUCH. ISKOP. AKAD. NAUK SSSR. [TGRG-A]
*MOSCOW 1, 1960-*
*LO/N13.*

**TRUDY INSTITUTA GIDROGEOLOGII I GIDROFIZIKI AKADEMII NAUK KAZAKHSKOJ SSR.**
++TR. INST. GIDROGEOL. I GIDROFIZ. AKAD. NAUK KAZ. SSR. [TIGD-B]
*ALMA-ATA 1, 1968-*
*BH/U-1.   OX/U-8. 2, 1969-*

TRUDY INSTYTUTU HEOLOHICHNYKH NAUK: SERIJA
HEOTEKTONIKY.                                           XXX
+ +TR. INST. HEOLOHICHNYKH NAUK, HEOTEKTONIKY.
AKADEMIJA NAUK UKRAJINS'KOJI RSR: INSTYTUT
HEOLOHICHNYKH NAUK.
  KIEV 10, 1962-
  PREV: TRUDY INSTYTUTU HEOLOHICHNYKH NAUK:
  SERIJA HEOTEKTONIKY I HEOFIZYKY FROM 3, 1958-
  9, 1959.
  LO/N13.

TRUDY INSTYTUTU HEOLOHICHNYKH NAUK: SERIJA
HEOTEKTONIKY I HEOFIZYKY.                               XXX
  SUBS (1962): TRUDY INSTYTUTU HEOLOHICHNYKH
  NAUK: SERIJA HEOTEKTONIKY.

TRUDY INSTYTUTU HEOLOHICHNYKH NAUK: SERIJA
ZAHAL'NOJI HEOLOHIJI.
+ +TR. INST. HEOLOHICHNYKH NAUK, ZAHAL'NOJI
  HEOLOHIJI.
  KIEV 1, 1962-
  LO/N-8.   LO/N13.

TRUDY INSTITUTA JAZYKA I LITERATURY AKADEMII
NAUK TURKMENSKOJ SSR.                                   XXX
  SUBS (1960): PART OF TRUDY INSTITUTA LITERAT-
  URY AKADEMII NAUK TURKMENSKOJ SSR; & (1962)
  TRUDY INSTITUTA JAZYKOZNANIJA AKADEMII NAUK
  TURKMENSKOJ SSR.

TRUDY INSTITUTA JAZYKOZNANIJA AKADEMII NAUK
TURKMENSKOJ SSR.                                        XXX
+ +TR. INST. JAZYKOZNANIJA AKAD. NAUK TURKM. SSR.
  AKHKHABAD 4, 1962-
  PREV: PART OF TRUDY INSTITUTA JAZYKA I LITER-
  ATURY AKADEMII NAUK TURKMENSKOJ SSR FROM 1,
  1956- 3, 1959.
  LO/N-3.   OX/U-1.

TRUDY INSTITUTA KIBERNETIKI AKADEMII NAUK
GRUZINSKOJ SSR.
+ +TR. INST. KIBERN. AKAD. NAUK GRUZ. SSR.
  TIFLIS 1, 1963-
  CA/U-2.

TRUDY INSTITUTA KOMPLEKSNYKH TRANSPORTNYKH
PROBLEM.
+ +TR. INST. KOMPLEKSN. TRANSP. PROBL.
  (RUSSIA USSR) GOSPLAN: INSTITUT KOMPLEKSNYKH
  TRANSPORTNYKH PROBLEM.
  MOSCOW 1, 1966-
  LO/U-3.   OX/U-1.

TRUDY INSTITUTA LITERATURY AKADEMII NAUK
TURKMENSKOJ SSR.                                        XXX
+ +TR. INST. LIT. AKAD. NAUK TURKM. SSR.
  AKADEMIJA NAUK TURKMENSKOJ SSR: INSTITUT
  LITERATURY.
  ASHKHABAD 4, 1960-
  PREV: PART OF TRUDY INSTITUTA JAZYKA I LITER-
  ATURY AKADEMII NAUK TURKMENSKOJ SSR FROM 1,
  1956- 3, 1959.
  LO/N-3.   OX/U-1.

TRUDY INSTITUTA PRIKLADNOJ GEOFIZIKI GLAVNOGO
UPRAVLENIJA GIDROMETEOROLOGICHESKOJ SLUZHBY.
+ +TR. INST. PRIKL. GEOFIZ. GL. UPR. GIDROMET-
  EOROL. SLUZHBY.
  MOSCOW 1, 1965-
  LO/N13.   XS/N-1.

TRUDY INSTITUTA PRIKLADNOJ MATEMATIKI, TBIL-
ISSKIJ GOSUDARSTVENNYJ UNIVERSITET.
+ +TR. INST. PRIKL. MAT. TBILIS. GOS. UNIV.
  TIFLIS 1, 1969-
  RUSS. WITH GEORG. SUMM.
  DB/S-1.   GL/U-1.   LO/U-2.

TRUDY INSTITUTA VODNOGO KHOZJAJSTVA.                    000
  SEE: PRACE INSTYTUTU GOSPODARKI WODNEJ.

TRUDY INSTITUTA VYSSHEJ NERVNOJ DEJATEL'NOSTI,
AKADEMIJA NAUK SSSR: SERIJA
FIZIOLOGICHESKAJA.                                      XXX
+ +TR. INST. VYSSH. NERV. DEJATEL'NOSTI, AKAD.
  NAUK. SSSR, FIZIOL.
  MOSCOW TOM 1, 1955- 7, 1962. //
  LO/M17.   LO/N-1.   LO/N13.   OX/U-1.

TRUDY INSTITUTA VYSSHEJ NERVNOJ DEJATEL'NOSTI,
AKADEMIJA NAUK SSSR: SERIJA
PATOFIZIOLOGICHESKAJA.
+ +TR. INST. VYSSH. NERV. DEJATEL'NOSTI, AKAD.
  NAUK SSSR, PATOFIZIOL.
  MOSCOW TOM 1, 1955- 10, 1962. //
  LO/N-1.   XY/N-1.
  0568-6059

TRUDY KAFEDR OBSHCHESTVENNYKH NAUK BARNAUL'-
SKOGO GOSUDARSTVENNOGO PEDAGOGICHESKOGO
INSTITUTA.
+ +TR. KAFEDR OBSHCHESTV. NAUK BARNAUL'SKOGO GOS.
  PEDAGOG. INST.
  BARNAUL 1, 1966-
  CC/U-1.   OX/U-1.

TRUDY, KAZAKHSKIJ POLITEKHNICHESKIJ INSTITUT.           XXX
+ +TR. KAZ. POLITEKH. INST.
  ALMA-ATA 21, 1960-
  PREV: SBORNIK NAUCHNYKH TRUDOV, KAZAKHSKIJ
  GORNO-METALLURGICHESKIJ INSTITUT FROM 1, 1938-
  20, 1959.  TITLE VARIES: VOL.21: SBORNIK
  NAUCHNYKH TRUDOV, KAZAKHSKIJ POLITEKHNICHESKIJ
  INSTITUT. VOLS 22(1962) & 25(1965): NAUCHNYE
  TRUDY, KAZAKHSKIJ POLITEKHNICHESKIJ INSTITUT.
  LO/N13.

TRUDY KAZAKHSKOGO FILIALA AKADEMII STROITEL'STVA
I ARKHITEKTURY SSSR.                                    XXX
  SUBS (1963): TRUDY ALMA-ATINSKOGO GOSUDARST-
  VENNOGO NAUCHNO-ISSLEDOVATEL'SKOGO INSTITUTA
  STROITEL'NYKH MATERIALOV.

TRUDY, KISHINEVSKIJ POLITEKHNICHESKIJ
INSTITUT.
+ +TR. KISHINEV. POLITEKH. INST.
  KISHINEV 1, 1964-
  LO/N13.

TRUDY, KRASNODARSKIJ NAUCHNO-ISSLEDOVATEL'-
SKIJ INSTITUT SEL'SKOGO KHOZJAJSTVA.
+ +TR. KRASNODARS. NAUCHNO ISSLED. INST. SEL'SK.
  KHOZ.
  KRASNODAR 1, 1963-
  TITLE VARIES SOME ISSUES: 'NAUCHNYE TRUDY'.
  LO/N13. 2, 1966-

TRUDY LABORATORII EVOLJUTSIONNOJ I EKOLOGI-
CHESKOJ FIZIOLOGII [IM. B.A. KELLERA], AKAD-
EMIJA NAUK SSSR.                                        XXX
+ +TR. LAB. EVOL.& EKOL. FIZIOL. [IM. B.A.
  KELLERA], AKAD. NAUK SSSR.
  MOSCOW TOM 4, 1962-
  PREV: TRUDY LABORATORII EVOLJUTSIONNOJ
  EKOLOGII RASTENIJ [IM. B.A. KELLERA] FROM 1,
  1940- 3, 1952.
  LO/N-2.

TRUDY LABORATORII EVOLJUTSIONNOJ EKOLOGII
RASTENIJ [IM. B. A. KELLERA].                           XXX
  SUBS (1962):  TRUDY LABORATORII EVOLJUTSIONNOJ
  I EKOLOGICHESKOJ FIZIOLOGII [IM. BA.
  KELLERA], AKADEMIJA NAUK SSSR.

TRUDY, LENINGRADSKIJ INSTITUT INZHENEROV
VODNOGO TRANSPORTA.                                     XXX
  SUBS (1960): TRUDY, LENINGRADSKIJ INSTITUT
  VODNOGO TRANSPORTA LIVT.

TRUDY LENINGRADSKIJ INSTITUT VODNOGO TRANS-
PORTA LIVT.                                             XXX
+ +TR. LENINGR. INST. VODN. TRANSP. LIVT.
  LENINGRAD 1, 1960-
  PREV: TRUDY, LENINGRADSKIJ INSTITUT INZHENEROV
  VODNOGO TRANSPORTA FROM 1, 1832- 26, 1959.
  LO/N13.

TRUDY MATEMATICHESKOGO INSTITUTA IMENI V.A.
STEKLOVA (ENGL. TRANSL.).                               000
  SEE: PROCEEDINGS OF THE STEKLOV INSTITUTE OF
  MATHEMATICS.

TRUDY I MATERIALY NAUCHNYKH KONGRESSOV I
SOVESHCHANIJ OPUBLIKOVANNYE ZA RUBEZHOM.
+ +TR. & MATER. NAUCHN. KONGR. & SOV. OPUBLIKO-
  VANNYE RUBEZHOM.
  AKADEMIJA NAUK SSSR: BIBLIOTEKA.
  LENINGRAD 1, 1960(1961)-
  CC/U-1.   LO/U-1.

TRUDY, MOLDAVSKIJ NAUCHNO-ISSLEDOVATEL'SKIJ
INSTITUT ZHIVOTNOVODSTVA I VETERINARII.
+ +TR. MOLD. NAUCHNO-ISSLED. INST. ZHIVOTNOVOD. &
  VET.
  KISHINEV 1, 1963-
  LO/N13.

TRUDY MORDOVSKOGO GOSUDARSTVENNOGO ZAPOVED-
NIKA.
+ +TR. MORD. GOS. ZAPOVED. [TMGZ-A]
  SARANSK 1, 1960-
  LO/N13.

**TRUDY MORDOVSKOGO NAUCHNO-ISSLEDOVATEL'SKOGO INSTITUTA JAZYKA, LITERATURY, ISTORII I EKONOMIKI.**    XXX
*++TR. MORD. NAUCH.-ISSLED. INST. JAZYKA LIT. ISTOR. EKON.*
MORDOVSKIJ NAUCHNO-ISSLEDOVATEL'SKIJ INSTITUT JAZYKA, LITERATURY, ISTORII I EKONOMIKI.
*SARANSK VYP. 20, 1960-*
PREV: ZAPISKI, NAUCHNO-ISSLEDOVATEL'SKIJ INSTITUT JAZYKA, LITERATURY, ISTORII I EKONOMIKI FROM 16, 1955- 19, 1958.
*LO/N-3. 23, 1962-*

**TRUDY MOSKOVSKOGO MEDITSINSKOGO STOMATOLOGICHESKOGO INSTITUTA.**    XXX
SUBS (1960): TEORIJA I PRAKTIKA STOMATOLOGII.

**TRUDY MURMANSKOJ BIOLOGICHESKOJ STANTSII.**    XXX
SUBS (1960): TRUDY MURMANSKOGO MORSKOGO BIOLOGICHESKOGO INSTITUTA.

**TRUDY MURMANSKOGO MORSKOGO BIOLOGICHESKOGO INSTITUTA.**    XXX
*++TR. MURM. MORSK. BIOL. INST.*
AKADEMIJA NAUK SSSR: MURMANSKIJ MORSKOJ BIOLOGICHESKIJ INSTITUT.
*MOSCOW; LENINGRAD 1(5), 1960-*
PREV: TRUDY MURMANSKOJ BIOLOGICHESKOJ STANTSII FROM 1, 1948- 4, 1958. CONT. NUMB. IN PARENTHESIS.
*LO/N13.*
*XS/R14. 10(14), 1966.*

**TRUDY MUZEJA AZERBAJDZHANSKOJ LITERATURY.**
*++TR. MUZ. AZERBA. LIT.*
AKADEMIJA NAUK AZERBAJDZHANSKOJ SSR: MUZEJ AZERBAJDZHANSKOJ LITERATURY.
*BAKU 1. 1961-*
RUSS. & AZERB.
*LO/N-3.**   OX/U-1.*

**TRUDY NAUCHNO-ISSLEDOVATEL'SKOGO INSTITUTA MEDITSINSKOJ PARAZITOLOGII I TROPICHESKOJ MEDITSINY.**
*++TR. NAUCHNO-ISSLED. INST. MED. PARAZITOL. & TROP. MED.*
AZERBAJDZHANSKIJ NAUCHNO-ISSLEDOVATEL'SKIJ INSTITUT MEDITSINSKOJ PARAZITOLOGII I TROPICHESKOJ MEDITSINY.
*TIFLIS 4, 1963-*
NO DATA AVAILABLE REGARDING VOLS 1- 3.
*LO/M10.*

**TRUDY RESPUBLIKANSKOGO RUKOPISNOGO FONDA.**
*++TR. RESP. RUKOPISNOGO FONDA.*
AKADEMIJA NAUK AZERBAJDZHANSKOJ SSR.
*BAKU 1, 1961-*
AZERB. & RUSS.
*LO/N-3.*

**TRUDY SEKTSII METALLOVEDENIJA I TERMICHESKOJ OBRABOTKI, NAUCHNO-TEKHNICHESKOE OBSHCHESTVO MASHINOSTROITEL'NOJ PROMYSHLENNOSTI.**    XXX
SUBS (1964): METALLOVEDENIE I TERMICHESKAJA OBRABOTKA.

**TRUDY SEVERO-VOSTOCHNOGO KOMPLEKSNOGO NAUCHNO-ISSLEDOVATEL'SKOGO INSTITUTA.**
*++TR. SEV.-VOST. KOMPLEKSN. NAUCHNO-ISSLED. INST [TSKI-A]*
AKADEMIJA NAUK SSSR (SIBIRSKOE OTDELENIE): SEVERO-VOSTOCHNYJ KOMPLEKSNYJ NAUCHNO-ISSLEDOVATEL'SKIJ INSTITUT.
*MAGADAN 1, 1962-*
*GL/U-1.   OX/U-1.*
*LO/N13. 3, 1963-**

**TRUDY SHEMAKHINSKOJ ASTROFIZICHESKOJ OBSERVATORII AKADEMII NAUK AZERBAJDZHANSKOJ SSR.**    XXX
SUBS (1965): SOOBSHCHENIJA SHEMAKHINSKOJ ASTROFIZICHESKOJ OBSERVATORII.

**TRUDY, TADZHIKSKIJ GOSUDARSTVENNYJ UNIVERSITET: SERIJA ISTORICHESKIKH NAUK.**
*++TR. TADZH. GOS. UNIV., ISTOR. NAUK.*
*DUSHANBE 2, 1966-*
*GL/U-1.   LO/U-3.   LO/U14.*

**TRUDY, TATARSKAJA RESPUBLIKANSKAJA GOSUDARSTVENNAJA SEL'SKOKHOZJAJSTVENNAJA OPYTNAJA STANTSIJA.**
*++TR. TATAR. RESP. GOS. S-KH. OPYTN. STN.*
*KAZAN' 1, 1961-*
*LO/N13.*

**TRUDY, TSELINOGRADSKIJ SEL'SKOKHOZJAJSTVENNYJ INSTITUT.**
*++TR. TSELINOGR. S-KH. INST.*
*TSELINOGRAD 1, 1963-*
*LO/N13.*

**TRUDY UCHENYKH FILOLOGICHESKOGO FAKUL'TETA MOSKOVSKOGO UNIVERSITETA PO SLAVJANSKOMU JAZYKOZNANIJU.**
*++TR. UCH. FILOL. FAK. MOSK. UNIV. SLAV. JAZYKOZNANIJU.*
MOSKOVSKIJ GOSUDARSTVENNYJ UNIVERSITET.
*MOSCOW 1, 1960-*
S/T: BIBLIOGRAFICHESKIJ UKAZATEL'.
*GL/U-1.   LA/U-1.   LO/N-3.   LO/U15.   NR/U-1.*

**TRUDY URAL'SKOGO NAUCHNO-ISSLEDOVATEL'SKOGO INSTITUTA CHERNYKH METALLOV.**
*++TR. URAL. NAUCHNO-ISSLED. INST. CHERN. MET.*
URAL'SKIJ NAUCHNO-ISSLEDOVATEL'SKIJ INSTITUT CHERNYKH METALLOV.
*SVERDLOVSK 1. 1961-*
*LO/N13.*

**TRUDY VOLGOGRADSKOGO OTDELENIJA GOSNIORKH.**
*++TR. VOLGOGR. OTD. GOSNIORKH.*
GOSUDARSTVENNYJ NAUCHNO-ISSLEDOVATEL'SKIJ INSTITUT OZERNOGO I RECHNOGO KHOZJAJSTVA (VOLGOGRADSKOE OTDELENIE).
*VOLGOGRAD 1, 1965-*
*LO/N13.*

**TRUDY, VOLZHSKO-KAMSKIJ GOSUDARSTVENNYJ ZAPOVEDNIK.**
*++TR. VOLZH.-KAMSKIJ GOS. ZAPOVEDNIK. [TVKG-B]*
*KAZAN 1, 1968-*
*LO/N13.*

**TRUDY VSESOJUZNOGO NAUCHNO-ISSLEDOVATEL'SKOGO INSTITUTA FIZIOLOGII I BIOKHIMII SEL'SKO-KHOZJAJSTVENNYKH ZHIVOTNYKH.**
*BOROVSK (MOSCOW) 1, 1964-*
SPONS. BODY ALSO: VSESOJUZNAJA AKADEMIJA SEL' SKOKHOZJAJSTVENNYKH NAUK.
*LO/N13.*

**TRUDY, VSESOJUZNYJ NAUCHNO-ISSLEDOVATEL'SKIJ INSTITUT MAGNITNOJ ZAPISI I TEKHNOLOGII RADIO-VESHCHANIJA I TELEVIDENIJA (VNIIRT).**    XXX
*++TR. VSES. NAUCHNO-ISSLED. INST. MAGN. ZAP. & TEKHNOL. RADIOVESHCHANIJA & TELEV. (VNIIRT).*
*MOSCOW 1(11), 1964-*
PREV: TRUDY, VSESOJUZNYJ NAUCHNO-ISSLEDOVATEL'SKIJ INSTITUT ZVUKOZAPISI FROM 1, 1957- 10, 1962.
*LO/N13.*

**TRUDY VSESOJUZNOGO NAUCHNO-ISSLEDOVATEL'SKOGO INSTITUTA PO PERERABOTKE SLANTSEV 'VNIIPS'.**    XXX
SUBS (1960): PART OF KHIMIJA I TEKHNOLOGIJA GORJUCHIKH SLANTSEV I PRODUKTOV IKH PERERABOTKI; & KHIMIJA I TEKHNOLOGIJA TOPLIVA I PRODUKTOV EGO PERERABOTKI.

**TRUDY, VSESOJUZNYJ NAUCHNO-ISSLEDOVATEL'SKIJ INSTITUT PO STROITEL'STVU MAGISTRAL'NYKH TRUBOPROVODOV (VNIIST).**    XXX
*++TR. VSES. NAUCHNO-ISSLED. INST. STROIT. MAGISTRAL'NYKH TRUBOPROVODOV (VNIIST).*
*MOSCOW 10, 1960-*
PREV: TRUDY VSESOJUZNOGO NAUCHNO-ISSLEDOVATEL'SKOGO INSTITUTA PO STROITEL'STVU OBEKTOV NEFTJANOJ I GAZOVOJ PROMYSHLENNOSTI FROM 1, 1950- 9, 1957.
*LO/N13.*

**TRUDY VSESOJUZNOGO NAUCHNO-ISSLEDOVATEL'SKOGO INSTITUTA PO STROITEL'STVU OBEKTOV NEFTJANOJ I GAZOVOJ PROMYSHLENNOSIT.**    XXX
SUBS (1960): TRUDY, VSESOJUZNYJ NAUCHNO-ISSLEDOVATEL'SKIJ INSTITUT PO STROITEL'-STVU MAGISTRAL'NYKH TRUBOPROVODOV (VNIIST).

**TRUDY, VSESOJUZNYJ NAUCHNO-ISSLEDOVATEL'SKIJ INSTITUT ZVUKOZAPISI.**    XXX
SUBS (1964): TRUDY, VSESOJUZNYJ NAUCHNO-ISSLEDOVATEL'SKIJ INSTITUT MAGNITNOJ ZAPISI I TEKHNOLOGII RADIOVESHCHANIJA I TELEVIDENIJA (VNIIRT).

TRUDY VSESOJUZNOGO NAUCHNO-ISSLEDOVATEL'SKOGO
I PROEKTNO-KONSTRUKTORSKOGO INSTITUTA DOBYCHI
UGLJA GIDRAVLICHESKOM SPOSOBOM 'VNIIGIDROUGOL'
I GORNOGO FAKUL'TETA SIBIRSKOGO METALLURGICH-
ESKOGO INSTITUTA.
VSESOJUZNYJ NAUCHNO-ISSLEDOVATEL'SKIJ I PROEK-
TNO-KONSTRUKTORSKIJ INSTITUT DOBYCHI UGLJA
GIDRAVLICHESKOM SPOSOBOM 'VNIIGIDROUGOL'.
*NOVOKUZNETSK 1, 1962-*
SPONS. BODY ALSO SIBIRSKIJ METALLURGICHESKIJ
INSTITUT.
*LO/N13.*

TRUDY, VYSOKOGORNYJ GEOFIZICHESKIJ INSTITUT
(NAL'CHIK).                                                      XXX
*++TR. VYSOKOGORN. GEOFIZ. INST. (NAL'CHIK).*
*[TVGI-B]*
*LENINGRAD 3, 1966-*
PREV: TRUDY EL'BRUSSKOJ VYSOKOGORNOJ KOMPLEK-
SNOJ EKSPEDITSII FROM 1, 1959- 2, 1961.
*BH/U-1.    LO/N13.\**

TRUE JACOBITE.
*[T.J. PUBL.]*
*LONDON NO.1, JA/F 1970-*
*OX/U-1.*
*ISSN 0049-4798*

TSIFROVAJA VYCHISLITEL'NAJA TEKHNIKA I PROGR-
AMMIROVANIE. SBORNIK STATEJ.
*++TSIFROVAJA VYCHISL. TEK. & PROGRAM.*
*MOSCOW 1, 1966-*
*LO/N13.*
*BH/U-1.   4(1968) ONLY.*

TSUYAMA KOGYO KOTO SENMON GAKKO KIYO.
TSUYAMA KOGYO KOTO SENMON GAKKO.
*TSUYAMA-SHI 1(1), 1963-*
SUMM. IN EUR. LANG.
*XN/S-1.*

TTG INTERNATIONAL.
*[TRAVEL TRADE GAZETTE]*
*LONDON NO.1, 1/JL 1968-*
*W.*
*ED/N-1.*
*ISSN 0039-8500*

TUB. ZEITSCHRIFT DER TECHNISCHEN UNIVERSITAT
BERLIN.
*BERLIN &C 1(1), 1969-*
*DB/U-2.   LD/U-1.   LO/N14.   LO/U12.   SH/U-1.*

TUBINGER BEITRAGE ZUR LINGUISTIK.
*++TUBINGER BEITR. LINGUIST.*
*TUBINGEN NO.1, 1969-*
*LO/N-1.*

TUL. TRANSPORTIEREN, UMSCHLAGEN, LAGERN.
*[HESTRA-VERLAG]*
*DARMSTADT 1, 1966-*
*LO/N14.*

TULANE STUDIES IN ZOOLOGY & BOTANY.\*
*++TULANE STUD. ZOOL. & BOT.*
TULANE UNIVERSITY.
*NEW ORLEANS 1, JE 1953-*
TITLE EXPANDED FROM TULANE STUDIES IN ZOOLOGY
FROM 15, 1969.
*LO/N-2.   LO/N13.   LO/S19.   LV/U-1.*

TULSA ANNALS.
*++TULSA ANN.*
TULSA GENEALOGICAL SOCIETY.
*TULSA 1, S 1966-*
*ED/N-1.   1, 1966- 2(3), 1967.*

TUNNELS & TUNNELLING.
*++TUNN. & TUNNELL.*
*[LOMAX, ERSKINE &CO.]*
*LONDON 1, MY/JE 1969-*
*ED/N-1.   LO/N14.   OX/U-8.*
*DB/U-2. 1973-                  LD/U-1. 3, 1971-*
*NW/U-1. N/D 1969-               SH/U-3. 2, 1970-*
*SW/U-1. 3(3), 1971-*
*ISSN 0041-414X*

TURBINE TECHNOLOGY.
*++TURBINE TECHNOL.*
*[GAS TURBINE PUBL. INC.]*
*STAMFORD (CONN.) 1, 1969- 5, 1973.*
SUBS: TURBINE TECHNOLOGY AND MARKETING NEWS.
*LO/N13.   LO/N14.*

TURTLE.
*LONDON 1, 1971-*
*6/A.*
*ED/N-1.   OX/U-1.*

TVVL.
NEDERLANDSE TECHNISCHE VERENIGING VOOR VERWARM-
ING EN LUCHTBEHANDELING.
*UTRECHT 1(1), JA 1972-*
*M.*
*XS/T10.*

TWENTIETH CENTURY STUDIES.                                      000
SEE: 20TH CENTURY STUDIES.

TWO THOUSAND.                                                   000
SEE: 2000.

TWO WHEELER DEALER.
NATIONAL ASSOCIATION OF CYCLE & MOTOR CYCLE
TRADERS LTD.
*TUNBRIDGE WELLS NO.1, 1970-*
*OX/U-1.*
*ISSN 0027-5891*

UCHENYE ZAPISKI, AZERBAJDZHANSKIJ GOSUDARST-
VENNYJ UNIVERSITET: SERIJA ISTORICHESKIKH I
FILOSOFSKIKH NAUK.
*++UCH. ZAP. AZERB. GOS. UNIV., ISTOR. & FILOS.*
*NAUK.*
AZERBAJDZHANSKIJ GOSUDARSTVENNYJ UNIVERSITET.
*BAKU 1, 1963-*
NAME OF THE SUB-SERIES VARIES FROM VOL. 1 &
3- 7: ISTORIJA. VOL.2: SERIJA 1: ISTORIJA I
FILOSOFIJA.
*LO/N13.*

UCHENYE ZAPISKI AZERBAJDZHANSKOGO SEL'SKO-
KHOZJAJSTVENNOGO INSTITUTA.
*++UCH. ZAP. AZERB. S-KH. INST.*
AZERBAJDZHANSKIJ SEL'SKOKHOZJAJSTVENNYJ
INSTITUT.
*KIROVABAD 1, 1963-*
*LO/N13.*

UCHENYE ZAPISKI, DAL'NEVOSTOCHNYJ GOSUDARST-
VENNYJ UNIVERSITET: SERIJA EKONOMICHESKAJA.
*++UCH. ZAP. DAL'NEVOST. GOS. UNIV., EKON.*
*[UZDG-B]*
*VLADIVOSTOK 1, 1963-*
*LO/U-3.   OX/U-1.*

UCHENYE ZAPISKI KAFEDR OBSHCHESTVENNYKH NAUK
VUZOV GORODA LENINGRADA: FILOSOFIJA.                            XXX
*++UCH. ZAP. KAFEDR OBSHCHESTV. NAUK VUZOV.*
*GORODA LENINGR., FILOS.*
VYSSHIE UCHEBNYE ZAVEDENIJA GORODA LENINGRADA.
*LENINGRAD 2, 1960-*
PREV. AS PART OF ABOVE MAIN TITLE FROM 1,
1959. THEN ISSUED IN SUBJECT SECTIONS WHICH
CONTINUE PREV. NUMBERING.
*CC/U-1.   LO/U-3.*
*BH/U-1. 5, 1964-               GL/U-1. 5, 1964-*

UCHENYE ZAPISKI KAFEDR OBSHCHESTVENNYKH NAUK
VUZOV GORODA LENINGRADA:  PROBLEMY NAUCHNOGO
KOMMUNIZMA.
*++UCH. ZAP. KAFEDR OBSHCHEST. NAUK VUZOV GORODA*
*LENINGRADA, PROBL. NAUCH. KOMMUNIZMA.*
VYSSHIE UCHEBNYE ZAVEDENIJA GORODA LENINGRADA.
*LENINGRAD VYP.1, 1967-*
*BH/U-1.   CC/U-1.   GL/U-1.   OX/U-1.*

UCHENYE ZAPISKI KAFEDRY SOVETSKOJ EKONOMIKI.
*++UCH. ZAP. KAFEDRY SOV. EKON.*
VYSSHAJA PARTIJNAJA SHKOLA PRI TSK KPSS.
*MOSCOW 1, 1964-*
*CC/U-1. 5, 1970-*

UCHENYE ZAPISKI, NAUCHNO-ISSLEDOVATEL'SKIJ
INSTITUT GEOLOGII ARKTIKI: PALENTOLOGIJA I
BIOSTRATIGRAFIJA.
*++UCH. ZAP. NAUCHNO-ISSLED. INST. GEOL. ARKTIKI,*
*PALENTOL. & BIOSTRATIGR.*
*LENINGRAD 1, 1963-*
*LO/N13.*
*CA/U12. 11, 1966-              LO/N-2. 13, 1966-*

UCHENYE ZAPISKI, NAUCHNO-ISSLEDOVATEL'SKIJ
INSTITUT GEOLOGII ARKTIKI: REGIONAL'NAJA
GEOLOGIJA.
*++UCH. ZAP. NAUCHNO-ISSLED. INST. GEOL. ARKTIKI,*
*REG. GEOL. [UGRG-A]*
*LENINGRAD 1, 1963-*
*LO/N13.*
*CA/U12. 1966-                  LO/N-2. 8, 1966-*

UCHENYE ZAPISKI, PENZENSKIJ POLITEKHNICHESKIJ
INSTITUT: ELEKTROIZMERITEL'NAJA TEKHNIKA.
*++UCH. ZAP. PENZ. POLITEKH. INST. ELEKTROIZMER.*
*TEKH.*
*PENZA VYP.1, 1962-*
*LO/N13.*

UCHENYE ZAPISKI, VIL'NJUSSKIJ GOSUDARSTVENNYJ
UNIVERSITET /IM. V. KAPSUKASA/; ...
 SEE: VILNIAUS VALSTYBINIS /V. KAPSUKO VARDO/
 UNIVERSITETAS, MOKSLO DARBAI; ...

UCHENYE ZAPISKI, VLADIMIRSKIJ GOSUDARSTVENNYJ
PEDAGOGICHESKIJ INSTITUT: SERIJA BOTANIKA.
+ +UCH. ZAP. VLADIMIRSKIJ GOS. PEDAGOG. INST.,
 BOT.
 VLADIMIR 1, 1968-
 LO/N13.

UCHUMI. JOURNAL OF THE ECONOMIC SOCIETY OF
TANZANIA.
 DAR ES SALAAM 1(1), [1969]-
 2/A.
 BT/U-1.    LO/U-8.    LO/U14.

UDS AIR QUALITY CONTROL DIGEST.                    XXX
 [UNIVERSITY DIGEST SERVICES]
 TROY, MICH. 2(7), 1971-
 PREV: AIR QUALITY CONTROL DIGEST FROM 1, 1969-
 2(6), 1971.
 LO/N14.

UDS METAL JOINING DIGEST.                          XXX
+ +UDS MET. JOIN. DIG.
 [UNIV. DIGEST SERVICES] .
 TROY, MICH 6(5), 1972-
 PREV: METAL JOINING DIGEST FROM 1, 1967- 6(4),
 1972.
 LO/N14.

UDS SURFACE COATINGS DIGEST.                       XXX
+ +UDS SURF. COAT. DIG.
 [UNIVERSITY DIGEST SERVICES]
 TROY, MICH. 4(2), 1972-
 PREV: & ALSO ENTITLED SURFACE COATINGS DIGEST
 FROM 1, 1968- 4(1), 1972.
 LO/N14.

UDS WATER QUALITY CONTROL DIGEST.                  XXX
+ +UDS WATER QUAL. CONTROL DIG.
 [UNIV. DIGEST SERVICES]
 TROY, MICH. 2(8), 1971-
 PREV: WATER QUALITY CONTROL DIGEST FROM 1,
 1969- 2(7), 1971.
 WOOD VILLAGE, KENT 1, D 1968-
 ED/N-1.

UGANDA NEWS REVIEW.
+ +UGANDA NEWS REV.
 (UGANDA) HIGH COMMISSION, LONDON.
 LONDON AP 1972- F 1974. //
 LO/S14.
 LO/N-1. JE 1972-            LO/U-3. MY 1973-

UHURU. JOURNAL OF THE ...
 UNIVERSITY OF LEEDS UNION: AFRICAN SOCIETY.
 LEEDS 1, 1968-
 LD/U-1.

UICC MONOGRAPH SERIES.
+ +UICC MONOGR. SER. (UNION INT. CONTRE CANCER).
 UNION INTERNATIONALE CONTRE LE CANCER.
 COPENHAGEN 1, 1967-
 OX/U-8.

UK SHIPPING NEWS.
 CHAMBER OF SHIPPING OF THE UNITED KINGDOM.
 LONDON OC/N 1970-
 6/A. SPONS. BODY ALSO BRITISH SHIPPING
 FEDERATION.
 LD/U-1.    OX/U-1.
 CR/U-1. NO.4, 1971-          XS/R10. NO.5, 1971-

U.K.A.E.A. METRIC GUIDE.
 UNITED KINGDOM ATOMIC ENERGY AUTHORITY.
 LONDON NO.1, 1969-
 LO/N14.

UKRAINS'KA LITERATURNA GAZETA.                     XXX
 SUBS (1961): PART SUCHASNIST'.

UKRAINSKIJ GEOMETRICHESKIJ SBORNIK.
+ +UKR. GEOM. SB.
 (UKRAINE) MINISTERSTVO VYSSHEGO I SREDNEGO
 SPETSIAL'NOGO OBRAZOVANIJA.
 KHAR'KOV 1, 1965-
 LO/N13.

UMFORMTECHNIK.
 ZENTRALINSTITUT FUR FERTIGUNGSTECHNIK: BEREICH
 UMFORMTECHNIK.
 ZWICKAU 1, 1967-
 'UBERSETZUNGEN AUS: KUZNECHNO-SHTAMPOVOCHNOE
 PROIZVODSTVO; VESTNIK MASHINOSTROENIJA; STANKI
 I INSTRUMENT.' PARENT BODY SOMETIMES LISTED
 AS: ZENTRALINST. FUR FERTIGINGSTECH. [DES
 MASCHINENBAUES].
 LO/N13.
 ISSN 0030-3167

UMWELT. FORSCHUNG, TECHNIK, SCHUTZ.
 [VEREIN DEUTSCHER INGENIEURE]
 DUSSELDORF 1, S 1970-
 2M. S 1970 ISSUE CALLED V.1, NO.0.
 LO/N14. 1971-
 ISSN 0041-6355

UNASYLVA. AN INTERNATIONAL REVIEW OF FOR-
ESTRY & FOREST PRODUCTS.
 FOOD & AGRICULTURE ORGANIZATION (UN).
 ROME 1(1), JL/AG 1947-
 PUBL. SUSPENDED FROM 1973- SPRING 1974.
 BN/U-2.    LO/U-3.    OX/U-3.
 RE/U-1. 20, 1966-
 LO/R-6. NO.104, 1972.
 ISSN 0041-6436

UNDERCURRENTS. THE MAGAZINE OF ALTERNATIVE
SCIENCE & TECHNOLOGY.
 [UNDERCURRENTS SYNDICATE]
 LONDON NO.1, 1972-
 Q.
 CA/U-1.    ED/N-1.
 LO/R-6. NO.4, 1973-

UNDERGROUND ENGINEERING.
+ +UNDERGROUND ENG.
 [A-Z PUBL CORP.]
 LOS ANGELES 1, JE/JL 1970-
 6/A.
 LO/N14.

UNDERWATER INFORMATION BULLETIN.                   XXX
+ +UNDERWATER INF. BULL.
 [IPC SCIENCE & TECHNOLOGY P.]
 GUILDFORD 6(1), F 1974-
 PREV: UNDERWATER JOURNAL INFORMATION BULLETIN
 FROM 3, 1971- 5(6), D 1973.
 ED/N-1.
 ISSN 0302-3478

UNDERWATER JOURNAL.                                XXX
+ +UNDERWATER J.
 [IPC SCIENCE & TECHNOLOGY P.]
 GUILDFORD 3, 1971-
 PREV: UNDERWATER SCIENCE & TECHNOLOGY JOURNAL
 FROM 1, 1969- 2, 1970.
 ED/N-1.    LO/N14.    MA/U-1.    SO/U-1.    XS/R10.
 GL/U-2. 4, 1972-                    LO/N14. 3, 1971-

UNDERWATER JOURNAL INFORMATION BULLETIN.           XXX
+ +UNDERWATER J. INF. BULL.
 [IPC SCIENCE & TECHNOLOGY P.]
 GUILDFORD 3, 1971- 5(6), D 1973 ...
 PREV: UNDERWATER SCIENCE & TECHNOLOGY
 INFORMATION BULLETIN FROM 1, 1969- 2, 1970.
 SUBS: UNDERWATER INFORMATION BULLETIN.
 SUPPL. TO UNDERWATER JOURNAL.
 ED/N-1.    LO/N14.    MA/U-1.    OX/U-1.    SO/U-1.
 XS/R10.
BULLETIN A, 1972-                                  XXX
+ +UNDERWAT. SCI. & TECHNOL. INF. BULL.
 [ILIFFE]
 GUILDFORD 1(1), F 1969- 2, 1970 ...
 SUBS: UNDERWATER JOURNAL INFORMATION BULLETIN.
 ED/N-1.    HL/U-1.    LO/N-2.    LO/N-4.    LO/N14.    LO/U-4.
 NR/U-1.    XS/R10.
 ISSN 0503-1737

UNDERWATER SCIENCE & TECHNOLOGY JOURNAL.           XXX
+ +UNDERWAT. SCI. & TECHNOL. J.
 [ILIFFE]
 GUILDFORD 1(1), JE 1969- 2, 1970 ...
 SUBS: UNDERWATER JOURNAL.
 BH/U-1.    ED/N-1.    HL/U-1.    LO/N-2.    LO/N-4.    LO/N14.
 LO/U-4.    NR/U-1.    NR/U-1.    OX/U-8.    SW/U-1.    XS/R10.
 XS/T-4. 2(1), 1970-

UNDEX. UNITED NATIONS DOCUMENTS INDEX:
SERIES A: SUBJECT INDEX.
 NEW YORK 1(1), JA 1970-
 LO/S14.    OX/U-1.

**UNDEX. UNITED NATIONS DOCUMENTS INDEX: SERIES B: COUNTRY INDEX.**
*NEW YORK 1(1), JA 1970-*
*LO/S14.    OX/U-1.*

**UNESCO TECHNICAL PAPERS IN MARINE SCIENCE.**
*+ +UNESCO TECH. PAP. MAR. SCI.*
*[PARIS] NO.1, 1965-*
*BN/U-2.\*\**
*LO/N-2. NO.5, 1966-*

**UNIDO NEWSLETTER.**
*+ +UNIDO NEWSL. (U.N. IND. DEV. ORG.)*
UNITED NATIONS INDUSTRIAL DEVELOPMENT ORGANI-
ZATION.
*NEW YORK NO.1, JE 1967-*
*2M.*
*ED/N-1.    LO/U-3.*
*ISSN 0049-5387*

**UNION OF BURMA JOURNAL OF LIFE SCIENCES.**
*+ +UNION BURMA J. LIFE SCI.*
BURMA MEDICAL RESEARCH INSTITUTE.
*RANGOON 1, JA 1968-*
*3/A.*
*CA/U-2.    LO/N-2.    LO/N12.*

**UNION OF BURMA JOURNAL OF SCIENCE & TECHNOL-OGY.**
*+ +UNION BURMA J. SCI. & TECHNOL.*
UNION OF BURMA APPLIED RESEARCH INSTITUTE.
*RANGOON 1(1), AP 1968-*
*LO/N-2.    LO/N12.    XS/R10.*

**UNION OF CONSTRUCTION & ALLIED TRADES TECHNIC-IANS JOURNAL.**                                    XXX
*+ +UNION CONSTR. & ALLIED TRADES TECH. J.*
*LONDON NO.3, JL 1972-*
PREV: WOODWORKERS & PAINTERS JOURNAL FROM
NO.1, 1970- NO.2, 1972.
*BH/P-1.*

**UNISA ENGLISH STUDIES.**
*+ +UNISA ENGL. STUD:*
UNIVERSITY OF SOUTH AFRICA: DEPARTMENT OF
ENGLISH.
*PRETORIA NO.1, MR 1968-*
*DB/U-2.    LO/N-1.    LO/N-3.    OX/U-1.*
*ISSN 0041-5359*

**UNISIST NEWSLETTER.**
*+ +UNISIST NEWSL.*
UNESCO: DIVISION OF SCIENTIFIC & TECHNOLOGICAL
INFORMATION & DOCUMENTATION.
*PARIS NO.1, 1973-*
*CA/U-1.    CA/U-2.    LO/N-1.    LO/N-2.    LO/N-4.    LO/N35.*
*LO/U-1.    OX/U-1.    XS/R10.*
*XS/N-1. NO.4, 1973-*
*LO/U-3. [CURRENT ISSUES ONLY]*

**UNITAR LECTURE SERIES.**
*NEW YORK [NO.]1, 1970-*
*LO/N-1.*

**UNITED ARAB REPUBLIC JOURNAL OF PHARMACEUTICAL SCIENCES.**                                   XXX
*+ +UAR J. PHARM. SCI.*
PHARMACEUTICAL SOCIETY OF EGYPT.
*CAIRO 11(1), 1970-*
PREV: JOURNAL OF PHARMACEUTICAL SCIENCES OF
THE UNITED ARAB REPUBLIC FROM 1(1), 1960-
10(1), 1969.
*BN/U-2.*

**UNITED ARAB REPUBLIC JOURNAL OF PHYSICS.**
*+ +UAR J. PHYS.*
NATIONAL INFORMATION & DOCUMENTATION CENTRE
(U.A.R.).
*CAIRO 1, 1970-*
EDITED BY THE EGYPTIAN PHYSICAL SOCIETY.
*LO/N14.*

**UNITED ARAB REPUBLIC JOURNAL OF SOIL SCIENCE.**                                               XXX
*+ +UAR J. SOIL SCI.*
SOCIETY OF SOIL SCIENCE (UAR).
*CAIRO 10(1), 1970-*
PREV: JOURNAL OF SOIL SCIENCE OF THE UNITED
ARAB REPUBLIC FROM 1(1), 1961- 9(2), 1969.
*BN/U-2.    CA/U11.*

**UNITED CHURCH REVIEW.**                                                                        XXX
**SUBS (1971): NORTH INDIA CHURCHMAN.**

**UNITED NIGERIA.**                                                                              XXX
*LONDON NO.1, JL 1968- 12, OC 1969. //*
PUBL. BY THE FEDERAL GOVERNMENT OF NIGERIA,
DISTRIB. BY NIGERIAN HIGH COMMISSION, LONDON.
*CB/U-1.    ED/N-1.    LO/U-3.*
*BH/P-1. [W. NO. 10]*

**UNITED SCOTSMAN.**
*[GLASGOW] 1, 1972-*
*ED/N-1.*

**UNITED STATES PATENTS REPORT.**
*+ +U.S. PAT. REP.*
[DERWENT PUBL. LTD.]
*LONDON S(1), 1971-*
VOLUMES LETTERED.
*LO/N14.    OX/U-8.*
*BH/U-1. 21, 1971-*

**UNIVERSAL ABSTRACTS.**                                                                         XXX
*+ +UNIVERS. ABSTR.*
NATIONAL EYE RESEARCH FOUNDATION (US).
*CHICAGO 1(1- 3), 1972.*
Q. SUBS. INCORP. IN: CONTACTO. S/T: CURRENT
WORLD WIDE LITERATURE PUBLISHED QUARTERLY
FOR THE OPHTHALMIC PROFESSION.
*BH/U-3.*

**UNIVERSITY OF BIRMINGHAM HISTORICAL JOURNAL.**                                                 XXX
**SUBS (1971): MIDLAND HISTORY.**

**UNIVERSITY BULLETIN, UNIVERSITY OF NAIROBI.**
*+ +UNIV. BULL. UNIV. NAIROBI.*
*NAIROBI [NO.1], N 1970-*
*LO/U-8.    LO/U14.    OX/U-9.*

**UNIVERSITY OF CALIFORNIA PUBLICATIONS IN AUTOMATIC COMPUTATION.**
*+ +UNIV. CALIF. PUBL. AUTOM. COMPUT.*
*BERKELEY, CALIF. NO.1, 1961-*
*LO/N14.*

**UNIVERSITY OF CALIFORNIA PUBLICATIONS: NEAR EASTERN STUDIES.**
*+ +UNIV. CALIF. PUBL., NEAR E. STUD.*
*BERKELEY, CALIF. 1, 1963-*
*MA/U-1.*

**UNIVERSITY OF CINCINNATI CLASSICAL STUDIES.**
*+ +UNIV. CINCINNATI CLASSICAL STUD.*
[PRINCETON U.P.]
*PRINCETON 1, 1967-*
*GL/U-1.*

**UNIVERSITY OF DUNDEE GAZETTE.**
*+ +UNIV. DUNDEE GAZ.*
*DUNDEE 1, 1969-*
*ED/N-1.    LO/N-1.*

**UNIVERSITY FILM JOURNAL.**                                                                     XXX
**SUBS (1968): UNIVERSITY VISION.**

**UNIVERSITY OF KENTUCKY LIBRARY NOTES.**
*·+ +UNIV. KY. LIBR. NOTES.*
*LEXINGTON, KY. 1(1), 1967-*
*OX/U-1.*
*LD/U-1. 1(3), 1970-*

**UNIVERSITY OF LANCASTER LIBRARY OCCASIONAL PAPERS.**
*+ +UNIV. LANC. LIBR. OCC. PAP.*
*LANCASTER NO.1, 1968-*
*BH/U-1.    GL/U-1.    LO/U-1.    OX/U-1.*

**UNIVERSITY OF PITTSBURGH LIBRARIES BIBLIO-GRAPHIC SERIES.**
*+ +UNIV. PITTSB. LIBR. BIBLIOGR. SER.*
UNIVERSITY OF PITTSBURGH: LIBRARY.
*PITTSBURGH [1, 1969]-*
*OX/U-1.*

**UNIVERSITY OF PITTSBURGH SERIES IN THE PHIL-OSOPHY OF SCIENCE.**
*+ +UNIV. PITTSBURG SER. PHIL. SCI.*
UNIVERSITY OF PITTSBURGH: CENTER FOR PHILOSOPHY
OF SCIENCE.
*LONDON &C 1, 1962-*
*AB/U-1.    OX/U-8.*

**UNIVERSITY OF QUEENSLAND PAPERS (COMPUTER CENTRE).**
*+ +UNIV. QUEENSL. PAP. (COMPUT. CENT.). [QUCP-A]*
*BRISBANE 1, MR 1968-*
*DB/S-1.*

**UNIVERSITY REVIEW (DUBLIN).**                                                                  XXX
**SUBS (1970): IRISH UNIVERSITY REVIEW.**

**UNIVERSITY OF SINGAPORE NEWS.**
++UNIV. SINGAPORE NEWS.
SINGAPORE 1, 1967-
LD/U-1.

**UNIVERSITY STUDIES, UNIVERSITY OF KARACHI.**
++UNIV. STUD. UNIV. KARACHI.
KARACHI 1, 1964-
LO/N-2.

**UNIVERSITY OF TASMANIA LAW REVIEW.**                    XXX
++UNIV. TASMANIA LAW REV.
UNIVERSITY OF TASMANIA: LAW SCHOOL.
HOBART 2, 1964-
PREV: TASMANIAN UNIVERSITY LAW REVIEW FROM 1,
JL 1958/1963.
LD/U-1.    OX/U15.

**UNIVERSITY VISION. THE JOURNAL OF THE ...**
++UNIV. VISION.
BRITISH UNIVERSITIES FILM COUNCIL.
LONDON NO.1, F 1968-
AD/U-1.    BL/U-1.    DB/U-1.    EX/U-1.    GL/U-2.    LD/U-1.
LO/U-1.    NO/U-1.
LO/N-2. NO.9, 1972-          LO/S10. NO.5, 1970-
ISSN 0042-0395

**UNIVERSITY WORKING PAPERS.**
++UNIV. WORK. PAP.
LONDON CES UWP 1, 1969-
MONOGR.
LO/N-1.    OX/U-1.

**UNIVERSO.**
SANTO DOMINGO 1, 1971-
OX/U-1.

**UNMUZZLED OX.**
NEW YORK 1, N 1971-
Q.
OX/U-1.
ISSN 0049-5557

**UNTERSUCHUNGEN ZUR ANTIKEN LITERATUR UND
GESCHICHTE.**
++UNTERS. ANTIKEN LIT. & GESCH.
[WALTER DE GRUYTER]
BERLIN 1, 1968-
LO/N-1.

**UNTERSUCHUNGEN UBER GRUPPEN UND VERBANDE.**
++UNTERS. GRUPPEN & VERB.
[DUNCKER & HUMBLOT]
BERLIN 1, 1964-
OX/U-1.
ISSN 0566-2753

**U.P. LIBRARIAN.**
++U.P. LIBR.
UNIVERSITY OF THE PHILIPPINES: OFFICE OF THE
UNIVERSITY LIBRARIAN.
QUEZON CITY NO.1, 1970-
LD/U-1.

**UPDATE. THE JOURNAL OF POSTGRADUATE GENERAL
PRACTICE.**
[UPDATE PUBL. LTD.]
LONDON 1(1), OC 1968-
MON.
CR/M-1. 3, 1971-          ED/N-1. 2(7), 1970-
LO/M-1. 1(2), 1968-       LO/N31. 3, 1971-
OX/U-8. 1(15), 1969-
XS/R10. 5(10), 1972-
ISSN 0301-5718

**UPDATE PLUS.**
[UPDATE PUBL. LTD.]
LONDON 1(1- 12), 1971.//
MON.
AD/U-1.    BL/U-1.    ED/N-1.    LO/N-1.    OX/U-8.

**URBAN ANTHROPOLOGY.**
++URBAN ANTHROPOL.
STATE UNIVERSITY OF NEW YORK: DEPARTMENT OF
ANTHROPOLOGY.
BROCKPORT, N.Y. 1(1), 1972-
2/A.
AD/U-1.    LO/S10.    LO/U14.

**URBAN ANTHROPOLOGY NEWSLETTER.**
++URBAN ANTHROPOL. NEWSL.
STATE UNIVERSITY OF NEW YORK: DEPARTMENT OF
ANTHROPOLOGY.
BROCKPORT, N.Y. 1(1), 1972-
LO/U14.

**URBAN DESIGN BULLETIN.**
++URBAN DES. BULL.
GREATER LONDON COUNCIL.
LONDON NO.1, MR 1970-
ED/N-1.    LO/N14.    OX/U-1.

**URBAN HISTORY REVIEW.**
++URBAN HIST. REV.
NATIONAL MUSEUM OF MAN (CANADA): HISTORY
DIVISION.
OTTAWA NO.1, F 1972-
S/T: RESOURCES FOR THE STUDY OF URBAN HISTORY
IN THE PUBLIC ARCHIVES OF CANADA.
ED/N-1.    SO/U-1.

**URBAN LIFE & CULTURE.**                    XXX
++URBAN LIFE & CULT.
[SAGE PUBL.]
BEVERLY HILLS, CALIF. 1(1), AP 1972- 3, 1974.
Q. SUBS: URBAN LIFE.
AD/U-1.    CA/U-1.    LO/S10.    LO/U-3.    MA/U-1.
SH/U-1. 2, 1973-
BD/U-1. 1(3), 1972-1(4), 1973.
ISSN 0049-5662

**URBAN & REGIONAL STUDIES.**
++URBAN & REG. STUD.
NATIONAL BUREAU OF ECONOMICS RESEARCH (US).
NEW YORK 1, 1972-
GL/U-1.
BL/U-1. 2, 1975.

**URBAN & SOCIAL CHANGE REVIEW.**                    XXX
++URBAN & SOC. CHANGE REV.
BOSTON COLLEGE: INSTITUTE OF HUMAN SCIENCES.
CHESTNUT HILL, MASS. 3(1), 1969-
PREV: REVIEW, INSTITUTE OF HUMAN SCIENCES,
BOSTON COLLEGE FROM 1(1), 1967- 2, 1969.
LO/N-1.
ISSN 0042-0832

**URETHANE ABSTRACTS.**
++URETHANE ABSTR.
FRANKLIN INSTITUTE RESEARCH LABORATORIES.
[TECHNOMIC PUBL. CO.]
WESTPORT, CONN. 1(1), JA 1972-
MON.
OX/U-8.

**URETHANE PLASTICS & PRODUCTS.**
++URETHANE PLAST. & PROD.
[TECHNOMIC PUBL. CO.]
STAMFORD, CONN 1, 1970-
LO/N14.
ISSN 0049-5700

**UROLOGY & NEPHROLOGY. AN INTERNATIONAL
QUARTERLY.**                    000
SEE: INTERNATIONAL UROLOGY & NEPHROLOGY.

**UR-SCHWEIZ.**                    XXX
SUBS (1970): HELVETIA ARCHAEOLOGICA.

**USPEKHI FIZIOLOGICHESKIKH NAUK (ENGL.TRANSL.)**                    000
SEE: PROGRESS IN PHYSIOLOGICAL SCIENCES.

**U.S.S.R. & THIRD WORLD.**
CENTRAL ASIAN RESEARCH CENTRE.
LONDON 1(1), D 1970/JA 1971-
10/A. S/T: A SURVEY OF SOVIET & CHINESE
RELATIONS WITH AFRICA, ASIA & LATIN AMERICA.
CV/C-1.    ED/N-1.    LO/N-1.    LO/S14.    LO/U-8.    MA/U-1.
OX/U-1.
AD/U-1. 2, 1972-          SW/U-1. 2, 1971/72-
ISSN 0041-5545

**UST LIBRARY BULLETIN.**
++UST LIB. BULL. (UNIV. SANTO TOMAS).
UNIVERSITY OF SANTO TOMAS: LIBRARY.
MANILA 1(1), 1968-
OX/U-1.

**UTILITAS MATHEMATICA.**
++UTIL. MATH.
WINNIPEG 1, 1972-
AD/U-1.    LO/N14.

**UTRECHT MICROPALEONTOLOGICAL BULLETINS.**
++UTRECHT MICROPALEONTOL. BULL.
[SCHOTANUS & JENS INC.]
UTRECHT [NO.]1, 1969-
LO/N-2.    LO/N13.    OX/U-8.

UTRECHTSE STERREKUNDIGE OVERDRUKKEN.
+ +UTRECHT. STERREK. OVERDR.
RIJKSUNIVERSITEIT TE UTRECHT: STERREWACHT.
*UTRECHT 1, 1966-*
BODY ALSO CALLED STERREWACHT 'SONNENBORGH'.
PUBL. WITH (THE UNIV.'S) LABORATORIUM VOOR
RUIMT OENDERZOEK.
*DB/S-1.     ED/R-3.  2, 1966-*

UTSUNOMIYA DAIGAKU KYOYOBU KENKYU HOKOKU: DAI
2BU.  BULLETIN OF THE FACULTY OF GENERAL
EDUCATION, UTSUNOMIYA UNIVERSITY: SECTION 2.
*TOKYO  NO.1, 1968-*
*LO/N13.*

UTSUNOMIYA DAIGAKU NOGAKUBU ENSHURIN HOKOKU.
BULLETIN OF THE UTSUNOMIYA UNIVERSITY FORESTS.
*UTSUNOMIYA  NO.1, 1961-*
JAP. WITH ENGL. SUMM.
*LO/N13.*

UURIMUSI EHITUSE ALALT.  ISSLEDOVANIJA PO
STROITEL'STVU.
EESTI NSV TEADUSTE AKADEEMIA.
*TALLIN  1, 1961-*
RUSS. WITH ENGL. & ESTONIAN SUMM.
*LO/N14.*

V MIRE KNIG.                                                          XXX
(RUSSIA, USSR) MINISTERSTVO KUL'TURY.
*MOSCOW  1, JA 1961-*
M. S/T: EZHEMESJACHNYJ KRITIKO-BIBLIOGRAFI-
CHESKI ZHURNAL. PREV: CHTO CHITAT' FROM
1958(1)- 1960(12).
*LO/N-3.     OX/U-1.*
*CC/U-1.  1966-*

VACHER'S EUROPEAN COMPANION.  A DIPLOMATIC,
POLITICAL & COMMERCIAL REFERENCE BOOK.
+ +VACHER'S EUR. COMPANION.
[A.S. KERSWILL LTD.]
*LONDON  NO.1, AP 1972-*
Q.
*ED/N-1.     GL/U-2.     LO/S14.     SH/U-1.*

VAKBLAD VOOR TEXTIELREINIGING.
+ +VAKBL. TEXTIELREINIG. [VKTX-A]
FEDERATIE VOOR DE WASINDUSTRIE.
*VOORBURG   1(1), JA 1964-*
*LO/N13.  2(5),1965-*
*ISSN 0042-224X*

VALUE ENGINEERING.                                                    XXX
+ +VALUE ENG.
[PERGAMON PRESS]
*OXFORD &C   1, AP 1968- 2(4), F 1970.*
*ED/N-1.     LO/N13.     MA/P-1.     OX/U-8.*

VALVE INFORMATION REPORT.                                            XXX
+ +VALVE INF. REP. [VAIR-A]
TECHNICAL ECONOMICS ASSOCIATION.
*ESTES PARK, COLO.  1962- F 1973.*
10/A.  SUBS: IMPACT.  VALVE REPORT.
*LO/N14.  1972-*
*ISSN 0042-2436*

VAND. TIDSSKRIFT FOR VANDKVALITET.
INTERNATIONAL ASSOCIATION ON WATER POLLUTION
RESEARCH: DANISH NATIONAL COMMITTEE.
[TEKNISK FORLAG]
*COPENHAGEN  1, 1971-*
*LO/N14.*

VARIA HISTORICA BRABANTICA.
+ +VARIA HIST. BRABANTICA.
WETENSCHAPPEN IN NOORD-BRABANT: HISTORISCHE
SECTIE.
*'S-HERTOGENBOSCH  NO.1, 1962-*
*LO/N-1.*

VARSTVO NARAVE.
ZAVOD ZA SPOMENSKO VARSTVO S.R. SLOVENIJE.
*LJUBLJANA  1, 1962-*
ANNU.  ENGL., FR., & GER. SUMM.  TITLE ALSO IN
ENGL.: PROTECTION OF NATURE.
*LO/N-2.     LO/R-5.*

VASA.  ZEITSCHRIFT FUR GEFASSKRANKHEITEN.                            XXX
[HUBER]
*BERN  1, 1972-*
PREV: ZENTRALBLATT FUR PHLEBOLOGIE FROM 1, F
1962- 10, 1971.
*LO/N13.*

VAT BULLETIN.                                                         XXX
(GREAT BRITAIN) CUSTOMS & EXCISE.
*LONDON  NO.1, 1972- 10, 1973.//*
*CA/U-1.     ED/N-1.     LO/N-6.     LO/N35.     LO/U-3.     RE/U-1.*
*SH/P-1.*

VAT NEWSLETTER.
+ +VAT NEWSL.
[NEWSLETTERS FOR BUSINESS]
*SOUTH HARROW  NO.1, MY 1972-*
*ED/N-1.     OX/U-1.*

VAXT-NARINGS-NYTT.                                                    XXX
GODSEL - OCH KALKINDUSTRIERNAS SAMARBETSDELEG-
ATION.
*STOCKHOLM  1, 1945- 26, 1970.//*
*XS/R12.*
*LO/N-6. 2, 1946-                     LO/N13.  16, 1960-*
OGICAL SOCIETY.
*NEW DELHI  1(1), 1971-*
*XS/N-1.*

VECTOR GENETICS.
+ +VECTOR GENET.
WORLD HEALTH ORGANIZATION.
*GENEVA  1, 1966-*
S/T: MUTATION & STOCK LIST OF ARTHROPOD
VECTORS.
*CA/U15.*

VEETEELT- EN ZUIVEL BERICHTEN.                                       XXX
SUBS (1970): BEDRIJFSONTWIKKELING. EDITIE
VEEHOUDERIJ.

VEGETARIAN: NS.                                                      XXX
VEGETARIAN SOCIETY OF THE UNITED KINGDOM, LTD.
*LONDON  NO.1, OC 1971-*
PREV: BRITISH VEGETARIAN FROM 1(1), JA/F 1959-
13(4), JL/AG 1971.
13(4), JL/AG 1971.
*BH/U-1.     ED/N-1.     LO/N-1.*

VEHICLE CLEANING NEWS.
+ +VEH. CLEAN. NEWS.
[TRADE & TECHNICAL P.]
*MORDEN  3(5), 1969-*
PREV: CARWASH & TRANSPORT CLEANING FROM
1, 1967.
*LO/N14.*
*ED/N-1.  3(5), 1969-*
*ISSN 0008-7084*

VEHICLE SYSTEM DYNAMICS.
+ +VEH. SYST. DYN.
[SWETS & ZEITLINGER]
*AMSTERDAM  1, 1972-*
*DB/U-2.     LD/U-1.     LO/N-4.     LO/N14.     SW/U-1.*
*ISSN 0042-3114*

VEL'KA SLOVENSKA GALERIA.
+ +VEL'KA SLOV. GALERIA.
*BRATISLAVA  1, 1966-*
*CA/U-1.     OX/U-1.*

VELKOMMEN TIL GRONLAND.                                               000
SEE: WELCOME TO GREENLAND.

VENTILATION BROADSHEET.
+ +VENT. BROADSH.
NATIONAL COAL BOARD (GB).
*LONDON  NO.1, N 1967-*
ISSUED BY THE BOARD'S  PRODUCTION DEPARTMENT.
*ED/N-1.     LO/N14.*

VENTURE. JOURNAL OF THE FABIAN COLONIAL
BUREAU.                                                               XXX
SUBS (1972): THIRD WORLD. SOCIALISM &
DEVELOPMENT.

VER SACRUM.
[VERLAG JUGEND & VOLK]
*VIENNA &C.  NO.1, 1970-*
ANNU.  S/T: NEUE HEFTE FUR KUNST UND LITERATUR
INTRODUCTORY ISSUE DATED 1969.
*LO/N-1.*

VERFASSUNG UND VERFASSUNGSWIRKLICHKEIT.
[WESTDEUTSCHER VERLAG]
*COLOGNE  1, 1966-*
A.
*OX/U-1.*

VERGE.
UNIVERSITY OF THE PHILIPPINES COLLEGE IN BAGUIO
*BAGUIO CITY  1(1), JE 1966-*
*OX/U-1.*
*ISSN 0042-3912*

VERHANDELINGEN, RIJKSINSTITUUT VOOR NATUUR-
BEHEER.
++VERH. RIJKSINST. NATUURBEHEER.
AMSTERDAM NR.1, 1970-
LO/N-2.     OX/U-8.

VERHANDLUNGEN, DEUTSCHE GESELLSCHAFT FUR
RHEUMATOLOGIE.
++VERH. DTSCH. GES. RHEUMATOL.
DARMSTADT 1, 1969-
OX/U-8.

VERNACULAR ARCHITECTURE.
++VERNACULAR ARCHIT.
VERNACULAR ARCHITECTURE GROUP.
YEOVIL NO.1, 1970-
ED/N-1.     LO/N-1.     OX/U-1.     SH/U-1.

VEROFFENTLICHUNGEN, ABTEILUNG UND LEHRSTUHL
FUR WASSERCHEMIE, INSTITUT FUR GASTECHNIK,
FEUERUNGSTECHNIK UND WASSERCHEMIE (KARLSRUHE).XX
++VEROFF. ABT. & LEHRSTUHL WASSERCHEM. INST.
GASTECH. FEUERUNGSTECH. & WASSERCHEM.(KARLSR.)
KARLSRUHE 1, 1966- 4, 1969 ...
SUBS: VEROFFENTLICHUNGEN, BEREICH UND LEHR-
STUHL FUR WASSERCHEMIE, ENGLER-BUNTE-INSTITUT.
LO/N14.*

VEROFFENTLICHUNGEN DER ARBEITSGEMEINSCHAFT
FUR WESTFALISCHE MUSIKGESCHICHTE.
++VEROFF. ARBEITSGEM. WESTFAL. MUSIKGESCH.
[BARENREITER-VERLAG]
CASSEL NO.1, 1969-
LO/N-1.

VEROFFENTLICHUNGEN, BEREICH UND LEHRSTUHL
FUR WASSERCHEMIE, ENGLER-BUNTE-INSTITUT.          xxx
++VEROFF. BEREICH & LEHRSTUHL WASSERCHEM.
ENGLER-BUNTE-INST.
KARLSRUHE 5, 1971-
PREV: VEROFFENTLICHUNGEN, ABTEILUNG UND LEHR-
STUHL FUR WASSERCHEMIE, INSTITUT FUR GASTECH-
NIK, FEUERUNGSTECHNIK UND WASSERCHEMIE FROM 1,
1966- 4, 1969.
LO/N14.

VEROFFENTLICHUNGEN DES BEZIRKSHEIMATMUSEUMS
POTSDAM.
++VEROFF. BEZIRKSHEIMATMUS. POTSDAM.
POTSDAM 1, 1962-
LO/N-1.

VEROFFENTLICHUNGEN, GEOPHYSIKALISCHES INSTITUT,
KARL-MARX-UNIVERSITAT, LEIPZIG: 2S: SPEZIAL-
ARBEITEN.                                          xxx
SUBS (1974) PART OF: GEOPHYSIK UND GEOLOGIE.
GEOPHYSIKALISCHE VEROFFENTLICHUNGEN DER KARL-
MARX-UNIVERSITAT, LEIPZIG.

VEROFFENTLICHUNGEN ZUR GESCHICHTE DES GLASES
UND DER GLASHUTTEN IN DEUTSCHLAND.
++VEROFF. GESCH. GLASES & GLASHUTTEN DTSCHL.
WIESBADEN 1, 1969-
OX/U-1.

VEROFFENTLICHUNGEN DER GREGORIANISCHE AKAD-
EMIE ZU FREIBURG: NF.
++VEROFF. GREGORIANISCHE AKAD. FREIB., NF.
FREIBURG 1, 1972-
PREV. SERIES FROM 1, 1903.
OX/U-1.

VEROFFENTLICHUNGEN DES HISTORISCHEN INSTITUTS
DER UNIVERSITAT SALZBURG.
++VEROFF. HIST. INST. UNIV. SALZBURG.
VIENNA NO.1, 1971-
LO/N-1.

VEROFFENTLICHUNGEN, KARLSRUHE STADTARCHIV.
++VEROFF. KARLSRUHE STADTARCH.
KARLSRUHE 1, 1965-
OX/U-1.

VEROFFENTLICHUNGEN DES SEMINARS FUR ETHNOL-
OGIE DER UNIVERSITAT BERN.
++VEROFF. SEMIN. ETHNOL. UNIV. BERN.
BERN NO.1, 1969-
MONOGR.
LO/N-1.

VEROFFENTLICHUNGEN DER SOCIETAS URALO-ALTAICA.
++VEROFF. SOC. URALO-ALTAICA.
[OTTO HARRASSOWITZ]
HAMBURG; WIESBADEN 1, 1969-
LO/N-1.     OX/U-1.

VEROFFENTLICHUNGEN DER STAATSBIBLIOTHEK
PREUSSISCHER KULTURBESITZ.
++VEROFF. STAATSBIBL. PREUSS. KULTURBESITZ.
BERLIN 1, 1972-
LO/N-1.

VEROFFENTLICHUNGEN DES ZENTRALINSTITUTS FUR
PHYSIK DER ERDE.
++VEROFF. ZENTRALINST. PHYS. ERDE.
POTSDAM NO.1, 1969-
BODY AS: ZENTRALINSTITUT PHYSIK DER ERDE
FROM NO.1, 1969- 16, 1972.
DB/S-1.     LO/N14.
LO/N-4. NO.2, 1969-
ISSN 0514-8790

VERSPREIDE OVERDRUKKEN, INSTITUUT VOOR
CULTUURTECHNIEK EN WATERHUISHOUDING.
++VERSPREIDE OVERDRUKKEN INST. CULTUURTECH.
WATERHUISHOUDING.
WAGENINGEN 1962-
BN/U-2.

VERSUS. QUADERNI DI STUDI SEMIOTICI.
MILAN 1, 1971-
Q. ENGL., FR., OR ITAL. COVER TITLE: VS.
CA/U-1.     LO/U-2.     OX/U-1.

VERTEBRATOLOGICKE ZPRAVY.
++VERTEBR. ZPR. [VTBZ-A]
CESKOSLOVENSKA AKADEMIE VED: USTAV PRO VYZKUM
OBRATLOVCU.
BRNO 1, 1967-
ANNU. S/T: NOTULAE VERTEBRATOLOGICAE.
DB/N-2.     DB/S-1.     LO/N-2.     LO/N13.

VERTIGO NEWSEXTRA.
[VERTIGO PUBL.]
CARDIFF NO.1, 1969-
OX/U-1.

VERZEICHNIS LIEFERBARER BUCHER.
++VERZ. LIEFERBARER BUCHER.
BOER-SENVEREIN DES DEUTSCHEN BUCHHANDELS.
[VERLAG DOKUMENTATION]
FRANKFURT AM MAIN 1971/72-
ANNU. TEXT IN ENGL. & GER. ENGL. TEXT HAS
TITLE: GERMAN BOOKS IN PRINT.
CO/U-1.     GL/U-1.     LO/U-1.

VESTNIK CESKOSLOVENSKE AKADEMIE ZEMEDELSKE.
++VESTN. CESK. AKAD. ZEMED.
PRAGUE 16(1), 1969-
ALSO AS ABOVE TITLE FROM 1, 1925- 25, 1951.
PREV: VESTNIK, USTREDI ZEMEDELSKEHO A POTRAV-
INARSKEHO VYZKUMU FROM 15(1), 1968- 15(12),
1968.
CA/U11.     LO/N14.

VESTNIK MASHINOSTROENIJA: (GER. TRANSL.)           000
SEE: UMFORMTECHNIK. [ARTICLES]

VESTNIK MOSKOVSKOGO UNIVERSITETA: SERIJA 13:
TEORIJA NAUCHNOGO KOMMUNIZMA.
++VESTN. MOSK. UNIV., 13.
MOSCOW 26, 1971-
2M. CONT. VOL. NUMB. OF THE OTHER SERIES OF
'VESTNIK ...'
CC/U-1.
LO/U-3. 1972- [W.MR- AG 1972]

VESTNIK OBSHCHESTVENNYKH NAUK, AKADEMIJA NAUK
ARMJANSKOJ SSR.                                    xxx
++VESTN. OBSHCHESTV. NAUK AKAD. NAUK ARM. SSR.
EREVAN 1(272), JA 1966-
M. PREV: IZVESTIJA AKADEMII NAUK ARMJANSKOJ
SSR: OBSHCHESTVENNYE NAUKI FROM 1946- 1965.
CONT. VOL. NUMBERING IN PARENTHESIS.
DB/S-1.     LO/N-3.     LO/U14.     OX/U-1.

VESTNIK, USTREDI ZEMEDELSKEHO A POTRAVINARSK-
EHO VYZKUMU.
++VESTN. USTREDI ZEMED. POTRAVIN. VYZK.
PRAGUE 15(1), 1968- 15(12), 1968...
PREV: VESTNIK VYZKUMNYCH USTAVU ZEMEDELSKYCH
FROM 9(4), 1962- 14(12), 1967. . SUBS: VESTNIK
CESKOSLOVENSKE AKADEMIE ZEMEDELSKE.
CA/U11.     LO/N14.

VESTNIK ZOOLOGII (KIEV).
++VESTN. ZOOL. (KIEV). [VEZO-A]
AKADEMIJA NAUK UKRAJINS'KOJI RSR: INSTYTUT
ZOOLOHIJI.
KIEV 1, 1967-
ENGL. SUMM., CONT. LISTS & TITLE: ZOOLOGICAL
RECORD.
LO/N-2.     LO/N13.

**VETERINARIA. REVISTA DE LA ...**
UNIVERSIDAD NACIONAL AUTONOMA DE MEXICO:
FACULTAD DE MEDICINA VETERINARIA Y ZOOTECNIA.
*MEXICO, D.F. 1(1), JA/MR 1970-*
Q.
LO/M18.

**VETERINARY CLINICS OF NORTH AMERICA.**
+ +VET. CLIN. NORTH AM.
[W.B.SAUNDERS CO.]
*PHILADELPHIA &C. 1(1), JA 1971-*
3/A.
CA/U-1.    GL/U-1.    LO/M18.

**VETERINARY DIGEST.**                                                    XXX
+ +VET. DIG.
VETERINARIANS' UNION.
*LONDON    1, JL 1967- 4, 1970.*
SUBS. INCORP. IN: VETERINARY DOCTOR.
DB/U-2.    ED/N-1.    LO/M15.
LO/N13.  [CURRENT BOX ONLY]

**VETERINARY DOCTOR.**                                                    XXX
+ +VET. DOCTOR.
VETERINARIAN'S UNION.
*LONDON  [1](1), OC 1968-*
FROM 2, 1971 INCORP: VETERINARY DIGEST.
ED/N-1.    OX/U-8.
LO/N13. 1(2), 1969-

**VETERINARY MEDICINE.**                                                  XXX
SUBS (1964): VETERINARY MEDICINE/SMALL ANIMAL
CLINICIAN.

**VETERINARY MEDICINE/SMALL ANIMAL CLINICIAN.**          XXX
+ +VET. MED./SMALL ANIM. CLIN.
[C.M. COOPER]
*BONNER SPRINGS, KANS. 59, 1964-*
PREV: VETERINARY MEDICINE FROM 1, 1905- 58,
1963. INCORP: SMALL ANIMAL CLINICIAN 1, 1961-
3, 1963, TO CONT. AS ABOVE TITLE.
LO/N13.
ISSN 0042-4889

**VETERINARY NEWS.**                                                      XXX
+ +VET. NEWS. [VTNW-A]
[MEDICAL PUBL.]
*LONDON  NO.1, JA 1966- 4(8), AG 1969.*
M.  SUBS: VETERINARY PRACTICE.
ED/N-1.

**VETERINARY PATHOLOGY.**                                                 XXX
+ +VET. PATHOL.
AMERICAN COLLEGE OF VETERINARY PATHOLOGISTS.
[KARGER]
*BASLE  8, 1971-*
PREV: PATHOLOGIA VETERINARIA FROM 1(1), 1964-
7(6), 1970.
GL/U-1.    LD/U-1.    LO/N13.

**VETERINARY PRACTICE.**                                                  XXX
+ +VET. PRACT.
[HAYMARKET P.]
*EWELL, SURREY.  1, S 1969-*
INCORP:VETERINARY NEWS, 1(1), 1966- 4(8), 1969
LO/N13.  CURRENT ISSUES ONLY.
ISSN 0042-4897

**VIATOR. MEDIEVAL & RENAISSANCE STUDIES.**
UNIVERSITY OF CALIFORNIA (LOS ANGELES): CENTER
FOR MEDIEVAL & RENAISSANCE STUDIES.
*BERKELEY  1, 1970-*
ANNU.
AD/U-1.    CB/U-1.    DB/U-2.    ED/N-1.    HL/U-1.    NO/U-1.
RE/U-1.    SH/U-1.    SO/U-1.    SW/U-1.

**VICKERS MAGAZINE.**
+ +VICKERS MAG.
*LONDON NO.1, 1969-*
OX/U-1.

**VICTORIA & ALBERT MUSEUM BROCHURE.**
*LONDON NO.1, 1972-*
CA/U-1.    LO/N-1.

**VICTORIA & ALBERT MUSEUM YEARBOOK.**
+ +VIC. & ALBERT MUS. YEARB.
*LONDON NO.1, 1969-*
AD/U-1.    BL/U-1.    BT/U-1.    CA/U-1.    HL/U-1.    LO/U-1.
OX/U-1.    RE/U-1.
LD/U-1. NO.4, 1974-              LO/N-4. NO.2, 1970
CB/C-1. NO.1, 1969.
GL/U-1. NO.1, 1969- 3, 1972.
MA/U-1. NO.1, 1969.

**VICTORIAN PERIODICALS NEWSLETTER.**
+ +VICTORIAN PERIOD. NEWSL.
INDIANA UNIVERSITY.
*BLOOMINGTON  NO.1, JA 1968-*
AT HEAD OF TITLE: VICTORIAN STUDIES.
DB/U-2.    GL/U-2.    LO/M24.    LO/U-3.    LO/U13.
NW/U-1.    OX/U17.    SO/U-1.    SW/U-1.
HL/U-1. NO.2, 1968-                    LO/U-1. NO.3, 1968-
NO/U-1. NO.3, 1968-
ISSN 0049-6189

**VICTORIAN STUDIES HANDLIST.**
+ +VICTORIAN STUD. HANDLIST.
UNIVERSITY OF LEICESTER: VICTORIAN STUDIES
CENTRE.
*LEICESTER  NO.1, 1969-*
BL/U-1.    GL/U-1.
HL/U-1. NO.1 1969.
LO/N-1. NO.1, 1969.

**VIDYODAYA. JOURNAL OF ARTS, SCIENCES & LETT-
ERS.**
VIDYODAYA UNIVERSITY OF CEYLON.
*GANGODAWILA, NUGEGODA  1, 1968-*
LD/U-1.

**VIERTELJAHRIGE REVUE UBER IMPLANTOLOGIE.**          000
SEE: REVUE TRIMESTRIELLE D'IMPLANTOLOGIE.

**VIETNAM INTERNATIONAL.**
+ +VIETNAM INT.
INTERNATIONAL CONFEDERATION FOR DISARMAMENT &
PEACE.
*LONDON  1(1), 1966-*
ALSO ISSUED IN A FR. ED.
ED/N-1.    LO/U-3.

**VIETNAM NEWSLETTER.**
+ +VIETNAM NEWSL.
VIETNAM (SOUTH) COUNCIL ON FOREIGN RELATIONS.
*SAIGON  1(1), OC 1969-*
LO/S14.

**VIEWPOINT.  AN IUD QUARTERLY.**
AMERICAN FEDERATION OF LABOR & CONGRESS OF
INDUSTRIAL ORGANIZATIONS: INDUSTRIAL UNION
DEPARTMENT.
*WASHINGTON, D.C.  1(1), SPRING 1971-*
OX/U16.    OX/U17.
ISSN 0042-5869

**VIEWPOINT.  LOOKING AT SOME ASPECTS OF
AUSTRALIA'S IMMIGRATION POLICY.**
IMMIGRATION CONTROL ASSOCIATION (AUSTRALIA).
*CROWS NEST, N.S.W.  NO.1, JE/JL 1970-*
LO/U-8.*

**VIEWPOINT.  A RADICAL NON-ZIONIST & INDEPENDENT
NEWS SERVICE & CRITICAL REVIEW.**
*JERUSALEM  NO.1, 1973-*
LO/U14.

**VIEWPOINT SERIES, AUSTRALIAN CONSERVATION
FOUNDATION.**
+ +VIEWPOINT SER. AUST. CONSERV. FOUND.
*CANBERRA  NO.1, 1967-*
LO/N-2.    LO/R-5.

**VIEWPOINTS.**                                                           XXX
INDIANA UNIVERSITY: SCHOOL OF EDUCATION.
*BLOOMINGTON, IND.  46(1), JA 1970-*
PREV: BULLETIN OF THE SCHOOL OF EDUCATION,
INDIANA UNIVERSITY FROM 1, 1924- 45, 1969.
LO/U-1.    OX/U-1.
ISSN 0019-6835

**VIGIL.**
*TACNA, PERU  1, 1972-*
OX/U-1.

**VIGILANTE.**
*CALGARY  1, 1970-*
OX/U-1.
ISSN 0042-5990

**VILNIAUS VALSTYBINIS /V. KAPSUKO VARDO/ UNI-
VERSITETAS, MOKSLO DARBAI; EKONOMIKA. =
UCHENYE ZAPISKI, VIL'NJUSSKIJ GOSUDARSTVENNYJ
UNIVERSITET /IM. V. KAPSUKASA/; EKONOMIKA.**     XXX
+ +VILNIAUS VALST. UNIV. MOKS. DARB., EKON.
*VILNIUS  [NO.]1, 1960...*
ALSO NUMBERED IN GEN. SERIES OF ABOVE MAIN
TITLE, 1 = 34. SUBS: LIETUVOS TSR AUKSTUJU
MOKYKLU MOKSLO DARBAI; EKONOMIKA. = UCHENYE
ZAPISKI VYSSHIKH UCHEBNYKH ZAVEDENIJ LITOVSKOJ
SSR; EKONOMIKA.
LO/N-3.

**VIP. THE MAGAZINE FOR VERY IMPORTANT PEOPLE.**
[VIP]
*BEDFORD NO.1, MR 1973-*
*CA/U-1.  ED/N-1.*

**VIRGINIA WOOLF QUARTERLY.**
*++VIRGINIA WOOLF Q.*
[CALIFORNIA STATE UNIV. P.]
*SAN DIEGO 1, 1972/73-*
*AD/U-1.  LO/U-1.  OX/U-1.*

**VIROLOGY MONOGRAPHS.**
*++VIROL. MONOGR.*
[SPRINGER]
*NEW YORK 1, 1968-*
*LO/M17.  LO/M25.  LO/N-4.  LO/N-6.  LO/N13.*
*LV/U-1.  OX/U-8.*

**VISHVESHVARANAND INDOLOGICAL JOURNAL.**
*++VISHVESHVARANAND INDOL. J.*
VISHVESHVARANAND VEDIC RESEARCH INSTITUTE.
*HOSHIARPUR 1(1), MR 1963-*
*ED/U-1.  4(1), MR 1966.*

**VISIBLE LANGUAGE.**                                    XXX
*++VISIBLE LANG.*
[P. OF WESTERN RESERVE UNIV.]
*CLEVELAND, OHIO 5, 1971-*
Q. PREV: JOURNAL OF TYPOGRAPHICAL RESEARCH
FROM 1(1), JA 1967- 4, 1970.
*BT/C-1.  DB/U-2.  ED/N-1.  LO/N14.  LO/N15.  RE/U-1.*
*ISSN 0022-2224*

**VISION. THE EUROPEAN BUSINESS MAGAZINE.**
*GENEVA NO.1, N 1970-*
*DB/U-2.*

**VISION INDEX.**
UNIVERSITY OF CALIFORNIA: VISUAL SCIENCE INFOR-
MATION CENTER.
*BERKELEY, CALIF. 1, MR 1971-*
Q.
*LO/N13.*
*ISSN 0049-6510*

**VISION OF MALAWI.**
(MALAWI) DEPARTMENT OF INFORMATION.
*BLANTYRE 1(1), 1970-*
*OX/U-9.*
*CA/U-1.  3(4), 1972-*

**VISION & VOICE.**
SUNDERLAND POLYTECHNIC: SCHOOL OF ART & DESIGN.
*SUNDERLAND NO.1, 1969-*
*ED/N-1.  OX/U-1.*
*ISSN 0042-6946*

**VISTAS IN RESEARCH.**
*++VISTAS RES.*
[GORDON & BREACH]
*NEW YORK &C. 1, 1967-*
ALSO ENTITLED: BROOKHAVEN NATIONAL LABORATORY
LECTURES IN SCIENCE.
*BL/U-1.  LO/N14.*
*OX/U-8.  4, 1969-*

**VIVALDIANA.**
CENTRE INTERNATIONAL DE DOCUMENTATION ANTONIO
VIVALDI.
*BRUSSELS NO.1, 1969-*
*LO/N-1.  LO/U-1.  OX/U-1.*

**VLAAMSE STAM. TYDSCHRIFT VOOR FAMILIE-
GESCHIEDENIS.**
*++VLAAM. STAM.*
*ANTWERP 1, 1965-*
*ED/N-1.*

**VNESHNJAJA POLITIKA SOVETSKOGO SOJUZA I MEZH-
DUNARODNYE OTNOSHENIJA. SBORNIK DOKUMENTOV.**
*++VNESHN. POLIT. SOV. SOJUZA & MEZHDUNAR.*
*OTNOSHENIJA.*
INSTITUT MEZHDUNARODNYKH OTNOSHENIJ.
*MOSCOW 1, 1961-*
ANNU.
*BH/U-1.  BT/U-1.  CC/U-1.  LA/U-1.  LD/U-1.  LO/S14.*
*LO/U-3.  NR/U-1.  SW/U-1.  XW/C-3.*

**VOCATIONAL TEACHERS VIEWS & NEWS.**
*++VOCAT. TEACH. VIEWS & NEWS.*
*DUBLIN 1, S 1972-*
*DB/U-2.  ED/N-1.*

**VODNOE KHOZJAJSTVO. RESPUBLIKANSKIJ MEZHVED-
OMSTVENNYJ NAUCHNO-TEKHNICHESKIJ SBORNIK.**     XXX
*++VODN. KHOZ.*
(UKRAINE) MINISTERSTVO MELIORATSII I VODNOGO
KHOZJAJSTVA.
*KIEV TOM 1, 1965- 5, 1966 ...*
SUBS: MELIORATSIJA I VODNOE KHOZJAJSTVO.

**VOEDINGSMIDDELENTECHNOLOGIE.**                  XXX
[VERENIGDE PERIODIEKE PERS NV]
*THE HAGUE 1, 1970-*
PREV: CONSERVA FROM 1, 1952- 18, 1969.
*LO/N14.*
*ISSN 0042-7934*

**VOGELWELT: BEIHEFTE.**
[DUNCKER & HUMBLOT]
*BERLIN 1, 1968-*
*LO/N13.*

**VOICE. A CHRISTIAN MAGAZINE FOR STUDENTS.**
INTER-VARSITY FELLOWSHIP.
*LONDON NO.1, 1970-*
*ED/N-1.  OX/U-1.*

**VOICE OF THE WEST.**
WEST COUNTRY ANTI-COMMON MARKET LEAGUE.
*LUSTLEIGH, DEVON. 1(1), 1972-*
*OX/U-1.*

**VOLE.**
*HITCHIN NO.1, 1972-*
6/A.
*ED/N-1.  OX/U-1.*

**VOPROSY ARKHIVOVEDENIJA.**                       XXX
SUBS (1966): SOVETSKIE ARKHIVY.

**VOPROSY BIOKHIMII MOZGA.**
*++VOPR. BIOKHIM. MOZGA. [VBIM-A]*
AKADEMIJA NAUK ARMJANSKOJ SSR: INSTITUT
BIOKHIMII.
*EREVAN 1, 1964-*
*XY/N-1.*
*LO/N13.  4, 1968-*

**VOPROSY BOR'BY S PRESTUPNOST'JU.**              XXX
*++VOPR. BOR'BY PRESTUPNOST'JU.*
VSESOJUZNYJ INSTITUT PO IZUCHENIJU PRICHIN I
RAZRABOTKE MER PREDUPREZHDENIJA PRESTUPNOSTI.
*MOSCOW 5, 1967-*
PREV: VOPROSY PREDUPREZHDENIJA PRESTUPNOSTI
FROM 1, 1965- 4, 1966.
*BH/U-1.  CC/U-1.  GL/U-1.  LO/U15.*

**VOPROSY DOZIMETRII I ZASHCHITY OT IZLUCHENIJ.**  XXX
*++VOPR. DOZIM. & ZASHCH. IZLUCH.*
MOSKOVSKIJ INZHENERNO-FIZICHESKIJ INSTITUT.
*MOSCOW 1, 1962-*
PREV: PRIBORY I METODY ANALIZA IZLUCHENIJ FROM
1, 1957- 3, 1962.
*LO/N13.*
*XS/R10.  9, 1969-*

**VOPROSY EKOLOGII I PRAKTICHESKOGO ZNACHENIJA
PTITS I MLEKOPITAJUSHCHIKH MOLDAVII.**
*++VOPR. EKOL. & PRAKT. ZNACHENIJA PTITS &*
*MLEKOPITAJUSHCHIKH MOLD.*
AKADEMIJA NAUK MOLDAVSKOJ SSR: INSTITUT
ZOOLOGII.
*KISHINEV [1] 1962-*
VOL.1 UNNUMBERED.
*LO/N-2.*
*LO/N13.  4, 1969-*

**VOPROSY EKONOMIKI I ORGANIZATSII SOTSIALIST-
ICHESKOGO PROIZVODSTVA.**
*++VOPR. EKON. & ORG. SOTS. PROIZVOD.*
TOMSKIJ GOSUDARSTVENNYJ UNIVERSITET: EKONOM-
ICHESKIJ FAKUL'TET.
*TOMSK 1, 1965-*
*CC/U-1.  GL/U-1.*

**VOPROSY ELEKTRONIKI SVERKHVYSOKIKH CHASTOT.**
*++VOPR. ELEKTRON. SVERKHVYS. CHASTOT.*
SARATOVSKIJ GOSUDARSTVENNYJ UNIVERSITET.
*MOSCOW 2, 1966-*
NO DATA AVAILABLE REGARDING VOL.1.
*LO/N13.*

**VOPROSY FILOSOFII I PSIKHOLOGII. SBORNIK
RABOT ASPIRANTOV.**
*++VOPR. FILOS. & PSIKHOL. [VFPS-A]*
LENINGRADSKIJ GOSUDARSTVENNYJ UNIVERSITET:
FILOSOFSKIJ FAKUL'TET.
*LENINGRAD 1, 1965-*
*BH/U-1.  CC/U-1.  GL/U-1.  OX/U-1.*

VOPROSY FILOSOFII I SOTSIOLOGII.
+ +VOPR. FILOS. & SOTSIOL.
LENINGRADSKIJ GOSUDARSTVENNYJ UNIVERSITET:
FILOSOFSKIJ FAKUL'TET.
  LENINGRAD 1, 1969-
  S/T: SBORNIK RABOT ASPIRANTOV FILOSOFSKOGO
  FAKUL'TETA LGU.
  BH/U-1.    CC/U-1.    GL/U-1.    OX/U-1.

VOPROSY GEOGRAFII KAMCHATKI.
GEOGRAFICHESKOE OBSHCHESTVO SSSR, KAMCHATSKOE
OTDELENIE.
  PETROPAVLOVSK-KAMCHATSKIJ  1963-
  LO/N-3.  2, 1964.
  SW/U-1.  5, 1967.

VOPROSY GOSUDARSTVA I PRAVA (MINSK).
+ +VOPR. GOS. & PRAVA (MINSK).
BELORUSSKIJ GOSUDARSTVENNYJ UNIVERSITET:
JURIDICHESKIJ FAKUL'TET.
  MINSK 1, 1969-
  BH/U-1.    GL/U-1.    LO/U-3.

VOPROSY ISTORII KOMMUNISTICHESKOJ PARTII
KAZAKHSTANA. (*)
+ +VOP. ISTOR. KOMMUNIST. PARTII KAZAKHSTANA.
KOMMUNISTICHESKAJA PARTIJA KAZAKHSTANA:
INSTITUT ISTORII PARTII.
  ALMA-ATA  [VYP.1], 1963-
  A.  INST. SUBORD. TO: TSENTRAL'NYJ KOMITET KP
  KAZAKHSTANA.  VYP. [1] & 2 ACTUALLY TITLED:
  VOPROSY ISTORII KOMPARTII KAZAKHSTANA.
  CC/U-1.    GL/U-1.    LO/U-3.    OX/U-1.
  BH/U-1.  4,1966-

VOPROSY ISTORII SIBIRI.
+ +VOPR. ISTOR. SIB.
TOMSKIJ GOSUDARSTVENNYJ UNIVERSITET.
  TOMSK 1, 1964-
  SUBSERIES OF THE UNIVERSITET'S 'TRUDY ...'
  GL/U-1.    LO/U-3.    LO/U15.    SW/U-1.

VOPROSY ISTORII SOTSIAL'NO-EKONOMICHESKOJ I
KUL'TURNOJ ZHIZNI SIBIRI I DAL'NEGO VOSTOKA.
+ +VOPR. ISTOR. SOTS.-EKON. & KUL'T. ZHIZNI SIB.
& DAL'NEGO VOSTOKA.
AKADEMIJA NAUK SSSR (SIBIRSKOE OTDELENIE):
INSTITUT ISTORII, FILOLOGII I FILOSOFII.
  NOVOSIBIRSK 1, 1968-
  SPONS BODY ALSO: GEOGRAFICHESKOE OBSHCHESTVO
  SSSR (NOVOSIBIRSKOE OTDELENIE): SEKTSIJA
  ISTORICHESKOJ GEOGRAFII.
  GL/U-1.    OX/U-1.    SW/U-1.

VOPROSY MAGNITNOJ GIDRODINAMIKI.                          XXX
+ +VOPR. MAGN. GIDRODIN.
AKADEMIJA NAUK LATVIJSKOJ SSR: INSTITUT FIZIKI.
  RIGA  3, 1963-
  A.  PREV: VOPROSY MAGNITNOJ GIDRODINAMIKI I
  DINAMIKI PLAZMY FORM 1, 1958- 2, 1962.
  LO/N13.

VOPROSY MAGNITNOJ GIDRODINAMIKI I DINAMIKI
PLAZMY.                                                    XXX
  SUBS (1963): VOPROSY MAGNITNOJ GIDRODINAMIKI.

VOPROSY MATEMATICHESKOJ EKSPLUATATSII VYCHIS-
LITEL'NYKH MASHIN.
+ +VOPR. MAT. EKSPL. VYCHISL. MASH. [VMEV-A]
AKADEMIJA NAUK SSSR: KOMISSIJA PO EKSPLUATATSII
VYCHISLITEL'NYKH MASHIN.
  MOSCOW 1, 1965-
  VOL.2 PUBL. IN 5 EDITIONS: 2 DATED 1965, 2
  DATED 1966, ONE DATED 1967.
  LO/N13.

VOPROSY NAUCHNOGO ATEIZMA.
+ +VOPR. NAUCHN. ATEIZMA.
AKADEMIJA OBSHCHESTVENNYKH NAUK PRI TSK KPSS:
INSTITUT·NAUCHNOGO ATEIZMA.
  MOSCOW 1, 1966-
  BH/U-1.    GL/U-1.    LO/U-3.    LO/U15.    NO/U-1.    OX/U-1.

VOPROSY NAUCHNOGO KOMMUNIZMA (MINSK).
+ +VOPR. NAUCHN. KOMMUN. (MINSK).
BELORUSSKIJ GOSUDARSTVENNYJ UNIVERSITET:
KAFEDRA NAUCHNOGO KOMMUNIZMA.
  MINSK 1, 1970-
  BH/U-1.    CC/U-1.

VOPROSY OBSHCHESTVENNYKH NAUK (KIEV).
+ +VOPR. OBSHCHESTV. NAUK (KIEV).
KYJIVS'KYJ DERZHAVNYJ UNIVERSYTET: INSTYTUT
PIDVYSHCHENNJA KVALIFIKATSII VYKLADACHIV
SUSPIL'NYKH NAUK.
  KIEV 1, 1970-
  LO/N-3.  2(1971).

VOPROSY PREDUPREZHDENIJA PRESTUPNOSTI.                     XXX
+ +VOPR. PREDUPREZHDENIJA PRESTUPNOSTI.  [VOPP-A]
VSESOJUZNYJ INSTITUT PO IZUCHENIJU PRICHIN I
RAZRABOTKE MER PREDUPREZHDENIJA PRESTUPNOSTI.
  MOSCOW 1, 1965- 4, 1966 ...
  SUBS: VOPROSY BOR'BY PRESTUPNOST'JU.
  BH/U-1.    CC/U-1.    GL/U-1.

VOPROSY PRIRODNOJ OCHAGOVOSTI BOLEZNEJ.
+ +VOPR. PRIR. OCHAGOVOSTI BOLEZN.
AKADEMIJA NAUK KAZAKHSKOJ SSR: INSTITUT
ZOOLOGII.
  ALMA-ATA 1, 1966-
  ENGL. CONT. LISTS & TITLE: CONTRIBUTIONS TO
  THE NATURAL NIDALITY OF DISEASES.
  XS/R14.    XY/N-1.
  LO/N13.  3, 1970-

VOPROSY RATSIONAL'NOGO PITANIJA.
+ +VOPR. RATSIONAL. PITAN.  [VPRP-B]
KYJIVS'KYJ NAUKOVO-DOSLIDNYJ INSTYTUT HIHIENY
ZHYVLENNJA.
  KIEV 1, 1964-
  S/T: RESPUBLIKANSKIJ MEZHVEDOMSTVENNYJ SBORNIK
  BH/U-1.  4, 1968-
  LO/N13.  5, 1969-

VOPROSY RUSSKOJ LITERATURY.
+ +VOP. RUSS. LIT.
CHERNIVETS'KYJ DERZHAVNYJ UNIVERSYTET.
  L'VOV VYP.1, 1966-
  ED/U-1.    HL/U-1.    LO/N-3.    SA/U-1.
  MA/U-1.  7, 1968-                SW/U-1.  7, 1968-
  CC/U-1.  1(9), 1972.

VOPROSY SUDEBNOJ PSIKHOLOGII.
+ +VOPR. SUD. PSIKHOL.
BELORUSSKIJ GOSUDARSTVENNYJ UNIVERSITET.
  MINSK 1, 1970-
  BH/U-1.    CC/U-1.    GL/U-1.

VOPROSY TEATRA.  SBORNIK STATEJ I MATERIALOV.
+ +VOPR. TEATRA.
(RUSSIA USSR) MINISTERSTVO KUL'TURY: INSTITUT
ISTORII ISKUSSTV.
  MOSCOW 1, 1965-
  ANNU.  SPONS. BODY ALSO: VSEROSSIJSKOE TEAT-
  RAL'OBSHCHESTVO.
  BH/U-1.    CC/U-1.    GL/U-1.    MA/U-1.    NO/U-1.    OX/U-1.
  SW/U-1.
  LO/U15.  1965- 1967; 1970.

VOPROSY TEKHNICHESKOJ ESTETIKI.
+ +VOP. TEKH. ESTETIKI.
VSESOJUZNYJ NAUCHNO-ISSLEDOVATEL'SKIJ INSTITUT
TEKHNICHESKOJ ESTETIKI.
  MOSCOW VYP. 1, 1968-
  BH/U-1.    CC/U-1.

VOPROSY TEORII I PRAKTIKI MASSOVYKH FORM
PROPAGANDY.                                                000
  SEE: VOPROSY TEORII I PRAKTIKI MASSOVYKH
  SREDSTV PROPAGANDY.

VOPROSY TEORII I PRAKTIKI MASSOVYKH SREDSTV
PROPAGANDY.                                                XXX
+ +VOPR. TEOR. & PRAKT. MASSOVYKH SREDSTV PROPAG.
AKADEMIJA OBSHCHESTVENNYKH NAUK PRI TSK KPSS:
SEKTSIJA ZHURNALISTIKI.
  MOSCOW 1, 1968- 4, 1971.
  ANNU.  VOL.1, 1968 PUBL. AS: VOPROSY TEORII I
  PRAKTIKI MASSOVYKH FORM PROPAGANDY. SUBS:
  VOPROSY.TEORII I METODOV IDEOLOGICHESKOJ
  ROBOTY.
  BH/U-1.    CC/U-1.
  LO/U15.  1969-

VORTRAGE, FORSCHUNGEN, BERICHTE, GRILLPARZER-
FORUM FORCHTENSTEIN.                                       000
  SEE: GRILLPARZER-FORUM FORCHTENSTEIN:
  VORTRAGE, FORSCHUNGEN, BERICHTE.

VOSPITANIE SHKOL'NIKOV.
+ +VOSPITAN. SHK.  [VOSH-A]
(RUSSIA RSFSR) MINISTERSTVO PROSVESHCHENIJA.
  MOSCOW 1(1), 1966-
  CC/U-1.    LO/N-3.    OX/U-1.
  ISSN 0042-8957

VOSTOCHNYJ SBORNIK.                                        000
  SEE: KAVKAZSKO-BLIZHNE-VOSTOCHNYJ SBORNIK.

VOSTOKOVEDCHESKIJ SBORNIK.
+ +VOSTOKOVEDCHESK. SB.
AKADEMIJA NAUK ARMJANSKOJ SSR: SEKTOR
VOSTOKOVEDENIJA.
  EREVAN 1, 1960-
  OX/U-1.

**VOX. BULLETIN OF THE VOLUNTARY COMMITTEE ON OVERSEAS AID & DEVELOPMENT.**
*LONDON 1(1), N 1966-*
MON.
*ED/N-1. 4(36), 1969-      OX/U-1. 4(28), 1969-*

**VOX EVANGELICA.**
LONDON BIBLE COLLEGE.
[EPWORTH P.]
*LONDON 1, 1962-*
S/T: BIBLICAL & HISTORICAL ESSAYS BY MEMBERS
OF THE FACULTY OF THE LONDON BIBLE COLLEGE.
*ED/N-1.      MA/U-1.*
*SH/U-1. 1965-*

**VRANJSKI GLASNIK.**
*+ +VRANJSKI GLAS.*
NARODNI MUZEJ VRANJE.
*LO/S30.      OX/U-1.      OX/U-1.      OX/U-2.*

**VREMENNIK PUSHKINSKOJ KOMISSII.**
*+ +VREMENNIK PUSHKINSKOJ KOM.*
AKADEMIJA NAUK SSSR: PUSHKINSKAJA KOMISSIJA.
*MOSCOW 1962-*
A. PUSHKINSKAJA KOMISSIJA SUBORD. TO OTDELENIE
LITERATURY I JAZYKA AN SSSR.
*CC/U-1.      EX/U-1.      HL/U-1.      LA/U-1.      LD/U-1.      LV/U-1.*
*NO/U-1.      NR/U-1.      SA/U-1.*      SW/U-1.*
*BH/U-1. 1966-*
*LO/N-3. 1966(1969).*

**VS.**                                                    000
SEE: VERSUS.

**VSPOMAGATEL'NYE ISTORICHESKIE DISTSIPLINY.**
AKADEMIJA NAUK SSSR: ARKHEOGRAFICHESKAJA
KOMISSIJA [LENINGRADSKOE OTDELENIE].
*LENINGRAD 1, 1968-*
*CC/U-1.      OX/U-1.*
*GL/U-1. 2, 1969-*

**VUOTO SCIENZA E TECNOLOGIA.**
*+ +VUOTO SCI. & TECNOL.*
ASSOCIAZIONE ITALIANA DEL VUOTO.
[TAMBURINI]
*MILAN 1, 1968-*
ITAL. OR ENGL. WITH SUMM. IN BOTH.
*LO/N-4.      LO/N14.*

**VYCHISLITEL'NAJA TEKHNIKA I VOPROSY KIBERNET-
IKI.**                                                    XXX
*+ +VYCHISL. TEKH. & VOPR. KIBERN.*
LENINGRADSKIJ GOSUDARSTVENNYJ UNIVERSITET:
KAFEDRA VYCHISLITEL'NOJ MATEMATIKI I
VYCHISLITEL'NYJ TSENTR LGU.
*LENINGRAD 5, 1968-*
PREV: VYCHISLITEL'NAJA TEKHNIKA I VOPROSY
PROGRAMMIROVANIJA FROM 1, 1962- 4, 1965.
*BH/U-1.*
*LO/N13. 7, 1970-*

**VYCHISLITEL'NAJA TEKHNIKA I VOPROSY PROGRAM-
MIROVANIJA.**                                             XXX
*+ +VYCHISL. TEKH. & VOPR. PROGRAM. [VTVP-A]*
LENINGRADSKIJ GOSUDARSTVENNYJ UNIVERSITET:
KAFEDRA VYCHISLITEL'NOJ MATEMATIKI I
VYCHISLITEL'NYJ TSENTR LGU.
*LENINGRAD 1, 1962- 4, 1965.*
SUBS: VYCHISLITEL'NAJA TEKHNIKA I VOPROSY
KIBERNETIKI.
*BH/U-1.*

**VYCHISLITEL'NYE SISTEMY. SBORNIK TRUDOV.**
*+ +VYCHISL. SIST.*
AKADEMIJA NAUK SSSR (SIBIRSKOE OTDELENIE):
INSTITUT MATEMATIKI.
*NOVOSIBIRSK 1, 1962-*
*LO/N13.*

**VYSOKOMOLEKULJARNYE SOEDINENIJA: SERIJA A.**           XXX
*+ +VYSOKOMOL. SOEDIN., A. [VYSA-A]*
AKADEMIJA NAUK SSSR.
*MOSCOW 9, 1967-*
PREV: AS PART OF ABOVE MAIN TITLE FROM 1,
1959- 8, 1966. THEN ISSUED IN TWO SERIES: A &
B.
*LO/S-3.      LO/U28.*

**VYSOKOMOLEKULJARNYE SOEDINENIJA. SERIJA B:
KRATKIE SOOBSHCHENIJA.**                                 XXX
*+ +VYSOKOMOL. SOEDIN., B. [VYSB-A]*
AKADEMIJA NAUK SSSR.
*MOSCOW 9, 1967-*
SEE NOTES FOR SERIES A.
*LO/S-3.      LO/U28.*

**WALIA.**
ETHIOPIAN WILDLIFE & NATURAL HISTORY SOCIETY.
*ADDIS ABABA NO.1, 1969-*
*LO/N-2.*

**WALLACE STEVENS NEWSLETTER.**
*+ +WALLACE STEVENS NEWSL.*
*CHICAGO 1(1), OC 1969-*
2/A.
*DB/U-2.      OX/U-1.*
*ISSN 0043-0110*

**WAR & SOCIETY NEWSLETTER.**
*+ +WAR & SOC. NEWSL.*
*EDINBURGH AP 1973-*
*LO/U-3.      OX/U-1.*

**WARME UND STOFFUBERTRAGUNG.**
*+ +WARME & STOFFUBERTRAG.*
*BERLIN 1(1), 1968-*
*LO/N-4.      LO/N14.      OX/U-8.*

**WARWICK RESEARCH IN INDUSTRIAL & BUSINESS
STUDIES.**
*+ +WARWICK RES. IND. & BUS. STUD.*
UNIVERSITY OF WARWICK: CENTRE FOR INDUSTRIAL &
BUSINESS STUDIES.
*COVENTRY NO.1, 1969-*
*DB/U-2.      LO/N-1.      OX/U-1.*
*NW/U-1. NO.3, 1970-*

**WARWICKSHIRE HISTORY. BULLETIN OF THE …**
*+ +WARKS. HIST.*
WARWICKSHIRE LOCAL HISTORY SOCIETY.
*WARWICK 1(1), 1969-*
*ED/N-1.      LO/U-1.      NO/U-1.      OX/U-1.*

**WASCHER + REINIGER.**                                   XXX
SUBS (1970): REINIGER + WASCHER.

**WASEDA DAIGAKU SEISAN KENKYUJO KIYO. BULLETIN
OF THE INSTITUTE FOR RESEARCH IN PRODUCTIVITY,
WASEDA UNIVERSITY.**
WASEDA DAIGAKU SEISAN KENKYUJO.
*TOKYO NO.1, 1970-*
JAP. OR ENGL.
*LO/N13.*

**WASSER UND ABWASSER IN FORSCHUNG UND PRAXIS.**
*+ +WASSER & ABWASSER FORSCH. & PRAX.*
[E. SCHMIDT]
*BIELEFELD 1, 1969-*
*LO/N14.*

**WATER, AIR & SOIL POLLUTION.**
*+ +WATER AIR & SOIL POLLUT.*
[REIDEL]
*DORDRECHT 1(1), N 1971-*
*EX/U-1.      GL/U-2.      LO/N-2.      LO/N-6.      LO/N14.      LO/R-5.*
*LO/U28.      OX/U-8.      XS/R10.      XY/N-1.*
*BL/U-1. 3, 1974-*
*ISSN 0049-6979*

**WATER IN BIOLOGICAL SYSTEMS.**
*+ +WATER BIOL. SYST.*
[CONSULTANTS BUREAU]
*NEW YORK 1, 1969-*
ARTICLES CONSIST OF RUSS. TRANSL.
*LO/N14.*

**WATER POLLUTION CONTROL RESEARCH SERIES.**
*+ +WATER POLLUT. CONTR. RES. SER.*
(UNITED STATES) FEDERAL WATER POLLUTION
CONTROL ADMINISTRATION.
*WASHINGTON, D.C. [NO.] ORD/1, 1969-*
*LO/N13.*

**WATER POLLUTION DIGEST.**                               000
SEE: WATER QUALITY CONTROL DIGEST.

**WATER QUALITY CONTROL DIGEST.**                         XXX
*+ +WATER QUAL. CONTR. DIG.*
*DETROIT 1, 1969- 2(7), 1971 …*
SUBS: UDS WATER QUALITY CONTROL DIGEST. ALSO
ENTITLED: WATER POLLUTION DIGEST.
*LO/N14.*
*ISSN 0043-1346*

**WATER RESOURCES ABSTRACTS.**
*+ +WATER RESOUR. ABSTR. (US)*
AMERICAN WATER RESOURCES ASSOCIATION.
*URBANA, ILL. 1, 1968-*
*HL/U-1.      LO/N14.*
*ISSN 0043-1362*

WATER RESOURCES BULLETIN.
+ +WATER RESOUR. BULL. (US)
AMERICAN WATER RESOURCES ASSOCIATION.
*URBANA, ILL. 1, 1965-*
*LO/N13.*
*DB/U-2. 9, 1973-*
*ISSN 0043-1370*

WATER RESOURCES NEWSLETTER.
+ +WATER RESOUR. NEWSL. (AUST.)
AUSTRALIAN WATER RESOURCES COUNCIL.
*CANBERRA NO.1, OC 1963-*
*2/A.*
*XS/R13.*
*LO/U-2. NO.15, 1970-*
*SO/U-1. CURRENT THREE YEARS ONLY.*
*ISSN 0043-1389*

WATER SPECTRUM.
+ +WATER SPECTR.
(UNITED STATES) ARMY: CORPS OF ENGINEERS.
*WASHINGTON, D.C. 1, 1969-*
*Q.*
*LO/N13.*
*ISSN 0043-1435*

WATER TOWER.                                                              XXX
SUBS (1972): CHI NEWS.

WATERSPORT & POWERBOAT.*
[LERNHURST PUBL.]
*LONDON [1], 1968- 2(1), 1969 ...*
TITLE EXPANDED FROM WATERSPORT WITH 2(1),
1969. SUBS: POWERBOAT & WATERSPORT.
*LO/N14.*

WATERWAYS NEWS.
BRITISH WATERWAYS BOARD.
*PORTSMOUTH NO.1, 1971-*
*OX/U-1.*
*ED/N-1. NO.2, 1971-*

WAVE. NEW POETRY.
[SONUS P.]
*HULL NO.1, 1970-*
*HL/U-1. OX/U-1.*

WEED RESEARCH (JAPAN).                                                   000
SEE: ZASSO KENKYU.

WEED SCIENCE.                                                            XXX
+ +WEED SCI. [WEES-A]
WEED SCIENCE SOCIETY OF AMERICA.
[HUMPHREY P.]
*GENEVA, N.Y. 16, 1968-*
*Q. PREV: WEEDS FROM 1, OC 1951- 15, OC 1967.*
*BH/U-1. DB/U-2. GL/U-1. LO/N14. RE/U-1. XS/R-2.*
*ISSN 0043-1745*

WEEDS.                                                                   XXX
SUBS (1968): WEED SCIENCE.

WEEK. A NEWS ANALYSIS FOR SOCIALISTS.                                    XXX
*LONDON 1(1), JA 1964- 9(13), MR 1968.*
SUBS: PART OF INTERNATIONAL. A SURVEY OF
BRITISH & WORLD AFFAIRS.
*LO/U-3.*
*BH/P-1. 3, 1965-          ED/N-1. 3(8), 1965-*

WELCOME TO GREENLAND. VELKOMMEN TIL GRONLAND.
GREENLAND PROVINCIAL COUNCIL.
*RUNGSTED KYST, DENMARK 1, 1971-*
*ANNU.*
*LO/N-1.*
*ISSN 0085-8056*

WELDING INTERNATIONAL. RESEARCH &
DEVELOPMENT.                                                             XXX
+ +WELD. INT.
WELDING INSTITUTE.
*CAMBRIDGE 1(1-4), 1971...*
*Q. SUBS: WELDING RESEARCH INTERNATIONAL.*
*ED/N-1. LO/N14.*

WELDING RESEARCH INTERNATIONAL.                                          XXX
+ +WELD. RES. INT.
WELDING INSTITUTE.
*CAMBRIDGE 2, 1972-*
PREV: WELDING INTERNATIONAL, RESEARCH & DEVEL-
OPMENT FROM 1, 1971.
*BL/U-1. LO/N14.*
*ED/N-1. 2, 1972-*
*LD/U-1. 3, 1973.*

WELL-BEING. A REVIEW OF HEALTH & EDUCATION.
WEST RIDING COUNTY COUNCIL.
*WAKEFIELD 1, 1968-*
*LD/U-1.*

WELSH MEDICAL GAZETTE. = CYLCHGRAWN MEDDYGOL
CYMRU.
+ +WELSH MED. GAZ.
*CARDIFF NO.1, 1970-*
*BL/U-1. DB/U-2. LD/U-1. SW/U-1.*

WELWYN DIGEST.
+ +WELWYN DIG.
WELWYN HALL RESEARCH ASSOCIATION.
*WELWYN 1, 1969-*
*BL/U-1. LO/N-7. LO/N14.*

WESLEYAN LIBRARY NOTES.
+ +WESLEYAN LIBR. NOTES.
WESLEYAN UNIVERSITY LIBRARY.
*MIDDLETOWN, CONN. NO.1, 1968-*
*LO/N-1.*

WEST AFRICAN ARCHAEOLOGICAL NEWSLETTER.                                  XXX
+ +WEST. AFR. ARCHAEOL. NEWSL.
UNIVERSITY OF IBADAN: INSTITUTE OF AFRICAN
STUDIES.
*IBADAN NO.1, D 1964- 12, 1970.*
ENGL. & FR. SUBS: WEST AFRICAN JOURNAL OF
ARCHAEOLOGY.
*LO/S10.*
*LO/U14. NO.5, 1966-*
*LO/N-3. NO.5, 1966.*

WEST AFRICAN JOURNAL OF ARCHAEOLOGY.                                     XXX
+ +WEST AFR. J. ARCHAEOL.
*IBADAN 1, 1971-*
PREV: WEST AFRICAN ARCHAEOLOGICAL NEWSLETTER
FROM NO.1, 1964- 12, 1970.
*AD/U-1. CA/U-3. OX/U-9.*
*LO/U-2. 4, 1974-*

WEST AFRICAN PHARMACIST.                                                 XXX
SUBS (1971): PART OF AFRICAN JOURNAL OF
PHARMACY & PHARMACEUTICAL SCIENCES.

WEST AFRICAN RELIGION.
+ +WEST AFR. RELIG.
UNIVERSITY OF NIGERIA: CROWTHER COLLEGE OF
RELIGION.
*NSUKKA NO.1, MY 1963-*
*BH/C-3.*
*ISSN 0083-8187*

WEST COAST DRUGGIST.*                                                    XXX
+ +WEST. COAST DRUG.
*LOS ANGELES 1, 1906-*
TITLE VARIES: INCORP. WESTERN PHARMACY TO
BECOME WEST COAST DRUGGIST & WESTERN PHARMACY
FROM 46(6), 1964- 48, 1968. THEN REVERTED TO
ABOVE FROM 49, 1967.
*LO/N14. 49, 1967-*
*ISSN 0043-3101*

WEST INDIAN JOURNAL OF ENGINEERING.
+ +WEST INDIAN J. ENG.
UNIVERSITY OF THE WEST INDIES: FACULTY OF
ENGINEERING.
*TRINADAD 1, 1967-*
*LO/N14.*

WEST LONDON SYNAGOGUE REVIEW.
+ +WEST LOND. SYNAGOGUE REV.
*LONDON NO.1, 1967-*
*SO/U-1.*

WEST MIDLANDS STUDIES.                                                   XXX
+ +WEST MIDL. STUD.
WOLVERHAMPTON POLYTECHNIC.
*WOLVERHAMPTON 3, 1969-*
PREV: JOURNAL OF WEST MIDLANDS REGIONAL
STUDIES FROM 1, 1967- 2, 1968. S/T: A JOURNAL
OF INDUSTRIAL ARCHAEOLOGY & BUSINESS HISTORY.
*BH/U-1. OX/U17. SO/U-1. SW/U-1.*
*LO/U-1. 4, 1971-          NW/U-1. 4, 1970/71-*

WEST ONE.
LONDON POLYTECHNIC: STUDENTS' UNION.
*LONDON 1(1), 1966-*
*OX/U-1.*

WESTERN AMERICAN LITERATURE.
+ +WEST. AM. LIT.
COLORADO STATE UNIVERSITY.
*[FORT COLLINS, COLO.] 1(1), 1966-*
*EX/U-1. LO/U-1.*
*ISSN 0043-3462*

WESTERN CANADIAN JOURNAL OF ANTHROPOLOGY.          XXX
+ + WEST. CAN. J. ANTHROPOL.
 EDMONTON, ALTA. 1, 1969-
 PREV: ALBERTA ANTHROPOLOGIST FROM 1(1), 1967-
 2(3), 1968.
 LO/S10.
 ISSN 0008-5340

WESTERN CANADIAN STUDIES IN MODERN LANGUAGES
& LITERATURE.
+ + WEST. CAN. STUD. MOD. LANG. & LIT.
UNIVERSITY OF SASKATCHEWAN: DEPARTMENT OF
MODERN LANGUAGES.
 REGINA [NO.]1, 1970-
 CB/U-1.    LO/U-1.    SW/U-1.

WESTERN CONSTRUCTION & BUILDING.                   XXX
 SUBS (1969): WESTERN CONSTRUCTION & INDUSTRY.

WESTERN CONSTRUCTION & INDUSTRY.                   XXX
+ + WEST. CONSTR. & IND.
[MERCURY PUBL.]
 WINNIPEG 21(9), 1969-
 PREV: WESTERN CONSTRUCTION & BUILDING FROM 1,
 JE 1949- 21(8), 1969.
 LO/N13.    LO/N14.
 ISSN 0043-3624

WESTERN EUROPEAN EDUCATION.
+ + WEST. EUR. EDUC.
[INTERNATIONAL ARTS & SCIENCES P.]
 WHITE PLAINS, N.Y. 1, 1969-
 S/T: A JOURNAL OF TRANSLATIONS.
 SW/U-1.
 AD/U-1. 1, 1969- 3, 1972.
 ISSN 0043-3675

WESTERN GEOGRAPHICAL SERIES.
+ + WEST. GEOGR. SER.
UNIVERSITY OF VICTORIA: DEPARTMENT OF
GEOGRAPHY.
 VICTORIA, B.C. 1, 1970-
 2/A.
 LO/S13.

WESTERN HISTORICAL QUARTERLY.
+ + WEST. HIST. Q.
WESTERN HISTORY ASSOCIATION.
[UTAH STATE UNIV. P.]
 LOGAN, UTAH 1, 1970-
 AD/U-1.    CB/U-1.    HL/U-1.    LO/N-1.    MA/U-1.
 ISSN 0043-3810

WESTERN ONTARIO LAW REVIEW.
+ + WEST. ONT. LAW REV.
UNIVERSITY OF WESTERN ONTARIO: FACULTY OF LAW.
 LONDON 6, 1967-
 PREV: WESTERN LAW REVIEW FROM 1, 1961-5, 1966.
 OX/U15.

WESTERN PHARMACY.                                  XXX
 SUBS (1967): PART OF WEST COAST DRUGGIST.

WESTERN PLASTICS.                                  XXX
+ + WEST. PLAST.
[BRESKIN COMMUNICATIONS INC.]
 SCOTTSDALE, ARIZ. 1, OC 1954- 19(4), 1972.//
 XS/N-1.
 LO/N14. 1959-
 ISSN 0043-406X

WESTMINSTER BANK REVIEW.                           XXX
 SUBS (968): PART OF QUARTERLY REVIEW, NAT-
 IONAL WESTMINSTER BANK.

WEXFORD BIRD REPORT.
+ + WEXFORD BIRD REP.
WILDBIRD CONSERVANCY: WEXFORD BRANCH.
 WEXFORD 1, 1970-
 DB/U-2.    LO/N13.

WHAT ? IDEAS FOR ACTION.
NATIONAL SUGGESTIONS CENTRE.
 LONDON 1, 1968-
 ED/N-1.    LO/N14.    OX/U-1.
 ISSN 0043-4493

WHEEL EXTENDED.  A TOYOTA QUARTERLY REVIEW.
 TOKYO 1(1), 1971-
 LD/U-1.
 ED/N-1. 1(2), 1971-              SO/U-1. 1(2), 1971-
 ISSN 0049-755X

WHERE: SUPPLEMENT.                                 XXX
ADVISORY CENTRE FOR EDUCATION.
 CAMBRIDGE NO.1, 1964- 17, 1969.//
 S/T: INFORMATION ON EDUCATION.
 LO/U-1.

WHICH COURSE?
[DOMINION P.]
 LONDON 1(1), 1971-
 5/A. S/T: JOURNAL FOR SCHOOL LEAVERS ENTER-
 ING FURTHER EDUCATION.
 CA/U-1. 2(2), 1972-              ED/N-1. 2(2), 1972-

WHICH UNIVERSITY?
+ + WHICH UNIV.
[CORNMARKET PRESS]
 LONDON  1964 (1963)-
 BH/U-1.    HL/U-1.    LO/M22.    LO/S22.    SO/U-1.
 XW/C-4.

WHITE RABITT PAPERS.
+ + WHITE RABITT PAP.
UNIVERSITY OF READING.
 READING NO.1, 1970-
 RE/U-1.

WHITE TRASH.
WHITE PANTHER PARTY.
[INTERNATIONAL TIMES]
 LONDON NO.1, SUMMER 1972-
 Q.
 CA/U-1. NO.3, 1972-           OX/U-1. NO.3, 1972-
 ED/N-1. AUTUMN 1972-

WHO DOES WHAT IN PARLIAMENT.
[MITCHELL & BIRT]
 LONDON [NO.1] 1970-
 LO/N-1.
 NW/U-1. NO.3, 1971-           OX/U17. NO.3, 1971-

WHO FOOD ADDITIVES SERIES.
+ + WHO FOOD ADDIT. SER.
WORLD HEALTH ORGANIZATION.
 GENEVA NO.1, 1972-
 CO/U-1.    GL/U-1.

WHO'S WHO OF BRITISH ENGINEERS.
+ + WHO'S WHO BR. ENG.
[MACLAREN]
 LONDON  1966-
 BH/U-1.**    LO/S22.**    LO/U20.**    SX/U-1.**    XW/C-4.**
 LO/N14. CURRENT ISSUE ONLY.

WHO'S WHO IN THE WORLD.
[MARQUIS WHO'S WHO INC.]
 CHICAGO 1ST 1971/1972(1970)-
 LO/N-3.    LO/N14.

WIADOMOSCI EKOLOGICZNE.                            XXX
+ + WIAD. EKOL.
POLSKA AKADEMIA NAUK: KOMITET EKOLOGICZNY.
 WARSAW 16, 1970-
 ENGL. SUMM.  ENGL. TITLE: ECOLOGICAL NEWS.
 PREV: EKOLOGIA POLSKA: SERIA B FROM 1, 1955-
 15, 1969.
 DR/U-1.    GL/U-1.    LO/N-2.    LO/N13.    LO/R-5.    XY/N-1.

WIADOMOSCI NARODOWEGO BANKU POLSKIEGO.             XXX
 SUBS (1970): BANK I KREDYT.

WIADOMOSCI TELEKOMUNIKACYJNE.
+ + WIAD. TELEKOMUN. [WDTE-A]
STOWARZYSZENIE ELEKTRYKOW POLSKICH.
 WARSAW 1, 1961-
 M. S/T: MIESIECZNIK POPULARNO-TECHNICZNY.
 LO/N13. 6, 1966-

WIENER ARBEITEN ZUR DEUTSCHEN LITERATUR.
+ + WIEN. ARB. DTSCH. LIT.
[HERMANN BOHLAUS]
 VIENNA &C. NO.1, 1970-
 CA/U-1.    LO/N-1.

WIENER BYZANTINISCHE STUDIEN.
+ + WIEN. BYZANTIN. STUD.
OSTERREICHISCHE AKADEMIE DER WISSENSCHAFTEN:
KOMMISSION FUR BYZANTINISTIK.
 VIENNA 1, 1964-
 LO/U-1.

WIENER ETHNOHISTORISCHE BLATTER.
+ + WIEN. ETHNOHIST. BL.
 VIENNA 1, 1970-
 CA/U-3.    LO/S10.

WIENER JAHRBUCH FUR PHILOSOPHIE.
+ + WIEN. JAHRB. PHIL.
[WILHELM BRAUMUELLER]
 VIENNA &C. 1, 1968-
 OX/U-1.

WILBOUR LIBRARY OF EGYPTOLOGY ACQUISITIONS
LIST.                                              XXX
 SUBS (1972): EGYPTOLOGY TITLES.

**WILDFOWL.**                                                                          XXX
WILDFOWL TRUST.
*SLIMBRIDGE, GLOS. NO.19, 1966/67(1968)-*
PREV: ANNUAL REPORT, WILDFOWL TRUST FROM
6TH, 1952/53(1954)- 18, 1965/66(1967).
*ED/N-1.     LO/N13.*

**WILDLIFE NEWS. NOUVELLES DE LA FAUNE.**
++*WILDL. NEWS.*
CANADIAN WILDLIFE FEDERATION.
*OTTAWA  1(1), 1965-*
*LO/N-1.*
*ISSN 0043-5503*

**WILDLIFE RESEARCH REPORT (US).**
++*WILDL. RES. REP. (US).*
(UNITED STATES) BUREAU OF SPORT FISHERIES &
WILDLIFE.
*WASHINGTON, D.C. NO.1, 1972-*
*LO/N13.     LO/R-5.*

**WILDLIFE SOCIETY BULLETIN.**                                                          XXX
++*WILDL. SOC. BULL.*
*LAWRENCE, KANS. 1, 1973-*
PREV: WILDLIFE SOCIETY NEWS.
*AD/U-1.    CA/U-1.    GL/U-1.    LO/N13.    SO/U-1.*

**WILDLIFE SOCIETY NEWS.**                                                              XXX
SUBS (1973): WILDLIFE SOCIETY BULLETIN.

**WILTSHIRE ARCHAEOLOGICAL & NATURAL HISTORY**                                          XXX
**SOCIETY: RECORDS BRANCH.**
SUBS (1969): WILTSHIRE RECORD SOCIETY.

**WILTSHIRE INDUSTRIAL ARCHAEOLOGY. TRANS-**
**ACTIONS OF THE ...**
++*WILTS. IND. ARCHAEOL.*
SALISBURY & SOUTH WILTSHIRE ARCHAEOLOGY SOCIETY
*TROWBRIDGE  NO.1, 1969-*
*ED/N-1.     LO/S13.*

**WILTSHIRE RECORD SOCIETY.**                                                           XXX
++*WILTS. REC. SOC.*
*DEVIZES  23, 1967 (1969)-*
PREV: WILTSHIRE ARCHAEOLOGICAL & NATURAL
HISTORY SOCIETY: RECORDS BRANCH FROM 1, 1939-
22, 1966 (1968).
*BH/U-1.    GL/U-1.    NO/U-1.*

**WINDLESS ORCHARD.**
[FORT WAYNE SCHOOL OF FINE ARTS P.]
*FORT WAYNE, IND.  NO.1, F 1970-*
*OX/U-1.*
*LO/U-2.  NO.6, 1971-*
*ISSN 0043-5716*

**WINDWARD.**
SOCIETY FOR NAUTICAL RESEARCH: SOUTHERN BRANCH.
*SOUTHAMPTON  NO.1, 1972-*
*LO/N-4.*

**WINTER'S CRIMES.**
[MACMILLAN]
*LONDON &C.  1, 1969-*
*OX/U-1.*

**WIRA NEWS.**
WOOL INDUSTRIES RESEARCH ASSOCIATION.
*LEEDS  NO.1, 1968-*
*OX/U-1.*
*ED/N-1.  NO.4, 1969-*
*XS/R10.  NO.23, 1973- (3 YEARS ONLY).*

**WIRA TEST METHOD.**
++*WIRA TEST METH. (WOOL IND. RES. ASS.)*
WOOL INDUSTRIES RESEARCH ASSOCIATION.
*LEEDS  NO.1, 1965-*
*ED/N-1.*

**WIRE JOURNAL.**
++*WIRE J.*
WIRE ASSOCIATION (U.S.).
[U.S. INDUSTRIAL PUBL. INC.]
*STAMFORD (CONN.)  1, 1968-*
*LO/N14.*
*ISSN 0043-602X*

**WISSENSCHAFTLICHE LANDESKUNDEN.**
++*WISS. LANDESKUNDEN.*
*DARMSTADT  1, 1968-*
*OX/U-1.*

**WITHERED ROOTS.**
*HAWICK  1, JL 1969-*
PROD. BY THREE HAWICK HIGH SCHOOL STUDENTS.
*ED/N-1.    OX/U-1.*

**WIVENHOE PARK REVIEW.**                                                               XXX
++*WIVENHOE PARK REV.*
UNIVERSITY OF ESSEX.
*COLCHESTER  NO.1, WINTER 1965- 2, 1967.*
PUBL. BY THE UNIV'S DEPT. OF ENGLISH. SUBS:
PARK.
*ED/N-1.     LO/U-2.*
*ISSN 0043-7107*

**WOLFENBUTTELER BEITRAGE.**
++*WOLFENBUTTELER BEITR.*
*FRANKFURT AM MAIN  1, 1972-*
*CA/U-1.    LD/U-1.    NO/U-1.    OX/U-1.*
*LO/U-1.  1, 1972.*

**WOLVERTON HISTORICAL JOURNAL.**                                                       XXX
++*WOLVERTON HIST. J.*
WOLVERTON & DISTRICT ARCHAEOLOGICAL SOCIETY.
*CHICHESTER  [1], 1970.*
PREV: JOURNAL, WOLVERTON & DISTRICT ARCHAEO-
LOGICAL SOCIETY FROM 1, 1968- 2, 1969. SUBS:
MILTON KEYNES JOURNAL OF ARCHAEOLOGY & HISTORY
*BH/U-1.    OX/U-2.*

**WOMEN STUDIES ABSTRACTS.**
++*WOMEN STUD. ABSTR.*
*RUSH, N.Y.  1, WINTER 1972-*
Q.
*ED/N-1.*
*ISSN 0049-7835*

**WOMEN, WIVES, WIDOWS.**                                                               XXX
ASSOCIATION OF WIDOWS IN IRELAND.
*DUBLIN  1(1-2), 1971. //*
*DB/U-2.*

**WOMEN'S REPORT.**
++*WOMEN'S REP.*
FAWCETT SOCIETY.
*LONDON  NO.1, N 1972/JA 1973-*
S/T: A BI-MONTHLY NEWS SHEET FOR WOMEN BY
WOMEN.  SPONS. BODY ALSO: WOMEN'S LOBBY.
*ED/N-1.    LO/U-3.    OX/U-1.*

**WOMEN'S STUDIES.**
++*WOMEN'S STUD.*
[GORDON & BREACH]
*LONDON  1(1), 1972-*
2/A.
*CA/U-1.    ED/N-1.    LO/U-4.    OX/U-1.*
*ISSN 0049-7878*

**WOOD.**                                                                               XXX
[BENN BROTHERS, LTD.]
*LONDON  1, 1936- 36(1), 1971.*
MON. SUBS. INCORP. IN: TIMBER TRADES JOURNAL.
*OX/U-3.*
*BH/P-1.  35, 1970-*
*BL/U-1.  31(5), 1966-*
*ISSN 0043-762X*

**WOOD & FIBER.**
SOCIETY OF WOOD SCIENCE & TECHNOLOGY.
*LAWRENCE, KANS.  1(1), 1969-*
*BN/U-2.    OX/U-3.*
*ISSN 0043-7654*

**WOOD SCIENCE.**
++*WOOD SCI.*
FOREST PRODUCTS RESEARCH SOCIETY.
*MADISON, WIS.  1, 1968-*
*LO/N14.    OX/U-3.*
*ISSN 0043-7700*

**WOOD WORLD.**                                                                         XXX
COUNCIL OF FOREST INDUSTRIES OF BRITISH
COLUMBIA.
*VANCOUVER  1, 1971-*
PREV: PLYWOOD WORLD FROM 1, 1961- 11, 1970.
*LO/N14.*

**WOODLANDS PAPERS.**                                                                   XXX
++*WOODLANDS PAP.*
PULP & PAPER RESEARCH INSTITUTE OF CANADA.
*POINTE CLAIRE  NO.1, AP 1968- 29, 1971.*
SUBS: WOODLANDS REPORTS.
*LO/N14.    OX/U-3.*

**WOODLANDS REPORTS.**                                                                  XXX
++*WOODL. REP.*
PULP & PAPER RESEARCH INSTITUTE OF CANADA.
*POINTE CLAIRE, P.Q.  WR/30, 1970- 44, 1972 ...*
PREV: WOODLANDS PAPERS FROM 1, 1968- 29, 1971.
SUBS: LOGGING RESEARCH REPORTS.
*LO/N14.**

**WOODROW WILSON ASSOCIATION MONOGRAPH SERIES
IN PUBLIC AFFAIRS.**
++WOODROW WILSON ASSOC. MONOGR. SER. PUBLIC
AFF.
WOODROW WILSON SCHOOL OF PUBLIC &
INTERNATIONAL AFFAIRS.
PRINCETON, N.J. NO.1, 1970-
BH/U-1.

**WOODWORKERS JOURNAL.**                                        XXX
SUBS (1970): WOODWORKERS & PAINTERS JOURNAL.

**WOODWORKERS & PAINTERS JOURNAL.**                            XXX
++WOODWORK. & PAINTERS J.
AMALGAMATED SOCIETY OF WOODWORKERS.
LONDON NO.1, 1970- NO.2, 1972 ...
PREV: WOODWORKERS JOURNAL FROM JA 1948- 1969.
SUBS: UNION OF CONSTRUCTION & ALLIED TRADES
TECHNICIANS JOURNAL.
BH/P-1.    HL/U-1.
ISSN 0049-7940
++WOODWORK. DIG.
[HITCHCOCK PUBL. CO.]
WHEATON, ILL. 68(1), JA 1966- 71, 1969 ...
PREV: HITCHCOCK'S WOOD WORKING DIGEST FROM
59(1), JA 1957- 67, 1965. SUBS: WOODWORKING
& FURNITURE DIGEST.
LO/N14.**

**WOODWORKING & FURNITURE DIGEST.**                            XXX
++WOODWORK. & FURNITURE DIG.
[HITCHCOCK PUBL. CO.]
WHEATON, ILL. 72, 1970-
PREV: WOODWORKING DIGEST FROM 68(1), JA 1966-
71, 1969.
LO/N14.
ISSN 0043-7778

**WORCESTERSHIRE ARCHAEOLOGY NEWSLETTER.**
WORCESTER CITY MUSEUM.
WORCESTER [NO.1], 1967-
SPONS. BODIES ALSO WORCESTERSHIRE ARCHAEOLOG-
ICAL SOCIETY; WORCESTER CITY ARCHAEOLOGICAL
RESEARCH GROUP.
OX/U-1.
CA/U-3. NO.6, 1970-          ED/N-1. NO.2, 1968-
SO/U-1. NO.7, 1971-

**WORDSWORTH CIRCLE.**
TEMPLE UNIVERSITY: DEPARTMENT OF ENGLISH.
PHILADELPHIA 1(1), 1970-
Q.
NW/U-1. 2, 1971-          SO/U-1. 1(2), 1970-
ISSN 0043-8006

**WORKERS' PRESS: THE DAILY ORGAN OF THE ...**                 XXX
SOCIALIST LABOUR LEAGUE: CENTRAL COMMITTEE.
LONDON 1, S 1969-
PREV: NEWSLETTER: TWICE-WEEKLY ORGAN OF THE...
HL/U-1.    LO/U-3.    OX/U-1.    OX/U17.
ED/N-1. NO.8, 8/OC 1969-

**WORKERS VANGUARD. MARXIST WORKING CLASS
MONTHLY JOURNAL.**
++WORK. VANGUARD.
SPARTACIST LEAGUE.
NEW YORK NO.1, OC 1971-
LO/U-3.

**WORKERS' WEEKLY.**
++WORK. WKLY.
BRITISH & IRISH COMMUNIST ORGANISATION.
BELFAST NO.1, AP 1972-
ED/N-1.    HL/U-1.

**WORKING DOCUMENT, COUNCIL ON BIOLOGICAL
SCIENCES INFORMATION.**
++WORK. DOC. COUNC. BIOL. SCI. INF.
BETHESDA, MD. NO.1, [1970]
LO/N-2.

**WORKING PAPERS IN ASIAN STUDIES.**
++WORK. PAP. ASIAN STUD.
ASIAN STUDIES.
NEDLANDS 1, JE 1967-
HL/U-1.    ·LO/N-1.

**WORKING PAPERS IN CULTURAL STUDIES.**
++WORK. PAP. CULT. STUD.
UNIVERSITY OF BIRMINGHAM: CENTRE FOR
CONTEMPORARY CULTURAL STUDIES.
BIRMINGHAM [NO.]1, 1971-
2/A. CENTRE SUBORD. TO DEPARTMENT OF ENGLISH.
BT/U-1.    ED/N-1.    GL/U-2.    LO/U-3.    MA/U-1.    OX/U-1.
OX/U16.    OX/U17.
GL/U-1. 1, 1971- 3, 1972.
ISSN 0049-7991

**WORKING PAPERS, HUNGARIAN-ENGLISH CONTRASTIVE
LINGUISTICS PROJECT.**
++WORK. PAP. HUNG.-ENGL. CONTRASTIVE LINGUIST.
PROJ.
BUDAPEST 1, 1972-
OX/U-1.

**WORKING PAPER, INTERNATIONAL PLANNED PARENT-
HOOD FEDERATION.**
++WORK. PAP. INT. PLANN. PARENTHOOD FED.
LONDON NO.1, 1967-
OX/U-1.

**WORKING PAPERS IN LINGUISTICS, DEPARTMENT OF
LINGUISTICS, UNIVERSITY OF HAWAII.**
++WORK. PAP. LINGUIST. DEP. LINGUIST. UNIV.
HAWAII.
HONOLULU 1, 1969-
LO/U14.

**WORKING PAPER, NATIONAL COUNCIL FOR EDUCAT-
IONAL TECHNOLOGY (GB).**
++WORK. PAP. NATL. COUNC. EDUC. TECHNOL. (GB).
LONDON NO.1, 1969-
OX/U-1.
GL/U-1. NO.3, 1970- [W.NO.4 &5]

**WORKING PAPER, TROPICAL FISH CULTURE RESEARCH
INSTITUTE (MALACCA).**
++WORK. PAP. TROP. FISH CULT. RES. INST.
(MALACCA).
MALACCA NO.1, 1968-
LO/N-2.

**WORKING PAPERS, URBAN SYSTEMS RESEARCH UNIT,
UNIVERSITY OF READING.**
++WORK. PAP. URBAN SYST. RES. UNIT UNIV. READING
READING 1, 1970-
UNIT SUBORD. TO DEPARTMENT OF GEOGRAPHY.
BL/U-1.    SO/U-1.

**WORKMEN'S COMPENSATION REPORTER.**
++WORKMEN'S COMPENS. REP.
(BRITISH COLUMBIA) WORKMEN'S COMPENSATION BOARD
VANCOUVER 1, 1973-
SH/U-1.

**WORKS. A QUARTERLY OF WRITING.**
[ARMS P., INC.]
NEW YORK 1(1), 1967-
OX/U-1.
ISSN 0043-812X

**WORKS ENGINEERING & FACTORY SERVICES.**                      XXX
++WORKS ENG. & FACT. SERV.
[TOTHILL P. LTD.]
LONDON 62(737), 1967-
PREV: POWER & WORKS ENGINEERING FROM 1, 1906.
FROM 1969 INCORP: ENGINEERING & BOILER HOUSE
REVIEW.
ED/N-1.    LO/N14.
BH/U-1. 62(737), 1967- 64(752), 1969. [W.
63(742-3), 1969]
ISSN 0043-8138

**WORKSHOP. A MAGAZINE OF NEW POETRY.**
LONDON [NO.]2, WINTER 1967/8-
PREV: WRITERS' WORKSHOP.
LO/U-2.
ED/N-1. 3,1968-

**WORLD ABSTRACTS ON PROTEIN COLLOIDS.**                       XXX
++WORLD ABSTR. PROTEIN COLLOIDS.
GELATINE & GLUE RESEARCH ASSOCIATION.
LONDON 21, 1970-
PREV: ABSTRACTS, GELATINE & GLUE RESEARCH
ASSOCIATION FROM 14(2), 1963- 20, 1969.
LO/N-4.    LO/N13.    LO/N14.

**WORLD AFFAIRS REPORT.**                                      XXX
++WORLD AFF. REP.
CALIFORNIA INSTITUTE OF INTERNATIONAL STUDIES.
STANFORD 3, 1973-
PREV: REPORT, CALIFORNIA INSTITUTE OF INTER-
NATIONAL STUDIES FROM 1, 1970- 2, 1972.
OX/U-1.

**WORLD ALUMINUM ABSTRACTS.**                                  XXX
AMERICAN SOCIETY FOR METALS.
METALS PARK, OHIO 3, 1970(1971)-
PREV: ALUMINIUM ABSTRACTS FROM 1, 1963- 8,
1970. VOLUMES NUMBERED IN REVISED SERIES.
LO/N14.
ISSN 0002-6697

**WORLD ANIMAL REVIEW.**
+ +WORLD ANIM. REV.
FOOD & AGRICULTURE ORGANIZATION (UN).
 ROME NO.1, 1972-
 S/T: A QUARTERLY JOURNAL DEVOTED TO WORLD
 DEVELOPMENTS IN ANIMAL PRODUCTION, ANIMAL
 HEALTH & ANIMAL PRODUCTS.
 CA/U-1.    CA/U11.    ED/N-1.    GL/U-2.    LO/N-2.    LO/N-6.
 LO/R-6.    NW/U-1.    RE/U-1.    SH/U-1.
 MA/P-1. NO.2, 1972-
 LO/U-3. CURRENT ISSUES ONLY.
 ISSN 0049-8025

**WORLD ARCHAEOLOGY.**
+ +WORLD ARCHAEOL.
[ROUTLEDGE & K. PAUL]
 LONDON 1(1), 1969-
 AD/U-1.    BH/U-1.    BL/U-1.    CA/U-3.    CR/U-1.    DB/S-1.
 DB/U-2.    GL/U-1.    LO/N-1.    LO/S-7.    LO/S10.    LO/U-2.
 LV/P-1.    MA/U-1.    NO/U-1.    OX/U-1.    OX/U-2.
 CA/U14. 7, 1975-              NW/U-1. 2, 1970-
 SO/U-1. 1, 1969- 2, 1970.
 ISSN 0043-8243

**WORLD BANK STAFF OCCASIONAL PAPERS.**
+ +WORLD BANK STAFF OCC. PAP.
INTERNATIONAL BANK FOR RECONSTRUCTION &
DEVELOPMENT.
 WASHINGTON 1, 1967-
 MA/U-1.

**WORLD BIENNIAL OF PSYCHIATRY & PSYCHOTHERAPY.**
+ +WORLD BIENNIAL PSYCHIATR. & PSYCHOTHER.
 NEW YORK; LONDON 1, 1971-
 LO/N-1.

**WORLD BUSINESS PERSPECTIVES.**
+ +WORLD BUS. PERSPECT.
NATIONAL INDUSTRIAL CONFERENCE BOARD (US).
 NEW YORK NO.1, 1970-
 OX/U-9.
 OX/U16. NO.9, JE 1972-
 ISSN 0084-1455

**WORLD DEVELOPMENT.**                                    XXX
+ +WORLD DEV.
[WORLD DEVELOPMENT (PUBL.) LTD.]
 OXFORD &C. 1(1/2), F 1973-
 MON. PREV: NEW COMMONWEALTH & WORLD DEVELOP-
 MENT FROM 49(10/11), OC 1970- NO.10/11/12,
 1972.
 ED/N-1.    LO/U11.    LO/R-6.    LO/S14.    MA/P-1.
 NW/U-1.    OX/U-1.
 LO/U-2. 2, 1974-

**WORLD DREDGING & MARINE CONSTRUCTION.**
+ +WORLD DREDG. & MAR. CONSTR.
[WORLD TRADE PUBL.]
 CONROE, TEX. 1, 1965-
 LO/N14.**
 SO/U-1. 9, 1973-
 LO/N-5. 6(12), 1970-
 ISSN 0043-8405

**WORLD FEEDS & PROTEIN NEWS.**                           XXX
BRITISH SULPHUR CORPORATION, LTD.
 LONDON NO.1, JA/F 1971- 11, 1972.
 SUBS. INCORP. IN: FEED & FARM SUPPLIES.
 ED/N-1.    LO/N-6.    LO/N14.    LO/R-6.    OX/U-8.    XS/F11.

**WORLD FISHERIES ABSTRACTS.**                            XXX
+ +WORLD FISH. ABSTR. [WFAB-A]
FOOD & AGRICULTURAL ORGANIZATION (UN).
 ROME 1, JA/F 1950- 23(4), 1972.//
 PROD. BY ORGANIZATION'S FISHERIES DIVISION.
 LO/U-3.
 LD/U-1. 13, 1962-          LO/R-6. 1(2), 1950-
 LO/U-2. 15(4), 1964-       MA/U-1. 17(2), 1966-
 ISSN 0043-8472

**WORLD INDEX OF SCIENTIFIC TRANSLATIONS & LIST
OF TRANSLATIONS NOTIFIED TO E.T.C.**                      XXX
+ +WORLD INDEX SCI. TRANSL. & LIST TRANSL.
 NOTIFIED E.T.C.
EUROPEAN TRANSLATIONS CENTRE.
 DELFT 6, 1972-
 PREV: WORLD INDEX OF SCIENTIFIC TRANSLATIONS
 FROM NO.1, JA/MR 1967- 5, 1971.
 LO/N14.
 GL/U-1. 7, 1973-

**WORLD OF IRISH NURSING.**
+ +WORLD IR. NURS.
IRISH NURSES ORGANISATION.
 DUBLIN 1(1), JA 1972-
 DB/U-2.

**WORLD IRRIGATION.**                                     XXX
+ +WORLD IRRIG. [WORI-B]
[H.L. PEACE PUBL.]
 NEW ORLEANS 17(6), OC/D 1967- 20, 1970.
 PREV: IRRIGATION ENGINEERING & MAINTENANCE
 FROM 1, 1951- 17(5), 1967. SUBS: IRRIGATION
 JOURNAL.

**WORLD MEETINGS: SOCIAL & BEHAVIORAL SCIENCES,
EDUCATION & MANAGEMENT.**
+ +WORLD MEET., SOC. & BEHAV. SCI. EDUC. & MANAGE
WORLD MEETINGS INFORMATION CENTER.
 CHESTNUT HILL, MASS. 1, JA 1971-
 Q.
 SF/U-1. 3, 1973-
 SH/P-1. [ONE YEAR]
 ISSN 0043-8685

**WORLD MINERALS & METALS.**
+ +WORLD MINER. & MET.
BRITISH SULPHUR CORPORATION LTD.
 LONDON NO.1, MY/JE 1971-
 FIRST TWO ISSUES ENTITLED WORLD MINERALS.
 LO/N14.    XS/R10.

**WORLD OF N.P.K.S.**                                     XXX
 SUBS (1969): PART OF FERTILIZER INTERNATIONAL.

**WORLD REPORT.**
+ +WORLD REP.
[EMPLOYMENT CONDITIONS ABROAD LTD.]
 LONDON 1(1), JA 1973-
 MON.
 ED/N-1.    OX/U-1.

**WORLD SURVEY.**                                         XXX
+ +WORLD SURV.
ATLANTIC EDUCATIONAL TRUST.
 LONDON NO.1, JA 1969-
 M. PREV: BRITISH SURVEY FROM NO.1, 1939- 237,
 D 1968.
 DB/U-2.    ED/N-1.    LO/N-1.    LO/N17.    LO/U-3.
 ISSN 0043-9096

**WORLD TEXTILE ABSTRACTS.**
+ +WORLD TEXT. ABSTR.
SHIRLEY INSTITUTE.
 MANCHESTER 1,1969-
 CONTINUES ABSTRACTS SECTION OF THE JOURNAL OF
 THE TEXTILE INSTITUTE.
 BH/U-1.    ED/N-1.    GL/U-2.    LO/N14.    LO/R-6.
 ISSN 0043-9118

**WORLD WEATHER WATCH PLANNING REPORT.**
+ +WORLD WEATHER WATCH PLANN. REP.
WORLD METEOROLOGICAL ORGANIZATION.
 GENEVA NO.1, 1966-
 LO/N13.*   XS/N-1.

**WORLD YEAR BOOK OF RELIGION.**
+ +WORLD YEAR BOOK RELIG.
[EVANS BROS.]
 LONDON 1, 1968(1969)-
 AD/U-1.    BH/U-1.    DB/U-2.    LO/U-1.    MA/U-1.    OX/U-1.
 SH/U-1.    SO/U-1.
 XS/C-2. 1, 1969.

**WORLDWIDE BIBLIOGRAPHY OF SPACE LAW & RELATED
MATTERS. BIBLIOGRAPHIE MONDIALE DE DROIT
SPATIAL ET MATIERES CONNEXES.**
+ +WORLDWIDE BIBLIOGR. SPACE LAW & RELAT. MATTERS
INTERNATIONAL INSTITUTE OF SPACE LAW.
 PARIS 1964-
 LO/N-1. JE 1968-

**WORLDWIDE NEWSPAPER COLLECTING & PRESS
HISTORY.**
+ +WORLDWIDE NEWSPAP. COLLECT. & PRESS HIST.
WORLDWIDE NEWSPAPER COLLECTORS CLUB.
 SALE, CHES. 1(1), OC/D 1970-
 Q.
 ED/N-1.    LO/U-3.    OX/U-1.
 ISSN 0043-938X

**WORM.**
UNIVERSITY OF READING.
 READING NO.1, 1969-
 RE/U-1.

**WORSHIP & PREACHING.**
+ +WORSHIP & PREACH.
[EPWORTH P.]
 LONDON 1(1), 1970-
 6/A.
 ED/N-1.    OX/U-1.
 ISSN 0032-7107

**WRITERS' WORKSHOP.**                                           XXX
*LONDON [NO.1, 1967]...*
SUBS: WORKSHOP.
*LO/U-2.    OX/U-1.*

**W.S.C.F. NEWSLETTER.**
*++W.S.C.F. NEWSL.*
WORLD STUDENT CHRISTIAN FEDERATION.
*GENEVA 1, 1973-*
*OX/U-1.*

**WYCHOWANIE OBYWATELSKIE.**
(POLAND) MINISTERSTWO OSWIATY.
*WARSAW 1, 1967-*
2M.  SUPPL. TO WIADOMOSCI HISTORYCZNE FROM
VOL.10(1), 1967.
*OX/U-1.*

**WYKLADY INAUGURACYJNE, UNIWERSYTET IM. ADAMA
MICKIEWICZA W POZNANIU.**
*++WYKLADY INAUG. UNIW. IM. ADAMA MICKIEWICZA
POZNANIU.*
*POZNAN 1, D 1962-*
MONOGR.
*BH/U-1.    BL/U-1.    LO/N-3.    OX/U-1.*

**XENOBIOTICA.  THE FATE OF FOREIGN COMPOUNDS
IN BIOLOGICAL SYSTEMS.**
[TAYLOR & FRANCIS]
*LONDON 1, 1971-*
*ED/N-1.    GL/U-2.    LO/M-3.    LO/N13.    LO/S-3.    LO/U-2.*
*LO/U28.*
*ISSN 0019-8254*

**X RAY ON CURRENT AFFAIRS IN SOUTHERN AFRICA.**
*++X-RAY CURR. AFF. SOUTH. AFR.*
AFRICA BUREAU.
*LONDON 1(1), JL 1970-*
M.
*ED/N-1.    LD/U-1.    LO/U-8.    LO/U14.    OX/U-9.*
*ISSN 0049-8238*

**X-RAY DIFFRACTION ABSTRACTS.**
*++X-RAY DIFFR. ABSTR.*
[SCIENCE & TECHNOLOGY AGENCY]
*LONDON 1(1), JL/S 1972-*
Q.
*CA/U-1.    ED/N-1.*

**X-RAY FLUORESCENCE SPECTROMETRY ABSTRACTS.**
*++X-RAY FLUORESC. SPECTROM. ABSTR.*
[SCIENCE & TECHNOLOGY AGENCY]
*LONDON 1, JA/MR 1970-*
Q.
*LO/N14.    SW/U-1.*
*CA/U-1. 3, 1972-*                    *ED/N-1. 3, 1972-*
*XS/R10. 1(4), 1970-*
*ISSN 0043-9851*

**X-RAY SPECTROMETRY.**
*++X-RAY SPECTROM.*
[HEYDEN]
*LONDON 1(1), JA 1972-*
Q.
*ED/N-1.    LO/N-2.    LO/N14.    LO/R-5.    MA/U-1.    OX/U-8.*
*SH/U-1.    SO/U-1.    SW/U-1.    XS/R10.*
*ISSN 0049-8246*

**YALE STUDIES IN THE HISTORY OF SCIENCE & MEDI-
CINE.**
*++YALE STUD. HIST. SCI. & MED.*
[YALE UNIV. P.]
*NEW HAVEN 1, 1965-*
*LO/U-1.*

**YALE/THEATRE.**
YALE UNIVERSITY: SCHOOL OF DRAMA.
*NEW HAVEN NO.1, 1968-*
*LO/N-1.    OX/U-1.*
*ISSN 0044-0167*

**YALOVA BAHCE KULTURLERI ARASTIRMA VE EGITIM
MERKEZI DERGI. JOURNAL OF THE YALOVA HORTI-
CULTURAL RESEARCH & TRAINING CENTER.**
*YALOVA 1, 1968-*
ENGL. SUMM.
*LO/N13.*

**YAMAGATA KENRITSU YAMAGATA CHUO KOTO GAKKO
KENKYU KIYO.**
*YAMAGATA 1, 1969-*
*LO/N13.*

**YASHIRO GAKUIN DAIGAKU KIYO.  ANNUAL REVIEW
OF YASHIROGAKUIN UNIVERSITY.**
YASHIRO GAKUIN DAIGAKU.
*KOBE  NO.1, 1970-*
ENGL. CONT. LISTS.
*LO/N13.*

**YEARBOOK OF AGRICULTURAL STATISTICS.**
*++YEARB. AGRIC. STAT.*
COMMISSION OF THE EUROPEAN COMMUNITIES.
*LUXEMBOURG  [NO.1], 1970(1971)-*
*BH/U-1.    OX/U16.    OX/U17.*

**YEARBOOK OF AIR & SPACE LAW.  ANNUAIRE DE
DROIT AERIEN ET SPATIAL.**
*++YEARB. AIR & SPACE LAW.*
MCGILL UNIVERSITY: INSTITUTE OF AIR & SPACE
LAW.
*MONTREAL  1965-*
*LO/U11.*
*ISSN 0084-3636*

**YEAR BOOK, ASSOCIATION OF COLLEGES FOR
FURTHER & HIGHER EDUCATION.**
*++YEAR BOOK ASSOC. COLL. FURTHER & HIGHER EDUC.*
*LONDON  1971/72(1971)-*
*OX/U-1.*

**YEAR BOOK OF CARDIOVASCULAR MEDICINE & SURGERY.**
*YEAR BOOK CARDIOVASC. MED. & SURG.*
[YEAR BOOK MEDICAL PUBL.]
*CHICAGO  1968-*
PREV: YEAR BOOK OF CARDIOVASCULAR & RENAL
DISEASE FROM 1961/62(1962).
*LD/U-1.*
*NW/U-1.  1969-*

**YEAR BOOK OF THE COMMONWEALTH.**                              XXX
*++YEAR BOOK COMMONW.*
(GREAT BRITAIN) FOREIGN & COMMONWEALTH OFFICE.
*LONDON  1969-*
PREV: COMMONWEALTH OFFICE YEAR BOOK FROM 1967.
*BH/U-1.    LO/N-1.    OX/U17.    RE/U-1.*

**YEARBOOK OF COMPARATIVE CRITICISM.**
*++YEARB. COMP. CRITICISM.*
[PENNSYLVANIA STATE UNIV. P.]
*UNIVERSITY PARK, PA.  1, 1968-*
*LO/U-1.*
*MA/U-1.  2, 1969-*

**YEARBOOK OF EAST-EUROPEAN ECONOMICS.**                        000
SEE:  JAHRBUCH DER WIRTSCHAFT OSTEUROPAS.

**YEARBOOK OF EDUCATIONAL & INSTRUCTIONAL
TECHNOLOGY.**
*++YEARB. EDUC. & INSTR. TECHNOL.*
ASSOCIATION FOR PROGRAMMED LEARNING AND EDUCAT-
IONAL TECHNOLOGY.
[CORNMARKET P.]
*LONDON  1969/70 (1969)-*
INCORP: PROGRAMMES IN PRINT.
*LO/N-1.    OX/U-1.    SH/U-1.    XS/C-2.    XS/R10.*
*ED/N-1.  1972/73-*
*MA/U-4. CURRENT ISSUE.*

**YEARBOOK OF ENGLISH STUDIES.**
*++YEARB. ENGL. STUD.*
MODERN HUMANITIES RESEARCH ASSOCIATION.
*BIRMINGHAM  1, 1971-*
*BH/U-1.    BT/U-1.    DB/U-2.    DN/U-1.    ED/N-1.    EX/U-1.*
*LD/U-1.    LN/U-2.    LO/N-1.    LO/U-2.    LO/U12.    MA/U-1.*
*NO/U-1.    NW/U-1.    OX/U-1.    RE/U-1.    SH/U-1.*
*SW/U-1.*

**YEARBOOK OF THE EUROPEAN UNIVERSITIES.**                      000
SEE:  CRE YEARBOOK.

**YEARBOOK OF THE FACULTY OF AGRICULTURE,
UNIVERSITY OF EGE.**
*++YEARB. FAC. AGRIC. UNIV. EGE.*
EGE UNIVERSITESI: ZIRAAT FAKULTESI.
*IZMIR  1, 1970-*
*LO/N13.*

**YEARBOOK OF THE FINNISH SOCIETY FOR ECONOMIC
RESEARCH.**                                                     000
SEE:  TALOUSTIETEELLISEN SEURAN VUOSIKIRJA.

**YEAR BOOK OF HIGHER EDUCATION.**
*++YEAR BOOK HIGHER EDUC.*
[ACADEMIC MEDIA]
*LOS ANGELES 1, 1969-*
*OX/U-9.  1970-*

**YEAR BOOK OF THE INDIAN NATIONAL SCIENCE**
**ACADEMY.**                                                                   XXX
*++YEAR BOOK INDIAN NAT. SCI. ACAD.*
*NEW DELHI 1970-*
PREV: YEAR BOOK OF THE NATIONAL INSTITUTE OF
SCIENCES OF INDIA FROM 1961- 1969.
*LD/U-1.*

**YEARBOOK OF INTERNATIONAL CONGRESS PROCEED-**
**INGS.**                                                                          XXX
*++YEARB. INT. CONGR. PROC.*
UNION OF INTERNATIONAL ASSOCIATIONS.
*BRUSSELS 1, 1960/1967(1969)-*
PREV: BIBLIOGRAPHY OF PROCEEDINGS OF INTER-
NATIONAL MEETINGS.
*AD/U-1.     GL/U-1.     HL/U-1.     LO/N-1.     LO/N14.     LO/S14.*
*LO/U-1.     LO/U-3.     OX/U-1.     SH/U-1.     SO/U-1.*
*NW/U-1. 2, 1969-*

**YEARBOOK, INTERNATIONAL FEDERATION FOR**
**DOCUMENTATION.**                                                     000
SEE: FID YEARBOOK.

**YEARBOOK OF ITALIAN STUDIES.**
*++YEARB. ITAL. STUD.*
ITALIAN CULTURAL INSTITUTE (MONTREAL).
[CASALINI LIBRI]
*MONTREAL & FLORENCE 1, 1971-*
*LO/U17.     RE/U-1.*
*SW/U-1. 1971.*

**YEARBOOK ON LATIN AMERICAN COMMUNIST AFFAIRS.**
*++YEARB. LAT. AM. COMMUNIST AFF.*
HOOVER INSTITUTION ON WAR, REVOLUTION & PEACE.
*STANFORD 1971-*
*LO/U-1.     LO/U-3.*

**YEARBOOK, NATIONAL COUNCIL FOR GEOGRAPHIC**
**EDUCATION.**                                                                 XXX
*++YEARB. NATL. COUNC. GEOGR. EDUC.*
*BELMONT, CALIF. [1], 1970(1969)-2, 1971*
*(1970).//*
*DB/U-2.     OX/U-1.*

**YEAR BOOK OF NEUROLOGY & NEUROSURGERY.**         XXX
*++YEAR BOOK NEUROL. & NEUROSURG. [YNNS-A]*
[YEAR BOOK MEDICAL PUBLISHERS]
*CHICAGO 1969-*
PREV: PART OF YEAR BOOK OF NEUROLOGY, PSYCH-
IATRY & NEUROSURGERY FROM 1947- 1967/68.
*LD/U-1.     SO/U-1.*

**YEAR BOOK OF NEUROLOGY, PSYCHIATRY &**
**NEUROSURGERY.**                                                           XXX
SUBS (1969): PART OF YEAR BOOK OF NEUROLOGY &
NEUROSURGERY; & (1970) YEAR BOOK OF PSYCHIATRY
& APPLIED MENTAL HEALTH.
SUBS (1963): COPPERBELT OF ZAMBIA MINING
INDUSTRY YEAR BOOK.

**YEAR BOOK OF PLASTIC & RECONSTRUCTIVE SURGERY.**
*++YEAR BOOK PLAST. & RECONSTR. SURG.*
[YEAR BOOK MEDICAL PUBL.]
*CHICAGO 1970-*
PREV. YEARBOOK OF ORTHOPEDICS & TRAUMATIC
SURGERY FROM 1969.
*NW/U-1.     OX/U-8.     SH/U-1.     SO/U-1.*
*BL/U-1. 1974-*
*ISSN 0084-3962*

**YEAR BOOK OF PSYCHIATRY & APPLIED MENTAL**
**HEALTH.**                                                                         XXX
*++YEAR BOOK PSYCHIATRY & APPL. MENT. HEALTH.*
[YEAR BOOK MEDICAL PUBL.]
*CHICAGO 1970-*
PREV: PART OF YEAR BOOK OF NEUROLOGY, PSYCH-
IATRY & NEUROSURGERY FROM 1947- 1967/68.
*NW/U-1.     OX/U-8.     SH/U-1.     SO/U-1.*

**YEAR BOOK OF SOCIAL POLICY IN BRITAIN.**
*++YEAR BOOK SOC. POLICY BR.*
[ROUTLEDGE & KEGAN PAUL]
*LONDON 1971/72-*
*BL/U-1.     CA/U-1.*

**YEARBOOK OF STATISTICS (SINGAPORE).**
*++YEARB. STAT. (SINGAPORE).*
(SINGAPORE) DEPARTMENT OF STATISTICS.
*SINGAPORE 1, 1967(1968)-*
*LO/N-1.*

**YEARBOOK, STOCKHOLM INTERNATIONAL PEACE RES-**
**EARCH INSTITUTE.**                                                      000
SEE: SIPRI YEARBOOK OF WORLD ARMAMENTS &
DISARMAMENTS.

**YEARBOOK, UNITED NATIONS COMMISSION ON**
**INTERNATIONAL TRADE LAW.**
*++YEARB. U.N. COMM. INT. TRADE LAW.*
*NEW YORK 1, 1968/70-*
*BH/U-1.     LO/N-1.     LO/U-3.     MA/P-1.     OX/U15.     SO/U-1.*

**YEARBOOK, VICTORIA & ALBERT MUSEUM.**                 000
SEE: VICTORIA & ALBERT MUSEUM ...

**YEARBOOK, WORLD WILDLIFE FUND.**                            XXX
*++YEARB. WORLD WILDL. FUND.*
*LONDON 1968(1969)-*
PREV: REPORT ... FROM 1ST, 1961/64(1965)-
2ND, 1965/67(1968).
*LO/N13.*

**YEATS STUDIES. AN INTERNATIONAL JOURNAL.**
*++YEATS STUD.*
UNIVERSITY COLLEGE, GALWAY.
[IRISH UNIVERSITY P.]
*BEALTAINE NO.1, 1971-*
2/A. SPONS. BODY ALSO ST. MICHAEL'S COLLEGE,
UNIVERSITY OF TORONTO.
*BH/P-1.     BL/U-1.     DB/U-1.     ED/N-1.     LO/N-1.     LO/U-2.*
*LO/U13.     MA/U-1.     NW/U-1.*
*ISSN 0044-0272*

**YELMO. REVISTA DEL PROFESOR DE ESPANOL.**
*MADRID 1, AG/S 1971-*
2M.
*MA/U-1.*
*ISSN 0006-6966*

**YERMO. CUADERNOS DE HISTORIA Y DE ESPIRIT-**
**UALIDAD MONASTICOS.**
SOCIEDAD DE ESTUDIOS MONASTICOS.
*MADRID 1, 1963-*
*OX/U-1.*

**YES.**
CHURCH MISSIONARY SOCIETY.
*LONDON NO.1, JA 1973-*
Q.
*ED/N-1.     OX/U-1.*

**YORK PAPERS IN LINGUISTICS.**
*++YORK PAP. LINGUIST.*
UNIVERSITY OF YORK: LINGUISTICS SOCIETY.
*YORK [NO.]1, MY 1971-*
*CA/U-1.     ED/N-1.     LO/U-3.*
*SA/U-1. 2, 1972-*

**YORKSHIRE BULLETIN OF ECONOMICS & SOCIAL**
**RESEARCH.**                                                                    XXX
SUBS (1971): BULLETIN OF ECONOMIC RESEARCH.

**YORKSHIRE & HUMBERSIDE INDUSTRIAL REVIEW.**
*++YORKS. & HUMBERSIDE IND. REV.*
[W. PARR & CO.]
*WILMSLOW 1(1), AP/JE 1971-*
*ED/N-1.     OX/U-1.     SH/C-5.*
*LD/U-1. 2, 1972-*
*SH/P-1. 1, 1971- 3(2), 1973.*

**YORKSHIRE TORY.**
*++YORKS. TORY.*
*[LEEDS] 1(1), 1965-*
PUBL. BY THE CONSERVATIVE ASSOCIATIONS OF
THE UNIVERSITIES OF HULL, LEEDS, SHEFFIELD
& YORK.
*LD/P-1.     OX/U-1.*

**YOUNG DRAMA.**
[THIMBLE P.]
*STROUD, GLOS. 1(1), F 1973-*
*ED/N-1.     GL/U-1.     HL/U-2.     OX/U-1.*

**YOUNG WRITER.**
YOUNG WRITER GROUP.
*ASHFORD COMMON, SURREY 1(1), 1969-*
*ED/N-1.     OX/U-1.*
*ISSN 0044-0957*

**YOUR ENIVRONMENT.**                                                  XXX
*++YOUR ENVIRON.*
*LONDON [1](1), 1969- 4(2), 1973. //*
Q.
*BH/U-1.     CR/N-1.     HL/U-1.     LO/N-6.     LO/N-7.     LO/S74.*
*LO/U-3.     LO/U12.     OX/U-1.*
*ED/N-1. 1(2), 1970-                      LO/N13. 1(2), 1970-*
*SH/C-5. 2, 1971-*

**YOUTH ACTION.**
INSTITUT INTERNATIONAL D'ETUDES SUR L'EDUCATION
*BRUSSELS 1(1), 1970-*
2M.
*LO/N-1. ISOLATED ISSUES.*
*ISSN 0049-8440*

**YOUTH TRAVELS.**
EDUCATIONAL INTERCHANGE COUNCIL.
*LONDON NO.1, 1969-*
*OX/U-1.*
*ED/N-1. NO.2, 1970-*

**YUATSU TO KUKIATSU. JOURNAL, JAPAN HYDRAUL-
ICS & PNEUMATICS SOCIETY.**
NIHON YUKUATSU KYOKAI.
*TOKYO 1, 1970-*
*LO/N13.*

**YUGOSLAV REVIEW OF INVENTIONS.**                                    000
SEE: JUGOSLOVENSKO PRONALAZASTVO.

**Z DEJIN VIED A TECHNIKY NA SLOVENSKU.**
*++Z DEJIN VIED TECH. SLOV. [ZDVT-A]*
SLOVENSKA AKADEMIA VIED: HISTORICKY USTAV
(ODDELENIE DEJIN VIED).
*BRATISLAVA 1, 1962-*
GER. & RUSS. SUMM.
*LO/M24. 6, 1972-*               *LO/N-4. 6, 1972-*

**Z DZIEJOW FORM ARTYSTYCZNYCH W LITERATURZE
POLSKIEJ.**
*++Z DZIEJOW FORM ARTYSTYCZNYCH LIT. POL.*
POLSKA AKADEMIA NAUK: INSTYTUT BADAN LITER-
ACKICH.
*WROCLAW 1, 1963-*
MONOGR.
*CA/U-1.   ED/N-1.   NO/U-1.*
*ISSN 0084-4411*

**Z PRAC SEKCJI HISTORYCZNEJ, INSTYTUT ZACHOD-
NIO-POMORSKI.**
*++Z PR. SEKC. HIST. INST. ZACHODNIO-POMOR.*
INSTYTUT ZACHODNIO-POMORSKI: SEKCJA HISTORYCZNA
*POZNAN 1, 1963-*
MONOGR.
*LO/U-3.   OX/U-1.*

**ZA TEKHNICHESKIJ PROGRESS.**
*++ZA TEK. PROG. [ZATP-A]*
(AZERBAJDZHANSKAJA SSR) MINISTERSTVO NEFTEDO-
BYVAJUSHCHEJ PROMYSHLENNOSTI.
*BAKU 1(1), 1961-*
RUSS. & AZERB. SPONS. BODY ALSO: GOSUDARST-
VENNYJ PLANOVYJ KOMITET.
*LO/N13. 2(13), 1962-*

**ZA VYSSI UROVEN PLANOVITEHO RIZENI.**
*++ZA VYSSI UROVEN PLAN. RIZENI.*
*PRAGUE 1, 1965-*
*BH/U-1.*

**ZAGADNIENIA DRGAN NIELINIOWYCH.**
POLSKA AKADEMIA NAUK: INSTYTUT PODSTAWOWYCH
PROBLEMOW TECHNIKI.
*WARSAW 1, JE 1960-*
ENGL. & RUSS. SUMM. ALSO ENGL. ED. ISSUED AS
NONLINEAR VIBRATION PROBLEMS.
*LO/N13.   LO/U-2.*

**ZAGADNIENIA NAUKOZNAWSTWA, STUDIA I MATERIALY.**
*++ZAGADNIENIA NAUK. STUD. & MATER.*
POLSKA AKADEMIA NAUK: KOMISJA NAUKOZNAWSTWA.
*WARSAW 1(1), 1965-*
ENGL. & RUSS. SUMM.
*OX/U-1.*

**ZAGADNIENIA ONTOGENEZY. PROBLEMS OF ONTOGEN-
ESIS.**
*++ZAGADNIENIA ONTOGEN.*
POLSKA AKADEMIA NAUK: ZAKLAD ANTROPOLOGII.
*WROCLAW 1, 1964-*
ENGL. SUMM. NUMBERED ALSO AS PART OF MAIN
SERIES: MATERIALY I PRACE ANTROPOLOGICZNE. NO.
1 OF ABOVE = NO. 68 OF MATERIALY...
*LO/N-2.   LO/N-3.*

**ZAKUPKI SEL'SKOKHOZJAJSTVENNYKH PRODUKTOV.**
*++ZAKUPKI S-KH. PROD.*
(RUSSIA USSR) SOVET MINISTROV: GOSUDARSTVENNYJ
KOMITET ZAGOTOVOK.
*MOSCOW 1962-*
MON.
*GL/U-1. 1967-*

**ZAMBEZIA. A JOURNAL OF SOCIAL STUDIES IN
SOUTHERN & CENTRAL AFRICA.**
UNIVERSITY COLLEGE OF RHODESIA.
*SALISBURY 1(1), JA 1969-*
*LD/U-1.   LO/U-3.   LO/U-8.   OX/U-9.*

**ZAMBIA LAW JOURNAL.**
*++ZAMBIA LAW J.*
UNIVERSITY OF ZAMBIA.
*LUSAKA 1, 1969-*
*BL/U-1.   CR/U-1.   ED/U-1.   OX/U15.*

**ZAMBIA MUSEUM PAPERS.**
*++ZAMBIA MUS. PAP.*
NATIONAL MUSEUMS BOARD OF ZAMBIA.
*LIVINGSTONE 1, 1967-*
*LO/N-2.   OX/U-8.*

**ZAMBIA MUSEUMS JOURNAL.**
*++ZAMBIA MUS. J.*
NATIONAL MUSEUMS BOARD OF ZAMBIA.
*LIVINGSTONE 1, 1970-*
*LO/N-2.*

**ZAMBIAN URBAN STUDIES.**
*++ZAMBIAN URBAN STUD.*
UNIVERSITY OF ZAMBIA: INSTITUTE FOR SOCIAL
RESEARCH.
*LUSAKA NO.1, 1969-*
*LO/N-1.*
*OX/U-9 NO.2, 1969-*
*ISSN 0044-1767*

**ZAPISKI, NAUCHNO-ISSLEDOVATEL'SKIJ INSTITUT
JAZYKA, LITERATURY, ISTORII I EKONOMIKI.**             XXX
SUBS (1960): TRUDY MORDOVSKOGO NAUCHNO-
ISSLEDOVATEL'SKOGO INSTITUTA JAZYKA,
LITERATURY, ISTORII I EKONOMIKI.

**ZAPISKI NAUCHNYKH SEMINAROV (ENGL. TRANSL.).**      000
SEE: SEMINARS IN MATHEMATICS.

**ZAPISKI NAUCHNYKH SEMINAROV LENINGRADSKOE
OTDELENIE MATEMATICHESKII INSTITUT IM. V.A.
STEKLOVA.**
*++ZAP. NAUCHN. SEMIN. LENINGR. OTD. MAT. INST.*
*IM. V.A. STEKLOVA. [ZNSL-A]*
*MOSCOW 1, 1966-*
ENGL. CONT. LISTS.
*LO/N13.   LO/U-2.*

**ZARUBEZHNYE LITERATURY I SOVREMENNOST'.**
*++ZARUBEZHNYE LIT. & SOVREM.*
[KHUDOZHESTVENNAJA LITERATURA]
*MOSCOW 1, 1970-*
*CC/U-1.   LO/U15.***

**ZASHCHITA METALLOV.**
*++ZASHCH. METAL.*
GOSUDARSTVENNYJ KOMITET PO KOORDINATSII NAUCHNO
*MOSCOW 1(1), 1965-*
2M.
*LO/S-3.*
*OX/U-1. 5(1), 1969-*
*ISSN 0044-1856*

**ZASHCHITNYE POKRYTIYA NA METALLAKH; (ENGL.
TRANSL.).**                                           000
SEE: PROTECTIVE COATINGS ON METALS.

**ZASSO KENKYU. WEED RESEARCH.**
NIHON ZASSO BOJO KENKYUKAI.
*TOKYO NO.1, 1962-*
ENGL. SUMM. FROM NO.6.
*LO/N13.*

**ZBORNIK RADOVA ZAVODA ZA STRANA ZITA.**
*++ZB. RAD. ZAVODA STRANA ZITA.*
*KRAGUJEVAC 1, 1966-*
*CA/U11.*

**ZBORNIK VEDECKYCH PRAC LESNICKEJ FAKULTY VYSO-
KEJ SKOLY LESNICKEJ A DREVARSKEJ VO ZVOLENE.**
*++ZB. VED. PR. LESN. FAK. VYS. SK. LESN. DREV.*
*ZVOLENE.*
*ZVOLEN 1, 1960-*
*OX/U-3. 11(1), 1969-*

**ZEITGEIST.**
[ZEITGEIST INC.]
*EAST LANSING, MICH. 1(1), 1965-*
Q.
*OX/U-1.*
*ISSN 0044-2119*

**ZEITSCHRIFT FUR ALLGEMEINE WISSENSCHAFTSTHEORIE.
= JOURNAL FOR GENERAL PHILOSOPHY OF SCIENCE.**
*++Z. ALLG. WISSENSCHAFTSTHEOR.*
[FRANZ STEINER]
*WIESBADEN 1, 1970-*
2/A. GER. & ENGL.
*LO/U-3.   OX/U-8.*
*ISSN 0044-2216*

ZEITSCHRIFT FUR ANALYTISCHE PSYCHOLOGIE UND IHRE
GRENZGEBIETE.
++Z. ANAL. PSYCHOL. & GRENZGEB.
[VERLAG DIAGNOSTISCHES ZENTRUM]
BERLIN 1970-
Q. ENGL. SUMM.
CA/U-1.
ISSN 0049-8580

ZEITSCHRIFT FUR ANGEWANDTE DRUCKLUFT TECHNIK.    XXX
++Z. ANGEW. DRUCKLUFT TECH.
[MARTONAIR DRUCKLUFTSTEUERUNGEN]
ALPEN 1966- 1971(1).
SUBS: BAR.
LO/N14.

ZEITSCHRIFT FUR ANGEWANDTE PHYSIK.    XXX
++Z. ANGEW. PHYS. [ZAPH-A]
DEUTSCHEN PHYSIKALISCHEN GESELLSCHAFT.
BERLIN 1, 1948- 32, 1972.//
BH/U-1.    MA/U-1.    SF/U-1.    SO/U-1.
ISSN 0044-2283

ZEITSCHRIFT FUR BIENENFORSCHUNG.    XXX
SUBS (1970): PART APIDOLOGIE.

ZEITSCHRIFT DER DEUTSCHEN MORGENLANDISCHEN
GESELLSCHAFT: SUPPLEMENTA.
++Z. DTSCH. MORGENLANDISCHEN GES. SUPPL.
[STEINER VERLAG GMBH]
WIESBADEN SUPPL. 1(1), 1969-
AD/U-1.    BN/U-1.

ZEITSCHRIFT FUR DIALEKTOLOGIE UND LINGUISTIK.
++Z. DIALEKTOL. & LINGUIST.
WIESBADEN 1, 1969-
PREV: ZEITSCHRIFT FUR MUNDARTFORSCHUNG FROM
11, 1935- 36(1), 1969.
NO/U-1.    NW/U-1.    SO/U-1.
ISSN 0044-1449

ZEITSCHRIFT FUR EISENBAHNWESEN UND VERKEHRS-
TECHNIK.    XXX
++Z. EISENBAHNWES. & VERKEHRSTECH.
[SIEMENS]
BERLIN 96, 1972-
CONTINUATION OF, & ALSO ENTITLED, GLASERS
ANNALEN FROM 1(1), 1877- JAHRG. 95, 1971.
LO/N14.

ZEITSCHRIFT FUR ELEKTRISCHE INFORMATIONS- UND
ENERGIETECHNIK.    XXX
++Z. ELEKTR. INF. & ENERGIETECH.
[AKAD. VERLAGSGES. GEEST & PORTIG]
LEIPZIG 1, 1971-
PREV: PART OF WZE FROM 1, 1963- 17, 1971; &
HOCHFREQUENZTECHNIK UND ELEKTROAKUSTIK FROM 1,
1907- 80, 1971 [SUSPENDED 1944- 1953].
LO/N14.

ZEITSCHRIFT FUR DIE GESAMTE TEXTIL-INDUSTRIE.    XXX
SUBS (1970): TEXTIL-INDUSTRIE.

ZEITSCHRIFT FUR KLINISCHE MEDIZIN.    XXX
SUBS (1966): PART OF ARCHIV FUR KLINISCHE
MEDIZIN.

ZEITSCHRIFT FUR KREBSFORSCHUNG.    XXX
SUBS (1971): ZEITSCHRIFT FUR KREBSFORSCHUNG
UND KLINISCHE ONKOLOGIE.

ZEITSCHRIFT FUR KREBSFORSCHUNG UND KLINISCHE
ONKOLOGIE.    XXX
++Z. KREBSFORSCH. & KLIN. ONKOL.
[SPRINGER; BERGMANN]
BERLIN &C. 76, 1971-
PREV: ZEITSCHRIFT FUR KREBSFORSCHUNG FROM´56,
1948- 75, 1971.
LO/N13.
ISSN 0084-5353

ZEITSCHRIFT FUR LATEINAMERIKA. FORSCHUNGEN,
BERICHTE, INFORMATION.
++Z. LATEINAM.
OSTERREICHISCHES LATEINAMERIKA-INSTITUT.
VIENNA NO.1, 1971-
LO/N-1.    OX/U-1.

ZEITSCHRIFT FUR LITERATURWISSENSCHAFT UND
LINGUISTIK.
++Z. LITERATURWISS. LINGUIST.
[ATHENAUM]
FRANKFURT 1, 1971-
BD/U-1.    LO/N-1.

ZEITSCHRIFT FUR MUNDARTFORSCHUNG.    XXX
SUBS (1969): ZEITSCHRIFT FUR DIALEKTOLOGIE
UND LINGUISTIK.

ZEITSCHRIFT FUR MUSIKTHEORIE.    000
SEE: ZFMTH.

ZEITSCHRIFT FUR NATIONALOKONOMIE: SUPPLEMENTUM.
JOURNAL OF NATIONAL ECONOMICS: SUPPLEMENT.
++Z. NATIONALOKON., SUPPL.
[SPRINGER]
VIENNA; NEW YORK NO.1, 1971-
LO/N-1.
ISSN 0084-537X

ZEITSCHRIFT FUR PARLAMENTSFRAGEN.
++Z. PARLAMENTSFRAGEN.
[WESTDEUTSCHER VERLAG]
OPLADEN 1, JE 1970-
OX/U17.
LO/U-3. 2, 1971-          OX/U-1. 4(3), 1973-

ZEITSCHRIFT FUR PHYSIKALISCHE MEDIZIN.
++Z. PHYS. MED.
DEUTSCHE GESELLSCHAFT FUR PHYSIKALISCHE
MEDIZIN.
[SCHATTAUER]
STUTTGART &C. 1(1), F 1970-
2/M.
LO/N13.
ISSN 0044-3344

ZEITSCHRIFT FUR RECHTSMEDIZIN. JOURNAL OF    XXX
LEGAL MEDICINE.
++Z. RECHTSMED.
DEUTSCHE GESELLSCHAFT FUR RECHTSMEDIZIN.
[SPRINGER]
BERLIN &C. 67, 1970-
PREV. PART OF: DEUTSCHE ZEITSCHRIFT FUR DIE
GESAMTE GERICHTLICHE MEDIZIN FROM 1, 1922-
66, 1969.
LD/U-1.    NW/U-1.
ISSN 0044-3433

ZEITSCHRIFT FUR RECHTSPOLITIK.
++Z. RECHTSPOLIT.
[C.H. BECK'SCHE VERLAGSBUCHHANDLUNG OSCAR BECK]
FRANKFURT/MAIN 1, 1968-
M. SUPPL TO: NEUE JURISTISCHE WOCHENSCHRIFT.
DB/U-2.    OX/U-15.
GL/U-1. 3, 1970-

ZEITSCHRIFT FUR SOZIOLOGIE.
++Z. SOZIOL.
UNIVERSITAT BIELEFELD: FAKULTAT FUR SOZIOLOGIE.
STUTTGART 1(1), JA 1972-
LO/N-1.

ZEITSCHRIFT FUR UNTERNEHMENS- UND GESELLSCHAFTS-
RECHT.
++Z. UNTERNEHMENS- & GESELLSCHAFTSRECHT.
FRANKFURT AM MAIN 1, 1972-
OX/U15.

ZEITSCHRIFT FUR VERERBUNGSLEHRE.    XXX
SUBS (1967): MOLECULAR & GENERAL GENETICS.

ZEITSCHRIFT FUR VERGLEICHENDE PHYSIOLOGIE.    XXX
SUBS (1972): JOURNAL OF COMPARATIVE PHYSIOLOGY

ZEITSCHRIFT FUR WERKSTOFFTECHNIK.
++Z. WERKST.
[VERLAG CHEMIE]
WEINHEIM/BERGSTR. 1, 1970-
LO/N14.
ISSN 0049-8688

ZEITSCHRIFT FUR WISSENSCHAFTLICHE MIKROSKOPIE
UND FUR MIKROSKOPISCHE TECHNIK.    XXX
SUBS (1971): MICROSCOPICA ACTA.

ZEITSCHRIFT FUR WISSENSCHAFTLICHE PHOTOGRAPHIE,
PHOTOPHYSIK UND PHOTOCHEMIE.    XXX
++Z. WISS. PHOTOGR. PHOTOPHYS. & PHOTOCHEM.
LEIPZIG 1, AP 1903- 64, 1970.//
SUSPENDED BETWEEN 1944 & JA 1948.
LO/N-4.*    LO/N14.    OX/U-8.

ZEMLJA RODNAJA.    XXX
(RUSSIA RSFSR) MINISTERSTVO SEL'SKOGO KHOZJAJST
MOSCOW 1, 1968-
PREV: SEL'SKOKHOZJAJSTVENNOE PROIZVODSTVO
NECHERNOZEMNOJ ZONY FROM 1(1), JA 1963-
5(12), 1967.
LO/N13.

ZENITH.
SAINT PATRICK'S COLLEGE (MAYNOOTH).
MAYNOOTH 1, 1971-
CO/U-1.    DB/U-1.
CA/U-1. 2, 1972-          ED/N-1. 2, 1972-

ZENTRALBLATT FUR DIE GESAMTE RECHTSMEDIZIN
UND IHRE GRENZGEBIETE.                                                          XXX
+ +ZENTRALBL. GES. RECHTSMED. & GRENZGEB.
DEUTSCHE GESELLSCHAFT FUR RECHTSMEDIZIN.
[SPRINGER]
  BERLIN &C. 1, 1970-
  PREV. PART OF: DEUTSCHE ZEITSCHRIFT FUR DIE
  GESAMTE GERICHTLICHE MEDIZIN FROM 1, 1922- 66,
  1969.
  LO/N13.    NW/U-1.

ZENTRALBLATT FUR PHARMAZIE, PHARMAKOTHERAPIE
UND LABORATORIUMSDIAGNOSTIK.                                               XXX
+ +ZENTRALBL. PHARM. PHARMAKOTHER. LABORATORIUMS-
DIAGN.
[VEB VERLAG VOLK UND GESUNDHEIT]
  BERLIN 109, 1970-
  PREV: PHARMAZEUTISCHE ZENTRALHALLE FROM 107,
  1968- 108, 1969.
  LO/N14.    LO/S-3.
  ISSN 0049-8696

ZENTRALBLATT FUR VETERINARMEDIZIN: REIHE C:
ANATOMIE, HISTOLOGIE, EMBRYOLOGIE.
+ +ZENTRALBL. VETERINARMED., C.
[PAREY]
  BERLIN 1, 1972-
  GL/U-1.    LO/M18.    LO/N13.

ZESZYTY HISTORYCZNE, INSTYTUT HISTORYCZNY
UNIWERSYTETU WARSZAWSKIEGO.                                            XXX
+ +ZESZ. HIST. INST. UNIW. WARSZ.
  WARSAW 1, 1960- 3, 1963.
  MONOGR. SUBS: FASCIULI HISTORICI.
  LO/S-9.

ZESZYTY NAUKOWE AKADEMII GORNICZO-HUTNICZEJ W
KRAKOWIE: AUTOMATYKA.
+ +ZESZ. NAUK. AKAD. GORN.-HUTN. KRAKOWIE, AUTOM.
AKADEMIA GORNICZO-HUTNICZA W KRAKOWIE.
  CRACOW 1, S 1966-
  ENGL. SUMM. NO. 1 OF AUTOMATYKA = NO. 112 OF
  ZESZYTY.
  LD/U-1.    XY/N-1.

ZESZYTY NAUKOWE AKADEMII GORNICZO-HUTNICZEJ W
KRAKOWIE: ROZPRAWY.
+ +ZESZ. NAUK. AKAD. GORN.-HUTN. KRAKOWIE, ROZPR.
[ZGKR-A]
AKADEMIA GORNICZO-HUTNICZA W KRAKOWIE.
  CRACOW 1, JE 1961-
  MONOGR. ENGL. SUMM. NO. 1 OF ROZPRAWY = NO.
  45 OF ZESZYTY...
  LO/S-9.    XY/N-1.

ZESZYTY NAUKOWE AKADEMII GORNICZO-HUTNICZEJ W
KRAKOWIE: ZAGADNIENIA TECHNICZNO-EKONOMICZNE.
+ +ZESZ. NAUK. AKAD. GORN.-HUTN. KRAKOW., ZAGAD-
NIENIA TECH.-EKON. [ZNKZ-A]
  CRACOW 1, 1961-
  ENGL. SUMM.
  LO/N13. 6, 1969-

ZESZYTY NAUKOWE POLITECHNIKI GDANSKIEJ:
FIZYKA.
+ +ZESZ. NAUK. POLITECH. GDANSK., FIZ.
  GDANSK 1, 1967-
  ENGL. SUMM.
  LO/N13.

ZESZYTY NAUKOWE POLITECHNIKI GDANSKIEJ:
MATEMATYKA.
  GDANSK 1, 1963-
  ENGL. SUMM.
  LO/N13. 2, 1964-

ZESZYTY NAUKOWE POLITECHNIKI POZNANSKIEJ:
FIZYKA.
+ +ZESZ. NAUK. POLITECH. POZNAN., FIZ. [ZNPO-A]
  POZNAN 1, 1964-
  ALSO NUMBERED AS PART OF MAIN SERIES: NO.1
  ABOVE = NO.25 OF MAIN SER.
  LO/N13.

ZESZYTY NAUKOWE POLITECHNIKI POZNANSKIEJ:
MATEMATYKA.
+ +ZESZ. NAUK. POLITECH. POZNAN., MAT.
  POZNAN 1, 1962-
  ALSO NUMBERED AS PART OF MAIN SERIES: NO.1
  ABOVE = NO.12 OF MAIN SERIES. SOME PAPERS IN
  ENGL.
  LO/N13.

ZESZYTY NAUKOWE POLITECHNIKI SLASKIEJ:
AUTOMATYKA.
+ +ZESZ. NAUK. POLITECH. SLASK., AUTOM.
  GLIWICE 1, 1961-
  SOME ENGL. SUMM. ALSO NUMBERED AS PART OF
  MAIN SEQUENCE OF POLYTECHNIC'S ZESZYTY NAUKOWE
  LO/N13. 12, 1969-

ZESZYTY NAUKOWE POLITECHNIKI SLASKIEJ: MAT-
EMATYKA-FIZYKA.
+ +ZESZ. NAUK. POLITECH. SLASK., MAT.-FIZ.
  GLIWICE 1, 1961-
  ENGL. SUMM. ALSO NUMBERED AS PART OF MAIN
  SEQUENCE OF POLYTECHNIC'S ZESZYTY NAUKOWE.
  LO/N13. 14, 1969-

ZESZYTY NAUKOWE POLITECHNIKI SZCZECINSKIEJ:
CHEMIA.
+ +ZESZ. NAUK. POLITECH. SZCZECIN., CHEM.[ZNSC-A]
POLITECHNIKA SZCZECINSKA.
  SZCZECIN Z.1, 1960-
  ENGL., GER., OR RUSS. SUMM. NO.1 OF CHEMIA =
  NO.14 OF ZESZYTY.
  LO/N14.

ZESZYTY NAUKOWE POLITECHNIKI WROCLAWSKIEJ:
FIZYKA.
+ +ZESZ. NAUK. POLITECH. WROCLAW., FIZ.
POLITECHNIKA WROCLAWSKA.
  WROCLAW 1, AP 1960-
  ENGL. & RUSS. SUMM. NUMBERED ALSO AS PART OF
  MAIN TITLE: NO.1 OF ABOVE = NO.35.
  LO/N13.

ZESZYTY NAUKOWE POLITECHNIKI WROCLAWSKIEJ:
INZYNIERIA SANITARNA.
+ +ZESZ. NAUK. POLITECH. WROCLAW., INZ. SANIT.
POLITECHNIKA WROCLAWSKA.
  WROCLAW NO.1, 1961-
  ENGL. & RUSS. SUMM. NUMBERED ALSO AS PART OF
  MAIN TITLE: NO.1 OF ABOVE = NO.40.
  LO/N13.

ZESZYTY NAUKOWE, SLASKI INSTYTUT NAUKOWY.
+ +ZESZ. NAUK. SLASK. INST. NAUK.
  KATOWICE [1], 1968-
  MONOGR. ENGL. & RUSS. SUMM. VOLS.1- 4 UNNUM-
  BERED. NUMBERING STARTS WITH VOL. 5, 1968.
  BH/U-1.    CA/U-1.    LO/N-3.

ZESZYTY NAUKOWE SZKOLY GLOWNEJ GOSPODARSTWA
WIEJSKIEGO: ROZPRAWY NAUKOWE.
+ +ZESZ. NAUK. SZK. GL. GOSPOD. WIEJSK., ROZPR.
NAUK.
  WARSAW 1, 1969-
  ENGL. SUMM.
  LO/N13.

ZESZYTY NAUKOWE SZKOLY GLOWNEJ GOSPODARSTWA
WIEJSKIEGO: TECHNOLOGIA DREWNA.
+ +ZESZ. NAUK. SZK. GL. GOSPOD. WIEJSK., TECHNOL.
DREWNA.
  WARSAW 1, 1967-
  ENGL. & RUSS. SUMM.
  LO/N13. 2, 1968-

ZESZYTY NAUKOWE SZKOLY GLOWNEJ GOSPODARSTWA
WIEJSKIEGO: TECHNOLOGIA ROLNO-SPOZYWCZA.
+ +ZESZ. NAUK. SZK. GL. GOSPOD. WIEJSK., TECHNOL.
ROLNO-SPOZYW.
  WARSAW 1, 1961-
  ENGL., GER. & RUSS. SUMM. NO.1 OF ABOVE PUBL.
  ALSO NUMBERED AS NO.4 OF: ZESZYTY NAUKOWE
  SZKOLY GLOWNEJ GOSPODARSTWA WIEJSKIEGO:
  ROLNICTWO.
  CA/U11.    ED/U-2.    LO/N13.    LO/S-9.    XS/R-6.    XY/N-1.

ZESZYTY NAUKOWE UNIWERSYTETU IM. ADAMA MICK-
IEWICZA: BIBLIOTEKA.                                                            XXX
+ +ZESZ. NAUK. UNIW. ADAMA MICKIEWICZA, BIBL.
UNIWERSYTET IM. ADAMA MICKIEWICZA W POZNANIU.
  POZNAN Z.1, 1960- 9, 1970.
  ZESZYT [VOL.] 1 PUBL. AS: ZESZYTY NAUKOWE...
  BIBLIOTEKA GLOWNA. Z.1 OF ABOVE = NO. 29 OF
  ZESZYTY. SUBS. PART OF: STUDIA O KSIAZCE.
  LO/N-3.    OX/U-1.
  GL/U-1. 8, 1969-

ZESZYTY NAUKOWE UNIWERSYTETU JAGIELLONSKIEGO:
PRACE ARCHEOLOGICZNE. ACTA SCIENTIARUM LITT-
ERARUMQUE, UNIVERSITAS JAGELLONICA CRACOVIEN-
SIS: SCHEDAE ARCHAEOLOGICAE.
+ +ZESZ. NAUK. UNIW. JAGIELLON., PR. ARCHEOL.
  CRACOW Z.1, JE 1960-
  NUMBERED ALSO AS PART OF MAIN SERIES: NO.1 OF
  ABOVE = NO.28 OF ZESZYTY ...
  BH/U-1.    GL/U-1.    LO/S-9.
  CA/U-1. 2, 1965-

ZESZYTY NAUKOWE UNIWERSYTETU JAGIELLONSKIEGO:
PRACE ETNOGRAFICZNE. ACTA SCIENTIARUM LITT-
ERARUMQUE, UNIVERSITAS JAGELLONICA CRACOVIEN-
SIS: SCHEDAE ETNOGRAPHICAE.
+ +ZESZ. NAUK. UNIW. JAGIELLON., PR. ETNOGR.
 CRACOW Z.1, 1963-
 ENGL. & RUSS. SUMM.   NUMBERED AS PART OF MAIN
 SERIES: NO.1 OF ABOVE = NO.53 OF ZESZYTY...
 BH/U-1.   GL/U-1.   LO/N-3.   LO/S-9.

ZESZYTY NAUKOWE UNIWERSYTETU JAGIELLONSKIEGO:
PRACE FILOZOFICZNE.
+ +ZESZ. NAUK. UNIW. JAGIELLON., PR. FILOZ.
 CRACOW 1, 1972-
 ENGL. SUMM.   TITLE ALSO IN LATIN: SCHEDAE
 PHILOSOPHICAE.
 CA/U-1.   OX/U-1.

ZESZYTY NAUKOWE UNIWERSYTETU JAGIELLONSKIEGO:
PRACE GEOGRAFICZNE, SERIE NOWA. ACTA SCIENT-
IARUM LITTERARUMQUE, UNIVERSITAS JAGELLONICA
CRACOVIENSIS: SCHEDAE GEOGRAPHICAE.
+ +ZESZ. NAUK. UNIW. JAGIELLON., PR. GEOGR. S.N.
 CRACOW Z.1, 1960-
 POL. & ENGL. MONOGR.   NUMBERED ALSO AS PART
 OF MAIN SERIES: NO.1 OF ABOVE = NO.32 OF
 ZESZYTY ...
 BH/U-1.   GL/U-1.   LO/S-9.   LO/U-2.

ZESZYTY NAUKOWE UNIWERSYTETU JAGIELLONSKIEGO:
PRACE Z HISTORII SZTUKI. ACTA SCIENTIARUM
LITTERARUMQUE, UNIVERSITAS JAGELLONICA CRACO-
VIENSIS: SCHEDAE AD ARTIS HISTORIAM PERTINEN-
TES.
+ +ZESZ. NAUK. UNIW. JAGIELLON., PR. HIST.
 SZTUKI.
 CRACOW Z. 1, 1962-
 NUMBERED ALSO AS PART OF MAIN SERIES.  NR.1
 OF ABOVE = NR.45 OF 'ZESZYTY ...'.  ENGL.,
 FR., OR RUSS. SUMM.
 CA/U-1.   ED/N-1.   ED/U-1.   LO/N-3.   LO/U17.   OX/U-1.

ZESZYTY NAUKOWE UNIWERSYTETU JAGIELLONSKIEGO:
PRACE HISTORYCZNE. ACTA SCIENTIARUM LITTER-
ARUMQUE, UNIVERSITAS JAGELLONICA CRACOVIENSIS:
SCHEDAE HISTORICAE.                                    XXX
+ +ZESZ. NAUK. UNIW. JAGIELLON., PR. HIST.
 CRACOW Z. 4, F 1960-
 PREV: ZESZYTY NAUKOWE UNIWERSYTETU JAGIELLON-
 SKIEGO: SERIA NAUK SPOLECZNYCH: HISTORIA FROM
 1, AP 1955- 3, 1958.  NUMBERED ALSO AS PART OF
 MAIN SERIES: NO.4 OF ABOVE = NO. 26 OF
 'ZESZTY ...'.
 BH/U-1.   CA/U-1.   GL/U-1.   LO/N-3.   LO/S-9.   OX/U-1.

ZESZYTY NAUKOWE UNIWERSYTETU JAGIELLONSKIEGO:
PRACE Z LOGIKI.
+ +ZESZ. NAUK. UNIW. JAGIELLON., PR. LOGIKI.
 CRACOW 1, 1965-
 ENGL. & RUSS. SUMM.
 OX/U-1.

ZESZYTY NAUKOWE UNIWERSYTETU JAGIELLONSKIEGO:
PRACE PSYCHOLOGICZNO-PEDAGOGICZNE. ACTA
SCIENTIARUM LITTERARUMQUE, UNIVERSITAS JAG-
ELLONICA CRACOVIENSIS: SCHEDAE PSYCHOLOGICAE
ET PAEDAGOGICAE.
+ +ZESZ. NAUK. UNIW. JAGIELLON., PR. PSYCHOL.-
 PEDAGOG.
 CRACOW Z. 2, F 1960-
 ZESZYT 1 PUBL. AS:  ZESZYTY NAUKOWE UNIWERSY-
 TETU JAGIELLONSKIEGO: SERIA NAUK SPOLECZNYCH:
 PSYCHOLOGIA I PEDAGOGIKA.  NUMBERED ALSO AS
 PART OF MAIN SERIES: Z. 2 OF ABOVE = Z. 29 OF
 'ZESZYTY ...'.
 BH/U-1.   CA/U-1. **   GL/U-1.   LO/N-3.   LO/S-9.

ZESZYTY NAUKOWE UNIWERSYTETU JAGIELLONSKIEGO:
SERIA NAUK SPOLECZNYCH: HISTORIA.                      XXX
 SUBS-(1960):  ZESZYTY NAUKOWE UNIWERSYTETU
 JAGIELLONSKIEGO: PRACE HISTORYCZNE.

ZESZYTY NAUKOWE UNIWERSYTETU LODZKIEGO: SERIA
3: NAUKIE EKONOMICZNE.
+ +ZESZ. NAUK. UNIW. LODZ., 3.
 LODZ 1, 1962-
 ENGL., FR. OR GER. SUMM.
 LO/N-3.

ZESZYTY NAUKOWE UNIWERSYTETU MIKOLAJA KOPER-
NIKA: NAUKI HUMANISTYCZNO-SPOLECZNE: ARCH-
EOLOGIA.
+ +ZESZ. NAUK. UNIW. MIKOLAJA KOPERNIKA, NAUK.
 HUM.-SPOLECZNE, ARCHEOL.
 TORUN 1, 1968-
 OX/U-1.

ZESZYTY NAUKOWE UNIWERSYTETU MIKOLAJA KOPER-
NIKA: NAUKI HUMANISTYCZNO-SPOLECZNE: EKONOMIA.
+ +ZESZ. NAUK. UNIW. MIKOLAJA KOPERNIKA, NAUK.
 HUM.-SPOLECZNE, EKON.
 TORUN 1, 1972-
 ENGL. SUMM.
 OX/U-1.

ZESZYTY NAUKOWE UNIWERSYTETU MIKOLAJA KOPER-
NIKA: NAUKI HUMANISTYCZNO-SPOLECZNE: FILOZ-
OFIA.
+ +ZESZ. NAUK. UNIW. MIKOLAJA KOPERNIKA, NAUK.
 HUM.-SPOLECZNE, FILOZ.
 TORUN 1, 1960-
 OX/U-1.

ZESZYTY NAUKOWE UNIWERSYTETU MIKOLAJA KOPER-
NIKA: NAUKI HUMANISTYCZNO-SPOLECZNE: HISTORIA.
+ +ZESZ. NAUK. UNIW. MIKOLAJA KOPERNIKA, NAUK.
 HUM.-SPOLECZNE, HIST.
 TORUN 1, 1965-
 CA/U-1.   OX/U-1.

ZESZYTY NAUKOWE UNIWERSYTETU MIKOLAJA KOPER-
NIKA: NAUKI HUMANISTYCZNO-SPOLECZNE: NAUKA O
KSIAZCE.                                               XXX
+ +ZESZ. NAUK. UNIW. MIKOLAJA KOPERNIKA, NAUK.
 HUM.-SPOLECZNE, NAUK. KSIAZCE.
 TORUN 1, 1962- 5, 1968.
 SUBS. PART OF: STUDIA O KSIAZCE.
 OX/U-1.

ZESZYTY NAUKOWE UNIWERSYTETU MIKOLAJA KOPER-
NIKA: NAUKI HUMANISTYCZNO-SPOLECZNE: NAUKI
POLITYCZNE.
+ +ZESZ. NAUK. UNIW. MIKOLAJA KOPERNIKA, NAUK.
 HUM.-SPOLECZNE, NAUK. POLIT.
 TORUN 1, 1967-
 OX/U-1.

ZESZYTY NAUKOWE UNIWERSYTETU MIKOLAJA KOPER-
NIKA: NAUKI HUMANISTYCZNO-SPOLECZNE:
PEDAGOGIKA.
+ +ZESZ. NAUK. UNIW. MIKOLAJA KOPERNIKA, NAUK.
 HUM.-SPOLECZNE, PEDAGOG.
 TORUN 1, 1971-
 GER. SUMM.
 OX/U-1.

ZESZYTY NAUKOWE UNIWERSYTETU MIKOLAJA KOPER-
NIKA: NAUKI HUMANISTYCZNO-SPOLECZNE: PRAWO.
+ +ZESZ. NAUK. UNIW. MIKOLAJA KOPERNIKA, NAUK.
 HUM.-SPOLECZNE, PRAWO.
 TORUN 1, 1961-
 OX/U-1. 2, 1961-

ZESZYTY NAUKOWE UNIWERSYTETU MIKOLAJA KOPER-
NIKA: NAUKI HUMANISTYCZNO-SPOLECZNE:
SOCJOLOGIA.
+ +ZESZ. NAUK. UNIW. MIKOLAJA KOPERNIKA, NAUK.
 HUM.-SPOLECZNE, SOCJOL.
 TORUN 1, 1972-
 ENGL. & FR. SUMM.
 OX/U-1.

ZESZYTY NAUKOWE UNIWERSYTETU MIKOLAJA KOPER-
NIKA: NAUKI HUMANISTYCZNO-SPOLECZNE: ZABYT-
KOZNAWSTWO I KONSERWATORSTWO.
 TORUN 1, 1966-
 OX/U-1.

ZESZYTY NAUKOWE WYZSZEJ SZKOLY EKONOMICZNEJ W
KRAKOWIE: SERIA SPECJALNA: ROZPRAWY HABILIT-
ACYJNE.
+ +ZESZ. NAUK. WYZSZ. SZK. EKON. KRAKOWIE, SER.
 SPEC. ROZPR. HABILIT.
 WYZSZA SZKOLA EKONOMICZNA W KRAKOWIE.
 CRACOW NO.1, 1961-
 MONOGR.  ENGL. & RUSS. SUMM.
 BH/U-1.   LO/S-9.   OX/U-1.

ZESZYTY NAUKOWE WYZSZEJ SZKOLY PEDAGOGICZNEJ
W GDANSKU: MATEMATYKA, FIZYKA, CHEMIA.
+ +ZESZ. NAUK. WYZSZ. PEDAGOG. GDANSKU, MAT. FIZ.
 CHEM.
 WYZSZA SZKOLA PEDAGOGICZNA W GDANSKU: WYDZIAL
 MATEMATYKI, FIZYKI I CHEMII.
 GDANSK 1, JE 1961-
 ENGL. & RUSS. SUMM.
 LO/N14.   LO/S-3.

ZETA. PHOTOCOLOURACTIONMAG.
 [MICHAEL GASSMAN PUBL.]
 LONDON 1(1), OC 1967-
 M.
 OX/U-1.

**ZFMTH. ZEITSCHRIFT FUR MUSIKTHEORIE.**
*STUTTGART 1, 1970-*
*LO/N-1.    OX/U-1.*

**ZHILISHCHNO-KOMMUNAL'NOE KHOZJAJSTVO.**                              XXX
*+ +ZHILISHCHNO-KOMMUNAL. KHOZJAJSTVO. [ZLKK-A]*
(RUSSIA, RSFSR) MINISTERSTVO KOMMUNAL'NOGO
KHOZJAJSTVA.
*MOSCOW 1951(1)- 1964(12) ...*
M.  SUBS: ZHILISHCHNOE I KOMMUNAL'NOE
KHOZJAJSTVO.
*BH/U-1.    LO/N-3.    SW/U-1.*

**ZHILISHCHNOE I KOMMUNAL'NOE KHOZJAJSTVO.**                          XXX
*+ +ZHILISHCHNOE KOMMUNAL. KHOZJAJSTVO.*
(RUSSIA, RSFSR) MINISTERSTVO KOMMUNAL'NOGO
KHOZJAJSTVA.
*MOSCOW 1965(1)-*
M.  PREV: ZHILISHCHNO-KOMMUNAL'NOE KHOZJAJST-
VO FROM 1951(1)- 1964(12).
*SW/U-1.*
*CC/U-1.  1968-*                      *OX/U-1.  1966(1)-*

**ZHIVOE SLOVO V RUSSKOJ RECHI PRIKAM'JA.**
*+ +ZHIVOE SLOVO RUSS. RECHI PRIKAM'JA.*
PERMSKIJ GOSUDARSTVENNYJ UNIVERSITET.
*PERM'  1, 1969-*
*CC/U-1.  1, 1969.*

**ZHIVOTNOVUDNI NAUKI.**
*+ +ZHIVOTNOVUD. NAUK. [ZHVN-A]*
AKADEMIJA NA SELSKOSTOPANSKITE NAUKI.
*SOFIA  1, 1964-*
ENGL., GER. & RUSS. SUMM. & CONT. LISTS.
ENGL. TITLE: ANIMAL SCIENCE.
*LO/N13.    ZS/U-1.*

**ZHURNAL EVOLJUTSIONNOJ BIOKHIMII I FIZIOLOGII.**
**JOURNAL OF EVOLUTIONARY BIOCHEMISTRY & PHYS-**
**IOLOGY.**
*+ +ZH. EVOL. BIOKHIM. & FIZIOL. [ZEBF-A]*
AKADEMIJA NAUK SSSR.
*MOSCOW &C.  1(1), JA/F 1965-*
ENGL. SUMM. & CONTENTS LIST.
*LO/N13.    LO/S-3.    XY/N-1.*

**ZHURNAL EVOLYUTSIONNOJ BIOKHIMII I FIZIOLOGII**
**(ENGL. TRANSL.).**                                                  000
SEE:  JOURNAL OF EVOLUTIONARY BIOCHEMISTRY &
PHYSIOLOGY.

**ZHURNAL MATERIALY REGISTRATSII INFORMATSII.**                       000
SEE: JOURNAL FUR SIGNALAUFZEICHUNGSMATERIALIEN

**ZHURNAL MOSKOVSKOI PATRIARKHII (ENGL. LANG.**
**ED.)**                                                              000
SEE: JOURNAL OF THE MOSCOW PATRIARCHATE.

**ZHURNAL NAUCHNOJ I PRIKLADNOJ FOTOGRAFII I**
**KINEMATOGRAFII (ENGL. TRANSL.).**                                   000
SEE: PHOTOGRAPHIC TECHNOLOGY USSR.

**ZHURNAL PRIKLADNOJ SPEKTROSKOPII, AKADEMIJA**
**NAVUK BELARUSKAJ SSR.**
*+ +ZH. PRIKL. SPEKTROSK. AKAD. NAVUK BELARUS.*
*SSR.*
AKADEMIJA NAUK BELORUSSKOJ SSR.
*MINSK TOM 1, S 1964-*
M.  ENGL. SUMM. & CONT. LISTS.
*CA/U-2. 2, 1965-*                      *DB/S-1.  4, 1966-*
*LO/N13. 2, 1965-*                      *LO/S-3.  2, 1965-*

**ZHURNAL VSESOJUZNOGO KHIMICHESKOGO**
**OBSHCHESTVA IMENI D.I. MENDELEEVA; (ENGL.**
**TRANSL.)**                                                          000
SEE: MENDELEEV CHEMISTRY JOURNAL.

**ZHURNAL YUGOSLAVSKIKH IZOBRETATELEV.**                              000
SEE: JUGOSLOVENSKO PRONALAZASTVO.

**ZHURNALIST.**                                                       XXX
*MOSCOW JA, 1967-*
MON. PREV: SOVETSKAJA PECHAT' FROM OC, 1955-
1966.
*BH/U-1.    GL/U-1.    LD/U-1.*
*CC/U-1.  1969-*

**ZITTELIANA.  ABHANDLUNGEN DER BAYERISCHEN**
**STAATSSAMMLUNG FUR PALAONTOLOGIE UND HISTOR-**
**ISCHE GEOLOGIE.**
*MUNICH 1, 1969-*
*LO/N-2.    LO/N13.    LO/U-2.*
*BR/U-1.  3, 1974-*

**ZOGRAF.  CASOPIS ZA SREDNJOVEKOVNU UMETNOST.**
GALERIJA FRESAKA.
*BELGRADE  BR.1, 1966-*
A.
*LO/N-3.  2,1967.*

**ZONE.  ENVIRONMENTAL ENGINEERING IN IRELAND.**
[PUBLISHING & PUBLICITY LTD.]
*DUBLIN  [NO.1] JA 1972-*
*DB/U-1.*
*ISSN 0044-5010*

**ZOO FEDERATION NEWS.**
*+ +ZOO FED. NEWS.*
FEDERATION OF ZOOLOGICAL GARDENS OF GREAT
BRITAIN & IRELAND.
*LONDON NO.1, 1971-*
*LO/N-2.    LO/N13.*
*ED/N-1.  4, F 1972-*

**ZOOLOGICA SCRIPTA.**                                                XXX
*+ +ZOOL. SCR.*
KUNGLIGA SVENSKA VETENSKAPSAKADEMIEN.
[ALMQVIST & WIKSELL]
*STOCKHOLM  1, 1971-*
PREV: ARKIV FOR ZOOLOGI FROM 1903.
*BL/U-1.    CA/U-1.    GL/U-1.    LD/U-1.    LO/N-2.    LO/N13.*
*NW/U-1.    OX/U-8.    SH/U-1.*
*ISSN 0300-3256*

**ZOOLOGICAL JOURNAL OF THE LINNEAN SOCIETY.**                        XXX
*+ +ZOOL. J. LINN. SOC.*
LINNEAN SOCIETY OF LONDON.
[ACADEMIC P.]
*LONDON 48, F 1969-*
PREV: JOURNAL OF THE LINNEAN SOCIETY- ZOOLOGY
FROM 1, 1855- 47, 1968.
*BN/U-2.    DB/S-1.    ED/N-1.    GL/U-1.  ·  LD/U-1.    LO/U-2.*
*RE/U-1.    SF/U-1.*
*ISSN 0024-4082*

**ZOOLOGICAL RECORD (KIEV).**                                         000
SEE: VESTNIK ZOOLOGII (KIEV).

**ZOOPHYSIOLOGY & ECOLOGY.**
*+ +ZOOPHYSIOL. & ECOL.*
[SPRINGER]
*BERLIN &C.  1, 1971-*
*LO/N-2.    LO/N-2.*

**ZPRAVY GEOGRAFICKEHO USTAVU CSAV.**
*+ +ZPR. GEOGR. USTAVU CSAV.*
CESKOSLOVENSKA AKADEMIE VED: GEOGRAFICKY USTAV.
*BRNO 1, 1964-*
VARIOUS LANG.
*CA/U-2.*
*OX/U-1.  1967-*

**ZRODLA DO DZIEJOW KLASY ROBOTNICZEJ NA ZIE-**
**MIACH POLSKICH.**
POLSKA AKADEMIA NAUK: INSTYTUT HISTORII.
*WARSAW TOM 1, F/JE 1962-*
MONOGR.  TEXT ALSO IN RUSS.
*BH/U-1.    LO/U-3.*

**ZUKA.  A JOURNAL OF EAST AFRICAN CREATIVE**
**WRITING.**
[OXFORD UNIV. PRESS]
*NAIROBI  NO.1, S 1967-*
*LD/U-1.    LO/S26.    LO/U-2.    LO/U14.*
*CB/U-1.  2,1968-*
*ISSN 0044-5444*

**ZWANGLOSE ABHANDLUNGEN AUS DEM GEBIET DER NOR-**
**MALEN UND PATHOLOGISCHEN ANATOMIE.**                                XXX
SUBS (1970):  NORMALE UND PATHOLOGISCHE ANA-
TOMIE.

**ZWIERZETA LABORATORYJNE.**
*+ +ZWIERZETA LAB.*
POLSKA AKADAMIA NAUK: ZAKLAD HODOWLI ZWIERZAT
LABORATORYJNYCH.
*WARSAW  1(1), 1963-*
ENGL. & RUSS. SUMM.  BODY PREV. AS: POLSKA
AKADEMIA NAUK: KOMISJA DO SPRAW ZWIERZAT LAB-
ORATORYJNYCH.
*LO/N13. 2(3), 1964-*

# Index of Sponsoring Bodies

ISB/ 1

**1320 CLUB.**
— CATALYST. FOR THE SCOTTISH VIEWPOINT.

**AARHUS UNIVERSITET: KULTURGEOGRAFISK INSTITUT.**
— KULTURGEOGRAFISKE SKRIFTER, KULTURGEOGRAFISK INSTITUT, AARHUS UNIVERSITET. = PUBLICATIONS OF THE INSTITUTE OF ECONOMIC & APPLIED GEOGRAPHY, UNIVERSITY OF AARHUS.

**ABBAYE DE SCOURMONT.**
— CISTERCIAN STUDIES.

**ABDULLAH BAYERO COLLEGE (KANO).**
— KANO STUDIES.

**ABERDEEN COLLEGE OF EDUCATION.**
— INKLINS.

**ABERDEEN UNIVERSITY LITERARY SOCIETY.**
— NEW NORTH.

**ACADEMIA DE CIENCIAS DE CUBA.**
— SERIE ARCHIVO NACIONAL, ACADEMIA DE CIENCIAS DE CUBA.

**ACADEMIA DE CIENCIAS DE CUBA: DEPARTMENTO DE ANTROPOLOGIA.**
— SERIE ANTROPOLOGICA, DEPARTMENTO DE ANTROPOLOGIA, ACADEMIA DE CIENCIAS DE CUBA.

**ACADEMIA DE CIENCIAS DE CUBA: INSTITUTO DE AGRONOMIA.**
— REVISTA DE AGRICULTURA (CUBA).

**ACADEMIA DE CIENCIAS DE CUBA: INSTITUTO DE DOCUMENTACION E INFORMACION CIENTIFICA Y TECNICA.**
— BOLETIN DE INFORMACION CIENTIFICA CUBANA.

**ACADEMIA DE CIENCIAS DE CUBA: INSTITUTO DE METEOROLOGIA.**
— SERIE METEOROLOGICA, INSTITUTO DE METEOROLOGIA, ACADEMIA DE CIENCIAS DE CUBA.

**ACADEMIA DE CIENCIAS DE CUBA, INSTITUTO DE OCEANOLOGIA.**
— SERIE OCEANOLOGICA, INSTITUTO DE OCEANOLOGIA, ACADEMIA DE CIENCIAS DE CUBA.

**ACADEMIA COLOMBIANA DE CIENCIAS EXACTAS, FISICAS Y NATURALES.**
— BOLETIN BIBLIOGRAFICO, ACADEMIA COLOMBIANA DE CIENCIAS EXACTAS, FISICAS Y NATURALES.

**ACADEMIA COLOMBIANA DE HISTORIA: SECCION DE ARCHIVOS Y MICROFILMES.**
— ARCHIVOS, SECCION DE ARCHIVOS Y MICROFILMES, ACADEMIA COLOMBIANA DE HISTORIA.

**ACADEMIA DE HISTORIA POTOSINA.**
— ARCHIVOS DE HISTORIA POTOSINA.

**ACADEMY OF KOREAN STUDIES.**
— KOREA OBSERVER.

**ACADEMIA NACIONAL DE CIENCIAS ECONOMICAS (PERU)**
— REVISTA DE LA ACADEMIA NACIONAL DE CIENCIAS ECONOMICAS (PERU).

**ACADEMIA NACIONAL DE CIENCIAS EXACTAS, FISICAS Y NATURALES (ARGENTINA).**
— ANALES DE LA ACADEMIA NACIONAL DE CIENCIAS EXACTAS, FISICAS Y NATURALES (ARGENTINA). SUPLEMENTO.

**ACADEMY OF PHARMACEUTICAL SCIENCES: PHARMACEUTICAL ANALYSIS & CONTROL SECTION.**
— ANALYTICAL PROFILES OF DRUG SUBSTANCES.

**ACADEMIA PORTENA DEL LUNFARDO (BUENOS AIRES).**
— BOLETIN, ACADEMIA PORTENA DEL LUNFARDO (BUENOS AIRES).

**ACADEMIA REPUBLICII POPULARE ROMINE.**
— REVUE ROUMAINE D'EMBRYOLOGIE ET DE CYTOLOGIE: SERIE DE CYTOLOGIE.
— REVUE ROUMAINE D'EMBRYOLOGIE ET DE CYTOLOGIE: SERIE D'EMBRYOLOGIE.

**ACADEMIA REPUBLICII SOCIALISTE ROMANIA.**
— IZVOARE ORIENTALE PRIVIND ISTORIA ROMANIEI.

**ACADEMIA REPUBLICII SOCIALISTE ROMANIA: CENTRUL DE DOCUMENTARE STIINTIFICA.**
— PROGRESELE STIINTEI.

**ACADEMIA REPUBLICII SOCIALISTE ROMANIA: INSTITUTUL DE ARCHEOLOGIE.**
— INVENTARIA ARCHAEOLOGICA.

**ACADEMIA REPUBLICII SOCIALISTE ROMANIA; INSTITUTUL DE ISTORIE 'N. IORGA'.**
— CRONICILE MEDIEVALE ALE ROMINIEI.
— CRONICILE MEDIEVALE ALE ROMINIEI, SUPLIMENT.
— INSCRIPTILE MEDIEVALE ALE ROMANIEI.

**ACADEMY OF SCIENCES OF THE USSR.**  000
SEE: AKADEMIJA NAUK SSSR.

**ACCADEMIA DELLA CRUSCA.**
— STUDI DI GRAMMATICA ITALIANA.

**ACCADEMIA LUCCHESE DI SCIENZE, LETTERE E ARTI.**
— STUDI E TESTI, ACCADEMIA LUCCHESE DI SCIENZE, LETTERE E ARTI.

**ACCADEMIA NAZIONALE DI SANTA CECILIA.**
— STUDI MUSICALI.

**ADELPHI UNIVERSITY: LATIN AMERICAN STUDIES PROGRAM.**
— NUEVA NARRATIVA HISPANOAMERICANA.

**ADVISORY CENTRE FOR EDUCATION.**
— WHERE: SUPPLEMENT.  XXX

**ADVISORY CENTRE FOR EDUCATION FOR PRIORITY.**
— PRIORITY NEWS.

**ADVISORY GROUP FOR AEROSPACE RESEARCH & DEVELOPMENT.**
— AGARD EXTENDED SUMMARIES.

**AER LINGUS: PUBLICITY DEPARTMENT.**
— CARA. TRAVEL MAGAZINE OF ...

**AERIAL ROPEWAY ENGINEERS SOCIETY.**
— LIFT. ELEVATOR LIFT & ROPEWAY ENGINEERING.  XXX

**AFRICA BUREAU.**
— X RAY ON CURRENT AFFAIRS IN SOUTHERN AFRICA.

**AFRICA INSTITUTE OF SOUTH AFRICA.**
— SOUTH AFRICAN JOURNAL OF AFRICAN AFFAIRS.

**AFRICAN BUREAU FOR THE 1973 JUSTICE FOR RHODESIA CAMPAIGN.**
— NEWSBRIEF RHODESIA '73.

**AFRICAN ACADEMY OF POLITICAL & SOCIAL SCIENCES.**
— AFRICAN SCHOLAR. JOURNAL OF RESEARCH & ANALYSIS.

**AFRICAN STUDIES ASSOCIATION.**
— AFRICAN STUDIES BULLETIN.  XXX
SUBS (1970): AFRICAN STUDIES REVIEW.
— AFRICAN STUDIES NEWSLETTER.*
— AFRICAN STUDIES REVIEW.  XXX
— ISSUE. A QUARTERLY JOURNAL OF OPINION.

**AFRICAN STUDIES ASSOCIATION OF THE WEST INDIES.**
— BULLETIN, AFRICAN STUDIES ASSOCIATION OF THE WEST INDIES.

**AFRICAN STUDIES CENTRE (CAMBRIDGE).**
— OCCASIONAL PAPERS, AFRICAN STUDIES CENTRE (CAMBRIDGE).

AFRICAN STUDIES CENTER (LOS ANGELES).　　　　000
　　SEE: UNIVERSITY OF CALIFORNIA AT LOS ANGELES:
　　AFRICAN STUDIES CENTER.

AFRICAN TRAINING & RESEARCH CENTRE IN ADMIN-　000
ISTRATION FOR DEVELOPMENT.
　　SEE: CENTRE AFRICAIN DE FORMATION ET DE RECH-
　　ERCHES ADMINISTRATIVES POUR LE DEVELOPPEMENT.

AFRO-ASIAN PEOPLE'S SOLIDARITY MOVEMENT.
　　— AFRO-ASIAN SOLIDARITY.　JOURNAL OF ...

AGE CONCERN.
　　— AGE CONCERN TODAY.　　　　　　　　　　　XXX

AGRARNI INSTITUT.
　　— SOCIOLOGIJA SELA.

AGRICULTURAL CENTRAL CO-OPERATIVE ASSOCIATION
LTD.
　　— FARMING BUSINESS.

AGRICULTURAL CHEMICAL SOCIETY OF JAPAN.　　000
　　SEE: NIHON NOGEI KAGAKKAI.

AGRICULTURAL COLLEGE OF ISHIKAWA PREFECTURE.　000
　　SEE: ISHIKAWA-KEN NOGYO TANKI DAIGAKU.

AGRICULTURAL DEVELOPMENT & ADVISORY SERVICE
(GB).　　　　　　　　　　　　　　　　　　　　XXX
　　— A.D.A.S.　QUARTERLY REVIEW.　　　　　　　XXX
　　— TECHNICAL REPORT, AGRICULTURAL DEVELOPMENT &
　　ADVISORY SERVICE (GB).　　　　　　　　　　　XXX

AGRICULTURAL ECONOMICS SOCIETY OF IRELAND.
　　— PROCEEDINGS, AGRICULTURAL ECONOMICS SOCIETY
　　OF IRELAND.

AGRICULTURAL EXPERIMENT STATION, BLACKSBURG,
VA.
　　— RESEARCH REPORT, AGRICULTURAL EXPERIMENT STA-
　　TION, BLACKSBURG, VIRGINIA.　　　　　　　　XXX
　　SUBS (1967):　RESEARCH REPORT, RESEARCH
　　DIVISION, VIRGINIA POLYTECHNIC INSTITUTE.

AGRICULTURAL EXPERIMENTAL STATION, CALHOUN, LA.
　　— HORTICULTURAL PROGRESS REPORT, AGRICULTURAL
　　EXPERIMENTAL STATION, CALHOUN, LOUISIANA.

AGRICULTURAL EXPERIMENT STATION, FORT COLLINS,
COLO.
　　— COLORADO FARM & HOME RESEARCH.　　　　XXX
　　SUBS (1969):　CSU RESEARCH.
　　— CSU RESEARCH.　　　　　　　　　　　　　XXX

AGRICULTURAL EXPERIMENT STATION, KINGSTON, R.I.
　　— RHODE ISLAND AGRICULTURE.　　　　　　　XXX
　　SUBS (1970):　RHODE ISLAND RESOURCES.
　　— RHODE ISLAND RESOURCES.　　　　　　　　XXX

AGRICULTURAL EXPERIMENT STATION, ORONO, MAINE.
　　— MAINE FARM RESEARCH.　　　　　　　　　XXX
　　SUBS (1968):　RESEARCH IN THE LIFE SCIENCES.
　　— RESEARCH IN THE LIFE SCIENCES.　　　　　XXX

AGRICULTURAL INSTITUTE OF CANADA.
　　— AGRICULTURAL INSTITUTE REVIEW.　　　　　XXX
　　SUBS (1969): A.I.C. REVIEW.
　　— AGROLOGIST.　　　　　　　　　　　　　　XXX
　　— A.I.C. REVIEW.　　　　　　　　　　　　　XXX

AGRICULTURAL LAND SERVICE (GB).　　　　　　XXX
　　— TECHNICAL REPORT, AGRICULTURAL LAND SERVICE
　　(GB).　　　　　　　　　　　　　　　　　　　XXX
　　SUBS (1971): TECHNICAL REPORT, AGRICULTURAL
　　DEVELOPMENT & ADVISORY SERVICE (GB).

AGRICULTURAL RESEARCH COUNCIL.
　　— ARC INDEX OF AGRICULTURAL & FOOD RESEARCH.　XXX
　　— INDEX OF AGRICULTURAL RESEARCH.　　　　XXX
　　SUBS (1972): ARC INDEX OF AGRICULTURAL &
　　FOOD RESEARCH.

AGRICULTURAL RESEARCH COUNCIL: SOIL SURVEY OF
GREAT BRITAIN.　　　　　　　　　　　　　　　000
　　SEE: SOIL SURVEY OF GREAT BRITAIN (ENGLAND &
　　WALES).

AHMADI NATURAL HISTORY & FIELD STUDIES GROUP.
　　— NEWSLETTER, AHMADI NATURAL HISTORY & FIELD
　　STUDIES GROUP.

AHMADU BELLO UNIVERSITY.
　　— SAVANNA.

AHMADU BELLO UNIVERSITY: INSTITUTE OF ADMIN-
ISTRATION.
　　— NIGERIAN JOURNAL OF PUBLIC AFFAIRS.

AICHI INSTITUTE OF TECHNOLOGY.　　　　　　000
　　SEE: AICHI KOGYO DAIGAKU.

AICHI KOGYO DAIGAKU.
　　— AICHI KOGYO DAIGAKU KENKYU HOKOKU. BULLETIN
　　OF AICHI INSTITUTE OF TECHNOLOGY.

AICHI-KEN AGRICULTURAL RESEARCH CENTER.　　000
　　SEE: AICHI-KEN NOGYO SOGO SHIKENJO.

AICHI-KEN NOGYO SOGO SHIKENJO.
　　— AICHI-KEN NOGYO SOGO SHIKENJO KENKYU HOKOKU: D:
　　SANGYO.　RESEARCH BULLETIN OF THE AICHI-KEN
　　AGRICULTURAL RESEARCH CENTER: SERIES D:
　　SERICULTURE.

AIR FORCE ASSOCIATION.
　　— AEROSPACE INTERNATIONAL.
　　— AIR FORCE/SPACE DIGEST INTERNATIONAL.　　XXX

AIR TRANSPORT & TRAVEL INDUSTRY TRAINING BOARD.
　　— AIR & TRAVEL TRAINING WORLD.　　　　　　XXX
　　— NEWS, AIR TRANSPORT & TRAVEL INDUSTRY TRAIN-
　　ING BOARD.　　　　　　　　　　　　　　　　XXX

AKADEMIA GORNICZO-HUTNICZA W KRAKOWIE.
　　— ZESZYTY NAUKOWE AKADEMII GORNICZO-HUTNICZEJ W
　　KRAKOWIE: AUTOMATYKA.
　　— ZESZYTY NAUKOWE AKADEMII GORNICZO-HUTNICZEJ W
　　KRAKOWIE: ROZPRAWY.
　　— ZESZYTY NAUKOWE AKADEMII GORNICZO-HUTNICZEJ W
　　KRAKOWIE: ZAGADNIENIA TECHNICZNO-EKONOMICZNE.

AKADEMIJA MEDITSINSKIKH NAUK SSSR.
　　— TOKSIKOLOGIJA NOVYKH PROMYSHLENNYKH KHIMICH-
　　ESKIKH VESHCHESTV.

AKADEMIJA NAUK ARMJANSKOJ SSR.
　　— IZVESTIJA AKADEMII NAUK ARMJANSKOJ SSR:
　　OBSHCHESTVENNYE NAUKI.　　　　　　　　　XXX
　　SUBS (1966): VESTNIK OBSHCHESTVENNYKH NAUK,
　　AKADEMIJA NAUK ARMJANSKOJ SSR.
　　— VESTNIK OBSHCHESTVENNYKH NAUK, AKADEMIJA NAUK
　　ARMJANSKOJ SSR.　　　　　　　　　　　　　XXX

AKADEMIJA NAUK ARMJANSKOJ SSR: INSTITUT
BIOKHIMII.
　　— VOPROSY BIOKHIMII MOZGA.

AKADEMIJA NAUK ARMJANSKOJ SSR: SEKTOR
VOSTOKOVEDENIJA.
　　— VOSTOKOVEDCHESKIJ SBORNIK.

AKADEMIJA NAUK AZERBAJDZHANSKOJ SSR.
　　— IZVESTIJA AKADEMII NAUK AZERBAJDZHANSKOJ SSR:
　　SERIJA NAUK O ZEMLE.
　　— SOVETSKAJA TJURKOLOGIJA.
　　— TRUDY RESPUBLIKANSKOGO RUKOPISNOGO FONDA.

AKADEMIJA NAUK AZERBAJDZHANSKOJ SSR: INSTITUT
ISTORII.
　　— AZERBAJDZHANSKIJ ETNOGRAFICHESKIJ SBORNIK.

AKADEMIJA NAUK AZERBAJDZHANSKOJ SSR: MUZEJ
AZERBAJDZHANSKOJ LITERATURY.
　　— TRUDY MUZEJA AZERBAJDZHANSKOJ LITERATURY.

AKADEMIJA NAUK AZERBAJDZHANSKOJ SSR: SEKTOR
FILOSOFII.
　　— OCHERKI PO ISTORII AZERBAJDZHANSKOJ FILOSOFII.

AKADEMIJA NAUK AZERBAJDZHANSKOJ SSR: SHEMAKH-
INSKAJA ASTROFIZICHESKAJA OBSERVATORIJA.
　　— SOOBSHCHENIJA SHEMAKHINSKOJ ASTROFIZICHESKOJ
　　OBSERVATORII.　　　　　　　　　　　　　　XXX
　　— TRUDY SHEMAKHINSKOJ ASTROFIZICHESKOJ OBSERVAT-
　　ORII AKADEMII NAUK AZERBAJDZHANSKOJ SSR.　XXX
　　SUBS (1965): SOOBSHCHENIJA SHEMAKHINSKOJ
　　ASTROFIZICHESKOJ OBSERVATORII.

AKADEMIJA NAUK BELORUSSKOJ SSR.
　　— ZHURNAL PRIKLADNOJ SPEKTROSKOPII, AKADEMIJA
　　NAVUK BELARUSKAJ SSR.

AKADEMIJA NAUK BELORUSSKOJ SSR: INSTITUT
GEOLOGICHESKIKH NAUK (MINSK).
　　— PALEONTOLOGIJA I STRATIGRAFIJA PRIBALTIKI I
　　BELORUSSII.　PALAEONTOLOGY & STRATIGRAPHY OF
　　THE BALTIC & THE BYELORUSSIA.　　　　　　　XXX

AKADEMIJA NAUK BELORUSSKOJ SSR: (INSTYTUT
HISTORYI).
　　— OCHERKI PO ARKHEOLOGII BELORUSSII.

AKADEMIJA NAUK GRUZINSKOJ SSR: GEOLOGICHESKIJ
INSTITUT.
— TRUDY GEOLOGICHESKOGO INSTITUTA AKADEMII NAUK
GRUZINSKOJ SSR: NOVAJA SERIJA.

AKADEMIJA NAUK GRUZINSKOJ SSR: INSTITUT
ELEKTRONIKI AVTOMATIKI I TELEMEKHANIKI.
— TRUDY, INSTITUT ELEKTRONIKI, AVTOMATIKI I
TELEMEKHANIKI AKADEMII NAUK GRUZINSKOJ SSR.

AKADEMIJA NAUK GRUZINSKOJ SSR: INSTITUT FIZIKI.
— ELEKTRONNYE I IONNYE PROTSESSY V TVERDYKH
TELAKH.

AKADEMIJA NAUK GRUZINSKOJ SSR: INSTITUT ISTORI.
— KAVKAZSKIJ ETNOGRAFICHESKIJ SBORNIK.
— KAVKAZSKO-BLIZHNE-VOSTOCHNYJ SBORNIK.

AKADEMIJA NAUK GRUZINSKOJ SSR: INSTITUT ISTORII
GRUZINSKOJ LITERATURY.
— GRUZINSKIJ FOL'KLOR, MATERIALY I ISSLEDO-
VANIJA.
— LITERATURNYE VZAIMOSVJAZI.  SBORNIK.

AKADEMIJA NAUK GRUZINSKOJ SSR: INSTITUT
KIBERNETIKI.
— TRUDY INSTITUTA KIBERNETIKI AKADEMII NAUK
GRUZINSKOJ SSR.

AKADEMIJA NAUK GRUZINSKOJ SSR: INSTITUT
ZOOLOGII.
— MATERIALY K FAUNE GRUZII.
— PARAZITOLOGICHESKIJ SBORNIK.

AKADEMIJA NAUK KAZAKHSKOJ SSR.
— IZVESTIJA AKADEMII NAUK KAZAKHSKOJ SSR:
SERIJA BIOLOGICHESKIKH NAUK.                    XXX
— IZVESTIJA AKADEMII NAUK KAZAKHSKOJ SSR:
SERIJA BOTANIKI I POCHVOVEDENIJA.               XXX
SUBS (1963): IZVESTIJA AKADEMII NAUK
KAZAKHSKOJ SSR:  SERIJA BIOLOGICHESKIKH
NAUK.

AKADEMIJA NAUK KAZAKHSKOJ SSR: INSTITUT
EKONOMIKI.
— PROBLEMY SOVREMENNOJ EKONOMIKI KAZAKHSTANA.

AKADEMIJA NAUK KAZAKHSKOJ SSR: INSTITUT GIDRO-
GEOLOGII I GIDROFIZIKI.
— TRUDY INSTITUTA GIDROGEOLOGII I GIDROFIZIKI
AKADEMII NAUK KAZAKHSKOJ SSR.

AKADEMIJA NAUK KAZAKHSKOJ SSR: INSTITUT
ZOOLOGII.
— VOPROSY PRIRODNOJ OCHAGOVOSTI BOLEZNEJ.

AKADEMIJA NAUK KAZAKHSKOJ SSR: SEKTOR FIZICH-
ESKOJ GEOGRAFII.
— GLJATSIOLOGICHESKIE ISSLEDOVANIJA V KAZAKHST-
ANE.

AKADEMIJA NAUK KIRGIZSKOJ SSR: INSTITUT FIZIKI,
MATEMATIKI I MEKHANIKI.
— ISSLEDOVANIJA PO INTEGRO-DIFFERENTSIAL'NYM
URAVNENIJAM V KIRGIZII.

AKADEMIJA NAUK KIRGIZSKOJ SSR: INSTITUT
GEOLOGII.
— MATERIALY PO GEOLOGII TJAN'-SHANJA.

AKADEMIJA NAUK LATVIJSKOJ SSR.                  000
SEE: LATVIJAS PSR ZINATNU AKADEMIJA.

AKADEMIJA NAUK LITOVSKOJ SSR.                   000
SEE: LIETUVOS TSR MOKSLU AKADEMIJA.

AKADEMIJA NAUK MOLDAVSKOJ SSR.
— IZVESTIJA AKADEMII NAUK MOLDAVSKOJ SSR:
SERIJA BIOLOGICHESKOKH I KHIMICHESKIKH NAUK.    XXX
— IZVESTIJA AKADEMII NAUK MOLDAVSKOJ SSR:
SERIJA FIZIKO-TEKHNICHESKIKH I MATEMATICHES-
KIKH NAUK.                                      XXX
— IZVESTIJA AKADEMII NAUK MOLDAVSKOJ SSR:
SERIJA OBSHCHESTVENNYKH NAUK.                   XXX

AKADEMIJA NAUK MOLDAVSKOJ SSR: INSTITUT BIO-
KHIMII I FIZIOLOGII RASTENIJ.
— INFEKTSIONNYE ZABOLEVANIJA KUL'TURNYKH
RASTENIJ MOLDAVII.

AKADEMIJA NAUK MOLDAVSKOJ SSR: INSTITUT
GEOLOGII I POLEZNYKH ISKOPAEMYKH.
— PALEONTOLOGIJA, GEOLOGIJA I POLEZNYE ISKOP-
AEMYE MOLDAVII.

AKADEMIJA NAUK MOLDAVSKOJ SSR: INSTITUT ISTORII
— ARKHEOLOGICHESKIE PAMJATNIKI MOLDAVII.
— BALKANSKIJ ISTORICHESKIJ SBORNIK.

AKADEMIJA NAUK MOLDAVSKOJ SSR; INSTITUT
JAZYKA I LITERATURY.
— KULTIVARIA LIMBII.

AKADEMIJA NAUK MOLDAVSKOJ SSR: INSTITUT
MATEMATIKI.
— MATEMATICHESKIE ISSLEDOVANIJA.

AKADEMIJA NAUK MOLDAVSKOJ SSR: INSTITUT MATEM-
ATIKI S VYCHISLITEL'NYM TSENTROM.
— PRIKLADNAJA MATEMATIKA I PROGRAMMIROVANIE.

AKADEMIJA NAUK MOLDAVSKOJ SSR: INSTITUT
ZOOLOGII.
— BIOLOGICHESKIE RESURSY VODOEMOV MOLDAVII.
— PARAZITY ZHIVOTNYKH I RASTENIJ.
— VOPROSY EKOLOGII I PRAKTICHESKOGO ZNACHENIJA
PTITS I MLEKOPITAJUSHCHIKH MOLDAVII.

AKADEMIJA NAUK MOLDAVSKOJ SSR: KOMISSIJA PO
OKHRANE PRIRODY.
— OKHRANA PRIRODY MOLDAVII.

AKADEMIJA NAUK MOLDAVSKOJ SSR: OTDEL
ENERGETICHESKOJ KIBERNETIKI.
— ELEKTROENERGETIKA I AVTOMATIKA.

AKADEMIJA NAUK MOLDAVSKOJ SSR: OTDEL GEOGRAFII.
— GEOGRAFIJA I KHOZJAJSTVO MOLDAVII.
— PROBLEMY GEOGRAFII MOLDAVII.

AKADEMIJA NAUK SSSR.
— EKOLOGIJA.
— FIZIKA I TEKHNIKA POLUPROVODNIKOV.
— FUNKTSIONAL'NYJ ANALIZ I EGO PRILOZHENIJA.
— GEOMAGNETIZM I AERONOMIJA.
— GEOMORFOLOGIJA.
— ITOGI NAUKI: ORGANIZATSIJA UPRAVLENIJA.
— IZVESTIJA AKADEMII NAUK SSSR: SERIJA EKONOM-
ICHESKAJA.
— KHIMIJA VYSOKIKH ENERGIJ.
— LESOVEDENIE.
— MIKOLOGIJA I FITOPATOLOGIJA.
— NAUKA I CHELOVECHESTVO.
— ONTOGENEZ.
— OPTIKA I SPEKTROSKOPIJA: SBORNIK STATEJ.
— PARAZITOLOGIJA.
— PROBLEMY REGIONAL'NOGO ZIMOVEDENIJA.
— RASTITEL'NYE RESURSY, AKADEMIJA NAUK SSSR.
— SOVETSKAJA TJURKOLOGIJA.
— TEORETICHESKAJA I MATEMATICHESKAJA FIZIKA.
— TEORETICHESKIE OSNOVY KHIMICHESKOJ TEKHNOLO-
GII.
— VYSOKOMOLEKULJARNYE SOEDINENIJA: SERIJA A.     XXX
— VYSOKOMOLEKULJARNYE SOEDINENIJA. SERIJA B:
KRATKIE SOOBSHCHENIJA.                          XXX
— ZHURNAL EVOLJUTSIONNOJ BIOKHIMII I FIZIOLOGII.
JOURNAL OF EVOLUTIONARY BIOCHEMISTRY & PHYS-
IOLOGY.

AKADEMIJA NAUK SSSR: ARKHEOGRAFICHESKAJA
KOMISSIJA [LENINGRADSKOE OTDELENIE].
— VSPOMAGATEL'NYE ISTORICHESKIE DISTSIPLINY.

AKADEMIJA NAUK SSSR: ASTRONOMICHESKIJ SOVET.
— NAUCHNYE INFORMATSII ASTRONOMICHESKOGO SOVETA
AKADEMII NAUK SSSR.

AKADEMIJA NAUK SSSR (BASHKIRSKIJ FILIAL):
INSTITUT ISTORII, JAZYKA I LITERATURY.
— ARKHEOLOGIJA I ETNOGRAFIJA BASHKIRII.

AKADEMIJA NAUK SSSR: BIBLIOTEKA.
— BIBLIOGRAFIJA INOSTRANNOJ BIBLIOGRAFII PO
KHIMII.
— TRUDY I MATERIALY NAUCHNYKH KONGRESSOV I
SOVESHCHANIJ OPUBLIKOVANNYE ZA RUBEZHOM.

AKADEMIJA NAUK SSSR: BOTANICHESKIJ INSTITUT.
— ARKTICHESKAJA FLORA SSSR.  FLORA ARCTICA URSS.
— NOVOSTI SISTEMATIKI NIZSHIKH RASTENIJ.  NOVI-
TATES SYSTEMATICAE PLANTARUM NON VASCULARIUM.
— NOVOSTI SISTEMATIKI VYSSHIKH RASTENIJ.  NOVI-
TATES SYSTEMATICAE PLANTARUM VASCULARIUM.

AKADEMIJA NAUK SSSR: (DAGESTANSKIJ FILIAL)
OTDEL EKONOMIKI.
— PROBLEMY RAZVITIJA EKONOMIKI DAGESTANA.

AKADEMIJA NAUK SSSR: EINSHTEINOVSKIJ KOMITET.
— EINSHTEINOVSKIJ SBORNIK.

**AKADEMIJA NAUK SSSR: GEOLOGICHESKIJ INSTITUT.**
— GEOTEKTONIKA.

**AKADEMIJA NAUK SSSR: INSTITUT AFRIKI.**
— AFRICA IN SOVIET STUDIES.
— AFRIKANSKIJ SBORNIK.
— BIBLIOGRAFIJA AFRIKI.

**AKADEMIJA NAUK SSSR: INSTITUT ARKHEOLOGII.**
— ARKHEOLOGICHESKIE OTKRYTIJA.
— KRATKIE SOOBSHCHENIJA O DOKLADAKH I POLEVYKH
ISSLEDOVANIJAKH INSTITUTA ARKHEOLOGII.*    XXX

**AKADEMIJA NAUK SSSR: INSTITUT EKONOMIKI.**
— METODY I PRAKTIKA OPREDELENIJA EKONOMICHESKOJ
EFFEKTIVNOSTI KAPITAL'NYKH VLOZHENIJ I
NOVOJ TEKHNIKI.

**AKADEMIJA NAUK SSSR: INSTITUT ETNOGRAFII.**
— RASY I NARODY.  SOVREMENNYE, ETNICHESKIE I
RASOVYE PROBLEMY.

**AKADEMIJA NAUK SSSR: INSTITUT FILOSOFII.**
— ESTETIKA I ZHIZN'.
— SOTSIALISTICHESKIJ REALIZM I PROBLEMY
ESTETIKI.

**AKADEMIJA NAUK SSSR: INSTITUT GEOGRAFII.**
— MATERIALY GLIATSIOLOGICHESKIKH ISSLEDOVANIJ.
[VARIOUS SUBSERIES].

**AKADEMIJA NAUK SSSR: INSTITUT GEOKHIMII I
ANALITICHESKOJ KHIMII.**
— PROBLEMY ANALITICHESKOJ KHIMII.

**AKADEMIJA NAUK SSSR: INSTITUT GEOLOGII I
RAZRABOTKI GORJUCHIKH ISKOPAEMYKH.**
— TRUDY, INSTITUT GEOLOGII I RAZRABOTKI GORJU-
CHIKH ISKOPAEMYKH AKADEMII NAUK SSSR.

**AKADEMIJA NAUK SSSR: INSTITUT GEOLOGII RUDNYKH
MESTOROZHDENIJ, PETROGRAFII, MINERALOGII I
GEOKHIMII.**
— PROBLEMY GEOLOGII MINERAL'NYKH MESTOROZHDENIJ,
PETROLOGII I MINERALOGII.

**AKADEMIJA NAUK SSSR: INSTITUT ISTORII ESTESTVO-
ZNANIJA I TEKHNIKI.**
— FIZIKO-MATEMATICHESKIE NAUKI V STRANAKH
VOSTOKA.    XXX
— SISTEMNYE ISSLEDOVANIJA.

**AKADEMIJA NAUK SSSR: INSTITUT ISTORII ESTESTVO-
ZNANIJA I TEKHNIKI (LENINGRADSKOE OTDELENIE).**
— IZ ISTORII BIOLOGICHESKIKH NAUK.  MEMORABILIA
HISTORIAE NATURALIS.    XXX

**AKADEMIJA NAUK SSSR: INSTITUT LATINSKOJ
AMERIKI.**
— LATINSKAJA AMERIKA.

**AKADEMIJA NAUK SSSR: INSTITUT MEKHANIKI.**
— INZHENERNYJ ZHURNAL: MEKHANIKA TVERDOGO TELA.    XXX
— IZVESTIJA AKADEMII NAUK SSSR: MEKHANIKA TVER-
DOGO TELA.    XXX

**AKADEMIJA NAUK SSSR: INSTITUT MEZHDUNARODNOGO
RABOCHEGO DVIZHENIJA.**
— MEZHDUNARODNOE RABOCHEE DVIZHENIE.

**AKADEMIJA NAUK SSSR: INSTITUT MINERALOGII,
GEOKHIMII I KRISTALLOKHIMII REDKIKH ELEMENTOV.**
— GEOKHIMICHESKIE ISSLEDOVANIJA.

**AKADEMIJA NAUK SSSR: INSTITUT MIROVOJ EKONOMIKI
I MEZHDUNARODNYKH OTNOSHENIJ.**
— MEZHDUNARODNYJ EZHEGODNIK - POLITIKA I EKON-
OMIKA.    XXX

**AKADEMIJA NAUK SSSR: INSTITUT NARODOV AZII.**
— LITERATURA O STRANAKH AZII I AFRIKI.
— PAMJATNIKI LITERATURY NARODOV VOSTOKA: PEREV-
ODY.    XXX
— PAMJATNIKI PIS'MENNOSTI VOSTOKA.    XXX

**AKADEMIJA NAUK SSSR: INSTITUT NAUCHNOJ INFOR-
MATSII.**
— ITOGI NAUKI:  GEOGRAFIJA SSSR.
— ITOGI NAUKI: MATEMATICHESKIJ ANALIZ.
— ITOGI NAUKI: ZOOLOGIJA.
— ITOGI NAUKI I TEKHNIKI - SERIJA: PROMYSHLENNYJ
TRANSPORT.

**AKADEMIJA NAUK SSSR: INSTITUT RUSSKOGO JAZYKA.**
— ETIMOLOGIJA.
— RUSSKAJA RECH'.
— RUSSKIJ JAZYK I SOVETSKOE OBSHCHESTVO.

**AKADEMIJA NAUK SSSR: INSTITUT VYSSHEJ NERVNOJ
DEJATEL'NOSTI.**    XXX
— TRUDY INSTITUTA VYSSHEJ NERVNOJ DEJATEL'NOSTI,
AKADEMIJA NAUK SSSR: SERIJA
FIZIOLOGICHESKAJA.    XXX
— TRUDY INSTITUTA VYSSHEJ NERVNOJ DEJATEL'NOSTI,
AKADEMIJA NAUK SSSR: SERIJA
PATOFIZIOLOGICHESKAJA.

**AKADEMIJA NAUK SSSR (KOMI FILIAL): INSTITUT
GEOLOGII.**
— TRUDY INSTITUTA GEOLOGII KOMI FILIALA AKAD-
EMII NAUK SSSR.

**AKADEMIJA NAUK SSSR: KOMISSIJA PO EKSPLUATATSII
VYCHISLITEL'NYKH MASHIN.**
— VOPROSY MATEMATICHESKOJ EKSPLUATATSII VYCHIS-
LITEL'NYKH MASHIN.

**AKADEMIJA NAUK SSSR: KOMISSIJA ISTORIKOV SSSR &
GDR.**
— EZHEGODNIK GERMANSKOJ ISTORII.

**AKADEMIJA NAUK SSSR: KOMISSIJA PO RENTGENO-
GRAFII MINERAL'NOGO SYR'JA.**
— RENTGENOGRAFIJA MINERAL'NOGO SYR'JA.

**AKADEMIJA NAUK SSSR: LABORATORIJA EVOLJUTS-
IONNOJ I EKOLOGICHESKOJ FIZIOLOGII.**
— TRUDY LABORATORII EVOLJUTSIONNOJ I EKOLOGI-
CHESKOJ FIZIOLOGII [IM. B.A. KELLERA], AKAD-
EMIJA NAUK SSSR.    XXX

**AKADEMIJA NAUK SSSR: MATEMATICHESKIJ INSTITUT
IM. V.A. STEKLOVA (LENINGRADSKOE OTDELENIE).**
— ZAPISKI NAUCHNYKH SEMINAROV LENINGRADSKOE
OTDELENIE MATEMATICHESKII INSTITUT IM. V.A.
STEKLOVA.

**AKADEMIJA NAUK SSSR: MURMANSKIJ MORSKOJ
BIOLOGICHESKIJ INSTITUT.**
— TRUDY MURMANSKOGO MORSKOGO BIOLOGICHESKOGO
INSTITUTA.    XXX

**AKADEMIJA NAUK SSSR: NAUCHNYJ SOVET PO PRIMEN-
ENIJU MATEMATICHESKIKH METODOV I VYCHISLITEL-
'NOJ TEKHNIKI V EKONOMICHESKIKH ISSLEDOVANIJAKH
I PLANIROVANII.**
— EKONOMIKO-MATEMATICHESKIE METODY.

**AKADEMIJA NAUK SSSR: OTDELENIE BIOLOGICHESKIKH
NAUK.**
— PROBLEMY KOSMICHESKOJ BIOLOGII.

**AKADEMIJA NAUK SSSR: OTDELENIE FIZIKO-KHIMII I
TEKHNOLOGII NEORGANICHESKIKH MATERIALOV.**
— FIZIKA I KHIMIJA OBRABOTKI MATERIALOV.

**AKADEMIJA NAUK SSSR: OTDELENIE MATEMATIKI.**
— MATEMATICHESKIE ZAMETKI.

**AKADEMIJA NAUK SSSR: OTDELENIE MEKHANIKI I
PROTSESSOV UPRAVLENIJA.**
— MEKHANIKA MASHIN.    XXX

**AKADEMIJA NAUK SSSR: PUSHKINSKAJA KOMISSIJA.**
— VREMENNIK PUSHKINSKOJ KOMISSII.

**AKADEMIJA NAUK SSSR (SIBIRSKOE OTDELENIE).**
— FIZIKO-TEKHNICHESKIE PROBLEMY RAZRABOTKI
POLEZNYKH ISKOPAEMYKH.
— IZVESTIJA SIBIRSKOGO OTDELENIJA AKADEMII
NAUK SSSR; SERIJA BIOLOGO-MEDITSINSKIKH NAUK.
— IZVESTIJA SIBIRSKOGO OTDELENIJA AKADEMII
NAUK SSSR; SERIJA KHIMICHESKIKH NAUK.
— IZVESTIJA SIBIRSKOGO OTDELENIJA AKADEMII
NAUK SSSR; SERIJA OBSHCHESTVENNYKH NAUK.
— IZVESTIJA SIBIRSKOGO OTDELENIJA AKADEMII
NAUK SSSR; SERIJA TEKHNICHESKIKH NAUK.

**AKADEMIJA NAUK SSSR (SIBIRSKOE OTDELENIE):
BURJATSKIJ INSTITUT OBSHCHESTVENNYKH NAUK.**
— TRUDY BURJATSKOGO INSTITUTA OBSHCHESTVENNYKH
NAUK.

**AKADEMIJA NAUK SSSR (SIBIRSKOE OTDELENIE):
BURJATSKIJ KOMPLEKSNYJ NAUCHNO-ISSLEDOVATEL'-
SKIJ INSTITUT.**
— ETNOGRAFICHESKIJ SBORNIK (ULAN-UDE).

**AKADEMIJA NAUK SSSR (SIBIRSKOE OTDELENIE):
INSTITUT GEOLOGII I GEOFIZIKI.**
— TRUDY INSTITUTA GEOLOGII I GEOFIZIKI, AKADEM-
IJA NAUK SSSR (SIBIRSKOE OTDELENIE).

**AKADEMIJA NAUK SSSR (SIBIRSKOE OTDELENIE): INSTITUT ISTORII, FILOLOGII I FILOSOFII.**
— VOPROSY ISTORII SOTSIAL'NO-EKONOMICHESKOJ I KUL'TURNOJ ZHIZNI SIBIRI I DAL'NEGO VOSTOKA.

**AKADEMIJA NAUK SSSR(SIBIRSKOE OTDELENIE): INSTITUT MATEMATIKI.**
— OPTIMAL'NOE PLANIROVANIE.                                          XXX
— VYCHISLITEL'NYE SISTEMY. SBORNIK TRUDOV.

**AKADEMIJA NAUK SSSR (SIBIRSKOE OTDELENIE): JAKUTSKIJ FILIAL INSTITUTA JAZYKA, LITERATURY I ISTORII.**
— DIALEKTOLOGICHESKIE MATERIALY PO GOVORAM EVENKOV JAKUTSKOJ ASSR.

**AKADEMIJA NAUK SSSR (SIBIRSKOE OTDELENIE): KOMISSIJA PO OKHRANE PRIRODY.**
— OKHRANA PRIRODY NA DAL'NEM VOSTOKE.

**AKADEMIJA NAUK SSSR (SIBIRSKOE OTDELENIE): SEVERO-VOSTOCHNYJ KOMPLEKSNYJ NAUCHNO-ISSLEDO-VATEL'SKIJ INSTITUT.**
— TRUDY SEVERO-VOSTOCHNOGO KOMPLEKSNOGO NAUCHNO-ISSLEDOVATEL'SKOGO INSTITUTA.

**AKADEMIJA NAUK SSSR: TSENTRAL'NYJ EKONOMIKO-MATEMATICHESKIJ INSTITUT.**
— EKONOMIKO-MATEMATICHESKIE MODELI.

**AKADEMIJA NAUK SSSR (URAL'SKIJ FILIAL): KOMIS-SIJA PO OKHRANE PRIRODY.**
— OKHRANA PRIRODY NA URALE.

**AKADEMIJA NAUK SSSR: VSESOJUZNYJ INSTITUT NAUCHNOJ I TEKHNICHESKOJ INFORMATSII.**
— ITOGI NAUKI I TEKHNIKI: METALLOVEDENIE I TER-MICHESKAJA OBRABOTKA.
— ITOGI NAUKI I TEKHNIKI: METALLURGIJA.
— REFERATIVNYJ SBORNIK: ORGANIZATSIJA UPRAVLENIJA PROMYSHLENNOST'JU.

**AKADEMIJA NAUK SSSR: VYCHISLITEL'NYJ TSENTR.**
— ALGORITMY I ALGORITMICHESKIE JAZYKI.
— SOOBSHCHENIJA PO VYCHISLITEL'NOJ TEKHNIKE.

**AKADEMIJA NAUK SSSR: ZOOLOGICHESKIJ INSTITUT.**
— ISSLEDOVANIJA FAUNY MOREJ.                                        XXX

**AKADEMIJA NAUK TADZHIKSKOJ SSR.**
— IZVESTIJA AKADEMII NAUK TADZHIKSKOJ SSR: OTD-ELENIE FIZIKO-MATEMATICHESKIKH I GEOLOGO-KHIM-ICHESKIKH NAUK.                                                     XXX
— IZVESTIJA AKADEMII NAUK TADZHIKSKOJ SSR: OTD-ELENIE FIZIKO-TEKHNICHESKIKH I KHIMICHESKIKH NAUK.                                                                XXX
— IZVESTIJA AKADEMII NAUK TADZHIKSKOJ SSR: OTDELENIE GEOLOGO-KHIMICHESKIKH I TEKHN-ICHESKIKH NAUK.                                                    XXX
  SUBS (1964): IZVESTIJA AKADEMII ...: OTDEL-ENIE FIZIKO-TEKHNICHESKIKH I KHIMICHESKIKH NAUK.

**AKADEMIJA NAUK TADZHIKSKOJ SSR: INSTITUT ISTORII.**
— MATERIAL'NAJA KUL'TURA TADZHIKISTANA.
— MATERIAL'NAJA KUL'TURA USTRUSHANY.

**AKADEMIJA NAUK TURKMENSKOJ SSR.**
— IZVESTIJA AKADEMII NAUK TURKMENSKOJ SSR: SERIJA BIOLOGICHESKIKH NAUK.                                       XXX
— IZVESTIJA AKADEMII NAUK TURKMENSKOJ SSR: SERIJA FIZIKO-TEKHNICHESKIKH, KHIMICHESKIKH I GEOLOGICHESKIKH NAUK.                                            XXX
— IZVESTIJA AKADEMII NAUK TURKMENSKOJ SSR: SERIJA OBSHCHESTVENNYKH NAUK.                                   XXX

**AKADEMIJA NAUK TURKMENSKOJ SSR: INSTITUT JAZYKOZNANIJA.**
— TRUDY INSTITUTA JAZYKOZNANIJA AKADEMII NAUK TURKMENSKOJ SSR.                                               XXX

**AKADEMIJA NAUK TURKMENSKOJ SSR: INSTITUT LITERATURY.**
— TRUDY INSTITUTA LITERATURY AKADEMII NAUK TURKMENSKOJ SSR.                                               XXX

**AKADEMIJA NAUK TURKMENSKOJ SSR: NAUCHNYJ SOVET PO PROBLEME PUSTYN'.**
— PROBLEMY OSVOENIJA PUSTYN'.

**AKADEMIJA NAUK UKRAJINS'KOJI RSR.**
— DOPOVIDI AKADEMIJI NAUK UKRAJINS'KOJI RSR: SERIJA A: FIZYKO-TEKHNICHNI TA MATEMATYCHNI NAUKY.                                                             XXX
— KATALIZ I KATALIZATORY.
— POLUPROVODNIKOVAJA TEKHNIKA I MIKROELEKTRONIKA.
— SLOV'JANS'KE LITERATUROZNAVSTVO I FOL'KLORYS-TYKA.

**AKADEMIJA NAUK UKRAJINS'KOJI RSR: FIZYKO-MEKHANICHNYJ INSTYTUT.**
— OTBOR I PEREDACHA INFORMATSII.

**AKADEMIJA NAUK UKRAJINS'KOJI RSR: FIZYKO-TEKHNICHNYJ INSTYTUT.**
— ISSLEDOVANIE PLAZMENNYKH SGUSTKOV.

**AKADEMIJA NAUK UKRAJINS'KOJI RSR: INSTYTUT ARKHEOLOHIJI.**
— SEREDNI VIKI NA UKRAJINI.

**AKADEMIJA NAUK UKRAJINS'KOJI RSR: INSTYTUT FIZIOLOHIJI ROSLYN.**
— MIKROELEMENTY V SEL'SKOM KHOZJAJSTVE I MEDIT-SINE.
— ROST I USTOJCHIVOST' RASTENIJ: SERIJA: FIZIOLOGIJA RASTENIJ.

**AKADEMIJA NAUK UKRAJINS'KOJI RSR: INSTYTUT HEOLOHICHNYKH NAUK.**
— KONSTITUTSIJA I SVOJSTVA MINERALOV.
— TRUDY INSTYTUTU HEOLOHICHNYKH NAUK: SERIJA HEOTEKTONIKY.                                                   XXX
— TRUDY INSTYTUTU HEOLOHICHNYKH NAUK: SERIJA HEOTEKTONIKY I HEOFIZYKY.                                        XXX
  SUBS (1962): TRUDY INSTYTUTU HEOLOHICHNYKH NAUK: SERIJA HEOTEKTONIKY.
— TRUDY INSTYTUTU HEOLOHICHNYKH NAUK: SERIJA ZAHAL'NOJI HEOLOHIJI.

**AKADEMIJA NAUK UKRAJINS'KOJI RSR: INSTYTUT HEOLOHIJI I HEOKHIMIJI HORJUCHYKH KOPALYN.**
— GEOLOGIJA I GEOKHIMIJA GORJUCHIKH ISKOPAEMYKH.

**AKADEMIJA NAUK UKRAJINS'KOJI RSR: (INSTITUT KIBERNETIKY).**
— KIBERNETIKA I VYCHISLITEL'NAJA TEKHNIKA(KIEV)

**AKADEMIJA NAUK UKRAJINS'KOJI RSR: INSTYTUT METALLOKERAMIKY I SPETSIAL'NYKH SPLAVIV.**
— POROSHKOVAJA METALLURGIJA.

**AKADAMIJA NAUK UKRAJINS'KOJI RSR: INSTYTUT ZOOLOHIJI.**
— PRIRODNAJA OBSTANOVKA I FAUNY PROSHLOGO.
— VESTNIK ZOOLOGII (KIEV).

**AKADEMIJA NAUK UKRAJINS'KOJI RSR: OTDELENIE MATEMATIKI, MEKHANIKI I KIBERNETIKI.**
— KIBERNETIKA, OTDELENIE MATEMATIKI, MEKHANIKI I KIBERNETIKI UKRAINSKOJ AKADEMII NAUK SSR.

**AKADEMIJA NAUK UKRAJINS'KOJI RSR: (OTDELENIE OBSHCHEJ BIOLOGII).**
— GIDROBIOLOGICHESKIJ ZHURNAL.

**AKADEMIJA NAUK UKRAJINS'KOJI RSR: VIDDIL LITERATURY, MOVY I MYSTETSVOZNAVSTVA.**
— MOVOZNAVSTVO. NAUKOVO TEORETYCHNYJ ZHURNAL.

**AKADEMIJA NAUK UKRAJINS'KOJI RSR: INSTITUT PROBLEM PROCHNOSTI.**
— PROBLEMY PROCHNOSTI.

**AKADEMIJA NAUK UZBEKSKOJ SSR.**
— GELIOTEKHNIKA, AKADEMIJA NAUK UZBEKSKOJ SSR.
— KHIMIJA PRIRODNYKH SOEDINENIJ.

**AKADEMIJA NAUK UZBEKSKOJ SSR: BOTANICZESKIJ SAD.**
— INTRODUKTSIJA I AKKLIMATIZATSIJA RASTENIJ.

**AKADEMIJA OBSHCHESTVENNYKH NAUK PRI TSK KPSS: INSTITUT NAUCHNOGO ATEIZMA.**
— VOPROSY NAUCHNOGO ATEIZMA.

**AKADEMIJA OBSHCHESTVENNYKH NAUK PRI TSK KPSS: KAFEDRA NAUCHNOGO KOMMUNIZMA.**
— NAUCHNOE UPRAVLENIE OBSHCHESTVOM.
— PROBLEMY NAUCHNOGO KOMMUNIZMA.

**AKADEMIJA OBSHCHESTVENNYKH NAUK PRI TSK KPSS: SEKTSIJA ZHURNALISTIKI.**
— VOPROSY TEORII I PRAKTIKI MASSOVYKH SREDSTV PROPAGANDY.                                                     XXX

AKADEMIJA PEDAGOGICHESKIKH NAUK RSFSR.
— NOVYE ISSLEDOVANIJA V PEDAGOGICHESKIKH
NAUKAKH.
— PSIKHOLOGIJA I TEKHNIKA.

AKADEMIJA NA SELSKOSTOPANSKITE NAUKI.
— DOKLADY AKADEMII SEL'SKO-KHOZJAJSTVENNYKH
NAUK V BOLGARII.
— FIZIOLOGIJA NA RASTENIJATA.
— GENETIKA & SELEKTSIJA. GENETICS & PLANT
BREEDING.
— GORSKOSTOPANSKA NAUKA.
— GRADINARSKA I LOZARSKA NAUKA.
— POCHVOZNANIE I AGROKHIMIJA. SOIL SCIENCE &
AGROCHEMISTRY.
— ZHIVOTNOVUDNI NAUKI.

AKADEMIJA NA SELSKOSTOPANSKITE NAUKI: VETERIN-
AREN INSTITUT PO VIRUSOLOGIJA.
— IZVESTIJA NA VETERINARNIJA INSTITUT PO VIRUS-
OLOGIJA.

AKADEMIJA NA SELSKOSTOPANSKITE NAUKI: VETERIN-
ARNOKHIGIENEN INSTITUT ZA ZHIVOTINSKI PRODUKTI.
— IZVESTIJA NA VETERINARNOKHIGIENNIJA INSTITUT
ZA ZHIVOTINSKI PRODUKTI.

AKADEMIE DER WISSENSCHAFTEN IN GOTTINGEN.
— NACHRICHTEN DER AKADEMIE DER WISSENSCHAFTEN
IN GOTTINGEN: PHILOLOGISCHE-HISTORISCHE
KLASSE.

AKADEMIE DER WISSENSCHAFTEN UND DER LITERATUR:
KOMMISSION FUR GESCHICHTE DES ALTERTUMS.
— FORSCHUNGEN ZUR ANTIKEN SKLAVEREI.

AKADEMIE DER WISSENSCHAFTEN UND DER LITERATUR:
MATHEMATISCH-NATURWISSENSCHAFTLICHE KLASSE.
— MIKROFAUNA DES MEERESBODENS.

AKITA FRUIT-TREE EXPERIMENT STATION.
— BULLETIN OF THE AKITA FRUIT-TREE EXPERIMENT
STATION.

ALABAMA MARINE RESOURCES LABORATORY.
— ALABAMA MARINE RESOURCES BULLETIN.*

(ALASKA) DEPARTMENT OF HEALTH & WELFARE.
— ALASKA'S HEALTH & WELFARE.*

ALASKA AGRICULTURAL EXPERIMENT STATION.
— AGROBOREALIS.

ALASKA GEOGRAPHIC SOCIETY.
— ALASKA GEOGRAPHIC.

ALBERT-FRANKENTHAL AG.
— ALBERT DTZ. DRUCKMASCHINENTECHNISCHE ZEIT-
SCHRIFT.

ALBISWERK ZURICH, A.G.                                              XXX
— ALBISWERK-BERICHTE.                                              XXX
SUBS (1972): SIEMENS-ALBIS BERICHTE.

ALFRED P. SLOAN SCHOOL OF MANAGEMENT.
— SLOAN MANAGEMENT REVIEW.                                        XXX

ALFRED UNIVERSITY.
— STUDIES IN BURKE & HIS TIME.                                    XXX

ALGEMENE NEDERLANDSE PHARMACEUTISCHE STUDENTEN
VERENIGING.
— FOLIA FARMACEUTIKA.                                             XXX
— FOLIA PHARMACEUTICA.                                            XXX
SUBS (1973): FOLIA FARMACEUTIKA.

(ALGERIA) METEOROLOGIE NATIONALE.
— CAHIERS DE LA METEOROLOGIE (ALGERIA).

ALIGARH MUSLIM UNIVERSITY: DEPARTMENT OF
HISTORY.
— MEDIEVAL INDIA.                                                 XXX
— MEDIEVAL INDIA QUARTERLY.                                       XXX
SUBS (1969): MEDIEVAL INDIA.

ALL INDIA AIR CONDITIONING & REFRIGERATION
ASSOCIATION.
— CLIMATE CONTROL.

ALLAHABAD LAW AGENCY.
— ALLAHABAD LAW REVIEW.

ALLGEMEINE GESCHICHTFORSCHENDE GESELLSCHAFT
DER SCHWEIZ.
— MONOGRAPHIEN ZUR SCHWEIZER GESCHICHTE. =
MONOGRAPHIES D'HISTOIRE SUISSE.

ALLYN MUSEUM OF ENTOMOLOGY.
— BULLETIN OF THE ALLYN MUSEUM.

ALMA-ATINSKIJ GOSUDARSTVENNYJ NAUCHNO-ISSLEDO-
VATEL'SKIJ INSTITUT STROITEL'NYKH MATERIALOV.
— TRUDY ALMA-ATINSKOGO GOSUDARSTVENNOGO NAUCHNO-
ISSLEDOVATEL'SKOGO INSTITUTA STROITEL'NYKH
MATERIALOV.                                                       XXX

ALUMINUM ASSOCIATION.
— WORLD ALUMINUM ABSTRACTS.                                       XXX

AMALGAMATED POWER ENGINEERING, LTD.
— APE ENGINEERING.                                                XXX
— APEX (BEDFORD).                                                 XXX

AMALGAMATED SOCIETY OF WOODWORKERS.
— WOODWORKERS & PAINTERS JOURNAL.                                 XXX

AMATEUR YACHT RESEARCH SOCIETY.
— A.Y.R.S. AIRS.                                                  XXX
— A.Y.R.S. PUBLICATION.                                           XXX
SUBS (1971): A.Y.R.S. AIRS.

AMERICAN ACADEMY OF ALLERGY.
— JOURNAL OF ALLERGY.                                             XXX
SUBS (1971): JOURNAL OF ALLERGY & CLINICAL
IMMUNOLOGY.
— JOURNAL OF ALLERGY & CLINICAL IMMUNOLOGY.                       XXX

AMERICAN ACADEMY OF APPLIED NUTRITION.
— MONTHLY NEWSLETTER JOURNAL, AMERICAN ACADEMY
OF APPLIED NUTRITION.                                             XXX
SUBS (1952): MODERN NUTRITION.

AMERICAN ACADEMY OF BENARES.
— BULLETIN OF THE AMERICAN ACADEMY OF BENARES.

AMERICAN ACADEMY OF CLINICAL TOXICOLOGY.
— CLINICAL TOXICOLOGY.

AMERICAN ACADEMY OF NUTRITION.
— MODERN NUTRITION.                                               XXX

AMERICAN ACADEMY OF PERIODONTOLOGY.
— JOURNAL OF PERIODONTOLOGY.                                      XXX
SUBS (1969): JOURNAL OF PERIODONTOLOGY -
PERIODONTICS.
— JOURNAL OF PERIODONTOLOGY - PERIODONTICS.                       XXX

AMERICAN AGRICULTURAL ECONOMICS ASSOCIATION.
— AMERICAN BIBLIOGRAPHY OF AGRICULTURAL ECON-
OMICS.
— AMERICAN JOURNAL OF AGRICULTURAL ECONOMICS.                     XXX
— JOURNAL OF FARM ECONOMICS.                                      XXX
SUBS (1968): AMERICAN JOURNAL OF
AGRICULTURAL ECONOMICS.

AMERICAN ANIMAL HOSPITAL ASSOCIATION.
— SMALL ANIMAL CLINICIAN.

AMERICAN ASSOCIATION OF BOTANICAL GARDENS
& ARBORETA.
— ARBORETUM & BOTANICAL GARDEN BULLETIN.                          XXX

AMERICAN ASSOCIATION OF NEUROLOGICAL SURGEONS.
— NEUROSURGICAL BIBLIO-INDEX.

AMERICAN ASSOCIATION OF PETROLEUM GEOLOGISTS.
— EARTH SCIENCES RESEARCH CATALOG.

AMERICAN ASSOCIATION OF SCHOOL LIBRARIANS.
— SCHOOL LIBRARIES.                                               XXX
SUBS (1972): SCHOOL MEDIA QUARTERLY.
— SCHOOL MEDIA QUARTERLY.                                         XXX

AMERICAN ASSOCIATION OF TEXTILE CHEMISTS &
COLORISTS.
— TEXTILE CHEMIST & COLORIST.

AMERICAN ASSOCIATION OF VARIABLE STAR OBSERVERS
— AAVSO JOURNAL.

AMERICAN ASTRONOMICAL SOCIETY.
— BULLETIN, AMERICAN ASTRONOMICAL SOCIETY.

AMERICAN BAR ASSOCIATION.
— FAMILY LAW QUARTERLY.

AMERICAN BAR ASSOCIATION: SECTION OF INTERNAT-
IONAL & COMPARATIVE LAW.
— INTERNATIONAL LAWYER.

AMERICAN BAR ASSOCIATION: SECTION OF NATURAL
RESOURCES LAW.
— NATURAL RESOURCES LAWYER.

AMERICAN BAR ASSOCIATION: SPECIAL COMMITTEE ON
ELECTRONIC DATA RETRIEVAL.
— JURIMETRICS JOURNAL.    XXX
— MULL. MODERN USES OF LOGIC IN LAW.    XXX
  SUBS (1966): JURIMETRICS JOURNAL.

AMERICAN BIBLIOGRAPHICAL CENTRE.
— ABC POL SCI. ADVANCE BIBLIOGRAPHY OF CONT-
  ENTS: POLITICAL SCIENCE & GOVERNMENT.

AMERICAN CERAMIC SOCIETY: CERAMIC-METAL SYSTEMS
DIVISION.
— CERAMIC-METAL SYSTEMS BIBLIOGRAPHY &
  ABSTRACTS.    XXX

AMERICAN CHEMICAL SOCIETY.
— ACCESS. KEY TO THE SOURCE LITERATURE OF THE
  CHEMICAL SCIENCES.    XXX
— ACCOUNTS OF CHEMICAL RESEARCH.
— ANNUAL REVIEWS OF INDUSTRIAL & ENGINEERING
  CHEMISTRY.
— CHEMICAL ABSTRACTS SERVICE SOURCE INDEX.    XXX
— CHEMICAL ABSTRACTS SERVICE SOURCE INDEX
  QUARTERLY.    XXX
— CHEMICAL-BIOLOGICAL ACTIVITIES.
— CHEMICAL TECHNOLOGY.    XXX
— INDUSTRIAL & ENGINEERING CHEMISTRY.    XXX
  SUBS (1971): CHEMICAL TECHNOLOGY.
— INFORMATION SCIENCE ABSTRACTS.    XXX
— JOURNAL OF PHYSICAL & CHEMICAL REFERENCE DATA.
— MACROMOLECULES.
— POLYMER SCIENCE & TECHNOLOGY: GUIDES TO THE
  JOURNAL & REPORT LITERATURE.    XXX
— POLYMER SCIENCE & TECHNOLOGY: GUIDES TO
  PATENT LITERATURE.

AMERICAN CHEMICAL SOCIETY: CHEMICAL ABSTRACTS
SERVICE.
— CAS REPORT.

AMERICAN COLLEGE (LOUVAIN).
— LOUVAIN STUDIES.

AMERICAN COLLEGE OF CHEST PHYSICIANS.
— CHEST. JOURNAL OF CIRCULATION, RESPIRATION &
  RELATED SYSTEMS.    XXX
— DISEASES OF THE CHEST.    XXX
  SUBS (1970): CHEST.

AMERICAN COLLEGE OF VETERINARY PATHOLOGISTS.
— VETERINARY PATHOLOGY.    XXX

AMERICAN COUNCIL OF LEARNED SOCIETIES DEVOTED
TO HUMANISTIC STUDIES: PLANNING GROUP ON
COMPARATIVE COMMUNIST STUDIES.
— NEWSLETTER ON COMPARATIVE STUDIES OF    XXX
  COMMUNISM.

AMERICAN DATA PROCESSING, INC.
— DATA PROCESSING MONOGRAPH SERIES.

AMERICAN DENTAL SOCIETY OF ANESTHESIOLOGY.
— ANESTHESIA PROGRESS.
— JOURNAL, AMERICAN DENTAL SOCIETY OF ANESTHES-    XXX
  IOLOGY.
  SUBS (1966): ANESTHESIA PROGRESS.

AMERICAN DIALECT SOCIETY.
— NEWSLETTER, AMERICAN DIALECT SOCIETY.

AMERICAN DOCUMENTATION INSTITUTE.
— AMERICAN DOCUMENTATION.    XXX
  SUBS(1970): JOURNAL OF THE AMERICAN    XXX
  SOCIETY FOR INFORMATION SCIENCE.
— INFORMATION SCIENCE ABSTRACTS.    XXX

AMERICAN ECONOMIC ASSOCIATION.
— JOURNAL OF ECONOMIC ABSTRACTS.    XXX
— JOURNAL OF ECONOMIC LITERATURE.    XXX

AMERICAN ETHICAL UNION.
— AEU REPORTS.

AMERICAN EUGENICS SOCIETY.
— EUGENICS QUARTERLY.    XXX
  SUBS (1969): SOCIAL BIOLOGY.
— SOCIAL BIOLOGY.    XXX

AMERICAN FARM BUREAU FEDERATION.
— AMERICAN FARMER.    XXX

AMERICAN FEDERATION OF LABOR & CONGRESS OF
INDUSTRIAL ORGANIZATIONS: INDUSTRIAL UNION
DEPARTMENT.
— VIEWPOINT. AN IUD QUARTERLY.

AMERICAN FISHERIES SOCIETY.
— HYDROBIOLOGICAL JOURNAL.

AMERICAN FORENSIC ASSOCIATION.
— JOURNAL OF THE AMERICAN FORENSIC ASSOCIATION.

AMERICAN GEOLOGICAL INSTITUTE.
— PALEONTOLOGICAL JOURNAL.

AMERICAN GEOPHYSICAL UNION.
— EOS. TRANSACTIONS, AMERICAN GEOPHYSICAL
  UNION.    XXX
— GEOTECTONICS.
— OCEANOLOGY (WASHINGTON, D.C.).    XXX
— REVIEWS OF GEOPHYSICS & SPACE PHYSICS.*
— TRANSACTIONS, AMERICAN GEOPHYSICAL UNION.    XXX
  SUBS (1960): EOS.

AMERICAN HEALTH FOUNDATION.
— PREVENTIVE MEDICINE.

AMERICAN HERITAGE SOCIETY.
— AMERICANA (1973).

AMERICAN HORTICULTURAL SOCIETY.
— AMERICAN HORTICULTURAL MAGAZINE.    XXX
— AMERICAN HORTICULTURALIST.    XXX

AMERICAN INDIAN HISTORICAL SOCIETY.
— INDIAN HISTORIAN.

AMERICAN INDUSTRIAL DEVELOPMENT COUNCIL.
— AIDC JOURNAL.

AMERICAN INSTITUTE OF AERONAUTICS & ASTRO-
NAUTICS.
— JOURNAL OF HYDRONAUTICS.

AMERICAN INSTITUTE OF CERTIFIED PUBLIC ACCOUNT-
ANTS.
— ACCOUNTING RESEARCH STUDY.

AMERICAN INSTITUTE OF CHEMICAL ENGINEERS.
— AICHE MONOGRAPH SERIES.    XXX
— CHEMICAL ENGINEERING PROGRESS MONOGRAPH
  SERIES.    XXX
  SUBS (1972): AICHE MONOGRAPH SERIES.
— INDUSTRIAL PROCESS DESIGN FOR POLLUTION
  CONTROL.    XXX
— INDUSTRIAL PROCESS DESIGN FOR WATER POLLUTION
  CONTROL.*    XXX

AMERICAN INSTITUTE OF INDUSTRIAL ENGINEERS.
— AIIE TRANSACTIONS.
— INDUSTRIAL ENGINEERING.

AMERICAN INSTITUTE OF ISLAMIC STUDIES.
— BIBLIOGRAPHIC SERIES, AMERICAN INSTITUTE OF
  ISLAMIC STUDIES.

AMERICAN INSTITUTE OF MINING, METALLURGICAL
& PETROLEUM ENGINEERS.
— ROCK MECHANICS ABSTRACTS.

AMERICAN INSTITUTE OF MINING, METALLURGICAL &
PETROLEUM ENGINEERS: METALLURGICAL SOCIETY.
— JOURNAL OF ELECTRONIC MATERIALS.

AMERICAN INSTITUTE OF PHYSICS.
— AIP INFORMATION PROGRAM NEWSLETTER.    XXX
  SUBS (1970): AIP INFORMATION & PUBLICATION
  NEWSLETTER.
— AIP INFORMATION & PUBLICATION NEWSLETTER.    XXX
— JOURNAL OF PHYSICAL & CHEMICAL REFERENCE DATA.
— SOVIET JOURNAL OF QUANTUM ELECTRONICS.

AMERICAN INSTITUTE OF PLANNERS.
— SMALL BUSINESS.

AMERICAN INSTRUMENT COMPANY: BIOCHEMICAL
INSTRUMENTATION DIVISION.
— FLUORESCENCE NEWS.

AMERICAN LESSING SOCIETY.
— LESSING YEARBOOK.

AMERICAN LIBRARIES BOOK PROCUREMENT CENTER
(CEYLON).
— ACCESSIONS LIST, AMERICAN LIBRARIES BOOK
  PROCUREMENT CENTER: CEYLON.

AMERICAN LIBRARIES BOOK PROCUREMENT CENTER
(EGYPT).
— ACCESSIONS LIST, AMERICAN LIBRARIES BOOK
  PROCUREMENT CENTER: MIDDLE EAST.

AMERICAN LIBRARIES BOOK PROCUREMENT CENTER
(INDIA).
— ACCESSIONS LIST, AMERICAN LIBRARIES BOOK
PROCUREMENT CENTER: INDIA.

AMERICAN LIBRARIES BOOK PROCUREMENT CENTER
(INDONESIA).
— ACCESSIONS LIST, AMERICAN LIBRARIES BOOK
PROCUREMENT CENTER: INDONESIA.

AMERICAN LIBRARIES BOOK PROCUREMENT CENTER
(ISRAEL).
— ACCESSIONS LIST, AMERICAN LIBRARIES BOOK
PROCUREMENT CENTER: ISRAEL.

AMERICAN LIBRARIES BOOK PROCUREMENT CENTER:
(NEPAL).
— ACCESSIONS LIST, AMERICAN LIBRARIES BOOK
PROCUREMENT CENTER: NEPAL.

AMERICAN LIBRARY ASSOCIATION.
— ALA BULLETIN.                                          XXX
  SUBS (1970):  AMERICAN LIBRARIES.
— AMERICAN LIBRARIES.  BULLETIN OF THE ...               XXX
— BOOKLIST.                                              XXX
— BOOKLIST & SUBSCRIPTION BOOKS BULLETIN.                XXX
  SUBS (1969):  BOOKLIST.

AMERICAN LIBRARY ASSOCIATION: INFORMATION
SCIENCE & AUTOMATION DIVISION.
— JOLA TECHNICAL COMMUNICATIONS.

AMERICAN LIBRARY ASSOCIATION: LIBRARY TECHNO-
LOGY PROGRAM.
— LTP PUBLICATIONS.

AMERICAN MATHEMATICAL SOCIETY.
— CONTENTS OF CONTEMPORARY MATHEMATICAL
  JOURNALS.
— INDEX OF MATHEMATICAL PAPERS.
— LECTURES ON MATHEMATICS IN THE LIFE SCIENCES.
— MATHEMATICS OF THE USSR - IZVESTIJA.
— MATHEMATICS OF THE USSR - SBORNIK.
— PROCEEDINGS OF THE STEKLOV INSTITUTE OF MATH-
  EMATICS.
— PROCEEDINGS OF SYMPOSIA IN APPLIED MATHEMAT-
  ICS OF THE AMERICAN MATHEMATICAL SOCIETY.            XXX
  SUBS (1969): SIAM-AMS PROCEEDINGS.
— REGIONAL CONFERENCE SERIES IN MATHEMATICS.
— SIAM-AMS PROCEEDINGS.                                 XXX

AMERICAN MEAT INSTITUTE FOUNDATION.
— MEAT SCIENCE REVIEW.

AMERICAN MEDICAL ASSOCIATION.
— ABRIDGED INDEX MEDICUS.
— AMA DRUG EVALUATIONS.                                 XXX
— NEW DRUGS.                                            XXX
— NEW & NON OFFICAL DRUGS.                              XXX
  SUBS (1965): NEW DRUGS.

AMERICAN METEOROLOGICAL SOCIETY.
— JOURNAL OF PHYSICAL OCEANOGRAPHY.

AMERICAN MUSEUM OF NATURAL HISTORY.
— BIBLIOGRAPHY & INDEX OF MICROPALEONTOLOGY.
— DEAN BIBLIOGRAPHY OF FISHES.

AMERICAN MUSICOLOGICAL SOCIETY, INC.
— AMS NEWSLETTER.

AMERICAN NUCLEAR SOCIETY.
— NUCLEAR APPLICATIONS & TECHNOLOGY.*
— NUCLEAR STANDARDS NEWS.
— NUCLEAR TECHNOLOGY.                                   XXX

AMERICAN NUMISMATIC SOCIETY.
— NUMISMATIC LITERATURE SUPPLEMENTS.

AMERICAN PHILOSOPHICAL SOCIETY.
— MENDEL NEWSLETTER.

AMERICAN PHYSICAL SOCIETY.
— ABSTRACTS OF ARTICLES TO BE PUBLISHED IN THE
  PHYSICAL REVIEW.                                      XXX
— PHYSICAL REVIEW ABSTRACTS.                            XXX

AMERICAN POLITICAL SCIENCE ASSOCIATION.
— PS. NEWSLETTER OF THE ...

AMERICAN PSYCHOLOGICAL ASSOCIATION.
— DEVELOPMENTAL PSYCHOLOGY.
— JOURNAL OF CONSULTING & CLINICAL PSYCHOLOGY.*         XXX

AMERICAN PUBLIC HEALTH ASSOCIATION.
— AMERICAN JOURNAL OF PUBLIC HEALTH.
— CURRENT BIBLIOGRAPHY OF EPIDEMIOLOGY.
— NATION'S HEALTH.                                      XXX

AMERICAN RHEUMATISM ASSOCIATION.
— INDEX OF RHEUMATOLOGY.

AMERICAN SCHIZOPHRENIA FOUNDATION.
— SCHIZOPHRENIA.

AMERICAN SCHOOL OF CLASSICAL STUDIES AT ATHENS.
— LERNA.

AMERICAN SCHOOL OF CLASSICAL STUDIES AT ATHENS:
GENNADIUS LIBRARY.
— GRIFFON.

AMERICAN SCHOOLS OF ORIENTAL RESEARCH.
— NEWSLETTER, AMERICAN SCHOOLS OF ORIENTAL RE-
  SEARCH.

AMERICAN SOCIETY OF AGRONOMY.
— JOURNAL OF ENVIRONMENTAL QUALITY.

AMERICAN SOCIETY OF CIVIL ENGINEERS.
— ENGINEERING ISSUES.                                   XXX

AMERICAN SOCIETY OF CLINICAL PATHOLOGISTS:
REGISTRY OF MEDICAL TECHNOLOGISTS.
— TECHNICAL BULLETIN, REGISTRY OF MEDICAL
  TECHNOLOGISTS, AMERICAN SOCIETY OF CLINICAL
  PATHOLOGISTS.                                         XXX
  SUBS. (1970) PART OF: LABORATORY MEDICINE.

AMERICAN SOCIETY OF CRIMINOLOGY.
— CRIMINALOGICA.

AMERICAN SOCIETY FOR ENGINEERING EDUCATION.
— ENGINEERING EDUCATION.                                XXX
— JOURNAL OF ENGINEERING EDUCATION.                     XXX
  SUBS (1969):  ENGINEERING EDUCATION.

AMERICAN SOCIETY FOR HORTICULTURAL SCIENCE.
— JOURNAL, AMERICAN SOCIETY FOR HORTICULTURAL
  SCIENCE.
— PROCEEDINGS, AMERICAN SOCIETY FOR HORTICULT-
  URAL SCIENCE.                                         XXX
  SUBS: (1969) JOURNAL, AMERICAN SOCIETY FOR
  HORTICULTURAL SCIENCE.

AMERICAN SOCIETY FOR INFORMATION SCIENCE.              XXX
— JOURNAL OF THE AMERICAN SOCIETY FOR INFORMA-
  TION SCIENCE.                                         XXX

AMERICAN SOCIETY OF LIMNOLOGY & OCEANOGRAPHY.
— SPECIAL SYMPOSIA, AMERICAN SOCIETY OF LIMNOL-
  OGY & OCEANOGRAPHY.

AMERICAN SOCIETY OF MAMMALOGISTS.
— MAMMALIAN SPECIES.
— RECENT LITERATURE OF MAMMALOGY.
— SPECIAL PUBLICATIONS, AMERICAN SOCIETY OF
  MAMMALOGISTS.

AMERICAN SOCIETY OF MECHANICAL ENGINEERS.
— HEAT TRANSFER-SOVIET RESEARCH.
— JOURNAL OF LUBRICATION TECHNOLOGY. (TRANS-
  ACTIONS OF THE ASME: SERIES F).

AMERICAN SOCIETY OF MECHANICAL ENGINEERS:
HEAT TRANSFER DIVISION.
— HEAT TRANSFER.  JAPANESE RESEARCH.

AMERICAN SOCIETY OF METALS.
— ASM NEWS.
— ASM NEWS QUARTERLY.
— ASM REVIEW OF METAL LITERATURE.                       XXX
  SUBS. (1968) PART OF: METALS ABSTRACTS; &
  METALS ABSTRACTS INDEX.
— INTERNATIONAL METALLURGICAL REVIEWS.                  XXX
— MATERIALS APPLICATION NEWS FOR DESIGN & MANU-
  FACTURING.
— METALLURGICAL TRANSACTIONS.                           XXX
— METALS ABSTRACTS.                                     XXX
— METALS ABSTRACTS INDEX.                               XXX
— TRANSACTIONS, AMERICAN SOCIETY FOR METALS.            XXX
  SUBS (1961):  TRANSACTIONS QUARTERLY ...
— TRANSACTIONS QUARTERLY, AMERICAN SOCIETY FOR
  METALS.                                               XXX
— WORLD ALUMINUM ABSTRACTS.                             XXX

AMERICAN SOCIETY FOR MICROBIOLOGY.                      XXX
— ABSTRACTS OF THE ANNUAL MEETING OF THE AMER-
  ICAN SOCIETY FOR MICROBIOLOGY.                        XXX
— INFECTION & IMMUNITY.

AMERICAN SOCIETY FOR OCEANOGRAPHY.
— PUBLICATION, AMERICAN SOCIETY FOR OCEANO-
  GRAPHY.

AMERICAN SOCIETY OF PAPYROLOGISTS.
— AMERICAN STUDIES IN PAPYROLOGY.

AMERICAN SOCIETY FOR PHARMACOLOGY & EXPERI-
MENTAL THERAPEUTICS.
— DRUG METABOLISM & DISPOSITION.
— PHARMACOLOGY FOR PHYSICIANS.                          XXX
— RATIONAL DRUG THERAPY.                                XXX

AMERICAN SOCIETY OF PSYCHOPATHOLOGY OF
EXPRESSION.
— PSYCHIATRY & ART.

AMERICAN SOCIETY FOR QUALITY CONTROL.
— JOURNAL OF QUALITY TECHNOLOGY.
— QUALITY PROGRESS.

AMERICAN SOCIETY FOR REFORMATION RESEARCH.
— ARCHIV FUR REFORMATIONSGESCHICHTE: BEIHEFT:
  LITERATURBERICHT.

AMERICAN SOCIETY FOR TESTING & MATERIALS.
— ASTM STANDARDIZATION NEWS.                            XXX
— JOURNAL OF TESTING & EVALUATION.
— TIRE SCIENCE & TECHNOLOGY.

AMERICAN SOCIETY OF TOOL ENGINEERS.
— TOOL & MANUFACTURING ENGINEER.                        XXX
  SUBS (1970): MANUFACTURING ENGINEERING &
  MANAGEMENT.

AMERICAN SOCIOLOGICAL ASSOCIATION.
— CONTEMPORARY SOCIOLOGY.
— JOURNAL OF HEALTH & SOCIAL BEHAVIOUR.                 XXX
— SOCIOLOGICAL METHODOLOGY.

AMERICAN TELEPHONE & TELEGRAPH CO.
— BELL JOURNAL OF ECONOMICS & MANAGEMENT
  SCIENCE.

AMERICAN UNIVERSITY OF BEIRUT.
— MISCELLANEOUS PAPERS IN THE NATURAL SCIENCES.

AMERICAN WATER RESOURCES ASSOCIATION.
— WATER RESOURCES ABSTRACTS.
— WATER RESOURCES BULLETIN.

AMNESTY INTERNATIONAL: BRITISH SECTION.
— BRITISH AMNESTY NEWS.

AMON CARTER MUSEUM OF WESTERN ART.
— TEXAS ARCHITECTURAL SURVEY.

ANAN KOGYO KOTO SENMON GAKKO.
— ANAN KOGYO KOTO SENMON GAKKO KENKYU KIYO.
  RESEARCH REPORTS OF THE ANAN TECHNICAL
  COLLEGE.

ANDERSONIAN LIBRARY.                    000
SEE: UNIVERSITY OF STRATHCLYDE: ANDERSONIAN
LIBRARY.

ANDOVER LOCAL ARCHIVES COMMITTEE.
— ANDOVER DOCUMENTS.

ANGEHORIGER DER TEXTILINDUSTRIE.
— MITTEX.                                               XXX

ANGLO-BYELORUSSIAN SOCIETY.
— JOURNAL OF BYELORUSSIAN STUDIES.

ANNAMALAI UNIVERSITY.
— AUARA.

ANSTEY COLLEGE OF PHYSICAL EDUCATION.
— PAPERS IN EDUCATION.

ANTHROPOS INSTITUTE: INDIAN BRANCH.
— PUBLICATIONS, INDIAN BRANCH, ANTHROPOS
  INSTITUTE.

ANTIQUARIAN BOOKSELLERS' ASSOCIATION OF THE
NETHERLANDS.                             000
SEE: NEDERLANDSCHE VEREENIGING VAN ANTIQUAREN

ANTWERPSE MYCOLOGISCHE KRING.
— STERBEECKIA.

APHID LABORATORY (SUWON).
— BULLETIN, APHID LABORATORY (SUWON).

APPLIED PROBABILITY TRUST.
— ADVANCES IN APPLIED PROBABILITY.

APPLIED PSYCHOLOGY ADVISORY SERVICE.
— TECHNICAL & RESEARCH REPORTS, APPLIED
  PSYCHOLOGY ADVISORY SERVICE.

APPLIED SCIENTIFIC RESEARCH CORPORATION OF
THAILAND.
— ASRCT NEWSLETTER.

AQUATIC RESEARCH INSTITUTE (STOCKTON, CALIF.)
— SPECIAL REPORT, AQUATIC RESEARCH INSTITUTE.

ARAB HORSE SOCIETY OF AUSTRALASIA.
— ARAB HORSE NEWS.

ARAB PETROLEUM RESEARCH CENTRE.
— ARAB OIL & GAS. PETROLE ET LE GAZ ARABES.

ARAB WOMEN'S INFORMATION COMMITTEE.
— FACTS ABOUT THE PALESTINE PROBLEM.

ARANETA INSTITUTE OF AGRICULTURE.
— ARANETA JOURNAL OF AGRICULTURE.                       XXX
  SUBS (1972): ARANETA RESEARCH JOURNAL.
— ARANETA RESEARCH JOURNAL.                             XXX

ARBEITSGEMEINSCHAFT FUR ALPENORNITHOLOGIE.
— MONTICOLA.

ARBEITSGEMEINSCHAFT ETHNOMEDIZIN.
— ETHNOMEDIZIN. ETHNOMEDICINE.

ARBEITSGEMEINSCHAFT FERNWARME.
— FERNWARME INTERNATIONAL.

ARBEITSGEMEINSCHAFT FUR FLORISTIK IN SCHLESWIG-
HOLSTEIN UND HAMBURG.
— KIELER NOTIZEN ZUR PFLANZENKUNDE SCHLESWIG-
  HOLSTEINS.

ARBEITSGEMEINSCHAFT FUR HISTORISCHE SOZIAL-
KUNDE.
— BEITRAGE ZUR HISTORISCHEN SOZIALKUNDE.

ARBEITSGEMEINSCHAFT FUR TIER- UND PFLANZENGEOG-
RAPHISCHE HEIMATFORSCHUNG IM SAARLAND.
— ABHANDLUNGEN, ARBEITSGEMEINSCHAFT FUR TIER-
  UND PFLANZENGEOGRAPHISCHE HEIMATFORSCHUNG IM
  SAARLAND.
— FAUNISTISCH-FLORISTISCHE NOTIZEN AUS DEM
  SAARLAND.

ARBEITSGEMEINSCHAFT FUR WESTFALISCHE MUSIK-
GESCHICHTE.
— VEROFFENTLICHUNGEN DER ARBEITSGEMEINSCHAFT
  FUR WESTFALISCHE MUSIKGESCHICHTE.

ARBEITSKREIS FUR OST-WEST-FRAGEN.
— MODERNE WELT.                                         XXX

ARCHAEOLOGICAL CENTRE.
— AGO. THE NEW ARCHAEOLOGICAL MAGAZINE.

ARCHITECTURAL ASSOCIATION.
— AA NOTES.
— AAQ. ARCHITECTURAL ASSOCIATION QUARTERLY.
— PAPER, ARCHITECTURAL ASSOCIATION.

ARCTIC INSTITUTE OF NORTH AMERICA.
— NEWSLETTER, ARCTIC INSTITUTE OF NORTH AMERICA.
— TECHNICAL PAPERS, ARCTIC INSTITUTE OF NORTH
  AMERICA.                                              XXX

(ARGENTINA) SECRETARIA DE DIFUSION Y TURISMO.
— ARGENTINA.

ARHEOLOSKI MUZEJ ISTRE.
— HISTORIA ARCHAEOLOGICA (PULA).

ARHEOLOSKO DRUSTVO JUGOSLAVIJE.
— LIMES U JUGOSLAVIJI.

ARIZONA PIONEERS' HISTORICAL SOCIETY.
— ARIZONIANA.                                           XXX
— JOURNAL OF ARIZONA HISTORY.                           XXX
— NEWSLETTER, ARIZONA PIONEERS' HISTORICAL
  SOCIETY.                                              XXX
  SUBS (1960): ARIZONIANA.

ARIZONA STATE UNIVERSITY: COLLEGE OF LAW.
— LAW & THE SOCIAL ORDER.                               XXX

ARIZONA STATE UNIVERSITY: DEPARTMENT OF
ANTHROPOLOGY.
— NEWSLETTER FOR COMPUTER ARCHAEOLOGISTS.              XXX
— NEWSLETTER OF COMPUTER ARCHAEOLOGY.                   XXX

ARKTICHESKIJ I ANTARKTICHESKIJ NAUCHNO-
ISSLEDOVATEL'SKIJ INSTITUT (LENINGRAD).
— TRUDY ARKTICHESKOGO I ANTARKTICHESKOGO
NAUCHNO-ISSLEDOVATEL'SKOGO INSTITUTA ...                    XXX

ARMAGH PLANETARIUM.
— PLANETARIUM.

ARMFIELD HYDRAULIC ENGINEERING CO. LTD.
— EDUCATIONAL FLUID MECHANICS.

ARMJANSKAJA PROTIVOCHUMNAJA STANTSIJA.
— TRUDY, ARMJANSKAJA PROTIVOCHUMNAJA STANTSIJA.

ARMJANSKIJ NAUCHNO-ISSLEDOVATEL'SKIJ INSTITUT
STROITEL'NYKH MATERIALOV I SOORUZHENIJ.
— NAUCHNYE SOOBSHCHENIJA, ARMJANSKIJ NAUCHNO-
ISSLEDOVATEL'SKIJ INSTITUT STROITEL'NYKH
MATERIALOV I SOORUZHENIJ.

ARNOLD BAX SOCIETY.
— BULLETIN, ARNOLD BAX SOCIETY.

ARQUIVO NACIONAL (BRAZIL).
— MENSARIO, ARQUIVO NACIONAL (BRAZIL).

ART INFORMATION REGISTRY.
— CATALYST (LONDON).

ART INSTITUTE OF CHICAGO.
— MUSEUM STUDIES.

ART LIBRARIES SOCIETY.
— ARLIS NEWSLETTER.

ART WORKERS' GUILD.
— ARTIFEX. JOURNAL OF THE CRAFTS.

ARTHUR SCHNITZLER RESEARCH ASSOCIATION.              000
SEE: INTERNATIONAL ...

ARTS COUNCIL OF GREAT BRITAIN.
— ARTS BULLETIN. (1970).

ARUP ASSOCIATES.
— ARUP JOURNAL.                                           XXX
— ARUP NEWSLETTER.                                        XXX
SUBS (1966): ARUP JOURNAL.

ASAHIKAWA KOGYO KOTO SENMON GAKKO.
— ASAHIKAWA KOGYO KOTO SENMON GAKKO KENKYU
HOBUN. JOURNAL OF THE ASAHIKAWA TECHNICAL
COLLEGE.

ASAHIKAWA TECHNICAL COLLEGE.                         000
SEE: ASAHIKAWA KOGYO KOTO SENMON GAKKO.

ASIAN BROADCASTING UNION.
— ABU TECHNICAL REVIEW.

ASIAN COCONUT COMMUNITY.
— COCOMUNITY.

ASIAN DEVELOPMENT BANK.
— QUARTERLY NEWSLETTER, ASIAN DEVELOPMENT BANK.

ASIAN INSTITUTE FOR ECONOMIC DEVELOPMENT &
PLANNING.                                            000
SEE: UNITED NATIONS: ...

ASIAN MASS COMMUNICATION  RESEARCH & INFORMAT-
ION CENTRE.
— ASIAN MASS COMMUNICATION BULLETIN.

ASIAN REGIONAL INSTITUTE FOR SCHOOL BUILDING
RESEARCH.
— BUILDINGS FOR EDUCATION.                                XXX
— TECHNICAL NOTES, ASIAN REGIONAL INSTITUTE
FOR SCHOOL BUILDING RESEARCH.

ASIAN TRADE UNION COLLEGE.                           000
SEE: INTERNATIONAL CONFEDERATION OF FREE
TRADE UNIONS: ASIAN ...

ASIATIC SOCIETY (CALCUTTA).
— JOURNAL OF THE ASIATIC SOCIETY.

ASLIB.
— ASLIB INFORMATION.                                      XXX
— ASLIB OCCASIONAL PUBLICATIONS.
— LIBRARY & INFORMATION SCIENCE ABSTRACTS.                XXX

ASLIB: BIOLOGICAL GROUP.
— NEWSLETTER, BIOLOGICAL GROUP, ASLIB.

ASLIB: COMPUTER INFORMATION GROUP.
— COMPUTER INFORMATION.

ASOCIACION ENTRERRIANA GENERAL URQUIZA.
— REVISTA DE HISTORIA ENTRERRIANA.

ASOCIACION ESPANOLA DE ORIENTALISTAS.
— BOLETIN DE LA ASOCIACION ESPANOLA DE ORIENT-
ALISTAS.

ASOCIACION KRAGLIEVIANA DEL URUGUAY.
— KRAGLIEVIANA.

ASOCIACION LATINO-AMERICANA DE FITOPATALOGIA.
— FITOPATALOGIA.

ASOCIACION DE MEDICOS VETERINARIOS DEL PERU.
— REVISTA, ASOCIACION DE MEDICOS VETERINARIOS
DEL PERU.

ASOCIACION DE SOCIOLOGOS DE LENGUA ESPANOLA Y
PORTUGUESA.
— ANUARIO DE SOCIOLOGIA DE LOS PUEBLOS IBERICOS.

(ASSIS, BRAZIL) FACULDADE DE FILOSOFIA,
CIENCIAS DE LETTRAS: DEPARTAMENTO DE HISTORIA.
— ANAIS DE HISTORIA.

ASSOCIACAO BRASILEIRA DE PESQUISAS SOBRE
PLANTAS AROMATICAS E OLEOS ESSENCIAIS.
— BOLETIM ESPECIAL, ASSOCIACAO BRASILEIRA DE
PESQUISAS SOBRE PLANTAS AROMATICAS E OLEOS
ESSENCIAIS.

ASSOCIATED GENERAL CONTRACTORS OF AMERICA.
— CONSTRUCTOR ANNUAL.

ASSOCIATED OCTEL COMPANY.
— TECHNICAL DEPARTMENT BULLETIN, ASSOCIATED
OCTEL COMPANY.

ASSOCIATION FOR ACADEMIC SURGERY.
— CURRENT TOPICS IN SURGICAL RESEARCH.

ASSOCIATION D'ACRIDOLOGIE.
— ACRIDA.

ASSOCIATION FOR THE ADVANCEMENT OF AGRICULTURAL
SCIENCES IN AFRICA.
— JOURNAL OF THE ASSOCIATION FOR THE ADVANCE-
MENT OF AGRICULTURAL SCIENCES IN AFRICA.

ASSOCIATION FOR AFRICAN MICROPALEONTOLOGY &
BIOSTRATIGRAPHY.
— NEWSLETTER OF THE ASSOCIATION FOR AFRICAN
MICROPALEONTOLOGY & BIOSTRATIGRAPHY.

ASSOCIATION OF AMERICAN GEOGRAPHERS.
— PROCEEDINGS, ASSOCIATION OF AMERICAN GEOG-
RAPHERS.

ASSOCIATION OF AMERICAN GEOGRAPHERS: COMMISSION
ON COLLEGE GEOGRAPHY.
— PUBLICATION, COMMISSION ON COLLEGE GEOGRAPHY,
ASSOCIATION OF AMERICAN GEOGRAPHERS.
— RESOURCE PAPER, COMMISSION ON COLLEGE GEOG-
RAPHY, ASSOCIATION OF AMERICAN GEOGRAPHERS.
— TECHNICAL PAPER, COMMISSION ON COLLEGE GEOGR-
APHY, ASSOCIATION OF AMERICAN GEOGRAPHERS.

ASSOCIATION DES AMIS D'ANDRE GIDE.
— BULLETIN D'INFORMATION, ASSOCIATION DES AMIS
D'ANDRE GIDE.
— CAHIERS ANDRE GIDE.

ASSOCIATION DES AMIS DE PIERRE TEILHARD DE
CHARDIN: CENTRE BELGE D'ETUDE ET D'INFORM.
— ETUDES TEILHARDIENNES.

ASSOCIATION OF APPLIED BIOLOGISTS.
— DESCRIPTIONS OF PLANT VIRUSES.

ASSOCIATION OF ARTS CENTRES IN SCOTLAND.
— TRENDS & TOPICS.

ASSOCIATION FOR ASIAN STUDIES.
— ASIAN STUDIES PROFESSIONAL REVIEW.
— BIBLIOGRAPHY OF ASIAN STUDIES.                          XXX

ASSOCIATION OF ASSISTANT LIBRARIANS: SUSSEX
DIVISION.
— OCCASIONAL PAPER, SUSSEX DIVISION,
ASSOCIATION OF ASSISTANT LIBRARIANS.

ASSOCIATION BELGE DE MALACOLOGIE, CONCHYLIOL-
OGIE ET PALEONTOLOGIE.
— BULLETIN MENSUEL, ASSOCIATION BELGE DE MALAC-
OLOGIE, CONCHYLIOLOGIE ET PALEONTOLOGIE.

ASSOCIATION OF BRITISH LIBRARY SCHOOLS.
— NEWSLETTER, ASSOCIATION OF BRITISH LIBRARY
SCHOOLS.

ASSOCIATION OF BURGLARY INSURANCE SURVEYORS.
— SECURITY SURVEYOR. JOURNAL OF THE ...

ASSOCIATION OF CANADIAN LAW TEACHERS.
— CANADIAN LEGAL STUDIES. = ETUDES JURIDIQUES
AU CANADA.

ASSOCIATION OF CERTIFIED & CORPORATE
ACCOUNTANTS.
— CERTIFIED ACCOUNTANT.                              XXX
— CERTIFIED ACCOUNTANTS JOURNAL.                     XXX
SUBS (1972): CERTIFIED ACCOUNTANT.

ASSOCIATION OF CLINICAL BIOCHEMISTS.
— ANNALS OF CLINICAL BIOCHEMISTRY.                   XXX
— SCIENTIFIC REPORT, ASSOCIATION OF CLINICAL
BIOCHEMISTS.

ASSOCIATION OF CLINICAL SCIENTISTS.
— ANNALS OF CLINICAL LABORATORY SCIENCE.

ASSOCIATION OF COLLEGES FOR FURTHER & HIGHER
EDUCATION.
— YEAR BOOK, ASSOCIATION OF COLLEGES FOR
FURTHER & HIGHER EDUCATION.

ASSOCIATION FOR COMMONWEALTH LITERATURE &
LANGUAGE STUDIES.
— BULLETIN, ASSOCIATION FOR COMMONWEALTH
LITERATURE & LANGUAGE STUDIES.
— NEWS SHEET, ASSOCIATION FOR COMMONWEALTH
LITERATURE & LANGUAGE STUDIES.                       XXX

ASSOCIATION OF COMMONWEALTH UNIVERSITIES.
— AWARDS FOR COMMONWEALTH UNIVERSITY STAFF.         XXX
— BULLETIN OF CURRENT DOCUMENTATION.

ASSOCIATION FOR COMPUTING MACHINERY.
— COMPUTING SURVEYS.

ASSOCIATION FOR COMPUTING MACHINERY: SPECIAL
INTEREST COMMITTEE ON NUMERICAL MATHEMATICS.
— SIGNUM NEWSLETTER.

ASSOCIATION OF CONTEMPORARY HISTORIANS.
— BULLETIN, ASSOCIATION OF CONTEMPORARY
HISTORIANS.

ASSOCIATION DE DROIT INTERNATIONAL ET DE RELAT-
IONS INTERNATIONALES DE LA REPUBLIQUE SOCIAL-
ISTE DE ROUMANIE.
— REVUE ROUMAINE D'ETUDES INTERNATIONALES.

ASSOCIATION FOR EDUCATION IN INTERNATIONAL
BUSINESS.
— JOURNAL OF INTERNATIONAL BUSINESS STUDIES.

ASSOCIATIONS FOR THE EDUCATION OF PUPILS FROM
OVERSEAS.
— MULTIRACIAL SCHOOL. JOURNAL OF THE ...           XXX

ASSOCIATION OF ETHIO-HELLENIC STUDIES.
— ABBA SALAMA.

ASSOCIATION POUR L'ETUDE DU MOUVEMENT DADA.        XXX
— REVUE DE L'ASSOCIATION POUR L'ETUDE DU
MOUVEMENT DADA.                                      XXX

ASSOCIATION POUR L'ETUDE DES SCIENCES HUMAINES
EN AFRIQUE DU NORD.
— REVUE DE L'OCCIDENT MUSULMAN ET DE LA
MEDITERRANEE.

ASSOCIATION FOR EVOLUTIONARY ECONOMICS.
— JOURNAL OF ECONOMIC ISSUES.

ASSOCIATION OF EXPLORATION GEOCHEMISTS.
— JOURNAL OF GEOCHEMICAL EXPLORATION.

ASSOCIATION FORET-CELLULOSE.
— (ASSOCIATION FORET-CELLULOSE).

ASSOCIATION FRANCAISE POUR L'AVANCEMENT DES
SCIENCES.
— REVUE DE L'ASSOCIATION FRANCAISE POUR
L'AVANCEMENT DES SCIENCES.

ASSOCIATION GENERALE DES HYGIENISTES ET TECH-
NICIENS MUNICIPAUX.
— TECHNIQUES ET SCIENCES MUNICIPALES - L'EAU.       XXX

ASSOCIATION OF HISTORY TEACHERS IN THE SOUTH
WEST.
— BULLETIN, ASSOCIATION OF HISTORY TEACHERS IN
THE SOUTH WEST.

ASSOCIATION POUR L'INFORMATION CULTURELLE
(BELGIUM).
— CLES POUR LES ARTS.
— CLES POUR LE SPECTACLE.

ASSOCIATION POUR L'INFORMATION MUSICALE
(BELGIUM).
— CLES POUR LA MUSIQUE.

ASSOCIATION INTERNATIONALE DE BIBLIOPHILIE.
— BULLETIN DU BIBLIOPHILE.                           XXX

ASSOCIATION INTERNATIONALE DES ETUDES BALKANIQ-
UES ET SUD-EST EUROPEENNES.
— ACTES DU PREMIER CONGRES INTERNATIONAL DES
ETUDES BALKANIQUES ET SUD-EST EUROPEENNES.

ASSOCIATION INTERNATIONALE DES ETUDES
BYZANTINES.
— BULLETIN D'INFORMATION ET DE COORDINATION,
ASSOCIATION INTERNATIONALE DES ETUDES
BYZANTINES.

ASSOCIATION INTERNATIONALE POUR L'ETUDE DE DADA
ET DU SURREALISME.                                   XXX
— CAHIERS DADA SURREALISME.                          XXX

ASSOCIATION INTERNATIONALE D'ETUDE PATRISTIQUES
— BULLETIN D'INFORMATION ET LIAISON.

ASSOCIATION INTERNATIONALE D'ETUDES DU
SUD-EST EUROPEEN.                                    000
SEE: INTERNATIONAL ASSOCIATION OF SOUTH-
EAST EUROPEAN STUDIES.

ASSOCIATION INTERNATIONALE POUR LA LIBERTE DE
LA CULTURE.
— PREUVES. LES IDEES QUI CHANGENT LE MONDE.

ASSOCIATION INTERNATIONALE DE SEMIOTIQUE.
— SEMIOTICA.

ASSOCIAZIONE ITALIANA DI AERONAUTICA E
ASTRONAUTICA.
— AEROTECNICA - MISSILI E SPAZIO.                    XXX

ASSOCIAZONE ITALIANA DI GENIO RURALE.
— RIVISTA DI INGEGNERIA AGRARIA.

ASSOCIATION DES JEUNES SCIENTIFIQUES.
— TRAVAUX DES JEUNES SCIENTIFIQUES.

ASSOCIATION OF LAW TEACHERS.
— JOURNAL OF THE ASSOCIATION OF LAW TEACHERS.

ASSOCIATION LIBANAISE DES SCIENCES POLITIQUES.
— REVUE LIBANAISE DES SCIENCES POLITIQUES.

ASSOCIATION OF LIBERAL COUNCILLORS.
— A.L.C. POLICY PAPERS.

ASSOCIATION FOR LITERARY & LINGUISTIC COMPUT-
ING.
— BULLETIN, ASSOCIATION FOR LITERARY & LING-
UISTIC COMPUTING.

ASSOCIATION OF MINING ELECTRICAL & MECHANICAL
ENGINEERS.
— MINING TECHNOLOGY.                                 XXX

ASSOCIATION OF MINNESOTA ENTOMOLOGISTS.
— NEWSLETTER, ASSOCIATION OF MINNESOTA
ENTOMOLOGISTS.

ASSOCIATION FOR MUTUAL INFORMATION.
— BLOOD GROUP NEWS.                                  XXX

ASSOCIAZIONE NAZIONALE ALLEVATORI DELLA RAZZA
BRUNA ALPINA (ITALY).
— BRUNA ALPINA.

ASSOCIAZIONE NAZIONALE ITALIANA PER
L'AUTOMAZIONE.
— RICERCHE DI AUTOMATICA.

ASSOCIATION OF OCCUPATIONAL THERAPISTS OF
IRELAND.
— O-T IRELAND.

ASSOCIATION DES OUVRIERS EN INSTRUMENTS DE
PRECISION.
— BIFLASH MESURES.

**ASSOCIATION DES PHARMACOLOGISTES.**
— JOURNAL DE PHARMACOLOGIE.

**ASSOCIATION FOR PHILOSOPHY OF MATHEMATICS.**
— PHILOSOPHIA MATHEMATICA.

**ASSOCIATION FOR PROGRAMMED LEARNING.**
— PROGRAMMED LEARNING NEWS.

**ASSOCIATION FOR PROGRAMMED LEARNING AND EDUCAT-
IONAL TECHNOLOGY.**
— YEARBOOK OF EDUCATIONAL & INSTRUCTIONAL
TECHNOLOGY.

**ASSOCIATION OF PSYCHIATRIC SOCIAL WORKERS.**
— BRITISH JOURNAL OF PSYCHIATRIC SOCIAL WORK.     XXX

**ASSOCIATION FOR PSYCHIATRIC TREATMENT OF
OFFENDERS.**
— INTERNATIONAL JOURNAL OF OFFENDER THERAPY.     XXX
   SUBS (1972): INTERNATIONAL JOURNAL OF
   OFFENDER THERAPY & COMPARATIVE CRIMINOLOGY.
— INTERNATIONAL JOURNAL OF OFFENDER THERAPY &
COMPARATIVE CRIMINOLOGY.     XXX

**ASSOCIATION OF PUBLIC HEALTH INSPECTORS.**
— ENVIRONMENTAL HEALTH (LONDON).     XXX
— MONOGRAPH SERIES, ASSOCIATION OF PUBLIC
HEALTH INSPECTORS.
— PUBLIC HEALTH INSPECTOR.     XXX

**ASSOCIATION DE RECHERCHE SUR LA POESIE FRANC-
AISE MODERNE ET CONTEMPORAINE.**
— CREATION (PARIS).

**ASSOCIATION OF RECOGNISED ENGLISH LANGUAGE
SCHOOLS.**
— ARELS JOURNAL.

**ASSOCIATION OF RESEARCH LIBRARIES: CENTER FOR
CHINESE RESEARCH MATERIALS.**
— NEWSLETTER, CENTER FOR CHINESE RESEARCH MATER-
IALS, ASSOCIATION OF RESEARCH LIBRARIES.

**ASSOCIATION OF RESEARCH LIBRARIES: SLAVIC BIBL-
IOGRAPHIC & DOCUMENTATION CENTER.**
— NEW SLAVIC PUBLICATIONS.
— NEWSLETTER, SLAVIC BIBLIOGRAPHIC & DOCUMENTAT-
ION CENTER, ASSOCIATION OF RESEARCH LIBRARIES.

**ASSOCIATION OF SCIENTIFIC SOCIETIES IN
RHODESIA.**
— RHODESIA SCIENCE NEWS.

**ASSOCIATION OF SCIENTIFIC, TECHNICAL &
MANAGERIAL STAFFS.**
— ASTMS JOURNAL.
— PRINT OUT. THE NEWSLETTER OF THE ...

**ASSOCIATION OF SCIENTIFIC WORKERS.**     XXX
— ASCW JOURNAL.     XXX
   SUBS (1968, PART OF): ASTMS JOURNAL.

**ASSOCIATION SCIENTIFIQUE DE COTE D'IVOIRE.**
— BULLETIN BIOLOGIQUE (IVORY COAST).

**ASSOCIATION SCIENTIFIQUE ET TECHNIQUE POUR
L'EXPLOITATION DES OCEANS.**
— OCEANS INFORMATION.

**ASSOCIATION FOR SCOTTISH LITERARY STUDIES.**
— OCCASIONAL PAPERS, ASSOCIATION FOR SCOTTISH
LITERARY STUDIES.
— SCOTTISH LITERARY NEWS. NEWSLETTER OF THE ...

**ASSOCIATION SENEGALAISE D'ETUDES ET DE
RECHERCHES JURIDIQUES.**
— REVUE SENEGALAISE DE DROIT.

**ASSOCIATION FOR SPECIAL EDUCATION: RESEARCH
COMMITTEE.**
— RESEARCH IN SPECIAL EDUCATION. ABSTRACTS &
INFORMATION.

**ASSOCIATION OF STORES & MATERIALS CONTROLLERS.**
— MATERIALS HANDLING & MANAGEMENT.

**ASSOCIATION FOR THE STUDY OF AFRICAN & ASIAN
AFFAIRS.**
— JOURNAL OF AFRICAN & ASIAN STUDIES.

**ASSOCIATION FOR THE STUDY OF ORIENTAL INSECTS.**
— ORIENTAL INSECTS.

**ASSOCIATION OF SUPERVISORY STAFFS EXECUTIVES
& TECHNICIANS.**     XXX
— ASSET.     XXX
   SUBS (1968, PART OF): ASTMS JOURNAL.

**ASSOCIATION OF TEACHERS OF ENGLISH.**
— ATE. JOURNAL OF THE ASSOCIATION OF TEACHERS
OF ENGLISH.

**ASSOCIATION OF TEACHERS OF ENGLISH TO PUPILS
FROM OVERSEAS.**
— ENGLISH FOR IMMIGRANTS.     XXX

**ASSOCIATION OF TEACHERS OF GEOLOGY.**
— GEOLOGY. JOURNAL OF THE ASSOCIATION OF ...

**ASSOCIATION OF TEACHERS OF MANAGEMENT.**
— A.T.M. BULLETIN.     XXX
— A.T.M. OCCASIONAL PAPERS.     XXX
— MANAGEMENT EDUCATION AND DEVELOPMENT.     XXX

**ASSOCIATION TECHNIQUE POUR LE DEVELOPPEMENT DES
LAITIERS DE HAUTS FOURNEAUX.**
— LAITIERS DE HAUTS FOURNEAUX.     XXX
— LAITIERS ET TARMACADAM.     XXX
   SUBS (1971): LAITIERS DE HAUTS FOURNEAUX.

**ASSOCIATION FOR TROPICAL BIOLOGY.**
— BIOTROPICA.

**ASSOCIATION OF UNIVERSITY PROFESSORS OF FRENCH.**
— CURRENT RESEARCH IN FRENCH STUDIES AT UNIV-
ERSITIES & UNIVERSITY COLLEGES IN THE UNITED
KINGDOM.     XXX

**ASSOCIATION VAROISE POUR LA SAUVEGARDE DE
L'AGRICULTURE, DE LA NATURE ET DE L'ENVIRONE-
MENT.**
— NATURE, AGRICULTURE, ENVIRONMENT.

**ASSOCIATION OF VETERINARY ANAESTHETISTS.**
— PROCEEDINGS OF THE ASSOCIATION OF VETERINARY
ANAESTHETISTS.

**ASSOCIATION OF WIDOWS IN IRELAND.**
— WOMEN, WIVES, WIDOWS.     XXX

**ASSOCIAZONE DEGLI AFRICANISTI ITALIANI.**
— BOLLETTINO, ASSOCIAZONE DEGLI AFRICANISTI
ITALIANI.

**ASSOCIAZIONE GEOTECNICA ITALIANA.**
— RIVISTA ITALIANA DI GEOTECNICA.

**ASSOCIAZIONE ITALIANA PER GLI STUDI DI POLIT-
ICA ESTERA.**
— AFFARI ESTERI.     XXX
— ESTERI.     XXX
   SUBS (1969): AFFARI ESTERI.

**ASSOCIAZIONE ITALIANA DEL VUOTO.**
— VUOTO SCIENZA E TECNOLOGIA.

**ASSOCIAZIONE PISCICOLTORI ITALIANI.**
— RIVISTA ITALIANA DI PISCICOLTURA E ITTIOPATO-
LOGIA.

**ASTRO-GATOR ASTRONOMY CLUB.**
— METEOR NEWS.

**ASTROLOGICAL ASSOCIATION.**
— CORRELATION.

**ASTRONOMICAL SOCIETY OF THE PACIFIC.**
— MERCURY. THE JOURNAL OF THE ...

**ASTRONOMISCHES RECHEN-INSTITUT (HEIDELBERG).**
— ASTRONOMY & ASTROPHYSICS ABSTRACTS.     XXX

**ASTRONOMISK SELSKAB.**
— ASTRONOMISK TIDSSKRIFT.     XXX
— NORDISK ASTRONOMISK TIDSSKRIFT.     XXX
   SUBS (1968): ASTRONOMISK TIDSSKRIFT.

**ATLANTIC EDUCATIONAL TRUST.**
— WORLD SURVEY.     XXX

**ATLANTIC INSTITUTE.**
— ATLANTIC PAPERS.

**ATLANTICHESKIJ NAUCHNO-ISSLEDOVATEL'SKIJ
INSTITUT RYBNOGO KHOZJAJSTVA I OKEANOGRAFII.**
— ATLANTICHESKIJ OKEAN. RYBOPOISKOVYE ISSLE-
DOVANIJA.

**ATOMIC ENERGY RESEARCH ESTABLISHMENT.**
— PHYSICO-CHEMICAL MEASUREMENT UNIT BULLETIN.
— QUALITY TECHNOLOGY.

**ATOMIC WEAPONS RESEARCH ESTABLISHMENT.**
— AWRE PAMPHLET.

**AUBURN UNIVERSITY.**
— SOUTHERN HUMANITIES REVIEW.

**AUSTRALASIAN INSTITUTE OF MINING & METALLURGY.**
— AUSTRALIAN GEOMECHANICS JOURNAL.

**AUSTRALASIAN NATIVE ORCHID SOCIETY.**
— ORCHADIAN.

**(AUSTRALIA) BUREAU OF AGRICULTURAL ECONOMICS.**
— COMMODITY RESEARCH REPORTS, BUREAU OF AGRI-
CULTURAL ECONOMICS (AUSTRALIA).
— FIBRE REVIEW.

**(AUSTRALIA) BUREAU OF CENSUS AND STATISTICS.**                    000
SEE: (AUSTRALIA) COMMONWEALTH BUREAU OF
CENSUS AND STATISTICS.

**(AUSTRALIA) COMMONWEALTH BUREAU OF CENSUS &
STATISTICS.**
— CAUSES OF DEATH (AUSTRALIA).
— FORESTS & FOREST PRODUCTS.
— GOVERNMENT PENSION & SUPERANNUATION SCHEMES
(AUSTRALIA).
— MINERAL EXPLORATION (AUSTRALIA).
— PUBLIC AUTHORITY FINANCE BULLETIN.

**(AUSTRALIA) COMMONWEALTH BUREAU OF CENSUS &
STATISTICS: SOUTH AUSTRALIA OFFICE.**
— SOUTH AUSTRALIAN YEAR BOOK.

**(AUSTRALIA) COMMONWEALTH BUREAU OF CENSUS &
STATISTICS: TASMANIAN OFFICE.**
— TASMANIAN YEAR BOOK.

**(AUSTRALIA) DEPARTMENT OF EXTERNAL TERRITOR-
IES.**                                                              XXX
— AUSTRALIAN EXTERNAL TERRITORIES.                                  XXX

**(AUSTRALIA) DEPARTMENT OF PRIMARY INDUSTRY:
FISHERIES BRANCH.**
— AUSTRALIAN FISHERIES.                                             XXX

**(AUSTRALIA) DEPARTMENT OF SOCIAL SECURITY.**
— SOCIAL SECURITY QUARTERLY.

**(AUSTRALIA) DEPARTMENT OF THE TREASURY.**
— ROUND-UP OF ECONOMIC STATISTICS.

**AUSTRALIAN ACADEMY OF FORENSIC SCIENCES.**
— AUSTRALIAN JOURNAL OF FORENSIC SCIENCES.

**AUSTRALIAN ACADEMY OF THE HUMANITIES.**
— MONOGRAPH, AUSTRALIAN ACADEMY OF THE
HUMANITIES.
— PROCEEDINGS, AUSTRALIAN ACADEMY OF THE
HUMANITIES.                                                         XXX

**AUSTRALIAN ACADEMY OF SCIENCE.**
— RECORDS OF THE AUSTRALIAN ACADEMY OF SCIENCE.

**AUSTRALIAN ASSOCIATION OF NEUROLOGISTS.**
— PROCEEDINGS, AUSTRALIAN ASSOCIATION OF NEURO-
LOGISTS.

**AUSTRALIAN BIOCHEMICAL SOCIETY.**
— PROCEEDINGS OF THE AUSTRALIAN BIOCHEMICAL
SOCIETY.

**AUSTRALIAN COMPUTER SOCIETY.**
— AUSTRALIAN COMPUTER JOURNAL.

**AUSTRALIAN CONSERVATION FOUNDATION.**
— HABITAT AUSTRALIA.
— SPECIAL PUBLICATION, AUSTRALIAN CONSERVATION
FOUNDATION.
— VIEWPOINT SERIES, AUSTRALIAN CONSERVATION
FOUNDATION.

**AUSTRALIAN ENTOMOLOGICAL SOCIETY.**
— HANDBOOK, AUSTRALIAN ENTOMOLOGICAL SOCIETY.
— JOURNAL, AUSTRALIAN ENTOMOLOGICAL SOCIETY.              XXX
— MISCELLANEOUS PUBLICATION, AUSTRALIAN ENTOMOL-
OGICAL SOCIETY.

**AUSTRALIAN GEOGRAPHY TEACHERS' ASSOCIATION.**
— GEOGRAPHICAL EDUCATION. JOURNAL OF THE ...

**AUSTRALIAN HUMANITIES RESEARCH COUNCIL.**
— REPORT, AUSTRALIAN HUMANITIES RESEARCH
COUNCIL.                                                            XXX
SUBS (1970): PROCEEDINGS, AUSTRALIAN ACAD-
EMY OF THE HUMANITIES.

**AUSTRALIAN INSTITUTE OF ABORIGINAL STUDIES.**
— CURRENT BIBLIOGRAPHY, AUSTRALIAN INSTITUTE OF
ABORIGINAL STUDIES.                                                 XXX

**AUSTRALIAN INSTITUTE OF ARCHAEOLOGY.**
— BURIED HISTORY. A QUARTERLY JOURNAL OF BIB-
LICAL ARCHAEOLOGY.

**AUSTRALIAN INSTITUTE OF METALS.**
— METALS AUSTRALIA.

**AUSTRALIAN INSTITUTE OF PARKS & RECREATION.**
— AUSTRALIAN PARKS.

**AUSTRALIAN MARINE SCIENCES ASSOCIATION.**
— AUSTRALIAN MARINE SCIENCES NEWSLETTER.

**AUSTRALIAN MATHEMATICAL SOCIETY.**
— BULLETIN OF THE AUSTRALIAN MATHEMATICAL SOC-
IETY.

**AUSTRALIAN MINERAL DEVELOPMENT LABORATORIES.**
— AMDEL BULLETIN.

**AUSTRALIAN NATIONAL RESEARCH COUNCIL.**
— AUSTRALIAN JOURNAL OF SCIENCE.                                    XXX
SUBS (1970): SEARCH.

**AUSTRALIAN NATIONAL UNIVERSITY: CENTRE OF
ORIENTAL STUDIES.**
— OCCASIONAL PAPERS, CENTRE OF ORIENTAL STUDIES,
AUSTRALIAN NATIONAL UNIVERSITY.

**AUSTRALIAN NATIONAL UNIVERSITY: DEPARTMENT OF
BIOGEOGRAPHY & GEOMORPHOLOGY.**
— MT. WILHELM STUDIES.

**AUSTRALIAN NATIONAL UNIVERSITY: DEPARTMENT OF
FAR EASTERN HISTORY.**
— PAPERS ON FAR EASTERN HISTORY.

**AUSTRALIAN NATIONAL UNIVERSITY: RESEARCH SCHOOL
OF PACIFIC STUDIES.**
— TERRA AUSTRALIS.

**AUSTRALIAN & NEW ZEALAND ASSOCIATION FOR THE
ADVANCEMENT OF SCIENCE.**
— SEARCH.                                                           XXX

**AUSTRALIAN & NEW ZEALAND ASSOCIATION FOR
MEDIEVAL & RENAISSANCE STUDIES.**
— BULLETIN, AUSTRALIAN & NEW ZEALAND ASSOCIA-
TION FOR MEDIEVAL & RENAISSANCE STUDIES.                            XXX
— PARERGON. BULLETIN OF THE AUSTRALIAN & NEW
ZEALAND ASSOCIATION FOR MEDIEVAL & RENAIS-
SANCE STUDIES.                                                      XXX

**AUSTRALIAN & NEW ZEALAND SOCIETY OF CRIMINOLOGY**
— AUSTRALIAN & NEW ZEALAND JOURNAL OF CRIMIN-
OLOGY.

**AUSTRALIAN NEWS & INFORMATION BUREAU.**
— AUSTRALIAN ECONOMIC NEWS DIGEST.

**AUSTRALIAN PETROLEUM EXPLORATION ASSOCIATION.**
— A.P.E.A. JOURNAL.

**AUSTRALIAN PHYSIOLOGICAL SOCIETY.**
— PROCEEDINGS, AUSTRALIAN PHYSIOLOGICAL SOCIETY.

**AUSTRALIAN PLANNING INSTITUTE.**                                  XXX
— AUSTRALIAN PLANNING INSTITUTE JOURNAL.                            XXX
SUBS (1970): ROYAL AUSTRALIAN PLANNING ...

**AUSTRALIAN RHODODENDRON SOCIETY.**
— RHODODENDRON.

**AUSTRALIAN SOCIETY OF ANAESTHETISTS.**
— ANAESTHESIA & INTENSIVE CARE.

**AUSTRALIAN SOCIETY FOR BIBLICAL ARCHAEOLOGY.**
— AUSTRALIAN JOURNAL OF BIBLICAL ARCHAEOLOGY.

**AUSTRALIAN SOCIETY FOR CLASSICAL STUDIES.**
— ANTICHTHON. JOURNAL OF THE ...

**AUSTRALIAN SOCIETY OF EXPLORATION GEOPHYSICISTS**
— BULLETIN, AUSTRALIAN SOCIETY OF EXPLORATION
GEOPHYSICISTS.

AUSTRALIAN SOCIETY FOR LIMNOLOGY.
— BULLETIN, AUSTRALIAN SOCIETY FOR LIMNOLOGY.

AUSTRALIAN SOCIETY FOR PARASITOLOGY.
— INTERNATIONAL JOURNAL OF PARASITOLOGY.

AUSTRALIAN WATER RESOURCES COUNCIL.
— TECHNICAL PAPER, AUSTRALIAN WATER RESOURCES
COUNCIL.
— WATER RESOURCES NEWSLETTER.

AUTOMATION COUNCIL (GB).                                    000
SEE: UNITED KINGDOM AUTOMATION COUNCIL.

(AZERBAJDZHANSKAJA SSR) MINISTERSTVO NEFTEDO-
BYVAJUSHCHEJ PROMYSHLENNOSTI.
— ZA TEKHNICHESKIJ PROGRESS.

AZERBAJDZHANSKIJ GOSUDARSTVENNYJ UNIVERSITET.
— UCHENYE ZAPISKI, AZERBAJDZHANSKIJ GOSUDARST-
VENNYJ UNIVERSITET: SERIJA ISTORICHESKIKH I
FILOSOFSKIKH NAUK.

AZERBAJDZHANSKIJ NAUCHNO-ISSLEDOVATEL'SKIJ
INSTITUT MEDITSINSKOJ PARAZITOLOGII I
TROPICHESKOJ MEDITSINY.
— TRUDY NAUCHNO-ISSLEDOVATEL'SKOGO INSTITUTA
MEDITSINSKOJ PARAZITOLOGII I TROPICHESKOJ
MEDITSINY.

AZERBAJDZHANSKIJ NAUCHNO-ISSLEDOVATEL'SKIJ
INSTITUT MEKHANIZATSII I ELEKTRIFIKATSII
SEL'SKOGO KHOZJAJSTVA.
— TRUDY AZERBAJDZHANSKOGO NAUCHNO-ISSLEDOVATEL'-
SKOGO INSTITUTA MEKHANIZATSII I ELEKTRIFIK-
ATSII SEL'SKOGO KHOZJAJSTVA.

AZERBAJDZHANSKIJ SEL'SKOKHOZJAJSTVENNYJ
INSTITUT.
— UCHENYE ZAPISKI AZERBAJDZHANSKOGO SEL'SKO-
KHOZJAJSTVENNOGO INSTITUTA.

BADISCHE ANILIN-UND SODA-FABRIK.
— BASF DIGEST.                                              XXX
— BASF REVIEW.
— SCHRIFTENREIHE DES FIRMENARCHIVS, BADISCHE
ANILIN-UND SODA-FABRIK.

BAKELITE XYLONITE LTD.
— BXL CROSSLINK.

BALAI PENJELIDIKAN PERUSAHAAN PERKEBUNAN GULA.
— BULLETIN, BALAI PENJELIDIKAN PERUSAHAAN
PERKEBUNAN GULA.  BULLETIN, INDONESIAN SUGAR
EXPERIMENT STATION.

BALINT SOCIETY.
— JOURNAL OF THE BALINT SOCIETY.

BALLET NACIONAL DE CUBA.
— CUBA EN EL BALLET.

BANCO CENTRAL DEL URUGUAY: DEPARTMENTO DE
INVESTIGACIONES ECONOMICAS.
— BOLETIN ESTADISTICO. (URUGUAY)

BANCO INTERAMERICANO DE DESARROLLO.                         000
SEE: INTER-AMERICAN DEVELOPMENT BANK.

BANCO DI ROMA.
— JOURNAL OF EUROPEAN ECONOMIC HISTORY.

(BANGLADESH) BUREAU OF STATISTICS.
— MONTHLY STATISTICAL BULLETIN OF BANGLADESH.

(BANGLADESH) MINISTRY OF FOREIGN AFFAIRS:
EXTERNAL PUBLICITY DIVISION.
— BANGLADESH DOCUMENTS.

BANGLADESH INSTITUTE OF DEVELOPMENT ECONOMICS.
— BANGLADESH ECONOMIC REVIEW.                               XXX

BANK OF CANADA.
— BANK OF CANADA REVIEW. = REVUE DE LA BANQUE
DU CANADA.                                                  XXX
— STATISTICAL SUMMARY, BANK OF CANADA.                      XXX
SUBS (1971): BANK OF CANADA REVIEW.

BANK OF CANADA: PUBLICATIONS COMMITTEE.
— STAFF RESEARCH STUDIES, BANK OF CANADA.

BANK OF ENGLAND.
— BANK OF ENGLAND STATISTICAL ABSTRACT.

BANK NEGARA MALAYSIA.
— QUARTERLY ECONOMIC BULLETIN, BANK NEGARA
MALAYSIA.

BANK OF SIERRA LEONE.
— OCCASIONAL PAPERS, BANK OF SIERRA LEONE.

BANK OF SUDAN.
— FOREIGN TRADE STATISTICAL DIGEST (SUDAN).

BANK OF UGANDA.
— QUARTERLY BULLETIN, BANK OF UGANDA.

BANK OF ZAMBIA.
— QUARTERLY STATISTICAL REVIEW, BANK OF ZAMBIA.

BANQUE CENTRALE DES ETATS DE L'AFRIQUE DE
L'OUEST.
— BIBLIOGRAPHIE, BANQUE CENTRALE DES ETATS DE
L'AFRIQUE DE L'OUEST.

BANQUE DE FRANCE.
— NOTE D'INFORMATION, BANQUE DE FRANCE.

BANQUE NATIONALE DE PARIS.
— REVUE ECONOMIQUE, BANQUE NATIONALE DE PARIS.

BARNAUL'SKIJ GOSUDARSTVENNYJ PEDAGOGICHESKIJ
INSTITUT: KAFEDRY OBSHCHESTVENNYKH NAUK.
— TRUDY KAFEDR OBSHCHESTVENNYKH NAUK BARNAUL'-
SKOGO GOSUDARSTVENNOGO PEDAGOGICHESKOGO
INSTITUTA.

BASILDON NATURAL HISTORY SOCIETY.
— BULLETIN, BASILDON NATURAL HISTORY SOCIETY.

BATTELLE-INSTITUT; GEMEINNUTZIGE LABORATORIEN
FUR VERTRAGSFORSCHUNG.
— BATTELLE INFORMATION.

BATTELLE MEMORIAL INSTITUTE: COLOMBUS LABORAT-
ORIES.
— BATTELLE RESEARCH OUTLOOK.                                XXX

BAYERISCHE STAATSSAMMLUNG FUR PALAONTOLOGIE
UND HISTORISCHE GEOLOGIE.
— ZITTELIANA.  ABHANDLUNGEN DER BAYERISCHEN
STAATSSAMMLUNG FUR PALAONTOLOGIE UND HISTOR-
ISCHE GEOLOGIE.

BAYLOR UNIVERSITY: ARMSTRONG BROWNING LIBRARY.
— BROWNING NEWSLETTER.

BECKMAN INSTRUMENTS INC.
— FLAME NOTES.

BECKMAN INSTRUMENTS, INC.: SPINCO DIVISION.
— FRACTIONS.  NEWS OF BIOCHEMICAL INSTRUMENTAT-
ION.

BEDFORD INSTITUTE (NOVA SCOTIA).
— COLLECTED CONTRIBUTIONS, BEDFORD INSTITUTE.

BEHAVIOR THERAPY SOCIETY.
— JOURNAL OF BEHAVIOR THERAPY & EXPERIMENTAL
PSYCHIATRY.

BELFAST NATURALISTS' FIELD CLUB.
— OCCASIONAL PUBLICATION, BELFAST NATURALISTS'
FIELD CLUB.

(BELGIUM) INSTITUT NATIONAL DE STATISTIQUE.
— STATISTIQUES FINANCIERES, INSTITUT NATIONAL
DE STATISTIQUE (BELGIUM).

(BELGIUM) SERVICE DE LA METROLOGIE.
— BULLETIN BELGE DE METROLOGIE.                             XXX
SUBS (1971): BULLETIN DE METROLOGIE.
— BULLETIN DE METROLOGIE.                                   XXX

(BELORUSSIA) MINISTERSTVO VYSSHEGO I SREDNEGO
SPETSIAL'NOGO OBRAZOVANIJA.
— PROGRESSIVNAJA TEKHNOLOGIJA MASHINOSTROENIJA.

BELORUSSKIJ GOSUDARSTVENNYJ UNIVERSITET:
JURIDICHESKIJ FAKUL'TET.
— VOPROSY GOSUDARSTVA I PRAVA (MINSK).
— VOPROSY SUDEBNOJ PSIKHOLOGII.

BELORUSSKIJ GOSUDARSTVENNYJ UNIVERSITET:
KAFEDRA NAUCHNOGO KOMMUNIZMA.
— VOPROSY NAUCHNOGO KOMMUNIZMA (MINSK).

BELORUSSKIJ POLITEKHNICHNICHESKIJ INSTITUT.
— PROGRESSIVNAJA TEKHNOLOGIJA MASHINOSTROENIJA.

BENDIX CORPORATION.
— BENDIX TECHNICAL JOURNAL.

BENELUX-MERKENBUREAU.
— BENELUX-MERKENBLAD. RECUEIL DES MARQUES
BENELUX.

BENNINGTON COLLEGE.
— BENNINGTON REVIEW. XXX

BEOGRADSKI UNIVERZITET.
— ANALI FILOLOSKOG FAKULTETA, BEOGRADSKI UNI-
VERZITET.
— DIJALEKTIKA. CASOPIS ZA OPSTE PROBLEME MATE-
MATICKIH, PRIRODNIH I TEHNICKIH NAUKA.

BERKELEY NUCLEAR LABORATORIES. 000
SEE: CENTRAL ELECTRICITY GENERATING BOARD: ...

BERMUDA BIOLOGICAL STATION FOR RESEARCH.
— NEWSLETTER, BERMUDA BIOLOGICAL STATION FOR
RESEARCH.
— SPECIAL PUBLICATIONS, BERMUDA BIOLOGICAL STA-
TION FOR RESEARCH.

BERTRAND RUSSELL ARCHIVES.
— RUSSELL. THE JOURNAL OF THE...

BERTRAND RUSSELL PEACE FOUNDATION.
— LONDON BULLETIN. XXX
— SPOKESMAN.

BEZIRKSHEIMATMUSEUM POTSDAM.
— VEROFFENTLICHUNGEN DES BEZIRKSHEIMATMUSEUMS
POTSDAM.

BIALOSTOCKIE TOWARZYSTWO NAUKOWE.
— PRACE BIALOSTOCKIEGO TOWARZYSTWA NAUKOWEGO.

BIBLE CHURCHMEN'S MISSIONARY SOCIETY.
— ON THE MOVE.

BIBLIOGRAPHICAL SOCIETY OF AUSTRALIA & NEW
ZEALAND.
— BULLETIN OF THE BIBLIOGRAPHICAL SOCIETY OF
AUSTRALIA & NEW ZEALAND.

BIBLIOGRAPHICAL SOCIETY OF CANADA.
— PAPERS, BIBLIOGRAPHICAL SOCIETY OF CANADA. XXX

BIBLIOTECA DEL MOVIMENTO OPERAIO ITALIANO.
— STUDI MEMORIE E DOCUMENTI, BIBLIOTECA DEL
MOVIMENTO OPERAIO ITALIANO.

BIBLIOTECA NACIONAL (PORTUGAL).
— REPERTORIO DAS PUBLICACOES PERIODICAS
PORTUGUESAS.

BIBLIOTECA NACIONAL (SALVADOR).
— SIGNO.

BIBLIOTECA NACIONAL (URUGUAY).
— REVISTA, BIBLIOTECA NACIONAL (URUGUAY).

BIBLIOTECA NACIONAL: CENTRO BIBLIOGRAFICO
VENEZOLANO.
— BIBLIOGRAFIA VENEZOLANA.

BIBLIOTEKA NARODOWA.
— BIULETYN INFORMACYJNY BIBLIOTEKI NARODOWEJ.
— ROCZNIK BIBLIOTEKI NARODOWEJ.

BIBLIOTHEQUE NATIONALE (ALGERIA).
— BIBLIOGRAPHIE DE L'ALGERIE.

BIBLIOTHEQUE NATIONALE (IVORY COAST).
— BIBLIOGRAPHIE DE LA COTE D'IVOIRE.

BIBLIOTHEQUE NATIONALE (QUEBEC).
— BIBLIOGRAPHIE DU QUEBEC.

BIHAR RESEARCH SOCIETY.
— INDIAN NUMISMATIC CHRONICLE.

BIO-CULT LABORATORIES LTD.
— TISSUE CULTURE ABSTRACTS, BIBLIOGRAPHY &
METHODS.

BIOCHEMICAL SOCIETY.
— BIOCHEMICAL JOURNAL: CELLULAR ASPECTS. XXX
— BIOCHEMICAL JOURNAL: MOLECULAR ASPECTS. XXX
— CLINICAL SCIENCE & MOLECULAR MEDICINE. XXX
— TRANSACTIONS, BIOCHEMICAL SOCIETY.

BIOLOGICAL RESEARCH CENTRE (BAGHDAD).
— PUBLICATIONS, BIOLOGICAL RESEARCH CENTRE
(BAGHDAD).

BIOLOGICAL SOCIETY OF NEVADA.
— MEMOIRES, BIOLOGICAL SOCIETY OF NEVADA.

BIOMEDICAL DOCUMENTATION CENTER.
— TERATOLOGY LOOKOUT.

BIOPHYSICAL SOCIETY OF JAPAN.
— ADVANCES IN BIOPHYSICS.

BIRKBECK COLLEGE.
— LIBRARY PUBLICATIONS, BIRKBECK COLLEGE,
UNIVERSITY OF LONDON.

BIRLA INSTITUTE OF TECHNOLOGY & SCIENCE.
— JOURNAL, BIRLA INSTITUTE OF TECHNOLOGY &
SCIENCE.

BIRMINGHAM LIBRARIES CO-OPERATIVE MECHANISATION
PROJECT.
— MASS WORKING PAPERS.

BIRMINGHAM POETRY CENTRE.
— MUSE.

BIRTH CONTROL CAMPAIGN.
— BULLETIN, BIRTH CONTROL CAMPAIGN.

BLACK KNIGHT ANARCHIST GROUP.
— BLACK PUDDING: MAGAZINE FOR FREE EXPRESSION.

BLACK WORLD FOUNDATION.
— BLACK SCHOLAR. JOURNAL OF BLACK STUDIES &
RESEARCH.

BLACKMORE SOCIETY.
— BLACKMORE STUDIES.

BLYTHSWOOD TRACT SOCIETY.
— BLYTHSWOOD TRACT SOCIETY MAGAZINE.

BOER-SENVEREIN DES DEUTSCHEN BUCHHANDELS.
— VERZEICHNIS LIEFERBARER BUCHER.

BOLIGINSTITUTTET FOR OSLO.
— PUBLIKASJONER, BOLIGINSTITUTTET FOR OSLO.

(BOLIVIA) MINISTERIO DE EDUCACION.
— REVISTA NACIONAL DE CULTURA (BOLIVIA).

BOLSA DE PRENSA.
— GUIA LATINOAMERICANA DE DIARIOS, REVISTAS Y
MEDIOS DE DIFUSION.

BOLUS HERBARIUM. 000
SEE: UNIVERSITY OF CAPE TOWN: BOLUS
HERBARIUM.

BORIS KIDRIC INSTITUTE OF NUCLEAR SCIENCES.
— PHYSICS OF SINTERING. XXX

BOROUGH OF TWICKENHAM LOCAL HISTORY SOCIETY.
— PAPERS, BOROUGH OF TWICKENHAM LOCAL HISTORY
SOCIETY.

BOSTON COLLEGE: INSTITUTE OF HUMAN SCIENCES.
— REVIEW, INSTITUTE OF HUMAN SCIENCES, BOSTON
COLLEGE. XXX
SUBS (1969): URBAN & SOCIAL CHANGE REVIEW.
— URBAN & SOCIAL CHANGE REVIEW. XXX

BOSTON UNIVERSITY: AFRICAN STUDIES CENTER.
— AFRICAN HISTORICAL STUDIES. XXX

BOTANICAL SOCIETY OF THE BRITISH ISLES.
— BSBI ABSTRACTS. ABSTRACTS OF LITERATURE
RELATING TO THE VASCULAR PLANTS OF THE
BRITISH ISLES.
— BSBI NEWS.

(BOTSWANA) NATIONAL LIBRARY SERVICE.
— NATIONAL BIBLIOGRAPHY OF BOTSWANA.

BOTSWANA CO-OPERATIVE DEVELOPMENT CENTRE. 000
SEE: INTERNATIONAL LABOUR ORGANIZATION:
BOTSWANA CO-OPERATIVE DEVELOPMENT CENTRE.

BOWDOIN COLLEGE.
— BRITISH STUDIES MONITOR.

BOYCE THOMPSON INSTITUTE FOR PLANT RESEARCH.
— CONTRIBUTIONS FROM BOYCE THOMPSON INSTITUTE
FOR PLANT RESEARCH. XXX

BRADFORD WRITER'S CIRCLE.
— QUARTO.

BRANDENBURGISCHEN LANDES- UND HOCHSHULBIBLIO-
THEK.
— FONTANE BLATTER. (KREIS DER FREUNDE THEODOR
FONTANES).

(BRAZIL) DEPARTAMENTO DE PESQUISAS E EXPER-
IMENTACAO AGROPECUARIAS.
— PESQUISA AGROPECUARIA BRASILEIRA.  XXX

(BRAZIL) MINISTERIO DA AGRICULTURA: ESCRITORIO
DE METEOROLOGIA.
— BOLETIM CLIMATOLOGICO (BRAZIL).

(BRAZIL) MINISTERIO DA AGRICULTURA: ESCRITORIO
DE PESQUISAS E EXPERIMENTACAO.
— PESQUISA AGROPECUARIA BRASILEIRA: SERIE
AGRONOMIA.  XXX
— PESQUISA AGROPECUARIA BRASILEIRA: SERIE
VETERINARIA.  XXX

(BRAZIL) MINISTERIO DA EDUCACAO E CULTURA:
DIRECTORIA DE DOCUMENTACAO E DIVULGACAO.
— CULTURA.
— EDUCACAO (BRAZIL).

(BRAZIL) MINISTERIO DA INDUSTRIA E DO COMERCIO.
— POLIMEROS.

(BRAZIL) SUPERINTENDENCIA DO DESENVOLVIMENTO
DO NORDESTE.
— SUDENE. BOLETIM DE RECURSOS NATURAIS.

BRECKNOCK COUNTY NATURALISTS' TRUST.
— BRECONSHIRE BIRDS.

BRESLAU POLITECHNIKA.
— OPTICA APPLICATA.

BRICK DEVELOPMENT ASSOCIATION.
— BDA RESEARCH NOTES.
— BDA TECHNICAL NOTE.

BRIGHAM YOUNG UNIVERSITY.
— SPECIAL PUBLICATIONS, BRIGHAM YOUNG UNIVER-
SITY GEOLOGY STUDIES.

BRISTOL ARTS CENTRE: POETRY CIRCLE.
— POETRY OF THE CIRCLE IN THE SQUARE.

BRISTOL INDUSTRIAL ARCHAEOLOGICAL SOCIETY.
— BIAS BULLETIN.
— BIAS JOURNAL. JOURNAL OF THE BRISTOL INDUST-
RIAL ARCHAEOLOGICAL SOCIETY.

BRITISH AGRICULTURAL & GARDEN MACHINERY
ASSOCIATION.
— AGRICULTURAL & GARDEN MACHINERY SERVICE.

BRITISH ALLERGY SOCIETY.
— CLINICAL ALLERGY. JOURNAL OF THE BRITISH
ALLERGY SOCIETY.

BRITISH ALUMINIUM CO. LTD.
— INDUSTRIAL ENGINEERING ABSTRACTS.

BRITISH ANIMAL NURSING AUXILIARIES ASSOCIATION.
— BANAA JOURNAL.

BRITISH ARACHNOLOGICAL SOCIETY.
— BULLETIN, BRITISH ARACHNOLOGICAL SOCIETY.  XXX
— NEWSLETTER, BRITISH ARACHNOLOGICAL SOCIETY.

BRITISH ASSOCIATION FOR THE ADVANCEMENT OF
SCIENCE.
— ADVANCEMENT OF SCIENCE.  XXX

BRITISH ASSOCIATION FOR AMERICAN STUDIES.
— BULLETIN OF THE BRITISH ASSOCIATION FOR
AMERICAN STUDIES: NS.  XXX

BRITISH ASSOCIATION FOR COMMERCIAL & INDUSTRIAL
EDUCATION.
— BACIE NEWS.  XXX

BRITISH ASSOCIATION OF GREEN CROP DRIERS.
— GRASS.

BRITISH ASSOCIATION OF INDUSTRIAL EDITORS.
— BAIE NEWSLETTER.
— NEWS OF THE BRITISH ASSOCIATION OF INDUSTRIAL
EDITORS.

BRITISH ASSOCIATION OF ORTHODONTISTS.
— ORTHODONTIST.  XXX

BRITISH ASSOCIATION OF PHYSICAL MEDICINE.
— RHEUMATOLOGY & PHYSICAL MEDICINE.  XXX

BRITISH ASSOCIATION FOR RHEUMATOLOGY &
REHABILITATION.
— RHEUMATOLOGY & REHABILITATION.  XXX

BRITISH ASSOCIATION OF SOCIAL WORKERS.
— BRITISH JOURNAL OF SOCIAL WORK.  XXX
— DISCUSSION PAPER, BRITISH ASSOCIATION OF SOC-
IAL WORKERS.
— PARLIAMENT & SOCIAL WORK.
— SOCIAL WORK TODAY. JOURNAL OF THE ...

BRITISH ASSOCIATION OF SPORT & MEDICINE.
— BRITISH JOURNAL OF SPORTS MEDICINE.

BRITISH BLIND & SHUTTER ASSOCIATION.
— BLINDMAKER.  XXX
SUBS (1972): BLINDS & SHUTTERS.
— BLINDS & SHUTTERS.  XXX

BRITISH BROADCASTING CORPORATION.
— BBC ENGINEERING.  XXX

BRITISH BROADCASTING CORPORATION: ENGINEERING
DIVISION.
— BBC ENGINEERING DIVISION MONOGRAPH.  XXX
SUBS (1970): BBC ENGINEERING.

BRITISH BROMELIAD SOCIETY.
— BROMELIADS. JOURNAL OF THE...

BRITISH BRYOLOGICAL SOCIETY.
— JOURNAL OF BRYOLOGY.  XXX
— TRANSACTIONS, BRITISH BRYOLOGICAL SOCIETY.  XXX
SUBS (1972): JOURNAL OF BRYOLOGY.

BRITISH BUREAU OF TELEVISION ADVERTISING.
— OCCASIONAL PAPERS, BRITISH BUREAU OF TELEVIS-
ION ADVERTISING.

BRITISH CAMPAIGN TO STOP IMMIGRATION.
— BRITISH PATRIOT.

BRITISH CELLOPHANE LTD.
— CELLOSCOPE.

BRITISH CERAMIC SOCIETY.
— TRANSACTIONS & JOURNAL, BRITISH CERAMIC
SOCIETY.  XXX

(BRITISH COLUMBIA) DEPARTMENT OF LABOUR:
RESEARCH BRANCH.
— LABOUR RESEARCH BULLETIN (BRITISH COLUMBIA).

(BRITISH COLUMBIA) WORKMEN'S COMPENSATION BOARD
— WORKMEN'S COMPENSATION REPORTER.

BRITISH COLUMBIA PROVINCIAL MUSEUM.
— SYESIS.

BRITISH COMPUTER SOCIETY.
— ARTIFICIAL INTELLIGENCE.
— COMPUTER BULLETIN.  XXX

BRITISH COUNCIL.
— BRITISH MEDICINE.  XXX

BRITISH DAIRY FARMERS' ASSOCIATION.  XXX
— JOURNAL, BRITISH DAIRY FARMERS' ASSOCIATION.  XXX
SUBS (1961): JOURNAL, ROYAL ASSOCIATION OF
BRITISH DAIRY FARMERS.

BRITISH DENTAL ASSOCIATION: WESTERN COUNTIES
BRANCH.
— CONTACT POINT.

BRITISH ECOLOGICAL SOCIETY.
— BULLETIN, BRITISH ECOLOGICAL SOCIETY.

BRITISH EDUCATIONAL ADMINISTRATION SOCIETY.
— EDUCATIONAL ADMINISTRATION BULLETIN.

BRITISH ENDODONTIC SOCIETY.
— JOURNAL OF THE BRITISH ENDODONTIC SOCIETY.

BRITISH ENTOMOLOGICAL & NATURAL HISTORY SOCIETY
— PROCEEDINGS & TRANSACTIONS OF THE BRITISH
ENTOMOLOGICAL & NATURAL HISTORY SOCIETY.  XXX

BRITISH EQUINE VETERINARY ASSOCIATION.
— EQUINE VETERINARY JOURNAL.

BRITISH ESPERANTO ASSOCIATION.
— NEWSLETTER, BRITISH ESPERANTO ASSOCIATION.

BRITISH GEOMORPHOLOGICAL RESEARCH GROUP.
— OCCASIONAL PAPERS, BRITISH GEOMORPHOLOGICAL
RESEARCH GROUP.  XXX
— TECHNICAL BULLETIN, BRITISH GEOMORPHOLOGICAL
RESEARCH GROUP.

BRITISH GERIATRICS SOCIETY.
— AGE & AGEING.

BRITISH GLUES & CHEMICALS LTD: AGRICULTURAL
DEPARTMENT.
— FEED FORUM.                                           XXX

BRITISH HEART FOUNDATION.
— HEART BULLETIN: NS (LONDON).                          XXX

(BRITISH HONDURAS) GOVERNMENT INFORMATION
SERVICE.
— NEW BELIZE.

BRITISH HUMANIST ASSOCIATION.
— HUMANIST NEWSLETTER.

BRITISH HYDROMECHANICS RESEARCH ASSOCIATION.
— CHANNEL.
— INDUSTRIAL AERODYNAMICS ABSTRACTS.
— PUMPS & OTHER FLUIDS MACHINERY ABSTRACTS.
— TRIBOS. TRIBOLOGY ABSTRACTS.

BRITISH INDUSTRIAL TRUCK ASSOCIATION.
— B.I.T.A. BULLETIN.

BRITISH INSTITUTE OF INTERNATIONAL & COMPARAT-
IVE LAW.
— QUARTERLY NEWSLETTER OF THE BRITISH INSTITUTE
OF INTERNATIONAL & COMPARATIVE LAW.

BRITISH INSTITUTE OF MANAGEMENT.
— B.I.M. NOTES FOR COLLECTIVE SUBSCRIBERS.           XXX
SUBS (1971): B.I.M. QUARTERLY REVIEW ...
— B.I.M. QUARTERLY REVIEW OF SERVICES FOR
COLLECTIVE SUBSCRIBERS.                                XXX
— OCCASIONAL PAPERS, BRITISH INSTITUTE OF MAN-
AGEMENT: NS.

BRITISH INSTITUTE OF MANAGEMENT: BRISTOL BRANCH
— DISCUSSION PAPER, BRISTOL BRANCH, BRITISH
INSTITUTE OF MANAGEMENT.

BRITISH INSTITUTION OF RADIO ENGINEERS: INDIAN
DIVISION.
— PROCEEDINGS, INDIAN DIVISION, BRITISH INSTIT-
UTION OF RADIO ENGINEERS.                              XXX

BRITISH INTERPLANETARY SOCIETY.
— JOURNAL OF THE BRITISH INTERPLANETARY SOCIETY.

BRITISH & IRISH ASSOCIATION OF LAW LIBRARIANS.
— LAW LIBRARIAN. BULLETIN OF THE ...

BRITISH & IRISH COMMUNIST ORGANISATION.
— WORKERS' WEEKLY.

BRITISH IRON & STEEL RESEARCH ASSOCIATION.
— ANNUAL REPORT, BRITISH IRON & STEEL RESEARCH
ASSOCIATION.                                           XXX
SUBS (1971): STEELRESEARCH.

BRITISH LEYLAND MOTOR CORPORATION LTD.
— HIGH ROAD.

BRITISH LIBRARY: LENDING DIVISION.                     XXX
— BLL ANNOUNCEMENT BULLETIN. A GUIDE TO BRITISH
REPORTS, TRANSLATIONS & THESES.                        XXX
— BLL REVIEW.                                          XXX
— INDEX OF CONFERENCE PROCEEDINGS RECEIVED BY
THE BLL.                                               XXX

BRITISH LIGHTING INDUSTRIES, LTD.
— LIGHTING JOURNAL.

BRITISH MEDICAL ASSOCIATION.
— PSYCHOLOGICAL MEDICINE.

BRITISH MEDICAL ASSOCIATION: DEPARTMENT OF
AUDIO VISUAL COMMUNICATION.
— INFORMATION, DEPARTMENT OF AUDIO VISUAL
COMMUNICATION, BRITISH MEDICAL ASSOCIATION.

BRITISH MEDICAL ASSOCIATION: PLANNING UNIT.
— PLANNING UNIT REPORT, BRITISH MEDICAL
ASSOCIATION.

BRITISH MEDICAL STUDENTS' ASSOCIATION.
— SCOPE.

BRITISH MENSA LTD.
— BRITISH MENSA MAGAZINE.

BRITISH MUSEUM SOCIETY.
— BRITISH MUSEUM SOCIETY BULLETIN.

BRITISH NATIONAL BIBLIOGRAPHY.
— PUBLICATIONS, BNB MARC DOCUMENTATION SERVICE.

BRITISH NATIONAL EXPORT COUNCIL.
— EXPORT CLUB NEWS.

BRITISH NON-FERROUS METALS RESEARCH ASSOCIATION
— BNF ABSTRACTS.                                       XXX
— BULLETIN, BRITISH NON-FERROUS METALS RESEARCH
ASSOCIATION.                                           XXX
SUBS (1970): BNF ABSTRACTS.

BRITISH NUCLEAR FORUM.
— BNF NEWS SHEET.

BRITISH NUTRITION FOUNDATION LTD.
— INFORMATION BULLETIN, BRITISH NUTRITION FOUN-
DATION LTD.

BRITISH PARENT EDUCATION INFORMATION CIRCLE.
— PARENT EDUCATOR.                                     XXX
— QUARTERLY BULLETIN OF THE BRITISH PARENT EDUC-
ATION INFORMATION CIRCLE.                              XXX

BRITISH PELARGONIUM & GERANIUM SOCIETY.
— BULLETIN, BRITISH PELARGONIUM & GERANIUM
SOCIETY.                                               XXX
— PELARGONIUM NEWS.                                    XXX

BRITISH PHARMACOLOGICAL SOCIETY.
— BRITISH JOURNAL OF PHARMACOLOGY.*

BRITISH PHYCOLOGICAL SOCIETY.
— BRITISH PHYCOLOGICAL BULLETIN.                       XXX
SUBS: (1969) BRITISH PHYCOLOGICAL JOURNAL.
— BRITISH PHYCOLOGICAL JOURNAL.
— NEWSLETTER, BRITISH PHYCOLOGICAL SOCIETY.

BRITISH PREMIUM MANUFACTURERS ASSOCIATION.
— BPMA NEWS.

BRITISH QUARRYING & SLAG FEDERATION.
— TECHNICAL REVIEW, BRITISH QUARRYING & SLAG
FEDERATION.

BRITISH RAILWAYS BOARD.
— TRAVELLING.

BRITISH RECORDS ASSOCIATION.
— ARCHIVES & THE USER.

BRITISH RED CROSS SOCIETY.
— CROSS TALK. MAGAZINE OF THE ...                     XXX

BRITISH RORSCHACH FORUM.
— BRITISH JOURNAL OF PROJECTIVE PSYCHOLOGY &
PERSONALITY STUDY.                                     XXX
— RORSCHACH NEWSLETTER.                                XXX
SUBS (1969): BRITISH JOURNAL OF PROJECTIVE
PSYCHOLOGY & PERSONALITY STUDY.

BRITISH SCHOOL OF ARCHAEOLOGY IN JERUSALEM.
— LEVANT. JOURNAL OF THE...

BRITISH SCIENTIFIC INSTRUMENT RESEARCH
ASSOCIATION.
— INSTRUMENT ABSTRACTS.                                XXX
SUBS(1968): SIRA ABSTRACTS & REVIEWS.
— METRON. SIRA MEASUREMENT & CONTROL ABSTRACTS
& REVIEWS.                                             XXX
— SIRA ABSTRACTS & REVIEWS.                            XXX

BRITISH SHIP RESEARCH ASSOCIATION.
— JOURNAL OF ABSTRACTS, BRITISH SHIP RESEARCH
ASSOCIATION.                                           XXX
— JOURNAL, BRITISH SHIP RESEARCH ASSOCIATION.*        XXX
SUBS (1968): JOURNAL OF ABSTRACTS, BRITISH
SHIP RESEARCH ASSOCIATION

BRITISH SHIPPING FEDERATION.
— UK SHIPPING NEWS.

BRITISH SOCIETY FOR AGRICULTURAL LABOUR SCIENCE
— JOURNAL OF AGRICULTURAL LABOUR SCIENCE.

BRITISH SOCIETY OF AUDIOLOGY.
— BRITISH JOURNAL OF AUDIOLOGY.                        XXX

BRITISH SOCIETY FOR EIGHTEENTH-CENTURY STUDIES.
— NEWSLETTER, BRITISH SOCIETY FOR EIGHTEENTH-
CENTURY STUDIES.

BRITISH SOCIETY FOR THE HISTORY OF PHARMACY.
— PHARMACEUTICAL HISTORIAN. NEWSLETTER OF ...
— TRANSACTIONS, BRITISH SOCIETY FOR THE HISTORY
OF PHARMACY.

**BRITISH SOCIETY FOR INTERNATIONAL UNDERSTANDING**
— BRITISH SURVEY.                                                                      XXX
  SUBS (1969): WORLD SURVEY.

**BRITISH SOCIETY OF MUSIC THERAPY.**
— BRITISH JOURNAL OF MUSIC THERAPY.

**BRITISH SOCIETY FOR PHENOMENOLOGY.**
— JOURNAL, BRITISH SOCIETY FOR PHENOMENOLOGY.

**BRITISH SOCIETY FOR RESEARCH ON AGEING.**
— AGE & AGEING.

**BRITISH SOCIETY FOR SOCIAL RESPONSIBILITY IN SCIENCE.**
— BSSRS NEWSHEET.

**BRITISH SOCIETY FOR SURGERY OF THE HAND.**
— HAND. JOURNAL OF THE BRITISH SOCIETY FOR SURGERY OF THE HAND.

**BRITISH STANDARDS INSTITUTION.**
— LIST OF OVERSEA STANDARDS.                                                 XXX
— OVERSEA & COMMONWEALTH STANDARDS.                                XXX
  SUBS (1969): LIST OF OVERSEA STANDARDS.

**BRITISH STEEL CORPORATION.**
— BRITISH STEEL.
— REPORTS ON ORGANISATION, BRITISH STEEL CORPORATION.
— SPECIAL STEELS REVIEW.                                                          XXX
— STEEL METRICATION BULLETIN.
— STEELRESEARCH.                                                                        XXX

**BRITISH STEEL CORPORATION: STRIP MILLS DIVISION**
— STRIP MILL PRODUCTS REVIEW.

**BRITISH SULPHUR CORPORATION.**
— FERTILIZER INTERNATIONAL.
— STATISTICAL SUPPLEMENT TO SULPHUR, NITROGEN & PHOSPHORUS & POTASSIUM.
— WORLD FEEDS & PROTEIN NEWS.                                              XXX
— WORLD MINERALS & METALS.

**BRITISH TAR INDUSTRY ASSOCIATION.**

**BRITISH THORACIC & TUBERCULOSIS ASSOCIATION.**
— B.T.T.A. REVIEW.

**BRITISH UNIVERSITIES FILM COUNCIL.**
— NEWSLETTER, BRITISH UNIVERSITIES FILM COUNCIL.
— UNIVERSITY VISION. THE JOURNAL OF THE ...

**BRITISH URBAN & REGIONAL INFORMATION SYSTEMS ASSOCIATION.**
— BURISA NEWSLETTER.

**BRITISH WATERWAYS BOARD.**
— WATERWAYS NEWS.

**BRITISH WATERWORKS ASSOCIATION.**
— BRITISH WATER SUPPLY.
— JOURNAL, BRITISH WATERWORKS ASSOCIATION.                          XXX
  SUBS (1969): BRITISH WATER SUPPLY.

**BROOKINGS INSTITUTION.**
— BROOKINGS PAPERS ON ECONOMIC ACTIVITY.

**BROOKLYN MUSEUM: WILBOUR LIBRARY OF EGYPTOLOGY.**                                                                           000
  SEE: WILBOUR LIBRARY OF EGYPTOLOGY.

**BROWN UNIVERSITY: PSYCHOLOGY DEPARTMENT.**
— LABORATORY PRIMATE NEWSLETTER.

**BRUNEI MUSEUM.**
— BRUNEI MUSEUM JOURNAL.

**BRUNEL INDUSTRIAL LIAISON BUREAU.**                                      000
  SEE: BRUNEL UNIVERSITY: BRUNEL INDUSTRIAL LIAISON BUREAU.

**BRUNEL UNIVERSITY: BRUNEL INDUSTRIAL LIAISON BUREAU.**
— NEWSLETTER, BRUNEL INDUSTRIAL LIAISON BUREAU.

**BUILD FOUNDATION.**
— BUILD INTERNATIONAL.

**BUILDING CENTRE (LONDON).**
— BUILDING CENTRE INTELLIGENCE REPORT.

**BUILDING CENTRE TRUST.**
— INTELLIGENCE REPORT, BUILDING CENTRE TRUST.

**BUILDING RESEARCH ESTABLISHMENT (G.B.): PRINCES RISBOROUGH LABORATORY.**
— TECHNICAL NOTE, PRINCES RISBOROUGH LABORATORY, BUILDING RESEARCH ESTABLISHMENT (GB).                            XXX

**BUILDING RESEARCH INSTITUTE (TOKYO).**
— BRI OCCASIONAL REPORT.                                                           XXX

**BUILDING RESEARCH STATION (GB).**
— BUILDING RESEARCH CURRENT PAPERS; CONSTRUCTION SERIES.
— BUILDING RESEARCH CURRENT PAPERS; ENGINEERING SERIES.

**(BULGARIA) MINISTERSTVO NA ENERGETIKATA I GORIVATA.**
— ENERGETIKA (SOFIA).                                                                 XXX

**(BULGARIA) MINISTERSTVO SUVET: TSENTRALNO STATISTICHESKO UPRAVLENIE.**
— FINANSOVA STATISTIKA, STATISTICHESKIJ SBORNIK.

**(BULGARIA) MINISTERSTVO NA TEZHKATA PROMISH-LENOST.**
— MASHINOSTROENIE.                                                                   XXX

**BULGARSKA AKADEMIJA NA NAUKITE: GEOLOGICHESKI INSTITUT.**
— IZVESTIJA NA GEOLOGICHESKIJA INSTITUT, BULGARSKA AKADEMIJA NA NAUKITE: SERIJA GEOTEKTONIKA, STRATIGRAFIJA I LITOLOGIJA.                    XXX
— IZVESTIJA NA GEOLOGICHESKIJA INSTITUT, BULGARSKA AKADEMIJA NA NAUKITE: SERIJA INZHENERNA GEOLOGIJA I KHIDROGEOLOGIJA.                      XXX
— IZVESTIJA NA GEOLOGICHESKIJA INSTITUT, BULGARSKA AKADEMIJA NA NAUKITE: SERIJA PALEONTOLOGIJA.                                                                 XXX
— TRUDOVE VURKHU GEOLOGIJATA NA BULGARIJA: SERIJA INZHENERNA GEOLOGIJA I KHIDROGEOLOGIJA.

**BULGARSKA AKADEMIJA NA NAUKITE: INSTITUT ZA BALKANISTIKA.**
— BULGARSKA AKADEMIJA NA NAUKITE: INSTITUT ZA BALKANISTIKA: SERIJA: IZVORI.

**BULGARSKA AKADEMIJA NA NAUKITE: INSTITUT ZA BULGARSKI EZIK.**
— TRUDOVE PO BULGARSKA DIALEKTOLOGIJA.

**BULGARSKA AKADEMIJA NA NAUKITE: (INSTITUT D'ETUDES BALKANIQUES).**
— BIBLIOGRAPHIE D'ETUDES BALKANIQUES.

**BULGARSKA AKADEMIJA NA NAUKITE: INSTITUT ZA IZKUSTVOZNANIE.**
— PROBLEMI NA IZKUSTVOTO.

**BULGARSKA AKADEMIJA NA NAUKITE: INSTITUT ZA LITERATURA.**
— PAMETNITSI NA STARATA BULGARSKA PISMENOST.

**BULGARSKA AKADEMIJA NA NAUKITE: OTDELENIE ZA KHIMICHESKI NAUKI.**
— IZVESTIJA NA OTDELENIETO ZA KHIMICHESKI NAUKI, BULGARSKA AKADEMIJA NA NAUKITE.                                       XXX

**BULGARSKA AKADEMIJA NA NAUKITE: PROBLEMNA KOMISIJA ZA IZUCHAVANE MINALOTO, BITA I KULTURATA NA NASELENIETO V RODOPITE.**
— RODOPSKI SBORNIK.

**BULGARSKA AKADEMIJA NA NAUKITE: ZOOLOGICHESKIJ INSTITUT S MUZEJ.**
— FAUNA NA TRAKIJA.

**BULGARSKA KOMUNISTICHESKA PARTIJA: OKRUZHEN KOMITET.**
— CHELEN OPIT V SELSKOTO STOPANSTVO.

**BULGARSKA KOMUNISTICHESKA PARTIJA: TSENTRALEN KOMITET.**
— IKONOMICHESKI ZHIVOT.

**BUNDA COLLEGE OF AGRICULTURE.**
— RESEARCH BULLETIN, BUNDA COLLEGE OF AGRICULTURE.

**BUNDESANSTALT FUR MATERIALPRUEFUNG.**
— DOKUMENTATION: VERSCHLEISS, REIBUNG UND SCHMIERUNG. DOCUMENTATION: WEAR, FRICTION & LUBRICATION.

**BUNDESANSTALT FUR VEGETATIONSKUNDE, NATURSCHUTZ & LANDSCHAFTSPFLEGE.**
— SCHRIFTENREIHE FUR VEGETATIONSKUNDE.

BUNYAD-I FARHANG-I IRAN.                                      000
  SEE: IRANIAN CULTURE FOUNDATION.

BUREAU FOR ECONOMIC POLICY & ANALYSIS (SOUTH
AFRICA).
  — PUBLICATION, BUREAU FOR ECONOMIC POLICY &
    ANALYSIS (SOUTH AFRICA).

BUREAU INTERNATIONAL DE L'EDITION MECANIQUE.
  — BULLETIN, BUREAU INTERNATIONAL DE L'EDITION
    MECANIQUE.                                               XXX
    SUBS (1968): BULLETIN, BUREAU INTERNATIONAL
    DES SOCIETES GERANT LES DROITS D'ENREGISTRE-
    MENT ET DE REPRODUCTION MECANIQUE.

BUREAU INTERNATIONAL DES POIDS ET MESURES.
  — RECUEIL DE TRAVAUX, BUREAU INTERNATIONAL DES
    POIDS ET MESURES.

BUREAU INTERNATIONAL DES SOCIETES GERANT LES
DROITS D'ENREGISTREMENT ET DE REPRODUCTION
MECANIQUE.
  — BULLETIN, BUREAU INTERNATIONAL DES SOCIETES
    GERANT LES DROITS D'ENREGISTREMENT ET DE REP-
    RODUCTION MECANIQUE.                                     XXX

BUREAU OF MEDICAL PRACTITIONER AFFAIRS.
  — MODERN MANAGEMENT & ADMINISTRATION IN GENERAL
    PRACTICE.

BUREAU DE RECHERCHES GEOLOGIQUES & MINIERES
(FRANCE).
  — BIBLIOGRAPHIE DES SCIENCES DE LA TERRE:
    CAHIER A: MINERALOGIE ET GEOCHIMIE.                      XXX
  — BIBLIOGRAPHIE DES SCIENCES DE LA TERRE:
    CAHIER B: GITOLOGIE ET ECONOMIE MINIERE.
  — BIBLIOGRAPHIE DES SCIENCES DE LA TERRE:
    CAHIER C: ROCHES CRISTALLINES.                           XXX
  — BIBLIOGRAPHIE DES SCIENCES DE LA TERRE:
    CAHIER D: ROCHES SEDIMENTAIRES.                          XXX
  — BIBLIOGRAPHIE DES SCIENCES DE LA TERRE: CAH-
    IER E: STRATIGRAPHIE ET GEOLOGIE REGIONALE.              XXX
  — BIBLIOGRAPHIE DES SCIENCES DE LA TERRE:
    CAHIER F: TECTONIQUE ET GEOPHYSIQUE.                     XXX
  — BIBLIOGRAPHIE DES SCIENCES DE LA TERRE:
    CAHIER G: HYDROGEOLOGIE ET GEOLOGIE DE
    L'INGENIEUR.                                             XXX
  — BIBLIOGRAPHIE DES SCIENCES DE LA TERRE: CAH-
    IER H: PALEONTOLOGIE.                                    XXX
  — BULLETIN DU BUREAU DE RECHERCHES GEOLOGIQUES
    ET MINIERES: 2S: SECTION 2. GEOLOGIE
    APPLIQUEE.                                               XXX
  — BULLETIN, BUREAU DE RECHERCHES GEOLOGIQUES ET
    MINIERES: 2S: SECTION 3: HYDROGEOLOGIE.
  — BULLETIN, BUREAU DE RECHERCHES GEOLOGIQUES ET
    MINIERES: 2S: SECTION 4: GEOLOGIE ET
    GENERALE.                                                XXX
  — CHRONIQUE D'HYDROGEOLOGIE.                               XXX

BUREAU.DES TEMPS ELEMENTAIRES.
  — ETUDE DU TRAVAIL.                                        XXX
    SUBS (1973): PRODUCTION ET GESTION: ETUDE
    DU TRAVAIL.
  — PRODUCTION ET GESTION : L'ETUDE DU TRAVAIL.              XXX

BURJATSKIJ KOMPLEKSNYJ NAUCHNO-ISSLEDOVAT-
EL'SKIJ INSTITUT: KOMISSIJA PO IZUCHENIJU MIK-
ROELEMENTOV.
  — MIKROELEMENTY V SIBIRI.

BURMA MEDICAL RESEARCH INSTITUTE.
  — UNION OF BURMA JOURNAL OF LIFE SCIENCES.

BURMAH-CASTRCL INDUSTRIAL LTD.
  — INDUSTRIAL OILS REVIEW.

BURNHAM ON CROUCH & DISTRICT LOCAL HISTORY
SOCIETY.
  — BULLETIN, BURNHAM ON CROUCH & DISTRICT LOCAL
    HISTORY SOCIETY.

BURROUGHS MACHINES LTD.
  — DECIMAL POINTS.

BUSINESS ARCHIVES COUNCIL OF SCOTLAND.
  — NEWSLETTER, BUSINESS ARCHIVES COUNCIL OF
    SCOTLAND.

BUTLER SOCIETY.
  — JOURNAL, BUTLER SOCIETY.

BUXTON FIELD CLUB.
  — REPORT, BUXTON FIELD CLUB.

BYDGOSKIE TOWARZYSTWO NAUKOWE.
  — BYDGOSTIANA.
  — PRACE WYDIALU NAUK HUMANISTYCZNYCH, BYDGOS-
    KIE TOWARZYSTWO NAUKOWE - SERIA B.

BYRON SOCIETY.
  — BYRON JOURNAL.

CAIRO UNIVERSITY HERBARIUM.
  — PUBLICATIONS, CAIRO UNIVERSITY HERBARIUM.

CALIFORNIA ACADEMY OF PERIODONTOLOGY.
  — PARODONTOLOGIE & ACADEMY REVIEW.

CALIFORNIA FIELD ORNITHOLOGISTS.
  — CALIFORNIA BIRDS.                                        XXX

CALIFORNIA INSTITUTE OF INTERNATIONAL STUDIES.
  — REPORT, CALIFORNIA INSTITUTE OF INTERNATIONAL
    STUDIES.                                                 XXX
  — WORLD AFFAIRS REPORT.                                    XXX

CALIFORNIA INSTITUTE OF TECHNOLOGY: JET
PROPULSION LABORATORY.
  — JPL QUARTERLY TECHNICAL REVIEW.

CAMBORNE-REDRUTH NATURAL HISTORY SOCIETY.
  — JOURNAL OF THE CAMBORNE-REDRUTH NATURAL
    HISTORY SOCIETY.

CAMBRIDGE & COUNTY FOLK MUSEUM.
  — MUSEUM BOOKLET, CAMBRIDGE & COUNTY FOLK
    MUSEUM.

CAMBRIDGE GROUP FOR THE HISTORY OF POPULATION
AND SOCIAL STRUCTURE.
  — LOCAL POPULATION STUDIES. MAGAZINE & NEWS-
    LETTER.

CAMBRIDGESHIRE COLLEGE OF ARTS & TECHNOLOGY:
GEOGRAPHY DEPARTMENT.
  — GEOPHILE.

(CANADA) COURTS.
  — REPORTS OF FAMILY LAW.

(CANADA) DEPARTMENT OF AGRICULTURE: ECONOMICS
BRANCH.
  — CANADIAN AGRICULTURAL OUTLOOK.
  — CANADIAN AGRICULTURAL SITUATION.

(CANADA) DEPARTMENT OF AGRICULTURE: RESEARCH
BRANCH.
  — CANADIAN AGRICULTURAL INSECT PEST REVIEW.               XXX
  — CANADIAN INSECT PEST REVIEW.                             XXX
    SUBS (1968): CANADIAN AGRICULTURAL INSECT
    PEST REVIEW.

(CANADA) DEPARTMENT OF ENERGY, MINES & RESOUR-
CES: MARINE SCIENCES BRANCH.
  — PAPERS, MARINE SCIENCES BRANCH, DEPARTMENT OF
    ENERGY, MINES & RESOURCES (CANADA).                      XXX

(CANADA) DEPARTMENT OF ENERGY, MINES &
RESOURCES: POLICY RESEARCH & CO-ORDINATION
BRANCH.
  — RESOURCE PAPER, POLICY RESEARCH & CO-ORDINAT-
    ION BRANCH, DEPARTMENT OF ENERGY, MINES &

(CANADA) DEPARTMENT OF THE ENVIRONMENT: MARINE
SCIENCES BRANCH.
  — MARINE SCIENCE PAPERS.                                   XXX

(CANADA) DEPARTMENT OF EXTERNAL AFFAIRS.
  — EXTERNAL AFFAIRS.                                        XXX
    SUBS (1972): INTERNATIONAL PERSPECTIVES.
  — INTERNATIONAL PERSPECTIVES.                              XXX

(CANADA) DEPARTMENT OF INDIAN AFFAIRS &
NORTHERN DEVELOPMENT.
  — TAWOW. CANADIAN INDIAN CULTURAL MAGAZINE.
  — TECHNICAL NOTES, DEPARTMENT OF INDIAN AFFAIRS
    & NORTHERN DEVELOPMENT (CANADA).

(CANADA) DEPARTMENT OF LABOUR.
  — LABOUR & INDUSTRIAL RELATIONS RESEARCH IN
    CANADA. = RECHERCHE SUR LE TRAVAIL ET LES
    RELATIONS INDUSTRIELLES AU CANADA.

(CANADA) DEPARTMENT OF NATIONAL HEALTH & WELF-
ARE: OFFICE OF PLANNING & DEVELOPMENT.
  — CANADA PENSION PLAN. STATISTICAL BULLETIN.

(CANADA) DEPARTMENT OF SUPPLY & SERVICES:
BUREAU OF MANAGEMENT CONSULTING.
  — OPTIMUM. A FORUM FOR MANAGEMENT.

(CANADA) DOMINION BUREAU OF STATISTICS.
— CONSTRUCTION MACHINERY & EQUIPMENT SALES.
— SYSTEM OF NATIONAL ACCOUNTS: FINANCIAL
  ACCOUNTS.

(CANADA) DOMINION BUREAU OF STATISTICS:
AGRICULTURAL BRANCH.
— COARSE GRAINS REVIEW.                                    xxx

(CANADA) DOMINION BUREAU OF STATISTICS:
INFORMATION DIVISION.
— STATISTICAL OBSERVER.

(CANADA) HIGH COMMISSION IN LONDON.
— CANADA TODAY.

(CANADA) LAW REFORM COMMISSION.
— ANNUAL REPORT OF THE LAW REFORM COMMISSION OF
  CANADA.

(CANADA) STATISTICS CANADA: CENSUS DIVISION.              xxx
— CENSUS DATA NEWS.

CANADIAN AERONAUTICS & SPACE INSTITUTE.
— CASI TRANSACTIONS.

CANADIAN AMPHIBIAN & REPTILE CONSERVATION SOC-
IETY.
— BULLETIN, CANADIAN AMPHIBIAN & REPTILE CONS-
  ERVATION SOCIETY.
— BULLETIN, CANADIAN AMPHIBIAN & REPTILE CONS-
  ERVATION SOCIETY: SUPPLEMENT.

CANADIAN ASSOCIATION OF AMERICAN STUDIES.
— CANADIAN REVIEW OF AMERICAN STUDIES.

CANADIAN ASSOCIATION FOR APPLIED SPECTROSCOPY.
— CANADIAN JOURNAL OF SPECTROSCOPY.                       xxx

CANADIAN ASSOCIATION FOR SOUTH ASIAN STUDIES.
— CONTRIBUTIONS TO ASIAN STUDIES.

CANADIAN AUDUBON SOCIETY.
— NATURE CANADA.                                          xxx

CANADIAN BAR ASSOCIATION.
— CANADIAN BAR JOURNAL.                                   xxx
  SUBS: (1970): JOURNAL OF THE CANADIAN BAR
  ASSOCIATION.
— JOURNAL OF THE CANADIAN BAR ASSOCIATION.               xxx

CANADIAN BOTANICAL ASSOCIATION.
— BULLETIN, CANADIAN BOTANICAL ASSOCIATION.

CANADIAN ECONOMICS ASSOCIATION.
— CANADIAN JOURNAL OF ECONOMICS. SUPPLEMENT. =
  REVUE CANADIENNE D'ECONOMIQUE. SUPPLEMENT.

CANADIAN HISTORICAL ASSOCIATION.
— CANADIAN ARCHIVIST.

CANADIAN INSTITUTE OF FOOD SCIENCE &
TECHNOLOGY.                                                xxx
— JOURNAL, CANADIAN INSTITUTE OF FOOD SCIENCE &
  TECHNOLOGY.                                             xxx

CANADIAN INSTITUTE OF FOOD TECHNOLOGY.
— JOURNAL, CANADIAN INSTITUTE OF FOOD
  TECHNOLOGY.                                             xxx

CANADIAN INSTITUTE OF INTERNATIONAL AFFAIRS.
— ETUDES INTERNATIONALES. REVUE TRIMESTRIELLE.
— INTERNATIONAL CANADA.

CANADIAN INTERNATIONAL DEVELOPMENT AGENCY.
— COOPERATION CANADA.

CANADIAN LIBERATION MOVEMENT.
— NEW CANADA.

CANADIAN LIBRARY ASSOCIATION.
— CANADIAN LIBRARY JOURNAL.                               xxx

CANADIAN MATHEMATICAL CONGRESS.
— CANADIAN MATHEMATICAL MONOGRAPHS.

CANADIAN MUSIC COUNCIL.
— CANADA MUSIC BOOK. CAHIERS CANADIENS DE
  MUSIQUE.

CANADIAN OCEANOGRAPHIC DATA CENTRE.
— LIMNOLOGICAL DATA REPORT: LAKE EYRIE.
— LIMNOLOGICAL DATA REPORT: LAKE HURON, LAKE
  SUPERIOR.

CANADIAN OPERATIONAL RESEARCH SOCIETY.
— INFOR. CANADIAN JOURNAL OF OPERATIONAL
  RESEARCH & INFORMATION PROCESSING.

CANADIAN PEACE RESEARCH INSTITUTE.
— PEACE RESEARCH.
— PEACE RESEARCH REVIEWS.

CANADIAN PHARMACEUTICAL ASSOCIATION.
— CANADIAN JOURNAL OF PHARMACEUTICAL SCIENCES.

CANADIAN PSYCHOLOGICAL ASSOCIATION.
— CANADIAN JOURNAL OF BEHAVIOURAL SCIENCE.
  =REVUE DES SCIENCES DU COMPORTEMENT.

CANADIAN RADIO-TELEVISION COMMISSION.
— ANNUAL REPORT, CANADIAN RADIO-TELEVISION COMM-
  ISSION.

CANADIAN SOCIETY OF EXPLORATION GEOPHYSICISTS.
— JOURNAL, CANADIAN SOCIETY OF EXPLORATION GEO-
  PHYSICISTS.

CANADIAN SOCIETY OF FORENSIC SCIENCE.
— JOURNAL, CANADIAN SOCIETY OF FORENSIC SCIENCE.

CANADIAN SOCIETY OF RADIOLOGICAL TECHNICIANS.
— CANADIAN JOURNAL OF RADIOGRAPHY, RADIOTHERAPY,
  NUCLEOGRAPHY.                                           xxx
— FOCAL SPOT.                                             xxx
  SUBS (1970): CANADIAN JOURNAL OF RADIO-
  GRAPHY, RADIOTHERAPY, NUCLEOGRAPHY.

CANADIAN UNIVERSITY SERVICE.
— NEW STATEMENTS.

CANADIAN WELFARE COUNCIL.
— CANADIAN JOURNAL OF CRIMINOLOGY & CORRECTIONS      xxx

CANADIAN WILDLIFE FEDERATION.
— WILDLIFE NEWS. NOUVELLES DE LA FAUNE.

CANADIAN WILDLIFE SERVICE.
— PROGRESS NOTES, CANADIAN WILDLIFE SERVICE.

CANBERRA COMMITTEE FOR SUPPORT OF BANGLADESH.
— SONAR BANGLIA.                                         xxx

CANON CAMERA CO., INC.                                   000
SEE: KYANON KAMERA K.K.

CANTERBURY BOTANICAL SOCIETY (NZ).
— JOURNAL, CANTERBURY BOTANICAL SOCIETY.

CAREERS RESEARCH & ADVISORY CENTRE.
— BRITISH JOURNAL OF GUIDANCE & COUNSELLING.
— CRAC COURSE COMPARISON BULLETIN.
— JOURNAL, CAREERS RESEARCH & ADVISORY CENTRE.

CAREERS RESEARCH & ADVISORY CENTRE (SCOTLAND).
— GUIDANCE SCOTLAND.

CARIBBEAN ARTISTS MOVEMENT.
— SAVACOU. A JOURNAL OF THE ...

CARIBBEAN ECONOMIC DEVELOPMENT CORPORATION.
— CURRENT CARIBBEAN BIBLIOGRAPHY.

CARIBBEAN RESEARCH INSTITUTE: VIRGIN ISLANDS
ECOLOGICAL RESEARCH STATION.
— CONTRIBUTIONS, VIRGIN ISLANDS ECOLOGICAL
  RESEARCH STATION, CARIBBEAN RESEARCH
  INSTITUTE.

CARLETON COLLEGE: RADICAL RESEARCH CENTER.
— ALTERNATIVE PRESS INDEX.

CARLETON UNIVERSITY.
— HISTOIRE SOCIALE. = SOCIAL HISTORY.

CARRIAGE ASSOCIATION.
— CARRIAGE JOURNAL.

CARWORTH EUROPE.
— COLLECTED PAPERS, CARWORTH EUROPE.

CASE WESTERN RESERVE UNIVERSITY.
— MEDIEVALIA ET HUMANISTA: NS.

CATCH SOCIETY OF AMERICA.
— JOURNAL OF THE CATCH SOCIETY OF AMERICA.

CATHOLIC BIBLICAL ASSOCIATION.
— SCRIPTURE BULLETIN.

CATHOLIC RECORD SOCIETY.
— MONOGRAPHS, CATHOLIC RECORD SOCIETY.

**CAVE DIVING GROUP.**
— TECHNICAL REVIEW, CAVE DIVING GROUP.

**CCM INFORMATION SCIENCES INC.**
— CURRENT INDEX TO JOURNALS IN EDUCATION.
— PANDEX CURRENT INDEX TO SCIENTIFIC & TECH
NICAL LITERATURE.

**CELTIC LEAGUE IN GLASGOW.**
— A' BHRATACH UR.  NEW BANNER.

**CEMENT & CONCRETE ASSOCIATION.**
— CEMENT TECHNOLOGY.                     XXX
— CONCRETE BUILDING & CONCRETE PRODUCTS.  XXX
  SUBS (1970): PRECAST CONCRETE.
— CONCRETE MATERIALS, TECHNOLOGY & CONSTRUCTION
  ABSTRACTS.
— PRECAST CONCRETE.                       XXX

**CEMENT RESEARCH INSTITUTE OF INDIA.**
— CRI ABSTRACTS.

**CENTENNIAL MUSEUM (VANCOUVER).**
— OCCASIONAL PAPERS, CENTENNIAL MUSEUM
  (VANCOUVER).

**CENTRE FOR ADMINISTRATIVE STUDIES.**          XXX
— CAS OCCASIONAL PAPER.                         XXX

**CENTRAL AFRICA HISTORICAL ASSOCIATION.**
— RHODESIAN HISTORY.

**CENTRAL AFRICA RESEARCH OFFICE.**
— CENTRAL AFRICA RESEARCH BULLETIN.

**CENTRE AFRICAIN DE FORMATION ET DE RECHERCHES
ADMINISTRATIVES POUR LE DEVELOPPEMENT.**
— CAFRAD NEWS.
— CAHIERS AFRICAINS D'ADMINISTRATION PUBLIQUE.
  AFRICAN ADMINISTRATIVE STUDIES.

**CENTER FOR APPLIED LINGUISTICS.**
— LANGUAGE & AUTOMATION.

**CENTRAL ASIAN RESEARCH CENTRE.**
— U.S.S.R. & THIRD WORLD.

**CENTRAL ASSOCIATION FOR HEAT ENGINEERING.**     000
SEE: CHUO NETSU KANRI KYOGIKAI.

**CENTRAL BANK OF CEYLON.**
— STAFF STUDIES, CENTRAL BANK OF CEYLON.

**CENTRAL BANK OF KENYA.**
— ECONOMIC & FINANCIAL REVIEW, CENTRAL BANK OF
  KENYA.

**CENTRAL BANK OF MALTA.**
— QUARTERLY REVIEW, CENTRAL BANK OF MALTA.

**CENTRE BELGE DE PEDAGOGIE DE LA MATHEMATIQUE.**
— NICO. REVUE PERIODIQUE DE CENTRE BELGE DE
  PEDAGOGIE DE LA MATHEMATIQUE.

**CENTRAL BUREAU FOR EDUCATIONAL VISITS &
EXCHANGES.**
— EDUCATIONAL EXCHANGE.

**CENTRO CAMUNO DI STUDI PREISTORICI.**
— BOLLETTINO DEL CENTRO CAMUNO DI STUDI PRE
  ISTORICI.

**CENTRE CANADIEN DES RECHERCHES GENEALOGIQUES.**
— FRENCH CANADIAN & ACADIAN GENEALOGICAL REVIEW.

**CENTER FOR COMPUTER ORIENTATED RESEARCH IN
BIBLICAL & RELATED ANCIENT LITERATURE.**
— ARITHMOI.  NEWSLETTER OF THE ...

**CENTRO DE COOPERACION CIENTIFICA PARA AMERICA
LATINA.**
— BOLETIN DEL CENTRO DE COOPERACION CIENTIFICA
  PARA AMERICA LATINA: NS.                      XXX

**CENTRAL COUNCIL FOR AGRICULTURAL & HORTICULT
URAL CO-OPERATION.**
— REPORT, CENTRAL COUNCIL FOR AGRICULTURAL &
  HORTICULTURAL CO-OPERATION.

**CENTRAL COUNCIL FOR THE DISABLED.**
— CONTACT (LONDON).

**CENTRAL COUNCIL FOR PHYSICAL RECREATION.**
— SPORTS DEVELOPMENT BULLETIN.

**CENTRO CULTURAL PORTUGUES (PARIS).**
— ARQUIVOS, CENTRO CULTURAL PORTUGUES.

**CENTRUL DE DOCUMENTAIRE AL INDUSTREI PETROLVLUI
SI CHIMENIE.**
— CHEMISTRY, OIL & GAS IN RUMANIA. NEWS & COM
  MENTARIES.

**CENTRE DE DOCUMENTATION DE L'ARMEMENT.**
— SELECTION DE SOMMAIRES DE LA PRESSE SCIENTIF
  IQUE ET TECHNIQUE DE LANGUE FRANCAISE.

**CENTRE DE DOCUMENTATION NATIONALE (TUNIS).**
— EVENEMENTS DU MOIS EN TUNISIE.

**CENTRE FOR EDUCATIONAL DEVELOPMENT OVERSEAS.**
— EDUCATIONAL BROADCASTING INTERNATIONAL.        XXX

**CENTRE FOR EDUCATIONAL TELEVISION OVERSEAS.**
— EDUCATIONAL TELEVISION INTERNATIONAL.          XXX

**CENTRAL ELECTRICITY GENERATING BOARD.**
— PFA TECHNICAL BULLETIN.

**CENTRAL ELECTRICITY GENERATING BOARD: BERKELEY
NUCLEAR LABORATORIES.**
— CE-BNL BIB.

**CENTRE ON ENVIRONMENT FOR THE HANDICAPPED.**
— CEH DESIGN GUIDE.

**CENTRE FOR ENVIRONMENTAL STUDIES.**
— ANNUAL REPORT, CENTRE FOR ENVIRONMENTAL
  STUDIES.
— UNIVERSITY WORKING PAPERS.

**CENTRO DE ESPLORO KAJ DOKUMENTADO PRI LA MONDA
LINGVO-PROBLEMO.**
— MONDA LINGVO-PROBLEMO.

**CENTRE D'ESSAI DES AUTEURS DRAMATIQUES DE
MONTREAL.**
— THEATRE QUEBEC.

**CENTRO DE ESTUDIOS ECONOMICOS Y SOCIALES
(BARCELONA).**
— ANALES DE SOCIOLOGIA.

**CENTRO DE ESTUDIOS EDUCATIVOS (MEXICO).**
— REVISTA DEL CENTRO DE ESTUDIOS EDUCATIVOS
  (MEXICO).

**CENTRO DE ESTUDIOS DE HISTORIA ARGENTINA.**
— NUESTRA HISTORIA.

**CENTRO DE ESTUDIOS LATINAMERICANO (HAVANA).**
— PENSAMIENTO CRITICO.

**CENTRO DE ETNOLOGIA PENINSULAR.**
— ETHNICA.  REVISTA DE ANTROPOLOGIA.

**CENTRE D'ETUDES ET DE DOCUMENTATION AFRICAINES.**
— CAHIERS DU CEDAF.

**CENTRE D'ETUDES ET DE DOCUMENTATION EUROPEENNES
(MONTREAL).**
— BULLETIN, CENTRE D'ETUDES ET DE DOCUMENTATION
  EUROPEENNES (MONTREAL).
— BULLETIN TRIMESTRIEL D'INFORMATION, CENTRE
  D'ETUDES ET DE DOCUMENTATION EUROPEENNES
  (MONTREAL).

**CENTRE D'ETUDES GEOGRAPHIQUES (METZ).**
— MOSELLA.

**CENTRE D'ETUDES ET D'INITIATIVE REVOLUTIONNAIRE**
— QUE FAIRE. CAHIERS DU CENTRE D'ETUDES ET
  D'INITIATIVE REVOLUTIONNAIRE.

**CENTRE D'ETUDE DES PLANTES MEDICINALES: FACULTE
MIXTE DE MEDICINE ET DE PHARMACIE.**
— PLANTES MEDICINALES & PHYTOTHERAPIE.

**CENTRE D'ETUDE DES PROBLEMES DE LA MER.**
— BULLETIN DE LIAISON, CENTRE D'ETUDES DES PROB
  LEMES DE LA MER.

**CENTRE D'ETUDES ET DE RECHERCHES DE L'INDUSTRIE
DU BETON MANUFACTURE.**
— MONOGRAPHIE, CENTRE D'ETUDES ET DE RECHERCHES
  DE L'INDUSTRIE DU BETON MANUFACTURE.

CENTRE D'ETUDES ET DE RECHERCHES DE L'INDUSTRIE
DES LIANTS HYDRAULIQUES.
— BULLETIN ANALYTIQUE, CENTRE D'ETUDES ET DE
  RECHERCHES DE L'INDUSTRIE DES LIANTS HYDRAUL-
  IQUES.                                                                                              XXX
— DOCUMENTATION BIBLIOGRAPHIQUE. BULLETIN DE
  DOCUMENTATION, CENTRE D'ETUDES ET DE
  RECHERCHES DE L'INDUSTRIE DES LIANTS HYDRAUL-
  IQUES.                                                                                              XXX
  SUBS (1969): BULLETIN ANALYTIQUE, CENTRE ...

CENTRE D'ETUDES THEORIQUES DE LA DETECTION ET
DES COMMUNICATIONS.
— REVUE DU CETHEDEC.

CENTRE D'INFORMATION DU COBALT.
— COBALT & COBALT ABSTRACTS.                                                                         XXX

CENTRE D'INFORMATION ET DE DOCUMENTATION
IVOIRIEN.
— MARCHE IVOIRIEN.                                                                                   XXX
— REALITES IVOIRIENNES.

CENTRE FOR INFORMATION ON LANGUAGE TEACHING.
— CILT REPORTS & PAPERS.
— SPECIALISED BIBLIOGRAPHY, CENTRE FOR
  INFORMATION ON LANGUAGE TEACHING.

CENTRE D'INFORMATION DU NIGER.
— PERSPECTIVES NIGERIENNES.

CENTRE FOR INFORMATION ON THE TEACHING OF
ENGLISH.
— CITE NEWSLETTER.

CENTRALINSTITUT FOR NORDISK ASIEN-FORSKNING.
— SPECIAL PUBLICATIONS, CENTRALINSTITUT FOR
  NORDISK ASIEN-FORSKNING.

CENTRO INTERAMERICANO DE DESARROLLO RURAL Y
REFORMA AGRARIA (COLOMBIA).
— DESARROLLO RURAL EN LAS AMERICAS.

CENTRO INTERAMERICANO DE PROMOCION DE
EXPORTACIONES.
— NUEVOS MERCADOS (BOGOTA).

CENTRO INTERNACIONAL DE AGRICULTURE TROPICAL.
— NOTI-CIAT.

CENTRO INTERNAZIONALE DELLE ARTI E DEL COSTUME.
— ALTO MEDIOEVO.

CENTRE INTERNATIONAL DE DEVELOPPEMENT DE
L'ALUMINIUM.
— WORLD ALUMINUM ABSTRACTS.                                                                          XXX

CENTRE INTERNATIONAL DE DOCUMENTATION ANTONIO
VIVALDI.
— VIVALDIANA.

CENTRE INTERNATIONAL DE HAUTES ETUDES AGRONO-
MIQUES MEDITERRANEENNES.
— MEDITERRANEA. REVUE DES PROBLEMES AGRONO-
  MIQUES MEDITERRANEENS.

CENTRO INTERNAZIONALE PER LO STUDIO DEI PAPIRI
ERCOLANESI.
— CRONACHE ERCOLANESI.

CENTRE INTERUNIVERSITAIRE D'ETUDE DE L'HISTOIRE
DE LA TAPISSERIE FLAMANDE.
— MEMOIRES ET RECUEILS DE DOCUMENTS, CENTRE
  INTERUNIVERSITAIRE D'ETUDE DE L'HISTOIRE DE
  LA TAPISSERIE FLAMANDE.

CENTRO DE INVESTIGACION DE BIOLOGIA MARINA
(ARGENTINA).
— CONTRIBUCION TECNICA, CENTRO DE INVESTIGACION
  DE BIOLOGIA MARINA.

CENTRO DE INVESTIGACION JUAN GAVALA.
— REVISTA ESPANOLA DE MICROPALEONTOLOGIA.

CENTRO ITALIANO DI SESSUOLOGIA.
— SESSUOLOGIA.

CENTRAL LEATHER RESEARCH INSTITUTE (INDIA).
— CURRENT LEATHER LITERATURE.

CENTRE LENINE (LAUSANNE).
— OCTOBRE. = OKTOBER. = OTTOBRE.

CENTRAL MARINE FISHERIES RESEARCH INSTITUTE
(INDIA).
— BULLETIN, CENTRAL MARINE FISHERIES RESEARCH
  INSTITUTE.

CENTRO NACIONAL DE INVESTIGACIONES METALURGICAS
(SPAIN).
— REVISTA DE SOLDADURA.

CENTRE NATIONAL DE DOCUMENTATION SCIENTIFIQUE
ET TECHNIQUE (BELGIUM).
— BELGIAN ENVIRONMENTAL RESEARCH INDEX.

CENTRE NATIONAL D'ETUDES SPATIALES (FRANCE).
— RAPPORT D'ACTIVITE, CENTRE NATIONAL D'ETUDES
  SPATIALES.

CENTRE NATIONAL DE LA RECHERCHE SCIENTIFIQUE.
— ANNALES D'EMBRYOLOGIE ET DE MORPHOGENESE.
— ANTIQUITES AFRICAINES.
— BULLETIN ANALYTIQUE DE LINGUISTIQUE FRANCAISE.
— ECONOMIE DE L'ENERGIE.
— PROCEDURES ALGOL EN ANALYSE NUMERIQUE.
— REVUE DE L'EST. ECONOMIE ET TECHNIQUES DE
  PLANIFICATION, DROIT ET SCIENCES SOCIALES.

CENTRE NATIONAL DE LA RECHERCHE SCIENTIFIQUE
(FRANCE): INSTITUT DE RECHERCHE ET D'HISTOIRE
DES TEXTES.
— REVUE D'HISTOIRE DES TEXTES.                                                                       XXX

CENTER FOR NEO-HELLENIC STUDIES (AUSTIN).
— NEO-HELLENIKA. ANNUAL PUBLICATION OF THE ...

CENTRAL NEW YORK GENEALOGICAL SOCIETY.
— TREE TALKS.

CENTRE FOR OVERSEAS PEST RESEARCH.
— TROPICAL PEST BULLETIN.

CENTRO PARAGUAYO DE ESTUDIOS SOCIOLOGICOS.
— REVISTA PARAGUAYA DE SOCIOLOGIA.

CENTRO DE PESQUISAS DO CACAU.
— REVISTA THEOBROMA.

CENTRO PIRENAICO DE BIOLOGIA EXPERIMENTAL
(SPAIN).
— PUBLICACIONES, CENTRO PIRENAICO DE BIOLOGIA
  EXPERIMENTAL.

CENTRAL PUBLIC HEALTH ENGINEERING RESEARCH
INSTITUTE (INDIA).
— INDIAN JOURNAL OF ENVIRONMENTAL HEALTH.                                                            XXX

CENTRE DE RECHERCHES ARCHEOLOGIQUES MEDIEVALES.
— ARCHEOLOGIE MEDIEVALE.

CENTRE DE RECHERCHES DE L'HISTOIRE DE LA SID-
ERURGIE(GENEVA).
— REVUE D'HISTOIRE DES MINES ET DE LA METALL-
  URGIE. REVUE SEMESTRIELLE...                                                                       XXX

CENTRE DE RECHERCHE SUR L'IMAGINAIRE.
— CIRCE. CAHIERS DU CENTRE ...

CENTRE DE RECHERCHE ET D'INFORMATION SOCIO-
POLITIQUES (BELGIUM).
— CAHIERS CONGOLAIS RECHERCHE ET DU DEVELOPPE-
  MENT.                                                                                              XXX
— ETUDES AFRICAINES.                                                                                 XXX

CENTRE DE RECHERCHES METALLURGIQUES (BELGIUM).
— METALLURGICAL REPORTS, CENTRE DE RECHERCHES
  METALLURGIQUES (BELGIUM).                                                                          XXX

CENTRE DE RECHERCHES SAHARIENNES.
— PUBLICATIONS DU CENTRE DE RECHERCHES SAHA-
  RIENNES: SERIE GEOLOGIE.                                                                           XXX

CENTRE DE RECHERCHES SUR LES ZONES ARIDES.
— PUBLICATIONS DU CENTRE DE RECHERCHES SUR LES
  ZONES ARIDES: SERIE GEOLOGIE.

CENTRE OF SCIENTIFIC & TECHNOLOGICAL INFORMA-
TION (ISRAEL).
— DESALINATION ABSTRACTS.

CENTRE SCIENTIFIQUE ET TECHNIQUE DE LA CONST-
RUCTION (BELGIUM).
— CSTC REVUE.

CENTRAL SILK BOARD (INDIA).
— INDIAN JOURNAL OF SERICULTURE.
— INDIAN SILK.

CENTER FOR THE STUDY OF DEMOCRATIC INSTITUTIONS
— CENTER DIARY.                                                                                      XXX
— CENTER MAGAZINE. A PUBLICATION OF THE ...                                                          XXX

CENTRO STUDI E DOCUMENTAZIONE SULL'ITALIA
ROMANA.
— ATTI, CENTRO STUDI E DOCUMENTAZIONE SULL'
  ITALIA ROMANA.

CENTRO STUDI PIEMONTESI.
— STUDI PIEMONTESI.

CENTRE FOR THE STUDY OF RELIGION & COMMUNISM.
— RELIGION IN COMMUNIST LANDS.

CENTRO DI STUDI E DI RICERCHE ECONOMICO-SOCIALI
DELLA TOSCANA.
— QUADERNO, CENTRO DI STUDI E DI RICERCHE
  ECONOMICO-SOCIALI DELLA TOSCANA.

CENTRE TECHNIQUE DES INDUSTRIES AERAULIQUES ET
THERMIQUES.
— DOCUMENTS SCIENTIFIQUES ET TECHNIQUES, CENTRE
  TECHNIQUE DES INDUSTRIES AERAULIQUES ET
  THERMIQUES.

CENTRE VOLTAIQUE DE LA RECHERCHE SCIENTIFIQUE.
— NOTES ET DOCUMENTS VOLTAIQUES.

CERAMICS GLASS & MINERAL PRODUCTS INDUSTRY
TRAINING BOARD.
— INFORMATION PAPER, CERAMICS GLASS & MINERAL
  PRODUCTS INDUSTRY TRAINING BOARD.

CESKOSLOVENSKA AKADEMIE VED.
— BIOLOGIZACE A CHEMIZACE VYZIVY ZVIRAT.
— STUDIE, CESKOSLOVENSKA AKADEMIE VED.

CESKOSLOVENSKA AKADEMIE VED: ANTROPOLOGICKE
ODDELENI.
— CRANIA BOHEMICA.  MATERIALY PREHISTORICKE A
  HISTORICKE ANTROPOLOGIE.

CESKOSLOVENSKA AKADEMIE VED: ARCHEOLOGICKY
USTAV.
— ARCHEOLOGICKE STUDIJNI MATERIALY.
— PAMATNIKY NASI MINULOSTI.

CESKOSLOVENSKA AKADEMIE VED (POBOCKA V BRNE):
ARCHEOLOGICKY USTAV.
— SBORNIK, ARCHEOLOGICKY USTAV (POBOCKA V BRNE)
  CESKOSLOVENSKA AKADEMIE VED.

CESKOSLOVENSKA AKADEMIE VED: GEOGRAFICKY USTAV.
— ZPRAVY GEOGRAFICKEHO USTAVU CSAV.

CESKOSLOVENSKA AKADEMIE VED: KABINET TEORIE
ARCHITEKTURY A TVORBY ZIVOTNEHO PROSTREDIA.
— ARCHITEKTURA A URBANIZMUS.

CESKOSLOVENSKA AKADEMIE VED: KOMISE PRO
HISTORICKOU DEMOGRAFII.
— HISTORICKA DEMOGRAFIE.

CESKOSLOVENSKA AKADEMIE VED: KOMISE PRO SOUPIS
RUKOPISU.
— STUDIE O RUKOPISECH.

CESKOSLOVENSKA AKADEMIE VED: MIKROBIOLOGICKY
USTAV.
— ALGOLOGICAL STUDIES.

CESKOSLOVENSKA AKADEMIE VED: USTAV PRO CESKOU
LITERATURU.
— ESTETIKA.  CASOPIS PRO ESTETIKU A TEORII
  UMENI.

CESKOSLOVENSKA AKADEMIE VED: USTAV PRO VYZKUM
OBRATLOVCU.
— VERTEBRATOLOGICKE ZPRAVY.

CESKOSLOVENSKA AKADEMIE ZEMEDELSKA.
— VESTNIK CESKOSLOVENSKE AKADEMIE ZEMEDELSKE.

CESKOSLOVENSKA AKADEMIE ZEMEDELSKYCH VED,
VYZKUMNY USTAV RYBARSKY VE VODNANECH.
— PRACE VYZKUMNEHO USTAVU RYBARSKEHO VE VODNAN-
  ECH.

CESKOSLOVENSKA SPOLECNOST ARCHEOLOGICKA.
— SBORNIK CESKOSLAVENSKE SPOLECNOSTI ARCHEOLOG-
  ICKE. = RECUEIL DES TRAVAUX DE LA SOCIETE
  PREHISTORIQUE TCHECOSLOVAQUE.

CESKOSLOVENSKA SPOLECNOST PRO DEJINY VED A
TECHNIKY.
— DEJINY VED A TECHNIKY.

CESKOSLOVENSKA SPOLECNOST PRO SIRENI POLITICK-
YCH A VEDECKYCH ZNALOSTI.
— CESKOSLOVENSKA VLASTIVEDA: DIL 1: GEOLOGIE,
  FIZICKY ZEMEPIS.
— CESKOSLOVENSKA VLASTIVEDA: DIL 2: DEJINY DO
  R.1781.
— CESKOSLOVENSKA VLASTIVEDA: DIL 3: LIDOVA
  KULTURA.

CESKOSLOVENSKY VYSKUMNY USTAV PRACE.
— SYNTEZA.

(CEYLON) GOVERNMENT INFORMATION DEPARTMENT.          XXX
— CEYLON TODAY.                                      XXX
  SUBS (1972): SRI LANKA TODAY.

(CEYLON) HIGH COMMISSION (LONDON).                   XXX
— CEYLON NEWS-LETTER.                                XXX
  SUBS (1973): SRI LANKA NEWS-LETTER.

CHAMBER OF MINES OF SOUTH AFRICA: RESEARCH
ORGANISATION.
— GOLD BULLETIN.
— UK SHIPPING NEWS.

CHARBONNAGES DE FRANCE.
— PRESENCE DU GROUPE CDF.

CHARTERED INSTITUTE OF PATENT AGENTS.
— CIPA JOURNAL.                                      XXX
— TRANSACTIONS, CHARTERED INSTITUTE OF PATENT
  AGENTS.                                            XXX
  SUBS (1971): CIPA JOURNAL.

CHARTERED INSTITUTE OF SECRETARIES & ADMINIST-
RATORS.
— PROFESSIONAL ADMINISTRATION.                       XXX

CHARTERED INSTITUTE OF TRANSPORT.                    XXX
— JOURNAL, CHARTERED INSTITUTE OF TRANSPORT.         XXX
— TRANSPORT RESEARCH BULLETIN.

CHARTERED INSURANCE INSTITUTE.
— OCCASIONAL PAPERS, CHARTERED INSURANCE INSTI-
  TUTE.

CHEMICAL ECONOMY RESEARCH INSTITUTE (JAP.)           000
SEE: KAGAKU KEIZAI KENKYUJO.

CHEMICAL RUBBER COMPANY (CLEVELAND).
— CRC CRITICAL REVIEWS IN ANALYTICAL CHEMISTRY.
— CRC CRITICAL REVIEWS IN BIOCHEMISTRY.
— CRC CRITICAL REVIEWS IN BIOENGINEERING.
— CRC CRITICAL REVIEWS IN CLINICAL LABORATORY
  SCIENCES.
— CRC CRITICAL REVIEWS IN CLINICAL RADIOLOGY &
  NUCLEAR MEDICINE.                                  XXX
— CRC CRITICAL REVIEWS IN ENVIRONMENTAL CONTROL.
— CRC CRITICAL REVIEWS IN FOOD TECHNOLOGY.
— CRC CRITICAL REVIEWS IN MACROMOLECULAR
  SCIENCE.                                           XXX
— CRC CRITICAL REVIEWS IN MICROBIOLOGY.
— CRC CRITICAL REVIEWS IN RADIOLOGICAL SCIENCES.
— CRC CRITICAL REVIEWS IN SOLID STATE SCIENCES.
— CRC CRITICAL REVIEWS IN TOXICOLOGY.

CHEMICAL SOCIETY.
— ALIPHATIC, ALICYCLIC, & SATURATED HETERO-
CYCLIC CHEMISTRY.                                    XXX
— ALKALOIDS.  A REVIEW OF THE LITERATURE.
— AMINO-ACIDS, PEPTIDES & PROTEINS.
— ANNUAL REPORTS ON THE PROGRESS OF CHEMISTRY:
SECTION A:  GENERAL, PHYSICAL & INORGANIC
CHEMISTRY.                                           XXX
— ANNUAL REPORTS ON THE PROGRESS OF CHEMISTRY:
SECTION B: ORGANIC CHEMISTRY.                        XXX
— AROMATIC & HETEROAROMATIC CHEMISTRY.
— BIOSYNTHESIS.  A SPECIALIST PERIODICAL REPORT.
— CARBOHYDRATE CHEMISTRY: A REVIEW OF THE
LITERATURE.
— CHEMICAL SOCIETY REVIEWS.                          XXX
— CHEMICAL THERMODYNAMICS.
— CHEMSCAN: RADIATION & PHOTOCHEMISTRY.              XXX
— CHEMSCAN: STEROIDS.                                XXX
— COLLOID SCIENCE.
— DIELECTRIC & RELATED MOLECULAR PROCESSES.
— ELECTROCHEMISTRY.  A SPECIALIST PERIODICAL
REPORT.
— ELECTRON SPIN RESONANCE.
— ELECTRONIC STRUCTURE & MAGNETISM OF INORGANIC
COMPOUNDS.
— FLUOROCARBON & RELATED CHEMISTRY.
— FOREIGN COMPOUND METABOLISM IN MAMMALS.
— INORGANIC CHEMISTRY OF THE TRANSITION ELEM-
ENTS.
— INORGANIC REACTION MECHANISMS.
— JOURNAL OF THE CHEMICAL SOCIETY: CHEMICAL
COMMUNICATIONS.                                      XXX
— JOURNAL OF THE CHEMICAL SOCIETY: DALTON TRANS-
ACTIONS: INORGANIC CHEMISTRY.
— JOURNAL OF THE CHEMICAL SOCIETY: PERKIN TRANS-
ACTIONS 1: ORGANIC & BIO-ORGANIC CHEMISTRY.
— JOURNAL OF THE CHEMICAL SOCIETY: PERKIN TRANS-
ACTIONS 2: PHYSICAL ORGANIC CHEMISTRY.
— MASS SPECTROMETRY.
— MOLECULAR SPECTROSCOPY.
— NUCLEAR MAGNETIC RESONANCE.
— ORGANIC COMPOUNDS OF SULPHUR, SELENIUM &
TELLURIUM.
— ORGANOMETALLIC CHEMISTRY.
— ORGANOPHOSPHORUS CHEMISTRY.
— PHOTOCHEMISTRY.  A REVIEW OF THE LITERATURE.
— RADIOCHEMISTRY.  (LONDON).
— SPECTROSCOPIC PROPERTIES OF INORGANIC &
ORGANOMETALLIC COMPOUNDS.
— STATISTICAL MECHANICS.
— SURFACE & DEFECT PROPERTIES OF SOLIDS.
— TERPENOIDS & STEROIDS.

CHEMICAL SOCIETY: FARADAY DIVISION.
— FARADAY SPECIAL DISCUSSIONS OF THE CHEMICAL
SOCIETY.                                             XXX
— JOURNAL OF THE CHEMICAL SOCIETY: FARADAY
TRANSACTIONS 1: [PHYSICAL CHEMISTRY].                XXX
— JOURNAL OF THE CHEMICAL SOCIETY: FARADAY
TRANSACTIONS 2: [CHEMICAL PHYSICS].                  XXX

CHEMICAL SOCIETY OF JAPAN.
— CHEMISTRY LETTERS.

CHEMICAL SPECIALTIES MANUFACTURERS ASSOCIATION.
— SOAP, COSMETICS, CHEMICAL SPECIALTIES.             XXX

CHEMISCHE GESELLSCHAFT IN DER DDR.
— JOURNAL FUR SIGNALAUFZEICHNUNGSMATERIALIEN.

CHEPSTOW SOCIETY.
— SEVERN & WYE REVIEW.

CHERNIVETS'KYJ DERZHAVNYJ UNIVERSYTET.
— VOPROSY RUSSKOJ LITERATURY.

CHESHIRE CONSERVATION TRUST.
— NEWS BULLETIN, CHESHIRE CONSERVATION TRUST.

CHESHIRE COUNTY COUNCIL.
— CHESHIRE HISTORY NEWSLETTER.

CHEST & HEART ASSOCIATION.
— CHEST & HEART.  NEWS BULLETIN OF ...

CHIBA-KEN AGRICULTURAL EXPERIMENT STATION.           000
SEE: CHIBA-KEN NOGYO SHIKENJO.

CHIBA-KEN NOGYO SHIKENJO.
— CHIBA-KEN NOGYO SHIKENJO TOKUBETSU HOKOKU.
SPECIAL BULLETIN OF THE CHIBA-KEN AGRICULTUR-
AL EXPERIMENT STATION.

CHICAGO BRIDGE & IRON COMPANY.
— CHI NEWS.                                          XXX
— WATER TOWER.                                       XXX
SUBS (1972): CHI NEWS.

CHICAGO LYING IN HOSPITAL.
— LYING IN.  THE JOURNAL OF REPRODUCTIVE MEDI-
CINE.                                                XXX

CHICHESTER POETS CO-OPERATIVE.
— ABOUT THIS ...

CHIGWELL LOCAL HISTORY SOCIETY.
— TRANSACTIONS, CHIGWELL LOCAL HISTORY SOCIETY.

CHILD POVERTY ACTION GROUP.
— POVERTY.  JOURNAL OF THE ...

CHILDREN'S SCIENCE BOOK REVIEW COMMITTEE.
— APPRAISAL.

CHINESE MEDICAL ASSOCIATION.
— CHINA'S MEDICINE.                                  XXX

CHINESE PETROLEUM CORPORATION: TAIWAN PETROLEUM
EXPLORATION OFFICE.
— PETROLEUM GEOLOGY OF TAIWAN.

CHRISTIAN-ALBRECHTS UNIVERSITAT.                     000
SEE: UNIVERSITAT KIEL.

CHRISTIAN BRETHREN RESEARCH FELLOWSHIP.
— CHRISTIAN BRETHREN RESEARCH FELLOWSHIP BROAD-
SHEET.

CHRISTIAN ENDEAVOUR UNION.
— ADVANCE.

CHRISTUS REX SOCIETY.
— CHRISTUS REX.                                      XXX
SUBS (1972): PART OF SOCIAL STUDIES.
— SOCIAL STUDIES.  IRISH JOURNAL OF SOCIOLOGY.       XXX

CHUNG-YANG T'U-SHU-KUAN (TAIWAN).
— CHUNG-HUA MIN-KUO CH'I-K'AN LUN-WEN SO-YIN.
MONTHLY INDEX TO PERIODICALS PUBLISHED IN
TAIWAN.

CHUO NETSU KANRI KYOGIKAI.
— NETSU KANRI.                                       XXX
SUBS (1971): NETSU KANRI TO KOGAI.
— NETSU KANRI TO KOGAI.                              XXX

CHURCH MISSIONARY SOCIETY.
— YES.

CHURCH OF SCIENTOLOGY.
— FREEDOM. INTERNATIONAL EDITION.
— FREEDOM SCIENTOLOGY.

CHURCH SERVICE SOCIETY.
— ANNUAL, CHURCH SERVICE SOCIETY.                    XXX
SUBS (1971): LITURGICAL STUDIES.
— LITURGICAL STUDIES.                                XXX

CHURCHES' COUNCIL OF HEALING IN IRELAND.
— CHRISTIAN HEALING.

CIBA.
— CIBA-BLATTER.                                      XXX
SUBS (1971): CIBA-GEIGY ZEITSCHRIFT.
— CIBA JOURNAL.                                      XXX
SUBS (1971): CIBA-GEIGY JOURNAL.
— CIBA-REVIEW.                                       XXX
SUBS (1971): CIBA-GEIGY REVIEW.
— CIBA-RUNDSCHAU.                                    XXX
SUBS (1971): CIBA-GEIGY RUNDSCHAU.

CIBA: AGROCHEMICALS DIVISION.
— TECHNICAL MONOGRAPH, AGROCHEMICALS DIVISION,
CIBA.

CIBA-GEIGY.                                          XXX
— CIBA-GEIGY JOURNAL.                                XXX
— CIBA-GEIGY REVIEW.                                 XXX
— CIBA-GEIGY RUNDSCHAU.                              XXX
— CIBA-GEIGY ZEITSCHRIFT.                            XXX

CIBA-GEIGY (UK), LTD.                                XXX
— CIBA-GEIGY TECHNICAL NOTES.                        XXX

CITY OF LONDON POLYTECHNIC: GEOGRAPHY SECTION.
— LONDONER.  JOURNAL OF THE GEOGRAPHY SECTION,
CITY OF LONDON POLYTECHNIC.

CITY UNIVERSITY (LONDON).
— ANNUAL REPORT, CITY UNIVERSITY (LONDON).

CITY UNIVERSITY OF NEW YORK.
— COMPARATIVE POLITICS.

CITY UNIVERSITY OF NEW YORK: QUEEN'S COLLEGE.
— AMERICAN CLASSICAL REVIEW.

CIVIL AIR TRANSPORT INDUSTRY TRAINING BOARD.
— CIVIL AIR TRANSPORT NEWS.

CIVIL ENGINEERING RESEARCH ASSOCIATION.
— CERA BULLETIN.                                                    XXX

CIVIL ENGINEERING RESEARCH COUNCIL.
— CERC BULLETIN.                                                    XXX

CIVIL SERVICE COLLEGE.                                              XXX
— OCCASIONAL PAPER, CIVIL SERVICE COLLEGE.                          XXX

CIVIL SERVICE SOCIETY.
— NEWSLETTER, CIVIL SERVICE SOCIETY.

CLAN MUNRO ASSOCIATION: AMERICAN BRANCH.
— MUNRO EAGLE.

CLEARINGHOUSE FOR FEDERAL SCIENTIFIC & TECH-
NICAL INFORMATION (U.S.).
— SELECTED WATER RESOURCES ABSTRACTS.

CLEMSON UNIVERSITY: DEPARTMENT OF FORESTRY.
— FOREST RESEARCH SERIES, DEPARTMENT OF FOR-
   ESTRY, CLEMSON UNIVERSITY.
— TECHNICAL PAPER, DEPARTMENT OF FORESTRY,
   CLEMSON UNIVERSITY.

CLERICAL & ADMINISTRATIVE WORKERS UNION.
— APEX (LONDON).                                                    XXX

CLEVELAND MUSEUM OF NATURAL HISTORY.
— KIRTLANDIA.

CLEVELAND & TEESSIDE LOCAL HISTORY SOCIETY.
— BULLETIN, CLEVELAND & TEESSIDE LOCAL HISTORY
   SOCIETY.

CLINICAL ELECTRON MICROSCOPY SOCIETY OF JAPAN.
— JAPANESE JOURNAL OF CLINICAL ELECTRON
   MICROSCOPY.

CLOTHING INSTITUTE.
— CLOTHING RESEARCH JOURNAL.                                        XXX
— TECHNOLOGICAL REPORT, CLOTHING INSTITUTE.                         XXX
   SUBS (1973): CLOTHING RESEARCH JOURNAL.

COCKBURN ASSOCIATION.
— NEWSLETTER, COCKBURN ASSOCIATION.

COLEGIO DE MEXICO.
— BIBLIOGRAFIA HISTORICA MEXICANA.
— DEMOGRAFIA Y ECONOMIA.
— ESTUDIOS ORIENTALES.

COLEGIO UNIVERSITARIO DE ALAVA.
— HISPANIA ANTIQUA.  REVISTA DE HISTORIA
   ANTIQUA.

COLLEGE OF AERONAUTICS (CRANFIELD).                                 XXX
— COA REPORT AERO.                                                  XXX
— COA REPORT E & C.
— COA REPORT M & P.
— COA REPORT MAT.
— REPORT, COLLEGE OF AERONAUTICS (CRANFIELD).                       XXX
   SUBS (1963):  COA REPORT AERO.

COLLEGE OF ESTATE MANAGEMENT.
— OCCASIONAL PAPERS IN ESTATE MANAGEMENT.                           XXX

COLLEGE OF EUROPE.
— STUDIES IN CONTEMPORARY EUROPEAN ISSUES.

COLLEGE OF LIBRARIANSHIP, WALES.
— LLYFRGELL.

COLLEGE OF PATHOLOGISTS OF AUSTRALIA.
— PATHOLOGY.  JOURNAL OF THE ...

COLLEZIONE INTERNAZIONALE DEL GESU.
— BIBLICAL THEOLOGY BULLETIN.
— CLARETIANUM.  COMMENTARIA THEOLOGICA.

(COLOMBIA) DEPARTMENTO NACIONAL DE PLANÉACION.
— REVISTA DE PLANEACION Y DESARROLLO.

COLOMBIA INFORMATION SERVICE.
— COLOMBIA TODAY.

(COLOMBIA) MINISTERIO DE JUSTICIA.
— BOLETIN DE INFORMACIONES SOCIO JURIDICAS
   (COLOMBIA).

(COLOMBIA) SERVICIO COLOMBIANO DE METEOROLOGIA
E HIDROLOGIA.
— BOLETIN CLIMATOLOGICO MENSUAL (COLOMBIA).
— BOLETIN METEOROLOGICO MENSUAL (COLOMBIA).

COLOMBO PLAN INFORMATION DEPARTMENT.
— COLOMBO PLAN NEWS LETTER.

COLORADO GEOLOGICAL SURVEY.
— SPECIAL PUBLICATION, COLORADO GEOLOGICAL
   SURVEY.

COLORADO MUSEUM OF NATURAL HISTORY.
— PROCEEDINGS OF THE COLORADO MUSEUM OF NATURAL
   HISTORY.                                                         XXX
   SUBS (1955): PROCEEDINGS OF THE DENVER
   MUSEUM OF NATURAL HISTORY.

COLORADO STATE UNIVERSITY.
— WESTERN AMERICAN LITERATURE.

COLORADO STATE UNIVERSITY: DEPARTMENT OF
ATMOSPHERIC SCIENCE.
— REPORT, DEPARTMENT OF ATMOSPHERIC SCIENCE,
   COLORADO STATE UNIVERSITY.

COLUMBIA UNIVERSITY.
— COLUMBIA FORUM: NS.                                               XXX
— COLUMBIA UNIVERSITY FORUM.                                        XXX
   SUBS (1968): COLUMBIA FORUM.

COLUMBIA UNIVERSITY: AFRICAN LAW CENTER.
— AFRICAN LAW STUDIES.

COLUMBIA UNIVERSITY: ANCIENT NEAR EASTERN
SOCIETY.
— JOURNAL OF THE ANCIENT NEAR EASTERN SOCIETY
   OF COLUMBIA UNIVERSITY.

COLUMBIA UNIVERSITY: GRADUATE SCHOOL OF
JOURNALISM.
— COLUMBIA JOURNALISM REVIEW.

COLUMBIA UNIVERSITY: INTERNATIONAL INSTITUTE
FOR THE STUDY OF HUMAN REPRODUCTION.
— COUNTRY PROFILES.

COLUMBIA UNIVERSTIY: SCHOOL OF INTERNATIONAL
AFFAIRS.
— COLUMBIA STUDIES IN ECONOMICS.

COLUMBIA UNIVERSITY: SCHOOL OF LAW.
— COLUMBIA SURVEY OF HUMAN RIGHTS LAW.                              XXX

COMISION CIENTIFICA DE PROTECCION DE LA
NATURALEZA (SPAIN).
— NATURALEZA.

COMISION INTERNACIONAL PERMANENTE DE FOLKLORE.
— PUBLICACIONES, COMISION INTERNACIONAL PERMAN-
   ENTE DE FOLKLORE.

COMISION DE INVESTIGACION CIENTIFICA (BUENOS
AIRES, PROVINCIA).
— MISCELANEA, COMISION DE INVESTIGACION CIENT-
   IFICA DE LA PROVINCIA DE BUENOS AIRES.
— PUBLICACION, COMISION DE INVESTIGACION CIEN-
   TIFICA (BUENOS AIRES, PROVINCIA).

COMITATO PER LE SCIENZE POLITICHE E SOCIALI.
— SCIENZE SOCIALI.

COMITE FRANCAISE D'HISTOIRE DE L'ART.
— REVUE DE L'ART.

COMITE FRANCE-AMERIQUE LATINE.
— BULLETIN PERIODIQUE, COMITE FRANCE-AMERIQUE
   LATINE.

COMITE NATIONAL FRANCAIS DE LIAISON POUR LA
READAPTATION DES HANDICAPES.
— CAHIERS DE LA VIE QUOTIDIENNE.

COMMISSARIAT A L'ENERGIE ATOMIQUE (FRANCE).
— INDEX DE LA LITTERATURE NUCLEAIRE FRANCAISE.

COMMISSION OF THE EUROPEAN COMMUNITIES.
— CAMAC BULLETIN.
— DEVELOPING COUNTRIES, PRODUCE & TRADE.
— EURO ABSTRACTS.
— GENERAL REPORT ON THE ACTIVITIES OF THE
   COMMUNITIES.                                                     XXX
— INTEGRATION.  BEITRAGE ZUR EUROPAFORSCHUNG.
— STATISTISCHE STUDIEN UND ERHEBUNGEN.
— YEARBOOK OF AGRICULTURAL STATISTICS.

**COMMISSION FOR THE GEOLOGICAL MAP OF THE WORLD.**
— BULLETIN, COMMISSION FOR THE GEOLOGICAL MAP
OF THE WORLD.

**COMMISSION GEOLOGIQUE DE FINLANDE.**
— BULLETIN, COMMISSION GEOLOGIQUE DE FINLANDE.          XXX
SUBS (1971): BULLETIN, GEOLOGICAL SURVEY OF
FINLAND.

**COMMISSION ON INDUSTRIAL RELATIONS (GB).**
— STUDIES, COMMISSION ON INDUSTRIAL RELATIONS
(GB).

**COMMISSION ROYALE BELGE DE FOLKLORE.**
— CONTRIBUTIONS AU RENOUVEAU DU FOLKLORE EN
WALLONIE.

**COMMITTEE FOR THE ADVANCEMENT OF KURDISTAN (GB)**
— KURDICA.

**COMMITTEE ON AFRICAN STUDIES IN CANADA.**
— CANADIAN JOURNAL OF AFRICAN STUDIES. = JOUR-
NAL CANADIEN DES ETUDES AFRICAINES.

**COMMITTEE OF CONCERNED ASIAN SCHOLARS.**
— BULLETIN OF CONCERNED ASIAN SCHOLARS.               XXX
— CCAS NEWSLETTER.                                     XXX
SUBS (1969): BULLETIN OF CONCERNED ASIAN
SCHOLARS.

**COMMITTEE ON DATA FOR SCIENCE & TECHNOLOGY.**
— CODATA BULLETIN.
— CODATA NEWSLETTER.

**COMMITTEE FOR DESCENDANTS OF BABYLONIAN JEWRY.**
— SCRIBE. JOURNAL OF THE DESCENDANTS OF BABY-
LONIAN JEWRY.

**COMMITTEE OF TEN.**
— AFRICAN STATESMAN.

**COMMITTEE OF VICE-CHANCELLORS & PRINCIPALS
OF THE UNIVERSITIES OF THE UNITED KINGDOM.**
— COMPENDIUM OF UNIVERSITY ENTRANCE REQUIRE-
MENTS FOR FIRST DEGREE COURSES IN THE UNITED
KINGDOM ...
— IN BRIEF. AN OCCASIONAL BULLETIN.

**COMMITTEE OF WEST PAKISTANIS IN SOLIDARITY WITH
BENGAL & KASHMIR.**
— JADD-O-JEHAD.

**COMMONWEALTH AGRICULTURAL BUREAU.**
— HELMINTHOLOGICAL ABSTRACTS: SERIES A: ANIMAL
& HUMAN HELMINTHOLOGY.                                 XXX
— HELMINTHOLOGICAL ABSTRACTS: SERIES B: PLANT
NEMATOLOGY.                                            XXX
— HORTICULTURAL REVIEW.

**COMMONWEALTH BUREAU OF ANIMAL HEALTH.**
— TECHNICAL COMMUNICATION, COMMONWEALTH BUREAU
OF ANIMAL HEALTH.

**COMMONWEALTH BUREAU OF CENSUS & STATISTICS
(AUSTRALIA).**                                         000
SEE: (AUSTRALIA) COMMONWEALTH BUREAU OF
CENSUS & STATISTICS.

**COMMONWEALTH BUREAU OF HORTICULTURE & PLANTA-
TION CROPS.**
— RESEARCH REVIEW, COMMONWEALTH BUREAU OF
HORTICULTURE & PLANTATION CROPS.

**COMMONWEALTH BUREAU OF PASTURES & FIELDCROPS.**
— MIMEOGRAPHED PUBLICATION, COMMONWEALTH BUREAU
OF PASTURES & FIELDCROPS.                              XXX
SUBS (1968) REVIEW SERIES, ...
— REVIEW SERIES, COMMONWEALTH BUREAU OF PAST-
URES & FIELD CROPS.

**COMMONWEALTH FOUNDATION.**
— PROGRESS REPORT, COMMONWEALTH FOUNDATION.

**COMMONWEALTH INDUSTRIES ASSOCIATION LTD.**
— BRITAIN & OVERSEAS.

**COMMONWEALTH INSTITUTE OF BIOLOGICAL CONTROL.**
— TECHNICAL COMMUNICATIONS, COMMONWEALTH INST-
ITUTE OF BIOLOGICAL CONTROL.

**COMMONWEALTH MYCOLOGICAL INSTITUTE.**
— DESCRIPTIONS OF PLANT VIRUSES.
— REVIEW OF PLANT PATHOLOGY.                           XXX

**COMMONWEALTH SECRETARIAT.**
— COMMONWEALTH DIARY OF COMING EVENTS.
— COMMONWEALTH RECORD OF RECENT EVENTS.
— EDUCATION IN DEVELOPING COUNTRIES OF THE COM-
MONWEALTH. ABSTRACTS OF CURRENT RESEARCH.
— IRON ORE & ALLOYING METALS.
— MINERALS QUARTERLY.

**COMMUNICATIONS SATELLITE CORPORATION.**
— COMSAT TECHNICAL REVIEW.

**COMMUNICATIONS TECHNOLOGY, INC.**
— HAM RADIO MAGAZINE.*

**COMMUNIST PARTY OF CANADA.**
— COMMUNIST VIEWPOINT.

**COMMUNIST PARTY OF CUBA.**
— GRANMA WEEKLY REVIEW.

**COMMUNIST PARTY OF GREAT BRITAIN: INTERNATIONAL
DEPARTMENT.**
— INTERNATIONAL AFFAIRS BULLETIN.

**COMMUNIST PARTY OF GREAT BRITAIN: SCOTTISH
COMMITTEE.**
— SCOTTISH MARXIST.

**COMMUNITY RELATIONS COMMISSION.**
— COMMUNITY. QUARTERLY JOURNAL OF ...                  XXX
— C.R.C. NEWS.                                         XXX
— EDUCATION FOR A MULTI-CULTURAL SOCIETY.
— NEW COMMUNITY.                                       XXX

**COMPAGNIE DES CONSEILS EN BREVETS D'INVENTION.**
— CBI INFORMATIONS.

**COMPAGNIE FRANCAISE PHILIPS.**
— TECHNIQUES PHILIPS.                                  XXX

**COMPRESSED AIR & GAS INSTITUTE.**
— CAGI TECHNICAL DIGEST.

**COMPUTER ARTS SOCIETY.**
— PAGE.

**COMPUTER EDUCATION GROUP.**
— COMPUTER EDUCATION.

**CONCHOLOGICAL SOCIETY OF GREAT BRITAIN & IRE-
LAND.**
— PAPERS FOR STUDENTS, CONCHOLOGICAL SOCIETY OF
GREAT BRITAIN & IRELAND.

**CONCRETE SOCIETY OF SOUTHERN AFRICA.**
— CONCRETE/BETON.

**CONFEDERATION OF BRITISH INDUSTRY.**
— BRITISH INDUSTRY WEEK.                               XXX
— CBI EDUCATION & TRAINING BULLETIN.
— CBI EUROPE BRIEF.
— CBI INDUSTRIAL RELATIONS BULLETIN.                   XXX
— CBI INDUSTRIAL TRENDS SURVEY.                        XXX
— CBI OVERSEAS TRADE BULLETIN.
— CBI REVIEW.
— CBI SMALLER FIRMS BULLETIN.
— INDUSTRIAL TRENDS SURVEY.                            XXX
— INDUSTRY WEEK. (LONDON).                             XXX

**CONFEDERACION GENERAL ECONOMICA: INSTITUTO
DE INVESTIGACIONES ECONOMICAS Y FINANCIERAS.**
— ESTUDIOS SOBRE LA ECONOMIA ARGENTINA.

**CONFEDERATION OF IRISH INDUSTRY.**
— CII EUROLETTER.
— ECONOMIC REVIEW (DUBLIN).
— ECONOMIC TRENDS.
— METRICATION BULLETIN.
— RECLAIM. CONSERVATION BULLETIN.

**CONFERENCE ON BRITISH STUDIES: PACIFIC NORTH-
WEST SECTION.**
— ALBION (SEATTLE).

**CONFERENCE OF BRITISH STUDIES, WEST VIRGINIA
UNIVERSITY.**
— ARCHIVES OF BRITISH HISTORY & CULTURE.

**CONFERENCE GROUP FOR SOCIAL & ADMINISTRATIVE
HISTORY.**
— SOCIETAS. A REVIEW OF SOCIAL HISTORY.

**CONFERENCE OF MUSLIM LECTURERS & SENIOR STAFF
OF ALL NIGERIAN UNIVERSITIES.**
— NIGERIAN JOURNAL OF ISLAM.

CONFERENCE OF SOCIALIST ECONOMISTS.
— BULLETIN OF THE CONFERENCE OF SOCIALIST
  ECONOMISTS.

CONGO (DEMOCRATIC REPUBLIC) OFFICE NATIONAL DE
LA RECHERCHE ET DU DEVELOPPEMENT.
— ANNEE POLITIQUE AU CONGO.

CONGREGATIONAL HISTORICAL SOCIETY.                              XXX
— TRANSACTIONS, CONGREGATIONAL HISTORICAL
  SOCIETY.                                                      XXX
  SUBS(1973): JOURNAL, UNITED REFORMED CHURCH
  HISTORY SOCIETY.

CONNECTICUT HERPETOLOGICAL SOCIETY.
— BULLETIN, CONNECTICUT HERPETOLOGICAL SOCIETY.

CONSEIL CANADIEN DE RECHERCHE EN SCIENCE
SOCIALES.                                                      000
 SEE: SOCIAL SCIENCE RESEARCH COUNCIL OF
 CANADA.

CONSEIL INTERNATIONAL DE LA LANGUE FRANCAISE.
— BANQUE DES MOTS.

CONSEIL INTERNATIONAL DES MONUMENTS ET DES
SITES.
— MONUMENTUM.

CONSEJO CIENTIFICO VETERINARIO (CUBA).
— REVISTA CUBANA DE CIENCIAS VETERINARIAS.

CONSEJO LATINOAMERICANO DE CIENCIAS SOCIALES.
— REVISTA LATINOAMERICANA DE ESTUDIOS URBANO
  REGIONALES.

CONSEJO NACIONAL DE CULTURA (CUBA): DEPARTA-
MENTO COLECCION CUBANA.
— ANUARIO MARTIANO.

CONSEJO SUPERIOR DE INVESTIGACIONES CIENTIFICAS
(SPAIN).
— CUADERNOS BIBLIOGRAFICOS.
— PROHEMIO. RIVISTA DE LINGUISTICA Y CRITICA
  LITERARIA.

CONSEJO SUPERIOR DE INVESTIGACIONES CIENTIF-
ICAS (SPAIN): INSTITUTO DE ESTUDIOS MADRILENOS.
— ANALES, INSTITUTO DE ESTUDIOS MADRILENOS,
  CONSEJO SUPERIOR DE INVESTIGACIONES
  CIENTIFICAS (SPAIN).

CONSEJO SUPERIOR DE INVESTIGACIONES CIENTIFICAS
(SPAIN): INSTITUCION FERNANDO EL CATOLICO.
— CUADERNOS DE ARAGON.
— FUENTES HISTORICAS ARAGONESAS.

CONSERVATIVE CENTRAL OFFICE.
— FOCUS ON LOCAL GOVERNMENT.

CONSILIUL SUPERIOR AL AGRICULTURII (RUMANIA).
— STUDII SI CERCETARI DE MECANICA AGRICOLA.

CONSTRUCTION INDUSTRY INFORMATION GROUP.
— CIIG BULLETIN.

CONSTRUCTION INDUSTRY RESEARCH & INFORMATION
ASSOCIATION.
— CIRIA.                                                       XXX
— CIRIA BULLETIN.                                              XXX
— CIRIA REPORT.                                                XXX
— CIRIA RESEARCH REPORT.                                       XXX
  SUBS (1969): CIRIA REPORT.
— TECHNICAL NOTE, CONSTRUCTION INDUSTRY RES-
  EARCH & INFORMATION ASSOCIATION.

CONSTRUCTION INDUSTRY TRANSLATION & INFORMATION
SERVICES.
— EUROPEAN CIVIL ENGINEERING ABSTRACTS.

CONTACT LENS ASSOCIATION OF OPHTHALMOLOGISTS.
— CONTACT LENS MEDICAL BULLETIN.

COOPER LABORATORIES INTERNATIONAL, INC.
— INDENT. JOURNAL OF INTERNATIONAL DENTISTRY.

COOPERATIVE EDUCATION ASSOCIATION.
— JOURNAL OF COOPERATIVE EDUCATION.

COOPERATIVE FEDERATION OF CEYLON.
— CEYLON COOPERATIVE REVIEW.

COOPERATIVE INVESTIGATION OF THE MEDITERRANEAN
(MONACO).
— NEWSLETTER OF THE COOPERATIVE INVESTIGATION
  OF THE MEDITERRANEAN. BULLETIN DE L'ETUDE EN
  COMMUN DE LA MEDITERRANEE.

COPPER DEVELOPMENT ASSOCIATION.
— TECHNICAL NOTE, COPPER DEVELOPMENT ASSOCIAT-
  ION.

COPPER INDUSTRY SERVICE BUREAU (ZAMBIA).
— COPPERBELT OF ZAMBIA MINING INDUSTRY YEAR
  BOOK.                                                        XXX
— MINDECO MINING YEAR BOOK.                                    XXX
— MINING YEAR BOOK OF ZAMBIA.                                  XXX

CORBY HISTORICAL SOCIETY.
— RESEARCH BULLETIN, CORBY HISTORICAL SOCIETY.

CORDON BLEU COOKERY SCHOOL.
— CORDON BLEU COOKERY COURSE.

CORN REFINERS ASSOCIATION.
— CORN.                                                        XXX
  SUBS (1970): CORN ANNUAL.
— CORN ANNUAL.                                                 XXX

CORNELL SOCIETY OF INTERNATIONAL LAW.
— CORNELL INTERNATIONAL LAW JOURNAL.

CORNELL UNIVERSITY.
— CORNELL LIBRARY JOURNAL.

CORNELL UNIVERSITY: DEPARTMENT OF SOCIOLOGY.
— CORNELL JOURNAL OF SOCIAL RELATIONS.

CORNELL UNIVERSITY: LABORATORY OF ORNITHOLOGY.
— BIO-ACOUSTICS BULLETIN.

CORNELL UNIVERSITY: LATIN AMERICAN STUDIES
PROGRAM.
— DISSERTATION SERIES, LATIN AMERICAN STUDIES
  PROGRAM, CORNELL UNIVERSITY.

CORNELL UNIVERSITY: NEW YORK STATE SCHOOL OF
INDUSTRIAL & LABOR RELATIONS.                                  000
 SEE:  NEW YORK STATE SCHOOL ...

CORNELL UNIVERSITY: SOCIETY FOR THE HUMANITIES.
— STUDIES IN THE HUMANITIES.

CORNISH NATIONAL MOVEMENT.
— CORNISH NATION.

CORPORACION DE DESAROLLO ECONOMICO DEL
CARIBE.                                                        000
 SEE: CARIBBEAN ECONOMIC DEVELOPMENT CORP.

CORPORACION VENEZOLANA DE GUAYANA (VENEZUELA).
— INFORME ANUAL, CORPORACION VENEZOLANA DE
  GUAYANA.

CORPORATION OF LLOYD'S.
— LLOYD'S LAW REPORTS.

CORPORATION FOR THE PUBLICATION OF ACADEMIC
STUDIES IN RELIGION IN CANADA.
— STUDIES IN RELIGION. SCIENCES RELIGIEUSES.                   XXX

COSMETIC, TOILETRY & FRAGRANCE ASSOCIATION.
— CTFA COSMETIC JOURNAL.                                       XXX

COSTAIN GROUP.
— CONSTRUCTION PROGRESS.

COSTUME SOCIETY.
— COSTUME.

COTTON RESEARCH CORPORATION.                                   XXX
— COTTON RESEARCH REPORTS.                                     XXX
— PROGRESS REPORTS FROM EXPERIMENT STATIONS,
  COTTON RESEARCH CORPORATION.                                 XXX

COUNCIL FOR ACADEMIC FREEDOM & DEMOCRACY.
— CAFD NEWSLETTER.                                             XXX

COUNCIL ON BIOLOGICAL SCIENCES INFORMATION.
— WORKING DOCUMENT, COUNCIL ON BIOLOGICAL
  SCIENCES INFORMATION.

COUNCIL FOR CULTURAL CO-OPERATION.
— EUROPEAN CURRICULUM STUDIES.

COUNCIL ON ENVIRONMENTAL QUALITY (US).
— ENVIRONMENTAL QUALITY.

COUNCIL OF EUROPE: DIRECTORATE OF INFORMATION.
— ICI L'EUROPE. BULLETIN D'INFORMATION DE LA
  DIRECTION DES AFFAIRES JURIDIQUES.

COUNCIL FOR EXCEPTIONAL CHILDREN.
— TEACHING EXCEPTIONAL CHILDREN.

**COUNCIL FOR EXCEPTIONAL CHILDREN: DIVISION OF MENTAL RETARDATION.**
— EDUCATION & TRAINING OF THE MENTALLY RETARDED.

**COUNCIL OF FOREST INDUSTRIES OF BRITISH COLUMBIA.**
— PLYWOOD WORLD.     XXX
— WOOD WORLD.     XXX

**COUNCIL FOR NATIONAL ACADEMIC AWARDS.**
— STATEMENT, COUNCIL FOR NATIONAL ACADEMIC AWARDS.

**COUNCIL FOR NAUTICAL ARCHAEOLOGY.**
— INTERNATIONAL JOURNAL OF NAUTICAL ARCHAEOLOGY & UNDERWATER EXPLORATION.

**COUNCIL ON NEW GUINEA AFFAIRS.**
— NEW GUINEA & AUSTRALIA, THE PACIFIC & SOUTH-EAST ASIA.

**COUNCIL FOR THE PRESERVATION OF RURAL ENGLAND: OXFORDSHIRE BRANCH.**
— BULLETIN, OXFORDSHIRE BRANCH, COUNCIL FOR THE PRESERVATION OF RURAL ENGLAND.

**COUNCIL OF RESEARCH IN MUSIC EDUCATION.**
— BULLETIN, COUNCIL OF RESEARCH IN MUSIC EDUCA-TION.

**COUNCIL OF SCIENTIFIC & INDUSTRIAL RESEARCH (INDIA).**
— CURRENT LITERATURE ON SCIENCE OF SCIENCE.
— INDIAN JOURNAL OF BIOCHEMISTRY & BIOPHYSICS.
— INDIAN JOURNAL OF MARINE SCIENCES.
— INDIAN JOURNAL OF RADIO & SPACE PHYSICS.

**COUNCIL ON SOCIAL WORK EDUCATION.**
— JOURNAL OF EDUCATION FOR SOCIAL WORK.

**COUNSELLING & REHABILITATION EMPLOYEES SERVICES.**
— ALCOHOLISM IN INDUSTRY.

**COUNTRYSIDE COMMISSION (GB).**
— COASTAL PRESERVATION & DEVELOPMENT: SPECIAL STUDY REPORTS.
— LONG DISTANCE FOOTPATH GUIDE.
— MANAGEMENT & DESIGN NOTES.

**COUNTRYSIDE COMMISSION FOR SCOTLAND.**
— REPORT, COUNTRYSIDE COMMISSION FOR SCOTLAND.

**COVENT GARDEN LABORATORY.**
— ANNUAL REPORT, DITTON & COVENT GARDEN LABORATORIES.     XXX

**CRAFTSMEN POTTERS ASSOCIATION OF GREAT BRITAIN.**
— CERAMIC REVIEW. MAGAZINE OF THE CRAFTSMEN POTTERS ASSOCIATION OF GREAT BRITAIN.

**(CRANBROOK) PUBLIC AFFAIRS OFFICE.**
— CRANBROOK MAGAZINE.

**CRANFIELD CENTRE FOR TRANSPORT STUDIES.**
— CRANFIELD CTS REPORT.

**CRANFIELD INSTITUTE OF TECHNOLOGY.**     XXX
— CRANFIELD REPORT AERO.     XXX
— CRANFIELD REPORT A.S.A.E.     XXX
— CRANFIELD REPORT E & C.     XXX
— CRANFIELD REPORT M & P.     XXX
— CRANFIELD REPORT MAT.     XXX

**CRANFIELD INSTITUTE OF TECHNOLOGY: SCHOOL OF MECHANICAL ENGINEERING.**
— CRANFIELD REPORT SME.

**CRIMINOLOGICA FOUNDATION.**
— ABSTRACTS ON CRIMINOLOGY & PENOLOGY.     XXX
— ABSTRACTS ON POLICE SCIENCE.

**CROATION ACADEMY OF AMERICA.**
— JOURNAL OF CROATIAN STUDIES.

**CROSBY PUBLIC LIBRARIES.**
— CROSBY HISTORICAL PUBLICATIONS.

**CROYDON NATURAL HISTORY & SCIENTIFIC SOCIETY.**
— BULLETIN, CROYDON NATURAL HISTORY & SCIENT-IFIC SOCIETY.

**CRYOGENIC DATA CENTER.**
— QUARTERLY PROGRESS REPORT, CRYOGENIC DATA CENTER.

**CRYSTALLOGRAPHIC DATA CENTRE.**
— MOLECULAR STRUCTURES & DIMENSIONS.

**CSIRO (AUSTRALIA).**
— AUSTRALIAN JOURNAL OF BOTANY: SUPPLEMENTARY SERIES.
— AUSTRALIAN JOURNAL OF ZOOLOGY: SUPPLEMENTARY SERIES.

**CSIRO (AUSTRALIA): DIVISION OF APPLIED CHEM-ISTRY.**
— TECHNICAL PAPER, DIVISION OF APPLIED CHEM-ISTRY, CSIRO (AUSTRALIA).

**CSIRO (AUSTRALIA): DIVISION OF APPLIED GEO-MECHANICS.**
— ABSTRACTS OF PUBLISHED PAPERS, DIVISION OF APPLIED GEOMECHANICS, CSIRO (AUSTRALIA).
— TECHNICAL REPORT, DIVISION OF APPLIED GEOMECH-ANICS, CSIRO (AUSTRALIA).     XXX

**CSIRO (AUSTRALIA): DIVISION OF APPLIED MINER-ALOGY.**
— TECHNICAL PAPER, DIVISION OF APPLIED MINERAL-OGY, CSIRO (AUSTRALIA).

**CSIRO (AUSTRALIA): DIVISION OF COAL RESEARCH.**
— ANNUAL REPORT, DIVISION OF COAL RESEARCH, CSIRO (AUSTRALIA).     XXX

**CSIRO (AUSTRALIA): DIVISION OF FOOD PRESERV-ATION.**     XXX
— TECHNICAL PAPER, DIVISION OF FOOD PRESERVAT-ION, CSIRO (AUSTRALIA).     XXX
SUBS (1972): TECHNICAL PAPER, DIVISION OF FOOD RESEARCH ...

**CSIRO (AUSTRALIA): DIVISION OF FOOD RESEARCH.**
— TECHNICAL PAPER, DIVISION OF FOOD RESEARCH, CSIRO (AUSTRALIA).     XXX

**CSIRO (AUSTRALIA): DIVISION OF HORTICULTURAL RESEARCH.**
— TECHNICAL PAPER, DIVISION OF HORTICULTURAL RESEARCH, CSIRO (AUSTRALIA).

**CSIRO (AUSTRALIA): DIVISION OF MINERAL CHEMISTRY.**
— ANNUAL REPORT, DIVISION OF MINERAL CHEMISTRY, CSIRO (AUSTRALIA).     XXX
— MINERAL CHEMISTRY RESEARCH REPORT, DIVISION OF MINERAL CHEMISTRY, CSIRO (AUSTRALIA).     XXX

**CSIRO (AUSTRALIA): DIVISION OF SOIL MECH-ANICS.**     XXX
— TECHNICAL REPORT, DIVISION OF SOIL MECHANICS, CSIRO (AUSTRALIA).     XXX

**CSIRO (AUSTRALIA): DIVISION OF SOILS.**
— TECHNICAL PAPER, DIVISION OF SOILS, CSIRO (AUSTRALIA).

**CSIRO (AUSTRALIA): DIVISION OF WILDLIFE RESEARCH.**
— TECHNICAL MEMORANDUM, DIVISION OF WILD LIFE RESEARCH, CSIRO (AUSTRALIA).

**CSIRO (AUSTRALIA): MARINE BIOCHEMISTRY UNIT.**
— ANNUAL REPORT, MARINE BIOCHEMISTRY UNIT, CSIRO (AUSTRALIA).

**CSIRO (AUSTRALIA): RANGELANDS RESEARCH UNIT.**
— REPORT, RANGELANDS RESEARCH UNIT, CSIRO (AUSTRALIA).     XXX

**CUMANN NA GAEILGE (NEW YORK).**
— FEINISC.

**CUMANN SEANCHAIS LONGFOIRT.**     000
SEE: LONGFORD HISTORICAL SOCIETY.

**CUMBERLAND, WESTMORLAND & CARLISLE JOINT ARCH-IVES COMMITTEE: RECORD OFFICE.**
— PUBLICATIONS, RECORD OFFICE, CUMBERLAND, WEST-MORLAND & CARLISLE JOINT ARCHIVES COMMITTEE.

**CURRENT AFFAIRS RESEARCH SERVICES CENTRE.**
— CONFLICT STUDIES.

**CUSHMAN FOUNDATION FOR FORAMINIFERAL RESEARCH.**
— CONTRIBUTIONS FROM THE CUSHMAN FOUNDATION FOR FORAMINIFERAL RESEARCH.     XXX
SUBS (1970): JOURNAL OF FORAMINIFERAL RES-EARCH.
— JOURNAL OF FORAMINIFERAL RESEARCH.     XXX

CYMDEITHAS EMYNAU CYMRU.
— BWELTIN, CYMDEITHAS EMYNAU CYMRU.

CYMDEITHAS EMYNWYR CYMRU.
— TRAFODION, CYMDEITHAS EMYNWYR CYMRU.

(CYPRUS) PUBLIC INFORMATION OFFICE.
— CYPRUS BULLETIN.

CYPRUS RESEARCH CENTRE.
— EPETERIS.

CZECHOSLOVAK ATOMIC ENERGY COMMISION.
— NUCLEAR SCIENCE ABSTRACTS OF CZECHOSLOVAKIA.

(CZECHOSLOVAKIA) CENTRAL OFFICE OF SCIENTIFIC,
TECHNICAL & ECONOMIC INFORMATION.
— CZECHOSLOVAK SCIENTIFIC & TECHNICAL
  PERIODICALS CONTENTS.

(CZECHOSLOVAKIA) MINISTERSTVO STAVEBNICTVI:
(RESEARCH INSTITUTE OF ENGINEERING,
BRATISLAVA).
— EUROPEAN CIVIL ENGINEERING.

(CZECHOSLOVAKIA) MINISTERSTVO VNITRA.
— SPRAVNI PRAVO.

(CZECHOSLOVAKIA) MINISTERSTVO ZEMEDELSTVI,
LESNIHO A VODNIHO HOSPODARSTVI.
— SOCIALISTICKE ZEMEDELSTVI, CASOPIS PRO
  VYROBNI ZEMEDELSKE SPRAVY A ORGANIZATORY
  VYROBY.

(CZECHOSLOVAKIA) MINISTERSTVO ZEMEDELSTVI,
LESNIHO A VODNIHO HOSPODARSTVI: USTAV
VEDECKOTECHNICKYCH INFORMACI.
— GENETIKA A SLECHTENI.
— SBORNIK UVTI: SOCIOLOGIE A HISTORIE
  ZEMEDELSTVI.

(CZECHOSLOVAKIA) URAD PRO NORMALIZACI A MERENI.
— MEROVA TECHNIKA.

DACHSHUND CLUB.
— DACHSHUND CLUB NEWSLETTER.

DAG HAMMARSKJOLD FOUNDATION.
— DEVELOPMENT DIALOGUE.

DAIDO KOGYO DAIGAKU.
— DAIDO KOGYO DAIGAKU KIYU.  BULLETIN OF DAIDO
  TECHNICAL COLLEGE.

DAIDO TECHNICAL COLLEGE.                                                000
  SEE:  DAIDO KOGYO DAIGAKU.

DAI-ICHI DANGYO BANK LTD.                                               000
  SEE: DAIICHI KANGYO GINKO.

DAIICHI KANGYO GINKO.
— DKB ECONOMIC REPORT.

DAL'NEVOSTOCHNYJ GOSUDARSTVENNYJ UNIVERSITET.
— UCHENYE ZAPISKI, DAL'NEVOSTOCHNYJ GOSUDARST-
  VENNYJ UNIVERSITET: SERIJA EKONOMICHESKAJA.

DAL'NEVOSTOCHNYJ TEKHNICHESKIJ INSTITUT RYBNOJ
PROMYSHLENNOSTI I KHOZJAJSTVA.
— TRUDY DAL'NEVOSTOCHNOGO TEKHNICHESKOGO INST-
  ITUTA RYBNOJ PROMYSHLENNOSTI I KHOZJAJSTVA.

DANIEL DE LEON LEAGUE.
— DE LEONIST.                                                          XXX

DANISH-SCOTTISH SOCIETY.
— NEWSLETTER, DANISH-SCOTTISH SOCIETY.

DANMARKS GEOLOGISKE UNDERSOGELSE.
— RAPPORT, DANMARKS GEOLOGISKE UNDERSOGELSE.

DANMARKS NATIONALMUSEET.
— MUSEUMSTEKNISKE STUDIER.  STUDIES IN MUSEUM
  TECHNOLOGY.

DANMARKS TEKNISKE HOJSKOLE: AFDELINGEN FOR
BAERENDE KONSTRUKTIONER.
— RAPPORT, AFDELINGEN FOR BAERENDE KONSTRUKT-
  IONER, DANMARKS TEKNISKE HOJSKOLE.                                  XXX

DANMARKS TEKNISKE HOJSKOLE: LABORATORIET FOR
BYGNINGSTEKNIK.
— RAPPORT, LABORATORIET FOR BYGNINGSTEKNIK,
  DANMARKS TEKNISKE HOJSKOLE.

DANSK METEOROLOGISK INSTITUT.
— KLIMATOLOGISKE MEDDELELSER.

DARESBURY NUCLEAR PHYSICS LABORATORY.
— ANNUAL REPORT, DARESBURY NUCLEAR PHYSICS LAB-
  ORATORY.                                                            XXX
— PROGRESS REPORT, DARESBURY NUCLEAR PHYSICS
  LABORATORY: 4 GE V ELECTRON SYNCHROTRON.                          XXX

DATA PROCESSING MANAGEMENT ASSOCIATION.
— DATA MANAGEMENT. (PARK RIDGE).                                     XXX

DECIMAL CURRENCY BOARD (GB).
— ANNUAL REPORT, DECIMAL CURRENCY BOARD (GB).
— DECIMAL CURRENCY BOARD NEWSLETTER.

DELAWARE MUSEUM OF NATURAL HISTORY.
— NEMOURIA.

DELFT HYDRAULICS LABORATORY.                                          000
  SEE:  WATERLOOPKUNDIG LABORATORIUM (DELFT).

DELTA TAU KAPPA.
— INTERNATIONAL BEHAVIOURAL SCIENTIST.

DEMBAR EDUCATIONAL RESEARCH SERVICES.
— ENVIRONMENTAL EDUCATION.

DENISON UNIVERSITY: DEPARTMENT OF VISUAL ARTS.
— BURMESE ART NEWSLETTER.

(DENMARK) UDENRIGSMINISTERIUM.
— DANISH FOREIGN OFFICE JOURNAL.                                     XXX
  SUBS (1969): DANISH JOURNAL.
— DANISH JOURNAL.                                                    XXX

DENVER MUSEUM OF NATURAL HISTORY.
— PROCEEDINGS, DENVER MUSEUM OF NATURAL HISTORY                      XXX

DEPAUW UNIVERSITY: AFRICAN STUDIES CENTRE.
— LIBERIAN STUDIES JOURNAL.

DEPUTAZIONE DI STORIA PATRIA PER LE VENEZIE.
— BIBLIOTECA DELL' 'ARCHIVIO VENETO'.

DERBYSHIRE ARCHAEOLOGICAL & NATURAL HISTORY
SOCIETY: INDUSTRIAL ARCHAEOLOGY SECTION.
— NEWSLETTER, INDUSTRIAL ARCHAEOLOGY SECTION,
  DERBYSHIRE ARCHAEOLOGICAL & NATURAL HISTORY
  SOCIETY.

DERZHAVNYJ KOMITET PO KOORDYNATSIJI NAUKOVO-
DOSLIDNYKH ROBIT URSR: INSTYTUT TEKHNICHNOJI
INFORMATSIJI.
— KHARCHOVA PROMYSLOVIST'.
— MASHINOSTROENIE. INFORMATSIONNYJ NAUCHNO-TEKHN-
  ICHESKIJ SBORNIK.                                                  XXX

DESIGN METHODS GROUP.
— DMG BULLETIN.
— DMG OCCASIONAL NEWSLETTER.
— DMG OCCASIONAL PAPER.

DESIGNERS & ART DIRECTORS ASSOCIATION OF
LONDON.
— DESIGN & ART DIRECTION ...

DEUTSCHE AKADEMIE DER LANDWIRTSCHAFTSWISSEN-
SCHAFT ZU BERLIN.
— ARCHIV FUR FORSTWESEN.                                             XXX
— ARCHIV FUR ZUCHTUNGSFORSCHUNG.

DEUTSCHE AKADEMIE DER WISSENSCHAFTEN ZU
BERLIN.                                                              XXX
— MONATSBERICHTE, DEUTSCHE AKADEMIE DER WISSEN-
  SCHAFTEN ZU BERLIN.                                                XXX
— SPEKTRUM.

DEUTSCHE AKADEMIE DER WISSENSCHAFTEN ZU BERLIN:
ZENTRALINSTITUT FUR WIRTSCHAFTSWISSENSCHAFTEN.
— SCHRIFTEN, ZENTRALINSTITUT FUR WIRTSCHAFTS-
  WISSENSCHAFTEN, DEUTSCHE AKADEMIE DER WISSEN-
  SCHAFTEN ZU BERLIN.

DEUTSCHES ARCHAOLOGISCHES INSTITUT: ABTEILUNG
KAIRO.
— ARCHAOLOGISCHE VEROFFENTLICHUNGEN, ABTEILUNG
  KAIRO, DEUTSCHES ARCHAOLOGISCHES INSTITUT.

DEUTSCHES ARCHAOLOGISCHES INSTITUT: ABTEILUNG
TEHERAN.
— ARCHAEOLOGISCHE MITTEILUNGEN AUS IRAN: NEUE
  FOLGE.

DEUTSCHES ARCHAOLOGISCHES INSTITUT: KOMMISSION
FUR ALTE GESCHICHTE UND EPIGRAPHIK.
— CHIRON. MITTEILUNGEN DER ...

**DEUTSCHER BUCHEREIVERBAND: ARBEITSSTELLE FUR DAS BUCHEREIWESEN.**
— MUSIKBIBLIOGRAPHISCHER DIENST.

**DEUTSCHE BUNDESBANK.**
— STATISTISCHE BEIHEFTE ZU DEN MONATSBERICHTEN DER DEUTSCHEN BUNDESBANK. REIHE I: BANKENSTATISTIK NACH BANKENGRUPPEN.

**DEUTSCHE DENDROLOGISCHE GESELLSCHAFT.**
— KURZMITTEILUNGEN, DEUTSCHE DENDROLOGISCHE GESELLSCHAFT.

**DEUTSCHE FORSCHUNGS- UND VERSUCHSANSTALT FUR LUFT- UND RAUMFAHRT.**
— DFVLR NACHRICHTEN.

**DEUTSCHE FORSCHUNGSANSTALT FUR LUFT- UND RAUMFAHRT.**												XXX
— BERICHT, DEUTSCHE FORSCHUNGSANSTALT FUR LUFT- UND RAUMFAHRT.												XXX
SUBS (1964): FORSCHUNGSBERICHT, DEUTSCHE LUFT- UND RAUMFAHRT.

**DEUTSCHE FORSCHUNGSGEMEINSCHAFT.**
— 'METEOR' FORSCHUNGSERGEBNISSE; REIHE A: ALLGEMEINES PHYSIK UND CHEMIE DES MEERES.
— 'METEOR' FORSCHUNGSERGEBNISSE; REIHE B: METEOROLOGIE UND AERONOMIE.
— 'METEOR' FORSCHUNGSERGEBNISSE: REIHE C: GEOLOGIE UND GEOPHYSIK.
— 'METEOR' FORSCHUNGSERGEBNISSE: REIHE D: BIOLOGIE.

**DEUTSCHE FORSCHUNGSGESELLSCHAFT FUR BLECHVERARBEITUNG UND OBERFLACHENBEHANDLUNG.**
— PRAKTISCHE WINKE FUR DIE BLECHVERARBEITUNG UND OBERFLACHENBEHANDLUNG.

**DEUTSCHE GESELLSCHAFT FUR FORSCHUNG IM GRAPHISCHEN GEWERBE.**
— FOGRA PRAXIS REPORT.

**DEUTSCHE GESELLSCHAFT FUR DIE GESAMTE HYGIENE, GESELLSCHAFT FUR GESUNDHEITSSCHUTZ.**
— MITTEILUNGEN, DEUTSCHE GESELLSCHAFT FUR DIE GESAMTE HYGIENE, GESELLSCHAFT FUR GESUNDHEITSSCHUTZ: SEKTION FUR GESCHICHTE DER MEDIZIN.

**DEUTSCHE GESELLSCHAFT FUR KRANKENHAUSGESCHICHTE**
— HISTORIA HOSPITALIUM. MITTEILUNGEN ...

**DEUTSCHE GESELLSCHAFT FUR MINERALOLWISSENSCHAFT UND KOHLECHEMIE.**
— ERDOL UND KOHLE, ERDGAS, PETROCHEMIE VEREINIGT MIT BRENNSTOFF-CHEMIE.*

**DEUTSCHE GESELLSCHAFT FUR OSTEUROPAKUNDE.**
— BULLETIN ZUR OSTRECHTSFORSCHUNG IN DEN LANDERN DES EUROPARATES.

**DEUTSCHE GESELLSCHAFT FUR PHYSIKALISCHE MEDIZIN.**
— ZEITSCHRIFT FUR PHYSIKALISCHE MEDIZIN.

**DEUTSCHE GESELLSCHAFT FUR PSYCHOLOGIE.**
— ARCHIV FUR DIE GESAMTE PSYCHOLOGIE.												XXX
SUBS (1970): ARCHIV FUR PSYCHOLOGIE.
— ARCHIV FUR PSYCHOLOGIE.												XXX

**DEUTSCHE GESELLSCHAFT FUR RECHTSMEDIZIN.**
— DEUTSCHE ZEITSCHRIFT FUR DIE GESAMTE GERICHTLICHE MEDIZIN.												XXX
SUBS. (1970) PART OF: ZEITSCHRIFT FUR RECHTSMEDIZIN; & ZENTRALBLATT FUR DIE GESAMTE RECHTSMEDIZIN UND IHRE GRENZGEBIETE.
— ZEITSCHRIFT FUR RECHTSMEDIZIN. JOURNAL OF LEGAL MEDICINE.												XXX
— ZENTRALBLATT FUR DIE GESAMTE RECHTSMEDIZIN UND IHRE GRENZGEBIETE.												XXX

**DEUTSCHE GESELLSCHAFT FUR RHEUMATOLOGIE.**
— VERHANDLUNGEN, DEUTSCHE GESELLSCHAFT FUR RHEUMATOLOGIE.

**DEUTSCHES INSTITUT FUR MILITARGESCHICHTE.**												XXX
— MILITARGESCHICHTE.												XXX

**DEUTSCHES INSTITUT FUR WIRTSCHAFTSFORSCHUNG.**
— DIW-BEITRAGE ZUR STRUKTURFORSCHUNG.

**DEUTSCHE LUFT- UND RAUMFAHRT.**
— FORSCHUNGSBERICHT, DEUTSCHE LUFT- UND RAUMFAHRT.												XXX

**DEUTSCHE MALAKOZOOLOGISCHEN GESELLSCHAFT.**
— MITTEILUNGEN, DEUTSCHE MALAKOZOOLOGISCHEN GESELLSCHAFT.

**DEUTSCHEN PHYSIKALISCHEN GESELLSCHAFT.**
— ZEITSCHRIFT FUR ANGEWANDTE PHYSIK.												XXX

**DEUTSCHE VERSUCHSANSTALT FUR LUFT- UND RAUMFAHRT.**												XXX
— BERICHT, DEUTSCHE VERSUCHSANSTALT FUR LUFT- UND RAUMFAHRT.												XXX
SUBS (1964): FORSCHUNGSBERICHT, DEUTSCHE LUFT- UND RAUMFAHRT.

**DEVELOPMENT BANK OF THE PHILIPPINES.**
— PHILIPPINE PROGRESS.

**D.H. LAWRENCE ASSOCIATION.**
— NETHERMERE NEWS.

**DIAMOND LEAD CO.**
— INDUSTRIA. JAPAN'S ECONOMY, INDUSTRY & TECHNOLOGY.

**DIESEL ENGINES INC.**
— DIESEL & GAS TURBINE PROGRESS - WORLDWIDE EDITION.

**DIFFUSION INFORMATION CENTER.**
— DIFFUSION MONOGRAPH SERIES.

**DIGITAL EQUIPMENT COMPUTER USERS SOCIETY.**
— DECUSCOPE. NEWSLETTER FOR DIGITAL EQUIPMENT COMPUTER USERS SOCIETY.

**DINERS CLUB OF GREAT BRITAIN.**
— DINERS CLUB MAGAZINE. (LONDON)												XXX
SUBS (1966): SIGNATURE.
— SIGNATURE.

**DIOCESE OF SOUTHWARK COMMISSION FOR THE LITURGY: SUB-COMMITTEE FOR THE PROMOTION OF THE LITURGY.**
— LITURGY BULLETIN.

**DISTRICT BANK.**												XXX
— DISTRICT BANK REVIEW.												XXX
SUBS (1968): PART OF QUARTERLY REVIEW, NATIONAL WESTMINSTER BANK.

**DITTON LABORATORY.**
— ANNUAL REPORT, DITTON & COVENT GARDEN LABORATORIES.												XXX
— ANNUAL REPORT, DITTON LABORATORY.

**DNEPROPETROVSKIJ GORNYJ INSTITUT [IM. ARTEMA].**
— GORNAJA ELEKTROMEKHANIKA I AVTOMATIKA.

**DNEPROPETROVSKIJ INSTITUT CHERNOJ METALLURGII.**
— TRUDY DNEPROPETROVSKOGO INSTITUTA CHERNOJ METALLURGII.												XXX

**DNIPROPETROVS'KYJ KHIMIKO-TEKHNOLOHICHNYJ INSTYTUT.**
— KHIMICHESKAJA TEKHNOLOGIJA.

**DOBOKU GAKKAI.**
— TRANSACTIONS OF THE JAPAN SOCIETY OF CIVIL ENGINEERS.

**DOBUTSU IYAKUHIN KENSAJO.**
— DOBUTSU IYAKUHIN KENSAJO NENPO. ANNUAL REPORT OF THE NATIONAL VETERINARY ASSAY LABORATORY.

**DOMESTIC HEATING SOCIETY.**
— DOMESTIC HEATING. THE JOURNAL OF THE ...

**DONCASTER ARTS & MUSEUM SOCIETY.**
— LOCAL HISTORY PUBLICATION, DONCASTER ARTS & MUSEUM SOCIETY.

**DONCASTER & DISTRICT DEVELOPMENT COUNCIL.**
— ANNUAL REPORT, DONCASTER & DISTRICT DEVELOPMENT COUNCIL.
— DEVELOPMENT DIGEST FOR YORKSHIRE & HUMBERSIDE.

**DONETSKIJ NAUCHNO-ISSLEDOVATEL'SKIJ INSTITUT CHERNOJ METALLURGII.**
— SBORNIK TRUDOV, DONETSKIJ NAUCHNO-ISSLEDOVATEL'SKIJ INSTITUT CHERNOJ METALLURGII.

**DONNER INSTITUTE FOR RESEARCH IN RELIGIOUS & CULTURAL HISTORY (ABO AKADEMI).**
— SCRIPTA INSTITUTI DONNERIANI ABOENSIS.

DORE VILLAGE SOCIETY.
— OCCASIONAL PUBLICATIONS, DORE VILLAGE SOCIETY.

DORMAN MUSEUM & MUNICIPAL ART GALLERY.
— REPORT, DORMAN MUSEUM & MUNICIPAL ART GALLERY.

DOUGLAS COMMUNICATIONS, INC.
— COMMUNICATIONS DESIGNER'S DIGEST.                    XXX

DOW CHEMICAL EUROPE.
— ELEMENTS.

DOWLING COLLEGE.
— MEDITERRANEAN REVIEW (NEW YORK).

DRUID ORDER.
— DRUID.

DRUSTVO PARAZITOLOGA JUGOSLAVIJE.
— ACTA PARASITOLOGICA IUGOSLAVICA.

DRZAVNI ARHIV NR BOSNE I HERCEGOVINE.
— GLASNIK ARHIVA I DRUSTVA ARHIVISTA BOSNE I
HERCEGOVINE.

DU PONT OF CANADA LTD.
— CREATIVE PLASTICS.

DU PONT DE NEMOURS & CO.
— DU PONT INNOVATION.

DUBLIN HISTORICAL ASSOCIATION.
— MEDIEVAL IRISH HISTORY SERIES.

DUMBARTON OAKS TRUSTEES.
— STUDIES IN PRE-COLUMBIAN ART & ARCHAEOLOGY.

DUNDEE MUSEUMS & ART GALLERIES DEPARTMENT.
— TAYMAG. NEWSLETTER OF THE CITY OF DUNDEE
MUSEUMS & ART GALLERIES DEPARTMENT.

DUQUESNE UNIVERSITY: DEPARTMENT OF MODERN
LANGUAGES.
— DUQUESNE HISPANIC REVIEW.

DURHAM COUNTY COUNCIL: PLANNING COMMITTEE.
— PLANNING IN DURHAM.

DURHAM UNIVERSITY ANTHROPOLOGICAL SOCIETY.
— DYN. THE JOURNAL OF THE ...

DURHAM UNIVERSITY GROUP FOR INDUSTRIAL ARCH-
AEOLOGY.
— INDUSTRIAL HERITAGE.

DURZHAVEN KOMITET ZA NAUKA I TEKHNICHESKI
PROGRES.
— AVTOMATIKA I IZCHISLITELNA TEKHNIKA.

DURZHAVNA STROITELNA ORGANIZATSIJA: KOMITET PO
LEKATA PROMISHLENOST.                                  XXX
— KOZHI, OBUVKI.                                        XXX

DUTCH ARCHAEOLOGICAL & HISTORICAL SOCIETY.
— TALANTA. PROCEEDINGS OF THE ...

EALING TECHNICAL COLLEGE: SCHOOL OF LIBRARIAN-
SHIP.
— EALING OCCASIONAL PAPERS IN THE HISTORY OF
LIBRARIES.
— STAMP OUT.

EAST AFRICAN AGRICULTURAL ECONOMIC SOCIETY.
— EAST AFRICAN JOURNAL OF RURAL DEVELOPMENT.

EAST AFRICAN FISHERIES RESEARCH ORGANIZATIONS.
— AFRICAN JOURNAL OF TROPICAL HYDROBIOLOGY &
FISHERIES.

EAST AFRICAN LITERATURE BUREAU.
— JOURNAL OF EASTERN AFRICAN RESEARCH &
DEVELOPMENT.

EAST AFRICAN MANAGEMENT FOUNDATION.
— EAST AFRICAN MANAGEMENT JOURNAL.

EAST AFRICAN RESEARCH INFORMATION CENTRE.
— EARIC INFORMATION CIRCULAR.

EAST LONDON ARTS MAGAZINE SOCIETY.
— PORTFOLIO.

EAST MIDLAND ART ASSOCIATION.
— LAURELS.

EAST RIDING ARCHAEOLOGICAL SOCIETY.
— EAST RIDING ARCHAEOLOGIST.

EAST RIDING ASSOCIATION FOR RURAL STUDIES.
— RURAL STUDIES: YORKSHIRE EAST RIDING.

EAST OF SCOTLAND COLLEGE OF AGRICULTURE:
ECONOMICS DEPARTMENT.                                  XXX
— REPORT, ECONOMICS DEPARTMENT, EAST OF
SCOTLAND COLLEGE OF AGRICULTURE.                    XXX

EASTBOURNE THEATRE COMPANY.
— FOOTLIGHTS.

EASTERN ARTS ASSOCIATION.
— EASTWORD.

EASTERN MICHIGAN UNIVERSITY: DEPARTMENT OF
ENGLISH.
— JOURNAL OF NARRATIVE TECHNIQUE.

EASTERN NEW MEXICO UNIVERSITY.
— STUDIES IN NATURAL SCIENCES.

EASTMAN KODAK.
— EASTMAN ORGANIC CHEMICAL BULLETIN.          XXX
— ORGANIC CHEMICAL BULLETIN.                   XXX
SUBS (1969): EASTMAN ORGANIC CHEMICAL
BULLETIN.

ECOLE FRANCAISE DE ROME.
— MELANGES D'ARCHEOLOGIE ET D'HISTOIRE.        XXX
SUBS (1971): PART OF MELANGES DE L'ECOLE
FRANCAISE DE ROME: MOYEN AGE - TEMPS
MODERNES; & MELANGES ... ROME: ANTIQUITE.
— MELANGES DE L'ECOLE FRANCAISE DE ROME:
ANTIQUITE.                                      XXX
— MELANGES DE L'ECOLE FRANCAISE DE ROME: MOYEN
AGE - TEMPS MODERNES.                           XXX

ECOLE NATIONALE SUPERIEURE D'AGRONOMIE ET DES
INDUSTRIES ALIMENTAIRES (FRANCE).               XXX
— BULLETIN, ECOLE NATIONALE SUPERIEURE D'AGRON-
OMIE ET DES INDUSTRIES ALIMENTAIRES (FRANCE).  XXX

ECOLE NATIONALE SUPERIEURE AGRONOMIQUE
(MADAGASCAR).
— TERRE MALGACHE. TANY MALAGASY.

ECOLE NATIONALE SUPERIEURE AGRONOMIQUE DE
NANCY.                                          XXX
— BULLETIN, ECOLE NATIONALE SUPERIEURE AGRONOM-
IQUE DE NANCY.                                  XXX
SUBS (1972): BULLETIN, ECOLE NATIONALE
SUPERIEURE D'AGRONOMIQUE ET DES INDUSTRIES
ALIMENTAIRES (FRANCE).

ECOLE NORMALE SUPERIEURE.
— SCOLIES. CAHIERS DE RECHERCHES DE ...

ECOLE PRATIQUE DES HAUTES ETUDES (PARIS):
CENTRE DE DOCUMENTATION SUR L'EXTREME-ORIENT.
— BULLETIN DE LIAISON POUR LES ETUDES CHINOISES
EN EUROPE.

ECOLE PRATIQUE DES HAUTES ETUDES (PARIS):
CENTRE DE DOCUMENTATION ET DE RECHERCHES.
— ASIE DU SUD-EST & MONDE INDONESIEN.

ECOLE PRATIQUE DES HAUTES ETUDES (PARIS):
CENTRE D'ETUDES DES COMMUNICATIONS DE MASSE.
— COMMUNICATIONS.

ECOLE PRATIQUE DES HAUTES ETUDES (PARIS):
CENTRE D'ETUDES PRE-ET PROTOHISTORIQUES.
— ARCHEOCIVILISATION: NS.                       XXX

ECOLE SUPERIEURE DE TRADUCTEURS ET D'INTER-
PRETES DE BRUXELLES.
— EQUIVALENCES. REVUE DE L'ECOLE SUPERIEURE DE
TRADUCTEURS ET D'INTERPRETES DE BRUXELLES.

ECOLOGICAL SOCIETY OF AUSTRALIA.
— PROCEEDINGS OF THE ECOLOGICAL SOCIETY OF
AUSTRALIA.

ECONOMICS ASSOCIATION: LONDON BRANCH.
— BRITISH ECONOMY SURVEY.

ECONOMIC ASSOCIATION OF MALAYSIA.
SEE: PERSATUAN EKONOMI MALAYSIA.

ECONOMICS CLUB OF KENYA.
— EAST AFRICAN ECONOMIC REVIEW. N.S.            XXX

ECONOMIC COUNCIL OF CANADA.
— ANNUAL REVIEW OF THE ECONOMIC COUNCIL OF
CANADA.

ECONOMIC DEVELOPMENT COMMITTEE FOR... [VARIOUS
SUBJECTS]                                                                                              000
   SEE: NATIONAL ECONOMIC DEVELOPMENT OFFICE(GB)

ECONOMIC RESEARCH COUNCIL (GB).
— ECONOMIC AGE.

ECONOMIC & SOCIAL RESEARCH INSTITUTE (DUBLIN).
— ESRI BROADSHEETS.

ECONOMIC & SOCIAL SCIENCE RESEARCH ASSOCIATION.
— ESSRA MAGAZINE.

ECONOMIC & SOCIAL STUDIES.
— ECONOMIC & SOCIAL REVIEW.

ECONOMIC SOCIETY OF AUSTRALIA & NEW ZEALAND:
QUEENSLAND BRANCH.
— ECONOMIC ANALYSIS & POLICY.

ECONOMIC SOCIETY OF TANZANIA.
— UCHUMI. JOURNAL OF THE ECONOMIC SOCIETY OF
  TANZANIA.

ECONOMIST INTELLIGENCE UNIT.
— INTERNATIONAL TOURISM QUARTERLY.
— MULTINATIONAL BUSINESS.
— QUARTERLY ECONOMIC REVIEW: THE ARABIAN
  PENINSULA & JORDAN.                                                                       XXX
— QUARTERLY ECONOMIC REVIEW: CONTINENTAL
  SOUTH EAST ASIA.                                                                          XXX
  SUBS. (1971) PART OF: QUARTERLY ECONOMIC
  REVIEW: INDOCHINA: SOUTH VIETNAM, NORTH
  VIETNAM, CAMBODIA, LAOS; & QUARTERLY
  ECONOMIC REVIEW: THAILAND, BURMA.
— QUARTERLY ECONOMIC REVIEW: CZECHOSLOVAKIA,
  HUNGARY.                                                                                   XXX
— QUARTERLY ECONOMIC REVIEW: EASTERN EUROPE,
  NORTH.
  SUBS (1971): PART OF QUARTERLY ... POLAND,
  EAST GERMANY; & ... CZECHOSLOVAKIA, HUNGARY.
— QUARTERLY ECONOMIC REVIEW: EASTERN EUROPE,
  SOUTH.                                                                                     XXX
  SUBS (1971): PART OF QUARTERLY ... RUMANIA,
  BULGARIA, ALBANIA; & ... CZECHOSLOVAKIA,
  HUNGARY.
— QUARTERLY ECONOMIC REVIEW: INDOCHINA: SOUTH
  VIETNAM, NORTH VIETNAM, CAMBODIA, LAOS.
— QUARTERLY ECONOMIC REVIEW: MOROCCO.                                                                  XXX
— QUARTERLY ECONOMIC REVIEW: OIL IN THE FAR
  EAST & AUSTRALASIA.
— QUARTERLY ECONOMIC REVIEW: OIL IN LATIN
  AMERICA & THE CARIBBEAN.
— QUARTERLY ECONOMIC REVIEW: OIL IN THE MIDDLE
  EAST.                                                                                      XXX
— QUARTERLY ECONOMIC REVIEW: POLAND, EAST
  GERMANY.                                                                                   XXX
— QUARTERLY ECONOMIC REVIEW: RUMANIA, BULGARIA,
  ALBANIA.                                                                                   XXX
— QUARTERLY ECONOMIC REVIEW: SAUDI ARABIA,
  ARABIA, JORDAN.                                                                            XXX
— QUARTERLY ECONOMIC REVIEW: THAILAND, BURMA.                                                          XXX

ECONOMISTS ADVISORY GROUP.
— GOVERNMENT & BUSINESS.

ECUMENICAL THEOLOGICAL RESEARCH FRATERNITY IN
ISRAEL.
— IMMANUEL.

EDGE HILL COLLEGE OF EDUCATION.
— EDGE HILL FORUM ON TEACHER EDUCATION.

EDINBURGH COLLEGE OF COMMERCE: LIBRARY.
— OCCASIONAL PAPER, LIBRARY, EDINBURGH COLLEGE
  OF COMMERCE.

EDINBURGH & EAST OF SCOTLAND COLLEGE OF
AGRICULTURE: ECONOMICS DEPARTMENT.                                                                     XXX
— BULLETIN, ECONOMICS DEPARTMENT, EDINBURGH &
  EAST OF SCOTLAND COLLEGE OF AGRICULTURE.                                                    XXX
  SUBS (1970): REPORT, ECONOMICS DEPARTMENT,
  EAST OF SCOTLAND ...
— ECONOMIC REPORT, ECONOMICS DEPARTMENT,
  EDINBURGH & EAST OF SCOTLAND COLLEGE OF
  AGRICULTURE.                                                                               XXX
  SUBS (1970): REPORT, ECONOMICS DEPARTMENT,
  EAST OF SCOTLAND ...

EDINBURGH UNIVERSITY DRAMATIC SOCIETY.
— MUST.

EDUCATIONAL INTERCHANGE COUNCIL.
— YOUTH TRAVELS.

EESTI NSV POLEVKIVI UURIMISE INSTITUUT.
— KHIMIJA I TEKHNOLOGIJA GORJUCHIKH SLANTSEV I
  PRODUKTOV IKH PERERABOTKI.                                                                 XXX

EESTI NSV TEADUSTE AKADEEMIA.
— SOVETSKOE FINNO-UGROVEDENIE.
— UURIMUSI EHITUSE ALALT. ISSLEDOVANIJA PO
  STROITEL'STVU.

EGE UNIVERSITESI: ZIRAAT FAKULTESI.
— YEARBOOK OF THE FACULTY OF AGRICULTURE,
  UNIVERSITY OF EGE.

EGYPTIAN SOCIETY OF GENETICS.
— EGYPTIAN JOURNAL OF GENETICS & CYTOLOGY.

EIDGENOSSISCHEN JODLER-DIRIGENTEN-VEREINIGUNG.
— BARGFRUEHLIG. MUSIKALISCH-VOLKSKUNDLICHE
  ZEITSCHRIFT DER ...

EIGHTEENTH-CENTURY SHORT-TITLE CATALOGUE
COMMITTEE.
— NEWSLETTER, EIGHTEENTH-CENTURY SHORT-TITLE
  CATALOGUE COMMITTEE.

(EIRE) DEPARTMENT OF EDUCATION.
— OIDEAS.

(EIRE) DEPARTMENT OF INDUSTRY & COMMERCE:
NATIONAL PRICE'S COMMISSION.
— OCCASIONAL PAPER, NATIONAL PRICE'S COMMISSION,
  DEPARTMENT OF INDUSTRY & COMMERCE (EIRE).

(EIRE) GEOLOGICAL SURVEY.
— BULLETIN, GEOLOGICAL SURVEY OF IRELAND.
— INFORMATION CIRCULAR, GEOLOGICAL SURVEY OF
  IRELAND.
— SPECIAL PAPERS, GEOLOGICAL SURVEY OF IRELAND.

(EIRE) GOVERNMENT INFORMATION BUREAU.
— EOLAS.

(EIRE) METEOROLOGICAL SERVICE.
— CLIMATOLOGICAL NOTE.

EIRE PHILATELIC ASSOCIATION.
— JOURNAL OF IRISH PHILATELY.

ELECTRIC CAR RACING ASSOCIATION.
— MODEL CARS.

ELECTRICAL, ELECTRONIC & TELECOMMUNICATION
UNION.
— CONTACT (BROMLEY).                                                                                   XXX

ELECTRICAL RESEARCH ASSOCIATION.
— ELECTROSTATICS ABSTRACTS.
— ERA JOURNAL. INNOVATION IN ELECTROTECHNOLOGY.                                                        XXX

ELECTRICITY SUPPLY INDUSTRY TRAINING BOARD
(G.B.).
— BULLETIN, ELECTRICITY SUPPLY INDUSTRY TRAIN-
  ING BOARD (G.B.).

EMERSON COLLEGE.
— DICKENS STUDIES.                                                                                     XXX

EMERSON SOCIETY.
— AMERICAN TRANSCENDENTAL QUARTERLY.
— EMERSON SOCIETY QUARTERLY.                                                                           XXX
  SUBS (1972): E.S.Q.
— E.S.Q.                                                                                               XXX

E.M.I. ELECTRONICS, LTD.
— ELECTRONICS POST.                                                                                    XXX

EMORY UNIVERSITY.
— CENTRAL EUROPEAN HISTORY.

EMPIRE COTTON GROWING CORPORATION.                                                                     XXX
— PROGRESS REPORTS FROM EXPERIMENT STATIONS,
  EMPIRE COTTON GROWING CORPORATION.                                                          XXX
  SUBS (1966): PROGRESS REPORTS FROM EXPER-
  IMENT STATIONS, COTTON RESEARCH CORPORATION.

ENGINEERING EMPLOYERS' FEDERATION.
— EEF NEWS.
— FEDERATION RESEARCH PAPER.

ENGINEERING INDUSTRY TRAINING BOARD (GB).
— BLUEPRINT.
— OCCASIONAL PAPER, ENGINEERING INDUSTRY TRAIN-
  ING BOARD (GB).

ENGLER-BUNTE-INSTITUT: BEREICH UND LEHRSTUHL
FUR WASSERCHEMIE.                                                XXX
— VEROFFENTLICHUNGEN, BEREICH UND LEHRSTUHL
FUR WASSERCHEMIE, ENGLER-BUNTE-INSTITUT.                    XXX

ENGLISH PLACE NAME SOCIETY.
— JOURNAL, ENGLISH PLACE NAME SOCIETY.

ENGLISH SPEAKING BOARD.
— SPOKEN ENGLISH.

ENTOMOLOGICAL SOCIETY OF AMERICA.
— ENVIRONMENTAL ENTOMOLOGY.

ENTOMOLOGICAL SOCIETY OF CANADA.
— BULLETIN OF THE ENTOMOLOGICAL SOCIETY OF
CANADA.

ENTOMOLOGICAL SOCIETY OF MANITOBA.
— MANITOBA ENTOMOLOGIST.

ENTOMOLOGICAL SOCIETY OF NEW ZEALAND.
— BULLETIN, ENTOMOLOGICAL SOCIETY OF NEW
ZEALAND.

ENTOMOLOGICAL SOCIETY OF NIGERIA.
— BULLETIN OF THE ENTOMOLOGICAL SOCIETY OF
NIGERIA.
— NIGERIAN ENTOMOLOGISTS' MAGAZINE.

ENTOMOLOGICAL SOCIETY OF QUEBEC.
— MEMOIRS, ENTOMOLOGICAL SOCIETY OF QUEBEC.

ENTOMOLOGISCHERVEREIN (STUTTGART).
— MITTEILUNGEN, ENTOMOLOGISCHERVEREIN (STUTT-
GART).

ENVIRONMENT INFORMATION CENTER.
— ENVIRONMENT INDEX.

ENVIRONMENT INFORMATION CENTER OF ECOLOGY FORUM
— ENVIRONMENT INFORMATION ACCESS.                            XXX

ENVIRONMENTAL MUTAGEN SOCIETY.
— NEWS LETTER, ENVIRONMENTAL MUTAGEN SOCIETY.               XXX

ENYO SUISAN KENKYUJO.
— ENYO SUISAN KENKYUJO KENKYU HOKOKU.  BULLETIN,
FAR SEAS' FISHERIES RESEARCH LABORATORY.

EREVANSKIJ GOSUDARSTVENNYJ PEDAGOGICHESKIJ
INSTITUT.
— BRJUSOVSKIE CHTENIJA.

ERNST-MORITZ-ARNDT UNIVERSITAT GREIFSWALD.
— NORDEUROPA. JAHRBUCH FUR NORDISCHE STUDIEN.

ESCOLA NACIONAL DE SAUDE PUBLICA E DE MEDICINA
TROPICAL (PORTUGAL).
— ANAIS DA ESCOLA NACIONAL DE SAUDE PUBLICA E
DE MEDICINA TROPICAL.                                       XXX

ESCUELA INTERAMERICANA DE BIBLIOTECOLOGIA.
— BIBLIOGRAFIA OFICIAL COLOMBIANA.

ESCUELA LATINOAMERICANA DE CIENCIA POLITICA Y
— REVISTA LATINOAMERICANA DE CIENCIA POLITICA.

ESCUELA NACIONAL DE CIENCIAS BIOLOGICAS
(MEXICO).
— BOLETIN BIBLIOGRAFICO DE LA ESCUELA NACIONAL
DE CIENCIAS BIOLOGICAS (MEXICO).

ESCUELA NACIONAL DE CIENCIAS BIOLOGICAS
(MEXICO): SEMINARIO DE ESTUDIOS BIOLOGICAS.
— BIOS. SEMINARIO DE ESTUDIOS BIOLOGICAS.                   XXX

ESCUELA POLITECNICA NACIONAL (ECUADOR).
— POLITECNICA.  REVISTA DE INFORMACION TECNICO-
CIENTIFICA.

ESSEX MAMMAL GROUP.
— ESSEX MAMMAL NEWS.                                         XXX

ESSEX UNIVERSITY: DEPARTMENT OF SOCIOLOGY.
— ORAL HISTORY.

ESSO PETROLEUM CO. LTD.
— SCIENCE ABSTRACTS.                                         XXX
— SCIENCE TEACHERS ABSTRACTS.

(ESTONIA) METSAMAJANDUSE JA LOODUSKAITSE
MINISTEERIUM.
— TRUDY GOSUDARSTVENNYKH ZAPOVEDNIKOV ESTONSKOJ
SSR.

(ESTONIAN SSR) RIIKLIK RAAMATUPALAT.
— EESTI NSV TRUKITOODANGU STATISTIKA. STATIST-
IKA PECHATI ESTONSKOJ SSR.

ESTUARINE & BRACKISH WATER SCIENCES
ASSOCIATION.
— ESTUARINE & COASTAL MARINE SCIENCE.

ESTUDOS GERAIS UNIVERSITARIOS DE MOCAMBIQUE.
— REVISTA DOS ESTUDOS GERAIS UNIVERSITARIOS DE
MOCAMBIQUE: SERIE 1: CIENCIAS MATEMATICAS,
FISICAS E QUIMICAS.                                          XXX

ETHIOPIAN WILDLIFE & NATURAL HISTORY SOCIETY.
— WALIA.

EUGENICS SOCIETY.
— BULLETIN, EUGENICS SOCIETY.

EURATOM.                                                      000
SEE: EUROPEAN ATOMIC ENERGY COMMUNITY.

EUROPEAN ASSOCIATION OF EARTH SCIENCE EDITORS.
— EDITERRA CIRCULAR LETTER.

EUROPEAN ASSOCIATION FOR INDUSTRIAL MARKETING
RESEARCH.
— INDUSTRIAL MARKETING MANAGEMENT.

EUROPEAN ASSOCIATION FOR MAXILLOFACIAL SURGERY.
— JOURNAL OF MAXILLOFACIAL SURGERY.

EUROPEAN ASSOCIATION FOR POTATO RESEARCH.
— EUROPEAN POTATO JOURNAL.                                   XXX
SUBS (1970):  POTATO RESEARCH.
— POTATO RESEARCH.                                           XXX

EUROPEAN-ATLANTIC MOVEMENT.
— CITIZENS OF EUROPE.  NS.

EUROPEAN ATOMIC ENERGY COMMUNITY.
— EURATOM. REVIEW OF THE EUROPEAN ATOMIC ENERGY
COMMUNITY.                                                   XXX
— EURATOM BULLETIN.  Q.                                      XXX
— EURATOM INFORMATION.                                       XXX
— EURO SPECTRA. SCIENTIFIC & TECHNICAL REVIEW
OF THE EUROPEAN COMMUNITIES.                                XXX

EUROPEAN BANKS' INTERNATIONAL COMPANY.
— EBIC BULLETIN.

EUROPEAN CENTRE FOR LEISURE & EDUCATION.
— SOCIETY & LEISURE.

EUROPEAN CENTRE FOR POPULATION STUDIES.
— EUROPEAN DEMOGRAPHIC INFORMATION BULLETIN.

EUROPEAN CHEMORECEPTION RESEARCH ORGANIZATION.
— CHEMORECEPTION ABSTRACTS.  CHEMICAL SENSE &
APPLIED TECHNIQUES.

EUROPEAN COAL & STEEL COMMUNITY: HIGH AUTHORITY
— ETUDES DE PHYSIOLOGIE ET DE PSYCHOLOGIE DE
TRAVAIL.

EUROPEAN COIL COATING ASSOCIATION.
— ORGANIC METAL COATING REVIEW.

EUROPEAN COMPUTER MANUFACTURERS ASSOCIATION.
— ECMA STANDARDS.

EUROPEAN CONSERVATION YEAR SECRETARIAT.
— ECY NEWSLETTER.                                            XXX

EUROPEAN CONSORTIUM FOR POLITICAL RESEARCH.
— EUROPEAN JOURNAL OF POLITICAL RESEARCH.

EUROPEAN ECONOMIC COMMUNITY.
— ECONOMIC SITUATION IN THE (EUROPEAN ECONOMIC)
COMMUNITY.

EUROPEAN & MEDITERRANEAN CEREAL RUSTS
FOUNDATION.
— CEREAL RUSTS BULLETIN.

EUROPEAN MOVEMENT.
— BRITISH EUROPEAN.                                          XXX

EUROPEAN NUCLEAR ENERGY AGENCY.
— INFORMATION BULLETIN ON ISOTOPIC GENERATORS.              XXX

EUROPEAN PHYSICAL SOCIETY.
— EUROPHYSICS NEWS.  BULLETIN OF THE...

EUROPEAN PROPERTY OWNERS ASSOCIATION.
— EUROPROPERTY.

EUROPEAN SCIENTIFIC ASSOCIATION OF APPLIED
ECONOMICS.
— EUROPEAN ECONOMIC REVIEW.

EUROPEAN SOCIETY FOR ANIMAL BLOOD GROUP
RESEARCH.
— ANIMAL BLOOD GROUPS & BIOCHEMICAL GENETICS.

EUROPEAN SOCIETY FOR CLINICAL INVESTIGATION.
— EUROPEAN JOURNAL OF CLINICAL INVESTIGATION.        XXX

EUROPEAN SOCIETY FOR EXPERIMENTAL SURGERY.
— EUROPEAN SURGICAL RESEARCH.

EUROPEAN SOCIETY OF LINGUISTICS.
— FOLIA LINGUISTICA. ACTA SOCIETATIS
  LINGUISTICAE EUROPAEAE.

EUROPEAN SOCIETY FOR OPINION SURVEYS &
MARKET RESEARCH.
— EUROPEAN MARKETING RESEARCH REVIEW.

EUROPEAN SPACE RESEARCH ORGANISATION.
— ELDO-ESRO SCIENTIFIC & TECHNICAL REVIEW.         XXX
— ELDO/ESRO TECHNICAL REVIEW. = REVUE TECHNIQUE
  CECLES/CERS.
— SCIENTIFIC NOTE, EUROPEAN SPACE RESEARCH ORG-
  ANIZATION.

EUROPEAN SPACE VEHICLE LAUNCHER DEVELOPMENT
ASSOCIATION.
— ELDO/ESRO SCIENTIFIC & TECHNICAL REVIEW.
— ELDO/ESRO TECHNICAL REVIEW. = REVUE TECHNIQUE
  CECLES/CERS.

EUROPEAN TERATOLOGY SOCIETY.
— TERATOLOGY LOOKOUT.

EUROPEAN TRANSLATIONS CENTRE.
— TRANSLATION NEWS.
— WORLD INDEX OF SCIENTIFIC TRANSLATIONS & LIST
  OF TRANSLATIONS NOTIFIED TO E.T.C.                XXX

EUROPEAN WHEAT ANEUPLOID CO-OPERATIVE.
— EUROPEAN WHEAT ANEUPLOID CO-OPERATIVE NEWSL-
  ETTER.

EVOLUTION PROTEST MOVEMENT.
— CREATION. JOURNAL OF THE ...

EWAC.                                                000
SEE: EUROPEAN WHEAT ANEUPLOID COOPERATIVE.

EXCERPTA MEDICA FOUNDATION.
— ADVANCES IN CONTACT LENSES.                       XXX
— ADVERSE REACTIONS TITLES.
— CARDIOLOGY TODAY.
— DRUG LITERATURE INDEX.
— EPILEPSY ABSTRACTS.
— EXCERPTA MEDICA, SECTION 28: UROLOGY
  & NEPHROLOGY.                                     XXX
— EXCERPTA MEDICA: SECTION 34: PLASTIC SURGERY.
— EXCERPTA MEDICA: SECTION 35: OCCUPATIONAL
  HEALTH & INDUSTRIAL MEDICINE.
— EXCERPTA MEDICA: SECTION 36: HEALTH ECONOMICS.
— EXCERPTA MEDICA: SECTION 46: ENVIRONMENTAL
  HEALTH.                                           XXX
— EXCERPTA MEDICA: SECTION 47: VIROLOGY.
— EXCERPTA MEDICA: SECTION 48: GASTROENTEROLOGY.
— PERSPECTIVES IN OPTHALMOLOGY.

FABIAN SOCIETY.
— THIRD WORLD. SOCIALISM & DEVELOPMENT.             XXX
— VENTURE. JOURNAL OF THE FABIAN COLONIAL
  BUREAU.                                           XXX
  SUBS (1972): THIRD WORLD. SOCIALISM &
  DEVELOPMENT.

FABIAN SOCIETY: TRADE UNION & INDUSTRIAL
RELATIONS COMMITTEE.
— INDUSTRIAL RELATIONS BULLETIN.

FACTORY MUTUAL ENGINEERING CORPORATION.            XXX
— FACTORY MUTUAL RECORD.                            XXX
  SUBS (1971): RECORD, FACTORY MUTUAL ENGIN-
  EERING CORPORATION.
— RECORD, FACTORY MUTUAL ENGINEERING CORPORAT-
  ION.                                              XXX

FACULDADE DE FILOSOFIA, CIENCIAS E LETRAS
(ASSIS, BRAZIL).
— REVISTA DE LETRAS (BRAZIL).

FACULDADE DE FILOSOFIA, CIENCIAS E LETRAS DE
MARILIA (BRAZIL).
— ESTUDOS HISTORICOS.

FACULDADE DE FILOSOFIA, CIENCIAS E LETRAS DE
SAO LEOPOLDO (BRAZIL).
— ESTUDOS LEOPOLDENSES.

FACULTAD LATINOAMERICANA DE CIENCIAS SOCIALES.
— ANALES DE LA FACULTAD LATINOAMERICANA DE
  CIENCIAS SOCIALES.

FACULTE DES LETTRES ET SCIENCES HUMAINES DE
BREST: CENTRE DE RECHERCHE BRETONNE ET CELTIQUE
— PUBLICATIONS DU CENTRE DE RECHERCHE BRETONNE
  ET CELTIQUE DE LA FACULTE DES LETTRES ET
  SCIENCES HUMAINES DE BREST.

FAIR ORGAN PRESERVATION SOCIETY.
— KEY FRAME.

FAMILY PLANNING ASSOCIATION.
— FAMILY PLANNING MISCELLANY.

FAR SEAS' FISHERIES RESEARCH LABORATORY
(JAPAN).                                             000
SEE: ENYO SUISAN KENKYUJO.

FARADAY SOCIETY.
— SPECIAL DISCUSSIONS OF THE FARADAY SOCIETY.       XXX
— SYMPOSIA OF THE FARADAY SOCIETY.
— TRANSACTIONS, FARADAY SOCIETY.                    XXX
  SUBS(1972): PART OF JOURNAL, CHEMICAL SOC-
  IETY: FARADAY TRANSACTIONS 1; & ... 2.

FARM ECONOMICS ASSOCIATION OF THE PHILIPPINES.
  DEVELOPMENT.

FARMACEUTSKO DRUSTVO VOJVODINE.
— FARMACEUT (NOVI SAD).

FARNHAM MUSEUM SOCIETY.
— QUARTERLY NEWSLETTER, FARNHAM MUSEUM SOCIETY.

AL-FATEH.                                            000
SEE: PALESTINE NATIONAL LIBERATION MOVEMENT.

FAWCETT SOCIETY.
— WOMEN'S REPORT.

FEDERAL RESERVE BANK OF BOSTON.
— NEW ENGLAND BUSINESS REVIEW.                      XXX
  SUBS (1969): NEW ENGLAND ECONOMIC REVIEW.
— NEW ENGLAND ECONOMIC REVIEW.                      XXX

FEDERATIE VOOR DE WASINDUSTRIE.
— VAKBLAD VOOR TEXTIELREINIGING.

FEDERATION OF BRITISH INDUSTRIES.                   XXX
— BRITISH INDUSTRY.                                 XXX
— INDUSTRIAL TRENDS ENQUIRY.                        XXX
  SUBS (1965): INDUSTRIAL TRENDS SURVEY.

FEDERATION DES ENTREPRISES DE BELGIQUE.
— BULLETIN DE LA FEDERATION DES ENTREPRISES DE
  BELGIQUE.                                         XXX

FEDERATION OF EUROPEAN BIOCHEMICAL SOCIETIES.
— FEBS LETTERS.
— PROCEEDINGS OF THE MEETINGS, FEDERATION OF
  EUROPEAN BIOCHEMICAL SOCIETIES.

FEDERATION FRANCAISE DE SPELEOLOGIE.
— QUOI DE NEUF.

FEDERATION DES INDUSTRIES BELGES.
— BULLETIN DE LA FEDERATION DES INDUSTRIES
  BELGES.                                           XXX
  SUBS (1973): BULLETIN DE LA FEDERATION DES
  ENTREPRISES DE BELGIQUE.

FEDERATION DES INDUSTRIES CHIMIQUES DE BELGIQUE
— BELGIAN PLASTICS.                                 XXX

FEDERATION INTERNATIONALE DE DOCUMENTATION.         000
SEE: INTERNATIONAL FEDERATION FOR DOCUMENTAT-
ION.

FEDERATION OF IRISH INDUSTRIES: CLOTHING SECTOR
— IRISH CLOTHING INDUSTRY.

FEDERATION OF MASTER BUILDERS.
— MASTER BUILDER (1971).                            XXX
— MASTER BUILDERS' JOURNAL.                         XXX
  SUBS (1971): MASTER BUILDER (1971).

FEDERATION NATIONAL DU MOVEMENT FRANCAIS POUR
LE PLANNING FAMILIAL.
— PLANNING FAMILIAL.

FEDERATION OF ZOOLOGICAL GARDENS OF GREAT
BRITAIN & IRELAND.
— ZOO FEDERATION NEWS.

FELLOWSHIP OF RECONCILIATION.
— FELLOWSHIP OF RECONCILIATION QUARTERLY.                               XXX
— RECONCILIATION QUARTERLY.                                            XXX

FERTILIZER INSTITUTE.
— FERTILIZER PROGRESS.

FIELD STUDIES ASSOCIATION (HULL & EAST YORK-
SHIRE).
— EAST YORKSHIRE FIELD STUDIES.

(FIJI) BUREAU OF STATISTICS.
— SOCIAL INDICATORS FOR FIJI.

(FIJI) DEPARTMENT OF AGRICULTURE.
— AGRICULTURAL JOURNAL, DEPARTMENT OF AGRICUL-
  URE (FIJI).                                                          XXX
  SUBS (1970): FIJI AGRICULTURAL JOURNAL: NS.
— FIJI AGRICULTURAL JOURNAL: NS.

(FIJI) DEPARTMENT OF FORESTRY.
— FIJI TIMBERS & THEIR USES.

(FIJI) GEOLOGICAL SURVEY.
— OCCASIONAL PAPERS, GEOLOGICAL SURVEY OF FIJI.

(FINLAND) MINISTRY FOR FOREIGN AFFAIRS.                                 000
SEE: (FINLAND) ULKOASAINMINISTERIO.

(FINLAND) ULKOASAINMINISTERIO.
— LOOK AT FINLAND.

FINNISH MEDICAL SOCIETY DUODECIM.                                       000
SEE: SUOMALAINEN LAAKARISEURA DUODECIM.

FINNISH SOCIETY FOR ECONOMIC RESEARCH.                                  000
SEE: TALOUSTIETEELLISEN SEURAN.

FINNISH SOCIETY OF PHOTOGRAMMETRY.
— PHOTOGRAMMETRIC JOURNAL OF FINLAND.

FINNISH TRAVEL ASSOCIATION.                                             000
SEE: SUOMEN MATKAILUYHDISTYS.

FIRE PROTECTION ASSOCIATION.
— FIRE PREVENTION.                                                     XXX
— FIRE PREVENTION SCIENCE & TECHNOLOGY.
— F.P.A. CENTRE. NEWS ABOUT FIRE PREVENTION
  INFORMATION & ACTIVITIES.                                            XXX
— F.P.A. JOURNAL.                                                      XXX
  SUBS (1971): FIRE PREVENTION.
— FPA NEWS.                                                            XXX
— PLANNING FOR FIRE SAFETY IN BUILDINGS SERIES.

FISHERIES RESEARCH & DEVELOPMENT AGENCY
(KOREA).                                                                000
SEE: KUNGNIP SUSAN CHINHUNGWON.

FISHERIES SOCIETY OF THE BRITISH ISLES.
— JOURNAL OF FISH BIOLOGY.

FISONS LTD.
— FISONS FERTILIZER & AGRICULTURAL NEWS.

F.L. ALLAN MEMORIAL TRUST.
— OCCASIONAL PAPERS, F.L. ALLAN MEMORIAL TRUST.

FLINDERS UNIVERSITY OF SOUTH AUSTRALIA: HISTORY
& POLITICS SOCIETY.
— FLINDERS JOURNAL OF HISTORY & POLITICS.

(FLORIDA) DEPARTMENT OF AGRICULTURE: DIVISION
OF PLANT INDUSTRY.
— ENTOMOLOGY CIRCULAR, DIVISION OF PLANT IND-
  USTRY, DEPARTMENT OF AGRICULTURE (FLORIDA).
— NEMATOLOGY CIRCULAR, DIVISION OF PLANT IND-
  USTRY, DEPARTMENT OF AGRICULTURE (FLORIDA).
— PATHOLOGY CIRCULAR, DIVISION OF PLANT IND-
  USTRY, DEPARTMENT OF AGRICULTURE (FLORIDA).

(FLORIDA) DEPARTMENT OF NATURAL RESOURCES:
MARINE RESEARCH LABORATORY.
— PROFESSIONAL PAPERS SERIES, MARINE RESEARCH
  LABORATORY, DEPARTMENT OF NATURAL RESOURCES
  (FLORIDA).                                                           XXX
— SPECIAL SCIENTIFIC REPORT, MARINE RESEARCH
  LABORATORY, DEPARTMENT OF NATURAL RESOURCES
  (FLORIDA).                                                           XXX

(FLORIDA) STATE BOARD OF CONSERVATION: MARINE
LABORATORY.
— PROFESSIONAL PAPERS SERIES, MARINE LABORATORY,
  STATE BOARD OF CONSERVATION (FLORIDA).                               XXX
  SUBS (1969): PROFESSIONAL PAPERS SERIES,
  MARINE RESEARCH LABORATORY, DEPARTMENT OF
  NATURAL RESOURCES (FLORIDA).
— SPECIAL SCIENTIFIC REPORT, MARINE LABORATORY,
  STATE BOARD OF CONSERVATION (FLORIDA).                               XXX
  SUBS (1969): SPECIAL SCIENTIFIC REPORT,
  MARINE RESEARCH LABORATORY, DEPARTMENT OF
  NATURAL RESOURCES (FLORIDA).

FLORIDA STATE MUSEUM.
— PLASTER JACKET.

FLORIDA STATE UNIVERSITY: CENTRE FOR SOCIAL
PHILOSOPHY.
— SOCIAL THEORY & PRACTICE.

FLORIDA STATE UNIVERSITY: DEPARTMENT OF ENGLISH
— PAPERS IN LINGUISTICS.

FLUGWISSENSCHAFTLICHE FORSCHUNGSANSTALT.                                XXX
— BERICHT, FLUGWISSENSCHAFTLICHE FORSCHUNGSAN-
  STALT.                                                               XXX
  SUBS (1964): FORSCHUNGSBERICHT, DEUTSCHE
  LUFT- UND RAUMFAHRT.

FLUID AMPLIFIER ASSOCIATES.
— FLUIDICS QUARTERLY.

FOLGER LIBRARY.
— FOLGER LIBRARY NEWSLETTER.

FOLKESTONE NATURAL HISTORY SOCIETY.
— NEWSLETTER, FOLKESTONE NATURAL HISTORY
  SOCIETY.

FONDATION MAEGHT.
— EPHEMERE. REVUE TRIMESTRIELLE.                                       XXX

FONDATION NATIONALE DES SCIENCES POLITIQUES
(FRANCE).
— BIBLIOGRAPHIES FRANCAISES DE SCIENCES
  SOCIALES.                                                            XXX
— TRAVAUX ET RECHERCHES DE SCIENCE POLITIQUE.

FONDAZIONE LUIGI EINAUDI.
— ANNALI DELLA FONDAZIONE LUIGI EINAUDI.

FOOD & AGRICULTURE ORGANIZATION (UN).
— AGRICULTURAL EDUCATION & TRAINING.
— BASIC TEXTS, FOOD & AGRICULTURE ORGANIZATION
  (UN).
— FAO FISHERIES SYNOPSIS.
— MARINE SCIENCE CONTENTS TABLES.                                      XXX
— UNASYLVA. AN INTERNATIONAL REVIEW OF FOR-
  ESTRY & FOREST PRODUCTS.
— WORLD ANIMAL REVIEW.
— WORLD FISHERIES ABSTRACTS.                                           XXX

FOOD & AGRICULTURAL ORGANIZATION (UN): AGRARIAN
RESEARCH & INTELLIGENCE SERVICE.
— INFORMATION ON LAND REFORM, LAND SETTLEMENT &
  COOPERATIVES.                                                        XXX

FOOD & AGRICULTURAL ORGANIZATION (UN): RURAL
INSTITUTIONS DIVISION.
— LAND REFORM, LAND SETTLEMENT & COOPERATIVES.

FOOD MANUFACTURERS' FEDERATION.
— FMF REVIEW.                                                          XXX
— FOOD WORLD.                                                          XXX

FOODGRAIN TECHNOLOGISTS' RESEARCH ASSOCIATION
OF INDIA.
— BULLETIN OF GRAIN TECHNOLOGY.

FOOTBALL LEAGUE.
— FOOTBALL LEAGUE REVIEW.

FORAS TALUNTAIS.
— FARM & FOOD RESEARCH.                                                XXX
— IRISH VEGETARIAN STUDIES.

FORD FOUNDATION.
— AFRICAN ABSTRACTS.                                                   XXX

FORENINGEN AF FULDBLODSOPDRAETTERE I DANMARK.
— FULDBLODSAVL.

FOREST MANAGEMENT INSTITUTE (CANADA).                                  XXX
— PROGRAM REVIEW, FOREST MANAGEMENT INSTITUTE
  (CANADA).                                                            XXX

**FOREST MANAGEMENT RESEARCH & SERVICES INSTITUTE (CANADA).**   XXX
— PROGRAM REVIEW, FOREST MANAGEMENT RESEARCH & SERVICES INSTITUTE (CANADA).   XXX

**FOREST PRODUCTS RESEARCH LABORATORY (GB).**
— TECHNICAL NOTE, FOREST PRODUCTS RESEARCH LABORATORY (GB).   XXX
— TIMBERLAB NEWS: NEWSLETTER OF THE...

**FOREST PRODUCTS RESEARCH SOCIETY.**
— WOOD SCIENCE.

**FOREST RESEARCH INSTITUTE (AUSTRALIA).**
— NEWSLETTER OF TREE IMPROVEMENT & INTRODUCTION.

**FOREST RESEARCH INSTITUTE (NEW ZEALAND).**
— NEW ZEALAND JOURNAL OF FORESTRY SCIENCE.

**FORESTRY ASSOCIATION OF NIGERIA.**
— NIGERIAN JOURNAL OF FORESTRY.

**FORESTRY COMMISSION (GB).**
— ELM NEWSLETTER.   XXX
— JOURNAL OF THE FORESTRY COMMISSION (GB).   XXX

**FOUNDATION FOR REFORMATION RESEARCH.**
— SIXTEENTH CENTURY ESSAYS & STUDIES.   XXX
— SIXTEENTH CENTURY JOURNAL.   XXX

**FOUNDATION FOR RESEARCH ON THE NATURE OF MAN.**
— FRNM. BULLETIN OF THE FOUNDATION FOR RESEARCH ON THE NATURE OF MAN.   XXX
— PARAPSYCHOLOGY BULLETIN.   XXX

**FOUNDATION FOR THE STUDY OF PLURAL SOCIETIES.**
— PLURAL SOCIETIES.

**FOUNDATION OF THANATOLOGY.**
— ARCHIVES, FOUNDATION OF THANATOLOGY.

**FOURAH BAY COLLEGE: DEPARTMENT OF MODERN EUROPEAN AFRICAN LANGUAGES.**
— AFRICAN LANGUAGE REVIEW.   XXX

**FOURTH INTERNATIONAL: EUROPEAN BUREAU.**
— EUROPEAN MARXIST REVIEW.

**(FRANCE) MINISTERE DE LA SANTE PUBLIQUE ET DE SECURITE SOCIALE.**
— BULLETIN DE STATISTIQUES DE SANTE ET DE SECURITE SOCIALE.

**(FRANCE) SECRETARIAT D'ETAT AUPRES DU PREMIER MINISTRE CHARGE DE L'INFORMATION.**
— POLITIQUE INTERIEURE DE LA FRANCE.

**FRANKLIN INSTITUTE RESEARCH LABORATORIES.**
— POWDER METALLURGY SCIENCE & TECHNOLOGY.
— URETHANE ABSTRACTS.

**FREEDOM FROM HUNGER COUNCIL OF IRELAND.**
— GORTA NEWS.

**FREIE UNIVERSITAT: INSTITUT FUR METEOROLOGIE UND GEOPHYSIK.**
— GEOPHYSIKALISCHE ABHANDLUNGEN.

**FREIGHT TRANSPORT ASSOCIATION LTD.**
— FREIGHT. JOURNAL OF THE ...

**FRITZ-THYSSEN-STIFTUNG.**
— STUDIEN ZUR PHILOSOPHIE UND LITERATUR DES NEUNZEHNTEN JAHRHUNDERTS.

**FRITZSCHE DODGE & OLCOTT, INC.**
— FRITZSCHE - D & O LIBRARY BULLETIN.   XXX
— FRITZSCHE LIBRARY BULLETIN.   XXX
  SUBS (1969): FRITZSCHE - D & O LIBRARY BULLETIN.

**F.U. RESEARCH INSTITUTE INC.**
— PARTICLES & NUCLEI.   XXX

**FUJI IRON & STEEL CO.**   000
SEE: FUJI SEITETSU K.K.

**FUJI SEITETSU K.K.**
— FUJI SEITETSU GIHO. TECHNICAL REPORT, FUJI STEEL.   XXX

**FUJIKURA CABLE WORKS, LTD.**
— FUJIKURA TECHNICAL REVIEW.

**FULLER THEOLOGICAL SEMINARY.**
— STUDIA BIBLICA ET THEOLOGICA.

**FULMER RESEARCH INSTITUTE.**
— FRI NEWSLETTER.

**FUND FOR THE REPLACEMENT OF ANIMALS IN MEDICAL EXPERIMENTS.**
— ABSTRACTS OF ALTERNATIVES TO LABORATORY ANIMALS.   XXX

**FUNDACAO CALOUSTE GULBENKIAN.**
— COLOQUOI LETRAS.

**FUNDEX LTD.**
— MONEY MANAGEMENT & UNITHOLDER.   XXX

**FUNDO DE DESENVOLVIMENTO DA MAO-DE-OBRA (PORTUGAL).**
— ESTATISTICAS INTERNAS.

**FURNITURE, TIMBER & ALLIED TRADES UNION.**
— FTAT RECORD.   XXX

**GALERIJA FRESAKA.**
— ZOGRAF. CASOPIS ZA SREDNJOVEKOVNU UMETNOST.

**GARDA SIOCHANA PENSIONERS ASSOCIATION.**
— SIOCHAIN.

**GAS CHROMATOGRAPHY DISCUSSION GROUP.**
— GAS & LIQUID CHROMATOGRAPHY ABSTRACTS.   XXX

**GATESHEAD & DISTRICT LOCAL HISTORY SOCIETY.**
— BULLETIN, GATESHEAD & DISTRICT LOCAL HISTORY SOCIETY.

**GATT INTERNATIONAL TRADE CENTRE.**
— INTERNATIONAL TRADE FORUM; SUPPLEMENT.

**GDANSKIE TOWARZYSTWO NAUKOWE.**
— SERIA ZRODEL, WYDZIAL I: NAUK SPOLECZNYCH I HUMANISTYCZNYCH, GDANSKIE TOWARZYSTWO NAUKOWE.

**GDANSKIE TOWARZYSTWO NAUKOWE, WYDZIAL 3: NAUK MATEMATYCZNYCH I PRZYRODNICZYCH.**
— ROZPRAWY WYDZIALU 3: NAUK MATEMATYCZNYCH I PRZYRODNICZYCH, GDANSKIE TOWARZYSTWO NAUKOWE.

**GELATINE & GLUE RESEARCH ASSOCIATION.**
— WORLD ABSTRACTS ON PROTEIN COLLOIDS.   XXX

**GENERAL ELECTRIC CO. LTD.**
— G.E.C. - A.E.I. JOURNAL OF SCIENCE & TECHNOLOGY.   XXX

**GENERAL ELECTRIC & ENGLISH ELECTRIC CO.**   XXX
— JOURNAL OF SCIENCE & TECHNOLOGY (1969).   XXX

**GENERAL LEGAL COUNCIL (GHANA).**
— REVIEW OF GHANA LAW.

**GENERAL STUDIES ASSOCIATION.**
— NEWSLETTER, GENERAL STUDIES ASSOCIATION.

**(GEOCHEMICAL SOCIETY OF JAPAN).**
— GEOCHEMICAL JOURNAL.

**GEOGRAFICHESKOE OBSHCHESTVO MOLDAVII.**
— PROBLEMY GEOGRAFII MOLDAVII.

**GEOGRAFICHESKOE OBSHCHESTVO SSSR.**
— DOKLADY OTDELENIJ I KOMISSIJ GEOGRAFICHESKOGO OBSHCHESTVA SSSR.

**GEOGRAFICHESKOE OBSHCHESTVO SSSR, KAMCHATSKOE OTDELENIE.**
— VOPROSY GEOGRAFII KAMCHATKI.

**GEOGRAFICHESKOE OBSHCHESTVO SSSR (NOVOSIVIRSKOE OTDELENIE): SEKTSIJA ISTORICHESKOJ GEOGRAFII.**
— VOPROSY ISTORII SOTSIAL'NO-EKONOMICHESKOJ I KUL'TURNOJ ZHIZNI SIBIRI I DAL'NEGO VOSTOKA.

**GEOGRAFICHESKOE OBSHCHESTVO SSSR (PERMSKIJ OTDEL).**
— PESHCHERY.   XXX

**GEOGRAFICHESKOE OBSHCHESTVO SSSR: ZABAJKAL'SKIJ OTDEL.**
— PROBLEMY REGIONAL'NOGO ZIMOVEDENIJA.

**GEOGRAFSKO DRUSTVO NA SR MAKEDONIJA.**
— GEOGRAFSKI RAZGLEDI.

**GEOGRAPHICAL ASSOCIATION.**
— TEACHING GEOGRAPHY.

GEOGRAPHICAL ASSOCIATION: KINGSTON BRANCH.
— KINGSTON GEOGRAPHER. JOURNAL OF ...

GEOGRAPHICAL ASSOCIATION OF TANZANIA.
— JOURNAL OF THE GEOGRAPHICAL ASSOCIATION OF
TANZANIA.

GEOLOGICAL, MINING & METALLURGICAL SOCIETY OF
LIBERIA.
— BULLETIN, GEOLOGICAL, MINING & METALLURGICAL
SOCIETY OF LIBERIA.

GEOLOGICAL SOCIETY OF AMERICA.
— ABSTRACTS WITH PROGRAMS, GEOLOGICAL SOCIETY
OF AMERICA.                                              XXX
— BIBLIOGRAPHY & INDEX OF GEOLOGY.*

GEOLOGICAL SOCIETY OF AUSTRALIA.
— SPECIAL PUBLICATION, GEOLOGICAL SOCIETY OF
AUSTRALIA.

GEOLOGICAL SOCIETY OF IRAQ.
— JOURNAL, GEOLOGICAL SOCIETY OF IRAQ.

GEOLOGICAL SOCIETY OF LONDON.
— JOURNAL, GEOLOGICAL SOCIETY OF LONDON.          XXX
— QUARTERLY JOURNAL, GEOLOGICAL SOCIETY OF
LONDON.                                                  XXX
SUBS (1971): JOURNAL ...
— SPECIAL REPORT, GEOLOGICAL SOCIETY OF LONDON.

GEOLOGICAL SOCIETY OF MALAYSIA.                          000
SEE: KESATUAN KAJIBUMI MALAYSIA.

GEOLOGICAL SOCIETY OF NORFOLK.
— BULLETIN, GEOLOGICAL SOCIETY OF NORFOLK.        XXX

GEOLOGICAL SOCIETY OF THE PHILIPPINES.
— JOURNAL, GEOLOGICAL SOCIETY OF THE PHILIP-
PINES.                                                   XXX

GEOLOGICAL SOCIETY OF SOUTH AFRICA.
— SPECIAL PUBLICATIONS, GEOLOGICAL SOCIETY OF
SOUTH AFRICA.

GEOLOGICAL SURVEY OF FINLAND.
— BULLETIN, GEOLOGICAL SURVEY OF FINLAND.         XXX

GEOLOGISCH-PALAONTOLOGISCHES INSTITUT (GOTTIN-
GEN).
— GOTTINGER ARBEITEN ZUR GEOLOGIE UND PALAONTO-
LOGIE.

GEOLOSKI ZAVOD U SARAJEVU.
— GEOLOSKI GLASNIK - POSEBNA IZDANJA.

GEOLOSKI ZAVOD (SKOPJE).
— POSEBNA IZDANJA, GEOLOSKI ZAVOD, SKOPJE.

GEORGE WASHINGTON UNIVERSITY: INTERNATIONAL
LAW SOCIETY.
— JOURNAL OF LAW & ECONOMIC DEVELOPMENT.          XXX
— STUDIES IN LAW & ECONOMIC DEVELOPMENT.          XXX

GEORGE WASHINGTON UNIVERSITY: NATIONAL LAW
CENTER.
— JOURNAL OF INTERNATIONAL LAW & ECONOMICS.       XXX

GEORGETOWN UNIVERSITY: INSTITUTE OF LANGUAGES &
LINGUISTICS.
— TESOL QUARTERLY. TEACHERS OF ENGLISH & SPEA-
KERS OF OTHER LANGUAGES.

GEORGETOWN UNIVERSITY: LAW CENTRE.
— LAW & POLICY IN INTERNATIONAL BUSINESS.

(GEORGIA) AGRICULTURAL EXPERIMENT STATIONS.
— ANNUAL REPORT, AGRICULTURAL EXPERIMENT STAT-
IONS (GEORGIA).                                          XXX
SUBS (1970): BIENNIAL REPORT, AGRICULTURAL
EXPERIMENT STATIONS (GEORGIA).
— BIENNIAL REPORT, AGRICULTURAL EXPERIMENT
STATIONS (GEORGIA).

GEORGIA ENTOMOLOGICAL SOCIETY.
— JOURNAL, GEORGIA ENTOMOLOGICAL SOCIETY.

(GEORGIA) GEOLOGICAL SURVEY.
— SPECIAL PUBLICATIONS, GEOLOGICAL SURVEY
(GEORGIA).

GEORGIA STATE COLLEGE: DEPARTMENT OF ENGLISH.
— STUDIES IN THE LITERARY IMAGINATION.

GEORGIA STATE UNIVERSITY: SCHOOL OF BUSINESS
ADMINISTRATION.
— JOURNAL OF INTERNATIONAL BUSINESS STUDIES.

GEOSCIENCE INFORMATION SOCIETY (US).
— PROCEEDINGS, GEOSCIENCE INFORMATION SOCIETY.

GERANIUM SOCIETY.
— BULLETIN, GERANIUM SOCIETY.                      XXX
SUBS (1965): BULLETIN, BRITISH PELARGONIUM
& GERANIUM SOCIETY.

(GERMANY, EAST) METEOROLOGISCHER DIENST.
— ANGEWANDTE METEOROLOGIE.                         XXX

(GERMANY, WEST) BUNDESMINSTER FUR BILDUNG UND
WISSENSCHAFT.
— SCHRIFTENREIHE TECHNOLOGIEN.

(GERMANY, WEST) STATISTISCHES BUNDESAMT.
— ALLGEMEINE STATISTIK DES AUSLANDES; LANDER-
BERICHTE: PAKISTAN.

GESCHIED- EN OUDHEIDKUNDIG GENOOTSCHAP VAN
ROESELARE EN OMMELAND.
— ROLLARIENSIA. JAARBOEK VAN ...

GESELLSCHAFT FUR KERNFORSCHUNG.
— PLUTONIUM - DOKUMENTATION.

(GHANA) CENTRAL BUREAU OF STATISTICS: ECONOMICS
LIBRARY.
— LIBRARY BULLETIN, ECONOMICS LIBRARY, CENTRAL
BUREAU OF STATISTICS (GHANA).

GHANA ACADEMY OF SCIENCES: CROP RESEARCH
INSTITUTE.
— GHANA JOURNAL OF AGRICULTURAL SCIENCES.

GHANA COMMERCIAL BANK.
— MONTHLY ECONOMIC BULLETIN, GHANA COMMERCIAL
BANK.

GHANA LIBRARY BOARD.
— GHANA NATIONAL BIBLIOGRAPHY.

GHANA SOCIOLOGICAL ASSOCIATION.
— GHANA JOURNAL OF SOCIOLOGY.

GIFU KOGYO KOTO SEMMON GAKKO.
— GIFU KOGYO KOTO SEMMON GAKKO KIYO. MEMOIR OF
GIFU TECHNICAL COLLEGE.

GIFU TECHNICAL COLLEGE.                                  000
SEE: GIFU KOGYO KOTO SEMMON GAKKO.

GLAMORGAN COUNTY NATURALISTS' TRUST.
— BULLETIN, GLAMORGAN COUNTY NATURALISTS' TRUST.

GLASGOW ARCHAEOLOGICAL SOCIETY.
— GLASGOW ARCHAEOLOGICAL JOURNAL.

GLASGOW SCHOOL OF ART.
— FACET.

GLAVNOE POLITICHESKOE UPRAVLENIE SOVETSKOJ
ARMII I VOENNO-MORSKOGO FLOTA.
— KOMMUNIST VOORUZHENNYKH SIL.                    XXX

GLAVNOE UPRAVLENIE GIDROMETEOROLOGICHESKOJ
SLUZHBY: INSTITUT PRIKLADNOJ GEOFIZIKI.
— TRUDY INSTITUTA PRIKLADNOJ GEOFIZIKI GLAVNOGO
UPRAVLENIJA GIDROMETEOROLOGICHESKOJ SLUZHBY.

GLAVNOE UPRAVLENIE GIDROMETEOROLOGICHESKOJ
SLUZHBY PRI SOVETE MINISTROV SSSR: GIDROMETEOR-
OLOGICHESKIJ NAUCHNO-ISSLEDOVATEL'SKIJ TSENTR
SSSR.
— TRUDY GIDROMETEOROLOGICHESKOGO NAUCHNO-ISSLE-
DOVATEL'SKOGO TSENTRA SSSR.

GLENBOW-ALBERTA INSTITUTE.
— GLENBOW. A NEWSLETTER OF THE GLENBOW-ALBERTA
INSTITUTE.

GLOUCESTERSHIRE COLLEGE OF ART.
— CHELTENHAM PAPERS.

GLOWNA BIBLIOTEKA LEKARSKA.
— INFORMACJA BIEZACA.

GODSEL - OCH KALKINDUSTRIERNAS SAMARBETSDELEG-
ATION.
— VAXT-NARINGS-NYTT.                                XXX

GOLDSMITHS' COLLEGE: CURRICULUM LABORATORY.
— IDEAS.

GOSPORT HISTORIC RECORDS & MUSEUM SOCIETY.
— GOSPORT RECORDS.

**GOSUDARSTVENNAJA BIBLIOTEKA SSSR IM. V.I. LENINA.**
— KHUDOZHESTVENNAJA LITERATURA, LITERATUROVED-
  ENIE, ISKUSSTVO.                                           XXX
— LITERATURA I ISKUSSTVO, GOSUDARSTVENNAJA
  BIBLIOTEKA SSSR IM. V.I. LENINA.                           XXX
— SVODNYJ UKAZATEL' BIBLIOGRAFICHESKIKH SPISKOV
  I KARTOTEK, SOSTAVLENNYKH BIBLIOTEKAMI SOVETS-
  KOGO SOJUZA : OBSHCHESTVENNYE NAUKI, KHUDOZ-
  HESTVENNAJA LITERATURA, ISKUSSTVO.

**GOSUDARSTVENNOE NAUCHNO-TEKHNICHESKOE IZDATEL'-
STVO NEFTJANOJ I GORNO-TOPLIVNOJ PROMYSHLEN-
NOSTI.**
— JADERNAJA GEOFIZIKA.

**GOSUDARSTVENNYJ GEOLOGICHESKIJ KOMITET SSSR:
INSTITUT GEOLOGII.**
— TRUDY INSTITUTA GEOLOGII, GOSUDARSTVENNYJ
  GEOLOGICHESKIJ KOMITET SSSR.

**GOSUDARSTVENNYJ KOMITET PO CHERNOJ I TSVETNOJ
METALLURGII PRI GOSPLANE SSSR: INSTITUT CHERNOJ
METALLURGII.**
— NAUCHNYE TRUDY, INSTITUT CHERNOJ METALLURGII.     XXX

**GOSUDARSTVENNYJ KOMITET PO ISPOL'ZOVANIJU
ATOMNOJ ENERGII SSSR.**
— IZOTOPY V SSSR.

**GOSUDARSTVENNYJ KOMITET KHIMICHESKOJ NEFTIANOJ
PROMYSHLENNOSTI GOSPLANA SSSR.**
— KHIMIJA V SEL'SKOM KHOZJAJSTVE.

**GOSUDARSTVENNYJ KOMITET PO KOORDINATSII NAUCHNO**
— ZASHCHITA METALLOV.

**GOSUDARSTVENNYJ KOMITET SOVETA MINISTROV GRUZ-
INSKOJ SSR PO KOORDINATSII NAUCHNO ISSLE-
DOVATEL'SKIKH RABOT: INSTITUT NAUCHNO-TEKHNICH-
ESKOJ INFORMATSII I PROPAGANDY.**
— CHAJ.  KULTURA I PROIZVODSTVO.

**GOSUDARSTVENNYJ KOMITET SOVETA MINISTROV SSSR
PO MATERIAL'NO-TEKHNICHESKOMU SNABZHENIJU.**
— MATERIAL'NO-TEKHNICHESKOE SNABZHENIE.

**GOSUDARSTVENNYJ KOMITET SOVETA MINISTROV SSSR
PO RADIOVESHCHANIJU I TELEVIDENIJU.**
— KRUGOZOR.

**GOSUDARSTVENNYJ KOMITET SOVETA MINISTROV
UKRAINSKOJ SSR PO KOORDINATSII NAUCHNO-ISSLE-
DOVATEL'SKIKH RABOT: INSTITUT TEKHNICHESKOJ
INFORMATSII.**
— ENERGETIKA I ELEKTROTEKHNICHESKAJA PROMYSHLEN-
  NOST'.                                                     XXX

**GOSUDARSTVENNYJ LITERATURNYJ MUZEJ.**
— NOVOE I ZABYTOE.

**GOSUDARSTVENNYJ MAKEEVSKIJ NAUCHNO-ISSLEDO-
VATEL'SKIJ INSTITUT.**
— BOR'BA S GAZOM I PYL'JU V UGOL'NYKH SHAKHTAKH.

**GOSUDARSTVENNYJ MEDITSINSKIJ INSTITUT.**
— TRUDY, GOSUDARSTVENNYJ MEDITSINSKIJ INSTITUT.   XXX

**GOSUDARSTVENNYJ NAUCHNO-ISSLEDOVATEL'SKIJ
INSTITUT MASHINOVEDENIJA.**
— MEKHANIKA MASHIN.

**GOSUDARSTVENNYJ NAUCHNO-ISSLEDOVATEL'SKIJ
INSTITUT OZERNOGO I RECHNOGO KHOZJAJSTVA
(VOLGOGRADSKOE OTDELENIE).**
— TRUDY VOLGOGRADSKOGO OTDELENIJA GOSNIORKH.

**GOSUDARSTVENNYJ PEDAGOGICHESKIJ INSTITUT:
LINGVISTICHESKOE OBSHCHESTVO.**
— SBORNIK DOKLADOV I SOOBSHCHENIJ LINGVISTICH-
  ESKOGO OBSHCHESTVA.

**GOSUDARSTVENNYJ PLANOVYJ KOMITET.**
— ZA TEKHNICHESKIJ PROGRESS.

**GOSUDARSTVENNYJ PROEKTNO-KONSTRUKTORSKIJ I
NAUCHNO-ISSLEDOVATEL'SKIJ INSTITUT MORSKOGO
TRANSPORTA.**
— TRUDY, GOSUDARSTVENNYJ PROEKTNO-KONSTRUKTOR-
  SKIJ I NAUCHNO-ISSLEDOVATEL'SKIJ INSTITUT
  MORSKOGO TRANSPORTA.                                       XXX

**GOSUDARSTVENNYJ VSESOJUZNYJ INSTITUT PO PRO-
EKTIROVANIJU I NAUCHNO-ISSLEDOVATEL'SKIM
RABOTAM 'JUZHGIPROTSEMENT'.**
— TRUDY, GOSUDARSTVENNYJ VSESOJUZNYJ INSTITUT
  PO PROEKTIROVANIJU I NAUCHNO-ISSLEDOVATEL'-
  SKIM RABOTAM 'JUZHGIPROTSEMENT'.

**GOTEBORGS KUNGLIGA VETENSKAPS- OCH VITTERHETS-
SAMHALLE.**
— ACTA REGIAE SOCIETATIS SCIENTIARUM ET LITTER-
  ARUM GOTHOBURGENSIS: BOTANICA.
— ACTA REGIAE SOCIETATIS SCIENTIARUM ET LITTER-
  ARUM GOTHOBURGENSIS:  GEOPHYSICA.
— ACTA REGIAE SOCIETATIS SCIENTIARUM ET LITTER-
  ARUM GOTHOBURGENSIS: HUMANIORA.

**GOTEBORGS UNIVERSITET.**
— GEOPHYSICA GOTHOBURGENSIA.

**GOTEBORGS UNIVERSITET: HISTORISKA INSTITUTIONEN**
— MEDDELANDEN, HISTORISKA INSTITUTIONEN, GOTEB-
  ORGS UNIVERSITET.

**GOTHIQUE FILM SOCIETY.**
— GOTHIQUE.

**GOTTFRIED-WILHELM-LEIBNIZ GESELLSCHAFT E.V.**
— STUDIA LEIBNITIANA.  VIERTELJAHRSCHRIFT FUR
  PHILOSOPHIE UND GESCHICHTE DER WISSENSCHAFTEN.

**GOVERNMENT COLLEGE (LAHORE): DEPARTMENT OF
ECONOMICS.**
— ECONOMIC JOURNAL.

**GOVERNMENT COLLEGE (LAHORE): DEPARTMENT OF
HISTORY.**
— JOURNAL OF HISTORY & POLITICAL SCIENCE.

**GOWER ORNITHOLOGICAL SOCIETY.**
— GOWER BIRDS.

**GRADSKI MUZEJ U SENJU: SENJSKO MUZEJSKO
DRUSTVO.**
— SENJSKI ZBORNIK.  PRILOZI ZA GEOGRAFIJU,
  ETNOLOGIJU, EKONOMIKU, POVIJEST I KULTURU.

**GRADUATE CENTRE FOR MANAGEMENT STUDIES (BIR-
MINGHAM).**
— DISCUSSION PAPERS IN BUSINESS & ORGANISATION.

**GRAPHIC ARTS TECHNICAL FOUNDATION, INC.**
— TECHNICAL SERVICE REPORT, GRAPHIC ARTS TECH-
  NICAL FOUNDATION, INC.

**GRASSLAND SOCIETY OF SOUTHERN AFRICA.**
— PROCEEDINGS, GRASSLAND SOCIETY OF SOUTHERN
  AFRICA.

**GRAVESEND HISTORICAL SOCIETY: SPRINGHEAD
EXCAVATION COMMITTEE.**
— SPRINGHEAD JOURNAL.

**(GREAT BRITAIN) BOARD OF TRADE.**                          XXX
— BOARD OF TRADE JOURNAL.                                    XXX
  SUBS (1970): TRADE & INDUSTRY.
— BUSINESS MONITOR; CIVIL AVIATION SERIES.

**(GREAT BRITAIN) CENTRAL OFFICE OF INFORMATION.**
— ANGLIJA, ZHURNAL O SEVODNJASHCHEJ ZHIZNI V
  VELIKOBRITANII.
— FACTSHEETS ON BRITAIN AND EUROPE.                          XXX
— HEALTH & SAFETY AT WORK.
— SURVEY OF CURRENT AFFAIRS.                                 XXX

**(GREAT BRITAIN) CENTRAL STATISTICAL OFFICE.**
— SOCIAL TRENDS.
— STUDIES IN OFFICIAL STATISTICS (GREAT BRIT-
  AIN): RESEARCH SERIES.

**(GREAT BRITAIN) CIVIL SERVICE DEPARTMENT.**                XXX
— MANAGEMENT SERVICES IN GOVERNMENT.                         XXX
— REPORT, CIVIL SERVICE DEPARTMENT (GB).

**(GREAT BRITAIN) CIVIL SERVICE DEPARTMENT:
CIVIL SERVICE COLLEGE.**
— CIVIL SERVICE COLLEGE STUDIES.

**(GREAT BRITAIN) COMMISSION ON INDUSTRIAL
RELATIONS.**                                                 000
SEE: COMMISSION ON INDUSTRIAL RELATIONS (GB).

**(GREAT BRITAIN) COMMONWEALTH OFFICE.**                     XXX
— COMMONWEALTH OFFICE YEAR BOOK.                             XXX

**(GREAT BRITAIN) COMMONWEALTH RELATIONS OFFICE.**
— COMMONWEALTH RELATIONS OFFICE LIST.    XXX
   SUBS (1966): COMMONWEALTH RELATIONS OFFICE
   YEAR BOOK.
— COMMONWEALTH RELATIONS OFFICE YEAR BOOK.    XXX

**(GREAT BRITAIN) CUSTOMS & EXCISE.**
— VAT BULLETIN.    XXX

**(GREAT BRITAIN) DEPARTMENT OF EDUCATION & SCIENCE.**
— EDUCATION PLANNING PAPER.
— JOURNAL OF EDUCATION FOR INDUSTRY & COMMERCE.
— SCIENCE POLICY & ORGANISATION BULLETIN.    XXX
— SCIENCE POLICY STUDIES.
— STATISTICS OF EDUCATION (GB): SPECIAL SERIES.
— STATISTICS OF SCIENCE & TECHNOLOGY.    XXX

**(GREAT BRITAIN) DEPARTMENT OF EDUCATION & SCIENCE: INTERNATIONAL SCIENTIFIC RELATIONS DIVISION.**
— OTTAWA NEWSLETTER.

**(GREAT BRITAIN) DEPARTMENT OF EMPLOYMENT.**
— DEPARTMENT OF EMPLOYMENT GAZETTE (GB).    XXX

**(GREAT BRITAIN) DEPARTMENT OF EMPLOYMENT: INFORMATION BRANCH.**
— BACKGROUND BRIEFING.

**(GREAT BRITAIN) DEPARTMENT OF EMPLOYMENT & PRODUCTIVITY.**
— HEALTH & SAFETY AT WORK.    XXX
— MANPOWER PAPERS.

**(GREAT BRITAIN) DEPARTMENT OF THE ENVIRONMENT.**
— CONSTRUCTION (LONDON).
— HOUSING & CONSTRUCTION STATISTICS (G.B.).    XXX
— LIBRARY BULLETIN, DEPARTMENT OF THE ENVIRON-
   MENT (GB).

**(GREAT BRITAIN) DEPARTMENT OF THE ENVIRONMENT: LIBRARY SERVICE.**    XXX
— CONSTRUCTION REFERENCES.    XXX

**(GREAT BRITAIN) DEPARTMENT OF HEALTH & SOCIAL SECURITY.**
— DIGEST OF HEALTH STATISTICS FOR ENGLAND &
   WALES.
— HEALTH TRENDS: A QUARTERLY REVIEW FOR THE
   MEDICAL PROFESSION.
— MANAGEMENT SERVICES (N.H.S.).
— REPORTS ON HEALTH & SOCIAL SUBJECTS (GB).    XXX
— REPORTS ON PUBLIC HEALTH & MEDICAL SUBJECTS.    XXX
   SUBS (1972): REPORTS ON HEALTH & SOCIAL
   SUBJECTS.

**(GREAT BRITAIN) DEPARTMENT OF HEALTH & SOCIAL SECURITY: SOCIAL SCIENCE RESEARCH UNIT.**
— STUDY, SOCIAL SCIENCE RESEARCH UNIT, DEPART-
   MENT OF HEALTH & SOCIAL SECURITY.

**(GREAT BRITAIN) DEPARTMENT OF TRADE & INDUSTRY.**
— CONTENTS OF RECENT ECONOMIC JOURNALS.
— FOR YOUR CURRENT INFORMATION: ECONOMICS.    XXX
— FOR YOUR CURRENT INFORMATION: INDUSTRY &
   MANAGEMENT.    XXX
— MOSCOW NEWSLETTER.
— REPORT ON OVERSEAS TRADE (GB).    XXX
— TECHNOLOGY & THE ENVIRONMENT.
— TRADE & INDUSTRY.    XXX

**(GREAT BRITAIN) FOREIGN OFFICE.**
— ARMS CONTROL & DISARMAMENT (LONDON).    XXX
— ARMS LIMITATION & DISARMAMENT.    XXX

**(GREAT BRITAIN) FOREIGN & COMMONWEALTH OFFICE.**
— YEAR BOOK OF THE COMMONWEALTH.    XXX

**(GREAT BRITAIN) FOREIGN & COMMONWEALTH OFFICE: OVERSEAS DEVELOPMENT ADMINISTRATION.**
— LAND RESOURCES BIBLIOGRAPHY.

**(GREAT BRITAIN) HOME OFFICE.**
— HOME OFFICE RESEARCH STUDIES.

**(GREAT BRITAIN) HOME OFFICE: DIRECTORATE OF TELECOMMUNICATIONS.**
— INTERCOM. THE JOURNAL OF THE ...

**(GREAT BRITAIN) MINISTRY OF AGRICULTURE, FISHERIES & FOOD.**
— AGRICULTURAL ENTERPRISE STUDIES IN ENGLAND &
   WALES: ECONOMIC REPORT.

**(GREAT BRITAIN) MINISTRY OF HEALTH.**
— MONTHLY BULLETIN OF THE MINISTRY OF HEALTH &    XXX
   THE PUBLIC HEALTH LABORATORY SERVICE.
   SUBS: (1969) HEALTH TRENDS.

**(GREAT BRITAIN) MINISTRY OF LABOUR.**
— SAFETY, HEALTH & WELFARE. NS.    XXX
   SUBS (1970): HEALTH & SAFETY AT WORK.

**(GREAT BRITAIN) MINISTRY OF OVERSEAS DEVELOP-MENT.**
— OVERSEAS DEVELOPMENT.

**(GREAT BRITAIN) MINISTRY OF OVERSEAS DEVELOP-MENT: LAND RESOURCES DIVISION.**
— LAND RESOURCE STUDY.
— TECHNICAL BULLETIN, LAND RESOURCES DIVISION,
   MINISTRY OF OVERSEAS DEVELOPMENT (GB).

**(GREAT BRITAIN) MINISTRY OF PUBLIC BUILDING & WORKS.**
— CONRAD. CONSTRUCTION RESEARCH & DEVELOPMENT
   JOURNAL.
— METRICATION IN THE CONSTRUCTION INDUSTRY.

**(GREAT BRITAIN) MINISTRY OF PUBLIC BUILDING & WORKS: COMMITTEE ON THE APPLICATION OF COMPUT-ERS IN THE CONSTRUCTION INDUSTRY.**
— BIBLIOGRAPHY ON THE APPLICATION OF COMPUTERS
   IN THE CONSTRUCTION INDUSTRY. SUPPLEMENT.

**(GREAT BRITAIN) MINISTRY OF PUBLIC BUILDING & WORKS: INTERDEPARTMENTAL SUB-COMMITTEE FOR COMPONENT CO-ORDINATION.**
— TECHNICAL NOTE, INTERDEPARTMENTAL SUB-COMM-
   ITTEE FOR COMPONENT CO-ORDINATION, MINISTRY
   OF PUBLIC BUILDING & WORKS (GB).

**(GREAT BRITAIN) MINISTRY OF PUBLIC BUILDINGS & WORKS: LIBRARY.**    **XXX**
— CONSOLIDATED BUILDING REFERENCES TO ARTICLES
   IN PERIODICALS.
   SUBS (1970) PART OF: CONSTRUCTION REFERENCES.

**(GREAT BRITAIN) MINISTRY OF TECHNOLOGY.**
— STUDIES IN TECHNOLOGICAL MANPOWER.

**(GREAT BRITAIN) MINISTRY OF TECHNOLOGY: INDUS-TRIAL OPERATIONS UNIT.**
— MANAGEMENT REPORTS OF THE INDUSTRIAL OPERA-
   TIONS UNIT, MINISTRY OF TECHNOLOGY (G.B.).

**(GREAT BRITAIN) SCOTTISH DEVELOPMENT DEPARTMENT**
— HOUSING & CONSTRUCTION STATISTICS (GB).    XXX

**(GREAT BRITAIN) SCOTTISH OFFICE.**
— DIGEST OF SCOTTISH STATISTICS.    XXX
   SUBS (1971): PART OF SCOTTISH ABSTRACT OF
   STATISTICS; & SCOTTISH ECONOMIC BULLETIN.
— SCOTTISH ABSTRACT OF STATISTICS.    XXX
— SCOTTISH ECONOMIC BULLETIN.    XXX

**(GREAT BRITAIN) TREASURY: INFORMATION DIVISION.**
— ECONOMIC PROGRESS REPORT. (GB).

**(GREAT BRITAIN) TREASURY: ORGANISATION & METHODS DIVISION.**    XXX
— O & M BULLETIN.    XXX
   SUBS (1973): MANAGEMENT SERVICES IN
   GOVERNMENT.

**(GREAT BRITAIN) WELSH OFFICE.**
— HEALTH TRENDS: A QUARTERLY REVIEW FOR THE
   MEDICAL PROFESSION.
— HOUSING & CONSTRUCTION STATISTICS (GB).    XXX

**GREATER LONDON ARTS ASSOCIATION.**
— ARTS DIARY.
— GREATER LONDON ARTS.

**GREATER LONDON COUNCIL.**
— ANNUAL ABSTRACT OF GREATER LONDON STATISTICS.
— DESIGN STUDY, GREATER LONDON COUNCIL.
— DEVELOPMENT & MATERIALS BULLETIN: 2S.
— URBAN DESIGN BULLETIN.

**GREATER LONDON COUNCIL: INTELLIGENCE UNIT.**
— HOUSING FACTS & FIGURES.

**(GREECE) GENERAL INSPECTORATE OF ANTIQUITIES & RESTORATION.**
— ARCHAIOLOGIKA ANALEKTA EX ATHENON. = ATHENS
   ANNALS OF ARCHAEOLOGY.    XXX

**(GREECE) TECHNICAL CHAMBER.**    **000**
SEE: TEHNIKON ERIMETETERION TES ELLADOS.

GREEK CHEMISTS ASSOCIATION: SCIENTIFIC
COMMITTEE.
— CHIMIKA CHRONIKA: NS.

GREENFIELD CENTER.
— GREENFIELD REVIEW.

GREENLAND PROVINCIAL COUNCIL.
— WELCOME TO GREENLAND. VELKOMMEN TIL GRONLAND.

GREGORIANISCHE AKADEMIE ZU FREIBURG.
— VEROFFENTLICHUNGEN DER GREGORIANISCHE AKAD-
EMIE ZU FREIBURG: NF.

GRILLPARZER-FORUM FORCHTENSTEIN.
— GRILLPARZER-FORUM FORCHTENSTEIN: VORTRAGE,
FORSCHUNGEN, BERICHTE.

GROUP FOR EUROPEAN SUPERCONDUCTING SYNCHROTRON
STUDIES.
— REPORT, GROUP FOR EUROPEAN SUPERCONDUCTING
SYNCHROTRON STUDIES.

GROUP FOR THE STUDY OF IRISH HISTORIC SETTLE-
MENT.
— BULLETIN OF THE GROUP FOR THE STUDY OF IRISH
HISTORIC SETTLEMENT.

GROUPE D'ETUDE SUISSE POUR LES IMPLANTS.
— REVUE TRIMESTRIELLE D'IMPLANTOLOGIE.
VIERTELJAHRIGE REVUE UBER IMPLANTOLOGIE.

GROUPE FRANCAIS DE RHEOLOGIE.
— CAHIERS DU GROUPE FRANCAIS DE RHEOLOGIE.

GROUPE FRANCO-HELLENIQUE DE RECHERCHES BIOL-
OGIQUE.
— BIOLOGIA GALLO-HELLENICA.

GROUPEMENT DES ACOUSTICIENS DE LANGUE FRANCAISE
— REVUE D'ACOUSTIQUE.

GRUZINSKIJ NAUCHNO-ISSLEDOVATEL'SKIJ INSTITUT
PISHCHEVOJ PROMYSHLENNOSTI.
— TRUDY, GRUZINSKIJ NAUCHNO-ISSLEDOVATEL'SKIJ
INSTITUT PISHCHEVOJ PROMYSHLENNOSTI.

GUILD OF AIR PILOTS & AIR NAVIGATORS.
— JOURNAL OF THE GUILD OF AIR PILOTS & AIR
NAVIGATORS.

GUILDFORD INSTITUTE OF FURTHER EDUCATION.
— LINK (GUILDFORD).

GUNMA DAIGAKU NAIBUNDI KENYUSHO.
— GUNMA SYMPOSIA ON ENDOCRINOLOGY.

GUSTAV ADOLFS AKADEMIEN FOER FOLKLIVS-
FORSKNING.                                                    000
SEE: KUNGLIGA GUSTAV ADOLFS AKADEMIEN.

GUYANA DEVELOPMENT CORPORATION.
— INDUSTRIAL REVIEW.                                         XXX

GUYANA INDUSTRIAL DEVELOPMENT CORPORATION.
— QUARTERLY NEWS BULLETIN, GUYANA INDUSTRIAL        XXX
DEVELOPMENT CORPORATION.

GUYANA INSTITUTE FOR SOCIAL RESEARCH & ACTION.
— GISPARK.
— GISRA.

(GUYANA) MINISTRY OF EXTERNAL AFFAIRS.
— GUYANA JOURNAL.

(GUYANA) MINISTRY OF INFORMATION & CULTURE.
— GUYNEWS.

GYPSUM PRODUCTS DEVELOPMENT ASSOCIATION.
— INTERGYPS.

HACETTEPE UNIVERSITY.
— HACETTEPE BULLETIN OF SOCIAL SCIENCES &
HUMANITIES.

HACHINOHE KOGYO KOTO SENMON GAKKO.
— HACHINOHE KOGYO KOTO SENMON GAKKO KIYO.
RESEARCH REPORTS, HACHINOHE TECHNICAL COLLEGE.

HACHINOHE TECHNICAL COLLEGE.                                 000
SEE: HACHINOHE KOGYO KOTO SEMMON GAKKO.

HAIGHT-ASHBURY MEDICAL CLINIC.
— JOURNAL OF PSYCHEDELIC DRUGS.

HAILE SELLASSIE I UNIVERSITY: INSTITUTE OF
ETHIOPIAN STUDIES.
— ETHIOPIAN PUBLICATIONS.

HAILEYBURY BIOLOGICAL SOCIETY.
— HART'S TONGUE.

HAKKO KENKYUJO.
— HAKKO KENKYUJO NEMPO. ANNUAL REPORT, INSTI-
TUTE FOR FERMENTATION (JAPAN).

HAMILTON NATURAL HISTORY SOCIETY.
— REPORTS, HAMILTON NATURAL HISTORY SOCIETY.

HAMPSHIRE ARCHIVISTS' GROUP.
— PUBLICATION, HAMPSHIRE ARCHIVISTS' GROUP.

HAMPSHIRE FIELD CLUB & ARCHAEOLOGICAL SOCIETY.
— NEWSLETTER, HAMPSHIRE FIELD CLUB &
ARCHAEOLOGICAL SOCIETY.                                      XXX

HAMPSHIRE & ISLE OF WIGHT NATURALIST'S TRUST
LTD.
— JOURNAL OF THE HAMPSHIRE & ISLE OF WIGHT
NATURALISTS' TRUST LTD.

HANGUK KISULSAHOE.
— KISULSA. JOURNAL OF THE KOREAN SOCIETY OF
PROFESSIONAL ENGINEERS.

HARLOW CONSUMER GROUP.
— HARLOW CONSUMER.

HARVARD UNIVERSITY.
— STUDIES IN PRE-COLUMBIAN ART & ARCHAEOLOGY.

HARVARD UNIVERSITY: INSTITUTE OF ECONOMIC
RESEARCH.
— DISCUSSION PAPER SERIES, INSTITUTE OF ECONO-
MIC RESEARCH, HARVARD UNIVERSITY.

HARVARD UNIVERSITY: LABORATORY FOR COMPUTER
GRAPHICS.
— CONTEXT.

HARVARD UNIVERSITY: LAW SCHOOL.
— HARVARD STUDIES IN EAST ASIAN LAW.

HARVARD UNIVERSITY: MUSEUM OF COMPARATIVE
ZOOLOGY.
— MCZ NEWSLETTER.

HARYANA AGRICULTURAL UNIVERSITY.
— JOURNAL OF RESEARCH, HARYANA AGRICULTURAL
UNIVERSITY.

HASKOLI ISLANDS.
— PUBLICATIONS IN LINGUISTICS, UNIVERSITY OF
ICELAND.

HAVERING POETRY GROUP.
— POETRY ...

HAWAIIAN HISTORICAL SOCIETY.
— HAWAIIAN JOURNAL OF HISTORY.

HAWKER SIDDELEY LTD.
— HARRIER COMMUNIQUE.
— HAWKER SIDDELEY TECHNICAL REVIEW.

HAWKESYARD PRIORY.
— SPODE HOUSE REVIEW.

HEAL ORGANISATION.
— FOURPOSTER.                                                XXX
— FOURPOSTER BROADSHEET.                                     XXX
SUBS (1962): FOURPOSTER.

HEALTH EDUCATION COUNCIL (GB).
— NEWSLETTER, HEALTH EDUCATION COUNCIL (GB).

HEBREW UNIVERSITY OF JERUSALEM.
— INDEX OF ARTICLES ON JEWISH STUDIES.
— SCOPUS REVIEW.

HEBREW UNIVERSITY OF JERUSALEM: DEPARTMENT OF
GEOGRAPHY.
— JERUSALEM STUDIES IN GEOGRAPHY.

HEBREW UNIVERSITY OF JERUSALEM: FOLKLORE RES-
EARCH CENTER.
— FOLKLORE RESEARCH CENTER STUDIES.

HEERESGESCHICHTLICHEN MUSEUM (VIENNA).
— MILITARHISTORISCHE SCHRIFTENREIHE.

HEIDELBERGER AKADEMIE DER WISSENSCHAFTEN: MATHEMATISCH-NATURWISSENSCHAFTLICHE KLASSE.
— MEDIZINISCHE LANDERKUNDE. GEOMEDICAL MONO-
GRAPH SERIES.

HELSINGIN YLIOPISTOLLISEN KESKUSSAIRAALAN PSYKIATRIAN KLINIKAN VUOSIKIRJA.
— PSYCHIATRICA FENNICA. FINNISH PSYCHIATRY.
SUOMALAISTA PSYKIATRICAA.

HELSINKI UNIVERSITY CENTRAL HOSPITAL: PSYCHIATRIC CLINIC.                                       000
SEE: HELSINGIN YLIOPISTOLLISEN KESKUSSAIRA-
ALAN PSYKIATRIAN KLINIKAN VUOSIKIRJA.

HERBARIUM AUSTRALIENSE.
— CONTRIBUTIONS, HERBARIUM AUSTRALIENSE.

HERBARIUM BRADEANUM (RIO DE JANEIRO).
— BRADEA.

HEREFORDSHIRE & RADNORSHIRE NATURE TRUST, LTD.
— NEWSLETTER, HEREFORDSHIRE & RADNORSHIRE
NATURE TRUST, LTD.

HERPETOLOGICAL ASSOCIATION OF AFRICA.
— JOURNAL, HERPETOLOGICAL ASSOCIATION OF AFRICA.

HERPETOLOGICAL ASSOCIATION OF RHODESIA.
— NEWSLETTER, HERPETOLOGICAL ASSOCIATION OF
RHODESIA.

HERTFORDSHIRE COUNTY COUNCIL: TECHNICAL LIBRARY & INFORMATION SERVICE.                           000
SEE: HERTIS.

HERTFORDSHIRE COUNTY LIBRARIES.
— PHOTOGRAPHY INDEX FOR AMATEURS.

HERTFORDSHIRE & MIDDLESEX TRUST FOR NATURE CONSERVATION.
— GREBE. JOURNAL OF HERTFORDSHIRE & MIDDLESEX
TRUST FOR NATURE CONSERVATION.

HERTIS.
— HERTIS OCCASIONAL PAPER.

HIGH PRESSURE DATA CENTER.
— BIBLIOGRAPHY ON HIGH PRESSURE RESEARCH.*

HIGHLANDS & ISLANDS DEVELOPMENT BOARD.
— REPORT, HIGHLANDS & ISLANDS DEVELOPMENT BOARD.
— SPECIAL REPORT, HIGHLANDS & ISLANDS DEVELOP-
MENT BOARD.

HIGHWAY RESEARCH BOARD (US).
— HIGHWAY RESEARCH CIRCULAR.
— TRANSPORTATION NOISE BULLETIN.

HIGHWAY RESEARCH INFORMATION SERVICE (US).
— HRIS ABSTRACTS.

HILLINGDON NATURAL HISTORY SOCIETY.
— JOURNAL, HILLINGDON NATURAL HISTORY SOCIETY.

HIRAM COLLEGE.
— HIRAM POETRY REVIEW.

HIROSHIMA INSTITUTE OF TECHNOLOGY.
— RESEARCH BULLETIN, HIROSHIMA INSTITUTE OF
TECHNOLOGY.

HISTORICAL ASSOCIATION.
— APPRECIATIONS IN HISTORY.
— HISTORY TEACHERS' NEWSLETTER.
— TEACHING HISTORY.

HISTORICAL ASSOCIATION OF TANZANIA.
— PAPERS, HISTORICAL ASSOCIATION OF TANZANIA.

HISTORICAL ASSOCIATION OF ZAMBIA.
— HISTORY IN ZAMBIA.

HISTORICAL MANUSCRIPTS COMMISSION.
— ARCHITECTURAL HISTORY & THE FINE & APPLIED
ARTS.

HISTORY OF EDUCATION SOCIETY.
— BULLETIN, HISTORY OF EDUCATION SOCIETY.
— HISTORY OF EDUCATION.

HOBART & WILLIAM SMITH COLLEGES: STUDENT ASSOCIATIONS.
— SENECA REVIEW.

HOCHSCHULE FUR MUSIK UND DARSTELLENDE KUNST IN GRAZ: INSTITUT FUR JAZZFORSCHUNG.
— BEITRAGE ZUR JAZZFORSCHUNG. STUDIES IN JAZZ
RESEARCH.
— JAZZFORSCHUNG. JAZZ RESEARCH.

HOFMANNSTHAL GESELLSCHAFT.
— HOFMANNSTHAL-BLATTER.

HOFSTRA UNIVERSITY: SCHOOL OF LAW.
— HOFSTRA LAW REVIEW.

HOKKAIDO DAIGAKU: BOTANIC GARDEN.
— SAPPORO BULLETIN.

HOKKAIDO DAIGAKU NOGAKUBU KONCHUGAKU KYOSHITSU.
— INSECTA MATSUMURANA: SUPPLEMENT.

HOKKAIDO DAIGAKU: RESEARCH INSTITUTE OF NORTH PACIFIC FISHERIES.
— COLLECTED REPRINTS, RESEARCH INSTITUTE OF
NORTH PACIFIC FISHERIES, HOKKAIDO UNIVERSITY.

HOKKAIDO JOSHI TANKI DAIGAKU.
— HOKKAIDO JOSHI TANKI DAIGAKU KENKYU KIYO.

HOKKAIDO KOGYO KAIHATSU SHIKENJO.
— HOKKAIDO KOGYO KAIHATSU SHIKENJO HOKOKU.
REPORTS OF THE GOVERNMENT INDUSTRIAL DEVELOP-
MENT LABORATORY.

HOKKAIDO UNIVERSITY: BOTANIC GARDEN                            000
SEE: HOKKAIDO DAIGAKU: BOTANIC GARDEN.

HOKKAIDO UNIVERSITY: ENTOMOLOGICAL INSTITUTE.
SEE: HOKKAIDO DAIGAKU NOGAKUBU KONCHUGAKU
KYOSHITSU.

HOKKAIDO UNIVERSITY: RESEARCH INSTITUTE OF NORTH PACIFIC FISHERIES.                               000
SEE: HOKKAIDO DAIGAKU: RESEARCH INSTITUTE OF
NORTH PACIFIC FISHERIES.

HOKURIKU AGRICULTURAL EXPERIMENT STATION.          000
SEE: HOKURIKU NOGYO SHIKENJO.

HOKURIKU NOGYO SHIKENJO.
— HOKURIKU NOGYO KENKYU SHIRYO.

HOLLAND SOCIETY OF SCIENCES.
— NETHERLANDS JOURNAL OF ZOOLOGY= ARCHIVES
NEERLANDAISES DE ZOOLOGIE.

HOLLANDSCHE MAATSCHAPPIJ DER WETENSCHAPPEN.        000
SEE: HOLLAND SOCIETY OF SCIENCES.

HOME-GROWN CEREALS AUTHORITY.
— CERES. THE JOURNAL OF THE ...                                XXX

HONEYWELL INC.: ELECTRONIC DATA PROCESSING DIVISION.
— HONEYWELL COMPUTER JOURNAL.

(HONG KONG) DEPARTMENT OF AGRICULTURE & FISHERIES.
— AGRICULTURAL SCIENCE, HONG KONG.

(HONG KONG) DEPARTMENT OF AGRICULTURE & FISHERIES: FISHERIES BRANCH.
— HONG KONG FISHERIES BULLETIN.

HONOLULU ORCHID SOCIETY.
— HAWAII ORCHID JOURNAL.                                        XXX

HOOSIER FOLKLORE SOCIETY.
— INDIANA FOLKLORE.

HOOVER INSTITUTION ON WAR, REVOLUTION & PEACE.
— JOURNAL OF THE NEW AFRICAN LITERATURE.
— YEARBOOK ON LATIN AMERICAN COMMUNIST AFFAIRS.

HOPKINS SOCIETY.
— HOPKINS RESEARCH BULLETIN.

HORACE BARKS REFERENCE LIBRARY & INFORMATION SERVICE.
— OCCASIONAL PAPERS, HORACE BARKS REFERENCE
LIBRARY & INFORMATION SERVICE.

(HORNSEY) COLLEGE OF ART; ADVANCED STUDIES GROUP.
— DESIGN EDUCATION.

HOSEI UNIVERSITY: DEPARTMENT OF GEOGRAPHY.
— CLIMATOLOGICAL NOTES, DEPARTMENT OF GEOGRAPHY,
HOSEI UNIVERSITY.

HOSHASEN IKUSHUJO.
— ACTA RADIOBOTANIKA ET GENETIKA.
— HOSHASEN IKUSHUJO TEKUNIKARU NYUSU. TECH-
NICAL NEWS, INSTITUTE OF RADIATION BREEDING
(JAPAN).

HOSPITAL RESEARCH & EDUCATIONAL TRUST.
— HEALTH SERVICES RESEARCH.

HOTEL & CATERING INDUSTRY TRAINING BOARD (GB).
— SERVICE. NEWSLETTER OF THE ...

HOUSE-BUILDERS FEDERATION ADVISORY SERVICE.
— DIGEST OF BUILDING LAND PRICES.

HOVERMAIL COLLECTORS' CLUB.
— HOVER COVER.

HOWEY FOUNDATION.
— EPOCH. ENVIRONMENT - POLLUTION + CONSERVATION =
HEALTH.

HRVATSKO FILOZOFSKO DRUSTVO.
— PRAXIS. FILIZOFSKI CASOPIS.

HSIN-SHE (SINGAPORE).
— HSIN-SHE HSUEH-PAO. JOURNAL OF THE ISLAND
SOCIETY (SINGAPORE).

HSIN-YA YEN-CHIU-SO.
— CHUNG-KUO HSUEH-JEN. CHINESE SCHOLARS.

HUBBARD SCIENTOLOGY ORGANIZATION.
— HORIZON. LONDON SCIENTOLOGY MAGAZINE.

HUDSON INSTITUTE.
— ARMS CONTROL & DISARMAMENT (NEW YORK).          XXX
— ARMS CONTROL & NATIONAL SECURITY.               XXX

HULL CITY COUNCIL: DEVELOPMENT COMMITTEE.
— CIVIC REVIEW.

HULL GEOLOGICAL SOCIETY.
— EAST YORKSHIRE FIELD STUDIES.

HULL SCIENTIFIC & FIELD NATURALISTS' CLUB.
— EAST YORKSHIRE FIELD STUDIES.

HUMAN SCIENCES RESEARCH COUNCIL (SOUTH AFRICA).
— ANNUAL REPORT, HUMAN SCIENCES RESEARCH
COUNCIL (SOUTH AFRICA).

HUNGARIAN SCIENTIFIC COUNCIL FOR WORLD
ECONOMY.                                          000
SEE: VILAGGAZDASAGI TUDOMANYOS TANACS.

HYDROBIOLOGISCHE VERENIGING.
— MEDEDELINGEN VAN DE HYDROBIOLOGISCHE
VERENIGINC.                                       XXX

HYDROGRAPHIC SOCIETY.
— JOURNAL OF THE HYDROGRAPHIC SOCIETY.            XXX

HYDRO-QUEBEC.
— FORCES.

IBERIAN SOCIAL STUDIES ASSOCIATION.
— IBERIAN STUDIES.

IBM CORPORATION: DATA PROCESSING DIVISION.
— COMPUTING REPORT IN SCIENCE & ENGINEERING.

ICEFIELD RANGES RESEARCH PROJECT.
— SCIENTIFIC RESULTS, ICEFIELD RANGES
RESEARCH PROJECT.

IDAHO BUREAU OF MINES & GEOLOGY.
— EARTH SCIENCE SERIES, IDAHO BUREAU OF MINES &
GEOLOGY.

ILKESTON & DISTRICT LOCAL HISTORY SOCIETY.
— OCCASIONAL PAPER, ILKESTON & DISTRICT LOCAL
HISTORY SOCIETY.

ILLINOIS STATE GENEALOGICAL SOCIETY.
— QUARTERLY, ILLINOIS STATE GENEALOGICAL
SOCIETY.

ILLINOIS STATE MUSEUM.
— DICKSON MOUNDS MUSEUM ANTHROPOLOGICAL STUDIES.
— INVENTORY OF COLLECTIONS, ILLINOIS STATE
MUSEUM.

(ILLINOIS) SUPERINTENDENT OF PUBLIC
INSTRUCTION.
— JOURNAL OF AESTHETIC EDUCATION.

ILLUMINATING ENGINEERING SOCIETY.
— LIGHTING RESEARCH & TECHNOLOGY.                 XXX

ILLUMINATING ENGINEERING SOCIETY (NEW YORK).
— ILLUMINATING ENGINEERING.                       XXX
SUBS (1971): PART OF JOURNAL, ILLUMINATING
ENGINEERING SOCIETY (NEW YORK); & LD & A.
LIGHTING DESIGN & APPLICATION.
— JOURNAL, ILLUMINATING ENGINEERING SOCIETY
(NEW YORK).                                       XXX
— LD & A. LIGHTING DESIGN & APPLICATION.          XXX

IMMIGRATION CONTROL ASSOCIATION (AUSTRALIA).
— VIEWPOINT. LOOKING AT SOME ASPECTS OF
AUSTRALIA'S IMMIGRATION POLICY.

IMPERIAL CHEMICAL INDUSTRIES: FARM ADVISORY
SERVICE.
— ICI GRASSLAND MANAGEMENT GUIDE.

IMPERIAL COLLEGE OF SCIENCE & TECHNOLOGY: ROCK
MECHANICS INFORMATION SERVICE.
— ROCK MECHANICS ABSTRACTS.

IMPERIAL TOBACCO GROUP LTD.
— IMPERIAL TOBACCO GROUP REVIEW.
— INFORMATION BROCHURE, IMPERIAL TOBACCO GROUP LTD

INCORPORATED ASSOCIATION OF ARCHITECTS &
SURVEYORS.
— FIRE SURVEYOR.

INCORPORATED COUNCIL OF LAW REPORTING FOR
ENGLAND & WALES.
— INDUSTRIAL COURT REPORTS.                       XXX

INCORPORATED COUNCIL OF LEGAL EDUCATION
(CEYLON).
— JOURNAL OF CEYLON LAW.

INCORPORATED LAW SOCIETY OF IRELAND.
— GAZETTE, INCORPORATED LAW SOCIETY OF IRELAND.

INDECO LTD.
— ENTERPRISE. THE INDECO JOURNAL.

INDEPENDENT BROADCASTING AUTHORITY.
— IBA TECHNICAL REVIEW.

INDEPENDENT TELEVISION AUTHORITY.
— ITV EDUCATION NEWS.

INDEPENDENT WORLD WIDE RIGHT-WING NEWS & INFOR-
MATION SERVICE.
— FACTUAL NEWS INFORMATION.

(INDIA) GEOLOGICAL SURVEY.
— NEWS, GEOLOGICAL SURVEY OF INDIA.

(INDIA) MINISTRY OF FOREIGN TRADE.
— ECONOMIC & COMMERCIAL NEWS (INDIA).

(INDIA) OFFICE OF THE REGISTRAR GENERAL.
— CENSUS CENTENARY MONOGRAPH.
— INDIAN DEMOGRAPHIC BULLETIN.                    XXX

(INDIA) PLANNING COMMISSION.
— ANNUAL PLAN (INDIA).

INDIAN ACADEMY OF WOOD SCIENCE.
— JOURNAL OF THE INDIAN ACADEMY OF WOOD SCIENCE.

INDIAN ASSOCIATION OF MANCHESTER.
— MANCUNIAN INDIAN.

INDIAN ASSOCIATION OF SPECIAL LIBRARIES &
INFORMATION CENTRES.
— INDIAN LIBRARY SCIENCE ABSTRACTS.

INDIAN COUNCIL OF AGRICULTURAL RESEARCH.
— INDIAN JOURNAL OF ANIMAL SCIENCES.              XXX
— INDIAN JOURNAL OF VETERINARY SCIENCE & ANIMAL
HUSBANDRY.                                        XXX
SUBS (1969): INDIAN JOURNAL OF ANIMAL
SCIENCES.

INDIAN COUNCIL OF SOCIAL SCIENCE RESEARCH.
— ICSSR NEWSLETTER.

INDIAN GEOLOGISTS ASSOCIATION.
— BULLETIN, INDIAN GEOLOGISTS ASSOCIATION.

INDIAN GEOTECHNICAL SOCIETY.
— INDIAN GEOTECHNICAL JOURNAL.                    XXX

INDIAN INSTITUTE OF ASIAN STUDIES.
— IFCEP JOURNAL OF MODERN INDIA. THE INDUSTRY, FINANCE, COMMERCE, EXPORT-PROMOTION EXPERIENCE OF INDIA.

INDIAN INSTITUTE OF FOREIGN TRADE.
— FOREIGN TRADE REVIEW (INDIA).

INDIAN INSTITUTE OF TECHNOLOGY.
— JOURNAL OF MATHEMATICAL & PHYSICAL SCIENCES.

INDIAN JUTE MILLS ASSOCIATION.
— JUTE CHRONICLE.

INDIAN LAW INSTITUTE.
— INDEX TO INDIAN LEGAL PERIODICALS.

INDIAN METEOROLOGICAL SOCIETY.
  OGICAL SOCIETY.

INDIAN NATIONAL CONGRESS.
— POLITICAL & ECONOMIC REVIEW.

INDIAN NATIONAL SCIENCE ACADEMY.                       XXX
— BULLETIN, INDIAN NATIONAL SCIENCE ACADEMY.           XXX
— INDIAN JOURNAL OF RADIO & SPACE PHYSICS.
— PROCEEDINGS, INDIAN NATIONAL SCIENCE ACADEMY:
  PART A: PHYSICAL SCIENCES.                            XXX
— PROCEEDINGS, INDIAN NATIONAL SCIENCE ACADEMY:
  PART B: BIOLOGICAL SCIENCES.                          XXX
— YEAR BOOK OF THE INDIAN NATIONAL SCIENCE
  ACADEMY.                                              XXX

INDIAN SCHOOL OF SOCIAL SCIENCES.
— SOCIAL SCIENTIST.

INDIAN SOCIETY OF AGRICULTURAL CHEMISTS.
— INDIAN JOURNAL OF AGRICULTURAL CHEMISTRY.

INDIAN SOCIETY FOR MALARIA & OTHER COMMUNICABLE DISEASES.
— BULLETIN OF THE INDIAN SOCIETY FOR MALARIA &
  OTHER COMMUNICABLE DISEASES.                          XXX
— JOURNAL OF COMMUNICABLE DISEASES.

INDIAN WIRE ASSOCIATION.
— INDIAN WIRE INDUSTRY JOURNAL.                          XXX

INDIANA ACADEMY OF SCIENCE.
— MONOGRAPHS, INDIANA ACADEMY OF SCIENCE.

INDIANA STATE UNIVERSITY: DEPARTMENT OF GEOGRAPHY & GEOLOGY.
— PROFESSIONAL PAPERS, DEPARTMENT OF GEOGRAPHY
  & GEOLOGY, INDIANA STATE UNIVERSITY.                  XXX

INDIANA UNIVERSITY.
— MIDWEST FOLKLORE.                                      XXX
  SUBS (1964): JOURNAL OF THE FOLKLORE
  INSTITUTE, INDIANA UNIVERSITY.
— VICTORIAN PERIODICALS NEWSLETTER.

INDIANA UNIVERSITY: DEPARTMENT OF MATHEMATICS.
— INDIANA UNIVERSITY MATHEMATICS JOURNAL.               XXX
— JOURNAL OF MATHEMATICS & MECHANICS.                   XXX
  SUBS (1970): INDIANA UNIVERSITY MATHEMAT-
  ICS JOURNAL.

INDIANA UNIVERSITY: FOLKLORE INSTITUTE.
— JOURNAL OF THE FOLKLORE INSTITUTE, INDIANA
  UNIVERSITY.                                           XXX

INDIANA UNIVERSITY: RESEARCH CENTER FOR THE LANGUAGE SCIENCES.
— LANGUAGE SCIENCES.

INDIANA UNIVERSITY: SCHOOL OF EDUCATION.
— BULLETIN OF THE SCHOOL OF EDUCATION, INDIANA
  UNIVERSITY.                                           XXX
  SUBS (1970): VIEWPOINTS.
— VIEWPOINTS.                                            XXX

INDO-BRITISH HISTORICAL SOCIETY.
— INDO-BRITISH REVIEW.

(INDONESIA) EMBASSY (GB).
— INDONESIAN NEWS.

INDONESIAN SUGAR EXPERIMENT STATION.                     000
  SEE: BALAI PENJELIDIKAN PERUSAHAAN PERKEBUNAN
  GULA.

INDUSTRIAL ARCHAELOGY GROUP FOR THE NORTH EAST.
— BULLETIN, INDUSTRIAL ARCHAEOLOGY GROUP FOR
  THE NORTH EAST.

INDUSTRIAL ARTS INSTITUTE (JAPAN).                       000
  SEE: SANGYO KOGEI SHIKENJO.

INDUSTRIAL DIAMOND INFORMATION BUREAU.
— DIAMOND RESEARCH.

INDUSTRIAL LAW SOCIETY.
— BULLETIN, INDUSTRIAL LAW SOCIETY.                      XXX
— INDUSTRIAL LAW JOURNAL.                                XXX

INDUSTRIAL MARKETING RESEARCH ASSOCIATION.
— INDUSTRIAL MARKETING RESEARCH ABSTRACTS.

INDUSTRIAL PRODUCTS RESEARCH INSTITUTE (JAP.)
  SEE: SEIHIN KAGAKU KENKYUJO.

INDUSTRIAL RELATIONS RESEARCH ASSOCIATION.
— REVIEW OF INDUSTRIAL RELATIONS RESEARCH.

INDUSTRIJA VISKOZNIH PROIZVODA 'VISKOZA'.
— HEMIJSKA VLAKNA.

INFORMATION CENTRE OF LITERATURE, ART & SCIENCE (SOFIA).
— BULGARIAN HORIZONS.

INFORMATION PROPAGANDE FRANCAISES.
— REVUE FRANCAISE DE RADIODIFFUSION ET DE TELE-
  VISION.                                               XXX
— REVUE TECHNIQUE DE RADIODIFFUSION ET DE TELE-
  VISION.                                               XXX

INGENIORSVETENSKAPSAKADEMIEN: PALKOMMISSIONEN.
— SARTRYCK OCH PRELIMINARA RAPPORTER.

IN'GU MUNJE YON'GUSO.
— IN'GU MUNJE NONJIP. JOURNAL OF POPULATION
  STUDIES.

INITIAL TEACHING ALPHABET FOUNDATION.
— ITA FOUNDATION PUBLICATION.

INNER LONDON EDUCATION AUTHORITY.
— ILEA CONTACT.

INNER LONDON TEACHERS' ASSOCIATION.
— CENTRE POINT.

INSTITUTE FOR ADVANCED STUDIES (VIENNA).
— INTERNATIONAL JOURNAL OF GAME THEORY.

INSTITUTION OF AGRICULTURAL ENGINEERS.                   XXX
— AGRICULTURAL ENGINEER.                                 XXX
— JOURNAL & PROCEEDINGS, INSTITUTION OF AGRI-
  CULTURAL ENGINEERS.                                    XXX

INSTITUTO DE ALTA CULTURA (PORTUGAL).
— ARQUIVOS DE HISTORIA DA CULTURA PORTUGUESA.

INSTITUT D'AMENAGEMENT ET D'URBANISME DE LA REGION PARISIENNE.
— BULLETIN D'INFORMATION DE L'INSTITUT D'AMEN-
  AGEMENT ET D'URBANISME DE LA REGION PARIS-
  IENNE.

INSTITUTO ANTARCTICO CHILENO.
— BOLETIN, INSTITUTO ANTARCTICO CHILENO.
— SERIE CIENTIFICA, INSTITUTO ANTARCTICO
  CHILENO.

INSTITUTE OF APPLIED ECONOMIC RESEARCH (AUSTRALIA).
— AUSTRALIAN ECONOMIC REVIEW.

INSTITUT FUR BAU VON LANDVERKEHRSWEGEN.
— MITTEILUNG, INSTITUT FUR BAU VON LANDVERK-
  EHRSWEGEN.                                            XXX

INSTITUT BELGE DES HAUTES ETUDES BOUDDHIQUES: CENTRE D'ETUDES BOUDDHIQUES ANANDA.
— SAMADHI. CAHIERS D'ETUDES BOUDDHIQUES.

INSTITUT BELGE DU PETROLE.
— ANNALES, INSTITUT BELGE DU PETROLE.

INSTITUT BELGE DE LA SOUDURE.
— NOTE TECHNIQUE, INSTITUT BELGE DE LA SOUDURE.

INSTITUTE FUR BIENENFORSCHUNG: ARBEITSGEMEINSCHAFT.
— APIDOLOGIE.                                           XXX

INSTITUTE OF BIOLOGY.
— BIOLOGIST.
— JOURNAL, INSTITUTE OF BIOLOGY.                        XXX
  SUBS (1969): BIOLOGIST.

INSTITUTE OF BIOLOGY: COMMITTEE ON BIOLOGICAL
INFORMATION.
— COBI NEWSLETTER.

INSTITUTO BOLIVIANO DE ESTUDIO Y ACCION SOCIAL.
— ESTUDIOS ANDINOS.

INSTITUTO BRASILEIRO DE BIBLIOGRAFIA E
DOCUMENTACAO.
— BIBLIOGRAFIA BRASILEIRA DE CIENCIAS AGRICOLAS.

INSTITUTO BRASILEIRO DE ESTATISTICA.
— BRASIL: SERIES ESTATISTICAS RETROSPECTIVAS.

INSTITUTION OF BRITISH AGRICULTURAL ENGIN-
EERS.                                                          XXX
— JOURNAL & PROCEEDINGS, INSTITUTION OF BRITISH
  AGRICULTURAL ENGINEERS.                                      XXX
  SUBS (1960): JOURNAL & PROCEEDINGS, INSTIT-
  UTION OF AGRICULTURAL ENGINEERS.

INSTITUTE OF BRITISH GEOGRAPHERS.
— AREA.
— SPECIAL PUBLICATIONS, INSTITUTE OF BRITISH
  GEOGRAPHERS.

INSTITUTE OF BRITISH GEOGRAPHERS: URBAN STUDY
GROUP.
— OCCASIONAL PUBLICATIONS, URBAN STUDY GROUP,
  INSTITUTE OF BRITISH GEOGRAPHERS.

INSTITUTET FOR BYGGDOKUMENTATION.
— BYGGREFERAT.                                                 XXX

INSTITUTO CATOLICO DE ESTUDIOS SOCIALES DE
BARCELONA.
— PERSPECTIVA SOCIAL.

INSTITUTUL CENTRAL DE CERCETARI AGRICOLE.
— BIBLIOGRAPHIE AGRICOLE COURANTE ROUMAINE.

INSTITUTUL CENTRAL DE DOCUMENTARE TEHNICA.
— ABSTRACTS OF ROMANIAN SCIENTIFIC & TECHNICAL
  LITERATURE.                                                  XXX

INSTITUTO CENTROAMERICANO DE INVESTIGACION Y
TECNOLOGIA INDUSTRIAL.
— PUBLICACIONES GEOLOGICAS DEL ICAITI.

INSTITUTUL DE CERCETARI PENTRU IMBUNATATIRI
FUNCIARE SI PEDOLOGIE.
— ANALELE, INSTITUTUL DE CERCETARI PENTRU
  IMBUNATATIRI FUNCIARE SI PEDOLOGIE:
  SERIA HIDROTECHNICA.

INSTITUTUL DE CERCETARI PENTRU NUTRITIE ANIMALA
— LUCRARILE STIINTIFICE, INSTITUTUL DE CERCET-
  ARI PENTRU NUTRITIE ANIMALA.

INSTITUTUL DE CERCETARI PENTRU POMICULTURA
PITESTI.
— ANALELE, INSTITUTUL DE CERCETARI PENTRU
  POMICULTURA PITESTI.

INSTITUTUL DE CERCETARI PENTRU VITICULTURA
SI VINIFICATIE.
— ANALELE, INSTITUTUL DE CERCETARI PENTRU
  VITICULTURA SI VINIFICATIE.

INSTITUTUL DE CERCETARI SI PROIECTARI PENTRU
PASTRAREA SI VALORIFICAREA LEGUMELOR SI
FRUCTELOR.
— LUCRARI STIINTIFICE ALE INSTITUTUL DE CERCET-
  ARI SI PROIECTARI PENTRU PASTRAREA SI VALOR-
  IFICAREA LEGUMELOR SI FRUCTELOR.

INSTITUTE OF CHARTERED ACCOUNTANTS IN
ENGLAND & WALES.
— ACCOUNTING AND BUSINESS RESEARCH.
— ACCOUNTING & DATA PROCESSING ABSTRACTS.                      XXX
— LIBRARIAN'S DIGEST OF ARTICLES, INSTITUTE OF
  CHARTERED ACCOUNTANTS IN ENGLAND & WALES.                    XXX
  SUBS (1970): ACCOUNTING & DATA PROCESSING
  ABSTRACTS.

INSTITUTE OF CHARTERED ACCOUNTANTS IN IRELAND.
— ACCOUNTANCY IRELAND.

INSTYTUT CHEMII OGOLNEJ.
— TLUSZCZE, SRODKI PIORACE, KOSMETYKI.                         XXX

INSTITUTE OF CHRISTIAN STUDIES.
— CHRISTIAN (LONDON).

INSTITUTE OF CHURCH GROWTH.
— CHURCH GROWTH BULLETIN.

INSTITUTO DE CIENCIA ANIMAL (CUBA).
— REVISTA CUBANA DE CIENCIA AGRICOLA.                          XXX

INSTITUTION OF CIVIL ENGINEERS.
— NEW CIVIL ENGINEER.
— PROCEEDINGS, INSTITUTION OF CIVIL ENGINEERS:
  PT 1, DESIGN & CONSTRUCTION.                                 XXX
— PROCEEDINGS, INSTITUTION OF CIVIL ENGINEERS:
  PT 2: RESEARCH & THEORY.                                     XXX

INSTITUTO COLOMBIANO AGROPECUARIO.
— REVISTA DEL INSTITUTO COLOMBIANO AGROPECUARIO.

INSTITUTO COLOMBIANO DE FOLCLOR.
— REVISTA COLOMBIANA DE FOLCLOR: SUPLEMENTO.

INSTITUTION OF COMPUTER SCIENCES.
— JOURNAL OF THE INSTITUTION OF COMPUTER
  SCIENCES.

INSTITUTE OF CONSTITUTIONAL & PARLIAMENTARY
STUDIES (INDIA).
— CONPARLIST.
— JOURNAL OF CONSTITUTIONAL & PARLIAMENTARY
  STUDIES (INDIA).

INSTITUTE OF CONSTITUTIONAL & PARLIAMENTARY
STUDIES (INDIA): CENTRE FOR THE STUDY OF LAW &
SOCIETY.
— LAW & SOCIETY NEWSLETTER.

INSTITUTE OF CONTEMPORARY ARTS.
— MAGAZINE OF THE INSTITUTE OF CONTEMPORARY
  ARTS.                                                        XXX

INSTITUTE OF CORN & AGRICULTURAL MERCHANTS.
— TECHNOLOGY IN AGRICULTURE.                                   XXX

INSTITUTE OF CORNISH STUDIES.
— BULLETIN, INSTITUTE OF CORNISH STUDIES.

INSTITUTO CUBANO DE INVESTIGACIONES DE LOS
DERIVADOS DE LA CANA DE AZUCAR.
— SOBRE LOS DERIVADOS DE LA CANA DE AZUCAR.

INSTITUTO DE CULTURA DOMINICANA: MUSEO DEL
HOMBRE DOMINICANO.                                             000
  SEE: MUSEO DEL HOMBRE DOMINICANO.

INSTITUTO DE CULTURA HISPANICA.
— ANUARIO DE SOCIOLOGIA DE LOS PUEBLOS IBERICOS.

INSTITUUT VOOR CULTUURTECHNIEK EN
WATERHUISHOUDING.
— VERSPREIDE OVERDRUKKEN, INSTITUUT VOOR
  CULTUURTECHNIEK EN WATERHUISHOUDING.

INSTITUT FUR DEUTSCHE SPRACHE.
— SPRACHE DER GEGENWART.

INSTITUTO DE DIREITO PUBLICO E CIENCIA POLITICA
(BRAZIL).
— REVISTA DE CIENCIA POLITICA.

INSTITUTE OF ECONOMIC AFFAIRS (GB).
— EATON PAPER.
— READINGS IN POLITICAL ECONOMY.

INSTITUTE OF ECONOMIC GROWTH (DELHI):
DEMOGRAPHIC RESEARCH CENTRE.
— CENSUS STUDIES.

INSTITUT ECONOMIQUE AGRICOLE (BELGIUM).
— SITUATION DE L'AGRICULTURE BELGE AU COURS DE
  L'ANNEE.

INSTITUT FUR EISENBAHNBAU UND STRASSENBAU.                     XXX
— MITTEILUNGEN, INSTITUT FUR EISENBAHNBAU UND
  STRASSENBAU.                                                 XXX
  SUBS (1970): MITTEILUNGEN, INSTITUT FUR BAU
  VON LANDVERKEHRSWEGEN.

INSTITUT FUR EISENBAHNWESEN, SPEZIALBAHNEN UND
VERKEHRSWIRTSCHAFT.
— ARBEITEN, INSTITUT FUR EISENBAHNWESEN, SPEZ-
  IALBAHNEN UND VERKEHRSWIRTSCHAFT.

INSTITUTE OF ELECTRICAL & ELECTRONICS ENGINEERS
— IEEE TRANSACTIONS ON COMMUNICATIONS. XXX
— IEEE TRANSACTIONS ON INDUSTRY APPLICATIONS. XXX
— IEEE TRANSACTIONS ON MAN-MACHINE SYSTEMS. XXX
— IEEE TRANSACTIONS ON MANUFACTURING TECHNOLOGY.
— IEEE TRANSACTIONS ON PARTS, HYBRIDS &
PACKAGING. XXX
— IEEE TRANSACTIONS ON PROFESSIONAL COMMUNICAT-
ION. XXX
— IEEE TRANSACTIONS ON SYSTEMS, MAN, & CYBERNET-
ICS. XXX
— IEEE TRANSACTIONS ON VEHICULAR COMMUNI-
CATIONS. XXX
— IEEE TRANSACTIONS ON VEHICULAR TECHNOLOGY.
— NEREM TECHNICAL APPLICATIONS PAPERS.

INSTITUTE OF ELECTRICAL & ELECTRONICS ENGIN-
EERS: COMPUTER SOCIETY.
— COMPUTER. XXX

INSTITUTE OF ELECTRICAL & ELECTRONICS ENG-
INEERS: NUCLEAR & PLASMA SCIENCES SOCIETY.
— IEEE TRANSACTIONS ON PLASMA SCIENCE.

INSTITUTE OF ELECTRICAL & ELECTRONICS ENGINEERS
: POWER ENGINEERING SOCIETY.
— SPECIAL PUBLICATION, POWER ENGINEERING SOC-
IETY, INSTITUTE OF ELECTRICAL & ELECTRONICS
ENGINEERS.

INSTITUTION OF ELECTRICAL & ELECTRONICS TECH-
NICIAN ENGINEERS.
— ELECTRICAL & ELECTRONICS TECHNICIAN ENGINEER. XXX
— ELECTROTECHNOLOGY (LONDON). XXX

INSTITUTION OF ELECTRICAL ENGINEERS.
— CURRENT PAPERS ON COMPUTERS & CONTROL. XXX
— CURRENT PAPERS ON CONTROL. XXX
— CURRENT PAPERS IN ELECTRICAL & ELECTRONICS
ENGINEERING.
— IEE MEDICAL ELECTRONICS MONOGRAPHS.
— INSPEC MATTERS.
— ISMEC BULLETIN. INFORMATION SERVICE IN MECH-
ANICAL ENGINEERING.

INSTITUTION OF ELECTRONIC & RADIO ENGINEERS:
INDIAN DIVISION.
— PROCEEDINGS, INDIAN DIVISION, INSTITUTION OF
ELECTRONIC & RADIO ENGINEERS. XXX

INSTITUTION OF ENGINEERS (AUSTRALIA).
— AUSTRALIAN GEOMECHANICS JOURNAL.

INSTITUTO DE ESTUDIOS FISCALES.
— HACIENDA PUBLICA ESPANOLA.

INSTITUTO DE ESTUDIOS SINDICALES, SOCIALES Y
COOPERATIVOS.
— ANUARIO DE SOCIOLOGIA DE LOS PUEBLOS IBERICOS.
— COMUNICADES, INSTITUTO DE ESTUDIOS SINDICALES,
SOCIALES Y COOPERATIVOS.
— ESTUDIOS SINDICALES Y COOPERATIVOS.

INSTITUT D'ETUDES SCIENTIFIQUES DE CARGESE.
— CARGESE LECTURES IN PHYSICS.

INSTITUT FUR EXPERIMENTELLE KUNST UND ASTHETIK.
— ASTHETIK UND KOMMUNIKATION.

INSTITUTY FIZICHESKOJ KUL'TURY.
— PROBLEMY PSIKHOLOGII SPORTA.

INSTITUTO FORESTAL DE CHILE.
— SERIE DE INVESTIGACION, INSTITUTO FORESTAL DE
CHILE.

INSTITUT FRANCAIS D'ETUDES ANDINES.
— BULLETIN DE L'INSTITUT FRANCAIS D'ETUDES
ANDINES.

INSTITUT FRANCAIS DE POLEMOLOGIE.
— ETUDES POLEMOLOGIQUES. XXX

INSTITUTE OF FUEL.
— ENERGY WORLD.

INSTITUT FUR GASTECHNIK, FEUERUNGSTECHNIK UND
WASSERCHEMIE (KARLSRUHE): ABTEILUNG UND LEHR-
STUHL FUR WASSERCHEMIE. XXX
— VEROFFENTLICHUNGEN, ABTEILUNG UND LEHRSTUHL
FUR WASSERCHEMIE, INSTITUT FUR GASTECHNIK,
FEUERUNGSTECHNIK UND WASSERCHEMIE (KARLSRUHE).XX

INSTITUTION OF GENERAL TECHNICIAN ENGINEERS.
— JOURNAL, INSTITUTION OF GENERAL TECHNICIAN
ENGINEERS. XXX

INSTITUT GEOGRAPHIQUE NATIONAL (FRANCE).
— ETUDES DE PHOTO-INTERPRETATION.

INSTITUTUL GEOLOGIC (BUCHAREST).
— STUDII TEHNICE SI ECONOMICE, INSTITUTUL GEO-
LOGIC: SERIA A: PROSPECTIUNI SI EXPLORARI
GEOLOGICE.
— STUDII TEHNICE SI ECONOMICE, INSTITUTUL GEO-
LOGIC: SERIA B: CHIMIE.
— STUDII TEHNICE SI ECONOMICE, INSTITUTUL GEO-
LOGIC: SERIA C: PEDOLOGIA.
— STUDII TEHNICE SI ECONOMICE, INSTITUTUL GEO-
LOGIC: SERIA D: PROSPECTIUNI GEOFIZICE.
— STUDII TEHNICE SI ECONOMICE, INSTITUTUL GEO-
LOGIC: SERIA F: GEOLOGIE TEHNICA.
— STUDII TEHNICE SI ECONOMICE, INSTITUTUL GEO-
LOGIC: SERIA H: GEOLOGIE.
— STUDII TEHNICE SI ECONOMICE, INSTITITUL GEO-
LOGIC: SERIA I: MINERALOGIE-PETROGRAFIE.
— STUDII TEHNICE SI ECONOMICE, INSTITUTUL GEO-
LOGIC: SERIA J: STRATIGRAFIE.

INSTITUTE OF GEOLOGICAL SCIENCES (GB).
— GEOMAGNETIC BULLETINS. XXX
— SEISMOLOGICAL BULLETIN, INSTITUTE OF GEOLOG-
ICAL SCIENCES (GB).

INSTYTUT GOSPODARKI MIESZKANIOWEJ: KOMITET
BUDOWNICTWA, URBANISTYKI I ARCHITEKTURY.
— SPRAWY MIESZKANIOWE.

INSTYTUT GOSPODARKI WODNEJ.
— PRACE INSTYTUTU GOSPODARKI WODNEJ. PROCEED-
INGS OF WATER ECONOMICS RESEARCH INSTITUTE.
TRUDY INSTITUTA VODNOGO KHOZJAJSTVA.

INSTITUTE OF GROUP ANALYSIS.
— GROUP ANALYSIS.

INSTITUTE OF HEALTH SERVICE ADMINISTRATORS.
— HOSPITAL & HEALTH SERVICES PURCHASING. XXX
— HOSPITAL & HEALTH SERVICES REVIEW. XXX

INSTITUTION OF HEATING & VENTILATING ENGINEERS.
— BUILDING SERVICES ENGINEER. XXX

INSTITUTION OF HIGHWAY ENGINEERS.
— HIGHWAY ENGINEER. XXX

INSTITUTE OF HISTORICAL STUDIES (CALCUTTA).
— QUARTERLY REVIEW OF HISTORICAL STUDIES.

INSTITUTUM HISTORICUM SOCIETATIS IESU.
— SOURCES & STUDIES FOR THE HISTORY OF THE
JESUITS.

INSTITUTE OF THE HISTORY OF SOCIALISM (CZECH.)
SEE: USTAV DEJIN SOCIALISMU.

INSTITUTE OF HOSPITAL ADMINISTRATORS.
— HOSPITAL PURCHASING. XXX

INSTITUTE OF HOSPITAL ADMINISTRATORS (EIRE).
— IRISH HOSPITAL. OFFICIAL JOURNAL OF THE ...

INSTITUTE OF HOSPITAL ENGINEERING.
— HOSPITAL ENGINEERING. XXX

INSTITUTE OF HUMAN BIOLOGY (PAPUA-NEW GUINEA).
— MONOGRAPH SERIES, INSTITUTE OF HUMAN BIOLOGY
(PAPUA-NEW GUINEA).

INSTITUT FUR IBEROAMERIKA-KUNDE: DOKUMENTAT-
IONSDIENST LATEINAMERIKA.
— BOLETIN DE DOCUMENTACION LATINOAMERICANA.

INSTITUTE FOR INDUSTRIAL RESEARCH & STANDARDS
(EIRE).
— FOOD PROGRESS.
— GUIDE TO EEC TECHNICAL DIRECTIVES.
— PACKAGING & PRINTING PROGRESS.
— TECHNOLOGY IRELAND.

INSTITUTO PARA LA INTEGRACION DE AMERICA
LATINA.
— DERECHO DE LA INTEGRACION.
— REVISTA DE LA INTEGRACION.

INSTITUT INTERNATIONAL D'ADMINISTRATION PUB-
LIQUE.
— BULLETIN, INSTITUT INTERNATIONAL D'ADMINIS-
TRATION PUBLIQUE.

INSTITUT INTERNATIONAL D'ETUDES SUR L'EDUCATION
— YOUTH ACTION.

**INSTITUT INTERNATIONAL D'ETUDES SOCIALES.**
— CAHIERS DE L'INSTITUT INTERNATIONAL D'ETUDES
SOCIALES.

**INSTITUT INTERNATIONAL D'HISTOIRE DE LA BANQUE.**
— REVUE INTERNATIONALE D'HISTOIRE DE LA BANQUE.
= RIVISTA INTERNAZIONALE DI STORIA DELLA
BANCA. = INTERNATIONAL REVIEW OF THE HISTORY
OF BANKING.

**INSTITUT FUR INTERNATIONALE POLITIK UND
WIRTSCHAFT.**
— IPW BERICHTE.

**INSTITUTO DE INVESTIGACAO AGRONOMICA DE ANGOLA.**
— SERIE CIENTIFICA, INSTITUTO DE INVESTIGACAO
AGRONOMICA DE ANGOLA: SELECTED SERIES.

**INSTITUTO DE INVESTIGACIONES AGROPECUARIAS
(CHILE).**
— INVESTIGACION Y PROGRESO AGRICOLA.

**INSTITUTO DE INVESTIGACIONES BIBLIOGRAFICAS
(MEXICO).**
— BOLETIN DEL INSTITUTO DE INVESTIGACIONES
BIBLIOGRAFICAS (MEXICO).

**INSTITUTO DE INVESTIGACAO CIENTIFICA DE ANGOLA.**
— BOLETIM DO INSTITUTO DE INVESTIGACAO CIENTI-
FICA DE ANGOLA.
— RELATORIOS E COMUNICACOES, INSTITUTO DE
INVESTIGACAO CIENTIFICA DE ANGOLA.

**INSTITUTO DE INVESTIGACAO CIENTIFICA DE MOCAM-
BIQUE.**
— TRABALHOS, INSTITUTO DE INVESTIGACAO CIENTIF-
ICA DE MOCAMBIQUE.

**INSTITUTO DE INVESTIGACIONES CIENTIFICAS Y
TECNICAS DE LAS FUERZAS ARMADAS (BUENOS AIRES).**
— ACTA CIENTIFICA, INSTITUTO DE INVESTIGACIONES
CIENTIFICAS Y TECNICAS DE LAS FUERZAS ARMADAS
(BUENOS AIRES).

**INSTITUTO DE INVESTIGACIONES FILOSOFICAS.**
— BIBLIOGRAFIA FILOSOFICA MEXICANA.

**INSTITUT ZA IZUCAVANJE RADNICKOG POKRETA.**
— PRILOZI ZA ISTORIJU SOCIJALIZMA.

**INSTITUTE OF JAMAICA: WEST INDIA REFERENCE
LIBRARY.**
— JAMAICAN ACCESSIONS.                               XXX
— JAMAICAN NATIONAL BIBLIOGRAPHY.                    XXX

**INSTITUTE OF JEWISH AFFAIRS.**
— BULLETIN ON SOVIET & EAST EUROPEAN JEWISH
AFFAIRS.                                             XXX
— CHRISTIAN ATTITUDES ON JEWS & JUDAISM.
— SOVIET JEWISH AFFAIRS.                             XXX
— SURVEY OF THE GERMAN PRESS.

**INSTITUTE OF JEWISH STUDIES (LONDON).**
— PAPERS OF THE INSTITUTE OF JEWISH STUDIES
LONDON.

**INSTITUTE OF JOURNALISTS.**
— NEWS LETTER, INSTITUTE OF JOURNALISTS.

**INSTITUTUM JUDAICUM DELITZSCHIANUM.**
— THEOKRATIA.

**INSTITUTE OF LANDSCAPE ARCHITECTS.**
— JOURNAL, INSTITUTE OF LANDSCAPE ARCHITECTS.      XXX
SUBS (1971): LANDSCAPE DESIGN.
— LANDSCAPE DESIGN.                                  XXX

**INSTITUTIONEN FOR LANTBRUKETS BYGGNADSTEKNIK.**
— INSTITUTIONEN FOR LANTBRUKETS BYGGNADSTEKNIK,
HANDLINGAR.                                          XXX

**INSTITUTE FOR LASER DOCUMENTATION (VANCOUVER).**
— JOURNAL OF CURRENT LASER ABSTRACTS.

**INSTITUTO DE LENGUAS ABORIGINES.**
— KUNAN/HICHA/AHORA.

**INSTITUT DE LITTERATURE ET DE TECHNIQUES ART-
ISTIQUES DE MASSE.**
— DISCOURS SOCIAL.

**INSTITUTION OF LOCOMOTIVE ENGINEERS.**             XXX
— JOURNAL, INSTITUTION OF LOCOMOTIVE ENGINEERS.    XXX
SUBS (1970): RAILWAY DIVISION JOURNAL,
INSTITUTION OF MECHANICAL ENGINEERS.

**INSTITUTO 'LUIS DE CAMOES.'**
— BOLETIM, INSTITUTO 'LUIS DE CAMOES.'

**INSTITUTE OF MANAGEMENT IN PRINTING LTD.**
— MANAGEMENT IN PRINTING.

**INSTITUTE OF MARINE ENGINEERS.**
— ABSTRACTS, INSTITUTE OF MARINE ENGINEERS:
MARINE ENGINEERING/SHIPBUILDING.
— MARINE ENGINEERS JOURNAL.                         XXX
— MARINE ENGINEERS REVIEW.                          XXX

**INSTITUT FUR MARXISTISCHE STUDIEN UND FORSCH-
UNGEN (FRANKFURT/MAIN).**
— MARXISMUS DIGEST.

**INSTITUTE OF MATERIALS HANDLING.**
— JOURNAL, INSTITUTE OF MATERIALS HANDLING.         XXX
SUBS (1968): MATERIALS HANDLING AND
MANAGEMENT.
— MATERIALS HANDLING & MANAGEMENT.                  XXX

**INSTITUTE OF MATHEMATICAL STATISTICS.**
— ANNALS OF PROBABILITY.                            XXX
— ANNALS OF STATISTICS.                             XXX
— BULLETIN, INSTITUTE OF MATHEMATICAL STATIST-
ICS.

**INSTITUTION OF MECHANICAL ENGINEERS.**
— ISMEC BULLETIN. INFORMATION SERVICE IN MECH-
ANICAL ENGINEERING.
— MECHANICAL ENGINEERING NEWS.
— MECHANICAL ENGINEERING SCIENCE.                   XXX
— REJ. THE RAILWAY ENGINEERING JOURNAL.             XXX
— TRIBOLOGY NEWS.

**INSTITUTION OF MECHANICAL ENGINEERS: AUTOMOBILE
DIVISION.**
— JOURNAL OF AUTOMOTIVE ENGINEERING.

**INSTITUTION OF MECHANICAL ENGINEERS: MEDICAL
ENGINEERING WORKING PARTY.**
— ENGINEERING IN MEDICINE.

**INSTITUTION OF MECHANICAL ENGINEERS: RAILWAY
DIVISION.**
— RAILWAY DIVISION JOURNAL, INSTITUTION OF
MECHANICAL ENGINEERS.                               XXX

**INSTITUTION OF MECHANICAL ENGINEERS: THERMO-
DYNAMICS & FLUID MECHANICS GROUP.**
— HEAT & FLUID FLOW.

**INSTITUTE OF MEDICAL LABORATORY TECHNOLOGY.**
— JOURNAL OF MEDICAL LABORATORY TECHNOLOGY.        XXX
SUBS (1971): MEDICAL LABORATORY TECHNOLOGY.
— MEDICAL LABORATORY TECHNOLOGY.                    XXX

**INSTITUTO DE MEDICINA TROPICAL (LISBON).**        XXX
— ANAIS DO INSTITUTO DE MEDICINA TROPICAL.          XXX
SUBS (1967): ANAIS DA ESCOLA NACIONAL DE
SAUDE PUBLICA E DE MEDICINA TROPICAL.

**INSTITUTE OF MEDIEVAL CANON LAW.**
— BULLETIN OF MEDIEVAL CANON LAW: NS.

**INSTITUT ZA MEDUNARODNU POLITIKU I PRIVREDU.**
— HRONIKA MEDUNARODNIH DOGADAJA.

**INSTITUT ZA MEHANIZACIJU POLJOPRIVREDE.**
— POLJOPRIVREDNA TEHNIKA.

**INSTITUTE OF METALS.**
— INTERNATIONAL METALLURGICAL REVIEWS.              XXX
— METALS ABSTRACTS.
— METALS ABSTRACTS INDEX.                           XXX

**INSTITUTUL DE METEOROLOGIE SI HIDROLOGIE.**
— METEOROLOGY & HYDROLOGY (RUMANIA).

**INSTITUT MEZHDUNARODNYKH OTNOSHENIJ.**
— VNESHNJAJA POLITIKA SOVETSKOGO SOJUZA I MEZH-
DUNARODNYE OTNOSHENIJA. SBORNIK DOKUMENTOV.

**INSTITUTE FOR MUSCLE BIOLOGY.**
— MUSCLE BIOLOGY.

**INSTITUTO NACIONAL DE ESTATISTICA (PORTUGAL).**
— INDICADORES ECONOMICO-SOCIAIS.                    XXX
— INDICADORES ESTATISTICOS A CURTO PRAZO. =
SHORT TERM STATISTICAL INDICATORS.                  XXX

**INSTITUTO NACIONAL DE ESTADISTICA Y CENSOS DE
REPUBLICA ARGENTINA.**
— COSTO DE LA CONSTRUCCION (EN LA CAPITAL
FEDERAL).

INSTITUTO NACIONAL DE GEOLOGIA (SPAIN).
— ACTA GEOLOGICA HISPANICA.

INSTITUTO NACIONAL DE INVESTIGACIONES Y
ARCHIVOS LITERARIOS (URUGUAY).
— FUENTES.

INSTITUTO NACIONAL DE INVESTIGACIONES
BIOLOGICO-PESQUERAS (MEXICO).
— ANALES DEL INSTITUTO NACIONAL DE INVESTIGA-
CIONES BIOLOGICO-PESQUERAS.

INSTITUTO NACIONAL DE LA PESCA (CUBA).
— MAR Y PESCA.

INSTITUTO NACIONAL DE PESCA DEL ECUADOR.
— BOLETIN CIENTIFICO Y TECNICO, INSTITUTO NA-
CIONAL DE PESCA DEL ECUADOR.

INSTITUTO NACIONAL DE PESQUISAS DA AMAZONIA
(BRAZIL).
— ACTA AMAZONICA.

INSTITUT NATIONAL DES INDUSTRIES EXTRACTIVES
(BELGIUM).
— BULLETIN TECHNIQUE, INSTITUT NATIONAL DES
INDUSTRIES EXTRACTIVES (BELGIUM): SECURITE ET
SALUBRITE.

INSTITUT NATIONAL DE LA RECHERCHE AGRONOMIQUE
(FRANCE).
— ANNALES DE L'ABEILLE.                                    XXX
SUBS (1970) PART OF: APIDOLOGIE.
— ANNALES DE EPIPHYTIES.                                   XXX
SUBS (1969) PART OF: ANNALES DE PHYTOPATH-
OLOGIE; & ANNALES DE ZOOLOGIE - ECOLOGIE
ANIMALE.
— ANNALES DE GENETIQUE ET DE SELECTION ANIMALE.
— ANNALES D'HYDROBIOLOGIE.                                 XXX
— ANNALES DE PHYTOPATHOLOGIE.                              XXX
— ANNALES DE RECHERCHES VETERINAIRES.
— ANNALES DE ZOOLOGIE - ECOLOGIE ANIMALE.                  XXX
— APIDOLOGIE.                                              XXX
— RECHERCHES D'HYDROBIOLOGIE CONTINENTALE.

INSTITUT NATIONAL DE LA RECHERCHE AGRONOMIQUE
(FRANCE): DEPARTEMENT D'ECONOMIE ET DE SOCIOL-
OGIE RURALES.
— RECHERCHES D'ECONOMIE ET DE SOCIOLOGIE
RURALES.

INSTITUT NATIONAL DE RECHERCHES FORESTIERES
DE TUNISIE.
— ANNALES DE L'INSTITUT NATIONAL DE RECHERCHES
FORESTIERES DE TUNISIE.

INSTITUT NATIONAL DE STATISTIQUE (BELGIUM).
— STATISTIQUES AGRICOLES (BELGIUM).
— STATISTIQUES DEMOGRAPHIQUES (BELGIUM).

INSTITUT NATIONAL DE LA STATISTIQUE ET DES
ETUDES ECONOMIQUES (FRANCE).
— ANNALES, INSTITUT NATIONAL DE LA STATISTIQUE
ET DES ETUDES ECONOMIQUES (FRANCE).
— ECONOMIE ET STATISTIQUE. REVUE MENSUELLE.
— TENDANCES DE LA CONJONCTURE.

INSTITUT NATIONAL DE LA STATISTIQUE ET DES
ETUDES ECONOMIQUES (FRANCE): DIRECTION REGION-
ALE DE DIJON.
— DIMENSIONS ECONOMIQUES DE LA BOURGOGNE.

INSTITUTE OF NAVIGATION.
— JOURNAL OF THE INSTITUTE OF NAVIGATION.          XXX
SUBS (1972): JOURNAL OF NAVIGATION.
— JOURNAL OF NAVIGATION.                           XXX

INSTITUTION OF NUCLEAR ENGINEERS.
— JOURNAL, INSTITUTION OF NUCLEAR ENGINEERS.       XXX
— NUCLEAR ENERGY.                                  XXX
SUBS (1971): JOURNAL, INSTITUTION OF
NUCLEAR ENGINEERS.

INSTITUTE OF OCEANOGRAPHY & FISHERIES (CAIRO).
— BULLETIN, INSTITUTE OF OCEANOGRAPHY & FISH-
ERIES (CAIRO).

INSTITUTO DE LA OPINION PUBLICA (SPAIN).
— REVISTA ESPANOLA DE LA OPINION PUBLICA.

INSTITUTO DE ORDENACION DE VERTIENTES A
INGENIERIA FORESTAL.
— INGENIERIA FORESTAL (ARGENTINA).

INSTITUT ORIENTALE FRANCAIS DU CAIRE.
— ANNUAIRE DE L'EGYPTOLOGIE.

INSTITUUT VOOR ORIENTALISTIEK (LOUVAIN).
— ORIENTALIA LOVANIENSIA PERIODICA.

INSTITUTE FOR PALESTINE STUDIES.
— INTERNATIONAL DOCUMENTS ON PALESTINE.
— JOURNAL OF PALESTINE STUDIES.

INSTITUTO PANAMERICANO DE GEOGRAFIA E HISTORIA:
COMISION DE GEOFISICA.
— GEOFISICA PANAMERICANA.                          XXX

INSTITUTE OF PAPER CHEMISTRY.
— GENETICS & PHYSIOLOGY NOTES.

INSTITUTE OF PARKS & RECREATION ADMINISTRATION.
— PARKS & RECREATION. OFFICIAL JOURNAL OF ...

INSTITUT PASTEUR (PARIS).
— ANNALES D'IMMUNOLOGIE.                           XXX
— ANNALES DE L'INSTITUT PASTEUR.                   XXX
SUBS (1973): PART OF: ANNALES D'IMMUNOLOGIE;
& ANNALES DE MICROBIOLOGIE.
— ANNALES DE MICROBIOLOGIE: A.                     XXX
— ANNALES DE MICROBIOLOGIE: B.                     XXX

INSTITUTO DE LA PATAGONIA.
— ANALES, INSTITUTO DE LA PATAGONIA.

INSTITUT PEDAGOGIQUE NATIONAL (FRANCE).
— REVUE FRANCAISE DE PEDAGOGIE.

INSTITUTO PEDAGOGICO NACIONAL (VENEZUELA).
— MONOGRAFIAS CIENTIFICAS 'AUGUSTO PI SUNER.'

INSTITUTE OF PERSONNEL MANAGEMENT.
— PERSONNEL MANAGEMENT (1969).                     XXX
— PERSONNEL REVIEW.

INSTITUTO DE PESQUISAS E EXPERIMENTACAO AGROP-
ECUARIAS DO NORTE (BRAZIL).
— INSTITUTO DE PESQUISAS E EXPERIMENTACAO AGROP-
ECUARIAS DO NORTE (BRAZIL): SERIE CULTURAS DA
AMAZONIA.                                          XXX
— INSTITUTO DE PESQUISAS E EXPERIMENTACAO AGROP-
ECUARIAS DO NORTE (BRAZIL): SERIE ESTUDOS
SOBRE BUBALINOS.                                   XXX
— INSTITUTO DE PESQUISAS E EXPERIMENTACAO AGROP-
ECUARIAS DO NORTE (BRAZIL): SERIE FITOTECNIA.      XXX
— INSTITUTO DE PESQUISAS E EXPERIMENTACAO AGROP-
ECUARIAS DO NORTE (BRAZIL): SERIE QUIMICA DE
SOLOS.                                             XXX
— INSTITUTO DE PESQUISAS E EXPERIMENTACAO AGROP-
ECUARIAS DO NORTE (BRAZIL): SERIE TECNOLOGIA.      XXX

INSTITUTE OF PETROLEUM.
— ABSTRACTS, INSTITUTE OF PETROLEUM.               XXX
— INTERNATIONAL PETROLEUM ABSTRACTS.               XXX
— PETROLEUM REVIEW.                                XXX
— REVIEW, INSTITUTE OF PETROLEUM.                  XXX
SUBS (1968): PETROLEUM REVIEW.

INSTITUTE OF PHYSICS (& THE PHYSICAL SOCIETY).
— BULLETIN OF THE INSTITUTE OF PHYSICS (& THE
PHYSICAL SOCIETY).                                 XXX
SUBS (1968): PHYSICS BULLETIN.
— JOURNAL OF PHYSICS; A: GENERAL. PROCEEDINGS
OF THE PHYSICAL SOCIETY.                           XXX
— JOURNAL OF PHYSICS; B: ATOMIC & MOLECULAR
PHYSICS. PROCEEDINGS OF THE PHYSICAL SOCIETY.
— JOURNAL OF PHYSICS: C: SOLID STATE PHYSICS.
PROCEEDINGS OF THE PHYSICAL SOCIETY.               XXX
— JOURNAL OF PHYSICS D: APPLIED PHYSICS.           XXX
— JOURNAL OF PHYSICS E: SCIENTIFIC INSTRUMENTS.    XXX
— JOURNAL OF PHYSICS: F: METAL PHYSICS.            XXX
— METAL PHYSICS (LONDON).                          XXX
— PHYSICS BULLETIN.                                XXX
— PHYSICS IN TECHNOLOGY.                           XXX

INSTITUTE OF PLUMBING.
— PLUMBING.                                        XXX

INSTITUTO PONTIFICIO DE TEOLOGIA.
— ESCRITOS DEL VEDAT.

INSTITUCION 'PRINCIPE DE VIANA'.
— CUADERNOS DE ETNOLOGIA Y ETNOGRAFIA DE
NAVARRA.

INSTITUTE OF PRINTING.                             XXX
— PRINTING TECHNOLOGY.                             XXX
SUBS (1973): PROFESSIONAL PRINTER.
— PROFESSIONAL PRINTER.                            XXX

INSTITUTO PROVINCIAL DE INVESTIGACIONES Y EST-
UDIOS TOLEDANOS.
— ANALES TOLEDANOS.

**INSTYTUT PRZEMYSLU TLUSZCZOWEGO.**
— TLUSZCZE I SRODKI PIORACE.　　　　　　XXX
　　SUBS: TLUSZCZE, SRODKI PIORACE, KOSMETYKI.

**INSTITUTE OF PSYCHOLOGY (DUBLIN).**
— PAPER, INSTITUTE OF PSYCHOLOGY (DUBLIN).

**INSTITUTION OF PUBLIC HEALTH ENGINEERS.**　　XXX
— JOURNAL, INSTITUTION OF PUBLIC HEALTH
　ENGINEERS.　　　　　　　　　　　　　XXX
　SUBS (1973): PUBLIC HEALTH ENGINEER.
— PUBLIC HEALTH ENGINEER.　　　　　　　XXX

**INSTITUTE OF RACE RELATIONS.**
— RACE RELATIONS ABSTRACTS.
— RACE RELATIONS BULLETIN.
— RACE RELATIONS BULLETIN: INDUSTRIAL SUPPLE-
　MENT.　　　　　　　　　　　　　　　XXX
— RACE TODAY.

**INSTITUTE OF RADIATION BREEDING (JAPAN).**　000
　SEE: HOSHASEN IKUSHUJO.

**INSTITUT FUR RATIONALISIERUNG UND ORGANISATION
DER ELEKTROINDUSTRIE.**
— RATIO. ZEITSCHRIFT FUR RATIONALISIERUNG MIT
　ELEKTROSTANDARD.

**INSTITUT DE RECHERCHES AGRONOMIQUES TROPICALES
ET DES CULTURES VIVRIERES (PARIS).**
— CAHIERS D'AGRICULTURE PRATIQUE DES PAYS
　CHAUDS.

**INSTITUT POUR LA RECHERCHE SCIENTIFIQUE EN
AFRIQUE CENTRALE (CONGO).**
— CHRONIQUE DE L'IRSAC. INFORMATIONS DE ...　XXX
— FOLIA SCIENTIFICA AFRICAE CENTRALIS.　　　XXX
　SUBS (1966): CHRONIQUES DE L'IRSAC.

**INSTITUTE OF REGISTERED ARCHITECTS.**
— REGISTERED ARCHITECT. JOURNAL OF THE ...

**INSTITUTE OF ROAD TRANSPORT ENGINEERS.**
— TRANSPORT ENGINEER.　　　　　　　　XXX

**INSTITUTUM ROMANUM FINLANDIAE.**
— ACTA INSTITUTI ROMANI FINLANDIAE.

**INSTITUTION OF THE RUBBER INDUSTRY.**
— JOURNAL, INSTITUTION OF THE RUBBER INDUSTRY.　XXX
— PROCEEDINGS, INSTITUTION OF THE RUBBER
　INDUSTRY.　　　　　　　　　　　　　XXX
　SUBS (1967) PART OF: JOURNAL, INSTITUTION
　OF THE RUBBER INDUSTRY.
— TRANSACTIONS, INSTITUTION OF THE RUBBER
　INDUSTRY.　　　　　　　　　　　　　XXX
　SUBS (1967) PART OF: JOURNAL, INSTITUTION
　OF THE RUBBER INDUSTRY.

**INSTITUTION OF SALES ENGINEERS.**
— SALES ENGINEER.　　　　　　　　　　XXX

**INSTITUT DES SCIENCES HUMAINES DU MALI.**
— ETUDES MALIENNES.

**INSTITUTE FOR SCIENTIFIC COOPERATION
(TUBINGEN).**
— PHILOSOPHY & HISTORY.

**INSTITUTE FOR SCIENTIFIC INFORMATION.**
— CURRENT ABSTRACTS OF CHEMISTRY & INDEX CHEM-
　ICUS.　　　　　　　　　　　　　　　XXX
— CURRENT CONTENTS: AGRICULTURAL, FOOD & VETER-
　INARY SCIENCES.
— CURRENT CONTENTS: BEHAVIORAL, SOCIAL & MANAG-
　EMENT SCIENCES.
— CURRENT CONTENTS: CHEMICAL SCIENCES.　　XXX
— CURRENT CONTENTS: CLINICAL PRACTICE.
— CURRENT CONTENTS: EDUCATION.
— CURRENT CONTENTS: ENGINEERING & TECHNOLOGY.
— CURRENT CONTENTS: PHYSICAL & CHEMICAL
　SCIENCES.　　　　　　　　　　　　　XXX
— CURRENT CONTENTS: PHYSICAL SCIENCES.　　XXX
　SUBS (1971): PART OF CURRENT CONTENTS:
　PHYSICAL & CHEMICAL SCIENCES.
— INDEX CHEMICUS.　　　　　　　　　　XXX

**INSTITUTE OF SOCIAL STUDIES (HAGUE).**
— DEVELOPMENT & CHANGE.

**INSTITUT DE SOCIOLOGIE DE RABAT.**
— ANNALES MAROCAINES DE SOCIOLOGIE. = MOROCCAN
　ANNALS OF SOCIOLOGY.

**INSTITUT DE SOCIOLOGIE SOLVAY: CENTRE D'ECON-
OMIE POLITIQUE.**
— STATISTIQUES INTERNATIONALES RETROSPECTIVES =
　INTERNATIONAL HISTORICAL STATISTICS.

**INSTITUTE OF SOUTH AFRICAN ARCHITECTS.**
— ISAA. SOUTH AFRICAN ARCHITECTURAL RECORD.　XXX
— PLAN (JOHANNESBURG).

**INSTITUTE OF SOUTHEAST ASIAN STUDIES
(SINGAPORE).**
— LIBRARY BULLETIN, INSTITUTE OF SOUTHEAST
　ASIAN STUDIES (SINGAPORE).
— NEWSLETTER, INSTITUTE OF SOUTHEAST ASIAN
　STUDIES (SINGAPORE).

**INSTITUT ZA SPOLJNU TRGOVINU.**
— JUGOSLOVENSKO VINOGRADARSTVO I VINARSTVO.
— PROBLEMI SPOLJNE TRGOVINE I KONJUNKTURE.

**INSTITUTE FOR STRATEGIC STUDIES (LONDON).**
— STRATEGIC SURVEY.
— STUDIES IN INTERNATIONAL SECURITY.

**INSTITUTE FOR THE STUDY OF DRUG ADDICTION.**
— INTERNATIONAL JOURNAL OF THE ADDICTIONS.

**INSTITUTE FOR THE STUDY OF DRUG DEPENDENCE.**
— DRUGS & SOCIETY.

**INSTITUTO SUPERIOR DE ADMINISTRACION PUBLICA
(ARGENTINA).**
— REVISTA DE ADMINISTRACION PUBLICA (ARGENTINA).

**INSTITUT SUPERIEUR DE GESTION DES ENTERPRISES
(TUNIS).**
— REVUE AFRICAINE DE MANAGEMENT.

**INSTITUT FUR TECHNOLOGIE DER GESUNDHEITSBAUTEN.**
— MITTEILUNGEN, INSTITUT FUR TECHNOLOGIE DER
　GESUNDHEITSBAUTEN.

**INSTYTUT TECHNOLOGII ELEKTRONOWEJ (WARSAW).**
— ELECTRON TECHNOLOGY.

**INSTITUTE FOR TELECOMMUNICATION SCIENCES.**
— OT/ITS RESEARCH REPORT.　　　　　　　XXX
— TELECOMMUNICATIONS RESEARCH & ENGINEERING
　REPORT.　　　　　　　　　　　　　XXX

**INSTITUT ZA TEORIJU KNJIZEVNOSTI I UMETNOSTI
(BELGRADE).**
— POSEBNA IZDANJA, INSTITUT ZA TEORIJU KNJIZEV-
　NOSTI I UMETNOSTI.

**INSTITUTE OF TIBETAN STUDIES.**
— SHAMBHALA. OCCASIONAL PAPERS OF THE INSTIT-
　UTE OF TIBETAN STUDIES.

**INSTITUTE OF TRADING STANDARDS ADMINISTRATION.**
— MONTHLY REVIEW, INSTITUTE OF TRADING STAND-
　ARDS ADMINISTRATION.　　　　　　　　XXX

**INSTITUT UNIVERSITAIRE DE HAUTES ETUDES INTER-
NATIONALES: ASSOCIATION DES ANCIENS.**
— ANNALES D'ETUDES INTERNATIONALES. ANNALS OF
　INTERNATIONAL STUDIES.

**INSTITUTO VENEZOLANO DE INVESTIGACIONES
CIENTIFICAS.**
— I.V.I.C. BOLETIN INFORMATIVO, INSTITUTO
　VENEZOLANO DE INVESTIGACIONES CIENTIFICAS.

**INSTITUTE OF WEIGHTS & MEASURES ADMINISTRATION.**
— MONTHLY REVIEW, INSTITUTE OF WEIGHTS & MEAS-
　URES ADMINISTRATION.　　　　　　　　XXX
　SUBS (1972): MONTHLY REVIEW, INSTITUTE OF
　TRADING STANDARDS ADMINISTRATION.

**INSTITUTE OF WORK STUDY PRACTITIONERS.**
— MONOGRAPH, INSTITUTE OF WORK STUDY PRACTIT-
　IONERS.

**INSTITUTE FOR WORKERS' CONTROL.**
— BULLETIN, INSTITUTE FOR WORKERS' CONTROL.
— INTERNATIONAL STUDIES IN INDUSTRIAL DEMOCRACY.

**INSTYTUT ZACHODNI (POZNAN).**
— DZIEJE POLSKIEJ GRANICY ZACHODNIEJ.
— STUDIA NAD ZAGADNIENIAMI GOSPODARCZYMI I
　SPOLECZNYMI ZIEM ZACHODNICH.

**INSTYTUT ZACHODNIO-POMORSKI: SEKCJA HISTORYCZNA**
— Z PRAC SEKCJI HISTORYCZNEJ, INSTYTUT ZACHOD-
　NIO-POMORSKI.

INSTITUT FUR ZEITGESCHICHTE (MUNICH).
— DEUTSCHE GESCHICHTE SEIT DEM ERSTEN WELTKRIEG.

INSTITUT ZA ZNANOST O KNJIZEVNOSTI: FILOZOFSKOG
FAKULTETA.
— CROATICA. PRINOSI PROUCAVANJU HRVATSKE
KNJIZEVNOSTI.

INSTRUMENT & CONTROL SOCIETY OF SOUTHERN AFRICA
— INSTRUMENT TECHNOLOGY IN SOUTHERN AFRICA.

INSTRUMENT SOCIETY OF AMERICA.
— INSTRUMENT MAINTENANCE MANAGEMENT.
— INSTRUMENTATION IN THE FOOD & BEVERAGE
INDUSTRY.
— INSTRUMENTATION TECHNOLOGY.
— ISA INSTRUMENTATION INDEX.
— ISA JOURNAL.                                                          XXX
SUBS (1967): INSTRUMENTATION TECHNOLOGY.

INTER-ACTION TRUST.
— PLAY.

INTERAMERICAN UNIVERSITY OF PUERTO RICO.
— REVISTA INTERAMERICANA. INTERAMERICANA
REVIEW.

INTERGOVERNMENTAL OCEANOGRAPHIC COMMISSION.
— [INFORMATION PAPER] INTERGOVERNMENTAL OCEAN-
OGRAPHIC COMMISSION.

INTERMEDIATE TECHNOLOGY DEVELOPMENT GROUP LTD.
— I.T.D.G. BULLETIN.

INTERMOUNTAIN FOREST & RANGE EXPERIMENT
STATION (US).
— GENERAL TECHNICAL REPORT, INTERMOUNTAIN
FOREST & RANGE EXPERIMENT STATION (US).

INTERNATIONAL AFRICAN INSTITUTE.
— AFRICAN ABSTRACTS.                                                    XXX

INTERNATIONAL AFRICAN INSTITUTE: RESEARCH
INFORMATION LIAISON UNIT.
— CURRENT AFRICANIST RESEARCH. INTERNATIONAL
BULLETIN. = RECHERCHE AFRICANISTE EN COURS.
BULLETIN INTERNATIONALE.
— INTERNATIONAL AFRICAN BIBLIOGRAPHY.                                   XXX

INTERNATIONAL AGENCY FOR RESEARCH ON CANCER.
— SCIENTIFIC PUBLICATIONS, INTERNATIONAL AGENCY
FOR RESEARCH ON CANCER.

INTERNATIONAL AIR TRANSPORT ASSOCIATION.
— IATA NEWS REVIEW.

INTERNATIONAL ALBAN BERG SOCIETY.
— NEWSLETTER, INTERNATIONAL ALBAN BERG SOCIETY.

INTERNATIONAL ANTONIO VIVALDI SOCIETY.
— INFORMATIONS, INTERNATIONAL ANTONIO VIVALDI
SOCIETY.

INTERNATIONAL ARTHUR SCHNITZLER RESEARCH
ASSOCIATION.
— MODERN AUSTRIAN LITERATURE.                                          XXX

INTERNATIONAL ASSOCIATION FOR CHILD PSYCHIATRY
& ALLIED PROFESSIONS.
— LIVRE ANNUEL INTERNATIONAL DE PSYCHIATRIE
INFANTILE ET DES PROFESSIONS ASSOCIEES.

INTERNATIONAL ASSOCIATION FOR DENTAL RESEARCH:
SCANDINAVIAN DIVISION.                                                  000
SEE: NORDISKA ODONTOLOGISKA FORENINGEN.

INTERNATIONAL ASSOCIATION FOR EARTHQUAKE
ENGINEERING.
— EARTHQUAKE ENGINEERING & STRUCTURAL DYNAMICS.
— INTERNATIONAL JOURNAL OF EARTHQUAKE ENGINEER-
ING & STRUCTURAL DYNAMICS.

INTERNATIONAL ASSOCIATION OF ENGINEERING
GEOLOGY.
— BULLETIN, INTERNATIONAL ASSOCIATION OF ENGIN-
EERING GEOLOGY.

INTERNATIONAL ASSOCIATION OF HYDROLOGICAL
SCIENCES.
— HYDROLOGICAL SCIENCES BULLETIN.                                       XXX

INTERNATIONAL ASSOCIATION OF LAW LIBRARIES.
— BULLETIN, INTERNATIONAL ASSOCIATION OF LAW
LIBRARIES.
— INTERNATIONAL JOURNAL OF LAW LIBRARIES.                              XXX

INTERNATIONAL ASSOCIATION FOR MATHEMATICAL
GEOLOGY.
— JOURNAL, INTERNATIONAL ASSOCIATION FOR MATHE-
MATICAL GEOLOGY.

INTERNATIONAL ASSOCIATION OF MICROBIOLOGICAL
SOCIETIES: VIROLOGY SECTION.
— INTERVIROLOGY.

INTERNATIONAL ASSOCIATION OF ORAL SURGEONS.
— INTERNATIONAL JOURNAL OF ORAL SURGERY.

INTERNATIONAL ASSOCIATION FOR RESEARCH IN
INCOME & WEALTH.
— REVIEW OF INCOME & WEALTH.

INTERNATIONAL ASSOCIATION OF SCIENTIFIC
HYDROLOGY.                                                              XXX
— BULLETIN OF THE INTERNATIONAL ASSOCIATION OF
SCIENTIFIC HYDROLOGY.                                                   XXX
SUBS (1972): HYDROLOGICAL SCIENCES BULLETIN.

INTERNATIONAL ASSOCIATION FOR SEMIOTIC STUDIES.
— APPROACHES TO SEMIOTICS.

INTERNATIONAL ASSOCIATION FOR SHELL & SPATIAL
STRUCTURES.
— BULLETIN, INTERNATIONAL ASSOCIATION FOR SHELL
& SPATIAL STRUCTURES.

INTERNATIONAL ASSOCIATION OF SOUND ARCHIVES.
— PHONOGRAPHIC BULLETIN.

INTERNATIONAL ASSOCIATION OF SOUTH-EAST
EUROPEAN STUDIES.
— BULLETIN, ASSOCIATION INTERNATIONALE D'ETUDES
DU SUD-EST EUROPEEN.
— ETUDES ET DOCUMENTS CONCERNANT LE SUD-EST
EUROPEEN.

INTERNATIONAL ASSOCIATION FOR THE STUDY OF
ANGLO-IRISH LITERATURE.
— NEWSLETTER, INTERNATIONAL ASSOCIATION FOR THE
STUDY OF ANGLO-IRISH LITERATURE.

INTERNATIONAL ASSOCIATION OF TAMIL RESEARCH.
— JOURNAL OF TAMIL STUDIES.

INTERNATIONAL ASSOCIATION OF TECHNOLOGICAL
UNIVERSITY LIBRARIES.
— IATUL NEWSLETTER.                                                     XXX
— IATUL PROCEEDINGS.

INTERNATIONAL ASSOCIATION OF TESTING &
RESEARCH LABORATORIES FOR MATERIALS &
STRUCTURES.
— MATERIALS & STRUCTURES: TESTING & RESEARCH. =
MATERIAUX ET CONSTRUCTIONS: ESSAIS ET RE-
CHERCHES.

INTERNATIONAL ASSOCIATION ON WATER POLLUTION
RESEARCH.
— PROGRESS IN WATER TECHNOLOGY.

INTERNATIONAL ASSOCIATION ON WATER POLLUTION
RESEARCH: DANISH NATIONAL COMMITTEE.
— VAND. TIDSSKRIFT FOR VANDKVALITET.

INTERNATIONAL ASSOCIATION OF WHALING COMPANIES.
— NORSK HVALFANGST-TIDENDE. = NORWEGIAN
WHALING GAZETTE.                                                        XXX

INTERNATIONAL ASTRONAUTICAL FEDERATION: INTER-
NATIONAL INSTITUTE OF SPACE LAW.                                        000
SEE: INTERNATIONAL INSTITUTE OF SPACE LAW.

INTERNATIONAL ATOMIC ENERGY AGENCY.
— ATOMIC ENERGY CONFERENCES.                                           XXX
SUBS (1969): MEETINGS ON ATOMIC ENERGY.
— ATOMINDEX.                                                            XXX
SUBS (1970): INIS ATOMINDEX.
— HEALTH PHYSICS RESEARCH ABSTRACTS.
— INIS ATOMINDEX.                                                       XXX
— INTERNATIONAL NUCLEAR INFORMATION SYSTEM REF-
ERENCE SERIES.
— MEETINGS ON ATOMIC ENERGY.                                           XXX

INTERNATIONAL BANK FOR RECONSTRUCTION &
DEVELOPMENT.
— WORLD BANK STAFF OCCASIONAL PAPERS.

INTERNATIONAL BAR ASSOCIATION.
— INTERNATIONAL BAR JOURNAL.                                           XXX

INTERNATIONAL BIO-ACOUSTICS COUNCIL.
— BIOPHON. BIO-ACOUSTICS BULLETIN.

INTERNATIONAL BIOLOGICAL PROGRAMME.
— BIOSPHERE. BULLETIN OF THE ...                    XXX
— IBP INTER-AMERICAN NEWS.

INTERNATIONAL BOOK INFORMATION SERVICE.
— NB: EDITION EUROPA.

INTERNATIONAL BRECHT SOCIETY.
— BRECHT HEUTE. BRECHT TODAY.

INTERNATIONALEN BRECHT-GESELLSCHAFT.               000
SEE: INTERNATIONAL BRECHT SOCIETY.

INTERNATIONAL BUREAU OF EDUCATION.
— BULLETIN, INTERNATIONAL BUREAU OF EDUCATION.      XXX
  SUBS (1971): EDUCATIONAL DOCUMENTATION &
  INFORMATION.
— EDUCATIONAL DOCUMENTATION & INFORMATION.          XXX

INTERNATIONAL BUREAU FOR THE PROTECTION OF
INDUSTRIAL PROPERTY.
— INDUSTRIAL PROPERTY. MONTHLY REVIEW OF THE
  INTERNATIONAL ...

INTERNATIONAL CENTER FOR ARID & SEMI-ARID LAND
STUDIES.
— ICASALS NEWSLETTER.
— PUBLICATION, INTERNATIONAL CENTER FOR ARID &
  SEMI-ARID LAND STUDIES.
— SPECIAL REPORT, INTERNATIONAL CENTER FOR
  ARID & SEMI-ARID LAND STUDIES.

INTERNATIONAL CIVIL AIRPORT ASSOCIATION.
— AIRPORTS INTERNATIONAL.

INTERNATIONAL COLLEGE OF PEDIATRICS.
— PAEDIATRICIAN.

INTERNATIONAL COLLEGE OF SURGEONS.
— INTERNATIONAL SURGERY.                            XXX
— JOURNAL, INTERNATIONAL COLLEGE OF SURGEONS.       XXX
  SUBS (1966): INTERNATIONAL SURGERY.

INTERNATIONAL COMMISSION OF JURISTS.
— REVIEW, INTERNATIONAL COMMISSION OF JURISTS.

INTERNATIONAL COMMISSION OF JURISTS: AUSTRALIAN
SECTION.
— JUSTICE.

INTERNATIONAL COMMITTEE ON BACTERIOLOGICAL
NOMENCLATURE; JUDICIAL COMMISSION.
— INTERNATIONAL JOURNAL OF SYSTEMATIC BACTERIO-
  LOGY.

INTERNATIONAL COMPRESSED AIR CORPORATION, LTD.
— COMPAIR JOURNAL.

INTERNATIONAL CONFEDERATION FOR DISARMAMENT &
PEACE.
— CZECHOSLOVAKIA INTERNATIONAL.
— VIETNAM INTERNATIONAL.

INTERNATIONAL CONFEDERATION OF FREE TRADE
UNIONS.
— FEATURES.

INTERNATIONAL CONFEDERATION OF FREE TRADE
UNIONS: ASIAN TRADE UNION COLLEGE.
— ASIAN TRADE UNIONIST.

INTERNATIONAL CONFEDERATION FOR THERMAL
ANALYSIS.
— THERMAL ANALYSIS ABSTRACTS.

INTERNATIONAL CONFERENCE ON LARGE ELECTRONIC
SYSTEMS.
— ELECTRA.                                          XXX

INTERNATIONAL COPPER COUNCIL.
— COPPER.

INTERNATIONAL COUNCIL FOR THE ADVANCEMENT OF
AUDIO-VISUAL MEDIA IN EDUCATION.
— AUDIO-VISUAL MEDIA. MOYENS AUDIO-VISUELS.         XXX

INTERNATIONAL COUNCIL ON ARCHIVES.
— ADPA. AUTOMATIC DATA PROCESSING FOR ARCHIVAL
  MANAGEMENT.
— NEWSLETTER, INTERNATIONAL COUNCIL ON ARCHIVES.

INTERNATIONAL COUNCIL ON ARCHIVES: SOUTHEAST
ASIAN REGIONAL BRANCH.
— SOUTHEAST ASIAN ARCHIVES. JOURNAL OF THE ...

INTERNATIONAL COUNCIL FOR BUILDING RESEARCH
STUDIES & DOCUMENTATION.
— BUILD INTERNATIONAL.
— BUILDING RESEARCH & PRACTICE.
— CIB BULLETIN.                                     XXX
  SUBS (1968): BUILD INTERNATIONAL.

INTERNATIONAL COUNCIL FOR EDUCATIONAL MEDIA.
— EDUCATIONAL MEDIA INTERNATIONAL.                  XXX

INTERNATIONAL COUNCIL OF MUSEUMS.
— ANNALES: MUSEES, EDUCATION, ACTION CULTUR-
  ELLE.
— ANNUAL, INTERNATIONAL COUNCIL OF MUSEUMS.         XXX
— MUSEUMS ANNUAL.                                   XXX

INTERNATIONAL COUNCIL OF NURSES.
— ICN CALLING. NEWSLETTER OF THE ...

INTERNATIONAL COUNCIL OF SCIENTIFIC UNIONS.
— GARP SPECIAL REPORT.

INTERNATIONAL COUNCIL OF SCIENTIFIC UNIONS:
COMMITTEE ON DATA FOR SCIENCE & TECHNOLOGY.        000
SEE: COMMITTEE ON DATA ...

INTERNATIONAL COUNCIL OF SCIENTIFIC UNIONS:
INTER-UNION COMMISSION ON SOLAR TERRESTRIAL
PHYSICS (ICSU).                         000
SEE: INTER-UNION COMMISSION ON SOLAR
TERRESTRIAL PHYSICS (ICSU).

INTERNATIONAL COUNCIL OF SCIENTIFIC UNIONS:
SPECIAL COMMITTEE FOR THE INTERNATIONAL YEARS
OF THE QUIET SUN.
— ANNALS OF THE IQSY.

INTERNATIONAL COURT OF JUSTICE.
— BULLETIN OF THE INTERNATIONAL COURT OF
  JUSTICE.

INTERNATIONAL CROCODILIAN SOCIETY.
— NEWSLETTER, INTERNATIONAL CROCODILIAN SOCIETY.

INTERNATIONAL DEVELOPMENT RESEARCH CENTRE.
— IDRC REPORTS.

INTERNATIONAL DOCUMENTATION CENTRE.
— IDC PROGRESS REPORT.

INTERNATIONAL FABRICARE INSTITUTE.                  XXX
— IFI BULLETIN SERVICE: FABRICS-FASHIONS
  BULLETIN.                                         XXX
— IFI BULLETIN SERVICE: PRACTICAL OPERATING
  TIPS BULLETIN.                                    XXX
— IFI BULLETIN SERVICE: TECHNICAL BULLETIN.         XXX

INTERNATIONAL FEDERATION FOR DOCUMENTATION.
— FID YEARBOOK.
— LINGUISTICS IN DOCUMENTATION: CURRENT AB-
  STRACTS.
— R & D PROJECTS IN DOCUMENTATION & LIBRARIAN-
  SHIP.

INTERNATIONAL FEDERATION FOR INFORMATION PRO-
CESSING: ADMINISTRATIVE DATA PROCESSING GROUP.
— IAG JOURNAL.                                      XXX

INTERNATIONAL FEDERATION OF LIBRARY ASSOCIAT-
IONS: COMMITTEE ON CATALOGUING.
— INTERNATIONAL CATALOGUING. QUARTERLY
  BULLETIN OF THE ...

INTERNATIONAL FOOD INFORMATION SERVICES.
— FOOD SCIENCE & TECHNOLOGY ABSTRACTS.

INTERNATIONAL FOUNDATION FOR TELEMETERING.
— TELEMETRY JOURNAL.

INTERNATIONALEN GESELLSCHAFT FUR JAZZFORSCHUNG.
— BEITRAGE ZUR JAZZFORSCHUNG. STUDIES IN JAZZ
  RESEARCH.

INTERNATIONALEN GESELLSCHAFT FUR PROSPEKTIVE
MEDIZIN.
— DATENVERARBEITUNG IN DER MEDIZIN. MITTEILUNGS-
  BLATT DER INTERNATIONALEN GESELLSCHAFT FUR
  PROSPEKTIVE MEDIZIN.

INTERNATIONAL HEINRICH SCHUTZ-GESELLSCHAFT.
— SAGITTARIUS. BEITRAGE ZUR ERFORSCHUNG UND
  PRAXIS ALTER UND NEUER KIRCHENMUSIK.

INTERNATIONAL HYDROLOGICAL DECADE.
— REPORTS ON WMO/IHD PROJECTS.

INTERNATIONAL HYDROLOGICAL DECADE: CANADIAN
NATIONAL COMMITTEE.
— BULLETIN, INTERNATIONAL FIELD YEAR FOR THE
   GREAT LAKES.

INTERNATIONAL HYDROLOGICAL DECADE: UNITED
STATES NATIONAL COMMITTEE.
— BULLETIN, INTERNATIONAL FIELD YEAR FOR THE
   GREAT LAKES.

INTERNATIONAL INSTITUTE OF ADMINISTRATIVE
SCIENCES.
— DEVELOPMENT ADMINISTRATION.

INTERNATIONAL INSTITUTE FOR AERIAL SURVEY &                  XXX
EARTH SCIENCES.
— ITC JOURNAL.                                               XXX
— PUBLICATIONS, INTERNATIONAL INSTITUTE FOR
   AERIAL SURVEY & EARTH SCIENCES: SERIES A:
   [PHOTOGRAMMETRY].                                         XXX
— PUBLICATIONS, INTERNATIONAL INSTITUTE FOR
   AERIAL SURVEY & EARTH SCIENCES: SERIES B:
   [PHOTO-INTERPRETATION].                                   XXX

INTERNATIONAL INSTITUTE FOR GEOTHERMAL RESEARCH
— GEOTHERMICS.

INTERNATIONAL INSTITUTE FOR LABOUR STUDIES.
— BULLETIN, INTERNATIONAL INSTITUTE FOR LABOUR
   STUDIES.

INTERNATIONAL INSTITUTE OF SEISMOLOGY &
EARTHQUAKE ENGINEERING.
— BULLETIN, INTERNATIONAL INSTITUTE OF
   SEISMOLOGY & EARTHQUAKE ENGINEERING.

INTERNATIONAL INSTITUTE OF SPACE LAW.
— WORLDWIDE BIBLIOGRAPHY OF SPACE LAW & RELATED
   MATTERS. BIBLIOGRAPHIE MONDIALE DE DROIT
   SPATIAL ET MATIERES CONNEXES.

INTERNATIONAL INSTITUTE FOR THE STUDY OF HUMAN
REPRODUCTION.
— REPORTS ON POPULATION / FAMILY PLANNING.

INTERNATIONAL INSTITUTE FOR THE UNIFICATION OF
PRIVATE LAW.
— NEWS BULLETIN, INTERNATIONAL INSTITUTE FOR
   THE UNIFICATION OF PRIVATE LAW.

INTERNATIONAL LABOUR ORGANISATION.
— ILO PUBLICATIONS.

INTERNATIONAL LABOUR ORGANIZATION: BOTSWANA
CO-OPERATIVE DEVELOPMENT CENTRE.
— TECHNICAL REPORT, BOTSWANA CO-OPERATIVE DEVEL-
   OPMENT CENTRE.

INTERNATIONAL LABOUR ORGANIZATION: TANZANIA
NATIONAL INDUSTRIAL TRAINING PROGRAMME.
— TECHNICAL REPORT, TANZANIA NATIONAL INDUST-
   RIAL TRAINING PROGRAMME.

INTERNATIONAL LEAD ZINC RESEARCH ORGANIZATION,
INC.
— LEAD RESEARCH DIGEST.                                      XXX
— RESEARCH DIGEST, INTERNATIONAL LEAD ZINC RE-
   SEARCH ORGANIZATION: PART 4: LEAD METALLURGY.             XXX
   SUBS (1971): PART OF LEAD RESEARCH DIGEST.
— RESEARCH DIGEST, INTERNATIONAL LEAD ZINC RE-
   SEARCH ORGANIZATION: PART 5: LEAD CHEMISTRY.              XXX
   SUBS (1971): PART OF LEAD RESEARCH DIGEST.

INTERNATIONALE LENAU-GESELLSCHAFT.
— LENAU-FORUM.

INTERNATIONAL MANAGEMENT ASSOCIATION OF JAPAN.
— MANAGEMENT JAPAN. IMAJ REVIEW.                             XXX
— QUARTERLY REVIEW OF MANAGEMENT.                            XXX
   SUBS (1967): MANAGEMENT JAPAN.

INTERNATIONAL MARXIST GROUP.
— INTERNATIONAL.

INTERNATIONAL METALLOGRAPHIC SOCIETY.
— METALLOGRAPHY. AN INTERNATIONAL JOURNAL.
— MICROSTRUCTURES.

INTERNATIONAL MODULAR GROUP.
— TRANSACTIONS, INTERNATIONAL MODULAR GROUP.                XXX
   SUBS (1971): PART OF OAP JOURNAL FOR THE
   BUILT ENVIRONMENT.

INTERNATIONAL MONETARY FUND.
— IMF SURVEY.
— SURVEYS OF AFRICAN ECONOMIES.

INTERNATIONAL MUSIC COUNCIL.
— MUSIC & COMMUNICATION.

INTERNATIONAL NICKEL LTD.
— INCO REPORTER.

INTERNATIONAL ORGANIZATION FOR ANCIENT LANG-
UAGES ANALYSIS BY COMPUTER.
— REVIEW, INTERNATIONAL ORGANIZATION FOR
   ANCIENT LANGUAGES ANALYSIS BY COMPUTER.

INTERNATIONAL ORGANIZATION FOR SEPTUAGINT &
COGNATE STUDIES.
— BULLETIN, INTERNATIONAL ORGANIZATION FOR
   SEPTUAGINT & COGNATE STUDIES.

INTERNATIONAL PACIFIC HALIBUT COMMISSION.
— TECHNICAL REPORT, INTERNATIONAL PACIFIC HALI-
   BUT COMMISSION.

INTERNATIONAL PEACE RESEARCH INSTITUTE.
— BULLETIN OF PEACE PROPOSALS.
— PEACE RESEARCH MONOGRAPHS.

INTERNATIONAL PEAT SOCIETY.
— BULLETIN, INTERNATIONAL PEAT SOCIETY.

INTERNATIONAL PERSONNEL MANAGEMENT ASSOCIAT-
ION.                                                         XXX
— PERSONNEL ADMINISTRATION & PUBLIC PERSONNEL
   REVIEW.                                                   XXX

INTERNATIONAL PHONETIC ASSOCIATION.
— JOURNAL OF THE INTERNATIONAL PHONETIC ASSOC-
   IATION.
— MAITRE PHONETIQUE.                                         XXX
   SUBS (1971): JOURNAL OF THE INTERNATIONAL
   PHONETIC ASSOCIATION.

INTERNATIONAL PLANNED PARENTHOOD FEDERATION.
— RESEARCH IN REPRODUCTION.
— WORKING PAPER, INTERNATIONAL PLANNED PARENT-
   HOOD FEDERATION.

INTERNATIONAL PROJECT IN THE FIELD OF FOOD
IRRADIATION.
— FOOD IRRADIATION INFORMATION. INFORMATIONS
   SUR L'IRRADIATION DES DENREES.                            XXX

INTERNATIONAL RAILWAY CONGRESS ASSOCIATION.
— RAIL INTERNATIONAL. MONTHLY REVIEW.                        XXX

INTERNATIONAL REMOTE SENSING INSTITUTE.
— JOURNAL OF REMOTE SENSING.

INTERNATIONAL REPERTORY OF MUSIC LITERATURE.
— RILM ABSTRACTS OF MUSIC LITERATURE.

INTERNATIONAL RESEARCH & TECHNOLOGY CORP-
ORATION.
— IR & T JOURNAL.                                            XXX
— IR & T NUCLEAR JOURNAL.                                    XXX

INTERNATIONAL ROAD FEDERATION.
— ROAD INTERNATIONAL.                                        XXX

INTERNATIONAL SEISMOLOGICAL CENTRE.
— P-NODAL SOLUTIONS FOR EARTHQUAKES.

INTERNATIONAL SELF-SERVICE ORGANISATION.
— SELF-SERVICE. = LIBRE-SERVICE. = SELBST-
   BEDIENUNG.

INTERNATIONAL SOCIAL SECURITY ASSOCIATION.
— BULLETIN OF THE INTERNATIONAL SOCIAL SECURITY
   ASSOCIATION.                                              XXX
— INTERNATIONAL SOCIAL SECURITY REVIEW.

INTERNATIONAL SOCIETY FOR ASTROLOGICAL RESEARCH
— CORRELATION.

INTERNATIONAL SOCIETY OF BIOMETEOROLOGY.
— BIOMETEOROLOGY.

INTERNATIONAL SOCIETY OF CHEMOTHERAPY.
— NEWSLETTER, INTERNATIONAL SOCIETY OF CHEMOTH-
   ERAPY.

INTERNATIONAL SOCIETY FOR CONTEMPORARY MUSIC.
— MUSIC NOW.

INTERNATIONAL SOCIETY FOR THE EVANGELIZATION
OF THE JEWS.
— FOCUS ON PRAYER.                                           XXX
— PRAYER FOCUS.                                              XXX

INTERNATIONAL SOCIETY FOR EXISTENTIAL
PSYCHIATRY.
— BEHAVIORAL NEUROPSYCHIATRY.                                    XXX

INTERNATIONAL SOCIETY FOR FLUORIDE RESEARCH.
— FLUORIDE.

INTERNATIONAL SOCIETY FOR HORTICULTURAL SCIENCE
— SCIENTIA HORTICULTURAE.

INTERNATIONAL SOCIETY OF ICHTHYOLOGY & HYDRO-
BIOLOGY.
— BULLETIN, INTERNATIONAL SOCIETY OF ICHTHY-
OLOGY & HYDROBIOLOGY.

INTERNATIONAL SOCIETY OF LYMPHOLOGY.
— LYMPHOLOGY.

INTERNATIONAL SOCIETY OF ORGANBUILDERS.
— ISO INFORMATION.

INTERNATIONAL SOCIETY FOR PLANT PATHOLOGY.
— INTERNATIONAL NEWSLETTER ON PLANT PATHOLOGY.

INTERNATIONAL SOCIETY OF ROCK MECHANICS.
— ROCK MECHANICS. = FELSMECHANIK. = MECANIQUE
DES ROCHES.
— ROCK MECHANICS. SUPPLEMENTUM.                                  XXX
— ROCK MECHANICS & ENGINEERING GEOLOGY: SUPPL-
EMENTUM.                                                          XXX

INTERNATIONAL SOCIETY FOR SOIL MECHANICS &
FOUNDATION ENGINEERING.
— GEOTECHNICAL ABSTRACTS.

INTERNATIONAL SOLID WASTES & PUBLIC CLEANSING
ASSOCIATION.
— INFORMATION BULLETIN, INTERNATIONAL SOLID
WASTES & PUBLIC CLEANSING ASSOCIATION.

INTERNATIONAL STATISTICAL INSTITUTE.
— INTERNATIONAL STATISTICAL REVIEW.  REVUE INT-
ERNATIONALE DE STATISTIQUE.                                      XXX
— REVIEW OF THE INTERNATIONAL STATISTICAL
INSTITUTE.                                                       XXX
SUBS (1972): INTERNATIONAL STATISTICAL
REVIEW.

INTERNATIONALER STIFTUNG MOZARTEUM.
— SCHRIFTENREIHE, INTERNATIONALER STIFTUNG
MOZARTEUM.

INTERNATIONAL STUDY GROUP FOR MATHEMATICS
LEARNING.
— JOURNAL OF STRUCTURAL LEARNING.

INTERNATIONAL STUDY GROUP FOR STEROID HORMONES.
— RESEARCH ON STEROIDS.

INTERNATIONAL THEATRE INSTITUTE: GREEK CENTER.
— THESPIS.

INTERNATIONAL TIN COUNCIL.
— STATISTICAL NOTES ON TIN.

INTERNATIONAL TRANSPORT WORKERS FEDERATION.
— ITF DOCUMENTATION.

INTERNATIONAL UNION OF BIOCHEMISTRY.
— BIOCHEMICAL EDUCATION.

INTERNATIONAL UNION FOR CHILD WELFARE: LIBRARY.
— LIST OF ARTICLES INDEXED, LIBRARY, INTER-
NATIONAL UNION FOR CHILD WELFARE.

INTERNATIONAL UNION OF CRYSTALLOGRAPHY.
— ACTA CRYSTALLOGRAPHICA.                                        XXX
— ACTA CRYSTALLOGRAPHICA: SECTION A.
— ACTA CRYSTALLOGRAPHICA: SECTION B.
— MOLECULAR STRUCTURES & DIMENSIONS.

INTERNATIONAL UNION OF GEOLOGICAL SCIENCES.
— GEOLOGICAL NEWSLETTER.                                         XXX

INTERNATIONAL UNION OF PURE & APPLIED CHEMISTRY
— INTERNATIONAL UNION OF PURE & APPLIED CHEM-
ISTRY INFORMATION BULLETIN.
— BULLETIN, INTERNATIONAL UNION OF RAILWAYS.
ENGL. ED.                                                        XXX
SUBS (1970) PART OF: RAIL INTERNATIONAL.

INTERNATIONAL WILDFOWL RESEARCH BUREAU.
— BULLETIN, INTERNATIONAL WILDFOWL RESEARCH
BUREAU.                                                          XXX
— NEWSLETTER, INTERNATIONAL WILDFOWL RESEARCH
BUREAU.                                                          XXX
SUBS (1970): BULLETIN, INTERNATIONAL WILD-
FOWL RESEARCH BUREAU.

INTERNATIONAL WORK GROUP FOR INDIGENOUS AFFAIRS
— I.W.G.I.A. DOCUMENTS.

INTER-UNION COMMISSION ON SOLAR TERRESTRIAL
PHYSICS (ICSU).
— STP NOTES.

INTER-UNIVERSITY INSTITUTE FOR INTERNATIONAL
LAW.
— NETHERLANDS YEARBOOK OF INTERNATIONAL LAW.

INTER-VARSITY FELLOWSHIP.
— VOICE.  A CHRISTIAN MAGAZINE FOR STUDENTS.

INTRA-SCIENCE RESEARCH FOUNDATION.
— BIBLIOGRAPHIES OF CHEMISTS.
— INTERNATIONAL JOURNAL OF SULFUR CHEMISTRY:
PART A: ORIGINAL EXPERIMENTAL & THEORETICAL
STUDIES.
— INTERNATIONAL JOURNAL OF SULFUR CHEMISTRY:
PART B: QUARTERLY REPORTS ON SULFUR CHEMISTRY.
— INTERNATIONAL JOURNAL OF SULFUR CHEMISTRY:
PART C: MECHANISMS OF REACTIONS OF SULFUR
COMPOUNDS.                                                       XXX
— INTRA-SCIENCE CHEMISTRY REPORTS.
— MECHANISMS OF REACTIONS OF SULFUR COMPOUNDS.

IOWA GENEALOGICAL SOCIETY.
— HAWKEYE HERITAGE.

IOWA GEOLOGICAL SURVEY.
— EDUCATIONAL SERIES, IOWA GEOLOGICAL SURVEY.

IOWA STATE HISTORICAL SOCIETY.
— STUDIES IN IOWA HISTORY.

IOWA STATE UNIVERSITY: GRADUATE COLLEGE.
— IOWA STATE JOURNAL OF RESEARCH.                                XXX

IOWA STATE UNIVERSITY: RARE-EARTH INFORMATION
CENTER.
— RARE-EARTH INFORMATION CENTER NEWS.

IOWA STATE UNIVERSITY OF SCIENCE & TECHNOLOGY.
— INTERNATIONAL STUDIES IN EDUCATION: MONOGRAPH.

IOWA STATE UNIVERSITY OF SCIENCE & TECHNOLOGY:
DEPARTMENT OF ECONOMICS & SOCIOLOGY.
— INTERNATIONAL STUDIES IN ECONOMICS: MONOGRAPH.

IOWA STATE UNIVERSITY OF SCIENCE & TECHNOLOGY:
ENGINEERING RESEARCH INSTITUTE.
— IOWA STATE ENGINEERING RESEARCH.

(IRAN) GEOLOGICAL SURVEY.
— SPECIAL PUBLICATION, GEOLOGICAL SURVEY OF
IRAN.

(IRAN) MINISTRY OF SCIENCE & HIGHER EDUCAT-
ION: IRANIAN DOCUMENTATION CENTRE.
— IRANDOC SCIENCE & SOCIAL SCIENCE ABSTRACT
BULLETIN.

IRISH ACTORS' EQUITY ASSOCIATION.
— EQUITY ANNUAL.

IRISH AGRICULTURAL ORGANISATION SOCIETY LTD.
— IRISH CO-OPERATIVE REVIEW.

IRISH ASSOCIATION FOR CURRICULUM DEVELOPMENT.
— COMPASS.

IRISH BAPTIST HISTORICAL SOCIETY.
— JOURNAL, IRISH BAPTIST HISTORICAL SOCIETY.

IRISH COLLEGES OF PHYSICIANS & SURGEONS.
— JOURNAL OF THE IRISH COLLEGES OF PHYSICIANS &
SURGEONS.                                                        XXX

IRISH COMMUNIST ORGANISATION.
— COMMUNIST COMMENT.
— IRISH COMMUNIST.

IRISH COUNCIL OF THE EUROPEAN MOVEMENT.
— OCCASIONAL PAPER, IRISH COUNCIL OF THE EUROP-
EAN MOVEMENT.

IRISH COUNCIL FOR ITINERANT SETTLEMENT.
— SETTLEMENT NEWS.

IRISH CREAMERY MANAGERS' ASSOCIATION.
— DAIRYNEWS.

IRISH DECIMAL CURRENCY BOARD.
— IRISH DECIMAL MONTHLY. = MIOSACHAN DEACHUIL.

IRISH FARMING NEWS COOPERATIVE SOCIETY LTD.
— IRISH FARMING NEWS.

IRISH HEART FOUNDATION.
— CROI. NEWSLETTER OF THE IRISH HEART
FOUNDATION.

IRISH HOUSEWIVES' ASSOCIATION.
— HOUSEWIVES' VOICE.

IRISH LIVESTOCK & MEAT BOARD.
— IRISH LIVESTOCK & MEAT IN THE COMMON MARKET.

IRISH MANAGEMENT INSTITUTE: SMALL BUSINESS
DIVISION.
— GROWTH.                                                              XXX

IRISH NATIONAL PRODUCTIVITY COMMITTEE.
— PROGRESS IN DISTRIBUTION BULLETIN.

IRISH NURSES ORGANISATION.
— WORLD OF IRISH NURSING.

IRISH PACKAGING INSTITUTE.
— IRISH PACKAGING & PRINTING.

IRISH PHILATELIC CIRCLE.
— JOURNAL OF IRISH PHILATELY.

IRISH PIGS & BACON COMMISSION.
— IRISH BACON NEWS.

IRISH PUBLISHERS' ASSOCIATION.
— STADCHLO. NEWSLETTER OF THE ...

IRISH SOCIETY FOR ARCHIVES.
— IRISH ARCHIVES BULLETIN.

IRISH SPELEOLOGICAL ASSOCIATION.
— IRISH SPELEOLOGY. JOURNAL OF THE ...                                 XXX

IRISH WILDBIRD CONSERVANCY.
— NEWSLETTER, IRISH WILDBIRD CONSERVANCY.                               XXX
— REPORT, IRISH WILDBIRD CONSERVANCY.

IRON & STEEL INSTITUTE.
— PUBLICATION, IRON & STEEL INSTITUTE.                                  XXX
— [SPECIAL REPORT], IRON & STEEL INSTITUTE.                             XXX
  SUBS (1966): PUBLICATION, IRON & STEEL INST-
  ITUTE.
— STEEL IN THE USSR.                                                    XXX

IRON & STEEL INSTITUTE: HISTORICAL METALLURGY
GROUP.                                                                  XXX
— BULLETIN, HISTORICAL METALLURGY GROUP, IRON &
  STEEL INSTITUTE.                                                      XXX

IRONBRIDGE GORGE MUSEUM TRUST LIMITED.
— IRONBRIDGE QUARTERLY.

ISHIKAWA PREFECTURE COLLEGE OF AGRICULTURE.            000
SEE: ISHIKAWA-KEN NOGYO TANKI DAIGAKU.

ISHIKAWAJIMA-HARIMA HEAVY INDUSTRIES COMPANY,
LTD.
— IHI ENGINEERING REVIEW.

ISHIKAWA-KEN NOGYO TANKI DAIGAKU.
— ISHIKAWA-KEN NOGYO TANKI DAIGAKU KENKYU
  HOKOKU. BULLETIN, ISHIKAWA PREFECTURE COLLEGE
  OF AGRICULTURE.
— ISHIKAWA-KEN NOGYO TANKI DAIGAKU TOKUBETSU
  KENKYU HOKOKU. SPECIAL BULLETIN OF THE AGRI-
  CULTURAL COLLEGE OF ISHIKAWA PREFECTURE.

ISLAM & THE MODERN AGE SOCIETY.
— ISLAM & THE MODERN AGE.

ISLAND SOCIETY (SINGAPORE).                            000
SEE: HSIN-SHE (SINGAPORE).

ISOTOPTEKNISKA LABORATORIET (STOCKHOLM).
— SKRIFTER, ISOTOPTEKNISKA LABORATORIET.

ISRAEL ACADEMY OF SCIENCES & HUMANITIES.
— PROCEEDINGS, SECTION OF SCIENCES, ISRAEL
  ACADEMY OF SCIENCES & HUMANITIES.

ISRAEL EXPLORATION SOCIETY.
— QADMONIOT QUARTERLY FOR THE ANTIQUITIES OF
  ERETZ-ISRAEL & BIBLICAL LANDS.

ISRAEL MALACOLOGICAL SOCIETY.
— ARGAMON.

ISRAEL MUSEUM.
— ISRAEL MUSEUM NEWS.

ISRAEL SOCIETY OF ENTOMOLOGY.
— ISRAEL JOURNAL OF ENTOMOLOGY.

ISTITUTO DELL'ATLANTE LINGUISTICO ITALIANO.
— PAROLE E METODI.

ISTITUTO CENTRALE DI STATISTICA.
— SINTESI GRAFICA DELLA VITA ECONOMICA
  ITALIANA.

ISTITUTO DI INDAGINI PSICOLOGICHE.
— RIVISTA INTERNAZIONALE DI PSICOLOGIA E IPNOSI.
— RIVISTA DI PSICOLOGIA DELLA SCRITTURA.                                XXX
  SUBS (1972): RIVISTA INTERNAZIONALE DI PSIC-
  OLOGIA E IPNOSI.

ISTITUTO ITALIANO PER LA STORIA DEI MOVIMENTI
SOCIALI E DELLE STRUTTURE SOCIALI.
— CAHIERS INTERNATIONAUX D'HISTOIRE ECONOMIQUE
  ET SOCIALE. QUADERNI INTERNAZIONALI DI
  STORIA ECONOMICA E SOCIALE. INTERNATIONAL
  JOURNAL OF ECONOMIC & SOCIAL HISTORY.                                 XXX

ISTITUTO ITALIANO PER LA STORIA DELLA TECNICA.
— MACHINE. BOLLETINO DELL' ...

ISTITUTO ITALIANO DI STUDI GERMANICI.
— STUDI GERMANICI. NS.

ISTITUTO NAZIONALE DELL'INFORMAZIONE.
— RIVISTA DELL'INFORMAZIONE. INFORMATION
  REVIEW.

ISTITUTO DI PSICO-SINTESI SCIENTIFICA.
— TOTUS HOMO. REVISTA SCIENTIFICA
  INTERDISCIPLINARE.

ISTITUTO ROMANO PER LA STORIA D'ITALIA DAL
FASCISMO ALLA RESISTENZA.
— QUADERNI, ISTITUTO ROMANO PER LA STORIA
  D'ITALIA DAL FASCISMO ALLA RESISTENZA.

ISTITUTO SPERIMENTALE AGRONOMICO (BARI).
— ANNALI, ISTITUTO SPERIMENTALE AGRONOMICO.

ISTITUTO SPERIMENTALE PER L'ASSESTAMENTO
FORESTALE E PER L'ALPICOLTURA (TRENTO).
— ANNALI, ISTITUTO SPERIMENTALE PER L'ASSES-
  TAMENTO FORESTALE E PER L'ALPICOLTURA.

ISTITUTO SPERIMENTALE PER LE COLTURE FORAGGERE.
— QUADERNI DI SPERIMENTAZIONE.

ISTITUTO SPERIMENTALE PER LA FRUTTICOLTURA.
— PUBBLICAZIONI DELL' ISTITUTO SPERIMENTALE PER
  LA FRUTTICOLTURA.

ISTITUTO SPERIMENTALE PER LA SELVICOLTURA.
— ANNALI DELL'ISTITUTO SPERIMENTALE PER LA
  SELVICOLTURA.

ISTITUTO SPERIMENTALE PER LA VALORIZZAZIONE
TECNOLOGICA DEI PRODOTTI AGRICOLI.
— ANNALI, ISTITUTO SPERIMENTALE PER LA VALORIZ-
  ZAZIONE TECNOLOGICA DEI PRODOTTI AGRICOLI.

ISTITUTO SPERIMENTALE PER LA ZOOTECNIA (ROME).
— ANNALI DELL' ISTITUTO SPERIMENTALE PER LA ZOO-
  TECNIA (ROME).                                                        XXX

ISTITUTO PER LA STORIA ECCLESIASTICA PADOVANA.
— FONTI E RICERCHE DI STORIA ECCLESIASTICA
  PADOVANA.

ISTITUTO PER LA STORIA DEL RISORGIMENTO
ITALIANO (COMITATO DI CATANIA).
— STUDI RISORGIMENTALI.

ISTITUTO DI STORIA E SOCIOLOGIA.
— QUADERNI STORICI.

ISTITUTO STORICO DELLA RESISTENZA IN TOSCANA.
— QUADERNI, ISTITUTO STORICO DELLA RESISTENZA
  IN TOSCANA.

ISTITUTO DI STUDI DANTESCHI.
— ANNALI DELL' ISTITUTO DI STUDI DANTESCHI.

ISTITUTO PER GLI STUDI ECONOMICI ED ORGANIZ-
ZATIVI: CENTRI MECCANOGRAFICI ED ELETTRONICI.
— CENTRI MECCANOGRAFICI ED ELETTRONICI.                                XXX

ISTITUTO PER GLI STUDI DI POLITICA INTERNAZ-
IONALI.
— QUADERNI DI RELAZIONI INTERNAZIONALI.

ISTITUTO DI ZOOLOGIA (PALERMO).
— ACTA EMBRYOLOGIAE EXPERIMENTALIS.                    XXX

ITA FOUNDATION.                                        000
SEE: INITIAL TEACHING ALPHABET FOUNDATION.

ITALIAN CULTURAL INSTITUTE (MONTREAL).
— YEARBOOK OF ITALIAN STUDIES.

(ITALY) CONSIGLIO DEI MINISTRI.
— ITALY; DOCUMENTS & NOTES.

(ITALY) SERVIZIO GEOLOGICO.                            000
SEE: SERVIZIO GEOLOGICO D'ITALIA.

IZDATEL'STVO POLITICHESKOJ LITERATURY.
— SPRAVOCHNIK PROPAGANDISTA-MEZHDUNARODNIKA.

JAKUDOKU SEI-PORIO-UIRUSU-WAKUCHIN KENKYU
KYOGIKAI.
— PORIO SEIWAKUCHIN KENKYU HOKOKU.

(JAMAICA) DEPARTMENT OF STATISTICS: DEMOGRAPHIC
& SOCIAL STATISTICS UNIT.
— DEMOGRAPHIC STATISTICS (JAMAICA).

(JAMAICA) GEOLOGICAL SURVEY.
— ECONOMIC GEOLOGY REPORT (JAMAICA).

JAMAICA INFORMATION SERVICE.
— JAMAICA TODAY.

JAMAICAN GEOGRAPHICAL SOCIETY.                         000
SEE: UNIVERSITY OF THE WEST INDIES: ...

JAMAICAN SOCIETY OF ARCHITECTS.
— JAMAICA ARCHITECT. A REVIEW OF ARCHITECTURE
  IN THE TROPICS.

JAMES COOK UNIVERSITY OF NORTH QUEENSLAND:
DEPARTMENT OF GEOGRAPHY.
— MONOGRAPH SERIES, DEPARTMENT OF GEOGRAPHY,
  JAMES COOK UNIVERSITY OF NORTH QUEENSLAND.

JAMES FORD BELL LIBRARY.                               000
SEE: UNIVERSITY OF MINNESOTA: LIBRARY.

JANOS BOLYAI MATHEMATICAL SOCIETY.
— PERIODICA MATHEMATICA HUNGARICA.

(JAPAN) AGRICULTURAL ENGINEERING RESEARCH          000
STATION.
SEE: NORIN-SHO NOGYO DOBOKU SHIKENJO.

JAPANESE ANTARCTIC RESEARCH EXPEDITION.
— JARE SCIENTIFIC REPORTS; SPECIAL ISSUE.

JAPAN ASSOCIATION FOR APPLIED SOLAR ENERGY.        000
SEE: NIHON TAIYO ENERUGI RIYO KYOKAI.

JAPAN ATOMIC ENERGY RESEARCH INSTITUTE.            000
SEE: KAGAKU GIJUTSUCHO GENSHIRYOKUKYOKU.

JAPAN CENTER FOR AREA DEVELOPMENT RESEARCH.
— AREA DEVELOPMENT IN JAPAN.

JAPANESE ELECTRIC METERS INSPECTION CORP.          000
SEE: NIHON DENKI KEIKI KENTEIJO.

JAPAN ENTOMOLOGICAL ACADEMY.
— BULLETIN, JAPAN ENTOMOLOGICAL ACADEMY.

(JAPAN) GOVERNMENT INDUSTRIAL DEVELOPMENT
LABORATORY.                                        000
SEE: HOKKAIDO KOGYO KAIHATSU SHIKENJO.

(JAPAN) GOVERNMENT INDUSTRIAL RESEARCH INSTI-
TUTE.                                              000
SEE: KYUSHU KOGYO GIJUTSU SHIKENJO.

JAPAN LIBRARY GROUP.
— NEWSLETTER, JAPAN LIBRARY GROUP.

(JAPAN) MINISTRY OF AGRICULTURE & FORESTRY:
AGRICULTURE, FORESTRY & FISHERIES RESEARCH
COUNCIL.                                           000
SEE: NORIN-SHO NORIN SUISAN GIJUTSU KAIGI.

(JAPAN) MINISTRY OF INTERNATIONAL TRADE & IND-
USTRY: GOVERNMENT RESOURCES RESEARCH INST-
ITUTE.                                             000
SEE: KOGYO GIJUTSUIN SHIGEN GIJUTSU SHIKENJO
SANGYO KOGAI BOSHI GIJUTSU-BU UKIMA BUNSHITSU

JAPAN MONOPOLY CORPORATION: MORIOKA TOBACCO
EXPERIMENT STATION.
— BULLETIN OF THE MORIOKA TOBACCO EXPERIMENT
  STATION.

(JAPAN) PATENT OFFICE.
— KOKAI JITSUYO SHINAN KOHO.

(JAPAN POLAR RESEARCH ASSOCIATION).
— POLAR NEWS.

JAPAN RADIOISOTOPE ASSOCIATION.
— JAPANESE NUCLEAR MEDICINE.

JAPAN SEA RESEARCH INSTITUTE.                      000
SEE: NIHON KAI-IKI KENKYUJO.

JAPANESE SOCIETY OF APPLIED ENTOMOLOGY &
ZOOLOGY.                                           000
SEE: NIPPON OYO-DOBUTSI-KONCHU GAKKAI.

JAPAN SOCIETY OF CIVIL ENGINEERS.                  000
SEE: DOBOKU GAKKAI.

JAPANESE SOCIETY OF DEVELOPMENTAL BIOLOGISTS.
— DEVELOPMENT, GROWTH & DIFFERENTIATION.          XXX

JAPANESE SOCIETY OF GASTROENTEROLOGY.
— GASTROENTEROLOGIA JAPONICA.

(JAPAN SOCIETY OF HISTOCHEMISTRY & CYTO-
CHEMISTRY).
— ACTA HISTOCHEMICA ET CYTOCHEMICA.

JAPANESE SOCIETY OF PEDIATRIC SURGEONS.            000
SEE: NIHON SHONI GEKKA GAKKAI.

JAPAN STATISTICAL SOCIETY.                         000
SEE: NIHON TOKEI GAKKAISHI.

JAPAN SURGICAL SOCIETY.
— JAPANESE JOURNAL OF SURGERY.

JAROSLAVSKIJ GOSUDARSTVENNYJ PEDAGOGICHESKIJ
INSTITUT.
— DOKLADY NA NAUCHNYKH KONFERENTSIJAKH, JARO-
  SLAVSKIJ GOSUDARSTVENNYJ PEDAGOGICHESKIJ
  INSTITUT.

JEWISH VEGETARIAN & NATURAL HEALTH SOCIETY.
— JEWISH VEGETARIAN.

JIDOSHA GIJUTSUKAI.
— BULLETIN OF JSAE.

JOINT COMMITTEE ON SLAVIC STUDIES.
— CURRENT ABSTRACTS OF THE SOVIET PRESS.

JOINT COUNCIL ON ECONOMIC EDUCATION.
— JOURNAL OF ECONOMIC EDUCATION.

JOINT FISHERIES RESEARCH ORGANIZATION (NORTHERN
RHODESIA & NYASALAND).                             XXX
— REPORT, JOINT FISHERIES RESEARCH ORGANIZATION
  (NORTHERN RHODESIA & NYASALAND).                XXX
  SUBS (1962): FISHERIES RESEARCH BULLETIN
  (ZAMBIA).

JOINT STANDING COMMITTEE ON LIBRARY COOPERATION
& BIBLIOGRAPHICAL SERVICES (MALAYA).
— INDEX TO CURRENT MALAYSIAN, SINGAPORE & BRUN-
  EI PERIODICALS.

JORDANHILL COLLEGE OF EDUCATION.
— RELEASE. THE MAGAZINE OF ...

JOSEPH HAYDN-INSTITUT (COLOGNE).
— HAYDN-STUDIEN.

JRDI LABORATORY.
— MATERIALS INFORMATION JAPAN.

JUGOSLAVENSKA AKADEMIJA ZNANOSTI I UMJETNOSTI.
— SUVREMENI EKONOMSKI PROBLEMI.

JUGOSLAVENSKA AKADEMIJA ZNANOSTI I UMJETNOSTI:
INSTITUT ZA KNJIZEVNOST I TEATROLOGIJU.
— CROATICA. PRINOSI PROUCAVANJU HRVATSKE
  KNJIZEVNOSTI.

JUGOSLAVENSKA AKADEMIJA ZNANOSTI I UMJETNOSTI:
INSTITUT ZA POVIJEST PRIRODNIH, MATEMATICKIH I
MEDICINSKIH NAUKA.
— RASPRAVE I GRADA ZA POVIJEST NAUKA.

JUGOSLAVENSKA AKADEMIJA ZNANOSTI I UMJETNOSTI,
ODJEL ZA SUVREMENU KNJIZEVNOST.
— FORUM. CASOPIS ODJELA ZA SUVREMENU KNJIZEV-
NOST JUGOSLAVENSKE AKADEMIJE ZNANOSTI I
UMJETNOSTI.

JUGOSLOVENSKI INSTITUT ZA TEHNOLOGIJU MESA.
— TEHNOLOGIJA MESA.

JUGOSLOVENSKO NAUCHNO VOCARSKO DRUSTVO.
— JUGOSLOVENSKO VOCARSTVO.

JUNIOR INSTITUTION OF ENGINEERS.
— JOURNAL & RECORD OF TRANSACTIONS, JUNIOR
INSTITUTION OF ENGINEERS.                          XXX
SUBS (1971): JOURNAL, INSTITUTION OF
GENERAL TECHNICIAN ENGINEERS.

JUNTA DE ESTUDIOS HISTORICOS DE BAHIA BLANCA.
— REVISTA, JUNTA DE ESTUDIOS HISTORICOS DE
BAHIA BLANCA.

JUSTUS LIEBIG-UNIVERSITAT IN GIESSEN; TROPEN
INSTITUT.
— GIESSENER BEITRAGE ZUR ENTWICKLUNGSFORSCHUNG;
REIHE 1: SYMPOSIEN.

JYVASKYLAN YLIOPISTO.
— JYVASKYLA STUDIES IN THE ARTS.

KAGAKU GIJUTSUCHO GENSHIRYOKUKYOKU.
— NUCLEAR SCIENCE INFORMATION OF JAPAN.          XXX

KAGAKU KEIZAI KENKYUJO.
— CHEMICAL ECONOMY & ENGINEERING REVIEW.         XXX
— JAPAN CHEMICAL QUARTERLY.                       XXX

KAGAKU KOGAKU KYOKAI.
— CHEMICAL ENGINEERING, JAPAN.                    XXX
— HEAT TRANSFER. JAPANESE RESEARCH.
— JOURNAL OF CHEMICAL ENGINEERING OF JAPAN.

KAGOSHIMA DAIGAKU KOGAKUBU.
— KAGOSHIMA DAIGAKU KOGAKUBU KENKYU HOKOKU.
RESEARCH REPORTS, FACULTY OF ENGINEERING,
KAGOSHIMA UNIVERSITY.

KAGOSHIMA KOGYO KOTO SENMON GAKKO.
— KAGOSHIMA KOGYO KOTO SENMON GAKKO KENKYU
HOKOKU. RESEARCH REPORT OF KAGOSHIMA TECH-
NICAL COLLEGE.

KAGOSHIMA TECHNICAL COLLEGE.                      000
SEE: KAGOSHIMA KOGYO KOTO SENMON GAKKO.

KAGOSHIMA UNIVERSITY: FACULTY OF ENGINEERING.
SEE: KAGOSHIMA DAIGAKU KOGAKUBU.

KAIYO SHUPPAN K.K.
— KAIYO KAGAKU. MARINE SCIENCES.

KAMMER DER TECHNIK (LEIPZIG).
— DEUTSCHE TEXTILTECHNIK.                         XXX
SUBS (1973): TEXTILTECHNIK.
— TEXTILTECHNIK.                                  XXX

KANAGAWA KENRITSU HAKUBUTSUKAN.
— KANAGAWA KENRITSU HAKUBUTSUKAN KENKYU HOKOKU:
SHIZEN KAGAKU.
— RESEARCH REPORT, KANAGAWA PREFECTURAL MUSEUM:
NATURAL HISTORY.

KANAWAGA PREFECTURAL MUSEUM.                      000
SEE: KANAGAWA KENRITSU HAKUBUTSUKAN.

KANSAS AGRICULTURAL EXPERIMENT STATION.
— RESEARCH PUBLICATION, KANSAS AGRICULTURAL EXP-
ERIMENT STATION.                                  XXX

KARL-MARX-UNIVERSITAT, LEIPZIG.
— GEOPHYSIK UND GEOLOGIE. GEOPHYSIKALISCHE
VEROFFENTLICHUNGEN DER KARL-MARX-UNIVERSITAT,
LEIPZIG.                                          XXX

KARL MARX-UNIVERSITAT (LEIPZIG); BIBLIOTHEK.
— INTERNATIONALE BIBLIOGRAPHIE DER ANTIQUARIATS-
AUKTIONS- UND KUNSTKATALOGE. (IBAK)

KARL-MAY-GESELLSCHAFT.
— JAHRBUCH DER KARL-MAY-GESELLSCHAFT.

KARLOVA UNIVERSITA V PRAZE.
— ACTA UNIVERSITATIS CAROLINAE: IURIDICA:
MONOGRAPHIA.
— ACTA UNIVERSITATIS CAROLINAE; PHILOLOGICA:
GERMANISTICA PRAGENSIA.
— ACTA UNIVERSITATIS CAROLINAE; PHILOLOGICA;
MONOGRAPHIA.
— ACTA UNIVERSITATIS CAROLINAE: PHILOSOPHICA
ET HISTORICA: MONOGRAPHIAE.
— CESKOSLOVENSKA DEFEKTOLOGIA.
— PRACE Z DEJIN UNIVERSITY KARLOVY.
— PSYCHOLOGIE V EKONOMICKE PRAXI. PSYCHOLOGY IN
ECONOMICS.
— SBIRKA PRAMENU A PRIRUCEK K DEJINAM UNIVER-
SITY KARLOVY.

KARLOVA UNIVERSITA V PRAZE: CENTRO DE ESTUDIOS
IBERO-AMERICANOS.
— IBERO-AMERICANA PRAGENSIA.

KARLOVA UNIVERSITA V PRAZE: PEDAGOGICKE FAKULTY
— SBORNIK PEDAGOGICKE FAKULTY UNIVERSITY
KARLOVY - HISTORIE.

KARLSRUHE STADTARCHIV.
— VEROFFENTLICHUNGEN, KARLSRUHE STADTARCHIV.

KARNATAK UNIVERSITY: INSTITUTE OF ECONOMIC
RESEARCH.
— JOURNAL, INSTITUTE OF ECONOMIC RESEARCH,
KARNATAK UNIVERSITY.

KASETSART UNIVERSITY (BANGKOK).
— KASETSART JOURNAL.                              XXX

KATOLICKI UNIWERSYTET LUBELSKI: TOWARZYSTWO
NAUKOWE.
— STUDIA HELLENSKIE.
— STUDIA HISTORYCZNE, TOWARZYSTWO NAUKOWE KATOL-
ICKIEGO UNIWERSYTETU LUBELSKIEGO.

KAWASAKI SEITETSU K.K.
— KAWASAKI SEITETSU GIHO. KAWASAKI STEEL TECH-
NICAL REPORT.

KAZAKHSKIJ NAUCHNO-ISSLEDOVATEL'SKIJ INSTITUT
— PROBLEMY OBSHCHEJ ENERGETIKI I EDINOJ ENERG-
ETICHESKOJ SISTEMY.
— PROBLEMY TEPLOENERGETIKI I PRIKLADNOJ TEPLOF-
IZIKI.

KAZAKHSKIJ POLITEKHNICHESKIJ INSTITUT.
— TRUDY, KAZAKHSKIJ POLITEKHNICHESKIJ INSTITUT.  XXX

KAZANSKIJ GOSUDARSTVENNYJ UNIVERSITET.
— MASTERSTVO OCHERKISTA.
— METEORNOE RASPROSTRANENIE RADIOVOLN.
— OCHERKI PO ISTORII RUSSKOGO JAZYKA I
LITERATURY XVIII VEKA (LOMONOVSKIE CHTENIJA).
— PRIEM I OBRABOTKA INFORMATSII V STRUKTURNO-
SLOZHNYKH INFORMATSIONNYKH SISTEMAKH.
— RAZNOCHINNO-DEMOKRATICHESKOE DVIZHENIE V
POVOLZH'E I NA URALE.

KAZANSKIJ GOSUDARSTVENNYJ UNIVERSITET: BIOLOGI-
CHESKIJ NAUCHNO-ISSLEDOVATEL'SKIJ INSTITUT.
— FIZIOLOGIJA VODOOBMENA I USTOJCHIVOSTI
RASTENIJ.

KEIKINZOKU ATSUEN KOGYOKAI.
— ARUMI EJI. ALUMINIUM AGE.

KEIO GIJUKU DAIGAKU FUJIHARA KINEN KOGAKUBU.
— KEIO ENGINEERING REPORTS.                       XXX
— KEIO GIJUKU DAIGAKU FUJIHARA KINEN KOGAKUBU
KENYU HOKOKU.                                     XXX
SUBS (1971): KEIO ENGINEERING REPORTS.

KEIO UNIVERSITY: FUJIHARA MEMORIAL FACULTY OF
ENGINEERING.                                      000
SEE: KEIO GIJUKU DAIGAKU FUJIHARA KINEN
KOGAKUBU.

KELVIN HUGHES DIVISION OF SMITHS INDUSTRIES,
LTD.
— KELVIN HUGHES REVIEW.*                          XXX

KENT STATE UNIVERSITY: LIBRARY.
— OCCASIONAL PAPERS, LIBRARY, KENT STATE UNIV-
ERSITY.

KENTUCKY HISTORICAL SOCIETY.
— KENTUCKY ANCESTORS.

KENYA ASSOCIATION OF MANUFACTURERS.
— EAST AFRICAN REPORT ON TRADE & INDUSTRY.

**(KENYA) BOARD OF ADULT EDUCATION.**
— KENYA JOURNAL OF ADULT EDUCATION.

**KENYA INSTITUTE OF ADMINISTRATION.**
— OCCASIONAL PAPERS, KENYA INSTITUTE OF ADMIN-
ISTRATION.

**KENYA TEA BOARD.**
— TEA IN EAST AFRICA.                                        XXX

**KENYON COLLEGE.**
— KENYON REVIEW.                                             XXX

**KERRY ARCHAEOLOGICAL & HISTORICAL SOCIETY.**
— JOURNAL, KERRY ARCHAEOLOGICAL & HISTORICAL
SOCIETY.

**KESATUAN KAJIBUMI MALAYSIA.**
— BULLETIN, GEOLOGICAL SOCIETY OF MALAYSIA.
— NEWSLETTER, KESATUAN KAJIBUMI MALAYSIA.

**KESTNER MUSEUM (HANOVER).**
— JAHRESBERICHT, KESTNER MUSEUM.

**KHAR'KOVSKIJ AVIATSIONNYJ INSTITUT.**
— SAMOLETOSTROENIE I TEKHNIKA VOZDUSHNOGO FLOTA.

**KHAR'KOVSKIJ GOSUDARSTVENNYJ UNIVERSITET.**
— OBRABOTKA METALLOV DAVLENIEM V MASHINOST-
ROENII.
— SUDOSTROENIE I MORSKIE SOORUZHENIJA.

**KHAR'KOVSKIJ INSTITUT GORNOGO MASHINOSTRO-
ENIJA, AVTOMATIKI I VYCHISLITEL'NOJ TEKHNIKI.**
— PRIBORY I SISTEMY AVTOMATIKI.

**KHAR'KOVSKIJ POLITEKHNICHESKIJ INSTITUT.**
— DINAMIKA I PROCHNOST' MASHIN.
— STANKI I REZHUSHCHIE INSTRUMENTY.

**KHAR'KOVSKIJ ZOOTEKHNICHESKIJ INSTITUT.**
— SBORNIK TRUDOV, KHAR'KOVSKIJ ZOOTEKHNICHESKIJ
INSTITUT.                                                    XXX
SUBS (1963): NAUCHNYE TRUDY, KHAR'KOVSKIJ
ZOOVETERINARNYJ INSTITUT.

**KHAR'KOVSKIJ ZOOVETERINARNYJ INSTITUT.**
— NAUCHNYE TRUDY, KHAR'KOVSKIJ ZOOVETERINARNYJ
INSTITUT.                                                    XXX

**KIEVSKIJ GOSUDARSTVENNYJ UNIVERSITET.**          000
SEE: KYJIVS'KYJ DERZHAVNYJ UNIVERSYTET.

**KIEVSKIJ INZHENERNO-STROITEL'NYJ INSTITUT.**
— PRIKLADNAJA GEOMETRIJA I INZHENERNAJA GRAFIKA.

**KIEVSKIJ TORGOVOEKONOMICHESKIJ INSTITUT.**
— SBORNIK NAUCHNYKH RABOT, KIEVSKIJ TORGOVO-
EKONOMICHESKIJ INSTITUT.

**KINGSTON COLLEGE OF TECHNOLOGY: GEOLOGY CLUB.**
— KINGSTON GEOLOGICAL REVIEW.

**KINGSTON LAW REVIEW ASSOCIATION.**
— KINGSTON LAW REVIEW.

**KINGSTON POLYTECHNIC: SCHOOL OF SOCIOLOGY.**
— NEW SOCIOLOGY.

**KINJO GAKUIN DAIGAKU.**
— KINJO GAKUIN DAIGAKU RONSHU KASEIGAKU
TOKUSHU. ANNUAL REPORT OF NATURAL SCIENCE &
HOME ECONOMICS, KINJO GAKUIN COLLEGE.

**KISHINEVSKIJ POLITEKHNICHESKIJ INSTITUT.**
— TRUDY, KISHINEVSKIJ POLITEKHNICHESKIJ
INSTITUT.

**KISHINEVSKIJ UNIVERSITET: KAFEDRA ALGEBRY I
GEOMETRII.**
— ISSLEDOVANIJA PO OBSHCHEJ ALGEBRE.

**KLASSILLUS-FILOLOGINEN YHDISTYS.**
— ARCTOS. ACTA PHILOLOGICA FENNICA. SUPPLEMEN-
TUM.

**KOBE MUNICIPAL OFFICE: SANITARY BUREAU.**       000
SEE: KOBE-SHI EISEI-KYOKU.

**KOBE-SHI EISEI-KYOKU.**
— KOBE-SHIRITSU BYOIN KIYO. = KOBE MUNICIPAL
HOSPITAL BULLETIN.

**KOBENHAVNS UNIVERSITET.**
— HAFNIA. COPENHAGEN PAPERS IN THE HISTORY OF
ART.

**KOBENHAVNS UNIVERSITET: ZOOLOGISKE MUSEUM.**
— STEENSTRUPIA.

**KODAK LTD.**
— FINISHER NEWS.
— INSTRUMENTATION INTELLIGENCE.                              XXX

**KOENIG-STEINER INSTITUT FUR KIRCHEN- UND
GEISTESGESCHICHTE DER SUDETENLAENDER.**
— ARCHIV FUR KIRCHENGESCHICHTE VON BOHMEN-
MAHREN-SCHLESIEN.

**KOGAI SHIGEN KENKYUJO.**
— KOGAI SHIGEN KENKYUJO HOKOKU.
— KOGAI SHIGEN KENKYUJO IHO. BULLETIN, NATION-
AL RESEARCH INSTITUTE FOR POLLUTION & RESOUR-
CES (JAPAN).

**KOGYO CHOSAKAI K.K.**
— DENSHI ZAIRYO. ELECTRONIC PARTS & MATERIALS.

**KOGYO GIJUTSUIN SHIGEN GIJUTSU SHIKENJO SANGYO
KOGAI BOSHI GIJUTSU-BU UKIMA BUNSHITSU.**
— KOGAI (HAKUA SHOBO). POLLUTION CONTROL.

**KOKURITSU BOSAI KAGAKU GIJUTSU SENTA.**
— KOKURITSU BOSAI KAGAKU GIJUTSU SENTA KENKYU
HOKOKU. REPORT OF THE NATIONAL RESEARCH
CENTER FOR DISASTER PREVENTION.

**KOKURITSU SHINJU KENKYUJO.**
— KOKURITSU SHINJU KENKYUJO SHIRYO. MATERIAL,
NATIONAL PEARL RESEARCH LABORATORY (JAPAN).

**KOKUSHIKAN DAIGAKU KOGAKUBU.**
— KOKUSHIKAN DAIGAKU KOGAKUBU KIYO.
TRANSACTIONS, DEPARTMENT OF ENGINEERING,
KOKUSHIKAN UNIVERSITY.

**KOLO LWOWIAN.**
— BIULETYN KOLA LWOWIAN.

**KOMITET PO LEKATA I KHRANITELNATA PROMISH-
LENOST.**                                                    XXX
— KOZHI, OBUVKI, KAUCHUK, PLASTMASI.                         XXX

**KOMMUNISTICHESKAJA PARTIJA KAZAKHSTANA:
INSTITUT ISTORII PARTII.**
— VOPROSY ISTORII KOMMUNISTICHESKOJ PARTII
KAZAKHSTANA. (*)

**KOMMUNISTICHESKAJA PARTIJA UZBEKISTANA.**
— KOMMUNIST UZBEKISTANA.

**KOMUNISTICKA STRANA CESKOSLOVENSKA.**
— OTAZKY MEZINARODNI POLITIKY.

**KONINKLIJK INSTITUUT VOOR TAAL-, LAND- EN
VOLKENKUNDE.**
— EXCERPTA INDONESICA.

**KONINKLIJK NEDERLANDS AARDRIJKSKUNDIG
GENOOTSCHAP.**
— GEOGRAFISCH TIJDSCHRIFT: NS.

**KONINKLIJKE INSTITUUT VOOR DE TROPEN:
(ANTHROPOLOGY DEPARTMENT).**
— TROPICAL MAN.                                              XXX

**KONINKLIJKE NEDERLANDSE AKADEMIE VAN WETEN-
SCHAPPEN: GENEESKUNDIGE RAAD.**
— RAPPORT, GENEESKUNDIGE RAAD, KONINKLIJKE
NEDERLANDSE AKADEMIE VAN WETENSCHAPPEN.

**KONINKLIJKE VERENIGING VOOR BOSKOOPSE CULTUREN.**
— DENDROFLORA.

**KONINKLIJKE VERENIGING VOOR NATUUR- EN STEDES-
CHOON.**
— NATUUR- EN STEDESCHOON.

**(KOREA, SOUTH) GEOLOGICAL SURVEY.**
— REPORT OF MARINE GEOLOGY & GEOPHYSICS (KOREA,
SOUTH).

**KOREA SCIENTIFIC & TECHNOLOGICAL
INFORMATION CENTER.**
— KOREAN MEDICAL ABSTRACTS.
— KOREAN SCIENTIFIC ABSTRACTS.

**KOREAN ASSOCIATION FOR THE PROTECTION OF NATURE**
— KOREAN NATURE.

**KOREAN INSTITUTE OF INTERNATIONAL STUDIES.**
— INTERNATIONAL STUDIES.

KOREAN SOCIETY OF PROFESSIONAL ENGINEERS.   000
  SEE: HANGUK KISULSAHOE.

KOSSUTH LAJOS TUDOMANYEGYETEM: MAGYAR
IRODALOMTORTENETI INTEZET.
  — STUDIA LITTERARIA.

KRASNODARSKIJ NAUCHNO-ISSLEDOVATEL'SKIJ
INSTITUT SEL'SKOGO KHOZJAJSTVA.
  — TRUDY, KRASNODARSKIJ NAUCHNO-ISSLEDOVATEL'-
    SKIJ INSTITUT SEL'SKOGO KHOZJAJSTVA.

KRISHNAMURTI FOUNDATION.
  — KRISHNAMURTI FOUNDATION BULLETIN.

KUJAWSKO-POMORSKIE TOWARZYSTWO KULTURALNE.
  — ROCZNIK KULTURALNY KUJAW I POMORZA.

KUNGLIGA BIBLIOTEKET (STOCKHOLM).
  — SUECANA EXTRANEA: BOCKER OM SVERIGE & OCH
    SVENSK SKONLITTERATUR PA FRAMMANDE SPRAK.

KUNGLIGA GUSTAV ADOLFS AKADEMIEN.
  — ETHNOLOGIA SCANDINAVICA.   XXX

KUNGLIGA SVENSKA VETENSKAPSAKADEMIEN.
  — AMBIO. A JOURNAL OF THE HUMAN ENVIRONMENT,
    RESEARCH & MANAGEMENT.
  — ARKIV FOR FYSIK.   XXX
    SUBS (1970): PHYSICA SCRIPTA.
  — CHEMICA SCRIPTA.   XXX
  — PHYSICA SCRIPTA.   XXX
  — ZOOLOGICA SCRIPTA.   XXX

KUNGLIGA TEKNISKA HOGSKOLAN: INSTITUTIONEN
FOR TEKNISK ELEKTROKEMI OCH KORROSIONSLARA.
  — KORROSION OCH METALLSKYDD.

KUNGLIGA UNIVERSITET I UPPSALA: NATURGEOGRAF-
ISKA INSTITUTIONEN.
  — RAPPORT, NATURGEOGRAFISKA INSTITUTIONEN, UNIV-
    ERSITET I UPPSALA.

KUNGNIP CHIJIL CHOSASO.
  — CHIJIL KWANGSANG. GEOLOGY & ORE DEPOSIT.

KUNGNIP KWAHAK SUSA YONGUSO.
  — KUNGNIP KWAHAK SUSA YONGUSO YONBO. ANNUAL
    REPORT OF THE NATIONAL INSTITUTE OF SCIEN-
    TIFIC INVESTIGATION.

KUNGNIP SUSAN CHINHUNGWON.
  — CHONGORI CHAWON CHOSA POGO. PROGRESS REPORT
    OF THE SARDINES RESOURCES INVESTIGATIONS.
  — KUNGNIP SUSAN CHINHUNGWON YONGU POGO. BULLE-
    TIN OF FISHERIES RESEARCH & DEVELOPMENT
    AGENCY (KOREA).

KURATORIUM FUR TECHNIK UND BAUWESEN IN DER
LANDWIRTSCHAFT.
  — FLUGSCHRIFT, KURATORIUM FUR TECHNIK UND
    BAUWESEN IN DER LANDWIRTSCHAFT.   XXX
  — KTBL-BAUSCHRIFTEN.

KURATORIUM FUR TECHNIK IN DER LANDWIRTSCHAFT.
  — FLUGSCHRIFT, KURATORIUM FUR TECHNIK IN DER
    LANDWIRTSCHAFT.   XXX
    SUBS (1970): FLUGSCHRIFT, KURATORIUM FUR
    TECHNIK UND BAUWESEN IN DER LANDWIRTSCHAFT.

KURGANSKAJA OBLASTNAJA GOSUDARSTVENNAJA SEL'-
SKOKHOZJAJSTVENNAJA OPYTNAJA STANTSIJA.
  — SBORNIK NAUCHNYKH RABOT, KURGANSKAJA OBLAST-
    NAJA GOSUDARSTVENNAJA SEL'SKOKHOZJAJSTVENNAJA
    OPYTNAJA STANTSIJA.

KUSHIRO JOSHI TANKI DAIGAKU.
  — KUSHIRO JOSHI TANKI DAIGAKU KIYO. BULLETIN
    OF KUSHIRO WOMEN'S JUNIOR COLLEGE.

KUSHIRO WOMEN'S JUNIOR COLLEGE.   000
  SEE: KUSHIRO JOSHI TANKI DAIGAKU.

KUWAIT MEDICAL ASSOCIATION.
  — JOURNAL, KUWAIT MEDICAL ASSOCIATION.

KUWAIT UNIVERSITY.
  — JOURNAL OF PALESTINE STUDIES.

KWAME NKRUMAH UNIVERSITY OF SCIENCE &
TECHNOLOGY: BUILDING RESEARCH GROUP.
  — PLANNING RESEARCH STUDIES, BUILDING RESEARCH
    GROUP, KWAME NKRUMAH UNIVERSITY OF SCIENCE &
    TECHNOLOGY.

KYANON KAMERA K.K.
  — KYANON KENKYU HOKOKU. RESEARCH REPORT OF
    CANON CAMERA CO., INC.

KYJIVS'KYJ DERZHAVNYJ UNIVERSYTET.
  — NAUKOVI PRATSI Z ISTORII KPRS.
  — PROBLEMY KOSMICHESKOJ FIZIKI.
  — PROGRAMMIROVANNOE OBUCHENIE. MEZHVEDOMSTVEN-
    NYJ NAUCHNYJ SBORNIK.

KYJIVS'KYJ DERZHAVNYJ UNIVERSYTET: INSTYTUT
PIDVYSHCHENNJA KVALIFIKATSII VYKLADACHIV
SUSPIL'NYKH NAUK.
  — VOPROSY OBSHCHESTVENNYKH NAUK (KIEV).

KYJIVS'KYJ INZHENERNO-BUDIVEL'NYJ INSTYTUT.
  — INZHENERNAJA GEODEZIJA.

KYJIVS'KYJ NAUKOVO-DOSLIDNYJ INSTYTUT HIHIENY
ZHYVLENNJA.
  — VOPROSY RATSIONAL'NOGO PITANIJA.

KYOTO AGRICULTURAL EXPERIMENT STATION.   000
  SEE: KYOTO FURITSU NOGYO SHIKENJO.

KYOTO DAIGAKU: BOSAI KENKYUJO.
  — ANNUAL REPORT OF HYDROLOGICAL RESEARCH IN THE
    AREA OF LAKE BIWA.

KYOTO DAIGAKU: COMMITTEE OF THE AFRICA PRIMAT-
OLOGICAL EXPEDITION.
  — KYOTO UNIVERSITY AFRICAN STUDIES.

KYOTO DAIGAKU: DEPARTMENT OF MATHEMATICS.
  — LECTURES IN MATHEMATICS, DEPARTMENT OF MATH-
    EMATICS, KYOTO UNIVERSITY.

KYOTO DAIGAKU: ENGINEERING RESEARCH INSTITUTE.
  SEE: KYOTO DAIGAKU: KOGAGU KENKYUJO.

KYOTO DAIGAKU: FARM POWER & MACHINERY
LABORATORY.
  — TECHNICAL REPORT, FARM POWER & MACHINERY LAB-
    ORATORY, KYOTO DAIGAKU.

KYOTO DAIGAKU: GENSHIRO JIKKENJO.
  — ANNUAL REPORTS OF THE RESEARCH REACTOR INST-
    ITUTE, KYOTO UNIVERSITY.

KYOTO DAIGAKU: INSTITUTE OF ATOMIC ENERGY.   XXX
  — RESEARCH ACTIVITIES, INSTITUTE OF ATOMIC
    ENERGY, KYOTO UNIVERSITY.   XXX
  — TECHNICAL REPORTS, INSTITUTE OF ATOMIC ENERGY,
    KYOTO UNIVERSITY.   XXX

KYOTO DAIGAKU: KOGAGU KENKYUJO.
  — RESEARCH ACTIVITIES OF THE ENGINEERING RES-
    EARCH INSTITUTE, KYOTO UNIVERSITY.   XXX
  — TECHNICAL REPORTS, ENGINEERING RESEARCH INST-
    ITUTE, KYOTO UNIVERSITY.   XXX
    SUBS (1971): TECHNICAL REPORTS, INSTITUTE
    OF ATOMIC ENERGY, KYOTO UNIVERSITY.

KYOTO DAIGAKU TONAN AJIA KENKYU SENTA.
  — REPORTS ON RESEARCH IN SOUTHEAST ASIA: SOCIAL
    SCIENCE SERIES.

KYOTO FURITSU NOGYO SHIKENJO.
  — KYOTO FURITSU NOGYO SHIKENJO KENKYU HOKOKU.
    BULLETIN OF THE KYOTO AGRICULTURAL EXPERIMENT
    STATION.

KYOTO UNIVERSITY: CENTER FOR SOUTHEAST ASIAN
STUDIES.   000
  SEE: KYOTO DAIGAKU TONAN AJIA KENKYU SENTA.

KYOTO UNIVERSITY: DEPARTMENT OF MATHEMATICS.   000
  SEE: KYOTO DAIGAKU: DEPARTMENT OF MATHEMATICS

KYOTO UNIVERSITY: ENGINEERING RESEARCH
INSTITUTE.   000
  SEE: KYOTO DAIGAKU: KOGAGU KENKYUJO.

KYOTO UNIVERSITY: FARM POWER & MACHINERY
LABORATORY.   000
  SEE: KYOTO DAIGAKU: FARM POWER & MACHINERY
    LABORATORY.

KYOTO UNIVERSITY: HYDROLOGY & WATER RESOURCES
RESEARCH GROUP.   000
  SEE: KYOTO DAIGAKU: BOSAI KENKYUJO.

KYOTO UNIVERSITY: INSTITUTE OF ATOMIC ENERGY.
  SEE: KYOTO DAIGAKU: INSTITUTE OF ATOMIC
    ENERGY.

KYOTO UNIVERSITY: RESEARCH REACTOR INSTITUTE                    000
SEE: KYOTO DAIGAKU: GENSHIRO JIKKENJO.

KYUSHU DAIGAKU NOGAKUBU FUZOKU HIKOSAN SEIBUT-
SUGAKU KENKYUSHO.
— ESAKIA. OCCASIONAL PAPERS OF THE HIKOSAN
  BIOLOGICAL LABORATORY IN ENTOMOLOGY.

KYUSHU DAIGAKU RIGAKUBU SHIMABARA KAZAN ONSEN
KENXYUSHO.
— KYUSHU DAIGAKU RIGAKUBU SHIMABARA KAZAN ONSEN
  KENKYUSHO KENKYU HOKOKU.

KYUSHU IMPERIAL UNIVERSITY: ZOOLOGICAL LABOR-
ATORY.
— OHMU: OCCASIONAL PAPERS OF THE ZOOLOGICAL
  LABORATORY, KYUSHU IMPERIAL UNIVERSITY.

KYUSHU INSTITUTE OF TECHNOLOGY.                                 000
SEE: KYUSHU KOGYO DAIGAKU.

KYUSHU KOGYO DAIGAKU.
— MEMOIRS OF THE KYUSHU INSTITUTE OF TECHNOLOGY:
  ENGINEERING.

KYUSHU KOGYO GIJUTSU SHIKENJO.
— KYUSHU KOGYO GIJUTSU SHIKENJO HOKOKU. REPORTS
  OF THE GOVERNMENT INDUSTRIAL RESEARCH INSTI-
  TUTE, KYUSHU.

KYUSHU UNIVERSITY: HIKOSAN BIOLOGICAL LABORA-
TORY IN ENTOMOLOGY.                                             000
SEE: KYUSHU DAIGAKU NOGAKUBU FUZOKU HIKOSAN
SEIBUTSUGAKU KENKYUSHO.

KYUSHU UNIVERSITY: SHIMBARA INSTITUTE OF VOL-
CANOLOGY & BALNEOLOGY.                                          000
SEE: KYUSHU DAIGAKU RIGAKUBA SHIMBARA KAZAN
ONSEN KENKYUSHO.

LABORATOIRE DE PALEONTOLOGIE (MONTPELLIER).
— PALAEOVERTEBRATA.

LABORATORIO DEL TRANSPORTE Y MECANICA DEL
SUELO (MADRID).
— MONOGRAFIA, LABORATORIO DEL TRANSPORTE Y
  MECANICA DEL SUELO (MADRID).

LABOUR PARTY (GB).
— INTERNATIONAL BRIEFING.                                       XXX
— OVERSEAS REVIEW.                                              XXX
  SUBS (1970): INTERNATIONAL BRIEFING.

LABOUR PARTY YOUNG SOCIALISTS (GB).
— LEFT. JOURNAL OF THE ...

LAFAYETTE NATURAL HISTORY MUSEUM.
— TECHNICAL BULLETIN, LAFAYETTE NATURAL HISTORY
  MUSEUM.

LAKEHEAD UNIVERSITY.
— LAKEHEAD UNIVERSITY REVIEW.

LANCASHIRE NATURALISTS' TRUST.
— NATURE IN LANCASHIRE. JOURNAL OF THE ...

LANCASTER CITY MUSEUM & ART GALLERY.
— HISTORY TRAIL.

LANDSCAPE RESEARCH GROUP.
— LANDSCAPE RESEARCH NEWS.

LANDSCHAFTVERBAND RHEINLAND.
— EPIGRAPHISCHE STUDIEN.

LANGUAGE ASSOCIATION OF EASTERN AFRICA.
— JOURNAL OF THE LANGUAGE ASSOCIATION OF EAST-
  ERN AFRICA.

LANTBRUKSHOGSKOLAN (SWEDEN).
— SWEDISH JOURNAL OF AGRICULTURAL RESEARCH.                     XXX

LATIN AMERICAN STUDIES ASSOCIATION.
— NEWSLETTER, LATIN AMERICAN STUDIES ASSOCIA-
  TION.

LATINAMERIKA-INSTITUTET I STOCKHOLM.
— IBERO-AMERICANA. RESEARCH NEWS & PRINCIPAL
  ACQUISITIONS OF DOCUMENTATION ON LATIN-
  AMERICA IN DENMARK, FINLAND, NORWAY & SWEDEN.
— PUBLICACIONES, LATINAMERIKA-INSTITUTET I
  STOCKHOLM: SERIES A: MONOGRAFIAS.
— PUBLICACIONES, LATINAMERIKA-INSTITUTET I
  STOCKHOLM: SERIES B: INFORMES.
— PUBLICACIONES, LATINAMERIKA-INSTITUTET I
  STOCKHOLM: SERIES C: ARS REDOGORELSAR.
— SKRIFTER UTGIVNA AV LATINAMERIKA-INSTITUTET I
  STOCKHOLM: SERIES C.

LATVIJAS PSR ZINATNU AKADEMIJA.
— KHIMIJA GETEROTSIKLICHESKIKH SOEDINENIJ.
— KHIMIJA GETEROTSIKLICHESKIKH SOEDINENIJ:
  SBORNIK.
— LATVIJAS PSR ZINATNU AKADEMIJAS VESTIS:
  KIMIJAS SERIJA. = IZVESTIJA AKADEMII NAUK
  LATVIJSKOJ SSR: SERIJA KHIMICHESKAJA.
— LATVIJSKIJ MATEMATICHESKIJ EZHEGODNIK.
— MAGNITNAJA GIDRODINAMIKA.
— MEKHANIKA POLIMEROV.

LATVIJAS PSR ZINATNU AKADEMIJA: ENERGETIKAS
INSTITUTAS.
— BESKONTAKTNYE ELEKTRICHESKIE MASHINY.

LATVIJAS PSR ZINATNU AKADEMIJA: INSTITUT
EKONOMIKI.
— MATEMATICHESKIE METODY V EKONOMIKE.
— TRUDY INSTITUTA EKONOMIKI AKADEMII NAUK
  LATVIJSKOJ SSR.

LATVIJAS PSR ZINATNU AKADEMIJA: INSTITUT ELEKT
RONIKI I VYCHISLITEL'NOJ TEKHNIKI.
— AVTOMATIKA I VYCHISLITEL'NAJA TEKHNIKA.

LATVIJAS UNIVERSITATE.
— LATVIJSKIJ MATEMATICHESKIJ EZHEGODNIK.

LAW ASSOCIATION FOR ASIA & THE WESTERN PACIFIC.
— LAWASIA.

LAW & SOCIETY ASSOCIATION.
— LAW & SOCIETY REVIEW.                                         XXX

LEAGUE OF ANGLICAN LOYALISTS.
— LOYALIST LINKS.

LEAGUE OF ARAB STATES: INFORMATION DEPARTMENT.
— PRESS RELEASES, INFORMATION DEPARTMENT, LEAG-
  UE OF ARAB STATES.

LEDERINDUSTRIE-BERUFS-GENOSSENSCHAFT.
— SICHERHEIT AM ARBEITSPLATZ.                                   XXX
— TECHNISCHER BERICHT, LEDERINDUSTRIE-BERUFS-
  GENOSSENSCHAFT.                                               XXX
  SUBS (1971): SICHERHEIT AM ARBEITSPLATZ.

LEEDS GEOLOGICAL ASSOCIATION.
— JOURNAL OF EARTH SCIENCES.                                    XXX
— TRANSACTIONS, LEEDS GEOLOGICAL ASSOCIATION.                   XXX
  SUBS (1970): JOURNAL OF EARTH SCIENCES.

LEGAL ACTION GROUP.
— LEGAL ACTION GROUP BULLETIN.

LEGON COMMITTEE ON NATIONAL RECONSTRUCTION.
— LEGON OBSERVER. ORGAN OF THE ...

LEHIGH UNIVERSITY (PA).
— JOURNAL OF DIFFERENTIAL GEOMETRY.

LEICESTERSHIRE COUNTY LIBRARY.
— REPORT SERIES, LEICESTERSHIRE COUNTY LIBRARY.

LEICESTERSHIRE LOCAL HISTORY COUNCIL.
— LEICESTERSHIRE HISTORIAN.

LEIDEN OBSERVATORY.
— ASTRONOMY & ASTROPHYSICS. SUPPLEMENT SERIES.

LEMBAGA PUSAT PERPUSTAKAAN BIOLOGI DAN PERTA-
NIAN.
— INDEKS BIOLOGI PERTANIAN INDONESIA. INDONES-
  IAN BIOLOGICAL & AGRICULTURAL INDEX.
— LEMBAGA PUSAT PERPUSTAKAAN BIOLOGI DAN PER-
  TANIAN SERI BIBLIOGRAFI.

LENINGRADSKIJ GOSUDARSTVENNYJ UNIVERSITET.
— AREALY RASTENIJ FLORY SSSR.
— ISSLEDOVANIJA PO GENETIKE.
— ISTORIJA RABOCHEGO KLASSA LENINGRADA. SBORNIK STATEJ.
— JADERNYJ MAGNITNYJ REZONANS.
— OCHERKI PO ISTORII LENINGRADSKOGO UNIVERSITETA.
— PRIMENENIE MATEMATIKI V EKONOMIKE.
— SEVERO-ZAPAD EVROPEJSKOJ CHASTI SSSR.
— STRUKTURA I ROL' VODY V ZHIVOM ORGANIZME.

LENINGRADSKIJ GOSUDARSTVENNYJ UNIVERSITET: FILOSOFSKIJ FAKUL'TET.
— VOPROSY FILOSOFII I PSIKHOLOGII. SBORNIK RABOT ASPIRANTOV.
— VOPROSY FILOSOFII I SOTSIOLOGII.

LENINGRADSKIJ GOSUDARSTVENNYJ UNIVERSITET: KAFEDRA VYCHISLITEL'NOJ MATEMATIKI I VYCHISLI-TEL'NYJ TSENTR LGU.
— METODY VYCHISLENIJ.
— VYCHISLITEL'NAJA TEKHNIKA I VOPROSY KIBERNET-IKI.                                                    XXX
— VYCHISLITEL'NAJA TEKHNIKA I VOPROSY PROGRAM-MIROVANIJA.                                               XXX

LENINGRADSKIJ GOSUDARSTVENNYJ UNIVERSITET: MATEMATIKO-MAKHANICHESKIJ FAKUL'TET.
— ISSLEDOVANIJA PO UPRUGOSTI I PLASTICHNOSTI.

LENINGRADSKIJ GOSUDARSTVENNYJ UNIVERSITET: NAUCHNO-ISSLEDOVATEL'SKIJ INSTITUT KOMPLEKSNYKH SOTSIAL'NYKH ISSLEDOVANIJ.
— CHELOVEK I OBSHCHESTVO.

LENINGRADSKIJ INSTITUT INZHENEROV VODNOGO TRANSPORTA.
— TRUDY, LENINGRADSKIJ INSTITUT INZHENEROV VODNOGO TRANSPORTA.                                           XXX
SUBS (1960): TRUDY, LENINGRADSKIJ INSTITUT VODNOGO TRANSPORTA  LIVT.

LENINGRADSKIJ INSTITUT VODNOGO TRANSPORTA LIVT.
— TRUDY LENINGRADSKIJ INSTITUT VODNOGO TRANS-PORTA LIVT.                                                XXX

LENINGRADSKIJ NAUCHNO-ISSLEDOVATEL'SKIJ
— SBORNIK NAUCHNO-ISSLEDOVATEL'SKIKH RABOT PO LESNOMU KHOZJAJSTVU.                                       XXX

LEPROSY MISSION.
— LEPROSY MISSION IN ACTION.

LIBERA UNIVERSITA INTERNAZIONALE DEGLI STUDI SOCIALI PRO DEO: INSTITUTO DI SOCIOLOGIA.
— RIVISTA DI SOCIOLOGIA.

(LIBERIA) DEPARTMENT OF PLANNING & ECONOMIC AFFAIRS.
— QUARTERLY STATISTICAL BULLETIN OF LIBERIA.

(LIBERIA) GEOLOGICAL SURVEY.
— BULLETIN, GEOLOGICAL SURVEY (LIBERIA).

LIBRARIES BOARD OF SOUTH AUSTRALIA.
— OCCASIONAL PAPERS IN ASIAN & PACIFIC STUDIES.

LIBRARY ACTION GROUP.
— LIBRARY ACTION.

LIBRARY ASSOCIATION.
— JOURNAL OF LIBRARIANSHIP.
— LIBRARY ASSOCIATION RESEARCH PUBLICATIONS.
— LIBRARY & INFORMATION SCIENCE ABSTRACTS.                XXX
— LIBRARY SCIENCE ABSTRACTS.                              XXX
SUBS (1969): LIBRARY & INFORMATION SCIENCE ABSTRACTS.

LIBRARY ASSOCIATION: BRANCH·& MOBILE LIBRARIES GROUP.
— OCCASIONAL PAPERS, BRANCH & MOBILE LIBRARIES GROUP, LIBRARY ASSOCIATION.
— SERVICE POINT.

LIBRARY ASSOCIATION: CATALOGUING & INDEXING GROUP.
— ANGLO-AMERICAN CATALOGUING RULES AMENDMENT BULLETIN.

LIBRARY ASSOCIATION: EAST MIDLANDS BRANCH.
— EAST MIDLANDS BIBLIOGRAPHY.                             XXX

LIBRARY ASSOCIATION: UNIVERSITY, COLLEGE & RESEARCH SECTION.
— ANNUAL BIBLIOGRAPHY OF SCOTTISH LITERATURE.

LIBRARY ASSOCIATION: YORKSHIRE BRANCH.
— STRESS. AN INFORMATION BULLETIN ON LIBRARIES & LOCAL GOVERNMENT REORGANISATION IN YORKSHIRE.

LIBRARY ASSOCIATION OF AUSTRALIA: UNIVERSITY & COLLEGE LIBRARIES SECTION.
— AUSTRALIAN ACADEMIC & RESEARCH LIBRARIES.

LIBRARY ASSOCIATION OF MALAYSIA.
— PERPUSTAKAAN.                                           XXX
— PERPUSTAKAAN MALAYSIA.                                  XXX

LIBRARY-COLLEGE ASSOCIATIONS, INC.
— LIBRARY-COLLEGE JOURNAL.

LIBRARY OF CONGRESS (US).
— AIR FORCE SCIENTIFIC RESEARCH BIBLIOGRAPHY.

LIETUVOS TSR AUKSTESNIS MOKYKLA.
— LIETUVOS TSR AUKSTUJU MOKYKLU MOKSLO DARBAI: EKONOMIKA. = UCHENYE ZAPISKI VYSSHIKH UCHEB-NYKH ZAVEDENIJ LITOVSKOJ SSR: EKONOMIKA.                 XXX
— LIETUVOS TSR AUKSTUJU MOKYKLU MOKSLO DARBAI: ELEKTROTECHNIKA IR AUTOMATIKA = NAUCHNYE TRUDY VYSSHIKH UCHEBNYKH ZAVEDENIJ LITOVSKOJ SSR: ELEKTROTEKHNIKA I AVTOMATIKA.                          XXX
— LIETUVOS TSR AUKSTUJU MOKYKLU MOKSLO DARBAI: ELEKTROTECHNIKA IR MECHANIKA = NAUCHNYE TRUDY VYSSHIKH UCHEBNYKH ZAVEDENIJ LITOVSKOJ SSR: ELEKTROTEKHNIKA I MEKHANIKA.                          XXX
— LIETUVOS TSR AUKSTUJU MOKYKLU MOKSLO DARBAI: FILOSOFIJA. = UCHENYE ZAPISKI VYSSHIKH UCHEB-NYKH ZAVEDENIJ LITOVSKOJ SSR.
— LIETUVOS TSR AUKSTUJU MOKYKLU MOKSLO DARBAI: GEOGRAFIJA IR GEOLOGIJA. = NAUCHNYE TRUDY VYSSHIKH UCHEBNYKH ZAVEDENIJ LITOVSKOJ SSR: GEOGRAFIJA I GEOLOGIJA.
— LIETUVOS TSR AUKSTUJU MOKYKLU MOKSLO DARBAI: ISTORIJA. = NAUCHNYE TRUDY VYSSHIKH UCHEBNYKH ZAVEDENIJ LITOVSKOJ SSR: ISTORIJA.
— LIETUVOS TSR AUKSTUJU MOKYKLU MOKSLO DARBAI: KALBOTYRA. = UCHENYE ZAPISKI VYSSHIKH UCHEB-NYKH ZAVEDENIJ LITOVSKOJ SSR: JAZYKOZNANIE.              XXX
— LIETUVOS TSR AUKSTUJU MOKYKLU MOKSLO DARBAI: LITERATURA. = NAUCHNYE TRUDY VYSSHIKH UCHEB-NYKH ZAVEDENIJ LITOVSKOJ SSR: LITERATURA.                XXX
— LIETUVOS TSR AUKSTUJU MOKYKLU MOKSLO DARBAI: MECHANIKA. = NAUCHNYE TRUDY VYSSHIKH UCHEB-NYKH ZAVEDENIJ LITOVSKOJ SSR: MEKHANIKA.
— LIETUVOS TSR AUKSTUJU MOKYKLU MOKSLO DARBAI: MECHANINE TECHNOLOGIJA.= NAUCHNYE TRUDY VYSSHIKH UCHEBNYKH ZAVEDENIJ LITOVSKOJ SSR: MEKHANICHESKAJA TEKHNOLOGIJA.

LIETUVOS TSR GEOGRAFINE DRAUGIJA: HIDROMETEOR-OLOGIJOS SKYRIUS.
— HIDROMETEOROLOGINIAI STRAIPSNIAI.

LIETUVOS TSR MOKSLU AKADEMIJA.
— LIETUVOS TSR MOKSLU AKADEMIJOS /IR JOS/ DAR-BUOTOJU KNYGU IR STRAIPSNIU BIBLIOGRAFIJA.               XXX
SUBS (1965): LIETUVOS TSR MOKSLU AKADEMIJOS LEIDINIU BIBLIOGRAFIJA.

LIETUVOS TSR MOKSLU AKADEMIJA: BOTANIKOS INSTITUTAS.
— BOTANIKOS KLAUSIMAI.

LIETUVOS TSR MOKSLU AKADEMIJA; CENTRINE BIBLIOTEKA.
— LIETUVOS TSR MOKSLU AKADEMIJOS LEIDINIU BIBLIOGRAFIJA. = BIBLIOGRAFIJA IZDANIJ AKADEMII NAUK LITOVSKOJ SSR.

LIETUVOS TSR MOKSLU AKADEMIJA ISTORIJOS.
— ACTA HISTORICA LITUANICA.

LIGHT METAL ROLLING INDUSTRY ASSOCIATION (JAPAN).                                                      000
SEE: KEIKINZOKU ATSUEN KOGYOKAI.

LIGUE DES BIBLIOTHEQUES EUROPEENNES DE RECHERCHE.
— BULLETIN, LIGUE DES BIBLIOTHEQUES EUROPEENNES DE RECHERCHE.

LINCOLNSHIRE METHODIST HISTORY SOCIETY.
— EPWORTH WITNESS & JOURNAL OF THE ...

LINDSEY COUNTY COUNCIL.
— HISTORY FROM THE ARCHIVES.

**LINNEAN SOCIETY OF LONDON.**
— BIOLOGICAL JOURNAL OF THE LINNEAN SOCIETY
  OF LONDON.
— BOTANICAL JOURNAL OF THE LINNEAN SOCIETY.
— BOTANICAL JOURNAL OF THE LINNEAN SOCIETY:
  SUPPLEMENT.
— JOURNAL OF THE LINNEAN SOCIETY. BOTANY.            XXX
  SUBS (1969): BOTANICAL JOURNAL OF THE LINN-
  EAN SOCIETY.
— JOURNAL OF THE LINNEAN SOCIETY. ZOOLOGY.          XXX
  SUBS (1969): ZOOLOGICAL JOURNAL OF THE LINN-
  EAN SOCIETY.
— PROCEEDINGS OF THE LINNEAN SOCIETY OF LONDON.     XXX
  SUBS (1969): BIOLOGICAL JOURNAL OF THE ...
— SYNOPSES OF THE BRITISH FAUNA: NS.
— ZOOLOGICAL JOURNAL OF THE LINNEAN SOCIETY.        XXX

**LINOTYPE & MACHINERY LTD.**
— L & M NEWS.                                       XXX
  SUBS (1970): LINOTYPE NEWS.
— LINOTYPE NEWS.                                    XXX

**LIST & INDEX SOCIETY.**
— SPECIAL SERIES, LIST & INDEX SOCIETY.

**(LITHUANIA) CENTRINE STATISTIKOS VALDYBA.**
— EKONOMIKA I KUL'TURA LITOVSKOJ SSR.

**(LITHUANIA) LIETUVOS TSR AUKSTOJO IR SPECIAL-
IOJO VIDURINIO MOKSLO MINISTERIJA.**
— LIETUVOS TSR AUKSTUJU MOKYKLU MOKSLO DARBAI:
  BIOLOGIJA.
— LIETUVOS TSR AUKSTUJU MOKYKLU MOKSLO DARBAI:
  MENOTYRA. = UCHENYE ZAPISKI VYSSHIKH UCHEBNYKH
  ZAVEDENIJ LITOVSKOJ SSR: ISKUSSTVOVEDENIE.
— LIETUVOS TSR AUKSTUJU MOKYKLU MOKSLO DARBAI:
  STATYBA IR ARCHITEKTURA.
— PROBLEMOS. FILOSOFIJOS, SOCIOLOGIJOS, LOGIKO-
  OS, ESTETIKOS, ETIKOS IR ATEIZMO MOKSLINIS
  LEIDINYS.

**LITOVSKOE OBSHCHESTVO DRUZHBY I KUL'TURNYKH
SVIAZEJ S ZARUBEZHNYMI STRANAMI.**
— LITVA SEGODNJA.

**LITTLEMORE LOCAL HISTORY SOCIETY.**
— LITTLEMORE JOURNAL.

**LIVERPOOL COUNCIL OF SOCIAL SERVICE.**
— CASTLE ST. CIRCULAR.

**LIVERPOOL PUBLIC RELATIONS OFFICE.**
— LIVERPOOL.

**LLOYD'S.**                                         000
SEE: CORPORATION OF LLOYD'S.

**LODZKIE TOWARZYSTWO NAUKOWE.**
— ACTA ARCHAEOLOGICA LODZIENSIA.                    XXX
— STUDIA PRAWNO-EKONOMICZNE, LODSKIE TOWARZYSTWO
  NAUKOWE. STUDIES IN LAW & ECONOMICS.
— SZLAKAMI NAUKI.

**LODZKIE TOWARZYSTWO NAUKOWE: WYDZIAT IV NAUK
LEKARSKICH.**
— FOLIA MEDICA LODZIENSIA.

**LODZKIE TOWARZYSTWO NAUKOWE: WYDZIALU V NAUK
TECHNICZNYCH.**
— PRACE WYDZIALU V: NAUK TECHNICZNYCH, LODZKIE
  TOWARZYSTWO NAUKOWE.

**LONDON BIBLE COLLEGE.**
— VOX EVANGELICA.

**LONDON BOROUGH OF CAMDEN: LIBRARIES & ARTS
DEPARTMENT.**
— SOUND VERDICT.

**LONDON CHAMBER OF COMMERCE.**
— COMMERCE. JOURNAL OF THE ...                       XXX
— COMMERCE INTERNATIONAL.                            XXX
— EASTERN EUROPE.

**LONDON ELECTRICITY BOARD.**
— LEB NEWS.

**LONDON MASTER PRINTERS ASSOCIATION.**
— LONDON PRINTER.

**LONDON MATHEMATICAL SOCIETY.**
— BULLETIN OF THE LONDON MATHEMATICAL SOCIETY.
— JOURNAL, LONDON MATHEMATICAL SOCIETY: 2S.
— LECTURE NOTE SERIES, LONDON MATHEMATICAL
  SOCIETY.

**LONDON POLYTECHNIC: STUDENTS' UNION.**
— WEST ONE.

**LONDON RECORD SOCIETY.**
— OCCASIONAL PUBLICATIONS, LONDON RECORD
  SOCIETY.
— PUBLICATIONS, LONDON RECORD SOCIETY.

**LONDON REGION FREE RADIO CAMPAIGN.**
— SCRIPT. MAGAZINE ON ALTERNATIVE RADIO.

**LONDON SCHOOL OF ECONOMICS & POLITICAL SCIENCE.**
— MILLENNIUM. A JOURNAL OF INTERNATIONAL
  STUDIES.

**LONDON SCHOOL OF ECONOMICS & POLITICAL SCIENCE
ANTHROPOLOGY SOCIETY.**
— KUNG. THE MAGAZINE OF THE LONDON SCHOOL OF
  ECONOMICS ANTHROPOLOGY SOCIETY.

**LONDON SCHOOL OF ECONOMICS & POLITICAL SCIENCE:
LAW SOCIETY.**
— CLAPHAM OMNIBUS. THE MAGAZINE OF LSE LAW
  SOCIETY.

**LONDON WRITERS & ARTISTS GROUP.**
— SUNBURST.

**LONG ASHTON RESEARCH STATION.**
— REPORT, LONG ASHTON RESEARCH STATION.

**LONG ISLAND HERPETOLOGICAL SOCIETY.**
— ENGELHARDTIA.

**LONGFORD HISTORICAL SOCIETY.**
— TEATHBHA. JOURNAL OF THE LONGFORD HISTORICAL
  SOCIETY.

**LOS ANGELES COUNTY MUSEUM OF NATURAL HISTORY.**
— BULLETIN, LOS ANGELES COUNTY MUSEUM OF
  NATURAL HISTORY: SCIENCE.

**LOUGHBOROUGH COLLEGE OF FURTHER EDUCATION.**
— LOUGHBOROUGH OCCASIONAL PAPERS IN SOCIAL
  STUDIES.

**LOUGHBOROUGH UNIVERSITY OF TECHNOLOGY: LIBRARY.**
— MASS WORKING PAPERS.

**LOUGHBOROUGH UNIVERSITY OF TECHNOLOGY: SOCIAL
SCIENCE SOCIETY.**
— FEEDBACK. JOURNAL OF THE ...

**LOUISIANA SOCIETY FOR HORTICULTURAL RESEARCH.**
— JOURNAL, LOUISIANA SOCIETY FOR HORTICULTURAL
  RESEARCH.                                          XXX
— LSHR NEWS LETTER.                                  XXX
— MONTHLY NEWS LETTER, LOUISIANA SOCIETY FOR
  HORTICULTURAL RESEARCH.                            XXX

**LOUISIANA STATE UNIVERSITY: COLLEGE OF BUSINESS
ADMINISTRATION.**
— MISSISSIPPI VALLEY JOURNAL OF BUSINESS &
  ECONOMICS.

**LOUISIANA STATE UNIVERSITY: SCHOOL OF GEO-
SCIENCE.**
— GEOSCIENCE & MAN.

**LOW COST AUTOMATION CENTRE.**
— LOW COST AUTOMATION REVIEW.

**LUBELSKIE TOWARZYSTWO NAUKOWE.**
— PRACE WYDZIALU HUMANISTYCZNEGO, LUBELSKIE TOW-
  ARZYSTWO NAUKOWE - MONOGRAFIE.

**LUDLOW MUSEUM.**
— PUBLICATIONS, LUDLOW MUSEUM.

**LUDWIG-BULTZMANN INSTITUT FUR GESCHICHTE DER
ARBEITERBEWEGUNG.**
— SCHRIFTENREIHE, LUDWIG-BULTZMANN INSTITUT FUR
  GESCHICHTE DER ARBEITERBEWEGUNG.

**LUGANSKIJ MASHINOSTROITEL'NYJ INSTITUT.**
— POLIMERY V MASHINOSTROENII. SBORNIK TRUDOV.

**LUNDS UNIVERSITET.**
— BIT. NORDISK TIDSKRIFT FOR INFORMATIONS-
  BEHANDLING.

**LUNDS UNIVERSITET: SLAVISKA INSTITUTET.**
— TEST- OCH MATERIALUTGAVOR, SLAVISKA
  INSTITUTET, LUNDS UNIVERSITET.

**L'VOVSKIJ GOSUDARSTVENNYJ UNIVERSITET.**
— TEORETICHESKAJA ELEKTROTEKHNIKA, L'VOVSKIJ
GOSUDARSTVENNYJ UNIVERSITET.

**L'VOVSKIJ GOSUDARSTVENNYJ UNIVERSITET: PROBLEM-
NAJA LABORATORIJA RADIOBIOLOGII.**
— BIOLOGICHESKOE DEISTVIE RADIATSII.

**L'VOVSKIJ POLITEKHNICHESKIJ INSTITUT.**
— AVTOMATIZATSIJA PROIZVODSTVENNYKH PROTSESSOV
V MASHINOSTROENII I PRIBOROSTROENII.

**MACAULEY INSTITUTE FOR SOIL RESEARCH.**
— BULLETIN, SOIL SURVEY OF SCOTLAND.

**MACHINE TOOL INDUSTRY RESEARCH ASSOCIATION.**
— PRODUCTION TECHNOLOGY. ABSTRACTS AND REPORTS
FROM EASTERN EUROPE.                               XXX

**MADRAS PSYCHOLOGY SOCIETY.**
— INDIAN JOURNAL OF EXPERIMENTAL PSYCHOLOGY.

**MAGYAR TUDOMANYOS AKADEMIA.**
— ACTA GEODAETICA, GEOPHYSICA ET MONTANISTICA.

**MAGYAR TUDOMANYOS AKADEMIA: REGESZET KUTATO
INTEZET.**
— MAGYARORSZAG REGESZETI TOPOGRAFIAJA.

**MAGYAR TUDOMANYOS AKADEMIA SZOCIOLOGIAI
BIZOTTSAGANAK FOLYOIRATA.**
— SZOCIOLOGIA.

**MAHATMA PHULE AGRICULTURAL UNIVERSITY.**
— RESEARCH JOURNAL, MAHATMA PHULE AGRICULTURAL
UNIVERSITY.

**MAINE HISTORICAL SOCIETY.**
— NEWSLETTER, MAINE HISTORICAL SOCIETY.

**MAIZURU KOGYO KOTO SENMON GAKKO.**
— MAIZURU KOGYO KOTO SENMON GAKKO KIYO.

**MAIZURU TECHNICAL COLLEGE.**                        000
SEE: MAIZURU KOGYO KOTO SENMON GAKKO.

**MAKERERE INSTITUTE OF SOCIAL RESEARCH.**
— OCCASIONAL PAPERS, MAKERERE INSTITUTE OF
SOCIAL RESEARCH.

**MAKERERE UNIVERSITY.**
— DHANA.

**MAKERERE UNIVERSITY: SOCIOLOGICAL SOCIETY.**
— SOCIOLOGICAL JOURNAL.

**MAKERERE UNIVERSITY COLLEGE: FACULTIES OF ARTS
& SOCIAL SCIENCES.**
— MAWAZO.

**(MALAWI) DEPARTMENT OF INFORMATION.**
— THIS IS MALAWI.
— VISION OF MALAWI.

**(MALAWI) GEOLOGICAL SURVEY.**                       XXX
— RECORDS OF THE GEOLOGICAL SURVEY OF MALAWI.       XXX

**(MALAWI) MINISTRY OF FINANCE.**
— QUARTERLY DIGEST OF STATISTICS (MALAWI).*         XXX

**(MALAYSIA) FEDERAL DEPARTMENT OF INFORMATION.**
— MALAYSIAN DIGEST.                                 XXX
— MALAYSIAN PRESS DIGEST.                           XXX

**(MALAYSIA) FOREST DEPARTMENT: FOREST RESEARCH
INSTITUTE.**
— MISCELLANEOUS PAPÉR, FOREST RESEARCH INSTIT-
UTE (MALAYSIA).

**MALAYSIAN INSTITUTE OF CHEMISTRY.**
— KIMIA.

**MALAYSIAN INSTITUTE OF MANAGEMENT.**
— MALAYSIAN MANAGEMENT REVIEW. JOURNAL OF THE...

**MALAYSIAN & SINGAPORE LAW STUDENT'S SOCIETY.**
— FIAT JUSTITIA.

**MALTA POETRY SOCIETY.**                              000
SEE: SOCJETA TAL-POEZIJA.

**MAMMAL SOCIETY OF THE BRITISH ISLES.**
— MAMMAL REVIEW.

**MANCHESTER BUSINESS SCHOOL.**
— CURRENT CONTENTS IN MANAGEMENT.                   XXX

**MANITOBA MUSEUM OF MAN & NATURE.**
— SPECIAL PUBLICATIONS, MANITOBA MUSEUM OF MAN
& NATURE.

**MARA INSTITUTE OF TECHNOLOGY.**
— QUARTERLY JOURNAL, MARA INSTITUTE OF TECHNOL-
OGY.

**MARBURGER UNIVERSITAT.**
— AFRICANA MARBURGENSIA.

**MARCONI'S WIRELESS TELEGRAPH COMPANY.**
— POINT TO POINT COMMUNICATION.                     XXX
— POINT TO POINT TELECOMMUNICATION.                 XXX
SUBS (1970): POINT TO POINT COMMUNICATION.

**MARINE HISTORICAL ASSOCIATION.**
— BIBLIOGRAPHY OF MARITIME & NAVAL HISTORY.

**MARINE TECHNOLOGY SOCIETY.**
— JOURNAL, MARINE TECHNOLOGY SOCIETY.

**MARKETING SOCIETY.**
— MARKETING WORLD. OFFICIAL JOURNAL OF THE ...

**MARTIN-LUTHER-UNIVERSITAT HALLE-WITTENBERG.**
— BEITRAGE ZUR ANALYSIS.

**MARXIST-LENINIST ORGANIZATION OF BRITAIN.**
— RED VANGUARD. JOURNAL OF THE THEORY &
PRACTICE OF MARXISM-LENINISM.

**MARY WASHINGTON COLLEGE: DEPARTMENT OF ENGLISH.**
— STUDIES IN BLACK LITERATURE.

**MARYLAND HERPETOLOGICAL SOCIETY.**
— BULLETIN, MARYLAND HERPETOLOGICAL SOCIETY.

**MASCHINENFABRIK AUGSBURG-NURNBERG, A.G.**
— M.A.N. RESEARCH, ENGINEERING, MANUFACTURING.

**(MASSACHUSETTS) DEPARTMENT OF NATURAL RE-
SOURCES, DIVISION OF MARINE FISHERIES.**
— MONOGRAPH SERIES, DIVISION OF MARINE FISH-
ERIES, DEPARTMENT OF NATURAL RESOURCES (MASS-
ACHUSETTS).

**MASSACHUSETTS INSTITUTE OF TECHNOLOGY: ALFRED
P. SLOAN SCHOOL OF MANAGEMENT.**                    000
SEE: ALFRED P. SLOAN ...

**MASSACHUSETTS INSTITUTE OF TECHNOLOGY: APPLIED
MATHEMATICS GROUP.**
— STUDIES IN APPLIED MATHEMATICS.                   XXX

**MASSACHUSETTS INSTITUTE OF TECHNOLOGY: SCHOOL
OF HUMANITIES & SOCIAL SCIENCES.**
— JOURNAL OF INTERDISCIPLINARY HISTORY.

**MASTIC ASPHALT COUNCIL & EMPLOYERS' FEDERATION.**
— TECHNICAL INFORMATION SHEET, MASTIC ASPHALT
COUNCIL & EMPLOYERS' FEDERATION.

**MATEMATICKI INSTITUT U BEOGRADU.**
— POSEBNA IZDANJA, MATEMATICKI INSTITUT U
BEOGRADU.

**MATHEMATICAL ASSOCIATION.**
— MATHEMATICS IN SCHOOL.

**MATHEMATICAL & PHYSICAL SOCIETY OF A.R.E.**
— PROCEEDINGS, MATHEMATICAL & PHYSICAL SOCIETY
OF A.R.E.                                           XXX

**MATICA HRVATSKA.**
— KOLO. CASOPIS ZA KNJIZEVNOST, UMJETNOST I
KULTURU: NS.

**MATICA SLOVENSKA V MARTINE.**
— BIBLIOGRAFIA SLOVENSKYCH BIBLIOGRAFII.
— SLOVENSKA NARODNA BIBLIOGRAFIA: SERIA A:
KNIHY.                                              XXX
— SLOVENSKA NARODNA BIBLIOGRAFIA: SERIA C:
CLANKY.                                             XXX

**MATSUE KOGYO KOTO SENMON GAKKO.**
— MATSUE KOGYO KOTO SENMON GAKKO KENKYU KIYO.
RESEARCH REPORTS OF MATSUE TECHNICAL COLLEGE.

**MATSUE TECHNICAL COLLEGE.**                         000
SEE: MATSUE KOGYO KOTO SENMON GAKKO.

**MATSUSHITA DENKO K.K.**
— MATSUSHITA DENKO GIHO. MATSUSHITA ELECTRIC
WORKS TECHNICAL REPORT.

MATSUSHITA ELECTRIC WORKS.                                          000
  SEE: MATSUSHITA DENKO K.K.

MATTHEWS WRIGHTSON GROUP OF COMPANIES.
  — MATTHEWS WRIGHTSON REVIEW.

MAURICE FALK INSTITUTE FOR ECONOMIC RESEARCH
IN ISREAL.
  — REPORT, MAURICE FALK INSTITUTE FOR ECONOMIC
    RESEARCH IN ISRAEL.

MAX-PLANCK-INSTITUT FUR AUSLANDISCHES UND
INTERNATIONALES PATENT- URHEBER-UND
WETTBEWERBSRECHT.
  — INTERNATIONAL REVIEW OF INDUSTRIAL PROPERTY &
    COPYRIGHT LAW.                                                  XXX

MAX-PLANCK-INSTITUTE FOR FOREIGN & INTERNAT-
IONAL PATENT, COPYRIGHT & COMPETITION LAW.         000
  SEE: MAX-PLANCK-INSTITUT FUR AUSLANDISCHES
  UND INTERNATIONALES PATENT-URHEBER-UND
  WETTBEWERBSRECHT.

MAZOWIECKI OSRODEK BADAN NAUKOWYCH.
  — PRACE, MAZOWIECKI OSRODEK BADAN NAUKOWYCH.

MCGILL UNIVERSITY: CENTRE FOR DEVELOPING-AREA
STUDIES.
  — MANPOWER & UNEMPLOYMENT RESEARCH IN AFRICA. A
    NEWSLETTER.
  — OCCASIONAL PAPER SERIES, CENTRE FOR DEVELOP-
    ING AREA STUDIES, MCGILL UNIVERSITY.

MCGILL UNIVERSITY: INSTITUTE OF AIR & SPACE
LAW.
  — YEARBOOK OF AIR & SPACE LAW. ANNUAIRE DE
    DROIT AERIEN ET SPATIAL.

MCGILL UNIVERSITY: LIBRARY.
  — OSLER LIBRARY NEWSLETTER.

MCMASTER UNIVERSITY: DEPARTMENT OF ENGLISH.
  — COPPERFIELD.

MCMASTER UNIVERSITY: MILLS MEMORIAL LIBRARY.
  — LIBRARY RESEARCH NEWS.

MEAT & LIVESTOCK COMMISSION.
  — ANNUAL REPORT, MEAT & LIVESTOCK COMMISSION.
  — BRITISH MEAT.

MEAT & LIVESTOCK COMMISSION: ECONOMIC
INFORMATION SERVICE.
  — ECONOMIC DIGEST, ECONOMIC INFORMATION SERVICE,
    MEAT & LIVESTOCK COMMISSION.

MEBYON KERNOW.                                                     000
  SEE: CORNISH NATIONAL MOVEMENT.

MECMAN LTD.
  — MECMAN TECHNIQUES.

MEDICAL LABORATORY TECHNOLOGISTS' ASSOCIATION.
  — IRISH MEDICAL LABORATORY TECHNOLOGIST.

MEDICAL RESEARCH SOCIETY.
  — CLINICAL SCIENCE & MOLECULAR MEDICINE.                         XXX

MEGURO KISEICHUKAN.
  — RESEARCH BULLETIN, MEGURO PARASITOLOGICAL
    MUSEUM.

MEGURO PARASITOLOGICAL MUSEUM.                                     000
  SEE: MEGURO KISEICHUKAN.

MEIJI DAIGAKU KAGAKU GIJUTSU KENKYUJO.
  — MEIJI DAIGAKU KAGAKU GIJUTSU KENKYUJO KIYO.
    MEMOIRS OF THE INSTITUTE OF SCIENCES & TECH-
    NOLOGY, MEIJI UNIVERSITY.

MEIJI UNIVERSITY: INSTITUTE OF SCIENCES &
TECHNOLOGY.                                                        000
  SEE: MEIJI DAIGAKU KAGAKU GIJUTSU KENKYUJO.

MEMORIAL UNIVERSITY OF NEWFOUNDLAND: MARINE
SCIENCES RESEARCH LABORATORY.
  — TECHNICAL REPORTS, MARINE SCIENCES RESEARCH
    LABORATORY, MEMORIAL UNIVERSITY OF NEWFOUND-
    LAND.

MENDELSSOHN-GESELLSCHAFT.
  — MENDELSSOHN STUDIEN.

MENTAL HEALTH ASSOCIATION OF IRELAND.
  — BULLETIN, MENTAL HEALTH ASSOCIATION OF IRE-
    LAND.
  — NEWSLETTER, MENTAL HEALTH ASSOCIATION OF
    IRELAND.

MERSEYSIDE POLITICS ASSOCIATION.
  — POLITIKS.

METAL INFORMATION SERVICES.
  — EAST EUROPEAN METALS REVIEW.

METALS & CERAMICS INFORMATION CENTER (U.S.).
  — REVIEW OF CERAMIC TECHNOLOGY.
  — REVIEW OF METALS TECHNOLOGY.

METHODIST CHURCH MUSIC SOCIETY.
  — BULLETIN, METHODIST CHURCH MUSIC SOCIETY.

METRICATION BOARD (GB).
  — ANNUAL REPORT, METRICATION BOARD (GREAT
    BRITAIN).
  — GOING METRIC.

METROPOLITAN MUSEUM OF ART (NEW YORK).
  — METROPOLITAN MUSEUM JOURNAL.

METROPOLITAN PENSIONS ASSOCIATION.
  — MPA REVIEW.

MICHIGAN ACADEMY OF SCIENCE, ARTS & LETTERS.
  — MICHIGAN ACADEMICIAN.                                          XXX
  — PAPERS OF THE MICHIGAN ACADEMY OF SCIENCE,        XXX
    ARTS & LETTERS.
    SUBS (1969): MICHIGAN ACADEMICIAN.

(MICHIGAN) DEPARTMENT OF NATURAL RESOURCES.
  — MICHIGAN CONSERVATION.                                         XXX
    SUBS (1969): MICHIGAN NATURAL RESOURCES.
  — MICHIGAN NATURAL RESOURCES.                                    XXX

MICHIGAN ENTOMOLOGICAL SOCIETY.
  — GREAT LAKES ENTOMOLOGIST.                                      XXX

MICHIGAN STATE UNIVERSITY: AFRICAN STUDIES
CENTER.
  — A.S.C. NEWSLETTER.
  — MAZUNGUMZO. STUDENT JOURNAL OF AFRICAN
    STUDIES.
  — RURAL AFRICANA. RESEARCH NOTES ON LOCAL
    POLITICS & POLITICAL ANTHROPOLOGY.

MICHIGAN STATE UNIVERSITY: AGRICULTURAL
EXPERIMENT STATION.
  — MICHIGAN SCIENCE IN ACTION.

MICHIGAN TECHNOLOGICAL UNIVERSITY: FORD
FORESTRY CENTER.
  — RESEARCH NOTES, FORD FORESTRY CENTER, MICHI-
    GAN TECHNOLOGICAL UNIVERSITY.

MICROINFO LTD.
  — MICROINFO. MICROGRAPHICS NEWS BULLETIN.

MIDCONTINENT AMERICAN STUDIES ASSOCIATION.
  — AMERICAN STUDIES. AN INTERDISCIPLINARY
    JOURNAL.                                                       XXX

MIDDLE EAST REGIONAL RADIOSCOPE CENTRE FOR
THE ARAB COUNTRIES.
  — ISOTOPE & RADIATION RESEARCH.

MIDLAND SOCIETY FOR THE STUDY OF MENTAL
SUBNORMALITY.
  — BRITISH JOURNAL OF MENTAL SUBNORMALITY.                        XXX

MIGRAINE TRUST.
  — HEMICRANIA. JOURNAL OF THE MIGRAINE TRUST.

MIE DAIGAKU NOGAKUBU.
  — MIE DAIGAKU NOGAKUBU ENSHURIN SHIRYO.
    RESEARCH DATA, MIE UNIVERSITY FORESTS.

MIE UNIVERSITY FORESTS.                                            000
  SEE: MIE DAIGAKU NOGAKUBU.

MILITARWISSENSCHAFTLICHES INSTITUT (VIENNA):
HEERESGESCHICHTLICHEN MUSEUM.                                      000
  SEE: HEERESGESCHICHTLICHEN MUSEUM (VIENNA).

MILWAUKEE PUBLIC MUSEUM.
  — OCCASIONAL PAPERS, MILWAUKEE PUBLIC MUSEUM:
    NATURAL HISTORY.
  — PRIMITIVE ART SERIES.
  — PUBLICATIONS IN MUSEOLOGY.

MINERALOGICAL SOCIETY OF GREAT BRITAIN &
IRELAND.
— BULLETIN, MINERALOGICAL SOCIETY OF GREAT
  BRITAIN & IRELAND.                                                            XXX
— NOTICES, MINERALOGICAL SOCIETY OF GREAT
  BRITAIN & IRELAND.
  SUBS (1969): BULLETIN, MINERALOGICAL
  SOCIETY OF GREAT BRITAIN & IRELAND.

MINERALS ENGINEERING SOCIETY.
— MINE & QUARRY.                                                               XXX

MINISTRY STUDIES BOARD (US).
— MINISTRY STUDIES.

MINNEAPOLIS FEDERAL RESERVE BANK.
— STUDIES IN MONETARY ECONOMICS.

MISSION BAY RESEARCH FOUNDATION OF SAN DIEGO.
— OCEANIC COORDINATE INDEX.                                                    XXX

MISSOURI LIBRARY ASSOCIATION.
— NEWSLETTER, MISSOURI LIBRARY ASSOCIATION.

MITSUBISHI JUKOGYO K.K.
— TECHNICAL REVIEW, MITSUBISHI JUKOGYO K.K.

MIYAKONOJO KOGYO KOTO SENMON GAKKO.
— MIYAKONOJO KOGYO KOTO SENMON GAKKO KENKYU. =
  MEMOIRS OF MIYAKONOJO TECHNICAL COLLEGE.

MIYAKONOJO TECHNICAL COLLEGE.                                                  000
SEE: MIYAKONOJO KOGYO KOTO SENMON GAKKO.

MODERN HUMANITIES RESEARCH ASSOCIATION.
— DISSERTATION SERIES, MODERN HUMANITIES
  RESEARCH ASSOCIATION.
— PUBLICATIONS, MODERN HUMANITIES RESEARCH
  ASSOCIATION.
— YEARBOOK OF ENGLISH STUDIES.

MODERN LANGUAGE ASSOCIATION OF AMERICA.
— FOREIGN LANGUAGE ANNALS.
— JOURNAL OF POPULAR CULTURE.
— MLA ABSTRACTS OF ARTICLES IN SCHOLARLY
  JOURNALS.
— SHAKESPEAREAN RESEARCH & OPPORTUNITIES.

MODERN LANGUAGE ASSOCIATION OF AMERICA: CENTER
FOR EDITIONS OF AMERICAN AUTHORS.
— CEAA NEWSLETTER.

MODERN LANGUAGE ASSOCIATION OF AMERICA: OLD
ENGLISH GROUP.
— OLD ENGLISH NEWSLETTER.

MODULAR SOCIETY.
— MODULAR QUARTERLY.                                                           XXX
— TRANSACTIONS, MODULAR SOCIETY.                                               XXX
  SUBS (1971): PART OF OAP JOURNAL FOR THE
  BUILT ENVIRONMENT.

MOLDAVSKIJ NAUCHNO-ISSLEDOVATEL'SKIJ INSTITUT
POCHVOVEDENIJA I AGROKHIMII.
— EFFEKTIVNOST' UDOBRENIJ V USLOVIJAKH MOLDAVII.

MOLDAVSKIJ NAUCHNO-ISSLEDOVATEL'SKIJ INSTITUT
ZHIVOTNOVODSTVA I VETERINARII.
— TRUDY, MOLDAVSKIJ NAUCHNO-ISSLEDOVATEL'SKIJ
  INSTITUT ZHIVOTNOVODSTVA I VETERINARII.

MOLOTOVSKIJ GOSUDARSTVENNYJ UNIVERSITEI:
ESTESTVENNO-NAUCHNYJ INSTITUT.
— SPELEOLOGICHESKIJ BJULLETEN'.                                                XXX
  SUBS (1961): PESHCHERY.

MONARCHIST PRESS ASSOCIATION.
— MONARCHIST BOOK REVIEW.

MONEYSAVERS ASSOCIATION.
— MONEYSAVERS.

MONGOLIA SOCIETY.
— MONGOLIA SOCIETY BULLETIN.                                                   XXX
— MONGOLIA SOCIETY NEWSLETTER.                                                 XXX

MONMOUTHSHIRE NATURALISTS TRUST, LTD.
— MONMOUTHSHIRE WILDLIFE REPORT.

MONOTYPE CORP. LTD.
— MONOTYPE BULLETIN.                                                           XXX

MONTREAL MUSEUM OF FINE ARTS.
— M. A QUARTERLY REVIEW OF THE ...

MORAVSKE MUZEUM V BRNE.
— FOLIA MENDELIANA.

MORAY HOUSE COLLEGE OF EDUCATION.
— PROGRAMMED LEARNING BULLETIN.

MORDOVSKIJ GOSUDARSTVENNYJ ZAPOVEDNIK.
— TRUDY MORDOVSKOGO GOSUDARSTVENNOGO ZAPOVED-
  NIKA.

MORDOVSKIJ NAUCHNO-ISSLEDOVATEL'SKIJ INSTITUT
JAZYKA, LITERATURY, ISTORII I EKONOMIKI.
— TRUDY MORDOVSKOGO NAUCHNO-ISSLEDOVATEL'SKOGO
  INSTITUTA JAZYKA, LITERATURY, ISTORII I EKON-
  OMIKI.                                                                        XXX

MORIOKA TOBACCO EXPERIMENT STATION.                                            000
SEE: JAPAN MONOPOLY CORPORATION: ...

MOSKOVSKAJA GIDROMETEOROLOGICHESKAJA OBSERV-
ATORIJA.
— SBORNIK RABOT MOSKOVSKOJ GIDROMETEOROLOGI-
  CHESKOJ OBSERVATORII.

MOSKOVSKAJA PATRIARKHIJA.
— BOGOSLOVSKIE TRUDY.  SBORNIK.

MOSKOVSKIJ GORODSKOJ SOVET DEPUTATOV TRUDJASH-
CHIKHSJA.
— ARKHITEKTURA I STROITEL'STVO MOSKVY.                                         XXX
  SUBS (1960): STROITEL'STVO I ARKHITEKTURA
  MOSKVY.
— STROITEL'STVO I ARKHITEKTURA MOSKVY.                                         XXX

MOSKOVSKIJ GOSUDARSTVENNYJ PEDAGOGICHESKIJ
INSTITUT INOSTRANNYKH JAZYKOV.
— TETRADI PEREVODCHIKA: UCHENYE ZAPISKI.

MOSKOVSKIJ GOSUDARSTVENNYJ UNIVERSITET.
— KOMPLEKSNYE ISSLEDOVANIJA PRIRODY OKEANA.
— PUBLIKATSII OTDELENIJA STRUKTURNOJ I PRI-
  KLADNOJ LINGVISTIKI, MOSKOVSKIJ GOS. UNIV.
— TRUDY UCHENYKH FILOLOGICHESKOGO FAKUL'TETA
  MOSKOVSKOGO UNIVERSITETA PO SLAVJANSKOMU
  JAZYKOZNANIJU.

MOSKOVSKIJ GOSUDARSTVENNYJ UNIVERSITET:
INSTITUT VOSTOCHNYJH JAZYKOV.
— KETSKIJ SBORNIK.  STUDIA KETICA.

MOSKOVSKIJ GOSUDARSTVENNYJ UNIVERSITET: KAFEDRA
GIDROLOGII.
— KOMPLEKSNYE ISSLEDOVANIJA VODOKHRANILISHCH.

MOSKOVSKIJ GOSUDARSTVENNYJ UNIVERSITET:
SEKTSIJA ISTORII ESTESTVOZNANIJA.
— ISTORIJA I METODOLOGIJA ESTESTVENNYKH NAUK.

MOSKOVSKIJ INSTITUT STALI I SPLAVOV.
— SBORNIK, MOSKOVSKIJ ... INSTITUT STALI I
  SPLAVOV.*

MOSKOVSKIJ INZHENERNO-FIZICHESKIJ INSTITUT.
— TEORIJA I RASCHET IMPUL'SNYKH I USILITEL'NYKH
  SKHEM NA POLUPROVODNIKOVYKH PRIBORAKH.
— VOPROSY DOZIMETRII I ZASHCHITY OT IZLUCHENIJ.                                XXX

MOSKOVSKIJ MEDITSINSKIJ STOMATOLOGICHESKIJ
INSTITUT.
— TEORIJA I PRAKTIKA STOMATOLOGII.                                             XXX

MOSKOVSKIJ UNIVERSITET: NAUCHNO-METODICHESKIJ
TSENTR RUSSKOGO JAZYKA.
— RUSSKIJ JAZYK ZA RUBEZHOM.

MOSS LANDING LABORATORIES.
— NEWSLETTER, MOSS LANDING LABORATORIES.

MOSS LANDING MARINE LABORATORIES.
— ANNUAL REPORT ON RESEARCH, MOSS LANDING MARINE
  LABORATORIES.
— NEWS, MOSS LANDING MARINE LABORATORIES.

MOSUL UNIVERSITY.
— BAYN AL-NAHRAYN.  MESOPOTAMIA QUARTERLY.

MOTOR INDUSTRY RESEARCH ASSOCIATION.
— AUTOMOBILE ABSTRACTS.                                                        XXX
— AUTOMOTIVE RESEARCH PUBLICATIONS.
— MIRA ABSTRACTS.                                                              XXX
— MIRA MONTHLY SUMMARY.                                                        XXX
— MONTHLY SUMMARY OF AUTOMOBILE ENGINEERING
  LITERATURE.                                                                  XXX
  SUBS (1967): MIRA MONTHLY SUMMARY.

MOUNT SINAI HOSPITAL (NEW YORK).
— JOURNAL OF THE MOUNT SINAI HOSPITAL.                                         XXX
  SUBS (1970): MOUNT SINAI JOURNAL OF
  MEDICINE.
— MOUNT SINAI JOURNAL OF MEDICINE.                                            XXX

**MOUNTAINEERING ASSOCIATION.**
— MOUNTAIN HOLIDAYS.

**MOUVEMENT NATIONAL DES QUEBECOIS.**
— QUEBEC NOUVEAU.

**MOVEMENT FOR DEMOCRACY IN RHODESIA.**
— MAJORITY RULE.

**MOVIMENTO NONVIOLENTO PER LA PACE.**
— AZIONE NONVIOLENTA.

**(MOZAMBIQUE) DIRECCAO PROVINCIAL DOS SERVICOS DE ESTATISTICA GERAL.**
— BOLETIM MENSAL DE ESTATISTICA (MOZAMBIQUE).**

**MPHALA CREATIVE SOCIETY.**
— JEWEL OF AFRICA. A LITERARY & CULTURAL MAGAZINE FROM ZAMBIA.

**MUSEE GUIMET.**
— ETUDE DES COLLECTIONS DU MUSEE.

**MUSEE DE MARIEMONT.**
— CAHIERS DE MARIEMONT. BULLETIN DU ...
— TRESORS INCONNUS DU MUSEE DE MARIEMONT.

**MUSEE NATIONAL DE VARSOVIE.**                                        000
SEE: MUZEUM NARODOWE W WARSZAWIE.

**MUSEI CIVICI DI STORIA ED ARTE (TRIESTE).**
— QUADERNO, MUSEI CIVICI DI STORIA ED ARTE (TRIESTE).

**MUSEO ARGENTINO DE CIENCIAS NATURALES 'BERNAR-DINO RIVADAVIA'.**
— COMUNICACIONES DEL MUSEO ARGENTINO DE CIEN-CIAS NATURALES 'BERNARDINO RIVADAVIA' E INST-ITUTO NACIONAL DE INVESTIGACION DE LAS CIEN-CIAS NATURALES: ECOLOGIA.
— COMUNICACIONES DEL MUSEO ARGENTINO DE CIEN-CIAS NATURALES 'BERNARDINO RIVADAVIA' E INST-ITUTO NACIONAL DE INVESTIGACION DE LAS CIEN-CIAS NATURALES: PALEONTOLOGIA.
— COMUNICACIONES DEL MUSEO ARGENTINO DE CIEN-CIAS NATURALES 'BERNARDINO RIVADAVIA' E INST-ITUTO NACIONAL DE INVESTIGACION DE LAS CIEN-CIAS NATURALES: PARASITOLOGIA.
— REVISTA, MUSEO ARGENTINO DE CIENCIAS NATUR-ALES 'BERNARDINO RIVADAVIA' E INSTITUTO NACIONAL DE INVESTIGACION DE LAS CIENCIAS NATURALES: ECOLOGIA.
— REVISTA, MUSEO ARGENTINO DE CIENCIAS NATUR-ALES 'BERNARDINO RIVADAVIA' E INSTITUTO NACIONAL DE INVESTIGACION DE LAS CIENCIAS NATURALES: ENTOMOLOGIA.
— REVISTA, MUSEO ARGENTINO DE CIENCIAS NATUR-ALES 'BERNARDINO RIVADAVIA' E INSTITUTO NACIONAL DE INVESTIGACION DE LAS CIENCIAS NATURALES: PARASITOLOGIA.

**MUSEO DE ARTES PLASTICAS (LA PLATA).**
— BOLETIN, MUSEO DE ARTES PLASTICAS (LA PLATA).

**MUSEO CANARIO.**
— CUADERNOS DE BOTANICA CANARIA.*

**MUSEO CIVICO DI STORIA NATURALE.**
— NATURA BRESCIANA.

**MUSEO DE HISTORIA NATURAL DE MONTEVIDEO.**
— COMUNICACIONES PALEONTOLOGICAS DEL MUSEO DE HISTORIA NATURAL DE MONTEVIDEO.

**MUSEO DEL HOMBRE DOMINICANO.**
— BOLETIN, MUSEO DEL HOMBRE DOMINICANO.

**MUSEO DEL MAR (COLOMBIA).**
— BOLETIN, MUSEO DEL MAR (COLOMBIA).

**MUSEO NACIONAL DE HISTORIA (PERU).**
— HISTORIA Y CULTURA.

**MUSEO PITRE.**
— QUADERNI DEL MUSEO PITRE.

**MUSEU RIO-GRANDENSE DE CIENCIAS NATURAIS.**
— IHERINGIA: ANTROPOLOGIA.
— IHERINGIA: SERIE GEOLOGIA.

**MUSEUM HEINEANUM.**
— NATURKUNDLICHE JAHRESBERICHTE, MUSEUM HEINEANUM.

**MUSEUM NATIONAL D'HISTOIRE NATURELLE (FRANCE): LABORATOIRE D'ETHNOBOTANIQUE.**
— HISTOIRE ET BIOLOGIE. CAHIERS DU CERCLE D'ETUDE HISTORIQUE DES SCIENCES DE LA VIE.

**MUSEUM OF NATURAL HISTORY (SANTA BARBARA, CALIF.).**
— CONTRIBUTIONS IN SCIENCE.

**MUSEUMS ACTION MOVEMENT.**
— MUSEUM NEWS.

**MUSEUMS ASSOCIATION.**
— MUSEUMS ASSOCIATION INFORMATION SHEET.

**MUSHROOM GROWERS' ASSOCIATION.**
— MGA BULLETIN.                                                       XXX
SUBS (1973): MUSHROOM JOURNAL.
— MUSHROOM JOURNAL.                                                   XXX

**MUSIC CRITICS ASSOCIATION.**
— AMERICAN MUSICAL DIGEST.

**MUSIC LIBRARY ASSOCIATION.**
— MLA INDEX SERIES.
— MUSIC CATALOGING BULLETIN.
— NEWSLETTER, MUSIC LIBRARY ASSOCIATION.

**MUZEUL ARHEOLOGIC (PIATRA NIAMT).**
— MEMORIA ANTIQUITATIS.

**MUZEUM NARODOWE W WARSZAWIE.**
— BULLETIN, MUZEUM NARODOWE W WARSZAWIE.

**MUZICKA AKADEMIJA U ZAGREBU: MUZIKOLOSKI ZAVOD.**
— ARTI MUSICES.

**(MYSORE) DEPARTMENT OF MINES & GEOLOGY.**
— GEOLOGICAL STUDIES.

**NACHRICHTENTECHNISCHE WERKE, A.G.**
— TECHNISCHE BERICHTE, NACHRICHTENTECHNISCHE WERKE, A.G.

**NACZELNA DYREKCJA ARCHIWOW PANSTWOWYCH: ARCHIWUM DOKUMENTACJI MECHANICZNEJ.**
— KATALOG MIKROFILMOW ARCHIWALNYCH.

**NAGASAKI DAIGAKU KOGAKUBU.**
— NAGASAKI DAIGAKU KOGAKUBU KENKYU HOKOKU. REPORTS, FACULTY OF ENGINEERING, NAGASAKI UNIVERSITY.

**NAGASAKI UNIVERSITY: FACULTY OF ENGINEERING.**       000
SEE: NAGASAKI DAIGAKU KOGAKUBU.

**NANKAI REGIONAL FISHERIES RESEARCH LABORATORY.**                                                   000
SEE: NANKAI-KU SUISAN KENKYUJO.

**NANKAI-KU SUISAN KENKYUJO.**
— NANKAI-KU SUISAN KENKYUJO HOKOKU RINJIGO. OCCASIONAL REPORT OF THE NANKAI REGIONAL FISH-ERIES RESEARCH LABORATORY.

**NANSEI KAIKU SUISAN KENKYUJO.**
— NANSEI KAIKU SUISAN KENKYUJO KENKYU HOKOKU. BULLETIN OF THE NANSEI REGIONAL FISHERIES RESEARCH LABORATORY.
— NANSEI KAIKU SUISAN KENKYUJO NENJI HOKOKU.

**NANSEI REGIONAL FISHERIES RESEARCH LABORATORY.**
SEE: NANSEI KAIKU SUISAN KENKYUJO.

**NANTIS.**                                                           000
SEE: NOTTINGHAM & NOTTINGHAMSHIRE TECHNICAL INFORMATION SERVICE.

**NANYANG UNIVERSITY.**
— JOURNAL OF NANYANG UNIVERSITY.

**NANYANG UNIVERSITY: DEPARTMENT OF MATHEMATICS.**
— NANTA MATHEMATICA.

**NARODNA BIBLIOTEKA 'KIRIL I METODY'.**
— BIBLIOGRAFIJA NA BULGARSKATA BIBLIOGRAFIJA, KNIGOZNANIE I BIBLIOTECHNO DELO.

**NARODNA BIBLIOTEKA SR SRBIJE.**
— BILTEN PREVODA JUGOSLOVENSKIH AUTORA I JUGOS-LAVIKE.

**NARODNI MUZEJ.**
— LESKOVACKI ZBORNIK.

**NARODNI MUZEJ VRANJE.**
— VRANJSKI GLASNIK.

NASSAU COMMUNITY COLLEGE.
— NASSAU REVIEW.

NATAL SOCIETY.
— NATALIA.

NATIONAL ACADEMY OF SCIENCES (US): DIVISION OF
EARTH SCIENCES.
— EARTH SCIENCES NEWSLETTER.

NATIONAL ACADEMY OF TELEVISION ARTS & SCIENCES
(US).
— TELEVISION QUARTERLY.

NATIONAL ADVISORY CANCER COUNCIL (US).
— PROGRESS AGAINST CANCER.

NATIONAL AERONAUTICS & SPACE ADMINISTRATION
(US).
— COMPUTER PROGRAM ABSTRACTS.

NATIONAL AGRICULTURAL ADVISORY SERVICE (GB).          XXX
— N.A.A.S. QUARTERLY REVIEW.                          XXX
    SUBS (1971): A.D.A.S. QUARTERLY REVIEW.

NATIONAL AGRICULTURAL ADVISORY SERVICE (GB):
REDESDALE EXPERIMENTAL HUSBANDRY FARM.                000
    SEE: REDESDALE ...

NATIONAL AGRICULTURAL SOCIETY OF CEYLON.
— JOURNAL, NATIONAL AGRICULTURAL SOCIETY OF
    CEYLON.

NATIONAL AIR POLLUTION CONTROL ADMINISTRATION
(US).
— AIR POLLUTION TRANSLATIONS.

NATIONAL ARCHIVES OF RHODESIA.
— LIST OF PUBLICATIONS DEPOSITED IN THE LIBRARY
    OF THE NATIONAL ARCHIVES (RHODESIA).             XXX
    SUBS (1968): RHODESIA NATIONAL BIBLIOGR.
— RHODESIA NATIONAL BIBLIOGRAPHY.

NATIONAL ARCHIVES (US).
— PROLOGUE.

NATIONAL ASSOCIATION OF ACCOUNTANTS (US).
— NAA RESEARCH STUDIES IN MANAGEMENT REPORTING.

NATIONAL ASSOCIATION FOR THE CARE & RESETTLE-
MENT OF OFFENDERS: SOUTH WALES & SEVERN VALLEY
REGION.
— FRONT SHEET.

NATIONAL ASSOCIATION OF CLINICAL TUTORS.
— BULLETIN OF THE NATIONAL ASSOCIATION OF
    CLINICAL TUTORS.

NATIONAL ASSOCIATION OF CORROSION ENGINEERS.
— MATERIALS PROTECTION & PERFORMANCE.*             XXX

NATIONAL ASSOCIATION OF CYCLE & MOTOR CYCLE
TRADERS LTD.
— TWO WHEELER DEALER.

NATIONAL ASSOCIATION OF CYCLE TRADERS.
— N.A. JOURNAL.

NATIONAL ASSOCIATION OF MENTAL HEALTH (GB).
— MENTAL HEALTH.                                    XXX
    SUBS (1971): MIND & MENTAL HEALTH MAGAZINE.
— MIND & MENTAL HEALTH MAGAZINE.                    XXX

NATIONAL ASSOCIATION OF PRISON VISITORS(GB).
— CONTACT. NEWSLETTER OF THE NATIONAL ASSOC-
    IATION OF PRISON VISITORS.

NATIONAL ASSOCIATION OF PROPERTY OWNERS.
— PROPERTY JOURNAL: NS.

NATIONAL ASSOCIATION OF PURCHASING AGENTS.
— JOURNAL OF PURCHASING.

NATIONAL ASSOCIATION OF SCHOOLMASTERS (GB).
— N.A.S. REPORT.

NATIONAL ASSOCIATION FOR SOVIET & EAST EUROPEAN
STUDIES.
— ABSEES. SOVIET & EAST EUROPEAN ABSTRACTS
    SERIES.                                         XXX

NATIONAL ASSOCIATION OF YOUTH CLUBS.
— TENNIS TALK.

NATIONAL AUDUBON SOCIETY.
— AMERICAN BIRDS.                                   XXX
— AUDUBON FIELD NOTES.                              XXX
    SUBS (1971): AMERICAN BIRDS.

NATIONAL AWAMI PARTY OF BANGLA DESH (IN GREAT
BRITAIN).
— BULLETIN, NATIONAL AWAMI PARTY OF BANGLA DESH
    (IN GREAT BRITAIN).

NATIONAL BENZOLE & ALLIED PRODUCTS ASSOCIATION.
— BENZOLE BIBLIOGRAPHY.                             XXX
— REVIEW OF BENZOLE TECHNOLOGY.                     XXX
    SUBS (1968): BENZOLE BIBLIOGRAPHY.

NATIONAL BOOK DEVELOPMENT COUNCIL OF SINGAPORE.
— SINGAPORE BOOK WORLD.

NATIONAL BUREAU FOR CO-OPERATION IN CHILD CARE.
— CONCERN.

NATIONAL BUREAU OF ECONOMIC RESEARCH (US).
— ANNALS OF ECONOMIC & SOCIAL MEASUREMENT.
— NATIONAL BUREAU REPORT.
— URBAN & REGIONAL STUDIES.

NATIONAL BUREAU OF STANDARDS (US).
— JOURNAL OF PHYSICAL & CHEMICAL REFERENCE DATA.

NATIONAL CACTUS & SUCCULENT SOCIETY (GB):
EPIPHYTIC PLANT STUDY GROUP.
— EPIPHYTES.

NATIONAL CANCER INSTITUTE (US).
— PROGRESS AGAINST CANCER.

NATIONAL CENTER FOR ATMOSPHERIC RESEARCH (US).
— FACILITIES FOR ATMOSPHERIC RESEARCH.             XXX

NATIONAL CENTRAL LIBRARY (TAIPEI).
— NEWSLETTER, NATIONAL CENTRAL LIBRARY (TAIPEI).

NATIONAL CENTRE FOR THE PERFORMING ARTS (INDIA)
— QUARTERLY JOURNAL, NATIONAL CENTRE FOR THE
    PERFORMING ARTS (INDIA).

NATIONAL CHRISTIAN EDUCATION COUNCIL.
— LINK (LONDON, 1971).

NATIONAL CITIZENS' ADVICE BUREAUX COUNCIL(GB).
— ABSTRACT, NATIONAL CITIZENS' ADVICE BUREAUX
    COUNCIL.

NATIONAL CLEARINGHOUSE FOR MENTAL HEALTH
INFORMATION (US).
— DRUG DEPENDENCE.
— MENTAL HEALTH DIGEST.
— MENTAL RETARDATION ABSTRACTS.

NATIONAL COAL BOARD (GB).
— VENTILATION BROADSHEET.

NATIONAL COAL BOARD (GB): CENTRAL ENGINEERING
ESTABLISHMENT.
— BRETBY BROADSHEET.                                XXX
— BRETBY REPORT.                                    XXX

NATIONAL COAL BOARD (GB): MINING RESEARCH &
DEVELOPMENT ESTABLISHMENT.
— MINING RESEARCH & DEVELOPMENT REVIEW.             XXX
— MRDE REPORT.                                      XXX

NATIONAL COMMERCIAL TEMPERANCE YOUTH LEAGUE:
YOUTH SERVICE INFORMATION CENTRE.
— OCCASIONAL PAPER, YOUTH SERVICE INFORMATION
    CENTRE, NATIONAL COMMERCIAL TEMPERANCE YOUTH
    LEAGUE.

NATIONAL COOPERATIVE HIGHWAY RESEARCH PROGRAM
(U.S.).
— RESEARCH RESULTS DIGEST, NATIONAL COOPERATIVE
    HIGHWAY RESEARCH PROGRAM (U.S).
— SYNTHESIS OF HIGHWAY PRACTICE.

NATIONAL COUNCIL OF APPLIED ECONOMIC RESEARCH
(INDIA).
— MARGIN: QUARTERLY JOURNAL OF THE NATIONAL
    COUNCIL OF APPLIED ECONOMIC RESEARCH.

NATIONAL COUNCIL FOR CIVIL LIBERTIES.
— SPEAK OUT.

NATIONAL COUNCIL FOR EDUCATIONAL TECHNOLOGY(GB)
— BRITISH JOURNAL OF EDUCATIONAL TECHNOLOGY.                    XXX
— JOURNAL OF EDUCATIONAL TECHNOLOGY.
— OCCASIONAL PAPER, NATIONAL COUNCIL FOR
  EDUCATIONAL TECHNOLOGY (GB).
— WORKING PAPER, NATIONAL COUNCIL FOR EDUCAT-
  IONAL TECHNOLOGY (GB).

NATIONAL COUNCIL FOR GEOGRAPHIC EDUCATION.
— YEARBOOK, NATIONAL COUNCIL FOR GEOGRAPHIC
  EDUCATION.                                                   XXX

NATIONAL COUNCIL OF THE PAPER INDUSTRY FOR AIR
& STREAM IMPROVEMENT (US).                                     XXX
— TECHNICAL BULLETIN, NATIONAL COUNCIL OF THE
  PAPER INDUSTRY FOR AIR & STREAM IMPROVEMENT
  (US).                                                        XXX

NATIONAL COUNCIL FOR QUALITY & RELIABILITY (GB)
— QUALITY MATTERS.  BULLETIN OF THE MEMBERS OF
  THE ...

NATIONAL COUNCIL OF SCIENCE EDUCATION (INDIA).
— INDIAN JOURNAL OF CHEMICAL EDUCATION.

NATIONAL COUNCIL FOR STREAM IMPROVEMENT OF THE
PULP, PAPER & PAPERBOARD INDUSTRIES (US).                      XXX
— TECHNICAL BULLETIN, NATIONAL COUNCIL FOR
  STREAM IMPROVEMENT OF THE PULP, PAPER & PAPER-
  BOARD INDUSTRIES (US).                                       XXX
  SUBS (1968): TECHNICAL BULLETIN, NATIONAL
  COUNCIL OF THE PAPER INDUSTRY FOR AIR &
  STREAM IMPROVEMENT (US).

NATIONAL COUNCIL OF TEACHERS OF ENGLISH (US).
— RESEARCH IN THE TEACHING OF ENGLISH.

NATIONAL COUNCIL OF WOMEN OF GREAT BRITAIN.
— COUNCIL.  NEWSLETTER OF THE ...

NATIONAL DAIRYING RESEARCH CENTRE (EIRE).
— DAIRY RESEARCH REVIEW SERIES.

NATIONAL ECONOMIC DEVELOPMENT OFFICE (GB).
— NEWSLETTER, ECONOMIC DEVELOPMENT COMMITTEE
  FOR FOOD MANUFACTURING.
— NEWSLETTER, ECONOMIC DEVELOPMENT COMMITTEE
  FOR MOTOR MANUFACTURING INDUSTRY.

NATIONAL EDUCATIONAL CONSULTANTS (US).
— ABSTRACTS & REVIEWS IN BEHAVIORAL BIOLOGY.                   XXX

NATIONAL ELECTRONICS COUNCIL (GB).
— NATIONAL ELECTRONICS REVIEW (GB).                            XXX
— NEC REVIEW.

NATIONAL ELECTRONICS RESEARCH COUNCIL (GB).
— NERC REVIEW.                                                 XXX

NATIONAL EYE RESEARCH FOUNDATION (US).
— UNIVERSAL ABSTRACTS.                                         XXX

NATIONAL FARMERS' UNION.
— BRITISH FARMER.                                              XXX
  SUBS (1971): PART OF BRITISH FARMER & STOCK-
  BREEDER; & N.F.U. INSIGHT.
— BRITISH FARMER & STOCKBREEDER.                               XXX
— FARMER & STOCKBREEDER.                                       XXX
  SUBS (1971): PART OF BRITISH FARMER & STOCK-
  BREEDER.
— N.F.U. INSIGHT.                                              XXX
— NORTH WALES FARMER.

NATIONAL FEDERATION OF CLAIMANTS UNIONS.
— JOURNAL OF THE NATIONAL FEDERATION OF CLAIM-
  ANTS UNIONS.

NATIONAL FEDERATION OF MEAT TRADERS'
ASSOCIATIONS (GB).
— MEAT TRADER.

NATIONAL FIRE PROTECTION ASSOCIATION.
— FIRE JOURNAL.                                                XXX
— QUARTERLY, NATIONAL FIRE PROTECTION ASSOCIA-
  TION.                                                        XXX
  SUBS (1965): FIRE JOURNAL.

NATIONAL FOUNDATION FOR EDUCATIONAL RESEARCH
IN ENGLAND & WALES.
— EDUCATIONAL RESEARCH NEWS.
— HIGHER EDUCATION MONOGRAPH SERIES.

NATIONAL FREIGHT FOUNDATION LTD.
— FREIGHTWAY.

NATIONAL FRUIT & CIDER INSTITUTE.                              000
SEE: LONG ASHTON RESEARCH STATION.

NATIONAL FUND FOR RESEARCH INTO CRIPPLING
DISEASES (GB): COMMITTEE FOR RESEARCH INTO
APPARATUS FOR THE DISABLED.
— ENGINEERING IN MEDICINE.

NATIONAL GAMING COUNCIL (US).
— GAMING NEWSLETTER.                                           XXX

NATIONAL GARDENS GUILD.
— NEWSLETTER OF THE NATIONAL GARDENS GUILD.

NATIONAL GYPSY COUNCIL.
— ROMANO DROM.  THE PAPER OF THE...

NATIONAL HIGHWAY SAFETY BUREAU (US).
— PERFORMANCE DATA FOR NEW PASSENGER CARS &
  MOTORCYCLES.

NATIONAL INDUSTRIAL CONFERENCE BOARD (US).
— WORLD BUSINESS PERSPECTIVES.

NATIONAL INDUSTRIAL SAFETY ORGANISATION (EIRE).
— SCIATH.  JOURNAL OF THE ...

NATIONAL INFORMATION & DOCUMENTATION CENTRE
(U.A.R).
— JOURNAL OF MICROBIOLOGY OF THE UNITED ARAB
  REPUBLIC.  MAGALLAT AL-MIKROBIYOLOCIYA LI-AL-
  GUMHURIYYAT AL-'ARABIYYAT AI-MUTTAHIDAH.
— UNITED ARAB REPUBLIC JOURNAL OF PHYSICS.

NATIONAL INSPECTION LABORATORY FOR FEEDS &
FERTILIZER (JAPAN).                                            000
SEE:  TOKYO HISHIRYO KENSAJO.

NATIONAL INSTITUTE OF AGRICULTURAL
ENGINEERING (GB).
— NIAE NEWSLETTER.

NATIONAL INSTITUTE OF ARTHRITIS & METABOLIC
DISEASES (U.S.).
— ENDOCRINOLOGY INDEX.

NATIONAL INSTITUTE OF CHILD HEALTH & HUMAN
DEVELOPMENT (US).
— CURRENT POPULATION RESEARCH.

NATIONAL INSTITUTE OF COMMUNITY DEVELOPMENT
(INDIA).
— BEHAVIOURAL SCIENCES & COMMUNITY DEVELOPMENT.

NATIONAL INSTITUTE OF DRYCLEANING (US).                        XXX
— BULLETIN SERVICE, NATIONAL INSTITUTE OF DRY-
  CLEANING: FABRICS-FASHIONS.                                  XXX
  SUBS (1972): IFI BULLETIN SERVICE: FABRICS-
  FASHIONS BULLETIN.
— BULLETIN SERVICE, NATIONAL INSTITUTE OF DRY-
  CLEANING: PRACTICAL OPERATING TIPS.                          XXX
  SUBS (1972): IFI BULLETIN SERVICE: PRACT-
  ICAL OPERATING TIPS.
— BULLETIN SERVICE, NATIONAL INSTITUTE OF DRY-
  CLEANING: TECHNICAL.                                         XXX
  SUBS (1972): IFI BULLETIN SERVICE: TECH-
  NICAL BULLETIN.

NATIONAL INSTITUTE OF ECONOMIC & SOCIAL
RESEARCH (G.B.).
— REGIONAL PAPERS, NATIONAL INSTITUTE OF ECON-
  OMIC & SOCIAL RESEARCH (G.B.).

NATIONAL INSTITUTE OF EDUCATION (UGANDA).
— TEACHER.  CURRENT IDEAS FOR UGANDA PRIMARY &
  SECONDARY SCHOOLS.

NATIONAL INSTITUTES OF HEALTH (U.S.).
— ENDOCRINOLOGY INDEX.

NATIONAL INSTITUTE FOR HIGHER EDUCATION (EIRE).
— BULLETIN, NATIONAL INSTITUTE FOR HIGHER
  EDUCATION (EIRE).

NATIONAL INSTITUTE OF MENTAL HEALTH (US).
— MENTAL HEALTH DIGEST.

NATIONAL INSTITUTE FOR METALLURGY (S. AFRICA).
— MINERALS SCIENCE & ENGINEERING.

NATIONAL INSTITUTE OF NEUROLOGICAL DISEASES &
STROKE (US).
— PARKINSON'S DISEASE & RELATED DISORDERS,
  CITATIONS FROM THE LITERATURE.

NATIONAL INSTITUTE FOR OCCUPATIONAL SAFETY &
HEALTH (US).
— TOXIC SUBSTANCES.  ANNUAL LIST.

NATIONAL INSTITUTE OF OCEANOGRAPHY (INDIA).
— MAHASAGAR.

NATIONAL INSTITUTE OF PUBLIC ADMINISTRATION
(PAKISTAN).
— ADMINISTRATIVE SCIENCE REVIEW.

NATIONAL INSTITUTE FOR RESEARCH IN DAIRYING.
— BIENNIAL REVIEWS, NATIONAL INSTITUTE FOR
RESEARCH IN DAIRYING.

NATiONAL INSTITUTE OF SCIENCES OF INDIA.          XXX
— BULLETIN, NATIONAL INSTITUTE OF SCIENCES OF
INDIA.                                            XXX
SUBS (1970): BULLETIN, INDIAN NATIONAL SCI-
ENCE ACADEMY.
— INDIAN JOURNAL OF PURE & APPLIED MATHEMATICS.
— PROCEEDINGS, NATIONAL INSTITUTE OF SCIENCES
OF INDIA: PART A: PHYSICAL SCIENCES.             XXX
SUBS (1970): PROCEEDINGS, INDIAN NATIONAL
SCIENCE ACADEMY: PART A: PHYSICAL SCIENCES.
— PROCEEDINGS, NATIONAL INSTITUTE OF SCIENCES
OF INDIA: PART B: BIOLOGICAL SCIENCES.           XXX
SUBS (1970): PROCEEDINGS, INDIAN NATIONAL
SCIENCE ACADEMY: PART B: BIOLOGICAL
SCIENCES.

NATIONAL INSTITUTE OF SCIENTIFIC INVESTIGATION
(KOREA).                                          000
SEE: KUNGNIP KWAHAK SUSA YONGUSO.

NATIONAL KIDNEY FOUNDATION (US).
— KIDNEY.

NATIONAL LENDING LIBRARY FOR SCIENCE &
TECHNOLOGY.
— LIST OF BOOKS RECEIVED FROM THE USSR (&
TRANSLATED BOOKS).                               XXX
— NLL ANNOUNCEMENT BULLETIN.                     XXX
— NLL REVIEW.                                    XXX

NATIONAL LIBRARY OF CANADA.
— NATIONAL LIBRARY NEWS. = NOUVELLES DE LA BIB-
LIOTHEQUE NATIONALE.

NATIONAL LIBRARY OF CANADA: RESEARCH & PLANNING
BRANCH.
— ACCESSIBLE.

NATIONAL LIBRARY OF MEDICINE (US).
— ABRIDGED INDEX MEDICUS.*
— INDEX OF TISSUE CULTURE.                       XXX
— MONTHLY BIBLIOGRAPHY OF MEDICAL REVIEWS.
— NEUROSURGICAL BIBLIO-INDEX.
— SELECTED REFERENCES ON ENVIRONMENTAL QUALITY
AS IT RELATES TO HEALTH.
— TOXICITY BIBLIOGRAPHY.

NATIONAL LIBRARY OF NIGERIA.
— NATIONAL LIBRARY OCCASIONAL PUBLICATION
(NIGERIA).

NATIONAL LIBRARY OF SCOTLAND.
— LIST OF FOREIGN ACCESSIONS, NATIONAL LIBRARY
OF SCOTLAND.

NATIONAL MARINE FISHERIES SERVICE (US).
— FISHERY FACTS (US),

NATIONAL MARITIME MUSEUM (G.B.).
— MARITIME MONOGRAPHS & REPORTS.

NATIONAL MICROFILM ASSOCIATION (U.S.).
— JOURNAL OF MICROGRAPHICS.                      XXX
— MICRO-NEWS BULLETIN.
— NATIONAL MICRO-NEWS.                           XXX
SUBS. (1967): NMA JOURNAL.
— NMA JOURNAL.                                   XXX

NATIONAL MUSEUM & ART GALLERY (BOTSWANA).
— BOTSWANA NOTES & RECORDS.

NATIONAL MUSEUM OF MAN (CANADA).
— PUBLICATIONS IN ARCHAEOLOGY, NATIONAL MUSEUM
OF MAN (CANADA).
— PUBLICATIONS IN ETHNOLOGY, NATIONAL MUSEUM OF
MAN (CANADA).
— PUBLICATIONS IN FOLK CULTURE, NATIONAL MUSEUM
OF MAN (CANADA).
— PUBLICATIONS IN HISTORY, NATIONAL MUSEUM OF
MAN (CANADA).

NATIONAL MUSEUM OF MAN (CANADA): ARCHAEOLOGICAL
SURVEY OF CANADA.
— PAPER, ARCHAEOLOGICAL SURVEY OF CANADA, NAT-
IONAL MUSEUM OF MAN (CANADA): MERCURY SERIES.

NATIONAL MUSEUM OF MAN (CANADA): CANADIAN
CENTRE FOR FOLK CULTURE STUDIES.
— PAPERS, CANADIAN CENTRE FOR FOLK CULTURE
STUDIES, NATIONAL MUSEUM OF MAN (CANADA):
MERCURY SERIES.

NATIONAL MUSEUM OF MAN (CANADA): ETHNOLOGY
DIVISION.
— PAPERS, ETHNOLOGY DIVISION, NATIONAL MUSEUM
OF MAN (CANADA): MERCURY SERIES.

NATIONAL MUSEUM OF MAN (CANADA): HISTORY
DIVISION.
— PAPERS, HISTORY DIVISION, NATIONAL MUSEUM OF
MAN (CANADA): MERCURY SERIES.
— URBAN HISTORY REVIEW.

NATIONAL MUSEUM OF NATURAL SCIENCES (CANADA).
— PUBLICATIONS IN BIOLOGICAL OCEANOGRAPHY, NAT-
IONAL MUSEUM OF NATURAL SCIENCES (CANADA).
— PUBLICATIONS IN BOTANY, NATIONAL MUSEUM OF
NATURAL SCIENCES (CANADA).
— PUBLICATIONS IN PALAEONTOLOGY, NATIONAL MUS-
EUM OF NATURAL SCIENCES (CANADA).
— PUBLICATIONS IN ZOOLOGY, NATIONAL MUSEUM OF
NATURAL SCIENCES (CANADA).
— SYLLOGEUS.

NATIONAL MUSEUM OF WALES.
— AMGUEDDFA. BULLETIN OF THE NATIONAL MUSEUM
OF WALES.

NATIONAL OBSERVATORY (GREECE): METEOROLOGICAL
INSTITUTE.
— BULLETIN OF ATMOSPHERIC ELECTRICITY.

NATIONAL OCEANIC ATMOSPHERIC ADMINISTRATION
(US).
— FISHERY FACTS (US).
— NOAA.

NATIONAL OLD PEOPLE'S WELFARE COUNCIL.
— QUARTERLY BULLETIN, NATIONAL OLD PEOPLE'S
WELFARE COUNCIL.                                 XXX
SUBS (1973): AGE CONCERN TODAY.

NATIONAL PEARL RESEARCH LABORATORY (JAPAN).      000
SEE: KOKURITSU SHINJU KENKYUJO.

NATIONAL PHYSICAL LABORATORY (G.B.): DIVISION
OF INORGANIC & METALLIC STRUCTURE.
— IMS REPORT.

NATIONAL POETRY FOUNDATION (US).
— PAIDEUMA.

NATIONALE POPULIEREN COMMISSIE (NETH.)
— POPULIER.

NATIONAL PORTS COUNCIL (GB).
— BULLETIN, NATIONAL PORTS COUNCIL (GB).

NATIONAL PROVINCIAL BANK.                        XXX
— NATIONAL PROVINCIAL BANK REVIEW.              XXX
SUBS (1968): PART OF QUARTERLY REVIEW,
NATIONAL WESTMINSTER BANK.

NATIONAL RADIOLOGICAL PROTECTION BOARD (GB).
— RADIOLOGICAL PROTECTION BULLETIN.

NATIONAL RECREATION & PARK ASSOCIATION (US).
— JOURNAL OF LEISURE RESEARCH.

NATIONAL REFERENCE LIBRARY OF SCIENCE &
INVENTION.
— AIDS TO READERS.
— PERIODICAL NEWS FROM THE NATIONAL REFERENCE
LIBRARY OF SCIENCE & INVENTION.                 XXX

NATIONAL REPROGRAPHIC CENTRE FOR DOCUMENTATION
(GB).
— DIRECTORY OF COMMERCIAL MICROFILM SERVICES IN
THE UNITED KINGDOM.
— NRCD BULLETIN.                                 XXX
— OCCASIONAL PAPERS, NATIONAL REPROGRAPHIC
CENTRE FOR DOCUMENTATION (GB).
— TECHNICAL EVALUATION REPORTS, NATIONAL
REPROGRAPHIC CENTRE FOR DOCUMENTATION.

NATIONAL RESEARCH CENTER FOR DISASTER PREVENT-
ION (JAPAN).                                     000
SEE: KOKURITSU BOSAI KAGAKU GIJUTSU SENTA.

**NATIONAL RESEARCH COUNCIL (CANADA).**
— CANADIAN JOURNAL OF FOREST RESEARCH.
— NRC RESEARCH NEWS.                                                  XXX
  SUBS (1969): SCIENCE DIMENSION.
— SCIENCE DIMENSION.

**NATIONAL RESEARCH COUNCIL (CANADA): ASTRO-
PHYSICS BRANCH.**
— PUBLICATIONS OF THE ASTROPHYSICS BRANCH,
  NATIONAL RESEARCH COUNCIL (CANADA).

**NATIONAL RESEARCH COUNCIL (CANADA): DIVISION
OF MECHANICAL ENGINEERING.**
— LABORATORY TECHNICAL REPORT, DIVISION OF
  MECHANICAL ENGINEERING, NATIONAL RESEARCH
  COUNCIL (CANADA).
— NEWSLETTER, DIVISION OF MECHANICAL ENGINEER-
  ING, NATIONAL RESEARCH COUNCIL (CANADA):
  COMPUTERS.
— NEWSLETTER, DIVISION OF MECHANICAL ENGINEER-
  ING, NATIONAL RESEARCH COUNCIL (CANADA):
  ENGINEERING & BIOLOGICAL CONTROL SYSTEMS.
— NEWSLETTER, DIVISION OF MECHANICAL ENGINEER-
  ING, NATIONAL RESEARCH COUNCIL (CANADA):
  GENERAL.
— NEWSLETTER, DIVISION OF MECHANICAL ENGINEER-
  ING, NATIONAL RESEARCH COUNCIL (CANADA):
  MANUFACTURING DEVELOPMENTS.
— NEWSLETTER, DIVISION OF MECHANICAL ENGINEER-
  ING, NATIONAL RESEARCH COUNCIL (CANADA):
  MEDICAL INSTRUMENTATION.
— NEWSLETTER, DIVISION OF MECHANICAL ENGINEER-
  ING, NATIONAL RESEARCH COUNCIL (CANADA):
  STANDARDS & STANDARDIZATION IN THE ENGINEERING
  INDUSTRIES.
— NEWSLETTER, DIVISION OF MECHANICAL ENGINEER-
  ING, NATIONAL RESEARCH COUNCIL (CANADA):
  TRANSPORTATION.

**NATIONAL RESEARCH COUNCIL (CANADA): NATIONAL
AERONAUTICAL ESTABLISHMENT.**
— LABORATORY TECHNICAL REPORT, NATIONAL AERO-
  NAUTICAL ESTABLISHMENT (CANADA).

**NATIONAL RESEARCH COUNCIL OF THAILAND.**
— LIST OF SCIENTIFIC REPORTS RELATING TO
  THAILAND.

**NATIONAL RESEARCH INSTITUTE OF FAMILY PLANNING
(PAKISTAN).**
— PAKISTAN JOURNAL OF FAMILY PLANNING.

**NATIONAL RESEARCH INSTITUTE FOR POLLUTION &
RESOURCES (JAPAN).**                                                  000
  SEE: KOGAI SHIGEN KENKYUJO.

**NATIONAL SCIENCE FOUNDATION (US).**
— HYGIENE & SANITATION.                                               XXX
— MOSAIC. QUARTERLY JOURNAL OF ...
— NSF FACTBOOK.

**NATIONAL SCIENCE MUSEUM TOKYO.**
— MEMOIRS OF THE NATIONAL SCIENCE MUSEUM TOKYO.

**NATIONAL SCIENCE TEACHERS ASSOCIATION (US).**
— JOURNAL OF COLLEGE SCIENCE TEACHING.

**NATIONAL SERVICE TO REGIONAL COUNCILS (US).**
— REGIONAL REVIEW QUARTERLY.

**NATIONAL SOCIETY FOR CLEAN AIR.**
— CLEAN AIR. JOURNAL OF THE ...
— SMOKELESS AIR.                                                      XXX
  SUBS (1971): PART CLEAN AIR.

**NATIONAL SUGGESTIONS CENTRE.**
— WHAT ? IDEAS FOR ACTION.

**NATIONAL TAIWAN UNIVERSITY: DEPARTMENT OF GEOG-
RAPHY & METEOROLOGY.**
— SCIENCE REPORTS, DEPARTMENT OF GEOGRAPHY &
  METEOROLOGY, NATIONAL TAIWAN UNIVERSITY.

**NATIONAL TECHNICAL INFORMATION SERVICE (US).**
— GOVERNMENT REPORTS ANNOUNCEMENTS (US).                              XXX
— GOVERNMENT REPORTS INDEX (US).                                      XXX

**NATIONAL UNION OF BANK EMPLOYEES.**
— NUBE NEWS. THE BANK OFFICER: JOURNAL OF ...

**NATIONAL UNION OF SHEET METAL WORKERS, COPPER-
SMITHS, HEATING & DOMESTIC ENGINEERS.**
— JOURNAL, NATIONAL UNION OF SHEET METAL WORK-
  ERS, COPPERSMITHS, HEATING & DOMESTIC ENGIN-
  EERS: N.S.

**NATIONAL UNION OF SOUTH AFRICAN STUDENTS.**
— NEWSLETTER, NATIONAL UNION OF SOUTH AFRICAN
  STUDENTS.

**NATIONAL UNION OF TEACHERS.**
— N.U.T. NEWS.
— SECONDARY EDUCATION.                                                XXX

**NATIONAL VETERINARY ASSAY LABORATORY (JAP.)**                       000
**SEE: DOBUTSU IYAKUHIN KENSAJO.**

**NATIONAL WESTMINSTER BANK GROUP.**
— NATIONAL WESTMINSTER. STAFF MAGAZINE OF...
— QUARTERLY REVIEW, NATIONAL WESTMINSTER BANK.

**NATIONAL YOUTH TEMPERANCE COUNCIL.**
— NOTES & NEWS, NATIONAL YOUTH TEMPERANCE
  COUNCIL.                                                            XXX
  SUBS (1967): TREND.
— TREND.

**NATO.**                                                             000
**SEE: NORTH ATLANTIC TREATY ORGANISATION.**

**NATURAL ENVIRONMENT RESEARCH COUNCIL (GB).**
— NERC NEWS JOURNAL.
— PUBLICATIONS, NATURAL ENVIRONMENT RESEARCH
  COUNCIL (GB): SERIES B.
— PUBLICATIONS, NATURAL ENVIRONMENT RESEARCH
  COUNCIL (GB): SERIES C.
— PUBLICATIONS, NATURAL ENVIRONMENT RESEARCH
  COUNCIL (GB): SERIES D.

**NATURAL HISTORY & ANTIQUARIAN SOCIETY OF MID
ARGYLL.**
— KIST. MAGAZINE OF THE...

**NATURE CONSERVANCY (US).**
— CONTRIBUTIONS, NATURE CONSERVANCY (US).

**NATURE CONSERVATION BRANCH (SOUTH AFRICA).**
— BULLETIN, NATURE CONSERVATION BRANCH (SOUTH
  AFRICA).

**NATURKUNDEMUSEUM IM OTTONEUM ZU KASSEL.**
— PHILIPPIA.

**NAUCHNO DRUZHESTVO NA KHIGIENISTI, EPIDEMIOL-
OZI, MIKROBIOLOZI, INFEKTSIONISTI I ORGANIZ-
ATORI NA ZDRAVEOPAZVANETO.**
— EPIDEMIOLOGIJA, MIKROBIOLOGIJA I INFEKTSIOZNI
  BOLESTI.

**NAUCHNO DRUZHESTVO NA ONKOLOZITE.**
— ONKOLOGIJA.

**NAUCHNO-ISSLEDOVATEL'SKIJ EKONOMICHESKIJ
INSTITUT.**
— OCHERKI PO SOVREMENNOJ SOVETSKOJ I
  ZARUBEZHNOJ EKONOMIKE.

**NAUCHNO-ISSLEDOVATEL'SKIJ INSTITUT ELEKTROFIZI-
CHESKOJ APPARATURY [IM. D.V. EFREMOVA].**
— ELEKTROFIZICHESKAJA APPARATURA.

**NAUCHNO-ISSLEDOVATEL'SKIJ INSTITUT GEOLOGII
ARKTIKI.**
— UCHENYE ZAPISKI, NAUCHNO-ISSLEDOVATEL'SKIJ
  INSTITUT GEOLOGII ARKTIKI: PALENTOLOGIJA I
  BIOSTRATIGRAFIJA.
— UCHENYE ZAPISKI, NAUCHNO-ISSLEDOVATEL'SKIJ
  INSTITUT GEOLOGII ARKTIKI: REGIONAL'NAJA
  GEOLOGIJA.

**NAUCHNO-ISSLEDOVATEL'SKIJ INSTITUT JAZYKA,
LITERATURY, ISTORII I EKONOMIKI.**
— ZAPISKI, NAUCHNO-ISSLEDOVATEL'SKIJ INSTITUT
  JAZYKA, LITERATURY, ISTORII I EKONOMIKI.                            XXX
  SUBS (1960): TRUDY MORDOVSKOGO NAUCHNO-
  ISSLEDOVATEL'SKOGO INSTITUTA JAZYKA,
  LITERATURY, ISTORII I EKONOMIKI.

**NAUCHNO-ISSLEDOVATEL'SKIJ INSTITUT METROLOGII
VYSSHIKH UCHEBNYKH ZAVEDENIJ.**
— TEKHNICHESKIE IZMERENIJA V MASHINOSTROENII.

**NAUCHNO-ISSLEDOVATEL'SKIJ INSTITUT PO PROEKTIR-
OVANIJU VYCHISLITEL'NYKH TSENTROV I SISTEM
EKONOMICHESKOJ INFORMATSII.**
— STATISTIKA & ELEKTRONNO-VYCHISLITEL'NAJA
  TEKHNIKA V EKONOMIKE. SBORNIK STATEJ.

**NAUCHNO-ISSLEDOVATEL'SKIJ INSTITUT STROITEL'NOJ
FIZIKI: OTDEL INFORMATSIONNO-IZDATEL'SKOJ I
PATENTNO-LITSENZIONNOJ RABOTY.**
— RESHENIE ZADACH STROITEL'NOJ FIZIKI NA
  TSIFROVYKH I ANALOGOVYKH MASHINAKH.

NAUCHNO-ISSLEDOVATEL'SKIJ INSTITUT TJAZHELOGO
MASHINOSTROENIJA.
— KONSTRUIROVANIE KRUPNYKH MASHIN.                                                            XXX

NAUCHNO-ISSLEDOVATEL'SKIJ I KONSTRUKTORSKO-
TEKHNOLOGICHESKIJ INSTITUT GORODSKOGO
KHOZJAJSTVA.
— NAUKA I TEKHNIKA V GORODSKOM KHOZJAJSTVE.

NAUCHNO-TEKHNICHESKOE OBSHCHESTVO ENERGOPROMY-
SHLENNOSTI UKRAINSKOJ SSR: OBLSTNYE PRAVLENIJA.
— ENERGETIKA I ELEKTRIFIKATSIJA.                                                                XXX

NAUCHNO-TEKHNICHESKOE OBSHCHESTVO MASHINO-
STROITEL'NOJ PROMYSHLENNOSTI: SEKTSIJA METAL-
LOVEDENIJA I TERMICHESKOJ OBRABOTKI.
— METALLOVEDENIE I TERMICHESKAJA OBRABOTKA.                                     XXX
— TRUDY SEKTSII METALLOVEDENIJA I TERMICHESKOJ
OBRABOTKI, NAUCHNO-TEKHNICHESKOE OBSHCHESTVO
MASHINOSTROITEL'NOJ PROMYSHLENNOSTI.                                                XXX
SUBS (1964): METALLOVEDENIE I TERMICHESKAJA
OBRABOTKA.

NAUCHNO-TEKHNICHESKOE OBSHCHESTVO RADIOTEKHNIKI
I ELEKTROSVJAZI: ANTENNAJA SEKTSIJA.
— ANTENNY. SBORNIK.

NEBRASKA ACADEMY OF SCIENCES.
— TRANSACTIONS OF THE NEBRASKA ACADEMY OF
SCIENCES.

NECESSITY FOR CHANGE INSTITUTE OF IDEOLOGICAL
STUDIES.
— LITERATURE & IDEOLOGY.
— LITERATURE & IDEOLOGY MONOGRAPH.

NEDERLANDS AKOESTISCH GENOOTSCHAP.
— PUBLIKATIE, NEDERLANDS AKOESTISCH GENOOTSCHAP.

NEDERLANDSE DIERKUNDIGE VERENIGING.                                                  000
SEE: NETHERLANDS ZOOLOGICAL SOCIETY.

NEDERLANDS HISTORISCH-ARCHEOLOGISCH INSTITUUT
IN HET NABIJE OOSTEN.
— ANATOLICA. ANNUAIRE INTERNATIONAL POUR LES
CIVILISATIONS DE L'ASIE ANTERIEURE.

NEDERLANDS HISTORISCH INSTITUUT TE ROME.
— ARCHEOLOGISCHE STUDIEN, NEDERLANDS HISTORISCH
INSTITUUT TE ROME.

NEDERLANDSE LIBELLENONDERZOEKERS.
— CONTACTBRIEF NEDERLANDSE LIBELLENONDERZOEKERS.

NEDERLANDSE ORGANISATIE VAN PLUIMVEEHOUDERS.
— PLUIMVEEHOUDERIJ.                                                                                   XXX

NEDERLANDSE TECHNISCHE VERENIGING VOOR VERWARM-
ING EN LUCHTBEHANDELING.
— TVVL.

NEDERLANDSCHE VEREENIGING VAN ANTIQUAREN.
— ANTIQUAAR. TIJDSCHRIFT VAN DE NEDERLANDSCHE
VEREENIGING VAN ANTIQUAREN.

NEDERLANDSE VERENIGING VOOR GEODESIE.
— NEDERLANDS GEODETISCH TIJDSCHRIFT.                                               XXX

NEDERLANDSE VERENIGING VOOR KOELTECHNIEK.
— KOELTECHNIEK (LEIDEN &C.).                                                               XXX
SUBS (1970): KOELTECHNIEK - KLIMAATREGELING.
— KOELTECHNIEK - KLIMAATREGELING.                                                        XXX

NEPAL ECONOMIC & COMMERCE RESEARCH CENTRE.
— COMMERCE (NEPAL).

(NEPAL) MINISTRY OF FORESTS: DEPARTMENT OF
MEDICINAL PLANTS.
— BULLETIN, DEPARTMENT OF MEDICINAL PLANTS,
MINISTRY OF FORESTS(NEPAL).

(NEPAL) MINISTRY OF INFORMATION & BROADCASTING.
— BIBLIOGRAPHY ON NEPAL.

NEPAL RASTRA BANK.
— QUARTERLY ECONOMIC BULLETIN, NEPAL RASTRA
BANK.

NETHERLANDS CHAMBER OF COMMERCE IN THE UNITED
KINGDOM.
— IN TOUCH.

NETHERLANDS HYDROGRAPHIC OFFICE.
— HYDROGRAPHIC NEWSLETTER.

(NETHERLANDS) MINISTERIE VAN LANDBOUW EN
VISSERIJ: DIRECTIE BEDRIJFSONTWIKKELING.
— BEDRIJFSONTWIKKELING. EDITIE AKKERBOUW.                                     XXX
— BEDRIJFSONTWIKKELING. EDITIE TUINBOUW.                                        XXX
— BEDRIJFSONTWIKKELING. EDITIE VEEHOUDERIJ.                                    XXX

NETHERLANDS NITROGEN FERTILIZER INDUSTRY
AGRICULTURAL BUREAU.
— NN. NETHERLANDS NITROGEN TECHNICAL BULLETIN.

NETHERLANDS ZOOLOGICAL SOCIETY.
— NETHERLANDS JOURNAL OF ZOOLOGY= ARCHIVES
NEERLANDAISES DE ZOOLOGIE.

NEUTRON DATA COMPILATION CENTRE.
— NEWSLETTER, NEUTRON DATA COMPILATION CENTRE.

NEW DEMOCRATIC PARTY OF ONTARIO.
— NEW DEMOCRAT.

NEW ENGLAND MARINE RESOURCES INFORMATION
PROGRAM.
— NEW ENGLAND MARINE RESOURCES INFORMATION.

NEW ENGLAND SCHOOL OF LAW.                                                                   XXX
— NEW ENGLAND LAW REVIEW.                                                                    XXX

NEW GLASGOW SOCIETY.
— NGS NEWS.

(NEW JERSEY) STATE MUSEUM.
— SCIENCE NOTES.

(NEW MEXICO) STATE BUREAU OF MINES & MINERAL
RESOURCES.
— HYDROLOGIC REPORT (NEW MEXICO).
— MINERAL RESOURCES REPORT (NEW MEXICO).

NEW MEXICO INSTITUTE OF MINING & TECHNOLOGY.
— MINERAL RESOURCES REPORT (NEW MEXICO).

NEW MEXICO ORNITHOLOGICAL SOCIETY.
— PUBLICATIONS, NEW MEXICO ORNITHOLOGICAL
SOCIETY.

NEW MEXICO STATE UNIVERSITY; OBSERVATORY.
— CONTRIBUTIONS OF THE OBSERVATORY, NEW
MEXICO STATE UNIVERSITY.

NEW MILLS NATURAL HISTORY SOCIETY.
— BULLETIN, NEW MILLS NATURAL HISTORY SOCIETY.

NEW NIPPON ELECTRIC CO.                                                                          000
SEE: SHIN NIHON DENKI K.K.

NEW ORLEANS CONSORTIUM.
— NEW ORLEANS REVIEW.

(NEW SOUTH WALES) DEPARTMENT OF AGRICULTURE:
ENTOMOLOGY BRANCH.
— INSECT PEST BULLETIN.

NEW TOWNS ASSOCIATION.
— NEW TOWNS BULLETIN.

NEW YORK C.S. LEWIS SOCIETY.
— BULLETIN, NEW YORK C.S. LEWIS SOCIETY.

NEW YORK GAELIC SOCIETY.                                                                         000
SEE: CUMANN NA GAEILGE (NEW YORK).

NEW YORK QUARTERLY POETRY REVIEW FOUNDATION,
INC.
— NEW YORK QUARTERLY.

NEW YORK SHAKESPEARE FESTIVAL PUBLIC THEATER.
— SCRIPTS. A MONTHLY OF PLAYS & THEATER PIECES.

NEW YORK (STATE) AGRICULTURAL EXPERIMENT
STATION.
— PLANT SCIENCES - ENTOMOLOGY.
— SPECIAL REPORT, AGRICULTURAL EXPERIMENT STAT-
ION, NEW YORK (STATE).

NEW YORK STATE COLLEGE.
— SATIRE NEWSLETTER.

NEW YORK STATE FLOWER GROWERS, INC.                                             XXX
— BULLETIN, NEW YORK STATE FLOWER GROWERS, INC.              XXX
SUBS (1970): NYSFI BULLETIN.

NEW YORK STATE FLOWER INDUSTRIES, INC.                                       XXX
— NYSFI BULLETIN.                                                                                    XXX

NEW YORK STATE SCHOOL OF INDUSTRIAL & LABOR
RELATIONS.
— ILR RESEARCH.                                                    XXX
  SUBS (1969): ISSUES IN INDUSTRIAL SOCIETY.
— ISSUES IN INDUSTRIAL SOCIETY.                                    XXX

NEW YORK UNIVERSITY: DEPARTMENT OF CLASSICS.
— MONOGRAPHS ON MEDITERRANEAN ANTIQUITY.

NEW YORK UNIVERSITY: INTERNATIONAL LAW SOCIETY.
— NEW YORK UNIVERSITY JOURNAL OF INTERNATIONAL
  LAW & POLITICS.

NEW ZEALAND AGRICULTURAL ENGINEERING INSTITUTE.
— ANNUAL REPORT, NEW ZEALAND AGRICULTURAL ENGIN-
  EERING INSTITUTE.
— EXTENSION BULLETIN, NEW ZEALAND AGRICULTURAL
  ENGINEERING INSTITUTE.
— RESEARCH PUBLICATION, NEW ZEALAND AGRICUL-
  TURAL ENGINEERING INSTITUTE.

NEW ZEALAND ASSOCIATION OF HEALTH, PHYSICAL
EDUCATION & RECREATION.
— NEW ZEALAND JOURNAL OF HEALTH, PHYSICAL EDU-
  CATION & RECREATION.

NEW ZEALAND GEOGRAPHICAL SOCIETY.
— NEW ZEALAND JOURNAL OF GEOGRAPHY.                                XXX
— PERSPECTIVE (N.Z.).
— RECORD OF PROCEEDINGS OF THE NEW ZEALAND GEO
  GRAPHICAL SOCIETY.                                               XXX
  SUBS (1969): NEW ZEALAND JOURNAL OF
  GEOGRAPHY.

NEW ZEALAND GEOGRAPHICAL SOCIETY: WAIKATO
BRANCH.
— PUBLICATIONS, WAIKATO BRANCH, NEW ZEALAND
  GEOGRAPHICAL SOCIETY.

NEW ZEALAND INSTITUTE OF CHEMISTRY.
— CHEMISTRY IN NEW ZEALAND.                                        XXX
— JOURNAL OF THE NEW ZEALAND INSTITUTE OF
  CHEMISTRY.                                                       XXX
  SUBS (1968): CHEMISTRY IN NEW ZEALAND.

NEW ZEALAND INSTITUTE OF ECONOMIC RESEARCH INC.
— PUBLICATIONS OF THE CONTRACT RESEARCH UNIT,
  NEW ZEALAND INSTITUTE OF ECONOMIC RESEARCH.

(NEW ZEALAND) MARINE DEPARTMENT: FISHERIES
RESEARCH DIVISION.
— FISHERIES RESEARCH BULLETIN.

NEW ZEALAND OCEANOGRAPHIC INSTITUTE.
— NZOI RECORDS.

(NEW ZEALAND) SOIL CONSERVATION & RIVERS
CONTROL COUNCIL.
— SOIL & WATER.

NEWBERRY LIBRARY.
— FAMILY IN HISTORICAL PERSPECTIVE.

NEWCASTLE N.S.W. FLORA & FAUNA PROTECTION
SOCIETY.
— HUNTER NATURAL HISTORY.

NEWCASTLE, N.S.W., PUBLIC LIBRARY.
— NEWCASTLE HISTORY MONOGRAPHS.

NEWCASTLE UPON TYNE POLYTECHNIC.
— BULLETIN OF EDUCATIONAL RESEARCH.

NIEDERSACHSISCHE LANDESZENTRALE FUR POLITISCHE
BILDUNG.
— SCHRIFTENREIHE, NIEDERSACHSISCHE LANDESZENT-
  RALE FUR POLITISCHE BILDUNG: BEITRAGE ZUR
  POLITISCHEN BILDUNG AN VOLKSSCHULEN.

(NIGERIA) FEDERAL FISHERIES SERVICE.
— FEDERAL FISHERIES OCCASIONAL PAPER (NIGERIA).

(NIGERIA) FEDERAL MINISTRY OF INFORMATION.
— TOWARDS ONE NIGERIA.

(NIGERIA) METEOROLOGICAL SERVICE.
— QUARTERLY METEOROLOGICAL MAGAZINE (NIGERIA).

NIGERIAN INSTITUTE OF INTERNATIONAL AFFAIRS.
— LECTURE SERIES, NIGERIAN INSTITUTE OF INTER-
  NATIONAL AFFAIRS.
— NIGERIA. BULLETIN ON FOREIGN AFFAIRS.

NIGERIAN INSTITUTE FOR OIL PALM RESEARCH.
— ANNUAL REPORT, NIGERIAN INSTITUTE FOR OIL
  PALM RESEARCH.

NIGERIAN MEDICAL ASSOCIATION.
— NIGERIAN MEDICAL JOURNAL.

NIGERIAN MINING, GEOLOGICAL & METALLURGICAL
SOCIETY.
— JOURNAL OF MINING & GEOLOGY.                                    XXX
— JOURNAL OF THE NIGERIAN MINING, GEOLOGICAL &
  METALLURGICAL SOCIETY.                                          XXX

NIGERIAN PHARMACEUTICAL & MEDICAL COMPANY.
— AFRICAN JOURNAL OF PHARMACY & PHARMACEUTICAL
  SCIENCES.

NIGERIAN SOCIETY OF CONTEMPORARY LAW.
— NIGERIAN JOURNAL OF CONTEMPORARY LAW.

NIGERIAN SOCIETY OF ENGINEERS.
— NIGERIAN ENGINEER.

NIHON ...
  NIHON ... & NIPPON ... HERE INTERFILED.

NIHON DENKI KEIKI KENTEIJO.
— DENKI KENTEIJO GIHO. JEMIC TECHNICAL REPORT.

NIHON HACHU RYOSEIRUI GAKKAI.
— HACHU RYOSEIRUIGAKU ZASSHI. ACTA HERPETO-
  LOGICA JAPONICA.

NIHON HACHURI GAKKAI.
— HACHURUIGAKU ZASSHI. ACTA HERPETOLOGICA
  JAPONICA.                                                       XXX

NIPPON INSTITUTE OF TECHNOLOGY.                                   000
  SEE: NIHON KOGYO DAIGAKU.

NIHON KAI-IKI KENKYUJO.
— NIHON KAI-IKI KENKYUJO HOKOKU. BULLETIN OF
  THE JAPAN SEA RESEARCH INSTITUTE.

NIHON KOGYO DAIGAKU.
— NIHON KOGYO DAIGAKU KENKYU HOKOKU. REPORT
  OF RESEARCHES, NIPPON INSTITUTE OF TECHNOLOGY.

NIHON NOGEI KAGAKKAI.
— KAGAKU TO SEIBUTSU. CHEMISTRY & BIOLOGY.

NIPPON OYO-DOBUTSI-KONCHU GAKKAI.
— APPLIED ENTOMOLOGY & ZOOLOGY.
— REVIEW OF PLANT PROTECTION RESEARCH.

NIHON SHONI GEKKA GAKKAI.
— NIHON SHONI GEKKA GAKKAI ZASSHI. JOURNAL OF
  THE JAPANESE SOCIETY OF PEDIATRIC SURGEONS.

NIHON SHOYU GIJUTSUKAI.
— SHOYU TO GIJUTSU. SHOYU & TECHNICS.                            XXX

NIPPON STEEL CORPORATION.                                        000
  SEE: SHIN NIHON SEITETSU K.K.

NIHON TAIYO ENERUGI RIYO KYOKAI.
— TAIYO ENERUGI. SOLAR ENERGY.                                   XXX

NIHON TOKEI GAKKAISHI.
— NIHON TOKEI GAKKAI.

NIHON YUKUATSU KYOKAI.
— YUATSU TO KUKIATSU. JOURNAL, JAPAN HYDRAUL-
  ICS & PNEUMATICS SOCIETY.

NIHON YUNIBAKKU SOGO KENKYUJO, K.K.
— NIHON YUNIBAKKU SOGO KENKYUJO, K.K. SOKEN
  KIYO.

NIHON ZASSO BOJO KENKYUKAI.
— ZASSO KENKYU. WEED RESEARCH.

NIIGATA DAIGAKU KYOYOBU.
— NIIGATA DAIGAKU KYOYOBU KENKYU KIYO. JOURNAL
  OF GENERAL EDUCATION DEPARTMENT, NIIGATA UNI-
  VERSITY.

NIIGATA DAIGAKU NOGAKUBU FUZOKU ENSHURIN.
— NIIGATA DAIGAKU NOGAKUBU ENSHURIN HOKOKU.
  BULLETIN OF THE NIIGATA UNIVERSITY FORESTS.

NIIGATA UNIVERSITY: GENERAL EDUCATION DEPART-
MENT.                                                            000
  SEE: NIIGATA DAIGAKU KYOYOBU.

NIIGATA UNIVERSITY FORESTS.                                      000
  SEE: NIIGATA DAIGAKU NOGAKUBU FUZOKU ENSHURIN

NIPPON ...                                                       000
  FILED AS: NIHON ...

NONDESTRUCTIVE TESTING CENTRE (HARWELL).
— INFORMATION BULLETIN, NONDESTRUCTIVE TESTING
CENTRE.                                                                                                          XXX
— NDT INFO. THE INFORMATION BULLETIN OF THE ...

NORDIC ASSOCIATION FOR AMERICAN STUDIES.                                               000
SEE: NORDISKA SALLSKAPET FOR AMERIKASTUDIER.

NORDISK INSTITUT FOR FOLKEDIGTNING.
— SKRIFTSERIE, NORDISK INSTITUT FOR FOLKEDIGTN-
ING.

NORDISKA ODONTOLOGISKA FORENINGEN.
— ODONTOLOGISK TIDSKRIFT.                                                                        XXX
SUBS (1970): SCANDINAVIAN JOURNAL OF DENTAL
RESEARCH.
— SCANDINAVIAN JOURNAL OF DENTAL RESEARCH.                                         XXX

NORDISKA SALLSKAPET FOR AMERIKASTUDIER.
— AMERICAN STUDIES IN SCANDINAVIA.

NORDISK SOCIALMEDICINSK FOERENING.
— ACTA SOCIO-MEDICA SCANDINAVICA.                                                           XXX
— SCANDINAVIAN JOURNAL OF SOCIAL MEDICINE.                                        XXX

NORFOLK ARCHITECTS ASSOCIATION.
— NORFOLK ARCHITECTS ASSOCIATION BROADSHEET.

NORFOLK REED GROWERS ASSOCIATION.
— MONOGRAPH, NORFOLK REED GROWERS ASSOCIATION.

NORGES ALMENVITENSKAPELIGE FORSKNINGSRAAD.
— MARINE INVERTEBRATES OF SCANDINAVIA.

NORGES BYGGFORSKNINGSINSTITUTT.
— BYGGFORSK INFORMERER OM BYGGSKADER.

NORGES LANDBRUKSOKONOMISKE INSTITUTT.
— DRIFTSFORMER I LANDBRUKET.

NORGES TEKNISK-NATURVITENSKAPELIGE FORSKNINGS-
RAD: TRANSPORTEKONOMISK INSTITUTT.
— SAMFERDSEL, TRANSPORTEKONOMISK INSTITUTT,
NORGES TEKNISK-NATURVITENSKAPELIGE FORSK-
NINGSRAD.

NORGES TEKNISKE HOGSKOLE: INSTITUTT FOR
FORBRENNINGSMOTORER.
— RAPPORT, INSTITUTT FOR FORBRENNINGSMOTORER,
NORGES TEKNISKE HOGSKOLE.

NORGREN FLUIDICS.
— NEWS SHEET, NORGREN FLUIDICS.

NORIN-SHO NOGYO DOBOKU SHIKENJO.
— NOGYO DOBOKU SHIKENJO GIHO; C: ZOKO. TECH-
NICAL REPORT OF THE AGRICULTURAL ENGINEERING
RESEARCH STATION; C: CONSTRUCTION ENGINEERING.
— NOGYO DOBOKU SHIKENJO HOKOKU.

NORIN-SHO NORIN SUISAN GIJUTSU KAIGI.
— JARQ. JAPAN AGRICULTURAL RESEARCH QUARTERLY.
— KOGAI KANKEI KENKYU SEIKA SHOROKU.
— TROPICAL AGRICULTURE RESEARCH SERIES (JAPAN).

NORSK LEPIDOPTERISK SELSKAP.
— ATALANTA NORVEGICA.*

NORTH ATLANTIC TREATY ORGANIZATION.
— NATO LETTER.                                                                                                  XXX
SUBS (1971): NATO REVIEW.
— NATO REVIEW.                                                                                                   XXX

NORTH ATLANTIC TREATY ORGANIZATION: INFORMATION
SERVICE.
— NATO LATEST.
— SPEAKERS' NOTES.

NORTH CAROLINA STATE UNIVERSITY AT RALEIGH:
SCHOOL OF ENGINEERING.
— FURNITURE INDEX.

(NORTH DAKOTA) GEOLOGICAL SURVEY.
— EDUCATIONAL SERIES, GEOLOGICAL SURVEY (NORTH
DAKOTA).

NORTH EAST DEVELOPMENT COUNCIL.
— NORTH EAST NEWS.

NORTH OF SCOTLAND COLLEGE OF AGRICULTURE.
— BULLETIN, NORTH OF SCOTLAND COLLEGE OF AGRI-
CULTURE.
— LEAFLET, NORTH OF SCOTLAND COLLEGE OF AGRI-
CULTURE. NS.
— REPORT, NORTH OF SCOTLAND COLLEGE OF AGRIC-
ULTURE.

NORTH OF SCOTLAND COLLEGE OF AGRICULTURE:
AGRICULTURAL ECONOMICS DIVISION.
— FARM MANAGEMENT REVIEW.                                                                 XXX

NORTH OF SCOTLAND COLLEGE OF AGRICULTURE:
GRASSLAND HUSBANDRY DIVISION.
— TECHNICAL REPORTS, GRASSLAND HUSBANDRY DIVIS-
ION, NORTH OF SCOTLAND COLLEGE OF AGRICULTURE.

NORTH STAFFORDSHIRE POLYTECHNIC.
— JOURNAL OF THE STAFFORDSHIRE INDUSTRIAL
ARCHAEOLOGY SOCIETY.

NORTH TEXAS STATE UNIVERSITY.

NORTH WALES ASSOCIATION FOR THE ARTS.
— MABON.

NORTHAMPTON MUSEUM & ART GALLERY.
— JOURNAL, NORTHAMPTON MUSEUM & ART GALLERY.

NORTHAMPTONSHIRE FEDERATION OF ARCHAEOLOGICAL
SOCIETIES.
— BULLETIN OF THE NORTHAMPTONSHIRE FEDERATION
OF ARCHAEOLOGICAL SOCIETIES.

NORTHAMPTONSHIRE NATURALISTS TRUST.
— BULLETIN, NORTHAMPTONSHIRE NATURALISTS TRUST.

NORTHEASTERN FOREST EXPERIMENT STATION (US).
— GENERAL TECHNICAL REPORT, NORTHEASTERN FOREST
EXPERIMENT STATION (US).

NORTHERN ARIZONA UNIVERSITY; SCHOOL OF FORESTRY
— ARIZONA FORESTRY NOTES.

NORTHERN CAVERN & MINE RESEARCH SOCIETY.
— MEMOIRS, NORTHERN CAVERN & MINE RESEARCH
SOCIETY.                                                                                                             XXX
— OCCASIONAL PUBLICATIONS, NORTHERN CAVERN &
MINE RESEARCH SOCIETY.                                                                              XXX

NORTHERN FOREST EXPERIMENT STATION (US).
— RESEARCH PAPER, NORTHERN FOREST EXPERIMENT
STATION (US).                                                                                                      XXX

NORTHERN ILLINOIS UNIVERSITY: DEPARTMENT OF
SOCIOLOGY.
— JOURNAL OF POLITICAL & MILITARY SOCIOLOGY.

NORTHERN ILLINOIS UNIVERSITY: EARTH SCIENCE
DEPARTMENT.
— PERSPECTIVES IN GEOGRAPHY.

NORTHERN IRELAND COMMUNITY RELATIONS COMMISSION
— COMMUNITY FORUM.

NORTHERN IRELAND LABOUR PARTY.
— LABOUR CHALLENGE.

NORTHERN POETRY WORKSHOP.
— STANZA. A MAGAZINE OF CONTEMPORARY POETRY &
CRITICISM.

NORTHERN RHODESIA CHAMBER OF MINES.
SUBS (1963): COPPERBELT OF ZAMBIA MINING
INDUSTRY YEAR BOOK.

NORTHUMBERLAND LOCAL HISTORY SOCIETY.
— NEWSLETTER, NORTHUMBERLAND LOCAL HISTORY
SOCIETY.

NORTH WESTERN ELECTRICITY BOARD.
— NORWEB NEWS.

NORTH-WESTERN POLYTECHNIC: GEOGRAPHY DEPARTMENT
— GRIFFIN. THE JOURNAL OF THE GEOGRAPHY
DEPARTMENT OF THE NORTH-WESTERN POLYTECHNIC.          XXX

NORTHWESTERN UNIVERSITY.
— TRI-QUARTERLY: SUPPLEMENT.

NORTHWESTERN UNIVERSITY: PROGRAM OF AFRICAN
STUDIES.
— PAN-AFRICANIST.

(NORWAY) ARBEIDSDIREKTORATET.
— PLAN OG ARBEID. TIDSSKRIFT FOR DISTRIKTS-
UTBYGGING, REGIONPLANLEGGING OG SYSSELSETTING.

NORWEGIAN CENTRE FOR INFORMATICS.
— SCANDINAVIAN SHIP ABSTRACT JOURNAL.

NORWEGIAN LEPIDOPTEROLOGICAL SOCIETY.
— ATALANTA NORVEGICA.

NORWICH SCHOOL OF ART: DEPARTMENT OF GRAPHIC DESIGN.
— E.G.

NOTO MARINE LABORATORY.                                    000
SEE:  NOTO RINKAI JIKKENJO.

NOTO RINKAI JIKKENJO.
— NOTO RINKAI JIKKENJO NEMPO.  ANNUAL REPORT OF
THE NOTO MARINE LABORATORY.

NOTRING DER WISSENSCHAFTLICHEN VERBANDE OSTERREICHS.
— GESAMTVERZEICHNIS OSTERREICHISCHER DISSERTATIONEN.

NOTTINGHAM LINGUISTIC CIRCLE.
— NOTTINGHAM LINGUISTIC CIRCULAR.

NOTTINGHAM & NOTTINGHAMSHIRE TECHNICAL INFOR-MATION SERVICE (NANTIS).
— NANTIS NEWS.

NOVA SCOTIA TECHNICAL COLLEGE: SCHOOL OF ARCHI-TECTURE.
— REPORT SERIES, SCHOOL OF ARCHITECTURE, NOVA
SCOTIA TECHNICAL COLLEGE.

NOVOSIBIRSKIJ GOSUDARSTVENNYJ UNIVERSITET.
— NAUCHNYE TRUDY, NOVOSIBIRSKIJ GOSUDARSTVENNYJ
UNIVERSITET: FILOSOFSKAJA SERIJA.
— NAUCHNYE TRUDY, NOVOSIBIRSKIJ GOSUDARSTVENNYJ
UNIVERSITET:  ISTORICHESKAJA SERIJA.
— NAUCHNYE TRUDY, NOVOSIBIRSKIJ GOSUDARSTVENNYJ
UNIVERSITET: SERIJA EKONOMICHESKAJA.

NOYES DEVELOPMENT CORPORATION.
— CHEMICAL PROCESS REVIEW.
— ELECTRONICS MATERIALS REVIEW.
— FOOD PROCESSING REVIEW.
— NEW CHEMICAL PRODUCTS QUARTERLY.

NUFFIELD ORTHOPAEDIC CENTRE: DEPARTMENT OF ORTHOPAEDIC SURGERY.
— ORTHOPAEDICS: OXFORD.

NUMAZU KOGYO KOTO SENMON GAKKO.
— NUMAZU KOGYO KOTO SENMON GAKKO KENKYU HOKOKU.
RESEARCH REPORTS OF NUMAZU TECHNICAL COLLEGE.

NUMAZU TECHNICAL COLLEGE.                                  000
SEE: NUMAZU KOGYO KOTO SENMON GAKKO.

NUMISMATIC SOCIETY OF IRELAND.
— OCCASIONAL PAPERS, NUMISMATIC SOCIETY OF
IRELAND.

(NYASALAND) GEOLOGICAL SURVEY.                             XXX
— RECORDS OF THE GEOLOGICAL SURVEY OF
NYASALAND.                                                 XXX
SUBS (1961): RECORDS OF THE GEOLOGICAL
SURVEY OF MALAWI.

NYU SAIENSU-SHA.
— KONCHU TO SHIZEN.  NATURE & INSECTS.

OAK RIDGE ASSOCIATED UNIVERSITIES.
— ANNUAL REPORT, OAK RIDGE ASSOCIATED UNIVER-
SITIES.

OBERLIN COLLEGE.
— FIELD. CONTEMPORARY POETRY & POETICS.

OBSERVATORIO ASTRONOMICO NACIONAL (COLOMBIA).
— PUBLICACIONES DEL OBSERVATORIO ASTRONOMICO
NACIONAL (COLOMBIA).

OBSHCHESTVENA KULTURNO-PROSVETNA ORGANIZATSIJA NA EVREITE V NARODNA REPUBLIKA BULGARIJA.
— GODISHNIK, OBSHCHESTVENA KULTURNO-PROSVETNA
ORGANIZATSIJA NA EVREITE V NARODNA REPUBLIKA
BULGARIJA.

OCEAN ENGINEERING INFORMATION SERVICE.
— OCEANIC INSTRUMENTATION REPORTER.

OCEANIC RESEARCH INSTITUTE (US).
— OCEANIC CITATION JOURNAL.                                XXX
— OCEANIC INDEX.                                           XXX
— OCEANIC INDEX - CITATION JOURNAL.                        XXX

OCEANOLOGICAL SOCIETY OF KOREA.
— JOURNAL, OCEANOLOGICAL SOCIETY OF KOREA.

ODENSE UNIVERSITET.
— ETUDES ROMANES DE L'UNIVERSITE D'ODENSE.
— ODENSE UNIVERSITY CLASSICAL STUDIES.
— ODENSE UNIVERSITY STUDIES IN ENGLISH.
— ODENSE UNIVERSITY STUDIES IN LINGUISTICS.
— ODENSE UNIVERSITY STUDIES IN LITERATURE.
— ODENSE UNIVERSITY STUDIES IN PHILOSOPHY.

ODENSE UNIVERSITETSBIBLIOTEK.
— NYANSKAFFET UDENLANDSK LITTERATUR.

ODESSKIJ GIDROMETEOROLOGICHESKIJ INSTITUT.
— METEOROLOGIJA, KLIMATOLOGIJA I GIDROLOGIJA.

ODESSKIJ POLITEKHNICHESKIJ INSTITUT.
— ELEKTROMASHINOSTROENIE I ELEKTROOBORUDOVANIE.

ODINIST COMMITTEE.
— RAVEN BANNER.  A FORUM FOR THE DISCUSSION &
PROPAGATION OF ODINIST PRINCIPLES.

OECD.
— ACTIVITIES OF OECD.
— CHANGES IN EMPLOYMENT STRUCTURE.
— OECD FINANCIAL STATISTICS.
— OECD POPULATION ABSTRACTS.
— SCIENCE POLICY INFORMATION.                             XXX
— SCIENCE POLICY NEWS.                                    XXX
— SOURCES & METHODS.

OECD: CENTRE FOR EDUCATIONAL RESEARCH & INNOVATION.
— INNOVATION IN EDUCATION.

OECD:  DEVELOPMENT CENTRE.
— LATEST INFORMATION ON NATIONAL ACCOUNTS OF
LESS DEVELOPED COUNTRIES.
— TECHNICAL PAPERS, DEVELOPMENT CENTRE, OECD.

OFFICE DE LA RECHERCHE SCIENTIFIQUE ET TECHNIQUE OUTRE-MER (FRANCE).
— CAHIERS ORSTOM:  SERIE GEOLOGIE.
— CAHIERS ORSTOM: SERIE SCIENCES HUMAINES.

OFFICE DE LA RECHERCHE SCIENTIFIQUE ET TECH-NIQUE OUTRE-MER(FRANCE): CENTRE DE NOUMEA. SECTION OCEANOGRAPHIE.
— RECUEIL DE TRAVAUX, SECTION OCEANOGRAPHIE,
CENTRE DE NOUMEA, OFFICE DE LA RECHERCHE
SCIENTIFIQUE ET TECHNIQUE OUTRE-MER.

OGOLNOPOLSKI ORGAN SZKOL WYZSZYCH.
— STUDIA O KSIAZCE.                                        XXX

OHIO BIOLOGICAL SURVEY.
— BIOLOGICAL NOTES, OHIO BIOLOGICAL SURVEY.

(OHIO) DEPARTMENT OF NATURAL RESOURCES; DIVISION OF WILDLIFE.
— GAME RESEARCH IN OHIO.

OHIO HERPETOLOGICAL SOCIETY.
— JOURNAL, OHIO HERPETOLOGICAL SOCIETY.           XXX
SUBS (1968):  JOURNAL OF HERPETOLOGY.

(OHIO) OFFICE OF OPPORTUNITY.
— OHIO OPPORTUNITY IN ACTION.

OHIO STATE UNIVERSITY: INSTITUTE OF POLAR STUDIES.
— NEWSLETTER, INSTITUTE OF POLAR STUDIES, OHIO
STATE UNIVERSITY.

OHIO UNIVERSITY.
— MUNDUS ARTIUM.  A JOURNAL OF INTERNATIONAL
LITERATURE & THE ARTS.

OHIO UNIVERSITY: BLACK STUDIES INSTITUTE.
— CONFRONTATION.

OHIO UNIVERSITY: DEPARTMENT OF ENGLISH.
— MILTON NEWSLETTER.                                      XXX
— MILTON QUARTERLY.                                       XXX

OIL & NATURAL GAS COMMISSION (INDIA).
— BULLETIN, OIL & NATURAL GAS COMMISSION(INDIA).

OKLAHOMA ACADEMY OF SCIENCE.
— ANNALS, OKLAHOMA ACADEMY OF SCIENCE.

OLD ATHLONE SOCIETY.
— JOURNAL OF THE OLD ATHLONE SOCIETY.

OLD CARLOW SOCIETY.
— CARLOVIANA. NS.  JOURNAL OF THE ...

OLD MOTOR CLUB.
— OLD MOTOR NEWS.

OLD WEXFORD SOCIETY.
— JOURNAL OF THE OLD WEXFORD SOCIETY.

ONTARIO COLLEGE OF PHARMACY.
— BULLETIN, ONTARIO COLLEGE OF PHARMACY.          XXX

(ONTARIO) DEPARTMENT OF EDUCATION.
— ONTARIO EDUCATION/1966.

(ONTARIO) DEPARTMENT OF LANDS & FORESTS.
— ONTARIO FISH & WILDLIFE REVIEW.

(ONTARIO) DEPARTMENT OF MINES.
— GEOLOGY & SCENERY. GEOLOGICAL GUIDE BOOK.

ONTARIO INSTITUTE OF CHARTERED CARTOGRAPHERS.
— CARTOGRAPHER.          XXX

ONTARIO INSTITUTE FOR STUDIES IN EDUCATION.
— INTERCHANGE. A JOURNAL OF EDUCATIONAL
STUDIES.
— ORBIT.

ONTARIO NURSERY TRADES ASSOCIATION.
— CANADIAN NURSERYMAN.

OPEN UNIVERSITY.
— SESAME. THE NEWSPAPER OF THE OPEN UNIVERSITY.

OPTICAL SOCIETY OF AMERICA.
— OPTICS & SPECTROSCOPY: SUPPLEMENT.
— SOVIET JOURNAL OF OPTICAL TECHNOLOGY.

OPTICAL SOCIETY OF INDIA.
— JOURNAL OF OPTICS.

ORANGE COUNTY (CALIFORNIA) GENEALOGICAL SOCIETY
— QUARTERLY, ORANGE COUNTY CALIFORNIA GENEAL-
OGICAL SOCIETY.

(OREGON) FISH COMMISSION.
— RESEARCH REPORTS, FISH COMMISSION (OREGON).

OREGON STATE COLLEGE: ENGINEERING EXPERIMENT
STATION.          XXX
— CIRCULAR, ENGINEERING EXPERIMENT STATION,
OREGON STATE COLLEGE.          XXX
SUBS (1962): CIRCULAR, ENGINEERING EXPER-
IMENT STATION, OREGON STATE UNIVERSITY.

OREGON STATE UNIVERSITY: ENGINEERING EXPERIMENT
STATION.          XXX
— CIRCULAR, ENGINEERING EXPERIMENT STATION,
OREGON STATE UNIVERSITY.          XXX

OREGON STATE UNIVERSITY: GENETICS INSTITUTE.
— GENETICS LECTURES, GENETICS INSTITUTE, OREGON
STATE UNIVERSITY.

ORGANIZATION FOR ECONOMIC CO-OPERATION &
DEVELOPMENT.          000
SEE: OECD.

ORGANISATION INTERNATIONALE POUR L'ETUDE DES
LANGUES ANCIENNES PAR ORDINATEUR.          000
SEE: INTERNATIONAL ORGANIZATION FOR
ANCIENT LANGUAGES ANALYSIS BY COMPUTER.

ORGANIZZAZIONE INTERNAZIONALE TRANSPORTI A
FUNE.
— LIFT. ELEVATOR LIFT & ROPEWAY ENGINEERING.

ORGANISATION & METHODS SOCIETY.
— MANAGEMENT IN ACTION.          XXX

ORGANISATION FOR POSTGRADUATE MEDICAL EDUCA-
TION: NEWCASTLE REGION.
— ADVERSE DRUG REACTION BULLETIN.

ORGANISATION OF REVOLUTIONARY ANARCHISTS.
— LIBERTARIAN STRUGGLE.

ORIJENTALNI INSTITUT U SARAJEVU.
— POSEBNA IZDANJA, ORIJENTALNI INSTITUT U
SARAJEVU.

ORKNEY FIELD CLUB.
— BULLETIN, ORKNEY FIELD CLUB.

ORNITHOLOGICAL SOCIETY OF TURKEY: FOREIGN
SECTION.
— BIRD REPORT, FOREIGN SECTION, ORNITHOLOGICAL
SOCIETY OF TURKEY.

ORSTOM (FRANCE).          000
SEE: OFFICE DE LA RECHERCHE SCIENTIFIQUE ET
TECHNIQUE OUTRE-MER (FRANCE).

OSAKA MUSEUM FOR NATURAL HISTORY.          000
SEE: OSAKA SHIRITSU SHIZEN KAGAKU HAKUBUTSU-
KAN.

OSAKA SHIRITSU SHIZEN KAGAKU HAKUBUTSUKAN.
— SHIZENSHI KENKYU.

OSSERVATORIO ASTRONOMICO DI TRIESTE.
— ANNUARIO ASTRONOMICO, OSSERVATORIO ASTRON-
OMICO DI TRIESTE.          XXX

OSTERREICHISCHE AKADEMIE DER WISSENSCHAFTEN.
— STUDIEN ZUR GESCHICHTE DER OSTERREICHISCH-
UNGARISCHEN MONARCHIE.

OSTERREICHISCHE AKADEMIE DER WISSENSCHAFTEN:
KOMMISSION FUR BYZANTINISTIK.
— WIENER BYZANTINISCHE STUDIEN.

OSTERREICHISCHES ARCHAOLOGISCHES INSTITUT.
— GRABUNGEN, OSTERREICHISCHES ARCHAOLOGISCHES
INSTITUT.

OSTERREICHISCHE BYZANTINISCHE GESELLSCHAFT.
— JAHRBUCH DER OSTERREICHISCHEN BYZANTINISCHEN
GESELLSCHAFT.          XXX
SUBS (1969): JAHRBUCH DER OSTERREICHISCHEN
BYZANTINISTIK.

OSTERREICHISCHE GESELLSCHAFT FUR MUSIK.
— BEITRAGE, OSTERREICHISCHE GESELLSCHAFT FUR
MUSIK.

OSTERREICHISCHE GESELLSCHAFT FUR POLITIKWISSEN-
SCHAFT.
— OSTERREICHISCHE ZEITSCHRIFT FUR POLITIKWISS-
ENSCHAFT.

OSTERREICHISCHE GESELLSCHAFT FUR SOZIOLOGIE.
— OSTERREICHISCHES JAHRBUCH FUR SOZIOLOGIE.

OSTERREICHISCHER INGENIEUR- UND ARCHITEKTEN-
VEREIN: LANDESVEREIN TIROL.
— BEITRAGE ZUR TECHNIKGESCHICHTE TIROLS.

OSTERREICHISCHES INSTITUT FUR WIRTSCHAFTS-
FORSCHUNG.
— FORSCHUNGSBERICHTE, OSTERREICHISCHES INSTITUT
FUR WIRTSCHAFTSFORSCHUNG.

OSTERREICHISCHE KULTURINSTITUT (CAIRO).
— SCHRIFTEN, OSTERREICHISCHE KULTURINSTITUT
(CAIRO).

OSTERREICHISCHES LATEINAMERIKA-INSTITUT.
— ZEITSCHRIFT FUR LATEINAMERIKA. FORSCHUNGEN,
BERICHTE, INFORMATION.

OSTERREICHISCHES NATIONALINSTITUT.
— NATIONSWERDUNG OSTERREICHS. SCHRIFTENREIHE
DES OSTERREICHISCHEN NATIONALINSTITUTS.

OSTERREICHISCHE STUDIENGESELLSCHAFT FUR
ATOMENERGIE.
— ISOTOPE IN INDUSTRIE UND LANDWIRTSCHAFT.

OSTEUROPA-INSTITUT (MUNICH).
— JAHRBUCH DER WIRTSCHAFT OSTEUROPAS. YEARBOOK
OF EAST-EUROPEAN ECONOMICS.

OTAGO MUSEUM.
— OTAGO MUSEUM BULLETIN.

OTANI COLLEGE OF TECHNOLOGY OF TOYAMA.          000
SEE: TOYAMA KENRITSU OTANI GIJUTSU TANKI
DAIGAKU.

OVERSEAS DEVELOPMENT COUNCIL (US).
— COMMUNIQUES ON DEVELOPMENT ISSUES, OVERSEAS
DEVELOPMENT COUNCIL (US).
— DEVELOPMENT PAPERS, OVERSEAS DEVELOPMENT
COUNCIL (US).
— MONOGRAPH SERIES, OVERSEAS DEVELOPMENT
COUNCIL (US).
— OCCASIONAL PAPER, OVERSEAS DEVELOPMENT
COUNCIL (US).

OWENS VALLEY RADIO OBSERVATORY.
— PUBLICATIONS OF THE OWENS VALLEY RADIO
OBSERVATORY.

OXFORD CITY & COUNTY MUSEUM.
— PUBLICATION, OXFORD CITY & COUNTY MUSEUM.

**OXFORD LIBERAL CLUB.**
— FRINGE. OXFORD'S RADICAL MAGAZINE.

**OXFORD POLYTECHNIC: DEPARTMENT OF ARCHITECTURE.**
— SYNTHESIS. ARCHITECTURAL RESEARCH REVIEW.

**OXFORD POLYTECHNIC: DEPARTMENT OF TOWN PLANNING**
— EDUCATION FOR PLANNING.
— FORMA.
— OXFORD WORKING PAPERS IN PLANNING & RESEARCH.

**OXFORD UNIVERSITY ADVANCED STUDIES IN EDUCATION SOCIETY.**
— JOURNAL OF APPLIED EDUCATIONAL STUDIES.

**OXFORD UNIVERSITY ANTHROPOLOGICAL SOCIETY.**
— JOURNAL OF THE ANTHROPOLOGICAL SOCIETY OF OXFORD.

**OXFORD UNIVERSITY CLASSICAL SOCIETY.**
— AREPO.

**OYAMA KOGYO KOTO SENMON GAKKO.**
— OYAMA KOGYO KOTO SENMON GAKKO KENKYU KIYO. RESEARCH REPORTS, OYAMA TECHNICAL COLLEGE.

**OYAMA TECHNICAL COLLEGE.**                                000
SEE: OYAMA KOGYO KOTO SENMON GAKKO.

**PACIFIC HORTICULTURAL CORPORATION.**
— CALIFORNIA HORTICULTURAL JOURNAL.              XXX

**PACIFIC NEWS COMMONWEALTH.**
— PACIFIC COMMUNITY. AN ASIAN QUARTERLY REVIEW.

**PACIFIC ORCHID SOCIETY**
— HAWAII ORCHID JOURNAL.

**PACIFIC ORCHID SOCIETY OF HAWAII.**
— BULLETIN OF THE PACIFIC ORCHID SOCIETY OF HAWAII.                                             XXX
SUBS (1972): HAWAII ORCHID JOURNAL.

**PADGATE COLLEGE OF EDUCATION.**
— STUDIES IN EDUCATION (FERNHEAD, LANCS.).

**PAHLAVI UNIVERSITY: ASIA INSTITUTE.**
— BULLETIN OF THE ASIA INSTITUTE OF PAHLAVI UNIVERSITY.

**PAKISTAN ADMINISTRATIVE STAFF COLLEGE.**
— PASC JOURNAL.                                   XXX
— QUARTERLY, PAKISTAN ADMINISTRATIVE STAFF COLLEGE.                                        XXX

**(PAKISTAN) BUREAU OF NATIONAL RESEARCH & REFERENCE.**
— CONTEMPORARY AFFAIRS: A QUARTERLY MAGAZINE.

**PAKISTAN COUNCIL OF SCIENTIFIC & INDUSTRIAL RESEARCH.**
— SCIENCE & INDUSTRY.

**PAKISTAN COUNCIL OF SCIENTIFIC & INDUSTRIAL RESEARCH: EAST REGIONAL LABORATORIES.**
— SCIENTIFIC RESEARCHES, EAST REGIONAL LABORATORIES, PAKISTAN COUNCIL OF SCIENTIFIC & INDUSTRIAL RESEARCH.                              XXX

**(PAKISTAN) HIGH COMMISSION, LONDON.**
— PAKISTAN BULLETIN.                              XXX
— PAKISTAN NEWS.                                  XXX
SUBS (1973): PAKISTAN BULLETIN.

**(PAKISTAN) LIBRARY PROMOTION BUREAU.**
— PAKISTAN LIBRARY BULLETIN. QUARTERLY JOURNAL OF THE ...

**(PAKISTAN) OFFICE OF THE ECONOMIC ADVISER.**
— PAKISTAN ECONOMIC SURVEY.

**PAKISTAN SOCIETY OF BIOCHEMISTS.**
— PAKISTAN JOURNAL OF BIOCHEMISTRY.

**PALACKEHO UNIVERSITA: FILOSOFICKA FAKULTA.**
— ACTA UNIVERSITATIS PALACKIANAE OLOMUCENSIS: HISTORICA.                                         XXX

**PALEONTOLOGICAL SOCIETY.**
— MEMOIR, PALEONTOLOGICAL SOCIETY.

**PALESTINE NATIONAL LIBERATION MOVEMENT.**
— FATEH. INFORMATION OF THE ...

**PALM SOCIETY.**
— PALMS.

**PAN-AFRICAN INSTITUTE.**
— PAN-AFRICAN JOURNAL.

**PAN AMERICAN INSTITUTE OF GEOGRAPHY & HISTORY: UNITED STATES NATIONAL SECTION.**
— SPECIAL PUBLICATIONS, UNITED STATES NATIONAL SECTION, PAN AMERICAN INSTITUTE OF GEOGRAPHY & HISTORY.                              XXX

**PAN-AMERICAN UNION.**
— STUDIES IN EXPORT PROMOTION.
— STUDIES IN EXPORT PROMOTION.

**PAN-AMERICAN UNION: DEPARTMENT OF SCIENTIFIC AFFAIRS.**
— SERIE DE BIOLOGIA, DEPARTMENT OF SCIENTIFIC AFFAIRS, PAN-AMERICAN UNION.
— SERIE DE FISICA, DEPARTMENT OF SCIENTIFIC AFFAIRS, PAN-AMERICAN UNION.
— SERIE DE MATEMATICA, DEPARTMENT OF SCIENTIFIC AFFAIRS, PAN-AMERICAN UNION.
— SERIE DE QUIMICA, DEPARTMENT OF SCIENTIFIC AFFAIRS, PAN-AMERICAN UNION.

**PANITIA KOORDINASI PENELITIAN PERTANIAN.**
— RINGKASAN PUBLIKASI DAN LAPORAN PENELITIAN PERTANIAN.

**PANSTWOWE MUZEUM ARCHEOLOGICZNE.**
— MATERIALY STAROZYTNE I WCZESNOSREDNIOWIECZNE       XXX

**PANSTWOWE WYDAWNICTWA EKONOMICZNE.**
— BANK I KREDYT.                                  XXX

**PAPER & PAPER PRODUCTS INDUSTRY TRAINING BOARD.**
— PAPER TRAINING NEWS.

**(PAPUA & NEW GUINEA) DEPARTMENT OF AGRICULTURE, STOCK & FISHERIES.**
— RESEARCH BULLETIN, DEPARTMENT OF AGRICULTURE, STOCK & FISHERIES (PAPUA & NEW GUINEA): CROP PRODUCTION SERIES.

**(PAPUA & NEW GUINEA) DEPARTMENT OF AGRICULTURE, STOCK & FISHERIES: WILDLIFE ECOLOGY UNIT.**
— REPORT, WILDLIFE ECOLOGY UNIT, DEPARTMENT OF AGRICULTURE, STOCK & FISHERIES (PAPUA & NEW GUINEA).

**(PAPUA & NEW GUINEA): DEPARTMENT OF FORESTS.**
— BOTANY BULLETIN, DEPARTMENT OF FORESTS (PAPUA & NEW GUINEA).

**PAPUA & NEW GUINEA SCIENTIFIC SOCIETY.**
— TRANSACTIONS, PAPUA & NEW GUINEA SCIENTIFIC SOCIETY.

**PAPUA & NEW GUINEA SOCIETY.**
— JOURNAL, PAPUA & NEW GUINEA SOCIETY.

**PARENTS NATIONAL EDUCATIONAL UNION.**
— PNEU. JOURNAL OF THE ...

**PARSON WOODFORDE SOCIETY.**
— QUARTERLY JOURNAL, PARSON WOODFORDE SOCIETY.

**PARTIDO REVOLUCIONARIO INSTITUCIONAL: COMITE EJECUTIVO NACIONAL.**
— POLEMICA. REFLEXIONES SOBRE TEMES SOCIALES DE MEXICO.

**PARTITO COMUNISTA ITALIANO.**
— FOREIGN BULLETIN OF THE ITALIAN COMMUNIST PARTY.                                            XXX
— ITALIAN COMMUNISTS.                             XXX

**PATENT OFFICE TECHNICAL SOCIETY (INDIA).**
— CALCUTTA JOURNAL.

**PATHOLOGICAL SOCIETY OF GREAT BRITAIN & IRELAND.**
— JOURNAL OF MEDICAL MICROBIOLOGY.
— JOURNAL OF PATHOLOGY.*

**PATRIARCHAL INSTITUTE FOR PATRISTIC STUDIES (THESSALONIKI).**
— KLERONOMIA.

**PATROCINADA POR CUBANOS EN EL DESTIERRO.**
— REVISTA CUBANA.

**PATTERN RECOGNITION SOCIETY.**
— PATTERN RECOGNITION. JOURNAL OF THE ...

**PEABODY FOUNDATION FOR ARCHAEOLOGY.**             000
SEE: ROBERT S. PEABODY ...

PEACE & CONFLICT RESEARCH PROGRAMME.
— NEWSLETTER, PEACE & CONFLICT RESEARCH
PROGRAMME.

PEACE PLEDGE UNION: YOUTH ASSOCIATION.
— STUDIES IN NONVIOLENCE.

PEDESTRIANS' ASSOCIATION FOR ROAD SAFETY.
— ARRIVE. QUARTERLY JOURNAL OF THE ...    XXX
— PEDESTRIAN.    XXX
SUBS (1970): ARRIVE.

PENDIK VETERINER KONTROL VE ARASTIRMA ENSTITUSU
— PENDIK VETERINER KONTROL VE ARASTIRMA ENSTI-
TUSU DERGI.

PENNSYLVANIA STATE UNIVERSITY.
— MODERN INTERNATIONAL DRAMA.

PENNSYLVANIA STATE UNIVERSITY; CENTER FOR
AIR ENVIRONMENT STUDIES.
— INDEX TO AIR POLLUTION RESEARCH.

PENNSYLVANIA STATE UNIVERSITY: DEPARTMENT OF
GEOGRAPHY.
— PAPERS IN GEOGRAPHY, DEPARTMENT OF GEOGRAPHY,
PENNSYLVANIA STATE UNIVERSITY.

PENNSYLVANIA-YALE EXPEDITION TO EGYPT.
— PUBLICATIONS, PENNSYLVANIA-YALE EXPEDITION TO
EGYPT.

PENZENSKIJ POLITEKHNICHESKIJ INSTITUT.
— UCHENYE ZAPISKI, PENZENSKIJ POLITEKHNICHESKIJ
INSTITUT: ELEKTROIZMERITEL'NAJA TEKHNIKA.

PEOPLE'S PROGRESSIVE PARTY (GUYANA).
— THUNDER. QUARTERLY THEORETICAL & DISCUSSION
JOURNAL OF THE PEOPLE'S PROGRESSIVE PARTY.

PEORIA ACADEMY OF SCIENCE.
— PROCEEDINGS, PEORIA ACADEMY OF SCIENCE.

PERIVALE BIRD SANCTUARY.
— NEWSLETTER, PERIVALE BIRD SANCTUARY.

PERKIN-ELMER, LTD.
— PERKIN-ELMER NMR QUARTERLY.

PERMANENT BUREAU OF AFRO-ASIAN WRITERS.
— AFRO-ASIAN WRITER.

PERMSKIJ GOSUDARSTVENNYJ UNIVERSITET.
— ZHIVOE SLOVO V RUSSKOJ RECHI PRIKAM'JA.

PERMSKIJ GOSUDARSTVENNYJ UNIVERSITET: INSTITUT
KARSTOVEDENIJA I SPELEOLOGII.
— PESHCHERY.

PERMSKIJ NAUCHNO-ISSLEDOVATEL'SKIJ UGOL'NYJ
INSTITUT.
— NAUCHNYE TRUDY, PERMSKIJ NAUCHNO-ISSLEDO-
VATEL'SKIJ UGOL'NYJ INSTITUT.

PERSATUAN EKONOMI MALAYSIA.
— KAJIAN EKONOMI MALAYSIA. MALAYSIAN ECONOMIC
STUDIES.

PERSATUAN PERPUSTAKAAN MALAYSIA.    000
SEE: LIBRARY ASSOCIATION OF MALAYSIA.

(PERU) DIRECCION GENERAL DE INVESTIGACIONES
AGROPECUARIAS.
— INVESTIGACIONES AGROPECUARIAS DEL PERU.

(PERU) OFICINA DE ESTADISTICA.
— ESTADISTICA CONTINUA: COMERCIO AGRARIO
EXTERIOR (PERU).

PETER WARLOCK SOCIETY.
— PETER WARLOCK SOCIETY NEWSLETTER.

PHARMACEUTICAL SOCIETY OF EGYPT.
— UNITED ARAB REPUBLIC JOURNAL OF
PHARMACEUTICAL SCIENCES.    XXX

PHILIPPINE ASSOCIATION OF ENTOMOLOGISTS.
— PHILIPPINE ENTOMOLOGISTS.

PHILIPPINE ATOMIC ENERGY COMMISSION.
— PHILIPPINES NUCLEAR JOURNAL.

PHOTOGRAPHIC SOCIETY OF IRELAND.
— LENS.

PHYSICAL EDUCATION ASSOCIATION OF GREAT
BRITAIN & NORTHERN IRELAND.
— OUTDOORS.

PHYTOCHEMICAL SOCIETY OF NORTH AMERICA.
— RECENT ADVANCES IN PHYTOCHEMISTRY.

PIERRE TEILHARD DE CHARDIN ASSOCIATION OF
GREAT BRITAIN & IRELAND.
— TEILHARD STUDY LIBRARY.

PINEAPPLE RESEARCH STATION (PEKAN NERIAS).
— MALAYSIAN PINEAPPLE.

PIRA.    000
SEE: RESEARCH ASSOCIATION FOR THE PAPER &
BOARD, PRINTING & PACKAGING INDUSTRIES.

PLAID CYMRU.
— ORIEL.

PLANNED ENVIRONMENT THERAPY TRUST.
— STUDIES IN ENVIRONMENT THERAPY.

PLANNED PARENTHOOD-WORLD POPULATION.
— FAMILY PLANNING PERSPECTIVES.

PLANT PESTS & DISEASES RESEARCH INSTITUTE
(IRAN).
— IRANIAN JOURNAL OF PLANT PATHOLOGY.

PLASTICS PIPE INSTITUTE.
— TECHNICAL REPORT, PLASTICS PIPE INSTITUTE.

POETRY SOCIETY OF AUSTRALIA.
— POETRY MAGAZINE.

(POLAND) GLOWNY URZAD STATYSTYCZNY.
— MASOWE BADANIA STATYSTYCZNE.    XXX
— ROCZNIK DOCHODU NARODOWEGO.
— ROCZNIK STATYSTYCZNY INWESTYCJI I SRODKOW
TRWALYCH.
— ROCZNIK STATYSTYCZNY SZKOLNICTWA.    XXX
— STATYSTYKA POLSKI: SPISY LUDNOSCI.    XXX
— STATYSTYKA POLSKI: SPISY MIESZKAN I BUDYNKOW.    XXX

(POLAND) GLOWNY URZAD STATYSTYCZNY POLSKIEJ
RZECZYPOSPOLITEJ LUDOWEJ.
— ROCZNIK STATYSTYCZNY GOSPODARKI MIESZKANIOWEJ
I KOMUNALNEJ.
— ROCZNIK STATYSTYKI HANDLU ZAGRANICZNEGO.
— ROCZNIK STATYSTYKI HANDLU ZAGRANICZNEGO:
SERIA ROCZNIKI BRANZOWE.
— STATYSTYKA POLSKI: SERIA L.
— STATYSTYKA POLSKI: SERIA M.
— STATYSTYKA POLSKI: SERIA R.

(POLAND) MINISTERSTWO OSWIATY.
— WYCHOWANIE OBYWATELSKIE.

(POLAND) MINISTERSTWO SPRAWIEDLIWOSCI: OSRODEK
BADAN PRZESTEPCZOSCI.
— PRZEGLAD PENITENCJARNY.

(POLAND) MINISTERSTWO SZKOLNICTWA WYZSZEGO:
MIEDZYUCZELNIANY ZAKLAD PODSTAWOWYCH PROBLEMOW
ARCHITEKTURY, URBANISTYKI I BUDOWNICTWA.
— MATERIALY I STUDIA, MIEDZYUCZELNIANY ZAKLAD
PODSTAWOWYCH PROBLEMOW ARCHITEKTURY, URBANIS-
TYKI I BUDOWNICTWA, MINISTERSTWO SZKOLNICTWA
WYZSZEGO: SERIA 1: ZAGADNIENIA LUDNOSCIOWE.
— MATERIALY I STUDIA, MIEDZYUCZELNIANY ZAKLAD
PODSTAWOWYCH PROBLEMOW ARCHITEKTURY, URBANIS-
TYKI I BUDOWNICTWA, MINISTERSTWO SZKONICTWA
WYZSZEGO: SERIA 4: ZAGADNIENIA SPOLECZNO-
GOSPODARCZE W KSZALTOWANIU PRZESTRZENNYM.
— MATERIALY I STUDIA, MIEDZYUCZELNIANY ZAKLAD
PODSTAWOWYCH PROBLEMOW ARCHITEKTURY, URBANIS-
TYKI I BUDOWNICTWA, MINISTERSTWO SZKOLNICTWA
WYZSZEGO: SERIA 6: ZAGADNIENIA TEORII
ARCHITEKTURY.

(POLAND) WOJEWODZKA RADA NARODOWA.
— ROCZNIK MAZOWIECKI.

POLICE FEDERATION.
— POLICE. THE MONTHLY JOURNAL OF THE ...

POLISH ACADEMY OF SCIENCES.    000
SEE: POLSKA AKADEMIA NAUK.

POLISH ASSOCIATION OF POLITICAL SCIENCES.    000
SEE: POLSKIE TOWARZYSTWO NAUK POLITYCZNYCH.

POLISH HISTOCHEMICAL & CYTOCHEMICAL SOCIETY.    000
SEE: POLSKIE TOWARZYSTWO HISTOCHEMIKOW I
CYTOCHEMIKOW.

**POLISH-UKRAINIAN SOCIETY IN LONDON.**                    000
SEE: TOWARZYSTWO POLSKO-UKRAINSKIE.

**POLITECHNIKA GDANSKA.**
— ZESZYTY NAUKOWE POLITECHNIKI GDANSKIEJ:
  FIZYKA.
— ZESZYTY NAUKOWE POLITECHNIKI GDANSKIEJ:
  MATEMATYKA.

**POLITECHNIKA POZNANSKA.**
— ZESZYTY NAUKOWE POLITECHNIKI POZNANSKIEJ:
  FIZYKA.
— ZESZYTY NAUKOWE POLITECHNIKI POZNANSKIEJ:
  MATEMATYKA.

**POLITECHNIKA SLASKA.**
— ZESZYTY NAUKOWE POLITECHNIKI SLASKIEJ:
  AUTOMATYKA.
— ZESZYTY NAUKOWE POLITECHNIKI SLASKIEJ: MAT-
  EMATYKA-FIZYKA.

**POLITECHNIKA SZCZECINSKA.**
— ZESZYTY NAUKOWE POLITECHNIKI SZCZECINSKIEJ:
  CHEMIA.

**POLITECHNIKA WARSZAWSKA: INSTYTUT MATEMATYKI.**
— DEMONSTRATIO MATHEMATICA.

**POLITECHNIKA WROCLAWSKA.**
— ZESZYTY NAUKOWE POLITECHNIKI WROCLAWSKIEJ:
  FIZYKA.
— ZESZYTY NAUKOWE POLITECHNIKI WROCLAWSKIEJ:
  INZYNIERIA SANITARNA.

**POLITICAL FREEDOM MOVEMENT.**
— PFM PAPER.

**POLITICS ASSOCIATION.**
— TEACHING POLITICS. JOURNAL OF THE POLITICS
  ASSOCIATION.

**POLSKA AKADEMIA NAUK: INSTYTUT AUTOMATYKI.**
— PRACE INSTYTUTU AUTOMATYKI POLSKIEJ AKADEMII
  NAUK.

**POLSKA AKADEMIA NAUK: INSTYTUT BADAN LITERAC-
KICH.**
— HISTORIA I TEORIA LITERATURY: STUDIA:
  HISTORIA LITERATURY.
— HISTORIA I TEORIA LITERATURY: STUDIA:
  TEORIA LITERATURY.
— STUDIA Z OKRESU OSWIECENIA.
— Z DZIEJOW FORM ARTYSTYCZNYCH W LITERATURZE
  POLSKIEJ.

**POLSKA AKADEMIA NAUK: INSTYTUT BIOLOGII
DOSWIADCZALNEJ IM. N. NENCKIEGO.**
— ACTA NEUROBIOLOGIAE EXPERIMENTALIS.            XXX

**POLSKA AKADEMIA NAUK: INSTYTUT FILOZOFII I
SOCJOLOGII.**
— ETYKA.
— STUDIA ESTETYCZNE.
— STUDIA SOCJOLOGICZNE.

**POLSKA AKADEMIA NAUK: INSTYTUT FIZYKI.**
— ACTA PHYSICA POLONICA: SERIES A: GENERAL
  PHYSICS, SOLID STATE PHYSICS, APPLIED PHYSICS.
— ACTA PHYSICA POLONICA: B: ELEMENTARY PARTICLE
  PHYSICS, NUCLEAR PHYSICS, THEORY OF RELAT-
  IVITY, FIELD THEORY.                           XXX

**POLSKA AKADEMIA NAUK: INSTYTUT HISTORII.**
— POLSKA LUDOWA. MATERIALY I STUDIA.            XXX
— STUDIA I MATERIALY Z DZIEJOW POLSKI W OKRESIE
  OSWIECENIA.                                    XXX
— STUDIA WARSZAWSKIE.
— ZRODLA DO DZIEJOW KLASY ROBOTNICZEJ NA ZIE-
  MIACH POLSKICH.

**POLSKA AKADEMIA NAUK: INSTYTUT HISTORII KULTURY
MATERIALNEJ.**
— STUDIA Z DZIEJOW OSADNICTWA.
— STUDIA Z DZIEJOW RZEMIOSLA I PRZEMYSLU.

**POLSKA AKADEMIA NAUK: INSTYTUT MASZYN
MATEMATYCZNYCH.**
— PRACE INSTYTUTU MASZYN MATEMATYCZNYCH, POLSKA
  AKADEMIA NAUK: SERIA A.
— PRACE INSTYTUTU MASZYN MATEMATYCZNYCH, POLSKA
  AKADEMIA NAUK: SERIA B.

**POLSKA AKADEMIA NAUK: INSTYTUT PODSTAWOWYCH
PROBLEMOW TECHNIKI.**
— ZAGADNIENIA DRGAN NIELINIOWYCH.

**POLSKA AKADEMIA NAUK: KOMISJA NAUK ROLNICZNYCH
I LESNYCH.**
— ACTA AGRARIA & SILVESTRIA: SERIA LESNA.
— ACTA AGRARIA & SILVESTRIA: SERIA ROLNICZA.

**POLSKA AKADEMIA NAUK: KOMISJA NAUKOZNAWSTWA.**
— ZAGADNIENIA NAUKOZNAWSTWA, STUDIA I MATERIALY.

**POLSKA AKADEMIA NAUK: KOMISJA POLONII ZAGRANI-
CZNEJ.**
— PROBLEMY POLONII ZAGRANICZNEJ.

**POLSKA AKADEMIA NAUK: KOMITET AKUSTYKI.**
— ARCHIWUM AKUSTYKI.

**POLSKA AKADEMIA NAUK: KOMITET EKOLOGICZNY.**
— WIADOMOSCI EKOLOGICZNE.                        XXX

**POLSKA AKADEMIA NAUK: KOMITET ELEKTRONIKI I
TELEKOMUNIKACJI.**                               XXX
— ELEKTRONIKA.

**POLSKA AKADEMIA NAUK: KOMITET HYDRO-TERMODYN-
AMIKI MASZYN I INZYNIERII CHEMICZNEJ.**
— INZYNIERIA CHEMICZNA.                          XXX

**POLSKA AKADEMIA NAUK: KOMITET MIKROBIOLOGI-
CZNY.**
— POSTEPY MIKROBIOLOGII.

**POLSKA AKADEMIA NAUK: KOMITET NAUK DEMOGRAFIC-
ZNYCH.**
— STUDIA DEMOGRAFICZNE.

**POLSKA AKADEMIA NAUK: KOMITET PRZESTRZENNEGO
ZAGOSPODAROWANIA KRAJU.**
— BIULETYN, KOMITET PRZESTRZENNEGO ZAGOSPODAROW-
  ANIA KRAJU POLSKIEJ AKADEMII NAUK.
— STUDIA KOMITETU PRZESTRZENNEGO ZAGOSPODARO-
  WANIA KRAJU POLSKIEJ AKADEMII NAUK.

**POLSKA AKADEMIA NAUK (ODDZIAL W KRAKOWIE);
KOMISJA ARCHEOLOGICZNA.**
— PRACE KOMISJI ARCHEOLOGICZNEJ, ODDZIAL W
  KRAKOWIE, POLSKA AKADEMIA NAUK.

**POLSKA AKADEMIA NAUK (ODDZIAL W KRAKOWIE):
KOMISJA CERAMICZNA.**
— PRACE KOMISJI CERAMICZNEJ, ODDZIAL W KRAKOWIE,
  POLSKA AKADEMIA NAUK: CERAMIKA.               XXX

**POLSKA AKADEMIA NAUK (ODDZIAL W KRAKOWIE):
KOMISJA FILOLOGII KLASYCZNEJ.**
— PRACE KOMISJI FILOLOGII KLASYCZNEJ, ODDZIAL W
  KRAKOWIE, POLSKA AKADEMIA NAUK.
— PRACE MONOGRAFICZNE, KOMISJA FILOLOGII
  KLASYCZNEJ, ODDZIAL W KRAKOWIE, POLSKA
  AKADEMIA NAUK.

**POLSKA AKADEMIA NAUK (ODDZIAL W KRAKOWIE):
KOMISJA GORNICZO-GEODEZYJNA.**
— PRACE KOMISJI GORNICZO-GEODEZYJNEJ, ODDZIAL W
  KRAKOWIE, POLSKA AKADEMIA NAUK: GEODEZJA.      XXX
— PRACE KOMISJI GORNICZO-GEODEZYJNEJ, ODDZIAL
  W KRAKOWIE, POLSKA AKADEMIA NAUK: GORNICTWO.   XXX

**POLSKA AKADEMIA NAUK (ODDZIAL W KRAKOWIE);
KOMISJA HISTORYCZNOLITERACKA.**
— PRACE KOMISJI HISTORYCZNOLITERACKIEJ, ODDZIAL
  W KRAKOWIE, POLSKA AKADEMIA NAUK.
— ROCZNIK KOMISJI HISTORYCZNOLITERACKIEJ, ODD-
  ZIAL W KRAKOWIE, POLSKA AKADEMIA NAUK.

**POLSKA AKADEMIA NAUK (ODDZIAL W KRAKOWIE):
KOMISJA JEZYKOZNAWSTWA.**
— PRACE KOMISJI JEZYKOZNAWSTWA, ODDZIAL W
  KRAKOWIE, POLSKA AKADEMIA NAUK.

**POLSKA AKADEMIA NAUK (ODDZIAL W KRAKOWIE):
KOMISJA METALURGICZNO-ODLEWNICZA.**
— PRACE KOMISJI METALURGICZNO-ODLEWNICZEJ,
  ODDZIAL W KRAKOWIE, POLSKA AKADEMIA NAUK:
  METALURGIA.                                    XXX

**POLSKA AKADEMIA NAUK (ODDZIAL W KRAKOWIE):
KOMISJA NAUK EKONOMICZNYCH.**
— FOLIA OECONOMICA CRACOVIENSIA.
— PRACE KOMISJI NAUK EKONOMICZNYCH, ODDZIAL W
  KRAKOWIE, POLSKA AKADEMIA NAUK.

**POLSKA AKADEMIA NAUK (ODDZIAL W KRAKOWIE),
KOMISJA NAUK GEOGRAFICZNYCH.**
— FOLIA GEOGRAPHICA. SERIES GEOGRAPHICA-
  OECONOMICA.
— FOLIA GEOGRAPHICA. SERIES GEOGRAPHICA-PHYSICA.

POLSKA AKADEMIA NAUK (ODDZIAL W KRAKOWIE): KOMISJA NAUK HISTORYCZNYCH.
— STUDIA HISTORYCZNE, KOMISJA NAUK HISTORY-CZNYCH, (ODDZIAL W KRAKOWIE) POLSKA AKADEMIA NAUK.                    XXX

POLSKA AKADEMIA NAUK (ODDZIAL W KRAKOWIE): KOMISJA NAUK PEDAGOGICZNYCH.
— ROCZNIK KOMISJI NAUK PEDAGOGICZNYCH, POLSKA AKADEMIA NAUK.

POLSKA AKADEMIA NAUK (ODDZIAL W KRAKOWIE): KOMISJA NAUK PRAWNYCH.
— KRAKOWSKIE STUDIA PRAWNICZE.

POLSKA AKADEMIA NAUK: OSRODEK ROZPOWSZECHNIANIA WYDANNICTW NAUKOWYCH.
— BIMONTHLY REVIEW OF SCIENTIFIC PUBLICATIONS.

POLSKA AKADEMIA NAUK: PRACOWNIA HISTORII CZASOPISMIENNICTWA POLSKIEGO XIX I XX WIEKU.
— MATERIALY I STUDIA DO HISTORII PRASY I CZASOPISMIENNICTWA POLSKIEGO.

POLSKA AKADEMIA NAUK: SEKCJA DEMOGRAFII HISTORYCZNEJ.
— PRZESZLOSC DEMOGRAFICZNA POLSKI. MATERIALY I STUDIA.

POLSKA AKADEMIA NAUK: ZAKLAD ANTROPOLOGII.
— MISCELLANEA, ZAKLAD ANTROPOLOGII POLSKIEJ AKADEMII NAUK.
— ZAGADNIENIA ONTOGENEZY. PROBLEMS OF ONTOGEN-ESIS.

POLSKA AKADEMIA NAUK: ZAKLAD HISTORII NAUKI I TECHNIKI.
— STUDIA COPERNICANA.

POLSKA AKADEMIA NAUK: ZAKLAD HISTORII ZSRR I EUROPY SRODKOWEJ.
— STUDIA Z DZIEJOW ZSRR I EUROPY SRODKOWEJ.

POLSKA AKADEMIA NAUK: ZAKLAD HODOWLI ZWIERZAT LABORATORYJNYCH.
— ZWIERZETA LABORATORYJNE.

POLSKI INSTYTUT SPRAW MIEDZYNARODOWYCH.
— POLISH YEARBOOK OF INTERNATIONAL LAW.

POLSKIE TOWARZYSTWO AKUSTYCZNE.
— ARCHIWUM AKUSTYKI.

POLSKIE TOWARZYSTWO GEOGRAFICZNE.
— POLSKI PRZEGLAD KARTOGRAFICZNY.

POLSKIE TOWARZYSTWO HISTOCHEMIKOW I CYTOCHEM-IKOW.
— FOLIA HISTOCHEMICA ET CYTOCHEMICA.
— FOLIA HISTOCHEMICA ET CYTOCHEMICA: SUPPLEMENT.

POLSKIE TOWARZYSTWO HISTORYCZNE: KOLO W PILE.
— ROCZNIK PILSKI.

POLSKIE TOWARZYSTWO NAUK POLITYCZNYCH.
— POLISH ROUND TABLE. YEARBOOK.

POLSKIE TOWARZYSTWO NAUTOLOGICZNE.
— NAUTOLOGIA.

POLSKIE TOWARZYSTWO PSYCHOLOGICZNE.
— POLISH PSYCHOLOGICAL BULLETIN.

PONTIFICIA FACOLTA TEOLOGICA DELL' ITALIA MERIDIONELLE (NAPLES): SEZIONE DI CAPODIMONTE.
— CAMPANIA SACRA. STUDI E DOCUMENTI.

PONTIFICIA UNIVERSIDADE CATOLICA DO RIO DE JANIERO: INSTITUTO DE ESTUDOS POLITICOS E SOCIAIS.
— SINTESE POLITICA, ECONOMICA, SOCIAL.                    XXX

POPULATION COUNCIL.
— REPORTS ON POPULATION / FAMILY PLANNING.
— STUDIES IN FAMILY PLANNING.

PORT OF LONDON AUTHORITY.
— PORT OF LONDON.                    XXX

PORTIA LAW SCHOOL.                    XXX
— PORTIA LAW JOURNAL.                    XXX
  SUBS (1969): NEW ENGLAND LAW REVIEW.

PORTLAND C.S. LEWIS SOCIETY.
— CHRONICLE, PORTLAND C.S. LEWIS SOCIETY.

PORTSMOUTH CITY COUNCIL.
— PORTSMOUTH PAPERS.

PORTSMOUTH COLLEGE OF TECHNOLOGY: GEOGRAPHICAL SOCIETY.
— SOUTH HAMPSHIRE GEOGRAPHER.

PORTSMOUTH COLLEGE OF TECHNOLOGY: INDUSTRIAL ARCHAEOLOGY SOCIETY.
— JOURNAL, INDUSTRIAL ARCHAEOLOGY SOCIETY, PORTSMOUTH COLLEGE OF TECHNOLOGY.

(PORTUGAL) PRESIDENCIA DO CONSELHO.
— III PLANO DE FOMENTO: PROGRAMA DE EXECUCAO.

PORTUGUESE NATIONAL TRADE OFFICE (LONDON).
— PORTUGAL ECONOMIC INFORMATION.

POSLOVNO ZDRUZENJE AVTOMACIJA.
— AVTOMATIKA. STROKOVNO GLASILO ZA AVTOMATI-ZACIJO.

POTATO MARKETING BOARD.
— POTATO QUARTERLY.
— RESEARCH PROJECTS & POSTGRADUATE STUDENTSHIP STUDIES SPONSORED BY THE POTATO MARKETING BOARD: REPORT.

POTATO MARKETING BOARD: SUTTON BRIDGE EXPER-IMENTAL STATION.                    000
SEE: SUTTON BRIDGE EXPERIMENTAL STATION.

POWDER ADVISORY CENTRE.
— PARTICLE SIZE ANALYSIS BIBLIOGRAPHY.
— PARTICLE TECHNOLOGY RESEARCH REVIEW.
— PARTICULATE MATTER.

POWDER METALLURGY PARTS MANUFACTURERS ASSOCI-ATION.
— P/M PARTS ENGINEERING.

POWELL DUFFRYN LTD.
— PD NEWS.

POZNANSKIE TOWARZYSTWO PRZYJACIOL NAUK: KOMISJA AUTOMATYKI.
— PRACE KOMISJI AUTOMATYKI, WYDZIAL NAUK TECH-NICZNYCH, POZNANSKIE TOWARZYSTWO PRZYJACIOL NAUK.

POZNANSKIE TOWARZYSTWO PRZYJACIOL NAUK: KOMISJA BUDOWNICTWA I ARCHITEKTURY.
— PRACE KOMISJA BUDOWNICTWA I ARCHITEKTURY, POZNANSKIE TOWARZYSTWO PRZYJACIOL NAUK.

POZNANSKIE TOWARZYSTWO PRZYJACIOL NAUK: KOMISJA BUDOWY MASZYN.
— PRACE KOMISJI BUDOWY MASZYN, WYDZIAL NAUK TECHNICZNYCH, POZNANSKIE TOWARZYSTWO PRZYJACIOL NAUK.

POZNANSKIE TOWARZYSTWO PRZYJACIOL NAUK: KOMISJA BUDOWY MASZYN I ELEKTROTECHNIKI.
— PRACE KOMISJI BUDOWY MASZYN I ELEKTROTECHNIKI, POZNANSKIE TOWARZYSTWO PRZYJACIOL NAUK.

POZNANSKIE TOWARZYSTWO PRZJACIOL NAUK: KOMISJA ETNOGRAFICZNA.
— PRACE KOMISJI ETNOGRAFICZNEJ, WYZIAL HISTORII I NAUK SPOLECZNYCH, POZNANSKIE TOWARZYSTWO PRZYJACIOL NAUK.

POZNANSKIE TOWARZYSTWO PRZYJACIOL NAUK: KOMISJA JEZYKOZNAWCZA.
— PRACE KOMISJI JEZYKOZNAWCZEJ, POZNANSKIE TOWARZYSTWO PRZYJACIOL NAUK.

POZNANSKIE TOWARZYSTWO PRZYJACIOL NAUK: KOMISJA NAUK EKONOMICZNYCH.
— PRACE KOMISJI NAUK EKONOMICZNYCH, WYDZIAL HISTORII I NAUK SPOLECZNYCH, POZNANSKIE TOWARZYSTWO PRZYJACIOL NAUK.

PRAZSKA INFORMACNI SLUZBA.
— PRAZSKY SBORNIK HISTORICKY.                    XXX
— PRAZSKY SBORNIK VLASTIVEDNY.                    XXX

PRE-RETIREMENT ASSOCIATION.
— RETIREMENT CHOICE.

PRESBYTERIAN HISTORICAL SOCIETY OF ENGLAND.                    XXX
— JOURNAL, PRESBYTERIAN HISTORICAL SOCIETY OF ENGLAND.                    XXX
  SUBS(1973): JOURNAL, UNITED REFORMED CHURCH HISTORY SOCIETY.

PRESERVATION OF THE RIGHTS OF PRISONERS.
— PROP.

PRESTRESSED CONCRETE DEVELOPMENT GROUP.
— RESEARCH NOTE, PRESTRESSED CONCRETE DEVELOP-
MENT GROUP.

PRIBALTIJSKAJA KOMISSIJA PO IZUCHENIJU
MIGRATSII PTITS.
— SOOBSHCHENIJA PRIBALTIJSKOJ KOMISSII PO
IZUCHENIJU MIGRATSII PTITS.

PRICE WATERHOUSE & CO.
— PW QUARTERLY.

PRICE'S (BROMBOROUGH), LTD.                              XXX
— TECHNICAL PUBLICATION, PRICE'S (BROMBOROUGH),
LTD.                                                    XXX
SUBS: TECHNICAL PUBLICATION, PRICE'S
CHEMICALS LTD.

PRICE'S CHEMICALS, LTD.                                  XXX
— TECHNICAL PUBLICATION, PRICE'S CHEMICALS, LTD.

PRINCETON UNIVERSITY: DEPARTMENT OF EAST ASIAN
STUDIES.
— SUNG STUDIES NEWSLETTER.

PRINCETON UNIVERSITY: WOODROW WILSON SCHOOL
OF PUBLIC & INTERNATIONAL AFFAIRS.
SEE: WOODROW WILSON...

PRINTING & PUBLISHING INDUSTRY TRAINING BOARD.
— NEWSLETTER, PRINTING & PUBLISHING INDUSTRY
TRAINING BOARD.
— PROSPECT.

PRIRODONAUCEN MUZEJ.
— POSEBNO IZDANJE, PRIRODONAUCEN MUZEJ.

PRIVATE LIBRARIES ASSOCIATION.
— PRIVATE LIBRARY: QUARTERLY JOURNAL OF THE
PRIVATE LIBRARIES ASSOCIATION. 2S.

PRIVREDNA KOMORA BOSNE I HERCEGOVINE.
— GLASNIK, PRIVREDNA KOMORA BOSNE I HERCEGOVINE.

PROGRAM DESIGN, INC.
— JOURNAL OF ADHESION.

PROGRESSIVE INTELLECTUALS' STUDY GROUP.
— SEEK TRUTH TO SERVE THE PEOPLE.
WETENSCHAPPEN IN NOORD-BRABANT: HISTORISCHE
SECTIE.
— VARIA HISTORICA BRABANTICA.

PROVINCIAL MUSEUM & ARCHIVES OF ALBERTA.
— MUSEUM & ARCHIVES NOTES, PROVINCIAL MUSEUM &
ARCHIVES OF ALBERTA.
— NATURAL HISTORY DIVISION INFORMATION,
PROVINCIAL MUSEUM & ARCHIVES OF ALBERTA.
— PUBLICATIONS, PROVINCIAL MUSEUM & ARCHIVES OF
ALBERTA.

PROVINCIALE BOND VAN RUNDVEEFOKVERENIGINGEN IN
NOORDHOLLAND.
— NOORDHOLLANDS GLORIE.                                 XXX

PSIONIC MEDICAL SOCIETY.
— PSIONIC MEDICINE.

PSYCHIC YOUTH GROUP.
— PSICON. MAGAZINE OF THE ...

PSYCHOLOGICAL SOCIETY OF IRELAND.
— IRISH JOURNAL OF PSYCHOLOGY.

PSYCHONOMIC SOCIETY.
— ANIMAL LEARNING & BEHAVIOR.                           XXX
— BEHAVIOR RESEARCH METHODS & INSTRUMENTATION.
— BULLETIN, PSYCHONOMIC SOCIETY.                        XXX
— MEMORY & COGNITION.                                   XXX
— PHYSIOLOGICAL PSYCHOLOGY.                             XXX

PUBLIC ENTERPRISE GROUP.
— PUBLIC ENTERPRISE.

PUBLIC MUSEUM & ART GALLERY OF PAPUA & NEW
GUINEA.
— RECORDS, PUBLIC MUSEUM & ART GALLERY OF PAPUA
& NEW GUINEA.

PUBLIC PERSONNEL ASSOCIATION.                           XXX
— PUBLIC PERSONNEL REVIEW.                              XXX
SUBS (1972): PERSONNEL ADMINISTRATION &
PUBLIC PERSONNEL REVIEW.

PULP & PAPER RESEARCH INSTITUTE OF CANADA.
— LOGGING RESEARCH REPORTS.                             XXX
— WOODLANDS PAPERS.                                     XXX
— WOODLANDS REPORTS.                                    XXX

(PUNJAB, PAKISTAN) DEPARTMENT OF AGRICULTURE.
— JOURNAL OF AGRICULTURAL RESEARCH.                     XXX

PUNJAB UNIVERSITY: CENTRE OF ADVANCED STUDY
IN GEOLOGY.
— PUBLICATION OF THE CENTRE OF ADVANCED STUDY
IN GEOLOGY, PUNJAB UNIVERSITY.

PUNJABI UNIVERSITY.
— PUNJAB PAST AND PRESENT.

PYE UNICAM, LTD.
— COLUMN. PYE UNICAM CHROMATOGRAPHY BULLETIN.
— SCAN. SPECTROPHOTOMETRY, CHROMATOGRAPHY,
ANALYTICAL NEWS.                                        XXX

QUEBEC (PROVINCE) MINISTERE DES AFFAIRES CULT-
URELLES.
— CULTURE VIVANTE.

QUEEN MARY COLLEGE LAW SOCIETY.
— ASSIZE. JOURNAL OF ...

QUEEN'S LANCASHIRE REGIMENT.
— LANCASHIRE LAD.

QUEEN'S UNIVERSITY OF BELFAST: ARCHITECTURE &
PLANNING INFORMATION SERVICE.
— APIS BULLETIN.

QUEEN'S UNIVERSITY OF BELFAST: PHYSICAL EDUCAT-
ION CENTRE.
— MONTHLY SELECTION OF RECENT PUBLICATIONS
(BOOKS, THESES ETC.) IN THE FIELDS OF SPORT,
PHYSICAL EDUCATION & RECREATION.
— SPORTS INFORMATION MONTHLY BULLETIN.

QUEEN'S UNIVERSITY (KINGSTON, ONT.).
— QUEEN'S PAPERS IN PURE & APPLIED MATHEMATICS.

QUEEN'S UNIVERSITY (KINGSTON, ONT.): FACULTY OF
LAW.
— INTRAMURAL LAW JOURNAL.                               XXX
— QUEEN'S INTRAMURAL LAW JOURNAL.                       XXX
— QUEEN'S LAW JOURNAL.                                  XXX

QUEENSLAND ORNITHOLOGICAL SOCIETY.
— SUNBIRD.

QUEKETT MICROSCOPICAL CLUB.
— NEWSLETTER, QUEKETT MICROSCOPICAL CLUB.

RACE RELATIONS BOARD (GB).
— RACE RELATIONS.

RACHELWOOD WILDLIFE RESEARCH PRESERVE.
— PUBLICATIONS, RACHELWOOD WILDLIFE RESEARCH
PRESERVE.

RADCLIFFE LOCAL HISTORY SOCIETY.
— PUBLICATIONS, RADCLIFFE LOCAL HISTORY SOCIETY.

RADICAL PHILOSOPHY GROUP.
— RADICAL PHILOSOPHY.

RADIO CORPORATION OF AMERICA.
— INDEX TO TECHNICAL PAPERS, RCA CORPORATION.         XXX

RADIO WOLNA EUROPA: ROZGLOSNIA POLSKA.
— NA ANTENIE.

RADIOCHEMICAL CENTRE (AMERSHAM).
— MEDICAL MONOGRAPHS.

RAILROAD ENGINEERING INDEX INSTITUTE.
— HIGH SPEED RAIL RESEARCH REPORT.

RANCHI UNIVERSITY: DEPARTMENT OF POLITICAL
SCIENCE.
— POLITICAL SCIENTIST.

RAND CORPORATION.
— GEOSCIENCES BULLETIN: SERIES A.
— SOVIET CYBERNETICS REVIEW.

REAL SOCIEDAD VASCONGADA DE LOS AMIGOS DEL
PAIS.
— BOLETIN DE ESTUDIOS HISTORICOS SOBRE SAN
SEBASTIAN.

REDESDALE EXPERIMENTAL HUSBANDRY FARM.
— ANNUAL REVIEW, REDESDALE EXPERIMENTAL
HUSBANDRY FARM.

REFORM SYNAGOGUES OF GREAT BRITAIN.
— LIVING JUDAISM.  JOURNAL OF THE ...                    XXX
— SYNAGOGUE REVIEW.                                       XXX
SUBS (1966):  LIVING JUDAISM.

REGIONAL COUNCIL FOR EDUCATION (NAIROBI).
— EDUCATION IN EASTERN AFRICA.

REGIONAL ENGLISH LANGUAGE CENTRE (SINGAPORE).
— R.E.L.C. JOURNAL.

REGIONAL SCIENCE ASSOCIATION (INDIA).
— INDIAN JOURNAL OF REGIONAL SCIENCE.

REGISTERED PLUMBERS ASSOCIATION.
— JOURNAL, REGISTERED PLUMBERS ASSOCIATION.       XXX
SUBS (1970): PLUMBING.

RENAISSANCE ENGLISH TEXT SOCIETY.
— PUBLICATIONS, RENAISSANCE ENGLISH TEXT
SOCIETY.

RENAISSANCE SOCIETY OF AMERICA.
— RENAISSANCE QUARTERLY.

REPERTOIRE INTERNATIONAL DE LA LITTERATURE
MUSICALE (RILM).                                          000
SEE: INTERNATIONAL REPERTORY OF MUSIC
LITERATURE.

RESEARCH ASSOCIATION FOR THE PAPER & BOARD,
PRINTING & PACKAGING INDUSTRIES.
— PIRA NEWS.
— PIRA PACKAGING JOURNAL.
— PIRA PAPER & BOARD ABSTRACTS.
— PIRA PAPER & BOARD JOURNAL.
— PIRA PATENT ABSTRACTS.
— PIRA PRINTING JOURNAL.

RESEARCH IN ELECTROCARDIOLOGY INC.
— JOURNAL OF ELECTROCARDIOLOGY.

RESEARCH INSTITUTE OF ASIAN ECONOMICS.
— ASIAN ECONOMIES.

RESEARCH INSTITUTE FOR NATURAL RESOURCES
(TOKYO).                                                  000
SEE: SHIGEN KAGAKU KENKYUSHO.

RESEARCH INSTITUTE FOR POLYMERS & TEXTILES
(JAPAN).                                                  000
SEE:  SENI KOBUNSHI ZAIRYO KENKYUJO.

RESEARCH LIBRARY ON AFRICAN AFFAIRS (ACCRA).
— GHANA. A CURRENT BIBLIOGRAPHY.

RESEARCH SOCIETY OF PAKISTAN.
— JOURNAL OF THE RESEARCH SOCIETY OF PAKISTAN.

RESERVE BANK OF MALAWI.
— ECONOMIC & FINANCIAL REVIEW, RESERVE BANK OF
MALAWI.

REUNION INTERNATIONALE DES LABORATOIRES
D'ESSAIS ET DE RECHERCHES SUR LES MATERI-
AUX ET LES CONSTRUCTIONS.                                 000
SEE: INTERNATIONAL ASSOCIATION OF TESTING
& RESEARCH LABORATORIES FOR MATERIALS &
STRUCTURES.

REVELATIONIST SOCIETY FOR PSYCHICAL & SPIRITUAL
STUDIES.
— REVELATION.

REVOLUTIONARY WORKERS PARTY.
— EUROPEAN MARXIST REVIEW.

RHODES UNIVERSITY: DEPARTMENT OF ICHTHYOLOGY.
— OCCASIONAL PAPER, DEPARTMENT OF ICHTHYOLOGY,
RHODES UNIVERSITY.
— SPECIAL PUBLICATION, DEPARTMENT OF ICHTHYO-
LOGY, RHODES UNIVERSITY.

(RHODESIA) MINISTRY OF INFORMATION, IMMI-
GRATION & TOURISM.
— RHODESIAN COMMENTARY.

RHODESIA LIBRARY ASSOCIATION.
— RHODESIAN LIBRARIAN.

RIEMENSCHNEIDER BACH INSTITUTE.
— BACH.  QUARTERLY JOURNAL OF THE ...

RIGAS POLITEHNISKAIS INSTITUTS.
— KIBERNETIKA I DIAGNOSTIKA.

RIJKSFACULTEIT LANDBOUWWETENSCHAPPEN TE GENT:
AFDELING VOOR BOSBOUW.
— SYLVA GANDAVENSIS. MEDEDELINGEN VAN DE AFDEL-
ING VOOR BOSBOUW, RIJKSFACULTEIT LANDBOUWWET-
ENSCHAPPEN TE GENT.

RIJKSINSTITUUT VOOR NATUURBEHEER.
— VERHANDELINGEN, RIJKSINSTITUUT VOOR NATUUR-
BEHEER.

RIJKSMUSEUM VAN GEOLOGIE EN MINERALOGIE.
— SCRIPTA GEOLOGICA.

RIJKSUNIVERSITEIT TE GENT: MUSEUM VOOR DE
GESCHIEDENIS VAN DE WETENSCHAPPEN.
— SARTONIA.

RIJKSUNIVERSITEIT TE LEIDEN: AFRIKA-STUDIE-
CENTRUM.
— AFRICAN SOCIAL RESEARCH DOCUMENTS.
— COMMUNICATIONS, AFRIKA-STUDIECENTRUM, RIJKS-
UNIVERSITEIT TE LEIDEN.

RIJKSUNIVERSITEIT TE UTRECHT: GEOGRAFISCH
INSTITUUT.
— BULLETIN, GEOGRAFISCH INSTITUUT, RIJKSUNIV-
ERSITEIT UTRECHT: SERIE II: SOCIALE GEOGRAFIE
ONTWIKKELINGSLANDEN.
— BULLETIN, GEOGRAFISCH INSTITUUT, RIJKSUNIV-
ERSITEIT UTRECHT: SERIE III: HISTORISCHE
GEOGRAFIE.

RIJKSUNIVERSITEIT TE UTRECHT: STERREWACHT.
— UTRECHTSE STERREKUNDIGE OVERDRUKKEN.

RILEM (REUNION INTERNATIONALE DES LABORA-
TOIRES D'ESSAIS ET DE RECHERCHES SUR LES
MATERIAUX ET LES CONSTRUCTIONS).                          000
SEE: INTERNATIONAL ASSOCIATION OF TESTING
& RESEARCH LABORATORIES FOR MATERIALS &
STRUCTURES.

RILEY COUNTY (KANSAS) GENEALOGICAL SOCIETY.
— KANSAS KIN.

RILM (REPERTOIRE INTERNATIONAL DE LA LITTE-
RATURE MUSICALE).                                         000
SEE: INTERNATIONAL REPERTORY OF MUSIC
LITERATURE.

RIZHSKIJ POLITEKHNICHESKIJ INSTITUT (RIGA).               000
SEE: RIGA POLITEHNISKAIS INSTITUTS.

ROAD TRANSPORT INDUSTRY BOARD.
— TRANSPORT TRAINING. NEWSPAPER OF THE ...

ROBERT OWEN BI-CENTENARY ASSOCIATION.
— BULLETIN OF THE ROBERT OWEN BI-CENTENARY
ASSOCIATION.

ROBERT S. PEABODY FOUNDATION FOR ARCHAEOLOGY.
— AYACUCHO ARCHAEOLOGICAL-BOTANICAL PROJECT:
REPORTS.

ROCKY MOUNTAIN MATHEMATICS CONSORTIUM.
— ROCKY MOUNTAIN JOURNAL OF MATHEMATICS.

ROEHAMPTON NEW ARTS CIRCLE.
— OCCASIONAL WINDHOVER.

ROLLS-ROYCE LTD.
— ROLLS-ROYCE JOURNAL.

ROMISCH-GERMANISCHES ZENTRALMUSEUM.
— ARCHAOLOGISCHES KORRESPONDENZBLATT.

ROTARY INTERNATIONAL OF GREAT BRITAIN &
IRELAND: DISTRICT 102.
— CHRONICLE.                                              XXX

ROYAL AERONAUTICAL SOCIETY.
— AERONAUTICAL JOURNAL.                                   XXX
— AEROSPACE.
— JOURNAL, ROYAL AERONAUTICAL SOCIETY.                    XXX
SUBS (1968): AERONAUTICAL JOURNAL.

ROYAL AGRICULTURAL SOCIETY OF ENGLAND.
— FARMING PRACTICE.                                       XXX
— PRACTICE WITH SCIENCE.
— RASE REVIEW.                                            XXX
SUBS: PRACTICE WITH SCIENCE.

ROYAL ANTHROPOLOGICAL INSTITUTE.
— ANTHROPOLOGICAL INDEX TO CURRENT PERIODICALS
  IN THE LIBRARY OF THE ROYAL ANTHROPOLOGICAL
  INSTITUTE.
— INDEX TO CURRENT PERIODICALS RECEIVED IN THE
  LIBRARY OF THE ROYAL ANTHROPOLOGICAL
  INSTITUTE.                                                          XXX

ROYAL ARCHITECTURAL INSTITUTE OF CANADA.
— ARCHITECTURE CANADA.                                               XXX
— ARCHITECTURE CANADA NEWSMAGAZINE.                                  XXX
— JOURNAL, ROYAL ARCHITECTURAL INSTITUTE OF
  CANADA.                                                            XXX
  SUBS (1966):  ARCHITECTURE CANADA.

ROYAL ARMY EDUCATIONAL CORPS.
— RAEC GAZETTE.

ROYAL ASIATIC SOCIETY OF GREAT BRITAIN & IRE-
LAND: HONG KONG BRANCH.
— JOURNAL, HONG KONG BRANCH, ROYAL ASIATIC SOC-
  IETY OF GREAT BRITAIN & IRELAND.

ROYAL ASIATIC SOCIETY OF GREAT BRITAIN &
IRELAND: KOREA BRANCH.
— MONOGRAPH SERIES, KOREA BRANCH, ROYAL ASIATIC
  SOCIETY OF GREAT BRITAIN & IRELAND.

ROYAL ASSOCIATION OF BRITISH DAIRY FARMERS.
  DAIRYING.                                                          XXX
— JOURNAL, ROYAL ASSOCIATION OF BRITISH DAIRY
  FARMERS.                                                           XXX

ROYAL AUSTRALASIAN COLLEGE OF PHYSICIANS.
— AUSTRALIAN & NEW ZEALAND JOURNAL OF MEDICINE.                      XXX

ROYAL AUSTRALASIAN ORNITHOLOGISTS' UNION.
— NEWSLETTER, ROYAL AUSTRALASIAN ORNITHOLOGISTS'
  UNION.

ROYAL AUSTRALIAN PLANNING INSTITUTE.                                 XXX
— ROYAL AUSTRALIAN PLANNING INSTITUTE JOURNAL.                       XXX

ROYAL BOTANICAL GARDENS (HAMILTON, ONT.).
— TECHNICAL BULLETIN, ROYAL BOTANICAL GARDENS
  (HAMILTON, ONT.).

ROYAL COLLEGE OF NURSING.
— NURSING BIBLIOGRAPHY.

ROYAL COMMISSION ON LOCAL GOVERNMENT IN
SCOTLAND.
— RESEARCH STUDIES, ROYAL COMMISSION ON LOCAL
  GOVERNMENT IN SCOTLAND.

ROYAL ENTOMOLOGICAL SOCIETY OF LONDON.
— JOURNAL OF ENTOMOLOGY: SERIES A: GENERAL ENT-
  OMOLOGY.                                                           XXX
— JOURNAL OF ENTOMOLOGY: SERIES B: TAXONOMY.                         XXX
— PROCEEDINGS, ROYAL ENTOMOLOGICAL SOCIETY OF
  LONDON: SERIES A: GENERAL ENTOMOLOGY.                              XXX
  SUBS (1971): JOURNAL OF ENTOMOLOGY: SERIES
  A: GENERAL ENTOMOLOGY.
— PROCEEDINGS, ROYAL ENTOMOLOGICAL SOCIETY OF
  LONDON: SERIES B: TAXONOMY.                                        XXX
  SUBS (1971): JOURNAL OF ENTOMOLOGY: SERIES
  B: TAXONOMY.

ROYAL GREEN JACKETS.
— ROYAL GREEN JACKETS CHRONICLE.

ROYAL INSTITUTE OF BRITISH ARCHITECTS: WEST
MIDLANDS REGION.
— ARCHITECTURE WEST MIDLANDS.

ROYAL INSTITUTION OF GREAT BRITAIN.
— PROGRESS REPORT, ROYAL INSTITUTION OF GREAT
  BRITAIN.

ROYAL INSTITUTE OF LINGUISTICS & ANTHROPOLOGY
(LEYDEN).                                                            000
  SEE: KONINKLIJK INSTITUUT VOOR TAAL-, LAND-
  EN VOLKENKUNDE.

ROYAL INSTITUTION OF NAVAL ARCHITECTS.
— NAVAL ARCHITECT.                                                   XXX
— TRANSACTIONS, ROYAL INSTITUTION OF NAVAL
  ARCHITECTS.                                                        XXX

ROYAL INSTITUTE OF PHILOSOPHY.
— LECTURES, ROYAL INSTITUTE OF PHILOSOPHY.

ROYAL INSTITUTE OF PUBLIC ADMINISTRATION:
LONDON REGIONAL GROUP.
— LONDON REVIEW OF PUBLIC ADMINISTRATION.

ROYAL INSTITUTE OF PUBLIC HEALTH & HYGIENE.
— COMMUNITY HEALTH.

ROYAL IRISH ACADEMY: COMMITTEE FOR THE STUDY
OF ANGLO-IRISH LANGUAGE & LITERATURE.
— HANDLIST, COMMITTEE FOR THE STUDY OF ANGLO-
  IRISH LANGUAGE & LITERATURE, ROYAL IRISH
  ACADEMY.

ROYAL MICROSCOPICAL SOCIETY.
— JOURNAL OF MICROSCOPY.
— JOURNAL OF THE ROYAL MICROSCOPICAL SOCIETY.                        XXX
  SUBS: (1969) JOURNAL OF MICROSCOPY.

ROYAL NATIONAL INSTITUTE FOR THE DEAF.
— BRITISH JOURNAL OF AUDIOLOGY.                                      XXX
— SOUND.  A QUARTERLY JOURNAL DEVOTED TO THE
  STUDY OF AUDIOLOGY.

ROYAL NATIONAL ROSE SOCIETY.
— ROSE BULLETIN.

ROYAL NETHERLANDS VETERINARY ASSOCIATION.
— NETHERLANDS JOURNAL OF VETERINARY SCIENCE.

ROYAL NEW ZEALAND INSTITUTE OF HORTICULTURE.
— ANNUAL JOURNAL, ROYAL NEW ZEALAND INSTITUTE
  OF HORTICULTURE.                                                   XXX
— JOURNAL, ROYAL NEW ZEALAND INSTITUTE OF
  HORTICULTURE:  NS.                                                 XXX

ROYAL ONTARIO MUSEUM.
— ROTUNDA.  THE BULLETIN OF THE ...

ROYAL REGIMENT OF FUSILIERS.
— FUSILIER.

ROYAL SOCIETY.
— SELECTED LECTURES OF THE ROYAL SOCIETY.

ROYAL SOCIETY FOR INDIA, PAKISTAN & CEYLON.
— ASIAN REVIEW.  THE JOURNAL OF THE ...

ROYAL SOCIETY OF MEDICINE.
— TROPICAL DOCTOR.

ROYAL SOCIETY OF NEW ZEALAND.
— JOURNAL OF THE ROYAL SOCIETY OF NEW ZEALAND.                       XXX
— TRANSACTIONS, ROYAL SOCIETY OF NEW ZEALAND:
  BIOLOGICAL SCIENCES.                                               XXX
— TRANSACTIONS, ROYAL SOCIETY OF NEW ZEALAND:
  EARTH SCIENCES.                                                    XXX
— TRANSACTIONS OF THE ROYAL SOCIETY OF NEW
  ZEALAND: GEOLOGY.                                                  XXX

ROYAL SOCIETY FOR THE PREVENTION OF ACCIDENTS.
— CARE IN THE HOME.
— INDUSTRIAL SAFETY BULLETIN.                                        XXX
— OCCUPATIONAL SAFETY BULLETIN.                                      XXX
— OCCUPATIONAL SAFETY & HEALTH.                                      XXX
— OCCUPATIONAL SAFETY & HEALTH: SUPPLEMENT.                          XXX

ROYAL SOCIETY FOR THE PREVENTION OF CRUELTY TO
ANIMALS.
— TODAY (1971).

ROYAL STUART SOCIETY.
— ROYAL STUART PAPERS.

ROYAL SWEDISH ACADEMY OF SCIENCES.                                   000
SEE: KUNGLIGA SVENSKA VETENSKAPSAKADEMIEN.

ROYAL TOWN PLANNING INSTITUTE.                                       XXX
— JOURNAL, ROYAL TOWN PLANNING INSTITUTE.                            XXX

ROYAL TROPICAL INSTITUTE (NETHERLANDS):
ANTHROPOLOGY DEPARTMENT.                                             000
SEE: KONINKLIJKE INSTITUUT VOOR DE TROPEN:
(ANTHROPOLOGY DEPARTMENT).

ROYAL UNITED SERVICE INSTITUTE FOR DEFENCE
STUDIES.                                                             XXX
— JOURNAL, ROYAL UNITED SERVICE INSTITUTE FOR
  DEFENCE STUDIES.                                                   XXX
— RUSI.  JOURNAL OF THE ROYAL UNITED SERVICES
  INSTITUTE FOR DEFENCE STUDIES.                                     XXX

ROYAL UNITED SERVICE INSTITUTION.                                    XXX
— JOURNAL, ROYAL UNITED SERVICE INSTITUTION.                         XXX
  SUBS(1971): JOURNAL, ROYAL UNITED SERVICE
  INSTITUTE FOR DEFENCE STUDIES.

ROYAL UNITED SERVICE INSTITUTION: LIBRARY.
— CACL.                                                              XXX

ROYAL YACHTING ASSOCIATION.
— RYA MAGAZINE.

ROYAL ZOOLOGICAL SOCIETY OF NEW SOUTH WALES.
— KOOLEWONG. PROCEEDINGS OF THE ROYAL ZOOLOG-
ICAL SOCIETY OF NEW SOUTH WALES.     XXX
— PROCEEDINGS OF THE ROYAL ZOOLOGICAL SOCIETY
OF NEW SOUTH WALES.     XXX
    SUBS (1972): KOOLEWONG.

ROYAL ZOOLOGICAL SOCIETY OF SCOTLAND: GANNET
CLUB.
— GANNET. NEWSLETTER OF THE GANNET CLUB OF THE
ROYAL ZOOLOGICAL SOCIETY OF SCOTLAND.

RUBBER & PLASTICS RESEARCH ASSOCIATION OF
GREAT BRITAIN.
— BIO-MEDICAL APPLICATIONS OF POLYMERS.
— RAPRA IN BRIEF.
— RAPRA LITERATURE BULLETIN.
— RAPRA MEMBERS JOURNAL.

(RUMANIA) DIRECTIA GENERALA FARMACEUTICA.
— PRACTICA FARMACEUTICA.

(RUMANIA) MINISTERUL SANATATII.
— PRACTICA FARMACEUTICA.

RUNNYMEDE TRUST.
— RACE RELATIONS BULLETIN.
— RACE RELATIONS BULLETIN: INDUSTRIAL SUPPLE-
MENT.     XXX
— RUNNYMEDE TRUST: EUROPEAN SUPPLEMENT.
— RUNNYMEDE TRUST: INDUSTRIAL SUPPLEMENT.     XXX
— RUNNYMEDE TRUST BULLETIN. A MONTHLY SUMMARY
OF RACE RELATIONS INFORMATION.     XXX

RURAL DISTRICT COUNCILS ASSOCIATION.
— DISTRICT COUNCILS REVIEW.     XXX
— RURAL DISTRICT REVIEW.     XXX
    SUBS (1972): DISTRICT COUNCILS REVIEW.

RUSKIN ASSOCIATION.
— RUSKIN NEWSLETTER.

RUSSELL SAGE COLLEGE.
— STUDIES IN THE 20TH CENTURY.

(RUSSIA, RSFSR) MINISTERSTVO KOMMUNAL'NOGO
KHOZJAJSTVA.
— ZHILISHCHNO-KOMMUNAL'NOE KHOZJAJSTVO.     XXX
— ZHILISHCHNOE I KOMMUNAL'NOE KHOZJAJSTVO.     XXX

(RUSSIA RSFSR) MINISTERSTVO PROSVESHCHENIJA.
— VOSPITANIE SHKOL'NIKOV.

(RUSSIA RSFSR) MINISTERSTVO SEL'SKOGO
KHOZJAJSTVA.
— SEL'SKOE KHOZJAJSTVO ROSSII.     XXX
— SEL'SKOKHOZJAJSTVENNOE PROIZVODSTVO NECHERNO-
ZEMNOJ ZONY.     XXX
— SEL'SKOKHOZJAJSTVENNOE PROIZVODSTVO POVOL-
ZH'JA.     XXX
— STEPNYE PROSTORY.
— ZEMLJA RODNAJA.     XXX

(RUSSIA RSFSR) MINISTERSTVO VYSSHEGO I SREDNEGO
SPETSIAL'NOGO OBRAZOVANIJA.
— SIBIR' I DAL'NYJ VOSTOK V PERIOD VOSSTANOV-
LENIJA NARODNOGO KHOZJAJSTVA.
— SOTSIALISTICHESKOE I KOMMUNISTICHESKOE STROIT-
EL'STVO V SIBIRI.

(RUSSIA RSFSR) VERKHOVNYJ SUD.
— BJULLETEN' VERKHOVNOGO SUDA RSFSR.

(RUSSIA USSR) GOSPLAN: INSTITUT KOMPLEKSNYKH
TRANSPORTNYKH PROBLEM.
— TRUDY INSTITUTA KOMPLEKSNYKH TRANSPORTNYKH
PROBLEM.

(RUSSIA USSR) MINISTERSTVO CHERNOJ METALLURGII.
— PROIZVODSTVO I ISSLEDOVANIE STALEJ I SPLAVOV.

(RUSSIA USSR) MINISTERSTVO KHIMICHESKOJ
PROMYSHLENNOSTI:
— KHIMIJA V SEL'SKOM KHOZJAJSTVE.
— LAKOKRASOCHNYE MATERIALY I IKH PRIMENENIE.

(RUSSIA USSR) MINISTERSTVO KHIMICHESKOJ PRO-
MYSHLENNOSTI: NAUCHNO-ISSLEDOVATEL'SKIJ INST-
ITUT TEKHNIKO-EKONOMICHESKIKH ISSEDOVANIJ.
— GAZOVAJA KHROMATOGRAFIJA. SBORNIK STATEJ.

(RUSSIA, USSR) MINISTERSTVO KUL'TURY.
— V MIRE KNIG.     XXX

(RUSSIA USSR) MINISTERSTVO KUL'TURY: INSTITUT
ISTORII ISKUSSTV.
— VOPROSY TEATRA. SBORNIK STATEJ I MATERIALOV.

(RUSSIA USSR) MINISTERSTVO MEDITSINSKOJ PROMY-
SHLENNOSTI USSR.
— KHIMIKO-FARMATSEVTICHESKIJ ZHURNAL.

(RUSSIA USSR) MINISTERSTVO PRIBOROSTROENIJA,
SREDSTV AVTOMATIZATSII I SISTEM UPRAVLENIJA ...
— PRIBORY I SISTEMY UPRAVLENIJA.

(RUSSIA USSR) MINISTERSTVO SEL'SKOGO
KHOZJAJSTVA.
— SEL'SKAJA NOV'.

(RUSSIA USSR) MINISTERSTVO VYSSHEGO I SREDNEGO
SPETSIAL'NOGO OBRAZOVANIJA USSR.
— PRIBOROSTROENIE, MEZHVEDOMSTVENNYJ RESPUBLIK-
AN SKIJ NAUCHNO-TEKHNNICHESKIJ SBORNIK.

(RUSSIA USSR) MINISTERSTVO ZDRAVOOKHRANENIJA.
— KOSMICHESKAJA BIOLOGIJA I MEDITSINA.     XXX
— PROBLEMY ENDOKRINOLOGII.     XXX

(RUSSIA USSR) SOVET MINISTROV: GLAVNOE
ARKHIVNOE UPRAVLENIE.
— SOVETSKIE ARKHIVY.     XXX

(RUSSIA USSR) SOVET MINISTROV: GOSUDARSTVENNYJ
KOMITET ZAGOTOVOK.
— ZAKUPKI SEL'SKOKHOZJAJSTVENNYKH PRODUKTOV.

RUTGERS UNIVERSITY.
— SOCIETY.     XXX

RUTGERS UNIVERSITY: DEPARTMENT OF GEOGRAPHY.
— DISCUSSION PAPERS, DEPARTMENT OF GEOGRAPHY,
RUTGERS UNIVERSITY.

RUTGERS UNIVERSITY: SCHOOL OF LAW.
— RUTGERS JOURNAL OF COMPUTERS & THE LAW.

SADDLEWORTH HISTORICAL SOCIETY.
— BULLETIN, SADDLEWORTH HISTORICAL SOCIETY.

SADLER'S WELLS OPERA.
— SADLER'S WELLS MAGAZINE.

SADO MARINE BIOLOGICAL STATION.     000
SEE: SADO RINKAI JIKENJO.

SADO RINKAI JIKENJO.
— SADO RINKAI JIKENJO KENKYU NEMPO.
ANNUAL REPORT, SADO MARINE BIOLOGICAL STATION.

SAFETY IN MINES RESEARCH ESTABLISHMENT.
— SMRE TECHNICAL PAPER.

SAFFRON WALDEN HISTORICAL & ARCHAEOLOGICAL
SOCIETY.
— OCCASIONAL PAPERS, SAFFRON WALDEN HISTORICAL
& ARCHAEOLOGICAL SOCIETY.

ST. ALBANS & HERTFORDSHIRE ARCHITECTURAL &
ARCHAEOLOGICAL SOCIETY.
— HERTFORDSHIRE ARCHAEOLOGY. TRANSACTIONS OF ...

ST. ANDREWS PRESBYTERIAN COLLEGE (LAURINBURG,
N.C.).
— ST. ANDREWS REVIEW.

ST. FRANCIS XAVIER UNIVERSITY: DEPARTMENT OF
ENGLISH.
— ANTIGONISH REVIEW.

ST. JOHN'S UNIVERSITY.
— REVIEW OF NATIONAL LITERATURES.

SAINT LOUIS COLLEGE.
— SAINT LOUIS QUARTERLY.     XXX

SAINT LOUIS UNIVERSITY (PHILIPPINES): GRADUATE
SCHOOL OF ARTS & SCIENCES.
— SAINT LOUIS UNIVERSITY RESEARCH JOURNAL.

ST. PATRICK'S COLLEGE (MAYNOOTH).
— BIBLE.
— ZENITH.

ST. PAUL INSTITUTE; SCIENCE MUSEUM.
— GUIDE LEAFLET, SCIENCE MUSEUM, ST. PAUL
INSTITUTE.
— MONOGRAPH OF THE SCIENCE MUSEUM OF MINNESOTA.

ST. PAUL UNIVERSITY: FACULTY OF THEOLOGY.
— EGLISE ET THEOLOGIE.

SAITAMA DAIGAKU; KYOYOBU.
— SAITAMA DAIGAKU KIYO; SHIZEN KAGAKU HEN. =
JOURNAL OF SAITAMA UNIVERSITY; NATURAL
SCIENCE.

SALISBURY & SOUTH WILTSHIRE ARCHAEOLOGY SOCIETY
— WILTSHIRE INDUSTRIAL ARCHAEOLOGY. TRANS-
ACTIONS OF THE ...

SALK INSTITUTE FOR BIOLOGICAL STUDIES.
— OCCASIONAL PAPERS, SALK INSTITUTE FOR
BIOLOGICAL STUDIES.

SALLSKAPET FOR FORSKNINGSINFORMATION.
— FORSKNING OCH FRAMSTEG.

SALMON NET FISHING ASSOCIATION OF SCOTLAND.
— SALMON NET. MAGAZINE OF THE ...

SAMEEKSHA TRUST.
— ECONOMIC & POLITICAL WEEKLY.

SAMENWERKENDE ELECTROTECHNISCHE FABRIEKEN HOLEC
N.V.
— HOLECTECHNIEK.

SAMFUNDET SVERIGE-ISLAND I LUND-MALMO.
— GARDAR. ARSBOK FOR SAMFUNDET SVERIGE-ISLAND
I LUND-MALMO.

SAMVIRKENDE DANSKE LANDBOFORENINGER.
— NYE DANSK LANDBRUG.                                                          XXX

SAN DIEGO COUNCIL FOR POETRY.
— LEMMING.

SAN DIEGO SHELL CLUB.
— FESTIVUS.

SAN FRANCISCO MARITIME MUSEUM.
— SEA LETTER.

SAN JOSE STATE COLLEGE: SCHOOL OF BUSINESS.
— REALTY REVIEW.

SANGYO KOGEI SHIKENJO.                                                         XXX
— SANGYO KOGEI SHIKENJO HOKOKU. BULLETIN OF
INDUSTRIAL ARTS INSTITUTE.                                                     XXX

SANTA BARBARA MALACOLOGICAL SOCIETY.
— TABULATA.

SARAJEVSKI UNIVERZITET: INSTITUT ZA RUDARSKA
I HEMIJSKO-TEHNOLOSKA ISTRAZIVANJA.
— ARHIV ZA RUDARSTVO I TEHNOLOGIJU.                                            XXX
— ARHIV ZA TEHNOLOGIJU. TECHNOLOGICA ACTA.                                     XXX

SARATOVSKIJ GOSUDARSTVENNYJ UNIVERSITET.
— ISSLEDOVANIJA PO TEORII CHISEL.
— VOPROSY ELEKTRONIKI SVERKHVYSOKIKH CHASTOT.

SARBICA-CONSAL REGIONAL MICROFILM CLEARING
HOUSE.
— SOUTHEAST ASIA MICROFILMS NEWSLETTER.

SARDAR PATEL INSTITUTE OF SOCIAL & ECONOMIC
RESEARCH.
— ANVESAK.

SAVEZ BIOLOSKIH DRUSTAVA JUGOSLAVIJE.
— ACTA BIOLOGICA JUGOSLAVICA: SERIJA D: EKOLO-
JIA.

SAVEZ DRUSTAVA HISTORICARA JUGOSLAVIJE
(ZAGREB).
— NASTAVA ISTORIJE.

SAVEZ DRUSTAVA ISTORICARA JUGOSLAVIJE.
— ACTA JUGOSLAVIAE HISTORICA.

SAVEZ DRUSTAVA ZA STRANE JEZIKE I KNJIZEVNOSTI
SFRJ.
— FILOLOSKI PREGLED. REVUE DE PHILOLOGIE.

SAVEZ EKONOMISTA SR SRBIJE ZA PITANJA EKONOMSKE
TEORIJE I PRAKSE.
— EKONOMSKA MISAO.

SAVEZ ISTORIJSKIH DRUSTAVA JUGOSLAVIJE.
— JUGOSLOVENSKI ISTORIJSKI CASOPIS.

SAVEZ KEMICARA I TEHNOLOGA HRVATSKE.
— CELULOZA - PAPIR - GRAFIKA.

SCANDINAVIAN INSTITUTE OF ASIAN STUDIES.
— NEWSLETTER, SCANDINAVIAN INSTITUTE OF ASIAN
STUDIES.
— SPECIAL PUBLICATIONS, SCANDINAVIAN INSTITUTE

SCANDINAVIAN ORNITHOLOGISTS' UNION.
— ORNIS SCANDINAVICA.

SCANDINAVIAN SOCIETY OF RHEUMATOLOGISTS.
— SCANDINAVIAN JOURNAL OF RHEUMATOLOGY.                                        XXX

SCHOOL LIBRARY ASSOCIATION, NORTHERN IRELAND
BRANCH.
— NEWS BULLETIN, NORTHERN IRELAND BRANCH,
SCHOOL LIBRARY ASSOCIATION.

SCHOOLS COUNCIL (GB).
— SATIS. SCIENCE & TECHNOLOGY INFORMATION
SOURCES FOR TEACHERS.

SCHOOLS COUNCIL (GB): PROJECT TECHNOLOGY.
— COMPUTER EDUCATION.

SCHOOLS COUNCIL (GB): SIXTH FORM MATHS PROJECT.
— READING AREA NEWS.

SCHWEIZER EVANGELISCHEN JUDENMISSION.
— SCHRIFTEN ZUR JUDENTUMSKUNDE.

SCHWEIZERISCHE GESELLSCHAFT FUR KOORDINATION
UND FORDERUNG DER BAUFORSCHUNG.
— SCHRIFTENREIHE DER SCHWEIZERISCHEN GESELL-
SCHAFT FUR KOORDINATION UND FORDERUNG DER
BAUFORSCHUNG.

SCHWEIZERISCHE GESELLSCHAFT FUR UR- UND
FRUHGESCHICHTE.
— HELVETIA ARCHAEOLOGICA.                                                     XXX

SCHWEIZERISCHE LANDESBIBLIOTHEK.
— BIBLIOGRAPHIE DER SCHWEIZERISCHEN AMTSDRUCK-
SCHRIFTEN.

SCHWEIZERISCHE VEREIN FUR PHYSIOLOGIE, PHYS-
IOLOGISCHE CHEMIE UND PHARMAKOLOGIE.
— HELVETICA PHYSIOLOGICA ET PHARMACOLOGICA ACTA.
— HELVETICA PHYSIOLOGICA ET PHARMACOLOGICA ACTA:
SUPPLEMENT.                                                                   XXX

SCHWEIZERISCHE ZENTRALE FUR HANDELSFORDERUNG.
— ELEGANCE SUISSE.

SCIENCE ASSOCIATES/INTERNATIONAL.
— SCIENTIFIC INFORMATION NOTES.

SCIENCE MUSEUM (ST. PAUL, MINN.).                                             000
SEE: SAINT PAUL INSTITUTE: SCIENCE MUSEUM.

SCIENCE POLICY FOUNDATION.
— SCIENCE POLICY.

SCIENCE REFERENCE LIBRARY.
— PERIODICALS NEWS FROM THE SCIENCE REFERENCE
LIBRARY.                                                                      XXX

SCIENCE RESEARCH COUNCIL (GB).
— QUEST. HOUSE JOURNAL OF THE SCIENCE RESEARCH
COUNCIL.

SCIENCE RESEARCH COUNCIL (GB): NEUTRON BEAM
RESEARCH COMMITTEE.
— TECHNICAL REPORT, NEUTRON BEAM RESEARCH
COMMITTEE, SCIENCE RESEARCH COUNCIL (GB).

SCIENCE RESEARCH COUNCIL(GB): NUCLEAR PHYSICS
BOARD.
— NEWSLETTER, NUCLEAR PHYSICS BOARD, SCIENCE
RESEARCH COUNCIL(GB).

SCIENCE OF SCIENCE FOUNDATION LTD.
— SCIENCE POLICY NEWS.                                                        XXX
— SCIENCE POLICY NEWS SUPPLEMENT: LIST OF
CURRENT NATIONAL PUBLICATIONS.
— SSF NEWSLETTER.                                                             XXX

SCIENCE & TECHNOLOGY AGENCY.
— ATOMIC ABSORPTION & FLAME EMISSION SPECTRO-
SCOPY ABSTRACTS.
— CZECHOSLOVAK CHEMISTRY ABSTRACTS.

SCIENTIFIC COMMITTEE ON OCEANIC RESEARCH.
— PROCEEDINGS, SCIENTIFIC COMMITTEE ON OCEANIC
RESEARCH.

SCIENTIFIC RESEARCH COUNCIL (JAMAICA).
— JOURNAL, SCIENTIFIC RESEARCH COUNCIL(JAMAICA).

SCIENTIFIC SURVEYS (OFFSHORE) LTD.
— OFFSHORE TECHNOLOGY.

SCOTLAND-CHINA ASSOCIATION.
— SINE. BULLETIN OF THE ...

SCOTT BADER & COMPANY: CRYSTIC RESEARCH CENTRE.
— CRYSTIC MONOGRAPH.

SCOTT POLAR RESEARCH INSTITUTE.
— RECENT POLAR LITERATURE.                                    XXX

SCOTTISH ASSOCIATION OF GEOGRAPHY TEACHERS.
— JOURNAL OF THE SCOTTISH ASSOCIATION OF
  GEOGRAPHY TEACHERS.

SCOTTISH ASSOCIATION FOR PUBLIC TRANSPORT.
— STUDY PAPER, SCOTTISH ASSOCIATION FOR PUBLIC
  TRANSPORT.

SCOTTISH CENTRE FOR MODERN LANGUAGES.
— MODERN LANGUAGES IN SCOTLAND.

SCOTTISH CIVIC TRUST.
— ENVIRONMENT SCOTLAND. THE MAGAZINE OF THE ...
— GRAPEVINE. NEWSLETTER OF THE SCOTTISH CIVIC
  TRUST.

SCOTTISH COUNCIL (DEVELOPMENT & INDUSTRY).
— SCOTTISH ECONOMIC REVIEW.

SCOTTISH COUNCIL FOR RESEARCH IN EDUCATION.
— RESEARCH IN EDUCATION (EDINBURGH).

SCOTTISH FARM BUILDINGS INVESTIGATION UNIT.
— FARM BUILDING REPORT.                                       XXX
— FARM BUILDING RESEARCH & DEVELOPMENT STUDIES.               XXX

SCOTTISH GEORGIAN SOCIETY.
— BULLETIN OF THE SCOTTISH GEORGIAN SOCIETY.

SCOTTISH INSTITUTE OF MISSIONARY STUDIES.
— BULLETIN OF THE SCOTTISH INSTITUTE OF MISS-
  IONARY STUDIES.

SCOTTISH LABOUR HISTORY SOCIETY.
— JOURNAL OF THE SCOTTISH LABOUR HISTORY
  SOCIETY.

SCOTTISH LIBRARY ASSOCIATION.
— SCOTTISH LIBRARY STUDIES.

SCOTTISH RECORD SOCIETY.
— [PUBLICATIONS] SCOTTISH RECORD SOCIETY. N.S.

SCOTTISH SOCIETY OF THE HISTORY OF MEDICINE.
— NEWSLETTER, SCOTTISH SOCIETY OF THE HISTORY
  OF MEDICINE.

SCOTTISH SOCIETY FOR INDUSTRIAL ARCHAEOLOGY.
— NEWSLETTER OF THE SCOTTISH SOCIETY FOR
  INDUSTRIAL ARCHAEOLOGY.

SCOTTISH TARTANS SOCIETY.
— PROCEEDINGS OF THE SCOTTISH TARTANS SOCIETY.

SCOTTISH TOURIST BOARD.
— REPORT, SCOTTISH TOURIST BOARD.

SCOTTISH WILDLIFE TRUST.
— NEWSLETTER, SCOTTISH WILDLIFE TRUST.

SCRIPTURE UNION.
— TODAY (1970).

SEATO.
— COMMUNITY DEVELOPMENT DIGEST.

SEIHIN KAGAKU KENKYUJO.                                        XXX
— SEIHIN KAGAKU KENKYUJO KENKYU HOKOKU. BULL-
  ETIN, INDUSTRIAL PRODUCTS RESEARCH INSTITUTE.             XXX
— SEIKAKEN NYUSU.

SEIKEI DAIGAKU.
— SEIKEI DAIGAKU KENKYU HOKOKU. BULLETIN OF
  THE SEIKEI UNIVERSITY.

SEIKEI UNIVERSITY.                                            000
  SEE: SEIKEI DAIGAKU.

SELAS CORPORATION.
— HEAT TECHNOLOGY.

SELBORNE SOCIETY.
— NEWSLETTER, SELBORNE SOCIETY.                               XXX
— PERIVALE NEWSLETTER.                                        XXX

SEMPAKU GIJUTSU KENKYUJO.
— SEMPAKU GIJUTSU KENKYUJO HOKOKU. REPORT OF
  SHIP RESEARCH INSTITUTE.

SEMPERVIVUM SOCIETY.
— JOURNAL, SEMPERVIVUM SOCIETY.

SENDAI SHIRAYURI JUNIOR COLLEGE.                              000
  SEE: SENDAI SHIRAYURI TANKI DAIGAKU.

SENDAI SHIRAYURI TANKI DAIGAKU.
— SENDAI SHIRAYURI TANKI DAIGAKU KIYO.
  MEMOIRS, SENDAI SHIRAYURI JUNIOR COLLEGE.

SENI KOBUNSHI ZAIRYO KENKYUJO.
— SENI KOBUNSHI ZAIRYO KENKYUJO KENKYU HOKOKU.
  BULLETIN OF RESEARCH INSTITUTE FOR POLYMERS
  &TEXTILES (JAPAN).                                          XXX

SENI KOGYO SHIKENJO.
— SENI KOGYO SHIKENJO KENKYU HOKOKU. BULLETIN          XXX
  OF THE TEXTILE RESEARCH INSTITUTE (JAPAN).
  SUBS (1969): SENI KOBUNSHI ZAIRYO KENKYUJO
  KENKYU HOKOKU.

SEOUL NATIONAL UNIVERSITY.
— FACULTY PAPERS, SEOUL NATIONAL UNIVERSITY:
  HUMANITIES & SOCIAL SCIENCES.

SERVIZIO GEOLOGICO D'ITALIA.
— STUDI ILLUSTRATIVI DELLA CARTA GEOLOGICA
  D'ITALIA: FORMAZIONI GEOLOGICHE.

SETO RINKAI JIKKENJO (KYOTO DAIGAKU).
— SPECIAL PUBLICATIONS FROM THE SETO MARINE
  BIOLOGICAL LABORATORY: SERIES 2.

SHEEP DEVELOPMENT ASSOCIATION LTD.
— ANNUAL REPORT, SHEEP DEVELOPMENT ASSOCIATION
  LTD.

SHEFFIELD PHILATELIC SOCIETY.
— SHEFFIELD PHILATELIST. N.S.

SHEFFIELD SURVEY OF LANGUAGE & FOLKLORE.
— LORE & LANGUAGE.

SHELL PETROLEUM CO.
— SCIENCE & TECHNOLOGY NEWSLETTER.

SHETLAND PONY STUD-BOOK SOCIETY.
— MAGAZINE, SHETLAND PONY STUD-BOOK SOCIETY.

SHIGEN KAGAKU KENKYUSHO.
— SHIGEN KAGAKU KENKYUSHO IHO. MISCELLANEOUS
  REPORTS, RESEARCH INSTITUTE FOR NATURAL
  RESOURCES.

SHIKOKU AGRICULTURAL EXPERIMENT STATION.                      000
  SEE: SHIKOKU NOGYO SHIKENJO.

SHIKOKU NOGYO SHIKENJO.
— SHIKOKU NOGYO NO SHIN GIJUTSU.

SHIMONOSEKI UNIVERSITY OF FISHERIES.
— DATA OF OCEANOGRAPHIC OBSERVATIONS & EXPLOR-
  ATORY FISHINGS.

SHIN NIHON DENKI K.K.
— SHIN NIHON DENKI GIHO. NEW NIPPON ELECTRIC
  TECHNICAL REVIEW.

SHIN NIHON SEITETSU K.K.
— NIPPON STEEL TECHNICAL REPORT OVERSEAS.

SHIP RESEARCH INSTITUTE.                                      000
  SEE: SEMPAKU GIJUTSU KENKYUJO.

SHIP STAMP SOCIETY.
— LOG BOOK.

SHIRLEY INSTITUTE.
— HAVE YOU READ THIS?
— SHIRLEY LINK.                                               XXX
— TEXTILES (MANCHESTER).                                      XXX
— WORLD TEXTILE ABSTRACTS.

SHIZUOKA PREFECTURE FORESTRY EXPERIMENT
STATION.                                                      000
  SEE: SHIZUOKA-KEN RINGYO SHIKENJO.

SHIZUOKA-KEN RINGYO SHIKENJO.
— SHIZUOKA-KEN RINGYO SHIKENJO KENKYU HOKOKU.
  BULLETIN OF THE SHIZUOKA PREFECTURE FORESTRY
  EXPERIMENT STATION.

**SHOCK & VIBRATION INFORMATION CENTER (US).**
— SHOCK & VIBRATION DIGEST.

**SHOE & ALLIED TRADES RESEARCH ASSOCIATION.**
— FOOTWEAR DIGEST.     XXX
— POROMERICS PROGRESS.     XXX
— SHOE MATERIALS PROGRESS.     XXX
— SHOEMAKING PROGRESS.

**SHOWA PHARMACEUTICAL COLLEGE.**     000
  SEE: SHOWA YAKKA DAIGAKU.

**SHOWA YAKKA DAIGAKU.**
— SHOWA YAKKA DAIGAKU KIYO. ANNUAL REPORT OF
  THE SHOWA PHARMACEUTICAL COLLEGE.

**SHOYU TECHNICAL SOCIETY OF JAPAN.**     000
  SEE: NIHON SHOYU GIJUTSUKAI.

**SHROPSHIRE CONSERVATION TRUST.**
— BULLETIN, SHROPSHIRE CONSERVATION TRUST.

**SIAM SOCIETY.**
— MONOGRAPH, SIAM SOCIETY.

**SIEMENS A.G.**
— SIEMENS FORSCHUNGS- UND ENTWICKLUNGSBERICHTE.

**SIEMENS UND HALSKE AG.**
— SIEMENS DATA REPORT.

**SIEMENS-ALBIS, A.G.**     XXX
— SIEMENS-ALBIS BERICHTE.     XXX

**SIERRA LEONE CHAMBER OF COMMERCE.**
— SIERRA LEONE CHAMBER OF COMMERCE JOURNAL.

**SIERRA LEONE PRODUCE MARKETING BOARD.**
— SLPMB RECORD. A NEWSLETTER FROM THE SIERRA
  LEONE PRODUCE MARKETING BOARD.

**(SIERRA LEONE) SUPREME COURT.**
— SIERRA LEONE LAW REPORTS.

**SILLIMAN UNIVERSITY.**
— RELIGIOUS STUDIES MONOGRAPHS.

**SIMON COMMUNITY.**
— SIMON STAR. NEWSLETTER OF THE SIMON
  COMMUNITY.     XXX

**SIMON COMMUNITY TRUST RESEARCH.**
— SOCIAL ACTION.

**SIMON POPULATION TRUST.**
— BIBLIOGRAPHY OF FAMILY PLANNING & POPULATION.

**SIMULATION COUNCILS, INC.**
— SIMULATION COUNCILS PROCEEDINGS SERIES.

**SIND MUSLIM LAW COLLEGE (KARACHI).**
— KARACHI LAW JOURNAL.

**(SINGAPORE) DEPARTMENT OF STATISTICS.**
— YEARBOOK OF STATISTICS (SINGAPORE).

**(SINGAPORE) MINISTRY OF HEALTH: PUBLIC HEALTH
DIVISION.**
— SINGAPORE PUBLIC HEALTH BULLETIN.

**(SINGAPORE) NATIONAL STATISTICAL COMMISSION.**
— SINGAPORE STATISTICAL BULLETIN.

**SINGAPORE NATIONAL ACADEMY OF SCIENCE.**
— JOURNAL, SINGAPORE NATIONAL ACADEMY OF
  SCIENCE.

**SINGAPORE NATIONAL INSTITUTE OF CHEMISTRY.**
— SNIC BULLETIN.

**SIRA.**     000
  SEE: BRITISH SCIENTIFIC INSTRUMENT RESEARCH
  ASSOCIATION.

**SKINNER & CO.**
— INTERNATIONAL TEXTILE MACHINERY.

**SLASKI INSTYTUT NAUKOWY.**
— GORNOSLASKIE STUDIA SOCJOLOGICZNE, SLASKI
  INSTYTUT NAUKOWY.
— ZESZYTY NAUKOWE, SLASKI INSTYTUT NAUKOWY.

**SLEZSKE MUSEUM.**
— CASOPIS SLEZSKEHO MUSEA: SERIE C: DENDROLOGIE.

**SLOAN SCHOOL OF MANAGEMENT.**     000
  SEE: ALFRED P. SLOAN ...

**SLOUGH CONSUMER GROUP.**
— SLOUGH CONSUMER.

**SLOVENSKA AKADEMIA VIED.**
— ARCHAEOLOGICA SLOVACA - CATALOGI.
— MATEMATICKY CASOPIS.     XXX

**SLOVENSKA AKADEMIA VIED: ENDOCRINOLOGICKY
USTAV.**
— ENDOCRINOLOGIA EXPERIMENTALIS.

**SLOVENSKA AKADEMIA VIED: FYZIKALNY USTAV.**
— FYZIKALNY CASOPIS.     XXX

**SLOVENSKA AKADEMIA VIED: HISTORICKY USTAV
(ODDELENIE DEJIN VIED).**
— Z DEJIN VIED A TECHNIKY NA SLOVENSKU.

**SLOVENSKA AKADEMIA VIED: LABORATORIUM RYBARSTVA**
— PRACE LABORATORIA RYBARSTVA, SLOVENSKA AKA-
  DEMIA VIED.

**SLOVENSKA AKADEMIA VIED: USTAV DEJIN UMENIA.**
— ARS.

**SLOVENSKA AKADEMIA VIED: USTAV STAVEBNICTVA A'
ARCHITEKTURY.**
— ARCHITEKTURA A URBANIZMUS.

**SLOVENSKA ARCHIVNA SPRAVA.**
— HISTORICKO-STATISTICKE PRAMENE A MONOGRAFIE.

**SLOVENSKY USTAV PRE DOSKOLOVANIE LEKAROV.**
— FARMACEUTICKY OBZOR.     XXX
— FARMACIA.     XXX
  SUBS(1961): FARMACEUTICKY OBZOR.

**SLOVENSKY USTAV PAMIATKOVEJ STAROSTLIVOSTI A
OCHRANY PRIRODY.**
— CESKOSLOVENSKA OCHRANA PRIRODY. NATURE CONS-
  ERVATION IN CZECHOSLOVAKIA.

**SLOVENSKA VYSOKA SKOLA TECHNICKA: CHEMICKA
FAKULTA.**
— SBORNIK PRAC CHEMICKEJ FAKULTY SVST.

**SMALL INDUSTRIES COUNCIL FOR RURAL AREAS OF
SCOTLAND.**
— CRAFTWORK. SCOTLAND'S CRAFT MAGAZINE.

**SMITHSONIAN INSTITUTION.**
— INFORMATION SYSTEMS INNOVATIONS.
— PACIFIC BIRD OBSERVER.
— SMITHSONIAN CONTRIBUTIONS TO BOTANY.
— SMITHSONIAN CONTRIBUTIONS TO THE EARTH
  SCIENCES.
— SMITHSONIAN CONTRIBUTIONS TO PALEOBIOLOGY.
— SMITHSONIAN CONTRIBUTIONS TO ZOOLOGY.

**SMITHSONIAN INSTITUTION: ASTROPHYSICAL
OBSERVATORY.**
— ASTRONOMICAL PAPERS TRANSLATED FROM THE
  RUSSIAN.

**SOAG MACHINE TOOLS LTD.**
— SOAG THEORY & PRACTICE.

**SOCIAL ADMINISTRATION ASSOCIATION.**
— JOURNAL OF SOCIAL POLICY.

**SOCIAL SCIENCE RESEARCH COUNCIL OF CANADA.**
— SOCIAL SCIENCES IN CANADA. SCIENCES SOCIALES
  AU CANADA.

**SOCIAL SCIENCE RESEARCH COUNCIL (GB).**
— RESEARCH SUPPORTED BY THE SSRC.

**SOCIALIST LABOUR LEAGUE: CENTRAL COMMITTEE.**
— NEWSLETTER, SOCIALIST LABOUR LEAGUE.     XXX
  SUBS (1969): WORKERS' PRESS.
— WORKERS' PRESS: THE DAILY ORGAN OF THE ...     XXX

**SOCIALIST MEDICAL ASSOCIATION.**
— MEDICINE TODAY & TOMORROW.     XXX
  SUBS (1967): SOCIALISM & HEALTH.
— SOCIALISM & HEALTH.     XXX

**SOCIALIST WOMAN GROUPS.**
— SOCIALIST WOMAN.

**SOCIETY FOR ADVANCEMENT OF ELECTROCHEMICAL
SCIENCE & TECHNOLOGY (INDIA).**
— TRANSACTIONS, SOCIETY FOR ADVANCEMENT OF
  ELECTROCHEMICAL SCIENCE & TECHNOLOGY (INDIA).

SOCIETY FOR THE ADVANCEMENT OF MATERIAL &
PROCESS ENGINEERING.
— SAMPE JOURNAL.                                           XXX
— SAMPE QUARTERLY.

SOCIETE AFRICAINE D'EDITION.
— REVUE FRANCAISE D'ETUDES POLITIQUES AFRICAINES.

SOCIETY FOR AMATEUR RADIO ASTRONOMERS.
— RADIO SKY.

SOCIETE DES AMIS DE JEAN COCTEAU.
— CAHIERS JEAN COCTEAU.

SOCIETY FOR ANALYTICAL CHEMISTRY.
— ANNUAL REPORTS ON ANALYTICAL ATOMIC SPECTROS-
COPY.
— SELECTED ANNUAL REVIEWS OF THE ANALYTICAL
SCIENCES.

SOCIETY FOR ANGLO-CHINESE UNDERSTANDING.
— CHINA NOW.

SOCIETY OF ANTIQUARIES OF NEWCASTLE-UPON-TYNE.
— PUBLICATIONS, SOCIETY OF ANTIQUARIES OF
NEWCASTLE-UPON-TYNE: RECORD SERIES.

SOCIETY FOR APPLIED BACTERIOLOGY.
— TECHNICAL SERIES, SOCIETY FOR APPLIED BACTER-
IOLOGY.

SOCIETE D'ARCHEOLOGIE ET D'HISTOIRE DE LA
MANCHE.
— PUBLICATIONS MULTIGRAPHIEES, SOCIETE D'ARCH-
EOLOGIE ET D'HISTOIRE DE LA MANCHE.

SOCIEDAD ARGENTINA DE INVESTIGADORES EN CIENCIA
DE LA INGENIERIA QUIMICA Y QUIMICA APLICADA.
— REVISTA LATINOAMERICANA DE INGENIERIA QUIMICA
Y QUIMICA APLICADA = LATIN AMERICAN JOURNAL
OF CHEMICAL ENGINEERING & APPLIED CHEMISTRY.

SOCIETY OF AUTOMOTIVE ENGINEERS, INC.
— AUTOMOTIVE ENGINEERING.                                  XXX
— SAE JOURNAL.                                             XXX
SUBS (1970):  AUTOMOTIVE ENGINEERING.

SOCIETY OF AUTOMOTIVE ENGINEERS OF JAPAN.          000
SEE: JIDOSHA GIJUTSUKAI.

SOCIETE BELGE D'HISTOIRE DES HOPITAUX.
— ANNALES, SOCIETE BELGE D'HISTOIRE DES HOPI-
TAUX.

SOCIETY OF BIOLOGICAL PSYCHIATRY.
— BIOLOGICAL PSYCHIATRY.                                   XXX
— PROCEEDINGS OF THE ANNUAL CONVENTION &
SCIENCE PROGRAM, SOCIETY OF BIOLOGICAL
PSYCHIATRY.                                                XXX
SUBS(1969): BIOLOGICAL PSYCHIATRY.
— PROCEEDINGS OF SCIENTIFIC SESSIONS, SOCIETY
OF BIOLOGICAL PSYCHIATRY.                                  XXX
SUBS(1969): BIOLOGICAL PSYCHIATRY.

SOCIETE DE BIOLOGIE HUMAINE ET ANIMALE DU
CENTRE.
— SYMBIOSES.

SOCIETE DE BIOMETRIE HUMAINE.
— REVUE DE LA SOCIETE DE BIOMETRIE HUMAINE
(BIOTYPOLOGIE).                                            XXX

SOCIEDAD BOLIVARIANA DE LIMA.
— BOLIVAR.

SOCIETA BOTANICA ITALIANA.
— INFORMATORE BOTANICO ITALIANO.

SOCIEDADE BRASILEIRA DE FISICA.
— REVISTA BRASILEIRA DE FISICA.
— REVISTA BRASILEIRA DE GEOCIENCIAS.

SOCIEDADE BRASILEIRA DE GEOLOGIA.
— PUBLICACAO, SOCIEDADE BRASILEIRA DE GEOLOGIA.

SOCIEDADE BRASILEIRA DE MATEMATICA.
— BOLETIM DA SOCIEDADE BRASILEIRA DE MATEMATICA.

SOCIEDADE BRASILEIRA DE MICROBIOLOGIA.
— REVISTA DE MICROBIOLOGIA.

SOCIETY OF BROADCAST ENGINEERS.
— BROADCAST JOURNAL.                                       XXX

SOCIETY OF CABLE TELEVISION ENGINEERS.            XXX
— CABLE TELEVISION ENGINEERING.                            XXX

SOCIETY OF CHEMICAL ENGINEERS (JAPAN).            000
SEE: KAGAKU KOGAKU KYOKAI.

SOCIETY OF CHEMICAL INDUSTRY.
— BRITISH POLYMER JOURNAL.
— CHEMISTRY & INDUSTRY.
— CHEMISTRY & INDUSTRY BULLETIN.
— JOURNAL OF APPLIED CHEMISTRY & BIOTECHNOLOGY.    XXX
— PESTICIDE SCIENCE.

SOCIETE DE CHIMIE BIOLOGIQUE.
— BIOCHIMIE.                                               XXX
— BULLETIN, SOCIETE DE CHIMIE BIOLOGIQUE.          XXX
SUBS (1971): BIOCHIMIE.

SOCIETY OF CIVIL ENGINEERING TECHNICIANS.
— CIVIL ENGINEERING TECHNICIAN.  JOURNAL OF ...

SOCIETY OF DESIGNER-CRAFTSMEN.
— NEWSLETTER, SOCIETY OF DESIGNER-CRAFTSMEN.

SOCIETY FOR DEVELOPMENTAL BIOLOGY.
— DEVELOPMENTAL BIOLOGY:  SUPPLEMENT.

SOCIEDAD DOMINICANA DE GEOGRAFIA.
— BOLETIN DE LA SOCIEDAD DOMINICANA DE
GEOGRAFIA.

SOCIETY OF DYERS & COLOURISTS.
— SDC NEWS.

SOCIETE D'ECOLOGIE.
— BULLETIN, SOCIETE D'ECOLOGIE (FRANCE).

SOCIETE DES EDITIONS RADIO.
— TELEVISION (PARIS).                                      XXX
SUBS (1970):  TELEVISION ET TECHNIQUES TELE-
VISUELLES.
— TELEVISION ET TECHNIQUES TELEVISUELLES.                  XXX

SOCIETA EDITRICE RIVISTE TECNICHE.
— ACQUA ED ARIA.

SOCIETY FOR EDUCATION IN FILM & TELEVISION.
— SCREEN.  JOURNAL OF THE...                               XXX
— SCREEN EDUCATION.                                        XXX
SUBS (1969): SCREEN.  JOURNAL OF THE...

SOCIETAS ENTOMOLOGICA SCANDINAVICA.
— ENTOMOLOGICA SCANDINAVICA.

SOCIETY OF ENVIRONMENTAL ENGINEERS.
— JOURNAL, SOCIETY OF ENVIRONMENTAL ENGINEERS.     XXX

SOCIEDAD ESPANOLA DE CERAMICA Y VIDRIO.           XXX
— BOLETIN, SOCIEDAD ESPANOLA DE CERAMICA Y
VIDRIO.                                                    XXX

SOCIEDAD ESPANOLA DE LINGUISTICA.
— REVISTA ESPANOLA DE LINGUISTICA.

SOCIEDAD DE ESTUDIOS MONASTICOS.
— YERMO.  CUADERNOS DE HISTORIA Y DE ESPIRIT-
UALIDAD MONASTICOS.

SOCIETE D'ETHNOGRAPHIE FRANCAISE.
— ARTS ET TRADITIONS POPULAIRES.                           XXX
SUBS (1971): ETHNOLOGIE FRANCAISE: NS.
— ETHNOLOGIE FRANCAISE: NS.                                XXX

SOCIETY FOR ETHNOMUSICOLOGY.
— SEM NEWSLETTER.
— SPECIAL SERIES IN ETHNOMUSICOLOGY.

SOCIETE D'ETUDES ALLEMANDES.
— REVUE D'ALLEMAGNE.

SOCIETE D'ETUDE ET DE DIFFUSION DES INDUSTRIES
THERMIQUES.
— PROMOCLIM.  INDUSTRIES THERMIQUES ET
AERAULIQUES.

SOCIETE D'ETUDES ET DE PUBLICATIONS ECONOMIQUES
— PREUVES.  LES IDEES QUI CHANGENT LE MONDE.

SOCIETE DES ETUDES RENANIENNES.
— BULLETIN, SOCIETE DES ETUDES RENANIENNES.
— CAHIERS RENANIENS.

SOCIETE DES ETUDES ROMANTIQUES.
— ROMANTISME.

SOCIETE D'ETUDE ET DE VULGARISATION DE LA
ZOOLOGIE AGRICOLE.
— REVUE DE ZOOLOGIE AGRICOLE ET DE PATHOLOGIE
VEGETALE.

SOCIEDADE EXCURSIONISTA E ESPELEOLOGICA
(BRAZIL).
— ESPELEOLOGIA.

SOCIETE D'EXPANSION TECHNIQUE ET ECONOMIQUE.
— HAUTS POLYMERES.

SOCIETY FOR THE EXPERIMENTAL ANALYSIS OF
BEHAVIOR.
— JOURNAL OF APPLIED BEHAVIOR ANALYSIS.
— REVUE DE ZOOLOGIE AGRICOLE ET APPLIQUE.      XXX
   SUBS (1969):  REVUE DE ZOOLOGIE AGRICOLE ET DE
   PATHOLOGIE VEGETALE.

SOCIETY OF FISHERIES TECHNOLOGISTS (INDIA).
— FISHERY TECHNOLOGY.

SOCIETE FRANCAISE D'ETUDE DU XVIIIE SIECLE.
— DIX-HUITIEME SIECLE.

SOCIETES FRANCAISE DE GENEALOGIE, D'HERALDIQUE
ET DE SIGILLOGRAPHIE.
— HERALDIQUE ET GENEALOGIE.  BULLETIN DES ...

SOCIETY FRANCAISE DE MALACOLOGIE.
— HALIOTIS.

SOCIETE FRANCAISE DE MICROBIOLOGIE.
— ANNALES DE MICROBIOLOGIE: A.                 XXX
— ANNALES DE MICROBIOLOGIE: B.                 XXX

SOCIETE FRANCAISE DE PHYSIQUE BIOLOGIQUE ET
MEDICALE.
— ANNALES DE PHYSIQUE BIOLOGIQUE ET MEDICALE.

SOCIETY FOR GEOGRAPHICAL STUDIES.
— GEOGRAPHICAL KNOWLEDGE.

SOCIETE GEOGRAPHIQUE DE LIEGE.
— BULLETIN, SOCIETE GEOGRAPHIQUE DE LIEGE.

SOCIETY FOR GERMAN-AMERICAN STUDIES.
— GERMAN-AMERICAN STUDIES.

SOCIETY OF GYNECOLOGIC ONCOLOGY.
— GYNECOLOGIC ONCOLOGY.

SOCIETE D'HISTOIRE ET D'ART DU DIOCESE DE
MEAUX.
— ETUDES & DOCUMENTS, SOCIETE D'HISTOIRE ET D'
   ART DU DIOCESE DE MEAUX.

SOCIETE D'HISTOIRE LITTERAIRE DE LA FRANCE.
— BIBLIOGRAPHIE DE LA LITTERATURE FRANCAISE DU
   MOYEN AGE A NOS JOURS.                        XXX

SOCIETY FOR THE HISTORY OF DISCOVERIES.
— TERRAE INCOGNITAE.  THE ANNALS OF THE ...

SOCIETY OF INDIAN ZOOLOGISTS.
— INDIAN ZOOLOGIST.

SOCIETY FOR INDUSTRIAL & APPLIED MATHEMATICS.
— SIAM JOURNAL ON COMPUTING.
— SIAM JOURNAL ON MATHEMATICAL ANALYSIS.
— STUDIES IN OPTIMIZATION.

SOCIETE DE L'INDUSTRIE MINERALE.
— INDUSTRIE MINERALE:  REVUE DE LA ...          XXX
— REVUE DE L'INDUSTRIE MINERALE.                XXX
   SUBS (1971): INDUSTRIE MINERALE.

SOCIETY FOR INFORMATION DISPLAY.
— INFORMATION DISPLAY.  JOURNAL OF THE ...      XXX

SOCIETE INTERNATIONALE DE CRIMINOLOGIE.
— ANNALES INTERNATIONALES DE CRIMINOLOGIE.
   INTERNATIONAL ANNALS OF CRIMINOLOGY.  ANALES
   INTERNACIONALES DE CRIMINOLOGIA.             XXX
— BULLETIN DE LA SOCIETE INTERNATIONALE DE
   CRIMINOLOGIE.                                 XXX
   SUBS (1962): ANNALES INTERNATIONALES DE
   CRIMINOLOGIE.

SOCIETE INTERNATIONALE D'EDITION MEDICALE.
— REVUE DE PHYSIOLOGIE SUBAQUATIQUE ET MEDECINE
   HYPERBARE. = REVIEW OF SUBAQUATIC PHYSIOLOGY &
   HYPERBARIC MEDICINE.

SOCIETAS INTERNATIONALIS ODONATOLOGICA.
— ODONATOLOGICA.

SOCIETY FOR INVESTIGATION & RESEARCH INTO
UNIDENTIFIED FLYING OBJECT SIGHTINGS.
— SIRIUS.

SOCIETY FOR IRANIAN CULTURE & SOCIAL STUDIES.
— IRANIAN STUDIES.

SOCIETA ITALIANA DI AGRONOMIA.
— RIVISTA DI AGRONOMIA.

SOCIETA ITALIANA DI FISICA.
— LETTERE AL NUOVO CIMENTO.  RIVISTA INTERNAZ-
   IONALE DELLA...
— RIVISTA DEL NUOVO CIMENTO.

SOCIETA ITALIANA DI GEOFISICA E METEOROLOGIA.
— GEOFISICA E METEOROLOGIA.                     XXX
   SUBS (1972): RIVISTA ITALIANA DI GEOFISICA.
— RIVISTA ITALIANA DI GEOFISICA.                XXX

SOCIETA ITALIANA DI MINERALOGIA E PETROLOGIA.
— RENDICONTI, SOCIETA ITALIANA DI MINERALOGIA
   E PETROLOGIA.                                 XXX

SOCIETA ITALIANA PER LO STUDIO DEL METABOLISMO
NORMALE E PATOLOGICO.
— METABOLISMO.

SOCIETE JULES VERNE.
— BULLETIN DE LA SOCIETE JULES VERNE: NS.

SOCIEDAD LATINOAMERICANA DE TUBEROSAS.
— NOTICIERO TUBEROSAS.

SOCIETY OF LEATHER TECHNOLOGISTS & CHEMISTS.  XXX
— JOURNAL OF THE SOCIETY OF LEATHER TECHNOLOG-
   ISTS & CHEMISTS.                              XXX

SOCIETY OF LEATHER TRADES' CHEMISTS.           XXX
— JOURNAL OF THE SOCIETY OF LEATHER TRADES'
   CHEMISTS.                                     XXX
   SUBS (1973): JOURNAL OF THE SOCIETY OF
   LEATHER TECHNOLOGISTS & CHEMISTS.

SOCIEDADE DE LINGUA PORTUGUESA.
— POESIA & FICCAO.

SOCIETE LINNEENNE DE BORDEAUX.
— BULLETIN, SOCIETE LINNEENNE DE BORDEAUX.

SOCIETY FOR LONG RANGE PLANNING.
— LONG RANGE PLANNING. JOURNAL OF THE ...

SOCIETY OF MANUFACTURING ENGINEERS.
— MANUFACTURING ENGINEERING & MANAGEMENT.      XXX

SOCIEDAD MEXICANA DE HISTORIA DE LA CIENCIA Y
DE LA TECNOLOGIA.
— ANALES DE LA SOCIEDAD MEXICANA DE HISTORIA
   DE LA CIENCIA Y DE LA TECNOLOGIA.

SOCIEDAD MEXICANA DE MICOLOGIA.
— BOLETIN INFORMATIVO, SOCIEDAD MEXICANA DE
   MICOLOGIA.

SOCIETY OF MULTIVARIATE EXPERIMENTAL PSYCHOLOGY
— MULTIVARIATE BEHAVIORAL RESEARCH.

SOCIETE NATIONALE FRANCAISE DE GASTROENTEROL-
OGIE.
— BIOLOGIE ET GASTRO-ENTEROLOGIE.

SOCIETE NATIONALE DE PROTECTION DE LA NATURE ET
D'ACCLIMATATION (FRANCE).
— COURRIER DE LA NATURE.

SOCIETA DEI NATURALISTI IN NAPOLI.
— MEMORIE DELLA SOCIETA DEI NATURALISTI IN
   NAPOLI.

SOCIETY FOR NAUTICAL RESEARCH: SOUTHERN BRANCH.
— WINDWARD.

SOCIETY FOR NEAR EASTERN STUDIES IN JAPAN.
— ORIENT.

SOCIETY OF NEMATOLOGISTS.
— JOURNAL OF NEMATOLOGY.
— SPECIAL PUBLICATIONS, SOCIETY OF
   NEMATOLOGISTS.

SOCIETE NOUVELLE D'EDITION ET DE DIFFUSION.
— MONDE MODERNE.

SOCIETE NOUVELLE D'EDITION GEOGRAPHIQUE ET
TOURISTIQUE.
— CONNAISSANCE DES VOYAGES.

SOCIETY FOR NUTRITION EDUCATION.
— JOURNAL OF NUTRITION EDUCATION.

SOCI

SOCIETE ODONTOLOGIQUE DES IMPLANTS-AIGUILLES.
— BOLLETTINO ODONTO-IMPLANTOLOGICO.

SOCIEDADE PAULISTA DE MEDICINA VETERINARIA E
DOS MEDICOS VETERINARIOS BRASILEIROS.
— REVISTA DE MEDICINA VETERINARIA (SAO PAULO).

SOCIETY FOR PERSONALITY ASSESSMENT.
— JOURNAL OF PERSONALITY ASSESSMENT.                    XXX

SOCIETY FOR PERSONALITY RESEARCH.
— PERSONALITY. AN INTERNATIONAL JOURNAL.

SOCIETE DE PHARMACIE DE NANCY.
— BULLETIN, SOCIETE DE PHARMACIE DE NANCY.              XXX
  SUBS (1973): SCIENCES PHARMACEUTIQUES ET
  BIOLOGIQUES DE LORRAINE.
— SCIENCES PHARMACEUTIQUES ET BIOLOGIQUES DE
  LORRAINE.                                             XXX

SOCIETY OF PHOTO-OPTICAL INSTRUMENTATION ENGIN-
EERS.
— OPTICAL ENGINEERING.                                  XXX

SOCIETY OF POLYMER SCIENCE (JAPAN).
— POLYMER JOURNAL (TOKYO).

SOCIETE PREHISTORIQUE DE L'ARDECHE.
— ETUDES PREHISTORIQUES (LYONS).

SOCIETE DE PRODUCTIONS DOCUMENTAIRES.
— ANALUSIS.                                             XXX
— CHIMIE ANALYTIQUE.                                    XXX
  SUBS (1972) PART OF: ANALUSIS.
— METHODS PHYSIQUE D'ANALYSE.                           XXX
  SUBS(1972) PART OF: ANALUSIS.

SOCIETY FOR THE PROMOTION OF CHRISTIAN KNOW-
LEDGE.
— CHURCH QUARTERLY.

SOCIETY FOR THE PROMOTION OF NATURE RESERVES.
— CONSERVATION REVIEW.

SOCIETY FOR THE PROMOTION OF ROMAN STUDIES.
— BRITANNIA.

SOCIETY FOR PSYCHICAL RESEARCH.
— S.P.R. NEWSLETTER.

SOCIETE DE PUBLICATIONS MECANIQUES.
— ENERGIE FLUIDE ET LUBRIFICATION.                      XXX

SOCIETE DES RECHERCHES AMERINDIENNES AU QUEBEC.
— RECHERCHES AMERINDIENNES AU QUEBEC. BULLETIN
  D'INFORMATION.

SOCIETY OF RELAY ENGINEERS.
— PROCEEDINGS, SOCIETY OF RELAY ENGINEERS.              XXX
  SUBS (1971): RELAY ENGINEER.
— RELAY ENGINEER.                                       XXX

SOCIETY FOR RESEARCH INTO HIGHER EDUCATION.
— INTERNATIONAL NEWSLETTER, SOCIETY FOR RE-
  SEARCH INTO HIGHER EDUCATION.

SOCIETY FOR RESEARCH IN PSYCHOLOGY OF MUSIC &
MUSIC EDUCATION.
— PSYCHOLOGY OF MUSIC.

(SOCIETE ROUMAINE DE LINGUISTIQUE ROMANE).
— BULLETIN DE LA SOCIETE ROUMAINE DE LINGUIS-
  TIQUE ROMANE.

SOCIETY OF ST. GREGORY.
— LIFE & WORSHIP. QUARTERLY OF ...                      XXX

SOCIETAS SCIENTIARUM FENNICA.
— COMMENTATIONES SCIENTIARUM SOCIALIUM.

SOCIETY FOR THE SCIENTIFIC STUDY OF SEX.
— JOURNAL OF SEX RESEARCH.

SOCIETY OF SOIL SCIENCE (UAR).
— UNITED ARAB REPUBLIC JOURNAL OF SOIL SCIENCE.         XXX

SOCIETATEA DE STIINTE BIOLOGICE DIN REPUBLICA
SOCIALISTA ROMANIA: SECTIA DE MICROBIOLOGIE.
— MICROBIOLOGIA.

SOCIETATEA DE STIINTE ISTORICE SI FILOLOGICE
DIN REPUBLICA SOCIALISTA ROMANIA.
— MAGAZIN ISTORIC.

SOCIETY FOR THE STUDY OF AMPHIBIANS &
REPTILES.
— HERPETOLOGICAL REVIEW.                                XXX
— JOURNAL OF HERPETOLOGY.                               XXX

SOCIETY FOR THE STUDY OF FERTILITY.
— JOURNAL OF REPRODUCTION & FERTILITY: SUPPLE-
  MENT.

SOCIETY FOR THE STUDY OF HUMAN EVOLUTION.
— PERSPECTIVES ON HUMAN EVOLUTION.

SOCIETY FOR THE STUDY OF REPRODUCTION.
— BIOLOGY OF REPRODUCTION.
— BIOLOGY OF REPRODUCTION: SUPPLEMENT.

SOCIETY FOR THE STUDY OF WELSH LABOUR HISTORY.
— LLAFUR. THE JOURNAL OF THE ...

SOCIETY OF UNIVERSITY CARTOGRAPHERS.
— BULLETIN, SOCIETY OF UNIVERSITY CARTOGRAPHERS.

SOCIETAS URALO-ALTAICA.
— MITTEILUNGEN, SOCIETAS URALO-ALTAICA.
— VEROFFENTLICHUNGEN DER SOCIETAS URALO-ALTAICA.

SOCIEDAD VENEZOLANA DE ESPELEOLOGIA: BIBLIOTECA
— BOLETIN INFORMATIVO DE LA BIBLIOTECA, SOCIE-
  DAD VENEZOLANA DE ESPELEOLOGIA.

SOCIETY FOR VETERINARY ETHOLOGY.
— PROCEEDINGS OF THE SOCIETY FOR VETERINARY
  ETHOLOGY.

SOCIETY OF WOOD SCIENCE & TECHNOLOGY.
— WOOD & FIBER.

SOCIEDAD ZOOLOGICA DEL URUGUAY.
— BOLETIN DE LA SOCIEDAD ZOOLOGICA DEL URUGUAY.

SOCIJALDEMOKRATSKA ZAJEDNICA JUGOSLOVENA VAN
OTADZBINE.
— BUDUCNOST. THE FUTURE.

SOCJETA TAL-POEZIJA.
— POEZIJA.

SOFIJSKIJA UNIVERSITET: KATEDRA POLITICHESKA
IKONOMIJA.
— GODISHNIK NA SOFIJSKIJA UNIVERSITET: KATEDRA
  POLITICHESKA IKONOMIJA.

SOIL ASSOCIATION.
— JOURNAL OF THE SOIL ASSOCIATION.                      XXX
— SOIL ASSOCIATION.                                     XXX
— SPAN. SOIL ASSOCIATION NEWS.                          XXX

SOIL SURVEY OF GREAT BRITAIN (ENGLAND & WALES).
— SPECIAL SURVEY, SOIL SURVEY OF GREAT BRITAIN.
— TECHNICAL MONOGRAPH, SOIL SURVEY OF GREAT
  BRITAIN.

SOJUZ BOR'BY ZA OSVOBOZHDENIE NARODOV ROSSII.
— S NARODOM - ZA NAROD.

SOJUZ PISATELEJ SSSR: LITERATURNYJ INSTITUT.
— PISATEL' I ZHIZN'.

SOJUZ PISATELEJ TADZHIKISTANA.
— PAMIR. LITERATURNO-KHUDOZHESTVENNYJ I OBSH-
  CHESTVENNO-POLITICHESKIJ ZHURNAL.

SOMERSET TRUST FOR NATURE CONSERVATION.
— NEWS LETTER, SOMERSET TRUST FOR NATURE
  CONSERVATION.

(SOUTH AFRICA) ADMINISTRATION OF SOUTH WEST
AFRICA: NATURE CONSERVATION & TOURISM BRANCH.
— MADOQUA. JOURNAL OF NATURE CONSERVATION RES-
  EARCH, SOUTH WEST AFRICA.

(SOUTH AFRICA) ATOMIC ENERGY BOARD.
— ISOTOPE.

(SOUTH AFRICA) BUREAU OF STATISTICS.
— ANTICIPATED CAPITAL EXPENDITURE OF THE PUBLIC
  SECTOR.
— SHORT TERM ECONOMIC INDICATORS (SOUTH AFRICA).
  = KORTTERMYN EKONOMIESE AANWYSERS.

(SOUTH AFRICA) DEPARTMENT OF AGRICULTURE.
— PHYTOPHYLACTICA.

(SOUTH AFRICA) DEPARTMENT OF INDUSTRIES.
— HYDROLOGICAL STATION LIST.

SOUTH AFRICA FOUNDATION.
— SOUTH AFRICA INTERNATIONAL.

SOUTH AFRICA WOOL TEXTILE RESEARCH INSTITUTE.
— SAWTRI BULLETIN.

SOUTH AFRICAN ARCHAEOLOGICAL SOCIETY.
— GOODWIN SERIES, SOUTH AFRICAN ARCHAEOLOGICAL
SOCIETY.

SOUTH AFRICAN COPPER DEVELOPMENT ASSOCIATION.
— COPPER INFORMATION: ARCHITECTURAL SERIES.
— COPPER INFORMATION: ENGINEERING SERIES.

SOUTH AFRICAN COUNCIL FOR SCIENTIFIC & INDUST-
RIAL RESEARCH.
— SOUTH AFRICAN JOURNAL OF ANTARCTIC RESEARCH.

SOUTH AFRICAN COUNCIL FOR SCIENTIFIC & IND-
USTRIAL RESEARCH: MICROBIOLOGY RESEARCH GROUP.
— BULLETIN, MICROBIOLOGY RESEARCH GROUP, SOUTH
AFRICAN COUNCIL FOR INDUSTRIAL RESEARCH.

SOUTH AFRICAN HUMAN SCIENCES RESEARCH COUNCIL.
— HUMANITAS. TYDSKRIF VIR NAVORSING IN DIE
GEESTESWETENSKAPPE.

SOUTH AFRICAN INSTITUTE OF ELECTRONIC & RADIO
ENGINEERS.
— ELECTRONICS IN SOUTHERN AFRICA.                          XXX

SOUTH AFRICAN INSTITUTE OF INTERNATIONAL
AFFAIRS.
— NEWSLETTER, SOUTH AFRICAN INSTITUTE OF INTER-
NATIONAL AFFAIRS.

SOUTH AFRICAN INSTITUTE FOR PRODUCTION
ENGINEERING.
— F.W.P. JOURNAL.                                          XXX

SOUTH AFRICAN INSTITUTE OF RACE RELATIONS.
— TOPICAL TALKS.

SOUTH AFRICAN SOCIETY OF DAIRY TECHNOLOGY.
— SOUTH AFRICAN JOURNAL OF DAIRY TECHNOLOGY.

SOUTH AFRICAN STATISTICAL ASSOCIATION.
— SOUTH AFRICAN STATISTICAL JOURNAL. = SUID-
AFRIKAANSE STATISTIESE TYDSKRIF.

SOUTH ASIA LIBRARY GROUP.
— SALG NEWSLETTER.

(SOUTH AUSTRALIA) GEOLOGICAL SURVEY.
— QUARTERLY GEOLOGICAL NOTES (AUSTRALIA).

(SOUTH AUSTRALIA) LIBRARIES BOARD.
— OCCASIONAL PAPERS IN LIBRARIANSHIP, LIBRARIES
BOARD OF SOUTH AUSTRALIA.

(SOUTH CAROLINA) STATE DEVELOPMENT BOARD:
DIVISION OF GEOLOGY.
— ENVIRONMENTAL GEOLOGY SERIES, DIVISION OF
GEOLOGY, STATE DEVELOPMENT BOARD (SOUTH
CAROLINA).

SOUTH-EAST ASIA LIBRARY GROUP.
— NEWSLETTER, SOUTH-EAST ASIA LIBRARY GROUP.

SOUTHEAST ASIAN MINISTERS OF EDUCATION COUNCIL.
— SOUTHEAST ASIAN JOURNAL OF TROPICAL MEDICINE
AND PUBLIC HEALTH.

SOUTHEAST ASIAN RESEARCH MATERIALS GROUP.
— NEWSLETTER, SOUTHEAST ASIAN RESEARCH MATER-
IALS GROUP.

SOUTHEAST ASIAN SOCIETY OF SOIL ENGINEERING.
— GEOTECHNICAL ENGINEERING.                                XXX
— JOURNAL, SOUTHEAST ASIAN SOCIETY OF SOIL
ENGINEERING.                                               XXX

SOUTHEAST ASIA TREATY ORGANISATION.                        000
SEE: SEATO.

SOUTHEASTERN CONFERENCE ON LATIN AMERICAN
STUDIES.
— ANNALS, SOUTHEASTERN CONFERENCE ON LATIN AMER-
ICAN STUDIES.

SOUTH EASTERN REGIONAL HOSPITAL BOARD
(SCOTLAND).
— SERHB MAGAZINE.

SOUTH LONDON ENTOMOLOGICAL & NATURAL HISTORY
SOCIETY.                                                   XXX
— PROCEEDINGS & TRANSACTIONS OF THE SOUTH LON-
DON ENTOMOLOGICAL & NATURAL HISTORY SOCIETY.              XXX
SUBS (1968): PROC. & TRANS. OF THE BRITISH
ENTOMOLOGICAL & NATURAL HISTORY SOCIETY.

SOUTH PACIFIC COMMISSION.
— INFORMATION CIRCULAR, SOUTH PACIFIC
COMMISSION.

SOUTH PACIFIC REGIONAL COLLEGE OF TROPICAL
AGRICULTURE.
— MONOGRAPH SERIES, SOUTH PACIFIC REGIONAL
COLLEGE OF TROPICAL AGRICULTURE.

SOUTH PACIFIC SOCIAL SCIENCES ASSOCIATION.
— PACIFIC PERSPECTIVE.

SOUTH PLACE ETHICAL SOCIETY.
— CONWAY PAPERS.

SOUTH OF SCOTLAND ELECTRICITY BOARD.
— SSEB NEWS.

SOUTH SEAS SOCIETY.
— NANYANG QUARTERLY.                                       XXX

SOUTH WEST AFRICA SCIENTIFIC SOCIETY.
— DINTERIA. BEITRAGE ZUR FLORA VON SUDWEST-
AFRIKA.

SOUTH WEST AFRICAN PEOPLES ORGANISATION IN
BRITAIN.
— NAMIBIA NEWS.

SOUTH WEST & CENTRAL SCOTLAND GRASSLAND
SOCIETIES.
— GREENSWARD. JOURNAL OF THE ...                          XXX

SOUTHWESTERN HERPETOLOGISTS' SOCIETY.
— HERPETON. JOURNAL OF THE ...

SOUTHWESTERN REGIONAL SCIENCE ASSOCIATION.
— REVIEW OF REGIONAL STUDIES.

SOUTHERN AFRICA RESEARCH OFFICE.
— RHODESIAN REVIEW.

SOUTHERN CALIFORNIA GENEALOGICAL SOCIETY.
— SEARCHER.

SOUTHERN ILLINOIS UNIVERSITY.
— PAPERS ON LANGUAGE & LITERATURE.

SOUTHERN ILLINOIS UNIVERSITY: CENTER FOR
VIETNAMESE STUDIES.
— SOUTHEAST ASIA. AN INTERNATIONAL QUARTERLY.

SOUTHERN ILLINOIS UNIVERSITY: PUBLIC AFFAIRS
RESEARCH BUREAU.
— PUBLIC AFFAIRS BULLETIN, PUBLIC AFFAIRS RES-
EARCH BUREAU, SOUTHERN ILLINOIS UNIVERSITY.

(SPAIN) MINISTERIO DE HACIENDA.
— PRESUPUESTO (SPAIN).

(SPAIN) SERVICIO METEOROLOGICO NACIONAL:
SECCION MARITIMA.
— REVISTA DE METEOROLOGIA MARITIMA (SPAIN).

SPANISH INFORMATION SERVICE.
— SPAIN TODAY (MADRID).

SPARTACIST LEAGUE.
— WORKERS VANGUARD. MARXIST WORKING CLASS
MONTHLY JOURNAL.

SPECIAL LIBRARIES ASSOCIATION.
— INFORMATION SCIENCE ABSTRACTS.                           XXX
— TRANSLATIONS REGISTER-INDEX.

SPECTRA-PHYSICS, INC.
— SPECTRA-PHYSICS LASER TECHNICAL BULLETIN.

SPELEOLOGICAL SOCIETY OF IRELAND.                          XXX
— JOURNAL OF THE SPELEOLOGICAL SOCIETY OF IRE-
LAND.                                                      XXX

SPERRY GYROSCOPE CO.                                       XXX
— SPERRY ENGINEERING REVIEW.                               XXX

SPERRY RAND CORPORATION.                                   XXX
— SPERRY RAND ENGINEERING REVIEW.                          XXX
— SPERRY TECHNOLOGY.                                       XXX

SPOJENE PODNIKY PRO ZDRAVOTNICKOU VYROBU.
— BIOLOGIZACE A CHEMIZACE VYZIVY ZVIRAT.

SRI AVINASHILINGHAM HOME COLLEGE.
— INDIAN JOURNAL OF NUTRITION & DIETETICS.          XXX

(SRI LANKA) GOVERNMENT INFORMATION DEPART-
MENT.                                               XXX
— SRI LANKA TODAY.                                  XXX

(SRI LANKA) HIGH COMMISSION (LONDON).               XXX
— SRI LANKA NEWS-LETTER.                            XXX

SRPSKA AKADEMIJA NAUKA I UMETNOSTI: BALKAN-
OLOSKI INSTITUT.
— BALCANICA.

SRPSKA AKADEMIJA NAUKA I UMETNOSTI: ISTORIJSKI
INSTITUT.
— POSEBNA IZDANJA, ISTORIJSKI INSTITUT, SRPSKA
ACADEMIJA NAUKA I UMETNOSTI, SERIJA 1:
JUGOSLOVENSKE ZEMIJE U XX VEKU. = MONOGRAPHIES,
INSTITUT D'HISTOIREA BEOGRAD - SERIE 1: LES
PAYS YOUGOSLAVES AU XX SIECLE.

STAATSBIBLIOTHEK PREUSSISCHER KULTURBESITZ.
— VEROFFENTLICHUNGEN DER STAATSBIBLIOTHEK
PREUSSISCHER KULTURBESITZ.

STADT-ARCHIV NURNBERG.
— NURNBERGER WERKSTUCKE ZUR STADT- UND LANDES-
GESCHICHTE NURNBERG.

STAFFORDSHIRE INDUSTRIAL ARCHAEOLOGY SOCIETY.
— JOURNAL OF THE STAFFORDSHIRE INDUSTRIAL
ARCHAEOLOGY SOCIETY.

STAMFORD SURVEY GROUP.
— REPORT, STAMFORD SURVEY GROUP.

STANDARD TELEPHONES & CABLES, LTD.
— STC QUARTERLY REVIEW.                             XXX
— STC REVIEW.                                       XXX

STANDING CONFERENCE FOR DEVON HISTORY.
— DEVON HISTORIAN.

STANDING CONFERENCE OF RECTORS & VICE-CHANCEL-
LORS OF THE EUROPEAN UNIVERSITIES.
— CRE YEARBOOK.

STANDING CONFERENCE ON SCHOOLS' SCIENCE &
TECHNOLOGY.
— SCSST NEWS.

STANDING CONSULTATIVE COUNCIL ON YOUTH &
COMMUNITY SERVICE.
— NEWSLETTER, STANDING CONSULTATIVE COUNCIL ON
YOUTH & COMMUNITY SERVICE.

STANFORD UNIVERSITY.
— SIMULATION/ GAMING/ NEWS.

STANFORD UNIVERSITY: HOOVER INSTITUTION ON WAR,
REVOLUTION & PEACE.                                 000
SEE: HOOVER INSTITUTION ON WAR, REVOLUTION &
PEACE.

STATE AGRICULTURAL UNIVERSITY AT GHENT: DEP-
ARTMENT OF SILVICULTURE.                            000
SEE: RIJKSFACULTEIT LANDBOUWWETENSCHAPPEN TE
GENT: AFDELING VOOR BOSBOUW.

STATE UNIVERSITY OF NEW YORK.
— ARETHUSA.
— CRIMINAL LAW BULLETIN.
— FORUM ITALICUM.

STATE UNIVERSITY OF NEW YORK: GRADUATE PHILO-
SOPHY ASSOCIATION.
— TELOS.
— URBAN ANTHROPOLOGY.
— URBAN ANTHROPOLOGY NEWSLETTER.

STATE UNIVERSITY OF NEW YORK: LOCKWOOD MEMORIAL
LIBRARY.
— CHRISTMAS BROADSIDE.

STATE UNIVERSITY OF NEW YORK; SOCIOLOGY CLUB.
— CATALYST (BUFFALO, N.Y.).

STATE UNIVERSITY OF NEW YORK COLLEGE AT POTSDAM
— AGORA. A JOURNAL IN THE HUMANITIES & SOCIAL
SCIENCES.

STATENS INSTITUT FOR BYGGNADSFORSKNING (SWEDEN).
— RAPPORT, STATENS INSTITUT FOR BYGGNADSFORSK-
NING: ENGLISH SUMMARIES.

STATENS LANTBRUKSKEMISKA LABORATORIUM (SWEDEN).
— METODIK REKOMMENDATION, STATENS LANTBRUKSKEM-
ISKA LABORATORIUM (SWEDEN).

STATION BIOLOGIQUE (BESSE-EN-CHANDESSE).
— ANNALES, STATION BIOLOGIQUE (BESSE-EN-CHAN-
DESSE).

STATION MARINE D'ENDOUME.
— TETHYS.

STATNI KNIHOVNA CSSR.
— BIBLIOGRAFIE EKONOMICKE LITERATURY: (KNIHY,
CLANKY, RECENZE).                                   XXX
— NOVINKY LITERATURY, PRIRODNI VEDY: RADA
CHEMICKA.
— NOVINKY LITERATURY, PRIRODNI VEDY: RADA
GEOLOGICKO-GEOGRAFICKA.
— NOVINKY LITERATURY, SPOLECENSKE VEDY: RADA 2:
BIBLIOGRAFIE EKONOMICKE LITERATURY.                 XXX

STATNI KNIHOVNA CSSR PRAZE.
— ROCENKA STATNI KNIHOVNY CSSR V PRAZE.

STAZIONE ZOOLOGICA DI NAPOLI.
— RAPPORT D'ACTIVITE DE LA STATION ZOOLOGIQUE
DE NAPLES.

STOCKHOLM CONFERENCE ON VIETNAM.
— INFORMATION LETTER, STOCKHOLM CONFERENCE ON
VIETNAM.

STOCKHOLM INTERNATIONAL PEACE RESEARCH INST-
ITUTE.
— SIPRI YEARBOOK OF WORLD ARMAMENTS & DISARM-
AMENTS.
— STOCKHOLM PAPERS.

STOCKHOLMS UNIVERSITET.
— STOCKHOLM STUDIES IN LINGUISTICS.
— STOCKHOLM STUDIES IN THEATRICAL HISTORY.

STOCKHOLMS UNIVERSITET: NATURGEOGRAFISKA
INSTITUTIONEN.
— FORSKNINGSRAPPORT, NATURGEOGRAFISKA INSTITUT-
IONEN, STOCKHOLMS UNIVERSITET.

STOCKHOLMS UNIVERSITET: STATSVETENSKAPLIGA
INSTITUTIONEN.
— STOCKHOLM STUDIES IN POLITICS.

STOWARZYSZENIE ELEKTRYKOW POLSKICH.
— WIADOMOSCI TELEKOMUNIKACYJNE.

STRATHSPEY RAILWAY ASSOCIATION.
— STRATHSPEY EXPRESS.                               XXX

STUDENT CHRISTIAN MOVEMENT.
— DESPATCH FROM IRELAND.

STUDIENGESELLSCHAFT ZUR FORDERUNG DER KERN-
ENERGIEVERWERTUNG IN SCHIFFBAU UND SCHIFFAHRT.
— BERICHTE DER STUDIENGESELLSCHAFT ZUR FORDER-
UNG DER KERNENERGIEVERWERTUNG IN SCHIFFBAU
UND SCHIFFAHRT.

STUDIESELSKAPET FOR NORSK INDUSTRI.
— ARTIKKELINDEKS FOR BYGG. SCANDINAVIAN BUILD-
ING ABSTRACTS.                                      XXX
— ARTIKKEL INDEKS FOR SKIP.
— ARTIKKEL-INDEKS, STUDIESELSKAPET FOR NORSK
INDUSTRI.                                           XXX
SUBS (1970): POLYTEKNISK ARTIKKEL-INDEKS.
— NORDISKT ARTIKELINDEX FOR BYGG.                   XXX
— POLYTEKNISK ARTIKKEL-INDEKS.                      XXX

STUDY GROUP ON EAST-WEST QUESTIONS (WOHRENDAMM)
— MODERN WORLD.

SUDAFRIKANISCHEN GERMANISTENVERBANDES.
— ACTA GERMANICA. ZUR SPRACHE UND DICHTUNG
DEUTSCHLANDS, OSTERREICHS UND DER SCHWEIZ.

SUDAN AGRICULTURAL SOCIETY.
— SUDAN AGRICULTURAL JOURNAL.

SUFFOLK RURAL COMMUNITY COUNCIL: SUFFOLK LOCAL
HISTORY COUNCIL.
— SUFFOLK LOCAL HISTORY NEWSLETTER.

SUGADAIRA BIOLOGICAL LABORATORY.               OOO
SEE: TOKYO UNIVERSITY OF EDUCATION: ...

SULPHUR INSTITUTE.
— JOURNAL, SULPHUR INSTITUTE.

SUMITOMO METAL INDUSTRIES, LTD.
— SUMITOMO SEARCH.

SUNDERLAND FOLK CENTRE.
— IMAGE.

SUNDERLAND POLYTECHNIC: SCHOOL OF ART & DESIGN.
— VISION & VOICE.

SUOMALAINEN LAAKARISEURA DUODECIM.
— ANNALS OF CLINICAL RESEARCH.                               XXX
— ANNALS OF CLINICAL RESEARCH. SUPPLEMENT.                   XXX
— ANNALES MEDICINAE INTERNAE FENNIAE.                        XXX
  SUBS (1969): PART OF ANNALS OF CLINICAL
  RESEARCH.
— ANNALES MEDICINAE INTERNAE FENNIAE. SUPPLE-
  MENTUM.
  SUBS (1969): ANNALS OF CLINICAL RESEARCH.
  SUPPLEMENT.
— ANNALES PAEDIATRIAE FENNIAE.                               XXX
  SUBS (1969): PART OF ANNALS OF CLINICAL RE-
  SEARCH.

SUOMEN KOTIELAINJALOSTUSYHDISTYS.
— NAUTAKARJA.

SUSSEX ARCHAEOLOGICAL SOCIETY.
— OCCASIONAL PAPER, SUSSEX ARCHAEOLOGICAL
  SOCIETY.
— SUSSEX ARCHAEOLOGICAL SOCIETY NEWSLETTER.

SUSSEX INDUSTRIAL ARCHAEOLOGY STUDY GROUP.
— SUSSEX INDUSTRIAL HISTORY.

SUSSEX NATURALISTS' TRUST, LTD.
— ANNUAL REPORT, SUSSEX NATURALISTS' TRUST, LTD.

SUTTON BRIDGE EXPERIMENTAL STATION.
— REPORT, SUTTON BRIDGE EXPERIMENTAL STATION.

SVAZ CESKOSLOVENSKYCH NOVINARU.
— REPORTER.

SVAZ CESKOSLOVENSKYCH SPISOVATELU.
— LISTY, SVAZ CESKOSLOVENSKYCH SPISOVATELU.              XXX
— LITERARNI LISTY.                                       XXX
— LITERARNI NOVINY.                                      XXX
  SUBS (1968): LITERARNI LISTY.

SVENSKA AB PHILIPS.
— TEKNIKA. PHILIPS TIDNING FOR ELEKTRONIK.

SVENSKA DRIFTPERSONALFORBUNDET.
— DRIFTTEKNIK.                                           XXX

SVENSKA ELEKTROINGENJORERS RIKSFORENING.
— ELTEKNIK MED AKTUELL ELEKTRONIK.                       XXX

SVENSKA GASFORENINGEN.
— GASNYTT.                                               XXX
— MANADSBLAD, SVENSKA GASFORENINGEN.*

SVENSK HAMNFORBUNDET.
— SVENSK HAMNTIDNING.

SVENSKA INTERPLANETARISKA SALLSKAPET.
— SIS RYMD-INFORMATION.

SVERIGES SKORSTENSFEJAREMASTARES RIKSFORBUND.
— SKORSTENSFEJARMASTAREN.

SVEUCILISTE U ZAGREBU.
— POLITICKA MISAO.

(SWAZILAND) DEPARTMENT OF STATISTICS.
— ANNUAL STATISTICAL BULLETIN, DEPARTMENT OF
  STATISTICS (SWAZILAND).

(SWEDEN) STATENS NATURVETENSKAPLIGA FORSKNINGS-
RAD: ECOLOGICAL RESEARCH COMMITTEE.
— BULLETIN, ECOLOGICAL RESEARCH COMMITTEE,
  NATURAL SCIENCE RESEARCH COUNCIL (SWEDEN).

SYDSVENSKA MEDICINHISTORISKA SALLSKAPET.
— ARSSKRIFT, SYDSVENSKA MEDICINHISTORISKA
  SALLSKAPET.

SYMPOSIUM ON FLUID DYNAMICS.
— FLUID DYNAMICS TRANSACTIONS.

SYNDICAT DES CONSTRUCTEURS DE TRANSMISSIONS
HYDRAULIQUES ET PNEUMATIQUES.
— ENERGIE FLUIDE ET LUBRIFICATION + HYDRAULIQUE,
  PNEUMATIQUE ET ASSERVISSEMENTS.                        XXX
— HYDRAULIQUE, PNEUMATIQUE ET ASSERVISSEMENTS.           XXX
— REVUE DES TRANSMISSIONS HYDRAULIQUES ET PNEU-
  MATIQUES ET DES ASSERVISSEMENTS.                       XXX
  SUBS (1964): HYDRAULIQUE, PNEUMATIQUE ET
  ASSERVISSEMENTS.

SZKOLA GLOWNA GOSPODARSTWA WIEJSKIEGO.
— ZESZYTY NAUKOWE SZKOLY GLOWNEJ GOSPODARSTWA
  WIEJSKIEGO: ROZPRAWY NAUKOWE.
— ZESZYTY NAUKOWE SZKOLY GLOWNEJ GOSPODARSTWA
  WIEJSKIEGO: TECHNOLOGIA DREWNA.
— ZESZYTY NAUKOWE SZKOLY GLOWNEJ GOSPODARSTWA
  WIEJSKIEGO: TECHNOLOGIA ROLNO-SPOZYWCZA.

SZKOLA GLOWNA PLANOWANIA I STATYSTYKI.
— PLANOWANIE GOSPODARKI NARODOWEJ W POLSCE
  LUDOWEJ. MATERIALY DO BIBLIOGRAFII.

TADZHIKSKIJ GOSUDARSTVENNYJ UNIVERSITET.
— IZ ISTORII KUL'TURNOGO STROITEL'STVA V TAD-
  ZHIKISTANE.
— TRUDY, TADZHIKSKIJ GOSUDARSTVENNYJ UNIVERS-
  ITET: SERIJA ISTORICHESKIKH NAUK.

TAIPEI NATIONAL PALACE MUSEUM.
— NATIONAL PALACE MUSEUM QUARTERLY.

TAIWAN SUGAR EXPERIMENT STATION.
— RESEARCH REPORT, TAIWAN SUGAR EXPERIMENT STA-
  TION.

TALOUSTIETEELLISEN SEURAN.
— TALOUSTIETEELLISEN SEURAN VUOSIKIRJA.
  YEARBOOK OF THE FINNISH SOCIETY FOR ECONOMIC
  RESEARCH.

TAMKANG COLLEGE OF ARTS & SCIENCES: WESTERN
LITERATURE RESEARCH INSTITUTE.
— TAMKANG REVIEW.

TAMPERE PEACE RESEARCH INSTITUTE.
— INSTANT RESEARCH ON PEACE & VIOLENCE.

(TANZANIA) MINISTRY OF INFORMATION & TOURISM.
— CIVIL SERVICE MAGAZINE, UNITED REPUBLIC OF
  TANZANIA.

TANZANIA LIBRARY ASSOCIATION.
— SOMENI.

TANZANIA TEA AUTHORITY.
— TEA IN EAST AFRICA.                                    XXX

TARTU RIIKLIK ULIKOOL: RAAMATUKOGU.
— TARTU RIIKLIK ULIKOOL, ILMUNUD TOODE BIBLIO-
  GRAAFIA.

TARTUSKIJ GOSUDARSTVENNYJ UNIVERSITET.
— REAKTSIONNAJA SPOSOBNOST' ORGANICHESKIKH
  SOEDINENIJ.

(TASMANIA) DEPARTMENT OF AGRICULTURE.
— INSECT PEST SURVEY (TASMANIA).

TATARSKAJA RESPUBLIKANSKAJA GOSUDARSTVENNAJA
SEL'SKOKHOZJAJSTVENNAJA OPYTNAJA STANTSIJA.
— TRUDY, TATARSKAJA RESPUBLIKANSKAJA GOSUDARST-
  VENNAJA SEL'SKOKHOZJAJSTVENNAJA OPYTNAJA
  STANTSIJA.

TATHATA CENTRE.
— TAT. SARVODAYA COMMUNITIES NEWSLETTER.

TBILISSKIJ GOSUDARSTVENNYJ UNIVERSITET:
INSTITUT PRIKLADNOJ MATEMATIKI.
— TRUDY INSTITUTA PRIKLADNOJ MATEMATIKI, TBIL-
  ISSKIJ GOSUDARSTVENNYJ UNIVERSITET.

TECHNI RESEARCH ASSOCIATES.
— PATENT LICENSING GAZETTE.                              XXX

TECHNICAL ECONOMICS ASSOCIATION.
— VALVE INFORMATION REPORT.                              XXX

TECHNICAL UNIVERSITY OF HELSINKI: INSTITUTE OF
PHOTOGRAMMETRY.
— PHOTOGRAMMETRIC JOURNAL OF FINLAND.

TECHNICON INSTRUMENTS CORPORATION.
— TECHNICON QUARTERLY.

TECHNISCHE AKADEMIE (WUPPERTAL).
— BERICHTE, TECHNISCHE AKADEMIE (WUPPERTAL).

TECHNISCHE HOCHSCHULE (HANNOVER): GEOLOGISCHES
INSTITUT.                                                              XXX
— MITTEILUNGEN AUS DEM GEOLOGISCHES INSTITUT
DER TECHNISCHE HOCHSCHULE (HANNOVER).                              XXX

TECHNISCHE HOCHSCHULE MUNCHEN: INSTITUT FUR
HYDRAULIK UND GEWASSERKUNDE.
— MITTEILUNGEN, INSTITUT FUR HYDRAULIK UND GEW-
ASSERKUNDE, TECHNISCHE HOCHSCHULE MUNCHEN.

TECHNISCHE HOCHSCHULE (VIENNA).
— DISSERTATIONEN, TECHNISCHE HOCHSCHULE(VIENNA).

TECHNISCHEN UNIVERSITAT BERLIN.
— TUB. ZEITSCHRIFT DER TECHNISCHEN UNIVERSITAT
BERLIN.

TECHNISCHE UNIVERSITAT HANNOVER: GEOLOGISCHEN
INSTITUT.                                                              XXX
— MITTEILUNGEN AUS DEM GEOLOGISCHEN INSTITUT
DER TECHNISCHE UNIVERSITAT HANNOVER.                              XXX

TEESSIDE INDUSTRIAL ARCHAEOLOGY GROUP.
— TRANSACTIONS, TEESSIDE INDUSTRIAL ARCHAEOLOGY
GROUP.

TEHNIKON ERIMETETERION TES ELLADOS.
— TEHNIKA HRONIKA. MENIAIA EKDOSIS TON TEHNIKON
ERIMETETERION TES ELLADOS.

TEL AVIV UNIVERSITY.
— ISRAEL ORIENTAL STUDIES.

TEL-AVIV UNIVERSITY: DEPARTMENT OF MUSICOLOGY.
— ORBIS MUSICAE.

TEL-AVIV UNIVERSITY: FACULTY OF LAW.
— ISRAEL YEARBOOK ON HUMAN RIGHTS.

TEL-AVIV UNIVERSITY: INSTITUTE OF CRIMINOLOGY &
CRIMINAL LAW.
— ISRAEL STUDIES IN CRIMINOLOGY.

TEL-AVIV UNIVERSITY: INSTITUTE FOR GERMAN
HISTORY.
— JAHRBUCH DES INSTITUTS FUR DEUTSCHE GESCH-
ICHTE.

TELECOMMUNICATION SOCIETY OF AUSTRALIA.
— ATR. AUSTRALIAN TELECOMMUNICATION RESEARCH.

TEMPLE UNIVERSITY.
— JOURNAL OF MODERN LITERATURE.

TEMPLE UNIVERSITY: DEPARTMENT OF ENGLISH.
— SCRIBLERIAN: A NEWSLETTER DEVOTED TO POPE,
SWIFT & THEIR CIRCLE.
— WORDSWORTH CIRCLE.

(TENNESSEE) DIVISION OF GEOLOGY.
— ENVIRONMENTAL GEOLOGY SERIES, DIVISION OF
GEOLOGY (TENNESSEE).

TENNESSEE VALLEY AUTHORITY.
— FERTILIZER ABSTRACTS.

TERATOLOGY SOCIETY.
— TERATOLOGY. JOURNAL OF ABNORMAL DEVELOPMENT.

TERMESZETTUDOMANYI MUZEUM.
— FRAGMENTA MINERALOGICA ET PALAEONTOLOGICA.

TERMITE CONTROL ASSOCIATION OF JAPAN.
— SHIROARI.

TERTIARY RESEARCH GROUP.
— TERTIARY TIMES.

TEXACO LTD.
— TEXACO QUARTERLY.

TEXAS HERPETOLOGICAL SOCIETY.
— NEWSLETTER, TEXAS HERPETOLOGICAL SOCIETY.

TEXAS ORNITHOLOGICAL SOCIETY.
— BULLETIN, TEXAS ORNITHOLOGICAL SOCIETY.

TEXAS RESEARCH FOUNDATION: HOBLITZELLE
AGRICULTURAL LABORATORY.
— RENNER RESEARCH REPORTS.

TEXAS STATE GENEALOGICAL SOCIETY.
— STIRPES.

TEXAS TECH UNIVERSITY: MUSEUM.
— OCCASIONAL PAPERS, MUSEUM, TEXAS TECH
UNIVERSITY.
— SPECIAL PUBLICATIONS, MUSEUM, TEXAS TECH
UNIVERSITY.

TEXTILE INSTITUTE.
— TEXTILE PROGRESS.

TEXTILE RESEARCH INSTITUTE (JAPAN).                              000
SEE: SENI KOGYO SHIKENJO.

(THAILAND) EMBASSY (GB).
— THAI NEWS.

THEATRE LIBRARY ASSOCIATION.
— THEATRE DOCUMENTATION.                                          XXX

THEMIS SOCIETY.
— PUBLIC OPINION.

THIRD WORLD FIRST EDUCATIONAL TRUST.
— INTERNATIONALIST.                                               XXX

THOMAS JEFFERSON CENTER FOR POLITICAL ECONOMY.
— PUBLIC CHOICE.                                                  XXX

THOMSON-CSF.
— REVUE TECHNIQUE, THOMSON-CSF.                                   XXX

TIDNINGSAKTIEBOLAGET SVENSK BOKHANDEL.
— SVENSK TIDSKRIFTSFORTECKNING.

TIERARZTLICHE HOCHSCHULE (VIENNA).
— DISSERTATIONEN, TIERARZTLICHE HOCHSCHULE
(VIENNA).

TISSUE CULTURE ASSOCIATION.
— CURRENT TISSUE CULTURE LITERATURE.                             XXX
— IN VITRO.
— INDEX OF TISSUE CULTURE.                                       XXX

TOC H.
— POINT THREE.
— TOC H JOURNAL.                                                 XXX
SUBS (1968): POINT THREE.

TOHOKU DAIGAKU: RESEARCH INSTITUTE FOR
STRENGTH & FRACTURE OF MATERIALS.
— REPORTS OF THE RESEARCH INSTITUTE FOR
STRENGTH & FRACTURE OF MATERIALS, TOHOKU
UNIVERSITY.

TOHOKU KOGYO DAIGAKU.
— KENCHIKU KEMPO.

TOILET GOODS ASSOCIATION.
— TGA COSMETIC JOURNAL.                                          XXX

TOKYO DAIGAKU.
— COLLECTED REPRINTS, UNIVERSITY OF TOKYO.

TOKYO DAIGAKU: COMPUTER CENTRE.
SEE: TOKYO DAIGAKU: OGATA KEISANKEI SENTA.

TOKYO DAIGAKU: DEPARTMENT OF GEOGRAPHY.
— BULLETIN OF THE DEPARTMENT OF GEOGRAPHY, UNI-
VERSITY OF TOKYO.

TOKYO DAIGAKU: OCEAN RESEARCH INSTITUTE.
— BULLETIN OF THE OCEAN RESEARCH INSTITUTE,
UNIVERSITY OF TOKYO.

TOKYO DAIGAKU: OGATA KEISANKEI SENTA.
— REPORT, COMPUTER CENTRE, TOKYO UNIVERSITY.

TOKYO HISHIRYO KENSAJO.
— TOKYO HISHIRYO KENSAJO SHIRYO KENKYU HOKOKU.
BULLETIN OF NATIONAL INSPECTION LABORATORY
FOR FEEDS & FERTILIZER.
— TOKYO HISHIRYO KENSAJO TOKUBETSU HOKOKU.
SPECIAL REPORT, NATIONAL INSPECTION LABORAT-
ORY FOR FEEDS & FERTILIZER.

TOKYO IKA SHIKA DAIGAKU IYO KIZAI KENKYUJO.
— TOKYO IKA SHIKA DAIGAKU IYO KIZAI KENKYUJO
HOKOKU. REPORTS OF THE INSTITUTE FOR MEDICAL
& DENTAL ENGINEERING, TOKYO MEDICAL & DENTAL
UNIVERSITY.

TOKYO MEDICAL & DENTAL UNIVERSITY: INSTITUTE
FOR MEDICAL & DENTAL ENGINEERING.                                000
SEE: TOKYO IKA SHIKA DAIGAKU IYO KIZAI
KENKYUJO.

**TOKYO METROPOLITAN INDUSTRIAL TECHNIC INSTITUTE.**                                          000
SEE: TOKYO TORITSU KOGYO GIJUTSU SENTA.

**TOKYO TORITSU KOGYO GIJUTSU SENTA.**                                                       XXX
— TOKYO TORITSU KOGYO GIJUTSU SENTA KENKYU
HOKOKU.  REPORT, TOKYO METROPOLITAN INDUST-
RIAL TECHNIC INSTITUTE.                                                                     XXX

**TOKYO TORITSU KOGYO SHOREIKAN.**                                                           XXX
— TOKYO TORITSU KOGYO SHOREIKAN HOKOKU.                                                      XXX
SUBS (1971): TOKYO TORITSU KOGYO GIJUTSU
SENTA KENKYU HOKOKU.

**TOKYO UNIVERSITY OF EDUCATION: SUGADAIRA BIOL-
OGICAL LABORATORY.**
— BULLETIN, SUGADAIRA BIOLOGICAL LABORATORY,
TOKYO UNIVERSITY OF EDUCATION.

**TOKYO WOMEN'S CHRISTIAN COLLEGE.**
— SCIENCE REPORTS OF THE TOKYO WOMEN'S CHRIST-
IAN COLLEGE.

**TOLKIEN SOCIETY.**
— MALLORN.

**TOMSKIJ GOSUDARSTVENNYJ UNIVERSITET.**
— GLJATSIOLOGIJA ALTAJA.
— REVOLJUTSIONNOE DVIZHENIE V SIBIRI I NA
DAL'NEM VOSTOKE.
— VOPROSY ISTORII SIBIRI.

**TOMSKIJ GOSUDARSTVENNYJ UNIVERSITET: EKONOM-
ICHESKIJ FAKUL'TET.**
— VOPROSY EKONOMIKI I ORGANIZATSII SOTSIALIST-
ICHESKOGO PROIZVODSTVA.

**TOWARZYSTWO IM. FRYDERYKA CHOPINA.**
— DOCUMENTA CHOPINIANA.

**TOWARZYSTWO MILOSNIKOW TORUNIA.**
— ROCZNIK TORUNSKI.

**TOWARZYSTWO NAUKOWE KATOLICKIEGO UNIWERSYTETU
LUBELSKIEGO: INSTYTUT GEOGRAFII HISTORYCZNEJ
KOSCIOLA W POLSCE.**
— MATERIALY ZRODLOWE DO DZIEJOW KOSCIOLA W
POLSCE.

**TOWARZYSTWO POLSKO-UKRAINSKIE.**
— BIULETYNE TOWARZYSTWA POLSKO-UKRAINSKIEGO.

**TOWARZYSTWO ROZWOJU ZIEM ZACHODNICH.**
— ROCZNIK ZIEM ZACHODNICH I POLNOCNYCH.

**TOWER INTERNATIONAL TECHNOMEDICAL INSTITUTE.**
— T.-I.-T. JOURNAL OF LIFE SCIENCES.

**TOWN & COUNTRY PLANNING ASSOCIATION.**
— BULLETIN OF ENVIRONMENTAL EDUCATION.

**TOWN PLANNING INSTITUTE.**                                                                 XXX
— JOURNAL, TOWN PLANNING INSTITUTE.                                                          XXX
SUBS (1971): JOURNAL, ROYAL ...

**TOYAMA KENRITSU OTANI GIJUTSU TANKI DAIGAKU.**
— TOYAMA KENRITSU OTANI GIJUTSU TANKI DAIGAKU
KENKYU HOKOKU.  BULLETIN OF RESEARCH, OTANI
COLLEGE OF TECHNOLOGY OF TOYAMA.                                                             XXX

**TRAMWAY MUSEUM SOCIETY.**
— TRAMS.                                                                                     XXX
— TRAMWAY TOPICS.

**TRENT RIVER AUTHORITY.**
— ANNUAL REPORT, TRENT RIVER AUTHORITY.

**TRIBHUVAN UNIVERSITY ECONOMIC SOCIETY.**
— AARTHIK JAGAT.  ECONOMIC JOURNAL OF THE ...

**TRINITY COLLEGE (DUBLIN).**
— DUBLIN UNIVERSITY LAW REVIEW.

**TROPICAL FISH CULTURE RESEARCH INSTITUTE
(MALACCA).**
— WORKING PAPER, TROPICAL FISH CULTURE RESEARCH
INSTITUTE (MALACCA).

**TROPICAL GRASSLAND SOCIETY OF AUSTRALIA.**
— TROPICAL GRASSLANDS.

**TROPICAL SCIENCE CENTER (COSTA RICA).**
— OCCASIONAL PAPERS, TROPICAL SCIENCE CENTER
(COSTA RICA).

**TROPICAL STORED PRODUCTS CENTRE.**
— TROPICAL STORAGE ABSTRACTS.

**TSELINOGRADSKIJ SEL'SKOKHOZJAJSTVENNYJ
INSTITUT.**
— TRUDY, TSELINOGRADSKIJ SEL'SKOKHOZJAJSTVENNYJ
INSTITUT.

**TSENTRAL'NAJA NAUCHNAJA SEL'SKOKHOZJAJSTVENNAJA
BIBLIOTEKA.**
— NOVOE V SEL'SKOKHOZJAJSTVENNOJ NAUKE I PRAK-
TIKE.
— SVODNYJ UKAZATEL' BIBLIOGRAFICHESKIKH SPISKOV
I KARTOTEK, SOSTAVLENNYKH BIBLIOTEKAMI SOVETS-
KOGO SOJUZA : SEL'SKOE KHOZJAJSTVO.

**TSENTRAL'NYJ NAUCHNO-ISSLEDOVATEL'SKIJ EKON-
OMICHESKIJ INSTITUT.**
— NAUCHNYE TRUDY, TSENTRAL'NYJ NAUCHNO-
ISSLEDOVATEL'SKIJ EKONOMICHESKIJ INSTITUT.

**TSENTRAL'NYJ NAUCHNO-ISSLEDOVATEL'SKIJ I PRO-
EKTNYJ INSTITUT TORGOVOGO I EKSPERIMENTAL'NOGO
PROEKTIROVANIJA ZHILISHCHA.**
— RABOTA KONSTRUKTSII ZHILYKH ZDANII IZ KRUP-
NORAZMERNYKH ELEMENTOV.

**TSUYAMA KOGYO KOTO SENMON GAKKO.**
— TSUYAMA KOGYO KOTO SENMON GAKKO KIYO.

**TSUYAMA TECHNICAL COLLEGE.**                                                               OOO
SEE: TSUYAMA KOGYO KOTO SENMON GAKKO.

**TUFTED CARPET MANUFACTURER'S ASSOCIATION.**
— T.C.M.A. NEWS.

**TULANE UNIVERSITY.**
— TULANE STUDIES IN ZOOLOGY & BOTANY.*

**TULSA GENEALOGICAL SOCIETY.**
— TULSA ANNALS.

**(TUNISIA) MINISTERE DE L'EDUCATION NATIONALE:
FACULTE D'AGRONOMIE.**
— BULLETIN DE LA FACULTE D'AGRONOMIE, MINISTERE
DE L'EDUCATION NATIONALE (TUNISIA).                                                          XXX

**TURKMENSKOE RESPUBLIKANSKOE DOBROVOL'NOE OB-
SHCHESTVO OKHRANY PAMJATNIKOV ISTORII I
KUL'TURY.**
— PAMJATNIKI TURKMENISTANA.

**TUSSOCK GRASSLANDS & MOUNTAIN LANDS INSTITUTE
(CHRISTCHURCH, NZ).**
— SPECIAL PUBLICATION, TUSSOCK GRASSLANDS &
MOUNTAIN LANDS INSTITUTE.

**UDRUZENJE EMAJLIRACA JUGOSLAVIJE.**
— EMAJL.  KERAMIKA-STAKLO.

**UDRUZENJE JUGOSLOVENSKIH PRONALAZACA.**
— JUGOSLOVENSKO PRONALAZASTVO.

**UDRUZENJE JUGOSLOVENSKIH ZELEZARA.**
— CELIK.  STEEL.  STAL.

**(UGANDA) HIGH COMMISSION, LONDON.**
— UGANDA NEWS REVIEW.

**(UGANDA) MINISTRY OF ANIMAL INDUSTRY, GAME &
FISHERIES: FISHERIES DEPARTMENT.**
— OCCASIONAL PAPERS, FISHERIES DEPARTMENT,
MINISTRY OF ANIMAL INDUSTRY, GAME & FISHERIES
(UGANDA).

**UGANDA TEA BOARD.**
— TEA IN EAST AFRICA.                                                                        XXX

**(UKRAINE) GOSPLAN: NAUCHNO-ISSLEDOVATEL'SKIJ
EKONOMICHESKIJ INSTITUT.**
— ORGANIZATSIJA I PLANIROVANIE OTRASLEJ NAROD-
NOGO KHOZJAJSTVA.

**(UKRAINE) MINISTERSTVO CHERNOJ METALLURGII
USSR.**
— METALLURGICHESKAJA I GORNORUDNAJA PROMYSHLEN-
NOST'.

**(UKRAINE) MINISTERSTVO MELIORATSII I VODNOGO
KHOZJAJSTVA.**
— MELIORATSIJA I VODNOE KHOZJAJSTVO.                                                         XXX
— VODNOE KHOZJAJSTVO.  RESPUBLIKANSKIJ MEZHVED-
OMSTVENNYJ NAUCHNO-TEKHNICHESKIJ SBORNIK.                                                    XXX

**(UKRAINE) MINISTERSTVO SIL'S'KOHO HOSPODARSTVA.**
— EKONOMIKA I ORGANIZATSIJA SIL'S'KOHO HOSPOD-
ARSTVA.

(UKRAINE) MINISTERSTVO TORGOVLI UKRAINSKOJ SSR.
— OBSHCHESTVENNOE PITANIE. MEZHVEDOMSTVENNYJ
RESPUBLIKANSKIJ NAUCHNO-TEKNICHESKIJ SBORNIK.

(UKRAINE) MINISTERSTVO VYSSHEGO I SREDNEGO
SPETSIAL'NOGO OBRAZOVANIJA.
— AVTOMOBIL'NYJ TRANSPORT. MEZHVEDOMSTVENNYJ
RESPUBLIKANSKIJ NAUCHNO-TEKHNICHESKIJ SBORNIK.
— KHOLODIL'NAJA TEKHNIKA I TEKHNOLOGIJA.
— LEGKAJA PROMYSHLENNOST'. MEZHVEDOMSTVENNYJ
RESPUBLIKANSKIJ NAUCHNO-TEKHNICHESKIJ SBORNIK.
— UKRAINSKIJ GEOMETRICHESKIJ SBORNIK.

(UKRAINE) MINISTERSTVO VYSSHOJI I SREDN'OJI
SPETSIAL'NOJI OS'VITY.
— DETALI MASHIN I POD'EMNO-TRANSPORTNYE MASHINY.
— GIDRAVLICHESKIE MASHINY.
— GIDRAVLIKA I GIDROTEKHNIKA.
— TEKHNOLOGIJA I AVTOMATIZATSIJA MASHINOSTROEN-
IJA.

(UKRAINE) MINISTERSTVO ZDRAVOOKHRANENIJA USSR:
KIEVSKIJ MEDITSINSKI INSTITUT.
— FILOSOFSKIE VOPROSY MEDITSINY I BIOLOGII.

UKRAINS'KE TOVARYSTVO ZAKORDONNYKH STUDII.
— SUCHASNIST'.

UKRAINSKIJ NAUCHNO-ISSLEDOVATEL'SKIJ INSTITUT
NAUCHNO-TEKHNICHESKOJ INFORMATSII I TEKHNIKO-
EKONOMICHESKIKH ISSLEDOVANIJ.
— TEKHNOLOGIJA I ORGANIZATSIJA PROIZVODSTVA.                            XXX

UKRAINSKIJ NAUCHNO-ISSLEDOVATEL'SKIJ INSTITUT
RYBNOGO KHOZJAJSTVA.
— RYBNOE KHOZJAJSTVO. RESPUBLIKANSKIJ MEZHVE-
DOMSTVENNYJ TEMATICHESKIJ NAUCHNYJ SBORNIK.

UKRAINSKIJ NAUCHNO-ISSLEDOVATEL'SKIJ INSTITUT
SPETSIAL'NYKH STALEJ, SPLAVOV I FERROSPLAVOV.
— PROIZVODSTVO I ISSLEDOVANIE STALEJ I SPLAVOV.

UKRAJINS'KE NAUKOVO-TEKHNICHNE TOVARYSTVO
KHARCHOVOJI PROMYSLOVOSTI.
— KHARCHOVA PROMYSLOVIST'.

UKRAJINS'KYJ NAUCHNO-DOSLIDNYJ INSTYTUT
OVOCHIVNYTSTVA I KARTOPLI.
— KARTOPLJA, OVOCHEVI TA BASHTANNI KUL'TURY.

UNESCO.
— AFRICAN ABSTRACTS.                                                    XXX
— ANNUAL SUMMARY OF INFORMATION ON NATURAL
DISASTERS.
— CASE STUDIES ON TECHNOLOGICAL DEVELOPMENT.
— IMS NEWSLETTER.                                                       XXX
— INTERNATIONAL EDUCATION YEAR 1970 BULLETIN.
— NEW TRENDS IN BIOLOGY TEACHING.
— NEW TRENDS IN CHEMISTRY TEACHING.
— NEW TRENDS IN PHYSICS TEACHING.
— PROSPECTS IN EDUCATION.                                               XXX
— TECHNICAL PAPERS IN HYDROLOGY.
— UNESCO TECHNICAL PAPERS IN MARINE SCIENCE.

UNESCO: CENTRO REGIONAL PARA EL FOMENTO DE LA
CIENCIA EN AMERICA LATINA.
— BOLETIN DEL CENTRO REGIONAL DE LA UNESCO PARA
EL FOMENTO DE LA CIENCIA EN AMERICA LATINA.                            XXX

UNESCO: DIVISION OF SCIENTIFIC & TECHNOLOGICAL
INFORMATION & DOCUMENTATION.
— UNISIST NEWSLETTER.

UNESCO: OFICINA DE CIENCIAS PARA AMERICA
LATINA.
— BOLETIN, OFICINA DE CIENCIAS DE LA UNESCO
PARA AMERICA LATINA.                                                    XXX

UNION OF AGRICULTURAL WORKING PEOPLE OF KOREA.
— AGRICULTURAL WORKING PEOPLE OF KOREA.

UNION OF AMERICAN EXILES IN BRITAIN.
— AMERICAN EXILE IN BRITAIN.

UNION BALKANIQUE DES MATHEMATICIENS.
— MATHEMATICA BALKANICA.

UNION OF BURMA APPLIED RESEARCH INSTITUTE.
— UNION OF BURMA JOURNAL OF SCIENCE & TECHNOL-
OGY.

UNION CENTRALE DES PRODUCTEURS SUISSES DE LAIT.
— INDUSTRIE LAITIERE SUISSE.                                            XXX
SUBS (1970): PRODUCTEUR DE LAIT.
— PRODUCTEUR DE LAIT.                                                   XXX

UNION FRANCAISE DES GEOLOGUES.
— GEOLOGUES. REVUE TRIMESTRIELLE DE L'...

UNION OF INTERNATIONAL ASSOCIATIONS.
— YEARBOOK OF INTERNATIONAL CONGRESS PROCEED-
INGS.                                                                   XXX

UNION INTERNATIONALE CONTRE LE CANCER.
— UICC MONOGRAPH SERIES.

UNIONE MALACOLOGICA ITALIANA.
— CONCHIGLIE.

UNIONE MATEMATICA ITALIANA.
— BOLLETTINO DELLA UNIONE MATEMATICA ITALIANA;
SERIE 4.                                                                XXX

UNION MOVEMENT.
— ALTERNATIVE.

UNION DES SYNDICATS AGRICOLES ROMANDS.
— REVUE SUISSE D'AGRICULTURE.

UNION DES TRANSPORTS PUBLICS URBAINS ET REG-
IONAUX.                                                                 XXX
— REVUE DES TRANSPORTS PUBLICS URBAINS ET REG-
IONAUX.                                                                 XXX

UNION DES VOIES FERREES ET DES TRANSPORTS
AUTOMOBILES.                                                            XXX
— INDUSTRIE DES VOIES FERREES ET DES TRANSPORTS
AUTOMOBILES.                                                            XXX
SUBS (1970): REVUE DES TRANSPORTS PUBLICS
URBAINS ET REGIONAUX.

UNION OF WRITERS OF TAJIKISTAN.
— SADOI SHARK.

(UNITED ARAB REPUBLIC) MINISTRY OF AGRICULTURE.
— TECHNICAL BULLETIN, MINISTRY OF AGRICULTURE
(U.A.R.).

UNITED KINGDOM ATOMIC ENERGY AUTHORITY.
— U.K.A.E.A. METRIC GUIDE.

UNITED KINGDOM ATOMIC ENERGY AUTHORITY:
AUTHORITY HEALTH & SAFETY BRANCH.
— AHSB (S) REPORT, UNITED KINGDOM ATOMIC
ENERGY AUTHORITY.                                                       XXX
SUBS (1971): SRD REPORT, UNITED KINGDOM
ATOMIC ENERGY AUTHORITY.

UNITED KINGDOM ATOMIC ENERGY AUTHORITY: SAFETY
& RELIABILITY DIRECTORATE.
— SRD REPORT, UNITED KINGDOM ATOMIC ENERGY
AUTHORITY.                                                              XXX

UNITED KINGDOM AUTOMATION COUNCIL.
— AUTOMATION COUNCIL NEWS.

UNITED KINGDOM CHEMICAL INFORMATION SERVICE.
— MACROPROFILE: RADIATION & PHOTOCHEMISTRY.                             XXX
— MACROPROFILE: STEROIDS.                                               XXX

UNITED KINGDOM NATIONAL DOCUMENTATION CENTRE
FOR SPORT, PHYSICAL EDUCATION & RECREATION.
— SPORTS INFORMATION MONTHLY BULLETIN.

UNITED KINGDOM READING ASSOCIATION.
— READING. A JOURNAL FOR THE STUDY & IMPROVE-
MENT OF READING & RELATED SKILLS.

UNITED KINGDOM SCIENTIFIC MISSION (US).
— ENVIRONMENTAL BULLETIN.
— TRANSPORTATION BULLETIN.

UNITED NATIONS.
— INDUSTRIAL DEVELOPMENT ABSTRACTS.
— UNDEX. UNITED NATIONS DOCUMENTS INDEX:
SERIES A: SUBJECT INDEX.
— UNDEX. UNITED NATIONS DOCUMENTS INDEX:
SERIES B: COUNTRY INDEX.

UNITED NATIONS: ASIAN INSTITUTE FOR ECONOMIC
DEVELOPMENT & PLANNING.
— OCCASIONAL PAPERS, ASIAN INSTITUTE FOR ECONO-
MIC DEVELOPMENT & PLANNING, UNITED NATIONS.

UNITED NATIONS: CENTRE FOR ECONOMIC & SOCIAL
INFORMATION.
— DEVELOPMENT FORUM.

UNITED NATIONS: CENTRE FOR HOUSING BUILDING &
PLANNING.
— HUMAN SETTLEMENTS.

UNITED NATIONS: COMMISSION ON INTERNATIONAL
TRADE LAW.
  — YEARBOOK, UNITED NATIONS COMMISSION ON
    INTERNATIONAL TRADE LAW.

UNITED NATIONS: COMMITTEE FOR CO-ORDINATION OF
JOINT PROSPECTING FOR MINERAL RESOURCES IN
ASIAN OFFSHORE AREAS.
  — TECHNICAL BULLETIN, COMMITTEE FOR CO-ORDINA-
    TION OF JOINT PROSPECTING FOR MINERAL RESOUR-
    CES IN ASIAN OFFSHORE AREAS (UN).

UNITED NATIONS: DEPARTMENT OF ECONOMIC &
SOCIAL AFFAIRS.
  — INTERNATIONAL SOCIAL DEVELOPMENT REVIEW.
  — JOURNAL OF DEVELOPMENT PLANNING.
  — NATURAL RESOURCES FORUM.
  — POPULATION NEWSLETTER.
  — SOCIAL DEVELOPMENT NEWSLETTER.

UNITED NATIONS: DEPARTMENT OF ECONOMIC & SOCIAL
AFFAIRS: STATISTICAL OFFICE.
  — GROWTH OF WORLD INDUSTRY.

UNITED NATIONS: DIVISION OF HUMAN RIGHTS.
  — HUMAN RIGHTS BULLETIN.

UNITED NATIONS: ECONOMIC COMMISSION FOR AFRICA.
  — AFRICAN ECONOMIC INDICATORS. = INDICATEURS
    ECONOMIQUES AFRICAINS.
  — AFRICA INDEX.  SELECTED ARTICLES ON SOCIO-
    ECONOMIC DEVELOPMENT.
  — AFRICAN POPULATION NEWSLETTER.
  — AFRICAN TARGET. = OBJECTIFS AFRICAINS.
  — INVESTMENT PROMOTION NEWSLETTER.
  — STATISTICAL BULLETIN FOR AFRICA.

UNITED NATIONS: ECONOMIC COMMISSION FOR ASIA &
THE FAR EAST.
  — ASIAN INDUSTRIAL DEVELOPMENT NEWS.
  — ASIAN POPULATION PROGRAMME NEWS.
  — INDUSTRIAL DEVELOPMENT IN ASIA & THE FAR EAST.
  — QUARTERLY BULLETIN OF STATISTICS FOR ASIA &
    THE FAR EAST.                                                               XXX

UNITED NATIONS: ECONOMIC COMMISSION FOR EUROPE.
  — ANNUAL BULLETIN OF GENERAL ENERGY STATISTICS
    FOR EUROPE.

UNITED NATIONS: ECONOMIC & SOCIAL OFFICE IN
BEIRUT.
  — STUDIES ON SELECTED DEVELOPMENT PROBLEMS IN
    VARIOUS COUNTRIES IN THE MIDDLE EAST.

UNITED NATIONS; HIGH COMMISSIONER FOR REFUGEES.
  — HCR BULLETIN.

UNITED NATIONS: INDUSTRIAL DEVELOPMENT ORGAN-
ISATION.
  — FOOD INDUSTRY STUDIES.
  — INDUSTRIAL RESEARCH & DEVELOPMENT NEWS.                                     XXX
  — INDUSTRIAL RESEARCH NEWS.                                                   XXX
  — TRAINING FOR INDUSTRY SERIES.
  — UNIDO NEWSLETTER.

UNITED NATIONS: INSTITUTE FOR TRAINING &
RESEARCH.
  — UNITAR LECTURE SERIES.

UNITED NATIONS: LIBRARY.
  — REFERENCE LISTS, LIBRARY, UNITED NATIONS.

UNITED NATIONS: OFFICE OF PUBLIC INFORMATION.
  — INTERNATIONAL YEAR FOR HUMAN RIGHTS NEWS-
    LETTER.
  — OBJECTIVE:  JUSTICE.

UNITED NATIONS: PROTEIN ADVISORY GROUP.
  — PAG BULLETIN.

UNITED NATIONS: RESEARCH INSTITUE FOR SOCIAL
DEVELOPMENT.
  — RESEARCH NOTES, RESEARCH INSTITUTE FOR SOCIAL
    DEVELOPMENT (UNITED NATIONS).

UNITED NATIONS STUDENTS ASSOCIATION: EDINBURGH
BRANCH.
  — SEED.

UNITED REFORMED CHURCH.
  — REFORM.

UNITED REFORMED CHURCH HISTORY SOCIETY.                                        XXX
  — JOURNAL, UNITED REFORMED CHURCH HISTORY
    SOCIETY.                                                                    XXX

(UNITED STATES) AIR FORCE: CAMBRIDGE RESEARCH
LABORATORIES.                                                                   XXX
  — PHYSICAL SCIENCES RESEARCH PAPERS.

(UNITED STATES) AIR POLLUTION CONTROL OFFICE:
ENVIRONMENTAL PROTECTION AGENCY.
  — AIR POLLUTION ABSTRACTS (RESEARCH TRIANGLE
    PARK).                                                                      XXX

(UNITED STATES) APPALACHIAN REGIONAL COMMISSION
  — APPALACHIA.

(UNITED STATES) ARMY: COLD REGIONS RESEARCH &
ENGINEERING LABORATORY.
  — CRREL IN ALASKA: ANNUAL REPORT.

(UNITED STATES) ARMY: CORPS OF ENGINEERS.
  — WATER SPECTRUM.

(UNITED STATES) ARMY: LOGISTICS MANAGEMENT
CENTRE.
  — ARMY LOGISTICIAN.

UNITED STATES ATOMIC ENERGY COMMISSION.
  — NEWS RELEASES, UNITED STATES ATOMIC ENERGY
    COMMISSION.

UNITED STATES ATOMIC ENERGY COMMISSION: DIVI-
SION OF TECHNICAL INFORMATION.
  — REACTOR & FUEL-PROCESSING TECHNOLOGY.                                       XXX
    SUBS (1970):  REACTOR TECHNOLOGY.
  — REACTOR TECHNOLOGY.  QUARTERLY TECHNICAL
    PROGRESS REVIEW.                                                            XXX

(UNITED STATES) BUREAU OF EMPLOYEES
COMPENSATION.
  — SAFETY STANDARDS.                                                           XXX
    SUBS (1972): JOB SAFETY & HEALTH.

(UNITED STATES) BUREAU OF INTELLIGENCE &
RESEARCH.
  — GEOGRAPHIC BULLETIN.

(UNITED STATES) BUREAU OF MINES.
  — TECHNICAL PROGRESS REPORT, BUREAU OF MINES
    (UNITED STATES).

(UNITED STATES) BUREAU OF SPORT FISHERIES &
WILDLIFE.
  — FISH DISTRIBUTION REPORT.
  — WILDLIFE RESEARCH REPORT (US).

(UNITED STATES) DEPARTMENT OF AGRICULTURE:
SOUTHERN MARKETING & NUTRITION RESEARCH DIV-
ISION.                                                                          XXX
  — PUBLICATIONS & PATENTS WITH ABSTRACTS, SOUTH-
    ERN MARKETING & NUTRITION RESEARCH DIVISION,
    DEPARTMENT OF AGRICULTURE (US).

(UNITED STATES) DEPARTMENT OF AGRICULTURE:
SOUTHERN UTILIZATION RESEARCH & DEVELOPMENT
DIVISION.                                                                       XXX
  — LIST OF PUBLICATIONS & PATENTS, SOUTHERN UTIL-
    IZATION RESEARCH & DEVELOPMENT DIVISION, DEP-
    ARTMENT OF AGRICULTURE (US).                                                XXX
    SUBS (1971): PUBLICATIONS & PATENTS WITH
    ABSTRACTS, SOUTHERN MARKETING & NUTRITION
    RESEARCH DIVISION, DEPARTMENT ...

(UNITED STATES) DEPARTMENT OF AGRICULTURE:
WESTERN MARKETING & NUTRITION RESEARCH
DIVISION.                                                                       XXX
  — LIST OF PUBLICATIONS & PATENTS WITH ABSTRACTS,
    WESTERN MARKETING & NUTRITION RESEARCH DIVIS-
    ION, DEPARTMENT OF AGRICULTURE (US).                                        XXX

(UNITED STATES) DEPARTMENT OF AGRICULTURE:
WESTERN UTILIZATION RESEARCH & DEVELOPMENT
DIVISION.                                                                       XXX
  — LIST OF PUBLICATIONS & PATENTS WITH ABSTRACTS,
    WESTERN UTILIZATION RESEARCH & DEVELOPMENT
    DIVISION, DEPARTMENT OF AGRICULTURE (US).                                   XXX
    SUBS (1970): LIST OF PUBLICATIONS & PATENTS
    WITH ABSTRACTS, WESTERN MARKETING & NUTRIT-
    ION RESEARCH DIVISION, DEPARTMENT OF AGRI-
    CULTURE (US).

(UNITED STATES) DEPARTMENT OF THE ARMY: OFFICE
OF THE CHIEF OF ENGINEERS.
  — ADVANCED TECHNOLOGY/LIBRARIES.                                             XXX

(UNITED STATES) DEPARTMENT OF COMMERCE.
  — COMMERCE TODAY.
  — FISHERY FACTS (US).

(UNITED STATES) DEPARTMENT OF HEALTH, EDUCATION
& WELFARE: PUBLIC HEALTH SERVICE.
— ENDOCRINOLOGY INDEX.
— HEALTH ASPECTS OF PESTICIDES: ABSTRACT
  BULLETIN.                                              XXX
— HYGIENE & SANITATION.                                 XXX

(UNITED STATES) DEPARTMENT OF HOUSING & URBAN
DEVELOPMENT.
— HUD CHALLENGE.

(UNITED STATES) DEPARTMENT OF THE INTERIOR.
— BIBLIOGRAPHY, DEPARTMENT OF THE INTERIOR (US).

(UNITED STATES) DEPARTMENT OF THE INTERIOR:
GEOLOGICAL SURVEY.
— JOURNAL OF RESEARCH OF THE UNITED STATES
  GEOLOGICAL SURVEY.

(UNITED STATES) DEPARTMENT OF LABOR MANPOWER
ADMINISTRATION.
— MANPOWER.

(UNITED STATES) EDUCATIONAL RESEARCH INFORMA-
TION CENTER.
— RESEARCH IN EDUCATION (WASHINGTON, D.C.).

(UNITED STATES) ENVIRONMENTAL PROTECTION
AGENCY: OFFICE OF RADIATION PROGRAMS.
— RADIATION DATA & REPORTS.                             XXX
— [REPORT] OFFICE OF RADIATION PROGRAMS, ENVIR-
  ONMENTAL PROTECTION AGENCY (US).

(UNITED STATES) ENVIRONMENTAL PROTECTION
AGENCY: SOLID WASTE MANAGEMENT OFFICE.
— ACCESSION BULLETIN, SOLID WASTE INFORMATION
  RETRIEVAL SYSTEM.

(UNITED STATES) ENVIRONMENTAL SCIENCE SERVICES
ADMINISTRATION.
— ESSA PROFESSIONAL PAPER.

(UNITED STATES) ENVIRONMENTAL SCIENCE SERVICES
ADMINISTRATION: OFFICE OF PUBLIC INFORMATION.
— ESSA.                                                 XXX
— ESSA WORLD.                                           XXX

(UNITED STATES) FEDERAL WATER POLLUTION
CONTROL ADMINISTRATION.
— WATER POLLUTION CONTROL RESEARCH SERIES.

(UNITED STATES) HEALTH SERVICE & MENTAL HEALTH
ADMINISTRATION.
— HSMHA HEALTH REPORTS.                                 XXX
— PUBLIC HEALTH REPORTS.                                XXX
  SUBS (1971): HSMHA HEALTH REPORTS.

(UNITED STATES) INFORMATION SERVICE (GB).
— LABOUR NEWS (US).                                     XXX

(UNITED STATES) MILITARY TRAFFIC MANAGEMENT &
TERMINAL SERVICE.
— TRANSLOG. JOURNAL OF MILITARY TRANSPORTA-
  TION MANAGEMENT.                                      XXX
— TRANSPORTATION PROCEEDINGS.                           XXX

(UNITED STATES) NATIONAL AIR POLLUTION CONTROL
ADMINISTRATION.
— NAPCA ABSTRACTS BULLETIN.                             XXX

(UNITED STATES) NATIONAL ARCHIVES.
— INVENTORY SERIES, NATIONAL ARCHIVES (US).

(UNITED STATES) NATIONAL MARINE FISHERIES
SERVICE.
— COMMERCIAL FISHERIES REVIEW.                          XXX
  SUBS (1972): MARINE FISHERIES REVIEW.
— MARINE FISHERIES REVIEW.                              XXX

(UNITED STATES) NATIONAL OCEANIC & ATMOSPHERIC
ADMINISTRATION.
— FISHERY BULLETIN OF THE NATIONAL OCEANIC &
  ATMOSPHERIC ADMINISTRATION (US).                      XXX

(UNITED STATES) NATIONAL OCEANIC & ATMOSPHERIC
ADMINISTRATION: ENVIRONMENTAL DATA SERVICE.
— ATMOSPHERIC TURBIDITY DATA FOR THE WORLD.

UNITED STATES NAVAL OCEANOGRAPHIC OFFICE.
— GEOMAGNETIC SURVEY INFORMATION.

(UNITED STATES) OCCUPATIONAL SAFETY & HEALTH
ADMINISTRATION.
— JOB SAFETY & HEALTH.                                  XXX

(UNITED STATES) OFFICE OF CHILD DEVELOPMENT:
CHILDREN'S BUREAU.
— CHILDREN TODAY.

(UNITED STATES) PACIFIC NORTHWEST FOREST &
RANGE EXPERIMENT STATION.
— GENERAL TECHNICAL REPORT, PACIFIC NORTHWEST
  FOREST & RANGE EXPERIMENT STATION (US).

(UNITED STATES) PUBLIC HEALTH SERVICE.
— RADIOLOGICAL HEALTH DATA & REPORTS.                   XXX

(UNITED STATES) PUBLIC HEALTH SERVICE: COM-
MUNICABLE DISEASE CENTER.
— CURRENT LITERATURE ON VENEREAL DISEASE:
  ABSTRACTS & BIBLIOGRAPHY.                             XXX

(UNITED STATES) ROCKY MOUNTAIN FOREST & RANGE
EXPERIMENT STATION.
— GENERAL TECHNICAL REPORT, ROCKY MOUNTAIN
  FOREST & RANGE EXPERIMENT STATION (US).

UNITED STATES CAPITOL HISTORICAL SOCIETY.
— CAPITOL STUDIES.

UNIUNE SOCIETATILOR DE STIINTE MEDICALE.
— INDEX AL ARTICOLELOR APARUTE IN CURSUL ANULUI
  ... IN REVISTELE MEDICALE PUBLICATE DE USSM.

UNIUNEA SCRIITORILOR DIN REPUBLICA SOCIALISA
ROMANIA.
— ROMANIA LITERARA.

UNIVERSITY OF ABERDEEN: CENTRE FOR SCOTTISH
STUDIES.
— NORTHERN SCOTLAND.

UNIVERSITY OF ABERDEEN: DEPARTMENT OF GEOGRAPHY
— O'DELL MEMORIAL MONOGRAPHS.

UNIVERSITE D'ABIDJAN.
— ANNALES DE L'UNIVERSITE D'ABIDJAN:
  SERIE D: LETTRES ET SCIENCES HUMAINES.
— ANNALES, UNIVERSITE D'ABIDJAN:  SERIE E:
  ECOLOGIE.                                             XXX
— ANNALES DE L'UNIVERSITE D'ABIDJAN:
  SERIE F: ETHNOSOCIOLOGIE.
— ANNALES, UNIVERSITE D'ABIDJAN: SERIE G: GEOGR-
  APHIE.
— ANNALES DE L'UNIVERSITE D'ABIDJAN:
  SERIE H: LINGUISTIQUE.
— BULLETIN, UNIVERSITE D'ABIDJAN.
— INTRODUCTIONS A LA BIOLOGIE AFRICAINE.

UNIVERSITE D'ABIDJAN: ECOLE DES SCIENCES.
— ANNALES, ECOLE DES SCIENCES, UNIVERSITE
  D'ABIDJAN.

UNIVERSITE D' ABIDJAN: FACULTE DE MEDECINE.
— ANNALES, FACULTE DE MEDECINE, UNIVERSITE
  D'ABIDJAN.

UNIVERSITE D'ABIDJAN: INSTITUTS DE RECHERCHE.
— BULLETIN DES INSTITUTS DE RECHERCHE DE L'
  UNIVERSITE D'ABIDJAN.                                 XXX

UNIWERSYTET IM. ADAMA MICKIEWICZA W POZNANIU.
— PRACE WYDZIALU BIOLOGII I NAUKI O ZIEMI,
  UNIWERSYTET IM. ADAMA MICKIEWICZA W POZNANIU,
  SERIA BIOLOGIA.
— PRACE WYDZIALU BIOLOGII I NAUK O ZIEMI,
  UNIWERSYTET IM. ADAMA MICKIEWICZA W POZNANIU:
  SERIA GEOGRAFIA.
— PRACE WYDZIALU BIOLOGII I NAUKI O ZIEMI,
  UNIWERSYTET IM. ADAMA MICKIEWICZA W POZNANIU,
  SERIA GEOLOGIA.
— PRACE WYDZIALU FILOLOGICZNEGO, UNIWERSYTET
  IM. ADAMA MICKIEWICZA W POZNANIU:  SERIA
  FILOLOGIA UGROFINSKA.
— SERIA PRAC Z ZAKRESU DZIEJOW UNIWERSYTETU
  POZNANSKIEGO.
— STUDIA ANGLICA POSNANIENSIA.
— WYKLADY INAUGURACYJNE, UNIWERSYTET IM. ADAMA
  MICKIEWICZA W POZNANIU.
— ZESZYTY NAUKOWE UNIWERSYTETU IM. ADAMA MICK-
  IEWICZA: BIBLIOTEKA.                                  XXX

UNIWERSYTET IM. ADAMA MICKIEWICZA W POZNANIU:
MIEDZYWYDZIALOWY ZAKLAD NOWYCH TECHNIK NAUCZAN-
IA.
— NEODIDAGMATA.

UNIWERSYTET IM. ADAMA MICKIEWICZA W POZNANIU:
OSRODEK METODYCZNY UNIWERSYTECKICH STUDIOW DLA
PRACUJACYCH.
— PRACE OSRODKA METODYCZNEGO UNIWERSYTECKICH
STUDIOW DLA PRACUJACYCH, UNIWERSYTET IM.
ADAMA MICKIEWICZA W POZNANIU.

UNIVERSIDAD AGRARIA, LIMA: INSTITUTO DE INVES-
TIGACIONES FORESTALES.
— REVISTA FORESTAL DEL PERU.

UNIVERSITY OF AGRICULTURAL SCIENCES (BANGALORE)
— MYSORE JOURNAL OF AGRICULTURAL SCIENCES.

UNIVERSITY OF AKRON: DEPARTMENT OF SPEECH
PATHOLOGY & AUDIOLOGY.
— ACTA SYMBOLICA.

UNIVERSITY OF ALASKA: INSTITUTE OF ARCTIC EN-
VIRONMENTAL ENGINEERING.
— NORTHERN ENGINEER.

UNIVERSITY OF ALASKA: INSTITUTE OF MARINE
SCIENCE.
— OCCASIONAL PUBLICATION, INSTITUTE OF MARINE
SCIENCE, UNIVERSITY OF ALASKA.

UNIVERSITY OF ALASKA: INSTITUTE OF SOCIAL,
ECONOMIC & GOVERNMENT RESEARCH.
— OCCASIONAL PAPERS, INSTITUTE OF SOCIAL,
ECONOMIC & GOVERNMENT RESEARCH, UNIVERSITY OF
ALASKA.

UNIVERSITY OF ALEPPO: FACULTY OF AGRICULTURE.
— RESEARCH PAMPHLETS, FACULTY OF AGRICULTURE,
UNIVERSITY OF ALEPPO.

UNIVERSITE D'ALGER: FACULTE DES LETTRES ET
SCIENCES HUMAINES.
— REVUE D'HISTOIRE ET DE CIVILISATION DU
MAGHREB.

UNIVERSITY OF ALLAHABAD: DEPARTMENT OF
CHEMISTRY.
— INDIAN JOURNAL OF AGRICULTURAL CHEMISTRY.

UNIVERSITY OF ALLAHABAD: MOTILAL NEHRU INSTIT-
UTE OF RESEARCH & BUSINESS ADMINISTRATION.
— QUARTERLY JOURNAL OF MANAGEMENT DEVELOPMENT.

UNIVERSITY OF ARKANSAS.
— STYLE.

UNIVERSITY OF ARKANSAS: WATER RESOURCES
RESEARCH CENTER.
— PUBLICATION, WATER RESOURCES RESEARCH CENTER,
UNIVERSITY OF ARKANSAS.

UNIVERSITIES ASSOCIATED FOR RESEARCH & EDUCAT-
ION IN PATHOLOGY.
— INDEX OF INVESTIGATIVE DERMATOPATHOLOGY &
DERMATOLOGY.                                          XXX

UNIVERSITY ASSOCIATION FOR CONTEMPORARY EUROP-
EAN STUDIES.
— NEWSLETTER, UNIVERSITY ASSOCIATION FOR CONT-
EMPORARY EUROPEAN STUDIES.

UNIVERSITY OF ASTON IN BIRMINGHAM.
— ANNUAL REPORT, UNIVERSITY OF ASTON IN
BIRMINGHAM.

UNIVERSITY OF AUCKLAND.
— NEW ZEALAND JOURNAL OF HISTORY.
— PRUDENTIA.

UNIVERSITY OF AUCKLAND: DEPARTMENT OF MATHEM-
ATICS.
— MATHEMATICAL CHRONICLE.

UNIVERSITY OF AUCKLAND: LAW STUDENTS' SOCIETY.
— AUCKLAND UNIVERSITY LAW REVIEW.

UNIVERSIDAD AUTONOMA DE SANTO DOMINGO: FACULTAD
DE HUMANIDADES.
— PEQUENO UNIVERSO.
— REVISTA DOMINICANA DE ARQUEOLOGIA Y ANTRO-
POLOGIA.

UNIVERSITY OF BAGHDAD: COLLEGE OF AGRICULTURE.
— IRAQI JOURNAL OF AGRICULTURAL SCIENCE.
— MESOPOTAMIA. JOURNAL OF AGRICULTURE &
FORESTRY RESEARCH.

UNIVERSIDAD DE BARCELONA.
— ACTA GEOBOTANICA BARCINONENSIA.
— ACTA PHYTOTAXONOMICA BARCINONENSIA.

UNIVERSIDAD DE BARCELONA: CATEDRA DE PALEONT-
OLOGIA.
— PUBLICACIONES, CATEDRA DE PALEONTOLOGIA,
UNIVERSIDAD DE BARCELONA.

UNIVERSIDAD DE BARCELONA: FACULTAD DE CIENCIAS.
— OPUSCULA SPARSA.

UNIVERSIDAD DE BARCELONA: INSTITUTO DE
ARQUEOLOGIA Y PREHISTORIA.
— PYRENAE. CRONICA ARQUEOLOGICA.

UNIVERSITA DI BARI; ISTITUTO DE GEOLOGIA
APPLICATA ALL'INGENERIA.
— GEOLOGIA APPLICATA E IDROGEOLOGIA.

UNIVERSITY OF BASRA: FACULTY OF ARTS.
— AL-MIRBAD. BULLETIN OF THE ...

UNIVERSITE DE BELGRADE.                               000
SEE: BEOGRADSKI UNIVERZITET.

UNIVERSITETET I BERGEN.
— ACTA UNIVERSITATIS BERGENSIS: SERIES MEDICA:
NS.

UNIVERSITETET I BERGEN: HISTORISK MUSEUM.
— ARKEOLOGISKE MEDDELELSER FRA HISTORISK MUSEUM,
UNIVERSITETET I BERGEN.

UNIVERSITAT BERN.
— VEROFFENTLICHUNGEN DES SEMINARS FUR ETHNOL-
OGIE DER UNIVERSITAT BERN.

UNIVERSITAT BIELEFELD: FAKULTAT FUR SOZIOLOGIE.
— ZEITSCHRIFT FUR SOZIOLOGIE.

UNIVERSITY OF BIRMINGHAM.
— DISCUSSION PAPERS, FACULTY OF COMMERCE &
SOCIAL SCIENCE, UNIVERSITY OF BIRMINGHAM;
SERIES E: SOCIAL SCIENCE METHODOLOGY.
— MIDLAND HISTORY.                                    XXX
— UNIVERSITY OF BIRMINGHAM HISTORICAL JOURNAL.       XXX
SUBS (1971): MIDLAND HISTORY.

UNIVERSITY OF BIRMINGHAM: CENTRE FOR
CONTEMPORARY CULTURAL STUDIES.
— WORKING PAPERS IN CULTURAL STUDIES.

UNIVERSITY OF BIRMINGHAM: CENTRE FOR RUSSIAN &
EAST EUROPEAN STUDIES.
— DISCUSSION PAPERS, CENTRE FOR RUSSIAN & EAST
EUROPEAN STUDIES, UNIVERSITY OF BIRMINGHAM:
SERIES RC/A.
— DISCUSSION PAPERS, CENTRE FOR RUSSIAN & EAST
EUROPEAN STUDIES, UNIVERSITY OF BIRMINGHAM:
SERIES RC/B.
— DISCUSSION PAPERS, CENTRE FOR RUSSIAN & EAST
EUROPEAN STUDIES, UNIVERSITY OF BIRMINGHAM:
SERIES RC/C: SOCIOLOGY & POLITICAL SCIENCE.

UNIVERSITY OF BIRMINGHAM: CENTRE FOR URBAN &
REGIONAL STUDIES.
— RESEARCH MEMORANDA, CENTRE FOR URBAN &
REGIONAL STUDIES, UNIVERSITY OF BIRMINGHAM.

UNIVERSITY OF BIRMINGHAM: CLEARINGHOUSE FOR
LOCAL AUTHORITY SOCIAL SERVICES RESEARCH.
— INLOGOV.

UNIVERSITY OF BIRMINGHAM: INSTITUTE OF JUDICIAL
ADMINISTRATION.
— ANNUAL REPORT, INSTITUTE OF JUDICIAL ADMINIS-
TRATION, UNIVERSITY OF BIRMINGHAM.

UNIVERSITY OF BIRMINGHAM: INSTITUTE OF LOCAL
GOVERNMENT STUDIES.
— LOCAL GOVERNMENT STUDIES.
— OCCASIONAL PAPERS, INSTITUTE OF LOCAL GOVERN-
MENT STUDIES, UNIVERSITY OF BIRMINGHAM,
SERIES A.

UNIVERSITY OF BIRMINGHAM: INSTITUTE FOR THE
STUDY OF WORSHIP & RELIGIOUS ARCHITECTURE.
— RESEARCH BULLETIN, INSTITUTE FOR THE STUDY OF
WORSHIP & RELIGIOUS ARCHITECTURE, UNIVERSITY
OF BIRMINGHAM.

UNIVERSITA DI BOLOGNA: CENTRO INTERFACOLTA DI
LINGUISTICA TEORICA ED APPLICATA.
— STUDI ITALIANI DI LINGUISTICA TEORICA ED
APPLICATA.

UNIVERSITA DI BOLOGNA: CENTRO DI MICROSCOPIA
ELETTRONICA.
— JOURNAL OF SUBMICROSCOPIC CYTOLOGY.

UNIVERSITA DI BOLOGNA: LABORATORIO DI ZOOLOGIA
APPLICATA ALLA CACCIA.
— RICERCHE DI BIOLOGIA DELLA SELVAGGINA.                XXX

UNIVERSITE DE BORDEAUX: INSTITUT DE
PREHISTOIRE.
— MEMOIRES, INSTITUT DE PREHISTOIRE, UNIVERSITE
DE BORDEAUX.

UNIVERSITE DE BORDEAUX: SECTION DE LA LANGUE ET
LITTERATURE FRANCAISE.
— REPERTOIRE ANALYTIQUE DE LITTERATURE
FRANCAISE.

UNIVERSITY OF BRADFORD.
— BRADFORD SEVEN.

UNIVERSITY OF BRADFORD LIBRARY.
— ACE. ARTICLES IN CIVIL ENGINEERING.

UNIVERSITY OF BRADFORD: MANAGEMENT CENTRE.
— EUROPEAN TRAINING.

UNIVERSITY OF BRISTOL: DEPARTMENT OF EXTRA-
MURAL STUDIES.
— GLOUCESTERSHIRE HISTORICAL STUDIES.

UNIVERSITY OF BRISTOL: LONG ASHTON RESEARCH
STATION.                                               000
SEE: LONG ASHTON ...

UNIVERSITY OF BRITISH COLUMBIA: BOTANICAL
GARDEN.
— DAVIDSONIA.

UNIVERSITE DE BUJUMBURA.
— REVUE, UNIVERSITE DE BUJUMBURA.                      XXX

UNIVERSITY OF CALCUTTA: DEPARTMENT OF ANCIENT
INDIAN HISTORY & CULTURE.
— JOURNAL OF ANCIENT INDIAN HISTORY.

UNIVERSITY OF CALCUTTA: DEPARTMENT OF COMPARA-
TIVE LITERATURE.
— JADAVPUR JOURNAL OF COMPARATIVE LITERATURE.

UNIVERSITY OF CALGARY.
— ARIEL. A REVIEW OF INTERNATIONAL ENGLISH
LITERATURE.

UNIVERSITY OF CALGARY: DEPARTMENT OF SOCIOLOGY
& ANTHROPOLOGY.
— JOURNAL OF COMPARATIVE FAMILY STUDIES.

UNIVERSITY OF CALIFORNIA.
— BIOPHYSICS SERIES, UNIVERSITY OF CALIFORNIA.
— JOURNAL OF SOCIAL HISTORY.
— UNIVERSITY OF CALIFORNIA PUBLICATIONS IN
AUTOMATIC COMPUTATION.
— UNIVERSITY OF CALIFORNIA PUBLICATIONS: NEAR
EASTERN STUDIES.

UNIVERSITY OF CALIFORNIA LIBRARY.
— SOUNDINGS.

UNIVERSITY OF CALIFORNIA: MEDICAL CENTER
PSYCHOPHARMACOLOGY STUDY GROUP.
— JOURNAL OF PSYCHEDELIC DRUGS.

UNIVERSITY OF CALIFORNIA: MUSEUM OF SYSTEM-
ATIC BIOLOGY.
— RESEARCH SERIES, MUSEUM OF SYSTEMATIC BIOLOGY,
UNIVERSITY OF CALIFORNIA.

UNIVERSITY OF CALIFORNIA: PACKAGING LIBRARY.
— CURRENT PACKAGING ABSTRACTS.                         XXX
— PACKAGING BULLETIN.                                  XXX

UNIVERSITY OF CALIFORNIA: SCHOOL OF CRIMINO-
LOGY.
— ISSUES IN CRIMINOLOGY.

UNIVERSITY OF CALIFORNIA: SCHOOL OF LAW.
— ECOLOGY LAW QUARTERLY.

UNIVERSITY OF CALIFORNIA: VISUAL SCIENCE INFOR-
MATION CENTER.
— VISION INDEX.

UNIVERSITY OF CALIFORNIA (LOS ANGELES): AFRI-
CAN STUDIES CENTER.
— AFRICAN ARTS. ARTS D'AFRIQUE.
— AFRICAN RELIGIOUS RESEARCH.

UNIVERSITY OF CALIFORNIA (LOS ANGELES): CENTER
FOR MEDIEVAL & RENAISSANCE STUDIES.
— VIATOR. MEDIEVAL & RENAISSANCE STUDIES.

UNIVERSITY OF CALIFORNIA (LOS ANGELES):
DEPARTMENT OF SPANISH & PORTUGUESE.
— MESTER.

UNIVERSITY OF CAMBRIDGE.
— LIBRARIES INFORMATION BULLETIN, UNIVERSITY OF
CAMBRIDGE.

UNIVERSITY OF CAMBRIDGE: AFRICAN STUDIES CENTRE
— AFRICAN SOCIAL RESEARCH DOCUMENTS.

UNIVERSITY OF CAMBRIDGE: CENTRE FOR LAND USE &
BUILT FORM STUDIES.
— LAND USE & BUILT FORM STUDIES REPORTS.

UNIVERSITY OF CAMBRIDGE: DEPARTMENT OF AGRICUL-
TURAL SCIENCE & APPLIED BIOLOGY.                       XXX
— MEMOIRS , DEPARTMENT OF AGRICULTURAL SCIENCE
& APPLIED BIOLOGY, UNIVERSITY OF CAMBRIDGE.            XXX

UNIVERSITY OF CAMBRIDGE: DEPARTMENT OF APPLIED
BIOLOGY.
— MEMOIRS, DEPARTMENT OF APPLIED BIOLOGY, UNIV-
ERSITY OF CAMBRIDGE.                                   XXX

UNIVERSITY OF CAMBRIDGE: DEPARTMENT OF LAND
ECONOMY.
— AGRICULTURAL ECONOMICS REPORT, DEPARTMENT OF
LAND ECONOMY, UNIVERSITY OF CAMBRIDGE.

UNIVERSITY OF CAMBRIDGE: FACULTY OF ORIENTAL
STUDIES.
— EGYPTOLOGY TITLES.                                   XXX

UNIVERSITY OF CAMBRIDGE: INSTITUTE OF EDUCAT-
ION.
— CAMBRIDGE JOURNAL OF EDUCATION.
— OCCASIONAL RESEARCH PAPERS, INSTITUTE OF EDUC-
ATION, UNIVERSITY OF CAMBRIDGE.

UNIVERSITY OF CAMBRIDGE: MAGDALENE COLLEGE.
— APPRENTICE. OXFORD & CAMBRIDGE POETRY.

UNIVERSITY OF CAMBRIDGE: SCHOOL OF AGRICULTURE.
— MEMOIRS, SCHOOL OF AGRICULTURE, UNIVERSITY OF
CAMBRIDGE.                                             XXX
SUBS (1970): MEMOIRS, DEPARTMENT OF
AGRICULTURAL SCIENCE & APPLIED BIOLOGY,
UNIVERSITY OF CAMBRIDGE.

UNIVERSITY OF CANTERBURY (NZ).
— BROADHEAD CLASSICAL LECTURES.

UNIVERSITY OF CANTERBURY: DEPARTMENT OF
PSYCHOLOGY & SOCIOLOGY.
— TOWN PLANNING REPORTS.

UNIVERSITY OF CANTERBURY: SCHOOL OF ENGINEERING
— CANTERBURY ENGINEERING JOURNAL.

UNIVERSITY OF CAPE TOWN.
— STUDIES IN ENGLISH, UNIVERSITY OF CAPE TOWN.

UNIVERSITY OF CAPE TOWN: BOLUS HERBARIUM.
— CONTRIBUTIONS FROM THE BOLUS HERBARIUM.

UNIVERSITY OF CAPE TOWN: DEPARTMENT OF OCEAN-
OGRAPHY.
— COLLECTED REPRINTS, DEPARTMENT OF OCEANOGR-
APHY, UNIVERSITY OF CAPE TOWN.

UNIVERSITY OF CAPE TOWN: RADICAL STUDENT'S
SOCIETY.
— RADICAL. A JOURNAL OF RADICAL THOUGHT & EXP-
RESSION.

UNIVERSITY OF CAPE TOWN: SCIENCE STUDENTS'
COUNCIL.
— IMPULSE (SOUTH AFRICA).

UNIVERSITY OF CAPE TOWN: STUDENTS REPRESENTA-
TIVE COUNCIL.
— DIALOGUE (CAPE TOWN).

UNIVERSITE CATHOLIQUE DE LOUVAIN.
— ANCIENT SOCIETY.

UNIVERSITE CATHOLIQUE DE LOUVAIN: CENTRE
D'HISTOIRE RURALE.
— PUBLICATIONS, CENTRE D'HISTOIRE RURALE DE
L'UNIVERSITE CATHOLIQUE DE LOUVAIN.

UNIVERSITE CATHOLIQUE DE LOUVAIN: EMG
LABORATORY.
— ELECTROMYOGRAPHY & CLINICAL NEUROPHYSIOLOGY.        XXX

UNIVERSITE CATHOLIQUE DE LOUVAIN: FACULTE DE
THEOLOGIE.
— REVUE THEOLOGIQUE DE LOUVAIN.
— TRAVAUX DE DOCTORAT EN THEOLOGIE ET EN DROIT
CANONIQUE.

UNIVERSITE CATHOLIQUE DE LOUVAIN: INSTITUT
D'ASTRONOMIE ET GEOPHYSIQUE GEORGES LEMAITRE.
— PUBLICATIONS DE L'INSTITUT D'ASTRONOMIE ET
GEOPHYSIQUE GEORGES LEMAITRE, UNIVERSITE
CATHOLIQUE DE LOUVAIN.

UNIVERSITE CATHOLIQUE DE LOUVAIN: INSTITUT
D'ETUDES DES PAYS EN DEVELOPPEMENT.
— CULTURES ET DEVELOPPEMENT. REVUE INTERNAT-
IONALE DES SCIENCES DU DEVELOPPEMENT.

UNIVERSITE CATHOLIQUE DE LOUVAIN: INSTITUT
SUPERIEUR D'ARCHEOLOGIE ET D'HISTOIRE DE L'ART.
— REVUE DES ARCHEOLOGUES ET HISTORIENS D'ART DE
LOUVAIN.

UNIVERSITE CATHOLIQUE DE LOUVAIN, SECTION DE
PHILOLOGIE ET HISTOIRE ORIENTALE.
— TRAVAUX, SECTION DE PHILOLOGIE ET HISTOIRE
ORIENTALE, UNIVERSITE CATHOLIQUE DE LOUVAIN.

UNIVERSIDAD CATOLICA ANDRES BELLO: CENTRO DE
ESTUDIOS DEL FUTURO DE VENEZUELA.
— PROSPECCION SIGLO XXI - VENEZUELA ANO 2000.

UNIVERSIDAD CATOLICA DE CHILE: CENTRO INTERDIS-
CIPLINARIO DE DESARROLLO URBANO Y REGIONAL.
— REVISTA LATINOAMERICANA DE ESTUDIOS URBANO
REGIONALES.

UNIVERSIDAD CATOLICA DE CHILE: FACULTAD DE
CIENCIAS JURIDICAS, POLITICAS Y SOCIALES.
— ESTUDIOS DE HISTORIA DE LAS INSTITUCIONES
POLITICAS Y SOCIALES.

UNIVERSIDADE CATOLICA DE PERNAMBUCO: INSTITUTO
DE GEOCIENCIAS.
— CADERNOS DE GEOCIENCIAS, INSTITUTO DE GEOCIEN-
CIAS, UNIVERSIDADE CATOLICA DE PERNAMBUCO.

UNIVERSIDAD CATOLICA DE VALPARAISO: DEPARTA-
MENTO DE GEOGRAFIA.
— REVISTA GEOGRAFICA DE VALPARAISO.

UNIVERSIDAD CATOLICA DE VALPARAISO: DIVISION
DE INVESTIGACIONES DEL MAR.
— INVESTIGACIONES MARINAS (CHILE).

UNIVERSIDAD CENTRAL DEL ECUADOR: INSTITUTO DE
ESTUDIOS ADMINISTRATIVOS.
— DESARROLLO ADMINISTRATIVO.

UNIVERSIDAD CENTRAL DE VENEZUELA: FACULTAD DE
MEDICINA.
— BIBLIOGRAFIA MEDICA DEL PROFESORADO DE LA
FACULTAD DE MEDICINA, UNIVERSIDAD CENTRAL DE
VENEZUELA.

UNIVERSIDAD CENTRAL DE VENEZUELA: INSTITUTO DE
ESTUDIOS POLITICOS.
— DOCUMENTOS. REVISTA DE INFORMACION POLITICA.
— POLITEIA.

UNIVERSITY OF CEYLON.
— CEYLON JOURNAL OF THE HUMANITIES.                    XXX
— MODERN CEYLON STUDIES.                               XXX

UNIVERSITY OF CHICAGO.
— SERAPIS.

UNIVERSITY OF CHICAGO: CENTER FOR URBAN STUDIES
— NEWSLETTER, CENTER FOR URBAN STUDIES, UNIVER-
SITY OF CHICAGO.

UNIVERSITY OF CHICAGO: LAW SCHOOL.
— JOURNAL OF LEGAL STUDIES.

UNIVERSIDAD DE CHILE: DEPARTMENTO DE HISTORIA.
— BOLETIN DE PREHISTORIA DE CHILE.

UNIVERSIDAD DE CHILE: ESTACION DE BIOLOGIA
MARINA.
— BIOLOGIA PESQUERA.

UNIVERSITY OF CINCINNATI.
— UNIVERSITY OF CINCINNATI CLASSICAL STUDIES.

UNIVERSITE DE CLERMONT-FERRAND: FACULTE DE
DROIT ET DES SCIENCES ECONOMIQUES.
— ANNALES, FACULTE DE DROIT ET DES SCIENCES
ECONOMIQUES, UNIVERSITE DE CLERMONT-FERRAND.

UNIVERSITY COLLEGE, ABERYSTWYTH: COLLEGE OF
LIBRARIANSHIP.
— STUDENTS PROJECTS, COLLEGE OF LIBRARIANSHIP,
UNIVERSITY COLLEGE, ABERYSTWYTH.

UNIVERSITY COLLEGE OF CAPE COAST.
— GAZETTE, UNIVERSITY COLLEGE OF CAPE COAST.

UNIVERSITY COLLEGE, CORK: ARTS SOCIETY.
— MOTUS. PERIODICAL OF THE ARTS.

UNIVERSITY COLLEGE, CORK: ENGINEERING SOCIETY.
— RECOIL.

UNIVERSITY COLLEGE, DAR-ES-SALAAM.
— TANZANIA ZAMANI.

UNIVERSITY COLLEGE, DAR-ES-SALAAM: DEPARTMENT
OF LITERATURE.
— DARLITE. A MAGAZINE OF ORIGINAL WRITING ...

UNIVERSITY COLLEGE, DAR-ES-SALAAM:
DEPARTMENT OF POLITICAL SCIENCE.
— AFRICAN REVIEW.
— TAAMULI. A POLITICAL SCIENCE FORUM.

UNIVERSITY COLLEGE, DAR-ES-SALAAM: FACULTY
OF LAW.
— EASTERN AFRICA LAW REVIEW.

UNIVERSITY COLLEGE, DAR-ES-SALAAM: INSTITUTE
OF PUBLIC ADMINISTRATION.
— CASE STUDIES IN AFRICAN DIPLOMACY.

UNIVERSITY COLLEGE, DUBLIN.
— INSTEAD. A PAPER BY & FOJ THE STAFF &
STUDENTS OF U.C.D.
— IRISH JURIST: NS.

UNIVERSITY COLLEGE, DUBLIN: COMPUTER LABORATORY
— FORMAT. COMPUTER LABORATORY NEWSLETTER.

UNIVERSITY COLLEGE, DUBLIN: DEPARTMENT OF
APPLIED AGRICULTURAL ECONOMICS.
— REPORT, DEPARTMENT OF APPLIED AGRICULTURAL
ECONOMICS, UNIVERSITY COLLEGE, DUBLIN.

UNIVERSITY COLLEGE, DUBLIN: DEPARTMENT OF
PSYCHOLOGY.
— THORNFIELD SERIES.

UNIVERSITY COLLEGE, DUBLIN: PSYCHOLOGICAL
SOCIETY.
— THORNFIELD JOURNAL.

UNIVERSITY COLLEGE, DUBLIN: SOIL SCIENCE
DEPARTMENT.
— SOIL BULLETIN (DUBLIN).

UNIVERSITY COLLEGE, DURBAN.
— JOURNAL OF THE UNIVERSITY COLLEGE, DURBAN.

UNIVERSITY COLLEGE, GALWAY.
— YEATS STUDIES. AN INTERNATIONAL JOURNAL.

UNIVERSITY COLLEGE, LONDON: DEPARTMENT OF
GEOGRAPHY.
— OCCASIONAL PAPERS, DEPARTMENT OF GEOGRAPHY,
UNIVERSITY COLLEGE, LONDON.

UNIVERSITY COLLEGE LONDON: DEPARTMENT OF TOWN
PLANNING.
— DISCUSSION PAPER SERIES, DEPARTMENT OF TOWN
PLANNING, UNIVERSITY COLLEGE LONDON.

UNIVERSITY COLLEGE, LONDON: FACULTY OF ENGIN-
EERING.
— TORQUE. FOR THE CULTURED DESPISERS & ADVO-
CATES OF TECHNOLOGY.

UNIVERSITY COLLEGE LONDON: GEOGRAPHICAL
SOCIETY.
— BLOOMSBURY GEOGRAPHER.

UNIVERSITY COLLEGE, LONDON: INSTITUTE OF JEWISH
STUDIES.
— BULLETIN OF THE INSTITUTE OF JEWISH STUDIES.

UNIVERSITY COLLEGE, LONDON: SCHOOL OF
ENVIRONMENTAL STUDIES.
— RESEARCH BULLETIN, SCHOOL OF ENVIRONMENTAL
STUDIES, UNIVERSITY COLLEGE, LONDON.

UNIVERSITY COLLEGE, NAIROBI: DEPARTMENT OF
ENGLISH.
— BUSARA.                                                                                                    XXX

UNIVERSITY COLLEGE, NAIROBI: DEPARTMENT OF
HISTORY.
— NAIROBI HISTORICAL STUDIES.

UNIVERSITY COLLEGE, NAIROBI: INSTITUTE FOR
DEVELOPMENT STUDIES.
— SOCIAL SCIENCE BULLETIN (KENYA).

UNIVERSITY COLLEGE OF NORTH WALES.
— RAM. A COLLECTION OF VERSE.

UNIVERSITY COLLEGE OF RHODESIA.
— ZAMBEZIA. A JOURNAL OF SOCIAL STUDIES IN
SOUTHERN & CENTRAL AFRICA.

UNIVERSITY COLLEGE OF RHODESIA: MENNELL SOCIETY
— DETRITUS.

UNIVERSITY COLLEGE OF SIERRA LEONE.
— AFRICAN LANGUAGE REVIEW.                                                                                   XXX

UNIVERSITY COLLEGE OF SOUTH WALES & MONMOUTH-
SHIRE.
— SOUNDINGS. A MUSIC JOURNAL.

UNIVERSITY COLLEGE OF SOUTH WALES & MONMOUTH-
SHIRE: FACULTY OF EDUCATION.
— EDUCATION FOR DEVELOPMENT. JOURNAL OF ...

UNIVERSITY COLLEGE, SWANSEA: BIOLOGICAL SOCIETY
— BIOS.

UNIVERSITY COLLEGE OF WALES: DEPARTMENT OF
GEOLOGY.
— PUBLICATIONS, DEPARTMENT OF GEOLOGY, UNIV-
ERSITY COLLEGE OF WALES.

UNIVERSITY COLLEGE OF WALES: DEPARTMENT OF LAW.
— CAMBRIAN LAW REVIEW.

UNIVERSITY OF COLOMBO: FACULTY OF LAW.
— COLOMBO LAW REVIEW.

UNIVERSITY OF COLORADO: INSTITUTE OF ARCTIC &
ALPINE RESEARCH.
— ARCTIC & ALPINE RESEARCH.

UNIVERSITY OF COLORADO (STATE).                                                                              000
SEE: COLORADO STATE UNIVERSITY.

UNIVERSITA COMMERCIALE LUIGI BOCCONI: FACOLTA
DI LINGUE E LETTERATURE STRANIERE.
— STUDI E RICERCHE DI LETTERATURA INGLESE E
AMERICANA.

UNIVERSIDAD DE CONCEPCION (CHILE): INSTITUTO
CENTRAL DE GEOGRAFIA.
— CUADERNOS GEOGRAFICOS DEL SUR (CHILE).

UNIVERSITY OF CONNECTICUT: SCHOOL OF LAW.
— CONNECTICUT LAW REVIEW.

UNIVERSITY OF COPENHAGEN.                                                                                    000
SEE: KOBENHAVNS UNIVERSITET.

UNIVERSITE DE DAKAR: FACULTE DES LETTRES ET
SCIENCES HUMAINES.
— ANNALES, FACULTE DES LETTRES ET SCIENCES
HUMAINES, UNIVERSITE DE DAKAR.

UNIVERSITY OF DELHI: DEPARTMENT OF POLITICAL
SCIENCE.
— INDIAN POLITICAL SCIENCE REVIEW.

UNIVERSITY OF DENVER: COLLEGE OF LAW.
— DENVER JOURNAL OF INTERNATIONAL LAW & POLICY.

UNIVERSITY OF DETROIT.
— BURKE NEWSLETTER.                                                                                          XXX
SUBS (1967): STUDIES IN BURKE & HIS TIME.

UNIVERSIDAD DE DEUSTO: FACULTAD DE FILOSOFIA
Y LETRAS.
— LETRAS DE DEUSTO.

UNIVERSITY OF DUNDEE.
— UNIVERSITY OF DUNDEE GAZETTE.

UNIVERSITY OF DUNDEE: TAY ESTUARY RESEARCH
CENTRE.
— RESEARCH REPORT, TAY ESTUARY RESEARCH CENTRE,
UNIVERSITY OF DUNDEE.

UNIVERSITY OF DURHAM: CENTRE FOR MIDDLE EASTERN
& ISLAMIC STUDIES.
— PUBLICATIONS, CENTRE FOR MIDDLE EASTERN &
ISLAMIC STUDIES, UNIVERSITY OF DURHAM.

UNIVERSITY OF EAST ANGLIA.
— KETT.
— PERIODICAL LITERATURE SURVEY IN THE FIELDS OF
GEOGRAPHY, GEOMORPHOLOGY & GEOLOGY: INTERIM
REPORT.

UNIVERSITY OF EAST ANGLIA: CLIMATIC RESEARCH
UNIT.
— CRUMB. CLIMATIC RESEARCH UNIT MONTHLY
BULLETIN.

UNIVERSITY OF EAST ANGLIA: SCHOOL OF ENVIRON-
MENTAL SCIENCES.
— COMPUTERS IN THE ENVIRONMENTAL SCIENCES.                                                                   XXX
— COMPUTERS IN GEOGRAPHY.                                                                                    XXX

UNIVERSITY OF THE EASTERN PHILIPPINES: RESEARCH
CENTRE.
— RESEARCHER.

UNIVERSITY OF EDINBURGH: CENTRE FOR TROPICAL
VETERINARY MEDICINE.
— TROPICAL ANIMAL HEALTH & PRODUCTION.

UNIVERSITY OF EDINBURGH: DRAMATIC SOCIETY.                                                                   000
SEE: EDINBURGH UNIVERSITY DRAMATIC SOCIETY.

UNIVERSITY OF EDINBURGH: SCHOOL OF SCOTTISH
STUDIES.
— TOCHER. TALES, MUSIC, SONG.

UNIVERSITY OF EDINBURGH: STUDENT PUBLICATIONS
BOARD.
— BUMP.
— NEW EDINBURGH REVIEW.

UNIVERSITY OF ESSEX.
— WIVENHOE PARK REVIEW.                                                                                      XXX

UNIVERSITY OF ESSEX: DEPARTMENT OF ECONOMICS.
— DISCUSSION PAPERS, DEPARTMENT OF ECONOMICS,
UNIVERSITY OF ESSEX.

UNIVERSITY OF EXETER: DEPARTMENT OF
AGRICULTURAL ECONOMICS.
— E.E.C. BEEF & VEAL CIRCULAR.

UNIVERSITY OF EXETER: DEPARTMENT OF CLASSICS.
— PEGASUS.

UNIVERSITY OF EXETER: INSTITUTE OF EDUCATION.
— THEMES IN EDUCATION.

UNIVERSITY OF EXETER: ST. LUKE'S COLLEGE OF
EDUCATION.
— STUDIES IN EDUCATION (EXETER).

UNIVERSITE FEDERALE DU CAMEROUN: FACULTE DES
LETTRES ET SCIENCES HUMAINES.
— ANNALES DE LA FACULTE DES LETTRES ET SCIENCES
HUMAINES, UNIVERSITE FEDERALE DU CAMEROUN.

UNIVERSITE FEDERALE DU CAMEROUN: SECTION DE
LINGUISTIQUE APPLIQUEE.
— CAMELANG. BULLETIN DE LA ...

UNIVERSIDADE FEDERAL DO CEARA: ESTACAO DE
BIOLOGIA MARINHA.
— ARQUIVOS, ESTACAO DE BIOLOGIA MARINHA, UNI-
VERSIDADE FEDERAL DO CEARA.                                                                                  XXX
SUBS (1969): ARQUIVOS DE CIENCIAS DO MAR.
— BOLETIM, ESTACAO DE BIOLOGIA MARINHA, UNIVER-
SIDADE FEDERAL DO CEARA.                                                                                     XXX

UNIVERSIDADE FEDERAL DO CEARA: LABORATORIO DE
CIENCIAS DO MAR.
— ARQUIVOS DE CIENCIAS DO MAR.                                                                               XXX
— BOLETIM DE CIENCIAS DO MAR.                                                                                XXX

UNIVERSIDADE FEDERAL DO PARA.
— REVISTA DA UNIVERSIDADE FEDERAL DO PARA.

UNIVERSIDADE FEDERAL DE PERNAMBUCO: INSTITUTO
DE CIENCIAS DO HOMEM.
— MONOGRAFIAS, INSTITUTO DE CIENCIAS DO HOMEM,
UNIVERSIDADE FEDERAL DE PERNAMBUCO.

UNIVERSIDADE FEDERAL DO RIO GRANDE DO NORTE:
INSTITUTO DE BIOLOGIA MARINHA.
— BOLETIM, INSTITUTO DE BIOLOGIA MARINHA, UNI-
VERSIDADE FEDERAL DO RIO GRANDE DO NORTE.

UNIVERSIDADE FEDERAL DO RIO GRANDE DO NORTE:
INSTITUTO DE CIENCIAS HUMANAS.
— ICH REVISTA.

UNIVERSIDADE FEDERAL DO RIO GRANDE DO SUL:
INSTITUTO DE GEOCIENCIAS.
— PESQUISAS, INSTITUTO DE GEOCIENCIAS, UNIV-
ERSIDADE FEDERAL DO RIO GRANDE DO SUL.

UNIVERSIDADE FEDERAL DE RIO DE JANEIRO:
DEPARTAMENTO DE BOTANICA.
— LEANDRA. REVISTA DE INFORMACAO CIENTIFICA.

UNIVERSIDADE FEDERAL DO RIO DE JANEIRO:
INSTITUTO GEOCIENCIAS.
— BOLETIM, INSTITUTO GEOCIENCIAS, UNIVERSIDADE
FEDERAL DO RIO DE JANEIRO: GEOLOGIA.

UNIVERSIDADE FEDERAL DE SANTA CATARINA:
CENTRO DE PESQUISAS E ESTUDOS BOTANICAS.
— INSULA. BOLETIM DO ...

UNIVERSITA DI FERRARA.
— MEMORIE GEOPALAEONTOLOGICHE DELL'UNIVERSITA
DI FERRARA.

UNIVERSITY OF FLORIDA.
— CARLETON NEWSLETTER.
— FLORIDA QUARTERLY.

UNIVERSITY OF FLORIDA: CENTER FOR LATIN
AMERICAN STUDIES.
— LATIN AMERICAN URBAN RESEARCH.

UNIVERSITY OF FLORIDA: FLORIDA STATE MUSEUM.                    000
SEE: FLORIDA ...

UNIVERSITY OF FORT HARE (S.AFR.)
— SPECULUM JURIS.

UNIVERSITE DE FRIBOURG: MEDIAEVISTISCHES
INSTITUT.
— SCRINIUM FRIBURGENSE.

UNIVERSITE DE GENEVE: ECOLE DES SCIENCES DE LA
TERRE.
— BULLETIN D'INFORMATION, ECOLE DES SCIENCES DE
LA TERRE, UNIVERSITE DE GENEVE.

UNIVERSITA DI GENOVA: ISTITUTO DI LINGUA E
LETTERATURA ITALIANA.
— PUBBLICAZIONI DELL'ISTITUTO DI LINGUA E LETT-
ERATURA ITALIANA, UNIVERSITA DI GENOVA.

UNIVERSITY OF GEORGIA: COLLEGE OF EDUCATION.
— JOURNAL OF RESEARCH & DEVELOPMENT IN EDUCAT-
ION.

UNIVERSITY OF GHANA: INSTITUTE OF AFRICAN
STUDIES.
— RESEARCH REVIEW, INSTITUTE OF AFRICAN STUDIES,
UNIVERSITY OF GHANA.

UNIVERSITY OF GLASGOW: DENTAL HOSPITAL & SCHOOL
— GLASGOW DENTAL JOURNAL. JOURNAL OF THE ...

UNIVERSITY OF GLASGOW: DEPARTMENT OF ENGLISH
LITERATURE.
— PHOENIX. POETRY & PROSE MAGAZINE FROM THE ...

UNIVERSITY OF GLASGOW: DEPARTMENT OF PSYCHOLOGY
— FEEDBACK. THE GLASGOW JOURNAL OF PSYCHOLOGY.

UNIVERSITY OF GLASGOW: GEOLOGICAL SOCIETY.
— OUTCROP. MAGAZINE OF THE ...

UNIVERSITY OF GLASGOW: INSTITUTE OF LATIN-
AMERICAN STUDIES.
— OCCASIONAL PAPERS, INSTITUTE OF LATIN-
AMERICAN STUDIES, UNIVERSITY OF GLASGOW.

UNIVERSITY OF GLASGOW: INSTITUTE OF SOVIET &
EAST EUROPEAN STUDIES.
— ABSEES. SOVIET & EAST EUROPEAN ABSTRACTS
SERIES.                                                        XXX

UNIVERSIDAD DE GRANADA: FACULTAD DE LETRAS.
— CUADERNOS DE ARTE Y LITERATURA.

UNIVERSITAT GRAZ; KUNSTHISTORISCHES INSTITUT.
— JAHRBUCH DES KUNSTHISTORISCHEN INSTITUTES
DER UNIVERSITAT GRAZ.

UNIVERSITAT GRAZ: LEHRKANZEL FUR WIRTSCHAFTS-
UND SOZIALGESCHICHTE.
— GRAZER FORSCHUNGEN ZUR WIRTSCHAFTS- UND
SOZIALGESCHICHTE.

UNIVERSITAT GREIFSWALD.                                         000
SEE: ERNST-MORITZ-ARNDT UNIVERSITAT GREIFS-
WALD.

UNIVERSITE DE GRENOBLE: LABORATOIRE DE GEOLOGIE
— GEOLOGIE ALPINE.                                             XXX

UNIVERSIDAD DE GUAYAQUIL: ESCUELA DE CIENCIAS
NATURALES.
— NATURALEZA ECUATORIANA.

UNIVERSITY OF GUELPH: DEPARTMENT OF GEOGRAPHY.
— GEOGRAPHICAL PUBLICATIONS, DEPARTMENT OF
GEOGRAPHY, UNIVERSITY OF GUELPH.

UNIVERSIDAD DE LA HABANA: INSTITUTO DE ECONOMIA
— ECONOMIA Y DESARROLLO.

UNIVERSITAT HAMBURG: INSTITUT FUR MEERESKUNDE.
— MITTEILUNGEN DES INSTITUTS FUR MEERESKUNDE,
UNIVERSITAT HAMBURG.

UNIVERSITAT HAMBURG: MATHEMATISCHES SEMINAR.
— HAMBURGER MATHEMATISCHE EINZELSCHRIFTEN: NS.

UNIVERSITAT HAMBURG: SEMINAR FUR ROMANISCHE
SPRACHEN UND KULTUR.
— HAMBURGER ROMANISTISCHE DISSERTATIONEN.

UNIVERSITY OF HARTFORD.
— HARTFORD STUDIES IN LITERATURE.

UNIVERSITY OF HAWAII: ASIAN STUDIES PROGRAM.
— EAST ASIAN OCCASIONAL PAPERS.

UNIVERSITY OF HAWAII: DEPARTMENT OF LINGUISTICS
— WORKING PAPERS IN LINGUISTICS, DEPARTMENT OF
LINGUISTICS, UNIVERSITY OF HAWAII.

UNIVERSITY OF HAWAII: INSTITUTE OF MARINE
BIOLOGY.
— CONTRIBUTIONS, HAWAII INSTITUTE OF MARINE
BIOLOGY, UNIVERSITY OF HAWAII.*

UNIVERSITY OF HAWAII: SOCIAL SCIENCE RESEARCH
INSTITUTE.
— CURRENT RESEARCH NOTES IN QUANTITATIVE &
THEORETICAL GEOGRAPHY.

UNIVERSITY OF HONG KONG: INSTITUTE OF MAINLAND
STUDIES.
— CHINA MAINLAND REVIEW.

UNIVERSITY OF HULL.
— OCCASIONAL PAPERS IN ECONOMIC & SOCIAL HIST-
ORY, UNIVERSITY OF HULL.

UNIVERSITY OF HULL: CENTRE FOR SOUTH-EAST
ASIAN STUDIES.
— INFORMATION-SHEET, CENTRE FOR SOUTH-EAST
ASIAN STUDIES, UNIVERSITY OF HULL.

UNIVERSITY OF HULL: DEPARTMENT OF GERMAN.
— NEW GERMAN STUDIES.

UNIVERSITY OF HULL: INSTITUTE OF EDUCATION.
— AIDS TO RESEARCH IN EDUCATION.

UNIVERSITY OF HULL: SUMATRA RESEARCH COUNCIL.
— BERITA KADJIAN SUMATERA. SUMATRA RESEARCH
BULLETIN.

UNIVERSITY OF IBADAN: DEPARTMENT OF LINGUISTICS
& NIGERIAN LANGUAGES.
— RESEARCH NOTES, DEPARTMENT OF LINGUISTICS &
NIGERIAN LANGUAGES, UNIVERSITY OF IBADAN.

UNIVERSITY OF IBADAN: DEPARTMENT OF RELIGIOUS
STUDIES.
— ORITA. IBADAN JOURNAL OF RELIGIOUS STUDIES.

UNIVERSITY OF IBADAN: INSTITUTE OF AFRICAN
STUDIES.
— WEST AFRICAN ARCHAEOLOGICAL NEWSLETTER.          XXX

UNIVERSITY OF ICELAND.                                         000
SEE: HASKOLI ISLANDS.

UNIVERSITY OF IDAHO: BUREAU OF BUSINESS &
ECONOMIC RESEARCH.
— MONOGRAPH, BUREAU OF BUSINESS & ECONOMIC
RESEARCH, UNIVERSITY OF IDAHO.

**UNIVERSITY OF IFE: FACULTY OF AGRICULTURE.**
— RESEARCH BULLETIN, FACULTY OF AGRICULTURE,
UNIVERSITY OF IFE.

**UNIVERSITY OF IFE: INSTITUTE OF ADMINISTRATION.**
— ADMINISTRATION. QUARTERLY REVIEW OF THE INST-
ITUTE OF ADMINISTRATION, UNIVERSITY OF IFE.

**UNIVERSITY OF IFE: LAW STUDENTS SOCIETY.**
— ADVOCATE. JOURNAL OF THE LAW STUDENTS ...

**UNIVERSITY OF ILLINOIS.**
— JOURNAL OF AESTHETIC EDUCATION.

**UNIVERSITY OF ILLINOIS: AVIATION RESEARCH
LABORATORY.**
— AVIATION RESEARCH MONOGRAPHS.

**UNIVERSITY OF ILLINOIS AT CHICAGO CIRCLE:
DEPARTMENT OF ENGLISH.**
— GENRE.

**UNIVERSITY OF ILLINOIS: DEPARTMENT OF ELECTR-
ICAL ENGINEERING.**
— INCREMENTAL MOTION CONTROL SYSTEMS & DEVICES
NEWSLETTER.

**UNIVERSITY OF ILLINOIS: GRADUATE SCHOOL OF
LIBRARY SCIENCE.**
— NEWSLETTER ON LIBRARY RESEARCH.

**UNIVERSITY OF INDIANA.**                                    000
SEE: INDIANA UNIVERSITY.

**UNIVERSITY OF IOWA: SCHOOL OF LETTERS & THE
GRADUATE COLLEGE.**
— IOWA REVIEW.

**UNIWERSYTET JAGIELLONSKI.**
— STUDIA ORAWSKIE.
— ZESZYTY NAUKOWE UNIWERSYTETU JAGIELLONSKIEGO:
PRACE ARCHEOLOGICZNE. ACTA SCIENTIARUM LITT-
ERARUMQUE, UNIVERSITAS JAGELLONICA CRACOVIEN-
SIS: SCHEDAE ARCHAEOLOGICAE.
— ZESZYTY NAUKOWE UNIWERSYTETU JAGIELLONSKIEGO:
PRACE ETNOGRAFICZNE. ACTA SCIENTIARUM LITT-
ERARUMQUE, UNIVERSITAS JAGELLONICA CRACOVIEN-
SIS: SCHEDAE ETNOGRAPHICAE.
— ZESZYTY NAUKOWE UNIWERSYTETU JAGIELLONSKIEGO:
PRACE FILOZOFICZNE.
— ZESZYTY NAUKOWE UNIWERSYTETU JAGIELLONSKIEGO:
PRACE GEOGRAFICZNE, SERIE NOWA. ACTA SCIENT-
IARUM LITTERARUMQUE, UNIVERSITAS JAGELLONICA
CRACOVIENSIS: SCHEDAE GEOGRAPHICAE.
— ZESZYTY NAUKOWE UNIWERSYTETU JAGIELLONSKIEGO:
PRACE Z HISTORII SZTUKI. ACTA SCIENTIARUM
LITTERARUMQUE, UNIVERSITAS JAGELLONICA CRACO-
VIENSIS: SCHEDAE AD ARTIS HISTORIAM PERTINEN-
TES.
— ZESZYTY NAUKOWE UNIWERSYTETU JAGIELLONSKIEGO:
PRACE HISTORYCZNE. ACTA SCIENTIARUM LITTER-
ARUMQUE, UNIVERSITAS JAGELLONICA CRACOVIENSIS:
SCHEDAE HISTORICAE.                                         XXX
— ZESZYTY NAUKOWE UNIWERSYTETU JAGIELLONSKIEGO:
PRACE Z LOGIKI.
— ZESZYTY NAUKOWE UNIWERSYTETU JAGIELLONSKIEGO:
PRACE PSYCHOLOGICZNO-PEDAGOGICZNE. ACTA
SCIENTIARUM LITTERARUMQUE, UNIVERSITAS JAG-
ELLONICA CRACOVIENSIS: SCHEDAE PSYCHOLOGICAE
ET PAEDAGOGICAE.
— ZESZYTY NAUKOWE UNIWERSYTETU JAGIELLONSKIEGO:
SERIA NAUK SPOLECZNYCH: HISTORIA.                          XXX
SUBS (1960): ZESZYTY NAUKOWE UNIWERSYTETU
JAGIELLONSKIEGO: PRACE HISTORYCZNE.

**UNIVERSITA J.E. PURKYNE V BRNE.**
— SBORNIK PRACI FILOSOFICKE FAKULTY BRNENSKE
UNIVERSITY: RADA HUDEBNEVEDNA H.

**UNIVERSITY OF KANSAS: CENTRE OF LATIN AMERICAN
STUDIES.**
— LATIN AMERICAN THEATRE REVIEW.

**UNIVERSITY OF KANSAS LIBRARIES.**
— BIBLIOGRAPHICAL CONTRIBUTIONS, UNIVERSITY OF
KANSAS LIBRARIES.

**UNIVERSITY OF KANSAS: MUSEUM OF NATURAL
HISTORY.**
— OCCASIONAL PAPERS, MUSEUM OF NATURAL HISTORY,
UNIVERSITY OF KANSAS.                                      XXX
— PUBLICATIONS, MUSEUM OF NATURAL HISTORY, UNIV-
ERSITY OF KANSAS.                                          XXX
SUBS (1971): OCCASIONAL PAPERS ...

**UNIVERSITY OF KARACHI.**
— UNIVERSITY STUDIES, UNIVERSITY OF KARACHI.

**UNIVERSITA KARLOVA (PRAGUE).**                            000
SEE: KARLOVA UNIVERSITA V PRAZE.

**UNIVERSITAT KARLSRUHE.**
— FRIDERICIANA. ZEITSCHRIFT DER...

**UNIVERSITI KEBANGSAAN MALAYSIA.**
— AKADEMIKA. JERNAL ILMU KEMANUSIAAN DAN SAINS
KEMASYARAKATAN.

**UNIVERSITY OF KEELE.**
— DISCUSSION PAPERS IN ECONOMICS, UNIVERSITY OF
KEELE.

**UNIVERSITY OF KENT: FACULTY OF HUMANITIES.**
— 20TH CENTURY STUDIES.

**UNIVERSITY OF KENTUCKY: COLLEGE OF BUSINESS &
ECONOMICS.**
— GROWTH & CHANGE. JOURNAL OF REGIONAL DEVEL-
OPMENT.

**UNIVERSITY OF KENTUCKY: LIBRARY.**
— UNIVERSITY OF KENTUCKY LIBRARY NOTES.

**UNIVERSITY OF KERALA: DEPARTMENT OF LINGUISTICS**
— INTERNATIONAL JOURNAL OF DRAVIDIAN LINGUISTICS.

**UNIVERSITY OF KHARTOUM: FACULTY OF LAW.**
— SUDAN LAW REPORTS: CIVIL CASES.

**UNIVERSITAT KIEL: ENGLISCHES SEMINAR.**
— LITERATUR IN WISSENSCHAFT UND UNTERRICHT.

**UNIVERZITA KOMENSKEHO (BRATISLAVA): FACULTATIS
RERUM NATURALIUM.**                                        000
SEE: UNIVERZITA KOMENSKEHO (BRATISLAVA):
PRIRODOVEDECKA FAKULTA.

**UNIVERZITA KOMENSKEHO (BRATISLAVA): FILOZO-
FICKA FAKULTA.**
— SBORNIK FILOZOFICKEJ FAKULTY UNIVERZITY KOM-
ENSKEHO: GRAECOLATINA ET ORIENTALIA.
— SBORNIK FILOZOFICKEJ FAKULTY UNIVERZITY
KOMENSKEHO: MARXIZMUS-LENINIZMUS.
— SBORNIK FILOZOFICKEJ FAKULTY UNIVERZITY
KOMENSKEHO: MUSAICA.
— SBORNIK FILOZOFICKEJ FAKULTY UNIVERZITY
KOMENSKEHO: OECONOMICA. (ORIG: POLITICKA
EKONOMIA).
— SBORNIK FILOZOFICKEJ FAKULTY UNIVERZITY
KOMENSKEHO: PHILOSOPHICA.
— SBORNIK FILOZOFICKEJ FAKULTY UNIVERZITY
KOMENSKEHO: PSYCHOLOGICA.

**UNIVERZITA KOMENSKEHO (BRATISLAVA): PRIRODO-
VEDECKA FAKULTA.**
— ACTA FACULTATIS RERUM NATURALIUM UNIVERS-
ITATIS COMENIANAE: GENETICA.
— ACTA FACULTATIS RERUM NATURALIUM UNIVERSIT-
ATIS COMENIANAE: PHYSIOLOGIA PLANTARUM.

**UNIVERSITY OF LAGOS.**
— ANNUAL LECTURES, UNIVERSITY OF LAGOS.
— JOURNAL OF BUSINESS & SOCIAL STUDIES.
— LAGOS NOTES & RECORDS.

**UNIVERSITY OF LAGOS LAW SOCIETY.**
— LAWYER (LAGOS). JOURNAL OF THE ...

**UNIVERSITY OF LANCASTER: DEPARTMENT OF EDUCAT-
IONAL RESEARCH.**
— HIGHER EDUCATION BULLETIN: NS.

**UNIVERSITY OF LANCASTER: DEPARTMENT OF SYSTEMS
ENGINEERING.**
— JOURNAL OF SYSTEMS ENGINEERING.

**UNIVERSITY OF LANCASTER: LIBRARY.**
— UNIVERSITY OF LANCASTER LIBRARY OCCASIONAL
PAPERS.

**UNIVERSITE LAVAL.**
— ETUDES LITTERAIRES.

**UNIVERSITY OF LEEDS.**
— HIGH TEMPERATURE INFORMATION BULLETIN.          XXX
— JOURNAL OF EDUCATIONAL ADMINISTRATION &
HISTORY.

**UNIVERSITY OF LEEDS: DEPARTMENT OF AGRICULTURAL
ECONOMICS.**
— MARKETING REPORT, DEPARTMENT OF AGRICULTURAL
ECONOMICS, UNIVERSITY OF LEEDS.

UNIVERSITY OF LEEDS: INFORMATION CENTRE ON HIGH
TEMPERATURE PROCESSES.
— HIGH TEMPERATURE BULLETIN.                                    XXX

UNIVERSITY OF LEEDS: POST GRADUATE STUDENTS'
REPRESENTATIVE COUNCIL.
— P.G. NEWSLETTER.

UNIVERSITY OF LEEDS: SCHOOL OF ENGLISH.
— LEEDS STUDIES IN BIBLIOGRAPHY & TEXTUAL CRIT-
ICISM: OCCASIONAL PAPER.
— LEEDS STUDIES IN ENGLISH. NS.                                 XXX

UNIVERSITY OF LEEDS UNION: AFRICAN SOCIETY.
— UHURU. JOURNAL OF THE ...

UNIVERSITY OF LEICESTER: DEPARTMENT OF ENGLISH
LOCAL HISTORY.
— OCCASIONAL PAPERS, DEPARTMENT OF ENGLISH
LOCAL HISTORY, UNIVERSITY OF LEICESTER: 2S.

UNIVERSITY OF LEICESTER: DEPARTMENT OF GEOLOGY.
— SPECIAL PUBLICATION, DEPARTMENT OF GEOLOGY,
UNIVERSITY OF LEICESTER.

UNIVERSITY OF LEICESTER: VICTORIAN STUDIES
CENTRE.
— VICTORIAN STUDIES HANDLIST.

UNIVERSITE LIBANAISE.
— PUBLICATIONS, UNIVERSITE LIBANAISE: SECTION
DES SCIENCES CHIMIQUES.

UNIVERSITE LIBANAISE: DEPARTEMENT DE GEOGRAPHIE
— HANNON. REVUE LIBANAISE DE GEOGRAPHIE.

UNIVERSITE LIBRE DE BRUXELLES: CENTRE D'ETUDE
DU SUD-EST ASIATIQUE ET DE L'EXTREME-ORIENT.
— ASIA QUARTERLY. A JOURNAL FROM EUROPE.         XXX

UNIVERSITE LIBRE DE BRUXELLES: INSTITUT D'ETUDE
EUROPEENNES.
— CHRONOLOGIE DES COMMUNAUTES EUROPEENNES.

UNIVERSITE LIBRE DE BRUXELLES: INSTITUT DE
PHONETIQUE.
— CONFERENCES ET TRAVAUX, INSTITUT DE PHONET-
IQUE, UNIVERSITE LIBRE DE BRUXELLES.

UNIVERSITY OF LIBYA: FACULTY OF SCIENCE.
— LIBYAN JOURNAL OF SCIENCE.

UNIVERSITE DE LIEGE: FACULTE DES SCIENCES
APPLIQUEES.
— COLLECTION DES PUBLICATIONS, FACULTE DES
SCIENCES APPLIQUEES, UNIVERSITE DE LIEGE.

UNIVERSITE DE LILLE: CENTRE D'ETUDES ET DE
RECHERCHES IRLANDAISES.
— ETUDES IRLANDAISES.

UNIVERSIDADE DE LISBOA: INSTITUTO DE ALTA
CULTURA.
— DO TEMPO E DA HISTORIA.

UNIVERSITY OF LIVERPOOL: CENTRE FOR LATIN
AMERICAN STUDIES.
— MONOGRAPH SERIES, CENTRE FOR LATIN AMERICAN
STUDIES, UNIVERSITY OF LIVERPOOL.

UNIWERSYTET LODZKI.
— ZESZYTY NAUKOWE UNIWERSYTETU LODZKIEGO: SERIA
3: NAUKIE EKONOMICZNE.

UNIVERSITY OF LONDON.
— BULLETIN OF THE UNIVERSITY OF LONDON.          XXX
— GAZETTE, UNIVERSITY OF LONDON.                 XXX
SUBS (1971): BULLETIN ...
— GEOLOGICAL NEWSLETTER, UNIVERSITY OF LONDON.

UNIVERSITY OF LONDON: BIRKBECK COLLEGE.          000
SEE: BIRKBECK COLLEGE.

UNIVERSITY OF LONDON: CENTRE OF SOUTH ASIAN
STUDIES.
— CENTRE OF SOUTH ASIAN STUDIES NEWSLETTER.

UNIVERSITY OF LONDON: GOLDSMITHS' COLLEGE.        000
SEE: GOLDSMITHS' COLLEGE.

UNIVERSITY OF LONDON: INSTITUTE OF EDUCATION.
— LONDON EDUCATIONAL REVIEW.

UNIVERSITY OF LONDON; INSTITUTE OF LATIN
AMERICAN STUDIES.
— BRITISH UNION CATALOGUE OF LATIN AMERICANA;
NEW LATIN AMERICAN TITLES.
— LATIN AMERICAN STUDIES IN THE UNIVERSITIES
OF THE UNITED KINGDOM.
— NEW LATIN AMERICAN TITLES.

UNIVERSITY OF LONDON: LONDON SCHOOL OF ECON-
OMICS & POLITICAL SCIENCE.                        000
SEE: LONDON SCHOOL ...

UNIVERSIDAD DE LOS ANDES.
— PITTIERIA.
— RAZON Y FABULA.

UNIVERSIDADE DE LOURENCO MARQUES.
— REVISTA DE CIENCIAS BIOLOGICAS: SERIE A.        XXX
— REVISTA DE CIENCIAS BIOLOGICAS: SERIE B.
— REVISTA DE CIENCIAS GEOLOGICAS: SERIE A.        XXX
— REVISTA DE CIENCIAS GEOLOGICAS: SERIE B.        XXX
— REVISTA DE CIENCIAS MATEMATICAS: SERIE B.       XXX
— REVISTA DE CIENCIAS VETERINARIAS: SERIE A.      XXX
— REVISTA DE CIENCIAS VETERINARIAS: SERIE B.      XXX
— REVISTA DE FISICA, QUIMICA E ENGENHARIA:
SERIE A.                                          XXX

UNIVERSIDADE DE LOURENCO MARQUES: FACULDADE
DE MEDICINA.
— REVISTA DE CIENCIAS MEDICAS. SERIE A.           XXX

UNIVERSIDADE DE LOURENCO MARQUES: INSTITUTO
SUPERIOR DE AGRONOMIA.
— REVISTA DE CIENCIAS AGRONOMICAS: SERIE A.       XXX

UNIVERSITE LOVANIUM DE KINSHASA.
— ETUDES D'HISTOIRE AFRICAINE.

UNIVERSITE LOVANIUM DE KINSHASA: CENTRE
D'ETUDES DES RELIGIONS AFRICAINES.
— CAHIERS DES RELIGIONS AFRICAINES.

UNIVERSIDADE DE LUANDA: FACULDADE DE CIENCIAS.
— CIENCIAS BIOLOGICAS.

UNIVERSITE DE LYON: DEPARTEMENT DES SCIENCES DE
LA TERRE.
— GEOBIOS.

UNIVERSITE DE MADAGASCAR.
— ANNALES MALGACHES: MEDECINE.
— REVUE ECONOMIQUE DE MADAGASCAR.

UNIVERSIDAD DE MADRID: DEPARTAMENTO DE BOTANICA
Y FISIOLOGIA VEGETAL.
— TRABAJOS DEL DEPARTAMENTO DE BOTANICA Y FIS-
IOLOGIA VEGETAL, UNIVERSIDAD DE MADRID.

UNIVERSIDAD DE MADRID: FACULTAD DE FILOSOFIA Y
LETRAS.
— CUADERNOS DE FILOLOGIA CLASICA.

UNIVERSITY OF MALAWI.
— CHANCELLOR COLLEGE FORUM.
— EXPRESSION (LIMBE).
— JOURNAL OF SOCIAL SCIENCE.

UNIVERSITY OF MALAWI: CHANCELLOR COLLEGE
ECONOMICS SOCIETY.
— ECONOMICA AFRICANA.

UNIVERSITY OF MALAYSIA: FACULTY OF AGRICULTURE.
— MALAYSIAN AGRICULTURAL RESEARCH.

UNIVERSITY OF MANCHESTER: DEPARTMENT OF EXTRA-
MURAL STUDIES.
— ROSCOE REVIEW.

UNIVERSITY OF MANCHESTER: INSTITUTE OF SCIENCE
& TECHNOLOGY.
— DESIGN RESEARCH REPORT.

UNIVERSITY OF MANCHESTER REGIONAL COMPUTER
CENTRE: LITERARY & LINGUISTIC GROUP.
— NEWSLETTER, LITERARY & LINGUISTIC GROUP,
UNIVERSITY OF MANCHESTER REGIONAL COMPUTER
CENTRE.                                           XXX

UNIWERSYTET MARII CURIE-SKLODOWSKIEJ.
— ANNALES UNIVERSITATIS MARIAE CURIE-SKLODOWSKA:
SECTIO H: OECONOMIA.

UNIVERSITY OF MARYLAND.
— CONRADIANA.

**UNIVERSITY OF MASSACHUSETTS: DEPARTMENT OF ANTHROPOLOGY.**
— RESEARCH REPORTS, DEPARTMENT OF ANTHROPOLOGY, UNIVERSITY OF MASSACHUSETTS.

**UNIVERSITY OF MASSACHUSETTS: DEPARTMENT OF ENGLISH.**
— ENGLISH LITERARY RENAISSANCE.

**UNIVERSITY OF MASSACHUSETTS: GRADUATE ENGLISH PROGRAM.**
— MASSACHUSETTS STUDIES IN ENGLISH.

**UNIVERSITY OF MELBOURNE.**
— HISTORICAL STUDIES.*                                                                    XXX

**UNIVERSITY OF MELBOURNE: DEPARTMENT OF RUSSIAN LANGUAGE & LITERATURE.**
— MELBOURNE SLAVONIC STUDIES.

**UNIVERSITY OF MIAMI: CENTER FOR ADVANCED INTER-NATIONAL STUDIES.**
— JOURNAL OF INTER-AMERICAN STUDIES & WORLD AFFAIRS.*

**UNIVERSITY OF MIAMI: INSTITUTE OF MARINE SCIENCE.**
— FAUNA CARIBAEA.

**UNIVERSITY OF MICHIGAN.**
— RACKHAM LITERARY STUDIES.

**UNIVERSITY OF MICHIGAN: BUREAU OF INDUSTRIAL RELATIONS.**
— MANAGEMENT OF PERSONNEL QUARTERLY.

**UNIVERSITY OF MICHIGAN: COOPERATIVE INFORMATION CENTRE FOR HOSPITAL STUDIES.**
— ABSTRACTS OF HOSPITAL MANAGEMENT STUDIES.

**UNIVERSITY OF MICHIGAN: GREAT LAKES RESEARCH DIVISION.**
— COLLECTED REPRINTS, GREAT LAKES RESEARCH DIVISION, UNIVERSITY OF MICHIGAN.

**UNIVERSITY OF MICHIGAN: INSTITUTE OF GERONTOLOGY.**
— OCCASIONAL PAPERS IN GERONTOLOGY.

**UNIVERSITY OF MICHIGAN: LAW SCHOOL.**
— PROSPECTUS: A JOURNAL OF LAW REFORM.                                  XXX

**UNIVERSITY OF MICHIGAN: MUSEUM OF ANTHROPOLOGY.**
— MEMOIRS, MUSEUM OF ANTHROPOLOGY, UNIVERSITY OF MICHIGAN.
— TECHNICAL REPORTS, MUSEUM OF ANTHROPOLOGY, UNIVERSITY OF MICHIGAN.

**UNIWERSYTETU MIKOLAJA KOPERNIKA.**
— ZESZYTY NAUKOWE UNIWERSYTETU MIKOLAJA KOPER-NIKA: NAUKI HUMANISTYCZNO-SPOLECZNE: ARCH-EOLOGIA.
— ZESZYTY NAUKOWE UNIWERSYTETU MIKOLAJA KOPER-NIKA: NAUKI HUMANISTYCZNO-SPOLECZNE: EKONOMIA.
— ZESZYTY NAUKOWE UNIWERSYTETU MIKOLAJA KOPER-NIKA: NAUKI HUMANISTYCZNO-SPOLECZNE: FILOZ-OFIA.
— ZESZYTY NAUKOWE UNIWERSYTETU MIKOLAJA KOPER-NIKA: NAUKI HUMANISTYCZNO-SPOLECZNE: HISTORIA.
— ZESZYTY NAUKOWE UNIWERSYTETU MIKOLAJA KOPER-NIKA: NAUKI HUMANISTYCZNO-SPOLECZNE: NAUKA O KSIAZCE.                                                                              XXX
— ZESZYTY NAUKOWE UNIWERSYTETU MIKOLAJA KOPER-NIKA: NAUKI HUMANISTYCZNO-SPOLECZNE: NAUKI POLITYCZNE.
— ZESZYTY NAUKOWE UNIWERSYTETU MIKOLAJA KOPER-NIKA: NAUKI HUMANISTYCZNO-SPOLECZNE: PEDAGOGIKA.
— ZESZYTY NAUKOWE UNIWERSYTETU MIKOLAJA KOPER-NIKA: NAUKI HUMANISTYCZNO-SPOLECZNE: PRAWO.
— ZESZYTY NAUKOWE UNIWERSYTETU MIKOLAJA KOPER-NIKA: NAUKI HUMANISTYCZNO-SPOLECZNE: SOCJOLOGIA.
— ZESZYTY NAUKOWE UNIWERSYTETU MIKOLAJA KOPER-NIKA: NAUKI HUMANISTYCZNO-SPOLECZNE: ZABYT-KOZNAWSTWO I KONSERWATORSTWO.

**UNIVERSITA DI MILANO: CENTRO DI CIBERNETICA E DI ATTIVITA LINGUISTICHE.**
— PENSIERO E LINGUAGGIO IN OPERAZIONI. THOUGHT & LANGUAGE IN OPERATIONS.

**UNIVERSITA DI MILANO: CENTRO G. ZAMBON.**
— APPLICAZIONI BIO-MEDICHE DEL CALCOLO ELET-TRONICO.

**UNIVERSITY OF MINNESOTA: INSTITUTE OF CHILD DEVELOPMENT.**
— MINNESOTA SYMPOSIA ON CHILD PSYCHOLOGY.

**UNIVERSITY OF MINNESOTA: LIBRARY.**
— MANIFEST. A NEWSLETTER FOR THE ASSOCIATES OF THE JAMES FORD BELL LIBRARY.

**UNIVERSITY OF MISSISSIPPI: DEPARTMENT OF ENGLISH.**
— STUDIES IN ENGLISH, DEPARTMENT OF ENGLISH, UNIVERSITY OF MISSISSIPPI.

**UNIVERSITY OF MISSOURI.**
— MUSEUM CONTRIBUTIONS.

**UNIVERSITY OF MISSOURI: DEPARTMENT OF GEOLOGY-GEOGRAPHY.**
— GEOGRAPHIC PUBLICATIONS, DEPARTMENT OF GEOL-OGY-GEOGRAPHY, UNIVERSITY OF MISSOURI.

**UNIVERSITY OF MONTANA.**
— NORTHWEST GEOLOGY.

**UNIVERSITE DE MONTPELLIER: FACULTAT DE LAS LETRAS E SCIENCIAS HUMAINES.**
— OBRADORS. QUASERNS D'INVENTARI DE LA CREACION LITERARIA OCCITANA.

**UNIVERSITE DE MONTPELLIER: FACULTE DE MEDECINE.**
— JOURNAL DE MEDECINE DE MONTPELLIER.                                  XXX
— MONTPELLIER MEDICAL.                                                            XXX
SUBS (1966): JOURNAL DE MEDECINE DE MONT-PELLIER.

**UNIVERSITE DE MONTREAL: DEPARTEMENT DE CRIMINOLOGIE.**
— ACTA CRIMINOLOGICA. ETUDES SUR LA CONDUITE ANTISOCIALE.

**UNIVERSITE DE MONTREAL: DEPARTEMENT DE MATHEM-ATIQUES.**
— SEMINAIRE DE MATHEMATIQUES SUPERIEURES.

**UNIVERSIDAD NACIONAL AUTONOMA DE MEXICO.**
— ANUARIO DE BIBLIOTECOLOGIA Y ARCHIVOLOGIA:S2.           XXX

**UNIVERSIDAD NACIONAL AUTONOMA DE MEXICO: CENTRO DE ESTUDIOS ANGLOAMERICANOS.**
— ANGLIA.

**UNIVERSIDAD NACIONAL AUTONOMA DE MEXICO: CENTRO DE ESTUDIOS DEL DESARROLLO.**
— ACTA SOCIOLOGICA, CENTRO DE ESTUDIOS DEL DES-ARROLLO, UNIVERSIDAD NACIONAL AUTONOMA DE MEXICO. SERIE PROMOCION SOCIAL.

**UNIVERSIDAD NACIONAL AUTONOMA DE MEXICO: CENTRO DE ESTUDIOS LATINOAMERICANOS.**
— LATINO AMERICA. ANUARIO ESTUDIOS LATINOAMER-ICANOS.

**UNIVERSIDAD NACIONAL AUTONOMA DE MEXICO: FACULTAD DE FILOSOFIA Y LETRAS.**
— ANUARIO DE BIBLIOTECONOMIA Y ARCHIVONOMIA.            XXX

**UNIVERSIDAD NACIONAL AUTONOMA DE MEXICO: FACULTAD DE MEDICINA VETERINARIA Y ZOOTECNIA.**
— VETERINARIA. REVISTA DE LA ...

**UNIVERSIDAD NACIONAL AUTONOMA DE MEXICO: INST-ITUTO DE GEOGRAFIA.**
— BOLETIN DEL INSTITUTO DE GEOGRAFIA, UNIVERS-IDAD NACIONAL AUTONOMA DE MEXICO.

**UNIVERSIDAD NACIONAL AUTONOMA DE MEXICO: INSTITUTO DE INVESTIGACIONES BIBLIOGRAFICAS.**
— BIBLIOGRAFIA FILOSOFICA MEXICANA.

**UNIVERSIDAD NACIONAL AUTONOMA DE MEXICO: INSTITUTO DE INVESTIGACIONES ECONOMICAS.**
— PROBLEMAS DEL DESARROLLO. REVISTA LATINOAMER-ICANA DE ECONOMIA.
**TUTO DE INVESTIGACIONES HISTORICAS.**
— SERIE DE CULTURAS MESOAMERICANAS.

**UNIVERSIDAD NACIONAL DE BUENOS AIRES: FACULTAD DE AGRONOMIA Y VETERINARIA.**
— BIBLIOGRAFIA ARGENTINA DE AGRONOMIA Y VETERINARIA.

**UNIVERSIDAD NACIONAL DEL CENTRO DEL PERU.**
— ANALES CIENTIFICOS, UNIVERSIDAD NACIONAL DEL CENTRO DEL PERU.

UNIVERSIDAD NACIONAL DEL CENTRO DEL PERU:
DEPARTAMENTO DE CIENCIAS SOCIALES.
— CIENCIA SOCIAL.

UNIVERSIDAD NACIONAL DE CORDOBA: FACULTAD DE
CIENCIAS EXACTAS, FISICAS Y NATURALES.
— LORENTZIA.

UNIVERSIDAD NACIONAL DE INGENIERIA (PERU).
— AMARU.

UNIVERSIDAD NACIONAL MAYOR DE SAN MARCOS:
INSTITUTO DE BOTANICA.
— RAYMONDIANA.

UNIVERSIDAD NACIONAL DE LA PLATA: BIBLIOTECA.
— BIBLIOGRAFIA ARGENTINA UNIVERSITARIA.

UNIVERSIDAD NACIONAL DE LA PLATA: ESCUELA
SUPERIOR DE BOSQUE.
— INGENIERIA FORESTAL (ARGENTINA).                    XXX

UNIVERSIDAD NACIONAL DEL SUR (ARGENTINA):
INSTITUTO DE HUMANIDADES.
— CUADERNOS DEL SUR.  TEXTOS COMENTADOS.

UNIVERSITY OF NAIROBI.
— UNIVERSITY BULLETIN, UNIVERSITY OF NAIROBI.

UNIVERSITY OF NAIROBI: FACULTY OF LAW.
— KENYA HIGH COURT DIGEST.

UNIVERSITE DE NANTES: CENTRE DE RECHERCHES SUR
L'HISTOIRE DE LA FRANCE ATLANTIQUE.
— ENQUETES ET DOCUMENTS, CENTRE DE RECHERCHES
SUR L'HISTOIRE DE LA FRANCE ATLANTIQUE, UNIV-
ERSITE DE NANTES.

UNIVERSITA DEGLI STUDI DI NAPOLI: ISTITUTO DI
STORIA ECONOMICA E SOCIALE.
— ANNALI DI STORIA ECONOMICA E SOCIALE, UNIVER-
SITA DEGLI STUDI DI NAPOLI.                           XXX

UNIVERSITY OF NATAL: SCIENCE STUDENT'S COUNCIL.
— NU SCIENCE.

UNIVERSITY OF NATAL: STUDENTS GEOLOGICAL
SOCIETY.
— PETROS.

UNIVERSITE NATIONALE DU ZAIRE: FACULTE DES
SCIENCES SOCIALES, POLITIQUES ET ADMINISTRAT-
IVES.
— CAHIERS ZAIROIS D'ETUDES POLITIQUES ET
SOCIALES.

UNIVERSIDAD DE NAVARRA.
— SCRIPTA THEOLOGICA.

UNIVERSIDAD DE NAVARRA: SECCION DE FILOSOFIA.
— ANUARIO FILOSOFICO.

UNIVERSITY OF NEBRASKA: DEPARTMENT OF GEOGRAPHY
— OCCASIONAL PAPERS, DEPARTMENT OF GEOGRAPHY,
UNIVERSITY OF NEBRASKA.

UNIVERSITY OF NEVADA: DEPARTMENT OF PSYCHOLOGY.
— BEHAVIORISM.  A FORUM FOR CRITICAL DISCUSSION.

UNIVERSITY OF NEW BRUNSWICK: DEPARTMENT OF
HISTORY.
— ACADIENSIS.  JOURNAL OF THE HISTORY OF THE
ATLANTIC REGION.

UNIVERSITY OF NEW ENGLAND: DEPARTMENT OF EDUC-
ATION.
— NEW ENGLAND PAPERS ON EDUCATION.

UNIVERSITY OF NEW SOUTH WALES.
— EDUCATIONAL PHILOSOPHY & THEORY.
— PH NEWS.

UNIVERSITY OF NEW SOUTH WALES: MINING &
GEOLOGICAL SOCIETY.
— JOURNAL, MINING AND GEOLOGICAL SOCIETY,
UNIVERSITY OF NEW SOUTH WALES.

UNIVERSITY OF NEW SOUTH WALES: WOLLONGONG UNI-
VERSITY COLLEGE.                                      000
SEE:  WOLLONGONG UNIVERSITY COLLEGE.

UNIVERSITY OF NEWCASTLE (N.S.W.).
— HISTORICAL JOURNAL.

UNIVERSITY OF NEWCASTLE (N.S.W.): DEPARTMENT
OF GEOGRAPHY.
— PUBLICATIONS IN GEOGRAPHY, DEPARTMENT OF
GEOGRAPHY, UNIVERSITY OF NEWCASTLE (N.S.W.)

UNIVERSITY OF NEWCASTLE UPON TYNE: AGRICULTURAL
ADJUSTMENT UNIT.
— BULLETIN, AGRICULTURAL ADJUSTMENT UNIT, UNIV-
ERSITY OF NEWCASTLE UPON TYNE.
— TECHNICAL PAPERS, AGRICULTURAL ADJUSTMENT
UNIT, UNIVERSITY OF NEWCASTLE UPON TYNE.

UNIVERSITY OF NEWCASTLE UPON TYNE: COMPUTING
LABORATORY.
— TECHNICAL REPORT SERIES, COMPUTING LABORATORY,
UNIVERSITY OF NEWCASTLE UPON TYNE.

UNIVERSITY OF NEWCASTLE UPON TYNE: DEPARTMENT
OF ADULT EDUCATION.
— ARCHAEOLOGICAL NEWSBULLETIN FOR NORTHUMBER-
LAND, CUMBERLAND & WESTMORLAND.

UNIVERSITY OF NEWCASTLE UPON TYNE: DEPARTMENT
OF AGRICULTURAL MARKETING.
— REPORT, DEPARTMENT OF AGRICULTURAL MARKETING,
UNIVERSITY OF NEWCASTLE UPON TYNE.

UNIVERSITY OF NEWCASTLE UPON TYNE: DEPARTMENT
OF GEOGRAPHY.
— PAPERS ON MIGRATION & MOBILITY IN NORTHERN
ENGLAND.

UNIVERSITY OF NEWCASTLE UPON TYNE:
INSTITUTE OF EDUCATION.
— ACHIEVEMENTS IN TEACHING.

UNIVERSITY OF NEWCASTLE UPON TYNE: SCHOOL OF
ARCHITECTURE.
— NEWCASTLE PAPERS IN ARCHITECTURE & BUILDING
SCIENCE.

UNIVERSITE DE NICE: FACULTE DES LETTRES ET
SCIENCES HUMAINES.
— ANNALES DE LA FACULTE DES LETTRES ET SCIENCES
HUMAINES, UNIVERSITE DE NICE.

UNIVERSITY OF NIGERIA: CROWTHER COLLEGE OF
RELIGION.
— WEST AFRICAN RELIGION.

UNIVERSITY OF NIGERIA: INSTITUTE OF AFRICAN
STUDIES.
— IKENGA.  JOURNAL OF AFRICAN STUDIES.
— IKORAK.  BULLETIN OF THE INSTITUTE ...

UNIVERZITET U NISU.
— GLASNIK UNIVERZITETA U NISU.

UNIVERSIDAD DEL NORTE: DEPARTAMENTO DE AGRICUL-
TURA.
— IDESIA.

UNIVERSITY OF NORTH CAROLINA: DEPARTMENT OF
ENGLISH.
— SOUTHERN LITERARY JOURNAL.

UNIVERSITY OF NOTRE DAME: LAW SCHOOL.
— AMERICAN JOURNAL OF JURISPRUDENCE.              XXX

UNIVERSITY OF NOTTINGHAM.
— COMPUTER APPLICATIONS IN THE NATURAL & SOCIAL
SCIENCES.
— HISTORY OF ECONOMIC THOUGHT NEWSLETTER.

UNIVERSITY OF NOTTINGHAM: DEPARTMENT OF ADULT
EDUCATION.
— LOCAL POPULATION STUDIES. MAGAZINE & NEWS-
LETTER.
— OCCASIONAL PAPERS IN SOCIAL RESEARCH.

UNIVERSITY OF NOTTINGHAM: DEPARTMENT OF
GEOGRAPHY.
— GEOMORPHOLOGICAL REPORT, DEPARTMENT OF
GEOGRAPHY, UNIVERSITY OF NOTTINGHAM.

UNIVERSIDAD DE ORIENTE (CUBA).
— SANTIAGO.  REVISTA DE LA UNIVERSIDAD DE
ORIENTE.

UNIVERSITET I OSLO: ZOOLOGISK MUSEUM.
— RHIZOCRINUS.  OCCASIONAL PAPERS [OF THE] ...

UNIVERSITY OF OTAGO: ANTHROPOLOGY DEPARTMENT.
— STUDIES IN PREHISTORIC ANTHROPOLOGY.

UNIVERSITY OF OTAGO: LAW STUDENTS ASSOCIATION.
— OTAGO LAW REVIEW.

UNIVERSITY OF OTAGO: POLITICAL SCIENCE SOCIETY.
— HISTORICAL & POLITICAL STUDIES.

UNIVERSITY OF OTTAWA.
— HISTOIRE SOCIALE. = SOCIAL HISTORY.
— OTTAWA LAW REVIEW.

UNIVERSITY OF OTTAWA: DEPARTMENT OF GEOGRAPHY.
— OCCASIONAL PAPERS, DEPARTMENT OF GEOGRAPHY,
UNIVERSITY OF OTTAWA.

UNIVERSITY OF OTTAWA: GEOGRAPHERS' ASSOCIATION.
— GEOSCOPE.

UNIVERSITY OF OXFORD: ANTHROPOLOGICAL SOCIETY.
SEE: OXFORD UNIVERSITY ...                    000

UNIVERSITY OF OXFORD: CATHOLIC CHAPLAINCY.
— FOCUS.

UNIVERSITY OF OXFORD: CORPUS CHRISTI COLLEGE.
— PELICAN.

UNIVERSITY OF OXFORD: INSTITUTE OF AGRICULTURAL
ECONOMICS.
— A.E.I. DISCUSSION PAPER.
— OXFORD AGRARIAN STUDIES.                    XXX

UNIVERSITY OF OXFORD: PENAL RESEARCH INSTITUTE.
— OCCASIONAL PAPER, PENAL RESEARCH INSTITUTE,
UNIVERSITY OF OXFORD.

UNIVERSITY OF OXFORD: SCHOOL OF GEOGRAPHY.
— RESEARCH PAPERS, SCHOOL OF GEOGRAPHY, UNIVER-
SITY OF OXFORD.

UNIVERSITY OF OXFORD SPECULATIVE FICTION GROUP.
— SFINX.

UNIVERSITA DEGLI STUDI DI PADOVA.
— COLLANA DI STUDI SULL'EUROPA ORIENTALE.

UNIVERSITA DEGLI STUDI DI PADOVA: ISTITUTO DI
FISICA TECNICA.
— QUADERNO, ISTITUTO DI FISICA TECNICA,
UNIVERSITA DEGLI STUDI DI PADOVA.

UNIVERSITA DEGLI STUDI DI PADOVA: ISTITUTO
PER LA STORIA.
— QUADERNI PER LA STORIA DELL'UNIVERSITA DI
PADOVA.

UNIVERSITA DI PALERMO: ISTITUTO DE AGRONOMIA
GENERALE E COLTIVAZIONI ERBACEE.
— QUADERNI AGRONOMIA, ISTITUTO DE AGRONOMIA
GENERALE E COLTIVAZIONI ERBACEE, UNIVERSITA
DI PALERMO.

UNIVERSITY OF THE PANJAB.
— JOURNAL OF RESEARCH, UNIVERSITY OF THE PAN-
JAB: HUMANITIES.

UNIVERSITY OF THE PANJAB: DEPARTMENT OF MATH-
EMATICS.
— PANJAB UNIVERSITY JOURNAL OF MATHEMATICS.

UNIVERSITY OF PAPUA & NEW GUINEA: DEPARTMENT
OF ANTHROPOLOGY & SOCIOLOGY.
— MAN IN NEW GUINEA.

UNIVERSITY OF PAPUA & NEW GUINEA: LAW FACULTY.
— MELANESIAN LAW JOURNAL.

UNIVERSITY OF PAPUA & NEW GUINEA: LIBRARY.
— NEW GUINEA PERIODICAL INDEX. GUIDE TO CURRENT
PERIODICAL LITERATURE ABOUT THE NEW GUINEA
ISLANDS.

UNIVERSITY OF PAPUA & NEW GUINEA: LINGUISTIC
SOCIETY.
— KIVUNG. JOURNAL OF THE ...

UNIVERSITE DE PARIS: DEPARTEMENT DE LITTERATURE
FRANCAISE.
— LITTERATURE.

UNIVERSITE DE PARIS: INSTITUT D'ETHNOLOGIE.
— MEMOIRES DE L'INSTITUT D'ETHNOLOGIE,
UNIVERSITE DE PARIS.

UNIVERSITA DI PARMA: ISTITUTO DI MICROBIOLOGIA
— SYNTHESIS MICROBIOLOGICA.

UNIVERSITY OF PARMA: X-RAY CRYSTALLOGRAPHY
GROUP.
— CRYSTAL STRUCTURE COMMUNICATIONS.

UNIVERSIDAD DE LA PATAGONIA SAN JUAN BOSCO.
— ANALES, UNIVERSIDAD DE LA PATAGONIA SAN JUAN
BOSCO.

UNIVERSITY, PENNSYLVANIA (STATE).             000
SEE: PENNSYLVANIA STATE UNIVERSITY.

UNIVERSITY OF THE PHILIPPINES: ASIAN LABOR
EDUCATION CENTER.
— ALEC REPORT.

UNIVERSITY OF THE PHILIPPINES COLLEGE IN BAGUIO
— VERGE.

UNIVERSITY OF THE PHILIPPINES: COLLEGE OF
BUSINESS ADMINISTRATION.
— PHILIPPINE REVIEW OF BUSINESS & ECONOMICS.

UNIVERSITY OF THE PHILIPPINES; INSTITUTE OF
ASIAN STUDIES.
— LIPUNAN.

UNIVERSITY OF THE PHILIPPINES: INSTITUTE OF
LIBRARY SCIENCE.
— JOURNAL OF PHILIPPINE LIBRARIANSHIP.

UNIVERSITY OF THE PHILIPPINES: OFFICE OF THE
UNIVERSITY LIBRARIAN.
— U.P. LIBRARIAN.

UNIVERSITY OF THE PHILIPPINES: TRAINING CENTER
FOR APPLIED GEODESY & PHOTOGRAMMETRY.
— PHILIPPINE JOURNAL OF GEODESY & PHOTOGRAM-
METRY.

UNIVERSITA DI PISA: ISTITUTO DI ELETTRONICA E
RADIO-CONTROLLI.
— PUBBLICAZIONE, ISTITUTO DI ELETTRONICA E
RADIO-CONTROLLI, UNIVERSITA DI PISA.

UNIVERSITA DI PISA: ISTITUTO DI LETTERATURA
SPAGNOLA E ISPANO-AMERICANO.
— PROHEMIO. RIVISTA DE LINGUISTICA Y CRITICA
LITERARIA.

UNIVERSITY OF PITTSBURGH: BLACK STUDIES DEP-
ARTMENT.
— BLACK LINES.

UNIVERSITY OF PITTSBURGH: CENTER FOR LATIN
AMERICAN STUDIES.
— CUBAN STUDIES NEWSLETTER.

UNIVERSITY OF PITTSBURGH: CENTER FOR PHILOSOPHY
OF SCIENCE.
— UNIVERSITY OF PITTSBURGH SERIES IN THE PHIL-
OSOPHY OF SCIENCE.

UNIVERSITY OF PITTSBURGH: DEPARTMENT OF HISTORY
— HISTORICAL METHODS NEWSLETTER.

UNIVERSITY OF PITTSBURGH: LIBRARY.
— UNIVERSITY OF PITTSBURGH LIBRARIES BIBLIO-
GRAPHIC SERIES.

UNIVERSITE DE POITIERS: CENTRE D'ETUDES
SUPERIEURES DE CIVILISATION MEDIEVALE.
— PUBLICATIONS DU C.E.S.C.M.

UNIVERSITE DE POITIERS: DEPARTEMENT D'ETUDES
PORTUGAISES ET BRESILIENNES.
— SILLAGES.

UNIVERSITY OF PUERTO RICO: DEPARTMENT OF
PHILOSOPHY.
— DIALOGOS. REVISTA DEL DEPARTAMENTO DE FILOS-
OFIA, UNIVERSIDAD DE PUERTO RICO.

UNIVERSITY OF QUEENSLAND.
— MAN IN SOUTHEAST ASIA.

UNIVERSITY OF QUEENSLAND: ANTHROPOLOGY MUSEUM.
— OCCASIONAL PAPERS, ANTHROPOLOGY MUSEUM OF THE
UNIVERSITY OF QUEENSLAND.

UNIVERSITY OF QUEENSLAND: COMPUTER CENTRE.
— UNIVERSITY OF QUEENSLAND PAPERS (COMPUTER
CENTRE).

UNIVERSITY OF QUEENSLAND: DEPARTMENT OF
GEOGRAPHY.
— PAPERS, DEPARTMENT OF GEOGRAPHY, UNIVERSITY
OF QUEENSLAND.                                XXX

UNIVERSITY OF RAJASTHAN: DEPARTMENT OF POLITI-
CAL SCIENCE.
— POLITICAL SCIENCE REVIEW.

UNIVERSITY OF RAJASTHAN: LIBRARY.
— INDEX INDIA.

UNIVERSITY OF RAJASTHAN: SOUTH ASIA STUDIES
CENTRE.
— SOUTH ASIAN STUDIES.

UNIVERSITY OF RAJSHAHI.
— RAJSHAHI UNIVERSITY STUDIES.

UNIVERSITY OF READING.
— BIBLIOGRAPHIES IN AGRICULTURAL HISTORY.
— DISCUSSION PAPERS IN ECONOMICS, UNIVERSITY
  OF READING.
— WHITE RABITT PAPERS.
— WORM.

UNIVERSITY OF READING: DEPARTMENT OF AGRICUL-
TURAL ECONOMICS.
— DEVELOPMENT STUDIES, DEPARTMENT OF AGRICUL-
  TURAL ECONOMICS, UNIVERSITY OF READING.

UNIVERSITY OF READING: DEPARTMENT OF GEOGRAPHY.
— READING GEOGRAPHER.

UNIVERSITY OF READING: DEPARTMENT OF GEOLOGY.
— GEOPHYSICAL REPORTS, DEPARTMENT OF GEOLOGY,
  UNIVERSITY OF READING.

UNIVERSITY OF READING: INSTITUTE OF AGRICULT-
URAL HISTORY.
— RESEARCH PAPER SERIES, INSTITUTE OF AGRICULT-
  URAL HISTORY, UNIVERSITY OF READING.

UNIVERSITY OF READING: LIBRARY.
— READING UNIVERSITY LIBRARY PUBLICATIONS.

UNIVERSITY OF READING: SIBLY HALL.
— GRAPEVINE.

UNIVERSITY OF READING: URBAN SYSTEMS RESEARCH
UNIT.
— WORKING PAPERS, URBAN SYSTEMS RESEARCH UNIT,
  UNIVERSITY OF READING.

UNIVERSIDADE DO RECIFE: INSTITUTO DE GEOLOGIA.
— PALEONTOLOGIA.

UNIVERSITE DE RENNES: FACULTE DES SCIENCES.
— TRAVAUX, FACULTE DES SCIENCES, UNIVERSITE DE
  RENNES: SERIE OCEANOGRAPHIE BIOLOGIQUE.

UNIVERSITE DE RENNES: LABORATOIRE DE BOTANIQUE.
— BOTANICA RHEDONICA: SERIE A.
— BOTANICA RHEDONICA: SERIE B.

UNIVERSIDAD DE LA REPUBLICA (URUGUAY): LABORA-
TORIO DE PALEONTOLOGIA DE VERTEBRADOS.
— BOLETIN, LABORATORIO DE PALEONTOLOGIA DE VER-
  TEBRADOS, UNIVERSIDAD DE LA REPUBLICA (URUG.).

UNIVERSITY OF RHODE ISLAND: AGRICULTURAL EXTEN-
SION SERVICE.
— RHODE ISLAND RESOURCES.                                                        XXX

UNIVERSITY OF RHODE ISLAND: DEPARTMENT OF
LANGUAGES.
— CLAUDEL NEWSLETTER.

UNIVERSIDADE DO RIO GRANDE DO SUL: CENTRO DE
INVESTIGACAO DO GONDWANA.
— GONDWANA NEWSLETTER.

UNIVERSITY OF RIYAD: FACULTY OF SCIENCE.
— BULLETIN OF THE FACULTY OF SCIENCE, UNIVER-
  SITY OF RIYAD.

UNIVERSITA DI ROMA: ISTITUTO DI GEOGRAFIA
ECONOMICA.
— NOTIZIARIO DI GEOGRAFIA ECONOMICA, ISTITUTO
  DI GEOGRAFIA ECONOMICA, UNIVERSITA DI ROMA.

UNIVERSITA DI ROMA: ISTITUTO DI PETROGRAFIA.
— QUADERNI, ISTITUTO DI PETROGRAFIA, UNIVERSITA
  DI ROMA.

UNIVERSITA DI ROMA: ISTITUTO DI TOPOGRAFIA
ANTICA.
— QUADERNI, ISTITUTO DI TOPOGRAFIA ANTICA, UNIV-
  ERSITA DI ROMA.

UNIVERSITA DI ROMA: MUSEO DELLE ORIGINI.
— ORIGINI. PREISTORIA E PROTOSTORIA DELLE
  CIVILTA ANTICHE.

UNIVERSITAT ROSTOCK: BOTANISCHEN INSTITUTS UND
DES BOTANISCHEN GARTENS.
— FLORISTISCHE MITTEILUNGEN DES BOTANISCHEN
  INSTITUTS UND DES BOTANISCHEN GARTENS DER
  UNIVERSITAT ROSTOCK.

UNIVERSITE SAINT-ESPRIT.
— MELTO. RECHERCHES ORIENTALES.                                                 XXX
— PAROLE DE L'ORIENT.                                                           XXX

UNIVERSITY, SAITAMA (JAP.)                                                       000
SEE: SAITAMA DAIGAKU.

UNIVERSIDAD DE SALAMANCA.
— STUDIA GEOLOGICA.

UNIVERSITAT SALZBURG: HISTORISCHE INSTITUT.
— VEROFFENTLICHUNGEN DES HISTORISCHEN INSTITUTS
  DER UNIVERSITAT SALZBURG.

UNIVERSITY OF SAN CARLOS (PHILIPPINES).
— JUNIOR PHILIPPINE SCIENTIST.
— SAN CARLOS PUBLICATIONS: SERIES B: NATURAL
  SCIENCES.

UNIVERSIDAD DE SAN MARCOS: CENTRO DE INVESTIG-
ACIONES DE SELVA.
— KIARIO.

UNIVERSITY OF SANTO TOMAS: LIBRARY.
— UST LIBRARY BULLETIN.

UNIVERSIDADE DE SAO PAULO: ESCOLA DE COMUNICA-
COES CULTURAIS.
— REVISTA, ESCOLA DE COMUNICACOES CULTURAIS,
  UNIVERSIDADE DE SAO PAULO.

UNIVERSIDADE DE SAO PAULO: FACULDADE DE
ODONTOLOGIA.
— REVISTA DA FACULDADE DE ODONTOLOGIA DA
  UNIVERSIDADE DE SAO PAULO.                                                     XXX

UNIVERSIDADE DE SAO PAULO: FACULDADE DE SAUDE
PUBLICA.
— REVISTA DE SAUDE PUBLICA (BRAZIL).

UNIVERSIDADE DE SAO PAULO: INSTITUTO DE ESTUDOS
BRASILEIROS.
— REVISTA DO INSTITUTO DE ESTUDOS BRASILEIROS,
  UNIVERSIDADE DE SAO PAULO.

UNIVERSIDADE DE SAO PAULO: INSTITUTO DE
GEOGRAFIA.
— BIOGEOGRAFIA.
— GEOMORFOLOGIA.

UNIVERSITY OF SASKATCHEWAN: DEPARTMENT OF
MODERN LANGUAGES.
— WESTERN CANADIAN STUDIES IN MODERN LANGUAGES
  & LITERATURE.

UNIVERSITY OF SASKATCHEWAN: MUSK-OX CIRCLE.
— MUSK-OX.

UNIVERSIDAD DE SEVILLA.
— HABIS.

UNIVERSITY OF SHEFFIELD.
— ASPERGILLUS NEWS LETTER.

UNIVERSITY OF SHEFFIELD: DEPARTMENT OF SOCIO-
LOGICAL STUDIES.
— SOCIOLOGICAL ANALYSIS.                                                        XXX

UNIVERSITY OF SHEFFIELD: INSTITUTE OF EDUCATION
— HUMANITIES NEWSLETTER.

UNIVERSITE DE SHERBROOKE: CENTRE D'ETUDE DES
LITTERATURES D'EXPRESSION FRANCAISE.
— PRESENCE FRANCOPHONE. REVUE SEMESTRIELLE DU
  CELEF.

UNIVERSITY OF SHIMANE: FACULTY OF AGRICULTURE.
— BULLETIN, FACULTY OF AGRICULTURE, UNIVERSITY
  OF SHIMANE.

UNIVERSITY OF SIND.
— SIND UNIVERSITY RESEARCH JOURNAL.

UNIVERSITA DI SIENA: ISTITUTO DI ZOOLOGIA.
— PUBBLICAZIONI, ISTITUTO DI ZOOLOGIA, UNI-
  VERSITA DI SIENA.

UNIVERSITY OF SIERRA LEONE: INSTITUTE OF
AFRICAN STUDIES.
— AFRICANA RESEARCH BULLETIN.

UNIVERSITY OF SINGAPORE.
— POETRY SINGAPORE.
— UNIVERSITY OF SINGAPORE NEWS.

UNIVERSITY OF SINGAPORE: ECONOMIC RESEARCH
CENTRE.
— RESEARCH BIBLIOGRAPHY SERIES, ECONOMIC RES-
EARCH CENTRE, UNIVERSITY OF SINGAPORE.

UNIVERSITY OF SINGAPORE: SOCIOLOGY SOCIETY.
— SOUTH EAST ASIAN JOURNAL OF SOCIOLOGY.                    XXX

UNIVERZITET SKOPJE: KATEDRA ZA ISTORIJA NA
KNIZEVNOSTITE NA NARODITE FNRJ.
— TRUDOVI NA KATEDRATA ZA ISTORIJA NA KNIZEV-
NOSTITE NA NARODITE NA FNR JUGOSLAVIJA.

UNIVERSITY OF SOUTH AFRICA.
— SEMITICS.

UNIVERSITY OF SOUTH AFRICA: DEPARTMENT OF
ENGLISH.
— UNISA ENGLISH STUDIES.

UNIVERSITY OF SOUTH AFRICA: DEPARTMENT OF
FINE ARTS.
— DE ARTE.

UNIVERSITY OF SOUTH AFRICA: DEPARTMENT OF
HISTORY.
— KLEIO.

UNIVERSITY OF SOUTH CAROLINA: DEPARTMENT OF
ENGLISH.
— BIBLIOGRAPHICAL SERIES, DEPARTMENT OF ENGLISH,
UNIVERSITY OF SOUTH CAROLINA.

UNIVERSITY OF SOUTHAMPTON: ELECTRONICS INSTRUM-
ENTATION CENTRE.
— QUARTERLY REPORTS, ELECTRONICS INSTRUMENTAT-
ION CENTRE, UNIVERSITY OF SOUTHAMPTON.

UNIVERSITY OF SOUTHAMPTON: INSTITUTE OF SOUND &
VIBRATION RESEARCH.
— ISVR TECHNICAL REPORT.

UNIVERSITY OF SOUTHAMPTON: LIBRARY.
— AD LIB. SOUTHAMPTON UNIVERSITY LIBRARY
INFORMATION BULLETIN.
— AUTOMATION PROJECT REPORT, LIBRARY,
UNIVERSITY OF SOUTHAMPTON.
— INFORMATION SHEET, LIBRARY, UNIVERSITY OF
SOUTHAMPTON.

UNIVERSITY OF SOUTHERN CALIFORNIA.
— STUDIES IN COMPARATIVE LITERATURE.

UNIVERSITY OF SOUTHERN CALIFORNIA: SCHOOL OF
POLITICS & INTERNATIONAL RELATIONS.
— STUDIES IN COMPARATIVE COMMUNISM.

UNIVERSITY OF SOUTHERN ILLINOIS.                             000
SEE: SOUTHERN ILLINOIS UNIVERSITY.

UNIVERSITY OF STIRLING.
— BRIG. JOURNAL OF THE ...

UNIVERSITE DE STRASBOURG.
— RECHERCHES GERMANIQUES.

UNIVERSITY OF STRATHCLYDE: ANDERSONIAN LIBRARY.
— HOLOGRAPHY INDEX.

UNIVERSITY OF STRATHCLYDE: ARCHITECTURAL &
BUILDING AIDS COMPUTER UNIT.
— BULLETIN OF COMPUTER-AIDED ARCHITECTURAL
DESIGN.

UNIVERSITY OF STRATHCLYDE: DEPARTMENT OF
APPLIED GEOLOGY.
— RESEARCH REPORT, DEPARTMENT OF APPLIED
GEOLOGY, UNIVERSITY OF STRATHCLYDE.

UNIVERSITY OF STRATHCLYDE: DEPARTMENT OF SOCIO-
LOGY.
— OCCASIONAL PAPER, DEPARTMENT OF SOCIOLOGY,
UNIVERSITY OF STRATHCLYDE.

UNIVERSITY OF STRATHCLYDE: SURVEY RESEARCH
CENTRE.
— OCCASIONAL PAPERS, SURVEY RESEARCH CENTRE,
UNIVERSITY OF STRATHCLYDE.

UNIVERSITY OF SUSSEX.
— SUSSEX AFRAS JOURNAL.

UNIVERSITY OF SUSSEX: CENTRE FOR CONTEMPORARY
EUROPEAN STUDIES & EUROPEAN COMMUNITY INFORM-
ATION SERVICE.
— EUROPEAN STUDIES. TEACHERS' SERIES.

UNIVERSITY OF SUSSEX: INSTITUTE OF DEVELOPMENT
STUDIES.
— BULLETIN, INSTITUTE OF DEVELOPMENT STUDIES,
UNIVERSITY OF SUSSEX.
— NEWSLETTER, INSTITUTE OF DEVELOPMENT STUDIES,    XXX
UNIVERSITY OF SUSSEX.

UNIVERSITY OF SYDNEY.
— AUSTRALIAN JOURNAL OF BIBLICAL ARCHAEOLOGY.
— HUMAN BIOLOGY IN OCEANIA.

UNIVERSITY OF SYDNEY: DEPARTMENT OF ECONOMICS.
— AUSTRALIAN ECONOMIC HISTORY REVIEW.              XXX

UNIVERSITY OF SYDNEY: DEPARTMENT OF INDONESIAN
& MALAYAN STUDIES.
— REVIEW OF INDONESIAN & MALAYAN AFFAIRS.

UNIVERSITY OF TAMPA.
— POETRY REVIEW.

UNIVERSITY OF TASMANIA: LAW SCHOOL.
— TASMANIAN UNIVERSITY LAW REVIEW.                 XXX
SUBS (1964): UNIVERSITY OF TASMANIA LAW
REVIEW.
— UNIVERSITY OF TASMANIA LAW REVIEW.               XXX

UNIVERSITY OF TENNESSEE: UNIVERSITY COMPUTING
CENTER.
— TECHNICAL REPORT, UNIVERSITY COMPUTING CENTER,
UNIVERSITY OF TENNESSEE.

UNIVERSITY OF TEXAS.
— JOURNAL OF ECONOMIC ISSUES.

UNIVERSITY OF TEXAS: AFRICAN & AFRO-AMERICAN
RESEARCH INSTITUTE.
— OCCASIONAL PUBLICATION OF THE AFRICAN & AFRO-
AMERICAN RESEARCH INSTITUTE, UNIVERSITY OF
TEXAS.
— RESEARCH IN AFRICAN LITERATURES.

UNIVERSITY OF TEXAS: DEPARTMENT OF GERMANIC
LANGUAGES.
— DIMENSION. CONTEMPORARY GERMAN ARTS & LETTERS.

UNIVERSITY OF TEXAS: HUMAN RESEARCH CENTER.
— HISTORY OF SCIENCE SERIES.

UNIVERSITY OF TEXAS: INSTITUTE OF LATIN
AMERICAN STUDIES.
— LATIN AMERICAN MONOGRAPHS (AUSTIN, TEX.).

UNIVERSITY OF TEXAS: SCHOOL OF ARCHITECTURE.
— TEXAS ARCHITECTURAL SURVEY.

UNIVERSITY OF TEXAS AT ARLINGTON.
— ARLINGTON QUARTERLY.

UNIVERSITY OF TEXAS AT ARLINGTON:
DEPARTMENT OF ENGLISH.
— AMERICAN LITERARY REALISM, 1870-1910.

UNIVERSITATII DIN TIMISOARA.
— ANALELE UNIVERSITATII DIN TIMISOARA: SERIA
STIINTE FIZICE-CHIMICE.                            XXX
— ANALELE UNIVERSITATII DIN TIMISOARA: SERIA
STIINTE MATEMATICE.                                XXX

UNIVERSITY OF TOKYO.                                000
SEE: TOKYO DAIGAKU.

UNIVERSITA DEGLI STUDI DI TORINO: FACOLTA DI
SCIENZE AGRARIE.
— ANNALI DELLA FACOLTA DI SCIENZE AGRARIE DELLA
UNIVERSITA DEGLI STUDI DI TORINO.

UNIVERSITA DEGLI STUDI DI TORINO: ISTITUTO DI
FILOLOGIA ROMANZA.
— [PUBLICATIONS] ISTITUTO DI FILOLOGIA ROMANZA,
UNIVERSITA DEGLI STUDI DI TORINO.

UNIVERSITY OF TORONTO: CENTRE FOR MEDIEVAL
STUDIES.
— TORONTO MEDIEVAL BIBLIOGRAPHIES.

UNIVERSITY OF TORONTO: DEPARTMENT OF GEOGRAPHY.
— DISCUSSION PAPER SERIES, DEPARTMENT OF GEOGR-
APHY, UNIVERSITY OF TORONTO.
— RESEARCH PUBLICATIONS, DEPARTMENT OF GEOG-
RAPHY, UNIVERSITY OF TORONTO.

UNIVERSITY OF TORONTO RENAISSANCE & REFORMATION
COLLOQUIUM.
— RENAISSANCE & REFORMATION.

UNIVERSITY OF TORONTO: ST. MICHAEL'S COLLEGE.
— YEATS STUDIES. AN INTERNATIONAL JOURNAL.

UNIVERSITE DE TOULOUSE: FACULTE MIXTE DE
MEDECINE ET DE PHARMACIE.
— REVUE DE MEDECINE DE TOULOUSE.

UNIVERSITA DI TRIESTE: ISTITUTO DI MATEMATICA.
— RENDICONTI DELL'ISTITUTO DI MATEMATICA
DELL'UNIVERSITA DI TRIESTE.

UNIVERSITY OF TULSA.
— BLAKE STUDIES.

UNIVERSITY OF TULSA: DEPARTMENT OF ENGLISH.
— MONOGRAPH SERIES, DEPARTMENT OF ENGLISH,
UNIVERSITY OF TULSA.

UNIVERSITY OF UDAIPUR.
— RESEARCH STUDIES, UNIVERSITY OF UDAIPUR.

UNIVERSITET I UPPSALA: NATURGEOGRAFISKA INST-
ITUTIONEN.
SEE: KUNGLIGA UNIVERSITET I UPPSALA: NATUR-
GEOGRAFISKA INSTITUTIONEN.

UNIVERSITY OF UTAH: DEPARTMENT OF ECONOMICS.
— INTERMOUNTAIN ECONOMIC REVIEW.

UNIVERSITY OF UTAH: DEPARTMENT OF MINING,
METALLURGICAL & FUEL ENGINEERING.
— INTERMET BULLETIN.

UNIVERSIDADE DO VALE DO RIO SINOS:
INSTITUTO ANCHIETANO DE PESQUISAS.
— PUBLICACOES AVULSAS, INSTITUTO ANCHIETANO DE
PESQUISAS UNIVERSIDADE DO VALE DO RIO DOS
SINOS.

UNIVERSIDAD DE VALENCIA: INSTITUTO DE GEOGRAFIA
— PUBLICACIONES DEL INSTITUTO DE GEOGRAFIA,
UNIVERSIDAD DE VALENCIA.

UNIVERSIDAD DE VALLADOLID: DEPARTAMENTO DE
INGLES.
— PUBLICACIONES, DEPARTAMENTO DE INGLES, UNIV-
ERSIDAD DE VALLADOLID.

UNIVERSIDAD DE VALLADOLID: SEMINARIO
AMERICANISTA.
— CUADERNOS PREHISPANICOS.

UNIVERSIDAD DEL VALLE: DEPARTAMENTO DE
BIBLIOTECAS.
— MACANA.
— MACANA: SUPLEMENTO.

UNIVERSIDAD DEL VALLE: DEPARTAMENTO DE
BIOLOGIA.
— BOLETIN, DEPARTAMENTO DE BIOLOGIA, UNIVER-
SIDAD DEL VALLE.

UNIVERSITY OF VICTORIA: DEPARTMENT OF
GEOGRAPHY.
— WESTERN GEOGRAPHICAL SERIES.

UNIVERSITY OF VICTORIA: MALTWOOD MUSEUM.
— STUDIES IN ARCHITECTURAL HISTORY.

UNIVERSITY OF VIRGINIA.
— NEW LITERARY HISTORY.

UNIVERSITY OF VIRGINIA: THOMAS JEFFERSON CENTER
FOR POLITICAL ECONOMY.                                                                 000
SEE: THOMAS JEFFERSON CENTER ...

UNIVERSITY OF WALES.
— PENTACOL. CHEMICAL JOURNAL OF THE UNIVERSITY
OF WALES.                                                                          XXX

UNIWERSYTET WARSZAWSKI.
— ROZPRAWY UNIWERSYTETU WARSZAWSKIEGO. DISSER-
TATIONES UNIVERSITATIS VARSAVIENSIS.

UNIWERSYTET WARSZAWSKI: INSTYTUT HISTORYCZNY.
— FASCICULI HISTORICI.                                                             XXX
— ZESZYTY HISTORYCZNE, INSTYTUT HISTORYCZNY
UNIWERSYTETU WARSZAWSKIEGO.                                                         XXX

UNIWERSYTET WARSZAWSKI: KATEDRA ARCHEOLOGII
SRODZIEMNOMORSKIEJ.
— STUDIA PALMYRENSKIE. = ETUDES PALMYRENIENNES.

UNIWERSYTET WARSZAWSKI: KATEDRA KLIMATOLOGII.
— PRACE I STUDIA INSTYTUTU GEOGRAFICZNEGO UNIW-
ERSYTETU WARSZAWSKIEGO.

UNIWERSYTET WARSZAWSKI: WYDZIAL GEOLOGII.
— BIULETYN GEOLOGICZNY.

UNIVERSITY OF WARWICK.
— GAZETTE, UNIVERSITY OF WARWICK.
— TRACKS.

UNIVERSITY OF WARWICK: CENTRE FOR INDUSTRIAL &
BUSINESS STUDIES.
— WARWICK RESEARCH IN INDUSTRIAL & BUSINESS
STUDIES.

UNIVERSITY OF WARWICK: DEPARTMENT OF GERMAN
STUDIES.
— OCCASIONAL PAPERS IN GERMAN STUDIES, UNIV-
ERSITY OF WARWICK.

UNIVERSITY OF WARWICK: LIBRARY.
— OCCASIONAL PUBLICATIONS, LIBRARY, UNIVERSITY
OF WARWICK.

UNIVERSITY OF WARWICK: MATHEMATICS INSTITUTE.
— MANIFOLD.

UNIVERSITY OF WASHINGTON: FAR EASTERN & RUSSIAN
INSTITUTE.
— PARERGA.

UNIVERSITY OF WASHINGTON: INSTITUTE OF FOREST
PRODUCTS.
— RESEARCH BULLETIN, INSTITUTE OF FOREST PROD-
UCTS, UNIVERSITY OF WASHINGTON.

UNIVERSITY OF WASHINGTON: SCHOOL OF LAW.
— ASIAN LAW SERIES, SCHOOL OF LAW, UNIVERSITY
OF WASHINGTON.

UNIVERSITY OF WASHINGTON (STATE).                                                  000
SEE: WASHINGTON STATE UNIVERSITY.

UNIVERSITY OF WATERLOO (ONTARIO).
— AEQUATIONES MATHEMATICAE.

UNIVERSITY OF WELLINGTON (NZ).                                                      000
SEE: VICTORIA UNIVERSITY OF WELLINGTON.

UNIVERSITY OF THE WEST INDIES: DEPARTMENT OF
GEOLOGY & GEOGRAPHY.
— OCCASIONAL PAPERS IN GEOGRAPHY, DEPARTMENT OF
OF GEOLOGY & GEOGRAPHY, UNIVERSITY OF THE
WEST INDIES.

UNIVERSITY OF THE WEST INDIES: DEPARTMENT OF
HISTORY.
— JOURNAL OF CARIBBEAN HISTORY.                                                    XXX

UNIVERSITY OF THE WEST INDIES: FACULTY OF
ENGINEERING.
— WEST INDIAN JOURNAL OF ENGINEERING.

UNIVERSITY OF THE WEST INDIES: INSTITUTE OF
EDUCATION.
— ROUND-UP NEWSLETTER.

UNIVERSITY OF THE WEST INDIES: INSTITUTE OF
SOCIAL & ECONOMIC RESEARCH.
— STUDIES IN REGIONAL ECONOMIC INTEGRATION.

UNIVERSITY OF THE WEST INDIES: JAMAICAN GEOG-
RAPHICAL SOCIETY.
— NEWSLETTER, JAMAICAN GEOGRAPHICAL SOCIETY.

UNIVERSITY OF THE WEST INDIES: NATURAL HISTORY
SOCIETY.
— BIOLOGICAL JOURNAL.
ASIAN STUDIES.
— WORKING PAPERS IN ASIAN STUDIES.

UNIVERSITY OF WESTERN ONTARIO: DEPARTMENT OF
ENGLISH.
— SPENSER NEWSLETTER.

UNIVERSITY OF WESTERN ONTARIO: FACULTY OF LAW.
— WESTERN ONTARIO LAW REVIEW.

UNIVERSITAT WIEN.
— BYZANTINA VINDOBONENSIA.

UNIVERSITY OF WISCONSIN (MILWAUKEE): CENTER FOR
LATIN AMERICAN STUDIES.
— CENTER DISCUSSION PAPERS, CENTER FOR LATIN
AMERICAN STUDIES, UNIVERSITY OF WISCONSIN
(MILWAUKEE).

UNIVERSITY OF WISCONSIN: DEPARTMENT OF AFRICAN LANGUAGES & LITERATURE.
— BA SHIRU.

UNIVERSITY OF WISCONSIN: DEPARTMENT OF COMPARATIVE LITERATURE.
— QUIXOTE.

UNIVERSITY OF WISCONSIN: DEPARTMENT OF ENGLISH.
— LITERARY MONOGRAPHS.

UNIWERSYTET WROCLAWSKI.
— ACTA UNIVERSITATIS WRATISLAVENSIS.                    XXX
— ANGLICA WRATISLAVIENSIA.
— ANTIQUITAS.
— BIBIOTEKOZNAWSTWO.                                    XXX
  SUBS (1970): PART OF STUDIA O KSIAZCE.
— LOGIKA, UNIWERSYTET WROCLAWSKI.
— ONOMASTICA SLAVOGERMANICA.
— PRACE GEOLOGICZNO-MINERALOGICZNE, UNIWERSYTET WROCLAWSKI.
— PRACE PSYCHOLOGICZNE, UNIWERSYTET WROCLAWSKI.
— PRZEGLAD PRAWA I ADMINISTRACJI.
— SLAVICA WRATISLAVIENSIA. (ACTA UNIVERSITATIS WRATISLAVIENSIS).
— STUDIA ARCHEOLOGICZNE, UNIWERSYTET WROCLAWSKI    XXX

UNIWERSYTET WROCLAWSKI: INSTYTUT NAUK POLITYCZNYCH.
— NAUKI POLITYCZNE.

UNIVERSITY OF WYOMING: COLLEGE OF LAW.
— LAND & WATER LAW REVIEW.

UNIVERSITY OF YORK: DEPARTMENT OF ECONOMICS.
— BULLETIN OF ECONOMIC RESEARCH.                       XXX

UNIVERSITY OF YORK: INSTITUTE OF ADVANCED ARCHITECTURAL STUDIES.
— RESEARCH PAPER, INSTITUTE OF ADVANCED ARCHITECTURAL STUDIES, UNIVERSITY OF YORK.

UNIVERSITY OF YORK: LINGUISTICS SOCIETY.
— YORK PAPERS IN LINGUISTICS.

UNIVERSITY OF ZAMBIA.
— ZAMBIA LAW JOURNAL.

UNIVERSITY OF ZAMBIA: INSTITUTE FOR SOCIAL RESEARCH.
— ZAMBIAN URBAN STUDIES.

UNIVERSIDAD DEL ZULIA: CENTRO DE INVESTIGACIONES BIOLOGICAS.
— BOLETIN DEL CENTRO DE INVESTIGACIONES BIOLOGICAS, UNIVERSIDAD DEL ZULIA.

URAL'SKIJ GOSUDARSTVENNYJ UNIVERSITET.
— SOTSIOLOGICHESKIE ISSLEDOVANIJA.

URAL'SKIJ GOSUDARSTVENNYJ UNIVERSITET [IM. A.M. GOR'KOGO].
— FILOSOFSKIE NAUKI, URAL'SKIJ GOSUDARSTVENNYJ UNIVERSITET [IM. A.M. GOR'KOGO].

URAL'SKIJ MASHINOSTROITEL'NYJ ZAVOD: NAUCHNO-ISSLEDOVATEL'SKIJ INSTITUT TJAZHELOGO MASHINOSTROENIJA.
— PROIZVODSTVO KRUPNYKH MASHIN.

URAL'SKIJ NAUCHNO-ISSLEDOVATEL'SKIJ INSTITUT CHERNYKH METALLOV.
— TRUDY URAL'SKOGO NAUCHNO-ISSLEDOVATEL'SKOGO INSTITUTA CHERNYKH METALLOV.

URBAN AMERICA.
— CITY.

URUGVAJA ESPERANTO-SOCIETO.
— KEMIO INTERNACIA.

USTAV DEJIN SOCIALISMU.
— HISTORY OF SOCIALISM YEARBOOK.
— REVUE DEJIN SOCIALISMU. PRISPEVKY K DEJINAM KSC.                                                     XXX

USTAV HYGIENY PRACE A CHOROB Z POVOLANI.
— INDEX RADIOHYGIENICUS.

USTAV PRO MEZINARODNI POLITIKU A EKONOMII.
— OTAZKY MEZINARODNICH VZTAHU.

USTAV PRE VYSKUM FINANCII V BRATISLAVE.
— FINANCNE STUDIE. CASOPIS PRE OTAZKY FINANCNEJ TEORIE A HOSPODARSKEJ POLITIKY.

USTREDI ZEMEDELSKEHO A POTRAVINARSKEHO VYZKUMU.
— VESTNIK, USTREDI ZEMEDELSKEHO A POTRAVINARSKEHO VYZKUMU.

UTAH GEOLOGICAL ASSOCIATION.
— PUBLICATIONS, UTAH GEOLOGICAL ASSOCIATION.

UTENTI MOTORI AGRICOLI.
— RIVISTA DI INGEGNERIA AGRARIA.

UTRIKESPOLITISKA INSTITUTET.
— SWEDISH STUDIES IN INTERNATIONAL RELATIONS.

UTSUNOMIYA DAIGAKU KYOYOBU.
— UTSUNOMIYA DAIGAKU KYOYOBU KENKYU HOKOKU: DAI 2BU. BULLETIN OF THE FACULTY OF GENERAL EDUCATION, UTSUNOMIYA UNIVERSITY: SECTION 2.

UTSUNOMIYA DAIGAKU NOGAKUBU.
— UTSUNOMIYA DAIGAKU NOGAKUBU ENSHURIN HOKOKU. BULLETIN OF THE UTSUNOMIYA UNIVERSITY FORESTS.

(UZBEKISTAN) MINISTERSTVO STROITEL'STVA I GOSSTROJA.
— STROITEL'STVO I ARKHITEKTURA UZBEKISTANA.*

UZBEKISTANSKOE GEOGRAFISCHESKOE OBSHCHESTVO.
— IZVESTIJA UZBEKISTANSKOGO GEOGRAFICHESKOGO OBSHCHESTVA.                                           XXX

UZBEKISTANSKOGO FILIALA GEOGRAFICHESKOGO OBSHCHESTVA SSSR.                                          XXX
— IZVESTIJA UZBEKISTANSKOGO FILIALA GEOGRAFICHESKOGO OBSHCHESTVA SSSR.                             XXX
  SUBS (1963): IZVESTIJA UZBEKISTANSKOGO GEOGRAFICHESKOGO OBSHCHESTVA.

VALE OF EVESHAM HISTORICAL SOCIETY.
— RESEARCH PAPERS, VALE OF EVESHAM HISTORICAL SOCIETY.

VALTION TEKNILLINEN TUTKIMUSKESKUS.
— BUILDING TECHNOLOGY & COMMUNITY DEVELOPMENT.

VANDERBILT UNIVERSITY: CENTER FOR SHAKESPEARE STUDIES.
— SHAKESPEARE STUDIES: MONOGRAPH SERIES.

VARENDRA RESEARCH MUSEUM.
— JOURNAL OF THE VARENDA RESEARCH MUSEUM.

VEGETARIAN SOCIETY OF THE UNITED KINGDOM LTD.
— GAZETTE, VEGETARIAN SOCIETY OF THE UNITED KINGDOM LTD.
— VEGETARIAN: NS.                                       XXX

(VENEZUELA) OFICINA CENTRAL DE INFORMACION.
— INDICE CULTURAL DE VENEZUELA.

VERBAND DER DEUTSCHEN HOHLEN- UND KARSTFORSCHER
— ABHANDLUNGEN ZUR KARST- UND HOHLENKUNDE: REIHE A: SPELAOLOGIE.
— ABHANDLUNGEN ZUR KARST- UND HOHLENKUNDE: REIHE F: GESCHICHTE DER SPELAOLOGIE, BIOGRAPHIEN.

VEREIN DEUTSCHER INGENIEURE.
— MEERESTECHNIK. MARINE TECHNOLOGY (DUSSELDORF).
— TECHNIKGESCHICHTE IN EINZELDARSTELLUNGEN.

VEREIN EHEMALIGER TEXTILFACHSCHULER ZURICH.
— MITTEX.                                               XXX

VEREIN FUR REFORMATIONSGESCHICHTE.
— ARCHIV FUR REFORMATIONSGESCHICHTE: BEIHEFT: LITERATURBERICHT.

VERENIGING TOT BEHOUD VAN NATUURMONUMENTEN IN NEDERLAND.
— NATUUREBEHOUD.

(VERMONT) DEPARTMENT OF WATER RESOURCES.
— STUDIES IN VERMONT GEOLOGY.

VERNACULAR ARCHITECTURE GROUP.
— VERNACULAR ARCHITECTURE.

VETERINARIANS' UNION.
— VETERINARY DIGEST.                                    XXX
— VETERINARY DOCTOR.                                    XXX

VETERINARY CONTROL & RESEARCH INSTITUTE PENDIK.                                                     000
SEE: PENDIK VETERINER KONTROL VE ARASTIRMA ENSTITUSU.

**VICKERS LTD.**
— VICKERS MAGAZINE.

**VICTORIA & ALBERT MUSEUM.**
— VICTORIA & ALBERT MUSEUM BROCHURE.
— VICTORIA & ALBERT MUSEUM YEARBOOK.

**VICTORIA UNIVERSITY OF WELLINGTON.**
— PACIFIC VIEWPOINT MONOGRAPH.

**VIDYODAYA UNIVERSITY OF CEYLON.**
— VIDYODAYA. JOURNAL OF ARTS, SCIENCES & LETT-
ERS.

**VIETNAM (SOUTH) COUNCIL ON FOREIGN RELATIONS.**
— VIETNAM NEWSLETTER.

**VILAGGAZDASAGI TUDOMANYOS TANACS.**
— ABSTRACTS OF HUNGARIAN ECONOMIC LITERATURE.

**VILLANOVA UNIVERSITY: AUGUSTINIAN INSTITUTE.**
— AUGUSTINIAN STUDIES.

**VILNIAUS ASTRONOMIJAS OBSERVATORIJA.**
— BIULETENIS, VILNIAUS ASTRONOMIJAS OBSERVATOR-
IJA.

**VILNIAUS VALSTYBINIS /V. KAPSUKO VARDO/
UNIVERSITETAS.**
— VILNIAUS VALSTYBINIS /V. KAPSUKO VARDO/ UNI-
VERSITETAS, MOKSLO DARBAI; EKONOMIKA. =
UCHENYE ZAPISKI, VIL'NJUSSKIJ GOSUDARSTVENNYJ
UNIVERSITET /IM. V. KAPSUKASA/; EKONOMIKA.                         XXX

**VIL'NJUSSKIJ GOSUDARSTVENNYJ UNIVERSITET.**              000
SEE: VILNIAUS VALSTYBINIS UNIVERSITETAS.

**VIOLA DA GAMBA SOCIETY.**
— CHELYS.

**(VIRGINIA) DEPARTMENT OF CONSERVATION & ECON-
OMIC DEVELOPMENT: DIVISION OF MINERAL RESOURCES**
— REPORT OF INVESTIGATIONS, DIVISION OF MINERAL
RESOURCES, DEPARTMENT OF CONSERVATION & ECON-
MIC DEVELOPMENT (VIRGINIA).

**VIRGINIA POLYTECHNIC INSTITUTE.**
— INSECTS OF VIRGINIA.

**VIRGINIA POLYTECHNIC INSTITUTE: RESEARCH DIV-
ISION.**
— MONOGRAPHS, RESEARCH DIVISION, VIRGINIA POLY-
TECHNIC INSTUTUTE.
— RESEARCH REPORT, RESEARCH DIVISION, VIRGINIA
POLYTECHNIC INSTITUTE.                                            XXX

**VISHVESHVARANAND VEDIC RESEARCH INSTITUTE.**
— VISHVESHVARANAND INDOLOGICAL JOURNAL.

**VISIBLE RECORD (EDP) SOCIETY.**
— COMPUTER EXECUTIVE. JOURNAL OF THE ...                          XXX
— JOURNAL OF THE VISIBLE RECORD (EDP) SOCIETY.                    XXX

**VISINDAFELAG ISLENDINGA.**
— SCIENCE IN ICELAND. = SCIENTIA ISLANDICA.

**VISOKA SKOLA ZA POLITICNE VEDE.**
— TEORIJA IN PRAKSA. REVIJA ZA DRUZBENA
VPRASANJA.

**VLADIMIRSKIJ GOSUDARSTVENNYJ PEDAGOGICHESKIJ
INSTITUT [IM. P.I. LEBEDEVA-POLJANSKOGO]**
— UCHENYE ZAPISKI, VLADIMIRSKIJ GOSUDARSTVENNYJ
PEDAGOGICHESKIJ INSTITUT: SERIJA BOTANIKA.

**VOLUNTARY COMMITTEE ON OVERSEAS AID & DEVELOP-
MENT: EDUCATION UNIT.**
— VOX. BULLETIN OF THE VOLUNTARY COMMITTEE ON
OVERSEAS AID & DEVELOPMENT.

**VOLZHSKO-KAMSKIJ GOSUDARSTVENNYJ ZAPOVEDNIK.**
— TRUDY, VOLZHSKO-KAMSKIJ GOSUDARSTVENNYJ
ZAPOVEDNIK.

**VORONEZHSKIJ GOSUDARSTVENNYJ UNIVERSITET.**
— SBORNIK RABOT ASPIRANTOV, VORONEZHSKIJ GOSUD-
ARSTVENNYJ UNIVERSITET.

**VSEROSSIJSKOE TEATRAL'NOE OBSHCHESTVO.**
— VOPROSY TEATRA. SBORNIK STATEJ I MATERIALOV.

**VSESOJUZNAJA AKADEMIJA SEL'SKOKHOZJAJSTVENNYKH
NAUK.**
— SEL'SKOKHOZJAJSTVENNAJA BIOLOGIJA.
— SVODNYJ UKAZATEL' BIBLIOGRAFICHESKIKH SPISKOV
I KARTOTEK, SOSTAVLENNYKH BIBLIOTEKAMI SOVETS-
KOGO SOJUZA : SEL'SKOE KHOZJAJSTVO.
— TRUDY VSESOJUZNOGO NAUCHNO-ISSLEDOVATEL'SKOGO
INSTITUTA FIZIOLOGII I BIOKHIMII SEL'SKO-
KHOZJAJSTVENNYKH ZHIVOTNYKH.

**VSESOJUZNOE ASTRONOMO-GEODEZICHESKOE
OBSHCHESTVO.**
— ASTRONOMICHESKIJ VESTNIK.
— BJULLETEN' VSESOJUZNOGO ASTRONOMO-GEODEZI-
CHESKOGO OBSHCHESTVA.                                             XXX
SUBS (1967): ASTRONOMICHESKIJ VESTNIK.

**VSESOJUZNYJ INSTITUT PO IZUCHENIJU PRICHIN I
RAZRABOTKE MER PREDUPREZHDENIJA PRESTUPNOSTI.**
— VOPROSY BOR'BY S PRESTUPNOST'JU.                                XXX
— VOPROSY PREDUPREZHDENIJA PRESTUPNOSTI.                          XXX

**VSESOJUZNYJ INSTITUT NAUCHNOJ I TEKHNICHESKOJ
INFORMATSII.**
— ITOGI NAUKI: ORGANIZATSIJA UPRAVLENIJA.
— NAUCHNO-TEKHNICHESKAJA INFORMATSIJA, VSESO-
JUZNYJ INSTITUT NAUCHNOJ I TEKHNICHESKOJ
INFORMATSII.
— NAUCHNO-TEKHNICHESKAJA INFORMATSIJA, VSESO-
JUZNYJ INSTITUT NAUCHNOJ I TEKHNICHESKOJ
INFORMATSII: SERIJA 1: ORGANIZATSIJA I METOD-
IKA INFORMATSIONNOJ RABOTY.
— NAUCHNO-TEKHNICHESKAJA INFORMATSIJA, VSESO-
JUZNYJ INSTITUT NAUCHNOJ I TEKHNICHESKOJ
INFORMATSII: SERIJA 2: INFORMATSIONNYE PROT-
SESSY I SISTEMY.

**VSESOJUZNYJ LENINSKIJ KOMMUNISTICHESKIJ SOJUZ
MOLODEZHI.**
— ROMASHKA.

**VSESOJUZNYJ LENINSKIJ KOMMUNISTICHESKIJ SOJUZ
MOLODEZHI: TSENTRAL'NYJ KOMITET.**
— FANTASTIKA.
— POZYVNYE ISTORII. UCHENYE ZAPISKI PO ISTORII
VLKSM.

**VSESOJUZNOE MINERALOGICHESKOE OBSHCHESTVO:
(UKRAINSKOE OTDELENIE).**
— KONSTITUTSIJA I SVOJSTVA MINERALOV.

**VSESOJUZNOE NAUCHNOE OBSHCHESTVO ENDOKRINOLOGOV**
— PROBLEMY ENDOKRINOLOGII.                                       XXX

**VSESOJUZNYJ NAUCHNO-ISSLEDOVATEL'SKIJ INSTITUT
FIZIOLOGII I BIOKHIMII SEL'SKOKHOZJAJSTVENNYKH
ZHIVOTNYKH.**
— TRUDY VSESOJUZNOGO NAUCHNO-ISSLEDOVATEL'SKOGO
INSTITUTA FIZIOLOGII I BIOKHIMII SEL'SKO-
KHOZJAJSTVENNYKH ZHIVOTNYKH.

**VSESOJUZNYJ NAUCHNO-ISSLEDOVATEL'SKIJ INSTITUT
KHIMICHESKIKH REAKTIVOV I OSOBO CHISTYKH KHIM-
ICHESKIKH VESHCHESTV.**
— METODY POLUCHENIJA KHIMICHESKIKH REAKTIVOV I
PREPARATOV.

**VSESOJUZNYJ NAUCHNO-ISSLEDOVATEL'SKIJ INSTITUT
MAGNITNOJ ZAPISI I TEKHNOLOGII RADIOVESHCHANIJA
I TELEVIDENIJA (VNIIRT).**
— TRUDY, VSESOJUZNYJ NAUCHNO-ISSLEDOVATEL'SKIJ
INSTITUT MAGNITNOJ ZAPISI I TEKHNOLOGII RADIO-
VESHCHANIJA I TELEVIDENIJA (VNIIRT).                              XXX

**VSESOJUZNYJ NAUCHNO-ISSLEDOVATEL'SKIJ INSTITUT
MINERAL'NOGO SYR'JA.**
— GEOLOGIJA MESTOROZHDENIJ TVERDYKH POLEZNYKH
ISKOPAEMYKH.
— RENTGENOGRAFIJA MINERAL'NOGO SYR'JA.

**VSESOJUZNYJ NAUCHNO-ISSLEDOVATEL'SKIJ INSTITUT
ORGANIZATSII, UPRAVLENIJA I EKONOMIKI NEFTE-
GAZOVOJ PROMYSHLENNOSTI.**
— EKONOMIKA NEFTEDOBYVAJUSHCHEJ PROMYSHLENNOSTI.
— GAZOVOE DELO. NAUCHNO-TEKHNICHESKIJ SBORNIK.                    XXX
— NEFTEGAZOVAJA GEOLOGIJA I GEOFIZIKA.                            XXX

**VSESOJUZNYJ NAUCHNO-ISSLEDOVATEL'SKIJ INSTITUT
PERERABOTKI I ISPOL'ZOVANIJA TOPLIVA.**
— KHIMIJA I TEKHNOLOGIJA TOPLIVA I PRODUKTOV
EGO PERERABOTKI.                                                 XXX

**VSESOJUZNYJ NAUCHNO-ISSLEDOVATEL'SKIJ INSTITUT
RADIATSIONNOJ TEKHNIKI.**
— RADIATSIONNAJA TEKHNIKA.

VSESOJUZNYJ NAUCHNO-ISSLEDOVATEL'SKIJ INSTITUT
PO STROITEL'STVU MAGISTRAL'NYKH TRUBOPROVODOV
(VNIIST).
— TRUDY, VSESOJUZNYJ NAUCHNO-ISSLEDOVATEL'SKIJ
INSTITUT PO STROITEL'STVU MAGISTRAL'NYKH
TRUBOPROVODOV (VNIIST).                                                 XXX
— TRUDY VSESOJUZNOGO NAUCHNO-ISSLEDOVATEL'SKOGO
INSTITUTA PO STROITEL'STVU OBEKTOV NEFTJANOJ
I GAZOVOJ PROMYSHLENNOSIT.                                              XXX
SUBS (1960): TRUDY, VSESOJUZNYJ NAUCHNO-
ISSLEDOVATEL'SKIJ INSTITUT PO STROITEL'-
STVU MAGISTRAL'NYKH TRUBOPROVODOV (VNIIST).

VSESOJUZNYJ NAUCHNO-ISSLEDOVATEL'SKIJ INSTITUT
TEKHNICHESKOJ ESTETIKI.
— VOPROSY TEKHNICHESKOJ ESTETIKI.

VSESOJUZNYJ NAUCHNO-ISSLEDOVATEL'SKIJ I PROEK-
TNO-KONSTRUKTORSKIJ INSTITUT DOBYCHI UGLJA
GIDRAVLICHESKOM SPOSOBOM 'VNIIGIDROUGOL'.
— TRUDY VSESOJUZNOGO NAUCHNO-ISSLEDOVATEL'SKOGO
I PROEKTNO-KONSTRUKTORSKOGO INSTITUTA DOBYCHI
UGLJA GIDRAVLICHESKOM SPOSOBOM 'VNIIGIDROUGOL'
I GORNOGO FAKUL'TETA SIBIRSKOGO METALLURGICH-
ESKOGO INSTITUTA.

VYBOR SOCIALISTICKE KULTURY.
— KULTURNI TVORBA.                                                      XXX
— POLITIKA. TYDENIK.                                                    XXX

VYSKUMNY USTAV PRE VINOHRADNICTVO A VINARSTVO.
— POKROKY VO VINOHRADNICKOM A VINARSKOM VYSKUME.

VYSOKA SKOLA CHEMICKO-TECHNOLOGICKA V PRAZE.
— SBORNIK VYSOKE SKOLY CHEMICKO-TECHNOLOGICKE
V PRAZE: POTRAVINARSKA TECHNOLOGIE.                                     XXX
SUBS (1966): SBORNIK VYSOKE SKOLY CHEMICKO-
TECHNOLOGICKE V PRAZE: POTRAVINY.
— SBORNIK VYSOKE SKOLY CHEMICKO-TECHNOLOGICKE
V PRAZE: POTRAVINY.                                                     XXX

VYSOKA SKOLA EKONOMICKA.
— SBORNIK VYSOKEJ SKOLY EKONOMICKEJ.

VYSOKA SKOLA LESNICKA A DREVARSKA: LESNICKA
FAKULTA.
— ZBORNIK VEDECKYCH PRAC LESNICKEJ FAKULTY VYSO-
KEJ SKOLY LESNICKEJ A DREVARSKEJ VO ZVOLENE.

VYSOKA SKOLA ZEMEDELSKA V BRNE.
— SBORNIK VYSOKE SKOLY ZEMEDELSKE V BRNE: RADA
D: SPISY FAKULTY PROVOZNE EKONOMICKE.                                   XXX

VYSOKOGORNYJ GEOFIZICHESKIJ INSTITUT (NAL'CHIK)
— TRUDY, VYSOKOGORNYJ GEOFIZICHESKIJ INSTITUT
(NAL'CHIK).                                                             XXX

VYSSHAJA PARTIJNAJA SHKOLA PRI TSK KPSS.
— UCHENYE ZAPISKI KAFEDRY SOVETSKOJ EKONOMIKI.

VYSSHIE UCHEBNYE ZAVEDENIJA GORODA LENINGRADA.
— UCHENYE ZAPISKI KAFEDR OBSHCHESTVENNYKH NAUK
VUZOV GORODA LENINGRADA: FILOSOFIJA.                                    XXX
— UCHENYE ZAPISKI KAFEDR OBSHCHESTVENNYKH NAUK
VUZOV GORODA LENINGRADA: PROBLEMY NAUCHNOGO
KOMMUNIZMA.

VYSSHIE UCHEBNYE ZAVEDENIJA LITOVSKOJ SSR.                              000
SEE: LIETUVOS TSR AUKSTESNIS MOKYKLA.

VYZKUMNY USTAV ZELEZORUDNYCH DOLU A HRUDKOVEN
N.P. EJPOVICE.
— SBORNIK PRACI, VYZKUMNY USTAV ZELEZORUDNYCH
DOLU A HRUDKOVEN N.P. EJPOVICE.

WAKE FOREST UNIVERSITY: OVERSEAS RESEARCH
CENTER.
— MEDICAL BEHAVIORAL SCIENCE.

WALTON & WEYBRIDGE HISTORICAL SOCIETY.
— PAPER, WALTON & WEYBRIDGE HISTORICAL SOCIETY.

WARNER ELECTRIC BRAKE & CLUTCH CO.
— INCREMENTAL MOTION CONTROL SYSTEMS & DEVICES
NEWSLETTER.

WARREN SPRING LABORATORY.
— REVIEW, WARREN SPRING LABORATORY.                                     XXX

WARSAW TECHNICAL UNIVERSITY: INSTITUTE OF
MATHEMATICS.                                                            000
SEE: POLITECHNIKA WARSZAWSKA: INSTYTUT
MATEMATYKI.

WARWICKSHIRE LOCAL HISTORY SOCIETY.
— NEWSLETTER, WARWICKSHIRE LOCAL HISTORY
SOCIETY.
— WARWICKSHIRE HISTORY. BULLETIN OF THE ...

WASEDA DAIGAKU SEISAN KENKYUJO.
— WASEDA DAIGAKU SEISAN KENKYUJO KIYO. BULLETIN
OF THE INSTITUTE FOR RESEARCH IN PRODUCTIVITY,
WASEDA UNIVERSITY.

WASEDA UNIVERSITY: INSTITUTE FOR RESEARCH
IN PRODUCTIVITY.                                                        000
SEE: WASEDA DAIGAKU SEISAN KENKYUJO.

WASHINGTON CENTER OF FOREIGN POLICY RESEARCH.
— STUDIES IN INTERNATIONAL AFFAIRS.

(WASHINGTON, STATE) DEPARTMENT OF FISHERIES.
— TECHNICAL REPORT, DEPARTMENT OF FISHERIES
(WASHINGTON, STATE).

WASHINGTON STATE ENTOMOLOGICAL SOCIETY.
— MELANDERIA.

WASHINGTON STATE UNIVERSITY: DEPARTMENT OF
ENGLISH.
— POE STUDIES.                                                         XXX

WASHINGTON STATE UNIVERSITY: DIVISION OF INDUS-
TRIAL RESEARCH.
— ABSTRACTS FOR THE ADVANCEMENT OF INDUSTRIAL
UTILIZATION OF CEREAL GRAINS.                                           XXX

WATER RESOURCES BOARD (GB).
— GROUND WATER YEARBOOK.                                               XXX
— PUBLICATION, WATER RESOURCES BOARD (GB).
— SURFACE WATER YEAR-BOOK OF GREAT BRITAIN.                            XXX
SUBS (1970): GROUND WATER YEARBOOK.

WATERLOOPKUNDIG LABORATORIUM (DELFT).
— HYDRO DELFT.

WATFORD & DISTRICT INDUSTRIAL HISTORY SOCIETY.
— JOURNAL OF THE WATFORD & DISTRICT INDUSTRIAL
HISTORY SOCIETY.

WAYNE STATE UNIVERSITY: CENTER FOR APPLICATION
OF SCIENCE & TECHNOLOGY.
— AIR QUALITY CONTROL DIGEST. = AIR POLLUTION
DIGEST.                                                                 XXX
— METAL JOINING DIGEST.                                                XXX
— SURFACE COATINGS DIGEST.                                             XXX
— WATER QUALITY CONTROL DIGEST.                                        XXX

WAYNE STATE UNIVERSITY: SCIENTIFIC & TECHNICAL
INFORMATION CENTER.
— INFORMATION SAMPLER DIGEST.

WEED SCIENCE SOCIETY OF AMERICA.
— WEED SCIENCE.                                                        XXX
— WEEDS.                                                               XXX
SUBS (1968): WEED SCIENCE.

WEED SOCIETY OF JAPAN.                                                  000
SEE: NIHON ZASSO BOJO KENKYUKAI.

WELDING INSTITUTE.
— METAL CONSTRUCTION & BRITISH WELDING JOURNAL.
— [TECHNICAL DISCLOSURE], WELDING INSTITUTE.
— WELDING INTERNATIONAL. RESEARCH &
DEVELOPMENT.                                                            XXX
— WELDING RESEARCH INTERNATIONAL.                                      XXX

WELWYN HALL RESEARCH ASSOCIATION.
— WELWYN DIGEST.

WERKGROEP VOOR TERTIAIRE EN KWARTAIRE GEOLOGIE.
— MEDEDELINGEN, WERKGROEP VOOR TERTIAIRE EN
KWARTAIRE GEOLOGIE.

WESLEY HISTORICAL SOCIETY: LANCASHIRE &
CHESHIRE BRANCH.
— JOURNAL, LANCASHIRE & CHESHIRE BRANCH, WESLEY
HISTORICAL SOCIETY.

WESLEYAN UNIVERSITY LIBRARY.
— WESLEYAN LIBRARY NOTES.

WESSEX CAVE CLUB.
— OCCASIONAL PUBLICATION, WESSEX CAVE CLUB:
SERIES 1.

WEST AFRICAN INSTITUTE FOR OIL PALM RESEARCH.
— ANNUAL REPORT, WEST AFRICAN INSTITUTE FOR OIL
PALM RESEARCH.                                                         XXX
SUBS (1965): ANNUAL REPORT, NIGERIAN INSTI-
TUTE FOR OIL PALM RESEARCH.

WEST COUNTRY ANTI-COMMON MARKET LEAGUE.
— VOICE OF THE WEST.

WEST COUNTRY TOURIST BOARD.
— ANNUAL REPORT, WEST COUNTRY TOURIST BOARD.
— INTO THE WEST COUNTRY.

WEST HAM COLLEGE OF TECHNOLOGY: DEPARTMENT OF
ELECTRICAL ENGINEERING.
— REPORT, DEPARTMENT OF ELECTRICAL ENGINEERING,
WEST HAM COLLEGE OF TECHNOLOGY.

WEST PAKISTAN UNIVERSITY OF ENGINEERING &
TECHNOLOGY.
— RESEACH BULLETIN, WEST PAKISTAN UNIVERSITY
OF ENGINEERING & TECHNOLOGY.

WEST PAKISTAN WATER & POWER DEVELOPMENT
AUTHORITY.
— INDUS.

WEST RIDING COUNTY COUNCIL.
— WELL-BEING.  A REVIEW OF HEALTH & EDUCATION.

WEST VIRGINIA UNIVERSITY: CONFERENCE OF BRITISH
STUDIES.                                                                                      000
    SEE: CONFERENCE OF BRITISH STUDIES ...

(WESTERN AUSTRALIA) DEPARTMENT OF AGRICULTURE.
— TECHNICAL BULLETIN, DEPARTMENT OF AGRICULTURE,
WESTERN AUSTRALIA.

(WESTERN AUSTRALIA) DEPARTMENT OF FISHERIES
& FAUNA.
— FAUNA BULLETIN.

(WESTERN AUSTRALIA) GEOLOGICAL SURVEY.
— REPORT, GEOLOGICAL SURVEY OF WESTERN AUSTRAL-
IA.

(WESTERN AUSTRALIA) GOVERNMENT CHEMICAL LABOR-
ATORIES.
— REPORT OF INVESTIGATIONS, GOVERNMENT CHEMICAL
LABORATORIES, WESTERN AUSTRALIA.

WESTERN AUSTRALIAN HERBARIUM.
— NUYTSIA.

WESTERN FOUNDATION OF VERTEBRATE ZOOLOGY.
— OCCASIONAL PAPERS OF THE WESTERN FOUNDATION
OF VERTEBRATE ZOOLOGY.

WESTERN HISTORY ASSOCIATION.
— WESTERN HISTORICAL QUARTERLY.

WESTERN MICHIGAN UNIVERSITY: DEPARTMENT OF
MATHEMATICS.
— MATHEMATICS REPORT, DEPARTMENT OF MATHEMATICS,
WESTERN MICHIGAN UNIVERSITY.

WESTERN REGIONAL SCIENCE ASSOCIATION.
— ANNALS OF REGIONAL SCIENCE.

WESTERN WASHINGTON STATE COLLEGE.
— ANNALS OF REGIONAL SCIENCE.

WESTERN WASHINGTON STATE COLLEGE: CENTER FOR
CROSS CULTURAL RESEARCH.
— JOURNAL OF CROSS CULTURAL PSYCHOLOGY.

WESTERN WASHINGTON STATE COLLEGE: ENGLISH
DEPARTMENT.
— CONCERNING POETRY.

WESTFALISCHE WILHELMS-UNIVERSITAT: GEOLOGISCH-
PALAONTOLOGISCHEN INSTITUT.
— ARBEITEN AUS DEM GEOLOGISCH-PALAONTOLOGISCHEN
INSTITUT, WESTFALISCHE WILHELMS-UNIVERSITAT.

WESTMINSTER BANK.                                                                    XXX
— WESTMINSTER BANK REVIEW.                                                  XXX
    SUBS (968): PART OF QUARTERLY REVIEW, NAT-
IONAL WESTMINSTER BANK.

WHITE FISH AUTHORITY.
— FISH INDUSTRY REVIEW.
— RESEARCH DEVELOPMENT BULLETIN, WHITE FISH
AUTHORITY.

WHITE PANTHER PARTY.
— CHAPTER.
— WHITE TRASH.

WHITEHALL MUSICAL & DRAMATIC SOCIETY.
— ANTHOS.  POETRY, REVIEWS, STORIES, ARTICLES.

WICKEN FEN GROUP.
— [REPORT] WICKEN FEN GROUP.

WILBOUR LIBRARY OF EGYPTOLOGY.
— EGYPTOLOGY TITLES.

WILDBIRD CONSERVANCY: WEXFORD BRANCH.
— WEXFORD BIRD REPORT.

WILDFOWL TRUST.
— ANNUAL REPORT, WILDFOWL TRUST.                                        XXX
    SUBS (1968): WILDFOWL.
— WILDFOWL.                                                                            XXX

WILDLIFE DISEASE ASSOCIATION.
— BULLETIN, WILDLIFE DISEASE ASSOCIATION.                          XXX
— JOURNAL OF WILDLIFE DISEASES.                                          XXX
— NEWSLETTER, WILDLIFE DISEASE ASSOCIATION.                    XXX
    SUBS:  BULLETIN, WILDLIFE ...

WILDLIFE SOCIETY (US).
— WILDLIFE SOCIETY BULLETIN.                                                XXX
— WILDLIFE SOCIETY NEWS.                                                      XXX
    SUBS (1973): WILDLIFE SOCIETY BULLETIN.

WILMINGTON COLLEGE.
— JOURNAL OF EAST AFRICAN STUDIES.

WILTSHIRE RECORD SOCIETY.
— WILTSHIRE RECORD SOCIETY.                                                XXX

WIRE ASSOCIATION (U.S.).
— WIRE JOURNAL.

WISCONSIN STATE UNIVERSITY: MUSEUM OF NATURAL
HISTORY.
— REPORTS ON THE FAUNA & FLORA OF WISCONSIN.

WISTAR INSTITUTE OF ANATOMY & BIOLOGY.
— TERATOLOGY.  JOURNAL OF ABNORMAL DEVELOPMENT.

WITCO CHEMICAL CO.
— ACTIVATED CARBON ABSTRACTS.                                          XXX

WOLLONGONG UNIVERSITY COLLEGE.
— RESEARCH REPORT, WOLLONGONG UNIVERSITY
COLLEGE.

WOLVERHAMPTON COLLEGE OF ART.
— POETRY WORKSHOP.

WOLVERHAMPTON COLLEGE OF TECHNOLOGY.
— JOURNAL OF WEST MIDLANDS REGIONAL STUDIES.                XXX

WOLVERHAMPTON CONSUMER GROUP.
— SERVICE.

WOLVERHAMPTON POLYTECHNIC.
— WEST MIDLANDS STUDIES.                                                    XXX

WOLVERTON & DISTRICT ARCHAEOLOGICAL SOCIETY.
— JOURNAL, WOLVERTON & DISTRICT ARCHAEOLOGICAL
SOCIETY.                                                                                    XXX
— WOLVERTON HISTORICAL JOURNAL.                                        XXX

WOMEN'S LIBERATION MOVEMENT.
— FOWNES STREET JOURNAL.

WOMEN'S LOBBY.
— WOMEN'S REPORT.

WOODROW WILSON SCHOOL OF PUBLIC &
INTERNATIONAL AFFAIRS.
— WOODROW WILSON ASSOCIATION MONOGRAPH SERIES
IN PUBLIC AFFAIRS.

WOOL INDUSTRIES RESEARCH ASSOCIATION.
— WIRA NEWS.
— WIRA TEST METHOD.

WORCESTER CITY ARCHAEOLOGICAL RESEARCH GROUP.
— WORCESTERSHIRE ARCHAEOLOGY NEWSLETTER.

WORCESTER CITY MUSEUM.
— WORCESTERSHIRE ARCHAEOLOGY NEWSLETTER.

WORCESTER FOUNDATION FOR EXPERIMENTAL BIOLOGY.
— RESEARCH IN PROSTAGLANDINS.

WORCESTERSHIRE ARCHAEOLOGICAL SOCIETY.
— WORCESTERSHIRE ARCHAEOLOGY NEWSLETTER.

WORCESTERSHIRE & SHERWOOD FORESTERS REGIMENT.
— FIRM & FORESTER.

WORKERS' EDUCATIONAL ASSOCIATION: FARNHAM
BRANCH.
— FARNHAM PAPERS.

WORKERS' PARTY OF SCOTLAND (MARXIST-LENINIST).
— SCOTTISH VANGUARD. JOURNAL OF THE ...

WORLD BANK.
SEE: INTERNATIONAL BANK FOR RECONSTRUCTION
AND DEVELOPMENT.

WORLD COUNCIL OF PEACE.
— PERSPECTIVES.

WORLD FEDERATION OF SCOTTISH SOCIETIES &
INDIVIDUALS.
— SCOTNEWS. NEWSLETTER OF THE ...

WORLD FUTURE SOCIETY.
— FUTURIST. A NEWSLETTER FOR TOMORROW'S WORLD.

WORLD HEALTH ORGANIZATION.
— VECTOR GENETICS.
— WHO FOOD ADDITIVES SERIES.

WORLD JEWISH CONGRESS.
— CHRISTIAN ATTITUDES ON JEWS & JUDAISM.

WORLD MEETINGS INFORMATION CENTER.
— WORLD MEETINGS: SOCIAL & BEHAVIORAL SCIENCES,
EDUCATION & MANAGEMENT.

WORLD METEOROLOGICAL ORGANIZATION.
— GARP SPECIAL REPORT.
— REPORTS ON MARINE SCIENCE AFFAIRS.
— REPORTS ON WMO/IHD PROJECTS.
— WORLD WEATHER WATCH PLANNING REPORT.

WORLD ORGANISATION FOR EARLY CHILDHOOD
EDUCATION.
— INTERNATIONAL JOURNAL OF EARLY CHILDHOOD.

WORLD PEACE THROUGH LAW CENTER: SECTION ON LAW
& COMPUTER TECHNOLOGY.
— LAW & COMPUTER TECHNOLOGY.

WORLD STUDENT CHRISTIAN FEDERATION.
— FEDERATION NEWS.
— W.S.C.F. NEWSLETTER.

WORLD UNION OF JEWISH STUDIES.
— NEWSLETTER, THE WORLD UNION OF JEWISH STUDIES.

WORLD WILDLIFE FUND.
— YEARBOOK, WORLD WILDLIFE FUND.                            XXX

WORLDWIDE NEWSPAPER COLLECTORS CLUB.
— WORLDWIDE NEWSPAPER COLLECTING & PRESS
HISTORY.

WORSHIPFUL COMPANY OF GOLDSMITHS.
— GOLDSMITH TODAY. BULLETIN OF THE ...

WRITERS & SCHOLARS INTERNATIONAL.
— INDEX. A RUNNING CHRONICLE OF CENSORSHIP &
THE SUPPRESSION OF FREE EXPRESSION AROUND THE
WORLD.

WROCLAWSKIE TOWARZYSTWO NAUKOWE.
— LITTERARIA. TEORIA LITERATURY, METODOLOGIA,
KULTURA, HUMANISTYKA.

WROCLAWSKIE WYDAWNICTWO PRASOWE RSW 'PRASA'.
— ODRA, MIESIECZNIK SPOLECZNO-KULTURALNY.

WURZWEILER SCHOOL OF SOCIAL WORK.
— JEWISH SOCIAL WORK FORUM.

WYE COLLEGE: DEPARTMENT OF ECONOMICS.
— BRITISH ISLES TOMATO SURVEY.

WYOMING GEOLOGICAL ASSOCIATION.
— EARTH SCIENCE BULLETIN.

(WYOMING) GEOLOGICAL SURVEY.
— MEMOIRS, GEOLOGICAL SURVEY OF WYOMING.

WYZSZA SZKOLA EKONOMICZNA W KRAKOWIE.
— ZESZYTY NAUKOWE WYZSZEJ SZKOLY EKONOMICZNEJ W
KRAKOWIE: SERIA SPECJALNA: ROZPRAWY HABILIT-
ACYJNE.

WYZSZA SZKOLA NAUK SPOLECZNYCH: KATEDRA HIST-
ORII POWSZECHNEJ I STOSUNKOW MIEDZYNARODOWYCH.
— MATERIALY I STUDIA, KATEDRA HISTORII POW-
SZECHNEJ I STOSUNKOW MIEDZYNARODOWYCH, WYZSZA
SZKOLA NAUK SPOLECZNYCH.

WYZSZA SZKOLA PEDAGOGICZNA W GDANSKU: WYDZIAL
MATEMATYKI, FIZYKI I CHEMII.
— ZESZYTY NAUKOWE WYZSZEJ SZKOLY PEDAGOGICZNEJ
W GDANSKU: MATEMATYKA, FIZYKA, CHEMIA.

WYZSZA SZKOLA ROLNICZA W SZCZECINIE.
— ROZPRAWY, WYZSZA SZKOLA ROLNICZA W SZCZECINIE.XX

YACIMIENTOS PETROLIFEROS FISCALES BOLIVIANOS:
BIBLIOTECA CENTRAL.
— BIBLIOGRAFIA DE YACIMIENTOS PETROLIFEROS
FISCALES BOLIVIANOS.

YALE UNIVERSITY: LIBRARY.
— BIBLIOGRAPHICAL SERIES, LIBRARY, YALE UNIVER-
SITY.

YALE UNIVERSITY: SCHOOL OF DRAMA.
— YALE/THEATRE.

YALOVA BAHCE KULTURLERI ARASTIRMA VE EGITIM
MERKEZI.
— YALOVA BAHCE KULTURLERI ARASTIRMA VE EGITIM
MERKEZI DERGI. JOURNAL OF THE YALOVA HORTI-
CULTURAL RESEARCH & TRAINING CENTER.

YALOVA HORTICULTURAL RESEARCH & TRAINING CENTRE
SEE: YALOVA BAHCE KULTURLERI ARASTIRMA VE
EGITIM MERKEZI.

YAMAGATA KENRITSU YAMAGATA CHUO KOTO GAKKO.
— YAMAGATA KENRITSU YAMAGATA CHUO KOTO GAKKO
KENKYU KIYO.

YASHIRO GAKUIN DAIGAKU.
— YASHIRO GAKUIN DAIGAKU KIYO. ANNUAL REVIEW
OF YASHIROGAKUIN UNIVERSITY.

YESHIVA UNIVERSITY: WURZWEILER SCHOOL OF
SOCIAL WORK.                                                        000
SEE: WURZEILER ...

YORK UNIVERSITY, TORONTO.
— PHILOSOPHY OF THE SOCIAL SCIENCES.

YORKSHIRE ANARCHIST FEDERATION.
— LIBERTY.                                                          XXX

YOUNG WRITER GROUP.
— YOUNG WRITER.

YUGOSLAV UNION OF BIOLOGICAL SCIENCES.                              000
SEE: SAVEZ BIOLOSKIH DRUSTAVA JUGOSLAVIJE.

ZAGREB MUSIC ACADEMY: INSTITUTE OF MUSICOLOGY.
— INTERNATIONAL REVIEW OF THE AESTHETICS &
SOCIOLOGY OF MUSIC.                                                 XXX
— INTERNATIONAL REVIEW OF MUSIC AESTHETICS &
SOCIOLOGY.

ZAKLAD NARODOWY IM. OSSOLINSKICH WE WROCLAWIU.
— MONOGRAFIE SLASKIE OSSOLINEUM.

(ZAMBIA) DEPARTMENT OF METEOROLOGY.
— AGROMETEOROLOGICAL REPORT.
— CLIMATE DATA PUBLICATION.

(ZAMBIA) DEPARTMENT OF WILDLIFE, FISHERIES &
NATIONAL PARKS: FISHERIES RESEARCH DIVISION.                        XXX
— FISHERIES RESEARCH BULLETIN (ZAMBIA).                            XXX

(ZAMBIA) MINISTRY OF NATURAL RESOURCES &
TOURISM.
— RESEARCH NOTES, DIVISION FOREST RESEARCH,
MINISTRY OF NATURAL RESOURCES & TOURISM.

ZAVOD ZA EKONOMSKE EKSPERTIZE.
— AUTOMATIZACIJA POSLOVANJA.

ZAVOD ZA SPOMENSKO VARSTVO S.R. SLOVENIJE.
— VARSTVO NARAVE.

ZAVOD ZA STRANA ZITA.
— ZBORNIK RADOVA ZAVODA ZA STRANA ZITA.

ZAVODY NA VYROBU LOZISK.
— FORUM. VYBER VEDECKYCH A TECHNICKYCH PRAC
ZVL.

ZENTRALES GEOLOGISHCHES INSTITUT (BERLIN).
— ABHANDLUNGEN, ZENTRALES GEOLOGISCHES INSTITUT
(BERLIN).
— JAHRBUCH FUR GEOLOGIE.

ZENTRALINSTITUT FUR FERTIGUNGSTECHNIK: BEREICH
UMFORMTECHNIK.
— UMFORMTECHNIK.

**ZENTRALINSTITUT FUR PHYSIK DER ERDE.**
— VEROFFENTLICHUNGEN DES ZENTRALINSTITUTS FUR
PHYSIK DER ERDE.

**ZENTRALINSTITUT FUR SCHWEISSTECHNIK DER
DEUTSCHEN DEMOKRATISCHEN REPUBLIK.**
— MITTEILUNGEN, ZENTRALINSTITUT FUR SCHWEISS-
TECHNIK DER DEUTSCHEN DEMOKRATISCHEN
REPUBLIK.

**ZESPOL DO SPRAW CHLODNICTWA I NACZELNA ORGAN-
IZACJA TECHNICZNA.**
— BIULETYN CHLODNICZY.                                    XXX
SUBS (1966): CHLODNICTWO.
— CHLODNICTWO.                                            XXX

**ZJEDNOCZENIE PRZEMYSLU CHEMII GOSPODARCZEJ.**
— TLUSZCZE, SRODKI PIORACE, KOSMETYKI.                    XXX

**ZONAL'NYJ NAUCHNO-ISSLEDOVATEL'SKIJ I
PROEKTNYJ INSTITUT TIPOVOGO I EKSPERIMENT-
AL'NOGO PROEKTIROVANIJA ZHILYKH OBSHCHEST-
VENNYKH ZDANIJ GORODA KIEVA.**
— STROITEL'STVO I ARKHITEKTURA (KIEV).

**ZOOLOGICAL MUSEUM (AMSTERDAM): ICHTHYOLOGY
DEPARTMENT.**
— BULLETIN OF AQUATIC BIOLOGY.

**ZOOLOGICAL SOCIETY OF PAKISTAN.**
— PAKISTAN JOURNAL OF ZOOLOGY.

**ZOOLOGICAL SURVEY OF PAKISTAN.**
— RECORDS, ZOOLOGICAL SURVEY OF PAKISTAN.

**ZOOLOGISCHES FORSCHUNGSINSTITUT.**
— MYOTIS. MITTEILUNGSBLATT FUER FLEDERMAUS.

# Index of Library Symbols

AB——— ABERYSTWYTH.

AB/N–1  NATIONAL LIBRARY OF WALES. L/A/P
AB/U–1  UNIVERSITY COLLEGE OF WALES, GENERAL
LIBRARY. L/*A
AB/U–2  WELSH PLANT BREEDING STATION, PLAS
GOGERDDAN, CARDS.


AD——— ABERDEEN.

AD/R–1  MACAULAY INSTITUTE FOR SOIL RESEARCH,
CRAIGIEBUCKLER. L/*A
AD/R–2  ROWETT RESEARCH INSTITUTE (REID LIBR.),
BUCKSBURN, ABERDEENSHIRE. ⟨JT. LIBR. WITH:
COMMONW. BUR. OF ANIM. NUTRITION⟩
AD/U1  UNIVERSITY OF ABERDEEN (UNIV. LIBR.),
KINGS COLLEGE. L/A/P
AD/U–2  MARISCHAL COLLEGE, ABERDEEN.


BD——— BRADFORD.

BD/U–1  UNIVERSITY OF BRADFORD (UNIV. LIBR.),
RICHMOND RD., BRADFORD, YORKS. BD7 1DP.


BH——— BIRMINGHAM.

BH/C–1  NOW AS BH/U–3, Q.V.
BH/C–2  CITY OF BIRM. COLLEGE OF COMMERCE,
ASTON ST., GOSTA GREEN, 4. L/A/XP
BH/C–3  SELLY OAK COLLEGES, 29. L/A/*P
BH/F–1  AUSTIN MOTOR CO. LTD. (TECHNICAL
INFORMATION BUREAU), BOX 41, GPO, L/A/*P
BH/P–1  BIRM. CITY LIBRARIES (REFERENCE LIBR.),
RATCLIFFE PLACE, 1. *L/A/P
BH/U–1  UNIVERSITY OF BIRM. (UNIV. LIBR.),
EDGBASTON, 15. L/*A/P
BH/U–2  INSTITUTE OF EDUCATION, UNIV OF BIRM.,
50, WELLINGTON RD., EDGBASTON, 15,. L/A/*P
BH/U–3  UNIVERSITY OF ASTON IN BIRMINGHAM,
GOSTA GREEN, 4 ⟨PREV: (BIRM.) COLL. OF
ADVANCED TECHNOLOGY⟩. XL/XF/A/P/M


BL——— BELFAST.

BL/C–1  STRANMILLIS COLLEGE, BELFAST, BT9 5DY.
*L/XF/A/P/XM
BL/P–1  BELF. PUBLIC LIBRARY, ROYAL AVE., 1. L/A/P
BL/U–1  QUEENS UNIVERSITY OF BELF. L/*A/P


BN——— BANGOR, NORTH WALES

BN/U–1  UNIVERSITY COLLEGE OF NORTH WALES.
L/*A/P
BN/U–2  UNIV. COLL. OF NORTH WALES (SCIENCE
LIBR.)


BR——— BRISTOL.

BR/C–1  BRIS. COLLEGE OF SCIENCE & TECHNOLOGY,
ASHLEY DOWN, 7. L/A/P
BR/F–1  IMPERIAL TOBACCO GROUP (RES. DEP. LIBR.),
RALEIGH RD., 3. L/*A/*P
BR/P–1  BRIS. CITY LIBRARIES (CENTRAL LIBR.),
COLLEGE GREEN, 1. L/A/P
BR/U–1  UNIVERSITY OF BRIS., 8. L/*A/P
BR/U–2  INSTITUTE OF EDUCATION, UNIV. OF BRIS.,
19 BERKELEY SQUARE, 8.
BR/U–3  ENGINEERING LABORATORIES, UNIV. OF BRIS.
UNIVERSITY WALK, 8.
BR/U–4  (LONG ASHTON) RESEARCH STATION, DEP.
OF AGRIC. & HORTIC., UNIV. OF BRIS., LONG ASHTON
L/*A/P


BT——— BRIGHTON.

BT/C–1  BRIGHTON COLLEGE: FACULTY OF ARTS &
DESIGN, GRAND PARADE, 7. L/A/*P
BT/U–1  UNIVERSITY OF SUSSEX, FALMER. L/*A/*P


CA——— CAMBRIDGE.

CA/M–1  DEP. OF PATHOLOGY, UNIV. OF CAMBRIDGE,
(KANTHACK LIBR.), TENNIS COURT RD. L/*A/*P
CA/M–2  PHYSIOLOGICAL LABORATORY, UNIV. OF
CAMB., DOWNING ST. *L/*A/P
CA/M–3  PSYCHOLOGICAL LABORATORY, DEP. OF
EXPERIMENTAL PSYCHOL., UNIV. OF CAMB.,
DOWNING ST. *L/*A/*P
CA/M–4  SCHOOL OF VETERINARY MEDICINE, UNIV.
OF CAMB., MADINGLEY RD. *L/*A/*P
CA/M–5  INSTITUTE OF ANIMAL PHYSIOLOGY
(AGRICULTURAL RESEARCH COUNCIL), BABRAHAM.
L/*A/*P
CA/M–7  SEE CA/M–8
CA/M–8  UNIVERSITY MEDICAL LIBRARY, ADDENBROOK'S
HOSPITAL, HILLS ROAD.
CA/P–1  CAMB. CITY LIBRARIES (CENTRAL LIBR.),
GUILDHALL. L/A/*P
CA/R–1  LOW TEMPERATURE RESEARCH STATION,
DOWNING ST. *L/*A/XP ⟨NOW FOOD RESEARCH
INSTITUTE, COLNEY LANE, NORWICH, & MEAT
RESEARCH INSTITUTE, LANGFORD, BRISTOL.⟩
CA/R–2  PLANT BREEDING INSTITUTE, TRUMPINGTON.
*L/*A
CA/S–1  TYNDALE LIBRARY FOR BIBLICAL RESEARCH
(TYNDALE FELLOWSHIP FOR BIBLICAL RES.),
TYNDALE HOUSE, 36 SELWYN GARDENS, CAMB.
XL/*A/XP/XM
CA/U–1  UNIVERSITY LIBRARY, CAMBRIDGE. *L/*A/P
CA/U–2  SCIENTIFIC PERIODICALS LIBRARY ⟨PREV:
CAMBRIDGE PHILOSOPHICAL LIBRARY⟩, BENE'T
STREET.
CA/U–3  FACULTY OF ARCHAEOLOGY &
ANTHROPOLOGY (HADDON LIBRARY), UNIV. OF
CAMBRIDGE, DOWNING ST. *L/*A/*P
CA/U–4  DEP. OF ENGINEERING, UNIV. OF CAMBRIDGE,
TRUMPINGTON ST. *L/*A/*P
CA/U–5  DEP. OF GEOGRAPHY, UNIV. OF CAMBRIDGE,
DOWNING PLACE. XL/*A/XP
CA/U–6  DEP. OF ZOOLOGY (BALFOUR LIBRARY),
UNIV. OF CAMBRIDGE, DOWNING ST. *L/*A/XP
CA/U–7  BOTANY SCHOOL, UNIV. OF CAMBRIDGE,
DOWNING ST. L/*A/*P
CA/U–8  CHRISTS COLLEGE. XL/*A/P
CA/U–9  INSTITUTE OF EDUCATION, UNIV. OF CAMB.,
SHAFTESBURY RD. *L/A
CA/U10  MOLTENO INSTITUTE OF BIOLOGY &
PARASITOLOGY, DOWNING ST. *L/*A/XP
CA/U11  DEPARTMENT OF AGRICULTURAL SCIENCE &
APPLIED BIOLOGY, UNIV. OF CAMBRIDGE. *L/*A/*P
CA/U12  SCOTT POLAR RESEARCH INSTITUTE.
LENSFIELD RD. *L/*A/P
CA/U13  SQUIRE LAW LIBR., OLD SCHOOLS. XL/*A/*P
CA/U14  SEDGWICK MUSEUM, DOWNING ST. XL
CA/U15  DEP. OF GENETICS, UNIV. OF CAMBRIDGE
CA/U37  INSTITUTE OF CRIMINOLOGY, UNIV. OF
CAMB., WEST RD., CB3 9DT.


CB——— CANTERBURY.

CB/U–1  UNIVERSITY OF KENT AT C'BURY. L/A/*P


CC——— COLCHESTER.

CC/U–1  UNIVERSITY OF ESSEX, P.O. BOX NO. 24,
WIVENHOE PARK, COLCHESTER, CO4 3UA.


CO——— CORK.

CO/U–1  UNIVERSITY COLLEGE, CORK. *L/*A/*P

CR —— CARDIFF.

CR/M–1  WELSH NATIONAL SCHOOL OF MEDICINE, HEATH PARK, CARDIFF, CF4 4XN.
CR/N–1  NATIONAL MUSEUM OF WALES. L/A
CR/S–1  CARDIFF NATURALISTS SOCIETY, C/O NAT. MUS. OF WALES. *L/*A/XP
CR/U–1  UNIVERSITY COLLEGE OF SOUTH WALES & MONMOUTHSHIRE, CATHAYS PARK. L/*A/*P

CV —— COVENTRY.

CV/C–1  LANCHESTER POLYTECHNIC. L/P/XM
CV/F–1  COURTAULDS LTD. (TECHNICAL INFORMATION BUREAU), FOLESHILL RD. L/*A/*P
CV/U–1  UNIVERSITY OF WARWICK. L/*A/XP

DB —— DUBLIN.

DB/S–1  ROYAL IRISH ACADEMY, 19 DAWSON ST., 2. L(THRU ICLS)/F(THRU ICLS)/*A/P/XM
DB/U–1  TRINITY COLLEGE LIBRARY, DUBLIN 2. XL/*A/P
DB/U–2  UNIVERSITY COLLEGE, DUBLIN, EARLSFORT TERRACE, 2. L/A/P

DN —— DUNDEE.

DN/R–1  SCOTTISH HORTICULTURAL RESEARCH INSTITUTE, MYLNEFIELD, INVERGOWRIE. L/*A/P
DN/U–1  UNIVERSITY OF DUNDEE, DD1 4HN. L/*A/XP

DR —— DURHAM.

DR/U–1  UNIVERSITY OF DURHAM (UNIV. LIBR.) L/*A/XP
DR/U–2  INSTITUTE OF EDUCATION, UNIV. OF DUR., OLD SHIRE HALL.

ED —— EDINBURGH.

ED/M–1  ROYAL COLLEGE OF PHYSICIANS OF EDINB., 9 QUEEN ST., 2. *L/A/P
ED/M–2  ROYAL (DICK) SCHOOL OF VETERINARY STUDIES, SUMMERHALL.
ED/N–1  NATIONAL LIBRARY OF SCOTLAND, 1. XL/*A/P
ED/P–1  EDINB. PUBLIC LIBRARIES (CENTRAL LIBR.), GEORGE IV BRIDGE, 1. *L/A/P
ED/R–1  POULTRY RESEARCH CENTRE (AGRIC. RES. COUN.), KINGS BUILDINGS, WEST MAINS RD., EDINB, 8. L/*A/P
ED/R–2  ANIMAL BREEDING LIBRARY, WEST MAINS RD., EDINB., 9. ⟨JT., LIBR. OF: ANIMAL BREEDING RES. ORG. (ARC): (&) COMMONW. BUR. OF ANIM. BREEDING & GENETICS⟩ L/*F/A/P
ED/R–3  ROYAL OBSERVATORY, BLACKFORD HILL, 9. L/*A/*P
ED/S–1  ROYAL SCOTTISH GEOGRAPHICAL SOCIETY, 10 RANDOLPH CRESCENT, 3. L/XA/P
ED/S–2  ROYAL SOCIETY OF EDINB., 22 GEORGE ST., EDINB., 2. L/A/P
ED/U–1  UNIVERSITY OF EDINB. (UNIV. LIBR.), OLD COLLEGE, SOUTH BRIDGE, 8. L/*A/*P
ED/U–2  EDINB. SCHOOL OF AGRICULTURE, WEST MAINS RD, 9. L/*A/*P
ED/U–3  HERIOT-WATT UNIVERSITY, CHAMBERS ST., 1. L/*A/*P

EX —— EXETER.

EX/U–1  UNIVERSITY OF EXETER (ROBOROUGH LIBR.) L/*A/*P
EX/U–2  INSTITUTE OF EDUCATION, UNIV. OF EX., GANDY ST.

GA —— GALWAY.

GA/U–1  UNIVERSITY COLLEGE, GALWAY. L/A/XP

GL —— GLASGOW.

GL/C–1  NOW AS GL/U–2, Q.V.
GL/C–2  NOW AS GL/U–3, Q.V.
GL/M–1  ROYAL COLLEGE OF PHYSICIANS & SURGEONS, 242 VINCENT ST., C2.
GL/P–1  MITCHELL LIBRARY, NORTH ST., C3. *L/A/P
GL/R–1  NATIONAL ENGINEERING LABORATORY, EAST KILBRIDE, BLLD (XY/N–1) MUST BE TRIED FIRST FOR ANY ITEM. *L/F/*A/*P/*M
GL/U–1  UNIVERSITY OF GLASGOW, W2. L/*A/P
GL/U–2  UNIVERSITY OF STRATHCLYDE (ANDERSONIAN LIBR.), MCCANCE BUILDING, RICHMOND ST., GLASGOW, G1 1XQ. *L/*A/P
GL/U–3  SCOTTISH COLLEGE, UNIV. OF STRATHCLYDE ⟨PREV: SCOTT. COLL. OF COMMERCE⟩ (COLL. LIBR.), PITT ST., C2. L/*A/P

HL —— HULL.

HL/P–1  KINGSTON UPON HULL PUBLIC LIBRARIES (CENTRAL LIBR.), ALBION ST. L/A/P
HL/U–1  UNIVERSITY OF HULL (BRYNMOR JONES LIBR.) COTTINGHAM RD. L/*A/P
HL/U–2  INSTITUTE OF EDUCATION, UNIV. OF HULL, 173 COTTINNGHAM RD. L/A/P

LA —— LANCASTER.

LA/U–1  UNIVERSITY OF LANCASTER (UNIV. LIBR.), BAILRIGG, LANCS. L/*A/*P

LB —— LOUGHBOROUGH, LEICS.

LB/C–1  LOUGHB. COLLEGE OF FURTHER EDUCATION. *L/A/*P ⟨PREV AS XE/C–1⟩
LB/U–1  LOUGHB. UNIVERSITY OF TECHNOLOGY. L/*A/*P ⟨PREV AS XE/C–2⟩

LC —— LEICESTER.

LC/C–1  CITY OF LEICESTER POLYTECHNIC L/A/P
LC/P–1  LEIC. CITY LIBRARIES, BISHOP ST. L/A/P
LC/U–1  UNIVERSITY OF LEIC., UNIVERSITY RD. *L/*A/*P
LC/U–2  SCHOOL OF EDUCATION, UNIV. OF LEIC., 21 UNIVERSITY RD. L/*F/A/*P/XM

LD —— LEEDS.

LD/P–1  LEEDS CITY LIBRARIES (CENTRAL LIBR.), 1. XL/A/P

*LD/T–1* COAL TAR RESEARCH ASSOCIATION, OXFORD ROAD, GOMERSAL. *L/*A/*P

*LD/T–2* WOOL INDUSTRIES RESEARCH ASSOCIATION, TORRIDON, HEADINGLEY LANE, 6. L/*F/*A/P/XM

*LD/U–1* UNIV. OF LEEDS (BROTHERTON LIBRARY), 2. L/*A/P

*LD/U–2* INSTITUTE OF EDUCATION, UNIV. OF LEEDS, LEEDS 2. L/*A/XP


**LN——— LONDONDERRY.**

*LN/U–1* MAGEE UNIVERSITY COLLEGE. L/A/*P


**LO ——— LONDON.**

*LO/C–1* ACTON TECHNICAL COLLEGE, HIGH ST., W3. L/*A

*LO/C–2* NOW AS *LO/U21*, Q.V.

*LO/C–3* POLYTECHNIC OF THE SOUTH BANK, BOROUGH RD., LONDON, SE1. *L/*A/*P

*LO/C–4* CHELSEA COLLEGE OF SCIENCE & TECHNOLOGY, MANRESA RD., SW3. L/*A/P

*LO/C–5* EALING TECHNICAL COLLEGE, ST. MARYS RD. W5. L/*A/XP

*LO/C–6* ENFIELD COLLEGE OF TECHNOLOGY, QUEENSWAY, ENFIELD, MIDDX. L/A/XP

*LO/C–7* HORNSEY COLLEGE OF ART, CROUCH END HILL, N8. L/*A/XP

*LO/C–8* ISLEWORTH POLYTECHNIC, LONDON RD., ISLEWORTH, MIDDX. L/A/P

*LO/C–9* JEWS COLLEGE, 11 MONTAGU PLACE, MONTAGU SQUARE, W1. *L/*A/XP

*LO/C10* KINGSTON COLLEGE OF TECHNOLOGY, PENRHYN RD., KINGSTON/THAMES, SURREY. L/A/*P

*LO/C11* NATIONAL COLLEGE OF FOOD TECHNOLOGY, ST GEORGES AVE., WEYBRIDGE, SURREY. *L/A/P

*LO/C12* NATIONAL COLLEGE FOR HEATING, VENTILATING, REFRIGERATION & FAN ENGINEERING, BORO POLYTECH, BOROUGH RD, SE1. L/A

*LO/C13* NOW AS *LO/U18*, Q.V.

*LO/C14* NORTHERN POLYTECHNIC, HOLLOWAY, N7. ⟨JT. LIBR. WITH NAT. COLL. RUBBER TECHNOL.⟩

*LO/C15* POLYTECHNIC OF CENTRAL LONDON, 309 REGENT ST., W1R 8AL.

*LO/C16* ST MARYS COLLEGE, STRAWBERRY HILL, TWICKENHAM. L/*A/XP

*LO/C17* NORTH EAST LONDON POLYTECHNIC, FOREST RD., LONDON, E17 4JB. L/A/P

*LO/C18* THAMES POLYTECHNIC, WELLINGTON ST., WOOLWICH, LONDON, SE18. L/XA/P

*LO/C19* NOW AS *LO/U20*, Q.V.

*LO/C20* MARIA ASSUMPTA TRAINING COLLEGE, 23 KENSINGTON SQ., W8. *L/*A

*LO/F–1* BRITISH INSULATED CALLENDERS CABLES LTD (RESEARCH DEP.), 38 WOOD LANE, W12. L/XA/*P

*LO/F–2* DECCA RADAR LTD. (RESEARCH LABS.), LYON RD., HERSHAM, WALTON/THAMES, SURREY. *L/*A/*P

*LO/F–3* EMI ELECTRONICS LTD. (EMI CENTRAL TECH. LIBR.), BLYTH RD., HAYES, MIDDX. L/*A/*P

*LO/F–4* ENGLISH ELECTRIC HOUSE, STRAND, WC2. *L/*A/*P

*LO/F–5* GEORGE WIMPEY & CO. LTD. (CENTRAL LAB.), LANCASTER RD., SOUTHALL, MIDDX. L/XA/*P

*LO/F–6* HAWKER SIDDELEY DYNAMICS LTD. (TECH. LIBR.), WELKIN HOUSE, CHARTERHOUSE SQ., EC1. L/XA/XP

*LO/F–7* IBM UNITED KINGDOM LTD., 101 WIGMORE STREET, W.1. *L/*A/*P

*LO/F–8* KODAK LTD. (RESEARCH LAB.), WEALDSTONE, HARROW, MIDDX. *L/XA

*LO/F–9* METAL BOX CO. LTD. (RESEARCH DIV.), KENDAL AVE., WESTFIELDS RD., W3. *L/XA/P

*LO/F10* BROOKE BOND OXO LIBRARY, 20 SOUTHWARK BRIDGE RD., SE1. L/*A/*P

*LO/F12* ILFORD LTD. (RESEARCH LIBR.), 7-9 RODEN ST., ILF., ESSEX. L/XA/*P

*LO/F13* LLOYDS & BOLSA INTERNATIONAL BANK LTD., 100 PALL MALL, SW1Y 5HP. XL/*A/*P/XM

*LO/F14* SHELL INTERNATIONAL PETROLEUM CO. LTD. (CENTRAL INF. SERVICES), SHELL CENTRE, SE1.

*LO/M–1* CHARING CROSS HOSPITAL MEDICAL SCHOOL (LIBRARY), FULHAM PALACE ROAD, W6 8RF. L/*A/P

*LO/M–2* GUYS HOSPITAL MEDICAL SCHOOL (WILLS LIBR.), SE1. L/*A/P (*L HOSP. DEPS.)

*LO/M–3* INSTITUTE OF CANCER RESEARCH, (CHESTER BEATTY RES. INST.), ROYAL CANCER HOSPITAL, FULHAM RD., SW3. L/*A/P

*LO/M–4* INSTITUTE OF CHILD HEALTH, HOSP. FOR SICK CHILDREN, GT. ORMOND ST., WC1. L/*A/*P

*LO/M–5* INSTITUTE OF DERMATOLOGY, ST. JOHNS HOSP. FOR DISEASES OF THE SKIN, LISLE ST., WC2. *L/*A/*P

*LO/M–6* INSTITUTE OF LARYNGOLOGY & OTOLOGY 330/2 GRAYS INN RD., WC1. XL/*A/*P

*LO/M–7* INSTITUTE OF PSYCHOANALYSIS, 63 NEW CAVENDISH ST., W1. *L/*A/XP

*LO/M–8* LISTER INSTITUTE OF PREVENTIVE MEDICINE, CHELSEA BRIDGE RD., SW1. L/*A/P

*LO/M–9* LONDON HOSPITAL MEDICAL COLLEGE, TURNER ST., E1. *L/*A/*P

*LO/M10* LONDON SCHOOL OF HYGIENE & TROPICAL MEDICINE, KEPPEL ST., WC1. *L/*A

*LO/M11* MIDDLESEX HOSPITAL MEDICAL SCHOOL, MORTIMER ST., W1. L/XA/P

*LO/M12* NATIONAL INSTITUTE FOR MEDICAL RESEARCH (MEDICAL RESEARCH COUNCIL), THE RIDGEWAY, MILL HILL, NW7. L/XA/P

*LO/M13* ROYAL COLLEGE OF PHYSICIANS OF LONDON, 11 ST. ANDREWS PLACE, NW1. *L/*A/P

*LO/M14* ROYAL COLLEGE OF SURGEONS OF ENGLAND, LINCOLNS INN FIELDS, WC2. L/*A/P

*LO/M15* ROYAL COLLEGE OF VETERINARY SURGEONS (MEMORIAL LIBR.), 32 BELGRAVE SQ., SW1 L/*A/P

*LO/M16* ROYAL FREE HOSPITAL SCHOOL OF MEDICINE, 8 HUNTER ST., WC1. L/XA/P

*LO/M17* ROYAL SOCIETY OF MEDICINE, 1 WIMPOLE ST., W1. XL/*A

*LO/M18* ROYAL VETERINARY COLLEGE, ROYAL COLLEGE ST., NW1. L/*A/*P

*LO/M19* ST. BARTHOLOMEWS HOSPITAL MEDICAL COLLEGE, WEST SMITHFIELD, EC1. L/*A/P

*LO/M20* ST. THOMAS'S HOSPITAL MED. SCHOOL, SE1. L

*LO/M21* SCHOOL OF DENTAL SURGERY (STOBIE MEMORIAL LIBR.), R. DENTAL HOSP. OF LONDON, LEICESTER SQ., WC2. *L/*A/*P

*LO/M22* SCHOOL OF PHARMACY, 29/39 BRUNSWICK SQ., WC1. L/*A/*P

*LO/M23* UNIVERSITY COLLEGE HOSPITAL MEDICAL SCHOOL, UNIVERSITY ST., WC1. *L/XA/*P

*LO/M24* WELLCOME HISTORICAL MEDICAL LIBRARY, EUSTON RD., NW1. *L/A/P

*LO/M25* WELLCOME RESEARCH LABORATORIES, LANGLEY COURT, BECKENHAM, KENT. *L/*A/*P

*LO/M26* CENTRAL VETERINARY LABORATORY, MIN. OF AGRIC., FISH & FOOD, NEW HAW, WEYBRIDGE, SURREY. L/*A/XP

*LO/M27* DEPARTMENT OF HEALTH & SOCIAL SECURITY, ALEXANDER FLEMING HOUSE, ELEPHANT & CASTLE, SE1.

*LO/M28* OFFICE OF HEALTH ECONOMICS, MERCURY HOUSE, 195 KNIGHTSBRIDGE, SW7. *L/*A/P

*LO/M29* MEDICAL RESEARCH COUNCIL LABORA-TORIES, WOODMANSTERNE RD., CARSHALTON, SY. *L/P

*LO/M30* ROYAL POSTGRADUATE MEDICAL SCHOOL OF LONDON, HAMMERSMITH HOSP., DUCANE RD., W12. L/*A

LO/M31   KINGS COLLEGE HOSPITAL MEDICAL SCHOOL, DENMARK HILL, SE5. L/*F/*A/P

LO/M32   BRITISH MEDICAL ASSOCIATION, TAVISTOCK SQUARE, WC1. XL/XF/*A/P

LO/M33   INSTITUTE OF PSYCHIATRY, DE CRESPIGNY PARK, DENMARK HILL, SE5. L/XA/XP

LO/M34   BRITISH DENTAL ASSOCIATION, 64 WIMPOLE ST., W1. L/*F/*A/P/XM

LO/N–1   BRITISH LIBRARY: REFERENCE DIVISION, GREAT RUSSELL ST., WC1 3DG. ⟨PREV: BRITISH MUSEUM⟩ XL/*A/P

LO/N–2   BRITISH MUSEUM (NATURAL HISTORY), CROMWELL RD., SW7. XL/*A/P

LO/N–3   NOW AS XY/N–1, Q.V.

LO/N–4   SCIENCE MUSEUM LIBRARY, SW7. XL/*A/P (*L THROUGH BLLD).

LO/N–5   DEPARTMENT OF INDUSTRY, KINGSGATE HOUSE, VICTORIA ST., SW1. ⟨PREV: MIN. OF TECHNOLOGY⟩

LO/N–6   MINISTRY OF AGRICULTURE, FISHERIES & FOOD (MAIN LIBR.), 3 WHITEHALL PLACE, SW1. L/A/XP

LO/N–7   SEE LO/N35

LO/N–8   INSTITUTE OF GEOLOGICAL SCIENCES ⟨PREV: GEOLOGICAL SURVEY & MUSEUM⟩ EXHIBITION ROAD, SW7. *L/A/P/M

LO/N–9   NOW AS LO/N14, Q.V.

LO/N10   DEPARTMENT OF INDUSTRY, 1 VICTORIA ST., SW1. ⟨PREV: BOARD OF TRADE⟩

LO/N11   DEPARTMENT OF EDUCATION & SCIENCE, 38 BELGRAVE SQUARE, SW1.

LO/N12   INDIA OFFICE LIBRARY, 197, BLACKFRIARS ROAD, SE1. *L/A/P

LO/N13   BRITISH LIBRARY: SCIENCE REFERENCE LIBRARY: BAYSWATER BRANCH, 10 PORCHESTER GARDENS, QUEENSWAY, W2 4DE. ⟨PREV: NATIONAL REFERENCE LIBRARY FOR SCIENCE AND INVENTION⟩ XL/A/P

LO/N14   BRITISH LIBRARY: SCIENCE REFERENCE LIBRARY: HOLBORN BRANCH ⟨PATENT OFFICE LIBRARY⟩, 25, SOUTHAMPTON BUILDINGS, CHANCERY LANE, WC2A 1AW. ⟨PREV: NATIONAL REFERENCE LIBRARY FOR SCIENCE AND INVENTION⟩ XL/A/P

LO/N15   VICTORIA & ALBERT MUSEUM, SW7

LO/N16   IMPERIAL WAR MUSEUM, LAMBETH RD., SE1.

LO/N17   FOREIGN & COMMONWEALTH OFFICE, SANCTUARY BUILDINGS, GREAT SMITH ST., SW1.

LO/N35   PROCUREMENT EXECUTIVE (MIN. DEFENCE), 1-13 ST. GILES HIGH ST., LONDON WC2H 8LD.

LO/P–1   BERMONDSEY DISTRICT LIBRARY (SOUTH-WARK PUB. LIBR.), SPA RD., SE16. L/A/*P

LO/P–2   CHELSEA PUBLIC LIBRARY (KENSINGTON & CHELSEA PUB. LIBR.), MANRESA RD., SW3. L/A/P

LO/P–3   EALING CENTRAL LIBRARY, WALPOLE PARK, W5. *L/A/*P

LO/P–4   EAST HAM LIBRARY (NEWHAM PUB. LIBR.), HIGH ST. SOUTH, E6. L/A/XP

LO/P–5   FINSBURY LIBRARY (ISLINGTON PUBLIC LIBRARIES), 245 ST. JOHN ST., EC1. L/A/*P

LO/P–6   GUILDHALL LIBRARY, EC2. *L/A/P

LO/P–7   HACKNEY CENTRAL LIBRARY, MARE ST., E8. L/A/*P

LO/P–8   HAMMERSMITH PUBLIC LIBRARIES (CENTRAL LIBR.), SHEPHERD'S BUSH RD., W6. L/A/P

LO/P–9   BARNET PUBLIC LIBRARIES (CENT. LIBR.), THE BURROUGHS, NW4. L/A/P

LO/P10   HOLBORN CENTRAL LIBRARY (CAMDEN PUB. LIBR.), 32/38 THEOBALDS RD., WC1. L/A/P

LO/P11   HORNIMAN MUSEUM & LIBRARY, LONDON RD., FOREST HILL, SE23. L/A/XP

LO/P12   LAMBETH PUBLIC LIBRARIES (TATE CENTRAL LIBR.), BRIXTON OVAL, SW2. *L/*A/*P

LO/P13   LEWISHAM PUBLIC LIBRARIES, 170 BROMLEY ROAD, SE6. L/A/P

LO/P14   PADDINGTON DISTRICT LIBRARY (WEST-MINSTER PUB. LIBR.), PORCHESTER RD., W2. L/A/P

LO/P15   WESTMINSTER PUBLIC LIBRARIES, CENTRAL LIBRARY, MARYLEBONE RD., NW1. L/A/P

LO/P16   SHOREDITCH DISTRICT LIBRARY (HACKNEY PUB. LIBR.), PITFIELD ST., N1. L/A/XP

LO/P17   NEWINGTON DISTRICT LIBRARY & CUMING MUSEUM (SOUTHWARK PUB. LIBR.), WALWORTH RD., SE17. L/A/P

LO/P18   TOTTENHAM PUBLIC LIBRARY (HARINGEY PUB. LIBR.), 391 HIGH RD., N17. L/A/P

LO/P19   WEST HAM LIBRARY (NEWHAM PUB. LIBR.), WATER LANE, STRATFORD, E15. L/A/P

LO/P20   WESTMINSTER PUBLIC LIBRARIES (CENTRAL REFERENCE LIBR.), ST. MARTINS ST., WC2. *L/A/P

LO/P21   WILLESDEN CENTRAL LIBRARY (BRENT PUB. LIBR.), HIGH RD., NW10. L/A/*P

LO/P22   WIMBLEDON PUBLIC LIBRARY (MERTON PUB. LIBR.), HILL RD., SW19. L/A/*P

LO/P23   WOOLWICH PUBLIC LIBRARY (GREENWICH PUB. LIBR.), CALDERWOOD ST., SE18. L/A/P

LO/P24   BATTERSEA PUBLIC LIBRARY (WANDSWORTH PUB. LIBR.), 265 LAVENDER HILL, SW11. L/A/P

LO/R–1   ANTI-LOCUST RESEARCH CENTRE, COLLEGE HOUSE, WRIGHTS LANE, W8. *L/*A/XP

LO/R–2   COMMONWEALTH INSTITUTE OF ENTO-MOLOGY, 56 QUEENS GATE, SW7. *L/*A/*P

LO/R–3   COMMONWEALTH MYCOLOGICAL INSTITUTE, FERRY LANE, KEW, SURREY. L/XA/P

LO/R–4   ⟨NATIONAL CHEMICAL LABORATORY, NOW INCORP. INTO NAT. PHYSICAL LABORATORY⟩

LO/R–5   NATURE CONSERVANCY COUNCIL, 19 BELGRAVE SQ., SW1.

LO/R–6   TROPICAL PRODUCTS INSTITUTE, 56-62 GRAYS INN RD., WC1.

LO/R–7   SCIENCE RESEARCH COUNCIL, STATE HOUSE, HIGH HOLBORN, WC1. L/F/*A/*P

LO/S–1   BRITISH INSTITUTE OF MANAGEMENT, 80 FETTER LANE, EC4. *L/*A/P

LO/S–2   CENTRE FOR EDUCATIONAL TELEVISION OVERSEAS, NUFFIELD LODGE, REGENTS PARK, NW8. L/XA/*P

LO/S–3   CHEMICAL SOCIETY, BURLINGTON HOUSE, W1. *L/*A/P

LO/S–4   INSTITUTE OF ACTUARIES, STAPLE INN HALL, HIGH HOLBORN, WC1. L/*A/XP

LO/S–5   INSTITUTION OF PRODUCTION ENGINEERS, 10 CHESTERFIELD ST., W1. *L/*A/*P

LO/S–6   LINNEAN SOCIETY OF LONDON, BURLINGTON HOUSE, W1. L/*A/P

LO/S–7   LONDON LIBRARY, 14 ST. JAMES'S SQ., SW1. *L/XA/*P

LO/S–8   METROPOLITAN POLICE LABORATORY, NEW SCOTLAND YARD, SW1. *L/*A

LO/S–9   POLISH LIBRARY, 9 PRINCES GARDENS, SW7. *L/A/P

LO/S10   ROYAL ANTHROPOLOGICAL INSTITUTE, 6 BURLINGTON GARDENS, LONDON W1X 2EX. L/*A/XP

LO/S12   ROYAL ENTOMOLOGICAL SOCIETY OF LONDON, 41 QUEENS GATE, SW7. *L/*A/P

LO/S13   ROYAL GEOGRAPHICAL SOCIETY, KENSING-TON GORE, SW7. L/*A/P

LO/S14   ROYAL INSTITUTE OF INTERNATIONAL AFFAIRS, CHATHAM HOUSE, 10 ST. JAMES'S SQ., SW1. XL/*A/P

LO/S15   ROYAL INSTITUTE OF PUBLIC ADMINISTRA-TION, 24 PARK CRESCENT, W1. L/XA/XP

LO/S16   ROYAL INSTITUTION OF CHARTERED SURVEYORS, 12 GREAT GEORGE ST., SW1. L/*A/*P

LO/S17   GEOLOGICAL SOCIETY OF LONDON, BURLINGTON HOUSE, W1. *L/*A/*P

LO/S18   TAVISTOCK LIBRARY (TAVISTOCK CLINIC & TAVISTOCK INST. OF HUMAN RELATIONS JT. LIBR.), 3 DEVONSHIRE ST., W1. L/*A/XP

LO/S19   ZOOLOGICAL SOCIETY OF LONDON, REGENTS PARK, NW1. *L/*A/XP

LO/S20   ROYAL INSTITUTION OF GREAT BRITAIN, 21 ALBEMARLE ST., W1. *L/*A/*P

LO/S21   INSTITUTION OF WELDING, 54 PRINCES GATE, SW7. L/A/P/ ⟨NOW THE WELDING INSTITUTE, ABINGTON HALL, ABINGTON, CAMB.⟩

LO/S22   ASLIB, 3 BELGRAVE SQ., SW1.

LO/S23   INTERNATIONAL WOOL SECRETARIAT, WOOL HOUSE, CARLTON GARDENS, SW1. L/*A/P

LO/S24  CHARTERED INSURANCE INSTITUTE, THE HALL, 20 ALDERMANBURY, EC2. L/XF/*A/XP/XM

LO/S25  ROYAL BOTANIC GARDENS, KEW, RICHMOND, SURREY. *L/A/*P

LO/S26  COMMONWEALTH INSTITUTE LIBRARY, KENSINGTON HIGH ST., W8. L/*F/A/*P/XM

LO/S27  HISPANIC & LUSO BRAZILIAN COUNCILS, CANNING HOUSE, 2 BELGRAVE SQ., SW1.

LO/S28  INSTITUTE OF BANKERS, 10 LOMBARD ST., EC3.

LO/S29  GERMAN INSTITUTE, 51 PRINCES GATE, SW7. L/A/XP

LO/S30  FOLKLORE SOCIETY, C/O UNIVERSITY COLLEGE LONDON, GOWER ST., WC1.

LO/S74  INTERNATIONAL PLANNED PARENTHOOD FEDERATION, 18–20 LOWER REGENT ST., LONDON, SW1. XL/XF/*A/P/XM

LO/T–1  NOW AS XS/N–2, Q.V.

LO/T–2  BRITISH LAUNDERERS RESEARCH ASSOCIATION LABS., HILL VIEW GARDENS, NW4. *L/*A/P

LO/T–3  GAS COUNCIL, WATSON HOUSE, PETERBOROUGH ROAD, SW6. L/XA/*P

LO/T–4  MINING RESEARCH ESTABLISHMENT (NATIONAL COAL BOARD), WORTON RD., ISLEWORTH, MIDDX. *L/XA/*P ⟨NOW CLOSED⟩

LO/T–5  RESEARCH ASSOCIATION OF BRITISH PAINT, COLOUR & VARNISH MANUFACTURERS, PAINT RESEARCH STATION, WALDEGRAVE RD., TEDDINGTON, MIDDX. L/*A/*P

LO/U–1  UNIVERSITY OF LONDON (GOLDSMITHS LIBR.), SENATE HOUSE, WC1. *L/*A/P

LO/U–2  UNIVERSITY COLLEGE LONDON, GOWER ST., WC1. L/*A/P

LO/U–3  LONDON SCHOOL OF ECONOMICS & POLITICAL SCIENCE (BR. LIBR. OF POLIT. & ECON. SCI.), HOUGHTON ST., WC2. L/*A/P

LO/U–4  BEDFORD COLLEGE, REGENTS PARK, NW1. L/*A/XP

LO/U–5  BIRKBECK COLLEGE, MALET ST., WC1. L/*A/XP

LO/U–6  IMPERIAL COLLEGE OF SCIENCE & TECHNOLOGY (LYON PLAYFAIR LIBR.), 180 QUEENS GATE, SW7. L/*A/*P

LO/U–7  INSTITUTE OF CLASSICAL STUDIES, UNIV. OF LOND., 31/34 GORDON SQ., WC1. L/*A/XP

LO/U–8  INSTITUTE OF COMMONWEALTH STUDIES, UNIV. OF LOND., 27 RUSSELL SQ., WC1. XL/*A/XP

LO/U–9  INSTITUTE OF EDUCATION, UNIV. OF LOND., 11-13 RIDGMOUNT ST., WC1.

LO/U10  INSTITUTE OF GERMANIC STUDIES, UNIV. OF LONDON., 29 RUSSELL SQ., WC1. XL/*A/*P

LO/U11  KINGS COLLEGE LONDON, STRAND, WC2. L/*A/*P

LO/U12  QUEEN MARY COLLEGE, MILE END RD., E1 L/*A/P

LO/U13  ROYAL HOLLOWAY COLLEGE, ENGLEFIELD GREEN, SURREY. L/*A/*P

LO/U14  SCHOOL OF ORIENTAL & AFRICAN STUDIES, UNIV. OF LOND., WC1. L/A/*P

LO/U15  SCHOOL OF SLAVONIC & EAST EUROPEAN STUDIES, UNIV. OF LOND., WC1. XL/*A/*P

LO/U16  WESTFIELD COLLEGE, NW3. *L/*A/*P

LO/U17  WARBURG INSTITUTE, WOBURN SQ., WC1.

LO/U18  THE CITY UNIVERSITY, ⟨PREV: NORTHAMPTON COLL. OF ADV. TECHNOL.⟩ (SKINNERS LIBR.), ST. JOHN ST., EC1. *L/*F/*A/P/XM

LO/U19  INSTITUTE OF HISTORICAL RESEARCH, UNIV. OF LOND., SENATE HOUSE, WC1. XI/XF/*A/P/M

LO/U20  BRUNEL UNIVERSITY ⟨PREV: BRUNEL COLL.⟩ KINGSTON LANE, UXBRIDGE, MIDDLESEX. L/*A/*P

LO/U21  UNIVERSITY OF SURREY, GUILDFORD SURREY. *L/*A/P

LO/U22  INSTITUTE OF UNITED STATES STUDIES, UNIV. OF LOND., 31 TAVISTOCK SQ., WC1.

LO/U23  INSTITUTE OF LATIN AMERICAN STUDIES, UNIV. OF LOND., 31 TAVISTOCK SQ., WC1.

LO/U24  INSTITUTE OF ADVANCED LEGAL STUDIES, UNIV. OF LOND., 25 RUSSELL SQ., WC1.

LO/U25  INSTITUTE OF ARCHAEOLOGY, UNIV. OF LOND., 31-34 GORDON SQ., WC1.

LO/U26  COURTAULD INSTITUTE OF ART, 20 PORTMAN SQ., W1.

LV——  LIVERPOOL.

LV/P–1  LIV. PUBLIC LIBRARIES (CENTRAL LIBR.), WILLIAM BROWN ST., 3. *L/A/*P

LV/U–1  UNIV. OF LIVERPOOL (UNIV. LIBRARY), 3. L/*A/*P

LV/U–2  INSTITUTE OF EDUCATION, UNIV. OF LIV., 1 ABERCROMBY SQUARE, 7.

MA——  MANCHESTER.

MA/C–1  NOW AS MA/U–3, Q.V.

MA/F–1  CARBORUNDUM CO. LTD., (TECHNICAL LIBR.), TRAFFORD PARK, 17. L/XA/P

MA/P–1  MANC. PUBLIC LIBRARIES (CENTRAL LIBR.), ST. PETERS SQUARE, 2. *L/A/P

MA/S–1  JOHN RYLANDS LIBRARY, DEANSGATE, 3. XL/*A/P

MA/T–1  TEXTILE INSTITUTE, 10 BLACKFRIARS ST., 3. *L/*A/*P

MA/T–2  COTTON, SILK & MAN-MADE FIBRES RESEARCH ASSOCIATION, (SHIRLEY INST.), DIDSBURY, MANC. 20. L(THRU BLLD)/*A/XP

MA/U–1  UNIVERSITY OF MANCHESTER (UNIV. LIBR.), OXFORD RD., 13. L/*A/P

MA/U–2  UNIV. (OF MANC.) SCHOOL OF EDUCATION.

MA/U–3  UNIVERSITY OF MANCHESTER INSTITUTE OF SCIENCE & TECHNOLOGY ⟨PREV: MANCHESTER COLL. OF SCI. & TECHNOL.⟩ SACKVILLE ST., MANC. 1.

MA/U–4  MANCHESTER BUSINESS SCHOOL, BOOTH ST. WEST, MANCHESTER, M15 6PB.

NO——  NOTTINGHAM.

NO/P–1  NOTTINGHAM CITY LIBRARY, SOUTH SHERWOOD ST. L/A/P

NO/T–1  HOSIERY & ALLIED TRADES RESEARCH ASS., 7 GREGORY BLVD. L/*A/P

NO/U–1  UNIVERSITY OF NOTTINGHAM, UNIVERSITY PARK. L/*A/P

NO/U–2  INSTITUTE OF EDUCATION, UNIV. OF NOTT., UNIVERSITY PARK.

NR——  NORWICH.

NR/P–1  NORWICH PUBLIC LIBRARIES (CENT. LIBR.), BETHEL ST. L/A/P

NR/U–1  UNIVERSITY OF EAST ANGLIA.

NW——  NEWCASTLE/TYNE.

NW/P–1  NEWC/TYNE CITY LIBRARIES (CENT. LIBR.), NEW BRIDGES ST., 1. *L/*A/*P

NW/U–1  UNIVERSITY OF NEWCASTLE UPON TYNE ⟨PREV: KINGS COLL. (UNIV. OF DURHAM)⟩, (UNIV. LIBR.). L/*F/*A/P/M

NW/U–2  INSTITUTE OF EDUCATION, UNIV. OF NEWC./ TYNE, ST. THOMAS ST. L/A/*P

# OX——— OXFORD.

OX/U–1   BODLEIAN LIBRARY. *L/*A/P
OX/U–2   ASHMOLEAN MUSEUM. XL/*A/P
OX/U–3   COMMONWEALTH FORESTRY INSTITUTE (&)
DEP. OF FORESTRY, UNIV OF OXFORD (JT. LIBR.),
SOUTH PARKS RD. *L/*A/*P
OX/U–4   DEP. OF AGRICULTURE, UNIV. OF OXFORD,
PARKS RD. L/*A/XP
OX/U–5   FACULTY OF HISTORY, UNIV. OF OXFORD,
MERTON ST. L/*A/XP
OX/U–6   INSTITUTE OF EDUCATION, UNIV. OF OXFORD,
15 NORHAM GARDENS.
OX/U–7   MUSEUM OF THE HISTORY OF SCIENCE, OLD
ASHMOLEAN BUILDING, BROAD ST. *L/*A/*P
OX/U–8   RADCLIFFE SCIENCE LIBRARY. *L/*A/P
OX/U–9   RHODES HOUSE. *L/*A/P
OX/U10   SCHOOL OF GEOGRAPHY, UNIV. OF OXFORD,
MANSFIELD RD. L/*A/*P
OX/U11   UNIVERSITY COLLEGE, OXFORD. *L/*A/XP
OX/U12   DEP. OF ZOOLOGY & COMPARATIVE
ANATOMY, UNIV OF OXFORD.
OX/U13   INDIAN INSTITUTE, UNIV. OF OXFORD.
OX/U14   INSTITUTE OF COMMONWEALTH STUDIES,
UNIV. OF OXFORD, QUEEN ELIZABETH HOUSE, 20/21
ST. GILES.
OX/15    LAW LIBRARY, (PART OF BODLEIAN LIBR.)
OX/U16   INSTITUTE OF ECONOMICS & STATISTICS,
UNIV. OF OXFORD 〈PREV: INST. OF STATISTICS〉,
ST. CROSS BLDG., MANOR RD. XL/*A/*P
OX/U17   NUFFIELD COLLEGE. *L/*A/*P
OX/U18   ST. ANTONY'S COLLEGE
OX/U19   TAYLOR INSTITUTION, UNIV. OF OXFORD, ST.
GILES ST., OXFORD.
OX/U24   INSTITUTE OF AGRICULTURAL ECONOMICS,
UNIV. OF OXFORD, DARTINGTON HOUSE, LITTLE
CLARENDON ST., OX1 2HP.

# RE——— READING.

RE/F–1   GILLETTE INDUSTRIES LTD. (RESEARCH LABS.),
454 BASINGSTOKE RD. L/*A/*P
RE/P–1   READING PUBLIC LIBRARIES, BLAGRAVE ST.
L/A/*P
RE/R–1   NATIONAL INSTITUTE FOR RESEARCH IN
DAIRYING, SHINFIELD.
RE/U–1   UNIVERSITY OF READING. *L/*A/XP
RE/U–2   INSTITUTE OF EDUCATION, UNIV. OF READ.

# SA——— ST. ANDREWS.

SA/U–1   UNIVERSITY OF ST. ANDREW'S, (UNIV. LIBR.)
L/A/P

# SF——— SALFORD, LANCS.

SF/U–1   UNIVERSITY OF SALFORD 〈PREV: ROYAL
COLL. OF ADV. TECHNOL〉. SALF. 5. XL/XF/A/P

# SH——— SHEFFIELD.

SH/C–5   SHEFFIELD POLYTECHNIC, CENT. LIBR.,
HOWARD ST., SHEFFIELD.
SH/P–1   SHEFFIELD CITY LIBRARIES (CENT. LIBR. GEN.
REF. LIBR.), SURREY ST., 1.
SH/T–1   BROWN-FIRTH RESEARCH LABORATORIES
(HATFIELD LIBR.), PRINCESS ST., 4. L/*A/*P
SH/T–2   JOINT LIBRARY OF GLASS TECHNOLOGY (BR.
GLASS IND. RES. ASS.: SOC. OF GLASS TECHNOL.:
DEP OF GLASS TECHNOL., UNIV. OF SHEFF.),
ELMFIELD, NORTHUMBERLAND RD., 10. *L/*A/P

SH/T–3   SAFETY IN MINES RESEARCH ESTABLISHMENT,
OFF BROAD LANE, 3. L/*A/*P
SH/U–1   UNIVERSITY OF SHEFFIELD (UNIV. LIBR.),
WESTERN BANK, 10. *L/*A
SH/U–2   INSTITUTE OF EDUCATION, UNIV. OF SHEFF.,
SHEFF. 10.
SH/U–3   UNIV. OF SHEFFIELD (APPLIED SCIENCE
LIBRARY), ST. GEORGE'S SQ., 1. L/*A/P
SL/U–1   FOR THIS SYMBOL READ SF/U–1 (SEE ABOVE).

# SO——— SOUTHAMPTON.

SO/F–1   BRITISH-AMERICAN TOBACCO CO. LTD. (RES.
& DEV. ESTAB.), REGENTS PARK RD.
SO/P–1   SOUTHAMPTON PUBLIC LIBRARIES (CENTRAL
LIBR.), CIVIC CENTRE. L/A/P
SO/U–1   UNIVERSITY OF SOUTHAMPTON. L/*A/P
SO/U–2   INSTITUTE OF EDUCATION, UNIV. OF SOUTH.,
L/*A/P

# SW——— SWANSEA.

SW/P–1   SWANSEA PUBLIC LIBRARIES (CENT. LIBR.),
ALEXANDRA RD. L/A
SW/U–1   UNIVERSITY COLLEGE OF SWANSEA,
SINGLETON PARK. L/*A/*P

# XE——— EAST MIDLANDS (LIBRARY) REGION.

XE/C–1   NOW AS LB/C–1, Q.V.
XE/C–2   NOW AS LB/U–1, Q.V.
XE/C–3   ROYAL AIR FORCE COLLEGE, TRENCHARD
HALL LIBR. 〈PREV: R.A.F. TECH. COLL., HENLOW,
BEDS.〉, CRANWELL, SLEAFORD, LINCS.
XE/F–1   FISONS LTD. (HEAD OFFICE), HARVEST HOUSE,
FELIXSTOWE, SUFFOLK. L/*A
XE/F–2   FISONS FERTILIZERS LTD., LEVINGTON RES.
STATION, IPSWICH, SUFFOLK. L/XA/P
XE/F–3   ENGLISH ELECTRIC DIESELS LTD., RUSTON
SUB-GROUP, P.O. BOX 46, LINCOLN. L/*A/P
XE/F–4   STAVELEY IRON & CHEMICALS CO. LTD. (RES.
DEP., TECH. LIBR.), NR. CHESTERFIELD. L/*A/*P
XE/P–1   ARNOLD (NOTTS.) PUBLIC LIBRARY. L/A/*P
XE/P–2   CHESTERFIELD PUBLIC LIBRARY, STEPHENSON
MEMORIAL HALL, CORPORATION ST., CHESTERFIELD,
DERBS. *L/A/XP
XE/P–3   GREAT YARMOUTH CENTRAL LIBRARY. L/A/*P
XE/P–4   NORTHAMPTON CENTRAL PUBLIC LIBRARY,
ABINGTON ST. L/A/XP
XE/P–5   WORKSOP (NOTTS.) PUBLIC LIBRARY &
MUSEUM. L/A/*P
XE/P–6   MANSFIELD (NOTTS) PUBLIC LIBRARY,
CENTRAL LIBR., LEEMING ST. L/A/XP
XE/R–1   HOUGHTON POULTRY RESEARCH STATION,
HOUGHTON, HUNTS. *L/*A/XP

# XL——— LANCASHIRE & CHESHIRE (NW LIBR. REGION).

XL/C–1   NOW AS SF/U–1, Q.V.
XL/F–1   FISONS PHARMACEUTICALS LTD. 〈PREV:
BENGER LABS〉, HOLMES CHAPEL, CHES. L
XL/M–1   DEVA HOSPITAL, MEDICAL LIBRARY,
LIVERPOOL RD., CHESTER. *L/*A/XP
XL/P–1   BARROW-IN-FURNESS PUBLIC LIBRARY. L/A/P
XL/P–2   BOOTLE PUBLIC LIBRARIES, CENT. LIBR.,
ORIEL RD., BOOTLE 20, LANCS. L/A/*P
XL/P–3   BURNLEY PUBLIC LIBRARIES, CENTRAL LIBR.,
GRIMSHAW ST. L/A/*P

XL/P–4  ECCLES PUBLIC LIBRARIES, CHURCH ST., ECCLES, LANCS. *L/*A/P

XL/P–5  MAYER PUBLIC LIBRARY, BEBINGTON, WIRRAL, CHES. L/A/XP

XL/P–6  ST. HELENS PUBLIC LIBRARIES, CENT. LIBR., ST. HELENS, LANCS. L/A/P

XL/P–7  SOUTHPORT PUBLIC LIBRARY, ATKINSON CENTRAL LIBR., LORD ST. *L/A/*P

XL/P–8  STOCKPORT PUBLIC LIBRARIES, CENT. LIBR., WELLINGTON RD. SOUTH. L/A/P

XL/P–9  WARRINGTON PUBLIC LIBRARY, MUSEUM ST. L/A/P

XL/P10  WIGAN CENTRAL LIBRARY, RODNEY ST. L/A/P

XL/P11  FLEETWOOD (LANCS.) CENTRAL LIBRARY, DOCK ST. L/A/XP

XL/T–1  UNITED KINGDOM ATOMIC ENERGY AUTHORITY, REACTOR GROUP HQ, LIBR. & INF. DEP., RISLEY, WARRINGTON, LANCS. L/XA/*P


XM———  MIDLANDS, WEST, (LIBRARY) REGION.

XM/F–1  ASSOCIATED ENGINEERING LTD., GROUP RES. & DEV., CAUSTON, RUGBY, WARWICKS. *L/*A/P

XM/F–2  GKN GROUP RESEARCH LAB., BIRMINGHAM NEW RD., LANESFIELD, WOLVERHAMPTON. L/*P

XM/P–1  OSWESTRY PUBLIC LIBRARY, ARTHUR ST., OSWESTRY, SALOP. L/A

XM/P–2  SHROPSHIRE COUNTY LIBRARY, WYLE COP, SHREWSBURY. L/A/*P

XM/P–3  SMETHWICK PUBLIC LIBRARIES, CENT. LIBR., SMETHWICK 41, STAFFS. L/A

XM/P–4  STOKE-ON-TRENT PUBLIC LIBRARIES, CENTRAL LIBRARY, BETHESDA ST., HANLEY. L/A/XP

XM/P–5  WALSALL CENTRAL LIBRARY, LICHFIELD ST. L/A/*P

XM/P–6  WARWICKSHIRE COUNTY LIBRARY, THE BUTTS, WARWICK. L/A/P

XM/P–7  WEST BROMWICH PUBLIC LIBRARY, HIGH ST., W. BROM., STAFFS. L/A/*P

XM/P–8  WOLVERHAMPTON PUBLIC LIBRARIES, CENTRAL LIBR., SNOW HILL, WOLV., STAFFS. L/A/XP

XM/P–9  DUDLEY PUBLIC LIBRARIES, CENT. LIBR., L/A/*P

XM/R–1  NATIONAL VEGETABLE RESEARCH STATION, WELLESBOURNE, WARWICKS. L/*A/*P

XM/T–1  BRITISH CERAMIC RESEARCH ASSOCIATION, MELLOR MEMORIAL LIBR., QUEENS RD., PENKHULL, STOKE/TRENT, STAFFS. L/*A/P


XN———  NORTHERN (LIBRARY) REGION.

XN/P–1  SUNDERLAND PUBLIC LIBRARIES, CENTRAL LIBR., BOROUGH RD. L/A/P

XN/R–1  FRESHWATER BIOLOGICAL ASSOCIATION, FERRY HOUSE, FAR SAWREY, AMBLESIDE, WESTMORL. *L/A/*P

XN/R–2  DOVE MARINE LABORATORY, CULLERCOATS, NORTH SHIELDS, NORTHUMB. *L/*F/*A/XP BUT P & M BY SENDING MATERIAL TO NW/U–1

XN/S–1  LIBRARY OF JAPANESE SCIENCE & TECHNOLOGY, 24 DUKE ST., WHITLEY BAY, NORTIIUMB. L/A/XP

XN/T–1  UNITED KINGDOM ATOMIC ENERGY AUTHORITY, REACTOR GROUP, WINDSCALE WORKS, SELLAFIELD, SEASCALE, CUMB. L/XA/*P


XS———  SOUTH EASTERN (LIBRARY) REGION.

XS/C–1  FIRE SERVICE COLLEGE, WOTTON HOUSE, ABINGER COMMON, DORKING, SURREY. L/*A

XS/C–2  HATFIELD POLYTECHNIC (& HERTFORDSHIRE COUNTY COUNCIL TECH. LIBR. INF. SERV.), HATFIELD, HERTS. *L/*A/P

XS/C–3  COLLEGE OF AERONAUTICS, CRANFIELD, BEDFORD. L/*A/P

XS/C–4  EWELL COUNTY TECHNICAL COLLEGE, REIGATE RD., EWELL, SURREY. L/A/P

XS/C–5  NOW AS XE/C–3, Q.V.

XS/F–1  COSSOR ELECTRONICS LTD., CENTR., LIBR., THE PINNACLES, HARLOW, ESSEX. L/XA

XS/F–2  ELLIOTT BROTHERS (LONDON) LTD., AIRPORT WORKS, TECH. LIBR., ROCHESTER, KENT. L/XA/*P

XS/F–3  GLAXO RESEARCH LTD., SEFTON PARK, STOKE POGES, BUCKS. L/XA/*P

XS/F–4  PLANT PROTECTION LTD., JEALOTT'S HILL RES. STN., BRACKNELL, BERKS. L/XA/XP

XS/F–5  JOHN LAING RESEARCH & DEVELOPMENT LTD., MANOR WAY, BOREHAM WOOD, HERTS. L/*A/*P

XS/F–6  MARCONI INSTRUMENTS LTD., LONGACRES, ST. ALBANS, HERTS. *L/XA/*P

XS/F–7  MILES LABORATORIES LTD., STOKES COURT, STOKE POGES, BUCKS. *L/XA/P

XS/F–8  PAN BRITANNICA INDUSTRIES LTD., BRITANNICA HOUSE, WALTHAM CROSS, HERTS. *L/*F/XA/*P/XM

XS/F–9  STANDARD TELECOMMUNICATION LABORATORIES LTD., TECH. LIBR., LONDON RD., HARLOW, ESSEX. L/*A

XS/F10  TATE & LYLE REFINERIES LTD., RESEARCH LAB., RAVENSBOURNE, WESTERHAM RD., KESTON, KENT. L/*A/P

XS/F11  BEECHAM RES. LAB., VITAMINS RES. STN., WALTON OAKS, TADWORTH, SURREY. L/XA/P

XS/F/12  WH ALLEN & SONS & CO. LTD., QUEENS ENGINEERING WORKS, TECH. LIBR., BEDFORD. L/*A/P

XS/F13  HAWKER SIDDELEY DYNAMICS LTD., TECH. LIBR., MANOR RD., HATFIELD, HERTS. *L/XA/*P

XS/F14  JOHN WYETH & BROTHER LTD., HUNTERCOMBE LANE SOUTH, TAPLOW, MAIDENHEAD, BERKS. L/XA/*P

XS/F15  VICKERS RESEARCH LTD., SUNNINGHILL, ASCOT, BERKS. L

XS/F16  SMITH KLINE & FRENCH LABORATORIES LTD., WELWYN GARDEN CITY, HERTS. L/XA/*P

XS/N–1  METEOROLOGICAL OFFICE, LONDON RD., BRACKNELL, BERKS. L/A/*P

XS/N–2  NAVAL SCIENTIFIC & TECHNICAL INFORMATION CENTRE (MIN. OF DEFENCE), BLOCK B, STATION SQ. HOUSE, ST. MARY CRAY, ORPINGTON, KENT. ⟨PREV: LO/T–1⟩

XS/P–1  BUCKINGHAMSHIRE COUNTY LIBRARY, HIGHBRIDGE RD., AYLESBURY, BUCKS. L/A/P

XS/P–2  DARTFORD PUBLIC LIBRARIES, CENTRAL PARK, DARTFORD, KENT. L/A/P

XS/P–3  ESSEX COUNTY LIBRARY, TECH. LIBR. SERV., GOLDLAY GARDENS, CHELMSFORD, ESSEX. L/A/P

XS/P–4  GILLINGHAM PUBLIC LIBRARY, CENT. LIBR., HIGH ST., GILL., KENT. L/A/*P

XS/P–5  THURROCK CENTRAL LIBRARY, ORSETT RD., GRAYS, ESSEX. L/A/P

XS/R–1  DITTON LABORATORY (AGRICULTURAL RESEARCH COUNCIL), LARKFIELD, MAIDSTONE, KENT. L/XA/*P

XS/R–2  EAST MALLING RESEARCH STATION (JT. LIBR. WITH: COMMONW. BUR. OF HORTICULTURE & PLANTATION CROPS), EAST MALLING, MAIDSTONE, KENT. L/*A/P

XS/R–3  FULMER RESEARCH INSTITUTE LTD., STOKE POGES, BUCKS. L/*A/*P

XS/R–4  GRASSLAND RESEARCH INSTITUTE, HURLEY, BERKS. XL/*A/XP

XS/R–5  JOHN INNES INSTITUTE, BAYFORDBURY, HERTFORD, HERTS. L/*A/P

XS/R–6  NATIONAL INSTITUTE OF AGRICULTURAL ENGINEERING, WREST PARK, SILSOE, BEDS. L/A/*P

XS/R–7  PEST INFESTATION LABORATORY, LONDON RD., SLOUGH, BUCKS. *L/*A/XP

XS/R–8  ANIMAL VIRUS RESEARCH INSTITUTE⟨PREV: RESEARCH INSTITUTE (ANIMAL VIRUS DISEASES)⟩. PIRBRIGHT, WOKING, SURREY. L/XF/*A/*P/XM

XS/R–9   WARREN SPRING LABORATORY, GUNNELS WOOD RD., STEVENAGE, HERTS. *L/*A/XP

XS/R10   ATOMIC ENERGY RESEARCH ESTABLISHMENT (UKAEA RESEARCH GROUP), HARWELL, DIDCOT, BERKS. *L/*A/*P

XS/R11   NATIONAL INSTITUTE OF OCEANOGRAPHY, WORMLEY, GODALMING, SURREY.

XS/R12   ROTHAMSTED EXPERIMENTAL STATION, HARPENDEN, HERTS. L/*F/A/P/M (SUPPLIES XEROX ONLY OF PER. ARTS. UP TO 10 PP.)

XS/R14   COMMONWEALTH BUREAU OF HELMINTHOLOGY, THE WHITE HOUSE, 103 ST. PETERS ST., ST. ALBANS.

XS/T–1   BREWING INDUSTRY RESEARCH FOUNDATION, NUTFIELD, REDHILL, SURREY. *L/*A/P

XS/T–2   BRITISH COAL UTILISATION RESEARCH ASSOCIATION, RANDALLS RD., LEATHERHEAD. SURREY. *L/*A/*P

XS/T–3   SIRA INSTITUTE, SOUTH HILL, CHISLEHURST, KENT. BR7 5EH. L/*A/*P

XS/T–4   ELECTRICAL RESEARCH ASSOCIATION (BR. ELEC. & ALLIED IND. RES. ASS.), CLEEVE RD., LEATHERHEAD, SURREY. *L/XA/*P

XS/T–5   MILITARY ENGINEERING EXPERIMENTAL ESTABLISHMENT, MEXE TECH. LIBR., BARRACK RD., CHRISTCHURCH, HANTS. L/XA/P

XS/T–6   PIRA (PRINTING & PACKAGING DIV.), RANDALLS RD., LEATHERHEAD, SURREY. *L/*A/P

XS/T–7   ROYAL AIRCRAFT ESTABLISHMENT, BEDFORD. L/XA

XS/T–8   SERVICES ELECTRONICS RESEARCH LABORATORY, BALDOCK, HERTS. L/*A/*P

XS/T–9   RADIOCHEMICAL CENTRE (UNITED KINGDOM ATOMIC ENERGY AUTHORITY), WHITE LION RD., AMERSHAM, BUCKS. L/XA/XP

XS/T10   HEATING & VENTILATING RESEARCH ASS., INFORMATION OFFICE, OLD BRACKNELL LANE, BRACKNELL, BERKS.

XS/T11   BRITISH FOOD MANUFACTURING INDUSTRIES RESEARCH ASS., LEATHERHEAD, SURREY.

XS/U–1   WYE COLLEGE, NR. ASHFORD, KENT. *L/*A


XW——— WESTERN, SOUTH (LIBRARY) REGION.

XW/C–1   HEYTHROP COLLEGE, CHIPPING NORTON, OXON. *L/*A/XP

XW/C–2   ROYAL AGRICULTURAL COLLEGE, CIRENCESTER, GLOUCS. L/*A/*P

XW/C–3   PORTSMOUTH POLYTECHNIC, HAMPSHIRE TCE., PORTSMOUTH, HANTS.

XW/C–4   ROYAL MILITARY COLLEGE OF SCIENCE, SHRIVENHAM, SWINDON, WILTS. *L/*A/*P

XW/P–1   BOURNEMOUTH PUBLIC LIBRARIES, CENTRAL LIBR., LANSDOWNE, BOURN., HANTS. L/A/P

XW/P–2   BRIDGWATER PUBLIC LIBRARY, BINFORD PLACE, BRIDGW., SOMERSET. L/A/P

XW/P–3   GLOUCESTER CITY LIBRARIES, BRUNSWICK RD. L/A/P

XW/P–4   HAMPSHIRE COUNTY LIBRARY HQ., NORTH WALLS, WINCHESTER. L/A/P

XW/P–5   SOMERSET COUNTY LIBRARY HQ., MOUNT ST., BRIDGWATER, SOMERSET. L/A/P

XW/P–6   SWINDON PUBLIC LIBRARIES, CENT. LIBR., REGENT CIRCUS, SWIN., WILTS. L/A/P

XW/P–7   TAUNTON PUBLIC LIBRARY, CORPORATION ST., TAUNTON, SOMERSET. L/A/P

XW/S–1   COMMONWEAL COLLECTION, 112 WINCHCOMBE ST., CHELTENHAM, GLOUCS. L/F/A/XP/XM

XW/T–1   ROYAL AIRCRAFT ESTABLISHMENT, FARNBOROUGH, HANTS. L/*A/P


XY——— YORKSHIRE (LIBRARY REGION).

XY/C–1   HUDDERSFIELD COLLEGE OF EDUCATION (TECHNICAL) ⟨PREV: TRAINING COLL. FOR TECHNICAL TEACHERS⟩, HOLLY BANK RD., LINDLEY. L/*A/*P

XY/F–1   BRITISH BELTING & ASBESTOS LTD., LIBR. & INF. SERV., CLECKHEATON, YORKS. L/*A/P

XY/N–1   BRITISH LIBRARY: LENDING DIVISION, BOSTON SPA WETHERBY, YORKS. LS23 7BQ. ⟨FORMED BY AMALGAMATION OF NATIONAL LENDING LIBRARY AND NATIONAL CENTRAL LIBRARY⟩ L/A/P

XY/P–2   TEESSIDE PUBLIC LIBRARIES, CENT. LIBR., VICTORIA SQUARE, MIDDLESBROUGH. L/A/P

XY/P–3   WEST RIDING COUNTY LIBRARY HQ, BALNE LANE, WAKEFIELD, YORKS. L/A/P

XY/P–4   ROTHERHAM PUBLIC LIBRARY, HOWARD ST., ROTH., YORKS. L/A/*P


YK——— YORK.

YK/U–1   UNIVERSITY OF YORK (J.B. MORRELL LIBR.), HESLINGTON, YORK. L/A/P


ZN——— NORTHERN IRELAND.

ZN/P–1   ARMAGH PUBLIC LIBRARY, ABBEY ST. *L/A/XP


ZS——— SCOTLAND.

ZS/F–1   BP CHEMICALS LTD., BO'NESS RD., GRANGEMOUTH, STIRLINGSHIRE. L/*A/P

ZS/P–1   CARNEGIE PUBLIC LIBRARY, AYR. L/A/XP

ZS/P–2   FRASERBURGH PUBLIC LIBRARY, KING EDWARD STREET, FRAS., ABERDEENSHIRE. L/A/*P

ZS/T–1   DOUNREAY EXPERIMENTAL REACTOR ESTABLISHMENT, THURSO, CAITHNESS. L/XA/P

ZS/T–2   SCIENTIFIC DOCUMENTATION CENTRE LTD., HALBEATH HOUSE, DUNFERMLINE, FIFE. L/*A/P

ZS/U–1   WEST OF SCOTLAND AGRICULTURAL COLLEGE, DONALD HENDRIE BUILDING, AUCHINCRUIVE, AYR. L/*A/*P


ZW——— WALES.

ZW/F–1   MIDLAND SILICONES LTD., BARRY, GLAMORGAN. L/XA/P

ZW/M–1   PNEUMOCONIOSIS RESEARCH UNIT (MEDICAL RESEARCH COUNCIL), LLANDOUGH HOSPITAL, PENARTH, GLAMORGAN. L/*A/P

ZW/P–1   NEWPORT (MON.) PUBLIC LIBRARY, CENTRAL LIBR., DOXK ST. L/A/P

ZW/P–2   WREXHAM PUBLIC LIBRARY, QUEEN SQUARE, WREXHAM, DENBS. L/A/XP